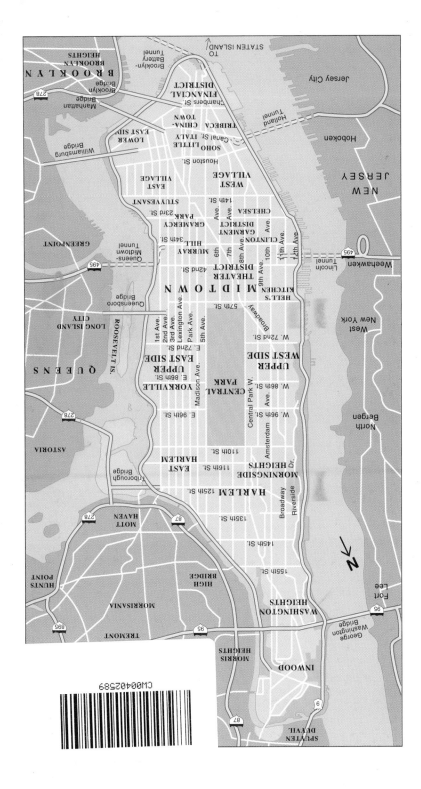

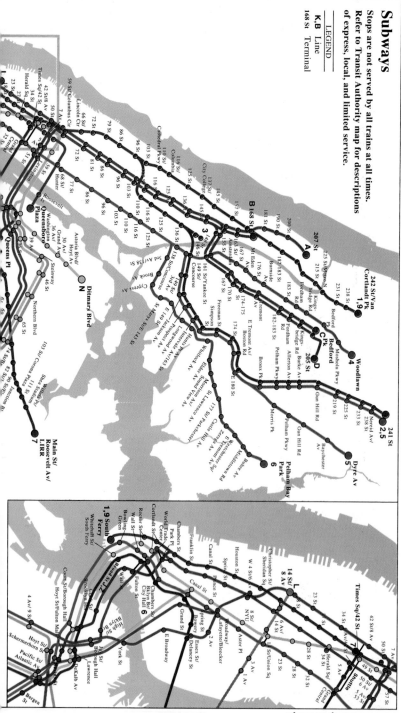

Subways

Stops are not served by all trains at all times.
Refer to Transit Authority map for descriptions
of express, local, and limited service.

New York City Subways

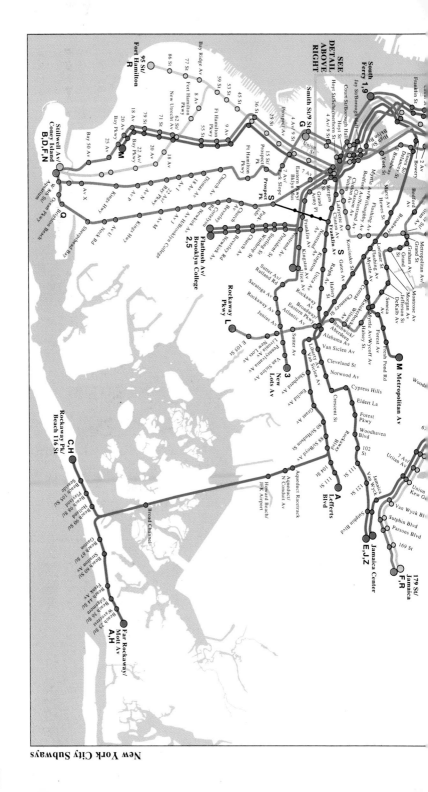

New York City Subways

N →

Holland Tunnel

West Side Hwy.

10th Ave.
9th Ave.
8th Ave.
Eighth Ave.
Seventh Ave.
Greenwich Ave.
Avenue of the Americas (Sixth Ave.)
Fifth Avenue
University Pl.
Broadway
Lafayette St.
Fourth Ave.
Third Avenue
Second Avenue
First Avenue
Avenue A
Avenue B
Avenue C
Avenue D

W. 14th St.
W. 15th St.
W. 13th St.
W. 12th St.
W. 11th St.
Bank St.
Bethune St.
Jane St.
Horatio St.
Gansevoort
Little W. 12th St.
ABINGDON SQUARE
GREENWICH VILLAGE
Charles St.
Perry St.
W. 10th St.
Christopher St.
Grove St.
W. 4th St.
Waverly Pl.
SHERIDAN SQUARE
Barrow St.
Morton St.
Leroy St.
Clarkson St.
W. Houston St.
Washington St.
Hudson St.
King St.
Charlton St.
Vandam St.
Spring St.
Broome St.
Dominick St.
Watts St.
Desbrosses St.
Vestry St.
Canal St.
Lispenard St.
Howard St.
Grand St.
TRIBECA
Varick St.

Greenwich St.
St. Luke's Pl.
Commerce St.
Bedford St.
Downing St.
Carmine St.
Bleecker St.
Jones St.
Cornelia St.
W. 4th St.
Minetta La.
Macdougal St.
Sullivan St.
Thompson St.
W. Houston St.
Prince St.
Spring St.
Wooster St.
Greene St.
Mercer St.
Crosby St.
Lafayette St.
Cleveland Pl.
Mulberry St.
Mott St.
Elizabeth St.
The Bowery
Chrystie St.
Forsyth St.
Eldridge St.
Allen St.
Orchard St.
Ludlow St.
Essex St.
Norfolk St.
Suffolk St.
Clinton St.
Ridge St.
Pitt St.
Willett St.
Columbia St.

SOHO
LITTLE ITALY
NOHO
EAST VILLAGE
LOWER EAST SIDE

Washington Square Park
New York University
La Guardia Pl.
W. 3rd St.
Bleecker St.
W. 8th St.
W. 9th St.
W. 10th St.
W. 11th St.
W. 12th St.
Astor Pl.
St. Marks Pl.
E. 7th St.
E. 6th St.
E. 5th St.
E. 4th St.
E. 3rd St.
E. 2nd St.
E. 1st St.
E. Houston St.
Stanton St.
Rivington St.
Delancey St.
Broome St.
Grand St.
Hester St.
Canal St.

COOPER SQUARE
Stuyvesant St.
Bond St.
Gt. Jones St.
Bleecker St.

Tompkins Square Park
E. 8th St.
E. 9th St.
E. 11th St.
E. 12th St.
E. 13th St.
E. 14th St.
E. 15th St.

UNION SQUARE

A.C.E.L.
1,2,3,9,L
F,L,Q
N,R
L,4,5,6
B,D,F,Q
N,R
A,C,E
6
F,J,M,Z
B,D,Q

East Broadway
Madison St.
Clinton St.
Montgomery St.
Jackson St.
Water St.
Lewis St.
Williamsburg Br.
FDR Drive

29 30 31 32 33 34 35 36 37 38 39 40 41 42 43 44 45 46 47

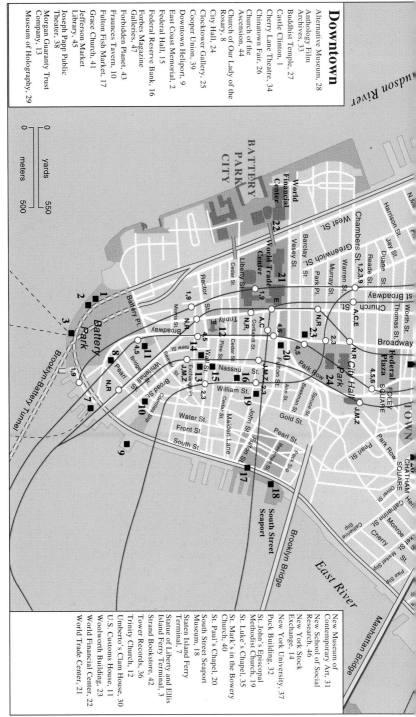

Downtown

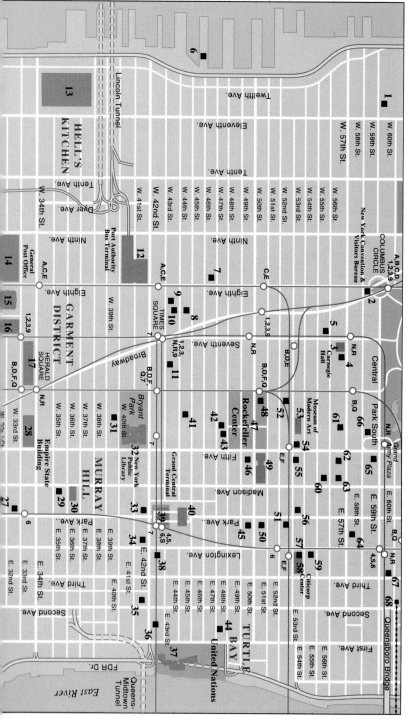

Midtown Manhattan

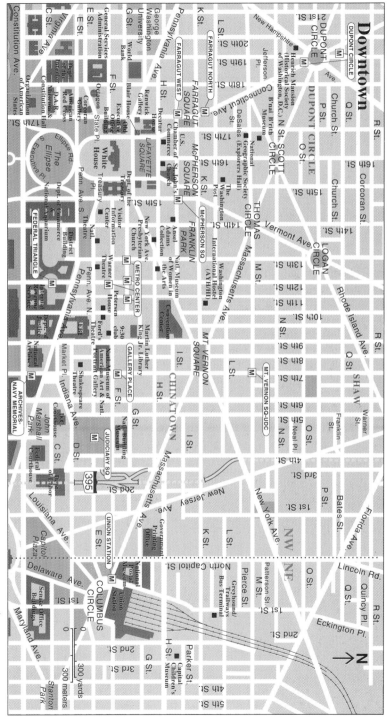

Downtown Washington, D.C.

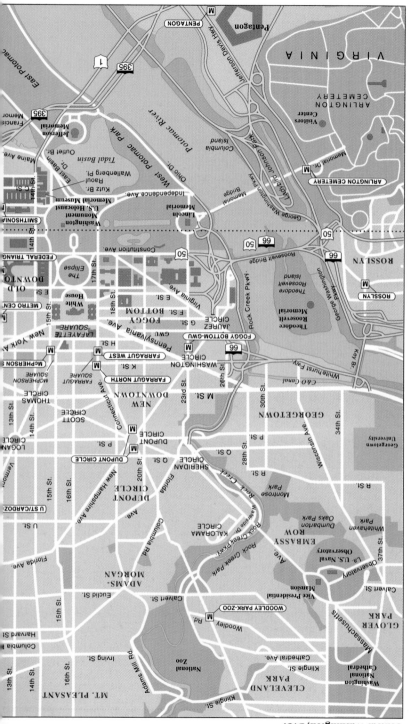

Central Washington, D.C.

Central Washington, D.C.

The Mall Area, Washington, D.C.

Mall Area

9:30 club, 13
Arts & Industries Building, 29
Bureau of Engraving & Printing, 25
Cannon House Office Building, 50
D.C. Courthouse, 17
Department of Agriculture, 26
Department of Commerce, 5
Department of Energy, 34
Department of Health & Human Services, 40
Department of Housing & Urban Development, 37
Department of Justice, 15
Department of Labor, 19
Department of Transportation, 38
Department of the Treasury, 3

Dirksen Senate Office Building, 46
District Building, 6
Federal Bureau of Investigation, 12
Federal Courthouse, 20
Folger Shakespeare Library, 48
Ford's Theatre, 11
Freer Gallery, 27
Hirshhorn Museum & Sculpture Garden, 32
Internal Revenue Service, 10
Interstate Commerce Commission, 7
L'Enfant Plaza, 36
Library of Congress, 49
Longworth House Office Building, 51
National Aquarium, 5

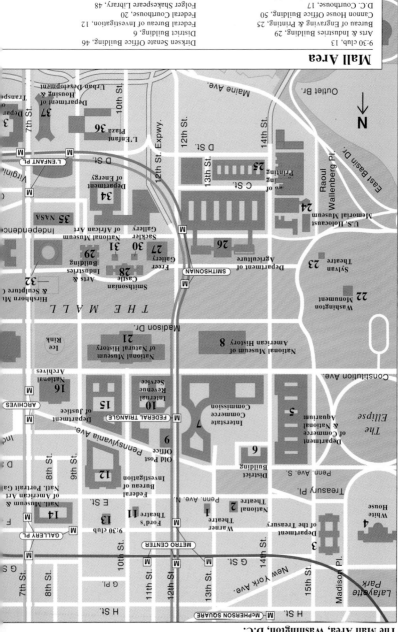

The Mall Area, Washington, D.C.

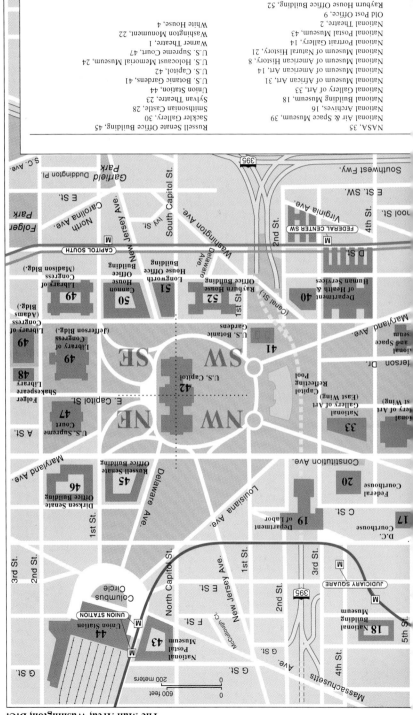

NASA, 35
National Air & Space Museum, 39
National Archives, 16
National Building Museum, 18
National Gallery of Art, 33
National Museum of African Art, 31
National Museum of American Art, 14
National Museum of American History, 8
National Museum of Natural History, 21
National Portrait Gallery, 14
National Postal Museum, 43
National Theatre, 2
Old Post Office, 9
Rayburn House Office Building, 52

Russell Senate Office Building, 45
Sackler Gallery, 30
Smithsonian Castle, 28
Sylvan Theatre, 23
Union Station, 44
U.S. Botanic Gardens, 41
U.S. Capitol, 42
U.S. Holocaust Memorial Museum, 24
U.S. Supreme Court, 47
Warner Theatre, 1
Washington Monument, 22
White House, 4

White House Area, Foggy Bottom, and Nearby Arlington

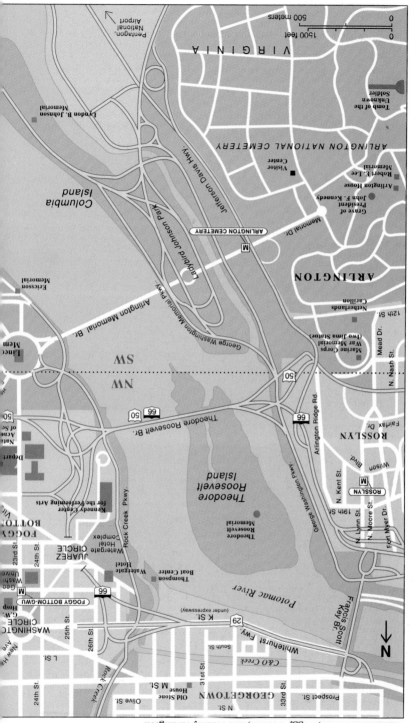

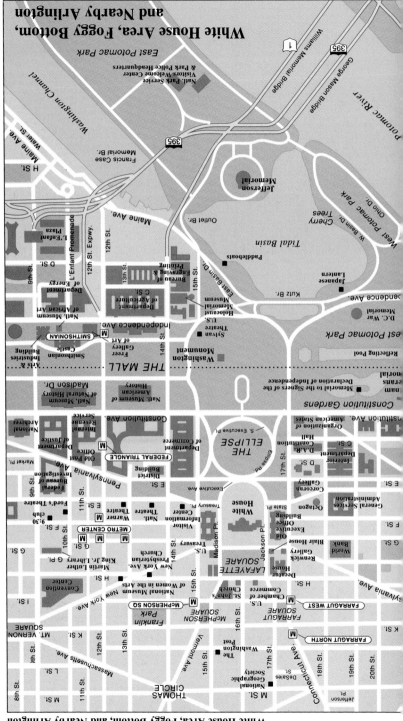

White House Area, Foggy Bottom, and Nearby Arlington

Metrorail System, Washington, D.C.

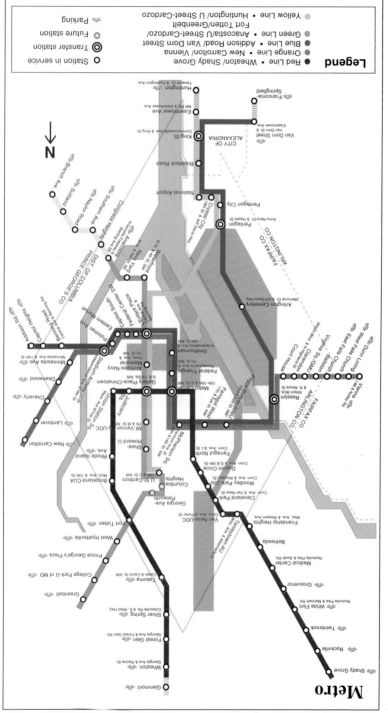

Metro

Legend

- ● Red Line • Wheaton/ Shady Grove
- ● Orange Line • New Carrollton/ Vienna
- ● Blue Line • Addison Road/ Van Dorn Street
- ● Green Line • Anacostia/U Street-Cardozo/ Fort Totten/Greenbelt
- ● Yellow Line • Huntington/ U Street-Cardozo

○ Station in service
◉ Transfer station
◯ Future station
⛿ Parking

Let's Go

USA & CANADA

is the best book for anyone traveling on a budget. Here's why:

▓ No other guidebook has as many budget listings.

In the USA and Canada we list over 10,000 budget travel bargains. We tell you the cheapest way to get around, and where to get an inexpensive and satisfying meal once you've arrived. We give hundreds of money-saving tips that anyone can use, plus invaluable advice on discounts and deals for students, children, families, and senior travelers.

▓ Let's Go researchers have to make it on their own.

Our Harvard-Radcliffe researcher-writers travel on budgets as tight as your own—no expense accounts, no free hotel rooms.

▓ Let's Go is completely revised each year.

We don't just update the prices, we go back to the place. If a charming café has become an overpriced tourist trap, we'll replace the listing with a new and better one.

▓ No other guidebook includes all this:

Honest, engaging coverage of both the cities and the countryside; up-to-the-minute prices, directions, addresses, phone numbers, and opening hours; in-depth essays on local culture, history, and politics; comprehensive listings on transportation between and within regions and cities; straight advice on work and study, budget accommodations, sights, nightlife, and food; detailed city and regional maps; and much more.

▓ Let's Go is for anyone who wants to see the USA and Canada on a budget.

Books by Let's Go, Inc.

EUROPE

Let's Go: Europe

Let's Go: Austria & Switzerland

Let's Go: Britain & Ireland

Let's Go: Eastern Europe

Let's Go: France

Let's Go: Germany

Let's Go: Greece & Turkey

Let's Go: Ireland

Let's Go: Italy

Let's Go: London

Let's Go: Paris

Let's Go: Rome

Let's Go: Spain & Portugal

NORTH & CENTRAL AMERICA

Let's Go: USA & Canada

Let's Go: Alaska & The Pacific Northwest

Let's Go: California

Let's Go: New York City

Let's Go: Washington, D.C.

Let's Go: Mexico

MIDDLE EAST & ASIA

Let's Go: Israel & Egypt

Let's Go: Thailand

Let's Go

The Budget Guide to

USA & CANADA

1995

Amelia Hollander Kaplan
Editor

Jeffrey Collins
Associate Editor

Sean K. Desmond
Associate Editor

Written by
Let's Go, Inc.
A subsidiary of
Harvard Student Agencies, Inc.

St. Martin's Press ■ **New York**

HELPING LET'S GO

If you have suggestions or corrections, or just want to share your discoveries, drop us a line. We read every piece of correspondence, whether a 10-page e-mail letter, a velveteen Elvis postcard, or, as in one case, a collage. All suggestions are passed along to our researcher-writers. Please note that mail received after May 5, 1995 will probably be too late for the 1996 book, but will be retained for the following edition.
Address mail to:

> **Let's Go: USA & Canada**
> **Let's Go, Inc.**
> **1 Story Street**
> **Cambridge, MA 02138**
> **USA**

Or send e-mail (please include in the subject header the titles of the *Let's Go* guides you discuss in your message) to:
> **letsgo@delphi.com**

In addition to the invaluable travel advice our readers share with us, many are kind enough to offer their services as researchers or editors. Unfortunately, the charter of Let's Go, Inc. and Harvard Student Agencies, Inc. enables us to employ only currently enrolled Harvard-Radcliffe students.

Maps by David Lindroth, copyright © 1995, 1994, 1993, 1992, 1991, 1990, 1989 by St. Martin's Press, Inc.

Distributed outside the U.S. and Canada by Macmillan.

ISBN: 0-312-11308-0

First edition
10 9 8 7 6 5 4 3 2 1

Let's Go: USA & Canada is written by the Publishing Division of Let's Go, Inc., 1 Story Street, Cambridge, MA 02138.

Let's Go® is a registered trademark of Let's Go, Inc.
Printed in the U.S.A. on recycled paper with biodegradable soy ink.

About Let's Go

Back in 1960, a few students at Harvard University got together to produce a 20-page pamphlet offering a collection of tips on budget travel in Europe. For three years, Harvard Student Agencies, a student-run nonprofit corporation, had been doing a brisk business booking charter flights to Europe; this modest, mimeographed packet was offered to passengers as an extra. The following year, students traveling to Europe researched the first full-fledged edition of *Let's Go: Europe*, a pocket-sized book featuring advice on shoestring travel, irreverent write-ups of sights, and a decidedly youthful slant.

Throughout the 60s, the guides reflected the times: one section of the 1968 *Let's Go: Europe* talked about "Street Singing in Europe on No Dollars a Day." During the 70s, *Let's Go* gradually became a large-scale operation, adding regional European guides and expanding coverage into North Africa and Asia. The 80s saw the arrival of *Let's Go: USA & Canada* and *Let's Go: Mexico*, as well as regional North American guides; in the 90s we introduced five in-depth city guides to Paris, London, Rome, New York City, and Washington, DC. And as the budget travel world expands, so do we; the first edition of *Let's Go: Thailand* hit the shelves last year, and this year's edition adds coverage of Malaysia, Singapore, Tokyo, and Hong Kong.

This year we're proud to announce the birth of *Let's Go: Eastern Europe*—the most comprehensive guide to this renascent region, with more practical information and insider tips than any other. *Let's Go: Eastern Europe* brings our total number of titles, with their spirit of adventure and reputation for honesty, accuracy, and editorial integrity, to 21.

We've seen a lot in 35 years. *Let's Go: Europe* is now the world's #1 best selling international guide, translated into seven languages. And our guides are still researched, written, and produced entirely by students who know first-hand how to see the world on the cheap.

Every spring, we recruit over 100 researchers and 50 editors to write our books anew. Come summertime, after several months of training, researchers hit the road for seven weeks of exploration, from Bangkok to Budapest, Anchorage to Ankara. With pen and notebook in hand, a few changes of underwear stuffed in our backpacks, and a budget as tight as yours, we visit every *pensione*, *palapa*, pizzeria, café, club, campground, or castle we can find to make sure you'll get the most out of *your* trip.

We've put the best of our discoveries into the book you're now holding. A brand-new edition of each guide hits the shelves every year, only months after it is researched, so you know you're getting the most reliable, up-to-date, and comprehensive information available. The budget travel world is constantly changing, and where other guides quickly become obsolete, our annual research keeps you abreast of the very latest travel insights. And even as you read this, work on next year's editions is well underway.

At *Let's Go*, we think of budget travel not only as a means of cutting down on costs, but as a way of breaking down a few walls as well. Living cheap and simple on the road brings you closer to the real people and places you've been saving up to visit. This book will ease your anxieties and answer your questions about the basics—to help *you* get off the beaten track and explore. We encourage you to put *Let's Go* away now and then and strike out on your own. As any seasoned traveler will tell you, the best discoveries are often those you make yourself. If you find something worth sharing, drop us a line. We're at Let's Go, Inc., 1 Story Street, Cambridge, MA, 02138, USA (e-mail: letsgo@delphi.com).

Happy travels!

Contents

▮ Maps

Researcher-Writers

Jace Clayton *Western Pennsylvania, Ohio, Illinois, Indiana, Kentucky, Missouri (St. Louis, Hannibal), North Carolina, Tennessee, Virginia (Virginia Beach)*

Belying his mild-mannered New England exterior, Jace throbbed, raved, and jived his way across the Blue Grass country from Chicago to Kentucky. From city to city, he grooved with expert copy and a purist's appreciation of Dada. Our funky-Americana finder ("We live in a strange country") hyped Ohiopyle and polished off his route with scarcely a hitch. Very in-tune, Jace jazzed up his route with chic cafés, Pere Ubu, and lots of funk.

Brandon Elizabeth Earp *Connecticut (Hartford), Massachusetts (Berkshires), Lower New York State, Ontario, Michigan, Northern Minnesota, Wisconsin*

Brandon camped her way across the Great Lakes, and sent back exhaustive coverage of every micro-brewery between Hartford and Madison ("I'm a beer fan!"). A future doctor, Brandon used surgical precision in checking every fact and covering every lake in the land—all 10,000 of them! Our dred-locked pro waxed prolific, impressively expanding coverage by hundreds of pages, and still took time to smell the roses ("I like flowers!"). For the second time, Brandon graced the U.S.A.

Anne Morrow Fulenwider *Northern Colorado, Idaho, Montana, Wyoming, Northern Utah*

Anne found paradise in Montana and oysters in the Rockies, bestowing us with the prettiest copy we ever did see. Four-color pen in hand, she partied down with Mormons while still finding time to list every campground above 5000 ft. A city rat from Massachusetts, Anne miraculously turned up sixteen cousins all living in Idaho, giving her the award for working the budget connections. A fantastic member of the U.S.A. team, Anne excelled in Denver and outdid herself in the Great Outdoors.

Caitlin M. Hurley *Alabama, Florida, Georgia, South Carolina*

Her car may have wheezed, but Caitlin whistled her way through Dixie. After sprinting through several new towns, she ran through Alabama and Georgia and paved the way for the '96 Olympics. After a fortunate rendezvous with her brother, Caitlin went on to do the beautiful Florida thing. The ocean breezes and pure-white crystals speedily seduced this Yankee, and we predict that by the time she reads this praise she'll be in Panama City Beach working on a hard-earned tan.

Stephen P. Janiak *Iowa, Kansas, Minnesota (Minneapolis/St. Paul), Missouri (Kansas City), Nebraska, North Dakota, Oklahoma, South Dakota, West Texas (Amarillo, El Paso, Big Bend), Wyoming (Devil's Tower)*

Stephen's love affair with Lincoln lasted longer than his car as he blew down the country from North Dakota to Texas. Our Texas native and postcard champion kept us abreast of his incredibly thorough and innovative research. After major car woes (abandoning his car in a parking lot) this valiant RW really took off, quickly earning the title of *Let's Go's* honorary Midwestern convert. Stephen, Oscar Wilde of the Great Plains, had a soft spot for Dairy Queen, crafted marginalia (that often needed to be censored), and still managed to master eleven states with panache.

Loren Geoffrey Soeiro *Arkansas, Louisiana, Mississippi, Tennessee (Memphis), East and South Texas*

Ren tented in Texas and sang the blues in the Bayou, protecting his copy from buses and finding a *Ren*oir in every art museum in the South. This future novelist ate fried alligator and turtle soup, used non-sexist terminology, saw Elvis, and found much material for his future epic. A mighty researcher, writing up copy by street lamp, Ren dominated the Big Easy, oversaw the Ozarks, did Dallas, and lived to tell the tale in his meticulous batches. We dedicate a certain NYC entry to the Blue Man himself.

Michael M. Stockman *Arizona, Southern Colorado, Nevada (Las Vegas), New Mexico, Southern Utah*

A budding Kerouac, Michael lived out his wanderlust and resurrected the Southwest. The Adjectival Kid swept through ghost towns and metaphysical oases, and got his kicks on Route 66. Master of the Metaphor added new places with ease and brought out the beauty of his route. Michael's copy might have been smoky, but his prose was sexy and his work excellent. Next year Michael will be on the road again writing the Great American Novel. We wish him the best of luck.

Michelle Catherine Sullivan *Atlantic Canada, Maine, New Hampshire, New York (Adirondacks, Thousand Island Seaway), Ontario (Ottawa), Québec, Vermont*

From Northern New England to Eastern Canada, Michelle mastered a route legendary for its difficulties. After selling her car to mountain men and enduring countless mishaps, Michelle reigned triumphant, becoming Goddess of *Let's Go*. Not only was her copy beautiful, but it was thorough, well-organized, and thoughtful. Her painstaking notes (even on her tearsheets) professed a perfectionism that translated into outstanding coverage of everywhere she went. A postcard runner up, Michelle wins for her introspective meditations. Have a screech and a Vermont mud bar on us.

Matthew L. Ware *Massachusetts (Boston Area and Cape Cod Area), Rhode Island, Eastern Pennsylvania, New Jersey, Delaware, Maryland, West Virginia, Virginia*

Matt left Boston pale and reticent, and returned six weeks later a bronzed Researcher-Warrior. Aside from an unfortunate run-in with the love child of Jabba the Hut in Philadelphia, he breezed through the mid-Atlantic, sending back fantastic copy and ever better marginalia. Furthermore, he survived whitewater rafting and a hair-raising five-dollar airplane ride. The punniest guy we ever met, we wish our Maine man a phantastic phuture.

Amara Balthrop-Lewis *California (Berkeley, San Francisco, Santa Cruz, Monterey, Carmel, Marin County, Wine Country)*

James Bronzan *Eastern Oregon and Washington*

Carrie Busch *Hawaii*

Colin Chant *Alaska (Wrangell-St. Elias , Fairbanks), Yukon (Whitehorse, Kluane)*

Meredith Fitzgerald *Alaska (Juneau, Anchorage, and Ketchikan)*

Ken Fleming *San Juan Islands, Washington (Seattle), Victoria, Vancouver, Jasper*

Kate Galbraith *Orgeon (Ashland, Eugene, Portland), Washington (Olympic Peninsula, Mount St. Helens)*

Rita A. Hao *Manhattan, New Haven*

Alexandra Jacobs *California (Los Angeles, Orange County, San Diego, Big Sur, Santa Barbara)*

Ericka Kostka *California (Big Bear, Joshua Tree, Palm Springs, San Diego, Kings Canyon and Sequoia National Parks, Sierra Nevada)*

Benjamin Peskoe *Manhattan, Queens, Staten Island, Long Island*

Katherine Raff *Washington, D.C., Annapolis, MD*

Patrick La Rivière *Washington, D.C., Baltimore, MD*

David Rodgers *California (Avenue of the Giants, Gold Country, Lava Beds, Sacramento, Redwoods National Park), Nevada (Reno, Lake Tahoe)*

Michael Sonnenschein *Manhattan, Brooklyn, Bronx, Atlantic City*

Michael Shapiro *Ciudad Juárez*

Acknowledgments

We offer our greatest thanks to the people who helped make this book a reality: Mark Moody, Maia Gemmill, and John Ruark, who left us an organized legacy, Kevin Groszkowski for his map prowess, super ME Matt Heid who took care of us and our researchers, Alexis and Liz for fighting the Courier war, Pete K., Anne Chisholm, Sales Group, Dan Glover and Luiza for Canada, our regional editors Brian, Amy, Brooke, and Mary, and city editors Jim, and Tim, and all the regional RWs for their fantastic contributions, Toby Pyle of Hostelling International, Mike of Merchants Car Rental, Jed, Natalie, Peter and Brent, Mimi, Mike Ng, readers who sent in suggestions, the domestic room for answering countless queries (esp. Eleni, Mike C., Michael F., and Rachel), everyone in the office who helped us do justice to their home states, and our intrepid researchers, who now understand firsthand the beauty of free local calls. **—AHK, JC, SKD**

This book, and my best thoughts, are dedicated to the memory of Meredith J. Frummer 1974-1994. I will forever celebrate her love of life and language. Jeff's wry style and subliminal whisperings of "cut, cut" are responsible for the highly polished prose before us. Sean beats Widener reference for finding football mascots in 3 seconds flat. Thanks also to Michelle for holding my hand after I held hers, Mary for saving my sanity, Tanya and Haneen for bellydancing bliss, the domestic room for answering my questions, Livy, Emily, Sucharita, Alexa, the Divas, Gene, Mark Moody for knowing an NJ girl would love the Midwest, Sarah Youssof for fishboils and Cafe Latte, Neil for knowing I could do it, my second mother Linnett, Du for forcing me off the beaten path, my wonderful friends, and my always-supportive family—Mom, Pop, Eve, NS&G, AB&UM—who never let me forget that as much as I may travel, I can always come home. You are my harshest editors and my best friends. **—AHK**

Just a few quick words of thanks, to Matt H., Mary, Michael, the rest of the folks in the domestic room, Michelle Sullivan, Matt Ware, Jace Clayton, Brandon Earp, Caitlin Hurley, and especially Sean and Amelia. **—JC**

Thanks go first to my parents for their wonderful gametes. Thanks to Heather for her care, compassion, and short stint managing the Yankees. Amelia "Queen Bee" Kaplan, who got snookered by my interview suit, guided this book like the mighty clipper ships of ole. Aaargh. Matt Heid—can anyone defeat us? My R-Ws were some of the best stuff on earth—Annie "Oakley" Fulenwider, "Renfield" Soeiro, Steve "Soda Jerk" Janiak, and Stocky Stockman. Finally, the good fellas: Peter "The Quiche" Keith, "Cadillac" Jeff Collins, "Sausage Egger" Mike Farbiarz, "Rhode Island" Wilson, Tim "T-Bone" Perlstein, Alexis "Scroll Queen" Averbuck, Roy "The Dragon" Prieb, Mary "The Mad Hawaiian" Sadanaga, and Marc "Boom Boom" Zelanko. For the tolpuddle martyrs in Dallas, Ricky "Cat Bite" Dowlearn, Rob "Moo Chicken" McGhee, and Carol "The French Lover" Lanoux. **—SKD**

■ Staff

Editor	Amelia Hollander Kaplan
Associate Editor	Jeffrey Collins
Associate Editor	Sean K. Desmond
Managing Editor	Matt Heid
Publishing Director	Pete Keith
Production Manager	Alexis G. Averbuck
Production Assistant	Elizabeth J. Stein
Financial Manager	Matt Heid
Regional Guide Staffs	
Alaska & the Pacific Northwest	Brain J. Erskine
	Amy E. Cooper
California	Brooke A. Rogers
	Mary T. Sadanaga
New York City	James Dylan Ebenhoh
Washington, D.C.	Timothy S. Perlstein
Assistant General Manager	Anne E. Chisholm
Sales Group Manager	Sherice R. Guillory
Sales Department Coordinator	Andrea N. Taylor
Sales Group Representatives	Eli K. Aheto
	Timur Okay Harry Hiçyılmaz
	Arzhang Kamerei
	Hollister Jane Leopold
	David L. Yuan
President	Lucienne D. Lester
General Manager	Richard M. Olken

How To Use This Book

Let's Go: USA and Canada is not meant to be read on your couch. Because we believe in choosing your own adventure, this book is meant to guide you with all the necessary basics for your life on the road. The three sections of this guide will bring you to the best sources that allow you to stand on the edge of the Grand Canyon, plan a whitewater rafting trip, hike a mountain, cruise a scenic highway, or beat the crowds at Graceland. From there, it's up to you.

The opening section, **Essentials,** will help you before you leave, giving information on **Useful Organizations, Documents, Money, Health, Work and Study, Packing,** and **Specific Concerns** for women, gays and lesbians, and seniors. Consult the **Mileage** and **Price Charts** for planning trips between major cities.

In the second portion of the book, the **United States,** we divide all 50 states into 12 geographic regions, presented contiguously from east to west: **New England,** the **Mid-Atlantic,** the **South,** the **Great Lakes,** the **Great Plains, Texas,** the **Southwest,** the **Rocky Mountains,** the **Pacific Northwest, California, Hawaii,** and **Alaska.** Within each region, the states are presented geographically. Under each state heading, the biggest or most accessible city is listed first and other destinations fan out accordingly. **American Essentials** consists of two parts: **USA Essentials,** which has U.S.-specific travel information, and **American Culture,** which describes U.S. history, literature, and art. **Trips and Trails** highlights America's best highways.

Canada, the third section, is organized like the U.S. The 11 provinces are presented east to west: **New Brunswick, Nova Scotia, Newfoundland and Labrador, Prince Edward Island, Québec, Ontario,** the **Prairie Provinces, Alberta, British Columbia,** and the **Yukon.** Within the provinces, we start with the largest city and proceed geographically. **Canadian Essentials** provides information specific to Canada. The main Essentials section also has important Canada-related material. **Canadian Culture** contains insights into Canadian history, literature, and music.

For all of the destinations within the U.S. and Canada we normally provide information on **Accommodations, Food, Camping, Sights,** and **Entertainment.** We also tell you all the **Practical Information** you will need as a budgeteer, including how to get there, and once there, where to seek aid, transportation, and welcome faces. If you use the PI for nothing else, use it to make your way to the town's tourist office. Tourist offices exist to help travelers find their way by offering free services and information, usually with a smile. Go there first—they often give out free maps too. Our **Near** sections list interesting daytrips usually right outside town.

If you intend to travel extensively, you should get one of our regional guides, *Let's Go: Alaska & The Pacific Northwest* and *Let's Go: California & Hawaii,* or either of our city guides, *Let's Go: New York City* and *Let's Go: Washington, D.C.*

A NOTE TO OUR READERS

The information for this book is gathered by *Let's Go*'s researchers during the late spring and summer months. Each listing is derived from the assigned researcher's opinion based upon his or her visit at a particular time. The opinions are expressed in a candid and forthright manner. Other travelers might disagree. Those traveling at a different time may have different experiences since prices, dates, hours, and conditions are always subject to change. You are urged to check beforehand to avoid inconvenience and surprises. Travel always involves a certain degree of risk, especially in low-cost areas. When traveling, especially on a budget, you should always take particular care to ensure your safety.

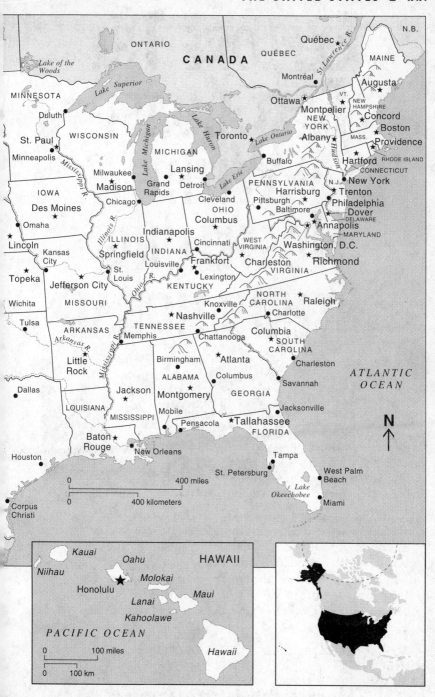

EXPLORE THE EAST COAST WITH HOSTELLING INTERNATIONAL

New York

Washington, DC

Miami Beach

With Hostelling International you can visit America's exciting East Coast at a budget price. Our low-cost, friendly hostels are great places to meet people from all over the world. You can stay in a landmark building on the dynamic Upper West Side of Manhattan, a highrise in the heart of the Nation's Capital or a historic masterpiece in Miami's Art Deco district in South Beach (SoBe), just two blocks from the ocean. For reservations call:

New York City .... (212) 932-2300
Washington, DC .... (202) 737-2333
Miami Beach .... (305) 534-2988

HOSTELLING INTERNATIONAL
The new seal of approval of the International Youth Hostel Federation.

ESSENTIALS

▓ Planning Your Trip

Every season is tourist season somewhere in the U.S. If you have a particular destination in mind, write to the local chamber of commerce or visitors bureau to find out about festivals which you might want to attend (or avoid if you're looking for a quiet vacation). Traveling during the off-season has its advantages, as transportation and accommodations may be cheaper, and sights won't be crawling with other tourists. Be sure to call ahead, because the sights might be closed. Also consider the weather when planning your vacation.

HOLIDAYS

Official holidays may mean extended hours at some tourist attractions, but many banks and offices will close for the day.

U.S. holidays in 1995 are: **New Year's Day,** Sun. Jan. 1; **Martin Luther King, Jr.'s Birthday,** Mon. Jan. 16 (observed); **Presidents Day,** Mon. Feb. 20 (observed); **Memorial Day,** Mon. May 29; **Independence Day,** Tues. July 4; **Labor Day,** Mon. Sept. 4; **Columbus Day,** Mon. Oct. 9; **Veterans Day (Armistice Day),** Fri. Nov. 10 (observed); **Thanksgiving,** Thurs. Nov. 23; **Christmas Day,** Mon. Dec. 25.

In **Canada,** official holidays for 1995 are: **New Year's Day,** Sun. Jan.1; **Easter Monday,** Mon. April 3; **Victoria Day,** Mon. May 22; **Canada Day,** Sat. July 1; **Thanksgiving,** Mon. Oct. 9; **Remembrance Day,** Fri. Nov. 10; **Christmas Day,** Mon. Dec. 25; **Boxing Day,** Tues. Dec. 26.

U.S. FESTIVALS

It can never be said the U.S. has passed up an opportunity to throw a party.
 New Year's Day (Jan. 1): Rose Bowl, Pasadena, CA; Orange Bowl, Miami, FL
 St. Patrick's Day (Mar. 17): St. Pat's Day Parade, New York City, NY.
 Mardi Gras (Feb. 7-14): New Orleans, LA.
 Independence Day (July 4): celebrations in Philadelphia, Boston, Washington, DC.
 Labor Day (Sept. 4): wherever the tourists are not.
 Thanksgiving (Nov. 23): Macy's Parade, New York City, NY.
 New Year's Eve (Dec. 31): Times Square, New York City, NY.

■■■ USEFUL ORGANIZATIONS AND PUBLICATIONS

As you plan your itinerary, read the section of the book which covers that region. Write to and visit **local chambers of commerce** and **visitors bureaus,** who will happily inundate you up with brochures, pamphlets, and other sorts of helpful information. There are also many organizations catering directly to budget travelers.

BUDGET TRAVEL SERVICES

Council on International Educational Exchange (CIEE), 5 E. 42nd St., New York, NY 10017 (212-661-1414). A private, not-for-profit organization, CIEE administers work, volunteer, academic, and professional programs around the world. They also offer identity cards (including the ISIC and the GO 25; see below) and a range of publications, among them the useful magazine *Student Travels* (free, postage $1) and *Going Places: The High School Student's Guide to*

Study, Travel, and Adventure Abroad ($13.95, postage $1.50). Call or write them for more information.

Council Travel, a subsidiary of CIEE, is an agency specializing in student and budget travel. They sell charter flight tickets, guidebooks, ISIC, ITIC, and GO 25 cards, hostelling cards, and travel gear. 41 U.S. offices, including Boston, Los Angeles, Chicago, Seattle, and the main office in **New York,** 205 E. 42nd St., New York, NY 10017 (212-661-1450). In the **United Kingdom,** contact 28A Poland St. (Oxford Circus), London WIV 3DB (tel. 0171 437 77 67). In **Canada** write to Travel CUTS (see below). Council Travel also has offices in **France,** 22 rue des Pyramides, Paris 75001 (tel. 1 44 55 55 44); and **Germany,** 18 Graf-Adolf-Strasse, 4000 Dusseldorf 1, (tel. 211 32 90 88).

STA Travel, 5900 Wilshire Blvd., Ste. 2110, Los Angeles, CA 90036 (800-777-0112). A student and youth travel organization with over 100 offices around the world offering discount airfare (for travelers under 26 and full-time students under 32), accommodations, tours, insurance, and ISICs. 11 offices in the U.S., including **Boston,** 297 Newbury St., MA 02116 (617-266-6014), **New York,** 48 E. 11th St., NY 10003 (212-447-7166), **Washington DC,** 2401 Pennsylvania Ave., 20037 (202-887-0912), and **San Francisco,** 51 Grant Ave., CA 94108 (415-391-8407). Internationally: **U.K.,** 86 Old Brompton Rd., London SW7 3LQ and 117 Euston RD., London NW1 2SX (tel. 0171 937 9971). **New Zealand,** 10 High St., Auckland (tel. 09 398 99 95). **Australia,** 222 Faraday St., Melbourne VIC 3053 (tel. 03 349 24 11).

Travel CUTS, 187 College St., Toronto, Ontario M5T 1P7 (416-798-CUTS, fax 416-979-8167). Canada's national student travel bureau and equivalent of CIEE, with 40 offices across Canada. Also in U.K., 295-A Regent St., London W1R 7YA (tel. 0171 637 31 61). Discounted domestic and international airfares open to all; special student fares to all destinations with valid ISIC. Issuing authority for ISIC, FIYTO, and HI hostel cards. Offers free *Student Traveller* magazine, as well as info on Student Work Abroad Program (SWAP).

Campus Travel, 52 Grosvenor Gardens, London SW1W 0AG (0171) 730 88 32; fax (0171) 730 57 39. 37 branches nationwide in the UK. Puts out booklets including travel suggestions, average prices, dates of local holidays, and other general information for British travelers in Europe and North America. Also offers a booking service via telephone: from London/Europe (tel. 0171 730 3402), from North America (tel. 0171 730 2101), worldwide (tel. 0171 730 8111).

Let's Go Travel, Harvard Student Agencies, Inc., 53-A Church St., Cambridge, MA 02138 (800-5-LETSGO or 617-495-9649). The world's largest student-run travel agency, Let's Go Travel is operated by the same students who published this book. Let's Go offers HI-AYH memberships, ISICs, International Teacher ID cards, FIYTO cards, every *Let's Go* book, maps, bargain flights, and a complete line of travel gear. All items available; call or write for a catalog (or see the color catalog in the center of *Let's Go: USA and Canada*).

PUBLICATIONS AND MAPS

Look for relevant publications and these useful sources in bookstores. If you're planning to drive in the U.S., good road maps and a U.S. atlas are essential. The maps in *Let's Go: USA and Canada* are intended for general orientation only.

Michelin Travel Publications, Michelin Tire Corporation, P.O. Box 19001, Greenville, SC 29602-90001 (800-423-0485, fax 803-458-5665). Publishes three major lines of travel-related material: Green Guides, for sight-seeing, maps, and driving itineraries; Red Guides, which rate hostels and restaurants; and detailed, reliable road maps and atlases. All three are available at bookstores in the U.S.

Travelling Books, P.O. Box 521491, Salt Lake City, UT 84152 (801-461-3345). Mail-order service specializing in travel guides, books, and accessories which make the armchair traveler weep with wanderlust. Call or write for a free catalog.

Rand McNally publishes one of the most comprehensive road atlases of the U.S., available in most bookstores for around $8, for mail orders call 800-333-0136; prices and postage vary.

Hippocrene Books, Inc., 171 Madison Ave., New York, NY 10016 (212-685-4371, orders 718-454-2366, fax 718-454-1391). Free catalog. Publishes travel reference books, travel guides, maps, and foreign language dictionaries.

Superintendent of Documents, U.S. Government Printing Office, P.O. Box 371954, Pittsburgh, PA 15250-7954 (202-783-3238, fax 202-272-2529). Publishes the helpful, regionally specific publication, *Tips for Travelers,* available for $1 from the address above.

Specialty Travel Index, 305 San Anselmo Ave., San Anselmo, CA 94960 (415-459-4900, fax 415-459-4974). Published twice yearly, this is an extensive listing of off-the-beaten-track and specialty travel opportunities. For copies or subscriptions, write to the address above.

■■■ DOCUMENTS & FORMALITIES

PASSPORTS

In case your passport is **lost or stolen,** be sure *before you leave* to photocopy the page of your passport that contains your photograph and identifying information. Especially important is your passport number. This information will facilitate the issuing of a new passport if your old one is lost or stolen. Put a copy of this information someplace far away from your passport, because in case of theft, you will still have the information. Lost or stolen passports require immediate notification of the local police and the nearest embassy or consulate of your government. Some consulates can issue new passports within two days if you give them proof of citizenship. In an emergency, ask for immediate temporary traveling papers that will permit you to return to your home country.

U.S. and Canadian citizens may cross the U.S.-Canada border with only proof of citizenship. U.S. citizens under 18 need the written consent of a parent or guardian; Canadian citizens under 16 need notarized permission from both parents.

Mexican citizens may cross into the U.S. with an I-186 form. Mexican border crossing cards (non-immigrant visas) prohibit you from staying more than 72 hours in the U.S., or traveling more than 25 mi. from the border.

British citizens can obtain a passport valid for 10 years (5 yrs. if under 16); apply in person or by mail to a passport office. There is an £18 fee. Children under 16 may be included on a parent's passport. Processing usually takes 4-6 weeks. The London office offers same-day, walk-in rush service; arrive early.

Irish citizens can apply for a passport by mail to the Department of Foreign Affairs, Passport Office, Setanta Centre, Molesworth St., Dublin 2 (tel. 01 671 1633). Passports cost £45 and are valid for 10 years. Citizens younger than 18 and older than 65 can request a 3-year passport that costs £10.

Australian citizens must apply for a passport in person at a local post office, a passport office, or an Australian diplomatic mission overseas. A parent may file an application for a child who is under 18 and unmarried. Application fees are adjusted every three months; call the toll-free info service for current details (tel. 13 12 32).

New Zealand offers passports good for 10 years. Contact the local Link Centre, travel agent, or New Zealand Representative for an application form, which must be completed and mailed to the New Zealand Passport Office, Documents of National Identity Division, Department of Internal Affairs, Box 10-526, Wellington (tel. 914 474 81 00). The application fee is NZ$130 (if under age 16, NZ$16).

U.S. AND CANADIAN ENTRANCE REQUIREMENTS

Foreign visitors to the United States and Canada are required to have a **passport, visa,** and **proof of intent to leave** (for example, an exiting plane ticket). To visit Canada, you must be healthy and law-abiding, and demonstrate ability to support yourself financially during your stay. To work or study in the U.S. or Canada, you must obtain special documents (see Work and Study).

Visas for the U.S.

Visitors from certain nations (including Japan and most of Western Europe) may enter the U.S. without visas through the **Visa Waiver Pilot Program.** Travelers qualify as long as they are traveling for business or pleasure, are staying for 90 days or less, have proof of intent to leave, and enter aboard particular air or sea carriers. Contact the nearest U.S. consulate for more information on visas.

Visas for Canada

Travelers who are staying for 90 days or less, have proof of intent to leave, and are citizens of Australia, the Bahamas, Barbados, Costa Rica, the EC, Singapore, Swaziland, the U.K., the U.S., Venezuela, Western Samoa, or Zimbabwe may enter Canada without visas. Contact the Canadian consulate for more info.

CUSTOMS

Passing customs should be routine, but take it seriously; don't joke around with customs officials or airport security personnel. To avoid problems when you transport prescription drugs, ensure that the bottles are clearly marked, and carry a copy of the prescription to show the customs officer. In addition, officials may seize articles made from protected species, such as certain reptiles and the big cats. It is also illegal to transport perishable food like fruit and nuts, which may carry pests.

Duty free, you may bring the following into the U.S.: $100 in gifts; 200 cigarettes, 50 cigars, or 2 kg of smoking tobacco; and personal belongings such as clothes and jewelry. Travelers ages 21 and over may also bring up to one liter of alcohol, although state laws may further restrict the amount of alcohol you can carry.

Money can be transported, but if you carry over $10,000, you'll need to report it. In general, customs officers ask how much money you're carrying and your planned departure date in order to ensure that you'll be able to support yourself while here.

HOSTEL MEMBERSHIP

Hosteling can be a fun and inexpensive way to travel. Some American hostels are independent, but many belong to the American Youth Hostels Association, which is associated with Hostelling International. The **International Booking Network** is a computerized reservation service available to HI members. With a call to any HI regional office or booking center, travelers can book overnight accommodations in over 120 hostels around the world (See Accommodations in Once There below).

Hostelling International (HI) is the new and universal trademark name adopted by the former International Youth Hostel Federation (IYHF). The more than 6000 official youth hostels worldwide will normally display the new HI logo (a blue triangle) alongside the symbol of one of the 70 national hostel associations. A one-year membership permits you to stay at youth hostels throughout the U.S. and Canada for between $5 and $22 a night. Travelers over 25 pay only a slight surcharge for a bed. You can save yourself potential trouble by procuring a membership card before you leave home, as some hostels do not sell them on the spot. For more information, contact HI or the affiliate in your country (listed below). For more information on hosteling, see Accommodations. **HI Headquarters,** 9 Guessens Rd., Welwyn Garden City, Hertfordshire, AL8 6QW, England (tel. 0171 33 24 87). This office publishes the *Hostelling North America Handbook,* a guide to hostels in the U.S. and Canada that is updated every year and free to members (available at bookstores, U.S.$6.95 for nonmembers).

Hostelling International-American Youth Hostels (HI-AYH), 733 15th St. NW, Suite 840, Washington, D.C., 20005 (202-783-6161; fax 202-783-6171); also has regional offices across the U.S. One-year membership $24, under 18 $10, over 54 $15. Contact HI-AYH for ISICs, student and charter flights, travel equipment, literature on budget travel, and info on summer positions as a group leader for domestic outings; to lead, you must first complete a seven-day, $350 course.

Hostelling International-Canada (HI-C), National Office, 400-205 Catherine St., Ontario, Canada K2P 1C3 (613-237-7884; fax 613-237-7884). Has 83 hostels. One-year membership CDN$26.75, under 18 CDN$12.84, two-year CDN$37.45.

Youth Hostels Association of England and Wales (YHA), Trevelyan House, 8 St. Stephen's Hill, St. Albans, Herts, AL1 2DY (tel. 44 727 855 215). Membership £9, under 18 £3.

An Oíge (Irish Youth Hostel Association), 61 Mountjoy Sq., Dublin 7, Ireland (tel. 01 304 555, fax 01 305 808). Membership £9, under 18 £3.

Australian Youth Hostels Association (AYHA), Level 3, 10 Mallett St., Camperdown, NSW, 2050 Australia (tel. 61 2 565 1699, fax 61 2 565 1253). Membership AUS$40, renewal AUS$24, under 18 AUS$12.

Youth Hostels Association of New Zealand (YHANZ), P.O. Box 436, 173 Gloucester St., Christ Church 1, New Zealand (tel. 64 3 379 99 70, fax 03 365 4476). Membership NZ$24.

YOUTH AND STUDENT IDENTIFICATION

Two main forms of student and youth identification are accepted worldwide; they are extremely useful, especially for the insurance packages that accompany them.

International Student Identity Card (ISIC) is $16. The 1995 card is valid from Sept. 1994-Dec. 1995. Present the card wherever you go, and ask about discounts even when none are advertised. Applicants must be 12 to 25 and attending a secondary or post-secondary school. The card provides accident insurance of up to $3000 as well as $100 per day of in-hospital care for up to 60 days. In addition, cardholders have access to a toll-free **Traveler's Assistance hotline** whose multilingual staff can provide help in medical, legal, and financial emergencies overseas. Many U.S. establishments will also honor an ordinary university student ID for student discounts, yet most overseas will not. See Useful Organizations above for some of the student travel offices which issue ISICs. When you apply for the card, ask for a copy of the *International Student Identity Card Handbook*, which lists some available discounts. Application requires current, dated proof of your degree-seeking student status (a letter on school stationery signed and sealed by the registrar or a photocopied grade report), a 1½" x 2" photo with your name printed and signed on the back, proof of your birthdate and nationality, and the name, address, and phone number of an insurance beneficiary.

International Youth Discount Travel Card or **Go 25 Card** is issued by the **Federation of International Youth Travel Organizations (FIYTO),** Bredgade 25H, DK-1260, Copenhagen K, Denmark (tel. 45 33 33 96 00, fax 45 33 93 96 76). Applicants must be under 26. The fee is $16, CDN$12, or £10. This One-year card offers many of the same benefits as the ISIC, and most organizations that sell the ISIC also sell the Go 25 Card. A brochure that lists discounts is free when you purchase the card. Application requires proof of birthdate (copy of birth certificate, a passport, or a valid driver's license) and a passport-sized photo with your name printed on the back.

INTERNATIONAL DRIVING PERMIT

Although not required in United States or Canada, the International Driving Permit can smooth out difficulties with American and Canadian police officers, and serves as an additional piece of identification. A valid driver's license from your home country must always accompany the IDP.

Your IDP must be issued in your own country before you depart (you can't get one here); check with your national automobile association. Also make sure you have proper insurance (required by law). Some foreign driver's licenses will be valid in the U.S. for up to one year (check before you leave). Members of national automobile associations affiliated with the American Automobile Association can receive services from the AAA while they're in the U.S. Check your club for details.

FOR THE BEST HOSTELS IN COLORADO CALL 303 442 0522 or FAX 303 442 0523

■■■ WORK AND STUDY

WORK

Job leads often come from local residents, hostels, employment offices, and chambers of commerce. Temporary agencies often hire for non-secretarial placement as well as for standard typing assignments. Marketable skills, i.e. touch-typing, dictation, computer knowledge, and experience with children, will prove very helpful (even necessary) in your search for a temporary job. Consult local newspapers and bulletin boards on local college campuses for job listings.

In The U.S.

Volunteer jobs are readily available almost everywhere in the U.S. Some jobs provide rooms and board in exchange for labor. Write to **CIEE** (see Useful Organizations) for *Volunteer! The Comprehensive Guide to Voluntary Service in the U.S. and Abroad* ($8.95 plus postage). CIEE also runs a summer travel/work program designed to provide students with the opportunity to spend their summers working in the U.S. University students studying in Australia, Canada, Costa Rica, the Dominican Republic, France, Germany, Ireland, Jamaica, New Zealand, Spain, and the United Kingdom are eligible: **Australia:** SSA, 200 Faraday St., 1st floor, Carlton 3053, (tel. 61 3 348 1930). **Canada:** CFS, 243 College St., Suite 500, Toronto, Ontario, M5T 2Y1 (416-977-3703). **Costa Rica:** OTEC, P.O. Box 323-1002, Paseo de los Estudiantes, San Jose, (tel. 506 22 08 66). **Dominican Republic:** Calle Luperon 51, esq. Hostos, Zona Colonial, 2nd floor, Santo Domingo, (809-687-7005). **France:** CIEE, Centre Franco-American Odeon, 1, place de l'Odeon, 87006 Paris, (tel. 33 1 44 41 74 74). **Germany:** CIEE, Thomas Mann Strasse 33, 53111 Bonn 1, (tel. 49 228 228 659 746 7). **Ireland:** USIT, 19 Aston Quay, Dublin 2, (tel. 353 1 778 117). **Jamaica:** JOYST, 9 Eureka Crescent, Kingston 5, (809-929-7928). **New Zealand:** STS (NZ), 10 High St., 1st floor, Auckland, (tel. 64 9 3099 723). **Spain:** CIEE, Carransa 7, 3-3 28004 Madrid, (tel. 34 1 594 1886). **United Kingdom:** BUNAC, 16 Bowling Green Lane, Clerkenwell, London EC1R OBD, (tel. 44 71 251 3472).

Foreign university-level students can get on-the-job technical training in fields such as engineering, computer science, agriculture, and natural and physical sciences from the **Association for International Practical Training,** which is the U.S. member of the **International Association for the Exchange of Students for Technical Experience (IAESTE).** You must apply through the IAESTE office at home; application deadlines vary. For more info, contact the local IAESTE or write to IAESTE, c/o AIPT, 10 Corporate Center, Suite 250, 10400 Little Patuxent Pkwy., Columbia, MD (410-997-2200). The **SCI-International Voluntary Service,** Rte. 2, Box 506B, Crozet, VA 22932 (804-823-1826), arranges placement in work camps in the U.S. for people over 16. Registration fees from $40 (U.S.) to $200 (former USSR).

Visa information: Working or studying in the U.S. with only a B-2 (tourist) visa is grounds for deportation. Before an appropriate visa can be issued to you, you must—depending on the visa category you are seeking—join a USIA-authorized Exchange Visitor Program (J-1 visa) or locate an employer who will sponsor you (usually an H-2B visa) and file the necessary paperwork with the Immigration and Naturalization Service (INS) in the United States on your behalf. In order to apply to the U.S. Embassy or Consulate for a J-1 visa, you must obtain an IAP-66 eligibility form, issued by a U.S. academic institution or a private organization involved in U.S. exchanges. The H-2 visa is difficult to obtain, as your employer must prove that there are no other American or foreign permanent residents already residing in the U.S. with your job skills. For more specific information on visa categories and requirements, contact the nearest U.S. embassy or consulate.

In Canada

Most of the organizations and the literature discussed above is not aimed solely at those interested in working in the U.S. Accordingly, many of the same programs which arrange volunteer and work programs in the U.S. are also active in Canada.

SEATTLE BACKPACKERS HOSTEL

WELCOMES YOU TO SEATTLE

Our Guests Receive:

- Free Parties
- Free Breakfast
- Free Coffee
- Free Linen
- Free Nightclub Passes
- Free Airport, Amtrak & Greyhound Pickup (From May - Sept. only)

Our Facilities Feature:

- Free Parking
- Coin Operated Laundry
- Equipped Kitchen with Microwave
- Central Location 10 Minutes from Downtown Seattle by Car or 15 Minutes by Foot.
- Cable TV
- No Curfew

♦ Dorm Room - $11, Single Room - $26, Double Room - $32 ♦

♦ Weekly Discounts ♦

♦ Visa, Mastercard & Traveler's Checks Accepted ♦

♦SEATTLE BACKPACKERS HOSTEL♦
1201 HOWELL STREET
SEATTLE, WASHINGTON 98102
(800) 600-2965 • (206) 720-2965

Write for the publications and contact the individual organizations which interest you most. **Travel CUTS** (see Budget Travel Services) may also help you out.

Visa information: If you intend to work in Canada, you will need an **Employment Authorization,** which must be obtained before you enter the country; visitors ordinarily are not allowed to change status once they have arrived. There is a $100 processing fee. Employment authorizations are only issued after it has been determined that qualified Canadian citizens and residents will not be adversely affected by the admission of a foreign worker. Your potential employer must contact the nearest **Canadian Employment Centre (CEC)** for approval of the employment offer. For more information, contact the consulate or embassy in your home country.

STUDY

If you are interested in studying in the U.S. or in Canada, there are a number of different paths you can take. One possibility is to enroll in a language education program, particularly if you are interested in a short-term stay. Contact **World Learning, Inc.,** P.O. Box 676, Brattleboro, VT 05302-0676 (802-257-7751), which runs the **International Students of English** program, offering intensive language courses at select U.S. campuses. The price of a four-week program averages $1800.

An excellent source of information on studying in the U.S., Canada, and abroad is the **Institute of International Education (IIE)** (212-883-8200), which administers many exchange programs. IIE publishes *Academic Year Abroad,* which describes over 2100 semester and academic-year programs offered by U.S. and foreign institutions in Canada and overseas ($43 plus $4 shipping), and *Vacation Study Abroad,* with information on 1500 short-term programs including summer and language schools ($37 plus shipping $4).

Visa information: Foreign students who wish to study in the U.S. must apply for either a J-1 visa (for exchange students) or a F-1 visas (for full-time students enrolled in an academic or language program). Neither the F-1 nor the J-1 visa specifies any expiration date; instead they are both valid for the duration of stay, which includes the length of your particular program and a brief grace period thereafter. Requests to extend a visa must be submitted 15-60 days before the departure date.

To study in Canada you will need a **Student Authorization** in addition to any entry visa you may need (see Documents and Formalities). To obtain one, contact the nearest Canadian Consulate or Embassy. Be sure to apply well ahead of time; it can take up to six months, and there is a fee of $75. You will also need to prove to the Canadian government that you are able to support yourself financially. A student authorization is good for one year. If you plan to stay longer, it is extremely important that you do not let it expire before you apply for renewal. Canadian immigration laws do permit full-time students to seek on-campus employment, but you will need to apply for an Employment Authorization. For specifics on official documentation, contact a Canadian Immigration Center (CIC) or consulate.

Residents of the U.S., Greenland, and St. Pierre/Miquelon may apply for Employment authorization or Student Authorization at a port of entry.

■ ■ ■ MONEY

Travelers should acquire some foreign currency before they leave home. This will allow you to breeze through the airport where exchange rates are generally abominable. Bank rates are usually preferable, but beware early closing hours. Most places in the U.S. do not accept foreign currency. Since you lose money with every transaction, it's wise to change larger sums of money less frequently.

TRAVELER'S CHECKS

Traveler's checks are the safest way to carry large sums of money. They are refundable if lost or stolen, and many issuing agencies offer additional services such as refund hotlines, message relaying, travel insurance, and emergency assistance. Buying checks in small denominations ($20 checks rather than $50 or higher) is safer

Don't forget to write.

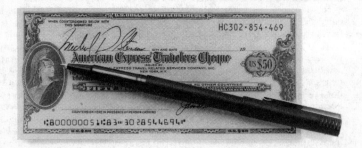

Now that you've said, "Let's go," it's time to say
"Let's get American Express® Travelers Cheques." If they are lost or
stolen, you can get a fast and full refund virtually anywhere you
travel. So before you leave be sure and write.

and more convenient. In less touristy regions have some cash on hand because smaller establishments may not accept traveler's checks. Bring along your passport any time you plan to use checks. Always keep your check receipts, a list of their serial numbers, and a record of which ones you've cashed separate from the checks themselves. This speeds up replacement if they are lost or stolen. Never countersign checks until you're prepared to cash them.

American Express (800-221-7282) in the U.S. and Canada; (tel. 0800 52 13 13) in the U.K., (tel. 00825 -902) in Australia, New Zealand, and the South Pacific. Elsewhere, call U.S. collect (801-964-6665). AmEx Travelers Cheques are the most widely recognized worldwide and easiest to replace if lost or stolen. Services are described in *The American Express Traveler's Companion* (free for customers). AmEx offices cash their own cheques commission-free. **American Automobile Association (AAA)** members can obtain AmEx Travelers Cheques commission-free at AAA offices.

Citicorp sells Visa traveler's checks. (800-645-6556) in the U.S. and Canada; from abroad call collect (813-623-17090. Commission is about 1-2% on check purchases. Check holders are automatically enrolled in **Travel Assist Hotline** (800-523-1199) for 45 days after checks are bought. This service provides travelers with English-speaking doctors, lawyers, and interpreter referrals as well as traveler's check refund assistance. Citicorp also has a **World Courier Service** which guarantees hand-delivery of traveler's checks anywhere in the world.

Mastercard International (800-223-9920) in the U.S. and Canada; from abroad call collect (609-987-7300). Commission varies from 1-2% for purchases depending on the bank. Issued in U.S. dollars only.

Thomas Cook (800-223-4030) for orders in the U.S; from elsewhere, call collect (212-974-5696). In cahoots with MC International, Thomas Cook handles the distribution of checks in U.S. dollars as well as ten other currencies. Some Thomas Cook Currency Services offices (located in major cities around the globe) do not charge any fee for purchase of checks.

CREDIT CARDS AND ATMS

Credit cards can be invaluable in a financial emergency. Foreign visitors can reduce conversion fees by charging a purchase instead of changing traveler's checks.

American Express (800-528-4800) has full service offers around the world and will honor personal checks of $1000-$5000 every seven days. Cardholders can also use AmEx offices as mailing stops for free. For lost or stolen cards call (800-528-4800). **Visa** and **Mastercard** sell credit cards through banks. For lost or stolen cards: Visa, (800-336-8472); Mastercard, (800-999-0454).

Automatic Teller Machines (abbreviated as ATMs) offer 24-hour service in banks, groceries, gas stations, and even in telephone booths across the U.S. Before you can use your bank card, be sure that your bank belongs to a network which has machines in the region you're headed for. The two largest networks are **PLUS** (800-843-7587) and **CIRRUS** (800-424-7787). ATMs often give one of the best rates of currency exchange, because they get the wholesale rate, which is generally 5% better than the retail rate most banks use.

SENDING MONEY

If you run out of money on the road, you can have more mailed to you in the form of **traveler's checks** bought in your name, a **certified check,** or through **postal money orders,** available at post offices (orders under $25, 75¢ fee; $700 limit per order; cash only). Certified checks are redeemable at any bank, while postal money orders can be cashed at post offices upon display of two IDs (one of which must be photo). Keep receipts since money orders are refundable if lost.

Wiring money, depending on the bank, costs about $30 for amounts less than $1000, plus the commission charged by your home bank. Once you've found a bank that will accept a wire, write or telegram your home bank with your account number, the name and address of the bank to receive the wire, and a routing num-

ber. Also notify the bank of the form of ID that the second bank should accept before paying the money. **Bank drafts** or **international money orders** are cheaper but slower. As a *very last* resort, **consulates** will wire home for you and deduct the cost from the money you receive.

Bank of America (800-346-7693) will **cable** money to any bank with a wire. Have someone bring cash, a credit card, or a cashier's check to the sending bank—you need not have an account. You can pick up the money with ID, and it will be paid out to you in U.S. currency. If you do not have a Bank of America account, there is a $40 fee for domestic cabling, $45 for international.

Western Union (800-325-6000) is a classic, time-honored, and expensive service. You or someone else can phone in a credit card number, or else bring cash to a Western Union office. As always, you need ID to pick up your money. Their charge is $29 to send $250, $40 for $500, $50 for $1000.

■■■ ALCOHOL AND DRUGS

You must be 21 to drink in the U.S. Even foreigners accustomed to no drinking age *will be carded* and will not be served without proper ID (preferably some government document; a driver's license suffices, but a passport is best). **In Canada, you must be 19,** except in Alberta, Manitoba, and Quebec, where you must be 18. Some areas of the United States are "dry," meaning they do not permit the sale of alcohol at all, while other places do not allow it to be sold on Sundays. Furthermore, some states require possession of a *liquor license.*

If you carry prescription drugs while you travel, it is vital to have a copy of the prescriptions itself readily accessible at country borders. The possession or sale of marijuana, cocaine, LSD, and most opiates are serious crimes in the U.S. and Canada.

■■■ HEALTH AND PACKING

In many places in the United States and Canada, **you can call 911 toll-free in case of medical emergencies.** In many rural areas, however, the 911 system has not yet been introduced; if 911 doesn't work, dial the **operator (0),** who will contact the appropriate emergency service.

BEFORE YOU GO

A **first-aid kit** should suffice for minor health problems on the road. Items to include are bandages, aspirin, antiseptic soap or antibiotic cream, a thermometer in a sturdy case, a Swiss Army knife with tweezers, moleskin (to prevent foot blisters), a decongestant, motion sickness remedy, medicine for diarrhea and stomach problems, sunscreen, insect repellent, burn ointment, and an elastic bandage.

Bring any **medication** you may need while away as well as a copy of the prescription and/or a statement from your doctor, especially if you will be bringing insulin, syringes, or any narcotics into the United States or Canada. Matching prescriptions with foreign equivalents may be difficult.

If you wear **glasses** or **contact lenses,** take an extra prescription and make plans with someone at home to send you a replacement pair in an emergency.

Any traveler with a medical condition that cannot be easily recognized (i.e. diabetes, epilepsy, heart conditions, allergies to antibiotics) may want to obtain a **Medic Alert Identification Tag.** Contact **Medic Alert Foundation,** P.O. Box 1009, Turlock, CA 95381-1009 (800-432-5378). Their internationally recognized tag indicates the nature of the bearer's problem and provides the number of Medic Alert's 24-hr. hotline which has information about the member's medical history. Lifetime membership (tag, annually updated wallet card, and 24-hr. hotline access) begins at $35.

Women on **birth control pills** should bring enough to allow for possible loss or extended stays. **Condoms** are widely available in the U.S. and Canada, but you may also want to stock up before you go. **Planned Parenthood** serves the U.S with counseling and birth control services. Call 800-230-7526 for the nearest clinic.

Abortion is legal in the U.S. and Canada. Some states restrict availability through waiting periods and parental consent requirements for minors. The **National Abortion Federation's hotline** (800-772-9100, Mon.-Fri. 9:30am-5:30pm) refers its callers to U.S. clinics that perform abortions.

The **HIV virus** that leads to AIDS is a concern for all travelers. AIDS is the leading cause of death among young men in New York City, Los Angeles, and San Francisco. The number of AIDS cases attributed to heterosexual contact has risen sharply in the past few years. Unprotected sex and sharing needles are leading causes for transmission. For more information call the **United States's Center for Disease Control's** main **AIDS hotline** (800-342-2437).

Before you leave, check and see whether your **insurance** policy (if you have one) covers medical costs incurred while traveling. Familiarity with your insurance policy can save you headaches and speed paperwork in cases of emergency. If you lack insurance, you may have trouble getting treated for conditions which are not emergencies. In an emergency, call the local hotline or crisis center listed in *Let's Go* under Practical Information for each area. Operators at these organizations have the numbers of public health organizations and clinics that treat patients without demanding proof that they can pay.

COMMON ILLS

Heatstroke is a real danger in warm weather travel. Heatstroke can begin without direct exposure to the sun. In the early stages of heatstroke, sweating stops, body temperature rises, and an intense headache develops, soon followed by mental confusion. To treat heatstroke, cool the victim off immediately with fruit juice or salted water, wet towels, and shade. In extreme cases, rush the victim to the hospital

In the desert, the body loses at least a gallon of liquid per day (two gallons during strenuous activity such as hiking), so keep drinking even when you're not thirsty. If you arrive from a cooler climate, allow yourself a couple of days to adjust to the heat. Thick-soled shoes and socks can help to keep feet comfortable on a hike during the summer as the sand can reach scorching temperatures. Whether you are driving or hiking, tote *two gallons of water per person per day*.

Before driving in the desert, make sure that your car has been recently serviced and carry water for the radiator.

Hypothermia is a result of exposure to cold and can occur even in the middle of the summer, especially in rainy or windy conditions. Body temperature drops rapidly, resulting in the failure to produce body heat. Other possible symptoms are uncontrollable shivering, poor coordination, and exhaustion followed by slurred speech, sleepiness, hallucinations, and amnesia. *Do not* let victims fall asleep if they are in advanced stages—if they lose consciousness, they might die.

Frostbite occurs in freezing temperatures. The affected skin will turn white, then waxy and cold. To counteract the problem, the victim should drink warm beverages, stay or get dry, and *gently and slowly warm* the frostbitten area in dry fabric or with steady body contact. NEVER rub frostbite—the skin is easily damaged.

Travelers in **high altitudes** should allow their body a couple of days to adjust to the lower atmospheric oxygen levels before engaging in any strenuous activity. Those new to high-altitude areas may feel drowsy, and one alcoholic beverage may have the same effect as three at a lower altitude.

For **diarrhea,** many people take with them over-the-counter remedies (such as Pepto-Bismol or Immodium). Since dehydration is the most common side effect of diarrhea, those suffering should drink plenty of fruit juice and pure water.

Lyme disease is a serious problem for hikers in the U.S., especially on the East Coast. Deer ticks carry Lyme disease, which is characterized by a circular rash of 2 inches or more around the bite. It can be treated with antibiotics if caught early on. Always *check your body for ticks* after any hike and avoid underbrush. Do not drink from mountain streams, because tapeworms and **giardia** can be acquired from untreated water. Giardia symptoms include swollen glands, fevers, rashes, digestive problems and anemia. Always boil your water or treat it with iodine, wear shoes, and spray on insect repellent.

PACKING

Before you leave, pack your bag and take it for a walk as if you're on the road already. At the slightest sign of heaviness, unpack something. A good general rule is to set out what you think you'll need, then take half of it.

A sturdy **backpack** with several external compartments is essential if you plan to cover a lot of ground on foot. Internal frames stand up to airline baggage handlers and can often be converted to shoulder bags; external frames distribute weight more evenly and lift the pack off your back. Whichever style you choose to buy, avoid extremely low economy prices (good packs usually cost at least $100). If checking a backpack on your flight, tape down loose straps, which can catch in the conveyer belt. A plastic bag packed inside your luggage will be useful for dirty laundry, as well as one to cover your knapsack when it rains. Wrap sharper items in clothing so they won't stab you or puncture your luggage, and pack heavy items along the inside wall if you're carrying a backpack.

A small **daypack** is also indispensable for plane flights, sight-seeing, carrying a camera and/or keeping some of your valuables with you. For more information on purchasing a backpack, see Camping and the Outdoors.

The **clothing** you bring will depend on when and where in the U.S. you're planning to travel. America is relatively casual clothing-wise, and any place formal enough to require a jacket and tie will likely be too expensive for a budget traveler anyhow. Weather more often than style will determine your mode of dress.

For warm, summer weather, t-shirts and shorts are the rule. Natural fibers and lightweight cottons are the best materials for hot weather. Start with several t-shirts, which take up virtually no space and over which you can wear a sweatshirt or sweater in case of a chilly night. Then pack a few pairs of shorts and jeans. Add underwear and socks, and you've got your essential wardrobe.

For colder, winter weather you need a few heavier layers. It's good to have at least one layer that will insulate while wet, such as polypropylene, polarfleece, or wool. Make sure your clothing can be washed in a sink and will survive a spin in the dryer.

In most parts of the U.S. and Canada, **rain gear** is essential; a rain poncho is cumbersome but lightweight.

Comfortable **shoes** are essential. In sunny climates, sandals or other light shoes serve well. It is often a good idea to bring an extra pair of walking shoes in case your first gets wet. For heavy-duty hiking, sturdy lace-up walking boots are necessary. Make sure they have good ventilation. Leather-reinforced nylon hiking boots are particularly good for hiking and for walking in general: they're lightweight, rugged and dry quickly. A double pair of **socks**—light absorbent cotton inside and thick wool outside—will cushion feet, keep them dry, and help prevent blisters. Bring a pair of light flip-flops for protection against the fungal floors of some stations and hostels.

There are many other useful items which you may not think you would need or might easily forget, including: flashlight, pens and paper, perhaps a travel journal, travel alarm, canteen or water bottle, Ziploc bags (for isolating damp or dirty clothing), garbage bags, sewing kit, string, safety pins, tweezers, a pencil with some electrical tape wound around it for patching tears, rubber bands, sturdy plastic containers (for soap and detergent, for example), a padlock, a pocketknife, earplugs for noisy hostels, waterproof, strike-anywhere matches, clothespins and a length of cord, sunglasses, sunscreen, toilet paper (not all bathrooms are well-equipped), and the other essential toiletries. A rubber squash ball or a golf ball is a universal sink stopper, and either liquid soap or shampoo will do for handwashing clothes.

■■■ SPECIAL CONCERNS

WOMEN AND TRAVEL

Women exploring any area on their own inevitably face additional safety concerns. In all situations it is best to trust your instincts: if you'd feel better somewhere else, don't hesitate to move on. You may want to consider staying in hostels which offer single rooms which lock from the inside, YWCAs, or religious organizations that offer rooms for women only. Stick to centrally located accommodations and avoid late-night treks or subway rides.

Hitchhiking is *never* safe for lone women, or even for two women traveling together. Choose train compartments occupied by other women or couples.

The less you look like a tourist, the better off you'll be. In general, dress conservatively, especially in more rural areas. If you spend time in cities, you may be harassed no matter how you're dressed. Look as if you know where you're going (even when you don't) and ask women or couples for directions if you're lost or if you feel uncomfortable. Your best answer to verbal harassment is no answer at all (a reaction is what the harasser wants). Wearing a conspicuous wedding band may help prevent such incidents. Don't hesitate to seek out a police officer or a passerby if you are being harassed. *Let's Go* lists emergency numbers (including rape crisis lines) and women's centers in the Practical Information section of most cities.

Stay in well-lit places and out of dark alleys and avoid late-night treks or subway rides. Always carry change for the phone and extra money for a bus or taxi. Carry a whistle or an airhorn on your keychain, and don't hesitate to use it in an emergency. All of these warnings and suggestions should not discourage women from traveling alone. Don't take unnecessary risks, but don't lose your spirit of adventure either.

As a general resource, the **National Organization for Women** can refer women travelers to rape crisis centers, counselling services, and provide lists of feminist events in the area. There are branches across the country including: 22 W 21st St., 7th floor, New York, NY 10010, (212-807-0721); 425 13th St. NW, Washington DC 20004 (202-234-4558); 3543 18th St., San Francisco, CA 94110 (415-861-8880). To read more about women traveling, check out these resources:

Places of Interest to Women, Ferrari Publications, P.O. Box 35575, Phoenix, AZ, (602-863-2408) $8.

Handbook for Women Travelers, by Maggie and Gemma Moss. Encyclopedic and well-written (£8.99), from Piaktus Books, 5 Windmill St., London W1P 1HF (tel. 0171 631-01710).

Wander Women, 136 N. Grand Ave., #237, West Covina, CA 91790, (818-966-8857). A travel networking organization for women over 40. Publishes the quarterly newsletter *Journal 'n Footnotes.* Membership US$29 per year.

Women Going Places is a women's travel and resource guide emphasizing women-owned enterprises. Geared toward lesbians, but offers advice appropriate for all women. US$14 from Inland Book Company, P.O. Box 12061, East Haven, CT 06512 (203-467-4257), or order from a local bookstore.

A Journey of One's Own, by Thalia Zepatos (Eighth Mountain Press $14.95). The latest source on the market, interesting and full of good advice, plus a specific and manageable bibliography of books and resources.

OLDER TRAVELERS AND SENIOR CITIZENS

Seniors are eligible for a wide range of discounts on transportation, museums, movies, theater, concerts, restaurants, and accommodations. Proof of age is usually required (e.g., a driver's license, Medicare card, or membership card from a recognized society of retired persons). Resources include:

AARP (American Association of Retired Persons), 601 E St. NW, Washington, DC 20049 (202-434-2277). U.S. residents over 50 and their spouses receive benefits including the AARP Travel Experience from American Express (800-927-

0111), the AARP Motoring Plan from Amoco (800-334-3300), and discounts on lodging, car rental, and sightseeing. Annual fee, US$8 per couple.

Golden Age Passport ($10 lifetime pass available at park entrance). Available to U.S. citizens 62 and over. Entitles you to free entry into all national parks and a 50% discount on recreational activities.

National Council of Senior Citizens, 1331 F St. NW, Washington, DC 20004 (202-347-8800). Memberships are US$12 a year, $30 for three years, or $150 for a lifetime. Individuals or couples can receive hotel and auto rental discounts, a senior citizen newspaper, use of a discount travel agency, supplemental Medicare insurance (if you're over 65), and a mail-order prescription drug service.

Unbelievably Good Deals and Great Adventures That You Absolutely Can't Get Unless You're Over 50, by Joan Rattner Heilman. A good read, with great tips on senior discounts and the like. Contemporary Books, US$7.95

Gateway Books, 2023 Clemens Rd., Oakland, CA 94602, (510-530-0299, fax 510-530-0497). Publishes *Get Up and Go: A Guide for the Mature Traveler* (US$10.95).

TRAVELERS WITH DISABILITIES

Planning a trip presents extra challenges to individuals with disabilities, but the difficulties are by no means insurmountable. Hotels and motels have become more and more accessible to disabled persons, and exploring the outdoors is often feasible. Call ahead to restaurants, hotels, parks, and other facilities to find out about the existence of ramps, the widths of doors, the dimensions of elevators, etc.

Hertz, Avis, and **National** car rental agencies have hand-controlled vehicles at some locations (see By Car). **Amtrak** trains and all **airlines** can better serve disabled passengers if notified in advance; tell the ticket agent when making reservations which services you'll need. **Greyhound** allows a traveler with disabilities and a companion to ride for the price of a single fare with a doctor's statement confirming that a companion is necessary. Wheelchairs, seeing-eye dogs, and oxygen tanks are not deducted from your luggage allowance. A free booklet entitled, *Access Travel: Air-*

ports, replete with info on the accessibility of airports across the globe, is available from Federal Consumer Information Center, Pueblo, CO 81009.

If you're planning to visit a national park, get a **Golden Access Passport** ($20) at the park entrance. This exempts disabled travelers and their families from the entrance fee and allows a 50% discount on recreational activity fees.

Directions Unlimited, 720 N. Bedford Rd., Bedford Hills, NY 10507 (800-533-5343 or 914-241-1700, fax 914-241-0243). Specializes in arranging individual and group vacations, tours, and cruises for those with disabilities.

The Guided Tour, Elkins Park House, Suite 114B, 7900 Old York Road, Elkins Park, PA 19117-2339 (215-635-2637 or 800-738-5841). Organizes travel programs, domestic and international, for persons with developmental and physical disabilities as well as those requiring renal dialysis.

Society for the Advancement of Travel for the Handicapped, 347 Fifth Ave., Suite 610, New York, NY 10016 (212-447-7284, fax 212-725-8253). Publishes quarterly travel newsletter *SATH News* and information booklets (free for members, $3 each for nonmembers). Advice on trip planning for people with disabilities. Annual membership $45, students and seniors $25.

Twin Peaks Press, P.O. Box 129, Vancouver, WA 98666 (206-694-2462, orders only 800-637-2256, fax 206-696-3210). *Travel for the Disabled* lists tips and resources for disabled travelers ($20). Also available are the *Directory for Travel Agencies of the Disabled* ($20) and *Wheelchair Vagabond* ($15). Postage US$2 for first book, $1 for each additional.

BISEXUAL, GAY, AND LESBIAN TRAVELERS

Prejudice against bisexuals, gays, and lesbians still exists in many areas of the U.S. and Canada. In many areas, public displays of homosexual affection are illegal. On the other hand, acceptance is growing. San Francisco, Los Angeles, New York, New Orleans, Atlanta, and Montréal have large, active gay and lesbian communities. Legislation to make discrimination on the basis of sexual orientation (in hiring, for example) a civil rights violation is being debated in several states.

Whenever available, *Let's Go* lists local gay and lesbian hotline numbers, which can provide counseling and crisis and social information for bisexual, gay, and lesbian visitors. *Let's Go* also lists local gay and lesbian hotspots whenever possible.

Ferrari Publications, P.O. Box 37887, Phoenix, AZ 85069 (602-863-2408). Publishes *Ferrari's Places of Interest* ($15), *Ferrari's for Men* ($14), *Ferrari's for Women* ($12), and *Inn Places: US and Worldwide Gay Accommodations* ($15).

Damron, P.O. Box 422458, San Francisco, CA 94142 (800-462-6654 or 415-255-0404). The *Damron Address Book* ($14) lists over 8000 bars, restaurants, guest houses, and services catering to the gay male community. Covers the U.S., Canada, and Mexico. *The Damron Road Atlas* ($13) includes color maps of 56 major U.S. and Canadian cities and gay and lesbian resorts, and listings of bars and accommodations. *The Women's Traveller* ($10) is a guide for the lesbian community, including maps of 50 major U.S. cities, and lists bars, restaurants, accommodations, bookstores, and services. Shipping is $4 per book in the U.S.

Gayellow Pages, available from Renaissance House, P.O. Box 533, Village Station, New York, NY 10014 (212-674-0120). USA/Canada edition $12. Lists accommodations, resorts, hotlines, and other items of interest to gay travelers.

Giovanni's Room, 345 S. 12th St., Philadelphia, PA 19107 (215-923-2960; fax 215-923-01813). International feminist, lesbian, and gay bookstore with mail-order service which carries many of the publications listed here.

KOSHER AND VEGETARIAN TRAVELERS

Travelers who keep **kosher** should contact synagogues in the larger cities for information on kosher restaurants; your own synagogue or college Hillel should have access to lists of Jewish institutions across the nation. If you are strict in your observance, consider preparing your own food. *The Jewish Travel Guide* lists Jewish institutions, synagogues, and kosher restaurants in over 80 countries and is available

SAN FRANCISCO

OFFICE 346·5786   GUEST 673·4048

THE GLOBETROTTER'S INN

NO CURFEW
NO LINEN FEE

FREE COFFEE

FRIENDLY
RELAXED ATMOSPHERE

·Clean rooms
·Fully equipped kitchen dining room and common room
·Laundry facilities

GREAT LOCATION ONLY ONE MINUTE WALK FROM BUS AND TUBE. ONE BLOCK FROM CABLE CARS AND UNION SQUARE. ACROSS STREET FROM AIRPORTER BUS, LEAVING EVERY TWENTY MINUTES.

$12 per person shared

$24 single

$75 weekly

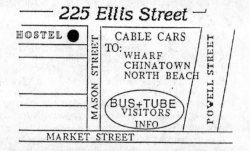

— 225 Ellis Street —

HOSTEL ●

MASON STREET

CABLE CARS TO: WHARF CHINATOWN NORTH BEACH

BUS+TUBE VISITORS INFO

POWELL STREET

MARKET STREET

WELCOME• WILKOMMEN• BIENVENUE

in the U.S. from Sepher-Hermon Press, 1265 46th St., Brooklyn, NY 11219 (718-972-9010), for $12 plus $1.75 shipping, and in the U.K. from Jewish Chronicle Publications, 25 Furnival St., London EC4A, England.

You should have no problem finding vegetarian cuisine in North America. Most restaurants have vegetarian selections on their menus, and some cater specifically to vegetarians. *Let's Go* notes restaurants with good vegetarian selections in the appropriate city listings. Contact the **North American Vegetarian Society** at P.O. Box 72, Dolgeville, NY 13329 (518-568-7970) for information.

Getting There and Getting Around

■■■ BY AIR

COMMERCIAL AIRLINES

When dealing with any commercial airline, buying in advance is best. To obtain the cheapest fare, buy a round-trip ticket and stay over at least one Saturday; traveling on off-peak days (Mon.-Thurs. morning) is usually $30-40 cheaper than traveling on the weekends. Any change in plans incurs a fee of between $25 (for some domestic flights) and $150 (for many international flights), even if only to change the date of departure or return. Since travel peaks June-August and around holidays, reserve a seat several months in advance for these times.

The commercial carriers's lowest regular offer is the **Advanced Purchase Excursion Fare (APEX);** specials advertised in newspapers may be cheaper, but may also have more restrictions and fewer available seats. APEX fares provide you with confirmed reservations and often allow "open-jaw" tickets (landing and returning from different cities). APEX tickets must usually be purchased two to three weeks ahead of the departure date. Be sure to inquire about any restrictions on length of stay (the minimum is most often seven days, the maximum two months; shorter or longer stays usually mean more money).

It is not wise to buy "free" tickets (i.e. **frequent-flyer coupons** given by airlines allowing the passenger named on them to fly a stated number of miles) from other people—it is standard policy on most commercial airlines to check a photo ID, and you could find yourself paying for a new, full-fare ticket.

Getting bumped: Airlines often overbook. If your travel plans are flexible, consider giving up your seat when the airline asks for volunteers—you will probably leave on the next flight and receive either a free ticket or a cash bonus.

Be sure to check with your travel agent for system-wide air passes and excursion fares, especially since these generally have fewer advance-purchase requirements than standard tickets. Consider **discount travel agencies** (see Useful Organizations, above), which sometimes have special deals that regular travel agents can't offer.

Within North America

There is *no smoking* on any flight under six hours within and between the U.S. states. There is no smoking on any aircraft registered in Canada, including international service from Canada.

Given the large distances between points within the United States and Canada, North Americans travel less on buses and trains and more on airplanes. Buses and trains take much longer and do not always confer a savings equal to the added trouble (a cross-country trip will take three or four days, compared with seven hours by

plane). Flying and driving are more common than riding buses and trains. A few major airlines serving the U.S. and Canada are listed below, together with sample fares:

America West, 4000 E. Sky Harbor Blvd. Phoenix, AZ 85034 (800-235-9292). In summer 1994, fares included NYC to LA $425 round-trip, flying mid-week with a 7-day advance purchase and Saturday stay.

Northwest Airlines, Customer Relations M.S. SC 5270, 5101 Northwest Dr., St. Paul, MN 55111 (800-225-2525). In summer 1994, round-trip fares included NYC to Los Angeles $418 with max. stay of 30 days; Los Angeles to Toronto $352 with 14-day advance purchase.

United Airlines, P.O. Box 66100, Chicago, IL 60666 (800-241-6522). Major domestic carrier. In summer 1994 London to NYC $740.

Air Canada, P.O. Box 14000, St. Laurent, Québec H4Y1H4 (800-776-3000). Ask about special discounts for ages 12-24 on stand-by tickets for flights within Canada. Discounts can be substantial, but youth tickets can be more expensive than advance purchase fares. In summer 1994, round-trip fares included Montréal to Seattle $551; Montréal to Halifax $295; Montréal to Vancouver $413. All tickets are 14-day advance purchases with Saturday stay and max. stay of 1 year.

Air Passes

Many major U.S. airlines offer special **Visit USA** air passes and fares to international travelers. You must purchase these passes in Europe, paying one price for a certain number of flight coupons. Each coupon is good for one flight segment on an airline's domestic system within a certain time period; typically, all travel must be completed within 30-60 days. Some cross-country trips may require two segments. The point of departure and the destination must be specified for each coupon at the time of purchase, and once in the U.S., any change in route will incur a fee of between $50 and $75. Dates of travel may be changed once travel has begun at no extra charge. **USAir** offers vouchers for the East coast ($589-649) and all 48 states ($649-679). **United, Continental, Delta,** and **TWA** also offer programs.

From Europe

Inexpensive seats are best found during the off-season, generally October until April. Higher peak rates take effect in mid-May or early June and run until mid-September. Take advantage of cheap off-season flights within Europe to reach an advantageous point of departure for North America. (London is a major connecting point for budget flights to the U.S.; New York City is often the destination.)

Charter agencies or ticket consolidators offer the cheapest tickets, but often with restrictions (see below). Commercial airlines provide greater reliability, security, and flexibility. Many major airlines offer reduced-fare options, such as youth (under 24) fares which can only be purchased within 72 hours of the time of the departure. **TWA** and **British Airways** both offer these fares on many international flights. Seat availability is known only a few days before the flight, although airlines will sometimes issue predictions. The worst crunch leaving Europe takes place from mid-June to early July, while August is uniformly tight for returning flights; at no time can you count on getting a seat right away. Call airlines for specific flight restrictions.

APEX is the lowest regular offer (see the beginning of this section). APEX normally requires a minimum stay of seven to 14 days and a maximum stay of 60 to 90 days. You must purchase your ticket between seven and 21 days in advance and it is almost always non-refundable. For summer travel, book APEX fares early; by June you may have difficulty getting the departure date you want. **American,** 15 Berkeley St., London W1A 6ND, often has good fares from London: 1994 rates included London to NYC for $629 peak-season and $348 off-season, with a maximum stay of one year. **British Airways,** P.O. Box 10, Heathrow Airport (London), Hounslow TW6 2JA, England (800-247-9297), has extensive service from London to North America. 1994 fares included London to NYC for $653 peak-season and $545 off-season; Lon-

don to Seattle $793/684; London to Montréal $717/576. Fares are 14- to 21-day advance purchase, leaving mid-week with a Saturday stop-over.

Smaller, budget airlines often undercut major carriers by offering bargain fares on regularly scheduled flights. Competition for seats on these smaller carriers during peak season is fierce—book early. Discount trans-Atlantic airlines include **Virgin Atlantic Airways** and **Icelandair.** Virgin Atlantic's fares from London to NYC range between $457-690, depending on the season, with 21-day advance purchase, mid-week travel and a Saturday stop-over; prices to Boston are equivalent. Icelandair flies heavily into and out of Luxembourg; all trans-Atlantic flights connect via Iceland.

From Australia and New Zealand

A good place to start searching for tickets is the local branch of one of the budget travel agencies listed under Useful Organizations. STA Travel is probably the largest international agency you will find: they have offices in Sydney, Melbourne, and Auckland. **Qantas, Air New Zealand, United,** and **Northwest** fly between Australia or New Zealand and the United States, and both **Canadian Pacific Airlines** and **Northwest** fly to Canada. Prices are roughly equivalent among the five (American carriers tend to be a bit less), but the cities they serve differ. A typical fare from Sydney to Los Angeles is $1457 peak-season and $1184 off-season, from Sydney to Toronto $2378/2004. Advance purchase fares from Australia have extremely tough restrictions. If you are uncertain about your plans, pay extra for an advance purchase ticket that has only a 50% penalty for cancellation. Travelers from Australia and New Zealand might also consider taking **Singapore Air** or another Far-East based carrier during the initial leg of their trip. Check with STA or another budget agency for more comprehensive information.

CHARTER FLIGHTS

Charter flights can save you a lot of money if you can afford to be flexible. Many charters book passengers up to the last minute—some will not even sell tickets more than 30 days in advance. However, many flights fill up well before their departure date. You must choose your departure and return dates when you book, and you will lose all or most of your money if you cancel your ticket. Charter companies themselves reserve the right to change the dates of your flight or even cancel the flight a mere 48 hours in advance. Delays are not uncommon. To be safe, get your ticket as early as possible, and arrive at the airport several hours before departure time. Many of the smaller charter companies work by contracting service with commercial airlines, and the length of your stay is often limited by the length of the company's contract. Prices and destinations can change (sometimes markedly) from season to season, so be sure to contact as many organizations as possible in order to get the best deal. For more information, contact **CIEE Travel Services** or **Travel CUTS** (see Budget Travel Services).

TICKET CONSOLIDATORS AND COURIERS

Ticket consolidators sell unbooked commercial and charter airline seats; tickets through them are both less expensive and more risky than those on charter flights. Companies work on a space-available basis which does not guarantee a seat; you get priority over those flying stand-by but below that of regularly-booked passengers. Although consolidators which originate flights in Europe, Australia, or Asia are scarce, the market for flights within North America is a good one, and growing. Consolidators tend to be reliable on these domestic flights, both in getting you on the flight and in getting you exactly where you want to go. Flexibility is often necessary, but all companies guarantee that they will put you on a flight or refund your money. On the day of the flight, the earlier you arrive at the airport the better, since ticket agents seat passengers in the order that they've checked them in. Courier services offer discount tickets, but allow space for carry-on luggage only.

WHO SAYS YOU NEED A CAR IN L.A. ?

At Hostelling International–Los Angeles/Santa Monica everything is convenient and hassle-free.

- Open 24 hours
- 1 block from one of California's legendary beaches
- 2 blocks from more than 100 chic sidewalk cafes and restaurants, comedy and movie theaters, popular pubs, and trendy shops
- $.75 bus ride from Los Angeles International Airport
- Daily doings at the hostel, including barbecues, movies and more
- Regularly scheduled trips to Disneyland and Universal Studios
- Couples rooms available with advance reservations
- Easy Reservations via telephone, fax, IBN

For information and reservations write Hostelling International–Los Angeles/Santa Monica, 1436 Second Street, Santa Monica, California USA 90401, FAX (310) 393-1769; or call (310) 393-9913

HOSTELLING INTERNATIONAL

The new seal of approval of the International Youth Hostel Federation. HOSTELLING INTERNATIONAL

Now Voyager, 74 Varick St. #307, New York, NY 10013 (212-431-1616), boasts reliability which rivals that of most charter companies (97% of customers get on their flights the first time), while its prices are still considerably less. Offers confirmed flights and voucher flights, where you pay $35 (deducted from ticket), go to airport with a list of flights, and try to get on stand-by. Also offers courier service, where you get 70% off a ticket, but are only allowed carry-on luggage. NYC to LA $125-200 each way; NYC to Chicago $75-104; NYC to San Francisco $203. Flights run out of and into NYC and Houston. (Phones open Mon.-Fri. 10am-5:30pm, Sat. noon-4:30pm, EST.)

Airhitch, 2472 Broadway #200, New York, NY 10025 (212-864-2000 on the East Coast; 310-394-0550 on the West Coast), works through more cities and to a greater number of destinations, although their prices are slightly higher and flights are less destination-specific (meaning that often you must list 2 or 3 cities within a given region which you are willing to fly to; Airhitch guarantees only that you will get to one of them). For domestic flights you must give a range of three days on either end within which you are willing to travel. Be sure to read *all* the fine print. The aptly named "Calhitch" program connects NYC with L.A. and San Francisco for $129; "Hawaiihitch" connects L.A. with Oahu and Maui for $129; "USAhitch" connects NYC with Miami ($79), Chicago ($79), San Juan (call for availability), and Orlando ($79). All fares are one way in either direction.

Air Tech, 584 Broadway #1007, New York, NY 10012 (212-219-7000). Domestic travelers must give a 2-day travel window. Flights primarily out of NYC (call for possible Boston departures). To: LA or San Francisco $129, Chicago $79, and Oct.-April Florida $79. To Europe $169 with a 5-day window.

Unitravel, 1177 N. Warson Rd., St. Louis, MO 63132 (800-325-2222, fax 314-569-2503). Specializes in trans-continental (mostly Europe). In the U.S., mostly coast-to-coast and to Florida. Restrictions depend upon the airline they contract.

■■■ BY TRAIN

Locomotion is still one of the cheapest ways to tour the U.S. and Canada. You can walk from car to car to stretch your legs, buy overpriced edibles in the snack bar, and shut out the sun to sleep in a reclining chair and avoid paying for a roomette or bedroom. It is essential to travel light on trains; not all stations will check your baggage and not all trains carry large amounts.

Amtrak (800-872-7245), 60 Massachusetts Ave. N.E., Washington D.C. 20002, is the main provider of train service. Most cities have Amtrak offices which directly sell tickets, but in some small towns with unmanned platforms, you must buy tickets through an agent. *Advance purchase is much cheaper, so plan ahead and make reservations early.* For price information to 19 major cities, see **Price Chart** below. Amtrak offers **discounts** off its full fares: children under 15 accompanied by a parent (½-fare); children under age two (free); senior citizens (15% off for travel Mon.-Thurs.) and travelers with disabilities (25% off); current members of the U.S. armed forces and active-duty veterans (25% discount) and their dependents (12.5% discount). Two-week advance purchase, circle trips, and special holiday packages can also save money. Keep in mind that discounted air travel, particularly on longer trips, may be cheaper than train travel. For up-to-date info and reservations, call your local Amtrak office or 800-872-7245 (use a touch-tone phone).

Amtrak's **All-Aboard America** fare divides the Continental U.S. into three regions—Eastern, Central, and Western. Amtrak charges the same rate for one-way and round-trip travel, with three stopovers permitted and a maximum trip duration of 45 days. During the summer, rates are $198 within one region, $278 within and between two regions, and $338 among three (late Aug.-mid-Dec. and Jan.-mid-June, rates are $178, $238, and $278). Drawing a line from Chicago south roughly divides the Eastern region from the Central; drawing a north-south line through Denver roughly divides the Central and Western regions. Your itinerary, including both cities and dates, must be set at the time the passes are purchased; the route may not be changed once travel has begun, though the times and dates may be changed at no

cost. All-Aboard fares are subject to availability; reserve two to three months in advance for summer travel.

The **USA Rail Pass,** a discount option available only to those who aren't citizens of North America, allows unlimited travel and unlimited stops over a period of either 15 or 30 days. As with All-Aboard America, the cost of this pass depends on the number of regions within which you wish to travel. The pass allowing 30 days of travel nationwide sells for $399 peak season/$319 off-season; the 15-day nationwide pass is $318/218. The 30-day pass which limits travel to the western region only (as far east as Denver) is $239/219; the 15-day pass for the western region is $188/168; the 30-day pass which limits travel to the eastern region (as far west as Chicago) is $239/219; and the 15-day pass for the eastern region is $188/168.

The **Air-Rail Travel Plan,** offered by Amtrak in conjunction with United Airlines, allows you to travel in one direction by train and then fly home, or to fly to a distant point and then return home by train. The train-portion of the journey allows up to three stopovers, and you have 180 days to complete your travel. The transcontinental plan, which allows coast-to-coast travel originating in either coast, sells for $550 peak season and for $463 off-season. The East Coast plan, which allows travel roughly as far west as Atlanta, is $381/337. The West Coast plan, allowing travel roughly as far east as Tucson, AZ, sells for $370/320. A multitude of variations on these plans are available as well; call for details.

For information on train travel in **Canada,** see the Canada Essentials Section.

■■■ BY BUS

Buses generally offer the most frequent and complete service between the cities and towns of the U.S. and Canada. Often they are the only way to reach smaller locales without a car. The exceptions are some rural areas and more open spaces where bus lines tend to be equally sparse. Your biggest challenge when you travel by bus is scheduling. *Russell's Official National Motor Coach Guide* ($12.80 including postage) is an indispensable tool for constructing an itinerary. Updated each month, *Russell's Guide* contains schedules of literally every bus route (except Greyhound) between any two towns in the United States and Canada. Russell's also publishes a semiannual *Supplement,* which includes a Directory of Bus Lines, Bus Stations, and Route Maps ($5 each). To order any of the above, write Russell's Guides, Inc., P.O. Box 278, Cedar Rapids, IA 52406 (319-364-6138, fax 319-364-4853).

Greyhound (800-231-2222 in the U.S.) P.O. Box 660362, Dallas, TX 75266-0362, operates the largest number of routes in both the U.S. and Canada, though local bus companies may provide more extensive services within specific regions. Schedule information can be obtained from any Greyhound terminal, or call (800-231-2222). For price information to 19 major cities, see **Price Chart** below. Greyhound is implementing a reservation system which will allow you to call and reserve a seat or purchase a ticket by mail. If you call seven days or more in advance and want to purchase your ticket with a credit card, reservations can be made and the ticket mailed to you. Otherwise, you may make a reservation up to 24 hours in advance. You can also buy your ticket at the terminal, but arrive early. *Advance purchase is much cheaper, so make reservations early.* A number of **discounts** are available on Greyhound's full-fare (restrictions apply): senior citizens (Mon.-Thurs. 10%, Fri.-Sat. 5% off); children ages two to 11 (50% off); travelers with disabilities and their companions together ride for the price of one; active and retired U.S. military personnel and National Guard Reserves, and their spouses and dependents, may (with valid ID) take a round-trip between any two points in the U.S. for $169.

Ameripass entitles you to unlimited travel for seven days ($250), 15 days ($350), or 30 days ($450); extensions for the seven- and 15-day passes cost $15 per day. The pass takes effect the first day used, so make sure you have a pretty good idea of your itinerary before you start. Before you purchase an Ameripass, total up the separate bus fares between towns to make sure that the pass is indeed more economical, or at least worth the unlimited flexibility it provides. **TNM&D Coaches, Vermont**

Transit, and **Adirondack Trailways** are actually Greyhound subsidiaries, and as such will honor Ameripasses. Check with the companies for specifics. Greyhound also offers an **International Ameripass** for those from outside North America. They are primarily peddled in foreign countries, but they can also be purchased in either of Greyhound's International Offices, located in New York City (212-971-0492) and Los Angeles (213-629-840). A seven-day pass sells for $175, a 15-day pass for $250, and a 30-day pass for $325.

If you are boarding at a remote "flag stop," be sure you know exactly where the bus stops. It's a good idea to call the nearest agency and let them know you'll be waiting at the flag-stop for the bus and at what time. Catch the driver's attention by standing on the side of the road and flailing your arms wildly—better to be embarrassed than stranded. If the bus speeds on by (usually because of over-crowding), the next less-crowded bus should stop. Greyhound allows passengers to carry two pieces of luggage (up to 45 lbs. total) and to check two pieces of luggage (up to 100 lbs.). Whatever you stow in compartments underneath the bus should be clearly marked; be sure to get a claim check for it, and watch to make sure your luggage is on the same bus as you.

Green Tortoise, 494 Broadway, San Francisco, CA 94133 (800-227-4766 or 415-956-7500, in Canada 800-867-8647), offers more unusual and social trips. These funky "hostels on wheels" are remodeled diesel buses done up with foam mattresses, sofa seats, stereos, and dinettes; meals are prepared communally. Bus drivers operate in teams so that one can drive and the other can point out sites and chat with passengers. Prices include transportation, sleeping space on the bus, and tours of the regions through which you pass. Deposits ($100 most trips) are generally required since space is tight. Trips run May to October.

Green Tortoise can get you to San Francisco from Boston or New York in 10-14 days for $279-349 (plus $71-81 for group "food fund"). For the vacation-oriented, Green Tortoise also operates a series of round-trip "loops" which start and finish in San Francisco and travel to Yosemite National Park, Northern California, Baja California, the Grand Canyon, and Alaska. The Baja trip (9 days, $249, plus $51 for food)

includes several days on the beach, with sea-kayaking provided for a fee. Much of Green Tortoise's charm lies in its low price and the departure it offers from the impersonality of Greyhound service. To be assured of a reservation, book one to two months in advance; however, many trips have space available at departure.

East Coast Explorer (718-694-9667 or 800-610-2680 outside NYC), is a new, inexpensive way to tour the East Coast between New York City and Boston and New York City and Washington DC (each leg is different). For $3-7 more than Greyhound, travel all day (10-11 hr.) with 13 other passengers on back roads, stopping at historic sites—a good bargain. Trips leaving from NYC to DC depart Thursday mornings and visit the Amish in Lancaster County; DC to NYC on Friday mornings; $32 each way. Buses traveling between NYC and Boston leave Mondays (northbound) and Tuesdays (southbound); $29 each way. The air-conditioned bus will pick up at most hostels and budget hotels; reservations required.

■■■ PRICE CHART

The following price chart gives one -way rates as of the fall of 1994. Prices may have changed. Travelers should note that, particularly on Amtrak, round-trip tickets are often not much more expensive than one-way tickets. *Major discounts are also available with advance purchase—usually 7 or 14-days.* For specific fare information, call Amtrak at 1-800-USA-RAIL/1-800-872-7245 or Greyhound at 1-800-231-2222. Amtrak rates are in the lower left triangle; Greyhound's are in the right one.

Amtrak Rates (lower left) and **Greyhound Rates** (upper right)

	Atl.	Bos.	Chi.	Dal.	L.A.	N.O.	NYC	Phila.	Port.	San F.	D.C.
Atl.		$112	$85	$99	$119	$59	$99	$89	$169	$159	$79
Bos.	$159		$112	$139	$179	$139	$30	$40	$179	$179	$40
Chi.	$171	$129		$111	$119	$92	$69	$91	$149	$149	$75
Dal.	$201	$247	$160		$119	$89	$139	$139	$149	$139	$129
L.A.	$247	$247	$217	$217		$119	$129	$169	$99	$29	$119
N. O.	$95	$172	$248	$248	$211		$115	$119	$169	$159	$112
NYC	$147	$57	$128	$247	$247	$160		$12	$169	$129	$26
Phila.	$136	$68	$121	$247	$247	$160	$32		$169	$169	$12
Port.	$474	$247	$217	$377	$157	$339	$247	$247		$69	$169
San F.	$247	$247	$217	$217	$67	$339	$247	$247	$131		$169
D.C.	$119	$101	$121	$247	$247	$160	$68	$35	$247	$247	

■■■ BY AUTOMOBILE

GETTING REVVED UP

If you'll be relying heavily on car travel, you might do well to join an automobile club. The **American Automobile Association (AAA),** 1050 Hingham St., Rocklin, MA 02370 (800-AAA-HELP/800-222-4357), offers free trip-planning services, roadmaps and guidebooks, discounts on car rentals, emergency road service anywhere in the U.S., free towing, and commission-free traveler's cheques from American Express. Your membership card doubles as a $5000 bail bond (if you wind up in jail) or a $1000 arrest bond certificate (which you can use in lieu of being arrested for any motor vehicle offense except drunk driving, driving without a valid license, or failure to appear in court on a prior motor-vehicle arrest). If someone in your household already owns a membership, you may be added on as an associate with full benefits for a cost of about $20-25 per year. AAA has reciprocal agreements with the auto associations of many other countries which often provide you with full benefits while in the U.S. AAA membership fees are $54 per year initially with $40 renewal yearly thereafter; $23 yearly for associate (a family member in household).

Other automobile travel service organizations include:

AMOCO Motor Club, P.O Box 9041, Des Moines, IA 50368 (800-334-3300). $50 annual membership enrolls you, your spouse, and your car. Services include 24-hr. towing (5 mi. free or free back to the tower's garage), emergency road service, trip planning and travel information, and car rental discounts. Premier membership ($75) brings 50 mi. free towing.

Mobil Auto Club, 200 N. Martingale Rd., Schaumbourg, IL 60174 (800-621-5581). $52 annual membership covers you and one other person of your choice. Benefits include locksmith, free towing (up to 10 mi.), and other roadside services, as well as car-rental discounts with Hertz, Avis, and National.

Montgomery Ward Auto Club, 200 N. Martingale Rd., Schaumbourg, IL 60173-2096 (800-621-5151). $52 annual membership includes you and your spouse in any car. Children (ages 16-23) $1.50 a month. Towing and roadside assistance.

If you'll be driving during your trip, make sure that your insurance is up-to-date and that you are completely covered. Car rental companies often offer additional insurance coverage, as does American Express if you use them to rent the car. *In Canada, automobile insurance with coverage of CDN$200,000 is mandatory.* If you are involved in a car accident and you don't have insurance, the stiff fine will not improve the experience. U.S. motorists are advised to carry the **Canadian Non-Resident Inter-Provincial Motor Vehicle Liability Card,** which is proof of coverage. The cards are available only through U.S. insurers. For information on the International Driver's License, see Documents and Formalities.

Let's Go lists U.S. highways in this format: "I" (as in "I-90") refers to Interstate highways, "U.S." (as in "U.S. 1") to United States Highways, and "Rte." (as in "Rte. 7") to state and local highways. For Canadian highways, "TCH" refers to the Trans-Canada Highway, "Hwy." or "autoroute" refers to standard autoroutes.

OUT ON THE ROAD

If you are driving in America, a **road atlas** will be your best friend. Splurge on a good one. **Carry a good map with you at all times.** Rand McNally publishes a comprehensive road atlas of the U.S. and Canada, available in bookstores for around $8.

Learn a bit about minor automobile maintenance and repair before you leave, and pack an easy-to-read manual—it may at the very least help you keep your car alive long enough to reach a reputable garage. Your trunk should contain the following **necessities:** a spare tire and jack, jumper cables, extra oil, flares, a blanket (several, if you're traveling in winter), extra water (if you're traveling in summer or through the desert), and a flashlight. If there's a chance you may be stranded in a remote area, bring an emergency food and water supply. Always have plenty of gas and check road conditions ahead of time when possible, particularly during the winter. **Gas** is generally cheaper in towns than at interstate service stops. When planning your budget, remember that the enormous travel distances of North America will require you to spend more on gas than you might expect. Burn less money by burning less fuel. Tune up the car, make sure the tires are in good repair, and have enough air, check the oil, and avoid running the air-conditioner unnecessarily.

Sleeping in a car or van parked in the city is *extremely* dangerous—even the most dedicated budget traveler should not consider it an option.

Be sure to **buckle up**—it's the law in many regions of the U.S. and Canada. Before you hit the road, check rental cars to make sure that the seatbelts work properly. In general, the speed limit in the U.S. is 55 mph, but rural sections of major interstates may well be 65 mph (when posted). Heed the limit; not only does it save gas, but most local police forces and state troopers make frequent use of radar to catch speed demons. The speed limit in Canada is 100kph.

In the 1950s, President Eisenhower envisioned an **interstate system,** a federally funded network of highways designed primarily to subsidize American commerce. Eisenhower's asphalt dream has been realized, and believe it or not, there is an easily comprehensible, consistent system for numbering interstates. Even-numbered interstates run east-west and odd ones run north-south, decreasing in number the further north or west they are. If the interstate has a three-digit number, it is a

branch of another interstate (i.e., I-285 is a branch of I-85), often a bypass skirting around a large city. An *even* digit in the *hundred's* place means the branch will eventually return to the main interstate; an *odd* digit means it won't. North-south routes begin on the West Coast with I-5 and end with I-95 on the East Coast. The southernmost east-west route is I-4 in Florida. The northernmost east-west route is I-94, stretching from Montana to Wisconsin.

RENTING

Although the cost of renting a car for long distances is often prohibitive, renting for local trips may be reasonable. **Auto rental agencies** fall into two categories: national companies with thousands of branches, and local agencies that serve only one city or region. National chains usually allow cars to be picked up in one city and dropped off in another (for a hefty charge). By calling a toll-free number you can reserve a reliable car anywhere in the country. Drawbacks include steep prices and high minimum ages for rentals (usually 25). If you're 21 or older and have a major credit card in your name, you may be able to rent where the minimum age would otherwise rule you out. Try **Thrifty** (800-367-2277; at some locations, ages 21-24 can rent with a credit card and an additional charge), **Alamo** (800-327-9633; ages 21-24 with a major credit card for $15 per day additional fee), **Dollar** (800-800-4000; ages 21-24 can rent with a credit card and an additional fee), **Budget** (800-527-0700; most branches ages 25 and older), **Hertz** (800-654-3131; ages 25 and older), **Avis** (800-331-1212; ages 25 and older), **National** (800-328-4567; generally ages 25 and older), or **Rent-A-Wreck** (800-421-7253; age policies vary). Companies in Boston, Dallas, and Los Angeles will rent to those over 18 (see Practical Information).

Local companies are often more flexible and cheaper than major companies, but you'll generally have to return the car to its point of origin. Some local companies will accept a cash deposit ($50-100) instead of a credit card. Companies such as **Rent-A-Wreck** (800-421-7253) supply cars that are long past their prime. Sporting dents and purely decorative radios, the cars sometimes get very poor mileage, but they run and they're cheap. *Let's Go* lists the addresses and phone numbers of local rental agencies in most towns and all cities.

Most packages allow you a certain number of miles free before the usual charge of 30-40¢ a mile takes effect; if you'll be driving a long distance (a few hundred miles or more), ask for an unlimited-mileage package. For rentals longer than a week, look into **automobile leasing,** which costs less than renting. Make sure, however, that your car is covered by a service plan to avoid outrageous repair bills.

AUTO TRANSPORT COMPANIES

Automobile transport companies match drivers with car owners who need cars moved from one city to another. Would-be travelers give the company their desired destination; the company finds the car. The only expenses are gas, food, tolls, and lodging. A security deposit covers any breakdowns or damage. You must be at least 21, have a valid license, and agree to drive about 400 mi. per day on a fairly direct route. Companies regularly inspect current and past job references, take your fingerprints, and require a cash bond. Cars are available between most points, although it's easiest to find cars for traveling from coast to coast; New York and Los Angeles are popular transfer points.

If offered a car, look it over first. Think twice about accepting a gas guzzler since you'll be paying for the gas. With the company's approval you may be able to share the cost with several companions. Contact **Auto Driveaway,** 310 S. Michigan Ave., Chicago, IL 60604 (800-346-2277), or **Anthony's Driveaway,** P.O. Box 502, 62 Railroad Ave., East Rutherford, NJ 07073 (201-935-8030, fax 201-935-2567).

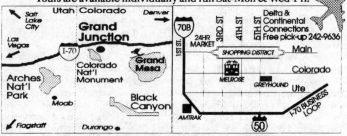

■ MILEAGE CHART

	Atlanta	Boston	Chic.	Dallas	Denver	L.A.	Miami	Mpls.	New O.	NYC	Phila.	Phnx.	St. L.	San F.	Seattle	Trnto.	Vanc.	Mont.
Atlanta		1108	717	783	1406	2366	653	1126	474	886	778	1863	560	2492	2699	959	2825	1240
Boston	22 hr		996	1794	1990	3017	1533	1437	1542	194	333	2697	1190	3111	3105	555	3242	326
Chicago	14 hr	20 hr		937	1023	2047	1237	410	928	807	767	1791	302	2145	2108	537	2245	537
Dallas	15 hr	35 hr	18 hr		794	1450	1322	963	507	1576	1459	906	629	1740	2112	1457	2255	1763
Denver	27 hr	38 hr	20 hr	15 hr		1026	2046	926	1341	1785	1759	790	860	1267	1313	1508	1458	1864
L.A.	45 hr	57 hr	39 hr	28 hr	20 hr		2780	2028	2005	2787	2723	371	1837	384	1141	2404	1285	2888
Miami	13 hr	30 hr	24 hr	26 hr	39 hr	53 hr		1789	856	1346	1214	2368	1197	3086	3368	1564	3505	1676
Mpls.	22 hr	28 hr	8 hr	19 hr	18 hr	37 hr	34 hr		1330	1547	1178	1796	608	2048	1661	948	1799	1196
New O.	9 hr	31 hr	18 hr	10 hr	26 hr	38 hr	17 hr	26 hr		1332	1247	1535	677	2331	2639	1320	2561	1654
NYC	18 hr	4 hr	16 hr	31 hr	35 hr	53 hr	26 hr	24 hr	27 hr		104	2592	999	2923	2912	496	3085	386
Phila.	18 hr	6 hr	16 hr	19 hr	33 hr	50 hr	23 hr	22 hr	23 hr	2 hr		2511	904	2883	2872	503	3009	465
Phoenix	40 hr	49 hr	39 hr	19 hr	17 hr	8 hr	47 hr	38 hr	30 hr	44 hr	44 hr		1503	753	1510	2069	1654	2638
St. Louis	11 hr	23 hr	6 hr	13 hr	17 hr	35 hr	23 hr	12 hr	13 hr	19 hr	16 hr	32 hr		2113	2139	810	2276	1128
San Fran.	47 hr	60 hr	41 hr	47 hr	33 hr	7 hr	59 hr	39 hr	43 hr	56 hr	54 hr	15 hr	45 hr		807	2630	951	2985
Seattle	52 hr	59 hr	40 hr	40 hr	25 hr	22 hr	65 hr	31 hr	50 hr	55 hr	54 hr	28 hr	36 hr	16 hr		2623	146	2964
Toronto	21 hr	11 hr	10 hr	26 hr	26 hr	48 hr	29 hr	19 hr	11 hr	13 hr	13 hr	48 hr	14 hr	49 hr	48 hr		4563	655
Vancvr.	54 hr	61 hr	42 hr	43 hr	27 hr	24 hr	67 hr	33 hr	54 hr	56 hr	56 hr	30 hr	38 hr	18 hr	2 hr	53 hr		4861
Montreal	23 hr	20 hr	17 hr	28 hr	39 hr	53 hr	32 hr	22 hr	31 hr	7 hr	9 hr	53 hr	23 hr	56 hr	55 hr	7 hr	55 hr	

ESSENTIALS

■■■ BY BICYCLE

Get in touch with a local biking club if you don't know a great deal about bicycle equipment and repair. Make your first investment in an issue of *Bicycling* magazine (published by Rodale Press; see below), which advertises low sale prices. When you shop around, compare knowledgeable local retailers to mail-order firms. If the disparity in price is modest, buy locally. Otherwise, order by phone or mail and make sure you have a local reference to consult. **Bike Nashbar,** 4111 Simon Rd., Youngstown, OH 44512 (800-627-4227), is the leading mail-order catalog for cycling equipment. They will beat any nationally-advertised price by 5¢, and will ship anywhere in the U.S. and Canada. They also have a techline (216-788-6464; open Mon.-Fri. 8am-midnight, Sat.-Sun. 8am-4pm) to answer questions about repairs and maintenance. An exceptional mail-order firm specializing in mountain bikes is **Supergo Bikes,** 1660 Ninth St., Santa Monica, CA 90404 (800-326-2453 or 310-450-2224).

Here are some good sources on bicycle touring and repair: **Rodale Press,** 33 E. Minor St., Emmaus, PA 18908 (215-967-5171) publishes *Mountain Biking Skills, Basic Maintenance and Repair, Bicycle Touring in the 90s* ($7 apiece), and other publications on prepping yourself and your bike for an excursion. *Bike Touring* ($11, Sierra Club) discusses how to equip and plan a bicycle trip. *Bicycle Gearing: A Practical Guide* ($9) is available from **The Mountaineers Books,** 1011 SW Klickitat Way #107, Seattle, WA 98134 (800-553-4453), and discusses in lay terms how bicycle gears work, covering everything you need to know in order to shift properly and get the maximum propulsion from the minimum exertion. *The Bike Bag Book* ($5 plus $3.50 shipping), available from **10-Speed Press,** Box 7123, Berkeley, CA 94707 (800-841-2665 or 510-524-1052), is a bite-sized manual with broad utility.

■■■ BY MOTORCYCLE

Bikers make up a strong sub-culture within the U.S. The **American Motorcyclist Association** (800-AMA-JOIN/262-5646) protects the right to ride, as well as has races, clubs, and promotions. **Americade** is an enormous week-long annual touring rally. In 1995 it will be held June 5-10 in Lake George, NY. Registration is $45 per person for the week or $12 per day. Call 518-656-3696 to register.

Bikers should avoid major highways, from which they are sometimes prohibited. Secondary roads are both more scenic and protect bikers from the dangerous drafts of trucks.

■■■ BY THUMB

Hitchhiking in the United States is dangerous. Let's Go urges you to consider the tremendous risks involved in hitchhiking before thumbing it. Hitching means entrusting your life to a random person who happens to stop beside you on the road. While this may be comparatively safe in some areas of Europe and Australia, it is generally *not* so in the United States. We do NOT recommend it. We strongly urge you to find other means of transportation. Hitching is especially risky and stupid in urban areas; even in small cities it can be extremely dangerous. Near metropoli like New York City and Los Angeles, hitching is insane and tantamount to suicide. In areas like rural Alaska and some island communities, hitching is reportedly less unsafe.

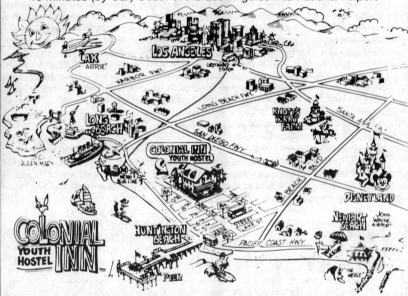

Once There

■■■ ACCOMMODATIONS

The cheapest accommodations in the U.S. are the motels, usually clustered off a main highway several miles outside of town. The closer to downtown, the higher the rates. Before you set out, try to locate places to stay along your route and *make reservations ahead of time,* especially if you plan to travel during peak tourist seasons. If you don't have the money for lodgings, call the **Traveler's Aid Society,** listed under Practical Information wherever it exists. The local crisis center hotline may also have a list of persons or groups who will house you in such an emergency.

HOTELS AND MOTELS

Many budget motels preserve single digits in their names (e.g. Motel 6), but the cellar-level price of a single room has matured to just about $27. Nevertheless, budget chain motels still cost significantly less than the chains catering to the next-pricier market, such as Holiday Inn. Chains usually adhere more consistently to a level of cleanliness and comfort than locally operated budget competitors; some budget motels even feature heated pools and cable TV. In bigger cities, budget motels are just off the highway, often inconveniently far from the downtown area, so if you don't have a car, you may well spend the difference between a budget motel and one downtown on transportation. Contact these chains for free directories:

Motel 6, 3391 S. Blvd., Rio Rancho, NM 87124 (505-891-6161).
Super 8 Motels, Inc., Box 4090, 1910 8th Ave. NE, Aberdeen, SD 57402-4090 (800-800-8000).
Choice Hotels International, 10750 Columbia Pike, Silver Springs, MD 20901-4494 (800-453-4511).
Best Western, P.O. Box 42007, Phoenix, AZ 85080-2007 (800-528-1234).

You may also want to consult one of several **omnibus directories,** like the *State by State Guide to Budget Motels* ($11) from Marlor Press, Inc., 4304 Brigadoon Drive, St. Paul, MN 55126 (800-669-4908 or 612-484-400), or the *National Directory of Budget Motels* ($7, shipping included), from Pilot Books, 103 Cooper St., Babylon, NY 11702 (516-422-2225 or 516-422-2227). If you are addicted to more expensive hotels like Hiltons and Hyatts, consider joining **Discount Travel International,** 114 Forrest Ave. #203, Narbeth, PA 19072 (215-668-7184). For an annual membership fee of $45, you and your household can have access to a clearing house of unsold hotel rooms (as well as airline tickets, cruises, car rentals, and the like) which can save you as much as 50%.

YOUTH HOSTELS

Youth hostels offer unbeatable deals on indoor lodging, and they are great places to meet traveling companions from all over the world; many hostels even have ride boards to help you hook up with other hostelers going your way. As a rule, hostels are dorm-style accommodations where the sexes sleep apart, often in large rooms with bunk beds. (Some hostels allow families and couples to have private rooms.) Hostels often have kitchens and utensils for your use, some have storage areas and laundry facilities, and a few have amenities like pools or sporting equipment.

Hostelling International/American Youth Hostels (HI-AYH), 733 15th St. NW, Suite 840, Washington DC 20005 (202-783-6161), maintains over 300 hostels in the U.S. and Canada. Basic HI-AYH rules (with some local variation): check-in between 5-8pm, check-out by 9:30am, max.-stay three days, no pets or alcohol allowed on the premises. All ages are welcome. Fees range from $7-14 per night, but are usually cheaper for HI-AYH members (membership fees $25, under 18 $10, seniors $15,

ESSENTIALS

families $35). The *AYH Handbook* is free with membership, and lists all AYH hostels. Hostels are graded according to the number of facilities they offer and their overall level of quality—consult *Let's Go* evaluations for each town. The **International Youth Hostel Federation (IYHF)** recently changed its name to **Hostelling International (HI).** HI memberships are valid at all HI-AYH hostels.

Many HI-AYH and HI-C hostels belong to the **International Booking Network (IBN).** The system allows participating hostels and booking centers to make reservations at other hostels worldwide up to six months in advance ($2 fee from a U.S. hostel, up to $5 from a booking center). Payment can be made in the local currency of the booking center, and a full refund is available for any cancellation made at least one week in advance. A complete listing of participating hostels and booking centers can be obtained from Hostelling International (see above).

Rucksackers North America, P.O. Box 90404 Santa Barbara, CA 20038, (301-469-5950), formerly the American Association of Independent Hostels (AAIH), is another hostelling organization. For only the cost of a self-addressed stamped envelope, they'll send you a free guidebook to RNA hostels.

BED AND BREAKFASTS

As alternatives to impersonal hotel rooms, bed and breakfasts (private homes with spare rooms available to travelers) range from the acceptable to the sublime. B&Bs may provide an excellent way to explore an area with the help of a host who knows it well, and some go out of their way to be accommodating by accepting travelers with pets or by giving personalized tours. The best part of your stay will often be a home-cooked breakfast (and occasionally dinner). However, many B&Bs do not provide phones, TVs, or private showers with your room.

Bed and Breakfast International, P.O. Box 282910, San Francisco, CA 94128-2910 (800-872-4500 or 415-696-1690, fax 415-696-1699) has information on B&Bs. CIEE's (212-661-1414) *Where to Stay USA* ($14) which includes listings for hostels, YMCAs, and dorms, along with B&Bs with singles under $30 and doubles under $35. Two useful guidebooks on the subject are *Bed & Breakfast, USA* ($14) available in bookstores or through Tourist House Associates, Inc., RR 1, Box 12-A, Greentown, PA 18426 (717-676-3222), and *The Complete Guide to Bed and Breakfasts, Inns and Guesthouses in the U.S. and Canada,* by Pamela Lanier, from Ten Speed Press, available in book stores or directly from Lanier Publications, P.O. Box 20467, Oakland, CA 94620 (510-644-2651).

Bed and Breakfast: The National Network (TNN) (800-884-4288, fax 401-847-7309) can book reservations at over 5600 B&Bs throughout America and Canada.

YMCAS AND YWCAS

Not all Young Men's Christian Associations (YMCAs) offer lodging; those that do are often located in urban downtowns, which can be convenient though a little gritty. Rates in YMCAs are usually lower than a hotel but higher than the local hostel and include use of the showers (often communal), libraries, pools, and other facilities. Economy packages that include lodging, some meals, and excursions are available in New York, New Orleans, and Hollywood. Many YMCAs accept women and families, but some (such as the Los Angeles chapters) will not accept ages under 18 without parental permission. Reservations (strongly recommended) usually require a small fee and key deposits are common; call the local YMCA in question to find out about fees. Payment for reservations must be made in advance, with a traveler's check (signed top and bottom), U.S. money order, certified check, Visa, or Mastercard. For information or reservations, write the **Y's Way to Travel,** 333 7th Ave., 15th floor, New York, NY 10001 (212-630-9600).

Most Young Women's Christian Associations (YWCAs) accommodate only women. Nonmembers are often required to join when lodging. For more information, write **YWCA-USA,** 726 Broadway, New York, NY 10003 (212-614-2700).

ALTERNATIVE ACCOMMODATIONS

Many **colleges and universities** open their residence halls to travelers when school is not in session—some do so even during term-time. These dorms are often close to the funky student areas and are usually very clean. No general policy covers all of these institutions, but rates tend to be low, and many offer free local calls. College dorms are popular with many travelers, so call or write ahead for reservations.

Students traveling through a college or university town while school is in session might try introducing themselves to friendly looking local students. At worst you'll receive a cold reception; at best, a good conversation might lead to an offer of a place to crash. International visitors may have especially good luck here. In general, college campuses are some of the best sources for information on things to do, places to stay, and possible rides out of town. In addition, dining halls often serve reasonably priced, marginally edible all-you-can-stomach meals.

Servas, another alternative, is an international cooperative system devoted to promoting peace and understanding by providing opportunities for more personal contacts among people of diverse cultures. Travelers are invited to share life in hosts's homes in over 100 countries. You are asked to contact hosts in advance, and you must be willing to fit into the household routine. Homestays are two nights. Prospective travelers must submit an application with references, have an interview, and pay a membership fee of $55, plus a $25 deposit for up to five host lists which provide a short description of each host member. Servas is a non-profit organization and no money passes between traveler and host. Write to U.S. Servas Committee, 11 John St. #407, New York, NY 10038-4009 (212-267-0252).

■■■ CAMPING & THE OUTDOORS

USEFUL PUBLICATIONS

For information about camping, hiking, and biking, write or call the publishers listed below to receive a free catalog.

Sierra Club Bookstore, 730 Polk St., San Francisco, CA 94109 (415-923-5500). Books on many national parks, as well as *The Best About Backpacking* ($11), *Cooking for Camp and Trail* ($12), *Learning to Rock Climb* ($14), and *Wildwater* ($12). Shipping $3.

The Mountaineers Books, 1011 Klickitat Way, Suite 107, Seattle, WA 98134 (800-553-4453 or 206-223-6303). Numerous titles on hiking (the *100 Hikes* series), biking, mountaineering, natural history, and environmental conservation.

Wilderness Press, 2440 Bancroft Way, Berkeley, CA 94704-1676 (800-443-7227 or 510-543-8080). Specializes in hiking guides and maps for the Western U.S. Also publishes *Backpacking Basics* ($11, including postage) and *Backpacking with Babies and Small Children* ($11).

Take advantage of *Woodall's Campground Directory* (Western and Eastern editions, $17 U.S./$19 Canada.) and *Woodall's Plan-It, Pack-It, Go...! Great Places to Tent, Fun Things to Do* (North American edition, $12 U.S./$14 Canada). If you can't find a copy locally, contact Woodall Publishing Company, P.O. Box 5000, 28167 N. Keith Dr., Box 5000, Lake Forest, IL 60045-5000 (800-323-9076 or 708-362-6700). For topographical maps, write the U.S. Geological Survey, Map Distribution, Box 25286, Denver, CO 80225 (303-236-7477) or the Canada Map Office, 615 Booth St., Ottawa, Ontario, K1A 0E9 (613-952-7000), which distributes geographical and topographical maps as well as aeronautical charts.

PARKS AND FORESTS

National parks protect some of the most spectacular scenery throughout North America. Though their primary purpose is preservation, the parks also have recreational activities like ranger talks, guided hikes, skiing, and snowshoe expeditions. Most national parks have backcountry with developed tent camping; others wel-

Grand Canyon
INTERNATIONAL HOSTEL

FLAGSTAFF, ARIZONA, USA

Southern Gateway to the Grand Canyon

Newly Constructed Hostel, only facility built specifically for a hostel and the backpacker's needs
Centrally located in quiet neighborhood away from sounds of trains and downtown.

Amenities include:

168 Beds, prices starting @ $10-12
Private Rooms for $30 (double)
Spacious Lounge area with TV's, pool tables, video games, sports bar, modern kitchen,
Free breakfast and nightly parties!
Library, Laundry, Free linen, hot tubs, bike rentals, basketball, and volleyball

Services:

Free pick up from Greyhound Station, Airport, and Amtrak Station.
Inexpensive shuttles and guided tours:

Grand Canyon	$26 Shuttle
	$36 All day guided tour
Sedona	$15 full day tour
Page	$15 one way to the beautiful Lake Powell Int'l Hostel

Also tours to other points of interest.

Location: Call **(602) 779-9421**
Truly the nicest facility in the Southwest-- Come and see for yourselves!
Member of Resort Hostels Network of America
Bunac Workers Welcome

DISCOVER THE WONDERS AND BEAUTY OF NORTHERN ARIZONA!

LAKE POWELL
International Hostel

In the centre of the Grand Circle, the best kept secret in the South West.

Hostel 2 miles from beautiful Lake Powell, where the water temperatures can reach as high as 84 degrees. The lake itself is 186 miles long with 1,986 miles of shoreline. . . more than the west coast of the U.S.! Surrounded by Navajo and Hopi Native American conservations. Only 2 hrs. from the North and South rim of the Grand Canyon, Manument Valley, and Zion national park, and 3 hr. from Mesa verde, Bryce canyon.

Amenities:

Bed $12-15
Free pick up from the airport-- fly direct to Page using your delta pass or take the $15 shuttle from the Grand Canyon International hostel in Flagstaff Arizona Free Shuttle to Lake Powell from the hostel, tea and coffee, free linens, indoor and outdoor cooking facilities, laundry, basketball and volleyball. Private rooms available.
Members of the Resort Hostels Network of America.

come RVs, and a few offer opulent living in grand lodges. Internal roads allow you to reach the interior and major sights even if you are not a hiker. For info on camping, accommodations, and regulations, contact the National Park Service (202-208-4747), Office of Public Inquiries. P.O. Box 37127, Washington D.C. 20013-7127.

Entry fees vary from park to park. The larger and more popular parks charge a $3-5 entry fee for vehicles and sometimes a nominal one for pedestrians and cyclists.

Golden Eagle Passport is an annual pass that allows a person free entry into all the national parks for $25; it can be bought at most national parks or. The **Golden Age Passport,** entitles visitors ages 62 and over to free entry and a 50% discount on recreational fees ($10); travelers with disabilities enjoy the same privileges with the **Golden Access Passport** (free). All passports are also valid at national monuments.

Many states and provinces have parks of their own, which are smaller than the national parks and serve primarily as recreation spots. Some offer the best camping around—handsome surroundings, elaborate facilities, and plenty of space. Prices for camping at public sites are almost always better than those at private campgrounds.

At the more popular parks in the U.S. and Canada, reservations are absolutely essential; make them through **MISTIX** (800-365-2267 in U.S.; 619-452-5956 outside the U.S.). Lodges and indoor accommodations are generally in the shortest supply and should be reserved months in advance. However, most campgrounds are strictly first-come, first-camped. Arrive early; many campgrounds, public and private, fill up by late morning. Some limit your stay and/or the number of people in a group (usually no more than 25).

National forests provide a purist's alternative to overdeveloped parks. While some have recreation facilities, most are equipped only for primitive camping—pit toilets and no water are the rule. Fees are nominal or nonexistent. Forests are generally less accessible than the parks, but are consequentially less crowded. Backpackers can take advantage of specially designated wilderness areas, which are even less accessible due to regulations barring all vehicles. Wilderness permits, required for backcountry hiking, can usually be obtained (sometimes for free) at parks; check ahead. Adventurers who plan to explore some real wilderness should always check in at a U.S. Forest Service field office before heading out. Write ahead for detailed maps. Contact a U.S. Forest Service field office for more information.

The U.S. Department of the Interior's **Bureau of Land Management (BLM)** offers a wide variety of outdoor recreation opportunities—including camping, hiking, mountain biking, rock climbing, river rafting, and wildlife viewing—on the 270 million acres it oversees in ten Western states and Alaska. These lands also contain hundreds of archaeological artifacts, such as ancient Indian cliff dwellings and rock art, and historic sites like ghost towns. For more information, write or call BLM Public Affairs, Washington D.C. 20240 (202-208-5717).

TENT CAMPING AND HIKING

Sleeping bags have ratings for specific minimum temperatures; pay attention to this index when shopping. If a bag's rating is not a temperature range but a seasonal description, keep in mind that "summer" translates to a rating of 30-40°F, "three-season" means 20°F, and "winter" refers to 0°F. It is also important to regard the material within the bag. Down are light weight and for cold camping, or synthetic, which are cheaper, heavier, more durable, and warmer when wet. The lowest prices for good sleeping bags s run $65-80 for a summer synthetic, $135-180 for a three-season, $170-225 for a down three-season, and upwards of $270-550 for a winter sleeping bag. **Sleeping bag pads** range from $15-30, while **air mattresses** go for about $25-50.

Tent size and shape should be your major considerations. The best tents are free-standing with their own frames and suspensions. They set up quickly and require no staking. Low-profile dome tents are the best all-around condition tents. When pitched, the inside space is almost entirely usable. Just be sure your tent has a rain fly and a plastic tarp for underneath. Good two-person tents start at about $135; $200 fetches a solid four-person. Usually you can find last year's model for about half

the price. Backpackers and hikers should look for small, lightweight models. Contact **Sierra Design,** 2039 4th St., Berkeley, CA 94710, which sells a two-person tent that weighs less than 4 lbs.

Frame backpacks ($200-300) are great for a lot of hiking or biking. Buy a backpack with an internal frame if you'll be hiking on difficult trails that require a lot of bending and maneuvering—internal-frame packs mold better to your back, keep a lower center of gravity, and have enough give to follow you through your contortions. An internal-frame backpack is also good as an all-around travel pack, something you can carry by hand when you return to civilization. An excellent choice is a conversion pack—an internal frame pack that converts into a suitcase. The size of a backpack is measured in cubic inches. Any serious backpacking requires at least 3300 of them, while longer trips require around 4000. Backpacks with many compartments can sometimes turn a large space into many unusable small spaces. Packs that load from the front rather than the top allow you access to your gear more easily (see Packing for more hints). Sturdy backpacks start anywhere from $50-125. This is one area where it doesn't pay to economize—cheaper packs may be less comfortable, and the straps are more likely to fray or rip quickly. Test-drive a backpack for comfort before you buy it. In addition to these basics, always have a battery-operated **lantern** (never gas) and a simple plastic **groundcloth.**

WILDERNESS CONCERNS

The first thing to preserve in the wilderness is you—health, safety, and food should be your primary concerns when you camp. See Health for information about basic medical concerns and first-aid. A comprehensive guide to outdoor survival is *How to Stay Alive in the Woods*, by Bradford Angier (Macmillan, $8). Most rivers, streams, and lakes are contaminated with bacteria such as **giardia,** which causes gas, cramps, loss of appetite, and violent diarrhea. To protect yourself from the effects of this invisible trip-wrecker, always boil your water vigorously before drinking it, or use an iodine solution made for purification. *Never go camping or hiking by yourself for any significant time or distance*. If you're going into an area that is not well-traveled or well-marked, let someone know where you're hiking and how long you intend to be out. If you fail to return on schedule or if you need to be reached for some reason, searchers will at least know where to look for you.

The second thing to protect while you are outdoors is the wilderness. The thousands of outdoor enthusiasts that pour into the parks every year threaten to trample the land to death. Because firewood is scarce in popular parks, campers are asked to make small fires using only dead branches or brush; using a campstove is the more cautious way to cook. Check ahead to see if the park prohibits campfires altogether. To avoid digging a rain trench for your tent, pitch it on high, dry ground. Don't cut vegetation, and don't clear campsites. If there are no toilet facilities, bury human waste at least four inches deep and 100 ft. or more from any water supplies and campsites. Always pack up your trash in a plastic bag and carry it with you until you reach the next trash can; burning and burying pollutes the environment.

BEAR NECESSITIES

A basic rule of thumb to follow is that if you're close enough for a bear to be observing you, you're too close. To avoid a grizzly experience, never feed a bear, or tempt it with such delectables as open trash cans. Keep your camp clean. Do not cook near where you sleep. Do not leave trash or food lying around camp.

When you sleep, don't even think about leaving food or other scented items (trash, toiletries) near your tent. The best way to keep your toothpaste from becoming a condiment is to **bear-bag**. Hang your delectables from a tree, out of reach of hungry paws. Park rangers can tell you how to identify bear trails (don't camp on them!). Bears are attracted to greasy foods and perfume smells; do without cologne, scented soap, and hairspray while camping. Leave your packs empty and open on the ground so that a bear can nose through them without ripping them to shreds.

FOR LESS THAN THE PRICE OF THIS BOOK, YOU COULD BE STAYING HERE.

For just $13-15 you could wake up in a National Park overlooking the San Francisco Bay and Golden Gate Bridge. Or stay in the heart of downtown San Francisco just a block from the big city excitement of Union Square. And for even less per night choose one of the other spectacular hostels in Northern California. Spend a night at a hostel and share experiences with travelers from around the world! For reservations call:

Pigeon Point Lighthouse 415/879-0633
San Francisco - Fort Mason ...415/771-7277
San Francisco Downtown 415/788-5804
Point Montara Lighthouse 415/728-7177
Point Reyes National Seashore 415/663-8811

Hidden Valley Ranch ..415/949-8648
Marin Headlands 415/331-2777
Redwood National Park 707/482-8265
Sacramento 415/443-1691

HOSTELLING INTERNATIONAL

The new seal of approval of the International Youth Hostel Federation.

HOSTELLING INTERNATIONAL®

Always shine a flashlight when walking at night: the bears will clear out before you arrive given sufficient warning. If you stumble upon a sweet-looking bear cub, leave immediately, lest its over-protective mother stumble upon you. If you are attacked by a bear, get in a fetal position to protect yourself, put your arms over the back of your neck, and play dead.

■■■ TIME

U.S. residents tell time on a 12-hour clock cycle. Hours before noon are "am" *(ante meridiem)*. Hours after noon are "pm" *(post meridiem)*. Due to the confusions of 12pm and 12am, *Let's Go* uses "noon" and "midnight" instead. The continental U.S. divides into four time zones (east to west): Eastern, Central, Mountain, and Pacific. Canada contains these four, plus Newfoundland and Atlantic to the east. Alaska, and Hawaii and the Aleutian Islands have their own time zones as well. Most of the U.S. and all of Canada observe **daylight saving time** from the last Sunday in April (April 30th in 1995) to the last Sunday in October (October 29th in 1995) by advancing clocks ahead one hour.

■■■ ELECTRICITY

Electric outlets throughout the U.S., Canada, and Mexico provide current at 117 volts, 60 cycles (Hertz). Appliances designed for the European electrical system (220 volts) will not operate without a transformer and a plug adapter (this includes electric systems for disinfecting contact lenses). Transformers are sold to convert specific wattages (e.g. 0-50 watt transformers for razors and radios; larger watt transformers for hair dryers and other appliances).

ESSENTIALS

■■■ MEASUREMENT

Although the metric system has made considerable inroads into American business and science, the English system of weights and measures continues to prevail in the U.S. The following is a list of U.S. units and their metric equivalents:

1 inch (in.) = 25 millimeters (mm)	1mm = 0.04 in.
1 foot (ft.) = 0.30 meter (m)	1m = a little less than 3 ft.
1 yard (yd.) = 0.92m	1m = 1.09 yd
1 mile (mi.) = 1.61 kilometers (km)	1km = 0.621 mi.
1 ounce (oz., mass) = 25 gram (g)	1g = 0.04 ounce
1 fluid ounce (fl. oz.; volume) = 29.6 milliliters (ml)	1ml = 0.34 fl. oz.
1 pound (lb.) = 0.45 kilograms (kg)	1kg = 2.2 lb.
1 liquid quart (qt.) = 0.94 liter (L)	1L = 1.057 qt.
1 U.S. gallon = 3.78L	1L = 0.27 U.S gallons

The U.S. uses the Fahrenheit temperature scale rather than the Centigrade (Celsius) scale. To convert Fahrenheit to Centigrade temperatures, subtract 32, then multiply by 5/9.

■ UNITED STATES

American culture is everywhere, but what is America? Reaching from below the Tropic of Cancer to above the Arctic Circle, America is a vast region which defies instant description or easy understanding. While tourists often reduce America to a sea of highways, fast food, and pop culture, residents have more trouble describing their country. From Alaska's tundra to Florida's Gulf Coast, from the bubbling pools of Yellowstone to the skyscrapers of Manhattan, the people of the United States of America have inhabited and flourished in the best and worst of environments.

Born in the tempest of revolution, America emerged on July 4, 1776 as a union representing and protecting the individual above all else. Over the next century, as the United States expanded its territory west of the Mississippi and beyond to the Pacific, the theme of the frontier became culturally emblematic. The self-sufficient pioneer, whether on the plains or on Wall Street, has been revered as the ultimate symbol of America. Throwing off Old World garb, this ideal American embraces the unknown, filled with possibility. It is this promise of a better life, of having a dream and achieving it, that has drawn millions of immigrants to American shores.

Whatever it is the traveler seeks—the cool jazz of New Orleans, the tropical swamps of the Everglades, the rolling hills of the Ozarks, or the tackiness of a Nebraskan Stonehenge made of cars—it can be found in the U.S. In many places the city blocks stretch on and on for endless miles, suburbs sleep with no city in sight, forests stand thick with evergreens, and stalks of grain rustle in the wind. There is just too much country to be represented by one image; America is both strip malls and rocky mountains. Some of the most solitary, beautiful vistas can be found just miles from cities packed with millions. One cannot know the U.S. from touring only the largest cities. To understand America, get off the highway and explore.

 # American Culture

HISTORY

In the Beginning

It is not known exactly when the first people set foot in the Americas. Until recently, scientists estimated that the first Americans crossed the Bering Sea from Siberia on a land bridge which arose during the last Ice Age, about 25,000 years ago. New archaeological finds, however, show evidence of even earlier habitation, leading experts to propose two waves of immigration. Whenever they arrived, these people multiplied, and their descendants spread to populate the entire continent. Little is known about the culture of the original tribes, since they possessed an oral rather than a written tradition. Those few who recorded their presence in writing did so only in indecipherable petroglyphs. Nevertheless, the heritage of these people has not been entirely lost—it reverberates still in the culture of the modern Native American tribes scattered throughout the United States and Canada.

European Exploration and Colonization

The exact arrival date of the first Europeans in North America is disputed. The earliest Europeans to alight upon the "New World" were likely sea voyagers blown off course by storms, but the first deliberate European visitors were probably Scandinavians. Vikings led by Leif Erikson explored the Atlantic coast around the year 1000, but left little trace of their visit. Europeans next stumbled upon the Americas in

1492, when Christopher Columbus found his voyage to the east blocked by Hispaniola in the Caribbean Sea. Believing he had reached the spice islands of the East Indies, Columbus fatefully dubbed the inhabitants "Indians." In recent years, revisionists have transformed Columbus from a much celebrated hero who brought civilization and religion to the Americas into a rapacious, greedy exploiter who ruthlessly destroyed the natives's paradise. Neither myth does full justice to the reality of Columbus. Whatever one may say about Christopher Columbus, his arrival and the arrival of those who followed him—such as the Spanish conquistador Hernando Cortez, who demolished the Aztec Empire in 1519—launched one of the most portentous culture clashes in human history.

Most of the Europeans who came to the Americas in search of gold and silver were unsuccessful. But European colonization persisted nonetheless. The Spanish boasted the most extensive American empire, based in South America but eventually spreading north into what are today New Mexico, Arizona, and Florida. St. Augustine, founded in Florida in 1565, was the first permanent European settlement in the present-day United States. Meanwhile, the French and Dutch founded more modest empires to the north. It was the English, however, who most successfully settled the vast New World. After a few unsuccessful attempts, like the "lost colony" at Roanoke, Virginia, the English finally managed to establish a colony at Jamestown in 1607. Malaria, hunger, and conflicts with the natives almost wiped out the original Jamestown colonists, until friendly Powahatans introduced them to a strain of Indian weed called tobacco. Tobacco achieved wild popularity in England and ensured the survival of the colony. Facing a labor shortage, it was not long before the English discovered the profitability of slave labor; the first black slaves were imported to Jamestown in 1619. Virginia thrived as an increasing number of Europeans became addicted to tobacco.

Not all English colonists sought wealth however. English Puritans, finding life intolerable under the Stuart reign, sailed to the New World in search of a place where they could found a godly community in their own vision. In 1620, they landed at Plymouth Rock in what is now Massachusetts. Native Americans helped them to survive in a harsh land and inspired one of the most treasured holidays in modern American culture, Thanksgiving. Though Britain's Empire grew to encompass 13 colonies down the eastern seaboard, the initial Puritan colonizers of New England exerted a political and cultural influence far in excess of their size until well after the Revolution.

Consolidation and Revolution

Throughout the first half of the 18th century, the English colonies expanded and grew as people moved outward into unsettled regions searching for more arable land. Fields were plowed, babies born, and valleys settled. The era was also marked by several military clashes with the French, who were expanding their own North American empire. The greatest of these encounters was the Seven Years War, known locally as the French and Indian War. From 1756-1763, English colonists and British troops fought the French and their Native American allies. The British emerged victorious, and the 1763 Peace of Paris ceded French Canada to King George III, securing the colonies's boundaries from French incursion.

But enormous debts accompanied Britain's victory. Determined to make the colonists help pay the debts incurred in assuring their safety, the British government levied a number of taxes in the 1760s and early 1770s. Two of the most hated were the Stamp Act, which placed a tax on paper products and documents, and the tax on tea. A movement arose to protest these taxes and the colonists, led by the Sons of Liberty (a semi-secret society which originated in Boston), boycotted many English goods. The colonists were angry at what they termed "taxation without representation." The British government repealed the Stamp Act in 1766, only to impose the so-called Townshend Duties a year later. Agitation over the taxes culminated with the Boston Tea Party in December of 1774, during which a group of colonists dressed as Native Americans dumped several shiploads of English tea into Boston

Harbor. The British response, known as the Intolerable Acts, was swift and harsh. Boston was effectively placed under siege and filled to the brim with red-coated British soldiers. Armed rebellion ensued. On July 4, 1776, the Continental Congress formally issued the Declaration of Independence, announcing the thirteen colonies's desire to be free of British rule. Though initially a mere guerilla army composed of home-spun militia known as Minutemen, the Continental forces eventually grew into an effective army under the leadership of George Washington. Despite many setbacks, the Continental forces prevailed, sealing their victory by vanquishing British General Lord Cornwallis at Yorktown, VA in 1781 with the help of the French fleet. Until 1787, the newly independent states were governed by a loose confederation of states. This proved unstable and problematic, so a Constitutional Convention was convened in Philadelphia to draw up a new plan of government which would provide for a stronger central government and a more powerful executive. The fruit of the work of the "Founding Fathers," the Constitution, is still the law of the land. Some states refused to ratify it without a number of immediate amendments, the first ten of which became known as the Bill of Rights. These rights, including the rights to free speech, freedom of the press, and freedom of religion, are inalienable and cannot be infringed upon by the government. The Constitution is itself a landmark political document, tapping the traditions of the French Enlightenment philosophers and English Commonwealth opposition tradition. It creates three separate branches of government—legislative, executive, and judicial—and a system of checks and balances which safeguard against domination by any one branch. It has been amended 26 times.

Onward and Outward: Manifest Destiny

With the original thirteen states under stable, federal rule, America began to expand westward. In 1803, President Thomas Jefferson purchased the Louisiana Territory (one-fourth of the present day United States) from Napoleon for the bargain price of three cents an acre. Curious about what lay in this tract, and eager to tap the northwest fur trade, Jefferson sent explorers Merriwether Lewis and William Clark to trek all the way to the Pacific coast. With the aid of a Native American woman called Sacajawea, they reached Seaside, OR in October, 1805.

After the War of 1812 (a war over trade with Great Britain), the westward movement gained momentum. Manifest Destiny, a belief that the United States was destined by God to rule the continent, captured the ideological imagination of the era. Droves of people moved west in search of cheap, fertile land, and a new life. America's annexation of Texas led Mexico to declare war in 1846. The U.S. won in 1848, forcing Mexico to cede most of the southwest and California. Soon after, the discovery of gold in California spurred mass migration.

White settlers continued moving west, requisitioning land rapidly. The Homestead Act of 1862, which distributed tracts of government land to settlers who would develop and live on that land, prompted the cultivation of the Great Plains. This large-scale settlement led to bloody battles with the Native Americans on whose lands they were intruding. Much of the legend of the Wild West revolves around stories of brave white settlers and stoic cowboys fending off attacks by Indians. These stories are largely distortions, created to justify the actions of the government in exploiting and displacing Native Americans. Nevertheless, expansion into wild, frontier territory retains its significance in the history of America's self-image.

Division over slavery and the Civil War

As the mid-19th century approached, it became increasingly difficult for the United States to ease the tensions created by the existence of slavery within its borders. Although the Declaration of Independence nobly asserted that "all men are created equal," slavery remained the basis of Southern agriculture, while the industrialized North was largely weaned from its dependence on slave labor by the mid-18th century. This hybrid nation, half-free, half-slave, was the fruit of compromises made in drawing up the Constitution. Cultural, economic, and political differences divided

North and South. The growing nation had to decide whether new territories would become free or slave states. Decisions like the Missouri Compromise of 1821 and "squatter sovereignty" in Kansas led to bloody fighting.

In 1861, the Southern states, outraged by the Northern demand for the end of the "peculiar institution," decided to secede from the Union and form a Confederacy which would permit the states greater autonomy and allow the South to pursue its agrarian, slave-based economy unmolested by Northern abolitionists. From 1861-1865, the country endured a savage and bloody war, fought by the North to restore the Union, and by the South to be free of the North and secure the slaveholding aristocracy. Brother fought against brother in the Civil War, which claimed more American men than any other war in U.S. history. The North, led by Abraham Lincoln, emerged victorious, slavery was ended in the Thirteenth Amendment, and the Union was preserved.

Industrialization and World War I

The period after the war, known as Reconstruction, also witnessed the high period of the American Industrial Revolution. Rapid investment by captains of industry such as Vanderbilt, Carnegie, and Rockefeller boosted the American economy and increased American influence abroad. This industrial expansion occurred at great cost to workers and farmers, and trade unions grew in response to poor working conditions and low wages. The 19th-century form of unabashed "free market" capitalism soon began to collapse under its own weight, as witnessed by the cyclical recessions of the 1870s, the 1890s, and particularly, the 1930s. The superficial high which the U.S. rode at the turn of the century is known as the Gilded Age.

Politically, the United States was coming of age. Through victory in the Spanish-American War in 1898, the United States acquired colonies in the Philippines, Puerto Rico, and Cuba. The imperial spirit was embodied in President Theodore Roosevelt, who assumed the office upon the assassination of President McKinley in 1901. Roosevelt also embraced another dominant turn-of-the century phenomenon: progressivism, a movement that sought to create a more just social order by attacking the monopolies and corruption of big business. The efforts of the progressivists resulted in such accomplishments as an increase in public works spending, the 1906 Pure Food and Drug Act, and the popular election of U.S. senators.

1912 brought the Democrat Woodrow Wilson to the White House. Wilson passed an economic reform program that was highlighted by the Clayton Anti-Trust Act and the establishment of the first peacetime income tax in American history.

The relative stability of the early years of the century was crushed beneath the steel weight of World War I. President Wilson overcame a strong neutrality sentiment among the people, and the United States eventually saw tardy but serious involvement in the war. When victory was won, Wilson was instrumental in drafting the peace, including creation of the League of Nations. But domestic opposition prevented the U.S. from ever joining the League, and the onerous terms imposed on Germany by the Versailles Treaty would bear bitter fruit in the coming decades.

The Roaring 20s, The Great Depression, and World War II

The decade following World War I, known as the Roaring 20s, brought many changes to American society. Women were granted the right to vote in 1920 by the 19th Amendment to the Constitution. The nation experimented, through the 21st Amendment, with the prohibition of alcohol, which proved a miserable failure. Progressivism gave way to pro-business, Republican policies. President Warren Harding drastically slashed corporate taxes and proved little more than a stooge for business. "Napping" Calvin Coolidge, who assumed the Presidency on Harding's death from a stroke in 1923, proclaimed that the "business of America is business," and proceeded to assume an arch-indifference toward the operation of the economy. A general (if false) prosperity settled in and fueled an unprecedented fit of conspicuous consumption. The economic euphoria of the 20s, however, was largely supported by overextended credit. It came tumbling down on Black Thursday, October 24,

1929, when the New York Stock Exchange crashed to the ground and launched the Great Depression. Compounding the industrial collapse, American agriculture suffered as the long-abused soil of the Great Plains blew away in one of the worst droughts in history, leaving a "dust bowl" and ruining thousands of farmers.

Under the firm hand of the reformer President Franklin D. Roosevelt, the United States began a slow recovery. His New Deal program created work for hundreds of thousands, building monuments, bridges, and parks with public funds. Out-of-work artists created paintings, sculptures, mosaics, and written and photographic records of the impoverished South and West. The New Deal also laid the ground-work for the modern system of social legislation, bringing the United States somewhat reluctantly into the era of the welfare state.

A crisis in foreign affairs again gripped the national attention late in the decade. Hitler and his murderous Nazi regime horrified the west, and his territorial gluttony in central Europe finally launched the second global war of the century. The Japanese attack on Pearl Harbor on December 7, 1941, a "day that will live in infamy" in the words of Roosevelt, unified the American people behind the allied cause. So America entered World War II. The sheer productive capacity of the nation's wartime economy was critical in assuring allied victory over the Axis powers. The war ended in September of 1945, after the United States had dropped two newly developed nuclear bombs on Japan, killing 80,000 civilians and launching the nuclear era. The United States emerged from the war as the most powerful nation on earth, but it was clear that the seeds of a potentially more devastating conflict had been sown.

Cold War and the New Frontier

Spared the war-time devastation of Europe and the East Asia, the U.S. economy boomed in the post-war era, solidifying the status of the United States as the world's foremost economic and military power. But an ideological polarity was developing between America and that other great power, the Soviet Union. Fears of Soviet expansion led to the Red Scare of the 1950s, when Congressional committees saw communists behind every tree and thousands of civil servants, writers, actors, and academics were blacklisted. Suspicion of communism had grown in the U.S. since the Russian Revolution in 1917, but the feverish intensity it gained during the Cold War ultimately led to American military involvement in Korea and Vietnam. Tensions between the U.S. and the U.S.S.R. culminated in 1962, when President John Kennedy and Nikita Khrushchev brought the world to the brink of nuclear war in a showdown over the deployment of Soviet nuclear missiles in Cuba.

Despite the nuclear shadow, the early 1960s were characterized domestically by an optimism embodied in the President himself. Kennedy's Peace Corps, NASA's program to place Americans on the moon, and the New Frontier to eliminate poverty and racism, all contributed to what must be seen as the nation's last period to date of large-scale activism. This optimistic mood eroded on account of the escalation of the Vietnam conflict, and was finally shattered by Kennedy's assassination in Dallas in 1963. The 60s were marked by increasing social unrest. The nation witnessed public protests against involvement in Vietnam and against the continuing discrimination against African-Americans. Dr. Martin Luther King, Jr. led peaceful demonstrations, marches, and sit-ins for civil rights. Unfortunately, these were often met with violence; civil rights activists were drenched with fire hoses, arrested, and sometimes even killed. Dr. King himself was assassinated in Memphis in 1968.

Accompanying the civil rights movement was the second wave of the women's movement. Sparked by Betty Friedan's landmark text, *The Feminine Mystique,* American women sought to change the delineation between men's and women's roles in society, demanding access to male-dominated professions and equal pay. The sexual revolution, fueled by the development of the birth control pill, brought a woman's right to choose to the forefront of national debate; the 1973 Supreme Court decision *Roe v. Wade* legalized abortion and began a battle between abortion opponents and pro-choice advocates which remains a major national divisor today.

Recent Times

In 1980, actor and former California governor Ronald Reagan was elected to the White House on a tidal wave of conservatism, and an ethic of materialism settled over the nation. College campuses became quieter and more conservative as graduates flocked to Wall Street to become investment bankers. Summing up the national mood, movie character Gordon Gekko (from Oliver Stone's *Wall Street*) declared "greed is good." Though the decade's conservatives did embrace certain right-wing social goals such as prayer in schools and the campaign against abortion, the Reagan Revolution was essentially economic. Reaganomics embraced business and tax breaks for the rich, spurred short term consumption, de-regulated Savings and Loans, and laid the ground work for economic disaster in the 1990s.

Today, America is dealing with a massive deficit, an insufficient education system, a crumbling infrastructure, and issues such as abortion, AIDS, gay rights, and racism. In an attempt to turn things around in 1992, Americans elected Democrat Bill Clinton president over incumbent George Bush and "billionaire populist" Ross Perot. Clinton's campaign promised a new era of governmental activism after years of laissez faire rule. The promise of universal health care, the most ambitious of Clinton's policy goals, best captured the new attitude, but by September 1994 objections from both Republicans and liberal Democrats put health care legislation at a standstill. It remains to be seen if America will be able to break the political standstill, form a consensus, and address the issues at hand.

LITERATURE

Like many things about America, its literature was a chance to begin anew. Starting in the mid-1800s, there was a collection of works that told the tale of the American individual—from the effusive nativist of Walt Whitman's *Leaves of Grass,* to the estranged and cynical Ishmael in Herman Melville's *Moby-Dick.* Even today, the most commonly taught novel in American literature remains Hawthorne's dark romance, *The Scarlet Letter.* It was during this literary "renaissance" that the philosophical essays of American thought were also written—Henry David Thoreau's *Walden* and Ralph Waldo Emerson's *Self-Reliance.* In the Midwest, humorists attempted to define the American soul in concocted fables and tall tales set in the landscapes of the new continent. Their captain was Mark Twain, whose *Adventures of Huckleberry Finn* explored coming-of-age on the Mississippi.

The pioneers traveled farther west, and with them authors like Willa Cather chronicled their trials and vices. Back along the East Coast, the aristocratic novels of Henry James and Edith Wharton portrayed the intricate mannerisms of high society.

The early 20th-century marked a reflective, self-examining point in American literature. F. Scott Fitzgerald's *Great Gatsby* tells of people who had "made it" but nonetheless lived in quiet desperation. Despite the anger and alcoholism many of them faced, this "lost generation" of American writers was its greatest: Hemingway, Faulkner, Welty, Eliot, Pound, Moore, Frost, and Stevens. The 20s also saw an important rise in black literature. Prefigured by the narratives of Fredrick Douglass, W.E.B. DuBois, and Booker T. Washington, the "Harlem Renaissance" matched the excitement of the Jazz Age with the works of Langston Hughes and Zora Neale Hurston.

The Beatniks of the 50s, spearheaded by cult heroes Jack Kerouac and Allen Ginsberg, raved wildly through postwar America's dull conformity—Kerouac's *On the Road* (1955), though dated, nonetheless makes a fine companion to this guidebook for the contemporary road scholar.

Over the last few decades there has been a scrutiny of the tensions of American life in literature itself but in the study and reception of literature as well. Books such as Ralph Ellison's *Invisible Man,* Richard Wright's *Black Boy,* Toni Morrison's *Beloved*, and Oliver LaFarge's portrayal of a Navajo youth, *Laughin' Boy,* all reflect this ongoing examination.

Wherever you go in the U.S., someone with pen and paper has been there before. Here's a list of some authors you can peruse as you ride through their region:

New England: Nathaniel Hawthorne, Emily Dickinson, Henry David Thoreau
Mid-Atlantic: Herman Melville, Edith Wharton, James Cooper, F. Scott Fitzgerald
The South: William Faulkner, Flannery O'Connor, Tennessee Williams, Kate Chopin, Harper Lee, Maya Angelou
The Midwest: Mark Twain, Willa Cather, Richard Wright, Garrison Keiler
The West: Jack London, John Steinbeck, John McPhee, Joan Didion, Amy Tan

MOVIES AND TELEVISION

From the days when viewers were amazed by Thomas Edison's 30-second film of a galloping horse, to today's stunning computer-generated special effects, Americans have been fascinated by movies (note: "cinema" is English—"movie" is American). The success of the American movie industry and its offspring, the movie-star-watching industry, is undisputed. Celebrated movies of each genre include: **sci-fi** (*Star Wars, Aliens, Blade Runner*), **high-tech** (*Jurassic Park, T2*), **thriller** (*Raiders of the Lost Ark, Silence of the Lambs*), **drama** (*Casablanca, The Godfather*), **cult** (*Easy Rider, Dazed and Confused, The Rocky Horror Picture Show*), and the "most American of them all," the **western** (*Unforgiven, Stagecoach, True Grit*).

There are television sets in almost 98% of U.S. homes, and the competition between the four national networks **(ABC, CBS, NBC**, and **Fox)** and cable television has led to an exponential growth in TV culture over the last few years. During prime time (8-11pm EST) you can find the most popular shows: the farcical yet popular *Melrose Place,* and *The Simpsons,* the wittiest animation ever to leave Springfield. On cable you'll discover around-the-clock channels offering news, sports, movies, kid shows, or weather. Then there's **MTV,** whose dazzling display of calculatedly random visceral images affords a glimpse into the psyche of the North American under-30 set.

MUSIC

The impact of broadcast and recording technology on the American music scene cannot be overstated. No longer do you have to lilt to the nearest concert hall to hear the classics, or journey to Chicago to hear true blues. Today, the full spectrum is available at your fingertips, in the forms of compact discs and radio waves, opening American music to all. Consider American music as the music written, performed, and heard in America. Its foundation rests upon the bedrock of the European classical tradition and the African roots of jazz and blues. The vast resources of the American classical musical industry has nurtured some great figures (Leonard Bernstein) and drawn others from Europe (Sir George Solti). The music of the American soul has been sounded by jazz greats like Louis Armstrong, Ella Fitzgerald, Miles Davis, Billie Holiday, Charlie Parker, John Coltrane, Wynton Marsalis, among many others. A baby of the blues, rock n' roll produced many of America's music icons—first Chubby Checker and Jerry Lee Lewis, and eventually the King of Rock, Elvis Presley. Today rock spans from punk to grunge to pop.

To hear some American music first hand, head to the halls, clubs, and stadiums of any American city, particularly the following:

Classical: New York, Boston, Philadelphia, Cleveland, Chicago, and St. Louis
Jazz or Blues: New Orleans, St. Louis, Chicago, Memphis, and New York
Country/Western: Nashville, Memphis, and Austin
Rock and Roll: New York, Boston, Seattle, Athens, GA, and Chapel Hill
Rap: New York, Los Angeles, Philadelphia, and Miami

THEATER

From rural summer stock to New York City's Broadway, there's a stage in almost every town, performing small plays and "visual pieces" to gargantuan operas and musicals (a U.S. original), made famous by Cole Porter, Rogers and Hammerstein), Stephen Sondheim, and George and Ira Gershwin. The budget traveler should not overlook the street theater, an inexpensive alternative.

VISUAL ART

American art is as broad as the experience it depicts. The works of artists in the 19th century such as Thomas Cole and Winslow Homer expressed the beauty and power of the primeval American continent. In the early twentieth century, Edward Hopper and Thomas Hart Benton explored the innocence and mythic values of the United States during its emergence as a superpower. The Abstract Expressionism of Arshile Gorky and Jackson Pollock displays both the swaggering confidence and frenetic insecurity of cold-war America. Pop Art, created by Jasper Johns, Robert Rauschenberg, Roy Lichtenstein, and Andy Warhol, uses as its subject matter the icons of American life and pop culture, satirizing what has become since 1945 the de facto world culture. Cindy Sherman and Robert Mapplethorpe have exposed Americans to personal-as-political photography, despite efforts of self-styled moral guardians to censor their work. However, contemporary American art runs a sometimes questionable gamut of expression that includes large white squares of minimalism and a wall of urinals passed off as "installation art."

New England: Winslow Homer, Mary Cassatt, Childe Hassam
Mid-Atlantic: Charles Willson Peale, Hudson River School, Thomas Eakins,
The South: Julian Onderdonk, William Aiken Walker, Ralph Earl
The Midwest: Thomas Hart Benton, Grant Wood, John Steuart Curry
The West: Georgia O'Keeffe, Charles M. Russell, Albert Bierstadt

ARCHITECTURE

The story of American architecture is its own tall tale. Louis Sullivan invented the skyscraper in the late 19th century in Chicago. It is, as Philip Johnson said, "the great American gift to the art of building." To get a taste of any local style, it is best to visit different cities and take numerous walking tours in city blocks. Most buildings in the southwest are made of clay-brick, while those of New England follow traditional patterns of ornamentation, down to the smallest cornice moulding or frame designs. Wrought iron was extremely popular in the south, especially on old plantation houses, for its stability, availability, and appearance.

■■■ TRIPS AND TRAILS

The best way to see America is to get off the highway and off the beaten path. For those who can't, *Let's Go: USA and Canada* offers a list of some of the most breathtaking and scenic driving routes—which can be seen as attractions themselves.

The Trails section is meant to familiarize the traveler with the recreational National Scenic Trails and the famous exploration routes memorialized by the National Historic Trails. For more info, contact the National Trails System Branch (202-343-3780), National Park Service, P.O. Box 37127, Washington, DC 20013.

THE BEST HIGHWAYS IN AMERICA

The Kancamagus Highway, ME Also known as Rte. 112, New England's only National Scenic Byway is a breathtaking drive winding 35 mi. east of I-93 in Lincoln to Conway on Rte. 16, through the White Mountain National Forest. Mountains soar above the trees like unexpected visitors, peeking out from the curves in the road. Don't miss the scenic viewing area which begs to be appreciated by a stop.

I-94 from Bismarck, ND to Billings, MT This amazing 300 mi. slice of I-94 is sparsely populated, but hosts an immense array of scenery. Journey from flatlands and low-lying prairies to hills and bedrock to dry riverbeds to badlands to larger hills to highland prairies to canyons to winding rivers to (finally) majestic mountains with snow-capped peaks. Buckle your seatbelt, turn off the radio, and enjoy the symphony of the land.

Blue Ridge Parkway If you don't believe that the best things in life are free, this ride could change your mind. The 469-mi. Blue Ridge Parkway runs through Virginia and North Carolina, connecting the **Shenandoah** and **Great Smoky Mountains National Parks** (see VA and TN respectively). Administered by the National Park Service, the parkway has hiking trails, picnic sites, and campgrounds. Every bit as scenic as the connecting Skyline Drive, the Parkway remains much wilder and less crowded, a non-stop parade of vistas, forests, and mountains.

Route 66 You can get your kicks on Rte. 66. Constructed in the 20s along long-established trading routes, the highway (also known as I-40) stretched from Chicago to Los Angeles. The construction of I-40 has outdated the highway and the colorful road culture it created. Left behind but not forgotten, Rte. 66 is a nostalgic detour into the American past. Roadside culture in its earliest forms thrived along this route. Today you can witness the decay of the Mom and Pop motel in the shadow of big chains. But the mystique lives on. In **Hackberry**, AZ, the **Old Route 66 Visitors Center and Preservation Foundation** (769-2605) makes its home in a general store.

The Loneliest Road in America, NV The vast stretch of U.S. 50 that slices east-west through central Nevada is known as the loneliest route in the U.S. Following the historic Pony Express route, this highway passes preserved railroad lines in Ely, the 77,000 acres of Great Basin National Park, and the Lehman Caves. Take a spiritual (and solitary—don't expect to see many cars) journey through the arid, mountainous beauty of the Silver State.

Route 1: The Pacific Coast Highway, CA Originating among the surfer beaches south of L.A., Rte. 1—or the Pacific Coast Highway (PCH)—sweeps grandly along the California coast. Never straying more than a few miles from the sea, the highway reaches from the beaches of L.A. to the magnificent redwood groves near Garberville, more than 200 mi. north of San Francisco. Along the way, its two lanes of blacktop offer a taste of the Californian experience. Across rolling hills filled with extravagant mansions, through cow pastures and fruit orchards, and past hip urban centers, the PCH traverses the best of the state's coastline.

Route 39 from Cedar Grove, WV to Rockbridge Baths, VA This backroad byway is a 45-mph voyage into America. You will find neither major metropoli nor rubbernecking tourists here. Instead, look for the forests, the grazing cows, the small towns with Main Streets and trailers painted red, white, and blue.

Northern Cascades Scenic Highway, WA Part of State Rte. 20 in Northern Washington, this highway makes impassable mountain ranges easily accessible. Far above the timber line, cutting through the mountains, this drive is breathtaking. But don't just stay on the highway — hike one of the moderate paths which wind further into the mountains from right off the road.

I-25 in NM Perhaps one of the nicest stretches of interstate in the country, I-25 from Albuquerque, NM to Truth or Consequences, NM follows the famous *El Camino Royal*, the trade route used by the Spanish settlers in the 16th century. As you drive, look for the signs that instruct you to turn your radio to an AM channel to hear history of the road. The austere beauty of the route is stunning. On this road one realizes the glory of the old West.

The Brockway Mountain Drive, MI Between Eagle Harbor, MI and Copper Harbor, MI, this drive rises 1000 ft. above sea level and is one of the most scenic drives in the Upper Peninsula and the country, supplying vistas of Lake Superior and the interior woodlands.

I-80 in Nevada Stretching from Reno to the Utah border, this route is known as the "Wagon Master Trail." This scenic highway cuts through cowboy country and sights such as the Buckaroo Hall of Fame in Winnemucca, and the town of Elke, one of the sites of the annual Cowboy Poetry Gathering. The road slices through the Paiute Reservation in its western end, passing very close to Pyramid Lake, the largest high desert lake in the state. I-80 also parallels the "Immigrant Trail," the former wagon route that hardy pioneers traveled on their way to California.

The Old San Antonio Road, TX This rough road has weathered the likes of explorers, missionaries, natives, traders, and settlers, all crossing the dusty plains from Louisiana down to Mexico. Scores of travelers and fortune seekers made their way on this historic route for over 300 years. Some of the route is still in use today.

The Hana Highway in Maui, HI The Hana may be the world's most beautiful stretch of road; carved from cliff faces and valley floors, its alternate vistas of smooth sea and lush terrain are made only somewhat less enjoyable by its tortuous curves. Wild ginger plants and fruit trees laden with mangos, guavas, and bananas perfume the air. Locals claim to have kept the best sights hidden, but they seem happy to tell enthusiastic hikers about many of them.

Route 101 in Oregon and Washington Hanging close to the shore, Rte. 101 earns the title of being one of the best coastal highways in the world. Rising in elevation, the highway will burst from the trees into the mist of the Pacific Ocean, rising above the fog and taking the driver's breath away. The highway laces together resort towns and small fishing villages, crossing hundreds of miles of state and national parks. There are even areas where you can leap from the highway onto the beach. And don't miss the seals, sea lions, and waterfowl, who lie right offshore.

The Natchez Trace Parkway When traveling, explore the lush forests, swamps, and countryside winding gracefully through the shade from Natchez, MS to Nashville, TN. This fantastic roadway passes through historic landmarks and a beautiful national park. And all the way, the mighty Mississippi River floats nearby, a gentle companion in the sleepy, scenic South.

Route 9 in the Ozarks of Arkansas Ozark culture survives most undiluted on Rte 9. The famous Ozark Folk Center north of Mountain View recreates a mountain village and the cabin crafts, music, and lore of the Ozarks. A melisma of mountain music also has long found its home here. Listen to some of the world's greatest fiddlers, or revel in the music of the Ozark-native dulcimer, a stringed instrument distinguished by a fret that extends the length of the instrument.

Apache Trail, AZ Starting in Apache Junction, the Apache Trail follows Rte. 88 into the steep, gray, and haunting Superstition mountains. Along the way, this road covers cliff dwellings, caves, canyon lakes, and ghost towns, then loops back to the Junction via U.S. 60. In the 1800s, the Apaches used this trail as an escape from the "settlers" and invading tribes. In the 1840s, a Mexican explorer found gold here, but was killed before he could reveal the location. In the 1870s, Jacob Waltz apparently found the mine and promptly died. As you drive, remember the still-lost gold mine of the Apache trail.

The Dempster Highway, Alaska The only public highway in North America to cross the Arctic Circle, the Dempster is more of a journey than an actual road. Often gravel, often axle-breaking, this route leads you to the top of the world. Below the big sky and the northern lights, this road is the only access to Canada's isolated Mackenzie Delta communities of Fort McPherson, Arctic Red River, and Inuvik in the Northwest Territories.

U.S. 50 in OH Dense green forests swathe southeastern Ohio's narrow valleys, steep hills, and ragged rock formations, which were carved into the land by Pleistocene glaciers. The southern route of the Buckeye trail snakes through this jagged terrain, roughly tracked by this spectacular road. Along the highway, which runs east from Cincinnati to Parkersburg, lie spectacular Native American burial grounds, gorges, cliffs, and caves. Look for the great state parks that cover the rugged terrain.

Scenic Drive in Palo Duro Canyon State Park, TX Follow a path leading into the "Grand Canyon of Texas." Mimic a river that left behind the truly inspiring and beautiful reds, yellows, and browns of this West Texas canyon. The 16,000-acres of Palo Duro makes it the largest state park in Texas. Not only stunning, Palo Duro is 50 miles southeast of Amarillo, a famous and fun stop-over on historic Route 66.

The Cabot Trail, Nova Scotia, Canada Named after English explorer John Cabot who landed in the Highlands in 1497, the trail is the most scenic marine drive in Canada—the Canadian answer to California's Rte. 1. The 300km-long loop winds precipitously around the perimeter of northern Cape Breton. A photographer's dream, the trail takes 7-10 hours to enjoy (allowing for a lunch break, stops at overlooks, and slow traffic).

NATIONAL SCENIC TRAILS

Appalachian National Scenic Trail (AT) 2144 mi. long, the AT covers the Appalachian Mountain range from Maine's Mt. Katahdin through New Hampshire's White Mountains, Massachusetts's Berkshires, New Jersey's Kittatinny Ridge, Pennsylvania's Blue Ridge, West Virginia's Harper's Ferry, Virginia's Shenandoah Valley, Tennessee and North Carolina's Smoky Mountains, and ends in Georgia's Springer Mountain. First envisioned in the 1920s, the AT was designed as an accessible wilderness, and accessible it is, since two-thirds of Americans live within 550 mi. of it. The AT is 96% protected by state and national parks, and is the longest continuous hiking trail in the country. Hikers can trek the AT for only day hikes or six-month wilderness jaunts. For more information, contact the **Appalachian Trail Conference,** P.O. Box 807, Harpers Ferry, WV 25425 (304-535-6331).

Continental Divide Trail 795 mi. from Canada along the Rocky Mountains all the way to Mexico. Through Montana and Idaho to Yellowstone National Park, the extremely rugged Divide Trail marks the line where the flow of water changes direction; on the eastern side to the Atlantic; on the western side to the Pacific.

Other National Scenic Trails include the **Florida Trail,** transversing America's only subtropical land from the Florida Panhandle to Big Cyprus National Preserve; the **Ice Age Trail,** covering Wisconsin from Lake Michigan to the St. Croix River; **North Country Trail,** connecting the Adirondack Mountains in NY with the Missouri River in North Dakota; **Pacific Crest Trail,** ranging over the Sierra Nevada Mountains from Canada to Mexico; and the **Potomac Heritage Trail,** tracking the Potomac River.

NATIONAL HISTORIC TRAILS

Oregon Trail As settlers went from the Midwest to Oregon in covered wagons, efficiency dictated following the same tracks. Since hundred of wagons would cross the plains together, the ruts were often very deep and in some places such as Scottsbluff National Monument in Nebraska, the actual marks are still preserved. You can recreate the pioneer experience with Historic Trails Expeditions, P.O. Box 428, Mills, WY 82604 (307-266-4868) offers wagon tours that follow the original Oregon Trail. Tours range from 3 hrs. ($25) to 5 days ($750), including all meals, overnight teepee, and sleeping pad.

Trail of Tears Under President Andrew Jackson's jurisdiction, against a Supreme Court proclamation, in 1838 the U.S. government forced 16,000 Cherokee Indians to march from the Southeast to west of the Mississippi. Many walked the 800 mi. at gunpoint, and by the end over a fourth of the Cherokees had died. The trail went from Chattanooga, TN to Tahlequah, OK. The excesses of American expansion and the mistreatment of the native population are some of the nation's greatest historical crimes.

Lewis and Clark Trail Commissioned by President Thomas Jefferson in 1804, Merriwether Lewis and William Clark set off from Independence, MO to reach the Pacific, which they were the first to do at the mouth of the Columbia River. Today you can trace the steps of these two intrepid adventurers as they crossed the Rocky Mountains and steered up the Missouri River over 3700 miles.

Santa Fe Trail Following the route carved by Native American traders going to Mexico from the Great Plains, this road linked the two countries economically and politically. The 1200 miles of dusty roads from Old Franklin, MO and Santa Fe, NM helped develop the American Southwest as a major link in the American economic chain. After the development of the Santa Fe Railroad in 1880, the trail lost its status as the road to Mexico. Today, some ruts are still visible, marking the way of thousands of pioneers and fortune-seekers.

Iditarod Trail In the late nineteenth and early twentieth centuries, gold-diggers and their dogs forged Iditarod trail in Alaska. The trail from Anchorage to Nome is still followed today during the famous Iditarod Sled Dog Race, which covers all 1150 miles of tundra and snow.

■ USA Essentials

■■■ CURRENCY AND EXCHANGE

CDN$1 = US$0.73	US$1 = CDN$1.36
UK£1 = US$1.54	US$1 = UK£0.65
IR£1 = US$1.52	US$1 = IR£0.66
AUS$1 = US$0.74	US$1 = AUS$1.35
NZ$1 = US$0.61	US$1 = NZ$1.66

U.S. currency uses a decimal system based on the **dollar ($)**. Paper money ("bills") comes in six denominations: $1, $5, $10, $20, $50, and $100. Bills of $2 are no longer printed, but are still acceptable as currency. Some restaurants and retail stores may not accept $50 bills or higher. The dollar divides into 100 cents (¢); fractions such as 35 cents are represented as 35¢. The penny (1¢), the nickel (5¢), the dime (10¢), and the quarter (25¢) are the most common coins. The half-dollar (50¢) and one-dollar coins are rare but valid.

It is nearly impossible to use foreign currency in the U.S., although in some regions near the Canadian border, shops may accept Canadian money at a very unfavorable rate of exchange. In some parts of the country you may even have trouble **exchanging your currency** for U.S. dollars. Convert your currency infrequently and in large amounts to minimize fees. Buy U.S. traveler's checks, which can be used instead of cash (when an establishment specifies "no checks accepted" this usually refers to personal checks drawn on a bank account). **Personal checks** can be very difficult to cash in the U.S.; most banks require that you have an account with them to cash one. You may want to bring a U.S.-affiliated credit card such as Interbank (MasterCard), Barclay Card (Visa), or American Express.

Sales tax is the U.S. equivalent of the Value Added Tax. Expect to pay 4-10% depending on the item and place. See the state introductions for information on local taxes. Some areas charge a hotel tax; ask in advance. In addition, a **tip** of 15% is expected by restaurant servers and taxi drivers, although restaurants sometimes include this service charge in the bill. Tip bellhops $1 per bag. It is also customary to tip barkeeps 25¢ to $1 for a drink.

■■■ KEEPING IN TOUCH

MAIL

Individual offices of the U.S. Postal Service are usually open Mon.-Fri. 9am-5pm and sometimes on Sat. until about noon; branches in many larger cities open earlier and close later. All are closed on national holidays. **Postcards** mailed within the U.S. cost 19¢ and **letters** cost 29¢ for the first ounce and 23¢ for each additional ounce. To Canada and Mexico, it costs 30¢ to mail a postcard, and 40¢ to mail a letter for the first ounce and 23¢ for each additional ounce. Postcards mailed to any other nation cost 40¢, and letters are 50¢ for a half-ounce, 95¢ for an ounce, and 39¢ for each additional half-ounce up to 64 ounces. **Aerogrammes** are available at post offices for 45¢. Domestic mail takes from two to five days to reach its destination. Mail to northern Europe, Canada, and Mexico takes a week to ten days; to Southern Europe, North Africa, and the Middle East, two weeks; and to South America or Asia, a week to 10 days. Of course, all of the above estimated times of arrival are dependent on the particular foreign country's mail service as well. Be sure to write "AIR MAIL" on the front of the envelope for the speediest delivery.

The U.S. is divided into postal zones, each with a five-digit ZIP code particular to a region, city, or part of a city. Writing this code on letters is essential for delivery. Some addresses have nine-digit ZIP codes, used primarily for business mailings to speed up delivery. The normal form of an address is as follows:

Ramón Heid (name)
Paquita School of Bellydancing (name of organization, optional)
1792 Desmond Drive, #14 (address, apartment number)
Collins, ME 94631(city, state abbreviation, ZIP)
USA (country, if mailing internationally)

If people want to get in touch with you, they can send mail **General Delivery** (or *Poste Restante*) to a city's main post office. Once a letter arrives it will be held for about 30 days; it can be held for longer at the discretion of the Postmaster if such a request is clearly indicated on the envelope. Label General delivery letters like this:

Dr. Guy D. Rough (underline last name for accurate filing)
c/o General Delivery
Main Post Office
1701 Americana Drive
Carhenge, NE 11475

Alternately, **American Express** offices throughout the U.S. and Canada will act as a mail service for cardholders, *if* you contact them in advance. Under this free "Client Letter Service," they will hold mail for 30 days, forward upon request, and accept telegrams. For a complete list of offices and how-to instructions, call 800-528-4800.

TELEPHONES

Telephone numbers in the U.S. consist of a three-digit area code, a three-digit exchange, and a four-digit number, written as 123-456-7890. Only the last seven digits are used in a **local call**. **Non-local calls** *within* the area code from which you are dialing require a "1" before the last seven digits, while **long-distance calls** *outside* the area code from which you are dialing require a "1" and the area code. For example, to call Harvard University in Cambridge, MA from Las Vegas, NV, you would dial 1-617-495-1000. Canada and much of Mexico share the same system. Generally, **discount rates** apply after 5pm on weekdays and Sunday and **economy rates** every day between 11pm and 8am. If you are unable to access an 800 number from your city, you can call the 800 operator (800-555-1212) who may be able to give you another number or the address. You can obtain a local number from the directory assistance operator of the appropriate city (area code plus 555-1212).

Pay phones are plentiful, often stationed on street corners and in public areas. Put your coins (10-25¢ for a local call depending on the region) into the slot and listen for a dial tone before dialing. If there is no answer or if you get a busy signal, you will get your money back after hanging up; if you connect with an answering machine, you won't. To make a long-distance direct call, dial the number. An operator will tell you the cost for the first three minutes; deposit that amount in the coin slot. The operator or a recording will cut in when you must deposit more money. A second, rarer variety of pay phone can be found in some large train stations and charges 25¢ for a one-minute call to any place in the continental U.S.

If you are at an ordinary telephone and don't have change, you may want to make a collect call (i.e., charge the call to the recipient). First dial "0" and then the area code and number you wish to reach. Tell the operator that you wish to place a **collect call** from Mr. Ed, or whatever your name happens to be; anyone who answers may accept or refuse the call. If you tell the operator you are placing a **person-to-person collect call** (more expensive than a regular collect call), you must give both your name and the receiving person's name; the benefit is that a charge appears only if the person with whom you wish to speak is there (and accepts the charges, of course). The cheapest method of reversing the charges is MCI's new plan; just dial 1-800-COLLECT, tell the operator what number you want to call (it can be anywhere in the world), and receive a 20-44% discount off normal rates; discounts are greatest when the rates are cheapest. Note that in some areas, particularly rural ones, you may have to dial "0" alone for any operator-assisted call.

You can place **international calls** from any telephone. To call direct, dial the international access code (011) followed by the country code, the city code, and the local number. Country codes and city codes may sometimes be listed with a zero in front (e.g. 033), but when using 011, drop succeeding zeros (e.g., 011-33). In some areas you will have to give the operator the number and he or she will place the call. Both AT&T and MCI offer calling services that allow you to place charges for international calls on an account; you must have a calling card to use these programs. For information on AT&T's **World Connect,** call 800-331-1140 within the U.S. For information on MCI's **WorldReach,** call 800-444-3333.

Travelers with British Telecom, Telecom Eireann, New Zealand Telecom, Telkom South Africa, or Telecom Australia accounts at home may wish to use special **access numbers** to place calls from the U.S. through their home systems. All companies except Telkom South Africa have different access numbers depending on whether their cooperative partner in the U.S. is AT&T, MCI, or Sprint. Access numbers are: **British Telecom** (800-445-5667 AT&T, 800-444-2162 MCI, 800-800-0008 Sprint); **Telecom Éireann** (800-562-6262 AT&T, 800-283-0353 MCI, 800-473-0353 Sprint); **New Zealand Telecom** (800-248-0064 AT&T, 800-666-5494 MCI, 800-949-7027 Sprint); **Telecom Australia** (800-682-2878 AT&T, 800-937-6822 MCI, 800-676-0061 Sprint); **Telkom South Africa** (800-949-7027).

NEW ENGLAND

New England, with its centuries-old commitment to education and its fascination with government, has been an intellectual and political center for the entire nation since before the States were even officially United. Students and scholars from across the country funnel into New England's colleges each fall, and town meetings still take place in many rural villages. Yet this region is an unlikely cradle for any sort of civilization: the soil is barren, the climate is harsh, the coast is rocky and treacherous, and the land is wrinkled with mountains.

Though the terrain gave the region's early settlers a tough time, it is kind to today's visitors. New England's dramatic coastline is a popular destination for summer vacationers; the slopes of the Green and White Mountains, with their many rivers and lakes, inspire skiers, hikers, cyclists, and canoers. In the fall, the "changing of the leaves" transforms the entire region into a giant kaleidoscope as the nation's most brilliant foliage bleeds and burns. Though largely rural, very little of New England (inland Maine excepted) is wild. Many vacation sites here are calculated to give you loads of human history—semi-old buildings, museums, battlegrounds, ubiquitous quaint inns, and famous-people sculptures dot the hillside hamlets. However, groups such as the Appalachian Mountain Club battle developers and tour promoters in their quest to preserve the privately owned backcountry.

Mark Twain once said that if you don't like the weather in New England, wait 15 minutes. Unpredictable at best, the region's climate can be particularly dismal in November and March. Watch out for black flies and swarming greenhead flies in summer, especially in Maine, and be warned that everything from rivers and state camprounds to tourist attractions may slow down or freeze up during the winter.

 # Maine

A sprawling evergreen wilderness dotted with lakes, swollen with mountains, and defined by a jagged shore, Maine is larger than the entire neat stack of New England states below. The Maine "Downeaster" is known for reticent humor, rugged pragmatism, and disdain for urban pretension. Maine's landscape is renowned for its deep wilderness and for rocky coastlines strewn with lighthouses and lobster shacks. It's also a bastion of New England preppiness. Few urban refugees can resist swathing themselves in plaid flannel in this green getaway.

"Vacationland," as Maine is known, lives by its waters and forests. Fishing communities along the coast and logging companies inland support the state's economy, and fresh-water fishing is a major Maine sport. The rapids of the Allagash Waterway challenge canoeists, and the remote backwoods lakes are perfect for hikers, bicyclists, and campers.

PRACTICAL INFORMATION

Capital: Augusta.
Maine Publicity Bureau, 325B Water St., Halowell (623-0363 or 800-533-9595). Send mail to P.O. Box 2300, Halowell 04347. **Bureau of Parks and Recreation,** State House Station #22 (1st floor Harlow Bldg.), Augusta 04333 (287-3821). **Maine Forest Service,** Bureau of Forestry, State House Station #22 (2nd floor Harlow Bldg.), Augusta 04333 (287-2791). All agencies open Mon.-Fri. 8am-5pm.
Time Zone: Eastern. **Postal Abbreviation:** ME
Sales Tax: 6%.

MAINE COAST

As the bird flies, the length of the Maine coast from Kittery to Lubec measures 228 mi., but if you untangled all of the convoluted inlets and rocky promontories, the distance would be a whopping 3478 mi. Fishing was the earliest business here, later augmented with a vigorous shipbuilding industry; both traditions retain visibility today. Lobster pounds are ubiquitous in coastal Maine; stop under one of the innumerable makeshift red wooden lobster signs which speckle the roadsides, set yourself down on a grey wooden bench and chow, but keep in mind that lobsters are most tasty before July, when most start to molt. Also be forewarned that lobster-poaching is treated seriously here; the color codings and designs on the buoy markers are as distinct as a cattle rancher's brand and serve the same purpose.

U.S. 1 hugs the coastline and strings the port towns together. Lesser roads and small ferry lines connect the remote villages and offshore islands. The best place for info is the **Maine Information Center** in Kittery (439-1319), 3 mi. north of the Maine-New Hampshire bridge (open daily 8am-6pm; mid-Oct.-June daily 9am-5pm). **Greyhound** (800-231-2222) serves points between Portland and Bangor along I-95, the coastal town of Brunswick, and connecting routes to Boston. Reaching most coastal points of interest is virtually impossible by bus; a car or bike is necessary.

■■■ SOUTH OF PORTLAND

Driving south on U.S. 1 out of Portland, you'll encounter nothing but traffic and stores until the town of **Kennebunk,** and, several miles east on Rte. 35, its coastal counterpart **Kennebunkport.** If you want to bypass busy U.S. 1, take the Maine Turnpike south of Portland to exit 3, then take Fletcher St. east into Kennebunk.

Both of these towns are popular hideaways for wealthy authors and artists. A number of rare and used bookstores line U.S. 1 just south of Kennebunk, while art galleries fill the town itself. The blue-blood (and blue-haired) resort of Kennebunkport has grown reluctantly famous as the summer home of former President Bush, who owns an estate on Walker's Point. The **Kennebunk-Kennebunkport Chamber of Commerce** (967-0857), at the intersection of Rte. 9 and 35 in Kennebunkport, has a free guide to area sights (open Mon.-Fri. 9am-8pm, Sat. 9am-6pm, Sun. 11am-4pm; mid-Oct. to June Mon.-Fri. 9am-5:30pm, Sat.-Sun. 10am-4pm).

Biking provides a graceful ride on the road past rocky shores and spares visitors the aggravation of fighting thick summer traffic. In nearby **Biddeford,** a few minutes north on U.S. 1, **Quinn's Bike and Fitness,** 140 U.S. 1 (284-4632), rents 10-, 5-, and 3-speeds ($30 per week, with $20 deposit). (Open Mon.-Thurs. and Sat. 9am-5:30pm, Fri. 9am-8pm.) You can get a copy of *25 Bicycle Tours in Maine* ($17) from the Portland Chamber of Commerce (see below).

A visit to Kennebunkport will cost. Buy groceries. The **Lobster Deck Restaurant** (967-5535), on Rte. 9 overlooking Kennebunk Harbor, serves lobster dinners ($18-20). (Open Memorial Day-Columbus Day daily 11am-10pm.) Camping is the most affordable lodging. **Salty Acres Campground** (967-8623), 4½ mi. northeast of Kennebunkport on Rte. 9, offers swimming, a grocery store, laundry, and a convenient location about 1 mi. from the beaches. (300 sites $16, with electricity and water $22, full hookup $24, $8 per additional adult after 2; $2 per additional child after 2. Open mid-May to mid-Oct.) A little farther out is the **Mousam River Campground** (985-2507), on Alfred Rd. just west of exit 3 off I-95 in West Kennebunk (115 sites $16; RV sites $19; free showers, open mid-May to mid-Oct.).

The **Rachel Carson National Wildlife Refuge** (646-9226), on Rte. 9 near U.S. 1, is a welcome escape from the tourist throngs west. A self-guided trail takes you through the salt marsh home of over 200 species of shorebirds and waterfowl. The refuge is a tribute to Rachel Carson, the naturalist and author of *Silent Spring,* a book that publicized the perils of chemical pollution and environmental waste and helped launch the environmental movement. (Open daily sunrise to sunset.)

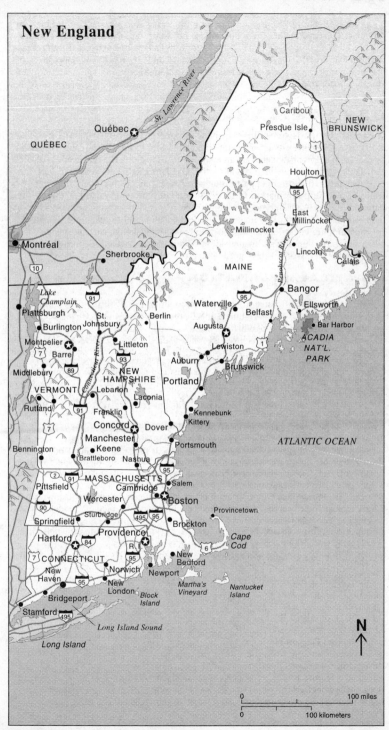

Ogunquit, south of Kennebunk, has a long, sandy strip of beach— the best on the coast. Nearby **Perkins Cove** charms the polo-shirt crowd with boutiques hawking sandshell sculptures and delicious lobster rolls ($9) from **Barnacle Billy's** restaurant, on Oar Weed Road (646-5575; open daily 11am-9:30pm). **Moody,** just south of Ogunquit, is home to some of the less expensive lodgings in the region. Ogunquit is summer home to a vibrant gay community.

■■■ PORTLAND

For a relatively tourist-free taste of the New England coast, go to Portland. Destroyed by a fire in 1866, the city rebuilt only to decline again in the 1960s. Lately, Portland profits from a downtown area advantageously located along the ocean and a revitalized fishing industry. Stroll in the attractive Old Port Exchange, where restaurants, taverns, and craft shops occupy former warehouses and 19th-century buildings, or follow the young population to more Bohemian haunts. Portland is among the nation's leaders in restaurants per capita. The reasonable location and low cost of living in Maine's largest city makes it an ideal base for sight-seeing and daytrips to the surrounding coastal areas, such as the Casco Bay Islands. Nearby Sebago Lake provides ample sunning and water-skiing opportunities, while Freeport, the outlet capital of the free world, offers ample budget shopping.

PRACTICAL INFORMATION

Emergency: 911.

Visitor Information Bureau, 305 Commercial St. (772-5800), at the corner of Center St. Open Mon.-Fri. 8am-6pm, Sat.-Sun. 10am-3pm; Oct. 16-May 14 Mon.-Fri. 9am-5pm, Sat.-Sun. 10am-3pm.

Buses: Concord Trailways, 161 Marginal Way (828-1151 or 800-639-5505), a 15-min. walk from downtown. Office open daily 7am-8:30pm. To: Boston (6 per day, 2 hr., $15); Bangor (3 per day, 2 hr., $20). A local Metro Bus (8) will transport you from the station to downtown, but you must call (774-0351). **Greyhound/Vermont Trailways,** 950 Congress St. (772-6587 or 800-231-2222), on the western outskirts of town. Be cautious here at night. Take the Congress St. bus (1) to downtown. Office open daily 6am-6pm. To: Boston (7 per day, 2 hr., $26); Bangor (5 per day, 2 hr., $19).

Prince of Fundy Cruises: P.O. Box 4216, 468 Commercial St. (800-341-7540 or 800-482-0955 in ME). Ferries to Yarmouth in southern Nova Scotia leave from the Portland Marine Terminal, on Commercial St. near the Million Dollar Bridge, May-late Oct. at 9pm. June 24-Sept. 20. $75, ages 5-14 $37.50; off-season $55 and $27.50. Cars $98, off-season $80. Reservations required. 50% off car fare on Tues. and Wed. 10% off stays in Portland International Hostel.

Local Bus: Metro Bus (774-0351) offers service within and beyond the downtown area. Most routes run only noon-7pm. $1, seniors and disabled 50¢, kids under 6 free, transfers free.

Help Lines: Rape Crisis, 774-3613. **Crisis Intervention Hotline,** 800-660-8500. Both operate 24 hrs.

Post Office: 125 Forest Ave. (871-8410). Open Mon.-Fri. 7:30am-7pm, Sat. 7:30am-5pm.

ZIP code: 04104.

Area Code: 207.

Downtown sits along Congress St. toward the bay between State and Franklin St. A few blocks south lies the Old Port on Commercial and Fore St. These two districts contain most of the city's sights and attractions. I-295 off I-95 forms the western boundary of downtown. Several offshore islands are served by regular ferries.

ACCOMMODATIONS AND CAMPING

Portland has some inexpensive accommodations, but prices jump during the summer season. You can always try exit 8 off I-95, where **Super 8** (854-1881) and other similar budget staples (singles around $40-45) proliferate.

Portland Youth Hostel, 645 Congress St. (874-3281). Centrally located in a university dorm. 48 beds in clean doubles with bath and shower. Poor lighting; no locks on closets. Kitchen, lounge with giant cable TV, laundry facilities, free breakfast. A helpful staff will store your stuff during lockout 11am-3pm (50¢). $14, nonmembers $17. Linen $2. Locks (bike locks will do) $2. Check-in 5pm-midnight. Check-out 7-10am. 5-day max. stay. Reservations recommended.

The Inn and St. John, 939 Congress St. (773-6481). Reasonable prices in a comfortable inn give way to discounts for hostelers when the hostel is full. Clean, attractive singles ($25, with private bath $40) and doubles ($35/45) with free local calls. Check-in after 10am. Displaced hostelers pay $20 per bed.

YWCA, 87 Spring St. (874-1130), downtown near the Civic Center. Women only. Small rooms verge on sterile, but an amiable atmosphere more than compensates. Fills up in summer. Lounge, pool, and kitchen (bring utensils). Check-out by 11am. Singles $25, doubles $40. Phone in reservations with a credit card.

YMCA, 70 Forest Ave. (874-1111), north side of Congress St., 1 block from the post office. Cash only. Men only. Check-in 11am-10pm. Access to kitchen, pool and exercise facilities. Singles $23 per night, $84 per week. Key deposit $10.

Hotel Everett, 51A Oak St. (773-7882), off Congress St. Central location. Old but clean singles $38, with bath $43; doubles $49/$53. Mid-Sept. to mid-June 10% cheaper. Weekly rates available. Reservations are recommended in summer.

Wassamki Springs, 855 Saco St. (839-4276), in Westbrook. Closest campground (15-min. drive) to Portland. Drive west down Congress St. (becomes Rte. 22, then County Rd.) about 6 mi., turn right on Saco St. Full facilities plus a sandy beach. Flocks of migrant Winnebagos nest here. Sites $20 for 2 people, $4 per additional person. Hook up $23. Showers 25¢. Open May to mid-Oct. Reservations recommended 4-6 weeks in advance, with $10 deposit per day, especially July-Aug.

FOOD

Seafood is, of course, the city's speciality. Check out the active port on Commercial St. for fresh clams, fish, and lobsters.

Raffles Café Bookstore, 555 Congress St. (761-3930), in the heart of downtown. Enjoy breakfast, a light lunch (soups made from scratch $2, sandwiches $3-4), or scrumptious desserts ($1-2.50) while doing heavy reading. Open Mon.-Tues. and Fri.-Sat. 8am-5:30pm, Wed.-Thurs. 8am-8pm, Sun. noon-5pm. Reopens Fri. 7-10pm for live music ($4).

Bella Bella, 606 Congress St. (780-1260). Specializes in ample servings of Italian specialties (entrees $7-10) served in an almost psychedelic flower-painted café. Open 5-10pm daily.

The Pepperclub, 78 Middle St. (772-0531). A colorful, casual café that features a diverse but always excellent selection of mostly vegetarian dishes and some chicken, fish, and organic beef items. The entree menu ($7-10) somehow manages to include the words Maine, Tunisian, Indonesian, Mexican, Bulgarian, and Italian. Open Sun.-Wed. 5-9pm, Thurs.-Sat. 5-10pm. Ample parking.

Seamen's Club, 375 Fore St. (772-7311), at Exchange St. in the Old Port with a harbor view. Top-notch seafood dining steeped in briny lore. Lunch entrees $6-11, dinner $9 and up. Fresh lobster year-round. Open Mon.-Thurs. 11am-10pm, Fri.-Sat. 11am-11pm, Sun. 10:30am-10pm.

SIGHTS

Many of Portland's most spectacular sights are to be found outside the city proper, along the rugged coast or on the beautiful, secluded islands a short ferry ride offshore. **Two Lights State Park** (799-5871), across the Million Dollar Bridge on State St. and south along Rte. 77 to Cape Elizabeth, is a wonderful place to picnic and relax; enjoy a rocky shore with a view of two lighthouses. (Open Memorial Day-Labor Day daily 9am-sunset. $2, ages 5-11 50¢, seniors and under 5 free.) **Casco Bay Lines** (774-7871), on State Pier near the corner of Commercial and Franklin), America's oldest ferry service, runs year-round to the nearby islands. Daily **ferries** depart approximately every hour (5:15am-midnight) for nearby **Peaks Island** ($4.50, seniors and kids 5-9 $2.25, under 5 free; bikes $3.40) where you can rent a bike at **Brad's Recycled Bike Shop,** 115 Island Ave. (766-5631), for $11 per day or $7 per 4 hrs. If your feet aren't up to pedaling, try the quiet, unpopulated beach on **Long Island.** (Departures daily 6am-9pm. $6.35, seniors and kids 5-9 $3.20. Bikes $4-6 extra.) Starting at Long Island allows for island hopping, by catching later ferries to other islands, for the same price. Start early and pay close attention to the schedule.

You may feel the call of the sea the instant you arrive in Portland, but the city does have a full slate of non-oceanic activities. The **Portland Museum of Art,** 7 Congress Sq. (775-6148), at the intersection of Congress, High, and Free St., collects American art by notables such as John Singer Sargent and Winslow Homer. (Open Tues.-Wed. and Fri.-Sat. 10am-5pm, Thurs. 10am-9pm, Sun. noon-5pm. $6, seniors and students $5, kids 6-12 $1, under 6 free. (First Sat. of month 9am-noon and every Thurs. 5-9pm free.) Down the street at 487 Congress St., the **Wadsworth-Longfellow House** (879-0427), a museum of social history and U.S. literature, zeroes in on late 18th- and 19th-century antiques as well as on the life of the poet. (Open June-Oct. Tues.-Sun. 10am-4pm. Tours every ½ hr. $4, under 12 $1. Purchase tickets at 489 Congress St. Gallery and museum store also open Oct.-June Wed.-Sat. noon-4pm.)

While the history of Portland's **Old Port Exchange** began in the 17th century, the area's shops, stores, and homes were rebuilt in Victorian style after the fire of 1866. The **Portland Observatory,** 138 Congress St. (772-5547), set atop a promontory east of downtown, went up in 1807. Climb 102 steps for a panoramic view of Casco Bay and the city. (Open July-Aug. Wed.-Thurs. and Sun. 1-5pm, Sat. 10am-5pm; June and Sept.-Oct. Fri.-Sun. 1-5pm. Closed if raining. $1.50, kids 50¢.)

ENTERTAINMENT AND NIGHTLIFE

After a brief respite, spanning back to its days as a Vaudeville venue, the **State Theater,** 609 Congress St. (879-1111; for tickets 879-1112) is back in business, presenting both concerts and theatrical productions. (Info line open 24 hrs.; box office open Mon.-Fri. 9am-5pm, Sat.-Sun., noon-showtime on performance days.)

The **Old Port Festival** (772-6828) begins the summer season with a bang in early June, spanning several blocks from Federal to Commercial St. and drawing as many as 50,000 people. On summer afternoons, enjoy the **Noontime Performance Series** (772-6828), in which bands from ragtime to Dixieland perform in Portland's Monument Square. (Late June-early July Mon.-Fri. noon-1:15pm.) The **6-Alive Sidewalk Arts Festival** (828-6666) lines Congress St. with booths featuring artists from all over the country, and is generally held around mid-August. From early October to late April, the **Portland Symphony,** under the direction of Toschiyuki Shimada, performs at the Portland City Hall on Myrtle Street. In February of 1995, rennovations on the hall will force the Symphony to relocate temporarily. Call for details. (Box office 773-8191, 800-639-2309 in ME and NH; tickets 50% off for students.)

For a taste of the hometown spirit, check out the **Portland Pirates** at 1 Civic Center Square (828-4665), Portland's own professional hockey team. The **Portland Seadogs** (874-9300), a new mid-April and early September.

After dark, head toward the Old Port area, especially **Fore Street** between Union and Exchange St., a stretch known as "the strip." At one end sits **Gritty MacDuff's,** 396 Fore St. (772-2739), which brews its own sweet beer for adoring locals—even the mayor drinks here. Tasty pints are a bargain at $2.50. (Open daily 11:30-1am, daily.) On the other end you'll find the atmosphere of an English pub at **Three Dollar Dewey's,** 446 Fore St. (772-3310), which serves 65 varieties of beer and ale (18 on tap at $3) along with great chili and free popcorn (open Mon.-Sat. 11am-1am, Sun. noon-1am). **Brian Boru,** 57 Center St. (780-1506), provides a kinder, gentler pub scene. Try the Irish nachos ($5.50). (Open daily noon-1am.) Find Portland's jazz at **Bebop's Café,** 548 Congress St. (828-6551), a funky little bistro which features live music on Wed. nights.

■■■ NORTH OF PORTLAND

Much like the coastal region south of Portland, the north offers the traveler sunny beaches and cool breezes—for a price. Lodgings are never cheap, but if you're either outfitted for camping or just passing through, you'll find fun and interesting shopping as well as ample access to the ocean. Much of the region is unserviced by public transportation; driving is rewarding, however. U.S. 1, running north along the coast, offers motorists a charming glimpse of woods and small towns.

Freeport About 20 mi. north of Portland on I-95, Freeport once garnered glory as the "birthplace of Maine": the 1820 signing of documents declaring the state's independence from Massachusetts took place at the historic **Jameson Tavern,** 115 Main St. (865-4196). Remember, historical does not mean economical. Dinner in the Jameson dining room costs $12-22, but lighter fare can be had in the tap room for $6-9. Freeport is now known as the factory outlet capital of the world, with over 100 downtown stores. The grandaddy of them all, **L.L. Bean,** began manufacturing Maine Hunting Shoes in Freeport in 1912. Bean sells diverse products from clothes epitomizing preppy *haute couture* to sturdy tenting gear. The bargain factory outlet is at 11 Depot St. (865-4761, ext. 2929), behind Bannister Shoes. The retail store, 95 Main St. (865-4761 or 800-341-4341), stays open 24 hrs., 365 days a year. Only three events have ever caused the store to close (and for only a few hours each time): a nearby fire in the late 1980s, the death of President Kennedy, and the death of L.L. Bean founder Leon Leonwood (no wonder he called himself L.L. Bean).

Heading up to **Penobscot Bay** (not in the town of Penobscot) from factory-outlet-land, be sure to stop at **Moody's Diner** (832-7468), on U.S. 1 in Waldoboro. Since business started in 1927, tourists and old salts rub shoulders over fantastic food. (Open Sun. 7am-Thurs. midnight, Fri.-Sat. 5am-11:30pm.)

Camden In summer, preppies flock to friendly Camden, 100 mi. north of Portland, to dock their yachts alongside the eight tall masted schooners in Penobscot Bay. Many of the cruises are out of the budgeteer's price range, but the Rockport-Camden-Lincolnville **Chamber of Commerce** (236-4404), on the public landing in Camden behind Cappy's Chowder House, can tell you which are most affordable. They also have info on a few rooms in local private homes for $30; otherwise expect to pay $50 or more. (Open Mon.-Fri. 9am-5pm, Sat. 10am-4pm, Sun. noon-4pm.) Cheaper still, the **Camden Hills State Park** (236-3109 out of state, 800-332-1501 for reservations in ME), 1¼ mi. north of town on U.S. 1, is almost always full in July and August, but you're fairly certain to get a site if you arrive before 2pm. This coastal retreat offers more than 25 mi. of trails; one leads up to Mt. Battie and has a harbor view. Make reservations by phone with a credit card. Showers are 25¢ and toilets are available. (Open May 15-Oct. 15. Day use $2. Sites $15, ME residents $11.)

Affordable to all and in the heart of downtown Camden is **Cappy's Chowder House,** 1 Main St. (236-2254), a kindly, comfortable hangout where the great seafood draws tourists and townspeople alike. Try the seafood pie ($8), made with scallops, shrimp, mussels, and clams. (Open daily 7:30am-midnight.) A little less central and a little less crowded, **The Harbor Café,** 1 Sharp's Wharf (236-6011), prepares fresh fish(with vegetable and potato $10). Eat it on the dockside patio. (Open Mon.-Thurs. 9am-2:30pm and 5-9pm, Fri.-Sat. 9am-2:30pm and 5-10pm, Sun. 5-9pm.)

The **Maine State Ferry Service** (789-5611), 5 mi. north of Camden in Lincolnville, takes you through the Bay to Isleboro Island (7-9 per day; fare $4, kids 5-11 $2, under 5 free, bike $2, auto $6.25). The ferry also has an agency in Rockland (596-2202; 517 A Main St.) on U.S. 1, running boats to North Haven, Vinalhaven, and Matinicus. Always confirm ahead of time; rates and schedules change with the weather.

Belfast For real-life coastal Maine, Belfast is the genuine article, 17 mi. north of Camden on U.S. 1. The **Belfast Area Chamber of Commerce,** 31 Front St. (338-5900), on the water, can help you with planning (open mid-May to mid.-Oct. daily 10am-6pm). When the chamber is closed for the season, call the director, Jim Lovejoy, at home at the **Hiram Alden Inn,** 19 Church St. (338-2151). Not only the home of an invaluable tourist helper, the inn is Belfast's most affordable accommodation, and a luxurious one at that. (Singles $30, doubles $45, additional adult $10; breakfast included; Oct.16-May deduct $5 from room prices.) Stroll by the waterfront and watch the fishing boats come in, or enjoy the innumerable antique sales, flea markets, and plain-old junk sales that line Rte. 1 in Belfast and the surrounding towns on summer weekends. **The Gothic,** 4 Main St. (338-4683), serves homemade baked goods and ice cream. If you're lucky, they'll have their blueberry sorbet ($1.20) while you're in town. (Open Mon.-Wed. 8am-6pm, Thurs.-Sat. 8am-9pm.)

Deer Isle South of Blue Hill on the other side of Penobscot Bay lies Deer Isle, a picturesque, forested island with rocky coasts accessible by bridge from the mainland. Off Main St. in Stonington, at the southern tip of Deer Isle, a **mailboat** (367-5193; mid-June to early Sept. Mon.-Sat. 2 per day) leaves for **Isle au Haut,** part of Acadia National Park. (Fare $9, kids under 13 $4.50.) Island exploration is done by foot or bike (no rental bikes available on the island). The only accommodations are five lean-tos, each of which can accommodate up to six people, at **Duck Harbor Campground** (no showers; sites $5; reservations necessary; open mid-May to mid-Oct.). Contact Acadia Park Headquarters (2883338; Mon.-Fri. 8am-4:30pm) or write P.O. Box 177, Bar Harbor 04609.

■■■ MOUNT DESERT ISLAND

In spite of its name, Mt. Desert is not barren. In summer, campers and tourists abound, drawn by mountains, rocky beaches, and spruce and birch forests. The Atlantic waters—calm in summer but stormy in winter—are too cold for all but the hardiest of souls. Wind-swept **Acadia National Park** features rugged headlands, fine beaches, plenty of tidal-pool critters, and a variety of naturalist activities. **Bar Harbor,** on Rte. 3 on the eastern side of the island, is a lively but crowded town packed with over 2400 (mostly expensive) guest rooms. The island's other towns, such as Seal and Northeast Harbors, are more relaxed but even more expensive.

PRACTICAL INFORMATION

Emergency: 911. **Acadia National Park,** 288-3369. **Mt. Desert Police,** 276-5111.

Acadia National Park Visitors Center (288-4932 or 288-5262), 3 mi. north of Bar Harbor on Rte. 3. Open May-June and mid-Sept.-Oct. daily 8am-4:30pm; July-mid-Sept. daily 8am-6pm. **Park Headquarters** (288-3338), 3 mi. west of Bar Harbor on Rte. 233. Open Oct.-May Mon.-Fri. 8am-4:30pm. **Bar Harbor Chamber of Commerce,** 93 Cottage St. (288-5103; open Mon.-Fri. 8am-5pm). **Mount Desert Island Joint Chamber of Commerce** (288-3411), on Rte. 3 at the entrance to Thompson Island. Info on the whole island and Frenton. Open July-Aug. daily 10am-8pm; May-June and Sept.-Oct. daily 10am-6pm. In the same building is an **Acadia National Park Information Center** (288-9702). Open June-Sept. daily 9:30am-2:30pm.

Ferries: Beal & Bunker, from Northeast Harbor on the town dock (244-3575). To: Cranberry Islands (5-7 per day, 25 min., $8, under 12 $4; open Mon.-Fri. 8am-4:30pm for info. **Marine Atlantic,** Bar Harbor (288-3395 or 800-341-7981). To: Yarmouth, Nova Scotia (1 per day June 24-Columbus Day, 3 per week Columbus Day to mid-March, 6 hr.; $39, seniors $29.50, kids 5-12 $20, car $51, bike $8.50; mid-Oct. to late June $27/$20/$13.50/$47/$6; $3 port tax per person).

Buses: Greyhound/ Vermont Transit (800-451-32922) leaves for Bangor daily at 6:45am in front of the Post Office, 55 Cottage St. ($8.50 June-Labor Day). Buy tickets at **Fox Run Travel,** 4 Kennebec St. (288-3366; open Mon.-Fri. 8:30am-5pm).

Taxis: Bar Harbor Taxi, 288-3914. $5 in zone; runs 5am-6pm daily.

Bike Rental: Bar Harbor Bicycle Shop, 141 Cottage St. (288-3886). Mountain bikes $9 per 4 hr., $14 per day, $79 per week. Rentals include helmet, lock, and map. Driver's license, cash deposit, or credit card required. Open June to mid-Sept. daily 8am-8pm, mid-Sept. to mid-Dec. daily 8am-6pm.

National Park Canoe Rentals (244-5854), north end of Long Pond off Rte. 102. Canoes $18 per 4 hr., $22 per day. Open May-Labor Day daily 8:30am-5pm.

Help Lines: Downeast Sexual Assault Helpline, 800-228-2470; **abused women crisis line,** 667-9489; **mental health crisis line,** 800-245-8889. All 24 hrs.

Post Office: 55 Cottage St. (288-3122), near downtown. Open Mon.-Fri. 8am-4:45pm, Sat. 9am-noon. **ZIP code:** 04609.

Area Code: 207.

Rte. 3 runs through Bar Harbor, becoming Mt. Desert St.; it and Cottage St. are the major east-west arteries. Rte. 102 circuits the western half of the island.

ACCOMMODATIONS AND CAMPING

Grand hotels with grand prices remain from Rockefeller's day, and you still have to be a Rockefeller to afford them. Nevertheless, a few reasonable establishments can be found, particularly on Rte. 3 north of Bar Harbor. Camping exists throughout the island; most campgrounds line Rtes. 198 and 102, well west of town.

Mt. Desert Island Hostel (HI-AYH), 27 Kennebec St., Bar Harbor (288-5587), behind the Episcopal Church, adjacent to the bus stop. Two large dorm rooms which can accommodate 24 in cheery red-and-white bunks. Common room, full kitchen, and a perfect location. Organized activities include movie nights and comedy performances. Curfew 11pm. Lockout 9am-5pm. $9, nonmembers $12. Linen $1.50. Reservations essential July-Aug. Open mid-June to Aug. 31.

Mt. Desert Island YWCA, 36 Mt. Desert St. (288-5008), near downtown. Extensive common space, full kitchen, laundry. Women only. Dorm-style singles in summer only with bath on hall $25 per night, $80 per week; doubles $36/$70; glassed-in porch with 7 beds $15/$60. $25 security deposit for stays of 1 week and longer. Fills in summer; make reservations early. Office open daily 9am-10pm.

Acadia Hotel, 20 Mt. Desert St., Bar Harbor (288-5721). Sweet, homey place overlooking the park. TV, private bath. Breakfast included. Room for 1 or 2 people $50-72 late June-early Sept.; $40-55 May-late June and early Sept.-Oct.

White Birches Campground, (244-3797), on Seal Cove Rd., 1½ mi. west of Rte. 102 in Southwest Harbor. Wooded sites offer an escape from the touristy areas. 60 sites, free hot showers, stove, bathrooms. $14 for up to 4 people, $18 with hookup. Weekly $84/108. $2 per additional person. Open May 15-Oct. 15 daily 8:30am-10pm for check-in.

Acadia National Park Campgrounds: Blackwoods (288-3274), 5 mi. south of Bar Harbor on Rte. 3. Over 300 sites mid-May to mid-June and mid-Sept. to mid-Oct. $11, mid-June to mid-Sept. $13, free other times. Reservations up to 8 weeks in advance; call 800-365-2267. **Seawall** (244-3600), Rte. 102A on the western side of the island, 4 mi. south of Southwest Harbor. Station open May-Sept. daily 8am-8pm, first-come, first-served. Walk-in sites $8, drive-in $11. Both campgrounds are within a 10-min. walk of the ocean and have toilets but no showers or hookups. Privately owned public-access showers available nearby for a fee. No reservations.

FOOD AND ENTERTAINMENT

Seafood is all the rage here. "Lobster pounds" sell the underwater crustaceans cheaply; cooking them is the only problem if you don't have access to a kitchen.

Beals's, Southwest Harbor (244-7178 or 244-3202), at the end of Clark Point Rd. The best price for lobster in an appropriate setting. Pick your own live lobster from a tank; Beals's does the rest ($7-8). Dining on the dock. A nearby stand sells munchies and beverages. Open daily 9am-8pm; Labor Day-May daily 9am-5pm.

The Lighthouse Restaurant (276-3958), in Seal Harbor. Fairly upscale during the day and even more so after 5pm when waiters don tuxes; a nice way to escape from the crowds at Bar Harbor. Sandwiches $4-9, entrees $9-15, lobster dinner $14. Open daily 9am-10pm.

Cottage St. Bakery and Deli, 59 Cottage St., (288-3010), Bar Harbor. Memorably delicious muffins (75¢), pancakes ($2.45), and breads (loaf $2.25-3.50) baked fresh on the premises. Open May-Oct. daily 6:30am-10pm.

Jordan's, 80 Cottage St. (288-3586). A blueberry smorgasbord specializing in muffins ($3.50 for 6) and pancakes ($2.75). Their popular breakfast is served all day. Open daily 5am-2pm.

The Colonels Deli Bakery and Restaurant, Main St., Northeast Harbor. The restaurant out back offers not very scenic outdoor seating and sandwiches so big you'll have to squash the fresh baked bread to get it into your mouth ($3-5). The desserts are unusual and delicious ($2-3). Open April-Oct. daily 6:30am-9pm.

Most after-dinner pleasures on the island are simple ones. For a treat, try **Ben and Bill's Chocolate Emporium,** 80 Main St. (288-3281), near Cottage, which boasts 24 flavors of homemade ice cream (cone $2) and a huge selection of fresh chocolates which will make you gasp (open March-Dec. daily 9:30am-11:30pm). **Benbow's Espresso Bar** (288-5271), at the **Alternative Market,** 99 Main St., features over 30 coffees roasted in house (75¢-$2.50). Try the German Chocolate Nut Cream for a change, or caramel mocha latte ($1.50), mocha ($1.75), espresso (75¢). Their seating is very limited and rather uncomfortable, but the waterfront and park are one block away. (Open daily 7am-11pm; Oct. 7am-9pm; late Oct.-May 7:30am-6pm.) **Geddy's Pub,** 19 Main St. (288-5077), is a three-tiered entertainment complex with bar, sporadic live music, and dancing. There is no cover. (Fri.-Sat. DJ nights. Open April-Oct. daily noon-1am.) Locals prefer the less-touristy **The Lompoc Café & Brew Pub,** 36 Rodick St. (288-9392), off Cottage St., which features live Jazz, blues, celtic, rock, or folk nightly. (Shows June-Sept. at 9pm, $1-2 cover charge. *Bar Harbor Real Ale* $2.50 for 12 oz., brewed on location. Open May-Oct. 11:30-1am, Nov. 11:30am-9pm.) The art-deco **Criterion Theatre** (288-3441), on Cottage St., was recently declared a national landmark and continues to show movies in the summer daily at 8pm. Matinees run on Sundays at 2pm. Don't be discouraged by the lines; the theater seats 891. Programs are available at the desk. ($6, kids under $12 $3.50, balcony seats $7; box office open ½ hr. before show.)

SIGHTS

Mt. Desert Island is shaped roughly like a lobster claw, 14 mi. long and 12 mi. wide. To the east on Rte. 3 lie Bar Harbor and Seal Harbor. South on Rte. 198 near the cleft is **Northeast Harbor,** and across Somes Sound, the only fjord in the continental U.S., on Rte. 102 is **Southwest Harbor,** where fishing and shipbuilding still thrive, without the taint of tacky tourism. **Bar Harbor** is by far the most crowded part of the island, sandwiched between the Blue Hill and Frenchmen Bays. Once a summer hamlet for the very wealthy, the town now harbors a motley melange of R&R-seekers. The wealthy have fled to the more secluded Northeast and Seal Harbor. **Little Cranberry Island,** out in the Atlantic Ocean south of Mt. Desert, has a spectacular view of Acadia as well as the area's cheapest uncooked lobster at the fishers' co-op.

The staff at the **Mt. Desert Oceanarium** (244-7330), at the end of Clark Pt. Rd. in Southwest Harbor, can teach you about the sea at each of their three facilities (the lobster hatchery 288-2334, and Salt Marsh Walk 288-5005, are located near Bar Harbor). The main museum—though resembling a grammar-school science fair—fascinates onlookers. (Open mid-May to late Oct. Mon.-Sat. 9am-5pm. Ticket for all 3 facilities $9.50, kids 4-12 $7.50, under 4 free; inquire about individual rates.) Cruises head out to sea from a number of points on the island. In Bar Harbor, the **Frenchman Bay Co.,** 1 West St., Harbor Place (288-3322), offers sailing trips (2 hr., $14.75, ages 5-15 $10.75), lobster fishing, seal-watching trips (1½ hr., $16.75, ages 5-15 $10.75, under 5 free), and whale watching (4 hr., $26, ages 5-15 $18, under 5 free. Open May-Oct. Reservations recommended, especially for whale watching. Call for details or schedule.) The **Acadian Whale Watcher,** Golden Anchor Pier, West St. (288-9794, 288-9776, or 800-421-3307), has slightly lower prices, guarantees sightings or you go again free, and has food and a full bar on board. Sunset and daylight whale-watching cruises ($25, seniors $20, ages 7-14 $14, under 7 free; open mid-May to mid-Oct.) leave 53 times a day. Bring extra clothing—the temperature can drop dramatically on the water.

From Northeast Harbor, the **Sea Princess Islesford Historical and Naturalist Cruise** (276-5352) brings you past an osprey nesting site and lobster buoys to Little Cranberry Island. You may be lucky enough to see harbor seals, cormorants, or pilot whales on the cruise. The crew takes you to the **Islesford Historical Museum** in sight of the fjord-like Somes Sound. (Four cruises per day July-Aug., 1-3 per day May-June and Sept.-Columbus Day, 2-3 hrs.; $10-12, ages 4-12 $7-8, under 4 free.)

Tourists can also explore the island by horse, the way Rockefeller intended. **Wildwood Stables** (276-3622), along the Park Loop Rd. in Seal Harbor, runs one- and two-hour carriage tours through the park (1 hr.; $10.50, seniors $9.50, ages 6-12 $6, ages 2-5 $3.50; 2 hr; $13.50/$12.50/$7/$4.50). Reservations are strongly suggested. No horses are available for rental on the island.

Acadia National Park The 33,000 acres that comprise **Acadia National Park** are a landlubber's dream, offering easy trails and challenging hikes which allow for an intimate exploration of Mt. Desert Island. More acres are available on the nearby **Schoodic Peninsula** and **Isle au Haut** to the west. Millionaire and expert horseman John D. Rockefeller funded half of the park's 120 mi. of trails out of fear that the park would someday be overrun by cars. These **carriage roads** make for easy walking, fun mountain biking, and pleasant horseback riding and are accessible to disabled persons.

Precipice Trail, closed June-late Aug. to accommodate nesting Peregrine falcons, and 24 other trails offer more advanced hiking. Be realistic about your abilities here; the majority of injuries in the park occur in hiking accidents. Swim in the relatively warm **Echo Lake,** which has on-duty lifeguards in summer. The 5 mi. **Eagle Lake Carriage Road** is graded for bicyclists. At the park visitors center, pick up the handy *Biking and Hiking Guide to the Carriage Roads* (free), which offers invaluable safety advice. Some of these paths are accessible only by mountain bike and can be dangerously desert-like and labyrinthine without a map. Touring the park by auto costs $5 per week , $2 per pedestrian or cyclist. Seniors and disabled are admitted free. About 4 mi. south of Bar Harbor on Rte. 3, take the **Park Loop Road** running along the shore of the island where great waves roll up against steep granite cliffs.

The sea comes into **Thunder Hole** at half-tide with a bang, sending plumes of spray high into the air and onto tourists. To the right just before the Loop Rd. turns back to the visitors center stands **Cadillac Mountain,** the highest Atlantic headland north of Brazil. A 7.4-mi. hiking trail to the summit starts at Blackwoods campground, 2 mi. east of Seal Harbor. The top of Mt. Cadillac, the very first place sunlight touches the U.S., makes a great place for an early breakfast—the sun rises between 4 and 4:30am in the summer.

New Hampshire

New Hampshire's farmers may have struggled for over two centuries with the state's rugged landscape, but a cultivator's *inferno* is a hiker's *paradiso*. The White Mountains dominate the central and northern regions, and nearly every part of the state identifies with some towering peak. Rising above them all, Mt. Washington is the highest point in the Appalachians (6288 ft.); from its summit you can view the Atlantic and five states. Aside from the stony beaches of the nation's shortest coastline (18 mi.), much of southeastern New Hampshire has succumbed to Boston's suburban invasion. Although the state motto and license-plate blazon "Live Free or Die," "Live Well or Die" may be more appropriate in these parts.

PRACTICAL INFORMATION

Capital: Concord.

Office of Travel and Tourism, Box 856, Concord 03302 (271-2666, 800-262-6660, or 800-258-3608). Recording provides fall foliage reports, daily ski conditions, weekly snowmobile conditions, and weekly special events. Operators available Mon.-Fri. 8am-4pm. **Fish and Game Department,** 2 Hazen Dr., Concord 03301 (271-3421) can provide information on hunting and fishing regulations and license fees. **U.S. Forest Service,** 719 Main St., mail to P.O. Box 638, Laconia 03247 (528-8721). Open Mon.-Fri. 8am-4:30pm.

Time Zone: Eastern. **Postal Abbreviation:** NH

Sales Tax: 0%. Live Tax-Free or Die. 8% tax on rooms and meals.

■■■ WHITE MOUNTAINS

In the late 19th century, the White Mountains became an immensely popular summer retreat for wealthy New Englanders. Grand hotels peppered the rolling green landscape, and as many as 50 trains per day bore tourists through the region. The mountains are not quite so busy or fashionable these days, and hiking and skiing have mostly replaced train travel. Unfortunately, the economics of vacationing here have not changed nearly so drastically. Affordable lodgings are as scarce as public transportation, and the notoriously unpredictable weather makes camping risky. The area is divided into notches, which are passes between the mountains.

Getting There and Getting Around Getting around the White Mountains can be problematic. **Concord Trailways** (228-3300 or 800-639-3317) runs from the Boston Peter Pan bus station at 555 Atlantic Ave. (617-426-8080) to Concord (Storrs St., 228-3300, open daily 5:15am-8pm, $11), Conway (First Stop store on Main St., 447-8444, open daily 5:30am-10pm. $25), and Franconia (Kelly's Foodtown, 823-7795, open daily 9am-9pm). **Vermont Transit** (800-451-3292) stops its Boston-to-Vermont buses in Concord at the Trailways terminal, 10 St. James Ave. (617-423-5810). The **Appalachian Mountains Club (AMC)** runs a **shuttle service** (466-2727) connecting points within the mountains. Consult **AMC's** *The Guide* for a complete map of routes and times. Reservations recommended for all stops and required for some, runs June 3-Oct. 10 8:45am-3:30pm. $5, nonmembers $7. See Useful Organizations below for more AMC information.

For **Trail and Weather Information** call the **Pinkham Notch Visitors Center** (466-2725) on Rte. 16. Regional **ZIP codes** include: Franconia, 03580; Jackson, 03846; and Gorham, 03587; **area code:** 603.

Useful Organizations Travel information can be obtained at local travel offices or from the **White Mountain Attraction Center** (745-8720) on Rte. 112 in North Woodstock (P.O. Box 10, N. Woodstock 03262). Those looking to bypass cities will have a much more relaxing time of it thanks to several superb organizations. One is the **U.S. Forest Service** (528-8721) whose main information station lies south of the mountains at 719 Main St., Laconia 03247. **Forest service ranger stations,** dotting the main highways through the forest, can also answer questions about trail locations and conditions: **Androscoggin** (466-2713) on Rte. 16, ½-mi. south of the U.S. 2 junction in Gorham (open Mon.-Fri. 7am-4:30pm); **Ammonoosuc** (869-2626) on Trudeau Rd. in Bethlehem west of U.S. 3 on U.S. 302 (open Mon.-Fri. 7am-4:30pm); **Saco** (447-5448) on the Kancamangus Hwy. in Conway 100 yards off Rte. 16 (open daily 8am-4:30pm). Each station provides a guide to the **backcountry facilities** in its area.

Another useful organization is the **Appalachian Mountains Club (AMC),** whose main base in the mountains is the Pinkham Notch Visitors Center on Rte. 16 between Gorham and Jackson (see Pinkham Notch below). The AMC is the area's primary supplier of information about camping, food, and lodging, and also provides hiking and camping equipment. The club runs two car-accessible lodgings in the White Mountains: the **Joe Dodge Lodge** (see Pinkham Notch) and the **Shapleigh Hostel** (846-7773), adjoining the **Crawford Notch Depot,** east of Bretton Woods on U.S. 302. The hostel has room for 24 people and provides toilets, metered showers, and a full kitchen. Bring your own sleeping bag and food. Curfew 9:30pm. Reservations recommended. ($10, non-AMC members $15.) The Depot sells trail guides, maps, food, camping necessities, and film, and has restrooms. (Open late May-Labor Day daily 9am-5pm.) The AMC also has a system of eight **huts** inaccessible by car or by phone; they are spaced about a day's hike apart along the Appalachian Trail. Either breakfast or dinner must be taken with each night's lodging, and guests must provide their own sleeping bags or sheets. Meals at the huts, though not as good as those back at the lodge, are said to be ample and appetizing. (Bunk with 2 meals for member $50, child member $20, nonmember $57/$27; $10 less for dinner only and $5 less for breakfast only.) All huts are open for **full service** June-Sept.; **self-service rates** (caretaker in residence but no meals provided) are available at other times ($10, non-AMC members $15). For all AMC information, consult AMC's *The Guide,* available at either visitors center.

Camping, Hiking, and Biking Camping is free in a number of areas throughout the **White Mountains National Forest (WMNF).** Neither camping nor fires are allowed above the tree line (approximately 4000 ft.), within 200 ft. of a trail, or within ¼ mi. of roads, huts, shelters, tent platforms, lakes, or streams. Rules often vary depending on forest conditions, so call the **U.S. Forest Service** (528-8721) before settling into a campsite. The Forest Service can also direct you to one of their 22 designated **campgrounds** (sites $8-12, bathrooms and firewood usually available). Call 800-280-2267 to reserve a site, especially in July and August.

If you plan significant **hiking,** invest in the invaluable *AMC White Mountain Guide,* available in most bookstores and huts ($17). The guide includes full maps and descriptions of all trails in the mountains; with these, you can pinpoint precisely where you are on the trail at any given time. *Never* drink untreated water from a stream or lake; all AMC outposts sell water-purification kits. Be prepared for sudden weather changes. Though often peaceful, the peaks can prove treacherous. Beware of black flies, particularly in June. Heightened dosages of B-complex vitamins for two weeks before your trip and continued use throughout should cut down bites significantly. Bug sprays containing DEET may also be helpful.

Next to hiking, **bicycling** offers the best way to see the mountains close up. According to some bikers, the approach to the WMNF from the north is slightly less steep than other approaches. Check the *New Hampshire Bicycle* guide/map, available at information centers, or *25 Bicycle Tours in New Hampshire* ($11), available in local bookstores and outdoor equipment stores.

■ FRANCONIA NOTCH AREA

Formed by glacial movements which began during an ice age 400 million years ago, Franconia Notch is more than just old. Imposing granite cliffs, waterfalls, endless woodlands, and the famous rocky profile "Old Man of the Mountain" attract droves of summer campers. The nearest town is Lincoln, just south of I-93 where Rte. 112 becomes the scenic Kancamagus Highway. The area's main attractions are the outstanding natural phenomena found within the Notch itself.

From Lincoln, the Kancamangus Hwy. (Rte. 112) branches east for a scenic 35 mi. through the **Pemigewasset Wilderness** to Conway. The large basin is rimmed by 4000-ft. peaks and attracts many backpackers and skiers. South of the highway, trails head into the **Sandwich Ranges,** including **Mount Chocorua** (south along Rte. 16 near Ossippee), a dramatic peak and a favorite of 19th-century naturalist painters

Sights and Activities The **Flume Visitors Center** (745-8391) off I-93 north of Lincoln has an excellent, free 15-minute film acquaints visitors with the landscape, (opens daily 9am). While at the center, purchase tickets to **The Flume,** a 2-mi. nature walk over hills, through a covered bridge, to a boardwalk above a fantastic gorge walled by 90-ft.-high granite cliffs ($6, ages 6-12 $3).

The westernmost of the notches, Franconia is best known for the **Old Man of the Mountain,** a 40-ft.-high human profile formed by five ledges of stone atop a 1200-ft. cliff north of The Flume. Hawthorne addressed this geological visage in his 1850 story "The Great Stone Face," and P.T. Barnum once offered to purchase the rock. Today the Old Man is rather doddering; his forehead is now supported by cables and turnbuckles. The best view of the old guy is from **Profile Lake,** a 10-minute walk from the base of the Cannon Mountain Aerial Tramway.

Unlike the Old Man, the **Great Cannon Cliff,** a 1000-ft. sheer drop into the cleft between **Mount Lafayette** and **Cannon Mountain,** is not just for onlookers. Hands-on types test their technical skill and climb the cliff via the "Sticky Fingers" or "Meat Grinder" routes, while less daring visitors might opt to let the 80-passenger **Cannon Mountain Aerial Tramway** (823-5563) do the work. (Open daily 9am-4:30pm, Nov.-mid-April Sat.-Sun. 9am-4:30pm; $8, ages 6-12 $4, one-way hike $6.) Tickets to the Flume and the Tramway may be purchased as a package ($11, ages 6-12 $5).

Myriad trails lead up into the mountains on both sides of the notch, providing excellent day hikes and spectacular views. Be prepared for severe weather, especially above 4000 ft. The **Lake Trail,** a relatively easy hike, wends its way one and a half miles from Lafayette Place to **Lonesome Lake,** where the AMC operates its westernmost summer hut (see White Mountains AMC huts above). The **Greenleaf Trail** (2½ mi.), which starts at the Cannon Tramway parking lot, and the **Old Bridle Path** (3 mi.), which starts at Lafayette Place, are much more ambitious; both lead up to the AMC's Greenleaf Hut near the summit of Mt. Lafayette. The hut overlooks Eagle Lake, a favorite destination for sunset photographers. From Greenleaf, you can trudge the next 7½ mi. east along **Garfield Ridge** to the AMC's most remote hut, the Galehead. Hikes from this base can keep you occupied for days. (Garfield Ridge campsite $4.) A number of other campsites, mainly lean-tos and tent platforms with no showers or toilets, are scattered throughout the mountains. Most run $4 per night on a first-come, first-served basis, but many are free. Contact the U.S. Forest Service or consult the AMC's two-page, free handout, *Backpacker Shelters, Tent sites, Campsites, and Cabins in the White Mountains.*

North of the southern end of Franconia Notch, the Basin, a waterfall in the Pemigewasset River, drops into a 15 ft. granite pool. **The Basin's** walls, smoothed by stones and sand for 25,000 years, seem almost too perfect to be natural. The Basin is one of Franconia Notch State Park's most popular attractions, and is fully accessible to the handicapped.

Besides hiking, take advantage of the nine miles of **bike paths** that begin off U.S. 3 and run through the White Mountain National Forest parallel to I-93. After any exertion, cool off at the lifeguard-protected beach on the northern shore of **Echo Lake State Park** (356-2672), just north of Franconia Notch. (Open daily mid-June-Sept. 9am-8pm. $2.50, NH residents, under 12 and over 65 free.)

Skiing Less renowned than the resorts of Mt. Washington Valley, the ski areas of Franconia Notch, collectively known as **Ski-93** (800-937-5493 or 745-8101, or write P.O. Box 517, Lincoln 13251), offer multiple-area packages. **Loon Mountain** (745-8111, 3 mi. east of I-93 on Rt. 112) has a free beginner's rope tow and, by limiting lift-ticket sales, promises crowd-free skiing. For cross-country skiing plus some great downhill, try **Waterville Valley** (236-8311). Home of the New England Ski Musuem, **Cannon Mountain** (823-5563) in the Notch on I-93, has decent slopes.

Camping At reasonable altitudes, you can camp at the **Lafayette Campground** (823-9513), in Franconia Notch State Park. (Open mid-May to mid-Oct., weather permitting; sites $14 for 2 people, $7 per extra person, showers available.) If Lafayette is full, try the more suburban **Fransted Campground** (823-5675), 1 mi. south of the village and 3 mi. north of the notch. (Sites $13, on the river $16. Each additional person $1. Showers and bathrooms available. Open May-Columbus Day.)

■ NORTH CONWAY

At first glance, North Conway, strung along the stretch of land shared by Rtes. 16 and 302, seems like just another strip of motels and fast food joints on the way to somewhere else. Look again. This town capitalizes on two of New Hampshire's most striking features: the taxes and the terrain. Factory outlet stores, including most major clothing labels, teem with voracious bargain-hunters. But shopping is not the town's only diversion; locals and tourists alike sing the praises of outdoor pastimes. While North Conway clearly shows the strain of being the largest city around, it also enjoys some of the benefits of that status. You'll find many affordable places to eat, the region's best outdoor equipment stores, and, within a short drive, a number of very good cross-country and downhill ski centers.

Accommodations and Food Four miles north of North Conway is the **Shamrock Village Hostel** (356-5153), on Rte. 16A in Intervale, off Rte. 16/302, which provides a bed, access to a kitchen and laundry facilities, and a free breakfast ($12, students or seniors $10). Call ahead. The **Maple Leaf Motel** (356-5388), on Main St., south of the North Conway city park, has clean, spacious rooms for reasonable rates. (Singles $58, doubles $62; spring $30/34; foliage and ski seasons $78/82.) Farther south, the **Sylan Pines Motel** (356-2878) rents rooms of a similar caliber and price. (Singles $35, doubles $40; foliage and ski seasons $70/80).

Breakfast and lunch spots line North Conway's Main St. **Gunther's** (356-5200) on Main St., serves up food devised by owner and cook George Gunther (meals $3-7, open daily 7am-2:30pm). The *après ski* crowd frequents **Café Rubine** (formerly Jackson Square), in the Eastern Slope Inn. Dinner is pricey but have inexpensive meals during happy hour. Dancing every Saturday. (Open daily 11:30am-10pm).

Skiing and Outdoor Activities Though close to many ski areas, North Conway is proudest of its own local mountain, **Cranmore** (800-543-9206; open mid-Dec.-April daily 9am-9pm). On winter Wednesdays, the slopes host a ski racing series; local teams also compete in the nationally known **Mountain Meisters,** open to the public. You can ski day ($35) or night ($15). Students receive a $3 discount with an ID. On U.S. 302, west of Rte. 16, **Attitash** (374-2368) boasts 98% snowmaking on its 28 trails (lift tickets Mon.-Fri. $29, Sat.-Sun. $36; children 6-12 $19/21). **Wildcat** (466-3326), known for having the area's largest lift capacity and a free novice skiing area, can be found on Rte. 16 just south of Pinkham Notch State Park (lift tickets Mon.-Fri. $19, Sat.-Sun. $35). All three areas offer special rates for groups and multi-day visitors; call ahead and ask about specials.

A number of stores in the North Conway area rent quality skis and other outdoor equipment. For downhill skis, try **Joe Jones** in North Conway on Main St. at Mechanic (356-9411; skis, boots and poles $15 per day, $25 per 2 days; open July-Aug. and Dec.-March daily 9am-9pm; off-season Sun.-Thurs. 9am-6pm, Fri.-Sat. 9am-9pm). **Eastern Mountain Sports (EMS),** Main St. (356-5433), on the premises of the Eastern Slope Inn, has free mountaineering pamphlets and excellent books on the area, including *25 Bicycle Tours in New Hampshire.* EMS rents tents and sleeping bags, and sells other camping equipment. The EMS staff gives knowledgable assistance and recommendations for climbing and hiking in North Conway. (Open June-Sept. daily 9am-9pm; off-season Sun.-Thurs. 9am-6pm, Fri.-Sat. 9am-9pm.)

■ PINKHAM NOTCH

Practical Information New Hampshire's easternmost notch lies in the shadow of Mt. Washington, between Gorham and Jackson on Rte. 16. The home of AMC's main information center in the White Mountains and the starting point for most trips up Mt. Washington, Pinkham Notch's practicality gets more publicity than its beauty. Both deserve renown. To get to Pinkham Notch from I-93 south, take exit 42 to U.S. 302 east, then follow Rte. 116 north to U.S. 2 east to Rte. 16 south. From I-93 north, take exit 32 to Rte. 112 east, then take Rte. 16 north. AMC's **Pinkham Notch Visitors Center** (466-2725 or 466-2727 for reservations, 10 mi. north of Jackson on Rte. 16) is the area's best source of information on weather and trail conditions. The center also makes reservations at any of the AMC lodgings and sells the complete line of AMC books, trail maps ($3, weatherproofed $5), and equipment for camping and hiking (open daily 6:30am-10pm).

The **post office** (383-6868) nearest to Pinkham Notch is on Rte. 16B in Jackson Village. (Open Mon.-Fri. 8am-5pm, Sat. 8:30am-12:30pm).

Mt. Washington Beginning just behind the center of Mountain Washington, and leading all the way to the summit, **Tuckerman's Ravine Trail** is a steep climb taking four to five hours each way. Be careful. Every year, Mt. Washington claims at least one life. A gorgeous day can suddenly turn into a chilling storm, with winds kicking up over 100 m.p.h. and thunderclouds ominously rumbling. It has never been warmer than 72°F atop Mt. Washington, and the *average* temperature on the peak is a bone-chilling 26.7°F. All risks aside, the climb *is* stellar, and the view well worth it. Non-climbers with cars can take the **Mount Washington Auto Road** (466-3988), a paved and dirt road that leads motorists 8 mi. to the summit. There they can buy bumper stickers boasting "This Car Climbed Mt. Washington" and thus cruise around impressing easily awed folks. The road begins at Glen House, a short distance north of the visitors center on Rte. 16. ($14 per driver, $5 per passenger, ages 5-12 $3. Road open mid-May to mid-Oct. daily 7:30am-6pm.) Guided van tours to the summit which give a 30-minute presentation on the mountain's natural history and then take a 30-minute trip back down are also available. ($18, kids 5-12 $10.) On the summit you'll find an information center, a snack bar, a museum (466-3347), strong wind, and the **Mt. Washington Observatory** (466-3388), all open the same hours as the visitors center.

Accommodations Just 1½ mi. from Mt. Washington's summit sits the **Lakes of the Clouds,** the largest, highest and most popular of the AMC's huts. Additional sleeping space for six backpackers is available here in a basement refuge room and can be reserved from any hut ($6 per night). For those who fancy a more leisurely climb, the **Hermit's Lake Shelter** is situated about 2 hours up the Tuckerman Ravine Trail. The shelter, which has bathrooms but no shower, sleeps 72 people in eight lean-tos and three tent platforms ($7 per night; buy nightly passes at the visitors center). **Carter Notch Hut** lies to the east of the visitors center, a 4-mile hike up the **Nineteen Mile Brook Trail.** At the **Joe Dodge Lodge,** immediately behind the visitors center, get a comfy bunk with a delicious and sizeable breakfast and dinner for $38 (children $20; nonmembers $45). One or both of the meals can be bypassed, thus lowering the price $5 without breakfast or $10 without dinner (lodging $5 more on Sat. and in Aug.; packages are available).

If all the AMC facilities are booked, head to the **Berkshire Manor** in Gorham, 133 Main St. (466-2186). Guests have access to a full kitchen, living room, large bedrooms, and hall bathrooms. Singles $20, doubles $30.

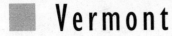# Vermont

Perhaps no state is as appropriately named as Vermont. The lineage of the name extends back to Samuel de Champlain, who in 1609 dubbed the area "green mountain" in his native French (*vert mont*). The Green Mountain range stretches the length of Vermont from north to south, and covers most of the state's width as well. Seemingly every town boasts its own local mountain, convenient for hiking, climbing, skiing, and sensational viewing. Vermont's economic fate has long been shaped by its mountanious terrain, which prevents the cultivation of many crops and has insulated the state from the encroachment of industry. The major agricultural activity for Vermonters is dairy farming, but much of the state's land has been preserved for public enjoyment in 30 state forests, 80 state parks, and one mammoth national forest; the Green Mountain National Forest covers 186,000 acres.

Vermonters have had a tradition of vigorous political participation, ranging widely from conservative (only Vermont and Maine rejected Franklin Roosevelt in all four of his elections) to liberal (Vermont's Congressman Bernie Sanders was once the socialist mayor of Burlington). Local activism today tends to be aimed at checking the excesses of the ex-urbanite yuppies who have invaded Vermont over the past few decades. There exists a constant tension between the original, pristine Vermont, and the packaged Vermont of organic food stores and mountaineering shops. Happily, the former still seems to prevail.

PRACTICAL INFORMATION

Capital: Montpelier.
Vermont Travel Division, 134 State St., Montpelier 05602 (828-3237; open Mon.-Fri. 7:45am-4:30pm). **Department of Forests, Parks and Recreation,** 103 S. Main St., Waterbury 05676 (241-3670; open Mon.-Fri. 8am-4:30pm). **Travel Division Fall Foliage Hotline** (828-3239) for fall colors information Sept.-Oct. **Vermont Snowline** (229-0531), Nov.-May 24-hr. recording on snow conditions.
Time Zone: Eastern. **Postal Abbreviation:** VT
Sales Tax: 5%; 7% on meals and lodgings.

SKIING

Twenty-four downhill resorts and 47 cross-country trail systems lace Vermont. For a free winter attractions packet, call the Vermont Travel Division (see Practical Information above. Also contact **Vermont Ski Areas Association,** 26 State St., Montpelier 05601 (223-2439; open Mon.-Fri. 8am-4:30pm). Contact the **Lake Champlain Regional Chamber of Commerce** (863-3489), P.O. Box 453, Burlington 05402 (open Mon.-Fri. 9am-5pm) about the **"Ski Vermont's Classics"** program, which offers a multi-area lift ticket usable at three Vermont resorts. (3-day ticket $145, 5-day ticket $200. Prices subject to holiday upgrades near Christmas at some resorts.)

Vermont's famous **downhill** ski resorts offer a great range of terrain and accommodations. Always inquire about shared rooms with bunks which cost significantly less than private rooms. Some better resorts include: **Killington** (773-1300; lodging 800-621-6867; 155 trails, 19 lifts, 6 mountains, and the most extensive snowmaking system in the world); **Stratton** (297-2200; lodging 800-843-6867; 92 trails, 12 lifts); **Sugarbush** (583-2381; lodging 800-537-8427; 110 trails, 16 lifts, 2 mountains); **Stowe** (253-3000; lodging 800-253-4754; 47 trails, 10 lifts); **Middlebury College Snow Bowl** (388-4356; lodging 388-7951, 14 trails; 3 lifts); and **Jay Peak** (800-451-4449; 37 trails, 6 lifts). **Cross-country** resorts include the **Trapp Family Lodge,** Stowe (253-8511; lodging 800-826-7000; 60 mi. of trails); **Mountain Meadows,** Killington (757-7077; 25 mi. of trails); **Woodstock** (457-2114; 47 mi. of trails); and **Sugarbush-Rossignol** (583-2301 or 800-451-4320; 30 mi. of trails).

■■■ BURLINGTON

The largest city in a state known for its outdoorsy entertainment and its granola-eater mentality, Burlington forges a harmonious union between its surrounding and its metropolitan status. In downtown, Burlington has taken the oxymoron "middle-class hippie" and made it not just a reality but a way of life, as bead stores coexist peacefully with elegant art galleries and designer clothing boutiques. Five local colleges, including the University of Vermont (UVM), endow the city with a large youthful population. Tucked between Lake Champlain and the Green Mountains, young and vibrant Burlington is a pleasant place to stay.

PRACTICAL INFORMATION

Emergency: 911.

Tourist Information: Lake Champlain Regional Chamber of Commerce, 60 Main St. (863-3489), provides free maps of the Burlington Bike Path and parks. Open year-round Mon.-Fri. 8:30am-5pm, June-Oct. also Sat.-Sun. 10am-2pm. More centrally located is the **Church St. Marketplace Information Gallery,** on the corner of Church and Bank St. Open May 15-June Mon.-Sat. 11am-4pm, July-mid-Oct. daily 11am-5pm.

Amtrak: 29 Railroad Ave., Essex Jct. (800-872-7245 or 879-7298), 5 mi. east on Rte. 15 from the center of Burlington. To: Montreal ($19); New York ($60). Station open daily 6am-6pm and 7pm-9pm. Local bus to downtown 75¢. Open Mon.-Sat. 6am-9:30pm bus every ½ hour.

Buses: Vermont Transit, 135 Saint Paul St. (864-6811), at Main St. Connections to: Boston ($44); Montreal ($23); White River Junction ($14.50); Middlebury ($7.50); Bennington ($19); Montpelier ($7.50); Albany ($31). Connections made with Greyhound. Sept.-May 25% discount for students with ID. Ameripasses accepted. Station open daily 7am-8pm. Tickets sold 7:30am-8pm.

Public Transport: Chittenden County Transit Authority (CCTA) (864-0211). Frequent, reliable service. Downtown hub at Cherry and Church St. Connections with Shelburne and other outlying areas. Buses operate every ½ hr. Mon.-Sat. 6:15am-9:20pm, depending on routes. Fare 75¢, seniors and disabled 35¢, under 18 50¢, under 5 free. **Special Services Transportation Agency** (655-7880), supplies information and advice about disabled and elderly travel.

Bike Rental: Ski Rack, 85 Main St. (658-3313), has road bikes ($5 per hr., $18 per day, $60 per week) and mountain bikes ($8/22/70). Helmet and lock included. Bike repairs guaranteed 48 hrs. or less; minor repairs while you wait. Open Mon.-Thurs. 10am-8pm, Fri. 9am-9pm, Sat. 9am-6pm, Sun. 11am-5pm.

Help Lines: Women's Rape Crisis Center, 863-1236. **Crises Services of Chittenden County,** 863-2400. Both open 24 hrs.

Post Office: 11 Elmwood Ave. (863-6033), at Pearl St. Open Mon.-Fri. 8am-5pm, Sat. 9am-noon. **ZIP code:** 05401.

Area Code: 802.

ACCOMMODATIONS AND CAMPING

See the Chamber of Commerce for a complete accommodations listings of area accommodations. Bed and Breakfasts are generally found in the outlying suburbs. Reasonably priced hotels and guest houses line Shelburne Rd. south of downtown. **Mrs. Farrell's Home Hostel (HI-AYH),** 27 Arlington (865-3730), three miles from downtown off Heineburg, has six beds: four in a clean, comfortable basement, and two on a screened-in porch amidst her garden's flowers. The adventurous owner is friendly, but not easy to reach on the phone. Call around 7-8am or 5-7pm in order to make an absolutely required reservation. Linens, showers, coffee, and bagels are free. Strict curfew begins at 10pm. ($15, nonmembers $17. Accessible by public transport. Handicapped-accessible room available for summer.) Close to downtown is **Howden Cottage,** 32 N. Champlain (864-7198), a charming B&B. The original art that adorns the walls and the daily, fresh-baked muffins are both created by the talented proprietor Bruce Howden. (Mid-May-mid-Oct. singles $39, doubles $49; off-season singles $35, doubles $45. Rates remain basically stable year-round at $45 for one of two double bedrooms with a shared bath. Reservations by credit card strongly recommended.) **North Beach Campsites** (862-0942) Institute Rd., is only 1½ mi. north of town on North Ave., along Lake Champlain. (Open mid-May-mid-Sept. 67 Sites. $14, $16 with electricity, $19 with full hookup. Vermont residents pay $4 less. Showers 25¢ per 5 min., beach free but closes at 9pm.) Take the CCTA North Ave. bus leaving from the main city terminal on Saint Paul St. **Shelburne Campground** (985-2540), Shelburne Rd., 1 mi. north of Shelburne and 5 mi. south of Burlington on Rte. 7, offers a pool, laundry facilities, and free showers. Buses en route to Shelburne South stop right next to the campground. (Open May-Oct. Sites for 2 people $16, $20 with hookup, $2 each additional person.)

PHISH FOOD

Immortalized by ex-regular Phish on their album *A Picture of Nectar's*, **Nectar's**, 188 Main St. (658-4771), serves inexpensive food in a relaxed setting. Burlington-famous fries $3. The place rocks with live music nightly with no cover. (Open Mon.-Fri. 5:30am-2am, Sat. 7am-1am, Sun. 7am-2am.) Upstairs dances **Club Metronome** (865-4563). **Bove's,** 28 Pearl St.(864-6651), serves authentic Italian food at more than affordable prices. Sandwiches range from $1.50-$3.50, dinner $5-8, and all drinks on the extensive cocktails menu are $2.30. Lines are common, so come before you're starving (open Tues.-Sat. 10am-10pm). **Henry's Diner,** 155 Bank St. (862-9010), has offered the ultimate American diner experience since 1925. (Sandwiches $2-4, full meals $5-10, breakfast offered all day. Open daily 6:30am-3:45pm.) Loads of booze and fun can be found at the **Vermont Pub and Brewery,** 144 College St. (865-0500), at Saint Paul's, which offers affordable sandwiches, delicious homemade beers, and English pub favorites like Cornish pasties—similar to a pot pie ($5). Should you want to learn more about Original Vermont Lager, the brewers would be happy to escort you on a free brewery tour given Wednesday at 8pm and Saturday at 4pm. (Open daily 11:30am-12-30am. Live entertainment Thurs.-Fri. 9:30pm.) Buy wine for $4 in the strong-smelling warehouse of the **Cheese Outlet,** 400 Pine St. (863-3968 or 800-447-1205; open daily 9am-7pm, Sun. 11am-5pm).

Top off any meal with the ultimate Vermont experience. Though the converted gas station has burned down, the first **Ben and Jerry's** (862-9620) still sits on its original site at 169 Cherry St. serving Cherry Garcia or Cookie Dough ice cream for $2 per cone. (Open Mon.-Fri. 11:30am-11pm, Sat.-Sun. 11:30am-midnight.)

SIGHTS AND ENTERTAINMENT

With its sprawling, low-lying suburbs, Burlington might not look like a cultural mecca. However, the city manages to provide the lively artistic entertainment characteristic of most cities, without compromising the natural advantages of its location. **Church Street Marketplace** downtown is a popular pedestrian mall; besides being a haven for tie-dye and ice-cream lovers, this historic district serves as a shopping center for modern northern Vermont and displays and sells the works of local artists. The history-inclined should also stroll through Victorian **South Willard Street,** which now houses **Champlain College,** and the campus of the **University of Vermont** (656-3480), founded in 1797. **City Hall Park,** in the heart of downtown, and **Battery Street Park,** on Lake Champlain near the edge of downtown, are beautiful places to relax and study the scenery.

Summer culture vultures won't want to miss the many festivities Burlington offers: the **Vermont Mozart Festival** (862-7352 or 800-639-9097) sends Bach, Beethoven, and Mozart to barns, farms, and meadows in July and early August; the **Discover Jazz Festival** (863-7992) features over 200 international and Vermont musicians in early to mid-June in both free and ticketed performances; and the **Champlain Valley Folk Festival** (656-5263) entertains in August. The Flynn Theatre Box Office, 153 Main St. (863-5966), handles sales for the Mozart and jazz performances. (Open Mon.-Fri. 10am-5pm, Sat. 11am-4pm.)

The **Shelburne Museum** (985-3346), 7 mi. south of Burlington, in **Shelburne,** houses one of the best collections of Americana in the country. Beside 35 buildings transported from all over New England, 45-acre Shelburne has a covered bridge from Cambridge, a steamboat and a lighthouse from Lake Champlain, and a bit of a local railroad. Don't miss the Degas, Cassatt, Manet, Monet, Rembrandt, and Whistler paintings. The museum really has one of the best collections of American art north of Boston; a surprising find in the middle of rural Vermont. Tickets are valid for two consecutive days; you'll need both to cover the mile-long exhibit. (Open daily 9am-5pm, mid-Oct.-mid-May Sat. only by reservation; $15, students $9, ages 6-14 $6.50, under 6 free.) 5 mi. farther south on U.S. 7, the **Vermont Wildflower Farm** (425-3500), has a seed shop and 6½ acres of wildflower gardens. (Open May-late Oct. daily 10am-5pm. $3, seniors and AAA members $2.50, under 12 free.)

The **Ethan Allen Homestead** (865-4556) rests northeast of Burlington on Rte. 127. In the 1780s, Allen, who forced the surrender of Fort Ticonderoga during the American Revolution and helped establish the state of Vermont, built his cabin in what is now the Winooski Valley Park. A multi-media show and tour give insight into the hero and his era. (Open Tues.-Sun. 1-5pm; mid-June-Labor Day Mon.-Sat. 10am-5pm, Sun. 1-5pm; last tour 4:15; Labor Day-late Oct. daily 1-5pm; $3.50, seniors $3, kids 5-17 $2, under 5 free.)

The **Burlington Community Boathouse,** at the base of College St. at Lake Champlain (865-3377), rents sailboats ($15 per hr.) and rowboats ($5 per hr. Open daily mid-May-Mid.-Sept. 9am-7pm).

■ NEAR BURLINGTON: CHAMPLAIN VALLEY

Lake Champlain, a 100-mi.-long lake between Vermont's Green Mountains and New York's Adirondacks, is often referred to as "Vermont's West Coast." Crisscrossing the lake is the **Lake Champlain Ferry** (864-9804), located on the dock at the bottom of King St., which will ship you across the lake or back from Burlington to Port Kent, NY. (Late June-Aug. daily 7:15am-7:45pm, 14 per day; Sept.-mid-Oct. 8am-5:30pm, 8-11 per day; $3, ages 6-12 $1, with car $12. Crossing time 1 hr. Return service available later.) You can also take a ferry from Grand Isle to Plattsburg, NY, or go 14 mi. south of Burlington and take one from Charlotte, VT, to Essex, NY (either fare $1.75, ages 6-12 50¢, with car $6.75). The Grand Isle Ferry is the only one that runs year-round.

The **Spirit of Ethan Allen** scenic cruise (862-9685) departs from Burlington's Perkins Pier at the bottom of Maple St. The boat cruises along the Vermont coast, giving passengers a close-up view of the famous Thrust Fault, invisible from land. (Late May-mid-Oct. daily at 10am, noon, 2pm, and 4pm. $7.75, ages 5-11 $3.75. Call about the more costly Captain's Dinner and Sunset Cruises.)

Mt. Philo State Park (425-2390), 15 mi. south on Rte. 7, offers outstanding viewpoints of the Champlain Valley and pleasant camping. The natural beauty of the spot somewhat makes up for its inconvenient location. (Open Memorial Day-Columbus Day daily 10am-sunset. Campsites $10. Lean-tos $14. Entrance fee $1.50, ages 4-14 $1.) Take the Vermont Transit bus from Burlington heading south along U.S. 7 toward Vergennes. There's a sign on the left for the park before you're out of Charlotte and directions are clearly marked from there. At the northern end of the Lake, near Swanton, VT, is the marsh of the **Missisquoi National Wildlife Refuge.** Also in the north part of the Lake is **Burton Island State Park** (524-6353), accessible only by ferry (8:30am-6:30pm) from Kill Kare State Park, 35 mi. north of Burlington and 3½ mi. southwest near St. Albans Bay, off U.S. 7. The campground has 46 lean-to and tent sites ($15.50 and $11 respectively, $3 per additional person in tent, $4 in lean-to). **Grand Isle** also has a state park with camping (372-4300), just off U.S. 2 north of Keeler Bay. (Open late May-mid-Oct. Sites $12, $3 each additional person after 4, lean-tos $16, $4 each additional person after 4.)

■■■ MIDDLEBURY

Unlike many Vermont towns, which seem to shy away from association with local colleges, Middlebury, "Vermont's Landmark College Town," is proud of the energy and culture stimulated by Middlebury College. The school and the town mix comfortably, and the result is an old Vermont atmosphere with an invigorating vitality, historical attractions, and an active nightlife.

Practical Information Middlebury is on U.S. Rte. 7, 42 mi. south of Burlington. Ask the friendly staff at the **Addison County Chamber of Commerce,** 2 Court St. (388-7951), in the historic Gamaliel Painter House, for area information, (open Mon.-Fri. 9am-5pm, summer Sat.-Sun. 1-4pm). **Vermont Transit** stops at Keeler's Gulf Station, 16 Court St. (388-4373), west of Main St. Buses run to Burlington ($7.50), Rutland ($7.50), Albany ($24), and Boston ($40). (Open Mon.-Sat. 6am-10pm, Sun. 7am-9pm.) There is no public transportation in Middlebury, but bikes can be rented at the **Bike and Ski Touring Center,** 74 Main St. (388-6666).
   Middlebury's **post office:** 10 Main St. (388-2681; open Mon.-Fri. 6am-5:40pm, Sat. 6am-4pm); **ZIP code:** 05753; **area code:** 802.

Accommodations and Camping Middlebury's best budget accommodations are all located several miles from the center of town. 3 mi. north of town on Rte. 7, Linda and Paul Horn rent one room, complete with private bath and country decor, out of their charming **Horn Farnsworth House** (388-2300). ($55, extra room available for large parties $25.) The **Sugar House Motor Inn** (388-2770 or 388-4330), just south of the Horn Farnsworth House on Rte. 7, rents basic motel rooms for average prices (singles $40, off season $84; during foliage season doubles $58/94). Arrive on the right night and, weather permitting, you can enjoy a campfire and free, fresh-roasted sweet corn. On the southern edge of Middlebury, 2 mi. south of the town center on Rte. 7, the **Greystone Motel** (388-4935) has 10 rooms, newly decorated and reasonably priced (singles $45-50, doubles $55-60). Situated on a lake, **Branbury State Park** (247-5925), 7 mi. south on U.S. 7, then 4 mi. south on Rte. 53, not only rents tent sites but also provides boats for the day ($3-5). (Open late May to mid Oct. Sites $11, lean-tos $14. Reservations recommended July-Aug.)

Restaurants and Nightlife Middlebury's many fine restaurants cater chiefly to those with large expense accounts, but the year-round presence of students assures the survival of cheaper places. **Calvi's,** 42 Main St. (388-4182), is an old-fashioned soda fountain with old-fashioned prices. Try their homemade ice cream in a cone ($1.30). (Open 8am-10pm, mid-Sept.-early June 8am-6pm, closed all Sundays.) Students also flock to **Mister Up's** (388-6724), on Bakery Lane just off Main St., for its impressively eclectic menu, which includes beer-boiled shrimp ($4.50), chicken picada ($13), sandwiches ($5-6), and an extensive salad bar ($6.50). (Open daily 11:30am-midnight.) Popular with students as well as locals is **Fire and Ice,** 26 Seymour St. (388-7166), down the hill from the Congregationalist Church downtown. Well-prepared American fare, and a great salad/bread bar. (Open Tues.-Fri. 11:30am-9pm, Sat.-Sun. 11:30am-9:30pm. Entrees $9.90-$17.50; lunch menu $5-12).
   Nightlife in Middlebury is surprisingly lively, thanks again to the college's proximity. Overlooking Otter Creek, the trendy **Woody's,** 5 Bakery Lane (388-4182), off Main St., offers delicious (if somewhat upscale) dishes and drinks. Lunch prices are reasonable ($4-7). (Open Mon.-Sat. 11:30am-midnight, Sun. 10:30am-3pm and 5-9:30pm.) **Amigos,** 4 Merchants Row (388-3624), serves up Mexican food ($2.50-$12) and live local music Friday and Saturday from 10pm-1am. Chow down on free spicy chicken wings between 4 and 6pm Monday to Thursday. (Open Mon.-Sat. 11:30am-10pm, Sun. 4-9pm. Bar open nightly until midnight.) **Noonie's Deli** (388-0014), in the Marbleworks building just behind Main St., serves up terrific sandwiches on homemade bread ($5 and up) and fresh baked desserts (open 9am-9pm).

NEW ENGLAND

Sights Visit the **Vermont State Craft Center** (388-3177) at Frog Hollow, which features exhibits and sells the artistic productions of Vermonters (open daily 10am-5pm). The nearby **Sheldon Museum,** 1 Park St. (388-2117), has an extensive and sometimes macabre collection of antiques and Americana, including a set of teeth extracted in the 19th century and a disturbingly well-preserved stuffed cat from the same period. (Open June-Oct. Mon.-Fri. 10am-5pm, Nov.-April Wed. and Fri. 1-4pm. $2.50, seniors and students $2, under 12 50¢.) **Middlebury College** provides access to a year-round calender of cultural events. The College's **Arts Center,** just outside of town, hosts a terrific concert series in its new concert hall, which is itself architecturally interesting and worth a visit. Call the campus **box office** (388-3711, ext. 7469) for details on plays and events sponsored by the college (open Tues.-Sat. 10am-4pm).

The **University of Vermont's Morgan Horse Farm** (388-2011) lies west of Middlebury on Rte. 23, 2 mi. from Rte. 125. Tour the farm and learn about breeding. (Open May-Oct. daily 9am-4pm.$2.50, teenagers $1, under 13 free.)

■■■ STOWE

Stowe winds gracefully up the side of Mount Mansfield (Vermont's highest peak, at 4393 ft.). The town is ostentatiously quaint, and fancies itself an American skiing hotspot on par with its ritzier European counterparts. Stowe does not want to be considered a bargain, but behind the facade, travelers can find some unbeatable values. Besides, no one can put a price on striking mountainous surroundings or the promise of a great downhill run.

Practical Information The ski areas all lie northwest of Stowe on Rte. 108. Stowe is 12 mi. north of I-89 exit 10, which is 27 mi. southwest of Burlington. **Vermont Transit** will only take you to **Vincent's Drug and Variety Store** off Park Row in Waterbury, 10 mi. from Stowe. (Open Mon.-Fri. 8:30am-7pm, Sat. 8:30am-6pm, Sun. 9am-3pm.) From there, **Lamoille County Taxi** (253-9433) will drive you to the center of Stowe village for $17. **The Stowe Trolley** (253-7585) has an irregular schedule, but runs between the important locations in the village ($1; every 30 min. 7:30-10:30am, 2-3pm; every hr. 11:30am-1:30pm).

In addition to providing information on area attractions, the **Stowe Area Association** (253-7321 or 800-247-8693) on Main St., in the center of the village, runs a free booking service for member hotels and restaurants. (Open Mon.-Fri. 9am-5pm, Sat. 10am-5pm, Sun. 10am-4pm; winter Mon.-Fri. 9am-9pm, Sat.-Sun. 10am-6pm.) This service is also provided by the **Stowe Mountain Resort's** booking service (253-3000). Stowe's **post office:** 105 Depot St. (253-7521), off Main St. (open Mon.-Fri. 8:30am-5pm, Sat. 7am-4:30pm); **ZIP code:** 05672; **area code:** 802.

Food, Accommodations, and Camping At the **Depot Street Malt Shoppe,** 57 Depot St. (253-4269), visitors can enjoy classic American diner fare in an artfully recreated 50s soda shop ($3-8, open daily 11am-9pm). For a filling meal try the **Sunset Grille and Tap Room** (253-9281), on Cottage Club Rd. off Mountain Rd., a friendly, down-home barbecue restaurant and bar with a vast selection of domestic beers and generous meals ($5-15). (Open daily 11:30am-midnight).

The town's best lodging bargain by far, the **Vermont State Ski Dorm** (253-4010), up 7 mi. into Mountain Rd., doubles as a hostel from April-December ($12.50 per night, breakfast $3.50, dinner $4; kitchen available). The rest of the year, manager and trained chef Jim Sanderson serves two meals a day with a room for $27.50. Make sure to reserve by phone far in advance for ski and foliage seasons. The friendly, eccentric host of the **Golden Kitz** (253-4217 or 800-548-7568), Mountain Rd., treats her "lovies" like family. Complete with room for "flirty dancing," this lodge/motel offers parlor areas, an art studio, and pleasant bedrooms varying in theme and price. Call ahead. (Singles with shared bath $20-$30 in lowest season, $40-50 during Christmas week and fall foliage; doubles with private bath $40-46/

$60-64. Multi-day packages available.) The committed budget traveler should ask if "dungeon" doubles are available ($30). The **Gold Brook Campground** (253-7683), 1½ mi. south of the town center on Rte. 100, provides the experience of camping without all of that wilderness stuff. (Showers, laundry, volleyball, badminton, horseshoes. Tent sites for 2 people $12, with varying degrees of hookup $16, $18, and $21; $3 per each additional person.) **Smuggler's Notch State Park** (253-4014) offers hot showers, lean-tos ($15 for 4 people, $4 per additional person up to max. of 8), and tent sites ($11 for 4 people, $3 per each additional person up to max. of 8. Open May 20-Oct.10; reservations suggested).

Skiing and Activities Stowe's ski offerings consist of the **Stowe Mountain Resort** (253-3000 or 800-253-4754) and **Smuggler's Notch** (664-8851 or 800-451-8752). Both areas are expensive; lift tickets are nearly $45 per day. The **Von Trapp Family Lodge,** (yes, *the* Trapp family of *Sound of Music* fame) Luce Hill Rd. (253-8511), offers the area's best cross-country skiing along with equipment rentals and lessons (trail fee $10, ski rentals $12, lessons $14; discounts for children). **AJ's Ski and Sports** (253-4593) at the base of Mountain Rd., rents virtually brand new ski and snow equipment (skis, boots, and poles: downhill $18 per day, 2 days $32; cross- country $12/20; snowboards with boots: $24 per day). Reserve equipment five days in advance for 20% off. (Open Nov.-April daily 8am-6pm; off-season 9am-6pm.)

In summer, Stowe's frenetic pace drops off—as do its prices. Rent **mountain bikes** at **Stowe Mountain Sports,** 1056 Mountain Rd. (253-4896; $6 for first hr., $5 for second hr., $13.50 for ½-day, $22 for full day; open daily 9am-5pm), and **roller blades** at **Front Four Sports,** 430 Mountain Rd. (253-9690; $8 per hr., $16 for 3 hr., $18 per day; open summer Mon.-Fri. 9am-5pm, Sat. 9am-4pm, Sun. 10am-4pm). Stowe's 5½-mi. asphalt recreation path, which starts behind the Community Church and roughly parallels the Mountain Road's ascent is smoothly suited for cross-country skiing in the winter, and biking, skating, or strolling in the summer.

Those interested in checking out the area's **fly-fishing** should head to the **Fly Rod Shop** (253-7346), 3 mi. south of Stowe on Rte. 100. The shop rents fly rods and reels ($12 per day), and rods with spinning reels ($6 per day). Watch the owner tie a fly or two; free fly-fishing classes are offered on the shop's own pond (April-Oct. Wed. 4-6pm, Sat. 9-10am). Fishing licenses are available (non-residents $18 per 3 days, $35 for season). If you're looking to canoe on the nearby Lamoille River, try **Umiak,** 1880 Mountain Rd. (253-2317), in Gale Farm Center. The store (its name is the Inuit word for "kayak") rents *umiaks* and canoes in the summer ($20 per ½-day, $30 per day) and offers a full-day river trip for $20 (rental and transportation to the river included). Located in a rustic red barn on Mountain Rd., **Topnotch Stowe** (253-8585) has summer horseback riding (guided tours, $22 per hr).

Entertainment Ski resorts have culture too. After a long day, unwind at a performance of the **Stowe Stage Company** (253-7944), the Playhouse, Mountain Rd. (performances June-October, 8pm). The sound of music fills the Trapp Family Concert Meadow on Sundays at 7pm for the Stowe Performing Arts's **Music in the Meadow.** (Tickets $15, under 19 $5.) **Noon Music in May,** each Wednesday at the Stowe Community Church, is free (call 253-7321 for info on both).

The absence of any significant body of water doesn't stop the **Stowe Yacht Club** at the Commodore's Inn (253-7131), just south of the village on Rte. 100, from hosting a full summer racing season, albeit with remote controlled models. The races are free and public (May 1-Oct. 31 Mon. and Wed. 5pm, Sun. 1pm).

■ SCOOPING LIBERALLY

In 1978, Ben Cohen and Jerry Greenfield enrolled in a Penn State correspondence course in ice cream making, converted a gas station into their first shop, and launched themselves on the road to the ice cream hall of fame. Today, **Ben and**

Jerry's Ice Cream Factory (244-5641), a few miles north of Waterbury on Rte. 100, is impossible to miss. At the factory, sample the flavors that made these two guys famous and learn the history of their operation on a 20-min. tour of the facilities ($1). The tour also showcases the social consciousness that their company is famous for. For instance, no individual worker in the company can make more than seven times the lowest paid worker. Those on an ice cream pilgrimage can sample the sweet success of the men who brought "Lemongrad" to Moscow and "Economic Chunk" to Wall Street after the 1987 stock market crash. (Open daily 9am-6pm, late June-Aug. 9am-9pm, tours every 30 min., every 15 min. late June-Aug.)

■■■ WHITE RIVER JUNCTION

Central Vermont is graced with quiet winding backroads and grazing cows in green pastures; if you enjoy rural rubbernecking, plan an east-west trip along U.S. 4, or a north-south trip on Rte. 100. Both routes are best reached from U.S. 5 or I-89, at the Connecticut River. White River Junction, however, receives more visitors today as a result of the nearby intersection of I-89 and I-91. Taking its name from its location at the confluence of the White and Connecticut rivers, the Junction once was the hub of railroad transportation in the northeastern U.S., and now serves as the major bus center for central and eastern Vermont. **Vermont Transit** (295-3011or 800-451-3292), on U.S. 5 adjoining the William Tally House Restaurant, has connections across New Hampshire and along the Connecticut River. (Office open Sun.-Fri. 7am-8:30pm, Sat. 7am-5pm. Students with ID 25% discount Sept.-May.) **Amtrak's** *Montrealer* train running south to New York City and Washington D.C., and north to Essex Junction (near Burlington) and Montréal, chugs through here daily (800-872-7245; station on Railroad Rd. off N. Main St.; open nightly 9:15pm-6am).

An **information booth** sits across Sykes Ave. from the bus station (intersection of Sykes and U.S. 5 off I-89 and 91; open June-Aug. Sat.-Sun. noon-5pm), and in town, the **Chamber of Commerce,** 12 Gates St. (295-6200), just off S. Main, will inform you on Vermont. (Open Mon. 9:30am-4:30pm, Wed.-Fri. 9:30am-5pm, June-Aug. Fri. and Sat. 5-8pm.) White River's **post office:** 9 Main St. (295-2803; open Mon.-Fri. 8-10am and 3-5pm and Sat. 8-10am) **ZIP code:** 05001; **area code:** 802.

For a quick bite, stop at the local favorite, the **Polkadot Restaurant,** 1 N. Main St. (295-9722), a diner authentic down to the gruff but likeable staff and incredible food. (Sandwiches $1.50-$4.50, 2 pork chops, applesauce, mashed potatoes, veggie, soup, rolls, slaw, dessert, and coffee $5.50. Open daily 5am-8pm.) The best, and virtually the only, bet for lodging is the old-style **Hotel Coolidge,** 17 S. Main St. (295-3118 or 800-622-1124), across the road from the retired Boston and Maine steam engine. From the bus station, walk to the right along U.S. 5, down the hill past two stop lights (about 1 mi.) into town. Renamed in honor of frequent guest "Silent Cal" Coolidge's pop, the Coolidge boasts neatly kept rooms at fair prices (singles from $40, doubles from $45). At the **Catamount Brewery,** 58 S. Main St. (296-2248), you can sample unpasteurized amber ale produced by British brewing methods (tours vary seasonally; call for details).

■■■ BRATTLEBORO

Southeastern Vermont is often accused of living too much in its colonial past, but Brattleboro seems to be more a captive of the Age of Aquarius than the War for Independence. Whether camouflaged in Birkenstocks and tie-dye or adorned more conventionally, visitors feel right at home in this town where the vibes are groovy and the organic produce is even better. Nature-worship peaks in the fall foliage season when a horde of tourists invades the area to take part in the ultimate earth fest.

Practical Information At the **Chamber of Commerce,** 180 Main St. (254-4565), get the *Brattleboro Main Street Walking Tour* and a detailed town map (open Mon.-Fri. 8am-5pm). In summer and foliage season, an information booth is open on the Town Common off Putney Rd. (257-1112; open Mon.-Fri. 9am-6pm). On the busiest summer weekends, an additional booth opens on Western Ave. just beyond the historic Creamery Bridge (257-4801; open Thurs.-Sun. 10am-6pm).

The **Amtrak** (800-835-8725) *Montrealer* train from New York City and Springfield stops in Brattleboro behind the museum on Vernon Rd. Trains go once daily to Montréal ($46), New York ($44), and Washington D.C. ($85). Arrange tickets and reservations at **Lyon Travel,** 10 Elliot St. (254-6033; open Mon.-Fri. 8:30am-5pm). **Greyhound** and **Vermont Transit** (254-6066) stop in the parking lot behind the Citgo station at the junction of U.S. 5, Rte. 9 and I-91 on Putney Rd. (Open Mon.-Fri. 8am-5pm, Sat. 8am-12:15pm, Sun. 10:30am-12:15pm, 2-3:30pm, and 6-7pm.) Brattleboro is on Vermont Transit's Burlington-New York City route (3 per day, $37). Other destinations include Springfield, MA (3 per day, $14) and White River Junction (3 per day, $11.50), with connections to Montpelier, Waterbury, Burlington, and Montréal. To get downtown from the Vermont Transit station, take the **Brattleboro Town Bus** (257-1761). Buses stop in front of the station and run on Putney Rd. to Main St. and then up High St. to West Brattleboro. (Buses run Mon.-Fri. 6:30am-5:45pm; fare 75¢, students 25¢.)

Brattleboro's **post office:** 204 Main St., (254-4100; open Mon.-Fri. 9am-5pm, Sat. 9am-noon); **ZIP code:** 05301; **area code:** 802.

Accommodations and Camping

Renovated in the 1930s, the Art-Deco **Latchis Hotel** (254-6300), on the corner of Flat and Main St., has decent rooms, (singles $49-62, doubles $55-72). The lobby decor outdoes that of the rooms, but the location is unbeatable. The **West Village,** 480 Western Ave. (254-5610), about 3 mi. out of town on Rte. 9 in West Brattleboro, caters more to the long-term visitor. Reservations cannot be made more than one week in advance. Some rooms have kitchenette and microwave. (Singles $40. Doubles $45, weekly $160.) If you are really in search of a bargain, grab your bug-repellant and flashlight and head for the **Vagabond Hostel (HI-AYH),** 25 min. north on Rte. 30, which offers decent bunks and extensive facilities, but not much lighting and many mosquitoes. (874-4096; open May 15-Nov. 16. $12, nonmembers $15. Group rates, 96 bunks, game room, kitchen.) **Fort Dummer State Park** (254-2610) 2 mi. south on U.S. 5, turn left on Fairground Ave. just before the I-91 interchange, and follow it around to South Main St., has campsites with fireplaces, picnic tables, and bathroom facilities, and one lean-to with disabled access. (Sites $10. Lean-tos $14. Firewood $2 per armload. Hot showers 25¢. Reservations accepted up to 21 days in advance; $3, non-refundable, min. stay 2 nights. Open May 21-Labor Day.) **Molly Stark State Park** (464-5460) is 15 mi. west of town on Rte. 9. (24 sites $10; 11 lean-tos $14; RV sites without hookups $10. Hot showers 25¢ per 5 min. Reservations $3, min. of 3 days in advance. Open Memorial Day-Columbus Day.) About 25 mi. west in Bennington, the **Greenwood Lodge (HI-AYH)** offers bunks and private rooms in a 50-bed lodge in the Prospect Cross-Country Ski Center (442-2547; dorm $14-19, private rooms for one or two $30-40; open May 20-Oct. 20). Tent sites with limited RV hookup are also available. (Site $11.55, each additional person $2.10. Water and electricity $2.10.)

Food and Nightlife

Just across Putney Rd. from the Connecticut River Safari is the **Marina Restaurant** (257-7563), which overlooks the West River, offering a cool breeze and a beautiful view. Try the chicken with fusilli ($7.75) or the eggplant parmesan ($6.75). (Open Wed. 4-10pm, Thurs.-Sat.4-10pm, Sun. 11am-2pm and 2:30pm-6:30pm.) The **Common Ground,** 25 Eliot St. (257-0855), where the town's laid-back "granolas" cluster, supports organic farmers by featuring a wide range of affordable veggie dishes. Soup, salad, bread, and a beverage for $4.25, or a good ol' PB&J for $3. (Open Mon. and Wed.-Sat. 11:30am-9pm, Sun. 10:30am-9pm.) The **Backside Cafe,** 24 High St. (257-5056), inside the Mid-town Mall, serves delicious food in an artsy loft with rooftop dining. Breakfast features farm-fresh eggs cooked to perfection. Create your own burrito ($5.25) or *chile rellenos* (2 for $5.50). (Open

Mon.-Fri. 7:30am-4pm, Sat. 8am-3pm, Sun. 10am-3pm; for dinner Mon.-Fri. 5-9pm. In winter, no lunch on Fri.) Neighboring the Latchis Hotel (see accommodations above) you'll find the **Latchis Grill**, 6 Flat St. (254-4747), where patrons dine in inexpensive elegance and sample beer brewed right on the premises by the **Windham Brewery.** (Lunch and dinner $5-8. Beer, 7 oz. sampler $1.75. Open daily 11:30am-midnight.) For locally grown fruits, vegetables, and cider, go to the **farmers market** (254-9657) on the Town Common, Main St. (June 12-Sept. 11, Wed. 10am-2pm) or on Western Ave. near the Creamery Bridge (open May 11-Oct. 12, Sat. 9am-2pm, Wed. 3-6pm). For some after dinner entertainment, **Mole's Eye Café** (257-0771), at the corner of High and Main St., has rock, R&B, blues, and reggae bands on Wed., Fri., and Sat. nights at 9pm. (open Mon.-Fri. 11:30am-1am, Sat. 4pm-midnight or 1am. Cover Fri.-Sat. $3.) Taste Duck Breath and Big Nose Blonde Ales at the younger **McNeill's Brew Pub**, 90 Elliot St. (254-2553;open daily 4pm-1am.)

Entertainment Brattleboro chills at the confluence of the West and Connecticut Rivers, both of which can be explored by **canoe.** Rentals are available at **Connecticut River Safari** (257-5008 or 254-3908) on Putney Rd., just across the West River Bridge. (Open mid-May to Oct. 31 daily 8:30am-6pm, 2-hr. minimum $8; $12 per ½-day, $19 per day. 2 not necessarily consecutive days $28.)

Housed in the old Union Railroad Station at the lower end of Main St. are the **Brattleboro Museum** and the new **Brattleboro Art Center** (257-0124; open mid-May-Oct. 31 Tues.-Sun. noon-6pm; $2, seniors and students $1). The **Windham Gallery,** 69 Main St. (257-1881), hosts local art openings on the first Friday of every month as well as poetry readings and discussions by artists about their work. (Open Fri.-Sat. noon-8pm, Sun. and Wed.-Thurs. noon-4pm; $1 suggested donation.)

Brattleboro's internationally renowned **New England Bach Festival** (257-4523) runs annually throughout the month of October. The Festival happily coincides with the high season for fall foliage, so plan a trip for both. Thousands cram the common for **Village Days,** the last weekend in July, and **Apple Days,** the last weekend in September, to browse through displays of local arts and crafts. Village Days also features **Riff-Raft Regatta,** where man-made, non-motorized rafts (two kegs strung together will do) race against each other.

■■■ BENNINGTON

Any history book can tell you about the famous Battle of Bennington, where British General "Gentleman Johnny" Burgoyne was forced to surrender his 8000-man army to the American colonists. What the book might not tell you is that the battle was actually not fought in Bennington, but 5 mi. away in Walloomsac, NY. Bennington locals recreate their town's history with monuments, festivals, and lots of lore.

Practical Information The **Bennington Area Chamber of Commerce** (447-3311) distributes free info packages, including a town map and brochures of historical sites. From Main St., go three blocks north on North St. (Open Mon.-Fri. 8:30am-5pm. After hours packages available in a box outside.)

Transportation around Bennington is relatively easy. **Vermont Transit, Peter Pan Trailways,** and **Bonanza Bus Lines** (442-4808) all operate at 126 Washington Ave., one block off Main St. Buses leave daily for Burlington ($19, 3 daily), Boston ($31, 3 daily), and New York ($33, five daily). (Open Mon.-Fri. 9am-noon, 1:30-4:30pm; Sat.-Sun. 9:30-11am, 2-4pm.) Free **local bus service** is provided by the American Red Cross (442-9458) along the major streets stopping on the hour at the municipal park on Pleasant St. (daily 8am-4pm).

Bennington's **post office:** 108 Elm St. (442-2421), one block south of Main St. (open Mon.-Fri, 8:30am-4:30pm, Sat. 8:30-noon); **ZIP code:** 05201; **area code:** 802.

Food, Accommodations, and Sights When it comes to food, the words **Blue Benn Diner** (442-5140) consistently spring to the lips of Bennington's residents. Located on North St., on the left after the first traffic light when coming from Main St., the diner serves up plentiful breakfasts ($5-6), and classic blue plates ($5-8). Check for Sonny's specialties, such as tofu enchiladas ($5.75). (Open Mon.-Tues. 6am-5pm, Wed.-Thurs. 6am-8pm, Sat. 6am-4pm, Sun. 7am-4pm.) **All Days and Onions,** 519 Main St. (447-0043), is very popular for its lunchtime sandwiches and salads ($5-7). (Open Mon. 7am-6pm, Tues.-Sat. 7am-8pm.)

The **Vermonter Motor Lodge** (442-2529 or 800-382-3175) allows guests to swim, fish, or boat at no extra charge 4 mi. west of Bennington's downtown on Rte. 9. The quilts are handmade and the view is spectacular. (Mid-Oct.-May $40, Sept.-mid-Oct. $58; double $45/63. Each additional guest $5. Closed Jan.-April.) Further from civilization is the **Red Mill Brook Campground** in the Green Mountain National Forest, 2 mi. off Rte. 9, 12 mi. east of Bennington. (Free camping up to a 15-day limit; open May 15-Dec. 15. Outhouses.)

The **Bennington Battle Monument** (447-0550), located 2 mi west of downtown in Old Bennington on Monument Ave., the 306'4" tall tower is hard to miss. Tours available by reservation, ($1; open daily April 1-Nov. 1 9am-5pm). Along with military and historical artifacts from the town, the **Bennington Museum** (447-1751) houses the world's largest public collection of the work of Grandma Moses and the school house Moses attended as a child. Located on West Main St., 1mi. west of downtown, the museum is a must for anyone interested in Americana. (Open daily March 1-Dec. 23 9am-5pm, Jan.-Feb. weekends and holidays only 9am-5pm. $5, student and seniors $4.50, children under 12 free.)

The apple wine of the **Joseph Cerniglia Winery,** 37 West Rd. (442-3531), is the only apple wine to be written up in the major wine publications. Cerniglia's potion is available at free tastings (daily 10am-5pm).

Massachusetts

Massachusetts considers itself the cerebral cortex of the national body, and the state certainly has credentials. Harvard, the oldest university in America, was founded in Cambridge in 1636. The nation's first public school was established soon after, in 1647. Countless literati have hocked their wares in this intellectual marketplace, from Hawthorne, Dickinson, Melville, Wharton, and the Jameses to Sylvia Plath, Robert Lowell, and Jack Kerouac. Many colleges and universities congregate in Massachusetts, drawing scholars from around the world and lending parts of this relatively small state a quirkily cosmopolitan flavor—espresso bars and leftist bookstores join Paul Revere statues and whitewashed churches on Main Street.

But there's more than the pale of academia in Massachusetts. A needlepoint charm blesses the rolling hills of the Berkshires in the west, resplendent during the fall foliage season. Boston, one of the oldest cities in America, attracts visitors with colonial legends, an Old World face, and an impressive array of cultural offerings. And on the Atlantic coast, from Newburyport to Nantucket, the great shipping ports and whaling centers of bygone days now lure tourists and leisured locals to summer homes and beachfront B&Bs.

PRACTICAL INFORMATION

Capital: Boston.

Massachusetts Division of Tourism, Department of Commerce and Development, 100 Cambridge St., Boston 02202 (727-3201; 800-632-8038 for guides). Can send you a complimentary, comprehensive *Spirit of Massachusetts Guidebook* and direct you to regional resources. Open Mon.-Fri. 9am-5pm.

Time Zone: Eastern. **Postal Abbreviation:** MA

Sales Tax: 5%.

BOSTON AREA

■■■ BOSTON

Boston, center of patriotic fervor during the American Revolution and of abolitionism during the Civil War, is rightly proud of its history. The city displays its past prominently, and any visitor to the nation's oldest city would be foolish not to take advantage of that fact. Still, there is more to Boston than history. Many first-time visitors stick to the familiar landmarks of the Freedom Trail, or the blue-blood and brownstone neighborhoods of Beacon Hill and Back Bay. Step off the Freedom Trail to explore Boston's less-touristy neighborhoods, from the Irish enclave of South Boston to the small-yet-vital Chinatown, to the Black Heritage Trail, which tells another part of the story of America.

The city's population is diverse, if somewhat incohesive. East Asians, Portuguese, Italians, Irish, West Indians, and African-Americans dominate particular neighborhoods. Plunked down in the middle of this sometimes uneasy mosaic are over 100,000 college students—drawn here in search of the $100,000 keg party, or enlightenment, whichever comes first. From September to June, the average age here dips into the mid-twenties, giving the city a youthful flavor, plenty of cheap eats, bookstores, and great (high or low) entertainment for the budget traveler.

PRACTICAL INFORMATION

Emergency: 911.

Visitor Information: Boston Common Information Center, 147 Tremont St., Boston Common. T: Park St. A good place to start a tour of the city. They dispense free maps and brochures of Boston, Freedom Trail maps ($1.50), and *The Official Guidebook to Boston* ($5), which comes with coupons you might actually use. Open Mon.-Sat. 8:30am-5pm, Sun. 9am-5pm. **Boston Visitor's Information,** 800 Boylston St., in the Prudential Plaza's customer service booth (536-4100). T: Prudential. Open Mon.-Fri. 9am-6pm, Sat. 10am-6pm, Sun. 11:30am-6pm. **National Historical Park Visitor's Center,** 15 State St. (242-5642). T: State. Info on historical sights and accommodations. Some rangers speak French, German, or Spanish. Open June-Aug. 9am-6pm; Sept.-May daily 9am-5pm.

Airport: Logan International (561-1800 or 800-235-6426), in East Boston. Easily accessible by public transport. The free **Massport Shuttle** connects all terminals with the "Airport" T-stop on the blue line. City Transportation (321-2282) runs shuttle buses between Logan and major downtown hotels (service daily every 15 min. 7:15am-9:15pm). $7.50 one way, under 12 free. A **water shuttle** from the airport to the Aquarium provides a more scenic journey, leaving from the waterfront downtown ($1).

Amtrak: (345-7442 or 800-872-7245), South Station, Atlantic Ave. and Summer St.. T: South Station. Station open daily 5:45am-10:30pm.

Buses: Greyhound, (800-231-2222), South Station. T: South Station. Station open 24 hrs. Also the station for **Vermont Transit** (802-862-9671). To: Burlington ($44). **Peter Pan** (426-7838), across from South Station at 155 Atlantic Ave. (T: South Station), runs to Western Massachusetts and Albany, NY ($22). Connections to New York City via Hartford ($25). Also home to **Concord Trailways** (800-639-3317), which goes north to New Hampshire, Concord ($11), and Portland ($15). Open daily 5:30am-12:30am. **Bonanza** (800-556-3815) operates out of the Back Bay Railroad Station at 145 Dartmouth St. (T: Back Bay), with frequent daily service to: Providence ($7.75), Fall River ($8), Newport ($12), Falmouth ($11), Woods Hole ($12). Open 24 hrs. **East Coast Explorer,** 245 Eighth Ave., NYC (718-694-9667), offers all-day, scenic budget bus trips between New York, Boston, and Washington D.C.

Ferry: Bay State Cruises, 723-7800. Ferry leaves from Long Wharf; the ticket office is a red building across from the Marriot Hotel. T: Aquarium. Cruises daily 10am-4pm on the hour, Memorial Day-Labor Day; call for schedule Labor Day-

NEW ENGLAND

Boston

1 Greyhound / Trailways
2 Bus Terminal
3 South Station
4 Post Office
5 Faneuil Hall / Quincy Market
6 Old State House
7 New England Aquarium
8 Museum of Science
9 Old South Meeting House
10 Granary Burying Ground
11 Mass. Genl. Hospital
12 Paul Revere House
13 Old North Church
14 North Station
15 Boston Garden
16 Children's Museum

Columbus Day. To: George's Island ($6, children and seniors $4), Provincetown ($29 same-day round trip.)

Public Transport: Massachusetts Bay Transportation Authority (MBTA).
The subway system, known as the "T," consists of the Red, Green, Blue, and Orange lines. Lines run daily 5:30am-12:30am. Fare 85¢, kids 5-11 40¢, seniors 20¢. Some automated T entrances in outlying areas require tokens and don't sell them; buy several tokens at a time and have them handy. Bus service reaches more of the city and suburbs; fare generally 60¢, but may vary depending on destination. Bus schedules available at Park St. or Harvard Sq. T-stations. A "T passport," sold at the Visitor's Center, offers discounts at local businesses and unlimited travel on all subway and bus lines and some commuter rail zones; the discount is only worth it if you use the T a lot. (1-day pass $5, 3-day $9; 7-day $18.)
MBTA Commuter Rail: Lines to suburbs and the North Shore leave from North Station, Porter Square, and South Station T-stops. For more information on any of these services call 722-3200 or 800-392-6100.

Taxi: Red Cab, 734-5000. **Checker Taxi,** 536-7000. Taxi from downtown to Logan $10-12; more if there's heavy traffic.

Car Rental: Merchants Rent a Car, 20 Rex Dr. (356-5656). T: Braintree. 18 and over can rent compact cars $25 per day, $150 per week, with unlimited mileage in New England. Customer must supply auto insurance or credit card with coverage. Under 21 25% surcharge per day. Open Mon.-Fri. 8am-6pm, Sat. 8am-noon. **Dollar Rent-a-Car,** 110 Mt. Auburn St. (354-6410), in the Harvard Manor House, Harvard Sq. T: Harvard. Sub-compact with unlimited mi. $37 per day; must stay within New England. Open Mon.-Thurs. 7:30am-6pm, Fri. 7:30am-7pm, Sat.-Sun. 8am-4pm. $20 extra per day for those under 25. Must have credit card. 10% discount for AAA members. Other offices throughout Boston, including the Sheraton Hotel (523-5098) and Logan Airport (569-5300).

Bike Rental: Community Bike Shop, 496 Tremont St. (542-8623). $20 per day. Open Mon.-Fri. 9:30am-8pm, Sat. 9:30am-6pm., Sun. noon-5pm (summer only). $5 per hr., $20 per day, $75 per week. Must have major credit card.

Help Lines: Rape Hotline, 492-7273. Open 24 hrs. **Gay and Lesbian Helpline,** 267-9001. Open Mon.-Fri. 4pm-11pm, Sat.-Sun. 6pm-11pm.

Post Office: 24 Dorchester Ave. (654-5327). Open Mon.-Fri. 8am-midnight, Sat. 8am-5pm, Sun. noon-5pm. **ZIP code:** 02205.

Area Code: 617.

Boston owes its layout as much to the clomping of colonial cows as to urban designers. Boston is compact and best explored on foot, so avoid driving along its bovine boulevards. The public transportation system is excellent, parking is expensive, and Boston drivers are somewhat maniacal. If you do choose to drive around the city, be defensive and alert; Boston's pedestrians can be as defiant as its drivers. Many street names (e.g. Harvard St.) are repeated within the city; others seem to disappear and reappear magically—ignore street names when in doubt and simply walk in as straight a line as possible. Ask for detailed directions wherever you go. Several outlying T stations offer park-and-ride services. Only a T ride (Red line to Kendall, Central, or Harvard) away, **Cambridge** (see next entry) offers excellent street musicians, bookstores, cafés, and people-watching.

ACCOMMODATIONS

Cheap accommodations are hard to come by in Boston. Early September is especially tight, when Boston fills with parents moving their college-bound children in; likewise the first week in June, when families move their graduated, unemployment-bound children out. Reserve a room six months to a year in advance during those times. Those with cars should investigate the motels along highways in outlying areas. **Boston Reservations,** 1643 Beacon St., #23, Waban, MA 02168 (332-4199, fax332-5751), presides over scores of Boston area accommodations. (Singles $70-100. Doubles $80-100. Open Mon.-Fri. 9am-5pm.)

Hostelling International-Boston (HI-AYH), 12 Hemenway St. (536-9455), in the Fenway. T: Hynes/ICA. This cheery, colorful hostel in a great location has clean and slightly crowded but liveable rooms, some with sinks. Hall bathrooms, some recently renovated. Lockers, common rooms, cafeteria, kitchens, and laundry. 190 beds in summer, 100 in winter. Planned activities nightly; ask about discounts. Check-in 24hrs. Check-out 11am. No lockout. $14, nonmembers $17. Membership required in summer. $5 deposit for sheets. Linens $2. Wheelchair-accessible. Reservations highly recommended. IBN reservations available.

Back Bay Summer Hostel (HI-AYH), 519 Beacon St. (352-6098). T: Copley. Back Bay picks up overflow from its sister in the Fenway. The hostel is situated in a pretty section of town. 80 beds. Check-in 5pm-2am. Check-out 7am-10am. Open mid-June to Aug. $14, membership required. 5-day max. stay, can shrink to 3 days in highest season. Reservations highly recommended.

Garden Halls Residences, 260 Commonwealth Ave. (267-0079, fax 536-1735), Back Bay. T: Copley. The rooms in these Boston brownstones are clean, bright, and attractively furnished. Just a few blocks from Copley Square, the location is outstanding. Vending machines, TV/VCR, laundry, microwaves, and linen service available. Singles, doubles, triples, and quads. Some private baths. Check-in 10am-4pm. No lockout or curfew. $30 per night, $190 per week, $450 per month. Key and linen deposit. Meals available: breakfast $2.75, lunch $3.75, dinner $4.75. Reservations recommended.

Berkeley Residence Club (YWCA), 40 Berkeley St. (482-8850). T: Arlington. Solid, industrial, clean accommodations for women. Men are not allowed above the lobby. Grand piano, patio, pool, TV room, sun deck, laundry, library. Hall baths. Some doubles with sinks are available (extra charge). 13-day max. stay. Check-out 11am. Members $30, nonmembers $32; ask for the recession rates. 2 weeks $110. Cafeteria ($2 breakfast, $5.25 dinner).

Greater Boston YMCA, 316 Huntington Ave. (536-7800). T: Northeastern. Down the street from Symphony Hall on Mass. Ave. Must be 18. Women accepted. Hall bathrooms. Elegant lobby, friendly atmosphere, partially used as overflow housing for Northeastern University students. Cafeteria, pool, and recreational facilities. Breakfast included. Key deposit $5. ID and luggage required for check-in. Check-out 11am. 10-day max. stay. Singles $36. Doubles $53. With hostel ID singles $33, doubles $48. Handicapped accessible. Office staffed 24 hrs.

Anthony's Town House, 1085 Beacon St. (566-3972), Brookline. T: Hawes on the Green Line. Very convenient to the T-stop. 12 rooms for 20 guests, who range from trim professionals to scruffy backpackers. Singles and doubles $30-60. Winter and off-season $5 less. Ask about weekly rates; mention *Let's Go* for 5% off the in-season rate. Noon check-out.

The Farrington Inn, 23 Farrington Ave. (787-1860 or 800-767-5337), Allston Station. T: Green Line-B, or 66 bus. Call for driving directions. Not fancy, but functional; prices include local phone, parking, and breakfast. Most rooms have TVs. Shared baths. Somewhat inconvenient location. Singles $45-50. Doubles $60.

The Irving House, 24 Irving St. (547-4600), in Cambridge, near Cambridge St. T: Harvard. Great location near Harvard Square. Singles $45-60, with bath $80. Doubles $60-85, with bath $110. Includes breakfast. Discounts for groups of 16 or more and for longer stays. Off-season rates about $10 less. Reservations required.

FOOD

Boston ain't called Beantown for nothing. Baked beans are a local favorite and you can sample a plate at local landmark **Durgin Park.** Durgin was a stronghold of Yankee cuisine in Faneuil Hall long before the tourist arrived, and it still maintains its integrity with such delights as Indian pudding ($2.50) and Yankee Pot Roast ($6.95). Durgin Park's **Oyster Bar** offers frequent, inexpensive seafood specials, including a modest lobster dinner for around $7. (T: Government Center, 227-2038.) Boston is also noted for its seafood, and rightly so: lobster, clams, cod, and other creatures from the briney deep abound. Numerous (mostly expensive) seafood restaurants line Boston Harbor by the wharf (T: Aquarium).

Beyond seafood and baked beans, Boston dishes out an impressive variety of international cuisines. The scent of garlic wafts from the **North End** (T: Haymarket), home to an endless array of Italian groceries, bakeries, cafés, and restaurants. Hanover and Salem Streets are lined with fine eateries. You haven't really sipped until you've sipped cappuccino at **Café Vittoria,** 294 Hanover St. (open daily 8am-midnight). **Chinatown** crowds a bevy of delectable restaurants into its several narrow blocks. A Sunday brunch of *Dim Sum* is an inexpensive Boston tradition. (T: Chinatown; be careful here at night). Wander through the open-air stalls at **Haymarket** and pick up produce, fresh fish, fruits, cheeses, and pigs' eyes at well-below supermarket prices. Try to get here early, especially during summer. (Indoor stores open daily dawn-dusk; outdoor stalls Fri.-Sat. only. T: Government Center or Haymarket.) Just up Congress St. from Haymarket, the restored **Quincy Market** houses a cornucopia of food booths peddling interesting but overpriced fare. Faneuil Hall and the surrounding shops will sell you anything from a stuffed whale to a massaging chair. The entire area provides a great spot to observe the shifting tides of tourists, and is home to a lively bar scene at night.

La Famiglia Giorgio's, 112 Salem St. (367-6711), in the North End. T: Haymarket. Head to La Famiglia for two meals: the one you'll eat in the restaurant and the one you'll take home. Portions are enormous and tasty; even the garden salad contains more than one head of lettuce. Plenty of vegetarian options, including a towering tribute to eggplant ($8). No reservations. Expect to wait, especially on weekends, but it's worth it. Entrees $4-18. Open daily 11am-11pm.

No Name, 15½ Fish Pier (423-2705), on the waterfront (T: South Station). This hole-in-the-pier restaurant has been serving up some of the best fried seafood in Boston for several decades. You'll get lots of fresh seafood, no fuss, and a small bill when it's over. The harbor view allow you watch tomorrow's dinner emerging from the boats. Entrees $5-15. No reservations. Open daily 11am-10pm.

Bob the Chef's, 604 Columbus Ave. (536-6204). T: Symphony or Mass. Ave. From either stop, exit onto Mass. Ave., walk away from the Symphony, and turn right onto Columbus Ave. Best (and damn near only) soul food in Boston. The chitterlings, fried fish, chicken livers, pigs feet, corn bread, and the famed "glorifried chicken" all have soul to spare. Bob will even serve you a fried chicken leg and waffle for breakfast. Vegetarians take caution! Entrees $7-10. Open Mon.-Sat. 8am-9pm, Sun. 9am-6pm.

Chau Chow, 52 Beach St. (426-6266). Chinatown. T: South Station. Follow Atlantic Ave. south to Beach St. No messing around here; you arrive, you wait in line, you sit down, you eat, you pay, and you leave. But you eat top-quality, award-winning Chinese food. They specialize in seafood, but the chicken with cashews and the vegetarian Buddha's Delight are also excellent. Most dishes hover around $6, and portions are huge. Open Sun.-Thurs. 10am-2am, Fri.-Sat. 10am-4am.

Addis Red Sea, 544 Tremont St. (426-8727). T: Back Bay. From station walk 5 blocks south on Clarendon St., then turn left on Tremont (10-min. walk). The best Ethiopian food in Boston is delicious, beautiful, and served on *mesobs,* woven tables which support a communal platter. Entrees $6-10, but go for the combination platters, which offer 5 different dishes for $10-12 (the Winnie Mandela Combination Platter commemorates her visit to the restaurant). Open Mon.-Thurs. 5-11pm, Fri. 5pm-midnight, Sat. noon-3pm and 5am-midnight, Sun. noon-11pm.

Ruby's, 280 Cambridge St. (367-3224). T: Charles. Walk toward the Holiday Inn from the T-stop; Ruby's is on your right about three blocks down. Locals stop into this small Beacon Hill spot before 10am weekdays and "Beat the House" for 75¢ — 2 eggs, home fries, and toast for less than a subway ride. Hearty sandwiches ($4.50) and very tasty burgers also available, but breakfast is the star attraction and is served all day. Open Mon.-Thurs. 7am-9pm, Fri.-Sun. 8am-11pm.

Sultan's Kitchen, 72 Broad St. (338-8509). T: Downtown Crossing. Follow Chauncy St., which will become Arch St. Turn right on Franklin St. and left on Broad St. Open only for lunch, this excellent Middle Eastern eatery has Turkish music, speedy service, and generous portions. 12 oz. soup with pita bread $2.85. Smooth Baba Ganoush $5.25. Open Mon.-Fri. 11am-5pm, Sat. 11am-3pm.

SIGHTS

Freedom Trail

The best introduction to the history and culture of Boston lies along the red -painted line of the Freedom Trail. This 2½ mile trail winds through Boston's crowded thoroughfares past many of the city's historic sights. Some of the sights charge admission, but the park service does offer free guided tours of the trail starting at their **visitors center,** 15 State St. (tours on the hr. 10am-3pm in summer). The Freedom Trail begins at the **visitors center** (where you can pick up a free map) on the **Boston Common** (T: Park Street). The Common was founded in 1634 and is today the oldest public park in America. The trail then runs uphill to the **Robert Gould Shaw and 54th Regiment Memorial** on Beacon St. Dedicated to the memory of the first black regiment of the Union Army during the Civil War, this memorial also begins the Black Heritage Trail (see below). The Freedom Trail next crosses the street to the **State House** (open Mon.-Fri. 9am-5pm; tours Mon.-Fri. 10am-4pm, every ½ hr. mornings, every hr. afternoons). Catch the Sacred Cod hanging in the House of Representatives. The trail proceeds to the **Park Street Church** where William Lloyd Garrison launched his abolitionist campaign. You'll next pass the **Old Granary Burial Ground.** If you look closely you'll find the graves of Mother Goose, John Hancock, John Adams, and Paul Revere among others. **King's Chapel and Burial Ground,** on Tremont St., is next. The church, founded in 1688, was Boston's first Anglican church. The burial ground is the permanent residence of Governor Bradford and William Dawes. (Open Mon.-Sat. 10am-4pm. $1, students and seniors 50¢, under 12 free.)

The Freedom Trail continues on past a statue of favorite son **Ben Franklin,** and then to the **Old Corner Bookstore,** which was once played host to the likes of Hawthorne, Emerson, Longfellow, and Oliver Wendell Holmes. Next encounter the **Old South Meeting House,** a Congregationalist church and cradle of insurrection which hosted the get together just before the Boston Tea Party (open June-Aug. 9am-6pm daily; Sept.-May 9am-5pm daily; $2.50, students $2, ages 6-18 $1). The **Old State House,** once the seat of British government in Boston, is now a museum (open daily 9:30am-5pm; $3, students and seniors $2, 6-18 $1.50). The Freedom Trail then proceeds past the site of the **Boston Massacre** (not to be confused with Fenway Park) and moves on to **Faneuil Hall.** The National Park Service operates a desk here and offers talks in the Great Hall (open daily 9am-5pm; talks every 30 min.). Heading into the North End, the trail next passes the **Paul Revere House** (open daily, $2.50, seniors and students $2, 5-17 $1). Paul is neighbor to the **Old North Church,** the church from which, as every school child should know, signal lanterns proclaimed whether the British were coming by land or by sea (open Mon.-Sat. 9am-5pm, Sun. services at 9am, 11am, 4pm). **Copp's Hill Burial Ground** is the final residence of many colonial Bostonians and offers a nice view of the Old North Church. Next, the Freedom Trail heads over the Charlestown Bridge to the **U.S.S. Constitution,** usually a highlight of the tour. The *Constitution* is, however, in drydock without masts until the spring of 1996. It is still open for limited touring (open daily 9:30-sunset). Finally, that obelisk on the hill is not on loan from Washington, it is the last stop on the Freedom Trail, the **Bunker Hill Monument.** The monument offers a grand view of the city and a misleading name. Nearby Breed's Hill was actually site of the Revolutionary Battle in question. If you want to enjoy the view, be prepared and do some stretches; the monument doubles as a Stairmaster (294 steps and no elevator). To return to Boston, follow the red line back over the bridge or hop on a water taxi from a pier by the Constitution (taxi leaves every 30 min. before 3:30pm, after 3:30 every 15 min.; $1, exact change needed).

Other Sights

In 1634, early inhabitants established the **Boston Common** (T: Park Street), bounded by Tremont, Boylston, Charles, Beacon, and Park St., as a place to graze their cattle. Now street vendors, not cows, live off the fat of this land. While many

NEW ENGLAND

stake claim to it in the daytime, the Common is dangerous at night—don't go here alone after dark. Across Charles St. from the Common waddle the title characters from the children's book *Make Way for Ducklings.* The bronze ducklings point the way to the **Swan Boats** (522-1966) in the fragrant and lovely **Public Gardens.** Here, pedal-powered boats glide around a quiet pond lined with shady willows and inhabited by live swans. (T: Arlington. Boats open mid-April to mid-June daily 10am-4pm; mid-June-Labor Day 10am-5pm; Labor Da to -mid-Sept. Mon.-Fri. noon-4pm, Sat.-Sun. 10am-4pm. $1.50, seniors $1.20, under 12 95¢.)

The city's neighborhoods cluster in a loose circle around the Common and Gardens. Directly above the Common lies **Beacon Hill,** a residential neighborhood settled by the Puritans. This exclusive bastion of Boston Brahmanism consists mainly of cobblestone streets and brick sidewalks lined with art galleries, antique shops, and cafés. The hill is significantly smaller than it was when the Puritans resided there - tons of earth were removed to fill in the marshes that are now the Back Bay. At the top of the hill is the State House (see Freedom Trail above). The **Harrison Gray Otis House,** 141 Cambridge St. (227-3956), is a Charles Bulfinch original. (Tours on the hr. Tues.-Fri. noon-4pm, Sat. 10am-4pm. $4, seniors $3.50, under 12 $2.) The nearby **Boston Athenaeum,** 10½ Beacon St. (227-0270), houses over 700,000 books, including most of George Washington's library, and offers tours of its library, art gallery, and print room. (Open Mon.-Fri. 9am-5:30pm, Sat. 9am-4pm; no Sat. hrs. in summer. Free tours Tues. and Thurs. at 3pm; reservations required for the tour.) Charles Street serves as the Hill's front door and is a fine avenue for a stroll.

Follow Cambridge St. east to the red brick plaza of **Government Center,** which, as its name indicates, proves a trifle less picturesque. The monstrous concrete **City Hall** (725-4000), designed by I.M. Pei, opens to the public Monday through Friday (T: Government Center). A few blocks south its more aesthetically pleasing precursor, the **Old State House,** 206 Washington St. (720-1713 or -3290). Built in 1713, it once rocked with revolutionary fervor. (See Freedom Trail above. T: State).

Downtown Crossing, south of City Hall at Washington St. (T: Downtown Crossing), is a pedestrian mall set amidst Boston's business district. Here, Filene's, 426 Washington St., a mild-mannered department store, conceals the chaotic bargain feeding frenzy that is **Filene's Basement.** (Budgeteers will appreciate that Filene's is good, cheap shopping.) The area shuts down after business hours. Directly southwest of the Common, Boston's **Chinatown** (T: Chinatown) demarcates itself with pagoda-style telephone booths and streetlamps, and an arch at its Beach St. entrance. Within this small area cluster many restaurants, food stores, and novelty shops where you can buy Chinese slippers and 1000-year-old eggs. Chinatown has two big celebrations each year. The first, **New Year,** usually falls on a Sunday in February, and festivities include lion dances, fireworks, and Kung Fu exhibitions. The **August Moon Festival** honors a mythological pair of lovers at the time of the full moon. Call 542-2574 for details.

The eastern tip of Boston contains the historic and vibrant **North End** (T: Haymarket). The city's oldest residential district, now an Italian neighborhood, overflows with windowboxes, Italian flags, fragrant pastry shops, crèches, Sicilian restaurants, and Catholic churches. The most famous of the last, **Old St. Stephens Church,** 401 Hanover St. (523-1230), is the classically colonial brainchild of Charles Bulfinch (open 8:30am-5pm daily). Down the street, the brilliant and sweet-smelling **Peace Gardens** try to drown out the honking horns of the North End with beautiful flora. (For more sights, see The Freedom Trail above.)

The **waterfront area,** bounded by Atlantic and Commercial St., runs along Boston Harbor from South Station to the North End Park. Stroll down Commercial, Lewis, or Museum Wharf for a view of the harbor and a breath of sea air. At the excellent **New England Aquarium** (973-5200; T: Aquarium), Central Wharf on the Waterfront, you can see cavorting penguins, giant sea turtles, and a bevy of briny beasts all in a 187,000 gallon tank. There's a tank outside the aquarium where you can watch harbor seals for free. Dolphins and sea lions perform in the ship *Discovery,* moored alongside the Aquarium. On weekends lines tend to be long. (Open

Mon.-Wed. and Fri. 9am-5pm, Thurs. 9am-8pm, Sat.-Sun. and holidays 9am-6pm; Sept.-June Mon.-Wed. and Fri. 9am-5pm, Thurs. 9am-8pm, Sat.-Sun. and holidays 9am-6pm. $8.50, seniors and students $7.50, ages 3-11 $4.50. $1 discount Thurs. after 4pm.) The aquarium also offers **whale-watching cruises** (973-5277) from April to October. (Sightings guaranteed; generally 2 trips daily; call for times. $24, seniors and students $19, ages 12-18 $17.50, ages 3-11 $16.50, under 36 inches not allowed. Reservations suggested.) The **Bay State Cruise Company** (723-7800) offers cheap lunch cruises of the harbor as well as longer cruises to the **Boston Harbor Islands** for a picnic and tour of Civil War Fort Warren. (See Practical Info).

Across Fort Point Channel from the waterfront, predominantly Irish-American **South Boston** has a unique accent. (T: South Station). "Southie" also has great seafood, two beaches, and a pub on every corner.

In **Back Bay,** north of the South End and west of Beacon Hill, three-story brownstone row houses line some of the only gridded streets in Boston. Originally the marshy, uninhabitable "back bay" on the Charles River, the area was filled in during the 19th century. Back Bay was filled in gradually, as reflected in its architectural styles, which run the gamut of 19th-century designs as you travel from east to west. **Commonwealth Avenue** ("Comm. Ave.") is a European-style boulevard with statues and benches punctuating its large and grassy median. **Newbury Street** is Boston's most flamboyant promenade; it's a good place to dye your poodle and ask yourself some serious questions about your credit rating. The dozens of small art galleries, boutiques, bookstores, and cafés that line the street are veritable bastions of exclusivity and swank. (T: Arlington, Copley, or Hynes/ICA.)

Beyond Back Bay, west on Commonwealth Ave., glows **Kenmore Square** (T: Kenmore), watched over by the huge landmark **Citgo sign.** The area around Kenmore Square. has more than its share of neon, containing many of the city's most popular nightclubs on **Landsdowne Street** (see Nightlife below). Near Kenmore Square, the **Fenway** area contains some of the country's best museums. Ubiquitous landscaper Frederick Olmsted of Central Park fame designed the **Fens** area at the center of the Fenway as part of his "Emerald Necklace" vision for Boston—a necklace he never completed. A gem nonetheless, the park's fragrant rose gardens and neighborhood vegetable patches make perfect picnic turf. The Fenway also houses Fenway Park (see Curse of the Bambino below).

You can see the rest of Olmsted's **Emerald Necklace Parks** by taking a five-hour walking tour given by the Boston Park Rangers (call 635-7383 for info). The parks that make up the Necklace can also be visited individually: the Boston Common (T: Park St.), the Public Garden (T: Arlington), Commonwealth Avenue Mall (T: Arlington), Back Bay Fens (T: Kenmore), Muddy River, Olmsted Park, Jamaica Pond, the Arnold Arboretum (T: Arborway), and Franklin Park. Call for info and directions.

The handsome **Copley Square** is in the Back Bay on commercial Boylston St. The square (T: Copley) accommodates a range of seasonal activities, including summertime concerts, folk dancing, a food pavilion, and people-watching. A permanent feature is the **Boston Public Library,** 666 Boylston St. (536-5400), a massive and imposing building, liberally inscribed with the names of hundreds of literati. Benches and window seats inside overlook a tranquil courtyard with fountain and garden. Relax here or in the vaulted reading room. The auditorium gives a program of lectures and films. (Open Mon.-Thurs. 9am-9pm, Fri.-Sat. 9am-5pm.) Across the square next to I.M. Pei's Hancock Tower (see below), is H.H. Richardson's Romanesque fantasy, **Trinity Church.** Many consider Trinity, built in 1877, a masterpiece of U.S. church architecture—the interior justifies this opinion. (T: Copley. Open Mon.-Sat. 8am-6pm.) **Copley Place** is a ritzy mall on the corner, and next door to the newly renovated **Prudential Building.** Both attract a steady stream of shoppers. The partially gentrified **South End,** south of Copley, makes for good brownstone viewing and casual dining.

Two blocks down Massachusetts Ave. from Boylston St. sits the Mother Church of the **First Church of Christ, Scientist,** 1 Norway St. (450-2000), at Mass. Ave. and Huntington, founded in Boston by Mary Baker Eddy. The lovely **Mother Church** is the world headquarters of the Christian Science movement, and its complex of buildings is appropriately vast and imposing. Both the Mother Church and the smaller, older church out back can be seen by guided tour only. (Tours every ½ hr. Tues.-Fri. 10am-4pm, Sat. noon-4pm, Sun. 11:15am-2pm.) In the Christian Science Publishing Society next door, use the catwalk to pass through the **Mapparium,** a 30-ft.-wide stained-glass globe with funky acoustics built in the 1930s. Whisper in the ear of Pakistan while standing next to Surinam. (Tours Tues.-Fri. 9:30am-4pm. Sat. noon-4pm. Free.)

At two lofty locations, you can map out the zones you want to visit or simply zone out as you take in the city skyline. A few blocks from the Mother Church, the **Prudential Skywalk,** on the 50th floor of the Prudential Center, 800 Boylston St. (236-3318), grants a full 360° view from New Hampshire to the Cape. (T: Prudential. Open Mon.-Sat. 10am-10pm, Sun. noon-10pm. $2.75, seniors, students with ID, and kids $1.75.) The **John Hancock Observatory,** 200 Clarendon St. (247-1977 recorded, 572-6429 live), refuses to be outdone, with 60 beefy floors and the distinction of being the highest building in New England (740 ft.). On good days, you can see New Hampshire. (T: Copley. Open Mon.-Sat. 9am-10pm, Sun. 10am-10pm. $3, age 5-15 and seniors $2.25.)

The Black Heritage Trail makes 14 fascinating stops, each marked by a red, black, and green logo. The tour begins at the **Boston African-American National Historic Site,** 46 Joy St. (T: Park Street), where you can pick up a free map before visiting the museum inside (742-1854; open daily 10am-4pm; small charge). The trail covers sights of importance to the development of Boston's African-American community, including: the **African Meeting House** (1805), the earliest black church in North America; the **Robert Gould Shaw and 54th Regiment Memorial** on the Common, dedicated to black soldiers who fought in the Union Army and to their white Boston leader memorialized in the movie *Glory*; and the **Lewis and Harriet Hayden House,** a station on the Underground Railroad.

Museums

Boston's intellectual and artistic community supports a higher concentration of museums than anywhere else in New England. Check the free *Guide to Museums of Boston* for details on the museums not mentioned here.

Museum of Fine Arts (MFA), 465 Huntington Ave. (267-9300). T: Ruggles/ Museum, Green line E train, near the intersection with Massachusetts Ave. The most famous of Boston's museums gathers one of the world's finest collections of Asian ceramics, outstanding Egyptian art, a good showing of Impressionists, and superb American art. Worth a gander are the two famous unfinished portraits of George and Martha Washington, painted by Gilbert Stuart in 1796. Open Tues. and Thurs.-Sun. 10am-4:45pm, Wed. 10am-9:45pm. West Wing only open Thurs.-Fri. 5-10pm. $7, seniors and students $6, kids $3.50. West Wing only, $5. Both free Wed. 4-10pm.

Isabella Stewart Gardner Museum, 280 Fenway (566-1401), a few hundred yards from the MFA. T: Museum. The eccentric Mrs. Gardner built the Venetian-style palace with a stunning courtyard. Unfortunately—in what ranks as the greatest art heist in history—a 1990 break-in relieved the museum of works by Rembrandt, Vermeer, Dégas, and others. Many masterpieces remain, and the courtyard garden soothes the weary budget traveler. Open Tues.-Sun. 11am-5pm. Chamber music on 1st floor Sept.-June Sat. and Sun. afternoons. $6, seniors and students $5, ages 12-17 free. Students $3 on Wednesday.

Museum of Science, Science Park (723-2500). T: Science Park. At the far eastern end of the Esplanade on the Charles River Dam. Contains, among other wonders, the largest "lightning machine" in the world. A multi-story roller-coaster for small metal balls purports to explain energy states, but is just fun to watch. Within the museum, the **Hayden Planetarium** features models, lectures, films, and laser and star shows; the **Mugar Omni Theatre** shows popular films of scientific interest on a gee-whiz-four-story-domed screen. Museum open Sat.-Thurs. 9am-

5pm (until 7pm in summer), Fri. 9am-9pm. Admission to museum or Omni (separate fees) $7, seniors, and ages 3-14 $5. Planetarium and laser show $6, seniors $4.50, ages 3-14). Museum, Omni, and Planetarium $17; seniors and ages 3-14 $12.50. Free Wed. afternoons Sept.-April 1-5pm.

Children's Museum, 300 Congress St. (426-8855), in south Boston on Museum Wharf. T: South Station. Follow the signs with the milk bottles on them. Here kids of all ages paw way-cool hands-on exhibits. Open July-Sept. Sat.-Thurs. 10am-5pm, Fri. 10am-9pm; closed Mon. during off-season. $7, seniors and ages 2-15 $6, kids age 1 $2, under 1 free; Fri. 5-9pm $1.

John F. Kennedy Presidential Library (929-4567), Columbia Point on Morrissey Blvd., Dorchester. T: JFK/UMass; free MBTA shuttle to the U Mass campus and from the library. Dedicated "to all those who through the art of politics seek a new and better world." Designed by I.M. Pei, the white cuboid oceanside edifice contains fascinating, sometimes trivial exhibits that employ mementos documenting the careers of President Kennedy and his brother, Robert Kennedy. Open daily 9am-5pm. $6, seniors $4, 6-16 $3, under 6 free.

Institute of Contemporary Art (ICA), 955 Boylston St. (266-5151 recorded message arts information line, 266-5153. T: Hynes/ICA. Boston's lone outpost of the avant-garde attracts major contemporary artists while aggressively promoting lesser-known work. Their innovative, sometimes controversial exhibits change every 8 weeks. The museum also presents experimental theater, music, dance, and film. Prices vary, so call for more info. Open Wed.-Thurs. noon-9pm, Fri.-Sun. noon-5pm. $5, students with ID $3, seniors and under 16 $2. Free Thurs. 5-9pm.

NIGHTLIFE

Boston's nightlife is tempered somewhat by remnants of the city's Puritan heritage ("blue laws" prohibit the sale of alcohol after certain hours and on Sundays), and the dearth of public transportation after midnight. Nearly all bars and most clubs close between 1 and 2am, and bar admittance for anyone under 21 is hard-won. Boston's local music scene runs the gamut from folk to funk; Beantown natives-gone-national include the Pixies, Aerosmith, Tracy Chapman, Dinosaur Jr., Lemonheads, Bobby Brown, and the Mighty Mighty Bosstones. National acts usually check in at the Orpheum, the Paradise, Avalon, the cavernous Boston Garden, or at one of the local colleges' theaters and arenas. Some of the liveliest areas in town are **Landsdowne St.** (T: Kenmore) and **Boylston Place** (T: Boylston). Peruse the weekly *Boston Phoenix* for its comprehensive "Boston-After-Dark" club and concert listings ($1.50, out on Thursdays). The *Phoenix* also operates a **club line:** 859-3300.

Avalon; Axis; Venus de Milo, 5-13 Lansdowne St. T: Kenmore. Upscale 80s-style pre-yuppie (262-2424); neo-punk/industrial (262-2437); relentlessly techno and outrageously attired (421-9595), respectively. All three clubs are open mid-week through the weekend 10pm-2am; exact hours for each club vary, as do cover charges. Axis and Venus have 18 plus nights; call for details. Avalon has live shows and is almost always over 21. If you are over 21, you can get in free (or for a smaller cover) from rowdy **Bill's Bar** (421-9678), next door.

Bull and Finch Pub, 84 Beacon St. (227-9605). T: Arlington. The super touristy bar inspired the TV show *Cheers*. Large crowds. Warning—the interior bears no resemblance to the set. No cover. Open Sun.-Fri. 11am-1:30am, Sat. 10am-1:30am.

Paradise, 967 Commonwealth Ave. (351-2526). T: Pleasant St. A young crowd flocks to this Back Bay hotspot for frequent live rock. Dancing on Saturdays. Most shows 18 and over. Open daily 8pm-2am. Cover varies.

Wally's Café, 427 Mass Ave. (424-1408). T: bus #1 (Dudley) to Columbus Ave. A great hole-in-the-wall bar frequented by Berklee School of Music's aspirants. Live music nightly with no cover. Open Mon.-Sat. 9am-2am, Sun. noon-2am.

Sticky Mike's, 21 Boylston Place (351-2583). T: Boylston. No pretensions at this new blues joint. Just lots of live blues by groups with names like D.D. and the Road Kings. Open Tues.-Sat. 8pm-2am, Sun. 9pm-2am.

Sunset Grill and Tap, 130 Brighton Ave. (254-1331), in Allston. T: 66 bus from Harvard to the corner of Harvard and Brighton Ave. One of the largest beer selections in the country (over 400, more than 70 on tap). College students dig the buenos nachos ($7). Free late-night buffets on Sun.-Tues. Open daily noon-1am.

Rathskeller, 528 Commonwealth Ave., Kenmore Sq. (536-2750). T: Kenmore. A somewhat faded legend on the Boston scene, the "Rat" still cultivates a grungy atmosphere to accompany its excellent program of grungy bands. Mosh pit. Open Mon.-Sat. 11am-2am, Sun. noon-2am. Live shows are 19 and over. Cover varies.

Nick's Comedy Stop, 100 Warrenton St. (482-0930), is very funny. Jay Leno, who is not, got his start here. Shows Tues.-Sat. 8:30pm and Sat. at 10:30pm.

For those seeking the gay scene, **Indigo's** clientele is predominantly women, and **Chaps, Club Café,** and **Sporters** are all gay clubs. **Club Café,** 209 Columbus Ave. (536-0966; T: Back Bay), has a largely yuppie clientele, live music nightly, and no cover. **Boston Ramrod,** 1254 Boylston St. (266-2986; T: Kenmore), behind Fenway Park on Boylston St., designates Thursday and Friday as official leather nights. **Campus/Manray,** 21 Brookline St. (864-0406; T: Central), in Cambridge's Central Square, features gay and mixed top-40 and progressive music. Also read *Bay Windows*.

ARTS AND ENTERTAINMENT

Musicians, dancers, actors, and *artistes* of every description fill Boston. Worth special mention is the large community of **street performers** ("buskers") who juggle steak knives, swallow torches, wax poetic, and sing folk tunes in the subways and squares of Boston and Cambridge. The *Boston Phoenix* and the "Calendar" section of Thursday's *Boston Globe* list activities for the coming week. Also check the *Where Boston* booklet available at the visitors center. What Boston doesn't have, Cambridge does (see Cambridge below). **Bostix,** a Ticket Master outlet in Faneuil Hall (723-5181), sells half-price tickets to performing arts events on the day of performance. (Service charge $1.50-2.50 per ticket. Cash and traveler's checks only. Open Tues.-Sat. 11am-6pm, Sun. 11am-4pm.)

Actors in town cluster around Washington St. and Harrison Ave., in the **Theater District** (T: Boylston). The **Wang Center for the Performing Arts,** 270 Tremont St. (482-9393), produces theater, classical music, and opera in its modern complex. The **Shubert Theater,** 265 Tremont St. (426-4520), hosts Broadway hits touring through Boston. Tickets for these and for shows at the **Charles Playhouse,** 74 Warrenton St. (426-6912), are costly (around $30). The area's professional companies are cheaper, and may provide a more interesting evening. The **New Theater,** 66 Marlborough St. (247-7388), and **Huntington Theater Co.,** 264 Huntington Ave. (266-7900; 266-0800 for box office), at Boston University have solid artistic reputations. (Tickets $8-35.) More affordable college theater is also available; during term-time, watch students trod the boards at **Tufts Theater Arena** (627-3493), the **BU Theater** (353-3320), the **MIT Drama Shop** (253-2908), and the **MIT Shakespeare Ensemble** (253-2903).

The renowned **Boston Ballet** (695-6950), one of the nation's best, annually brings to life such classics as the *Nutcracker* and *Swan Lake*. The ballet performs at the Wang Center (see above). The **Boston Symphony Orchestra,** 201 Mass. Ave. (266-1492; T: Symphony), at Huntington, holds its concert season from October to April ($20-57). Rush seats ($7) go on sale three hours before concerts (tickets for 8pm concerts available at 5pm; Fri. 2pm concert tickets available at 9am).

The riverside **Esplanade** (T: Charles) is a park extending from the Longfellow Bridge to the Harvard Bridge. Boston's quasi-pseudo-beach on the Charles, the Esplanade fills in the summer with sun-seekers and sail-boaters; but don't go in the water unless you like tetanus shots. Bikers and rollerbladers, upholding Boston's tradition of good road manners, try to mow down pedestrians on the walkway. The bike path, which follows the river to the posh suburb of **Wellesley,** makes a terrific afternoon's ride. The Esplanade also hosts some of Boston's best-loved cultural events—the concerts of the **Boston Pops Orchestra** (266-1492), at the mauve **Hatch Shell** (727-9547). The Pops play here during the first week of July. Concerts are free and begin at 8pm; arrive early so you can sit within earshot of the orchestra. On the **4th**

of July, hundreds of thousands of patriotic thrillseekers pack the Esplanade to hear the Pops concert (broadcast by loudspeaker throughout the area) and watch the ensuing terrific fireworks display. Arrive before noon for a seat on the Esplanade, although you can watch the fireworks from basically anywhere along the river. The regular Pops season at **Symphony Hall,** 301 Mass. Ave. (266-1200 box office and concert info; 266-2378 recorded message), runs mid-May through July when the BSO is in Tanglewood. (Tickets $11-35. Box office open Mon.-Sat. 10am-6pm, Sun. 1-6pm on concert days, but the best way to get tickets is to call 266-1200.)

The **Berklee Performance Center,** 136 Mass. Ave. (266-7455; box office 266-1400, ext. 261), an adjunct of the Berklee School of Music, holds concerts featuring students, faculty, and jazz and classical luminaries.

For information on other special events, such as the **St. Patrick's Day Parade** (March 17), **Patriot's Day** celebrations (April 19), the week-long **Boston Common Dairy Festival** (June), the **Boston Harbor Fest** (early July), the North End's **Festival of St. Anthony** (mid-August), and **First Night** (New Year's Eve), see the *Boston Phoenix* or *Globe* calendars.

Singing Beach is 40 min. on the commuter line to Manchester-by-the-Sea (see Practical Info). Make the beach literally sing by dragging your feet through the deep, dry sand (free). It's very cool. We like to do it. You can swim too. Park your car in town and walk the ½ mi. to the beach (entrance fee $1). Take Rte. 127 to exit 16.

THE CURSE OF THE BAMBINO AND OTHER SPORTS

Ever since the Red Sox traded Babe Ruth to the Yankees in 1918, Boston sports fans have learned to take the good with the bad. They have seen more basketball championships than any other city (16) but haven't boasted a World Series title in over 75 years. Yet through it all they follow their teams with a puritanical fervor. On summer nights, thousands of baseball fans make a pilgrimage to **Fenway Park.** Home of the "Green Monster," Fenway is the nation's oldest Major League ballpark and center stage for the perennially heart-rending **Boston Red Sox** baseball club, which if given a chicken filet, would find a bone to choke on. Still, there's no better place to watch a baseball game. (Box office 267-8661; open Mon.-Fri. 9am-5pm, Sat. 9:30am-2pm, or until game time if the team's in town. T: Kenmore.) Most grandstand tickets sell out far in advance, but bleacher seats are often available on game day.

Boston Garden (T: North Station), located off the JFK Expressway between the West and North Ends, hosts the storied **Boston Celtics** basketball team (season Oct.-May; 227-3200 for info) and **Boston Bruins** hockey team (season Oct.-April; call 227-3200 for info). A fair distance outside Boston, **Foxboro Stadium,** 16 Washington St., Foxboro, hosts the **New England Patriots** NFL team.

In October, the **Head of the Charles** regatta, the largest such single-day event in the U.S., attracts rowing clubs, white baseball caps, and beer-stained college sweatshirts from across the country. The 3-mi. boat races begin at Boston University Bridge; the best vantage points are on the Weeks footbridge and Anderson Bridge near Harvard University. On April 19, 10,000 runners competing in the **Boston Marathon** battle Boston area boulevards, including the infamous Heartbreak Hill. Call the **Massachusetts Division of Tourism** (727-3201) for details. .

■■■ CAMBRIDGE

Cambridge, founded in 1630 by the Puritans, has played almost as significant a historical role as its larger neighbor Boston. It was in Cambridge that George Washington assumed command of the Continental Army during the Revolution, and from Cambridge that he conducted the siege of Boston that eventually forced the evacuation of General Gage and his British force. Cambridge began its career as an intellectual and publishing center in the colonial era. Harvard, the nation's first university, was founded here in 1638. MIT (founded in 1861 in Boston) moved to Cambridge in 1916, giving the small city two academic heavyweights. A planned merger of the two (favored by William James) fell through soon after, and a rivalry was born. The city takes on the character of both universities. Around MIT radiate bio-tech labs and computer science buildings in Kendall Square. Harvard Square offers Georgian buildings, stellar bookstores, coffee houses, street musicians, and people-watching.

Though the Cambridge economy and landscape is dominated by its universities and high-tech labs, the city offers other neighborhoods. Central Square, sandwiched between MIT and Harvard, boasts inexpensive restaurants and clubs where students, working-class, and yuppies of all cultures mix. Inman Square is home to Portuguese and Brazilian enclaves, with no-nonsense retail stores as well as vintage clothing shops, coffeehouses, and sushi bars. Budget travelers will find kindred spirits in the rich slacker culture that extends its tendrils throughout the city.

PRACTICAL INFORMATION

See Boston: Practical Information, above, for a complete listing. The **Cambridge Discovery Booth** (497-1630), in Harvard Square, has the best and most comprehensive information about Cambridge, as well as MBTA bus and subway schedules. Pick up the *Old Cambridge Walking Guide*, an excellent self-guided tour ($1). Walking tours of Harvard and the surrounding area are given in summer. (Open mid-June to Aug. Mon.-Sat. 9am-6pm, Sun. 1-6pm; Sept. to mid-June Mon.-Sat. 9am-5pm, Sun. 1-5pm.) The **Harvard University Information Center,** 1350 Mass. Ave. (495-1573), Holyoke Center, in Harvard Square, has free guides to the university and museums, and offers tours of the university Mon.-Fri. at 10am and 2pm; two additional tours per day Mon.-Fri. and two Saturdays in summer.

Let's Go's compendium **The Unofficial Guide to Life at Harvard** ($8) has the inside scoop and up-to-date listings of Boston/Cambridge area restaurants, history, entertainment, sights, transportation and services, as well as a fine chapter on beer and its uses. It's the closest thing to a *Let's Go Boston,* and is available in Square bookstores and the Discovery Booth.

Cambridge's **post office:** 770 Mass. Ave. (876-0620; open Mon.-Fri. 7:30am-6:45pm, Sat. 8am-2pm), Central Sq. T: Central; **ZIP code:** 02139; **area code:**617.

Massachusetts Avenue ("Mass. Ave.") is Cambridge's major artery. Most of the action takes place in "squares" (that is, commercial areas which are of every geometric shape *except* square) along Mass. Ave. and the Red Line of the T. **MIT** is just across the Mass. Ave. Bridge from Boston at **Kendall Square,** on the Red Line. The Red Line continues outbound through: **Central Square,** the heart of urban Cambridge; frenetic, eclectic **Harvard Square; and Porter Square. Inman Square** is off the Red Line, but is accessible via the 69 Lechmere bus. Cambridge is a 10-min. T-ride from the heart of Boston.

FOOD

Nightly, thousands of college students renounce cafeteria fare and head to the funky eateries of Harvard Square. Ask a student where to go. **The Garage** at 36 Kennedy St. is a mall of restaurants. Pick up the weekly *Square Deal,* usually shoved in your face by distributors near the T-stop, for coupons and discounts on local fare. Frequented by insomniac Harvard students and the only 24-hour place in Harvard Sq., is the **Tasty Sandwich Shop,** 2 JFK St., Harvard Square (354-9016). T: Harvard. More than just a 12-seater, fluorescent lit, formica-countered, all-night diner, The Tasty is there for you. Tonight and forever. (Entrees $1-7. Open 24 hrs.)

The Middle East, 472 Mass. Ave. (354-8238), beyond Tandoor House in Central Sq. In this pink restaurant is served the best and most innovative Middle Eastern cuisine around. Huge sandwiches $3-4, dinner entrees $7-10. Go early with a two-for-one coupon from the *Square Deal* (mentioned above). Food served in the bakery; live alternative music in the evenings downstairs. Open Sun.-Wed. 11am-1am, Thurs.-Sat. 11:30am-2am.

Border Café, 32 Church St. (864-6100). "The Border" has tasty and filling entrees ($5-10), and even longer lines. No reservations. The chips and salsa flow loudly and freely. Open Sun. noon-11pm, Mon.-Wed. 11am-11pm, Sat. 11am-2pm.

Tandoor House, 991 Mass. Ave. (661-9001), between Harvard and Central. The best Indian restaurant in Cambridge. Vegetarians should not miss the Shahi Baingan Bharta, a miracle made with a little eggplant and a lot of love. Entrees $6-12; lunch specials from $3.25. Open daily 11:30am-2:30pm and 5-10:30pm.

Brookline Lunch, 9 Brookline St. (354-2983). T: Central. Two blocks toward Boston on Mass. Ave. Hip diner serving huge portions at dirt-cheap prices. Breakfast includes french toast ($2.75) and an incredible veggie omlet ($3.50). Dinner-like beef and chicken dishes are $4.95. Open daily 7am-5pm.

Boca Grande, 1728 Mass. Ave. (354-7400), between Harvard and Porter, the opposite direction on Mass. Ave. from Tandoor House. Award-winning Mexican food made to order, including enchiladas ($5), spicy tamales ($4), and burritos grandes ($3.50). The burritos grandes are certainly *grande,* but your bill here will be *muy poco.* Open Sun.-Wed. 10am-9pm, Thurs. 10am-9:30pm, Fri.-Sat. 10am-10pm.

Jake and Earl's Dixie BBQ, 1273 Cambridge St., Inman Sq. Take the 69 Lechmere bus from Harvard Sq.; look for the laughing pigs and the Elvis bust in the window (491-7427; for delivery call Vidi-Go at 547-0000). Next door to the East Coast Grill. They slop up masterfully spiced barbecue which includes coleslaw, baked beans, and a slice of watermelon, here at this tiny, award-winning BBQ joint. Mostly take-out. Entrees $4-7.50. Cash only. Open daily 11:30am-11pm.

Herrell's, 15 Dunster St., Harvard Sq. (497-2179). After dinner head for the "Best Ice Cream in Boston." Drown in lusciousness inside a vault painted to resemble the watery depths. (Open daily noon-midnight).

NIGHTLIFE AND ENTERTAINMENT

In warm weather, Cambridge entertainment is free. Street musicians ranging from Andean folk singers to jazz trios staff every streetcorner of Harvard Square. Cafes crowd at all times of year for lunch or after-hours coffee. The low-ceilinged, smoke-and-Heidegger-filled **Café Pamplona,** 12 Bow St., might be too angst-ridden for you; in summer escape to its outdoor tables. (Open Mon.-Sat. 11am-1am, Sun. 2pm-1am.) **Algiers Coffee House,** 40 Brattle St. (492-1557), has two beautiful floors of airy, wood-latticed seating, and exceptional food to boot (open Mon.-Thurs. 8am-midnight, Fri.-Sat. 8am-1am, Sun. 9am-midnight).

Harvard sponsors any number of readings and lectures each week; check the kiosks that fill Harvard Yard for posters. The renowned **American Repertory Theater,** in the Loeb Drama Center, 64 Brattle St. (547-8300), produces shows from September-June. (Tickets $17-38; box office open daily 10am-5:30pm).

Cambridge can also accommodate those whose idea of nightlife is something other than an evening with Umberto Eco: both the **Middle East** (a three-stage nirvana for the musically adventurous; see Food above), and **Johnny D's,** 17 Holland St. (776-9667), in neighboring Somerville (T: Davis), are fine venues for live music. The **House of Blues,** 96 Winthrop St. (491-2583), in Harvard Square, is a blues club-*cum*-theme park and restaurant masterminded by Isaac "Hard Rock Cafe" Tigrett and Blues "Brother" Dan Aykroyd. HOB has at least brought local and national blues *musicians* to attention (the music *is* stellar). The expensive food will give you the blues. (Entrees $6.50-17. Open Sun.-Wed. 11:30am-1am, Thurs.-Sat. 11:30am-2am, cover varies.) The **Dungeon Bar** downstairs has no cover.

T.T. The Bear's Place, 10 Brookline St., Central Sq. (492-0082). Brings really live, really loud rock bands to its intimate, seemingly makeshift stage. Open Mon.-Thurs. 8pm-1am, Fri.-Sun. noon-1am. Cover rarely exceeds $6. Really.

Ryles, 212 Hampshire St. (876-9330), in Inman Square. Take the 69 Lechmere bus. A Boston jazz-scene standby, with nightly live music and a jazz brunch on Sun. noon-4pm. Open Sun.-Thurs. 5pm-1am, Fri.-Sat. 5pm-2am.

Cantab Lounge, 738 Mass. Ave., Central Sq. (354-2684). For over 10 years, Little Joe Cook and his blues band have been packing the place with local fans and recently enlightened college students. Cover Thurs. $3, Fri.-Sat. $5. Open Mon.-Wed. 8am-1am, Thurs.-Sat. 8am-2am, Sun. noon-1am.

Passim, 47 Palmer St., Harvard Sq. (492-9653). Just off Church St. across from the Border Café. This legendary basement no-alcohol coffeehouse carries the folk-

NEW ENGLAND

music torch proudly on weekends; during the week, Passim is a restaurant. Cover $6-9. Open Tues.-Sat. noon-5:30pm, evening hours vary.

SIGHTS

Aside from the paunchy professors, ubiquitous yuppies, hippies, homeless, and highschoolers, there are also a number of fascinating attractions in Cambridge. **The Massachusetts Institute of Technology (MIT)** campus buildings are a huge slice in the I.M. Pei. MIT also has an impressive collection of modern outdoor sculpture, and an "infinite corridor" ¼ mi. long, second only to the Pentagon's. Tours are available weekdays at 10am and 2pm from the Rogers Building, or "Building Number 7" as the students here term it. Contact **MIT Information** at 77 Mass. Ave. (253-1000; open Mon.-Fri. 9am-5pm). The **MIT Museum,** 265 Mass. Ave. (253-4444), contains a slide rule collection and wonderful photography exhibits, including the famous stop-action photos of Harold Edgerton. (Open Tues.-Fri. 9am-5pm, Sat.-Sun. 1-5pm. $2, seniors and kids under 12 free.)

Up Mass. Ave., **Harvard University** resides in red brick-and-ivied dignity. The oldest university in the country, Harvard (founded in 1636) is home to nobel laureates, students from around the world, and, contrary to popular belief, an occasional party. **Radcliffe College,** founded in 1879 and once an all-female institution, is now joined with Harvard, but maintains its own name, alumnae group, and sports teams. The college formerly lodged in **Radcliffe Yard,** a verdant collection of garden and lawns between Garden and Brattle Streets, now houses the admissions office and a theater. **The Schlesinger Library** in Radcliffe Yard has the nation's largest collection of women-related literature. (Open to the public Mon.-Fri. 9am-8pm, Sat. 10am-5pm.)

The university revolves around **Harvard Yard,** where, try as you might, you won't be able to pahk your cah. The Yard is a grassy oasis of serenity amid the Cantabridgian bustle. The Yard's eastern half holds classroom buildings, **Memorial Church,** and **Widener Library** (495-2411). Widener, named after its benefactor who perished on the Titanic, is the largest academic library in the world and contains 4½ million of the university's 12 million books. While visitors can't browse among Widener's shelves, they are welcome to examine Harvard's Gutenberg Bible and other rare books in the Harry Elkins Widener Memorial Reading Room, or to take in the John Singer Sargent murals. In the western half ("The Old Yard"), some of the school's first buildings still stand. Today Harvard students live in the Yard during their first year of study; John F. Kennedy lived in Weld, while Emerson and Thoreau resided in Hollis.

The oldest of Harvard's museums, the **Fogg Art Museum,** 32 Quincy St. (495-9400), gathers a considerable collection of works ranging from ancient Chinese jade to contemporary photography, as well as the largest Ingres collection outside of France. The limited display space around its uplifting Italian Renaissance courtyard frequently rotates well-planned exhibits. Across the street, the modern exterior of the **Arthur M. Sackler Museum,** 485 Broadway (495-9400), belies a rich collection of ancient Asian and Islamic art. The third of Harvard's art museums, the **Busch-Reisinger Museum,** 32 Quincy St. (495-9400), displays Northern and Central European sculpture, painting, and decorative arts. (All three museums open daily 10am-5pm. Admission to each $5, students and seniors $4. Free Sat. mornings.) Peering down at the Fogg, Le Corbusier's guitar-shaped **Carpenter Center,** 24 Quincy St. (495-3251), shows student and professional work with especially strong photo exhibits, not to mention a great film series at the **Harvard Film Archives.** (Open Mon.-Sat. 9am-midnight, Sun. noon-10pm.) Included in the **Museums of Natural History,** 24 Oxford St. (495-3045), are the **Peabody Museum of Archaeology and Ethnology,** which houses treasures from prehistoric and Native American cultures, and the **Mineralogical and Geological Museums,** containing gems, minerals, ores, and meteorites. But the Ware collection of "glass flowers" at the **Botanical Museum** draws the largest crowds. A German glassblower and his son created these remarkably accurate, enlarged reproductions of over 840 plant species. (Open

Mon.-Sat. 9am-4:15pm, Sun. 1-4:15pm. $4, students and seniors $3, ages 5-15 $1. Admission includes all the natural history museums.)

George Washington worshiped at **Christ Church** on Garden St., the oldest church in Cambridge, which had its organ pipes melted down for Revolutionary bullets. Soldiers felled in the struggle are buried in the 17th-century **Old Burying Ground** or "God's Acre" on Garden St., also the final resting place of colonial settlers and early Harvard presidents. Behind Garden St., on 105 Brattle St., is the restored **Longfellow House** (876-4491), headquarters of the Continental Army during the early stages of the Revolution, later home of the poet Henry Wadsworth Longfellow and now a National Historic Site. The staff can give you info on local historic sights. (Tours daily 10:45am-4pm. Admission $2, seniors and under 17 free.) The **Mt. Auburn Cemetery** lies about 1 mi. up the road at the end of Brattle St. This first botanical-garden/cemetery in the U.S. has 170 acres of beautifully landscaped grounds fertilized by Louis Agassiz, Charles Bulfinch, Dorothea Dix, Mary Baker Eddy, and H.W. Longfellow among others

■■■ LEXINGTON AND CONCORD

Lexington "Listen, my children and you shall hear," wrote Henry Wadsworth Longfellow, "of the midnight ride of Paul Revere." The opening salvo of the American Revolution between the British Redcoats and the colonial minutemen was exchanged in downtown Lexington, and while the **Battle Green** is no longer guarded by colonial soldiers, it is defended by the **Minuteman Statue.** The **Buckman Tavern,** 1 Bedford St (862-5598), has been restored to the 1775 form in which it headquartered the Minutemen on the eve of their fateful battle, although now information is provided instead of spirits. The **Hancock-Clarke House,** 36 Hancock St. (861-0928), and the **Munroe Tavern,** 1332 Mass. Ave. (674-9238), also played significant roles in the birth of the Revolution. (House and Taverns open mid April to Oct. Mon.-Sat. Must be seen on a 30-min. tour that runs continuously. $3 per house for adults, $1 for ages 6-16, under 6 free. A combination ticket $7, kids $2.) An excellent model and description of the Battle of Lexington is on display at the **visitors center,** 1875 Mass. Ave. (862-1450), behind the Buckman Tavern (open May-Oct. daily 9am-5pm; Nov. 10am-4pm; Dec.-Feb. Mon.-Fri. 10am-2pm; March-April 10am-4pm). You can also survey an exhibit on the Revolution at the **Museum of Our National Heritage,** 33 Marrett Rd. (861-6559), which also features exhibits on historical and popular American life (open Mon.-Sat. 10am-5pm, Sun. noon-5pm; handicapped accessible; free).

Lexington is easily accessible by two-and four-wheeled vehicles. Drive straight up Mass. Ave. from Boston or Cambridge, or bike up the **Minuteman Commuter Bike Trail,** which runs rights into downtown Lexington, and beyond (access off Mass. Ave. in Arlington). When the minutemen retreated from Lexington they made their way to Concord via the **Battle Road.** The road now forms the spine of **Minuteman National Historical Park.** The **Battle Road Visitors Center** (862-7753) on Rte 2A in Lexington offers talks, distributes maps, and screens a film that sets the stage for the Revolutionary War, the second conflict of which occurred up the road in Concord. (Open April-Oct. daily 9am-5:30pm.) Lexington's **area code:** 617.

Concord Concord garnered fame both for its military history and its status as an American literary and intellectual capital of the 19th century. Muster your strength for a brief march from the parking lot on Monument St. across the **Old North Bridge.** As you troop past **The Minuteman** and shoot over the bridge, you'll pass the spot where "the shot heard round the world" rang out. This general area is historic as well as scenic and a five-minute walk brings you to the **North Bridge Visitors Center,** 174 Liberty St. (369-6793), where rangers will gladly surrender hosts of pamphlets and brochures. (Open April-Oct. daily 9am-5:30pm, call for winter hrs.)

The Alcotts and the Hawthornes once inhabited **Wayside,** 455 Lexington Rd. (369-6975), while Emerson himself lived down the road during the later half of the century. Now a part of the **Minute Man National Historical Park,** the house is open for public viewing. (Open May-Oct. Tues. noon-4pm, Fri-Sun. noon-4pm. Must be on a tour. Tours leave on the hour. $3, under 17 free.) The **Concord Museum** (369-9763), directly across the street from the house, houses a reconstruction of Emerson's study alongside Paul Revere's lantern and items from Henry David Thoreau's cabin. (Open April-Dec. Mon.-Sat 10am-5pm, Sun. 1-5pm; Jan-March Mon.-Sat. 11am-4pm, Sun. 1-4pm. $6, seniors $5, students and children $3.) Emerson, Hawthorne, Alcott, and Thoreau are reunited on "Author's Ridge" in the **Sleepy Hollow Cemetery** on Rte. 62, three blocks from the center of town. Concord's **area code:** 508.

Lexington and Concord are easy daytrips from Boston. Concord, 20 mi. north, is served by **MBTA** trains from North Station ($2.75). MBTA buses from Alewife station in Cambridge run several times daily to Lexington (60¢).

Walden Pond In 1845, Thoreau retreated 1½ mi. south of Concord on Rte. 126, "to live deliberately, to front only the essential facts of life." He did so, and produced his famous *Walden.* Any questions or comments about Thoreau can be directed to the **Thoreau Lyceum,** 156 Belknap St. (369-5912), where members of the Thoreau society will banter with you. The Lyceum also has a library and a replica of Thoreau's cabin on display. (Open March-Jan. Mon.-Sat. 10am-5pm, Sun. 2-5pm. $2, students $1.50, kids 50¢.) Thoreau wrote that "the mass of men lead lives of quiet desperation." Well, at the **Walden Pond State Reservation,** Rte. 126 (369-3254), they aren't all that quiet. This lovely locale is popular with picnickers, swimmers, and boaters; though the park is lovely, the solitude that inspired Thoreau is hard to get. (Open daily 5am-sunset. Parking $2 daily during the summer, and on weekends in the spring.) The Pond only holds 1000 visitors; rangers will turn you away, so call before coming out. When Walden Pond swarms with crowds, head down Rte. 62 east from Concord center to **Great Meadows National Wildlife Refuge,** (443-4661), Monson Rd., another of Thoreau's haunts (open daily dawn-dusk).

■■■ SALEM

Salem presents its history every witch way you turn. Along with the sensational **witch trials** of 1692, the town, which was once the sixth largest city in the U.S., has historic homes, a robust maritime heritage, and a literary history. Salem hexes 20 mi. northeast of Boston; take the Rockport/Ipswich commuter train from North Station (745-3527; $2.50) or the #450 bus from Haymarket ($2.25). Salem's **area code:** 508.

Salem's **Peabody Museum,** in East India Sq. (745-1876, for recorded info 745-9500), recalls the port's former leading role in Atlantic whaling and merchant shipping. You can also relax for free on sunny days in the museum's Oriental Garden, just beside the Museum on Liberty St. (Daily guided tour at 2pm; in summer also at 11am. Open Mon.-Sat. 10am-5pm, Sun. noon-5pm. $6, seniors and students $5, ages 6-18 $3.50.) Down by the waterfront, the **Salem Maritime National Historic Site,** three wharves and several historic buildings along Derby St., are worth exploring. Derby Wharf, a highlight of the site, is under construction for the next few years to restore it to its 19th century appearances. You can still walk to the lighthouse on the end. Federal officials, including Nathaniel Hawthorne, collected import duties until 1917 at the **Customs House,** 174 Derby St. (744-4323), where the narrator of Hawthorne's novel claims to find *The Scarlet Letter* (open daily 9am-6pm; off-season 9am-5pm). Hawthorne lost his desk job here thanks to the spoils system; he later took the customs beauraucrats to task in his writing.

The gothic **Witch Museum,** 19½ Washington Square (744-1692—notice the numerology), presents a melodramatic but informative multi-media presentation that fleshes out the history of the trials. (Open daily July-Aug. 10am-7pm; daily Sept.-June 10am-5pm. $4, seniors $3.50, ages 6-14 $2.50.) Never actually a dungeon, the **Witch Dungeon,** 16 Lynde St. (741-3570), has actresses present skits about the trials which amplify the toil and trouble of the proceedings. (Open April-Dec. daily 10am-5pm, shows every 30 min., $4, seniors $3.50, ages 6-14 $2.50.)

NEW ENGLAND

Salem boasts the "second most famous house in America," the **House of Seven Gables,** 54 Turner St. (744-0991), built in 1668 and made famous by Nathaniel Hawthorne's Gothic romance of the same name. (Open July-Aug. daily 9am-6pm; Sept.-June Mon.-Sat. 10am-4:30pm, Sun. noon-4:30pm. $6.50, ages 13-17 $4, ages 6-12 $3.) Prices are steeper than the famed roof, but the tour is thorough and informative. (Open daily 10am-4:30pm; July-Aug. Fri.-Wed. 9:30am-5:30pm, Thurs. 9:30am-8:30pm. Tour $6.50, ages 6-17 $4, access to grounds $1, although you can see all 7 gables from the street for free.)

Salem has two **information centers:** one at 2 Liberty St. (741-3648; open daily 9am-5pm), which presents a movie on three screens about Salem and Essex county, and one at Derby Wharf (745-1470; open daily 9:30am-5pm). Both provide a free map of historic Salem. A 1.3-mi. **Heritage Trail** traces an easy footpath past all the main sights in town, marked clearly by a painted red line on the pavement. Pull up a stone and sit for a spell at the **Witch Trials Memorial,** off Charter St., where simple engraved stones provide reflection on the trials amidst the sea of witch kitsch. Salem is packed to the belfries during Halloween with a week-long festival called **Haunted Happenings.** Book months in advance for Halloween.

■■■ CAPE ANN

Rockport Rockport is the picturesque quaint New England fishing village. Some downtown parking meters sell 15 min. for a penny and a lobster boat may disgorge its payload while you're strolling along the harbor. Check out the **Headlands** above town for a nice harbor view, or stroll through the bayberries and take a gander at the old granite quarries at **Halibut Point State Park,** (546-2997) Gott Ave. off Rte. 127. (Open June-Sept., sunrise-8pm daily; Oct.-May sunrise-sunset daily. Parking $2 per car.) Interaction with the ocean on **Long Beach,** off Thatcher Ave., from which you can spy the islands off the Cape. Sunset is the best time to visit. At high tide the beach virtually disappears. A free boat to **Thatcher Island,** one of only a few islands in the U.S. with twin lighthouses, leaves T Wharf in Rockport.

B&Bs proliferate in the area's historic homes. Call or stop by the **Rockport Visitors Center,** Rte. 127 (546-6575) for more info (open mid-May to mid-Oct. Mon.-Sat. 11am-5pm, Sun. noon-4pm). Dining here is largely seafood, but why would you want anything else? After all, Cape Ann produced one of America's great culinary masterpieces: the **fried clam.** Dine on lobster at picnic tables by the sea at **The Lobster Pool,** 327 Granite St. (546-7808), 3 mi. outside of town on Beach St. (open daily May-Aug. 11:30am-8:30pm.)

Rockport is accessible via **Rte. 128** from Boston or the **Commuter Rail** (800-392-6100 from North Station ($4). Once on Cape Ann, you can get around by using the **Salt Water Trolley** (283-7916. Runs June-min Sept. Sat 10am-11pm, Sun. and holidays 10am-10pm. $4, seniors and students $2 for an unlimited daily ticket), or the Cape Ann Transportation Authority **buses** (283-7916. Runs Mon.-Fri. 6am-6pm, Sat. 9am-6pm. 60¢ in the town, 75¢ between Rockport, and its salty sister Gloucester.) Rte. 127 also links Rockport and Glocester. Rockport's **post office:** 39 Broadway (508-546-2304: Mon.-Fri. 8:30am-5pm, Sat. 8:30am-2pm; **area code:** 508.

Gloucester As the oldest fishing port in the nation, Gloucester has long drawn on the plentiful life of the Atlantic, although today it counts on whales, not cod, for its livelihood. **Whale watching** is a hugely popular local industry. You can pick up more information on whale and Gloucester watchs at the **Visitors Center,** 33 Commercial St. (283-1601). Gloucester also draws visitors to the ocean views that inspired the artists of **Rocky Neck,** the oldest art colony in the United States. Rocky Neck is a stop on the **Maritime Trail,** which leads walkers around the sights of Gloucester. You can pick up a map at the visitors center or follow the red line on the streets. Check out the painted oars and the scale model of Gloucester harbor at the **Cape Ann Historical Museum,** 27 Pleasant St. (283-0455; open March-Jan. Tues.-Sat. 10am-5pm, Sun. 10am-1pm. $3.50, seniors $3, students $2, under 6 free.)

If you tire of boats and buoys, check out the **Hammond Castle,** 80 Hesperus Ave., off Rte. 127 (283-8079). This medieval-style manse was constructed by the inventor of the remote control, John Hammond. (Open summer, daily 10am-5pm; call for winter hours. $5.50, seniors and students $4.50, 4-12 $3.50.)

Gloucester is accessible via **Rte. 128** from Boston or the **Commuter Rail** (800-392-6100 from North Station ($4). Once on Cape Ann, you can get around by using the **Salt Water Trolley** (283-7916. Runs June-min Sept. Sat 10am-11pm, Sun. and holidays 10am-10pm. $4, seniors and students $2 for an unlimited daily ticket), or the Cape Ann Transportation Authority **buses** (283-7916. Runs Mon.-Fri. 6am-6pm, Sat. 9am-6pm. 60¢ in the town, 75¢ between towns.) Gloucester's **post office:** Dale Ave., (283-0474; Mon.-Fri. 8am-5pm, Sat. 8am-2pm); **area code:** 508.

■■■ PLYMOUTH

Despite what American high school textbooks say, the Pilgrims did *not* first step ashore onto the New World at Plymouth—they first stopped at Provincetown, but left because the soil was inadequate. **Plymouth Rock** itself is a rather anti-climactically diminutive stone that has dubiously been identified as the actual rock on which the Pilgrims disembarked. Since that first Puritan foot was credited to the rock, it has served as a symbol of liberty during the American Revolution, been moved three times, and been chipped away by tourists before landing at its current home beneath an extravagant portico on Water St., at the foot of North St. The **Plymouth Visitor's Information Center,** 130 Water St. (800-USA-1620), hands out brochures and useful maps, and has hotel and B&B information. Considering the proximity of Cape Cod's soft sand beaches, you won't want to spend more than a day here.

Plimoth Plantation (746-1622 for recording), on Warren Ave., superbly recreates the early settlement. In the **Pilgrim Village** costumed actors impersonate actual villagers carrying out their daily tasks based on William Bradford's record of the year 1627. Camping is available. The adjacent **Wampanoag Summer Encampment** recreates a Native American village of the same period. Admission to the plantation includes entry to the **Mayflower II,** built in the 1950s to recapture the atmosphere of the original ship. (Ship docked off Water St., 4 blocks south of the info center. Open July-Aug. daily 9am-7pm, April-June and Sept.-Nov. 9am-5pm. Separate admission $5.75, kids $3.75. Plantation open April-Nov. daily 9am-5pm. $18.50, ages 5-12 $11, seniors and students $16.50; admission good for 2 consecutive days.)

If you're feeling bogged down in history, head for **Cranberry World,** 225 Water St. (747-2350), which glorifies one of only four indigenous American fruits (the others are the tomato, the blueberry, and the Concord grape). Exhibits show how cranberries are grown, harvested, and sold, and include a small cranberry bog in front of the museum. They also provide free juice. (Open May-Nov. 9:30am-5pm. Free.) The nation's oldest museum in continuous existence, the **Pilgrim Hall Museum,** 75 Court St. (746-1620), houses Puritan crafts, furniture, books, paintings, and weapons (open daily 9:30am-4:30pm; $5, seniors $4 ages 6-15 $2.50)

Majestic **Myles Standish Forest** (866-2526), 7 miles south of Plymouth via Rte. 3, offers wooded ground (sites $5, with showers $6). The cheapest beds in Plymouth by far are found at the **Bunk and Bagel,** 51 Pleasant St. (830-0914) which offers hostel and bed and breakfast rooms. Go for the hostel; you still get a nice breakfast. (5-8 hostel beds, common bath. Breakfast and linens provided. Open May-Nov. Office open daily 7-9:30am and 5-10pm. $15.) .

CAPE COD AREA

Henry David Thoreau once said: "At present [this coast] is wholly unknown to the fashionable world, and probably it will never be agreeable to them." Think again Henry. In 1602, when English navigator and Jamestown colonist Bartholomew Gosnold landed on this peninsula in southeastern Massachusetts, he named it in honor of all the codfish he caught in the surrounding waters. In recent decades, it is tourists who have filled the waters. Within this small strip of land you can find a great diversity of delicate landscapes—long unbroken stretches of beach, salt marshes, hardwood forests, deep freshwater ponds carved by glaciers, and desert-like dunes sculpted by the wind. The fragility of the environment is visibly depleting; every year chunks of the Cape's delicate ecosystem wash away into the ocean, and sand dunes recede under the relentless pressures of ocean and humanity. The Cape's natural landscape has been protected by the establishment of the **Cape Cod National Seashore,** so this magnificent seaside is safe from the tide of commercialism. Blessed with an excellent hostel system, Cape Cod is an ideal budget seaside getaway, and is used by many cross-country travelers as a place to rest and relax after cramming in the cultural sights of urban America. It also serves as the gateway to **Martha's Vineyard** and **Nantucket.**

In a bit of confusing terminology, the part of Cape Cod closer to the mainland is called the **Upper Cape,** which is suburbanized and the most developed area on the Cape. As you proceed away from the mainland, you travel "down Cape" until you get to the **Lower Cape;** the National Seashore encompasses much of this area. Cape Cod resembles a bent arm, with **Woods Hole** at its armpit, **Chatham** at the elbow, and **Provincetown** at its clenched fist.

Cycling is the best way to travel the Cape's gentle slopes. The park service can give you a free map of trails or sell you the detailed **Cape Cod Bike Book** ($2.50; also available at most of the Cape's bookstores). The 135-mi. **Boston-Cape Cod Bikeway** connects Boston to Provincetown at land's end. Some of the most scenic bike trails in the country line either side of the **Cape Cod Canal** in the National Seashore, and the 14-mi. **Cape Cod Rail Trail** from Dennis to Eastham.

Cape Cod's **area code:** 508.

■■■ UPPER CAPE

■ HYANNIS

Hyannis is not the Cape Cod most people expect. JFK spent his summers on the beach in nearby Hyannisport, but the town is really more of a transportation hub than a scenic destination. Island ferries and cape bus service emanant from Hyannis, and you'll probably want to hop on one and get out of town: the Kennedys *aren't* going to meet you at the bus station.

Hyannis is tattooed midway across the Cape's upper arm, 3 mi. south of U.S. 6 on Nantucket Sound. The **Hyannis Area Chamber of Commerce,** 1481 Rte. 132 (775-2201), about 3 mi. up the road from the bus station, can help and hands out the *Hyannis Guidebook.* (Open Mon.-Thurs. 9am-5pm, Fri. 9am-7pm, Sat. 9am-4:30pm, Sun. 11am-3pm. Closed Sun. Sept.-May.)

Plymouth & Brockton (775-5524) runs a Boston-to-Provincetown bus five times a day with a ½-hr. layover at the **Hyannis Bus Station,** 17 Elm St. (775-5524), which also stops in Plymouth, Sagamore, Yarmouth, Orleans, Wellfleet, Truro, and elsewhere. (Boston to Hyannis: 3½ hr., $10. Hyannis to Provincetown: 1½ hr., $9.) **Bonanza Bus Lines** (800-556-3815) operates a line to New York City (6 per day, 6 hr., $39, with stop in Providence). **Amtrak,** 252 Main St. (800-872-7245), sends a direct train from New York City to Hyannis on Friday, and one from Hyannis to New York on Monday (6 hr., $65). For info on **ferries** to Martha's Vineyard and Nantucket, see the listings for those islands. **ZIP code:** 02601.

There is nowhere cheap to stay in Hyannis. The closest affordable places are the campgrounds near **Sandwich** (see listing), about 15 mi. from Hyannis, and the hostel in **Eastham** (see listing). Also contact the **Hyannis Chamber of Commerce.**

■ SANDWICH

The oldest town on the Cape, Sandwich cultivates a charm unmatched by its neighbors on the Upper Cape. Sandwich glass became famous for its beauty and workmanship when the Boston & Sandwich Glass Company was founded here in 1825. The original company is gone, but you can still see master glassblowers shaping their works of art from blobs of molten sand at **Pairpoint Crystal** on Rte. 6A, just across the town border in Sagamore (888-2344; open Mon.-Sat. 9am-6pm, Sun. 10am-6pm, glass blowing Mon.-Fri. 8:30am-4:30pm; free).

Practical Information and Camping Sandwich lies at the intersection of Rte. 6A and 130, about 13 mi. from Hyannis. The Plymouth and Brockton bus makes its closest stop in Sagamore, 3 mi. west. You can also reach Sandwich from Hyannis via the **Cape Cod Railroad** (771-3788), a scenic 2-hr. ride through cranberry bogs and marshes (3 per day round trip to the Cape Cod Canal from Main and Center St. in Hyannis; $10.50, kids $6.50; July-Aug. $11.50, kids $7.50).

Across the Sagamore Bridge, **Scusset Beach** (888-0859), right on the canal near the junction of U.S. 6 and Rte. 3, offers fishing and camping. (Sites—mostly for RVs—$16, hookup $19, day use $2 per carload.) The **Shawme-Crowell State Forest** (888-0351), on Rte. 130 and U.S. 6, has 280 wooded campsites with showers and campfires, but no hookups. (Open April-late Nov.; $6, including parking at Scusset Beach.) **Peters Pond Park Campground** (477-1775), Cotuit Rd. in south Sandwich, offers aquatic activities, a grocery store, showers, and a few prime waterside sites ($18-31, open mid-April to mid-Oct.)

Sights The **Sandwich Glass Museum** 129 Main St. (888-0251), in Sandwich Center, has old, beautiful glass and lots of it (open daily 9:30am-4:30pm; Nov.-March Wed.-Sun. 9:30am-4pm; $3, under 12 50¢). The **Thornton W. Burgess Museum** (888-6870) on Water St. pays tribute to the Sandwich-born naturalist who wrote tales about Br'er Rabbit and the "dear old briar patch." (Open Mon.-Sat. 10am-4pm, Sun. 1pm-4pm. Donations accepted.) Ask for directions to **The Green Briar Nature Center and Jam Kitchen,** 6 Discovery Rd. (888-6870). Wander through the real briar patch, trails, and wildflower gardens, or watch jam-making in the center kitchen Wed. and Sat. (Open Mon.-Sat. 10am-4pm, Sun. 1-4pm; Jan.-March Tues.-Sat. 10am-4pm. Donations accepted.) **Sandy Neck Beach,** 3 mi. east of Sandwich on Sandy Neck Rd. off Rte. 6-A, is the best beach on the Upper Cape. Stroll 6 mi. along Cape Cod Bay on beautifully polished egg-sized granite pebbles, or hike out through the verdant dunes (only on the marked trails; the plants are very fragile).

■ ■ ■ LOWER CAPE

Much less suburbanized than the Upper Cape, the Lower Cape preserves the weathered-shingle, dirt-road atmosphere of yore. In some towns, the majority of the land belongs to the National Seashore. On the whole, development here has been mercifully restrained, leaving an unsullied paradise for generations of vacationers to discover anew. To see the area you need to leave the highway behind. Make your way down a back lane by car, bike, or foot, and you'll find the rolling dunes, solitary lighthouses, and sweeping seascapes that make the Cape such a special place.

The Lower Cape towns of **Orleans, Eastham, Wellfleet,** and **Truro** shine, thanks to unspoiled beaches, pine-scented forests, and soft light. You may even be inspired to throw up a canvas or jot down some verse to capture the beauty that has inspired so many other artists. When searching for life after dark, head to Provincetown.

Accommodations, Camping, and Food There are two hostels in or near the national seashore. **Truro Hostel (HI-AYH)** (349-3889), at the far end of North Pamet Rd., Truro, 1½ mi. from a bus stop, is a gem. The hostel itself is spacious, with a large kitchen, lots of common space, and great ocean views. It also has access to a secluded beach. (Office open 7:30-10:30am and 5-10pm. $12, nonmembers $15. Reservations essential. Open late June-early Sept.) The **Mid-Cape Hostel (HI-AYH)** (255-2785) is a popular spot with Cape bikers. This quiet, wooded setting has six cabins, a kitchen, and a relaxed atmosphere that attracts a lot of groups. The location is convenient to the rest of the Cape. On the Plymouth-Brockton bus to Provincetown, ask to be let off oat the traffic circle in Orleans (*not* the Eastham stop), walk out on the exit to Rock Harbor, turn right on Bridge Rd., and take a right onto Goody Hallet Rd., ½ mi. from U.S. 6. (Office open daily 7:30-9:30am and 5-10:30pm. $10, nonmembers $13. Reservations essential July-Aug. Open mid-May to mid-Sept.) Also have Provincetown accommodations.

There are seven private campgrounds on the Lower Cape; pick up a free campground directory at the **Cape Cod Chamber of Commerce** in Hyannis. One of the best places to pitch a tent is **Nickerson State Park** (896-3491) on Rte. 6A to the Cape's elbow in Brewster; it's also on the Cape Cod Rail Trail bike path. There are two large ponds with a boat rental on the waterfront, showers, flush toilets, but no hookups. (Sites $6, waterfront $7. 150 sites reservable, 267 first-come, first-served; sites fill up quickly—call a couple weeks in advance or get there early.) About 7 mi. southeast of Provincetown on U.S. 6, several popular campgrounds nestle among the dwarf pines by the dunelands of North Truro and Truro. **North Truro Camping Area** (487-1847), on Highland Rd.½-mi. east of U.S. 6., has small sandy sites. ($15 for 2 people, hookup $20. Each additional person $7. Open year-round.) Other **Cape Campgrounds** include: **Atlantic Oaks** in Eastham (255-1457); **Coastal Acres** in Provincetown (487-1700); **Dune's Edge** in Provincetown (487-9815); **Horton's Park** in North Truro (487-1220); **Maurice's** in South Wellfleet (349-2029); **North of Highland** in North Truro (487-1191); **Paine's** in South Wellfleet (349-3007); **Shady Knoll** in Brewster (869-3002); **Sweetwater Forest** in Brewster (896-3773).

Located right at the oceanfront at the end of Cahoon Hollow Rd. off U.S. 6, the **Beachcomber** (349-6055) serves up large baskets of fish and chips ($6), and burgers and fries ($5), and attracts a young crowd of bathing-suit clad beachmongers (open in summer daily noon-1am). At the **Bayside Lobster Hut**, 91 Commercial St. (349-6333), in Wellfleet, you can "see 'em swim" and while it's questionable how enticing that is, this casual, usually crowded spot offers cheap lobster and picnic tables (open July-Aug. noon-10pm, June and Sept. 4:30-9pm).

Sights and Activities Cape Cod is dotted with historic houses and buildings, most of which are older than the United States. Built in 1680, the **Eastham Windmill,** Rte. 6 at Samoset Rd., Eastham, still has its nose to the grindstone. It continues to function, and demonstrates how the native American crop of corn was put to use by industrious Cape Codders. (Open July-Aug. Mon.-Sat. 10am-5pm, Sun. 1-5pm; free.) The **First Congregation Parish of Truro** (United Church of Christ) will transport you back to the 19th century. The church, built in 1827, has changed little since its construction; electricity was installed just 30 years ago, and the outhouse still serves in place of new-fangled toilets. Take the Bridge Rd. exit off U.S. 6 and turn right onto Town Hall Rd. (Sunday morning services at 10am.)

The best activities on the lower cape involve exploring the wonderful natural setting of the region. **Fort Hill,** off Rte. 6 in Eastham, grants a panoramic view of Nauset Marsh and the surrounding forest and ocean, as well as paths on which to explore them. **Nauset Light,** Salt Pond Rd. in Eastham, offers a windswept survey of dunes and sea, and **Marconi Station,** off Rte. 6 in Wellfleet, lets you gaze across the breadth of the Cape.

Take a walk on the **Cranberry Bog Trail,** North Pamet Rd. in Truro near the hostel, a picturesque path in a secluded, spectacular setting, which criss-crosses the National Seashore. Get a map at the visitors center. You can take a dip in the waves on some swell beaches. You can also immerse yourself in fresh water in one of the Cape's "kettle ponds." One of the best in which to paddle is **Gull Pond,** off Gull Pond Rd. in Wellfleet, which connects by a series of shallow channels to three more secluded ponds. From Higgins Pond you can see the home of the Wellfleet Oysterman, where Thoreau stayed and about which he wrote a chapter in *Cape Cod.* In the spring you can catch the unique spectacle of the **herring run.** The amorous creatures clog the rivers of the Cape as they head inland to spawn, blindly ignoring the glut of fish around them. Funny how it resembles July on Rte. 6.

■ CAPE COD NATIONAL SEASHORE

As early as 1825, the Cape was so heavily damaged by the hand of man that the town of Truro mandated that local residents plant beach grass and keep their cows off the dunes; the sea was threatening to wash the sandy town away and make Provincetown an island. This fragile environment is easily disturbed, and conservation efforts culminated in 1961 with the creation of the Cape Cod National Seashore, which includes much of the Lower Cape from Provincetown south to Chatham.

This beautiful stretch of land lures visitors with over 30 mi. of soft, wide, uninterrupted sandy beaches, tucked under tall clay cliffs spotted with 19th-century lighthouses. Besides worshipping the sand, you can explore salt marshes, home to migrating and native waterfowl, bicycle through quiet forests and grassy dunes, or contemplate a sunrise or a sunset reflecting off broad expanses of water. There are even warm, fresh-water ponds where you can escape for a dip when the waves or the crowds at the beach become too intense; try Gull or Long Pond in Wellfleet, or Pilgrim Lake in Truro.

Thanks to conservationists, this area has largely escaped the condo-strip boardwalk commercialism that afflicts most seacoasts in America. A 20-min. walk on the beach away from the lifeguards can take you away from the hordes of umbrella- and cooler-luggers. Or hike one of the under-used nature trails. You'll be impressed by the wide variety of habitats that huddle together on this narrow slice of land.

Beachgoers face one eternal question: ocean or bay. The ocean beaches attract with whistling winds and surging surf; the water on the bay side is calmer, a bit warmer, and better for swimming. The National Seashore oversees six beaches: **Coast Guard** and **Nauset Light** in Eastham; **Marconi** in Wellfleet; **Head of the Meadow** in Truro; **Race Point** and **Herring Cove** in Provincetown. Parking costs $5 per day and $15 per season. Walkers and riders are supposed to pay a $3 entrance fee.

To park at any other beach, you'll need a town permit. Each town has a different beach-parking policy, but permits usually cost $25-30 per week, $75 per season, or $10 per day. Beaches can be miles from any other legal parking and police with tow trucks roam the area like vultures, so call the appropriate Town Hall first. On sunny days, parking lots fill up by 11am or earlier. It's better to rent a bike and ride in. Most town beaches do not require bikers and walkers to pay an entrance fee. All ocean beaches are worth visiting, but Wellfleet and Truro are great examples of the Cape's famous, endangered sand dunes. **Cahoon Hollow Beach** in Wellfleet stands out with spectacular, cliff-like dunes, particularly young crowd, and day parking.

Nine self-guiding **nature trails** wind through an extraordinary range of landscapes. One of the best is the **Great Island Trail** in Wellfleet, an 8-mi. loop through pine forests, grassy marshes, and a ridge with a view of the bay and Provincetown. The **Buttonbush Trail,** a ¼-mi. walk, starts at the Salt Pond Visitors Center, is designed for the blind, and has braille guides and a guide rope. Also inquire at the visitors center about the three park **bike trails:** Nauset Trail (1.6 mi.), Head of the Meadow Trail (2 mi.), and Province Lands Trail (5 mi.). Start your exploration at the **National Seashore's Salt Pond Visitors Center** (255-1301), at Salt Pond, off U.S. 6 in Eastham (open daily 9am-6pm, Sept.-June 9am-4:30pm). The center offers info and advice on the whole seashore, as well as free 10-min. films every half-hour and a free museum which has excellent exhibits on the Cape's human and natural history.

Camping is *illegal* on the public lands of the national seashore. See Lower Cape for accommodations in the area.

■ PROVINCETOWN

Provincetown is where Cape Cod ends and the wide Atlantic begins. Two-thirds of "P-Town" is conservation land protected by the National Seashore; the inhabited sliver touches the harbor on the south side of town. Commercial Street, the city's main drag, has seen the whalers of yesteryear replaced by shops, Portuguese bakeries, restaurants, art galleries, clubs, and lots of people.

For over a century, Provincetown has been known for its broad acceptance of many different lifestyles, and a widely known gay and lesbian community has flowered here. Over half the couples on the street are same-sex, and a walk here makes it quietly plain that sexual orientation does not adhere to any stereotype of size, shape, color, or dress.

Practical Information Provincetown rests in the cupped hand at the end of the Cape Cod arm, 123 mi. away from Boston as the crow drives, or 3 hr. by ferry across Massachusetts Bay. Parking spots are always rare, and virtually cease to exist on grey days when the Cape's frustrated sun-worshippers flock to Provincetown, its wild stores, and fascinating people-watching scene. **Bradford Street** is the town's auto-friendly thoroughfare; follow the parking signs to dock your car for $5-7 per day. **MacMillan Wharf** is at the center of town, just down the hill from the Pilgrim Monument. Whale-watching boats, the Boston ferry, and buses all leave from here. **Emergency** is 911. The **Provincetown Chamber of Commerce** sits at 307 Commercial St. (487-3424), MacMillan Wharf (open mid-June to late Sept. daily 9am-5pm; April to mid-June and late Sept. to Nov. Mon.-Sat. 10am-4pm). Acquire info on the national seashore and free guides to the nature and bike trails at **Province Lands Visitors Center,** Race Point Rd. (487-1256; open July-Aug. daily 9am-6pm; mid-April-June and Sept.-Nov. daily 9am-4:30pm). Instead of Greyhound, hop on a **Plymouth and Brockton Bus** (746-0378), which stops at MacMillan Wharf, behind Provincetown Chamber of Commerce (with schedules and information). (Four buses per day in summer to Boston. 3½ hr., $19). Also at the Chamber of Commerce is **Bay State Cruises** (617-723-7800; operates mid-June and Labor Day-Columbus Day weekends only; summer daily.) Ferries to Boston (1 per day, 3 hr., $16, same-day round-trip $29). To get around in Provincetown and Herring Cove Beach, take the **Provincetown Shuttle Bus** (487-3353). One route travels the length of Bradford St., the other from MacMillan Wharf to Herring Cove Beach. (Operates late June-early Sept. daily 8am-11pm; 10am-6pm for the beach. Fare $1.25, seniors 75¢. 1 bus per hr.) Or, rent a bike at **Arnold's,** 329 Commercial St. (487-0844. $2.75-4 per hr., $10-12 per day, deposit and ID required; credit cards accepted; open daily 8:30am-5:30pm). Provincetown's **post office:** 211 Commercial St. (487-0163; open Mon.-Fri. 8:30am-5pm, Sat. 9:30-11:30am); **ZIP code:** 02657.

Accommodations and Camping Provincetown is filled with many expensive places to lay your head. Your best affordable bet is the wonderful hostel 10 mi. away in nearby Truro (see Lower Cape). The cheapest bed in town is at **The Outermost Hostel,** 28 Winslow St. (487-4378), barely 100 yards from the Pilgrim monument. $14 gets you 1 of 30 beds in 5 cramped cottages, a kitchen, free parking, and no curfew. (Key deposit $5. Linen rental $2. Office open 8-10am and 6-10pm. Hostel open mid-May to mid-Oct. Reservations recommended for weekends.) In the quiet east end of town, the **Cape Codder,** 570 Commercial St. (487-0131, call 9am-3pm or 9-11pm), welcomes you back with archetypal Cape Cod decor, right down to the wicker furniture, and access to a private beach. (Mid-June to mid-Sept. singles $26-36, doubles $36-52; off-season about $10 less. Light continental breakfast included. Open May-Oct.) **Alice Durham's Guest House,** 3 Dyer St. (487-3330), has four rooms available upstairs in a pleasant Victorian House near the beach and only five minutes walk from the center of Provincetown. (Single $38, doubles $48-52, rates variable on holidays; 1 free nights stay per week; check-out 11am.)

Camping is expensive here. The western part of **Coastal Acres Camping Court** (487-1700), a 1-mi. walk from the center of town, west on Bradford or Commercial St. and right on West Vine St., has over 100 crowded sites; try to snag one on the waterside. (Sites $20, with electricity and water $27; campground open May-Oct. Office open 8am-4pm and 8pm-9:30pm daily.) For more accommodations in the area see Truro, Wellfleet, Eastham, and Orleans, on the Lower Cape.

Food Sit-down meals in Provincetown will cost you a pretty penny. Grab a bite at one of the Portuguese bakeries on Commercial St., or at a seafood shack on Mac-Millan Wharf. Since 1921, the **Mayflower Family Dining,** 300 Commercial St. (487-0121), gives you walls lined with ancient caricatures and a stomach lined with solid food. Choose from Portuguese ($6-8.50) and Italian ($5-8) entrees, or Puritan sea-food meals ($7-10). (Open daily 11:30am-10pm.) **George's Pizza,** 275 Commercial St. (487-3744), serves up excellent deep-dish pizza ($5-7.50). Stare at the stars while eating your pie on the outdoor deck. (Open daily 11am-1am.) If you are hankering for a blue plate special, dine at **Dodie's Diner,** 401½ Commercial St. (487-3868), where they dish up offerings like meatloaf and chicken-fried steak that would make a mother smile. (Entrees $7-10; open daily 8am-10pm.)

Sights Provincetown has long been a refuge for artists and craftsmen; you can look but not touch at any of over 20 galleries—most are free and can be found east of **MacMillan Wharf** on Commercial St. (Most are open in the afternoon and evening until 11pm, but take a 2-hr. break for dinner. Get the free *Provincetown Gallery Guide* for complete details.) The kingpin of the artsy district is the **Provincetown Art Association and Museum,** 460 Commercial St. (487-1750), established in 1914. Alongside the permanent 500-piece collection, it exhibits works by new Provincetown artists. (Open late June-Sept. daily noon-5pm and 9-10pm. $2, seniors and kids $1.)

Contrary to popular belief, the Pilgrims first landed at Provincetown, not Plymouth. They moved on two weeks later in search of better farmland. The **Pilgrim Monument** (487-1310) on High Pole Hill commemorates that 17-day Puritan layover, and as the nation's tallest granite structure (255 ft.) serves as a useful navigation aid to mariners. You can view a gorgeous panorama of the Cape by ascending the 255 ft. on stairs and ramps. The **Provincetown Museum** at its base exhibits a broad swath of Cape history, from whaling artifacts to dollhouses. (Museum and monument open July-Aug. 9am-7pm daily; mid-March to June and Sept.-Oct. daily 9am-5pm. $5, ages 4-12 $3.) At the **Provincetown Heritage Museum,** 356 Commercial St. (487-7098), you can see a half scale model of a fishing schooner, complemented by paintings and other exhibits of Provincetown's past. (Open mid-June to mid-Oct. daily 10am-6pm. $3, under 12 free.)

Activities and Entertainment Whales are still hunted by Provincetown seamen, but now it's telephoto lenses and not harpoons that shoot these briney behemoths. **Whale-watch cruises** are some of P-town's most popular attractions, and several companies offer essentially the same service. They ride out to the feeding waters in about 40 min., and then cruise around them for about two hours. The companies claim that whales are sighted on 99% of the journeys. Tickets cost about $18, but look for discounts—since competition is fierce you may be able to successfully haggle the price down. Four of your options are **Dolphin Fleet** (255-3857 or 800-826-9300), **Portuguese Princess** (487-2651 or 800-442-3188), and **Ranger V** (487-3322 or 800-992-9333), which leave from and operate ticket booths on Mac-Millan Wharf, and **Superwhale** (800-942-5334), which runs off Fisherman's pier.

Back on *terra firma,* one of Provincetown's most entertaining attractions can be found sporadically at the corner of Commercial and Standish St. There, police officer extraordinaire Donald Thomas directs traffic to the rhythm of his whistle, whirling arms, and dancing feet. Watch for his trademark spin.

Provincetown has a nightlife with no holds barred; a local bumper sticker reads "Your place, then mine." The scene is almost totally gay- and lesbian-oriented, but open to all. Most of the nightlife lines up on Commercial St. and brings along cover charges and a 1am shutdown. Uninhibited dancing shakes the ground nightly for a mixed crowd at the **Backroom,** 247 Commercial St. (487-1430; open 10pm-1am, $5 cover). Live music jams at **Club Euro** in the Euro Island Grille, 258 Commercial St. (487-2505). Saturday nights have free live reggae. (Open May-Oct. daily 11am-2am.) The **Atlantic House,** 6 Masonic Ave. (487–3821), offers dancing and two bars to a predominantly gay crowd, and is proud to be the "oldest gay bar on the oldest seacoast" (dancing cover $3-5; open daily 9pm-1am; bars open daily noon-1am). The town rocks for a week in late August during **Carnival Week.**

■■■ MARTHA'S VINEYARD

In 1606, British explorer Bartholomew Gosnold named Martha's Vineyard after his daughter and the wild grapes that grow here. In the 18th century, the Vineyard prospered as a port, with sheepherding as the main occupation. This is an island of "quaintness," from the dunes of the beaches to the inland woods, to the pastel houses alongside weathered, salty, grey cottages. The captivating and comforting country landscape has converted many vacationers, including President Clinton.

The Vineyard is even welcoming to budget travelers. The best times to visit are in fall, when the tourist season wanes and the foliage waxes with color. Seven communities comprise Martha's Vineyard. The western end of the island is called "up island," from the nautical days when sailors had to tack upwind to get there. The three largest towns, Oak Bluffs, Vineyard Haven, and Edgartown, are "down island" and have flatter terrain. Oak Bluffs and Edgartown are the only "wet" towns.

Oak Bluffs, 3 mi. west of Vineyard Haven on State Rd., is the most youth-oriented of the Vineyard villages. Tour **Trinity Park** near the harbor and see the famous "Gingerbread Houses" (minutely detailed, elaborately pastel Victorian cottages), or Oak Bluffs' **Flying Horses Carousel,** on Circuit Ave., the oldest in the nation (built in 1876), containing 20 handcrafted horses with real horsehair tails and manes. (Open daily 10am-10pm. Fare $1.) A "wet" town.

Edgartown, 7 mi. south of Oak Bluffs, displays a waterfront cluster of stately Federal-style homes built for whaling captains; skip the shops and stores here and visit the town's historic sights maintained by **Dukes County Historical Society,** School and Cooke St. (627-4441). A "wet" town.

West Tisbury, 12 mi. west of Edgartown on the West Tisbury-Edgartown Rd., hosts the only vineyard on the Vineyard, the **Chicama Vineyards,** on Stoney Hill Rd. (693-0309), off State Rd. Free tasting follows the tour. (Open Jan.-April Fri.-Sat. 1-4pm; May Mon.-Sat. noon-5pm; June-Oct. Mon.-Sat. 11am-5pm, Sun. 1-5pm. Free.) The town supplies a well-stocked general store.

Gay Head, 12 mi. off West Tisbury, offers just about the best view in all of New England. The local Wampanoag frequently saved sailors whose ships wrecked on the breath-taking **Gay Head Cliffs.** The 100,000-year-old precipice contains a collage of brilliant colors with 1 of 5 lighthouses on the island.

Menemsha and Chilmark, a little northeast of Gay Head, gives good coastline, claiming the only working fishing town on the island, where tourists can fish off the pier or purchase fresh lobster.

Vineyard Haven has more tacky t-shirt shops and fewer charming old homes than other towns. It is also the port for the Woods Hole ferry.

Practical Information Though only about 30 mi. across at its widest point, the Vineyard is blessed with 15 beaches and one state forest. A good free map and info are available at the **Martha's Vineyard Chamber of Commerce,** Beach Rd.,

Vineyard Haven (693-0085; open Mon.-Fri. 9am-5pm, Sat. 10am-2pm; Sept.-May Mon.-Fri. 9am-5pm; or write P.O. Box 1698, Vineyard Haven 02568).

Ferries serve the island from Hyannis (778-2600 or 693-0112); New Bedford (997-1688); Falmouth (548-4800); and Nantucket (778-2600), but the shortest and cheapest ride, as well as the only one to transport cars, leaves from Woods Hole on Cape Cod by the **Steamship Authority** (477-8600), which sends 10 boats per day on the 45-min. ride. (One way $4.75, car $38; reservation necessary weeks in advance; bike $3, kids $2.40.) The ferry company has three parking lots ($8 per day) and provides a shuttle service to the dock. The **On Time Ferry** (627-9427) runs between Edgartown Town Dock and Chappaquidick Island (runs daily, June-mid Oct. 7:30-midnight; mid-Oct. to May reduced hours; round trip $4 car and driver, $2.50 bicycle and rider, $3.50 motorcycle and rider, $1 individual). **Bonanza** buses (800-556-3815) stop at the Ferry Terminal in Wood's Hole and depart, via Bourne, for Boston (11 per day, 1¾ hr., $12) and New York (6 per day, 6 hr., $39).

The Vineyard is designed for bicycles. Bring or rent one at **Martha's Vineyard Scooter and Bike** (693-0782), at the Steamship Authority Dock in Vineyard Haven (open daily July-Aug. 8am-8pm, off-season Mon.-Fri. 8am-6pm, Sat.-Sun. 8am-8pm.); **Vineyard Bike and Moped** (693-4498), Circuit Ave. Exit in Oak Bluffs (open daily 9am-6pm); or **R.W. Cutler,** Main St., Edgartown (627-4052; open April 7-Oct. 15 daily 8am-6pm). All three charge $10-12 per day for a three-speed, $15-18 per day for a mountain bike or hybrid. A deposit may be required. Trail maps are available at R.W. Cutler. Most **taxis** are vans and fares are negotiable; set a price before you get in. In Oak Bluffs, call 693-0037; in Edgartown 627-4677, in Vineyard Haven 693-3705. The **Island Transport** (693-0058) runs shuttle buses that connect Vineyard Haven (Union St.), Oak Bluffs (Ocean Park), and Edgartown (Church St.) every 15 min. from 10am-6pm, and every 30 min. from 8-10am and 6pm-midnight ($1.50). Buses run late June-Aug. Martha Vineyard's **area code: 508**.

Accommodations and Camping The cheapest beds on the island are found at America's first hostel, the fantastic **Martha's Vineyard Hostel (HI-AYH),** Edgartown-West Tisbury Rd., West Tisbury (693-2665). This popular hostel offers 78 beds located right on the bike path, a great kitchen with an illuminated stained glass earth, nice common space, and lots of recreation. (Open April-mid-May 7am-9:30am and 5pm-10:30pm. 11pm curfew. $12, nonmembers $15. Linen $2. Reservations essential. IBN reservations available.) The Chamber of Commerce provides a list of inns and guest houses; all recommend reservations in July and August, especially for packed weekends. For relatively inexpensive rooms, try the **Sea Horse Guests** (693-0594), on Lambert's Cove Rd. in West Tisbury. (Singles $45, doubles $55. Open mid-May -mid-Oct.)

Martha's Vineyard Family Campground, 1 mi. from Vineyard Haven on Edgartown Rd. (693-3772), has 180 sites. Groceries are available nearby. Metered showers. (Sites $24 for 2 people. Each additional person $9. Open mid-May to mid-Oct.) **Webb's Camping Area** (693-0233), Barnes Rd., Oak Bluffs , is more spacious, with 150 shaded sites. (Sites $23-25, depending on degree of privacy, for 2 people. Each additional person $8. Open mid-May-mid-Sept.)

Food and Entertainment Cheap sandwich and lunch places speckle the Vineyard—the traveler who watches the bottom line rather than the waistline may have the best luck in Vineyard Haven and Oak Bluffs. Fried-food shacks across the island sell clams, shrimp, and potatoes generally costing at least $15. A glorious exception is **Louis'** (693-3255), State Rd., Vineyard Haven, serving Italian food in a country-style atmosphere with unlimited bread and salad bar. (Lunch $4-5. Dinner $9-15. Open Mon.-Thurs. 11am-9pm, Fri.-Sat. 11am-9:30pm, Sun. 4-9pm.) **Shindigs,** 32 Kennebec Ave. (696-7727), in Oak Bluffs, serves generous portions of tasty BBQ ($6-7) and sandwiches ($4-7). (Open daily 10am-10pm.) Prospective revelers should note that on the Vineyard, alcohol is tightly controlled. Edgartown and Oak Bluffs are the only "wet" towns on the island.

Considering the outdoor beauty, you may want to grab your food and run at one of a number of take-out joints. At the **Black Dog Bakery** (693-4786), on Beach St. Exit in Vineyard Haven, you can sample a range of creative and delicious pastries and breads (75¢-$3.50) but for the love of God, please don't buy another sweatshirt. (Open daily 5:30am-9pm.) An island institution, **Mad Martha's** scoops out home-made ice cream and frozen yogurt. The main store (693-9151) is on Circuit Ave. in Oak Bluffs (open daily 11am-midnight), but there are seven other locations throughout the island (two more are in Oak Bluffs). Several **farm stands** on the island sell inexpensive produce; the free chamber of commerce map shows their locations.

Sights Exploring the Vineyard should involve much more than hamlet-hopping. Take time to head out into the countryside, or hit the beach. Great walking trails are found at several locations. **Felix Neck Wildlife Sanctuary** (627-4850), on the Edgartown-Vineyard Haven Rd., offers a variety of terrains and habitats for exploration (open 7am-7pm; $3, under 12 $2, seniors $1). **Cedar Tree Neck** on the western shore provides trails across 250 acres of headland off Indian Hill Rd., while the **Long Point** park in West Tisbury preserves 550 acres and a shore on the Tisbury Great Pond. **Camp Pogue Wildlife Refuge and Wasque Reservation** (627-7260) on Chappaquiddick is the largest conservation area on the island.

Two of the best beaches on the island are free and public. **South Beach**, at the end of Katama Rd. 3 mi. south of Edgartown, boasts sizeable surf and an occasionally nasty undertow. Parts of *Jaws* were filmed at the gentler **State Beach,** Beach Rd. between Edgartown and Oak Bluffs. The surf is smaller and the water warmer. For the best sunsets on the island make for fantastic **Gay Head** or the **Manemsha Town Beach,** where you can enjoy sundown with seafood from nearby stands.

■■■ NANTUCKET

The island of Nantucket is a secluded outpost of privilege and establishment. It is also, however, a land of entrancing beauty and charm. Furthermore, contrary to reputation, it is very possible to enjoy a stay on Nantucket without holding up a convenience store to do so. Bike the dirt roads through the heath, catch a bluefish on the beach, go sea-kayaking, explore Nantucket Town's cobblestone streets and weathered fishing shacks, or sit on the docks that were once the scene of the busiest whaling port in the world. If possible, visit during the last weeks of the tourist season, when prices drop. Only a few places stay open during the cold, rainy winter months, when awesome storms churn the slate-blue seas.

Practical Information The **visitor services center,** 25 Federal St. (228-0925), has a full complement of brochures and can help you find a place to stay (open Mon.-Sat. 9am-10pm, Sun. 9am-6pm). **Hyline** (778-2600) provides ferry service to Nantucket from Hyannis (6 per day, $11) and from Martha's Vineyard (3 per day, $11). **Steamship Authority** (540-2022) runs ferries from Hyannis only (6 per day, $10). Both charge $5 for bikes and take about 2 hours. The Steamship Authority docks are on Steamboat Wharf, and the Hy-line docks are on Straight Wharf.

It's said that hitch-hiking is the best way to get around Nantucket. For those who prefer to pedal, rent bikes at **Young's Bicycle Shop** (228-1151), Steamboat Wharf. Three-speeds are $10 per day, mountain bikes $18 (it's worth the extra dough to get the mountain bike—you'll want to travel dirt roads through the heath). Young's distributes free, decent maps of the island, but for an extended stay buy the *Complete Map of Nantucket* ($3). (Open daily 8am-8pm.) Alternatively, **Barrett's Bus Lines,** 20 Federal St. (228-0174), opposite the visitors center, runs buses on sunny days only to Jetty's Beach (every ½ hr. 10am-5pm, $1), Surfside Beach (hourly, 10am-5pm, roundtrip and Sconset (every hr. 10:10am-4:10pm, $5 round-trip kids $2.50). Nantucket's **ZIP code:** 02554; **area code:** 508.

Accommodations and Food **Nantucket Hostel (HI-AYH),** 31 Western Ave. (228-0433), is surfside at Surfside Beach 3½ mi. from town at the end of the Surfside Bike Path. (Open late April-mid Oct. daily 7:30am-9:30am and 5pm-11pm. 11pm curfew, lockout 9:30am-5pm. 49 beds; full kitchen. $12, nonmembers $15; linens $2; reservations essential.) The **Nesbitt Inn,** 21 Broad St. (228-2446), is right in the heart of Nantucket Town. This Victorian guest house offers 13 rooms, each with a sink and shared baths as well as a common room with a fireplace and friendly, attentive owners. (Office open daily 7am-10pm. Inn open year round. Check-in noon, check-out 11am. Singles $45, doubles $65-75, off season $8-10 less. Extra person in room $15-20. Reservations essential; deposit required.)

Nantucket restaurants do not operate with the budget traveler in mind. The standard entree is about $12-14, but the frugal gourmet can still dine well. Steal away to the **Brotherhood of Thieves,** 23 Broad St., which is a subterranean haven for those who don't like light to interfere with their meals. (Entrees $7-8; open Mon. 11:30am-11pm, Tues.-Thurs. 11:30am-midnight, Fri.-Sat. 11:30am-12:30am, Sun. noon-midnight.) **Black Eyed Susan's,** Indian St., offers a rotating breakfast and dinner menu with such interesting dishes as sourdough french toast with orange Jack Daniel's butter (full order $6.50, short $5). (Breakfast daily 6am-2pm, dinner Fri.-Wed. 6-10pm.) To avoid restaurant prices altogether, buy groceries at the **A&P,** on Commercial St. at Washington St. (Open Mon.-Sat. 7am-midnight, Sun. 8am-8pm.)

Sights and Activities Nantucket is an island of incredible beauty; enjoy it now before developers consign it to the subdivided fate of Cape Cod. For a great **bike trip,** head east from Nantucket Town on Milestone Rd. and turn left onto a path that looks promising. Head across beautiful moors of heather, huckleberries, bayberries, and wild roses. Those who want adventure in the water should go to **Sea Nantucket** (228-7499), at the end of Washington St. at the waterfront, and rent a **sea kayak** ($25 for 4½ hr.; open daily 9am-7pm). It is easy to learn how to maneuver the kayaks, and they are not too physically demanding; take one out to a nearby salt marsh, or head across the harbor to one of the isolated beaches on the Coatue peninsula and enjoy a picnic undisturbed by other beachgoers. If you prefer to stand on the strand between land and sea, rent **surf fishing** equipment from **Barry Thurston's** (228-9595), at Harbor Square near the A&P, for $15 for 24 hours. (Open Mon.-Sat. 8am-9pm, Sun. 9am-1am.) The **Maria Mitchell Association,** 2 Vestal St. (228-5982), named after the nation's first female astronomer, runs nature classes and trips for children and operates an observatory on Nantucket. From mid-July to August, the observatory has open nights when the public can come and gaze at the stars. ($2, children $1, family $5; call 228-5982 for observatory's open hrs.)

The fascinating **Nantucket Whaling Museum** (228-1736), Broad St. in Nantucket Town, recreates the old whaling community with exhibits on whales and whaling methods. The museum contains, among other things, a reconstructed candle shop and a complete whale skeleton. The **Museum of Nantucket History** (228-3889), in the Thomas Macy Warehouse, will help you appreciate the island's boom years as a whaling port and also describes other island industries such as candlemaking and sheep raising. Catch a lecture by a genuine Nantucket old-timer. (Check for times; $4, children $2. Both museums open late April-early June and mid-Oct. to early Dec. Sat.-Sun. 11am-3pm; early daily June to mid-Oct. 10am-5pm.) The best deal is a visitor's pass ($8, children $4) that gets you into both museums and 8 other sights run by the historical association as well. Pick up a free copy of *Yesterday's Island* for listings of nature walks, concerts, lectures, art exhibitions, and more.

THE BERKSHIRES

Famous for cultural events in the summer, rich foliage in the fall, and skiing in the winter, the Berkshire Mountains have long been a vacation destination for Boston and New York urbanites seeking a relaxing country escape. Filling approximately the western third of Massachusetts, the Berkshire Region is bordered to the north by Rte. 2 (the Mowhawk Trail) and Vermont, to the west by Rte. 7 and New York, to the south by the Mass. Pike and Connecticut, and to the east by I-91. A host of affordable B&Bs, restaurants, and campgrounds can be found throughout the Berkshires, making them both financially and logistically accessible for the budget traveler.

■■■ BERKSHIRE COUNTY

Practical Information With the exception of Rte. 2 and the Massachusetts Turnpike (Rte. 90), just about everything in Berkshire County runs north-south: the mountain range giving the county its name (a southern extension of the Green Mountains of Vermont); the 80 mi. of the **Appalachian Trail** that wind through Massachusetts; the Hoosac and the Housatonic rivers; and **U.S. 7**, the region's main artery. To see sights located far from the town centers, you'll have to drive. The roads are slow and often pocked with potholes, but certainly scenic. **Pete's Rent-a-Car** (445-5795), on the corner of Fenn and East St., offers some of the lowest local prices ($25 per day; 150 free mi., 24¢ each additional mi.; must be at least 23). **Berkshire Regional Transit Association** (499-2782), known as "the B," spans the Berkshires from Great Barrington to Williamstown. Buses run every hour at some bus stops (Mon.-Sat. 6am-6pm); fares (60¢ a zone up to $3.60) depend on the route you take. System schedules are available on the bus and at some bus stops. The **Berkshire Visitors Bureau,** 2 Berkshire Common, Place Level, Pittsfield (443-9186 or 800-237-5747) is open Mon.-Fri. 8:30-4:40pm. An **information booth** on the east side of **Pittsfield's** rotary circle can give more information on restaurants and accommodations in Pittsfield and the surrounding cities along U.S. 7 (open mid-June-Oct Mon.-Thurs. 9am-5pm, Fri-Sat. 9am-8pm, Sun. 10am-2pm, weekends only Labor Day- Columbus Day). Berkshire county's dozen state parks and forests cover 100,000 acres and offer numerous campsites and cabins. For info about the parks, stop by the **Region 5 Headquarters,** 740 South St. (442-8928), or write to P.O. Box 1433, Pittsfield 01202. (Open Mon.-Fri. 8am-5pm, Sat.-Sun. 8am-4:30pm.) The Berkshires' **area code** is 413.

The Mohawk Trail Perhaps the most famous highway in the state, the Mohawk Trail (Rte. 2) provides a meandering and scenic route showcasing the beauty of the Berkshires. During fall foliage weekends, the awe-inspiring reds and golds of the surrounding mountains draw crowds of leaf-peepers. For information on the Trail area, write or call the Mowhawk Trail Association, P.O. Box 722 Charlemont, MA 01339 (644-6256). **Millers Falls**, MA is the trail's eastern terminus. Next along the way comes **Greenfield,** at the intersection with I-91. **Peter Pan Trailways** (800-343-9999) has a bus stop at Barrett and Baker, 310 Main St. (413-774-7926), making Greenfield a minor transportation hub in the area. Farther West, the Mowhawk Trail is dotted with affordable campgrounds and lodgings. In **Shelburne Falls,** a hilltown of dairy farms and maple sugar houses, the only hostel in the region, the **Open Hearth Home Hostel,** RR #1, Box 16 (625-9638) opens its doors to travelers. Reservations should be made 48 hrs. in advance ($12).

Five miles west of **Charlemont,** off Rte. 2, lies the **Mohawk Trail State Forest** (339-5504), which offers campsites along a river ($6) and rents cabins (no electricity; large $20, small $16). (Bathrooms and showers available. Call for reservations.) **Whitewater Rafting** on the **Deerfield River** can be done through Crabapple Whitewater, located in Claremont (800-553-7238; trip times vary; multiple skill levels; call for prices and times.) Continuing west along the trail, one enters **North Adams,** home to the **Western Gateway** (663-6312), on Furnace St. Bypass of Rte. 8, is a railroad museum and one of Massachusetts' five **Heritage State Parks.** The Parks areserve as models of urban environmental design and historic preservation. The North Adams site has an extensive visitors center to guide you. On summer Thursdays at 7pm, free live music is played in the park. (Open daily 10am-4:30pm; Labor

Day-Memorial Day Thurs.-Mon. 10am-4:30pm; free, donations encouraged). The **Freight Yard Pub** (663-6312) within the Western Gateway park is a good bargain, serving salads ($2-6) and "Berkshire's best" french dip sandwiches ($7.95). (Open Sun.-Wed. 11:30am-1am, Thurs.-Sat. 11:30am-2am. Café dining available outside.) On Rte. 8 ½-mi. north is the **Natural Bridge** (663-6392 or 663-6312), a white marble bridge formed during the last Ice Age and the only natural, water-eroded bridge on the continent. There is a 1-mi. self-guided walking tour. (Open Memorial Day-Columbus Day, Mon.-Fri. 8:30am-4pm, Sat.-Sun. 10am-6pm; $5 per vehicle.)

Mt. Greylock, the highest peak in Massachusetts (3491 ft.), is south of the Mohawk Trail, accessible by Rte. 2 to the north and U.S. 7 to the west. By car, take Notch Rd. from Rte. 2 between North Adams and Williamstown, or take Rockwell Rd. from Lanesboro on U.S. 7. Hiking trails begin from nearly all the towns around the mountain; get free maps at the **Mount Greylock Visitors Information Center,** Rockwell Rd. (499-4262; open daily 9am-5pm). Once at the top, climb the **War Memorial** for a breathtaking view. Sleep high in nearby **Bascom Lodge** (743-1591), built from the rock excavated for the monument (bunks for members of the Appalachian Mountain Club Sun.-Fri. $23, Sat. $28, nonmembers $30/35, member children under 12 $12/17, nonmember kids $19/24; no member discount in Aug.). The lodge offers breakfast ($5) and dinner ($10). Snackbar open daily 10am-5pm.

The Mohawk Trail ends in **Williamstown** at its junction with U.S. 7; here, an **information booth** (458-4922) provides an abundance of free local maps and seasonal brochures, and can help you find a place to stay in one of Williamstown's many reasonably-priced **B&Bs** (open 24 hrs., staffed by volunteers Fri.-Sun. mid-May-Oct. 10am-6pm). At **Williams College,** the second oldest in Massachusetts (est. 1793), lecturers compete with the beautiful scenery of surrounding mountains for their students' attention. Campus maps are available from the **Admissions Office,** 988 Main St. (597-2211; open Mon.-Fri. 8:30am-4:30pm; tours at 10am, 11:15am, 1:15pm, 3:30pm, and in Aug. at 9am and 2:30pm). First among the college's many cultural resources, **Chapin Library** (597-2462) in Stetson Hall displays a number of rare U.S. manuscripts, including early copies of the Declaration of Independence, Articles of Confederation, Constitution, and Bill of Rights (open Mon.-Fri. 10am-noon and 1-4:30pm; free). The small but impressive **Williams College Museum of Art** (597-2429), off Main St. (Rte. 2) between Spring and Water St., merits a visit; rotating exhibits have included Soviet graphic art, postmodern architecture, and Impressionist works (open Mon.-Sat. 10am-5pm, Sun. 1-5pm; free). Also free in Williamstown, the **Sterling and Francine Clark Art Institute,** 225 South St. (458-9545), houses many impressionist paintings and collections of silver and sculpture. (Open Tues.-Sun. 10am-5pm.) A good place to eat near campus is **Pappa Charlie's Deli,** 28 Spring St. (458-5969), a popular, well-lit deli offering sandwiches ranging from the "Dick Cavett" to the "Dr. Johnny Fever." (Under $4; open Mon.-Sat. 8am-11pm, Sun. 9am-11pm.)

Williamstown's surrounding wooded hills beckon from the moment you arrive. The **Hopkins Memorial Forest** (597-2346) has over 2250 acres open free to the public for hiking and cross-country skiing. Take U.S. 7 north, turn left on Bulkley St., go to the end and turn right onto Northwest Hill Rd. **Spoke Bicycles and Repairs,** 618 Main St. (458-3456), rents 10-speed bikes ($15 per day) and can give you advice on good area rides. (Open Mon.-Fri. 10-6pm, Sat. 10am-5pm.

Route 7 South of Williamstown, the first major town along Rte. 7 is Pittsfield, the county seat of Bershire County and the town credited with the creation of the county fair. Recreational possibilities abound at the **Pittsfield State Forest,** 4 mi. northwest of town, off Rte. 20 (442-8992). The Forest offers modern campsites and schedules outdoor activities ($8-10). The Berkshire's rich literary history can be sampled at Herman Melville's home **Arrowhead,** 780 Holmes Rd. (442-1793), 3 ½ mi. south of Pittsfield. The headquarters of the Berkshire County Historical Society has displays on 19th century country life and the role of women on the farm. (Open Memorial Day - Labor Day daily 10am-5pm, Labor Day - Oct. Mon., Thurs.-Sat. 10am-

4:30pm Sun. 11am-3:30pm, May Sat.-Sun. 10am-5pm. Tours of the house are conducted every ½-hour. Admission $4.50, seniors $4, kids 6-16 $3.) The **Berkshire Museum,** 39 South St. in Pittsfield (443-7171), displays Hudson River School paintings, natural history exhibits, and an aquarium. (Open July-Aug. Mon.-Sat. 10am-5pm, Sun. 1-5pm; Sept.-June Tues.-Sat. 10am-5pm, Sun. 1-5pm; $3, seniors/students $2, children $1. Free Wed. and Sat. 10am-noon.) **The Bershire Museum's Little Corner** screens some of the finest U.S. and foreign films (mid June-Sept. Sun.-Fri. 8:15pm, Sat. 7pm and 9pm, Mon. matinee at 2pm.)

Tanglewood, the famed summer home of the **Boston Symphony Orchestra,** is one of the Berkshires' greatest treasures. South on Rte 7, a short distance west of Lenox Center on Rte. 183 (West St.), Tanglewood concerts show off a variety of music, from Ray Charles to Wynton Marsalis to James Taylor, but its bread-and-butter is world-class classical music. Buy a lawn ticket, bring a picnic dinner, and listen to your favorites under the stars or in the Sunday afternoon sunshine. Orchestral concerts held July-Aug. Fri. 8:30pm, with 6:30 prelude, Sat. 8:30pm, Sun. 2:30pm. (Tickets $13.50-67, on the lawn $11.50-12.50. Open rehearsals are held Sat. 10:30am. Call for schedules of special events and prices. Summer info 413-637-1940, recorded concert line 413-637-1666. Schedules available through the mail from the BSO, Symphony Hall, Boston, 02115.) There are also chamber concerts on Thursday evenings and the Boston Pops give two summer concerts as well. The summer concludes with a jazz festival over Labor Day weekend.

At the junction of Rte. 7 and 7A in Lenox is the **Edith Wharton Restoration at the Mount,** home of the great turn of the century Pulitzer Prize winner. Tours on the hour. ($6, seniors $5.50, 13-18 $4.50; open May 28-Sept. Tues.-Sun. 10am-3pm, Sept.-Oct. Fri.-Sun. 10am-3pm.)

Following Rte. 7 south will take you past the **Wagon Wheel Motel,** at the junction with Rte. 20 (445-4532). Rooms off-season $35 and on summer weekdays $44. Summer weekend rates are high throughout the Berkshires (starting at $100.) A cheaper option is to continue north on US 20, 3 mi. until you reach **October Mountain State Forest,** sites $6. Toilets and showers available (243-1778).

Slightly father toward the equator on Rte 7, **Stockbridge** is home to the **Norman Rockwell Museum** (298-4100), located on Rte. 183 (½ mi. south of the junction between Rte. 7 and 102.) Containing more that 1000 items, including many of Rockwell's *Saturday Evening Post* covers, the museum is a must-see for visitors to the area (Open May-Oct. daily 10am-5pm; $8, children $2; Nov.-April Mon.-Fri. 11am-4pm; Sat.-Sun. 10am-5pm, $7.50, children $2.)

Routes 90 and 91 The last two sides of the Berkshire square are major interstate roads and therefore, while saving time, the driver loses much natural scenery. An alternate Rte. for the Mass. Pike (Rte. 90) is Rte. 20, which weaves above and below it, crossing the Pike numerous times. In the north-south direction, Rte. 91 can be substitutes with Rtes. 47 and 63, which snake along the Connecticut River.

On Rte. 91, about 15 min. north of Springfield, the towns of **Northampton** and **Amherst** offer educational meccas with many attractions. Northampton is a beautiful town, former home of President Calvin Coolidge, current home to **Smith College,** and a place that boasts a surprising number of restaurants and shops for a small New England town. For more information on the area, visit or call the **Greater Northampton Chamber of Commerce,** 62 State St. (584-1900). The **Peter Pan Trailways** terminal is located at 1 Roundhouse Plaza (536-1030).

In Northampton, the **Smith College Museum of Art,** on Elm St. at Bedford Terrace, has a nice collection of 19th and 20th century European and American paintings. Tours and gallery talks are available. Free to the public. (open Tues.-Sat. noon-5pm, Sun. 2-5pm.) **Look Memorial Park** (584-5457), on the Berkshire Trail (Rte. 9) not far from downtown Northampton, is bordered by the Mill River. Its 200 acres make a pleasant picnic spot. (Open daily dawn-dusk; facilities open Memorial Day-Labor Day daily 11am-6pm; $2/vehical Sat.-Sun., $1 Mon.-Fri.) For excellent wood-

NEW ENGLAND

fired brick over pizza, head to **Pizzeria Paradiso,** 12 Crafts Ave. (586-1468), which offers gourmet vegetable, meat, and seafood creations ($6-7).

Farther north on Rte 91, travelers will run into Deerfield, home of **Historical Deerfield** (774-5581), 5 mi. south of Greenfield on U.S. 5. This idyllic, 18th century village contains 14 fully restored buildings. You can wander around outside them for free, or you can pay admission to go inside. Each building conducts its own ½ hour guided tour; admission is good for two consecutive days. (Open daily 9:30am-4:30pm. $10, ages 6-17 $5, under 6 free.))

Rhode Island

Rhode Island, the smallest state in the Union, is indeed smaller than some ranches in Texas, some icebergs in Antarctica, some parks in Wyoming, and some dogs in Newfoundland. Most Rhode Islanders are, however, proud of their compact, non-conformist heritage. From founder Roger Williams, a religious outcast during colonial days, to Buddy Cianci, convicted felon and two-time mayor of Providence, spirited Rhode Island has always lured a different crowd.

Outside the two main cities, coastal Rhode Island and Providence Plantations (the official state name, longest in the Union) is eminently explorable. Numerous small and provincial spots dot the shores down to Connecticut, while the inland roads are quiet, unpaved thoroughfares lined with family fruit stands, marshes, and ponds. Working ports derive their lifeblood from the fish of Narragansett Bay and Block Island Sound, and Block Island itself is a must-see.

PRACTICAL INFORMATION

Capital: Providence.
Rhode Island Division of Tourism, 7 Jackson Walkway, Providence 02903 (800-556-2484 or 277-2601). Open Mon.-Fri. 8:30am-4:30pm. **Department of Environmental Management** (State Parks), 9 Hayes St., Providence 02908 (277-2771). Open Mon.-Fri. 8:30am-4pm.
Time Zone: Eastern. **Postal Abbreviation:** RI
Sales Tax: 7%.

■■■ PROVIDENCE

Like Rome, Providence sits aloft seven hills. Unlike Rome, its residents are students (Brown University and Rhode Island School of Design), starving artists (Brown and RISD students), and business suits (not Brown and RISD students). This state capital has cobbled sidewalks and colonial buildings, but also a college-town identity, with more than its share of bookstores and cafés. Cheap college students support cheap restaurants and interesting shops, so head for the area around the colleges for the best of Providence. But the city also possesses a working-class grit, ensuring that it isn't merely an enclave of academia.

Practical Information The state capitol and the downtown business district cluster just east of the intersection of I-95 and I-195. **Brown University** and the **Rhode Island School of Design (RISD)** (RIZZ-dee) pose on top of a steep hill, a 10-min. walk east of downtown.

Emergency is 911. For a self-guided walking tour map and tourist literature, head to the **Greater Providence Convention and Visitors Bureau,** 30 Exchange Terrace (274-1636 or 800-233-1636), on the first floor, next to City Hall (open Mon.-Fri. 8:30am-5pm). The **Providence Preservation Society,** 21 Meeting St. (831-7440), at the foot of College Hill, gives detailed info on historic Providence. A self-guided tour map cost $1, audio-cassette tour $5 (open Mon.-Fri. 9am-5pm).

Amtrak operates from a gleaming white structure behind the state capitol at 100 Gaspee St. (800-872-7245; open daily 5:30am-8:30pm and 9pm-11pm), a 10-min. walk to Brown or downtown. (To: Boston $14; New York $46). **Greyhound** and **Bonanza,** 1 Bonanza Way (751-8800), off exit 25 of I-95, have very frequent service to Boston (1 hr., $7.75) and New York (4 hr., $29). (Open 5am-11:15pm.) Bonanza accepts Ameripass. All buses make a stop at the Kennedy Plaza downtown, where Bonanza also has a ticket office (open daily 7am-6pm). **Rhode Island Public Transit Authority (RIPTA),** 265 Melrose St. (781-9400, from Newport 847-0209), has an **information booth** on Kennedy Plaza across from the visitors center which provides in-person route and schedule assistance, as well as free maps of the bus system, which has service to points south, including Newport ($2.50). The fare ranges from 25¢ to $2.50; within Providence, fares are generally 85¢. Seniors ride free on weekends all day, weekdays 4:30am-7am, 9am-3pm and 6pm-midnight. Buses operate daily 4:30am-midnight. (Open Mon.-Sat. 8:30am-6pm. Info booth open Mon.-Fri. 7am-6pm.) For help, contact **Traveler's Aid** (351-6500 or 800-367-2700; 24 hrs.). Providence's **post office,** 2 Exchange Terrace (421-4361; open Mon.-Fri. 7am-5:30pm, Sat. 8am-2pm); **ZIP code:** 02903; **area code:** 401.

Accommodations and Camping The lack of a youth hostel combined with the high rates of motels downtown make Providence an expensive overnight stay, unless you have a friend at one of the local universities. Rooms are booked far in advance for the graduation season in May and early June; don't expect vacancy signs to be lit during that time. The friendly **International House of Rhode Island,** 8 Stimson Ave. (421-7181), near the Brown campus, has two comfortable rooms that usually book up. (Office open Mon.-Fri. 9:30am-5pm; singles $45, students $30; doubles $50/$35. If staying at least 5 nights, discount $5 off every price. Reservations required.) The cheapest room around is at the **New Yorker Motor Lodge,** 400 Newport Ave., East Providence (434-8000; single $40, double $44). A 30-min. drive from downtown reaches the dozen nearest campgrounds. **Colwell's Campground** (397-4614) is one of the closest; from Providence, take I-95 south to exit 10, then head west 8.5 mi. on Rte. 117 to Coventry. The campground has showers and hookups, and is on the shore of the Flat River Reservoir. (Tent sites $10-15 depending on waterfront proximity.) If you really want to expose yourself to nature, try **Dyer Woods Nudist Campground,** 114 Johnson Rd. (397-3007), 3 mi. south of U.S. 6. You can relax and get in touch with yourself, or get the skinny on the hot tub, sauna, volleyball, and badminton facilities (14 sites, $30; open May-Sept.).

Food Good food in Providence emanates from three areas: Atwells Avenue in the Italian district, (on Federal Hill just west of downtown); the student hangouts on Thayer Street, (on College Hill to the east); and the city's beautiful old diners near downtown. **Louis' Family Restaurant,** 286 Brook St. (861-5225), is a friendly venue that has made the entire community its family. Students swear by its prices, donating the artwork on the walls in return. Try the famous #1 special —two eggs, homefries, toast, coffee— for $2.30. (Open daily 5:30am-3pm.) **Thayer Street** is densely populated with bookstores, offbeat boutiques, and ethnic restaurants. A smiling sandwich presides over 60 different bread and ingredient combinations at **Geoff's,** 178 Angel St. (751-9214). Combos are $2-6 (open Mon.-Fri. 8am-10pm, Sat.-Sun. 10am-10pm). A 20 min. drive north on Rte. 95 brings you to Pawtucket and the **Modern Diner,** 364 East Ave. (726-8390). This timeless relic of simpler days gives you a dining experience last seen in Des Moines, Iowa in 1958. Break out that "I Like Ike" button and sit down to some down home American food. (Open Mon.-Wed. 6am-3pm, Thurs.-Fri. 6am-8pm, Sat. 7am-4pm, Sun. 7am-2pm; dinners $5-7.50.)

Sights and Entertainment Providence's most notable historic sights cluster on **College Hill,** a 350-year-old neighborhood. **Brown University,** established in

1764, claims several 18th-century buildings, and provides the best information about the area. The Office of Admissions, housed in the historic Carliss-Brackett House, 45 Prospect St. (863-2378), gives a free walking tours of the campus daily at 10 and 11am, and 1, 3, and 4pm. (Open Mon.-Fri. 8am-4pm.) In addition to founding Rhode Island, Roger Williams founded the *first* **First Baptist Church of America** (454-3418), built in 1775 and standing at 75 N. Main St. (open Mon.-Fri. 9am-4pm; free). Looking down from the hill, you'll see the **Rhode Island State Capitol** (277-2357), crowned with one of the only three free-standing marble domes in the world. (Free guided tours Mon., Tues., Thurs. at 10 and 11am; free self-guide booklets available in room 218. Building open Mon.-Fri. 8:30am-4:30pm.)

The nearby **RISD Museum of Art,** 224 Benefit St. (454-6500), gathers a fine collection of Greek, Roman, Asian, and Impressionist art, and a gigantic, 10th-century Japanese Buddha. (Open Wed.-Sat. noon-5pm; Sept.-June Tues.-Wed. and Fri.-Sat. 10:30am-5pm, Thurs. noon-8pm, Sun. 2-5pm. $2, seniors and ages 5-18 50¢. Free on Sat.) The New England textile industry was born in 1793 when Samuel Slater used plans smuggled out of Britain to build the first water-powered factory in America. The **Slater Mill Historic Site** (725-8638), on Roosevelt Ave. in Pawtucket, preserves this fiber heritage with operating machinery. ($5, kids 6-14 $3. Open June-Aug. Tues.-Sat. 10am-5pm, Sun. 1-5pm; March-May and Sept.-Dec. Sat. and Sun. 1pm-5pm. Must be seen on a tour that leaves every 2 hours.)

Brownies, townies, and RISDs rock the night away at several hot spots throughout town. **The Living Room,** 23 Rathbone St. (521-5200), welcomes lots of alternative bands and also has dancing. **Club Babyhead,** 73 Richmond St. (421-1698), is "loud, dark, and dirty." What more could you ask for in an alternative club?

Other attractions particular to the Providence proximity include the nationally acclaimed **Trinity Repertory Company,** 201 Washington St., (351-4242), and the **Providence Performing Arts Center,** 220 Weybosset St. (421-2787), which hosts a variety of concerts and Broadway musicals. The **Cable Car Cinema,** 204 S. Main St., Providence (272-3970), with an attached café, shows art and foreign films in an unusual setting—patrons recline on couches instead of regular seats ($6). Read the *New Paper,* distributed free Thursday, check the "Weekend" section of the *Friday Providence Journal,* or consult the *Providence Pheonix* for film, theater, and nightlife listings. Finally, if you're in the mood for a little hardball, check out the **Pawtucket Red Sox** (AAA farm team for their Boston big brothers), who play in Pawtucket's McCoy Stadium, 1 Columbus Ave. (724-7300; season April-Sept. box seats $5.50, under 12 and seniors $4.50; general admission $4/$3). Stock cars race at the **Seekonk Speedway** (336-8488), a few miles east on Rte. 6 in Massachusetts (1756 Fall River Ave.; $15, 12 and under $5).

■■■ NEWPORT

Money has always found its way into Newport. The city was once supported by triangle trade booty and later became the summer homes of society elite, who constructed some of the most opulent mansions in the nation. Today, the city attracts beautiful people (with deep pockets) from all over the world. But keep in mind that there is a 25-year waiting period to get a slip at the marina, so plan ahead.

Practical Information Emergency: 911. **Newport County Convention and Visitors Bureau,** 23 America's Cup Ave. (849-8048 or 800-326-6030), in the Newport Gateway Center, has free maps. (Open Mon.-Fri. 9am-6pm, Sat.-Sun. 9am-7pm; early Sept.-June daily 9am-5pm.) Pick up *Best-Read Guide Newport* and *Newport This Week* for current listings. Also out of the center runs **Bonanza Buses** (846-1820). The buses of **Rhode Island Public Transit Authority (RIPTA),** 1547 W. Main Rd. (847-0209 or 800-221-3797), leave from the Newport Gateway Center daily 7am-7pm. Fare is 85¢. Ride free on most routes Mon.-Fri. 9am-3pm and 6-7pm, all day Sat.-Sun. Frequent service to Providence (1 hr., $2.50) and points between on Rte. 114. (Office open daily 6am-7pm.) Rent bikes at **Ten Speed Spokes,** 18 Elm St.

(847-5609). Surprisingly, no 10-speeds. (Mountain bikes $5 per hr., $25 per day. Must have credit card and photo ID. Open daily 9:30am-6pm.) Newport's **post office:** 320 Thames St. (847-2329), opposite Perry Mill Market; open Mon.-Fri. 8:30am-5pm, Sat. 9am-1pm); **ZIP code:** 02840; **area code:** 401.

Accommodations, Camping, and Food Guest houses are the bulk of Newport's accommodations, and most offer bed and continental breakfast with colonial intimacy. Those willing to share a bathroom or forego a sea view might find a double for $60. Singles are practically nonexistent. Be warned that many hotels and guest houses are booked solid two months in advance for summer weekends. **Bed and Breakfasts of Rhode Island, Inc.,** 50 Thames St. (849-1298), can make a reservation for you for about $65 per night.

Camping is actually available at **Fort Getty Recreation Area** (423-7264), on Conanicut Island, walking distance from the Fox Hill Salt Marsh, a good spot for birdwatching. (125 sites. Showers and beach access; sites $17, hookup $22.)

Most of Newport's restaurants line up on **Thames St.** At 448 Thames St. you can tie up at **Dry Dock Seafood** (847-3974), a local seafood joint that fries 'em and serves 'em with a minimum of fuss. (Entrees $5-11. Open Sun.-Thurs. 11am-10pm, Fri.-Sat. 11am-11pm.) Shack up with some choice mollusks at **Flo's Clam Shack,** oceanside, across from Newport Beach (847-8141), where you can enjoy the clam product of your choice beside a severely incapacitated lobster boat. (Entrees $6-10. Open Thurs.-Sun. 11am-9pm.) A booth and some solid food await you at the **Franklin Spa,** 229 Franklin St. You can get a cheap, hearty breakfast or lunch for $1.50-7. (Open Mon.-Sat. 6:30am-3pm, Sun. 6:30am-2pm.)

Sights Newport takes "keeping up with the Joneses" to new heights. The Jones in question is George Noble Jones, who built the first "summer cottage" here in 1839 and thereby kicked off an extravagant string of palatial summer estates. The best way to see Newport's mansions is on a self-guided walking tour or one by the **Preservation Society of Newport** (847-1000). The colonial buildings downtown are more unassuming than the mansions, but make interesting studies nonetheless. The 1765 **Wanton-Lyman Hazard House,** 17 Broadway (846-0813), the oldest standing house in Newport, has been restored in different period styles (open mid June to July Fri.-Sat. 10am-4pm; $4). The **White Horse Tavern,** on Marlborough and Farewell St. (849-3600), the oldest drinking establishment in the country, dates from 1673, but the father of William Mayes, a notorious Red Sea pirate, first opened it as a tavern in 1687 (beer $2-4). The **Touro Synagogue,** 85 Touro St. (847-4794), a beautifully restored Georgian building and the oldest synagogue in the U.S., dates back to 1763. It was to the Newport congregation that George Washington wrote his famous letter promising that the U.S. would give "to bigotry no sanction, to persecution no assistance." (Can visit only in free tour; every ½-hr. in summer. Open mid June to Aug. Sun.-Thurs. 10am-5pm, Fri. 10am-3pm; Sept.-late Nov. Mon., Wed., and Fri 11am-1pm, Sun. 1pm-3pm; late Nov. to mid-June, Sun. 1-3pm.)

Tennis anyone? If you're a fan of the game, you're in luck. It is somehow appropriate that the **Tennis Hall of Fame**, 194 Bellevue Ave. (849-3990), is located in Newport. The Hall hosts grass court tournaments and runs a museum about the game. (Open daily 10am-5pm year-round. $6, under 16 $3, family $12.)

After a few hours of touring Newport, you might think of escaping to the shore. Unfortunately, the beaches crowd as frequently as the streets. The most popular is **First Beach** (847-6875), or Easton's Beach, on Memorial Blvd., with its wonderful old beach houses and carousel. (Open Memorial Day-Labor Day daily 8am-5pm. Parking $7, weekends $10.) Those who prefer hiking over dunes to building sandcastles should try **Fort Adams State Park** (847-2400), south of town on Ocean Dr., 2½ mi. from Gateway Center, with showers, picnic areas, and two fishing piers (entrance booth open daily 9am-4pm, park open sunrise to sunset; parking $4). Other good beaches line Little Compton, Narragansett, and the shore between

Watch Hill and Point Judith. For more details, consult the free *Ocean State Beach Guide*, available at the visitors center (see Practical Information above).

Entertainment   In July and August, lovers of classical, folk, and jazz each have a festival to call their own. The **Newport Jazz Festival** is the oldest and best-known jazz festival in the world; Duke Ellington, Count Basie, and many of their "peers" made their break here. Bring your beach chairs and coolers to Fort Adams State Park in mid-August (after May, 847-3700; $28.50, children $12.50). The **Newport Music Festival** (846-1133) in mid-July attracts pianists, violinists, and other classical musicians from around the world, showcasing them in the ballrooms and on the lawns of the mansions for two weeks of concerts. Tickets are available through Ticketron (800-382-8080; $25 daytime, $30 evening). In August, folksingers like Joan Baez and the Indigo Girls entertain at the legendary **Newport Folk Festival** (June-Aug. 847-3709), which runs two days, noon to dusk, rain or shine (tickets $28 per day).

Newport's nightlife is easy to find but relatively subdued. Down by the water at **Pelham East** (849-9460), at the corner of Thames and Pelham, they tend to play straight rock'n' roll. (Live music nightly. Open daily noon-1am. Weekend cover $5.) Those longing for disco should visit **Club Maximillian,** 108 William St. (849-4747), a popular video-enhanced dance club across from the Tennis Hall of Fame (open Wed.-Sat. year round. Hours and cover vary). **Bad Bob's** (848-9840) rocks the boat at Waite's Wharf with a DJ and live bands playing rock, soul, and reggae on board a boat (open June to mid.-Sept. Thurs.-Mon. 8pm-1am, $5 cover, Mondays free.)

■ NEAR NEWPORT: BLOCK ISLAND

A popular daytrip 10 mi. southeast of Newport in the Atlantic, sand-blown **Block Island** is endowed with weathered shingles, gorgeous untamed nature, and serenity. One quarter of the island is protected open space; local conservationists hope to increase that to 50%. You can bike or hike 4 mi. north from Old Harbor to the **National Wildlife Refuge,** bring a picnic, head due south from Old Harbor where the ferry lets you off, and hike 2 mi. south to the **Mohegan Bluffs.** Those who are adventurous, careful, and strong can wind their way down to the Atlantic waters 200 ft. below. The **Southeast Lighthouse,** high in the cliffs, has warned fog-bound fisherfolk since 1875; its beacon shines the brightest of any on the Atlantic coast. The **Block Island Chamber of Commerce** (466-2982) advises at the ferry dock in Old Harbor Drawer D, Block Island 02807 (open Mon.-Fri. 9am-3pm, Sat. 9am-1pm; mid-Oct. to mid-May Mon.-Fri. approximately 10am-2pm). Rhode Island Rest stop info centers supply the free *Block Island Travel Planner.*

No camping is allowed on the island, so make it a daytrip unless you're willing to shell out $50 or more for a room in a guest house. Most restaurants are close to the ferry dock in Old Harbor; several cluster at New Harbor 1 mi. inland.

Cycling is the ideal way to explore the tiny (7 mi. by 3 mi.) island. Try the **Old Harbor Bike Shop** (466-2029), to the left of where you exit the ferry. (10-speeds and mountain bikes $3 per hr., $15 per day; single mopeds $15/$45-55 weekdays, $20/$55 weekends; license required. Car rentals $60 per day, 20¢ per mi. Must be 21 with credit card. Open daily 9am-7pm.)

The **Interstate Navigation Co.** (783-4613) provides year-round **ferry service** to Block Island from Point Judith, RI (8 per day in summer, 1-4 per day in winter, 1¼ hr., $6.60, under 12 $3, cars by reservation $20.25, bikes $1.75), and summer service from Newport, RI (1 per day late June-early Sept., 2 hr., $6.45), New London, CT (1 per day mid-June to mid-Sept., 2 hr., $13.50), and Montauk, NY (mid-May to Oct.). If possible, leave from Galilee State Pier in Point Judith; it's the most frequent, cheapest, and shortest ride. **Coast Guard:** 466-2086. .

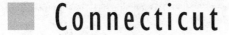

Connecticut

Connecticut's first European colonists were immigrants from the Massachusetts Bay Colony. They followed the Reverend Thomas Hooker and settled along the fertile banks of the Connecticut River in the 1630s. From the start, "nutmeggers" were independently minded—their remarkably democratic colonial government, dating back as early as 1639, foreshadowed the future political history of America and earned Connecticut fame as the "Constitution State." In the late 18th century, New England's first mills started operating in Hartford and manufacturing has continued to be the largest contributor to the state economy. In addition to industrialized cities such as Hartford, New Haven, and New London, Connecticut boasts a long coastline with numerous sandy beaches, an extensive network of rivers, and large stretches of farmland. A few more modern claims to fame add to Connecticut's identity: both the lollipop and the pay phone were born here.

PRACTICAL INFORMATION

Capital: Hartford.
Tourist Information Line: 800-282-6863. Call for vacation guides. **Bureau of State Parks and Forests,** 165 Capitol Ave. #265, Hartford 06106 (566-2304), will mail you an application for a permit to camp in the state parks and forests and also sends brochures describing sites. **Connecticut Forest and Park Association,** 16 Meriden Rd., Rockfall 06481 (346-2372), has outdoor activities info.
Time Zone: Eastern. **Postal Abbreviation:** CT
Sales Tax: 6%.

■■■ HARTFORD

Although currently the state capital, Hartford has not always been a law-abiding city. In 1687, the English governor demanded the surrender of the charter that Charles II had granted them 25 years before. Obstinate, Hartfordians hid the charter in a tree trunk until the infuriated governor returned to England. Today, the spot is marked with a plaque on Charter Oak Place. In the intervening three centuries, Hartford has grown into the world's insurance capital; the city's skyline is marked by architectural wonders financed by some of the larger firms, including the Boat Building, America's first two-sided building.

Practical Information Hartford lies at the intersection of I-91 and I-84. The **Greater Hartford Convention and Visitors Bureau** is located at the Hartford Civic Center, 1 Civic Center Plaza (728-6789 or 800-446-7811). There is another Bureau on Main St. in the Pavilion (522-6766). Both offer dozens of maps, booklets, and guides to local resorts, campgrounds, and historical sights. (Open Mon.-Fri. 10am-6pm, Sat. 10am-5pm). The **Greater Hartford Tourism District,** 1 Civic Center Plaza (520-4480 or 800-793-4480), can also be helpful. For information on the streets, look for one of the red-capped Hartford guides, all of whom are knowledgable about the history, services, events, and geography of the city. (Guides on duty Mon.-Sat. from mid-morning until late night. Guides have police radios.) In front of the Old State House, **Connecticut Transit's Information Center** (525-9181), at State and Market Streets, provides helpful downtown maps and public transportation info (basic fare 95¢). Union Place is home to **Amtrak** (727-1776 or 800-872-7245), which runs eight trains daily both north and south (office open daily 5:30am-9pm), and **Peter Pan Trailways** (800-237-8747), which offers buses north and south (ticket office open daily 5:45am-10pm). **Greyhound** at Union Place (800-231-2222) offers 17 buses daily to NYC and eight to Boston (office open daily 7am-10:30pm).

Hartford's **post office:** 141 Weston St. (524-6001; open Mon.-Fri. 7am-6pm, Sat. 7am-3pm); **ZIP code:** 06101; **area code:** 203.

Accommodations and Food Within the city, the **YMCA,** 160 Jewell St. (522-4183), provides the most affordable rates. (Singles $16.50 with a shared bath, $20.50 with a private bath. Gym, pool, cafeteria, and racquet courts. No reservations accepted.) Just north of Hartford, the **Windsor Youth Hostel (HI-AYH)** (683-2847) is located in Connecticut's oldest town. Reservations are essential and directions are available upon reservation confirmation (4 beds available, $11-13). For camping enthusiasts who don't mind a 30-min. drive out of the city, **Burr Road State Park,** five min. north of Torrington on Rte. 8 (379-0172), provides 40 wooded sites with showers and swimming.

Food courts abound within Hartford, offering cheap, typical, chain food. However, many delectable Hartford-specific restaurants can be found within a few blocks of the downtown area. The **Municipal Café,** 485 Main St. (278-4844), at Elm, is a popular and friendly place to catch a good breakfast or lunch. (Sandwiches under $4, hot dinners $6.) At night, the "Muni" is big, big, big on the local music scene. (Open daily 7am-2:30pm with breakfast and lunch menu, and from 7pm with bar menu; bands usually Wed.-Sat. 9pm-1:30am. For entertainment info call 527-5044.) **The Hartford Brewery, Ltd.,** 35 Pearl St. (246-2337), Connecticut's only brew-pub, serves up sandwiches ($5-6.50) and burgers ($6.50) which can be polished off with any of six freshly brewed beers. Tours of the brewery are available. (Open Mon.-Thurs. 11:30am-1am, Fri. 11:30am-2am, Sat. noon-2am.) For brick-oven pizza ($5), head to the **Original Pub,** 358 Asylum Ave. (278-0368). Try a half yard of beer (domestic $4.50, imported $6.50; open Mon.-Fri. 11:30am-2am, Sat. 10:30am-2am). Live entertainment can be found downtown at the **Russian Lady,** 191 Ann St. (525-3003), the oldest bar in Hartford. Dance away on the roof garden. The cover varies. (Open Sun. and Wed. 5pm-1am, Thurs. 3pm-1am, Fri. 3pm-2am, Sat. 4pm-2am.)

Sights Designed by Charles Bullfinch in 1796, the gold-domed **Old State House,** 800 Main St., housed the state government until 1914; it is under renovation through Nov. 1994. While it is under construction, the **Renovation Headquarters** (522-6766), located across the plaza in the **Pavilion,** are housing the State House's historical exhibits (open Mon.-Fri. 10am-6pm, Sat. 10am-5pm). Call for an update.

Thomas Hooker once preached across Main St., at the **Center Church and Ancient Burying Grounds,** 675 Main St., and you can see the centuries-old tombstones of his descendants in the graveyard. A block or so west, park-n-ride at **Bushnell Park,** the first public American park, on one of the country's few extant handcrafted merry-go-rounds. The **Bushnell Park Carousel** (246-7739), built in 1914, spins 48 horses and two lovers' chariots to the tunes of a 1925 Wurlitzer Organ. (Open April and Sept. Sat.-Sun. 11am-5pm; May-Aug. Tues.-Sun. 11am-5pm. Admission 50¢.) The **State Capitol,** 210 Capitol Ave. (240-0222), overlooks the park. Also gold-domed, this beautiful building houses Lafayette's camp bed and a war-ravaged tree trunk from the Civil War's Battle of Chickamauga, among other historic artifacts. Free one-hour tours begin at the west entrance of the neighboring **Legislative Office Building,** behind which is free parking. (Tours Mon.-Fri. 9:15am-1:15pm, Sat. tours 10:15am-2:15pm, begin at the SW entrance to the capitol.)

Lovers of American literature won't want to miss engaging tours of the **Mark Twain House**, 351 Farmington Ave. (493-6411), and **Harriet Beecher Stowe House**, 79 Forest St. (525-9317), both located just west of the city center on Farmington Ave.; from the Old State House take any Farmington Ave. bus east. The rambling and richly colored Victorian Mark Twain Mansion housed the Missouri-born author for 17 years; Twain composed his masterpiece *Huckleberry Finn* here. Harriet Beecher Stowe lived next door on Nook Farm after the publication of *Uncle Tom's Cabin*, from 1873 until her death. (Both houses open Tues.-Sat. 9:30am-4pm. Admission $6.50 at either house, $2.75 for children.)

Farther out Farmington Ave. in the colonial village of **Farmington** lies the **Hill-Stead Museum** (677-4787). Hill-Stead is a Colonial Revival "country house" built by Alfred Pope around 1900 to house his Impressionist Collection. Pieces by Manet, Monet, Degas, Cassat, and Whistler are on display. Hill-Stead is one of the very few places in the country where Impressionist masterpieces are shown in a domestic setting. (1-hr. guided tour only. Open Tues.-Sun. 10am-4pm. Tours every ½ hr. $6, seniors and students $5, kids 6-12 $3.)

Another must-see for the aesthetically inclined is the **Wadsworth Atheneum,** 600 Main St. (278-2670), the oldest public art museum in the country. The museum has absorbing collections of contemporary and Baroque art, including Monet, Renoir, Degas, as well as one of only three Caravaggios in the United States. (Open Tues.-Sun. 11am-5pm. $5, seniors and students $4, under 13 free. Free all day Thurs., and Sat. before noon. Tours Thurs. at 1pm and Sat.-Sun. noon-2pm.)

Hockey enthusiasts will enjoy catching the NHL's **Hartford Whalers** face off at the **Civic Center,** 242 Trumball St. (728-6637 or 800-WHALERS; tickets $20-35).

■■■ NEW HAVEN

Today New Haven is simultaneously university town and depressed city. Academic types and a working-class population live somewhat uneasily side by side—bumper stickers proclaiming "Tax Yale, Not Us" embellish a number of street signs downtown. Yalies tend to stick to their campus, further widening the rift between town and gown. The gap between the wealthy academic environment and the rest of the town is apparent in every facet of the city, from architecture to safety.

Practical Information The **Greater New Haven Convention and Visitors Bureau,** 1 Long Wharf Dr. (777-8550 or 800-332-7829) provides free maps and current event info. For weekly recorded events update, call 498-5050, ext. 1310. (Open Mon.-Fri. 9am-5pm.) For free campus maps, head to the **Yale Information Center,** Phelps Gateway, 344 College St. (432-2300), facing the Green. Pick up a 75¢ walking guide and *The Yale,* a guide to undergraduate life ($3). Bus maps and a New Haven bookstore guide are available. (Open daily 10am-3:30pm. Free one-hour tours Mon.-Fri. at 10:30am and 2pm, Sat.-Sun. at 1:30pm.) **Amtrak** (800-872-7245), Union Station, Union Ave., runs out of a newly renovated station, but the area is unsafe at night. (Trains to: New York $22, Boston $36, and Washington, D.C $73.) Also at Union Station is **Greyhound** (547-1500). Frequent service to New York ($13.50), Boston ($22), and Providence ($19). (Ticket office open daily 8:30am-7:30pm.) New Haven's **area code:** 203.

New Haven lies at the intersection of I-95 and I-91, 40 mi. from Hartford. At night, don't wander too freely out of the immediate downtown and campus areas, as surrounding sections are notably less safe. New Haven is laid out in nine squares. The central one is the **Green,** which, despite the fact that it lies between **Yale University** and City Hall, is a pleasant escape from the hassles of city life. A small but thriving business district of bookstores, boutiques, cheap sandwich places, and other services catering to students and professors, borders the Green.

Accommodations and Food Inexpensive accommodations are sparse in New Haven. The hunt is especially difficult around Yale Parents Weekend (mid-Oct.) and commencement (early June). Two decent places are **Hotel Duncan,** 1151 Chapel St. (787-1273) with the oldest elevator in CT (singles $40, doubles $55; reservations recommended on weekends), and **Nutmeg Bed & Breakfast,** 222 Girard Ave. (236-6698), Hartford. They reserve doubles ($35-45) in New Haven B&Bs (open Mon.-Fri. 9am-5pm). The nearest camping is **Hammonasset Beach** (245-2755; sites $12), 20 min. away, and **Cattletown** (264-5678; sites $10), 40 min. away.

Food in New Haven is reasonably cheap. The pride of New Haven is its superb pizza. Started by a Yale Alum, the **Daily Caffe,** 376 Elm St. (776-5063), is becoming the haunt of the university's coffee-and-cigarette set. (Open Mon.-Sat. 8am-1am, Sun.

8am-midnight.) Yale students hang out obsessively at **Naples Pizza,** 90 Wall St. (776-9021 or 776-6214), serves up interesting pies with broccoli, pineapple, or white clams ($7.25). Pitcher of beer costs $5.50. (Open Mon.-Wed. 7-10pm, Thurs.-Fri. 7-11pm; Sept.-May Sun.-Thurs. 7pm-1am, Fri.-Sat. 7pm-2am.)

Sights and Entertainment Yale's campus was modeled after Oxford. Architects here took great pains to artificially age the campus' buildings. Bricks were buried in different soils to give them that Industrial Revolution look, windows were shattered, and acid was sprayed, giving Yale that wonderful aura of going-to-shambles. James Gambel Rodgers, a firm believer in the sanctity of printed material, designed **Sterling Memorial Library,** 120 High St. (432-1775). The building looks so much like a monastery that even the telephone booths are shaped like confessionals. Rodgers spared no expense in making Yale's library look "authentic," even decapitating the figurines on the library's exterior to replicate those at Oxford, which, because of decay, often fall to the ground and shatter. (Open Mon.-Wed. and Fri. 8:30am-5pm, Thurs. 8:30am-10pm, Sat. 10am-5pm; Sept.- June Mon.-Thurs. 8:30am-midnight, Fri. 8:30am-5pm, Sat. 10am-5am, Sun. 1pm-midnight.)

The massive **Beinecke Rare Book and Manuscript Library,** 121 Wall St. (432-2977), has no windows. Instead this intriguing modern structure is paneled with Vermont marble cut thin enough to be translucent; supposedly its volumes (including one Gutenberg Bible and an extensive collection of William Carlos Williams's writings) can survive a nuclear war. (Open Mon.-Fri. 8:30am-5pm, Sat. 10am-5pm.) Along New Haven's own Wall St., between High and Yale St., the Neo-Gothic gargoyles perched on the **Law School** building are in fact cops and robbers.

Most of New Haven's museums are on the Yale campus. The **Yale University Art Gallery,** 1111 Chapel St. (432-0600), open since 1832, claims to be the oldest university art museum in the Western Hemisphere. Its collections of John Trumbull paintings and Italian Renaissance works are especially notable. (Open Tues.-Sat. 10am-5pm, Sun. 2-5pm. Closed Aug. Suggested donation $3.) The **Yale Center for British Art,** 1080 Chapel St. (432-2800), sponsors some thought-provoking exhibits—two years ago they displayed a collection of snuff boxes. This museum, filled with portraits of famous British folk, is a must for Anglophiles. (Open Tues.-Sat. 10am-5pm, Sun. noon-5pm. Free.) The **Peabody Museum of Natural History,** 170 Whitney Ave. (recorded message 432-5050), houses Rudolph F. Zallinger's Pulitzer Prize-winning mural, which portrays the North American continent as it appeared 70 to 350 million years ago. Other exhibits range from Central American cultural artifacts to a dinosaur hall displaying the skeleton of a *brontosaurus*. (Open Mon.-Sat. 10am-5pm, Sun. noon-5pm. $4, seniors $3, ages 3-15 $2.50. Free Mon.-Fri. 3-5pm.)

Toad's Place, 300 York St. (562-5694, recorded info 624-8623), has hosted gigs by Bob Dylan and the Stones and still has great live shows. (Box office open daily 11am-6pm; buy tickets at the bar after 8pm. Bar open Sun.-Thurs. 8pm-1am, Fri.-Sat. 8pm-2am.) The **Anchor Bar,** 272 College St. (865-1512), off the Green, has the area's best jukebox. (Open Mon.-Thurs. 11am-1am, Fri.-Sat. 10am-2am.)

Once a famous testing ground for Broadway-bound plays, New Haven's thespian community carries on today on a lesser scale. The **Schubert Theater,** 247 College St. (526-5666 or 800-228-6622), a significant part of the town's on-stage tradition, still mounts shows. (Box office open Mon.-Fri. 10am-5pm, Sat. 11am-3pm.) Yale itself accounts for an impressive part of the city's theater activity.

The **Yale Repertory Theater,** 222 York St. (432-1234) has turned out such illustrious alums as Meryl Streep, Glenn Close, and James Earl Jones, and continues to produce excellent shows (open Oct.-May; tickets under $8). In summer, the city hosts concerts on the Green (787-8956) like the free **New Haven Symphony** concerts (865-0831), the **New Haven Jazz Festival** (787-8228), and other free series. .

MID-ATLANTIC STATES

Ranging from the sleepy, almost-Southern state of Maryland, home to Edgar Allen Poe, through the experiment in Federal Democracy that is the District of Columbia, up to the vast melting pot of New York City, the diverse and densely populated states along the Eastern seaboard tell the story of the nation's creation and development. Constitutional democracy and free speech are still celebrated in Philadelphia, the nation's first capital, and the tradition of religious individualism persists as Mennonites and Amish maintain their dissenting ways and shun materialism. The presence of some of the nation's oldest and finest universities alongside large rural areas reflect the origins of the U.S. in an educated yeomanry. The mid-Atlantic witnessed heavy fighting in both the American Revolution and the Civil War. Around the turn of the century, the coal of Appalachia and the steel of Pittsburgh transformed the United States into a global economic power. The ethnically diverse populations of the Mid-Atlantic demonstrate how differences can contribute to the vitality of national identity, or mire it in hopeless conflict.

In spite of the concentration of urban centers in the Mid-Atlantic, there is plenty of outdoor fun. The celebrated Appalachian Trail treks through the area; in northern New York, the Adirondacks reign as the largest park in the U.S. outside of Alaska. The wilds of Pennsylvania's Allegheny Mountains provide a setting where you can raft, backpack, and even be chased by bears in truly remote areas. Wildlife refuges scattered along the Atlantic coast and its bays protect birdlife and wild ponies alike.

 ## New York

There are seven cities on earth with larger populations than New York City, but the Big Apple can arguably claim to be grander than them all. The city includes a staggeringly diverse population, a spectacular skyline, towering financial power, and a range of cultural enterprises that is matched by few. But there's more to the Empire State than its biggest city. Half of the state population lives outside NYC, and many of those are proud to rarely set foot there. Upstate New York is stunning. The peaceful Catskills, beautiful Finger Lakes, and awesome Niagara Falls all provide a stark contrast to the super-metropolis to the south.

■■■ NEW YORK CITY

Nowhere in America is the rhythm of urban life more pronounced than in the City. Cramped into tiny spaces, millions of people find themselves confronting each other every day. Perhaps because of the crush of the populace, people here are some of the loudest, pushiest, most neurotic, and loneliest in the world. Much that is unique, attractive, and repulsive about the Big Apple is a function of its scale. The city is just too big, too heterogeneous, too jumbled, and too exciting.

The colony was founded in 1624 by the Dutch West Indies Company as a trading post. In 1626, in a particularly shrewd transaction, Peter Minuit bought Manhattan from the natives for 60 guilders, or just under 24 bucks. Because the early colonists were less than enthralled by Dutch rule, they put up only token resistance when the British finally invaded the settlement in 1664. By the late 1770s the city had become an active port with a population of 20,000. New York's primary concern was maintaining that prosperity, and it reacted apathetically to the first whiffs of revolution. The new American Army—understandably—made no great efforts to protect the city. New York fell to the British in September of 1776 and remained in their hands until late November 1783.

Throughout the political turmoil, the city continued to grow. New York emerged as the nation's pre-eminent city in the 19th century. Manhattan went vertical to house the growing population streaming in from Western Europe. Escaping famine, persecution, and political unrest, immigrants faced the perils of the sea for the promise of America, landing on the shore of Ellis Island in New York Harbor. Post-WWII prosperity brought still more immigrants, especially African-Americans from the rural South and Hispanics from the Caribbean, and businesses into the city. However, by the 60s, crises in public transportation, education, and housing fanned the flames of ethnic tensions and fostered the rise of a criminal element. City officials raised taxes to improve services, but in the process drove away middle-class residents and corporations.

In the 80s, New York rebounded. Wall Street in the 80s was a tragically hip place to be, but as the rosy blush of the 80s fades to grey 90s malaise, the city is confronted once again with old problems—too many people, too little money, and not enough consideration for each other. The first African-American mayor, David Dinkins, was elected in 1989 on a platform of harmonious growth, but this "melting pot" of New York continued to burn, smolder, and belch. The election of Rudy Giuliani as mayor in 1993 split the city once again along racial lines. Still, there are signs of life and renewed commitment in the urban blightscape.

New York scoffs at other cities. It boasts the most immigrants, the tallest skyscrapers, the trickiest con artists. Even the vast blocks of concrete have charm. "There is more poetry in a block of New York than in 20 daisied lanes," said O. Henry, returning from rural Westchester. As do many New Yorkers, so agrees former Mayor Ed Koch, "New York is not a problem. New York is a stroke of genius."

For the ultimate coverage of New York City, see our city guide, *Let's Go: New York City*, available wherever fine books are sold.

PRACTICAL INFORMATION

Emergency: 911.

Police: 212-374-5000. Use this for inquiries that are not urgent. 24 hrs.

Visitor Information: New York Convention and Visitors Bureau, 2 Columbus Circle (397-8222 or 484-1200), 59th St. and Broadway. Subway: #1, 9 or A, B, C, D to 59th St.-Columbus Circle. Multilingual staff helps with directions, hotel listings, entertainment ideas, safety tips, and "insiders" descriptions of neighborhoods. Try to show up in person; the phone lines tend to be busy, the maps and brochures worthwhile. Open Mon.-Fri. 9am-6pm, Sat.-Sun. and holidays 10am-3pm.

Travelers' Aid Society: 1481 Seventh Ave. (944-0013), between 42nd and 43rd St.; and at JFK International Airport (718-656-4870), in the International Arrivals Building. JFK office provides general counseling and referral to travelers, as well as emergency assistance (open Mon.-Thurs. 10am-7pm, Fri. 10am-6pm, Sat. 11am-6pm, Sun. noon-6pm). Times Sq. branch specializes in crisis intervention services for stranded travelers or crime victims (open Mon.-Fri. 9am-6pm, but it's best to call first as they can sometimes close unexpectedly). Call the **Victims Service Agency** at 577-7777, a 24-hr. source. Subway: #1, 2, 3, 7, 9 or N, R, S to 42nd St.

Consulates: Australian, 630 Fifth Ave. (245-4000). **British,** 845 Third Ave. (745-0202). **Canadian,** 1251 Sixth Ave. (768-2400). **German,** 460 Park Ave. (308-8700). **Israeli,** 800 Second Ave. (351-5200). **Japanese,** 299 Park Ave. (371-8222). **South African,** 333 E. 38th St. (213-4880).

American Express: Multi-task agency providing tourists with traveler's checks, gift checks, cashing services, you name it. Branches in Manhattan include: **American Express Tower,** 200 Vesey St. (640-2000), near the World Financial Center (open Mon.-Fri. 9am-5pm); **Macy's Herald Square,** 151 W. 34th St. (695-8075), at Seventh Ave. inside Macy's (open Mon.-Sat. 10am-6pm); **150 E. 42nd St.** (687-3700), between Lexington and Third Ave. (open Mon.-Fri 9am-5pm); in **Bloomingdale's,** 59th St. and Lexington Ave. (705-3171; open Mon.-Wed. and Fri.-Sat.

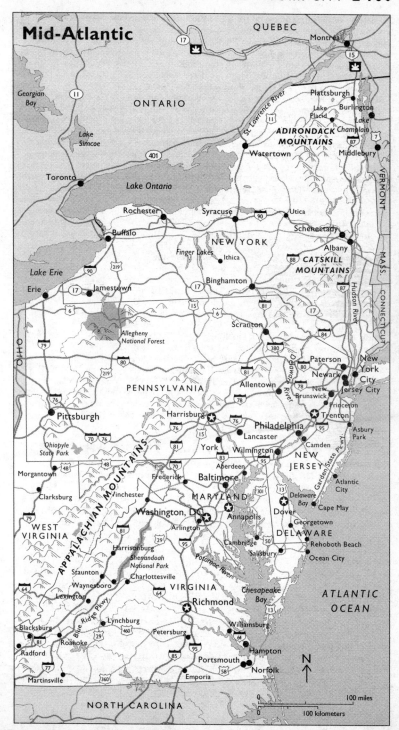

Mid-Atlantic

10am-6pm, Thurs. 10am-8pm); **822 Lexington Ave.** (758-6510), near 63rd St. (open Mon.-Fri. 9am-6pm, Sat. 10am-4pm).

Taxis: Radio-dispatched taxis 718-361-7270. Most people in Mahattan hail yellow (licensed) cabs on the street: $1.50 base, 25¢ each one-fifth mi. or every 75 seconds; passengers pay for all tolls. Don't forget to tip. Ask for a receipt, which will have the taxi's ID number. This is necessary to trace lost articles or to make a complaint to the **Taxi Commission,** 221 W. 41st St. (221-8294).

Car Rental: All agencies have min. age requirements and ask for deposits. Call in advance to reserve, especially near the weekend. **Nationwide,** 220 E. 9th St. (867-1234), between Second and Third Ave. Reputable nationwide chain. Mid-sized domestic sedan $59 per day, $289 per week, unlimited mileage. Open Mon.-Fri. 8am-6pm. Must be 23 with a major credit card.

Auto Transport Companies: New York serves as a major departure point. The length of time for application processing varies from place to place; these 2 process immediately. Nearly all agencies require references and a refundable cash deposit. **Dependable Car Services,** 801 E. Edgar Rd., Linden, NJ (840-6262 or 908-474-8080). Must be 21, have 3 personal references, and a valid license without major violations. $150-200 deposit. Open Mon.-Fri. 8:30am-4:30pm, Sat. 9am-1pm. **Auto Driveaway,** 264 W. 35th St., Suite 500 (967-2344); 33-70 Prince St., Flushing, Queens (718-762-3800). Must be 21, with 2 local references and a valid driver's license. $250 deposit, $10 application fee. Open Mon.-Fri. 9am-5pm.

Bicycle Rentals: May-Oct. weekdays 10am-3pm and 7-10pm and from Fri. 7pm to Mon. 6am, Central Park closes to cars, allowing bicycles to rule its roads. **Gene's,** 242 E. 79th St. (249-9344), near Second Ave. 3-speeds for $3 per hr., $10.50 per day; mountain bikes and rollerblades $6 per hr., $21 per day. $20 deposit required for 3-speeds, $40 for mountain bikes, plus driver's license and credit card. Both available for overnight rentals ($8 plus cash deposit of $100 or $250). 2-hr. minimum. Open Mon.-Fri. 9:30am-8pm, Sat.-Sun. 9am-7pm.

Help Lines: Crime Victim's Hotline, 577-7777; 24-hr. counseling and referrals. **Sex Crimes Report Line,** New York Police Dept., 267-7273; 24-hr.

Walk-in Medical Clinic, 57 E. 34th St. (683-1010), between Park and Madison. Open Mon.-Fri. 8am-6pm, Sat. 10am-2pm. Affiliated with Beth Israel Hospital.

Post Office: Central branch, 421 Eighth Ave. (967-8585 Mon.-Fri. 8:30am-5pm), across from Madison Square Garden (open 24 hrs.). For General Delivery, mail to and use the entrance at 390 Ninth Ave. C.O.D.s, money orders, and passport applications are also processed at some branches. **ZIP code:** 10001.

Area Codes: 212 (Manhattan); 718 (Brooklyn, Bronx, Queens, Staten Island.)

GETTING THERE: PLANE, BUS, TRAIN AND CAR

Airplane Three airports service the New York Metro Region. **John F. Kennedy Airport (JFK)** (718-244-4444), 12 mi. from Midtown in southern Queens, is the largest, handling most international flights. **LaGuardia Airport** (718-533-3400), 6 mi. from midtown in northwestern Queens, is the smallest, offering domestic flights and air shuttles. **Newark International Airport** (201-961-6000 or 201-762-5100), 12 mi. from Midtown in Newark, NJ, offers both domestic and international flights at better budget fares (though getting to and from Newark can be expensive).

JFK to midtown Manhattan can easily be covered by public transportation. Catch a brown and white JFK long-term parking lot bus from any airport terminal (every 15 min.) to the **Howard Beach-JFK subway station,** where you can take the A train to the city (1 hr.). Or you can take one of the city buses (Q10 or Q3; $1.25, exact change required) into Queens. The Q10 and Q3 connect with subway lines to Manhattan. Ask the bus driver where to get off, and make sure you know which subway line you want. Those willing to pay more can take the **Carey Airport Express** (718-632-0500), a private line that runs between JFK and Grand Central Station and the Port Authority Terminal (leaves every 30 min. from 5am-1am, 1 hr., $13).

LaGuardia to Manhattan journey can be done two ways. If you have extra time and light luggage, you can take the MTA Q33 bus ($1.25 exact change or token) to the 74th St./Broadway/Roosevelt Ave./Jackson Hts. subway stop in Queens, and from there, take the #7, E, F, G or R train into Manhattan ($1.25). Allow at least 90

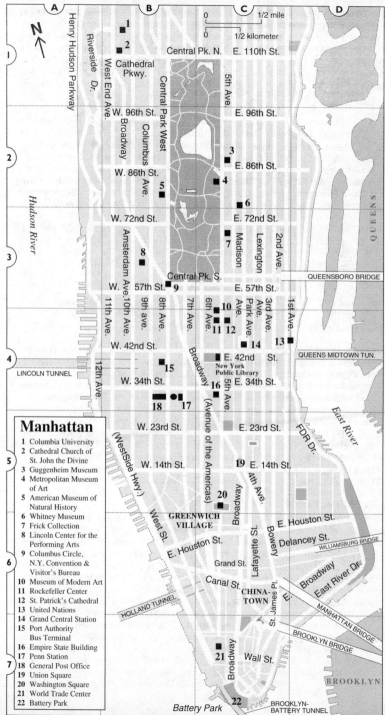

Manhattan

1 Columbia University
2 Cathedral Church of
   St. John the Divine
3 Guggenheim Museum
4 Metropolitan Museum
   of Art
5 American Museum of
   Natural History
6 Whitney Museum
7 Frick Collection
8 Lincoln Center for the
   Performing Arts
9 Columbus Circle,
   N.Y. Convention &
   Visitor's Bureau
10 Museum of Modern Art
11 Rockefeller Center
12 St. Patrick's Cathedral
13 United Nations
14 Grand Central Station
15 Port Authority
   Bus Terminal
16 Empire State Building
17 Penn Station
18 General Post Office
19 Union Square
20 Washington Square
21 World Trade Center
22 Battery Park

min. travel time. The second option, the Carey bus, stops at Grand Central Station and the Port Authority Terminal (every 30 min., 30 min., $9).

Newark Airport to Manhattan takes about as long as from JFK. **New Jersey Transit (NJTA)** (201-762-5100 or 212-629-8767) runs a fast, efficient bus (NJTA #300) between the airport and Port Authority every 15 min. during the day, less often at night ($7). For the same fare, the **Olympia Trails Coach** (212-964-6233) travels between the airport and either Grand Central or the World Trade Center (every 20 min. daily 5am-11pm; 25-45 min. depending on traffic; $7).

Bus Greyhound (800-231-2222), grooves out of their major Northeastern hub, the **Port Authority Terminal**, 41st. and Eighth Ave. (435-7000; Subway: A, C, or E to 42nd St.-Port Authority). Port Authority has good info, but be careful—with so many tourists, there are plenty of scam artists around. *This neighborhood is especially sleazy at night.* Avoid the terminal's bathrooms at all times. To: Boston (4½ hr., $26); Philadelphia (2 hr., $12); Washington, DC (4½ hr., $26); Montréal (8 hr., $70). **East Coast Explorer,** 245 Eighth Ave. (718-694-9667), offers budget full-day, scenic bus trips between New York, Boston, and Washington D.C. (NYC to Boston $32).

Train Train service in New York is primarily through two stations. On the East side, **Grand Central Station,** 42nd St. and Park Ave. (Subway: #4, 5, 6, 7, or S to 42nd St./Grand Central), handles **Metro-North** (800-638-7646, 532-4900) commuter lines to Connecticut and New York suburbs. Longer routes run from the West Side's **Penn Station,** 33rd St. and Eighth Ave. (Subway: #1, 2, 3, 9, A, C, or E to 34th St./Penn Station), as well as **Amtrak** (800-872-7245 or 582-6875), serving most major cities in the U.S., especially in the Northeast. (To: Washington, DC (4 hr., $52). Also from Penn station is the **Long Island Railroad (LIRR)** (718-822-5477), and **PATH** to New Jersey (800-234-7284 or 435-7000, Mon.-Fri. 8am-5pm).

Driving From New Jersey there are three ways to reach the city. The **George Washington Bridge,** which crosses the Hudson River into northern Manhattan, gives easy access to either Harlem River Drive or the West Side Highway. From the N.J. turnpike you'll probably end up going through Weehawken, N.J. at the **Lincoln Tunnel,** which exits in midtown in the West 40s. The **Holland Tunnel** connects to lower Manhattan, exiting into the SoHo and TriBeCa area. Coming from New England or Connecticut on I-95, follow signs for the **Triboro Bridge.** From there get onto FDR Drive, which runs along the east side of Manhattan and exits onto city streets every 10 blocks or so. Another option is to look for the **Willis Avenue Bridge exit** on I-95 to avoid the toll, and enter Manhattan north on the FDR Drive.

Hitchhiking is illegal in New York state and cops strictly enforce the law within NYC. *Hitching in and around New York City is suicidal.* Don't do it.

ORIENTATION

Five **boroughs** comprise New York City: Brooklyn, the Bronx, Queens, Staten Island, and Manhattan. For all its notoriety, **Manhattan** Island's length is only half that of a marathon; 13 mi. long and 2.5 mi. wide, and it houses only the third largest population of the five boroughs, after Brooklyn and Queens. Yet though small, Manhattan has all the advantages; it is surrounded by water and adjacent to the other four boroughs. **Queens,** the largest and most ethnically diverse of the boroughs, is located to the east of midtown Manhattan. **Brooklyn** lies due south of Queens and is even older than Manhattan. **Staten Island,** to the south of Manhattan, has remained defiantly residential, similar to the suburban communities of outer Long Island. North of Manhattan nests the **Bronx,** the only borough connected by land to the rest of the U.S., home of the lovely suburb Riverdale as well as New York's most depressed area, the South Bronx.

Manhattan's Neighborhoods

Glimpsed from the window of an approaching plane, New York City can seem a monolithic concrete jungle. But up close, New York breaks down into manageable neighborhoods, each with history and personality. Boundaries between these neighborhoods can often be abrupt.

The city began at the southern tip of Manhattan, in the area around **Battery Park** where the first Dutch settlers made their homes. The nearby harbor, now jazzed up with the **South Street Seaport** tourist magnet, provided the growing city with the commercial opportunities that helped it succeed. Historic Manhattan, however, lies in the shadows of the imposing financial buildings around **Wall Street** and the civic offices around **City Hall.** A little farther north, neighborhoods rich in the cultures brought by late 19th-century immigrants rub elbows below Houston Street— **Little Italy, Chinatown,** and the southern blocks of the **Lower East Side.** Formerly the home of Eastern European and Russian Jews, Delancey and Elizabeth Streets now offer pasta and silks. To the west lies the newly fashionable **TriBeCa** ("Triangle Below Canal St."). **SoHo** (for "South of Houston"), a former warehouse district west of Little Italy, has transformed into a pocket of art studios and galleries. Above SoHo thrives **Greenwich Village,** where jumbled streets, trendy shops, and cafés have for decades been home to intense political and artistic activity.

A few blocks north of Greenwich Village, stretching across the west teens and twenties, lies **Chelsea,** the late artist Andy Warhol's favorite hangout and former home of Dylan Thomas and Arthur Miller. East of Chelsea, presiding over the East River, is **Gramercy Park,** a pastoral collection of elegant brownstones immortalized in Edith Wharton's *Age of Innocence.* **Midtown Manhattan** towers from 34th to 59th St., where traditional and controversial new skyscrapers share the skies, supporting over a million elevated offices. Here department stores outfit New York while the nearby **Theater District** attempts to entertain the world, or at least people who like musicals. North of Midtown, **Central Park** slices Manhattan into East and West. On the **Upper West Side,** the gracious museums and residences of Central Park West neighbor the chic boutiques and sidewalk cafes of Columbus Ave. On the **Upper East Side,** the galleries and museums scattered among the elegant apartments of Fifth and Park Ave. create an even more rarefied atmosphere.

Above 97th St., the Upper East Side's opulence ends with a whimper where commuter trains emerge from the tunnel and the *barrio* begins. Above 110th St. on the Upper West Side sits majestic **Columbia University** (founded as King's College in 1754), an urban member of the Ivy League. The communities of **Harlem** and **Morningside Heights** produced the Harlem Renaissance of black artists and writers in the 1920s and the revolutionary Black Power movement of the 1960s. Now torn with crime, these areas are historically interesting, but not to be explored after dark. **Washington Heights,** just north of St. Nicholas Park, is home to Fort Tryon Park, the Medieval Cloisters museum, and a community of Old World immigrants.

Manhattan's Street Plan

New York's east/west division refers to an address's location in relation to the two borders of Central Park—**Fifth Avenue** along the east side and **Central Park West** along the west. Below 59th St. where the park ends, the West Side begins at the western half of Fifth Ave. **Midtown** is between 34th and 59th St. **Uptown** (59th St. and *up*) refers to the area north of Midtown. **Downtown** (34th St. and *down*) means the area south of Midtown. **Streets run east-west. Avenues run north-south.**

Manhattan's grid makes calculating distances fairly easy. **Three streets are equivalent to one avenue.** Numbers also increase from south to north along the avenues, but you always should ask for a cross street when you getting an avenue address. This plan does not work in the Village or in lower Mahattan; you must get a good map and ask directions.

GETTING AROUND

(For info on **Taxis** and **Biking,** see Practical Information.) Get a free subway map from station token booths or the visitors bureau, which also has a free street map (see Practical Information above). For a more detailed program of interborough travel, find a Manhattan Yellow Pages, which contains detailed subway, PATH, and bus maps. In the city, the round-the-clock staff at the **Transit Authority Information Bureau** (718-330-1234) dispenses subway and bus info.

Subways The fare for **Metropolitan Transit Authority (MTA)** subways and buses is a hefty $1.25; groups of four or more may find cabs cheaper for short rides. Once inside you may transfer to any train without restrictions. Most buses have access ramps, but steep stairs make subway transit more difficult for disabled people. Call for specifics on public transport Mon.-Fri 9am-5pm.

In crowded stations (notably those around 42nd St.), pickpockets find plenty of work; in deserted stations, more violent crimes can occur. *Always watch yourself and your belongings.* Try to stay in lit areas near a transit cop or token clerk. When boarding the train, make sure to pick a car with a number of other passengers on it—for long subway rides, the first car is usually the best idea.

For safety, avoid riding the subways between 11pm and 7am, especially above E. 96th St. and W. 120th St. and outside Manhattan. Riding the subway at night is dangerous—don't ride alone. During rush-hour you'll be fortunate to find air, let alone seating—on an average morning, more commuters take the E and the F than use the entire rapid-transit system of Chicago (the nation's second-largest system). Buy several tokens at once at the booth or, preferably, at the new token-vending machines now at most stations: You'll not only avoid a long line, but you'll be able to use any station—some token booths close at night.

Buses The **Metropolitan Transit Authority (MTA)** also runs buses for $1.25 a ride. Because buses sit in traffic, during the day they often take twice as long as subways, but they also stay relatively safe, clean—and always windowed. They'll also probably get you closer to your destination, since they stop roughly every two blocks and run crosstown (east-west), as well as uptown and downtown (north-south), unlike the subway which mostly travels north-south. The MTA transfer system provides north-south bus riders with a slip good for a free east-west bus ride, or vice-versa. Just ask the driver for a transfer slip when you pay. Ring when you want to get off. A yellow-painted curb indicates bus stops, but you're better off looking for the blue signpost announcing the bus number or for a glass-walled shelter displaying a map of the bus's route and a schedule of arrival times. Either exact change ($1.25) or a subway token is required; drivers will not accept dollar bills.

ACCOMMODATIONS

If you know someone who knows someone who lives in New York—get that person's phone number. The cost of living in New York is out of sight. Don't expect to fall into a hotel; if you do, odds are it will be a pit. At true full-service establishments, a night will cost you around $125 plus the hefty 14.25% hotel tax. However, some choices are available for under $60 a night, but it depends on your priorities. People traveling alone may want to spend more to stay in a safer neighborhood. The outgoing may prefer a crowded budget-style place; honeymooning couples will not.

Hostels and Student Organizations

New York International HI-AYH Hostel, 891 Amsterdam Ave. (932-2300, fax 932-2574), at 103rd St. Subway: #1, 9, B, or C to 102nd St. Located in a block-long, landmark building designed by Richard Morris Hunt, this is the largest hostel in the U.S., with 90 dorm-style rooms and 480 beds. Shares its site with the **CIEE Student Center** (666-3619), an info depot for travelers, as well as a Council Travel office. Spiffy new carpets, blondewood bunks, spotless bathrooms. Members's kitchens and dining rooms, coin-operated laundry machines ($1), communal TV lounges, and a large outdoor garden. Walking tours and outings. Key-card entry to individual rooms. Secure storage area and individual lockers. 29-day max. stay, 7-day in summer. Open 24 hrs. Check-in any time, check-out 11am (late check-out fee $5). No curfew. Members $22-25 per night, depending on number of beds in room ($3 more for nonmembers). Family room $60. Groups of 4-12 may get private rooms. Linen rental $3. Towel $2. Excellent wheelchair access.

International Student Center, 38 W. 88th St. (787-7706, fax 580-9283), between Central Park West and Columbus Ave. on the Upper West Side. Subway: B or C to 86th St. **Open only to foreigners (but not Canadians) aged 18-30;** you must show a foreign passport to be admitted. A welcoming brownstone on a cheerful, tree-lined street. Single-sex, no-frills bunk rooms. TV lounge with satisfied guests. 7-day max. stay when full. Open daily 8am-11pm. No curfew. $12. Key deposit $5. No reservations, and generally full in summer, but call by 10pm and they'll hold a bed for you for two hours. No wheelchair access.

International Student Hospice, 154 E. 33rd St. (228-7470), between Lexington and Third Ave. in Murray Hill. Subway: #6 to 33rd St. Up a flight of stairs in an inconspicuous converted brownstone with a brass plaque saying "I.S.H." Homey hostel with helpful and knowledgeable owner, exudes friendliness and community. Predominantly European backpacker crowd. Good location. 20 very small rooms with bunk beds. The ceilings are crumbling and the stairs slant precariously, but the house is slowly being restored by residents. Rooms for 2-4 people and hall bathroom. Large common room, lounge, and enough dusty books to last a summer. Strict midnight curfew. $25, some weekly discounts.

Banana Bungalow, 250 W. 77th St. (800-6-HOSTEL or 769-2441, fax 877-5733), between Broadway and Eleventh Ave. Subway: #1 or 9 to 79th St. Walk 2 blocks south and turn right. A continually expanding hostel, with sun deck on the top floor, a tropical-themed lounge/kitchen, and dorm-style rooms sleeping 4-7, each with its own bathroom. Beds $10-15. Reservations available by fax or writing with your Visa or Mastercard number and expiration date. Wheelchair access.

De Hirsch Residence, 1395 Lexington Ave. (415-5650 or 800-858-4692, fax 415-5578), at 92nd St. Subway: #6 to 96th St. Affiliated with the 92nd St. YMHA/YWHA. Large, clean, and convenient. Huge hall bathrooms, kitchens, and laundry machines on every other floor give this hostel a collegiate feel. Single-sex floors, strictly enforced. A/C $3. Access to the many facilities of the 92nd St. Y—free Nautilus and reduced rates for concerts. Organized activities such as video nights in the many common rooms and walking tours of New York. Singles $280 per week; beds in doubles $210 per week. 3-day min. stay. Long-term stays from 2 mo. to 1 yr. available for $595 per month for singles, $420-500 per month for beds in doubles. Application required at least a month in advance; must be a student or working in the city, and must supply references. Wheelchair access.

Sugar Hill International House, 722 Saint Nicholas Ave. (926-7030, fax 283-0108) at 146th St. Subway A, B, C, or D to 145th St. Located on Sugar Hill in Harlem, across from the subway station. Neighborhood's safety questionable. Converted brownstone with huge, well-lit, comfortable rooms. 2-10 people per room in sturdy bunkbeds, hand-built by the owners. Staff is stunningly helpful, with a vast knowledge of NYC and the Harlem area. Kitchens, TV, stereo, and paperback library. Beautiful garden in back. All-female room available. Check-in 9am-10pm. No lockout. $12 per person. Call in advance. The owners of Sugar Hill also run the new 4-floor hostel next door at 730 Saint Nicholas Ave., the **Blue Rabbit Hostel** (491-3892, 800-610-2030). Similar to the Sugar Hill, but with more doubles and hence more privacy. Backyard garden, common room, and kitchen. Spacious rooms. Check-in 9am-10pm. $12, $14 for a private room. Call in advance.

Chelsea International Hostel, 251 W. 20th St. (647-0010), between Seventh and Eighth Ave. Subway: #1, 9, C, or E to 23rd St. The congenial staff at this new 47-bed hostel offers their guests free beer and pizza on Wed. nights, and free beer (bring your own pizza) on Sun. Cramped but adequate 4-person dorm rooms $18; private rooms $35. Reservations recommended; call ahead.

Gershwin Hotel, 3 E. 27th St. (545-8000, fax 684-5546), between Fifth and Madison Ave. Subway: N or R to 28th St. Bright sculptures and European travellers congregate in this airy hotel, while a rooftop garden beckons to sun-seekers.

Passport or ID proving out-of-state or foreign residence required. Free tea and coffee. 20-day max. stay. 24-hr. reception. Check-out 11am. No curfew. 4-bed dorms $17. Doubles $55. Triples $70 Breakfast $2.50. All dorms have lockers.

Big Apple Hostel, 119th W. 45th St. (302-2603, fax 533-2603) between 6th and 7th Ave. Subway: #1,2,3,9,N, or R to 42nd St.; or B,D, or E to Seventh Ave. Centrally located, this hostel offers clean, comfortable, carpeted rooms, a full kitchen with refrigerator, a big back deck, and laundry facilities. Passport nominally required; Americans accepted with out-of-state photo ID or some other convincing means of proving themselves tourists. Open 24 hrs. Bunk in dorm-style room with shared bath $20. Private room with double bed and bath $45-50. Lockers in some rooms, but bring your own lock. No reservations accepted July-Aug., but they'll hold a bed if you call after 11am on the day you want to arrive. Reservations accepted Sept.-June; make them in advance for June.

Mid-City Hostel, 608 Eighth Ave. (704-0562), between 39th and 40th St. on the 3rd and 4th floors. Subway: #1,2,3,9,N, or R to 42nd St.-Seventh Ave.; or A,C, or E to 42nd St.-Ninth Ave. On the east side of Eighth Ave. No sign: just look for the street number on the small door. Don't be intimidated by the seedy neighborhood that surrounds this comfortable hostel. Caters to an international backpacking crowd—a passport and ticket out of the country are required. Americans may be able to talk themselves in. Small breakfast included. 5-day max. stay in summer. Lock-out noon-6pm. Curfew Sun.-Thurs. midnight, Sat.-Sun. 1am. Bunk in dorm-style room with shared bath $18 ($15 Oct.-late June). Reservations will be taken over the phone and should be made weeks in advance for summer.

YMCA—Vanderbilt, 224 E. 47th St. (756-9600, fax 752-0210), between Second and Third Ave. Subway: #6 to 51st St. or E, F to Lexington-Third Ave. 5 blocks from Grand Central Station. Convenient and well-run, with reasonable prices and vigilant security. Clean, brightly-lit lobby bustles with jabbering internationals and internal-frame backpacks. Rooms are quite small, and bathroom-to-people ratio is pretty low, but the perks! Lodgers get free run of the copious athletic facilities (Stairmasters, aerobics classes, Nautilus machines, pool, and sauna), safe-deposit boxes, and guided tours of the city. 25-day max. stay; no NYC residents. Check-in 1-6pm; after 6pm must have major credit card to check in. Check-out at noon, but luggage storage until departure ($1/bag). Five shuttles daily to the airports. Singles $45. Doubles $55. Key deposit $10. Make reservations a week or two in advance and guarantee them with a deposit. Wheelchair access.

YMCA—West Side, 5 W. 63rd St. (787-4400, fax 580-0441). Subway: #1, 9, A, B, C, or D to 59th St.-Columbus Circle. Small, well-maintained rooms but dilapidated halls in a big, popular Y with an impressive, Islamic-inspired facade. Free access to 2 pools, indoor track, racquet courts, and Nautilus equipment. Showers on every floor and spotless bathrooms. A/C and cable TV in every room. Check-out noon; lockout 11pm. Singles $42, with bath $65. Doubles $55, with bath $75. Reservations recommended. A few stairs, otherwise wheelchair-friendly.

Chelsea Center Hostel, 313 W. 29th St. (643-0214), between Eighth and Ninth Ave. Subway: #1, 2, 3, 9, A, C, E to 34th St. Gregarious, knowledgeable staff will help you out with New York tips in multiple languages (including Irish). 25 bunks in a low-ceilinged room make for a cramped setup. Only one shower. Tiny backdoor garden. Check in anytime, but lockout 11am-5pm. Dorm beds $20 in summer, $18 in winter, light breakfast included. Call ahead; usually full in summer.

Hotels

Carlton Arms Hotel, 160 E. 25th St. (684-8337, for reservations 679-0680), between Lexington and Third Ave. Subway: #6 to 23rd St. Each room was designed by a different avant-garde artist. Singles $44. Doubles $57, with bath $65. Triples with bath $78. Pay for 6 nights up front and get the 7th free. Confirm reservations at least 10 days ahead. Student and foreigner discounts.

Pickwick Arms Hotel, 230 E. 51st St. (355-0300 or 800-PICKWIK, fax 755-5029), between Second and Third Ave. Subway: #6 to 51st St. or E, F to Lexington-Third Ave. Business types congregate in this extremely well-located and well-priced mid-sized hotel. Chandeliered marble lobby filled with the silken strains of "Unforgettable You" contrasts with small rooms and microscopic hall bathrooms.

Roof garden and airport service available. Check-in 2pm; check-out 1pm. Singles $45, with shared bath $55. Doubles with one bed and bath $90, two beds $100. Studios (up to four people) $100. Additional person $12. Make reservations.

Roger Williams Hotel, 28 E. 31st St. (684-7500, reservations 800-637-9773, fax 576-4343), at Madison Ave. in the pleasant Murray Hill neighborhood. Subway: #6 to 33rd St. You won't be able to cook up a feast on the 2-burner stove in every room, but the spacious, clean rooms are a steal anyway. Small refrigerators will hold leftovers from the many take-out restaurants lining Madison Ave. All rooms with toilet, bath, cable TV, phone, and kitchenette. 24-hr. security. Singles $65, doubles $70, two twin beds $75, triples $80, and quads $90. Approximately 15% off regular rates with student ID, except for June through mid-July.

Portland Square Hotel, 132 W. 47th St. (382-0600 or 800-388-8988, fax 382-0684), between Sixth and Seventh Ave. Subway: B, D, F, Q to 50th St.–Sixth Ave. Rooms are carpeted, clean, and entirely comfortable, with A/C and cable TV, but the hotel's main asset is its great location. Attracts mostly foreigners. Singles with shared bath $40, with private bath $60. Doubles $85. Triples $90. Quads $95.

Herald Square Hotel, 19 W. 31st St. (279-4017 or 800-727-1888), at Fifth Ave. Subway: B, D, F, N, or R to 34th St. In the original Beaux Arts home of *Life* magazine (built in 1893). The reading cherub entitled the "Winged Life," carved by Philip Martiny, above the entrance was a frequent presence on the pages of early *Life* magazines. Work by some of America's most noted illustrators adorns the lobby, halls, and rooms. Tiny, clean rooms with TV and A/C. Singles with shared bath $40, with private bath $50. Doubles $55/80. Reservations recommended.

Hotel Wolcott, 4 W. 31st St. (268-2900, fax 563-0096), between Fifth and Sixth Ave. Subway: B, D, F, N, or R to 34th St. An ornately mirrored and marbled hall leads into this inexpensive, newly renovated hotel. New furniture and carpeting, cable TV, and efficient A/C. Singles $40, with bath $55-60. Doubles $45/55-65. Triples $65-75. Make summer reservations a month or more in advance.

Washington Square Hotel, 103 Waverly Pl. (777-9515, 800-222-0418, fax 979-8373), at MacDougal St. Subway: A, B, C, D, E, F, or Q to W. 4th St. Fantastic location. Glitzy marble and brass lobby, with a pretty cool medieval gate in front. TV, A/C, and key-card entry to individual rooms. Clean and comfortable; friendly and multilingual staff. Singles $58. Doubles $85. Two twin beds $95. Quads $112. Reservation required 2-3 weeks in advance.

Hotel Iroquois, 49 W. 44th St. (840-3080 or 800-332-7220, fax 398-1754), near Fifth Ave. Subway: B, D, or F to 47th St.-Rockefeller Ctr. Pink and blue, slightly worn but spacious rooms in an old prewar building. This hotel once hosted James Dean and is now the stop of choice for Greenpeace and other environmental activists when in town. Check-out noon. Singles and doubles $75-100. Suites (up to 5 people) $125-150. Student discounts available, and all prices negotiable during winter. Reservations advisable a few weeks in advance during the summer.

Mansfield Hotel, 12 W. 44th St. (944-6050 or 800-255-5167, fax 740-2508), at Fifth Ave. Subway: B, D, or F to 47th St.-Rockefeller Ctr. A dignified establishment housed in a turn-of-the-century building with comfortable leather couches in the lobby and beautiful oak doors in the hallways. Rooms in process of renovation; the new ones have new lighting, paint, and furniture, and some of the larger ones have whirlpool tubs. Be sure to request a renovated room specifically when making reservations (1 month in advance for summer). Check-out noon. Singles $65. Doubles $75. Triples $85. Quads $100. Large suites $120 for 5 people, $140 for 6.

Hotel Remington, 129 W. 46th St. (221-2600, fax 764-7481), between Broadway and Sixth Ave. Subway: B, D, or F to 47th St.-Rockefeller Ctr.; or #1, 2, 3, 9, N, or R to 42nd St.-Times Sq. Centrally located. Plush carpeting, bedspread, and curtains in matching orange hang in reasonably large rooms. All rooms with TV and A/C. Singles $60, with bath $75. Doubles $60/80. Triples $65/85.

Broadway-American Hotel, 222 W. 77th St. (362-1100, 800-446-4556), at Broadway. Subway: #1 or 9 to 79th St. Cool, clean, and ultra-modern with few right angles and lots of charcoal-gray; if it were roomier, it'd be a corporate law office. All rooms have refrigerators and TV; kitchen available for all guests. Singles $45, with bath $79. Doubles $65/89. Triples $75/99. Reservations recommended.

Riverview Hotel, 113 Jane St. (929-0060), near West St. on the Hudson in Greenwich Village, and between W. 12th and W. 14th St. Subway: #1 or 9 to Christopher St. Moderately safe area, particularly for two or more. Clean and friendly, but no frills. Singles are cramp-inducingly small but doubles are decent. No deadbolts on room doors. Shared co-ed bathrooms on the hall. Singles $25. Doubles $39.

Senton Hotel, 39-41 W. 27th St. (684-5800), at Broadway. Subway: R to 28th St. Comfortable beds in spacious quarters. TV, including HBO, cable, and dirty movies. Basic accommodations—spartan but newly renovated, with a shockingly incongruous bright-blue paint job. Not the best of neighborhoods at night, but the hotel has 24-hr. security and guests are not allowed. Singles with communal hall bath $40. Doubles $60. Suites (2 double beds) $65.

Hotel Grand Union, 34 E. 32nd St. (683-5890), fax 689-7397), between Madison and Park Ave. Subway: #6 to 33rd St. Centrally located and reasonably priced. Big, comfy rooms equipped with cable, phone, A/C, a mini-fridge, and full bathroom. 24-hr. security. Singles $70. Doubles $90. Will allow extra people in a room.

FOOD

This city takes its food seriously. New York will dazzle you with its stupendous culinary bounty, serving the needs of its diverse (and hungry) population. Ranging from mom-and-pop diners to elegant five-star restaurants, the food offered here will suit all appetites and pocketbooks. With thousands of restaurants opening and closing every year, the budget traveler can do some research of his or her own. Listed below are some choice places divided by neighborhood, but feel free to venture out, explore, and take a bite out of the Big Apple yourself.

East Midtown

East Midtown teems with restaurants. Around noon to 2pm, the many delis and cafés become swamped with harried junior executives trying to eat quickly and get back to work. The 50s on **Second Ave.** and the area immediately surrounding Grand Central Station are filled with good, cheap fare. You might also check out grocery stores, such as the **Food Emporium,** 969 Second Ave. (593-2224), between 51st and 52nd, **D'Agostino,** Third Ave. (684-3133), between 35th and 36th, or **Associated Group Grocers,** 1396 Second Ave., between E. 48th and E. 49th St. This part of town has many public spaces (plazas, lobbies, parks) to picnic; try **Greenacre Park,** 51st St. between Second and Third; **Paley Park,** 53rd St. between Fifth and Madison; or the **United Nations Plaza,** 48th St. at First Ave.

Dosanko, 423 Madison Ave. (688-8575), at E. 47th St. Very cheap, very fast, and very good Japanese food. The ramen is the dish to get ($5.30-7, depending on the toppings). Sit-down a few blocks up at 217 E. 59th St. (752-3936), between Second and Third Ave. Open Mon.-Fri. 11:30am-11pm, Sat.-Sun. noon-8pm.

Fortune Garden, 845 Second Ave. (687-7471), between E. 45th and E. 46th St. The prices in the restaurant are sky-high ($15-20), but take-out is much cheaper. Weekday lunch is two appetizers and an entree (beef and broccoli, General Gao's chicken, or 16 other choices) for $6. Dinner $7-11. Open daily 11:30am-3am.

Oyster Bar and Restaurant (490-6650), in Grand Central Station. Excellent seafood for the weary traveler. The prices are a little high, but the chowder is a great deal—$3.25 for a huge bowl. Open Mon.-Fri. 11:30am-9:30pm.

West Midtown

Your best bets here are generally along Eighth Ave. between 34th and 59th St. in the area known as **Hell's Kitchen.** Although once deserving of its name, this area has given birth to an array of ethnic restaurants. The area's cheapest meals can be had in the **fast food** variety, on the east side of **Seventh Ave.** between 33rd and 34th Those whose resources reach down deep should take a meal on **Restaurant Row,** on 46th St. between Eighth and Ninth Ave., which offers a solid block of dining primarily to a pre-theater crowd (arriving after 8pm will make getting a table easier).

Sapporo, 152 W. 49th St. (869-8972), near Seventh Ave. A Japanese translation of the American diner, with the grill in full view. A favorite snack spot for Broadway cast members, suits, and Japanese locals. Portions are huge and flavors astounding. Open Mon.-Fri. 11am-1am, Sat.-Sun. 11:30am-11:45pm.

Carnegie Delicatessen, 854 Seventh Ave. (757-2245), at 55th St. One of New York's great delis. Eat elbow-to-elbow at long tables, and chomp on huge sandwiches and free pickles. Gargantuan cheesecake $5.45. Open daily 6:30am-4am.

Ariana Afghan Kebab, 769 Ninth Ave. (307-1612 or 307-1629), between 51st and 52nd St. Excellent Afghani food at reasonable prices. Try the *beef tikka kebab*, chunks of marinated beef cooked over wood charcoal and served with rice, bread, and salad ($7.50). Open Mon.-Sat. noon-10pm.

Uncle Vanya Café, 315 W. 54th St. (262-0542), between Eighth and Ninth Ave. Delicacies of czarist Russia range from *borscht* ($3) to *teftley*, Russian meatballs in sour cream sauce ($5.50) to caviar (market price). Undiscovered, homey, and very good. Open Mon.-Sat. noon-11pm, Sun. noon-10pm.

Lower Midtown and Chelsea

Straddling the extremes, the lower Midtown dining scene is neither fast-food commercial nor *haute cuisine* trendy. East of Fifth Ave. on **Lexington,** Pakistani and Indian restaurants battle for customers. Liberally sprinkled throughout are Korean corner shops that are equal parts grocery and buffet hot and cold salad bars.

Finding food in Chelsea isn't always easy. Good food tends not to be cheap, and cheap food is rarely good. The neighborhood is dotted with fake-retro diners that offer unexceptional $6 hamburgers and $7 omelettes. The best offerings are the products of the large Mexican and Central American community in the southern section of the neighborhood. **Eighth Avenue** provides the best restaurant browsing.

Jai-ya, 396 Third Ave. (889-1330), at 28th St. Thai and Oriental food that critics rave over. *Pad thai* $8—a definite steal. Also at 81-11 Broadway in Elmhurst, Queens. Open daily Mon.-Fri. 11:30am-midnight, Sat. noon-midnight, Sun. 5pm-midnight.

Daphne's Hibiscus, 243 E. 14th St. (505-1180 and 505-1247), between Second and Third Ave. Dim lighting and intricate woodwork give this Caribbean restaurant an authentic Jamaican feel. Try the chicken cooked in coconut milk ($11), the jerk pork ($9), or the special meat-filled pastries called "patties." Most entrees $7.50-9.50. The plantains make an excellent side dish. Happy hour Mon.-Fri. 5-7pm.

Zen Palate, 34 E. Union Sq. (614-9345, fax 614-9401), across from the park. Gourmet veggie food, with an Asian twist. Stir-fried rice fettucini $6.50. Moo shu, Mexican style $7.45. Open Mon.-Sat. 11:30am-3pm and 5-11pm, Sun. 5-10:30pm. Also at 46th st. and 9th Ave. (582-1669)

Kitchen, 218 Eighth Ave. (243-4433), near W. 21st St. This take-out kitchen specializes in Mexican food, with hot red peppers dangling from the ceiling. There's no dining room here. Open Sun.-Thurs. 11:30am-9:30pm, Fri.-Sat. 11:30am-10pm.

Upper East Side

Unless you feel like eating a large bronze sculpture or an Armani suit, you won't find many dining opportunities on Museum Mile along Fifth and Madison Ave., aside from some charming cappuccino haunts, brunch breweries, and near-invisible ritzy restaurants. For less glamorous and more affordable dining, head east of Park Ave. Hot dog hounds shouldn't miss the 100% beef "better than filet mignon" $1.50 franks and exotic fruit drinks at **Papaya King,** 179 E. 86th St. (369-0648), off Third Ave. (open Sun.-Thurs. 8am-1am, Fri.-Sat. 9am-3am). For the best New York bagels, try **H&H East,** 1551 Second Ave. (734-7441), between 80th and 81st St., which bakes them round-the-clock. Don't feel confined to restaurant dining; you can buy provisions at a grocery store or deli and picnic in honor of frugality in Central Park.

ecco'la, 1660 third ave. (860-5609), corner of 93rd st. if you don't mind waiting with the rest of the neighborhood, you're in for a treat. Eat fresh pasta pockets filled with lobster, mushrooms, and scallions in an avocado cream sauce ($9). Open Sun.-Thurs. noon-11:45pm, Fri.-Sat. noon-12:30am.

Tang Tang Noodles and More, 1328 Third Ave. (249-2102/3/4), at 76th St. Cheap, hot, tasty Chinese noodles and dumplings. Not one noodle dish over $5.75—most around $5. Dense crowds but quick service, and very authentic food. Open Sun.-Thurs. 11:30am-11pm, Fri.-Sat. 11:30am-midnight.

El Pollo, 1746 First Ave. (996-7810), between 90th and 91st. This secret Peruvian dive has mastered the practice of cooking chicken and potatoes, which they serve with complimentary wine in their cramped bowling alley of a restaurant. Plump chickens are marinated and spit-roasted, topped with a variety of sauces. The corkscrew fries ($2.50) alone make it worth the trip. The *quinoa* pudding is quite a taste treat for dessert. Half chicken $5. BYOB. Open daily 11:30am-11pm.

EJ's Luncheonette, 1271 Third Ave. (472-0600), at 73rd St. Eternally crowded; huge portions of good food. Blueberry-strawberry on buttermilk pancakes $6.50. Hamburgers also a great deal ($5.75, fries included). Open Mon.-Thurs. 8am-11pm, Fri.-Sat. 8am-midnight, Sun. 8am-10:30pm.

Upper West Side

Unlike many other New York neighborhoods, the Upper West Side lacks a definitive typology of restaurants. Cheap pizza joints often neighbor chic eateries; street vendors hawk sausages in the shadow of pricey specialty stores. **Columbus Avenue** provides lots of options within a budgeters realm. Wander down the tempting aisles of **Zabar's,** 2245 Broadway (787-2002), at 81st, the gourmet deli and grocery that never ends. The original **H&H Bagels,** 2239 Broadway (595-8000), at 80th, bakes the best bagels in NYC (a noble title) all day, every day. Get a hot one.

La Caridad, 2199 Broadway (874-2780), at 78th St. Feed yourself and a pack of burros with one entree at this successful Chinese-Spanish hybrid. *Arroz con pollo* (¼-chicken with yellow rice) $5.55. Fast-food ambience, but so what? Lunch and dinner rushes cause lines. Open Mon.-Sat. 11:30am-1am, Sun. 11:30am-10:30pm.

Mingala West, 325 Amsterdam Ave. (873-0787), at 75th St. Burmese cooking uses rice noodles, peanut sauces, coconuts, and curries. Generous $5 lunch specials Mon.-Fri. noon-4pm; $6-9 "light meal" samplers 4:30-6:30pm. Open Mon.-Thurs. noon-11pm, Fri.-Sat. noon-midnight.

Empire Szechuan Gourmet, 2574 Broadway (663-6004/5/6), at 97th St. A favorite of Upper West Siders. Exhaustive menu features low-calorie entrees, hors d'oeuvres, *dim sum* ($1-6, Mon.-Fri. 10:30am-3:30pm and Sat.-Sun. 10am-3:30pm), a sushi bar, and Japanese dishes. Generous lunch specials $5 (Mon.-Fri. 11:30am-3pm). Dinner coupons on take-out menus in front of the restaurant. Open Mon.-Tues. 10:30am-midnight, Wed.-Sun. 10:30am-2am.

Diane's Uptown, 251 Columbus Ave. (799-6750), near 71st St. Large portions and reasonable prices make Diane's a popular hangout. Diane's is known for her burgers ($4.50). Frequently, burgers and omelettes are $1 off. Open daily 11am-2am.

Greenwich Village

Whatever your take is on the West Village's bohemian authenticity, it's undeniable that all the free-floating artistic angst does result in many creative (and inexpensive) food venues. The aggressive and entertaining street life makes stumbling around and deciding where to go almost as much fun as eating. Try the major avenues for cheap, decent food. The European-style bistros of **Bleecker Street** and **MacDougal Street,** south of Washington Square Park, have perfected the homey "antique" look. You can't eat inside the **Murray Cheese Shop,** 257 Bleecker St. (243-3289; open Mon.-Sat. 8am-7pm, Sun. 9am-5pm), at Cornelia St., but the 400-plus kinds of cheese justify a picnic. Try the camembert in rosemary and sage ($4), and get the bread next door at **A. Zito Bread.** Late night in the Village is a unique New York treat: as the sky grows dark, the streets quicken. Don't let a mob at the door make you hesitant about sitting over your coffee for hours and watching the spectacle. Explore twisting side streets and alleyways where you can drop into a jazz club or join Off-Broadway theater-goers as they settle down over a burger and a beer to write their own reviews. Or ditch the high life and slump down 8th St. to **Sixth Ave.** to find some of the most respectable pizza in the city at **John's** (see below).

John's Pizzeria, 278 Bleecker St. (243-1680), at Jones St. Loud NYU hangout caters to fratboys, freaks, and even U.S. presidents, if you believe the handwriting on the wall. The pizza's cooked in a brick oven and has thin, crispy crust and just enough cheese. Pizza for two or three costs $9. If the place is full, they'll find room for you at **John's Too** next door. No slices; table service only. Open Mon.-Sat. 11:30am-11:30pm, Sun. noon-midnight. John's also has locations at 4877 Broadway (942-7288), 408 E 64th (935-2895), and 43 W 64th (721-7001).

Cucina Stagionale, 275 Bleecker St. (924-2707), at Jones St. Unpretentious Italian dining in a clean, pretty environment. Packed with loyals on weekends—the lines reach the street at times. Sample the soft *calamari* in spicy red sauce ($6) or the pasta *putanesca* ($7) to realize why. Pasta dishes all under $8, meat dishes under $10. Open Sun.-Thurs. noon-midnight, Fri.-Sat. noon-1am.

Elephant and Castle, 68 Greenwich Ave. (243-1400), near Seventh Ave. Their motto is *"j'adore les omelettes,"* and boy, are those omelettes adorable ($5-7). The apple, cheddar, and walnut creation is weird but good. Open Mon.-Thurs. 8:30am-midnight, Fri. 8:30am-1am, Sat. 10am-1am, Sun. 10am-midnight.

Tea and Sympathy, 108 Greenwich Ave. (807-8329), between Jane and W. 13th St. An English tea house—high tea, cream tea, and good old-fashioned British cuisine. Filled with kitschy teacups and salt shakers, fading photos of obviously English families, and beautiful chipped china. Afternoon tea (the whole shebang—sandwiches, tea, scones, rarebit) $11, cream tea (tea, scones, and jam) $6, shepherd pie $6.75. Open daily approximately 11:30am-8:30pm.

Caffé Reggio, 119 MacDougal St. (475-9557), south of W. 3rd St. Celebs and wanna-bes crowd the oldest café in the Village. Good cappuccino ($2.25) and pastries ($2.50-3.50). Open Sun.-Thurs. 10am-2am, Fri.-Sat 10am-4am.

SoHo and TriBeCa

In SoHo, food, like life, is all about image. Most of the restaurants here tend to be preoccupied with decor, and most aim to serve a stylishly healthful cuisine. Expect a lot of lean meats and fresh vegetables, prepared with wonderful and unusual sauces, served in sizable portions. With the image lifestyle, of course, comes money, so don't be surprised if you find it hard to get a cheap meal. Often the best deal in SoHo is brunch, when the neighborhood shows its most good-natured front.

Dining in TriBeCa is generally a much funkier (and blessedly cheaper) experience than in chic SoHo. The style of choice here has a dressed-down, folksy, flea marketish flavor. TriBeCa is much more industrial than SoHo, and restaurants are often hidden like little oases among the hulking warehouses and decaying buildings.

Arturo's Coal Oven Pizza, 106 W. Houston St. (677-3820). While the decor seems guided by a definite "Old and Dark" motif, the coal-oven pizza is truly delicious. You'll find artsy types and other regulars here along with a full bar. Pianist plays dinner jazz nightly 8pm-1am. A number of tables outside allow outdoor dining. Pizzas $10-16, pasta $8-10, other Italian entrees $10-14, wine $7-9 by the carafe. Open Mon.-Thurs. 4pm-1am, Fri.-Sat. 4pm-2am, Sun. 4pm-midnight.

Bubby's, 120 Hudson St. (219-0666), between Franklin and N. Moore St. The rough brick walls with white woodwork, unupholstered wooden window benches, and the two walls of windows all add to the stylish simplicity of this small café/restaurant. Great scones, muffins, and pies keep this place packed with locals, but lunch and dinner are excellent as well; try the half-spicy jerk chicken with homemade mashed potatoes and greens ($8.75). Expect a wait on weekend mornings. Open Mon.-Wed. 7am-10:30pm, Thurs.-Fri. 7am-11pm, Sat.-Sun. 9am-11pm.

Abyssinia, 35 Grand St. (226-5959), at Thompson St. Terrific Ethiopian restaurant which seats you on low-to-the-ground, hand-carved stools at tables made of woven fibers akin to wicker. Scoop up the food with pieces of dense and spongy *injara* bread. Vegetarian entrees $6-8, meat dishes $8.50-12. Open Mon.-Thurs. 6-11pm, Fri. 6pm-midnight, Sat. 1pm-midnight, Sun. 1-11pm.

East Village, Lower East Side, and Alphabet City

The neighborhood took in the huddled masses, and, in return, immigrant culture after immigrant culture has left its residue in the form of cheap restaurants. Culinary cultures clash on the lower end of the East Side, where pasty-faced punks and starving artists dine alongside an older generation conversing in Polish, Hungarian, and Yiddish. **First** and **Second Avenues** are the best for restaurant-exploring, and sidewalk cafés and bars line **Avenue A.** Check out **6th St.** between First and Second Ave., a block composed of several Indian restaurants offering $3 lunch specials. For kosher eating, head on down to the Lower East Side south of East Houston St. **Kossar's Hot Bialys,** 367 Grand St. at Essex St. (473-4810; open 24 hrs.), makes bialys that recall the heyday of the Lower East Side.

Katz's Delicatessen, 205 E. Houston St. (254-2246), near Orchard. Classic informal deli established in 1888. The fake-orgasm scene in *When Harry Met Sally* took place here. Have an overstuffed corned beef sandwich with a pickle for $6.65. Mail-order department enables you to send a salami to a loved one (or, perhaps, an ex-loved one). With testimonial letters from Carter and Reagan, how could it be bad? Open Sun.-Wed. 8am-9pm, Thurs. 8am-10pm, Fri.-Sat. 8am-11pm.

Ratner's Restaurant, 138 Delancey St. (677-5588), just west of the Manhattan Bridge. The most famous of the kosher restaurants, partly because of its frozen-food line. Despite the run-down surroundings, this place is large, shiny, and popular. Jewish dietary laws are strictly followed and only dairy food is served; you will have to go elsewhere for a pastrami sandwich. Feast on fruit blintzes and sour cream ($9). Open Sun.-Thurs. 6am-midnight, Fri. 6am-3pm, Sat. sundown-2am.

Dojo Restaurant, 24 St. Mark's Pl. (674-9821), between Second and Third Ave. One of the most popular restaurants and hangouts in the East Village, and rightly so. Healthful, delicious, and inexpensive food. Tasty soyburgers, brown rice, and salad $3.20. Outdoor tables. Open Sun.-Thurs. 11am-1am, Fri.-Sat. 11am-2am.

Al Hamra, 203 First Ave. (505-6559), between 12th and 13th St. This phenomenally cheap and undiscovered restaurant serves huge plates of Indian and Pakistani food, all for under $5. No decor to speak of—oh well. Open 24 hrs.

Second Ave. Delicatessen, 156 Second Ave. (677-0606), at 10th St. The definitive New York deli, established in 1954. People come into the city just to be snubbed by the waiters here. Have pastrami (reputed to be the best in the city) or tongue on rye bread for $7.50. Note the Hollywood-style star plaques embedded in the sidewalk outside: this was once the heart of the Yiddish theater district. Open Sun.-Thurs. 8am-midnight, Fri.-Sat. 8am-2am.

Ukrainian East Village Restaurant, 140 Second Ave. (529-5024), between 8th and 9th St. More genuine Ukrainians than in the other East Village borscht-houses. Potato *pirogi* $4.75, cheese or meat *pirogi* $5, stuffed cabbage with potato and mushroom gravy $6. Open Sun.-Thurs. noon-11pm, Fri.-Sat. noon-midnight.

Chinatown

If you're looking for cheap, authentic Asian fare, join the crowds that push through the narrow, chaotic streets of one of the oldest Chinatowns in the U.S. In the numerous small stores that operate here, you can find rare items like Chinese housewares, hermetically sealed whole fish, roots, and spices of all stripes. The neighborhood's 200-plus restaurants cook up some of the best Chinese, Thai, and Vietnamese cooking around. Once-predominantly Cantonese cooking has now burgeoned into different cuisines from the various regions of China: hot and spicy Hunan or Szechuan food, the sweet and mildly spiced seafood of Soochow, or the hearty and filling fare of Beijing. Cantonese *dim sum* is still a Sunday afternoon tradition, when waiters roll carts filled with assorted dishes of bite-sized goodies up and down the aisles. Simply point at what you want (beware of "Chinese Bubblegum," a euphemism for tripe), and the end of the meal, the empty dishes on your table are tallied up.

Excellent Dumpling House, 111 Lafayette St. (219-0212 or 219-0213), just south of Canal St. Terrific vegetarian and meat dumplings fried, steamed, or boiled ($4 for 8 sizeable pieces). Lunch specials (served Mon.-Fri. 11am-3pm) include entree such as shredded pork with garlic sauce or chicken with black bean sauce, choice of soup, fried rice and a wonton (all specials $5.50). Open daily 11am-9pm.

HSF (Hee Sheung Fung), 46 Bowery (374-1319), just south of Canal St. Tasteful, large, and crowded. Well-known for its fantastic *dim sum* (served daily 7:30am-5pm) and for its "Hot Pot buffet." The Hot Pot is a sort of Asian equivalent to fondue, in which a huge pot of boiling broth is placed in the center of your table with a platter of more than 50 raw ingredients spread around it; you dip each piece into the flavored broth, and then into one of several sauces. All ingredients are unlimited ($18 per person). Open daily 7:30am-5am.

House of Vegetarian, 68 Mott St. (226-6572), between Canal and Bayard St. Faux chicken, faux beef, faux lamb, and faux fish comprise the huge menu; all the animals are made from soy and wheat. Most entrees $6-10. An ice-cold lotus seed or lychee drink ($2) hits the spot on hot summer days. Open daily 11am-11pm.

Road to Mandalay, 380 Broome St. (226-4218), at Mulberry St. A rare Burmese pearl washed up on the Italian shores of Mulberry St. Start with the coconut noodle soup ($3.50) and the 1000-layered pancake, a delicate Burmese bread ($2.50). Entrees $8-11.50. Open Mon.-Fri. 4-11pm, Sat.-Sun. 11am-11pm.

Little Italy

A chunk of Naples seems to have migrated to this lively yet very compact quarter roughly bounded by Canal, Lafayette, Houston St., and the Bowery. **Mulberry Street** is the main drag and the appetite avenue of Little Italy. Stroll here after 7pm to catch street life but arrive earlier to get one of the better tables. For the sake of variety and thrift, dine at a restaurant but get your just desserts at a café.

Ballato, 55 E. Houston St. (274-8881), at Mott St. As much a child of SoHo as of Little Italy, Ballato serves its impeccable southern Italian cooking to a thankful crowd. Pasta $9-12. Open daily noon-11pm; closed June-Aug. Sun. noon-5pm.

La Mela, 167 Mulberry St. (431-9493), between Broome and Grand St. If Little Italy believed in cult restaurants, La Mela would be the kingpin. People travel from as far as Rapid City for the famed chicken *scarpariello*. Outdoor seating, complete with a guitar-touting bard. Entrees $12-15. Open daily noon-11pm.

Paolucci's, 149 Mulberry St. (226-9653), between Grand and Hester St. Family-owned restaurant with a penchant for heaping portions. Chicken *cacciatore* with salad and spaghetti $12. Daily lunch specials (11:30am-5pm) $5-9.50. Open Sun. 11:30am-10pm, Mon.-Thurs. 11:30am-10:30pm, Fri.-Sat. 11:30am-11:30pm.

La Bella Ferrara, 110 Mulberry St. (966-1488). Named after the city that brought you turbo power, La Bella Ferrara maintains one of the largest selection of pastries around. Pastries $1.50-2. Definitely worth a visit; you can sit outside on the patio and enjoy your cannoli in peace. Open Sun.-Thurs. 9am-1am, Fri.-Sat. 9am-2am.

Financial District

Lower Manhattan is luncheon heaven to sharply-clad Wall St. brokers and bankers—it offers cheap food prepared lightning-fast at ultra-low prices and always available as take-out. Bargain-basement cafeterias here can fill you up with everything from gazpacho to Italian sausages. Fast-food joints pepper Broadway near Dey and John St. just a few feet from the overpriced offerings of the Main Concourse of the World Trade Center. In the summer, ethnic food pushcarts form a solid wall along Broadway between Cedar and Liberty St.

Zigolini's, 66 Pearl St. (425-7171), at Coenties Alley. One of the few places in the area where indoor air-conditioned seating abounds, this authentically Italian restaurant serves huge and filling sandwiches ($5-7), as well as some great pasta dishes. Open Mon.-Fri. 7am-7pm.

Frank's Papaya, 192 Broadway (693-2763), at John St. Excellent value, quick service. Very close to the World Trade Center. Hot dog 70¢. Breakfast (egg, ham, cheese, coffee) $1.50. Open Mon.-Sat. 5:30am-10pm, Sun. 5:30am-5:30pm.

Broadway Farm, 181 Broadway (587-1105 or 227-0701), between John and Cortland St. A salad bar the size of a Winnebago—choose your favorite greens and fruit, along with lots of hot pasta and Chinese dishes ($4 per lb.). Open 24 hrs.

Brooklyn

Ethnic flavor changes every two blocks in Brooklyn. **Brooklyn Heights** offers nouvelle cuisine, but specializes in pita bread and *baba ghanoush.* **Williamsburg** is dotted with kosher and cheap Italian restaurants, **Greenpoint** is a borscht-lover's paradise, and **Flatbush** serves up Jamaican and other West Indian cuisine. Brooklyn now has its own Chinatown in Sunset Park.

El Gran Castillo de Jagua, 345 Flatbush Ave. (718-622-8700), at Carlton St. near Grand Army Plaza. Subway: D or Q to 7th Ave. Terrific for cheap, authentic Spanish food. Meat dinners with rice and beans or plantains and salad $5-7. *Mofungo* (crushed plantains with roast pork and gravy) $3.50. Open daily 7am-midnight.

Primorski Restaurant, 282 Brighton Beach Ave. (718-891-3111), between Brighton Beach 2nd St. and 3rd St. Subway: D or Q to Brighton Beach, then 4 blocks east on Brighton Beach Ave. Populated by Russian-speaking Brooklynites, this restaurant serves the best Ukrainian borscht ($2.25) in the Western hemisphere. Many of the waiters struggle with English, but every dish is tasty. Lunch special is the best lunch deal in NYC—your choice of among three soups and about 15 entrees, bread, salad, and coffee or tea. (Mon.-Fri. 11am-5pm, Sat.-Sun. 11am-4pm; $4) Nightly entertainment, including disco music. Open daily 11am-2am.

Donna's Jerk Chicken, 3125 Church Ave. (718-287-8182), between 31st and 32nd St. in Flatbush. Subway: #2 or 5 to Church Ave. and 2 blocks east. Jerk chicken is a Jamaican specialty—crispy chicken roasted with a sweet and very peppery marinade. Enticing entrees ($5-9). Open daily 11am-midnight.

Junior's, 986 Flatbush Ave. Extension (718-852-5257), across the Manhattan Bridge at De Kalb St. Subway: #2, 3, 4, 5, B, D, M, N, Q, or R to Atlantic Ave. Lit up like a jukebox, Junior's feeds classic roast beef and brisket to hordes of loyals. Dinner specials $10. Suburbanites drive for hours to satisfy their cheesecake cravings here (plain slice $3.50). Open Sun.-Thurs. 6:30am-12:30am, Fri.-Sat. 6:30am-2am.

Moroccan Star, 205 Atlantic Ave. (718-643-0800), in Brooklyn Heights. Subway: #2, 3, 4, 5, M, or R to Borough Hall, then down 4 blocks on Court St. Ensconced in the local Arab community, this restaurant serves delicious and reasonably cheap food. Try the *pastello,* a delicate semi-sweet chicken pie with almonds ($8.75). Open Sun. noon-10pm, Tues.-Thurs. 10am-11pm, Fri.-Sat. 11am-11pm.

Stylowa Restaurant, 694 Manhattan Ave. (718-383-8993), between Norman and Nassau Ave. in Greenpoint. Subway: G to Nassau Ave. Polish at its best and cheapest. Entrees ($3-8) served with a glass of compote (pink, apple-flavored drink). Open Mon.-Thurs. noon-9pm, Fri. noon-10pm, Sat. 11am-10pm, Sun. 11am-9pm.

Tom's Restaurant, 782 Washington Ave. (718-636-9738), at Sterling Pl. Subway: #2 or 3 to Brooklyn Museum. Walk a ½-block east to Washington St. and then 1½ blocks north. The best breakfast place in Brooklyn—an old-time luncheonette with a soda fountain and 50s-style hyper-friendly service. Famous golden challah french toast $2.75. Breakfast served all day. Open Mon.-Sat. 6:30am-4pm.

Queens

With nearly every ethnic group represented in Queens, this often overlooked borough offers visitors authentic and reasonably priced international cuisine away from Manhattan's urban neighborhoods. **Astoria** specializes in discount shopping and cheap eats. Take the G or R train to Steinway St. and Broadway and start browsing— the pickings are good in every direction. In **Flushing,** excellent Chinese, Japanese, and Korean restaurants flourish, often making use of authentic ingredients such as skatefish, squid, and tripe. **Bell Boulevard** in Bayside, out east near the Nassau border, is the center of Queens nightlife for the young, white, and semi-affluent; on most weekends you can find crowds of natives bar-hopping here. **Jamaica Avenue** in downtown Jamaica and **Linden Blvd.** in neighboring St. Albans are lined with restaurants specializing in African-American and West Indian food.

Pastrami King, 124-24 Queens Blvd. (718-263-1717), near 82nd Ave., in Kew Gardens. Subway: E or F to Union Tpke./Kew Gardens. Exit station following sign that says "Courthouse" and "Q10 bus;" then go left following the sign to the north side of Queens Blvd.; it's 2 blocks ahead and across the street. Everything here, from the meats to the coleslaw to the pickles, is made on the premises. The home-cured pastrami and corned beef are among the best in New York. Take out a 3-inch-thick pastrami on rye for $6. Open Sun.-Fri. 11am-9pm, Sat. 11am-10pm.

Uncle George's, 33-19 Broadway, Astoria (718-626-0593), at 33rd St. Subway: N to Broadway, then 2 blocks east; or G or R to Steinway St., then 4 blocks west. This popular Greek restaurant, known as *"Barba Yiogis O Ksenihtis"* to the locals, serves inexpensive and hearty Greek delicacies around the clock. Almost all entrees are under $10; try the roast leg of lamb with potatoes ($8), or, if you're feeling intrepid, the octopus sauteed with vinegar ($7). Open daily 24 hrs.

Jack 'n' Jill's, 187-29 Linden Blvd., St. Albans (718-723-9344), near Mexico St. Subway: E, J, or Z to Jamaica Ctr., then the Q4 bus to St. Albans and Linden Blvd.; ask to be let off at Farmers Blvd. and then backtrack 1 block. The BBQ in this small joint will give you a good dose of Southern harmony. Open daily noon-9pm.

Bronx

When Italian immigrants settled the Bronx, they brought their recipes and a tradition of hearty communal dining. While much of the Bronx is a culinary disaster zone, the New York *cognoscenti* soon discovered the few oases along **Arthur Avenue.** With a sexy interior, and inviting outdoor tables, **Egioio Pastry Shop,** 622 E. 187th St., makes the best *gelato* in the Bronx.

Ann & Tony's, 2407 Arthur Ave. (933-1469), at 187th St. Typical of Arthur Ave., this bistro has not only an understated and comfortable decor but excellent food as well. Ann & Tony's has specials for dinner that run as low as $6, salad included. For lunch, sandwiches begin at $5. Open Tues.-Thurs. 11:30am-10pm, Fri. 11:30am-11pm, Sat. noon-midnight, Sun. 2-9pm.

Mario's, 2342 Arthur Ave. (584-1188), near 186th St. Five generations of the Migliucci *famiglia* have worked the kitchen of this celebrated southern Italian *trattoria.* Mario's appears in the pages of Puzo's *Godfather.* Celebrities pass through, among them the starting lineups for the Yankees and the Giants. Try *spiedini alla romana,* a deep-fried sandwich made with anchovy sauce and mozzarella ($8). Open Sun. and Tues.-Thurs. noon-10:30pm, Fri.-Sat. noon-midnight.

Caffè Margherita, 689 E. 187 St., near Arthur Ave. In the late '70s the *New York Times* called Margherita's cappuccino the "best in the world." On hot summer nights, retreat from the city into the fantasies offered by this *caffè,* complete with an outdoor jukebox with tunes ranging from Sinatra and Madonna to Italian folk music. Open daily 8am-midnight.

SIGHTS

You can tell tourists in New York City a mile away by a single feature—they are looking up. The internationally famous New York skyline is an optical illusion; while it can be seen miles away, the tallest skyscraper seems like just another building when you're standing next to it. This sightseeing quandary may explain why many New Yorkers have never visited some of the major sights in their hometown. In this densely-packed city, even the most mind-boggling landmarks serve as backdrops for everyday life. The beauty of New York City is not found solely in its museums, parks, and sights. New York's attraction is found in being able to get anything you could want, need, or dream of within a few city blocks. Explore, explore, explore. The city moves faster than we do—there will always be something new around the corner. Seeing New York takes a lifetime.

East Midtown and Fifth Avenue

Empire State Building, on Fifth Ave. between 33rd and 34th St. (736-3100), has style. It retains its place in the hearts and minds of New Yorkers even though it is no longer the tallest building in the U.S., or even the tallest building in New York (stood up by the twin towers of the World Trade Center). It doesn't even have the best looks (the Chrysler building is more delicate, the Woolworth more ornate). But the Empire State remains New York's best-known and best-loved landmark and dominates the postcards, the movies, and the skyline. The limestone and granite structure, with glistening mullions of stainless steel, stretches 1454 ft. into the sky; its 73 elevators run on 2 mi. of shafts. The nighttime view will leave you gasping. The Empire State was among the first of the truly spectacular skyscrapers, benefiting from innovations like Eiffel's pioneering work with steel frames and Otis's perfection of the "safety elevator." In Midtown it towers in relative solitude, away from the forest of monoliths that has grown around Wall St. ($3.75, children and seniors $1.75; observatory open daily 9:30am-midnight, tickets sold until 11:30pm.) It's within walking distance of Penn and Grand Central Stations. The nearest subway stations are at 34th St. (subway: B, D, F, N, Q, and R), 33rd St. (#6), and 28th St. (R).

In the **Pierpont Morgan Library,** 29 E. 36th St. (685-0610), a Low Renaissance-style *palazzo*, you can see the book raised to the status of a full-fledged fetish object in a stunning collection of rare books, sculpture, and paintings gathered by the banker and his son, J.P. Morgan, Jr. (Subway: #6 to 33rd St. Open Tues.-Sat. 10:30am-5pm, Sun. 1-5pm. Suggested contribution $5, seniors and students $3. Free tours on various topics Tues.-Fri. 2:30pm.)

The **New York Public Library** (661-7220) reposes on the west side of Fifth Ave. between 40th and 42nd St., near Bryant Park. On sunny afternoons, throngs of people perch on the marble steps, which are dutifully guarded by the mighty lions Patience and Fortitude. This is the world's seventh-largest research library; witness the immense third-floor reading room. Free tours Tues.-Sat. at 11am and 2pm. (Open Mon. and Thurs.-Sat. 10am-6pm, Tues.-Wed. 11am-7:30pm.)

Spreading out against the back of the library along 42nd St. to Sixth Ave. is soothing **Bryant Park.** Site of the World's Fair in 1853, the park has recently undergone renovations, and in the afternoon people of all descriptions crowd into the large, grassy, tree-rimmed expanse to talk, relax, and sunbathe. The stage that sits at the head of the park's big, grassy field plays host to a variety of free cultural events throughout the summer, including screenings of classic films, jazz concerts, and live comedy. Call 397-8222 for an up-to-date schedule of events.

To the east along 42nd St., **Grand Central Terminal** sits where Park Ave. would be, between Madison and Lexington Ave. A former transportation hub where dazed tourists first got a glimpse of the glorious city, Grand Central has since been partially supplanted by Penn Station and the Wright Brothers, but it maintains its dignity nonetheless. The massive Beaux Arts front, with the famed 13-ft. clock, gives way to the Main Concourse, a huge lobby area which becomes zebra-striped by the sun falling through the slatted windows. Constellations are depicted on the sweeping, arched expanse of green roof, while egg-shaped ribbed chandeliers light the secondary apses to the sides. (Free tours Wed. at 12:30pm from the Chemical Bank in the Main Concourse, and Fri. from the Phillip Morris building across the street.)

The New York skyline would be incomplete without the familiar Art Deco headdress of the **Chrysler Building,** at 42nd and Lexington, built by William Van Allen as a series of rectangular boxes and topped by a spire modeled on a radiator grille. When completed in 1929, this elegantly seductive building stood as the world's tallest. The Empire State Building topped it a year later. Walk east on 42nd St. about 1½ blocks; between Park and Second Ave. the **Daily News Building** delivers itself with smug, self-important pomp. Home to the country's first successful tabloid, the building was the inspiration for the *Daily Planet* of Superman fame. The lobby is dominated by a gigantic rotating globe and a clock for every time zone in the world.

Feel like leaving the country? The **United Nations Building** (963-4475) is actually not located along New York City's First Ave. between 42nd and 48th St.—this area is international territory and thus not subject to the laws and jurisdiction of the U.S. Outside, a multicultural rose garden and a statuary park provide a lovely view of the East River. Inside, go through security check and work your way to the back of the lobby for the informative tours of the **General Assembly.** (Tours about 40 min., leaving every 15 min. from 10am to 4:15pm daily, available in 20 languages. $6.50, seniors over 60 and students $4.50, under 16 $3.50. **Visitor's entrance** at First Ave. and 46th St.) You must take the tour to get past the lobby. Sometimes free tickets to G.A. sessions can be obtained when the U.N. is in session (Oct.-May); call 963-1234.

Between 48th and 51st St. and Fifth and Sixth Ave. stretches **Rockefeller Center,** a monument to the conjunction of business and art. On Fifth Ave., between 49th and 50th St., the famous gold-leaf statue of Prometheus sprawls out on a ledge of the sunken **Tower Plaza** while jet streams of water pulse around it. The Plaza serves as an overpriced open-air cafe in the spring and summer and as an ice-skating rink in the winter. The 70-story **RCA Building,** seated at Sixth Ave., remains the most accomplished artistic creation in this complex. Every chair in the building sits less than 28 feet from natural light. Nothing quite matches watching a sunset from the 65th floor as a coral burnish fills the room. The **NBC Television Network** makes its headquarters here, allowing you to take a behind-the-scenes look at their operations. Currently opens three shows to guests: *Saturday Night Live*, *The Phil Donahue Show*, and the new *Late Night with Conan O'Brien*. Call 664-3055 for general information. (Open daily 9:30am-4:30pm. Tours leave every 15 min.; maximum 17 per group; tickets are first come, first served, so buy in advance. $8.25, children under 6 not admitted.) The stores on Fifth Ave. from Rockefeller Center to Central Park are the ritziest and most expensive in the city.

Despite possessing an illustrious history and a wealth of Art Deco treasures, **Radio City Music Hall** (632-4041) was almost demolished in 1979 to make way for new office high-rises. However, the public rallied and the music hall was declared a national landmark. First opened in 1932, at the corner of Sixth Ave. and 51st St., the 5874-seat theater remains the largest in the world. The brainchild of Roxy Rothafel (originator of the Rockettes), it was originally intended as a variety showcase. Yet the hall functioned primarily as a movie theater; over 650 feature films debuted here from 1933 to 1979, including *King Kong, Breakfast at Tiffany's,* and *Doctor Zhivago*. The Rockettes, Radio City's chorus line, still dance on. Tours of the great hall are given daily 10am-5pm. ($9, children 6 and under $4.50)

At 25 W. 52nd St., the **Museum of Television and Radio** (621-6800) works almost entirely as a "viewing museum," allowing visitors to attend schedules screenings in one of its theaters or to choose and enjoy privately a TV or radio show from its library of 60,000. Continue over a block down W. 53rd St. towards Sixth Ave. and take in masterpieces in the **American Craft Museum** and the **Museum of Modern Art** (see Museums). Rest your tired feet with a visit to the sculpture garden of the MoMA, featuring the works of Rodin, Renoir, Miró, Lipschitz, and Picasso.

St. Patrick's Cathedral (753-2261), New York's most famous church and the largest Catholic cathedral in America, stands at 51st St. and Fifth Ave. Designed by James Renwick, the structure captures the essence of great European cathedrals like Reims and Cologne yet retains its own spirit. The twin spires on the Fifth Ave. facade streak 330 ft. into the air.

One of the monuments to modern architecture, Ludwig Mies Van der Rohe's dark and gracious **Seagram Building,** is over at 375 Park Ave., between 52nd and 53rd St. Pure skyscraper, with no frills or silly froufrou like the buildings near Grand Central, the Seagram stands as a paragon of the austere International Style. Van der Rohe envisioned it as an oasis from the tight canyon of skyscrapers on Park Ave. He set the tower back 90 ft. from the plaza and put two great fountains in the foreground. This design has inspired many other nearby plazas and atriums.

Reclaim that inner child at **F.A.O. Schwarz,** 767 Fifth Ave. (644-9400) at 58th St. Worth a browse, if only to remark on the opulence of one of the world's largest toystores, including complex Lego constructions, environmentally-responsible toys, life-sized stuffed animals, and a separate annex exclusively for Barbie dolls. (Open Mon.-Wed. and Fri.-Sat. 10am-7pm, Thurs. 10am-8pm, Sun. noon-6pm.)

On Fifth Ave. and 59th St., at the southeast corner of Central Park, sits the legendary. **Plaza Hotel,** built in 1907 at the then-astronomical cost of $12.5 million. Its 18-story, 800-room French Renaissance interior flaunts five marble staircases, countless ludicrously named suites, and a two-story Grand Ballroom. Past guests and residents have included Frank Lloyd Wright, the Beatles, F. Scott Fitzgerald, and, of course, the eminent Eloise. *Let's Go* recommends the $15,000-per-night suite.

West Midtown

Pennsylvania Station, at 33th St. and Seventh Ave., is one of the less engrossing pieces of architecture in West Midtown, but, as a major subway stop and train terminal, it can at least claim to be highly functional. (Subway: #1, 2, 3, 9, A, C, or E to 34th St./Penn Station). The original Penn Station, a classical marble building modeled on the Roman Baths of Caracalla, was demolished in the 60s. The railway tracks were then covered with the equally uninspiring **Madison Square Garden** complex. Facing the Garden at 421 Eighth Ave., New York's immense main post office, the **James A. Farley Building,** luxuriates in its 10001 ZIP code. A lengthy swath of Corinthian columns shoulders broadly across the front, and a 280-ft. frieze on top of the broad portico bears the bold, Cliff Clavenesque-motto of the U.S. Postal Service: "Neither snow nor rain nor heat nor gloom of night stays these couriers from the swift completion of their appointed rounds."

East on 34th St., between Seventh Ave. and Broadway, stands monolithic **Macy's** (695-4400). This giant, which occupies a full city block, was recently forced to relinquish its title as the "World's Largest Department Store" and change its billing to the "World's Finest Department Store" when a new store in Germany was built one square foot larger. With nine floors (plus a lower level) and some two million sq. ft. of merchandise, Macy's has come a long way from its beginnings in 1857, when it grossed $11.06 on its first day of business. Recently, however, it was forced to revisit its humble roots when it filed for bankruptcy, and its fate still remains uncertain. The store sponsors the **Macy's Thanksgiving Day Parade,** a New York tradition buoyed by helium-filled 10-story Snoopies and other such cultural-icon blobs, marching bands, floats, and general hoopla. (Open Mon. and Thurs.-Fri. 10am-8:30pm, Tues.-Wed. and Sat. 10am-7pm, Sun. 11am-6pm. Subway: #1, 2, 3, or 9 to Penn Station, or B, D, F, N, Q, or R to 34th St.)

The streets of **Times Square** flicker at the intersection of 42nd St. and Broadway. Although probably still considered the dark and seedy core of the Big Apple by most New Yorkers, the Square has worked hard in the past few years to improve its image. Robberies are down by 40%, pick-pocketing and purse-snatching by 43%, and the number of area porn shops has plummeted by more than 100 from its late-70s climax of 140. The historic Victory Theater is undergoing restoration and will be the site of a new children's theater, and Disney has big plans for the aging New Amsterdam Theater, where the Ziegfeld Follies performed their original chorus line routine for more than twenty years. Still, Times Square is Times Square. Teens continue to roam about in search of fake IDs, hustlers are still as eager as ever to scam suckers, and every New Year's Eve, millions booze and schmooze and watch an electronic ball drop. One-and-a-half million people pass through Times Square every day. Lots of subway lines stop in Times Square (#1, 2, 3, 7, and 9, and A, C, E, N, R, and S).

On 42nd St. between Ninth and Tenth Ave. lies **Theater Row,** a block of renovated Broadway theaters. The nearby **Theater District** stretches from 41st to 57th St. along Broadway, Eighth Ave., and the streets which connect them. Approximately 37 theaters remain active, most of them grouped around 45th St.

How do you get to **Carnegie Hall?** Practice, practice, practice. This venerable institution at 57th St. and Seventh Ave. was founded in 1891 and remains New York's foremost soundstage. Tchaikovsky, Caruso, Toscanini, and Bernstein have played Carnegie; as have the Beatles and the Rolling Stones. Other notable events from Carnegie's playlist include the world premiere of Dvorák's *Symphony No. 9 (From the New World)* on December 16, 1893, and an energetic lecture by Albert Einstein in 1934. Carnegie Hall was facing the wrecking ball in the 1950s, but outraged citizens managed to stop the impending destruction through special legislation in 1960. Tours are given Mon., Tues., Thurs., and Fri. at 11:30am, 2pm, and 3pm

($6, students and seniors $5). Carnegie Hall's **museum** displays artifacts and memorabilia from its illustrious century of existence (open daily 11am-4:30pm; free).

Lower Midtown and Chelsea

Madison Avenue ends at 27th St. and **Madison Square Park.** The park, opened in 1847, originally served as a public cemetery. The area near the park sparkles with funky architectural gems. Off the southwest corner of the park is another member of the "I-used-to-be-the-world's-tallest-building" club—the eminently photogenic **Flatiron Building,** often considered the world's first skyscraper. It was originally named the Fuller Building, but its dramatic wedge shape, imposed by the intersection of Broadway, Fifth Ave., 22nd St., and 23rd St., quickly earned it its current *nom de plume.* St. Martin's Press, publisher of such fine books as *Let's Go: USA and Canada,* currently occupies roughly half the building's space.

    Gramercy Park, located at the foot of Lexington Ave. between 20th and 21st St., was built in 1831 by Samuel B. Ruggles, a developer fond of greenery. He drained an old marsh and then laid out 66 building lots around the periphery of the central space. Buyers of his lots received keys to enter the private park; for many years, the keys were made of solid gold. Residents of the buildings now pay annual maintenance fees for the upkeep of the park and can obtain keys to the park's heavy iron gate from their buildings's doormen. The park, with its wide gravel paths, remains the only private park in New York, immaculately kept by its owners.

    Home to some of the most fashionable clubs, bars, and restaurants in the city, **Chelsea** has lately witnessed something of a rebirth. A large and visible gay and lesbian community and an increasing artsy-yuppie population have given Chelsea, which lies west of Fifth Ave. between 14th and 30th St., the flavor of a lower-rent West Village. The historic **Hotel Chelsea,** 222 W. 23rd St. between Seventh and Eighth, has sheltered many a suicidal artist, most famously Sid Vicious of the Sex Pistols. Edie Sedgwick made pit stops here between Warhol films and asylums before lighting the place on fire with a cigarette. Countless writers, as the plaques outside attest, spent their final days searching for inspiration and mail in the lobby. Arthur Miller, Vladimir Nabokov, and Dylan Thomas all made use of the hotel.

Upper East Side

The Golden Age of the East Side society epic began in the 1860s and progressed until the outbreak of World War I. Scores of wealthy people moved into the area and refused to budge, even during the Great Depression when armies of the unemployed pitched their tents across the way in Central Park. These days parades, millionaires, and unbearably slow buses share Fifth Avenue. Fifth Ave. in the 80s and 90s becomes **Museum Mile,** which includes the Metropolitan, the Guggenheim, the ICP, the Cooper-Hewitt, and the Jewish Museum, among others (see Museums).

    The Upper East Side, land of decadence, drips with money the length of the Park. Start your journey at 59th St. and Third Ave., where **Bloomingdale's** sits in regal splendor. **Madison Avenue** graces New York with luxurious boutiques and most of the country's advertising agencies. **Gracie Mansion,** at the northern end of Carl Schurz Park, between 84th and 90th St. along East End Ave., has been the residence of every New York mayor since Fiorello LaGuardia moved in during World War II. Now Rudolph Giuliani occupies this hottest of hot seats. To make a reservation for a tour, call 570-4751 (tours Wed. only; suggested admission $3, seniors $2.)

Central Park

Central Park rolls from Grand Army Plaza all the way up to 110th between Fifth and Eighth Ave. Twenty years of construction turned these 843 acres, laid out by Frederick Law Olmsted and Calvert Vaux in 1850-60, into a compressed sequence of infinite landscapes. The park contains lakes, ponds, fountains, skating rinks, ball fields, tennis courts, a castle, an outdoor theater, a bandshell, and two zoos.

    The Park may be roughly divided between north and south at the main reservoir; the southern section affords more intimate settings, serene lakes, and graceful promenades, while the northern end has a few ragged edges. Nearly 1400 species of trees, shrubs, and flowers grow here, the work of distinguished horticulturist Ignaz Anton Pilat. When you wander amidst the shrubbery, look to the nearest lamppost for guidance, and check the small metal four-digit plaque bolted to it. The first two digits tell you what street you're nearest (e.g., 89), and the second two whether you're on the east or west side of the Park (even numbers mean east, an odd west). In an emergency, call the 24-hr. Park hotline from boxes in the park (570-4820).

At the renovated **Central Park Zoo** (861-6030), Fifth Ave. at 64th St., the monkeys effortlessly ape their visitors. ($2.50, seniors $1.25, children 3-12 50¢. Open Mon.-Fri. 10am-5pm, Sat.-Sun. 11:30am-5:30pm.) The Dairy building now houses the **Central Park Reception Center** (794-6564). Pick up the free map of Central Park and the seasonal list of events. (Open Tues.-Thurs. and Sat.-Sun. 11am-5pm, Fri. 1-5pm; Nov.-Feb. Tues.-Thurs. and Sat.-Sun. 11am-4pm, Fri. 1-4pm.) The **Wollman Skating Rink** (517-4800) doubles as a **miniature golf course** in late spring. (Ice- or roller-skating $6, kids and seniors $3, plus $3.25 skate rental or $6.50 rollerblade rental; 9-hole mini-golf $6, kids $3; bankshot $6, kids $3; discounts for combining activities. Whole megillah open Mon. 10am-5pm, Tues. 10am-9:30pm, Wed.-Thurs. 10am-6pm and 7:30-9:30pm, Fri.-Sat. 10am-11pm, Sun. 10am-9:30pm.)

The **Friedsam Memorial Carousel** (879-0244) is located at 65th St. west of Center Dr. The 58-horsepower carousel was brought from Coney Island and fully restored in 1983. (Open Mon.-Fri. 10:30am-5pm, Sat.-Sun. 10:30am-6pm. Thanksgiving to mid-March Sun. 10:30am-4:30pm. 90¢.) Directly north of the Carousel lies **Sheep Meadow,** from about 66th to 69th St. on the western side of the Park. This is the largest chunk of greensward, exemplifying the pastoral ideals of the Park's designers and today's teenage crowds. It is not uncommon to join a stranger's game of frisbee, but ask first. Spreading out to the west, the **Lake** is still a dramatic sight in the heart of the City. The 1954 **Loeb Boathouse** (517-2233) supplies all necessary romantic nautical equipment. (Open daily late March-Nov. Mon.-Fri. noon-5pm, Sat.-Sun. 10am-5:30pm, weather permitting. Rowboats $10 per hr., $20 deposit.)

Strawberry Fields, sculpted as Yoko Ono's memorial to John Lennon, is located to the west of the Lake at 72nd St. and West Dr., directly across from the Dakota Apartments where Lennon was assassinated and where Ono still lives. Ono battled valiantly for this space against city-council members who had planned a Bing Crosby memorial on the same spot. Picnickers and 161 varieties of plants now inhabit the rolling hills around the star-shaped "Imagine" mosaic on sunny spring days. On John Lennon's birthday on October 9th, in one of the largest unofficial Park events, thousands gather here to remember—or as time passes, to "imagine"—what the legend was really like.

The **Swedish Cottage Marionette Theater** (988-9093), at the base of Vista Rock near the 79th St. Transverse, puts on regular puppet shows. (Shows Sat. at noon and 3pm. $5, children $4.) Up the hill from the Cottage Theater lies the round wooden space of the **Delacorte Theater,** hosting the wildly popular **Shakespeare in the Park** series each midsummer. These plays often feature celebrities and are always free. Come early: the theater seats only 1936 lucky souls (see Theater). North of the theater lies the **Great Lawn,** where large concerts often take place. Paul Simon sang here, the Stonewall 25 marchers rallied here, and the New York Philharmonic and the Metropolitan Opera Company frequently give free summer performances here.

Upper West Side

Broadway leads uptown to **Columbus Circle,** 59th St. and Broadway, the symbolic entrance to the Upper West Side and the end of Midtown—with a statue of Christopher himself. One of the Circle's landmarks, the **New York Coliseum,** has been relatively empty since the construction of the **Javits Center** in 1990.

Broadway intersects Columbus Ave. at **Lincoln Center,** the cultural hub of the city, between 62nd and 66th St. The seven facilities that constitute Lincoln Center—Avery Fisher Hall, the New York State Theater, the Metropolitan Opera House, the Library and Museum of Performing Arts, the Vivian Beaumont Theater, The Walter

Reade Theater, and the Juilliard School of Music—accommodate over 13,000 spectators at a time. At night, the Metropolitan Opera House lights up, making its chandeliers and huge Chagall murals visible through its glass-panel facade. **Columbus Avenue** is great for people-watching and moderately-priced eats, and leads up to the Museum of Natural History (see museums). The Upper West Side is covered with residential brownstones, scenic enough for a pleasant (and free) stroll. See Upper West Side food section for info on **Zabars,** a sight as well as a store.

Harlem

Half a million people are packed into the 3 square mi. that make up greater Harlem. On the East Side above 96th St. lies **Spanish Harlem,** known as El Barrio ("the neighborhood"), and on the West Side lies Harlem proper, stretching from 110th to 155th St. West of Morningside Ave. and south of 125th St. is the Columbia University area, known more commonly as **Morningside Heights** than as a part of Harlem. All these neighborhoods heat up with street activity, not always of the wholesome variety; visit Harlem during the day or go there with someone who knows the area. If you lack the street wisdom or can't find your own guide, opt for a commercial tour.

It is a colossal misconception that Harlem is merely a crime-ridden slum. Although an extremely poor neighborhood, it is culturally rich; and, contrary to popular opinion, much of it is relatively safe. Known as the "city within the City," Harlem is considered by many to be the black capital of the Western world. Over the years Harlem has often been viewed as the archetype of America's frayed cities—you won't believe that hype after you've visited. The 1920s were Harlem's Renaissance; a thriving scene of artists, writers, and scholars lived fast and loose, producing cultural masterworks in the process. The Cotton Club and the Apollo Theater, along with numerous other jazz clubs, were on the musical vanguard.

New York's Ivy Leaguer, **Columbia University,** chartered in 1754, is tucked between Morningside Dr. and Broadway, 114th and 120th St. Now co-ed, Columbia also has cross-registration across the street with all-female **Barnard College.**

The **Cathedral of St. John the Divine** (316-7540), along Amsterdam Ave. between 110th and 113th, promises to be the world's largest cathedral when finished. Construction, begun in 1812, is still going on and is not expected to be completed for another century or two. Near Columbia, at 120th St. and Riverside Dr., is the **Riverside Church.** The observation deck in the tower commands an amazing view of the bells within and the expanse of the Hudson River and Riverside Park below. You can hear concerts on the world's largest carillon (74 bells), the gift of John D. Rockefeller, Jr. (Open Mon.-Sat. 9am-4:30pm, Sun. service 10:45am. Tours of the tower given Sun. 12:30pm; call for tickets.) Diagonally across Riverside Dr. lies **Grant's Tomb** (666-1640). Once a popular monument, it now attracts only a few brave souls willing to make the hike. (Open daily 9am-5pm. Free.)

125th Street, also known as Martin Luther King Jr. Boulevard, spans the heart of traditional Harlem. Fast-food joints, jazz bars, and the **Apollo Theater** (222-0992, box office 749-5838) keep the street humming day and night. 125th has recently resurged as a center of urban life. Off 125th St., at 328 Lenox Ave., **Sylvia's** (966-0660) has magnetized New York for 22 years with enticing soul-food dishes (open Mon.-Sat. 7am-10pm, Sun. 1-7pm). The silver dome of the **Masjid Malcolm Shabazz,** where Malcolm X was once a minister, glitters on 116th St. and Lenox Ave. (visit Fri. at 1pm and Sun. at 10am for services and information, or call 662-2200).

In Washington Heights, north of 155th St., the **George Washington Bridge** has spanned the Hudson since 1931, connecting NY with New Jersey.

Greenwich Village and Washington Square Park

In "The Village," bordered by 14th St. to the north and Houston to the south, bohemian cool meets New York neurosis, resulting in the "downtown" approach to life. The buildings here do not scrape the skies, the street grid dissolves into geometric whimsy, and the residents revel in countercultural logic. Pop culture and P.C. politics thrive here, but both are the secret slaves to the real arbiter of cool: fashion.

"Greenwich Village" or "The Village" refers to the West Village and the rest of the area west of Broadway, including Washington Square Park and its environs. The East Village has a separate identity. An ongoing yuppification campaign has purged the Village of most of its aspiring artists, although the Christopher St. neighborhood is home to a vibrant (and upscale) gay and lesbian scene. The Village stays lively all day and most of the night. Those seeking propriety should head uptown immediately. Everyone else should revel in the funky atmosphere, stores, and people-watching.

The bulk of Greenwich Village lies west of Sixth Ave., thriving on the new and different. In spite of rising property prices, the West Village still boasts an eclectic summer street life and excellent nightlife. The West Village has a large and visible gay community around **Sheridan Square.** This is the native territory of the Guppie (Gay Urban Professional), although many gay males and lesbians shop, eat, and live here. **Christopher Street,** the main byway, swims in novelty restaurants and specialty shops. (Subway: #1 or 9 to Christopher St./Sheridan Sq.) A few street signs refer to Christopher St. as "Stonewall Place," alluding to the **Stonewall Inn,** the club where police raids in 1969 prompted riots that sparked the U.S. Gay Rights Movement

Washington Square Park has been the universally acknowledged heart of the Village since the district's days as a suburb. (Subway: A, B, C, D, E, F, or Q to W. 4th St./Washington Sq.) The marshland here served first as a colonial cemetery, but in the 1820s the area was converted into a park and parade ground. Soon high-toned residences made the area the center of New York's social scene. Society has long since gone north, and **New York University** has moved in. The country's largest private university and one of the city's biggest landowners (along with the city government, the Catholic Church, and Columbia University), NYU has dispersed its buildings and eccentric students throughout the Village.

In the late 1970s and early 80s Washington Square Park became a base for low-level drug dealers, and a rough resident scene. The mid-80s saw a noisy clean-up campaign that has made the park fairly safe and allowed a more diverse cast of characters to return. Today concerts play, defiant punks congregate, homeless people try to sleep, pigeons strut on the lawn, and children romp in the playground. In the southwest corner of the park, a dozen perpetual games of chess wend their ways toward ultimate checkmate. The fountain in the center of the park provides an amphitheater for comics and musicians of widely varying degrees of talent.

On the south side of Washington Square Park, at 133 MacDougal St., is the **Provincetown Playhouse,** a theatrical landmark. Originally based on Cape Cod, the Provincetown Players were joined by the young Eugene O'Neill in 1916 and went on to premiere many of his works. Farther south on MacDougal are the Village's finest coffeehouses, which had their glory days in the 1950s when Beatnik heroes and coffee-bean connoisseurs Jack Kerouac and Allen Ginsberg attended jazz-accompanied poetry readings at **Le Figaro** and **Café Borgia.** These sidewalk cafes still provide some of the best coffee and people-watching in the city.

The north side of the park, called **The Row,** showcases some of the most renowned architecture in the city. Built largely in the 1830s, this stretch of elegant Federal-style brick residences soon became an urban center roamed by 19th-century professionals, dandies, and novelists. Up Fifth Ave., at the corner of 10th St., rises the **Church of the Ascension,** a fine 1841 Gothic church with a notable altar and stained-glass windows (open daily noon-2pm and 5-7pm). Many consider the block down **10th St. between Fifth and Sixth Ave.** the most beautiful residential stretch in the city. This short strip plays out innumerable variations in brick and stucco, layered with wood and iron detailing, with ivy clothing the buildings.

At Fifth Ave. and 11th St. is **The Salmagundi Club,** New York's oldest club for artists. Founded in 1870, the club's building is the only remaining mansion from the area's heyday at the pinnacle of New York society. (Open during exhibitions. Call 255-7740 for details.) The corner of Fifth Ave. and 12th St. is dominated by the eccentric **Forbes Magazine Galleries** (206-5548), Malcolm Forbes's vast collection of random *stuff.* (Open Tues.-Sat. 10am-4pm. Free.)

SoHo and TriBeCa

SoHo ("South of HOW-ston Street") is bounded by Houston St., Canal, Lafayette, and Sullivan St. The architecture here is American Industrial (1860-1890), notable for its cast-iron facades. SoHo has become the high-priced home of New York's artistic community. Here, galleries reign supreme. More than just a place for galleries, the street is filled with experimental theaters and designer clothing stores. This is a great place for star-gazing, too, but don't bother celebrities—they really don't like that.

Greene Street offers the best of SoHo's lofty architecture. If you're looking for genuine starving artists, you probably won't find them in SoHo. But you may find a few in **TriBeCa** ("Triangle Below Canal St."), an area bounded by Chambers St., Broadway, Canal St., and the West Side Highway. Admire the cast-iron edifices lining White St., Thomas St., and Broadway, the 19th-century Federal-style buildings on Harrison Street, and the shops, galleries, and bars on Church and Reade Streets.

East Village and Alphabet City

The East Village, a comparatively new creation, was carved out of the Bowery and the Lower East Side as rents in the West Village soared and its residents sought accommodations elsewhere. Allen Ginsberg, Jack Kerouac, and William Burroughs all eschewed the Village establishment to develop their junked-up "beat" sensibility east of Washington Square Park. A fun stretch of Broadway runs through the Village, marking the western boundary of the East Village, although it is now very touristy.

Grace Church, constructed in 1845, asserts its powerful Gothic presence at 800 Broadway between 10th and 11th. The church used to be *the* place for weddings. The dark interior has a distinctly Medieval feel. (Open Mon-Thurs. 10am-5pm, Fri. 10am-4pm, Sat. noon-4pm.) One of the world's most famous bookstores is the **Strand,** at the corner of 12th St. and Broadway, which bills itself as the "largest used bookstore in the world" with over two million books on 8 mi. of shelves.

The intersection of **Astor Place** (at the juncture of Lafayette, Fourth Ave., Astor Pl., and E. 8th St.) is distinguished by a sculpture of a large black cube balanced on its corner. Astor Place prominently features the rear of the **Cooper Union Foundation Building,** 41 Cooper Sq. (254-6300), built in 1859 to house the Cooper Union for the Advancement of Science and Art, a tuition-free technical and design school founded by the self-educated industrialist Peter Cooper. The school's free lecture series has hosted practically every notable American since the mid-19th century. Cooper Union was the first college intended for the underprivileged and the first college to offer free adult-education classes. Across from a church at 156 Second Ave. stands a famous Jewish landmark, the **Second Avenue Deli** (677-0606). This is all that remains of the "Yiddish Rialto," the stretch of Second Ave. between Houston and 14th St. that comprised the Yiddish theater district in the early part of this century. The Stars of David embedded in the sidewalk in front of the restaurant contain the names of some of the great actors and actresses who spent their lives entertaining the poor Jewish immigrants of the city. (Also see Lower East Side food).

St. Mark's Place, running from Third Avenue at 8th Street down to Tompkins Square Park, is the geographical and spiritual center of the East Village. In the 1960s, the street was the Haight-Ashbury of the East Coast, full of pot-smoking flower children waiting for the next concert at the Electric Circus. In the late 1970s it became the King's Road of New York, as mohawked youths hassled the passers-by from the brownstone steps off Astor Place. Today things are changing again: a Gap store sells its color-me-matching combos across the street from a shop stocking "You Make Me Sick" T-shirts. Though many "Village types" now shun the commercialized and crowded street, St. Mark's is still central to life in this part of town.

In **Alphabet City,** east of First Ave., south of 14th St., and north of Houston, the avenues run out of numbers and take on letters. This part of the East Village has so far escaped the escalating yuppification campaign that has claimed much of St. Mark's Place; in the area's heyday in the 60s, Jimi Hendrix would play open-air shows to bright-eyed Love Children. There has been a great deal of drug-related crime in the recent past, although the community has done an admirable job of making the area livable. Alphabet City is generally safe during the day, and the addictive nightlife on Avenue A ensures some protection there, but try to avoid straying east of Avenue B at night. Alphabet City's extremist Boho activism has made the neighborhood chronically ungovernable in the last several years. A few years ago, police officers set off a riot when they attempted to forcibly evict a band of the homeless and their supporters in **Tompkins Square Park,** at E. 7th St. and Ave. A. The park has just reopened after a two-year hiatus, and still serves as a psycho-geographical epicenter for many a churlish misfit.

Lower East Side

South of Houston and east of the Bowery, in the somewhat deserted Lower East Side, you can still find some excellent kosher delis and a few old-timers who remember the time when the Second Ave. El ran. Two million Jews arrived on the Lower East Side in the 20 years before World War I. Today the Lower East Side continues to be a neighborhood of immigrants, now mostly Asian and Hispanic. Chinatown has expanded across the Bowery and along the stretch of East Broadway, one of the district's main streets. A number of East Village-type artists and musicians have recently moved in as well, especially near Houston St.

Despite the population shift, remnants of the Jewish ghetto that inspired Jacob Riis's compelling work *How the Other Half Lives* still remain. New York's oldest synagogue building, the red-painted **Congregation Anshe Chesed** at 172-176 Norfolk St., just off Stanton St., now houses a Hispanic social service organization. Further down Norfolk, at #60 between Grand and Broome St. sits the **Beth Hemedash Hagadol Synagogue,** the best-preserved of the Lower East Side houses of worship. From Grand St., follow Essex St. three blocks south to **East Broadway.** This street epitomizes the Lower East Side's flux of cultures. You will find Buddhist prayer centers next to (mostly boarded up) Jewish religious supply stores, and the offices of several Jewish civic organizations.

The area around Orchard and Delancey Streets is one of Manhattan's bargain shopping centers. At 97 Orchard St., between Broome and Delancey St., you can visit the **Lower East Side Tenement Museum** (431-0233), a preserved tenement house of the type that proliferated in this neighborhood in the early part of the century. Buy tickets at 90 Orchard St. at the corner of Broome St. ($3, seniors $2, students $1, free Tues.) The museum gallery at 90 Orchard St. offers slide shows, exhibits, and photographs documenting Jewish life on the Lower East Side (included in admission price). Guided historical tours are offered on Sundays (call for information; open Tues.-Fri. 10am-2pm, Sun. 11am-5pm).

Lower Manhattan

Many of the city's superlatives congregate at the southern tip of Manhattan. The Wall Street area is the densest in all New York. Wall Street itself measures less than a ½-mi. long. Along with density comes history: lower Manhattan was the first part of the island to be settled. Touring here won't cost much. Parks, churches, and temperature-controlled cathedrals of commerce such as the New York Stock Exchange and City Hall charge no admission. Visit during the work week.

Battery Park, named for a battery of guns that the British stored there from 1683 to 1687, is now a chaotic chunk of green forming the southernmost toenail of Manhattan Island. The #1 and 9 trains to South Ferry terminate at the southeastern tip of the park; the #4 and 5 stop at Bowling Green, just off the northern tip. On weekends the park is often mobbed with people on their way to the Liberty and Ellis Island ferries, which depart from here.

Once the northern border of the New Amsterdam settlement, **Wall Street** takes its name from the wall built in 1653 to shield the Dutch colony from a British invasion from the north. By the early 19th century, it had already become the financial capital of the United States. At Wall and Broad St. meet **Federal Hall** (264-8711), the original City Hall, where the trial of John Peter Zenger helped to establish freedom of the press in 1735. On the southwestern corner of Wall and Broad St. stands the current home of the **New York Stock Exchange** (656-5168; open to the public Mon.-Fri. 9:15am-4pm). The Stock Exchange was first created as a marketplace for handling the $80 million in U.S. bonds that were issued in 1789 and 1790 to pay Revolutionary War debts. Arrive early in the morning, preferably before 9am, because tickets usually run out by around 1pm. The real draw is the observation gallery that overlooks the exchange's zoo-like main trading floor.

Around the corner, at the end of Wall St., rises the seemingly ancient **Trinity Church** (602-0800). Its Gothic spire was the tallest structure in the city when first erected in 1846. The vaulted interior feels positively medieval.

Walk up Broadway to Liberty Park, and in the distance you'll see the twin towers of the city's tallest buildings, the **World Trade Center.** Two World Trade Center has an **observation deck** (435-7377) on the 107th floor. (Open daily June-Sept. 9:30am-11:30pm, Oct.-May 9:30am-9:30pm. $4.75, seniors $2.75, children $2.)

North on Broadway is City Hall Park and **City Hall** itself, which still serves as the focus of the city's administration. The Colonial chateau-style structure, completed in 1811, may be the finest piece of architecture in the city. North of the park, at 111 Centre St., between Leonard and White St., sits the **Civil Court Building,** which now actually serves mainly as a venue for criminal hearings and proceedings. You can sit in on every kind of trial from misdemeanor to murder here—visit the clerk's office in Room 927 for a schedule of what's taking place where, or call 374-8076.

Towering at 233 Broadway, off the southern tip of the park, is the Gothic **Woolworth Building,** one of the most sublime and ornate commercial buildings in the world. Erected in 1913 by F.W. Woolworth to house the offices of his corner-store empire, it stood as the world's tallest until the Chrysler Building opened in 1930. The lobby of this five-and-dime Versailles is littered with Gothic arches and flourishes, including a caricature of Woolworth himself counting change. A block and a half farther south on Broadway, **St. Paul's Chapel** was inspired by London's St. Martin-in-the-Fields. St. Paul's is Manhattan's oldest public building in continuous use. For information on the chapel, call the office of the Trinity Museum (602-0773; open Mon.-Fri. 8am-4pm, Sun. 7am-3pm).

Turn left off Broadway onto Fulton St. and head to the **South Street Seaport.** New York's shipping industry thrived here for most of the 19th century. The process of revitalization recently turned the historic district, in all its fishy and foul-smelling glory, into the ritzy South Street Seaport complex, with an 18th-century market, graceful galleries, seafaring schooners, and **Pier 16,** a shopping mall and food court. At the end of Fulton St., as the river comes suddenly into view, so does the smell of dead fish pass through your nostrils. The stench comes from the **Fulton Fish Market,** the largest fresh-fish mart in the country, hidden right on South St. on the other side of the overpass. Those who can stomach wriggling scaly things might be interested in the behind-the-scenes tour of the market given some Thurs. mornings June-Oct. (market opens at 4am). The Pier 16 kiosk, the main ticket booth for the seaport, is open 10am-7pm (open 1 hr. later on summer weekends).

The Statue of Liberty and Ellis Island

The renovated **Statue of Liberty** (363-3200) is a landmark of decades of immigrant crossings. The statue was given by the French in 1886 as a sign of goodwill. Since it has stood at the entrance to New York Harbor, the Statue of Liberty has welcomed millions of immigrants to America. Today, the statue welcomes tourists galore, as everyone and their sixteen cousins make the ferry voyage to Liberty Island. The **American Museum of Immigration,** located under the green lady's bathrobe, enshrines the dreams of all those who have come to look for America. The other ferry stop is **Ellis Island.** Once the processing center for the 15 million Europeans who came to the U.S via New York, Ellis Island was shut down after the large waves of immigration were over. Recently redone, Ellis Island now houses a museum telling the tale of many Americans's ancestors. Two **ferries bring** you to and from Liberty and Ellis islands. One runs Manhattan-Liberty-Ellis, and the other Liberty State

Park/Jersey City-Ellis-Liberty. Both run daily every ½-hr., 9:15am-4:30pm. (Ferry info 269-5755. $6, seniors $5, children 2-17 $3.)

Brooklyn

When romantics ponder Brooklyn, they conjure up images of the rough stickball players who grew up to become the Brooklyn Dodgers. What goes on in Brooklyn tends to happen on the streets and out of doors, whether it's neighborhood banter, baseball games in the park, ethnic festivals, or gang violence. The Dutch originally settled the borough in the 17th century. When asked to join New York in 1833, Brooklyn refused, saying that the two cities shared no interests except common waterways. Not until 1898 did Brooklyn decide, in a close vote, to become a borough of New York City. The visitors bureau publishes an excellent free guide to Brooklyn's rich historical past that outlines 10 walking tours of the borough.

Head south on Henry St. after the Brooklyn Bridge, then turn right on Clark St. toward the river for a synapse-shorting view of Manhattan. Many prize-winning photographs have been taken here from the **Brooklyn Promenade,** overlooking the southern tip of Manhattan and New York Harbor. George Washington's headquarters during the Battle of Long Island, now-posh **Brooklyn Heights** has advertised itself to many authors, from Walt Whitman to Norman Mailer, with its beautiful old brownstones, tree-lined streets, and proximity to Manhattan. Continuing south, soon you'll be at **Atlantic Avenue,** home to a large Arab community, with second-hand stores and inexpensive Middle Eastern bakeries and grocery stores. Atlantic runs from the river to Flatbush Ave. At the Flatbush Ave. Extension, pick up the **Fulton Street** pedestrian mall.

Williamsburg, several blocks north of downtown Brooklyn, has retained its Hasidic Jewish culture more overtly than Manhattan's Lower East Side. The quarter encloses Broadway, Bedford, and Union Avenues. It closes on *shabbat* (Saturday), the Jewish holy day.

Prospect Park, designed by Frederick Law Olmsted in the mid-1800s, was supposedly his favorite creation. He was even more pleased with it than with his Manhattan project—Central Park. At the north corner of the park stands **Grand Army Plaza,** an island in the midst of the borough's busiest thoroughfares, designed by Olmsted to shield surrounding apartment buildings from traffic. (Subway: 2 or 3 to Grand Army Plaza.) The nearby **Botanic Gardens** (718-622-4433) seem more secluded and include a lovely rose garden (Open April-Sept. Tues.-Fri. 8am-6pm, Sat.-Sun. and holidays 10am-6pm; Oct.-March Tues.-Fri. 8am-4:30pm, Sat.-Sun. and holidays 10am-4:30pm. Free). The gardens are behind the mammoth **Brooklyn Museum** (718-638-5000; open Wed.-Sun. 10am-5pm. Suggested donation $4, students $2, seniors $1.50).

Sheepshead Bay lies on the southern edge of Brooklyn, name to both a body of water (really part of the Atlantic) and a mass of land. Walk along Emmons Ave. and peruse menus for daily seafood specials. Nearby **Brighton Beach,** nicknamed "Little Odessa by the Sea," has been homeland to Russian emigrés since the turn of the century. (Subway: D or Q.)

Once a resort for the City's elite, made accessible to the rest of the Apple because of the subway, fading **Coney Island** still warrants a visit. The **Boardwalk,** once one of the most seductive of Brooklyn's charms, now squeaks nostalgically as tourists are jostled by roughnecks. Enjoy a hot dog and crinkle-cut fries at historic **Nathan's,** Surf and Sitwell. The **Cyclone,** 834 Surf Ave. (718-266-3434), at W. 10th St., built in 1927, was once the most terrifying roller coaster ride in the world (open daily mid-June to Labor Day noon-midnight; Easter weekend to mid-June Fri.-Sun. noon-midnight). Enter its 100-second-long screaming battle over nine hills of rickety wooden tracks—the ride's well worth $3. Go meet a walrus, dolphin, sea lion, shark, or other ocean critter in the tanks of the **New York Aquarium,** Surf and West 8th (718-265-3400; open daily 10am-5pm, holidays and summer weekends 10am-7pm; $6.75, children and seniors $2).

The **Brooklyn Bridge** spans the East River from lower Manhattan to Brooklyn. Built in 1883, the bridge was one of the greatest engineering feats of the 19th century. The 1-mi. walk along the pedestrian path (make sure to walk on the left side, as the right is reserved for bicycles) will show you why every New York poet feels compelled to write at least one verse about it, why photographers snap the bridge's airy spider-web cables, and why people jump off. Once on the bridge, you can look straight up at the cables and Gothic arches. To get to the entrance on Park Row, walk a couple of blocks west from the East River to the city hall area. Plaques on the bridge towers commemorate John Augustus Roebling, its builder, who, along with 20 of his workers, died during its construction.

Queens

In this urban suburbia, the American melting pot bubbles away with a more than 30% foreign-born population. Immigrants from Korea, China, India, and the West Indies rapidly sort themselves out into neighborhoods where they try to maintain the memory of their homeland while living "the American Dream."

Queens is easily New York's largest borough, covering over a third of the city's total area. You need to understand Queens's kaleidoscope of communities to understand the borough. If you visit only one place in Queens, let it be **Flushing.** Here you will find some of the most important colonial neighborhood landmarks, a bustling downtown, and the largest rose garden in the Northeast. (Subway: #7 to Main St., Flushing.) Nearby **Flushing Meadows-Corona Park** was the site of the 1964-1965 World's Fair, and now holds Shea Stadium (home of the Mets) and some museums.

Bronx

While the media presents "Da Bronx" as a crime-ravaged husk, the borough offers its few tourists over 2000 acres of parkland, a great zoo, turn-of-the-century river-front mansions, grand boulevards more evocative of Europe than of late 20th-century America, and thriving ethnic neighborhoods, including a Little Italy to shame its counterpart to the south. If you're not heading for Yankee Stadium, stay out of the South Bronx unless you're in a car and with someone who knows the area.

The most obvious reason to come to the Bronx is the **Bronx Zoo,** also known as the New York Zoological Society. The largest urban zoo in the United States, it houses over 4000 animals. You can explore the zoo on foot or ride like the king of the jungle aboard the Safari Train, which runs between the elephant house and Wild Asia ($1). Soar into the air for a funky cool view of the zoo from the **Skyfari** aerial tramway that runs between Wild Asia and the Children's Zoo (one-way $2, children $1). The **Bengali Express Monorail** glides round Wild Asia (20 min.; $2). If you find the pace too hurried, saddle up a camel in the Wild Asia area ($3). Call 220-5142 three weeks in advance to reserve a place on a **walking tour.** Pamphlets containing self-guided tours are available at the Zoo Center for 75¢. Parts of the zoo close down during the winter (Nov.-April); call 718-367-1010 or 718-220-5100 for more info. (Open Mon.-Fri. 10am-5pm, Sat.-Sun. 10am-5:30pm; Nov.-Jan. daily 10am-4:30pm. Free Wed., otherwise $5.75, seniors and children $2. For disabled-access, call 718-220-5188. Subway: #2 or 5 to E. Tremont Ave.)

North across East Fordham Rd. from the zoo sprawls the **New York Botanical Garden** (718-817-8705). Snatches of forest and virgin waterways allow you to imagine the area's original landscape. (Garden grounds open Tues.-Sun. 10am-7pm; Nov.-March 10am-6pm. Suggested donation $5, seniors, students, and children $3. Parking $4. Subway: #4 or D to Bedford Park Blvd. and Bx26 bus 8 blocks east.)

Wave Hill, 675 W. 252nd St. (718-549-2055), in Riverdale, is an estate that was home to Samuel Clemens (Mark Twain), Arturo Toscanini, and Teddy Roosevelt. Picnic in the world-famous gardens with an astonishing view of the Hudson and the Palisades. (Gardens open Wed.-Sun. 9am-5:30pm. $4, seniors and students $2.

The **Museum of Bronx History** (881-8900), at Bainbridge Ave. and 208th St. (Subway: D to 205th St., or #4 to Mosholu Pkwy. Walk 4 blocks east on 210th St. and then south a block) is run by the Bronx Historical Society on the premises of the landmark Valentine-Varian House. The museum presents historical narratives of the borough of the Bronx. (Open Sat. 10am-4pm, Sun. 1-5pm, $2.)

Staten Island

Getting there is half the fun. At 50¢ (round-trip), the half-hour ferry ride from Manhattan's Battery Park to Staten Island is as unforgettable as it is inexpensive. Or you can drive from Brooklyn over the **Verrazano-Narrows Bridge,** the world's second-longest (4260 ft.) suspension span. Because of the hills and the distances (and some very dangerous neighborhoods in between), it's a bad idea to walk from one site to the next. Make sure to plan your excursion with the bus schedule in mind.

The most concentrated number of sights on the island cluster around the beautiful 19th-century **Snug Harbor Cultural Center,** at 1000 Richmond Terrace. Picnic and see its catch: the **Newhouse Center for Contemporary Art** (718-448-2500), a small gallery displaying American art with an indoor/outdoor sculpture show in the summer (open Wed.-Sun. noon-5pm; free); the **Staten Island Children's Museum** (718-273-2060), with participation exhibits for the five- to 12-year-old in you (open Tues.-Sun. noon-5pm; $3); and the **Staten Island Botanical Gardens.**

MUSEUMS AND GALLERIES

For museum and gallery listings consult the following publications: *New Yorker* (the most accurate and extensive listing), *New York,* the Friday *New York Times* (in the Weekend section), the *Quarterly Calendar,* (available free at any visitors bureau) and *Gallery Guide,* found in local galleries. Most museums and all galleries close on Mondays, and are jam-packed on the weekends. Many museums require a "donation" in place of an admission fee—you can give less than the suggested amount. Most museums are free one weeknight; call ahead to confirm.

Major Collections

Metropolitan Museum of Art, Fifth Ave. (879-5500), at 82nd St. Subway: 4, 5, 6 to 86th St. If you see only one, see this. The largest in the Western Hemisphere, the Met's art collection encompasses 3.3 million works from almost every period through Impressionism; particularly strong in Egyptian and non-Western sculpture and European painting. Contemplate infinity in the secluded Japanese Rock Garden. When blockbuster exhibits tour the world they usually stop at the Met— get tickets in advance through Ticketron. Open Sun. and Tues.-Thurs. 9:30am-5:15pm, Fri.-Sat. 9:30am-8:45pm. Donation $6, students and seniors $3.

Museum of Modern Art (MoMA), 11 W. 53rd St. (708-9400), off Fifth Ave. in Midtown. Subway: E, F to Fifth Ave./53rd St. One of the most extensive contemporary (post-Impressionist) collections in the world, founded in 1929 by scholar Alfred Barr in response to the Met's reluctance to embrace modern art. Cesar Pelli's structural glass additions flood the masterpieces with natural light. See Monet's sublime *Water Lily* room, and many Picassos. Sculpture garden good for resting and people-watching. Open Sat.-Tues. 11am-6pm, Thurs.-Fri. noon-8:30pm. $7.50, seniors and students $4.50, under 16 free. Films require free tickets in advance. Pay-what-you-wish Thurs.-Fri. 5:30-8:30pm.

The Frick Collection, 1 E. 70th St. (288-0700), at Fifth Ave. Subway: #6 to 68th St. Robber baron Henry Clay Frick left his house and art collection to the city, and the museum retains the elegance of his French "Classic Eclectic" château. Impressive grounds. The Living Hall displays 17th-century furniture, Persian rugs, Holbein portraits, and paintings by El Greco, Rembrandt, Velázquez, and Titian. After exploring what may be NYC's least exhausting museum, relax in a courtyard inhabited by elegant statues surrounding the garden pool and fountain. Open Tues.-Sat. 10am-6pm, Sun. 1-6pm. $3.50, students and seniors $3. Ages under 10 not allowed, under 16 must be accompanied by an adult.

Guggenheim Museum, 1071 Fifth Ave. and 89th St. (recording 423-3500, human being 423-3600, TDD 423-3607). Many have called this controversial construction a giant turnip, Frank Lloyd Wright's joke on the Big Apple. The museum closed from 1990-92 while a ten-story "tower gallery" sprouted behind the original structure, allowing the museum to show more of its permanent collection of mostly

20th-century art. Open Sun.-Wed. 10am-6pm, Fri.-Sat. 10am-8pm. $7, seniors and students $4, under 12 free. Pay what you wish Fri. 6-8pm. Two-day pass to this museum and **Guggenheim Museum SoHo,** 575 Broadway (423-3500) at Prince St. in Greenwhich Village. Open Sun. and Wed.-Fri. 11am-6pm, Sat. 11am-8pm. $5, students and seniors $3, and children under 12 free.

American Museum of Natural History, Central Park West (769-5100), at 79th to 81st St. Subway: B or C to 81st St. The largest science museum in the world, in a suitably imposing Romanesque structure. Locals recommend seeing things from a new perspective by lying down under the whale in the Ocean Life room. J.P. Morgan's Indian emeralds blaze in the Hall of Minerals and Gems. Open Sun.-Thurs. 10am-5:45pm, Fri.-Sat. 10am-8:45pm. Donation $5, seniors and students $3, kids $2.50. Free Fri.-Sat. 5-8:45pm. The museum also houses **Naturemax** (769-5650), a cinematic extravaganza on New York's largest (4 stories) movie screen. Admission for museum visitors $5, students and seniors $4, kids $2.50, Fri.-Sat. double features $7, kids $3.50. The **Hayden Planetarium** (769-5700) offers outstanding multi-media presentations. Seasonal celestial light shows twinkle in the dome of its **Theater of the Stars,** accompanied by astronomy lectures. Admission $5, seniors and students $4, kids $2.50. Electrify your senses with the theater's **Laser Rock** Fri.-Sat. nights, $8.50.

Whitney Museum of American Art, 945 Madison Ave. (570-3676), at 75th St. Subway: #6 to 77th St. Futuristic fortress featuring the largest collection of 20th-century American art in the world, with works by Hopper, Soyer, de Kooning, Motherwell, Warhol, and Calder. Controversial political art has infiltrated what was once a bastion of high-modernist aestheticism, with food, trash, and video becoming accepted media. Open Wed. 11am-6pm, Thurs. 1pm-8pm, Fri.-Sun. 11am-6pm. $7, students and seniors $5, under 12 free. Thurs. 6pm-8pm $3.50.

Cooper-Hewitt Museum, 2 E. 91st St. (860-6868), at Fifth Ave. Subway: #4, 5, 6 to 86th St. Andrew Carnegie's majestic, Georgian mansion now houses the Smithsonian Institution's National Museum of Design. The playful special exhibits have considerable flair, focusing on such topics as doghouses and the history of the pop-up book. Open Tues. 10am-9pm, Wed.-Sat. 10am-5pm, Sun. noon-5pm. $3, seniors and students $1.50, under 12 free. Free Tues. 5-9pm.

Smaller and Specialized Collections

American Craft Museum, 40 W. 53rd St. (956-3535), across from MoMA. Subway: E, F to Fifth Ave.-53rd St. Offering more than quilts, this museum revises the notion of crafts with its modern media, including metal and plastic. Open Tues. 10am-8pm, Wed.-Sun. 10am-5pm. $4.50, seniors and students $2.

The Cloisters (923-3700), Fort Tryon Park, upper Manhattan. Subway: A through Harlem to 190th St. This monastery, built from pieces of 12th- and 13th-century French and Spanish cloisters, was assembled at John D. Rockefeller's behest by Charles Collens in 1938 as a setting for the Met's medieval art collection. Highlights include the Unicorn Tapestries, the Cuxa Cloister, and the Treasury, with 15th century playing cards. Open Tues.-Sun. 9:30am-5:15pm. Museum tours Tues.-Fri. 3pm, Sun. noon, in winter Wed. 3pm. Donation $6, students and seniors $3 (includes admission to the Metropolitan Museum of Art).

New Museum of Contemporary Art, 583 Broadway (219-1222), between Prince and Houston St. Subway: R to Prince, #6 to Bleecker, or B, D, F to Broadway/Lafayette. Dedicated to the destruction of the canon and of conventional ideas of "art," the New Museum supports the hottest, the newest, and the most controversial. Many works deal with fashionable politics of identity—sexual, racial, and ethnic. Once a month, an artist sits in the front window and converses with passersby. Open Wed.-Fri. and Sun. noon-6pm, Sat. noon-8pm. $3.50, artists, seniors, and students $2.50, children under 12 free. Sat. 6-8pm free.

International Center of Photography, 1130 Fifth Ave. (860-1777), at 94th St. Subway: #6 to 96th St. Housed in a landmark townhouse built in 1914 for *New Republic* founder Willard Straight. The foremost exhibitor of photography in the city, and a gathering-place for its practitioners. Historical, thematic, contemporary, and experimental works, running from fine art to photo-journalism. Midtown branch at 1133 Sixth Ave. (768-4680), at 43rd St. Both open Tues. 11am-8pm, Wed.-Sun. 11am-6pm. $4, seniors and students $2.50.

Jacques Marchais Center of Tibetan Art, 338 Lighthouse Ave., Staten Island (718-987-3478). Take bus S74 from Staten Island Ferry to Lighthouse Ave., turn right and walk up the hill. One of the finest Tibetan collections in the U.S. Exuding serenity, the center is a replica of a Tibetan temple set amid sculpture gardens. Open April-Nov. Wed.-Sun. 1-5pm; $3, seniors $2.50, children $1.

Museum of the American Indian (283-2420) at Broadway and 155th St. in Harlem. Subway: #1 to 157th St. The world's largest collection of Native American artifacts. In recent years, the museum has been faced with demands by Native American groups seeking the return of many exhibits; for now at least, you can still see Geronimo's warrior cap and cane, Sitting Bull's war club, and Crazy Horse's headdress. The museum is moving to the old U.S. Custom House in lower Manhattan at some point in 1995, so call ahead. Open Tues.-Sat. 10am-5pm, Sun. 1-5pm. $1.50, seniors and students with ID $1.

Museum of Television and Radio, 25 W. 52nd St. (621-6600), between Fifth and Sixth Ave. Subway: B, D, F, Q to Rockefeller Center, or E, F to 53rd St. Boob tube relics and memorabilia, as well as over 50,000 programs in the museum's permanent collection. With admission you can watch or listen to anything from the *Twilight Zone* to *Saturday Night Live.* Open Tues.-Wed. and Fri.-Sun. noon-6pm, Thurs. noon-8pm. $6, students $4, seniors and children $3.

Intrepid Sea-Air-Space Museum, Pier 86 (245-0072), at 46th St. and Twelfth Ave. Bus: M42 or M50 to W. 46th St. One ticket admits you to the veteran World War II and Vietnam War aircraft carrier *Intrepid,* the Vietnam War destroyer *Edson,* the only publicly displayed guided-missile submarine, *Growler,* and the lightship *Nantucket.* A breathtaking wide-screen flick puts the viewer on a flight deck as jets take off and land. The Iraqi tanks parked near the gift shop were captured in the Gulf War. Open Memorial Day-Labor Day daily 10am-5pm; Labor Day-Memorial Day Mon.-Fri. 10am-5pm. $7, seniors $6, children 6-11 $4, under 6 free.

The Jewish Museum, 1109 Fifth Ave. (423-3200), at 92nd St. Subway: #6 to 96th St. Over 14,000 works detail the Jewish experience throughout history. Open Sun.-Mon. and Wed.-Thurs. 11am-5:45pm, Tues. 11am-8pm. $6, seniors and students $4, children under 12 free; Tues. pay what you wish after 5pm.

El Museo del Barrio, 1230 Fifth Ave. (831-7272), at 104th St. Subway: #6 to 103rd St. El Museo del Barrio is the only museum in the U.S. devoted exclusively to the art and culture of Puerto Rico and Latin America. Open Wed.-Sun. 11am-5pm. Suggested contribution $4, students and senior $2.

The Museum for African Art, 593 Broadway (966-1313), between Houston St. and Prince St. in SoHo. Subway: N or R to Prince and Broadway. Formerly the Center for African Art, the museum has changed its name and expanded to feature two major exhibits of stunning African and African-American art. Open Tues.-Fri. 10am-5:30pm, Sat.-Sun. noon-6pm. $4, students and seniors with ID $2.

Museum of the City of New York (534-1672), 103rd St. and Fifth Ave. in East Harlem next door to El Museo del Barrio. Subway: #6 to 103rd St. Premier museum about New York City, it tells the city's story from the 16th century to the present through historical paintings, Currier and Ives prints, period rooms and artifacts. Open Wed.-Sat. 10am-5pm, Sun. 1-5pm. Contribution requested.

ENTERTAINMENT AND NIGHTLIFE

New York's incomparable nightlife presents the traveler with a welcome problem: finding the "right show" from among the city's dizzyingly broad selection of entertainment. New York's cultural activity does not revolve around a nuclear institution; instead, hundreds of independent venues compete for attention and credibility, each claiming greater artistry than the others but all equally (well, nearly equally) responsible for New York's premiere cultural status. **Publications** with especially noteworthy sections on nightlife include the *Village Voice, New York* magazine, and the Sunday edition of the *New York Times.* The most comprehensive survey of the current theater scene can be found in *The New Yorker.* An **entertainment hotline** (360-3456; 24 hrs.) runs down the week by both borough and genre.

Only a short train ride away, **Hoboken, NJ** hosts happening nightlife (see Maxwells below) as well as a trendy, less expensive bar scene. For longer NYC stays, it's worth the foray, if only to see the tremendous skyline view from across the Hudson. To get to Hoboken, take the B, D, F, N, Q, or R train to 34th St., then the PATH train ($1) to the 1st stop in Hoboken. (The PATH train also leaves from the 23rd and 14th St. stations of the F train, as well as from its own stations at 9th St./Sixth Ave. and Christopher St./Greenwich St.) The streets around the PATH station and from 1st to 4th St. bustle with activity.

Theater

Broadway is currently undergoing a revival—ticket sales are booming, and mainstream musicals are receiving more than their fair share of attention. Dorky, old-fashioned productions such as *Crazy For You* and *Guys and Dolls* are very popular, and tickets can be hard to get. Broadway tickets cost about $50 each when purchased through regular channels. **TKTS** (768-1818 for recorded info) sells half-priced tickets to many Broadway shows on the same day of the performance. TKTS has a booth in the middle of Duffy Square (the northern part of Times Square, at 47th and Broadway). TKTS tickets are usually about $25 each plus a $2.50 service charge per ticket. (Tickets are sold Mon.-Sat. 3-8pm for evening performances, Wed. and Sat. 10am-2pm for matinees, and Sun. noon-8pm for matinees and evening performances.) For information on shows and ticket availability, call the **NYC/ON STAGE** hotline at 768-1818 or **Ticket Central** between 1 and 8pm at 279-4200. **Ticketmaster** (307-7171) deals in everything from Broadway shows to mud-truck races; they charge at least $2 more than other outlets, but take most major credit cards. *Listings*, a weekly guide to entertainment in Manhattan ($1), has listings of Broadway, Off-Broadway, and Off-Off-Broadway shows.

Off-Broadway theaters have between 100 and 499 seats; only Broadway houses have over 500. Off-Broadway houses frequently offer more offbeat or quirky shows, with shorter runs. Occasionally these shows have long runs or jump to Broadway houses. Tickets cost $10-20. The best of the Off-Broadway houses huddle in the Sheridan Square area of the West Village. TKTS also sells tickets for the larger Off-Broadway houses. **Off-Off-Broadway** means cheaper, younger theaters.

For years, the **Joseph Papp Public Theater,** 425 Lafayette St. (598-7150), was inextricably linked with its namesake founder, one of the city's leading producers. The theater recently produced an exhaustive and exhausting Shakespeare Marathon, which includes every single one of the Bard's plays down to *Timon of Athens*. Tickets cost $15-35. About one quarter of the seats are sold for $10 on the day of performance (starting at 6pm for evening performances and 1pm for matinees). Papp also founded **Shakespeare in the Park** (861-7277), a New York summer tradition. From June through August, two Shakespeare plays are presented at the **Delacorte Theater** in Central Park, near the 81st St. entrance on the Upper West Side, just north of the main road. Tickets are free, but lines form early. Call for info.

Movies

If Hollywood is *the* place to make films, New York City is *the* place to see them. Most movies open in New York weeks before they're distributed across the country, and the response of Manhattan audiences and critics can shape a film's success or failure nationwide. Dozens of revival houses show motion picture classics and independent filmmakers from around the reel world come to New York to flaunt their work. Big-screen fanatics should check out the cavernous **Ziegfeld,** 141 W. 54th St. (765-7600), one of the largest screens left in America, which shows first-run films. **MoviePhone** (777-FILM/3456) allows you to reserve tickets for most major movie-houses and pick them up at showtime from the theater's automated ticket dispenser; you charge the ticket price plus a small fee over the phone. **The Kitchen,** 512 W. 19th St. (255-5793), between Tenth and Eleventh Ave., subway C or E to 23rd St., is a world-renowned showcase for the off-beat from New York-based struggling artists (prices vary). See eight screens of alternative (not quite underground) cinema at the **Angelika Film Center,** 18 W. Houston St. (995-2000), at Mercer St. Subway: #6 to Bleecker St. or B, D, F, Q to Broadway-Lafayette. The cafe upstairs has excellent espresso. **Anthology Film Archives,** 32 Second Ave. (505-5181) at E. 2nd St. Subway: F to Second Ave., is a forum for independent filmmaking.

Opera and Dance

Lincoln Center (875-5000) is New York's one-stop shopping mall for high-culture consumers; there's usually opera or dance at one of its many venues. Write Lincoln Center Plaza, NYC 10023, or drop by its Performing Arts Library (870-1930) for a full schedule and a press kit as long as the *Ring* cycle. The **Metropolitan Opera Company** (362-6000), opera's premier outfit, plays on a Lincoln Center stage as big as a football field. Regular tickets run as high as $100—go for the upper balcony (around $15; the cheapest seats have an obstructed view) unless you're prone to vertigo. You can stand in the orchestra ($14) along with the opera freakazoids who've brought along the score, or all the way back in the Family Circle ($15). (Regular season runs Sept.-April Mon.-Sat.; box office open Mon.-Sat. 10am-8pm, Sun. noon-6pm.) In the summer, watch for free concerts in city parks (362-6000).

At right angles to the Met, the **New York City Opera** (870-5570) has a new sound under the direction of Christopher Keene. "City" now has a split season (Sept.-Nov. and March-April) and keeps its ticket prices low year-round ($15-73). For rush tickets, call the night before and wait in line the morning of. In July, look for free performances by the **New York Grand Opera** (360-2777) at Central Park Summerstage every Wednesday night. Check the papers for performances of the old warhorses by the **Amato Opera Company,** 319 Bowery (228-8200; Sept.-May). Music schools often stage opera as well; see Music for further details.

The New York State Theater (870-5570) is home to the late, great George Balanchine's **New York City Ballet,** the country's oldest and most famous dance company. Decent tickets for the *Nutcracker* in December sell out almost immediately. (Performances Nov.-Feb. and April-June. Tickets $12-57, standing room $8.) The **American Ballet Theater** (477-3030), under Mikhail Baryshnikov's guidance, dances at the Met every May and June (tickets $16-95). The **Alvin Ailey American Dance Theater** (767-0940) bases its repertoire of modern dance on jazz, spirituals, and contemporary music. Often on the road, it always performs at the **City Center** in December. Tickets ($15-40) can be difficult to obtain. Write or call the City Center, 131 W. 55th St. (581-7907), weeks in advance. Look for ½-price tickets at the Bryant Park ticket booth (see below). The **Joyce Theater,** 175 Eighth Ave. (242-0800), between 18th and 19th St., has experimental dance troupes (tickets $15-40).

Other companies include the **Martha Graham Dance Co.,** 316 E. 63rd St. (832-9166), performing original Graham pieces during its October New York season, and the **Merce Cunningham Dance Company** (255-8240), of John Cage fame. Half-price tickets for many music and dance events can be purchased on the day of performance at the **Bryant Park** ticket booth, 42nd St. (382-2323), between Fifth and Sixth Ave. (Open Tues.-Sun. noon-2pm and 3-7pm; cash and traveler's checks only.) Concert tickets to Monday shows are available on the Sunday prior.

Classical Music

Begin with the ample listings in the *New York Times, The New Yorker,* or *New York* magazine. Remember that many events, like outdoor music, are seasonal.

The **Lincoln Center Halls** have a wide, year-round selection of concerts. The **Great Performers Series,** featuring famous and foreign musicians, packs the Avery Fisher and Alice Tully Halls and the Walter Reade Theater, from October until May (call 721-6500; tickets from $11). **Avery Fisher Hall** (875-5030; wheelchair accessible) paints the town ecstatic with its annual Mostly Mozart Festival. Show up early; there are usually pre-concert recitals beginning 1 hr. before the main concert and free to ticketholders. The festival runs July-Aug., with tickets to individual events $12-30. The **New York Philharmonic** (875-5656) begins its regular season in mid-September. (Tickets $10-60, call 721-6500 Mon.-Sat. 10am-8pm, Sun. noon-

8pm.) Students and seniors can sometimes get **$5 tickets;** call ahead for availability (Tues.-Thurs. only). Anyone can get $10 tickets for the odd morning rehearsal; again, call ahead. In late June for a couple of weeks, Kurt Masur and friends lead the posse at **free concerts** (875-5709) on the Great Lawn in Central Park, in Prospect Park in Brooklyn, in Van Cortland Park in the Bronx, and elsewhere. Free outdoor events at Lincoln Center occur all summer; call 875-4000.

Carnegie Hall (247-7800), Seventh Ave. at 57th St., is still the favorite coming-out locale of musical debutantes. (Box office open Mon.-Sat. 11am-6pm, Sun. noon-6pm; tickets $10-60.) One of the best ways for the budget traveler to absorb New York musical culture is to visit a **music school.** Except for opera and ballet productions ($5- 12), concerts at the following schools are free and frequent: The **Juilliard School of Music,** Lincoln Center (769-7406), the **Mannes School of Music** (580-0210), the **Manhattan School of Music** (749-2802).

Jazz

The **JVC Jazz Festival** (787-2020) blows into the city in June. All-star performances have included Ray Charles and Mel Torme. Tickets go on sale in early May.

Augie's, 2751 Broadway (864-9834), between 105th and 106th St. Subway: #1 or 9 to 103rd St. Small and woody. Jazz until 3am. The saxophonist sits on your lap and the bass rests on your table. Quality musicians and an unpretentious crowd. No cover; $3 drink min. Sets start around 10pm. Open daily 6pm-4am.

Blue Note, 131 W. 3rd St. (475-8592), near MacDougal St. Subway: A, B, C, D, E, F, or Q to Washington Sq. The Carnegie Hall of jazz clubs. Now a commercialized concert space with crowded tables and a sedate audience. Often books top performers. Sets Sun.-Thurs. 9pm and 11:30pm, Fri.-Sat. 9pm, 11:30pm, and 1:30am.

Apollo Theatre, 253 W. 125th St. (749-5838, box office 864-0372), between Frederick Douglass Blvd. and Adam Clayton Powell Blvd. Subway: #1, 2, 3, or 9 to 125th St. Historic Harlem landmark has heard Duke Ellington, Count Basie, Ella Fitzgerald, and Billie Holliday. *Don't go here alone at night.* Legendary Amateur Night (where the audience boos acts off the stage, à la *Gong Show*) $5.

Birdland, 2745 Broadway (749-2228), at 105th St. Subway: #1 or 9 to 103rd St. Reasonably good food and top jazz. Cover Fri.-Sat $5 plus $5 min. per set at bar, $10/$15 at tables; Sun.-Thurs. $5 plus $5 min. per set at tables; no cover at bar. No cover for brunch Sun. noon-4pm. Open Mon.-Sat. 4pm-4am, Sun. noon-4pm and 5pm-4am. First set nightly at 9pm.

Rock & Pop Clubs

In addition to the two venues listed below, check the *Village Voice* for shows at the **Bottom Line** (228-7880), the **Mercury Lounge** (260-4700), the **Knitting Factory** (219-3055), and **Wetlands** (966-4225), all fine clubs for live music of all varieties.

CBGB/OMFUG (CBGB's), 313 Bowery (982-4052), at Bleecker St. Subway: #6 to Bleecker St. The initials stand for "country, bluegrass, blues, and other music for uplifting gourmandizers," but everyone knows that since 1976 this club has been all about punk rock. Blondie and the Talking Heads got their starts here, and the club continues to be *the* place to see great alternative rock. Shows nightly at around 8pm, Sun. (often hardcore) matinee at 3pm. Cover $5-10.

Maxwell's, 1039 Washington St. (201-798-4064), in nearby Hoboken, NJ. Subway: B, D, F, N, Q, or R to 34th St., then PATH train ($1), or simply take the PATH train ($1) to the Hoboken stop; walk down Washington to 11th St. High-quality underground rockers from America and abroad have plied their trade in the back room of a Hoboken restaurant for about 15 years. Cover $5-10; shows sometimes sell out, so get tix in advance from Maxwell's or Ticketmaster.

Bars

Automatic Slims, 733 Washington St. (645-8660), at Bank St. Subway: A, C, or E to 14th St. Simple bar in the West Village; best selection of blues and screamin' soul.

Diverse crowd packs on weekends. American cooking 6pm-midnight. Entrees $7.50-14. Open Sun.-Mon. 5:30pm-2:30am, Tues.-Sat. 5:30pm-4:30am.

The Ear Inn, 326 Spring St. (226-9060), near the Hudson. Established in 1817 and once a big bohemian/activist hangout, this bar now tends to the TriBeCa young-and-wistful crowd. Mellow jazz and blues at low volume so as not to stem the flow of conversation. Good American food served from 11am-4:30pm and 6pm-1am every day. Appetizers and salads $2-6. Bar open till 4am.

Sophie's, 507 E. 5th St. (228-5680), between Ave. A and B. Subway: F to Second Ave. or #6 to Astor Pl. Packed with leather jackets, T-shirts, jeans, and baseball-caps on weekends. Cheap cheap cheap. Draft beer $1 for a large mug. Mixed drinks start at $2.50. Pool table and soulful jukebox. Open daily noon-4am.

The Shark Bar, 307 Amsterdam Ave. (496-6600), at 75th. High-class and enjoyable bar and soul-food restaurant. Well-dressed after-work crowd nurses stiff drinks. Live jazz on Tues. with a $5 cover; "gospel brunch" Sat. 12:30pm and 2pm (no cover). Reasonable drink prices (bottled beer from $3). Entrees from $11. Open Mon.-Fri. 11:30am-2am, Sat.-Sun. 11:30am-4:30pm and 6:30pm-4am.

Max Fish, 178 Ludlow St. (529-3959), at Houston St. in the Lower East Side. Subway: F to Delancey St. or J, M, Z to Essex St. The crowd is hip, if a bit pretentious, and the all-CD jukebox is easily the best in town: The Fall, The Minutemen, Super-chunk, and the Gordons. Beer $2.50 per glass. Open daily 5:30pm-4am.

Polly Esther's, 21 E. 8th St. (979-1970), near University Pl. Grab those bell-bottoms and funky platform shoes—it's a bar dedicated to the 1970s! Two-for-one happy hour 1-9pm on weekdays and 1-7pm on weekends. Open Mon.-Fri. 11am-2am, Sat.-Sun. 11am-4am. Another location at 249 W. 26th St. (929-4782).

The Slaughtered Lamb Pub, 182 Bleecker St. (627-5262), at Jones St. A rather sin-ister-looking English pub dedicated to the werewolf. 80 types of beer ($5-20 per bottle), yards of ale, darts and billiards in the "dungeon." Open 4pm-4am.

Dance Clubs

Tunnel, 220 Twelfth Ave. (695-7292), near 28th St. Subway: C or E to 23rd St. Immense club; 3 floors packed with 2 dance floors, lounges, glass-walled live shows, and a skateboarding cage. Enough room for a multitude of parties in this labyrinthine club. Open Fri.-Sat.; Sat. nights are gay. Cover $20.

Webster Hall, 125 E. 11th St. (353-1600), between Third and Fourth Ave. Subway: #4, 5, 6, N, or R to Union Sq.-14th St. Walk 3 blocks south and a block east. New and popular club offers several floors of dancing, a reggae room and a coffeeshop. "Psychedelic Thursdays" often feature live bands. Open Wed.-Sun. Cover $5-15.

Limelight, 47 W. 20th St. (807-7850), at Sixth Ave. Subway: F or R to 23rd St. Huge club in a converted church. Several rooms for dancing. Big suburban crowd. Men may have trouble getting in without women. Queer Wed. and Fri. nights. Sun. night is live heavy metal. Cover $15, but look for discount fliers everywhere.

Nell's, 246 W. 14th St. (675-1567), between Seventh and Eighth Ave. Subway: #1, 2, 3, or 9 to 14th St. A legendary hotspot; some faithful admirers hang on even through its decline. Dingy neighborhood belies the opulence of the huge Victo-rian-style sitting room inside. Angular dance floor downstairs. Not a gay club, but a popular gay spot. Cover Mon.-Wed. $7, Thurs.-Sun. $15. Open daily 10pm-4am.

Palladium, 126 E. 14th St. (473-7171), at Third Ave. Subway: #4, 5, 6, L, N, or R to 14th St. Once Madonna and her friends set the pace, now big hair has replaced big crowds. But the music is still good and the space is still cool. Look in Village stores for discount invites. Open Fri.-Sat. 10pm-4am. Cover $20.

Gay and Lesbian Clubs

Clit Club, 432 W. 14th St. (529-3300), at Washington St. This is *the* place to be for young, beautiful, queer grrls. Host Julie throws the hottest party around every Fri. night. Cover $3 before 11pm, $5 after 11pm. Doors open at 9:30pm.

Jackie 60, 432 W. 14th St. (366-5680), at Washington St. Drag queens and some-times celebrity crowd works Cover $10. Open at 10pm.

Uncle Charlie's, 56 Greenwich Ave. (255-8787), at Perry St. Subway: #1 or 9 to Christopher St. Biggest and best-known gay club in the city. Guppies galore. Women welcome, but few come. Open daily 4pm-4am. No cover.

The Pyramid, 101 Ave. A (420-1590), at 6th St. Subway: #6 to Astor Pl. Also known by its street address, this dance club mixes gay, lesbian, and straight folks. Vibrant drag scene. Fri. is straight night. Cover $5-10. Open daily 9pm-4am.

Hipster Hangouts and Must-Sees

Nuyorican Poets Café, 236 E. 3rd St. (505-8183), between Ave. B and Ave. C. Subway: F to Second Ave. Walk 3 blocks north and 3 blocks east. New York's leading venue for the currently in-vogue "poetry slams" and spoken word performances. Don't walk in this area alone at night. Cover $5-10.

Collective Unconscious, 28 Ave. B (505-8991), between 2nd and 3rd St. Subway: F to Second Ave. Walk 3 blocks east and 2 blocks north. Plays, rock shows, and other performances (cover usually $5-7). Open mike night Sun. at 9pm ($3). Ongoing serial play on Sat. at 8pm ($5). Bring your own refreshments.

Blue Man Group-Tubes, at the Astor Place Theater, 434 Lafayette St. (254-4370). Not a hangout, but a hilarious off-Broadway show with a cult following. Definitely worth the ticket price.

Sports

While most cities would be content to field a major-league team in each big-time sport, New York opts for the Noah's Ark approach: two baseball teams, two hockey teams, and two NFL football teams. In addition to local teams' regularly scheduled games, New York hosts a number of celebrated world-class events. Get tickets 3 months in advance for the prestigious **United States Open** (718-271-5100; tickets from $12), held in late Aug. and early Sept. at the USTA Tennis Center in Flushing Meadows, Queens. On the third Sunday in Oct., two million spectators witness the 22,000 runners of the **New York City Marathon** (only 16,000 finish). The race begins on the Verrazzano Bridge and ends at Central Park's Tavern on the Green.

On the **baseball** diamond, the **New York Mets** bat at **Shea Stadium** in Queens (718-507-8499; tickets $6.50-15). The legendary but mortal **New York Yankees** play ball at Yankee Stadium in the Bronx (293-6000; tickets $6.50-17). Both the **New York Giants** and the **Jets** play **football** across the river at **Giants Stadium** (201-935-3900) in East Rutherford, NJ. Tickets from $25. The **New York Knickerbockers** (that's the Knicks to you) dribble the **basketball** at **Madison Square Garden** (465-6751, 751-6130 off-season; tickets from $12). The **New York Rangers** play **hockey** at **Madison Square Garden** (465-6741 or 308-6977); the **New York Islanders** hang their skates at the **Nassau Coliseum** (516-794-9300), Uniondale, Long Island. Tickets from $12 and $14, respectively.

■■■ LONG ISLAND

For some, Long Island evokes images of sprawling suburbia dotted with malls and office parks; others see it as the retreat for privileged New Yorkers, a summer refuge of white sand and open spaces. Yet between the malls and beaches lie both vital cultural centers and pockets of poverty. Although New York City boroughs of Brooklyn and Queens are technically part of the island, practically speaking Nassau and Suffolk Counties constitute the real Long Island. East of the Queens-Nassau line, people back the Islanders, not the Rangers, and they enjoy their role as neighbor to, rather than part of, the great metropolis. The Hamptons, on the South Fork, are mainly ritzy summer homes. The North Fork is mainly agricultural. Besides great beaches, Long Island offers good camping just outside the City. The Long Island Expressway (LIE, officially State Highway 495), includes 73 exits on the 85-mi. stretch from Manhattan to Riverhead. Traffic jams are seemingly incessant on the expressway during rush hour (which basically extends from 7am to midnight). Many Islanders still commute to the city by train, but the sights of Long Island are most easily accessible by car.

PRACTICAL INFORMATION

Get Long Island info at the **Long Island Convention and Visitors Bureau** (794-4222), which operates a visitors booth on the LIE South between Exits 51 and 52 in Commack, and on the Southern State Pkwy. between exits 13 and 14. The Island's main public transportation, **Long Island Railroad (LIRR)** (822-5477), has five central lines. Depending on how far you want to go, peak fares range from $4.25 to 14, and off-peak fares range from $3 to 9.50. Call for connection directions from NYC subways. Daytime bus service is provided by **Metropolitan Suburban Bus Authority (MSBA)** in Queens, Nassau, and western Suffolk (542-0100, bus information 766-6722). The routes are complex and irregular—make sure you confirm your destination with the driver. (Fare $1.50, crossing into Queens an additional 50¢, transfers 25¢. Disabled travelers and senior citizens pay ½-fare.) The MSBA has daily service to and from Jones Beach during the summer months. The S-92 bus of **Suffolk Transit** (852-5200; open Mon.-Fri. 8am-4:30pm) loops back and forth between the tips of the north and south forks, with nine runs daily, most of them between East Hampton and Orient Point. Call to confirm stops and schedules. The route also connects with the LIRR at Riverhead, where the forks meet. (No service Sun. Fare $1.50, senior and the disabled 50¢, under 5 free. Transfers 25¢.) **Hampton Express** (212-861-6800, on Long Island 874-2400), runs to and through the South Fork, while **Sunrise Express** (800-527-7709, in Suffolk 477-1200), covers the North Fork. Long Island's **area code:** 516.

ACCOMMODATIONS AND CAMPING

Finding a place to stay on the island can be daunting. Daytrippers in Nassau do best to return to the city. Suffolk County provides a wider variety of mostly touristy accommodations. In Montauk, sleep at **Montauket,** Tuthill Rd. (668-5992). Follow the Montauk Hwy. to Montauk; at the traffic circle take Edgemere, then left onto Fleming, then another left. Make reservations for summer weekends starting March 1st—it fills up quickly. (Doubles $35, with private bath $40.) For **camping,** dig your trenches at **Battle Row** (572-8690), in Bethpage, Nassau. Eight tent sites, and 50 trailer sites available on first-come, first-served basis. Electricity, restrooms, showers, grills, and a playground available. (Tent sites $6.75 for Nassau residents, $8.50 for visitors. Trailer sites $10 for residents, $15 for visitors.) Also try **Heckscher Park** (800-456-2267 or 581-4433), in East Islip, Suffolk. Take LIE exit 53 and go south on the Sagtikos State Pkwy. Follow signs onto the Southern State Pkwy. east, and follow this as it turns south and becomes the Heckscher Spur Pkwy. The Park is at the end of the Pkwy. The state-run facility has 69 tent and trailer sites, restrooms, showers, food, grills, a pool, and a beach. ($12.50 for the first night and $11 per additional night. Make reservations at least 7 days in advance. Open May-Sept.) **Wildwood Park** (800-456-2267 or 929-4314), at Wading River. LIE exit 68 and go north onto Rte. 46 (Wm. Floyd Pkwy.): follow it to its end and go right (east) on Rte. 25A. Follow the signs from there. Former estate of Charles and John Arbuckle, multi-millionaire coffee dealers, has 300 tent sites and 80 trailer sites with full hook-ups, restrooms, showers, food, and a beach. (Sites $11.50 first night and $10 each additional night; sites with a concrete platform $12.50/11. Reservations urged for summer weekends and must be made at least a week in advance). **A Reasonable Alternative, Inc.** (928-4034), offers rooms in private homes all along the shores of Nassau and Suffolk. (Singles or doubles $50-100.)

SIGHTS

Nassau At **Old Westbury Gardens** (333-0048), on Old Westbury Rd., nature overwhelms architecture. The elegant house, modeled after 19th-century English country manors, sits in the shadow of its surroundings of gardens and tall evergreens. A vast rose garden adjoins a number of theme gardens. (Open Wed.-Mon. 10am-5pm. House and garden $10, seniors $7, children $6. Take LIE to Exit 39S (Glen Cove Rd.), turn right on Old Westbury Rd., and continue a ¼ mi.)

Jones Beach State Park (785-1600) is the best compromise between convenience and crowd for city daytrippers. There are nearly 2500 acres of beachfront here and the parking area accommodates 23,000 cars. Only 40 min. from the city, Jones Beach packs in the crowds during the summer months. Along the 1½-mi. boardwalk you can find deck games, roller-skating, miniature golf, basketball, and nightly dancing. The **Marine Theater** in the park hosts big-name rock concerts. There are eight different bathing areas on the rough Atlantic Ocean and the calmer Zach's Bay, plus a number of beaches restricted to residents of certain towns in Nassau County. In the summer you can take the LIRR to Freeport or Wantaugh, where you can get a bus to the beach. Call 212-739-4200 or 212-526-0900 for information. **Recreation Lines** (718-788-8000) provides bus service straight from mid-Manhattan. If you are driving, take the LIE east to the Northern State Pkwy., go east to the Meadowbrook (or Wantaugh) Pkwy., and then south to Jones Beach.

Suffolk   The peaceful villages of Suffolk County, only a few hours's drive from Manhattan, are New York's version of the tradition-steeped towns of New England. Many of Suffolk's colonial roots have been successfully preserved, and the county offers some fine colonial house-museums. Salty old towns, full of shady streets—refreshing retreats from the din of New York—line the lazy coast.

After shopping at the **Walt Whitman Mall,** the nearby **Walt Whitman's Birthplace,** 246 Old Walt Whitman Rd. (427-5240), will seem a more appropriate memorial to the great American poet. (Open Wed.-Fri. 1-4pm, Sat.-Sun. 10am-4pm. Free. Take LIE to Exit 49N, drive 1¾ mi. on Rte. 110, and left on Old Walt Whitman Rd.)

Fire Island   A 32-mi.-long barrier island buffering the South Shore from the roaring waters of the Atlantic, Fire Island has both summer communities and federally protected wilderness. Cars are allowed only on the easternmost and westernmost tips of the island; there are no streets, only "walks." Fire Island was a hip counterculture spot during the 60s and still maintains a laid-back atmosphere. The **Fire Island National Seashore** (289-4810 for the headquarters in Patchogue) is the main draw here, and in summer it offers fishing, clamming, and guided nature walks. The facilities at **Sailor's Haven** (just west of the Cherry Grove community) include a marina, a nature trail, and a famous beach. Similar facilities at **Watch Hill** (597-6455) include a 20-unit **campground,** where reservations are required. **Smith Point West,** on the eastern tip of the island, has a small visitor-information center and a nature trail with disabled access (281-3010; center open daily 9am-5pm). Here you can spot horseshoe crabs, whitetail deer, and monarch butterflies, which flit across the country every year to winter in Baja California. **Wilderness camping** is available near Smith Point West on Fire Island. Camping is free but requires a hike of about 1½ mi. to get into the camping area. You must pick up a permit from Smith Point Visitors Center (281-3010; open daily 9am-5pm) on the day you go down. To get to Smith Point, take exit 68, head south, and follow the signs.

The **Sunken Forest,** so called because of its location down behind the dunes, is another of the Island's natural wonders. Located directly west of Sailor's Haven, its soils support an unusual and attractive combination of gnarled holly, sassafras, and poison ivy. From the summit of the dunes, you can see the forest's trees laced together in a hulky, uninterrupted mesh.

To get to Fire Island: From **Bay Shore** (665-3600), ferries sail to Fair Harbor, Ocean Beach, Ocean Bay Park, Saltaire, and Kismet. (Round-trip fare $10.50, children under 12 $5.) From **Sayville** (589-8980), ferries leave for Sailor's Haven (round-trip fare $8, children under 12 $4.50) and Cherry Grove and Fire Island Pines (round-trip fare for either $10, children under 12 $5). From **Patchogue** (475-1665), ferries go to Davis Park and Watch Hill (round-trip to either $10, children under 12 $5.50). LIRR stations lie within a short distance of the 3 ferry terminals, making access from New York City relatively simple. (All ferries May-Nov.)

THE MID-ATLANTIC

Wine Country Long Island does not readily conjure up images of plump wine-grapes just waiting to be plucked by epicurean Islanders. But a visit to one of the North Fork's 40 vineyards can be a pleasant and interesting surprise. The wineries and vineyards here produce the best Chardonnay, Cabernet Sauvignon, Merlot, Pinot Noir, and Riesling in New York State. Many of the Island wineries offer free tours and tastings. To get to there, take the LIE to its end (Exit 73), then Rte. 58, which becomes Rte. 25 (Main Rd.). North of and parallel to Rte. 25 is Rte. 48 (North Rd. or Middle Rd.), which claims a number of wineries. Road signs announce tours and tastings. Of note is **Palmer Vineyards,** 108 Sound Ave. (722-9463), in Riverhead. Take a self-guided tour of the most advanced equipment on the Island and see a tasting room with an interior assembled from two 18th-century English pubs. At the junction of Rte. 43 and Sound Ave., **Berezny's Farm Stand** (722-3823) sells inexpensive, locally grown produce. (Open late May-Nov.) West on Sound Ave. takes you to **Briermere Farm,** 79 Sound Ave. (722-3931), which cooks up famous fruit pies and delicious breads (Open daily 8am-6pm; closed Jan. to mid-Feb.)

Hamptons Composed of **West, South, Bridge,** and **East Hampton,** this area is famous for its ritzy homes for rich New Yorkers who "summer" and great beaches. Each town offers a quaint Main street with shops, restaurants, and good people watching in the summer. Historians and sadists alike should check out the **Southampton Historical Museum** (283-1612), located near the center of town at the corner of Meeting House Lane and Main St. Start with the pillory, where thieves and those *accused* of adultery were publicly flayed. Or try your neck in the stocks, the clever device used to humiliate (and hurt) the drunkards and disrespectful children of old Southampton. (Open in summer Tues.-Sun. 11am-5pm. $2, children 6-11 50¢. Take Rte. 27E to Southampton Center.) The **Guild Hall Museum** 158 Main St. (324-0806), in East Hampton, specializes in well-known artists of the eastern Island region, from the late-19th century to the present. (Open June-Aug. daily 11am-5pm, Sept.-May Wed.-Sun. 11am-5pm. $5, seniors $2.) The East Hampton beach is known as being one of the most beautiful in the world.

East Hampton Bowl, 71 Montauk Hwy. (324-1950) just west of East Hampton, offers a great escape from the area's big-money scene. And yes—it is a spot for nightlife: the bowling alley and attached bar stay open until at least midnight every night, and Sat. nights feature "Rock-'n'-Bowl." (Bowling $3.40 per game; shoe rental $2.)

Sag Harbor Out on the South Fork's north shore droops Sag Harbor, one of the best-kept secrets of Long Island. Founded in 1707, this port used to be more important than New York Harbor since its deep shore made for easy navigation. The legacy of Sag Harbor's former grandeur survives in the second-largest collection of Colonial buildings in the U.S., and in the cemeteries lined with the gravestones of Revolutionary soldiers and sailors. Check out the **Sag Harbor Whaling Museum** (725-0770). Enter the museum through the jawbones of a whale. Note the antique 1864 washing-machine and the excellent scrimshaw collection. (Open May-Sept. Mon.-Sat. 10am-5pm, Sun. 1-5pm. $3, children $1. Call for tours.)

Montauk At the easternmost tip of the south fork, Montauk is one of the most popular destinations on Long Island. And with good reason, considering the thrill of looking out at the Atlantic Ocean and realizing that there is nothing but water between you and Limerick. The trip from Manhattan takes 4 hr. by car. Take the LIE to Exit 70 (Manorville), then go south to Sunrise Hwy. (Rte. 27), which becomes Montauk Hwy., and drive east.

The **Montauk Point Lighthouse and Museum** (668-2544) is the high point of a trip here. The 86-ft. structure went up by special order of President George Washington. On a clear day, you should climb the 138 spiralling steps to the top, where you can see across the Long Island Sound to Connecticut and Rhode Island. The best seasons for viewing are spring and fall; the thick summer air can haze over the view. But even on a foggy day, you may want to climb up to see if you can spot the

Will o' the Wisp, a ghostly clipper ship sometimes sighted on hazy days under full sail with a lantern hanging from its mast. Experts claim that the ship is a mirage resulting from the presence of phosphorus in the atmosphere, but what do they know? (Open May-June and Oct.-Nov. Sat.-Sun. 10:30am-4pm; June-Sept. daily 10:30am-6pm; Sept.-Oct. Fri.-Mon. 10:30am-5pm. $2.50, children $1, plus $3 to park a car.)

Try **Viking** (668-5700) or **Lazybones'** (668-5671) for half-day fishing cruises ($20-25). **Okeanos Whale Watch Cruise** (728-4522) offers excellent six-hour trips for spotting fin, minke, and humpback whales ($30 and up).

Shelter Island Shelter Island bobs in the protected body of water between the north and south forks. Accessible by ferry or by private boat, this island of about 12 sq. mi. offers wonderful beaches (locals tend to favor Wades Beach and Hay Beach) and a serene sense of removal from the intrusions of the city. A detailed map of the island is available from most inns and other places of business. **The Belle Crest House,** 163 North Ferry Rd. (749-2041), in Shelter Island Heights just up the hill from the north ferry, is a beautiful old country home with large rooms—a great spot for a romantic getaway. (From May 1 to Oct. 31: Mon.-Thurs. doubles $65-70 with shared bath, $95 with private bath; Fri.-Sun. $80 and $165. Two night min. for summer weekends. Off-season rates dip as low as $45.) **North Fork: Greenport Ferry** (749-0139), North Ferry Rd., on the dock, takes passenger and driver for $6.50, round-trip $7, each additional passenger $1, walk-on (without a car) $1. Ferries run daily every 15 min., with the first ferry leaving Greenport at 6am and the last ferry departing the island at 11:45pm. **South Fork: North Haven Ferry** (749-1200), 3 mi. north of Sag Harbor on Rte. 114, on the dock, takes car and driver for $6 one-way, $6.50 round-trip, additional passengers $1 each, walk-ons $1 round-trip. Ferries run daily at approximately 10 min. intervals 6am-1:45am.

■■■ TARRYTOWN

A convenient day trip from NYC, Tarrytown is a sleepy suburban hollow near the Tappan Zee bridge on the Hudson River. This area provided the inspiration for Washington Irving's famous tales of *Rip Van Winkle* and Ichabod Crane and the headless horseman in *The Legend of Sleepy Hollow.* Irving's home, **Sunnyside,** Sunnyside Lane (591-8763), in Irvington, is a small cottage surrounded by pretty grounds on what was once, well, a neck of land in the Hudson. (Open March-Dec. Wed.-Mon. 10am-5pm, $6, seniors $5, 6-17 $3, grounds only $3.) Near Sunnyside is **Lyndhurst,** 635 South Broadway (631-4481), the sumptuous summer palace of various New York tycoons. This stately manor has wonderful grounds, including a rose garden, a carriage house (*sans* horsemen), and the remains of what was once the largest greenhouse in America. The house itself is nice, but if you're looking to save a few bucks, skip it and just enjoy the magnificent grounds. (Open May-Oct. Tues.-Sun. 10am-5pm; Nov.-April Sat.-Sun. 10am-3:30pm. $7, seniors $6, child $3, grounds $3; join tickets for Sunnyside and Lyndhurst $10, seniors $8.) Head over to neighboring **North Tarrytown** (just down Rte. 9) to **Philipsburg Manor** (631-3992), which is a neat living history venue that features a working waterwheel on a replicated, but functioning, colonial farm.(Open March-Dec. Wed.-Mon. 10am-5pm; Jan.-Feb. Sat.-Sun. 10am-5pm; $6, seniors $5, ages 6-14 $3, students $3.)

For a nature break, roll out to **Rockefeller State Park Reserve,** Rte. 117, 1 mi. off Rte. 9 (631-1470), where you can bike, fish, or ride a horse (permit and head required). (Open daily 9am-sunset. Free.) The real must-see of the entire region, however, is the stupendous **Rockwood,** Rte. 117 (631-1470). Here you can climb over the foundations of a former Rockefeller estate and enjoy views of the Hudson River Valley that are head and shoulders, well, shoulders anyway, over any other around. Or you can picnic in the hillside meadows and fall asleep under a tree (but don't be alarmed by a tappanzee shoulder, they don't want any more 100-year naps.) The park is always open and free. All the fixin's for a picnic in one of the lovely spots in Tarrytown are available at the **Grand Union,** 1 Courtland Ave. and Wilton St. (Mon.-Sat. 7am-11pm, Sun.. 9am-8pm.)

Tarrytown is accessible from New York by a scenic ride on the **Metro-North Commuter Rail** (800-METRO-INFO) which runs from Grand Central Station. (Train runs 6:20am-1:20am, $5 offpeak, $6.75 rush hour.) **Area code:** 914.

■■■ CATSKILLS

These lovely mountains have captivated city-dwellers since long before Washington Irving celebrated them in his short stories. Yet if Rip Van Winkle were to choose a napping place, he couldn't find a more peaceful spot than the Catskill Mountains. Aside from the resorts, visitors can find serenity and natural beauty in the state-managed Catskill Preserve, home to quiet villages, sparkling streams, and miles of hiking and skiing trails. But these mountains provide not only recreation and relaxation. The Catskills are functional and, occasionally, radical; they hosted Woodstock, the 1969 concert that rocked the nation, are home to the state capital, and house the Ashokan reservoir, which supplies New York City with much of its drinking water.

Practical Information **Adirondack Pine Hill Trailways** provides excellent service through the Catskills. The main stop is **Kingston,** 400 Washington Ave. (914-331-0744 or 800-225-6815) on the corner of Front St. Buses run to: New York City (11 per day, 2 hr., $18.50, $25 same-day roundtrip; Ameripass accepted). Other stops in the area include Woodstock, Pine Hill, Saugerties, and Hunter; each connects with New York City, Albany, and Utica. (Ticket office open Mon.-Thurs. 5:30am-8:15pm; Fri. and Sun. 5:30am-11pm, Sat. 5:30am-10pm.) The **Ulster County Public Information Office,** 244 Fair St. (914-331-9300, ext. 436 or 800-342-5826), six blocks from Kingston bus station, has a helpful travel guide and a list of Catskill trails (open Mon.-Fri. 9am-5pm). Three **tourist cabooses** are also available, located at the traffic circle in Kingston, on Rte. 28 in Shandaken, and on Rte. 209 in Ellenville (open summer months Fri.-Sun; hours vary depending on volunteer availability). The **visitor centers** at rest stops along U.S. 87 can also advise well.

■ CATSKILL FOREST PRESERVE

The 250,000-acre **Catskill Forest Preserve** contains many small towns, such as **Phoenicia, Kingston,** and **Woodstock,** which are ready to host and equip the travelers who come to enjoy the outdoors. The slow-moving town of **Phoenicia,** accessible by bus from Kingston, makes a good place to anchor your trip. The **Esopus River,** just to the west, is great for trout fishing and for late-summer inner-tubing. Rent tubes at **The Town Tinker** (914-688-5553), on Bridge St. in Phoenicia. (Inner tubes $7 per day, with a seat $10. Driver's license or $15 required as a deposit. Transportation $3. Life jackets available and required. Open May-Sept. daily 9am-6pm, last rental 4:30pm.) Take a dive at the 65-ft. **Sundance Rappel Tower,** Rte. 214 (914-688-5640). Four levels of lessons are available: beginner $20 for 3-4 hr. Reservations required. Lessons are only given when a group of four is available. If you plan to go fishing, you need to buy a **fishing permit** (5 days, non-NY resident $16), available in any sporting goods store. To camp in the backcountry for more than three days, you must obtain a permit from the nearest ranger station. Trails are maintained year-round; available lean-tos are sometimes dilapidated and crowded. Boil or treat water with chemicals, and pack your garbage. To reach the head of your chosen trail, take an **Adirondack Trailways** bus from Kingston—drivers will let you out anywhere along the bus routes (914-331-0744).

Also in Phoenicia, the **Empire State Railway Museum** (688-7501) on High St. off Rte. 28, has artifacts from the late 19th century glory days of the steam engine. A 1910 locomotive is being restored and will eventually run on the tracks of the former Ulster and Delaware. (Open weekends and holidays 10am-6pm.)

When heading to Kingston, take a detour and stop in at the town of **Woodstock**, a haven for artists and writers since the turn of the century, but perhaps best known for the massive summer of 1969 concert which bore its name. Today, a few lonely protesters still picket in town, but most of the tie-dye legacy has faded and Woodstock has become an expensive, rather touristy place. Check out the galleries that line the main street in town. Just a few miles away, those seeking peace with nature can join in meditation at the **Zen Mountain Monastery**, S. Plank Rd., P.O. Box 197PC, Mt. Tremper, NY 12457 (914-688-2228), a short walk from Mt. Tremper. (Free meditation sessions Wed. 7:30pm and Sun. 9am; weekend retreats $165.) Back in Kingston, head to the **Woodstock Brewing Company**, 20 St. James St. (331-2810), for a taste of beer brewed right in the Hudson Valley. Nat Collins, the owner and brewmaster, will give you a free tour on Saturdays (along with a free tasting) of his (and the state's only) complete microbrewery.

Camping and Accommodations One of the many **state campgrounds** can serve as a base for your adventures. Reservations (800-456-2267) are vital during the summer, especially Thurs.-Sun. (Sites $15. Open May-Sept.) Call the rangers at the individual campgrounds for the best info on sites in the area. For brochures on state campgrounds call the **Office of Parks** (518-474-0456). **North Lake**, Rte. 23A (518-589-5058), 3 mi. northeast of Haines Falls in Greene County, rents canoes and has showers and good hiking trails. **Kenneth L. Wilson** (914-679-7020), a 4-mi. hike from Bearsville bus stop, has showers, a pond-front beach, and a family atmosphere ($11 per site). **Woodland Valley** (914-688-7647), 5 mi. southeast of Phoenicia, has flush toilets and showers, and sits on a good 16-mi. hiking trail (sites $9).

If you prefer sleeping in the midst of civilization, go to the **Super 8 Motel**, 487 Washington Ave. (914-338-3078), two blocks from the Kingston bus station (singles from $49, doubles from $53; reserve for summer weekends). In Phoenicia, the **Cobblestone Motel**, Rte. 214 (688-7871), has an outdoor pool and wellworn but very clean rooms from $44.

The **Belleayre Hostel** (914-254-4200), on Rte. 28 off exit 19 of the New York State Throughway, offers bunks and private rooms in a natural setting not far from Kingston. All rooms have sinks and radios, and access to a kitchen, picnic area, and sporting equipment. Call ahead. (Bunks $9 in summer, $12 in winter; private rooms $20/25; efficiency cabins for up to 4 $35/45.)

■■■ ALBANY

Although the English took Albany in 1664, the city was actually founded in 1614 as a trading post for the Dutch West Indies Company, and is the oldest continuous European settlement in the original 13 colonies (established six years before the Pilgrims landed on the New England shore). Albany (once named Fort Orange) became New York's state capital in 1797, but it never matched the growth of its southern sibling, the Big Apple. Today, Albany can justly claim the status of a major metropolis. Located at the confluence of the Mohawk and Hudson Rivers, the city serves as a transportation hub for the northeast. Recent efforts to stimulate tourism have led to the creation of a sprawling, urban cultural park in this, the site of the largest state government in the nation.

Practical Information The **Albany Visitors Center**, 25 Quackenbush Sq. (434-5132), at Clinton Ave. and Broadway, runs trolley tours (Thurs.-Fri. July-Sept. $4, children and seniors $2, free tours daily June-Sept. at 11:30am; call 434-6311 for info). **Amtrak** (800-872-7245 or 462-5763), is on East St. in Rensselaer across the Hudson from downtown Albany (open Mon.-Fri. 5:30am-11pm, Sat.-Sun. 6am-midnight). **Greyhound**, 34 Hamilton St. (434-8095), offers student discounts on selected routes. (Station open 24 hrs., but use caution when walking in this area at night.) One block away at 360 Broadway, **Adirondack Trailways** (436-9651) connects to other upstate locales: Lake George (3-5 per day, 1 hr., $9); Lake Placid (1-2

THE MID-ATLANTIC

per day, 4 hr., $22); Tupper Lake (1 per day, 4 hr., $26). Senior and college-student discounts are available for some routes. (Open daily 5:30am-midnight.) For local travel, the **Capital District Transit Authority (CDTA)** (482-8822) serves Albany, Troy, and Schenectady (fare 75¢). CDTA has a confusing schedule; call the main office for information. Albany's **post office:** 30 Old Karner Rd. (452-2499); **ZIP code:** 12201; **area code:** 518.

Accommodations and Food For reasonable accommodations, try the **College of Saint Rose,** Lima Hall, 366 Western Ave. (For reservations contact Tonita Nagle at Student Affairs, Box 114, 432 Western Ave., 454-5171; after hours 454-3069. Open May 15-Aug. 15 daily 8:30am-4:30pm.) You'll find large rooms and clean bathrooms in student dorms on a safe campus. The dining hall is open for use. (Singles $35, shared doubles $25 per person.) Nice accommodations in a safe neighborhood are available at **Pine Haven,** 531 Western Ave. (482-1574). Pine Haven is no longer an AYH affiliated hostel, but the proprietor still gives members a substantial discount. From the bus station, walk by the State University of New York offices on Broadway and turn left on State St. From the stop in front of the Hilton, take bus 10 up Western Ave. and get off at N. Allen St. Pine Haven is on your right, at the convergence of Madison and Western Ave. Parking is in the rear. (AYH members $30, $10 each additional; nonmembers $49 single, $64 double; shared bath.) Nearby Schenectady (accessible via Albany's public transportation system), also provides a cheap overnight stay. The **YWCA,** 44 Washington Ave. (374-3394), has single rooms ($20) with a shared bath for women only. Men should walk around the corner to the **YMCA,** 13 State St. (374-9136), which provides similar accommodations for men only ($21.50). Reservations for either should be made in advance. To get to the "Y's" from Albany, take bus #55. **Thompson's Lake State Park** (518-872-1674), on Rte. 157, 4 mi. north of East Berne, provides the closest outdoor living (18 mi. southwest of Albany). 140 sites ($10) boast many natural perks, including nearby fishing, hiking trails, and a swimming beach.

Downtown Albany closes up early when the suits head home. However, Malden St., just off North Pearl St., has a few terrific sandwich shops. **Barlee's,** 34 Malden St. (462-0535), offers excellent sandwiches ($2.50-3.50; open Mon.-Fri. 7am-2:30pm). Up the hill from downtown, sustenance becomes both affordable and plentiful. Head to Lark St., between Madison and Western, and find **Shades of Green** (434-1830), located in a small nook at 185½ Lark St. Delicious vegetarian cuisine (try the Tempeh Reuben, $4.25) can be washed down with a cool fruit or vegetable shake ($3). (Open Mon.-Fri. 11am-7pm, Sat. 11am-5pm.) **Next Door,** 142 Washington St. (434-1616), has a half-sandwich special with soup and salad ($4), and great chocolate chip cookies (55¢). (Open Mon.-Fri. 11am-6pm, for drinks until 10pm.)

Sights Albany offers about a day's worth of sight-seeing activity. The **Rockefeller Empire State Plaza,** State St., is a $1.9 billion towering, modernist Stonehenge. It houses, aside from state offices, any sort of store or service one might want, including a bus terminal, post office, cleaners, a cafeteria, and the **New York State Museum** (474-5877; museum open daily 10am-5pm; $2 suggested donation). The museum has exhibits on the history of the state's different regions and on Native America, and even displays an original set for "Sesame Street." Lining the walls throughout the plaza, the **Empire State Collection** features works by innovative New York School artists such as Jackson Pollock, Mark Rothko, and David Smith (the concourse level is open daily 6am-11pm; tours by appointment; free). The huge flying saucer at one end of the Empire State Plaza is the **Empire Center for the Performing Arts** (473-1845; box office open Mon.-Fri. 11am-3pm, Sat. noon-3pm, and 90 min. prior to all shows). For a bird's-eye view of Albany, visit the observation deck on the 42nd floor of the **Corning Tower** (open Mon.-Fri. 9am-4pm).

The modern plaza provides a striking contrast to the more traditional architectural landscape of the rest of the city. Within walking distance on Washington Ave. are **City Hall,** 24 Eagle St., an earthy Romanesque edifice (open Mon.-Fri. 8am-5pm,

Wed. until 8pm; free tours by appointment Mon.-Fri., call 434-5132), and the gothic **Capitol Building** (474-2418), (free tours on the hr. Mon.-Fri. 9am-4pm, Sat.-Sun. 10am-4pm). Both buildings were designed by H. H. Richardson. Colonial statesman and capitalized Philip Schuyler (SKY-ler) owned the **Schuyler Mansion,** 32 Catherine St. (434-0834), an elegant Georgian home built in 1761. Here George Washington and Benjamin Franklin dined, and here Alexander Hamilton married Schuyler's daughter. (Open April-Oct. Wed.-Sun. 10am-5pm; free.) The **First Church in Albany** (463-4449), on the corner of Orange and N. Pearl, was founded in 1642. Its present building was constructed in 1798 and houses both the oldest known pulpit and weather vane in America. (Open Mon.-Fri. 8:30am-3:30pm.)

Knickerbocker Arena, 51 South Pearl St. (487-2000), puts on large musical shows and hosts sporting events. Catch the Albany Roverats or Firebirds in action (call Ticketmaster at 476-1000 for info on events). Bikers should check out the **Mohawk-Hudson Bikeway,** which passes along old railroad grades and canal towpaths as it weaves through the capital area (maps available at the visitors center).

Albany blossoms in a colorful rainbow of music, dancing, food, and street-scrubbing in early May when it celebrates its Dutch heritage during the **Tulip Festival** (434-2032). The state sponsors free concerts and big-band dancing at the plaza every other Wednesday night in July and August (call 473-0559 for info). **Washington Park,** bounded by State St. and Madison Ave. north of downtown, has tennis courts, paddle boats, and verdant fields. From July to mid-August, the **Park Playhouse** (434-2035) stages free theater, including **Actor's Shakespeare** (436-3983) in Washington Park. On Thursdays during the summer, come **Alive at Five** (434-2032) to the sound of free concerts at the **Tercentennial Plaza** across from Norstar on Broadway. For a list of events, call the **Albany Alive Line** (434-1217, ext. 409).

■■■ COOPERSTOWN

Cooperstown is a village rich in American mythology. In fact, few cities can claim a more prominent place in the nation's collective idea of how America used to be. Two former residents are responsible—author James Fenimore Cooper and soldier Abner Doubleday. Cooper's novels, collectively known as the Leatherstocking Tales, are perhaps the first true pieces of American folklore. Civil War hero Doubleday was the inventor of baseball according to legend; the 1905 Mills Commission finally settled the matter. Tourists invade every summer to visit the Baseball Hall of Fame, buy baseball memorabilia, eat in baseball-theme restaurants, and sleep in baseball-theme motels.

Take me out to the **National Baseball Hall of Fame and Museum** (547-7200 or 547-9988) on Main St., an enormous monument to America's favorite pastime: baseball. Among the historic bats, balls, uniforms, and plaques are exhibits on women and minorities in baseball, a display on how a baseball is made, and remarkably life-like wooden statues of Babe Ruth and Ted Williams. The annual ceremonies for new hall inductees are held in **Cooper Park,** next to the building (late July-early Aug.; call ahead). There are special exhibits for hearing and visually impaired fans. The Hall of Fame is an engaging museum even for the tepid baseball fan. (Open daily 9am-9pm; Oct.-April 9am-5pm. $8, ages 7-15 $3, under 7 free. Combination tickets with the Farmers' Museum and Fenimore House $17.50, or $13 for 2 sites.)

Practical Information Cooperstown is accessible from I-90 and I-88 via Rte. 28. Street parking barely exists in Cooperstown; your best bets are the three free parking lots just outside of town near the Fenimore House, on Rte. 28 south of Cooperstown, and on Glen Ave. From these, take a trolley into town (runs daily July-Sept. 8:30am-9pm; weekends only Memorial Day-June and Labor Day-Columbus Day; all-day pass $1.50). **Adirondack Trailways** (800-225-6815) runs two buses per day from New York City (6 hr., $4, Ameripasses honored). The **Cooperstown Area Chamber of Commerce,** 31 Chestnut St. (547-9983), on Rte. 80 near Main St., has maps, brochures, and hotel and B&B listings; it also can make lodging reservations. (Open daily 9am-6:45pm.) Cooperstown's **post office:** 40 Main St. (225-6815; open Mon.-Fri. 8:30am-5pm, Sat. 9:30am-1pm); **ZIP code:** 13326; **area code:** 607.

Accommodations and Food Camping is the way to go in Cooperstown; lodging in the summertime is hideously expensive, although the Chamber of Commerce can help out. **Glimmerglass State Park,** RD2 Box 580 (547-8662 or 800-456-2267), Otsego County Rte. 31 (Main St. within Cooperstown) on the east side of Ostego Lake, 8 mi. north of Cooperstown, has 39 pristine campsites in a gorgeous lakeside park. You can swim, fish, and boat from 11am-7pm. (Sites $11.50; showers, dumping station, handicapped accessible, no hookups.) **Cooperstown Beaver Valley Campground,** Box 704 Cooperstown (293-7324 or 800-726-7314), never fills up, even in high season. Take Rte. 28 south 4 mi., turn right on to Seminary Rd. Two **bunkhouses** are available (bring your own linen), 110 sites, three ponds, and laundry facilities. Friday-Sunday, the owner personally buses campers into town. (Bunkhouse $12 per person, 4 person minimum; tent site for 4 $20; paddleboat rental $5 per hr. Open mid-May to mid-Sept.) Indoor accommodations are available at the **Ringwood Farms Campground,** RD #2, Box 721 (547-2896 or 800-231-9114), on Rte. 80 east, 8 mi. north of Cooperstown. Bunks are available (bring bedding) in a new year-round hostel ($15; tent sites $16; hostel reservations required). The **Lindsay House,** 56 Chestnut St. (547-5618), is a B&B with A/C near the center of town, only a short walk from Main St. (Rooms $35 and up; reservations essential.)

For decent food, an amusing baseball atmosphere, and a souvenir shop, check out **T.J.'s Place** (547-4040), on Main St. across from Doubleday Field. (Dinners $5-10; open daily 8am-9pm.) The **Pioneer Patio,** on Pioneer Alley off Pioneer St. (547-5601), serves up affordable American and German fare. Try the bratwurst ($3.95) while enjoying their outdoor patio. (Dinners $7-10; open daily 11am-10pm.)

■■■ ITHACA AND THE FINGER LAKES REGION

According to Iroquois legend, the Great Spirit laid his hand upon the earth, and the impression of his fingers made the Finger Lakes: Canandaigua, Keuka, Seneca, Cayuga, Owasco, and Skaneateles, among others. Others credit the glaciers of the last Ice Age for these formations. But, regardless of their creation, the lakes and the nearby waterfalls, hills, and gorges make for spectacular scenery, and, with the acclaimed regional wineries, afford travelers a sublime vacation.

PRACTICAL INFORMATION

Emergency is 911. The **Tompkins County Convention and Visitors Bureau,** 904 E. Shore Dr., Ithaca 14850 (272-1313 or 800-284-8422), has a tremendous number of brochures on upstate New York, hotel and B&B listings, and the best map of the area ($3). (Open Mon.-Fri. 9am-5pm, Sat.-Sun. 10am-5pm; Labor Day-Oct. Mon.-Sat. 9am-5pm; Nov.-Memorial Day Mon.-Fri. 9am-5pm.) **The Finger Lakes Association,** 309 Lake St. Pennyon, NY 14527 (800-548-4386 or 315-536-7488), can also guide the displaced traveler. For $2, they'll send you a copy of their *Finger Lakes Travel Guide.* **Ithaca Bus Terminal** (272-7930), W. State and N. Fulton St., houses **Short Line** and **Greyhound** (800-231-2222). (To: New York City 8 per day, Philadelphia 3 per day, Buffalo 3 per day.) Call for frequently-changing fares. (Open daily 7:30am-6:30pm.) **Tomtran (Tompkins County Transportation Services Project) (**272-7433), covers a wider area than Ithaca Transit, including Trumansburg and Ulysses, both northwest of Ithaca on Rte. 96, and Cayuga Heights and Lansing Village, both north of Ithaca on Rte. 13. Tomtron is your only choice for getting out to the Finger Lakes. Buses stop at Ithaca Commons, westbound on Seneca St., and eastbound on Green. (60¢, $1.25 for more distant zones. Mon.-Fri. only.) Rent a bike at **Pedal Away,** 700 W. Buffalo St. (272-5425), near the commons ($20 per day). Take Ithaca

Transit to the Tompkins County Trust, west end branch. (Open daily 10am-8pm.) Ithaca's **post office:** 213 N. Tioga St. (272-5455), at E. Buffalo (open Mon.-Fri. 8:30am-5:30pm, Sat. 8:30am-1pm); **ZIP code:** 14850; **area code:** 607.

ACCOMMODATIONS AND CAMPING

The Tompkins County Visitors Bureau (see Practical Information above) has full Ithaca area motel and B&B listings.

Podunk House Hostel (HI-AYH), Podunk Rd. (387-9277), in Trumansburg about 8 mi. northwest of Ithaca. Take 96 north, turn left on Cold Springs Rd. and proceed until it ends at Podunk Rd. Greyhound has eliminated its Trumansburg flag stop, and you can only take the Tomtran Mon.-Fri. Venture into the land of Oz, friendly owner of the hostel. Finnish sauna fired up twice a week, but if you miss it, the serenity of his 30-acre farm is sure to relax your body. Chilly mountain creek, hiking trails and cross-country skiing accessible. Beds in the loft of a homestead barn. No kitchen; refrigerator and hot plate only. Members only, $6. Linen $1.50. Open April-Oct. Call ahead before 9pm.

The Wonderland Motel, 654 Elmira Rd. (272-5252), is one of the most affordable and accessible motels in Ithaca. Winter singles $28, doubles $36. Summer singles from $36, doubles from $45. Outdoor pool.

Elmshade Guest House, 402 S. Albany St. (273-1707), at Center St., 3 blocks from the Ithaca Commons. From the bus station, walk up State St. and turn right onto Albany. Impeccably clean, well-decorated, good-sized rooms with shared bath. You'll feel like a guest at a rich relative's house. TV in every room, refrigerator, microwave in hall. Singles $35. Doubles $40; prices may rise. Morning coffee, rolls, and fruit included. Reservations recommended.

Camping options in this area are virtually endless. Ten of the 16 state parks in the Finger Lakes region have campsites, and nine have cabins. The brochure *Finger Lakes State Parks* contains a description of each park's location and services; pick it up from any tourist office, park, or the **Finger Lakes State Park Region,** 2221 Taughannock Park Rd., PO Box 1055, Trumansburg 14886 (607-387-7041. Sites $9-15.) Whatever your plans, reserve ahead. Summer weekends often fill up.

FOOD

Restaurants cluster in Ithaca along Aurora St. and the Ithaca Commons. For more options, pick up the *Ithaca Dining Guide* pamphlet at the Tompkins County Visitors Center (see above).

Moosewood Restaurant (273-9610), Seneca and Cayuga St., in Ithaca. Legendary! The *Moosewood Cookbook* originated here. Creative, well-prepared vegetarian, fish, and pasta dishes. Lunches $5-6, dinners $9-11. Open Mon.-Sat. 11:30am-2pm and 5:30-9pm, Sun. 5:30-9pm; winter Sun.-Thurs. 5:30-8:30pm.

Joe's Restaurant, 602 W. Buffalo St. (273-2693), at Rte. 13 (Meadow St.), 10-min. walk from Ithaca Commons. Italian and American food. Original Art-deco interior dates from 1932; this is a *big* student spot. Entrees $7-15. Open 4-10pm.

Just a Taste, 116 N. Aurora (277-9463), near Ithaca Common. The place to taste an extensive list of fine wines (2½ oz. $1.75-3.75) and savor *tapas,* the Spanish "little dishes" ($3.50-5.50). Individual pizzas from $3.50. 80 beers also available. Entrees $9-12. Open Sun.-Wed. 11:30am-10pm, Thurs.-Sat. 11:30am-midnight. Bar open Mon.-Wed. until midnight, Thurs.-Sat. until 1am, Sun. until 11pm.

Rongovian Embassy to the USA (387-3334) Rte. 96, in the main strip of Trumansburg about 10 mi. out of Ithaca. Worth the drive. Amazing Mexican entrees in a classic restaurant/bar. Plot your next trip to "Beefree," "Nearvarna," or "Freelonch" on their huge wall map. Tacos $2.50. Dinners $8-12. Mug of beer $1.50. Live bands Fri.-Sun., cover $4-6. Food served Tues.-Thurs. and Sun. 5-9pm, Fri.-Sat. 5-10pm. Bar open Mon.-Sat. 4pm-1am, Sun. 1pm-1am.

Station Restaurant, 806 W. Buffalo (272-2609), a plushly, renovated train station which serves as a National Historical Landmark. Tasty dishes make for a worthwhile culinary journey. Pasta, poultry, and seafood specials $9-14. Open Mon.-Sat. 4pm-9:30pm, Sun. noon-9:30pm.

SIGHTS AND ATTRACTIONS

The expansive Finger Lakes Region offers a virtual cornucopia of cultural attractions, outdoor activities, and scenic vistas. Numerous museums, dealing with subjects from country music to photography to architecture, are nestled throughout; frequently a wrong turn may find you a historical treasure, hidden to those who fail to venture off the main routes. Commercial sailing, ballooning, fishing, and other excursions can be enjoyed as well. Each county publishes an *I Love NY* county guide, which lists specific local sights and is available at area Information Centers.

The fertile soil of the Finger Lakes area makes this region the heart of New York's wine industry. Wine tasting and vineyard touring is a relaxing way to pass a day. There are three **wine trails:** the **Cayuga,** eight wineries located along Rte. 89 between Seneca Falls and Trumansburg; the **Seneca,** 14 wineries split into the east side of the lake (Rte.414) and the west side (Rte. 14); and the **Keuka,** seven wineries along Rte. 54 and Rte. 76. Locals say that the fall harvest is the best time to visit. All of the vineyards on the Cayuga Wine Trail (P.O. Box 123, Fayette, NY 13065; write for their brochure) offer picnic facilities and free tastings, though some require purchase of a glass ($1.50-2). **Americana Vineyards Winery,** 4367 East Covert Rd., Interlaken (387-6801), ferments 1 mi. from Trumansburg, accessible by Greyhound and Tomtran. A family of four operates this winery from grape-picking to bottle-corking; one of them will give you a personal tour and free tasting. Pick up a bottle for about $5. (Open May-Oct. Mon.-Sat. 10am-5pm, Sun. noon-5pm; April and Nov.-Dec. weekends only; if you're driving, take Rte. 96 or 89 north of Trumansburg to E. Covert Rd.) Held in late August, the **Finger Lakes Wine Festival** is the largest regional wine festival east of the Rockies. The annual event offers wines from over 30 vineyards. ($15, for info write PO Box 145, Fayette 13065, or call 869-9962.)

Cornell University, youngest of the Ivy League schools, sits atop a hill in downtown Ithaca. Its campus contains impressive stone masonry and the nation's largest indoor climbing wall. A stroll along Fall Creek and Beebe Lake makes for a fine time. The **Information and Referral Center** is located in the Day Hall Lobby (254-4636; open Mon.-Sat. 8am-5pm). **Ithaca College,** located on South Hill, also offers cultural, sporting, and recreation entertainment (274-3011 for campus info).

Considered the birthplace of the women's rights movement, **Seneca Falls** hosted the 1848 Seneca Falls Convention. Elizabeth Cady Stanton and Amelia Bloomer, two leading suffragists who lived here, organized a meeting of those seeking the vote for women. Today, the **Women's Rights National Historical Park** commemorates their efforts, preserving the area for those who have benefited so greatly from their courage and initiative. Begin at the **visitors center,** 116 Fall St. (315-568-2991; open daily 9am-5pm; free talks and walking tours are scheduled June-Sept.; guided tours of the Elizabeth Cady Stanton House may be taken June-Sept. daily 9am-5pm, and Oct.-May daily noon-4pm.) Visit the **National Women's Hall of Fame,** 76 Fall St. (315-568-8060), where photographs and biographies commemorate 38 outstanding U.S. women (open Mon.-Sat. 10am-4pm, Sun. noon-4pm; donation requested).

The town of **Corning** bakes 40 mi. outside Ithaca on Rte. 17 west off Rte. 13 south, home to the Corning Glass Works. The **Corning Glass Center** (607-974-2000), in the Centerway, was built in honor of the Glass Works' Centenary in 1951, and chronicles the 3500-year history of glass-making, displaying over 20,000 pieces (open July-Aug. daily 9am-8pm; Sept.-June daily 9am-5pm; $6, seniors $5, under 18 $4). The nearby **Rockwell Museum,** 111 Cedar St. Rte. 17 (607-937-5386), displays glass pieces by Frederick Carder, founder of the Steuben Glass Works, and an excellent collection of American Western art. (Open Mon.-Sat. 9am-5pm, Sun. noon-5pm; July-Aug. Mon.-Sat. until 7pm, Sun. noon-5pm. $3, seniors $2.50, under 18 free.)

In the Lakes region, a car provides the easiest transportation, but biking and hiking allow more intimate contact with this beautiful country. Reach out and touch the **Finger Lakes State Park Region** (see Practical Information above) for free maps and tips. Write the **Finger Lakes Trail Conference,** P.O. Box 18048, Rochester 14618 (716-288-7191), for free maps of the **Finger Lakes Trail,** an east-west footpath from the Catskills westward to the Allegheny Mountains. This 350-mi. trail and its 300 mi. of branch trails link several state parks, most with camping facilities. Bicyclists can buy *25 Bicycle Tours in the Finger Lakes* ($9) or write to the publisher: The Countryman Press, Inc., PO Box 175, Woodstock, VT 05091. In the immediate Ithaca area, 2 state parks, **Buttermilk Falls,** Rte. 13 (273-5761), and **Robert H. Treman** (273-3440) Rte. 327, offer swimming, fishing, hiking, and recreation programs for those who want close access to nature. (Park entrance fees vary; some weekdays are free; call parks for specifics.)

■■■ NIAGARA FALLS

One of the seven natural wonders of the world, Niagara Falls also claims the title of one of the world's largest sources of hydro-electric power. Originally, 5½ billion gallons of water per hour tumbled over the falls; now ¾ of this volume is diverted to supply the United States and Canada with power. This work by hydro-electricians to regulate water flow has slowed the erosion which was eating away at the falls at an alarming rate. It is believed that the falls now move back at a rate of 1 ft. per decade, down from 6 ft. per year. Admired not only for their beauty, the Falls have attracted thrill-seeking barrel-riders since 1901, when 63 year-old Annie Taylor successfully conquered them. Modern day adventurers beware—heavy fines can be levied for barrel attempts, and, as park officials note, "the chances for survival are slim."

PRACTICAL INFORMATION

Emergency: 911.

Visitor Information: Niagara Falls Convention and Visitors Bureau, 310 4th St., Niagara Falls, NY (285-2400 or 800-421-5223; 24-hr. Niagara City Events Line 285-8711) will send you the excellent *Niagara USA* travel guide. Open daily 9am-5pm. In Niagara, the **information center** that adjoins the bus station on 4th and Niagara is the place to visit (284-2000). It's a 10-min. walk from the Falls, with free 1-hr. parking. (Open mid May to mid-Sept. daily 8am-8pm, mid-Sept. to mid-May daily 9am-5pm.) The state runs a **Niagara Reservation State Park Visitors Center** (278-1750) right in front of the Falls' observation deck. Open May-Sept. daily 8am-10pm, Oct.-Dec. 8am-8pm, Dec.-April 8am-6:30pm. The **Niagara Falls Canada Visitor and Convention Bureau,** 5433 Victoria Ave., Niagara Falls, Ont. L2E 3L1 (905-356-6061), will send info on the Canadian side. (Open summer Mon.-Fri. 8:30am-8pm, Sat.-Sun. 10am-8pm; winter Mon.-Fri. 9am-5pm.) Also, the **Ontario Travel Information Center** at 5355 Stanley Ave. (905-358-3221), at Rte. 420 can help with tourism questions on the entire province.

Amtrak: 27th St. and Lockport, Niagara Falls, 1 block east of Hyde Park Blvd. Take #52 bus to the Falls/downtown. (800-872-7245 or 285-4224. Open Thurs.-Mon. 6:20am-11:30pm, Tues.-Wed. 6:20am-3pm. Closed 10:45-11:30am for lunch.

Greyhound: Niagara Falls Bus Terminal (282-1331), 4th St. and Niagara St. only sells tickets for use in Buffalo (open Mon.-Fri. 8am-4pm). To get to the Buffalo bus station, take bus #40 from the Niagara Falls bus terminal (12-17 per day, 1 hr., $1.70) to the **Buffalo Transportation Center,** 181 Ellicott St. (800-231-2222; open daily 6:30am-11:45pm). To: New York City (9 per day, 8 hr., $51); Boston (4 per day, 12 hr., $72); Chicago (6 per day, 12 hr., $77); Rochester (8 per day, 2 hr., $8); and Albany (5 per day, 7 hr., $29).

Public Transport: Niagara Frontier Metro Transit System, 343 4th St. (285-9319), provides local city transit and free map of bus routes. **ITA Buffalo Shuttle,** 800-551-9369. Service from Niagara Falls info center and major hotels to Buffalo Airport ($15). A **taxi** from Buffalo Airport to Niagara is $40, so take the bus.

Taxi:Rainbow Taxicab, 282-3221;**United Cab,** 285-9331. Both $1.50 base, $1.10/mi.

Post Office: Niagara Falls, 615 Main St. (285-7561), in Niagara Falls, NY. Open Mon.-Fri. 7:30am-5pm, Sat. 9am-2pm. **ZIP code:** 14301.

Area Code: 716 (New York), 905 (Ontario).

Niagara Falls falls in both America and Canada. Visitors approaching Niagra Falls, NY should take exit 3 (Rte. 62) which skirts the tolls and delivers you directly to the falls. Within town, Niagara St. is the main east-west drag; it ends on the western side in Rainbow Bridge, which crosses to Canada. Note that each crossing costs pedestrians 25¢, cars 75¢. Outside town, Rte. 62 (Niagara Falls Blvd.) is lined with stores, restaurants, and motels. Falls Park is at the western edge of the city. North-south streets are numbered; numbers increase west to east. Parking in the city is plentiful. Most lots near the Falls charge $3, but you can park in an equivalent spot for less on streets bordering the park. A free parking lot on Goat Island fills up early in the day.

ACCOMMODATIONS AND CAMPING

Niagara Falls International Hostel (HI-AYH), 1101 Ferry Ave., Niagara Falls, NY 14301 (282-3700). From bus station, walk east on Niagara St., turn left on Memorial Pkwy.; hostel is at corner of Ferry Ave. If walking from the falls, try to avoid the area on Ferry Ave., 4th and 5th St., particularly at night. Good facilities, with kitchen, TV lounge. 44 beds. Travelers without cars given first priority; nonmembers turned away when space is short, as it usually is in summer. Owners will shuttle you to airport, train, or bus station on request; rate depends on size of group going. Limited parking available. Bike rental $10 per day. The Sunset Tour, offered daily (weather and interest permitting), takes you north by the Power Project to Fort Niagara State Park, where you can watch sunsets over Lake Ontario ($4). Check-in 7:30-9:30am and 5-11pm. Lockout 9:30am-4pm. Curfew 11:30pm. Lights out midnight. $13, $11 in winter, nonmembers $16, $14 in winter. Required sheet sacks $1.50. Reservations essential. Open Jan. 4-Dec. 16.

Niagara Falls International Hostel (HI-C), 4699 Zimmerman Ave., Niagara Falls, Ontario (416-357-0770). Pleasant brick Tudor building 2½ mi. from the Falls, about 2 blocks from the Canada bus station and VIA Rail. Beautiful kitchen, dining room, lounge, peaceful backyard. 58 beds; can be cramped when full. Young, friendly manager leads bike trips and hikes along the Niagara gorge. Bike rentals $10 per day. Laundry facilities and plentiful parking. Open 9-11am and 7pm-midnight. Check-out at 11am. Curfew midnight. CDN$12, nonmembers CDN$16.28. 50¢ returned for doing morning chore. Linen $1. Reservations recommended.

YMCA, 1317 Portage Rd., Niagara Falls, NY (285-8491), a 20-min. walk from falls; at night take a bus from Main St. 58 beds. 24-hr. check-in, no laundry. Fee includes use of full YMCA facilities. Dorm rooms for men only (single $25, $10 key deposit). Men and women can sleep on mats in gym ($15).

Olde Niagara House, 610 4th St. (285-9408), is a country B&B just four blocks from the falls. Free pickup at the Amtrak or bus stations. Rooms (summer $45-55, winter $35-45) also come with a delicious, hearty breakfast. Student discount (summer singles $25-35, winter $20-25). Per person rates available ($12-15).

Henri's Motel, 4671 River Road, Niagara Falls, Ontario (905-358-6573). The first motel in Niagara Falls (est. 1938) is still run by the same friendly family. Clean rooms with a variety of arrangements to accommodate families or couples. Rooms start at CDN$17. Owners run a store featuring handmade Canadian arts and crafts. Call for reservations. Open April-Oct.

Four Mile Creek State Park (716-745-3802) Robert Moses parkway, 4 mi. east of Youngstown in the Ft. Niagara Area. Offers affordable camping ($10) as well as hiking and fishing. A scenic 10 mi. drive from the falls.

Niagara Falls Motel and Campsite, 2405 Niagara Falls Blvd., Wheatfield, NY (731-3434), 7 mi. from downtown. Nice-sized rooms with A/C, color TV, private bath. Singles $39-45, off-season $24-29; doubles $29-35; cheapest double in high season is $55. Sites $15, with hookup $18-22. Free pool.

Niagara Glen-View Tent & Trailer Park, 3950 Victoria Ave., Niagara Falls, Ontario (800-263-2570). Closest camp to the Falls; hiking trail across the street. Ice, showers, laundry available. Shuttle runs from driveway to bottom of Clifton Hill during the day every ½ hr. Sites $18.50, with full hookup $23.50. Open May to mid-Oct. Reception every 8am-11pm.

FOOD

Ferraro's, 626 Niagara St. (282-7020), has belly-filling Italian food. Pasta dishes with salad and bread are $6 (open Mon.-Thurs. 11:30am-8pm, Fri. 11:30am-9pm, Sat. 4-9pm). Decidedly more upscale (and expensive) are the flagship restaurants of Niagara Falls's vibrant Little Italy. Try **The Como,** 2220 Pine Ave. (285-9341), which has hosted a galaxy of stars and has the photographs to prove it. Entrees run $8-10. **The Press Box Bar,** 324 Niagara St. (284-5447), between 3rd and 4th St., is a popular spot; add a dollar bill to the several thousand taped to the wall. Every winter the owner takes them down and gives them to a cancer-fighting charity. Monday to Wednesday go for the spaghetti special (99¢, meatballs 25¢ each). Otherwise, burgers ($1.65) are a good bet, but the Porterhouse steak ($8.50) is the trademark dinner. Head straight into the kitchen and write down your order. (Food served Sun.-Thurs. 11:30am-11:30pm, Fri.-Sat. until 12:30am. Bar open until 2am Sun.-Thurs., until 3am Fri.-Sat.) **Sinatra's Sunrise Diner,** 829 Main St. (284-0959), serves filling cuisine just a few blocks from the falls (two eggs and toast 99¢, sandwiches $2-4; open Mon.-Tues. 7am-3pm, Wed.-Fri. 7am-8pm, Sat. 7am-3pm, Sun. 8am-3pm.) Food on the run can be found at the food court of the **Rainbow Centre Factory Outlet Mall,** 302 Rainbow Blvd., just one block from the falls (free parking; shops open Mon.-Sat. 10am-9pm, Sun. noon-5pm). Or stroll through **Tops Friendly Market,** 7200 Niagara Falls Blvd. (283-3100), one of the nation's largest (24 hrs.). For a bite on the Canadian side, there's **Simon's Restaurant,** 4116 Bridge St., Niagara Falls, Ontario (416-356-5310), directly across from the whirlpool bridge, the oldest restaurant in Niagara Falls. Enjoy hearty diner fare and big breakfasts, but the real attraction is the homemade giant muffins (CDN 74¢). (Open Mon.-Sat. 5:30-9pm, Sun. 5:30am-3pm.) Farther inland, **Basell's Restaurant,** 4880 Victoria Ave. (356-7501), offers full-course meal specials ($6-7). (Open daily 6am-11pm.)

SIGHTS AND ENTERTAINMENT

The Canadian-U.S. border, naturally created by the Niagara River, divides the attractions at the falls. Either side can be seen in about an afternoon. The immediate vicinity surrounding the American side of the falls has been a state reservation park since 1885, making it the oldest in the U.S. Consequently, the tourism industry has been less able to exploit the natural resources here than it has those on the opposite shore. Regardless, tourist snares abound on both sides; stick to the official sights and you'll get more for your money. On the American side, the entrance to the visitors center is marked with beautiful gardens.

American Side **Niagara Wonders** (278-1792), an interesting 20 min. show on the falls, can be viewed in the info center. (Shown on the hr. in the summer, daily 10am-8pm; in the fall and early spring, daily 10am-6pm. $2, seniors $1.50, ages 6-12 $1.) The Master Pass, available in the park visitors center, is only worth the price if you plan to visit every single sight. One pass provides admission to the observation tower, the Cave of the Wind, the theater, and the geological museum, plus discounts on Maid of the Mist tours and free parking. (Pass $13, kids $8.) Catch the **Maid of the Mist Tour** (284-8897), a 30-min. boat ride to the foot of both Falls. Don't bring anything that isn't waterproof; you'll get wet. (Tours every 15 min., 9:15am-8pm, daily in summer, 10am-8pm during winter. $7.50, ages 6-12 $4, under 6 free.) The **Viewmobile** (278-1730), an open-sided people transporter, provides a guided tour of the park, including stops at Goat Island, the brink of the falls, the visitors center, the Schoellkopf Museum, and the Aquarium (runs every 15 min.; 10am-8pm daily during summer, 10am-6:30pm in winter; $3.50, children $2.50). The Viewmobile can drop you off at the **Caves of the Wind Tour,** on Goat Island, which will outfit you with a yellow raincoat and take you on a thrilling body-soaking tour to the base of the Bridal Veil Falls. Adventurous souls can climb to the Hurricane Deck to test their nerve. The **Schoellkopf's Geological Museum** in Prospect Park (278-1780) depicts the birth of the Falls with slide shows every half hour. (Open daily 9:30am-7pm; Labor Day-Oct. daily 10am-5pm; Nov.-Memorial Day Thurs.-Sun.

10am-5pm. 50¢.) If you're going to all of the activities above, the **Master Pass,** available at the park visitors center, will save you $3. The pass provides admission to all of these attractions, and includes free parking ($15, 6-12 $10).

Outside the park, the **Aquarium,** 701 Whirlpool St. (285-3575), provides waterlovers with yet another outlet. Sharks, penguins, otters, and other marine mammals strut their stuff ($6.25, ages 4-12 $4.25; open daily 9am-5pm, Labor Day-Memorial Day until 7pm). Continuing north, the admission-free **Niagara Power Project,** 5777 Lewiston Rd. (285-3211, ext. 6660), features interactive demonstrations, short videos, and displays on energy, hydropower, and local history. There's even a fishing platform from which to catch salmon, trout, and bass. Take Robert Moses Pkwy. north to 104. (Open Sept.-June 10am-5pm, July-Labor Day 9am-6pm.) Nearby, the 200-acre state **Artpark** (800-659-PARK), at the foot of 4th St., focuses on visual and performing arts, offering workshops, classes, and demonstrations on a variety of artistic topics. The theater presents opera, pops concerts, and blues and jazz festivals. (Open Tues.-Sun. July-August. Call for schedule.)

Three different flags (French, British, and American) have flown over **Old Fort Niagara** (716-745-7611), which once guarded the entrance to the Niagara River. Its French Castle was built in 1726. (Box 169, Youngstown, NY 14174; follow Robert Moses Pkwy. north from Niagara Falls. (Open July-Labor Day 9am-6:30pm; hours vary off-season. $6, seniors $4.75, ages 6-12 $3.75.) **The Turtle,** 25 Rainbow Blvd. South (284-2427), between Winter Garden and the river, boasts an impressive collection of regional Iroquois arts and crafts. (Open daily 9am-6pm; Oct.-April Tues.-Fri. 9am-5pm, Sat.-Sun. noon-5pm. $3.50, seniors $3, kids and students $2.) Wander into **Artisans Alley,** 10 Rainbow Blvd. (282-0196), at 1st St., to see the works of over 600 American craftsmen. (Open May-Dec. daily 10am-9pm; Jan.-April 10am-5pm. Free.) NFL fans will want to venture south to Rich Stadium in Orchard Park to catch the 4-time AFC Champ/Super Bowl bust **Buffalo Bills** in action. (Ticket info 716-649-0015, or write: Buffalo Bills Ticket Office, One Bills Dr., Orchard Park, NY 14127.)

Canadian Side On the Canada side of Niagara Falls (across the Rainbow Bridge), **Queen Victoria Park** provides the best view of the Horseshoe Falls. The falls are illuminated for 3 hrs. every night, starting one hr. after sunset. Parking costs CDN$8, however. To beat this system, park at Rapids View at the southern end of the Niagara Parkway and take **People Movers** (357-9340). These air-conditioned buses run along 19 miles of the falls area and have drop-off points throughout. (CDN$3.50 buys a day pass, children $1.75; buses run early May to mid-Oct.) The highest view of the Falls (775 ft. up) is from the **Skylon Tower,** 5200 Robinson St. (356-2651), in Canada. On a clear day you can see as far as Toronto. (CDN$6, kids CDN$3.50.) Daily brunch in summer in revolving dining room (CDN$13). From the base of the **Observation Deck** (75¢) head up 282 ft. to access an unhindered view of the falls (open daily 8am-11pm, winter open daily 8am-9pm). Canada's version of the Master Pass is called the **Explorer's Passport Plus** (CDN$15.75, children CDN$7.90) and includes passage to **Journey Behind the Falls,** a gripping tour behind the rushing waters of Horseshoe Falls (354-1551, CDN$5.25, children CDN$2.65,) to **Great Gorge Adventure,** a descent into the Niagara River Rapids (374-1221, open late April-late Oct., $4.23, children $2.13), and to the **Spanish Aero Car,** an aerial cable ride over the turbulent whirlpool waters (354-5711; open mid March-Nov., CDN$4.50, children CDN$2.25). People Movers transportation is also included. The **Falls Incline Railway** transports visitors between the Table Rock Scenic Tunnels area and the falls view location. (One way 85¢.)

From late November to early January, Niagara Falls holds the annual **Festival of Lights.** Bright bulbs line the trees and create brilliant animated and outdoor scenes. Illumination of the falls caps the spectacle. (Animated display areas open Sun.-Thurs. 5-10pm. Fri.-Sat. 5-11pm; exterior display areas nightly 5-11pm.) Also every Friday at 10pm, fireworks explode over the falls (July-Labor Day).

For Niagara Fun with an alcohol slant, local beers and wines may be sampled and their respective facilities toured. The **Niagara Falls Brewing Company,** 6863

Lindy's Lane (374-1166), is open Sundays and most holidays for free touring and tasting. **Brights Winery,** Canada's oldest and largest, 4887 Dorchester Rd. (357-2400), provides tours as well (May.-Oct., Mon.-Sat. at 10:30am, 2pm and 3:30pm, Sun. at 2pm and 3:30pm, Nov.-April daily at 2pm and Sat.-Sun. at 3:30pm. CDN$2 to taste 4 wines.) Bikers, rollerbladers, and leisurely walkers will enjoy the 56km **Niagara River Recreation Trail,** which runs from Ft. Erie to Ft. George and passes many interesting historical and geological spots.

NORTHERN NEW YORK

■■■ THE ADIRONDACKS

One hundred and three years ago the New York State legislature, demonstrating uncommon foresight, established the **Adirondacks State Park**—the largest U.S. park outside Alaska and one of the few places left where hikers can spend days without seeing other people. Unfortunately, in recent years pollution and development have left a harsh imprint. Acid rain has damaged the tree and fish populations, especially in the fragile high-altitude environments, and tourist meccas like **Lake George** have continued to expand rapidly. Despite these urban intrusions, much of the area retains the beauty visitors have enjoyed for over a century.

Of the six million acres in the Adirondacks Park, 40% is open to the public. Two thousand miles of trails traverse the forest and provide the best access to the spectacular mountain scenery, whether you're hiking, snow-shoeing, or cross-country skiing. An interlocking network of lakes and streams makes the gentle Adirondack wilds a perennial favorite of canoers. Mountain-climbers may wish to surmount **Mt. Marcy,** the state's highest peak (5344 ft.), at the base of the Adirondacks, and skiers can choose from any of a dozen well-known alpine ski centers. Less natural attractions are also readily available. **Lake Placid** hosted the winter Olympics in 1932 and 1980, and frequently welcomes national and international sports competitions (see Lake Placid below). **Tupper Lake** and Lake George have carnivals every January and February, and Tupper hosts the Tin Man Triathlon in July. In September, the hot air balloons of the Adirondack Balloon Festival in Glens Falls race the trees to be the first to provide fall color.

Practical Information The best source of information on hiking and other outdoor activities in the region is the **Adirondack Mountain Club (ADK).** The ADK is in its 73rd year and has over 19,000 members, with offices at RR3, Box 3055, Lake George 12845 (668-4447) and at Adirondack Loj Rd., P.O. Box 867, Lake Placid 12946 (523-3441). Call the Lake Placid number for information on outdoors skills classes such as canoeing, rock climbing, whitewater kayaking, and wilderness medicine. The ADK's **High Peaks Information Center,** 3 mi. south of Lake Placid on Rte. 73, then 5 mi. down Adirondack Loj Rd., has the latest in backcountry info, sells basic outdoor equipment, trail snacks, and the club's extremely helpful regionalized guides to the mountains ($18). The Center also has washrooms (open daily 8am-7pm). Those interested in rock climbing should consult the **Mountaineer** (576-2281; in Keene Valley between I-87 and Lake Placid on Rte. 73). All employees here are experienced mountaineers, and the store is a good source of weather forecasts, equipment, and advice. Rent snowshoes for $15 per day, and ice-climbing equipment (boots and crampons) for $20 per day. Longer rentals should have lower rates. (Open Mon.-Fri. 9am-5:30pm, Sat. 8am-5:30pm, Sun. 10am-5:30pm.) Though less equipped to give details than the ADK or the Moutaineer, the **State Office of Parks and Recreation** (474-0456) Agency Bldg. 1, Empire State Place, Albany 12238, can provide basic information on the conditions and concerns of backwoods travel.

The Adirondacks are served by **Adirondacks Trailways,** with frequent stops along I-87. From Albany buses go to Lake Placid, Tupper Lake, and Lake George. From the Lake George bus stop, at the Mobil station, 320 Canada St. (668-9511; 800-858-8555 for bus info), buses reach Lake Placid (1 per day, $12.45), Albany (1 per day, $9.30), and New York City ($36.30). (Open June-Nov. Mon.-Wed. 7am-10pm, Thurs. 7am-midnight, Fri.-Sun. 7am-2am. The gas station may close Dec.-May but buses still run.) Adirondacks' **area code: 518.**

Accommodations and Camping Two lodges near Lake Placid are also run by the ADK. The **Adirondack Loj** (523-3441), 8mi. east of Lake Placid off Rte. 73, is a beautiful log cabin on Heart Lake with comfortable bunk facilities and a family atmosphere. Guests can swim, fish, canoe, and use rowboats on the premises (canoe or boat rental $5). In winter, explore the wilderness trails on rented snowshoes ($15 per day) or cross-country skis ($20 per day). (B&B $30, with dinner $41. Linen included. Tent sites for two people $14, winter $8, each additional $1.50; Lean-tos for two people $16, winter $12; each additional $2.50.) Call ahead for weekends and during peak holiday seasons. For an even better mix of rustic comfort and wilderness experience, hike 3½ mi. to the **John's Brook Lodge** from the closest trailhead, in Keene Valley 16 mi. southeast of Lake Placid off Rte. 73 (call the Adirondack Loj for reservations). From Placid, follow Rte. 73 15 mi. through Keene to Keene Valley, turning right at the Ausable Inn. The hike is slightly uphill, and the food is well worth the exertion; the staff packs in groceries every day and cooks on a gas stove. A great place to meet friendly New Yorkers, John's Brook is no secret; beds fill completely on weekends. Make reservations at least one day in advance for dinner, longer for a weekend. Bring sheets or a sleeping bag. (B&B $26, with dinner $37. Lean-tos $10. Open mid-June-early Sept. From Memorial Day-June 12 and from Labor Day-Columbus Day, bunks $9 weekdays, $12 weekends; full kitchen access.)

If ADK facilities are too pricey, try the **High Peaks Base Camp,** P.O. Box 91, Upper Jay 12987 (946-2133), a charming restaurant/lodge/campground just a 20-minute drive from Lake Placid. Take Rte. 86 N. to Wilmington, turn right on Fox Farm Rd., just before the Hungry Trout Tackle Shop, then go right 3½ mi. on Springfield Rd.; $15 (Sun.-Thurs.) or $18 (Fri.-Sat.) buys you a bed for the night and a huge breakfast. (Check-in until 10pm, later with reservations. Sites $5, each additional person $3. Free hot shower. Cabins $30 for 4 people.) Transportation is tough without a car but sometimes rides can be arranged from Keene; call ahead. **Free camping** abounds; in the forest, you can use the free shelters by the trails. Always inquire about their location before you plan a hike. Better still, camp for free anywhere on public land in the **backcountry,** as long as you are at least 150 ft. away from a trail, road, water source, or campground, and stay below 4000 ft. altitude. The State Office of Parks and Recreation (see Practical Information above) has more details.

In **Lake George,** 45 mi. south of the junction of Rte. 73 and I-87, off of I-87 exit 22, the **Lake George Youth Hostel (HI-AYH)** is located in the basement of **St. James Episcopal Church Hall,** P.O. Box 176, Lake George 12845 (668-2634), on Montcalm St. at Ottawa, several blocks from the lake. From the bus terminal, walk south one block to Montcalm, turn right and go one block to Ottawa for the slightly musty bunkroom with a decent kitchen. (Check-in 5-9pm, later only with reservations. Curfew 10pm. $10, nonmembers $13. Sleepsack required, rental $2. Open late May-early Sept.; spring and fall with reservations.)

■■■ LAKE PLACID

Home of the Olympic Winter Games in both 1932 and 1980, Lake Placid keeps the memory and the dream of Olympic glory alive. World class athletes train year-round in the town's extensive sporting facilities, lending an international flavor which distinguishes Lake Placid from its Adirondack neighbors. Meanwhile, the natural setting in the Adirondack High Peaks Region at the intersection of Rte. 86 and Rte 73, draws droves of hikers and backpackers each year.

Practical Information The Olympic past clearly makes its presence felt in Lake Placid, with a number of venues scattered in and just outside the town. The **Olympic Regional Development Authority** (523-1655 or 800-462-6236), 216 Main St., Olympic Center, operates the sporting facilities and sells tickets for self-guided tours (available daily 9am-4pm, July to mid-Oct $15, seniors and children 5-12 $12, under 5 free). Information on food, lodging, and area attractions can be obtained from the **Lake Placid-Essex County Visitors Bureau** (523-2445), also in Olympic Center (open Mon.-Sat. 9am-5pm, Sun. 9am-4pm.) **Adirondack Trailways** has extensive service in the area, stopping at the **326 Main St. Deli** (523-4309 for bus info). Buses run to New York City (1 per day, $48.75) and Lake George (1 per day, $12.45). Lake Placid is at the intersection of Rte. 86 and Rte. 73. For **weather** info, call 523-1363 or 523-3518. Lake Placid's **post office:** 201 Main St. (523-3071; open Mon.-Fri. 9am-5pm, Sat. 9am-12:30pm). **ZIP code:** 12946; **area code:** 518.

Accommodations and Camping As long as you avoid the resorts on the west end of town, both accommodations and food can be had cheaply in Lake Placid. The **White Sled** (523-9314; on Rte. 73 between the Sports Complex and the ski jumps) is the best bargain around: for $16 you get a comfortable, clean bed in the bunkhouse, which includes a full kitchen, living room, and entertainment by the friendly, Francophone hosts. The **Hotel St. Moritz,** 31 Saranac Ave. (523-9240), one block from Main St., offers "Old World Charm at an Affordable Price." A decent room for one or two and a full breakfast is $35. Prices hiked up for weekends and seasonal holidays. The closest campgrounds to Lake Placid are **Meadowbrook State Park** (891-4351; 5 mi. west on Rte. 86 in Ray Brook), and **Wilmington Notch State Campground** (946-7172; off Rte. 86 between Wilmington and Lake Placid). Both offer sites without hookups ($10.50 first night, $9 each additional night) which can accommodate two tents and up to six people.

Food Main Street in Lake Placid Village offers pickings to suit any palate, and prices are generally reasonable. Lunch buffet (Mon.-Sat. noon-2pm) at the **Hilton Hotel,** 1 Mirror Lake Dr. (523-4411), buys a sandwich and all-you-can-eat soup and salad ($4.75). At the **Black Bear Restaurant,** 157 Main St. (523-9886), enjoy a $5 lunch special and a $2.75 Saranac lager (the Adirondack's own beer) in the company of a stuffed bobcat, an otter, a fox, and three deer heads. Bottomless Java 80¢ (open Sun.-Thurs. 6:30am-10pm, Fri.-Sat. 24 hrs.) **The Cottage,** 5 Mirror Lake Dr. (523-9845), has relatively inexpensive meals (sandwiches and salads $4-6) with Lake Placid's best views of Mirror Lake; watch the U.S. canoe and kayaking teams practice on the water. (Meals served daily 11:30am-9pm. Bar open daily 11:30am-1am.) **Mud Puddles,** 3 School St. (523-4446), below the speed skating rink, is popular with the pop music crowd (open Wed.-Sun. 9pm-3am; cover $1.50).

Sights You can't miss the 70 and 90m runs of the Olympic ski jumps, which, with the **Kodak Sports Park,** make up the **Olympic Jumping Complex,** just outside of town on Rte. 73. The $6 admission fee includes a chairlift and elevator ride to the top of the spectator towers, where you might catch summer (June-mid-Oct.) jumpers flipping and sailing into a swimming pool. (Open daily 9am-5pm, Sept.-June 9am-4pm.) Three mi. farther along Rte. 73, the **Olympic Sports Complex** (523-4436) at Mt. Van Hoevenberg has a summer trolley coasting to the top of the bobsled run ($3, mid-June-mid-Oct.). In the winter (Dec.-March Tues.-Sun. 1-3pm) you can bobsled down the Olympic run ($25), or try the luge ($10). Contact the Olympic Regional Development Authority (see above) in order to tour the facilities.

The west branch of the **Ausable River,** just east of Lake Placid, lures anglers to its shores. **Fishing licenses** for non-New Yorkers are $20 for five days (season $35); for residents $6 for three days (season $14)and are sold in at Town Hall, 301 Main St. (523-2162), or Jones Outfitters, 37 Main St. (523-3468). Jones rents the necessary equipment as well (open daily 9am-6pm). Call the "Fishing Hotline" (891-5413) for an in-depth recording of the hot fresh-water fishing spots. The **Lake Placid Center** for the Arts (523-2512), on Saranac Ave. just outside town at Fawn Ridge, houses a local art gallery and hosts theater, dance, and musical performances. (Open daily 1-5pm; winter Tues.-Sat. Gallery free; call for prices and listings of performances.)

■■■ THOUSAND ISLAND SEAWAY

The Thousand Island region of St. Lawrence Seaway spans 100 mi. from the mouth of Lake Ontario to the first of the many man-made locks on the St. Lawrence River. Some 250 tree-covered islands and countless rocky shoals make navigation tricky in this area. Locals divide people into two groups: those who *have* hit a shoal and those who *will* hit a shoal. But don't let this dire prediction deter you; the Thousand Island Region has much to offer, from the extravagant homes of long-departed millionaires and some of the world's best bass and muskellunge fishing, to the more simple accolade of being the only area in the nation with a namesake salad dressing.

Practical Information The three main cities of the region are **Clayton, Alexandria Bay,** and **Cape Vincent.** Write or visit the **Clayton Chamber of Commerce,** 403 Riverside Dr., Clayton 13624 (686-3771), for the *Clayton Vacation Guide* and the *Thousand Islands Seaway Region Travel Guide;* both are free (open daily 9am-4pm). The **Alexandria Bay Chamber of Commerce** (482-9531) Market St., Alexandria Bay 13607, is just off James St. on the right. (Open daily 9am-5pm. Closed Wed. and Sun. during the winter). The **Cape Vincent Chamber of Commerce** (654-2481) receives mail and visitors at James St., Cape Vincent 13618, down by the ferry landing. (Open Sun.-Mon. 10am-3pm, Tues.-Sat. 9am-5pm.) Access the region by bus through **Greyhound,** 540 State St., Watertown (788-8110). To New York City (2 per day, 8 hr., $50), Syracuse (2 per day, 1¾ hr., $13), and Albany (1 per day, 5½ hr., $34). From the same station, **Thousand Islands Bus Lines** (287-2782) runs to Alexandria Bay and Clayton at 1pm (Mon.-Fri., $5.60 to Alexandria, $3.55 to Clayton); return trips leave from Clayton at the **Nutshell Florist,** 234 James St. (686-5791), at 8:45am, and from Alexandria at the **Dockside Cafe,** 17 Market St. (482-9849), at 8:30am. (Station open 9:15am-2:30pm and 6-8pm.)

Clayton and the Thousand Islands region are just two hours from Syracuse by way of I-81 N. For Welleslet Island, Alexandria Bay, and the eastern 500 islands, stay on I-81 until you reach Rte. 12 E. For Clayton and points west, take exit 47 and follow Rte. 12 until you reach 12 E.

Clayton's **post office:** 236 John St. (686-3311; open Mon.-Fri. 9am-5pm, Sat. 9am-noon); **ZIP code:** 13624. Alexandria Bay's **post office:** 13 Bethune St (482-9321; open Mon.-Fri. 8:30am-5:30pm, Sat. 8:30am-1pm); **ZIP code:** 13607. Cape Vincent's **post office:** 360 Broadway St. (654-2424; open Mon.-Fri. 8:30am-1pm, 2-5:30pm); **ZIP code:** 13618. Thousand Island's **area code:** 315.

Accommodations and Camping Cape Vincent, on the western edge of the seaway, keeps one of the most idyllic youth hostels in the country. **Tibbetts Point Lighthouse Hostel (HI-AYH),** RR1 Box 330 (654-3450), strategically and scenically situated where Lake Ontario meets the St. Lawrence, has two houses with 31 beds; choose between a riverfront or a lakefront view, and watch the ships glide past spectacular sunsets. A large, full kitchen with microwave is available, and the hosts George and Jean Cougler are like certified grandparents. Take Rte. 12 E. into town, turn left on Broadway, and follow the river until the road ends. There is no public transportation to Cape Vincent, but with enough advance notice, George or Jean will pick you up in Clayton. (Curfew 10pm. Check-in 5-9:30pm. $10, nonmembers $13. Open May 15-Oct. 31. Linen rental $2.) **Burnham Point State Park** (654-2324) on Rte. 12 E. 4 mi. east of Cape Vincent and 11 mi. west of Clayton, sports 50 tent sites which each can accommodate two tents and six people. Boat docking facilities available. (No showers. $10.50 first night, $9 each additional night. Hookup $12.50. Open Memorial Day-Labor Day daily 8am-9pm.) **Keewaydin State Park** (482-3331), just south of Alexandria Bay, has 41 sites along the St. Lawrence River.

An Olympic-size swimming pool is free for campers. (Open Memorial Day-Labor Day, $11.50 first night, $10 each additional night. Showers available. No hookups.)

Exploring the Seaway Any of the small towns dotting Rte. 12 can serve as a good base for exploring the region, though Clayton and Cape Vincent tend to be less expensive than Alexandria Bay. **Uncle Sam Boat Tours** in Clayton (686-3511) 604 Riverside Dr. or in **Alexandria Bay** (482-2611), James St., gives a good look at most of the islands and the plush estates situated atop them. (Open daily April-Dec. Tours 2¼ hrs. long. From Clayton $12.50, children 4-12 $7.25. From Alexandria Bay $11.50, children 4-12 $6.25. Seniors $1 off.) Tours highlight **Heart Island** and its famous **Boldt Castle** (482-9724 or 800-847-526), make unlimited stops to allow visitors to stay as long as they would like, but do not cover the price of admission to the castle. George Boldt, former owner of New York City's elegant Waldorf-Astoria Hotel, financed this six-story replica of a Rhineland castle as a gift for his wife, who died before its completion. In his grief, Boldt stopped construction on the 365-bed-room, 52-bathroom behemoth, which remains unfinished today. After extensive renovations, this exorbitant monument is now open to the public. (Open May-Oct. $3.25, ages 6-12, $1.75, seniors $1.75.) **Rental boats** are available in Clayton, Alex-andria Bay, and Cape Vincent. In Clayton, **French Creek Marina,** 98 Wahl St. (686-3621), rents 14-ft. fishing boats ($45/day) and pontoon boats ($110/day); launches boats ($5); and provides overnight docking ($15/night). In Alexandria Bay, **O'Brien's U-Drive Boat Rentals,** 51 Walton St. (482-9548), rents 16-ft fishing boats ($50/day, $50 deposit) and 18-ft runabouts ($150/day, $300 deposit). (Open April-Oct.; mechanic on duty daily.) In Cape Vincent, the **Sunset Trailer Park** (654-2482), 2 mi beyond town on 12 E., rents motor boats for $40/day. This location is especially convenient if staying at the nearby Tibbets Point Hostel.

Fishing licenses (non-NY residents: season $30, 5 days $20; NY residents: season $14, 3 days $6) are available at sporting goods stores or the **Town Clerk's Office,** 405 Riverside Dr., Clayton (686-3512; open Mon.-Fri. 9am-noon and 1-4pm). No local store rents equipment, so bring your own rods and reels or plan to buy them.

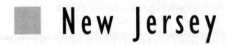

New Jersey

New Jersey was once called the Garden State for a reason, but with the advent of suburbia (NJ serves both New York City and Philadelphia), and tax-free shopping (giving rise to outlets and major mall country), travelers who refuse to get off the interstates envision the state as a conglomeration of smog, belching chemical plants, endless ranch houses, and ocean beaches strewn with garbage and gamblers. This picture, however, belies the state's quieter delights (off the highway). A closer look reveals that there is more to New Jersey than commuters, chemicals, and craps.

The Garden State was the sight of nearly 100 Revolutionary War battles, but today the interior blooms with countless fields of corn, tomatoes, and peaches, sandy beaches, wide pine forests, and verdant countryside. The state also shelters quiet hamlets and the Pine Barrens forest, as well as two world-class universities: Rutgers and Princeton. Atlantic City continues its gaudy existence, the New Jersey Turnpike remains road warrioresque, but those who stray a bit from the asphalt of the major highways will be pleasantly surprised; New Jersey can be a nice place to visit.

PRACTICAL INFORMATION
Capital: Trenton.
State Division of Tourism: CN 826, Trenton 08625 (609-292-2470). **New Jersey Department of Environmental Protection and Energy, State Park Service,** CN 404, Trenton, 08625-0404.

Time Zone: Eastern. **Postal Abbreviation:** NJ
Sales Tax: 6%; no tax on clothing.

■■■ PINE BARRENS

The Pine Barrens forest area in the middle of New Jersey is as large as it is unexpected. Further, Pine Barrens is anything but barren. The region was originally termed barren because of the lack of arable land, but today the area supports wide stretches of pine trees and scores of crop fields. The New Jersey Devil, the 13th child of some woman who was sick of kids and cursed him, supposedly retaliated by flying out the window and now haunts the hundreds of thousands of acres of the Pine Barrens. If you decide to explore the Barrens on one of the hundreds of sandy roads that criss-cross the region, ask for directions from the locals (known as Pineys), and go on foot unless your car has four wheel drive and a winch.

The town of **Hammonton,** at the junction of U.S. 206 and U.S. 30, makes a good starting point for entering the Barrens. It is the only town in the region served by public transportation and is also an entry point for **Wharton State Forest.** This 109,000 acre forest is the center-piece of the Barrens and offers fishing, boating, hiking, camping, and other nature-intensive activities year-round. You can pick up information about day use activities and the park's nine camping areas from the **Atsion Ranger Station,** R.D. 2, Vincetown (609-268-0444), 10 mi. north of Hammonton on U.S. 206, or from **Batsto Village** (609-561-3262), east of Hammonton on Rte. 542. (Atsion open Sun.-Thurs. 9am-4:30pm, Fri.-Sat. 9am-9pm; Batsto open daily 9am-4:30pm) These offices dispense nature knowledge and camping permits. **Camping** ranges from wilderness to cabins with showers, toilets, and fireplaces (sites $8, cabins $28 for four people, $56 for eight people. Book in January or February for cabins.) **Canoe trips** can be arranged through a number of private companies (the ranger stations can furnish a list). One of the most convenient is **Adams Canoe Rental,** 1055 Atsion Rd. (268-0189), off U.S. 206 near the Atsion Ranger Station ($27 a day on the lake, $35 a day on the river).

Before starting into the forest, fill your feed bag at **Acme,** Rte. 30 in Hammonton (open Mon.-Sat. 7am-10pm, Sun. 7am-9pm), or at one of the many **produce stands** that sprout up along the roads of central New Jersey. **New Jersey Transit** operates **train** service out of an unmanned station on 11th St., off Egg Harbor Rd. in Hammonton (800-228-7246 in N.J., 215-569-3752 out of state; Hammonton to Atlantic City $2.80). They also operate **buses** from Tapper's Stationery on 2nd St. and Bellevue Ave. (Buses run around the clock. $3.15 to Atlantic City.)

■■■ ATLANTIC CITY

The riches-to-rags-to-riches tale of Atlantic City began half a century ago when the beachside hotspot was tops among resort towns. Vanderbilts and Girards graced the boardwalk that inspired *Monopoly,* the Depression-era board game for coffee-table high rollers. But the opulence has faded. With the rise of competition from Florida resorts, the community chest closed. Atlantic City suffered decades of decline, unemployment, and virtual abandonment.

In 1976, state voters gave Atlantic City a reprieve by letting it legalize gambling. Casinos soon rose out of the rubble of Boardwalk. Those who enter soon forget the dirt and dank outside. Each velvet-lined temple of tackiness has a dozen restaurants, big-name entertainment, even skyways connecting it to other casinos. The chance to win big draws everyone to Atlantic City, from international jet-setters to seniors clutching plastic coin cups. One-third of the U.S. population lives within 300 mi. of Atlantic City, and fortune-seeking foreigners flock to its shore to toss the dice. Budgeteers can even take a casino-sponsored bus from Manhattan—pay $15 for the trip and get it all back in quarters upon arrival. How can you lose?

PRACTICAL INFORMATION

Emergency: 911.
Visitor Information: Atlantic City Convention Center and Visitors Bureau, 2314 Pacific Ave. (348-7130, 800-262-7395). Personal assistance daily 10am-6pm; leaflets available 24 hrs.
Airport: Atlantic City International (645-7895, 800-728-4322). Located just west of Atlantic City in Pamona with service to Washington, Philadelphia, and New York (around $50 one way).
Amtrak: (800-872-7245) at Kirkman Blvd. near Michigan Ave. Follow Kirkman to its end, bear right, and follow the signs. To New York (1 per day, 2½ hr., $28). Open Sun.-Fri. 9:30am-7:40pm, Sat. 9:30am-10pm.
Buses: Greyhound (345-6617). Buses every hr. to New York (2½ hr., $19). **New Jersey Transit** (800-582-5946). Runs 6am-10pm. Hourly service to New York City ($21). Also runs along Atlantic Ave. (base fare $1). Both lines operate from **Atlantic City Municipal Bus Terminal,** Arkansas and Arctic Ave. Both offer casino-sponsored round-trip discounts, including cash back on arrival in Atlantic City. Bally's has a particularly good deal—you get your full fare ($15) back in quarters upon arrival. Terminal open 24 hrs.
Help Lines: Rape and Abuse Hotline (646-6767). 24-hr. counseling, referrals, and accompaniment. **Gambling Abuse** (800-GAMBLER/800-426-2537). 24-hr. help for gambling problems.
Post Office: (345-4212), at Martin Luther King and Pacific Ave. Open Mon.-Fri. 8:30am-5pm, Sat. 10am-noon. **ZIP code:** 08401.
Area Code: 609.

Atlantic City lies about half-way down New Jersey's coast, accessible via the **Garden State Parkway** and the **Atlantic City Expressway,** and easily reached by train from Philadelphia and New York. Gamblers' specials make bus travel a cheap, efficient way to get to Atlantic City. Many casinos will give the bearer of a bus ticket receipt $10-15 in quarters and sometimes a free meal. **Gray Line Tours** in New York, 900 Eighth Ave. (397-2600), between 53rd and 54th St., offers several round-trip excursions daily to Atlantic City ($21, $23 on weekends). At press time, Caesar's, the Taj Mahal, and TropWorld had the best offers ($15 in cold, flexible cash).

Atlantic City's attractions cluster on and around the **Boardwalk,** which runs east-west along the Atlantic Ocean. All but two of the casinos overlook this paradise of soft-serve ice cream and fast food. Running parallel to the Boardwalk, Pacific and Atlantic Ave. offer cheap restaurants, hotels, and convenience stores. Getting around Atlantic City is easy on foot. When your winnings become too heavy to carry, you can hail a **Rolling Chair,** quite common along the Boardwalk. The less exotic and less expensive **yellow tram** runs continuously for $2 one-way or $5 for an all-day pass. On the streets, catch a **jitney** ($1.25), which runs 24 hrs. up and down Pacific Ave., or a NJ Transit Bus ($1) covering Atlantic Ave.

ACCOMMODATIONS AND CAMPING

Large, red-carpeted beachfront hotels have bumped smaller operators out of the game. Smaller hotels along **Pacific Avenue,** a block from the Boardwalk, have rooms for less than $60, and rooms in the city's guest houses are reasonably priced, though facilities there can be dismal. Reserve ahead, especially on weekends.

Irish Pub and Inn, 164 St. James Pl. (344-9063), near the Boardwalk, directly north of Sands Casino. Clean, cheap rooms fully decorated with antiques. Laundry in basement. Singles $29. Doubles $40, with private shower $60. Quads $60. Cot in room $10. Key deposit $5. Breakfast and dinner $10, children $8. Open Feb.-Nov.
Hotel Cassino, 28 Georgia Ave. (344-0747), at Pacific Ave. A little run-down, but no sleaze. Strictly a family business. Rates negotiable. Singles $30-45. Doubles $35-50. Key deposit $10. Open May-early Nov.
Birch Grove Park Campground (641-3778), Mill Rd. in Northfield. About 6 mi. from Atlantic City, off Rte. 9. 50 attractive and secluded sites $15 for 2 people, with hookup $18.

FOOD

After cashing in your chips, you can visit a **casino buffet** (about $10 for dinner; $6-7 for lunch). The town provides higher-quality meals in a less noxious atmosphere. For a complete rundown of local dining, pick up a copy of *TV Atlantic Magazine, At the Shore,* or *Whoot* (all free) from a hotel lobby, a restaurant, or a local store.

Your best bet for cheap dining in Atlantic City is the **Inn of the Irish Pub,** at 164 St. James Pl. (345-9613), which serves hearty, modestly priced dishes like deep-fried crab cakes ($4.25), honey-dipped chicken ($4.25), and Dublin beef stew ($5). Pacific Avenue is cramped with steak, sub, and pizza shops. Celebrity supporters of the **White House Sub Shop,** Mississippi and Arctic Ave. (345-1564, 345-8599), include Bill Cosby, Johnny Mathis, and Frank Sinatra, who is rumored to have these immense subs flown to him while he's on tour ($6-8, half-subs $3-4; open Mon.-Sat. 10am-midnight, Sun. 11am-midnight). For renowned Italian food, including the best pizza in town, hit **Tony's Baltimore Grille,** 2800 Atlantic Ave. at Iowa Ave. (345-5766). (Pasta around $5, pizza $5-8. Open daily 11am-3am; bar open 24 hrs.)

CASINOS, BEACHES, AND THE BOARDWALK

You don't have to spend a penny to enjoy yourself in Atlantic City's casinos; their vast, plush interiors and spotless, marble bathrooms can entertain a resourceful and voyeuristic budget traveller for hours. Watch people shove quarter after quarter in the slot machines with vacant, zombie-like stares. Gaze in admiration at those dressed in polyester, trying to act like James Bond at the blackjack tables. The luring rattle of chips, clicking of slot machines, and clacking of coins never stops. Open nearly all the time, casinos lack windows and clocks, denying you the time cues that signal the hours slipping away. To curb inevitable losses, stick to the cheaper games like blackjack or slot machines. Stay away from the cash machines. Keep your eyes on your watch or you'll have spent five hours and five digits before you know what hit you. The minimum gambling age of 21 is strictly enforced.

The casinos on the Boardwalk all fall within a dice toss of one another. Your best bet for sheer gaudiness and bombast is the **Taj Mahal** (449-1000) at Pennsylvania Ave.—Donald Trump's meditation on sacred Indian art and architecture.Trump has two other casinos, each a towering tribute to his meglomania: the **Trump Castle** (441-2000) and **Trump Plaza** (441-6000). Don't miss **Caesar's Boardwalk Resorts** (348-4411) at Arkansas Ave. (look for the giant statue of Julius beckoning you to come, see, and conquer), which features "Pompeii's Pasta Pavilion" and "Circus Maximus," an auditorium graced by the likes of Natalie Cole and Chicago. (Unfortunately, the performers are not fed to the lions.) The newly expanded **Sands** (441-4000) at Indiana Ave. is a close third in the big-and-ostentatious sweepstakes with its pink and green seashell motif. The other casinos are also worth exploring: **Bally's Park Place** (340-2000), **Harrah's Marina Hotel** (441-5000), the **Claridge** (340-3400) at Indiana Ave., **Showboat** (343-4000) at States Ave., and **TropWorld Casino** (340-4000) at Iowa Ave. Be sure to check out the celebrity handprints at the main entrance of Merv Griffin's **Resorts International** (344-6000).

Atlantic City squats on the northern end of long, narrow **Absecon Island,** which has seven miles of beaches—some pure white, some lumpy gray. The **Atlantic City Beach** is free and often crowded. Walk, jog, or bike west to adjacent **Ventnor City's** sands, which are quieter. The legendary **Boardwalk** of Atlantic City has given itself over to junk-food stands, souvenir shops, and carnival amusements.

■■■ CAPE MAY

Cape May is both the geographic and cultural extreme of the Jersey shore. It lies at the southernmost tip of New Jersey's coastline, and has also passed on the rampant boardwalk commercialism adopted by the rest of New Jersey's beachfront communities. Instead, Cape May has stuck to its Victorian roots and relies on century-old cottages, a lovely beach, and quiet tree-lined avenues to draw visitors. But like the rest of the Jersey shore, Cape May does attract visitors by the thousands, so plan ahead for a summer vacation and expect competition for your spot on the sand.

Practical Information Despite its geographic isolation, Cape May is easily accessible. By car from the north, Cape May is literally the end of the road—follow the **Garden State Parkway** south as far as it goes, watch for signs to Center City, and you'll end up on Lafayette St. From the south, take a 70-minute **ferry** from Lewes, DE (terminal 302-645-6346) to Cape May (886-9699; for recorded schedule info 800-643-3779). In summer months, 13 to 16 ferries cross daily; in the off-season 5-9. (Toll $18 for vehicle and driver, Dec.-March $15; passengers $4.50, ages 6-12 $2.25, motorcyclists $15, bicyclists $8. Adult round-trip $8.50) From Cape May, take a **shuttle** to the ferry ($1) from the Cape May Bus Depot.

The **Welcome Center,** 405 Lafayette St. (884-9562), provides a wagonload of friendly info about Cape May, and free hotlines to B&Bs (open daily 9am-4:30pm). As its name indicates, the **Chamber of Commerce and Bus Depot,** 609 Lafayette St. (884-5508), near Ocean St. across from the Acme, provides tourist info and a local stop for **New Jersey Transit** (800-582-5946; northern NJ 800-772-2222). Buses to: Atlantic City (2 hr., $3.50), Philadelphia (3 hr., $13.50), and New York City (4½ hr., $27). (Terminal open mid-May to mid-Oct, Mon.-Fri. 9am-8pm, Sat. 9am-5pm; mid-Oct. to mid-May Mon.-Thurs. 9am-5pm, Fri. 9am-8pm.) Pick up wheeled transportation at the **Village Bike Shop** (884-8500), Washington and Ocean St., right off the mall. Also ask about the four-person tandem bike. (Bikes $3.50 per hr., $9 per day. Open daily 6:30am-8pm.) But no riding on the beach!

Cape May's **post office:** 700 Washington St. (884-3578; open Mon.-Fri. 9am-5pm, Sat. 9am-noon); **ZIP code:** 08204; **area code:** 609.

Accommodations and Camping Many of the seaside homes now take in nightly guests, but they mostly cater to the B&B set. Still, some reasonable inns persevere. The **Hotel Clinton,** 202 Perry St. (844-3993; in winter 516-799-8889), at Lafayette St., has decent-sized singles ($30-35) and doubles ($40-45) with shared bath. (Open mid-June to Sept. 16 rooms. Reservations recommended.) The **Parris Inn,** 204 Perry St. (884-8015 or 884-6363), near Lafayette St., has simple rooms, some with private baths. (Singles $45, doubles $55; ask about *Let's Go* discount. Reservations recommended.) Also look for specials at the hotels lining Beach Drive.

Campgrounds line U.S. 9 from Atlantic City to the Cape. The two closest to town are **Cold Springs Campground,** 541 New England Rd. (884-8717; 450 fairly private sites $16.50, with hookup $20; open May to mid-Oct.), and **Cape Island Campground,** 709 U.S. 9 (884-5777; sites with water and electricity $26, with full hookup $31; open May to mid-Dec.; pool, store, and athletic facilities).

Food Cape May's cheapest food is the pizza and burger fare along **Beach Ave.,** and you're going to have to shell out a lot of clams for a sit-down meal. **The Ugly Mug,** 426 Washington St. (884-3459), a bar/restaurant in the mall, serves a dozen ugly clams for half as many dollars. (Open Mon.-Sat. 11am-2am, Sun. noon-2am. Food served until 11pm. Sandwiches $4.50-6, platters $7-17.) **Carney's,** 401 Beach Ave. (884-4424), is the self-proclaimed "best bar in town," with live bands nightly. A mug of beer costs $1.75, sandwiches $6-8. (Open Mon.-Sat. 11:30am-10pm, Sun. noon-10pm, last call daily 2am. Cover varies.) Stock your cooler at the **Acme,** in the Victorian Shopping Center bounded by Lafayette, Washington, and Ocean St. (Open Mon.-Sat. 7am-11pm, Sun. 8am-11pm.)

Hitting the Beach The entire Jersey shore is blessed with fine beaches, but the sand at Cape May literally glistens, dotted with some of the famous Cape May diamonds (actually quartz pebbles that glow when cut and polished). When you unroll your beach towel on a city-protected beach (off Beach Ave.), make sure you have the **beach tag** which beachgoers over 12 must wear June-Sept. 10am-5pm.

Pick up a tag (daily $3, weekly $8, seasonal $15) from the vendors roaming the shore. For more info, call the Beach Tag Office (884-9522).

The **Mid-Atlantic Center for the Arts,** 1048 Washington St. (884-5404), offers a multitude of tours and activities. Pick up *This Week in Cape May* in any of the public buildings or stores for a detailed listing. (Guided walking and trolley tours $4.40, children $2.25.) The **Cape May Light House** in **Cape May Point State Park** (884-2159), west of town at the end of the point, guides tourists, not ships. Built in 1859, the lighthouse offers a magnificent panorama of the New Jersey and Delaware coasts from the top of a 199-step stairwell. ($3.50 adults, $1 kids.) Free summer concerts enliven the town's bandstand.

Prevailing winds and geographic location have also made Cape May an important spot on a migration other than that of summer tourists. Hundreds of thousands of birds make a pit stop in Cape May every year on their way to greener pastures. The **Cape May Bird Observatory,** 707 E. Lake Dr. (884-2736), on Cape May Point, serves as the information center for this "bird watching mecca of North America." They give out bird maps and information, and run field trips and workshops. (Open Tues.-Sun. 9am-5pm. For a recorded birding hotline, call 884-2626.)

■ Pennsylvania

Driven to protect his fellow Quakers from persecution, William Penn, Jr. petitioned the English Crown for a slice of North America in 1680. In 1681, King Charles II, who owed the Penns a considerable sum of money, granted the Quakers a vast tract of land between what is now Maryland and New York. By making his colony a bastion of religious tolerance, Penn attracted all types of settlers. As a result, Pennsylvania's towns flourished. The Revolutionaries chose Philadelphia as the site of the First Continental Congress, the birthplace of the Declaration of Independence, and the country's first capital. However, other cities soon overshadowed Philadelphia— New York City rapidly grew into the nation's most important commercial center, and Washington, D.C. became the national capital.

But Pennsylvania, a state accustomed to revolution, has rallied in the face of adversity. In 1976, Philadelphia groomed its historic shrines for the nation's bicentennial celebration, and they have remained immaculate ever since. Even Pittsburgh, a city once dirty enough to fool streetlights into burning during the day, has initiated a cultural renaissance. Between the two cities, Pennsylvania's landscape, from the farms of Lancaster County to the deep river gorges of the Allegheny Plateau, retains much of the natural beauty that the area's first colonists discovered centuries ago.

PRACTICAL INFORMATION

Capital: Harrisburg.
Bureau of Travel Marketing, 453 Forum Bldg., Harrisburg 17120 (800-237-4363). Info on hotels, restaurants, and sights. **Bureau of State Parks,** P.O. Box 1467, Harrisburg 17120 (800-631-7105). The detailed *Recreational Guide* is available at no charge from all visitors centers.
Time Zone: Eastern. **Postal Abbreviation:** PA
Sales Tax: 7%.

■■■ PHILADELPHIA

Textbooks will tell you that Philadelphia is one of America's great historic treasures. They will detail the pivotal role the city played in forging the fledgling nation; both the Declaration of Independence and the Constitution were drafted here. What the books don't mention is the city that surrounds the historic red brick and cracked

THE MID-ATLANTIC

Delaware River

Port of History Museum
Gazela of Philadelphia
U.S.S. Olympia

Penn's Landing

Spring Garden Sta.
Front St.
2nd St.
676

Delaware   Ave.
Barnegar
U.S.S. Becuna

Betsy Ross House
Christ Church
Franklin Court

Sheraton
SOCIETY HILL
Dock St.
Mattis St.
Front St.

3rd St.
Callowhill St.
Benjamin Franklin Bridge
Elfreth's Alley

4th St.
U.S. Mint
Indep. St.
Christ Church Burial Ground (Ben. Franklin's Grave)
5th St.
Carpenter's Hall
Head House Sq.

5th St.
Franklin St.
6th St.
Independence National Historical Park

Free Quaker Meeting House
Liberty Bell Pavilion

WASHINGTON SQUARE

7th St.
8th St.

Tomb of the Unknown Soldier

200 yards
200 meters

9th St.
8th and Market St. Sta.
Independence Hall and Congress Hall
Norman Rockwell Museum

Race St.
Afro-American Historical and Cultural Museum
Bus Depot
Lombard St.
South St.

10th St.
11th St.
Filbert St.
13th St. Sta.
Walnut St.
Spruce St.
Pine St.

12th St.
Arch St.
13th St.
Juniper St.

Spring Garden Sta.
611
Broad St.
City Hall
S. Penn Sq.
Lombard South Sta.

Pennsylvania Academy of Fine Arts
Philadelphia Visitors Center

15th St.
City Hall Sta.
15th St. Sta.
16th St.
17th St.

Callowhill St.
30
Market St.
18th St.
RITTENHOUSE SQUARE
Spruce St.
Pine St.
Lombard St.
South St.

19th St.

Free Library of Philadelphia
Logan Circle
Parkway
Benjamin Franklin

Spring Garden St.
Hamilton St.
Rodin Museum
Academy of Natural Sciences
20th St.
21st St.
Chestnut St.
Walnut St.
Locust St.
22nd St.
Rosenbach Museum and Library
23rd St.
South St.

Franklin Institute /Science Museum
Please Touch Museum
Race St.
Arch St.
John F. Kennedy Blvd.
Mütter Museum
23rd St.
25th St.

Philadelphia Museum of Art
Spring Garden St. Bridge
Schuylkill
River
676
76

Arch St.
Amtrak/ 30th St. Station
30th St. Sta.
Post Office
Drexel University

3
3
30th St.
Sta.

N
2

Downtown Philadelphia

bell. Philly has produced the geniuses behind the soft pretzel and the cheese steak, contains a marvelous conglomeration of museums, concert halls, galleries, universities, and is home to a vibrant, multicultural population. It's true that Philadelphia has a star-spangled past, but the city is also very much alive today.

PRACTICAL INFORMATION

Emergency: 911.

Visitor Information, 1525 John F. Kennedy Blvd. (636-1666), at 16th St. Pick up a free *Philadelphia Visitor's Guide* and the *Philadelphia Quarterly Calendar of Events.* Open Labor Day-Memorial Day daily 9am-6pm; off-season daily 9am-5pm. **Directory Events Hotline,** 377-7777, ext. 2540. **National Park Service Visitors Center,** (597-8974; 627-1776 for recording), between Chestnut and Walnut St. Info on **Independence Park,** including maps, schedules, and the film *Independence.* Also distributes the *Visitor's Guide* and the *Quarterly Calendar of Events.* Open daily 9am-5pm; July-Aug. 9am-6pm. Film shown 9:30am-4pm. Tour assistance for non-English-speaking and disabled travelers.

Traveler's Aid: 311 Juniper St. (546-0571). Open daily 8:30am-4:30pm.

Airport: Philadelphia International, 8 mi. SW of Center City on I-76 (info line 492-3181, 24 hrs.). The 20-min. **SEPTA Airport Rail Line** runs from Center City to the airport. Trains leave every 30 min. daily 5:25am-11:25pm from 30th St. Station, Suburban Station, and Market East ($5 at ticket window, $7 on train). Last train from airport 12:10am. Cab fare downtown $20, but **Airport Limelight Limousine** (342-5557) will deliver you to a hotel ($8 per person) or a specific address downtown.

Amtrak: 30th St. Station (349-2153 or 800-872-7245), at 30th and Market St., in University City. Office open Mon.-Fri. 5:10am-10:45pm, Sat.-Sun. 6:10am-10:45pm. Station open 24 hrs. *See Mileage Chart.* To get to NYC, take the SEPTA commuter train to Trenton, NJ ($4-5), then hop on a New Jersey Transit train to NYC through Newark ($7.75).

Buses: Greyhound (931-4075), 10th and Filbert St., 1 block north of Market near the 10th and Market St. subway/commuter rail stop in the heart of Philadelphia. Station open 7am-1am daily. *See Mileage Chart.* In the same station, **New Jersey Transit** (800-582-5946 or 569-3752). To: Atlantic City ($10), Ocean City ($10.60), and other points on the New Jersey Shore. Operates Mon.-Wed. 6am-9:30pm, Thurs.-Sun. 6am-10:30pm.

Public Transport: Southeastern Pennsylvania Transportation Authority (SEPTA) (580-7800). Most buses operate 5am-2am, some all night. Extensive bus and rail service to suburbs. Two major subway routes: the **Market St. line** running east-west (including 30th St. Station and the historic area), and the **Broad St. line** running north-south (including the stadium complex in south Philadelphia). Subway is unsafe after dark, but buses are usually okay. Buses serve the 5-county area. Subway connects with commuter rails—the Main Line local runs through the western suburb of Paoli ($3.50), and SEPTA runs north as far as Trenton, NJ ($4). Pick up a SEPTA system map ($2) and a good street map at any subway stop. Fare $1.50, 2 tokens for $2.10, transfers 40¢. Unlimited all-day pass (for buses and subway) $5.

Taxi: Yellow Cab, 922-8400. **United Cab,** 238-9500. $1.80 base and $1.80 per mi.

Car Rental: Courtesy Rent-a-Car, 7704 Westchester Pike (446-6200). $19 per day, unlimited mileage. Must be 21 with major credit card.

Help Lines: Gay Switchboard, 546-7100; **Suicide and Crisis Intervention,** 686-4420; **Youth Crisis Line,** 800-448-4663.

Post Office: 2970 Market, at 30th St., across from the Amtrak station. Open 24 hrs. **ZIP code:** 19104.

Area Code: 215.

William Penn, Jr., a survivor of London's great fire in the 1660s, planned his city as a logical and easily accessible grid pattern of wide streets. The north-south streets ascend numerically from the **Delaware River,** flowing near **Penn's Landing** and **Independence Hall** on the east side, to the **Schuylkill River** (pronounced SKOOL-kill) on the west. The first street is **Front,** and the others follow consecutively from

2 to 69. **Center City** runs from 8th Street to the Schuylkill River. From north to south, the primary streets are Race, Arch, JFK, Market, Chestnut, and South. The intersection of Broad (14th St.) and Market marks the focal point of Center City. The **Historic District** stretches from Front to 8th St. and from Vine to South St. The **University of Pennsylvania** sprawls on the far side of the Schuylkill River, about 1 mi. west of Center City. **University City** includes the Penn/Drexel area west of the Schuylkill River. When getting directions, make sure they include numbered streets.

ACCOMMODATIONS AND CAMPING

Downtown Philadelphia is saturated with luxury hotels, so anything inexpensive is popular. If you make arrangements even a few days in advance, however, you should be able to find comfortable lodging close to Center City for under $50. **Bed and Breakfast Center City,** 1804 Pine St., Philadelphia 19103 (735-1137 or 800-354-8401), will find you a room in a private home. **Bed & Breakfast Connections/ Bed & Breakfast of Philadelphia,** at 610-687-3565 in Devon, PA, will also book you a room in Philadelphia or throughout southeastern Pennsylvania. No exterior sign. (Singles $40-75, doubles $45-80. Check-in 3-7pm, make reservations a week ahead. Best to call 9am-9pm.) **Philadelphia Naturist and Work Camp Center,** P.O. Box 4755 (634-7057), rents rooms to foreign visitors ($5 with light breakfast). They also arrange free room and board on nearby farms in exchange for doing daily chores.

Bank Street Hostel, 32 S. Bank St. (922-0222 or 800-392-4678), is a great hostel in a great location. Located in the historic district, it has A/C, TV, free coffee and tea, laundry facilities, kitchen, a free pool table, and a musical morning wakeup. From the bus station, walk down Market St. and it's between 2nd and 3rd. From the train, take the Market-Frankfort line east to 2nd. Lockout 10am-4:30pm. 54 beds. Curfew Sun.-Thurs. midnight, Fri.-Sat. 1am. $14. Linen $2.

Chamounix Mansion International Youth Hostel (HI-AYH), (878-3676 or 800-379-0017), West Fairmount Park. Take bus #38 from Market St. to Ford and Cranston Rd., follow Ford to Chamounix St., then turn left and follow the road to the hostel (about a 20-min. walk). Former country estate built in 1802. A hostel-deluxe with clean, beautifully furnished rooms with lots of perks, showers, kitchen, coin-operated laundry, a nice chess table, and a piano. Some basic groceries for sale. Extraordinarily friendly and helpful staff. 44 beds. Free parking. Check-in 8-11am, 4:30pm-midnight. Lockout 11am-4:30pm. Curfew midnight. $10, nonmembers $13. Linen $2.

Old First Reformed Church (922-4566), 4th and Race St., in Center City 1 block from the Independence Mall and 4 blocks from Penn's Landing. Historic church that converts its social hall to a youth hostel sleeping around 30. Foam pads on the floor, showers. 3-night max. stay. Check-in 5-10pm. Curfew 11pm. $11. Breakfast included. Ages 18-26 only. Open July and Aug.

The Divine Tracy Hotel, 20 S. 36th St. (382-4310), near Market St. in University City. Immaculately clean, quiet, and well-maintained rooms. Women must wear skirts and stockings at all times in the public areas of the hotel; men, long pants and socks with their shirts tucked in. Strictly single-sex floors. No smoking, vulgarity, obscenity, or blasphemy. Fans and TVs for rent. Check-in 7am-11pm. Check out 1pm. Singles $28-30, with private bath $33-40. Shared doubles $20-25 per person. The management does not permit alcohol or food (except small snacks) in the rooms, but the **Keyflower Dining Room** (386-2207) offers incredibly cheap and healthy, although bland, food. Entrees $3.85 per lb., salad $2.85 per lb. Open to the public Mon.-Fri. 11:30am-2pm and 5-8pm.

The closest camping is across the Delaware River in New Jersey. Try the **Timberline Campground,** 117 Timber Lane, Clarksboro, NJ 08020 (609-423-6677), 15 mi. from Center City. Take 295 S. to exit 18A (Clarksboro), turn left and then right at Cohawkin Rd. Go ½-mi. and turn right on Friendship Rd. Timber Lane is one block on the right. (Sites $16, with hookup $19.) In Pennsylvania, try the **Baker Park Campground,** 400 East Pothoure Rd. (933-5865), 45 min. to Rte. 76 west to Rte. 23 through Valley Forge Park. (Sites $14, with electricity $16. Open May-Oct.)

FOOD

Philly phood is phantastic. This is a city that likes to eat, and eat well. If you do nothing else in this city, try a **cheesesteak, hoagie,** or **soft pretzel,** all Philly specialities. Cheap food fills the city in the carts of the ubiquitous street vendors, and also gathers in several specific areas: very hip **South Street,** between Front and 7th; **Sansom Street,** between 17th and 18th; and **2nd Street,** between Chestnut and Market. All are home to affordable food. **Chinatown,** bounded by 11th, 8th, Arch, and Vine St., is near downtown and is loaded with great places serving up lots of cheap eats. **South Philadelphia** is also stocked with an abundance of inexpensive spots. The universities of Drexel and Penn share **University City,** west of the Schuylkill River, and support many student hangouts.

For fresh fruit, suckling pigs, fish heads, live chickens, and some other food stuff that you probably won't ever need, visit the **Italian Market,** on 9th St. below Christian St. The **Reading Terminal Market** (922-2317), at 12th and Arch St., is by far the best place to go for lunch in Center City. Food stands have clustered in this indoor market since 1893, selling fresh produce and meats. (Open Mon.-Sat. 8am-6pm.)

Historic District

Pat's Steaks and **Geno's Steaks,** 9th and Passyunk (both are on the same corner). A cheesesteak at Pat's or Geno's is perhaps the quintessential Philadelphia dining experience. These guys are the big cheese in the world of steaks and share a bitter rivalry; signs urge dinners not to eat a "misteak." Go have a steak and decide for yourself who serves the best. Basic cheesesteak: $4.66 (open 24 hrs.).

Famous 4th St. Delicatessen, (292-3274), 4th and Bainbridge St. This deli has been a Philadelphia landmark since 1923. They have a pickel barrel, egg creams from a soda fountain ($1.50), knishes ($1.50), matzos ($5), and a devoted following. Open Mon.-Sat. 7am-6pm, Sun. 7am-4pm.

Cedar's, 616 2nd St. (945-4950), between South and Bainbridge. This Lebanese restaurant right off South St. is popular with locals who come for the quiet atmosphere, good food, and good prices. Get the friendly waiter's recommendation from the authentic menu, but for a unique flavor try the mango juice with yogurt. Entrees $6-11. Open daily 11:30am-10:30pm.

Center City

Rangoon, 145 N. 9th St. (829-8939), Chinatown. This intimate Chinatown restaurant serves wonderful Burmese food. The three female proprietors share a love of good food, low prices, and spice. Entrees $3.50-9, most around $6.50. Open Mon.-Tues. 11:30am-3pm and 5-10pm, Fri. 11:30am-10pm, Sat. 1pm-10pm, Sun. 1pm-9pm.

Seafood Unlimited, 270 S. 20th St. (732-3663). Very fresh (still has scales) seafood $6-10. Open Mon.-Thurs. 11am-9pm, Fri.-Sat. 11am-10pm.

Harmony, 135 N. 9th St. (627-4520), Chinatown. The chefs in this small, popular Chinatown establishment masterfully dupe carnivores with a variety of meatless Chinese dishes, including imitation beef, poultry, seafood, and pork. Most entrees $7-8. Open Sun.-Thurs. 11:30am-10pm, Fri.-Sat. 11:30am-11:30pm.

Lee's Hoagie House, 44 S. 17th St. (564-1264). Authentic hoagies ($3.75-6) since 1953. The 3-ft. hoagie is an all day affair. Open Mon.-Fri. 10:30am-6pm, Sat. 10:30am-5pm.

University City

Smoky Joe's, 208 S. 40th St. (222-0770), between Locust and Walnut. An unofficial branch of Penn, "smokes" has been giving students a place to hang out for over 50 years. Try Rosie's Homemade Chili ($4) or a 10-oz. burger ($4.25). Open daily 11am-2am; occasional live music.

Tandoor India Restaurant, 106 S. 40th St. (222-7122). Northern Indian cuisine cooked in a clay oven. All-you-can-eat lunch buffet ($6), dinner buffet ($9). Open daily noon-3pm for lunch; Mon.-Thurs. 4:30-10pm for dinner.

Le Bus, 3402 Sansom St. (387-3800), serves eclectic gourmet college food. You'll think you stumbled into the dining hall when you have to grab a tray, but good food awaits. Sandwiches $3-5.50, entrees $6-8. Open Mon.-Sat. 7:30am-9pm, longer during the school year.

SIGHTS

Independence Hall and The Historic District

The buildings of the **Independence National Historical Park** (597-8974), bounded by Market, Walnut, 2nd, and 6th St. (open daily 9am-5pm; in summer 9am-9pm, all free), witnessed events that have become landmarks of U.S. history. The park **visitors center** makes a good starting point. Site of the signing of the Declaration of Independence in 1776, and the drafting and signing of the Constitution in 1787, **Independence Hall** lies between 5th and 6th St. on Chestnut. (Free guided tours daily every 15-20 min., arrive before 11am in summer to avoid an hour-long line.) The U.S. Congress first assembled in nearby **Congress Hall** (free self-guided tour), while its predecessor, the First Continental Congress, convened in **Carpenters' Hall,** (597-8974) 3rd St., in the middle of the block bounded by 3rd, 4th, Walnut and Chestnut. (925-0167; open Tues.-Sun. 10am-4:30pm). North of Independence Hall lies the **Liberty Bell Pavilion.** The cracked **Liberty Bell** itself, one of the most famous U.S. symbols, once tolled for presidents but is today silent.

The remainder of the park contains preserved residential and commercial buildings of the Revolutionary era. To the north lies Ben Franklin's home in **Franklin Court** to the north, on Market between 3rd and 4th St. The home includes an underground museum, a 20-min. movie, and phones for you to confer with long-dead political luminaries. (Open daily 9am-5pm. Free.) At nearby **Washington Square,** an eternal flame commemorates the **Tomb of the Unknown Soldier** of the Revolutionary War. Across from Independence Hall is Philadelphia's branch of the **U.S. Mint,** (597-7350), 5th and Arch St. A self-guided tour explains the mechanized coin-making procedure. No free samples here. (Open Mon.-Sat. 9am-4:30pm; July-Aug. daily 9am-4:30pm; off-season Mon.-Fri. 9am-4:30pm. Free.)

Just behind Independence Hall is the **Norman Rockwell Museum** (922-4345), 6th and Sansom St., which houses many of the artist's *Saturday Evening Post* covers. (Open Mon.-Sat. 10am-4pm, Sun. 11am-4pm; $2, seniors $1.50, under 12 free.) Near the mint, walk onto the **Benjamin Franklin Bridge,** just off Race and 5th. From this powder blue marvel observe boat traffic on the Delaware, get a great view of both Philadelphia and Camden, NJ, and wonder exactly how safe it is to put so much faith in engineers. Not for those with vertigo. (Open daily 6am-7pm; free.)

Tucked away near 2nd and Arch St. is the quiet, residential **Elfreth's Alley,** allegedly "the oldest street in America," along which a penniless Ben Franklin walked when he arrived in town in 1723. On Arch, near 3rd St., sits the tiny **Betsy Ross House** (627-5343), where Ross supposedly sewed the first flag of the original 13 states. (Open Tues.-Sun. 10am-5pm, $1 donation requested, 25¢ for kids.) **Christ Church** (922-1695), on 2nd near Market, hosted the Quakers who sought a more fashionable way of life in colonial Philadelphia. Ben Franklin lies buried in the nearby **Christ Church cemetery** at 5th and Arch St. Also see the Quaker meeting houses: the original **Free Quaker Meeting House** at 5th and Arch St., and a new, larger one at 4th and Arch St. (open Tues.-Sun. noon-4pm).

Mikveh Israel, the first Jewish congregation of Philadelphia, has a burial ground on Spruce near 8th St. The **Afro-American Historical and Cultural Museum** (574-0381), 7th and Arch St., stands as the first U.S. museum devoted solely to the history of African-Americans. (Open Tues.-Sat. 10am-5pm, Sun. noon-6pm. Admission $4; seniors, students, handicapped, and children $2.)

On the corner of 8th and Race St. is the Pennsylvania College of Podiatric Medicine, which contains the **Shoe Museum** (629-0300, ext. 185). This 6th floor collection contains footwear fashions from famous feet such as Reggie Jackson, Lady Bird Johnson, Dr. J, Nancy Reagan, and more. (Open Mon.-Thurs. 9am-5pm, Fri. 9am-3:30pm; free.)

Society Hill proper begins where the park ends, on Walnut St. between Front and 7th St. Now Philadelphia's most distinguished residential neighborhood, housing both established blue-bloods and a new yuppie crowd, the area was originally a tract of land owned by the Free Society of Traders, a company formed to help William Penn, Jr. consolidate Pennsylvania. Federal-style townhouses dating back 300 years line picturesque cobblestone walks, illuminated by old-fashioned streetlights. **Head House Square,** 2nd and Pine St., held a marketplace in 1745 and now houses restaurants, boutiques, and craft shops. An outdoor flea market occurs here over summer weekends.

South of Head House Square are two museums dedicated to life's more artistic side. The **Mario Lanza Museum,** 416 Queen St. (468-3623), is a shrine-like collection of artifacts and memorabilia from the life of opera singer Mario Lanza. (Mon.-Fri. 10am-4:30pm; free.) Even farther south is the **Mummer's Museum,** (336-3050) 2nd and Washington Ave., which is one of the few places where you can see evidence of construction workers, policemen, and other macho types dressed in feathers and sequins and generally looking like Liberace on a bad day. Chronicles the sordid tradition of Philly's mummers and their bizarre New Years Day parade. (Open July-Aug. Tues.-Sat. 9:30am-5pm; Sept.-June Tues.-Sat. 9:30am-5pm, Sun. noon-5pm. $2.50, seniors and under 12 $2.)

Located on the Delaware River, **Penn's Landing** (923-8181) is the largest freshwater port in the world. Among other vessels it holds the *Gazela,* a three-masted, 178-ft. Portuguese square rigger built in 1883; the *U.S.S. Olympia,* Commodore Dewey's flagship during the Spanish-American War (922-1898; tours daily 10am-5pm; admission $5, children $2); and the *U.S.S. Becuna,* a WWII submarine. The **Port of History,** (823-7280) Delaware Ave. and Walnut St., has frequently changing exhibits (open Wed.-Sun. 10am-4pm; admission $2, ages 5-12 $1). The **Delaware Landing** is a great spot to soak up sun. For $1.50 (under 12 75¢) you can jump on **Penn's Landing Trolley** (627-0807), Delaware Ave., between Catharine and Race St., for a guided tour along the waterfront (Thurs.-Sun. 11am-dusk).

Center City

Center City, the area bounded by 12th, 23rd, Vine, and Pine St., bustles with activity. **City Hall** (686-1776), Broad and Market St., an ornate structure of granite and marble with 20-ft.-thick foundation walls, is the nation's largest municipal building. Until 1908, it reigned as the tallest building in the U.S., with the help of the 37-ft. statue of William Penn, Jr. on top. A municipal statute prohibited building higher than the top of Penn's hat until entrepreneurs in the mid-80s overturned it, finally launching Philadelphia into the skyscraper era. You can enjoy almost the same view Billy does by taking an elevator up the tower for a commanding view of the city. (686-9074; Tower open Mon.-Fri. 10am-3pm. Last elevator at 2:45. Call ahead for tickets or you may have to wait. Free.) The **Pennsylvania Academy of Fine Arts** (972-7600), Broad and Cherry St., the country's first art school and one of its first museums, has an extensive collection of American and British art, including works by Charles Wilson Peale, Thomas Eakins, Winslow Homer, and some contemporary artists. (Open Tues.-Sat. 10am-5pm, Sun. 11am-5pm. Tours daily 12:15 and 2pm. $5, seniors and students $3, under 5 free. Free Sat. 10am-1pm.) Also near City Hall is the **Masonic Temple,** 1 N. Broad St. (988-1917), which contains numerous halls of various architectural styles. The building itself is a mammoth. (Must be seen on a 45-min. tour. Mon.-Fri. 10am, 11am, 1pm, 2pm, 3pm, Sat. 10am, 11am; free.)

Just south of **Rittenhouse Square,** 2010 Delancey St., the **Rosenbach Museum and Library** (732-1600) houses rare manuscripts and paintings, including some of the earliest-known copies of Cervantes' *Don Quixote,* the original manuscript of James Joyce's *Ulysses,* and the original *Yankee Doodle Dandy.* (Open Sept.-July Tues.-Sun. 11am-4pm. Guided tours $3.50, seniors, students, and kids $2.50. Exhibitions only, $2.) The nearby **Mütter Museum,** 19 S. 22nd St. (563-3737) between Chestnut and Market St., of Philadelphia's College of Physicians displays such fascinating medical treasures as a wall of skulls, a tumor removed from President Cleveland's jaw, part of John Wilkes Booth's thorax, and assorted other skeletons and body parts. (Open Tues.-Fri. 10am-4pm. $1 suggested donation.) Ben Franklin founded the **Library Company of Philadelphia,** 1314 Locust St. (546-3181), near 13th St., over 250 years ago, as a club the members of which pay for books from England. (Open Mon.-Fri. 9am-4:45pm. Free.)

Benjamin Franklin Parkway

Nicknamed "America's Champs-Elysées," the Benjamin Franklin Parkway is a wide, diagonal deviation from William Penn's original grid pattern of city streets. Built in the 1920s, this tree- and flag-lined street connects Center City with Fairmount Park and the Schuylkill River. It is flanked by elegant architecture, such as the twin buildings at Logan Square, 19th and Parkway, that house the **Free Library of Philadelphia** and the **Municipal Court.**

The **Franklin Institute** (448-1200), at 20th and Parkway, houses the fantastic **Science Center,** which amazes visitors with four floors of gadgets and games depicting the intricacies of space, time, motion, and the human body. A 20-ft. **Benjamin Franklin National Memorial** statue divines lightning at the entrance. In 1990, to commemorate the 200th anniversary of Franklin's death, the Institute unveiled the **Futures Center;** glimpses of life in the 21st century including simulated zero gravity and a timely set of exhibits on the changing global environment. (Futures Center open Mon.-Wed. 9:30am-5pm, Thurs.-Sat. 9:30am-9pm. Sun. 9:30am-6pm; Science Center daily 9:30am-5pm. Admission to both $9.50, seniors and kids $8.50.) The **Omniverse Theater** provides 180° and 4½ stories of optical oohs and aahs. (Shows daily on the hr., Mon.-Fri. 10am-4pm, Sat. 5 and 7-9pm, Sun. 5-6pm; also Thurs. 7-8pm, Fri. and Sat. 7-9pm. $7, seniors and kids $6.) **Fels Planetarium** boasts an advanced computer-driven system that projects a simulation of life billions of years beyond. (Shows daily 11:15am-4:15pm hourly. $7, seniors and kids $6.) See the exhibits and a show for $12, $10.50 seniors and kids; or see the exhibits and both shows for $14.50, seniors and kids $12.50. The rock music, multi-colored laser shows shown Friday and Saturday nights are very groovy. Call for details.

A casting of the *Gates of Hell* outside the **Rodin Museum** (684-7788), 22nd St., guards the portal of the most complete collection of the artist's works this side of the Seine, including one of the gazillion versions of *The Thinker* (Open Tues.-Sun. 10am-5pm; donation). Try your hand at the sensuous **Please Touch Museum,** 210 N. 21st St. (963-0666), designed specifically for grabby kids under eight (open daily 9am-4:30pm; $6.50).

The **Academy of Natural Sciences** (299-1000), 19th and Parkway, showcases an exhibit of precious gems and a 65 million year old dinosaur skeleton. (Open Mon.-Fri. 10am-4:30pm, Sat.-Sun. and holidays 10am-5pm; $6, kids $5). Farther down 26th St., the **Philadelphia Museum of Art** (763-8100) harbors one of the world's major art collections, including Rubens's *Prometheus Bound,* Picasso's *Three Musicians,* and Duchamp's *Nude Descending a Staircase,* as well as extensive Asian, Egyptian, and decorative art collections. (Open Tues. 10am-5pm, Wed. 10am-8:45pm, Thurs.-Sun. 10am-5pm. $6, seniors and students under 18 $3. Free Sun. 10am-1pm.) The **Free Library of Philadelphia** (686-5322) has a tremendous library of orchestral music, and one of the nation's largest rare book collections (open Mon.-Wed. 9am-9pm, Thurs.-Fri. 9am-6pm, Sat. 9am-5pm, Sun. 1-5pm).

Fairmount Park sprawls behind the Philadelphia Museum of Art on both sides of the Schuylkill River. Bike trails and picnic areas abound, and the famous **Philadelphia Zoo** (243-1100) at 34th St. and Girard Ave., the oldest in the U.S., houses 1500 species in one corner of the park, including America's first white lions (open daily 9:30am-5pm; $8, seniors and kids $5.50). **Boathouse Row,** which houses the shells of local crew teams, is particularly beautiful at night, when its buildings twinkle with lights. During the day, hikers and non-hikers alike may wish to venture out to the northernmost arm of Fairmount Park, where trails leave the Schuylkill River and wind along secluded Wissahickon Creek for 5 mi. The **Horticultural Center** (685-

0096), off Belmont Ave. (open daily 9am-3pm), blooms with greenhouses, Japanese gardens, and periodic flower shows ($2 suggested donation).

West Philadelphia (University City)

West Philly is home to both the **University of Pennsylvania (UPenn)** and **Drexel University,** located across the Schuylkill from Center City, within easy walking distance of the 30th St. Station. Benjamin Franklin founded UPenn in 1740. Fifteen years later the country's first medical school was founded, and students have been pulling all-nighters ever since. The Penn campus provides a cloistered retreat of green lawns, red-brick quadrangles, and rarefied air. Ritzy shops line Chestnut St. and boisterous fraternities line Spruce; warm weather brings out a variety of street vendors along the Drexel and Penn borders. Some of the area surrounding University City is not the best —it is better not to travel alone or at night.

Penn's **University Museum of Archeology and Anthropology** (898-4000), 33rd and Spruce St., houses an outstanding archeological collections. (Open June-Aug. Tues.-Sat. 10am-4:30pm; Sept.-May Tues.-Sat. 10am-4:30pm, Sun. 1-5pm); $5, seniors and students $2.50.) In 1965, Andy Warhol had his first one-man show at the **Institute of Contemporary Art** (898-7108), 34th and Walnut St., and today, the gallery remains cutting edge. (Open Thurs.-Sun. 10am-5pm, Wed. 10am-7pm. $3, seniors, children, and students $1. Free Sun. 10am-noon.)

ENTERTAINMENT AND NIGHTLIFE

Check Friday's weekend magazine section in the Philadelphia *Inquirer* for entertainment listings. *City Paper,* distributed on Thursdays, and the *Welcomemat,* distributed on Wednesdays, are free at newsstands and markets and have weekly listings of city events. *Au Courant,* a gay and lesbian weekly newspaper, lists and advertises events throughout the Delaware Valley region. The younger crowd frequents the bar scene in University City. Along **South Street,** there is a wide variety of live music and dance clubs on weekends. The **Khyber Pass Pub,** 56 S. 2nd St. (440-9683), is one of Philly's best live music venues, bringing in a variety of alternative bands. (Open Tues.-Sat.; hours and cover vary.) Nearby **Penn's Landing** (923-8181) has free concerts in summer.

Along Penn's Landing runs **Columbus Boulevard,** which has recently become a local hot spot with lots of nightclubs and restaurants, and makes for a great stroll on a warm summer night. The **Old City,** Chestnut to Vine and Front to 4th St., also comes alive on the first Friday of every month (Oct.-June) for the fantastic **First Friday** celebration. The streets are filled with people and the music of live bands, and the area's many art galleries open their doors with available art and free food. Formerly under the direction of the late Eugene Ormandy, and now under Ricardo Muti, the **Philadelphia Academy of Music** (893-1930), Broad and Locust St., houses the **Philadelphia Orchestra,** among the best in the U.S. The academy was modeled after Milan's *La Scala.* The season runs September-May. General admission tickets ($2) go on sale at the Locust St. entrance 45 min. before Friday and Saturday concerts. Check with the box office for availability (regular tickets $12-23). The **Mann Music Center,** (878-7707), George's Hill, near 52nd St. and Parkside Ave. in Fairmount Park, has 5000 seats under cover, 10,000 on outdoor benches and lawns—and hosts summer Philadelphia Orchestra, jazz, and rock events. Pick up free lawn tickets for the orchestra June-August on the day of performance from the visitors center at 16th St. and JFK Blvd. (See Practical Information above.) For the big-name shows, sit just outside the theater and soak in the sounds gratis. The **Robin Hood Dell East** (477-8810), Strawberry Mansion Dr., in Fairmount Park, brings in top names in pop, jazz, gospel, and ethnic dance in July and August. The Philadelphia Orchestra holds several free performances here in summer, and as many as 30,000 people gather on the lawn. Inquire at the visitors center (636-1666) about upcoming events. During the school year, the outstanding students of the **Curtis Institute of Music,** 1726 Locust St. (893-5279) give free concerts on Mondays, Wednesdays, and Fridays at 8pm. (Concerts run mid-Oct to April.) **Merriam The-**

ater, 250 S. Broad St., Center City (732-5446), stages a variety of dance, musical, and comedy performances September through May.

Philly has four professional sports teams. The **Phillies** (baseball; 463-1000) and **Eagles** (football; 463-5500) play at **Veterans Stadium,** Broad St. and Pattison Ave., while the **Spectrum,** Broad St. and Pattison Ave., houses the **76ers** (basketball; 339-7676) and the **Flyers** (hockey; 755-9700). Baseball and hockey general admission tickets run $5-20 while football and basketball tickets go for more, $15-50. Take the Broad St. line of the subway.

■ NEAR PHILADELPHIA: VALLEY FORGE

American troops during the Revolutionary War fought a fierce battle at Valley Forge, but it wasn't against the British. During the winter of 1777-78, the 12,000 men under General George Washington spent agonizing months fighting starvation, bitter cold, and disease. Only 8000 survived. Nonetheless, inspired by Washington's fierce spirit and the news of an American alliance with France, the troops left Valley Forge stronger and better trained, going on to victories in New Jersey, eventually reoccupying Philadelphia, and becoming a free and independent nation.

The park today encompasses over 3600 acres. (Open daily 6am-10pm.) Self-guided tours begin at the **visitors center** (783-1077), which also has a museum and film (twice per hr. 9am-4:30pm, 15 min.). (Center open daily 9am-5pm.) The tour features Washington's headquarters, reconstructed soldier huts and fortifications, and the Grand Parade Ground where the army drilled. Admission to the historic buildings of the park, such as **Washington's headquarters,** is $2 (under 17 free), but the grounds of the park are free to all. Audio tapes rental $8. The park has three picnic areas. There is no camping within the park, but the visitors center distributes a list of nearby campgrounds. A 5-mi. bike trail winds through the hills of the park.

To get to Valley Forge, take the Schuylkill Expressway westbound from Philadelphia for about 12 mi. Get off at the Valley Forge exit, then take Rte. 202 S. for 1 mi. and Rte. 422 W. for 1½ mi. to another Valley Forge exit. SEPTA runs buses to the visitors center Monday through Friday only. Catch #125 at 16th and JFK ($3.10).

■ ■ ■ LANCASTER COUNTY

Lancaster County is the home to the Pennsylvania Dutch, who should really be called the Pennsylvania Germans. The Amish, the Mennonites, and the Brethren are three groups of German Anabaptists who fled persecution in Deutschland (thus the misnomer by confused locals) and sought freedom to pursue their own religion in the rolling countryside of Lancaster County. They successfully escaped persecution, but they have not escaped attention. Thousands of visitors flock to this pastoral area every year to take a gander at the way life used to be. The Amish, in particular, eschew modern conveniences like motorized vehicles, electricity, and The Gap, in favor of a more traditional lifestyle. Their way of life is not for show, however, and visitors should be considerate of them; they do not wish to be photographed.

PRACTICAL INFORMATION

Visitor Information: Lancaster Chamber of Commerce and Industry, 100 Queen St. (397-3531), in the Southern Market Center. Pick up guided walking tours of Lancaster City (April-Oct. Mon.-Sat. 10am and 1:30pm, Sun. and holidays 10am, 11am, 1:30pm; adults $4, kids $3) or buy a worthwhile self-guided booklet ($1.50). To reserve a tour off-season call 653-8225 or 394-2339. (Open Mon.-Fri. 9am-5pm, Sat. 9am-4pm, Sun. 10am-3pm.) **Pennsylvania Dutch Visitors Bureau Information Center,** 501 Greenfield Rd. (299-8901), on the east side of Lancaster City just off Rte. 30, has walls of brochures and free phone lines to most area inns and campsites. (Open June-Aug. Mon.-Sat. 8am-6pm, Sun. 8am-5pm; Sept.-May daily 9am-5pm.) **Mennonite Information Center,** 2209 Millstream Rd. (299-0954; open Mon.-Sat. 8am-5pm), just off Rte. 30. Guides for a 2-hr. tour $23; call for times.

Amtrak: 53 McGovern Ave. (291-5080 or 800-872-7245; reservations 24 hrs.), in Lancaster City. 8trains per day to Philadelphia (1 hr., $12).

Capitol Trailways: 22 W. Clay St. (397-4861). 3 buses per day between Lancaster City and Philadelphia (2 hr., $12.35). Open daily 7am-4:45pm.

Public Transportation: Red Rose Transit, 45 Erick Rd. (397-4246), serves Lancaster and the surrounding countryside. Pick up route maps at the office. Base fare $1, seniors free Mon.-Fri. 9am-3:30pm and all day on weekends.

Post Office: 1400 Harrisburg Pike (396-6900). **ZIP code:** Lancaster City, 17604.

Area Code: 717.

Lancaster County—even the concentrated spots of interest to tourists—covers a huge area. Cars are the vehicle of choice for most visitors. You can pay a guide to hop in and show you around. If you'd rather go it alone, pick up maps at Lancaster City or Pennsylvania Dutch visitors bureaus (see above), veer off U.S. 30, and explore the winding roads. The most famous local towns lie along these scenic byways. You always thought **Intercourse** would lead to **Paradise,** and on the country roads of Lancaster County, it does.

ACCOMMODATIONS

Hundreds of hotels, B&Bs, and campgrounds cluster in this area. Don't search for accommodations without stopping by the **Pennsylvania Dutch Visitors Bureau Information Center** (see above). There seem to be as many **campgrounds** as cows in this lush countryside. All the campgrounds have laundry and showers.

Shirey's Youth Hostel (HI-AYH), P.O. Box 49, Geigertown 19523 (215-286-9537). Near French Creek State Park off Rte. 82. This hostel, located in a beautiful, though remote, area, has a full kitchen and showers. Transportation from Reading, 15 mi. away, might be arranged if you call ahead. Open March-Nov. Check out 9:30am, curfew 11pm. $9, nonmembers $12, sleepsack rental $1.

Old Millstream Camping Manor, 2249 U.S. 30 E. (299-2314). The closest year-round facility, 4 mi. east of Lancaster City. Office open daily 8am-8pm. Sites $16, with hookup $19. Reservations recommended.

Roamers Retreat, 5005 Lincoln Hwy. (442-4287 or 800-525-5605), off U.S. 30, 7½ mi. east of Rte. 896, open April-Oct. Call for reservations. Sites $18, hookup $20.

Shady Grove, P.O. Box 28, Adamstown 19501 (215-484-4225), on Rte. 272 at Rte. 897, 264 W. Swartzville Rd. 80 sites, with electricity $16, full hookup $18.

FOOD

Just about everyone passing through Lancaster County expects a taste of real German cuisine—and a flock of high priced "family-style" restaurants have sprouted up to please them. If you have the cash (all-you-can-eat meals $12-16) try any of the huge restaurants such as **The Amish Barn,** 3029 Old Philadelphia Pike (768-8886), open daily 7:30am-9pm, which are thick on Rte. 340 in Bird-in-Hand. Lancaster City dishes up more varied fare. **Isaac's,** 44 N. Queen St. (394-5544), creates imaginative sandwiches ($4-6 with avian names). Don't miss the **Central Market,** in the northwest corner of Penn Square, a huge food bazaar vending inexpensive meats, cheeses, vegetables, and sandwiches since 1899. (Open Tues. and Fri. 6am-4:30pm, Sat. 6am-2pm.) Many fun, interesting, and inexpensive restaurants surround the market. If you try nothing else in Lancaster County, at least sample a **whoopie pie** (75¢).

SIGHTS

A good place to start is the **People's Place** (768-7171), on Main St./Rte. 340, in Intercourse, 11 mi. east of Lancaster City. The film *Who Are the Amish* runs every half hour 9:30am-5pm. ($3.50, children $1.75.) The Place spans an entire block with bookstores, craft shops, and an art gallery. (Open Mon.-Sat. 9:30am-9:30pm; Nov.-March from 9:30am-4:30pm.) If you have specific questions, seek out friendly locals at the Mennonite Information Center (see above), which also shows the film *Por-*

traits of Our Heritage and Faith. Memorial Day to Labor Day, People's Place also shows another film titled *Hazel's People* ($5, under 12 $2.50). **Amish World,** also in Intercourse, has charming hands-on exhibits on Amish and Mennonite life, from barn-raising to hat-styles. (Admission to one $3.50, kids $1.75. To both $6.50, kids $3.25.) Note to Americana lovers: there is nothing cooler than a postcard that says "I am in Intercourse, having a good time, and wish you were here." Hell, send us one.

County seat **Lancaster City,** in the heart of Dutch country, has clean, red-brick row houses huddled around historic **Penn Square** in the city center. The **Quilt Museum,** Main St. (768-7171), in Intercourse, has a lovely patchwork of Amish quilts. (Open Mon.-Sat. 9am-5pm; $4, 12 and under $2.)

■ HERSHEY'S CANDYLAND

Milton S. Hershey, a Mennonite resident of eastern Pennsylvania farms, failed in his first several jaunts into the confectionery world. Then he found chocolate. Today the company that bears his name operates the world's largest chocolate factory, in **Hershey,** just across the northeastern border of Lancaster. Here, street lights are shaped like candy kisses, and streets are named Chocolate and Cocoa. East of town at **Hershey Park** (800-437-7439), the **Chocolate World Visitors Center** (534-4900) presents a free, automated tour through a simulated chocolate factory. After viewing the processing of the cacao bean from tropical forests past the Oompa-Loompas of Willy Wonka fame to final packaging, visitors emerge with two free Hershey Kisses in hand into a pavilion full of chocolate cookies, discounted chocolate candy, chocolate milk, and fashionable Hershey sportswear. (Open Sept. to mid-June daily 9am-5pm; mid-June to Labor Day Sun.-Fri. 9am-10pm, Sat. 9am-7:45pm.)

Hershey Park's **amusement center** (534-3900) has short lines and heart-stopping rides. Don't miss Sidewinder, the Comet, or the SooperdooperLooper. (Open late May-early Sept. daily 10am-10pm. $24, ages 3-8 and over 55 $15.) Camp 8 mi. from Hershey and 15 mi. from Lancaster City at **Ridge Run Campground,** 867 Schwanger Rd., Elizabethtown 17022 (367-3454). Schwanger Rd. connects Rte. 230 and Rte. 283. (Office open Mon.-Fri. 9am-9pm, Sat.-Sun. 9am-10pm; sites $17, with water and electricity $8.15, full hookup $19.) **Greyhound** (397-4861) goes to Hershey from Lancaster City (1 per day, 3 hr., $19), stopping at 337 W. Chocolate St.

■ ■ ■ GETTYSBURG

In early July of 1863, Union and Confederate forces met at Gettysburg in one of the bloodiest and most decisive battles of the Civil War. The ultimate victory of the Union forces dealt a dire blow to the hopes of the South, and the battle instantly earned a privileged place in the national memory. But the victory exacted a horrible price: over 50,000 casualties. Four months later, President Lincoln arrived in Gettysburg to dedicate a national cemetery and to give "a few appropriate remarks." Lincoln urged preservation of the union in a speech that, though only two minutes long, was a watershed in American history. Lincoln's *Gettysburg Address,* and the brutality of the battle which necessitated it, have entrenched Gettysburg as the most famous battlefield in America. Each year thousands of visitors head for these Pennsylvania fields, heeding the great President's call to "resolve that these dead shall not have died in vain."

Practical Information and Sights Before attacking Gettysburg's Civil War memorabilia, get your bearings at the **National Military Park Visitors Information Center** (334-1124), 1 mi. south of town on Taneytown Rd. (open daily 8am-6pm; Labor Day-Memorial Day 8am-5pm). Go on your own, letting the free map navigate you, or pay a park guide to show you the sights ($20 for a 2-hr. tour). Rangers also lead free guided walking tours. The same building houses a 750-square-foot **electric map.** This representation of the area as it was in 1863 lights up in coordination with a taped narration and is a must when trying to bring the great sweep of the battle into brighter focus ($2, seniors $1.50, under 15 free). The **Cyclorama Center** next door has the second draft of Lincoln's speech, exhibits, and a 20-minute film on the battle. The Cyclorama Center also houses the cyclorama itself, a huge painting (356x26 ft.) representing this turning point of the Civil War. Stand in the middle and you're back in 1863. A sound and light show is presented every thirty minutes. (Open daily 9am-5pm. $2, seniors $1.50, under 15 free.) For an excellent view of the area, walk over to the **National Tower** (334-6754), across from the Cyclorama Center, where high-speed elevators whisk you up 300 ft. (Open daily 9am-6:30pm. $4.35, seniors $3.85, ages 6-15 $2.25.)

Across the street from the visitors center is **Gettysburg National Cemetery,** where Lincoln delivered his speech. Many of the Union soldiers who fought in the battle are buried in this Pennsylvanian plain where they fell. Pick up a free self-guided walking tour at the visitors center. (Open daily dawn-dusk; free.) The lone non-Civil War sight in the area is the **Eisenhower National Historic Site,** bordering the military park, which brings in busloads of Ike-liking tourists. You can tour this farm that was the retirement home of Eisenhower, his wife, and his extensive collection of trinkets collected from foreign dignitaries. You can only get there on a shuttle bus from the visitors center. (Open March-Dec. daily 9am-4:15pm. $3.60, ages 13-16 $1.60, 6-12 $1.05, Golden Age and Golden Eagle passholders $1.60.)

The best way to see the **battlefields** is on the 18-mi. self-guided auto tour. A free map at the visitors center details the monuments, landmarks, and locations along the tour. Biking is also an excellent way to do the tour.

Gettysburg is in south-central PA, off U.S. 15 about 30 mi. south of Harrisburg. When the Union and Confederacy decided to lock horns here, they didn't have the traveler in mind. Neither Greyhound nor Amtrak services Gettysburg. You can rent a **bike** at Artillery Ridge campground, 610 Taneytown Rd. (334-1288; $4 per hour, $10 half day, $16 full day). Gettysburg's **post office:** 115 Buford Ave. (337-3781; open Mon.-Fri. 8am-4:30pm, Sat. 9am-noon); **ZIP code:** 17325; **area code:** 717.

Food, Accommodations, and Camping Gettysburg's eateries run the gamut from organic to historic. The candle-lit **Springhouse Tavern,** 89 Steinwehr Ave. (334-2100), lies in the basement of the **Dobben House,** Gettysburg's first building (c. 1776), once an Underground Railroad shelter for runaway slaves during the Civil War. Try the "Mason's Mile High" ($5.75) or create your own grilled burger ($6; open daily 11:30am-9pm). **Food for Thought,** 46 Baltimore St. (337-2221), is a café purveying huge salads, sandwiches, and other organic offerings for $3.50-5. (Open Tues.-Thurs. 8:30am-9pm, Fri.-Sat. 8:30am-11pm, Sun. 10am-6pm.)

The best place to sleep in Gettysburg remains the roomy and cheerful **Gettysburg International Hostel (HI-AYH),** 27 Chambersburg St. (334-1020), on U.S. 30 just west of Lincoln Square in the center of town. Amenities include kitchen, stereo, living room, laundry, library, and piano. (Check-in 7-9am and 5-9:30pm. Check-out 9:30am. $10, nonmembers $13. Sleepsack rental $1.) This remarkably friendly hostel usually has space, but if you want a motel, the **Gettysburg Travel Council,** 35 Carlisle St. (334-6274), Lincoln Sq., stocks a full line of brochures, as well as maps and information on local sights (open daily 9am-5pm). There are also **campgrounds** in the area. **Artillery Ridge,** 610 Taneytown Rd. (334-1288), 1 mi. south on Rte. 134, has showers, a riding stable, laundry, and a pool (sites $12.50 for 2 people, with hookup $16-19; open April-Oct.). Further down the road, the **Round Top Campground,** 180 Knight Rd. (334-9565) has everything Artillery Ridge does—plus a mini golf course (open year-round; $11 for 2 people, with hookup $16).

■■■ PITTSBURGH

Charles Dickens called this city "Hell with the lid off" for a reason. As late as the 1950s, smoke from area steel mills made street lamps essential even during the day. However, the decline of the steel industry has meant cleaner air and rivers. A similar renaissance has occurred in Pittsburgh's economy. Private-public partnerships have produced some shiny urban architecture like Phillip Johnson's Pittsburgh Plate Glass Building, a gothic black-glass cathedral. Admittedly, some of the character of old, sooty Pittsburgh has retreated to the suburbs. However, in a city of monumental change, most of the city's small neighborhoods have maintained strong identities. One needs only to view downtown from atop Mount Washington, accessible via the Duquene Incline, to see how thoroughly Pittsburgh has entered a new age.

PRACTICAL INFORMATION

Emergency: 911.

Visitor Information: Pittsburgh Convention and Visitors Bureau, 4 Gateway Ctr. (281-7711), downtown in a little glass building on Liberty Ave., across from the Hilton. Their city maps won't get you past downtown. Open Mon.-Fri. 9:30am-5pm, Sat.-Sun. 9:30am-3pm; Nov.-April Mon.-Fri. 9:30am-5pm, Sat. 9:30am-3pm.

Travelers Aid: two locations: **Greyhound Bus Terminal** (281-5474), 11th St. and Liberty Ave., and the **airport** (472-3599). Good maps, advice, and help for stranded travelers. Open Mon.-Fri. 9am-9pm, Sat.-Sun. 9am-5pm.

Airport: Pittsburgh International, (472-3525), 15 mi. west of downtown by I-279 and Rte. 60 in Findlay Township. Serves most major airlines. **Airline Transportation Company** (471-2250) serves downtown (daily, every 30 min., 6am-1pm; every 20 min., 1-7pm; every hr., 7-10pm, $10 one way, $17 round-trip), Oakland (Mon.-Fri., every hr., 9am-9pm; every 2 hr. Sat.-Sun., $18 round-trip), and Monroeville (daily, every 2 hr., 6am-2pm, every hr., 2pm-7pm, $15 round-trip).

Amtrak: Liberty and Grant Ave. (800-872-7245 for reservations; 471-6170 for station info), on the northern edge of downtown next to Greyhound and the post office. Safe and very clean inside, but be cautious about walking from here to the city center at night. To: Philadelphia ($64, 7 hrs.), Chicago ($81, 9 hrs.). Open 24 hrs. Ticket office open daily 8:30am-5:15pm and 11pm-4am.

Greyhound: (391-2300), 11th St. at Liberty Ave. near Amtrak. Large and fairly clean with police on duty. To: Philadelphia ($41, 8 hrs.), Chicago ($70, 13 hrs.). Station and ticket office open 24 hrs.

Public Transport: Port Authority of Allegheny County (PAT), General info 442-2000. Bus rides free within the Golden Triangle until 7pm, 75¢ after 7pm. For the rest of the city and inner suburbs, $1.25; weekend daily pass $3. The **subway's** 3 downtown stops are free. Taking the subway beyond the confines of the Triangle $1.60-1.95. Schedules and maps at most department stores and in the Community Interest section of the yellow pages.

Taxi: Yellow Cab, 665-8100; **Peoples Cab** 681-3131.

Car Rental: Rent-A-Wreck, 1200 Liberty Ave. (488-3440), 1block up from Liberty tunnels. $28 per day; 50 free mi., 18¢ each additional mi. Must be 21 with major credit card or $150 cash deposit. Open daily 8am-6pm.

Help Lines: General Help Line, 255-1155. **Rape Action Hotline,** 765-2731, emergencies 392-2472. Both open 24 hrs. **Pittsburgh Office for International Visitors,** 624-7800. Aid for non-English speakers. Open Mon.-Fri. 9am-5pm, Sat. 9am-1pm.

Post Office: (642-4472; general delivery 642-4478), 7th and Grant St. Open Mon.-Fri. 7am-6pm, Sat. 7am-2:30pm. **ZIP code:** 15219.

Area Code: 412.

The downtown area is the **Golden Triangle** formed by two rivers—the Allegheny on the north and the Monongahela to the south—flowing together to form a third, the Ohio. Parallel to the Monongahela, streets in the downtown triangle number 1 through 7. The **Hill District** just northeast of downtown has the reputation of being rather rough. **Oakland,** east of the Triangle, is home to the University of Pittsburgh and Carnegie-Mellon University.

THE MID-ATLANTIC

ACCOMMODATIONS AND CAMPING

Reasonable accommodations aren't very easy to find in Pittsburgh, but downtown is fairly safe, even at night. Pittsburgh has one of the lowest crime rates in the nation for a city of its size.

Point Park College (HI-AYH), 201 Wood St. (392-3824), 8 blocks from the Greyhound Station, corner of Blvd. of the Allies and Wood St. Closer to a hotel than a hostel; clean rooms, some with private baths. Office hours 8am-4pm. Check-in until 11pm (tell the guards you're a hosteler). 3-day max. stay; members only; $10. No kitchen but all-you-can-eat breakfast ($4) served in the third-floor cafeteria 7-9:30am. Reservations recommended. Open May 15-Aug. 15.

Red Roof Inn, 6404 Stubenville Pike (787-7870), south on I-279, past Rte. 22-Rte. 30 junction, at the Moon Run exit. From the Greyhound station, take bus #26F. Clean and quiet chain motel. Check in anytime; check out by noon. (Singles $41, doubles $48.) Call more than a week in advance in the summer.

Pittsburgh North Campground, 6610 Mars Rd., Evans City 16033 (776-1150). The nearest camping—still 20 mi. from downtown. Take I-79 to the Mars exit. 226 campsites. Facilities include tents and swimming. Sites $17 for 2 people, $3 per extra adult, $2 per extra child. Hookup $20.50.

FOOD

Aside from the pizza joints and bars downtown, **Oakland** is your best bet for a good, inexpensive meal. **Forbes Ave.,** around the University of Pittsburgh, is packed with collegiate watering holes and cafés. **Walnut St.** in Shadyside and **East Carson St.** on the Southside are also lined with colorful eateries and shops. The **Strip District** on Penn Ave. between 16th and 22nd Street (north of downtown along the Allegheny) bustles with Italian, Greek, and Asian cuisine, vendors, grocers and craftsmen. Saturday mornings are busiest as produce, fresh fish, and street performers vie for business.

Original Hot Dog Shops, Inc., 3901 Forbes Ave., at Bouquet St. in Oakland. A rowdy (actually, very rowdy), greasy Pittsburgh institution with lots and lots of fries, burgers, dogs, and pizza. Call it "the O" like a local. 16" pizza $3.99. Open Sun.-Wed. 10am-3:30am, Thurs. 10am-4:30am, Fri.-Sat. 10am-5am.

Beehive Coffeehouse and Theater, 3807 Forbes Ave. (683-4483), a few steps from the "O". The Beehive is a quirky coffeehouse brimming with cool wall paintings, cool staff, cool clientele, and hot cappuccino ($1.60). The theater in the back features current films and an occasional open-mike improv night. (Hours vary, closes at 10pm.)

The Elbow Room, 5744 Ellsworth Ave. (441-5222). Relaxed clientele take advantage of the garden seating, free refills, and crayolas for the tablecloths. Spicy chicken sandwiches ($6) and hybrid southwest and front parlor decoration make it worth the trip. Open daily 11am-2am.

Harris' Grill-A Cafe, at 5747 Ellsworth Ave. (363-0833) is across the street. Inexpensive Greek specialties ($3-9) on an outdoor deck. Open daily 11:30am-2am.

SIGHTS

The **Golden Triangle,** formed by the Allegheny and Monongahela rivers, is home to **Point State Park** and its famous 200-ft. fountain. A ride on the **Duquene Incline,** 1220 Grandview Ave. on the Southside (381-1665), affords a spectacular view of the city. (Fare $2, children 6-11 $1, under 6 free.) The **Fort Pitt Blockhouse and Museum** (281-9285) in the park dates back to the French and Indian War. (Open Tues.-Sat. 10am-4:30pm, Sun. noon-4:30pm. $4, seniors $3, kids $2.) The **Phipps Conservatory** (622-6915) conserves 2½ acres of happiness for the flower fanatic, about 3 mi. east along the Blvd. of the Allies in Schenley Park. (Open daily 9am-5pm. $3.50, seniors and kids $1.50, $1 more for shows. Reserve tours at 622-6958.) Founded in 1787, the **University of Pittsburgh** (624-4141; for tours call 624-7488) now stands in the shadow of the 42-story **Cathedral of Learning** (624-6000) at Bigelow Blvd. between Forbes and 5th Ave. The "cathedral," an academic building dedicated in 1934, features 23 "nationality classrooms" designed and decorated by artisans from each of Pittsburgh's ethnic traditions. **Carnegie-Mellon University** (268-2000) runs right down the street.

An intelligent concentration of Pittsburgh native Andy Warhol's prolific output is housed in the new **Andy Warhol Musuem,** 117 Sandusky St. (237-8300), on the North Side. The museum has seven exhaustive floors of Warhol's material; from Pop portraits of Marilyn, Jackie, and Grace to continuous screenings of films with titles like *Blowjob* and *Sleep*. (Open Thurs.-Sat. 11am-8pm, Wed. and Sun. 11am-6pm. $5, seniors $4, students and children $3.) A 20-min. walk farther into the North Side is **The Mattress Factory** (231-3169) 500 Sampsonia Way. This modern museum specializes in site-specific installations, art that surrounds and engages the audience. Current exhibits include the work of Damien Hirst in a piece involving the entire fourth floor, several monochrome paintings, and nearly half a million houseflies. (Open Tues.-Sat. 10am-5pm, Sun. 1pm-5pm. Free.)

Two of America's greatest financial legends, Andrew Carnegie and Henry Clay Frick, made their fortunes in Pittsburgh. Their bequests to the city have enriched its cultural scene. The most spectacular of Carnegie's gifts are the art and natural history museums, together called **The Carnegie,** 4400 Forbes Ave. (622-3328; 622-3289 for guided tours), across the street from the Cathedral of Learning. The natural history section is famous for its 500 dinosaur specimens, including an 84-ft. giant named for the philanthropist himself—*Diplodocus Carnegii.* The modern wing hosts an impressive collection of Impressionist, Post-Impressionist, and 20th-century art. (Open Tues.-Sat. 10am-5pm, Sun. 1-5pm. Take any bus to Oakland and get off at the Cathedral of Learning. $5, seniors $4, students and children $3.)

While most know Henry Clay Frick for his art collection in New York, the **Frick Art Museum,** 7227 Reynolds St., Point Breeze (371-0600), displays some of his early, less famous acquisitions. The permanent collection contains Italian, Flemish, and French works from the 13th to 18th centuries. Chamber music concerts are held Oct.-April. (Open Tues.-Sat. 10am-4pm, Sun. noon-6pm. Free.)

Other city sights lie across the three rivers. To the west of Allegheny Sq. soars the tropical **Pittsburgh Aviary** (323-7234; open daily 9am-4:30pm; admission $4, seniors $3, kids under 12 $2.50; take bus #16D or the Ft. Duquesne bridge).

Northward across the Allegheny, steal a look at **Three Rivers Stadium,** where four-time Super Bowl champs, the Steelers, and baseball's Pirates play. For **Steelers** tickets call 323-1200. For **Pirates** tickets call 323-5028.

ENTERTAINMENT

Most restaurants and shops carry the weekly *In Pittsburgh*, a great source for free, up-to-date entertainment listings, nightclubs, and racy personals. The internationally-acclaimed **Pittsburgh Symphony Orchestra** performs October through May at **Heinz Hall,** 600 Penn Ave. downtown, and gives free summer evening concerts outdoors at Point State Park (392-4835 for tickets and information). The **Pittsburgh Public Theater** (323-8200) is widely renowned, and tickets cost a pretty penny ($23.50-$33.50). Visitors with thin wallets should check out the **Three Rivers Shakespeare Festival** (624-0933), at University of Pittsburgh's Steven Foster Memorial Theater, near Forbes Ave. and Bigelow Blvd. in Oakland. The troupe, consisting of both students and professionals, performs from late May to mid-August. Seniors and students can line up a half hour before show time for half-price tickets. The box office (624-7529) is open Monday to Saturday 10am-8pm, and Sunday noon-3pm. (Tickets $12 to14.) All-student casts perform with the **Young Company** at City Theater (tickets $9). Clubberi should check out **The Metropol**, 1600 Small St. (261-4512), a spacious warehouse in the strip district which fills with raving natives as the night marches on.

THE MID-ATLANTIC

■■■ ALLEGHENEY NATIONAL FOREST

Containing half a million acres of woodland stretching 40 mi. south of the New York state border, the Allegheny National Forest offers year-round recreational opportunities such as hunting, fishing, trail-biking, and cross-country skiing. The forest makes an excellent stopover on a cross-state jaunt; its southern border is only 20 miles from I-80, and the park is never as crowded as the Poconos or Catskills.

Practical Information The forest divides into four quadrants, each with its own ranger station providing maps and information about activities and facilities within its region. **NE: Bradford Ranger District** (362-4613), on Rte. 59 west of Marshburg (open Mon.-Fri. 7am-4:30pm, Sat.-Sun. 9am-5:30pm). **NW: Sheffield Ranger District** (968-3232), on U.S. 6 (open Mon.-Fri. 8am-4pm). **SE: Ridgway Ranger District** (776-6172), on Montmorenci Rd. (open Mon.-Fri. 8am-4:30pm). **SW: Marienville Ranger District** (927-6628), on Rte. 66 (open Mon.-Sat. 7:30am-4pm). For forest info call the Bradford ranger station or write to **Forest Service, USDA,** P.O. Box 847, Warren, PA 16365. **Greyhound** no longer serves the area. When driving in the forest, be very careful during wet weather; about half the region is served only by dirt roads. Get good maps of the area ($3) at any ranger station. Allegheny's **area code:** 814.

Accommodations and Camping From whatever direction you approach the Allegheny Forest, you'll encounter a small community near the park that offers groceries and accommodations. **Ridgway,** 25 mi. from I-80 (exit 16) at the southeast corner, and **Warren,** on the northeastern fringe of the forest where U.S. 6 and 62 meet, have comparable services. There are 16 **campgrounds** in the park, 10 open year-round, albeit with no services in the winter. Sites are $7-15, depending on the location and time of year. There is also a $3 parking fee. **Red Ridge, Dew, and Kiasutha** are the most popular areas. You can call 800-288-2267 to reserve sites ($7.50), but the park keeps 50% of them on a first-come, first-served basis. You don't need a site to camp in the Allegheny; stay 1500 ft. from a major road or body of water and you can pitch a tent anywhere.

Sights and Activities Each summer, the **Allegheny Reservoir,** located in the northern section of the forest, is stocked with fish and tourists. Here you can enjoy fishing, boating, swimming, or touring the **Kinzua Dam.** The six boat-accessible camping sites along the 95-mi. shore of the reservoir are free and do not require reservations or a permit (fresh water, toilets, no showers). Anglers should dial the 24-hr. fishing hotline for tips (726-0164). **Hikers** should pick up the free 14-page pamphlet describing the 10 trails in the forest. **Buzzard Swamp,** near Marienville, has 8 mi. of trails through a wildlife refuge where no motor vehicles are permitted. **Kinzua Boat Rentals and Marina** (726-1650), on Rte. 59, 4 mi. east of Kinzua Dam, rents canoes ($5 per hr., $18 per day), rowboats ($5.50 per hr., $20 per day), and motorboats ($12 per hr., $50 per day). **Allegheny Outfitters** (723-1203) at Market St. Plaza in Warren provides canoe rentals for the reservoir and the Allegheny River.

■■■ OHIOPYLE STATE PARK

In southwestern Pennsylvania lie some of the loveliest forests in the East, lifted by steep hills and cut by cascading rivers. Native Americans dubbed this part of the state "Ohiopehhle" ("white frothy water"), because of the grand Youghiogheny River Gorge (pronounced yock-a-gay-nee—"The Yock" to locals). The river provides the focal point of Pennsylvania's Ohiopyle State Park. The park's 18,000 acres offer hiking, fishing, hunting, whitewater rafting, and a complete range of winter activities. The latest addition to the banks of the Yock is a gravelled bike trail. Converted from a riverside railroad bed, the trail winds 28 miles north from the town of Confluence to Connellsville. When this ingenious "rails to trails" project is complete, a bicycle trail will extend from Pittsburgh to Washington, DC.

Practical Information, Accommodations, and Food In order to do just about anything in the river you'll need a launch permit (free on weekdays, $2.50 on weekends). The **Park Information Center** (329-8591), just off Rte. 381 on Dinnerbell Rd., P.O. Box 105 (open daily 8:30am-5pm; Nov.-April Mon.-Fri. 8:30am-5pm), recommends calling at least 30 days in advance. You must also purchase a $2 token for the park's shuttle bus to return you to the launch area. Fishing licenses ($25) are required in the park and are available at Falls Market (see below). The 226 **campsites** in Ohiopyle also require advanced booking—especially for summer weekends. (Pennsylvania residents $9, out-of-staters $11, $3 reservation fee.)

Motels around Ohiopyle are sparse but the excellent **Ohiopyle State Park Hostel (HI-AYH)**, P.O. Box 99 (329-4476), sits right in the center of town off Rte. 381. Bob Utz has 24 bunks, a kitchen, a great yard, a washer and dryer, and an extreme fondness for chess. Unbeatable. ($8, nonmembers $11. Check-in 6-9pm.) Just down the street, **Falls Market and Overnight Inn** (329-4973) P.O. Box 101, rents singles ($25) and doubles ($40) with shared baths. The downstairs store has a decent grocery selection and a restaurant/snackbar. Burgers are $1.55, pancakes are $2.25. (Open daily 7am-9pm).

Ohiopyle is on Rte. 381, 64 mi. southeast of Pittsburgh via Rte. 51 and U.S. 41. The closest public transport is to **Uniontown**, a large town 20 mi. to the west on U.S. 40. **Greyhound** serves Uniontown from Pittsburgh (twice daily, 1½ hr., $11). Ohiopyle's **post office:** 47 E. Fayette St. (438-2522; open Mon.-Fri. 8am-6pm, Sat. until noon); **ZIP code:** 15470; **area code:** 412.

Sights and Activities Ohiopyle's white water rafting is some of the best in the East and draws throngs of tourists yearly. The rapids are 8 mi. long, class III, and take about five hours to conquer. Lined up in a row on Rte. 381 in "downtown" Ohiopyle are four outfitters: **White Water Adventurers** (800-992-7238); **Wilderness Voyageurs** (800-272-4141); **Laurel Highlands River Tours** (800-472-3846); and **Mountain Streams and Trails** (800-245-4090). Guided trips on the Yock vary dramatically in price ($20-170 per person per day), depending on length of trip, the season, day of week, and difficulty. If you're an experienced river rat (or if you just happen to *enjoy* flipping boats) any of the above companies will rent you equipment. (Rafts about $9 per person, canoes $15, "duckies"—inflatable kayaks—about $15.) Bike rentals vary with bike styles (peaking at $4 per hr. and $16 per day). **Youghiogheny Outfitters** (P.O. Box 21, 329-4549) and **Ohiopyle Trading Post** (P.O. Box 94, 329-1450) offer comparable prices but do rental business only.

Near Ohiopyle **Fort Necessity National Battlefield**, on U.S. 40 near Rte. 381 (329-5512), is a replica of the original, which was built by founding father George Washington. Young George, then of the British army, was trounced in a sneak attack that left commanding officer General Braddock dead, and opened the French and Indian War. Check on the fort's **Visitors Information Center** (open daily 8:30am-5pm; Labor Day-Memorial Day 10:30am-5pm; admission $2, 16 and under free). **Braddock's Grave** is 2 mi. northwest of the fort on U.S. 40, and if you travel another mile you can experience the singular **Museum of Early American Farm Machines and Very Old Horse Saddles with a History** (438-4500), which exhibits rusted and zany Americana strewn about a motel lawn.

Fallingwater (329-8501), 8 mi. north of Ohiopyle on Rte. 381, is the cantilevered masterpiece by the father of modern architecture, Frank Lloyd Wright. Designed in 1936 for the wealthy Kaufmann family, Fallingwater is perched over a waterfall. The stunning effect this yields has made this home "the most famous private residence ever built." (Open Tues.-Sun. 10am-4pm; Nov.-March weekends only. Admission Tues.-Fri. $6, Sat.-Sun. $10.)

THE MID-ATLANTIC

Delaware

Delaware is limited in size, but not in ingenuity. This is the second smallest state in the Union, but has given itself the dubious title "first state" on the basis of its trend-setting ratification of the Constitution in 1787. This is also the state that has long produced such chemical marvels as nylon, which made its shiny appearance here in 1938. There is more to Delaware than nicknames and nylon though, and its quiet seaside communities and rolling dunes lure vacationers from all along the east coast.

PRACTICAL INFORMATION

Capital: Dover.
State Visitors Service: P.O. Box 1401, 99 King's Hwy., Dover 19903 (800-441-8846 outside DE). 800-282-8667 in DE. Open Mon.-Fri. 8am-4:30pm. **Division of Fish and Wildlife,** P.O. Box 1401, 89 King's Hwy., Dover 19901 (739-4431).
Time Zone: Eastern. **Postal Abbreviation:** DE
Sales Tax: 0%. You gotta love it.

■■■ DELAWARE SEASHORE

Lewes Founded in 1613 by the Zwaanendael colony from Hoorn, Holland, **Lewes** (LOO-IS) touts itself as Delaware's first town. The reserved atmosphere of this seaside retreat contrasts starkly with the usual boardwalk fare. The beaches remain clean, the air stays salty, and the people are quiet and friendly.

East of Lewes, on the Atlantic Ocean, is tucked the secluded **Cape Henlopen State Park** (645-8983), home to a seabird nesting colony, sparkling white "walking dunes," and a beach with a bath house. (645-2103; $5 per car, bikes, and walkers free. Open daily 8am-sunset.) Sandy campsites are available on a first-come, first-served basis. (Sites $14; open April-Oct.) Enjoy a sandwich ($2-4) and a banana espresso ($2) at the aromatic **Oby Lee Coffee Roasters and Café,** 2nd St. (open Sun.-Fri. 7:30am-10pm, Sat. 7:30am-11pm). Stop by the **Lewes Chamber of Commerce** (645-8073), in the Fisher Martin House on King's Hwy. (open Mon.-Sat. 10am-5pm). **Carolina Trailways** serves Lewes with buses to Washington D.C. (3½ hr., $28), Baltimore (3½ hr., $26), and Philadelphia (4 hr., $30). Lewes makes up one end of the 70-min. **Cape May, NJ/Lewes, DE Ferry** route (Lewes terminal 645-6313). The Delaware Resort Transit **shuttle bus** runs from the ferry to Lewes, Rehoboth, and Dewey Beach. ($1 good for all day; runs June-Aug. daily 6:30-4am.)

Rehoboth Beach You can convene at the sand reefs of gay hotspot **Rehoboth Beach** on summer weekends to tan, mix, and mingle. The **beach** is the main attraction here. Follow Rehoboth Ave. until it hits the water at Rehoboth Beach, or follow Rte. 1 south to **Dewey Beach.** For more info, visit the **Rehoboth Beach Chamber of Commerce,** next to the lighthouse at 501 Rehoboth Ave. (800-441-1329 or 227-2233; open Mon.-Fri. 9am-4:30pm, Sat. 9am-1pm.)

At the **Country Squire,** 17 Rehoboth Ave. (227-3985), enjoy a lot of good, cheap food (open daily 7am-1am). **Thrasher's** has served fries and only fries, in enormous paper tubs ($3.50-6) for over 60 years. Don't expect ketchup; these fries only come with vinegar and salt. Locations on both sides of the main drag, at 7 and 10 Rehoboth Ave., make it easy to find. (Open daily 11am-11pm.) For those who stay up late, the **Blue Moon,** 35 Baltimore Ave. (227-6515), rises at 4pm every day and rocks a predominantly gay crowd until 2am (no cover).

For inexpensive lodging, walk one block from the boardwalk to **The Lord Baltimore,** 16 Baltimore Ave. (227-2855), which has clean, antiquated, practically beachfront rooms. (Singles and doubles $25-60. A/C. Call ahead; it's popular.) Or walk a little farther from the beach to the cluster of guest houses on the side lanes off First St., just north of Rehoboth Ave. **The Abbey Inn,** 31 Maryland Ave. (227-7023), is a decorous and friendly inn; there's always a local and a conversation on the front porch. Call for reservations at least one week in advance, especially in the summer. (2-day minimum stay. Doubles from $30, weekends $35.) The **Big Oaks Family Campground,** P.O. Box 53 (645-6838), sprawls at the intersection of Rte. 1 and 270. (Sites with hookup $19.50.)

Carolina Trailways 251 Rehoboth Ave., runs to Rehoboth Beach (227-7223). Buses run to: Washington, D.C. (3½ hr., $28), Baltimore (3½ hr., $26), and Philadelphia (4 hr., $30). To get around within Rehoboth, use the Delaware Resort Transit **shuttle bus** which runs between Lewes and the ferry terminal, Rehoboth, and Dewey Beach. (June-Aug. daily 6:30am-4am. $1 good for all day.)

Rehoboth's **post office:** 179 Rehoboth Ave. (227-8406; open Mon.-Fri. 9am-5pm, Sat. 9am-noon); Lewes and Rehoboth's **ZIP code:** 19971; **area code:** 302.

 # Maryland

Maryland is a small but varied state. In Baltimore, it boasts one of the more prominent cities of the mid-Atlantic, but beyond the Baltimore-Washington arey, one finds rolling hill country and the sleepy fishing villages of the Chesapeake Bay. The state was founded as the first and only Catholic colony in rabidly Protestant America. For generations fishing dominated the state economy; then the federal government expanded, industry shrank, and Maryland had a new economic base: not the bay, but the Baltimore-Washington Parkway. Baltimore has shed what was once a poor reputation and is now thought to be one of the more engaging cities to visit on the east coast. But take the time to venture beyond the city and see the rest of the state: the charming towns of the eastern shore particularly are worth a visit.

PRACTICAL INFORMATION

Capital: Annapolis.
Office of Tourist Development, 217 E. Redwood St., Baltimore 21202 (333-6611) or 800-543-1036). **Forest and Parks Service,** Dept. of Natural Resources, Tawes State Office Building, Annapolis 21401 (974-3771).
Time Zone: Eastern. **Postal Abbreviation:** MD
Sales Tax: 5%.

■■■ BALTIMORE

Once a center of East Coast shipping and industry, "Bawlmer" (pop. 751,000) declined structurally and economically from the late 1950s to the mid-'70s. Its renaissance began as then-mayor Donald Schaefer launched a program to clean up pollution, restore old buildings, and convert the Inner Harbor into a tourist playground. Modern Baltimore still serves as Maryland's urban core. Near the downtown skyscrapers, old ethnic neighborhoods like Little Italy front Baltimore's signature rowhouses, whose unique facades are microcosms of the larger city—polished marble stoops represent the shiny Inner Harbor, while straightforward brick fits the proud and gritty urban environs.

PRACTICAL INFORMATION

Emergency: 911.
Visitor Information: Baltimore Area Visitors Centers, 300 W. Pratt St. (837-INFO or 800-282-6632), at S. Howard St. 4 blocks from Harborplace. The visitors center will be moving sometime in early Oct.; call for new address (phone num-

bers will remain the same). Pick up a map and a *Quick City Guide*, a quarterly glossy with excellent maps and events listings. Open daily 9am-5:30pm.

Airport: Baltimore-Washington International (BWI), 859-7111. On I-195 off the Baltimore-Washington Expressway (I-295), about 10 mi. south of the city center. Take MTA bus #17 to the N. Linthicum Light rail station. Airport shuttles to hotels (859-0800) run daily every ½ hr. 6am-midnight ($8 to downtown Baltimore). For D.C., shuttles leave every 1½ hrs. between 7am-8:30pm (Sat. every 2½ hrs. from 8:30am-6:30pm) and drop passengers off at 16th and K St. NW ($14). Trains from BWI Airport run to Baltimore ($5); MARC trains are considerably cheaper ($3,) but also slower and only run Mon.-Fri. Trains to Washington, D.C. ($10); MARC ($4.50). BWI train office 410-672-6167.

Amtrak: Penn Station, 1500 N. Charles St. (800-872-7245), at Mt. Royal Ave. Easily accessible by bus 3, or 11 from Charles Station downtown. Trains run about every ½ hour to: New York ($62, Metroliner $91); Washington D.C. ($12, Metroliner $17); Philadelphia ($28, Metroliner $44). Ticket window open daily 5:30am-9:30pm, self-serve machines open 24 hrs. (credit card only).

Greyhound: (800-231-2222). Two locations: downtown at 210 W. Fayette St. (752-0868), near N. Howard St.; and at 5625 O'Donnell St. (744-9311), 3 mi. east of downtown near I-95. Frequent buses to: New York ($30.50); Washington, D.C. ($8.50); Philadelphia ($18.50). Open 24 hrs.

Public Transport: Mass Transit Administration (MTA), 300 W. Lexington St. (333-3434, recording 539-5000), near N. Howard St. Bus and rapid-rail service to most major sights in the city; service to outlying areas is more complicated. Bus #17 serves the airport. Some buses run 24 hr. **Metro** operates Mon.-Fri. 5am-midnight, Sat. 8am-midnight. Base fare for bus and metro $1.25; transfers 10¢. The **Water Taxi** (563-3901) makes stops every 8-18 min. at the harbor museums, Harborplace, Fell's Point, and more. An easy and pleasant way to travel, especially in summer when service continues until 11pm. Full-day pass $2-3.25.

Help Lines: Sexual Assault and Domestic Violence Center (828-6390). **Gay and Lesbian Information** (837-8888).

Post Office: 900 E. Fayette St. (655-9832). **ZIP code:** 21233.

Area Code: 410.

Baltimore dangles in central Maryland, 100 mi. south of Philadelphia and about 150 mi. up the Chesapeake Bay from the Atlantic Ocean. The Jones Falls Expressway (I-83) halves the city with its southern end at the Inner Harbor, while the Baltimore Beltway (I-695) circles it. I-95 cuts across the southwest corner of the city.

Baltimore is plagued by one-way streets. **Baltimore Street** (runs east across the Inner Harbor) and **Charles Street** (running north from the west side of the Harbor) divide the city into quarters. Streets parallel to Baltimore St. get "West" or "East" tacked onto their names, depending on their side of Charles St. Sreets are dubbed "North" or "South" according to their relation to Baltimore St.

ACCOMMODATIONS AND CAMPING

Baltimore International Youth Hostel (HI-AYH), 17 W. Mulberry St. (576-8880), at Cathedral St. Near bus and Amtrak terminals. Take MTA bus #3, 11, or 18. Elegant, centrally located 19th-century brownstone provides 48 beds in dorms. Kitchen, laundry, and lounge with baby grand piano. Friendly managers are a great source of information about Baltimore. 3-night max. stay, longer with manager's approval. Lockout noon-5pm. Curfew 11pm, but house keys available for rent ($2). Chores required. $10, nonmembers $13. Sheet rental $2. Reservations recommended, especially in the summer.

Duke's Motel, 7905 Pulaski Highway (686-0400), in Rosedale off the Beltway. Don't worry about the bulletproof glass in the front office—all the motels around here have them. Simple, clean rooms and probably the best deal on the Pulaski Hwy. motel strip, though slightly more expensive. Suitable only for people with cars. Cable TV. Singles $36, doubles $41. $2 key deposit and ID required.

Abbey Schaefer Hotel, 722 St. Paul St. (332-0405), near E. Madison St. Right on the bus route from Penn Station. The plaster's chipped, the wallpaper's peeling, and the carpets are stained, but the plumbing works and the location is great. Decaying rooms with A/C and cable TV $29, with shower $35. Key deposit $5.

FOOD AND DRINK

Virginia may be for lovers, but Maryland is for crabs—every eatery here serves **crab cakes.** The Light Street Pavilion at **Harborplace,** Pratt and Light St. (332-4191), has multifarious foodstuffs to suit every tourist—hence the long lines. **Phillips'** serves some of the best crabcakes in Baltimore; buy them cheaper from the cafeteria-style Phillips' Express line. (Harborplace open Mon.-Sat. 10am-9pm, Sun. 10am-6pm.) **Lexington Market,** 400 W. Lexington at Eutaw St., provides an endless variety of produce, fresh meat, and seafood, often at cheaper prices (open Mon.-Sat. 8am-6pm; take the subway to Lexington Station or bus #7).

Bertha's Dining Room, 734 S. Broadway (327-5795), at Lancaster. Obey the bumper stickers and "Eat Bertha's Mussels." Gorge yourself on the black-shelled bivalves ($7.50) while sitting at butcher-block tables, and don't miss the chunky vegetable mussel chowder (cup $1.75). Come for afternoon tea (Mon.-Sat.; make a reservation): share a platter of scones and assorted tarts with homemade whipped cream for only $7.50. Locals of all ages crowd in to hear jazz bands play Mon.-Wed. and Fri.-Sat. nights. Twelve kinds of beer and ale ($1.50-6). Kitchen open Sun.-Thurs. 11:30am-11pm, Fri.-Sat. 11:30am-midnight. Bar until 2am.

Obrycki's, 1727 E. Pratt St. (732-6399), near Broadway; take bus #7 or 10. Some of Balto's best crabs served every and any way—steamed, broiled, sauteed, or in crab cakes for $20-46 per dozen depending on size. Expect lines on weekends. Don't walk here alone at night. Open Mon.-Sat. noon-11pm, Sun. noon-9:30pm.

Buddies, 313 N. Charles St. (332-4200). Extensive salad bar with over 80 items ($3 per lb.; open Mon.-Fri. 11am-2:30pm) and sandwiches ($5-7). Jazz quartet draws in loyal locals and visitors of all ages (Thurs.-Sat. 9:30pm-1am). Happy hour 4-7pm with an assortment of free foodstuffs and 2-for-1 drinks. Wed. is Karaoke. Open Mon.-Thurs. 11am-1am, Fri. 11am-2am, Sat. 1pm-2am.

Haussner's, 3242 Eastern Ave. (410-327-8365), at S. Clinton; take bus #10. An East Baltimore institution. 700 original oil paintings crowd the huge dining room, including some copies of Rembrandt, Gainsborough, Whistler, and Homer. Central European cuisine like fresh pig knuckle and *sauerbraten* (meat stewed in vinegar and juices) $9.30, sandwiches $4 and up; big portions. Try the famous strawberry pie ($3.65), or get other freshly baked goods to go. Long pants preferred after 3pm; lines for dinner on weekends. Open Tues.-Sat. 11am-10pm.

Hellmands, 806 N. Charles St. (752-0311). Don't let the white linen on the tables frighten you away: there's nary a thing on the menu over $10. Acclaimed by some local magazines as one of the ten best restaurants in the city, Hellmands serves exquisite Afghan dishes in which meat garnishes vegetables and yogurt sauces garnish all. To start, try the *kaddo borani,* pan-fried and baked baby pumpkin in a yogurt-garlic sauce. Open Sun.-Thurs. 5-10pm, Fri.-Sat. 5-11pm.

Baltimore Brewing Co., 104 Albermarle St. (837-5000), just west of the Inner Harbor on the outskirts of Little Italy. Brewmaster Theo de Groen has captured the hearts and livers of Baltimoreans with his original and distinctive lagers, brewed right on the premises in the large brass turns that loom behind the bar. The Weizen and Märzen styles are especially good, but keep an eye out for the spicy seasonals. Open Mon.-Thurs. 11:30am-11pm, Fri.-Sat. 11:30am-midnight.

Cat's Eye Pub, 1730 Thames St. (276-9866), in Fells Point. *Playboy* thinks this is the best bar in Fells Point, and so do the regulars who pack it every night for live blues, jazz, folk, or traditional Irish music. No cover, but drink prices rise when the band strikes it up. Over 25 drafts and 60 bottled beers. Bands every night and twice Sat.-Sun. Happy hour 4-7pm. Open Mon.-Fri. 11am-2am, Sat.-Sun. 8am-2am.

The Hippo, 1 W. Eager St. (547-0069). Baltimore's largest and most popular gay bar, with pool tables, videos, and a packed dance floor. The first Sun. of every month is Ladies' Tea (6-10pm); Thurs. is Men's Night. Cover Thurs.-Fri. $3, Sat. $5. Happy hour Mon.-Fri. 4-8pm. Saloon open daily 3pm-2am. Dance bar open Wed.-Sat. 10pm-2am. Video bar open Thurs.-Sat. 10pm-2am.

THE MID-ATLANTIC

SIGHTS

Most tourists start at the Inner Harbor, a five-square block of water bounded by the National Aquarium, Harborplace, the Science Museum, and a fleet of boardable ships. Visitors should not neglect the *real* neighborhoods to the east and north.

The **National Aquarium,** Pier 3, 501 E. Pratt St. (576-3800), makes the whole Inner Harbor worthwhile. Multi-level exhibits and tanks show off rare fish, big fish, red fish, and blue fish along with the biology and ecology of oceans, rivers, and rainforests. The Children's Cove (level 4) lets visitors handle intertidal marine animals. (Open Mon.-Thurs. 9am-5pm, Fri.-Sun. 9am-8pm; Nov.-Feb. Sat.-Thurs. 10am-5pm, Fri. 10am-8pm. $11.50, seniors $9.50, children 3-11 $7.50, under 3 free; Oct.-March Fri. 5-8pm $3.50.)

Several ships bob in the harbor, among them the **U.S.S. Constellation,** the first commissioned U.S. Navy ship, which sailed from 1797 until 1945, serving in the War of 1812, the Civil War, and as flagship of the Pacific Fleet during WWII. The *Constellation* will likely spend the summer of 1995 in dry dock for much-needed repairs; call to see if it may be visited. (Open daily 10am-5pm; winter 10am-4pm. $2.50, seniors $2, ages 6-15 $1, military $1, children under 6 free.) Also moored in the harbor are the submarine *U.S.S. Torsk,* the lightship *Chesapeake,* and the Coast Guard cutter *Taney.* These vessels make up the **Baltimore Maritime Museum** at Piers 3 and 4. (Open Mon.-Fri. 10am-5pm, Fri.-Sat. 9:30am-6pm; winter Fri.-Sun. 9:30am-5pm. $4.50, seniors $4, children under 13 $1.75, active military free.)

At the Inner Harbor's far edge lurks the **Maryland Science Center,** 601 Light St. (685-5225), where kids can learn chemistry and physics through hands-on games. The IMAX Theater's 5-story screen stuns audiences. On summer weekends, come in the morning while lines are short. (Open Mon.-Thurs. 10am-6pm, Fri.-Sun. 10am-8pm; Sept.-May Mon.-Fri. 10am-5pm, Sat.-Sun. 10am-6pm. $8.50, kids 4-17, seniors and military $6.50, under 3 free. IMAX schedule posted as you come in.)

The **Baltimore Museum of Art,** N. Charles and 31st St. (396-7100), exhibits a fine collection of modern art (including pieces by Andy Warhol), and paintings and sculpture by Matisse, Picasso, Renoir and Van Gogh. Two adjacent sculpture gardens highlight 20th-century works and make wonderful picnic grounds. The museum's **Baltimore Film Forum** shows classic and current American, foreign, and independent films (Thurs.-Fri. 8pm, $5, students and seniors $4); get schedules at the museum or call 889-1993. (Open Wed.-Fri. 10am-4pm, Sat.-Sun. 11am-6pm. $5.50, seniors and students $3.50, kids 7-18 $1.50, under 7 free; Thurs. free.)

Baltimore's best museum, the **Walters Art Gallery,** 600 N. Charles St. (547-9000), at Centre, keeps one of the largest private collections in the world, spanning 50 centuries. The museum's apex is the Ancient Art collection (level 2); its seven marble sarcophagi with intricate relief carvings are of a type found in only two known collections (the other is the National Museum in Rome). Other high points are the Italian works and Impressionists, including Manet's *At the Café* and Monet's *Springtime,* as well as rare early Buddhist sculptures from China and Japanese decorative arts of the late 18th and 19th centuries. (Open Tues.-Sun. 11am-5pm. $4, seniors $3, students and kids under 18 free; Sat. free before noon.)

Druid Hill Park (396-6106) off Jones Falls Parkway on Druid Park Lake Drive, contains the **Baltimore Zoo** (366-5466), featuring elephants in a simulated savannah, Siberian tigers, and a waterfall. The Children's Zoo imports animals (otters and crafty woodchucks) from the Maryland wilds. (Open Mon.-Fri. 10am-4pm, Sat.-Sun. 10am-5:30pm; winter daily 10am-4pm. $6.50, seniors and kids 2-15 $3.50, under 2 free. Kids under 15 free on the first Sat. of each month 10am-noon.) **Fort McHenry National Monument** (962-4290) at the foot of E. Fort Ave. off Rte. 2 (Hanover St.) and Lawrence Ave. (take bus #1), commemorates the victory against the British in the War of 1812. This famous battle inspired Francis Scott Key to write the "Star Spangled Banner," but the flag isn't still there (it's in the Smithsonian now). Admission ($2, seniors and under 17 free) includes entrance to the museum, a way-too-long film, and a fort tour. (Open daily 8am-8pm; Sept.-May 8am-5pm.)

Itself once a station for the Baltimore & Ohio Railroad, the **B&O Railroad Museum,** 901 W. Pratt St. (752-2388; take bus #31), looks out on train tracks where dining cars, Pullman sleepers, and mail cars park themselves for your touring frenzy. The Roundhouse captures historic trains and a replica of the 1829 "Tom Thumb," the first American steam-driven locomotive. Don't miss the extensive model-train display. (Open daily 10am-5pm. $6, seniors $5, kids 5-12 $3, under 5 free. Train rides on weekends for an additional $2.)

Baltimore also holds the **Edgar Allen Poe House,** 203 N. Amity St. (396-7932; open Wed.-Sat. noon-3:45pm, Aug.-Sept. Sat. only; $3, under 13 $1), and the **Babe Ruth Birthplace and Baltimore Orioles Museum,** 216 Emory St. (727-1539; open daily 10am-5pm, Nov.-March 10am-4pm; $5, seniors $3.50, kids 5-16 $2, under 4 free). The sparkling new **Oriole Park at Camden Yards** (547-6234) sits just west of the Inner Harbor at Eutaw and Camden St. (Tours leave hourly Mon.-Fri. 11am-2pm, Sat. 10am-2pm, Sun. at 12:30pm and 1-3pm. $5, seniors and kids under 12 $4.)

To get a feel for Baltimore's historic districts, take bus #7 or 10 from Pratt St. to Abermarle St. and see **Little Italy,** or ride the same buses to Broadway and walk four blocks to **Fells Point.** The neighborhood around Abermarle, Fawn, and High St. is still predominantly Italian, even if the restaurant clientele no longer are; many of the brownstones have been in the same family for generations. Fell's Point imitates the past with cobblestone streets, quaint shops, and historic pubs.

ENTERTAINMENT

The **Showcase of Nations Ethnic Festivals** (837-4636, 800-282-6632) celebrate Baltimore's ethnic neighborhoods with a different culture each week June-Sept. Though somewhat generic, the fairs are fun, vending international fare and the inescapable crab cakes and beer. Most events are at **Festival Hall,** W. Pratt and Sharp St. The **Pier Six Concert Pavilion** (625-4230) at—where else?—Pier 6 at the Inner Harbor presents big-name musical acts at night from late July-Sept. Sit on Pier 5, near Harborplace, and overhear the music for free. The **Left Bank Jazz Society** (466-0600) sponsors jazz shows from Sept.-May; call for info. The **Theatre Project,** 45 W. Preston St. near Maryland St. (752-8558), experiments with theater, poetry, music, and/or dance Wednesday to Saturday at 8pm and Sunday at 3pm. (Ticket prices $5-14). Box office open Tues. noon-5pm, Wed.-Sat. 1-9pm, Sun. noon-4pm.)

The beloved **Baltimore Orioles** (685-9800) play baseball at **Camden Yards,** just a few blocks from the Inner Harbor at the corner of Russell and Camden St.

■■■ ANNAPOLIS

Settled in 1649, the capital of Maryland boasts a historic waterfront and narrow streets flanked by 18th-century brick antique and gift shops. Annapolis's Georgian townhouses once held Colonial aristocrats (and their slaves). The city made real history when the 1783-84 Continental Congress here ratified the Treaty of Paris, and again in 1790 during its stint as temporary capital of the U.S.

Practical Information Annapolis lies near U.S. 50 (a.k.a. U.S. 301) 30 mi. east of Washington, D.C. and 30 mi. southeast of Baltimore. From D.C. take U.S. 50 east to Rte. 70 (Rowe Blvd.) and follow signs to the historic district. From Baltimore, follow Rte. 3 south to U.S. 50 west, cross the Severn River Bridge, then take Rte. 70. Park at the corner of Calvert and Northwest St. as Rte. 70 enters historic Annapolis ($4-8 per day). Baltimore's **Mass Transit Administration** (539-5000) links Baltimore and Annapolis. (Express bus #210 runs Mon.-Fri., 1 hr., $2.85. Local bus #14 Mon.-Sun., 90 min., $2.25. Call for times.) **Greyhound/Trailways** buses (800-231-2222) connect Annapolis with D.C. (2 per day, 40 min., one-way $10, round-trip $20) and with towns on the far side of Chesapeake Bay. The **Annapolis Department of Public Transportation,** 160 Duke of Gloucester St. (263-7964), operates a web of buses connecting the historic district with the rest of town (Mon.-Sat. 5:20am-9:50pm, shorter hrs. on Sun.). Contact the **Annapolis and Anne Arundel**

County Conference & Visitor's Bureau, 26 West St. (280-0445), for brochures and information (open Mon.- Fri. 9am-5pm). **Information desks** field questions at the State House (974-3000; open Mon.-Fri. 9am-5pm) and the dockside visitors booth (268-8687; open daily 10am-5pm). The city's interesting quarter extends south and east from two landmarks: Church Circle, home of St. Anne's Episcopal Church, and State Circle, site of the Maryland State House. School St., in a blatantly unconstitutional move, connects Church and State. Annapolis is compact and easily walkable, but finding a parking space can be tricky.

Accommodations and Food Hostels and motels are few. The Visitor's Information Centers have brochures for B&Bs and hotels. Reserve in advance, especially in summer. **Amanda's Bed and Breakfast Regional Reservation Service** (410-225-0001, 800-899-7533; open Mon.-Fri. 8:30am-5:30pm, Sat. 8:30am-noon), can help arrange accommodations. Two people share a room for only $10 more than the single rate in most B&Bs. Rates fluctuate depending on demand; ask around and sound like you need convincing. **Middleton Tavern** (263-3323), 2 Market Space at Randall St., was established in 1750 and frequented by members of the Continental Congress. Seafood lasagna $8. Nightly music; raw bar features oysters until 1am. (Open Mon.-Fri. 11:30am-1:30am, Sat. 11am-1:30am, Sun. 10am-1:30am. Food served until midnight.) **Chick & Ruth's Delly** (269-6737), 165 Main St., offers dishes named, often satirically, for politicians. Try the Al Gore ($4). (Open 24 hrs.)

Sights and Activities The corinthian-columned **State House** offers maps and houses the state legislature, a fine silver collection, and other exhibits. The *Treaty of Paris* was signed here on January 14, 1784. (Open daily 9am-5pm; free tours, 11am and 3pm.) Restaurants and tacky tourist shops line the waterfront at **City Dock,** where Naval Academy ships ply the waters and civilian yachtsmen congregate and flex. Main Street, full of tiny shops and eateries, stretches from here back up to Church Circle. Stop by the **Maritime Museum** (268-5576), 77 Main St. at Compromise St., before heading up to the circle. From Church Circle, walk along College Ave. past St. John's St. to find **St. John's College** (founded in 1696). The **U.S. Naval Academy** squats at the end of King George St. Tours begin at the **Ricketts Hall** Visitors Center (263-6933) inside the academy gates at the end of Maryland Ave. (Call for times. $3, kids 6-12 $1, under 6 free.) Sailors flock to **Marmaduke's Pub** (269-5420), on Severn Ave. at 3rd, on Wed. nights to watch videos of their races. (Open daily 11:30am-2am. Weekend piano bar, cover $5.)

■■■ EASTERN SHORE

The Eastern Shore is a long arm of land separated from its mother states of Maryland and Virginia by more than just the Chesapeake Bay. The gulf is also a cultural one. The Eastern Shore still supports a lifestyle last seen in most of Virginia and Maryland decades ago. Sleepy burgs and long expanses of fields punctuate the forests and dunes of this quiet and beautiful stretch of land. Tractors are more common on the road than commuters and wild ponies still run free.

The states of Maryland and Virginia divvy up the Eastern Shore. Maryland claims the northern half while Virginia takes the south. For more information, contact the visitor information center in the respective state.

Assateague, MD and Chincoteague, VA A few centuries ago, some miserly mainland farmers put their horses out to graze on Assateague Island to avoid taxes and fencing expenses. The descendents of those horses, the famous wild ponies, now roam free across the unspoiled beaches and forests of the island.

Assateague Island is divided into three parts. The **Assateague State Park** (410-641-2120), Rte. 611 in southeast Maryland, is a 2-mi. stretch of picnic areas, beaches, hot-water bathhouses, and campsites. (Park open daily April-Oct. 8am-sunset daily. $2 per person for day use, seniors free. Campsite registration 7am-11pm. Sites $20.)

The **Assateague Island National Seashore** claims most of the long sandbar north and south of the park and has its own campground (sites $10; winter $8), beaches, and ranger station providing free back country camping permits. Arrive by 2pm for the backcountry permits (401-641-3030). The **Barrier Island Visitors Center** (641-1441), Rte. 611, provides an introduction to the park and gives day-use information. (Visitors center open daily 9am-5pm. Park open 8am-9pm daily. $4 per car, per week.) Fire rings illuminate some relatively challenging (4 to 13-mi.) hikes; otherwise it's just you and nature. Bring plenty of insect repellent. The mosquitoes are bad. Very bad. Bring gallons.

The **Chincoteague National Wildlife Refuge** stretches across the southern Virginia side of the island. This refuge provides a temporary home for the threatened migratory peregrine falcon, a half million Canadian and snow geese, and the beautiful Chincoteague ponies. At low tide, on the last Thursday in July, the wild ponies are herded together and made to swim from Assateague Island to Chincoteague Island, where the local fire department auctions off the foals. The adults swim back to Assateague and reproduce, providing next year's crop of ponies. To get more information on the refuge, swing by the **Chincoteague Visitor's Center,** on the island (804-336-6122; open daily 9am-4pm). The **Wildlife Loop** begins in the visitor's center parking lot and is your best chance to see the ponies (open 5am-sunset; open to cars 3pm-sunset). If all of this nature still isn't remote enough for you, explore space...the final frontier, at the **NASA Visitors Center** (804-824-1344), Chincoteague Rd. Informative, interactive exhibits allow visitors of all ages to space out. (Open daily 10am-4pm; Sept.-June Thurs.-Mon. 10am-4pm. Free.)

To get to Assateague Island, take **Carolina Trailways** to Ocean City, via daily express or local routes from Greyhound Stations in Baltimore ($22) and Washington, D.C. ($36.50). To get to Assateague Island from Ocean City, take a taxi (289-8164; about $15). Carolina Trailways buses from Salisbury, MD, and Norfolk, VA, stopping on U.S. 13 at **T's Corner** (804-824-5935), 11 mi. from Chincoteague. For more area info, call or write to **Chincoteague Chamber of Commerce,** P.O. Box 258 (Maddox Blvd.), Chincoteague, VA 23336 (804-336-6161; open summer daily 9am-5pm, after Labor Day Mon.-Sat. 9am-4:30pm.).

■■■ OCEAN CITY

Ocean City is a lot like a kiddie pool. It's shallow and plastic, but can be fun if you're the right age. This 10-mile strip of land packs endless bars, all-you-can-eat buffets, hotels, mini-golf courses, and tourists into a thin region between the Atlantic Ocean and a bay. Tourism is the town's only industry; in-season the population rises from 12,000 to 300,000. If you go for flashing lights, lots of action, and beer, this is the place to go. But if go-karts and boardwalks make you itch, head for quieter shores.

Practical Information Ocean City runs north-south with numbered streets connecting the ocean to the bay. A good first stop is the **Ocean City Visitor's Center,** 40th St. (800-626-2326), in the Convention Center (open Mon.-Sat. 8am-6pm, Sun. 9am-5:30pm; Sept.-May daily 8:30am-5:30pm.) To get to Ocean City ride **Carolina Trailways** (289-9307), which operates at 2nd and Philadelphia Ave. They send seven buses per day to Baltimore ($22) and Washington D.C. ($36.50). (Station open daily 7am-8am and 10am-5pm; Sept.-May daily 10am-3pm.) Once in town, **the bus** (723-1607) is by far the best way to get around ($1 unlimited riding for the day). The bus runs 24 hrs. and travels the length of the town. **Parking** in Ocean City is a nightmare. If you have a car, you can park free during the day at the Convention Center, 40th St., or try to find a spot on the street. If you're in town for more than one day, get up early one morning and find a free spot on the street. Ocean City's **post office:** 408 N. Philadelphia Ave. at 5th St. (289-9307; open Mon.-Fri. 9am-5pm, Sat. 9am-noon); **ZIP code:** 21842; **area code:** 410.

THE MID-ATLANTIC

Accommodations and Food If you're going to stay in Ocean City, make every effort to secure a room at the **Summer Place Youth Hostel,** 104 Dorchester St. (289-4542), in the south end of town. This friendly establishment has all private rooms, a kitchen, TV, common area, a dock, and a grill. ($18 per person; no lockout, shared bath, no reservations; open April-Oct.) If the hostel's full, try **Whispering Sands,** 45th St. (289-5759), oceanside. The amenable proprietor rents out rooms to students with kitchen access for $15. (Open May-Oct.) You can also pitch a tent at **Assateague National Seashore,** (641-1441) Rte. 611, where campground sites are $10 in summer or $8 in winter, and backcountry camping permits are free (see a ranger). There is a $4 fee to get into the park as well. The **Assateague State Park,** Rte. 611 (641-2120), has a campground, bath houses, and picnic areas. (Sites $20, open April-Oct.) See Assateague Island for more information.

Dining in Ocean City is a glutton's delight. The streets are lined with seemingly identical restaurants hosting all-you-can-eat specials. Be sure to try Maryland's specialty: crabs. **Hooper's Crab House,** (213-1717) Rte. 50, just over the bridge, serves lots and lots of crabs with a nice bay location. $13 all-you-can-eat crabs. (Open daily 11:30am-midnight.) A good, old-fashioned grocery store in Ocean City is the **Food Lion,** (514-9039) 120th St., bayside (open daily 6am-midnight).

Sights and Entertainment Ocean City's star attraction is its **beach.** And a beautiful beach it is. It runs the entire 10 mi. length of town and is wide and sandy the entire way. It's free and open 6am-10pm. You might have better luck avoiding the crush of beach goers if you go uptown, away from the boardwalk. Volleyball, surfing, fishing, tanning, and flexing are favorite beach activities. When the sun goes down the hard-earned tans are put to work at Ocean City's league of bars and nightclubs. The best of the bunch is **Seacrets,** 49th St. (524-4900), bayside. This huge complex brings a taste of Jamaica to the mid-Atlantic. Barefoot barflies wander between floats to the strains of reggae. There are live bands every night. (Cover $3-5. Open Mon.-Sat. 11am-2am, Sun. 12:30pm-2am.)

Washington, D.C.

Washington, D.C.'s strange experiment—an infant nation building a capital city from scratch—has matured into one of America's most influential, most compelling, and most visited cities. Monuments, museums, and the power of politics draw visitors from around the world to tour Chelsea Clinton's new hometown.

After winning independence from Great Britain in 1783, the United States was faced with the challenge of finding a home for its fledgling government. Both Northern and Southern states wanted the capital on their turf. The final location—100 sq. mi. pinched between Virginia and Maryland—was a compromise resulting in what President Kennedy later termed "a city of Northern charm and Southern efficiency."

Nineteenth-century Washington was a "city of magnificent distances"—a smattering of slave markets, elegant government buildings, and boarding houses along the absurdly large-scale avenues designed by French engineer Pierre L'Enfant. The city had hardly begun to expand when the British torched it in 1814; a post-war vote to give up and move the capital failed in Congress by just eight votes. Washington continued to grow, but so did its problems—a port city squeezed between two plantation states, the district was a logical first stop for slave traders, whose shackled cargo awaited sales on the Mall and near the White House. Foreign diplomats were properly disgusted. It took the Civil War to transform Washington from the Union's embarrassing appendix to its jugular vein.

During the 1960s, Washington became the nation's "March Central" by hosting a series of demonstrations advocating civil rights and condemning America's role in

THE MID-ATLANTIC

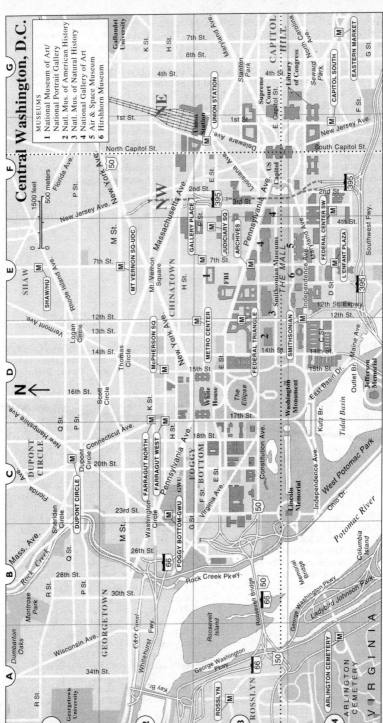

Central Washington, D.C.

MUSEUMS
1 National Museum of Art/
  National Portrait Gallery
2 Natl. Mus. of American History
3 Natl. Mus. of Natural History
4 National Gallery of Art
5 Air & Space Museum
6 Hirshhorn Museum

Vietnam. Martin Luther King, Jr. delivered his "I Have a Dream" speech in 1963 to 250,000 people of all races gathered on the Mall. In 1968, an anti-war gathering ringed the Pentagon with chants and shouts. Later the same year, riots touched off by King's assassination torched parts of the city; some blocks still await rebuilding. 1993 saw the inauguration of Bill Clinton, America's first baby boomer president. First-time tourists will undoubtedly want to visit his house, along with the Capitol, the Smithsonian museums, and Washington's other tourist staples.

Savvy travelers, however, will eventually want to escape the white marble gauntlet to explore the rest of the city. The arts thrive in Dupont Circle, while youngsters spar for turf and great budget meals in Adams-Morgan. The Kennedy Center bows and pirouettes with high culture almost every night, while local clubs throb to high-quality, honest tunes. There are also neighborhoods a tourist would rather not stumble upon, where poor tenements are devastated by crack, guns, and institutional neglect, but the rewards for venturing beyond the conventional grade-school-tour-group attractions are well worth the effort.

> For the ultimate in Washington, D.C. budget coverage, see *Let's Go: Washington, D.C.,* available from discerning booksellers everywhere.

PRACTICAL INFORMATION

Emergency: 911

Visitor Information: Visitor Information Center, 1455 Pennsylvania Ave. NW (789-7038), is a very helpful first stop. Ask for the *Washington Visitor Map,* which shows Metro stops near points of interest, and *Washington's Attractions.* Language-bank service in over 20 tongues. Open Mon.-Sat. 9am-5pm. **International Visitors Information Service (IVIS),** 1630 Crescent Pl. NW (667-6800). Call or write for brochures in a variety of languages. Open Mon.-Fri. 9am-5pm.

Embassies: Australia, 1601 Massachusetts Ave. NW (797-3000); **Canada,** 501 Pennsylvania Ave. NW (682-1740); **Ireland,** 2234 Massachusetts Ave. NW (462-3939); **New Zealand,** 37 Observatory Circle NW (328-4800); **Great Britain,** 3100 Massachusetts Ave. NW (462-1340).

Airport: National Airport (703-419-8000). It's best to fly here from within the U.S., since National is on the Metro and closer to Washington. Metro: National Airport, then walk or take a shuttle. Taxi $10-15 from downtown. **Dulles International Airport** (703-419-8000) is Washington's international airport and much further away; some domestic flights also land here. Taxi to Dulles over $40. No Metro near the airport, but the **Dulles Express Bus** (703-685-1400) runs from the West Falls Church Metro every 20-30 min. ($8 one-way; Mon.-Fri. 6am-10:30pm, Sat-Sun. 7:30am-10:30pm; last bus from Metro 11pm). The **Washington Flyer Express** (703-685-1400) shuttles between National, Dulles, and 1517 K St. NW. Buses run roughly every ½-hr. 6am-10:30pm Mon.-Fri., every hr. 6am-1pm Sat.-Sun. National one-way $8, round-trip $14; Dulles one-way $16, round-trip $26.

Trains: Amtrak (800-872-7245; 800-523-8720 for Metroliner) departs from Union Station, 50 Massachusetts Ave. NE (484-7540). Frequent daily service to: New York City (Metroliner: 3 hr., $96; regular: 3½ hr., $68); Baltimore (Metroliner: 30 min., $15; regular: 40 min., $12); Philadelphia (Metroliner: 1½ hr., $53; regular: 2 hr., $35); Boston (8 hr., round-trip $108). Less frequent service to: Richmond ($21); Williamsburg ($29); Virginia Beach ($42). **MARC** (800-325-7245), Maryland's commuter rail, also leaves Union Station for Baltimore ($5.25), Harper's Ferry, and Martinsburg, WV.

Greyhound: 1005 1st St. NE (800-231-2222) at L St., over a rather decrepit neighborhood. To: Philadelphia ($13); New York City ($26); Baltimore ($6). **East Coast Explorer,** 245 Eighth Ave., NYC (718-694-9667), offers all-day, scenic bus trips between New York, Boston, and Washington. (Bus departs for NY on Fri.)

Public Transportation: Metrorail, main office, 600 5th St. NW, (637-7000; open daily 6am-11:30pm). Clean, quiet, carpeted trains with A/C; the system is nearly crime-free. Computerized fare card must be bought from machines. If you plan to use the Metro several times, buy a $10 or more farecard; you will get a 5% bonus. Trains run daily 5:30am-midnight. Fare $1-2, depending on distance traveled; during peak-hour $1-$3.15. **Flash Pass** allows unlimited bus (and sometimes Metro) rides for 2-weeks ($20-34, depending on the zone it's good for). 1-day Metro pass $5. To make a bus transfer, get a pass from machines on the platform *before* boarding the train. The extensive **Metrobus** (same address, phone, and hours as Metrorail) system reliably serves Georgetown, downtown, and the suburbs. Fare $1. A comprehensive bus map is available from the main Metro office.

Taxi: Yellow Cab (544-1212). Fares are not based on a meter but on a map which splits the city into five zones and 27 subzones. Zone prices are fixed; ask how much the fare will be at the beginning of your trip. Max. fare within D.C. $10.20.

Car Rental: Easi Car Rentals, 2485 S. Glebe Rd. (703-521-0188), in Arlington. From $15 per day, plus 10¢ per mi. Weekly rates from $105, with 200 free mi. Must be 21 or older with major credit card or $300 cash deposit. Reservations advised. Open Mon.-Fri. 9am-7pm, Sat. 9am-2pm. **Bargain Buggies Rent-a-Car,** 912 N. Lincoln St. (703-841-0000), in Arlington. $20 per day and 10¢ per mi.; $110 per week (local rental) with 200 free mi. Must be 18 or older with major credit card or cash deposit of $300. Those under 21 need full insurance coverage of their own. Open Mon.-Fri. 8am-7pm, Sat.-Sun. 9am-3pm.

Bike Rental: Big Wheel Bikes, 315 7th St. SE (543-1600). Mountain bikes $5 per hr., $25 per business day; 3-hr. min. charge. For an extra $5, you can keep the bike overnight. Major credit card, driver's license, or $150 cash deposit per bike required. Open Tues.-Fri. 11am-7pm, Sat. 10am-6pm, Sun. 11am-5pm.

Help Lines: Gay and Lesbian Hotline: 833-3234. 7pm-11pm. **Rape Crisis Center:** 333-7273. **Information, Protection, and Advocacy Center for Handicapped Individuals:** 966-8081, TDD 966-2500.

Post Office: 900 Brentwood Rd. NE (682-9595). Open Mon.-Fri. 8am-8pm, Sat. 10am-6pm, Sun. noon-6pm. **ZIP code** 20066

Area Code: 202

D.C. is ringed by the **Capital Beltway,** or I-495 (except where it's part of I-95); the Beltway is bisected by **U.S. I,** and is intruded upon via Virginia by **I-395. I-95** shoots up from Florida, links Richmond, VA, to Washington and Baltimore, then rockets up the East Coast past Boston. The high-speed **Baltimore-Washington Parkway** connects D.C. to Baltimore. **I-595** trickles off the Capital Beltway and scenically east to Annapolis. **I-66** heads west through Virginia.

ORIENTATION

Pierre L'Enfant's street design operates with a simple and understandable logic (at least downtown). The city is roughly diamond-shaped, with the four tips of the diamond pointed at the four compass directions, and the street names and addresses split up into four quadrants: NW, NE, SE, and SW, as defined by their relation to the U.S. Capitol, Washington's geographic as well as spiritual heart. The names of the four quadrants distinguish otherwise identical addresses—pay very, *very* close attention to them. They matter. The basic street plan is a rectilinear grid. Streets running from east to west are named in alphabetical order running north and south from the Capitol, from two A Streets two blocks apart (nearest the Capitol) out to two W Streets dozens of blocks apart. (There is no A or B St. in NW and SW, and no J St. anywhere.) After W St., east-west streets take on two-syllable names, then three-syllable names, then (at the north end of NW) names of trees and flowers in alphabetical order (roughly—some letters get repeated, and others skipped entirely). Streets running north-south get numbers (1st St., 2nd St., etc.). Numbered and lettered streets sometimes disappear for a block, then keep going as if nothing happened. Addresses on lettered streets indicate the numbered cross street (1100 D St. SE will be between 11th and 12th St.). L'Enfant's plan also includes a sheaf of state avenues radiating outward from the U.S. Capitol or the White House or otherwise crossing downtown. The city added streets as the U.S. added space, and ultimately acquired avenues named for all 50 states. (Well, almost. CA has a "street" instead.)

Some **major roads** are **Pennsylvania Ave.,** which runs SE-NE from Anacostia to Capitol Hill to the Capitol, through downtown, past the White House (#1600), and

THE MID-ATLANTIC

ends finally at 28th and M St. NW in Georgetown; **Connecticut Ave.**, which runs north-northwest from the White House through Dupont Circle and past the Zoo; **Wisconsin Ave.**, north from Georgetown past the Cathedral to Friendship Heights; **16th St. NW,** which zooms from the White House north through offices, townhouses, Adams-Morgan, and Mt. Pleasant; **K St. NW,** a major artery downtown; **Constitution and Independence Ave.,** just north and south of the Mall; **Massachusetts Ave.,** from American University past the Cathedral, then through Dupont and Old Downtown to Capitol Hill; **New York Ave.,** whose principal arm runs from the White House through NE; and high-speed **North Capitol St.**

D.C. isn't just for fat-cat congressmen and their hangers-on. Over 600,000 residents inhabit the federal city; rich and poor, black, white, Asian, and Latino are all well-represented. Escape the grassy, touristy **Mall** to get a true feel for the city. **Capitol Hill** extends east from the Capitol; its townhouses and bars mix white- and blue-collar locals with legislation-minded pols. The **Southwest** quadrant of the city, south of the Mall, begins as federal offices, then passes under I-395 and becomes a low-income neighborhood (to the east) and the waterfront area (to the west). North of the Mall, **Old Downtown** goes about its business accompanied by **Foggy Bottom** (sometimes called the "West End") on the other side of the White House and **New Downtown** around K St. west of 15th St. NW. **Georgetown** draws crowds and sucks away bucks nightly from its center at Wisconsin and M St. NW. Business and pleasure, embassies and streetlife, straight and gay converge around **Dupont Circle;** east of 16th St. the Dupont Circle character changes to struggling **Logan Circle,** then to rundown **Shaw,** and then to Howard University and **LeDroit Park,** an early residence for Washington's African-American elite. A strong Hispanic community coexists with black, white, and cool in **Adams-Morgan,** north of Dupont and east of Rock Creek Park. West of the park begins **upper Northwest,** a big stretch of spread-out (mostly residential) territory that includes the National Zoo and the Cathedral. Across the Anacostia River, the **Southeast** (including **Anacostia**), has been damaged and further isolated by poverty, crack, and guns.

Parts of NE, SE, and NW (east of 14th St.) are unsafe. Use common sense at all times: avoid public parks after dark, walk on busy, well-lit streets whenever possible, and don't go out alone at night.

ACCOMMODATIONS

Business travelers desert D.C. during the summer months, leaving business hotels to discount deeply and swell with tourists on summer weekends. No less busy during the summer are the hostels, guest houses, and university dormitories that round out the selection of D.C.'s temporary residences. If you're lucky enough to hit the District without a car and you don't want a hostel, the guest houses around Dupont Circle and Adams-Morgan should be your first try. Check the *New York Times* Sunday Travel section for summer weekend deals before you go, and feel free to bargain. D.C. automatically adds an 11% occupancy surcharge and another $1.50 per room per night to your bill. Prices listed below *do not* include taxes, unless otherwise noted. **Bed & Breakfast Accommodations, Ltd.,** P.O. Box 12011, Washington, D.C. 20005 (328-3510), reserves rooms in private home with an interesting array of hosts (singles start at $35, doubles at $45; $15 per additional person).

Washington International Hostel (HI-AYH), 1009 11 St. NW 20001 (737-2333). Metro: Metro Center; take the 11th St. exit, then walk 3 blocks north. International travelers appreciate the college-aged staff, bunk beds, bulletin boards, kitchen, and common rooms. Rooms with A/C hold 4-12 beds, accessible by elevator. Lockers, game room, and laundry facilities. No alcohol or drugs. Relatively safe neighborhood, but less so to the northeast. Open 24 hrs. $17, nonmembers $20. Call at least 48 hrs. in advance; written reservations must be received 3 weeks in advance. Wheelchair accessible.

Washington International Student Center, 2452 18th St. NW (265-6555), near Columbia Rd. (on "restaurant row") in the heart of Adams-Morgan. Metro: Woodley Park-Zoo, then a 10-min. walk along Calvert St. 3 very clean but somewhat cramped rooms. The friendly managers are helpful and eager to please. Free linen, A/C, kitchen facilities. Laundromat nearby on Columbia Road. Alcohol permitted, smoking on balcony. No curfew. $15. Call 1-2 weeks ahead.

Simpkins' Bed & Breakfast, 1601 19th St. NW (387-1328), at the corner of Q in the heart of Dupont Circle. Metro: Dupont Circle. Washington's newest hostel. Unbeatable location. For travelers carrying passports (U.S. or foreign) or public-interest professionals, shared-room rates are $15 for a single bed, $20 for double bed, or $25 total for double occupancy of a double bed; private single $40, private double $50. No breakfast included with this discount rate; pre-paid reservations required. Without passport or public-interest affiliation, rates are 100% higher, but breakfast is included. Linen $5, or BYO. Reserve 2-3 weeks ahead.

Kalorama Guest House at Kalorama Park, 1854 Mintwood Place NW (667-6369) and **at Woodley Park,** 2700 Cathedral Ave. NW (328-0860). Metro (both): Woodley Park-Zoo. Well-run, impeccably decorated guest rooms in Victorian townhouses; the first is in the upscale western slice of Adams-Morgan near Rock Creek Park, the second in a high-class neighborhood near the zoo. Both have laundry facilities and free local calls. Free continental breakfast. Mintwood location also has a fireplace and refrigerator space. Rooms with shared bath $40-65, $5 per additional person. Rooms with private baths $55-85. Reserve 1-2 weeks in advance; office open Mon.-Fri. 8am-8pm, Sat.-Sun. 8:30am-7pm.

Adams Inn, 1744 Lanier Place NW (745-3600 or 800-578-6807), near Ontario Rd. behind Columbia Rd. 2 blocks from the center of Adams-Morgan. Metro: Woodley Park-Zoo, then a 12 min. walk; or #42 bus to Columbia Rd. from Dupont Cir. Elaborate and elegant Victorian townhouses. Patio, coin laundry facilities, and pay phones. TV in common room. Shared-bath singles $45, private bath $60; doubles $55/70. Breakfast included. Weekly singles with shared bath $220, with private bath $275; doubles $295/350. Breakfast not included for weekly rentals. Prices include taxes. Office open Mon.-Sat. 8am-9pm, Sun. 1-9pm.

Tabard Inn, 1739 N St. NW (785-1277, fax 785-6173), at 17th St. Metro: Dupont Circle. Romantic inn offers complimentary breakfast in a maze of darkened lounges. Singles $58-79, with private bath $99-130. Each additional person $12.

Connecticut Woodley Guest House, 2647 Woodley Rd. NW (667-0218). Metro: Woodley Park-Zoo. Modest furnishings in plain yet tidy rooms. Singles with shared bath $39-43, with private bath $49-56; doubles $45-48/54-61. Group, family, and long-term rates available. Office open daily 7:30am-midnight.

Davis House, 1822 R St. NW (232-3196, fax 232-3197), near 19th St. Metro: Dupont Circle. Charming and spacious wood-floored building. Common room, sun room, patio, fridge, and microwave. Accepts international visitors, staff of Quaker organizations, and "representatives of other organizations working on peace and justice concerns." Other visitors occasionally accepted on a same-day, space-available basis. Singles $35, doubles $60 (both with hall bath). One night's deposit required. Reserve early. No credit cards. Office open daily 8am-10pm.

Brickskeller Inn, 1523 22nd St. NW (293-1885), between P and Q St. Metro: Dupont Circle. Small, clean rooms, usually with private sinks and shared hall bathrooms. Some rooms with private bath, A/C, and TV. Singles from $40, doubles from $60 (including taxes). Weekly: singles from $140, doubles from $160.

Swiss Inn, 1204 Massachusetts Ave. NW (371-1816, 800-955-7947). Metro: Metro Center. 4 blocks from Metro Center; close to downtown. 7 clean, quiet studio apartments with refrigerator, private bath, high ceilings, kitchenettes, and A/C. Free local phone calls and laundry. International crowd welcomed by French, German, Portuguese, and Spanish-speaking managers. Singles and doubles $98; 20% discount for travel-club members (including HI-AYH), *Let's Go*-readers, and adults 60 and over. Weekly rates: singles and doubles $68 per night. Parking $4.50 per day weekdays (free weekends), or call the managers from the bus stop, Metro station, or downtown airport terminal and they'll come pick you up.

Allen Lee Hotel, 2224 F St. NW (331-1224, 800-462-0128), near 23rd St. and George Washington University. Metro: Foggy Bottom-GWU. Large, rickety, blue hallways. Rooms vary widely in size, furnishings, and state of repair. Singles $32, with private bath $40. Doubles $40, with private bath $51. Twins $42, with private bath $55. Reserve a few days in advance in summer.

2005 Columbia Guest House, 2005 Columbia Rd. NW (265-4006), near 20th St., ½-block from the Washington Hilton Hotel; southwest of central Adams-Morgan. An old senator's house, with a creaky central staircase and 7 rooms featuring faded decor and sometimes lumpy beds. 3 free swimming pools and tennis courts within walking distance. Singles $19-26, doubles $28-39. Weekly rates available. Summertime discounts for students and youth hostel members. Dubious security.

University Dorms: Georgetown University Summer Housing: available only for summer educational pursuits; they gladly take college-aged interns but *cannot house self-declared tourists.* Housing is single-sex. 3-week min. stay. Singles $18, with A/C $19. Doubles with A/C $16, with bath $17. Available early June-early Aug. Woe to those stranded without A/C. Contact G.U. Office of Housing and Conferences Services 20057 (687-4560). **American University Summer Housing:** Write to 407 Butler Pavilion, 4400 Massachusetts Ave. NW 20016-8039, attn.: Housing Management (885-2598). Metro: Tenleytown-AU. Simple dorm rooms with A/C for students and interns (late May-mid-Aug). Doubles only, with hall bathrooms $98 per week per person; come with a friend or they'll find one for you. *3-week min. stay.* Valid ID from any university and full payment for stay must be presented at check-in. Reserve early for check-in dates in early June; after that you can call 24 hrs. ahead and get a room if the dorms aren't full.

Cherry Hill Park, 9800 Cherry Hill Rd. (301-937-7116). Metrobus from the Metro-rail runs to and from the grounds every 30 min., every 15 min. during rush hour. Call for directions by car. The closest campground to Washington. Most of the 400 sites are for RVs. Cable hookup available; coin-operated laundry; heated swimming pool with whirlpool and sauna. Pets allowed. Tent site $25; RV site with electricity, water, and sewer $33. Extra person $2. $25 deposit required. Reserve at least 5 days ahead (call 9am-8pm).

FOOD

D.C. makes up for its days as a "sleepy Southern town" with a kaleidoscope of international restaurants. Smithsonian-goers should plan to eat dinner far away from the triceratops and the biplanes; visitors to the Mall get stuffed into mediocre institutional cafeterias mere blocks from the respectable food on Capitol Hill. You can eat for $4 or eat well for $7 at many places in D.C. Adams-Morgan is famous for budget restaurants; Dupont Circle and the Hill are worth the Metro rides as well. It's an open secret among interns that **happy hours** provide the cheapest dinners in Washington. Bars desperate to attract early-evening drinkers set up plates, platters, and tables of free appetizers; the trick is to munch lots but drink little. The best seem to concentrate, along with the interns, on Capitol Hill or south of Dupont Circle.

Capitol Hill

The Hill's residential character means neighborhood establishments outnumber obnoxious chains. On weekends, local farmers hawk their wares in the block-long red-brick bustle of **Eastern Market** on 7th St. SE (Metro: Eastern Market; open Sat. 7am-6pm, Sun. 9am-4pm). Over 50 eateries proffer burgers, pizza, sushi, bagels, and fruit shakes for under $5 in the lower level of **Union Station** (Metro: Union Station).

Head's, 400 1st St. SE (546-4545). On the corner of D St., right across from the Capitol South Metro stop. *Washingtonian* magazine thinks proprietor Nelson Head serves up the best barbecue in the District, and the bustling crowds at lunch and dinner seem to agree. This place is so popular with Congressfolk and their staffs that it keeps a few TVs tuned to C-SPAN at all times. If you see diners rush out in mid-bite, you know a vote has been called in the House or Senate. Barbecued pork, beef, or chicken sandwiches $6, platters $7. Open Mon.-Sat. 11:30am-12:30am (kitchen closes at 10:30pm).

Le Bon Café, 210 2nd St. SE (547-7200). Metro: Capitol South. Pick up a newspaper from the café's neat stack of abandoned ones and find out what's going on in the buildings all around you. A stone's throw from the Capitol and the Supreme Court, this café serves exquisite food. Breakfast pastries 95¢. Sandwiches $4-6. Elegant salads $3-6. Open Mon.-Fri. 7:30am-7:30pm, Sat.-Sun. 9am-4pm.

The Market Lunch, 225 7th St. SE (547-8444), in the Eastern Market. Metro: Eastern Market. Smells of fish waft over a dozen stools. Crab cakes ($6-9) are the local specialty, but the Blue Bucks (buckwheat blueberry pancakes $3) have people lined up around the corner on Sat. mornings. Open Tues.-Sat. 7:30am-2:30pm.

Misha's Deli, 210 7th St. SE (547-5858), north of Pennsylvania Ave. on 7th St. Metro: Eastern Market. Inexpensive, authentic Russian and Eastern European food. Practice your Russian with the friendly immigrant owner. Tasty knishes just $2, blintzes $1.75. Special $5 lunch plate: pick 1 entree and any 4 salads. Open Mon.-Thurs. 8am-6:30pm, Fri. 8am-7pm, Sat. 8am-6:30pm, Sun. 9am-5pm.

Provisions, 218 7th St. SE (543-0694), across from the Eastern Market. Metro: Eastern Market. A handful of tables crouch in a two-story red brick alcove with a wall-to-wall skylight. Gourmet sandwiches $4-6. Try the ever-popular "218" sandwich, a sumptuous concoction of smoked ham and lingonberry jam ($5.25). Daily coffee specials. Open Mon.-Fri. 10am-7pm, Sat. 8am-6pm, Sun. 10am-4pm.

Taverna the Greek Islands, 307 Pennsylvania Ave. SE (547-8360). Metro: Capitol South. Chef's specials include at least 3 options from $6. Dinners $9 and up. Order the *Saganaki alla Paros* ($5) to see 8-ft. flames shoot from your plate. Frequent **Kennedy sightings.** Happy hour (Mon.-Fri. 3-7pm) features drink specials and, after 6pm, free appetizers. Open Mon.-Sat. 11am-midnight, Sun. 4-11pm.

Old Downtown

American Café, 1331 Pennsylvania Ave. NW (626-0770), in the Shops at National Place at 13th and F St. NW. Metro: Metro Center. Choose your genre: deli, café, or restaurant. Cafe/deli open daily 8am-9pm. Restaurant open daily 11am-11pm.

Dixie Grill, 518 10th St. NW (628-4800), next to the Petersen House. Metro: Metro Center. A hot spot for drinks after work. Enjoy Karo corn fritters ($2.50), a hot chicken cornbread sandwich ($7.25), or the lunch special ($5). Open Mon. 11:30am-10pm, Tues.-Fri. 11:30am-1am, Sat. noon-1:30am, Sun. noon-10pm.

Capitol City Brewing Company, 1100 New York Ave. NW (628-2222); enter on the corner of 11th and H St. Metro: Metro Center. Reportedly the first brewery in the District of Columbia since Prohibition. New beers on tap every night, so check *City Paper* to find out what's brewin'. Pints $3.50-4.25. Hearty pseudo-Germanic grub around $9. Pub open daily 11am-2am.

Chinatown

You don't have to dig a hole to China to find authentic Chinese food and groceries. Don't be turned off by a decrepit exterior; dives often serve wonderful food.

Burma Restaurant, upstairs at 740 6th St. NW (393-3453). Burma's rare cuisine replaces soy sauce with pickles, mild curries, and spices. Make it your mission to try the *Kaukswe Thoke*, rice noodles with ground shrimp, fried onion, hot pepper, garlic, and lemon juice ($6.50). Open Mon.-Thurs. 11am-3pm and 6-9:30pm, Fri. 11am-3pm and 6-10:30pm, Sat. noon-3pm and 6-10:30pm, Sun. 6-9:30pm.

Li Ho Food Restaurant, 501 H St. NW (289-2059). Cantonese specialties—chicken wrapped in rice paper, unsealed salted shrimp, a fish head simmered in a clay pot ($8), and clams in black-bean sauce. 7 meal-size variations on the "noodles in soup" theme for under $5. Honey-glazed barbecued pork ($5). Lunch specials: 1, 2, or 3 entrees with fried rice $3.75-5.30. Open daily 10:30am-11pm.

Tony Cheng's Mongolian Restaurant, upstairs at 619 H St. NW (842-8669). Load your bowl with beef, leeks, mushrooms, sprouts, and such, then watch the cooks make it sizzle (1 serving $6, all-you-can-eat $14). 2 or more can stir up their own feast in charcoal hotpots provided by the restaurant. Platter $5 per person; more meat extra. Open Sun.-Thurs. 11am-11pm, Fri.-Sat. 11am-midnight.

White House Area/Foggy Bottom

Jonathan's Gourmet Deli/Market, 2142 L St. NW (331-8458 or 331-8497). Metro: Foggy Bottom-GWU. Hearty breakfasts $3.40 and under; gourmet sandwiches $1.90-4.40. Salad bar $3.80/lb. Open Mon.-Fri. 7am-8pm, Sat. 8am-3:30pm.

Lindy's Bon Apétit, 2040 I St. NW (452-0055), near Pennsylvania Ave. and Tower Records. Metro: Foggy Bottom-GWU. Ronald Reagan said that life at GWU was not complete without a bone burger from this carry-out deli. Breakfast sandwiches $1.85. Open Mon.-Fri. 7am-8pm, Sat.-Sun. 11am-4pm.

Treviso, 2138½ Pennsylvania Ave. NW (338-5760). Metro: Foggy Bottom-GWU. Quality Italian *pollo, pesce,* and *paste* $7-10. Open Mon.-Thurs. 11:30am-2:30pm and 5:30-10pm, Fri.11:30am-2:30pm and 5:30-10:30pm, Sat. 5:30-10:30pm.

Georgetown

Georgetown's restaurants have got pretension if you want it: tourists can feed with the powerful and boring at inflated prices amid brass rails and autographed photos. On the other hand, some of the best food comes from the smaller ethnic restaurants: Indian, Ethiopian, Thai, and Vietnamese are well-established in Georgetown.

Aditi, 3299 M St. NW (625-6825), at 33rd St. The Sanskrit name translates as "creative power"; here it means great food. Try the vegetarian (or non-vegetarian) Thali, $7-8. Lunch special $5. Open Mon.-Thurs. 11:30am-2:30pm and 5:30-10pm, Fri.-Sat. 11:30am-2:30pm and 5:30-10:30pm, Sun. noon-2:30pm and 5:30-10pm.

Au Croissant Chaud/Au Pied du Cochon/Aux Fruits de Mer, 1329 and 1335 Wisconsin Ave. NW (333-7700, 333-5440, and 333-2333), at Dumbarton St. Au Pied serves up casual French fare like salads and crepes amidst photos and rustic copper pots; Aux Fruits offers fish and seafood in a maritime setting with an aquarium. For $10, catch the lavish early-bird dinner at Au Pied from 3-8pm and at Aux Fruits from 5-8pm. Grab an 80¢ you-know-what at Au Croissant. Au Croissant open Mon.-Wed. 6am-9pm, Thurs. 6am-midnight, Fri.-Sat. 24 hr., Sun. 6am-8pm. Au Pied open daily 24hr. Aux Fruits open Mon.-Wed. approx. 6am-11pm, Thurs.-Sat. 24 hr., Sun. approx. 6am-11pm.

Booeymonger, 3265 Prospect St. NW (333-4810), at Potomac St. Georgetown students and residents stop by for breakfast ($3 special) or a quick, giant sandwich (under $5). Highlights include vegetarian pita pockets, Booey's Philly cheesesteak, and kosher hotdogs. Create your own sandwich for up to $4 with a choice of 15 fillings, 8 breads, and 13 condiments. Open daily 8am-midnight.

Quick Pita, 1210 Potomac St. NW (338-PITA or 338-7482), near M St. Good, cheap Middle Eastern fare, perfect for a Quick Snack or takeout. All sandwiches under $4. Felafel $2.75, miniature pies for under $1. Free delivery in the Georgetown area after 6pm ($12 min. order). Open Mon.-Sun. 11:30am-4am.

Sarinah, 1338 Wisconsin Ave. NW (337-2955), near O St. Delicious Indonesian food includes *satays,* grilled and skewered lamb, beef, chicken, or shrimp with spicy sauces ($9-10); vegetarian entrees also. Lots of exotic desserts ($3.25-4.25). Lunch special $6. Open Tues.-Sat. noon-3pm and 6-10:30pm, Sun. 6-10:30pm.

Sushi-Ko, 2309 Wisconsin Ave. NW (333-4187), below Calvert St. D.C.'s first sushi bar: authentic, no-frills Japanese food prepared before your eyes. Try the *Maki-sushi Nigiri* or *Temaki-sushi* (over 20 kinds), under $5. Open Mon. 6-10:30pm, Tues.-Fri. noon-2:30pm and 6-10:30pm, Sat. 5-10:30pm, Sun. 5-10pm.

Thomas Sweet, 3214 P St. NW (337-0616), at Wisconsin Ave. The best ice cream in D.C. by a light-year. Single-scoop $1.70. Hefty helpings of yogurt or ice cream mixed with fruit or candy $3.75. Open June-Aug. Mon.-Thurs. 9:30am-midnight, Fri.-Sat. 9:30am-1am, Sun. 11am-midnight; Sept.-May closes 1 hr. earlier.

New Downtown

Eye St. Café, 1915 I St. NW (457-0773). Metro: Farragut West. Middle Eastern/Italian. Restaurant setting and food at café prices. Pepper salad $6. Take-out available. Open Mon.-Thurs. 11am-3pm and 5:30-9pm, Fri. 11am-3pm and 5:30-10pm.

Tokyo Terrace, 1025 Vermont Ave. NW (628-7304), near K St. Metro: McPherson Square. Join every sushi-lover in New Downtown. $7.85 ($4 for children) buys all-you-can-eat sushi rolls plus salad, vegetable roll, and miso soup Fri., 6-9pm and Sat., noon-9pm. Open Mon.-Thurs. 9am-7:30pm, Fri. 9am-9pm, Sat. noon-9pm.

Whatsa Bagel, 1216 18th St. NW (293-8990). Metro: Farragut North. 50¢ bagels come in wacky varieties like sundried tomato, cheese, banana nut, granola, and "everything." Offbeat "overstuffed" bagel sandwiches around $2. Open Mon.-Fri. 7am-8pm, Sat. 7:30am-6pm, Sun. 8am-4:30pm.

Dupont Circle

Cheap coffee shops, one-of-a-kind American restaurants, health-food stores, and a pricey *patisserie* or two complement Dupont Circle's mostly ethnic assortment. Many restaurants hang together along P St. and Connecticut Ave. on both sides of the circle. Metro: Dupont Circle, for all of the following.

Bua, 1635 P St. NW (265-0828, delivery 546-8646), near 17th St. Award-winning Thai cuisine in a cool, spacious dining room or on the patio. Dinner entrees $7-13; lunch entrees $6-7.50. Happy hour Mon.-Fri. 5-7pm serves up selected beers for $2. Open Mon.-Thurs. 11:30am-2:30pm and 5-10:30pm, Fri. 11:30am-2:30pm and 5-11pm, Sat. noon-4pm and 5-11pm, Sun. noon-4pm and 5-10:30pm.

Café Petitto, 1724 Connecticut Ave. NW (462-8771), between R and S St. Excellent and popular Italian regional cooking. Start with the delicious pizza-like *focaccia* ($4.50), then move on to one of the house pastas ($9-11). Sample all of their delicious antipasto for free during happy hour at **Capo's** next door. Open Mon.-Thurs. 11:30am-11pm, Fri.-Sat. 11:30am-1am, Sun. 11:30am-10:30pm.

Food for Thought, 1738 Connecticut Ave. NW (797-1095), 3 blocks north of the circle. Veggie-hippie-folknik mecca with good, healthy food in a 60s atmosphere. 10 different vegetable and fruit salads; 25 sandwiches. Local musicians strum in the evenings, open mike every Mon. 9-11:30pm. Blues jam first Sun. of every month. Bulletin boards announce everything from rallies to beach parties to rides to L.A. Pool table upstairs. Lunch combos $4.75-6.75 (Mon.-Fri. until 4:30pm), dinner $6-10. Open Mon. 11:30am-2:30pm and 5pm-12:30am; Tues.-Thurs. 11:30am-12:30am, Fri. 11:30am-2am, Sat. noon-2am, Sun. 4pm-12:30am.

Pizzeria Paradiso, 2029 P St. NW (223-1245), near 21st St. Long lines herald the best pizza in the city. The toppings are tasty and traditional—basil, prosciutto, capers—but the crispy crust is the real star. The popular Bosco pizza, with tomato, mushrooms, spinach, red onion, and mozzarella, is $8.50 for one person, $15 for two. All meals come with a small bowl of black and green olives. Open Mon.-Thurs. 11am-11pm, Fri.-Sat. 11am-midnight, Sun. noon-10pm.

The Pop Stop, 1513 17th St. NW (328-0880), near P St. When business is slow, the price of a cup of coffee can buy several hours in the easy chairs upstairs at this hippest of D.C. cafés. Tables downstairs are within easy reach of the well-stocked magazine rack; the streetside patio is for serious people-watching. This structural diversity attracts a diverse crowd, though it's weighted toward the local, gay, and young. The café serves a wide range of coffee drinks ($1-3) and a handful of sandwiches (with chips $4). Open Sun.-Thurs. 7:30am-2am, Fri.-Sat. 7:30am-4am.

Shaw

The immediate vicinity of 14th and U St. NW, on the area's edge near the U St.-Cardozo Metro stop, is a safe source for supreme soul food, a uniquely African-American cuisine. Come during the day. Metro: U St.-Cardozo, for all of the following.

Florida Avenue Grill, 1100 Florida Ave. NW (265-1586), at 11th St. From the U St.-Cardozo Metro stop, walk east on U to 11th St., then north up 11th St. to Florida Ave.; or take the Metrobus that runs up 11th St. Small, enduring (since 1944) diner once fed black leaders and famous entertainers. Awesome Southern-style food: breakfast with salmon cakes or spicy half-smoked sausage, eggs, grits, hotcakes, or southern biscuits ($4-7). Lunch and dinner dishes served with choice of 2 vegetables ($6-9). Various dishes featuring pig's foot. Open Tues.-Sat. 6am-9pm.

Hogs on the Hill, 2001 14th St. NW (332-4647), at U St. Fast-food joint decor offsets enticing smells from the kitchen. Big portions, too. Half chickens $4, whole chickens $7. Platters served with corn bread and choice of collard greens, potato salad, cole slaw, or red beans and rice, or fries, $3.50-8. Open Mon.-Thurs. 11am-10pm, Fri.-Sat. 10am-11pm, Sun. noon-9pm.

Adams-Morgan

Adams-Morgan has justifiably become D.C.'s preferred locale for budget dining, with a jambalaya of cultures to satisfy all sorts of unusual tastes, from Latin American

THE MID-ATLANTIC

to Ethiopian to Caribbean—all for around $10. The action radiates from 18th, Columbia, and Calvert St. NW uphill along Columbia or down 18th.

Calvert Café, 1967 Calvert St. NW (232-5431), right at the foot of the Duke Ellington Bridge. Metro: Woodley Park-Zoo, then hoof it down Calvert for 10 min. Look for the brown and gold tiles; though it looks boarded-up, this landmark has lasted nearly 40 years. Huge, unadorned platters of Middle Eastern food. Appetizers $2-3.50, dinner entrees $6-8.50. Open daily 11:30am-11:30pm.

The Islander, 1762 Columbia Rd. NW (234-4955), easy to miss above a shoe store. Small Trinidadian and Caribbean restaurant has been winning regulars for over 15 years with its exotic but unpretentious cuisine. Curried goat or Calypso chicken, $8.50. 9 kinds of *roti* (thin pancakes stuffed with vegetables and meat) $3.50-7. Wash it all down with sweet ginger beer ($1.50). Open Mon. 5-10pm, Tues.-Thurs. noon-10pm, Fri.-Sat. noon-11pm.

Meskerem, 2434 18th St. NW (462-4100), near Columbia Rd. The best-looking Ethiopian place in Adams-Morgan. Cheery yellow 3-level interior with an upstairs dining gallery. Appetizers $2.50-4.75, meat entrees $8.75-11, vegetarian entrees $7-8.75. Try the *meskerem tibbs* (lamb with vegetables, $11) or *yemisir watt* (lentils in hot sauce, $8.50). Open daily noon-midnight.

Mixtec, 1792 Columbia Rd. NW (332-1011), near 18th St. A refreshing bastion of authentic Mexican food in a city overrun with greasy Tex-Mex. A neon sign flashes the specialty, tacos al carbon. The $3 version offers 2 small tortillas filled with beef and served with 3 garnishes. Mind-bending chicken *mole* $9. All-you-can-eat buffet Sat.-Sun. 11:30am-3pm ($10): the only authentic Mexican brunch on the East Coast. Open Sun.-Thurs. 11am-11:30pm, Fri.-Sat. 11am-12:30am.

Red Sea, 2463 18th St. NW (483-5000), near Columbia Rd. The first of Adams-Morgan's famous Ethiopian restaurants and still among the best. The red-painted exterior is weather-beaten but enticing. Placemats describe Ethiopian cuisine and customs—like the fact that you don't eat with utensils. Instead, use the traditional pancake bread, *injera,* to scoop up spicy lamb, beef, chicken, and vegetable *wats* (stews). Entrees $5.55-10. Open daily 11:30am-midnight.

Tom Tom's, 2333 18th St. NW (588-1300), at Belmont St. Well-pressed folks in well-pressed clothes vie for rooftop tables to feast on Mediterranean *tapas,* carefully prepared little dishes of anything from roasted peppers to lamb kebabs. A few such dishes make for a satisfying meal and a reasonable bill. Nothing on the menu, not even a bottle of wine, is over $10, and most tapas are under $5. Kitchen open Sun.-Thurs. 5-11pm, Fri.-Sat. 5pm-midnight. Bar open Sun.-Thurs. 5pm-1:30am, Fri.-Sat. 5pm-2:30am.

SIGHTS

OK, every first-time visitor has to go to the Capitol and the Smithsonian. But away from the grassy expanses of the manicured Mall, the rest of D.C. is a veritable thicket of art museums, ethnic communities, parks, public events, and bustling streets. Adams-Morgan, Dupont Circle, Connecticut Ave., and Georgetown are all good bets for those sick of the standard tourist circuit.

If you're pressed for time, however, or like riding around in unusual vehicles, **Tourmobile Sight-seeing,** 1000 Ohio Drive SW, near the Washington Monument (554-7950 or 554-5100 for recorded info), offers one of the most popular standard tours (9am-6:30pm, mid-Sept.-mid-March 9:30am-4:30pm; standard 18-sight loop $9, kids 3-11 $4; buy tickets from booth or drivers). **Scandal Tours** (783-7212) schleps tourists from one place of infamy to the next, including Gary Hart's townhouse, Watergate, and the Vista Hotel, where Mayor Barry was caught with his pants down (75 min., $27). Capitol Entertainment Services (636-9203) specializes in a **Black History Tour** through Lincoln Park, Anacostia, and the Frederick Douglass home. (Tours begin at area hotels. 3 hr.; $15, children 5-12 $10.)

Capitol Hill

The scale and style of the **U.S. Capitol** (operator 224-3121) grandly evoke the power of the republic (Metro: Capitol South.) The **East Front** faces the Supreme

Court; from Jackson (1829) to Carter (1977), most Presidents were inaugurated here. For Reagan's 1981 inauguration, Congress moved the ceremony to the newly fixed-up **West Front,** overlooking the Mall. If there's light in the dome at night, Congress is still meeting. The public East Front entrance brings you into the 180-ft.-high **rotunda.** Statesmen from Lincoln to JFK have lain in state in its center; recently, in his much-publicized "Living Will," late President Richard Nixon opted to forgo this highest of national honors. You can get a **map** from the tour desk here (free guided **tours** begin here daily every 20 min. 9am-3:45pm). Downstairs, ceremony and confusion reign in the **crypt** area; most of the functioning rooms are upstairs. For a spectacle, but little insight, climb to the **House and Senate visitors galleries.** Americans should request a gallery pass (valid for the whole 2-year session of Congress) from the office of their representative, delegate, or senator. Foreign nationals may get one-day passes by presenting a passport, driver's license, or birth certificate (or photocopies thereof) at the desk immediately outside the House visitors gallery (for a House pass) or at the "Appointments desk" located at the extreme North End of the main hallway of the crypt level (for a Senate pass). Expect to see a few bored-looking elected officials failing to listen to the person on the podium, who is probably speaking for the exclusive benefit of home-district cable TV viewers. The real business of Congress is conducted in **committee hearings.** Most are open to the public; check the *Washington Post's* "Today in Congress" box for times and locations. The **Senate Restaurant** on crypt (first) floor is also open to the public. The free **Capitol subway** shuttles between the basement of the Capitol and the House and Senate office buildings; a buzzer and flashing red lights signal an imminent vote. (Open daily 9am-4:30pm, Memorial Day-Labor Day daily 8am-8pm.)

The nine justices of the **Supreme Court,** 1 1st St. NE (479-3000), hold forth in their own building across from the East Front of the Capitol building. (Metro: Capitol South or Union Station.) Oral arguments are open to the public; show up early (before 8:30am) to be seated, or walk through the standing gallery to hear 5 min. of the argument. (Court is in session Oct.-June Mon.-Wed. 10am-3pm for 2 weeks each month.) The *Washington Post's* A-section can tell you what case is up. Hoof through the courtroom itself when the Justices are on vacation. Brief lectures cover the history, duties, and architecture of the court and its building (July-Aug. every hr. on the ½-hr. 9:30am-3:30pm). (Open Mon.-Fri. 9am-4:30pm. Free.)

The **Library of Congress,** 1st St. SE (707-5000; recorded events schedule 707-8000), between East Capitol and Independence Ave. (Metro: Capitol South), is the world's largest library, with 26 million books and over 80 million other holdings occupying three buildings: the 1897 Beaux Arts Jefferson Building; the 1939 Adams Building across 2nd St.; and the 1980 Madison Building. The entire collection, including rare items, is open to those of college age or older with a legitimate research purpose, but anyone can take the tour (irregular hours), which starts in the Madison Building lobby. After a brief film, the tour scuttles through tunnels to the Jefferson Building, which is otherwise closed for renovations. The octagonal Main Reading Room, under a spectacular dome, remains open to scholars despite renovations. (Most reading rooms open Mon.-Fri. 8:30am-9:30pm, Sat. 8:30am-5pm.)

Although the **Folger Shakespeare Library,** 201 East Capitol St. SE (544-4600), houses the world's largest collection of Shakespeareana (about 275,000 books and manuscripts), most of it is closed to the public. You can see the Great Hall exhibition gallery and the theater, which imitates the Elizabethan Inns of Court indoor theaters where Shakespeare's company performed. The Folger also sponsors readings, lectures, and concerts such as the PEN/Faulkner poetry and fiction readings and the Folger Consort, a chamber music group specializing in Renaissance music. (Exhibits open Mon.-Sat. 10am-4pm; library open Mon.-Sat. 8:45am-4:45pm.) Stop for a rest in the authentic Elizabethan **"knot" garden,** on the building's 3rd St. side.

The trains run on time at **Union Station,** 50 Massachusetts Ave. NE (371-9441), two blocks north of the Capitol (Metro: Union Station). Daniel Burnham's monumental Beaux Arts design took 4 years (1905-1908) to erect. Colonnades, archways, and huge domed ceilings equate Burnham's Washington with imperial Rome; today the station is a spotless ornament in the crown of capitalism, with a food court, chic stores, and mall rats aplenty (shops open Mon.-Sat. 10am-9pm, Sun. noon-6pm).

Directly west of Union Station is the new **National Postal Museum,** 1st St. and Massachusetts Ave. NE (357-2700), on the lower level of the City Post Office (Metro: Union Station). The Smithsonian's collection of stamps and other philatelic materials was relocated here in July 1993. The collection includes such postal floatsam as airmail planes hung from the ceiling in the 90-ft.-high atrium, half of a fake mustache used by a train robber, goofy mail boxes, and the letter-carrier uniform worn by everyone's favorite oedipal oddity, Cliff Claven in TV's *Cheers.* (Open daily 10am-5:30pm. Free.) Northeast of Union Station is the red-brick **Capital Children's Museum,** 800 3rd St. NE (675-4125; Metro: Union Station). Touch and feel every exhibit in this huge interactive experiment of a museum; walk through the life-sized cave, learn how a printing press works, grind and brew your own hot chocolate, a wander through the room-sized maze, or just watch cartoons. (Open daily 10am-5pm. $6, children under 2 free. All kids must be accompanied by an adult.)

The **Sewall-Belmont House,** 144 Constitution Ave. NE (546-3989; Metro: Union Station), one of the oldest houses in D.C. and headquarters of the National Woman's Party, now houses a museum of the U.S. women's movement. (Open Tues.-Fri. 11am-3pm, Sat.-Sun. noon-4pm; ring the bell—tours are unscheduled. Free.)

Southeast

Three museums and a boardable destroyer stay ship-shape among the booms at the **Washington Navy Yard,** at 9th and M St. SE (Metro: Navy Yard). *Use caution in this neighborhood.* The best of the lot, the **Navy Museum,** Building 76 (433-4882), should buoy anyone let down by the admire-but-don't-touch Air & Space Museum on the Mall. Climb inside the space capsule, play human cannonball inside huge ship guns, jam yourself into a bathysphere used to explore the sea floor, or give orders on the bridge. (Open Mon.-Fri. 9am-5pm, Sat.-Sun. 10am-5pm; Sept.-May Mon.-Fri. 9am-4pm, Sat.-Sun. 10am-5pm.) Tour the **U.S.S. Barry,** a decommissioned destroyer, docked a few steps from the Navy Museum (open daily 10am-5pm). The **Marine Corps Historical Museum,** Building 58 (433-3534), marches in Marine Corps time from the American Revolution to the present, touting the actions, guns, uniforms, swords, and other memorabilia of marines from the halls of Montezuma to the shores of Kuwait (open Mon.-Thurs. and Sat. 10am-4pm, Fri. 10am-8pm, Sun. noon-5pm; Sept.-May Mon.-Sat. 10am-4pm, Sun. noon-5pm).

After the Civil War, one-acre plots sold by the Freedmen's Bureau drew freed slaves to **Anacostia.** Despite the opening of the Anacostia Metro and community struggles to overcome drug-related violence, this neglected neighborhood remains largely unattractive to tourists. If you prefer exploring on foot, do so here only during the day and with a friend or two. The **Anacostia Museum,** 1901 Fort Place SE (287-3369, Sat.-Sun. 357-2700), focuses on African-American history and culture. (Take the W-1 or W-2 bus from Howard Rd. near the Metro Station to Fort Place.) Pick up a flyer at the Smithsonian Castle to see what's showing at the museum. (Open daily 10am-5pm; free.) Cedar Hill, the **Frederick Douglass Home,** 1411 W St. SE (426-5960), was the final residence of Abolitionist statesman, orator, and autobiographer Frederick Douglass, who escaped from slavery in 1838, published the *North Star* newspaper in the 1840s, and served in the 1880s as a D.C. official and as the U.S. Ambassador to Haiti. (Take the Mt. Ranier B-2 bus from Howard Rd. near the Metro station to the home.) Tours (every ½-hr. 9am-4pm) begin with a movie. (Open daily 9am-5pm; Nov.-March 9am-4pm. Free.)

Museums on the Mall

The **Smithsonian** is the catalogued attic of the United States. The world's largest museum complex (11 buildings) stretches out along Washington's longest lawn, the Mall. **Constitution Ave.** (on the north) and **Independence Ave.** (on the south) fence the double row of museums. All Smithsonian museums are free and wheelchair-accessible; all offer written guides in various languages. Allow no less than three days to see the Smithsonian—it would take a lifetime to "finish." For museum info, call 357-2700; for info on tours, concerts, lectures, and films, call 357-2020.

The National Mall, the U.S.'s taxpayer-supported national backyard, is a sight in itself. On any sunny day hundreds of natives and out-of-towners sunbathe and lounge, play frisbee or football, knock down their little brothers, or go fly a kite. The **Smithsonian Castle,** 1000 Jefferson Dr. SW (357-2700, recording 357-2020), holds no real exhibits, but it does have info desks, a (very) thorough 20-min. movie, and James Smithson's body (open daily 9am-5:30pm).

The National Museum of American History: Henry Ford said "History is bunk." This museum thinks history is junk—several centuries' worth of machines, textiles, photographs, vehicles, harmonicas, hats, and uncategorizable American detritus reside here. When the Smithsonian inherits a quirky artifact of popular history, like Dorothy's slippers from *The Wizard of Oz* or Archie Bunker's chair, it usually ends up here. The original "Star Spangled Banner" hangs behind Foucault's pendulum. Open daily 10am-6:30pm; Sept.-May daily 10am-5:30pm.

The Museum of Natural History: This golden-domed, neoclassical museum considers the earth and its life in 2½ big, crowded floors of exhibits. Corridors, cases, dioramas, and hanging specimens reflect the Victorian mania to collect, catalogue, and display (and sometimes nail). Inside, the largest African elephant ever "captured" (i.e., killed) stands under dome-filtered sunshine. Dinosaur skeletons dwarf it in a nearby gallery. Upstairs, cases of naturally-occurring crystals (including glow-the-dark rocks) make the final plush room of cut gems anticlimactic, despite the famously cursed Hope Diamond. The Insect Zoo pleases with an array of live creepy-crawlies, from cockroaches to walking sticks. Open daily 10am-6:30pm; Sept.-May daily 10am-5:30pm.

The National Gallery of Art: West Building (737-4215) houses and hangs its jumble of pre-1900 art in a domed marble temple to Western Tradition, including important works by El Greco, Raphael, Rembrandt, Vermeer, and Monet. Leonardo da Vinci's earliest surviving portrait, *Ginevra de' Benci,* the only da Vinci in the U.S., hangs amid a fine collection of Italian Renaissance Art. Other highlights include Jan Van Eyck's *The Annunciation,* a hall of Dutch masters, a bevy of French Impressionist pieces, and works by John Singer Sargent, George Bellows, and Winslow Homer. Open Mon.-Sat. 10am-5pm, Sun. 11am-6pm.

The National Gallery Of Art: East Building (737-4215) houses the museum's plentiful 20th-century collection in I. M. Pei's celebrated spacious, sunlit structure. The National Gallery owns works by a veritable parade of modern artists, including Picasso, Matisse, Mondrian, Miró, Magritte, Pollock, Warhol, Lichtenstein, and Rothko. Don't expect to see all of them, however; the East Building constantly rearranges, closes, opens, and remodels parts of itself for temporary exhibits. Open Mon.-Sat. 10am-5pm, Sun. 11am-6pm.

The National Air and Space Museum (357-2700) is gigantic, and the world's most popular museum to boot, with 7.5 million visitors per year. Airplanes and space vehicles dangle from the ceiling; the Wright brothers' biplane in the entrance gallery looks intimidated next to all its younger kin. The space-age atrium holds a moon rock, worn smooth by two decades of tourists' fingertips. Walk through the Skylab space station, the Apollo XI command module, and a DC-7. A full-scale lunar lander has touched down outside the cafeteria. A new exhibit entitled "Where Next, Columbus?" brings a historical perspective to issues dealing with space-exploration, while another gallery test-flies the *U.S.S. Enterprise* from *Star Trek.* The gift shop is a blast. IMAX movies on Langley Theater's 5-story screen are so realistic that some viewers suffer motion sickness. Films 9:30am-6:45pm. Tickets $3.25; kids, students, and seniors $2; available at the box office on the ground floor. Open daily 10am-6:30pm; Sept.-June daily 10am-5:30pm.

Hirshhorn Museum and Sculpture Garden (357-2700): This four-story, slide-carousel-shaped brown building has outraged traditionalists since 1966. Each floor consists of 2 concentric circles, an outer ring of rooms and paintings, and an inner corridor of sculptures. The Hirshhorn's best shows feature art since 1960; no other gallery or museum in Washington even pretends to keep up with the

Hirshhorn's avant-garde paintings, mind-bending sculptures, and mixed-media installations. The museum claims the world's most comprehensive set of 19th- and 20th-century Western sculptures, including small works by Rodin and Giacometti. Outdoor sculpture shines in the museum's courtyard. Museum open daily 10am-5:30pm. Sculpture Garden open daily 7:30am-dusk.

The Arts and Industries Building is an exhibition of an exhibition, the 1876 Centennial Exhibition of American technology in Philadelphia. Pause for the exterior: a polychromatic, multi-style chaos of gables, arches, rails, shingles, and bricks. Inside, furniture and candy-making equipment congregate near the Mall entrance; further back, heavy machinery will delight steam fans. Open daily 10am-5:30pm.

The National Museum of African Art, underground at 950 Independence Ave. SW (357-4600), displays artifacts from Sub-Saharan Africa such as masks, textiles, ceremonial figures, and fascinating musical instruments like a harp made partly of pangolin scales. One permanent display contains bronzes from what is today Nigeria; another focuses on pottery. Open daily 10am-5:30pm.

The Arthur M. Sackler Gallery, underground at 1050 Independence Ave. SW (357-2041), showcases an extensive collection of art from China, South and Southeast Asia, and Persia, including illuminated manuscripts; Chinese and Japanese painting; jade miniatures; carvings and friezes from Egypt, Phoenicia, and Sumeria; Hindu statues; and the Sackler Library. Open daily 10am-5:30pm.

The Freer Gallery of Art is the small, delicate pearl on a Mall-encircling necklace of big, showy gems. The Freer displays Asian and Asian-influenced art, including Chinese bronzes, precious manuscripts, jade carvings, and James McNeill Whistler's opulent *Peacock Room.* Open daily 10am-5:30pm. Free tours at 1:30pm.

South of the Mall

Exotic foliage from all continents and climates vegetates inside and outside the **U.S. Botanical Garden** (225-7099), 1st St. and Maryland Ave. SW (Metro: Federal Center SW). Cacti, bromeliads, and other odd-climate plants flourish indoors. (Open daily 9am–5pm. 40 min. guided tours at 10am and 2pm; call ahead.) Farther west, the **Bureau of Engraving and Printing** (a.k.a. the Mint) (662-2000), 14th St. and C St. SW, offers cramped tours of the presses that annually print over $20 billion worth of money and stamps. Money love has made this the area's longest line; arrive mega-early or expect to grow old waiting. (Open Mon.-Fri. 9am-2pm; free.)

The **U.S. Holocaust Memorial Museum,** 100 Raoul Wallenberg Place SW (488-0400; Metro: Smithsonian), opened in April 1993 after more than a decade of preparation. The new museum is uniquely suited to its audience; its displays move beyond mere historical narrative and force visitors to experience events from a more personal perspective. The **permanent exhibit** gives the whole story, beginning on the fourth floor with "Nazi Assault," which chronicles the rise of Nazism, the events leading up to the war in Europe, and the history of anti-semitism. "The Final Solution," on the third floor, shows films of barbaric Nazi "medical" experiments. Still photos and dioramas depict Jews and others being rounded up and sent to concentration camps, then exterminated in gas chambers or at gunpoint. The second floor chronicles the "Aftermath—1945 to the Present." Films show Soviet, British, and American troops entering the concentration camps, shocked by the mass graves and emaciated prisoners they encounter. A wall lists the names of those who heroically defied the Nazis to save Jewish lives, while more films and tapes bear the testimony of Holocaust survivors. The **Hall of Remembrance** contains an eternal flame. This museum draws immense crowds; get in line before 9am to acquire same-day tickets. (Open daily 10am-5:30pm. Free.)

South of G Street SW, along Maine Ave. Water St., yachts congregate at the **Washington Marina,** under the noses of the high-priced seafood restaurants and hordes of joggers. In the summer, huge fairs reel in hundreds of Washingtonians, kids in tow, to check out the T-shirts and food and to ogle the boats. The oldest open-air seafood market in the U.S., **Wharf Seafood Market,** hangs out between 9th and 11th St. SW and Maine Ave. NW (next to the Memorial Bridge; Metro: Waterfront). Sellers have been at it here since 1794; during low tide you'll find yourself looking down at mounds of ice cubes, coral lobsters, crawling crabs, and people in aprons. (Open 8am-9pm.)

Monuments and West of the Mall

The **Washington Monument** (Metro: Smithsonian) is a vertical altar to America's first president. The stairs up the monument were a famous (and strenuous) tourist exercise until the Park Service closed them after heart attacks (on the way up) and vandalism (on the way down). The experts say the thing could withstand a super-tornado blowing at 145 mi. per hour—we'd still like to see that . At the top, tiny windows offer lookout points. The line takes 45 min. to circle the monument; people with disabilities can bypass it. (Open daily 8am-midnight; Sept.-March daily 9am-5pm. Free.) The **Reflecting Pool** reflects Washington's obelisk in 7 million gallons of lit-up water 24hrs. a day—if you lean far enough over, it might reflect you too. Free.

Maya Ying Lin, who designed the **Vietnam Veterans Memorial,** south of Constitution Ave. at 22nd St. NW (Metro: Smithsonian or Foggy Bottom/GWU), called it "a rift in the earth—a long, polished black stone wall, emerging from and receding into the earth." 58,132 Americans died in Vietnam, and each of their names is chiseled onto the memorial's stark black edifice. Books at both ends of the structure serve as indexes to the memorial's numbered panels. Families and veterans come here to ponder and to mourn; many make rubbings of their loved ones' names from the walls. Other visitors leave letters or flowers. (Open 24 hrs.)

Anyone with a penny already knows what the **Lincoln Memorial** looks like, at the west end of the Mall (Metro: Smithsonian or Foggy Bottom/GWU); the design copies the rectangular grandeur of Athens' Parthenon. From these steps, Martin Luther King Jr. gave his "I Have a Dream" speech to the 1963 March on Washington. Daniel Chester French's seated Abe Lincoln presides over the memorial from the inside, keeping watch over protesters and Fourth of July fireworks. You can read his Gettysburg address on the wall to the left of the statue. Climbing the 19-ft. president is a federal offense; a camera will catch you if the rangers don't. (Open 24 hrs.)

A 19-ft. hollow bronze Thomas Jefferson stands enshrined in the domed, open-air rotunda of the **Jefferson Memorial,** surrounded by massive Ionic columns. The memorial's design pays tribute to Jefferson's home, Monticello, which he himself designed. Interior walls quote from Jefferson's writings: the *Declaration of Independence,* the *Virginia Statute of Religious Freedom, Notes on Virginia,* and an 1815 letter. The sentence around the dome's top rebukes those who wrongly called Jefferson an atheist. (Open 24 hrs.) The memorial overlooks the **Tidal Basin,** where pedalboats ripple in and out of the memorial's shadow; walk to it along the Basin's rim from Independence Ave. or 14th St. SW. (Metro: L'Enfant Plaza or Smithsonian.)

Downtown and North of the Mall

It's only proper that an architectural marvel should house the **National Building Museum,** which towers above F St. NW between 4th and 5th St. (Metro: Judiciary Square). Montgomery Meigs' Italian-inspired edifice remains one of Washington's most beautiful; the Great Hall is big enough to hold a 15-story building. "Washington: Symbol and City," one of the NBM's first permanent exhibits, covers D.C. architecture. Other highlights include rejected designs for the Washington Monument and the chance to design your own Capitol Hill rowhouse. (Open Mon.-Sat. 10am-4pm, Sun. noon-4pm. Tours Mon.-Fri. 12:30pm, Sat.-Sun. 12:30pm, 1:30pm. Free.)

The **National Museum of American Art** and the **National Portrait Gallery** (357-2700) share the Old Patent Office Building, a neoclassical edifice 2 blocks long (American Art entrance at 8th and G St., Portrait Gallery entrance at 8th and F; Metro: Gallery Place-Chinatown). The NMAA's corridors contain a diverse collection of major 19th- and 20th-century painters, as well as folk and ethnic artists. D.C. janitor James Hampton stayed up nights in an unheated garage for 15 years to create the *Throne of the Third Heaven of the Nations' Millennium General Assembly,* to the right of the main entrance. "Art of the American West" puts the U.S.'s westward expansion in perspective, while Edward Hopper competes with the abstractions of

THE MID-ATLANTIC

Franz Kline on the third floor. (Open daily 10am-5:30pm; tours Mon.-Fri. noon, Sat.-Sun. 2pm. Free.) The wide range of media, periods, styles, and people represented make the National Portrait Gallery a museum of the American character (open daily 10am-5:30pm; tours Mon.-Fri. 10am-3pm by request, Sat.-Sun. 1pm; free).

The U.S.'s founding documents can still be found at the **National Archives** (501-5000, guided tours 501-5205), 8th St. and Constitution Ave. NW (Metro: Archives-Navy Memorial). Visitors line up outside to view the original *Declaration of Independence, U.S. Constitution,* and *Bill of Rights.* Humidity-controlled, helium-filled glass cases preserve and exhibit all three documents in the central rotunda. Also on display is H. Ross Perot's 13-century copy of the *Magna Carta* (insert your own joke here). (Exhibit area open daily 10am-9pm, Sept.-March 10am-5:30pm. Free.) The **Federal Bureau of Investigation** (324-3000) still hunts Commies, freaks, druggies, and interstate felons with undiminished vigor. Tour lines form on the beige-but-brutal J. Edgar Hoover building's outdoor plaza (tour entrance from 10th St. NW at Pennsylvania Ave.; Metro: Federal Triangle or Archives-Navy Memorial). Real FBI agents sport walkie-talkies as they speed you through gangster paraphernalia and photos, confiscated drugs, gun displays, and mugshots of the nation's 10 most wanted criminals. John Dillinger's death mask hangs alongside his machine gun. At the tour's end, a marksman shreds cardboard evildoers; tellingly, the mostly American audience applauds vigorously. (Tours Mon.-Fri 8:45am-4:15pm; free.)

"Sic semper tyrannis!" said assassin John Wilkes Booth after shooting President Abraham Lincoln during a performance at **Ford's Theatre,** 511 10th St. NW (426-6924; Metro: Metro Center). National Park rangers narrate the events of the April 14, 1865 assassination. (Open daily 9am-5pm; talks every hr. 9am-noon and 2-5pm; Feb.-June every 30 min. Free.) Lincoln passed away the next day at the **Petersen House,** 526 10th St. NW (426-6830; open daily 9am-5pm). The **Old Post Office** (523-5691), at Pennsylvania Ave. and 12th St. NW, sheathes a shopping mall in architectural wonder (Metro: Federal Triangle). Its arched windows, conical turrets, and 315-ft. clock tower rebuke its sleeker contemporary neighbors. The National Park Service can show you around the clock tower; the view from the top may be D.C.'s best.(523-5691; tours meet on the patio). (Tower open 8am-11pm; mid-Sept.-mid-April 10am-6pm. Shops open Mon.-Sat. 10am-8pm, Sun. noon-6pm.)

The **National Museum of Women in the Arts,** 1250 New York Ave. NW (783-5000; Metro: Metro Center), houses works by the likes of Mary Cassatt, Georgia O'Keeffe, Lilla Cabot Perry, Frida Kahlo, and Alma Thomas in a former Masonic Temple. The hunt for the museum's permanent collection, which begins on the third floor (elevator access), is something like an initiation rite. (Open Mon.-Sat. 10am-5pm, Sun. noon-5pm. Suggested donation $3; seniors, students, and kids $2.)

White House and Foggy Bottom

The **White House,** 1600 Pennsylvania Ave. NW (456-7041), isn't Versailles; the President's house, with its simple columns and expansive lawns, seems a compromise between patrician lavishness and democratic simplicity. The President's personal staff works in the West Wing, while the First Lady's cohort occupies the East Wing. Get a free ticket for a short tour at the ticket booth at the northeast corner of the **Ellipse,** the park due south of the White House. Get in line for a ticket *before* 7:30am; expect a 2½ hr. wait afterwards. (Tours Tues.-Sat. 10am-noon; tickets distributed starting at 8am.) American citizens can arrange a better tour of the White House through their Congresspeople. Sometimes it's hard to tell the homeless, the political demonstrators, and the statues apart in **Lafayette Park,** across Pennsylvania Ave. from the White House. All three are more-or-less permanent presences.

At 17th St. and Pennsylvania Ave. NW, the **Renwick Gallery** (357-1300) is filled with "American crafts" (Metro: Farragut West). The first floor's temporary exhibits often show fascinating mixed-media sculptures and constructions by important contemporary artists. (Open daily 10am-5:30pm. Free.) Once housed in the Renwick's mansion, the **Corcoran Gallery** (638-3211) is now in much larger quarters on 17th St. between E St. and New York Ave. NW (Metro: Farragut West). The Corcoran shows off American artists like John Singer Sargent, Mary Cassatt, and Winslow Homer. Thomas Cole's 1841 *Return from the Tournament* provides an air of romance. The gallery's temporary exhibits seek the cutting edge of contemporary art. (Open Mon., Wed. and Fri.-Sun. 10am-5pm, Thurs. 10am-9pm. Suggested donation $3, families $5, students and seniors $1, under 12 free.)

The **Organization of American States** (458-3000, museum 458-6016), 17th St. and Constitution Ave. NW, is a Latin American extravaganza (Metro: Farragut West). The main-floor art gallery displays 20th-century art from Central and South America. Upstairs are the OAS meeting rooms, which holds formal sessions. The meetings, held largely in Spanish, welcome tourists; they even have translation machines. Outside, the path through the Aztec Garden leads to the Museum of the Americas, a collection of art from the member states. (Open Tues.-Sat. 10am-5pm. Free.)

The **National Academy of Sciences** (334-2000), 21st and C St. NW, holds scientific and medical exhibits. Pay homage to the statue of Albert Einstein outside, and note that the man who formulated the Theory of Relativity seems to be wearing Tevas. (Open Mon.-Fri. 8:30am-5pm.)

Above Rock Creek Parkway, the **John F. Kennedy Center for the Performing Arts** (tickets and info 467-4600; entrance off 25th St. and New Hampshire Ave. NW) rises like a marble sarcophagus (Metro: Foggy Bottom-GWU). Built in the late 60s, the center boasts four major stages and a film theater. The flag-decked Hall of States and Hall of Nations lead to the Grand Foyer, which could swallow the Washington Monument with room to spare. A rather unsavory 7-ft. bronze bust of JFK stares up and away at 18 Swedish chandeliers. In the Opera House, snowflake-shaped chandeliers require 1735 electric light bulbs. The terrace has an unbeatable view of the Potomac. (Open daily 10am-11pm. Tours 10am-1pm. Free.)

Georgetown

The best sights in Georgetown are the people, an odd mixture of funky and preppy, most of them wealthy. Oooh. Aaah. Work it, work it.

When Archbishop John Carroll learned where the new capital would be built, he rushed to found **Georgetown University** (main entrance at 37th and O St.), which opened in 1789 as the U.S.'s first Catholic institution of higher learning. Students live, study, and party together in the townhouses lining the streets near the university. Georgetown's basketball team, the Hoyas, are perennial contenders for the national college championship. Buy tickets through Ticketmaster (432-7328), the campus Ticket Office (687-4692), or Athletic Department (687-2449).

Philip Johnson's 1963 gallery, **Dumbarton Oaks,** 1703 32nd St. NW (recorded info 338-8278, tour info 342-3212), between R and S St., holds a collection of beautifully-displayed carvings, tools, and other art from the Aztec and Mayan civilizations. In 1944, the Dumbarton Oaks Conference, held in the Music Room, helped write the United Nations charter. (Collections open Tues.-Sun. 2-5pm; "suggested contribution" $1.) Save at least 1 hr. for the lush, Edenic gardens (open daily 2-6pm, Nov.-March 2-5pm; $3, seniors and kids $2; Nov.-March free).

Retired from commercial use since the 1800s, the **Chesapeake & Ohio Canal** (301-299-3613) extends 185 mi. from Georgetown to Cumberland, MD. The benches under the trees around 30th St. make a prime city lunch spot.

Dupont Circle and New Downtown

Dupont Circle used to be called Washington's most diverse neighborhood; then it turned expensive and Adams-Morgan turned cool. Nevertheless, the Circle and its environs remain a haven for Washington's artsy, international, and gay communities. Unless otherwise stated, the closest Metro to these sites is Dupont Circle. Massachusetts Ave. between Dupont Circle and Observatory Circle is also called **Embassy Row**. Identify an embassy by the national coat-of-arms or flag out front.

The **Phillips Collection,** 1600 21st St. (387-2151), at Q St. NW, was the first museum of modern art in the U.S. Everyone gapes at Auguste Renoir's masterpiece *Luncheon of the Boating Party,* in the Renoir room. Among the other few perma-

THE MID-ATLANTIC

nent exhibitions are the Rothko room and the Klee room. A stroll up the annex and down through original mansion is a delightful parade of Delacroix, Matisses, Van Goghs, Mondrians, Degas, Miros, Gris, Kandinskys, Turners, Courbets, Daumiers, Prendergasts, O'Keefes, and Hoppers—to name a few. (Open Mon.-Sat. 10am-5pm, Sun. noon-7pm. Sat.-Sun. $6.50, students and seniors $3.25, required Sat.-Sun. and suggested Mon.-Fri. Under 18 free.)

The **Bethune Museum and Archives,** 1318 Vermont Ave. NW (333-1233; Metro: McPherson Square), commemorates the life of educator, leader, and civil rights activist Mary McLeod Bethune. One of 17 children of former slaves, Bethune grew up to be the founder of a college, FDR's head of Minority Affairs, and Vice-President of the NAACP. The museum also houses the extensive **Archives for Black Women's History.** (Open Mon.-Fri. 10am-4:30pm, Sat. 10am-4pm; Aug. 29-June 4 Mon.-Fri. 10am-4:30pm. Archives open by appointment. Free.)**B'nai B'rith Klutznick National Jewish Museum,** 1640 Rhode Island Ave. NW (857-6583; Metro: Farragut North), contains Jewish cultural and ritual objects, including George Washington's famous letter to a Newport, Rhode Island, synagogue. The bulletproof glass isn't just evidence of paranoia: terrorists held over 100 people hostage in the B'nai B'rith building in 1977. (Open Sun.-Fri. 10am-4:30pm. Suggested donation $2, seniors and children $1.) **Anderson House,** 2118 Massachusetts Ave. NW (785-2040), retains the robber-baron decadence of U.S. ambassador Larz Anderson, who built it in 1902-5. The Society of the Cincinnati makes this mansion its home base. (Open Tues.-Sat. 1-4pm. Free.) The **Textile Museum,** 2320 S St. NW (667-0441), houses exhibits of rare or intricate textiles; ethnographic displays alternate with shows of individual artists (open Mon.-Sat. 10am-5pm, Sun. 1-5pm; admission by contribution). Flags line the entrance to the **Islamic Center,** 2551 Massachusetts Ave. NW (332-8343), a brilliant white building whose stunning designs stretch to the tips of its spired ceilings. No shorts; women must cover their heads and wear sleeved clothing (no short dresses). (Open daily 10am-5pm. Donation requested.)

The **National Geographic Society Explorer's Hall,** past M St. on 17th St. NW, conquers the first floor of its black-and-white pin-striped building. (857-7588, group tours 857-7689, N.G. Society 857-7000; Metro: Farragut North). The museum offers interactive films, a live parrot, a miniature tornado that you can touch, a huge globe, and fascinating changing exhibits, often by *National Geographic* magazine's crack photographers. (Open Mon.-Sat. 9am-5pm, Sun. 10am-5pm.) Picnic to the (occasional) summer sounds of flute duets and jazz sax players in **Farragut Square,** 3 blocks south of Connecticut Ave. on 17th St. between I and K St. NW.

Elsewhere

In the late 80s, the mantle of multicultural hipness passed to **Adams-Morgan,** when cool kids and the cool at heart arrived alongside immigrants from Mexico and El Salvador. A wreath of awesome ethnic food circles 18th, Columbia, and Calvert St. NW, and street carts and secondhand stores line Columbia Rd. east of 18th St. From the Woodley Park-Zoo Metro, walk to Calvert St., turn left, and hoof east. Don't go to Adams-Morgan in search of a specific establishment; plan to wander around. The neighborhood is a cornucopia of Hispanic, Caribbean, and international coolness any city would envy. From the central intersection, walk south along 18th or east along Columbia to soak in the flavor and eat well. Stay west of 16th St. (bring a friend at night), and safety should be simply a matter of common sense.

Ailing **Shaw** was once the address of choice for important African-American senators (Reconstruction-era Sen. Blanche K. Bruce), poets (Jean Toomer and Langston Hughes), musicians (Duke Ellington), journalists, and lawyers. The **Lincoln Theater,** at 1215 U St., hosted such acts as Pearl Bailey and Duke Ellington and was the first theater in the area to show movies to an integrated audience. The Lincoln was bought and restored by the city and reopened in February of 1994. Excersise caution in this area. Shaw can become deserted away from its business center; areas around housing projects are especially dangerous. At night, Shaw is not safe for the lone traveler or even small groups (especially for touristy types).

Legend has it that "pandemonium" entered the vernacular when the first giant pandas left China for **Washington's National Zoological Park** (673-4800) as a gift from Mao to Nixon. But after years of unsuccessful attempts to birth a baby panda in captivity, Ling-Ling sadly died; her life-mate Hsing-Hsing remains in the Panda House. The zoo spreads east from Connecticut Ave. a few blocks uphill from the Woodley Park-Zoo Metro; follow the crowds to the entrance at 3000 Connecticut Ave. NW. Forested paths—sometimes very steep—and flat walks near the entrance pass plenty of outdoor exhibits in fields and cages, which visitors seeking the big attractions often ignore. Valley Trail (marked with blue bird tracks) connects the bird and sealife exhibits, while the red Olmsted Walk (marked with elephant feet) links land-animal houses. (Grounds open daily 8am-8pm, Oct. 16-April 14 8am-6pm; buildings open daily 9am-6pm, Sept. 16-April 9am-4:30pm. Free.)

The **Cathedral Church of Saint Peter and Saint Paul**, also called the **Washington National Cathedral** (537-6200; recording 364-6616), at Massachusetts and Wisconsin Ave. NW (Metro: Tenleytown, then take the #30, 32, 34 or 36 bus toward Georgetown; or walk up Cathedral Ave. from the equidistant Woodley Park-Zoo Metro), took over 80 years (1907-90) to build, though the cathedral's interior spaces have been in use for decades. Rev. Martin Luther King Jr. preached his last Sunday sermon from the Canterbury pulpit; more recently, the Dalai Lama spoke here. Take the elevator to the Pilgrim Observation Gallery and see Washington from the highest vantage point in the city (open daily 10am-3:15pm). Angels, gargoyles, and grotesques glower outside. (Open Mon.-Fri. 10am-9pm, Sat. 10am-4:30pm, Sun. 12:30-4pm; Sept.-April Mon.-Sat. 10am-4:30pm, Sun. 12:30-4pm. Free.) Children and families "build" parts of their own cathedrals at the **Medieval Workshop** (537-2930) on the Cathedral grounds. Carve stone, see how a stained-glass window is created, mold a gargoyle out of clay—bring the kids to the workshop before visiting the cathedral so they'll appreciate the artwork (open Sat. 11am- 2pm).

The **National Arboretum** (475-3825), 24th and R St. NE (Metro: Stadium-Armory, then a B2 bus), is the U.S.'s living library of trees and flowers. Experts go berserk over the arboretum's world-class stock of *bonsai* (dwarf trees). Azaleas and azalea-watchers clog the place each spring. Be careful in the surrounding area; come in a car, if possible. (Open daily 8am-5pm; July-March Mon.-Fri. 8am-5pm, Sat.-Sun. 10am-5pm. Bonsai collection open daily 10am-3:30pm. Free.) Across the Anacostia River from the National Arboretum, **Kenilworth Aquatic Gardens,** Kenilworth Ave. and Douglas St. NE (426-6905; Metro: Deanwood), dozens of ponds sacrifice their surfaces to thousands of lilies, lotuses, and hyacinths. The gardens look best in summer, when the tropical plants bloom; come in the morning unless you have a fondness for unadorned lily pads. From the Deanwood Metro, tramp over a green-cage bridge, walk down Douglas St., and cross the parking lot. The entrance is at Anacostia Ave. and Douglas St. (Open daily 9am-5pm. Tours Sat.-Sun., 9am, 11am, 1pm.)

Pedestrians won't miss the **Basilica of the National Shrine of the Immaculate Conception** (526-8300), located on the edge of the Catholic U. campus at Michigan Ave. and 4th St. NE. (Metro: Brookland-CUA.) It's the eighth largest church in the world, and the largest Catholic Church in the Western Hemisphere. The shrine's striking, boundary-crossing architecture catches eyes too, as Romanesque arches support stark, Byzantine-flavored façades and a blue-and-gold onion dome that seems straight from Kiev. The bell tower beside the main entrance is cleverly disguised as an Islamic minaret. Some 60 kneeling chapels dedicated to the Virgin Mary line the walls of the main Church and crypt level, many decorated with stained-glass windows and colorful, intricate mosaics—part Byzantine, part Romanesque, and part neither. Free parking; non-free **cafeteria** (open daily 8am-2pm). (Basilica **tours** Mon.-Sat. 9am, 11am, 1pm, and 3pm; Sun. 1:30pm and 4pm. Free.)

The silence of **Arlington National Cemetery** (Metro: Arlington Cemetery) honors those who sacrificed their lives in war. The 612 acres of hills and tree-lined avenues hold the bodies of U.S. military veterans from five-star generals to unknown soldiers. Before you enter the main gate, get a map from the visitors center. The Kennedy Gravesites hold both President John F. Kennedy, his brother, Robert F.

Kennedy and newly joined by Jacqueline Kennedy Onassis.. The Eternal Flame flickers above JFK's simple memorial stone. The Tomb of the Unknowns honors all servicemen who died fighting for the United States and is guarded by delegations from the Army's Third Infantry (changing of the guard every ½-hr., Oct.-March every hr. on the hr.). Robert E. Lee's home, **Arlington House,** overlooks the cemetery. Enter the pastel-peach mansion at the front door; tours are self-guided. Head down Custis Walk in front of Arlington House and exit the cemetery through Weitzel Gate to get to the **Iwo Jima Memorial,** based on Joe Rosenthal's Pulitzer Prize-winning photo of 6 Marines straining to raise the U.S. flag on Mount Suribachi. (Cemetery open daily 8am-7pm, Oct.-March daily 8am-5pm.)

The **Pentagon,** the world's largest office building, shows just how huge a military bureaucracy can get. (Metro: Pentagon.) To take the guided tour, sign in, walk through a metal detector, get X-rayed, and show proper identification. The guide keeps the pace of the tour so brisk that it's like a military music video. (Tours every ½-hr. Mon.-Fri. 9:30am-3:30pm, Oct.-May no tours at 10:30am, 1:30, and 3pm. Non-U.S. citizens should bring their passports for the security check. Free.)

George Washington slept at **Mount Vernon** (703-780-2000), in Fairfax County. The tours, exhibits, and restorations at are staid and worshipful even by Virginia standards. (Metro: Huntington, then take the Fairfax Connector 101 bus at the north end of the station (call 703-339-7200 for schedule information). To drive, take the Beltway (I-495) to the George Washington Parkway and follow it to Mount Vernon.) A key to the Bastille, a gift from the Marquis de Lafayette, is on display in the main hall. Upstairs, see the bedroom of George and Martha Washington. A gravel path outside leads to their tomb. Don't expect to get too close; George and Martha rest in a mausoleum behind a sturdy iron gate. The markerless "slave burial ground" is nearby. The estate also has 18th-century gardens; its fields once grew corn, wheat, tobacco, and marijuana. (Open daily 8am-5pm, Sept.-Oct. and March 9am-5pm, Nov.-Feb. 9am-4pm. $7, over 61 $6, kids 6-11 $3.)

ENTERTAINMENT AND NIGHTLIFE

Just about everyone should be able to find a play, performance, concert, club, or flick to suit his or her taste among D.C.'s variegated scenes. Major culture purveyors, especially the Kennedy Center, make up for high ticket prices with student discounts and frequent low-cost or free events.

Alternatively, just hang out. Cruise around **Georgetown** and watch the beautiful people. In the early evening, most of the excitement is outside; throngs of students, interns, and young professionals share the sidewalk with street performers. Stroll down to **Washington Harbor** and watch those harbor lights at twilight time.

D.C. hosts dozens of annual festivals celebrating the nation's heritage, various ethnic cultures, all genres of music, war veterans, civil rights activists, and flying kites. A parade (789-7000) and fireworks on the Mall accompany the **4th of July,** which commemorate the signing of the *Declaration of Independence* and the nation's birthday. For a complete listing of annual events, consult the **D.C. Committee to Promote Washington,** 1212 New York Ave. NW, Ste. 200 (724-4091)

Theater and Film

At 25th St. and New Hampshire Ave., the **Kennedy Center** (416-8000) has zillions of performing-arts spaces. Tickets get expensive ($10-65), but most productions offer ½-price tickets the day of performance to students, seniors, military, and handicapped persons; call 467-4600 for details. Free events dot the Kennedy calendar.

The prestigious **Shakespeare Theater,** 450 7th St. NW (box office 393-2700; Metro: Archives-Navy Memorial), at the Lansburgh on Pennsylvania Ave., puts on... Shakespeare. Call for ticket prices, show times, and discounts for students and seniors. Standing-room tickets ($10) are available 2 hr. before curtain.

Thespians thrive in Washington's **14th St. theater district,** where tiny repertory companies explore and experiment with truly enjoyable results. *City Paper* provides great coverage of this scene. **Woolly Mammoth,** 1401 Church St. NW (393-

3939), **Studio Theater,** 1333 P St. NW (332-3300), and **The Source Theater,** 1835 14th St. NW (462-1073), all hang out in this borderline dangerous neighborhood near Dupont Circle (tickets $16-29; call for info on student discounts).

The excellent **American Film Institute** (828-4000), at the Kennedy Center, shows classic American, foreign, and avant-garde films, usually two per night. **Biograph,** 2819 M St. NW (333-2696), in Georgetown, shows first-run independents, foreign films, and classics. Film festivals are frequent; the eclectic is the norm. ($6, seniors and kids $3). **Key Theatre,** 1222 Wisconsin Ave. NW (333-5100), near Prospect St. (1 block north of M St.) features first-run art films. Subtitled films offer plenty of chances to polish up your French. ($6.50, over 65 $4, kids $3, matinees $3.50.)

Classical Music

D.C. is home to the well-respected **National Symphony Orchestra,** which performs in the **Kennedy Center** (416-8000), 25th St. and New Hampshire Ave. NW. Tickets are normally expensive ($18-45), but ½-price tickets are available (see above). The NSO also gives concerts in celebration of Memorial Day, the Fourth of July, and Labor Day. The **Washington Opera** (416-7890) also calls the Kennedy Center home. For a schedule of free events, call 467-4600.

The **Library of Congress,** 1st St. SE (concert line 707-5502), sponsors concerts in the Coolidge Auditorium, one of the finest chamber music performance spaces in the world. Concerts are currently being held elsewhere while the auditorium is being renovated. The **Phillips Collection,** 1600 21st St. (387-2151), at Q St. NW, provides an appropriate setting for chamber music and classical piano concerts (Sept.-May Sun. 5pm; free with museum admission).

Jazz

A free lunchtime summer jazz series takes place downtown at the **Corcoran Gallery** (638-3211), 17th St. between E St. and New York Ave. NW, in the Hammer Auditorium every Wed. at 12:30pm. (Metro: Farragut West.)

  Blues Alley, 1073 Rear Wisconsin Ave. NW (337-4141), in an actual alley, below M St. Cool jazz in an intimate supper club dedicated to the art. Past performers include Mary Wilson of the Supremes and Wynton Marsalis. Tickets $13-35. $7 food-or-drink min. Snacks ($2-9) served after 9:30pm. Upscale casual dress; some sport tuxes on big nights. Call for reservations and showtimes.

  One Step Down, 2517 Pennsylvania Ave. NW (331-8863), near M St. More casual and less expensive than Blues Alley. Jukebox well-stocked with jazz. Local jazz Wed.-Mon.; out-of-town talent Fri.-Sat. Free jam-sessions Sat.-Sun. 3:30-7:30pm. Cover $5; up to $17 for out-of-towners. Beers start at $3; happy hour Mon.-Fri. 3-7pm. Showtimes vary. Open Mon.-Fri. 10:30am-2am, Sat.-Sun. noon-3am.

Rock, Punk, Funk, R&B, Dance, Bars, and Karaoke

If you don't mind a young crowd, squeeze into a *local* rock-and-roll show; the D.C. punk scene is, or at least was, one of the nation's finest. To see what's up with local bands, check *City Paper.* George Washington University sponsors shows in **Lisner Auditorium** (994-1500), 21st and H St. NW, which hosts plays and rock concerts by well-known "alternative" acts. Tickets are sometimes free and never more than $25.

In summer on Sat. and Sun., jazz and R&B shows occupy the outdoor **Carter-Barron Amphitheater** (426-6837), in Rock Creek Park up 16th St. and Colorado Ave. NW (tickets about $13.50). From late June-Aug., rock, punk, and metal pre-empt soccer-playing at **Fort Reno Park** (282-0018 or 619-7225), at Chesapeake and Belt St. NW above Wisconsin Ave. (Metro: Tenley Circle.)

  9:30 club, 930 F St. NW (393-0930 or 638-2008). Metro: Metro Center. D.C.'s best local and alternative rock since the legendary d.c. space closed down. $3 to see 3 local bands; $5-20 for nationally known acts, which often sell out weeks in advance. Box office open Mon.-Fri. 1-6pm, as well as door time (Sun.-Thurs. 7:30-11:30pm, Fri.-Sat. 8:30-11:30pm). Under 21 admitted and hand-stamped.

Kilimanjaro, 1724 California St. NW (328-3839), between Florida Ave. and 18th St. Dimly lit, big-deal club for international music—African, Latin, and Caribbean groups; ju-ju, reggae, and salsa DJs (reggae on Sun.). Karaoke Tues. night, international music Wed.-Thurs. No sneakers, shorts, sweats, torn jeans, or tank tops on weekends. No cover Tues.-Thurs.; $5 Fri.-Sat. before 10pm, $10 after 10pm. Up to $20 for live bands. Open Tues.-Thurs. 5pm-2am, Fri. 5pm-4am, Sat. 8pm-4am.

Fifth Colvmn, 915 F St. NW (393-3632), near 9th St. Metro: Gallery Place-Chinatown. Euro-crowd brings serious disco into the trendy 90s. House music shakes the basement; quieter bar upstairs. Look for the 4 stone columns outside: the line to get in is the 5th. Cover $5-10 for anything from hip-hop and alternative industrial to acid jazz and New York freestyle. Open Mon. 9pm-2am, Tues.-Thurs. 10pm-2am, Fri.-Sat. 10pm-3am.

Club Heaven and **Club Hell,** 2327 18th St. NW (667-4355), near Columbia Rd. Hell's downstairs, Heaven's upstairs, so the ground-floor Italian restaurant must be *Purgatorio.* In Hell, smoke blurs the funky gold tables and loud music emanates from spooky, yellow-backlit masks. Heaven looks rather like an old townhouse: scuffed wood floor, comfy couches, a small bar, and TVs, but the dance floor throbs to pounding beats. No cover unless a band is playing. Domestic beer $3, imports $3.75. Dancing starts about 10pm. Heaven open Sun.-Thurs. 10pm-2am, Fri.-Sat. 10pm-3am. Hell open Sun.-Thurs. 6pm-2am, Fri.-Sat. 6pm-3am.

Brickskeller, 1523 22nd St. NW (293-1885), between P and Q St. Metro: Dupont Circle. "The world's largest selection of beer"—over 500 brands from the Ivory Coast, Togo, Belgium, South America, and elsewhere. Bi-monthly beer-tasting events ($24 for the night; call ahead for reservations). Must be 21 after 10pm. Open Mon.-Thurs. 11:30am-2am, Fri. 11:30am-3am, Sat. 6pm-3am, Sun. 6pm-2am.

The Front Page, 1333 New Hampshire Ave. NW (296-6500). Metro: Dupont Circle. Well-known among the intern crowd for its generous happy hours featuring free chicken wings or taco bar (Mon.-Fri. 4-7pm). Open daily 11:30am-1:30am.

Cities, 2424 18th St. NW (328-7194). This packed restaurant n' bar stays hip, or tries to, by changing decor and menu every 8 months or so to mimic a different city. They'll be Hong Kong until Feb. 1995; after that, who knows? Appetizers $3.50-6. Beer from $3.75. No cover. Open Mon.-Fri. 5pm-2am, Sat. 5pm-3am, Sun. 11am-2am. Restaurant closes at 11pm.

Chief Ikes Mambo Room, Chaos, and Pandemonium, 1725 Columbia Rd. (Chief Ikes 332-2211, Chaos and Pandemonium 797-4637), near Ontario Rd., about 2½ blocks from 18th St. At Chief Ikes, pub-style food ($4-10) accompanies live R&B Mon.-Tues., and DJ Wed.-Sat. Up a staircase, Chaos and Pandemoniums feature alternative music and pseudo-Japanese decor. Usually no cover. Must be 21. Chief Ikes open Mon.-Thurs. and Sun. 4pm-2am, Fri.-Sat. 4pm-3am. Chaos and Pandemonium open Mon.-Thurs. and Sun. 6pm-2am, Fri.-Sat. 6pm-3am.

Andalusian Dog, upstairs at 1344 U St. NW (986-6364), near 13th St. Metro: U St.-Cardozo. The place with the big Dali clocks melting off the roof, about to slip onto the pavement below. More surrealism awaits you inside, this time via Magritte. The tiled bar was inspired by the Spanish architect Gaudi. Live bands most Sun. and some Wed. for just $3-5; other nights, enjoy free jazz, poetry readings, or open mike. Dance for free on Thurs.-Sat. nights. Happy hour Mon.-Fri. 5-8pm, Sat.-Sun. 6-8pm: $1 Rolling Rock, $2 Andalusian Ale (made by Sam Adams). Open Mon.-Thurs. 5pm-1:30am, Fri. 5pm-2:30am, Sat. 6pm-2:30am, Sun. 6pm-1:30am.

J.R.'s, 1519 17th St. NW (328-0090). Metro: Dupont Circle. An upscale brick and varnished-wood bar, with a DJ in a choir stall overlooking the tank of "guppies." Open Mon.-Thurs. 2pm-2am, Fri. 2pm-3am, Sat. noon-3am, Sun. noon-2am.

Sports

Opportunities for sports addicts abound in the D.C. area. The Georgetown Hoyas (basketball) pack the **USAir Arena** (formerly the Capital Centre). Their professional counterparts, the **Bullets,** also fire away here, as do the **Capitals** (hockey). Call USAir Arena at 301-350-3400, located between Landover Rd. and Central Ave. in Landover, MD. Take the Beltway (I-95) to exits 15A or 17A and follow signs. Fans flock religiously to **RFK Stadium** to see the **Redskins** (546-2222) play football.

THE SOUTH

The American South has always fought to maintain a unique identity in the face of the more economically powerful North. That tension, of course, produced the most bloody war in the nation's history. The culture battle isn't fought with guns anymore (they tried that), but with stereotypes and conventional wisdom. Today's South has adopted the industry and urbanity of the North while retaining notions of hospitality, an easy-going pace, and a *carpe diem* philosophy. Northern stereotypes of rednecks, racists, and impoverished hayseeds are being countered by the rapid economic growth of the southern metropoli—Atlanta, Nashville, and New Orleans—infusing much of the region with a modern flavor. But the past lingers on both in the division of wealth beneath the white and black and in the genuine warmth of southern hospitality.

This region's history and culture, a mélange of Anglo, African, French, and Spanish, are reflected in its architecture, cuisine, geography, language, and people. From time immemorial—before people began creating their rich histories here—nature blessed the region with overwhelming mountains, lush marshlands, and sparkling beaches. From the Atlantic's Sea Islands to the rolling Ozarks, the Gulf's bayous to the Mississippi Delta, the South's beauty will awe, entice, and enchant.

 # Virginia

Virginia is the home of some of the most historic turf on the American landscape. The permanent colonization of British North America began here with Jamestown colony in 1607. Thirteen years later, the New World's first African slaves set foot on Virginia's shores. Williamsburg burgeoned with the influx of plantation labor and made its fortune on tobacco. The Virginian braintrust of Thomas Jefferson, George Washington, James Madison, James Monroe, and others formed a veritable colonial aristocracy and shepherded America through its inaugural years. Generations later, after slavery had become a political wedge between North and South, the Confederacy chose Richmond as its capital and favorite Virginian son Robert E. Lee as its defender.

Much of the state is rolling farmland, with tobacco still a major crop. But Virginia ain't just whistlin' *Dixie* these days. Charlottesville, Lexington, and Williamsburg are home to some of the finest schools in the nation. The world's most sophisticated military technology docks in Norfolk and checks in with the Pentagon in Arlington.

PRACTICAL INFORMATION

Capital: Richmond.

Virginia Division of Tourism, Bell Tower, Capitol Sq., 101 N. 9th St., Richmond 23219 (800-847-4882 or 786-4484). **Division of State Parks,** 1201 Washington Bldg., Richmond 23219 (786-1712). For the free *Virginia Accommodations Directory,* write to Virginia Travel Council, 7415 Brook Rd., P.O. Box 15067, Richmond 23227.

Time Zone: Eastern. **Postal Abbreviation:** VA

Sales Tax: 4.5%.

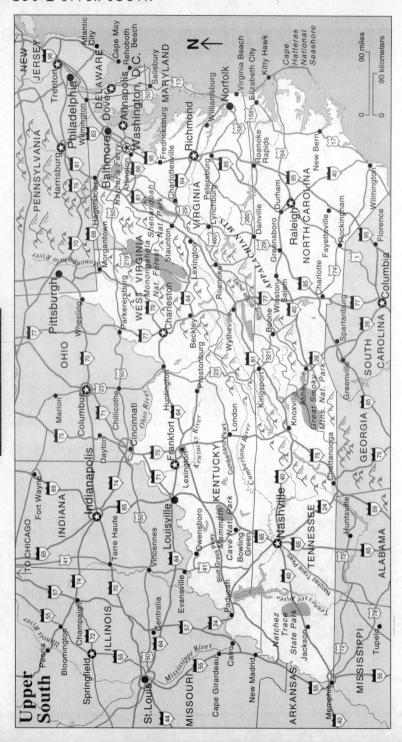

Upper South

Lower South

THE SOUTH

■■■ RICHMOND

The former capital of the Confederate States of America, Richmond is almost obsessively proud of its Civil War past, which is showcased in numerous museums and restored houses. Everything from troop movements to tablecloths belonging to Confederate President Jefferson Davis is on display. But in districts like the sprawling, beautiful Fan, and formerly industrial Shockoe Bottom, Richmond shows its kinder 20th-century face.

PRACTICAL INFORMATION

Emergency: 911.

Visitor Information: Richmond Visitors Center, 1700 Robin Hood Rd. (358-5511), exit 78 off I-95/64, in a converted train depot. Helpful 6-min. video introduces the city's attractions. Walking tours and maps of downtown and the metro region. Can also arrange discounts on accommodations. Open Memorial Day-Labor Day daily 9am-7pm; off-season 9am-5pm.

Traveler's Aid: 643-0279 or 648-1767.

Amtrak: Far away at 7519 Staple Mills Rd. (264-9194 or 800-872-7245). To: Washington, DC (8 per day, 2 hr., $21); Williamsburg (1¼ hr., $9); Virginia Beach (3 hr., $18, the last third of the trip is on a shuttle; New York City (8 per day, 7 hr., $81); Baltimore (3 hr., $29); Philadelphia (8 per day, 4¾ hr., $45). Taxi fare to downtown $12. Open 24 hrs.

Greyhound: 2910 N. Boulevard (254-5910 or 800-231-2222). To get downtown, walk 2 blocks or take GRTC bus 24 north. To: Washington, D.C. (16 per day, 2½ hr., $26.50), Charlottesville (6 per day, 1½ hr., $18), Williamsburg (7 per day, 1 hr., $9), and Norfolk (7 per day, 3 hr., $13).

Public Transport: Greater Richmond Transit Co., 101 S. Davis St. (358-4782). Maps available in the basement of City Hall, 900 E. Broad St., and in the Yellow Pages. Buses serve most of Richmond infrequently, downtown frequently; most leave from Broad St. downtown. Bus 24 goes south to Broad St. and downtown. Fare $1, transfers 10¢. Free trolleys provide dependable, if limited, service to downtown and Shockoe Slip 10am-4pm daily, with an extended Shockoe Slip schedule from 5pm-midnight.

Taxi: Colonial Cab, 264-7960. **Town and County Taxi,** 271-2211.

Help Lines: Rape Crisis, 643-0888. **Gay Information,** 353-3626.

Post Office: 10th and Main St. (783-0825). Open Mon.-Fri. 7:30am-5pm. **ZIP code:** 23219.

Area Code: 804.

Richmond is divided into several regions dubbed with interesting names. **Carytown** is an upscale district in the northwest between Thompson St. and the Boulevard. The **Fan** neighborhood, bounded by the Boulevard, I-95, Monument Ave., and Virginia Commonwealth University, holds many of Richmond's oldest homes and is named for its dubious resemblance to a lady's fan. **Jackson Ward,** in the heart of downtown, and **Shockoe Slip** and **Shockoe Bottom** farther to the east, are more urban sections of town. **Broad Street,** not Main St., is the city's central artery, and the numbered streets that cross it increase from west to east.

ACCOMMODATIONS AND CAMPING

Budget motels in Richmond cluster on **Williamsburg Road,** on the edge of town, and along **Midlothian Turnpike,** south of the James River; public transport to these areas is infrequent at best. As usual, the farther away from downtown you stay, the less you pay. The visitors center can reserve accommodations at ($10-20) discounts.

Massad House Hotel, 11 N. 4th St. (648-2893), 4 blocks from the capitol, near town. Shuttles guests via a 1940s elevator to clean, spacious rooms with shower, A/C, and TV. The only inexpensive rooms downtown. Singles $34, doubles $38.

Motel 6, 5704 Williamsburg Rd. (222-7600), Sandston, about 6 mi. east on U.S. 60, across from the airport. Get there by Bus 7 ("Seven Pines"). Ah, Motel 6; there's one in every city in the nation. Singles $30, doubles $34.

Red Carpet Inn, 5215 W. Broad St. (288-4011), 3 mi. from the center of town; take Bus 6. Offers grand (by motel standards) but slightly faded rooms and a pool/health club. Singles $41, doubles $44.

The closest **campground, Pocahontas State Park,** 10301 Beach Rd. (796-4255), 10 mi. south on Rte. 10 and Rte. 655 in Chesterfield, offers showers, biking, boating, lakes, and a huge pool. (Sites $9.50. No hookups. Pool admission $2.25, ages 3-12 $1.75.) (Open year-round.) Free reservations at 225-3867 in Richmond or 800-933-7275 outside the Richmond area.

FOOD AND ENTERTAINMENT

As both a college town and an old Southern capital, Richmond offers both cheap student eateries and affordable down-home fare. For the student haunts, head for the area around Virginia Commonwealth University (VCU), just west of downtown. For fried apples, grits, and cornbread, make your way downtown.

3rd St. Diner (788-4750), at the corner of 3rd and Main St., offers a taste of Richmond day or night. Enjoy the $2.25 breakfast special (2 eggs, biscuit or toast, and homefries, grits, or Virginia fried apples) on the mint green balcony. Old-time locals served by tattooed waitresses in combat boots. Open 24 hrs.

Texas-Wisconsin Border Café, 1501 W. Main St. (355-2907). Stetsons sporting stuffed steer survey a selection of specialities ranging from salsa to sauerkraut. At night the café becomes a popular bar. Lunches $5-7. Dinners $6-10. Open daily 11am-2am.

Perly's, 11 E. Grace St. (649-2779). Sample some authentic chow in booths beneath the portraits of the bewigged fathers of Richmond. Look for the distinctive sign. Breakfast $1.25-$5. Lunch $5-7. Open Mon.-Fri. 7am-3pm.

Coppola's, 2900 W. Cary St. (359-6969). This popular deli and food market has good and inexpensive Italian food. Dinners $5-7 and fantastic sandwiches $3-6. Open Mon.-Wed. 10am-8pm, Thurs.-Sat. 10am-9pm.

The Ocean Restaurant, 414 E. Main St. (643-9485), serves excellent, filling breakfast and lunch. Everything under $4. Open Mon.-Fri. 6:30am-4pm, Sat. 9am-3pm.

The Shockoe Slip district from Main, Canal, and Cary St. between 10th and 14th St. features fancy shops in restored warehouses, but few bargains. **Cary Street,** from the boulevard to Thompson St., is crowded with vintage clothing stores, antique shops, and entertaining crowds. At the **farmers market,** outdoors at N. 17th and E. Main St., pick up fresh fruit, vegetables, meat, and maybe even a pot swine. Free concerts abound here in the summer; check *Style Weekly,* a free magazine available at the visitors center.

Nightlife crowds Shockoe Slip and sprinkles itself in a less hectic manner throughout the Fan. The **Tobacco Company Club,** 1201 E. Cary St. (782-9555), smokes with top-40 music. (Rarely a cover.) (Open Tues.-Sat. 8pm-2am.) **Matt's British Pub and Comedy Club,** 1045 12th St. (643-5653), next door, pours out a bit of Brit wit with stand-up comedy at 8 and 11pm. (Open daily 11am-2am.) **The Factory,** 727 W. Broad St. (649-4952), assembles local industrial and progressive bands and also goes to work on the dance floor two nights a week. (Open daily 8pm-midnight. Cover varies.) **Flood Zone,** 11 S. 18th St. (643-6006), south of Shockoe Slip, offers a combination of big-name and off-beat rock bands. (Ticket office open Tues.-Fri. 10am-6pm. Tickets $6-20, depending on the show.)

The marvelous old **Byrd Theater,** 2908 W. Cary St. (353-9911), is a fantastically preserved music palace where you are sold your ticket by a tuxedoed agent, ushered into an opulent, chandeliered theater, and treated to a pre-movie concert on an ornate and cavernous Wurlitzer organ that rises out of the floor. All shows are 99¢ and there's a balcony which is open on Saturdays for an extra buck.

THE SOUTH

SIGHTS

Ever since Patrick Henry declared "give me liberty or give me death" in Richmond's **St. John's Church,** 2401 E. Broad St. (648-5015), this river city has been quoting, memorializing, and bronzing its heroes. Summer Sundays at 2pm, an actor recreates the famous 1775 speech. (Tours only; given Mon.-Sat. 10am-3:30pm, Sun. 1-3:30pm. $2, students $1.) The **State Capitol,** 9th and Grace St. (786-4344), is a neoclassical masterpiece that served as the home of the rebel government during the Civil War, and today houses the only statue of George Washington for which he ever posed. (Open April-Oct. daily 9am-5pm; Dec.-March Mon.-Sat. 9am-5pm, Sun. 1-5pm.) For a trip down Richmond's memory lane, follow Franklin Ave. from the capitol until it becomes **Monument Avenue.** This impressive boulevard is lined with stately trees, gracious old houses, and towering statues of Confederate heroes. The marble likeness of Robert E. Lee, who survived the Civil War, faces his beloved South, while that of Stonewall Jackson, who didn't, scowls at the victorious Yankees.

The **Court End** district stretches north and east of the capitol to Clay and College St., and guards Richmond's most distinctive historical sights. The **Museum of the Confederacy,** 1202 E. Clay St. (649-1861), is the world's largest Confederate artifact collection. The main floor leads visitors through the military history of the "Great War of Northern Aggression" (!); the basement displays guns and flags of the Confederacy; and the top floor houses temporary exhibits on such topics as slave life in antebellum South. The museum also runs one-hour tours through the **White House of the Confederacy** next door (ask at the museum desk). Statues of Tragedy, Comedy, and Irony grace the front door of the White House; decide for yourself which applies. (Museum open Mon.-Sat. 10am-5pm, Sun. 1-5pm; tours of the White House Mon., Wed., and Fri.-Sat. 10:30am-4:30pm, Tues. and Thurs. 11:30am-4:30pm, Sun. 1:15-4:30pm. Admission to museum or tour $4, students $2.50, under 13 $2.25; for both: $7/ $5/ $3.50.)

The **Valentine Museum,** 1015 E. Clay St. (649-0711), greets visitors with exhibits on Southern social and cultural history. Tours through the museum are self-guided, but the admission price includes a tour of the recently renovated **Wickham-Valentine House** next door. (Museum open daily 10am-5pm; house tours on the hour 10am-4pm; $5, seniors and students $4, ages 7-12 $3.) Combination tickets to the Museum of the Confederacy, White House of the Confederacy, Valentine Museum, and **John Marshall House,** 818 E. Marshall St. (648-7998; open Tues.-Sat. 10am-5pm, Sun. 1-5pm)—all within easy walking distance of each other—are $11 (seniors and students $10, ages 7-12 $5) and are available at any of the sights.

East of the capitol, follow your tell-tale heart to the **Edgar Allan Poe Museum,** 1914 16 E. Main St. (648-5523). Poe memorabilia stuffs the five buildings, including the **Stone House,** the oldest standing structure within the original city boundaries. (Open Tues.-Sat. 10am-4pm, Sun.-Mon. 1-4pm. $5, seniors $4, students $3.)

Four blocks from the intersection of Monument Ave. and N. Boulevard reposes the Southeast's largest art museum, the **Virginia Museum of Fine Arts,** 2800 Grove Ave. (367-0844). An outstanding art gallery, the museum boasts a gorgeous collection of Fabergé jewelry made for the Russian czars (the largest outside Russia) and what might just be the largest collection of horse sculpture and painting in North America outside Kentucky. (Open Tues.-Sat. 11am-5pm, Thurs. 11am-8pm in the North Wing Galleries, Sun. 1-5pm. Donation requested.)

The **Maggie L. Walker National Historic Site,** 110½ E. Leigh St. (780-1380), commemorates the life of an ex-slave's gifted daughter. Physically disabled, Walker advocated black women's rights and succeeded as founder and president of a bank. (Tours Wed.-Sun. 9am-5pm. Free.) The **Black History Museum and Cultural Center of Virginia,** 00 Clay St. (780-9093), is also worth a visit. (Open Tues., Thurs.-Sat. 11am-4pm. $2, children $1; showcases rotating exhibits about black life in Virginia.)

To the west lies the **Science Museum of Virginia,** 2500 W. Broad St. (367-1080), which is a fun museum heavy on the hands-on side of science. The Museum also contains the **Universe Theater,** which doubles as a planetarium and an OmniMax.

(Museum open Mon.-Fri. 9:30am-5pm, Sat. 9:30am-9pm, Sun. noon-5pm. Planetarium and Omni shows daily, call for times and fees. $4.50, seniors and ages 4-17 $4.)

Overlooking the James River rests the **Hollyrood Cemetery,** Cherry and Albemarle St., the final resting home of the first Civil War battle casualty, of Presidents Monroe and Tyler, and of Jefferson Davis, president of the Confederacy. (Open Mon.-Sat. 7am-6pm, Sun. 8am-6pm. Free.) Civil War buffs should brave the trip to the city's boundaries and the **Richmond National Battlefield Park,** 3215 E. Broad St. (226-1981). The **Chimborazo Visitors Center,** located in a former Civil War hospital, has exhibits on the Civil War, as well as maps detailing the battlefields and fortifications surrounding the city. (Open daily 9am-5pm. Free.)

■■■ WILLIAMSBURG

At the end of the 17th century, Williamsburg was the capital of Virginia. During the Revolutionary War, the capital moved to Richmond, and much of Williamsburg's grandeur went with it. John D. Rockefeller, Jr. came to the city's rescue in 1926, when he poured money into the complete restoration of a large chunk of the historic district. His foundation still runs the restored section, a five-by-seven-block town-within-a-town called **Colonial Williamsburg,** where fife-and-drum corps parade and cobblers, bookbinders, blacksmiths, and clockmakers go about their tasks using 200-year-old methods.

Street-side Punch and Judy shows, evenings of 18th-century theater, and militia reviews are just part of everyday business in Williamsburg. Though the fascinating and beautiful ex-capital claims to be a faithfully restored version of its 18th-century self, don't look for dirt roads, open sewers, or African slaves. Williamsburg also prides itself on William and Mary, the second-oldest college in the United States, and itself a lovely collection of colonial architecture. Outside Williamsburg, Virginia's other big tourist sights lie in wait; history buffs should visit Yorktown, Jamestown, or one of the restored plantations, while the adrenaline-minded should head to nearby **Busch Gardens** amusement park.

PRACTICAL INFORMATION

Emergency: 911.
Visitor Information: Tourist Visitors Center, (800-447-8679), Rte. 132-132y 1 mi. northeast of the train station. Tickets and transportation to Colonial Williamsburg. Maps and guides to the historic district, including a guide for the disabled, available upstairs. Info on prices and discounts on Virginia sights available downstairs. Open daily 8am-8pm.
Amtrak: 408 N. Boundary St. (229-8750 or 800-872-7245). To: New York City ($82, 7 hr.); Washington, D.C. ($29, 3½ hr.); Richmond ($9, 1½ hr.); Virginia Beach ($13, 2 hr.). Open Fri.-Mon. 7:15am-9:30pm; Tues.-Wed. 7:15am-2:45pm, Thurs. 7:15am-3:45pm.
Greyhound: (229-1460), also in the Transportation Center. To: Richmond ($9, 1 hr.); Norfolk ($12, 2 hr.); Washington, D.C. ($28, 4 hr.).Ticket office open Mon.-Fri. 7:30am-5:30pm, Sat.-Sun. 7:30am-3pm.
Public Transport: James City County Transit (JCCT), 220-1621. Service along Rte. 60, from Merchants Sq. in the Historic District west to Williamsburg Pottery or east past Busch Gardens. No service to Yorktown or Jamestown. Operates Mon.-Sat. 6:15am-6:20pm. $1 plus 25¢ per zone-change; exact change required.
Bike Rentals: Bikes Unlimited, 759 Scotland St. (229-4620), rents for $10 per day, with $5 deposit. Open Mon.-Fri. 9am-7pm, Sat. 9am-5pm, Sun. noon-4pm.
Post Office, 425 N. Boundary St. (229-4668). Open Mon.-Fri. 8am-5pm, Sat. 10am-2pm. **ZIP code:** 23185.
Area Code: 804.

Williamsburg lies some 50 mi. southeast of Richmond between **Jamestown** (10 mi. away) and **Yorktown** (14 mi. away). The Colonial Parkway, which connects Williamsburg, Jamestown, and Yorktown, has no commercial buildings along its route, helping to preserve the unspoiled atmosphere. Travelers should visit in late fall or early spring to avoid the crowds, high temperature, and summer humidity.

ACCOMMODATIONS AND CAMPING

A hardworking group of older women single-handedly keep Williamsburg an affordable place to stay. They operate guest houses out of their homes and provide a comfortable, friendly, and cheap alternative to hotels; some don't require reservations, but all expect you to call ahead and most expect you to behave like house guests. Some budget hotels line Rte. 60 west and Rte. 31 south. Avoid the exorbitant rates of the hotels operated by the Colonial Williamsburg Foundation.

Only five min. from the historic district, **Lewis Guest House,** 809 Lafayette St. (229-6116), rents several comfortable rooms, including an upstairs unit with private entrance, kitchen, and bath ($25 for 1 or 2 people). A few doors down is the **Carter Guest House,** 903 Lafayette St. (229-1117). Carter's has two spacious rooms, each with two beds and a shared bath (singles $25, doubles $28). Couples be forewarned: Mrs. Carter will not let unmarried men and women sleep in the same bed. Hotels close to the historic district do not come cheap. A few campsites service the area. **Anvil Campgrounds,** 5243 Moretown Rd. (526-2300), 3 mi. north of the Colonial Williamsburg Information Center on Rte. 60, boasts a swimming pool, bathhouse, recreational hall, and store. (Sites $14-15, with hookup $21).

The closest hostel, **Sangraal-by-the-Sea Youth Hostel (HI-AYH)** (776-6500), Rte. 626, near Urbanna, is 30 mi. away. It does provide rides to bus or train stations during business hours, but don't expect a daily ride to Williamsburg. (Singles $10, nonmembers more. Call ahead.)

FOOD AND NIGHTLIFE

Colonial Williamsburg proper contains several authentic-looking "taverns" which are often expensive and packed with tourists. For a fraction of the price, you can still get a colonial culinary experience by looking at the exteriors of the buildings over a picnic from one of the area supermarkets: try the **Williamsburg Shopping Center,** at the intersection of Richmond Rd. and Lafayette St.

Beethoven's Inn, 467 Merrimac Trail (229-7069). Try the Unnamed Sub, a combination of ham, salami, bologna, and Swiss cheese ($4.35). Play a variety of board games while you wait for your food. Open Mon.-Sat. 11am-9pm, Sun. noon-8pm.

Paul's Deli Restaurant and Pizza, 761 Scotland St. (229-8976). A lively summer hangout for errant, leftover William & Mary students. Sells crisp stromboli for 2 ($5.50-8.75) and filling subs ($3-5). Great jukebox. Open daily 11am-2am.

Chowning's Tavern, on Duke of Gloucester St. If you really want to eat in the historic district, you can wait in line for stew, sandwiches, or the Welsh rarebit—bread in cheese and beer sauce with ham (entrees from $6.25). Miss the expensive dinner and instead join in after 9pm: costumed waiters serve sandwiches, sing 18th-century ballads, and teach patrons how to play dice and card games. Open daily 11am-3:30pm and 4pm-1am.

The Old Chickahominy House, 1211 Jamestown Rd. (229-4689), is over a mile from the historic district. Miss Melinda's "complete luncheon" of Virginia ham served on hot biscuits, fruit salad, a slice of delectable homemade pie, and iced tea or coffee will fill you up for hours ($4.50). Expect a 20-30-min. wait for lunch. Open daily 8:30-10:15am and 11:30am-2:15pm.

Greenleaf Café (220-3405), next door to Paul's Deli, cultivates a subdued atmosphere, serves sandwiches ($3.50-5.50), and sways after 9pm on Tues. to the quiet sounds of live folk music. Cover $2. Locals and students eat at a 20% discount. Open daily 11am-2am.

SIGHTS

Unless you plan to apply to William and Mary, you're probably here for the restored gardens and buildings, crafts, tours, and costumed actors found in the historic district known as **Colonial Williamsburg.** The Colonial Williamsburg Foundation

(CWF) owns nearly everything in the historic district, from the **Governor's Palace** to the lemonade stands and even most of the houses marked "private home." A Patriot's Pass gains admission for one year to all the town's attractions and museums, including a half hour guided tour ($29, kids 6-12 $17), and to nearby Carter's Grove Plantation. A One-day Basic Admission Ticket lets you into any of the historic-area exhibits and includes a 30 min. introductory tour but gives you none of the museums ($24, kids 6-12 $14.25). Buy them at the CWF Visitors Center or from booths in town.

"Doing" the historic district without a ticket definitely saves money; for no charge you can walk the streets, ogle the buildings, march behind the fife-and-drum corps, lock yourself in the stocks, and even use the restrooms. Some old-time shops that actually sell goods—notably **McKenzie Apothecary,** by the Palace Green—are open to the public. Two of the buildings on the CWF map, the **Wren Building** and the **Bruton Parish Church,** are made to appear like regular exhibits but in fact are free. Outdoor events, including a mid-day cannon-firing, are listed in the weekly *Visitor's Companion,* given away to ticket-holders—many of whom conveniently leave it where non-ticket-holders can pick it up.

Guided **walking tours** trample Colonial Williamsburg night and day. The fascinating "Other Half" tour relates the experience of Africans and African-Americans (tours March-Sept.; separate ticket ostensibly required). The two-hour "Stepping into the Past" tour is designed especially for families (daily; $3).

Those willing to pay shouldn't miss the **Governor's Palace,** on the Palace Green. This mansion housed the appointed governors of the Virginia colony until the last one fled before the American Revolution in 1775. Reconstructed Colonial sidearms and ceremonial sabers line the restored walls. The extensive and wonderful gardens include a hedge maze. (Open daily 9am-5pm. Separate admission $15.) Most sights in town are open from 9:30am-5:30pm, but a complete list of hours is listed in the *Visitor's Companion.*

Spreading west from the corner of Richmond and Jamestown Rd. is the other focal point of Williamsburg, **The College of William & Mary,** is the second-oldest college in the U.S. Chartered in 1693, the college schooled Presidents Jefferson, Monroe, and Tyler. The **Sir Christopher Wren Building,** also restored with Rockefeller money, is the oldest classroom building in the country. The Wren building faces the old capitol, 1 mi. away, at the other end of Colonial Williamsburg's main drag, **Duke of Gloucester Street.** Nearby, the shops at **Merchant Square** border the historic district. Park here and walk straight into the restored town proper.

■ NEAR WILLIAMSBURG

Jamestown and Yorktown These historical re-creations are both part of U.S. colonial history. The National Park System runs the **Colonial National Park,** consisting of exhibits and visitors centers (with helpful and free guides) at both Jamestown and Yorktown. The state of Virginia operates the flashier **Yorktown Victory Center** and **Jamestown Settlement.** Combination tickets to Yorktown Victory Center and Jamestown Settlement are available at either site ($9, kids under 13 $4.40).

At the **Jamestown National Historic Site** you'll see remains of the first permanent English settlement (1607) as well as exhibits explaining colonial life. At the **visitors center** (229-1733), skip the hokey film and catch a "living history" walking tour on which a guide portraying one of the colonists describes the Jamestown way of life. Call ahead for info since "living history" guides get occasional off-days. (Open daily 9am-6pm; off-season 8am-5:30pm. The park opens and closes a half hour before the visitors center. Entrance fee $8 per car, $3 per hiker or bicyclist.) Also sniff around at the nearby **Jamestown Settlement** (229-1607), a museum commemorating the settlement with changing exhibits, a reconstruction of James Fort, a Native American village, and full-scale replicas of the three ships that brought the original settlers to Jamestown in 1607. The 20-min. "dramatic film" lives up to its name and fills tourists in on the settlement's history, including an embarrassed treatment of settler relations with the indigenous Powhatan tribe. (Open daily 9am-5pm. Admission $7.50, kids under 13 $3.75.)

The British defeat at **Yorktown** signaled the end of the Revolutionary War. British General Charles Lord Cornwallis and his men seized the town for use as a port in 1781, but were stranded when the French fleet blocked the sea approaches. Colonists and French troops attacked and the British soldiers surrendered, dealing a devastating blow to the British cause. The Yorktown branch of **Colonial National Park** (898-3400) vividly recreates this last significant battle of the war with an engaging film, dioramas, and a smart-looking electric map (behind the information center). Take a 7-mi. automobile journey around the battlefield; you can rent a tape cassette and recorder for $2 at the visitors center to listen to while you drive (**visitors center** open daily 8:30am-6pm; last tape rented at 5pm). The **Yorktown Victory Center** (887-1776), one block from Rte. 17 on Rte. 238, offers a museum brimming with Revolutionary War items and an intriguing "living history" exhibit: in an encampment in front of the center, a troop of soldiers from the Continental Army of 1781 takes a well-deserved break from active combat. (Open daily 9am-5pm. $3.75, kids under 13 $1.75.)

Without a car, you won't find a cheap way to get to Jamestown or Yorktown; since the "towns" are tourist sights, guided tours provide almost the only transportation. With **Williamsburg Limousine** (877-0279), a group of at least four people can see both Jamestown attractions in the morning ($19.50 per person), or both Yorktown sights in the afternoon ($17.50 per person), or take the whole day and see it all ($35, admission fees included). Williamsburg Limousine also offers daily round-trip tours from Colonial Williamsburg to Carter's Grove Plantation ($8), but if you can, bike from South England St. in Colonial Williamsburg along the one-way, 7-mi., wooded **Carter's Grove Country Road.** The unlined **Colonial Parkway** to both Jamestown and Yorktown makes a beautiful biking route.

James River Plantations Built near the water to facilitate the planters' commercial and social lives, these country houses buttressed the slave-holding Virginia aristocracy. Tour guides at **Carter's Grove Plantation,** 6 mi. east of Williamsburg on Rte. 60, show off the restored house and fields. The last owners doubled the size of the original 18th-century building while trying to keep its colonial "feel." The complex also includes reconstructed 18th-century slave quarters and, in front of the house, an archaeological dig. The brand-new **Winthrop Rockefeller Archaeological Museum,** built unobtrusively into a hillside, provides a fascinating case-study look at archaeology. (Plantation open daily 9am-5pm; Nov.-Dec. 9am-4pm. Museum and slave quarters open daily 9am-5pm. Country Road open daily 8:30am-4pm; Nov.-Dec. 8:30am-3pm. $13, kids 6-12 $8, free with CWF Patriot's Pass.) **Berkeley Plantation** (829-6018), halfway between Richmond and Williamsburg on Rte. 5, saw the birth of President William Henry Harrison. Union Soldiers camped on the grounds here in 1862; one of them wrote the famous bugle tune *Taps.* Pause at the terraced box-wood gardens which stretch from the original 1726 brick building to the river. (House open daily 9am-5pm; grounds open daily 8am-5pm. House and grounds $8, seniors $7.20, kids 6-16 $5. Grounds only $4, seniors $3.60, kids 6-16 $2.)

Busch Gardens When you have filled your colonial quotient, head to **Busch Gardens: The Old Country** (253-3350), 3 mi. east of Williamsburg on Rte. 60. You'll be flung, splashed, and throttled by the various shows and rides. Each section of the park represents a European nation; trains and sky-cars connect the sections. **Questor,** a new ride, brings roller coasters into the video age, while **Drachen Fire** provides timeless thrills. The **Loch Ness Monster Rollercoaster** is an enduring classic. Limousine and local buses serve Busch Gardens (see Williamsburg Practical Information above). (Open mid-March to mid-June daily 10am-7pm; mid-June to Aug. Sun.-Fri. 10am-10pm, Sat. 10am-midnight; Sept.-Oct. daily 10am-7pm. $28, children 3-6 $22. After 5pm, $5 off.)

■■■ VIRGINIA BEACH

Ahhh, the beach. Gaze upon endless miles of water, sand, and sky; inhale the perfume of the tide; listen to the insistent rhythm of the waves. Then turn around and face the boardwalk. Virginia Beach is unabashedly dedicated to the rows of hotels and motels, ice cream stands, surf shops, and fast-food joints which flank the golden coastline and cater to cruising college students and tourists.

PRACTICAL INFORMATION

Emergency: 911.

Visitor Information: Virginia Beach Visitors Center 22nd and Parks Ave. (425-7511 or 800-446-8038). Info on budget accommodations and area sights. Open daily 9am-8pm; Labor Day-Memorial Day daily 9am-5pm.

Greyhound: 1017 Laskin Rd. (422-2998), connects with Norfolk, Williamsburg, and Richmond, and with MD via the Bridge Tunnel. To: Washington, D.C. ($29, 6½ hrs.); Richmond ($23, 3½ hrs.); Williamsburg ($14, 2½ hr.).

Amtrak: (245-3589 or 800-872-7245). The nearest station, in Newport News, provides free 45-min. bus service to and from the Radisson Hotel at 19th St. and Pavilion Drive in Virginia Beach, but you must have a train ticket to get on the bus. To: Washington, D.C. ($42, 5½ hrs.); New York City ($85, 9 hrs.); Philadelphia ($70, 8 hrs.); Baltimore ($49, 7 hrs.); Richmond ($18, 3 hrs.); Williamsburg ($13, 2hrs.).

Public Transportation: Virginia Beach Transit/Trolley Information Center (428-3388) provides info on area transportation and tours, including trolleys, buses, and ferries. The **Atlantic Avenue Trolley** runs from Rudee Inlet to 42nd St. (Summer daily noon-midnight; 50¢, seniors and disabled 25¢.) Other trolleys run along the boardwalk, the North Seashore, and to Lynnhaven Mall.

Bike Rental: North End Cyclery, at Laskin Rd. and Arctic Ave. Bikes $3.50 per hr., $15 per day. Open daily 10am-7pm. **Moped Rentals, Inc.,** 21st St. and Pacific Ave. Open summer daily 9am-midnight. Mopeds $22.50 per 1½ hr.

Post Office: (428-2821), 24th and Atlantic Ave. Open Mon.-Fri. 8am-4:30pm. **ZIP code:** 23458.

Area Code: 804.

Virginia Beach is confusing to get to, but easy to get around in. Drivers from the north can take I-64 east from Richmond through the Bay Bridge Tunnel into Norfolk, then get on Rte. 44 (the Virginia Beach-Norfolk Expressway., toll 25¢), which delivers them straight to 22nd St. and the beach. In Virginia Beach east-west streets are numbered; north-south avenues parallel the beach.

ACCOMMODATIONS

The number of motels in Virginia Beach is unreasonably high; unfortunately, so are their rates (with the exception of Angie's). Atlantic Ave. and Pacific Ave. run parallel to the oceanfront, buzz with activity during the summer, and boast the most desirable hotels; reserve as far in advance as possible. If you're traveling in a group, look for "efficiency rate" apartments, which are rented cheaply by the week.

Angie's Guest Cottage-Bed and Breakfast and HI-AYH Hostel, 302 24th St. (428-4690), still ranks as the best place to stay on the entire Virginia Coast. Barbara Yates (who also answers to "Angie") and her team welcome guests with exceptional warmth. They'll pick you up from the train station (call before leaving with the time of your bus or train arrival). (Open April 1-Oct. 1, March with reservations. Memorial Day-Labor Day $11.50, nonmembers $14.80. Off-season $8, nonmembers $11. Overflow camping at off-season rates. Linen $2. Kitchen and lockers available.) In the bed and breakfast, breakfast is (duh) included (doubles $48-68). Accommodating accommodations are also available at the **Ocean Palms Motel** (428-8362), 30th St. and Arctic Ave., where 2-room apartments with refrigerators are $35-45. At the **Islander** (425-8300), 29th and Pacific Ave, $60-82 will get a two-room apartment with dishes, cooking utensils, and mattresses enough to sleep six.

You can **camp** at the **Seashore State Park** (481-2131, reservations 490-3939), about 8 mi. north of town on U.S. 60, which has some juicy spots ($14). Because of its desirable location amid sand dunes and cypress trees, the park is very popular, so call two to three weeks ahead (during business hours) for reservations. (Park open 8am-dusk; take the North Seashore Trolley.) **KOA**, 1240 General Booth Blvd. (428-1444), runs a quiet campground with free bus service to the beach and boardwalk (sites $26, with hook-up $31; comfortable and spacious 1-room cabins $46).

FOOD AND NIGHTLIFE

Junk-food slughogs will love Virginia Beach, thanks to the jumble of fast-food joints along the boardwalk and the main drags. But beyond the neon glare, **The Jewish Mother,** 3108 Pacific Ave. (422-5430), dotes on her customers with quiche, omelettes, crepes ($5-9), deli sandwiches ($4-6), and desserts ($2-4). At night it's a popular (and cheap) bar with live music. (Open Mon.-Tues 9:30pm-2am, Wed.-Fri 9:30-3am, Sat. 8-3am, Sun. 9:30-2am.) **The Raven,** 1200 Atlantic Ave. (425-1200), lays out tasty seafood and steaks in a tinted-glass greenhouse. You can eat outdoors when it's warm. (Sandwiches and burgers $5-7, dinners $12-17. Open daily 11am-2pm.) **Giovanni's Pasta Pizza Palace,** 2006 Atlantic Ave. (425-1575), serves tasty Italian pastas, pizzas, and hot grinders. (Lunches and dinners $5-8. Open daily noon-11pm.)

Buy produce at the **Virginia Beach Farmer's Market,** 1989 Landstown Rd. (427-4395; open daily 9am-6:30pm; in winter until dark). At 31st St. (Luskin Rd.) and Baltic Ave., the **Farm Fresh Supermarket** salad bar, stocked with fresh fruit, pastas, and frozen yogurt ($2.39 per 2 lbs.), is a cheap alternative (open 24 hrs.).

On summer nights, women should avoid walking the boardwalk alone. In darkness the beach becomes a haunt for lovers, while singles hover around the bars and clubs between 17th and 23rd St. along Pacific and Atlantic Ave. Locals favor **Chicho's** (422-6011) and the **Edge,** along Atlantic Ave. between 20th and 21st Streets. (Dress code: T-shirts, shorts, tight dresses, tanned skin.) Bartenders shout to one another underneath videos of surfing competitions and bungee jumping, while hopeful patrons run their eyes up and down their neighbors' figures. (Chicho's open Mon.-Fri. 5pm-2am, Sat.-Sun. 1pm-2am; no cover charge. The Edge open daily 4pm-1:30am; no cover.) Clubs like **Peabody's,** at the corner of 21st St. and Pacific Ave., feature neon lighting and a variety of live bands (open daily 7pm-2am; cover $5). **Peppermint,** 15th and Atlantic (491-2582), draws local crowds by booking solid area and national bands. Music starts at 9pm or later. (Call for usually inexpensive cover.)

SIGHTS

Virginia Beach is biker-friendly, with **bike paths** along the boardwalk and some of the larger streets. Rent a bike at one of the many stands near the boardwalk (about $5 per hr.), then ask for the Virginia Beach Bikeway Map at the Visitors Center. If you're feeling athletic, bike south down the coast to **Sandbridge Beach,** where the locals hang out to avoid crowds of tourists; take the bike trail through the **Back Bay National Wildlife Refuge.** Or bike north to **Seashore State Park.** On the way back from Seashore State Park, test your psychic ability at the **Edgar Cayce Association for Research and Enlightenment** (428-3588), 67th St. and Atlantic Ave., dedicated to psychic potential and holistic health (open Mon.-Sat. 9am-8pm, Sun. 1-8pm).

■■■ CHARLOTTESVILLE

This college town in the Blue Ridge foothills proudly bears the stamp of its patron, Thomas Jefferson. The college he founded, the University of Virginia, dominates the town economically, geographically, and culturally, supporting a community of writers such as Peter Taylor and Pulitzer Prize-winning poet Rita Dove—not to mention a community of pubs. Visitors are steered to Monticello, the cleverly constructed classical mansion Jefferson designed and lived in. Even Charlottesville's friendly, hip, and down-to-earth populace seems to embody the third U.S. President's dream of a well-educated citizenry living close to the land.

PRACTICAL INFORMATION

Emergency: 911. **Campus Police:** Dial 4-7166 on a UVA campus phone.

Visitor Information: Chamber of Commerce, 415 E. Market St. (295-3141), within walking distance of Amtrak, Greyhound, and historic downtown. Open Mon.-Fri. 9am-5pm. **Charlottesville/Albermarle Convention and Visitors Bureau,** P.O. Box 161 (977-1783), Rte. 20 near I-64. Take bus #8 ("Piedmont College") from 5th and Market St. They can make same day accommodation arrangements at a discounted rate. Discounted combo tickets to Monticello, Michie Tavern, and Ash Lawn-Highland ($17; seniors $15.50, under 12 $7.50). Open daily 9:30am-4:45pm. Students answer questions and distribute brochures in **Newcomb Hall** (924-3363), on UVA campus. Open daily 7am-10pm. The larger **University Center** (924-7166) is off U.S. 250 west—follow the signs. Transport schedules, entertainment guides, and hints on budget accommodations. Campus maps. Open 24 hrs.

Amtrak: 810 W. Main St. (800-872-7245 or 296-4559), 7 blocks from downtown. To: Washington, D.C. (1-2 per day, 3 hr., $23); New York City (1-2 per day, 7-8 hr., $83); Baltimore (1 per day, $38); Philadelphia ($58). Open daily 5:30am-9pm.

Greyhound: 310 W. Main St. (295-5131), within 3 blocks of historic downtown. To: Richmond (1 per day, $182), Washington, D.C. (2 per day, 3 hr., $27.50), Norfolk (1 per day, 4 hr., $32). Open Mon.-Sat. 7am-8:30pm, Sun. noon-8:30pm.

Public Transport: Charlottesville Transit Service (296-7433). Bus service within city limits, including most hotels and UVA campus locations. Maps available at both info centers, the Chamber of Commerce, and the UVA student center. Buses operate Mon.-Sat. 6am-6:30pm. Fare 60¢, seniors and disabled 30¢, under 6 free. The more frequent University of Virginia buses hypothetically require UVA ID but the merely studious-looking usually ride free.

Taxi: Yellow Cab, 295-4131. 90¢ first sixth mi., $1.50 each additional mi. To Monticello $8.

Help Lines: Region 10 Community Services Hotline, 972-1800. **Lesbian and Gay Hotline,** 971-4942. UVA-affiliated.

Post Office: 513 E. Main St. (978-7648). Open Mon.-Fri. 8:30am-5pm, Sat. 10am-1pm. **ZIP code:** 22902.

Area Code: 804.

Charlottesville streets number east to west, using compass directions; 5th St. N.W. is 10 blocks from (and parallel to) 5th St. N.E. Streets running east-west across the numbered streets are neither parallel nor logically named. Charlottesville has two downtowns: one on the west side near the university called **The Corner,** and **Historic Downtown,** about a mile east. The two are connected by **University Avenue,** running east-west, which becomes **Main Street** after the Corner ends at a bridge.

ACCOMMODATIONS AND CAMPING

Budget Inn, 140 Emmet St. (U.S. 29) (293-5141), near the university. 40 comfortable, hotel-quality rooms. Senior discounts. Single $33, double $36. $1 off in winter. Office open 8am-midnight. Each additional person $5.

Econo Lodge, 400 Emmet St. (296-2104). 60 typical rooms and a pool. Singles $39, doubles $43. Office open 24 hrs.

Charlottesville KOA Kampground, Rte. 708 (296-9881 or 800-336-9881 for reservations). Get on Rte. 708 off 29 south, go 5 mi.; the campground's on the left. All campsites are shaded. Recreation hall with video games, a pavilion, and a pool (open Mon.-Sat. 10am-8pm). Fishing (not wading or swimming) allowed. Check-in after noon, check-out before noon. Sites $16, hook-up $22. Camping season is March 15-Nov. 15.

FOOD AND NIGHTLIFE

The Corner neighborhood near UVA has bookstores and countless cheap eats, with good Southern grub in C-ville's unpretentious diners. The town loves jazz, likes rock, and has quite a few pubs. Around the Downtown Mall, ubiquitous posters and the free *Charlottesville Review* can tell you who plays where and when.

Macado's, 1505 University Ave. (971-3558). Great sandwiches (around $4), a handful of entrees ($5-7), homemade desserts, and long hours. Upstairs is a rockin' bar where Edgar Allen Poe once lived. Amontillado is the specialty of the house ($5). Open Sun.-Thurs. 9am-1am, Fri.-Sat. 9am-2am.

Coupe DeVille's, 9 Elliewood Ave. (77-3966). College students dig this popular bar and restaurant. ½ rotisserie chicken $6.50. Open Mon.-Fri. 11:30am-2pm and 5:30-10pm, Sat. 5:30-10pm. Pub only Mon.-Sat. 10pm-2am.

White Spot, University Ave. Lots of hard core locals. Dirt cheap—this very small diner has nothing on the menu over $3. Open Mon.-Thurs. 6am-2am, Fri.-Sat. 6am-2:30am, Sun. 7-2am.

The Hardware Store, 316 E. Main St. (977-1518), near the middle of the outdoor "mall." Slightly off-beat atmosphere: beers served in glass boots, appetizers in microcosmic basketball courts, and condiments in toolboxes. American grille and an eclectic set of entrees, from *ratatouille gratinée* ($5) to crêpes both sweet ($2-5) and savory ($6-7). Sandwiches ($5-7). Quality desserts. Open Mon.-Thurs. 11am-9:45pm, Fri.-Sat. 11am-10:30pm.

Littlejohn's, University Ave. (977-0588). This 24-hr. deli has answered the prayers of many UVA students-cum-late-night eaters with great sandwiches ($4-5). Open 24 hrs.

SIGHTS AND ENTERTAINMENT

Most activity on the spacious **University of Virginia (UVA)** campus clusters around the **Lawn** and fraternity-lined **Rugby Road.** Jefferson watched the University being built through his telescope at Monticello, and you can return the gaze with a glimpse of Monticello from the Lawn, a terraced green carpet that is one of the prettiest spots in American academia. Professors live in the Lawn's pavilions; Jefferson designed each one in a different architectural style. Lawn tours, led by students, leave from the Rotunda on the hour from 10am-4pm; self-guided tour maps are provided for those who prefer to find their own way. **The Rotunda** (924-7969) once housed a bell that was shot for the crime of waking students up too early. (Free tours given daily, call for times. Open daily 9am-4:45pm.) The **Old Cabell Building,** across the Lawn from the Rotunda, houses an auditorium with impressive acoustics. On its wall, a reproduction of Raphael's *The School of Athens* echoes Jefferson's vision of student-faculty harmony. The **Bayley Art Museum** (924-3592), Rugby Rd., features visiting exhibits and a small permanent collection including one of Rodin's castings of *The Kiss.* (Open Tues.-Sun. 1-5pm).

The **Downtown Mall,** about five blocks off E. Main St., is a brick thoroughfare lined with restaurants and shops catering to a diverse crowd. A kiosk near the fountain in the center of the mall has posters with club schedules. At 110 E. Main, **The Movie Palace** shows current flicks for only $2. Other diversions run the gamut from live folk music to homemade ice cream.

Thomas Jefferson oversaw every stage of the development of his beloved home **Monticello** (984-9800), and the house reflects the personality of its creator. Monticello is a neo-classical jewel loaded with fascinating innovations collected by or conceived by Jefferson. A unique all-weather passage links the kitchen with the dining room so that neither rain nor snow nor gloom of night could keep dinner from its appointed rounds, and an indoor compass registers wind direction using a weathervane on the roof. The grounds are also cleverly laid out and afford good strolling and views. There is often a hefty wait for the house tour, but you can explore the grounds in the interim. Arrive before 9am to beat the heat and crowds. Lovely silver souvenirs marked with Jefferson's profile are available for 5¢ at every store in America. (Open daily 8am-5pm; Nov.-Feb. 9am-4:30pm. Tickets $8, seniors $7, ages 6-11 $4, students $3 March-Oct., $1 Nov.-Feb.)

Ashlawn (293-9539), the 500-acre plantation home of President James Monroe, is minutes away (take a right turn to Rte. 795). Jefferson assisted with the building of Ashlawn as well, but made the front door short so that Monroe was always obliged to bow to his neighbor at Monticello. More quaint and less imposing than Monticello, Ashlawn has outdoor views to rival those of its domed neighbor. The current owner, the College of William and Mary, has turned Ashlawn into a museum honoring its former owner. A colorful, dainty garden lines the pathway to the house, where a guide offers facts about President Monroe. Ashlawn's peacocks proudly stroll the gardens and lawns. (Open daily 9am-6pm; Nov.-Feb. 10am-5pm. Tour $6, seniors $5.50, ages 6-11 $3.)

In the **Box Gardens** behind Ashlawn, English-language opera and musical theater highlight the **Summer Festival of the Arts.** (Box office 293-4500; open Tues.-Sun. 10am-5pm. Tickets $16, seniors $13, students $10, plus $2 on Sat.) A 45-min. intermission allows for a picnic supper ($8-12), which you can order from **Boar's Head Caterers** (972-2220) or provide yourself. Ashlawn also hosts **Music at Twilight** on Wednesdays ($10, seniors $9, students $6), including New Orleans jazz, Cajun music, blues, and swing.

Down the road from Monticello on Rte. 53 is **Michie** (Mick-ee) **Tavern** (977-1234), a 200 year-old establishment with an operating grist mill and a general store (open daily 9am-5pm; tours $5, under 6 $1). Jefferson's daughter supposedly fled the tavern after improperly teaching a waltz to a man in the ballroom. **The Ordinary,** located in the tavern, serves up a fixed buffet of fried chicken, beans, cornbread, and other dishes ($9.25, ages 6-11 $4). Eat outside in good weather. (Open 11:15am-3:30pm.) To visit these sites at a discount price, purchase the President's Pass at the Charlottesville/Albemarle Convention and Visitors Bureau (see Practical Information above).

■■■ SHENANDOAH NATIONAL PARK

Shenandoah National Park is a monumental testament to restoration. Before Congress established a national park here in 1926, the land was occupied by thread-bare farms and peopled by reclusive mountain folk. Today, the residents are not-so-reclusive deer, bear, and other critters, and their home is the lush forest that has reclaimed the area. The rocky fields have given way to spectacular ridgetop preserves. The Shenandoah is home to more plant species than all of Europe. A trip along its spine via Skyline Drive provides glimpses of the Blue Ridge mountain majesty. Shenandoah's natural beauty comes in the form of sweeping vistas and abundant life. On clear days drivers and hikers can look out over miles of unspoiled ridges and treetops. In the summer, cool mountain air offers a respite from Virginia's typical heat and humidity. Go early in June to see mountain laurel blooming in the highlands. In the fall, Skyline Drive and its lodges are choked with tourists who come to enjoy the magnificent fall foliage.

PRACTICAL INFORMATION

Emergency: 800-732-0911, or contact the nearest ranger.
Visitor Information: 999-2243, 999-2266 for 24-hr. recorded message. Mailing address: Superintendent, Park Headquarters, Shenandoah National Park, Rte. 4, P.O. Box 348, Luray, VA 22835. **Dickey Ridge Visitors Center,** Mile 4.6 (635-3566), closest to the north entrance. Daily interpretative programs. Open April-Nov. daily 9am-5pm. **Byrd Visitors Center,** Mile 50 (999-3283), in the center of the park. Movie explains the history of the Blue Ridge Range and its mountain culture. Open April-Oct. daily 9am-5pm. Both stations offer changing exhibits on the park, free pamphlets, daily posted weather updates, and ranger-led nature hikes.
Area Code: 703.

Shenandoah's technicolor mountains—bluish and covered with deciduous flora in summer, smeared with reds, oranges, and yellows in the fall—can be surveyed from overlooks along **Skyline Drive,** which runs 105 mi. south from Front Royal to Rockfish Gap. (See below for info on the adjoining Blue Ridge Parkway.) The overlooks provide picnic areas for hikers. Map boards also carry data about trail conditions. The drive closes during and after bad weather. Most facilities also hibernate in the winter. (Entrance $5 per vehicle, $3 per hiker, biker, or bus passenger; pass good for 7 days; disabled persons free.)

Miles along Skyline Dr. are measured north to south, beginning at Front Royal. **Greyhound** sends buses to Waynesboro, near the park's southern entrance, once each morning from Washington, D.C. ($38), but neither buses nor trains serve Front Royal.

When planning to stay more than a day, purchase the *Park Guide* ($2), a booklet containing all the park regulations, trail lists, and a description of the area's geological history. Another good guide which doubles as a souvenir is *Exploring Shenandoah National Park* ($2). The essential book to guide you here is the *Guide to Shenandoah National Park and Skyline Drive* (the "Blue Bible" in Ranger parlance—$6.50), which provides detailed info on accommodations, activities, and hikes. The free *Shenandoah Overlook* newspaper reports seasonal and weekly events. All four publications are available at the visitors centers.

ACCOMMODATIONS AND CAMPING

The **Bear's Den (HI-AYH)** (554-8708), located 35 mi. north of Shenandoah on Rte. 601 South, provides a woodsy stone lodge for travelers with two 10-bed dorm rooms. Drivers should exit from Rte. 7 onto Rte. 601 south and go about ½ mi., turn right at the stone-gate entrance, and proceed up the hostel driveway for another ½ mi. No bus or train service is available. The hostel has a dining room, kitchen, on-site parking, and a laundry room. Ask the friendly staff for activities info. (Check-in 5-9pm. Front gate locked and quiet hours begin at 10pm. Check-out by 9:30am. $9, nonmembers $12. Camping $4 per person. Reservations recommended; write Bear's Den HI-AYH, Postal Route 1, Box 288, Bluemont, VA 22012.)

The park maintains three lodges with motel-esque rooms in cabin-esque structures. **Skyland** (999-2211 or 800-999-4714), mile 42 on Skyline Drive, offers brown and green wood-furnished cabins ($43-$77, $5 more in Oct.; open April-Dec.) and slightly more upscale motel rooms. **Lewis Mountain,** mile 57 (999-2255 or 800-999-4714), also gets cabin fever with a set of its own ($50, $7 more in Oct.). Both locations charge an extra $2 or more Fridays or Saturdays. Reservations are necessary up to six months in advance for the fall season.

The park service operates three major campgrounds: **Big Meadows** (Mile 51), **Lewis Mountain** (Mile 58), and **Loft Mountain** (Mile 80). All three have stores, laundry facilities, and showers (no hookups). Heavily wooded and uncluttered by mobile homes, Lewis Mountain makes for the happiest tenters. The sites at Lewis Mountain and Loft Mountain check in at $12, and the sites at Big Meadows are $13. You can reserve sites only at Big Meadows (800-365-2267). Call a visitors center (see Practical Information above) to check availability.

Back-country camping is free, but you must obtain a permit at a park entrance, visitors center, ranger station, or the **park headquarters** (see Practical Information above), halfway between Thornton Gap and Luray on U.S. 211. Back-country campers must set up 25 yards from a water supply and out of sight of any trail, road, overlook, cabin, or other campsite. Since open fires are prohibited, bring cold food or a stove; you'll want to bring your own water or boil it because mountain streams are brimming with all sorts of unpleasant bacteria. Illegal camping carries a hefty fine. Hikers on the **Appalachian Trail** can make use of primitive open shelters, three-sided structures with stone fireplaces which are strewn along the trail at approximately 7-mi. intervals. At full shelters, campers often will move over to make room for a new arrival. These shelters are reserved for hikers with three or more nights in different locations stamped on their camping permits; casual hikers are banned from them ($1 donation per night). The **Potomac Appalachian Trail Club (PATC)** maintains five cabins in backcountry areas of the park. You must reserve them in advance by writing to the club at 118 Park St., SE, Vienna, VA 22180 (242-0693), and bring your own lanterns and food. The cabins contain bunk beds, water, and stoves. (Sun.-Thurs. $3 per person, Fri.-Sat. $14 per group; 1 person must be 21.)

HIKES AND ACTIVITIES

The **Appalachian Trail** runs the length of the park. In fact, it runs the length of the Appalachian Mountains, which include the peaks of the Shenandoah. The Appalacian Range is a national scenic trail, a continuous path between Georgia and Maine, and an American legend. (See Trails section in Essentials.) Only about 150 hardy souls each year complete the entire journey, but if you'd like to be among the 1500 or so who annually try to accomplish the feat, trail maps and the PATC guide can be obtained at the visitors center (see Practical Information above). The PATC puts out three different topographical maps (each $5) of three different parts of the park. When purchased as a package, the maps come with a trail guide, descriptions, and suggestions for budgeting time ($16). Brochures that cover the popular hikes are free. Campers must avoid lighting fires; use stoves instead and leave no litter whatsoever. Overnight hikers should remember the unpredictability of mountain weather. Be sure to get the park service package of brochures and advice before a long hike.

    Old Rag Mountain, 5 mi. from Mile 45, is 3291 ft.—not an intimidating summit—but the 7.2-mi. loop up the mountain is deceptively difficult. The hike is steep, involves scrambling over and between granite, and at many points offers disappointing "false summits." Bring lots of water, energy, food, and gumption, and you'll be rewarded with a hard-earned panorama. The **Whiteoak Canyon Trail** beckons from its own parking lot at Mile 42.6. The trail to the canyon is easy; the waterfalls and trout-filled streams below them are spectacular. Waysides vends 5-day fishing licenses ($6). From Whiteoak Canyon, the **Limberlost** trail slithers into a hemlock forest. At Mile 51.4, **Lewis Spring Falls Trail** takes only ¾-mi. to reach a gorgeous array of falls—the closest to Skyline Drive in the whole park. The trail descends farther (about an hour's walk) to the base of the falls, where water drops 80 ft. over the crumbling stone of an ancient lava flow. **Hogback Overlook,** from Mile 20.8 to Mile 21, bristles with easy hikes and idyllic views of the smooth Shenandoah River; on a clear day, you can see 11 bends in the river. Check out the setting for many of the park postcards at **Dark Hollow Falls,** mile 50.7. A 1.5-mile hike takes you to the base of the cascades.

    Take a break from hiking or driving at one of Shenandoah's seven **picnic areas,** located at Dickey Ridge (Mile 5), Elkwallow (Mile 24), Pinnacles (Mile 37), Big Meadows (Mile 51), Lewis Mountain (Mile 58), South River (Mile 63), and Loft Mountain (Mile 80). All have tables, fireplaces, water fountains, and comfort stations. When you forget to pack a picnic basket, swing by the **Panorama Restaurant** (800-999-4714 or 999-2265), at Mile 31.5, for a meal and a view. (Sandwiches $3-5, entrees $7.50-9. Open April-Nov. daily 9am-5:30pm.)

    Outside the park, the **Shenandoah Caverns** (477-3115) tout an iridescent collection of stalactites and stalagmites, with Rainbow Lake and amusing Capitol Dome among the underground formations prospering in the year-round 56°F air. Take U.S. 211 to Newmarket, get on I-81 north, go 4 mi. to the Shenandoah Caverns exit, and follow the signs to the caverns—not the town of the same name. (Accessible to disabled persons. $7, ages 8-14 $3.50, under 8 free.) **Skyline Caverns** (635-4545 or 800-635-4599), in Front Royal, built a reputation on its anthodites, whose white spikes defy gravity and grow in all directions at the rate of an inch every 7000 years. The caverns are 15 min. from the junction of Skyline Drive and U.S. 211. ($9, ages 6-12 $4, under 6 free. Open mid-June to Aug. daily 9am-6pm; spring and fall Mon.-Fri. 9am-5pm, Sat.-Sun. 9am-6pm; winter daily 9am-4pm.)

    If a scenic paddle floats your boat, the **Downriver Canoe Co.,** Rte. 613 (Indian Hollow Rd.), Bentonville (635-5526), is for the serious canoer. Canoe trips stretch from 3 mi. to 120-plus mi. From Skyline Drive Mile 20 follow U.S 211 west for 8 mi., then north onto U.S. 340, 14 mi. to Bentonville. Turn right onto Rte. 613 and go 1 mi. (Prices vary with length of trip. 3-mi. trips $29 per canoe; 3-day trip $122 per canoe; 25% discount midweek.)

■■■ BLUE RIDGE PARKWAY

If you don't believe that the best things in life are free, this ride could change your mind. The 469-mi. Blue Ridge Parkway, continuous with Skyline Drive, runs through Virginia and North Carolina, connecting the **Shenandoah** and **Great Smoky Mountains National Parks** (see Tennessee). Administered by the National Park Service, the parkway joins hiking trails, campsites, and picnic grounds. Every bit as scenic as Skyline Drive, the Parkway remains much wilder and less crowded. Don't expect to get anywhere fast on this Parkway, however—the speed limit is 45 mph. Also beware of fog during mornings and afternoons. From Shenandoah National Park, the road winds south through Virginia's **George Washington National Forest** from Waynesboro to Roanoke. The forest beckons motorists off the road with spacious campgrounds, canoeing opportunities, and swimming in cold, clear mountain water at **Sherando Lake** (Mile 16).

Self-guided nature trails range from the **Mountain Farm Trail** (Mile 5.9), a 20-minute hike to a reconstructed homestead, to the **Rock Castle Gorge Trail** (Mile 167), a 3-hr. excursion. At **Mabry Mill** (Mile 176.1) you can visit a mountain farm, and at **Crabtree Meadows** (Mile 339) you can purchase local crafts. **Humpback Rocks** (mile 5.8) is an easy hike with a spectacular view. Of course, real go-getters will venture onto the **Appalachian Trail,** which will take you in scenic style all the way to Georgia. In addition to these trails, the Park Service hosts a variety of ranger-led interpretive activities. Information is available at the visitors centers (see below).

Practical Information For general info on the parkway, call **visitor information**. For additional details call the park service in Roanoke, VA (703-982-6458), or in Montebello, VA (703-857-2490). For info write to **Blue Ridge Parkway Headquarters,** 200 BB&T Bldg., Asheville, NC 28801 (704-271-4779). Eleven **visitors centers** line the parkway at Miles 5.8, 63.8, 86, 169, 217.5, 294, 304.5, 316.4, 331, 364.6, and 382, and there are also seven stands where you can pick up brochures. Located at entry points where major highways intersect the Blue Ridge, the centers offer various exhibits, programs, and information facilities. Pick up a free copy of the helpful *Milepost* guide. (Most open daily 9am-5pm, a few 9am-6pm.)

Greyhound provides access to the major towns around the Blue Ridge. Buses run to and from Richmond, Waynesboro, and Lexington; a bus serves Buchanan and the Natural Bridge between Roanoke and Lexington once daily. For info, contact the station in Charlottesville (see Charlottesville Practical Information) or Greyhound, 26 Salem Ave. S.W. (703-343-5436. Ticket office open daily 7am-1am, terminal open daily 3:15-10pm), in Roanoke.

In an **emergency** call 800-727-5928 anywhere in VA or NC. Be sure to give your location to the nearest mile.

Accommodations The **Blue Ridge Country HI-AYH Hostel,** Rte. 2, P.O. Box 449, Galax 24333 (236-4962), rests only 100 ft. from the parkway at Mile 214.5. ($11, nonmembers $14, which includes $3 stamp redeemable for membership. This reproduction of a 1690 colonial building houses 22 beds and is located in the world capital of old-time mountain music. (Lockout 9:30am-5pm, curfew 11pm. Open Feb.-Dec.) (For North Carolina hostels, see Asheville and Boone, NC.) There are nine **campgrounds** along the parkway, each with water and restrooms, located at Miles 61, 86, 120, 167, 239, 297, 316, 339, and 408. (Fee $9, reservations not accepted.) Contact the parkway for info on free backcountry and winter camping.

The cities and villages along the parkway offer a range of accommodations. For a complete listing, pick up a *Blue Ridge Parkway Directory* at one of the visitors centers. The communities listed have easy access to the parkway and many, such as Asheville, NC, Boone, NC, and Charlottesville, VA, have attractions of their own.

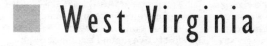 West Virginia

History and geography have conspired to keep West Virginia among the poorest and most isolated states in the Union. The Appalachians are at their highest and most rugged here, a fact which physically walls off the state. Historically, West Virginia mining was synonymous with the worst excesses of industrial capitalism. But West Virginia isn't without its proud moments. The area was one of the birthplaces of the American Labor movement, and the state itself was formed from the Virginian counties that remained loyal to the Union and shunned the Confederacy during the Civil War.

With the decline of heavy industry in the last 30 years, however, West Virginia has started cashing in on another resource—abundant natural beauty. Thanks to great skiing, hiking, fishing, and the best whitewater rafting in the eastern U.S., tourism has become one of the main sources of employment and revenue. West Virginians remain noticeably attached to traditional ways and despite the tourist onslaught, continue their long-standing penchant for hospitality and optimism.

PRACTICAL INFORMATION

Capital: Charleston.
Visitor Information: Travel Development Division, 1900 Washington St., State Capitol Complex, Bldg. 6, #B654, Charleston 25305 (348-2286 or 800-225-5982). **Division of Parks and Recreation,** 1900 Washington St., State Capitol Complex, Bldg. 6, #451, Charleston 25305. (800-CALL-WVA). **U.S. Forest Service Supervisor's Office,** 200 Sycamore St., Elkins 26241 (636-1800).
Time Zone: Eastern. **Postal Abbreviation:** WV
Sales Tax: 6%.
Area code: 304.

■■■ HARPER'S FERRY NATIONAL HISTORICAL PARK

Harper's Ferry sits at the junction of the Potomac and the Shenandoah rivers, and is itself a mixture of currents. A divided history and peaceful scenery intermingle at this beautiful spot. In 1859, the town witnessed abolitionist John Brown's famous attempt to capture the U.S. Armory, with the hope of launching a slave insurrection. Although General Robert E. Lee shot most of his raiders, including Brown's three sons, Brown's actions were not in vain. Brown was executed for treason against Virginia, but his acclaimed heroism helped spark the Civil War. Emerson said that Brown would "make the gallows as glorious as the cross," and Thoreau considered Brown a "crucified hero." Brown became a symbol dividing North from South. Yet aside from its bloody past, Harper's Ferry rests in a spectacular location and provides wonderful hiking, biking, canoeing, floating, and plain old gazing. Thomas Jefferson called the view from a Harper's Ferry overlook "worth a voyage across the Atlantic."

Practical Information Make your first stop at the **visitors center** (535-6298), just inside the park entrance off Rte. 340, and get maps and info about the park. The visitors center also provides free 30- to 90-min. **tours** guided by park rangers (in summer daily 10am-3pm) and occasional summer evening programs. If you drive, park near the visitors center; you'll get ticketed any closer to town. A shuttle bus between the parking lot and Shenandoah St. in town runs every 15 min. (Park and visitors center open daily 8am-5pm; Sept.-May 8am-5pm. $5 per car, $3 per hiker or bicyclist; good for 7 consecutive days.) **Amtrak** (800-872-7245) goes to Harper's Ferry from Washington, D.C. once a day (call for reservations, $14). Cheaper than Amtrak is the **Maryland Rail Commuter (MARC)** (800-325-7245), which runs (Mon.-Fri.) in the morning and three return times in the afternoon. ($6.75; seniors, disabled, children 5-15 $3.50; ticket office open Mon., Wed., and Fri. 6-9pm, Tues. and Thurs., 5-8am.) The closest **Greyhound** stations are ½-hr. drives away in Winchester, VA, and Frederick, MD. **River & Trail Outfitters,** 604 Valley Rd. at Rte. 340, (695-5177), at the blinking light, rents canoes, inner tubes, and rafts, and organizes guided trips (canoes $45 per day person, raft trips $28.50 per person, tubing $22.50 per day). In winter it runs cross-country skiing trips. Harper's Ferry's **ZIP code:** 25425; **area code:** 304. Knoxville, MD's **ZIP code:** 21758; **area code:** 301.

Accommodations and Food Hikers can try the **Harper's Ferry Hostel (HI-AYH),** 19123 Sandy Hook Rd. (301-834-7652), at Keep Tryst Rd. in Knoxville, MD, 2 mi. from Harper's Ferry, WV. This former auction house above the Potomac has 36 beds in two dormitory rooms. (Lockout 9:30am-5pm. Check-in 5-9pm. Curfew 11pm. Limited parking. $9, nonmembers $12. Camping $4, nonmembers $7.)

Camp free along the C&O Canal, where sites are 5 mi. apart, or in one of the five Maryland state-park campgrounds within 30 miles of Harper's Ferry. **Greenbrier State Park** (301-791-4767), a few mi. north of Boonsboro on Rte. 66 between exits 35 and 42 on I-70 (sites for $12; open April-Nov.)is a good bet for campers. Try the much closer **Camp Resort** (535-6895), on Rte. 3, adjacent to the entrance of Harper's Ferry National Historical Park (sites $20 for 2 people, with water and electricity $23; $4 per additional person, under 17 $2; registration fee $3 per person; open April-Oct.).

On High St. off Shenadoah St., you'll overload on "old tyme" crafts and souvenir shops. Instead, try **Potomac St.** for food. Both on Potomac, the **Little Ponderosa,** (535-2168) Potomac St., serves barbecue in a little red train car ($5-7; open Mon.-Thurs. 8am-5pm, Fri. 8am-8pm, Sat.-Sun. 7:30am-6pm.), and the **Back Street Café** (725-8019) has burgers and hot dogs for under $2.25 (open daily 10am-5pm).

Sights and Activities Recalling the days when the town flourished with a population of 3,200 (today only 360), **Harper's Ferry National Historical Park** has restored many of the town's buildings to their original, 19th-century form, including a renovated blacksmith's shop, ready-made clothing store, and general store. High St. holds some of the more interesting exhibits. **Black Voices** uses narration on phones to tell the story of the black population of Harper's Ferry. The **Civil War Story** plots the town's Civil War role with displays and a 20-ft. timeline. The Backstreet Café (see above) also doubles as an offbeat guide service; "Ghost Tours" of the town are offered weekend nights (tours May-Nov. 8 Fri.-Sun. 8pm; reservations recommended in Oct; $2).

The stairs on High St. follow the Appalachian Trail uphill to **upper Harper's Ferry.** The path passes **Harper's House,** home of town-founder Robert Harper, **St. Peter's Church,** where a sagacious pastor flew the Union Jack during the Civil War to protect the Church, and **Jefferson's Rock,** where Jefferson had his Atlantic-crossing inspiration. At the top of the climb moulders the abandoned campus of **Storer University,** one of America's first black colleges.

Those who prefer to mix nature and history can get both magnificent views and Civil War memories on the **Maryland Heights Trail,** the **Louden Heights Trail,** and in **Bolivar Heights.** Ask at the visitors center for details. The **Appalachian Trail Conference Headquarters** (535-6331), at Washington and Jackson St., offers trail information and a maildrop for hikers. (Open Mon.-Fri. 9am-5pm, Sat.-Sun. 9am-4pm; Nov.-April Mon.-Fri. 9am-5pm. Membership $25, seniors and students $18.

Write to P.O. Box 807 or call.) The less adventurous can walk along the **Chesapeake & Ohio Canal Towpath**.

Antietam National Battlefield A few miles north of Harper's Ferry, the bloodiest one-day battle of the Civil War was fought after skirmishing at Harper's Ferry. On September 17, 1862, 12,410 Union and 10,700 Confederate soldiers lost their lives as Confederate General Robert E. Lee tried and failed to overcome the army of Union General George B. McClellan. McClellan's typical failure to follow the retreating Confederates and crush them decisively tainted the victory, but the nominal Union triumph provided President Lincoln with the opportunity to issue the Emancipation Proclamation, freeing all slaves in those states still in rebellion against the United States on January 1, 1863. The **visitors center** (301-432-5124) has a museum of artifacts used in the battle, free maps for self-guided tours of the battlefield, tapes for rent ($4) with a detailed account of the battle, and an introductory film on the battle (film 9am-5pm on the hr.; center open daily 8:30am-6pm; battlefield fee $2, family $4). To get to Antietam from Harper's Ferry, take Rte. 340 N. to Rte. 67 heading toward Boonsboro. Stay on Rte. 67 N. until you reach Rte. 65; follow 65 to Antietam.

■■■ NEW RIVER GORGE

The New River Gorge is a mixture of raw beauty, raw resources, and raw power. The land has seen decades of environmental pillaging at the hands of coal magnates and timber barons who bled the natural abundance of the region until the coal and timber disappeared in the early and middle parts of this century. Today, the park capitalizes on its greatest resource: natural beauty. One of the oldest rivers in the world, the New River, cuts a narrow gouge in the Appalachian Mountains. The valley walls tower to an average of 1000 ft. above the river and whitewater that attracts rafters from across the country. The **New River Gorge National Park** protects the area and oversees the fishing, hiking, climbing, and boating that go on in the gorge. The park operates three visitors centers: **Canyon Rim,** off Rte. 19 near Fayatteville (574-2115); **Grandville,** Rte. 9 near Beckley (763-3715); **Hinton,** Rte. 20 (466-0417). Canyon Rim is at the northern extreme of the park and is the most full service center. They have info on all activities in the park, including free, detailed hiking guides, and an 11 minute slide presentation that's not to be missed. (Open June-Aug. daily 9am-8pm; Sept.-May daily 9am-5pm.) Popular gorge activities include rock climbing the superior walls of the gorge, mountain biking, and canoeing. There are also a number of excellent hiking trails in the park, among them the **Kaymoor Trail,** which is a 1.8 mile hike into the abandoned town and mines of Kaymoor. Complete information on all activities is at the visitors center.

The main draw to the area is **whitewater rafting.** Nearly 20 outfitters operate on the New River and the nearby Gauley River and rafting has risen to become one of the state's leading industries. All of the outfitters can be contacted by calling 800-225-5982. The best deal on the river is the express trip run by **American Whitewater Tours,** Rte. 1, Fayatteville (574-3655 or 800-346-7238). These trips skip the overpriced cold cut lunch and the waterfights and just run that baby. Trip takes 2½ to three hours in the summer, 45 min. in the spring; four trips on the New River daily ($39, $49 Saturday). American Whitewater also runs express trips on the rowdier **Gauley River,** which is only open six weeks in the fall. Some of the country's wildest whitewater is on the Upper Gauley. ($55 Sun.-Mon., $65 Sat.; experience required. A complete list of outfitters is available at the visitors center.

The natural beauty of the gorge is complemented by the engineered grace of the **New River Gorge Bridge,** which ferries Rte. 19 across the river at the park's northern end. It is definitely worth the walk down to the overlook at the Canyon Rim Visitors Center for a look. On **Bridge Day,** the third Saturday of October, you can walk across the bridge and parachute off it. From high above ground, you can go subterranean at the **Beckly Exhibition Coal Mine,** New River Park (256-1747), in Beckley.

Old time coal miners lead you down into the actual mine. (Open April-Oct. daily 10am-5:30pm. $5, kids $3.) The best money you can spend in the area, however, is out at the **Fayatte Airport**, Nickellville Rd. in Fayetteville. Built, owned, and operated by "five dollar" Frank, the airport is home to the small planes Frank uses to give tours of the New River Gorge for $5. Frank is the self-described Hillbilly #1 and will give you his unique perspective on local politics and foreign policy or recite poetry (his own or requests). Don't be alarmed by the gas gauge that registers an eighth of a tank. It's plenty . . .

Camping abounds in the area. Many of the raft companies operate private campgrounds and four public campgrounds are scattered in the general area. The most central is **Babcock State Park** (800-225-5982) Rte. 41, south of U.S. 60, 15 miles west of Rainelle. Shaded, sometimes slanted sites ($10). Backcountry camping in the park is free. stop by the visitors center for more info. **Greyhound** runs to Beckley. 105 Third St. (253-8333; open Mon.-Fri. 7am-8:15pm, Sat. 7-9am and 4:30-8:15pm). **Amtrak** serves Prince, Rte. 41 north (253-6651). Trains run Sun., Wed., and Fri. (open Sun., Wed., and Fri. 9am-1pm. Thurs. and Sat. 7am-3:30pm.) **Area code:** 304.

■■■ MONONGAHELA NATIONAL FOREST

Mammoth **Monongahela National Forest,** popular with canoers and spelunkers, enshrouds deer, bears, wild turkeys, and magnificent limestone caverns. But camping is the main attraction here. 600 miles of prize hiking trails and over 500 campsites to lure the outdoor adventurer. The forest is divided into six districts, each with its own campground and recreation area. A complete list of sites and fees can be obtained by contacting the forest **Supervisor's Office,** Monongahela National Forest, 200 Sycamore St., Elkins, WV 26241-3962 (636-1800; open Mon.-Fri. 8am-4:45pm). Base prices for established campsites are $12 or less, but the bold can sleep in the backcountry for free. If you're going into the back country, drop by the **Cranberry Visitor's Center** (304-653-4826), at the junction of Rte. 150 and Rte. 39/55; they like to know you're out there (open June-Aug. daily 8am-4:30pm; Sept.-May Mon.-Fri. 8am-4:30pm). Sites with electricity or group facilities will cost $5-10 extra. Much of West Virginia's most scenic country is encompassed here, relatively unspoiled by noisy crowds. The forest's **Lake Sherwood Area** (536-3660), 25 mi. north of I-64 on Rte. 92, in the south of the Forest, offers fishing, hunting, swimming, hiking, and boating, as well as campgrounds, mostly undisturbed by roving Merry Men. The campsites often fill on summer weekends. (2-week maximum stay. Sites $12.) **Cranberry Mountain** (846-2695), in the Gauley district approx. 6 mi. west of U.S. 219 on Rte. 39/55, has campgrounds (sites $5) and hiking trails through cranberry bogs. If you prefer something slightly more civilized, the **Middle Mountain Cabins,** Rte. 10 (636-1800), offer fireplaces, kitchen facilities, drinking water, and resident field mice. There are three cabins that sleep a total of 11 people and are rented as a group, regardless of whether all the cabins will be in use. Call 456-3335 for reservations ($30 per night, $168 per week; one week maximum stay; open May-Oct).

The only public transportation into the forest area comes into White Sulphur Springs at the forest's southern extreme. **Greyhound** has a flag stop at the Village Inn, 38 W. Main St. (one eastbound and one westbound bus per day). **Amtrak** comes in to an unmanned station on W. Main St. across from the Greenbriar on Sun., Wed., and Fri. (Washington $48, Charlottesville $26).

Kentucky

Kentucky's intermediary position between the North and South and between the East and Midwest lends the state more than its share of paradoxes. Although Kentucky is renowned for its bourbon distilleries, dry laws prevent the purchase of liquor in 90 of the state's 120 counties. Much of the countryside is genuine Appalachia, with problems still lingering from mining and 19th-century industrialization; gracious Southern-style mansions rise amidst this crushing penury. Despite borders on seven different states, about 75% of Kentucky's residents were born in-state. Even its signature city, Louisville, has a complex identity. It hosts the aristocratic, eminently Southern Kentucky Derby but is also an important site for labor historians—the legacy of the coal boom during World War I.

PRACTICAL INFORMATION

Capital: Frankfort.
Kentucky Department of Travel Development, 500 Metro St., #2200, Frankfort 40601 (502-564-4930 or 800-225-8747). **Department of Parks,** 500 Metro St., #1000, Frankfort 40601-1974 (800-255-7275).
Time Zones: Eastern and Central. **Postal Abbreviation:** KY
Sales Tax: 6%.

■■■ LOUISVILLE

Perched on the Ohio River, hovering between the North and the South, Louisville (LOU-uh-vul) is an immigrant town imbued with both grace and industry as beautiful Victorian neighborhoods surround smokestacks and the enormous meat-packing district of Butchertown. This laid-back city has riverfront parks and excellent cultural attractions fostered by the University of Louisville. The year's main event is undoubtedly the Kentucky Derby, the nation's most prestigious horse race. The Derby caps a week-long extravaganza which lures over half a million visitors who pay through the teeth for a week-long carnival, fashion display, and equestrian show, all culminating in a two-minute gallop that you'll miss if you're standing in line for mint juleps. The $15 million wagered on Derby Day alone proves that Kentuckians are deadly serious about their racing. An innovative place, Louisville was also home of John Colgan, the inventor of chewing gum, and Thomas Edison, inventor of just about everything else.

PRACTICAL INFORMATION

Emergency: 911.
Visitor Information: Louisville Convention and Visitors Bureau, 400 S. 1st St. (584-2121; 800-633-3384 outside Louisville; 800-626-5646 outside KY), at Liberty downtown. The standard goodies, including some bus schedules. Open Mon.-Fri. 8:30am-5pm, Sat. 9am-4pm, Sun. 11am-4pm. Visitors centers also in Standiford Field airport and in the Galleria Mall at 4th and Liberty St. downtown.
Traveler's Aid: 584-8186. Open Mon.-Fri. 9:30am-5pm.
Airport: Standiford Field (367-4636), 15 min. south of downtown on I-65. Take bus #2 into the city.
Greyhound: 720 W. Muhammad Ali Blvd. (800-231-2222), at 7th St. To: Indianapolis (8 per day, 2 hr., $21); Cincinnati (6 per day, 2 hr., $18); Chicago (8 per day, 6 hr., $57, $29 special); Nashville (12 per day, 3 hr., $29); Lexington (1 per day, 2 hr., $13.50). Storage lockers $1 first day, $3 per additional day. Open 24 hrs.
Public Transport: Transit Authority River City (TARC), 585-1234. Extensive system of thoroughly air-conditioned buses serves most of the metro area; buses run daily, some 4am-1am. Fare 80¢ during peak hours (Mon.-Fri. 6:30-8:30am and

3:30-5:30pm), 50¢ other times. Disabled access. Also runs a trolley on 4th Ave. from River Rd. to Broadway (free).

Taxi: Yellow Cab, 636-5511. Base fare $1.50 plus $1.50 per mi.

Car Rental: Dollar Rent-a-Car (366-6944), in Standiford Field airport. Weekends from $27 per day, weekdays $45. Must be 21 with credit card. Additional $6 per day for ages under 25. Open daily 6am-midnight. **Budget Rent-a-Car,** 4330 Crittenden Dr. (363-4300). From $40 per day, from $27 on weekends. Must be 21 with a major credit card or 25 without one. Open daily 6:30am-9pm.

Help Lines: Rape Hot Line, 581-7273. **Crisis Center,** 589-4313. Both 24 hrs. **Gay/Lesbian Hotline,** 897-2475. Open daily. 6-10pm.

Time Zone: Eastern.

Post Office: 1420 Gardner Lane (454-1650). Take the Louisville Zoo exit off I-264. Open Mon.-Fri. 7:30am-7pm, Sat. 7:30am-1pm. **ZIP code:** 40231.

Area Code: 502.

Major highways through the city include I-65 (north-south expressway), I-71, and I-64. The **Watterson Expressway,** also called I-264, is an easily accessible freeway that circles the city. The central downtown area is defined north-south by **Main Street** and **Broadway,** and east-west by **Preston** and **19th Street.**

Aside from theater and riverfront attractions, much activity in Louisville takes place outside the central city, but the fairly extensive bus system goes to all major areas. Call TARC (see above) for help since written schedules are incomplete and sometimes confusing.

ACCOMMODATIONS

Though easy to find, accommodations in Louisville are not particularly cheap. If you want a bed during Derby Week, make a reservation at least six months to a year in advance; be prepared to pay high prices. The visitors center (see Practical Information above) will help after March 13. If you don't choose one of the few affordable downtown options, try one of the many cheap motels that line I-65 just north of town. **Kentucky Homes Bed and Breakfast** (635-7341) offers stays in private homes from $65. Call seven to ten days ahead. **Newburg** (6 mi. away) and **Bardstown** (39 mi. away) are also likely spots for budget accommodations.

Collier's Motor Court, 4812 Bardstown Rd. (499-1238), south of I-264. 30 min. from downtown by car, or take bus #17. Inconvenient, but well-maintained and cheap. Singles $34. Doubles $38.50.

Motel 6, 3304 Bardstown Rd. (456-2861), is in the middle of the heavy traffic zone near the junction of Bardstown Rd. and 264. Noisy, but they do leave that light on for you. Prices start at a hard-to-beat $25.

KOA, 900 Marriot Dr., Clarksville, IN (812-282-4474), across the river from downtown. Follow I-65 north across the bridge and take the Stansifer Ave. exit. A great place to stay if only for the free use of the next door motel pool, grocery, playground, mini-golf and a fishing lake across the street. Sites $6 for 2 people. Each additional person $4, under 18 $2.50. Kamping kabins (for 2) $29.50. RV sites $21.

FOOD

Louisville's chefs whip up a wide variety of cuisines, though prices can be steep. Butchertown and the Churchill Downs area have several cheap delis and pizza places. **Bardstown Rd.** near Eastern Pkwy. offers cafés, budget pizzas, and more expensive French cuisine.

The Rudyard Kipling, 422 W. Oak St. (636-1311), just south of downtown. Take bus #4. Eclectic menu includes French, Mexican, and vegetarian entrees, Kentucky burgoo (a regional stew), and other creative fare ($5-13). Half-jungle, half-back porch. Fun and easy-going. Nightly entertainment is mainly music (ranging from Celtic to bluegrass to reggae) with an occasional poetry reading piece. Call for events calender. Open Mon.-Thurs. 11:30am-2pm and 5:30pm-midnight, Fri. 11:30am-around midnight, Sat. 5:30pm-midnight.

Ditto's, 1114 Bardstown Rd. (581-9129). Large burgers ($4-5.50), pastas ($5-5.50) and delicious pizzas ($6) served in a spacious area with eclectic dino deco. Open Mon.-Thurs. 11am-11pm, Fri.-Sat. 11am-midnight, Sun. 9am-10pm.

Pita Palace, 2345 Frankfort Ave. (899-7396). A hole-in-the-wall Middle Eastern treat serving cheap and tasty cuisine (falafel or hummus $1.80).

Miller's Cafeteria, 429 S. 2nd St. (582-9135), downtown. Serve yourself a full breakfast or lunch (entree, pie, 2 vegetables, and drink) for $3-4. Big, comfortable dining room built in 1826 is barely older than most of the customers. Open Mon.-Fri. 7am-2:30pm, Sun. 10am-2:30pm.

Highland Grunds, 919 Baxter Ave. (459-6478), rises above other Louisville coffeehouses due to the theater in the back. Free entertainment most nights. During the weekly Biff Banger Show throw sponges are $1. (Garden burger $3.50. Kiwi-tangerine quibell $1.) Open Mon.-Thurs. 8am-midnight, Fri. 8am-2am, Sat. 11am-2am, Sun. 11am-midnight.

NOT JUST A ONE-HORSE TOWN

Running along Baxter/Bardstown, bounded by Broadway and Trevilian Way in the south, is the **Highlands** strip. Bus #7 will take you to this "anti-mall" of unfranchised (well, *nothing* is immune to fast-food chains), independent establishments. Strollers are lured by cafés, pizza pubs, antique shops, record stores, and even an alternative culture outlet that allows you to surf the internet for 25¢ each 15 min. (**Diverse Media,** 1609 Bardstown Rd.; 459-5748). Between downtown and the university, **Old Louisville** harbors interesting Victorian architecture and a high crime rate. Farther south, in University of Louisville territory, the **J.B. Speed Art Museum,** 2035 S. 3rd St. (636-2893), has an impressive collection of Dutch paintings and tapestries, Renaissance and contemporary art, and a sculpture court. (Open Tues.-Sat. 10am-4pm, Sun. noon-5pm. Free. Parking $2. Take bus #4.)

The **Kentucky Center for the Arts,** 5 Riverfront Plaza (information and tickets 584-7777 or 800-283-7777), off Main St. is Louisville's newest entertainment complex. The KCA hosts the **Louisville Orchestra** and other major productions. The **Lonesome Pines** series showcases indigenous Kentucky music, including bluegrass. Ticket prices vary as wildly as the music, but student discounts are available.

Down a few stairs waits the **Belle of Louisville,** an authentic stern-wheeler. Ohio River cruises leave from Riverfront Plaza at the foot of 4th St. (Departs May 27-Sept. 2 Tues.-Sun. at 2pm. Sunset cruises Tues. and Thurs. 7-9pm; nighttime dance cruise Sat. 8:30-11:30pm. Boarding begins 1 hr. before the ship leaves; arrive early especially in July. $7, seniors $6, under 13 $3. Dance cruise $12.)

The **Louisville Science Center,** 727 W. Main St. (561-6100), downtown, emphasizes hands-on exhibits. Press your face against an Apollo space capsule, then settle back and enjoy the four-story screen at the new IMAX theater. (Open Mon.-Thurs. 10am-5pm, Fri.-Sat. 10am-9pm, Sun. noon-5pm. $6.50, kids $5; price includes IMAX tickets.) The **Louisville Zoo,** 1100 Trevilian Way (459-2181), between Newbury and Poplar Level Rd. across I-264 from Louisville Downs (take bus #18 or 43), exhibits the animals in neo-natural settings. Ride on an elephant's back or on the tiny train that circles the zoo. (Open daily 10am-6pm; Sept.-April 10am-4pm. Last entry 1 hr. before closing. $5.50, seniors $3.50, kids $2.75.)

Downtown is the **Actors Theater,** 316 W. Main St. (584-1265), a Tony award-winning repertory company, giving performances September to mid-June at 8pm and some matinees. (Tickets start at $15, with $7 student and senior rush tickets available 15 min. before each show.) Bring a picnic dinner to **Shakespeare in the Park** (583-8738), in Central Park, weekends June 19 to August 4. (Performances at 8:30pm.) Call the **Louisville Visual Arts Association,** 3005 Upper River Rd. (896-2146), for information on local artists' shows and events.

Butchertown Pub, 1335 Story Ave. (583-2242), has three stages where solid original music from local bands and national labels can be heard (open Mon. 4-10pm, Tues. 4pm-1am, Wed.-Sat. 4pm-2am. Cover free-$3).**The Brewery,** 426 Baxter Ave.

(583-3420), hosts folks like the Proclaimers and the Smithereens (open Sun.-Thurs. 11am-2am, Fri.-Sat. 11am-4am. Cover for live shows only.) **Phoenix Hill Tavern,** 644 Baxter Ave. (589-4957), cooks with blues and rock, scarce all-ages shows (open Wed.-Thurs. and Sat.-Sun. 8pm-4am, Fri. 5pm-4am, cover varies). Members of the Techno Alliance take heart, **Sparks,** 104 W. Main St. (587-8566), throbs and thumps til the early morn (open Sun.-Sat. 10pm-4am, cover Fri.-Sat. $3-5, Sun. $2).

IN THE NEIGH-BORHOOD

Even if you miss the Kentucky Derby, you can still visit **Churchill Downs,** 700 Central Ave. (636-4400), 3 mi. south of downtown. Take bus #4 (4th St.) to Central Ave. Bet, watch a race, or just admire the twin spires, colonial columns, gardens, and sheer scale of the track. (Grounds open in racing season daily 10am-4pm. Races April-June Tues.-Fri. 3-7:30pm, Sat.-Sun. 1-6pm; Oct.-Nov. Tues.-Sun. 1-6pm. Grandstand seats $2.50, clubhouse $3.50, reserved clubhouse $5.50. Parking $2.)

The **Kentucky Derby Festival** commences the week before the Derby and climaxes with the prestigious **Run for the Roses** the first Saturday in May. Balloon and steamboat races, concerts, and parades fill the week. Tickets for the Derby have a five-year waiting list. On Derby morning tickets are sold for standing-room-only spots in the grandstand or infield. Get in line early lest the other 80,000 spectators get there first.

The **Kentucky Derby Museum** (637-1111) at Churchill Downs offers a slide presentation on a 360° screen, tours of the stadium, profiles of famous stables and trainers (including the African-Americans who dominated racing early on), a simulated horse-race for betting practice, and tips on exactly what makes a horse a "sure thing." (Open daily 9am-5pm. $4, seniors $3, ages 5-12 $1.50, under 5 free.)

The **Louisville Downs,** 4520 Poplar Level Rd. (964-6415), south of I-264, hosts harness racing most of the year. (There are three meets: July-Sept. Mon.-Sat., Sept.-Oct. and Dec.-April Tues.-Sat. Post time 7:30pm; 10-12 races per night. $3.50 clubhouse, $2.50 grandstand. Minimum bet $2. Parking $2. Take bus #43 from downtown.)

If you're tired of spectating, go on a trail ride at **Iroquois Riding Stable,** 5216 New Cut Rd. (363-9159; $10 per hr.). Take 3rd St. south to Southern Parkway or ride bus #4 or 6 to Iroquois Park. **Hillerich and Bradsby Co.,** 1525 Charleston-New Albany Rd., Jeffersonville, IN (585-5226), 6 mi. north of Louisville, manufactures the famous "Louisville Slugger" baseball bat. (Go north on I-65 to exit for Rte. 131, then turn east. Tours Mon.-Fri. 8-10am and 1-2pm on the hr. except on national holidays and Good Friday. Free.)

■ NEAR LOUISVILLE: BARDSTOWN, MAMMOTH CAVE, AND HONEST ABE

Bardstown Kentucky's second oldest city, hosts **The Stephen Foster Story** (800-626-1563 or 348-5971), a mawkish, heavily promoted outdoor musical about America's first major songwriter, the author of "My Old Kentucky Home." (Performances mid-June-Labor Day Tues.-Sun. at 8:30pm, plus Sat. at 3pm. $12, $6 for ages 12 and under).

In 1791, Kentucky Baptist Reverend Elijah Craig left a fire unattended. He was heating oak boards in which to barrel his aging whiskey. He returned, undaunted, and built and used a charred barrel. Thus, bourbon was born, and Bardstown became the "Bourbon Captial of the World." Ninety percent of the nation's bourbon hails from Kentucky, and 60% of that is distilled in Nelson and Bullitt Counties. At **Jim Beam's American Outpost** (543-9877), in Clermont, 15 mi. west of Bardstown, Booker Noe, Jim Beam's grandson and current "master distiller," narrates a film about bourbon. Don't miss the free lemonade and sampler bourbon candies. From Louisville, take I-65 south to exit 112, then Rte. 245 east for 1½ mi. (Open Mon.-Sat. 9am-4:30pm, Sun. 1-4pm. Free.) You can't actually tour Beam's huge distillery, but you can visit the **Maker's Mark Distillery** (865-2099), in Loretto, 19 mi. southeast of Bardstown, for an investigation of 19th-century bourbon production. Take Rte. 49

south to Rte. 52 east. (Tours Mon.-Sat. every hr. on the ½ hr. 10:30am-3:30pm; Jan.-Feb. Mon.-Fri. only. Free.) Neither site has a license to sell its liquors. The **Bardstown Visitors Center,** 107 E. Stephen Foster Ave. (348-4877 or 800-638-4877), gives a 1½ hr. free tour, taking visitors by **Old Kentucky Home** and **Heaven Hill Distillery** in an open-air trolley. (Summer only 9:30am-1:30pm; center open Mon.-Sat. 8am-7pm, Sun. noon-5pm, off-season Mon.-Sat. 8am-5pm.)

Mammoth Cave Hundreds of enormous caves and narrow passageways wind through **Mammoth Cave National Park** (758-2328 or 800-967-2283), 80 mi. south of Louisville off I-65, west on Rte. 70. Mammoth Cave comprises the world's longest network of cavern corridors—over 325 mi. in length. Devoted spelunkers (ages 16 and over) will want to try the 6-hour "Wild Cave Tour" in summer ($25); also available are 2-hour, 2-mi. historical walking tours ($4, seniors and kids $2) and 90-min. tours for people with disabilities ($4). Since the caves stay 54°F year-round, bring a sweater. (**Visitors center** open daily 7:30am-7:30pm; off-season 7:30am-5:30pm.) **Greyhound** serves **Cave City,** just east of I-65 on Rte. 70, but the national park still lies miles away. **Gray Line** (637-6511; ask for the Gray Line) gives tours for groups of more than five people ($30 per person) and bus rides to the caves; call a few days ahead (tours April 10-Labor Day).

Abraham Lincoln's Birthplace This national historic site sits 45 mi. south of Louisville near Hodgenville on U.S. 31 east. From Louisville, take I-65 down to Rte. 61; public transportation does not serve the area. Fifty-six steps representing the 56 years of Lincoln's tragically foreshortened life lead up to a stone monument sheltering the small log cabin that was the scene of his birth. Only a few of the Lincoln logs that you see are believed to be original. A plodding film describes Lincoln's ties to Kentucky. (358-3874; open June-Aug. daily 8am-6:45pm; Labor Day-Oct. and May 8am-5:45pm; Nov.-April 8am-4:45pm. Free.)

■■■ LEXINGTON

Kentucky's second-largest city, Lexington is rich in Southern heritage, and even recent growth spurts have not changed its atmosphere from town to city, nor have they divorced it from the rest of the largely rural state. Historic mansions downtown aren't overshadowed by skyscrapers, and a 20-min. drive from the city will set you squarely in bluegrass country.

Like the rest of Kentucky, Lexington is horse-crazy—the Kentucky Horse Park is heavily advertised, and the shopping complexes and "lite" industries whose presence clutters the outskirts of town still share space with quaint, green, rolling horse farms. The 150-odd farms gracing the Lexington area have nurtured such equine greats as Citation, Lucky Debonair, Majestic Prince, and Whirlaway.

PRACTICAL INFORMATION

Emergency: 911.

Visitor Information: Greater Lexington Convention and Visitors Bureau, 430 W. Vine St. (800-848-1224 or 233-1221), in the civic center. Brochures and maps. Open Mon.-Fri. 8:30am-5pm, Sat. 10am-5pm. Information centers also located at I-75 north and south of Lexington.

Airport: Blue Grass Field, 4000 Versailles Rd. (255-7218). Serves regional airlines/flights; often easier to fly to Louisville's Standiford Field.

Greyhound: 477 New Circle Rd. N.W. (299-8804). Lets passengers off north of Main St. Take Lex-Tran bus #6 downtown. Open daily 7:30am-11:00pm. To: Louisville (1 per day, 1½ hr., $16); Cincinnati (5 per day, 1½ hr., $18); Knoxville (4 per day, 3 hr., $41).

Public Transport: Lex-Tran, 109 W. London Ave. (253-4636). Modest system serving the university and city outskirts. Buses leave from the **Transit Center,**

220 W. Vine St. between Limestone and Quality. Fare 80¢, transfers free. Bus service can be erratic but is continuous.

Taxi: Lexington Yellow Cab, 231-8294. Base fare $1.90 plus $1.35 per mi.

Transportation for People with Disabilities: WHEELS, 233-3433. Open Mon.-Fri. 6:30am-11pm, Sat. 6:30-8pm. 24-hr. notice required.

Help Line: Rape Crisis, 253-2511. Open 24 hrs. **GLSO Gayline,** 231-0335.

Time Zone: Eastern.

Post Office: 1088 Nandino Blvd. (231-6700). Take bus #2. Open Mon.-Fri. 8:30am-5pm, Sat. 9am-1pm. **ZIP code:** 40511. General delivery at Barr and Limestone.

Area Code: 606.

New Circle Road highway (Rte. 4/U.S. 60 bypass), which is intersected by many roads that connect the downtown district to the surrounding towns, corrals the city. **High, Vine,** and **Main Streets** are the major east-west routes downtown; **Limestone Street** and **Broadway** the north-south thoroughfares.

ACCOMMODATIONS AND CAMPING

The concentration of horse-related wealth in the Lexington area tends to push accommodation prices up. The cheapest places are outside the city beyond New Circle Rd. **Dial-A-Accommodations,** 430 W. Vine St. #363 (233-7299), will locate and reserve a room free of charge in a requested area of town and price range. (Open Mon.-Fri. 8:30am-5pm, Sat. 10am-5pm.)

University of Kentucky, Apartment Housing, 700 Woodland Ave. (257-3721). Full kitchen and private bathroom in University of Kentucky apartments. Rooms also available during the school year, space permitting. Talk to Mrs. Anderson well in advance because rooms are sparse. You can only stay for a few days but the price ($21) is unbeatable. Call ahead on a weekday and explain that you only want a short stay; longer-term rentals are for U of K affiliates only.

Microtel, 2240 Buena Vista Dr. (299-9600), near I-75 and Winchester Rd. New, bright motel rooms. Singles $33.50. Doubles $39.

Bryan Station Inn, 273 New Circle Rd. (299-4162). Take bus #4 or Limestone St. north from downtown and turn right onto Rte. 4. Clean, pleasant rooms in the middle of a motel/fast-food strip. No phones. Singles or doubles $28. Rates decrease the longer you stay. Must be 21.

Kimball House Motel, 267 S. Limestone St. (252-9565), between downtown and the university. The grungy sign conceals a number of quiet rooms in the basement. Some singles (1st floor, no A/C, shared bath) $28. Ask for them specifically; they often fill by late afternoon. Otherwise, cheapest singles $34. Doubles $38. Key deposit $5. Parking in back.

Good, cheap **campgrounds** can be found around Lexington; unfortunately, you'll need a car to reach them. The **Kentucky Horse Park Campground,** 4089 Ironworks Pike (233-4303), 10 mi. north off I-75, has laundry, showers, tennis, basketball and volleyball courts, swimming pool, more lawn than shade, and a free shuttle to the KY Horse Park and Museum (see Horses and Seasonal Events). (2-week max. stay. Sites $10, with hookup $14.50.)

FOOD

Lexington specializes in good, down-home feed-bags, and the lefty (college) side of town contributes some vegetarian and other wholesome options.

Everybody's Natural Foods and Deli, 503 Euclid Ave. (255-4162). This pleasant health-food store has a few tables where they serve excellent gazpacho, sandwiches ($2.50-3.50), and a daily lunch special ($3.75). Open Mon.-Sat. 9am-8pm, Sun. noon-6pm.

Parkette Drive-In, 1216 New Circle Rd. (254-8723). 50s-style drive-up eatery. No rollerskates on the waitresses, though, as they bring out your "Poor Boy" ($2.50) or chicken boxed lunch. Usually empty, there are a few booths inside for folks without cars. (Open Mon.-Thurs. 5-11pm. Fri.-Sat. 6pm-1am.)

Alfalfa Restaurant, 557 S. Limestone St. (253-0014), across from Memorial Hall at the university. Take bus #2A. Fantastic international and veggie meals. Complete dinners with salad and bread under $10. Filling soups and salads from $2. Live music on weekends. Open for lunch Mon.-Fri. 11am-2pm, Sat.-Sun. 10am-2pm. Dinner Tues.-Thurs. 5:30-9pm, Fri.-Sat. 5:30-10pm.

Ramsey's Diner, 496 E. High St. (259-2708). Real Southern grease. Vegetarians beware: authenticity means that even the vegetables are cooked with pork parts. Sandwiches under $5, entrees around $8, 4 vegetables for $6. Open Mon.-Sat. 11am-1am, Sun. 11am-11pm.

SIGHTS AND NIGHTLIFE

To escape the stifling swamp conditions farther south, antebellum plantation owners built beautiful summer retreats in milder Lexington. The most attractive of these stately houses preen only a few blocks northeast of the town center in the **Gratz Park** area near the public library. In addition to their past, the wrap-around porches, wooden minarets, stone foundations, and rose-covered trellises distinguish these estates from the neighborhood's newer homes.

The **Hunt Morgan House,** 201 N. Mill St. (253-0362), stands at the end of the park across from the library. Built in 1814 by John Wesley Hunt, the first millionaire west of the Alleghenies, the house later witnessed the birth of Thomas Hunt Morgan, who won a Nobel Prize in 1933 for proving the existence of the gene. The house's most colorful inhabitant, however, was Confederate General John Hunt Morgan. Chased by Union troops, the general rode his horse up the front steps and into the house, leaned down to kiss his mother, and rode out the back door. What a guy. (Tours Tues.-Sat. 10am-4pm, Sun. 2-5pm. $4, kids $2.)

Kentucky's loyalties divided sharply in the Civil War. Mary Todd, who grew up five blocks from the Hunt-Morgan House, later married Abraham Lincoln. The **Mary Todd Lincoln House** is at 578 W. Main St. (233-9999; open April 1-Dec. 15 Tues.-Sat. 10am-4pm; $4, kids 6-12 $1).

In Victorian Square on the west side of downtown, the **Lexington Children's Museum,** 401 W. Main St. (258-3255), puts kids in a variety of simulated contexts for fun and undercover education. (Open Mon.-Fri. 10am-6pm, Sat. 10am-5pm, Sun. 1-5pm; early Sept.-late May closed Mon. Kids $1.50, grown-ups $2.50.) The **Lexington Cemetery,** 833 W. Main St. (255-5522), serves another stage in the life cycle. Henry Clay and John Hunt Morgan are buried here. (Open daily 8am-5pm. Free.) At the corner of Sycamore and Richmond Rd., you can admire **Ashland** (266-8581), the 20-acre homestead where statesman Henry Clay lived before he moved to the cemetery. The mansion's carved ash interior came from trees grown on the property. (Open Tues.-Sat. 10am-4:30pm, Sun. 1-4:30pm. $5, kids $2. Take bus #4A.)

The sprawling **University of Kentucky** (257-7173) gives free campus tours in "Old Blue," an English double-decker bus, at 10am and 2pm weekdays and on Saturday mornings (call 257-3595). The university's specialties include architecture and (surprise!) equine medicine. For updates of U of K's arts calendar, call 257-7173; for more info about campus attractions, call 257-3595.

Lexington's nightlife is pretty good for a town its size. **Sundance** showcases lively times and music at 509 W. Main St. (255-2822). **The Brewery** is a friendly country-Western bar (both open daily 8am-1am). **Comedy on Broadway,** 144 N. Broadway (259-0013), features stand-up comics most nights. **The Bar,** 224 E. Main St. (255-1551), is a disco popular with gays and lesbians. (Open Sun.-Fri. until 1:30am, Sat. until 3:30am. Cover $3 on weekends.) **The Wrocklage,** 361 W. Short St. (231-7655), serves up alternative and punkish rock, and **Lynagh's** (259-9944), in University Plaza at Woodland and Euclid St., is a great neighborhood pub with superlative burgers ($4.35) and live music Tues.-Sat. Meet fraternity-sorority types at **Two Keys Tavern,** 333 S. Limestone (254-5000). *Ace* magazine tells what to do in the area; *The*

Bar is a key to events in Lexington's substantial gay and lesbian community. The "Weekender" section of Friday's *Heraldleader* also has useful entertainment ideas.

HORSES AND SEASONAL EVENTS

A visit to Lexington is not complete without a close encounter of the quadruped kind. Try **Spendthrift Farm,** 884 Ironworks Pike (624-5590), 8 mi. northeast of downtown. (Free tours Feb.-July Mon.-Sat. 10am-noon; Aug.-Jan. Mon.-Sat. 10am-2pm. Take Broadway until it becomes Paris Pike, turn left onto Ironworks.)

The **Kentucky Horse Park,** 4089 Ironworks Pike (233-4303), exit 120, 10 mi. north on I-75, is a highly touristy state park with full facilities for equestrians, a museum, two films, and the Man O' War Monument. (Open daily 9am-5pm. $9, ages 7-12 $5. Horse-drawn vehicle tours included.) The **American Saddle Horse Museum** (259-2746), on the park grounds, continues the celebration of Lexington's favorite animal. (Open daily 9am-6pm; Labor Day-Memorial Day reduced hrs. $2, seniors $1.50, ages 7-12 $1.)

If horse racing is more your style, visit **Keeneland Race Track,** 4201 Versailles Rd. (254-3412 or 800-354-9092), west on U.S. 60. (Races Oct. and April; fall post time 1pm, spring post at 7:30pm; $2.50.) Workouts open to the public. The final prep race for the Kentucky Derby occurs here in April. The **Red Mile Harness Track,** 847 S. Broadway (255-0752; take bus #3 on S. Broadway), has racing April to June and also late September to early Oct. (Post time 7pm.) The crowds run the gamut from wholesome families to seasoned gamblers. ($3, programs $2; parking free.) Morning workouts (7:30am-noon) are open to the public in racing season.

In June, the **Festival of the Bluegrass,** at the Kentucky Horse Park, attracts thousands. Camping at the festival grounds is free. The **Lexington Junior League Horse Show** (mid-July; 252-1893), the largest outdoor show in the nation, unfolds its pageantry at the Red Mile (see above).

■ NEAR LEXINGTON

The Shakers, a 19th-century celibate religious sect, practiced the simple life between Harrodsburg and Lexington, about 25 mi. southwest on U.S. 68, at the **Shaker Village** (734-5411). The 5000-acre farm features 27 restored Shaker buildings. A tour includes demonstrations of everything from apple-butter-making to coopering (barrel-making). (Open daily 9am-6pm. $8.50, $4 for students 12-17, ages 6-11 $2.) Although the last Shaker to live here died in 1923, you can still eat and sleep in original though somewhat altered Shaker buildings. (Dinner $13-18. Singles $46-90. Doubles $56-100. All rooms have A/C and private bath. Reservations required.)

Nestled 32 mi. southeast of Lexington on U.S. 68 lies an architectural treasure known as **Harrodsburg.** Daniel Boone founded Fort Harrod in 1774, the oldest permanent English settlement west of the Alleghenies. The fort soon became Harrodsburg, but its legacy can be re-lived at **Old Fort Harrod State Park,** P.O. Box 156 (734-3314). At this active replica, crafts people clothed in 18th century garb demonstrate tasks such as blacksmithing and quilting. The sheep, turkey, and cattle in the fort corral, while clothed in authentic garb, appear to demonstrate very little. (Open 8:30am-5pm, off-season 8am-4:30pm; $3.50, 6-11 $1.) Downtown Harrodsburg invites you to take a historic walking tour in this small, well-preserved community. The comprehensive tour booklet comes complete with a glossary so you can distinguish the cornices from the cupolas in this rustic community. This and other goodies are available at the **visitors center,** corner of U.S. 68 and Main (606-734-2364). Greyhound bus #350 runs to Harrodsburg, 7 mi. from the village (see Lexington: Practical Information).

The **Red River Gorge,** in the northern section of the Daniel Boone National Forest, approximately 50 mi. southeast of Lexington, draws visitors from around the country. A day outing from Lexington will show why song and square dance have immortalized this spacious land of sandstone cliffs and stone arches. **Natural Bridge State Park** (663-2214), 2 mi. south of Slade, highlights the major attraction of the upper valley. The Red River Gorge highlights the lower valley. Greyhound bus #296 (see Lexington: Practical Information) will get you to Stanton (10 mi. west of Slade) and a **U.S. Forest Service Office** (663-2853). If you're driving, take the Mountain Parkway (south off I-64) straight to Slade, and explore the region bounded by the scenic loop road, Rte. 715. Camp at **Natural Bridge State Resort Park** (800-325-1710). The campground, complete with pool, facilities for disabled people, and organized square dances, hosts the **National Mountain Style Square Dance and Clogging Festival,** a celebration of Appalachian folk dances. (Square dance tickets $1-3. Tent sites $8.50, with hookup $10.50.)

In **Richmond,** exit 90 off I-75, is **White Hall** (623-9178), home of the abolitionist (not the boxer) Cassius M. Clay, Senator Henry Clay's cousin. This elegant mansion really consists of two houses, one Georgian and one Italianate. The 45-min. tour covers seven different living levels. (Open April-Oct. daily 9am-4:30pm; Labor Day-Oct. 31 Wed.-Sun; open briefly in winter for a Christmas celebration. Guided tours only. $3, under 13 $2, under 6 free.) The Richmond pre-packaged tourism experience also includes **Fort Boonesborough** (527-3328), a re-creation of one of Daniel Boone's forts. The park has samples of 18th-century crafts, a small museum, and films about the pioneers. (Open April-Aug. daily 9am-5:30pm; Sept.-Oct. Wed.-Sun. 9am-5:30pm. $4, ages 6-12 $2.50, under 6 free. Combination White Hall/Boonesborough tickets available.)

■■■ CUMBERLAND GAP

Stretching from Maine to Georgia, the majestic Appalachian Mountain Range proved to be a formidable obstacle to early American settlers, but not to buffalo. It was by following buffalo herds that the Native Americans learned of the Cumberland Gap, a natural break in the mountains allowing passage to the west. Frontiersman Daniel Boone and the Gap itself became famous when he blazed the Wilderness Trail through it in 1775, opening the west to colonization. Today, the **Cumberland Gap National Historic Park** sits on 20,000 acres shared by Kentucky, Virginia, and Tennessee. It is best reached by U.S. 25E from Kentucky, or U.S. 58 from Virginia. The Cumberland Gap **visitors center** (606-248-2817) on U.S. 2 SE in Middleboro, KY, presents a brief slide presentation and displays on the history of the Gap. The park and visitors center are open daily 8am-6pm, until 5pm in winter. Nearby Middleboro, KY has sparse accommodations. Newly refurbished **Parkview Motel** (606-248-4516), U.S.2 SE, delivers clean rooms with refrigerators and a view of the highway. (Singles $31, doubles $36.) The Park has a 160-site **campground** on U.S. 58 in Virginia. Primitive campground is accessible by foot (site $8, requires a permit). For more information contact: Superintendent, Cumberland Gap NHP, Box 1848, Middlesboro, KY 40965.

▪ Tennessee

Tennessee, the last state to secede from the Union and the first to rejoin, boasts a landscape noticeably free of the antebellum plantations that seem to blanket every other Southern state. Industry has been the moving force in this state rather than agriculture—the state leads the South in production of commercial machinery, chemicals, and electronics. Tennessee defies other regional stereotypes as well. In 1920, it provided the final vote needed to enshrine women's suffrage in the Constitution, and Oak Ridge—pivotal in the development of the A-bomb—still houses one of the world's most sophisticated military laboratories. Tennessee has also added to the musical culture of the world; country music twangs from Nashville, and the blues wail from Memphis. Both cities offer a veritable treasure trove of modern diversions for the tourist. Balance seems to be the rule in Tennessee—home to the famous original Jack Daniels whiskey distillery as well as the largest Bible producing business in the world. After a spell here, you too will be singin' "there ain't no place I'd rather be than the grand ol' state of Tennessee."

PRACTICAL INFORMATION

Capital: Nashville.
Visitor Information: Tennessee Dept. of Tourist Development, P.O. Box 23170, Nashville 37202 (741-2158). Open Mon.-Fri. 8am-4:30pm. **Tennessee State Parks Information,** 701 Broadway, Nashville 37203 (742-6667).
Time Zones: Central and Eastern. **Postal Abbreviation:** TN
Sales Tax: 5.5-8.25%.

■■■ NASHVILLE

Long-forgotten Francis Nash is one of only four Revolutionary War heroes honored with U.S. city names (the others being Washington, Wayne and Knox). Nashville has been the capital of Tennessee since 1843. Despite its minor link with America's fight for independence, Nashville is better known for its country music than for its foothold in history. Banjo pickin' and foot stompin' have entrenched themselves securely in Tennessee's central city, providing Nashville with non-stop performances and the Country Music Hall of Fame. Behind this musical harmony resonates "the Wall Street of the South," a slick financial hub. The city headquarters the Southern Baptists alongside centers of the fine arts and higher learning like Fisk University and Vanderbilt. Nashville is a large, eclectic, unapologetically heterogeneous place.

PRACTICAL INFORMATION

Emergency: 911.
Visitor Information: Nashville Area Chamber of Commerce, 161 4th Ave. N. (259-4700), between Commerce and Church St. downtown. Ask for the free *Hotel/Motel Guide,* the *Nashville Dining & Entertainment Guide*, and a *Calendar of Events*. Information booth in main lobby open Mon.-Fri. 8am-5pm. **Nashville Tourist Information Center,** (259-4747) I-65 at James Robertson Pkwy., exit 85, about ½ mi. east of the state capitol, just over the bridge. Take bus 3 ("Meridian") east on Broadway. Complete maps marked with all the attractions. Open daily 8am-8pm.
Traveler's Aid: (780-9471). Lost your wallet? Travelers checks? Plane ticket? This is the place to go. With characteristic Southern warmth, Traveler's Aid helps the stranded find their way home. Open Mon.-Fri. 8am-4pm.
Airport: Metropolitan (275-1675), 8 mi. south of downtown. Airport shuttle operating out of major downtown hotels. $8 one way, taxis $15-17, MTA buses at 75¢ are cheap but unreliable and infrequent.
Greyhound: 200 8th Ave. S. (800-231-2222), at Demonbreun St., 2 blocks south of Broadway downtown. Borders on a rough and rowdy neighborhood, but the station is bright, and open 24 hrs. One youth under 21 can travel free with each adult. *See Mileage Chart.*
Public Transport: Metropolitan Transit Authority (MTA) (242-4433). Buses operate Mon.-Fri. 5am-midnight, less frequent service Sat.-Sun. Fare $1.15, transfers 10¢. The **Nashville Trolley** (242-4433) runs daily starting at 11am in the downtown area every 10 min. for 75¢.
Taxi: Nashville Cab, 242-7070. 90¢ base fare, $1.50 each mi.
Car Rental: Alamo Rent-A-Car, (800-327-9633). At the airport. $30 per day, $20 per day on weekends. $6 per day extra for those under 25.
Help Lines: Crisis Line, 244-7444. **Rape Hotline,** 256-8526. Both open 24 hrs. **Gay and Lesbian Switchboard,** 297-0008, opens at 5pm.
Post Office: 901 Broadway (255-9447), across from the Park Plaza Hotel and next to Union Station. Open Mon.-Fri. 8am-6pm, Sat. 8am-noon. **ZIP code:** 37202.
Area Code: 615.

Nashville's streets are fickle: many are one-way, they are often interrupted by curving parkways, and the names constantly change without warning. **Broadway,** the main east-west thoroughfare, spawns **West End Avenue** just outside downtown at Vanderbilt University and I-40, and later becomes **Hillsboro Pike.** Downtown, numbered avenues run north-south, parallel to the Cumberland River. The curve of **James Robertson Parkway** encloses the north end, becoming **Main Street** on the other side of the river (later **Gallatin Pike**), and **McGavock St.** at the south end. The area south of Broadway between 2nd and 7th Ave., and the region north of James Robertson Parkway, are both unsafe at night.

ACCOMMODATIONS AND CAMPING

Finding a room in Nashville is not difficult, just expensive. Most cheap places are within 20 mi. of downtown. Make reservations well in advance, especially for weekend stays (which will take a bigger toll on your budget). A dense concentration of budget motels line **W. Trinity Lane** and **Brick Church Pike** at I-65, north of downtown, off exit 87B. Even cheaper hotels inhabit the area around **Dickerson Rd.** and **Murfreesboro,** but the neighborhood is seedy at best. Closer to downtown (but still seedy) are several motels huddled on **Interstate Dr.** just over the Woodland Street Bridge. **Bed and Breakfast of Middle Tennessee** (331-5244) offers singles for $30, and doubles for $50, kitchenettes, and free continental breakfast.

The Cumberland Inn (226-1600), I-65 North and Trinity Lane has cheerful, fragrant rooms with bright, modern furnishings, unlimited local calls, laundry facilities, and a free continental breakfast. No pets. Singles $31. Doubles $40. Prices rise on weekends.

The Liberty Inn, 2400 Brick Church (228-2567), has tables and chairs in each room. Stall showers only. Singles $32. Doubles $47. Prices increase on weekends.

Hallmark Inns, 309 Trinity (800-251-3294), has inns in the Nashville area. Free continental breakfast. Generally cheaper than national chains but fill quickly. Singles start at $28, doubles $50; prices may vary with location.

Motel 6, 3locations. 311 W. Trinity Lane (227-9696), at exit 87B off I-24/I-65; 323 Cartwright St., Goodlettsville (859-9674), off Long Hollow Pike west from I-65; 95 Wallace Rd. (333-9933), off exit 56 from I-24. Tidy rooms with stall showers, and free local calls. Singles $31.50. Doubles $36. 18 and under free with parents. Wallace St. location is slightly more expensive.

You can reach three campgrounds near Opryland USA via public transport from 5th St. For the **Fiddler's Inn North Campground** (885-1440, sites $19.50), the **Nashville Travel Park** (889-4225, site for 2 $19.50, full hookup $33), and the **Two Rivers Campground** (883-8559, $23 for 2 people with full hookup), take the Briley Pkwy. north to McGavock Pike, and exit west onto Music Valley Dr. Ten min. north of Opryland is the **Nashville KOA,** 708 N. Dickerson Rd. (859-0075), off of I-65 in Goodlettsville, exit 98 (sites $22 with full hookup).

FOOD

In Nashville, music even influences the local delicacies. Pick up a Goo-Goo cluster (peanuts and pecans, chocolate, caramel, and marshmallow), sold at practically any store, and you'll bite into the initials of the Grand Ole Opry. Pecan pie is another favorite dessert, perfect after spicy barbecue or fried chicken. Nashville's food, however, is hardly parochial, and the finger-lickin' traditional joints are interspersed with varied and affordable international cuisines. Restaurants for collegiate tastes and budgets cram West End Ave. and the 2000 block of Elliston Place, near Vanderbilt. The **farmers market,** north of the capitol between 3rd and 7th Ave., sells fresh fruits and vegetables until sunset.

Slice of Life, 1811 Division St. (329-2526), next to music studios. Yuppie hangout featuring fresh bread and wholesome Tex-Mex with a large vegetarian selection. Veggie chili ($4), carrot and kale juice ($2). Try the bakery for giant cookies and muffins ($1). Some are even macrobiotic. Open Mon. 7am-4pm, Tues.-Thurs. 7am-9pm, Fri. 7am-10pm, Sat. 8am-10pm, Sun. 8am-4pm. Favorable location for sighting country musicians.

Calypso, 2424 Elliston (321-3878), near Vanderbilt, and 4910 Thoroughbred in Brentwood (370-8033). Lively, fresh, and easy on the pocket. Tasty Caribbean food like Jamaican chicken, and corn and coconut muffins ($1.25). Open Mon.-Thurs. and Sat. 11am-9pm, Fri. 11am-10pm, Sun. noon-8pm.

The World's End, 1713 Church St. (329-3480). Huge, airy gay restaurant. Standard burgers and salads ($5-8). Open Sun.-Thurs. 4pm-12:30am, Fri.-Sat. 4pm-1:30am.

International Market, 2010-B Belmont Blvd. (297-4453). Asian grocery with a large Thai buffet ($4-6). Crowded at lunch. Open daily 10:30am-9pm.

Granite Falls, 2000 Broadway (327-9250). For a classier, if costlier, dining experience, Granite Falls offers herb-roasted chicken, grilled fish sandwiches, and other dishes ($6-12). Open daily 11am-11pm.

SIGHTS

Music Row, home of Nashville's signature industry, fiddles around Division and Demonbreun St. from 16th to 19th Ave. S., bounded to the south by Grand Ave. (take bus #3 to 17th Ave. and walk south). After surviving the mobs outside the **Country Music Hall of Fame,** 4 Music Sq. E. (256-1639), at Division St., you can marvel at classic memorabilia like Elvis' "solid gold" Cadillac, his 24-karat gold piano, as well as evocative photos from the early days of country music and aggressively colored outfits from more recent performances. Though Tennessee is the birthplace of bluegrass, the Hall of Fame shows off Cajun, cowboy, western-swing, and honky-tonk styles of country music as well. (Open Mon.-Sat. 8am-7pm, Sun. 9am-5pm.) Included in the admission is a tour of RCA's historic **Studio B,** where stars like Dolly Parton and Chet Atkins recorded their first hits. ($7.50, kids 6-16 $2, under 6 free.) When you want to record your own hit, the **Recording Studio of America,** 1510 Division St. (254-1282), underneath the **Barbara Mandrell Country Museum,** lets you do your own vocals on pre-recorded 24-track backgrounds to popular country and pop tunes. Choose a set and make a video, too. (Audio $13, video $20. Open Sun.-Thurs. 9am-6pm, Fri. and Sat. 9am-8pm.) For a taste of southern extravagance, marvel at Webb Pierce's Silver Dollar car (adorned with 150 silver dollars with a pistol as a hood ornament) at **World Famous Car Collectors' Hall of Fame,** 1534 Demonbreun St. (255-6804; open daily 8am-10pm; $5, kids 4-11 $3.25).

Centennial Park, a 15-min. walk west from Music Row along West End Ave.,will bring you to Nashville's pride and joy. The "Athens of the South" boasts a full-scale replica of the **Parthenon** (862-8431), complete with a towering Athena surrounded by her fellow Olympians. Originally built as a temporary exhibit for the Tennessee Centennial in 1897, the Parthenon met with such Olympian success that the model was rebuilt to last. The Nashville Parthenon also houses the **Cowan Collection of American Paintings** in the basement galleries, refreshing but erratic. Watch Shakespeare-in-the-park performed on the steps in mid-July and August. (Open Tues.-Sat. 9am-4:30pm, Sun. 12:30-4pm. $2.50, kids and seniors $1.25, under 4 free.) The park area also includes the **Upper Room Chapel Museum,** 1908 Grand St. (340-7200), off 21st Ave. S. The floor-to-ceiling stained glass window with over 9000 pieces of glass is spectacular. (Open Mon.-Sat. 8am-4:30pm.)

A walk through the downtown area reveals more of Nashville's eclectic architecture. The **Union Station Hotel,** at 1001 Broadway, next to the post office, displays a full stained-glass arched ceiling and evokes the glamour of turn-of-the-century railroad travel with old-time schedules and clocks. The **Ryman Auditorium,** 116 5th Ave. N. (254-1445), off Broadway at 5th, is better known as the "Mother Church of Country Music." In previous incarnations, it has housed a tabernacle and the Grand Ole Opry. (Tours daily 8:30am-4:30pm. $5, kids 6-12 $2.) Turn up 2nd Ave. from Broadway to study the cast-iron and masonry facades of handsome late 19th century commercial buildings. Now known as **Market Street,** the area has been gentrified with restaurants and nightspots.

The **Tennessee State Capitol,** (741-0830) Charlotte Ave., is the comely Greek Revival structure atop the hill next to downtown, offering free guided tours of, among other things, the tomb of James Knox Polk (tours hourly Mon.-Fri. 9-11am and 1-3pm). Across the street, the **Tennessee State Museum,** 505 Deaderick (741-2692), depicts the history of Tennessee from the early Native American era to the time of "overlander" pioneers. Imaginative and interactive displays enhance this sometimes whitewashed version of Tennessee history. (Open Tues.-Sat. 10am-5pm, Sun. 1-5pm. Free.)

The **Museum of Tobacco Art and History,** 800 Harrison St. (271-2349), off 8th Ave., attests to Tennessee's most important crop. From the dual-purpose Indian pipe/tomahawk (a slow and a quick way to death), to the giant glass-blown pipes, museum exhibits expound upon the unexpectedly captivating history of tobacco, pipes, and cigars. (Open Mon.-Sat. 9am-4pm. Free.)

Also check out Fisk University's **Van Vechten Gallery** (329-8543), corner of Jackson St. and D.B. Todd Blvd. off Jefferson St. (gallery entrance does not face street), which exhibits a distinguished collection of American art. The gallery owns a portion of the Alfred Steiglitz Collection, donated to Fisk by Georgia O'Keeffe, Steiglitz's partner. Other exhibits feature O'Keeffe's work and a range of photography and African art. (Open Tues.-Fri.10am-5pm, Sat.-Sun. 1-5pm. Free, but donations accepted.)

If you tire of the downtown area, rest at the **Cheekwood Botanical Gardens and Fine Arts Center** (356-8000) Forest Park Dr., 7 mi. southwest of town. The well-kept, leisurely, Japanese rose and English-style gardens are a welcome change from Nashville glitz. Take bus 3 ("West End/Belle Meade") from downtown to Belle Meade Blvd. and Page Rd. (Open Mon.-Sat. 9am-5pm, Sun. 1-5pm. $5, seniors and students $4, kids 7-17 $1.)

Dubbed "The Queen of Tennessee Plantations," the nearby **Belle Meade Mansion,** 5025 Harding Rd. (356-0501), provides a second respite. This 1853 plantation has the works: gorgeous grounds, smokehouse, dollhouse, and dairy (most buildings can be toured). Belle Meade was also the site of the nation's first thoroughbred and Tennessee walking horse breeding farm. (Two wonderful tours per hr. led by guides in period costumes; last tour at 4pm. Open Mon.-Sat. 9am-5pm, Sun. 1-5pm. $5.50, kids 13-18 $3.50, 6-12 $2.)

The **Hermitage** is at 4580 Rachel's Lane (889-2941); take exit 221 off I-40 (13 mi. from downtown). Andrew Jackson, the 7th U.S. president and famous populist, built his beautiful manor house atop 625 gloriously shaded acres. The grounds make an ideal spot for a picnic. Beware the crowds in the summer months. (Open daily 9am-5pm. $7, seniors $6.50, kids 6-18 $3.50.)

Set aside the first weekend in June for the outdoor **Summer Lights** downtown, when top rock, jazz, reggae, classical, and, of course, country performers, all jam simultaneously. (Open Mon.-Thurs. 4pm-12:30am.) For information on **Nashville Symphony** tickets and performances, call Ticketmaster (741-2787).

ENTERTAINMENT AND NIGHTLIFE

Whether it be a corner honkey-tonk joint or the Grand Ole Opry, Nashville offers a wealth of opportunities to hear country and western, jazz, rock, bluegrass, or folk. There are entertainment listings in the *Tennessean* on Friday and Sunday, and in the *Nashville Banner* Thursday afternoon.

The Nashville *Key,* available at the chamber of commerce, opens many entertainment doors. Comprehensive listings for all live music and events in the area abound in free copies of *Nashville Scene.* Muse over these publications plus many more at **Moskós,** 2204-B Elliston Place (327-2658), while stalling at their tasty muncheonette (open Mon.-Fri. 7am-midnight, Sat. 8am-midnight, Sun. 8:30am-midnight).

Opryland USA (889-6611) cross-pollinates Las Vegas schmaltz and Disneyland purity, or vice versa, with the best in country music thrown in. This amusement park contains all the requisite family attractions, from the Wabash Cannonball roller coaster to cotton candy, and it stages a dozen live music shows daily. Sometimes a soundtrack of piped-in country music cascades through the park. Tune your radio to 580AM for more info. (Open April-May Sat.-Sun.; May-early Oct. daily. $25, 2 days $38; kids 4-11 $14. Concert series $5.) The **Grand Ole Opry,** setting for America's longest-running radio show, moved here from the town center in 1976. *The* place to hear country music, the Opry howls every Friday and Saturday night ($16). Matinees are added on various days during peak tourist season (3pm April-Oct., $14). Reserve tickets from Grand Ole Opry, 2808 Opryland Dr., Nashville 37214 (615-889-3060). General admission tickets can also be purchased at the box office, starting at 9am on Tuesday for weekend shows. Check the Friday morning *Tennessean* for a list of performers.

Blue Bird Café, 4104 Hillsboro Rd. (383-1461), in Green Hills. This bird sings original country, blues, and folk. Women traveling solo will feel safe in this mellow, clean-cut establishment. Garth Brooks got his start here. Dinner of salads and sandwiches ($4-6.50) until 11pm. Early shows at 7pm; cover begins around 9:30pm ($6). Open Mon.-Sat. 5:30pm-1am, Sun. 8pm-midnight. Cover $4-5.

Tootsie's Orchid Lounge, 422 Broadway (726-0463). Many stars got their start here; it still has good C&W music and affordable drinks. For years owner Tootsie Bess lent money to struggling musicians until they could get on the Ole Opry. Women should think twice about going to this rather rowdy bar alone at night. Open Mon.-Sat. 9:30am-3am, Sun. noon-3am.

Lucy's Record Shop, 1707 Church St. (321-0882), vends vinyl during the day to the same young crowd that catches the indie and local bands at night. Small cover. In case of a dull act, hop next door to **The Edge** (329-3480), a new dance venue. Open Thurs.-Sat. 10pm-3am. No cover before midnight, $3 after. Must be 21.

Vortex, 909 Church St. (259-2220). This mixed crowd receives its dose of techno through nightly injections of tribal, trance, and industrial. Thurs.-Sun 18 and up.

Ace of Clubs, 114 2nd St. (254-2237), in a huge downtown warehouse, packs 'em in for grand ol' rock n' roll. Open daily. Music around 9pm. Cover $10.

Station Inn, 402 12th Ave. S. (255-3307), blues some serious grass. Open Tues.-Sun. 7pm-late. Music starts at 9pm. Cover $4-6. Free Sun. night jam session.

■■■ CHATTANOOGA

Chattanooga snuggles against the Tennessee River, a thriving city that has cultivated much more than its dominant choo-choo image. What began as a trading post in 1815 has kept the commercial tradition and has evolved into a major factory outlet center. For an educational afternoon, the **Hunter Museum of Art,** 10 Bluff View (267-0968), houses the South's most complete American art collection and also hosts impressive travelling exhibits. ($5, seniors $4, children 3-12 $2.50; open Tues.-Sat. 10am-5pm, Sun. 1-5pm, closes at 7pm on Wed.) The **riverwalk** pathway connects the museum to the **Tennessee Aquarium** (800-262-0695 and 265-0695), on Ross's Landing, one of the world's largest aquariums (2 living forests, 5 stores, 7000 animals), with special attention paid to fresh water life and regional rivers. (Open daily 10am-6pm.) The **artsline** (756-2787) gives 24 hr. info on current cultural offerings.

A few miles outside Chattanooga, you can ride the world's steepest passenger railway (it reaches the ridiculous grade of 72.7 degrees; $6, children $3) to **Lookout Mountain,** where seven states can be seen on a clear day. Atop and around the mountain are several attractions, from the **Battles for Chattanooga Museum** (821-2812; $4, children $2), to an **alpine slide** (825-5666; $4, children $3.50). Tickets for all these attractions can be purchased in the ultra-modern **visitors center,** 1001 Market St. (800-322-3344 or756-8687), next to the Aquarium. Here touch-sensitive screens will print out info for you, and direct phonelines allow you to make reservations at a number of hotels and restaurants. (Open daily 8:30am-5:30pm.) Unfortunately, most accommodations have inflated prices; **Broad St.**, at the base of Lockout Mountain is a good place to do your comparison shopping. **Campgrounds** are abundant; **KOA-S. Chattanooga** (906-937-4166), is the closest to town but within 24 mil., there are two lakes, Chickamauga and Nickajack, each equipped with campgrounds. A **free shuttle** scuttles from the Chattanooga Choo Choo Holiday Inn to the Aquarium, with stops on every block (Mon.-Thurs. 10am-7pm, Fri.-Sun. 10am-8:30pm; daily 10am-7pm in off-season; summer service is available to Lookout Mountain; $1, children 50¢). Chattanooga's **area code: 615.**

■■■ GREAT SMOKY MOUNTAINS NATIONAL PARK

The largest wilderness area in the eastern U.S., the Great Smoky Mountains National Park encompasses a half-million acres of gray-green Appalachian peaks bounded on either side by misty North Carolina and Tennessee valleys. Bears, wild hogs, white-tailed deer, groundhogs, wild turkeys, and more than 1500 species of flowering plants make their homes here. Whispering conifer forests line the mountain ridges at elevations of over 6000 feet. Rhododendrons burst into their full glory in June and July, and by mid-October the sloping mountains become a giant crazy-quilt of color.

Practical Information Start any exploration of the area with a visit to one of the park's three visitors centers. **Sugarlands** (436-1200), on Newfound Gap Rd., 2 mi. south of Gatlinburg, TN, is next to the park's headquarters (open daily 8am-7pm; spring and fall 8am-6pm; winter 8am-4:30pm). **Cades Cove** (436-1275) is in the park's western valley, 15 mi. southwest of Sugarlands on Little River Rd., 7 mi. southwest of Townsend, TN (open in summer daily 9am-7pm; fall and spring 9am-6pm). The **Oconaluftee Visitors Center** (704-497-9147), 4 mi. north of Cherokee, NC, serves travelers entering the park from the Blue Ridge Parkway and all points south and east (open daily April 1-15 8am-4:30pm; April 16-May 8am-6pm; summer 8am-7pm, fall 8am-6pm). The park's **information line** (615-436-1200; open daily 8:30am-4:30pm) links all three visitors centers. The rangers can answer travel questions and trace lost equipment. Park **emergency** can be reached at 615-436-1230.

At each visitors center you'll find displays amplifying the park's natural and cultural resources, bulletin boards displaying emergency messages, brochures and films, and comfort stations. Be sure to ask for *The Smokies Guide*, a newspaper offering a comprehensive explanation of the park's changing natural graces. The helpful journal also includes information on tours, lectures, and other activities, such as rafting or horseback riding. The standard park service brochure provides the best driving map in the region. Hikers should ask the visitors center staff for assistance in locating an appropriately detailed backcountry map. You can also tune your car radio to 1610AM at various marked points for information.

Sleeping and Eating After a Long Day of Hiking There are 10 campgrounds in the park, each with tent sites, limited trailer space, water, tables, and comfort stations (no showers or hookups). **Smokemont, Elkmont,** and **Cades Cove** accept reservations; the rest are first-come, first-served. (Sites $11.) For those hauling a trailer or staying at one of the campgrounds near the main roads during the summer, reservations are a must. Obtain them at least eight weeks in advance by writing to Ticketron, P.O. Box 617516, Chicago, IL 60661 (800-452-1111).

Both **Cherokee** and **Gatlinburg** have many small motels. The prices vary widely depending on the season and the economy. In general, the cheaper motels are in Cherokee, and the nicer ones are in Gatlinburg, where the best deals are off Main St., especially by street light #6. Expect to pay at least $35 in Cherokee ($10 more on weekends) and at least $40-45 in Gatlinburg (again weekends are more expensive). Three youth hostels are located in the area around the park. The closest is **Bell's Wa-Floy Retreat,** 3610 East Pkwy (615-436-5575), 10 mi. east of Gatlinburg on Rte. 321, at mile marker 21. From the center of Gatlinburg catch the east-bound trolley (25¢) to the end of the line. From there, it's a 5-mi. walk to Wa-Floy. If driving, be careful not to hit the ducks and peacocks: the lovely grounds are complete with a pool, tennis courts, meditation area, chapel, and bubbling brook. Friendly proprietor Mrs. Floy both recites poetry and rents space in her apartment-style buildings; reservations are necessary. (AYH members $10, others $12 first night, $8 each additional night; linens $1. Check-in before 10pm. Midnight curfew.) **Smoky Mountain Ranch Camp (HI-AYH),** 3248 Manis Rd. (800-851-6715 or 429-8563), in Sevierville, is a small hostel under new management just 2 mi. from the park. Curfew 11pm. Office open 8am-noon and 4-10pm. Linens $1. $12, nonmembers $14.

Farther south, near Wesser, NC in the **Nantahala National Forest,** the bustling **Nantahala Outdoor Center (NOC),** 13077 Hwy. 19 W., Bryson City, NC (704-488-2175), 80 mi. from Gatlinburg and 13 mi. from downtown Bryson City, offers cheap beds. The "base camp" on the far side of the river, has bunks in simple wooden cabins as well as fairly large-sized motel rooms with kitchenettes. Showers, kitchen, and laundry facilities are included. ($10. Call ahead.) NOC offers white-water rafting (see Activities below). The center is not at all convenient to the GSM park or Gatlinburg.

After a full day of rafting, relish in the heavenly smell of freshly baked bread at **Maxwell's Bakery** (704-586-5046), Dillsboro exit off U.S. 74. (Open Mon.-Sat. 6am-6pm, Sun. 8am-6pm.) In Cherokee, **My Grandma's** (704-497-9801), U.S. 19 and U.S. 441, serves up home-cookin' at down-low prices ($2-4) (open daily 7am-3pm).

Sights and Activities Over 900 mi. of hiking trails and 170 mil. of road traverse the park. Ask the rangers at the visitors centers to help you devise a trip appropriate to your physical ability. Driving and walking routes are clearly charted. To hike off the marked trails, you must ask for a free backcountry camping permit. Otherwise, just choose a route, bring water, and DON'T FEED THE BEARS. Some of the most popular trails are the 5 mi. to **Rainbow Falls,** the 4 mi. to **Chimney Tops,** and the 21½ mi. to **Laurel Falls.** For a splendid drive with beautiful scenery, visitors can enjoy **Cades Cove loop,** which circles the last vestiges of a mountain community that occupied the area from the 1850s to the 1920s when the GSM national park materialized. What was once a living, breathing settlement today displays splendid grassy, open fields against peaceful mountain backdrops. Deep green forests enhance the pastoral aura of Cades Cove, as do the horses, deer, bears, and other animals. The 50¢ tour guide available at the entrance to the 11-mi. loop shares detailed, well-written descriptions of the old churches and homesteads. In the summer months, visit **Mingus Mill,** located 1 mi. north of the Oconaluftee visitors center along Newfound Gap Road. This 1876 Turbine mill boasts 107-year-old wooden tools and machinery which still operate. Watch corn and wheat being ground, or browse through the book of old photos to see the last miller, John Jones, hard at work. The **Pioneer Farmstead,** next door to the Oconaluftee center, recreates a turn of the century settlement, including a blacksmith shop and a corncrib. The 25¢ pamphlets give informative illustrations of the grounds. (Both sights are free and open the same hours as the visitors center.)

Great Smoky Mountains National Park straddles the Tennessee/North Carolina border. On the Tennessee side, the city of **Gatlinburg,** just 2 mi. from Sugarlands, appears and vanishes within the blink of a driver's eye, but is jam-packed enough to keep you dizzy with amazement for an evening or a day. Touristic hordes flood the towns sights, ranging from **Dollywood,** a theme park devoted to Dolly Parton, to a wax museum dedicated to President Bush. Also in Gatlinburg, **Christus Gardens** bills itself as America's #1 religious attraction, and **Ober Gatlinburg** has America's largest cable car. Between all these attractions are endless rows of hotels and motor inns. For more guidance and specific listings of accommodations and campgrounds, stop in at the **Tourist Information Center,** 520 Pkwy. (615-436-4178; open Mon.-Sat. 8am-8pm, Sun. 9am-5pm; Nov.-April Mon.-Sat. 8am-6pm, Sun. 9am-5pm).

The **Cherokee Indian Reservation** (800-438-1601) lies on the North Carolina side of the Mountains (a scenic 1 hr. drive south on U.S. 441), 1 mi. from the Oconaluftee Visitors Center. The reservation offers a guided tour of a re-created mid-18th century Indian village, an outdoor drama about the Cherokee tribe, and an informative museum. Invest your time and money for a ticket to "Unto these Hills," an outdoor drama that retells the story of the Cherokees and climaxes with a moving reenactment of the Trail of Tears. (Evening shows June-Aug.. Mon.-Sat. $8. children and under $5.) At the **Museum of the Cherokee Indian** (704-497-3481), on Drama Rd. off U.S. 441, you can hear the Cherokee language spoken, view artifacts and films, and learn about the past and the present of the Cherokee. Fascinating and well worth a visit. (Open Mon.-Sat. 9am-8pm, Sun. 9am-5pm; Sept. to mid-June daily 9am-5pm. $3.50, under 13 $1.75.) The **Cherokee Visitors Center** (800-438-1601), on U.S. 19, is open daily from 9am-5pm.

The **NOC** has 2½-hr. whitewater rafting expeditions which are pricey, but you can rent your own raft for a self-designed trip down the Nantahala River. (Sun.-Fri. $15, Sat. $22. 1-person inflatable "duckies" $27 weekdays, $30 on Sat. Group rates available. Higher prices on "premium Saturdays," July-Aug.) The NOC also rents canoes and kayaks and offers instruction. Most trips have minimum age or weight limits; daycare service is available at the center. Trip prices include transportation to the put-in site and all necessary equipment. Hike on the **Appalachian Trail** to explore some of the old forest service roads. The NOC staff will gladly assist if you need help charting an appropriate daytrip. The NOC also maintains seasonal "outposts" on the **Ocoee, Nolichucky, Chattoga,** and **French Broad Rivers;** a rafting expedition on any of these rivers makes a satisfying daytrip if you have a car. NOC has 20% discounts in March and April.

■■■ MEMPHIS

Up from "Blues Route" Highway 61, in the southwestern corner of Tennessee, follow the sound of soulful melodies to Memphis, home of the blues and the birthplace of rock n' roll. Decades after W.C. Handy was the first to publish a blues piece on legendary Beale Street in 1912, Elvis Presley (also a Memphean) became the "King of Rock 'n' Roll" with the help of his gyrating pelvis and amazingly versatile voice. Though the King *may* be dead, his image lives on throughout the city. Every year roadtrippers from around the country make a pilgrimage to the mecca of tack—Graceland, Elvis's former home.

Beyond music, Memphis stimulates all of the senses. Visitors can feast their eyes on both national and local history in the many museums around town, or focus instead on a live performance given by one of the city's increasingly sophisticated theaters. Noses and taste buds will be tempted by barbecue, a Memphis specialty. Travelers' blue suede shoes may feel sore after trekking, but even jaded visitors to Memphis will agree that this town will love you true (or then again, maybe not).

PRACTICAL INFORMATION
Emergency: 911.
Visitor Information: Visitor Information Center, 340 Beale St. (543-5333), 2 blocks south on 2nd St. and 2 blocks east on Beale from the Greyhound station. Open Mon.-Sat. 9am-6pm, Sun. noon-6pm; in the summer Mon.-Sat. 9am-5pm.
Airport: Memphis International, 2491 Winchester Rd. (922-8000), south of the southern loop of I-240. Taxi fare to the city $16—negotiate in advance. Hotel express shuttles run about $8. Public transport to and from the airport only $1.10, but sporadically available and a tough trip for a traveler unfamiliar with the area.
Amtrak: 545 S. Main St. (526-0052 or 800-872-7245), at Calhoun on the southern edge of downtown. *Take a taxi—the area is very unsafe* even during the day, downright hellish at night. *See Mileage Chart.* Open Sun.-Thurs. 9:20pm-2pm, Fri.-Sat. 9:20pm-6:20am.
Greyhound: 203 Union Ave. (523-7676), at 4th St. downtown. Unsafe area at night, but it beats the Amtrak station. *See Mileage Chart.* Open 24 hrs.
Public Transport: Memphis Area Transit Authority (MATA) (274-6282), corner of Union and Main. Extensive bus routes cover most suburbs, but buses don't run very frequently. The two major downtown stops are at Front and Jefferson St. and at 2nd St. and Madison Ave. Operates Mon.-Fri. 6am-7pm, Sat. 10am-6pm,

Sun. 11am-4pm. Fare $1, transfers 10¢. MATA recently refurbished original Portuguese trolley cars from the 19th century. They cruise Main St. Mon.-Thurs. 6:30am-9pm., Fri. 6:30am-1am, Sat. 9:30am-1am, Sun. 10am-6pm; 50¢.
Taxi: Yellow Cab, 526-2121. $2.35 first mi., $1.10 each additional mi.
Crisis Line: 458-8772. Open 24 hrs. Also refers to other hotlines.
Time Zone: Central (1 hr. behind Eastern).
Post Office: 1 N. Front St. (521-2140), at Madison St. Open Mon.-Fri. 8am-5pm.
  ZIP code: 38101.
Area Code: 901.

Downtown, named avenues run east-west and numbered ones north-south. **Madison Avenue** bifurcates north and south addresses. Two main thoroughfares, **Poplar** and **Union Avenues,** pierce the heart of the city from the east; 2nd and 3rd Streets arrive from the south. **I-240** and **I-55** join hands to encircle the city with brotherly love. **Bellevue** becomes **Elvis Presley Blvd.** and leads you straight to Graceland. If traveling by car, take advantage of the free, unmetered parking along the river.

SINCE M'BABY LEFT ME, I FOUND A NEW PLACE T'DWELL

Two hostels and a handful of motels downtown should render unnecessary the seedier, more distant, and expensive strip along Elvis Presley Blvd. and Brooks Rd. During the celebration of the earth-shattering days of Elvis's birth (early Jan.) and death (mid-Aug.), book way in advance. The visitors center has a thorough listing of lodgings. Contact **Bed and Breakfast in Memphis,** P.O. Box 41621, Memphis 38174 (726-5920; 800-336-2087 for reservations), for guest rooms in Memphean homes. French- and Spanish-speaking hosts are available (singles and doubles $40-60).

Lowenstein-Long House/Castle Hostelry, 1084 Poplar and 217 N. Waldran (527-7174). Take bus #50 from 3rd St. Beautiful grounds surround an elegant Victorian mansion. The hostel's institutionally tidy rooms are in a small red brick building out back. Women's rooms on the 3rd floor are pleasant and homey. Mens' rooms are a bit less neat. Towels $1, laundry $2. Hostel bed $10, key deposit $10. Beautiful B&B rooms in the mansion start at $60. Tent-people welcome on the big lawn out back, $5 each set of sideburns.

Admiral Benbow Inn, 1220 Union (725-0630), at S. Bellevue. A monstrous tribute to 70s architecture, these rooms are clean and close to downtown. Singles $30, doubles $34, all rooms $34 on weekends.

Motel 6, 1360 Springbrook Rd. (396-3620), just east of intersection of Elvis and Brooks Rd. near Graceland. A holler away lies another at 1117 E. Brooks Rd. (346-0492), but the neighborhood could be better. Both have pools and small, clean rooms with movies and free local calls. Singles $26, doubles $32.

Hernando Inn, 900 E. Commerce St. (601-429-7811, is just across the Mississippi border in Hernando (about 15 mi. south of Memphis). Take exit 280 off I-55. Singles $34, doubles $38.

Also off exit 280 lie the verdant pastures that will give you repose at the **Memphis South Campground,** 460 Byhalia Rd., Hernando, MS (601-429-1878). This ex-KOA provides a pool, laundry, and tent sites for $12. Water and wattage is $15, full hookup is $17. The campsites at **Memphis/Graceland KOA,** 3691 Elvis Presley Blvd. (396-7125), are right next to Graceland, so you can hear hound dog howlin' all night long (sites $15, full hookup $24).

MEALS FIT FOR THE KING

Memphis barbecue is as common here as rhinestone-studded jumpsuits. The city even hosts the World Championship Barbecue Cooking Contest in May. But don't fret if gnawing on ribs isn't your thing—Memphis has plenty of other Southern-style restaurants with down-home favorites like fried chicken, catfish, chitlins, and grits.

The Rendezvous (523-2746), Downtown Alley, in the alley across from the Peabody Hotel off Union St. between the Ramada and Days Inns. A Memphis legend, serving large portions of ribs ($6.50-10), and cheaper sandwiches ($3-4). Open Tues.-Thurs. 4:30pm-midnight, Fri.-Sat. noon-midnight.

The North End, 346 N. Main St. (526-0319 or 527-3663), downtown. A happening place with an extensive menu specializing in tamales, wild rice, stuffed potatoes, and creole dishes ($3-8). Wonderful rabbit-food and alternative to BBQ. Entrees $3-10. Hot fudge pie known as "sex on a plate," $3.25. Happy Hour daily 4-7pm. Live music starts at 10:30pm Wed.-Sun. with a $2 cover. Open daily 10:30am-3am. Next door, **Jake's Place** (527-2799) offers stir-fry specialties and breakfast.

P and H Cafe, 1532 Madison Ave. (726-0906). The initials aptly stand for Poor and Hungry. "The beer joint of your dreams" serves huge burgers, plate lunches, and grill food ($3-5); try the patty melt with grilled onions. The waitresses are a friendly Memphis institution—look at the wall murals and stuffed jackalope. Local bands occasionally play Sat. nights. Open Mon.-Fri. 11am-3am, Sat. 5pm-3am.

Jim Neely's Interstate BBQ, 2265 S. 3rd St. (775-2304), has hoppin', heapin' pig and cow sandwiches shellacked with sauces containing "herbs a lot of people never heard of," all under $5. Vegetarians can get BBQ spaghetti; 12 oz. for $2.

Front St. Delicatessen, 77 S. Front St. (522-8943). Lunchtime streetside deli in the heart of downtown with almost no room inside. Patio dining in sunny weather. Hot lunch specials ($2-4). Open Mon.-Fri. 7am-3pm, Sat. 11am-3pm.

Western Steakhouse, 1298 Madison (725-9896), slaps down some fine steaks. The back corner was graced by the King. Grilled cheese $2.25-$4.50. Open Tues.-Sun. 4pm-midnight. Live music Fri. and Sat. nights.

Corky's, 5259 Poplar Ave. (685-9744), about 25 min. from downtown. Very popular with the locals and justifiably so. BBQ dinner and ribs are served with baked beans, coleslaw, and homemade bread ($3-9) and are top notch, as are the pies and cobbler. Arrive early and expect a long wait, or use the drive-thru. Open Mon.-Thurs. 11am-10pm, Fri.-Sat. 11am-10:30pm, Sun. noon-10pm.

Squash Blossom Market, 1720 Poplar Ave. (725-4823), at White Station Rd. This huge health food store/cafe is slightly out of place in a city dripping with sauces, grease, and above all, meat. Try the Sunday brunch where veggie delights run about $4. Open Mon.-Fri. 9am-9pm, Sat. 9am-8pm, Sun. 11am-6pm.

ELVIS SIGHTINGS

Graceland (332-3322 or 800-238-2000), or rather "GRACE-lin," as the tour guides drawl, is Elvis Presley's home and the paragon of Americana that every Memphis visitor must see. But any desire to learn about the man, to share his dream, or to feel his music may go unrealized even by those who venture to his monumental home; the complex has been built up to resemble an amusement park that shuffles visitors from one room to another. It seems that the employees adhere to the Elvis motto "Taking Care of Business in a Flash." Despite the monotony of the tours, you'll never forget the mirrored ceilings, carpeted walls, and yellow-and-orange decor of Elvis' 1974 renovations. Elvis bought the mansion when he was only 22, and his daughter Lisa Marie inherited it. Be sure to gawk at the Trophy Building where hundreds of gold and platinum records line the wall. Around the corner, an enormous portrait of the King, in white, chuckles back at you. The list of exhibits is crazy: a collection of guns includes his favorite turquoise-handled Colt 45. The King and his court are buried next door in the **Meditation Gardens,** where you can seek the Buddha while reciting a mantra to the tune of "You're So Square." (Open Memorial Day-Labor Day, 7:30am-6pm; rest of the year 8:30am-5pm, mansion closed on Tues. from Nov.-Feb. $8, children 5-12 $5.)

If you love him tender, love him true, visit several Elvis museums, and several more Elvis souvenir shops. The **Elvis Presley Automobile Museum** proves to be the most worthwhile Elvis option. A huge hall houses a score of pink and purple Elvis mobiles, and an indoor drive-in movie theater shows clips from 31 Elvis movies ($4.50, seniors $4, kids $2.75). *If I Can Dream* is a free 20-min. film with performance footage which, unfortunately for Elvis, contrasts the early (otherwise known as slim) years with the later ones. **Elvis' Airplanes** features—you got it—the two Elvis planes: the *Lisa Marie* (named for the Elvis daughter) and the tiny *Hound Dog II* Jetstar. The cost of visiting these planes is overpriced at $4.25 (seniors $3.80, kids

THE SOUTH

$2.75), but the cost of seeing **Elvis' Tour Bus** is a bargain at $1. The **Sincerely Elvis** exhibit gives you a glimpse of Elvis's private side by presenting some books he read, some shirts he wore, and his Social Security card ($2.75).

There are three different combination tickets available: (1) all attractions except the mansion for $10 (seniors $9, kids $7); (2) all attractions except the bus and planes for $13 (seniors $12, kids $8); (3) all the attractions for $16 (seniors $14.50, kids $11). To get there, take Lauderdale/Elvis Presley bus #13 from 3rd and Union.

Every year from August 8-16, millions of the King's cortege get all shook up for **Elvis Week,** an extended celebration that includes a pilgrimage to his junior high school and a candlelight vigil. You can also make the bus trip to the two-room house in **Tupelo, MS** where it all began.

MORE MEMPHIS MUSIC AND MARVELS THAN THE MAN

Long before Sam Phillips and the tiny **Sun Studio,** 706 Union Ave. (521-0664), first produced Elvis, Jerry Lee Lewis, U2, and Bonnie Raitt (30-min. tours every hr. on the ½ hr.; open daily 9am-6:30pm; $5, kids $4.50), historic **Beale St.** saw the invention of the blues. After a long period of neglect, the neighborhood has music literally pouring from almost every door once again. The **W.C. Handy Home and Museum,** 352 Beale (527-2583), exhibits the music and photographs of the man, the myth, the legend who first put a blues melody to paper (open Tues.-Sat. 10am-5pm, Sun. 1-5pm; $2, kids free; call for an appointment). Earphones that spew blues hits litter the **Memphis Music Museum,** 97 S. 2nd St. (525-4007), as do photographs and TV footage of actual performances. If you like to sing, listen to, or watch the blues, this is the place to go. (Open Mon.-Sat. 10am-6pm, Sun. 10am-9pm. $5, seniors $4, kids 1-12 $2.) The **Center for Southern Folklore,** 130 Beale St. (525-3655), documents various aspects of music history, including a tribute to Memphis's WDIA—the nation's first all-black radio station where notables like B.B. King and Rufus Thomas began their musical careers. (Open Mon.-Thurs. 10am-8pm, Fri.-Sat. 10am-10pm, Sun. 11am-8pm; open later in summer. Admission by donation.) Call the center for info on the **Music and Heritage Festival** on the 3rd weekend of July. The festival is on 2nd and Madison and presents gospel, country, blues, and jazz with dancing troupes and craft booths. Some booths offer oral histories on everything from life on the Mississippi to playing in the Negro baseball leagues. (Festival runs 11am-11pm.)

Mud Island, a quick tram-ride over the picturesque Mississippi, has it all: a swimming pool, a museum, and a five-block scale model of the Mississippi River you can stroll along. (Call for hours. Entrance to the island $2.) At the **Mississippi River Museum,** 125 N. Front St. (576-7241), you can experience history first-hand by strolling on the decks of an indoor steamboat, relaxing to the blues in the Yellow Dog Cafe, or spying on a union ironclad gunboat from the lookout of a confederate bluff. (Museum and grounds $6, seniors and children under 12 $4.) In the summer, visitors can swim in the enormous pool that doubles as the Gulf of Mexico at the base of the Mississippi River sculpture. Also on Mud Island rests the renowned World War II B-17 **Memphis Belle.** Free tours of the Riverwalk and Memphis Belle Pavilion run several times daily, depending on the size of the crowds. Thursday evenings on the island are free; arrive before 6pm and catch the sunset.

William Faulkner once said of Memphis that "the Delta meets in the lobby of the **Peabody Hotel,"** 149 Union St. (529-4000), in the heart of downtown. Try the French Strawberry Cheesecake while you're there ($4). Now that the hotel keeps ducks in its indoor fountain, every day at 11am and 5pm the management rolls out the red carpet and the ducks waddle to and from the elevator with piano accompaniment. Get there early; sometimes the ducks are impatient.

The Great American Pyramid (526-5177), overlooking the waterfront, is the latest Memphis extravaganza. You won't be able to miss the 32-story-high, six-acre-wide shining pyramid that holds the American Music Hall of Fame, the Memphis Music Experience, the College Football Hall of Fame, and a 20,000-seat arena. (Open Mon.-Fri. 8:30am-5:30pm, tours 10am-4pm. $3.75, seniors $2.75.)

A. Schwab, 163 Beale St. (523-9782), a five-and-dime store run by the same family since 1876, still offers old-fashioned bargains. A "museum" of relics-never-sold gathers dust on the mezzanine floor, including an array of voodoo potions, elixirs, and powders. Elvis bought some of his flashier ensembles here. (Open Mon.-Sat. 9am-5pm. Free guided tours.) Next door on Beale St., the **Memphis Police Museum** (528-2370) summons visitors to gawk at 150 years of confiscated drugs, homemade weapons, and officer uniforms (open 24 hrs.; free).

The **National Civil Rights Museum,** housed at the site of Martin Luther King Jr.'s assassination at the **Lorraine Motel,** 450 I Saw It All On Mulberry St. (521-9699), at 2nd, serves as a reminder of the suffering African Americans have endured and as a tribute to their movement for change. A 10-min. movie, graphic photographs of lynching victims, live footage, and life-size exhibits vividly trace the progress of the Civil Rights Movement. Preserved in their original condition, rooms 306 and 307, where King's entourage stayed, can be toured. (Open Mon.-Sat. 10am-5pm, Sun. 1-5pm; summer Mon. and Wed.-Sat. 10am-6pm, Sun. 1-6pm. $5, seniors and students with ID $4, kids 6-12 $3. Free Mon. 3-5pm.)

The people of Memphis are hardly only black and white; the Native American presence is culturally rich as well. The **C.H. Nash Museum-Chucalissa,** 1987 Indian Village Dr. (785-3160), recaptures the 16th century with its reconstructed Choctaw village and historical and archaeological museum. Take Winchester which becomes Mitchell which becomes Indian Village Dr. in T.O. Fuller State Park. Local Choctaw sell pottery and beaded jewelry at reasonable prices. (Open Tues.-Sat. 9am-5pm, Sun. 1-5pm. $3, kids $2.) During the third weekend in June, the **Native American Pow-Wow and Crafts Fair** (789-9338) draws people from across the country to celebrate Native American heritage with food, dance, and music.

The **Pink Palace Museum and Planetarium,** 3050 Central Ave. (320-6320), which is, by the way, gray, details the natural history of the mid-South and expounds upon the development of Memphis. Check out the sharp and sparkling crystal and mineral collection. An IMAX theatre is scheduled to open in late '94. (Open Mon.-Sat. 10am-5pm, Sun. 1-5pm. $3, kids $2. $10 for the museum, IMAX, and planetarium.) On the corner of Central Ave. and Hollywood mirthfully stands the **Children's Museum,** a wonderfully fun option for kids (open Tues.-Sat. 9am-5pm, Sun. 1-5pm; $5, kids 1-12 $4).

The **Victorian Village** consists of 18 mansions in various stages of restoration and preservation. The **Mallory-Neeley House,** 652 Adams Ave. (523-1484), one of the village's two mansions open to the public, was built in the mid-19th century. Most of its original furniture remains intact for visitors to see. (Open Tues.-Sat. 10am-4pm, Sun. 1-4pm. $4, seniors and students $3.) For a look at a different lifestyle during the same era, visit the **Magevrney House,** 198 Adams Ave. (526-4464), which once held the clapboard cottage of Eugene Magevrney, who helped establish Memphis's first public schools (open Tues.-Sat. 10am-4pm; free; reservations required). French Victorian architecture and an antique/textile collection live on in the **Woodruff-Fontaine House,** 680 Adams Ave. (526-1469; open Mon.-Sat. 10am-4pm, Sun. 1-4pm; $5, students, seniors, and GIs with the blues $2).

The **Memphis Brooks Museum of Art** (722-3500), in Overton Park, houses a mid-sized collection of Renaissance and modern art (open Tues.-Sat. 10am-5pm, Sun. 11:30am-5pm; $4, seniors, students, and kids $2; free Fri.). The **Memphis Zoo and Aquarium,** 2000 Galloway Ave. (726-4787), squawks and splashes next door. Check out cat country where tigers prowl among the pillars of a ruined Egyptian temple. (Open daily 9am-5pm. $5, seniors and kids $3; free Mon. after 3:30pm.)

Memphis has almost as many parks as museums, each offering a slightly different natural setting. Brilliant wildflowers and a marvelous heinz of roses (57 varieties) bloom and grow forever at the **Memphis Botanical Garden,** 750 Cherry Rd. (685-1566), in Audubon Park off Park Ave. (Open Tues.-Sat. 9am-sunset, Sun. 11am-6pm. $2, kids 6-17 $1.) Across the street, the **Dixon Galleries and Garden,** 4339 Park Ave. (761-5250), flaunts its manicured landscape (open Mon.-Sat. 10am-5pm, Sun. 1pm-5pm; $5, seniors $4, students $3, kids 1-12 $1). The **Lichterman Nature Center,**

5992 Quince Rd. off Perkins (767-7322), is a wildscape with virgin forests and wildlife. A picnic area is available. (Open Tues.-Sat. 9:30am-5pm, Sun. 1-5pm. $2, students and seniors $1.)

ARE YOU LONELY TONIGHT?

If you don't know what to do while you're walkin' in Memphis, the visitors center's *Key* magazine, the free *Memphis Flyer*, or the "Playbook" section of the Friday morning *Memphis Commercial Appeal* will give you an idea of what's goin' down 'round town. Also go to the **Sun Cafe**, 710 Union Ave. (521-9820), adjacent to the Sun Studios, for a tall, cool glass of lemonade ($1.75) and a talk with the young waiters and cashiers about what to do (open daily 9am-7pm; Sept.-May 10am-6pm).

The most happening place is **Beale Street.** Blues waft nightly up and down the street; you could save a few bucks by buying a drink at one of the many outdoor stands and just meandering from doorway to doorway, park to park. **B.B. King's Blues Club,** 1413 Beale (527-5464), where the club's namesake still makes appearances, happily mixes young and old, tourist and native. (Open daily from 11:30am 'til the show stops. Suthun' cuisine served on Sun. from 3pm on. Cover $5 and up.) While the clientele at the **Rum Boogie Cafe,** 182 Beale (528-0150), may be more transplanted, the music is certainly homegrown. (Open daily 11:30am-2am. Cover $5.) For pool, **Peoples,** 323 Beale (523-7627), is open from noon until at least 2am, and charges $7.35 ($8.40 on weekends) for a table. **Silky O'Sullivan's,** 183 Beale St. (522-9596), is an old Irish bar behind the facade of an almost completely razed historic landmark. Play "beach" volleyball and listen to folk music outside, munch on burgers ($4-6), and hear some Memphis blues inside next door. (Open daily 11am-2:30am. Cover $3-5 after 7pm.) Sexy, saxy jazz can be found at the brand-new **This is It,** 167 Beale (so new it doesn't even have a phone yet).

Off Beale St., the **Antenna Club,** 1588 Madison Ave. (276-4052), showcases hip progressive rock. Up, up, and away to the **Daily Planet,** 3439 Park (327-1270), which throbulates with R&B. For a collegiate atmosphere, try the Highland St. strip near Memphis State University, with hopping bars like **Newby's,** 539 S. Highland St. (452-8408), which has backgammon tables and hosts alternative bands on Wednesdays at 9pm. Just up the street from Sun Studio is **"616,"** 600 Marshall (526-6552). The joint has a huge dance floor, and occasional 10¢ longnecks. (Cover around $8.) A hot gay spot, **J. Wags** has been open 24 hrs. since way back. (Live music Fri.-Sat. Drag shows Fri.-Sun. from 11:20pm-1am.) Otherwise, **Zippers,** 235 Union Ave. (527-6879), is hoppin'. (Drag shows Tues.-Sat. Cover after 8pm, Mon.-Wed. $3, Thurs. and Sun. $4, Fri.-Sat. $5. Happy Hour 3-8pm, open daily 3pm-3am.)

The majestic **Orpheum Theater,** 203 S. Main St. (525-3000), is a dignified movie palace, complete with 15-ft.-high chandeliers and a pipe organ. The theater shows classic movies on weekends along with an organ prelude and a cartoon, and occasionally live music in the summer. **Memphis in May** (525-4611) is a month-long celebration with concerts, art exhibits, food contests, and sports events. Book hotel reservations early. The **Memphis Chicks,** 800 Home Run Ln. (272-1687), near Libertyland, are a big hit with fans of Southern League baseball ($5, box seats $6).

■ NEAR MEMPHIS: OXFORD, MS

Southeast of Hwy. 61 and Memphis, you'll find Oxford, home to **University of Mississippi (Ole Miss).** Over the years, Oxford has seen several periods of bitter racial unrest. First a stop on the Trail of Tears, Oxford later came to the country's attention in 1962 when a federal court ruled that James Meredith should be the first black student to enroll at the university. The news resulted in rioting and the death of three civil rights workers, and the outrage of the entire country. Today, tensions on the Ole Miss campus have ceased and it is now home to a **Blues Archive** (601-232-7753) which holds thousands of recordings of the region's music.

Oxford also boasts the South's most august writer, **William Faulkner,** who lived here from 1930 to 1962. You can see his old home at **Rowan Oak** (601-234-3284) on Old Taylor Rd. (Home and grounds open Tues.-Sat. 10am-noon and 2-4pm, Sun. 2-4pm.) For the low down on the rest of Oxford, head to the **tourist information center,** 107 S. Lamar (601-232-2419), in the Square. While perusing the sound and fury that is Oxford, order something off the phonetically-spelled menu at **Smitty's Cafe,** 208 S. Lamar (601-234-9111). Most entrees are under $6, but be sure to have the cornbread. (Open Mon.-Sat. 6am-9pm, Sun. 8am-9pm.)

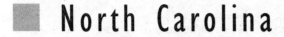

North Carolina

North Carolina splits neatly into thirds: the west's down-to-earth mountain culture, the mellow sophistication of the Raleigh/Durham/Chapel Hill Research Triangle in the state's center, and the placidity of the eastern coast and the Outer Banks. Whatever their cultural differences, these three regions share one similarity—an unmatched beauty apparent the moment you cross the state border. Even the occasional urban area complements Carolina's fertile resplendence. The streets are unlittered, the buildings well-spaced, the businesses clean, and the universities spacious.

PRACTICAL INFORMATION

Capital: Raleigh.
Travel and Tourism Division, 430 N. Salisbury St., Raleigh 27611 (919-733-4171 or 800-847-4862). **Department of Natural Resources and Community Development,** Division of Parks and Recreation, P.O. Box 27287, Raleigh 27611 (919-733-4181).
Time Zone: Eastern. **Postal Abbreviation:** NC
Sales Tax: 6%.

■■■ RALEIGH, DURHAM, AND CHAPEL HILL

The Research Triangle, a region embracing Raleigh, Durham, and Chapel Hill, contains more PhDs per capita than any other part of the nation. Durham, the former tobacco mecca of the world, is now, ironically, a city devoted to medicine, sprinkled with hospitals and diet clinics. It also houses Duke University, one of the most prestigious universities in the nation. Chapel Hill, just 20 mi. down the road, holds its own in education as the home of the nation's first public university, the University of North Carolina. The college population has catalyzed the area: environmentalism abounds (as evidenced in the number of bicycles), and the Hill's music scene thrives with several bands getting attention nationally. Raleigh, the state capital, is an easygoing, historic town, as well as the home of North Carolina State University.

PRACTICAL INFORMATION

Emergency: 911.
Visitor Information: Raleigh Capitol Area Visitors Center, 301 N. Blount St. (733-3456). Focuses on the capitol area. Open Mon.-Fri. 8am-5pm, Sat. 9am-5pm, Sun. 1-5pm. **Durham Convention Center and Visitors Bureau,** 101 E. Morgan (687-0288; open Mon.-Fri. 8:30am-5pm, Sat. 10am-2pm). **Chapel Hill Chamber of Commerce,** 104 S. Estes Dr. (967-7075); open Mon.-Fri. 9am-5pm.
Airport: Raleigh-Durham, 15 mi. northwest of Raleigh on U.S. 70 (829-1477). Many hotels and rental car agencies provide free airport limousine service (596-2361) if you have reservations. Pick up helpful complimentary maps of Raleigh and Durham at the **information counter** on the airport's lower level.

Amtrak: 320 W. Cabarrus, Raleigh (833-7594 or 800-872-7245). To: Miami (1 per day, 16 hr., $148); Washington, D.C. (2 per day, 6 hr., $46); Richmond (2 per day, 4 hr., $34). Open daily 9am-9:30pm.

Greyhound: In Raleigh: 314 W. Jones St. (828-2567). To: Durham (6 per day, 40 min., $6); Chapel Hill (5 per day, 80 min., $7); Richmond (6 per day, 3½ hr., $34). North Charleston (2 per day, 8 hr., $36 if reservations made 7 days in advance). Open 24 hrs. **In Durham:** 820 Morgan St. (687-4800), 1 block off Chapel Hill St. downtown. 2½ mi. northeast of Duke University. To: Chapel Hill (5 per day, ½ hr., $4). Washington, D.C. (4 per day, 7 hr., $40). Open daily 7am-11pm. **In Chapel Hill:** 311 W. Franklin St. (942-3356), 4 blocks from the UNC campus. Open Mon.-Fri. 9am-4pm, Sat.-Sun. 8am-3:30pm.

Public Transport: Capital Area Transit, Raleigh (828-7228). Operates Mon.-Sat., fewer buses on Sat. Fare 50¢. **Duke Power Company Transit Service,** Durham (688-4587). Most routes start at the 1st Federal Bldg. at Main St. on the loop, downtown. Buses run daily; hours vary for each route. Fare 60¢, transfers 10¢.

Taxi: Safety Taxi, 832-880., **Cardinal Cab,** 828-3228. Both $2.85 plus $1.50 each mi., 24-hr. service.

Help Lines: Rape Crisis, 828-3005. 24 hrs.

Post Office: Raleigh: 310 New Bern Ave. (831-3661). Open Mon.-Fri. 7am-6pm, Sat. 8am-noon. **ZIP code:** 27611. **Durham:** 323 E. Chapel Hill St. (683-1976). Open Mon.-Fri. 8:30am-5pm. **ZIP code:** 27701. **Chapel Hill:** 179 E. Franklin St. (967-6297). Open Mon.-Fri. 9am-5pm, Sat. 9:30am-12:20pm. **ZIP code:** 27514.

Area Code: 919.

ACCOMMODATIONS AND CAMPING

Carolina-Duke Motor Inn (286-0771 or 800-438-1158 for reservations), I-85 at Guess Rd. in Durham. Clean rooms, with duck pics on the walls. Free Movie Channel, swimming pool, and laundry facilities available. Free shuttle to Duke University Medical Center on the main campus. 10% discount for *Let's Go* users, seniors, and AAA cardholders. Singles $32, doubles $39. $3 for each additional person. The Wabash Express (286-0020) next door serves cheap and filling breakfasts (6 pancakes $2.75). Sat.-Sun. 8-11am.

YMCA, 1601 Hillsborough St. (832-6601), in Raleigh, 5 blocks from Greyhound station. Comfortable rooms in a communal atmosphere. Free recreational facilities. Singles $17, with bath $20. Key deposit $2. Call ahead for reservations.

Motel 6, 3921 Arrow Dr. (782-7071), in Raleigh. U.S. 70 at Crabtree Valley. Same as the last one you stayed in: pool, A/C, movie channel. Singles $34, doubles $38.

Umstead State Park (787-3033), U.S. 70, 2 mi. northwest of Raleigh. Tent and trailer sites. Large lake for fishing and hiking. Open 8am-9pm; Sept.-May shorter hrs. Sites $9. Closed to camping Mon.-Wed.

FOOD

The restaurants near the universities are well-suited to the budget traveler. In Raleigh, **Hillsborough Street,** across from North Carolina State University, has a wide array of inexpensive restaurants and bakeries staffed largely by students. The same can be said of **9th Street** in Durham and **Franklin Street** in Chapel Hill. The **Well Spring Grocery,** 737 9th St., in Durham, at Franklin and Eliot in Chapel Hill, and the Ridgewood Shopping Center in Raleigh (286-2290), is a health food grocery with fruits, vegetables, and whole grain baked goods. (Open daily 9am-9pm.)

Ramshead Rath-Skellar, 157-A E. Franklin St., Chapel Hill (942-5158), directly across from the campus. A student hang-out featuring pizza, sandwiches, and hot apple pie Louise. Ship mastheads, German beer steins, and old Italian wine bottles adorn 8 different dining rooms with names such as the "Rat Trap Lounge." "Flukey" Hayes, here since 1963, may cook your steak. Full meals $7-8. Open Mon.-Sat. 11am-2:30pm and 5-10:30pm, Sun. 11am-11pm.

Side Street, 225 N. Bloodworth St., Raleigh (828-4927), at E. Lane St. 3 blocks from the capitol. A classy place with antique furniture, botanical prints, flower table settings, and wholesome sandwiches. Salads too. All selections under $5. Open Mon.-Fri. 11am-3pm and 5-9pm, Sat.-Sun. 11am-8pm.

Skylight Exchange, 405½ W. Rosemary St., Chapel Hill (933-5550). An eclectic den where sandwiches can be eaten ($2-3), used books and records can be purchased, and live music can be heard on the weekends. Effortlessly hip hangout. Open Mon.-Thurs. 10am-11pm, Fri-Sat. 11am-midnight, Sun. 1-11pm.

The Ninth Street Bakery Shop, 754 9th St., Durham (286-0303). More than a bakery: sandwiches from $4. Try the dense bran or blueberry muffins (baked goods start at $1). Weekend nights see veggie/seafood dinners 6-9pm and acoustic music 9-11pm. Open Mon.-Tues. 7am-6pm, Wed.-Thurs. 7am-9pm, Fri. 7am-11pm, Sat. 8am-11pm, Sun. 8am-4pm.

Clyde Cooper's Barbeque, 109 E. Davie, Raleigh (832-7614), 1 block east of the Fayetteville Street Mall downtown. If you like BBQ, this is the place to try it NC-style. The local favorites are the baby back ribs ($5 per lb.) or the barbeque chicken ($4.75). Open Mon.-Sat. 10am-6pm.

Francesca's Dessert Café, 709 9th St., Durham (286-4177). A delectable local favorite with homemade ice cream and pastries served in a chic interior. Open Sun.-Thurs. 11:30am-11:30pm, Fri.-Sat. 11:30am-midnight.

SIGHTS AND ENTERTAINMENT

While the triangle's main attractions are universities, Raleigh has its share of historical sights. The **capitol building,** in Union Square at Edenton and Salisbury, was built in 1840. (Open Mon.-Fri. 8am-5pm, Sat. 9am-5pm. Tours available for large groups. Free.) Across from the capitol at 1 E. Edenton is the new **North Carolina Museum of History** (715-0200), exhibiting memorabilia from the state's Roanoke days to the present. (Open Tues.-Sat. 9am-5pm, Sun. 1-6pm. Free.) Pick up a brochure at the visitors center for a self-guided tour of the renovated 19th-century homes of **Historic Oakwood,** where eight North Carolina governors are buried. Across the street and around the corner at Bicentennial Square is the **Museum of Natural Sciences** (733-7450), which has fossils, gems, and animal exhibits including a live 17-ft. Burmese python named George. (Open Mon.-Sat. 9am-5pm, Sun. 1-5pm. Free.) The **North Carolina Museum of Art,** 2110 Blue Ridge Blvd. (833-1935), off I-40 (Wade Ave. exit), has eight galleries, which includes works by Raphael (the painter, not the turtle), Botticelli, Rubens, Monet, Wyeth, and O'Keeffe, as well as some ancient Egyptian artifacts. (Tours Tues.-Sun. at 1:30pm. Open Tues.-Thurs. 9am-5pm, Fri. 9am-9pm, Sun. 11am-6pm. Free.) A tour of **North Carolina State University** on Hillsborough St. (737-3276), includes the **Pulstar Nuclear Reactor.** (Free tours during the semester Mon.-Fri. at noon, leaving from the Bell Tower on Hillsborough St.) Barring a nuclear accident, none of these sights is all that glowing.

For less urban entertainment, visit Chapel Hill, where the **University of North Carolina** (962-2211), the oldest state university in the country, sprawls over 729 acres. Astronauts practiced celestial navigation until 1975 at the university's **Morehead Planetarium** (962-1236), which houses one of twelve $2.2 million Zeiss Star projectors. The planetarium puts up six different shows yearly, each involving a combination of films and Zeiss projections. These shows are conceived and produced while you watch. The best part is the staff of friendly UNC students, some of whom are Zeissmeisters; they will give advice to travelers—celestial and otherwise. (Open daily 12:30-5pm and 6:30-9:30pm, Sat. noon-5pm and 6:30-9:30pm. $3, seniors, students, and kids $2.50.) Call the university (962-2211) for info on sporting events and concerts at the Smith Center (a.k.a. the Dean Dome).

In Durham, **Duke University** is the major attraction. The **admissions office,** at 2138 Campus Dr. (684-3214), doubles as a visitors center (open Mon.-Fri. 8am-5pm, Sat. 10am-1pm). The **Duke Chapel** (tours and info 684-2572) at the center of the university has more than a million pieces of stained glass in 77 windows depicting almost 900 figures. The Duke Memorial Organ inside has 5000 pipes. Show up around lunchtime and you might catch a free personal concert. (Open daily Sept.-June 8am-10pm.) To the left is the walkway to the **Bryan Center,** Duke's labyrinthine student center, with a gift shop, a café, a small art gallery, and the info desk. Near West Campus on Anderson St. are the **Sarah Duke Gardens** (684-3698), with over 15 acres of landscaped gardens and tiered flower beds. (Open daily 8am-dusk.)

THE SOUTH

Take the free Duke campus shuttle bus to East Campus, where the **Duke Museum of Art** (684-5135) hangs with a small but impressive collection. (Open Tues.-Fri. 9am-5pm, Sat. 11am-2pm, Sun. 2-5pm. Free.) Also take time to enjoy Duke's 7700-acre **forest,** and its more than 30 mi. of trails and drivable roads.

On the other side of Durham, up Guess Rd., is the **Duke Homestead,** 2828 Duke Homestead Rd. (477-5498). Washington Duke first started in the tobacco business here and went on, with the help of his sons, to fund what would become Duke University. The beautiful estate is still a small working farm. (Open Mon.-Sat. 9am-5pm, Sun. 1-5pm; Nov.-March Tues.-Sat. 10am-4pm, Sun. 1-4pm. Free.)

At night, students frequent bars along **Franklin Street** in Chapel Hill, and **9th Street** in Durham, but to hear the emerging Chapel Hill and national talent, go to the **Cat's Cradle,** 300 E. Main St., Carroboro (967-9053), the quasi-legendary rock club where R.E.M. and Pearl Jam once played (inexpensive cover). Or you can catch a **Durham Bulls** (688-8211) baseball game. The **Durham Bulls,** a class A farm team for the Atlanta Braves, became famous after the 1988 movie *Bull Durham* was filmed in their ballpark. (Reserved tickets $6, general admission and under 18 $3, students and seniors $2.50.)

The Research Triangle area always offers something to do, whether it's a concert, guest lecture, exhibit, or going to a bar and getting super-trashed. For a complete listing, pick up free copies of both the *Spectator* and *Independent* weekly magazines, available at most restaurants, bookstores, and hotels.

■■■ CHARLOTTE

In 1799, some fortunate fellow happened upon a gold nugget in the new town of Charlotte. A large and ungainly gold nugget, exactly the kind of nugget you wouldn't want to stub your toe on—basically, a 17-pound nugget. Gold speculation boomed, mines sprung up, and prospectors poured in. The rush lasted about 50 years until some folks in California began to find smaller nuggets, but in larger quantities. The 19th-century mines are gone, but Charlotte, which began as a village along the Catawba Indian trade route, is now the largest city in the Carolinas and the nation's third largest banking center.

Orientation and Practical Information Visitor Information, E. Stonewall St. (331-2700 or 800-231-4636), awaits your brochure browsing uptown between S. Tyron and College St. (Open Mon.-Fri. 8:30am-5pm, Sat. 10am-4pm, Sun. 1-4pm. The **Traveler's Aid Society** can be contacted at 334-7288. **Amtrak:** 1914 N. Tryon St. (376-4416; open daily 7am-12:30pm and 1:30-3:30pm, 7:45pm-4am; call 800-872-7245 for route and schedule information). **Greyhound Trailways:** 601 W. Trade St. (527-9393; open 24 hrs.). For public transportation, ride **Charlotte Transit,** 901 N. Davidson St. (336-3366; 80¢ within city, $1.15 for outlying areas; transfers free). Charlotte's **post office:** 201 N. McDowell (333-5135); **ZIP code:** 28202; **area code:** 704.

Accommodations and Food Charlotte's budget motels thrive off I-85, exit 41, clustered around Sugar Creek Road and the I-85 Service Road. **Econolodge** (597-0470 or 800-424-6473) offers big rooms, a pool, and low prices. (Singles or doubles $29.50; $5 key deposit.) After exit 41, take a left onto Sugar Creek, then another left on the Cricket Inn corner. This puts you on the service road. Nearby **Continental Inn** (597-8100) has new, nicely furnished rooms, but you must be 21 or older to stay. (Singles $31.50, doubles $45; $5 key deposit.)

South of Uptown, the **Dilworth** neighborhood cooks with a generous number of independent restaurants ranging from ethnic cuisine to pizza pub fare. Part yuppie, part gay, and continuously upbeat, the area and its residents are well-heeled, but there are still a few places that are easy on the wallets of unwashed backpackers. Also, the **Charlotte Regional Farmer's Market,** 1715 Yorkmont Rd. (357-1269), hawks local produce, baked goods, and crafts from April to December (Tues.-Sat. 8am-5pm).

Talley's Green Grocery and Café Verde, 1408-C East Blvd. (334-9200), Dilworth Gardens Shopping Center, is an environmental supermarket where you can get your milk, meats, and veggies without the addition of growth hormones, antibiotics, nitrates, pesticides, factory-farming, or anything else. (Deli Express sandwiches $2-3. Grocery open Mon.-Sat. 9am-9pm, Sun. 10am-7pm; café open Mon.-Sat. 11:30am-7pm, Sun. 11:30am-5pm.) **300 East,** 300 East Blvd. (332-6507), is an airy, tidy, American eatery. (Entrees $10-12, sandwiches $5-6; any one of their 6 baked stuffed potatoes $6; open Mon.-Thurs. 11:30am-10:30pm, Fri.-Sat. 11:30am-midnight, Sun. 11am-10pm.) **Café 541,** 521 N. College St. (377-9100), is a coffeehouse with outstanding lunchtime fare. 541 has a killer euro image and paper tablecloths and crayons adorn every table. (Dishes $4-6.) Small portions will leave you hungry for more, but everything comes with free bread and a balsamic vinegar and olive oil dipping sauce. (Open Mon.-Fri. 11:30am-3:30pm, daily 5pm-1am, bar closes at 2am.)

Sights and Entertainment The **Mint Museum of Art,** 2830 Randolph Rd. (337-2000), a five-min. drive from uptown, is particularly proud of its exhaustive pottery and porcelain collection and its American art. (Free tours daily at 2pm; $2, 12 and under free; open Tues. 10am-10pm, Wed.-Sat. 10am-5pm, Sun. 1-6pm; free on Tues. after 5pm and on the 2nd Sun. of every month.) The **Discovery Place,** 301 N. Tryon St. (800-935-0553 or 845-6664), draws crowds with its hands-on science and technology museum, OmniMax theater, aquarium, and planetarium. Tickets for OmniMax, planetarium, or exhibit halls are $5 (ages 6-18 and seniors $4, 3-5 $2.50). Tickets for any two events are $7, $6, and $4 respectively. (Open Mon.-Sat. 9am-6pm, Sun. 1-6pm, off-season Mon.-Fri. 9am-5pm, Sat. 9am-6pm, Sun. 1-6pm.) The **Charlotte Knights** play minor league baseball at Knights Castle, E 77 at Exit 88 (332-3746; tickets $4.50, youths and seniors $3.00; season April-July).

Paramounts Carowinds Entertainments Complex (588-2606), 10 mi. south of Charlotte off exit 90 of I-77, is an amusement park featuring the new theme area, **Wayne's World,** where you can ride the "hurler" roller coaster. ($25, seniors and children 4-6 $13.50, 3 and under free; $3 parking; open weekends March-May and Sept., 10am-8pm; June-August 10am-8pm on weekdays, and until 10pm weekends.)

To get nightlife, arts, and entertainment listings, grab a free issue of *Creative Loafing* or *Break* in your travels through Charlotte shops and restaurants. The **Moon Room,** 433 S. Tryon St. (342-2003), has live music on weekends and explodes into bohemian funkiness with theme nights on Sunday (tarot readers on Psychic Night and wacky films on Movie Night). **Dilworth Brewing Co.,** 1301 East Blvd. (377-2739), pours homemade brew while local rock and blues play on weekends. **Heretics/Aardvark,** 5600 Old Concord Rd. (596-1342), has local talent on-stage and all-ages in the crowd. Late night (until 4am on Fri. and Sat.) dancing is provided by **The Edge,** 4369 S. Tryon (525-3343), a "progressive dance complex" for those 19 and up with nights like Disco Hump and College Quake. Call for details.

THE CAROLINA MOUNTAINS

The sharp ridges and endless rolling slopes of the southern Appalachian range creates some of the most spectacular scenery in the Southeast. At one time, North Carolina's verdant highlands provided an exclusive refuge for the country's rich and privileged. The Vanderbilts owned a large portion of the 500,000-acre Pisgah National Forest, which they subsequently willed to the U.S. government. Today the Blue Ridge, Great Smoky, Black, Craggy, Pisgah, and Balsam Mountains that comprise the western half of North Carolina beckon budget travelers, not millionaires. Campsites blanket the region, coexisting with elusive but inexpensive youth hostels and ski lodges. Enjoy the area's rugged wilderness while backpacking, canoeing, whitewater rafting, or cross-country skiing. Motorists and cyclists can follow the **Blue Ridge Parkway** to some unforgettable views.

The Blue Ridge Mountains divide into two areas. The northern area is the **High Country,** which includes the territory between the town of Boone and the town of Asheville, 100 mi. to the southwest. The second area comprises the **Great Smoky Mountains National Park** (see Great Smoky Mountains National Park, TN) and the **Nanatahala National Forest.**

■■■ BOONE AND BLOWING ROCK

Named for famous frontiersman Daniel Boone, who built a cabin here in the 1760s on his journey into the western wilderness, the town of **Boone** continues to evoke (and profit from) its pioneer past with shops such as the Mast General Store and the Candy Barrel. Boone is not just a tourist town, though, and Appalachian State University's sprawling campus and youthful inhabitants lend a relaxed and funky atmosphere, bookshops, coffee houses, and hole-in-the-wall restaurants. **Blowing Rock,** 7 mi. south at the entrance to the Blue Ridge Parkway, is a folk artists' colony. Its namesake overhangs **Johns River Gorge**; chuck a piece of paper (biodegradable, of course) over the edge and the wind will blow it back in your face.

PRACTICAL INFORMATION

Emergency: 911. **National Park Service/Blue Ridge Parkway Emergency,** 259-0701 or 800-727-5928.

Visitor Information: Boone Area Chamber of Commerce, 208 Howard St. (800-852-9506 or 264-2225), turn from Rte. 321 onto River St., drive behind the university, turn right onto Depot St. then take the first left onto Howard St. Info on accommodations and sights. Open daily 9am-5pm. The **Blowing Rock Chamber of Commerce** (295-7851) is housed in the town hall (open Mon.-Sat. 9am-5pm). **North Carolina High Country Host Visitor Center,** 1700 Blowing Rock Rd. (264-1299 or 800-438-7500). Pick up copies of the *High Country Host Area Travel Guide,* an informative and detailed map of the area, and the *Blue Ridge Parkway Directory,* a mile-by-mile description of all services and attractions located on or near the Parkway. Open daily 9am-5pm.

Greyhound: (262-0501.) At the AppalCart station on Winkler's Creek Road, off Rte. 321. Flag stop in Blowing Rock. One per day to most points east, south, and west. Open Mon.-Fri. 8am-5pm, Sat.-Sun. 10am-4:30pm.

Public Transport: Boone AppalCart (264-2278), on Winkler's Creek Rd. Local bus and van service; 3 main routes. The Red Route links downtown Boone with ASU and the motels and restaurants on Blowing Rock Rd. The Green Route serves Rte. 421. Crosstown route between the campus and the new marketplace. The Red Route operates Mon.-Fri. every hr. 7am-6:30pm; Green Mon.-Fri. every hr. 7am-8pm; crosstown Mon.-Fri. 7am-11pm, Sat. 8am-8pm. Fare 50¢ in town, charged by zones for the rest of the county (25-75¢). AppalCart goes to the Blowing Rock Town Hall from Boone twice daily.

Post Office: 637 Blowing Rock Rd. (264-3813), and 103 W. King St. (262-1171). Open Mon.-Fri. 9am-5pm, Sat. 9am-noon. Lobby sells stamps until 10pm. **ZIP code:** 28607.

Area Code: 704.

ACCOMMODATIONS, CAMPING, AND FOOD

Catering primarily to wealthy visitors, the area fields more than its share of expensive motels and B&Bs. Scratch the lodging surface, however, and you will also find enough inexpensive motels, hostels, and campsites to answer one's financial woes.

Blowing Rock Assembly Grounds, P.O. Box 2530, Blowing Rock (295-7813), near the Blue Ridge Parkway, has clean rooms, communal bathrooms, sports facilities, and a cheap cafeteria, all in a gorgeous setting with access to hiking trails. Ask the bus driver to let you off at Blowing Rock Town Hall or at the Rte. 321 bypass and Sunset Dr., depending on the direction you're traveling—it's about 2 mi. from both points. Call the hostel for a pick-up, or stay on Rte. 321 and drive south to Goforth Rd. on the left, near a huge white building; follow along the golf course until you see the "BRAG" signs. Primarily a retreat for religious groups. (Check-in after 4pm, check-out before noon. Desk open daily 9am-5pm. Package rates available. No laundry facilities. $15; linens $1.50. Reservations required.)

The **Boone Trail Motel,** U.S. 421, south of downtown (264-8839), exists in a price range all its own ($21 singles, doubles $28). If the rooms are too budget for you, then apartments are available from $33 per night. Most inexpensive hotels are concentrated along **Blowing Rock Rd.** (Rte. 321), or Rte. 105. The red-brick **Red Carpet Inn** (264-2457) has spacious rooms that come with remote TV, a playground, and a pool. Prices may vary with seasonal availability. Some holiday weekends have a two-night minimum stay. (All credit cards accepted; reservations not required; no laundry facilities; singles around $47, doubles $57.) The **High Country Inn** (264-1000 or 800-334-5605), Rte. 105, also has a pool, jacuzzi, sauna, and exercise room. They even have a watermill. (Standard-sized, comfortable rooms; check-in 4pm, check-out 11am; mid-range prices: singles $37. doubles $42. Weekend rates $10 more. Ask about seasonal prices. Breakfast and dinner packages available.)

Boone and **Pisgah National Forest** offer developed and well-equipped **campsites** as well as **primitive camping** options for those who are looking to rough it. Along the Blue Ridge Pkwy., spectacular sites without hookups are available for $8 at the **Julian Price Campground,** Mile 297 (963-5911); **Linville Falls,** Mile 316 (963-5911); and **Crabtree Meadows,** Mile 340 (675-4444; open May-Oct. only). Cabins in **Roan Mountain State Park** (772-3314) comfortably sleep six and are furnished with linens and cooking utensils (Sun.-Thurs. $62, Fri.-Sat. $85, weekly $419). The state park offers pool and tennis facilities and tends to attract smaller crowds than the campgrounds on the parkway. May through September visitors can unwind from a day of hiking at the park's "Summer in the Park" festival featuring cloggers and storytellers. Call the **Roan Mountain Visitors Center** (772-3314 or 772-3303) for info.

Fast food restaurants' deep-fat options fry on both sides of Rte. 321. College students and professors alike hang out on **West King Street** (U.S. 441/ U.S. 221). **Our Daily Bread,** 629 West King St. (264-0173), serves sandwiches, salads, and super vegetarian specials for $3-5 (open Mon.-Fri. 8am-6:30pm, Sat. 9am-5pm). Down the block, the **Appalachian Soda Shop,** 651 West King St. (262-1500), lays the grease on thicker, but the prices are lower. Huge, juicy burgers for under $2.80, "famous" BBQ for $3-5 (open Mon.-Sat. 9am-5pm). The **Daniel Boone Inn** (264-8657), junction routes 321 and 421, serves hefty, country sit-down, family-style, all-you-can-eat, meals. (Open daily, dinner 11am-9pm, $10; breakfast Sat.-Sun. only, $6.) **Piccadeli's,** 818 Blowing Rock Rd. (704-262-3500), has homemade soups and sandwiches ($3-5). Italian specialties like spaghetti from $5. (Open daily 11am-10pm.)

SIGHTS AND ACTIVITIES

In an open air amphitheater, **Horn in the West** (264-2120), located near Boone off Rte. 105, presents an outdoor drama of the American Revolution as it was fought in the southern Appalachians. (Shows Tues.-Sun. at 8:30pm. Tickets $8-12, children under 13 ½-price. Group rates upon request. Reservations recommended.) Adjacent to the theater, the **Daniel Boone Native Gardens** celebrate mountain foliage, while the **Hickory Ridge Homestead** documents 18th-century mountain life. **An Appalachian Summer** (800-843-2787) is a month-long, high-caliber festival of music, art, theater, and dance sponsored by Appalachian State University.

In Blowing Rock, stop by **Parkway Craft Center,** Mile 294 (295-7938), 2 mi. south of Blowing Rock Village in the Cone Manor House, where members of the Southern Highland Handicraft Guild demonstrate their skills and sell their crafts. The craft center is on the grounds of the **Moses H. Cone Memorial Park,** 3600 acres of shaded walking trails and magnificent views including a picture-postcard view of Bass Lake. Check out the National Park Service desk in the center for a copy of "This Week's Activities." (Open May-Oct. daily 9am-5:30pm; free.) To see the Moses H. Cone Park from another perspective, take the $15 per hour guided horseback ride. Tours leave the **Blowing Rock Stables** from the L.M. Tate Showgrounds, "home of the oldest continuous horse show in America." Get off the Blue Ridge Pkwy. at the Blowing Rock sign, turn left onto Yonahlossee Rd. and look for the "Blowing Rock Stables" sign on the right; call a day in advance for reservations (295-7847; open April-Dec. daily). The **Cosmic Coffee House** (295-4762), N. Main St., brews wonderful coffee, shows the artwork of local artists, and hosts local bands several times a month (open Mon. and Wed.-Sat. 8am-11pm, Tues. and Sun. 8am-9pm).

Hikers should arm themselves with the invaluable large-scale map *100 Favorite Trails* ($3.50). Consider joining one of the guided expeditions led by the staff of **Edge of the World**, P.O. Box 1137, Banner Elk (898-9550), on Rte. 184 downtown. A complete outdoor equipment/clothing store, the Edge rents equipment and gives regional hiking information. They also lead day-long backpacking, whitewater canoeing, spelunking, and rock climbing trips throughout the High Country for about $65. (Open Mon.-Sat. 9am-10pm, Sun. 9am-1pm.)

Downhill skiers can enjoy the Southeast's largest concentration of alpine resorts. Four converge on the Boone/Blowing Rock/Banner Elk area: **Appalachian Ski Mountain**, P.O. Box 106, Blowing Rock 28604 (800-322-2373; lift tickets $35, $25 on weekdays, full rental $13); **Ski Beech**, 1007 Beech Mt. Parkway, Beech Mountain 28605 (800-438-2093 or 387-2011; lift tickets weekends $35, weekdays $25, rentals $16/12); **Ski Hawknest**, Town of Seven Devils, 1605 Skyland Dr., Banner Elk (800-822-4295 or 963-6561; lift tickets weekends $20, weekdays $10, with rentals $30/$16); and **Sugar Mountain**, P.O. Box 369, Banner Elk (898-4521; lift tickets weekends $38, weekdays $25, rentals $15/$12). AppalCart (264-2278) runs a daily shuttle in winter to Sugar Mountain and four times per week to Ski Beech. Call the High Country Host (264-1299) for ski reports. It is best to call ahead to the resort for specific prices of ski packages.

The 5-mi. auto road to **Grandfather Mountain** (800-468-7325) reveals an unparalleled view of the entire High Country area. At the top you'll find a private park featuring a one mile-high suspension bridge, a nature museum with minerals, bird, and plant life indigenous to NC, and a small zoo ($9, kids $5, under 4 free). To hike or camp on Grandfather Mt. you need a permit ($4 per day, $8 per night for camping—available at the Grandfather Mountain Country Store on Rte. 221 or at the park entrance). Pick up a trail map at the entrance to learn which trails are available for overnight use. Also contact the **Backcountry Manager,** Grandfather Mt., Linville 28646. Mountain open daily 8am-7pm; Dec.-March 9am-5pm, weather permitting.)

■■■ ASHEVILLE

A drive along the winding Blue Ridge Parkway reveals the scenic vistas of Asheville's hazy blue mountains, deep valleys, spectacular waterfalls, and plunging gorges. The people of this Appalachian Mountain hub rival nature in their diversity and excitement. Students at UNC-Asheville, nature lovers, a thriving gay and lesbian community, and artists make the city itself as intriguing as the mountains that surround it. The sheer number of attractions—the Vanderbilt Biltmore Estate, campgrounds and trails, Cherokee museums and cultural exhibitions less than an hour to the south, and almost continuous year-round festivals—disperses tourists and leaves the streets relatively uncluttered.

PRACTICAL INFORMATION

Emergency: 911.

Visitor Information: Chamber of Commerce, 151 Haywood St. (258-3858 or 800-257-1300 in NC), off I-240 on the northwest end of downtown; just follow the frequent signs. Ask at the desk for a detailed city and transit route and a comprehensive sight-seeing guide. Open Mon.-Fri. 8:30am-5:30pm, Sat.-Sun. 9am-5pm.

Greyhound: 2 Tunnel Rd. (253-5353), 2 mi. east of downtown, near the Beau-catcher Tunnel. Asheville Transit bus 13 or 14 run to and from downtown every ½-hr. Last bus at 5:50pm. To: Charlotte (5 per day, 3 hr., $22); Knoxville (7 per day, 3 hr., $24.50); Atlanta ($44). Open daily 8am-10pm.

Public Transport: Asheville Transit, 360 W. Haywood (253-5691). Service within city limits. All routes converge on Pritchard Park downtown. Buses oper-ate Mon.-Fri. (and some Sat.) 5:30am-7pm, most at ½-hr. intervals. Fare 60¢, trans-fers 10¢. Special fares for seniors, disabled, and multi-fare tickets.

Post Office: 33 Coxe Ave. (257-4112), at Patton Ave. Open Mon.-Fri. 8am-5pm, Sat. 9am-noon. **ZIP code:** 28802.

Area Code: 704.

ACCOMMODATIONS AND CAMPING

Asheville's many reasonably priced motels cluster in two spots—several indepen-dent motels lie on **Merrimon Avenue** near downtown (take bus #2), while **Tunnel Road** east of downtown (take buses 4 or 12) also sports many chain motels. The **American Court Motel,** 85 Merrimon Ave. (253-4427 or 800-233-3582 for reserva-tion desk only), has bright, cozy, and well-kept rooms with cable, A/C, pool, and laundromat. (No pets. Singles $47, doubles $53.) The **Down Town Motel,** 65 Merri-mon Ave. (253-9841), on Merrimon St. just north of the I-240 expressway, is a 10-min. walk from downtown (or take bus #2), with cable, A/C, renovated rooms, new furniture, and bathrooms. Prices are seasonal, starting at $33. Ask about long-term (several days) discounts. As of press time, the Down Town was still being reno-vated, and on-season rates may rise. **In Town Motor Lodge,** 100 Tunnel Rd. (252-1811), provides clean rooms with cable, A/C, pool, and free local calls (singles $37, doubles $42; weekends $53). The **Skyway Motel,** 131 Tunnel Rd. (253-2631), daz-zles with its daintily painted walls and decorative prints in simple rooms. (In-season singles $31, doubles $38; weekend rates are higher. Group and long-term rates available.)

With the Blue Ridge Pkwy., Pisgah National Forest, and the Great Smokies easily accessible by car, you can find a campsite to suit any taste. Close to town is **Bear Creek RV Park and Campground,** 81 S. Bear Creek Rd. (253-0798). Take I-40 exit 47, and look for the sign at the top of the hill. (Pool, laundry, groceries, and game room. Tent sites $17.50. RV sites with hookup $25.) In Pisgah National Forest, the nearest campground is **Powhatan,** off Rte. 191, 12 mi. southwest of Asheville. (All sites along the Pkwy. $8. Open May-Sept.)

FOOD

You'll find greasy links in most major fast-food chains on **Tunnel Road** and **Biltmore Avenue.** The **Western North Carolina Farmers Market** (253-1691), at the inter-section of I-40 and Rte. 191, near I-26, hawks fresh produce and crafts. Take bus 16 to I-40, then walk ½-mi. (Open daily 8am-6pm.)

Malaprops Bookstore/Café, 61 Haywood St. (254-6734), downtown in the base-ment of the bookstore. Gourmet coffees, bagels, and great smells that emanate throughout the store. Check out the cerebral readings and the Malaprops staff art on the walls. Open Mon.-Thurs. 9am-8pm, Fri.-Sat. 9am-10pm, Sun. noon-6pm.

Superette, 78 Patton Ave. (254-0255), in the heart of the downtown, serves Mid-dle Eastern food good, fast, and cheap. Salads from $1.50, sandwiches $2.50-$3.50. Open Mon.-Fri. 8am-5pm, Sat. 10am-4pm.

Beanstreets, 3 Broadway (255-8180). Quality art hangs next to protruding, fake body parts in this swank café. Excellent for breakfast with Belgian waffles, blue-berry scones ($1.50), and crunchy granola and fruit ($2.50). Open Mon.-Wed. 8am-1pm, Tues., and Fri. 8am-midnight, Sat. 9am-midnight, Sun. 9am-3pm.

Five Points Restaurant, 258 Broadway (252-8030), at the corner of Chestnut 2 blocks from Merrimon. For home cookin' close to several motels, this unremark-able-looking diner cannot be beat. So inexpensive it's almost unbelievable. You can get a full dinner (entree, salad, and two veggies) for $3-5, and sandwiches from $1.70. Open Mon.-Fri. 6am-8pm, Sat. 6am-5pm, Sun. 6am-2:30pm.

SIGHTS AND FESTIVALS

Elvis's Southern mansion, Graceland, has nothing on the Vanderbilt family's **Biltmore Estate,** 1 North Pack Square (255-1700 or 800-543-2961). Take exit 50 off I-40, and go three blocks north. A tour of this French Renaissance-style castle can take all day if it's crowded; try to arrive early in the morning. The ostentatious abode was built in the 1890s and is the largest private home in America. The self-guided tour winds through a portion of the 250 rooms, enabling one to view an indoor pool, a bowling alley, rooms lined with Sargent paintings and Dürer prints, and immense rare-book libraries. Tours of the surrounding gardens, which were designed by Central Park planner Frederick Law Olmsted, and the Biltmore winery (with sour-wine tasting for those over 21) are included in the hefty admission price. (Open daily 9am-5pm. Winery open Mon.-Sat. at 11am, Sun. at 1pm. Estate admission $25, ages 10-15 $19, under 9 free. Ticket prices rise $2-3 in Nov.-Dec. in order to defray the cost of Christmas decorations.) Be sure to get your ticket validated—if you decide to return the next day, your visit will be free. Also, pay a visit to **Biltmore Village,** the quaint shopping district that George Vanderbilt had built right outside the gates of his chateau. It contains craft galleries, antique stores, and a music shop. On Memorial Day, July 4th, and Labor Day weekends, the Village hosts outdoor jazz. September always brings the International Exposition overflowing with food and music.

Past travelers like Henry Ford, Thomas Edison, and F. Scott Fitzgerald all stayed in the towering **Grove Park Inn** (252-2711), on Macon St. off Charlotte St. Look for the bright red-tile roof peeking through the trees. Made of stone quarried from the surrounding mountains, the still-operating hotel has many pieces of original early-20th-century furniture and fireplaces so immense you can walk into them. Walk to the right wing of the inn and you will happen upon the **Biltmore Industrial Museum** (253-7651) where looms loom large and homespun handicrafts used on the Biltmore Estate gather dust (open daily 10am-6pm). Next door is the **Estes-Winn Memorial Museum,** which houses about 20 vintage automobiles ranging from a Model T Ford to a 1959 Edsel. Check out the 1922 candy-red America La France fire engine. On the way out, peruse the door engraving: "Doing a common thing uncommonly well often brings success." (Both open Mon.-Sat. 10am-5pm, Sun. 1-5pm. Free.)

The **Thomas Wolfe Memorial,** 48 Spruce St. (253-8304), between Woodfin and Walnut St., site of the novelist's boyhood home, was a boarding house run by his mother. Wolfe depicted the "Old Kentucky Home" as "Dixieland" in his first novel, *Look Homeward, Angel.* (Open Mon.-Sat. 9am-5pm, Sun. 1-5pm; hours vary in winter. Tours given every ½-hr. $1, students and kids 50¢.) The **Riverside Cemetery,** Birch St. off Montford Ave., north of I-240, houses (permanently) writers Thomas Wolfe and O. Henry.

Asheville's artistic tradition remains as strong as its literary one; visit the **Folk Art Center** (704-298-7928), east of Asheville at mile 382 on the Blue Ridge Pkwy., north of U.S. 70, to see the outstanding work of the **Southern Highland Handicraft Guild**. (Open daily 9am-5pm. Free.) Each year around mid-July the Folk Art Center sponsors a **Guild Fair** (298-7928) at the Asheville Civic Center, off I-240 on Haywood St. Both the Folk Art Center and the chamber of commerce have more info on this weekend of craft demonstrations, dancing, and music.

Scrutinizing observers may catch the next Houston Astros' baseball star at **McCormick Field** (258-0428), at the intersection of Biltmore Ave. and S. Charlotte St. This stadium houses the Astros' farm team and "the greatest show on dirt" ($3.75, students with ID $3, ages 3-12 $2).

THE SOUTH

OUTER BANKS

England's first attempt to colonize North America took place on the shores of North Carolina in 1587. This ill-fated adventure ended when Sir Walter Raleigh's Roanoke Island settlement inexplicably vanished. Since then, a succession of pirates, patriots, and secessionists has brought adventure to the North Carolina coast. Blackbeard called Ocracoke home in the early 18th century until a savvy serviceman struck down the buccaneer at Pamlico Sound. Few seafarers fare well here; over 600 ships have foundered on the Banks' southern shores. Though they were the site of the deaths of countless sailors, the Outer Banks also saw the birth of powered flight—the Wright Brothers flew the first airplane at Kitty Hawk in 1903.

The Outer Banks descend from touristy beach towns southward into heavenly wilderness. Highly developed Bodie Island, on the Outer Banks' northern end, holds the towns of Nags Head, Kitty Hawk, and Kill Devil Hills. Crowds become less overpowering as you travel south on Rte. 12 through magnificent wildlife preserves and across Hatteras Inlet to Ocracoke island and its isolated beaches.

PRACTICAL INFORMATION

Emergency: 911, north of the Oregon Inlet. In **Ocracoke,** 928-4831.

Visitor Information: Aycock Brown Visitors Center (261-4644), off U.S. 158, after the Wright Memorial Bridge, Bodie Island. Info on accommodations, picnic areas, and National Park Service schedules. Open daily 8:30am-6:30pm; in winter Mon.-Fri. 9am-5pm.

Cape Hatteras National Seashore Information Centers: Bodie Island (441-5711), Rte. 12 at Bodie Island Lighthouse. Info and special programs. Open Memorial Day-Labor Day daily 9am-5pm. **Hatteras Island** (995-4474), Rte. 12 at Cape Hatteras. Camping info, demonstrations, and special programs. Open daily 9am-6pm; off-season daily 9am-5pm. **Ocracoke Island** (928-4531), next to the ferry terminal at the south end of the island. Info on ferries, camping, lighthouses, and wild ponies. Open daily 9am-5pm, mid-June to Aug. daily 9am-6pm.

Ferries: Toll ferries operate to Ocracoke from **Cedar Island,** east of New Bern on U.S. 70 (4-8 per day, 2¼ hr.), and **Swan Quarter,** on the northern side of Pamlico. $10 per car (reserve in advance), $2 per biker, $1 on foot. Cedar Island 225-2551, Swan Quarter 926-1111, Ocracoke 928-3841. All open daily 5:30am-8:30pm. Free ferry across Hatteras Inlet between Hatteras and Ocracoke (daily 5am-11pm, 40 min.).

Taxi: Beach Cab, 441-2500. Serves Bodie Island and Manteo. $1.50 first mi., $1.20 each additional mi.

Car Rental: National, Mile 6, Beach Rd. (800-328-4567 or 441-5488), Kill Devil Hills. $55 per day. 75 free mi., 30¢ each additional mi. Must be 25 with major credit card. Open Mon.-Fri. 9am-5pm, Sat. 9am-3pm.

Bike Rental: Pony Island Motel (928-4411) and the **Slushy Stand** on Rte. 12, both on Ocracoke Island. $1 per hr., $7 per day. Open daily 8am-dusk.

ZIP codes: Manteo 27954, Nags Head 27959, Ocracoke 27960.

Area Code: 919.

Four narrow islands strung north-to-south along half the length of the North Carolina coast comprise the Outer Banks. **Bodie Island** includes the towns of **Kitty Hawk, Kill Devil Hills,** and **Nags Head,** and is accessible via U.S. 158 from Elizabeth, NC, and Norfolk, VA. **Roanoke Island** lies between Bodie and the mainland on U.S. 64, and includes the town of **Manteo. Hatteras Island,** connected to Bodie by a bridge, stretches like a great sandy elbow. **Ocracoke Island,** the southernmost, is linked by free ferry to Hatteras Island, and by toll ferry to towns on the mainland. **Cape Hatteras National Seashore** encompasses Hatteras, Ocracoke, and the southern end of Bodie Island. On Bodie Island, U.S. 158 and Rte. 12 run parallel to each other until the beginning of the preserve. After that, Rte. 12 (also called Beach Rd.) continues south, stringing Bodie, Hatteras, and Ocracoke together with free bridges and ferries. Addresses on Bodie Island are determined by their distance in miles from the Wright Memorial Bridge.

Nags Head and Ocracoke lie 76 mi. apart, and public transportation is virtually nonexistent. Hitching, though common, is not recommended, and may require lengthy waits. The flat terrain makes hiking and biking pleasant, but the Outer Banks' ferocious traffic calls for extra caution.

ACCOMMODATIONS AND CAMPING

Most motels cling to Rte. 12 in the costly town of Nags Head. For budget accommodations, try **Ocracoke.** On all three islands the in season usually lasts from mid-June to Labor Day, and rates are much higher during those months. Reserve seven to ten days ahead for weekday stays and up to a month for weekends. Rangers advise campers to bring extra-long tent spikes because of the loose dirt as well as tents with extra-fine screens to keep out the flea-sized, biting "no-see-ums." Strong insect repellent is also helpful. Sleeping on the beach is illegal.

Kill Devil Hills

The Ebbtide, Mile 10, Beach Rd. (441-4913), Kill Devil Hills. A family place with spruce, wholesome rooms. Cable TV, A/C, refrigerator, microwave, pool. Offers "inside track" on local activities. Singles or doubles $54-74; off-season $32-47. $1 breakfast. Open April-Oct.

Nettlewood Motel, Mile 7, Beach Rd. (441-5039), Kill Devil Hills, on both sides of the highway. Private beach access. Don't let the uninviting exterior prevent you from enjoying this clean, comfortable motel. TV, A/C, pool, refrigerator. Singles or doubles $37-65; off-season: $30-46. Free day for week-long stays.

Ocracoke

Sand Dollar Motel (928-5571), off Rte. 12. Turn right at the Pony Island Inn, right at the Back Porch Restaurant, and left at the Edwards Motel. Accommodating owners make you feel at home in this breezy, quiet, immaculate motel. Singles $47, doubles $58. Off-season $33/40.

Edwards Motel (928-4801), off Rte. 12, by the Back Porch Restaurant. Fish-cleaning facilities on premises. Bright assortment of accommodations, all with A/C and TV. Rooms with 2 double beds $44, with 2 double beds and 1 single bed $49; efficiencies $63; cottages $82-93. Off-season $40, $46, $58, and $71-77, respectively.

Oscar's House (928-1311), on the ocean side of Rte. 12, 1 block from Silver Lake harbor. Charming B&B with 4 rooms, shared baths. Memorial Day-June singles $47, doubles $60; July-Labor Day singles $55, doubles $66; off-season singles $44, doubles $55. Full vegetarian breakfast and use of their bicycles included.

Four oceanside **campgrounds** on Cape Hatteras National Seashore are all open mid-April to mid-October. **Oregon Inlet** lies on the southern tip of Bodie Island; **Cape Point** (in Buxton), and **Frisco** near the elbow of Hatteras Island; and **Ocracoke** in the middle of Ocracoke Island. All have restrooms, cold running water, and grills. All sites (except Ocracoke's) cost $11, and are rented on a first-come, first-served basis. Ocracoke sites ($12) can be reserved through **MISTIX** (800-365-2267 or 619-452-5956). For info, contact Cape Hatteras National Seashore, Rte. 1, P.O. Box 675, Manteo, NC 27954 (473-2111).

SIGHTS AND ACTIVITIES

The **Wright Brothers National Memorial,** Mile 8, U.S. 158 (441-7430), marks the spot in Kill Devil Hills where Orville and Wilbur Wright made the world's first sustained, controlled power flight in 1903. You can see models of their planes, hear a detailed account of the day of the first flight, chat with the flight attendants, and view the dramatic monument the U.S. government dedicated to the brothers in 1932. (Open daily 9am-7pm; winter 9am-5pm. Presentations every hr. 10am-5pm. $1, $3 per car, free with seniors.) In nearby **Jockey's Ridge State Park** (441-7132), home of the East Coast's largest sand dunes, hang-gliders soar in the wind that Orville and Wilbur first broke.

On **Roanoke Island,** the **Fort Raleigh National Historic Site,** off U.S. 64, offers separately run attractions in one park. In the **Elizabeth Gardens** (473-3234), antique statues and fountains punctuate a beautiful display of flowers, herbs, and trees. (Open daily 9am-8pm; off-season 9am-5pm. $2.50, under 12 free.) Behind door number two lies the theater where *The Lost Colony,* the longest-running outdoor drama in the U.S., has been performed since 1937 (473-3414 or 800-488-5012; performed Mon.-Sat. mid-June to late Aug. at 8:30pm; $12, seniors and disabled people $10, under 12 $6; bring insect repellent). **Fort Raleigh** (473-5772) is a reconstructed 1585 battery—basically a pile of dirt. The nearby **visitors center** contains a tiny museum and plays Elizabethan music as part of its losing battle to recall the earliest days of English activity in North America. (Open Mon.-Sat. 9am-8pm, Sun. 9am-5pm.) Lay your hands on a horseshoe crab and make faces at marine monsters in the Shark, Skate, and Ray Gallery at the **North Carolina Aquarium** (473-3493), 1 mi. west of U.S. 64. A full slate of educational programs keeps things lively. (Open Mon.-Sat. 9am-5pm, Sun. 1-5pm. $3, seniors $2, 6-17 $1.)

On **Ocracoke Island,** historic sights give way to the incessant, soothing surf. With the exception of the town of Ocracoke on the southern tip, the island remains an undeveloped national seashore. Speedy walkers or meandering cyclists can cover the town in less than an hour. Pick up a walking tour pamphlet at the visitors center (see Practical Information above). Better yet, stroll or swim along the waters that lick the pristine shore. At the **Soundside Snorkel,** park rangers teach visitors to snorkel. Bring tennis shoes and a swimsuit. (Wed. and Fri. at 2:30pm. Equipment rental $1. Make reservations at the Ocracoke Visitors Center from 9am the day before until 2:30pm the day of program.)

South Carolina

The first state to secede from the Union in 1860, South Carolina continues to take great pride in its Confederate history. Civil War monuments dot virtually every public green or city square. South Carolina strangely supports a mix of the progressive and reactionary. The state is periodically plagued by Confederate "patriots," who vehemently protest any legislative effort to remove the Confederate flag from the state flag, but also hosts an annual and well-attended gay-right parade. The capital, Columbia, is slow-paced with little to see—Sherman ruined its tourist-town potential by burning it to the ground—but Charleston, despite a recent hurricane, still boasts beautiful, stately, antebellum charm. You'll want to do the Charleston for a few days and take in the city's favors and flavors.

PRACTICAL INFORMATION

Capital: Columbia.
Department of Parks, Recreation, and Tourism, Edgar A. Brown Bldg., 1205 Pendleton St. #106, Columbia 29201 (734-0122). **U.S. Forest Service,** P.O. Box 970, Columbia 29202 (765-5222).
Time Zone: Eastern. **Postal Abbreviation:** SC
Sales Tax: 6%.

■■■ CHARLESTON

Dukes, barons, and earls once presided over Charleston's great coastal plantations, leaving in their wake an extensive historic downtown district. However, in recent years natural disasters, including five fires and 10 hurricanes, have ruled Charleston, leaving destruction in their wake. The reconstruction after the latest natural mishap—Hurricane Hugo's rampage in September, 1989—is nearly complete; fresh paint, new storefronts, and tree stumps mix with beautifully refurbished antebellum homes, old churches, and hidden gardens. The Charleston area also offers visitors access to the nearby Atlantic coastal islands. Most noticeably, the people of Charleston are some of the friendliest people you will meet on your journeys in the South. They survive and flourish with a smile.

PRACTICAL INFORMATION

Emergency: 911.

Visitor Information: Charleston Visitors Center, 375 Meeting St. (853-8000), across from the Charleston Museum. Walking tour map ($4.50) has historical info and good directions. The film *Forever Charleston* gives an overview of Charleston past and present. Tickets $3, children $1.50. Open daily 8:30am-5:30pm.

Amtrak: 4565 Gaynor Ave. (744-8263), 8 mi. west of downtown. The "Durant Ave." bus will take you from the station to the historic district. To Richmond ($84, 8 hr.), Savannah ($25, 2 hr.), Washington D.C. ($108, 8 hr.). Open daily 4:15am-9:30pm.

Greyhound: 3610 Dorchester Rd. (722-7721), in N. Charleston near I-26—try to avoid this area at night. To: Savannah (#28, 3 hr.), Charlotte ($40, 6 hr.). To get into town, take the **South Carolina Electric and Gas** bus, marked "Broad St." or "South Battery," that stops right in front of the station, and get off at the intersection of Meeting St. and Calhoun St. To get back to the station from town, pick up the bus marked "Navy Yard: 5 Mile Dorchester Rd." at the same intersection. There are two "Navy Yard" buses, so be sure to take this one; it's the only one that stops in front of the station. Open daily 6am-10pm.

Public Transport: South Carolina Electric and Gas Company (SCE&G) City Bus Service, 2469 Leeds Ave. (747-0922). Operates Mon.-Sat. 5:10am-1am. Fare 75¢. **Downtown Area Shuttle (DASH)** also operates Mon.-Fri. 8am-5pm. Fare 75¢, transfers to other SCE&G buses free.

Car Rental: Thrifty Car Rental, 3565 W. Montague Ave. (552-7531 or 800-367-2277). $32 per day with unlimited mi. Must be 25 with major credit card. Open daily 5:45am-11:30pm.

Bike Rental: The Bicycle Shoppe, 283 Meeting St. (722-8168). $3 per hr., $15 per day. Open Mon.-Sat. 9am-8pm, Sun. 1-5pm.

Taxi: North Area Taxi, 554-7575. Base fare $1.

Help Lines: Hotline, 744-4357. 24 hrs. General counseling and information on transient accommodations. **People Against Rape,** 722-7273. 24 hrs.

Post Office: 83 Broad St. Open Mon.-Fri. 8:30am-5pm, Sat. 8:30am-noon. **ZIP code:** 29402.

Area Code: 803.

Old Charleston is confined to the southernmost point of the mile-wide peninsula below **Calhoun Street. Meeting, King,** and **East Bay Streets** are major north-south routes through the city. North of Calhoun St. runs the **Savannah Hwy. (U.S. 17).**

ACCOMMODATIONS AND CAMPING

Motel rooms in historic downtown Charleston are expensive. All the cheap motels are far out and not a practical option for those without cars. Investigate the tiny accommodations just across the Ashley River on U.S. 17 south; several offer $15-20 rooms. The best budget option in town is the **Rutledge Victoria Inn,** 114 Rutledge Ave. (722-7551), a beautiful historic home with shared rooms and free coffee or tea ($20 per person first day, $15 each additional day). The friendly manager will not let you set foot in Charleston until she's given you a full orientation. This deal, however, is only valid May 15 through August. They have discount rooms with shared bath and full continental breakfast for $50 during the non-summer months. (Only 6 beds available, so call ahead for reservations. Lockout 10:30am-4:30pm.) If she can't house you, try **Charleston East Bed and Breakfast,** 1031 Tall Pine Rd. (884-8208), in Mt. Pleasant, east of Charleston off U.S. 701; they will try to place you in one of 15

private homes. (Rooms $20-80. Prior reservations recommended—call 9am-10pm.)
Motel 6, 2058 Savannah Hwy. (556-5144), 4 mi. out at 7th Ave., is clean and pleasant but far from downtown and frequently filled. (Singles $28, additional person $6. Call ahead; fills up quickly in summer months.)

There are several inexpensive campgrounds in the Charleston area, but none are near downtown. 8 mi. south on U.S. 17, **Oak Plantation Campground** has 350 sites (766-5936; sites $9, with hookup $13.75; office open daily 7:30am-9pm). Also look for **Pelican's Cove,** 97 Center St. (588-2072), at Folly Beach (sites with full hookup $17; office open daily 8am-9pm).

FOOD AND NIGHTLIFE

Most restaurants in the revamped downtown area are expensive. If you choose to eat out, try lunch, since most restaurants serve their dinner selections at noonday at discounted prices.

- **Hyman's Seafood Company,** 215 Meeting St. (723-0233). Kudos to the proprietor, who manages to serve about 15 different kinds of fresh fish daily ($8). If you like shellfish, the snow crabs ($10) are a must. Open daily 11am-11pm.
- **Marina Variety Store/City Marina,** 17 Lockwood Blvd. (723-6325). Pleasant view of the Ashley River. Crowded with locals. Good shellfish and great nightly specials under $7. Open daily 6:30am-3pm and 5-10pm; closed Sun. night.
- **Henry's,** 54 N. Market St. (723-4363), at Anson. A local favorite. Not cheap, but the food is good, especially the grilled shrimp ($8). On weekends, live jazz upstairs starts at 9pm, followed by a late-night breakfast. Open Mon.-Wed. 11:30am-10:30pm, Thurs.-Sun. 11:30am-1am.
- **T-Bonz Grill and Grill,** 80 N. Market St. (517-2511). Typical steak and seafood in an atypical atmosphere. Live music on Tues. nights is a local favorite. Lunch or dinner $3-12. Potato stuffed with chili $2.95. Open daily 11am-midnight.
- **Craig Cafeteria** (953-5539), corner of St. Philip and George St., the place to chow in Chaz. During the school year, serves all-you-can-eat buffets for breakfast (7-9am, $3.75), lunch (11am-2pm, $4), and dinner (4:30-6:30pm, $4.25). Open for dinner only in the summer.
- **Magic Wok,** 219 Meeting St. (723-8163), has dirt cheap, tasty Chinese food. Specials $6-8. Open daily 11am-10pm.

Before going out in Charleston, pick up a free copy of *Poor Richard's Omnibus,* available at grocery stores and street corners all over town; the *PRO* lists concerts and other events. Locals rarely dance the *Charleston* anymore, and the city's nightlife has suffered accordingly. Most bars and clubs are in the **Market Street** area. **Cafe 99,** 99 S. Market St. (577-4499), has live entertainment, strong drinks ($2-4), and reasonably priced dinners ($5-10). (Open daily 11:30am-2am. No cover.) For fun, live jazz, and beer, try **Henry's,** 54 Market St., also the oldest restaurant in town. (Wed. is ladies night. Happy hour Mon.-Fri. 4-7pm. Open Mon.-Fri. 4pm-2am, Sat.-Sun. noon-2am.) Find live eclectic music at the **Acme Bar and Grill,** 5 Faber St. (577-7383; open Mon.-Fri. 4pm-wee hours, Sat.-Sun. 7pm-2am), and the **Music Farm,** 32 Ann St. (853-3276; hours and cover vary, so call ahead).

SIGHTS AND EVENTS

Charleston's ancient homes, historical monuments, churches, galleries, and gardens can be seen on foot, by car, bus, boat, trolley, or carriage. Ask about these organized tours at the visitors center. The bus tours provide the best overview of the city. **Talk of the Towne** (795-8199) has tours thrice a day and will even pick you up from your hotel (75 min. tour $11, 2-hr. tour $17.50). **Trolley Tours** (795-3000) captures the charm and nostalgia of historic Charleston by touring the narrow streets in real trolley cars (75 min. tours depart from the City Market at "Quarter Hill" every hr. and from the visitors center on the hr. 9am-5pm; $12.50, children $6.50). **Gray Line Water Tours** (722-1112) gives you your money's worth. Their 2-hr. boat rides leave daily at 10am, 12:30pm, and 3pm ($9, ages 6-11 $4.25; reservations recommended).

The **Gibbes Museum of Art,** 135 Meeting St. (722-2706), has a fine collection of portraits by prominent American artists (open Sun.-Mon. 1-5pm, Tues.-Sat. 10am-5pm; $3, seniors and students $2, under 13 50¢).

The **Nathaniel Russell House,** 51 Meeting St. (724-8481), features a magnificent staircase that spirals without support from floor to floor. The house gives an idea of how Charleston's wealthy merchant class lived in the early 19th century. (Open Mon.-Sat. 10am-5pm; Sun. 2-5pm.) The **Edmonston-Allston House,** 21 E. Battery St. (722-7171), looks out over Charleston Harbor (open Tues.-Sat. 10am-5pm, Sun.-Mon. 1:30-5pm; 1 house $6, to both $10; last tour at 4:40pm, tours given every 10 min.) Founded in 1773, the **Charleston Museum,** 360 Meeting St. (722-2996), maintains a collection of knick-knacks ranging from natural history specimens to old sheet music (open Mon.-Sat. 9am-5pm, Sun. 1-5pm). The museum also offers combination tickets for the museum itself and the historic homes that are within easy walking distance: the 18th-century **Heyward-Washington House,** 87 Church St., and the **Joseph Manigault House,** 350 Meeting St. (for info on all three tours call 722-2996). The Washington House includes the only 18th-century kitchen open to the public in Charleston. Hope they hide those dirty dishes. (Washington, and Manigault homes open Mon.-Sat. 10am-5pm, Sun. 1-5pm. Admission to museum and two homes $10, children $5.)

A visit to Charleston just wouldn't be complete without a **boat tour** to **Fort Sumter** (722-1691) in the harbor. The Civil War was touched off when rebel forces in South Carolina, the first state to secede, attacked this Federal fortress on April 12, 1861. Over seven million pounds of metal were fired against the fort before those inside finally fled in February 1865. Tours leave several times daily from the Municipal Marina, at the foot of Calhoun St. and Lockwood Blvd. ($9, ages 6-12 $4.50). **Fort Sumter Tours,** a company that runs tour boats to the fort, also offers tours to **Patriots' Point,** the world's largest naval and maritime museum. Here you can walk the decks of the retired U.S. aircraft carrier *Yorktown,* or stroke the destroyer *Laffey's* huge fore and aft cannon.

If you are feeling a tad gun-shy, visit the open-air **City Market,** downtown at Meeting St., which vends everything from porcelain sea lions to handwoven sweetgrass baskets daily from 9:30am to sunset.

Magnolia Gardens, (571-1266), 10 mi. out of town on Rte. 61 off U.S. 17, is the 300-year-old ancestral home of the Drayton family, and treats visitors to 50 acres of gorgeous gardens with 900 varieties of camellia and 250 varieties of azalea. Get lost in the hedge maze. You'll probably want to skip the manor house, but do consider renting bicycles ($2 per hr.) to explore the neighboring swamp and bird sanctuary. (Open daily 9:30am-5pm. $8, seniors $7, teens $6, kids $4.)

From mid-March to mid-April, the **Festival of Houses and Gardens** (724-8481) celebrates Charleston's architecture and traditions; many private homes open their doors to the public. Music, theater, dance, and opera converge on the city during **Spoleto Festival U.S.A.** (722-2764) in late May and early June. The **Charleston Maritime Festival** in mid-Sept. celebrates America's water heritage with parades, a regatta, and artists. During **Christmas in Charleston** (853-8000), tours of many private homes and buildings are given, and many motels offer special reduced rates.

■■■ COLUMBIA

This quiet, unassuming city sprung up when Charleston bureaucrats decided in 1786 that their territory needed a proper capital. Surveyors found some land by the Congaree River and soon over 1000 people had poured into one of America's first planned cities. President Woodrow Wilson called Columbia home during his boyhood; now thousands of University of South Carolina (USC) students do the same. In many ways, Columbia's pervasive college-town flavor overshadows its state politics.

Practical Information Emergency is 911. The **Columbia Metropolitan Convention and Visitors Bureau,** 1012 Gervais St. (254-0479), is open Mon.-Fri.

THE SOUTH

9am-5pm, Sat. 10am-4pm. The **University of South Carolina Information Desk,** 1400 Green St. in Russell House Union, 2nd floor (777-3196), stocks campus maps and has shuttle schedules, and the low-down on campus events. If you get stranded in the area or need transportation in a hurry, contact **Traveler's Aid,** 1924 Taylor St. (343-7071; open Mon.-Fri. 9am-5pm).

Most buses running along the East Coast stop here. The **Congaree River** marks the western edge of the city. **Assembly Street** and **Sumter Street** are the major north-south arteries downtown; **Gervais Street** and **Calhoun Street** cut east-west. **Columbia Metropolitan Airport** is at 3000 Aviation Way (822-5000). Taxis from the airport to downtown run $10-$12. **Amtrak,** 850 Pulaski St. (252-8246 or 800-872-7245), has trains once per day to Washington, DC (10 hr., $90), Miami (13 hr., $124), and Savannah (2 hr., $32). The northbound train leaves daily at 4:55am, the southbound at 12:33am. (Open Mon.-Sat. 6am-4:30pm and 10:30pm-6:30am, Sun. 10:30pm-6:30am.) **Greyhound,** 2015 Gervais St. (779-4091 or 800-231-2222), at Harden, about 1 mi. east of the capital. Buses run to: Charlotte (3 per day, 2 hr., $24), Charleston (4 per day, 2 hr., $24), Atlanta (9 per day, 6 hr., $48). (Open 24hrs.)

South Carolina Electric and Gas (748-3019) operates local buses (fare 75¢). Most routes start from the transfer depot at the corner of Assembly and Gervais St. Local **help lines** are **Helpline of the Midlands** (790-4357) and **Rape Crisis** (771-7273), both 24 hrs. Columbia's **post office:** 1601 Assembly St. (733-4647; open Mon.-Fri. 7:30am-5pm); **ZIP code:** 29201; **area code:** 803.

Accommodations and Camping Just outside of downtown across the Congaree River, a number of inexpensive motels line Knox Abbot Dr. **Econo Lodge,** 491 Piney Grove Rd. (731-4060), has bright rooms, a swimming pool, A/C, and a movie channel. (Singles $37, doubles $41.) Only 3 mi. from downtown, **Economy Inn of America** (798-9210), at I-26 and St. Andrews Rd. (exit 106), provides clean rooms, a pool, and free movies. (Singles $31, doubles $38.) Inaccessible by public transportation is the **Sesquicentennial State Park** (788-2706), which has 87 sites with electricity and water ($13). Take I-20 to the Two Notch Rd. (Rte. 1) exit, and head northeast 4 mi. Gate locked at 9pm.

Sights, Food, and Nightlife Columbia's 18th-century aristocratic elegance has been preserved in the **Robert Mills Historic House and Park,** 1616 Blanding St. (252-3964), three blocks east of Sumter St. (tours Tues.-Sat. 10:15am-3:15pm, Sun. 1:15-4:15pm; $3, students $1.50). Mills, one of America's first federal architects, designed the Washington Monument and 30 of South Carolina's public buildings. Across the street at #1615 is the **Hampton-Preston Mansion** (252-0938), which was both used by Sherman's Union forces as headquarters during the Civil War and was also once home of Confederate general Wade Hampton. (Open Tues.-Sat. 10:15am-3:15pm, Sun. 1:15-4:15pm. Tours $3, students $1.50, under 6 free.) Stroll through USC's **Horseshoe,** at the junction of College and Sumter St., which holds the university's oldest buildings, dating from the beginning of the 19th century. The **McKissick Museum** (777-7251), at the top of the Horseshoe, showcases scientific, folk, and pottery exhibits, as well as selections from the university's extensive collection of Twentieth Century-Fox newsreels. (Open Mon.-Fri. 9am-4pm, Sat. 10am-5pm, Sun. 1-5pm. Free.) One of the finest in the country, **Riverbanks Zoo** (779-8730), on I-26 at Greystone Blvd. northwest of downtown, takes visitors through a rainforest, desert, undersea kingdom, and a southern farm. Over 2000 animals roam in open habitats. (Open Mon.-Thurs. 9am-4pm, Fri. 9am-8:30pm, Sat.-Sun. 9am-5pm. $4.75, seniors $3.25, students $3.50, ages 3-12 $2.25, Fri. after 5pm $1 for all.)

The **South Carolina State Museum,** 301 Gervais St. (737-4921), beside the Gervais St. Bridge, is inside the historic Columbia Mills building. Exhibits include a great white shark and a Confederate submarine—the first submarine ever to sink an enemy ship. Allow two hours for a complete visit. (Open Mon.-Sat. 10am-5pm, Sun.

1-5pm. $4, seniors and students with ID $3, ages 6-17 $1.50, free for all first Sunday of the month, under 6 always free.)

The **Five Points** business district, at the junction of Harden, Devine, and Blossom St. (from downtown, take the "Veterans Hospital" bus), caters to Columbia's large student population with bars, nightclubs, and coffeehouses. **Groucho's,** 611 Harden St. (799-5708), in the heart of Five Points, is a Columbia institution and anomaly—a New York-style Jewish deli. (large sandwiches $4-6; open Mon.-Wed. 11am-4:30pm, Thurs.-Fri. 11am-9pm, Sat. 11am-4pm). Award-winning **Yersterday's Restaurant and Tavern,** 2030 Devine St., serves homemade and healthy American food. (Confederate fried steak with muffin and veggies $5.50; open Sun.-Tues. 11:30am-1am, Wed.-Sat. 11:30am-2am.) Down Main St. from the State House lies USC's renowned deli, **Stuffy's Famous,** 629 S. Main St. (771-4098), frequented by students and locals (cheeseburger, fries, and iced tea $3.25). Happy hour (Mon.-Fri. 4-7pm) offers 15¢ wings. (Open Mon.-Fri. 10am-11pm, Sat. 11am-11pm, Sun. noon-10pm.) The **Columbia State Farmers Market** (253-4041), Bluff Rd. across from the USC Football Stadium, is a good place to stock up on fresh Carolina produce (open Mon.-Sat. 6am-9pm).

■■■ MYRTLE BEACH AND THE GRAND STRANDS

Stretching 60 mi. from Little River near the North Carolina border to the tidelands of historic Georgetown, the Grand Strand is exactly that—a long, wide ribbon of land containing beaches, tourists, restaurants, and small villages. In the middle of it all lies Myrtle Beach, full of golf courses, tennis courts, water parks, and sand. During spring break and in early June, Myrtle Beach (especially North Myrtle Beach) becomes jam-packed with leering, sun-burned students who revel in the area's bungee jumping, crazy golf, cheap buffets, and the call of the deep blue.

South of Myrtle Beach lies **Murrell's Inlet,** a quaint port stocked with good fish restaurants, and **Pawley's Island,** a secluded and leisurely resort that plantation owners used to frequent. **Georgetown** distinguishes itself with a rich past, housing a 32-block historic district complete with museums and 18th-century homes, while farther out of town lie old rice and indigo plantations.

PRACTICAL INFORMATION

Emergency: 911.
Visitors Information: Myrtle Beach Chamber of Commerce, 1301 N. Kings Hwy. (626-7444), provides area info including events listings, coupons, and accommodations details.
Greyhound: 508 9th Ave. (448-2471). Open daily 8:30am-1pm and 3-7:30pm.
Public Transportation: Minimal transportation is provided by **Costal Rapid Public Transit (CRPTA)** buses (626-9138 in Myrtle Beach). Local fare 75¢ one way; Conway to Myrtle Beach is $1.25.
Bike Rental: The Bike Shoppe, 711 Broadway (448-5103), rents sturdy 1-speeds cheaply at $5 for 3hr. License or credit card required. Open daily 8am-6pm.
Post Office: 505 N. Kings Hwy. (626-9533). Open Mon.-Fri. 8:30am-5pm, Sat. 9am-noon. **ZIP code:** 29577.
Area code: 803.

U.S. 17, also called **Kings Highway,** is the main north-south thoroughfare through the entire Grand Strand. In Myrtle Beach, **Ocean Blvd.** parallels Rte. 17, and is lined with pricier motels, hotels, and reasonably priced restaurants. **Rte. 501** runs west in the direction of Conway and leads to U.S. 95 and, more importantly, to the popular factory outlet stores.

ACCOMMODATIONS AND CAMPING

Summer is the most expensive season to visit the Myrtle Beach area, when couples and families take over. Many motels and campgrounds, in fact, only accept families or couples. Cheap motels are found just west of the beach in the 3rd St. area or on U.S. 17. You can often bargain for a lower hotel rate. Don't forget that prices plunge from Oct.-March, and they want your business. An easy, free way to find the most economical rates is to call the **Beach Hotel and Motel Reservation Service,** 1551 21st Ave. N. Suite #20 (626-7477 or 800-626-7477). For the best deals, ask for the "second row" string of hotels across the street from the ocean front. (Open daily 8am-8pm.) The Grand Strand has been called the "camping capital of the world." Myrtle Beach is laden with nine campgrounds and two state parks.

Sea Banks Motor Inn, 2200 S. Ocean Blvd. (448-2434 or 800-523-0603), across the street from the ocean. A friendly, family-run establishment with laundry, pool, TV, and phones. Rates for a double bed vary from $23 (March, Sept.-Oct.) to $39 in mid-summer.

Grand Strand Motel, 1804 S. Ocean Blvd. (448-1461 or 800-433-1461), is similar to Sea Banks and has small rooms with double bed (2 adults) at $15 in the winter, up to $51 in the summer.

Lazy G Motel 405 27th Ave. N. (448-6333 or 800-633-2163), has A/C, TV, refrigerators, a large pool, phones, comfortable rooms, and is convenient to golfing, shopping, and the beach. 2 double beds with oceanview range from $23 (mid-Oct.- mid-March) to $61 in the summer.

Myrtle Beach State Park Campground (238-5325), 3 mi. south of town off U.S. 17 and across from the air force base, has 312 acres of unspoiled land and a cool beach. 350 sites. Call ahead. First come, first served. Fishing, pool, nature trail. Each site has full hookup. Showers and bathrooms are close by. Sites $15, $11 Oct.-March 31. Office open Mon.-Fri. 9am-5pm, Sat.-Sun. 11am-noon, 4-5pm.

Huntington Beach State Park Campground (237-4440), 3 mi. south of Murrell's Inlet on U.S. 17, has a diverse natural environment with lagoons, salt marshes, and, of course, a beach. 127 sites with full hookup and convenient showers and rest rooms. Sites $15, $11 Oct.-March 31. Office open Mon.-Fri. 9am-5pm, Sat.-Sun. 11am-noon. Call ahead for reservations.

ALL-YOU-CAN-EAT

Over 1600 restaurants, serving anything you could dream of, can be found (or, can't be missed) on the Grand Strand. Massive, family-style, all-you-can-eat joints are at every traffic light. Seafood is best on Murrell's Inlet, while Ocean Blvd. and Hwy. 17 offer endless steakhouses, fast food spots, and buffets.

River City Café, 404 21st Ave. N. (448-1990), serves up juicy burgers ($2.95), homemade fries, beer, and free peanuts (toss the shells on the floor) in a young, fun, collegiate atmosphere. Open Mon.-Sat. 11am-10pm, Sun. 11:30am-9pm.

Mammy's Kitchen, 11th Ave. N. at King's Hwy., (448-7242), has quite a breakfast special of hashbrowns, toast, eggs, and bacon ($2.19). Open daily 7am-1pm and 4:30-9:30pm.

Big Sam's Diner (651-0280), in Murrell's Inlet on McDowell Shortcut and Bypass Hwy. 17. Locals come here and all know each other. They are friendly and love to chat. Cheap, fresh, and tasty food. Three-decker clubs with cold slaw and salad $3.95. Open Mon.-Sat. 6am-2:30pm and 6-9pm, Sun. 6am-3pm.

The Filling Station has two locations, Hwy. 17 at 17th Ave. N. (626-9435), and on the Alabama Theater side of Bearfoot Landing (272-7034). One great menu idea: all-you-can-eat pizza, soup, sandwich bar, and dessert. Fill 'er up here at lunch ($4.89) or dinner ($7.29). Children $2-3, including drink.

'TIL HER DADDY TAKES HER T-BIRD AWAY

The cheapest and most amusing form of entertainment here is people watching. Families, newlyweds, foreigners, and students flock to this incredibly popular spot

THE SOUTH

to lay in the sun, eat out, and live American pop culture. The boulevard and the length of the beach is called the **strand.** Cruising it at night is a must.

The white sand beaches and refreshing water are still Myrtle Beach's main attraction. The mind-boggling number of golf and mini-golf spots (45!), and amusement and water parks (13) makes even Walleyworld seem passé. The largest amusement park in the area is the **Myrtle Beach Pavilion** (448-6456), on Ocean Blvd. and 9th Ave. N. (Unlimited rides $17.25, under 42" $11. Each ticket 50¢, and each ride uses 2-7 tickets, depending on the number of loops, drops, and spins; open daily 1pm-midnight.) If you're hot, try the **Myrtle Waves Water Park,**,10th Ave. N and Hwy. 17 by-pass, (448-1026). Come out water logged after riding their 30 water rides, including the world's largest tubular slide. ($16, under 42 inches $10. Open daily 10am-7pm.)

Myrtle Beach is a mecca for country music shows, including the **Gatlin Brothers Theater** and the **Myrtle Beach Opry.** It's worth the price of admission to see the characters around you git riled up (you may enjoy it, in fact). The **Alabama Theater at Barefoot Landing,** 4750 U.S. 17 S. (272-1111), has it all—singin', swingin', and comedy, complete with an aptly named production, the American Pride Show. ($15-16, ages 3-11 $7. Concert series with celebrities $20-30. Reservations required. Shows begin at 8pm, celebrity concerts at 7pm.)

Massive nightclubs slam every night. **2001,** 920 Lake Arrowhead Rd. (449-9434), in Restaurant Row, is 3 clubs in 1: a piano bar with live entertainment nightly, a lively beach club, and a top 40 club. (Must be 21; cover $8. Open daily 8pm-3am.) **Studebakers,** 2000 N. Kings Hwy. (448-9747), is a casual, hip hang-out with a young, fun crowd. Contests and ladies night held often (call for details). 18 and up. (Cover $5. Open nightly 8pm-2am.) Pick up a free copy of *Beachcomber* and *Kicks* at the Chamber of Commerce for up-coming events. Big-time fests include **Canadian-American Days Festival** in mid-March, a huge **Sun Fun Festival** in early June, and Christmas partying starting in November.

■ # Georgia

Where else can you find great state roads, restaurants serving pre-sweetened iced tea, and TV programs on how to fish? From the North Georgia mountains to the coastal plains and swamps, Georgia thrives on such alliterative industries as paper products, popcorn, peanuts, pecans, peaches, poultry, and politicians. President Jimmy Carter's hometown and the only house ever owned by President Franklin D. Roosevelt both stand on red Georgia clay. Coca-Cola was invented here in 1886; since then, it has gone on to carbonate and caffeinate the rest of the world. Ted Turner and CNN have brought world news and folks from all over the globe, making the capital a diverse, sophisticated metropolis.

As 1996 nears, Atlanta gears up to host the Olympic Games. Sharing the spotlight are coastal Savannah, a city with stately, romantic antebellum homes and colonial city blocks, and Athens, home of the Bulldogs and REM. The state blooms in the spring, glistens in the summer, and mellows in the autumn, all the while welcoming y'all with peachy Southern hospitality. Stay here long and you'll *never* be able to shake Georgia from your mind.

PRACTICAL INFORMATION

Capital: Atlanta.

Department of Industry and Trade, Tourist Division, 285 Peachtree St., Atlanta 30301 (656-3590), across from Atlanta Convention and Visitors Bureau. Write for or pick up the comprehensive *Georgia Travel Guide.* Open Mon.-Fri. 8am-5pm.

Department of Natural Resources, 205 Butler St. SE, Atlanta 30334 (800-542-

7275; 404-656-3530 in GA). **U.S. Forest Service,** 1720 Peachtree Rd. NW,
Atlanta 30367 (347-2384), has info on the Chattahoochee and Oconee National
Forests. Open Mon.-Fri. 10am-4:30pm.
Time Zone: Eastern. **Postal Abbreviation:** GA
Sales Tax: 4-6%, depending on county.

■■■ ATLANTA

Unlike other southern cities which are defined by their Civil War past, Atlanta
defines itself in terms of its ever-expanding present. Not even Union General Sherman's "scorched earth" burning of Atlanta to the ground in 1864 could quench its
spirit which, like its seal (the phoenix) and its motto (*resurgens*), arose from the
ashes to soar today as the largest metropolis in the Southeast. A nationwide economic powerhouse, Atlanta contains the world's largest airport complex, the headquarters of Coca-Cola and CNN, and offices of 400 of the Fortune 500 corporations.
Nineteen institutions of higher learning, including Georgia Tech, Morehouse College, Spelman College, and Emory University, call "Hotlanta" home.

Fame and prosperity have diluted Atlanta's Old South flavor. An influx of transplanted Northerners and Californians, the third-largest gay population in the U.S.,
and a host of ethnicities contribute to the city's cosmopolitan air. It is the birthplace
of Martin Luther King, Jr., and witnessed unrest and activism during the 1960s.

As host of the 1996 summer Olympics, Atlantans are already burning with Olympic fever. The city is besieged by new construction at nearly every turn.

PRACTICAL INFORMATION

Emergency: 911.
Visitor Information: Atlanta Convention and Visitors Bureau, 233 Peachtree
St. NE, #200 (222-6688), Peachtree Center, 20th floor of Harris Tower, downtown; stop by to pick up a free copy of *Atlanta and Georgia Visitors' Guide* ($3
at newsstands). Open Mon.-Fri. 9am-5pm. Also at **Underground Atlanta** (577-
2148), Pyror and Alabama St. Open Mon.-Sat. 10am-9pm, Sun. noon-6pm.
Olympics Information: 224-1996, event locations, schedules, and ticket prices
should be available in Jan. 1995. Open Mon.-Sat. 10am-9:30pm, Sun. noon-6pm.
Airport: Hartsfield International (530-6600 for general info; international services and flight info 530-2081), south of the city. Headquarters of **Delta Airlines**
(756-5000 or 800-325-1999). Get phone assistance in 6 languages at the **Calling
Assistance Center** in the international terminal. MARTA (see Public Transport
below) is the easiest way to get downtown, with 15-min. rides departing every 8
min., daily 5am-1am with baggage space available, fare $1.25. **Atlanta Airport
Shuttle** (525-2177) runs vans from the airport to midtown, downtown, Emory,
and Lenox Sq. ($8-12). **Northside Airport Express** (768-7600) serves Stone
Mountain, Marietta, and Dunwoody. Buses run daily 7am-7pm ($15-30). Taxi to
downtown $15.
Amtrak: 1688 Peachtree St. NW (881-3060), 3 mi. north of downtown at I-85.
Take bus #23 to and from the "Arts Center" MARTA station. *See mileage chart.*
Open daily 6:30am-9:45pm.
Greyhound: 81 International Blvd. (584-1728), 1 block from Peachtree Center.
MARTA: Peachtree Center. *See mileage chart.* Open 24 hrs.
Public Transport: Metropolitan Atlanta Rapid Transit Authority (MARTA)
(848-4711; schedule info Mon.-Fri. 6am-10pm, Sat.-Sun. 8am-4pm). Combined rail
and bus system serves virtually all area attractions and hotels. Operates Mon.-Sat.
5am-1:30am, Sun. 6am-12:30am in most areas. Fare $1.25 exact change or buy a
token at station machines; transfers free. Unlimited weekly pass $11. Pick up a
system map at the **MARTA Ride Store,** Five Points Station downtown, or at one
of the satellite visitors bureaus. If you get confused, just find the nearest MARTA
courtesy phone in each rail station.
Taxi: Checker, 351-1111. **Rapid,** 222-9888. Base fare $1.50, $1.20 per mi.
Car Rental: Atlanta Rent-a-Car, 3185 Camp Creek Pkwy. (763-1160), just inside
I-285, 3 mi. east of the airport. 9 other locations in the area including Cheshire

Bridge Rd. and I-85, 1 mi. west of the Lindberg Center Railstop. Rates from $20 per day. 100 free mi., 19¢ each additional mi. Must be 21 with major credit card. **Help Lines: Rape Crisis Counseling,** 659-7273. Open 24 hrs. **Gay/Lesbian Help Line,** 892-0661. Open daily 6-11pm. Center located at 63 12th St. (876-5372). **Post Office:** 3900 Crown Rd. (768-4126). Open 10am-4pm. **ZIP code:** 30321. **Area Code:** 404.

Atlanta sprawls across the northwest quadrant of the state, 150 mi. east of Birmingham, AL and 113 mi. south of Chattanooga, TN, at the junctures of I-75, I-85, and I-20, and is circumscribed by I-285 ("the perimeter").

Getting around is confusing—*everything* seems to be named Peachtree. However, of the 40-odd roads bearing that name, only one, **Peachtree Street,** is a major north-south thoroughfare, as are **Spring Street** and **Piedmont Avenue. Ponce De León Avenue** and **North Avenue** are major east-west routes. In the heart of downtown, the area to the west of I-75/85, south of International Blvd. and north of the capitol, where angled streets and shopping plazas run amok, navigation is difficult.

Most tourists frequent **Underground Atlanta** and **Peachtree Center,** shopping and entertainment complexes. But Atlanta has more than mall walking to offer. The **Midtown** area (from Ponce de Leon Ave. to 26th St.) holds Atlanta's art museums. Directly southwest of downtown is the **West End**—a black residential area and the city's oldest historical quarter. North of Auburn Ave. lies the **Little Five Points** (L5P) district, which brims with galleries, theaters, bookstores and a plethora of restaurants and nightclubs.

ACCOMMODATIONS AND CAMPING

If you're an international student and plan to stay for more than a few days, check with the **International Youth Travel Program (IYTP)** (212-206-7307). Travelers should pick up coupon books like *Look at Atlanta Now* at the convention and visitors bureau (see Practical Information), which will also help locate a single for a reasonable price. The IYTP is your cheapest bet besides the YMCA and the hostels. Unfortunately, some options are not available to women from the U.S. **Bed and Breakfast Atlanta,** 1801 Piedmont Ave. NE (875-0525; call Mon.-Fri. 9am-noon or 2-5pm), offers singles from $50 and doubles from $55-65 in over 80 establishments.

Hostelling International Atlanta (HI-AYH), 223 Ponce de León Ave. (875-9449). From MARTA: North Ave. station, exit onto Ponce de León, about 3½ blocks east on the corner of Myrtle St. Part of a converted Victorian B&B in the middle of historic downtown. Clean, dorm-style rooms ½ mi. from the Olympic village. Kitchen and showers at no charge. Linens $1. Sheets $1. No sleeping bags allowed, but they distribute free blankets. A/C. Free local calls and rides to city sights in van. Luggage storage $1. Free city magazine and map, and occasional free passes to city attractions. Alcohol allowed on patio only. Free coffee and doughnuts 8-10am. No curfew, but if out past midnight, you need a key ($1 deposit). Reservations recommended. $13.25, nonmembers $16.25.

Atlanta Dream Hostel, 222 E. Howard Ave. (370-0380) From MARTA: Decatur, go right on Church St. for 2 blocks and then left on Howard). A funky communal joint complete with 2 peacocks, a bus that serves as an Elvis shrine, and a biergarten, it is a hostel for the adventurous soul. Reception daily 8am-11pm; no curfew, $12 a night with linen, showers, kitchen, TV and local calls.

Motel 6, 4 perimeter locations: 3585 Chamblee Tucker Rd. in Chamblee exit 27 (455-8000); 6015 Oakbridge Pkwy. (446-2311), in Norcross exit 37; 4100 Wendell Dr. SW (696-0757), exit 14; and 2565 Weseley Chapel Rd. (288-6911), in Decatur exit 36. All locations $29-32, $6 per additional person. Each location offers free movie channel, free local calls, and kids under 18 stay free with their parents.

Atlanta Midtown Manor, 811 Piedmont Ave., NE, (872-5846), is located in a safe spot, convenient to downtown. Singles $30-40. Doubles $45-55.

Days Inn Atlanta, 2910 Clairmont Rd. (633-8411), recently renovated and near downtown. Singles $39. Doubles $44. Also at 2788 Forest Hills Dr. (768-7750) offering spacious rooms close to the airport. Singles $34. Doubles $38.

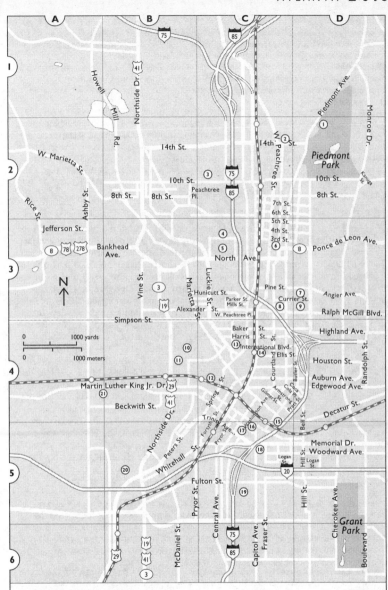

THE SOUTH

Downtown Atlanta

1 Atlanta Botanical Garden
2 Peachtree Community Playhouse
3 Alexander Memorial Coliseum
4 Georgia Institute of Technology
5 Grant Field / Bobby Dodd Stadium
6 Fox Theatre
7 Exhibition & SciTrek Museum
8 Civic Center
9 Atlantic Civic 3 Center
10 World Congress Center

11 Georgia Dome
12 CNN Center
13 Greyhoun Bus Depot
14 Peachtree Center
15 Georgia State University
16 State Capitol
17 City Hall
18 Georgia Dept. of Archives & History
19 Atlanta Fulton County Stadium

20 Spelman College
21 Clark Atlanta
University

Villages Lodge, 144 14th St. NW (873-4171). A fence separates you from the highway. Tidy rooms in a dark decor. Chinese restaurant. Optional phone ($10 deposit); local calls 30¢. Laundry facilities. Friendly management. Mexican restaurant. Pool. Singles $35. Doubles $40. Key deposit $5.

Red Roof Inn, 1960 Druid Hills (321-1653), exit 31 off I-85, offers rooms with clean, modern decor and pleasant tree-cloistered location. Convenient to downtown. Look carefully for the sign, it's partially hidden by branches. Singles $37. Doubles $40.

KOA South Atlanta (957-2610), Mt. Olive Rd. in McDonough exit 72 off I-75, offers tent sites with water for $15, add $2 for electricity. Showers, pool, laundry, and fishing pond on the premises. You can also try **KOA West Atlanta,** 2420 Old Alabama Rd. I (941-7485), in Austell, 3 mi. west of Six Flags Amusement Park.

Stone Mountain Family Campground (498-5710), on U.S. 78 16 mi. east of town. Exit 30-B off I-285 or subway to Avondale then "Stone Mountain" bus. Part of state park system. Tent sites. RV sites with water and electricity and $1 for dump. Reservations not accepted. Entrance fee $5 per car.

FOOD

From Russian to Ethiopian, al fresco to underground, Atlanta dining provides a torrent of treats to tantalize tourists' tastebuds. But since y'all are here you may want to savor some home-style cookin'. Some favorite dishes to sample include fried chicken, black-eyed peas, okra, sweet-potato pie, and mustard greens. Dip a hunk of cornbread into "pot likker," water used to cook greens, and enjoy. For a cheap breakfast, you can't beat the Atlanta-based **Krispy Kreme Doughnuts** whose baked delights are a Southern institution. The original company store is at 295 Ponce de León Ave. NE (876-7307; open 24 hrs.). Southern restaurants are easily recognized by name, like **Aunt Fanny's Cabin,** 2155 Campbell Rd. SE, in Smyrna, or **The Beautiful Restaurant,** 397 Auburn Ave. (505-0271), where soul food warms the body and mind. (Dinner under $5, vegetarian platter $2.50. Open daily 7am-8:30pm.)

Do-it-yourself-ers can procure produce and regionally popular items such as chitlins, pork cracklin', sugar cane, collards, and yams at the **Atlanta Municipal Market** (659-1665), 209 Edgewood St. at Butler St. This market also houses inexpensive deli stalls such as the **Snack Bar** where the adventurous visitor can munch on a hot pig ear sandwich ($1.25). For a more international arena, shoppers should take the subway to Avondale and then the "Stone Mountain" bus to the **Dekalb County Farmers Market,** 3000 E. Ponce De León Ave. (377-6400), where the famished can run the gustatory gamut from Chinese to Middle Eastern and everything in between. For heaps of fresh fruit and vegetables in the middle of nowhere, head for the 80 acres of **Atlanta's State Farmers Market,** 16 Forest Pkwy. (366-6910), exit 78 off I-75 south. (Take "Farmers Market" bus from the airport. Open daily 8am-5pm.)

Bridgetown Grill, 1156 Euclid Ave. (653-0110), also in L5P. Reggae and salsa make for a hopping hole in the wall. Jerk chicken dinner ($7.95). Open Sun.-Thurs. 11:30am-10:30pm, Fri.-Sat. 11:30am-midnight.

Manuel's Tavern, 602 N. Highland Ave. (525-3447), prime spot between L5P and Virginia-Highlands. English pub style. Jimmy and Rosalyn Carter are regulars. Open Mon.-Sat. 10:30am-2am, Sun. 3-11pm.

American Roadhouse, 842 N. Highland Ave. (872-2822), fashioned after 19th century roadhouse. Hearty breakfasts and blue plates. Georgia Trout with sides ($7.50). Open Sun.-Thurs. 7am-11pm, Fri.-Sat. 7am-midnight.

Eat Your Vegetables Café, 438 Moreland Ave. NE (523-2671), in L5P area. Vegetarian entrees $7-8, including macrobiotic dinner special. Open Mon.-Thurs. 11:30am-10pm, Fri. 11:30am-10:30pm, Sat. 11am-10:30pm, Sun. 11am-3pm.

Einstein's, 1077 Juniper St. (876-7925) at 14th St. in Midtown. Fresh quantum coffee and deli delights (8 oz. burger and fries $6.25). Open Sun.-Thurs. 11:30am-midnight, Fri.-Sat. 11:30am-1am.

Mary Mac's Tea Room, 224 Ponce De León Ave. (876-1800) at Myrtle NE. Take the "Georgia Tech" bus north. 40s atmosphere with amazing home-made cornbread and peach cobbler. Open Mon.-Fri. 11am-3pm, 5pm-9pm.

The Varsity, 61 North Ave. NW (881-1706), at I-85. Take MARTA to North Ave. station. The world's larges drive-in. Best known for chili dogs ($1-2) and the greasiest onion rings in the South ($1). Ice cream cones (80¢). Open Sun.-Thurs. 7am-12:30am, Fri.-Sat. 7am-2am.

Touch of India, 962 Peachtree St. (876-7777) and 2065 Piedmont Rd. (876-7775). 3-course lunch specials $5. Dinners $8-10. Open Mon.-Sat. 11:30am-2:30pm and 5:30-10:30pm.

Nicola's, 1602 Lavista Rd. NE (325-2524), cooks, bakes, and dishes up the most savory and authentic Lebanese cuisine in Atlanta. Look for raw kibby, a Lebanese delicacy, on Sat. nights. Open daily 5:30-10:30pm.

Everybody's, 1040 N. Highland Ave. (873-4545), Locals love the mouth-watering pizza. Large pie $10.50. Open daily, 11:30am-11pm, Fri.-Sat. 11:30am-1am.

SIGHTS

Atlanta's sights may seem scattered, but the effort it takes to find them usually pays off. The **Atlanta Preservation Center,** 156 7th St. NE (876-2040), offers ten walking tours of popular areas: Fox Theatre District, West End and the Wren's Nest, Historic Downtown, Miss Daisy's Druid Hills, Inman Park, Underground and Capitol area, Ansley Park, and Sweet Auburn, Piedmont Park and Vine City—from April through November. The 1½-hr. Fox Theater tour is given year-round. ($5, students $3, seniors $4. Call for more info.)

Hopping on MARTA and taking in the sites on your own is the cheapest and most rewarding tour option. An intimate part of southern history can be explored at the **Ebenezer Baptist Church,** 407 Auburn Ave. (688-7263), where Martin Luther King, Jr. was pastor from 1960 to 1968. The church is now a visitors center for the National Park Service and a new church for the local congregation is located across the street. (Open Mon.-Fri. 9am-4:30pm. Call for weekend hours.)

The church, birthplace, grave, and museum are all part of a 23½-acre **Martin Luther King, Jr. National Historic Site.** The Queen Anne style **birthplace** of MLK offers guided tours every ½ hr., daily 9am-5pm (during summer open until 7:30pm).

Plaques line Sweet Auburn pointing out the Queen Anne architecture and eminent past residents of this historically African-American neighborhood. King is buried at the **Martin Luther King Center for Nonviolent Social Exchange,** 449 Auburn Ave. NE (524-1956), which also holds a collection of King's personal effects and a film about his life. Take bus #3 from Five Points. (Open daily 9am-5:30pm, until 8pm from early April through October. Entrance and film are free.)

The **APEX Museum,** 135 Auburn Ave. (521-2739), recognizes the cultural heritage of African-Americans rising from slavery to help build this country. (Open Tues.-Sat. 10am-5pm, Wed. until 6pm, Sun. 1-5pm. $2, students $1, seniors and children, under 5 free.)

In the **West End**—Atlanta's oldest neighborhood, dating from 1835—hovers the **Wren's Nest,** 1050 R.D. Abernathy Blvd. (753-5835), home to Joel Chandler Harris who popularized the African folktale trickster Br'er Rabbit through the stereotypical slave character Uncle Remus. Take bus #71 from West End Station South. (Open Tues.-Sat. 10am-4pm, Sun. 1-4pm. Tours $3, teens and seniors $2, ages 4-12 $1, storytelling $1 extra.) The **Hammonds House,** 503 Peeples St. SW (752-8730) displays a fantastic collection of African-American art. Take bus #71 from West End Station South to the corner of Oak and Peeples. (Open Tues.-Fri. 10am-6pm, Sat.-Sun. 1-5pm; $2, students and seniors $1). Also worth a look is the **Herndon Home,** 587 University Place NW (581-9813), a 1910 Beaux Arts Classical mansion built by slave-born Alonzo F. Herndon, a prominent barber before becoming Atlanta's wealthiest African-American in the early 1900s. Take bus #3 from Five Points station to the corner of Martin Luther King, Jr. Dr. and Maple, and walk one block north. (Open Tues.-Sat. 10am-4pm.Tours every hour. Free.)

A drive through **Buckhead** (north of midtown off Peachtree near W. Paces Ferry Rd.) uncovers the "Beverly Hills of Atlanta"—the sprawling mansions of Coca-Cola CEOs and the like. It is also a hub of local grub and grog (see Entertainment below). One of the most exquisite residences in the Southeast, the Greek Revival **Gover-**

nor's Mansion, 391 W. Paces Ferry Rd. (261-1776; take bus #40 "West Paces Ferry" from Linbergh Station), has elaborate gardens and furniture from the Federal period. (Tours Tues.-Thurs. 10-11:30am. Free.)

In the same neighborhood, discover the **Atlanta History Center/Buckhead,** 130 W. Paces Ferry Rd. NW (814-4000). On the grounds are the **Swan House,** a lavish Anglo-Palladian Revival home, and the **Tullie Smith House,** an antebellum farmhouse. Don't miss the intriguing *"Atlanta Resurgens"* exhibit. The **New Museum of Atlanta History** features a fine Civil War Gallery. (Tours every ½ hr. Open Mon.-Sat. 9am-5:30pm, Sun. noon-5:30pm. $7, seniors and students $5, kids $4, under 6 free. Free Thurs. after 1pm.)

North of mid-town but south of Buckhead sprawls **Piedmont Park,** home to the 60-acre **Atlanta Botanical Garden** (876-5858), Piedmont Ave. at the Prado. Stroll through five acres of landscaped gardens, a 15-acre hardwood forest with walking trails, and an exhibition hall. The **Dorothy Chapman Fugua Conservatory** houses hundreds of species of rare tropical plants. Take bus #36 "North Decatur" from the Arts Center subway stop. (Open Tues.-Sun. 9am-7pm, closed Mon. Admission $6, seniors $4.75, students $3. Thurs. free after 1pm.)

Near the park lies **Scitrek** (The Science and Technology Museum of Atlanta), 395 Piedmont Ave. NE (522-5000; take bus #31 or 16 from Five points Station and walk a block north along Piedmont). Over 100 interactive exhibits for all ages make Scitrek one of the top ten science centers in the country. (Open Tues.-Sat. 10am-5pm, Sun. noon-6pm, call for summer hrs. $6.50, seniors and students $4.25.)

Just to the west of the park, the **Woodruff Arts Center,** 1280 Peachtree St. NE (892-3600; take the subway to Arts Center), houses the **High Museum of Art** (892-HIGH), Richard Meier's award-winning building of glass, steel, and white porcelain. (Open Tues.-Sat. 10am-5pm, Fri. until 9pm, Sun. noon-5pm. $5, seniors and students with ID $3, kids $1. Free Thurs. 1-5pm.) The museum branch at **Georgia-Pacific Center** (577-6940), one block south of Peachtree Center Station, is free (open Mon.-Sat. 10am-5pm).

A different mode of culture prances at the **Center for Puppetry Arts,** 1404 Spring St. NW (873-3089 or 873-3391 for tickets), at 18th St., whose museum features Wayland Flower's "Madame," traditional Punch and Judy figures, Asian hand-carved puppets, and some of Jim Henson's original Muppets. (Museum open Mon.-Sat. 9am-4pm. Admission $3, ages 2-13 $2. Shows are $5.50, ages 2-13 $4.50, museum free with show tickets.)

True fans of Rhett Butler and Scarlett O'Hara can visit the Margaret Mitchell Room in the **Atlanta-Fulton Public Library,** 1 Margaret Mitchell (730-1700), to peruse memorabilia such as autographed copies of her famous novel (open Mon.-Thurs. 9am-9pm, Fri.-Sat. 9am-6pm, Sun. 2-6pm), or they can drive by the dilapidated three-story house on the corner of 10th and Crescent where Mitchell used to live. The most hard-core fans can witness the graves of Mitchell (and golfer Bobby Jones) at **Oakland Cemetery,** 248 Oakland Ave. SE (658-6019), directly below Piedmont Park. Open daily sunrise-sunset. Free.) Take bus #3.

Directly south, in **Grant Park,** off Cherokee Ave., revolves the **Cyclorama** (624-1071), a massive panoramic painting (42 ft. high and 358 ft. around) recreating the 1864 Battle of Atlanta with 3-D light and sound effects. (Open June-Sept. daily 9:20am-5:30pm; Oct.-May 9:20am-4:30pm. $3.50, students and seniors $3, ages 6-12 $2.) Next door growls **Zoo Atlanta,** 800 Cherokee Ave. SE (624-5600), whose entertaining animal displays stress conservation and environmental awareness. Among the special exhibits are the Masai Mara, Mzima Springs, and the Ford African Rain Forest. (Open daily 10am-4:30pm, until 5:30pm on weekends during Daylight Savings Time. $7.75, seniors $6.75, ages 3-11 $5.75, under 3 free.)

Outside of these historical and culture-preserving sights, high-tech "Hotlanta" reigns with multinational business powerhouses situated in business section of **Five Points District. Turner Broadcasting System** offers an insider's peek with its **Cable News Network (CNN) Studio Tour** (827-2300), corner of Techwood Dr. and Marietta St. Witness anchorpeople broadcasting live while writers toil in the background. (Open daily 9am-5:30pm; 50-min. tours given on the ½ hr. $5, seniors $4, kids 5-12 $3.50. Take MARTA west to the Omni/Dome/GWCC Station at W1.)

Redeveloped **Underground Atlanta** gets down with six subterranean blocks filled with over 120 shops, restaurants, and night spots in 19th-century Victorian-style storefronts. Descend the entrance beside the Five Points subway station. (Shops open Mon.-Sat. 10am-9:30pm, Sun. noon-6pm. Bars and restaurants open later.) **Atlanta Heritage Row,** 55 Upper Alabama St. (584-7879), Underground, documents the city's past and looks into the future with exhibits and films (open Tues.-Sat. 10am-5pm, Sun. 1-5pm; $3, seniors and students over 12 $2.50, kids $2).

Adjacent to the shopping complex is the **World of Coca-Cola Pavilion,** 55 Martin Luther King, Jr. Dr. (676-5151). The $15 million facility highlights "the real thing's" humble beginnings in Atlanta with over 1000 artifacts and interactive displays. (Open Mon.-Sat. 10am-9:30pm, Sun. noon-6pm. $2.50, seniors $2, ages 6-12 $1.50. The lines around the block suggest you make reservations.)

The political-minded can revel in the **Georgia State Capitol** (656-2844; MARTA: 1 block south of Georgia State station), Capitol Hill at Washington St., which offers tours (Mon.-Fri. on the hr. 10am-2pm except noon. Open Mon.-Fri. 8am-5pm. Free.). Delight in the **Carter Presidential Center,** 1 Copenhill (331-3942), north of Little Five Points, which documents the Carter Administration (1977-1981) through exhibits and films. Take bus #16 to Cleburne Ave. (Open Mon.-Sat. 9am-4:45pm, Sun. noon-4:45pm. $2.50, seniors $1.50, under 16 free.)

A respite from the city is available at **Stone Mountain Park** (498-5600), 16 mi. east on U.S. 78, where the fabulous Confederate Memorial is carved into the world's largest mass of granite. The "Mount Rushmore of the South" features Jefferson Davis, Robert E. Lee, and Stonewall Jackson and measures 90 ft. by 190 ft. Surrounded by a 3200-acre recreational area and historic park, the mountain dwarfs the enormous statue. Check out the dazzling laser show on the side of the mountain every summer night at 9:30pm (free). Take bus #120 "Stone Mountain" from the Avondale subway stop (buses leave Mon.-Fri. only at 4:30 and 7:50pm). (Park gates open daily 6am-midnight; attractions open daily 10am-9pm; off-season 10am-5:30pm; $5 per car. Admission to beach complex $4.)

The **Fernbank Museum of Natural History,** 767 Clifton Rd. NE (370-0960), has a forest, science center, and IMAX theater. (Open Mon.-Sat. 9am-6pm, Sun. noon-6pm. Museum or IMAX theater $5.50, students and seniors $4.50, combination passes $9.50, students and seniors $7.50.)

Olympics Information should be available in January 1995. For event locations, schedules, and ticket prices, call 224-1996.

ENTERTAINMENT AND NIGHTLIFE

For sure-fire fun in Atlanta, buy a MARTA pass (see Practical Information above) and pick up one of the city's free publications on music and events. *Creative Loafing, Music Atlanta,* the *Hudspeth Report,* or "Leisure" in the Friday edition of the *Atlanta Journal* will all give you the low-down. *Southern Voice* also has complete listings on gay and lesbian news and nightclubs throughout Atlanta. Stop by **Charls,** 419 Moreland Ave. NE (524-0304), for your free copy (open Mon.-Sat. 10:30am-6:30pm, Sun. 1-6pm). Look for free summer concerts in Atlanta's parks.

The outstanding **Woodruff Arts Center,** 1280 Peachtree St. NE (892-3600), houses the Atlanta Symphony, the Alliance Theater Company, Atlanta College of Art, and the High Museum of Art. For more plays and movies check the Moorish and Egyptian Revival Movie Palace, the **Fox Theatre,** 660 Peachtree St. (249-6400), or the **Atlanta Civic Center,** 395 Piedmont St. (523-6275), home to the Atlanta ballet.

For drink or dance, hotspots center in **Little Five Points; Virginia Highlands,** a neighborhood east of downtown with trendy shops and a hip atmosphere; **Buckhead;** and **Underground Atlanta.** A college-age crowd usually fills Little Five Points heading for **The Point,** 420 Moreland Ave. (659-3522) where there's always live music. (Open Mon.-Fri. 4pm-4am, Sat. 1pm-3am, Sun. 1pm-4am. Cover $4-5.) For blues, go to **Blind Willie's,** 828 N. Highland Ave. (873-2583), a dim, usually packed club with Cajun food and occasional big name acts (live music 10pm-2am; open daily at 8pm; cover $5-8).

Rub elbows and hob-nob with the Buckhead hoi polloi near Peachtree and Lenox Rd. Try the **Good Old Boys,** 3013 Peachtree Rd. (266-2597), for light fare and relaxed hanging out; closing times vary (open Tues.-Fri. 5pm-1am, Sat. 11am-3am, Sun. 11am-until). For dancing, nearby **Oxygen,** 3065 Peachtree St. (816-6522), at Bolling Way will leave you breathless. Then cool off with a 60-oz. industrial strength goblet margarita at **Lu Lu's Bait Shack,** 3057 Peachtree Rd. (262-5220).

Kenny's Alley, a street in The Underground, is composed solely of bars—a blues club, a dance emporium, a jazz bar, a country/western place, a New Orleans-style daiquiri bar, and an oldies dancing spot. Towards downtown, **Masquerade,** 695 North Ave. NE (577-8178), is housed in an original turn-of-the-century mill. The bar has three different levels: heaven, with live hard-core music; purgatory, a more laid-back coffee house; and hell, offering progressive dance music. (Open Wed.-Sun. 9pm-4am. Cover $4-8 or more, depending on band. 18 and over.) **Backstreet,** 845 Peachtree St. NE (873-1986), a 24-hr., hot, gay dance spot which prides itself on being straight-friendly, stays open all night. (Thurs.-Sun. at midnight plays an extra-special hoppin' cabaret. Cover Sun.-Thurs. $2 after midnight; Fri.-Sat. $5.)

Six Flags, 7561 Flags Rd. SW (948-9290), at I-20W, is one of the largest theme amusement parks in the nation, and includes several rollercoasters and a plethora of rides. Take bus #201 ("Six Flags") from Hightower Station. (Open summer Sun.-Thurs. 10am-10pm, Fri.-Sat. 10am-midnight. 1-day admission $28, kids from ages 3-9, $19; be sure to check local grocery stores and soda cans for discounts.)

■■■ ATHENS

Home to over 30,000 University of Georgia (UGA) students and the host for '96 Olympic soccer, Athens challenges its Hellenic namesake in cultural prowess. History and legend aside, Athens has nurtured a prolific music scene—REM, the B-52s, Love Tractor, and Pylon, to name a few.

Practical Information 70 mi. northeast of Atlanta, Athens can be reached from I-85 via U.S. 316 (exit 4) which runs into U.S. 29. Two blocks north of the UGA campus is the **Athens Welcome Center,** 280 E. Dougherty St. (353-1820), located in the Church-Brumby House, the city's oldest surviving residence. The **Athens Transit System** (613-3430) runs buses every half hour on the hour Mon.-Fri. 6am-7pm, Sat. 7:30am-7pm). Schedules are available at the UGA Tate Center, City Hall, and the bus garage on Pound St. and Prince Ave. (fare 75¢, children and seniors 35¢). The **Athens-Atlanta Airport** (725-5573 or 800-354-7874) flies commuters six times a day to Atlanta for $25 (open 24 hrs.). **Greyhound,** 220 W. Broad St. (549-2255), has service to Atlanta thrice daily (open daily 7:30am-5:45pm). The **Rape Crisis Line** (353-1912) takes calls 7pm to 7am daily. The **health center** (546-5526) is open by appointment (Mon.-Fri. 8:30am-5pm). **Post office:** 575 Olympic Dr. (613-2695); **ZIP Code:** 30601; **area code:** 706.

Accommodations and Sights The **Downtowner Motor Inn,** 1196 S. Milledge Ave. (549-2626), has affordable rooms near campus (singles $30, doubles $36). In nearby Watkinsville, the **Hawkes-Nest Hostel (HI-AYH),** 1716 McRee Mill Rd. (769-0563), offers wooden cabins with private baths ($10, groups $16).

For a walking tour of Athens's historical neighborhood pick up a copy of *Athens of Old* at the Welcome Center. The **Georgia Museum of Art,** in historic North University Campus off Jackson St. (542-3255; open Mon.-Sat. 9am-5pm, Sun. 1-5pm), houses a collection of over 7000 works. With the **State Botanical Gardens of Georgia,** 2450 S. Milledge Ave. (542-1244; open daily 8am-sunset), close by, Athens is a paradise for aesthete and botanist alike. Some bizarre Athenian lore include a double-barreled cannon at City Hall Plaza that never worked and the **"The Tree That Owns Itself."** Prof. W.H. Jackson deeded that the white oak standing at the corner of Dearling and Finley streets should own itself and its 8-ft. radius of shade. The original oak died in 1942 but was reborn by one of its own acorns.

Food and Nightlife The **Athens Coffeehouse**, 301 E. Clayton St. (208-9711), serves the sophisticated palate (open Mon.-Thurs. 11am-11pm, Fri. 11am-2am, Sat.-Sun. 9am-2pm). A simulated French Quarter restaurant, **Harry Bissett's New Orleans Café and Oyster Bar,** 279 E. Broad St. (353-7065), has a terrific oyster and beer bar and a more secluded dining area for sampling Creole cuisine (open Mon.-Fri. 11:30am-3pm and 5:30-10pm, Sat.-Sun. 11:30am-3:30pm and 5:30-11pm).

Those on an REM pilgrimage must check out the **40 Watt Club,** 285 W. Washington St. (549-7871), where the group started out and where many bands today are following their lead. For southern R&B, the **Georgia Theatre** (549-9918), at the corner of Lumpkin and Clayton St., is happening. With Guinness on tap and a smoke-free zone on the second floor, **The Globe,** 199 N. Lumpkin St. (353-4721), has the feel of a pub from the old country (open Mon.-Sat. 4pm-1am).

■■■ SAVANNAH

In February of 1733, General James Oglethorpe and his rag-tag band of 120 colonists founded the state of Georgia at Tamacraw Bluff on the Savannah River. Since then the city has had a stint as the capital of Georgia, housed the first girl scout troop in the U.S., and provided enough inspiration for Eli Whitney, longtime Savannah resident, to invent the cotton gin.

When the price of cotton crashed at the turn of the century, many of the homes and warehouses along River St. fell into disrepair, and the townhouses and mansions that lined Savannah's boulevards became boarding houses or rubble. In the mid-1950s, a group of concerned citizens mobilized to restore the downtown area, preserving the numerous Federalist and English Regency houses as historic monuments. Today, four historic forts, broad streets, and trees hung with Spanish moss enhance the city's classic Southern aura. This beautiful backdrop will serve as the site for the boating and yachting events during the 1996 Olympic Summer Games.

PRACTICAL INFORMATION

Emergency: 911.

Visitor Information: Savannah Visitors Center, 301 Martin Luther King, Jr. Blvd. (944-0456), at Liberty St. in a lavish former train station. Excellent free maps and guides and 15-min. slide show about Savannah past and present (every 30 min., $1, kids 6-12 50¢). Open Mon.-Fri. 8:30am-5pm, Sat.-Sun. 9am-5pm. The **Savannah History Museum,** in the same building, has exhibits depicting the city's history. Open daily 8:30am-5pm. $3, seniors $2.50, ages 6-12 $1.75.

Amtrak: 2611 Seaboard Coastline Dr. (234-2611 or 800-872-7245), 4 mi. outside the city. Taxi fare to city about $5. To: Charleston, SC (2 per day; 2 hr.; $22); Washington, DC (4 per day; 11 hr.; $112). Open 24 hrs.

Greyhound: 610 E. Oglethorpe Ave. (232-2135), convenient to downtown. To: Jacksonville (11 per day, 3 hr., $27); Charleston, SC (4 per day, 3 hr., $28); Washington, DC (6 per day, 14 hr., $98). Open daily 5am-9pm.

Public Transport: Chatham Area Transit (CAT), 233-5767. Operates daily 6am-midnight. Fare $1, transfers 5¢. **C&H Bus,** 530 Montgomery St. (232-7099). The only public transportation to Tybee Beach. Buses leave from the civic center in summer at 8:15am, 1:30pm, and 3:30pm, returning from the beach at 9:25am, 2:30pm, and 4:30pm. Fare $1.75.

Help Line: Rape Crisis Center, 233-7273. 24 hrs.

Post Office: 2 N. Fahm St. (235-4646). Open Mon.-Fri. 8:30am-5pm. **ZIP code:** 31402.

Area Code: 912.

Savannah smiles on the coast of Georgia at the mouth of the **Savannah River,** which runs along the border with South Carolina. Charleston, SC, lies 100 mi. up the coast;

Brunswick, GA lies 90 mi. to the south. The city stretches south from bluffs overlooking the river. The restored 2½-square-mi. **downtown historic district,** bordered by East Broad, Martin Luther King, Jr. Blvd., Gwinnett Street, and the river, is best explored on foot. **Tybee Island,** Savannah's beach, is 18 mi. east on U.S. 80 and Rte. 26. Try to visit at the beginning of spring, the most beautiful season in Savannah.

ACCOMMODATIONS AND CAMPING

Make your first stop in Savannah the visitors center (see Practical Information), where a wide array of coupons offer 15-20% discounts on area hotels. The downtown motels cluster near the historic area, visitors center, and Greyhound station. Do not stray south of Gwinnett St., where the historic district quickly deteriorates into an unsafe and seedy area. For those with cars, Ogeechee Rd. (U.S. 17) has several independently owned budget options.

Savannah International Youth Hostel (HI-AYH), 304 E. Hall St. (236-7744), far and away the best deal in town. 2 blocks from the historic district, 2 blocks east of Forsyth Park. Check-in 7:30-10am and 5-10pm. Call the friendly manager, Brian, for late check-in. $11, nonmembers $13. A/C, kitchen, laundry facilities. Located in a restored Victorian mansion. No curfew; lockout 10am-5pm. Private rooms $22; flexible 3-night max. stay.

Bed and Breakfast Inn, 117 W. Gordon St. (238-0518), at Chatham Sq. in the historic district. 10 pretty little rooms with TV, A/C, phones, shared bath, and full southern breakfast. Singles $35, doubles $49. Add $10 on weekends. Reservations requested.

Sanddollar Motel, 11 16th St. (786-5362), at Tybee Island, 1½ mi. south on Butler Ave. A small, family-run motel practically on the beach. Most rooms rented weekly for $125. Singles may be available for $30, Fri.-Sat. $45.

Skidaway Island State Park (598-2300), 13 mi. southeast of downtown off Diamond Causeway. Inaccessible by public transportation. Follow Liberty St. east out of downtown; soon after it becomes Wheaton St., turn right on Waters Ave. and follow it to the Diamond Causeway. Bathrooms and heated showers. Sites $17, each additional night $15. Fall-spring $15/12. Check-in before 10pm.

Richmond Hill State Park (727-2339), off Rte. 144, ½ hr. south of downtown; take exit 15 off I-95. Quieter than Skidaway and usually less crowded. Sites $12. Parking $2. Check-in before 10pm. Office open daily 8am-5pm.

FOOD AND NIGHTLIFE

In Savannah, cheap food and frozen alcoholic delights are easy to come by. Try the waterfront area (E. River St.) for budget meals in a pub-like atmosphere. The early-bird dinner specials at **Corky's,** 407 E. River St. (234-0113), range from $4-6. **Kevin Barry's Irish Pub,** 117 W. River St. (233-9626), has live Irish folk music (Wed.-Sun. after 9pm), as well as cheap drinks during happy hour. For a drink that will keep you on your ear for days, check out **Wet Willies,** 101 E. River St. (233-5650), which has casual dining, young folks, and irresistible frozen daiquiris (open Sun.-Thurs. 11am-1am, Fri.-Sat. 11am-2am). Local college students usually hang out at **City Market,** where an array of shops, restaurants, and bars are clustered. One hot spot is **Malone's Bar and Grill,** 27 Barnard St (234-3059), with dancing, drinks, live jazz, and rock Friday and Saturday nights (happy hour 4-8pm daily; open daily 11:30am-1am). Hustlers will enjoy **B&B Billiards,** 411 W. Congress St. (233-7116), which was recently renovated by local art students and has a new stock of 10 Gandi pool tables and over 80 types of beer. (Open Mon.-Sat. noon-3am.)

Olympia Cafe, 5 E. River St. (233-3131). On the river, great Greek specialities, including salads and pizzas. Lunch or dinner $4-10. Open Sun.-Thurs. 10am-10pm, Fri.-Sat. 10am-midnight.

Clary's Café, 404 Abercorn St. (233-0402). Open since 1903, this local family spot has a famous weekend brunch and friendly service. Malted waffle $3.50. Open Mon.-Fri. 6:30am-4pm, Sat. 8am-1pm, Sun. 9am-2pm.

Mrs. Wilkes Boarding House, 107 W. James St. (232-5997), is truly a southern institution. Let grandma make you lunch. Sit with friendly strangers around a large table and help yourself to luscious fried chicken, sweet potatoes, spinach, beans, and spaghetti. All you can eat (and then some) $8. No sign, so just join the line. Lunch only, at 11am. Get there early, the wait can be up to 2 hr.

Morrison's Cafeteria, 15 Bull St. (232-5264), near Johnson Sq. downtown. Traditional U.S. and southern cooking. Full meals $4-6. Whole pies $2. The food is guaranteed—if you don't like it, you don't pay for it. Open daily 7:30am-8pm.

SIGHTS AND EVENTS

In addition to restored antebellum houses, the downtown area includes over 20 small parks and gardens. The **Historic Savannah Foundation,** 210 Broughton St. (233-7703; call 233-3597 for reservations; 24 hrs.), offers a variety of guided 1- and 2-hr. tours ($7-14). You can also catch any number of bus, horse carriage, or van tours ($7-12) leaving about every 10-15 min. from outside the visitors center (see Practical Information above). Ask inside for details.

The best-known historic houses in Savannah are the **Owens-Thomas House,** 124 Abercorn St. (233-9743), on Oglethorpe Sq. (open Feb.-Dec. Sun.-Mon. 2-5pm, Tues.-Sat. 10am-5pm; last tour at 4:30pm; $5, students $3, under 13 $2), and the **Davenport House,** 324 E. State St. (236-8097), a block away on Columbia Sq. The Owens-Thomas House is one of the best examples of English Regency architecture in the U.S. The Davenport House typifies the Federalist style and contains an excellent collection of Davenport china. Earmarked to be razed for a parking lot, its salvation in 1955 marked the birth of the Historic Savannah Foundation and the effort to restore the city. There are guided tours of the first floor every 15 min.; explore the second and third floors at your leisure. (Open Mon.-Sat. 10am-4:30pm, Sun. 1:30-4:30pm. Closed Thurs. Last tour at 4pm. $5.) Another famous house is the **Green Meldrim House,** 1 W. Maco St. (233-3845), on Madison Sq., a gothic revival mansion and General Sherman's headquarters throughout the Civil War (open Tues. and Thurs.-Sat. 10am-4pm; $3 donation requested).

Lovers of Thin Mints, Scot-teas, and, of course, Savannahs, should make a pilgrimage to the **Juliette Gordon Low Girl Scout National Center,** 142 Bull St. (233-4501), near Wright Square. The association's founder was born here on Halloween, 1860, possibly explaining the Girl Scouts' door-to-door treat-selling technique. The center's "cookie shrine," in one of the most beautiful houses in Savannah, contains an interesting collection of Girl Scout memorabilia. (Open Mon.-Sat. 10am-4pm, Sun. 12:30-4:30pm, closed Wed. $4, under 18 $3, group and Girl Scout discount rates.) The burial obelisk of Revolutionary War hero Nathaniel Green is 1 block down in **Johnson Square,** at the intersection of Bull and E. Saint Julian St.; a plaque bears an epitaph by the Marquis de Lafayette. Juliette Gordon Low lived in the **Andrew Law House,** 329 Abercorn St. (233-6854), facing Lafayette Sq. (open Mon.-Wed. and Fri. 10:30am-4pm, Sun. noon-4pm; $5, kids 12-17 $2, under 12 and Girl Scouts $1). The **Telfair Mansion and Art Museum,** 124 Abercorn St. (232-1177), is a distinguished collection of decorative arts in an English Regency house (open Tues.-Sat. 10am-5pm, Sun. 2-5pm; $3, students $1, kids 6-12 50¢, under 6 free).

For a less conventional view of Savannah's history, follow the **Negro Heritage Trail,** visiting African-American historic sights from early slave times to the present. Three different tours are available on request from the Savannah branch of the **Association for the Study of Afro-American Life and History,** King-Tisdell Cottage, Negro Heritage Trail, 520 E. Harris St. (234-8000). Tours originate at the visitors center (Mon.-Sat. 10am and 1pm; 1-day notice necessary; $10, children $5).

Savannah's four forts once protected the city's port from Spanish, British, and other invaders. The most interesting is **Fort Pulaski National Monument** (786-5787), 15 mi. east of Savannah on U.S. 80 and Rte. 26, which marks the Civil War battle site where walls were first pummeled by rifled cannon, making Pulaski and similar forts obsolete (open daily 8:30am-6:45pm; off-season 8:30am-5:15pm; $2, over 62 and under 16 free). Built in the early 1800s, **Fort Jackson** (232-3945), also along U.S. 80 and Rte. 26, contains exhibits on the Revolution, the War of 1812, and the Civil War. Like Fort Pulaski, it makes a quick detour on a daytrip to Tybee Beach. (Open daily 9am-7pm; Sept.-June 9am-5pm. $2, seniors and students $1.50.)

Special events in Savannah include the **Hidden Garden of the Nogs Tour** (238-0248), in mid-April, when private walled gardens are opened to the public. The free, three-day **St. Patrick's Day Weekend Music Fest** (232-4903) blares jazz, blues, and rock and roll from noon to midnight, Friday through Sunday in the City Market.

■■■ BRUNSWICK AND ENVIRONS

■ BRUNSWICK

Beyond its hostel and the nearby beaches, laid-back Brunswick is of little interest to the traveler except as a relaxing layover between destinations. The Okefenokee Swamp and the Golden Isles make interesting on-the-road daytrips.

Greyhound, 1101 Glouster St. (265-2800; open Mon.-Sat. 8am-1pm and 2-7pm), offers service to Jacksonville (6 per day, 1½ hr., $16) and Savannah (6 per day, 1½ hr., $13). Brunswick's **area code:** 912.

The fantastic **Hostel in the Forest (HI-AYH)** (264-9738, 265-0220, or 638-2623) is located 9 mi. west of Brunswick on U.S. 82, just past a small convenience store. Take I-95 to exit 6 and travel west on U.S. 82/84 about 1½ mi. from the interchange until you see a white-lettered wooden sign set back in the trees along the eastbound lane. The hostel itself is ½ mi. back from the highway; every effort is made to keep the area surrounding the complex of geodesic domes and treehouses as natural as possible. The low-key managers will shuttle you to the Brunswick Greyhound station for $2. They can usually be convinced to make daytrips to Savannah, the Okefenokee Swamp, and the coastal islands. If possible, arrange to stay in one of the three treehouses at the hostel, each complete with a 25-square-ft. picture window and a spacious double bed. Bring insect repellent in the summertime; mosquitoes and yellow, biting flies abound. In addition to a peahen named Cleopatra and numerous chickens, the hostel has an extensive patch of blueberry bushes; you can pick and eat as many berries as you wish in May and June. (No lockout, no curfew, and few rules. $8, nonmembers $10.)

Twin Oaks Pit Barbecue, 2618 Norwick St. (265-3131), 8 blocks from downtown Brunswick across the Southern Bell building, features a chicken-and-pork combination ($6). The breaded french fries ($1) are deep fried and deeeeelicious. (Open Mon.-Thurs. 10am-8:30pm, Fri.-Sat. 10am-10pm.)

■ OKEFENOKEE SWAMP

The Okefenokee Swamp Park, 5700 Okefenokee Swamp Rd. (912-283-0583), on U.S. 1, 8 mi. south of Waycross, is a haven for snoozing alligators, snakes, and birds. Interpretive talks, 25-min. guided boat trips, a ½-mi. wilderness walkway to an observation tower, and swamp life exhibits are all included in the admission price ($10, children 5-11 $7). You can literally walk on water, or at least over a web of weeds. Real adventurers can take their chances renting a canoe ($9 daily, must be 18 or accompanied by an adult). (Open daily summer 9am-6:30pm; rest of year daily 9am-5:30pm.)

■ GOLDEN ISLES

Including **St. Simon's Island, Jekyll Island,** and **Sea Island,** the Golden Isles have miles of white sand beaches. Near the isles, **Cumberland Island National Seashore** is 16 mi. of salt marsh, live-oak forest, and sand dunes laced with a network of trails and disturbed only by a few decaying mansions. Reservations (by phone only; call 882-4335 daily 10am-2pm) are necessary for overnight visits, but the effort is often rewarded; you can walk all day on the beaches without seeing another person. Sites are also available on a stand-by basis 15 min. before ferry departures to Cumberland Island. The **ferry** (2 per day, 45 min., $10, children $6) leaves from St. Mary's on the mainland at the terminus of Rte. 40, at the Florida border (departures daily 9am and 11:45am, returning 10:15am and 4:45pm; off-season Thurs.-Mon. only).

Florida

Ponce de León landed on the Florida coast in 1513, near what would soon be St. Augustine, in search of the elusive Fountain of Youth. Although the multitudes who flock to Florida today aren't desperately seeking fountains, many find their youth restored in the Sunshine State—whether they're dazzled by Orlando's fantasia Disney World or bronzed by the sun on the state's seductive beaches. Droves of senior citizens also migrate to Florida, where they thrive in comfortable retirement communities, leaving one to wonder whether the unpolluted, sun-warmed air isn't just as good as Ponce de León's fabled magical elixir.

But a dark shadow hangs over this land of the winter sun. Anything as attractive as Florida is bound to draw hordes of people, the nemesis of natural beauty. Florida's population boom is straining the state's resources; commercial strips and tremendous development in some areas have turned pristine beaches into tourist traps. Nevertheless, it is possible to find a deserted spot on this peninsula. Sit yourself down, grease yourself up, and pay homage to the sun.

PRACTICAL INFORMATION

Capital: Tallahassee.
Florida Division of Tourism, 126 W. Van Buren St. Tallahassee 32301 (487-1462). **Department of Natural Resources—Division of Recreation and Parks,** 3900 Commonwealth Blvd. #506, Tallahassee 32399-2000 (488-9872).
Time Zones: Eastern and Central (westernmost part). **Postal Abbreviation:** FL
Sales Tax: 6%.

■■■ SAINT AUGUSTINE

Spanish adventurer Juan Ponce de León founded St. Augustine in 1565, making it the first European colony in North America and the oldest city in the United States. Although he never found the legendary Fountain of Youth, Ponce de León did live to age 61, twice the expected life span at that time. Much of St. Augustine's original Spanish flavor remains intact, thanks to the town's preservation efforts. Word-of-mouth has propelled this old-world village into a bustling tourist port. Historic sights, good food, and friendly people make St. Augustine rejuvenating and well worth a few days.

PRACTICAL INFORMATION

Emergency: 911.
Visitor Information: Visitors Center, 10 Castillo (825-1000), at San Marco Ave. From the Greyhound station, walk north on Ribeira, then right on Orange. Pick up hotel coupons and the free *Chamber of Commerce Map,* a comprehensive city guide. A worthwhile (it took 7 yrs. to research) 52-min. video presentation gives the visitor a glimpse of early life in St. Augustine. Open daily 8:30am-5:30pm, summer 8am-7:30pm.
Greyhound: 100 Malaga St. (829-6401). To: Jacksonville (5 per day, 1 hr., $6.50); Daytona Beach (6 per day, 1 hr., $8). Open daily 7:30am-8:30pm.
Taxi: Ancient City Taxi, 824-8161. From the bus station to San Marco about $2.
Help Lines: Rape Crisis, 355-7273 (24 hrs).

Post Office: King St. (829-8716), at Martin Luther King Ave. Open Mon.-Fri. 8:30am-5pm, Sat. 10am-1pm. **ZIP code:** 32084.
Area Code: 904.

Unfortunately, the city has no public transportation, though most points of interest are within walking distance of one another. Historic St. Augustine, concentrated in the area between the **San Sebastian River** and the **Matanzas Bay** to the east, is easily covered on foot. **King Street,** running along the river, is the major east-west axis and crosses the bay to the beaches. **St. George Street,** also east-west, is closed to vehicular traffic and contains most of the shops and many sights in St. Augustine. **San Marco Avenue** and **Cordova Street** travel north-south. Winter brings a surge of activity to nearby **Vilano, Anastasia,** and **St. Augustine Beaches.**

ACCOMMODATIONS AND CAMPING

St. Augustine Hostel (HI-AYH), 32 Treasury St. (829-6163), at Charlotte, 6 blocks from the Greyhound station. Large, dormitory-style rooms with shower and fans. Kitchen available. 1 block from historic Saint George St. with cool view from roof deck. Private singles $12, nonmembers $15. Doubles $25, nonmembers $30. No curfew, but get a combination for the lock. Reservation advised but not necessary. Open for reservations 8-10am and 5-10pm. 10am-5pm access to common room for storage, but no access to sleeping rooms. Day fee $3.

American Inn, 42 San Marco Ave. (829-2292), near the visitors center. Owner won't take your money until you've inspected your room. When a car is available he also provides transportation to and from the bus station. Big, clean singles and doubles $35-45, weekends $50-60. Check visitors center (see Practical Information) for coupons.

Seabreeze Motel, 208 Anastasia Blvd. (829-8122), just over the Bridge of Lions east of the historic district. Clean rooms with A/C, TV, pool. Good restaurants nearby. Singles $30. Doubles $35.

The St. Francis Inn, 279 Saint George St. (824-6068), at Saint Francis St., 2 doors down from the Oldest House. Built in 1791, a charming 16-room inn with a jungle of flowers and a tucked-away pool. Much of its original 18th-century interior has been preserved. Iced tea and juice served all day. Complimentary sangria in the summer and sherry in the winter. Free bike use. Rooms $49-95. Cottage on premises with full kitchen and living room, $140 for 4 people, $10 each additional person. Continental breakfast included.

Anastasia State Recreation Area (461-2033), on Rte. A1A, 4 mi. south of the historic district. From town, cross the Bridge of Lions and bear left just beyond the Alligator Farm. Open daily 8am-8pm. Sites $19, with electricity $21. Make weekend reservations.

FOOD

The flood of daytime tourists and abundance of budget eateries make lunch in St. Augustine's historic district a delight. Stroll **St. George St.** to check the daily specials scrawled on blackboards outside each restaurant; locals prefer those spots clustered at the southern end of St. George near King St. Finding a budget dinner in St. Augustine is trickier, since the downtown is deserted after 5pm. However, an expedition along Anastasia Blvd. should unearth good meals for under $6. The seafood-wise will seek out the surf-'n'-turf dinners ($15) at **Captain Jack's,** 410 Anastasia Blvd. (829-6846; open Mon.-Fri. 11:30am-9pm, Sat.-Sun. noon-9pm).

Café Camacho, 11-C Aviles St. (824-7030), at Charlotte St., 1 block from Saint George St. in the historic district. Cozy Cuban café displaying local artwork. Serves delicious fruit shakes, sandwiches, vegetarian dishes, and daily breakfast and lunch specials ($5-6). Open Mon.-Fri. 8am-9pm, Sat.-Sun. 8am-10pm.

The Bunnery Café, 35 Hypolita St. (829-6166). Sit outside and devour an enormous cinnamon roll ($1.29). Ask for icing on top and they'll generously heap it on till you say the magic word. Oversized portions. Lunch specials and ice cream as well. Open daily 9am-5:30pm.

Florida Peninsula

GEORGIA

Jacksonville

TO TALLAHASSEE

St. Augustine

Gainesville

ATLANTIC OCEAN

Ocala

Daytona Beach

Ocala National Forest

Cedar Keys

NASA Kennedy Space Center

Walt Disney World

Orlando

Cape Canaveral

Tampa

Tampa Bay

St. Petersburg

Manatee R.

Sarasota

Florida's Turnpike

Fort Pierce

Peace R.

Kissimmee R.

Lake Okeechobee

Caloosahatchee R.

West Palm Beach

Fort Myers

Palm Beach

Loxahatchee Nat. Wildlife Refuge

GULF OF MEXICO

Seminole Indian Reservation

Naples

Big Cypress National Preserve

Fort Lauderdale

Miami

Miami Beach

Biscayne Bay

Everglades National Park

Florida City

THE SOUTH

N

0   100 miles

0   100 kilometers

Florida Bay

Key Largo

Florida Keys

Key West

St. George Pharmacy and Restaurant, 121 Saint George St. (829-5929). Museum, luncheonette, and bookstore. Cheap sandwiches from $1.50; dinners from $3. Try the grilled cheese with a thick chocolate malt ($4). Breakfast special (egg, bacon, grits, toast or biscuit, and jelly) $2. Open Mon.-Sat. 7am-5:30pm, Sun. 7:30am-5pm.

New Dawn, 110 Anastasia Blvd. (824-1337). A health-conscious grocery store with a sandwich and juice counter. Delicious vegetarian sandwiches; try the tofu salad surprise ($3.25). Banana smoothies $2.25. Open Mon.-Sat. 9am-5:30pm.

SIGHTS AND ENTERTAINMENT

Saint George St. is the center of the **historic district,** which begins at the Gates of the City near the visitors center and runs south past Cadiz St. and the Oldest Store. Visit **San Agustín Antiguo** (825-6830), Gallegos House on Saint George St., St. Augustine's authentically restored 18th-century neighborhood, where artisans and villagers in period costumes describe the customs and crafts of the Spanish New World. (Open daily 9am-4pm. $5, seniors $3.75, students and ages 6-18 $2.50.) The oldest masonry fortress in the continental U.S., **Castillo de San Marcos,** 1 Castillo Dr. (829-6506), off San Marco Ave., has 14-ft. thick walls built of coquina, the local shellrock. The fort itself is a four-pointed star complete with drawbridge and a murky moat. Inside you'll find a museum, a large courtyard surrounded by guard-rooms, livery quarters for the garrison, a jail, a chapel, and the original cannon brought overseas by the Spanish. A cannon-firing ceremony occurs four times per day on the weekend. (Open daily 8:45am-4pm. $2, over 62 and under 16 free.)

St. Augustine has several old stores and museums. The self-described **Oldest House,** 14 Saint Francis St. (824-2872), has been occupied continuously since its construction in the 1600s. (Open daily 9am-5pm. $5, seniors $4.50, students $2.50.) The **Oldest Store Museum,** 4 Artillery Lane (829-9729), has over 100,000 odds and ends from the 18th and 19th centuries. (Open Mon.-Sat. 9am-5pm, Sun. noon-5pm. $4, ages 6-12 $1.50.) Also in the old part of the city is the coquina **Cathedral of St. Augustine,** begun in 1793. Although several fires have destroyed parts of the cathedral, the walls and facade are original.

Six blocks north of the info center is the **Mission of Nombre de Dios,** 27 Ocean St. (824-2809), a moss- and vine-covered mission which held the first Catholic service in the U.S. on September 8, 1565. Soaring over the structure is a 208-ft. steel cross commemorating the founding of the city. (Open daily 8am-6pm in winter; 7am-8pm in summer. Mass Mon.-Fri. at 8:30am, Sat. at 6pm, Sun. at 8am. Admission by donation.) No trip to St. Augustine would be complete without a trek to the **Fountain of Youth,** 155 Magnolia Ave. (829-3168). Go right on Williams St. from San Marco Ave. and continue a few blocks past Nombre de Dios. (Open daily 9am-5pm. $4, seniors $3, ages 6-12 $1.50.) In addition to drinking from the spring that Ponce de León mistakenly thought would give him eternal youth, you can see a statue of the explorer that does not age.

Though oil and water don't usually mix, Henry Flagler, co-founder of Standard Oil and a good friend of the Rockefellers, retired to St. Augustine. He built two hotels in the downtown area that the rich and famous once frequented, making St. Augustine the "Newport of the South." The former Ponce de León Hotel, at King and Cordova St., is now **Flagler College.** In summer, the college is deserted, but during the school year students enliven the town. Free 20-25 min. tours of some recently restored rooms in the old hotel are available in the summer. (Tours given daily on the hour 10am-4pm.) In 1947, Chicago publisher and lover of *objets d'art* Otto Lightner converted the Alcazar Hotel into the **Lightner Museum** (824-2874), with an impressive collection of cut, blown, and burnished glass (open daily 9am-5pm; $4, ages 12-18 and college students with ID $1).

Visitors can tour St. Augustine by land or by sea. **St. Augustine Sight-Seeing Trains,** 170 San Marcos Ave. (829-6545), offer a variety of city tours (1-8 hr.; open daily 8:30am-4:30pm). The one-hour tour ($9, ages 6-12 $4), a good introduction to the city, starts at the front of the visitors center (see Practical Information). **Colée**

Sight-Seeing Carriage Tours (829-2818) begin near the entrance to the fort, take about an hour, and cover the historic area of St. Augustine ($9, ages 4-11 $4; open daily 8:30am-10pm). The **Victory II Scenic Cruise Ships** (824-1806) navigate the emerald Matanzas River from the City Yacht Pier, a block south of the Bridge of Lions (leaves at 11am and 1, 2:45, 4:30, 6:45, and 8:30pm; $7.50, under 12 $3).

On Anastasia Island, at **Anastasia State Park,** you can see Paul Green's *Cross and Sword,* Florida's official state play, telling St. Augustine's story with a large cast, booming cannon, and swordfights. ($8, ages 6-12 and students $4.)

With a penchant for loudness and liquid, St. Augustine has an impressive array of bars. **Scarlett O'Hara's,** 70 Hypolita St. (824-6535), at Cordova St., is popular with locals. The barbecue chicken sandwiches ($4.50) are filling and juicy, the drinks ample and cool. Live entertainment begins at 9pm nightly. (Happy hour 5:30-6:30pm Mon.-Fri. Cover on Fri. and Sat. nights only, $1. Tues. and Thurs. ladies nights. Open daily 11:30am-1am.) Try the **Milltop,** 19½ Saint George St. (829-2329), a tiny bar situated above an old mill in the restored area. Local string musicians play on the tiny stage (daily 11am-midnight, no cover). On St. Augustine Beach, **Panama Hattie's,** 361 A1A Beach Blvd. (471-2255), caters to the post-college crowd (open daily 1pm-midnight, no cover). **The Oasis Deck and Restaurant,** 4000 A1A Beach Blvd. (471-3424), is the new hot spot for the young beach crowd (complimentary sunsets daily). Nightly live entertainment and happy hour (Mon.-Fri. 4-7pm). Try the Whaler sandwich ($5). (Open daily 6:30am until when y'all go home.) Pick up a copy of the *Today Tonight* newspaper, available at most grocery and convenience stores, for a complete listing of current concerts, events, and dinner specials.

■■■ DAYTONA BEACH

Daytona's 500-ft. wide beach is the city's *raison d'etre.* During spring break, students from practically every college in the country come here to get a head and body start on summer. The beach itself resembles a traffic jam; dozens of cars, motorcycles, and rental dune buggies crawl along the hot sand. During any season, hundred of cars roll along the beach within feet of sunbathers, or cruise the Atlantic Avenue strip. Hotels and fast food restaurants line the streets. If you're looking for scenery in Daytona Beach, go a few miles north to picturesque Ormond Beach. If not, slap on some sunscreen and enjoy.

PRACTICAL INFORMATION

Emergency: 911.

Visitor Information: The Daytona Beach Area Convention and Visitors Bureau, at the chamber of commerce, 126 E. Orange Ave., on City Island (255-0415 or 800-854-1234). Open Mon.-Fri. 9am-5pm. **Traveler's Aid,** 300 Magnolia Ave. (252-4752). Open Mon.-Fri. 8:30am-4:30pm, call 24 hrs.

Airport: Daytona Beach Regional, 189 Midway Ave. (255-8441). The **Daytona-Orlando Transit Service (DOTS)** shuttle (257-5411) runs between Orlando's airport and Daytona every 1½ hrs. Departing Orlando for Daytona 7am-11:30pm, Daytona for Orlando 6am-7:30pm. $25; $46 roundtrip. Call one day ahead for reservations.

Amtrak: 2491 Old New York Ave., Deland (734-2322 or 800-872-7245), 24 mi. west on Rte. 92. Open daily 1-10pm.

Greyhound: 138 Ridgewood Ave. (800-231-2222), 4 mi. west of the beach. Catch any of the several different routes to the beach at the Volusia County Terminal. Open Mon.-Sat. 8am-10pm, Sun 10am-7pm.

Public Transportation: Voltran Transit Co. (761-7700), at the corner of Palmetto and 2nd Ave. on the mainland. Buses operate Mon.-Sat. 5:30am-6:30pm. 75¢, transfers free. Free system maps available at hotels.

Taxi: A&A Cab Co. (253-2522). $1.80 for first ½ mi., $1.20 each additional mi.

Car Rental: Alamo (255-1511 or 800-327-9633) at the airport. Subcompact $25 per day, $95 per week with unlimited mileage. Free drop-off in Jacksonville or Ft. Lauderdale. Must be 21 with credit card. $6 extra if under 25.

THE SOUTH

Help Line: Rape Crisis and Sexual Abuse, 254-4106; 24 hrs.
Post Office: 220 N. Beach St., Daytona Beach (253-5166). Open Mon.-Fri. 8am-5pm. Sat. 9am-noon.
ZIP code: 32176.
Area Code: 904.

Daytona Beach is 53 mi. northeast of Orlando and 90 mi. south of Jacksonville on Florida's northeast coast. **Atlantic Avenue,** or **Rte. A1A,** is lined with budget motels, tanning oil, surf shops, and bars in **Beachside,** the main strip of land. **East International Speedway Blvd.** (U.S. 92) divides Atlantic Ave. north-south. Pay attention when hunting down street addresses, as the north-south streets often change number passing through the various towns.

To avoid the inevitable gridlock on the beach, you'll have to arrive early (6 or 7am) and leave early (3pm or so). You'll pay $5 to drive onto the beach (permitted from sunrise to sunset), and police strictly enforce the 10 mph speed limit.

ACCOMMODATIONS AND CAMPING

Almost all of Daytona's accommodations are on Atlantic Ave. (Rte. A1A), either on the beach or across the street; those off the beach offer the best deals. During spring break and big race weekends, even the worst hotels become ridiculously overpriced. Look for cheaper and quieter hotels along Ridgewood Ave. In summer and fall, prices plunge and most hotels offer special deals in June. Don't plan to sleep on these well-patrolled shores.

Daytona Beach International Youth Hostel (Rucksackers), 140 S. Atlantic Ave. (258-6937), 1 block north of E. International Speedway Blvd. Pink stucco hostel with 36 rooms, 100 beds, and close proximity to the beach. Clean kitchen facilities and recreation room. Usually full of international students. All rooms have A/C and phones with free local calls. HI-AYH members $12, nonmembers $16 (though hostel is not AYH affiliated). Weekly $70. Key deposit $5. Lockers $1-2.

Camelia Motel, 1055 N. Atlantic Ave. (252-9963), across the street from the beach, has cozy rooms decorated with furniture built by Joe, the Czech owner. All rooms have cable TV, A/C, and some have kitchens for an extra $6. Singles $20, doubles $25, each additional person $4, except during spring break when singles are a negotiable $60 plus $10 for each additional.

Monte Carlo Beach Motel, 825 S. Atlantic Ave. (255-0461). A friendly Italian family runs this pink and white motel surrounded by palm trees on the beach. Rooms with cable TV, A/C, phone, and a pool. Singles $20. Doubles $25. During spring break a negotiable $60-75, with $100 deposit. Kitchen use $5.

Nova Family Campground, 1190 Herbet St. (767-0095), in Port Orange south of Daytona Beach, 10 min. from the shore. Take bus #7 or #15 from downtown or from the beach. Shady sites, pool, grocery store. Open Sun.-Thurs. 8am-7pm, Fri.-Sat. 8am-8pm. Sites $17, $18 with hookup. Open sites posted after hours; register the next day.

Tomoka State Park, 2099 N. Beach St. (676-4050), 8 mi. north of Daytona and 70 min. to Disneyworld. Take bus #3 ("North Ridgewood") to Domicilio and walk 2 mi. north. Nature trails, a museum, and lots of shade. Open daily 8am-7:45pm. 100 sites, $9, $11 with hookup.

FOOD

B&B Fisheries, 715 E. International Speedway Blvd. (252-6542). Family owned business almost lives up to its motto: "if it swims . . . we have it." Take-out broiled flounder or sea trout lunches under $4.40. Lobster specials for under $10. Open Mon.-Sat. 11am-8:30pm. Take-out service Mon.-Sat. 11:30am-8:30pm.

Oyster Pub, 555 Seabreeze Blvd. (255-6348). A huge square bar where locals drink, eat hearty meat sandwiches ($2-4), or slurp up the raw oysters served all day. Open daily 11:30am-3am. Happy hour 4-7pm.

St. Regis Bar and Restaurant, 509 Seabreeze Blvd. (252-8743), in a historic home. Serves up an eclectic array of edibles and cocktails. Cool veranda and live music Fri.-Sat. nights (9pm-midnight). Open Mon.-Fri. 11:30am-2pm, and 5:30-10pm. Sat. 5:30-10pm. Happy hour 4:30-6pm with free hors d'oeuvres.

Triple S Supermarket, 167 S. Atlantic Ave (252-8431), across from the youth hostel. Features deli sandwiches and subs ($3-4) during spring break. Stock up for the beach. Open daily 9am-9pm.

EVENTS AND ENTERTAINMENT

If you grow tired of racing around Daytona's beaches, try an actual racing event at the **Daytona International Speedway,** 1801 International Blvd. (254-2700). Call 254-2700 for general info and 253-RACE for tickets to a race. February 1-16 is Speed Week (general admission $20-25) and includes the **Daytona 500** (Feb. 19), the **Goody's 300** (Feb. 18), and the **ARCA 200 World Championship Race** (Feb. 12). The **Daytona Racefest** and the **Pepsi 400 NASCAR Winston Cup Series** kick into gear at the beginning of July (tickets $20-45) and during the first weekend in March. Motorcycle Week culminates with the **Daytona 200 Motorcycle Classic** (tickets $10). The speedway has daily 30-min. tours 9am-5pm ($2, children $1) when no races are scheduled, and houses a huge collection of historic racing memorabilia and a cool "video wall" featuring early racing films. Finally, the **Birthplace of Speed Museum,** 160 Granada Blvd. (672-5657), depicts the history of racing in the Daytona Beach area. (Open Tues.-Sat. 1-5pm, $1, children 50¢.)

During spring break, concerts, hotel-sponsored parties, and other events cater to students questing for fun. Word of mouth is the best way to find out about these transient events and parties, but also check out the *Calendar of Events* and *SEE the Best of Daytona Beach,* available at the Chamber of Commerce.

As if you needed more outlets for sin, you sickos. Fine, have **600 North Attitudes,** 600 N. Atlantic Ave. (255-4471), and **Kokomos,** 100 North Atlantic Ave. (254-8200), two hot spots during spring break. **Razzel's,** 611 Seabreeze Blvd. (257-6236), boasts free drinks between 8am-10pm for those wearing miniskirts, and **Finky's,** 600 Grandview (255-5059), motto is "I got kinky at . . . "

For more mellow nights, head for the boardwalk where you can play volleyball, pinball, listen to music at the Oceanfront Bandshell, or park (ahem) for $3 on the beach until 1am .

■■■ ORLANDO: THE LAND OF AMUSEMENT PARKS

■ ORLANDO

Although Orlando likes to tout itself as "the world's vacation center" and one of the country's fastest-growing cities, millions annually descend on this central Florida city for just one reason: **Disney World,** the most popular tourist attraction on earth. Walt Disney selected the area south of Orlando as the place for his sequel to California's Disneyland. Disney has since augmented the Magic Kingdom with the Epcot Center and the new Disney-MGM Studios theme park.

A number of parasitic attractions, such as expensive water parks, abound in the area to scavenge the left-overs of Disney tourism. Be warned: there are many ways to blow your dough in this land of illusions. Usually you are best off spending your time and money at Disney first.

PRACTICAL INFORMATION

Emergency: 911.

Visitor Information: Orlando-Orange County Visitors and Convention Bureau, 8445 International Dr. (363-5871), several mi. southwest of downtown at the Mercado (Spanish-style mall). Take bus #8, and ask the bus driver to drop you off at the Mercado. Maps and info on nearly all of the amusement park attractions in the area. Pick up a free bus system map. Open daily 8am-8pm.

THE SOUTH

Amtrak: 1400 Sligh Blvd. (425-9411 or 800-872-7245). Three blocks east of I-4. Take S. Orange Ave., turn west on Columbia, then right on Sligh. To Tampa ($18, 2 hrs.), Jacksonville ($30, 3 hrs.). Open 7:45am-9:15pm.

Greyhound: (292-3424 for 24-hr. fare and ticket info.) 555 N. Magruder Blvd. across from John Young Parkway. To Tampa ($16, 3 hrs.), Jacksonville ($22, 4 hrs.). Open 24 hrs.

Public Transport: LYNX, 438 Woods Ave. (841-8240 for info Mon.-Fri. 6:30am-6:30pm, Sat. 7:30am-6pm, Sun. 8am-4pm). Downtown terminal between Central and Pine St., 1 block west of Orange Ave. and 1 block east of I-4. Schedules available at most shopping malls, banks, and at the downtown terminal. Serves the airport (bus #11 at "B" terminal luggage claim), Sea World, and Wet 'n' Wild. Buses operate daily 6am-9pm. Fare 75¢, under 18 25¢, transfers 10¢.

Mears Motor Shuttle: 324 W. Gore St. (423-5566). Has a booth at the airport for transportation to most hotels, including the Airport Hostel (see Accommodations below). Cheapest transport besides city bus #11 if you're alone and can't split taxi fare. Also runs from most hotels to Disney (cost depends on proximity to the park $7-14). Open 24 hrs. Call day in advance to reserve seat to Disney.

Taxi: Yellowcab, 422-4455. $2.65 first mi., $1.40 each additional mi.

Car Rental: Alamo, 8200 McCoy Rd. (857-8200 or 800-327-9633), near the airport. $25 per day, $122 per week. Under 25 $10 extra per day. Open 24 hrs. Must have major credit card or a $50 deposit and book through a travel agent.

Help Lines: Rape Hotline, 740-5408. **Crisis Information:** 648-3028. Both 24 hrs.

Post Office: 46 E. Robinson St. (843-5673), at Magnolia downtown. Open Mon.-Fri. 8am-5pm, Sat. 9am-noon. **ZIP code:** 32801.

Area Code: 407.

Orlando proper lies at the center of hundreds of small lakes and amusement parks. **Lake Eola** reclines at the center of the city, east of I-4 and south of Colonial Dr. Streets divide north-south by **Route 17-92 (Orange Blossom Trail)** and east-west by **Colonial Drive.** I-4, supposedly an east-west expressway, actually runs north-south through the center of town. To reach either downtown youth hostel (see Accommodations) by car, take the Robinson St. exit and turn right. **Disney World** and **Sea World** are 15-20 mi. south of downtown on I-4; **Cypress Gardens** is 30 mi. south of Disney off U.S. 27 near Winter Haven. Transportation out to the parks is simple—most hotels offer a shuttle service to Disney, but you can take a city bus or call Mears Motor Shuttle (see above).

ACCOMMODATIONS AND CAMPING

Orlando does not cater to the budget traveler. Prices for hotel rooms rise exponentially as you approach Disney World; plan to stay in a hostel or in downtown Orlando. Reservations are a good idea December to January, March to April, and on holidays. Or try **Kissimmee,** a few mi. east of Disney World along U.S. 192, which has some of the cheapest places around to camp. One city park and four Orange County parks have campsites ($11, with hookup $14). Contact **Orange County Parks & Recreation Department,** 118 W. Kaley St. (836-4290), or **Orlando Parks Department,** 1206 W. Columbia (246-2283), for more info (both open Mon.-Fri. 8am-8pm).

Orlando International Youth Hostel at Plantation Manor (HI-AYH), 227 N. Eola Dr. (843-8888), at E. Robinson, downtown on the east shore of Lake Eola. Usually full July-Oct., so make reservations. Porch, TV room, A/C in most rooms, kitchen facilities, (negotiable) midnight curfew Mon.-Tues. Rooms sleep 4-8. Hostel beds $13, nonmembers $14.50. Private rooms $29. Breakfast $2, linen $2, key deposit $5. The friendly managers will take you to the theme park of your choice for $10 round-trip.

Airport Hostel, 3500 McCoy Rd. (859-3165 or 851-1612), off Daetwiler Rd. behind the La Quinta Motel. Take "Airport" bus #11 from the airport or downtown. Little glamour, but very homey, with tropical fruit trees out back. Kitchen facilities, pool access, no curfew. Check-in by 10pm. $10, $60 per week. Breakfast and linen included.

Women's Residential Counseling Center (HI-AYH), 107 E. Hillcrest St. (425-1076), at Magnolia, 4 blocks from Plantation Manor right behind the Orlando Sentinel. Take bus #10 or 12; staff recommends a taxi. Women only. Clean, safe, and friendly. Pool. Flexible 3-night max. stay. $10. Linen $2. Good breakfast $2, dinner $4. No reservations. No curfew. Office open 7am-3pm.

Sun Motel, 5020 W. Irlo Bronson Memorial Hwy. (396-6666 or 800-541-2674), in Kissimmee. Very reasonable considering proximity to Disney World (4 mi.). Cable TV, phone, pool, A/C. Singles $45, doubles $60. Off-season singles $28, doubles $35.

KOA, U.S. 192 (396-2400; 800-331-1453), down the road from Twin Lakes. Kamping kabins $38. Pool, tennis, store (open 7am-11pm). Even in season you're bound to get a site, but arrive early. Free buses twice per day to Disney. Office open 24 hrs. Tent sites with hookup $22 for up to 2 people, $4 each additional.

Stage Stop Campground, 700 W. Rte. 50 (656-8000), 8 mi. north of Disney in Winter Garden. Take exit 80 off the Florida Turnpike N., then left on Rte. 50. Office open daily 8am-8:30pm. 248 sites with full hookup $17. Weekly: $102.

FOOD

Lilia's Grilled Delight, 3150 S. Orange Ave. (351-9087), 2 blocks south of Michigan St., 5 min. from the downtown business district. Small, modestly decorated Polynesian restaurant—one of the best-kept secrets in town. Don't pass up the Huli Huli Chicken, a twice baked delight (½ chicken for $3.95). Lunch $4-6, dinner $5-9. Open Mon.-Sat. 11am-9pm.

Numero Uno, 2499 S. Orange Ave. (841-3840). A #1 local favorite serving tasty Cuban specialties in a casual setting. Roast pork dinner with rice, plantains, and black beans about $9. Open Mon.-Wed. 11am-3pm, Thurs.-Fri. 11am-3pm and 5-10pm, Sat. 1-10pm.

Deter's Restaurant and Pub, 17 W. Pine St.(839-5975), just up from Orange St. near the Church Street Mall. German-American cuisine in an after-work-let's-have-a-beer atmosphere. Try the amazing chicken in *riesling* sauce ($10). Live entertainment Fri.-Sat. nights. No cover. Open Mon.-Thurs. 11am-11pm, Fri.-Sat. 11am-2am.

Ronnie's Restaurant, 2702 Colonial Plaza (894-2943), at Bumby St. just past the Colonial Plaza mall. Art-Deco booths and counters from the 50s. Mix of Jewish, Cuban, and American cuisine. The famous breakfast special (eggs, rolls, juice, coffee, and more) may fill you up for a few days ($5). Steak dinner $11, fresh breads, swell pancakes. Open Sun.-Thurs. 7am-11pm, Fri.-Sat. 7am-1am.

Nature's Table, 8001 South Orange Blossom Trail (857-5496). Vegetarian and healthful specialties. Tasty fruit and protein powder shakes ($1-2), yogurt, juice. Mongo sandwiches under $4. Open Mon.-Sat. 10am-9:30pm., Sun. 9:30am-6pm.

ENTERTAINMENT

The **Church Street Station,** 129 W. Church St. (422-2434), downtown on the corner of Church and Garland Streets, is a slick, block-long entertainment, shopping, and restaurant complex (open 11am-2am). If you're low on funds, try the $3 dinner platter at the **Chinese Cafe,** Listen to free folk and bluegrass music at **Apple Annie's Courtyard,** or boogie down (and enjoy 5¢ beers on Wed. from 6:30-7:30pm) at **Phineas Phogg's Balloon Works** (enforced 21 age restriction). Or pay $16 to go to the three theme shows. **Rosie O'Grady's** is the most popular show, featuring Dixieland and can-can girls. **Cheyenne Saloon and Opera House** has a country and western show, while rock and roll rules at the **Orchid Garden Ballroom.** For less expensive nightlife, explore **Orange Avenue** downtown. Several good bars and clubs have live music and dancing at very reasonable prices.

■ DISNEY WORLD

Disney: the mother of all amusement parks, a sprawling three-park labyrinth of kiddie rides, movie sets, and futuristic world displays. If bigger is better, Disney World certainly wins the prize for best park in the U.S. (824-4321 for info daily 8am-10pm). Disney World is divided into three parts: the **Magic Kingdom,** with seven theme regions; the **Epcot Center,** part science fair, part World's Fair; and the newly completed **Disney-MGM Studios,** a pseudo movie and TV studio with Magic Kingdom-style rides. All are located a few mi. from each other in the town of **Lake Buena Vista,** 20 mi. west of Orlando via I-4.

A one-day entrance fee of $36 (ages 3-9 $29) admits you to *one* of the three parks; it also allows you to leave and return to the same park later in the day. A four-day **Value Pass** ($124, ages 3-9 $97) allows you one day at each park, plus an extra day at one of them. A four-day **Park-Hopper Pass** ($134, ages 3-9 $107) admits you to all three parks and includes unlimited transportation between attractions on the Disney monorail, boats, buses, and trains. You can opt for a five-day **World-Hopper Pass** ($179, ages 3-9 $143), which also admits you to all other Disney attractions. Multi-day passes need not be used on consecutive days. Those Disney attractions that charge separate admissions (unless you have the five-day Pass) are: **River Country** ($14, ages 3-9 $11); **Discovery Island** ($9.50, ages 3-9 $5.25); **Typhoon Lagoon** ($21.50, ages 3-9 $16.50); and **Pleasure Island** ($15, over 18 only unless with adult). For descriptions, see Other Disney Attractions below.

Gray Line Tours (422-0744) and **Mears Motor Shuttle** (423-5566) offer transport from most hotels to Disney (depart hotel at 9am, depart Disney at 7pm; $14 roundtrip). Major hotels and some campgrounds provide their own shuttles for guests. **Cyclists** are stopped at the main gate and driven by security guards to the inner entrance where they can stash their bikes free of charge.

Disney World opens its gates 365 days a year, but hours fluctuate according to season. It's busy during the summer when school is out, but the enormously crowded "peak times" are Christmas, Thanksgiving, spring break, and the month around Easter. More people visit between Christmas and New Year's than at any other time of year. Since the crowd hits the main gates at 10am, arrive before the 9am opening time and seek out your favorite rides or exhibits before noon. During peak period (and often during the rest of the year), the Disney parks actually open earlier than the stated time. Begin the day at the rear of a park and work your way to the front. You'll have more fun at the distant attractions while lines for those near the entrance are jammed. Persevere through dinner time (5:30-8pm), when a lot of cranky kids head home. Regardless of tactics, you'll often have to wait anywhere from 45 min. to two hrs at big attractions.

Magic Kingdom Seven "lands" comprise the Magic Kingdom. You enter on **Main Street, USA,** meant to capture the essence of turn-of-the-century hometown U.S. In a potpourri of styles, architects employed "forced perspective" here, building the ground floor of the shops 9/10 of the normal size, while the second and third stories get progressively smaller. Walt describes his vision in the "Walt Disney Movie" at the Hospitality House, to the right as you emerge from under the railroad station. The Main Street Cinema shows some great old silent films. Late afternoons on Main Street turn gruesome when the not-so-impressive "All America Parade" marches through at 3pm; take this chance to ride some of the more crowded attractions. Near the entrance, you'll find a steam train that huffs and puffs its way across the seven different lands.

Tomorrowland has rides and early-70s exhibits of space travel and possible future lifestyles. Tease the workers who have to wear hideous blue-and-orange polyester jumpsuits. The very cool indoor roller coaster **Space Mountain** proves the high point of this section, if not the whole park, and is worth the extensive wait.

The golden-spired Cinderella Castle marks the gateway to **Fantasyland,** where you'll find Dumbo the Elephant and a twirling teacup ride. **20,000 Leagues Under**

the Sea sinks to new depths of brilliant premise but flawed implementation. The chilly temperatures in **It's A Small World** are the ride's only redeeming feature. Don't ride this until the end of the day. You may never, ever, get the evil tune out of your head. Catch "Magic Journeys," a plotless 3-D movie with extraordinary effects.

Liberty Square and **Frontierland** devote their resources to U.S. history and a celebration of Mark Twain. History buffs will enjoy the Hall of Presidents, which has been recently updated (President Clinton is represented, Maya Angelou narrates) and focuses on our nation's quest for equality. Adventurers should catch the rickety, runaway **Big Thunder Mountain Railroad** rollercoaster or the truly cool **Splash Mountain,** which takes you on a voyage with Br'er Rabbit that will leave you chilled inside and out. **Haunted Mansion** is both spooky and dorky. A steamboat ride or a canoe trip both rest your feet from the seemingly endless trek. Also be sure to stop and watch the entertaining animatronics at the **Country Bear Jamboree.**

Adventureland is a home away from home for those who feel the White Man's Burden. **The Jungle Cruise** takes a tongue-in-cheek tour through tropical waterways populated by not-so-authentic-looking wildlife. **Pirates of the Caribbean** explores caves where animated buccaneers battle, drink, and sing. The Swiss Family Robinson tree house, a replica of the shipwrecked family's home, provides more mental than adrenal excitement.

Epcot Center In 1966, Walt dreamed up an "Experimental Prototype Community Of Tomorrow" (EPCOT) that would evolve constantly, never be completed, and incorporate new ideas from U.S. technology—functioning as a self-sufficient, futuristic utopia. At present, Epcot splits into **Future World** and **World Showcase.** For smaller crowds, visit the former in the evening and the latter in the morning.

The 180-ft.-high trademark geosphere forms the entrance to Future World and houses the **Spaceship Earth** attraction, where visitors board a "time machine" for a tour through the evolution of communications. The **CommuniCore** highlights new technologies and offers several "hands-on" displays. The **World of Motion** traces the evolution of transportation, and the **Universe of Energy** traces (in a somewhat outdated fashion, since it glorifies the Alaskan port of Valdez—site of the 1989 Exxon oil spill) the history of energy. The **Wonders of Life** takes its visitors on a tour of the human body (with the help of a simulator) and tells us all where babies come from. **Horizons** lamely presents the lifestyles of the 21st century, but has a fabulous movie sequence on a huge screen extending above and below you, only ten feet away. **The Land** has a thought-provoking film about people's relationship with the land, and takes visitors on a tour of futuristic agrarian methods serenaded by another nifty Disney tune. **The Living Seas** tries to recreate an underwater research station. Finally, the ever-popular **Journey Into Imagination** pavilion features the 3-D "Captain Eo" (starring moon-walking, sequin-sporting rock star Michael Jackson), with interesting laser pen demonstrations.

The rest of Epcot is the **World Showcase** series of international pavilions surrounding an artificial lake. An architectural style or monument, as well as typical food, represents each country. People in costumes from past and present perform dances, theatrical skits, and other "cultural" entertainment at each pavilion. Before setting out around the lake, pick up a schedule of daily events at **Epcot Center Information** in Earth Station. Three of the best attractions are the two 360° films made in China and Canada and the 180° film made in France. They all include spectacular landscapes, some national history, and an inside look at the people of the respective countries. **The American Adventure** gives a very enthusiastic and patriotic interpretation of American history. Save your pesos by shopping at your local Pier 1 store rather than the marked-up Mexican marketplace. Norwegian life must be more exciting than the fishing, sailing, and oil exploring shown by the boat ride in the Norway Pavilion. Every summer night at 9pm, Saturday 10pm (off-season Saturday only), Epcot has a magnificent show called **Illuminations,** which features music from the represented nations accompanied by dancing, lights, and fireworks.

The World Showcase pavilions also offer regional cuisine. Make reservations first thing in the morning at the Earth Station World Key Terminal, behind Spaceship Earth. At the **Restaurant Marrakesh** in the Moroccan Pavilion, for example, head chef Lahsen Abrache cooks delicious *brewat* (spicy minced beef fried in pastry) and *bastilla* (sweet and slightly spicy pie). A belly dancer performs in the restaurant every evening. (Lunch $10-15. Dinner $15-20.) The Mexican, French, and Italian pavilions also serve up excellent food at similar prices.

Disney-MGM Studios Disney-MGM Studios has successfully created a "living movie set." Many familiar Disney characters stroll through the park, as do a host of characters dressed as directors, starlets, gossip columnists, and fans. A different has-been movie star leads a parade across Hollywood Boulevard every day. Events such as stunt shows and mini-theatricals take place continually throughout the park.

The Great Movie Ride, inside the Chinese Theater, takes you on a simple but nostalgic trip through old and favorite films; the interactive ride varies by your selection of the first or second set of cars. **Superstar Television** projects members of the audience alongside TV stars, and the **Monster Sound Show** requires volunteers to add special effects to a short movie. The biggest attractions at this park are the **Indiana Jones Epic Stunt Spectacular,** in which you watch stuntmen and audience volunteers pull off amazing moves, and the **Star Tours** Star Wars ride, in which you feel the jerk of your space cargo ship dodging laser blasts.

Other Disney Attractions For those who did not get enough amusement at the three main parks, Disney also offers several other attractions on its grounds with different themes and separate admissions (see Disney World above). The newest is **Typhoon Lagoon,** a 50-acre water park centered around the world's largest wave-making pool. Surf the 7-ft. waves that occasionally appear out of nowhere, or snorkel in a salt water coral reef stocked with tropical fish and harmless sharks. Besides eight water slides, the lagoon has a creek on which you can take a relaxing inner-tube ride, an anomaly at Disney. Built to resemble a swimming hole, **River Country** offers water slides, rope swings, and plenty of room to swim. Both parks fill up early on hot days, and you might get turned away. Across Bay Lake from River Country is **Discovery Island,** a zoological park. Those seeking more (relatively) sinful excitations should head at night to **Pleasure Island,** Disney's attempt to draw students and the thirtysomething set. Those over 17 can roam freely between the theme nightclubs; those under 18 can enter if they remain with their guardians.

■ SEA WORLD, CYPRESS GARDENS, SPLENDID CHINA, AND UNIVERSAL STUDIOS, FL

Sea World One of the country's largest marine parks, **Sea World** (407-351-3600 for operator; 407-351-0021 for recording), 19 mi. southwest of Orlando off I-4 at Rte. 528, has neat attractions that will take about six hours to see. Shows feature marine mammals such as whales, dolphins, sea lions, seals, and otters. Though the Seal and Otter Show and the USO waterski show are enjoyable, the killer whales Baby Shamu and Baby Namu are the big stars. Not only do they share the stage (or pool) with two beautiful white whales and two Orcas, the trainers actually mix it up with the huge creatures and take rides on their snouts. People in the park gravitate towards Shamu Stadium before the show; arrive early to get a seat. After your brow gets sweaty, visit the air-conditioned **Fantasy Theater,** an educational show with live characters in costume. The smallest crowds come in February and September to October. Most hotel brochure counters and hostels have coupons for $2-3 off regular admission prices. (Open daily 8:30am-10pm; off-season daily 9am-10pm. $35, ages 3-9 $30. Sky Tower ride $3 extra. Guided tours $6, kids $5. Take bus #8.)

Cypress Gardens In Winter Haven, Cypress Gardens (813-324-2111) is a botanical garden with over 8000 varieties of plants and flowers, "the Gardens of the

World" features plants, flowers, and sculptured mini-gardens depicting the horticultural styles of many countries and periods. Winding walkways and electric boat rides take you through the foliage. The main attraction is a water-ski show performed daily at 10am, noon, 2pm, and 4pm. (813-324-2111; open daily 9:30am-5:30pm; in winter daily 9am-7pm. $25, ages 3-9 $16.50). Take I-4 southwest to Rte. 27 south, then Rte. 540 west. **Greyhound** stops here once a day on its Tampa-West Palm Beach schedule ($20 from Tampa to Cypress Gardens). Look for coupons at motels and visitors centers (see Orlando).

Splendid China Florida's newest theme park, Splendid China has no rides (or lines) to make your heart ache. Instead enjoy a relaxing, educational day by walking through beautiful Chinese gardens and seeing over 60 miniatures of China's best known sites. Shows, movies, and good food abound. Located at 3000 Splendid Blvd., right off Rte. 192 two miles west of Disney World. (396-7111; open daily 9am-8pm. $24, ages 5-12 $14, under 5 free.)

Universal Studios Florida Opened in 1990, Universal Studio's is a two-in-one park containing a number of theme rides: **Kongfrontation,** where King Kong will roughhouse your cable car; the **E.T. Adventure** bike ride; and **Jaws,** a boat trip where you can see the shark used in the movie. Also look for **Back to the Future...The Ride,** with seven-story high OMNI-MAX surround screens and spectacular special effects.

Since the park serves as a working studio making films, stars abound. Recently, Steve Martin played a dad in *Parenthood* here, and John Goodman starred in *Matinee* and *The Flintstones.* Nickelodeon TV programs are in continuous production. Universal also has a number of back-lot locations that you may have seen before in the movies—displaying Hollywood, Central Park, and Beverly Hills, as well as the infamous Bates Motel from *Psycho.* (363-8000) 435 N. State Rd. and Vineland Rd., ($38, ages 3-9 $31. Open Mon.-Sat. 9am-10pm, Sun. 9am-9pm, off-season daily 9am-7pm.)

■■■ COCOA BEACH AND CAPE CANAVERAL

Known primarily for its rocket launches, space shuttle blast-offs, and enormous **NASA** space center complex, the "Space Coast" also has uncrowded golden sand beaches and vast wildlife preserves. Even during spring break the place remains placid because most vacationers and sunbathers are neighborly Florida or Space Coast residents.

The Cocoa Beach area, 50 mi. east of Orlando, consists of mainland towns Cocoa and Rockledge, oceanfront towns Cocoa Beach and Cape Canaveral, with Merritt Island in between. **Route A1A** runs through Cocoa Beach and Cape Canaveral, and **North Atlantic Avenue** runs parallel to the beach. Inaccessible by bus, Cocoa Beach also lacks local public transport. Cocoa, 8 mi. inland, is serviced by **Greyhound,** 302 Main St. (636-3917). From the bus station, **taxi** fare to Cocoa Beach is about $14 (call 783-8294). A **shuttle** service (784-3831) connects Cocoa Beach with Orlando International Airport, Disney World (round-trip $75 for 1 or 2 people), and the Kennedy Space Center (round-trip only $45, 1 or 2 people). Make reservations one day in advance and ask about special rates for groups of five or more.

Try the **Cocoa Beach Chamber of Commerce,** 400 Fortenberry Rd. (459-2200; open Mon.-Fri 8:30am-5pm), Merritt Island, or the **Brevard County Tourist Development Council** (455-1309 or 800-872-1969), at Kennedy Space Center, for area info (open Mon.-Fri. 8:30am-5pm, Sat. 8:30am-noon). **Post office:** 25 N. Brevard Ave. (783-2544); **ZIP code:** 32931; **area code:** 407.

THE SOUTH

Food and Accommodations **Herbie K's Diner,** 2080 N. Atlantic Ave. (783-6740), south of Motel 6. A shiny chrome reproduction of a 50s diner, serves mac and cheese, chicken pot pie, "happy haw" (apple sauce), great malts, and hamburgers ($4-7). (Open Sun.-Thurs. 6am-10pm, Fri.-Sat. 24 hrs.) At the beach, **Motel 6,** 3701 N. Atlantic Ave. (783-3103), has a pool and large, clean rooms with cable TV and A/C. (Singles $38, Feb.-March $42. Each additional person $4.) If Motel 6 is full, try farther down N. Atlantic Ave. at the **Luna Sea,** 3185 N. Atlantic Ave. (783-0500 or 800-348-0348; singles $39, Jan.-March $42 each additional person $4). If you need a place to spend the night between bus connections, walk right behind the Greyhound station to the **Dixie Motel,** 301 Forrest Ave. (632-1600), one block east of U.S. 1, which has big, clean rooms, a swimming pool, and A/C. (Singles $28. Doubles $34. Key deposit $10.) Or pitch your tent at scenic **Jetty Park Campgrounds,** 400 East Jetty Rd. (868-1108), Cape Canaveral. (Sites $15, with hookup $18.50. Reservations recommended before shuttle launches.)

Beam Me Up Scotty The **Kennedy Space Center,** 18 mi. north of Cocoa Beach, is the site of all of NASA's shuttle flights. The Kennedy Center's **Spaceport USA** (452-2121 for information) provides a huge welcoming center for visitors. There are two different two-hour bus tours of the complex. The **red tour** takes you around the space sites, the **blue tour** on a visit to the Cape Canaveral Air Force Station. There are also three IMAX films projected on 5½-story screens: *The Blue Planet* is about environmental issues, and *The Dream is Alive* tells the story of human and robotic space exploration. Tours depart from Spaceport USA daily from 9:45am to 6pm every 15 min. ($7, ages 3-11 $4. Movie tickets $4, ages 3-11 $2). Buy tickets to both immediately upon arrival at the complex to avoid a long line. The center itself is free, as are the movies at the Spaceport Theater. Also worth visits are the **Rocket Garden** and the **Astronauts Memorial,** which is the newest national memorial in the country (open winter 9am-6pm, spring and fall 9am-7:30pm, summer 9am-8:30pm.) The **NASA Parkway,** site of the visitors center, is accessible only by car via State Rd. 405. From Cocoa Beach, take Rte. A1A north until it turns west into Rte. 528, then follow Rte. 3 north to the Spaceport. With NASA's ambitious launch schedules, you may have a chance to watch the space shuttles *Endeavor, Columbia, Atlantis,* or *Discovery* thunder off into the blue skies above the cape. In Florida, call 800-KSC-INFO (800-572-4636) for **launch information.**

Surrounding the NASA complex, the marshy **Merritt Island Wildlife Refuge** (861-0667) stirs with deer, sea turtles, alligators, and eagles (open daily 8am-sunset). Just north of Merritt Island is **Canaveral National Seashore** (867-2805), 67,000 acres of undeveloped beach and dunes, home to more than 300 species of birds and mammals. (Take Rte. 406 east off U.S. 1 in Titusville; open daily 6am-sunset.) Closed 3 days before and 1 day after NASA launches.

■ ■ ■ FORT LAUDERDALE

Fort Lauderdale was once the unrivaled Spring Break Capital of America, but since the city cracked down on student excess several years ago, it is no longer the destination for the lust-crazed spring masses. The title has moved to other cities like Daytona Beach and Panama City Beach. Fort Lauderdale today is a laid back beach community, dubbed the "Venice of America" because of its intricate intra-coastal waterway with over 165 miles of navigable waters. If you find your SPF 15 sunblock failing you, there are plenty of non-beach activities around. Serious shoppers head to Sawgrass Mills, the world's largest outlet mall, 9mi west of the city. Boutiques, cafés, and restaurants line Los Olas Blvd.

PRACTICAL INFORMATION

Emergency: 911.
Visitor Information: The **Greater Fort Lauderdale Convention and Visitors Bureau,** 200 E. Los Olas Blvd., suite 1500 (765-4466), offers friendly advice and

pamphlets galore. For published information, call 1-800-222-SUNY (7869). Also try the **Chamber of Commerce,** 512 NE 3rd Ave. (462-6000), 3 blocks off Federal Hwy. at 5th St. Pick up the helpful *Visitor's Guide.* Open Mon.-Fri. 8am-5pm.

Airport: Fort Lauderdale/Hollywood International, 359-6100. 3½ mi. south of downtown on U.S. 1, at exits 26 and 27 on I-95. **American, Continental, Delta, TWA, Northwest, United,** and **USAir** all serve this airport.

Amtrak: 200 SW 21st Terrace (487-6692 or 800-872-7245), just west of I-95, ¼-mi. south of Broward Blvd. Take bus #9, 10, or 81 from downtown. Daily service on "The Floridian" to Miami (2 per day, 45 min., $6), Orlando (1 per day, 4 hr., $44). Open daily 7:30am-8:45pm.

Greyhound: 513 NE 3rd St. (764-6551), 3 blocks north of Broward Blvd., downtown. Unsavory location, especially unfriendly at night. To: Orlando (9 per day, 4½ hr., $35); Daytona Beach (6 per day, 6 hr., $28); Miami (14 per day, 1 hr., $6). Open daily 6am-midnight.

Public Transport: Broward County Transit (BCT), 357-8400 (call Mon.-Fri. 7am-8:30pm, Sat. 7am-8pm, Sun. 8:30am-5pm). Extensive regional coverage. Most routes go to the terminal at the corner of 1st St. NW and 1st Ave. NW, downtown. Operates daily 6am-9pm every ½-hr. on most routes. Fare 85¢, seniors 40¢, students with ID 40¢, transfers 10¢. 7-day passes $8, available at beachfront hotels. Pick up a handy system map at the terminal. **Tri-Rail** (800-874-7245 or 728-8445) connects West Palm Beach, Ft. Lauderdale, and Miami. Trains run Mon.-Sat. 5am-9:30pm. Pick up schedules at the airport or at Tri-Rail stops. Fare $3, students and seniors with ID $1.50.

Car Rental: Alamo, 2601 S. Federal Hwy. (525-4715 or 800-327-9633). Cheapest cars $18 per day, $70 per week. Unlimited mileage, free drop-off in Daytona and Miami. Shuttle to airport $3. Must be 21 with credit card or deposit of $50 per day or $200 per week for out-of-state renters. Under 25 surcharge $15.

Bike Rentals: International Bicycle Shop, 1900 E. Sunrise Blvd. at N. Federal Hwy. (764-8800). Take bus #10 from downtown or bus #36 from A1A north of Sunrise. $10 per day, $35 per week. $150 deposit. Open Mon.-Fri. 10am-9pm, Sat. 9am-9pm, Sun. 11am-5pm. Must be 18. Avoid the expensive joints on the beach.

Taxi: Yellow Cab (565-5400) and **Public Service Taxi** (587-9090), both $2.45 plus $1.75 per mi.

Help Line: Crisis Hotline, 746-2756. 24 hrs.

Post Office: 1900 W. Oakland Park Blvd. (527-2028). Open Mon.-Fri. 7:30am-7pm, Sat. 8:30am-2pm. **ZIP code:** 33310.

Area Code: 305.

I-95 runs north-south, connecting West Palm Beach, Ft. Lauderdale, and Miami. Rte. 84/I-75 (Alligator Alley) slithers 100 mi. west from Ft. Lauderdale across the Everglades to Naples and other small cities on the Gulf Coast of Southern Florida. Ft. Lauderdale is bigger than it looks. The place is huge. The city extends westward from its 23 mi. of beach to encompass nearly 450 square miles of land area. Roads are divided into two categories: streets and boulevards (east-west) and avenues (north-south). All are labeled NW, NE, SW, or SE according to the quadrant. **Broward Boulevard** divides the city east-west, **Andrews Avenue** north-south. The unpleasant downtown centers around the intersection of **Federal Highway (U.S. 1)** and **Las Olas Boulevard,** about 2 mi. west of the oceanfront. Between downtown and the waterfront, yachts fill the ritzy inlets of the **Intracoastal Waterway.** The strip (variously called Rte. A1A, N. Atlantic Blvd., 17th St. Causeway, Ocean Blvd., and Seabreeze Blvd.) runs along the beach for 4 mi. between **Oakland Park Boulevard** to the north and Las Olas Blvd. to the south. Las Olas Blvd. is the pricey shopping street; **Sunrise Boulevard** has most shopping malls. Both degenerate into ugly commercial strips west of downtown.

ACCOMMODATIONS AND CAMPING

Hotel prices vary from slightly unreasonable to absolutely ridiculous, increasing exponentially as you approach prime beachfront and spring break. High season runs from mid-February to early April. Investigate package deals at the slightly worse-for-wear hotels along the strip in Ft. Lauderdale. Many hotels offer off-season deals for under $35. Small motels crowd each other one or two blocks off the beach area; many offer small kitchenettes. Look along **Birch Rd.,** one block back from Rte. A1A. **The Broward County Hotel and Motel Association** (462-0409) provides a free directory of area hotels (open Mon.-Fri. 9am-5pm). Scan the *Ft. Lauderdale News* and the Broward Section of the *Miami Herald* for occasional listings of local residents who rent rooms to tourists in spring. Sleeping on the well-patrolled beaches is impossible between 9pm and sunrise.

Ft. Lauderdale Youth Hostel, Sol-y-Mar (Rucksackers), 2839 Vistamar St. (305-566-1023 or 565-1419). Very nice hostel with plenty of amenities and an excellent location in a wooded area near the beach. Close to the clubs as well. 80 beds. Pool. Cable TV and refrigerator in every room. Common kitchen and entertainment room with big screen TV. Wild but friendly monkeys make regular appearances out back. Open 7am-midnight. Reservations recommended. $11 per night.

HI-International House (HI-AYH), 3811 N. Ocean Blvd. (568-1615). Take bus #10 to Coral Ridge Mall, then pick up bus #72 east; it will stop at the hostel. Shuttle service throughout Florida. Rooms with 6 beds, showers, A/C, cable TV, kitchen. Pool. 96 beds. $12, nonmembers $15. $5 key deposit. $2 linen fee. One block from beach. For guests with SCUBA certification, dive trips offered $35-40. Private rooms $26.

Floyd's Youth Hostel, (462-0631), call ahead for address. A recently opened home-like hostel catering to international travelers. 10 beds (4 bedrooms, 3 bathrooms), two separate kitchen and living room areas, and a quiet, friendly atmosphere. Free rice, tea, sugar, and pick-up service from bus station or airport. No curfew. Open 24 hours. $10.

Estoril Apartments, 2648 NE 32nd St. (563-3840; 800-548-9398 reservations only). From downtown, take bus #20, 10, 55, or 72 to Coral Ridge Shopping Center and walk 2 blocks east on Oakland. Students can probably persuade the proprietors to pick them up from the bus station or airport. A 10-min. walk to the beach. Very clean rooms with A/C, TV, and small kitchenette. Pool and barbecue. Students with *Let's Go* receive 10% discount. Office closes about 11pm. Singles $26. Jan.-April singles $42-47. Additional person $6 off-season, $10 in season. Reservations recommended.

Motel 6, 1801 State Rd. 84 (760-7999), 3 blocks east of I-95 and 3 mi. southwest of downtown. Take bus #14 to Rte. 84 and SW 15th Ave. and walk 3 blocks west. Far from the action. Clean. A/C, HBO. Singles $30, doubles $36; Nov.-April singles $38, doubles $44.

Easterlin County Park, 1000 NW 38th St. (938-0610), Oakland Park, less than 4 mi. west of the strip and 3 mi. north of downtown. Take bus #14 to NW 38th St. or #72 along Oakland Park to Powerline Rd. By car take Oakland Park exit from I-95. 2-week max. stay. Registration open 24 hrs. Sites with electricity, barbecue pits, and picnic table $17.

Quiet Waters County Park, 6601 N. Powerline Rd. (NW 9th Ave.) (360-1315), Pompano Beach, 10 mi. north of Oakland Park Blvd. I-95 exit 37B. Take Hillsboro Blvd. west to Powerline Rd. From downtown, take bus #14. Cramped, commercialized, but friendly. Bizarre 8-person "boatless water skiing" at the end of a cable and other water sports. No electricity. Check-in 2-6pm. Fully equipped campsites (tent, mattresses, cooler, grill, canoe) for up to 6 people, Sun.-Thurs. $17, Fri.-Sat. $25 plus $20 refundable deposit.

FOOD

The clubs along the strip offer massive quantities of free grub during happy hour: surfboard-sized platters of wieners, chips, and hors d'oeuvres, or all-you-can-eat pizza and buffets. However, these bars have hefty cover charges (from $5) and expect you to buy a drink once you're there (from $2). In addition, these bars are nightclubs, not restaurants, and the quality of their cuisine proves it. In contrast, the restaurants listed below serve "real" food.

La Spada's, 4346 Seagrape Drive (776-7893). Two blocks from the beach, off Commercial Blvd. Best, and biggest, subs in southern Florida. The foot-long Italian sub ($6.50) is an absolute must. Open Mon.-Sat. 10am-8pm, Sun. 11am-8pm.

Golden Chopsticks, 4350 N. Federal Hwy. (776-0953). Some of the best Chinese food in town. For a treat, try the steak kew ($12). Most of the uniformly delicious food is more reasonably priced. Open Mon.-Thurs. 11:30am-midnight, Fri. 11:30am-1am, Sat. 1pm-1am, Sun.1pm-11pm.

Southport Raw Bar, 1536 Cordova Rd. (525-2526), by the 17th St. Causeway behind the Southport Mall on the Intracoastal Waterway. Take bus #40 from the strip or #30 from downtown. Aggressively marine decor. Spicy conch chowder $2.25, fried shrimp $5.25. Tasty custom sandwiches. Open Mon.-Sat. 11am-2am, Sun. noon-2am.

Tina's Spaghetti House, 2110 S. Federal Hwy. (522-9943), just south of 17th St. Take bus #1 from downtown. Authentic red-checkered tablecloths, hefty oak furniture, and bibs. Popular with locals since 1951. Lunch specials $4-5. Spaghetti dinner $6-7. Open Mon.-Thurs. 11:30am-10pm, Fri. 11:30am-11pm, Sat. 4-11pm, Sun. 4-10pm.

SIGHTS AND ACTIVITIES

To see why Ft. Lauderdale is called the "Venice of America," take a tour of its waterways aboard the **Jungle Queen,** located at the **Bahia Mar Yacht Center** (462-5596), on Rte. A1A three blocks south of Las Olas Blvd. (3-hr. tours daily at 10am, 2pm, and 7pm. $7.50, kids $5.) A fun way to dine in style or simply to take a different mode of transportation to town is by taking the **Water Taxi,** 1900 E. 15th St. (565-5507; $5 one way, $3 for children under 12. All day, unlimited service $13, $8 for children. Call 10 minutes before desired pick-up.) For more intimate acquaintance with the ocean, **Water Sports Unlimited,** 301 Seabreeze Blvd. (467-1316), offers equipment for a variety of water sports. Located on the beach, Water Sports offers wave runners ($35 per ½-hr., $55 per hr.), motor boats ($40 per hour, $220 per day), and parasailing trips ($42 per ride). Landlubbers can get closer to nature too, with a visit to **Butterfly World,** 3400 W. Sample Rd. (977-4400), just west of the Florida Turnpike in Coconut Creek, 3 acres of tropical gardens with thousands of Sun. 1-5pm.)

SIN

Ft. Lauderdale offers all kinds of licit and illicit entertainment. Planes flying over the beach hawk hedonistic happy hours at local watering holes. Students frequent the night spots on the A1A strip along the beach, with an emphasis on "strip." When going out, bring a driver's license or a passport as proof of age; most bars and nightclubs don't accept college IDs. Be warned that this is *not* the place for cappuccino and conversation but for nude jello wrestling and similarly lubricated entertainment.

For those who prefer garbed service, several popular nightspots line N. Atlantic Blvd. next to the beach. Try **Banana Joe's on the Beach,** 837 N. Atlantic Blvd. (565-4446), at Sunrise and A1A. (Open Mon.-Fri. 7am-2am, Sat. 7am-3am, Sun. noon-2am. Kitchen open 11:30am-7pm.) For off-the-beach entertainment, Ft. Lauderdale's new hotspot is **Crocco's World Class Sports Bar,** 3339 N. Federal Hwy. (566-2406). Built in an old movie theater, this gargantuan club has lines out the door almost every night (cover varies). (Open Sun.-Fri. 4pm-2am, Sat. noon-3am.) **Mombasa Bay,** 3051 NE 32nd Ave. (561-8220), is a new club on the Intracoastal Waterway. (Live R&B Thurs., live reggae Fri.-Mon.; open Sun.-Fri. 11:30am-2am, Sat. 11:30am-3am. Concerts start at 9:30pm.)

■■■ MIAMI

Long a hot spot for stars and a popular setting for TV shows and movies, Miami's international flavor and Latin beat pulses with the largest Cuban population outside of Cuba. Most tourists lie-and-fry by day, then move inland about 400 meters to dance the night away. Only 7½ square miles, Miami Beach has an unbelievable number of hotels, which together can accommodate three times the city's usual population. The rest of Miami is relatively residential and made up of many smaller cultures: Little Havana, a well-established Cuban community; Coconut Grove, with its village-in-the-swampland bohemianism; placid, well-to-do Coral Gables, one of the country's earliest planned cities; and the African-American communities of Liberty City and Overtown. Wherever you find yourself in Miami, a knowledge of Spanish is always helpful and sometimes necessary.

PRACTICAL INFORMATION

Emergency: 911.

Visitor Information: Greater Miami Convention and Visitors Bureau, 701 Brickell Ave. (539-3000 or 800-283-2707 outside Miami), 27th floor of the Barnett Bank building downtown. Open Mon.-Fri. 8:30am-5pm. A tourist information booth is located outside of Bayside Marketplace, downtown at 401 Bisscaayne Blvd. (539-2980). Free maps and advice. (Open daily 10am-6:30pm.) **Coconut Grove Chamber of Commerce,** 2820 McFarlane Rd. (444-7270). Mountains of maps and advice. Open Mon.-Fri. 9am-5pm. The **Miami Beach Resort Hotel Association,** 407 Lincoln Rd. #10G (531-3553), can help you find a place on the beach. Open 24 hrs.

Airport: Miami International (876-7000), located at Le Jeune Rd. and NW 36th Ave 7 mi. northwest of downtown. Bus #20 is the most direct public transportation into downtown (bus #3 is also usable); from there, take bus C, K, or S to South Miami Beach. Helpful maps of Miami and the Public Transportation systems available at the **information** booth for free.

Amtrak: 8303 NW 37th Ave. (835-1221 or 800-872-7245), not far from the Northside station of Metrorail. Bus L goes directly to Lincoln Rd. Mall in South Miami Beach. See mileage chart. Open Tues., Thurs., Sat., and Sun. 6:15am-7:15pm; Mon., Wed., and Fri. 6:15pm-midnight. Ticket office open 6:30am-9:45pm.

Greyhound: Miami Beach Station, 7101 Harding Ave. (538-0381 for fare and schedule info). See mileage chart. Station open 6:30am-9:45pm.

Public Transport: Metro Dade Transportation (638-6700; 6am-11pm for info.) Complex system; buses tend to be quite tardy. The extensive **Metrobus** network converges downtown; most long bus trips transfer in this area. Lettered bus routes A through X serve Miami Beach. After dark, some stops are patrolled by police (indicated with a sign). Service daily 6am-8pm; major routes until 11pm or midnight. Fare $1.25. Transfers 10¢. Futuristic **Metrorail** elevated train service downtown. Fare $1.25, rail to bus transfers 25¢. The **Metromover** loop downtown, which runs 6am-midnight, is linked to the Metrorail stations (25¢, free if transferring from Metrorail). **Tri-Rail** (800-874-7245) connects Miami, Ft. Lauderdale, and West Palm Beach. Trains run Mon.-Sat. 5am-9:30pm. Fare $2.50, $5 daily, $18 weekly. 50% off for seniors and students.

Taxis: Yellow Cab, 444-4444 (easy enough). **Metro Taxi,** 888-8888 (really easy). **Central Cab,** 532-5555 (not too hard). $1.75 per mile.

Car Rental: Value Rent-a-Car, 1620 Collins Ave. (532-8257), Miami Beach. $27 per day, $129 per week. Unlimited free mileage. Drivers under 25 pay $12 additional daily charge. Open daily 8am-6pm. Must be 21 with credit card. Also Value Rent-a-Car at the **airport,** 2875 NW Le Jeune Rd. (871-6761). $15 a day, $61 a week. Unlimited mileage. Open 24 hrs.

Auto Transport Company: Dependable Car Travel, 162 Sunny Isles Blvd. (945-4104). Open Mon.-Fri. 8:30am-5pm, Sat. 8:30am-noon. Must be 18 with credit card or $150 deposit and passport and foreign license. A free service. Call a week in advance.

Bike Rental: Miami Beach Bicycle Center, 923 W. 39th St. (531-4161), Miami Beach. $5 first hr., $3 each additional. $12 per day, $40 per week. Open Mon.-Fri. 9:30am-6pm, Sat. 9:30am-5pm. Must be 18 with credit card or $40 deposit. **Dade Cycle Shop,** 3216 Grand Ave., Coconut Grove (443-6075). $3-7 per hr., $15-22 per day. Open daily 9:30am-5:30pm. Must have $100 deposit, driver's license, or credit card.

Help Lines: Crisis Hotline, 358-4357. **Rape Treatment Center and Hotline,** 1611 NW 12th Ave. (585-6949). **Gay Community Hotline,** 759-3661. All 24 hrs.

Post Office: 500 NW 2nd Ave. (371-2911). Open Mon.-Fri. 8:30am-5pm, Sat. 8:30am-12:30pm. **ZIP code:** 33101.
Area Code: 305.

ORIENTATION

Three highways criss-cross the Miami area. Just south of downtown, I-95, the most direct route north-south, runs into **U.S. 1 (Dixie Highway).** U.S. 1 goes as far as the Everglades entrance at Florida City and then all the way out to Key West as the Overseas Highway. **Route 836,** a major east-west artery through town, connects I-95 with the **Florida Turnpike,** passing the airport in between. Take Rte. 836 and the Turnpike to Florida City to avoid the traffic on Rte. 1.

When looking for street addresses, pay careful attention to the systematic street layout; it's *very* easy to confuse North Miami Beach, West Miami, Miami Beach, and Miami addresses. Streets in Miami run east-west, avenues north-south, and both are numbered. Miami divides into NE, NW, SE, and SW sections; the dividing lines (downtown) are **Flagler Street** (east-west) and **Miami Avenue** (north-south). Some numbered streets and avenues also have names—i.e., Le Jeune Rd. is SW 42nd Ave., and SW 40th St. is called Bird Rd. Try to get a map with both numbers and names in order to solve this conundrum.

Several four-lane causeways connect Miami to **Miami Beach**. The most useful is **MacArthur Causeway,** which feeds onto 5th St. in Miami Beach. Numbered streets run across the island, with numbers increasing as you go north; the main north-south drag is **Collins Avenue.** In South Miami Beach, **Washington Avenue,** one block to the west, is the main commercial strip, while **Ocean Avenue,** actually on the waterfront, lies one block east. The **Rickenbacker Causeway** is the only connection to Key Biscayne.

ACCOMMODATIONS AND CAMPING

Finding cheap rooms in Miami is easy. Several hundred art-deco hotels in South Miami Beach stand at your service. For safety, convenience, and security, stay north of 5th St. A "pullmanette" (in 1940s lingo) is a room with a refrigerator, stove, and sink; getting one and some groceries allows you to save money on food. In South Florida, many inexpensive hotels are likely to have two- to three-inch cockroaches ("palmetto bugs"), so try not to take them as absolute indicators of quality. In general, high season for Miami Beach runs late December to mid-March, but is always busy.

Camping is not allowed in Miami. Those who can't bear to put their tents aside for a night or two should head on to one of the nearby national parks.

Miami Beach International Travelers Hostel (9th Street Hostel), 236 9th St. (534-0268), at the intersection with Washington Ave. From the airport, take J bus to 41st and Indian Creek, then transfer to bus C to 9th and Washington. Relaxed international atmosphere, central location, kitchen, laundry, common room. No curfew. 29 clean and comfortable rooms, all with A/C and private bath. Hostel rooms $12 (max. 4 people) for any hostelling membership or student ID. Nonmembers $14. Private rooms $28 single or double.

Miami Beach International Hostel (HI-AYH), 1438 Washington Ave. (534-2988), in the historic Clay Hotel. Take bus C or K from downtown. Cheerful chaos reigns in the 7 Mediterranean-style buildings. Located in the heart of the Art Deco district. Kitchen, laundry facilities, and a useful ride board. International crowd. Most rooms have 4 beds; 2 rooms share a bathroom. 24-hr. A/C. 230 beds. Near nightlife. IBN reservations available. No curfew. Members $10, winter $11. Nonmembers $14, winter $15. Hotel singles $28. Doubles $33. Key deposit $5.

The Tropics, 1550 Collins Ave. (531-0361). Across the street from the beach, clean hostel rooms with 4-8 beds, A/C, private baths. $12. No curfew. Private rooms $35 single or double.

Kent Hotel, 1131 Collins Ave. (531-6771), one block from the beach. Beautifully renovated rooms and friendly staff. TV, A/C, fridge, kitchen, and breakfast. Singles or doubles May 1-Oct. 15 $50-55, Oct. 15-May 1 $70-75. Ocean view $10 more.

Tudor Hotel, 1111 Collins Ave. (534-2934). Beautiful renovations make this one of the nicest hotels in Miami Beach, in all pastels with flamingo murals and deco-period lighting. Rooms have refrigerator, microwave, cable TV, A/C, phone. Singles/doubles.$55, weekly $210. Oct. 15-May 1 $75, weekly $390.

Miami Sun Hotel, 226 NE 1st Ave. (375-0786 or 800-322-0786). Near downtown, restaurants, and Bayside Marketplace. Spacious, comfortable rooms with Art Deco decor. 88 rooms, cable TV, hot tub, guest laundry room. Dec. 16-April 15 $42-47. April 16-Dec.15, $28-35.

Miami Airways Motel, 5001 36th St. (883-4700). Will pick you up at nearby airport for free. Clean, small rooms, breakfast, A/C, pool, HBO, but pretty far from the action. Singles $36. Doubles $42.

Larry & Penny Thompson Memorial Campground, 12451 SW 184th St. (232-1049), a long way from anywhere. By car, drive 20-30 min. south along Dixie Hwy. Pretty grounds in a grove of mango trees. Laundry, store, and all facilities, plus artificial lake with swimming beach, beautiful park, and even water slides. For further lake info, call 255-8251. Office open daily 8am-7pm but takes late arrivals. Lake open daily 10am-5pm. Sites with hookup $17, $90 weekly.

FOOD

If you eat nothing else in Miami, be sure to try Cuban food. Specialties include *media noche* sandwiches (a sort of Cuban club sandwich on a soft roll, heated and compressed); *mamey,* a bright red ice cream concoction; rich *frijoles negros* (black beans); and *picadillo* (shredded beef and peas in tomato sauce, served with white rice). For Cuban sweets, seek out a *dulcería,* and punctuate your rambles around town with thimble-sized shots of strong, sweet *café cubano* (25¢).

Cheap restaurants are not common in Miami Beach, but an array of fresh bakeries and fruit stands can sustain you with melons, mangoes, papayas, tomatoes, and carrots for under $3 a day.

An entirely different atmosphere prevails on the bay south of downtown in self-consciously rustic **Coconut Grove** (take bus #1 or Metrorail from downtown). The grove centers around the intersection of Grand Ave. and Main Hwy. Drop into a watering hole like **Señor Frog's,** 3008 Grand Ave. (448-0999), home of bang-up tables and phenomenal *salsa.* Be prepared to speak Spanish! (Open Sun.-Thurs. 10:30am-1am, Fri.-Sat. 10:30am-2am.)

Irish House (534-5667) 14th St. and Alton Rd., Miami Beach. A favorite hangout for local journalists, politicos and beach-goers. Noted for its buffalo wings ($3.50) and cheeseburgers ($4.50). Open Mon.-Sat. 11am-2am, Sun. 2am-2am—this place never closes on Saturday night.

La Rumba, 2008 Collins Ave. (534-0522), Miami Beach, between 20th and 21st St. Good, cheap Cuban food and noisy fun. Try their *arroz con pollo* (chicken with yellow rice, $6) or a banana milkshake ($1.75). Open daily 7:30am-midnight.

The Versailles, 3555 SW 8th St. (444-0240). Good Cuban fare; recommended by locals. Entrees about $10. Open daily 8am-2am.

Renaissance Cafe, 410 Española Way (672-5539), attached to the Clay Hotel. Try the big burgers ($3.95) or the pizza ($4-6). Open 8am-2am daily.

Flamingo Restaurant, 1454 Washington Ave. (673-4302), right down the street from the hostel. Friendly service, all in Spanish. Peck at the grilled chicken with pinto beans and rice ($5.50). Open Mon.-Sat. 7am-7:30pm.

King's Ice Cream, 1831 SW 8th St. (643-1842), on Calle Ocho. Tropical fruit *helado* (ice cream, $2) flavors include coconut (served in its own shell), *mamey,* and banana. Also try *churros* (thin Spanish donuts, 10 for $1) or *café cubano* (10¢). Open Mon.-Sat. 10am-11pm, Sun. 2pm-11pm.

SIGHTS

The best sight in Miami is the beach. When you get too burned and are in need of some shade, try the **Seaquarium,** 4400 Rickenbacker Causeway (361-5703), Virginia Key, just minutes from downtown. Take "B" bus from downtown toward Key Biscayne. While not on par with Sea World in Orlando, it has an impressive array of shows, including obligatory dolphins, hungry sharks, and Lolita, the killer whale. The aquarium also displays tropical fish. (Open daily 9:30am-6pm; ticket office closes 4:30pm. $18, kids $13, under 3 free, police officers $1.)

South Miami Beach or **South Beach,** between 6th and 23rd St., teems with hundreds of hotels and apartments whose sun-faded pastel facades recall what sunthirsty northerners of the 1920s thought a tropical paradise should look like. The Art Deco palaces constitute the country's largest national historic district and the only one which has preserved 20th-century buildings. A fascinating mixture of people populates the area, including large retired and first-generation Latin communities; knowing Spanish is a big advantage here. **Walking tours** of the historic district are offered Saturdays at 10:30am ($6). **Bike tours** available Sundays at 10:30am ($5, rental $5 extra). Call 672-2014 the point of departure.

On the waterfront downtown is Miami's newest attraction, the **Bayside** shopping complex, with fancy shops (many beyond the realm of the budget traveler), exotic food booths, and live reggae or *salsa* on Friday and Saturday nights. Near Bayside, visit the **Police Hall of Fame and Museum,** 3801 Biscayne Blvd. (891-1700), and learn more than you ever wanted to know about the police. Watch in your rearview mirror for the police car suspended alongside the building. (Open daily 10am-5:30pm. $6, seniors and children $3.)

Little Havana lies between SW 12th and SW 27th Ave. (Take bus #3, 11, 14, 15, 17, 25, or 37.) The street scenes of **Calle Ocho** (SW 8th St.) lie at the heart of this district; the corresponding section of W. Flagler St. is a center of Cuban business. The changing exhibits at the **Cuban Museum of Arts and Culture,** 1300 SW 12th Ave. (858-8006), reflect the bright colors and rhythms of Cuban art. Take bus #27. (Open Wed.-Sun. 1-5pm. Admission by donation.) At **La Gloria Cubana,** 1106 SW 8th St. (858-4162), you can witness firsthand Cuban cigars being made (open Mon.-Fri. 8am-6pm, Sat. 9am-4pm; free).

On the bayfront between the Grove and downtown stands **Vizcaya,** 3251 S. Miami Ave. (250-9133), set in acres of elaborately landscaped grounds. Built in 1916 by International Harvester heir James Deering, the four facades of this 70-room Italianate mansion hide a hodgepodge of European antiques. There are 10 lush acres of gardens. (Open daily 9:30am-5pm; last admission 4:30pm. $8, ages 6-12 $4. Take bus #1 or Metrorail to Vizcaya.) Across the street from Vizcaya, the **Museum of Science** and its **Planetarium,** 3280 S. Miami Ave. (854-4247; show info 854-2222), offer laser shows and their ilk. Both congest with kids. (Open daily 10am-6pm. $6, ages 3-12 and seniors $4. Shows $6 extra.) Farther south, **Fairchild Tropic Garden,** 10901 Old Cutler Rd., Coral Gabels (667-1651). The largest tropical botanical garden in the United States, this paradise garden covers 83 acres and features winding paths, a rain forest, a sunken garden, and a narrated train tour. (Open daily 9:30am-4:30pm. $7, under 13 free.)

ENTERTAINMENT

The Art Deco district in South Miami Beach is filled with clubs; many have one hot night, so call ahead. Ocean Blvd., on the beach, is crowded with a young, rowdy set nearly every night of the week. For beautiful people and slammin' DJs, try **The Spot,** 216 Espanola Way (532-1682) or **Velvet,** 634 Collins Ave. (532-0313), Miami Beach (open nightly 10pm-5am. Cover $5 Thurs.-Sat., $3 Sun., free other nights). More swiggin', swingin', and sin happens at the **Baja Beach Club,** 3015 Grand Ave. (445-0278), Coconut Grove. Thursday is college night and Wednesday is ladies night (free entrance). (Open 9pm-5am daily. $7 cover; free with a Florida ID.) **Café Europa,** 3159 Commodore Plaza (448-5723), Cocount Grove, is a laid-back Latin bar. Thursday is salsa night. Live music Friday to Sunday. (Open 5pm-2am.)

After the money's gone, head for **Friday Night Live** (673-7224 for info; Mon.-Fri. 8:30am-5pm), at South Point Park, the very southern tip of Miami Beach, which features free city-sponsored concerts 8-11pm. Down Washington Ave. at Española Way, the **Cameo Theater** (532-0922 for showtimes and prices) has a huge, multi-leveled dance floor. For those with dance fever, this is the only place to go for disco on Sunday night. Friday and Saturday women over 18 free. (Cover $5-7; open daily 9am-5am.) For gay nightlife, check out **Warsaw Ballroom,** 1450 Collins Ave (531-4555), Miami Beach (open Wed.-Sun. 9:30pm-5am), or **Uncle Charlie's,** 3673 Bird Rd. (442-8687), just off Dixie Hwy. (cover $3 Mon.-Wed., $4 Thurs.-Sun.).

Performing Arts and Community Education (PACE) (681-1470; open Mon.-Fri. 9am-5pm) offers more than 1000 concerts each year (jazz, rock, soul, dixieland, reggae, *salsa,* and bluegrass), most of which are free. For more information on what's happening in Miami, check *Miami-South Florida Magazine,* the "Living Today," "Lively Arts," and Friday "Weekend" sections of the *Miami Herald,* or the *Miami New Times,* which comes out every Tuesday and can be found on street corners and in alleyways (free), and in establishments in Miami Beach.

■■■ THE EVERGLADES

■ EVERGLADES NATIONAL PARK

The country's largest remaining subtropical wilderness, the **Everglades National Park** contains more than 1.5 million acres of natural habitat, including Cape Sable, the southernmost point on the U.S. mainland. Named "pahoyokee" (grassy waters) by Native Americans, the glades are a haven for wildlife; the trees and flowers are like those found in Cuba and the West Indies. Visit the park in winter or spring, when heat, humidity, storms, and bugs are at a minimum and when wildlife congregates around the water. *Always* bring mosquito repellent to the Everglades; you'll need it. **Shark Valley** (a 15 mi. loop) is accessible on the northern boundary of the park via the **Tamiami Trail (U.S. 41),** and offers a two-hour tram tour, several self-guided walking tours, and bike rentals for those who want to experience the loop more quietly. (Shark Valley admission $4 percar, $2 for bike or on foot; tram tours 305-221-8455; daily 9am-4pm, tours on the hour; $7.30, seniors $6.50, under 12 $3.65. Reservations required.) Most visitors tour the largely inaccessible park by taking the main park road (Rte. 9336) out of Florida City. **Rte. 9336** runs 40 mi. through the flat grasslands to **Flamingo,** on Florida Bay, stopping at the various nature trails and pullouts along the way. (Park entrance fee $5.) Stop at the main **visitors center,** 40001 State Rd. 9336, Homestead 33034 (305-242-7700), by the park headquarters just inside the entrance, to pick up maps and information (open daily 8am-5pm). The visitors center also sponsors a variety of hikes, canoe trips, and amphitheater programs. One of the many ways to get face-to-snout with an alligator is to amble down the **Anhinga Trail,** at **Royal Palm,** 4 mi. beyond the park's entrance. Naturalists offer 50-min. strolls and can spot alligators with their eyes closed on the **Mahogany Hammock** trail, boasts the largest living mahogany tree in the U.S. **Pa-hay-okee Overlook** affords a terrific view of the "river of grass" for which the Park is named.

There are a number of options for campers in the Everglades. The park **campgrounds** at **Long Pine Key** and **Flamingo** have drinking water, grills, and restrooms. The Flamingo site has showers, but neither site has RV hookups (sites free in summer, $8 in winter). Flamingo has walk-in tent sites which offer a picturesque view of the bay ($4). The park also has lots of primitive backcountry campsites, accessible by boat, foot, or bicycle. Free permits for backcountry camping are available at ranger stations. For heavy nature bonding, acquire a permit for a Chickee—no, not a baby bird, a Chickee is a wooden platform elevated above the water in a mangrove swamp. Canoe rental ($7 per hr., $20 per ½ day, $25 per day) is available at the **Flamingo Marina** (305-253-2241) in Flamingo. Adventure through the **Nine Mile Pond** canoe loop and paddle through alligator ponds, mazes of mangrove trees, and open sawgrass areas (allow 3-4 hr.) **Gulf Coast Visitors Center** (813-695-3311), near Everglades City, is a popular park entrance due to its proximity to Tampa and St. Petersburg. Explore the area's 10,000 islands and see a manatee from a boat or canoe (1½-hr. guided boat tour $11, $7 for children).

Dozens of private **airboat** concessionaires line the northern and eastern park borders, especially along the Tamiami Trail. Cruises into Florida Bay are offered daily at the Flamingo Marina ($8.50, ages 6-12 $4.50, under 6 free). Catch the **Sunset Cruise** (1½ hr.) for a gorgeous end to the day.

The **park headquarters** and after hours **emergency** number is 305-242-7700. Park information on the radio, turn your dial to AM1610. If you're not a camper, or just grow weary of swatting mosquitoes in a tent, the **Flaming Lodge** (305-253-2241) offers hip rooms with A/C, TV, private baths, and a pool. (Singles and doubles $59, Nov.-Dec. $74, Jan.-March $87.) There are cheaper motels on SR 997 in Homestead and Florida City, a one-hr., drive from Flamingo.

Everglades City has a number of motels, RV parks, and campgrounds. The **Barron River Villa, Marina, and RV Park** (813-695-3591) has easy access to the areas 10,000 islands and to the Gulf of Mexico. The park has 67 RV sites, 29 of which are on the river. (Summer RV sites $16, $18 on water; $22/$27 in winter. Full hookups and bathhouse.) **Glades Haven RV Park** (813-695-2746), overlooking Chokoloskee Bay near the Gulf Coast Ranger Station in Everglades City, has pleasant and safe sites with shower facilities (RV sites $20, tents $15).

■ BIG CYPRESS NATIONAL PRESERVE

Adjacent to the Everglades lies **Big Cypress National Preserve,** easily accessible on Rte. 41 between Miami and Naples. Information can be obtained at the **Big Cypress National Preserve Visitors Center,** HCR 61, Box 11, Ochopee, FL 33943 (813-695-4111), on the Tamiami Trail near Everglades City. There is no entrance fee at Big Cypress, and several free, primitive campgrounds for RVs and tents line U.S. 41. Two of these campgrounds are located along the scenic **Florida Trail,** a wet but popular trek that takes hikers through 31 mi. of wildlife. Winter is the best time to brave the trail, because the dry weather brings out more of the indigenous animals. The **campgrounds** at **Dona Drive,** which boast potable water and picnic tables, and **Monument Lake** will charge starting winter 1995. Free **Burns Lake** campground has good fishing and abundant wildlife. Most campgrounds have a portajohn and dumpster. For accommodations just outside the preserve or other sights near the preserve, check with the **Everglades City Chamber of Commerce** (813-695-3941).

THE FLORIDA KEYS

The coral rock islands, mangrove trees, and relaxed attitude of the residents make the Florida Keys pleasant places to visit. With a character quite different from anywhere else in the U.S., these islands off the coast are a nation unto themselves. The Keys are more Caribbean than Floridian, with cool breezes at night, wild tropical rainstorms, and a sun hot enough to roast a turkey. When the sun *does* set, clouds, heat lightning, and the surrounding ocean provide an incredible accompaniment. Approximately 6 mi. offshore from these islands, a 100-yd. wide barrier reef parallels the Keys, running from Key Largo south to Key West. Adored by divers, these reefs harbor some of the ocean's most diverse and colorful marine life as well as hundreds of wrecked ships and legendary lost treasure. And contrary to popular belief, there are very few sharks.

The Keys run southwest into the ocean from the southern tip of Florida, accessible by the **Overseas Highway (U.S. 1). Mile markers** divide the highway into sections and replace street addresses to indicate the location of homes and businesses.

They begin with Mile 126 in Florida City and count down to zero on the corner of Whitehead and Fleming St. in Key West.

Greyhound runs buses to Key West from Miami ($26), stopping in Perrine, Homestead (247-2040), Key Largo (451-2908), Marathon (743-3488), Big Pine Key (872-4022), and Key West (296-9072). If there's a particular mile marker where you need to get off, most bus drivers can be convinced to stop at the side of the road. Biking along U.S. 1 across the swamps between Florida City and Key Largo is impossible because the road lacks shoulders. Bring your bike on the bus.

■■■ KEY LARGO

After traversing the thick swamps and crocodile marshland of Upper Florida Bay, Key Largo opens the door to the Caribbeanesque islands. Spanish explorers named the island "long island" because, at 30 mi., it is the largest of the Florida keys. Home to John Pennekamp, the nation's first underwater state park, Key Largo is a good place to begin exploring the deep. Without a car it can be difficult to get around, although everything of importance lies within a 6-mi. range. Many travelers pass right through Key Largo, rushing to see the sunset or catch the action in Key West. Slow down and enjoy incredible snorkeling, scuba, and funky bars.

Practical Information The **Key Largo Chamber of Commerce/Florida Keys Welcome Center,** Mile 105.5 (451-1414), has info on local and other Key attractions. Look for a large turquoise awning at the 106 Plaza in Key Largo. Also offers free phone calls to hotels, restaurants, and attractions. (Open daily 9am-6pm.) The dramatic mailroom scene from *Key Largo* was filmed at the **post office:** Mile 100 (451-3155; open Mon.-Fri. 8am-4:30pm); **ZIP code:** 33037; **area code:** 305.

Accommodations and Food After the **John Pennekamp State Park Campground** fills up (see below), try crowded but well-run **Key Largo Kampground,** Mile 101.5 (451-1431 or 800-KAMP-OUT/526-7688; 110 RV and tent sites, heated pool, game room, laundry and a bath house; $20-35, extra person $5). The **Calusa Camp Resort,** (451-0232 or 800-457-CAMP/2267) on the bay side of mile 101.5, has 400 sites (some waterfront), a pool, tennis courts, two bathhouses, and a marina ($23-29, extra person $3). For beautiful sunsets, a warm reception, and reasonable rates, check out the **Seafarer Fish and Dive Resort** (852-5349 or 800-599-7712) mile 97.8, 97820 Overseas Highway. The Seafarer also offers a free jacuzzi, and free use of boats and kayaks ($40 summer, $46 winter, $6 for extra person). The **Hungry Pelican,** Mile 99.5 (451-3576), boasts beautiful bougainvillea vines in the trees and friendly managers Larry and Dana. Stuff your beak full in a clean, cozy trailer or room with a double bed ($40-55, $10 for extra person).

The **Italian Fisherman,** Mile 104 (451-4471), has it all—fine food and a spectacular view of Florida Bay. Formerly an illegal gambling casino, this restaurant was the locale for some scenes from Bogart and Bacall's movie *Key Largo.* (Lunch $4-8, dinner $7-15. Open daily 11am-10pm.) The seafood and 99-beer selection at **Crack'd Conch,** Mile 105 (451-0732), is superb. Try the "sorry Charlie" tuna fish sandwich ($4.50) or an entire key lime pie ($7.50), once called "the secret to world peace and the alignment of the planets." (Open Thurs.-Tues. noon-10pm.) From two locations, **Perry's,** at Mile 102 (451-1834), serves fresh local seafood and charbroiled steaks; and from its most famous location at Key West, 3800 N. Roosevelt Blvd. (294-8472). (Lunch $4-10, dinner $10-23.) (Open daily 9am-10:30pm.) They also offer a "you hook 'em, we cook 'em" service for $3.50. Other scenes from *Key Largo* were filmed at the **Caribbean Club,** Mile 104 (451-9970), a friendly local bar. The in-house band Blackwater Sound plays a variety of rock for the locals Thursday-Sunday evenings; snapshots of Bogart and Bacall grace the walls. (Beer $1.50, drinks $2. Open daily 7am-4am.)

THE SOUTH

John Pennecamp State Park The nation's first underwater sanctuary, Key Largo's **John Pennecamp State Park,** Mile 102.5 (451-1202), 60 mi. from Miami, protects a 120-square-mile stretch of coral reef that runs the length of the Florida Keys (park admission $3.75 for driver, 50¢ per extra passenger up to 8). The park's **visitor center**, about ¼ mi. past the entrance gate, provides maps of the reefs, information on boat and snorkeling tours, three aquariums, and introductory films on the park (open daily 8am-5pm, 451-1202). To see the reefs, visitors must take a boat or rent their own. **Boat rentals**, unfortunately, are rather expensive (19' motor boat $22 per hr, 2 hr. minimum; refundable deposit required, 451-1621 to reserve a boat). **Scuba trips** (9:30am and 1:30pm) are $37 per person for a two tank dive. A **snorkeling tour** allows you to experience underwater tranquility (3 trips daily, 9am, noon, and 3pm; $25, under 18 $20; 2½ hr. total, 1½ hr. water time). If you're up for a longer snorkeling tour, ask about the combined sailing/snorkeling trip, which takes about half a day and is about the same price as the shorter trip. For a crystal clear view of the reefs without wetting your feet, the **Glass Bottom Boat Tours** (451-1621) are the way to go (daily 9:15am, 12:15pm, and 3pm; $14, under 12 $9, 2 children free with an adult for 9:15am tour). The tours leave from the park shore at mile 102.5.

Camping in the park is extremely popular, so reservations are a must. The sites are clean, convenient, and well worth the effort required to obtain one ($26, with hookup $28.)

■■■ KEY WEST

This is the end of the road. When searching for a tropical paradise, you can do no better than Key West. The island's pastel clapboard houses, hibiscus and bougainvillea vines, year-round tropical climate, and gin-clear waters make it a beautiful spot to visit in summer or winter.

Key West's relaxed atmosphere, hot sunshine, and spectacular sunsets have attracted travelers and famous authors like Tennessee Williams, Ernest Hemingway, Elizabeth Bishop, and Robert Frost. Today, an easygoing diversity continues to attract a new generation of writers, artists, gays, recluses, adventurers, and eccentrics. Yet before you off and throw yourself into the Key West sun, beware—the island lies as far south as the Bahamas, and the tropical sun will scald you if you don't take precautions. Especially if you're getting to the farthest key via the Overseas Highway, the sun reflecting off the water is powerful.

Situated only 90 mi. northwest of Cuba, Key West is closer to Havana than Miami, and Key West was once a haven for Cuban political exiles. Originally, Key West was a burial ground for the Caloosa tribe of native Americans and was known as Cayo Hueso, or "Island of Bones." Ages later, and in a somewhat different spirit, Henry Flager brought the first true tourists to the Keys on his Overseas Railroad, which operated from 1912 to 1935. Today, it takes 3-3½ hours to reach Key West from Miami (155 mi.).

PRACTICAL INFORMATION

Emergency: 911.
Visitor Information: Key West Chamber of Commerce, 402 Wall St. (294-2587 or 800-648-626), in old Mallory Sq. Useful *Guide to the Florida Keys* available here. List of popular gay accommodations. Open daily 8:30am-5pm. **Key West Welcome Center,** 3840 N. Roosevelt Blvd. (296-4444 or 800-284-4482), just north of the intersection of U.S. 1 and Roosevelt Blvd. Arranges housing, theater tickets, and reef trips if you call in advance. Open daily 9am-5pm.
Airport: Key West International Airport, (296-5439) on the southeast corner of the island. Serviced by **American Eagle, U.S. Air Express,** and **Vintage** airlines. No public bus service.

Greyhound: 615½ Duval St. (296-9072). Obscure location in an alley behind Antonio's restaurant. To Miami, stopping along all the Keys. Open Mon.-Fri. 7am-12:30pm and 2:30-5pm, Sat. 7am-noon.

Public Transport: Key West Port and Transit Authority, (292-8161), City Hall. One bus ("Old Town") runs clockwise around the island and Stock Island; the other ("Mallory St.") runs counterclockwise. Pick up a clear, helpful, and free map from the Chamber of Commerce (see above) or any bus driver. Service Mon.-Sat. 6:10am-10:35pm, Sun. 6:40am-6:40pm. Fare 75¢, seniors and students 35¢. **Handicapped Transportation,** 292-3515.

Taxi: Keys Taxi, 296-6666, $1.40 plus $1.75 per mi.

Car Rental: Alamo, Ramada Inn, 3420 N. Roosevelt Blvd. (294-6675 or 800-327-9633), near the airport. $30 per day, $115 per week. Under 25 $15 extra. Must be 21 with major credit card or $50 deposit. Miami drop-off costs a prohibitive $55.

Bike Rental: Key West Hostel, 718 South St. (296-5719). $4 per day, $30 per week. Open daily 8-11am. Credit card and deposit required.

Help Line: 296-4357, everything from general info to crises. 24 hr.

Post Office: 400 Whitehead St. (294-2557), 1 block west of Duval at Eaton. Open Mon.-Fri. 8:30am-5pm. **ZIP code:** 33040.

Area Code: 305.

Just 4 mi. long and two wide, Key West resides at the southernmost point of the continental U.S. and at the end of Rte. 1, 160 mi. southwest of Miami. Only 90 mi. north of Cuba, Key West dips farther south than much of the Bahamas.

Divided into two sectors, the eastern part of the island, called "New Town" by some, harbors tract houses, chain motels, shopping malls, and the airport. **Old Town,** the west side of town below White St., is cluttered with beautiful old conch houses. **Duval Street** is the main north-south thoroughfare in Old Town, **Truman Avenue** the major east-west route. Key West is cooler than mainland Florida in summer and much warmer in winter.

ACCOMMODATIONS AND CAMPING

Beautiful weather resides year-round in Key West alongside beautiful tourists. As a result, good rooms at the nicer hotels go for up to $400 per day, especially during the winter holidays. There is no "off-season." Key West remains packed virtually year-round, with a lull of sorts from mid-September to mid-December; even then, don't expect to find a room for less than $40.

Try to bed down in **Old Key West;** the beautiful, 19th-century clapboard houses capture the flavor of the Keys. Some of the guest houses in the Old Town offer complimentary breakfasts and some are for gay men exclusively. Do *not* park overnight on the bridges—this is illegal and dangerous.

Key West Hostel, 718 South St. (296-5719), at Sea Shell Motel in Old Key West, 3 blocks east of Duval St. Call for airport or bus station pickup. Rooms with 4-6 beds, shared bath. A/C at night. Famous $1 dinners and $2 breakfasts. Kitchen open until 9pm. No curfew. Office open daily 9am-10pm. Members $13, nonmembers $16. Key deposit $5. Motel rooms in summer $45, in winter $50-100. Call ahead to check availability; also call for late arrival. 24-hr. check-in.

Caribbean House, 226 Petronia St. (296-1600 or 800-543-4518), at Thomas St. in Bahama Village. Brand-new, Caribbean-style rooms with cool tile floors, A/C, TV, fridge, and ceiling fans. Comfy double beds. Free continental breakfast. Norman, the friendly manager, may be able to place you in a completely furnished Caribbean cottage (sleeps 6) or an unfurnished low-rent apartment for comfortable summer living. Rooms $69, cottage $79-89. In summer: rooms $39, cottage $59. No reservations—first come, first served, so rooms are usually available.

The Spindrift, 1212 Simonton St. (298-3432), between Truman Ave. and United St. Simple, clean, rooms with bathroom, cable TV, A/C, a pool, and individual refrigerators. Summer single and doubles $49, winter $89.

Eden House, 1015 Fleming St. (296-6868 or 800-533-5397). Bright, clean, friendly hotel with very nice rooms, just 5 short blocks from downtown. Cooool rooms with private or shared bath, some with balconies. Pool, jacuzzi. In-season $75-105, summer $50-70.

Boyd's Campground, 6401 Maloney Ave. (294-1465), on Stock Island. Take bus to Maloney Ave. from Stock Island. 12 acres on the ocean. Full facilities, including showers. $25 summer, $31 winter. $5 each additional camper. Water and electricity $5 extra, A/C or heat $5 extra. Waterfront sites $5 extra.

FOOD

Expensive restaurants line festive **Duval Street.** Side streets offer lower prices and fewer crowds. Sell your soul and stock up on supplies at **Fausto's Food Palace,** 522 Fleming St. (296-5663), the best darn grocery store in Old Town. (Open Mon.-Sat. 8am-8pm, Sun. 8am-6pm.) Although the genuine article with a tangy yellow filling is hard to come by (key limes are not green), don't leave Key West without having a sliver of (or even a whole) **key lime pie.**

Half-Shell Raw Bar, Land's End Village (294-7496), at the foot of Margaret St. on the waterfront 5 blocks east of Duval. Rowdy and popular with tourists. Great variety of seafood dinners $10-14. Famed for its spring conch chowder ($2.95). Open Mon.-Sat. 11am-11pm. Sun. noon-11pm.

El Cacique, 125 Duval St. (294-4000). Cuban food at reasonable prices. Homey and colorful. Filling lunch specials with pork or local fish, black beans, and rice for $6-10, dinner $11-15. Try fried plantains, conch chowder, or bread pudding as side dishes, and flan for dessert. Open daily 8am-10pm.

Blue Heaven Fruit Market, 729 Thomas St. (296-8666), 1 block from the Caribbean House. Hemingway used to drink beer and referee boxing matches here when it was a pool hall. Dinners $8-12. Open Mon.-Sat. 3-11pm.

SIGHTS

Biking is a good way to see Key West, but you might want to take the **Conch Tour Train** (294-5161), a narrated ride through Old Town, leaving from Mallory Sq. at 3840 N. or from Roosevelt Blvd. next to the Quality Inn. This touristy 1½ hour trip costs $12 (kids $6), but guides provide a fascinating history of the area. (Operates daily 9am-4:30pm.) **Old Town Trolley** (296-6688) runs a similar tour, but you can get on and off throughout the day ($14, kids $6; full tour 1¾ hr.).

The glass-bottomed boat *Fireball* takes two-hour cruises to the reefs and back (296-6293; tickets $19, ages 3-12 $9.50). One of a few cruise specialists, the **Coral Princess Fleet,** 700 Front St. (296-3287), offers snorkeling trips with free instruction for beginners (1 per day, leaves 1:30pm returns 5:30pm, $20; open daily 8:30am-6:30pm). For a landlubber's view of the fish of Key West, the **Key West Aquarium,** #1 Whitehead St. (296-2051), in Mallory Square, offers a 50,000 gallon Atlantic shore exhibit as well as a touch pool and shark feedings. ($6.50, seniors, students, and military $5.50, children 8-15 $3.50, under 7 free; open daily 9am-6pm. Sun. 10am-6pm).

Long a mecca for artists and writers, the **Hemingway House,** 907 Whitehead St. (294-1575), off Olivia St., is where "Papa" wrote *For Whom the Bell Tolls* and *A Farewell to Arms.* Tours of the house are available; grin and bear it, or traipse through the house on your own. About 50 cats (descendants of Hemingway's cats) make their home on the grounds; ask their names from the tour guides and be mildly amused. (House open daily 9am-5pm. $6, kids 6-12 $1.50.) The **Audubon House,** 205 Whitehead St. (294-2116), built in the early 1800s, houses some fine antiques and a private collection of the works of ornithologist John James Audubon. (Open daily 9:30am-5pm. $6, ages 6-12 $4, under 6 $2.)

Down Whitehead St., past Hemingway House, you'll come to the **southernmost point** in the continental U.S. and the adjacent **Southernmost Beach**. A small, conical monument and a few conchshell hawkers mark the spot. The **Monroe County Beach,** off Atlantic Ave., has an old pier allowing access past the weed line. The **Old U.S. Naval Air Station** offers deep water swimming on Truman Beach ($1). **Mel Fisher's Treasure Exhibit,** 200 Greene St. (294-2633), will dazzle you with glorious gold. Fisher discovered the sunken treasures from the shipwrecked Spanish vessel, *Atocha.* A *National Geographic* film is included in the entrance fee. (Open daily 9:30am-5pm. $5, students $4, under 12, $1.50, under 6 free.)

The **Wrecker's Museum,** 322 Duval St. (294-9502), was built in 1829 and is known as the "Oldest House." A "wrecker" was a daring sea captan who risked arm and limb for the promise of money and adventure. The museum details the colorful history of wrecking, and its exhibits include such interesting artifacts as a black list of wreckers caught in an insurance scam. (Open daily 10am-4pm, $3, under 12 $2.)

The **San Carlos Institute,** 516 Duval St., built in 1871, is a freshly restored paragon of Cuban architecture that shines with majorca tiles from Spain and houses a research center for Hispanic studies. The **Haitian Art Company,** 600 Frances St. (296-8932), six blocks east of Duval St., is crammed full of vivid Caribbean artworks. (Open daily 10am-6pm. Free.)

Watching a sunset from the **Mallory Square Dock** is always a treat. Magicians, street entertainers, and hawkers of tacky wares work the crowd, while swimmers and speedboaters show off; the crowd always cheers when the sun slips into the Gulf with a blazing red farewell.

Every October, Key West holds a week-long celebration known as **Fantasy Fest,** culminating in an extravagant parade. The entire population turns out for the event in costumes that stretch the imagination. In April, the **Conch Republic** celebrates with bed races, and the January to March **Old Island Days** features art exhibits, a conch shell-blowing contest, and the blessing of the shrimp fleet.

ENTERTAINMENT

Check out the daily *Key West Citizen* (sold in front of the post office) and the weekly *Solares Hill* (available at the Key West Chamber of Commerce) for events on the island. Nightlife in Key West revs up at 11pm and winds down very late.

Rick's, 208 Duval St. (296-4890). This place rocks, especially when the **Terry Cassidy Band** plays (Tues.-Sat. 5-11pm). Ask bartender Mike about the house specials, including the $1.50 draft. Open daily 11am-4am.

Sloppy Joe's, 201 Duval St. (294-5717), at Greene. Reputedly one of "Papa" Hemingway's preferred watering holes; the decor and rowdy tourists would probably now send him packing. Originally located in Havana but moved to "Cayo Hueso" (i.e. Key West) when Castro rose to power. The bar's usual frenzy heightens during the Hemingway Days Festival in mid-July. Drafts $2.25. R&B day and night. Open daily 9am-4am.

Captain Tony's Saloon, 428 Greene St. (294-1838). The oldest bar in Key West. Tony Tarracino, the owner, usually shows up at 9pm. Open Mon.-Thurs. 10am-1am, Fri.-Sat. 10am-2am, Sun. noon-1am.

■■■ TAMPA AND ST. PETERSBURG

The Gulf Coast communities of Tampa and St. Petersburg enjoy a less raucous atmosphere than Florida's Atlantic Coast vacation destinations. The two cities offer quiet beaches, beautiful harbors, and perfect weather year-round unpoisoned by droves of tourists. One of the nation's fastest-growing cities and largest ports, Tampa contains thriving financial, industrial, and artistic communities. Across the bay, St. Petersburg caters to a relaxed, attractive community, made up of retirees and young singles alike. The town enjoys 28 mi. of soft white beaches, emerald water, beautiful sunsets, and approximately 361 days of sunshine yearly. The high season on the Gulf Coast runs from October to April.

PRACTICAL INFORMATION

Emergency: 911.
Visitor Information: Tampa/Hillsborough Convention and Visitors Association, 111 Madison St. (223-1111 or 800-826-8358). Open Mon.-Sat. 9am-5pm. **St.**

Petersburg **C.O.C.,** 100 2nd Ave. N. (821-4069). Open Mon.-Fri. 9am-5pm. **The Pier Information Center,** 800 2nd Ave. N. (821-6164). Open Mon.-Sat. 10am-7:30pm. Sun. 11am-6pm.

Traveler's Aid: Tampa, 273-5936. St. Pete, 823-4891. Open Mon.-Fri. 8:30am-4:30pm.

Airport: Tampa International: (870-8700), 5 mi. west of downtown. HARTline bus #30 runs between the airport and downtown Tampa. **St. Petersburg Clearwater International** (539-7491) sits right across the bay. **The Limo Inc.** (572-1111 or 800-282-6817) offers 24-hr. service from both airports to the cities and to all the beaches between Ft. De Soto and Clearwater ($9.50 from St. Pete, $12 from Tampa). Make reservations 6 hr. in advance.

Amtrak: In Tampa, 601 Nebraska Ave. (221-7600 or 800-872-7245), at Twiggs St. 1 block north of Kennedy. Open daily 7:45am-7:15pm. No trains go south of Tampa. In St. Pete, 3101 37th Ave. N. (522-9475 or 800-872-7245). Amtrak will transport you to Tampa by bus ($7). There is no direct train link between Tampa and St. Petersburg. Open 9:30am-7:15pm.

Greyhound: In Tampa, 610 E. Polk St. (229-2174 or 800-231-2222), next to Burger King downtown. Open 24 hrs. In St. Pete, 180 9th St. N. (898-1496), downtown. Open 6·15am-11:30pm.

Public Transport: In Tampa, **Hillsborough Area Regional Transit (HARTline),** 254-4278. Fare 85¢, transfers 10¢. To reach St. Pete, take bus #100 express from downtown to the Gateway Mall ($1.50). Has free shuttle that loops through downtown. The **Tamp Town Ferry** has pick-up and drop-off points throughout downtown. $6 round-trip. In St. Pete, **Pinnellas Suncoast Transit Authority (PSTA),** 530-9911. Most routes depart from Williams Park at 1st Ave. N. and 3rd St N. Fare 90¢, transfer 10¢.

Help Lines: In Tampa, **Rape Crisis,** 238-8821. 24 hrs. **Gay/Lesbian Crisis Line,** 229-8839. In St. Petersburg, **Rape Crisis,** 530-7233. 24 hrs.

ZIP codes: Tampa 33601, St. Pete 33731.

Post Office: The main Tampa office is at the airport, 5201 W. Spruce Rd. (879-1600). Open 24 hrs. In St. Petersburg: 3135 1st Ave. N. (323-6516). Open Mon.-Fri. 8am-6pm, Sat. 8am-12:30pm.

Area Code: 813.

Tampa divides into quarters with **Florida Avenue** running east-west and **Kennedy Boulevard,** which becomes **Frank Adams Drive** (Rte. 60), running north-south. Numbered avenues run east-west and numbered streets run north-south. You can reach Tampa on I-75 from the north, or I-4 from the east.

In St. Petersburg, 22 mi. south, **Central Avenue** runs east-west. **34th Street** (U.S. 19) cuts north-south through the city and links up with the **Sunshine-Skyway Bridge,** connecting St. Pete with the Bradenton-Sarasota area to the south. The St. Pete beachfront is a chain of barrier islands accessible by bridges on the far west side of town, and extends from **Clearwater Beach** in the north to **Pass-a-Grille Beach** in the south. Many towns on the islands offer quiet beaches and reasonably priced hotels and restaurants. From north to south, these towns include: **Clearwater Beach, Indian Rocks Beach, Madiera Beach, Treasure Island,** and **St. Pete Beach.** The stretch of beach past the Don Cesar Hotel (luxury resort-cum-pink monstrosity recently declared a historical landmark) in St. Pete Beach and Pass-a-Grille Beach has the best sand, a devoted following, and the least pedestrian and motor traffic.

ACCOMMODATIONS AND CAMPING

Inexpensive, convenient lodgings are rare in Tampa, but St. Petersburg has two youth hostels as well as many cheap motels lining 4th St. N. and U.S. 19. Some establishments advertise singles for as little as $16, but these tend to be ancient and dirty. To avoid the worst neighborhoods, stay on the north end of 4th St. and the south end of U.S. 19. Several inexpensive motels also line the St. Pete beach. In Tampa, you can contact the **Overseas Information Center** at the University of South Florida (974-3933) for help in finding accommodations.

Tampa

Motel 6, 333 E. Fowler Ave. (932-4948), off I-275 near Busch Gardens and the Tom Bodett Memorial. On the northern outskirts of Tampa, 30 mi. from the beach. Clean, small rooms. Singles $29. Each additional person $6.

Holiday Inn, 2708 N. 50th St. (621-2081). From I-4, take Exit #3. Pool, whirlpool, spa, and cable. Breakfast buffet $5, lunch buffet $6, Mon.-Fri. 1-4 people $58.

St. Petersburg

St. Petersburg Youth Hostel, 326 1st Ave. N. (822-4141), downtown in the McCarthy Hotel. Small, clean singles, doubles, and quads, all with private showers. Common room with kitchen, TV, A/C. $11 with any youth hostel card, without a card $13, not including $2 linen fee. 11pm curfew. If staying here Thurs.-Sat., check out **Jannus Landing** a block away (corner of 1st Ave. N. and 1st St.) for some great live music or $2 drafts.

Clearwater Beach International Hostel (Rucksakers), 606 Bay Esplande Ave. (443-1211), 20 mi. out of town, but just 2 blocks from a superb white-sand beach. Bunk in shared room $11, nonmembers $13. Linen $2. Kitchen, common room, free bikes and tennis rackets, ping pong. Private rooms available (call for rates).

Kentucky Motel, 4246 4th St. N. (526-7373). Large, clean rooms with friendly owners, cable TV, refrigerator in each room, and free postcards. Singles $24. Doubles $28. Jan.-March rooms $10 more.

Grant Motel, 9046 4th St. (576-1369), 4 mi. north of town on U.S. 92. Pool. Clean rooms with A/C; most have a fridge. Singles $30, doubles $32. Jan.to mid-April singles $39, doubles $43.

Treasure Island Motel, 10315 Gulf Blvd. (367-3055). Across the street from beach, big rooms with A/C, fridges, and color TV. Pool. Singles and doubles $30. Jan.-Feb. $52/$53 respectively. Each additional person $4. Pirates not allowed.

Fort De Soto State Park (866-2662), composed of five islands at the southern end of a long chain of keys and islands, has the best camping. A wildlife sanctuary, the park makes a great oceanside picnic spot (2-day min. stay; curfew 10pm, front gate locked at 9pm; no alcohol; 147 sites, $16.50). Disregard the "no vacancy" sign at the toll booth (85¢) by the Pinellas Bayway exit. However, from January to April, you may want to make a reservation in person at the St. Petersburg County Building, 150 5th St. N. #146, or at least call ahead (892-7738).

FOOD AND NIGHTLIFE

Cheap Cuban and Spanish establishments dot Tampa. Black bean soup, gazpacho, and Cuban bread usually yield the best bargains. For Cuban food, **Ybor City** definitely has superior prices and atmosphere. St. Petersburg's cheap, health-conscious restaurants cater to its retired population—and generally close by 8 or 9pm. Those hungry later should try St. Pete Beach and 4th St.

Ice cold brew is never far away; most hotels have beachside bars or tiki huts where you can enjoy a drink while watching a brilliant red sunset.

Tampa

JD's, 2029 E. 7th Ave. (247-9683), in Ybor City. Take bus #12. Soups, sandwiches, and Cuban food in a roomy, low-key restaurant. Breakfast $2.50. Lunch $4. Open Mon.-Fri. 9am-2pm.

Cepha's, 1701 E. 4th Ave. (247-9022), has cheap Jamaican specialties. Red snapper or curry chicken $4-7. Colorful garden in back and reggae shows throughout the summer. Open Mon.-Wed. 11:30am-10pm, Thurs. 11:30am-1am, Fri.-Sat. 11:30am-3am.

The Loading Dock, 100 Madison St. (223-6905), downtown. Sandwiches $3-5. Try the "flatbed" or the "forklift" for a filling diesel-fueled meal. Open Mon.-Fri. 8am-8pm, Sat. 10:30am-2:30pm.

Yucatan Liquor Stand, 4811 W. Cypress (289-8454). Spacious bar, tiki bar, and volleyball courts. No cover. Open Mon.-Fri. 4pm-3am, Sat.-Sun. 6pm-3am. Weeknight happy hour 4-9pm.

THE SOUTH

St. Pete

Crabby Bills, 5100 Gulf Blvd. (360-8858), Indian Rocks Beach. Cheap, extensive menu. Ultra-casual atmosphere. 6 blue crabs $5.50. Open Mon.-Thurs. 11am-10pm, Fri.-Sat. 11am-11pm.

Tangelo's Bar and Grille, 226 1st Ave. NE (894-1695), St. Pete. Try a tasty crab burger ($4.50) or gazpacho soup ($2). Open Mon.-Sat. 11am-9pm.

Beach Nutts, 9600 W. Gulf Blvd. (367-7427), Treasure Island. Not much selection, but Oh! what an atmosphere. Right on the beach. Live reggae Sat. and Sun. 4-8pm, bands every night. Open daily 9am-2am.

SIGHTS AND ACTIVITIES

Tampa

Bounded roughly by 22nd Street, Nebraska Avenue, 5th Avenue, and Columbus Drive, **Ybor City** is Tampa's Latin Quarter. Walking tours of Ybor City's two square miles are available (233-1111, ext. 46). The area expanded rapidly after Vincent Martínez Ybor moved his cigar factories here from Key West in 1886. Although cigar manufacturing has since been mechanized, some people still roll cigars by hand and sell them for $1 in **Ybor Square,** 1901 13th St. (247-4497), three 19th-century cigar factories converted into an upscale retail complex. (Open Mon.-Sat. 9:30am-5:30pm, Sun. noon-5:30pm.) **Ybor City State Museum,** 1818 9th Ave. (247-6323), at 21st St., traces the development of Ybor City, Tampa, the cigar industry, and Cuban migration (open Tues.-Sat. 9am-noon and 1-5pm; 50¢). The **Three Birds Bookstore and Coffee Room,** 1518 7th Ave. (247-7041), contributes artsily to Ybor City. Sip orange zinger tea or get a slice of black forest cheesecake while you read the latest Paris Review. (Open Mon.-Thurs. 11am-6pm, Fri.-Sat. 11am-10pm.) Aside from the square, the Ybor City area has remained relatively unsullied by the rapid urban growth that typifies the rest of Tampa; **East 7th Avenue** still resembles an old neighborhood. Keep an ear out for jazz and a nose out for Cuban cuisine. Be careful not to stray more than two blocks north or south of 7th Ave. since the area can be extremely dangerous, even during the daytime. Buses #5, 12, and 18 run to Ybor City from downtown.

Now part of the University of Tampa, the Moorish **Tampa Bay Hotel,** 401 W. Kennedy Blvd., once epitomized fashionable Florida coast hotels. Teddy Roosevelt trained his Rough Riders in the backyard before the Spanish-American War. The small **Henry B. Plant Museum** (254-1891), in a wing of the University of Tampa building, is an orgy of rococo craftsmanship and architecture; the exhibits themselves, which include Victorian furniture and Wedgewood pottery, pale in comparison. (Guided tours at 1:30pm. Open Tues.-Sat. 10am-4pm. Admission by donation.)

Downtown, the **Tampa Museum of Art,** 601 Doyle Carlton Dr. (223-8130), houses the Joseph Veach Nobre collection of classical and modern works. (Open Tues.-Sat. 10am-5pm, Sun. 1-5pm. Free.) Across from the University of South Florida, north of downtown, the **Museum of Science and Industry,** 4801 E. Fowler Ave. (985-6300), features a simulated hurricane. (Open Sun.-Thurs. 9am-4:30pm, Fri.-Sat. 9am-9pm. $4, ages 5-15 $2.) The **Museum of African American Art,** 1308 N. Marion St. (292-2466), features the art history and culture of the classical Barnett-Aden collection. (Open Tues.-Sat. 10am-4pm and Sun. 1-4:30pm. $2 donation requested.)

The **waterfront** provides much of Tampa's atmosphere. *"Day-O! Day-O! Daylight come and me wanna go home."* Banana boats from South and Central America unload and tally their cargo every day at the docks on 139 Twiggs St., near 13th St. and Kennedy Blvd. Every year in February the *Jose Gasparilla,* a fully rigged pirate ship loaded with hundreds of exuberant "pirates," "invades" Tampa and kicks off a month of parades and festivals, such as the **Gasparilla Sidewalk Art Festival.** (Pick up a copy of the visitors guide for current info on various events and festivals.)

Tampa's **Busch Gardens—The Dark Continent** (971-8282), E. 3000 Busch Blvd. and NE 40th St. is a fascinating park with a different theme; African animals rule this kingdom. Take I-275 to Busch Blvd., or take bus #5 from downtown. Not only are people confined to trains, boats, and walkways while giraffes, zebras, ostriches, and antelope roam freely across the park's 60-acre plain, but Busch Gardens has two of only 50 white Bengal tigers in existence. The park also has rides that will leave you breathless. Try the Rumba, the largest and fastest steel roller coaster in the South East. (Open daily 9am-8pm; off-season daily 9:30am-6pm. $29, Parking $3.) A visit to the **Anheuser-Busch Hospitality House** inside the park provides a sure-fire way to make your afternoon more enjoyable. You must stand in line for each beer, with a three-drink limit.

About ¼ mi. northeast of Busch Gardens at 4500 Bougainvillea Ave. is **Adventure Island** (971-7978), a 13-acre water theme park. ($15. For those under 48 inches $12. Open 10am-5pm with extended hours in summer.)

St. Petersburg

St. Petersburg's main attraction is its coastline. **Pass-a-Grille Beach** may be the nicest, but with parking meters, it exacts a toll. The **Municipal Beach** at Treasure Island, accessible from Rte. 699 via Treasure Island Causeway, offers free parking. When you're too sunburned to spend another day on the sand, head for **Sunken Gardens,** 1825 4th St. N. (896-3186), home of over 7000 varieties of exotic flowers and plants. A new alligator wrestling show adds to the thrill of green-thumbing (be careful where you put that thumb!) (Open daily 9am-5:30pm. $7, ages 3-11 $4.)

Hello Dalí! The **Salvador Dalí Museum,** 1000 3rd St. S. (823-3767), in Poynter Park on the Bayboro Harbor waterfront, contains the world's most comprehensive collection of Dalí works and memorabilia—94 oil paintings, 1300 graphics, and even works from a 14-year-old Dalí. The tours are worthwhile. (Tours 45 min. and five times daily. Open Tues.-Sat. 9:30am-5:30pm, Sun. noon-5:30pm. $5, seniors $4, students $3.50, under 10 free.) **Great Explorations,** 1120 4th St. S. (821-8992), is a museum with six areas of exhibits to fondle. Test your strength at the **Body Shop,** where you can compare your muscles with scores taken from around the country. (Open Mon.-Sat. 10am-5pm, Sun. 1-5pm. $4.50, seniors $4, ages 4-17 $3.50.) The **Pier** (821-6164), at the end of 2nd Ave. NE, downtown, extends out into Tampa Bay from St. Pete, ending in a five-story inverted pyramid complex that contains a shopping center, aquarium, restaurants and bars. (Open Mon.-Thurs. 10am-9pm, Fri.-Sat. 10am-10pm, Sun. 11am-7pm; bars and restaurants open later. Free trolley service from the parking area

■■■ PANAMA CITY BEACH

Where the boys are has moved. Panama City Beach, where suntan oil is the perfume of choice, has become *the* spring break spot. Situated on the Gulf Coast, a few hours from New Orleans, the city is becoming the new mecca of the Gulf's meat markets Quartz crystals, washing down from the Appalachian Mountains, break into millions of glistening shards, blessing PCB with miles of snow white sand. But geology would not be the main subject at the U of PCB—try comparative anatomy.

Practical Information Emergency is 911. **Panama City Beach Convention and Visitors Bureau,** 12015 Front Beach Rd. (233-5070 or 800-PCBEACH; open daily 8am-5pm). Taxis run on grid system. **AAA Taxi** (785-0533) or **Yellowcab** (763-4691). Airport to strip $14.25. **Help Lines: Domestic Violence and Rape Crisis Hotline** (763-0706), **Crisis and Mental Health Emergency Hotline** (769-941), both 24 hrs. **Post Office,** 275 Hwy. 79 (234-8888). **Zip Code:** 32407. **Area Code:** 904.

After crossing Hathaway Bridge, Rte. 98 splits. Everything centers on **Front Beach Road,** also known as the Strip or Miracle Mile. To bypass the hubbub, take some of the smaller roads off Rte. 98.

Accommodations and Camping Depending on the time of year and strip location, rates range from moderate to exorbitant. The end of April until early September is high season, with much cheaper rates in fall and winter. **La Brisa Inn,**

9424 Front Beach Rd. (235-1122 or 800-523-4369), is off the beach, but has free coffee and doughnuts and free local calls. On-season singles or doubles $54-60. Off-season singles $28. **Fiesta Motel,** 13623 Front Beach Rd. (235-1000 or 800-833-1415), is quieter than most, but still close to the "wild." Prices vary. (On-season singles $60, doubles $80. Family suite $90.) **The Reef,** 12011 Front Beach Rd.(234-3396 or 800-847-7286), near the visitors center. (Singles $50-65.) Camp on the beach at **St. Andrews State Recreation Area,** 4415 Thomas Dr. (233-5140), 3 mi. east of PCB on Rte. 392. (177 sites. $16.35. Water and electricity $21.) **Panama City Beach KOA,** 8800 Thomas Dr. (234-5731), 2 blocks south of Rte. 98 on the Gulf, but not beachside. (114 sites; showers, laundry, and a pool. $19, with electricity $23.)

Food, Sights, and Entertainment Buffets abound on the strip. **JP's Restaurant and Bar,** 4701 Front Beach Rd. (769-3711), has original recipes in abundant portions. (Fettuccini and clams $9; open daily 11am-10:30pm). **Mikato,** 7724 Front Beach Rd. (235-1338), has sumptuous Japanese seafood. (Complete dinner $9; open Sun.-Thur. 4-10:30pm, Fri.-Sat. 4pm-midnight.) More pricey is **Captain Anderson's Restaurant,** 5551 N. Lagoon Dr. (234-2225), off Thomas Dr. Renowned in PCB for its superb seafood and panoramic view. (Open daily 4-10pm.)

The **St. Andrews State Recreation Area** (see Accommodations) consists of more than 1260 acres of gators, nature trails, and beaches. Take a glass bottom boat trip to **Shell Island** at **Treasure Island Marina** (234-8944) on Thomas Dr. (Call for hours; $9-11.) Explore the deep at the **Museum of the Man in the Sea,** 17314 Back Beach Rd. (235-4101l; open daily 9am-5pm. $4, ages 6-16 $2, seniors $3.60.)

Meat-market Miracle Mile is meant for the cruisers and those wanting to be cruised. **Spinnaker,** 8795 Thomas Dr. (234-7882), **Club LaVela,** 8813 Thomas Dr. (234-3866), and **Salty's Beach Bar,** 11073 Front Beach Rd. (234-1913), will get ya on the good foot. Call for hours. Bungee jumping, parasailing, and scuba diving are everyday activities here. Check out the **Miracle Strip Amusement Park** (234-5810), adjacent to the **Shipwreck Island Water Park,** 2000 Front Beach Rd. (234-0368). Nearby **Alvin's Magic Mountain Mall,** 12010 Front Beach Rd. (234-3048), houses a 30,000 gallon tank replete with sharks and alligators.

Alabama

The "Heart of Dixie" has matured since the 1960s and 1970s when Governor George Wallace fought a vicious campaign opposing African-American advancement. During decades of internal racial strife, Alabama was the home to bigotry but also to dynamic civil rights leaders like Reverend Dr. Martin Luther King, Jr., whose amazing patience and fortitude helped spawn the first real changes in race relations.

Today, Alabama's larger cities attract a cosmopolitan populace as art museums, concerts, and ethnic restaurants appear. A coastal city, Mobile has grown from one of the Gulf's first settlements to one of the busiest ports in the nation. Though plantation estates endure throughout the countryside, King Cotton now shares his throne with mineral ores and one of the largest beds of white marble in the world.

While modern attractions can keep you busy, the most compelling reasons to visit Alabama remain the monuments and legacies of a divided past: from the poignant statues in Birmingham's Kelly Ingram Park commemorating the struggles of the 1950s to Booker T. Washington's pioneering Tuskegee Institute (now University).

PRACTICAL INFORMATION

Capital: Montgomery.

Alabama Bureau of Tourism and Travel, 401 Adams Ave. (242-4670; 800-252-2262 outside AL). Open Mon.-Fri. 8am-5pm. **Travel Council,** 702 Oliver Rd.

#254, Montgomery 36117 (271-0050). Open Mon.-Fri. 8am-5pm. **Division of Parks,** 64 N. Union St., Montgomery 36130 (800-252-7275). Open daiily 8:30am-4:30pm.
Time Zone: Central (1 hr. behind Eastern). **Postal Abbreviation:** AL
Sales Tax: 4% plus county tax.

■■■ MONTGOMERY

A look into Montgomery's history unveils a concatenation of firsts and beginnings: the first capital of the Confederacy, the first operating electric streetcar in 1886, and the first Wright Brothers' flight school in 1910. This is also the city where Dr. Martin Luther King, Jr. began his ministry. In late 1955, King went on to lead bus boycotts here that introduced the nation to his nonviolent approach to gaining equal rights for African-Americans. With its nationally acclaimed Alabama Shakespeare Festival and the recently completed Arts Museum, Montgomery lures culture-seekers. Retaining an ambience of easygoing lifestyles, the capital of Alabama celebrates its rural past alongside a busy, diverse present.

PRACTICAL INFORMATION

Emergency: 911.
Visitor Information: Visitor Information Center, 401 Madison Ave. (262-0013). Open Mon.-Fri. 8:30am-5pm, Sat.-Sun. 9am-4pm. **Chamber of Commerce,** 401 Adams Ave. (242-4670). Open Mon.-Fri. 8:30am-5pm.
Traveler's Aid: 265-0568. Operated by Salvation Army. Open Mon.-Fri. 9am-5pm.
Greyhound: 210 S. Court St. (800-231-2222), south of downtown. From Court Square Fountain on Washington St., take a left on Court St. and 2 blocks ahead. Open 24 hrs.
Amtrak: 335 Coosa St. (277-9400), in Riverfront Park. Northwest of downtown, Coosa St. is at Madison and Bibb. Take Coosa across the railroad tracks; station is on your left. Open Mon.-Fri. 9am-6pm, Sat. 10am-4pm.
Public Transport: Montgomery Area Transit System (MATS), 701 N. McDonough St. (262-7321). Operates throughout the metropolitan area Mon.-Sat. 5am-5pm. Fare $1, transfers 10¢.
Taxi: Yellow Cab, 262-5225. $2.60 first mi., $1.10 each additional mi.
Help Lines: Council Against Rape, 286-5987. **Help-A-Crisis,** 279-7837. Both open 24 hrs.
Post Office: 135 Catoma St. (244-7576). Open Mon.-Fri. 7am-5:30pm, Sat. 8am-noon. **ZIP code:** 36104.
Area Code: 205.

Downtown Montgomery follows a grid pattern: **Madison Avenue** and **Dexter Avenue** are the major east-west routes; **Perry Street** and **Lawrence Street** run north-south.

ACCOMMODATIONS AND FOOD

Those with a car will find it easy to procure accommodations; **I-65** at the Southern Blvd. exit overflows with cheap beds. Two well-maintained budget motels centrally located downtown are the **Capitol Inn,** 205 N. Goldthwaite St. (265-3844), at Heron St., with spacious, clean, and comfortable rooms and a pool, near the bus station on a hill overlooking the city (singles $30, doubles $38) and the comfortable **Town Plaza,** 743 Madison Ave. (269-1561), at N. Ripley St. (singles $22, doubles $26). Off exit 168 on I-65 sleep a slew of budget motels. **Budget Inn,** 995 W. South Blvd. (284-4004), has a pool, clean, big rooms, and lots of funky light switches (singles $33, doubles $36). **The Inn South,** 4243 Inn South Ave. (288-7999), has very nicely decorated rooms and a lobby with a grand double staircase and chandelier (singles $29, doubles $33). For an alternative to these inns, contact **Bed and Breakfast Montgomery,** P.O. Box 1026, Montgomery 36101 (264-0056). **KOA Campground**

(288-0728), ¼ mi. south of Hope Hull exit, 4 mi. from town, has a pool, laundry, and showers (tent sites $12, with water and electricity $18, with A/C add $2.50).

Martha's Place, 458 Sayre St. (263-9135), is a new but soon-to-be-legendary, family-run, down-home restaurant with a daily country-style buffet ($5.50). Read the articles on the wall and discover a real-life American dream come true. (Open Mon.-Fri. 11am-3pm, Sun. brunch 11am-3pm.) A 70-year-old Montgomery institution, **Chris's Hot Dogs,** 138 Dexter Ave. (265-6850), has a carnivorous following. This small diner serves stuffed-silly hot dogs (under $2) and thick Brunswick stew ($1.65). (Open Mon.-Thurs. 8:30am-7pm, Fri. 8:30am-8pm, Sat. 10am-7pm.) At **The China Bowl,** 701 Madison Ave. (832-4004), 2 blocks from the Town Plaza Motel, large portions include a daily special of one entree, fried rice, egg roll, chicken wing, and a fried wonton for $4.20; take-out available (open Mon.-Thurs. 11am-9pm, Fri. 11am-9:30pm). For a great snack, make your way over to the **Montgomery State Farmers Market** (242-5350), at the corner of Federal Dr. (U.S. 231) and Coliseum Blvd., and snag a bag of peaches for $1 (open spring and summer daily 7am-8pm). For a more filling meal, right next door there is never an empty seat for the Southern cooking at **The Farmer's Market Cafeteria,** 315 N. McDonough St. Free iced tea with every inexpensive meal ($4-5). (Open Mon.-Fri. 5am-2pm.)

SIGHTS AND ENTERTAINMENT

Montgomery's newest sight is the **Civil Rights Memorial,** 400 Washington Ave. (264-1968), at Hull St. Maya Lin, the architect who designed the Vietnam Memorial in Washington, D.C., also designed this dramatically minimalist tribute to 40 of the men, women, and children who died fighting for civil rights. The outdoor monument bears names and dates of significant events on a circular black marble table over which water and flowers of remembrance continuously flow; a wall frames the table with Martin Luther King's words, "...Until Justice rolls down like waters and righteousness like a mighty stream." (Open 24 hrs. Free.)

The legacy and life of African-American activism and faith can also be seen one block away at the **Dexter Avenue King Memorial Baptist Church,** 454 Dexter Ave. (263-3970), where King first preached. At this 112-year-old church, Reverend King and other Civil Rights leaders organized the 1955 Montgomery bus boycott; 10 years later, King led a nationwide Civil Rights march past the church to the capitol building. The basement mural chronicles King's role in the nation's struggle during the 1950s and 60s. (Tours Mon.-Thurs. 10am and 2pm, Fri. 10am, Sat. every 45 min. beginning at 10am.)

Three blocks north is **Old Alabama Town,** 310 N. Hull St. (246-4500), at Madison, a historic district of 19th-century buildings. The complex includes a pioneer homestead, an 1892 grocery, a schoolhouse, and an early African-American church. Renowned Alabama storyteller Kathryn Tucker Windham artfully recounts her family's past as she leads you through the quaint, reconstructed village. (Open Mon.-Sat. 9:30am-3:30pm, last tour at 3:30pm; Sun. 1-3:30pm. $5, kids 6-18 $2.)

After years of restoration, the **State Capitol** (242-3750), Bainbridge St. at Dexter Ave., is once again open for public viewing (open Mon.-Fri. 8am-5pm for free, self-guided tours; make an appointment for a guide; free). You can also visit the nearby **Alabama State Archives and History Museum,** 624 Washington Ave. (242-4363). On exhibit are many Native American artifacts along with early military swords and medals. Stop by **Grandma's Attic** where you can try on antique furs and play with antique sewing machines and typewriters in a wooden-frame attic replica. (Open Mon.-Fri. 8am-5pm, Sat. 9am-5pm. Free.) Next door to the Archives is the elegant **First White House of the Confederacy,** 644 Washington Ave. (242-1861), which contains many original furnishings from Jefferson Davis's presidency (open Mon.-Fri. 8am-4:30pm, Sat.-Sun. 9am-4:30pm; free). Another restored home of interest is the **F. Scott and Zelda Fitzgerald Museum,** 919 Felder Ave. (264-4222), off Carter Hill Rd. Zelda, originally from Montgomery, lived here with F. Scott from October 1931 to April 1932. The museum contains a few of her paintings and some of his original manuscripts, as well as their strangely monogrammed bath towels. (Open Wed.-Fri. 10am-2pm, Sat.-Sun. 1-5pm.)

Country music fans might want to join the hundreds who make daily pilgrimages to the **Hank Williams Memorial,** 1304 Upper Wetumpka Rd., located in the Oakwood Cemetery Annex off Upper Wetumpka Rd. near dowtown. Oversize music notes flank the gravestone upon which rests a stone cowboy hat and engravings of guitars, cowboy boots, and titles of his most famous hits. Green astro-turf carpets the holy ground. (Open daily 7am-sunset.) For more live entertainment, turn to the renowned **Alabama Shakespeare Festival,** (800-841-4ASF) staged at the **State Theatre** on the grounds of the 250-acre private estate, **Wynton M. Blount Cultural Park.** Go 15 min. southeast of the downtown area onto Woodmere Rd. via East Blvd. Broadway shows and other plays are also staged. Nearby, off Woodmere Blvd., the **Montgomery Museum of Fine Arts,** 1 Museum Dr. (244-5700), houses a substantial collection of 19th- and 20th-century paintings and graphics, as well as ART-WORKS, a hands-on gallery and art studio for children. (Open Tues.-Wed. and Fri-Sat. 10am-5pm, Thurs. 10am-9pm, Sun. noon-5pm. Free.)

Montgomery shuts down fairly early, but if you're in the mood for some blues and beers, try **1048,** 1048 E. Fairview Ave. (834-1048), near Woodley Ave. (open Mon.-Sat. 6pm-until the cow walks in the door). For further information on events in the city, call the Chamber of Commerce's 24-hr. **FunPhone** (240-9447).

■ NEAR MONTGOMERY: TUSKEGEE

After Reconstruction, Southern states still segregated and disenfranchised "emancipated" African-Americans. Booker T. Washington, a former slave, believed that blacks could best combat repression and racism by educating themselves and learning a trade, as opposed to pursuing the classical, more erudite education which W.E.B. Dubois proposed. Therefore, the curriculum at the college Washington founded, **Tuskegee Institute,** revolved around such practical endeavors as agriculture and carpentry, with students constructing almost all of the campus buildings. Washington raised money for the college by giving lectures on social structure across the country. Artist, teacher, and scientist George Washington Carver became head of the Agricultural Department at Tuskegee, where he discovered many practical uses for the peanut, including axle grease and peanut butter.

Today, a more academically oriented Tuskegee University consists of over 160 buildings on 1500 acres and offers a wide range of subjects; the buildings of Washington's original institute also comprise a national historical site. A walking tour of the campus begins near the entrance to the university at the **Carver Museum,** with the **Visitor Orientation Center** (727-3200) inside (both open daily 9am-5pm; free). Down the street from the museum on old Montgomery Rd. is **The Oaks,** a restored version of Washington's home. Free tours from the museum begin on the hour.

For a filling, delicious, and inexpensive meal after your touring, just cross the street from campus to **Thomas Reed's Chicken Coop,** 527 Old Montgomery Rd. (727-3841). Chicken is sold by the piece or as a full dinner (all under $5). And you *will* lick your fingers. (Open daily 9am-5pm.)

To get to Tuskegee, take I-85 toward Atlanta and exit at Rte. 81 south. Turn right at the intersection of Rte. 81 and Old Montgomery Rd. onto Rte. 126. **Greyhound** (727-1290) also runs frequently from Montgomery (1 hr., $8). Tuskegee's **ZIP code:** 36083; **area code:** 205.

■■■ BIRMINGHAM

This city literally sprang up from the ground. Like its English namesake, Birmingham sits on soil rich in coal, iron ore, and limestone—responsible for its lightning transformation into a premier steel industry center. No longer an industrial town, the city's largest employer is now the University of Alabama, home to one of the best cardiology hospitals in the world. With an urban version of Southern charm and hospitality, arts festivals and museums may suffice in drawing visitors, but the most compelling sights of the area hark back to less idyllic times. Birmingham has been "A Place of Revolution and Reconciliation," trying in recent decades to heal the wounds left by Eugene "Bull" Connor, firehoses, bombings, and police dogs, whose images were spread all over the American news media during the civil rights protests of the early 1960s.

PRACTICAL INFORMATION

Emergency: 911.
Visitor Information: Birmingham Visitors Center, 1200 University Blvd. (458-8001), at 12 St., I-65 exit 259. Maps, calendars, and coupons for accommodations. Open Mon.-Sat. 8:30am-5pm, Sun. 1-5pm. Another location on the lower level of **Birmingham Municipal Airport** (458-8002). Open 24 hrs. **Greater Birmingham Convention and Visitors Bureau,** 2200 9th Ave. N., 3rd floor (252-9825), downtown. Open Mon.-Fri. 8:30am-5pm.
Amtrak: 1819 Morris Ave. (324-3033 or 800-872-7245), downtown.
Greyhound: 618 N. 19th St. (800-231-2222). Open 24 hrs.
Public Transport: Metropolitan Area Express (MAX), 252-0101. Runs Mon.-Sat. 7am-6pm. Fare 80¢. **Downtown Area Runabout Transit (DART),** 252-0101. Runs Mon.-Fri. 10am-4pm. Fare 25¢.
Taxi: Yellow Cab, 252-1131. Base fare $2.95, $1.20 each additional mi.
Help Lines: Crisis Center, 323-7777. Open 24 hrs.
Post Office: 351 24th St. N. (521-0209). Open Mon.-Fri. 7:30am-7pm. **ZIP code:** 35203.
Area Code: 205.

The downtown area grid system has avenues running east-west and streets running north-south. Each numbered avenue has a north and a south. Major cultural and government buildings surround **Linn Park,** located between 19th and 21st St. N. on 7th Ave. N. The **University of Alabama in Birmingham (UAB)** extends along University Blvd. (8th Ave. S.) from 11th to 20th St.

ACCOMMODATIONS AND CAMPING

Passport Inn, 821 20th St. S. (252-8041), 2 blocks from UAB. Large, clean rooms and tasteful decor in a convenient location. Pool. Singles $32. Doubles $34.
Ranchhouse Inn, 2125 7th Ave. S. (322-0691). Near busy bars and restaurants. Pleasant rooms with cable TV and wood paneling. Check out the cowboy tiling in each bathroom. Local calls 25¢ each. Singles $30. Doubles $36.
Budgetel Inn, 513 Cahaba Park Circle (995-9990). Good area. Free movies and cable. Senior discount, under 18 with adult stay free. Singles $37. Doubles $44.
Oak Mountain State Park (620-2527), 15 mi. south of Birmingham off I-65 in Pelham (exit 246). Alabama's largest state park with nearly 10,000 heavily forested acres. Horseback rides, golf, hiking, and an 85-acre lake. Sites $8.50 for 1-4 people, with electricity $13.

FOOD

Barbecue remains the local specialty, although more ethnic variations have sprung up downtown. The best places to eat cheaply (and meet young people) are at **Five Points South,** located at the intersection of Highland Ave. and 20th St. S. Choose from pesto pizza with sun-dried tomatoes ($3 per slice) at **Cosmo's Pizza,** 2012 Magnolia Ave. (930-9971; open Mon.-Thurs. 11am-11pm, Fri.-Sat. 11am-midnight, Sun. noon-10pm), or health-conscious veggie lunches and groceries at **The Golden Temple,** 1901 11th Ave. S. (933-6333; open Mon.-Fri. 8:30am-7:30pm, Sat. 9:30am-5:30pm, Sun. noon-5:30pm; kitchen open daily 11:30am-2pm).

For barbecue, locals will tell you to "just look for the pig." The swine symbolizes **Johnny Ray's Bar-B-Que,** 316 Valley Ave (945-7437), and 3 other perimeter locations in Colonnade (967-0099), Vestaria (823-7437), and Hueytown (491-2345). You may oink when you leave, but the J.R. Triple Decker Pork and Beef Combo with slaw and beans ($4.60), followed by a sumptuous slice of Honey's (Johnny's wife) famous chocolate pies ($1.50) will suffice for pigging out.

The Mill, 1035 20th St. S. (939-3001), sits at the center of Five Points South, serving tasty pizzas ($6-8) and sandwiches ($5-6). Microbrewery, bakery, and restaurant in one, this sidewalk café/restaurant/bar is the perfect place for any gastronomic need. Live entertainment Wed.-Sun. (cover on weekends $2). Open Sun.-Wed. 6:30am-midnight, Thurs.-Sat. 6:30am-2am.

Café Bottega, 2240 Highland Ave. S. (939-1000). High-ceilinged and sophisticated, this café serves fresh bread to dip in olive oil and Italian specialties brimming with fresh vegetables and herbs. Marinated pasta with sweet peas and mint $5.25. Entrees $5-12. Open Mon.-Sat. 11am-11pm. Bar open until "everyone goes home."

Bogue's, 3028 Clairmont Ave. (254-9780). A short-order diner with true delicious Southern fare (cheese omelette and biscuit $3). Always busy weekend mornings. Open Mon.-Fri. 6am-2pm, Sat.-Sun. 6-11:30am.

Ollie's, 515 University Blvd. (324-9485), near Green Springs Hwy. Bible Belt dining in an enormous circular 50s-style building. Pamphlets shout "Is there really a Hell?" while you lustfully consume your beef. BBQ sandwich $2, homemade pie $1.50. Diet plates available. Open Mon.-Sat. 10am-8pm.

SIGHTS

A prominent part of Birmingham's efforts towards reconciliation has culminated in the **Black Heritage Tour** of the downtown area. The **Birmingham Civil Rights Institute,** 520 16th St. N. (328-9696), at 6th Ave. N., rivals the museum in Memphis (see Memphis, TN) in thoroughness, and surpasses it in visual and audio evocations, depictions, and footage of African-American history and the turbulent events of the Civil Rights Movement. The Institute intends to display exhibits on human rights across the globe, and to serve as a research facility open to the public. A trip to Birmingham would be incomplete without a more than cursory tour. (Open Tues.-Sat. 10am-6pm, Sun. 1-5pm. Free.) Other significant sights include the **Sixteenth Street Baptist Church,** 1530 6th Ave. N. (251-9402), at 16th St. N. (in the lower level), where four African-American girls died in a September 1963 bombing by white segregationists after a protest push which culminated in Dr. Martin Luther King Jr.'s "Letter From a Birmingham Jail." The deaths spurred many protests in nearby **Kelly-Ingram Park,** corner of 6th Ave. and 16th St., where a bronze statue of Dr. Martin Luther King, Jr. and granite scupltures of oppression, revolution, and reconciliation grace the green lawns.

Remnants of Birmingham's steel industry are best viewed at the gigantic **Sloss Furnaces National Historic Landmark** (324-1911), adjacent to the 1st Ave. N. viaduct off 32nd St. downtown. Though the blast furnaces closed 20 years ago, they stand as the only preserved example of 20th-century iron-smelting in the world. Ballet and drama performances and music concerts are often held here at night. (Open Tues.-Sat. 10am-4pm, Sun. noon-4pm; free guided tours Sat.-Sun. at 1, 2, and 3pm.) To anthropomorphize the steel industry, Birmingham cast the **Vulcan** (Roman god of the forge) who overwhelms the skyline as the largest cast-iron statue in the world. Visitors can watch over the city from its observation deck. The Vulcan's glowing torch burns red when a car fatality has occurred that day, green when none occur. (Open daily 8am-10:30pm. $1, kids 6 and under free.)

The **Alabama Sports Hall of Fame** (323-6665), corner of Civic Center Blvd. and 22nd St. N., honors the careers of outstanding sportsmen like Bear Byrant Jesse Owens, Joe Louis, Joe Namath, and Willie Mays (open Mon.-Sat. 9am-5pm, Sun. 1-5pm. $5, seniors $4, students $3). A few blocks down from the Hall of Fame blooms the refreshing **Linn Park,** across from the **Birmingham Museum of Art,** 2000 8th Ave. N. (254-2565). The museum displays U.S. paintings and English Wedgewood ceramics, as well as a superb collection of African textiles and sculptures. (Open Tue.-Sat. 10am-5pm, Sun. noon-5pm. Free.)

For a breather from the downtown scene, revel in the marvelously sculpted grounds of the **Birmingham Botanical Gardens,** 2612 Lane Park Rd. (879-1227), whose spectacular floral displays, elegant Japanese gardens, and enormous greenhouse vegetate on 68 acres (open daily dawn-dusk; free).

Antebellum **Arlington,** 331 Cotton Ave. (780-5656), southwest of downtown, houses a fine array of Southern decorative arts from the 19th century. Go west on 1st Ave. N., which becomes Cotton Ave., to reach the stately white **Greek Revival** building, which also hosts craft fairs throughout the year. (Open Tues.-Sat. 10am-4pm, Sun. 1-4pm. $3, ages 6-18 $2.)

To learn more about the geology of the area, visit the **Red Mountain Museum and Cut,** 1421 22nd St. S. (933-4104). You can wander a walkway above the highway to see different levels of rock formation inside Red Mountain. The museum indoors has various exhibits on the prehistoric inhabitants of Alabama. The **Discovery Place,** 1320 22nd St. S (939-1176), next door, invites children of all ages to explore body mechanics, the ins and outs of cities, brainteasers, channels of communication, and much more. (Both sites open Mon.-Fri. 9am-3pm, Sat. 10am-4pm, Sun. 1-4pm. Museum free, admission to Discovery Place $3, kids $2.)

Music lovers lucky or smart enough to visit Birmingham in the middle of June for **City Stages** (251-1272) will hear everything from country to gospel to big name rock groups, with headliners like James Brown, the Indigo Girls, and George Jones. The three-day festival also includes food, crafts, and children's activities. (Daily pass $10, weekend pass $14.)

ENTERTAINMENT AND NIGHTLIFE

Historic **Alabama Theater,** 1817 3rd Ave. N. (251-0418), shows old movies on occasional weekends throughout the year. Their organ, the "Mighty Wurlitzer," entertains the audience before each showing. ($4, seniors $3, under 12 $2.) Pick up a free copy of *Fun and Stuff* or see the "Kudzu" in the Friday edition of *The Birmingham Post Herald* for listings of all movies, plays, and clubs in the area.

The **Five Points South (Southside)** has a high concentration of nightclubs. On cool summer nights many people grab outdoor tables in front of their favorite bars or hang out by the fountain. Use caution here, and avoid parking or walking in dark alleys near the square. For the hippest licks year-round check out **The Nick,** 2514 10th Ave. S. (322-7550). The poster-covered exterior asserts "the Nick...rocks." (Open Mon.-Sat. Live music nightly. Cover $2-5.)

Louie Louie's, 2001 Highland Ave. (933-2778), at 21st St., is good for a cheap drink and tunes. Opens at 9pm, closes late when the music stops. **The Burly Earl,** 2109 7th Ave. S. (322-5848), specializes in fried finger-foods and local acoustic, blues, and rock sounds. Sandwiches are $3-5. (Restaurant open Mon.-Thurs. 10am-midnight, bar open until midnight; Fri.-Sat. 10am-1am, bar open until 2am. Wed.-Thurs. live folk from 8:30pm-midnight; Fri.-Sat. rock bands 9:30pm-2am. No cover.)

■■■ MOBILE

Situated on the Gulf of Mexico, Mobile (mo-BEEL) reflects its checkered past under English, French, and Spanish dominion through its distinctive and diverse architectural styles. Antebellum mansions, Italianate dwellings, Spanish and French historical forts, and Victorian homes line the azalea-edged streets of Alabama's oldest major city. Mobile is also awash with museums and gardens that further enhance its color. Site of the first U.S. Mardi Gras, with fresh seafood, a moderate climate, and white sandy beaches, Mobile resembles New Orleans and the Mississippi Coast more than it does the rest of Alabama.

PRACTICAL INFORMATION

Emergency: 911.
Visitor Information: Fort Condé Information Center, 150 S. Royal St. (434-7304), in a reconstructed French fort near Government St. Open daily 8am-5pm. **Mobile Convention and Visitors Bureau,** 1 S. Water St. (415-2100). Open Mon.-Fri. 8am-5pm.

Traveler's Aid: 438-1625. Operated by the Salvation Army; ask for Traveler's Services. Lines open Mon.-Fri. 8am-3:30pm.

Amtrak: 11 Government St. (432-4052 or 800-872-7245). The "Gulf Breeze" blows from Mobile to New York via Birmingham ($66); Atlanta ($74); Greenville, S.C. ($116); Washington, DC ($155).

Greyhound: 2545 Government St. (478-9793), at S. Conception downtown. To: Montgomery (8 per day, 4 hr., $27); New Orleans (15 per day, 3 hr., $26); Birmingham (6 per day, 6 hr., $39). Open 24 hrs.

Public Transport: Mobile Transit Authority (MTA), 344-5656. Major depots are at Bienville Sq., St. Joseph, and Dauphin St. Operates Mon.-Sat. 5am-7pm. Fare 75¢, seniors and disabled 35¢, transfers 10¢.

Taxi: Yellow Cab, 476-7711. Base fare $1.30, $1.20 each additional mi.

Help Lines: Rape Crisis, 473-7273. **Crisis Counseling,** 666-7900. Both 24 hrs.

Post Office: 250 Saint Joseph St. (694-5917). Open Mon.-Fri. 7am-5pm, Sat. 9am-4pm. **ZIP code:** 36601.

Area Code: 205.

The downtown district fronts the Mobile River. **Dauphin Street** and **Government Boulevard** (U.S. 90), which becomes Government Street downtown, are the major east-west routes. **Royal Street** and **St. Joseph Street** are the north-south byways. Some of Mobile's major attractions lie outside downtown. The *U.S.S. Alabama* is off the causeway leading out of the city; **Dauphin Island** is 30 mi. south.

ACCOMMODATIONS AND CAMPING

If you're stuck here inside of Mobile, don't get the Memphis blues again. Accommodations are both reasonable and accessible, but stop first at the Fort Condé Information Center (see above; they can make reservations for you at a 10-15% discount). The MTA runs a "Government St." bus regularly which reaches the Government St. motels listed below, but they are all about a 15-min. walk from downtown.

Economy Inn, 1119 Government St. (433-8800). Big beds, clean sheets, and a pool. Singles and doubles $30. Key deposit $5. $5 each additional humanoid.

Motel 6, 400 Beltline Hwy. (343-8448). Small, dark rooms with tidy furnishings. Free movie channel, pool. $30 for 1 person, $6 per additional person.

Family Inns, 900 S. Beltline Rd. (344-5500), I-65 at Airport Blvd., sports new carpets, firm beds, and general comfort. Singles $27. Doubles $35.

I-10 Kampground, 6430 Theodore Dawes Rd. E. (653-9816), 7½ mi. west on I-10 (exit 13 and turn south). No public transportation. Pool, kiddie playground, laundry, and bath facilities. Sites $12, $1 per additional person. $14.50 full hookup.

FOOD AND NIGHTLIFE

Mobile's proximity to the Gulf makes seafood and Southern cookin' regional specialties. Well-known for its atmosphere and its seafood, **Wintzels,** 605 Dauphin St., (433-1004), six blocks west of downtown, offers a dozen oysters on the half shell "fried, stewed, and nude" for $4 (open Mon.-Thurs. and Sat. 11am-9pm, Fri. 11am-9:45pm). Next to the *U.S.S. Alabama,* **Argiro's,** 1320 Battleship Pkwy. (626-1060), is a quick-stop deli that provides cheap hot dogs and sandwiches ($2-5) and Southern specialties such as red beans and rice (open Mon.-Tues. and Sat. 8am-3:45pm, Wed.-Fri. 8am-4:45pm). **Weichman's All Seasons,** 168 S. Beltline Hwy. (344-3961), has excellent tender crab ($6.50-9.50) and key lime pie ($2.25). (Open Mon.-Fri. 11am-3pm and 5-10pm, Sat. 5-10pm, Sun. 11am-3pm and 5-9pm.) **Port City Brewery,** 225 Dauphin St. (438-2739), has vats and vats to drive you bats. There's rock and reggae at **G.T. Henry's,** 462 Dauphin St. (432-0300), with crawfish boils on Sundays (open Wed.-Sun. 5:30pm until everyone leaves; cover $2-5).

SIGHTS

Mobile encompasses four historic districts: **Church Street, DeToni Square, Old Dauphin Way,** and **Oakleigh Garden.** Each offers a unique array of architectural styles. The information center provides maps for walking or driving tours of these former residences of cotton brokers and river pilots as well as the cottages of their servants. (Package tour available at the center; $10 for four house museums.)

Church St. divides into east and west subdistricts. The homes in the venerable **Church Street East District** showcase popular U.S. architectural styles of the mid- to late 19th century, including Federal, Greek Revival, Queen Anne, and Victorian. While on Church St., be sure and pass through the **Spanish Plaza,** Hamilton and Government St., which honors Mobile's sibling city—Málaga, Spain—while recalling Spain's early presence in Mobile. Also of interest in this area is the **Christ Episcopal Church,** 115 S. Conception St. (433-1842), opposite the tourist office at Fort Condé. Dedicated in 1842, the church contains beautiful German, Italian, and Tiffany stained glass windows. Call the office (weekdays 8am-4pm) or wander in when the church is open on weekends (Sunday services at 8 and 10am).

In the **DeToni Historical District,** north of downtown, tour the tastefully restored **Richards-DAR House,** 256 North Joachim St. (434-7320), whose red Bohemian stained glass and rococo chandeliers blend beautifully with its antebellum Italianate architecture and ornate "Iron Lace." On slow days, the staff may invite you in for tea and cookies. (Open Tues.-Sat. 10am-4pm, Sun. 1-4pm. Tours $3, kids $1.) Brick townhouses with wrought-iron balconies fill the rest of the district.

One of Mobile's most elegant buildings is **Oakleigh,** 350 Oakleigh Place (432-1281), off Government St., with a cantilevered staircase and enormous windows that open onto all the balconies upstairs. Inside, a museum contains furnishings of the early Victorian, Empire, and Regency periods. (Tours every ½ hr.; last tour at 3:30pm. $5, seniors $4.50, students $2, kids 6-18 $1.) Also part of the museum system are the simple **Cox-Deasy House** and the **Carlen House** (470-7768), Carlen St. off Dauphin St., a six-room restored Creole cottage. The **Phoenix Fire Museum,** 203 S. Claiborne St. (434-7554), displays several antique fire engines including an 1898 steam-powered one. (All open Tues.-Sat. 10am-5pm, Sun. 1-5pm. Free.)

The famous **Fine Arts Museum of the South (FAMOS),** 4850 Museum Dr. (343-2667), displays some fascinating African-American art (open Tues.-Sun. 10am-5pm; free). The **Exploreum,** 1906 Springhill Ave. (476-6873), offers scientific diversions geared to children with hands-on investigations and experiments (open Tues.-Fri. 9am-5pm, Sat.-Sun. 1-5pm; $3, kids 2-17 $2).

The battleship *U.S.S. Alabama,* which fought in every major World War II Pacific battle, is permanently moored at **Battleship Park** (433-2703). The park is at the entrance of the Bankhead Tunnel, 2½ mi. east of town on I-10. Berthed along the port side of this intriguing ship is the famous submarine, the *U.S.S. Drum.* (Open daily 8am-sunset. Admission to both vessels $5, kids 6-11 $2.50. Parking $2.)

Gray Line of Mobile (432-2228) leads interesting tours of Battleship Park and **Bellingrath Gardens** from the Fort Condé Information Center; call for details. For a lengthier excursion, travel south on Rte. 193 to **Dauphin Island,** where you can fish or just lounge around. No swimming though, not even if you're the dauphin.

■ Mississippi

Understandably known as the "Magnolia State," Mississippi's flora and fauna defy the humid, wilting heat for which the South is so famous. When traveling here, steer off the interstate onto the Natchez Trace Parkway and explore the lush forests, swamps, and countryside winding gracefully through the shade from Natchez, MS to Nashville, TN, passing through historic landmarks and a beautiful national park.

The beauty of this roadway and the Mississippi River contrasts with the many disturbing years of racial conflicts and appalling economic conditions for which the state is notorious. Mississippi's green hills provided the backdrop for major Civil

War Battles. Unfortunately, the Union's victory at Vicksburg in 1863 was only the beginning of the battle for civil rights—the state would see many more years of racial strife. Mississippi's culture is strongly influenced by its African-American heritage. The blues, born in Mississippi, was derived from slave songs. Mississippians W.C. Handy, Bessie Smith, Robert Johnson, and B.B. King brought the blues up the "Blues Highway," U.S. 61, to Memphis, Chicago, and the world.

PRACTICAL INFORMATION

Capital: Jackson.
Division of Tourism, 1301 Walter Siller Bldg., 550 High St. (359-3414 or 800-647-2290). Open Mon.-Fri. 8am-5pm. **Bureau of Parks and Recreation,** P.O. Box 10600, Jackson 39209.
Time Zone: Central (1 hr. behind Eastern). **Postal Abbreviation:** MS
Sales Tax: 7-8%.

■■■ JACKSON

A sleepy Deep South town the size of a sunbelt city, Mississippi's capital offers travelers a glimpse into southern life without overwhelming them with the usual plastic and pricey tourist traps. The lush homes and posh country clubs of North Jackson root Mississippi's commercial and political capital in its southern heritage. Jackson has shaded campsites, cool reservoirs, national forests, and Native American burial mounds only minutes away. Combining history with natural beauty, the Natchez Trace Parkway can lead you north to Nashville or south to Natchez.

PRACTICAL INFORMATION

Emergency: 911.
Visitor Information: Visitor Information Center, 1150 Lakeland Dr. (981-0019), off I-55 Lakeland East exit. Open Mon.-Sat. 9am-5pm. **Convention and Visitors Bureau,** 921 N. President St. (960-1891), downtown. Open Mon.-Fri. 8:30am-5pm.
Airport: Jackson Municipal (932-2859), east of downtown off I-20. Cab fare to downtown about $15.
Amtrak: 300 W. Capitol St. (355-6350 or 800-872-7245). Neighborhood is deserted at night. To: Memphis (1 per day, 4 hr., $46) and New Orleans (1 per day, 4 hr., $42). Open Mon.-Fri. 8am-1pm and 2-7pm, Sat.-Sun. 8-11am and 4:30-7pm.
Greyhound: 201 S. Jefferson (353-6342). Be cautious walking in the area at night. To: Dallas (5 per day, 10 hr., $72); Montgomery (3 per day, 7 hr., $46); Memphis (5 per day, 4½ hr., $37); New Orleans (4 per day, 4½ hr., $36). Open 24 hrs.
Public Transport: Jackson Transit System (JATRAN) (948-3840), in the Federal Bldg. downtown. Limited service. Bus schedules and maps posted at most bus stops. Buses run Mon.-Fri. 5am-7pm, Sat. 7am-6pm. Fare 75¢, transfers free.
Help Lines: First Call for Help, 352-4357. **Rape Hotline,** 982-7273.
Taxi: City Cab, 355-8319. Base fare $1.10, $1 per mi.
Post Office: 401 E. South St. (968-1612). Open Mon.-Fri. 7am-7pm, Sat. 8am-noon.
ZIP code: 39201.
Area Code: 601.

Downtown, just west of I-55, is bordered on the north by **High St.,** on the south by **Pascagoula,** and on the west by **Farish St.** North-south **State St.** cuts the city in half.

ACCOMMODATIONS

There are few motels downtown, but with a car, head for the motels along I-20 and I-55; price is directly related to proximity and comfort. Camping is the most inexpensive, not to mention aesthetically pleasing, option in Jackson.

Sun n' Sand Motel, 401 N. Lamar St. (354-2501), downtown. Large, newly-renovated rooms with 50s orange n' aqua—even a Polynesian room. Cable TV. Pool.

Lounge/restaurant in motel serves $5 lunch buffet. Close to dowtown. Singles $27.50. Doubles $34. $5 each additional person.

Admiral Benbow Inn, 905 N. State St. (948-4161), downtown. Large, comfortable rooms, TV, pool. Singles/doubles $36-48. Frequent $29 specials.

Motel 6, (2 locations) 970 I-20 Frontage Rd. (969-3423). Tidy, small rooms. Singles $30. Doubles $36. Also 61455 I-55N, exit 103 (956-8848). Similar rooms closer to downtown. Singles $27.50. Doubles $34.

Parkside Inn, 3720 I-55N, exit 98B (982-1122), close to downtown. Drab, worn rooms with full amenities: pool, cable TV, restaurant/lounge, free local calls. Currently being renovated. Singles $25. Doubles $30.

Timberlake Campgrounds (992-9100), off Old Fanon Rd., stays busy throughout the summer. Pool, video games, pool tables. Tent sites $9; full hookup $14.

FOOD AND NIGHTLIFE

The Iron Horse Grill, 320 W. Pearl St. (355-8419), at Gallatin. A huge converted smokehouse with a waterfall trickling from the 2nd floor. Primarily Tex-Mex ($8-11); steak and seafood more expensive. A pianist accompanies lunch and dinner. Open Mon.-Thurs. 11am-10pm, Fri.-Sat. 11am-11pm.

Primo's, 4330 N. State St. (982-2064), is part of a 40-year Jackson tradition. Burgers and sandwiches $4-8. Open Mon.-Sat. 11am-10pm, Sun. 11am-2:30pm.

The Elite Cafe, 141 E. Capitol (352-5606). Egalitarian lunch spot with great home-made cornbread, rolls, and steaks. Plate lunch specials with 2 vegetables and bread under $4.50. Be prepared to wait in line during lunch rush. Dinner slightly pricier. Open Mon.-Fri. 7am-9:30pm, Sat. 5-9:30pm.

Soak up some music and fun at **Hal & Mal's Restaurant and Oyster Bar,** 200 Commerce St. (948-0888), which entertains in a converted warehouse. Everything from reggae to innovative rock bands plays Friday and Saturday nights. (Restaurant open Mon.-Thurs. 10am-9pm, Fri. 10am-10:30pm, Sat. 5-10:30pm; bar open Fri.-Sat. until 1am. Cover $2-12.) If you'd rather mellow out with the artsy crowd or some college students, stop by **Cups,** 2757 Old Canton Rd. (362-7422), for a cappuccino and conversation. (Open Mon.-Thurs. 7am-11pm, Fri.-Sat. 7am-midnight.)

SIGHTS AND ENTERTAINMENT

Rich in history, Jackson hardly neglects the wonders of the present. Built in 1840, the **Old State Capitol** (359-6920), at the intersection of Capitol and State St., houses an excellent museum of Mississippi's turbulent history, including artifacts from original Native American settlements and documentaries on the Civil Rights Movement. (Open Mon.-Fri. 8am-5pm, Sat. 9:30am-4:30pm, Sun. 12:30-4:30pm. Free.) The **War Memorial Building,** 120 S. State St. (354-7207), depicts a gruesome narrative of American wars and the Mississippians who fought, were honored, and often died in them. (Open Mon.-Fri. 8am-4:30pm. Free.) For a more upbeat presentation on nature and wildlife try the **Mississippi Museum of Natural Science** (354-7303), on Jefferson St. across from the fairground (open Mon.-Fri. 8am-5pm, Sat. 9:30am-4:30pm; free). The Greek Revival **Governor's Mansion,** 300 E. Capitol St. (359-3175), is an enlightening introduction to Mississippi politics (open Mon.-Fri. 9:30-11am). For a more in-depth look at some fine architecture, visit the **Manship House,** 420 E. Fortification (961-4724), a short walk north from the New Capitol. Charles Henry Manship, Jackson's Civil War mayor, built this Gothic Revival "cottage villa," now restored to its 19th-century condition. (Open Tues.-Fri. 9am-4pm, Sat. 1-4pm. Free.) Sherman occupied both Manship and Jackson's oldest house, **The Oaks,** 823 N. Jefferson St. (353-9339), during the siege of the city in 1863. Enjoy a delightful tour by the current loquacious tenant. (Open Tues.-Sat. 10am-4pm, Sun. 1:30-4pm. $2, students $1.)

The state legislature's current home is the beautiful **New State Capitol** (359-3114), at Mississippi and Congress, completed in 1903. A huge restoration project preserved the *beaux arts* grandeur of the building, complete with a gold-leaf-covered eagle perched on the capitol dome, carnival-like colors, and strings of lights which brighten the spacious inside. (Open Mon.-Fri. 8am-5pm. Guided 1-hr. tours Mon.-Fri. at 9am, 10am, 11am, 1:30pm, 2:30pm, and 3:30pm. Free.) For more priceless beauty, **The Mississippi Museum of Art,** 201 E. Pascagoula (960-1515), at Lamar St., has a fabulous collection of Americana and a fun participatory Impression Gallery for kids. (Open Tues.-Sun. noon-5pm. $3, kids $2, students free Tues. and Thurs.) Next door is the **Russell C. Davis Planetarium** (960-1550), considered one of the most stellar worldwide. (Galactic and musical shows Mon.-Fri. at noon, Sat. at 2pm and 8pm, Sun. at 2pm, 4pm, and 8pm. $4, seniors and kids $2.50.)

African-Americans have been some of the main contributors to agricultural progress in this Deep South state since the 18th century. Witness the struggles and achievements of Mississippi's African-Americans at the **Smith-Robertson Museum and Cultural Center,** 528 Bloom St. (960-1457), directly behind the Sun n' Sand Motel. This large, expanding museum once housed the state's first black public school, which *Black Boy* author Richard Wright attended until the eighth grade. Now it displays folk art, photographs, and excellent exhibits on the Civil Rights Movement, particularly the role of African-American women in Mississippi history. (Open Mon.-Fri. 9am-5pm, Sat. 9am-noon, Sun. 2-5pm. $1, kids 50¢.) Every Labor Day, the surrounding neighborhood celebrates African-American culture through art, theater, crafts, and great food at the **Farish Street Festival** (355-ARTS).

The **Agriculture and Forestry Museum/National Agricultural Aviation Museum,** 1150 Lakeland Dr. (354-6113), near the visitors center, does the plant/plane thing. (Open Mon.-Sat. 9am-5pm, Sun. 1-5pm. $3, seniors $2.75, children $1.) The **New Jackson Zoo,** 2918 W. Capitol St. (352-2582), has a fair-sized collection of spots, stripes, paws, and wings. (Open daily 9am-6pm; Labor Day-Memorial Day 9am-5pm. $3.50, seniors and children $1.75.) The ever-blooming **Mynelle Gardens,** 4736 Clinton Blvd. (960-1894 or 960-1814), relaxes the mind with its fragrant beauty. (Call for hrs.; $2, kids 50¢.)

For a different perspective on southern history and culture, take a trip to the **Museum of the Southern Jewish Experience** (362-6357 or 885-6042), on the grounds of the UAHC Henry S. Jacobs Camp in Utica, 40 mi. south of Jackson. (Open for tours by appointment. $3, seniors and children $1.50.)

■■■ VICKSBURG

Started as a mission by Rev. Newit Vick in 1814, Vicksburg is best known for its role in the Civil War. President Abraham Lincoln called this town the "key," and maintained that the war "can never be brought to a close until that key is in our pocket." Its verdant hills and prime Mississippi River location proved extremely strategic for the Confederate forces, though not strategic enough; the "Gibraltar of the South" fell to Union forces on July 4, 1863, after valiant resistance to a 47-day bombardment. Although the loss of this critical river city augured death for the Confederacy, the city itself proved more buoyant. Although the siege devastated the area, today Vicksburg has put its trying history to good use, welcoming visitors to recapture and relive the battle through historic homes, salvaged ships, and restored battlefields.

Practical Information The **Tourist Information Center** (636-9421 or 800-221-3536), across the street from the park, has many pamphlets with discount coupons for area hotels and restaurants, as well as copies of *The Newcomer's Guide* and *Southland Explorer.* (Open daily 8am-5pm; in winter 9am-4pm.) Unfortunately, you'll need a car to see most of Vicksburg—the bus station, the information center, downtown, and the far end of the sprawling military park are at the city's four extremes. The **Greyhound** station (636-1230) is inconveniently located at 1295 S. Frontage Rd. (open daily 7am-8:30pm). **Crisis Hotline** (800-222-8000), and the **Rape and Sexual Assault Service** (638-0031) are both 24 hrs.

Vicksburg's **post office:** (636-1822) on U.S. 61 at Pemberton Blvd. (open Mon.-Fri. 8:30am-5pm, Sat. 9am-noon); **ZIP code:** 39180; **area code:** 601.

THE SOUTH

Accommodations, Food, and Nightlife Inexpensive accommodations are easily found in Vicksburg, except over the July Fourth weekend, when the military park's war reenactment brings thousands of tourists and inflated hotel rates. The **Hillcrest Motel,** 40 Hwy. 80E (638-1491), has a pool and rooms with plastic furniture. (Singles $24, doubles $28.) Most hotels are near the park; don't expect to stay downtown, unless you choose the **Dixiana Motel,** 4033 Washington St. (636-9876). (Rooms $25-35.) The **Beachwood Motel,** 4449 Rte. 80E (636-2271), has no pool but offers cable and newly furnished rooms. (Singles $30, doubles $35.) **The Vicksburg Battlefield Campground,** 4407 I-20 Frontage Rd. (636-9946), has a pool, bathrooms, and laundry accompanying small, hilly sites.

While downtown, chow down at the **Burger Village,** 1220 Washington St. (638-0202),with good meals under $5 (open Mon.-Thurs. 9am-6pm, Fri.-Sat. 9am-7pm). The **New Orleans Café,** 1100 Washington St. (638-8182), serves mouth-watering sandwiches for under $6, delectable Cajun specialties, seafood, and more. (Specials $6-16. Popular with the locals. Open Mon.-Thurs. 11am-10pm, Fri.-Sat. 11am-2am.) On the weekends, the café's **Other Side Lounge** is a popular nightspot with live bands (open Fri.-Sat. 5:30pm-2am). Across the street is **Miller's Still Lounge,** 1101 Washington St. (638-8661), a real Southern watering hole with live entertainment Thurs.-Sun. (Open Mon.-Sat. 3pm-2am. No cover.)

Sights Markers of combat sites and prominent memorials riddle the grass-covered 1700-acre **Vicksburg National Military Park** (636-0583; 800-221-3536 out-of-state) that blockades the eastern and northern edges of the city. If possible, drive to the battlefield, museums, and cemetery, east of town on Clay St. at exit 4B off I-20. ($4 per car, $2 per person on bus, kids under 16 free; tickets are valid for 7 days.) The visitors center at the entrance provides maps that detail a brief history of the siege as well as prominent sights along the 16-mi. loop. Take a guide with you on a two-hour driving tour ($20) of the military park, or drive the trail yourself. (Open summer daily 8am-5pm.) Within the park, visit the **National Cemetery** and the **U.S.S. Cairo Museum** (636-2199): The museum's centerpiece is the restored Union iron-clad gunboat *U.S.S. Cairo,* the first vessel sunk by an electronically detonated mine. Check around the *Cairo* for the 100-yr.-old artifacts preserved within it when the ship sank in the Yazoo River. (Open daily 9:30am-6pm; off-season 8am-5pm. Free with park admission.) Learn more about the battle at Vicksburg by catching **"Vanishing Glory,"** 717 Clay St. (634-1863), a multi-media theatrical panorama. (Shows daily on the hr. 10am-5pm. $3.50, ages 6-18 $2.) Preserving a more comprehensive history of the time when this house was divided, the **Old Courthouse Museum,** 1008 Cherry St. (636-0741), presides over the town center, 3 mi. from the park's entrance. Many consider it one of the South's finest Civil War museums, with everything from newspapers printed on wallpaper to Jefferson Davis's tie to an interpretation of Klan activities. (Open spring and summer Mon.-Sat. 8:30am-5pm, Sun. 1:30-5pm; fall and winter Mon.-Sat. 8:30am-4:30pm, Sun. 1:30-4:30pm. $2, seniors $1.50, under 18 $1.) Next door, **Toys and Soldiers, A Museum,** 1100 Cherry St. (638-1986), offers 32,000 toy soldiers from all over the world. (Open Mon.-Sat. 9am-4:30pm, Sun. 1:30-4:30pm. $2, kids $1.50, families $5.)

The Battle of Vicksburg was not alone in focusing its energies on the magnificent Mississippi River. A free tour, either by yourself or guided, of the **U.S. Army Engineer Waterways Experiment Station,** 3909 Halls Ferry Rd. (634-2502), the largest in the nation, explains the role of the Mississippi River in urban and rural development and the functions of locks and dams. The entire floor of one room is a scale model of the dam system of Niagara Falls. (Open daily 7:45am-4:15pm, guided tours at 10am and 2pm. Free.) For a taste of the lighter side of Vicksburg history, two blocks away, lie the **Museum of Coca-Cola History and Memorabilia** and the **Biedenharn Candy Company,** 1107 Washington St. (638-6514), which first bottled the soft drink. Though the two-room museum displays Coke memorabilia from as far back as 1894, the admission fee seems steep for 10 min. it takes to admire the artifacts. Coke floats and over 100 different Coca-Cola items are sold. (Open Mon.-Sat. 9am-5pm, Sun. 1:30-4:30pm. $1.75, kids under 12 $1.25. Disabled access.)

Escape from the downtown heat during a walk along the well-preserved tree-lined streets showing off several fine antebellum homes. The **Duff Green Mansion,** 1114 First East St. (638-6968), hosted numerous social events before it was converted into a war-time hospital during the siege of Vicksburg. (Open daily 9am-5pm. $5, kids 5-12 $3.) The **Martha Vick House,** 1300 Grove St. (638-7036), was the home of an unmarried daughter of Reverend Vick, founder of the city. (Open Mon.-Sat. 9am-5pm. $5, kids under 12 free.) Slightly farther away, **McRaven,** 1445 Harrison St. (636-1663), was once featured in *National Geographic* as a "time capsule of the South." (Open Mon.-Sat. 9am-5pm, Sun. 10am-5pm. 1½-hr. guided tours $5, seniors $4.50, ages 12-18 $3, ages 6-11 $2.50.)

Drive south on Washington St. to the **Louisiana Circle,** a secluded overview serving truly breathtaking vistas of the great Mississippi River. For a glimpse of Americana, visit **Holidays Washateria and Lanes,** 2900 Clay St. (636-9682), near the park entrance on Rte. 80 across from the KFC. It's a bowling alley, pool room, and laundromat all in one! Enjoy yourself and clean your socks at the same time. (Open Sun.-Thurs. 3-11pm, Fri. 3pm-midnight, Sat. 10am-2am.)

If billiards don't get your juices, maybe riverboat gambling will (watch your pockets, budget travelers). Part of a growing national fad, Vicksburg is home to the **Isle of Capri,** 3990 Washington Blvd. (800-THE ISLE), a "player's paradise" open 24 hrs., and **Harrah's,** 1310 I Saw It On Mulberry St.

MISSISSIPPI DELTA

■■■ NATCHEZ

Just before the Civil war, Natchez preened as one of the wealthiest settlements on the Mississippi. Of the thirteen millionaires in Mississippi at the time, eleven built their cotton plantation estates here. The custom then was to fashion the home on the Mississippi side of the River, and till the soil on the Louisiana side. Although the cotton-based economy has waned, nowadays Ol' Man River continues to bring wealth into Natchez's arms in the shape of floating casinos off the shoreline.

Practical Information The **Mississippi Welcome Center,** 370 Sergeant Prentiss Dr. (442-5849), housed in an antique-filled home, does its thing southern style—no comfort is missed. Pick up maps, discount books, suggested tours, and even have them book your hotel! (Open daily 8am-7pm; in winter 8am-5pm.)

Make connections to Vicksburg ($13.50) and Baton Rouge ($19.50) at the **Natchez Bus Station,** 103 Lower Woodville Rd. (445-5291; open daily 8am-5:30pm). In-town transportation is available at the **Natchez Ford Rental** (445-0076), with rates of $38 per day plus 20¢ per mi. ($250 deposit or major credit card required, must be at least 21 years old). The **Natchez Bicycling Center,** 334 Main St. (446-7794), rents wheels. ($7.50 for 1-3 hrs., $10 for 3-5 hrs., $14 for all day. Must be at least 14 years old accompanied by an adult or 18 unaccompanied. Open Tues.-Fri. 10am-3pm, Sat. 10am-4pm. Other times by appointment.) Natchez's **post office:** 214 N. Canal St. (442-4361; open Mon.-Fri. 8:30am-5pm, Sat. 10am-2pm); **ZIP code:** 39120; **area code:** 601.

Accommodations and Food The most economical way to visit Natchez is as a daytrip from either Vicksburg, MS, or Baton Rouge, LA. If you prefer to stay in Natchez, **Scottish Inns** (442-9141 or 800-251-1962), on U.S. 61, has fully furnished rooms with newly painted facilities and a pool. (Singles $28, doubles $35.) **Days Inn** (800-524-4892), has singles ($42) and doubles ($47). Call for possible discounts. If you want to go whole hog and stay in a plantation home, rest easy at the **Wensel House,** 206 Washington St. (9445-8577), for $50, breakfast included. Make B&B reservations through the welcome center. If you'd prefer a secluded **campground,** head for **Natchez State Park** (442-2658), less than 10 mi. north of Natchez on U.S. 61 in Stanton. (Full hookups $10, primitive camping $6. Watch for signs.)

Satisfying your stomach is less costly; inexpensive cafes and diners abound in Natchez. **Cock of the Walk,** 200 N. Broadway (446-8920), has certainly earned its title and stature with spicy catfish and baked potatoes. (Catfish fillet, $9. Open Mon.-Thurs. 5-9pm, Fri.-Sat. 5-10pm, Sun. 5-8pm.) **Local Color,** 112 N. Commerce St. (442-6886), has po'boys ($4-7) and other deli-style sandwiches (open daily 10am-10pm). At **Fat Mama's Tamales,** 500 S. Canal St. (442-4548), Cajun boudin, chili, and peanut butter pie are served in a log cabin. Try a "knock-you-naked" margarita ($3.25). (Open Mon.-Wed. 11am-7pm, Thurs.-Sat. 11am-9pm, Sun. noon-5pm.)

Sights Open for public tours, the manorial restorations of the "white gold" days are under the supervision of the efficient **Natchez Pilgrimage Tours,** P.O. Box 347 (446-6631; 800-647-6742), on the corner of Canal St. and State St. Pick up free tour schedules, maps, pamphlets, and a guidebook about the homes and their histories ($5). (Open daily 8:30am-5pm.) Cotton tycoons acquired these homes as early as their 13th birthdays. Although tickets can be purchased at individual houses for $5, Pilgrimage Tours offers packages of 3 houses for $14, 4 houses for $17, and 5 houses for $19 (children always ½ price).

The largest octagonal house in America, **Longwood,** 140 Lower Woodville Rd. (442-5193), astounds visitors with its creative, elaborate decor and imaginative floor plan designed to be an "Arabian palace." The six-story edifice remains unfinished because the builders, hired from the North, abandoned work at the beginning of the Civil War so that they could fight for the Union. They never returned, and their discarded tools and undisturbed crates still lie as they were left. (Open daily 9am-5pm, tours every 20 min.) **Stanton Hall,** 401 High St. (442-6282), on the other hand, arose under the direction of local Natchez architects and artisans. Completed in 1857, this mansion regales the visitor with French mirrors, Italian marble mantels, and specially-cut chandeliers (open daily 9am-4:30pm, tours every ½ hr).

For centuries before the rise of such opulence, the Natchez Indians flourished on this fertile land. The arrival of the French incited warfare in the 1720s and 1730s; French military successes were the death knell for the thriving Natchez community. Their memory lives on in the town's name and at the **Grand Village of the Natchez Indians,** 400 Jefferson Davis Blvd. (446-6502), where stupendously large burial mounds dominate green, grassy fields. According to historical documentation, when the Great Sun, or chief, of the tribe died, his wife and others who so desired were strangled and buried also. The house of the chief's successor was supposed to sit atop the mound. A museum documenting the history and culture of the Natchez sits there today. (Open Mon.-Sat. 9am-5pm, Sun. 1:30-5pm. Free.)

Historic **Jefferson College** (442-2901), off U.S. 61 near U.S. 84E, stands 6 mi. east of Natchez as the first educational institution in the Mississippi Territory. Incorporated in 1802, the peaceful grounds and buildings are the site where Aaron Burr, Vice-President under Thomas Jefferson, was tried for treason in 1807. Fortunately for Burr, the judges couldn't be found for sentencing, and Burr escaped in the night. (He was later acquitted in Virginia.) (Grounds open sunrise-sunset, buildings open Mon.-Sat. 9am-5pm, Sun. 1-5pm. Free.)

■■■ HAVE IT OUT ON HWY. 61

Winding its way through small-town Mississippi and the Delta, **Highway 61** is a sunscorched stretch richer in history than scenery. This **"blues route"** was the road that brought the blues to Memphis. Blues greats such as Bessie Smith, W.C. Handy, Muddy Waters, and John Lee Hooker rolled down this road to stardom.

Clarksdale, once the home of "Father of the Blues" W.C. Handy, now pays tribute to his memory with the **Delta Blues Museum,** 114 Delta Ave. (624-4461). The museum is chock full of photos, paintings, recordings, and books of blues artists. In the corner stands a life-size replica of Muddy Waters. (Open Mon.-Fri. 9am-5pm, Sat. 10am-5pm. Free, but please donate.) Clarksdale also supports a rollicking **blues festival** (624-4461) during the first week of August. Otherwise mosey down to one of Clarksdale's **juke joints** which focus on music above everything else. **Red's South End Disco** (627-9366) is on the corner of Sunflower and Martin Luther King St. Don't bother looking for a sign, it's the inside that counts. Otherwise try **Mr. Johnnie's,** 347 Issaquena (637-3392), to hear that twang and shake ya thang.

Greenville is another home of the blues as you head south from Clarksdale into the heart of the Delta. From Thursday until Saturday during the third weekend in September, Greenville has its own **blues and jazz festival.** Why not get things started at the **Jim Henson Museum** (686-2687), at the intersection of Rte. 82 and S. Deer Creek, 7 mi. east in Leland. The late great Jim Henson was born in Greenville and his fuzzy, original creations can be viewed here. (Open Mon.-Fri. 10am-4pm, Sat.-Sun. 1-5pm. Not open Labor Day-Memorial Day. Free, but please donate.)

■■■ BILOXI AND THE MISSISSIPPI COAST

For more than a century, Biloxi's shores have served it well—providing sustenance first through the thriving seafood and canning industries and now as "America's Riviera." Today, the gambling industry expands quicker than the roll of the dice, both reinvigorating the local economy and drawing record numbers of fortune-seeking tourists to its flashy floating casinos. Biloxi's picturesque small-town charm still resonates with sun-drenched history; the fine, sandy shores still soothe bathers and swarm with scrumptious seafood. But as Biloxi surfs into the 21st century, it is likely to become famed for its nice dice and hot slots.

Practical Information The **Biloxi Chamber of Commerce,** 1048 Beach Blvd. (374-2717), across from the lighthouse, eagerly aids tourists (open Mon.-Fri. 8:30am-noon and 1-5pm). The **Biloxi Tourist Information Center,** 710 Beach Blvd. (374-3105), is down the street from the bus station (open Mon.-Fri. 8am-5pm, Sat. 9am-5pm, Sun. noon-5pm). For more info contact the **Mississippi Gulf Coast Convention and Visitors Bureau,** 135 Courthouse Rd. (896-6699 or 800-237-9493; open Mon.-Fri. 8am-5pm), or tune your radio to 1490 AM for beach and tourist info.

Getting into and out of Biloxi is rarely problematic; buses service the town well. **Greyhound,** 166 Main St. (436-4335), offers frequent service to New Orleans (8 per day, 2½ hr., $19) and Jackson (2 per day, 4 hr., $31). (Open daily 6:30am-10pm.) **Amtrak,** 860 Esters Blvd. (800-872-7245), is a few blocks from U.S. 90. Trains run 3 times per week to New Orleans ($32) and Los Angeles ($214). (Unstaffed station; call to reserve tickets.) **Coast Area Transit** (896-8080) operates buses (marked "Beachcomber") along the beach on U.S. 90 (Beach Blvd.) from Biloxi to Gulfport. Nine other lines serve the gulf coast area. (Buses operate Mon.-Sat. every 30 min. Board at any intersection. Fare $1, students 75¢, seniors 50¢.) **Casino shuttle buses** will pick you up from anywhere for free to lure you to their den of iniquity. Call 436-RIDE to reach the Gold Shore Casino's shuttle service.

Biloxi's **post office:** 135 Main St. (432-0311), near the bus station (open Mon.-Fri. 8:30am-5pm, Sat. 9am-noon); **ZIP code:** 39530; **area code:** 601.

Accommodations and Food Rooms with a coastal view will cost you a pretty penny, but just a few blocks from the beach (and the casinos, the bus, the train, restaurants, bars, and stores), the brand new **Biloxi International Hostel,** 128 Fayard St. (435-2666), 2 blocks north of Beach Blvd. and east of I-10, welcomes travelers with literally open doors. The spotless and homey accommodations are surpassed only by the incredible warmth of proprietors J.D. and Julie. (Comfy living room, kitchen, laundry. $11 per person. Key deposit $2.) Since hotel/motel prices fluctuate according to complex laws, your best bet for cheap rates is to ask at the visitors center or flip through a current copy of *The Traveler Discount Guide* distributed there. Sun.-Thurs. is cheaper, as is the off-season which runs from Labor Day to Jan.-Feb. About 15 mi. from dowtown, the **Red Creek Colonial Inn** (452-3080 or 800-729-9670) has very comfortable beds furnished with lovely antiques. (Singles $39-59, doubles $49-69.) Take exit 28 south off I-10; make a right onto Red Creek Rd. immediately after the railroad tracks. **Camping** is a less expensive alternative; rates go from $10-15 depending on the season. The most convenient site is the **Biloxi Beach Campground,** 1816 W. Beach Blvd. (432-2755; $12 per site, $17 full hookup, for 2 people; $2 per additional person).

Biloxi swims with seafood restaurants, but they're often pricey. For fried, stuffed crabs ($7.50), or fresh, half-shell oysters ($6 per dozen), sail into **McElroy's Harbor House** (435-5001), in the small craft harbor on Beach Blvd. (open daily 7am-10pm). **Mary Mahoney's** (374-0163), a 24-hr. sidewalk cafe at the Magnolia Mall on Beach Blvd., offers reasonable and filling po'boys ($4-6) and sandwiches ($3-5).

Sights and Activities

Sights and Activities Although the 26-mi. snow-white, sandy beaches of Biloxi today sport a few too many souvenir shops, the "natural beauty" of this—the longest man-made beach in the world—still attracts throngs of sun worshipers and beachcombers. If jet skis and sand volleyball sound too hectic, travel west on I-90 toward **Gulfport's** sparsely populated beaches with views of lovely historic homes. The Spanish moss hanging from the oak trees along the road (actually neither Spanish nor moss, but a relative of the pineapple plant) and the old **antebellum mansions** in the **historic district** also merit more than a glance. Between Biloxi and Gulfport you'll find the garden and grounds of **Beauvoir,** 2244 Beach Blvd. (388-1313), at Beauvoir Rd. Jefferson Davis's last home, it is now a shrine in his honor, containing a Confederate Museum, a Davis Family Museum, and a Confederate Veterans Cemetery with the tomb of the Unknown Confederate Soldier. Each October, Beauvoir is also the site of a Confederate boot camp simulation, complete with drills. (Open daily 9am-5pm. $4.75, kids $2.50.) Also along the shoreline is the **Biloxi Lighthouse** (435-6293), the South's first cast-metal lighthouse; it has shone since 1848 and is now seasonally open for tours. The visitors center offers a free, self-guided **Historic Heart of Biloxi Walking Tour** (about 1 hr.). Amble through quiet streets to the **Tullis-Toledano Manor,** 360 Beach Blvd. (435-6293), a summer retreat for wealthy New Orleans cotton merchants in the 19th century (open Mon.-Fri. 10am-noon and 1-5pm; last tour 4:30pm).

Take a spin through the **Mississippi Museum of Art, Gulf Coast,** 136 George E. Ohr St. (374-5547), off Beach Blvd., and check out the bizarre yet functional pottery of Ohr, the Mad Potter of Biloxi (open Tues.-Sat. 10am-5pm, Sun. 1-5pm; free).

To learn more about Biloxi's fishy past, visit the **Seafood Industry Museum** (435-6320), at Point Cadet Plaza; turn off U.S. 90 onto Myrtle Rd. at the foot of the Biloxi-Ocean Springs Bridge. The museum traces Biloxi's growth from a French colony to its current "Seafood Capital" status. (Open Mon.-Sat. 9am-5pm. $2.50, seniors and kids 6-16 $1.50.) Drop by the **Farmer's Market** next door (open Tues.-Thurs. 6am-6pm) or try to catch your own shrimp, horseshoe crabs, and other marine life in the "touch tank" at the **J.L. Scott Marine Education Center and Aquarium,** 115 Beach Blvd. (374-5550), next to the Isle of Capri Casino. The largest public aquarium in the state, the center's cynosure is a 42,000-gallon Gulf of Mexico tank in which sharks, sea turtles, eels, and larger residents frolic and feed. (Open Mon.-Sat. 9am-4pm. $3, seniors $2, kids 3-17 $1.50.)

Evening brings cool breezes off the gulf and beaches ripe for moonlit strolls. Yet new destinations, namely the recently legalized "floating" casinos, interrupt the sand. Starting with the **Grand Casino,** 265 Beach Blvd. (800-WIN-2-WIN), in Gulfport, these gaming hotspots moved east along Beach Blvd. with the **Presidents Casino,** 2110 Beach Blvd. (388-7737), next, then **Biloxi Belle** (800-BILOXI-7),

Casino Magic, and the **Isle of Capri** (800-THE-ISLE). All are open 24 hrs. for those 21 and over. A little tamer, and a lot easier on the pocket, the **Silver Screen,** 2650 Beach Blvd., shows second-run films for $1, $2 after 6pm, and even offers a movie and all-you-can-eat pizza for $5. For show times call 388-9200.

Gulf Islands National Seashore The tranquil Gulf Islands are the natural antidote to Biloxi's wheelin' and dealin'. The Islands are protected seashore—by alligators mostly, seeing how the area is a salt marsh. Swimming is forbidden, but the fishing is fine. Birdwatchers will cry fowl at the sight of ospreys and blue herons. **Camping** in the park costs $10, $14 for water and wattage. The U.S. Park Service can be found on **West Ship Island.**

  Ship Island floats 12 mi. off the Mississippi Coast, far enough out to sea to exempt it from federal bans on liquor and gambling in the 1920s. Crystal blue waters and white sandy beaches are the lures today, as visitors swim, fish, and explore. Defending the island is **Fort Massachusetts** (875-0821), which served as both a Confederate and Union command center at different points during the Civil War (free). Ship Island has had two parts, East and West, since it was sliced in two by Hurricane Camille in 1969. To get to West Ship Island, where overnight camping is prohibited, take the Skrmetta family **ferry service** that leaves from Biloxi's **Point Cadet Marina** (432-2197), Beach Blvd. near Isle of Capri (2 ferries per day leave for the island at 9am and noon; arriving back in Biloxi 4 and 7pm; 70min.; round-trip $12, kids $6). A different kind of cruise is the **Biloxi Shrimping Trip** (374-5718). The *Sailfish* departs from the Biloxi Small Craft Harbor at 9am, 11am, and noon, giving passengers an opportunity to see what trawling between the Biloxi shore and nearby Deer Island will yield ($9, kids $5. Call for reservations.)

 # Louisiana

Cross the Mississippi into Louisiana and you'll enter a state markedly different from its Southern neighbors. Here empires, races, and cultures mix in a unique and spicy jambalaya. The battlefields and old forts that liberally pepper the state—some dating back to the original French and Spanish settlers—illustrate the bloody succession of Native American, French, Spanish, and American acquisition. Early Catholic settlers spawned the annual celebrations of Mardi Gras which flavor every February with festivities and parades throughout the state. Louisiana also cooks with Acadians ("Cajuns"), descendants of French Nova Scotians. Exiled by the British in 1755, Cajuns created a culture that contributes the Creole dialect, zydeco music, swampy folklore, and spicy cuisine that enliven the simmering, lazy Southern atmosphere. African-Americans, brought here as plantation laborers, became an integral part of this culture. The French tolerance in antebellum southern Louisiana combined with a cosmopolitan sensibility to produce a black aristocracy unique in the old South.

PRACTICAL INFORMATION
  Capital: Baton Rouge.
  State Travel Office, P.O. Box 94291, Capitol Station, Baton Rouge 70804 (800-633-6970). Open Mon.-Fri. 9am-5pm. **Office of State Parks,** P.O. Box 1111, Baton Rouge 70821. Open Mon.-Fri. 9am-5pm.
  Time Zone: Central (1 hr. behind Eastern). **Postal Abbreviation:** LA
  Sales Tax: 4%.

■■■ NEW ORLEANS

New Orleans is a country unto itself. Originally explored by the French, *La Nouvelle Orleans* changed ownership secretly to the Spanish in 1762 (the citizens didn't realize until 4 years later). Shortly after the American Revolution, Spain returned the city to France just in time for Thomas Jefferson to purchase it in 1803. N'Awlins stayed faithful and in 1812 Louisiana was admitted to the Union. Multiculturalism rules here as Spanish courtyards, Victorian verandas, Acadian jambalaya, Caribbean Gumbo, and French beignets mix and mingle. Don't try to place the accent of its people—it's a combination found nowhere else. Similarly unique is internationally-renowned New Orleans jazz, a fusion of African rhythms and modern brass.

In the 19th century, the Red-Light District known as "Storyville" flared. Today, New Orleans, with a legal drinking age of 18, is still a city that loves to party. Come late February there's no escaping the month-long celebration of Mardi Gras, the apotheosis of the city's already festive atmosphere. Anxious to accrue as much sin as spirit and flesh will allow before Lent, perfect strangers, in all stages of undress, embrace each other with the "purpose" of acquiring multi-colored beads and doubloons. The "city that care forgot" promenades, shuffles, sings, and swigs until midnight of Mardi Gras itself. Afterwards, the soulful jazz melodies play on, comforting those who have forsaken drunken cavorting for the next 40 long and Lenten days.

PRACTICAL INFORMATION

Emergency: 911.

Visitor Information: To plan your vacation before you leave home, write or call the very helpful **New Orleans/Louisiana Tourist Center,** 529 St. Ann, (568-5661), Jackson Square, in the French Quarter. Free city and walking tour maps. Open daily 10am-6pm. **Greater New Orleans Tourist and Convention Commission,** 1520 Sugar Bowl Dr., New Orleans 70112 (566-5011), on the main floor of the Superdome. Open Mon.-Fri. 8:30am-5pm.

Traveler's Aid: 846 Barone St. (525-8726). Assists stranded people by providing temporary shelter, food, and counseling. Come early for the best service. Open Mon.-Fri. 8am-4pm.

Airport: Moisant International (464-0831), 15 mi. west of the city. Served by the major domestic airlines as well as by larger Latin American carriers. Cab fare to the Quarter, $21 for 2 people. **Louisiana Transit Authority** (737-9611; office open 4am-6pm) runs between the airport and downtown at Elk and Tulane every hour for $1.10 in exact change (travel time approx. 45 min. to downtown). Pick-up on the upper level, near the exit ramp.

Amtrak: Good morning America, how are ya! (528-1631 or 800-872-7245) at Union Passenger Terminal, 1001 Loyola Ave., a 10-min. walk to Canal St. via Elk. *See Mileage Chart.* Station open 24 hrs.; ticket office open Sun.-Thurs. 6am-11pm, Fri.-Sat. 6am-8:30pm. Dontcha ya' know me, I'm your native son.

Greyhound: (525-9371), also at Union Passenger Terminal. *See Mileage Chart.* Open 24 hrs.

Public Transport: Regional Transit Authority (RTA), 700 Plaza Dr. (569-2700), has bus schedules and transit info. Office open Mon.-Fri. 8:30am-5pm. Phone line provides 24-hr. route information. All buses pass by Canal St., at the edge of the French Quarter. Major buses and streetcars run 24 hrs. Fare $1, transfers 10¢, disabled and elderly 40¢. 1- and 3-day passes are also available.

Those with an eastern accent: It's not pronounced (NU or-lEEEEns); work on (NU-or-lens — like a *new* contact *lens*).

Taxi: United Cabs 522-9771. **Checker Yellow Cabs,** 943-2411. **Classic Cabs,** 835-CABS. Base fare $1.70, each additional mi. $1.

Car Rental: Budget, 1317 Canal (467-2277), and 4 other locations. $37 per day. 100 free mi. Open daily 7:30am-5:30pm. Airport branch only closed 1-5am. Must be 25 with credit card. Reservations suggested.

Bike Rental: Michael's, 622 Frenchman (945-9505), a few blocks west of the Quarter. $3.50 per hr., $12.50 per day. Weekly rates. Open Mon.-Sat. 10am-7pm, Sun. 10am-5pm. Car racks available. Must have major credit card for deposit.

New Orleans

Help Lines: Crisis Line, 523-2673. **Rape Hotline,** 483-8888. Both open 24 hrs.
Post Office: 701 Loyola Ave. (589-1111 or 589-1112), near the Union Passenger
Terminal. Open Mon.-Fri. 8am-6pm, Sat. 8am-noon. **ZIP code:** 70113.
Area Code: 504.

It's easy to get lost in New Orleans even though it is fairly small. The main streets of
the city follow the curve of the **Mississippi River.** Directions from locals will show
watery influences—north is lakeside, referring to **Lake Ponchartrain,** and south is
riverside. Uptown means west, up river; downtown means down river. There are
many one-way streets, and drivers must sometimes make U-turns to cross intersections. The major tourist area is the small **French Quarter (Vieux Carré),** bounded
by the Mississippi River, **Canal Street, Esplanade Avenue,** and **Rampart Street.**
Streets in the French Quarter follow a grid pattern; traveling there on foot is easy.
The **Garden District** grows west of downtown. Buses to all parts of the city pass by
Canal St. at the edge of the Quarter.

Parts of New Orleans are unsafe, particularly the tenement areas directly to the
north of the French Quarter and those directly northwest of Lee Circle. Even quaint-
looking side streets in the Quarter can be dangerous at night—stick to busy, well-lit
thoroughfares and try to look as little like a tourist as possible (don't wear shorts).
Take a cab back to your lodgings when returning late at night from the Quarter.

ACCOMMODATIONS

Finding inexpensive yet decent accommodations in the French Quarter is as difficult as finding a sober person on Mardi Gras. But then, the French Quarter isn't the

only happenin' place in the city. Several **hostels** dot the area, as do **bed and break-fasts** near the Garden District, which often cater to the young and almost penniless. About the only way to get accommodations for Mardi Gras is to reserve them a year in advance. **Jazzfest** held at the end of April, attracts 4000 musicians worldwide and makes budget rooms scarce. Pay close attention to warnings under individual lodgings regarding the safety of its location; avoid areas where you feel at all uncomfortable, and do not walk around alone at night anywhere in this city. During peak times, proprietors will rent out any extra space—be sure you know what you're paying for.

Marquette House New Orleans International Hostel (HI-AYH), 2253 Carondelet St. (523-3014), provides the cleanest hostelling experience in New Orleans. Call to inquire about reservations since a recent fire burnt half of their main building. 196 new, comfy beds. Clean, homey kitchens, study rooms, no lockout. No alcohol permitted; smoking only in the courtyard; no curfew. Exceptionally quiet for a hostel. $12.50, nonmembers $15.50. Linens $2.50. Key deposit $5.

India House, 124 S. Lopez St. (821-1904), entertains as it accommodates. The decorated rooms may lack luxury and order, but if you've come to New Orleans for its bawdy reputation, this bohemian haunt is party central. The common room, kitchen, and dining areas are supplemented with a bar/coffee shop and pool. $10 per night. Also two Cajun cabins ($25) complete with Spanish moss, and a tiny mock-swamp with two very real (baby) alligators. Key deposit $5, free linens, no curfew or lockout. Best to walk in groups at night.

Longpre House (RNA), 1726 Prytania St. (501-4440), a block off the streetcar route. 25-min. walk from the Quarter. Attracts travelers with relaxed atmosphere in a 150-year-old house. Free coffee. Check-in 8am-10pm. Dorm rooms $12 per person. Singles and doubles $35 with shared bath, $40 for private scrub-a-dub.

St. Vincent's Guest House, 1507 Magazine (566-1515), same management as Prytania Inn. This magnificent, renovated, 19th-century building was formerly an orphanage. Notice their photos on the wall near the entrance. Book in advance. Singles $30-45, doubles $35-55. Rooms discounted in off-season.

St. Charles Guest House, 1748 Prytania St. (523-6556), in a serene neighborhood near the Garden District and St. Charles streetcar. Free breakfast. Lovely pool, sunbathing deck, and grounds. Backpackers's singles $25, doubles $50.

Hotel LaSalle, 1113 Canal St. (523-5831 or 800-521-9450), 4 blocks from Bourbon St. downtown. Attractive lobby with coffee around the clock on an antique sideboard. Ample rooms and free movies. Laundry 50-75¢. Singles $29, with bath $46. Doubles $34, with bath $51. Reservations recommended.

Old World Inn, 1330 Prytania St. (566-1330). Multi-colored carpeting and walls covered with paintings create a slightly tacky but comfortable atmosphere. Complimentary continental breakfast. Singles from $30. Doubles from $45.

Prytania Inn, 1415 Prytania St. (566-1515), includes 3 restored 19th-century homes about 5 blocks from each other. Breakfast $5; served Mon.-Fri. 8-10am, Sat.-Sun. until 10:30am). Reasonable prices, multilingual staff (German, French, Italian, Spanish, and Japanese). Singles $30-45, doubles $35-55; rooms are discounted in off-season. Double check reservations. Book in advance for the peaks.

Cheap motels line the seedy and sometimes *very* scary Tulane Ave. off I-10. Public buses run along the length of the street, but a car is recommended for safety. *Lone travelers and women may feel uncomfortable in this area.* One of the best choices is **Rose Inn,** 3522 Tulane Ave. (484-7611), exit 232 off I-10, 4 blocks from S. Carrollton, with older but spacious rooms. (Pool. Extra charge for phone. Singles $25. Doubles $28.) Another option for lads and lassies is the **Scottish Inn Motel,** 6613 West Bank Expressway (347-1502 or 800-251-1962), in Marrero. (Standard rooms with usable bathrooms. New management is renovating. Fenced-in pool, HBO, free adult movies (quit lookin' up me kilt!). Singles $22, doubles $25.)

French Quarter

CAMPING

The several campgrounds near New Orleans are tough to reach via public transportation. Try to enjoy Louisiana's beautiful forests, lakes, and bayous anyway, if only to be voracious. **Golden Pelican passes,** available at state parks, allow you to stay in state campgrounds for $6 per night ($30 for Louisianians, $50 for others).

Bayou Segnette State Park (736-7777), Westbank Expressway at Drake (flashing yellow light), 7 mi. from the French Quarter. RTA transport available. Cabins on the bayou $65 for up to 8 people, terrific vista and wave pool included. Big, grassy campsites with water and electricity $12.

KOA West, 11129 Jefferson Hwy., River Ridge 70123 (467-1792), off I-10. RTA bus transport available. Pool, laundry facilities. Bathrooms new and very clean. Tent sites for 2 $22. Full hookup $26 for 2 people. Shuttle to French Quarter $3.

St. Bernard State Park, P.O. Box 534, Violet 70092 (682-2101), 14 mi. southeast of New Orleans. Take Rte. 46 south and go right on Rte. 39. Nearest public transport to New Orleans ½ mi. away. Registration til 8pm, weekends 10pm. Sites $12.

Willow Mar Travel Park, 10910 Chef Menteur Hwy. (242-6611; 800-788-6787 outside LA), 3 mi. east of the junction of I-10 and U.S. 90 (Chef Menteur Hwy.). Near public transport into the city. Pool, showers, and laundry facilities. Sites $12, full hookup $16.

Parc D'Orleans Travel Park, 7676 Chef Menteur Hwy. (241-3167 or 800-535-2598), near the intersection of U.S. 90 and I-10. 71 small but orderly sites. Pool. Sites $14 with water and electricity. Full hookup $16.

FOOD

You will find more restaurants per capita in New Orleans than in any major city in the world outside of Paris. Acadian refugees, Spaniards, Italians, African-Americans, and Native Americans have all contributed to the fray. Here, the Acadian hot, spicy, **Cajun** culinary style—like a good stew—has a bit of everything thrown in. Cajun cult members gather to worship the "holy trinity": bell peppers, onions, and celery. **Jambalaya**—a jumble of rice, shrimp, oysters, and ham or chicken mixed with spices—and the African stew-like gumbo grace practically every menu in New Orleans. A southern breakfast of grits, eggs, bacon, and corn bread will satisfy even the biggest of eaters. Also, sample the regional delights—**Creole,** a mixture of Spanish, French, and Carribean cuisine is famous for its red beans and rice, seafood **po'boys** (a french-bread sandwich filled with fried oysters and shrimp), and shrimp or crawfish **étouffé.** And you may *not* leave New Orleans without dining on **beignets** and **café au lait** (or chocolate milk) at the world-famous, 1862 **Café du Monde.**

If the eats in the Quarter prove too trendy, touristy, or tough on your budget, take a jaunt down **Magazine St.,** where cafes, antique stores, and book fairs abound, or hop on the St. Charles streetcar to the **Tulane University** area for some late-night grub and collegiate character.

Cool off in the summer months and "air condition your tummy" with a snow-blitz sundae from **Hansen's Snow-Blitz Sweet Shop,** 481 Tchoupitoulas St. (891-9788), where if the 50¢- or $1-size cups can't quench your need for a "Hansen's fix," then trash-can-size servings are available for only $200. Always expect a line. (Open Tues.-Fri. and Sun. 3-8pm.) Indulge in **Creole pralines** (90¢); some of the best and cheapest bake at **Laura's Candies,** 600 Conti (525-3880) and 155 Royal St. (525-3886; open daily 9am-7pm). The **French Market,** between Decatur and N. Peters St. on the east side of the French Quarter, sells pricey fresh vegetables. The grocery stores on Decatur St. have the rest of the fixins' you'll need for a picnic.

French Quarter

Acme Oyster House, 724 Iberville (522-5973). Slurp fresh oysters shucked before your eyes (6 for $3.75, 12 for $6.50) or sit at the red checkered tables for a good ol' po'boy ($5-6). Open Mon.-Sat. 11am-10pm, Sun. noon-7pm.

Quarter Scene Restaurant, 900 Dumaine (522-6533). This elegant cornerside cafe serves delicious salads and seafood and pasta entrees ($6-13) along with 31 flavors of ½-lb. burgers ($4-5.25). A tasty surprise is the *Dumaine* ($4), a peanut butter and banana sandwich topped with nuts and honey. Open 24 hrs., except Tues. closes at 11:30pm, reopening Wed. at 7:30am.

Café du Monde (587-0835), French Market at the intersection of Decatur and St. Ann St. The consummate people-watching paradise since 1862. Drink café au lait (90¢) and down perfectly prepared hot beignets with powdered sugar (3 for 75¢). Open 24 hrs.

Central Grocery, 923 Decatur St. (523-1620). Try an authentic **muffuletta** at the place that invented them. Half $3.75 serves 1, whole $7 serves 2 or some big ole guy. Open daily 8am-5:30pm.

Olde N'awlins Cookery, 729 Conti (529-3663), between Bourbon and Royal. Mouth-watering crawfish étouffé $15.50, entrees $14-19 but well worth it. Sincere turtle soup $3.50. Open daily 11am-11pm.

Gumbo Shop, 630 St. Peter (525-1486). Sit under a broad-leafed pam and savor a bowl of seafood okra gumbo or chicken andouille gumbo (both $5.50). Entrees $5.50-15. Expect a line. Recipes available. Open daily 11am-11pm.

Croissant d'Or, 617 Ursuline St. (524-4663). In a historic building that was the first ice cream parlor in New Orleans. Delicious, reasonably-priced French pastries (75¢-$2). Courtyard seating. Open daily 7am-5pm.

Outside The Quarter

Mother's Restaurant, 401 Poydras (523-9656), 4 blocks southwest of Bourbon St. Yo Mama has been serving up roast beef and ham po'boys ($6-9) to locals for almost half a century. Be daring and try the crawfish or shrimp *étouffé* omelette

($8). Tremendous entrees and your mother $6-15. Open Mon.-Sat. 5am-10pm, Sun. 7am-10pm.

P.J.'s, 7624 Maple St. (866-7031), soothes the throat and the spirit. A college hang-out. Pastries and muffins under $2. Some say the best iced mocha on the planet. Open Mon.-Fri. 7am-11pm, Sat.-Sun. 8am-11pm.

All Natural, 5517 Magazine St. (891-2651). This friendly neighborhood health store cooks up fabulous and healthy sandwiches, pizzas, and hot specials ($3-5). Probably the only place in the world serving vegetarian jambalaya ($5 with salad). Open Mon.-Sat. 10am-7pm, Sun. 10am-5pm.

Tee Eva's, 4430 Magazine St. (899-8350), goes for the no-frills look but attracts locals with peerless pies and sizzlin' soul food. 3-in. sweet potato, cream cheese pecan, or plain pecan pies $1.10. Large 9-in. pies $8-12 by order only. Soul food lunches change daily and cost $5 a plate. Open daily 11am-8pm.

Dunbar's, 4927 Fieret, (899-0734), at Robert St., has breakfast, lunch, and dinner soul-food style. Sit next to the Tulane football team and gorge yourself on cabbage and candied yams ($4), or all-you-can-eat red beans and chicken ($4). Kind of a risky area, so go when the sun shines.

Franky and Johnny's, 321 Arabella (899-9146), southwest of downtown towards Tulane off Tchoupitoulas. A hole-in-the-wall with great onion rings ($3.25) and boiled crayfish ($3.75 for 2 lbs., Nov.-June). Open Mon.-Thurs. 11am-11pm, Fri.-Sat. 11am-midnight, Sun. 11am-10pm.

Taqueria Corona, 5932 Magazine (897-3734), between State and Nashville. Excellent Mexican cuisine with throngs each and every night. Try the char-broiled shrimp taco ($2.45) and flan, fabulous flan for dessert ($1.80). Open for lunch Mon.-Sat. 11:30am-2pm

Camellia Grill, 626 S. Carrollton Ave. (866-9573). Take the St. Charles streetcar away from the Quarter to the Tulane area. One of the finest diners in America and the safest, best, late-night bet. Have the chef's special omelette ($5.25) or partake of the pecan pie ($2). Expect a wait on weekend mornings. Open Sun.-Wed. 8am-1am, Thurs.-Sat. 8am-2am.

O'Henry's, has 3 area locations, 634 S. Carrollton (866-9741—a pick-up spot), 3020 Cevern (888-9383), and 301 Baronne (522-5242). Knosh on burgers and sandwiches ($4-6) and fresh peanuts (you can throw shells on the floor). Open Sun.-Wed. 11am-midnight, Thurs.-Sat. 11am-2am. Trade your hair in for a set of combs.

SIGHTS

French Quarter

Allow yourself *at least* a full day (some take a lifetime) in the Quarter. The oldest section of the city, it is famous for its ornate wrought-iron balconies, French, Spanish, and uniquely New Orleans architectures, and joyous atmosphere. Known as the **Vieux Carré** (view-ca-RAY), meaning Old Square, the historic district of New Orleans offers interesting used book and record stores, museums, and shops that pawn off ceramic masks and cheap t-shirts to innocent tourists. The farther you get from the main drag of **Bourbon Street,** the more clearly you'll be able to hear the variety of street musicians. Stroll down **Royal Street** to **Madame Lalaurie's** **"haunted house,"** at 1140 Royal, a socialite's mansion in which firefighters discovered slaves chained and tortured in the attic. A mob ran Madame Lalaurie out of town, but rumor has it that the screams of slaves can still be heard. Less thrilling but pretty houses can be found in the residential section down **Dumaine Street.** Stop in at a neighborhood bar. Tourists are taken in stride here, and should feel welcome.

North of the Quarter, one block past the **Esplanade** in the **Marigny,** New Orleans's large gay community lives, eats, parties, and reads. Stop in at **Faubourg Marigny Books,** 600 Frenchman St. (943-9875), to find out what's happening and where to go. (Open Mon.-Fri. 10am-8pm, Sat.-Sun. 10am-6pm.)

The heart of the Quarter beats at **Jackson Square,** whose center boasts a bronze equestrian statue of General Andrew Jackson, victor of the Battle of New Orleans. While the square boogies with artists, mimes, musicians, psychics, magicians, and con artists, the **St. Louis Cathedral**, 615 Pere Anoine Alley (525-9585), presides at its head. Across the street, the **Jackson Brewery Rivermarket** (586-8021) is marked by the vuglar red neon sign, "JAX." The complex offers fast food and over-priced shopping (open Sun.-Thurs. 10am-9pm, Fri.-Sat. 10am-10pm). Try the bundles of flea market paraphernalia, jewelry, and leather goods amassed at the **French Market** (522-2621) instead (open daily 9am-8pm).

The rich cultural history of the French Quarter has made it a National Historic Park, and free tours and interpretive programs are given by the **Jean Lafitte National Historical Park,** 916-918 North Peters (589-2636), located in the back section of the French Market at Decatur and St. Phillip St. Free 90-min. tours at 10:30am, 11:30am, and 2:30pm emphasize various aspects of New Orleans's cultural, ethnic, and environmental history. Garden District tours are at 2:30pm and require reservations. Call ahead for specific info.

The Park Service no longer conducts tours of the city cemeteries because these areas have been deemed unsafe. Visitors foul in heart and experienced with evil eyes should dare to take a tour led by the **New Orleans Historic Voodoo Museum,** 724 Dumaine St. (523-7685), which offers tour packages including graveyards ($12-18) and haunted plantations ($59) as well as other tours of the Atchafalaya Swamp ($58). (Open daily 10am-dusk. Museum admission $5.) Be careful here; ghosts may not bother you, but other shady characters might. Tourists of pure heart and naive to the evil that lurks on the dark side should opt for the **Hidden Treasures Cemetery Tour** (529-4507 or 522-5629) of New Orleans's original St. Louis cemetery #1. Tours ($12) depart at 9am daily from The Ultimate Coffee Shop, 417 Bienville St. (524-7417). Free coffee for those who live to see the next sunrise.

Before you die, read this: Being dead in New Orleans has always been a problem. Because the city lies 4 to 6 ft. below sea level, a 6-ft. hole in the earth fills up with 5 ft. of water. Coffins used to literally **float in the grave,** so cemetery workers had to push them down into the grave with long wooden poles. One early solution to this problem was to **bore holes in the coffins,** allowing them to sink. Unfortunately, the sight of a drowning coffin coupled with the **awful gargling sound** of its immersion proved too much for the squeamish families of the departed. Instead burial became obsolete and stiffs were laid to rest in beautiful raised stone tombs instead. This makes for miles and miles of marble tombs that are creepy and cool.

Outside The Quarter

New Orleans has more to see than just the French Quarter. In the southernmost corner of the Quarter, at the "foot of Canal St." where the riverboats dock, stands the **World Trade Center**, 2 Canal St. (525-2185), where you can take in New Orleans from 31 flights up ($2, ages 6-12 $1, seniors $1.50; open daily 9am-5pm) and then grab a snack at **Riverview Cafeteria** on the third floor (open Mon.-Fri. 7am-2 pm). In this same area ambles the **Riverwalk,** a multi-million dollar conglomeration of over-priced shops overlooking the port. For entertainment and an unbeatable meal, let the **Cookin' Cajun New Orleans Cooking School,** 116 Riverwalk (586-8832), prepare a Cajun or Creole meal before your eyes. Call ahead for the menu of the day, or just drop by and sample one of the 18 hot sauces. (Open Mon.-Sat. 11am-1pm, $15 for 2 hrs.) You can take the free **Canal Street Ferry** to Algiers Point until about 9pm for a 25-minute view of the Mississippi River and a bite of African-American history. Algiers of old housed many of New Orleans's free people of color.

Relatively new in the downtown area, the **Warehouse Arts District,** on Julia St. between Commerce and Baronne, contains historic architecture and contemporary art galleries housed in revitalized warehouse buildings. Exhibits range from Southern folk art to experimental sculpture. Maps of the area are available in each gallery. Be sure to check out the **Contemporary Arts Center,** 900 Camp St. (523-1216), an old brick building with a modern glass and chrome facade. The exhibits range from cryptic to puzzling, but you will always enjoy the amazing architecture that flourishes within. (Open Tues.-Sun. 11am-5pm. $3, students, seniors, and over 12 $2.)

Though much of the Crescent City's fame derives from the **Vieux Carré,** as you move "uptown" (i.e. upriver), you certainly don't move away from the beauty or the action. The streetcar named "Desire" had its date long ago, but you can take the **St. Charles Streetcar** to the west of the French Quarter to view some of the city's finest buildings, including the elegant, mint-condition 19th-century homes along **St. Charles Avenue.** The old-fashioned train takes you through some of New Orleans's most beautiful neighborhoods at a leisurely pace for a mere $1. Be sure to disembark at the **Garden District,** an opulent neighborhood between Jackson and Louisiana Ave. The legacies of French, Italian, Spanish, and American architecture create an extraordinary combination of magnificent structures, rich colors, ironworks, and, of course, exquisite gardens. Many are raised several feet above the ground as protection from the swamp on which New Orleans was built.

The St. Charles Street Car runs all the way to **Audubon Park,** across from Tulane University. Designed by Frederick Law Olmsted—the same architect who planned New York City's Central Park—Audubon contains lagoons, statues, stables, and the awesome and award-winning **Audubon Zoo** (861-2537), with its re-created Louisiana swamp harboring the world's only white alligators. A free museum shuttle glides from the Audubon Park entrance (streetcar stop #36) to the zoo. (Zoo open daily 9:30am-5pm. $7.75, seniors and ages 2-12 $3.70.) If you happen to have a good rapport with pirhanas, swim on over to the brand spanking new **Aquarium of the Americas** (861-2538), Waldenberg Park by the World Trade Center. Among the 500 species you'll see black-footed penguins, endangered sea turtles, and the world's only white alligators. (Wait a second...) The steamboat **John Audubon** (586-8777) shuttles four round-trips a day between the aquarium and the zoo (leaves the aquarium 10am, noon, 2pm, 4pm; leaves the zoo 11am, 1pm, 3pm, 5pm; round-trip fares $11.50, $5.75 kids; one-way cruise $9.50, kids $4.75; package tours including cruise, zoo, and aquarium range from $17-25, kids $9-13).

If animals, fish, and much water don't quench your thirst for nature, a 10-min. drive north from the Quarter will lead you to **City Park** (482-4888; call for hours), at the corner of City Park Ave. and Marconie Dr., accessible by the Esplanade or City Park bus. This 1500-acre park is one of the five largest city parks in the U.S. In addition to the **Museum of Art** (see Museums below), it contains a botanical garden, golf courses, tennis courts, 800-year-old oak trees under which gentlemen dueled years ago, lagoons, and a miniature train.

One of the most unique sights near New Orleans, the coastal wetlands that line Lake Salvador make up a segment of the **Jean Lafitte National Historical Park** called the **Barataria Unit** (589-2330). Unfortunately, the park can only be reached with a car, but the park service swamp tours almost warrant renting one. Guided tours leave at 10am and 2pm and cost $35, children 3-12 $20 with transportation. Without, tours are $20, $10 for the kiddies. The park is off the West Bank Expressway across the Mississippi River down Barataria Blvd. (Rte. 45). Birdwatcher, fisherman, geologist, and environmentalist John Nielson knows his nature and will share it with you on **Nielson's** (241-5994 or 531-7884), one of the best swamp tours around. (Rte. 90 at E. Pearl River Bridge in Slidell off I-10E. Adults $20, kids under 12 $10; double the price for round-trip transportation. Ask for the 10% *Let's Go* discount for 10 or more people.)

MUSEUMS

Louisiana State Museum, P.O. Box 2448 (568-6968), oversees 4 separate museums: the **Old U.S. Mint,** 400 Esplanade; the **Cabildo; Presbytère;** and **1850 House.** They contain artifacts, papers, and other changing exhibits on the history of Louisiana and New Orleans. All open Tues.-Sun. 10am-5pm. Pass to all 4 buildings, $10, seniors $7.50; pass to one $4, seniors $3, ages 12 and under free.

New Orleans Museum of Art (488-2631), City Park. Take the Esplanade bus from Canal and Rampart. Recently expanded to a space of 130,000 sq. ft., this magnificent museum houses the arts of North and South America, a small collection of local decorative arts, opulent works by the jeweler Fabergé, and a strong collection of French paintings including works by Degas. Guided tours available. Open Tues.-Sat. 10am-5pm, Sun. 1-5pm. $6, seniors and kids ages 2-17 $3.

Historic New Orleans Collection, 533 Royal St. (523-4662), boasts extensive facilities and offers 2 guided tours ($2 each). The History Tour explores New Orleans's past, while the interesting Williams Residence Tour showcases the eclectic home furnishings of the collection founders, General and Mrs. L. Kemper Williams. The downstairs gallery displays varying exhibitions. Open Tues.-Sat. 10am-4:45pm; tours at 10am, 11am, 2pm, and 3pm. Gallery free; guided tours $2.

Musée Conti Wax Museum, 917 Conti St. (525-2605). One of the world's finest houses of wax. The voodoo display and haunted dungeon are perennial favorites, along with a mock up of Madame Lalaurie's torture attic. Open daily 10am-5:30pm, except Mardi Gras. $5.75, under 17 $3.50, seniors $5.25.

Civil War Museum, 929 Camp St. (523-4522), just west of Lee Circle in an ivy-covered building. An extensive collection of Civil War records and artifacts. Warning: They root for the South. Open Mon.-Sat. 10am-4pm. $4, kids under 16 $2.

K&B Plaza, 1055 St. Charles Ave.(568-5661), on Lee Circle, houses the outstanding contemporary collection of art and sculpture from the Virlane Foundation, including sculpture by Henry Moore, mobiles by Alexander Calder, and a bust by Renoir. Sculpture garden open 24 hrs. Building open Mon.-Fri. 8am-5pm. Free.

Louisiana Children's Museum, 428 Julia St. (523-STAR). Invites kids to star on their own news show, shop at a mini-mart, pretend to be a streetcar driver, and much more. They can play and learn. Cool. Kids under 12 must be accompanied by an adult. Open Tues.-Sun. 9:30-4:30pm. $4, under 12 free.

Louisiana Nature and Science Center, 11000 Lake Forest Blvd. (246-5672), in Joe Brown Memorial Park. Hard to reach without a car, but a wonderful escape from the debauchery of the French Quarter. Trail walks, exhibits, planetarium shows, laser shows, and 86 acres of natural wildlife preserve. Open Tues.-Fri. 9am-5pm; $2, seniors and kids $1; Sat.-Sun. noon-5pm $3, seniors and kids $2.

NASA Michoud Assembly Facility, 13800 Old Gentilly Rd. (257-1310). Fascinating tours of the facility that builds Space Shuttle External Tanks. Walk the factory and gape at the 154-ft. long, 28-ft. diameter tanks. Reservations must be made and you must be a U.S. citizen to visit the museum. Call for an appointment.

HISTORIC HOMES AND PLANTATIONS

Called the "Great Showplace of New Orleans," **Longue Vue House and Gardens,** 7 Bamboo Rd. (488-5488), off Metairie Rd., epitomizes the grand Southern estate with lavish furnishings and opulent decor. The sculpted gardens are startlingly beautiful, dating back to the turn of the century. Tours available in English, French, Spanish, Italian, and Japanese. (Open Mon.-Sat. 10am-4:30 pm, Sun. 1-5pm. House and garden $6, students $3; gardens only $3, students $1.) Take the Metairie Rd. exit off I-10 and take a peak at the 85-ft.-tall monument among the raised tombs in the Metairie Cemetery. **River Road,** a winding street that follows the Mississippi River, holds several preserved plantations from the 19th century. Pick up a copy of *Great River Road Plantation Parade: A River of Riches* at the New Orleans or Baton Rouge visitors centers for a good map and descriptions of the houses. Free and frequent ferries cross the Mississippi at Plaquemines, White Castle, and between Lutcher and Vacherie. A tour of all the privately-owned plantations would be quite expensive. Those below are listed in order from New Orleans to Baton Rouge.

Hermann-Grima Historic House, 820 St. Louis St. (525-5661), exemplifies early American architecture from around the 1830s and features the only working Creole kitchen and private stable in the area. Also has period garden and interior restorations. Open Mon.-Sat. 10am-4pm. $4, students $3.

Gallier House Museum, 1118-1132 Royal St. (523-6722), French Quarter. This elegant restored residence brings alive the taste and lifestyle of mid-19th century New Orleans. Tours every ½ hr., last tour at 4 pm. Open Mon.-Sat. 10am-4:30pm. $4, seniors and students $3, children $2.25.

San Francisco Plantation House (535-2341), Rte. 44 2 mi. north of Reserve, 23 mi. from New Orleans on the north bank of the Mississippi. Beautifully restored plantation built in 1856. Galleried in the old Creole style with the main living room on the 2nd floor. Exterior painted 3 different colors with many colorfully decorated ceilings. Tours daily 10am-4pm. $6.50, students $3.75, children free.

Houmas House (522-2262), River Rd., Burnside, just over halfway to Baton Rouge on the northern bank of the Mississippi on Rte. 942. Setting for the movie *Hush, Hush, Sweet Charlotte,* starring Bette Davis and Olivia DeHavilland. Built in two sections, the rear constructed in the last quarter of the 18th century, the Greek Revival mansion in front in 1840. Beautiful gardens and furnishings. "Southern Belle" guides tours in authentic antebellum dress. Open Feb.-Oct. daily 10am-5pm; Nov.-Jan. 10am-4pm. $7, ages 13-17 $5, ages 6-12 $3.50.

Nottoway (545-2730), Rte. 405, between Bayou Goula and White Castle, 18 mi. south of Baton Rouge on the southern bank of the Mississippi. Largest plantation home in the South; often called the "White Castle of Louisiana." An incredible 64-room mansion with 22 columns, a large ballroom, and a 3-story stairway. The first choice of David O. Selznick for filming *Gone with the Wind,* but the owners frankly didn't give a damn and simply wouldn't allow it. Open daily 9am-5pm. Admission and 1-hr. guided tour $8, kids $3.

ENTERTAINMENT AND NIGHTLIFE

The drinking laws in New Orleans are sketchy. Some say you are legal at 18, others at 21. (You only have to be 18 to enter a bar, but 21 to buy alcohol (they will card at a liquor store). Needless to say, life in New Orleans is a party. On any night of the week, at any time of year, multitudes of people join the constant fete of the French Quarter. **Bourbon Street,** though technically an automobile thoroughfare, is so clogged with revelers that car passage is quite a chore. Unfortunately, the many bars and clubs on Bourbon tend toward the sleazy and clothing optional. After exploring the more traditional jazz, blues, and brass sound of the Quarter, assay the rest of the city for less tourist-oriented bands playing to a more local clientele. Check *Off Beat* for maps of the clubs; try opening *Gambit,* the free weekly entertainment newspaper, or the Friday edition of the *Times-Picayune's* entertainment guide *Lagniappe* to find out who's playing where. The Quarter supports a large gay community here; check out local newsletters *Impact* and *Ambush* for more information on gay events and nightlife.

Traditional New Orleans jazz, born here at the turn of the century in **Armstrong Park,** can still be enjoyed at tiny, dimly lit, historic **Preservation Hall,** 726 Saint Peter St. (523-8939). This is jazz in its most fundamental and visceral element. Arrive early or be prepared for a lengthy wait in line, poor visibility, and sweaty standing-room only ($3). Beverages are not sold. Doors open at 8pm; music begins at 8:30pm and goes on until midnight. If you don't get a seat, wait outside and hear for free.

Keep your ears open for **Cajun** and **zydeco** bands. Using accordions, washboards, triangles, and drums, they perform hot dance tunes (to which locals expertly two-step) and sappy waltzes. Their traditional fare is the *fais do-do,* a lengthy, wonderfully sweaty dance. Anyone who thinks couple-dancing went out in the 50s should try one of these; just grab a partner and throw yourself into the rhythm. The locally based **Radiators** do it up real spicy-like in a rock-cajun-zydeco style.

The ever-expanding annual **New Orleans Jazz Festival** (522-4786) attracts 4000 musicians from around the country to the fairgrounds in the end of April. The likes of Aretha Franklin, Bob Dylan, Patti LaBelle, Wynton Marsalis, and others have graced this slightly "classier" fest, which features music played simultaneously on 11 stages, as well as a Cajun food and crafts festival. Though exhilarating fun, the festival grows more zoo-like each year. Book a room early.

French Quarter

New Orleans bars stay open late, and few bars adhere to a strict schedule. In general, they open around 11am and close around 3am. Many bars in the area are very expensive, charging $3-5 for drinks. Yet on most blocks, you can find cheap draft beer and "Hurricanes," sweet drinks made of juice and rum; also try local Abita beer. Visitors can totter around the streets, get pleasantly soused, and listen to great music without going broke. A walk down Bourbon St. after midnight is so crowded it feels like noon. Music pours out of the bars, and bouncers beckon you inside. Beware of con-men and always bring ID—the party's fun, but the law is enforced.

The Napoleon House, 500 Chartres St. (524-9752), is one of the world's great watering holes. Located on the ground floor of the Old Girod House, it was built as an exile home for Napoleon in a plan to spirit him away from St. Helena. Setting for the opening scene of Oliver Stone's *JFK*. New Orleans fare ($3-9). Open Mon.-Thurs. 11am-midnight, Fri.-Sat. 11am-1am, Sun. 11am-7pm.

The Old Absinthe House, 240 Bourbon St. (525-8108). Reasonably priced drinks for the French Quarter, with a blues band. Has irrigated the likes of Mark Twain, Franklin D. Roosevelt, the Rolling Stones, and Humphrey Bogart. Bet you've never heard those four names together in the same sentence! The Absinthe Frappe is a re-invention of the infamous drink with anisette or Pernod liqueur ($4.75). Open daily noon-3am, since 1806. Music begins at 5:30pm.

Pat O'Brien's, 718 Saint Peter St. (525-4823). The busiest bar and best in the French Quarter, bursting with happy (read: drunk) tourists. You can listen to the pianos in one room, mix with local students in another, or lounge beneath fans near a fountain in the courtyard. Home of the original Hurricane; purchase your first in a souvenir glass ($6.75). Open daily 10:30am-4am, weekends until 5am.

Bourbon Pub/Parade, 801 Bourbon St. (529-2107). This gay dance bar sponsors a "tea dance" on Sun. with all the beer you can drink for $5. Open 24 hrs. Dancing nightly 9pm until they run out of gas.

Old Absinthe Bar, 240 Bourbon St. (523-3181). The marble absinthe fountain inside has been dry since absinthe was outlawed. Reputed to be the oldest bar in the U.S., having opened in 1807; the Absinthe House right down the street (est. 1806) shows up its story. Today Herbsaint liquor is basically absinthe without the delectable wormwood. Open daily 10am-2am.

Outside The Quarter

Mid City Lanes, 4133 S. Carrolton Ave. (482-3133), at Tulane, is "Home of Rock n' Bowl;" bowling alley by day, dance club by night. (Don't worry, you can bowl at night too.) Featuring local zydeco, blues, and rock n' roll, this is where the locals party. Every Thursday is a wild zydeco night. Music starts at 9:30 or 10pm. Cover $3-5. Pick up a *Rock n' Bowlletin* for specific band info (and a list of the regulars' birthdays). Lanes cost $8 per hr. on weekday nights, $10 per hr. on weekends.

Cooter Brown's Tavern and Oyster Bar, 509 S. Carrolton Ave. (866-9104). A blues bar which lofts over 200 beers including a 3-liter Belgian ale for $60. Ground cow on a bun too ($4-7). Open Sun.-Mon. 11am-2am, Tues.-Thurs. 11am-3am, Fri-Sat. 11am-4am.

Checkpoint Charlie's, 501 Esplanade (947-0979), in the Marigny, grunges it up like the best of Seattle. Do your laundry while you listen to live rockin' music 7 nights a week. Open 24 hrs. No cover.

Tipitina's, 501 Napoleon Ave. (897-3943 concert line; 895-8477 regular line). This renowned establishment attracts the best local bands and some big names. The Neville Brothers and Harry Connick Jr. are regulars. Favorite bar of late jazz pianist and scholar Professor Longhair; his bust now graces the front hall. Call ahead for times and prices. Cover $4-15.

Maple Leaf Bar, 8316 Oak St. (866-9359), near Tulane University. The best local dance bar offers zydeco and Cajun music; everyone does the two-step. Poetry readings Sun. at 3pm. Open Mon.-Sat. 11am-4am, Sun. 1pm-4am. The party begins Sun.-Thurs. at 10pm, Fri.-Sat. at 10:30pm. Cover $3-5.

F&M Patio Bar, 4841 Tchoupioulas (895-6784), near Napolean. A mellow twenty-something crowd mixed with doctors, lawyers, and ne'er-do-wells. Show up late. Open Mon.-Thurs. 1pm-4am, Fri. 1pm-6am, Sat. 3pm-6am, Sun. 3pm-4am.

Ms. Mae's, 5535 Magazine St. (891-9974). The cheapest beer in town, possibly the world. Long-neck $1.25, mixed drinks $1-2. Open 24 hrs.

Michaul's, 701 Magazine St. (522-5517), at Girnod. A huge floor for Cajun dancing; they'll even teach you how. Open Mon.-Sat. 6pm-midnight.

Muddy Water's, 8301 Oak St. (966-7174), near Tulane. Live music nightly, mostly blues. Burgers and seafood ($3-10). Open daily 11am to whenever. Cover $4-5.

Snug Harbor, 626 Frenchman St. (949-0696), just east of the Quarter near Decatur. Blues vocalists Charmaine Neville and Amasa Miller sing here regularly, giving 2 shows per night at 9pm and 11pm. Ellis Marsalis also performs here. The cover is no bargain ($6-14), but Mon. evening with Ms. Neville is worth it. You can also hear, but not see, the soulful music from the bar in the front room. Bar open daily 5pm-2am; restaurant open Sun.-Thurs. 5-11pm, Fri.-Sat. 5pm-midnight.

■■■ BATON ROUGE

Native Americans once marked their tribal hunting boundaries with a "red stick." From those beginnings, Baton Rouge has hosted the French, English, Spanish, and Acadians. Baton Rouge was little more than a backwoods, (red)stick-in-the-mud village until a group of evangelical Louisiana politicians, concerned that the state government was wallowing in a hotbed of debauchery in the "Big Easy," picked Baton Rouge, 60 mi. away, as the new capital.

Baton Rouge fuses its aggressive Mississippi River industry with a quieter plantation country, yielding a hybrid culture alive with trade, historical museums, and homes. Its research university, a progressive music scene, and a thriving gay community in Spanish Town attest to a cosmopolitan temperament enriched by eclectic architecture and a rambunctious political history. Baton Rouge was home to "Kingfish" Huey P. Long—a Depression-era populist demagogue who, until his assassination, was considered Franklin D. Roosevelt's biggest political threat. Current governor Edwin Edwards, a flamboyant Cajun Democrat, survived two federal indictments and regained the governorship for a third time by defeating "ex-"Ku Klux Klansman David Duke.

PRACTICAL INFORMATION

Emergency: 911.

Visitor Information: Baton Rouge Area Visitors Center (342-7317), 1st floor of the State Capitol, off I-110 on U.S. 61, west to 3rd St. and north to the sky-scraping capitol. Pick up info here not only on Baton Rouge, but the rest of Louisiana as well. Open Mon.-Fri. 8am-4pm.

Greyhound: 1253 Florida Blvd. (800-231-2222), at 13th St. A short walk from downtown. Unsafe area at night. To: New Orleans (11 per day, 2 hr., $15) and Lafayette (7 per day, 1 hr., $12). Open 24 hrs.

Public Transport: Capital City Transportation, 336-0821. Terminal at 22nd and Florida Blvd. Buses run Mon.-Sat. 6:30am-6:30pm. Service to LSU decent, otherwise unreliable and/or infrequent. Fare $1, transfers 25¢.

Help Lines: Crisis Intervention/Suicide Prevention Center, 924-3900. **Rape Crisis,** 383-7273. Both open 24 hrs.

Post Office: 750 Florida Blvd. (381-0713), off River Rd. Open Mon.-Fri. 8:30am-4:30pm, Sat. 9-11am. **ZIP code:** 70821.

Area Code: 504.

The state capitol sits on the east bank of the river; the city spreads eastward. The heart of downtown, directly south of the capitol, runs until **Government Street. Highland Road** leads south from downtown directly into Louisiana State University. Avoid the area known as "the bottom," if you value your rear. Down on Highland Rd. there is an area of streets named after presidents that is dangerous at night.

ACCOMMODATIONS, FOOD, AND NIGHTLIFE

Budget hotel seekers should head out of town along Florida Blvd. (U.S. 190) or Airline Hwy. (U.S. 61). **Louisiana State University (LSU)** provides inexpensive accommodations at their on-campus hotel run out of Pleasant Hall (387-0297). Take bus #7 ("University") from North Blvd. behind the Old State Capitol. Pleasant Hall is quite pleasant—a room with 2 beds (for up to four people) costs $42. The concierge

($50) or the suite ($60) offers greater luxury. **Motel 6,** 9901 Airport Hwy. (924-2130), has cookie-cutter rooms with good security, hard beds, soft water, HBO, ESPN, and a pool to boot. (Singles $30, doubles $36.) The **Alamo Plaza Hotel Courts,** 4243 Florida Blvd. (924-7231), has spacious rooms (some with kitchenettes) in a less safe downtown area. Take bus #6 ("Sherwood Forest") east on Florida Blvd. from the Greyhound station. (Singles $20, doubles $25-28.) The **KOA Campground,** 7628 Vincent Rd. (664-7281), 12 mi. east of Baton Rouge (Denham Springs exit off I-12), has well-maintained sites including clean facilities and a big pool. (Sites $14.50 for 2 people, with hookup $19.50.)

Near LSU on (and off) **Highland Rd.,** you can find all the sustenance you need. **Louie's Café,** 209 W. State (246-8221), a 24-hr. grill, has been lauded in *Rolling Stone* for fabulous stir-fried vegetable omelettes served all the time ($5). On the corner of Chimes and Highland behind Louie's, local favorite **The Bayou,** 124 W. Chimes (346-1765), is site of the bar scene from *Sex, Lies, and Videotape.* Free pool daily 5-8pm. (Open Mon.-Sat. 2pm-2am; 5pm-2am in the summer.) Downtown, you can't miss the **Frostop Drive-In,** 402 Government (344-1179); a giant frothy root beer mug spinning on a post outside welcomes diners for delicious root beer floats crafted with homemade root beer ($2). Sandwiches run $1-3. (Open Mon.-Fri. 9am-4pm, Sat. 10am-4pm.) For power dining at a grassroots price, join the state lawmakers at the **House of Representatives Dining Hall,** in the basement of the state capitol. (Entrees $2-3. Open daily 7-10:30am and 11am-2pm.)

SIGHTS

The most prominent building in Baton Rouge is also the first sight you should visit. In a move reminiscent of Ramses II, Huey Long ordered the building of the unique **Louisiana State Capitol** (342-7317), a magnificent, modern skyscraper, completed in a mere 14 months in 1931-32. The front lobby alone merits a visit, but visitors should also go to the free 27th-floor observation deck. (Open daily 8am-4pm.) One of the most interesting in the U.S., the building attests to the staying power of Long's personality. Look for the bullet holes in a back corridor near the plaque indicating the site of his assassination; the place of his burial is under the statue in front. Right across the lawn fires the **Old Arsenal Museum,** whose smoky smell originates from the powder barrels and other wartime equipment on display. (Open Tues.-Fri. 9am-4pm, Sat. 10am-4pm, Sun. 1-4pm. $1, kids 50¢, seniors free.) Also tour the great white **Governor's Mansion** by appointment; call Betty George at 342-5855 from 8am-4pm. Check at the visitors center for the hours of the newly-renovated **Old State Capitol,** at River Rd. and North Blvd., an eccentric Gothic Revival castle ($5, $3 for seniors, $2 for kids). Just south of downtown, the **Beauregard District** boasts typically ornate antebellum homes. Walk down North Blvd. from the Old State Capitol to the visitors center to take in the beauty of this neighborhood.

A block away from the Old State Capitol on River Rd. floats the **Riverside Museum** of the Louisiana Arts and Science Center, 100 S. River Rd. (344-LASC). Climb on the old steam engine and train cars parked next door. The museum also has a varied collection of works by contemporary Louisiana artists. (Open Tues.-Sat. 10am-3pm, Sat. 10am-4pm, Sun. 1-4pm. $2, seniors and students, $1.) The museum runs the **Old Governor's Mansion,** the chief executive's residence from 1930-1963, at North Blvd. and St. Charles St., a planetarium, and various art exhibits. (Open Sat. 10am-4pm, Sun. 1-4pm. $2, seniors, students and kids $1.)

The **LSU Rural Life Museum,** 6200 Burden Lane (765-2437), off Perkins Rd., re-creates everyday rural life in pre-industrial Louisiana. The authentically furnished shops, cabins, and storage houses adjoin meticulously-kept rose and azalea gardens. (Open Mon.-Fri. 8:30am-4pm, Sat. 9:30am-4pm, Sun. 1-4pm. $3, kids $2.)

Tour the harbor in the **Samuel Clemens** steamboat (929-8490), which departs from Florida Blvd. at the river for one-hour cruises. (Tours April-Aug. daily at 10am, noon, and 2pm; Sept.-Dec. and March Wed.-Sun. at 10am, noon, and 2pm. $6, kids $4. Dinner cruises Tues., Thurs., and Sat. 7-9pm, with all-you-can-eat catfish and hushpuppies. $15, kids $10.) Open for inspection, the *U.S.S. Kidd* (342-1942), a

WWII destroyer, stands guard on the river just outside the **Louisiana Naval War Memorial Museum** (Open daily 9am-5pm. Ship and museum admission $5, seniors $4.50, kids 5-18 $3.50. Museum only $3, kids $2.) Alongside the ship museum and beneath a A-7 Corsair bomber, the **Louisiana Memorial Plaza** commemorates the deaths of Louisianians from the Revolutionary War to the Persian Gulf. Baton Rouge commemorates life with the annual **Blues Festival** (800-LA-ROUGE) in late August.

Within the varied cultural centers of the state, the Baton Rouge region is known as "Plantation Country." For a taste of these stately old homes in the downtown area, visit the well-restored **Magnolia Mound Plantation,** 2161 Nicholson Dr. (343-4955), the only plantation on the regular bus line. (Open Tues.-Sat. 10am-4pm, Sun. 1-4pm; last tour at 3:30pm. $3.50, seniors $2.50, students $1.50.) Another mansion, **St. Francisville,** is a mere 25 mi. to the north on U.S. 61. Among its notable estates is the **Oakley House,** where John Audubon painted his famous depictions of nature, on Rte. 965. Call the **West Feliciana Historical Society Museum** (504-635-6330) for more info and maps. (Open Mon.-Sat. 9am-5pm, Sun. 9:30am-5pm. Free.)

■■■ NATCHITOCHES

Founded in 1714, Natchitoches (NAK-a-tish) is the oldest European settlement in the Louisiana Purchase. At first a French outpost, it soon became a soothing small town of houses with old "iron lace" balconies. To meander peacefully through town, stroll along **Front Street** next to the **Cane River Lake.**

The town's most famous novelist lived 20 mi. south on Rte. 1 at the aptly-named **Kate Chopin House** (318-379-2253), where the author retreated after the censure of her novel *The Awakening.* The grounds also house a **Bayou Folk Museum** and a century-old blacksmith's shop.

Natchitoches boasts several unusual plantations such as the **Melrose** (318-379-2431). The nine-building complex includes the **African House,** home of the nativist artist, and Clementine Hunter. Nearby, the **Big House,** which was once owned by "Miss Cammie" Henry, drew literary visitors the likes of Faulkner, Steinbeck, and Erskine Caldwell. (Open daily noon-4pm. Take Rte. 1 south 14 mi., turn left onto Rte. 493 and go 2 mi.) If you need some orienting, stop by the **tourist information office,** 781 Front St. (800-259-1714), for the low down on driving tours in the area, especially **Kisatchie National Forest.**

■ NEAR NATCHITOCHES: NACOGDOCHES, TX

Legend has it that Nacogdoches (na-co-DOE-chez), the "oldest town in Texas" and Natchitoches, the "oldest town in Louisiana" were founded by twin brothers of a Native American tribe. Today, Nacogdoches sits as a small, sunny, college town in east Texas. Check out the **Stonefort Museum** (568-2408) on the campus of **Stephen F. Austin University** at College and Griffith. Built in 1780, the museum examines the early Spanish and Mexican history of Texas. (Open Tues.-Sat. 9am-5pm, Sun. 1-5pm. Free.) Mosey around and about **Millard's Crossing,** 6020 North St., for a look at the history behind the 19th-century homes of Nacogdoches. Also along North St. the **chamber of commerce** (564-7351) has more info on the town's **walking tours** and **antique shops.**

ACADIANA

In 1755, the English government expelled French settlers from their homes in New Brunswick. Migrating down the Atlantic coastline and into the Caribbean, the so-called *Acadiens* received a hostile reception; people in Massachusetts, Georgia, and South Carolina made them indentured servants. The Acadians (Cajuns) soon realized that their only hope for freedom lay in reaching the French territory of Louisiana and settling on the Gulf Coast. Many of the present-day inhabitants of St. Martin, Lafayette, Iberia, and St. Mary parishes are descended from these settlers.

Since their exodus began, many factors have threatened Acadian culture with extinction. Louisiana passed laws in the 1920s forcing Acadian schoolchildren to speak English. The oil boom of the past few decades has also endangered the survival of Acadian culture. Oil executives and developers envisioned Lafayette—a center of Acadian life—as the Houston of Louisiana, threatening to flood this small town and its neighbors with mass culture. However, the proud people of southern Louisiana have resisted homogenization, making the state officially bilingual and establishing a state agency to preserve Acadian French in schools and in the media.

Today "Cajun Country" spans the southern portion of the state, from Houma in the east to the Texas border. Mostly bayou and swampland, this unique natural environment has intertwined with Cajun culture. The music and the cuisine especially symbolize the ruggedness of this traditional, family-centered society. This is the place to try some crawfish or to dance the two-step to a fiddle and an accordion.

■■■ LAFAYETTE

The official capital of Acadiana, Lafayette is a perfect place to sample the zydeco music, boiled crawfish, and *pirogues* (carved cypress boats) that characterize Cajun culture. With all of its homey culture and small-town atmosphere, Lafayette is still a sizeable city of almost 100,000. In addition to the Acadian sites and historical villages, you can find everything from museums to chain motels. Even so, be sure to take some time to sit under a cypress on the bayou at sunset.

Practical Information The **Lafayette Parish Tourist Information Bureau,** 1400 Evangeline Thruway (232-3808), can swamp you with information (open Mon.-Fri. 8:30am-5pm, Sat.-Sun 9am-5pm). Lafayette provides a railroad stop for **Amtrak's** "Sunset Limited," linking the city with New Orleans (3 per week, 4 hr., $29); Houston (3 per week, 5 hr. $52), and Los Angeles ($211). Buy your tickets in advance from a travel agent; the train station is at 133 E. Grant St., near the bus station. **Greyhound,** 315 Lee Ave. (235-1541), connects Lafayette to New Orleans (7 per day, 3½ hr., $22.50) and Baton Rouge (7 per day, 1 hr., $10), as well as to small towns such as New Iberia (2 per day, ½ hr., $4). Open 24 hrs. The **Lafayette Bus System,** 400 Dorset Rd. (261-8570), runs infrequently and not on Sundays (fare 45¢, handicapped, seniors, and kids 5-12, 20¢). You'll need a car to really explore Acadiana and the Gulf Coast bayou country. **Thrifty Rent-a-Car,** 401 E. Pinhook Rd. (237-1282), usually has the best deals ($25 per day for a compact, 100 free mi.; must be 25 with major credit card). **Rape Crisis Center** (233-7273), is open Mon.-Fri. 8:30am-4:30pm. Lafayette's **post office:** 1105 Moss St. (269-4800; open Mon.-Fri. 8am-5:30pm, Sat. 8am-12:30pm); **ZIP code:** 70501; **area code:** 318.

Lafayette stands at Louisiana's major crossroads. I-10 leads east to New Orleans (130 mi.) and west to Lake Charles (76 mi.); U.S. 90 heads south to New Iberia (20 mi.) and the Atchafalaya Basin; U.S. 167 runs north into central Louisiana.

Accommodations and Camping Inexpensive chain and local hotels line the **Evangeline Thruway,** just off I-10. Several motels are a $3 cab fare from the bus station. The close **Travel Host Inn South,** 1314 N. Evangeline Thruway (233-2090 or 800-671-1466), has large, attractive rooms, cable TV, and a pool. Vibro-beds are available. (Singles $27, doubles $33.) The **Super 8,** 2224 N. Evangeline Thruway (232-8826 or 800-800-8000), just off I-10, has ample, plain-looking rooms, a pool, and a stunning view of the highway. (Singles $27, doubles $33.) Also off the main drag is the **Travelodge Lafayette,** 1101 W. Pinhook Rd. (234-7402), with free breakfast, free local calls, and your own coffee maker and beans. If it is not a full moon, steal a glimpse at the graveyard off Pinhook, with its raised marble crypts.

Campgrounds include the lakeside **KOA Lafayette** (235-2739), 5 mi. west of town on I-10 (exit 97), with a komplete store, a mini-golf course, and a pool. (Sites

$14.50, a few small kabins $25.) Closer to town is **Acadiana Park Campground,** 11201 E. Alexander (234-3838), off Louisiana, with tennis courts, a soccer field, and a **nature station** (261-8348) offering trail guides and maps. (All sites including full hookups $8. Office open Mon.-Thurs. 9am-5pm, Fri.-Sat. 8am-8pm, Sun. 9am-5pm.)

Food and Nightlife Cajun restaurants with live music and dancing have popped up all over Lafayette. Unfortunately, they tend to be expensive since they cater to the tourist crowd. **Mulates** (MYOO-LOTS), 325 Mills Ave. (332-4648), Breaux Bridge, calls itself the most famous Cajun restaurant in the world, and the autographs on the door corroborate its claim. Slap down some fried alligator ($5) or the special catfish ($14). (Open Mon.-Sat. 7am-10:30pm, Sun. 11am-11pm. Music nightly 7:30-10pm, and Sat.-Sun. noon-2pm as well.) In central Lafayette, visit **Chris' Po'Boys,** 4 locations including 1941 Moss St. (237-1095) and 631 Jefferson St. (234-1696), which (not surprisingly) offers po'boys ($4-5) and seafood platters (open Mon.-Thurs. 10:30am-9pm, Fri. 10:30am-10pm, Sat. 11am-9pm). If you have time to find it, **Prejeans,** 3480 U.S. 167N. (896-3247), is another Cajun restaurant (dinners $8-12) with savory food and nightly Acadian entertainment at 7pm. Check out the 14-ft. alligator by the entrance. Take Frontage Rd. which parallels Evangeline Rd. (Open Mon.-Thurs. 11am-9:30pm, Fri.-Sat. 11am-11pm, Sun. 11am-10pm. Nightly entertainment at 7pm.)

Sights and Activities Full of music, crafts, and food, **Vermilionville,** 1600 Surrey St. (233-4077 or 800-992-2968), is a historic bayou attraction that educates as it entertains. This re-creation of an Acadian settlement invites guests to dance the two-step, ride an Acadian skiff, make a cornhusk doll, and more. (Open daily 9am-5pm. $8, seniors $6.50, ages 6-18 $5.) A folk-life museum of restored 19th-century homes, **Acadian Village,** 200 Greenleaf Rd. (981-2364 or 800-962-9133), 10 mi. from the tourist center, offers another view of Cajun life. Take U.S. 167 north, turn right on Ridge Rd., left on Mouton, and then follow the signs. (Open daily 10am-5pm. $5.50, seniors $4.50, kids $2.50.) The **Lafayette Museum,** 1122 Lafayette St. (234-2208), exhibits heirlooms, antiques, and Mardi Gras costumes. (Open Tues.-Sat. 9am-5pm, Sun. 3-5pm. $3, seniors $2, students and kids $1.) The **Acadiana Park Nature Station and Trails** (235-6181), E. Alexander St., snakes through 50 acres of bottomland forest. The station has presentations on the environment. (Open Mon.-Fri. 9am-5pm, Sat.-Sun. 11am-3pm. Free, as nature should be.)

But don't lose sight of the trees for the forest. Check out **St. John's Cathedral Oak,** in the yard of St. John's Cathedral, 914 St. John St. This 450-year-old tree—one of the largest in the U.S.—shades the entire lawn with its gargantuan, spidery limbs creating a spread of 210 ft. The weight of a single limb is estimated at 72 tons. When that bough breaks, boy, does that cradle fall (free).

If you can't quite swing the tree-climbing thing, you can watch the experts at the **Zoo of Acadiana** (837-4325), 4 mi. south of Broussard on Rte. 182, known locally as "the little zoo that could." (Open daily 9am-5pm. $6, kids $3.) While the zoo tends to its live animals, the **Lafayette Natural History Museum and Planetarium,** 637 Girard Park Dr. (268-5544), pays homage to their ancestors, their environments, and the cosmos itself. (Open Mon., Wed., Fri. 9am-5pm, Tues. 9am-9pm, Sat.-Sun. 1-5pm. $3.50, kids $2, families $6.)

Pick up a copy of *The Times,* available at restaurants and gas stations, to find out about what's going on. Lafayette has a surprising variety of after-hours entertainment, including **Randol's,** 2320 Kaliste Saloom Rd. (981-7080), which romps with live music nightly, and doubles as a restaurant. (Open Sun.-Thurs. 5-10pm, Fri.-Sat. 5-10:30pm.) Lafayette kicks off spring and fall weekends with **Downtown Alive!,** a series of free concerts featuring everything from new wave to Cajun and zydeco (all concerts Fri. at 5:30pm; call 268-5566 for info). The **Festival International de Louisiane** (232-8086) in late April blends the music, visual arts, and cuisine of this region into a francophone tribute to southwestern Louisiana. The latest addition to Lafayette is fast-paced thorougbred racing. **New Evaneline Downs** (896-7223 or 800-

256-1234), on I-49, has opened its gates. (Races April 1-Sept. 1, Mon., Thurs, Fri. at 6:45pm. Admission $2, $2.50 more for a seat. Call for more info.)

Atchafalaya Basin While driving through south-central Louisiana, chances are, you're driving over the Atchafalaya (a-CHAH-fa-LIE-a) Basin. **The Atchafalaya Freeway** (I-10) stretches over 32 mi. of swamp and sloping cypress trees. How'd they build an interstate over such muck? Exit at Henderson and follow the signs to **McGee's Landing.** This family-run establishment sends four **boat tours** into the basin each day (10am, 1pm, 3pm, 5pm). If you see turtles and think "Hmmm, I'd like to eat one" head out to the **Atchafalaya Café** (228-7555). Turtle étoufée is $10. (Open Mon. 11am-5pm, Tues.-Wed. 11am-8pm, Thurs.-Sun. 11am-10pm.)

■ ■ ■ NEW IBERIA AND ENVIRONS

While oil magnates invaded Lafayette in the 70s and 80s, trying to build the town into a Louisiana oil-business center, New Iberia kept right on about its daily business. Although its attractions are less numerous, this small bayou town with picturesque streets and quiet neighborhoods is a gem worth discovering.

Practical Information New Iberia lies 21 mi. southeast of Lafayette on U.S. 90. **Amtrak** (800-872-7245) serves New Iberia between New Orleans and Lafayette. Trains run to: Lafayette ($6) and New Orleans ($27). **Greyhound** (364-8571) pulls into town at 101 Perry St. Buses run to: Morgan City ($10), New Orleans ($22), and Lafayette ($5) three times per day. The **Iberia Parish Tourist Commission,** 2704 Rte. 14 (365-8246), offers maps (open daily 9am-5pm). New Iberia's **post office:** 817 E. Dale St. (364-4568; open daily 8am-4:30pm); **ZIP code:** 70560; **area code:** 318.

Sights and Activities While other plantations made their fortunes off cotton, most plantations in southern Louisiana grew sugarcane. Today most of these stay in private hands, but **Shadows on the Teche,** 317 E. Main St. (369-6446), is open to the public. A Southern aristocrat saved the crumbling mansion, built in 1831, from neglect after the Civil War. (Open daily 9am-4:30pm. $5, kids 6-11 $3.)

Avery Island, 7 mi. away on Rte. 329 off Rte. 90, sizzles the world-famous **Tabasco Pepper Sauce factory,** where the McIlhenny family has produced the famous condiment for nearly a century. Guided tours include a sample taste. *OOOOOeeeeeee!!!!* (Open Mon.-Fri. 9am-4pm, Sat. 9am-noon. Free. 50¢ toll to enter the island.) Nearby crawl the **Jungle Gardens** (369-6243), 250 acres developed in the 19th century that include waterways, herons, egrets, alligators, and an 800-year-old statue of the Buddha. (Open daily 9am-6pm. $5.25, kids $3.75.) For a fast-paced, bugs-in-ya-teeth look at swamp and bayou wildlife, take an **Airboat Tour** (229-4457) of Lake Fausse Point and the surrounding area. (Tickets $10.)

Protruding from the lake next to **Live Oak Gardens,** 5505 Rip Van Winkle Rd. (365-3332), you'll see a lone chimney. This is all that remains of a mansion which was devoured by a whirlpool that resulted when an oil rig ruptured a huge salt mine in 1980. Oh well. Today the peaceful gardens and scenic boat tours belie this hectic past. (Open daily 9am-5pm. $10, kids $5.)

The best stuff to see in this region, however, is Acadiana's lush wilderness, a subtropical environment of marsh, bottomland hardwoods, and stagnant backwater bayous. You'll want to plan a daytrip to the **Attakapas Wildlife Area,** in southern St. Martin and Iberia Parishes, 20 mi. northwest of Morgan City and 10 mi. northeast of Franklin. Flat swampland comprises most of this hauntingly beautiful area, which includes a large amount of raised land used as a refuge by animals during flooding. In Attakapas cypress, tupelo, oak, maple, and hackberry grow on the high ground, and a cornucopia of swamp plants and animals slog about in the wetlands. Squirrel, deer, and rabbit hunting is popular here. The area can be reached by boat; public launches leave from Morgan City on Rte. 70. No camping is allowed. Bring bug repellant. Primitive campsites are available at **Atchafalaya Delta Wildlife Area** at the mouth of the Atchafalaya River in St. Mary Parish. The preserve encompasses bayous, potholes, low and high marsh, and dry ground. Access it by boat launch from Morgan City near the Bayou Boeuf locks.

 # Arkansas

Most Americans have probably heard by now of a place called Hope, birthplace of a man called Clinton. Arkansas's offerings, however, hardly end with the nation's latest president. Even as you zip over the Mississippi River from the east, you can feel nature's expanse widen—the landscape transforms into green fields that sparkle with the last rain. "The Natural State," as its license plates proclaim, certainly lives up to its boast, encompassing the ascents of the Ozarks, the clear waters of Hot Springs, the miles of twisting highway through the lush pine forests, and the natural friendliness of its people.

PRACTICAL INFORMATION

Capital: Little Rock.
Arkansas Dept. of Parks and Tourism, 1 Capitol Mall, Little Rock 72201 (501-682-7777 or 800-643-8383). Open Mon.-Fri. 8am-5pm.
Time Zone: Central (1 hr. behind Eastern). **Postal Abbreviation:** AR
Sales Tax: 5.5%.

■■■ LITTLE ROCK

Once upon a time, a little rock jutting into the Arkansas River served as an important landmark for boats pushing their way upstream. Over time, that rock was overshadowed by the big city that grew up around it.

Trouble swept the city in 1957 when Little Rock became the focus of a nationwide civil rights controversy. Governor Orval Faubus led a violent segregationist movement, using troops to prevent nine black students from enrolling in Central High School; they entered only under protection from troops sent by President Eisenhower. As years passed, the racial tension cooled and Little Rock became the integrated cultural center that it is today.

PRACTICAL INFOMATION

Emergency: 911.
Visitor Information: Arkansas Dept. of Parks and Tourism, 1 Capitol Mall (800-628-8725; 682-7777 in-state), in a complex directly behind the capitol building. Open Mon.-Fri. 8am-5pm. **Little Rock Convention and Visitors Bureau,** 100 W. Markham St. (376-4781 or 800-844-4781), next door to the Excelsior Hotel. Also dispenses useful information. Open Mon.-Fri. 8:30am-5pm.
Airport: Little Rock Regional (372-3430), 5 mi. east of downtown off I-440. Easily accessible to downtown (taxi $5-10, bus 80¢).
Amtrak: Union Station, 1400 W. Markham (372-6841 or 800-872-7245), at Victory St. downtown. One train per day to: St. Louis (7 hr., $70); Dallas (7 hr., $83); Malvern, 20 mi. east of Hot Springs (40 min., $12). Open Mon. and Wed. 6am-10pm, Tues. and Thurs. 6am-2pm and 5pm-1am, Fri.-Sat. 6am-2pm, Sun. 5pm-1am.
Greyhound: 118 E. Washington St. (372-1871), across the river in North Little Rock. Use the walkway over the bridge to get downtown. To: St. Louis ($63); New Orleans ($72); Memphis ($19). Tickets are more expensive on the weekends, but 14-day advance purchases come with a 25% discount. Open 24 hrs.
Public Transportation: Central Arkansas Transit (375-1163). Little Rock has a fairly comprehensive local transport system (although no evening hours), with 21 bus routes running through the city Mon.-Sat. 6am-6pm.

Taxi: Black and White Cabs, 374-0333. $1.10 pickup, $1 per mi.
Car Rental: Budget Car and Truck Rental (375-5521 or 800-527-0700), at the
airport, does its thing for $37.50 per day, 150 free mi., 25¢ per additional mi., or
$165 per week, 700 free mi., 25¢ per additional mi. No extra charge for ages 21-
25. Open Mon.-Sat. 6am-midnight, Sun. 7am-10pm.
Help Lines: Rape Crisis, 663-3334. Open 24 hrs. **First Call for Help,** 376-4567.
Open Mon.-Fri. 8am-5pm.
Post Office: 600 E. Capitol (371-1888). Open Mon.-Fri. 7:30am-5:30pm. **ZIP code:**
72201.
Area Code: 501 which covers all of Arkansas.

Most of Little Rock's streets were "planned" with no apparent pattern in mind,
although downtown is relatively grid-like. **Broadway** and **Main** are the major north-
south arteries running to and from the river. **Markham** and all streets numbered one
to 36 run east-west. **Third St.** turns into **W. Markham St.** as it moves west.

ACCOMMODATIONS

Inexpensive motels in Little Rock tend to cluster around **I-30,** which is right next to
downtown, and **University Ave.** at the intersection of I-630 and I-430, a 5-10-min.
drive from downtown. A few motels in town are cheaper but shabbier.

Master's Inn Economy (372-4392 or 800-633-3434), I-30 (exit 140) and 9th St.,
almost in downtown. Locations in North Little Rock as well. Spacious, well-lit,
newly furnished rooms with a lovely pool, restaurant, and even room service; this
chain is unbeatable. Singles $26, $6 per extra person; under 18 free with adult.
Mark 4000 Motel, 4000 W. Markham (664-0950). Don't be fooled by the dingy
exterior—recently renovated rooms boast comfortable and attractive decor. Be
careful at night in the surrounding neighborhood. Singles $28. Doubles $32.
Little Rock Inn (376-8301), 6th and Center St., half a block downtown and
includes a pool, saloon, laundry room, and spacious but worn rooms without TV
and telephone. $33 per night for 1-2 people, $75-90 per week with $20 security
deposit. Call 2 days ahead.
KOA Campground (758-4598), on Crystal Hill Rd. in North Little Rock, 7 mi. from
downtown between exit 12 on I-430 and exit 148 on I-48. You can "rough it" outdoors by the pool (sites $19, with hookup $25, kabins $28).

FOOD AND NIGHTLIFE

Vino's, 923 W. 7th (375-8466), at Chester, the only micro-brewery in Little Rock,
gives Italian food a good name and a good price (pizza 95¢ a slice, calzones $5).
This youthful hangout is also a mecca for the night owl—weekends bring live
music, poetry, plays, and film showings. Open Mon.-Wed. 11am-10pm, Thurs.-Fri.
11am-midnight, Sat. noon-midnight.
Juanita's, 1300 S. Main (372-1228), at 13th. Scrumptious Mexican food on the
pricey side (dinner $8-12), but wonderfully prepared. If it's beyond your budget,
the live nightly music may not be; call or stop by for a jam-packed schedule. Open
Mon.-Thurs. 11am-2:30pm and 5:30-10pm, Fri. 11am-2:30pm and 5:30-10:30pm,
Sat. noon-10:30pm, Sun. 5:30-9pm.
The Oyster Bar, 3003 W. Markham St. (666-7100). Reasonably priced seafood and
po'boy sandwiches ($4-5). Big screen TV, pool, cheap draft beer, and a laid-back
atmosphere where paper towels take the place of napkins. Open Mon.-Thurs.
11am-9:30pm, Fri.-Sat. noon-10:30pm. Happy Hour Mon.-Fri. 3-6:30pm.
Wallace Grill Café, 103 Main St. (3722-3111), near the visitors center. Generous
portions of rib-stickin' cuisine. $1.70 for a BLT, fried catfish for $5.25. Open Mon.-
Fri. 6am-2:30pm, Sat. 6am-noon.
Terri Lynn's Delicatessen, 406 Louisiana (376-2226), provides standard deli fare.
"Killer" hot dogs ($2.65), sasparilla 69¢. Open Mon.-Fri. 11am-2:30pm.
Backstreet, 1021 Jessie Rd. (664-2744), near Riverfront Rd. and Cantrell Rd., is a
popular gay bar for both men and women complete with a fun game room. Open
daily 7pm-5am. Next door is another gay bar, the **Discovery** (664-4784).

SIGHTS

Tourists can visit the legendary "Little Rock, " which once jutted into the Arkansas River and spurred the development of this big city at **Riverfront Park,** a pleasant place for a walk. Pay close attention; the rock has had a hard life and is (oddly enough) *little* and easy to miss. For quick access, cut through the back of the Excelsior Hotel at Markham and Center St. The town celebrates the waterway at **Riverfest** (call 376-4787 for info), with arts and crafts, a number of bands, lots of food, and a fireworks display on the last evening of Memorial Day weekend.

One block from the visitors bureau resides the refined **Old State House,** 300 W. Markham St. (324-9685), which served as the capitol from 1836 until the ceiling collapsed in 1899 while the legislature was in session. The restored building now displays the gowns of first ladies, and an exhibit devoted to President Clinton. (Open Mon.-Sat. 9am-5pm, Sun. 1-5pm. $2, kids $1.) The functioning **state capitol** (682-5080), at the west end of Capitol St., may look very familiar—it's actually a replica of the U.S. Capitol in Washington, DC. Take a free self-guided tour or one of the 45-min. group tours given on the hour. (Schedule in advance. Open Mon.-Fri. 9am-4pm.) To glimpse President Clinton's previous life, you might want to swing by the **Governor's Mansion,** at S. Center and 18th, in the middle of a gorgeous historic district. For a look at the history of the townspeople of 19th-century Little Rock, visit the **Arkansas Territorial Restoration,** 200 E. Third St. (324-9351). Tours of four restored buildings include an old-fashioned print shop. Though long, the tours are varied and fascinating; the tour guides have done all the research themselves and are not merely hired robots. (Open Mon.-Sat. 9am-5pm, Sun. 1-5pm. 1-hr. tours every hr. on the hr. $2, seniors $1, kids 50¢. Free first Sun. of each month.)

On the eastern edge of town lounges **MacArthur Park,** elegant home to the **Museum of Science and History** (324-9231). Particularly suited to kids, the museum houses exhibits on Arkansas history, including a walk-through bear cave and an entire room of stuffed birds. (Open Mon.-Sat. 9am-4:30pm, Sun. 1-4:30pm. $1, kids under 12 and seniors 50¢, free on Mon.) Next door poses the **Arkansas Art Center** (372-4000), featuring outstanding collections by both the old European masters and contemporary artists (open Mon.-Sat. 10am-5pm, Sun. noon-5pm; admission by donation). Just a block or so north of Riverfront Park, the **Decorative Arts Museum** (372-4000), 7th and Rock St., polishes innovative silverware and furniture designs which demonstrate that art can be functional. (Tours given Wed. at noon, Sun. at 1:30pm. Open Mon.-Sat. 10am-5pm, Sun. noon-5pm. Free.) The **War Memorial Park,** northwest of the state capitol off I-30 at Fair Park Blvd., houses the 40-acre **Little Rock Zoo,** 1 Jonesboro Dr. (666-2406), which simulates animals's natural habitats (open daily 9:30am-5pm; $2, kids under 12 $1).

The opening scene of *Gone With the Wind* features **Old Mill Park** (758-2400), Lakeshore Dr. at Fairway Ave. in North Little Rock, which has been turning and grinding since the Depression. (Open daily dawn 'til frankly I-don't-give-a-damn dusk. Free.) The opening scene of the TV show "Designing Women" features **The Villa Marre,** 1321 Scott (374-9979), a restored 19th-century house and museum (open Mon.-Fri. 9am-1pm, Sun. 1-5pm; $3, seniors and kids $2).

The **Toltec Mounds State Park** (961-9442), 15 mi. east of North Little Rock on Rte. 386, brings you back to 700AD. The Mounds were the political and religious center of the Plum Bayou Native Americans. (Open Tues.-Sat. 8am-5pm, Sun. noon-5pm. 1-hr. guided tours every ½ hr. starting at 9:30am. $2.64, kids $1.32.)

■■■ THE OZARKS

Up from the bayous and swamps of Louisiana, west of the muddy Mississippi, and east of Texas's dusty plains, road-trippers will find a terrain that is as beautiful as it is different. The verdant hills of the **Ozark Mountains** have lorded over the fertile resplendence of southern Missouri and northern Arkansas for many a moon. Not towering or jagged, they gently ripple over the land. Yet as docile as the hills appear, the scenic highways that traverse them expose curving, twisting danger as well as great beauty. These roads are now opening access to the Ozarks, crossing the natural boundaries that isolated the lives and customs of American mountain natives. Though diluted by the tourist trade, the simple lifestyle in the Ozarks survives.

Few buses venture into the area, and hitching is *not* recommended. Drivers should follow U.S. 71, or Rtes. 7 or 23 for best access and jaw-dropping views. Eureka Springs to Huntsville on Rte. 23 south is a scenic 1-hr. drive. Also head east or west on U.S. 62 from Eureka Springs for attractive stretches of road. The **Arkansas Department of Parks and Services** (800-643-8383) can help with your trip. For hiking, the **Ozark National Forest** presents a myriad of opportunities. If you want to paddle a portion of the **Buffalo National River,** call the ranger station for camping and canoe rental info (449-4311; canoe rental $25 per day, cabin $45 per day), or contact Buffalo Point Concessions, HCR, P.O. Box 388, Yellville 72687 (449-6206). The **Eureka Springs Chamber of Commerce** (253-8737; 800-643-3546 outside AR) also has vacation-planning info.

■ MOUNTAIN VIEW

Mountain View tries hard to maintain its authentic Ozark flavor. Home to a Pizza Hut, a picturesque courthouse square, and much surrounding beauty, this village (pop. 2439) succeeds. Be sure to visit the nearby **Ozark Folk Center.**

Practical Information Mountain View's **Chamber of Commerce** (269-8068), is located on Main St. (open Mon.-Sat. 8am-5pm). Pick up one of their essential and easy-to-read maps. **Rental cars** are available at **Lackey Motors Car Rental** (269-3211), at the corner of Main St. and Peabody Ave. ($25 per day plus 25¢ per mi.; open Mon.-Sat. 8am-5:30pm). The brand-new "vintage" **shuttle bus** (269-4423), reminiscent of a 1935 Ford, services all the major sights and downtown (every hr. 9am-noon; fare $1). The **Mental Health and Rape Crisis Hotline** (800-592-9503) and **Crisis Intervention** (800-542-1031) are both open 24 hrs. In **emergencies,** dial 911. Mountain View's **post office** (269-3520), is located in courthouse square; **ZIP code:** 72560; **area code:** 501.

Accommodations and Food Mountain View has enough lodgings for the budget traveler. The **Mountain View Motel,** 407 E. Main St. (269-3209), offers rustic but clean rooms with hot pots of free coffee. (Singles $26. Doubles $28.) The charming bed and country breakfast **Inn at Mountain View** (269-4200 or 800-535-1301), on Washington St., is an elegant Victorian home just off the town square. The reasonable price of its plushly decorated rooms and suites (all with private baths) includes a seven-course homemade breakfast. (Rooms and suites $44-91; 10% discount in the off-season.) Visitors who choose to sleep at the **Dry Creek Lodge** (269-3871 or 800-264-3655), at the Ozark Folk Center, will enjoy a cottage with simple country furnishings and convenience to the folk center ($45-50 plus $5 per additional person, 13 and under free with an adult). Soon to undergo new ownership and a name change, the **Scottish Inn** (269-3287 or 800-252-1962), on Main St. at the junction of Rtes. 5, 9, and 14 (a central corner), has a pool, clean rooms, and new furniture. (Singles $26, doubles $45; call for changing rates.)

Because Mountain View lies only 5-10 mi. south of the Ozark National Forest, the cheapest way to stay in the area is free **camping.** Pitching a tent anywhere is free and legal (and usually safe) as long as the campsite does not block any road, path, or thoroughfare. Campgrounds around the Blanchard Springs caverns include **Blanchard Springs Recreation Area** (32 sites, $8), **Gunner Pool Recreation Area** (27 sites, $5), and **Barkshed Recreation Area** (5 sites, free, but beware of young idlers who bring their drink and wickedness). For more information about the caverns, camping, and the fabulous hiking trails through the Ozark Forest, consult the **Ozark National Sylamore Ranger District** at P.O. Box 1279, Mountain View (269-3228); their office is on Rte. 14, a few blocks from Main.

The **Catfish House** (269-3820), Rte. 14 to School Dr. to Senior Dr., runs out of the gym of an old school complex and dishes up Mountain View's "Best Food in the Worst Location" for $5-8, as well as nightly hoedowns with banjo and fiddle music, clogging, and "Ozark humor" (open daily 11am-9pm). **The Hearthstone Bakery** (269-3297), next door to the Inn at Mountain View, provides culinary delights including cookies and danishes for under $1, and loaves of homemade bread for $2. Specialty diet breads are also available. **Joshua's Mountain View** (269-4136) serves daily lunch specials and several different buffets (sandwiches $2-3, dinner $6-8; open Sun.-Wed. 6am-2pm, Thurs.-Sat. 6am-9pm).

Sights and Entertainment Ozark culture survives most undiluted on the lush grounds of the **Ozark Folk Center** (269-3851), just minutes north of Mountain View off Rte. 9N. The center recreates a mountain village and the cabin crafts, music, and lore of the Ozarks. For those who shudder at the steep walk to the center, a tram transports visitors from the central parking lot (free). Among the 20 artisans practicing their trades in the **Crafts Forum** are a blacksmith, a basket weaver, a potter, a gunsmith, and a furniture maker. Visitors can taste freshly baked biscuits prepared in an antique kitchen for free, or dip their own candles in the chandler's shop (50¢). A wood carver sculpts faces from dried apples and a local herbalist concocts medicines from a garden beside the cottage. Musicians fiddle, pluck, and strum at lunchtime and nightly in the auditorium (shows at 7:30pm) while dancers implore the audience to jig and clog along. (Open May-Oct. daily 10am-5pm. Crafts area $5.50, ages 6-12 $3.25. Evening musical performances $6, kids 6-12 $4. Combination tickets and family rates available.) The center's seasonal events include the **Arkansas Folk Festival,** the **Mountain and Hammered Dulcimer Championships** from April 15-17, the **Banjo Weekend** in late May, the **Arkansas Old-Time Fiddlers Association State Championship** from Sept. 23-24, and the **SPBGMA National Fiddle Championships** from Nov. 4-6. While the devil may have gone down to Georgia, the **Fiddlers Championships** is right here—hundreds of experienced fiddlers, young and old, play the authentic music of the Ozarks.

A melisma of mountain music has long found its home in this region. The **dulcimer,** a stringed instrument distinguished by a fret that extends the length of the instrument, is native to the Ozarks. To dull some more, Mountain View boasts one of the finest dulcimer shops in the world, the **Dulcimer Shoppe,** P.O. Box 1230 (269-4313), on Rte. 9N, where observers can watch craftsmen fashion this mellow music maker and can even hammer a few strings themselves (open Mon.-Fri. 9am-5pm, Sat. 10am-5pm). Call the folk center (269-3871) for information on the annual **October Beanfest** which draws cooks from all over Arkansas, and guarantees free samples from cast-iron pots full of beans. Winter nights find the town wrapped around a **community bonfire,** while during March and April, thousands of people from around the world arrive to celebrate spring with parades, square and jig dancing, clogging, and musical tributes. In the meantime, visitors can revel in the musical charisma of triple Grammy Award winner Jimmy Driftwood, the quintessential Ozark artist, at the **Jimmy Driftwood Barn and Folk Museum** (269-8042), also on Rte. 9N. (shows Fri. and Sun. 7:30pm until whenever; free).

To catch some slightly different sounds, check out the **Old Mill** (269-4514), on Main St. This renovated 1914 grist mill still grinds some very fine flour for its museum visitors. (Open April-Oct. Wed.-Sun. 9am-5pm. Free.)

The areas around Mountain View abound with recreational activities. Fishing and rafting on the **White River** are popular diversions. Fishing licenses can be purchased at the Wal-Mart (269-4395) in Mountain View for around $10. If your legs ache from hiking, climb on a horse and experience the Ozarks from a saddle for $10 per hour at either **Sylamore Trail Rides,** P.O. Box 210, Mountain View (585-2231; open Wed.-Mon. 8:30am-5pm), or the **OK Trading Post** (585-2217), on Rte. 14 approximately 3½ mi. from the entrance to Blanchard Spring Caverns. Both places offer hour-long or overnight trips and all-day rides by reservation. If you have your own horse, Sylamore horse trail maps are available at the Sylamore Ranger Station.

Daytrips from Mountain View to **Buffalo River** (about 45 min. northwest) add the option of **canoeing** down the river for about $25 per day. Rent equipment at **Dodd's Float Service** (800-423-8731) or **Bennett's Canoe Rental** (449-6431). These businesses also provide paddles, life jackets, and shuttle service to Take-Out Point. For the adventurous hiker, the town of **Rush,** part of the Buffalo National Park River District, slowly decays about 30 mi. northwest of Mountain View off Rte. 14. Once a zinc ore mining hub, Rush is now a ghost town. Primitive camping areas with vault toilet, fire grates, and water are available year-round; Rush also has river access.

Blanchard Springs Caverns (757-2291), on the southern border of the Ozark Forest, glow and drip with exquisite cave formations and glassy, cool springs. Guided trails navigate the caverns (tours every 15 min., last spelunk ½ hr. before closing; open daily 9am-6pm; winter Mon.-Fri. 9am-5pm; $8, seniors and kids 6-15 $4).

■ EUREKA SPRINGS

In the early 19th century, the native Osage spread reports of a wonderful spring with magical healing powers. White settlers came to the site and quickly established a small town from which they sold bottles of the miraculous water. Tourists still flock to this tiny town in northwest Arkansas, but the springs are hardly the main attraction. Eureka has become the Lourdes of the South—today thousands flock to see the Passion Play or to feel the healing powers of the springs and the seven-story statue of Christ of the Ozarks.

For basic info, visit the **chamber of commerce** (800-643-3546 or 253-8737), located on U.S. 62 just north of Rte. 23 (open Mon.-Sat. 9am-5:30pm, Sun. 9am-5pm; Nov.-April Mon.-Fri. 9am-5pm). Eureka's **post office:** (253-9850), located on the historic loop (open Mon.-Fri. 8:15am-4:15pm); **ZIP code:** 72632; **area code:** 501.

Eureka Springs has more hotel beds than it does residents. Daily fluctuations in supply and demand determine the price of a room. The clean rooms of the **Frontier Motel** (253-9508), on Rte. 62E, are standard fare for the area. (Singles and doubles $32, two beds $38.) Prices drop on Mondays and Thursdays, when Passion Players take a break. **Kettle Campgrounds** (253-9100), on the eastern edge of town on Rte. 62, provides tent and hookup sites ($10/15).

The town is filled with tourist-oriented restaurants. Get away from the fast food and tourist glitz at the **Wagon Wheel,** 84 S. Main St. (253-9934), a country-western bar decorated with antiques (open Mon.-Fri. 10am-2am, Sat. 10am-midnight). Upstairs, dine at the **Chuck Wagon,** serving "sandwiches stacked like Mae West" ($3.25-$5.50) on a cozy patio jutting over a cliff. (Open Tues.-Sat. 11am-5pm.)

Built on piety, holy water, and slick marketing, the **Great Passion Play** (253-9200 or 800-882-PLAY), a production modeled after Germany's *Oberammergau* Passion Play, has begun to draw crowds, at times hordes, to its depiction of Jesus Christ's life and death. (Performances April 24-Oct. 26 Tues.-Wed. and Fri.-Sun. 8:30pm. Tickets $10-12, kids 4-11 ½-price. For reservations write P.O. Box 471, Eureka Springs 72632.) The amphitheater is off U.S. 62, on Passion Play Road. The chamber of commerce (253-8737) operates a trolley service which runs to the play, local churches, and the downtown historic loop ($3.50 for any 1 of the 6 routes for the entire day, 9am-8pm in the summer, 9am-5pm otherwise; kids 6 and under free). The loop is chock full with what might once have been charming old-style buildings but are now crammed with trinkets and souvenirs. The **Christ of the Ozarks** statue is seven stories of the messianic schtick, hallejuah, hallejuah...

■ FAYETTEVILLE

The young Bill Clinton and Hillary Rodham first shacked up here. Even though the First Couple have found classier digs, Fayetteville still ranks as one of America's top ten places to live. This is a real city where people live and work and it just happens to be in the beautiful Ozarks and to entertain a number of attractions worth seeing. **Prairie Grove Battlefield State Park** (846-2990), a 130-acre historic park located 8 mi. west of Fayetteville off Rte. 62, evokes the Civil War history of Fayetteville—the battle, the manner of life, and the buildings in which it all occurred (open daily 8am-10pm; free).

For more modern history, the **Arkansas Air Museum** (521-4947), Northwest Hangar, Drake Field, will lift your spirits with its soaring exhibits of aviation history (open daily 9:30am-4:30pm; free). Check out the cultural goings-on at the **Walton Arts Center** (443-5600), on Dixon St. For more info, call or visit the **Fayetteville Chamber of Commerce,** 123 W. Mountain St. (800-766-4626).

■■■ HOT SPRINGS NATIONAL PARK

Don't let the alligator farms, gift shops, wax museums, and amphibious tour-buses and boats turn you away. Despite the ubiquitous commercialism, Hot Springs delivers precisely what it advertises—cleansing, soothing relaxation. Once you've bathed in one of the many coils of these 143° springs and dined in one of several fine and friendly eateries, don't be surprised if you forget the tourist trade.

Practical Information Before touring Hot Springs, stop by the **visitors center,** 600 Central St. (321-2277, 800-772-2489, or 800-543-2284), downtown at Reserve St., and pick up the free *Hot Springs Pipeline* (open Mon.-Sat. 9:30am-5pm, Sun. 1-5pm). Hot Springs is especially crowded during the horse racing season at nearby **Oaklawn** (623-4411 or 800-722-3652 for racetrack info; Feb.-April; admission $1). Hot Springs's **post office:** 100 Reserve St. (623-7703), at the corner of Central in the Federal Reserve Building; **ZIP code:** 71901; **area code:** 501.

Accommodations and Food Not far from dowtown, the **Hot Springs Youth Hostel,** 435 Convention Blvd. (623-5223), has rooms in an old colonial house. (Office open daily 8-10am and 5-10pm.) Walk into a fairy tale at the **Best Motel,** 630 Ouachita (624-5736), which has gingerbread-like cabins. (Singles $20. Doubles $35.) The **Margarete Motel,** 217 Fountain St., offers an excellent deal with large rooms, each with kitchenette. (Singles $24-26. Doubles $26-28.) Rooms at the **Parkway Motel,** 815 Park Ave. (624-2551), start at $18. The motels clustered along Rtes. 7 and 88 have similar prices, but rates rise during the tourist season (Feb.-Aug.); camping is far cheaper (see Nearby Parks below).

Snack on *beignets* (3 for 90¢) and *café au lait* (95¢) at **Café New Orleans,** 210 Central Ave. (624-3200). At dinnertime, the café serves New Orleans's best, including po'boys ($4.25-6) and seafood selections ($5-10). (Open Sun.-Thurs. 11am-9pm, Fri.-Sat. 11am-10pm.) For good ol' country food, try **Granny's Kitchen,** 322 Central Ave. (624-6183), with full dinners and veggie plates under $6, and a damn good blackberry cobbler for only $2 (open daily 6:30am-8pm). Also try **Magee's Cafe,** 362 Central (623-4091), which costs a bit more ($5-8), but serves a fabulous chicken-fried steak ($7); be sure to have the Mississippi mud pie ($2) for dessert (open Sun.-Thurs. 8:30am-9:30pm, Fri.-Sat. 8:30am-11pm).

Sights and Entertainment For info on **Hot Springs National Park,** contact the **Fordyce Bathhouse Visitors Center,** 300 Central Ave. (623-1433), which offers fascinating tours on the surrounding wilderness areas and on the bathhouse itself. Seeing how Hot Springs was the "boyhood home" of Bill Clinton, Fordyce has recently constructed an exhibit of his rise to fame. (Open daily 9am-5pm.) The **Buckstaff** (623-2308), in "Bathhouse Row" on Central, retains the dignity and elegance of Hot Springs's heyday in the 1920s. Baths are $11,50, whirlpool $1.50 extra, massages $11.75. (Open Mon.-Fri. 7-11:45am and 1:30-3pm, Sat. 7-11:45am.) Around the corner is the rather unconventional **Hot Springs Health Spa,** N. 500 Reserve (321-9664). Not only does the spa offer the only coed baths in town, but you can stay as long as you like and meander among the many baths. Note the late hours. (Bath $11, massage $11-13; open daily 9am-9pm.) The **Downtowner,** at Central and Park, gives the cheapest hands-on, full treatment baths with no difference in quality. (Bath $9.50, whirlpool $1.50 extra, massage $10. Open Mon.-Fri. 7-11:30am and 1:30-3:30pm, Sat. 7-11:30am and 2-4:30pm, closed Wed. afternoons.) The handy guide at the visitors center lists all the hours and prices around town.

Hot Spring is full of natural beauty. You can gaze up at the green-peaked mountains or cruise Lake Hamilton on the **Belle of Hot Springs** (525-4438), with 1-hr. narrated tours alongside the Ouachita Mountains and Lake Hamilton mansions ($8, kids $4). In town, the **Mountain Valley Spring Water Company,** 150 Central Ave. (623-6671 or 800-643-1501), offers free samples and tours of its national headquarters (open Mon.-Fri. 9am-5pm, Sat.-Sun. 10am-4pm). From the **Hot Springs Mountain Observatory Tower** (623-6035), located in the national park (turn off Central Ave. to Rte. 7), you can view the beautiful panorama of the surrounding mountains and lakes. (Open May 16-Labor Day daily 9am-9pm; Nov.-Feb. 9am-5pm; March-Oct. 9am-6pm. $2.75, kids $1.75.) A more horizontal escape from the bustling town center is **Whittington Park,** on Whittington off Central, where shops and bathhouses quickly give way to an expanse of trees, grass, and shaded picnic tables.

Nighttime family entertainment percolates throughout Hot Springs. **The Famous Bath House Show,** 701 Central Ave. (623-1415), performs a smattering of every possible type of music (well, perhaps not industrial-funk-hip-hop) around. (Shows nightly 8pm. May-Sept. $9.45, children $5. Reservations recommended.) A short drive out of town is the **Music Mountain Jamboree,** 2720 Albert Pike (767-3841), also called U.S. 270W. Family-style country music shows take place nightly during the summer, and at various times throughout the rest of the year (shows at 8pm; $9, kids $4.50; reservations recommended).

■ NEARBY PARKS

The closest **campgrounds** can be found at **Gulpha Gorge** (part of Hot Springs National Park); follow Rte. 70 to 70B, about 3 mi. northeast of town (sites $6, seniors $3, no hookups, no showers).

Lake Ouachita Park (767-9366) encompasses 48,000 acres and the largest of three clear, beautiful, artificial lakes near Hot Springs. Travel 3 mi. west on U.S. 270, then 12 mi. north on Rte. 227. Numerous islands promise an escape from civilization in quiet coves and rocky beaches. Campers pay $6-14 per day, depending on the beauty of the site and the facilities available; fishing boats rent for $10 per day.

Lake Catherine Park (844-4176), covers over 2000 acres of the Ouachita Mountains and stretches along the shores of beautiful Lake Catherine. Campsites start at $12 per day. Take exit 97 off I-30 at Malvern. (Canoe rentals $3.50 per hr., power boats $18 per ½ day, $25 per day.) **Shore Line Campground,** 5321 Central Ave. (525-1902), just south of town on Lake Hamilton, has full RV hookups, a pool, restrooms, showers, and laundry facilities ($12 per day, $72 per week). Call for reservations. Houseboats are permitted.

■ LEAVING ARKANSAS: TEXARKANA

For those not adept at etymology, Texarkana straddles the border between Texas and Arkansas. Stand on the median of **Stateline Avenue** and you'll have a foot in each state. The **Texarkana Historical Museum,** 219 State Line Ave. (793-4831), has exhibits on the area's Native Americans and Texarkana's most famous entertainer, **Scott Joplin.** (Open Tues.-Fri. 10am-4pm, Sat. noon-3pm, Sun. 1-3pm. $1, kids 50¢.) On the corner of 3rd and Main St. you can see a **mural** of the father of ragtime.

Have a neat whiskey at the **Ace of Clubs House,** 420 Pine St. (793-7108). Financed from the winnings of an 1885 card game, the joint is built in the shape of a club. Every Memorial and Labor Day, Texarkana hosts the **Strange Family Bluegrass Festival** at the Strange Family Park. Take U.S. 59 south to Farm Rd. 989 to Farm Rd. 2516 to George Thomas Rd. During the holiday season, Texarkana glows with yuletide spirit in the **Twice as Bright Light Festival.** Texarkana's **area codes:** Texas: 903, Arkansas: 501.

THE GREAT LAKES

When the glaciers retreated from the northern border of the United States, they left behind a fertile, flat bed, filled with small pockets of water. The region is now covered with the five Great Lakes and thousands upon thousands of shallow pools. Northernmost Lake Superior, the largest freshwater lake in the world, has the least populated and most scenic coasts, and dances with one of the only significant wolf populations left in the contiguous United States. Lake Michigan, bordering on four states, is a sports-lover's paradise, offering deep-water fishing, swimming, sailing, and sugar-fine sand dunes. Lake Erie, connecting the east to the midwest, has suffered the most from industrial pollution, but thanks to vigilant citizens and strict regulations, the shallowest Great Lake is gradually reclaiming its former beauty. Lake Huron and Ontario provide splashing around and great fishing for both Americans and Canadians.

The deep forests of the Great Lakes region were home to some of the earliest Native Americans, who blessed the fertile soil for its natural abundance. Since then much of the land has been taken, cultivated, and the once pristine splendor bears the scars of industrial boom and rust. In the 19th and early 20th centuries, millions of immigrants came here to search their fortune in the land of the region by farming the rich soil, mining the lodes of iron and copper, and logging the dense forests. Soon, natural resources were exhausted, and the economies of the region had to either change or collapse. Most areas weathered the shift by transporting and manufacturing rather than supplying raw materials. However, in the wake of modernization and adaptation, cities like Cleveland and Detroit were left behind, forced to retool their economic base and recapture a spirit of growth.

Today, the Great Lakes region has the strongest draw for the hostel-and-campground crowd, with its multitudinous water and wilderness opportunities in places where the talons of "progress" never reached. But the sophisticated urban traveler should not despair—Minneapolis/St. Paul has all the artsy panache of any coastal metropolis (minus the accompanying angst), and Chicago remains the focal point for Midwestern activity, with world-class music, architecture, and cuisine.

 # Ohio

Ohio is best known for rust-belt industrial cities like Cincinnati and Cleveland, thought to combine the pollution of the East Coast with the cultural blandness of the Midwest. In reality, these cities have cleaned themselves up, Midwestern blandness is a misrepresentation, and the majority of the state lies outside metropoli in gentle, quintessentially middle-American farmland. Here rolling green wooded hills, verdant river valleys, the Great Lake shore, and enchanting small towns entice you to re-evaluate the mythos of the Midwest.

By the way—never, *ever* confuse Ohio with Iowa or Idaho, or the Tri-State Name Council will place you on their widely-distributed blacklist, and residents of all three otherwise friendly states will scorn and publicly humiliate you. Just a warning.

PRACTICAL INFORMATION
Capital: Columbus.
Tourist Information: State Office of Travel and Tourism, 77 S. High St., P.O. Box 1001, Columbus 43215 (614-466-8844). **Greater Columbus Convention and Visitors Bureau,** 1 Columbus Bldg., 10 W. Broad St. #1300, Columbus

43215 (614-221-2489 or 800-234-4386). Open Mon.-Fri. 8am-5pm. **Ohio Tourism Line:** 800-282-5393.

Time Zone: Eastern. **Postal Abbreviation:** OH

Sales Tax: 5.5%.

■■■ CLEVELAND

"Just drive north until the sky and all the buildings turn gray. Then you're in Cleveland." One of Cleveland's many critics uttered this quote hoping to achieve the "city cliche" honors normally reserved for Mark Twain. Alas, this witticism's author has remained obscure, much as has any praise for poor, beleaguered Cleveland. Business leaders are working to creatively convert its resources into new and vital forms. Cleveland's old warehouses on the Cuyahoga River have been reworked into raving nightclubs, and the much-anticipated Rock and Roll Hall of Fame will soon open, drawing scads of youthful tourists. With skillful management, Cleveland could change from a popular joke to a pop culture haven.

PRACTICAL INFORMATION

Emergency: 911.

Visitor Information: Cleveland Convention and Visitors Bureau, 3100 Tower City Ctr. (621-4110 or 800-321-1001), 31st floor in Terminal Tower at Public Square. Free maps. Write for a copy of the mind-boggling *Greater Cleveland Official Visitors Guide,* which gives info on every attraction conceivable. Open Mon.-Fri. 8:30am-5pm.

Cleveland Hopkins International: (265-6030) in Brookpark, 10 mi. west of downtown; take the RTA airport rapid #66X ("Red Line") to Terminal Tower ($1.25).

Amtrak: 200 Cleveland Memorial Shoreway N.E. (696-5115 or 800-872-7245), across from Municipal Stadium, east of City Hall. To: New York City ($97, 11 hrs.), Chicago ($76, 6 hrs.). Open Mon.-Sat. 11am-3:30pm, Sun. 11pm-8am.

Greyhound: 1465 Chester Ave. (781-0520), at E. 14th St. near RTA bus lines and about 7 blocks east of Terminal Tower. To: New York City ($63, 10 her.), Chicago ($29, 6 hrs.), Pittsburgh ($19, 4 hrs.).

Regional Transit Authority (RTA): 315 Euclid Ave. (566-5074), across the street from Woolworth's. Schedules for city buses and rapid transit lines. Bus lines, connecting with the Rapid stops, provide public transport to most of the metropolitan area. 24-hr. **answerline** (621-9500) accessible from touch-tone phones. Trains $1.50, buses $1.25 ("local" service, free transfers—remember to ask), $1.50 express. Office open Mon.-Fri. 7am-6pm. Service daily 4:30am-12:30am.

Taxi: Yellow Cab, 623-1550; 24 hrs. **Americab,** 429-1111; 24 hrs. $2.40 first mi., $1.20 each additional ¼ mi.

Help Line: Rape Crisis Line, 391-3912; 24 hrs. **Ohio Aids Hotline,** 800-3222437.

Post Office: 2400 Orange Ave. (443-4199 or 443-4096). Open Mon.-Fri. 8am-7pm. **ZIP code:** 44101. **Area Code:** 216.

Terminal Tower in **Public Square** cleaves the land into east and west. North-south streets are numbered and given an east-west prefix, e.g. E. 18th St. is 18 blocks east of the Terminal Tower. To reach Public Square from I-90 or I-71, follow the Ontario Ave./Broadway exit. From I-77, take the 9th St. exit to Euclid Ave., which runs into the Square. From the Amtrak station, follow Lakeside Ave. and turn onto Ontario, which leads to the tower. Almost all of the RTA trains and buses run downtown.

ACCOMMODATIONS AND CAMPING

For cheap lodgings, travelers are better off staying in the suburbs. Hotel taxes, not included in the prices listed below, are a hefty 10%,. If you know your plans well in advance, try **Cleveland Private Lodgings,** P.O. Box 18590, Cleveland 44118 (321-3213), which places people in homes around the city for as little as $35. All arrangements must be made through the office. Leave two to three weeks for a letter of confirmation. (Open Mon.-Tues. and Thurs.-Fri. 9am-noon and 3pm-5pm.)

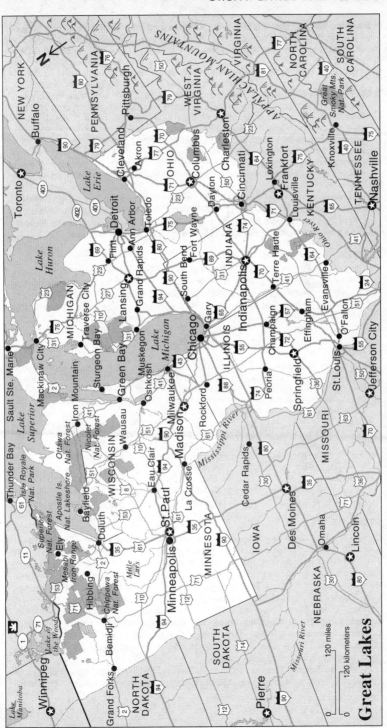

Great Lakes

Stanford House Hostel (HI-AYH), 6093 Stanford Rd. (467-8711), 22 mi. south of
Cleveland in Peninsula. Exit 12 off I-80. Take bus #77F to Ridgefield Holiday Inn
(the last stop) and call the hostel for a ride. Located in a beautifully restored 19th-
century Greek Revival farmhouse in the Cuyahoga Valley National Recreation
Area. It's a great hostel, but somewhat distant. One-week max. stay. Check-in 5-
10pm. 30 beds. Curfew 11pm. Everybody pays, $10. Reservations recommended.

Cleveland YMCA, 2200 Prospect Ave. (344-3822), a 15 min. walk from downtown, at the corner of Prospect and E. 22nd. If you plan on sticking around Cleveland for a week and can bring a recent paycheck stub as proof of employment,
then this is worth investigating. The room quality varies by floor, so investigate in
person. Weekly $93.70, daily $28. Office open Mon.-Fri. 8:30am-4pm.

Lakewood Manor Motel, 12020 Plympton Ave. (226-4800), about 3 mi. west of
downtown in Lakewood. Take bus #55CX. Neat and clean. TV, central A/C. Complimentary coffee daily and donuts on weekends. Singles $32. Doubles $34.

Two **campgrounds** are 40 min. east of downtown, off I-480 in Streetsboro: **Wood-
side Lake Park,** 2256 Frost Rd. (626-4251; tent sites for 2 $17.50, with electricity
$18.50; $2 per additional guest, ages 3-17 75¢); and **Valley View Lake Resort,**
8326 Ferguson (626-2041; tent sites $19, water and hookup available).

FOOD

You'll find Cleveland's culinary treats in tiny neighborhoods surrounding the downtown area. To satiate that lust for hot corned beef, step into one of the bakers' dozens of delis in the city center. There are a cluster of Italian cafés and restaurants in
Little Italy around **Mayfield Road.** Over 100 vendors sell produce, meat, cheese and
other groceries at the indoor-outdoor **West Side Market** at W. 25th St. and Lorain
Ave. (Open Mon. and Wed. 7am-4pm, Fri.-Sat. 7am-6pm.) For an extensive listing of
restaurants, turn to the monthly magazine *Live* ($2).

Brewed Awakenings, 1859 Prospect Ave. (696-5530), a short walk from the Terminal Tower. Hip café action downtown where you can contemplate a stairway
leading into the ceiling and a psychedelic VW "bug" while sipping cappuccino
($2) or munching on a deli sandwich ($4-5). Open Mon.-Thurs. 7am-8pm, Fri.
7am-midnight, Sat. 9am-midnight, Sun. 10am-2pm.

Tommy's, 182 Coventry Rd. (321-7757), just up the hill from University Circle.
Take bus #9X east to Mayfield and Coventry Rd. Did someone say hummus? Sample any of Tommy's delicious and creative Eastern-based dishes. Healthful pita
bread sandwiches ($2.60-$6). Try the Brownie Monster ($1.85) for dessert. Open
Mon.-Fri. 7:30am-9:45pm, Sat. 7:30am-11pm, Sun. 9am-9:45pm.

Mama Santa's, 12305 Mayfield Rd. (421-2159), in Little Italy, just east of University
Circle. Sicilian food served beneath subdued lighting. Medium pizza $3.70, spa-
ghetti $4.50. Open Mon.-Thurs. 10:30pm-11:45pm, Fri.-Sat. 10:30am-12:45am.

SIGHTS

Downtown Cleveland has escaped the hopeless blight which has struck other Great
Lakes cities such as Detroit and Erie. Capital is moving into the town rather than out.
The Cleveland Indians now play at brand-new Jacobs Field, and the Rock and Roll
Hall of Fame, a new theater in Playhouse Square, and the Great Lakes Museum of Sci-
ence are all about to open. 1990 witnessed the opening of the long-awaited **Tower
City Center** (771-6611), a three-story shopping complex in the Terminal Tower.
Although essentially a luxury mall with prices to match, Tower Center is a notable
emblem of the tremendous renovation and revitalization of downtown Cleveland.
Cleveland Lakefront State Park (881-8141), two mi. west of downtown and
accessible from Lake Ave. or Cleveland Memorial Shoreway, is a mi.-long beach with
great swimming and picnicking areas.

Playhouse Square Center, 1519 Euclid Ave. (771-4444), a 10-min. walk east of
Terminal Tower, is the third-largest performing arts center in the nation. The **Cleve-**

land Opera (575-0900) and the famous **Cleveland Ballet** (621-2260) perform from September to May nearby at 1375 Euclid Ave.

University Circle, 4 mi. east of the city, is a cluster of 75 cultural institutions. Check with the helpful visitors bureau (see Practical Information above) for details on museums, live music, and drama. The world-class **Cleveland Museum of Art,** 11150 East Blvd. (421-7340), in University Circle, exhibits fine French and American Impressionist paintings, as well as a version of Rodin's "The Thinker." A beautiful plaza and pond face the museum. (Open Tues. and Thurs.-Fri. 10am-5:45pm, Wed. 10am-9:45pm, Sat. 9am-4:45pm, Sun. 1-5:45pm. Free.) Nearby is the **Cleveland Museum of Natural History,** Wade Oval (231-4600), where you can see the only existing skull of the fearsome Pygmy Tyrant *(Nanatyrannus)*. (Open Mon.-Sat. 10am-5pm, Sun. 1-5pm. Admission $5, seniors $3. Free after 2pm Tues. and Thurs.) The renowned **Cleveland Orchestra,** one of the nation's best, bows, plucks and blows in University Circle at Severance Hall, 11001 Euclid Ave. (231-7300; tickets $11-25, student rush available the preceding Friday). During the summer, the orchestra performs at **Blossom Music Center,** 1145 W. Steels Corners Rd., Cuyahoga Falls (920-8040), about 45 min. south of the city (lawn seating $10). University Circle itself is safe, but some of the nearby areas can be rough, especially at night.

In a nicer area east of University Circle sits the **Dobama Theatre,** 1846 Coventry Rd., Cleveland Hts. (932-6838). This intimate theater gives terrific, inexpensive (free-$15) performances in a living-room atmosphere. **The Rock and Roll Hall of Fame** will not be finished until October 1995, but the impatient may call 781-7625 for details. Fun-seekers flock to **Cedar Point Amusement Park** (see Sandusky, OH). Peruse the monthly *Live* or the daily *Plain Dealer* for entertainment listings.

The **Cleveland Indians** play baseball at brand-new, beautiful Jacobs Field (861-1200, tickets $4-18), while the **Cavaliers** hoop it up at the Arena (659-9100, tickets $17 and up). In the fall, catch the orange-helmeted **Browns** in all their gridiron glory at Municipal Stadium (891-5000, tickets $20 and up).

NIGHTLIFE

A great deal of Cleveland's nightlife is focused in the **Flats,** the former industrial core of the city along both banks of the Cuyahoga River. The northernmost section of the Flats, just west of Public Square, contains several nightclubs and restaurants. On weekend nights, expect large crowds and larger traffic jams. On the east side of the river, you can watch the sun set across the water through the steel frames of old railroad bridges from the deck at **Rumrunners,** 1124 Old River Rd. (696-6070). Live bands play (Thurs.-Sun.), and draft beer is $1.75. (Open Wed.-Thurs. 7pm-2:30am, Fri. 4pm-2:30am, Sat. and Sun. 1pm-2:30am. $3 cover.) **Fagan's,** 996 Old River Rd. (241-6116), looks like a South Florida beachside resort, not a den of iniquity which trains hungry English waifs to pickpocket. "Please, sir. Can I have some $6-9 sandwiches or entrees starting at $11?" Yes, son, you can, but please tell your friends not to do dance numbers on the gorgeous riverside deck. On the west side of the river are several other clubs, including **Shooters,** 1148 Main Ave. (861-6900), a bar and restaurant with a great view of the river and Lake Erie. Prices are high (dinners $11-20), but you can capture the flavor of Cleveland nightlife inexpensively by taking your drink to the in-deck pool. (Open Mon.-Sat. 11:30am-2am, Sun. 11am-2am.)

■ NEAR CLEVELAND

Cedar Point Amusement Park, 65 mi. from Cleveland in **Sandusky,** is *cool as all hell.* Cedar Point provides the country with the "best amusement park in the world," earning its superlatives over and over. Catering to thrill seekers with 11 rollercoasters, from the world's highest and fastest inverted rollercoasters (riders are suspended from above) to a "training coaster" for kids, Cedar Point offers fun for all levels of courage. (419-627-2350, off U.S. 6 near Sandusky; open mid-May to mid-Sept. daily 10am-10pm, with 8pm close in May and midnight close on summer weekends. $26, senior $15, children 4 and older under 48" $10.)

Holmes County's Amish communities lie within an hour's drive from Cleveland. Outsiders can visit the **Amish Farm** (893-2951) in **Berlin,** which offers a film presentation, demonstrations of non-electrical appliances, and a tour of the grounds. (Open April-Oct. Mon.-Fri. 10am-5pm, Sat. 10am-6pm. Tours $2.25, children $1. Buggy ride $2.75.) Unserved by public transportation, Berlin lies 70 mi. south of Cleveland on Rte. 39, 17 pastoral miles west of I-77. For demonstrations of electrical appliances which provoke raw fear, visit **Geauga Lake Amusement Park,** 1060 Aurora Rd. (800-THE-WAVE or 843-9283), 30 mi. southeast of Cleveland in Aurora. Those over 55" tall can experience the brand new Texas Twister ride. $17.95, children under 42" free. Nearby **Sea World,** 1100 Sea World Drive, off Rte. 43 at Rte. 91 (800-63-SHAMU or 637-4268), has Shark Encounter, sequel to the less menacing Penguin Encounter. ($21.95, children 3-11 $17.95. Parking $3.) Farther south (60 mi. from town) is the **Pro Football Hall of Fame,** 2121 George Halas Dr. N.W. (456-8207), in Canton (take exit 107a at the junction of I-77 and U.S. 62), has memorabilia and films of American football. (Open 9am-8pm, Labor Day-Memorial Day 9am-5pm. $6, over 62 and children 6-14, $2.50.

The Lake Erie Coast around Sandusky is lined with numerous 50s-era roadside "amusements." **Train-O-Rama,** 6732 E. Harbor Rd. (734-5856), in Marblehead, is a diorama of a miniature landscape built with 1½ mi. of track, 1001 lights, 9,500 lbs. of plaster, and 200 miniature buildings (open Memorial Day-Labor Day, Mon.-Sat. 10am-6pm, Sun. 1-6pm. $3.50, children 4-11 $2.50))

■■■ LAKE ERIE ISLANDS

The Lake Erie Islands, off the coast of northern Ohio, are among those unusual land formations known as resort islands. Unlike the ordinary island, everything costs twice as much and the air has a "peppiness" that smothers the land. **Sandusky,** on the mainland on Rte. 2, 55 mi. west of Cleveland, is the starting point for the islands and home to **Cedar Point Amusement Park** (see Near Cleveland above). Once the last stop in the United States for escaped slaves fleeing to Canada through the Underground Railroad, Sandusky now supplies lots of fast food and motels. The **Visitors and Convention Center Bureau,** 231 W. Washington Row, Sandusky OH, 44870 (800-255-3743) has info on the area. **Greyhound,** 6513 Milan Rd., Sandusky (625-6907) runs on U.S. 250 south of Rte. 2. Sandusky's **area code:** 419.

South Bass Island, or Put-In-Bay as it is commonly known, is the lively, exciting island with a party atmosphere. The town of **Put-In-Bay** is packed on weekend with those frequenting the bizarre bars. The **Round House** (285-4595) in—you guessed it—a round house, attracts guzzlers with buckets of beer ($22.50). The bucket holds 13 glasses, provided you don't spill any—plus you get to keep the nifty plastic bucket. Refills are $17.50, making it the best bulk beer bargain ever. Just a few steps down Lorain Ave., the **Beer Barrel Saloon** (285-2337) can probably find you elbow room at its bar, the longest in the world at 405 ft. 10 in. (glasses $2.50). (Both open 11am-12:30am; both feature live music daily in the early afternoon, with evening shows on weekends.) Under-21sters will find fun at **Kimberly's Carousel** downtown, one of just 100 carousels with wooden horses left in America (75¢; open summer only). On the eastern edge of Put-in Bay, **Perry's Victory and International Peace Memorial,** (285-2184) honoring Commodore Oliver Hazard Perry's 1813 victory over the British in the Battle of Lake Erie and the 100 years of peace between the U.S. and Canada, rises 352 ft. above lake-level, the tallest Doric column in the world. (Elevator to the top $2.) In the center of the island, at the corner of Catawba Ave. and Thompson Rd., the **Heineman Winery** (285-2811) ferments a fun time. Tours of wine-making $3.50 and include a sampling. (Tours daily every hr. 11am-5pm; bottle of wine $5.) While digging for a well, they discovered the **largest geode ever discovered;** a look at it is included in the winery tour. Keep in mind that the average geode is only baseball-sized.

Rooms on the island start at $55; the **South Bass Island State Park** (419-797-4530). on the western edge, offers 136 **campsites** and charges $12 per night (showers, no hookup, no reservations). On weekends arrive before 8:30am on Friday.

The most enjoyable activity on the islands is a leisurely bike ride (both islands are about 3 mi. in diameter). Both islands run **trams** between the dock, the sights, and the campground ($1). The **Miller Boat Line** (800-500-2421 or 285-2421) ferries passengers and cars to South Bass Island from Catawba Point (June-Sept. 7:30am-7:30pm every ½-hr., less frequently in April, May, Oct. and Nov.; $4 one way, children 6-11 $1, bike $1.50, car $8). (Exit Rte. 2, follow Rte. 53 north to the end. Park at one of the ferry's free lots; be careful of the ones that charge.) **Sonny S. Water Taxi** (285-8774) runs from Put-in Bay to **Lonz Winery** on Middle Bass Island. ($5 round-trip, winery tours $1.50.) Miller Boat Line also serves Middle Bass from Catawba Point ($4.50 one way). At the ferry dock, **Island Bike Rental** (285-2016) rents one-speeds ($2.50 per hr., $7.50 per day). Pick up a free map of the island a few yards away at **E's Golf Carts** (285-5553; carts $8 per hr., $45 per day).

Kelleys Island, though still less developed than South Bass, is rapidly becoming the more popular of the two. **Kelleys Island Ferry Boat Lines, Inc.,** 510 Main St., Marblehead (798-9763 or 800-876-1907; runs April-Nov. From late June-early September, the ferry departs every hour Mon.-Thurs., 7;30am-7pm, and Fri.-Sat., 7am-11pm. Adults $7.80, children 6-11 $4.50, automobiles $14, bicycles $2.50. The **Neuman Boat Line,** Foot of Frances St., Marblehead (798-5800), runs late June-early September, $7.80, children 6-11 $4.50, and automobiles $14. Departure times vary, so calling ahead. Neuman boats rarely leave past 9pm.

The island was once a large source of limestone; you can wander around abandoned, water-filled quarries, the best of which is **East Quarry** in the center of the island. The quarries are great places to watch people try to dodge the security guards for a dive into the crystal-clear coolness. The **Kelleys Island State Park** (419-797-4530), has 129 sites $12. No reservations; arrive by early afternoon on Friday for weekend spots. (Showers, toilets, a beach, and allows pets.) Accommodations on Kelleys include cottages, inns, and B&Bs, but you're not likely to find anything below $60 a night. The **West Bay Inn**, 1230 West Lakeshore Dr. (746-2207), on the west side of the island has burgers $2.75, Mama's Big Lovin' apple pie $2.50. (Open Mon.-Fri 11am-9pm, Sat.-Sun. 11am-10pm.) Several rental shops supply bicycles ($8 and up) and golf carts.

■■■ COLUMBUS

This college town looks more like a city, as it is home to Ohio State University, the largest university in the country. The main drag, High Street, heads north from the towering office complexes of downtown, through the thriving galleries and gay community in Short North, and finally to the collegiate coolness that OSU and its unwieldy student population of 60,000 bring. Along with the overwhelming cultural options that unfold along High St., this state capital also boasts the Sciotto river, whose banks allow relaxing picnics, and Bexley, lawnscaped suburbia at its best.

Practical Information Visitors to the city can contact the **Greater Columbus Visitors Center** (800-345-4386 or 221-2489), located in downtown's **City Center Mall** on the third floor. *The Other, Columbus Alive,* and *The Guardian* are free weekly papers with listings of art and entertainment options, available in many shops and restaurants. **Greyhound,** 111 E. Town St. (221-5311), offers the most frequent and complete service from downtown. To: Cincinnati ($15.50-19); Cleveland ($15-23); Chicago ($60). Public transportation in the city is run by the **Central Ohio Transit Authority (COTA),** 177 S. High St. (228-1776); offices Mon.-Fri. 8:30am-5:30pm; fare $1, express $1.35); **ZIP code:** 43216; **area code:** 614.

Accommodations and Food The **Heart of Ohio Hostel (HI-AYH),** 95 E. 12th Ave. (294-7157), one block from OSU, has outstanding facilities, a helpful manager named Clint, and organized activities: biking, hiking, rock climbing, and more. ($8, nonmembers $11. Weekly rates available. Check-in 5-11pm. Curfew 11pm.) Rooms in apartment houses near campus are cheap, abundant, and well advertised during the summer, when OSU students vacate. The **Greater Columbus Bed and Breakfast Cooperative** (967-6060) includes B&Bs with rates around $35.

The following are all located on Columbus' main drag, High St. **Bernie's Bagels and Deli,** 1896 N. High St. (291-3448), for a variety of sandwiches in a grunge rock cellar atmosphere ($3-6). There are live shows nightly. (Opens Mon.-Tues. 8:30am-1am, Wed.-Fri. 8:30am-2am, Sat. 9:30am-2am, Sun. 9:30am-1am.) **Bermuda Onion Delicatessen,** 660 N. High St. (221-6296), specializes in sandwiches ($4-7) like grilled provolone on challah with herb mayo, sprouts, and tomato. (Open Mon.-Thurs. 8:30am-10pm, Fri. 8:30am-11pm, Sat. 9am-11pm, Sun. 9am-10pm.) Downtown, **Katzinger's Delicatessen** (228-3354), Third at Livingston, has served such luminaries as President Clinton. Over 80 sandwiches to choose from. (Open Mon.-Thurs. 8:30am-8:30pm, Fri. 8:30am-9:30pm, Sat.-Sun. 9am-8:30pm.) At **Firdous,** 1538 N. High (299-1844), you can set up at the counter and order fresh falafel or shish-kebab from this small and well-loved Middle Eastern restaurant/grocery.

Sights **Ohio State University (OSU)** looms 2 mi. north of downtown Columbus. Its enrollment of over 60,000 students makes it the largest in the United States. **Visitor Information** is at the Ohio Union, 1839 N. High St. (292-0428 or 292-0418). The well-respected, heavily endowed, and architecturally outstanding **Wexner Center for the Arts** (292-3535), N. High St. at 15th Ave., displays avant-garde exhibits and films, and hosts progressive music, dance, and other performances. The Bookstore (292-1807) has an exhaustive selection of art books and gifts. (Exhibits open Tues., Thurs., and Fri. 10am-6pm, Wed. and Sat. 10am-8pm, Sun. noon-5pm. Free. Ticket office open Mon.-Fri. 9am-5pm; call 292-2354 for prices.)

In 1991, the **Columbus Museum of Art,** 480 E. Broad St. (221-6801), acquired the Sirak Collection of Impressionist and European Modernist works. (Open Tues., Thurs., and Fri. 11am-4pm, Wed. 11am-9pm, Sat. 10am-5pm, Sun. 11am-5pm. Permanent collection free, traveling exhibits have a small fee.) Ohio's **Center of Science and Industry (COSI),** 280 E. Broad St. (288-2674), ½ mi. west of I-71 and Broad St., will wow kids with such hands-on exhibits as a mock coal mine. (Open Mon.-Sat. 10am-5pm, Sun. noon-5:30pm. $5, students, children, seniors $3.) Across the street is the first ever **Wendy's** restaurant. Just west is the lighthearted **Thurber House,** 77 Jefferson Ave. (464-1032), where rooms of James Thurber's childhood home are decorated with cartoons by the famous author and *New Yorker* cartoonist. Memorabilia from his life and times on display. (Open daily noon-4pm, free.)

Nature lovers can enjoy the **Columbus Zoo,** 9990 Riverside Dr. (645-3400), in Powell. (Open Thurs.-Tues. 9am-6pm, Wed. 9am-8pm; Labor Day-Memorial Day daily 9am-5pm. $5, kids 2-11 $3, under 2 free. Parking $2.) The expansive **Franklin Park Conservatory,** 1777 E. Broad St. (645-8733), has a mammoth collection of self-contained environments including rain forests, deserts, and Himalayan mountains. (Tues.-Sun. 10am-5pm, Wed. 10am-8pm. $4, students and seniors $3, kids $2.)

Just south of Capitol Square is the **German Village,** first settled in 1843 and now the largest privately-funded historical restoration in the U.S. Visitors can tour stately brick homes and patronize old-style beer halls. At **Schmidt's Sausage Haus,** 240 E. Kossuth St. (444-6808), the oom-pah bands **Schnickelfritz** and **Schnapps** lead polkas Tues.-Sat. 8:30pm. (Open Sun.-Mon. 11am-10pm, Tues.-Thurs. 11am-11pm, Fri.-Sat. 11am-midnight.) Call or visit the helpful **German Village Society,** 634 S. 3rd St. (221-8888; open Mon.-Fri. 9am-4pm, Sat. 9am-3pm, Sun. noon-3pm).

Entertainment and Nightlife On the first Saturday night of each month, Columbus hosts the roaming art-party known as **The Gallery Hop,** where galleries in the Short North display new exhibitions while socialites and art collectors admire the works (and each other) until early Sunday morning. The **Riley Hawk Galleries,** 642 N. High St. (228-6554), are among the world's finest for glass sculpture.

Bar bands are a Columbus mainstay; it's hard to find a bar that *doesn't* have live music on the weekend. **Bernie's Distillery**, pounds with live acts all week ($1 cover on weekends). The once-industrial **Brewery District** now houses a majority of the bars. **High Beck**, 564 S. High St. (224-0886), moves to jazz and blues, while **Hosters Brewing Co.**, 564 S. High St. (228-6066), attracts locals with its homemade brew.

If rocking bars aren't your flavor, check out the phat Transylvanian coffeehouse, **Idiot Bou Café**, 2153 N. Hight St. (421-7722), serving up "coffee, cakes, and funky freshness" from 9am-6am daily. On Thurs. nights (11pm-4am), the DJ spins, and around midnight area rappers start freestylin' on the open mic. **Paradigm**, 163 N. High St., provides house, tribal, acid jazz, and all the thumping club fare found between (no cover Wednesday nights). For a more mellow evening, many Columbians (Columbusians?) head for the cafés. **Luna's Coffeehouse**, 1655 N. Hight St. (291-5060), is student-run and presents an occasional poetry slam or rock act. **Cup O' Joe**, 627 S. 3rd St. (221-1563) in German Village, adorns itself with a cubist Cup o' Joe interpretation on one wall, futuristic lamps, green and fuzzy loft disc bolted to the ceiling, and a high level of yuppie pretention left over from the Reagan Years.

■ NEAR COLUMBUS

Dense green forests swathe southeastern Ohio's narrow valleys, steep hills, and ragged rock formations, which were carved into the land by Pleistocene glaciers. The southern route of the Buckeye trail snakes through this jagged terrain, roughly tracked by **U.S. 50.** Along the highway, which runs east from Cincinnati to Parkersburg, lie spectacular Native American burial grounds, constructed by Adena, Hopewell, and Fort Ancient "Moundbuilders." Among the most interesting is the **Mound City Group National Monument** (774-1125), on Rte. 104, 3 mi. north of Chillicothe. Within a 13-acre area swell 24 still-enigmatic Hopewell burial mounds. The adjoining museum elucidates theories about Hopewell society based upon the mounds' configuration. (Museum open daily 8am-5pm. $1, $4 per carload, seniors and under 17 free.) Check with park officials for info on other nearby mounds. Visit **Chillicothe** to see Greek Revival mansions that grace the Northwest Territory's first capital. From mid-June to early September, see **Tecumseh** (614-775-0700), an outdoor drama re-enacting the life and death of the Shawnee leader. (Mon.-Sat. 8pm. $13, 10 and under $6.) If you're curious about how the stunt men dive headfirst off the 21 ft. cliff, a $3.50 behind-the-scenes tour is available hourly from 2pm-5pm. 10 mi. south of Chillicothe off U.S. 23, camp at **Scioto Trail State Park** (663-2125; 24-hr.; primitive camping free; designated sites $4, with electricity $8).

About 30 mi. east of Chillicothe, U.S. 50 passes near **Hocking Hills State Park,** accessible by Rte. 93 north or Rte. 56 west. Waterfalls, gorges, cliffs, and caves scar the rugged terrain within the park. **Ash Cave,** east of South Bloomingville on Rte. 56, gouges 80 acres out of a horseshoe-shaped rock. A trickling stream falls over the edge of this cliff to a pool at the cave entrance. **Cantwell Cliffs,** southwest of Rockbridge on Rte. 374, is another horseshoe-shaped precipice. Camp at **Old Man's Cave** (385-6165), off Rte. 664 (primitive camping $5; designated sites with pool $6, with electricity and pool $11). **Greyhound,** 193 E. Main St. (775-3013), inside Parceland Post Express, at the corner of Hickory St., serves Chillicothe from both Cincinnati ($30) and Columbus ($18.50). Chillicothe's **area code:** 614.

■■ CINCINNATI

Longfellow called it the "Queen City of the West." In the 1850s, more prosaic folk tagged it "Porkopolis," alluding to its position as the planet's premier pork-packer. Winged pigs guarding the entrance of downtown's Sawyer Point Park remind visitors of the divine swine of yore. Today, pigs no longer snort through the streets, and the frontier has moved on to parts west; the city instead parades an excellent collection of museums, a renowned zoo, a pleasantly designed waterfront, and a PLETH-

ORA of parks. Hidden in a valley surrounded by seven rolling hills and the Ohio River, Cincinnati has always been surprisingly insulated despite its prosperity.

PRACTICAL INFORMATION

Emergency: 911.

Visitor Information: Cincinnati Convention and Visitors Bureau, 300 W. 6th St. (621-2142 or 800-344-3445). Open Mon.-Fri. 9am-5pm. Pick up an *Official Visitors Guide.* **Information Booth** in Fountain Sq. Open Mon.-Sat. 8:30am-5:30pm. **Info Line,** 421-4636. Lists plays, opera, and symphonies.

Airport: Greater Cincinnati International, in Kentucky, 13 mi. south of Cincinnati. **Jetport Express** (606-283-3702) shuttles to downtown ($10).

Amtrak: (651-3337 or 800-872-7245). To: Indianapolis ($30) and Chicago ($61). Open Mon.-Fri. 9:30am-5pm, Tues.-Sun. 11pm-6:30am. Avoid the neighborhood north of the station.

Greyhound: 1005 Gilbert Ave. (352-6000), just past the intersection of E. Court and Broadway. To: Indianapolis ($20.50); Louisville, KY ($19.50); Cleveland ($39); Columbus ($18.50). Open daily 7:30am-6:30am.

Public Transport: Queen City Metro, 122 W. Fifth St. (621-4455). Office has schedules and information. Telephone info Mon.-Fri. 6:30am-6pm, Sat.-Sun. 8am-5pm. Most buses run out of Government Sq., at 5th and Main, to outlying communities. Peak fare 65¢, other times 50¢, weekends 35¢, extra 30¢ to suburbs.

Taxi: Yellow Cab, 241-2100. Base fare $1.50, $1.20 per mi.

Weather Line: 241-1010.

Help Lines: Rape Crisis Center, 216 E. 9th St. (381-5610), downtown. **Gay/Lesbian Community Switchboard:** 221-7800.

Post Office: 525 Vine (684-5667), located in the Skywalk. Open Mon.-Fri. 8am-5pm, Sat. 8am-1pm. **ZIP code:** 45203.

Area Code: 513; Kentucky suburbs 606.

Fountain Square, E. 5th at Vine St., is the focal point of the downtown business community. Cross streets are numbered and designated East or West, with Vine Street as the divider. **Riverfront Stadium,** the **Serpentine Wall,** and the **Riverwalk** are down by the river. The **University of Cincinnati** spreads out from Clifton, north of the city. Overlooking downtown from the east, **Mt. Adams,** adjoining Eden Park, harbors Cincinnati's most active nightlife.

ACCOMMODATIONS AND CAMPING

Cincinnati's only hostel is shutting down, but budget accommodations can be found sprinkled about outside the heart of the city.

College of Mount St. Joseph, 5701 Delhi Pike (244-4327 or 244-4327), about 8 mi. west of downtown off U.S. 50. Take bus #32. Immaculate rooms available year-round in a quiet, remote location. Excellent facilities. Cafeteria lunch $3.50. Singles $15. Doubles $25.

Evendale Motel, 10165 Reading Rd. (563-1570). Take a ride on the Reading bus #43 north to Reading and Columbia, then walk ½ hr. north on Reading. Dark but clean rooms. Singles or doubles $24.

Yogi Bear's Camp Resort (800-832-1133), I-71 exit 25 at Mason. Pricey ($23.50, with water and electricity $30.50) but within a stone's throw of Kings Island. Reservations recommended.

Rose Gardens Resort—KOA Campgrounds (606-428-2000), I-75 exit 166, 30 mi. south of Cincinnati. Tent sites $16. Cabins $25, with water and electricity.

FOOD

The city that gave us the first soap opera, the first baseball franchise (the Redlegs), and the Heimlich maneuver presents as its great culinary contribution **Cincinnati chili.** It's an all-pervasive ritual in local culture, though somehow no other city but Louisville, KY seems to have caught this gastronomical wave. Meat sauce, spaghetti, and cheese are the basic ingredients. Chili is cheap; antacid tablets cost extra.

Skyline Chili, everywhere. This chain has over 50 locations, including 9254 Plain-field Rd. (793-3350). Better than other chains. Secret ingredient debated for years. Some say chocolate, but curry is more likely. Open Mon.-Fri. 11am-1am, Sat.-Sun. 11am-3am. 5-way jumbo chili $4.80, cheese coney (hot dog) $1.15.

Graeter's, 41 E. 4th St. (381-0653), downtown, and 10 other locations. Since 1870, Graeter's has been pleasing sweet-toothed locals with candy and ice cream made with giant chocolate chips. (Not very) small cone $1.50, $1.60 with chips; larger size 50¢ extra. Open Mon.-Sat. 11am-5:30pm.

Izzy's, 819 Elm St. (721-4241), also 610 Main St. A Cincinnati institution founded in 1901. Overstuffed sandwiches and potato pancake $3-4. Izzy's famous reuben $5. Open Mon.-Fri. 7am-5pm, Sat. 10am-5pm; Main St. site open Mon.-Sat. 7am-9pm.

Mulane's, 723 Race St. (381-1331). A street-side café and restaurant with terrific vegetarian food. Out-of-this world meatless entrees ($4-6), and hearty salads. Live music weekly. Chicken or ham can be added to entrees for $2. Not to be missed. (Open Mon.-Thurs. 11:30am-11pm, Fri. until midnight, Sat. 5pm-midnight.)

Findlay Market, (861-5530) 18th at Elm St., 1½ mi. north of downtown. Produce and picnic items $3-5. Open Wed. 7am-1:30pm, Fri.-Sat. 7am-6pm.

SIGHTS AND EVENTS

Downtown Cincinnati orbits around the **Tyler Davidson Fountain,** an ideal spot to people-watch while admiring this florid 19th-century masterpiece. If you squint, you can almost see Les Nesman rushing to WKRP to deliver the daily hog report. Check out the expansive gardens at **Proctor and Gamble Plaza,** just east of Fountain Square, or walk along **Fountain Square South,** a shopping and business complex connected by a series of second-floor skywalks. When the visual stimuli exhaust you, pick up your ears for a free concert in front of the fountain, produced by **Downtown Council,** (579-3191), Carew Tower (open Mon.-Fri. 8:30am-5pm).

Close to Fountain Square, the **Contemporary Arts Center,** 115 E. 5th St., 2nd floor (721-0390), by Walnut, has earned a strong reputation among the national arts community. It continues to change its exhibits frequently, offering evening films, music, and multi-media performances. (Open Mon.-Sat. 10am-5pm, Sun. 1-5pm. $2, seniors and students $1. Sun. and Mon. free.) The **Taft Museum,** 316 Pike St. (241-0343), also downtown, has a beautiful collection of painted enamels, as well as pieces by Rembrandt and Whistler. (Open Mon.-Tues. and Thurs.-Sat. 10am-5pm, Sun. 1-5pm. $3, seniors and students $1.)

Cincinnati's answer to Paradise is **Eden Park,** northeast of downtown. Among the park's bounteous fruits is the **Cincinnati Art Museum** (721-5204), with a permanent collection spanning 5000 years, including musical instruments and Near Eastern artifacts. Take bus #49 to Eden Park Dr. Open Tues.-Sat. 10am-5pm, Sun. 11am-5pm. $5, seniors $4, students $4, under 17 free.) The **Krohn Conservatory** (421-5707), one of the largest public greenhouses in the world, illustrates an indoor Eden. (Open daily 10am-5pm. $2, seniors and under 18 $1.)

The **Union Terminal,** 1031 Western Ave. (241-7257), 1 mi. west of downtown near the Ezzard Charles Dr. exit off I-75 (take bus #1), functions more as a museum than as a bus terminal. The building itself is a fine example of Art Deco architecture and boasts the world's largest permanent half-dome. Cool down in the Ice-Age world of simulated glaciers inside the **Museum of Natural History** (287-7021), or investigate the carefully constructed artificial cavern, featuring a colony of real live bats. On the other side of the dome, stroll about a model of a pre-1860 Cincinnati street at the **Cincinnati Historical Society** (287-7031), which houses an **Omni-max Theater** (shows Mon.-Thurs. hourly 11am-4pm and 7-8pm, Fri. 11am-4pm and 7-9pm, Sat. 11am-5pm and 7-9pm, Sun. 11am-5pm and 7-8pm). (Museums open Mon.-Sat. 9am-5pm, Sun. 11am-6pm; admission to either museum $5, ages 3-12 $3; to both $8/4; to Omnimax $6/4; combo ticket $12/7.)

The **Cincinnati Zoo,** 3400 Vine St. (281-4700), at Forest Ave., can be reached by car (take Dana Ave. off I-75 or I-71), or by bus (#78 or 49 from Vine and 5th St.). *Newsweek* called it one of the world's "sexiest zoos" (this sort of thing presumably turns them on); the lush greenery and cageless habitats evidently encourage the zoo's gorillas and famous white Bengal tigers to reproduce like animals. (Open daily 9am-dusk, usually 8pm; Labor Day-Memorial Day daily 9am-5pm. Children's Zoo open 9am-8pm. $7.50, seniors $5, under 12 $4.50. Parking $4.)

Cincinnati is fanatical about sports. The **Reds** major league baseball team (421-7337) and the **Bengals** NFL football team (621-3550) both play in **Riverfront Stadium.** The **Riverfront Coliseum** (241-1818), a Cincinnati landmark, hosts other sports events and concerts year-round. In early June **Summerfair** (531-0050), an art extravaganza, is held at **Coney Island,** 6201 Kellogg Ave. (232-8230).

The city basks in its German heritage during **Oktoberfest-Zinzinnati** (579-3191), held the third weekend in September. The **International Folk Festival** fests two months later. Labor Day's **Riverfest** (352-4000) memorializes the roles of the river and steamboats in Cincinnati's history. For more info on festivals, contact the Convention and Visitors Bureau (see Practical Information).

ENTERTAINMENT AND NIGHTLIFE

The cliff-hanging communities that line the steep streets of Mt. Adams also support a vivacious arts and entertainment industry. Perched on its own wooded hill is the **Playhouse in the Park,** 962 Mt. Adams Circle (421-3888), a theater-in-the-round remarkably adaptable to many styles of drama. The regular season runs mid-Sept. to June, plus special summer programs. Performances daily Tuesday to Sunday. (Tickets $19-31, 15 min. before the show student and senior rush tickets $12.)

For a drink and a voyage back to the 19th century, try **Arnold's,** 210 E. 8th St. (421-6234), Cincinnati's oldest tavern, between Main St. and Sycamore downtown. After 9pm, Arnold's does that ragtime, traditional jazz, and swing thing while serving sandwiches ($4-5) and dinners ($6-10). (Open Mon.-Fri. 11am-1am.) Check out the antique toys inside or listen to jazz and blues in the courtyard at **Blind Lemon,** 936 Hatch St. (241-3885), at St. Gregory St. in Mt. Adams. (Open Mon.-Sat. 5pm-2:30am, Sat.-Sun. 3pm-2:30am. Music at 9:30pm.) The **City View Tavern,** also in Mt. Adams at 403 Oregon St. (241-8439), off Monastery St., is hard to find but worth the effort. This down-to-earth local favorite is one of the best dives in Cincinnati. The deck in back offers a great view of the city's skyline and the Ohio River. Locally brewed draft beer 90¢. (Open Mon.-Sat. noon-1am, Sun. 2-11pm.)

The University of Cincinnati's **Conservatory of Music** (556-9430) often gives free classical recitals. A tad more upscale, the **Music Hall,** 1243 Elm St. (721-8222), hosts the **Cincinnati Symphony Orchestra** (381-3300) Sept.-May (tickets $10-50). A summer season is held at **Riverbend** on Old Coney Island in June and July (tickets $12.50-28). Other companies performing at the Music Hall are the **Cincinnati Ballet Company** (621-5219; Oct.-May, tickets $9-48) and **Cincinnati Opera** (241-2742; limited summer schedule). For updates, call **Dial the Arts** (751-2787).

◼ NEAR CINCINNATI

If you can't get to California's Napa or Sonoma Valleys, the next best thing may be **Meiers Wine Cellars,** 6955 Plainfield Pike (891-2900). Take I-71 to exit 12 or I-75 to Galbraith Rd. Free tours of Ohio's oldest and largest winery allow you to observe the entire wine-making operation and taste the fermented fruits of their labor. (Free tours June-Oct. Mon.-Sat. every hr. 10am-3pm; otherwise by appointment.)

Mason, 24 mi. north of Cincinnati off I-71 at exit #24, boasts the **Paramount's Kings Island** (800-288-0808) is an amusement park which cages **The Beast.** Admission entitles you to unlimited rides, attractions, and the opportunity to buy expensive food. Lines shrink after dark. (Open May 27-Sept. 4, Sun.-Fri. 10am-10pm, Sat. 10am-11pm. $26, seniors and ages 3-6 $16.)

Michigan

Bordered by four Great Lakes and enclosing over 11,000 inland lakes, Michigan lives a fertile existence. Michigan's vast forests first attracted furriers who set up trading posts along the coasts of the Great Lakes. Eventually, the Astor Company came to dominate the trade from Mackinac. However, it wasn't until a century later that the production of the automobile put Michigan on the map. Detroit and Flint rose as perfecters of the assembly line. But the post-war decline has eroded these areas to shells of their former selves. Today what attracts people to Michigan is the unspoiled nature, with miles of outstanding coastline, 10 national and state forests, and innumerable recreation possibilities.

PRACTICAL INFORMATION

Capital: Lansing.
Michigan Travel Bureau, 333 S. Capitol Suite F, Lansing 48909 (517-335-1876 or 800-543-2937), has the week's events and festivals. **Department of Natural Resources,** Information Services Center, P.O. Box 30028, Lansing 48909 (517-373-1270), offers info on state parks, forests, campsites, and other facilities. Entry to all state parks requires a motor vehicle permit. Day pass $4, annual pass $18.
Time Zones: Eastern and Central. **Postal Abbreviation:** MI
Sales Tax: 4%.

■■■ DETROIT

An author recently proclaimed Detroit "America's first Third-World city," and indeed, the city has witnessed a quarter-century of hardship. In the 60s, as the country grooved to Motown's beat, the city erupted into some of the era's most violent race riots. Massive white flight to the suburbs has been the norm ever since; the population has more than halved since 1967, turning some neighborhoods into ghost towns. The decline of the auto industry in the late 70s exacerbated problems, and economic disempowerment has caused frustration, violence, and hopelessness among the city's residents. Downtown Detroit is virtually empty—boarded up businesses line the streets. The *really* high crime areas are located in the suburbs. Most gang violence takes place southwest of the city.

The five towers of the Renaissance Center symbolize the hope that a city-wide comeback is possible. However, without a growing job base and a shift in housing patterns, Detroit will remain in the doldrums.

PRACTICAL INFORMATION

Emergency: 911.
Visitor Information: Detroit Convention and Visitors Bureau, 100 Renaissance Center, #1900 (259-4333 or 800-338-7648). Pick up the free *Metro Detroit Visitors Guide.* Open Mon.-Fri. 9am-5pm; phone after hours to hear a recorded list of entertainment events.
Traveler's Aid: 211 W. Congress at Shelby, 3rd floor (962-6740). Emergency assistance. Open Mon.-Thurs. 8:30am-5pm, Fri. 8:30am-4:30pm.
Airport: Detroit Metropolitan (942-3550 or 800-351-5466), 21 mi. west of downtown off I-94 at Merriman Rd., Romulus. **Commuter Transportation Company** (941-3252) runs shuttles downtown, stopping at major hotels (45 min.; $13 one way; 6am-midnight by reservation). Make reservations; taxi to downtown $25.
Trains: Amtrak, 11 W. Baltimore at Woodward (873-3442 or 800-872-7245). To: Chicago ($28, 5hr.), New York ($107, 14 hrs.). Open daily 6am-11:30pm. For Canada destinations, use: **VIA Rail,** 298 Walker Rd., Windsor, Ont. (800-387-1144), across the river in Canada.

THE GREAT LAKES

Greyhound: 1001 Howard St. (961-8011). To: Chicago ($29, 8hr.), St. Louis ($52, 17 hrs.). Open 24 hrs.; ticket office open daily 6:30am-1am.

Public Transport: Detroit Department of Transportation (DOT), 1301 E. Warren (925-4910 or 933-1300 for customer service). Carefully policed public transport system. Serves the downtown area, with limited service to the suburbs. Many buses now stop service at midnight. Fare $1.25, transfers 25¢. **People Mover,** Detroit Transportation Corporation, 150 Michigan Ave. (224-2160 or 9622-RAIL). Ultramodern elevated tramway facility circles the Central Business District with 13 stops on a 2.7-mi. loop. Worth a ride just for the view. Fare 50¢. **Southeastern Michigan Area Regional Transit (SMART),** 962-5515. Bus service to the suburbs. Fare $1-2.50, transfers 10¢. Pick up a free map of the SMART bus system at their office on the first floor of the First National Bank at Woodward and Fort. Buses run 4am-midnight; $1.50 daily. **Tunnel Bus** (519-944-4111) transportation from downtown Detroit to downtown Windsor. $1.50 one-way. **Detroit Trolley** (933-1300 or 933-8020). See Detroit the old-fashioned way. Operates year-round, weather permitting. Daily 8am-5pm. Fare 50¢.

Taxi: Checker Cab, 963-7000. Flat fee $1.40 per mi.

Car Rental: Thrifty Rent-a-Car, 29111 Wick Rd. (946-7830), in Romulus. $44 per day; weekend specials from $25 per day. Must be 21 with credit card. $10 surcharge if under 25.

Help Lines: 24-hr. Crisis Hotline, 224-7000. **Gay and Lesbian Switchboard Line,** 398-4297. Sun.-Fri. 4:30-11pm. **Sexual Abuse Helpline,** 800-551-0008 or 800-234-0038. 24 hrs.

Time Zone: Eastern.

Post Office: 201 Michigan (965-1719) handles general delivery; Open Mon.-Fri. 7:45am-5pm, Sat. 7:45am-noon. **ZIP code:** 48226.

Area Code: 313.

Detroit lies on the Detroit River, which connects Lakes Erie and St. Clair. South across the river, the town of Windsor, Ontario, can be reached by tunnel, just west of the Renaissance Center, or by the Ambassador Bridge, 3500 Toledo St. Detroit is a tough town—one T-shirt reads "I'm so bad I vacation in Detroit"—but if you stay inside the loop encompassed by the People Mover, you shouldn't have trouble.

Detroit's streets form a grid. Major east-west arteries are the **Mile Roads. Eight Mile Road** is the city's northern boundary and beginning of the suburbs. **Woodward Avenue** heads northwest from downtown, dividing city and suburbs into "east side" and "west side." **Gratiot Avenue** flares out northeast from downtown, and **Grand River Avenue** shoots west. **I-94** and **I-75** pass through downtown.

ACCOMMODATIONS AND CAMPING

Avoid hotels near the bus station. Camping is only an attractive option if you don't mind a 45-min. commute to get into the city. Many budget chain motels are found in Detroit's suburbs. The *Detroit Metro Visitor's Guide* has extensive listings of accommodations. Car travelers should consider staying in hip Ann Arbor.

Park Avenue Hotel (HI-AYH), 2305 Park Ave. (961-8310), at Montcalm, one block west behind the Fox Theater and the police academy. Do not walk in this area alone at night. Sparkling rooms, new wooden beds, lounge, TV, laundry, parking in guarded lot ($1 when there is no show, $5 during showtimes), and delicatessen on the 1st floor. Check-in 24 hrs., but preferred before 11pm. Bring a lock for lockers. Bring own linen. Beds $12, nonmembers $14, private rooms for 1 or 2 $20. Full apartments from $75 per week.

Shorecrest Motor Inn, 1316 E. Jefferson Ave. (800-992-9616). Unbeatable location 3 blocks east of the Renaissance Center. Rates from $48.

Metro Inn - Detroit Metro Airport, 8230 Merriman Rd. (729-7600), Romulus. Clean, cheap rooms from $25. Free airport shuttle.

Country Grandma's Home Hostel, (753-4901), located in New Boston, about half-way between Detroit and Ann Arbor. This small, friendly hostel features a kitchen and on-site parking, $9, nonmembers $11.

Algonac State Park (765-5605) sits on the shore of the Detroit River, 35 mi. from downtown. Take I-94 north, then Rte. 29 north., for about 15 mi. Watch the big ships cruise the river at night, carrying cargo to and from Detroit, the fifth largest port in the U.S. (Sites $10, riverside sites $14.)

FOOD AND NIGHTLIFE

Although many of the restaurants downtown have migrated to the suburbs, the budget traveler still has some in-town dining options. **Greektown,** at the Greektown People Mover stop, has Greek restaurants and excellent bakeries on Monroe St., all on one block near Beaubien St. **Cyprus Taverna,** 579 Monroe St. (961-1550), is a local Greek favorite (open Sun.-Thurs. 11am-2am, Fri.-Sat. 11am-3:30am). **Trapper's Alley** (963-5445), in Greektown, is an old tannery converted into a four-story mall of food and retail shops (open Mon.-Thurs. 11am-9pm, Fri.-Sat. 11am-11pm, Sun. noon-7pm). **Mexican Town,** a lively neighborhood south of Tiger Stadium, also has some terrific restaurants, but be somewhat wary in the surrounding area. **Rivertown,** east of the Renaissance Center in the old warehouse district, has been reclaimed and now hosts some of the city's best nightlife. **American Coney Islands** (961-7758) and **Lafayette Coney Islands** (964-8198), 114 and 118 W. Lafayette, just west of Cadillac Square, are known for the Coney: hot dog, chili, mustard, and chopped onion ($1.75). (Both open 24 hrs.).

Soup Kitchen Saloon, 1585 Franklin St. (259-1374). Once home to a speakeasy and brothel, this Rivertown building today features the best live blues music in town. Fresh seafood, steaks, and BBQ. Huge beer selection. Open Mon.-Thurs. 11am-midnight, Fri. 11am-2am, Sat. 4pm-2am, Sun. 4pm-midnight. Cover varies.

The Clique Restaurant, 1326 East Jefferson St. (259-0922), is heralded city-wide for its fast service and fabulous breakfasts. French toast $2.75, 3-egg omelette $4.50. Open Mon.-Fri. 6am-10pm, Sat.-Sun. 7am-10pm.

Xochimilco, 3409 Bagley St. (843-0179), has brought its chefs from Mexico to give customers an authentic but inexpensive taste. 3meat tacos, enchiladas, or burritos with rice and beans for $4.75-5. Free chips and salsa. Open daily 11am-4am. No reservations on weekends, so come early. From downtown, take the Baker St. Bus to Lafayette and Washington Blvd., or spring for the $7 cab ride.

Union Street, 4145 Woodward St. (831-3965). Spicy, mouthwatering cuisine in a popular mid-town beer hall. A favorite is the Rasta wings with hellfire sauce ($7.25). Open Mon.-Thurs. 11am-midnight, Fri. 11am-1am, Sat.-Sun. 4pm-1am.

SIGHTS

The colossal **Henry Ford Museum & Greenfield Village,** 20900 Oakwood Blvd., is off I-94 in nearby Dearborn; take SMART bus 200 or 250 (271-1620 or 271-1976; open 24 hrs.). These exhibits alone justify a trip to Detroit. The museum—a 12-acre room—has a comprehensive exhibit on the importance of the automobile in America, including the Lunar Rover used by the Apollo mission and the limousine in which President Kennedy was riding on the day of his murder. The museum also exhibits artifacts of industrialization, from 19th-century typewriters to farm machinery and underwater cables. Over 80 historic homes, workplaces, and community buildings from around the country have been moved to **Greenfield Village,** a 240-acre park next to the museum. Visit the workshop of the Wright Brothers or the factory where Thomas Edison used systematic research and development methods (98% perspiration, 1% inspiration, and 1% deep-seated desire to best rival genius C.G. Steimetz). (Open daily 9am-5pm. Museum or Village admission $11.50, seniors $10.50, ages 5-12 $5.75. Both sights, over 2 days, $20, ages 5-12 $10.)

Detroit's Cultural Center, at Woodward and Warren St. (take bus #53), consists of public and private cultural institutions such as the **Detroit Institute of Arts (DIA)** (833-7900), and the **Museum of African-American History,** which explores the history of the Underground Railroad. One of the nation's finest art museums, the **Detroit Institute of Arts,** 5200 Woodward (833-7900), houses Van Gogh's "Self-Portrait" and the nation's largest historic puppet collection. (Open

THE GREAT LAKES

Wed.-Fri. 11am-4pm, Sat.-Sun. 11am-5pm. Suggested donation $4, children $1.) Good for a stroll through history, the **Detroit Historical Museum,** 5401 Woodward Ave. (833-1805), contains an outstanding costume gallery as well as a reconstruction of the city's main roadway. (Open Wed.-Fri. 9:30am-4pm, Sat.-Sun. 10am-5pm. Suggested donation $3, seniors $2, children $1.) Explore the African-American experience and struggle at the **Museum of African American History,** 301 Frederick Douglas Rd. (833-9800). (Open Wed.-Sat. 9:30am-5pm, Sun. 1-5pm. Suggested donation $2, children $1.) The **Detroit Science Center,** 5020 John R. St. (577-8400), provides great entertainment in the state's only Omnimax Theater. (Open Mon.-Fri. 10am-5pm. $6.50, children $4.50.)

Compact downtown Detroit can be explored easily in one day. The futuristic, gleaming, steel-and-glass **Renaissance Center** provides a shocking contrast to the downtown wasteland. A five-towered complex of office, hotel, and retail space, the Ren Cen encloses a maze of concrete walkways and spiraling stairs. Thrill to the **World of Ford** on level 2, or ride to the top of the 73-story **Westin Hotel,** the tallest hotel in North America, for a towering view of the city ($3; open Sun.-Thurs. 11am-11pm, Fri.-Sat. 11am-1:30am; for general Ren Cen info call 568-5600; tour information 341-6810; lines open daily 9am-5pm). Difficult to reach by public transportation, the sights are now accessible by an **attractions shuttle** (800-225-5389), which runs daily 10am-7:45pm (mid-May to mid-Aug.; $3 ticket good all day).

Although Berry Gordy's Motown Record Company has moved to Los Angeles, the **Motown Museum,** 2648 W. Grand Blvd. (875-2264), preserves its memories. Downstairs, shop around the primitive studio in which the Jackson Five, Marvin Gaye, Smokey Robinson, and Diana Ross recorded their celebrated tunes. (Open Mon.-Sat. 10am-5pm; Sun. 2-5pm. $3, under 12 $2.) The museum is east of Rosa Parks Blvd., about 1 mi. west of the Lodge Freeway (Rte. 10). Take the "Dexter Avenue" bus to the museum from downtown.

The **Holocaust Memorial Center,** 6602 W. Maple Rd. (810-661-0840), West Bloomfield, is a historical and educational memorial to the victims of the Nazis. Rare documentary films and propaganda of the times can be viewed. (Free; open Sun.-Thurs. 10am-3:30pm, tours Sun. 1pm.)

One of Detroit's favorite escapes is **Belle Island** (267-7121), 3 mi. from downtown via the MacArthur Bridge, and home to many attractions, including a conservatory, nature center, aquarium, and a small zoo. The first to largely remove the bars from its exhibits, the **Detroit Zoo,** 8450 W. Ten Mile Rd., Royal Oak (398-0900), prides itself on naturalistic animal environments. The chimps are a popular draw, but don't miss the penguinarium or the elephants. (Open summer daily 10am-5pm, winter Wed.-Sun. 10am-4pm. $6, seniors $4, under 12 $3, parking $3.) No budget traveler should miss the **Eastern Market** at Gratiot Ave. and Russell St. (833-1560). This 11-acre farmers market sells virtually every edible imaginable. (Open Mon.-Fri. 5am-noon, Sat. 5am-5pm.)

Detroit, the "city of champions," is home to the **Pistons,** who shoot hoops at the Palace of Auburn Hills, 3777 Lapeer Rd. (810-377-8200), Auburn Hills. The pucklovin' **Red Wings** face off in the Joe Louis Arena, 600 Civic Center Dr. (567-6000). The **Tigers** catch fly balls and hit home runs at Tiger Stadium, on Michigan and Trumball Ave. (962-4000). The **Lions** punt, pass, and tackle at the Pontiac Silverdome, 1200 Featherstone Rd. (810-335-4151), Pontiac.

FESTIVALS AND ENTERTAINMENT

Millions come to Detroit for its multitude of festivals. Jazz fans jet to Hart Plaza during Labor Day weekend for the four-day **Montreux-Detroit Jazz Festival** (963-7622). With more than 100 free open-air concerts, it's the largest on the continent. The **Michigan State Fair** (368-1000 or 369-8250), the nation's oldest, gathers bake-offs, art exhibits, and livestock at Eight Mile Rd. and Woodward (10 days long, late Aug.-early Sept.). The international **Freedom Festival** (923-7400), a two-week extravaganza in late June, held jointly with Windsor, Ontario, celebrates the friendship between Canada and the U.S. and marks the birthdays of both nations. The world's largest annual fireworks display takes place over the Detroit River near the Ren Cen. What would the city of automobiles be without a festival of cars? The **Concours d'Elegance** is an exhibit of elegant classic cars at the Meadow Brook Hall, held in early August (810-370-3140). The **North American International Auto Show** showcases the new models, prototypes, and concept cars from manufacturers around the world. The show is held in January in the Cobo Center on One Washington Blvd. (224-1010 or 886-6750). The **Detroit Grand Prix** zooms for three days in June, when Belle Isle's streets are turned into a race course (393-7749). The Friday before the race weekend when trial runs are free to all spectators. Detroit's **African World Festival,** brings over a million people to Hart Plaza in mid-August for an open-air market and free reggae, jazz, blues, and gospel concerts (833-9800).

Newly renovated and restored, Detroit's theater district (around Woodward and Columbia) is witnessing a cultural revival. The **Fox Theater,** 2211 Woodward Ave. (567-6000), near Grand Circus Park, features high-profile performers (drama, comedy, and musicals) and some Broadway shows. As the nation's largest movie theater, the Fox occasionally shows epic films. The **State Theater,** 2115 Woodward Ave. (961-5450), brings in a variety of popular concerts and dancing. **Orchestra Hall** (962-9107), Woodward at Parsons St., houses the Detroit Symphony Orchestra. The **Masonic Temple,** 500 Temple Ave. (832-7100), houses three theaters in a classic gothic building. Events include Broadway plays and concerts. The **Michigan Opera Theater,** 6519 Second Ave. (874-7850), has five main stage productions annually. Everybody performs at the **Music Hall for the Performing Arts,** 350 Madison Ave. (963-7622). Pick up a copy of the weekly *Metro Times* for complete entertainment listings. Get concert or sports tickets from **Ticketmaster** (645-6666).

■ NEAR DETROIT: FRANKENMUTH

Take exit 136 northbound or 144 southbound off I-75 between Flint and Saginaw to experience the incomparable **Frankenmuth.** The kitsch capital of Michigan is an uproarious Bavarian knock-off village which has become a gargantuan tourist draw. The **Frankenmuth Convention and Visitors Bureau,** 625 S. Main St. (652-8666 or 800-386-8696), awaits to answer your questions (open Mon.-Sat. 8am-8pm, Sun. noon-8pm). Frankenmuth's claim to fame is the **Bavarian Inn Restaurant,** 713 South Main St. (652-9941), where all-you-can-eat chicken dinners ($12.25) have been wolfed down since 1888 (open daily 11am-9:30pm). Get samples at the **Frankenmuth Brewery,** 425 S. Main St. (517-652-6183 or 517-652-2088. Tours $1.75 per person; summer tours Mon.-Fri. 11am-4pm, Sat. 11am-6pm, Sun. noon-5pm, on the hour. Winter hours vary.) Viewers can witness Michigan's only hard pretzels being made at the **Frankenmuth Pretzel Company,** 333 Market Strasse (517-652-2050). Tours daily at 11am and 1pm. .

■■■ ANN ARBOR

Named after Ann Rumsey and Ann Allen, wives of the area's first two pioneers, Ann Arbor has certainly made tracks. In 1837 the University of Michigan moved to town, and since then, this gargantuan, well-respected institution has created a a hip collage of leftists, granolas, yuppies, and middle America.

Practical Information The **Ann Arbor Convention and Visitors Bureau** (995-7281) provides info on the city and U of M at 120 W. Huron St. at Ashley (open Mon.-Fri. 8:30am-5pm). **University of Michigan Information** (764-1817) can provide assistance as well (open Sun.-Mon. 9am-1am, Tues.-Sat. 7am-2am). **Amtrak,** 325 Depot St. (994-4906 or 800-872-7245), offers train service to Chicago ($41-43) and Detroit ($15-$20). (Open daily 7:30am-11:30pm.) **Greyhound,** 116 W. Huron St. (662-5511), runs buses to Detroit ($8) and Chicago ($29). (Office open Mon.-Sat. 9am-6:30pm.) The **Ann Arbor Transportation Authority (AATA),** at the Blake Transit Center, 331 South 4th Ave. (996-0400 or 973-6500), serves Ann Arbor and a

THE GREAT LAKES

few neighboring towns. Buses run Mon.-Fri. 6:45am-10:15pm, Sat.-Sun. 8am-6:15pm. (Station open Mon.-Fri. 7:30am-9:30pm, Sat. noon-6:15pm. Fare 75¢, seniors and students 35¢.) **Nightride** (663-3888), run by the AATA, provides safe transportation between 10pm and 6am. (Reservations accepted up to 24 hrs. in advance. Fare varies.) **Commuter Transportation Company** (941-9391 or 800-488-7433) runs frequent shuttle service between Ann Arbor and Detroit Metro Airport. Vans depart from Ann Arbor 5am-7pm and from the airport 7am-midnight. ($14.50 one-way and $26 round-trip; door-to-door service for 4-6 passengers $34.) The 24-hr. **sexual assault crisis line:** 483-7273 (U. Michigan sexual assault line 936-3333); **gay crisis line** (open Mon.-Fri. 9am-7pm): 662-1977 (U. Michigan gay/lesbian hotline 763-4186); **emergency** is 911; Ann Arbor's **post office:** 2075 W. Stadium Blvd. (665-1100; open Mon.-Fri. 7:30am-5pm); **ZIP code:** 48106; **area code:** 313.

Ann Arbor is a well-planned grid. **Main Street** divides the town east-west and **Huron Street** cuts it north-south. The central campus of the University of Michigan lies four blocks east of Main St., south of E. Huron (a 5-min. walk from downtown).Although street meter parking is plentiful, the authorities ticket ruthlessly.

Accommodations Expensive hotels, motels, and B&Bs dominate Ann Arbor due to the many business travelers and sports fans flocking to the town. Reasonable rates can be found at discount chains farther out of town or in Ypsilanti. The **YMCA,** 350 S. Fifth Ave. (663-0536), provides clean, dorm-style singles with shared bath for men and women ($27, key deposit $5; check-out 11am, no curfew; weekly or monthly rentals available); and the **Embassy Hotel,** 200 E. Huron at Fourth Ave. (662-7100), offers singles for $25 and doubles for $30. **Camping** is an accessible option, with seven campgrounds within a 20-mi. radius of Ann Arbor. Call the campground offices of the **Pinckney Recreation Area,** 8555 Silver Hill (426-4913), Pinckney, or the **Waterloo Recreation Area,** 16345 McClure Rd. (475-8307), Chelsea.

Food and Nightlife Where there are students, there are cheap eats; check out **State Street** and **S. University Street**, where the sidewalks are lined with restaurants. The **Cottage Inn,** 512 E. William St. (663-3379) at Thompson St., serves up what was voted the "best pizza" by readers of *Ann Arbor News*. (Expect long lines for dinner. Open Mon.-Thurs. 11am-midnight, Fri.-Sat. 11am-1am, Sun. noon-midnight.) **Angelo's,** 1100 Catherine St. (761-8996), can't be beat for breakfast. Their raisin bread french toast is thick and heavenly ($4.50). A tradition at the University since the 1950s. (Open Mon.-Fri. 6am-4pm, Sat. 6am-3pm, Sun. 7am-2pm.) **Del Rio,** 122 W. Washington (761-2530), at Ashley, brings locals in for the cheap Mexican food and burgers (burrito $2.50). Sunday night is jazz night (no cover). Del Rio is managed cooperatively by its employees—a vestige of a fast-dying Ann Arbor tradition. (Open Mon.-Fri. 11:30am-2am, Sat. noon-2am, Sun. 5:30am-2am.) **The Blind Pig,** 208 S. First St. (996-8555), showcases the rock-'n-roll, reggae, and blues offerings of local bands and acts from all over the country. (Cover varies.) Friday from 6-9pm is happy hour (no cover). (Open Mon.-Sat. until 2am.) **Rick's American Café,** 611 Church St. (996-2747), has live music almost nightly on a packed dance floor: Ann Arbor's home of blues. (Varying cover, open daily.)

Sights and Entertainment The university offers a handful of free museums. The **University of Michigan Arts Museum** (UMAM), 525 S. State St. (764-03395), at the corner of University St., houses a small but impressive collection of works from around the world (open Tues.-Sat. 10am-5pm, Sun. 1-5pm). Just down the street, the **Kelsey Museum of Archaeology,** 434 S. State St. (764-9304), presents pieces recovered from digs in the Middle East, Greece, and Italy. (Open Sept.-April Mon.-Fri. 9am-4pm, Sat.-Sun. 1-4pm; May-Aug. Tues.-Fri. 11am-4pm, Sat.-Sun. 1-4pm.) The **University of Michigan Exhibit Museum,** Geddes at Washtenaw (763-6085), displays a Hall of Evolution and other exhibits on Michigan wildlife, astronomy, and rock and minerals. (Open Mon.-Sat. 9am-5pm, Sun. 1-5pm.) The **Planetarium** (764-0478 or 763-6085) features star-gazing weekend entertainment ($2.50). Outside the

University, the **Ann Arbor Hands-On Museum,** 219 E. Huron (995-5437), takes an unusual attitude toward learning—all the exhibits are meant to be felt, turned, and pushed. (Open Tues.-Fri. 10am-5:30pm, Sat. 10am-5pm, Sun. 1-5pm; $3.50, seniors, students, and children $2.50.) Don't miss the **farmers market,** 315 Detroit St. (761-1078), at Kerrytown, where visitors can purchase fresh produce straight from the growers. (Open May-Dec. Wed. and Sat. 7am-3pm, Jan.-April Sat. 8am-3pm.) At the same location on Sundays from May to Dec. (11am-4pm), an **artisan market** displays the creations of numerous local artists.

As tens of thousand of students depart for the summer (and rents plummet), locals indulge in a little celebrating of their own. During late July, thousands pack the city to view the work of nearly 600 artists at the **Ann Arbor Summer Art Fair** (662-2787). Also drawing crowds from mid-June to early July, the **Ann Arbor Summer Festival** (747-2278) assembles humorous dance and theater productions, performances by musicians ranging from jazz artists to country to classical, and outdoor movies every night at **Top of the Park** (on top of the Heath Service Building on Fletcher St.). The free monthly entertainment magazine, *Current* (668-4044), can steer your toward upcoming events. For classical music contact the **University Musical Society** (764-2538), in the Burton Memorial Clock Tower at N. University and Thouper, which sponsors 40 to 50 professional concerts per season. (Tickets $10-50; open Mon.-Fri. 10am-6pm.) The city prides itself on live jazz performances; call the University Activities Office (763-1107).

■■■ LAKE MICHIGAN SHORE

The 350-mi. eastern shore of Lake Michigan stretches from the Indiana border north to the Mackinaw Bridge. It can be reached in less than two hours from downtown Chicago, and has been a vacation spot for over a century with its dunes of sugary sand, superb fishing, abundant fruit harvests, and deep winter snows. The region was one of Lake Michigan's shipping centers before the railroad to Chicago was completed, and though the harbors today welcome more pleasure boats than freighters, merchant vessels are still a common sight along the coast.

Many of the region's attractions are in small coastal towns, with the highest concentration located around **Grand Traverse Bay** in the north. Visitors will soon discover that coastal accommodations can be exorbitantly expensive and a better bet is to head for cheaper inland lodging. **Traverse City,** at the south tip of the bay, is famous as the "cherry capital of the world." Fishing is best in the **Au Sable** and **Manistee Rivers.** However, the rich **Mackinac Island Fudge,** sold in numerous specialty shops, seems to have the biggest pull on tourists, whom locals dub "fudgies." The main thoroughfare north-south along the coast is **U.S. 31.** Numerous detours take winding routes closer to the shoreline, providing an excellent way to explore the coast. The **West Michigan Tourist Association,** 136 E. Fulton, Grand Rapids 49503 (616-456-8557), offers free literature on this area (open Mon.-Fri. 8:45am-5pm). Michigan Coast's **time zone:** Eastern; **area code:** 616.

■ SOUTHERN MICHIGAN SHORE

Grand Rapids The biggest and cleanest city in the area, Grand Rapids is the hub of local bus routes. **Greyhound,** 190 Wealthy St. (456-1707), in the Grand Rapids Station, connects to Detroit, Chicago, Holland, and Grand Haven. (Open daily 6:30am-9:30pm; to Detroit: $27.) **Amtrak** (800-872-7245), at Wealthy and Market (open only when trains pass through), has service to the south and west (to Chicago: $41). For eastern service, travelers must catch the train at the Kalamazoo Station, 459 N. Burdick St., open daily 9am-9pm (to Detroit: $26). Motels line the junction of 28th St. and Rte. 96, but only men have the luck with the **YMCA,** 33 Library St. N.E. (458-1141), for $10 a night (men only - key deposit $10). The **Main Street Inn,** 5175 28th St. SE (956-6601 or 800-533-3714), at I-96, has rooms from $34, free local calls, and an outdoor pool. There's plenty of camping in the area;

THE GREAT LAKES

your best guide to these is the *West Michigan Travel Planner.* Write or call the West Michigan Tourist Association (see above) for a copy. Also available is the *MAR-VAC RV and Campsite Guide,* or the *Michigan Campground Directory,* both of which list state and private sites. For general area info, head to the **Grand Rapids-Kent County Convention and Visitors Bureau,** 140 Monroe Center NW (459-8287 or 800-678-8959; open Mon.-Fri. 10am-5:30pm, Sat. 10am-2pm), or the **West Michigan Tourist Association,** 136 E. Fulton (456-8557; open Mon.-Fri. 8:45am-5pm).

The stellar **Grand Rapids Public Museum** (456-3977), in its new complex along the river at Pearl and Front St. (as of Nov. 1994), will continue to dazzle with its indoor "Gaslight Village" restoration, a giant 1905 steam engine, a 50-animal 1928 carousel, the world's largest whale skeleton, and a brand-new planetarium. (Call for hours and prices.) Next door, the **Gerald R. Ford Museum,** 303 Pearl St. NW, traces the life and public service work of the nation's 38th (and only unelected) President. (Open Mon.-Sat. 9am-4:45pm, Sun. noon-4:45pm. $2, seniors $1.50, under 15 free.)

For good food and home-brewed beer, head to the **Grand Rapids Brewing Company,** 3689 28th St. SE (285-5970; burgers $5; tours available upon request).

Holland Southwest of Grand Rapids, off I-96, Holland was founded in 1847 by Dutch religious dissenters and remained mostly Dutch until well into the 20th century. Today the town cashes in on its heritage with a wooden shoe factory, **Windmill Island** (396-5433), **Netherlands Museum** (392-9084), **Veldheer Tulip Gardens** (399-1900), and a recreated **Dutch Village** (396-1475). Explore these places (admission $1-4) or simply wander around downtown to get a sense of how this tightly-knit community has survived. The **Wooden Shoe Motel** (392-8521), U.S. 31 Bypass at 16th St., has singles starting at $45, doubles for $54, and a putt-putt course out back. For more info head for the **Holland Convention and Visitors Bureau,** 171 Lincoln Ave. (396-4221 or 800-968-8590; open Mon.-Fri. 9am-5pm).

Grand Haven Grand Haven, 25 mi. west of Grand Rapids off I-96, has perhaps the best beach on Lake Michigan: several miles of fine sugary sand so pure that auto manufacturers use it to make cores and molds for engine parts. A cement "boardwalk" connects the beach to the small downtown. The action centers on Washington St. **Smitty's Deli,** 200 S. Harbor Ave. (846-1550), has meal-sized sandwiches for $5 (open Sun.-Thurs. 9am-11pm, Fri.-Sat. 9-2am). The **Bij De Zee Motel,** 1030 Harbor Ave. (846-7431), has rooms from $45, the cheapest near the beach. State Parks line the coast between Saugatuck and Muskegon. Campground sites run $10-14.

■ CENTRAL MICHIGAN SHORE

Ludington, Manistee, and Interlochen Ludington is a popular fishing center at the center of Michigan's western coast. The **Lake Michigan Car Ferry** (800-841-4243) transports people and cars between Ludington and Manitowoc, WI, crossing Lake Michigan in about 4 hours. (Two trips each way daily in summer; one daily in spring and fall, $33, seniors $30, ages 5-15 $15, autos $45.) The **White Pine Village,** 1687 S. Lakeshore Dr. (843-4808), off Old U.S. 31, recreates 19th-century Michigan life with 20 historic buildings. (Open mid-June to Labor Day Tues.-Sun. 11am-4:30pm. $4, under 18 $3.) Pick a pint at the 32-acre **Blueberry Patch,** Fischer Rd. (843-9561 or 843-9619), off Hwy. 10 (open daily 9am-6pm Aug. to mid-Sept.).

Continuing north, **Manistee** beckons tourists with Victorian shtick. The **A.H. Lyman Store,** 425 River St. (723-5531), recreates a turn-of-the-century store ($1. Open Mon.-Sat. 10am-5pm; Oct.-May Tues.-Sat. 10am-5pm.) **Manistee National Forest** has copious camping (sites $5-9) with hookup or primitive sites, and puts on a tremendous National Forest Festival in July. Call the **Manistee Ranger Station,** 1658 Manistee Hwy. (723-2211 or 800-999-7677 for more info; open Mon.-Fri. 8am-5pm. Sat.-Sun. 8am-4:30pm). Boaters should try the **Riverside Motel,** 520 Water St. (723-3554). Rooms range from $50-60; winter rates drop to $28. The motel backs right up to the river and has dock space available. The **Manistee County Chamber of Commerce,** 11 Congress St. (723-2575), can also assist with local attractions.

The renowned **Interlochen Center for the Arts** (276-7200) lies between two lakes 17 mi. south of Traverse City on Rte. 137, in **Interlochen.** Here, the high-powered **National Music Camp** instructs over 2000 young artists and musicians. Faculty and student concerts are free. The **International Arts Festival** is held late June-early Sept. (Tickets from $10, student discounts available).

Sleeping Bear Dunes Along the western shores of the Leelanau Peninsula lie the Sleeping Bear Dunes. According to legend, the mammoth sand dunes, which lie 20 mi. west of Traverse City on M-72, are a sleeping mother bear, waiting for her cubs—the **Manitou Islands**—to finish a swim across the lake. Local legend does not explain why the cubs didn't just take the ferry which services the islands from Leland. (**Manitou Island Transit,** 256-9061. Daily trips to South Manitou, 3 per week to North Manitou, the larger and more wild of the pair. Check-in 9:30am. Round-trip $18, under 12 $13.) Camping is free on both islands; no cars allowed.

The islands are just one part of the **Sleeping Bear Dunes National Lakeshore** (326-5134), which also includes 25 mi. of lakeshore on the mainland. The dunes are ancient glacial remains perilously hanging on steep cliffs. These mountains of fine sand rise to a precipitous 450 ft. above Lake Michigan. You can make the gritty climb to the top at the **Dune Climb,** 5 mi. north of Empire on M-109, or you can hike one of the two trails, which are 2.8 and 3.5 mi. long. The less adventurous can motor to an overlook along the **Pierce Stocking Scenic Drive,** off M-109 just north of Empire. Here, the truly rugged and courageous can run down a 450 ft. sand cliff to the cool water below. The climb up is extremely rigorous and can prove very tiring (but rewarding). (Open mid-May to mid-Oct. daily 9am-10pm.) Call the National Parks Service **visitors center** (326-5134), on M-72 in Empire, for more info (open daily 9am-6pm, 9:30am-4pm in winter). The Platte River at the southern end and the Crystal River at the northern, near Glen Arbor, are suitable for canoeing. **Crystal River Canoes** (334-3090), Empire, will equip you with a canoe and pick you up at the end of a 3-hr. paddle ($20). Find the same service and price on the Platte at **Riverside Canoes,** 5042 Scenic Hwy. Honor (325-5622), off Hwy. M-22 at the Platte River Bridge. Call the visitors center for maps and info on the numerous trails for **cross-country skiing, hiking,** and **mountain biking.**

Sleeping Bear Dunes has 4 campgrounds: **DH Day** (334-4634; $8, no showers), in Glen Arbor; **Platte River** (325-5881; $10, $15 with hookup; has showers), in Honor; and two free backcountry campgrounds; no water or reservations.

Traverse City In summer, vacationers head to Traverse City, for its sandy beaches and annual **Cherry Festival** (947-4230), held the first full week in July. The Traverse City area produces 50% of the nation's sweet and tart cherries, and they won't let you forget it—the cherry theme is emblazoned on everything. The nearby sparkling bay and ancient sand dunes make this region a Great Lakes paradise, though a crowded and expensive one. In summer, Grand Traverse Bay is the focal point for swimming, boating, and scuba diving. Free beaches and public access sites dot its shores. The Leeanau Peninsula pokes up between Grand Traverse Bay and Lake Michigan. Explore the coastline on scenic **M-22,** which will channel you to **Leland,** a charming one-time fishing village which now launches the Manitou Island ferries (see above). Five orchards near Traverse City let you pick your own cherries. One of them is **Amon Orchards** (938-9160), 10 mi. east on U.S. 31.

There are many **campgrounds** around Traverse City—in state parks, the National Lakeshore (see below), and various townships. The West Michigan Tourist Association's guide gives a comprehensive list of public and private sites. State parks usually charge $10-14. As usual, the national forests are the best deal ($5-8). The cheapest beds in Traverse City get made at **Northwestern Michigan Community College,** East Hall, 1701 E. Front St. (922-1406), which offers dorms with shared bath. (Singles $25; doubles $35. Reservations required at least one week in advance. Open

THE GREAT LAKES

late June-Aug.) At the **Fox Haus Motor Lodge,** 704 Munson Ave. (947-4450), frequent specials cut the price of a double from $80 to $45.

For visitor info, contact the **Traverse City Area Chamber of Commerce** (947-5079), corner of Grand View Ave. and Cass, P.O. Box 387, Traverse City 49685 (open Mon.-Fri. 9am-5pm). Ask for the *Traverse City Guide.* For local events and entertainment, pick up the weekly *Traverse City Record-Eagle Summer Magazine.* Also check out the **Traverse City Convention and Visitors Bureau,** 415 Munson Ave., suite 200 (800-940-1120 or 947-1120 open Mon.-Fri. 9am-5pm). From 3233 Cass Rd., **Greyhound** (946-5180) ties Traverse City to the Upper Peninsula and southern Michigan ($44 to Detroit; 2 per day; open Mon.-Fri.7:45am-12:45pm, 1:45-5pm, Sat.-Sun. 7:45am-noon), and the **Bay Area Transportation Authority** (941-2324), runs buses once per hour on scheduled routes and every 20 min. within the city ($1.50 per ride) and can provide for group outings (buses run Mon.-Sat. 6am-5:30pm in Traverse City, Mon.-Fri. 6am-5:30pm outside the city). Traverse City's **post office:** 202 S. Union St. (946-9616; open Mon.-Fri. 8am-5pm); **ZIP code:** 49684; **area code:** 616.

■ NORTHERN MICHIGAN SHORE

Charlevoix and Petoskey Hemingway set some of his Nick Adams stories on the stretch of coast near Charlevoix (SHAR-le-voy), north of Traverse City on U.S. 31. The town, which lies on a ½-mi.-wide ribbon of land between Lake Michigan and Lake Charlevoix, attracts more tourists today than in Hemingway's time. Downstaters triple Charlevoix's population in summer. For visitor info, head to the **Charlevoix Chamber of Commerce,** 408 Bridge St. (616-547-2101; open year-round Mon.-Fri. 9am-5pm, Sat. 10am-5pm). **Sailing** is Charlevoix's specialty. Several companies offer cruises of Lake Charlevoix, some stopping 32 mi. away on **Beaver Island,** the largest island on Lake Michigan. Camping, RV stations, and cottages are available at **Uhrick's Lincoln Log Motel and Campground,** 800 Petoskey Ave., (547-4881) on U.S. 31. Prices vary, but warm cottage rooms start at $32. (Don't expect anything less than $48 on summer weekends; tent or RV sites $15.)

Petoskey is famed for its **Petoskey Stones,** fossilized coral from a long-gone sea, now found in heaps along the lakeshores. For info on these beaches and other local attractions, including canoeing, orchards, and walking tours, head to the **Petoskey Regional Chamber of Commerce,** 401 E. Mitchell (347-4150 or 800-845-2828), in Petoskey, 18 mi. north of Charlevoix (open during summer Mon.-Fri. 8am-6pm, Sat. 10am-3pm; during winter Mon.-Fri. 8am-5pm). **Greyhound** has a flag stop at the **Bookstop,** 301 W. Mitchell (347-4400). Petoskey's **Gaslight District,** one block from the Chamber of Commerce, has local crafts and foods in period shops. **Symon's General Store,** 401 E. Lake St. (347-2438), has a large wine selection and gourmet delights. Try the chicken and herb pizza ($1.95). (Open summer daily 8:30am-7:30pm; winter daily 8:30am-6pm.) Vegetarians can head to **Grain Train Natural Foods Co-op,** 421 Howard St. (347-2381), for such daily-changing delectable creations as soy pizza ($2.50-3.50). (Open Mon.-Thurs. 9am-7pm, Fri. 9am-8pm, Sat. 9am-8pm, Sun. 11am-5pm.)

Petosky is definitely the place on the western coast to find affordable accommodations. **North Central Michigan College,** 1515 Howard St. (616-348-6611), offers single dorm rooms off of a suite for $22.50 ($28 for two). Linens are provided. Make reservations at 348-6612;e little walk-in traffic is accepted. Outdoors, camping options abound. The **Petoskey State Park,** 2 mi. east of town off Rte. 31 (616-347-2311), has sites on Little Traverse Bay for $13.

Rte. 119 is an excellent driving detour for those heading north from Petoskey. The road curves along the coast, passing through a Tunnel of Trees. While cruising Rte. 119, stop by the **Legs Inn** (616-526-2281) in Cross Village. This landmark has a rather expensive restaurant serving the only food for miles. Polish and American cuisine ($9-16) daily 11am-10pm. Live music and dancing on Fri.-Sun.

Straits of Mackinac Further north, colonial **Fort Michilimackinac** (436-5563) guards the straits between Lake Michigan and Lake Superior, just as it did in the 18th century, though **Mackinaw City,** the town that grew up around the fort, is now out to trap tourists, not invading troops. (Tours of the fort mid-May to mid-June and Labor Day to mid-Oct. 10am-4pm; mid-June to Labor Day 9am-6pm. $6.50, ages 6-12 $4.) The **Mackinaw City Chamber of Commerce,** 706 S. Huron (436-5574), can assist you with visitor info. (Open summer Mon.-Fri. 9am-7:30pm, Sat.-Sun. 9am-2pm; winter Mon.-Fri. 9am-2pm.) Campers can pitch their tents or park their RVs at the 600-site **Mackinaw Mill Creek Campground** (436-5584), 3 mi. south on Rte 23, which offers some sites within feet of the lake (basic site $11, nominal fees for amenities.) You can also head to the **Wilderness State Park** (436-5381), 11 mi. west on Wilderness Park Drive, where sites run $14. Indoor lodging will force you to reach much deeper into your wallet; the least expensive lodging in town, the **Nicolet Inn,** 725 S. Nicolet (436-7311), has rooms from $46.

Mackinac Island (which prohibits cars) offers **Fort Mackinac** (906-847-3328), many Victorian homes, and the **Grand Hotel** (906-847-3331; open mid-June to Labor Day, daily 9am-6pm, otherwise varies May to mid-June and Labor Day-Oct; $6.50, ages 6-12 $4), an elegant, gracious summer resort with the world's longest porch and where rooms rent for upwards of $310 per night. This snooty abode charges $5 for non-guests to enter the grounds, and proper attire (skirts for women) is mandatory after 6pm. Horse-drawn **carriages** cart guests all over the island (906-847-3325; $11.50 per person, children 4-11 $6; open daily 8:30am-5pm). Saddle horses ($20 per hr.) and bikes ($3 per hr.) are also available to rent. Encompassing 80% of the island, **Mackinac Island State Park** offers a circular 8.2-mi. shoreline road for biking and hiking (free). The **Mackinac Island Chamber of Commerce** can help you plan your trip (906-847-3783; open daily year-round, hours vary. Summer hours 8:30am-7pm). Tourist-tempting **fudge** shops originated on the island. **Ferries** leave Mackinaw City and St. Ignace (June-Sept. every ½ hr.; May and Sept.-Oct. every hr.; round-trip $11.50, ages 5-12 $6.50, bike passage $3). **Greyhound** has a flag stop at the Standard gas station in downtown Mackinaw City. The **Michigan Dept. of Transportation Welcome and Travel Information Center** (436-5566), off I-75, is loaded with brochures (open summer daily 8am-8pm; winter 9am-5pm). The **Mackinaw Bridge** leads to St. Ignace (toll $1.50.) .

■■■ UPPER PENINSULA

A multi-million-acre forestland bordered by three of the world's largest lakes, Michigan's Upper Peninsula (U.P.) is one of the most scenic and unspoiled stretches of land in the Great Lakes region. But in 1837, after losing the Toledo War against Ohio in Congress, Michigan only grudgingly accepted this "wasteland to the north" as part of an unpopular deal in which Michigan gained statehood. Since then, U.P.'s extensive natural resources, spectacular waterfalls, and miles of coastline have won over the hearts of most Michiganders. One hundred years ago the region was almost completely deforested, its timber destined for houses and fences on the treeless Great Plains and for the fireplaces of voracious Chicago; these woodlands are only now returning to their former grandeur.

If you want to experience small-town America, this is the place. The largest town in the U.P. has a population of 25,000; the region is a paradise for fishing, camping, hiking, snowmobiling, and getting away from it all. For regional cuisine, stick to the Friday night fish-fry: a mess o' perch, walleye, or whitefish, available everywhere for about $7-10. Try the local ethnic specialty, a meat pie imported by Cornish miners in the 19th century called a pastie (PASS-tee).

Hikers will enjoy numerous treks, including Michigan's 875 mi. of the **North Country Trail,** a national scenic trail extending from New York to North Dakota. (Contact the North Country Trail Association, P.O. Box 311, White Cloud, MI 49349.) Half a dozen rivers in the U.P. beckon canoers. Those who heed the call of the rapids should write to **Michigan Recreational Canoe Association,** P.O. Box

668, Indian River 49749 (616-238-7868). The peninsula has 200 **campgrounds,** including those at both national forests. Sleep with your dogs or bring extra blankets; temperatures in these parts can drop to 40°F even in July. **Welcome centers** guard the U.P. at the six main entry points: **Ironwood, Iron Mountain, Menominee, St. Ignace, Sault-Ste. Marie,** and **Marquette.** Pick up their handy-dandy *Upper Peninsula Travel Planner.* Write to the **U.S. Forestry Service,** 2727 N. Lincoln Rd., Escanaba 49829 (786-4062), for help planning a trip into the wilderness; or contact **Upper Peninsula Travel and Recreation Association** (800-562-7134).

The region's isolation and large distances make travel very difficult without a car. **Greyhound** (632-8643 or 800-800-2814) has just three routes: Sault-Ste. Marie to St. Ignace and points south; St. Ignace to Rapid River, Iron Mountain, and Ironwood along U.S. 2; and Calumet south to Marquette, Rapid River, and Green Bay on U.S. 41. (All routes run once per day.) Carless travelers should rent in one of the gateway cities (Green Bay from the west or Grand Rapids from the east), or bike the area. Outside the major tourist towns, motel rooms can be had from $20. The vibrant spectrum of leaves make autumn a beautiful time to hike; by winter, x-county skiers have replaced hikers. Upper Peninsula's **area code:** 906.

■ SAULT STE. MARIE

In 1855, entrepreneurs built the first lock at Sault Ste. Marie (the "SOO"), easing the costly burden of moving between Lake Huron and Lake Superior (the water level difference between the two lakes is 22 vertical feet). Today the city's four locks are the busiest in the world, floating over 12,000 ships annually. The U.S. Army Corps of Engineers, which operates the locks, maintains a good **visitors center** (10 Portage St.; 632-0888; open mid-May to early Nov., during the summer daily 7am-11pm, during the spring and fall 8am-10pm). Ask for info on boat and train tours of the Locks. The **Locks Park Historic Walkway** parallels the water for 1 mi., showcasing the Locks Overlook, Plank Alley, Fort Brady, and the Johnston Homestead. To tour a freighter, head to the waterfront at the end of Johnston St., where the *Valley Camp* (632-3658), a 1917 steam-powered freighter, has been converted into a museum (open mid-May to mid-Oct. 10am-6pm, July-Aug. 9am-9pm; $5.95, seniors $5.45, ages 6-16 $3.50). Just up the block from the water, the **Tower of History,** 326 E. Portage St. (632-3658) affords a panoramic view of the locks, bridges, and ships. (Open May 15-Oct. 15 daily 10am-6pm; $2.95, seniors $2.50, kids 6-16 $1.75.)

In Sault Ste. Marie, bed down at the **King's Inn Motel,** 3755 I-75 Business Spur (635-5061), which has rooms from $42. **Tahquamenon Falls State Park,** a 90-min. drive, 10 mi. west of Paradise (492-3415), has hookups at three of the four areas (modern sites $10, rustic sites $6). Lower falls has canoe and rowboat rentals.

About 10 mi. north of Paradise, at the end of Hwy. 123, **Whitefish Point,** known as the "Graveyard of the Great Lakes," has its history of violent shipwrecks grippingly documented at the **Great Lakes Shipwreck Historical Museum** (635-1742; open mid-May to mid-Oct. daily 10am-6pm; $4, ages 6-18 $3). Over 500 vessels have found a watery grave just off the point (today protected as an Underwater Preserve), affording divers exceptional opportunities to search for **sunken treasure.**

■ MIDDLE OF THE PENINSULA

One of the U.P.'s two huge **national forests,** the **Hiawatha,** 2727 N. Lincoln Rd., Escanaba (786-4062) blankets central and eastern U.P. Campsites are available throughout both forests ($6-8). Also visit the lovely **Ottawa National Forest,** 2100 E. Cloverland Dr., Ironwood, MI 49938 (932-1330). The **Seney National Wildlife Refuge,** off M-77 between Seney and Germfask, 12 mi. north of U.S. 2, is a 95,000-acre sanctuary (open during daylight; free). Go beyond the **visitors center** (open mid-May to mid-Oct. daily 9am-5pm) and see over 200 different species of beaver. There are also 70 mi. of trails for hiking and biking and a 7-mi. drive. **Canoeing** and **fishing** are permitted in certain areas at specific times, but overnight camping is not. A state **fishing permit** ($9 per day, out-of-state $20; available from any convenience store, grocery store, or tackle shop) is required if you want to fish. The best time for viewing wildlife is in the early morning and the early evening.

In **Shingleton,** 20 mi. west of the refuge, you can observe snowshoes being hand-made at the **Iverson Snowshoe Company's** "factory," in a garage on Maple St. off Hwy. 28 (452-6370; open Mon.-Fri. 8am-3:30pm).

Drop a penny and watch it sink all the way to the bottom of the 45-ft. deep **Big Spring** (341-2355), at Palms Book State Park on M-149, 10 mi. north of U.S. 2. This pellucid natural spring, called Kitch-iti-Kipi ("mirror of heaven") by the native Americans, gushes 10,000 gallons per minute. Hop on the self-propelled raft, haul yourself to the center of the pool, and observe the billows of silt where the water streams in.($4 per carload, open daily 9am-7pm.) According to folklore, Paul Bunyan, who performed such legendary feats as creating a riverbed by dragging his axe, was born in **Manistique**. As you drive through on U.S. 2, you can't miss the 20-ft.-tall fiberglass statue of the man himself. Camp at **Indian Lake State Park,** 5 mi. west of town; take U.S. 2 west, then M-149 north. (Sites $12). Contact the Park Office (341-2355; open daily 8am-noon, 1-5pm) for more info.

West along Rte.2, then south on Rte. 183, the town of **Fayette** guards the peninsula at Big Bay de Noc. There, **Fayette State Historic Park** (644-2603) displays the historic townsite, a preserved ghost town, an opera house, company store, hotel, and machine shop. (Open June-Labor Day daily 9am-5pm, Labor Day to mid-Oct daily 9am-5pm.) The park also offers scuba diving, hiking, semi-modern camping ($8; no showers), and boat tours past the limestone cliffs of Snail Shell Harbor ($6, children $4, depart continuously from the townsite dock).

On the U.P.'s northern shore, the scenic beauty and recreational opportunities are concentrated at the **Pictured Rocks National Lakeshore,** which stretches for 40 mi. along Lake Superior between Munising and Grand Marais. The **Pictured Rocks** have been sculpted by wind, rain, and ice for millennia. The kaleidoscopic beauty of their arches and columns is hard to appreciate from land, but an overlook at **Miner's Castle** off Miner's Castle Rd. from H58, gives a decent perspective of the stone formations. The best way to see the carved cliffs is the **Pictured Rocks Boat Cruise** (387-2379), a 2-hr. and 40 min. tour which leaves from Munising. (Memorial Day-June, and Sept. to mid-Oct., 2 per day; July-late Aug. 7 per day; $19, under 12 $9.50). The **Twelve Mile Beach** and **Grand Sable Dunes** occupy the other half of the lakeshore. Enjoy the sand and rock beaches, but don't plan to swim unless you have a layer of blubber; Lake Superior is f-f-f-reezing year-round. Hwy. 58, an oft-bumpy, unpaved gem of a road, weaves along the lakeshore, affording some outstanding views as well as access to trailheads and campsites in the area. The **North Country Trail,** which winds from Port Henry, NY to Lake Sakakawea, ND, passes along the lakeshore. You can hike on the trail and sleep at primitive campsites on the way (get free permit at Grand Marais, Manistique, or Munising visitors centers).

The lakeshore is accessible from **Munising** or **Grand Marais;** in both towns you can find food, supplies, and lodging. In Grand Marais, take a detour and stop by the **Maritime Museum** (494-2669) at Coast Guard Point on Canal St. (July-early Sept.open Fri.-Sun. 1-5pm.) At the other end of Munising, take a ferry (387-2379) out to **Grand Island** (2-3 daily during summer, $10, under 12 $5) to enjoy an afternoon hike or picnic. Camping and biking are also allowed; limited motor vehicle access may be granted. For more info contact the **Grand Sable Visitor Center** (494-2660), H-58, 1 mi. west of Grand Marais (open mid–May to mid-June and mid-Sept., daily 9am-5pm; mid-June to mid-Sept. daily 9am-7pm.)

■ KEWEENAW PENINSULA

The curved finger of land in the Northwest corner of the U.P., known as the Keweenaw Peninsula, first beckoned speculators in 1843 when the discovery of a rich lode of copper ore set off the nation's first mining boom. Unfortunately, the mines never proved very profitable and by 1969 had been silenced, leaving behind a barren, exploited land. Through reforestation efforts and government support, the

THE GREAT LAKES

area has recovered and become a tourist destination. Comb the agate beaches, see the Northern Lights, dive to explore the multitudes of offshore shipwrecks, and in winter, ski, snowmobile, snowshoe, or take a dog sled ride over the 250 inches of snow the region receives each year. At the base of the peninsula, along the shore of Lake Superior, **Porcupine Mountain Wilderness State Park** (885-5275), with 80 mi. of flash-marked trails, is one of the best places to hike in the U.P. The park is on the western side of the U.P., 16 mi. west of Ontonagon off M-107. The **Lake of the Clouds** glistens high in the mountains of this 58,000-acre preserve. **Campgrounds** both modern ($10) and rustic ($6), and a visitors center with slide shows and exhibits (open 10am-6pm daily during summer), enhance the travelers' stay at this, the state's largest wilderness park. North along Hwy. 26, the **Seaman Mineral Museum** (487-2512), on the fifth floor of the Electrical Resources Center at Michigan Technological University, houses one of the continent's premier crystal collections, along with minerals from the copper days of the Keweenaw. (Open July-Oct. Mon.-Fri. 9am-4:30pm, Sat. noon-4pm; $4, under 18 $1.)

Farther north in **Calumet,** the **Coppertown U.S.A. Mining Museum** (337-4354), west off U.S. 41 on Calumet Ave., displays the tools, techniques, and history behind the mining of raw materials. (Open Mon.-Sat. 10am-5pm; also Sun. 1-4pm July-Sept.; $2, children and seniors $1.) The nation's newest park, **Keweenaw National Historical Park,** showcases the culture, industry, and resultant prosperity of the Copper Age, with a self-guided tour of the historic sites, homes, buildings of the period.

Between 1847 and 1887, prospectors came to the **Delaware Copper Mine** (289-4688), south of Eagle Harbor and 11 mi. southwest of Copper Harbor on U.S. 41, and extracted 8 million pounds of copper from the earth. Now, tourists plunk down coppers to pay for the daily 45-min. guided tour through shafts still lined with copper veins (June-Aug. 10am-6pm; May, and Sept.-Oct. 10am-5pm; $6, under 13 $3.50). A must for all visitors, the **Brockway Mountain Drive** between Eagle Harbor and Copper Harbor rises 1000 ft. above sea level and is one of the most scenic drives in the U.P., supplying vistas of Lake Superior and the interior woodlands.

The northernmost town in Michigan, **Copper Harbor** functions as the main gateway to **Isle Royale National Park** (see below). In Copper Harbor, stop by the country's oldest active one-room schoolhouse where 13 students (K-8) study algebra and the alphabet. **Estivant Pines,** the largest remaining stand of virgin pines in Michigan, has been preserved near Copper Harbor, 3 mi. out on Lake Manganese Rd. These trees average more than 500 years old, with a girth of 4½ feet.

■■■ ISLE ROYALE NATIONAL PARK

Isle Royale's tourist literature reminds you that "more people visit Yellowstone National Park in one day than visit Isle Royale in the whole year"; if you're seeking backcountry seclusion, this is the real McCoy. Isle Royale (ROY-al) is an island. 45 mi. long and 10 mi. wide, which runs parallel to the northwestern coast of Lake Superior. The 99% wilderness island has no cars, telephones, and medical service, and is accessible only by boat (or by sea plane, for the thick of wallet); visitors should plan ahead, leaving time to explore Isle Royale as a living wilderness.

The island was home to quiet fisherfolk until it was made a national park in 1940. The inhabitants were allowed to remain on the island until they left or died, at which point their property reverted to the park. Howard Sivertson's paintings and his book *Once Upon an Isle* document his childhood in this now-defunct community. The remains of human history in the lighthouses and millennia-old Native American copper pit mines are now merely roaming grounds for the island's newer inhabitants: moose, which presumably swam from Canada around the turn of the century, and wolves, which crossed an ice bridge in 1948.

Practical Information Experienced seapersons with boats longer than 20 ft.. can navigate to Isle Royale on their own (contact the park headquarters for advice in plotting a course or determining the feasibility of making the attempt; Lake Superior is big, cold, and treacherous), but the largest share of visitors come on the government operated *Ranger III* (906-482-0984) boat from Houghton, MI, which departs early June to mid-September Tuesday and Friday at 9am (return trip leaves Rock Harbor Wed. and Sat. 9am), and takes 6½ hours. (Round-trip $85, children under 12 $40. Extra charge to transport a boat.) The *Isle Royale Queen III* (operated by **Isle Royale Ferry Service,** The Dock, Copper Harbor, MI 49918, 906-289-4437; off-season 108 Center St., Hancock MI 49930, 906-482-4950) makes 4½-hour trips from Copper Harbor, MI, starting at 8am, and return the same afternoon. (Mid-May to mid-June and Labor Day-end of Sept. Mon. and Fri.; mid-June to the end of June Mon.-Tues. and Thurs.-Sat.; July Thurs.-Tues.; Aug.-Labor Day daily. Round-trip fare $68, children under 12 $34. Extra charge for canoes, kayaks, and suchlike; 10% discount for generally pointless same-day round-trips.) Both of these boats land at **Rock Harbor,** on the island's eastern end, where the most services are available. All times are EST. From **Grand Portage, MN,** near the northern end of Minnesota's Superior North Shore, the **Grand Portage-Isle Royale Transportation Line Inc.,** 1507 N. First St., Superior, WI (715-392-2100) sends the *Voyager II* to Windigo (100-min. trip), making "pit stops" at various trail heads around the island, and reaching Rock Harbor after six hours. (Departures from Grand Portage early May to Memorial Day and Labor Day to late Oct. Wed. and Sat. 9:30am, Thurs. and Sun. 8am, Memorial Day to Labor Day Mon., Wed., and Sat. 9:30am; Tues., Thurs., Sun. 8am. Round-trip to Rock Harbor $80, under 12 $50, other fares vary.) Also, the **Wenonah** chugs to Windigo mid-June to Labor Day three hour, round-trip $35, under 12 $17.50).

The **ranger stations** include: **Windigo** on the western tip of the island; **Rock Harbor** on the eastern tip of the island and **Malone Bay** near **Siskiwit Lake,** on the south shore, midway between Windigo and Rock Harbor. Despite its closer proximity to the Ontario and Minnesota mainland, the park is part of Michigan, and its headquarters are located in **Houghton,** on the Upper Peninsula (mailing address: Isle Royale National Park, Houghton, MI 49931; 906-482-0984).

Camping There are numerous **campgrounds** scattered around the island; required permits are free and available at any ranger station. Some campgrounds have three-sided, screened-in shelters, but they're popular and can't be reserved; bring your own tent just in case. Nights are always cold (mid-40s°F in June); bring warm clothes. Mosquitoes, gnats, and other far nastier biting bugs peak in June and July, so come prepared with plenty of insect repellent. Use a 25-micron filter or boil water for at least two min., as it is infested with a nasty tapeworm; iodine tablets or charcoal purification are insufficient. Wood fires are greatly restricted; bring a self-contained fuel store instead. Some pit toilets are available on the island, otherwise, be sure to follow the guidelines for digging your own mini-toilet. Campers can buy supplies and groceries at Rock Harbor and in limited amounts at Windigo. Indoor accommodations are available at Rock Harbor; they tend to be nice but expensive. Housekeeping cottages at **Rock Harbor Lodge,** P.O. Box 405, Houghton (906-337-4993), start at $60 per day. (Available late May to mid-Sept.)

Activities Hiking most of the length of the island from Rock Harbor to Windigo on some of the 170 mi. of trails in the park is a two-day journey through forests recovered from 19th-century logging, with plenitudes of streams and lakes. Sturdy, broken-in boats, a minimalistic packing style, and topographic maps are recommended for all hikers. The **Greenstone Ridge Trail** follows the backbone of the island from Rock Harbor Lodge. **Ojibway Lookout,** on Mt. Franklin, affords a good view of the Canadian shore 15 mi. away. **Monument Rock,** 70 ft. tall, challenges even experienced climbers. **Lookout Louise,** also on the trail, offers one of the most beautiful views in the park. Really serious backpackers will want to conquer the **Minong Ridge Trail,** which runs parallel to the Greenstone Trail to the north for

THE GREAT LAKES

30 mi. from McCargoe Cove to Windigo. Shorter hikes near Rock Harbor include **Scoville Point,** a 4.2-mi. loop out a jut of land surrounded on three sides by water, and **Suzy's Cave,** a 3.8 mile loop to an inland sea arch. Every day at 1:30pm, there is a one-hour **ranger-led interpretive walk,** giving an island overview at Rock Harbor.

Transportation between places on the island can be accomplished by boat. The *Voyager II* (see above) makes several stops as it circumnavigates Isle Royale. Also, the *M.V. Shady* offers daily trips. Prices and lengths of trips vary. Inquire at the lodge about water charter. **Canoeing** and **kayaking** afford access to otherwise unreachable parts of the island. For a superlative time, go to **Ryan Island** in **Siskiwit Lake,** the largest island in the largest freshwater lake in the world. **Boat** and **canoe rentals** are available at both Rock Harbor and Windigo. (Motor rentals $12 for ½ day, $20 full day. Boat and canoe rentals $10.50 for ½ day, $18 full day.) **Scuba diving** possibilities off the island include numerous shipwrecks which lie just off-shore. Registration. Dive flags are mandatory. Air tanks cannot be refilled at the island, so bring a compressor. On Lake Superior, a Michigan fishing license is mandatory.

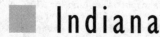

Indiana

The contrast between two popular explanations for Indiana's nickname of "Hoosier" typifies the dichotomy between the state's rural and industrial traditions. The first explanation holds the name to be a corruption of the pioneer's call to visitors at the door, "Who's there?"; the second claims that it spread from Louisville, where labor contractor Samuel Hoosier employed Indiana workers. Visitors still encounter two Indianas: the heavily industrialized northern cities, and the slower-paced agricultural southern counties.

Most tourists identify Indiana as either the state of Gary's smokestacks and the Indianapolis 500, or as home of rolling hills thick with cornstalks. Don't try to choose between the farms and the factories; it is precisely this combination that makes Indiana interesting. Visit the athletic, urban mecca of Indianapolis, but don't miss the rural beauty downstate. The state that produced TV celebrities David Letterman and Jane Pauley, and basketball great Larry Bird, also has beautiful scenery, especially when the fall foliage around Columbus explodes in a profusion of colors.

PRACTICAL INFORMATION

Capital: Indianapolis.
Indiana Division of Tourism, 1 N. Capitol #700, Indianapolis 46204 (232-8860; 800-289-6646 in IN). **Division of State Parks,** 402 W. Washington Room: W-298, Indianapolis 46204 (232-4124).
Time Zones: Eastern and Central. In summer, most of Indiana does not observe Daylight Savings Time. **Postal Abbreviation:** IN
Sales Tax: 5%; 10% hotel tax.

■■■ INDIANAPOLIS

On the seam of the Rust Belt and the Corn Belt, Indianapolis focuses more on the former, embracing the drastically unenvironmental but All-American "sport" of automobile racing as its civic symbol. Its midwestern location produces a city that is All-American almost to the point of being nondescript, but like every good-sized American city, Indianapolis has its points of interest: buildings, museums, ethnic festivals, the nightlife area of Broad Ripple, a local celebrity (one-time meteorologist David Letterman, who was laughed out of town for warning of hail "the size of canned hams"), and, of course, a passion for sports. This reaches its apotheosis each Memorial Day weekend when the Indy 500 fuses exhaust and exhaustion in the world's largest single-day sporting event.

PRACTICAL INFORMATION

Emergency: 911 or 632-7575.

Visitor Information: Indianapolis City Center, 201 S. Capital St. (237-5200), in the Pan Am Plaza across from the Hoosier Dome. Open Mon.-Fri. 10am-5:30pm, Sat. 10am-5pm. Sun. noon-5pm. Also try 800-233-INDY/4639.

Airport: Indianapolis International (487-7243), 7 mi. southwest of downtown near I-465. To get to the city center, take bus #9 ("West Washington").

Amtrak: 350 S. Illinois (263-0550 or 800-872-7245), behind Union Station. In a somewhat deserted but relatively safe area. Trains travel east-west only, with almost all connecting in Chicago ($28) or Washington, D.C. ($95). *See mileage chart.* Station hours are erratic and vary daily, so call ahead.

Greyhound: 127 N. Capital Ave. (800-231-2222), downtown at E. Ohio St. 1 block from Monument Circle. Fairly safe area. To Chicago ($28, 4hr.), Cincinnati (#21, 2 hrs.), Louisville ($25, 2 hrs.). Open 24 hrs. **Indiana Trailways** operates out of the same station and serves cities within the state.

Public Transport: Metro Bus, 36 N. Delaware St. (635-3344), across from City County building. Open Mon.-Fri. 7:30am-5:30pm. Fare 75¢, rush hour $1. Transfers 25¢. For disabled service call 632-3000.

Taxi: Yellow Cab, 487-7777; $2.45 first mi., $1.50 each additional mi.

Car Rental: Thrifty, 5860 Fortune Circle West (636-5622), at the airport. Daily $31 with 150 free mi., weekly $133 with 1050 free mi. Must be 21 with major credit card. $3 daily surcharge for under 25. Open Sun.-Fri. 8am-11pm, Sat. 8am-5pm.

Post Office: 125 W. South St. (464-6000), across from Amtrak. Open Mon.-Wed. and Fri. 7am-5:30pm, Thurs. 7am-6pm. **ZIP code:** 46206.

Area Code: 317.

I-465 laps the city and provides access to downtown. I-70 cuts through the city east-west and passes by the Speedway. The center of Indianapolis is just south of **Monument Circle** at the intersection of **Washington Street** (U.S. 40) and **Meridian Street.** Washington St. divides the city north-south; Meridian St. east-west.

ACCOMMODATIONS AND CAMPING

Budget motels in Indianapolis cluster around the I-465 beltway, 5 mi. from downtown. They are particularly concentrated in the west near the Speedway; buses from downtown to this area cost an extra 25¢. Motels jack up their rates for the Indy 500 in May; make reservations a year in advance.

Fall Creek YMCA, 860 W. 10th St. (634-2478), just north of downtown. Small, clean rooms for both men and women include access to all recreational facilities and pool. Singles $25, with private bath $35; weekly $66/$76; student weekly rate $52.

Motel 6 (293-3200) I-465 at Exit 16A, 3 mi. from the Indy Speedway and 10 mi. from downtown, or take the #13 bus. Clean, bright rooms with a really nice outdoor pool which *isn't* in the parking lot. Singles $31, doubles $37.

Dollar Inn (788-9561) I-465 at Harding St. or at Speedway (248-8500). Take #13 bus. Convenient to the Speedway and Eagle Creek Park. Singles $24, doubles $30. Key deposit $2.

Medical Tower Inn, 1633 N. Capitol Ave. (925-9831), in the tall building across from the Methodist Hospital. Luxurious 2-room suites with decor you wouldn't mind in your own home. Singles $47, doubles $57. With student ID $2 less.

Indiana State Fairgrounds Campgrounds, 1202 E. 38th St. (927-7510). 133 nice sites $10.50, full hookup $12.60. Open year-round. The State Fair is mid-Aug., so make reservations well in advance.

FOOD AND NIGHTLIFE

Tourists and residents alike head for **Union Station,** 39 Jackson Pl. (267-0700), near the Hoosier Dome and four blocks south of Monument Circle. This 13-acre maze of restaurants, shops, dance clubs, bars, and hotels sells many edible goodies in an authentically refurbished rail depot. The second-level bustles with a moderately priced food court. Entrees average $2.50-5. (Open Mon.-Thurs. 10am-9pm, Fri.-Sat. 10am-10pm, Sun. 11am-6pm.) Another place to food-window-shop is **The City Market** 222 E. Market St., two blocks east of Monument Circle, a renovated 19th-century building with produce stands and 15 ethnic markets. (Open Mon.-Sat. 6am-6pm; but individual stalls usually close earlier, so go weekdays 10am-3pm.)

Bazbeaux Pizza, 334 Massachusetts Ave. (636-7662) and 832 E. Westfields Boulevard (255-5712). Indulge in Indianapolis's favorite pizza either downtown or at Broad Ripple. Try the Xchoupitoulas pizza, a cajun masterpiece, or construct your own culinary wonder with any of 53 toppings. Pizzas $5-18. Open Mon.-Thurs. 11am-10pm, Fri. 11am-11pm, Sat. noon-11pm, Sun. 4:30-10pm.

Acapulco Joe's, 365 N. Illinois (637-5160). The first Mexican restaurant in Indianapolis greets its guests with a sign saying: "Acapulco Joe's has sold over 5 million tacos—do you realize that represents *over 6 pounds of ground beef?*" Heavy on flavor, atmosphere, and popularity. Entrees $7.65 and under. Open Mon.-Thurs. 7am-9pm, Fri.-Sat. 7am-10pm.

Café Angst, 326 E. Vermont St. (237-0363). Cool basement coffeehouse under a yellow awning equipped with boardgames, books, nightly music, and a killer kiwi creme soda ($1.50). Healthy vegetarian fare from baguettes ($1.40) to vegie stromboli ($4.50). Occasional live music and poetry readings. Open Sun.-Thurs. 1:30pm-midnight, Fri.-Sat. 1:30pm-1am.

Nightlife undulates 6 mi. north of the downtown area at **Broad Ripple,** at College Ave. and 62nd St., an area typically swamped with students and yuppies. The area has charming ethnic restaurants (many have lunch specials) and art studios in original frame houses, as well as artsy and sports bars and dance clubs. **The Vogue,** 6259 N. College Ave. (255-2828), hosts mid-sized national acts, with techno nights (usually Sat.). Nearby the **Patio,** 6303 Guilford Ave. (255-2828), attracts solid local talent with low cover charges ($2 or under—free dancing on Wed.). Many places ask for several forms of identification to verify your 21+ years of existence.

SIGHTS

The **State House** (232-3131), bounded by Capitol and Senate, looks like any other capitol from the outside, but enter and see an amazing marble palace with a majestic stained-glass inside. Self-guided tour brochures are available inside. (Open daily 8am-5pm, on weekends tour main floor only.) "Please touch" is the motto of the **Children's Museum,** 3000 N. Meridian St. (924-5431), one of the largest in the country. Kids help run hands-on exhibits, which include a turn-of-the-century carousel, a huge train collection, petting zoos, and high-tech electronic wizardry. (Open daily 10am-5pm, closed Mon. Sept.-April. $6, seniors $5, ages 2-17 $3. Free Thurs. 5-8pm.) The **Indianapolis Museum of Art,** 1200 W. 38th (923-1331), houses a large collection of Turner paintings and watercolors as well as Robert Indiana's *LOVE* sculpture. The museum sits among 154 acres of park, beautifully landscaped with gardens and nature trails. (Open Tues.-Wed. and Fri.-Sat. 10am-5pm, Thurs. 10am-8:30pm, Sun. noon-5pm. Free, except special exhibits, which are free only on Thurs.) Stunning African and Egyptian decor graces the **Walker Theatre,** 617 Indiana Ave. (236-2099). Erected in 1927, the theater commemorates Madame Walker, America's first self-made woman millionaire, and symbolizes Indianapolis' African-American community, hosting jazz greats as Louis Armstrong and Dinah Washington. The complex also sponsors plays and dance performances. Upstairs in the ballroom, the **Jazz on the Avenue** series offers live music every Friday night. The **Indiana Film Society** (239-2099) has an annual fall film festival, with some movies shown in the Walker.

Indianapolis has a host of musical, theatrical, and cultural productions. The **Indiana Repertory Theater,** 140 W. Washington (635-5252), is Indiana's only full-season professional company, performing classical and modern plays (tickets $6-30). The **Pride of Indy Barbershop Harmony Chorus,** 426 N. Harbison (897-0872), meets for free open rehearsals every Monday at 7:30pm at the Broad Ripple United Methodist Church, 62nd and Guilford Ave.

THE INDIANAPOLIS 500: ALL I WANT TO DO IS VROOM VROOM VROOM

The **Indianapolis Motor Speedway,** 4790 W. 16th St. (481-8500), is the quintessential Indianapolis tourist site. Take the Speedway exit off I-465 or catch bus #25 ("West 16th"). Except in May, you can take a bus ride around the 2½-mi. track for $2. The adjacent **Speedway Museum** (Indy Hall of Fame) houses a collection of Indy race cars and antique autos, as well as racing memorabilia and videotapes highlighting historic Indy moments. (Open daily 9am-5pm. $2, under 16 free.)

The country's passion for the automobile reaches a speeding frenzy during the **500 Festival** (636-4556), a month of parades, a mini-marathon, and lots of hoopla, leading up to the day when 33 aerodynamic, turbocharged race cars circle the track at speeds exceeding 225 mph. Beginning with the "time trials" (the two weekends in mid-May preceding the race), the party culminates with a big blowout on the Sunday of Memorial Day weekend (weather permitting). Book hotel reservations early and buy tickets in advance. For ticket info, call 481-8500 (open daily 9am-5pm). The 500 isn't the only race in town; call for information on other auto events at the **Indianapolis Raceway Park,** 9901 Crawfordsville Rd. (293-7223), near the intersection of I-74 and I-465. Another huge racing event is NASCAR's **Brickyard 400** (800-822-4639), which sends stockcars zooming down the speedway in early August.

■■■ BLOOMINGTON

Bloomington maintains a masterful balance between a rural Indiana community and a fresh-minded, frenetic college town. Home to the 35,000 students of Indiana University (IU), this town offers punks, frat boys, and Bible-thumping fundamentalists, as well as lakes, parks, and safe streets.

Orientation and Practical Information Bloomington is south of Indianapolis on Rte. 37. An **American Trailways** bus station, 535 N.Walnut (332-1522), serves the town four blocks from the center of downtown. (Open Mon.-Sat. 4:30am-5:30pm, Sun. open during bus times only.) **Bloomington Transit** transports the populace on seven routes. Service is infrequent, so call 332-5688 for info. (Fare 50¢, children 5-17 and seniors 25¢.) The **visitors center** is located at 2855 N. Walnut (334-8900 or 800-800-0037; open Mon.-Fri. 8am-5pm, Sat. 9am-4pm, Sun. 10am-3pm; 24-hr. brochure area.) Bloomington's **post office:** Fourth St., two blocks east after Walnut (open Mon. 8am-6pm, Tues.-Thurs. 8am-5:30pm, Fri. 8am-6pm, Sat. 8am-1pm); **ZIP code:** 47401; **area code:** 812.

Accommodations and Food Bloomington's budget hotels cluster around the intersection of N. Walnut St. and Rte. 46. A block north, the **University Inn,** 2601 N. Walnut (332-9453), supplies a pool, free breakfast, free local calls, and rooms equipped with refrigerators and microwaves. (Singles $33, doubles $44.) On Maplegrove Rd. off Rte. 46 just west of town stands **Bauer House,** 4595 N. Maple Grover Rd. (336-4383). In this family-run B&B, $50 will secure a room that sleeps up to four people and a country breakfast prepared by Mrs. Bauer. (Open May-Oct.) Reservations recommended around the start and end of the scholastic year. For campers, the **Lake Monroe Village Campgrounds,** 8107 S. Fairfax Rd. (824-2267), 8 mi. south of Bloomington, are within walking distance of the lake. (Sites $16, with full hookup $23.)

The **Downtown Square** of Bloomington holds a wealth of restaurants in a two-block radius. A half block west of the square is the **Irish Lion,** 212 Kirkwood (336-9076), serving pub grub (fish and chips $4.25) and full entrees (ballydebob halibut $12), but locally famous for its half-yard glasses of beer ($5). (Open Sun.-Thurs. 11am-midnight, Fri.-Sat. 11am-1am.) Cheap eateries mark Kirkwood Ave. as it approaches U of I on the east end of town. **Jiffy-Treet,** 425 E. Kirkwood (332-3502), produces homemade ice-cream.

Sights and Entertainment IU's **Art Museum,** Fine Arts Plaza, E. 7th St. (855-5445), maintains an excellent university collection including a rather likeable Dada enclave. Marcel Duchamp's famous *Fountain,* a urinal with "R. Mutt" scrawled on its surface, and Man Ray's *Gift,* an iron with several small nails affixed to the bottom, are proof that Dada *still* kicks you in the butt and you *still* like it. (Open Wed.-Fri. 10am-5pm, Sat. and Sun. noon-5pm. Free.) Downtown, the **Antique Mall,** 311 W. 7th St. (332-2290), invites browsing among three floors of antiques. (Open Mon.-Thurs. and Sat. 10am-5pm, Fri. 10am-8pm, Sun. noon-5pm.) Frolic at **Lake Monroe,** 10 mi. south of Bloomington. **The Crazy Horse,** 214 W. Kirkwood (336-8877), offers a selection of 80 beers from Jamaica to Japan. (Open Mon.-Thurs. 11am-1am, Fri.-Sat. 11am-2am, Sun. 11am-midnight.) The **Bluebird,** 216 N. Walnut (336-2473), caters to those with a taste for rock or 10¢ drafts. For further info on the Bloomington scene, consult the *Bloomington Voice* for listings, the *Village Vine* for general info, and *Bam* for band descriptions.

The 4th St. **Festival of the Arts and Crafts** draws hundreds of Midwestern artisans to a Labor Day weekend artfest. **A Taste of Bloomington** in June gives local restaurants a chance to gather under a single tent and entice hungry festival-goers amidst music of Bloomington bands. **Unidentified Flying Octave** is another June gathering, this one involving primitive camping and a "solar electric sound stage."

Illinois

Once rolling prairies, Illinois has since been thoroughly plowed and mined—it is now the largest producer of both soybeans and coal, giving the 21st state diversity. The state is bounded by water on three sides and is an important railroad connection; if something is moving cross-country, chances are good that it goes through Illinois. And with 11½ million people, Illinois is as important for politics as it is for provisions. Most of the state is farmland; only Iowa produces more corn. The southern tip, known as Little Egypt for its resemblance to the fertile Nile Valley, is especially rich with cottonfields and southern lifestyle. Clashing against the amber waves of grain is Chicago. America's third largest city, Chicago throbs as the energetic and tough-minded cultural center of the Midwest.

PRACTICAL INFORMATION
Capital: Springfield.
Office of Tourism, 620 E. Adams St., Springfield 62701 (217-782-7500).
Time Zone: Central (1 hr. behind Eastern). **Postal Abbreviation:** IL
Sales Tax: 6.25%.

■■■ CHICAGO

The Windy City is aptly named, due not only to the sharp gusts that roll off Lake Michigan, but also to the multitudes who have blown through the third largest city in the U.S. Chicago, since its founding in 1833, has been an urban center in a rural setting. With the explosion of the railroad in the mid-19th century, Chicago became

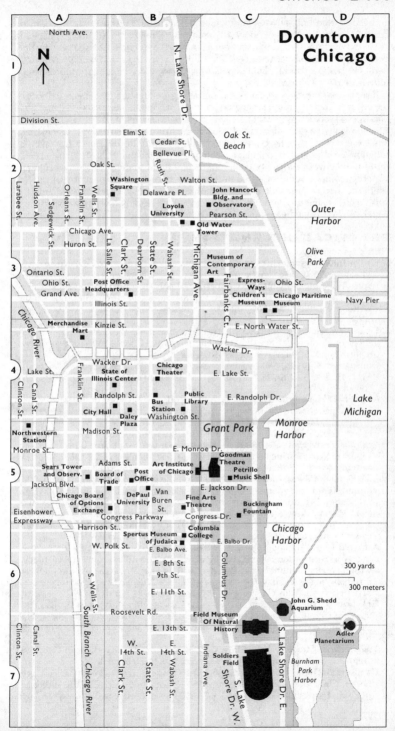

Downtown Chicago

a transportation hub, moving large quantities of natural resources from coast to coast. When industrialists developed assembly-line slaughterhouses and refrigerated rail cars, which allowed meat to be moved during the summer, Chicago became the country's premier slaughterhouse. Unfortunately, de-industrialization has struck hard. The stockyards and freight depots which made the Armours and Pullmans rich have been closed for decades.

In a place where every building is a contrasting architectural statement, so too are the city's distinctive products and personalities: Al Capone, Jesse Jackson, Jane Addams, the skyscraper, Cracker Jack, deep dish pizza, Ebony magazine, and Playboy. Chicago is a complex interplay of modern highrises and burned out tenements. Since racial minorities have now become the majority in Chicago, it has taken a tough breed of politician to find cohesion here. Chicago pulses as the financial center of the Midwest, captain of commodities and futures trading. The city's cultural variety includes a score of major museums, and impressive collection of public sculpture, one of the world's finest symphony orchestras, excellent (and radical) small theaters, and the University of Chicago, which has employed more Nobel laureates than any other university in the world.

PRACTICAL INFORMATION

Emergency: 911.

Visitor Information: Chicago Visitor Information Center, 163 E. Pearson (744-2400 or 800-487-2446), in the Water Tower Pumping Station. Open daily 9:30am-5pm. The **Chicago Cultural Center,** Randolph St. at Michigan Ave. Pick up a copy of the *Chicago Visitors Guide.* Open Mon.-Sat. 9am-5pm, Sun. 11am-5pm. Write or call the **Chicago Office of Tourism,** 806 N. Michigan Ave., Chicago 60611 (744-2000).

Traveler's and Immigrant's Aid: Travelers should use the O'Hare Airport (686-7562; open Mon.-Fri. 8:30am-5pm) and Greyhound (629-4500; open Mon.-Fri. 8:30am-5pm) locations, which provide over 20 different programs.

Consulates: Canada, 180 N. Stetson Ave. (616-1860); **Ireland,** 400 N. Michigan Ave. (337-1868); **U.K.,** 33 N. Dearborn St. (346-1810). Hours vary, so call specific consulate to verify.

Airport: O'Hare International, (686-2200) off I-90. Inventor of the layover, the holding pattern and the headache. Depending on traffic, a trip between downtown and O'Hare can take up to 2 hrs. The **Rapid Train** runs between the Airport El station and downtown ($1.50). The ride takes from 40 min. to 1 hr. **Continental Air Transport** (454-7800) connects the airport to selected downtown and suburban locations, including the Marriot Hotel at Michigan and Rush. Runs every 5-10 min. 6am-11:30pm from each baggage terminal. Fare $14.75. The ride takes 60-75 min. **Midway Airport** (767-0500), on the western edge of the South Side, often offers less expensive flights. To get downtown, take CTA bus #54B to Archer St., then ride bus #62 to State St. For an extra 25¢, the 99M express runs from Midway downtown 6-8:15am and from downtown to Midway during the afternoon rush hour 3:55-6pm. Continental Air Transport costs $10.50 and runs every 15 min., 6am-10:30pm. Airport baggage lockers $1 per day.

Amtrak: Union Station (558-1075 or 800-872-7245), Canal and Adams St. across the river, west of the Loop. Take the El to State and Adams, then walk 7 blocks west on Adams. Amtrak's main hub may look familiar; it was the backdrop for the final baby-buggy scene of *The Untouchables.* See *Mileage Chart.* Station open 24 hrs.; tickets sold daily 6:15am-9pm. Baggage lockers $1 per day.

Greyhound: 630 W. Harrison St. (800-231-2222), at Jefferson and Desplaines. Take the El to Linton. The hub of the central U.S. Also serves as home base for several smaller bus companies covering the Midwest. *See Mileage Chart.* Station open 24 hrs., ticket office open 5am-2am.

Taxi: Yellow Cab, 829-4222; **Flash Cab,** 561-1444; **American United Cab,** 248-7600. Taxis average fare $1.50 for flag drop plus $1.20 per mile.

Car Rental: Dollar Rent-a-Car (800-800-4000), at O'Hare and Midway; P.O. Box 66181, Chicago, IL 60666. $35 per day, $174 per week; age 21-25, $12 surcharge per day. **Thrifty Car Rental** (800-367-2277), from O'Hare and Midway. $37 per day, $178 per week with unlimited mileage in state and bordering states; age 21-25, $10 surcharge per day. Must be 21 with major credit card for both.

Auto Transport Company: National U-Drive, 3626 Calumet Ave., Hammond, IN (219-852-0134). 20 min. from the Loop. Call for rates.

Help Lines: Rape Crisis Line, 708-872-7799. 24 hrs. **Gay and Lesbian Hotline,** 871-2273. 24 hrs. **Police,** 744-4000 (non-emergency).

Medical Emergency: Cook County Hospital, 1835 W. Harrison (633-6000). Take the Congress A train to the Medical Center Stop.

Medical Walk-in Clinic: Doctor's Office Center, 3245 N. Halsted Ave. (528-5005). Non-emergency medical care. Open Mon.-Fri. 8am-8pm, Sat. 9am-3pm.

Post Office: 433 W. Van Buren St. (765-3210), 2 blocks from Union Station. Open Mon.-Fri. 7am-9pm, Sat. 8am-5pm, 24-hr. self-service available. **ZIP code:** 60607.

Area Code: 312 for numbers in Chicago, 708 for numbers outside Chicago's municipal boundaries. All numbers listed here without area code are for 312 area.

ORIENTATION

Encompassing the entire northeastern corner of Illinois, Chicago runs north-south along 29 mi. of southwest Lake Michigan shorefront. A focal point of the Midwest, Chicago serves as a transportation connection between the coasts; most cross-country road, rail, and airplane trips in the northern U.S. will pass through the city.

Chicago is a machine that accepts immigrants and produces Americans. Arriving with little or nothing but a foreign tongue, loads of newcomers have found jobs, apartments, and a new start here. To ease the transition, many remain in ethnic communities which sustain Old-World traditions in churches, social clubs, and local bars. The Chicago immigrant paradigm is a familiar one. Once established, immigrant children move to the suburbs to become middle class, and the neighborhood evaporates. Later, *their* children move back to the city as young professionals, gentrifying worn-out districts and rejoining the churn and bustle of this living city. This cycle continues today, and Chicago's neighborhoods are always in a state of flux. An area that illustrates the first step in this sequence is **Uptown,** whose new name is **New Chinatown;** it centers at Broadway and Argyle and is the center of the Southeast Asian influx into the city. It also has a strong Indian and Arab presence. The areas that were once **Greektown** (Halsted St. at Madison) and **Little Italy** (Taylor St. between Morgan and Racine) have reached middle-age; their residents have begun the exodus to the suburbs. Though it still exists, Greektown is fading; Little Italy is no more. In all, Chicago neighborhoods are neither discrete nor fixed; the city constantly evolves.

The Chicago River on the north and west, Lake Michigan on the east, and the elevated train enclose the **Loop,** the downtown area and business hub which contains many of America's architectural treasures. Just south of the Loop lies **Pilsen,** a center for Chicago's Latino community, and unfortunately *not* a safe place to venture at night. North of the Loop across the river are **Near North,** an area with more office buildings, and the glitzy shopping district known as the **Magnificent Mile:** Michigan Ave. between Grand Ave. and Division St. The north side of Chicago—a broad term subsuming all the territory north of the river—is generally safe during the day, with active commercial streets bounding residential areas. There are over a dozen neighborhoods with fairly ambiguous boundaries; the *Rand McNally Chicago Visitor's Guide and Map* labels them all. The **Gold Coast,** an elite residential area, glitters on North Lake Shore Drive. Farther north along the lake is **Lincoln Park,** a 19th-century English-style park which includes a zoo, a conservatory, and beaches. The neighborhood around Clark St., Lincoln Ave., and Halsted St. sprawls with bohemian cafés and used bookstores. Sharing vague boundaries with Lincoln Park is **Lakeview,** the city's most concentrated gay area, with cheap restaurants and funky shops. The streets surrounding Wrigley Field at Clark and Addison are known as **Wrigleyville,** a fun area full of sports bars and ethnic restaurants. South of the Loop, **Chinatown** preserves a sliver of China on Cermak Rd. at Wentworth; there are oodles of noodle restaurants, bakeries, and touristy shops. It can be dangerous at night; it is wisest to go there for lunch. The city's sizable Polish community has an enclave near **Oak Park.** Further south, at about 57th St., lies **Hyde Park,** home of the University of Chicago. Although Hyde Park is reasonably safe, especially during the day, avoid neighboring **Near South Side,** one of the country's most dangerous urban ghettos. Parts of the **West Side** are also extremely unsafe. In general, don't go south of Cermak or east of Halsted St. at night.

TRANSPORTATION

The **Chicago Transit Authority,** part of the **Regional Transit Authority** (836-7000), runs rapid transit trains, subways, and buses. The El runs 24 hrs., but late-night service is infrequent and unsafe in some areas, especially the South Side. Some buses do not run all night. Call CTA for schedules. Maps are available at many stations, the Water Tower Information Center, and the RTA Office. It is worthwhile to get one of these maps and to spend a few minutes deciphering the system of bus routes and trains. Directions in *Let's Go* are generally given from the downtown area, but obviously there are several ways of getting to any destination.

The **elevated rapid transit train** system, called the **El,** bounds the major downtown section of the city, the **Loop.** Some of the downtown routes are underground, but are still referred to as the El. Trains marked "A," "B" or "all stops" may run on the same route, stopping only at designated stations. Also, different routes may run along the same tracks in some places. Train fare is $1.50. Bus fare $1.25, from 6-10am and 3-7pm, $1.50; 10 tokens good for one train or bus ride each at any time of day cost $12.50. Remember to get a transfer (30¢) from the driver when you board the bus or enter the El stop, which will get you up to two more rides on a different route during the following two hours. A $18.50 weekly pass (valid Sun.-Sat.) is available in many supermarkets and at the "Checks Cashed" storefronts with the yellow signs. A $72 monthly pass is available in many supermarkets.

METRA operates a vast commuter rail network with 11 rail lines and four downtown stations snaking far out to the suburbs to the north, west, and south. (For route information call 836-7000 daily 5am-1am.) Schedules and maps are free at their office at 547 W. Jackson. Fare is based on distance ($1.75-5). **PACE** (836-7000) is the suburban bus system.

Avoid **driving** in the city as much as possible. Daytrippers can leave the car in one of the suburban subway lots for 24 hrs. ($1.75). There are a half-dozen such park-and-ride lots; call CTA (see above) for information. Parking downtown costs $8 per day for most lots; most residential areas in the north side have street parking for residents only (look for signs).

ACCOMMODATIONS

If you're in the mood for a "nap," Chicago has its share of hotels that charge by the hour. For a full night's sleep at a decent price, stop at one of the hostels, which are farther from downtown but social and worth the trek. If you have a car, there are moderately priced motels on Lincoln Ave., such as **Acres Motel,** (5600 N. Lincoln Ave. at Bryn Mawr Ave.; 561-7777). Free parking. Single or double $40. Motel chains have locations off the interstates, about an hour's drive from downtown; they're inconvenient and expensive ($35 and up), but a reliable option for late night arrivals. **Chicago Bed and Breakfast,** P.O. Box 14088, Chicago 60614 (951-0085), is a referral service with over 150 rooms of varying prices throughout the city and outlying areas. None have parking, but the majority are near public transit; street parking is occasionally available. (Singles $65 and up, doubles $75 and up; 2 night min.)

Chicago International Hostel, 6318 N. Winthrop (262-1011). Take Howard St. northbound train to Loyola Station. Walk south 2 blocks on Sheridan Rd., then east 1 block on Sheridan Rd. (the road zigs) to Winthrop, then ½ block south. Clean rooms are well worth the 30-min. train ride from the Loop, 20 min. by #147 express bus. Free parking in the rear. 2-8 beds per room. Good place to meet traveling students. Kitchen, laundry room. Bike rentals $8 per day. Lockers $1. Key deposit $5. Check-in 7-10am, 4pm-midnight. Curfew on winter weekdays midnight; winter weekends and summer 2am. Reservations recommended.

Arlington House (AAIH, ISIC, IYHF), 616 Arlington Pl. (929-5380 or 800-467-8355). Take the El to Fullerton, walk 2 blocks east to Orchard, turn right on Arlington Place; it's on the right. Parking is a hassle. Crowded rooms in a basement; shares a building with a senior citizens home. Laundry room, kitchenette. No curfew. Dorm-style rooms with 4, 6, or 10 beds each, $13, nonmembers $16. Linens $2. Open 24 hrs.

International House (HI-AYH), 1414 E. 59th St. (753-2270), Hyde Park, off Lake Shore Dr. Take the Illinois Central Railroad to 59th St. and walk ½ block west. Part of the University of Chicago. Isolated from the rest of the city, the neighborhood can be dangerous at night. 200 comfortable dorm-style rooms; good price if you *need* privacy. Shared bath, linens provided, cheap cafeteria with outdoor cafe area. $16, nonmembers $31. Open year round; reservations recommended.

Garden Youth Hostel (HI-AYH), 5340 South Maplewood (925-0447). Small hostel southwest of the city, near the intersection of 38th and California. 10 beds. Shared bath, linens provided. Kitchen access, coin-operated laundry. TV lounge with VCR movie selection. $10, nonmembers $13. Call ahead.

Hotel Wacker, 111 W. Huron (787-1386), Near North Side. Insert your own joke—you lecherous swine. Convenient to downtown, no parking. No reservations; often fills on summer weekends. Clean, good sized rooms. 24-hr. check-in. Singles $40. Doubles $45. Weekly: $80-85. Key and linen deposit $5.

Hotel Cass, 640 N. Wabash (787-4030), just north of the Loop. Take subway to Grand St. Convenient location; clean functional rooms with cable. No parking. Singles $45, doubles $45, $5 extra with TV. A/C $5. Key deposit $5. International student ID card, $5 off. Reservations recommended.

Leaning Tower YMCA, 6300 W. Touhy, Niles, 60714 (708-647-8222). From Jefferson Park El stop, take bus #85A; 1 hr. from the Loop. Look for an extraordinary half-scale replica of the Leaning Tower of Pisa (it's a water tower, not the residence hall itself). Private baths, cafeteria, use of YMCA facilities, including swimming pool, gym, and other recreational facilities. Coed. Must be over 21. It's worth the commute if you want *more* than just a place to stay. Unavailable by public transport evenings and Sundays. Free parking. Singles $30, doubles $32. Key deposit $5. Off-season $4-5 less. Call ahead for summer reservations.

FOOD

Cooks of every nation stir the melting pot of Chicago. With new restaurants opening and closing almost daily, the city often seems ready to bubble over in this abundance and variety of victuals. Investigate this phenomenon on **Wrigleyville** on the blocks just south of Wrigley Field, especially on N. Clark St., where you can find chow that spans the globe from Ethiopia to Mexico to Mongolia. Those who are dexterous with chopsticks should visit **Chinatown** at the Cermak El stop or, more conveniently, **New Chinatown** at Argyle and Sheridan at the Argyle El stop. Most of the original Greeks have left **Greektown,** on Halsted St. at Monroe, but their restaurants linger. Tourist brochures still call Taylor St. "**Little Italy,**" but most of the Italian-Americans have said *ciao,* and their restaurants, except for three or four fairly expensive joints, have split as well. It's also worth noting that good, cheap Thai restaurants are opening up all over the city. Chicago is famous for its deep dish pan pizza, but the latest innovation is stuffed pizza, a tasty reworking with the toppings lodged underneath a thin crust topped with melted cheese and tomatoes. *Chicago* magazine includes an extensive restaurant guide which is cross-indexed by price, cuisine, and quality.

Pizza

Pizzeria Uno, 29 E. Ohio (321-1000), and **Due,** 619 N. Wabash (943-2400). As the hordes of tourists waiting for a table remind us, Uno is where it all began. In 1943, owner Ike Sewall introduced Chicago-style deep dish pizza, and though the graffiti-stained walls have been painted over and the restaurant is franchised across the nation, the pizza remains damn good. Younger sister Due sits right up the street, with a terrace and more room than Uno's, but without the attendant legend. Pizzas $3.75-16. Uno open Mon.-Fri. 11:30am-1am, Sat. 11:30am-2am, Sun. 11:30am-11:30pm; Due open Sun.-Thurs. 11:30am-1:30am, Fri. 11:30am-2:30am, Sat. noon-2:30am.

Giordano's, 747 N. Rush St. (951-0747). Indulge in a Chicago specialty-stuffed pizza ($8.50-17.50). The first bite will assure you it's worth the 35 min. wait. Lunchtime specials (small is large) $4. Call ahead to start the pizza's journey toward your stomach. Open Mon.-Thurs., Sun. noon-midnight, Fri.-Sat. 11am-1am

Loop

For a cheaper alternative to most Loop dining, try the surprisingly good fast-food pizza, fish, potato, and burger joints in the basement of the State of Illinois Building at Randolph and Clarke St., where entrees run $3-6.

Heaven on Seven, 111 N. Wabash (263-6443). Hidden, with no exterior sign. The diligent who makes it to the 7th floor will be rewarded with zesty Cajun fare. The vanilla coke ($1.35) washes down sandwiches ($3.25-6) or entrees ($7.50-10). Collard greens, grits, and about 2 dozen spices on each table. Cash only. Open Mon.-Fri. 7am-5pm, Sat. 7am-3pm.

The Berghoff, 17 W. Adams (427-3170). Moderately priced German and American fare. Wash down the corned beef ($3.90) with a home-brewed beer (stein $2.10). Open Mon.-Thur. 11am-9:30pm, Fri. 11:30am-9:30pm, Sat. noon-10pm.

Morry's Old Fashioned Deli, 345 S. Dearborn (922-2932). Deli favorites sustain lunch-bound tourists and locals alike. Open Mon.-Fri. 7am-7pm, Sat. 8am-5pm.

Near North

Billy Goat's Tavern, 430 N. Michigan (222-1525), underground on lower Michigan Ave. Descend through a seeming subway entrance in front of the Tribune building. The gruff service was the inspiration for *Saturday Night Live*'s legendary "Cheezborger, cheezborger—no Coke, Pepsi" greasy spoon. Cheezborgers $2.40. Butt in anytime Mon.-Sat. 10am-midnight, Sun. 11am-2am.

Foodlife, 835 N. Michigan Ave. (335-3663), in Water Tower Place, mezzanine level. High concept food court with large selection from Asian stir-fry to pizza to Mother Earth Pasta. Good sized entrees $6-9. Open daily 11am-10pm.

The Original A-1, 401 E. Illinois (644-0300), in North Pier. After a hard day on the trail, this Texas-style chuckwagon is close to nightlife. Durango burger $6.50. Open Mon.-Fri. 11:30am-10pm, Sat. noon-midnight, Sun. noon-9pm.

Uptown (New Chinatown)

Mekong, 4953 N. Broadway (271-0206), at Argyle St. Busy, spotless Vietnamese restaurant. All you can eat lunch buffet on weekdays 11am-2:30pm for $5. Tasty soups $3.50-4. Open Sun.-Thurs. 10am-10pm, Fri.-Sat. 10am-11pm.

Gin Go Gae, 5433 N. Lincoln Ave. (334-3894). Korean place, popular with locals. *Be bim bob,* steamed rice with marinated beef, spinach, kim-chee, and an egg, $7.25. Lunch specials $5.50. Open daily 11am-10:30pm.

Chinatown

Hong Min, 221 W. Cermak (842-5026). El to Cermak. Attention paid to the food, *not* the furnishings—unlike some Chinese restaurants nearby. Dinner entrees $6-12, excellent seafood. Open daily 10am-2am.

Three Happiness, 2130 S. Wentworth Ave. (791-1228). Reliable and predictable, a "far-east experience" (or so they promise). Entrees $4.50-9. Dim sum $1.70 Mon.-Fri. 10am-2pm, Sat.-Sun. 10am-3pm. Open daily 10am-midnight.

Little Italy

The Rosebud, 1500 W. Taylor (942-1117). This neighborhood staple serves huge portions of pasta ($9.95) that easily feed three. Free parking, reservations recommended. Open for lunch Mon.-Fri. 11am-3pm; dinner Mon.-Thurs. 5-10:30pm, Fri.-Sat. 5:30-11:30pm.

Al's Italian Beef, 1079 W. Taylor St. (226-4717), at Aberdeen near Little Italy. Take a number, please. Al's is sleazy in a harmless way with no tables or chairs. Italian beef sandwich $3.15. Open Mon.-Sat. 9am-1am.

Mario's Italian Lemonade, 1074 W. Taylor St., across from Al's. Sensational Italian ices 60¢-$4.50 (tub size) every flavor you can think of in this classic neighborhood stand. Open mid-May-mid-Sept. 10am-midnight.

Greektown

The Parthenon, 314 S. Halsted St. in Greektown (726-2407). Enjoy anything from gyros ($6) to *saganaki* (cheese flamed in brandy, $3.25). Try the combination dinner to sample *moussaka,* lamb, *pastitsio,* and *dolmades.* Dinners $4.25-13.50. Open daily 11am-1am.

Greek Islands, 200 S. Halsted (782-9855). Walk under the grape leaf awning and enter this native favorite. No reservations, so expect a wait on weekends. *Spanakopita* $5.50. Open daily 11am-midnight.

North Side

Potbelly's, 2264 N. Lincoln (528-1405). Unbelievable sub sandwiches $3.60. Open daily 11am-11pm.

Kopi, A Traveller's Café, 5317 N. Clark (989-5674). A 10-min. walk from the Berwyn El. Peruse a travel guide on the socks-only section of this artful cafe. Occasional free live music. Open Mon.-Thur. 8am-11pm, Fri. 8am-midnight, Sat. 9am-midnight, Sun. 10am-11pm.

Café Ba-Ba-Reeba! 2024 N. Halsted (935-5000). *Buena comida.* Hearty Spanish cuisine with subtle spices. Entrees $6-10. Try the *paella valenciana* ($10) on the outdoor terrace. Open Tues.-Sat. 11:30am-2:30pm, Mon.-Thurs. 5:30-11pm, Fri. 5:30pm-midnight, Sat. 5pm-midnight, Sun. 5:30-10:30pm.

Addis Abeda, 3521 N. Clark, (929-9383) near Wrigley Field. Communal Ethiopian cuisine; it's not just food, it's an adventure. No utensils; scoop up dinner with a slap of spongy *injera* bread. Entrees $5-9. Open Mon.-Thurs. 5-10pm, Fri.-Sat. 5-11pm, Sun. 4-10pm.

Café Voltaire, 3231 N. Clark (528-3136). Cabaret coffeehouse with couches, patio and live performances nightly. Open Sun.-Thur. 11am-1am, Fri.-Sat. 11am-3am.

Downtown

Wishbone, 1001 W. Washington (850-2663). In this converted tire warehouse they serve a southern cuisine extravaganza, with cornbread and banana bread on every table. Homemade pies $6.95. Cafeteria-style lunch Mon.-Fri. 11:30am-2pm and dinner Mon. 5-8pm; sit-down breakfast 7-11am and dinner 5-10:30pm. Sat.-Sun. brunch 8am-2:30pm.

Frontera Grill, 445 N. Clark (661-1434). Avant-Tex-Mex. For $10 you can get a plate of excellent Mexican. Open Tues.-Sat. after 9am.

SIGHTS

Chicago is truly massive, and its sights cannot be exhausted; there is always another hole-in-the-wall restaurant, another architectural delight, another museum exhibit to discover. Chicago is a prime walking city, with lakefront, parks, residential neighborhoods, and commercial districts all awaiting exploration. Use the public transportation system liberally, though, or you'll spend all your time walking. Avoid touristy and expensive bus tours which zip you past sights. For the price of one of these tours you can buy a pass and ride the city bus for a week.

Museums

Admission to each of Chicago's major museums is free at least one day a week. The "Big Five" exhibit everything from Monet to mummies to marine mammals; a handful of smaller collections represent diverse ethnic groups and professional interests. For more information, pick up the informative pamphlet *Chicago Museums* at the tourist information office (see Practical Information).

The Art Institute of Chicago, (443-3500) Michigan Ave. at Adams St. in Grant Park. The city's premier art museum. Finest collection of French Impressionist paintings west of Paris, which even the novice can enjoy. Also works by El Greco, Chagall, Van Gogh, Picasso, and Rembrandt. Call for information on temporary exhibits. Open Mon. and Wed.-Fri. 10:30am-4:30pm, Tues. 10:30am-8pm, Sat. 10am-5pm, Sun. and holidays noon-5pm. Donation of any amount required (you can pay a nickel if you want to). Free Tues.

Museum of Science and Industry, 5700 S. Lake Shore Dr. (684-1414), housed in the only building left from the 1893 World's Columbian Exposition. In Hyde Park; take the Jeffrey Express, Bus #6 to 57th St. Hands-on exhibits ensure a crowd of grabby kids, overgrown and otherwise. Highlights include the Apollo 8 command module, a German submarine, a life-sized replica of a coal mine, and a new exhibit on learning disabilities. OmniMax Theatre shows; call for showtimes and prices. Open Memorial Day-Labor Day daily 9:30am-9pm; off-season Mon.-Fri. 9:30am-4pm, Sat.-Sun. 9:30am-5:30pm. $5, seniors $4, ages 5-12 $2. Free Thurs.

The Oriental Institute, 1155 E. 58th St. (702-9521), take Jeffrey Express, Bus #6, to the University of Chicago campus. Houses an extraordinary collection of ancient Near Eastern art and archeological treasures. Open Tues. and Thurs.-Sat. 10am-4pm, Wed. 10am-8:30pm, Sun. noon-4pm. Free.

Field Museum of Natural History (922-9410), Roosevelt Rd. at Lake Shore Dr., in Grant Park. Take Bus #146 from State St. Geological, anthropological, botanical, and zoological exhibits. Don't miss the Egyptian mummies, the Native American Halls, the Hall of Gems, and the dinosaur display. Open daily 9am-5pm. Admission $5, seniors, students, and children $3, families $16. Free Wed.

The Adler Planetarium, 1300 S. Lake Shore Dr. (322-0300), in Grant Park. Astronomy exhibits, a sophisticated skyshow, and the $4-million Astro-Center. 5 skyshows per day in summer, less frequently in winter. Open daily 9am-5pm, Fri. until 9pm. Exhibits free. Skyshow daily at 10am and 1-4pm on the hour. $4, seniors and ages 4-17 $2.

Shedd Aquarium 1200 S. Lake Shore Dr.(939-2438), in Grant Park. The world's largest indoor aquarium with over 6600 species of fresh and saltwater fish in 206 exhibition tanks, including a replicated Caribbean reef. The Oceanarium features small whales, dolphins, seals, and other marine mammals. Check out exhibits on Asian rainforests and the Pacific Ocean, complete with simulated crashing waves. Parking available. Open March-Oct. daily 9am-6pm; Nov.-Feb. 10am-5pm. Feedings weekdays 11am and 2pm. Combined admission to Oceanarium and Aquarium $8, children and seniors $6; Thurs. free to Aquarium, but not Oceanarium. Buy weekend tickets in advance through Hot Tix or Ticketmaster.

The Museum of Contemporary Art, 237 E. Ontario (280-5161). A decent collection; exhibits change often. One gallery devoted to local artists. Open Tues.-Sat. 10am-5pm, Sun. noon-5pm. $4, seniors and students $2. Free Tues.

Chicago Historical Society, (642-4600) N. Clark St. at North Ave. A research center for scholars with a good museum open to the public. The Society was founded in 1856, just 19 years after the city was incorporated, like a kid who keeps a diary for future biographers. Permanent exhibits on America in the age of Lincoln, plus changing exhibits. Open Mon.-Sat. 9:30am-4:30pm, Sun. noon-5pm. $3, students and seniors $2. Free Mon.

Terra Museum of American Art, (664-3939) 666 N. Michigan Ave. at Eric St. Excellent collection of American art from colonial times to the present, with a focus on 19th-century American Impressionism. Open Tues. noon-8pm, Wed.-Sat. 10am-5pm, Sun. noon-5pm. $3, seniors $2, teachers, children, and students with ID free. Free public tours noon and 2pm daily.

Museum of Broadcast Communications, at Michigan and Washington, in the Loop (629-6000). Celebrate couch-potato culture with these exhibits on America's favorite pastime: watching the tube. Open Mon.-Sat. 10am-4:30pm, Sun. noon-5pm. Free.

The Loop

When Mrs. O'Leary's cow kicked over a lantern and started the Great Fire of 1871, Chicago's downtown was turned into a pile of ashes. The city rebuilt with a vengeance, turning the functional into the fabulous and creating one of the most concentrated clusters of architectural treasures in the world.

The downtown area, the Loop, is hemmed in by the Chicago River and Lake Michigan, so its buildings spread up rather than out. Take a few hours to explore this street museum either by yourself or on a **walking tour** organized by the Chicago Architectural Foundation. Tours start from the foundation's bookstore/gift shop at 224 S. Michigan Ave. (922-3432). Learn to recognize Louis Sullivan's arch, the Chicago window, and Mies van der Rohe's glass and steel; geometrically rigorous boxes which refashioned the concept of the skyscraper. Two tours are offered: one of early skyscrapers, another of modern. ($9 for one, $15 for both. Call for tour schedules. Weekdays one each morning and one each afternoon.)

Long ago, the city's traders developed the concept of a graded commodity, so that a real-life bag of wheat, once evaluated, could henceforth be treated as a currency unit. Today, the three exchanges coexist within a few blocks and are worth a visit. You can watch the frantic trading of Midwestern farm goods at the world's oldest and largest commodity, the **Futures Exchange** (open Mon.-Fri. 9am-2pm, free) or at the **Chicago Board of Options Exchange,** both located in **The Board of Trade Building,** 400 S. LaSalle (435-3455). The building has a huge monument to Ceres, Greek goddess of grain, standing 609 ft. above street level. The third exchange, the **Chicago Mercantile Exchange** (930-8249) is at Wacker and Madison.

In the late 19th century, Sears and Roebuck, along with competitor Montgomery Ward, created the mail-order catalog business, undercutting many small general stores and permanently altering the face of American merchandising. Today, although the catalog business is over, the **Sears Tower**, 233 W. Walker (875-9696), is more than just an office building; at 1707 ft., it stands as a monument to the insatiable lust of the American consumer. You can view the city from the top of this, the tallest building in the world. (Open March-Sept. 9am-11pm, Oct.-Feb. 9am-10pm. $6.50, seniors $4.75, children $3.25, family $18. Lines can be long.) **The First National Bank Building and Plaza** stands about two blocks northeast, at the corner of Clark and Monroe St. The world's largest bank building compels your gaze skyward with its diagonal slope. Marc Chagall's vivid mosaic, *The Four Seasons,* lines the block and sets off a public space often used for concerts and lunchtime entertainment.

State and Madison is the most famous block of "State Street that great street" and the focal point of the Chicago street grid. Louis Sullivan's **Carson Pirie Scott** store building is adorned with exquisite ironwork and the famous extra-large Chicago window (though the grid-like modular construction has been altered by additions). Also visit Sullivan's other masterpiece, the **Auditorium Building,** several blocks south at the corner of Congress and Michigan. Beautiful design and flawless acoustics highlight this Chicago landmark.

Chicago has one of the country's premier collections of outdoor sculpture. Many downtown corners are punctuated by large, abstract designs. The most famous of these is a Picasso at the foot of the **Daley Center Plaza,** Washington and Dearborn (346-3278), beside which there is free entertainment daily in the summer. Across the street rests Joan Miró's *Chicago,* the sculptor's gift to the city. A great Debuffet sculpture is across the way in front of the **State of Illinois Building,** a post modern version of a town square designed by Helmut Jahn in 1985. Take the elevator all the way up, where there is a thrilling (and free) view of the sloping atrium, circular floors, and hundreds of employees at work. Worth a look. A few years ago, the city held a contest to design a building in honor of the late mayor for only $144 million. The result is the **Harold Washington Library Center,** 400 S. State St. (747-4300), a researcher's dream and an architectural delight. (Tours Mon.-Sat. noon, 2pm; Open Mon. 9am-7pm, Tues. and Thurs. 11am-7pm, Wed., Fri.-Sat. 9am-5pm.)

North Side

Extending north of Diversey Ave., the North Side offers an amalgam of ethnically diverse neighborhoods. Stroll the streets here and you'll find fresh-baked pita bread, vintage clothing stores, elite apartment buildings, and humble two-story abodes.

Though they finally lost their battle against night baseball in 1988, **Wrigleyville** residents remain, like much of the North Side, fiercely loyal to the Chicago Cubs. Just east of Graceland, at the corner of Clark and Addison, tiny, ivy-covered **Wrigley Field** at 1060 W. Addison is the North Side's most famous institution, well worth a pilgrimage for the serious or simply curious baseball fan, as well as for the *Blues Brothers* nuts who want to visit their falsified address. After a game, walk along Clark St. in one of the city's busiest nightlife districts, where restaurants, sports bars, and music clubs abound. It's well worth the trip to explore the neighborhood, window shop in the funk, junk, and 70s revival stores, or, if you prefer, people-watch.

Outdoors

A string of lakefront parks fringes the area between Chicago proper and Lake Michigan. On a sunny afternoon, a cavalcade of sunbathers, dog walkers, roller skaters, and skateboarders storm the shore, yet everyone still has room to stake out a private little piece of paradise. The two major parks, both close to downtown, are Lincoln and Grant, operated by the Recreation Department (294-2200). **Lincoln Park,** which extends across 5 mi. of lakefront on the north side of town, rolls in the style of a 19th-century English park: winding paths, natural groves of trees and asymmetrical open spaces. The **Lincoln Park Conservatory** encloses fauna from desert to jungle environments under its glass palace (249-4770). Great apes, snow leopards, and a rhinoceros (among others) call the **Lincoln Park Zoo,** 2200 N. Cannon Drive (294-4600), home. (Both zoo and conservatory are free and open daily 9am-5pm.)

Grant Park, covering 14 blocks of lakefront east of Michigan Ave., follows the proper 19th-century French park style: symmetrical, ordered, with squared corners, a fountain in the center, and wide promenades. The **Petrillo Music Shell** hosts many free concerts here during the summer, great for mellowing under the stars with a bottle of wine, cheese, and a blanket; check the papers.

Kiss someone under the colored lights that illuminate **Buckingham Fountain** each night at 9-11pm. The **Field Museum of Natural History,** the **Shedd Aquarium,** and the **Adler Planetarium** beckon museum-hoppers to the southern end of the park (take the #146 bus, it's a 1-mi. walk from the park center), while the **Art Institute** houses its collection on the northern side of the park, east of **Adams St.** Grant Park is also a good place to view the downtown skyline.

Lake Michigan lures swimmers to the **Lincoln Park Beach** and the **Oak Street Beach,** on the North Side. Both crowded, popular swimming spots soak in the sun. The beaches are patrolled 9am-9:30pm and are unsafe after dark. The rock ledges are restricted areas, and swimming from them is illegal. Call the Chicago Parks District for further information (294-2200).

Hyde Park and Oak Park

Seven mi. south of the Loop along the lake, the **University of Chicago's** (702-1234) beautiful campus dominates the **Hyde Park** neighborhood. A former retreat for the city's artists and musicians, the park became the first U.S. community to undergo urban renewal in the 50s and is now an island of intellectualism in a sea of dangerous neighborhoods. Don't stray south of Midway Plaisance, west of Cottage Grove, or north of Hyde Park Blvd. Lakeside Burnham Park, to the east of campus, is relatively safe during the day but dangerous at night. On campus, U. of Chicago's architecture ranges from knobby, gnarled, twisted Gothic to neo-streamlined high-octane Gothic. Check out Frank Lloyd Wright's famous **Robie House,** 5757 S. Woodlawn (702-8374) at the corner of 58th St.; tours ($3, students and seniors $1 on Sun.) depart daily at noon. Representative of the Prairie school, this large house blends into the surrounding trees; its low horizontal lines now house university offices. From the Loop, take bus #6 ("Jefferson Express") or the Illinois Central Railroad

LET'S GO® TRAVEL

TRAVEL

C A T A L O G

1 9 9 5

WE GIVE YOU THE WORLD... AT A DISCOUNT

**Discounted Flights, Eurail Passes,
Travel Gear, Let's Go™ Series Guides,
Hostel Memberships... and more**

Let's Go Travel

a division of

**Harvard Student
Agencies, Inc.**

**Bargains
to every
corner of
the world!**

Travel Gear

A Let's Go T-Shirt..$10
100% combed cotton. Let's Go logo on front left chest. Four color printing on back. L and XL. Way cool.

B Let's Go Supreme..........$175
Innovative hideaway suspension with parallel stay internal frame turns backpack into carry-on suitcase. Includes lumbar support pad, torso, and waist adjustment, leather trim, and detachable daypack. Waterproof Cordura nylon, lifetime gurantee, 4400 cu. in. Navy, Green, or Black.

C Let's Go Backpack/Suitcase....................$130
Hideaway suspension turns backpack into carry-on suitcase. Internal frame. Detachable daypack makes 3 bags in 1. Waterproof Cordura nylon, lifetime guarantee, 3750 cu. in. Navy, Green, or Black.

D Let's Go Backcountry I..$210
Full size, slim profile expedition pack designed for the serious trekker. New Airflex suspension. X-frame pack with advanced composite tube suspension. Velcro height adjustment, side compression straps. Detachable hood converts into a fanny pack. Waterproof Cordura nylon, lifetime guarantee, main compartment 3375 cu. in., extends to 4875 cu. in.

E Let's Go Backcountry II............................$240
Backcountry I's Big Brother. Magnum Helix Airflex Suspension. Deluxe bi-lam contoured shoulder harness. Adjustable sterm strap. Adjustable bi-lam Cordura waist belt. 5350 cubic inches. 7130 cubic inches extended. Not pictured.

Discounted Flights

Call Let's Go now for inexpensive airfare to points across the country and around the world.

EUROPE • SOUTH AMERICA • ASIA • THE CARRIBEAN • AUSTRALIA •

AFRICA

Eurail Passes

Eurailpass (First Class)

15 days.....................................$498
1 month (30 days)....................$798
2 months (60 days)................$1098

Unlimited rail travel anywhere on Europe's 100,000 mile rail network. Accepted in 17 countries.

Eurail Flexipass (First Class)

A number of individual travel days to be used at your convenience within a two-month period.

Any 5 days in 2 months.............$348
Any 10 days in 2 months...........$560
Any 15 days in 2 months...........$740

Eurail Youthpass (Second Class)

15 days.....................................$398
1 month (30 days)....................$578
2 months (60 days)..................$768

All the benefits of the Eurail Pass at a lower price. For those passengers under 26 on their first day of travel.

Eurail Youth Flexipass (Second Class)

Eurail Flexipass at a reduced rate for passengers under 26 on their first day of travel.

Any 5 days in 2 months.............$255
Any 10 days in 2 months...........$398
Any 15 days in 2 months...........$540

Europass (First & Second Class)

First Class starting at................$280
Second Class starting at............$198
For more details......................CALL

Discounted fares for those passengers travelling in France, Germany, Italy, Spain and Switzerland.

Hostelling Essentials

F Undercover Neckpouch............$9.95
Ripstop nylon with soft Cambrelle back. Three pockets. 6 x 7". Lifetime guarantee. Black or Tan.

G Undercover Waistpouch.........$9.95
Ripstop nylon with soft Cambrelle back. Two pockets. 5 x 12" with adjustable waistband. Lifetime guarantee. Black or Tan.

H Sleepsack................................$13.95
Required at all hostels. 18" pillow pocket. Washable poly/cotton. Durable. Compact.

I Hostelling International Card
Required by most international hostels. For U.S. residents only. Adults, $25. Under 18, $10.

J Int'l Youth Hostel Guide.......$10.95
Indispensable guide to prices, locations, and reservations for over 4000 hostels in Europe and the Mediterranean.

K ISIC, ITIC, IYTC..........$16, $16, $17
ID cards for students, teachers and those people under 26. Each offers many travel discounts.

800-5-LETSGO

Order Form

Last Name	First Name	Date of Birth

Street (We cannot ship to P.O. boxes)		

City	State	Zip

Country	Citizenship	Date of Travel

( )   -

Phone	School (if applicable)

Item Code	Description, Size & Color	Quantity	Unit Price	Total Price
			SUBTOTAL:	

Domestic Shipping & Handling		Shipping and Handling (see box at left):	
Order Total:	Add:	Add $10 for RUSH, $20 for overnite:	
Up to $30.00	$4.00	MA Residents add 5% tax on books and gear:	
$30.01 to $100.00	$6.00		
Over $100.00	$7.00	GRAND TOTAL:	
Call for int'l or off-shore delivery			

MasterCard / VISA Order

CARDHOLDER NAME _____

CARD NUMBER _____

EXPIRATION DATE _____

Enclose check or money order payable to:
Harvard Student Agencies, Inc.
53A Church Street
Cambridge, MA 02138

Allow 2-3 weeks for delivery. Rush orders guaranteed within
one week of our receipt. Overnight orders sent via FedEx the same afternoon.

Missing a Let's Go Book from your collection?
Add one to any $50 order at 50% off the cover price!

Let's Go Travel
1-800-5-LETSGO

(617) 495-9649   Fax: (617) 496-8015
53A Church Street
Cambridge MA 02138

from the Randolph St. Station south to 57th St. The Oriental Institute, Museum of Science and Industry, and DuSable Museum are all in or border on Hyde Park.

Ten mi. west of downtown on the Eisenhower Expressway (I-290) sprouts **Oak Park.** Frank Lloyd Wright endowed the community with 25 of his spectacular homes and buildings. Wright pioneered a new type of home, the Prairie House, which sought to integrate the house with the environment, eliminating the discrete break between indoors and out. (Robie House is the finest example.) The **visitors center,** 158 Forest Ave. (708-848-1500), offers maps and guidebooks. (Open daily 10am-5pm.) Don't miss the **Frank Lloyd Wright House and Studio,** 951 Chicago Ave. (708-848-1500), with his beautiful 1898 workplace and original furniture. Two tours daily. The exterior tour is self-guided only, with a tape recording. ($6 each, $9 combined.) Call for directions.

Near West Side

The **Near West Side,** bounded by the Chicago River to the east and Ogden Ave. to the west, is a fascinating assembly of tiny ethnic enclaves. Farther out, however, looms the West Side, one of the most dismal slums in the nation. Dangerous neighborhoods lie alongside safe ones, so always be aware of where you stray. **Greektown** might not be overly Greek anymore, but several blocks of authentic restaurants (north of the Eisenhower on Halsted) remain, and still draw people from all over the city.

A few blocks down Halsted (take the #8 Halsted bus), Jane Addams devoted her life to historic **Hull House.** This settlement house stands as testament to Chicago's role in turn-of-the-century reform movements. Hull House has been relocated to 800 S. Halsted, but painstaking restoration has made the **Hull House Museum** (413-5353) a fascinating part of a visit to Chicago. (Open Mon.-Fri. 10am-4pm, Sun. noon-5pm. Free.) **Ukrainian Village,** at Chicago and Western, is no longer dominated by ethnic Ukrainians, but now that the Ukraine has regained its independence, you may have even more reason to visit the **Ukrainian National Museum** at 2453 W. Chicago Ave. (276-6565), and the **Ukrainian Institute of Modern Art** at 2318 W. Chicago Ave. (227-5522; donations suggested).

Near North

The city's ritziest district lies above the Loop along the lake, just past the Michigan Ave. Bridge. Overlooking this stretch is the **Tribune Tower,** 435 N. Michigan Ave., a Gothic skyscraper that resulted from a hotly-contested international design competition in the 20s. The building houses Chicago's largest newspaper, *The Chicago Tribune*; quotations exalting the freedom of the press adorn the inside lobby. Roam the **Merchandise Mart** (entrances on N. Wells and Kinzie; 644-4664), the largest commercial building in the world, 25 stories high and two city blocks long. The first two floors are a mall open to the public; the rest of the building contains showrooms where design professionals converge from around the world to choose home and office furnishings, kitchen products, and everything else that goes into a building, right down to the "restroom" signs. (Public tours Mon.-Fri. 10am and 1:30pm. $7, seniors and students over 15 $6.)

Chicago's **Magnificent Mile,** along Michigan Ave. north of the Chicago River, is a conglomeration of chic shops and galleries. Several of these retail stores, including the recently opened Banana Republic and Crate & Barrel, were designed by the country's foremost architects. Hiding among them is the **Chicago Water Tower and Pumping Station** (467-7114), at the corner of Michigan and Pearson Ave. Built in 1867, these two structures were among the few to survive the Great Chicago Fire. The pumping station, which supplies water to nearly 400,000 people on the North Side, houses the multimedia show and tourist center *Here's Chicago.* Across the street is **Water Tower Place,** the first urban shopping mall in the U.S., full of expensive and trendy stores.

Beautiful old mansions and apartment buildings fill the streets between the Water Tower and Lincoln Park. Known as the **Gold Coast,** the area has long been the elite residential enclave of the city. Early industrialists and city founders made their homes here and, lately, many families have moved back from the suburbs. Lake Michigan and the Oak St. Beach shimmer a few more blocks east.

Urban renewal has made **Lincoln Park,** a neighborhood just west of the park of the same name, a popular choice for upscale residents. Bounded by Armitage to the south and Diversey Ave. to the north, lakeside Lincoln Park is a center for recreation and nightlife, with beautiful harbors and parks and some of the liveliest clubs and restaurants along North Halsted and Lincoln Ave.

If you hear the bells of St. Michael's Church, you're in **Old Town,** a neighborhood where eclectic galleries, shops, and nightspots crowd gentrified streets. Absorb the architectural atmosphere while strolling the W. Menomonee and W. Eugenie St. area. In early June, the **Old Town Art Fair** attracts artists and craftsmen from across the country. Many residents open their restored homes to the public. (Take bus #151 to Lincoln Park and walk south down Clark or Wells St.)

Farther Out

The **Pullman Historic District** on the southeast side was once considered the nation's most ideal community. George Pullman, inventor of the sleeping car, hired British architect Solon S. Beman in 1885 to design a model working town so that his Palace Car Company employees would be "healthier, happier, and more productive." The **Hotel Florence,** 1111 S. Forrestville Ave. (785-8181) houses a museum and restaurant. Tours leave from the hotel the first Sun. of each month May-Oct. $4, seniors and students $3. By car, take I-94 to W. 111th St.; by train, take the Illinois Central Gulf Railroad to 111th St. and Pullman.

In **Wilmette,** the **Baha'i House of Worship** (708-256-4400), at Shendan Rd. and Linden Ave., is an 11-sided Near Eastern-styled dome modeled on the House of Worship in Haifa, Israel. (Open daily 10am-10pm; Oct.-May 10am-5pm.) **Chicago Botanical Gardens** (708-835-5440), Lake Cook Rd. ½-mi. from I-94, in Glencoe, IL, celebrates flora and fauna 25 mi. from downtown.

The **Brookfield Zoo** (708-485-0263), First Ave. and 31st St., Brookfield (about 20 mi. from the Loop), is a nationally renowned, superb zoo. **Six Flags Great America** (708-249-1776), I-94 at Route 132 E., Gurnee, IL, is the largest amusement park in the Midwest. **Arlington International Racetrack** (708-255-4300), Route 53 at Euclid, Arlington Heights, has thoroughbred racing at cheap—or not so cheap—prices. It's up to you to decide, at the betting windows.

Steamboat Gambling has been embraced by the Midwest as a way to bet around anti-betting laws. Joliet, IL centers Chicago's operation. **Empress River Cruises,** 2300 Empress Dr. (708-345-6789), Rte. 6 off I-55 and I-80, has six cruises daily. **Harrah's Casino Cruises** (800-342-7724) accommodates more than 1000 "guests."

ENTERTAINMENT

To stay on top of Chicago events, grab a copy of the free weekly *Chicago Reader,* published on Thursday and available in many bars and restaurants. *Chicago* magazine has exhaustive club listings. The Friday edition of the *Chicago Tribune* includes a thick section with full music, theater, and cultural listings.

Theater

Chicago is one of the foremost theater centers of North America, as well as the home of Improv and the Improvorgy. For a local experience, visit one of the intimate, smaller theaters that stage home-grown productions. At one point last summer, over 100 shows were running, ranging in respectability from *Exit the King* to *The Postman Always Shoots Twice.* The "Off-Loop" theaters on the North Side specialize in original drama, with tickets in the $15 and under range.

Victory Gardens Theater, 2257 N. Lincoln Ave. (871-3000). 3 theater spaces. Drama by Chicago playwrights. Tickets $14-27.

Center Theatre, 1346 W. Devon Ave. (508-5422). Solid, mainstream work. Tickets vary show to show, $15-18.

Annoyance Theatre, 3747 N. Clark (929-6200). Different show each night of the week, original works that play off pop culture; they launched *The Real-Life Brady Bunch.* In the center of an active gay neighborhood and currently showing participatory comedy.

Bailiwick Repertory, 1225 W. Belmont Ave. (327-5252) in the Theatre building. A mainstage and experimental studio space. Tickets from $6.

Live Bait Theatre, 3914 N. Clark St. (871-1212). Shows with titles like *Food, Fun, & Dead Relatives* and *Mass Murder II.* Tickets $6-12.

Most theater tickets are expensive, although half-price tickets are available on the day of performance at **Hot Tix Booths,** 108 N. State St. (977-1755), downtown. Buy them in person only; show up 15-20 min. before booth opens to get first dibs. (Open Mon. noon-6pm, Tues.-Fri. 10am-6pm, Sat. 10am-5pm. Tickets for Sun. shows on sale Sat.) Phone **Curtain Call** (977-1755) for information on ticket availability, schedules, and Hot Tix booths. **Ticket Master** (559-8989) supplies tickets for many theaters. Check with theaters box offices for half-price student rush tickets 30 min. before showtime.

Two Chicago theaters are especially well-known, with prices to match their fame: the **Steppenwolf Theater,** 1650 N. Halsted (335-1650), where David fucking Mamet got his goddamn start, and the **Goodman Theatre,** 200 S. Columbus Dr. (443-3800); both present consistently good original works. (Tickets $20-40.) The big-name presentation house that hosts Broadway touring productions is the **Shubert Theater,** 22 W. Monroe St. (902-1500). The monthly *Chicago* and the weekly *Chicago Reader* review all major shows, with show times and ticket prices.

Comedy

Chicago boasts a giggle of comedy clubs, the most famous being **Second City,** 1616 N. Wells St. (337-3992), with its satirical spoofs of Chicago life and politics. Second City graduated Bill Murray, and the late greats John Candy, John Belushi and Gilda Radner, among others. (Shows Mon.-Thurs. 8:30pm, Fri.-Sat. at 8:30 and 11pm, Sun. at 8pm. Tickets $10-15. Reservations recommended; during the week you can often get in if you show up 1 hr. early.) Most nights a free improv session follows the show. **Second City ETC.** (642-8189) offers yet more comedy next door (same times and prices). The big names drop by and make it up as they go along at **The Improv,** 504 N. Wells (782-6387). (Shows Sun., Thurs. 8pm, Fri.-Sat. 7pm, 9:30pm, and midnight. Tickets $10-13.50 depending on day.)

Dance, Classical Music, and Opera

Chicago philanthropists have built the network of high-priced, high-art performance centers that are expected in a major metropolis. The **Chicago City Ballet** pirouettes under the direction of Maria Tallchief at the **Auditorium Theater,** 50 E. Congress Parkway (922-2110). From October to May, the **Chicago Symphony Orchestra,** conducted by Daniel Barenboim, performs at **Orchestra Hall,** 220 S. Michigan Ave. (435-6666). The **Lyric Opera of Chicago** performs from September to February at the **Civic Opera House,** 20 N. Wacker Dr. (332-2244). The **Grant Park Music Festival** is more attractive to the budget traveler. From mid-June to late August, the acclaimed **Grant Park Symphony Orchestra** gives a few free evening concerts a week at the Grant Park Petrillo Music Shell. (Usually Wed.-Sun.; schedule varies. Call 819-0614 for details.) *Chicago* magazine has complete listings of music, dance, and opera performances throughout the city.

Seasonal Events

Like Chicago's architecture, the city's summer celebrations are executed on a grand scale. The **Taste of Chicago** festival cooks the eight days up through July Fourth, when over 70 restaurants set up booths with endless samples at Grant Park (free). Big name bands also come to perform. The first week in June, the **Blues Festival** celebrates the city's soulful, gritty music; the **Chicago Gospel Festival** hums and hollers in mid-June, the **Viva! Chicago** Latin music festival swings in mid-September, and the **Chicago Jazz Festival** scats Labor Day weekend, all at the Grant Park Petrillo Music Shell. Call the Mayor's Office Special Events Hotline (800-487-2446) for info on all five free events.

Chicago also offers several free summer festivals on the lakeshore, including the **Air and Water Show** in late August, when Lake Shore Park, Lake Shore Dr., and Chicago Ave. are the scene of several days of boat races, parades, hang gliding, and stunt flying, as well as aerial acrobatics by the Blue Angels precision fliers.

The regionally famous **Ravinia Festival** (728-4642), in the northern suburb of Highland Park, runs from late June to late September. The Chicago Symphony Orchestra, ballet troupes, folk and jazz musicians, and comedians perform throughout the festival's 14-week season. (Shows Mon.-Sat. 8pm, Sun. 7pm. $15-40. $7 rents you a patch of ground for a blanket and picnic.) Round-trip on the train (METRA) about $7; the festival runs charter buses for $12. The bus ride is 1½ hrs. each way.

Sports

The National League's **Cubs** play baseball at gorgeous Wrigley Field, at Clark St. and Addison (831-2827), one of the few ballparks in America that has retained the early grace and intimate feel of the game; it's definitely worth a visit, especially for international visitors who haven't seen a baseball game. (Tickets $8-19.) The **White Sox**, Chicago's American League team, swings at the South Side at the new Comiskey Park, 333 W. 35th St. (800-347-2827). Da **Bears** play football at Soldier's Field Stadium, McFetridge Dr. and S. Lake Shore Dr. (708-615-BEAR/2327). The **Blackhawks** hockey team skates and the **Bulls** basketball team slam-dunks at United Center, 1901 W. Madison (Blackhawks 733-5300; tickets $15-75. Bulls 943-5800; tickets $15-30). Beware of scalpers who illegally sell tickets at inflated prices outside of sports events. For current sports events, call **Sports Information** (976-1313).

Nightlife

"Sweet home Chicago" takes pride in the innumerable blues performers who have played here (a strip of 43rd St. was recently renamed Muddy Waters Drive). For other tastes, jazz, folk, reggae, and punk clubs throbulate all over the **North Side**. **Bucktown**, west of Halsted St. in North Chicago, stays open late with bucking bars and dance clubs. Aspiring pick-up artists swing over to Rush and Division, an intersection that has replaced the stockyards as one of the biggest meat markets of the world. To get away from the crowds, head to a little neighborhood spot for atmosphere. **Lincoln Park** is full of bars, cafes, and bistros, and is dominated by the gay scene, as well as singles and young married couples. For more raging, raving, and discoing, there are plenty of clubs in River N. and Riverwest, and on Fulton St. Refer to *Chicago* magazine or *ChicagoLife* for descriptions of current hip spots.

Blues

B.L.U.E.S. etcetera, 1124 W. Belmont Ave. (525-8989), El to Belmont then 3 blocks west on Belmont. Cover $4 weekdays, $7 weekends. With the aid of a dance floor, it's a more energetic blues bar than its sibling location **B.L.U.E.S.,** 2519 N. Halsted St. (528-1012), El to Fullerton, then westbound Fullerton bus. Cramped, but the music is unbeatable. Music starts at both joints Mon.-Thurs. at 9pm, Fri.-Sun. at 9:30pm. Open Sun.-Fri. 8pm-2am, Sat. 8pm-3am. Cover Sun.-Thurs. $5, Fri.-Sat. $7.

Kingston Mines, 2548 N. Halsted St. (477-4646). Shows 6 nights per week. Watch for the "Blue Monday" jam session. Music starts at 9:30pm. Open Sun.-Fri. 8pm-4am, Sat. until 5am. Cover Sun.-Thurs. $8, Fri.-Sat. $10.

Other Nightlife

Cabaret Metro, 3730 N. Clark (549-0203). *The* place for live alternative music. The action heats up downstairs at the dance club **Smart Bar** (549-4140). Opening times vary (around 10pm) and close around 5am on weekends. Cover $5-13.

Shelter, 564 W. Fulton (528-5500). Club kids congregate on several dance floors. Opens around 10pm and raves until the wee hours. Cover $8-10.

Wild Hare & Singing Armadillo Frog Sanctuary, 3350 N. Clark (327-0800), El to Addison. Near Wrigley Field. Live Rastafarian bands play nightly to a packed house. Open daily until 2-3am. Cover $3-5.

Butch McGuires, 20 W. Division St. (337-9080), at Rush St. Originator of the singles bar. Owner estimates that "over 2400 couples have met here and gotten married" since 1961—he's a little fuzzier on divorce statistics. Once on Rush St., check out the other area hang-outs. Drinks $2-5. Open Sun.-Thurs. 9:30am-2am, Fri. 10am-4am, Sat. 10am-5am.

Jazz Showcase, 636 S. Michigan (427-4846), in the Blackstone Hotel downtown. #1 choice for serious jazz fans. During the jazz festival, big names heat up the elegant surroundings with impromptu jam sessions. No smoking allowed. Music Tues.-Thurs. at 8 and 10pm, Fri.-Sat. at 9 and 11pm, Sun. at 4 and 8pm. Closing time varies; cover $5-10.

Tania's, 2659 N. Milwaukee Ave. (235-7120). Exotic dinner and dancing adventure with hot *salsa cumbia* and *merengue* bands. No jeans or sneakers. Live music Wed.-Sun. after 10:30pm. Open Sun.-Fri. 11am-4am, Sat. 11am-5am.

■■■ SPRINGFIELD

Springfield didn't even exist when Illinois became a state in 1818, but 15 years later the city was designated the state capital. As the home of Abraham Lincoln from 1837 until he entered the White House in 1860, the whole city is geared towards reliving and relishing the memory of the great man. Stephen Douglas is also revered, if only for his rivalry with Lincoln. Welcome to Lincolnsville, USA.

Practical Information Start your visit by checking out the office for visitor information: **Springfield Convention and Visitors Bureau,** 109 N. 7th St. (789-2360 or 800-545-7300; open Mon.-Fri. 8am-5pm). Write ahead and request information and they'll send you an exhaustive packet on food, lodgings, and events. Springfield is accessible via **Amtrak,** at 3rd and Washington St. (800-872-7245), near downtown. To: Chicago (4 per day, 4 hr., $34) and St. Louis (3 per day, 2½ hr., $21). (Open daily 6am-9:30pm.) **Greyhound** has a station at 2351 S. Dirksen Pkwy. (544-8466), on the eastern edge of town. Walk or take a cab ($3 flat rate) to the nearby shopping center, where you can catch the #10 bus. To: Chicago (Mon.-Thurs. $24, Fri.-Sun. $26); Indianapolis ($42); St. Louis ($16). (Open Mon.-Fri. 7:30am-7pm, Sat. 7:30am-5pm. Lockers $1 per day.) The **Springfield Mass Transit District,** 928 S. 9th St. (522-5531), is the best way to get around town. Pick up maps at transit headquarters or at the tourist office on Adams. All 13 lines serve the downtown area on Capitol between 6th and 7th, or Monroe St., near the Old State Capitol Plaza. (Fare 50¢, transfers free. Buses operate Mon.-Sat. 6am-6pm.) For taxi service, try **Lincoln Yellow Cab** (523-4545 or 522-7766; $1.25 base, $1.50 each additional mile). Springfield's **post office:** 2105 E. Cook St. (788-7200), at Wheeler St. (Open Mon.-Fri. 7:45am-5:30pm, Sat. 8am-noon); **ZIP code:** 62703; **area code:** 217.

Accommodations and Food Most inexpensive places are off I-55 and U.S. 36 on Dirksen Parkway; bus service from downtown is limited. More expensive downtown hotels may be booked solid on weekdays when the legislature is in session; ask the visitors bureau (see Practical Information above) about finding reasonable weekend packages. Make reservations on holiday weekends and during the State Fair in mid-August.

The **Dirksen Inn Motel,** 900 N. Dirksen Pkwy. (522-4900; take #3 "Bergen Park" bus to Milton and Elm, then walk a few blocks east), has clean rooms in good condition (singles $28, doubles $30; office open 24 hrs.). **Motel 6,** 3125 Wide Track Dr. (789-1063), near Dirksen Pkwy. at the intersection of I-90 and State Rte. 29, is, well, Motel 6, but with a nice pool (singles $28, doubles $34). **Mister Lincoln's Campground,** 3045 Stanton Ave. (529-8206), next to the car dealership 4 mi. southeast of

THE GREAT LAKES

downtown, has a large area for RVs, a field for tents, and showers. Take bus #10. (Sites $7 per person, with electricity $9, full hookup $17.)

Horseshoe sandwiches are a Springfield original. Although they may look more like what ends up on horseshoes than horseshoes, these tasty concoctions consist of ham on prairie toast smothered with cheese sauce and french fries. Depending on your personal taste, you may end up saying "neigh" to them. Springfield has a host of restaurants that are lunch only, or breakfast and lunch only. In and around the **Vinegar Hill Mall,** at 1st and Cook St., are a number of moderately priced restaurants, including **A Capitol City Bar and Grill,** which has inexpensive horseshoes ($5) and five types of homemade brew (open Mon.-Fri.11am-10pm, Sat. noon-10pm, 753-5720). **The Feed Store,** 516 E. Adam S. St. (528-3355), across from the old state capitol, has inexpensive deli sandwiches ($2.75-4.50) and a no-choice special—sandwich, soup, and drink, $4.65. (Open Mon.-Sat. 11am-3pm.) **Saputo's,** 801 E. Munroe at 8th St. (522-0105), two blocks from Lincoln's home, has tasty southern Italian cuisine. Try the baked lasagna ($4.75). (Open Mon.-Fri. 10:30am-midnight, Sat. 5pm-midnight, Sun. 5-10pm.)

Sights Re-creating Lincoln's life is Springfield's business, and it goes about it zealously. The best way to see Lincoln is to park the car and walk from sight to sight—retracing the steps of the man himself (or so they keep telling you). The Visitors Bureau prints an excellent street map of all the sights. Happily, all Lincoln sights are free. A quick call to 800-545-7300 will verify site hours (winter weather often forces curtailed hours). The **Lincoln Home Visitors Center,** 426 S. 8th St. at Jackson (492-4150), shows an 18-minute film on "Mr. Lincoln's Springfield" and doles out free tour tickets to see the **Lincoln Home** (492-4150), the only one Abe ever owned and *the* main Springfield attraction, sitting at 8th and Jackson in a restored 19th-century neighborhood. (10-min. tours every 5-10 min. from the front of the house. Open daily 8am-8pm. Arrive early to avoid the crowds. Free.)

A few blocks northwest, at 6th and Adams right before the Old State Capitol, the **Lincoln-Herndon Law Offices** (785-7289) let visitors experience where Abe honed his skills practicing law until he left for the Presidency. (Open for tours only; daily 9am-5pm; last tour at 4:15pm. Free.) Around the corner to the left across from the Downtown Mall stands the magnificent limestone **Old State Capitol** (785-7691). It was here that, in 1858, Lincoln delivered his stirring and prophetic "House Divided" speech, warning that the nation's contradictory pro-slavery and abolitionist government risked dissolution. The manuscript copy of Lincoln's "Gettysburg Address" is on display in the rotunda. The capitol was also the sight of the famous Lincoln-Douglas debates which bolstered Lincoln to national prominence. (Tours daily. Open daily 9am-5pm. Free.) The **New State Capitol,** four blocks away at 2nd and Capitol (782-2099), opened in 1877, is a beautiful example of the Midwestern State Capitol complete with murals of Illinois pioneer history and an intricately designed dome. Sneak a closer peek at the facade through the free sidewalk telescopes in the front of the building. (Tours Mon.-Fri. 8am-4pm, Sat.-Sun. 9am-3:30pm. Building open Mon.-Fri. 8am-4pm, Sat.-Sun. first floor only 9am-3:30pm.) The **Lincoln Tomb** (782-2717) at Oak Ridge Cemetery is his final resting place, as well as that of his wife and three sons (open daily 9am-5pm).

Springfield also contains the **Dana-Thomas House,** 301 E. Lawrence Ave. (782-6776), six blocks south of the Old State Capitol. This stunning and well-preserved 1902 home resulted from Frank Lloyd Wright's early experimentation in the Prairie School style. The furniture and fixtures are also Wright originals. (Open Wed.-Sun. 9am-5pm. Tours $3, children $1.) The **Illinois State Museum,** Spring and Edwards St. (782-7386), has displays on the area's original Native American inhabitants and contemporary Illinois art. (Open Mon.-Sat. 8:30am-5pm, Sun. noon-5pm. Free.)

In June, the **Thomas Rees Carillon** in **Washington Park Botanical Gardens** hosts the world's only **International Carillon Festival.** Springfield's renowned Fourth of July shebang is called (of course) **Lincolnfest** and more than doubles the town's population with fireworks, and plenty of patriotism.

THE GREAT LAKES

 Wisconsin

Cultivation, industrialization, and fermentation are the sturdy pillars of Wisconsin's economy. The state is the nation's foremost producer of milk, cheese, and butter. But "America's Dairyland" also offers outdoor sporting thrills. In a land of almost 15,000 lakes, including Lake Superior to the north and Lake Michigan to the east, this Great Lakes state is a natural playland.

French fur trappers first explored the area in search of lucrative furry creatures. Later, hearty Norsemen lumbered to the logging and lead mining camps of this frontier. By the time the virgin forests had fallen and the mines had been exhausted, immigrant German farmers arrived. Discovering local barley, they made the state the beer capital of the nation. Wisconsin celebrates these ethnic roots in its food and drink. Fishboils—feasts fit for Thor—are a celebrated tradition dating back to the 19th century. This welcoming state explodes in the summer with ethnic fêtes, each with the local flavors of food, music, and (of course) oceans of beer.

PRACTICAL INFORMATION

Capital: Madison.
Division of Tourism, 123 W. Washington St., P.O. Box 7606, Madison 53707 (266-2161, 266-6797, or 800-372-2737 in Wisconsin; 800-432-8748 elsewhere).
Time Zone: Central (1 hr. behind Eastern). **Postal Abbreviation:** WI
Sales Tax: 5½%.

■■■ MILWAUKEE

A mecca of drink and festivals, Milwaukee is a city given to celebration. The influx of immigrants, especially German and Irish, gave the city its reputation for *gemütlichkeit* (hospitality), and is responsible for the outstanding number of churches dotting the city. The ethnic communities take turns throwing city-wide parties each summer weekend. This self-proclaimed "City of Fabulous Festivals" has top-notch museums, quality arts organizations, *baklava*, bagpipes, and excellent frozen custard. And since Jacob Best, a German emigré, introduced lager, the state's large barley supply has been used to make beer. As the nation's largest per capita producer and with over 1500 bars and taverns, there is *lots* of beer.

PRACTICAL INFORMATION

Emergency: 911.
Visitor Information: Greater Milwaukee Convention and Visitors Bureau, 510 W. Kilbourne (273-7222, 273-3950, or 800-231-0903), downtown. Open Mon.-Fri. 8am-5pm, during the summer also open Sat. 9am-4pm. Also at Grand Avenue Mall at 3rd St. (open Mon.-Fri. 10am-8pm, Sat. 10am-7pm, Sun. 11am-5pm). Pick up a copy of *Greater Milwaukee Official Visitor's Guide.*
Airport: General Mitchell International, 5300 S. Howell Ave. (747-5300). Take bus #80 from downtown (30 min.).
Amtrak: 433 W. St. Paul Ave. (271-0840 or 800-872-7245), at 5th St., 3 blocks from the bus terminal. To: Chicago ($17, 2 hr.); Madison ($33). Ticket office open Mon.-Sat. 5:30am-9pm, Sun. 7am-9pm. Fairly safe during the day, less so at night.
Buses: Greyhound, 606 N. 7th St. (800-231-2222), off W. Michigan St. downtown. To: Chicago ($12, 2 hrs.), Madison ($10, 2 hrs.). Ticket office open daily 6:30am-11:15pm; station open 24 hrs. **Wisconsin Coach,** in the Greyhound terminal (544-6503 or 542-8861), has service to southeast Wisconsin. **Badger Bus,** 635 N. 7th St. (276-7490), is across the street. To: Madison (6 per day; $8). Open daily 6:30am-10pm. Stations not very safe at night.
Public Transport: Milwaukee County Transit System, 1942 N. 17th St. (344-6711). Efficient service in the metro area. Most lines run 4:30am-2am. Fare $1.25,

seniors 60¢ with Medicare card. Weekly pass $9.25. Pick up free map at the library or info center at the Grand Ave. Mall. Call for schedules and information.

Taxi: City Veteran Taxi, 291-8080. Base rate $1.50, plus $1.25 per mi., 50¢ each additional passenger.

Airport Limo Service: Limousine Service (769-9100 or 800-236-5450). 24-hr. pickup/dropoff with reservation from most downtown hotels. One way $7.50, round-trip $14.

Car Rental: Sensible Car Rental, 5150 S. 27th St. (282-1080). Free airport pickup. $9.95 per day if car remains in Milwaukee; $18.95 per day if car is driven outside the city. $7 per day for insurance. Must be 22 with a credit card or a $500 deposit. Weekend specials available. Open Mon.-Fri. 9am-9pm, Sat. 9am-6pm.

Auto Transport Company: Auto Driveaway Co., 9039A W. National Ave. (962-0008 or 327-5252), in West Alice. Must be 21 with good driving record. $250 cash deposit refunded at destination; driver pays for gas. Call in advance for availability. Open Mon.-Fri. 8:30am-5pm, Sat. 8am-noon.

Help Lines: Crisis Intervention, 257-7222. 24 hrs. **Rape Crisis Line,** 542-3828. 24 hrs. **Gay People's Union Hotline,** 562-7010. Open daily 7-10pm.

Traveler's Aid: At the airport, upper level (747-5245). Open daily 9am-9pm.

Post Office: 345 W. St. Paul Ave. (291-2544), south along 4th Ave. from downtown, next to the Amtrak station. Open Mon.-Fri. 7:30am-8pm. **ZIP code:** 53203. **Area Code:** 414.

Milwaukee is constructed in an organized grid pattern, with address numbers increasing as you get farther away from **Second Street** and **Wisconsin Ave.** Downtown Milwaukee starts at **Lake Michigan** and runs west to about 10th St.

ACCOMMODATIONS

Sleeping rarely comes cheap in downtown Milwaukee, but there are two attractive hostels nearby, as well as the convenient University of Wisconsin dorms. **Bed and Breakfast of Milwaukee** (277-8066) is a reservation service which finds rooms (from $55) for in-area B&Bs.

University of Wisconsin at Milwaukee (UWM): Sandburg Halls, 3400 N. Maryland Ave. (229-4065 or 299-6123). Take bus #30 north to Hartford St. Nice rooms. Laundry, cafeteria, free local calls available, no kitchen. Convenient to nightlife and east-side restaurants. Private singles with shared bath $22, doubles $30. Open May 31-Aug. 15. Parking for 24hrs. is $4. 2-day advance reservations required.

Hotel Wisconsin, 720 N. 3rd St. (271-4900), across from the Grand Avenue Mall. 250 very nice rooms at a convenient downtown location with free parking, private bath, and cable TV. Singles $59, doubles $62, $8 each extra adult. Key deposit $5. Availability varies, so make reservations early.

Red Barn Hostel (HI-AYH), 6750 W. Loomis Rd. (529-3299), in Greendale, 13 mi. southwest of downtown via Rte. 894, exit Loomis. Take bus #10 or 30 west on Wisconsin Ave., get off at 35th St., and transfer to bus #35 south to the Loomis and Ramsey intersection; then walk ¾mi. south on Loomis. Musty, dark rooms in an enormous red barn; bathroom is campground-quality. Full kitchen. A trek, almost not worth it without a car, but the price is right ($8). Nonmembers $11. The bus ride out is not very safe at night. Check-in 5-10pm. Open May-Oct.

Wellspring Hostel (HI-AYH), 4382 Hickory Rd., (675-6755), Newburg. Take Hwy. 43 north to Hwy. 33 west to Newburg. Hickory Rd. intersects Newburg's Main St. 25 beds ($12), kitchen, on-site parking. Office open daily 8am-8pm; reservations required.

Belmont Hotel, 751 N. 4th St. (271-58880), at Wells downtown. Single rooms to rent in a mainly residential hotel with an exceptional location. Not as safe at night. Shared bath. Rooms $20-25.50. Key deposit $3.

Wisconsin State Fair Park's RV Park (266-7035), just off Hwy. 94 at 84th St. Offers showers, toilets, electricity, dump station, and 24-hr. police patrol for $14 per night. 7-night max-stay. No tent camping.

FOOD

Milwaukee is a premier town of food and drink. German brewery masterminds took a gold liquid which has been around since 4000 BC and industrialized it with refrigeration, glass bottles, cans, and lots of PR, making beer available to all. In this dairy state, French ice cream, better known as frozen custard, is a renowned treat. There are stands all over the city with specialties like Snow Job and Grand Marnier Blueberry Crisp. To top it off, Milwaukeeans take advantage of their proximity to Lake Michigan with the Friday night fish fry, a local favorite.

Brady Street has many Italian restaurants and the **South Side** is heavily Polish. The **Grand Avenue Mall's** third floor, a huge *Speisegarten* ("meal garden") on Wisconsin Ave. between 2nd and 4th St., cultivates reasonable ethnic and fast-food places. **East Side** eateries are a little more cosmopolitan, and good Mexican food sambas at S. 16th St. and National.

Abu's Jerusalem of the Gold, 1978 N. Farwell (277-0485), at Lafayette on the East Side. Exotic tapestries and plenty of trinkets adorn this tiny corner restaurant. Try the rosewater lemonade, (85¢). Plenty of veggie entrees, including falafel sandwich ($2.50) or Manazeleh (a baked eggplant and rice dish, $7). In case you want to try it at home, next door is Abu's Academy of Arabian Bites (277-0485). Open Mon.-Thurs. 11:30am-9pm, Fri.-Sat. 11:30am-11pm, Sun. noon-9pm.

Leon's, 3131 S. 27th St. (383-1784), has the colorful neon lights and famous custard. Rumored to have served as the model for Al's Place on *Happy Days.* Prices also seem historic. Double-dip cone 90¢, hot dog 89¢. Open Sun.-Thurs. 11am-midnight, Fri. 11am-12:30am, Sat 11am-1am.

Three Brothers, 2414 St. Clair St. (481-7530), #15 bus to Conway and walk 4 blocks east, crossing the railroad track. One of the best known of Milwaukee's famed Serbian restaurants, this family-owned business serves dishes such as *burek,* a strudel puff pastry filled with beef or chicken ($11.95). Open Tues.-Thurs. 5-10pm, Fri.-Sat. 4-11pm, Sun. 4-10pm. Reservations recommended.

Bangkok Orchid, 2239 N. Prospect Ave. (223-3333), 1 block south of the intersection with North Ave. Flexible, innovative menu and friendly staff allow diners to create their own Thai dishes. Open Mon.-Fri. 4-10pm, Sat. 4-11pm, Sun. 4-9pm.

Balisterer's (475-1414), 68th and Wells, a delectable-smelling Italian fare restaurant with excellent (and huge) pizza ($6.95 small). Open Mon.-Thurs. 11am-1am, Fri.11am-2am, Sat. 3pm-2am, Sun. 3pm-midnight.

SIGHTS

Although many of Milwaukee's breweries have left, the city's name still conjures up images of a cold one. No visit to the city would be complete without a look at the yeast in action. **The Miller Brewery,** 4251 W. State St. (931-2337), offers free one-hour tours with free samples from the corporate giant that produces 43 million barrels of beer annually. (2 tours per hr. Mon.-Sat. 10am-3:30pm. Under 19 accompanied by adult.) **Pabst Brewing Company,** 915 W. Juneau Ave. (223-3709), offers free 35- to 40-min. tours with a free tasting in a magnificent stone courtyard (on the hr., Mon.-Fri., 10am-3pm, Sat. 10am-2pm Sept.-May closed Sat.). The **Lakefront Brewery,** 818 E. Chambers St. (372-8800), produces four year-round beers and several seasonal specials including pumpkin beer and cherry lager. (Tours Sat. 1:30pm, 2:30pm and 3:30pm.($2 donation requested.)

You've seen the t-shirts and the bikes, now see the factory. **Harley-Davidson Inc.,** 11700 W. Capitol Dr. (342-4680), assembles their engines here. (1-hr. tours Mon.-Fri. at 9am, 10:30am, and 12:30pm. Groups larger than 7 must make reservations.) Would-be journalists and news-lovers will enjoy the free 75-min. tour of the **Milwaukee Journal and Milwaukee Sentinel,** which visits the newsrooms, pressrooms, and production departments. (Tours Mon.-Fri. at 9:15am, 11am, 12:30pm, and 2pm. Must be older than 8; reservations required. Call 224-2120 for details.)

Milwaukee is graced with several excellent museums. The **Milwaukee Public Museum,** 800 W. Wells St. (278-2700; 278-2702 for recorded info), at N. 8th St., allows visitors to walk through exhibits on the streets of Old Milwaukee and a European village, complete with cobblestones and two-story shops. Other exhibits include a skeleton of a tyrannosaurus, Native American artifacts, and a replicated Costa Rican rain forest. (Parking available. Open daily 9am-5pm. $4.50, seniors and students $3, kids $2.50.) The lakefront **Milwaukee Art Museum,** 750 N. Lincoln Memorial Dr., (224-3200), in the War Memorial Building, houses Haitian art, 19th-century German art, and American sculpture and painting, including two of Warhol's soup cans. (Open Tues.-Wed. and Fri.-Sat. 10am-5pm, Thurs. noon-9pm, Sun. noon-5pm. $4, seniors, students, and persons with disabilities $2.) Park free along the Lincoln Memorial Drive, or pay $2 to use the Museum lot. The **Charles Allis Art Museum,** 1801 N. Prospect Ave. (278-8295), at Royal Ave., one block north of Brady, is an English Tudor mansion with a fine collection of Chinese, Japanese, Korean, Persian, Greek, and Roman artifacts, as well as American and European furniture. (Open Wed. 1-5pm and 7-9pm, Thurs.-Sun. 1-5pm. $2. Take bus #30 or 31.) The stone-and-ivy **Milwaukee County Historical Center,** 910 N. Old World 3rd St. (273-8288), details the early years of the city. (Open Mon.-Fri. 9:30am-5pm, Sat. 10am-5pm, Sun. 1-5pm. Free.)

The **Mitchell Park Horticultural Conservatory,** 524 S. Layton Blvd. (649-9800), at 27th St., better known as "The Domes," recreates a desert, a rain forest, and seasonal displays in a series of three seven-story conical glass domes. (Open daily 9am-5pm. $2.50, seniors, kids, and persons with disabilities $1.25. Take bus #27.) 4 mi. west, you'll find the **Milwaukee County Zoo,** 10001 W. Bluemound Rd. (256-5412), where zebras and cheetahs eye each other across a moat in the only predator-prey exhibit in the U.S. Also look for the elegant, misunderstood black rhinos and the trumpeter swans. Many shows are free with admission. (Open May-Labor Day Mon.-Sat. 9am-5pm, Sun. 9am-6pm; daily 9am-4:30pm the rest of year. $6, children 3-12 $4. Parking $4. Take bus #10.) The **Boerner Botanical Gardens,** 5879 S. 92nd St. (425-1130), in Whitnall Park between Grange and Rawsen St., boasts billions of beautiful blossoms. (Open May-Oct. 8am-sunset daily. Free.) County parks line much of Milwaukee's waterfront, providing free recreational areas for all. Bikers will revel in the many trails by the lake. Those needing to rent wheels should head to **High Roller Bike and Skate Rental** (273-1343), at McKinley Marina in Veteran's Park, where roller blades are $5 per hour. (Open daily in winter 10am-8pm; must have one form of ID and be over 18 years old.) Skaters of the ice-persuasion can pirouette at **Pettit National Ice Center,** 500 S. 84th St. (266-0100), by the State Fairgrounds, where a trip to the ice will cost $2. (Hours vary; call for info.)

Historic Milwaukee, Inc. (277-7795), P.O. Box 2132, offers walking tours focusing on ethnic heritage, original settlements, and architecture ($4, students $2). Ask about Milwaukee's many beautiful churches, including **St. Josaphat's Basilica,** 2333 S. 6th St. (645-5623), a turn-of-the-century landmark with a dome larger than the Taj Mahal's (doors open daily 10am-2pm; make phone arrangements to see the church at other times). The **Milwaukee County Transit System** runs four-hour **bus tours** that include a stop at a brewery and the domes. (Mid-June to Aug. Mon.-Sat. departing 12:15pm from the Grand Ave. 2nd St. entrance. $10, children and seniors $8; call 344-6711 for details.)

EVENTS AND ENTERTAINMENT

Milwaukee is festival-happy, throwing a different city-wide party almost every summer weekend. The tourist office is overflowing with pamphlets and brochures on every kind of event. **Summerfest** (273-3378; outside Milwaukee 800-837-3378), the largest and most lavish, lasts over 11 days in late June and early July. Daily life is put on hold as a potpourri of musical acts, culinary specialities, and an arts and crafts bazaar take over at Maier Festival Park. The **Rainbow Summer** (273-7206) is a series of free lunchtime concerts throughout the summer which run the spectrum from jazz and bluegrass to country music. Concerts are held weekdays from noon to 1:15pm in the Peck Pavilion at the Performing Arts Center (see below). Milwaukeeans line the streets for **The Great Circus Parade** (273-7877) in mid-July, an authentic re-creation of turn-of-the-century processions, with trained animals, daredevils, costumed performers, and 75 original wagons. In early August the **Wisconsin State Fair** (266-7000) rolls into the fairgrounds, toting big-name entertainment, 12 stages, exhibits, contests, rides, fireworks, and of course, a pie-baking contest ($5, seniors and disabled $4, under 11 free). Pick up a copy of the free weekly entertainment magazine, *Downtown Edition,* for the full scoop on festivals. There are ethnic festivals every weekend; the most popular are **Polishfest** (529-2140), in mid-June; **Festa Italiana** (223-2180), in mid-July; **Bastille Days** (271-1416), near Bastille Day (July 14); and **German Fest** (464-9444), in late July (tickets $6, children under 12 free). Downtown at the riverfront in **Pére Marquette Park,** between State and Kilbourn, **River Flicks** (286-5700) presents free movies every Thursday in August at dusk.

For quality arts performances, visit the modern white stone **Performing Art Center (PAC),** 929 N. Water St. (273-7206 or 800-472-4458), across the river from Pére Marquette Park. The PAC hosts the Milwaukee Symphony Orchestra, First Stage Milwaukee, a Ballet Company, and the Florentine Opera Company. (Symphony tickets $13-50; ballet and symphony offer ½-price student and senior tickets on the day of any show.) **The Milwaukee Repertory Theater,** 108 East Wells St. (224-9490), features a three-stage complex which hosts contemporary, classical, cabaret, and holiday shows from September to May. (Tickets $8-26, students $1 off if purchased in advance; rush tickets available ½ hr. before all shows for ½ price.)

The **Milwaukee Brewers** baseball team plays at County Stadium, 201 S. 46th St. and the interchange of I-94 and Rte. 41 (933-9000 or 800-933-7890), as do the **Green Bay Packers** (342-2717) for some of their home games. The **Milwaukee Bucks** (227-0500), the local basketball team, as well as the **Marquette University Warriors** (288-7127), lock horns with opponents at Bradley Center, 1001 N. 4th St. (227-0700); the **Milwaukee Admirals** (227-0550) also skate there.

NIGHTLIFE

In this land of over 15,000 lakes, it sometimes seems there's more beer flowing than water. With a bar almost always in sight, Milwaukee doesn't lack for *something* to do after sundown. Downtown gets a little seedy at night; the best nightlife district is on North Ave. on the East Side, near the UW campus.

Downtown, come in from the cold to **Safehouse,** 779 N. Front St. (271-2007), across from the Pabst Theater. Step through a bookcase passage and enter a bizarre world of spy hideouts, James Bond music, and a phone booth with 90 sound effects. A brass plate labeled "International Exports, Ltd." marks the entrance. Draft beer (code name: "liquid gold") costs $1.50, simple dinners are $6-12. (Open Mon.-Sat. 11:30am-2am, Sun. 4pm-midnight. Cover $1-2.) For British-style drinking fun, dip into **John Hawk's Pub,** 101 E. Washington Ave. (272-3199). A beautiful oak bar complements the riverside view. (Imported beer $3; open Sun.-Thurs. 10am-midnight, Fri.-Sat. 10am-2am; live jazz Sat. 8:30-9:30pm and some Fridays at 5pm. Open daily 10am-2am. No cover.)

On North Ave. on the East Side, there are a slew of bars and clubs. **Von Trier's,** 2235 N. Farwell (272-1775), at North, is very cool and definitely the nicest. Authentic German-American artifacts adorn the walls; check out the ceiling painting of the town of Trier. Twenty draft and 74 bottled beers (mostly imported) along with numerous hot drinks and coffees are served in the lavish German interior or on the large outdoor patio. (Open Sun.-Thurs. 4pm-2am, Fri.-Sat. 4pm-3am.) **Hooligan's,** a block or so south at 2017 North Ave. (273-5230), at Farwell, is smaller, louder, and—as the name might suggest—rowdier. (Open Sun.-Thurs. 11am-2am, Fri.-Sat 11am-2:30am. Live music Sept.-June on Mon. at 9:30pm. Cover $2-4.) **Café Melange,** 720 Old World 3rd St. (291-9889), in the Hotel Wisconsin, highlights a variety of entertainment, including Monday poetry readings, open mike nights, tap dance, and jazz, blues, and Latin music ensembles. (Open Mon. 11am-3pm and 9pm-2am, Tues.-Thurs. 11am-2am, Fri.-Sat. 11am-2:30am, Sun. 5pm-2am.) **Comedy Sportz,** 126 N. Jefferson (272-8888), in 3rd Ward, has a restaurant, bar, and great entertainment. (Shows Thurs.-Sun. at 7:30pm, additional show Fri.-Sat. at 10pm. Bar open Sun.-Thurs. 5pm-midnight, Fri.-Sat. 5pm-2am.

THE GREAT LAKES

■■■ MADISON

Sandwiched between Lake Mendota and Lake Monona, Madison is best known for its urban attractions, almost all of which lie within a mile of the state capitol building. This college town, home to the University of Wisconsin, has a youthful atmosphere and an abundance of ethnic restaurants and coffee houses.

Practical Information The **Greater Madison Convention and Visitors Bureau,** 615 Washington Ave. (255-2537 or 800-373-6376), will provide travel information. (Open Mon.-Fri. 8am-5pm.) The **Greyhound Station,** 2S. Bedford St. (257-3050 or 800-231-2222), is open daily from 5:45am-10pm. Use the **Madison Metro Transit System,** 1101 E. Washington Ave. (266-4466), which offers an extensive, efficient system serving downtown, the UW campus, and surrounding area. ($1; free travel Mon.-Sat. 10am-3pm within the capitol and UW campus.) **Post office:** 3902 Milwaukee Ave. (246-1249; open Mon.-Fri. 7:30am-6pm, Sat. 8:30am-2pm); **ZIP code:** 53714; **area code:** 608.

Accommodations Travelers on government business drive up the accommodations prices in Madison. E. Washington Ave. and the Beltline Hwy. are slightly less convenient than downtown, but save pennies for the budget travelers. **Langdon Residence Hall,** 126 Langdon St. (257-8841 or 800-634-1460), at the UW Campus, sometimes has vacant dorm rooms during the summer months ($22). Alternatively, the **Select Inn,** 4845 Haynes Rd. (249-1815), near the junction of I-90 and Hwy. 151, provides clean, comfortable budget lodging and free local calls (rooms $29-36). Campers should head south on Hwy. 90 to Stoughton, where **Lake Kegonsa State Park,** 2405 Door Creek Rd. (873-9695), has sites for $8 ($6 for Wisconsin residents; no showers).

Food and Nightlife Good restaurants are dispersed throughout Madison. For downtown eats, head to **State Street,** by the University, where food of all flavors bombards visitors. Farm-fresh produce can be found Saturdays (April-Nov. 6am-2pm at the Capitol Square) (563-5031). **The Opera House,** 126 S. Pickney St. (284-8466), creates innovative cuisine like blackened bluefish with pineapple salsa ($6.50), all served in a jazzy atmosphere (open Mon.-Fri. 11am-midnight, Sat. 5pm-midnight; bar open until 2am Mon.-Sat.). **Dotty's Dumpling Dowry,** 116 N. Fairchild (255-3175), prides itself on award-winning cheeseburgers ($3.80). This is not just an ordinary burger. (Open Mon.-Wed. 11am-10pm, Thurs.-Sat. 11am-midnight, Sun. noon-9pm.) **Himal Chuli,** 318 State St. (251-9225), is a popular spot for a taste of the Himalayas (primarily vegetarian dishes). (Open Mon.-Sat. 11am-9pm.) The **Crystal Corner Bar,** 1302 Williamson St. (256-2953), showcases live bands on Thursdays at 9pm, and Saturdays at 10pm. (Draught beers $1.10-2, bottles $1.90-3.50. Open Mon.-Thurs. 11am-2am, Fri.-Sat. 11am-2:30am, Sun. noon-2am. Cover $5.40.) The **Terrace** (255-INFO), at Memorial Union, on UW Campus, offers free jazz, folk, and local bands from Thursday to Saturday at 9:30pm.

Sights and Entertainment Madison claims a number of terrific museums and visitors have the good fortune of being able to walk to almost all of them. On weeknights and weekends, garage parking along the "museum mile" costs only $1. The **State Capitol** (266-0382), in Capitol Square, is the center of downtown from which streets radiate outward. This magnificent structure can be self-toured daily from 6am-8pm (free guided tours depart from the ground floor info desk Mon.-Sat on the hr. 9am-3pm, except noon, and Sun. on the hour 1-3pm). Also on Capitol Square, the **Wisconsin Veterans Museum,** 30 W. Mifflin St. (264-6086), honors the state's soldiers who served the nation. The 19th- and 20th-century galleries cover America's military involvement. (Open Tues.-Sat. 9:30am-4:30pm; also April-Sept. Sun. noon-4pm. Free.) The history of Wisconsin's Native American population is explored at the **State Historical Museum,** 30 N. Carroll St. (264-6555; open Tues.-Sat. 10am-5pm, Sun. noon-5pm; free.)

The **Madison Civic Center,** 211 State St. (266-6550), houses much of the city's arts and performing entertainment. Call for details (office open Mon.-Fri. 8am-4:30pm). The **Madison Art Center** (257-0158) exhibits modern and contemporary art (open Tues.-Thurs. 11am-5pm, Fri. 11am-9pm, Sat. 10am-5pm, Sun. 1-5pm; $1, students 50¢). The **Madison Repertory Theatre,** 122 State St., #201 (256-0029), performs classic and contemporary musical productions in the **Isthmus Playhouse** at the Civic Center (performance times and ticket prices vary; call.) For up-to-date entertainment news, pick up a free copy of the weekly *Isthmus* (printed Thurs.).

The **University of Wisconsin,** one of the best public universities in the United States, has a few fantastic museums. The **UW Visitors Center** is on Park St. on the west side of the Memorial Union. Particularly interesting are the UW **Geology Museum,** 215 W. Dayton (262-2399; open Mon.-Fri. 8:30am-4:30pm, Sat. 9am-noon); and the **Elvehjem Museum of Art,** 800 University Ave. (263-2246; Open daily 9am-5pm; free). Slightly farther away, the **Henry Villas Zoo,** 702 S. Randall Ave. (266-4732), near the intersection of W. Washington and Park, provides habitats for over 800 animals from the American Bison to elephants (grounds open June-Labor Day weekend daily 9:30am-8pm, Sept.-May daily 9:30am-5pm; free).

Circus World Museum, 426 Water St. (356-8341, 356-0800 for recorded info), in Baraboo, is the place for circus lovers. Take exit 106 off Hwy. 90/94 (45-min. drive from Madison). This former home of the Ringling Brothers Circus continues the fun-loving, clown-filled, carefree tradition of the big top with 50 acres of circus attractions, including horses, an elephant barn, flea circus paraphernalia, parade wagons, and more. Mesmerizing shows take place throughout the day. (Open May-Sept. 5 daily 9am-6pm, some nights until 10pm. $10.95, seniors $9.95, ages 3-12 $5.95; after 4pm $6.95, kids $3.95.) Also in Baraboo, the **International Crane Foundation,** E-11376 Shady Lane Rd. (356-9462), offers a close-up at the tallest flying birds in the world. (Open May-Oct. 9am-5pm, tour Memorial Day-Labor Day daily 10am, 1pm, and 3pm; weekend tours May and Sept.-Oct. $5, seniors $4.50, ages 5-11 $2.50.)

■■■ DOOR COUNTY

Jutting 40 mi. out into Lake Michigan, Door Peninsula boasts 250 mi. of shoreline, parks, lakes, apple and cherry orchards, and backroad bicycle routes. Ever since the area was settled by Scandinavians, fishboils—fabulous feasts of fish—topped with homemade cherry pie have been *the* food. Door County swings open to visitors, providing stores, restaurants, and parks, and yet so far has managed to protect its home-town feel from reckless developers.

Practical Information Emergency is 911. **Door County Chamber of Commerce,** 6443 Green Bay Rd. (743-4456 or 800-52-RELAX), on Rte. 42/57 entering Sturgeon Bay, has free brochures for every village on the peninsula as well as biking maps. Outside, a free **Triphone** allows you to call hotels, restaurants, police, a weather line, and a fishing hotline. (Open Mon.-Fri.8:30am-5pm, Sat. 10am-4pm; Nov.-May. Mon.-Fri. 8:30am-4:30pm). Each village has a visitors center.

The closest **Greyhound** is 50 mi. away at 800 Cedar, in Green Bay (414-432-4883). The closest station to Door County is about 50 mi. from Sturgeon Bay. (Open Mon.-Fri. 6:30am-5:15pm, Sat. 6:30am-noon, Sun. 9am-noon.) You can rent a car at **Advantage,** 1629 Velp, (414-497-2152), Green Bay 50 mi. from Sturgeon Bay, 3 mi. from the Greyhound station. ($14 per day, $89 per week, 10¢ per mi., extra $5 insurance. Must be 25 years old with credit card. Open Mon.-Fri. 8:30am-5:30pm, Sat. 8am-3pm.) **Edge of Park Bike Rentals,** 4007 Hwy. 41, (868-3344), Fish Creek at the entrance to Peninsula State Park, has six speed bikes for $5 per hour or $20 per day; mopeds for $20 per hr. **Kurtz Corral,** 5712 Howard Ln., (743-6742), Sturgeon Bay, 3 mi. east of Carlsville on C.R. "I" has horseback riding on 300 acres. Hour-long trail rides $20-35. (Trails open daily 9am-3pm.) Door County's **post office:** 359 Louisiana (743-2681), at 4th St. in Sturgeon Bay (open Mon.-Fri. 8:30am-5pm, Sat. 9:30am-noon); **ZIP code:** 54235; **area code:** 414.

The real Door County begins north of **Sturgeon Bay,** where Rtes. 42 and 57 converge and then split again—Rte. 57 running up the eastern coast of the peninsula, Rte. 42 up the western side. The peninsula is 200 mi. northeast of Madison and 150 mi. north of Milwaukee; there is no land access except via Sturgeon Bay. Summer is high season in Door's 12 villages, the biggest of which are **Fish Creek** (rhymes with "fish stick"), **Sister Bay,** and **Ephraim.** There is no public transportation on the peninsula. The eastern side is less commercial than the western; the county is less developed and more traditional the farther north you go. Wherever in the area you are, dress warmly; temperatures can dip to 40°F at night in July.

Accommodations and Camping An abundance of lodgings, most which cater to the family-with-boat crowd, charge $60 and up per night. Camping is your best option. The **Camp-Tel Family Campground,** 8164 Hwy. 42 (868-3278), 1 mi. north of Egg Harbor, sports A-frame cabins, each with two sets of bunks, a loft, heat and electricity, and accommodating a family of six or two couples ($28). Tent sites are $14. Cozy and affordable rooms can be found at **Billerbecks,** 9864 Hidden Spring Rd. (854-2528), off Hwy. 42 in Ephraim, which offers three rooms with a shared bath ($24-27). The **Century Farm Motel** (854-4069), on Rte. 57, 3 mi. south of Sister Bay, is a really nifty place located on a farm complete with cows and chickens; the individual cottages have pine walls, showers, and cozy bedspreads and curtains. The friendly owner lives in a log cabin built by his great-grandfather a century ago. (Cottage for 2 $40, for 5 $55. Open May-Oct. Reserve 1 week ahead, more for holiday weekends.) Check out the proprietress' collection of several thousand dolls, including 700 Barbies, at the **Chal-A Motel,** 3910 Rte. 42/57 (743-6788), 3 mi. north of the bridge in Sturgeon Bay. In the same barn her husband shows off 24 vintage automobiles, ranging from a 1924 Model T to a 1983 DeLorean. Large rooms in a serene setting. (July-Oct. singles $39, doubles $49; Nov.-June $24/34.)

Camping is the way to go in Door County, and four out of the five **state parks** (all except Whitefish Dunes State Park) have sites ($12, Wisconsin residents $10). Parks also require a $6 entrance fee for any motor vehicle (good for 24 hrs.). An annual admission sticker for motor vehicles is $24 and permits access to all state parks. **Peninsula State Park,** P.O. Box 218, Fish Creek 54212 (868-3258), by Fish Creek village on Rte. 42, is the largest, with 472 sites. Make reservations way ahead of time (i.e. 6 months), or come in person and put your name on the waiting list for one of the 127 sites reserved for walk-ins. Peninsula has showers and flush toilets, 20 mi. of shoreline, a spectacular view from Eagle Tower, and 17 mi. of hiking. **Potawatomi State Park,** 3740 Park Dr., Sturgeon Bay 54235 (746-2890), just outside Sturgeon Bay off Rte. 42/57, has 125 campsites, half of which are open to walk-ins. Write for reservations. **Newport State Park,** a wildlife preserve at the tip of the peninsula, 7 mi. from Ellison Bay off Rte. 42, has only 16 sites; vehicles are allowed, but sites are accessible only by hiking. To get to **Rock Island State Park** (847-2235), take the ferry from Gill's Rock to Washington Island (see Sights and Activities below), and then another ferry (847-2252; $6 round-trip) to Rock Island. (40 sites, open mid-April to mid-Nov.) Private **Path of Pines,** 3709 Hwy. F (868-3332), in Fish Creek, has scenic sites and free showers 1 mi. east of the perennially packed Peninsula, off Rte. 42. (91 sites; tents $12, with hookup $16, Fri.-Sat. $3 more.)

Food and Drink Many people come to Door County just for **fishboils,** not a trout with blemishes but a Scandinavian tradition dating back to 19th-century lumberjacks. Fifty meals are cooked at a time in a steaming cauldron over a wood fire. To remove the fish oil from the top of the water, the boilmaster throws a can of kerosene into the fire, producing a massive fireball; this causes the cauldron to boil over and signals chow time. The best fishboils are at: **Edgewater Restaurant** (854-4034), in Ephraim (May-Oct. Mon.-Sat. at 5:30pm, 6:45pm, and 8pm; $12.25, kids under 12 $8.25; reservations recommended); and **The Viking** (854-2998), in Ellison

Bay (mid-May to Nov. 4:30-8pm, every ½ hr.; $10.50, child $7.50). Cherries are another county tradition, and most fishboils conclude with a big slice of cherry pie.

Al Johnson's Swedish Restaurant (854-2626), in Sister Bay on Rte. 42, down the hill and two blocks past the information center on the right, has excellent Swedish food ($7-16) along with goats who dine daily on the thick sod roof. (Open daily 6am-9pm; winter Mon.-Sat. 6am-8pm, Sun. 7am-8pm.) **Bayside Tavern** (868-3441), Fish Creek on Rte. 42, serves serious burgers ($2.50-3.50) and a delicious Friday perch fry ($8). Also a hip bar. (Beer $1.00.) After 10pm, minors should be with an adult. (Open daily 11am-2am. Kitchen open until 10pm.)

Sights and Activities Door County is best seen by bike; ask for free bike maps at the tourist offices. **Cave Point County Park** offers the most stunning views on the peninsula. The park is on Cave Point Rd. off Rte. 57, just south of Jacksonport (open daily 6am-9pm; free). Next door is **Whitefish Dunes State Park,** with hikin' a-plenty through a well-kept wildlife preserve (open daily 8am-8pm; $6 per vehicle). Visit the small public beaches along Door's 250-mi. shoreline; one of the nicest is **Lakeside Park** at **Jacksonport.** The beach is wide and sandy, backed by a shady park and playground (open daily 6am-9pm; free). While on the beaches, look for the many lighthouses which flank the peninsula's perimeter. **Peninsula State Park,** a few miles south of Ephraim in Fish Creek, has 3763 acres of forested land (open daily 6am-11pm; $6 per motorized vehicle). Ride a moped or bicycle along the 20 mi. of shoreline road, rent a boat for aquatic exploration, or sunbathe at **Nicolet Beach** in the park. From the immense Eagle Tower 1 mi. east of the beach, 110 steps up, you can see clear across the lake to Michigan.

Kangaroo Lake, the largest of the eight inland lakes on this thin peninsula, offers warmer swimming and a less intimidating stretch of water than Lake Michigan. Kangaroo Lake Rd., south of Bailey's Harbor off Rte. 57, provides lake access; follow the county roads around the lake to find your own secluded swimming spot. The **Ridges Sanctuary** (839-2802), north of Bailey's Harbor off County Rte. Q, has an appealing nature trail that leads to an abandoned lighthouse (open Mon.-Sat. 9am-4pm, Sun. 1-4pm; free). **Newport State Park,** 6 mi. east of Ellison Bay on Newport Dr. off Rte. 42, provides more satisfying hiking than Peninsula (no vehicles). Newport has an expansive 3000-ft. swimming beach and 13 mi. of shoreline on Lake Michigan and on inland Europe Lake. Three free Maritime Museums, at Gills Rock, Sturgeon Bay, and Cana Island and Lighthouse document the water industries of the Great Lakes. (Open Memorial Day to mid-Oct.; hours vary.) Tours and tastings can be had at the **Door Peninsula Winery,** 5806 Hwy. 42 (743-7431 or 800-551-5049).

Green Bay, the largest city near Door County, has pollution, noise, and lots of industry. A shipping and packing town, home of the aptly named (and oldest) NFL team, the **Green Bay Packers,** this city has plenty of bars and a little gambling. **The Oneida Bingo and Casino,** (414-497-8118), County Rte. GG southwest of downtown, is on a Native American reservation. Watch Native Americans call the shots for a change; (free; 18 and older only). The **National Railroad Museum,** 2285 S. Broadway, (414-435-7245), Green Bay, exhibits trains (surprise!) (open May-Oct. daily 9am-5pm; $5.50, kids $2.75).

■■■ APOSTLE ISLANDS

The Apostle Islands, product of a million years of scourging glacial activity, float majestically off the northern coast of Wisconsin, some 90 mi. from Duluth. The rich cultural heritage and natural beauty of this area has been variously claimed by Native Americans, loggers, quarreymen, and fishermen. Apostle Island is now protected as a National Lakeshore, encompassing 21 of the 22 islands and a 12-mi. stretch along the mainland shore. Summer tourists visit the caves by the thousands, camping on unspoiled sandstone bluffs and hunting for wild blueberries and raspberries. Legend has it that the islands were named in the 18th century when a band of pirates called the Twelve Apostles hid out on Oak Island.

Free camper's permits are available at the **National Lakeshore Headquarters Visitors Center,** 410 Washington Ave. (779-3397), Bayfield, see Bayfield Practical Info). The permit allows you to camp on 19 of the 22 islands. The Headquarters gives hiking and camping info. Due to the extreme cold, swimming is not recommended in Lake Superior, and campers should be sure to boil lake water for at least two min. before drinking.

Besides Bayfield and Madeline Island (see below), the 21 other islands have subtle charms of their own. The sandstone quarries of Basswood and Hermit Islands, as well as the abandoned logging and fishing camps on some of the other islands, are mute reminders of a more vigorous era. The restored **lighthouses** on Sand, Raspberry, Michigan, Outer, and Devils Islands offer spectacular views of the surrounding country. Sea caves, carved out by thousands of years of winds and water, pocket the shores of some of the islands; a few on Devil's Island are large enough to explore by boat. An easy way to visit all of these sights is on one of three narrated three-hr. cruises provided by the **Apostle Islands Cruise Service** (779-3925 or 800-323-7619; tours depart mid-May to mid-Oct. daily 10am from Bayfield City Dock $20, kids $9). From late June to late August, the cruise service runs other trips ($19) from which passengers can disembark to camp on the islands and then be picked up the next time the cruise schedule brings the boat to that island. At other times, up to six people can charter a **Water Taxi** (779-5153) to the nearest (round-trip $56) or farthest ($272) island. The **Catchyn-Sun Charter Co.** (779-3111) offers two 3½-hr. trips daily, leaving at 9:30am and 1:30pm ($40 per person).

■ BAYFIELD

Practical Information All Apostle Islands excursions begin in the sleepy mainland town of **Bayfield,** in the northwest part of Wisconsin on the Lake Superior coast. The few remnants of Bayfield's glory days as the main shipping port for brownstone can be witnessed in the elegant well-kept mansions set into the hill, overlooking the lake. These days, apples are the area's claim to fame, and the town comes vibrantly alive in early October for the **Apple Festival.** For that fresh-picked orchard taste, make your way to the **Bayfield Apple Company,** (779-5700), on Betzold Rd. (Open Sept.-Jan. daily 9am-6pm). The nearest **bus** station is in **Ashland,** 101 2nd St. (682-4010), 22 mi. southeast of Bayfield on U.S. 2 (to Duluth, 1per day 1½ hr., $15). The **Bay Area Rural Transit (BART),** 300 Industrial Park Rd., (682-9664), Ashland offers a shuttle to Bayfield (4 per day, Mon.-Fri., $1.80, seniors $1.10, students $1.50). The **Bayfield Chamber of Commerce,** 42 S. Broad St. (779-3335 or 800-447-4094), has helpful info on the area (open daily 9am-5pm). The **Apostle Islands National Lakeshore Headquarters Visitors Center,** 410 Washington Ave. (779-3397), features exhibits and a theater, runs nature programs, and dispenses info and free camping permits for the islands (open summer daily 8am-6pm; winter Mon.-Fri. 8am-4:30pm). Bayfield's **post office:** open Mon.-Fri. 8:30am-6pm, Sat. 8:30am-12:30pm; **ZIP code:** 54814; **area code:** 715.

Accommodations and Food There are numerous campgrounds in the area. **Red Cliff** (779-3743), a Chippewa settlement 3 mi. north on Rte. 13, offers tourists a campground with modern conveniences ($10, tents with electricity $11, trailers with electricity $12). Talk to the Native Americans for a different perspective on the area and its offerings. **Dalrymple Park** (779-5712), ¼ mi. north of town on Rte. 13, offers 30 sites under tall pines right on the Lake, but no showers ($7, $8 with electricity). **Apostle Islands View Campground** (779-5524), County Rd. J, off Rte. 13, ½ mi. south of Bayfield, offers modern sites overlooking the islands. Some electric and water hookups. (Sites $10, showers 25¢, check-out 2pm.) For those who prefer indoors, the **Frostman Home,** 24 N. 3rd St. (779-3239), has three spotless and comfortable rooms (two with lake views) for $22.50 each (open mid-June to mid-Sept.). Down the street and around the corner, **Greunke's First Street Inn,** 17 Rittenhouse Ave. (779-5480 or 800-245-3072), has pleasant rooms for $30-75.

In early summer, Bayfield's basket overflows with berry pies. **Maggie's,** 257 Manypenny Ave. (779-5641), also has sandwiches and burgers ($4.50). Trout and whitefish ($9.95) are specialties of the house. (Open May-Oct. daily 6am-midnight; Nov.-April Sun.-Thurs. 11am-9pm, Fri.-Sat. 11am-10pm.) The **Bayfield Deli,** 201 Manypenny (779-5566), slices up huge sandwiches ($1.50-6). (Open daily 7am-9pm.) **Greunke's Restaurant,** 17 Rittenhouse Ave. (779-5480), at 1st St., is locally famous for its fishboils, held every summer night at 6:30 and 7:30pm ($10.50 per person; open daily 6am-10pm).

■ MADELINE ISLAND

A few hundred years ago, the Chippewa came to **Madeline Island** from the Atlantic in search of the *megis shell,* a light in the sky that was purported to bring prosperity and health. Today, the island maintains its allure, drawing thousands of visitors in the summer, all seeking the clean and sandy beaches of this relaxing island retreat.

Practical Information The **Madeline Island Chamber of Commerce,** (747-2801), Main St., is especially helpful concerning accommodations (open daily 10am-4pm). Street addresses aren't necessary on Madeline Island; there are only about five streets. Ferry service between Bayfield and **La Pointe,** on Madeline Island, is provided by **Madeline Island Ferry Line** (747-2051 or 747-6801; summer ferries daily every 30 min. 7am-11pm; less frequently March-June and Sept.-Dec.; one way $3, ages 6-11 $1.75, bikes $1.50, cars $6.75; less off-season). The 2.6-mi. trip takes about 20 min. During the winter (Jan.-March), the crossing is made by windsled, snowmobile, on foot, or by car. Transport on Madeline Island is by foot, car, or bicycle. Rent a moped at **Motion to Go,** 102 Lake View Pl. (747-6585), about one block from the ferry. ($10 per hr., $45 per day. Mountain bikes $5 per hr., $18 per day. Open mid-May to early Oct. 10am-8pm.) La Pointe's **post office:** (747-3712), just off the dock on Madeline Island (open Mon.-Fri. 9am-4:20pm, Sat. 9:30am-12:50pm); **ZIP code:** 54850.

Accommodations and Food Madeline Island has two campgrounds. **Big Bay Town Park** (747-6913) is 6½ mi. from La Pointe out Big Bay Rd., right next to beautiful Big Bay Lagoon (sites $9, with electric hookup $16). Across the lagoon, **Big Bay State Park** (747-6425; Bayfield office 779-3346) has 55 primitive sites for $8-12. Sites can be reserved by mail for an extra $3. A daily vehicle permit ($6, $4 for Wisconsinites) is also required. The **Madeline Island Motel** (747-3000) offers clean rooms named for personalities in the island's history. (July-Labor Day singles $51, doubles $56; May-June and Labor Day-Nov. $41 and $45; Dec.-April all rooms $31.) Rooms in the area are scarce during the summer; call ahead for reservations.

The **Beach Club** (747-3955), just off the ferry in La Pointe, has a relaxed atmosphere, a view of the lake, superlative shortcake ($3.50), and a superb shrimp basket with fries ($7). (Open summer daily 11:30am-3:30pm and 5:30-9:30pm.) The **Island Café** (747-6555), one block to the right when exiting the ferry, serves up big meals (ham and cheese omelette $4.25) and lunch ($4-6). Dinner selection changes daily, but always includes many vegetarian dishes. Check-out the all-you-can-eat fish fry ($6.95). (Open daily 8am-10:30pm.)

Sights The **Madeline Island Historical Museum** (747-2415), right off the dock, accompanies the legend of Madeline with other historical information on 19th-century agriculture, mining, fishing, and logging. (Open late May to mid-July and Sept.-early Oct. daily 10am-5pm; mid-July to Aug. 9am-8pm. $3, seniors $2.70, ages 5-12 $1.25.) The **Indian Burial Ground** 1 mi. south of La Pointe has dirt paths that lead to the graves of early settlers and christianized Chippewa, including Chief Great Buffalo. Towards the end of the day, head to **Sunset Bay** on the island's north side. **Madeline Island Bus Tours** (747-2051) offers two-hr. tours of the island (June 18-

24, daily 10:30am and 1pm; June 25 to mid-Aug. 10:30am, 1pm, and 3:15pm; tickets $6.75, ages 6-11 $3.75).

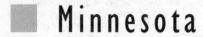

Minnesota

Minnesota is a fabulous melange of images. Folklore has it that Minnesota's 11,000 lakes were formed by the footprints of Paul Bunyan's ox, Babe. The Jolly Green Giant stands tall over the evergreen forests and 20 million acres of farmland as the Pillsbury doughboy chuckles with the captains of industry and technology. Charles Schulz's Snoopy plays with the artists of the twin cities, while Bob Dylan, Prince, and Hüsker Dü provide a soundtrack. Loons and wolves fill Lake Superior's North Shore and inland forests with their own music while the spirit of the Native American presides over them. Tonka trucks drive slowly but surely over the Mesabi Iron Range. Together, the natural and cultural beauty create the rhapsody of Minnesota.

PRACTICAL INFORMATION

Capital: St. Paul.
Minnesota Office of Tourism, 100 Metro Sq., 121 7th Pl. E., St. Paul 55101-2112 (296-5029 or 800-657-3700). Open Mon.-Fri. 9am-4:30pm.
Time Zone: Central (1 hr. behind Eastern). **Postal Abbreviation:** MN
Sales Tax: 6.5-7%.

■■■ MINNEAPOLIS AND ST. PAUL

The Twin Cities born of the Mississippi are more fraternal than identical. St. Paul, the slightly elder of the two, began as a settlement near Fort Snelling. With the influx of settlers, this sister grew to be an important steamboat port and Minnesota's capital. Minneapolis was born across a suspension bridge as the soldiers built lumber and flour mills. The twin cities share a fondness for the arts, celebrating them with large-scale sculptures and hole-in-the-wall galleries and cafes. Theater is especially beloved here, with off-beat and relatively cheap productions abounding. The thousands of lakes within the metropolitan area, and the nightly summertime music and events in all of the cities's parks, are enough to send anyone outdoors.

PRACTICAL INFORMATION

Emergency: 911.
Visitor Information: Minneapolis Convention and Visitors Association, 1219 Marquette Ave. (348-4313). Open Mon.-Fri. 8am-5:30pm. Also in the **City Center Shopping Area,** 2nd level skyway. Open Mon.-Fri. 10am-8pm, Sat. 10am-6pm, Sun. noon-5pm. **St. Paul Convention and Visitors Bureau,** 101 Northwest Center, 55 E. 5th St. (297-6985 or 800-627-6101). Open Mon.-Fri. 8am-5pm. **Cityline** (645-6060) and **The Connection** (922-9000) are 24-hr. local event hotlines.
Airport: Twin Cities International, south of the cities, on I-494 in Bloomington (726-8100). **Airport Express** (726-6400) runs to downtown and suburban hotels, leaving from the lower level near baggage claim. Open 5am-midnight; $8 to St. Paul, $10 to Minneapolis. Take bus #35 to Minneapolis. ($1.75, $1.50 off-peak; service to the airport 6-8am and to downtown Minneapolis 3-4:45pm.) Otherwise, take bus #7 to Washington Ave. in Minneapolis, or transfer at Fort Snelling for bus #9 to downtown St. Paul. Taxis are $20 to Minneapolis, $17 to St. Paul.
Amtrak: 730 Transfer Rd. (800-872-7245), on the east bank off University Ave. S.E., between the Twin Cities. A nice station, but a fair distance from both downtowns. Take bus #7. Open daily 6am-12:30am.
Greyhound: In **Minneapolis,** 29 9th St. at 1st Ave. N. (371-3325), 1 block northwest of Hennepin Ave. Very convenient. Open 24 hrs. with security. In **St. Paul,**

7th St. at St. Peter (222-0509), 3 blocks east of the Civic Center in a somewhat unsafe area of town. Open daily 5:45am-8:15pm.

Public Transport: Metropolitan Transit Commission, 560 6th Ave. N. (349-7700). Call for information and directions. Open Mon.-Fri. 6am-11pm, Sat.-Sun. 7am-11pm. Bus service for both cities. Some buses operate 4:30am-12:45am, others shut down earlier. Fare $1.25 during the peak hours of 6-9am and 3:30-6:30pm, $1 off-peak, under 18 25¢, off-peak express 50¢ extra. #16 bus connects the 2 downtowns (50-min.); the #94 freeway express bus is much faster (25-30 min.). **University of Minnesota Bus,** (625-9000). Buses run 7am-9pm. Free for students to campus locations. Off-campus routes $1.80, off-peak $1.30.

Car Rental: Affordable Rent-A-Car, 6405 Cedar Ave. S. (861-7545), Minneapolis, near the airport. Used cars from $25 per day with 150 free mi., weekly from $149. Open Mon.-Fri. 9am-6pm, Sat. 11am-3pm. Must be 23 with major credit card. **Thrifty Car Rental,** 160 E. 5th St. (227-7690), $38 with 200 free mi., 20¢ each additional mi., $159 per week with 1000 free mi. Must be 21 with major credit card; $5 surcharge per day if under 25.

Taxi: Yellow Taxi (824-4444) in Minneapolis. **Yellow Cab** (222-4433) in St. Paul. Base rate $1.75, $1.30 per mi.

Help Lines: Crime Victim Center, 822 S. 3rd St., St. Paul (340-5400). Open 24 hrs. **Rape/Sexual Assault Line,** 825-4357. **Gay-Lesbian Helpline,** 822-8661 or 800-800-0907; open Mon.-Fri. noon-midnight, Sat. 4pm-midnight. **Gay-Lesbian Information Line,** 822-0127.

Post Office: In Minneapolis, 1st St. and Marquette Ave. (349-4957), next to the Mississippi River. General Delivery open Mon.-Fri. 8am-5pm, Sat. 9am-noon. **ZIP code:** 55401. In **St. Paul,** 180 E. Kellogg Blvd. (293-3011). General Delivery open Mon.-Fri. 6am-6pm, Sat. 6am-8:30am. **ZIP code:** 55101.

Area Code: 612.

Many downtown streets in both cities parallel the curving Mississippi, so it is wise to acquire a good street map. Remember that Minneapolis is west of St. Paul. **I-94** connects the two cities' downtowns. **I-35** (north-south) splits in the Twin Cities with **I-35W** serving Minneapolis and **I-35E** serving St. Paul. In Minneapolis, the streets run east-west and avenues run north-south. **Hennepin Avenue** is an important line which crosses the Mississippi and goes through downtown, curving **south** towards uptown. **Lake St.** also traverses the city, crossing the Mississippi and becoming **Marshall St.** From Marshall, it is easy to get to **Cleveland** and **Snelling Avenue,** major **north-south** thoroughfares. **Grand Avenue** is the major east-west road. A second-story tunnel system called **Skywalks** connects more than ten square blocks of buildings in each downtown area, protecting workers from the winter cold.

ACCOMMODATIONS AND CAMPING

While cheap hotels abound in the Twin Cities, most are of dubious cleanliness and safety. The convention and visitors bureaus have useful lists of **B&Bs.** The **University of Minnesota Housing Office** (624-2994; see Practical Information), has a list of rooms around the city that rent on a daily ($13-45) or weekly basis. The closest state park camping is in the **Hennepin Parks** system, 25 miles outside the cities.

College of St. Catherine, Caecilian Hall (HI-AYH), 2004 Randolph Ave. (690-6604), St. Paul. Take St. Paul bus #7 or 14, or call for directions. 60 simple and quiet dorm rooms near the river in a nice and generally safe neighborhood. Shared bath, kitchenette. Free local calls. Singles $14. Doubles $26. Triples $33. Max. stay 2 weeks. Open June to mid-Aug.

City of Lakes International House, 2400 Stevens Ave. S. (871-3210). Nice, large house in an awesome location across from the Institute of Arts. No curfew, afternoon check-out, and free local calls. $14, singles $22 (only 2 available).

Kaz's Home Hostel (822-8286), in South Minneapolis. Call for directions. 1 room with 2 beds. Check-in 5-9pm. Curfew 11pm, check-out 9am. Max. stay 3 nights. $10. Reservations absolutely required.

THE GREAT LAKES

Evelo's Bed and Breakfast, 2301 Bryant Ave. (374-9656), in South Minneapolis. A 15-min. walk from uptown; take bus #17 from downtown. Three comfortable rooms with elegant wallpaper and furnishings in a beautiful house filled with Victorian artifacts. Friendly owners. Singles $40. Doubles $50. Reservations required.

Town and Country Campground, 12630 Boone Ave. S. (445-1756), 15 mi. south of downtown Minneapolis. From I-35W., go west on Rte. 13 to Rte. 101 for ½ mi., then left onto Boone Ave. 65 sites. Well-maintained, with laundry and pool; quiet, but clearly close to an urban area. Sites $12.50 for 2, with electricity $16.50, full hookup $17.50. Each additional person $1.

Minneapolis Northwest I-94 KOA (420-2255), on Rte. 101 west of I-94 exit 213, 15 mi. north of Minneapolis. Pool, sauna, and showers. Sites for 2 $15.50, with water and electricity $18.50. Each additional person $2, $1 for kids.

FOOD

The Twin Cities's love of music and art carries over to their culinary choices—small cafés with nightly music and poetry readings are very popular. Enjoy a thick slice of cake and any variation of mocha, or just sit and people watch. **Uptown** Minneapolis has plenty of funky and eclectic restaurants and bars, without high prices. The **Warehouse District,** near downtown Minneapolis, and **Victoria Crossing** (at Victoria and Grand St.) in St. Paul, serve the dessert crowd with pastries (a meal in themselves). **Dinkytown** and the **West Bank** cater to student appetites with many low-end, dark, and intriguing places.

Minneapolis

The Loring Café, 1624 Harmon Pl. (332-1617), next to Loring Park and the Loring Theater. A truly beautiful café with extraordinary pasta and pizza ($8-11), and desserts ($3-5). A great place for dinner, or just for drinks or coffee. A good bar, too, with live music and no cover. Open Sun.-Thurs. 11am-11pm, Fri.-Sat. 11am-2am.

Annie's Parlor, 313 14th Ave. S.E. (379-0744), in Dinkytown; 406 Cedar Ave. (339-6207), West Bank; and 2916 Hennepin Ave. (825-4455), uptown. Fantastic, super-filling malts ($3.50) and great hamburgers ($3.50-4.50). Open Mon.-Thurs. 11am-11pm, Fri.-Sat. 11am-12:30am, Sun. 11am-10pm.

Cafe Wyrd, 1600 W. Lake St. (827-5710). Great coffee, soups, salads, and pastries. Fun atmosphere. Open daily 7am-1am.

Lowry's, 1934 Hennepin Ave. S. (871-0806). Elegant pasta, pizza, risotto, and polenta ($8-12). Open Mon.-Thurs. 11am-10pm, Fri. 11am-11pm, Sat. 10am-11pm, Sun. 10am-9pm.

Mud Pie, 2549 Lyndale Ave. S. (872-9435), at 26th. Ask your server at this vegetarian/Mexican restaurant about their renowned veggie burger ($4.75). Excellent black cherry *kefir* ($1). Open Mon.-Thurs. 11am-10pm, Fri. 11am-11pm, Sat. 8am-11pm, Sun. 8am-10pm. Breakfast served weekends only.

Ruby's Cafe, 1614 Harmon Pl. (338-2089). Good breakfast ($1.70-5), and lunch ($2.50-5.50). Open Mon.-Sat. 7am-2pm, Sun. 8am-2pm.

St. Paul

Café Latté, 850 Grand Ave. (224-5687), near Victoria Crossing. Absolutely fabulously delicious and enormous chocolate cakes $2.25. *The Editor's Pick.* Try a steaming milk drink called a Hot Moo ($1.65); the Swedish Hot Moo with cinnamon, cardamom, and maple syrup is especially good. Lines usually long. Open Mon.-Thurs. 10am-11pm, Fri. 10am-midnight, Sat. 9am-midnight, Sun. 9am-10pm.

Ciatti's, 850 Grand Ave. (292-9942). Popular Italian restaurant next to Café Latté. Chicken parmesan $11. Open Mon.-Thur. 11am-10pm, Fri.-Sat. 11am-11pm, Sun. 10am-2pm and 2:30-10pm.

Table of Contents and **Hungry Mind Bookstore,** 1648 Grand Ave. (699-6595). An awesome bookstore attached to this classy cafe. Wafer crust pizza $4.50. Regular poetry readings. Open Mon.-Thurs. 9am-10pm, Fri.-Sat. 9am-11:30pm, Sun. 10am-6pm.

Mickey's Dining Car, 36 W. 7th St. (222-5633), kitty-corner to the Greyhound station. Small, cheap, and convenient; a great spot for wee-hour munchie runs. Steak and eggs from $5, lunch and dinner from $3. Open 24 hrs.

St. Paul Farmers Market, 5th St. (227-6856), at Wall Market downtown. Fresh produce and baked goods. Call to verify hours. Open Sat. 6am-1pm and May-Oct. Sun. 8am-1pm.

SIGHTS

Minneapolis

Situated in the land of 10,000 lakes, Minneapolis boasts a few of its own. Ringed by stately mansions, **Lake of the Isles,** off Franklin Ave., about 1½ mile from downtown, is an excellent place to meet Canadian geese. **Lake Calhoun,** on the west end of Lake St. south of Lake of the Isles, is a hectic social and recreational hotspot. Rent skates and rollerblades at **Rolling Soles,** 1700 W. Lake St. (823-5711; skates $3 per hr., $7.50 per day; blades $5 per hr., $10 per day; open Mon.-Fri. 10am-9pm, Sat.-Sun. 9am-9pm, weather permitting). The **Minneapolis Park and Recreation Board** (661-4875) rents canoes ($5 per hr.) at the northeast corner of Lake Calhoun. Situated in a more residential neighborhood, **Lake Harriet** has a tiny paddleboat and a stage with occasional free concerts. The city provides 28 miles of trails along these lakes for cycling, roller skating, roller blading, jogging, or strolling on a sunny afternoon. Take bus #28 to all three lakes.

Minneapolis is an art hub, home to two of the country's premiere art museums. The **Minneapolis Institute of Arts,** 2400 3rd Ave. S (870-3131; take bus #9) contains an outstanding collection of international art including the world-famous *Doryphoros*, a Roman sculpture of a perfectly proportioned man from the first century (free; open Tues.–Sat. 10am-5pm, Thurs. until 9pm, and Sun. noon-5pm). The **Walker Art Center,** 725 Vineland Place (375-7622), a few blocks from downtown, draws thousands with daring exhibits of Lichtenstein and Warhol. (Open Tues.-Sat. 10am-8pm, Sun. 11am-5pm. $3, ages 12-18 and students with ID $2, seniors free. Free on Thurs.) Next to the Walker is the beautiful **Minneapolis Sculpture Garden.** An attempt to bring art to the masses, the Garden displays dozens of sculptures and a fountain in a maze of landscaped trees and flowers. **St. Anthony Falls and Upper Locks,** 1 Portland Ave. (333-5336), downtown, has a free observation deck that overlooks the Mississippi River (open April-Nov. daily 9am-10pm). Several miles downstream, Minnehaha Park provides a view of **Minnehaha Falls,** immortalized in Longfellow's *Song of Hiawatha* (take bus #7 from Hennepin Ave. downtown).

Mall of America, about 10 miles outside Minneapolis, 60 E. Broadway, Bloomington (883-8800), is the largest mall in the U.S. With almost 2 miles of stores, this monument to the American consumer is mind-blowing and one of the most active tourist spots in the U.S. Normally, malls are not tourist fare, but have you ever seen one with an indoor roller coaster and carousel? Take I-35E south to I-494W to the 24th Ave. exit and follow signs. (Open Mon.-Sat. 10am-9:30pm, Sun. 11am-7pm.)

St. Paul

The capital city of Minnesota boasts many curious architectural sites. West of downtown, Summit Avenue reaches from the Mississippi to the capitol, displaying the nation's longest continuous stretch of Victorian homes, most built with railroad money. See the home of an old railroad magnate at the **James J. Hill House,** 240 Summit Ave. (297-2555; tours Wed.-Sat. 10am-3:30pm, reservations recommended; $3, children $1). Also look for the Governor's Mansion and a former home of American novelist F. Scott Fitzgerald. Overlooking the capitol on Summit Ave. stands **St. Paul's Cathedral,** 239 Selby Ave. (228-1766), a scaled-down version of St. Peter's in Rome (open Thurs.-Tues. 7:30am-5:45pm). Battle school fieldtrips to see the golden horses atop the ornate **State Capitol** (296-3962 or 297-1503) at Cedar and Aurora St. (Open Mon.-Fri. 9am-5pm, Sat. 10am-4pm, Sun. 1-4pm. Tours on the hour Mon.-Fri. 9am-4pm, Sat. 10am-3pm, Sun. 1-3pm.) The nearby **Minnesota History Cen-**

ter, 345 Kellogg Blvd. W. (296-1430), an organization older than the state itself, houses a café and gift shop, as well as three exhibit galleries on Minnesota history (open Tues.-Sat. 10am-5pm, Thur. until 9pm, Sun. noon-5pm; free). The society also recreates life in the fur trapping era at **Fort Snelling,** Rte. 5 and 55 (725-2413). At the site of the original French settlement, this park teems with costumed role-playing artisans and guides (open Mon.-Sat. 10am-5pm, Sun. noon-5pm. $3, under 16 $1). Housing the **Minnesota Museum of Art** is the historic **Landmark Center,** 75 W. 5th St. (292-3225), a grandly restored 1894 Federal Court building replete with towers and turrets, a collection of pianos, art exhibits, a concert hall, and four restored courtrooms. (Open Mon.-Wed. and Fri. 8am-5pm, Thurs. 8am-8pm, Sat. 10am-5pm, Sun. 1-5pm. Free. Tours Thurs. 11am and Sun. 2pm.) The Minnesota Museum of Art houses other collections in the **Jemne Building** at St. Peter and Kellogg Blvd. The **Science Museum,** 30 E. 10th St. (221-9454), near Exchange and Wabasha St. has an interesting paleontology exhibit. The **McKnight-3M Omnitheater** (221-9400) inside presents mind-swelling gigantic films. (Museum open Mon.-Fri. 9:30am-9pm, Sat. 9am-9pm, Sun. 10am-9pm. Exhibit-only tickets $5.50, seniors and under 13 $4.50; with theater $6.50, seniors and children $5.50.)

ENTERTAINMENT

With more theaters per capita than any U.S. city outside New York, the Twin Cities' theater scene shines. The brightest star in this constellation is the **Guthrie Theater,** 725 Vineland Pl. (377-2224), just off Hennepin Ave. in Minneapolis, adjacent to the Walker Art Center. The Guthrie Repertory Company performs here from June to March. (Box office open Mon.-Sat. 9am-8pm, Sun. 11am-7pm. Tickets $9-38, rush tickets 10 min. before show $8.)

The **Children's Theater Company,** 3rd Ave. at 24th S. (874-0400), by the Minneapolis Institute of Arts, stages classics and innovative productions for all ages between September and June. (Box office open Mon.-Sat. 9am-5pm, Sun. noon-5pm. Tickets $13.50-22, seniors, students, and kids $9-16. Rush tickets 15 min. before performance $8.)

In July and early August, **Orchestra Hall,** 1111 Nicollet Mall (371-5656) in downtown Minneapolis, hosts the **Sommerfest,** a month-long celebration of Viennese music performed by the **Minnesota Orchestra.** (Box office open Mon.-Sat. 10am-6pm. Tickets $10-30. Rush tickets 30 min. before show $6.75.) Don't miss the free coffee concerts at nearby **Peavey Plaza,** in Nicollet Mall.

St. Paul's glass-and-brick **Ordway Music Theater,** 345 Washington St. (224-4222), is a beautiful public space for music. The **St. Paul Chamber Orchestra,** the **Schubert Club,** and the **Minnesota Opera Company** all perform here. (Box office open Mon.-Sat. 10am-9pm. Tickets $10-50.) Some other notable players are the **Theatre de la jeune lune** ("Theater of the young moon"), which performs (in English) at the **Loring Playhouse,** 1645 Hennepin Ave. (333-6200; tickets $8-17), and the **Penumbra Theatre Company,** 270 N. Kent St., St. Paul (224-3180), Minnesota's only professional African-American theater company, which performs many early plays of former St. Paul resident August Wilson.

The Twin Cities are filled with parks. Almost all feature free summertime evening concerts. For information on dates and locations, check at one of the visitors centers. The **Harriet Bandshell** (348-7275) hatches rock, blues, jazz, and high school bands and choirs throughout the summer (take bus #28). Also popular are **Loring Park's** Monday evening events (348-8226), featuring free local bands, followed by vintage films, on the hill toward the north edge. Take bus #1, 4, 6, or 28 going south. The **Rooftop Cinema** (824-1240) at Calhoun Square, Lake and Hennepin, shows classic films on the side of a building every Wed. night at dusk. (Free.)

A giggle of comedy and improvisational clubs make the Twin Cities a downright hilarious place to visit. Dudley Riggs's **Brave New Workshop,** 2605 Hennepin Ave. (332-6620), stages consistently good musical comedy shows in an intimate club. (Box office open Thurs.-Sun. Call for performance times. Tickets $12-15.) The

Comedy Gallery, 219 Main St., S.E., Minneapolis, and Galtier Plaza, 175 E. 5th St., St. Paul (331-5653; tickets $5) features stand-up comedians.

Minnesota-bred artists from all genres have emerged from local status to make their mark on international stages. The man formerly known as **Prince** still casts the greatest shadow; his state-of-the-art **Paisley Park** studio complex outside the city draws bands from all over to the Great White North. The post-punk scene thrives in the Land of 10,000 Aches: Soul Asylum, and Hüsker Dü, as well as the best bar band in the world, The Replacements, rocked here before it all went big (or bad).

For great live music with high and low-profile bands, try the **Uptown Bar and Café,** 3018 Hennepin (823-4719; open 8am-1am. Shows at 10:30pm. Weekend cover varies. For band information, call 823-5704.) The **400 Bar,** 4th St. (332-2903), at Cedar Ave. on the West Bank, is a great place, featuring live music nightly on a minuscule stage. (Open daily noon-1am. Occasional $2 cover.) Prince's old court— **First Avenue and 7th St. Entry,** 701 N. First Ave., Minneapolis (332-1775), rocks with live music several nights a week; even Prince occasionally turns up. (Open Mon.-Sat. 8pm-1am; cover $1-5, for concerts $7-18.) The Purple One's latest haunt is the **Glam Slam,** 110 N. 5th St., Minneapolis (338-3383; has live music Mondays, cover $3-10; open Mon.-Sat. 8pm-1am). **St. Anthony Main,** 1 Main St., is an enclosed area with multiple bars making bar-hopping quite easy. Most importantly, these hangouts are country music places and hop at night. **The Gay 90s,** Hennepin Ave. (333-7755), at 4th St., is a popular gay nightspot (open daily 8pm-3am). The Twin Cities card hard, even for cigarettes, so carry your ID with you. After 1am, many clubs open their doors to the 18+ crowd; call clubs for specifics.

For general information on the local music scene and other events, pick up the free *City Pages* or *Twin Cities Reader* available throughout the cities. In January, the 10-day **St. Paul Winter Carnival,** near the state capitol, cures cabin fever with ice sculptures, ice fishing, parades, and skating contests. On the Fourth of July, St. Paul celebrates **Taste of Minnesota** on the Capitol Mall. Following this, the nine-day **Minneapolis Aquatennial** begins, with concerts, parades, art exhibits, and kids dripping sno-cones on their shirts. (Call **The Connection,** 922-9000, for information on all of these events.) During late August and early September, spend a day at the **Minnesota State Fair,** at Snelling and Como, or the **Renaissance Festival** (445-7361) in Shakopee, MN. The **Minnesota Zoo** (432-9000; go south on 35E to 77S) houses a wide variety of well-maintained habitats. (Open Mon.-Sat. 10am-6pm, Sun. 9am-8pm; off-season daily 10am-4pm. $8, seniors $5, ages 3-12 $4.50.) **Paddleford Boats** (227-1100) lets you explore the mighty Mississippi River on a paddle boat ($8.50, seniors $7.50, children $6.50).

The **Hubert H. Humphrey Metrodome,** 501 Chicago Ave. S. (332-0386), in downtown Minneapolis, houses the Minnesota **Twins,** the Twin Cities' baseball team, and the Minnesota **Vikings,** the resident football team. The **Timberwolves** kindle basketball hardwood at the **Target Center,** 600 1st Ave. (673-0900).

■■■ DULUTH

With over 49 mi. of dock line, Duluth claims the crown as King of the Great Lake ports. Although the area's population has declined in recent decades, and many local mines have closed, Duluth still ships out over one billion dollars worth of iron ore annually. Increasingly, however, Duluth is projecting itself as a tourist gateway to the northern wilderness. Minnesota's "refrigerated city," known for its unbelievably cold weather and pea-soup fog, is a great place to gear up for fishing, camping, or driving excursions into northwestern Minnesota. It retains an honest, raw, unpredictable quality born of its harsh climate.

Practical Information The **Convention and Visitors Bureau,** at Endion Station, 100 Lake Place Dr. (722-4011) in Canal Park (open Mon.-Fri. 9am-4:30pm), and the **Summer Visitors Center** (722-6024) on the waterfront at Harbor Dr. (open mid-May to mid-June and Labor Day to mid-Oct. Mon.-Fri. 10am-3pm, Sat.-Sun.

THE GREAT LAKES

10am-5pm; mid-June to Labor Day, daily 8:30am-8pm) have an ample supply of brochures and Duluth maps. **Greyhound,** 2212 W. Superior (722-5591; 722-6193 for recorded information), runs 2 mi. west of downtown. Take "Piedmont" bus (#9) from downtown. (Ticket office open daily 7am-5pm.) The **Duluth Transit Authority,** 2402 W. Michigan St. (722-7283), runs buses throughout the city. (Fare during peak hours $1, students 75¢; off-peak 50¢.) **Port Town Trolley** (722-7283) serves the downtown area, canal park, and the waterfront and runs Memorial Day to Labor Day daily from 11am-7pm, and weekends in September (50¢). Help lines include a **24-hour Sexual Assault Crisis Line** (726-1931) and **Gay/Lesbian Information** (722-4903). Duluth's **post office:** 2800 W. Michigan St. (723-2590), six blocks west of the Greyhound station (open Mon.-Fri. 8am-4:30pm, Sat. 10am-12:30pm); **ZIP code:** 55806; **area code:** 218.

Accommodations and Camping Duluth motels, dependent for their livelihood on the summer migration of North Shore-bound tourists, raise their prices and are booked early during the warm months; call as far ahead as possible. The **College of St. Scholastica,** 1200 Kenwood Ave. (723-6396, ask for the housing director), has large, quiet dorm rooms with phones, kitchen access, and laundry, available for stays early June to mid-August ($19). Group rates and week-long apartment rentals are available. Reservations are essential. The **Willard Munger Inn,** 7408 Grand Ave. (624-4814 or 800-982-2453), at the base of Sprint Mountain across from the zoo, offers clean, comfortable rooms (singles $30-41, doubles $39-49) just off the Willard Munger State Trail. Bikes and rollerblades are rented at the inn for use on the trail. Some relatively reasonable motels lie on **London Road,** west of downtown; the **Chalet Motel,** 1801 London Rd. (728-4238 or 800-235-2957), has singles for $29-41, doubles for $39-59 (depending on the season). **Jay Cooke State Park** (384-4610), southwest of Duluth off exit 242 of I-35, has 80 campsites (21 with electricity) in a pretty setting near the dramatic St. Louis River valley. (Open daily 9am-9pm. July-Sept. $12, with electricity $14.50; Oct.-June, $10/$12.50. Vehicle permit $4.) **Spirit Mountain,** 9500 Spirit Mountain Pl. (628-2891 or 800-642-6377), near the ski resort of the same name, is 10 mi. south on I-35 (exit 249). (Sites $12, with electricity $15, with electricity and water $17.) **Buffalo Valley** (624-9901), exit 245 off I-35 South, has sites with showers and bathrooms only 15 mi. from Duluth. (Open June-Aug. 11am-1am; off-season 3pm-1am. Sites $8, electricity and water $14.)

Food The restored **Fitger's Brewery Complex,** 600 E. Superior St. (722-8826 or 800-726-2982), and the **Canal Park** region south from downtown along **Lake Avenue,** have plenty of pleasant eateries. **Sir Benedict's Tavern on the Lake,** 805 E. Superior St. (728-1192), occupies a cottage overlooking the lake, and serves soups ($1.65-2.50) and sandwiches ($3-4.50) with an English flair. Try the vegetarian Sir Melt or the British Dip. A wide variety of imported and microbrewery beer is also available ($2-3). Those under 21 are not admitted. (Live music Wed. and sometimes on weekends are free of cover.; open Sun. 11am-11pm, Mon.-Tues. and Sat. 11am-midnight, Wed.-Fri. 11am-12:20am; winter Sun. 11am-10pm, Mon.-Tues. 11am-11pm, Wed.-Sat. 11am-midnight.) The **Blue Note Café,** 357 Canal Park Dr. (727-6549), creates delicious sandwiches ($4-5) in a moody coffeehouse setting. Live music plays Wednesday to Saturday from 8-11pm during summer, Wednesday 6-8pm and Friday to Saturday 8-11pm during winter. (Open for food Mon.-Thurs. 9am-9pm, Fri.-Sat. 9am-11pm, Sun. 9am-6pm; winter Mon.-Thurs. 9am-6pm, Fri.-Sat. 9am-11pm, Sun. 9am-5pm.) **Grandma's,** 522 Lake Avenue S. (727-4192), serves large portions. Dante's Inferno ($6.45) and the Original Godfather ($5.95) are popular sandwiches. A free sand volleyball court, which becomes an ice-hockey rink in winter, is available for post-dining activity. Those under 21 must be accompanied by an adult. **Kegler's Bar & Grill,** 601 W. Superior St. (722-0671), in Incline Station, offers food like taco pizza ($5.95) and fresh pressure-fried chicken ($3.95), and even has a 24-lane bowling alley. (Open daily 7am-11pm. Bowling $2.50, pool tables 75¢.)

Sights The best thing about Duluth is its proximity to majestic **Lake Superior.** Visitors should head to the **Waterfront Canal Park** to see the big ships go by. The **Boatwatcher's Hotline** (722-6489) has up-to-the-minute information on ship movements in the area. The unique **Aerial Lift Bridge** climbs 138 ft. in 55 seconds to allow vessels to pass to and from the world's largest inland harbor. Crossing the bridge takes you to **Park Point,** where sandy beaches provide excellent swimming areas. Within **Canal Park,** the **Marine Museum** (727-2497), run by the U.S. Army Corps of Engineers, features extensive exhibits on commercial shipping in Lake Superior. (Open April to mid-June Mon.-Fri. 10am-4:30pm, Fri.-Sat. until 6pm; mid-June to mid-Sept. daily 10am-9pm; mid-Sept. to mid-Dec. Mon.-Fri. 10am-4:30pm; mid-Dec to March Fri.-Sun. 10am-4:30pm.) Throughout the park, international sculpture and art line the paths. Pick up a free self-guided walking tour brochure at any information center. Farther west on the waterfront, **Bayfront Park** hosts many events and festivals, including the **International Folk Festival** (722-7425) on the first Saturday in August, and the **Bayfront Blues Festival** in mid-August.

The **Ore Docks Observation Platform,** part of the Duluth, Messabe, and Iron Range Railway Co., extends out into the harbor, allowing for outstanding views of the shiploading process and the harbor itself. Linking West Duluth to Jay Cooke State Park is the **Willard Munger State Trail,** an excellent 14-mi., paved bike trail providing a scenic, traffic-free riding area for those without motors. Rising high above this shoreline (approximately 600 ft.), the 30-mi. **Skyline Drive** affords scenic views of the city and harbor. At **Hawk Ridge,** 4 mi. north of downtown off Skyline Blvd., perches a birdwatcher's paradise. In order to avoid flying over open water, hawks veer their migration over Duluth; in September and October they fly in flocks past this bluff. **Enger Tower,** 18th Ave. W. on Skyline Parkway, sits on the highest land in Duluth. The Japanese flower gardens make a beautiful picnic area.

The **Lake Superior Zoo,** 7210 Fremont St. (723-3747), off Grand Ave. (Hwy. 23) at 71st Ave. W., boasts polar bears, leopards, and the usual lions and tigers. If you're lucky the porcupines will show off and climb trees for you. (Open April-Sept. daily 9am-6pm; Oct.-March 9am-4pm. $1, ages 4-11 75¢.)

For indoor entertainment, visit **The Depot,** 506 W. Michigan St. (727-8025), in the old Amtrak station. The several museums located there include the **Lake Superior Museum of Transportation,** featuring antique locomotives restored to shining splendor by retired railway workers. (Open May to mid-Oct. daily 10am-5pm; mid-Oct. to April Mon.-Sat. 10am-5pm, Sun. 1-5pm. $5 includes all museums, families $15, ages 3-11 $3.) The Depot also is home to four preforming arts organizations, including the **Duluth-Superior Symphony Orchestra** (727-7429; tickets $14.50-20; student rush tickets are available for $6.50). The **Tweed Museum of Art** (726-8222), at the University of Minnesota-Duluth, presents over 40 changing exhibits annually (open Tues. 9am-8pm, Wed.-Fri. 9am-4:30pm, Sat.-Sun. 1-5pm). **Glensheen,** 3300 London Rd. (724-8864), north towards the outskirts, is a 39-room neo-Jacobean mansion; one way to really annoy the tour guides is to ask where the double-murder, which apparently occurred in the house during the early 1970s, actually took place. (Hours vary. $7, seniors $5.50, under 12 $3.50. Tours of grounds only $3. Make reservations for summer visits up to 2 weeks in advance.)

■■■ VOYAGEURS NATIONAL PARK

Voyageurs is the only National Park accessible almost solely by boat. Named for the daring, knowledgable French-Canadian fur traders who once traversed this area, Voyageurs invites voyagers to leave the automobile-dominated world behind and push off into the this vast network of waterways. Preservation efforts have kept the area much as it was in the late 18th century, and wolves, bear, deer, and moose roam freely. While some hiking trails exist, boats and canoes are the predominant means for transportation within the park. In the winter, when ice freezes to more than 1½ft. thick, it is frequently possible to drive through plowed parts of the park. Many fish in these waters contain mercury and must be specially cleaned before eating. Drinking water should be boiled for two min. before consumption. Lyme-disease-bearing ticks have been found in the area, and visitors should take precautions. For more information, see Health in the Essentials section.

The park can be accessed through **Crane Lake, Ash River,** or **Kabetogama Lake,** all of which lie east of Hwy. 53, and through **International Falls,** which lies along Hwy. 11 east. Outside the park, call **Crane Lake Visitor and Tourism Bureau** (993-2234 or 800-362-7405 Mon.-Fri. 9am-5pm), or visit the **International Falls Visitors and Convention Bureau,** 200 Fourth St. (800-325-5766; open daily 8am-5pm). Within the park, three visitors centers offer information: **Rainy Lake** (286-5258), 12 mi. east of International Falls at the end of Hwy. 11 (open mid-May to mid-Oct. daily 9am-5pm); **Ash River** (374-3221), 7 mi. west of Hwy. 53 on Hwy. 129, then 4mi. north (open mid-May to August, daily 10am-5pm); **Kabetogama Lake** (875-2111), take Hwy. 122 to Hwy. 53, then follow signs (open mid-May to Sept., daily 9am-5pm). Both Rainy Lake and Kabetogama Lake offer cruises in addition to free walks and programs. Cruise tour schedules vary and prices range from $7.50 to $32.50. For **boat information** call Rainy Lake at 286-5470, or Kabetogama at 875-2111.

Camping is abundant within the park, but most of the park is accessible only by water. Car-accessible sites can be found in state forest campgrounds, including **Wooden Frog** (757-3274), about 4 mi. from Kabetogama Visitors Center Rd. 122, and **Ash River** (757-3274), 3 mi. from the visitors center, then 2 mi. east on Hwy. 129 ($7, no showers). In International Falls, camp at the **Rocky Pine Campground** (286-3500), 9 mi. east of town ($10, with shower and toilets). Indoor accommodations can be found at the **Hilltop Motel** (283-2505 or 800-322-6671), Hwy. 53 on International Falls, where singles run $24, doubles $34, and three beds $39. In Crane Lake, sleep tight at the **Lakeview Motel,** 7533 Gold Coast Rd. (993-2398; in winter 749-3635), where basic rooms rent for $30 (May-Sept.).

Aside from the park, **International Falls** also has some interesting historical sites. The **Grand Mound History Center** (279-3332), 17 mi. west of town on Hwy. 11, is the state's largest prehistoric burial ground, supposedly dating from 2000 BC. (Open May-Aug. daily 10am-5pm. Free.) Also visit the **Smokey Bear Park,** home of the 26-ft., 82-ton giant who asks you to help fight forest fires, and a 22-ft. tall thermometer. Another little-known fact about International Falls is that it was the inspiration for Frostbite Falls, hometown of Rocky and Bullwinkle.

■■■ CHIPPEWA NATIONAL FOREST

The Norway pine forests, interspersed with lovely strands of birch, thicken as you move north into **Chippewa National Forest,** source of the Mississippi River and nesting ground to more eagles than anywhere else in the U.S. These majestic symbols of our country can be frequently viewed soaring overhead near the Mississippi River between Cass Lake and Lake Winnie (mid-March to Nov.). Nearly half of this forest is wetlands and lakes, making camping and canoeing the popular activities. Leech, Cass, and Winnibigoshish (win-nuh-buh-GAH-shish or simply "Winnie") are the largest of the lakes.

The national forest shares territory with the **Leech Lake Indian Reservation,** home of 4560 members of the Minnesota Chippewa tribe, the fourth largest tribe in the U.S. The Chippewa migrated from the Atlantic coast, through the Great Lakes, and into this area in the early 1700s, successfully pushing out the local Sioux. In the mid-1800s, the government seized most of the Chippewa's land, setting up reservations like Leech Lake.

Use the town of **Walker** on Leech Lake as a gateway to the Chippewa National Forest. Travelers, especially walkers, can find information at the **Leech Lake Area Chamber of Commerce** (547-1313 or 800-833-1118) on Rte. 371 downtown (open Mon.-Sat. 8:30am-5pm). Material on abundant, cheap outdoor activities is available just east of the Chamber of Commerce, heading away from town, at the

Forest Office (547-1044; open Mon.-Fri. 7:30am-5pm). The head forest superintendent's office is in Cass Lake (335-8600). In Walker, lodge indoors at the **Lakeview
Inn** (800-252-5073 or 547-1212), overlooking Walker Bay next to the tourist office,
where singles start at $35, doubles at $41. Camping is available at various stages of
modernization for varying fees (over 400 are free). See the forest office for information. Private campgrounds can be found in the Cass Lake region; try **Camper Landing, Inc.,** (335-9941), Country Road 92, which offers sites for $12 with showers, a
community room, and free movies. **Greyhound** (722-5591) runs from Minneapolis
to Walker (5½ hr., $21), stopping at the **Lake View Laundrette** (547-9585), 1st and
Michigan St. just east of the Chamber of Commerce. Buses leave to the cities daily at
9:20am and arrive from the cities at 3:20pm. Tickets are purchased on the bus.
Chippewa National Forest Area's **area code: 218.**

The **Headwaters of the Mississippi** trickle out of **Lake Itasca State Park,** 30 mi.
west of Walker on Rte. 200, the only place where mere mortals can wade easily
across the Mississippi. The comfortable **Mississippi Headwaters HI-AYH-Hostel**
(266-3415), located in a renovated log building, has 34 beds with some four bedrooms for families. It's open in the winter to facilitate access to the park's excellent
cross-country skiing. (Memorial-Labor Day and winter weekends $13, nonmembers
$16; rest of the year $11/14. 2-night min. stay on certain weekends; key deposit $5;
check-in daily 5-10pm , until 11pm Fri.-Sat.; check-out 10am Mon.-Fri., 1pm Sat.-Sun;
linen $2-4.) The park itself has **campgrounds** with showers. (Sites $12, with electricity $14.50. 2-day vehicle permit $4; annual permit $18.) The **Itasca State Park
Office** (266-3654), through the north entrance and down County Rd. 38, has more
info (office open daily 8am-4:30pm, park open daily 8am-10pm, ranger on call after
hours). **Bicycles** and **boats** are available from **Itasca Sports Rental** (266-3654, ext.
150) in the park. (Open May-Oct. daily 7am-9pm.)

Bemidji, famous for its life-size statue of Paul Bunyan, lumbers northeast of Lake
Itasca. The statue sits in the parking lot of the **Bemidji Chamber of Commerce,**
(751-3541 or 800-458-2223), Paul Bunyan Drive at 3rd St.; open Mon.-Fri. 9am-7pm,
Sat. 9am-5pm, Sun. noon-5pm). **Greyhound** runs from 902½ Paul Bunyan Dr. (751-
7600; open Mon.-Sat. 8am-2pm and 3-5pm, Sun. 7:45-8:15am and 12:30-1:30pm;
Duluth to Bemidji, 2½ hr., $18.30), but there is no bus from the town to the park. In
Bemidji, you can stay at the **Sunrise Lodge,** 5416 Birchmont Dr. (751-1370), where
a motel room with two double beds runs $30. Cottages, which start at $65, come
with daily use of an 18-ft. core craft boat for your fishing or relaxing pleasure.
Stoney Point Resort (335-6311 or 800-332-6311), 16 mi. east of town on Hwy. 2 in
Cass Lake, has a bunkhouse which rents for $25 and sleeps up to four people. Tent
sites are also available ($12; water, electricity, and sewer $1 each).

■■■ THE IRON RANGE

Inland from the North Shore lies the **Iron Range,** home to ore boom-towns and hills
that once fed the nation's steel mills, providing about 75% of the ore needed for the
two world wars. Now largely silent, this area, adjacent to the Superior National Forest and Boundary Waters Canoe Area Wilderness, offers natural beauty as well as an
interesting perspective on the history of technology.

Ely, Soudan, and Chisholm Serving as a launching pad both into the Boundary Waters Canoe Area Wilderness (BWCAW) and the Iron Range, Ely provides
many wilderness outfitters. Head to the **Chamber of Commerce,** 1600 E. Sheridan
St. (365-6123 or 800-777-7281), for BWCAW permits and brochures on various
guides. (Open summer Mon.-Sat. 9am-6pm, Sun. noon-4pm; winter Mon.-Fri. 9am-
5pm.) The **International Wolf Center,** 1396 Rte. 169 (365-4685), has informative
displays on history, habitat, and behaviors of these creatures. (Open July-Aug. daily
9am-7pm, May-June and Sept. to mid-Oct. daily 9am-5pm; mid-Oct. to April Tues.
and Fri.-Sat. 10am-5pm, Sun. 10am-3pm.) Also in Ely, learn about the "root beer
lady" who made between 11,000 and 12,000 bottles of the sweet beer annually, at

the **Dorothy Molter Museum,** next to the Wolf Center (365-4451; open May-Sept. daily 10am-6pm; $2, child $1). **Kring's Kabins and Kampgrounds,** (365-6637), 60 W. Lakeview Pl., Ely, has a tidy loft full of bunks for $10 per night, including linen and showers (tent sites $6, RV $10, water and electricity $1.50 each). While in town, don't miss the **Chocolate Moose,** 101 N. Central (356-6343), a favorite of locals and canoeists alike. Breakfast, served from 6-11am, draws crowds with its blueberry pancakes ($4). Friday and Saturday nights feature a BBQ with ribs ($10) and chicken ($9.25). (Open daily 6am-9pm, ice cream until 10pm.)

The **Soudan Underground Mine** (753-2245), in Soudan west of Ely on Rte. 1, was retired in the middle of digging the 27th level, a full ½-mi. below the surface. Visitors take a 60-min. tour down the 11°-from-the-vertical mineshaft and are shown the principles and techniques of underground iron mining. ($5, ages 5-12 $3, plus state park vehicle fee.) Tours Memorial Day-Labor Day every ½ hr., 9:30am-4pm, gates open until 6pm. Off-season tours scheduled by reservation only.) A little past the mine on the same road is **McKinley Park Campground** (753-5921), overlooking gorgeous Vermilion Lake (sites $7.50, electricity and water $9).

Chisholm, to the southwest on U.S. 169, is home to **Ironworld USA** (254-3321 or 800-372-6437), a mining theme park which also contains displays on the area's ethnic groups. (Open Memorial Day-Labor Day daily 10am-7pm; $6.25, seniors $5.25, ages 7-17 $4.) The **Chisholm KOA** (254-3635) camps nearby. (Open May-early Oct. Tent sites $13, with water and electricity $15, with cable TV $18.)

Hibbing, Calumet, and Grand Rapids Hometown to Bob Dylan, **Hibbing,** a few miles south of Chisholm, has made a park out of the open-pit **Hull Rust Mahoning Mine** (262-4900; open mid-May to Sept. daily 9am-7pm). Take Third Ave. E. to the north until it ends. Carless travelers in particular may wish to pay tribute at the **Greyhound Bus Origin Center,** (262-3895) 23rd St. and 5th Ave. E., which features model buses and more bus cartoons than you ever knew existed. Greyhound's puppyhood was spent here as a transport for miners in the Hibbing area. (Open mid-May to Sept. Mon.-Sat. 9am-5pm. $1, ages 6-12 50¢.) Bed down in a beautiful Tudor style B&B called **Adams House,** 201 E. 23rd St. (263-9742), which has rooms for $37. Campers can pitch their tents ($4) or park their RVs ($10) at **Forest Heights,** (263-5782) 2240 E. 25th St., Hibbing. The **Hibbing Chamber of Commerce** is at 211 East Howard St. (218-262-3895; open Mon.-Fri. 8am-5pm).

Calumet plays home to the **Hill Mine Annex State Park** (247-7215), a now-retired intact natural iron ore pit mine. An exceptional 1½-hour, tour brings visitors through the buildings and shops, all the way into the 500-ft.-deep mine, where guides who once worked this mine relive their experience for visitors. A well-spent $5 (child 5-12 $3). **Grand Rapids,** a paper mill town of 8000, houses the **Forest History Center,** 2609 Country Rd. 76 (327-4482), off Hwy. 2 west or 169 south, with informative exhibits in the Interpretive Center and a recreated turn-of-the-century logging camp. ($3, ages 6-15 $1, family max. $10. Open mid-May to mid-Oct. Mon.-Sat. 10am-5pm, Sun. noon-5pm; interpretive center and trails also open mid-Oct. to mid-May daily noon-4pm.) Grand Rapids is the hometown of Judy Garland, and celebrates this with its own Yellow Brick Road and the world's largest collection of Garland memorabilia, in the **Judy Garland Historical Center,** located in the Central School, 10 5th St. NW, (326-6431; open Mon.-Sat. 10am-5pm, plus Sun. 11am-4pm, between Memorial Day and Labor Day), and a **Judy Garland Festival** (326-6431) every June around her birthday on the 10th.

Motel Americana, 1915 Hwy. 2 west (326-0369 or 800-533-5148), is the cheapest, most convenient indoor lodging (singles $25, doubles $29). The **Prairie Lake Campground** (326-8486), 400 Wabana Rd., 6½ mi. north of Grand Rapids on Rte. 38 has a nice, shady waterfront location with showers, flush toilets, and canoe/paddleboat rentals. (Tent sites $8.75, RV with electricity $11.75, add $1 each for water and sewer, full hookup at 16 of 40 sites $15.75.) To get to the area, take **Triangle Bus Lines** from Duluth ($12.35) and Minneapolis ($29) to the **Redding Bus Depot,** 21 E. Forth St. (326-37226; open daily 9am-5pm). Iron Range's **area code: 218.**

■■■ LAKE SUPERIOR NORTH SHORE

The North Shore begins with the majestic **Sawtooth Mountains** just north of Duluth and extends 150 wild and woody miles to Canada. This stretch, defined by **Rte. 61 (North Shore Drive),** encompasses virtually all of Minnesota's Superior lakeshore and supports bear, moose, and the largest U.S. wolf range in the lower 48 states. Each break in the trees lets the driver catch glimpses of Lake Superior, inviting exclamations that the lake is aptly named. Summer brings a human tide to the area, as flocks of tourists drawn by the cool and breezy weather migrate north to fish, camp, hike, and canoe. Beautiful beaches do exist, but Superior's waters remain brisk year-round, discouraging even arctic-loving swimmers. Bring warm clothes, since even summer temperatures can drop into the low 40s° at night.

Most towns along the North Shore of the lake have small information centers, but visitors should take note of a couple of the larger ones. The **Gunflint Ranger Station** (387-2451; open summer daily 6am-6pm), ¼ mi. south of town, offers information on Superior National Forest (a 3-million-acre wilderness including 2000 lakes) and issues permits for individual ports of entry into the **Boundary Waters Canoe Area Wilderness (BWCAW),** a unique area including over two million acres of forests and 1100 lakes. For info about the area, go to the **Lake County Information Center,** (218-834-4005 or 800-554-2116), 8 Hwy. 61 east, Two Harbors (open mid-May to mid-October. Mon.-Thurs. 10am-6pm, Fri.-Sat. 10am-8pm, Sun. noon-4pm), or the **Arrowhead Visitors Information Center** (387-2524), Broadway and 1st Ave. (Open summer Mon.-Sat. 8:30am-7pm, Sun. 11am-7pm. Call for winter hours.).

There are no roads, phones, electricity, or private dwellings here; motorized vehicle access is limited. Permits are required to enter the BWCAW from May to September. **Grand Marais** serves as the hub of North Shore activity. The 60 mi. **Gunflint Trail,** now widened into an auto road, begins in Grand Marais and continues northwest into the BWCAW. **Happy Trails** runs one bus per day up the shore, leaving from the **Duluth Greyhound Station,** 2122 W. Superior St. (722-5591; to Grand Marais $17.50; open daily 7am-9pm). North Shore's **area code: 218.**

Reward yourself at the end of the trail with a stay in the well-kept cabins at **"Spirit of the Land" Island HI-AYH Hostel** (388-2241 or 800-454-2922), on an island in Seagull Lake. The hostel is run by **Wilderness Canoe Base,** which leds canoe trips and summer island camps for various groups. Call from Grand Marais to arrange a boat pick-up. (Mon.-Thurs. nights $13, Fri.-Sun. nights $15, nonmembers $2 extra. Meals $4-6. Showers $2. Closed Nov. and April.) The **Cobblestone Cabins** (663-7957), off Hwy. 61 in Tofte, offer pine-paneled cabins that sleep from One-12 people ($35-80). A cobblestone beach and woodburning sauna are available; some cabins have cooking facilities. The elegant **Naniboujou Lodge** (387-2688), 15 mi. east of Grand Marais on Rte. 61, has rooms with shared baths for summer/fall family rates ($45, doubles $60).

The **South of the Border Café** (387-1505), 4 W. Hwy. 61, Grand Marais, is cheap and popular with fishermen. Grand Marais' specialty bluefin herring sandwich is $2.75. (Open daily 4am-2pm, Sept. to mid-May 5am-2pm.)

THE GREAT LAKES

THE GREAT PLAINS

Between the big cities of the East and West Coast, the Rocky Mountains and the Great Lakes, lies the Heartland of the United States—a vast land of prairies and farms, less developed and less appreciated than the rest of the country. It is from these Great Plains, or the "Bread Basket," that American farmers feed the country and much of the world. Nearly 200 years ago, a newborn nation stretched westward across the Mississippi into what was then the Louisiana Territory, bought from the French at just 2¢ an acre! Here was forged the mythic American frontier. This is the stomping ground of Huckleberry Finn, Buffalo Bill, Laura Ingalls Wilder, and Chief Crazy Horse—the legend, the cowboy, the pioneer farmer, and the native.

Once ruled by the Cheyenne, Sioux, Kansas, Pawnee, Arapaho, Crow and other Native Americans who enjoyed this fertile territory, the Homestead Act of 1862, brought land-hungry settlers to the Great Plains. No longer seen as simply a huge, flat barrier to be crossed en route to the fertile valleys of the West Coast, the states west of the Mississippi River were now viewed as a main prize. The new law and the transcontinental railroad brought bloody struggles over land rights and later over slavery. But it also began an economic boom that did not bust until poor land management and a drought during the Great Depression of the 1930s turned the region into a devastated Dust Bowl. Modern farming techniques have since tamed the soil, and the region now produces most of the nation's grain and livestock; cities such as Des Moines, Omaha, and Dodge City thrive once more on the trading of farm commodities.

The land still rules here; some of the most staggering sights in the region, and the country, are those created without the touch of a human hand—the Badlands of the Dakotas, the prairies of North Dakota, the vast caverns of Missouri, the rolling hills of Iowa, the Willa Cather Memorial Prairie in Nebraska, and the Black Hills majestically rising to mark the transition from plains to mountains. Others overwhelm the visitor with the combined effort of earth and man—Mount Rushmore and the insanely gigantic Crazy Horse National Monument. The great Missouri and Mississippi Rivers trace their way through small town America—alive and thriving in the Plains. And covering the area, the "amber waves of grain" quietly reign as perhaps the greatest of all symbols of America.

North Dakota

Although long occupied by the Dakota Sioux, North Dakota was sold to the U.S. in 1803 as part of the Louisiana Purchase. Even after joining the Union in 1889, North Dakota and most of its windswept terrain remained a mystery to both foreign and domestic travelers. Those who do visit often pass like wildfire through the eastern prairie to the "badlands," the pock-marked buttes that dominate the western half of the state. Blessed solitude rewards those who savor the tranquil expanses of farmland before moving on to the tourist-filled western towns.

PRACTICAL INFORMATION

Capital: Bismarck.
Tourism Promotion Division, Liberty Memorial Bldg., Capitol Grounds, Bismarck 58505 (224-2525; 800-437-2077 outside ND). **Parks and Recreation Department,** 1424 W. Century Ave. #202, Bismarck 58502 (221-5357). Both open Mon.-Fri. 8am-5pm.

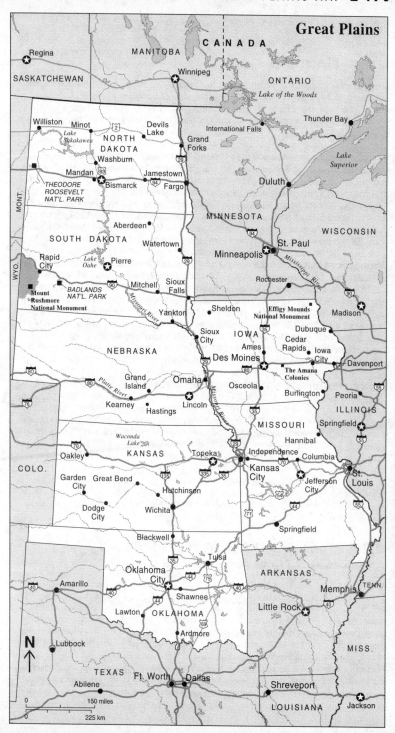

Great Plains

Time Zones: Central and Mountain. **Postal Abbreviation:** ND
Sales tax: 6%.

■■■ FARGO

Originally the hub of the North Pacific Railroad in the 1870s, Fargo is now the largest city in North Dakota, and the largest urban area between Minneapolis and Spokane. Much of the city's economy comes from farming, but Fargo is also a happening college town—home to the University of North Dakota, Concordia, and nearby Moorhead State.

Practical Information Fargo's **Main Street** runs east-west and intersects I-29, **University Ave.**, and **Broadway.** The **Fargo-Moorhead Convention and Visitors Bureau,** 2001 44th St. SW (282-3653 or 800-235-7654) is open daily 7am-9pm, Sept.-April daily 8am-6pm. **Amtrak** chugs at 402 4th St. N (232-2197; open daily 11:30am-7pm, Mon.-Wed. 7:30am-3pm). **Greyhound** runs from 402 Northern Pacific Ave. (293-1222; open daily 6:30am-6:30pm and 10:30pm-4:30am). **Crisis Line,** 235-7335, is 24 hrs. Fargo's **post office:** 657 2nd Ave. N. (241-6100) is open Mon.-Fri. 9am-5pm; **ZIP code:** 58103; **time zone:** Central; **area code:** 701.

Accommodations and Food There's a plethora of cheap motels on Main St. and 13th Ave. **The Sunset Motel,** 731 W. Main in West Fargo (282-3266 or 800-252-2207), offers clean, spacious rooms with free cable, spa, and fitness rooms. (Singles $20, doubles $30.) Stunning **Lindenwood Park** (232-3987) merits a visit even if you don't take advantage of the campgrounds. (Sites along the Red River $8, with water and electricity $12.50.) Great burgers at **Old Broadway,** 2200 Broadway (237-6161). After 11pm it's a popular nightspot. (Open daily 11am-1am.) For a good breakfast, **Pannekoeken,** 3340 13th Ave. SW (237-3559), has filling, oven-baked pancakes for $4-6 (open Sun.-Thurs. 6am-10pm, Fri.-Sat. 6am-11pm).

Sights and Entertainment The **Plains Art Museum,** 521 Main Ave. (218-236-7383), in Moorhead, has a collection of Native American art, as well as African sculpture. (Open Tues.-Wed., Fri.-Sat. 10am-5pm, Thurs. 10am-9pm, Sun. noon-5pm. Free.) **Bonanzaville USA,** on Main Ave. in West Fargo (282-2822), is a restored pioneer village (open daily 9am-5pm, winter hours vary). **Borrowed Buck's Roadhouse** (232-1535), off 13th Ave., is a great old-fashioned country bar that looks like a 60s gas station. (Open Mon.-Fri. 4pm-1am, Sat. noon-1am.) **Rooter's Bar,** 107 Broadway (232-1012), is a popular sports bar. Take exit 343 from I-94. (Open daily 4pm-1am.) The **Fargo-Moorhead Symphony** (233-8397) performs at the NDSU concert hall. (Tickets $6-15.) **Trollwood Park,** 37th Ave. N (241-8160), offers picnic spots, plays, and events. In mid-July, the **Red River Valley Fair** brings live music and ethnic food to Fargo.

■■■ THEODORE ROOSEVELT NATIONAL PARK

President Theodore Roosevelt appreciated the beauty of the Badlands's red- and brown-hued lunar formations so much that he bought a ranch here. After his mother and his wife died on the same day, he came here seeking "physical and spiritual renewal." Today's visitor can achieve the same rejuvenation among the quiet canyons and dramatic rocky outcroppings which earned the park the nickname "rough-rider country." The park is split into southern and northern units, and bisected by the border between Mountain and Central time zones.

A park entrance fee is collected in the summer ($4 per vehicle, $2 per pedestrian) and is valid for seven days entrance to *both* units of the park. The more popular **south unit** (time zone: Mountain) maintains a mini-museum at its **visitors center**

(623-4466), in Medora. See Teddy's guns, spurs and old letters, and a beautiful film of winter Badlands scenes. Copies of *Frontier Fragments,* the park newspaper, with listings of ranger-led talks, walks, and demonstrations, are available here. (Open daily 8am-8pm; winter hours vary. Inquire at desk for film times.) A 36-mi. **scenic automobile loop** is a great way to see the park; many hiking trails start from the loop and penetrate into the wilderness. **Wind Canyon,** located on the loop, is a constantly mutating canyon formed by winds blowing against the soft clay. The world's third largest **petrified forest** lies 14 mi. into the park and is worth the hike. **Painted Canyon Overlook,** 7 mi. east of Medora, has its own **visitors center** (575-4020; open daily 8am-6pm, closed winters), picnic tables, and a breathtaking view of the Badlands. Get a free camping permit at the visitors center or try the state's **Cottonwood Campgrounds** in the park (sites $8).

The **north unit** of the park (time zone: Central) is 75 mi. from the south unit on U.S. 85. Most of the land is wilderness. Fewer people visit than in the south, but it's becoming more popular. This combination results in virtually unlimited backcountry hiking possibilities. Check in at the **visitors center** (842-2333; open daily 8am-6pm) for information and a free overnight camping permit, or try **Squaw Creek Campground,** 5 mi. west of the north unit entrance (sites $8). For more information, write to Theodore Roosevelt National Park, Medora 58645.

■ MEDORA

The entrance to the better-developed **south unit** (time zone: Mountain) is just north of I-94 in the historic frontier town of Medora. Restored with tourist dollars in mind, Medora now resembles a strip town not big enough for the both of us. Accommodations are expensive. The **Sully Inn,** 401 Broadway (623-4455), offers clean and tiny rooms at the lowest rates in town. (Singles $25, doubles $40.) Check out authentically restored **Joe Ferris' General Store** (623-4447; open daily 8am-8pm; closed winter). The **Chuckwagon Restaurant** (623-4820), is cafeteria style, but excellent. (Open daily 4:30-7pm.) The **Museum of the Badlands,** on 3rd and Main St. (623-4451), exhibits Plains Indians's artifacts and local natural history. (Open daily 9am-8pm; closed winters; admission $2, kids $1.) Take a horse-drawn carriage ride from in front of the museum for $2. The **Medora Musical** (623-4444) in the Burning Hills Amphitheater downtown, stages different shows nightly from early June through early Sept. **Greyhound** serves Medora from the Sully Inn, with three buses daily to Bismarck ($20.25). Medora's **post office:** 355 3rd Ave., is open Mon.-Fri. 8am-noon, 12:30-4:30pm, Sat. 8:15-9:45am.

South Dakota

From the forested granite crags of the Black Hills to the glacial lakes of the northeast, the Coyote State has more to offer than casual passers-by might expect. WALL DRUG. In fact, with only 10 people per square mile, South Dakota has the highest ratio of sights-to-people in all the Great Plains. Stunning natural spectacles like the Black Hills, the Badlands, and the Wind and Jewel Caves, as well as colossal manmade attractions such as Mt. Rushmore and the Crazy Horse Monument, have made tourism the state's largest industry after agriculture. WALL DRUG. Camera-toting tourists in search of nature have brought both dollars and development to South Dakota, which struggles to keep its balance between playground and parking lot. Weatherwise too, South Dakota is a land of extremes. Temperatures during the year oscillate between Arctic frigidity and Saharan heat. YOU ARE NOW ONLY A HALF-PAGE FROM WALL DRUG.

PRACTICAL INFORMATION

Capital: Pierre.

Division of Tourism, 221 S. Central, in Capitol Lake Plaza, P.O. Box 1000, Pierre 57051 (773-3301 or 800-952-2217; 800-843-1930 outside SD). Open Mon.-Fri. 9am-5pm. **U.S. Forest Service,** Custer 57730 (673-4853). Provides camping stamps for the national forest, Golden Eagle passes for those over 62, and Black Hills National Forest maps ($3). Open Mon.-Fri. 8am-7pm. **Division of Parks and Recreation,** Capitol Bldg., Pierre 57501 (773-3371). Information on state parks and campgrounds. Open Mon.-Fri. 8am-6pm.

Time Zones: Central and Mountain. **Postal Abbreviation:** SD

Sales Tax: 4-7% depending on the city.

■■■ BADLANDS NATIONAL PARK

Some 60 million years ago, when much of the Great Plains was under water, tectonic shifts thrust up the Rockies and the Black Hills. Mountain streams deposited silt from these nascent highlands into what is now known as the Badlands, fossilizing in layer after pink layer the remains of wildlife that once wandered these flood plains. Erosion has carved spires and steep gullies into the land of this area, creating a landscape that contrasts sharply with the prairies of eastern South Dakota. The Sioux called these arid and treacherous formations "Mako Sica," or "bad land"; General Alfred Sully—the opposition—simply called them "hell with the fires out."

The Badlands still smolder about 50 mi. east of Rapid City on I-90. Highway 240 winds through the wilderness in a 32-mi. detour off I-90 (take exit 131 or 110). There is almost no way to visit the park by highway without being importuned by advertisements from **Wall Drug,** 510 Main St. (279-2175), in Wall; the store is a towering monument to the success of saturation advertising. After seeing billboards for Wall Drug from as far as 500 mi. away, travelers feel obligated to make a stop in Wall to see what all the ruckus is about, much as they must have done 60 years ago when Wall enticed travelers on the parched Plains by offering free water. The "drug store" itself hawks souvenirs and other kitsch. (Open daily 6:30am-10pm; Dec.-April daily 7am-6pm.) All in all the town is just another brick in the...well, forget it.

From Wall, take Rte. 240, which loops through the park and returns to I-90 30 mi. east of Wall in Cactus Flat. From Rapid City, take Rte. 44 and turn northeast at Scenic, where it leads to Sage Creek and Rte. 240. There are ranger stations at both entrances off I-90, although the western portion of the park is much less developed. **Jack Rabbit Buses** (348-3300) makes two stops daily at Wall from Rapid City ($19). Entrance to the park costs $2 per person, $5 per carload.

The **Ben Reifel Visitors Center** (433-5361), 5 mi. inside the park's eastern entrance, is more convenient than **White River Visitors Center** (455-2878), 55 mi. southwest, off Rte. 27 in the park's less-visited southern section. (Ben Reifel open daily 7am-8pm; Sept.-May hours vary. White River open May 31-Sept. 9am-5pm.) Both of the visitors centers offer potable water. The Badlands experience extreme temperatures in midsummer and winter, but in late spring and fall offer pleasant weather and few insects. Always watch (and listen) for rattlesnakes.

ACCOMMODATIONS, CAMPING, AND FOOD

On your way there, you may want to spend the night at **Welsh's Motel** (279-2271) located near the beginning of Rte. 240. Clean comfy singles go for $30, doubles for $46. Two campgrounds lie within the park. The **Ben Reifel Campground,** near the visitors center, has shaded picnic tables and a bathroom with running water, but no showers (sites $8). The **Sage Creek Campground,** 11 mi. from the Pinnacles entrance south of Wall, is free. It is merely an open field with no toilets, no water, and it does *not* allow fires. What do you expect for nothing? Try backcountry camping for an intimate intro to this austere landscape, but don't cozy up to the bison, especially in spring when nervous mothers become, shall we say, overprotective.

For tenderfoot tourists, the **Cedar Pass Lodge** (433-5460) next to the visitors center, has air-conditioned cabins. (Singles with showers $37, doubles $41. Each additional person $4. Open mid-April-mid-Oct.) Try a buffalo burger ($3.25) at the lodge's mid-priced restaurant (the only one in the park; open June-Aug. daily 7am-8pm). The **Cedar Pass Campground,** the only campground in the main north site, is $8 a night and very close to the lodge.

SIGHTS AND ACTIVITIES

The 244,000-acre park protects large tracts of prairie along with the stark rock formations. The Reifel Visitors Center has a video on the Badlands, and the park rangers lead **nature walks** which leave from the Cedar Pass amphitheater. The free walks (at 8am and 6pm, 1½ hr.) provide an easy way to appreciate the Badlands—you may find Oligocene fossils right at your feet. A 3-hr. hike leaves from the fossil exhibit daily at 6:30am. In the evening, the amphitheater slide program narrates Badlands history. A 1-hr. night-prowl or sky-trek (stargazing) follows the program.

You can also hike through the Badlands on your own. Pick up a trail guide at one of the visitors centers. If you're planning an overnight hike, be certain to ask for their **backcountry camping** information. Try the short but steep **Saddle Pass Trail** or the less hilly **Castle Trail** (10 mi. round-trip). If you'd rather drive than hike, follow **Loop Road** and pull over at the overlooks. Highlights of Loop Road are **Robert's Prairie Dog Town** and the **Yellow Mounds Overlook,** where red and yellow formations relieve the ubiquitous Badland bleached rose. Keep your eyes peeled along Sage Creek Rd. for the park's herd of about 400 bison. It is easy to lose your bearings in this convoluted territory, so consult with a ranger or tote a map.

BLACK HILLS

The Black Hills, named for the dark hue that distance lends the green pines covering the hills, have long been considered sacred by the Sioux. The Treaty of 1868 gave the Black Hills and the rest of South Dakota west of the Missouri River to the Sioux, but the U.S. government broke it during the gold rush of 1877-79. Today, white residents dominate the area, which contains a trove of treasures, including Mount Rushmore, Crazy Horse Monument, Custer State Park, Wind Cave National Park, Jewel Cave National Monument, and the Black Hills National Forest.

I-90 skirts the northern border of the Black Hills from Spearfish in the west to Rapid City in the east. The interconnecting road system through the hills is an attraction in its own right, but is difficult to navigate without a good map; pick up one for free almost anywhere in the area.

Take advantage of the excellent and informative **Grayline** tours (342-4461). Tickets can be purchased at Rapid City motels, hotels, and campgrounds. Make reservations, or call 1 hr. before departure; they will pick you up at your motel. Tour #1 is the most complete Black Hills tour, going to Mt. Rushmore, Black Hills National Forest, Custer State Park, Needles Highway, and the Crazy Horse Monument (mid-May-mid-Oct. daily, 8-hr., $36).

■■■ BLACK HILLS NATIONAL FOREST

The majority of the land in the Black Hills area is part of the National Forest. Like other national forests, the Black Hills adhere to the principle of "multiple use"; mining, logging, ranching, and tourism all take place in close proximity. "Don't miss" attractions like reptile farms and Flintstone Campgrounds lurk around every bend in the Black Hills's narrow, sinuous roads. Because all the area's attractions are in a close area, travelers can use **Spearfish, Hot Springs,** or **Rapid City** as a base to explore the monuments and parks. The forest itself offers unlimited opportunities for backcountry hiking and camping, as well as park-run campgrounds and private tent sites. Contact the **Black Hills Forest Service Center** (343-8755) on I-385 at Pactola Lake for details on backcountry camping.

Camping Camping in the national forest is free. To save money the adventurous way, disappear down one of the many dirt roads (make sure it isn't someone's driveway) and set up camp. There are a few rules to follow: you can't park on the side of the road, your campsite must be at least 1 mi. away from any campground or visitors center, and you can't build a campfire. Watch for poison ivy and afternoon thundershowers. The most popular established campgrounds include **Bear Gulch** and **Pactola** (343-4283), on the Pactola Reservoir just south of the junction of Rte. 44 and U.S. 385 (sites $10-12). You must register for sites at the **Pactola Campground** (on 385 South, 1 mi. past the visitors center; turn right at sign for the Black Forest Inn). They fill quickly, so call for reservations up to 10 days in advance. Other favorites include **Sheridan Lake Campground** (574-2873 or 800-283-2267), east of Hill City on U.S. 385 (sites $10-12), which provides picnic tables, pit toilets, water hydrants, movies, and talks on Saturday at 8pm. For more information, contact the Pactola or Spearfish Ranger District (see Spearfish). The Black Hills National Forest extends into Wyoming, with a ranger station (307-283-1361; open daily 8am-5pm, winter Mon.-Fri. 8am-5pm) in Sundance. The Wyoming side is sparsely visited, horses are permitted in more places, and campfires are allowed. Maps are $3. Contact the **Black Hills Forest Service Visitors Center** (343-8755) on I-385S., at Pactola Lake.

■■■ MOUNT RUSHMORE NATIONAL MONUMENT

South Dakota historian Doane Robinson originally conceived this "shrine of democracy" in 1923 as a memorial for local Western heroes like Lewis and Clark and Kit Carson. By its completion in 1941, the monument portrayed the 60-ft.-tall faces of George Washington, Thomas Jefferson, Abraham Lincoln, and Theodore Roosevelt. Think about it: these heads have nostrils large enough to snort a man! Millions have stared in awe at the four stony-faced patriarchs, designed and sculpted by chiseler extraordinaire Gutzon Borglum. The work remains unfinished—Borglum envisioned the presidents's torsos carved into the mountain as well as an area behind the heads to house a museum of American history. Imagine: these heads are meant to fit 465-ft.-tall bodies. The monument proves that Americans do take great men for granite. There's no fee to view the heads, because they are, after all, just heads.

From Rapid City, take U.S. 16 to Keystone and Rte. 16A up to the mountain. The **visitors center** (574-2523) has exhibits as well as braille brochures and wheelchairs. Programs for the disabled are held daily at 9pm (open daily 8am-10pm; Sept. 18-May 14 daily 8am-5pm). **Borglum's Studio,** in the visitors center, holds the plaster model of the carving, as well as his tools and plans. (Ranger talks in summer hourly 10am-4:30pm; studio open daily 9am-5pm.) Also in the visitors center is **Mount Rushmore Memorial Amphitheater,** the location of the evening monument-lighting programs. (May 14-Sept. 4 program at 9pm, monument lit 9:30-10:30pm; trail lights off at 11pm.) For nearby accommodations, try the **Hill City-Mount Rushmore KOA** (574-2525), 5 mi. west of Mount Rushmore on Rte. 244. With kabins ($58) come use of showers, stove, heated pool, laundry facilities, and free shuttle service to Mt. Rushmore. (Office open daily 7am-11pm, Oct.-April 8am-10pm. Kampsites $18 for 2 people, $20 with water and electricity.)

■■■ CRAZY HORSE NATIONAL MONUMENT

If you thought Mount Rushmore was big, think again. This monument is a wonder-of-the-world-in-progress; an entire mountain is being transformed into a 500-ft.-high memorial sculpture of the great Lakota chief Crazy Horse. When finished, this will relegate the denizens of Rushmore to the status of smurfs—one nostril of the chief will be large enough to lodge a five story building. The project began in 1947 and receives no government funding of any kind; the sculptor, Korczak Ziolkowski, believed in the American spirit of free enterprise, and twice refused $10 million in federal funding. Crazy Horse himself was a resolute Native American war chief who fought against the U.S. government to protect his people's land, rights, and pride. He was stabbed in the back (literally) by an American soldier in 1877, while at Fort Robinson, NE, under a flag of truce. Viewing the monument reminds one that this land was home to Native Americans long before the Europeans usurped the territory. The Monument, on Rte. 16/385, 14 mi. south of Mt. Rushmore, includes the **Indian Museum of North America** as well as the mountain statue. (Open daily 7am-10pm, Sept.-May 8am-5pm. $6, $15 per carload, $3 for AAA members, under 6 free.) For information or to make a tax-deductible donation, write: Crazy Horse Memorial, Crazy Horse, SD 57730-9506, or call 673-4681.)

■■■ CUSTER STATE PARK

Imagine a herd of buffalo grazing in fields with a bubbling brook nearby. This is Custer country. Peter Norbeck, governor of South Dakota during the late 1910s, loved to hike among the thin, towering rock formations that haunt the area south of Sylvan Lake and Mt. Rushmore. Norbeck not only created Custer State Park, but spectacular **Needles Highway** as well, which follows his favorite hiking route. He purposely kept the highway narrow and winding so that newcomers could experience the pleasures of discovery. This steep and curvy highway does not have guard rails, so slow and cautious driving is essential; watch out for mountain goats and big-horn sheep among the rocky spires. For information, contact HC 83, P.O. Box 70, Custer SD 57730 (255-4515; open Mon.-Fri. 7:30am-5pm). There is a daily entrance fee ($3 per person, $8 per carload for a 5-day pass). At the entrance, ask for a copy of *Tatanka* (meaning "buffalo"), the informative Custer State Park newspaper. The **Peter Norbeck Welcome Center** (255-4464), on U.S. 16A 1 mi. west of the State Game Lodge, is the park's info center (open May-Sept. daily 8am-8pm). All six **campgrounds** charge $8-10 per night; some have showers and restrooms. Restaurants and concessions are available at all four park lodges, but you can save money by shopping at the local general stores in Custer, Hermosa, or Keystone.

Sylvan Lake, on Needles Hwy. (Rte. 87), is a lovely place to hike, fish, ride horseback, paddle boat, or canoe. Horse rides are available at **Blue Bell Lodge** (255-4531, stable 255-4571). Rides are $14.50 per hr., under 12 $12.50, $22 per 2 hrs., under 12 $20. Paddle and row boat rentals are offered at **Legion Lake Lodge** (255-4521; paddleboats $3.50 per person for ½-hr). All lakes and streams permit fishing, with a daily license ($6.75). Five-day nonresident licenses are $14.75. There is a limit of eight trout per day, six times per summer. Summer fishing is the best. Rental equipment is available at the four area lodges.

■■■ WIND CAVE AND JEWEL CAVE

In the cavern-riddled Black Hills, the subterranean scenery often rivals what lies above-ground. Private concessionaires will attempt to lure you into the holes in their backyards, but the government owns the area's prime real estate. **Wind Cave National Park** (745-4600), adjacent to Custer State Park on Rte. 87, and **Jewel Cave National Monument** (673-2288), 14 mi. west of Custer on Rte. 16A, are in the

THE GREAT PLAINS

southern hills. There is no public transportation to the caves. Bring a sweater on all tours—Jewel Cave remains a constant 47°F, Wind Cave 53°F.

Wind Cave Though discovered in 1881, most of Wind Cave is still unexplored. The cave lies 12 mi. north of Hot Springs on Rte. 385. Wind Cave Park offers five **tours.** The **Garden of Eden Tour** gives an overview of the cave's interior (6 per day 8:40am-5:30pm; $3, seniors and under 15 $1.50). The **Natural Entrance Tour** leaves on the hour, 9am-6pm, and covers ½-mi. of the cave ($5, ages 6-15 $2.50). The more strenuous, 2-hr. **Fairgrounds Tour** snakes ½ mi. through two levels of the cave (9:40am-4:20pm, $7, ages 6-15 $3.50). The four-hour **Spelunking Tour,** limited to 10 people ages 16 and over, leaves at 1pm ($10, reservations required). Finally, the **Candlelight Tour** is $7, minimum age 8. To make reservations for these tours, contact Wind Cave National Park, Hot Springs SD 57747 (745-4600; open daily 8am-7pm; Aug. 24-June 4 daily 8am-5pm).

Jewel Cave Sprawling underground in one of the largest labyrinths in the world, Jewel Cave, the second largest cave in the U.S., is formed of the same limestone as Wind Cave, but is covered by a layer of gray calcite crystals. Rangers sponsor four different tours during the summer. The ½-mi. **Scenic Tour** takes you over 700 stairs (every 30 min., 80-min. long; $4, ages 6-15 $2). Make reservations for the **Spelunking Tour,** limited to 10 people ages 16 and over, and be sure to wear sturdy foot gear (Sun., Tues., Thurs., and Sat., $8). The **visitors center** (638-2288) is open in the summer daily 8am-6pm and in the winter 9am-4pm. Tours run in the summer from 8:30am-5:30pm. The scenic tour runs once a day in the winter.

■■■ RAPID CITY

Rapid City's location, approximately 40 mi. east of Wyoming, makes it an ideal base from which to explore the Black Hills and the Badlands. Every summer the area welcomes about 2.2 million tourists, over 40 times the city's permanent population.

PRACTICAL INFORMATION

Emergency: 911.

Rapid City Chamber of Commerce, Visitors Bureau, 444 Mt. Rushmore Rd. N. (343-1744), in the Civic Center. Visitors Bureau (343-8531) open May 16-Oct 15 daily 7:30am-6pm; Chamber of Commerce open year-round Mon.-Fri. 9am-5pm, racks in lobby during other times, but no one working; call ahead.

Buses: Milo Barber Transportation Center, 333 6th St. (348-3300), downtown. **Jack Rabbit Lines** runs east from Rapid City. To: Pierre (11:30am, 3 hr., $52); Sioux Falls (11:30am, 8 hr., $97). **Powder River Lines** services Wyoming and Montana. To: Billings (5pm, 9 hr., $53); Cheyenne (5pm, 8½ hr., $61). Station open Mon.-Fri. 7:30am-5pm, Sat.-Sun. 10am-2pm, 3-5pm.

Public Transport: Milo Barber Transportation Center, 394-6631. City bus transportation available by reservation for disabled travelers. Call 24 hrs. in advance. $1, seniors 50¢. Buses run 6am-6pm, call for specific routes. Office open Mon.-Fri. 8am-4pm.

Taxi: Rapid Taxi, 348-8080. Base fare $2.20, $1.20 per mi.

Help Line: Rape and Assault Victims, 341-4808. Open Mon.-Fri. 7:30am-10:30pm, Sat. 1-7pm.

Time Zone: Mountain (2 hr. behind Eastern).

Post Office: 500 East Blvd. (394-8600), several blocks east of downtown. Open Mon. and Fri. 7:30am-5:30pm, Tues.-Thurs. 8am-5pm, Sat. 9am-12:30pm. **ZIP code:** 57701.

Area Code: 605.

Orienting yourself may be difficult at first, but the main east-west roads are **St. Joseph, Kansas City,** and **Main,** which is also **business loop 90. Mount Rushmore Rd.** (also Rte. 16) is the main north-south thoroughfare.

ACCOMMODATIONS, CAMPING, AND FOOD

Rapid City accommodations are considerably more expensive during the summer. Make reservations, since budget motels often fill up weeks in advance.

The **Rapid City YMCA Hostel (HI-AYH),** 815 Kansas City St. (342-8538), downtown in the YMCA, consists of 12 cots, with no separation between men and women. Access to YMCA facilities (pool, gym, game room) is free, kitchen facilities are available, and sheet rental is $2.50; Cots are $10; curfew is at midnight. If the hostel is full and you have a sleeping bag, you can sleep on the floor for $5.

The **Tip Top Motel,** 405 St. Joseph St. (800-341-8000) has small, clean singles, cable, and a pool (singles $40, doubles $45). **Tradewinds Motel,** 420 E. North St. (342-4153), has larger rooms but is farther away at exit 59 on I-90 (singles $38, doubles $48). The **Berry Patch Campground,** 1860 E. North St. (341-5588), 1 mi. east of I-90 off exit 60, has 15 nice campsites, a gameroom, playground, showers, and swimming. (Sites $15.50 for 2, with hookup $17.50 from end of May-Labor Day.)

The **Atomic Cafe,** 515 7th St. (399-1922) offers exotic beverages like Italian cream soda ($1), and more traditional espresso (75¢). A cool place to hang out with occasional live music (open daily 8am-2am, 8am-midnight during the winter). **Sixth St. Bakery and Delicatessen,** 516 6th St. (342-6660), serves up delectable sandwiches ($3-4). Try Paul's fudge brownies (90¢). **Tally's,** 530 6th St. (342-7621), downtown under the faded orange awning, serves traditional Mexican and country meals (fajitas $4.25, chicken-fried steak $6.25; open Mon.-Sat. 7am-8pm).

SIGHTS AND ENTERTAINMENT

Tourism rears its flashing neon head in Rapid City. If you got dem walkin' blues, take the **Rapid City Walking Tour** of the historic and well-preserved downtown area; pick up a guidebook at the visitors center. **The Museum of Geology,** 501 E. St. Joseph St. (394-2467), in the administration building of the School of Mines and Technology, just east of Main St., houses an impressive collection of minerals and fossils including rare casts of prehistoric eggs. (Open Mon.-Sat. 8am-6pm, Sun. noon-6pm; Labor Day-Memorial Day Mon.-Fri. 8am-5pm, Sat. 9am-2pm, Sun. 1-4pm. Free.) In the same building sits the **Museum in Motion** with exhibits for kids (open summers only, Mon.-Fri. 10am-5pm, $2). The **Dahl Fine Arts Center** (394-4101), 7th and Quincy St., houses rotating exhibits of local and Native American art. (Open Mon.-Thurs. 9am-7pm, Fri.-Sat. 9am-5pm, Sun. 1-5pm. Free.) The **Sioux Indian Museum** and the **Pioneer Museum** (both 348-0557) cohabitate at 515 West Blvd., between Main and St. Joseph St. in Halley Park. The two museums present interesting but limited exhibits. (Open Mon.-Sat. 9am-5pm, Sun. 1-5pm; Oct.-May Tues.-Sat. 10am-5pm, Sun. 1-5pm. Free.)

For nightlife, try **Main Street** between 9th and Mt. Rushmore St. **The Firehouse Brewing Co.,** 610 Main St. (348-1915), is *the* bar in Rapid City. Located in a restored 1915 firehouse, the place makes its own beer; dinner runs about $5-6. (Open Mon.-Thurs. 10am-midnight, Fri.-Sat. 11am-2am, Sun. 4-10pm.) **The Uptown Grill,** 615 Main St. (343-1942), serves food ($2-7) and beer. (Open Mon.-Thurs. 11am-10pm, Fri.-Sat. 11am-2am. Live bands on the weekends with occasional cover.) For boot-stompin', knee-slappin' country-western music and dancing, head to **Boot Hill,** 526 Main St. (343-1931), where live bands perform nightly (open Mon.-Sat. 4pm-2am, occasional $5 cover on weekends).

■■■ SPEARFISH, LEAD, AND DEADWOOD

Spearfish A picturesque community in the Hills, Spearfish is a great area to hike or camp, especially **Rte. 14A.** This beautiful road winds through 32 mi. of forest, **Spearfish Canyon,** and the site where Kevin Costner filmed *Dances with Wolves.* Follow the signs to the film site and travel another mile past it—there is a secluded public campsite nestled among the hills.

For free maps and help with hiking plans stop by the **Spearfish Ranger District,** 2014 N. Main St. (642-4622; open Mon.-Fri. 8am-5pm). The weary traveler can rest at **Bell's Motor Lodge** (642-3812) on Main St., a great deal with free local calls, TV, and a pool (singles $24, doubles $32). The **Canyon Gateway Hotel** (642-3402) on Rte. 14A offers large rooms with hardwood paneling (singles $32, doubles $42).

For an eclectic menu try **Bay Leaf Cafe,** 126 W. Hudson (642-5462), right off Main and across from the only **ATM** machine in the area (entrees $3-13). The **Valley Cafe,** 608 Main St. (642-2423), has standard fare cheap (3 big ol' flapjacks $2.25).

Lead About 20 mi. from Spearfish on Rte. 14a is Lead (LEED), an old 1870s gold mining town. Now a hardrock minerals mining town, the few interesting things left to see are the **Open Cut,** a huge chasm where a mountain once stood, and the **Black Hills Mining Museum,** 323 W. Main St. (584-1605), where you can tour fake mines (every 20 min.) and try your hand at panning for gold (open May 20-Oct. 10 daily 9am-5pm; $3.50, students $2.50, under 6 free).

Deadwood Continue down Main St. from Lead for about a mile and you'll find yourself in Deadwood. Gunslingers **Wild Bill Hickock** and **Calamity Jane** sauntered into town during the height of the Gold Rush. Bill stayed just long enough—two months—to spend an eternity here. Legend has it that Deadwood was home to the saloon where Hickock was shot holding **aces and eights,** the infamous "dead man's hand." Visit Bill and Jane at **Mt. Moriah Cemetery** on Boot Hill (open daily 7am-8pm, $1). The main attraction in Deadwood is **gambling,** with casinos lining **Main Street.** There isn't any budget lodging in Lead or Deadwood, so stay in nearby Spearfish or Rapid City. Or try **Wild Bill's Campground** (578-2800), on Rte. 385 about 3 mi. south of Lead and Deadwood (sites $12.50, $14.50 with water and hookup). For food, head to **Mama Leon's,** 638 Main St. (578-2440), in the rear of the Lucky Wrangler Casino. Yummy Italian food is $7-13 (open Mon.-Sat. noon-10pm).

■■■ HOT SPRINGS

Located on scenic **Rte. 385,** people used to come from all over to bathe in the mineral waters of this quaint town. Hot Springs is a charming and inexpensive location from which to explore the southern Black Hills. **Wind Cave National Park** is just outside of town, but Hot Springs has a few sights of its own. For information, stop at the **visitors center,** 801 S. 6th St. (745-4140 or 800-325-6991) on Rte. 385, which runs right through downtown.

Swim in one of the area's oldest pools at **Evan's Plunge** (745-5165) also on Rte. 385. The Sioux and Cheyenne used to fight over possession of the spring. (Open daily 5:30am-9:45pm. $7 for an all day swimming pass and access to the waterslides, ages 3-12 $5.) Rumored to have healing powers, visit Kidney Spring at the **Kidney Spring Gazebo,** across the river from 6th St. You can also drink from the public fountain or bring a jug and take some mineral water home.

30,000 years ago mammoths got trapped in a sinkhole and were fossilized near Hot Springs. See their bones as they lie, at the **Mammoth Site** (745-6017) on Rte. 18, (open daily 8am-8pm, $4.25, seniors $3.95, kids 6-12 $2.25). About 15 mi. west of Hot Springs on Rte. 18, you can view 300 wild mustangs roaming the **Black Hills Wild Horse Sanctuary** (800-252-6652; open daily dawn to dusk).

Clean rooms and cable fly at the **Skyline Motel** (745-6980) on Rte. 385N, (singles $26, doubles $34). **Hide Away Cabins,** 442 S. Chicago St. (745-5683), has rooms with kitchenettes (singles $30, doubles $40). For cheap eats, try generic **Family Restaurant,** 745 Battle Mountain St. (745-3737), across from Evan's Plunge, where you can find buffalo burgers for $2.75 (open daily 6am-9pm). The place to schmooze with booze in Hot Springs is **Yogi's Den,** 225 N. River St. (745-5949) where the casino and lounge open daily 7am-2am.

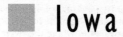 # Iowa

Depending on your perspective, "Iowa" evokes images of patchwork corn and soybean farmland, idyllic "fields of dreams," the sandman, or Hicksville, U.S.A. To see Iowa's real beauty, exit the freeway and meander along the old country roads. Here, far from the beaten and pummeled concrete path, you can cast your line into one of the state's innumerable fishing streams, bike 52 mi. along the Cedar Valley Nature Trail, see the dust-created Loess Hills in the west, or travel back in time at one of the many traditional communities dotting the area.

PRACTICAL INFORMATION

Capital: Des Moines.
Iowa Department of Economic Development, 200 E. Grand Ave., Des Moines 50309 (515-281-3100 or 800-345-4692).
Time Zone: Central (1 hr. behind Eastern). **Postal Abbreviation:** IA
Sales Tax: 5%.

■■■ DES MOINES

French explorers originally named the Des Moines river the "Rivière des Moingouenas," for a local Native American tribe, but then shortened the name to "Rivière des Moings." Because of its identical pronunciation (mwan), later French settlers called their river and city by a name much more familiar to them: Des Moines (of the monks). Today, Des Moines (pronounced "da moyne" like "da loin") shows neither Native American nor monastic influence, but rather the imprint of the agricultural state that spawned it. The World Pork Expo is a red letter event on the Iowan calendar and the city goes hog-wild for the Iowa State Fair every August. If Iowa's capital city is a meat market, it's a cosmopolitan one; it's the third-largest insurance center in the world, after London and Hartford. Des Moines also boasts a great art museum and hosts many local festivals and events. Despite the horrendous flooding of 1993, the city has rebuilt with a vengeance, even inspiring an up-and-coming club scene.

PRACTICAL INFORMATION

Emergency: 911.
Visitor Information: Des Moines Convention and Visitors Bureau, 2 Ruan Center #222 (286-4960 or 800-451-2625), near the Kaleidoscope and Locust Malls downtown. Open Mon.-Fri. 8:30am-5pm.
Airport: Des Moines International (256-5857), Fleur Dr. at Army Post Rd., about 5 mi. southwest of downtown. Take bus #8 ("Havens").
Greyhound: 1107 Keosauqua Way (800-231-2222), at 12th St. just northwest of downtown. Open 24 hrs. Taxi to downtown $10.
Public Transport: Metropolitan Transit Authority (MTA), 1100 MTA Lane (283-8100), just south of the 9th St. viaduct. Open Mon.-Fri. 8am-5pm. Get maps at the MTA office or any Dahl's market. Routes converge at 6th and Walnut St. Buses run Mon.-Fri. 6:20am-6:15pm, Sat. 6:45am-5:50pm. Fare 75¢, transfers 5¢.
Taxi: Capitol Cab, 282-8111. **Yellow Cab,** 243-1111. $1.50 base rate.
Car Rental: Budget (287-2612), at the airport. $32, 150 free mi. per day, 25¢ per additional mi. Open Sun.-Fri. 6am-11pm, Sat. 6am-10pm. Must be 21 with major credit card. Under 25 add $10 per day.
Help Lines: Gay Resource Center, info line 277-1454. Open Mon.-Thurs. 4-10pm, Sun. 4-8pm. **Rape/Sexual Assault Line,** 288-1750. Open 24 hrs.
Post Office: 1165 2nd Ave. (283-7500), just north of I-235, downtown. Open Mon.-Fri. 8:30am-5:30pm. **ZIP code:** 50318.
Area Code: 515.

Des Moines idles on the northwest side at the junction of I-35 and I-80. Numbered streets run north-south, named streets east-west. Numbering begins at the **Des Moines River** and increases east or west, starting at **South Union** where the river twists east. **Grand Avenue** divides addresses north-south along the numbered streets. Other east-west thoroughfares are **Locust Street, Park Avenue, Douglas Avenue, University Avenue,** and **Hickman Road.** Most downtown buildings are connected by **Skywalk,** passages above the street.

ACCOMMODATIONS AND CAMPING

Finding cheap accommodation in Des Moines is usually no problem, though you should make reservations for visits in March (high school sports tournament season) and in August, when the State Fair comes to town. Several cheap motels cluster around **I-80** and **Merle Hay Rd.,** 5 mi. northwest of downtown. Take bus #4 ("Urbandale") or #6 ("West 9th") from downtown.

Econo Lodge, 5626 Douglas Ave. (278-1601), across from Merle Hay Mall, with the bus stop in front. Large rooms with cable TV, free coffee, juice, rolls, and newspaper. Spa and sauna available. Singles $40, doubles $44.

YMCA, 101 Locust St. (288-2424), at 1st St. downtown on the west bank of the river. Small, somewhat clean rooms with a communal bathroom, convenient downtown location. Lounge, laundry, athletic facilities, including pool. Men only. Key deposit $5. Singles $19.70, $61 per week.

YWCA, 717 Grand Ave. (244-8961), across from the Marriott Hotel downtown. In a fairly safe area. Women only. Moderately clean dorm-style rooms with access to lounge, kitchen, laundry, and pool. All rooms shared; its main purpose is to provide social services and emergency shelter. $8 per day, $44 per week.

Iowa State Fairgrounds Campgrounds, E. 30th St. (262-3111), at Grand Ave. Take bus #1 or 2 to the Grand Ave. gate 2000 (yes, *2000*). Sites with water and electricity. At fairtime, 2500 additional primitive sites are squeezed in. No fires. Open mid-May to mid-Oct. $8 per vehicle; fee collected in the morning.

Walnut Woods State Park, S.W. 52 Ave. (285-4502), 4 mi. south of the city on Rte. 5. Secluded campground with horse and hiking trails nearby, not accessible by public transportation. Floods occasionally; if the front gate is locked, it's for a good reason. Primitive sites $5, with electricity $7.

FOOD

Spaghetti Works, 310 Court Ave. (243-2195). A huge converted warehouse with portions to match. Unlimited salad bar and free soda refills $5-8. Open Sun.-Thurs. 11:15am-10pm, Fri.-Sat. 11:15am-11pm; half-price drinks daily 3-6pm.

Porky's, 444 Douglas Ave. (270-6058). Good burgers $2. On Saturdays, about 30 vintage cars are on display outside the restaurant. Open daily 10am-10pm.

A Taste of Thailand, 215 E. Walnut St. (243-9521), east of downtown. Authentic Thai food in American setting, and 71 zillion different kinds of beer. Dinners around $8. Open Mon.-Sat. 11am-2pm and 5-9pm.

SIGHTS

The copper- and gold-domed **state capitol** (281-5591), on E. 9th St. across the river and up Grand Ave., is a beautiful building with an excellent view of the city. Note the "please walk in" sign on the Secretary of State's door. (Free tours Mon.-Sat., call in the morning for schedule. Building open Mon.-Fri. 8am-4:30pm, Sat.-Sun. 8am-4pm.) Take bus #5 ("E. 6th and 9th St."), #1 ("Fairgrounds"), #2, 4 or 7. Farther downhill sits the **Iowa State Historical Museum and Archives** (281-5111), at Pennsylvania and Grand Ave., a modern building with three floors exhibiting Iowa's natural, industrial, and social history, including an exhibit addressing the environmental overdevelopment of Iowa—once the state had three million acres of prairie, now only a few thousand. (Open Tues.-Sat. 9am-4:30pm, Sun. noon-4pm. Free. Take any bus that goes to the capitol.) Also related to Iowan government is the grandiose Victorian mansion **Terrace Hill,** 2800 Grand Ave. (281-3604), built in 1869 and currently the gubernatorial mansion. (Tours Feb.-Dec. Tues.-Sat. 10am-1:30pm every 30 min. Tickets $3, kids 80¢.) The geodesic greenhouse dome of the **Botanical Center,** 909 E. River Dr. (238-4148), next to I-235 and not far from the capitol, encompasses a wide array of exotic flora. (Open Mon.-Thurs. 10am-6pm, Fri. 10am-9pm, Sat.-Sun. 10am-5pm. $1.50, ages 6-18 25¢, under 6 free.)

Most cultural sights cluster west of downtown. The **Des Moines Art Center,** 4700 Grand Ave. (277-4405), is acclaimed for its wing of stark white porcelain tile designed by I.M. Pei. Impressive modern works include George Segal's *To All Gates,* with which every wayworn traveler can identify. (Open Tues.-Wed. and Fri.-Sat. 11am-5pm, Thurs. 11am-9pm, Sun. noon-5pm. $2, seniors and students $1. Free all day Thurs. and until 1pm Fri.-Wed. Take bus #1.) Flapper-era cosmetics manufacturer Carl Weeks realized his aristocratic aspirations after he had salvaged enough ceilings, staircases, and artifacts from English Tudor mansions to complete **Salisbury House,** 4025 Tonawanda Dr. (279-9711), Grand Ave. to 42 St. (public tours Mon.-Thurs. at 2pm, Fri. 10am, or by appointment; $3, kids $1).

In **Indianola,** 12 mi. south on U.S. 69, the **Des Moines Metro Opera** (961-6221) produces three full-scale operas every summer in the Blank Performing Arts Center at Simpson college. (Tickets $25-50.) Also in Indianola, the **National Balloon Museum,** 1601 N. Jefferson (961-3714), is rumored to derive its hot air from the operatic performers and holds balloon regattas. (Open Mon.-Fri. 9am-4pm, Sat. 10am-4pm, Sun. 1-4pm.) **Pella,** 25 mi. east of Des Moines on Rte. 163, hosts a famous festival, **Tulip Time** (628-4311), the second weekend in May. At other times the town maintains a tangible Dutch presence and several great Dutch bakeries.

ENTERTAINMENT

Juke Box Saturday Night, 206-208 3rd St. (284-0901). Hot spot for fun and drink. Decorative '57 Chevy motif. Drinks average $2.50. Thurs. pay $3 and beers are 5¢. Summer Fri.-Sat. 7-11pm, cover $2. Open daily 5pm-2am.

Johnny's Hall of Fame Bar & Grill, 300 Court St. (280-6679), has live bands Fri.-Sat. nights. Cover $1. Beer 75¢ Mon.-Sat. 4-6pm. Open Mon.-Sat. 11am-2am.

Hairy Mary's, 200 SW 2nd (237-9915). Alternative club with pool tables, pinball, and loud rock in a warehouse. Cover $2-5. Open Mon.-Sat. 8pm-2am.

The Garden, 112 SE 4th St. (243-3965). A fun gay dance and video bar. Free beer Sat. 8-10pm. Wednesdays all-you-can-drink $6. Open daily 6pm-2am.

Noodles Comedy Club, 210 Court St. (243-2195), in the rear of Spaghetti Works, you may just laugh yours off. Comedians perform Fri. 8:30pm, Sat. 7:30 and 10pm. Reservations recommended. $6.

The **Iowa State Fair,** one of the largest in the U.S., captivates Des Moines for 10 days during the middle of August with prize cows, crafts, cakes, and corn. For info contact the 24-hr. info line at the Administration Building, Iowa State Fair Grounds, Des Moines 50306 (262-3111). At the end of May many clubs host live bands with $1 cover each from 5pm to midnight to celebrate the **Court Avenue River Party.** Early June the party repeats with the **Blues on Court** festival. **Seniom Sed** (Des Moines spelled backwards) is a sort of block party that occurs 4:45-7pm on Fridays, May to September. The **Civic Center,** 200 SW 2nd (237-9915), sponsors theater and concerts. Call for ticket info. For lots of free event listings, pick up a copy of *Cityview,* the free local weekly paper.

■■■ IOWA CITY

Iowa City, the capital of Iowa until 1857, is now a classic college town; housing the main University of Iowa campus, it's complete with bars, frozen yogurt, street musicians, and hordes of students. But more importantly, Iowa City is a mecca of liberalism in a conservative state. Each weekend, whole communes of Iowans make a pilgrimage to the city in order to burn incense, bar-hop, and cheer on the Hawkeyes, the University's football team.

THE GREAT

Practical Information The city lies on I-80, about 112 mi. east of Des Moines. The downtown is bounded by east-west **Madison** and **Gilbert** and north-south **Market** and **Burlington**. From the **Convention and Visitors Bureau**, 325 E. Washington St. (337-6592 or 800-283-6592), 2nd floor, you can walk to the main downtown. Downtown, take **Iowa City Transit** (356-5151; runs Mon.-Fri. 6am-10:30pm, Sat. 6am-6:30pm; 50¢, seniors 25¢, monthly pass $18). The free **Cambus** also connects the campus to downtown. Check out the University of Iowa's **Campus Information Center** (335-3055) for area information. (Open Mon.-Fri. 8am-9pm, in the Iowa Memorial Union. See Accommodations below.) **Greyhound** and **Burlington Trailways** are both located at 404 E. College St. (337-2127), at Gilbert. Buses run to: Des Moines (6 per day, $16.50; open Mon.-Sat. 6am-8pm, Sun. 10:30am-3pm, 5-8pm). **Help lines** include the **24-hour Crisis Line** (335-6000) and **Gay and Lesbian Helpline** (335-3877), which operates Tuesday and Thursday evenings. Iowa City's **post office:** 400 S. Clinton St. (354-1560; open 8:30am-5pm, Sat. 9:30am-1pm). **ZIP code:** 52240; **area code:** 319.

Accommodations and Food There are cheap motels in **Coralville**, 2 mi. west of downtown on I-80, off exit 242. Off one wing of the **Iowa Memorial Union** (335-3055), the huge U of I student center at Madison and Jefferson, is **Iowa House** (335-3513), a pricey but classy hotel with good location. (Free parking. Singles $52, doubles $58. Reservations recommended, especially for football and parents weekends.) The Union also has cheap dining, a Ticketmaster, a mini-post office, an excellent bookstore, and many other services. (Open Mon.-Thurs. 7am-11pm, Fri.-Sat. 7am-midnight.) Less expensive, but very much a hole-in-the-wall is **Wesley House Hostel (HI-AYH),** 120 N. Dubuque St. (338-1179), at Jefferson. (Check in 7-9:45pm only, and must be out again by 9am. Strict curfew is 10pm. 7 beds in two cramped rooms. $10 Members only.) For camping try **Kent Park Campgrounds** (645-2315), 9 mi. west on U.S. 6W, a very pretty area with meadows and 86 nice sites. $4, with electricity $8. First-come, first-served.

The downtown is loaded with good, cheap restaurants and bars. **Vito's,** 118 E. College (338-1393), is a restaurant and bar with cajun chicken fettucine ($8). (Open daily 11am-1:30am.) **Bushnell's Turtle,** 127 E. College (351-5536), serves the lunch crowd sandwiches ($3-7). (Open Mon.-Sat. 11am-7pm.) At **The Kitchen,** 215 E. Washington (358-9524), you can devise your own pasta concoction ($5.25 and up). (Open Mon.-Sat. 11am-2:30pm and 5-9:30pm.)

Sights and Entertainment The **Old Capitol** building (335-0548), at Union and Iowa St., which has been restored almost beyond recognition, is still the main attraction (open Mon.-Sat. 10am-3pm, Sun. noon-4pm; free, including tours). The capitol is also the focal point of the **Pentacrest,** at Clinton and Iowa, a five-building formation with a center green perfect for hanging out. One of the five is the **Museum of Natural History** (335-0480), which has interesting exhibits on the Native Americans of Iowa. (Open Mon.-Sat. 9:30am-4:30pm, Sun. 12:30-4:30pm; free.) Five blocks west is the **Museum of Art,** 150 N. Riverside Drive (335-1727), housing an internationally acclaimed collection of African art. (Open Tues.-Sat. 10am-5pm, Sun. noon-5pm. Free.)

Bars and nightspots cover the downtown. **The Union Bar and Grill,** 121 E. College St. (339-7713), is the largest bar in a Big Ten college town. (Open Tues.-Sat 7pm-2am.) **The Sanctuary,** 405 S. Gilbert (351-5692), is a popular jazz club (open daily 4pm-2am). **Hancher Auditorium,** North Riverside Dr. (800-426-2437 or 335-1130), hosts top-notch performances; ask for student and senior discounts. Street musicians and shopping can be found in the open-air **Pedestrian Mall.**

■■■ THE AMANA COLONIES

In 1714, German fundamentalists disillusioned with the established church formed the Community of True Inspiration. Facing persecution, they fled to the U.S. in

1843. Settling near Buffalo, NY, their community grew too large, so they migrated—this time to the rich promised land along the Iowa River, where they founded the Amana Colonies ("Amana" means "to remain true"). There they lived a communal lifestyle where everyone was equal and everything shared. Eventually, the people became tired of the sacrifices for such living and in 1932 they went capitalist. Some joined to form the Amana Society, Inc., which now owns most of the area's land and mills; another member started the hugely successful Amana Refrigeration Co. Unlike the Amish, the Inspirationists did not believe that technology or material wealth obstructed personal piety. Although the colonies have become a large tourist attraction, it is important to realize that most of the stores are run by colonists' descendents (and some former commune members themselves), and many are still active in the Church, proving that there is living history behind the chintz.

Until 1994 there were no addresses in the colonies, only place names. Anything that isn't on the road leading into town is easily found by following signs that point to attractions off the main thoroughfare, the **Amana Trail,** which runs off U.S. 151 and goes through all seven colonies. **Main Amana** is the largest and most touristy of the seven Amana villages. The farther out you go into the smaller villages, the easier it is to imagine what life must have been like for the colonists.

Practical Information and Orientation The Amana Colonies lie 10 mi. north of I-80, clustered around the intersection of U.S. 6, Rte. 220, and U.S. 151. From Iowa City, take U.S. 6 west to U.S. 151; from Des Moines, take exit 225 off I-80 to U.S. 151. There is no public transportation in the Colonies. The **Amana Colonies Visitors Center** (622-6262 or 800-245-5465), just west of Amana on Rte. 220, shows an informative film. (Open Mon.-Wed. 9am-5pm, Thurs.-Sat. 9am-10pm, Sun. 10am-5pm, call for winter hrs.) A private car caravan tour covering six villages is given every Saturday at 10am, leaving from the visitors center (622-6178; 3 hr., $7, 12 and under $3.50). Throughout the colonies look for the helpful *Visitors Guide.* Main Amana's **post office:** 101 2nd St. (622-3019), off I-51 (open Mon.-Fri. 7:30-11am and noon-4:30pm, Sat. 8:30-9:30am); **ZIP code:** 52203; **area code:** 319.

Accommodations and Camping Most lodging options consist of pricey but personal B&Bs, including the **Dusk to Dawn Bed and Breakfast** (622-3029), in Middle Amana, which offers attractive rooms, a hot tub, and a great breakfast. (Singles and doubles $41.50.) The **Guest House Motor Inn** (622-3599) in downtown Main Amana is a converted 126 year-old communal kitchen house with 38 clean rooms. (Singles $35, doubles $47.) **Sudbury Court Motel** (642-5411) has clean, comfortable rooms with A/C and TV. Take exit 216 off I-80 and go 7 mi. north on U.S. 6. Camp at the **Amana Community Park** in Middle Amana (622-3732. Sites $3 per vehicle, $4.50 with electricity and water; no showers.)

Food Restaurants throughout the colonies serve huge portions of heavy food family-style. One of the best deals is the **Colony Inn** (622-6270) in Main Amana, which serves up hefty portions of delicious German and American food. Dinners ($10-15) and lunches ($5.50-9) are served with cottage cheese, bread, diced ham, sauerkraut, fruit salad, and mashed potatoes. Breakfast ($6) is also an all-you-can-eat orgy. (Open Mon.-Sat. 7am-10:30pm, Sun. 11am-7:30pm.) Middle Amana's **Hahn's Hearth Oven Bakery** (622-3439) sells the scrumptious products of the colonies' only functional open-hearth oven (open April-Oct. Tues.-Sat. 7am to sell-out around 4:30pm, Nov.-Dec. and March Wed. and Sat. only). Sample some dandelion wine at the **Heritage Wine and Cheese Haus** (622-3379) in Main Amana, which has delicious local goods, and free samples galore (open Mon.-Wed. 9am-6pm, Thurs.-Sat. 9am-5pm, Sun. 10am-5pm).

Sights The **Museum of Amana History** (622-3567) helps explain what life was like for the colonists (open April 15-Nov. 15 Mon.-Sat. 10am-5pm, Sun. noon-5pm; $2.50, ages 6-17 $1). At the **Woolen Mill,** visitors can watch the machinery run on weekdays (622-3051; open Mon.-Sat. 8am-6pm, Sun. 11am-5pm). Down the street, watch artisans craft in the open workshop at the **Amana Furniture and Clock Shop** (622-3291; open Mon.-Sat. 9am-5pm, Sun. noon-5pm). Beyond the **Amana Refrigeration Plant,** in Middle Amana, tour the **Communal Kitchen Museum** (622-3567), the former site of all local food preparation (open May-Oct. daily 9am-5pm; $1.50, kids 75¢). **Miniature Americana** (622-3058), in South Amana on 220 trail, has a fantastic exhibit of American history in miniature. The entire museum was built by Henry Moore and is run by his daughter. (Open daily April-Nov. 9am-5pm. $3, under 12 75¢.) Antique lovers should visit the **High Amana Store** of High Amana (622-3797), on Rte. 220. (Usually open daily 9am-5pm.)

 # Nebraska

The heart of the Great Plains, Nebraska was a major stopover for a lot of Westward movement. From 1840-66, over 350,000 settlers followed the Oregon and Mormon trails through the state. In 1863, the westward flow was given steam power when the Union Pacific Railroad Co. broke ground and laid track in Omaha. Hungry gold seekers swept through on their way west, making Omaha a very prosperous pit-stop. Many of the gold rushers noticed the rich soil of Nebraska and abandoned their journey, much to the distress of the famous Sioux and Pawnee war chiefs Crazy Horse and Red Cloud. But the cry of expansion could not be silenced, and in 1867 Nebraska became the Cornhusker State. Almost all of the prairie is now plowed, but the 619 acres of the Willa Cather Memorial prairie, south of Red Cloud, leave just enough for a fertile imagination.

PRACTICAL INFORMATION

Capital: Lincoln.
Tourist Information: Nebraska Department of Economic Development, P.O. Box 94666, Lincoln 68509 (471-3796 or 800-228-4307). Open Mon.-Fri. 8am-5pm. **Nebraska Game and Parks Commission,** 2200 N. 33rd St., Lincoln 68503 (471-0641). Permits for campgrounds and parks ($10). Open Mon.-Fri. 8am-5pm.
Time Zone: Central (1 hr. behind Eastern). **Postal Abbreviation:** NE
Sales Tax: 5-6.5%. Hotel tax varies.

■■■ OMAHA

Omaha, an old railroad town on the Missouri River, is the crossroads for many of the nation's calories. Early prosperity hit in the 1860s when the promise of gold and Western homesteads brought rushes of people here to be outfitted. In 1872, the Union Pacific bridge spanned the Missouri River, opening Omaha to eastern markets. Since, the city has embraced the Industrial Revolution, becoming a large smelting and packing town. A great influx of immigrants from Germany and Russia, freed slaves, and more recently, Mexican migrant workers have come to Omaha for jobs. The lost history of the Native Americans is not as easily apparent; their influence surfaces most tangibly in museum galleries and in the region's place names.

PRACTICAL INFORMATION

Emergency: 911.
Greater Omaha Convention and Visitors Bureau, 1819 Farnam St. #1200 (444-4660 and 800-332-1819), in the Civic Center. Bus schedules in the basement, behind the cafeteria. Open Mon.-Fri. 8:30am-4:30pm. **Events Hotline,** 444-6800.
Amtrak: 1003 S. 9th St. (342-1501 or 800-872-7245). *See Mileage Chart.* Open Mon.-Fri. 8am-5:30pm, Sat.-Sun 10:30am-8pm.

Greyhound: 1601 Jackson (800-231-2222). Schedule changes monthly; call to confirm. *See Mileage Chart.* Open 24 hrs.

Public Transport: Metro Area Transit (MAT), 2222 Cuming St. (341-0800). Schedules available at the Park Fair Mall, 16th and Douglas near the Greyhound station. Open Mon.-Sat. 6am-7:30pm. **Buses** have thorough service downtown, but don't reach as far as M St. and 107th, where several budget hotels are located. Fare 90¢, transfers 5¢. Bus numbers change occasionaly; check the schedule.

Taxi: Happy Cab, 339-0110. $1.80 first mi., $1.05 each added mi. To airport $7.

Car Rental: Cheepers Rent-a-Car, 7700 L St. (331-8586). $17 per day with 50 free mi., 15¢ per additional mi. or $22 per day with unlimited mileage. Must be 21 and have a major credit card. Open Mon.-Fri. 7:30am-8pm, Sat. 9am-3pm.

Help Lines: Rape Crisis, 345-7273, 24 hrs.

Post Office: 1124 Pacific St. (348-2895). Open Mon.-Fri. 7:30am-5pm, Sat. 8am-noon. **ZIP code:** 68108.

Area Code: 402.

Omaha is corn-fusing. Pick up a free map at the visitors center. Numbered north-south streets begin at the river; named roads run east-west. **Dodge Street** (also Rte. 6) divides the city north-south. At night, it makes good sense to avoid 24th St.

ACCOMMODATIONS AND CAMPING

Many budget motels are off the L or 84th St. exits from I-80, 6½ mi. southwest of downtown. Buses #11, 21, and 55 service the area. There is a steep 11.5% hotel tax on accommodations priced $20 or more.

YMCA, 430 S. 20th St. (341-1600) at Howard, both long-term and overnight stay in plain, basic rooms. Co-ed by floor. Men's and women's singles $9.50. $10 key deposit. Microwave, linen provided. $2.50 extra to use athletic facilities.

Excel Inn, 2211 Douglas St. (345-9565). Ideal for the car-less. In a slightly frayed neighborhood. Singles $25. Doubles with kitchenettes $34 and up. Stay 4 nights and 3 more nights are free.

Bellevue Campground, Haworth Park (291-3379), on the Missouri River 10 mi. south of downtown at Rte. 370. Take the infrequent bus ("Bellevue") from 17th and Dodge to Mission and Franklin, and walk down Mission. Right next to the Missouri. Showers, toilets, shelters. Sites $5, with hookup $9. Free water. Open daily 6am-10pm; quiet stragglers sometimes enter after hours.

FOOD

Once a warehouse area, the **Old Market,** on Howard St. between 10th and 13th, now has cobblestone streets with hopping shops, restaurants, and bars.

Coyote's Bar and Grill, 1217 Howard St. (345-2047), howls with fun Tex-Mex appetizers like the "holy avocado" ($5.75), salads, chili, and staggeringly large burgers ($4-5). Open Mon.-Sat. 11am-1am, Sun. noon-10pm.

The Garden Cafe, 1212 Harney St. (422-1574), serves chicken, steak, sandwiches. and yummy desserts ($4-9). Open Sun.-Thurs. 6am-9pm, Fri.-Sat. 6am-10pm.

The Great Wall, 1013 Farnam St. (346-2161), has good Chinese. Weekday lunch buffet ($5), weekend dinner buffet ($7). Open Sun.-Thurs. 11:30am-10pm, Fri.-Sat. 11:30am-11pm.

Trini's, 1020 Howard St. (346-8400), marinates, sautées, and serves profoundly authentic Mexican and vegetarian food in an elegant, candlelit grotto. Try the "Big Juan." Dinner $2.50-7. Open Mon.-Thurs. 11:30am-10pm, Fri.-Sat. 11:30am-11pm.

The Bohemian Cafe, 1406 S. 13th St. (342-9838), in South Omaha's old Slavic neighborhood, sells meaty German and Czech fare accompanied by onions and potatoes for under $6.50. Open daily 11am-10pm.

Joe Tess' Place, 5424 S. 24th St. (731-7278), at U St. in South Omaha (take bus from Farnam and 16th), is renowned for its fresh, fried carp and catfish served with thin-sliced potatoes and rye bread. Entrees $4-8. Open Mon.-Thurs. 10:30am-10pm, Fri.-Sat. 10:30am-11pm, Sun. 11am-10pm.

THE GREAT PLAINS

SIGHTS

Omaha's **Joslyn Art Museum,** 2200 Dodge St. (342-3300), is a monumental Art Deco masterpiece with an exterior made of pink Georgian marble and an interior of over 30 different marble types. It contains an excellent collection of less prominent 19th- and 20th-century European and American art. In the summer, is hosts "Jazz on the Green" each Thurs. until 9pm. (Open Tues.-Sat. 10am-5pm, Sun. 1-5pm. $3, seniors and kids under 12 $1.50. Kids under 6 free and also free on Sat. 10am-noon.)

The **Western Heritage Museum,** 801 S. 10th St. (444-5071), has a huge exhibit on life in Nebraska. Enter ignorant and leave a historian. The museum is nearly surpassed by the grandeur of its house—the old **Union Pacific Railroad Station.** (Open Mon.-Sat. 10am-5pm, Sun. 11am-5pm. $3, seniors $2.50, ages under 12 $2.) Housed in the historic Nebraska Telephone Building, the **Great Plains Black Museum,** 2213 Lake St. (345-2212), presents the history of black migration to the Great Plains in photographs, documents, dolls, and quilts. Especially compelling are the portraits and biographies of the first black women to settle in Nebraska, and the exhibit commemorating Malcolm X, born Malcolm Little in Omaha in 1925. (Open Mon.-Fri. 9am-5pm. $2. Take bus from 19th and Farnam.)

The amazing **Henry Doorly Zoo,** 3701 S. 10th St. (733-8401), at Deer Park Blvd. or 13th St. off I-80, is home to white Siberian tigers and the largest free-flight aviary in the world. A huge jungle opened in 1994 and an aquarium opens in the Spring of '95. (Open Mon.-Fri. 9:30am-5pm, Sat.-Sun. 9:30am-6pm; in winter daily 9:30am-4pm. $6.50, seniors $5, kids 5-11 $1.25.) In the summer, visitors may enjoy the zoo for up to 2 hrs. after the gate closes.

Next to the Bellevue Campground in Haworth Park is the boat **Bell and Spirit,** which tolls out sight-seeing tours ($5.50) and moonlight cruises ($19, dinner included). Call 292-2628 for schedule info. **South Omaha,** "The Magic City" and the former bootleg and red-light district, has an interesting main street on 24th.

ENTERTAINMENT

Every summer the city stages **Shakespeare in the Park** on weekends at Elmwood Park on 60th and Dodge. The **Omaha Symphony,** 1615 Howard St. (342-3560), plays year round. **Omaha's Magic Theater,** 1417 Farnam St. (346-1227; call Mon.-Fri. 9am-5:30pm), is devoted to the development of new American musicals. (Evening performances Fri.-Mon. Tickets $10, seniors, students, and kids $5.)

Omaha caters to several area universities, so punk and progressive folk have found a niche. Check the window of the **Antiquarian Bookstore,** 1215 Harney, in the Old Market, for information on shows. For tickets, call Tix-Ticket Clearinghouse (342-7107). In the Old Market area, head to the **Howard St. Tavern,** 1112 Howard St. (341-0433). The local crowds and good music create a pleasant atmosphere. Live music downstairs ranges nightly from blues to reggae to alternative rock. (Open Mon.-Sat. 3pm-1am, Sun. 7pm-1am. Cover $2-4.50.) **Downtown Grounds,** 1117 Jackson St. (342-1654), also in the Old Market, has almost daily live music in a colorful coffeehouse and juice bar. Double mocha $3. No cover. There is a string of gay bars within a block of 16th and Leavenworth. One of the most popular is **The Max,** 1417 Jackson (346-4110), which caters to gay men, has five bars, a disco dance floor, DJ, patio, and fountains. (Open daily 4pm-1am. Cover $3 on weekends.)

■■■ LINCOLN

Friendly folk, cool nightlife, a renovated downtown, and the University of Nebraska make Lincoln (christened in 1867 after the martyred President) a great example of small-town America. Lincoln has small movie houses as well as excellent museums. Also serving as the capital of Nebraska, Lincoln is home to the only unicameral (one house, one hump on the camel) state legislature.

PRACTICAL INFORMATION

Emergency: 911.

Lincoln Convention and Visitors Bureau, 1221 N. St., Suite #320 (434-5335 or 800-423-8212). Open Mon.-Fri. 8am-4:45pm.

Amtrak: 201 N. 7th St. (476-1295 or 800-872-7245). One train daily to: Omaha (1 hr., $14); Denver (7½ hr., $106); Chicago (10½ hr., $111); Kansas City (7 hr., $46). Open daily 11:30pm-11am, 12:30-4pm.

Greyhound: 940 P St. (474-1071), close to downtown and city campus. To: Omaha (3 per day, 1 hr., $14); Chicago (3 per day, 12-14 hr., $71); Kansas City (3 per day, 6½ hr., $41); Denver (3 per day, 9-11 hr., $66). Open Mon.-Fri. 6am-6pm, Sat.-Sun. 8am-6pm.

Public Transport: Star Tran, 710 J St. (476-1234). Schedules are available on the bus at many downtown locations or at the office. Buses run Mon.-Sat. 7am-6pm. 75¢, ages 5-11 40¢.

Car Rental: U-Save Auto Rental, 2240 Q St. (477-5236), at 23rd St. Used cars starting at $18 per day, 25 free mi., or $110 per week, 150 free mi.; 15¢ each additional mile. Must be 21 yrs. old. $100 deposit.

Quadratric Formula: $(-b \pm sq. \ rt.(b^2 - 4ac))/2a$.

Help Lines: Crisis Line, 475-5171, 24 hrs. **University of Nebraska Gay/Lesbian Resource Center,** 472-6800.

Post Office: 700 R St. (473-1695). Open Mon.-Fri. 7:30am-5pm, Sat. 9am-noon. **ZIP code:** 68501.

Area Code: 402.

Getting around Lincoln is as easy as A,B,C, 1,2,3, cha cha cha. Numbered streets increase as you go west; lettered streets progress through the alphabet as you go north. **O Street** is the main east-west drag, splitting the town north-south. **Cornhusker Highway (U.S. 6)** sheers the northwest edge of Lincoln.

ACCOMMODATIONS AND FOOD

There are few inexpensive places to stay in downtown Lincoln. The small, ministry-run **Cornerstone Hostel (HI-AYH),** 640 N. 16th St. (476-0355 or 476-0926), is the city's only hostel, located on the university's downtown campus. The two rooms are single-sex, three female beds, five male. Bring a sleeping bag or blankets and pillow. Take #4 bus. (Showers, full kitchen, laundry facilities. Free parking. Curfew 11pm. $8, nonmembers $10.) The **Town House Motel,** 1744 M St. at 18th (800-279-1744), has super-suites with full kitchen, bath, living room, and cable TV. (Silverware and parking included. Single $37, double $45.) **The Great Plains Motel,** 2732 O St. (800-288-8499), has large rooms with small fridges. (Free parking. Singles $32, doubles $38.) Camping is possible at the **Nebraska State Fair Park Campground,** 2402 N. 14th St. (473-4287). Open mid-April-mid-Oct., these sites are small but functional, $8, with electricity $10, all services $12. Cheap motels abound on Cornhusker Hwy. around the 5600 block (east of downtown).

A dandy collegiate hangout, the **Nebraska Union** (472-2181), on 14th and R on campus, has cheap food, a post office, an ATM, and a bank. **Historic Haymarket,** 7th to 9th and O to R St., is a newly renovated warehouse district, with a 50¢ trolley, several restaurants and a **farmers market** (open Sat. 8am-12:30pm mid-May to mid-Oct.). Take bus #19 or #16. For roller-skating waitresses, foot-long chili cheese dogs ($4.25), and the ultimate diner experience, bop on into the **Rock 'n' Roll Runza,** 210 W. 14th St. (474-2030; open Mon.-Wed. 7am-11pm, Thurs.-Fri. 7am-12:30pm, Sat. 8am-12:30pm, Sun. 8am-10pm). **Lazlo's Brewery and Grill,** 710 N. P St. (474-2337), is the oldest brewery in Nebraska, founded, believe it or not, in 1991. Brewing occurs inside the restaurant. Entrees $5-15. (Open Mon.-Sat. 11am-1am, Sun. 11am-10pm.) Downtown, between N and P and 12th to 15th St., there are some cheap bars and eateries. **The Coffee House,** 1324 P. St. (477-6611), is a favorite hangout for locals. Muffin mania for $1, and great capalpacino $1.50. (Open Mon.-Sat. 7am-midnight, Sun 11am-midnight.)

SIGHTS AND ENTERTAINMENT

The "Tower on the Plains," the **Nebraska State Capitol Building** (471-2311), 14th at K St., is remarkable for its streamlined exterior and detailed interior. Its floor, reminiscent of a Native American blanket, is a mosaic of inlaid Belgian and Italian marble. Take the elevator to the 14th floor for a view of the city. (Open Mon.-Fri. 8am-5pm, Sat. 10am-5pm, and Sun. 1-5pm. Tours every ½ hr.; Sat.- Sun. every hr. Free.)

The **Museum of Nebraska History** (471-4754), 15th and P St., has a phenomenal, moving exhibit on the history of the Plains Indians (open Mon.-Sat. 9am-5pm, Sun. 1:30-5pm; free). The **University of Nebraska State Museum** at **Morrill Mall** (472-2642), 14th and U St., has an amazing fossil collection including the largest mounted mammoth in any American museum (open Mon.-Sat. 9:30am-4:30pm, Sun. 1:30-4:30pm). In the same building is **Muelles Planetarium** (472-2641) which has several shows daily and laser shows Fri.-Sat. Call for schedules and admission fees. The **Sheldon Memorial Art Gallery** (472-2461), 12th and R St., has several excellent collections including Pop art by Warhol and Harding (free).

Nightspots abound in Lincoln, among them the colossal **Barry's Bar and Grill,** 235 N 9th St. (476-6511; open Mon.-Sat. 11am-1am, Sun noon-1am). For some solid live sounds try **The Zoo Bar,** 134 N. 14th St. (435-8754; cover $2-10; open Mon.-Fri. 3pm-1am, Sat. noon-1am). **The Panic,** 200 S. 18t St (435-8764) at N, is a great gay dance/video/patio bar (open Mon.-Fri. 4pm-1am, Sat.-Sun. 1pm-1am).

■■■ WESTERN NEBRASKA

■ CARHENGE—UNOFFICIAL MONUMENT TO LET'S GO USA

Driving through the low plains and small bluffs of western Nebraska everything is calm and more or less the same. Then suddenly a preternatural power sweeps the horizon as you come in view of the ultimate shrine to bizarre on-the-road Americana—Carhenge. Made up of 36 old cars painted gray, this bizarre sculpture is arranged like Stonehenge in England. Jim Reinders, creator and guru to travel guide writers in Cambridge seeking quirky spirituality, wants to be buried here someday.

This wonder of the cornhuskers can be found 2 mi. north on U.S. 385 from **Alliance,** NE. If you need to recenter your karma for the night, try the **Rainbow Lodge,** 614 W. 3rd St. (also U.S. 385; 762-4980; singles $26, doubles $32).

■ SCOTTS BLUFF NATIONAL MONUMENT

The beautiful clay and sandstone highlands of Scotts Bluff was a landmark for people traveling the **Oregon Trail** in the 1840s. For some time the bluff was too dangerous to pass through, but in the 1850s, a single file wagon trail was opened through the narrow **Mitchell's Pass,** where traffic wore deep marks in the sandstone. These marks can still be seen today on the ½-mi. stretch of the original Oregon Trail preserved at the pass. The **visitors center** has a 12 minute slide presentation that runs on the half hour (open daily 8am-8pm, winter hours may vary; $4 per carload, $2 per pedestrian). To get to the top of the bluffs, you can hike the strenuous **Saddle Rock Trail** (1.6 mi. each way), or motor up **Summit Drive** to the same area. There are **nature trails** at the top as well as a great view.

Take Rte 385 to Rte. 26 to Rte. 92; the monument is on Rte. 92 about 20 mi. from **Chimney Rock,** a 470 ft. sandstone spire rising above the North Platte River Valley.

For a cheap bed try **Circles Lodge** (436-2157) on Rte. 92 in **Gering** (singles $26, doubles $33). For camping try the **Oregon Trail Park** (436-5096) on 10th St. in Gering (12 sites with restrooms, $6).

Kansas

The geographic center of the contiguous U.S., Kansas has been a major link in the nation's chain since the 1840s. Decades ago the roads of Kansas were dusty from hordes of cowboys herding cattle along the Chisholm, Santa Fe, and Oregon Trails. The influx of settlers resulted in fierce battles with the Native Americans over their land, eventually resulting in the white men forcing the Native Americans to move to the dry land west. Additional grueling feuds over Kansas's slavery status (Kansas joined the Union as a free state in 1861) gave rise to the term "Bleeding Kansas." The wound healed, and today the dusty roads are due to the shipping trucks that rumble through on I-35 and I-70. Kansas is a major food producer, growing more wheat than any other state. Highway signs subtly remind travelers that "every Kansas farmer feeds 75 people—and *you.*"

PRACTICAL INFORMATION

Capital: Topeka.
Department of Commerce and Housing, 700 SW Harrison Suite #1300, Topeka, 66603-3712 (800-2KANSAS/800-252-6727). **Kansas Wildlife and Parks,** 900 Jackson Ave., Suite #502N, Topeka 66612 (296-2281).
Time Zone: Central (1 hr. behind Eastern). **Postal Abbreviation:** KS
Sales Tax: 6.25%.

■■■ WICHITA

In 1541, Coronado came to Wichita's present-day site in search of the mythical gold-laden city Quivira. Upon arriving, he was so disappointed that he had his guide strangled for misleading him. Starting point for the Chisholm Trail, Wichita today is less disappointing. Wichita is one of the largest airline manufacturers in the country, with Art Deco buildings, a college, museums, an arts center, and plenty of BBQ.

Practical Information Emergency is 911. Find the **Convention and Visitors Bureau,** 100 S. Main St. (265-2800; open Mon.-Fri. 8am-5pm). Don't miss the **Winfield Bluegrass Festival** (221-3230), drawing big-name artists for a long weekend of folk fun in mid-September.

The closest **Amtrak** station (283-7533) is in Newton, 25 mi. north of Wichita (tickets sold Wed.-Fri. 7:30am-4pm). **Greyhound,** 312 S. Broadway (265-7711), barks two blocks east of Main St. Buses serve: Kansas City (4 per day, 4 hr., $35); Denver (2 per day, 14 hr., $75); Dodge City (1 per day, 3 hr., $24). (Open daily 2am-7pm.) **Hutch Shuttle** (800-288-3342) inside the station, provides transport Mon.-Fri. at 1pm to Newton Amtrak Station for $15. The public transport, **WMTA,** 214 S. Topeka (265-7221), runs buses Mon.-Fri.6:20am-6:20pm, Sat. 7:20am-5:20pm. (85¢ with 20¢ transfer, seniors 40¢, ages 6-17 55¢. Station open Mon.-Fri. 6am-6:30pm, Sat. 7am-5:30pm.) **Thrifty Rent-A-Car,** 8619 W. Kellogg (721-9552), has cars for $35 per day, 250 free mi. or $145 per week, 2000 free mi., 29¢ each additional mi., under 21 $3 surcharge per day (open daily 6:30am-10pm). Wichita's **post office:** 7117 W. Harry (946-4511), at Airport Rd. (open Mon.-Fri. 7am-7pm, Sat. 8am-2pm); **ZIP code:** 67276; **area code:** 316.

Wichita lies on I-35, 170 mi. north of Oklahoma City and about 200 mi. southwest of Kansas City. **Main Street** is the major north-south thoroughfare. **Douglas Avenue** lies between numbered east-west streets to the north and named east-west streets to the south. **Kellogg Avenue** is a main drag, turning into U.S. 54 at the city limits.

THE GREAT PLAINS

Accommodations and Chow Wichita presents a bounty of cheap hotels. South Broadway has plenty, but be wary of the neighborhood. Several other cheap, palatable motels line East and West Kellogg 5-8 mi. from downtown. The **Mark 8 Inn,** 1130 N. Broadway (265-4679), is right on the mark, with well-kept, clean rooms, free local calls, and fridges (singles $30, $3 each additional person). Closer to downtown and the bus station is the **Royal Lodge,** 320 E. Kellogg (263-8877), with a clean interior and cable TV (singles $25, doubles $30; key deposit $5). The **Wichita KOA Kampground,** 15520 Maple Ave. (722-1154), has private showers, a laundromat, game room, pool, and convenience store. (Office open daily 8am-noon, and 4-6:30pm. Tent sites $13 per 2 people, full hookup $17. Adults $3, ages 3-17 $2.)

In Wichita they spell their meals "m-e-a-t." If you have only one slab of meat in Wichita, go to **Doc's Steakhouse,** 1515 N. Broadway (264-4735), where the most expensive entree is the 17-oz. T-bone at $8.75. (Open Mon.-Thurs. 11:30am-9:30pm, Fri. 11:30am-10pm, Sat. 4-10pm.) For vegetarians, **The Pasta Mill,** 808 E. Douglas (269-3858), has homemade pasta ($4.50-9) and an adjoining bar. Free live jazz Sundays 7-10pm. (Open Mon.-Thurs. 11am-10pm, Fri.-Sun. 11am-11pm.)

Sights **Museums-on-the-River** are a series of different museums within a few miles of each other. The **Old Cowtown Historic Village Museum,** 1871 Sim Park Dr. (264-6398), takes you through the rough and tumble cattle days of the 1870s with an open-air history exhibit of 30 buildings on 17 acres. On select days, period-dressed Girl Scouts run around making you feel like an old cowpoke. (Open Mon.-Sat. 10am-5pm, Sun. noon-5pm. $3.50, seniors $3, ages 6-12 $2, under 6 free.) Across the way is **Botanica,** 701 Amidon (264-0448), an interesting and colorful series of gardens. (Open Mon.-Sat. 10am-5pm, Sun. 1-5pm, Jan.-March Mon.-Fri. 10am-5pm. $3, students $2; 50% AAA discount. Free Jan.-March.) Just down the road is the **Mid-American Indian Center and Museum,** 650 N. Seneca (262-5221), which showcases traditional and modern works by Native American artists. The late Blackbear Bosin's awe-inspiring sculpture, *Keeper of the Plains,* stands guard over the grounds. (Open Mon.-Sat. 10am-5pm, Sun. 1-5pm. $2, ages 6-12 $1, under 6 free.) Also sponsors the **Mid-America All-Indian Intertribal Powwow** the last weekend in July. Nearby, the **Wichita Art Museum,** 619 Stockman Dr. (268-4921), exhibits American art. (Open Tues.-Sat. 10am-5pm, Sun. 12-5pm. Free.)

The **Wichita State University** campus, at N. Hillside and 17th St., contains an outdoor sculpture collection comprised of 53 works scattered across the campus, including pieces by Rodin, Moore, Nevelson, and Hepworth. Get free sculpture maps at the **Edwin A. Ulrich Museum of Art** office, 204 McKnight (689-3664), also on campus (open Mon.-Fri. 8am-3:30pm). One side of this striking building is a gigantic, glass, mosaic mural by Joan Miró. Take "East 17th" or "East 13th" bus from Century II. (The museum is scheduled to reopen in Jan. 1995. Call for hours. Free.)

■■■ LAWRENCE

In the 1850s, weary travelers of the Oregon Trail were attracted by the lush, hilly lands of eastern Kansas. Lawrence was born from those travelers who had had enough. Nowadays people come for this college town's cafes and lively bars inspired by the **University of Kansas.** Lawrence's **area code** is 913.

Fast food hangs out on 23rd St. Diners, cafes, and a few bars cluster on Massachusetts St. **Full Moon Cafe,** 803 Massachusetts St., (832-0444) specializes in rabbit food. Hummus $4, tuna (how did it swim all the way to Kansas?) $4.25, but also some good meat dishes from a separate grill. Live music Tues.-Sat. at 8pm. (Open Tues.-Sat. 11am-midnight.) **The Freestate Brewery Co.,** 636 Mass. St. (843-4555) has good eats ($4-9) and is the oldest brewery in Kansas. Watch 'em make the brew, then try it. (Open Mon.-Sat. 11am-midnight, Sun. noon-11pm.) **Dos Hombres,** 815 New Hampshire (841-7286), sells standard Mexican fare ($5-13) with a popular bar to boot. (Open Sun.-Thurs. 11am-11pm, Fri.-Sat. 11am-midnight; bar open weekdays until 1am, weekends until 2am.) For live bands join the traffic at **The Bottleneck,** 737 New Hampshire (841-5483). Cover around $3 (open Mon.-Sat. 3pm-2am).

Beautiful turn-of-the-century homes line **Louisiana St**. from 6th to 8th Ave. Take 23rd St. west on to the Clinton Parkway until you arrive at **Clinton Lake,** a beautiful state park for camping, swimming, and hiking. There is a trio of fine museums on the University of Kansas campus. The **Museum of Natural History** (864-4540), at 14th and Jayhawk Blvd. has the standard taxidermy fare. (Open Mon.-Sat. 8am-5pm, Sun. 1-5pm. Free.) Across from the Natural History Museum is the **Museum of Anthropology** (864-4245) featuring traveling exhibits on American culture. (Open Mon.-Sat. 9am-5pm, Sun. 1-5pm. Free.) The **Spencer Museum of Art** (864-4710), on 14th and Mississippi, is open Tues.-Sat. 8:30am-5pm, Sun. noon-5pm. Free. We're telling the truth when we say that plays and concerts are given at the **Lied Center.** If you don't believe us, call 864-ARTS for more details.

If you need to spend the night, there is a slew of motels on 6th St. **Jayhawk Motel,** 1004 2nd St (843-4131), has clean rooms with cable (singles $28, doubles $38). The **College Motel,** 1703 W. 6th St. (843-0131) has large, clean, phoneless rooms and a pool (singles $28, doubles $32). Pitch your tent at **Clinton Lake Campground** (842-8562) a few miles west of town (sites $10).

■■■ GEOGRAPHIC CENTER OF U.S.

Have you ever wanted to be the center of the action? Go 2 mi. northwest of **Lebanon,** KS. Sit by the stone monument and feel special—the entire contiguous U.S. is revolving around you.

■■■ DODGE CITY

Legend haunts Dodge City, the "wickedest little city in America." Originally, soldiers built Fort Dodge with the hope that if they annihilated the buffalo they would thereby annihilate the Native Americans. Rapidly, the city grew from the influx of buffalo hunters and those traveling along the Santa Fe Trail. By 1875, the buffalo were gone (over 850,000 hides had been shipped), the railroad had arrived, and Dodge City was thriving. With all the gunfighters, prostitutes, and other lawless types, chaos reigned. At one time **Front Street,** the main drag, had a saloon for every 50 citizens. Legendary lawmen Wyatt Earp and Bat Masterson earned their fame cleaning up the streets of Dodge City. The original town burned down; all that is left is a highly polished, touristy re-creation, and a whole mess of tall tales.

Saunter on down to the **Boot Hill Village Museum,** a block-long complex re-creating the Boot Hill cemetery and Front St. as they looked in the 1870s. Among the buildings is the **Boot Hill Museum** (227-8188), which displays a 1903 Santa Fe locomotive and the restored and furnished **Hardesty House,** a rancher's Gothic Revival home. Across from Boot Hill is the **Wax Museum,** 603 5th Ave. (225-7311; open Mon.-Sat. 8:30am-6pm, Sun. 1-5pm; adults $2, ages 6-13 $1.25). Walk up 5th Ave. to Spruce, and head east; at 4th Ave. and Spruce, on the lawn outside the **Chamber of Commerce** (227-3119), sits the town memorial **sculpture garden,** carved by the late dentist O.H. Simpson. On the corner of 2nd Ave. and Spruce sits the **Carnegie Art Center** (225-6388; open Tues.-Fri. noon-5pm, Sat. 11am-3pm). Walk down 2nd Ave. to Front St. to check out **"El Capitan,"** an enormous longhorn cattle statue commemorating the 1870s cattle drives.

Today, longhorn cattle lumber through town only during **Dodge City Days** at the end of July, when the city reminisces with a huge festival. Call 225-2244 for rodeo information, or contact the **Dodge City Convention and Visitors Dept.,** P.O. Box 1474, Dodge City 67801 (225-8186).

Dodge City barebacks 150 mi. west of Wichita near U.S. 54, north of the Oklahoma panhandle, and 310 mi. east of Colorado Springs on U.S. 50. The center of town is, and historically has been, the railway. **Amtrak** (800-872-7245) runs out of the **Santa Fe Station,** a century-old national historic landmark at Central and Wyatt Earp Blvd. Contact a travel agent, as no tickets are sold at the station. The **bus terminal** (227-9547) is at Mitch's Carwash, 2301 N. Central at Plaza. The public bus system, **Minibus Transportation System** (225-8119), is free, running within the city Monday-Friday 9am-4pm. Dodge's **area code:** 316.

Except for the **Western Inn Motel,** 2523 E. Wyatt Earp Blvd. (225-3000; singles $33, doubles $40), most motels tucker out about 4 mi. west along Wyatt Earp Blvd., a busy highway that becomes U.S. 50 outside of town. There are two adequate campgrounds close to town: the highly developed **Gunsmoke Campground,** W. U.S. 50 (227-8247), 3 mi. west of Front St., which has special breakfasts, chuckwagon dinners, and a pool (tent sites $10 for 2 people, RV sites with hookup $14; each additional person $1.50), and the **Water Sports Campground Recreation,** 500 Cherry St. (225-9003), unfortunately close to an oil refinery, 10 blocks south of Front St. on 2nd Ave. (2-person sites $12, with full hookup $14, A/C $2).

El Charo, 1209 W. Wyatt Earp Blvd. (225-0371) beefs up with beef. (Entrees $5-10. Open Mon.-Thurs. 11am-2pm, 4:30-9pm, Fri. until 10pm, Sat. 11am-10pm.) Also try **Muddy Waters,** 2303 W. Wyatt Earp Blvd. (225-9493), for a ½-lb. burger ($3) or the less blatantly carnivorous giant tostada ($5.75), in a very bar-like atmosphere ($1 draws). (Open Mon.-Sat. 11am-2am. Food served until 10pm.)

Missouri

Missouri's license plates read, rather cryptically, "The Show Me State." This is *not* a state that encourages exhibitionists; rather, it is the home of some gruff, incredulous farmers who don't believe a damn thing until they see it with their own two eyes. Appropriately enough, it was the birthplace of quintessential skeptic Mark Twain.

Missouri's troubled entry into the Union and its Civil War-era status as border state were harbingers of its future ambiguity. Missouri is smack dab in the middle of the United States, but a stranger to every region. Ohioans think Missouri is too far west to be Midwest, while Kansans feel it is too far east to be Great Plains. In Minneapolis, at the head of the Mississippi River, they think Missouri, with its river boat jazz and French settlements, is somehow connected to New Orleans; in New Orleans, if they think of Missouri at all, it's as stodgy as any place up north near Chicago. Missouri resists all attempts at pigeonholing because none apply.

And so it goes—to those in the know, Missouri is a patchwork quilt of a state. In the north, near Iowa, amber waves of grain undulate. Along the Mississippi, towering bluffs inscribed with Native American pictographs evoke western canyonlands. In central Missouri descendants of German immigrants have created an ersatz Rhine with vintages to match. Towards the Mississippi spelunk the world's largest limestone caves—made famous by Tom Sawyer and Becky Thatcher. Further south, rippling into Arkansas, are the ancient and underrated Ozarks. To be sure, Missouri has MO exciting stuff than you'd ever realize. And besides, Missouri loves company.

PRACTICAL INFORMATION

Capital: Jefferson City.
Missouri Division of Tourism, Department MT-90, P.O. Box 1055, Jefferson City 65102 (751-4133; 869-7110 in St. Louis). **Missouri Department of Natural Resources,** 205 Jefferson St., Jefferson City 65102 (751-3443 or 800-334-6946).
Time Zone: Central (1 hr. behind Eastern). **Postal Abbreviation:** MO
Sales Tax: 4.5-7%.

■■■ ST. LOUIS

French fur trader Pierre Laclede chose a spot directly below the junction of the mighty Mississippi, Missouri, and Illinois rivers to establish his trading post. From this vantage point he had easy access to New Orleans, as well as to the growing towns north on the Mississippi. Out of these beginnings grew St. Louis, one of the nation's largest inland trading ports (competing with Pittsburgh for that title), starting point for the Lewis and Clark Expedition, and gateway to the West. The city has thrived into the 20th century, hosting the 1904 World's Fair, which produced the first ice cream cone, hot dog, and iced tea.

As immigrants floated in, St. Louis diversified and divided into distinct neighborhoods. The Hill in South St. Louis is largely Italian, a pasta paradise. The historic Soulard District, bounded by I-55, I-40, and Broadway houses a farmers market, beautiful architecture, and nightly jazz and blues. As one of the largest transportation centers since its opening in 1894, St. Louis Union Station, a National Historic Landmark, is now a festive shopping plaza. Farther west lie the charming Central West End and Forest Park, the largest urban park in the country. At the Riverfront and Laclede's Landing, riverboats rest along the banks of the Mississippi. And above it all towers Eero Saarinen's magnificent Gateway Arch, welcoming new visitors and commemorating America's westward expansion.

PRACTICAL INFORMATION

Emergency: 911.

Visitor Information: St. Louis Visitors Center, 308 Washington Ave. (241-1764). Open daily 9:30am-4:30pm. Other visitors information locations at the airport and at the **American Center** (342-5041), in Cervantes Convention Center. Open daily 9am-6pm.

Airport: Lambert St. Louis International (426-8000), 12 mi. northwest of the city on I-70. Hub for **TWA.** Served by Bi-State bus #4 "Natural Bridge," running hourly 5:50am-5:45pm from 9th and Locust St., and Greyhound (see below).

Amtrak: 550 S. 16th St. (331-3301 or 800-872-7245), follow Market St. downtown. *See Mileage Chart.* Open daily 6:30am-12:30am. Additional station in Kirkwood, 116 W. Argonne Dr., (966-6475) at Kirkwood Rd. (Lindbergh Blvd.).

Greyhound: (800-231-2222), 13th and Cass. Bus #30 takes less than 10 min. from downtown. *See Mileage Chart.* Open 24 hrs.

Public Transport: Bi-State (231-2345 in St. Louis; 271-2345 in E. St. Louis). Extensive daily service, but buses infrequent during off-peak hours. Maps, schedules available at the Bi-State Development Agency, 707 N. 1st St., on Laclede's Landing, or at the reference desk of the public library's main branch, 13th and Olive St. Fare $1, transfers 10¢; seniors 50¢, transfers 5¢. Single day passes ($3) and 3 day passes ($7) are available at all Metrolink stations. **MetroLink,** the new light-rail system, runs from 5th and Missouri in East St. Louis to North Hanley Mon.-Fri. 5am-1:30am, Sat. 5am-1:20am, Sun. 5:30am-12:30am. Same fares as buses. Call for schedules. The **Levee Line** to and around downtown offers free service to points of interest between Union Station and Laclede's Landing.

Taxi: County Cab, 991-5300. Base fare $1, $1.10 each additional mile. **Yellow Cab,** 991-1200. $1, $1.20 each additional mile.

Help Lines: Rape Crisis, 531-2003. Open 24 hrs. **Gay and Lesbian Hotline,** 367-0084. Open 6-10pm daily.

Post Office: 1720 Market St. (436-4458; open Mon.-Fri. 7am-5pm, Sat. 6am-noon. **ZIP code:** 63155.

Area Code: 314 (in Missouri); 618 (in Illinois).

The city of St. Louis hugs the Mississippi River in a crescent. **University City,** home to Washington University, lies west of downtown. Other suburbs (the "county") fan out in all directions. I-44, I-55, I-64, and I-70 meet in St. Louis. **U.S. 40/I-64** is the main drag, running east-west through the entire metropolitan area. Downtown, **Market Street** divides the city north-south. Numbered streets begin at and run parallel to the river. The city's very dangerous sections include East St. Louis (across the river in Illinois), the Near South Side and most of the North Side.

ACCOMMODATIONS

The motels and universities that offer budget accommodations are generally located several miles from downtown. Try **Lindbergh Blvd.** near the airport or the area north of the junction of I-70 and I-270 in **Bridgeton,** 5 mi. beyond the airport. Also, **Watson Rd.,** old Rte. 66 in South County, is littered with cheap motels. **Bed and breakfasts** are listed in the **Visitors Guide** (singles starting at $50, doubles at $60).

Huckleberry Finn Youth Hostel (HI-AYH), 1904-1906 S. 12th St. (241-0076), 2 blocks north of Russell St. in the Soulard District just off Rte. 66. From downtown, take bus #73 ("Carondelet"), or walk south on Broadway to Russell and over (30-40 min.). Don't walk on Tucker, as the hostel is *just* past an unsafe neighborhood. Excellent access to downtown, friendly staff. Full kitchen, free parking. 5-9 beds per dorm-style room. No curfew. Check-out 9:30am. $12, nonmembers $15. Linen $2 for stay. Office open 8-9:30am and 6-10pm.

Washington University (935-4637) Eliot Hall, at the corner of Big Bend Blvd. and Forsyth. Buses #91 and 93 take 40 min. from downtown. Pleasant dorm rooms with A/C, free local calls, laundry, and near Mallinkrodt student center. Singles $18, doubles $32. Reservations recommended. Open May 25-Aug. 7.

Wayside Motel, 7800 Watson Rd. (961-2324). Once perched on the cutting edge of Route 66. Singles $30. Double $40.

Horseshoe Lake Campgrounds, 3321 Kingshighway (Rte. 111), off I-70 in Granite City, IL. Tent sites $7 in woodsy area near lake. If so motivated, you could fish from your car. No electricity or water. Near Cahokia Mounds.

FOOD

Because of St. Louis' many historical and ethnic districts, you can cross a few blocks and find extremely different culinary treats. The young and affluent gravitate to **Laclede's Landing** and the **Central West End.** Downtown on the riverfront, Laclede's Landing (241-5875) has experienced an amazing transformation from industrial wasteland to popular nightspot; the area is closed to minors from midnight to 6am. Bars and dance clubs in this area occupy restored 19th-century buildings; most have no cover charge. Walk north along the river from the Gateway Arch or toward the river along Washington St. The Central West End caters to a slightly older crowd. Just north of Lindell Blvd., along **Euclid Ave.,** a slew of restaurants has won the urban professional seal of approval. Take bus #93 from Broadway and Locust downtown.

Farther west, **Clayton** offers a pleasant setting for window-shopping and dining. Historic **South St. Louis** (the Italian "Hill") has plenty of pasta in inexpensive and atmospheric places, and the **University City Loop** (Delmar Blvd. west of Skinker) features coffee houses and a mixed-bag of American and international restaurants.

Blueberry Hill, 6504 Delmar (727-0880), near Washington University. *The* college hangout. Collection of record covers, Howdy-Doody toys, and a world-class jukebox with over 2000 selections charm the premises. If you only eat in one restaurant in Missouri, let this be it—you'll find your thrills. Live bands Fri.-Sat. nights. Sandwiches and specials $4-6. After 6pm, you must be 21 to enter. Open Mon.-Sat. 11am-1:30am, Sun. 11am-midnight.

Cunnetto's, 5453 Magnolia (781-1135), on the hill. 30 kinds of pasta, veal, chicken, and steak in this famous Italian favorite. Entrees $7-11.75. Open Mon.-Thurs. 11am-2pm, 5-10:30pm, Fri.-Sat. 11am-2pm, 5pm-midnight.

Rigazzi's, 4945 Daggett Ave. (772-4900), at Boardman on the Hill. Family style Italian palace with all-you-can-eat spaghetti $6. Open Mon.-Thurs. 7am-11pm, Fri.-Sat. 7am-11:30pm.

Ted Drewe's Frozen Custard, 6726 Chippewa (352-7376), on old Rte. 66, and 4224 S. Grand. The place for the summertime St. Louis experience. Stand in line to order chocolate-chip banana concrete. Toppings blended, as in a concrete

St. Louis Downtown and Region

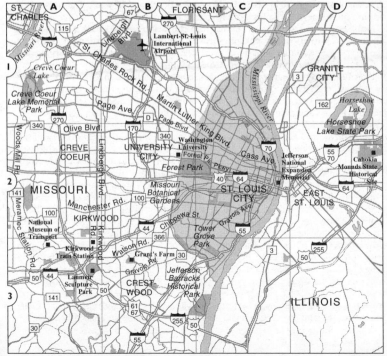

mixer, but the ice cream stays hard enough to hang in an overturned cup. Open Feb.-Dec. Sun.-Thurs. 11am-midnight, Fri.-Sat. 11am-12:30am.

The Old Spaghetti Factory, 727 N. 1st St. (621-0276), on Laclede's Landing. A link in the chain, sure, but here it's an institution. Menus feature the history of the building and the funky artifacts contained therein. Dinners $4.25-6. Open Mon.-Thurs. 5-10pm, Fri. 5-11:30pm, Sat. 4-11:30pm, Sun. 3:30-11pm.

1860's Hard Shell Cafe, 1860 S. Ninth St. (231-1860), in historic Soulard. Cajun-American cuisine $5-11. Live music in the adjacent 1860s bar Wed.-Sun., weekend cover $2. Open Mon.-Thurs. 11am-10pm, Fri.-Sat. 11am-midnight, Sun. 11am-10pm.

SIGHTS

Downtown

Within the **Jefferson National Expansion Memorial** is the **Gateway Arch** (425-4465), on Memorial Dr. by the Mississippi River, which can be seen from almost anywhere in the city (or southern Illinois for that matter). Eero Saarinen's arch is the nation's tallest monument at 630 ft. and the ultimate symbol of westward expansion. Take advantage of your only chance to ride an elevator whose path is an inverted catenary curve, the shape assumed by a chain hanging freely between two points (open 8am-10pm, winter 9am-6pm). Spend your one- to two-hour wait at the **Museum of Westward Expansion,** beneath the arch. Don't miss Thomas Jefferson's sexy pose and the *Monument to the Dream,* a half-hour documentary chronicling the sculpture's construction (17 showings per day in summer), or a film at the **Odyssey Theater** shown on a 4-story screen (shown every hr. on the ½-hr.). (Museum hours same as arch's. Tickets for 1 event $5, children $2; 2 events $7.50/3, 3 events $9.50/3.50; all 4 events $11/4.)

Within walking distance, across the highway from the arch is the **Old Courthouse,** 11 N. 4th St. (425-4468). As a slave, Dred Scott first sued for his freedom here in 1847. (Open daily 8am-4:30pm. Tour hours vary. Free.) The **Old Cathedral,** 209 Walnut St. (231-3250), is St. Louis' oldest church at 155 years. The museum is around the corner (25¢). Masses daily; call for schedule.

Sightseers can also view St. Louis from the water with **Gateway Riverboat Cruises** (621-4040), one hour cruises leave from docks on the river right in front of the arch. (Daily summer departures every 1½ hr. beginning at 10:15am; spring and fall every 1½ hr. beginning at 11am. Cruise $7, children $3.50.)

North of the arch, on the riverfront, is historic **Laclede's Landing,** the birthplace of St. Louis in 1764. The cobblestone streets of this district are bordered by restaurants, bars, and two museums. The **Wax Museum,** 720 N. Second St. (241-1155), features heroes and anti-heroes of all kinds; be sure to see the Chamber of Horrors. ($4, ages 6-12 $3. Open Mon.-Sat. 10am-10pm, Sun. noon-8pm.) The **National Video Game and Coin-Op Museum,** 801 N. Second St. (621-2900), charts the development of video games and pinball machines (you can play the exhibits!); you'll feel really old when you see Space Invaders, Pac-Man, and Donkey Kong treated as historic artifacts. Admission includes four game tokens. (Open Mon.-Sat. 10am-10pm, Sun. noon-8pm. $3, ages 12 and under $2.) Stroll down the lane to the **National Bowling Hall of Fame and Museum,** 111 Stadium Plaza (231-6340), across from Busch Stadium. This intelligently laid-out museum is lined with funny panels on bowling's history and development, with titles like "real men play quills and throw cheeses." For $2 you can play four frames in the old-fashioned lanes downstairs. (Open Mon.-Sat. 9am-5pm, Sun. noon-5pm; on baseball game days open until 7pm. $4, seniors $3, children under 13 $1.50. Free after 4pm and on Sun.) The **Dog Museum,** 1721 Mason Rd. (821-DOGS/3647), between Manchester and Clayton, depicts the history of the canine. (Open Tues.-Sat. 9am-5pm, Sun. 1-4pm. $3, seniors $1.50, kids $1.) Travelers should transport themselves to the **National Museum of Transport,** 3015 Barrett Station Rd. (965-7998), full of stationary trains, planes, ferries, and more. (Open daily 9am-5pm. $4, seniors and kids 5-12 $1.50.)

South St. Louis

Walk south of downtown on Broadway or 7th St. or take bus #73 ("Carondelet") to **South St. Louis.** The city proclaimed this area a historic district in the early 70s; it once housed German and East European immigrants, great numbers of whom worked in the breweries. Young couples and families are revitalizing South St. Louis but have not displaced the older generation of immigrants. The historic Soulard district surrounds the **Soulard Farmers Market,** 1601 S. 7th St. (622-4180), which claims a 200-plus-year tradition, but the produce is *still* fresh. (Open Tues.-Fri. 8am-5:30pm, Sat. 6:30am-6pm.) The end of 12th St. in the historic district features the **Anheuser-Busch Brewery,** 1127 Pestalozzi St. (577-2626), at 13th and Lynch, the largest brewery in the world. Take bus #40 ("Broadway") or 73 from downtown. Watch the beer-making process from barley to bottling and meet the famous Clydesdale horses. The 70-min. tour stops in the hospitality room, where guests can sample each beer Anheuser-Busch produces. Don't get too excited about the free brew, bucko—you'll get booted after 15 min. (Summer tours Mon.-Sat. 9am-5pm; off-season 9am-4pm. Pick up tickets at the office. Free.) Historic **Union Station,** at 18th and Market, 1 mi. west of downtown, retains its magnificent structure while housing a modern shopping mall, food court, and entertainment center. Take Levee bus.

   Laumeier Sculpture Park, 12580 Rott Rd. (821-1209), 12 mi. southwest of downtown, off the Lindbergh Blvd. exit of I-44, awaits discovery. 96 partially wooded acres are graced with quiet trails and contemporary sculpture. Enter into the charmed space of Beverly Pepper's **Cromlech Glen,** a shapely glen with modest spruce and pine log stairs emerging from its grassy surface, an ageless and moving combination of nature, art, and utility. Continuous exhibitions of contemporary art can be found inside the museum. (Park open daily 8am-30 min. after sunset, museum Tues.-Sat. 10am-5pm, Sun. noon-5pm; Free.)

   Built in South St. Louis, on grounds left by botanist Henry Shaw, thrive the internationally acclaimed **Missouri Botanical Gardens,** 4344 Shaw (800-642-8842), north of Tower Grove Park. From downtown, take bus #99 ("Lafayette") from 4th and Locust St. going west, or take I-44 by car; get off at Shaw and Tower Grove. The gardens display flora and fauna from all over the globe; the Japanese Garden truly soothes the weary budget traveler. (Open Memorial Day-Labor Day daily 9am-8pm; winter 9am-5pm. $3, seniors $1.50, under 12 free. Free Wed. and Sat. until noon.)

Forest Park Area

West of downtown is **Forest Park,** home of the 1904 World's Fair and St. Louis Exposition. Take bus #93 ("Lindell") from downtown. The park contains two museums, a zoo, a planetarium, a 12,000-seat amphitheater, a grand canal, countless picnic areas, pathways, and flying golf balls. All are connected by a $1 shuttle on the Metrolink. At the **St. Louis Science Center** (289-4400) one can learn how a laser printer works, watch an old Star Trek episode, or practice surgery. Lots of hands-on exhibits, an OmniMax, and planetarium. (Exhibits free; call for show schedules and prices. Museum open Sun.-Thurs. 9:30am-5pm, Wed.-Fri. 9:30am-9pm.) Marlin Perkins, the late great host of the TV show *Wild Kingdom,* turned the **St. Louis Zoo** (781-0900) into a world-class institution. At the "Living World" exhibit, view computer-generated images of future human evolutionary stages. (Open Memorial Day-Labor Day Sun. 9am-5:30pm, Mon. and Wed.-Sat. 9am-5pm, Tues. 9am-8pm, off-season daily 9am-5pm. Free.) The **History Museum** (746-4599), at the corner of Lindell and DeBaliviere on the north side of the park, is filled with U.S. memorabilia including an exhibit devoted to Charles Lindbergh's flight across the Atlantic in the *Spirit of St. Louis.* (Open Tues.-Sun. 9:30am-5pm. Free.) Atop **Art Hill,** just to the southwest, stands an equestrian statue of France's Louis IX, the city's namesake and the only Louis of France to achieve sainthood. The king beckons with his raised sword toward the **St. Louis Art Museum** (721-0067), which contains masterpieces of Asian, Renaissance, and Impressionist art. (Open Tues. 1:30-8:30pm, Wed.-Sun. 10am-5pm. Free except for special exhibits.) From Forest Park, head north a few blocks to gawk at the residential sections of the Central West End, where every house is a turn-of-the-century version of a French château or Tudor mansion.

Near Forest Park, **Washington University** livens things up with a vibrant campus. The **Washington University Gallery of Art** (935-5490), in Steinberg Hall at the corner of Skinker and Lindell, has a diverse collection including a few Warhols and Conrad Atkinson's *Critical Mats,* which proffers an inviting welcome to "the seductiveness of the end of the world." (Open summer Tues.-Fri. 10am-5pm, Sat.-Sun. 1-5pm, in winter Mon.-Fri. 10am-5pm, Sat.-Sun. 1-5pm. Free.) The **Cathedral of St. Louis,** 4431 Lindell Ave. (533-2824), just north of Forest Park at Newstead, strangely combines Romanesque, Byzantine, Gothic, and Baroque styles. Gold-flecked mosaics depict 19th-century church history in Missouri. (Free tour Sun. at 1pm. Open daily 6:30am-6pm. Take "Lindell" bus #93 from downtown.)

The **KATY Trail State Park** (800-334-6946) is an old 1890's railroad route that has been converted into a hiking and biking trail. The 200 mi. include towering bluffs, wetlands, and lots of wildlife, which even Lewis and Clark stopped to admire. The route begins in St. Charles and ends in Kansas City. Call for more info.

ENTERTAINMENT

In the early 1900s, showboats carrying ragtime and brassy Dixieland jazz regularly traveled to and from Chicago and New Orleans. St. Louis, a natural stopover, fell head over heels in love with the music and continues to nurture it happily. Float down the Mississippi while listening to jazz on **Gateway Riverboat Cruises'** (621-4040) old-fashioned paddle-boats. (1-2½ hr. cruises Tues.-Sun. 11am and 7pm. $7, kids $3.50; rates higher at night. Open June-Oct.) For other seasonal events, check *St. Louis Magazine,* published annually, or the comprehensive calendar of events put out by the Convention and Visitors Bureau.

For year-round musical entertainment, head to Laclede's Landing. Bars and restaurants featuring jazz, blues, and reggae fill "the landing." Try **Kennedy's Second Street Co.,** 612 N. Second St. (421-3655), for cheap food (burgers $3.25-4.75) and varied bands. (Cover $2-5. Shows for all ages often at 8pm; the 11:15pm show is for 21-plus only. Open Mon.-Fri. 11:30am-3am, Sat.-Sun. 1pm-3am.) Or take your pick of one of the dozens of clubs and bars lining the narrow streets. **Tasmania,** 118 Morgan (621-1160), features late-night dancing and ladies drink free on Tuesday and Thursday before 1am (open Mon.-Sat. 9pm-3am). Historic Soulard is also a groovy nightspot, where bars and pubs abound. **McGurk's** (776-8309), 12th and Russell, has live Irish music nightly (cover $3). (Open Mon.-Fri. 11am-1:30am, Sat. 11:30am-1am, Sun. 1pm-1am.)

Founded in 1880, the **St. Louis Symphony Orchestra** is one of the finest in the country. **Powell Hall,** 718 N. Grand (534-1700), which houses the 101-member orchestra, is acoustically and visually magnificent. (Performances Sept.-May Thurs. 8pm, Fri.-Sat. 8:30pm, Sun. 3pm and 7:30pm. Box office open Mon.-Sat. 9am-5pm and before performances. Tickets $12-53. Sometimes half-price student rush tickets are available the day of the show. Take bus #97 to Grand Ave.)

St. Louis offers theater-goers many choices. The outdoor **Municipal Opera** (361-1900), the "Muny," performs hit touring musicals in Forest Park during the summer. The back rows provide 1400 free seats on a first-come, first-served basis; the gates open at around 6:30pm. Otherwise, tickets cost $5-29. Bring a picnic (no bottles). Hot dogs and beer are also sold at moderate prices. Other regular productions are staged by the **St. Louis Black Repertory,** 2240 St. Louis Ave. (534-3807), and the **Repertory Theatre of St. Louis,** 130 Edgar Rd. (968-4925). Call for current show information. Tour the Fabulous **Fox Theatre** (534-1678; $2.50, under 12 $1.50; Tues., Thurs., and Sat. at 10:30am; call for reservations), or pay a little more for Broadway shows, classic films, Las Vegas, country, and rock stars. Renovated and reopened in 1982, the Fox was originally a 1930s movie palace.

Six Flags over Mid-America (938-4800) is a popular area amusement park, located 30 min. southwest of St. Louis on I-44 at Exit 261. Thrilling rides and shows (admission $19.95 to $24.95). **St. Louis Cardinals** baseball games (421-3060; tickets $4-12) are played at **Busch Stadium,** downtown. **Blues** hockey games (781-5300; tickets $30-50, limited view $13) blow at the **Kiel Center** at 14th and Clark.

■ NEAR ST. LOUIS: CAHOKIA MOUNDS

The **Cahokia Mounds State Historic Sight** (618-346-5160), in Collinsville, IL, are the amazing earthen remains of the extremely advanced city of Cahokia inhabited by early Mississippian Native Americans from 700-1500 AD. They built over 120 mounds of, well, dirt as foundations and protection for important buildings. You can climb the largest, Monk's Mound, which took 300 years to complete. Interestingly, they encountered the same problems of pollution, overcrowding (at one time housing 20,000 people), and depletion of resources that we do today, which might help explain their mysterious Roanokian disappearance. The **Interpretive Center** has an incredible 15 min. slide show illustrating this "City of the Sun" which runs every hr. 10am-4pm. The mounds site is open 8am-dusk. The Interpretive Center is open daily 9am-5pm. All free and definitely worth the trip. (Go 8 mi. east of downtown on I-55/70 East to Kingshighway (Rte. 111), only 15 min. from the city.)

■■■ HANNIBAL

Hannibal hugs the Mississippi River 100 mi. west of Springfield and 100 mi. northwest of St. Louis. Founded in 1819, this town remained a sleepy village until Samuel Clemens (a.k.a. Mark Twain) roused the world's attention to his boyhood home, setting for the renowned saga of prepubescence, *The Adventures of Tom Sawyer.* Hannibal now draws tourists to the town like gullible boys to a white-washed fence. Each year the town's population sextuples as 100,000 tourism-hungry fans converge for the **Tom Sawyer Days** festival (July 1-4).

White-washed sights abound here. The **Mark Twain Boyhood Home and Museum,** 208 Hill St. (221-9010), highlights the **historic district** of downtown Hannibal with its restored rooms, one of Twain's trademark white suits, and an assortment of memorabilia from his life. Across the street, the **Pilaster House** and **Clemens Law Office** complete the experience. (All 3 sites $4, children $2; open daily 8am-6pm, spring and fall 8am-5pm, winter 10am-4pm.) Browse in the **Becky Thatcher Bookshop,** 211 Hill St. (221-0822), held in restored rooms where the real-life Becky was admired by the boy next door.

The **Mark Twain Riverboat Co.** (221-3222), Center St. Landing, provides an opportunity to steam down the Mississippi on a 1-hr. sightseeing cruise. (3 times daily, June-Sept. $7, children $4. More expensive dinner cruises are also available.) 1 mi. south of Hannibal on Hwy. 79 is the **Mark Twain Cave** (221-1656; 1-hr. tours $8, children $4, under 12 free. Open 8am-8pm, winter 9am-4pm.)

The **Hannibal Visitors and Convention Bureau,** P.O. Box 624 (221-2477), publishes a detailed booklet (open daily 8am-5pm, weekends only April-May and Sept.-Oct.). Hannibal is serviced by **Trailway Bus Lines,** 308 Mark Twain (221-0033), from a Citgo Station. A northbound bus leaves at 5am and a southbound bus at 9:30pm (open daily 5am-10pm). Hannibal's **post office:** 801 Broadway (221-0957); open Mon.-Fri. 8:30am-5pm, Sat. 8:30am-noon); **ZIP code:** 63401; **area code:** 314.

Motels and hotels swarm about Hannibal, particularly on Mark Twain Ave. (Rte. 36) and on Hwy. 61 around its junction with Rte. 36. Numerous **bed and breakfasts** are located downtown, but these tend to be costlier (singles $50, doubles $60.) The best bet is the pleasant **Hannibal House Inn,** 601-11 McMaster Ave. (221-7950), where U.S. 36 and 61 meet. (Pool, A/C, and cable. Singles $30, doubles $36; prices jump $14 higher on weekends). 1 mi. south of Hannibal on Hwy. 79 is the **Mark Twain Cave Campgrounds,** P.O. Box 913 (221-1656), which is convenient to the cave itself. ($11, full hookup $14, $1.50 charge for every extra person after the second.) 4 mi. south of Hannibal on Hwy. 61, the youth-oriented **Injun Joe Campground,** (985-3581) lures with mini-golf, go-carts, an arcade, and a water slide. ($12, full hookup $16, each extra person after the second $1.)

Cheap diners and fast food joints litter Hannibal, but the **Mark Twain Family Restaurant,** 400 N. 3rd St. (221-5511) cooks up local fare with homemade root beer served in a frosty mug (95¢) (open Sun.-Thurs. 6am-10pm, Fri.-Sat. 6am-11pm).

■■■ KANSAS CITY

Once a heavily trafficked trading post situated on both the Oregon and Santa Fe Trails, Kansas City enjoyed an almost mystical reputation in the early 1850s as an island of civilization amidst a wild frontier. The KC of today is mainly a cattle trading and distribution center that spans over seven counties in two states—the more plush residential area in Kansas (KCKS) and the quicker-paced commercial one in Missouri (KCMO). Immortalized in the song from *Oklahoma!,* "Ev'rythin's up to date in Kansas City," this burg has business, blues, and barbecue galore.

PRACTICAL INFORMATION

Emergency: 911.

Visitors Center, 1100 Main St. #2550 (221-5242 or 800-767-7700), in the City Center Square Bldg. downtown. Pick up *A Visitor's Guide to Kansas City.* Open Mon.-Fri. 8:30am-5pm.

Airport: Kansas City International (243-5237) 18 mi. northwest of KC off I-29. The **KCI Shuttle** (243-5000) departs every 30-45 min., servicing downtown, Westport, Overland Park, Mission, and Lenexa ($10-15 one-way).

Amtrak: 2200 Main St. (421-3622 or 800-872-7245), directly across from Crown Center. To: St. Louis ($40, 6 hrs.), Chicago ($77, 9 hrs.). Open 24 hrs.

Greyhound: 1101 N. Troost (800-231-2222 or 221-2885). To: St. Louis ($31, 4 hrs.), Chicago ($49, 12 hrs.). Open daily 5:30am-1:30am.

Kansas City Area Transportation Authority (Metro): 1350 E. 17th St. (221-0660; open Mon.-Fri. 8am-4:45pm), at Brooklyn. Excellent downtown coverage. Fare 90¢, plus 10¢ for crossing zones, seniors half-price, for KCKS, $1. Free transfers; free return receipt available downtown. Pick up maps and schedules at headquarters, airport gate #62, or buses. Buses run Mon.-Fri. 7am-5:30pm.

Taxi: Yellow Cab, 471-5000. Base $1.30 plus $1.10 per mi. Fare about $25-30 from airport to downtown.

Car Rental: Thrifty Car Rental, 2001 Baltimore (842-8550 or 800-367-2277), 1 block west of 20th and Main St.; also at KCI airport (464-5670). $30 per day, 250 mi. free, 29¢ per mi. thereafter. Drivers under 25 add $5. Must be 21 with major credit card. Open daily 5:30am-midnight.

Post Office: 315 W. Pershing Rd. (374-9275), near the train station. Open Mon.-Fri. 8am-6:30pm, Sat. 8am-2:30pm. **ZIP code:** 64108.

Area Codes: 816 in Missouri, 913 in Kansas.

Most sights worth visiting in KC lie south of the Missouri River on the Missouri side of town. The KC metropolitan area sprawls across two states, and travel may take a while, particularly without a car. Most sights are *not* located downtown. All listings are for Kansas City, MO, unless otherwise indicated. KCMO is organized like a grid with numbered streets running east-west and named streets running north-south. **Main Street,** the central artery, divides the city east-west.

ACCOMMODATIONS

Kansas City is a big convention center and can usually accommodate everyone who needs a room. The least expensive lodgings are near the interstate highways, especially I-70. Downtown, most hotels are either expensive, uninhabitable, or unsafe—sometimes all three. Most on the Kansas side require a car. The Westport area is lively, but prices can be steep. **Bed and Breakfast Kansas City** (888-3636) has over 40 listings at inns and homes throughout the city ($40 and up).

Interstate Inn (229-6311) on Woods Chapel Rd., off I-70, exit 18. Large, clean rooms with cable and a great price. Free local calls. Singles $17. Doubles $24.

American Inn has several locations off I-70. Clean, cheap rooms with outdoor pool. The Woods Chapel Rd. location (229-1080, exit 18) has singles $20, doubles $29. The Noland Rd. location (373-8300, exit 12) has singles $28 and doubles for $32, but some rooms go as low as $23. The 78th St. location (244-2999) has singles for $25, doubles for $32.

Motel 6 (228-9133) on the access road at exit 19. The standard board with singles $25, doubles $33.

FOOD

Kansas City rustles up a herd of meaty, juicy barbecue restaurants that serve unusually tangy ribs. For fresh produce year-round, visit the large and exceptional **farmers market,** in the River Quay area, at 5th and Walnut St. Arrive in the morning, especially on Saturday.

Arthur Bryant's, 1727 Brooklyn St. (231-1123). Take the Brooklyn exit off I-70 and turn right. Down-home, sloppy BBQ. The thin, orange, almost granular sauce is a spectacular marriage of southern and western influences. Huge portions, like the beef sandwich and fries for under $6.50. Open Mon.-Thurs. 10am-9:30pm, Fri.-Sat. 10am-10pm, Sun. 10am-8pm.

Stephenson's Old Apple Farm Restaurant, 16401 E. U.S. 40 (373-5400), right off I-70, exit 14, several mi. from downtown. The hickory-smoked specialties are worth the trip and the prices. Awesome apple fritters. (Sunday brunch $11, kids 6-10 $6.) Open Mon.-Fri. 10am-10pm, Sat. 11:30am-11pm, Sun. 10am-9pm.

BB's BBQ, 1205 E. 85th St. (8BB-RIBS/822-7427). This stuff is so good it will stick to your ribs. Go for the ½ slab pork ribs with side ($8.50, $5 on Thurs.). Live music with no cover Thurs.-Sun. nights. Open Tues.-Sun. 11am-10:30pm.

Strouds, 1015 E. 85th St. (333-2132), off Troost. Sign proclaims: "We choke our own chickens." Don't choke on the incredible fried chicken with cinnamon rolls, biscuits, and honey. Enormous dinners ($9-16) in a weathered wooden hut. Open Mon.-Thurs. 4-10pm, Fri. 11am-11pm, Sat. 2-11pm, Sun. 11am-10pm. Also at 5410 N. Oak Ridge Blvd. (454-9600). Open Mon.-Thurs. 5-9:30pm, Fri. 11am-10:30pm, Sat. 2-10:30pm, Sun. 11am-9:30pm.

SIGHTS

For a taste of KC masterpieces, try the **Nelson-Atkins Museum of Fine Art** (751-1278 or 561-4000), located at 45th Terrace and Rockhill, 3 blocks east of Country Club Plaza. The museum contains one of the best East Asian art collections worldwide. (Open Tues.-Thurs. 10am-4pm, Fri. 10am-9pm, Sat. 10am-5pm, Sun. 1-5pm. $4, students $2, kids 6-18 $1. Sat. free, also free tours Tues.-Sat. 10:30am, 11am, 1pm, and 2pm; Sun. 1:30 and 2:30pm.) **Black Archives of Mid-America,** 2033 Vine (483-1300), is a large and fine collection of paintings and sculpture by African-American artists (open Mon.-Fri. 9am-4:30pm).

A few blocks to the west, the **Country Club Plaza** (known as "the plaza") is the oldest and perhaps most picturesque U.S. shopping center. The plaza is modeled after buildings in Seville, Spain, replete with fountains, sculptures, hand-painted tiles, and the reliefs of grinning gargoyles. A Country Club Plaza bus runs downtown until 11pm. Just south of the plaza is the luxurious **Mission Hill** district.

Crown Center, 2450 Grand Ave. (274-8444), is 2 mi. north of the Plaza at Pershing. The center is the headquarters of Hallmark Cards, as well as houses a maze of restaurants and shops. Also in the Crown Center are the **Coterie Children's Theatre** (474-6552) and the **Ice Terrace** (274-8411), KC's only public ice skating rink. (Open mid-Nov. to mid-March. Take bus #40, 56, or 57, or any trolley from downtown; $4, ages 6-12 $3.) The Crown Center has **Free Concerts in the Park** (274-8411) every Fri. at 7:30pm) during the summer. Run through a huge fountain designed for exactly that purpose—you can't have more fun on a hot summer night with your clothes on. To the west stands **Liberty Memorial,** 100 W. 26th St. (221-1918), a tribute to those who died in World War I. Pay to ride the elevator to the top for a fantastic view, then visit the free museum. (Open Wed.-Sun. 9:30am-4:30pm.

THE GREAT PLAINS

$2, under 12 free.) The memorial is also a big gay hangout. The newly remodeled **Kansas City Zoo** (871-5700) is in Swope Park at 63rd St. (Open daily 10am-8pm, 9am-4pm in the winter, $3, kids 6-12 $2.)

ENTERTAINMENT AND NIGHTLIFE

The **Missouri Repertory Theatre** (235-2700) stages productions all year. (Ticket office is open Mon.-Fri. 10am-5:30pm, Sat.-Sun. 12pm-5:30pm.) Be a Huck Finn wanna-be and cruise on the **Missouri River Queen** (281-5300 or 800-373-0027; $7, seniors $6.30, ages 3-13 $3.50).

Formerly the crossroads of the Santa Fe, Oregon, and California Trails, and an out-fitting post for travelers to the West, the restored **Westport** area (931-3586), located near Broadway and Westport Rd. ½-mi. north of the plaza, is now packed with noisy nightspots. **Blayney's,** 415 Westport Rd. (561-3747), in a small base-ment, hosts live bands six nights a week, offering reggae, rock, or jazz. (Open Mon.-Thurs. 8pm-3am, Fri.-Sat. 6pm-3am. Max. cover $1-3 on weekends.)

In the '20s, Kansas City was a jazz hot spot. Count Basie and his "Kansas City Sound" reigned at the River City bars, while Charlie "Bird" Parker spread his wings and soared in the open environment. Stop by the **Grand Emporium,** 3832 Main St. (531-7557), voted best live jazz club in KC for the last eight years and twice voted the #1 blues night club in the U.S., to hear live jazz Tues.-Sat.; weekdays feature rock, blues, and reggae bands (open Mon.-Sat. 10am-3am). **Kiki's Bon-Ton Maison,** 1515 Westport Rd. (931-9417), features KC's best in-house soul band, the Bon-Ton Soul Accordion Band Wed. 9-11pm and Sat. at 10:30pm. Kiki's serves up cajun food with zydeco and hosts the annual Crawfish Festival (complete with a "Crawfish Look-Alike Contest") the last weekend in May. (Open Mon.-Thurs. 11am-10pm, Fri. 11am-midnight, Sat. 11am-11pm. Food until 10pm.) **City Lights,** 7425 Broadway (444-6969), is dependable and fun with live bands Tues.-Sat. 7pm-12am. (Open Mon.-Sat. 4pm-1:30am. Cover $4.) **The Edge,** 323 W. 8th St. (221-8900) is a popular gay bar and dance club (open daily 9pm-3am, occasional weekend cover).

Sports fans will be bowled over by the **Arrowhead Stadium,** 1 Arrowhead Dr. (924-3333), home to football's **Chiefs** (924-9400). Next door, the water-fountained, artificial turf-clad wonder of **Royals Stadium,** 1 Royal Way (921-8000), houses the **Royals** baseball team. The stadium express bus runs from downtown on game days.

■■■ BRANSON

The tourists, the shops, and the inns are all in Branson for one reason: the music. Plentiful and nationally acclaimed, Branson has become *the* place for country musi-cians to set up house and theater in the 90s. The **Grand Palace,** 2700 Country Music Blvd. (334-7263 or 800-572-5223), hears regularly from the likes of Kenny Rogers, Glen Campbell, and the Oak Ridge Boys (April-Dec., $15-26, children 4-11 $9-11, except for limited engagements). For a lesser known but locally renowned enter-tainment experience, Shoji Tabuchi fiddles, sings, and jokes away at none other than the **Shoji Tabuchi Show,** Shepherd of the Hills Expwy. near Rte. 76 (Country Music Blvd.) (334-7469). Tickets May-Dec. $24, senior citizens $23, children $15. Ever wonder what happened to the Osmond Brothers? Wonder no longer—they're still jammin' at the **Osmond Family Theater** in Branson, Rte. 76 and Rte. 165 (336-6100); Mid Feb.-Dec.; tickets $15.50, children under 13 $5. And these are a mere smattering of the full repertoire. Others include the **Andy Williams' Show** (334-4500), **Presley's** (334-4874) for a bit of Ozark humor, and the **John Davidson The-ater** (334-0773 or 800-444-8497). Full listings at the Chamber of Commerce.

If country music isn't your *thang,* and you're in Branson anyway, never fear—this is the Ozarks, after all. Table Rock Lake, Lake Taneycomo, and a criss-crossing sys-tem of streams and creeks are perfect for canoeing, fishing, or just splashing along the shoreline. Canoes run about $30 per day; call **Beaver Canoe Rental** (796-2336 or 796-2406), which sensibly admonishes, "Take only pictures, kill only time." Bea-ver Canoe is on Rte. 26, 33 mi. east of Branson (canoes $28 per day).

The **Branson Chamber of Commerce,** junction of Rtes. 248 and 65 (334-4136), not only has brochures, but also a computer/telephone system that can help arrange your whole stay. Open Mon.-Fri. 8am-7pm, Sat. 8am-5pm, Sun. 10am-4pm. **Greyhound** (800-321-2222) runs one bus per day to: Springfield (1hr., $9); Kansas City (5½ hrs., $40); Memphis (7 hrs., $52). The bus drops off and picks up from **Rapid Robert's Amoco** station on Rte. 76W. Call **911** in an **emergency**. **Rape Crisis,** 889-4357 in Springfield. Branson's **post office**: 327 S. Commercial St. (334-3366; open Mon.-Fri. 8:30am-5pm, Sat. 9am-1pm); **ZIP code:** 65616; **area code:** 417.

 Oklahoma

Between 1831 and 1835, President Andrew Jackson ordered the forced relocation of "The Five Civilized Tribes" from Florida and Georgia to the designated Oklahoma Indian Territory. Tens of thousands of Native Americans died of hunger and disease on the brutal, tragic march that came to be known as the "Trail of Tears." The survivors rebuilt their decimated tribes in Oklahoma, only to be moved again in 1889 to make way for whites rushing to stake claims on newly opened settlement lands. Those who slipped in and claimed plots before the first official land run were called "sooners"—what Oklahomans have been dubbed ever since. Ironically, when the territory was admitted to the union in 1907, it did so with a Choctaw name. Oklahoma means "land of the red man" and despite the serious mistreatment of the Native Americans, many street names carry Indian names, and cultural life seems to center around Native American heritage and experiences. There are reenactments and interpretations of the Trail of Tears throughout Oklahoma, and the world's largest collection of American art in Tulsa features 250,000 Native American artifacts.

PRACTICAL INFORMATION

Capital: Oklahoma City.
Oklahoma Tourism and Recreation Department, 500 Will Rogers Bldg., Oklahoma City 73105 (521-2409 or 800-652-6552 out of state), in the capitol.
Time Zone: Central (1 hr. behind Eastern). **Postal Abbreviation:** OK
Sales Tax: 4.5-7%, depending on city.

■■■ TULSA

First settled by Creeks arriving from the "Trail of Tears," Tulsa's location on the banks of the Arkansas River made it a logical trading outpost for Europeans and Native Americans. The discovery of huge oil deposits catapulted the city into the oil capital of America by the 1920s. The city's varied heritage is visible today in its Art Deco skyscrapers, French villas, and Georgian mansions, as well as its Native American community, the second largest among U.S. metropolitan areas.

PRACTICAL INFORMATION

Emergency: 911.
Visitor Information: Convention and Visitors Division, Metropolitan Tulsa Chamber of Commerce, 616 S. Boston (585-1201 or 800-558-3311).
Greyhound: 317 S. Detroit (800-231-2222). To: Oklahoma City (8 per day, 2 hr., $19); St. Louis (9 per day, 7½-9½ hr., $67); Kansas City (4 per day, 6-8 hr., $38); Dallas (5 per day, 7 hr., $48). Lockers $1. Open Mon.-Fri. 8am-5pm.
Public Transport: Metropolitan Tulsa Transit Authority, 510 S. Rockford (582-2100). Buses start running 5-6am and stop 6-7pm. Fare 75¢, transfers 5¢, seniors and disabled (disabled card available at bus offices) 35¢, ages 5-18 60¢, under 5

free with adult. Maps and schedules are widely available and at the main office (open Mon.-Fri. 7am-5:30pm, Sat. 8:30am-3:30pm) but are not always reliable.

Taxi: Yellow Cab, 582-6161. $1.25 base fare, $1 per mi., $1 per passenger.

Car Rental: Thrifty, 1506 N. Memorial Dr. (481-1818), $27 per day, $132 per week. Unlimited mileage. Must be 21 with major credit card. Open Mon.-Wed. 10am-7pm, Thurs.-Sun. 9am-9pm.

Bike Rental: River Trail Sports Center, 6861 S. Peoria (743-5898). 5-speeds $4 per hr., $12 per day. Rollerblades $5 per hr., $10 per day. Open Mon.-Sat. 9am-7pm, Sun. 11am-6pm. Credit card deposit.

Help Line: 583-4357, for information, referral, crisis intervention. Open 24 hrs. **Gay Information Line,** 743-4297. Open daily 8am-10pm.

Post Office: 333 W. 4th St. (599-6800). Open Mon.-Fri. 8:30am-5pm. **ZIP code:** 74101.

Area Code: 918.

Tulsa is divided into blocks of one square mile. Downtown lies at the intersection of **Main Street** and **Admiral Boulevard.** Admiral divides addresses north and south; numbered streets lie in increasing order as you move away from Admiral. Named streets stretch north to south in alphabetical order. Those named after western cities are on the west side of Main St.; after eastern cities on the east side of it. Every time the alphabetical order reaches the end, the cycle begins again.

ACCOMMODATIONS AND CAMPING

Generally, the downtown motels are unclean and unsafe. The best downtown bet is the **Darby Lane Inn,** 416 W. 6th St. (584-4461). Clean, spacious rooms with cable TV. (Singles $39, doubles $45.) A better bet are the budget motels which are plentiful along I-44 and I-244. To reach the **Gateway Motor Inn,** 5600 W. Skelly Dr. (446-6611), take bus #17 and get off at Rensor's Grocery. Clean rooms replete with large beds, HBO, and cable. (Singles $24, doubles $28.) Trusty **Motel 6** also has two locations, identical to every other Motel 6 in America: I-40 at exit 235 (234-6200) and I-44 at exit 222a (445-0223). (Singles $24, doubles $30.)

The **KOA Kampground,** 193 East Ave. (266-4227), ½ mi. west of the Will Rogers Turnpike Gate off I-44, has a pool, laundry, showers, and game room (sites $15 for 2 people, with hookup $17). **Keystone State Park** (865-4991) offers three campgrounds along the shores of Lake Keystone, 20 mi. west of Tulsa on the Cimarron Turnpike (U.S. 64). The wooded park offers hiking, swimming, boating, and excellent catfish and bass fishing. (Sites $10, with hookup $14. Tent camping $6.) Four-person cabins with kitchenettes available ($48).

FOOD AND NIGHTLIFE

Take a gander at the gaggle of restaurants and bars on **S. Peoria.** Many downtown restaurants close at 3pm weekdays and 1pm Saturdays. The **Blue Rose Cafe,** 3421 S. Peoria has cheap, great food with an outdoor patio equipped with a misting machine. Burgers are fine and dandy ($3-5). (Live music Mon.-Thurs. at 9pm. No cover. Open Mon.-Sat. 11am-2am.) **Nelson's Buffeteria,** 514 S. Boston (584-9969), takes you on a sentimental journey through Tulsa's past. Operating since 1929 and now run by Nelson Jr., this old-style diner's walls are blanketed with mid-American memorabilia. Try a blue plate special (two scrambled eggs, hash browns, toast and jam, $2) or the famous chicken-fried steak ($4.50). Ask for extra gravy. (Open Mon.-Fri. 6am-2:30pm.) Only three blocks from the YMCA is the **Little Ancient Denver Grill,** 112 S. Denver (582-3790). Lunch specials ($4) include a salad, fresh rolls, and a choice of vegetables. (Open Mon.-Sat. 6am-8pm, Sun. 8am-4pm.) Restaurants on Rte. 66 (between Main and Lewis) welcome hungry budget travelers. Inconspicuous but unrivaled among them is the **Route 66 Diner,** 2639 E. 11th St. (592-6666). Run by a couple with old Tulsa blood and a long culinary tradition, the diner is a great bargain for lunch ($3-6). Try the are-you-sure-you're-*that*-hungry double burger ($5.50) or daily special ($4.75). (Open Tues.-Sun. 7am-2pm.)

At night, head to the bars along 15th St. east of Peoria, or in the 30s along S. Peoria. Down at the **Sunset Grill,** 3410 S. Peoria (742-4242), catch nightly rowdy rock bands (open daily 6pm-2am; must be 21; no cover). The city's most popular gay club is **Metropole,** 1902 E. 11th (587-8811; open Fri.-Sun. 4pm-2am).

SIGHTS AND ENTERTAINMENT

The most frequented tourist attraction in Tulsa, **Oral Roberts University,** 7777 S. Lewis (495-6161), was founded in 1964 when Oral had a dream in which God commanded him to "Build Me A University." The ultra-modern, gold-mirrored architecture rising out of an Oklahoma plain, the 80-ft.-high praying hands sculpture guarding the campus, and the hordes of believers flocking to visit make this kitschy experience a must. The university is about 6 mi. south of downtown Tulsa between Lewis and Harvard Ave. Take bus #9. (Visitors center open Mon.-Sat. 10:30am-4:30pm, Sun. 1-4:30pm.)

The **Fenster Museum of Jewish Art,** 1223 E. 17th Pl. (582-3732), housed in B'nai Emunah Synagogue, contains an impressive if oddly located collection of Judaica dating from 2000 BC to the present (open Sun.-Thurs. 10am-4pm; free). The **Philbrook Art Center,** 2727 S. Rockford Rd. (749-7941), displays exquisite exhibits in the former Renaissance villa of an oil baron, houses a collection of Native American pottery and artifacts alongside Renaissance art.Take bus #16 ("S. Peoria") from downtown. (Open Tues.-Wed. and Fri.-Sat. 10am-5pm, Thurs. 10am-8pm, Sun. 11am-5pm. $4, seniors and students $2, ages 12 and under free.) Perched atop an Osage foothill 2 mi. northwest of downtown, the **Thomas Gilcrease Museum,** 1400 Gilcrease Museum Rd. (596-2700), houses one of the world's largest collections of American art. Designed as an anthropological study of North America from pre-history to the present, the museum contains 250,000 Native American artifacts and more than 10,000 paintings and sculptures by artists such as Remington and Russell. Take bus #7 ("Gilcrease") from downtown. (Open Mon.-Sat. 9am-5pm, Sun. 1-5pm. Donation requested.)

Rodgers and Hammerstein's *Oklahoma!* continues its run under the stars at the **Discoveryland Amphitheater** (245-0242), 10 mi. west of Tulsa on 41st St., accessible only by car. It features what is now the state song and commemorates the suffering of the Okie farmers in the 19th century. (Shows June-Aug. Mon.-Sat. at 8pm. Mon.-Thurs. $12, seniors $11, kids under 12 $7; Fri.-Sat. $14, seniors $13, kids under 12 $5.) Arrive early for the pre-show barbecue, starting at 5:30pm. ($7, seniors $6.50, kids $4.50.) A moving commemoration of Native American heritage is the **Trail of Tears Drama,** a show reenacting the Cherokees' tragic march, performed in Tahlequah, 66 mi. east of Tulsa on Rte. 51. (Performances June-Sept. 2 Mon.-Sat. 8pm. For tickets, call 456-6007, or write P.O. Box 515, Tahlequah 74465; reservations recommended. $9, under 13 $4.50.) For more cultural enlightenment, the **Tulsa Philharmonic** (747-7445) and **Tulsa Opera** (582-4035) perform year-round. The **Tulsa Ballet** (585-2573), acclaimed as one of America's finest regional troupes, performs at the **Performing Arts Center** (596-7111), at the corner of 3rd St. and Cincinnati. (Ticket office open Mon.-Fri. 10am-5:30pm, Sat. 10am-3pm.)

The best times to visit Tulsa are during annual special events like the **International Mayfest** (745-6024) in mid-May. This outdoor food, arts, and performance festival takes place in downtown Tulsa over a 10-day period. The **Pow-Wow** (835-8699), held the first weekend in June at the Tulsa Fairground Pavilion, attracts Native Americans from dozens of different tribes. The three-day festival features Native American food, arts and crafts exhibits, and nightly dancing contests which visitors may attend ($1, kids under 10 free.)

■■■ OKLAHOMA CITY

At noon on April 22, 1889, a gunshot sent settlers scrambling into Oklahoma Territory to claim land. By sundown, Oklahoma City, set strategically on the tracks of the Santa Fe Railroad, had a population of over 10,000 homesteaders. The city became the state capital in 1910. The 1928 discovery of oil modernized the city, and elegant homes rose with the oil derricks. As the wells dried up and the oil business slumped, Oklahoma City fell on hard times.

PRACTICAL INFORMATION

Emergency: 911.

Visitor Information: Chamber of Commerce Tourist Information, 4 Santa Fe Plaza (278-8900), at the corner of Gaylord. Open Mon.-Fri. 8:30am-5pm.

Airport: Will Rogers Memorial (681-5311), southwest of downtown. **Airport Limousine, Inc.,** 3910 S. Meridian (685-2638), has van service to downtown ($9 for 1 person; $3 per additional person).

Greyhound: 427 W. Sheridan Ave. (235-6425), at Walker. In a rough part of town. Take city bus #4, 5, 6, 8, or 10. To: Tulsa (7 per day, 2 hr., $19.50); Dallas (4 per day, 5 hr., $39); and Kansas City (6 per day, 10 hr., $64). Open 24 hrs.

Public Transport: Oklahoma Metro Area Transit, main terminal at 20 E. Greenham (235-7433). Bus service Mon.-Sat. 6am-6pm. All routes radiate from the station at Reno and Gaylord, where maps are available for 50¢. Route numbers vary depending on the direction of travel. Fare 75¢, seniors and kids 35¢.

Taxi: Yellow Cab, 232-6161. $2.50 base, $1.25 per mi. To airport, $12.50.

Car Rental: Rent-A-Wreck, 2930 N.W. 39th Expressway (946-9288). Used cars $28 per day with 150 free mi., 25¢ each additional mi. Open Mon.-Fri. 8am-6pm, Sat. 8am-noon. Must be 25 with major credit card. The state of Oklahoma does *not* honor the International Driver's License.

Bike Rental: Miller's Bicycle Distribution, 215 W. Boyd. (321-8296). 10-speeds and mountain bikes $5 per day for first 3 days, $3 per day thereafter. Open Mon.-Sat. 9am-6pm, Sun. noon-5pm. They may ask for a credit card deposit.

Help Lines: Contact, 848-2273 or 840-9396 for referrals and crisis intervention. **Rape Crisis,** 943-7273. Open 24 hrs.

Post Office: 320 S.W. 5th St. (278-6300). Open Mon.-Fri. 8:30am-5:30pm, Sat. 9am-midnight. Emergency window open 24 hrs. **ZIP code:** 73125.

Area Code: 405.

Main Street divides the town north-south. Traveling by car is the best way to go; almost all of the city's attractions are outside the city center, but are accessible by the all-encompassing Metro Transit. Use caution with public transportation, especially downtown after dark.

ACCOMMODATIONS, CAMPING, AND FOOD

Accommodations in OKC leave something to be desired. Somewhat clean and somewhat safe, the **YMCA,** 125 N.W. 5th St. (232-6101), has rooms with shared bath for men only. Facilities include pool, gym, and TV. (Singles $14, $52.50 per week. Key deposit $5.) **The Economy Inn,** 501 N.W. 5th St. has singles for $25, doubles for $35. **Motel 6** also has 7 locations in the OKC area; call 946-6662 for info. (Singles range $21-28, doubles $27-35.) **I-35** near Oklahoma City is lined with inexpensive hotels that offer singles for under $25. Oklahoma City has two accessible campgrounds. **RCA,** 12115 Northeast Expwy. (478-0278), next to Frontier City Amusement Park 10 mi. north of the city on I-35, has a pool, laundry room, showers, and lots of fast-food restaurants nearby (open 8am-9pm; sites $16). The nearest state-run campground roosts on Lake Thunderbird, 30 mi. south of OKC at **Little River State Park** (360-3572 or 364-7634). Take I-40 East to Choctaw Rd., then south until the road ends, and make a left. Set up a tent, and a collector will come for your money. (Sites $6, $7 in area with gate attendant; showers included. RV sites $10, $11 in area with gate attendant. Seniors and disabled pay ½-price. Open 8am-5pm.)

Since Oklahoma City contains the largest feeder cattle market in the U.S., beef tops most menus. Established in 1926, **Cattleman's Steak House,** 1309 S. Agnew (236-0416), is a classic diner a block away from the stockyards. Try the chopped sirloin dinner ($6) or the navy bean soup with cornbread ($1.50). (Open Sun.-Thurs. 6am-10pm, Fri.-Sat. 6am-midnight.) **Yippie Yi Yo Cafe,** 4723 N. Western (542-5282), will give you the standard cup of java plus pastries. (Open Mon.-Tues. 7am-6pm, Wed.-Thurs. 7am-10pm, Fri.-Sat. 7am-midnight, Sun. 9am-3pm.) **Sweeney's Deli,** 900 N. Broadway (232-2510), serves up tasty dishes in a friendly atmosphere; play pool or watch the big-screen TV. (Sandwiches $3-4, burgers $2.20, hot plates $4. Open Mon.-Fri. 11am-11pm.) Downtown, the **Century Center Plaza,** 100 Main St., is inundated with cheap lunch spots (open Mon.-Sat. 11am-3pm).

SIGHTS AND ENTERTAINMENT

The **Oklahoma City Stockyards,** 2500 Exchange Ave. (235-8675), are the busiest in the world. Cattle auctions, held here Mon.-Wed., begin at 7-8am and sometimes last into the night. Mon.-Tues. are the busiest days; Mon. morning is *the* time to visit. Visitors enter free of charge via a calfwalk over pens, leading from the parking lot east of the auction house. Take bus #12 from the terminal to Agnon and Exchange.

The plight of Native Americans along the "Trail of Tears" is commemorated by James Earle Fraser's *The End of the Trail.* Ironically, his sculpture of a man slumped over an exhausted pony is on display at the **National Cowboy Hall of Fame and Western Heritage Center,** 1700 N.E. 63rd St. (478-2250). The Hall commemorates pistol-packin' frontiersmen. Every summer, the museum showcases 150 works of the National Academy of Western Art. Take bus #22 from downtown. (Open daily 8:30am-6pm; Labor Day-Memorial Day daily 9am-5pm. $6, seniors $5, ages 6-12 $3.) The **State Capitol,** 2300 N. Lincoln Blvd. (521-3356), is the world's only capitol building surrounded by working oil wells. Completed in 1917, the Greco-Roman structure was inadvertently but appropriately built atop a large reserve of crude oil. (Open 24 hrs. Guided tours 8am-3pm. Free.)

The **Kirkpatrick Center Museum Complex,** 2100 N.E. 52nd St. (427-5461), is a sort of educational amusement park. It looks like a mall but it's actually a pastiche of eight separate museums. Highlights are the **Air and Space Museum, International Photography Hall of Fame,** and the **Omniplex,** a hands-on science museum with free planetarium shows. Take bus #22. (Open Mon.-Sat. 9am-6pm, Sun. noon-6pm; Labor Day-Memorial Day Mon.-Fri. 9:30am-5pm, Sat. 9am-6pm, Sun. noon-6pm. Admission to all 8 museums $6, seniors $4, ages 3-12 $3.50, under 3 free.)

Nightlife in Oklahoma City is as rare as the elusive jackalope. For ideas, pick up a copy of the *Oklahoma Gazette.* The **Oklahoma Opry,** 404 W. Commerce (632-8322), is home to a posse of country music stars (regular performances Sat. at 8pm; tickets $6, seniors $5, kids $2).

■ NEAR OKLAHOMA CITY

Anadarko, a short one-hour drive through the Great Plains, is home to **Indian City USA** (247-5661), a museum which has reconstructed villages of seven Native American tribes. During the summer, each tour begins with a performance of Native American dances by prize-winning dancers. Drive 40 mi. south from Oklahoma City on I-44 to exit #83, take a right on Rte. 9W, go about 20 mi. to Anadarko, take a left on Rte. 8S, and go 2 mi. to the museum entrance. (Open daily 9am-6pm; off-season 9am-5pm. First tour at 9:30am, last tour at 4:15pm. $7, kids 6-11 $4, under 6 free.)

For those in search of a home where the buffalo roam, check out the **Wichita Mountain Wildlife Refuge** (429-3222), an hour south of Anadarko. Created in 1905 by Teddy Roosevelt, the refuge is home to 625 buffalo, thousands of deer and Texas longhorns, and various other wildlife. **Mount Scott** offers a stupendous vista those who drive or hike to the top. Camping is permitted in certain areas of the park. Take exit #49 off I-44. (Open daily; some areas close at dusk.)

Texas

Texas

Spanning an area as wide as Wisconsin to Montana and as long as North Carolina to Key West, Texas is more like its own country than a state. In fact, after revolting from the Spanish in 1821, the Republic of Texas stood alone until 1845, when it entered the Union as the 28th state.

Tumbleweed, cowboy hats, and patriotic braggarts may pin-point the Texas of the past, but today, Texas provides its tourists with an environment of cosmopolitan cities, industries, and businesses in an incredibly diverse setting. Mexican influence is unmistakable in architecture, place names, and cuisine. Though cotton, cattle, and oil are the natural resources that built Texan fortune, the state's growing technology and tourism industries will serve as the building blocks of its future. Regional cuisine, like most of Texan culture, is enriched by the state's Mexican heritage. "Tex-Mex" is a restaurant epidemic ranging from 39¢ taco stands to elegant border cafés. Mexican pastries, longhorn beef, and chicken-fried steak are staples. And of course, BBQ with plenty of sauce.

PRACTICAL INFORMATION

Capital: Austin.

Texas Division of Tourism, P.O. Box 12728, Austin 78711 (800-888-8839). **U.S. Forest Service,** 701 N. First St., Lufkin 75901 (409-639-8501). **State Parks and**

Recreation Areas, Austin Headquarters Complex, 4200 Smith School Rd., Austin 78744 (512-389-8950).
Time Zones: Central and Mountain. **Postal Abbreviation:** TX
Sales Tax: 6-8%.

■■■ DALLAS

Dallas offers a little country, a little rock n' roll, too many businessmen in Stetsons, and a stampede of cowgirls all tossed together in a "metroplex" mishmash of skyscrapers, neon lights, modern shopping malls, and miles and miles of suburbs. In 1841 founding father John Neely Bryan, an ambitious Irish immigrant, built a tiny little loghouse outpost in the hopes that one day it would grow into a bustling metropolis. Dallas rose to prominence in the 1870s when a major north-south railroad crossed a transcontinental east-west line just south of the town. Converging waves of settlers lured by prospects of black gold caused the population to swell.

The eighth-largest city in America, Dallas today has attracted droves of immigrants from the Far East and Latin America. While the city's legendary preoccupation with commerce is evident, recent campaigns for historic preservation have restored many run-down urban areas to their pre-petro glory.

PRACTICAL INFORMATION
Emergency: 911.
Visitor Information: Dallas Convention and Visitors Bureau, 1201 Elm St., #24, 20th floor. (746-6677). **Dallas Visitors Center,** 1303 Commerce (746-6603). Both open Mon.-Thurs. 8am-5:30pm, Fri. 8am-5pm. **Special Events Info Line,** 746-6679. 24 hrs.
Airport: Dallas-Ft. Worth International (574-8888), 17 mi. northwest of downtown, take #300 bus. **Love Field** (670-6080; take bus #39) has mostly intra-Texas flights. To get downtown from either airport, take the **Super Shuttle,** 729 E. Dallas Rd. (817-329-2001; in terminal, dial 02 on phone at ground transport services). 24-hr. service. Shuttle or taxi from DFW airport to downtown $25, Love Field to downtown $15.
Amtrak: 400 S. Houston Ave. (653-1101 or 800-872-7245), in Union Station. *See mileage chart.* Open daily 9am-6pm.
Greyhound: 205 S. Lamar (800-231-2222), 3 blocks east of Union Station. *See mileage chart.* Open 24 hrs.
Public Transport: Dallas Area Rapid Transit (DART), 601 Pacific Ave. (979-1111). Serves most suburbs; routes radiate from downtown. Service 5am-midnight, to suburbs 5am-8pm. Base fare 75¢, $1.75 to suburbs. Info desk open Mon.-Fri. 8:30am-4:45pm. Maps available at Main and Akard St. (open Mon.-Fri. 8am-5pm), or at Elm and Ervay St. (open Mon.-Fri. 7am-6pm). **Hop-a-Bus** (979-1111) is DART's downtown Dallas service, with a park-and-ride system. Three routes (blue, red, and green) run about every 10 min. Fare 25¢, transfers free. No Hop-A-Bus service on weekends.
Taxi: Yellow Cab Co., 426-6262. $2.70 first mi., $1.20 each additional mi.
Car Rental: All-State Rent-a-Car, 3206 Live Oak (741-3118). $23 per day with 100 free mi., 16¢ per additional mi. Open Mon.-Sat. 7:30am-6pm. Must be 21 with major credit card.
Bike Rental: Bicycle Exchange, 11716 Ferguson Rd. (270-9269). Rates from $60 per week. Open Mon.-Fri. 9am-7pm, Sat. 9am-5pm. Must have a credit card.
Help Lines: Rape Crisis and Child Abuse Hotline, 653-8740; **Suicide and Crisis Center,** 828-1000; **Contact 214** (general counseling), 233-2233. All three open 24 hrs. **Dallas Gay and Lesbian Community Center,** 2701 Reagan (528-4233). Open Mon.-Fri. 9am-9pm, Sat. 10am-6pm, Sun. noon-6pm.
Time Zone: Central (1 hr. behind Eastern).
Post Office: 400 N. Ervay St. (953-3045), near Byran St. downtown. Open Mon.-Fri. 8am-6pm. **ZIP code:** 75201; General Delivery, 75221.
Area Code: 214.

TEXAS

ACCOMMODATIONS AND CAMPING

Cheap accommodations of the non-chain motel type are hard to come by; big events like the Cotton Bowl (Jan. 1) and the State Fair in October exacerbate the problem. If you can afford it, the **Bed and Breakfast Texas Style,** 4224 W. Red Bird Ln. (298-5433 or 298-8586), will place you at a nice home, usually near town, with friendly residents who are anxious to make y'all as comfortable as possible. Just give them a call (from 8:30am-4:30pm) and they'll direct you to your host. Good deal for two. (Singles $60-75, doubles from $65.)

For the tighter wallet, try the **Delux Inn,** 3111 Stemmons Fwy. (637-0060). Accessible by bus #49, the inn has balconies, a pool, free coffee, free local calls, cable and HBO. Fast food restaurants and banks are only blocks away (singles $24, doubles $34). Major credit cards accepted. **U.S. 75 (Central Expressway), I-635 (LBJ Freeway),** and the suburbs of **Irving** and **Arlington** also have many inexpensive motels. Try **Motel 6** (505-891-6161), singles $30, with 11 locations in the Dallas area, or **Excel Inns** (800-356-8013; singles $32-35).

If you have a car and camping gear, and are given to whistling while you work, try the **Hi-Ho Campground,** 200 W. Bear Creek Rd. (223-8574), south of town. Take I-35 14½ mi. to exit 412, turn right, and go 2 mi. (Sites $12 for 2 people, with hookup $18.50, $1.50 per additional person.) RV drivers might stop by **Sandy Lake Campground** with its 270 trailer sites, a grocery store, game room, and two laundries. (RV rates $15-19, dependent on size. Office hours Mon.-Fri. 7:30am-8pm, Sat. 8am-8pm, Sun. 1-6pm.)

FOOD

Dallas is full of cheap 'n cheesy taco joints, but for the culinary low-down, pick up a copy of the Friday weekend guide of the *Dallas Morning News.* For fast Tex-Mex food and a variety of small touristy shops, explore the **West End Marketplace,** 603 Munger St. (748-4801). The **Farmers Produce Market,** 1010 S. Pearl Expressway (748-2082), between Pearl and Central Expressway near I-30 (open daily 5am-6pm), is a veggie haven in beef country. For gourmet restaurants and low-priced authentic barbecue joints, mosey down **Greenville Avenue.**

Snuffer's, 3526 Greenville (826-6850). Has good burgers ($4.25) amidst cacti and peppy music. Nice all-wooden interior with friendly service and fun crowd. The cheddar fries ($3.95) are miraculous, but also like putting a sledgehammer to your heart. Cash bar. Other dishes range from $5-7. Open daily 11am-2am.

Bubba's, 6617 Hillcrest Ave. (373-6527). A remodeled, 50s-style diner near the heart of SMU. Serves awful good fried chicken and chicken-fried steak dinners ($5-6). Open daily 6:30am-10pm.

Terilli's, 2815 Greenville Ave. (8727-3993). Sexy atmosphere with low-lit lamps. Some of the best jazz in Dallas is here. The emphasis is on "creative Italian," with terrific antipasto and vegetarian dishes. Try the veggie lasagna ($7.50), and wash it down with a specialty martini ($5.50). Open daily 11:30am-2am.

Sonny Bryan's Smokehouse, 302 N. Market St. (744-1610). Located at the threshold of the historic West End, this landmark defines Dallas BBQ. $6 for one meat on a bun, $16 for a combo of all 7 smokehouse meats. Some vegetables. Open Mon.-Thurs. 11am-10pm, Fri.-Sat. 11am-11pm, Sun. noon-9pm.

Sticky's, 427 Thompkins St. (363-9639). Serving the best Cajun in Big D for 23 years. Try Chef Lanoux's *senip amgems,* a special bayou broth with a salty, sour kick ($6). The Tolpuddle Possum ($4.50) is just a pseudonym for the greasy burger. Open Mon.-Sat. 11am-until Rick the bartender passes out.

SIGHTS

Most of historic Dallas remains in present-day downtown and lends itself well to a walking tour. A replica of the 1841 log cabin of **John Neely Bryant,** the City's founder, can be found in the heart of Dallas at Elm and Market St. The city's layout can be viewed from 50 stories up, atop **Reunion Tower,** 300 Reunion Blvd. (651-

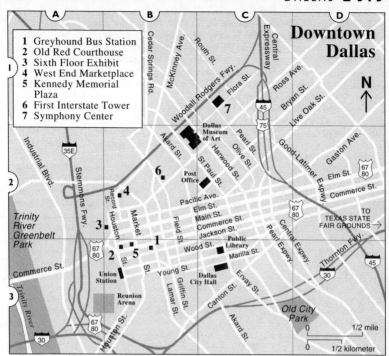

Downtown Dallas

N ↑

1 Greyhound Bus Station
2 Old Red Courthouse
3 Sixth Floor Exhibit
4 West End Marketplace
5 Kennedy Memorial Plaza
6 First Interstate Tower
7 Symphony Center

1234). This is a good place to start a walking tour and to get acquainted with the city. (Open Sun.-Thurs. 10am-10pm, Fri.-Sat. 9am-midnight; $2, seniors and kids $1.)

On your way out of Reunion Tower, take the underground walkway to the adjoining **Union Station,** 400 S. Houston Ave., and explore one of the city's few grand old buildings. Upon exiting the building, walk north along Houston, and you'll come upon the **West End Historic District and Marketplace** with broad sidewalks and funky shops, restaurants, and bars. (Open Tues.-Thurs. 11am-10pm, Fri.-Sat. and Mon. 11am-midnight, Sun. noon-6pm.)

Two blocks down and six flights up on Elm is the notorious **Sixth Floor** of the former **Texas School Book Depository** (653-6666), from which Lee Harvey Oswald *allegedly* fired the fatal shot at President John F. Kennedy on November 22, 1963. This floor, now a museum devoted to the Kennedy legacy, traces the dramatic and macabre moments of the assassination in various media. (Open Mon.-Thurs. 9am-8pm, Fri.-Sun. 9am-8pm. Last ticket sold one hour before closing. Self-guided tour $4, seniors and kids 6-18 $2. Audio tour with cassette $2.) Down from the depository, Elm St. runs through **Dealey Plaza,** a national landmark and site of the infamous grassy knoll, where the limo was passing when the shots were fired. The area has not changed much and the likeness to Abraham Zapruder's film of the assassination is eerie. Philip Johnson's illuminating **Memorial to Kennedy** looms nearby, at Market and Main St.

At the corner of Houston and Main St. is the old **Dallas County Courthouse,** nicknamed "Old Red" for its unique Pecos red sandstone and frightening gargoyles. Just east on the corner of Ross Ave. and Field St. stands Dallas's most impressive skyscraper, **The First Interstate Tower,** a multi-sided prism towering above a glistening water garden. Walking farther east along Ross Ave. leads you to the new **Arts District,** the centerpiece of which is the **Dallas Museum of Art,** 1717 N. Harwood St. (922-1200). The museum offers Egyptian, impressionist, modern, and decorative art. (Open Tues.-Wed. 11am-4pm, Thurs.-Fri. 11am-9pm, Sat.-Sun. 11am-5pm. Free.)

TEXAS

Walking south from the museum on St. Paul, toward the downtown area, turn right on Bryan St. and walk one block to **Thanksgiving Square** (969-1977), a triangular park beneath massive towers. Below the park's sunken gardens and waterfalls lies a small museum devoted to the history of Thanksgiving in all religions. (Open Mon.-Fri. 9am-5pm, Sat.-Sun. and holidays 1-5pm.) Continue south from the square along Ervay St. to the imposing **Dallas City Hall,** 100 Marilla St. (670-3957), designed by the ubiquitous I.M. "Everywhere" Pei.

About nine blocks south of City Hall on Ervay St. is **Old City Park** (421-5141)**,** at Gano St. The park is both the oldest and the most popular recreation area and lunch spot in the city. (Park open daily 9am-6pm. Exhibit buildings open Tues.-Sat. 10am-4pm, Sun. noon-4pm. Admission $5, seniors $4, kids $2, families $12. Free on Mon., when exhibits are closed.)

Fair Park (670-8400), southeast of downtown on 2nd Ave., has been home to the state fair since 1886. The national landmark is the largest collection of 30s Art Deco style architecture in the U.S. The park is home to the Cotton Bowl, numerous museums, and during the fair (Sept.-Oct.) **Big Tex** stands Texas tall. The park's **Museum of Natural History** (670-8457) has a small permanent display on prehistoric life. (Open Mon.-Sat. 9am-5pm, Sun. 11am-5:30pm; $3, students and seniors $2, kids under 12 $1, kids under 3 free.) Other buildings include the **Aquarium** (670-8443; open daily 9am-4:30pm; $1); the **Age of Railroad Steam Museum** (428-0101; open Thurs.-Fri. 10am-3pm, Sat.-Sun. 11am-5pm; $3, under 12 $1.50); the **Science Place** (428-5555; open daily 9:30am-5:30pm; $5.50, seniors and kids 3-16 $2.50, under 3 free); the **African-American Life and Culture Museum,** (565-9026), a multi-media collection of folk art and sculpture, (open Tues.-Thurs. noon-5pm, Fri. noon-9pm, Sat. 10am-5pm, Sun. 1-5pm); and the **Dallas Garden Center** (428-7476; open Tues.-Sat. 10am-5pm, Sun. 1-5pm).

Nearby **White Rock Lake** is safe for walking, biking, or rollerblading. On the eastern shore of the lake is the **Dallas Arboretum,** 8525 Garland Rd. (327-8263), a 66-acre botanical heaven on earth with resplendent flowers and trees. Take the #60N bus from downtown. To gaze upon Dallas's mansions, drive up the **Swiss Avenue Historic District** or through the streets of the **Highland Park** area.

ENTERTAINMENT

Most Dallas establishments cater to the night owl, since restaurant, bars, and fast food joints are typically open until 2am. The free weekly *Dallas Observer* (out Wednesdays) will help you to sort your entertainment options. Enjoy free summer theater July-Aug. at the **Shakespeare in the Park** festival (599-2778), at Samuel-Grand Park just northeast of State Fair Park. Two plays are performed annually; each runs about two weeks. The **Music Hall** (565-1116) in Fair Park houses the **Dallas Civic Opera** (443-1043) Nov.-Feb. (tickets $20-95) and **Dallas Summer Musicals** June-Oct. (Performances nightly, $5-45; call 565-1116 for information, 373-8000 for tickets, 696-4253 for ½-price tickets on performance days.) The **Dallas Symphony Orchestra** (692-0203) orchestrates at the new **Morton H. Meyerson Symphony Center,** at Pearl and Flora St. in the arts district. Take in a show if only to marvel at the world-renowned acoustics. (Tickets $12-50.)

For alternative nightlife, head to **Deep Ellum,** east of the downtown. A blues haven in the 20s for the likes of Blind Lemon Jefferson, Lightnin' Hopkins, and Robert Johnson, it was revitalized by early 80s bohemians. Like almost everything in Dallas, it has since become commercialized, but is still enjoyable. **Trees,** 2079 Elm St. (748-5009), a converted warehouse with pool tables in the loft, is the best music venue in the city. (Open daily 8pm-2am; cover $2-10, 17 and over.) **Club Dada,** 2720 (744-3232), former haunt of Edie Brickell, has upscaled with an outdoor patio, and live local acts. (Open daily 8pm-2am; cover $3-5). For more info on Deep Ellum, call the **What's Up Line** (747-3337) or ask Rob McGhee (800-MOO-CHICKEN).

The trendy **West End** offers **Dallas Alley,** 2019 N. Lamar (988-0581), an ensemble of clubs with a single ($3-5) cover charge. The **Outback Pub** (761-9355) and **Dick's Last Resort** (747-0001), both at 1701 N. Market, are locally popular bars with no cover, good beer selections, and raucous crowds. (Both open daily 11am-2am.) On weekends, and occasionally during the week, various bands perform free concerts out on the red brick marketplace.

Greenville Avenue may be a refreshing change from the downtown crowds. **Poor David's Pub,** 1924 Greenville (821-9891), stages live music for an older crowd that leans towards folk and blues. (Open Mon.-Sat. 7:30pm-2am. Tickets available after 5pm at the door (cash only) or from Ticketmaster.) The **Greenville Bar and Grill,** 2821 Greenville (823-6691), is a classic R&B bar (dollar beers, Mon.-Fri. 4-7pm, open daily 11am-2am; pianist Fri. 5-8pm). Popular nightspots conveniently line **Yale Blvd.,** home of Southern Methodist University's fraternity row. The current bar of choice is **Green Elephant,** 5612 Yale (750-6625), a pseudo-60s extravaganza complete with lava lamps and tacky tapestries (open daily 11pm-2am). **Oak Lawn,** north of downtown, is home to many gay clubs, notably the cover-free **Roundup,** 3912 Cedar Springs Rd., at Throckmorton (522-9611; open daily 1pm-2am).

In Dallas, the moral order is God, country, and the **Cowboys.** Football devotees flock to **Cowboys Stadium** at the junction of Loop 12 and Rte. 183, west of Dallas in **Irving** (579-5000; open Mon.-Fri. 9am-4pm for tickets).

Sports fans will want to visit the brand, spanking new **Ballpark in Arlington,** 1000 Ballpark Way (817-273-5100), in Arlington between Dallas and Fort Worth, home of the Texas **Rangers.** Also in Arlington, **Six Flags Over Texas** (817-640-8900), 15 mi. from downtown off I-30 in Arlington, is the original link in the nationwide amusement park chain. The name alludes to the six different ruling states that have flown their flags over Texas. But the thrills don't come cheap—look for discounts on soda cans and in grocery stores. ($25, over 55 years or under 4 ft. $19—includes unlimited access to all rides and attractions. Open June-Aug. Sun.-Thurs. 10am-10pm, Fri.-Sat. 10am-midnight; Sept.-Jan. Sat.-Sun. 10am-midnight. Parking $5.)

■ NEAR DALLAS: FORT WORTH

If Dallas is the last Eastern city, Fort Worth is undoubtedly the first Western one; a daytrip here (40 min., west on I-30) is worth your while if only for the **Stockyards District** (625-9715). At the corner of N. Main and E. Exchange Ave., the stockyards host weekly rodeos (625-1025, April-Sept. 17 Sat. 8pm, $8) and **Pawnee Bill's Wild West Show** (625-1025, Sat. at 2 and 4pm), which features sharpshooting, bulldoggin, and a stagecoach robbery. At night in the Yards you can't miss **Billy Bob's.** At 100,000 square ft. it is billed as the world's largest honky tonk, with a bull ring, a BBQ restaurant, pool, video games, and a country and western dance club with 42 bar stations. Professional bull-riding Fri.-Sat. 9 and 10pm. (Open Mon.-Sat. 11am-2am, Sun. noon-2am. Cover $3 after 6pm Sun.-Thurs., $5 on the weekends.) Although cattle is auctioned via satellite these days, you can still see **hog auctions,** next to Billy Bob's, (624-0679, Mon. and Tue. afternoons).

The **Tarantula** steam train (800-952-5717), takes the rider on a nostalgic journey through the Old West and on a comprehensive tour of downtown. The train leaves from 8th Avenue downtown and the Stockyards, ($10, seniors $8, kids under 12, $5.50). The stockyards also hosts the **Chisholm Round-Up,** a three-day jamboree during the second weekend of June commemorating the heroism of cowhands who led the long cattle drive to Kansas during the Civil War. Also check out the **Hog and Armadillo Races** (625-7005), in which grandfather and grandson work together to blow the beast to move.

Down Rodeo Plaza, you'll find **Exchange St.,** a thoroughfare to the wild west. The district's frontier feeling is accessorized by numerous western bookstores, restaurants, and saloons. For more on the Stockyards, go to the **visitor information center,** 130 Exchange Ave. (624-4741; open Mon.-Sat. 10am-5pm, Sun noon-6pm).

Culturally light-years from the Stockyards warps the **Kimbell Art Museum,** 3333 Camp Bowie Blvd. (332-8451), a beautiful building designed by Louis Kahn. Inside is one of the best collections of pre-20th-century European art in the South. (Open daily 10am-6pm, Fri. until 8pm; $5, seniors $3, kids under 11 $1.) For American and

Western art, check out the **Amon Carter Museum,** 3501 Camp Bowie Blvd. (738-1933) nearby. (Open Tues.-Sat. 10am-5pm, Sun. noon-5pm. Free.) Round-up some culture at the **Modern Art Museum,** 1309 Montgomery Rd. (738-9215; open Tues.-Fri. 10am-5pm, Sat. 11am-5pm, Sun. noon-5pm; free), and the **Museum of Science and History,** 1501 Montgomery (732-1631), which houses an OmniMax theater and planetarium. (Open Tues.-Thurs. 9am-8pm, Fri.-Sat 9am-9pm, Sun. noon-9pm; $3, children $1.) Fort Worth's **area code** is 817.

■ ■ ■ AUSTIN

In some ways, Austin doesn't seem like Texas; in other ways, it typifies the best about the Lone Star State. Somehow Austin houses the hustle and bustle of state politics while holding onto a laid-back attitude. Here you can walk the streets with honky tonks on one side and cafes on the other. At the center of rugged conservatism lies The University of Texas (UT), home to a slacker sub-culture and people who take their motto "Hook 'em Horns" seriously.

PRACTICAL INFORMATION

Emergency: 911.

Visitor Information: Austin Convention Center/Visitor Information, 201 E. 2nd St. (474-5171 or 800-926-2282). Open Mon.-Fri. 8am-5pm, Sat. 9am-5pm, Sun. noon-5pm. **University of Texas Information Center,** 471-3434. **Texas Parks and Wildlife,** 389-4800 or 800-792-1112. Open Mon.-Fri. 8am-5pm. Call for info on camping outside Austin. Or contact **Texas Parks and Wildlife Dept.,** 4200 Smith School Rd., Austin 78744.

Airport: Robert Mueller Municipal, 4600 Manor Rd. (480-9091), 4 mi. northeast of downtown. Taxi to downtown $8-10.

Amtrak: 250 N. Lamar Blvd. (800-872-7245). To: Dallas (7 per week, 6 hr., $35), San Antonio (7 per week, 3 hr., $15, continues to Houston), and El Paso (4 per week, 10 hr., $122). Open daily 8am-10pm.

Greyhound: 916 E. Koenig (800-231-2222), several mi. north of downtown off I-35. Easily accessible by public transportation. Buses #15 and 7 to downtown stop across the street. To: San Antonio (11 per day, 2-3 hr., $11); Houston (11 per day, 4 hr., $18); Dallas (11 per day, 5 hr., $20); San Antonio (11 per day, 13 hr., $11); El Paso (5 per day, 14 hr. $80). Open 24 hrs.

Public Transport: Capitol Metro, 504 Congress (474-1200; line open daily 8:30am-5:30pm, Sat. 6am-8pm, Sun. 7am-6pm). Maps and schedules available Mon.-Fri. 8am-5pm or at the green kiosk at 5th and Congress. Fare 50¢, seniors, kids, students, and disabled 25¢. The **Armadillo Express** connects major downtown points and runs every 10-15 min. in green trolley cars Mon.-Fri. 6:30am-7pm, Sat. 11am-7pm. Free. The **University of Texas Shuttle Bus** serves the campus area. Officially only for UT affiliates, but drivers rarely ask for ID.

Taxi: Yellow Cab, 472-1111. Base fare $1.25, $1.25 per mi.

Car Rental: Rent-A-Wreck, 6820 Guadalupe (454-8621). $20-40 per day, 50 free mi. with cash deposit; 100 free mi. with credit card deposit, 25¢ per additional mi. Open Mon.-Fri. 8am-7pm, Sat. 9am-5pm, Sun. 10am-2pm. Ages 18-21 $10 surcharge per day.

Bike Rental: Bicycle Sports Shop, 1426 Toomey St. (477-3472), at Jesse. Up to 2 hrs. $8, 3-5 hrs. $14, full day $20 (overnight $9 extra), 24 hrs. $26, 48 hrs. $48, 3 or more days $16 per day, 1 week $80. $100 deposit or credit card required. And they don't accept American Express. Open Mon.-Fri. 10am-8pm, Sat. 9am-6pm, Sun. 11am-8pm.

Help Lines: Crisis Intervention Hotline, 472-4357; **Austin Rape Crisis Center Hotline,** 440-7273. Both 24 hrs. **Outyouth Gay/Lesbian Helpline,** 800-96-YOUTH. Open daily 5:30-9:30pm for referrals and counseling.

Time Zone: Central (1 hr. behind Eastern).

Post Office: 8225 Cross Park Dr. (929-1253). Open Mon.-Fri. 8am-5pm. **ZIP code:** 78767.

Area Code: 512.

UT students inhabit central **Guadalupe St.** ("The Drag"), where numerous music stores and cheap restaurants thrive on their business. A few blocks to the southeast is the state capitol; south of it lies **Congress Ave.** and its upscale eateries and classy shops. **6th St.** houses a plethora of bars and live-music clubs, giving Austin its nickname of "the live music capitol of the world." Some of the nightlife, however, has headed to the **Warehouse Area,** around 4th St., west of Congress. Away from the urban gridiron is **Town Lake** which is the athletic supporter to the town's joggers, rowers, and cyclists.

ACCOMMODATIONS AND CAMPING

Cheap accommodations can be found on **I-35,** running north and south of Austin, but three co-ops run by **College Houses** (476-5678) at UT rent rooms to hostelers, which include three meals per day. Those who are interested in staying at these co-ops should call College Houses, not the individual co-ops, for information. Particularly ideal for young travelers, the co-ops welcome everyone. Patrons have access to all their facilities including a fully-stocked kitchen. Unfortunately, UT houses are only open during the summer.

Austin International Youth Hostel (HI-AYH), 2200 S. Lakeshore Blvd. (444-2294). From Greyhound station take bus #7 ("Duval") to Lakeshore Blvd. and walk about ½ mi. From I-35 east, exit at Riverside, head east, and turn left at Lakeshore Blvd. About 3 mi. from downtown on Town Lake. Kitchen, A/C; located near grocery store. Barrack-style, single-sex rooms. Breakfast $3, dinner $5. Can work in kitchen for a bed. No sleeping bags allowed, sleepsacks $1. $12, nonmembers $15. No curfew. Open daily 9-11am, 5-10pm.

21st St. Co-op, 707 W. 21st St. (476-1857), has carpeted, air-conditioned rooms. To get here from the bus station, take bus #15 to 7th and Congress St., walk down 7th to Colorado, and take #3 to 21st and Nueces St. $10 per person, plus $5 for three meals and kitchen access. Fills up rapidly in summer.

Pearl Street Co-op, 2000 Pearl St. (476-9478). Large, clean, sparsely furnished rooms. Laundry, kitchen, and a beautiful courtyard pool. Open and friendly atmosphere. Rooms include 3 square meals, Shared bath, no curfew, TV/VCR room. Max. stay 2 weeks. Singles $13, doubles $17.

Taos Hall, 2612 Guadalupe (474-6905), 6 blocks up Guadalupe, at 27th St. Same deal as the other co-ops. You're most likely to get a private room here, and when you stay for dinner, the friendly residents will give you a welcoming round of applause. Stay a week and be voted in a member. Three meals and a bed $15.

The Goodall Wooten, 2112 Guadalupe (472-1343). The "Woo" has private rooms with a small fridge, plus access to a TV room, laundry, and basketball courts. Call ahead. Singles $20, doubles $30.

Motel 6, 9420 N. I-35 (339-6161), at the Rundberg exit, 12 mi. north of the capitol off N. Lamar and E. Rundberg Lane. Take bus #7 or 25 to Fawnridge and walk four blocks. Clean, air-conditioned rooms. Pool, TV, HBO, and free local calls. Singles $28, $6 per additional adult, kids under 17 free. Call ahead, open 24 hrs.

Camping is a 15-45-min. drive away. The **Austin Capitol KOA** (444-6322), 6 mi. south of the city along I-35, offers a pool, game room, laundry, grocery, and playground. Some cabins (for up to six) are available. (Sites $22, each additional person 18 and over $3; cabins $32 for four people, $42 for six.) **Emma Long Metropolitan Park,** 1600 City Park Rd. (346-1831), is a large preserve in the bend of the Colorado River. Take I-35 north to the 2222 junction at City Park Rd. The park is 6½ mi. south. Hookup, boat ramp, and a concession stand. (Open 7am-10pm. Park entry fee $3, $5 on weekends. Sites $6. Full hookups $10.)

FOOD

Scores of fast-food joints line the west side of the UT campus on **Guadalupe Street.** The second district clusters around **Sixth Street,** south of the capitol. Here the battle for happy hour business rages with unique intensity; three-for-one drink specials and free *hors d'oeuvres* are common. You might also want to try the area along **Barton Springs Rd.,** which is a bit removed from downtown, but offers a diverse selection of inexpensive restaurants, including Mexican and Texas-style barbecue joints. The **Warehouse District** offers safe bets for seafood or Italian chow.

Trudy's Southern Star, 409 W. 30th St. (477-2935). Fine Tex-Mex dinner entrees $5.25-8, and a fantastic array of margaritas. Famous for *migas,* a corn tortilla soufflé ($4). Open Mon.-Thurs. 7am-midnight, Fri.-Sat. 7am-2am, Sun. 8am-midnight.

Dos Hermanos, 501 E. Oltorf (445-5226), west of Oltorf I-35 exit. Fantastic, very cheap Mexican food. Try the carne guisada taco $1.45. Open Mon.-Sat. 7am-9pm, Sun. 7am-7pm.

Mongolian BBQ, 117 San Jacinto Blvd. (476-3938) at 2nd St., where you can create your own stir-fry. Lunch $5, dinner $7. All you can eat $2 extra; no added cost for herbivores. Open Mon.-Fri. 11am-3pm, 5-9:30pm, Sat. 11:30am-3:30pm, 5-10pm.

Texadelphia, 2422 Guadalupe (480-0107), on the drag across from UT. Great burgers and steak sandwiches ($3-6). Open Mon.-Sat. 11am-9pm.

Sholz Garden, 1607 San Jacinto (477-4171), near the capitol. An Austin landmark recognized by the legislature for "epitomizing the finest traditions of the German heritage of our state." German only in name, though. Great chicken-fried steaks and Tex-Mex meals $5-6. Live country-rock music. Open Mon.-Thurs. 11am-midnight, Fri.-Sat. 11am-2am.

Quackenbush's, 2120 Guadalupe (472-4477), at 21st St. Cafe/deli popular with UT students for a cup of espresso or other stylish drink ($1-2.50). Open Sun.-Thurs. 7am-midnight, Fri.-Sat. 8am-1am.

SIGHTS

Not to be outdone by Washington, D.C., Texans built their **state capitol,** Congress Ave. (463-0063), 7 ft. higher than the national one. (Open daily 7am-10pm. Free tours every 15 min. Mon.-Fri. 8:30am-4:30pm, Sat. 9:30am-4:30pm, Sun. 12:30-4:30pm.) A **tourist information center** (463-8586; open daily 8am-5pm) is in the south foyer of the capitol. Across the street at 11th and Colorado St., sleeps the **Governor's Mansion** (463-5516), built in 1856. Former residents include Governor Hogg and his daughter Ima (Ura was just a myth). (Free tours every 20 min. Mon.-Fri.10-11:40am.)

The **University of Texas at Austin (UT),** the wealthiest public university in the country, forms the backbone of Austin's cultural life. With 50,000 plus students, UT is the second largest university in the country. There are two **visitors information centers,** one in Sid Richardson Hall at 2313 Red River (471-6498), and the other in the Nowtony building at the corner of I-35 and Martin Luther King, Jr. Blvd. (471-1420). Campus tours leave from the base of the Tower (Mon.-Sat. at 11am and 2pm). Campus highlights include the **Lyndon B. Johnson Library and Museum,** 2313 Red River St. (482-5279), which houses 35 million documents (open daily 9am-5pm; free), and the **Harry Ransom Center** (471-8944), where a copy of the Gutenberg Bible rests. The center also hoards a vast collection of manuscripts and correspondences of Aleister Crowley, Woolf, Joyce, Faulkner, D.H. Lawrence, and Evelyn Waugh. (Open Mon.-Sat. 9am-5pm, Sun. noon-5pm. Free.)

The **Laguna Gloria Art Museum,** 3809 W. 35th St. (458-8191), 8 mi. from the capitol in a Mediterranean villa-lookalike, is an exemplary blend of art, architecture, and nature in Austin. With rolling, spacious grounds that overlook **Lake Austin,** the Laguna displays 20th-century artwork and hosts **Fiesta Laguna Gloria,** a May arts and crafts festival, as well as inexpensive evening concerts and plays. Take bus #21. (Group tours Aug.-June by appt. Open Tues.-Wed, Fri.-Sat. 10am-5pm, Thurs. 10am-9pm, Sun. 1-5pm. $2, seniors and students $1, under 16 free. Free to all Thurs.)

On hot afternoons, many zip to riverside **Zilker Park,** 2201 Barton Springs Rd., just south of the Colorado River. **Barton Springs Pool** (476-9044), in the park, is a popular swimming hole flanked by walnut and pecan trees. The natural spring-fed pool is 1000 ft. long and 200 ft. wide with wooden decks. Beware: the pool's temperature rarely rises above 60°F. You can get away from the crowd and avoid the fee by walking upstream (take an inner tube) and swimming at any spot that looks nice. (Open March-Oct. Mon. 9am-7:30pm, Tue.-Wed, 9am-dusk, Thurs. 9am-7:30pm, Fri.-Sun. 9am-dusk. $1.75, Sat.-Sun. $2, ages 12-18 50¢, under 12 25¢.) For more fun and sun, drive to the **Windy Point,** a picturesque sandy park on **Lake Travis,** and try your hand (and body) at windsurfing or scuba-diving. The park is on Comanche Rd., 3 mi. west off the I-620 intersection.

Just before dusk, head to the Congress Ave. Bridge and watch for the thousands of **bats** that emerge from their roosts. The bats make their appearance from mid-March until November, reaching a peak in August. For questions call Bat Conservation International (327-9721).

ENTERTAINMENT

On weekends fans from around the city and nearby towns converge to swing to a wide range of music. **Sixth Street** is bespeckled with warehouse nightclubs, fancy bars, a tattoo workshop, and an Oriental massage parlor. The *Weekly Austin Chronicle* provides detailed listings of current music performances, shows, and movies.

Famous for its blues, **Antone's,** 2915 Guadalupe (474-5314), at 29th St., features all sounds and draws some big names. Stevie Ray Vaughan and B.B. King have graced the stage. (Open daily 4pm-2am, shows at 7 and 10pm. Cover $3-6.) A good alternative is **Hole in the Wall,** 2538 Guadalupe (472-5599), at 28th St. (open 11-2am, Sat.-Sun. noon-2am; cover $3-5). The **Chicago House,** 607 Trinity (473-2542), also off 6th St., plays a different tune on weekends and hosts the occasional poetry reading. (Open Mon.-Sat. 5pm-2am, Thurs. 8pm-2am. $7, students and seniors $6.) Stumble along 6th St. (the street is closed to traffic after 7pm daily), especially on weeknights when there are neither crowds nor cover charges, to sample the bands from the sidewalk. For raunchy Texas-style rock n' roll and cheap beer, try **Joe's Generic Bar,** 315 E. 6th St. (480-0171; open daily 11am-until the wayward crawl home). It's well known that Nashville is the queen of country music, but Austin is a renegade, funky princess with suitors including the likes of Willie Nelson, Waylon Jennings, and more recently Stevie Earle. On campus, the **Cactus Cafe** (471-8228), 24th and Guadalupe, hosts different musicians almost every night. Specializing in folk rock, and the "New Country" sound which came out of Austin, the Cactus gave Lyle Lovett his start. (Hours vary; usually 9am-1am. Cover $2-15.) Next door, the **Texas Tavern** (471-5651) favors country twang and fast food. (Hours vary; usually 11:30am-1:45am. Cover $2-5.) Dance the night to a different beat at **Paradox** (469-7615), on the corner of 5th and Trinity. (Cover around $5. 18 and over. Open daily 4pm-3am.) **404,** 404 Colorado (476-8297) is the city's most popular gay dance club. (Cover for over 21 $5, under 21 $10. Open Wed.-Sun. 10pm-4am.)

Hippie Hollow About 15 mi. northwest of downtown Austin, Hippie Hollow (266-1644) boasts the only **nude swimming** and sunbathing in Texas. The water of beautiful **Lake Travis** is nestled in the heart of Texas Hill Country. The **entrance fee** is $5 a car in the summer and spring, free other times. Take **Mopac (Loop 1)** north to the exit for F.M. 2222. Take 2222 west and turn onto Oasis Bluff.

■■■ HOUSTON

Houston arose in the wake of Texas's battle for independence from Mexico when two New York speculators bought 2000 acres of land on Buffalo Bayou. Named after the quintessential Texan, Sam Houston, the city sprawls over almost 500 sq. miles. But while Houston's glass and steel skyscrapers provide dazzling reflections of the Texas sun and skies, the city itself has little inner substance.

PRACTICAL INFORMATION

Emergency: 911.
Visitor Information: Greater Houston Convention and Visitors Bureau, (227-3100) 810 Congress St., at Milam, uptown.

TEXAS

Airport: Houston Intercontinental (230-3000), 25 mi. north of downtown. Get to the city center via the **Airport Express** (523-8888). Buses depart every 30 min. beginning at 7am. Last bus leaves airport Sun.-Fri. at 11:50pm, Sat. at 11:10pm ($15-17, kids $5). **Hobby Airport** is 9 mi. south of downtown, just west of I-45. Take bus #73 to Texas Med Center and then catch any bus to downtown.

Amtrak: 902 Washington Ave. (224-1577 or 800-872-7245), in a rough neighborhood. During the day, catch a bus west on Washington (away from downtown) to its intersection with Houston Ave. At night, call a cab. To San Antonio ($44, 5 hrs.), New Orleans ($73, 8 hrs.). Station and ticket office open Sat.-Wed. 7am-midnight, Thurs.-Fri. 7am-6pm.

Greyhound: 2121 S. Main St. (800-231-2222), on or near local bus routes. All late-night arrivals should call a cab—this is an unsafe area. To: Dallas ($24, 5 hrs.), Sante Fe ($119, 24 hrs.), San Antonio ($19, 4 hrs.). Open 24 hrs. Lockers $1.

Public Transport: Metropolitan Transit Authority (METRO Bus System), (635-4000). Operates Mon.-Fri. 5am-10pm, Sat.-Sun. 8am-8pm, less frequently on weekends. An all-encompassing system that can take you from NASA (15 mi. southeast of town) to Katy (25 mi. west of town). Get system maps at the Customer Services Center, 813 Dallas St. (658-0180; open Mon.-Fri. 8am-5pm) and individual route maps from Metro headquarters, 1201 Louisiana; the Houston Public Library, 500 McKinney at Bagby (236-1313; open Mon.-Fri. 9am-9pm, Sat. 9am-6pm; Sun. 2-6pm); or from the Metro Ride Store at 813 Dallas and 405 Main, where packs of 10 tokens ($6.80) are available. Fare 85¢; students, seniors, and persons with disabilities with an ID ½ fare; express service $1.20; transfers free.

Taxi: Yellow Cab, 236-1111. Base rate $2.70; $1.35 per mi. Be *sure* to ask for a flat rate in advance.

Car Rental: Cash Plus Car Rental, 5819 Star Lane (977-7771). $24-35 per day with 200 free mi., 25¢ each additional mi. Open Mon.-Fri. 9am-5pm, Sat. 10am-2pm. Must be 21; $350 cash deposit.

Help Lines: Crisis Center Hotline, 228-1505. **Rape Crisis,** 528-7273. Both open 24 hrs. **Gay and Lesbian Switchboard of Houston,** 529-3211. Counseling, medical and legal referrals, and entertainment info. Open daily 3pm-midnight. **Women's Center Hotline,** 528-2121. Open daily 9am-9pm.

Time Zone: Central (1 hr. behind Eastern).

Post Office: 401 Franklin St. (227-1474). Open Mon.-Fri. 6am-7pm, Sat 8am-noon. **ZIP code:** 77052.

Area Code: 713.

The flat Texan terrain supports several mini-downtowns. True downtown Houston, a squarish grid of interlocking one-way streets, borders the Buffalo Bayou at the intersection of I-10 and I-45. The shopping district of **Westhermes Boulevard** grows more ritzy as you progress west. Restaurants and shops line **Kirby Street** and **Richmond Street** nearby. The south and east areas of Houston contain some risky neighborhoods; while the upper portion of Kirby Street winds through some of Houston's most spectacular mansions. **The Loop (I-610)** lassoes the city center with a radius of 6 mi. Anything inside The Loop is easily accessible by car or bus. Find rooms on the southern side of the city—near Montrose Ave., the museums, Hermann Park, Rice University, and Perry House—for easy access to bus lines and points of interest.

ACCOMMODATIONS AND CAMPING

Houston has plenty of cheap motels southwest of downtown along the **Katy Freeway** (I-10 west), but better and more convenient rooms are along **South Main Street.** Singles dip to $22, doubles to $24. Be mindful that these parts of town can be quite dangerous at night. (Buses #8 and 9 go down S. Main; #19, 31, and 39 go out along the Katy Freeway.)

Perry House, Houston International Hostel (HI-AYH), 5302 Crawford (523-1009), at Oakdale. From Greyhound station, take bus #8 or 9 south to Southmore St. (Bank of Houston) stop. Walk 5 blocks east to Crawford and 1 block south to

Houston

N ←

2.5 miles
2.5 kilometers
0
0

Maxey Rd.
Federal Rd.
Shaver St.
Holand Ave.
East Frwy.
Market St. Rd.
Wallisville Rd.
Clinton Dr.
Houston Ship Channel
225
Allen-Genoa Rd.
TO HOBBY AIRPORT
610
Broadway
McCarthy Dr.
Liberty Rd.
Clinton Dr.
90
10
Navigation Blvd.
Lawndale
Wayside
35
45
75
TO HOUSTON INTERCONTINENTAL AIRPORT
Cavalcade
Harrisburg Blvd.
Gulf Frwy.
alt 90
75
59
610
Elysian St.
Moody Park
North Main
Preston
Dallas Ave.
Crawford St.
Elgin
Scott
University of Houston
Mac Gregor Park
Old Spanish Trail
Cullen Blvd.
South Loop Frwy.
518
45
75
Louisiana
288
610
North Loop Frwy.
E. 11th St.
Washington
Buffalo Bayou
W. Gray
Montrose
Main
Hermann Park
Almeda Dr.
alt 90
Astroworld/ Water World
Shepherd Dr.
Westheimer Rd.
Richmond Ave.
59
Kirby Dr.
Rice University
Astrodome
Kirby Dr.
Katy Frwy.
Memorial Dr.
Buffalo Speedway
Holcombe Blvd.
South Main St.
Weslayan
Stella Link Rd.
Memorial Park
610
Hempstead Rd.
290
90
10
West Loop Frwy.
San Felipe
Chimney Rock Rd.
S.W. Freeway
Belfaire Blvd.
Bissonet
Beechnut
Hillcroft Rd.

A B C D E F G
1 2 3 4

Oakdale. The neighborhood toughens 2 blocks east of the hostel. Friendly management and nice rooms near Hermann park. Owners sometimes offer makeshift city tours; ask about nighttime version. Closed 10am-5pm; you can show up during lock-out and hang out in TV room. $11.25, nonmembers $14.25. Linen $1.50.

Houston Hostel, 5530 Hillman #2 (926-3444). Take bus #36 to Lawndale at Dismuke. This converted apartment has one 6-bed, co-ed bedroom. No curfew, even for the several cats who live there. $7 per bunk, linen $1.

YMCA, 1600 Louisiana Ave. (659-8501), between Pease and Leeland St. An excellent YMCA. Good downtown location only blocks from Greyhound. Clean rooms with daily maid service, TV, wake-up calls, common baths. Rooms $17.45, key deposit $5. Another branch at 7903 South Loop (643-4396) is farther out but less expensive. Take Bus #50 at Broadway. $13, plus key deposit $10.

Little House Cottage Hostel, 13609 Hooper Rd. (649-4748 and leave a message). Close to Hobby Airport but more than an hour from downtown. From the bus station, take Rte. 288S to exit Almeda/Genoa. Make a right go several blocks and make a left on to Hooper. Pick-up from bus station and Hobby available if you call ahead of time. 10 min. from Astroworld, 45 min. from NASA. Linen $1. Coin-op laundry across the street. Check in 6-10:30pm only. 6 beds in two rooms, $10.

The Roadrunner, 8500 S. Main St. (666-4971). One of 2 locations in Houston. Friendly and helpful management. Cable TV, mini pool, free coffee, local calls, and free ACME catalogs. Large, well-furnished rooms, but be careful of falling rock formations. Singles $24. Doubles $30. Meep! Meep!

Grant Motor Inn, 8200 S. Main St. (668-8000), near the Astrodome. Clean and relatively safe. Satellite TV, swing-set, and pool. Maid service and free continental breakfast. Big ole rooms surround an amoeba-shaped pool shaded by palm umbrellas. Singles $32, $35 for 2 people. Doubles $43.

Two campgrounds grace the Houston area, but both are out in the boondocks, inaccessible by METRO Bus. **KOA Houston North,** 1620 Peachleaf (442-3700), has a pool and showers. From I-45, go east on Beltway 8N, then turn right on Aldine-Westfield Road and then right again on Peachleaf (tent sites for 2 $16, with electricity $18, full hookup $22; $2 per additional adult). Or try the **Houston Campground,** 710 State Hwy. 6 S. (493-2391) off I-10. ($13 per 2-person tent site, $15 with water and electricity, and $17 for full hookup; $3 per additional adult.)

FOOD

A port town, Houston has witnessed the arrival of many immigrants (today its Indochinese population is the second largest in the nation), and its restaurants reflect this diversity. Houston's cuisine mingles Mexican and Vietnamese food. Look for reasonably priced restaurants among the shops and boutiques along **Westheimer St.,** especially near the intersection with Montrose. This area, referred to as "Montrose," is popular with gay men. Bus #82 follows Westheimer from downtown to well past The Loop. For great Vietnamese cuisine, go to **Milam St.,** where it intersects Elgin St., just south of downtown.

Goode Company BBQ, 5109 Kirby Dr. (522-2530) near Bissonet. Might be the best BBQ (and the most popular) in Texas, with honky-tonk atmosphere to match. Sandwiches $3, dinner $5-6. Check out the "bully bags" (bull scrotums) hanging above the cash register, and the jackalope mounted over the feeding line. *No hay pollo aquí.* Open daily 11am-10pm. Expect a line.

Hobbit Hole, 1715 S. Shepherd Dr. (528-3418). A reddish, 2-story, dimly-lit diner with a nice backyard patio. A few blocks off Westheimer. Take bus #82 and get off at Shepard Drive intersection. *Lord of the Rings* paraphernalia abounds. Owners known to ride black horses, disappear into the forest, rap with Ents, and sing "Ramble On." For the herbivorous adventurer. Entrees $5-9. Open Mon.-Thurs. 11am-10:30pm, Fri.-Sat. 11am-11:30pm, Sun. 11:30am-10pm.

Van Loc, 3010 Milam St. (528-6441) at Elgin. Yummy Vietnamese and Chinese food (entrees $5-8). Have one of the lunch specials for dinner and eat cheaper ($3-4).

Open Sun.-Thurs. 9:30am-11:30pm, Fri.-Sat. 9:30am-12:30am. Downtown location, 825 Travis St., has a similar buffet but charges a bit more. Same hrs.

Cadillac Bar, 1802 N. Shepherd Dr. (862-2020), at the Katy Freeway (I-10), northwest of downtown. Take bus #75, change to #26 at Shepherd Dr. and Allen Pkwy. Wild fun and authentic Mexican food. Tacos and enchiladas $5-7; heartier entrees $5-13. Drinks with sexy names $4. Open Sun.-Thurs. 10am-10:30pm, Sat. 10am-midnight, Sun. 10am-10pm.

Luther's Bar-B-Q, 8777 S. Main St. (432-1107). One of 12 locations in the Houston area. Good Texas BBQ entrees ($5-7). Open Sun.-Thurs. 11am-10pm, Fri.-Sat. 11am-11pm.

SIGHTS

Amid Houston's sprawling sauna of oil-related establishments and food chains are a few worthy sights. Focus on **downtown,** the nexus of nearly all the city's bus routes.

In the southwest corner of the downtown area is **Sam Houston Park,** just west of Bagby St. between Lamar and McKinney St. **Saint John's Lutheran Church** (373-0503), built in 1891 by German farmers, contains the original pulpit and pews. Catch the one-hour tour to see four buildings in the park. (Tours on the hr. Mon.-Sat. 10am-3pm, Sun. 1-4pm. Tickets $4, students and seniors $2.)

Central downtown is a shopper's subterranean paradise. Hundreds of shops and restaurants line the **Houston Tunnel System,** which connects all the major buildings in downtown Houston, extending from the Civic Center to the Tenneco Building and the Hyatt Regency. On hot days, duck into the air-conditioned passageways via any major building or hotel. To navigate the tunnels, pick up a map ($1.50) at the Public Library, Pennzoil Place, Texas Commerce Bank, the Hyatt Regency, or call Tunnel Walks at 840-9255.

Antique-lovers will want to see the collection of 17th- to 19th-century American decorative art at **Bayou Bend Museum of Americana,** 1010 Milam (526-2600), in **Memorial Park.** The collection is housed in the palatial mansion of millionaire Ima Hogg (we *swear*), daughter of turn-of-the-century Texas governor Jim "Boss" Hogg. The museum houses some of the more obscure Remington paintings. (Open for tours Tues.-Fri. 1-2:45pm, $3. Open house Sat. 10am-1pm. Garden open Tues.-Sat. 10am-5pm, Sun. 1-5pm. Call for price information.)

Back toward downtown, just east of Montrose, are two of the city's more highly acclaimed museums. The **de Menil Collection,** 1515 Sul Ross (525-9400), is an eclectic collection of African and Asian artifacts and 20th-century European and American paintings and sculpture. Be sure to see Magritte's hilarious *Madame Récamier.* (Open Wed.-Sun. 11am-7pm. Free.) One block away, the **Rothko Chapel,** 3900 Yupon (524-9839), houses some of the artist's paintings. Fans of modern art will delight in Rothko's ultra-simplicity; others will wonder where the actual paintings are (open daily 10am-6pm). The **Houston Fire Museum,** 2403 Milam (524-2526) at McIlhenny, will ignite your imagination. Featuring exhibits from the bucket brigades to *Backdraft* (open Tues.-Sat. 10am-4pm. $2, kids and seniors $1).

Most of Houston's museums lie 3 to 4 mi. south of downtown. On Main St. lies the beautifully landscaped **Hermann Park,** and the **Houston Museum of Natural Science** (639-4600), which offers a splendid display of gems and minerals, permanent exhibits on petroleum, a hands-on gallery geared toward grabby children, and a planetarium and IMAX theater. (Open Tues.-Sat. 9am-6pm, Sun. noon-6pm; $3, over 62 and under 12 $2; combined museum and IMAX admission $7.50, over 62 and under 12 $5.) Flutter from your city worries and visit the **Cockrell Butterfly Centre** in the museum. In a tropical paradise of 80° you'll find yourself surrounded by more than 2000 butterflies. Wear bright colors to attract them, *but don't eat 'em.* (Open Mon.-Fri. 9am-6pm, Sun. noon-6pm. $3, kids $2, seniors $1.50.) The **Houston Zoological Gardens** (525-3300) feature small mammals, alligators, and hippopotami eating spicy hippoplankton food (open daily 10am-6pm; $2.50, seniors $2, ages 3-12 50¢). The **Museum of Fine Arts,** 1001 Bissonet (639-7300), adjoins the north side of Hermann Park. Designed by Mies van der Rohe, the museum boasts a collection of

TEXAS

Impressionist and post-Impressionist art, as well as a slew of Remingtons. (Open Tues.-Wed, Fri.-Sat. 10am-5pm, Thurs. 10am-9pm, Sun. 12:15-6pm. $3, seniors and students $1.50. Free Thurs.) Across the street, the **Contemporary Arts Museum,** 5216 Montrose St. (526-0773), has multi-media exhibits. (Open Tues.-Fri. 10am-5pm, Sat.-Sun. noon-5pm; free, but admission to Gallery 1 costs $3, seniors and students $1, under 12 and on Thurs. free.) Also on the park grounds are sports facilities, a zoo, a kiddie train, a Japanese garden, and the Miller Outdoor Theater (see Entertainment below). The **University of Houston, Texas Southern University,** and **Rice University** all study in this part of town.

The **Astrodome,** Loop 610 at Kirby Dr. (799-9555), a mammoth indoor arena the first of its kind, is the home of **Oilers** (799-1000) and **Astros** (526-1709; tours daily 11am, 1pm, and 3pm; $4, seniors and students $3, under 7 free; parking $4). At these prices, you're better off paying admission to a game.

Wander down Space Age memory lane at NASA's **Lyndon B. Johnson Space Center** (483-4321), where models of Gemini, Apollo, Skylab, and the space shuttle are displayed in a free walk-through museum. Houston is home of Mission Control, which is still HQ for modern-day Major Toms; when astronauts ask, "Do you read me, Houston?" the folks here answer. (Control center open daily 9am-7pm. $10, kids $6.) Arrive early to secure a *space* in mission control and allow 3-4 hrs. to orbit the complex. For launch info call 483-8600. By car, drive 25 mi. south on I-45. The car-less should take the Park and Ride Shuttle #246 from downtown.

Terminus of the gruesomely polluted Houston Ship Channel (known from time to time to catch on fire), the **Port of Houston** leads the nation in foreign trade. Free 90-min. guided harbor tours are offered on the inspection boat *Sam Houston* (tours Tues.-Wed. and Fri.-Sat. at 10am and 2:30pm, Thurs. and Sun. at 2:30pm). Reservations for these tours should be made in advance, but you can join one if the boat doesn't reach its 90-person capacity. Call to make last-minute reservations between 8:30am and 12:30pm. To reach the port, drive 5 mi. east from downtown on Clinton Dr., or take bus #30 ("Clinton/Clinton Drive") at Capital and San Jacinto to the Port Authority gate. For more info or reservations, write or call the Port of Houston Authority, P.O. Box 2562, Houston 77252 (670-2416; open Mon.-Fri. 8am-5pm).

The most important monument to Lone Star independence is the **San Jacinto Battleground State Historical Park,** 21 mi. east on Rte. 225, then 3 mi. north on Rte. 134. The battle which ultimately brought Texas independence from Mexico was fought here on April 21, 1836. The view from the top of the 50-story-high **San Jacinto Monument and Museum of Natural History** (479-2421) is amazing (open daily 9am-6pm; elevator $2.50, under 12 $1; slide show $3.50, under 12 $2).

ENTERTAINMENT

The **Westheimer** strip offers the largest variety of places for no cover. Rub elbows with venture capitalists and post-punks alike at **The Ale House,** 2425 W. Alabama (521-2333), at Kirby. The bi-level bar and beer garden offers over 130 brands of beer. Upstairs you'll find old-time rock n' roll or the blues on Sat. nights. (Open Mon.-Sat. 11am-2am, Sun. noon-2am.) Listen to live jazz at **Cody's Restaurant and Club,** penthouse of 3400 Montrose St. (522-9747; open Tues.-Fri. 4pm-2am, Sat. 6pm-2am). **Sam's Place,** 5710 Richmond Ave. (781-1605), is your typical spring-break-style Texas hangout. On Sunday afternoons a band plays outdoors (5-10pm), and various booths proffer different beers. (Happy Hour Mon. 2pm-closing, Tues. 2-8pm, Wed.-Fri. 2-9pm, Sat. 11am-5pm. Open Mon.-Sat. 11am-2am, Sun. noon-2am.) **The Red Lion,** 7315 Main St. (795-5000), features cheap beer and nightly acoustic sets (open daily 11am-2am; bar open 2:30pm-2am).

Houston offers ballet, opera, and symphony at **Jones Hall,** 615 Louisiana Blvd. Tickets for the **Houston Symphony Orchestra** (227-ARTS/2787) cost $8-50. The season runs Sept.-May. During July, the symphony gives free concerts Monday, Wednesday, and Saturday at noon in the Miller Theater. The **Houston Grand Opera** (546-0200) produces seven operas each season, with performances Oct.-May (tickets $15-110, 50% student discount ½ hr. before performance). Call 227-2787 for info on the ballet, opera, or symphony. If you're visiting Houston in the summer, take advantage of the **Miller Outdoor Theater** (520-3290), in Hermann Park. The symphony, opera, and ballet companies and various professional theaters stage free concerts here on the hillside most evenings April-Oct., and the annual **Shakespeare Festival** struts and frets upon the stage from late July to early August. For an event update call 520-3292. The downtown **Alley Theater**, 615 Texas Ave. (228-8421), stages Broadway-caliber productions at moderate prices (tickets $22-40, student rush seats the day of the show ½ price).

■ NEAR HOUSTON: GALVESTON ISLAND

The narrow, sandy island of **Galveston** (pop. 65,000), 50 mi. southeast of Houston on I-45, offers not only a beach resort's requisite t-shirt shops, ice cream stands, and video arcades, but also beautiful vintage homes, antique shops, and even a few deserted beaches. In the 19th century, Galveston was Texas's most prominent port and wealthiest city, earning the nickname "Queen of the Gulf." Yet the crippled shipping industry could not be protected from the refocus of commerce along the Houston Ship Channel, completed in 1914. Wealthy residents disembarked, leaving the former port and austere mansions behind.

Practical Information Emergency is 911. The **Strand Visitors Center**, 2016 Strand (765-7834; open daily 9:30am-6pm), provides info about island activities. Galveston's streets follow a grid; lettered streets (A to U) run north-south, numbered streets run east-west, with **Seawall** following the southern coastline. Most streets have two names; Avenue J and Broadway, for example, are the same thoroughfare. **Texas Bus Lines**, a **Greyhound** affiliate, operates out of the station at 613 University (765-7731), providing service to Houston (5 per day, 1½ hr., $9). Galveston's **post office:** 601 25th St. (763-1527; open Mon.-Fri. 9:30am-5pm, Sat. 9am-12:30pm); **ZIP code:** 77550; **area code:** 409.

Accommodations and Food Money-minded folk should avoid lodging in Galveston. Accommodation prices fluctuate by season and can rise to exorbitant heights during holidays and weekends. The least expensive option is to make Galveston a daytrip from Houston. Nevertheless, RVs can rest at any of several parks on the island. The **Bayou Haven Travel Park**, 6310 Heards Lane off 61st St. (744-2837), is the closest to downtown and located on a peaceful waterfront with laundry facilities and bug-free restrooms and showers. (Full hookup $14 for 2 people, waterfront sites $17 for 2, each additional person $3.) You can pitch a tent at **Galveston Island State Park** (737-1222), on 13 Mile Rd. about 10 mi. southwest of the trolley-stop visitors center (sites $12). The few cheap motels along Seawall are shabby. Perhaps the best is **Treasure Isle Inn,** 1002 Seawall (763-8561), with TV, pool, and A/C. (Singles $29. Doubles $35. Seniors receive a 10% discount.)

Seafood and traditional Texas barbecue abound in Galveston. Plenty of eateries line Seawall and the Strand. For seafood, go to **Benno's on the Beach,** 1200 Seawall (762-4621), and try a big bowl of the shrimp gumbo ($4), or order a plate of whole crabs ($7-8.50 in the summertime; open Sun.-Thurs. 11am-10pm, Fri.-Sat. 11am-11pm). A popular place, **El Nopalito,** 614 42nd St. (763-9815), sports cheap Mexican breakfast and lunch. Its early afternoon closing time may be sensible, seeing how the restaurant is located in a seedy area (entrees $3.75-5; open Tues.-Fri. 6:30am-2pm, Sat.-Sun 6:30am-4pm). After a day at the beach, indulge your sweet tooth with a Cherry Phosphate ($1) at **LaKing's Confectionery,** 2323 Strand (762-6100), a large, old-fashioned ice cream and candy parlor. (Open Mon.-Fri. 10am-9pm, Sat. 10am-10pm, Sun. 10am-9pm.) If your pockets are starting to fill with lint, try the **H-E-B Supermarket,** 6013 Stewart St. at 61st St. (734-0064).

Sights and Activities Finding your favorite beach is not difficult in tiny Galveston. Just stroll along the seawall and choose a spot. Immerse yourself in partying teenagers and high-spirited volleyball games at **Stewart Beach,** near 4th and Sea-wall. For a kinder, gentler student crowd, try **Pirates Beach,** about 3 mi. west of 95th and Seawall. There are three **Beach Pocket Parks** on the west end of the island, east of Pirates Beach, with bathrooms, showers, playgrounds, and a conces-sion stand (parking $3). **Apfel Park,** on the far eastern edge of the island, is a quiet, clean beach with a good view of ships entering and leaving the port (entry $5).

The historic **Strand,** near the northern coastline, between 20th and 25th St., is a national landmark with over 50 Victorian buildings; today the preserved district houses a range of cafes, restaurants, gift shops, and clothing stores. The **Galveston Island Trolley** takes visitors to the seawall area and all the beaches (trains leave every 30 min., hourly Oct.-April.; $2, seniors and kids $1). You can take the trolley from the Strand Visitors Center or the Visitors Bureau (see above), or take a two-hour cruise in Galveston harbor aboard the **Colonel** (763-4900), a Victorian paddle-wheel boat. The Colonel leaves from **Moody Gardens,** a collection of touristy spas and restaurants. The area distinguishes itself with a 10-story glass pyramid enclosing a tropical rainforest and 2000 exotic species of flora and fauna.

■■■ SAN ANTONIO

Tourist office propaganda says that every Texan has two homes—his own and San Antonio. As tourist capital of Texas, San Antonio has a vast array of sights; the his-toric Missions, the Riverwalk, the Tower of the Americas, a hopping nightlife, and one of the country's most impressive zoos. Since most of downtown San Antonio was built before 1930, the architectural mixture is as varied as periods and materials allowed. Though Native Americans and Germans alike once claimed the city as their own, today the Spanish-speaking community outnumbers any other group.

PRACTICAL INFORMATION

Emergency: 911.
Visitor Information: 317 Alamo Plaza (270-8748), downtown across from the Alamo. Open daily 8:30am-6pm.
Airport: San Antonio International, 9800 Airport Blvd. (821-3411), north of town. Served by I-410 and U.S. 281. Cabs to downtown $7-11. By bus, take #12 at Commerce and Navarro or Market and Alamo.
Amtrak: 1174 E. Commerce St. (223-3226 or 800-872-7245), off the I-37 E. Com-merce St. exit. To: Houston ($44, 5 hrs.), Dallas ($44, 9hrs.) Ticket office open Sun.-Wed. 11pm-4am, Thurs.-Fri. 6:30am-4pm and Sat. 6:30am-4pm, 11pm-4am.
Greyhound: 500 N. Saint Mary's St. (800-231-2222). To: Houston ($24, 4 hrs.), Dal-las ($32, 8hrs.). Lockers $1. Terminal open 24 hrs.
Public Transport: VIA Metropolitan Transit, 800 W. Myrtle (227-2020), between Commerce and Houston. Buses operate 5am-10pm, but many routes stop at 5pm. Inconvenient service to outlying areas. Fare 40¢ (more with zone changes), express 75¢. Cheap (10¢), dependable, and frequent old-fashioned **streetcars** operate downtown at varying hours. Call the office for info, open Mon.-Sat. 5:30am-8pm.
Taxi: Yellow Cab, 226-4242. $2.90 for first mi., $1.30 each additional mi.
Car Rental: Chuck's Rent-A-Clunker, 3249 SW Military Dr. (922-9464). Lives up to its name! $18-25 per day with 100 free mi., vans $35-45 per day. Must be 19 with a major credit card or cash deposit with reference check. Open Mon.-Fri. 8am-7pm, Sat. 9am-6pm, Sun. 10am-6pm.
Help Lines: Rape Crisis Center, 349-7273. 24 hrs. **Presa Community Service Center,** 532-5295. Referrals and transport for elderly and disabled. Open Mon.-Fri. 8:30am-noon and 1-4pm. **Gay/Lesbian Switchboard,** 733-7300 for referral and entertainment info 24 hrs., or the **Lesbian Info San Antonio,** 828-5472.
Time Zone: Central (1 hr. behind Eastern).
Post Office: 615 E. Houston (227-3399), 1 block from the Alamo. Open Mon.-Fri. 8:30am-5:30pm. **ZIP code:** 78205.
Area Code: 210.

ACCOMMODATIONS AND CAMPING

Since San Antonio is a popular city, downtown hotel managers have no reason to keep prices low to meet the needs of budget travelers. Furthermore, San Antonio's dearth of rivers and lakes makes for few good campsites. But cheap motels are bountiful along Roosevelt Ave., an extension of St. Mary's, only 2 mi. from downtown, accessible by the VIA bus (see Practical Information), and near the missions. Inexpensive motels also clutter Broadway between downtown and Breckenridge Park. Drivers should follow I-35 north to find cheaper and often safer accommodations within 15 mi. of town.

Bullis House Inn San Antonio International Hostel (HI-AYH), 621 Pierce St. (223-9426), 2 mi. northeast of the Alamo, across the street from Fort Sam Houston. From downtown take bus #11 at Market and St. Mary's to Grayson St. and get off at Grayson and Palmetto, then walk 1 block over to Pierce. Friendly hostel in a quiet neighborhood. Pool, kitchen. $13, nonmembers $16. Private rooms for 1-2 people $27, nonmembers from $30. Sheets $2. Fills rapidly in summer. Office open daily 7:30-11pm.

Elmira Motor Inn, 1126 E. Elmira (222-9463), about 3 blocks east of St. Mary's, a little over 1 mi. north of downtown—take bus #8 and get off at Elmira St. Very large and well-furnished rooms—the cleanest you'll get at this price. However, it is not in a safe area of town. TV, laundry service, and 5 free local calls. Caring management. Singles $26, doubles $32. Key deposit $2.

Navarro Hotel, 116 Navarro St. (223-8453). Some rooms have cracked plaster and most are irregularly shaped. Some have A/C, some don't. Some people stay here, some don't. Nonetheless, it's in the heart of town. Singles $37, doubles $45.

El Tejas Motel, 2727 Roosevelt Ave. (533-7123), at E. South Cross, 3 mi. south of downtown near the missions. Take bus #42. Family-run, with TV and a pool. Rooms have thin walls. Open 24 hrs. Singles start at $30, doubles at $36.

Alamo KOA, 602 Gembler Rd. (224-9296), 6 mi. from downtown. Take bus #24 ("Industrial Park") from the corner of Houston and Alamo downtown. Showers, laundry, A/C, pool, playground, movies, fishing pond. Sites $14, full hookup $17.75 for 2 people, $2 each additional person over age 3. Open daily 7:30am-10:30pm. Lots of shade and each site has a BBQ grill and patio.

Traveler's World RV Park, 2617 Roosevelt Ave. (532-8310 or 800-755-8310), at South Cross 3 mi. south of downtown. Sites are large and have tables and benches. Showers, laundry, pool, hot tub, playground. Next to golf course and restaurants. Open Mon.-Sat. 8am-7pm, Sun. 9am-6pm. Tent sites $10 for 2; RV sites $18 for 2, $16 in winter. Each additional person $1, $2 in winter.

FOOD

Explore the area east of S. Alamo and S. Saint Mary's St., for the best Mexican food and BBQ. The **Riverwalk** abounds with expensive cafes and restaurants. Breakfast alone could clean you out, if you don't settle for just a muffin and coffee. **Pig Stand** (227-1691) diners offer decent, cheap food all over this part of Texas; the branch at 801 S. Presa, off S. Alamo, is open 24 hrs. North of town, many old Asian restaurants line Broadway across from Brackenridge. The best fast-food Mexican is **Taco Cabana** with many locations across downtown. Visit the one at 101 Alamo Plaza (224-6158), at Commerce.

Josephine St. Steaks/Whiskey (224-6169), Josephine St. at McAllister. Off the beaten track—away from the more touristy spots along the riverwalk. Entrees $5-11. Josephine's specializes in Texan steaks, but offers an assortment of chicken, seafood, and pork entrees. Great home-baked desserts; try the carrot cake or cookie pie (both $2.50). Open Mon.-Thurs. 11am-10pm, Fri.-Sat. 11am-11pm.

Rio Rio Cantina, 421 E. Commerce (CAN-TINA/226-8462), offers funky upscale Mexican in a fancy, shaka-shaka setting. Order up a huge naked José Iguana ($8.50)—a 27 oz. combo of every chemical with an alcohol ring, and a splash of delightful 7Up. After you eat, check out Iggy, the live iguana on the premises. Open Sun.-Thurs. 11am-11pm., Fri.-Sat. 11am-1am. Live music Fri. and Sat.

TEXAS

Sulema's Mexican Kitchen, 319 E. Houston (222-9807), at Presa St. Cheap lunch and breakfast entrees. Lunch plates $4-5 with free iced tea or coffee. Breakfast specials under $2.50. Open Mon.-Sat. 7am-8pm.

Hung Fong Chinese and American Restaurant, 3624 Broadway (822-9211), at Queen Anne, 2 mi. north of downtown. Take bus #14. The oldest Chinese restaurant in San Antonio. Consistently good and crowded. Big portions. Try the egg rolls and lemon chicken. Meals $3-5. Open Mon.-Thurs. 11am-10:45pm, Fri. 11am-11:45pm, Sat. 11:30am-12:45am, Sun. 11:30am-10:45pm.

SIGHTS

Much of historic San Antonio lies in present-day downtown and surrounding areas. The city may seem diffuse, but almost every major site and park is within a few miles of downtown and accessible by public transportation.

The Missions

The five missions along the San Antonio River once formed the soul of San Antonio; the city preserves their remains in the **San Antonio Missions National Historical Park.** To reach the missions, follow the blue-and-white "Mission Trail" signs beginning on S. Saint Mary's St. downtown. **San Antonio City Tours** (520-8687), at the Alamo's Visitors Center on Crockett St., offers full-day tours ($38), half-day ($24), and mini, pocket size tours ($12) of the city. Bus #42 stops right in front of Mission San José, within walking distance of Mission Concepción. (All missions open daily 9am-6pm; Sept.-May 8am-5pm. For general info on the missions, call 229-5701.)

Mission Concepción, 807 Mission Rd. (229-5732), 4 mi. south of the Alamo off E. Mitchell St. Oldest unrestored church in North America (1731). Traces of the once-colorful frescoes still visible. Active parish sanctuary.

Mission San José, 6539 San José Dr. (229-4770). The "Queen of the Missions" (1720), with its own irrigation system, a church with a gorgeous sculpted rose window, and numerous restored buildings. The largest of San Antonio's missions, it provides the best sense of the self-sufficiency of these institutions. Catholic services (including a noon "Mariachi Mass") are held 4 times Sun.

Mission San Juan Capistrano (534-3161) and **Mission San Francisco de la Espada** (627-2064), both off Roosevelt Ave., 10 mi. south of downtown as the Texas swallows fly. Smaller and simpler than the other missions, these two are best at evoking the isolation such outposts once knew.

Remember the Alamo!

"Be silent, friend, here heroes died to blaze a trail for other men." Disobeying orders to retreat with their cannons, the defenders of the Alamo, outnumbered 20 to one, held off the Mexican army for 12 days. Then, on the morning of the 13th day, the Mexicans commenced the infamous *deguello* (throat-cutting). Forty-six days later General Sam Houston's small army defeated the Mexicans at San Jacinto amidst cries of "Remember the Alamo!" Now phalanxes of tourists attack the **Alamo** (225-1391), at the center of Alamo Plaza by the junction of Houston and Alamo St., and sno-cone vendors are the only defenders. A single chapel and barracks preserved by the state are all that remain of the former Spanish mission. (Open Mon.-Sat. 9am-6:30pm, Sun. 10am-5:30pm. Free.) The **Long Barracks Museum and Library,** 315 Alamo Plaza, houses Alamo memorabilia (open Mon.-Sat. 9am-6:30pm). Next door, the **Clara Driscoll Theater** shows an historical documentary titled "The Battle of the Alamo." (Shows run every 20 min. Mon.-Sat. 9am-5:30pm.)

Heading southwest from the Alamo, black signs indicate access points to the **Paseo del Río (Riverwalk),** with shaded stone pathways following a winding canal built in the 1930s by the WPA. Lined with picturesque gardens, shops, and cafes, and connecting most of the major downtown sights, the Riverwalk is well-patrolled, safe, and beautiful at night, when it becomes the hub of San Antonio's nightlife. Ride the entire length of the Riverwalk by taking a boat (222-1701; $3, kids under 4 ft. $1) from the front of the Hilton and Mariott Hotels. The **Alamo IMAX Theater** (225-

4629), in Rivercenter Mall, shows "The Price of Freedom," a 45-min. docudrama Alamo film, on its six-story screen. (8 shows 9am-6pm. $6.25, kids under 11 $4.) A few blocks south, a cluster of 27 restored buildings called **La Villita**, 418 Villita (299-8610), houses restaurants, crafts shops, and art studios. (Open daily 10am-6pm.)

To take a self-guided tour of downtown, hop on an **old-fashioned street car** (10¢; see Practical Information), and spend at least an hour tooting by the sites. The purple-line street car has the more extensive route, stretching from the Alamo to the Spanish Governor's Mansion to La Villita.

Hemisfair Plaza (229-8570), on S. Alamo, the site of the 1968 World's Fair, is another top tourist spot. The city often uses the plaza, surrounded by restaurants, museums, and historic houses, for special events. The **Tower of the Americas,** 600 Hemisphere Park (299-8615), rises 750 ft. above the dusty plains, dominating the meager skyline. Get a view of the city from the observation deck on top (open daily 8am-11pm; $2.50, seniors $1.25, ages 4-11 $1). Stroll through the free museums in the plaza, including the **Institute of Texan Cultures** (558-2300; open Tues.-Sun. 9am-5pm; parking $2), and the **Mexican Cultural Institute** (227-0123), filled with modern Mexican art (open Tues.-Fri. 10am-5pm, Sat.-Sun. 11am-5pm).

Near Hemisfair on Commerce St., across from the San Antonio Convention Center, German immigrants erected **St. Joseph's Church** (226-1413) in 1868. Since this beautiful old church refused to move, a local store chain built their establishment around it. (Sun. mass 8am and 11am in English, 9:30am and 12:30pm in Spanish.)

Walk west to the **Main Plaza** and **City Hall,** between Commerce and Dolorosa St. at Laredo. Directly behind the City Hall lies the **Spanish Governor's Palace,** 105 Plaza de Armas (224-0601). Built in Colonial Spanish style in 1772, the house has carved doors and an enclosed, shaded patio and garden. (Open Mon.-Sat. 9am-5pm, Sun. 10am-5pm. $1, kids under 14 50¢, kids under 7 free.)

Market Square, 514 W. Commerce (229-8600), sells both schlocky souvenirs and handmade local crafts. The walkway **El Mercado** continues the block-long retail stretch. At the nearby **Farmers Market** (299-8596) you can buy produce, Mexican chiles, candy, and spices. Come late in the day when prices are lower and vendors more willing to haggle. (Open daily 10am-8pm; Sept.-May daily 10am-6pm.)

The brand-new **Alamodome** (207-3600), at Montana and Hoefgen downtown, resembles a Mississippi riverboat. It's home to the San Antonio **Spurs** and sports column-free viewing and the world's largest retractable seating system (wow!). (Tours $3, kids under 12 $1.50.)

San Antonio North and South

Head to **Brackenridge Park,** 3900 N. Broadway (734-5401), 5 mi. north of the Alamo, for a day of unusual sight-seeing. From downtown, take bus #8. The 343-acre showground includes a Japanese garden, playgrounds, a miniature train, and an aerial tramway ($2). (Open Mon.-Fri. 9am-5pm, Sat.-Sun. 9am-5:30pm.) Directly across the street is the **San Antonio Zoo,** 3903 N. Saint Mary's St. (734-7183). The zoo is one of the country's largest, housing over 3500 animals from 800 species in reproductions of their natural settings, including an extensive African mammal exhibit. (Open daily 9:30am-6:30pm; Nov.-March daily 9:30am-5pm. $6, seniors $4, kids 3-11 $4.) Nearby **Pioneer Hall,** 3805 N. Broadway (822-9011), contains a splendid collection of artifacts, documents, portraits, and cowboy accessories related to early Texas history. Three exhibit rooms are separately devoted to the Pioneers, the Texas Rangers, and the Trail Drivers. (Open Tues.-Sun. 10am-5pm, Sept.-April Wed.-Sun. 11am-4pm. $1, kids 6-12 25¢.) Next door, at the **Witte Museum** (rhymes with city), 3801 Broadway (820-2111), permanent exhibits focus on Texas wildlife. (Open Mon. and Wed.-Sat. 10am-5pm, Tues. 10am-9pm, Sun. noon-5pm; off-season closes at 5pm. $4, seniors $2, ages 4-11 $1.75. Free Tues. 3-9pm.) The 38-acre **Botanical Center,** 555 Funston Pl. (821-5115), 1 mi. east of Brackenridge Park, includes the largest conservatory in the Southwest (open Tues.-Sun. 9am-6pm; $3, seniors $1.50, kids $1).

TEXAS

The **San Antonio Museum of Art,** 200 W. Jones Ave. (978-8100), just north of the city center, inhabits the restored Lone Star Brewery building. Towers, turrets, and spacious rooms decorated with ornate columns house Texan furniture and pre-Columbian, Native American, Spanish Colonial, and Mexican folk art. (Open Mon. and Wed.-Sat. 10am-5pm, Tues. 10am-9pm, Sun. noon-5pm. $4, seniors and collegiates with ID $2, kids 4-11 $1.75. Free Tues. 10am-9pm. Free parking.) The former estate of Marion Koogler McNay, the **McNay Art Institute,** 6000 N. New Braunfels (824-5368), displays a collection of mostly post-Impressionist European art. It also has a charming inner courtyard with sculpture fountains and meticulous landscaping (open Tues.-Sat. 10am-5pm, Sun. noon-5pm; free).

The **Lone Star Brewing Company,** 600 Lone Star Blvd. (226-8301), is about 2 mi. south of the city. Trigger-happy Albert Friedrich had managed to accumulate a collection of 3500 animal heads, horns, and antlers when he opened the Buckhorn in 1887. What better place to put them than in his bar? Now you can pity his prey on tours which leave every hour and provide beer samples (open daily 9:30am-5pm; $5, seniors $4, ages 6-12 $1.75).

To get out of the sun head north 40 min. on I-35 to **Natural Bridge Caverns** (651-6101; you can't miss the signs). Discovered only 35 years ago, the caverns are a dizzying delight with phallic formations that will knock your socks off.

Watch killer whale Shamu at **Sea World of Texas** (523-3611). Take U.S. 90 to Rte. 151 west then follow the signs to Sea World. (Open Jun 11-Aug.14 10am-10pm, and 10am-6pm for weekends the rest of the year.)

ENTERTAINMENT AND NIGHTLIFE

During the last 10 days of April, **Fiesta San Antonio** ushers in spring with concerts, parades, and plenty of Tex-Mex to commemorate the victory at San Jacinto and honor the heroes at the Alamo. But San Antone's nocturnal thrills come much more often than just once a year. For fun after dark any time, any season, stroll down the Riverwalk. Peruse the Friday *Express* or the weekly *Current* which will guide you to concerts and entertainment. **Floore's Country Store,** 14464 Old Bandera Rd. (695-8827), toward the northwestern outskirts, is an old hangout of scruffy but lovable country music star Willie Nelson. Dancing takes place outside on a large cement platform. Cover $5-15. Dancing 8pm-midnight on Fri. (Open Mon.-Fri. 11am-8pm, Sat. 3pm-11pm, Sun. 3-11pm, lunch until 2pm. Winter hours same except free dancing on Sun. 6-10pm.) Some of the best Mexicali blues in the city play at **Jim Cullen's Landing,** 123 Losoya (222-1234), in the Hyatt downtown. The music inside starts at 9pm and goes until around 2am. A jazz quartet performs on Sunday nights. The Riverside Saloon outside opens at 11am. For rowdy rock n' roll beat, stroll along **North Mary's Street** about 15 blocks from downtown.

■ NEAR SAN ANTONIO: NEW BRAUNFELS

Like Venice, New Braunfels depends on its waterways to attract its visitors. But don't go looking for gondolas, this is the land of the innertube. Rent one and float along the pea-green waters of the Guadalupe River, but be sure to hitch your beer supply with care. Besides tubing, New Braunfels is home to a bastion of German Texans. As you peruse the cafes and restaurants that pepper the town, a German accent and Texas twang will greet you with a "Wilkommen y'all."

The river runs through it on **Gruene** (GREEN) **Street** off Rte. 46 west where swimming, rafting, and tubing abound. If the Guadalupe don't float your boat seek and ye shall find the **Schlitterbahn,** 305 W. Austin St. (625-2351), the granddaddy of all water parks with 17 water slides, 5 giant hot tubs, and more than 65 acres of moist extravaganza ($18 a day, kids 3-11 $15). The **visitors information center,** 390 Seguin St. (800-572-2626; open Mon.-Fri. 8am-5pm, Sat. 9:30am-4pm, Sun. 10am-2pm), is a helpful friend. **Greyhound,** 235 Trade Center Dr. (629-3181), just off Seguin St., runs buses to Austin (5 buses per day, 1 hr., $9) and San Antonio (5 per day, 45 min., $6). New Braunfels's **ZIP code:** 78730; **area code:** 210.

Lay your sleepy head to rest, and dontcha cry no more at the **Shafer Inn** (625-6266), I-35 at the Lake McQueeny exit. (A/C, TV, HBO, and a pool. Singles Sun.-Thurs. $29, Fri.-Sat. $58.) Find immediate "toobin'" access at the **Rock n' River Campground**, 135 River Terrace (629-4867, for reservations 629-999), off Rte. 46 west 30 has shady sites next to the green Guadalupe. (Office open daily 8am-dusk in summer. During the winter, rent-collectors come by twice daily at 8am and 6pm.)

Krause's Café, 1148 S. Castell (625-7587), at San Antonio St., serves German cuisine and BBQ alike. The sauerbraten entrees ($5.50-7) and big portions will have you weeping for the fatherland (open 6:30am-8:30pm, until 9pm in the summer). If you prefer to douse yourself in beer, the **Watering Hole** at McQueeney and Perryman next to the Shafer Inn, has a bar, dance, and sports joint with four satellites and 42 TVs including one 12 ft. tall. Ask Bob, the tattooed owner, about Willie Nelson's 50th birthday party which he attended. Or sit at the Attorney's Table, which contains real bullshit visible under glass.

■■■ PADRE ISLAND AND CORPUS CHRISTI

■ PADRE ISLAND NATIONAL SEASHORE

Bounded on the north by North Padre Island's string of condos and tourists and on the south by the Mansfield ship channel, which separates the national seashore from **South Padre Island** (a haven for hundreds of thousands of rowdy spring breakers every year), the **Padre Island National Seashore (PINS)** is a flawless gem, with over 60 mi. of perfectly preserved beaches, dunes, and a wildlife refuge. The seashore is an excellent place for windsurfing, swimming, or even surf-fishing—an 850-lb. shark was once caught at the southern, more deserted end of the island.

Practical Information Motorists enter the PINS via the JFK Causeway, which runs through the Flour Bluff area of Corpus Christi. PINS is difficult to reach by public transportation. Corpus Christi bus #29 (2 trips per day, 8:45am and 1:45pm Mon.-Fri., 50¢) takes you to the tip of the Padre Isles (get off at Padre Isles Park-n-Ride near the H-E-B supermarket). This bus also stops at the visitors center. To reach the national seashore, call the **Yellow Checker Cab Co.** (884-3211; base fare $1.35, $1.25 each additional mi.). Round-trip distance from the bus stop to the visitors center is over 26 mi. The PINS **ZIP code:** 78418; **area code:** 512.

Entry into PINS costs $4. For just a daytrip to the beach, venture toward the beautiful and uncrowded **North Beach** (24 mi. from Corpus Christi), which lies just before the $4 checkpoint. The **PINS Visitors Center,** 9405 S. Padre Island Dr. (937-2621; open Mon.-Fri. 8am-4:30pm), provides info on sight-seeing opportunities in nearby **Mustang State Park** and **Port Arkansas.** Within the national seashore, the **Malaquite Visitors Center** (949-8068), about 14 mi. south of the JFK Causeway turn-off, supplies similar info plus exhibits and wildlife guidebooks (open daily 9am-6pm; Sept.-May daily 9am-4pm).

Camping and Activities Nothing beats camping on the beach at PINS, where crashing waves will lull you to sleep. Bring insect repellant, or you will awake to the slurping noise of thousands of mosquitoes sucking you dry. The **PINS Campground** (949-8173) consists of an asphalt area for RVs, restrooms, and cold-rinse showers—no soap permitted on PINS. Five miles of beach is devoted to primitive camping (RV and tent sites $5). Free camping is permitted wherever vehicle driving is allowed. Near the national seashore is the **Balli County Park** (949-8121), on Park Rd. 22, 3½ mi. from the JFK Causeway. Running water, electricity, and hot showers are available. (3-day max. stay. Full hookup $10. Key deposit $5.) Those who value creature comforts should head a few miles farther north to the **Mustang State Park Campground** (749-5246), on Park Rd. 53, 6 mi. from the JFK Causeway, for electricity, running water, dump stations, restrooms, hot showers, shelters, trailer sites, and picnic tables. Make reservations; there's often a waiting list. (Entry fee $2. Sites $9. Overnight camping on the beach $4.)

Hiking and driving are also popular activities at PINS. Those with four-wheel-drive vehicles can make the 60-mi. trek to the **Mansfield Cut,** the most remote and untraveled area of the seashore. Loose sands prevent vehicles without four-wheel drive from venturing far on the beach. Although the seashore has no hiking trails, the **Malaquite Ranger Station** (949-8173), 3½ mi. south of the park entrance, conducts hikes and programs throughout the year (call 949-8060 for info on group programs). They also provide first aid and emergency assistance.

■ CORPUS CHRISTI

After you've taken in all of Corpus Christi's sights—in other words, after half an hour—you may wonder what you're doing in the town named for the "body of Christ." Yet once you hit the beach, you will understand why this area is divine.

Practical Information Emergency is 911. The **Convention and Visitors Bureau,** 1201 N. Shoreline (882-5603), where I-37 meets the water, has piles of pamphlets, bus schedules, and local maps (open Mon.-Fri. 8:30am-5pm). Info is also available at the **Corpus Christi Museum,** 1900 N. Chaparral (883-2862; open Mon.-Sat. 10am-6pm, Sun. 1-6pm). Major airlines serve the **Corpus Christi International Airport,** 1000 International Dr. (289-2675), 15 min. west of downtown, bordered by Rte. 44 (Agnes St.) and Joe Mireur Rd. Taxi to downtown for about $12. **Greyhound,** 702 N. Chaparral (882-2516), at Starr downtown, runs to Dallas (5 per day, 8 hr., $41); Houston (12 per day, 5 hr., $19); Austin (5 per day, 6 hr., $27). (Open daily 6am-2:30am. Lockers $1.) **Regional Transit Authority (The "B")** (289-2600) runs buses on a varying schedule; pick up route maps and schedules at the visitors bureau (see above). Central transfer points are at City Hall and Six Points. (Fare 50¢, seniors, disabled, students, and kids 25¢, 10¢ during off-peak hours. All buses 25¢ on Sat.) **The Corpus Christi Beach Connector** runs along the shoreline and to the aquarium daily 6:40am-6:30pm. (Same fares as buses.) **Help Lines: Bay View Hospital,** 993-9700 for counselling and crisis service. **Battered Women and Rape Victims Shelter,** 881-8888. Both open 24 hrs. Corpus Christi's **post office:** 809 Nueces Bay Blvd. (886-2200; open Mon.-Fri. 7:30am-5:30pm, Sat. 8am-noon); **ZIP code:** 78469; **area code:** 512.

Touristy Corpus Christi (pop. 225,000) follows **Shoreline Drive,** which borders the Gulf coast, 1 mi. east of the downtown business district. Some downtown clubs are on **Water St.** Food can be found farther out on **Staples St.**

Accommodations, Food, and a Club Cheap accommodations are scarce downtown. Much of the scenic and convenient shoreline is gilded with posh hotels and expensive motels. Overshadowed by the plethora of expensive lodgings, the **Sand and Sea Budget Inn,** 1013 N. Shoreline Dr. (882-6518), surfs five blocks from the Greyhound station, across the street from the visitors bureau. Brick-walled rooms with TV and sliding glass doors. On weekends and holidays, make reservations in advance. (Singles $24. Doubles $35, with a view of the bay $45.) For the best motel bargains, drive several miles south on Leopard St. (served by bus #27) or I-37 (served by #27 Express). Sleep at the **Ecomotel,** 6033 Leopard St. (289-1116). Exit I-37 north at Corn Products Rd., turn left and go to the second light (at Leopard St.), and take another left. Generic rooms with cable TV, game room, and pool. (Singles $28. Doubles $36.) Campers should head to **Padre Island National Seashore** or **Mustang State Park** (see Padre Island National Seashore). Also, **Nueces River City Park** (241-1464), north on I-37 (exit 16 at Nueces River), has free tent sites and three-day RV permits, but no restrooms or showers.

The mixed population and seaside locale of Corpus Christi have resulted in a wide range of cuisine. **La Bahía,** 224 Chaparral, serves simple but rib-sticking Mexican breakfasts and lunches. Try *nopalitos* (cactus and egg on a tortilla $1.10) or a taco and two enchiladas with rice, beans, tea, and dessert ($4). (Open Mon.-Fri. 7am-4pm, Sat. 7am-3pm, Sun. 8am-2pm.) Around the corner, the **Water St. Seafood Company,** 309 N. Water St. (882-8683), has moderate to pricey edible marine life, like oyster in a quartet of styles ($5.50; entrees $7-13). (Open Sun.-Thurs. 11am-10pm, Fri.-Sat. 11am-11pm.) **Howard's BBQ,** 120 N. Water St. (882-1200), shells out a meat, an all-you-can-graze salad bar, and a drink for $5. The city shuts down early, but the **Yucatan Beach Club,** 208 N. Water St. (888-6800), easily spotted by its fluorescent blue and pink exterior, has live music nightly.

Sights Corpus Christi's most significant sight is the shoreline, which is bordered for miles by wide sidewalks with graduated steps down to the water. Recently built lighthouses along the shoreline make the night view spectacular. The piers are filled with overpriced seaside restaurants, sail and shrimp boats, and hungry seagulls. Feeding these birds will produce a Hitchcockian swarm; wear a hat and prepare to run for your life. Almost all of the beaches on **North Shoreline Dr.** are open for swimming; just follow the signs, or call the Beach Services (949-7023) for directions.

The **Texas State Aquarium** (881-1200) focuses on marine life in the Gulf of Mexico and the Caribbean Sea. It is located on the **Corpus Christi Beach,** a five-minute walk from downtown. This undersea adventureland is worth the time and money to visit. (Open Mon.-Sat. 9am-6pm, Sun. 10am-6pm; $7, seniors $5, kids $3.75.) Just offshore floats the aircraft carrier **U.S.S. Lexington,** a World War II relic now open to the public. (Open daily 9am-6pm; $7, children $3.75, seniors and active military personnel $5.) To eke out a little culture after a day in the sun, your only option is on the north end of Shoreline Dr., at the **Art Museum of South Texas,** 1902 N. Shoreline (884-3844), whose small but impressive collection includes works by Matisse, Rembrandt, Goya, and Ansel Adams. (Open Tues.-Sat. 10am-5pm, Sun. 1-5pm. Suggested donation $2, kids 12 and under 50¢.) The **Texas Jazz Festival** (883-4500) jams for three days in early July, drawing hundreds of musicians and thousand of fans from around the country (most performances free).

WEST TEXAS

On the far side of the Río Pecos lies a region whose extremely stereotypical Texan character verges on self-parody. This is the stomping ground of Pecos Bill—a mythical cowpoke raised by coyotes whose exploits included lassoing a tornado. The land here was colonized in the days of the Texan Republic, during an era when the "law west of the Pecos" meant a rough mix of vigilante violence and frontier gunslinger machismo. The border city of El Paso, and its Chihuahuan neighbor, Ciudad Juárez, beckon way, *wayyyy* out west—700 mi. from the Louisiana border.

■■■ AMARILLO

Named for the yellow clay of a nearby lake, Amarillo was at the head of the massive cattle stampedes of the western expansion. Cattle is still the name of the game today, but panhandle oil has become an equal partner of commerce and wealth. A stop-over on historic Route 66, Amarillo still retains the feel of a small western town with sights such as the Palo Duro Canyon, and the arid prairie of the panhandle.

Practical Information Amarillo sprawls at the intersection of I-27, I-40, and U.S. 287/87—the only way to explore this expansive city is with a car. The city is basically contained within Rte. 335 (the Loop); Amarillo Blvd. (Historic Rte. 66) runs east-west, parallel to I-40.

Emergency is 911. The **Texas Travel Info Center,** 9400 I-40E (335-1441), at exit 76, is open daily 8am-5pm. Or try **Amarillo Chamber of Commerce,** 1000 S. Polk

TEXAS

(373-7800), and **Amarillo Convention and Visitors Bureau** (374-1497 or 800-692-1338; open Mon.-Fri. 8am-5pm). Swoop down to **Amarillo International Airport,** 10801 Airport Blvd. (335-1671). Cab fare to the hotel strip on I-40 $4-6; to downtown $12-13. Go go go **Greyhound** from 700 S. Tyler (374-5371) to: Oklahoma City ($37), Albuquerque ($50), Dallas ($50), Santa Fe ($51). Get around in Amarillo on **Amarillo City Transit** (378-3094). Buses run daily 6am-6pm; fare is 60¢. Or ride like a king with **Royal Cab Co.** (376-4276; base fare $1.30, $1 per mi). Amarillo's **post office:** 505 E. 9th Ave. (379-2148), in Downtown Station at Buchanan St.; **ZIP code:** 79109; **area code:** 806.

Accommodations, Camping, and Food   Cheap motels can be found along the outskirts of town on I-40. Be prepared to pay more as you near the downtown area. One of the best off I-40 is **Camelot Inn,** 2508 I-40E (373-3600), at exit 72A. ($25 for 1-4 people.) **Motel 6** (374-6444 or 359-7651) has two joints along I-40. (Singles $27. Doubles $33.) The **KOA Kampground,** 111 Folsom St. (335-1792), is 6 mi. east of downtown (sites $16, full hookup $22). Take exit 75 to Rte. 60E. Or the **RV Park,** 1414 Sunrise (335-1742), off exit 74 (sites for $15, $18 full hookup).

Beef is what's for dinner at **The Big Texan** (372-6000 or 800-657-7177) at the Lakeside exit of I-40. Signs from miles around remind you that a 72 oz. steak is free if you can eat it in an hour. To date 17,476 have tried, 3,672 have succeeded. The portions are whopping, but the bill won't whip you. (Try the rattlesnake appetizer for $3. Burgers are $5-10. Texas steaks go for $12-22. The restaurant, gift shop, bar, and game room are open Sun.-Thurs. 10:30am-10:30pm. Free Texas Opry concerts on Tuesday, but you must call and reserve.) Do not offer to gladly pay next Tuesday at **Wimpy's,** 1210 Amarillo Blvd. (372-5041), for cheap burgers ($2) or hot dogs (50¢). (Open daily 10am-8pm.)

Sights   The outstanding **Panhandle-Plains Historical Museums,** 2401 4th Ave. in nearby **Canyon,** has fossils, an old drilling rig, and exhibits galore about the local history and geology. (Open Mon.-Sat. 9am-5pm, Sun. 1-6pm. Free.) The **Amarillo Zoo** (374-6141) is 20 acres of open prairie with bison, roadrunners, and other Texas fauna. Take the Thompson Park exit on U.S. 287. (Open daily 9am-5pm. Free.) The **American Quarter Horse Heritage Center and Museum** (376-5181), at I-40 exit 72a, is a monument to the less-thoroughbred. Sitting on the world's largest supply of helium, Amarillo deserves its **Helium Monument,** 1200 Strait Dr. (355-4547). Get in some ropin', brandin', and ridin' at Figure 3 Ranch's **Cowboy Morning** (658-2613; $19, $14.50 for the cowpokes). Go for a 20-min. wagon ride and have a chuck-wagon dinner followed by an old West show at **Creekwood Ranch** (356-4256 or 800-658-6673; $28, kids $14, under 6 free). Seen by over two million people, the musical drama *Texas* is staged under the stars in an outdoor amphitheater. (Runs Mon.-Sat. at 8:30. Tickets $6-14. Call 655-2181 for reservations.) If you're in town in early August, mosey over to the Civic Center for **Old West Days..**

Palo Duro Canyon State Park   Palo Duro, 50 mi. southeast of Amarillo, is at 16,000-acres the largest state park in Texas. Take I-27 to Texas Rte. 217. The entrance fee is $5, and the **Interpretive Center** (488-2227) is open daily from 9am-5pm and can answer your queries. There is a **scenic drive** of this "Grand Canyon of Texas" through the red, yellow, and browns of the canyon that is truly inspiring and beautiful. Of the two hiking trails, the 3-hr., 5-mi. **Lighthouse Trail** is the better but is *very* strenuous. **Backcountry hiking** is allowed and encouraged. Temperatures in the canyon can frequently climb to 100°F; *always* take water on your hike. **Horseback riding** (48-8-2231) is a popular way of exploring the park. (Open daily 8am-7pm; in the winter 8am-dusk.) There is a **refreshment center** (488-2760) with **bike rentals** ($6.50 per hr.), **hayrides** ($5.50 per hr.), and a **restaurant** (burgers $2.30). **Backcountry camping** is allowed in designated areas; primitive sites are $13.

■■■ GUADALUPE MOUNTAINS NATIONAL PARK

The Guadalupe Mountains rising out of the vast Texas desert carry with them a legacy of unexplored grandeur. Early westbound pioneers avoided the area, fearful of the climate and the Mescalero Apaches who controlled the range. By the 1800s, when the Apaches had been driven out, only a few homesteaders and *guano* miners inhabited this rugged region. The national park covers 86,000 acres of desert, canyons, and highlands. With over 70 mi. of trails, the mountains ensure challenging hikes in a mostly desert environment for those willing to journey to this remote part of the state. The passing tourist who hopes to catch only the most established sights should stop to see **El Capitán,** a 2000-ft. limestone cliff, and **Guadalupe Peak,** at 8749 ft. the highest point in Texas. Less hurried travelers should hike to **McKittrick Canyon,** with its spring-fed stream and amazing variety of vegetation. **The Bowl,** a stunning high-country forest of Douglas fir and ponderosa pine, is quite a hike.

Practical Information There is no gas in the park, so gas up ahead. Guadalupe Park is less than 40 mi. west of Carlsbad Caverns in New Mexico and 115 mi. east of El Paso. **TNM&O Coaches** (808-765-6641), an affiliate of **Greyhound,** runs along U.S. 62/180 between Carlsbad, NM and El Paso, passing Carlsbad Caverns National Park and Guadalupe National Park en route. This line makes flag stops at the park in each direction ($25, $47.50 round-trip). Guadalupe Mountains National Park is in the **Mountain time zone** (2 hr. behind Eastern). For further info, write: Guadalupe Mountains National Park, HC60, P.O. Box 400, Salt Flat, TX 79847-9400 (828-3251). Guadalupe's **area code:** 915.

Hiking and Camping Most major trails begin at the **Headquarters Visitors Center** (828-3215), right off U.S. 62/180 where the bus drops you. Guadalupe Peak is an easy 3 to 5-hr. hike, depending on your mountaineering ability, while the McKittrick Canyon and the Bowl can be hiked in a full day. (Open daily 7am-6pm; Sept.-May 8am-4:30pm. After-hours info is posted on the bulletin board outside.) The trail leading to the historic Pratt Cabin in the Canyon begins at the **McKittrick Visitors Center,** off U.S. 62/180.

The **Pine Springs Campgrounds** (828-3251), just past the headquarters directly on the highway, has water and restrooms but no hookups (sites $6). **Dog Canyon Campground** (505-981-2418), just south of the New Mexico state line at the north end of the park, can be reached only by a 110-mi. drive from Carlsbad, NM, on Rte. 137. Dog Canyon also lacks hookups but provides water and restrooms (sites $6). Free backcountry hiking is permitted. The 2½-mi., 1½-hr. **Spring Trail** is a cheap, quick hike to a mountain spring. The trail starts at the **Frijole Ranch,** about 1 mi. north of the visitors center. You should use **Carlsbad, NM** as a base. The town, 55 mi. northeast of the park, has several cheap motels, campgrounds, and restaurants.

Food and Gas Guadalupe National Park's lack of development may be a bonus for backpackers, but it makes daily existence tough. Bring water for even the shortest, most casual hike. *Hundreds of people run out of gas every season, so gas up before you enter the park.* There are no places to eat in or around the park. The only place to eat is **Texas Border Outpost** (828-3227) right at the border of TX/NM, 19 mi. from Carlsbad. Meals run $1-5. (Open Tues.-Sat. 7am-9pm, Sun. 8am-8pm.)

■■■ EL PASO

The largest of the U.S. border towns (pop. 60,000), El Paso grew up in the 17th century as a stop-over on the only navigable wagon route through the Rocky Mountains. Hispanic culture undoubtedly defines the regional flavor of El Paso—El Paso, along with the bordering Mexican city of Juárez, forms a bi-national metropolis unlike any of Texas's other urban centers; Spanish is spoken here as often as

English. Besides its cultural connection with Juárez, El Paso also provides its visitors with a collegiate atmosphere thanks to the University of Texas-El Paso.

PRACTICAL INFORMATION

Emergency: 911. **Juárez Police,** 248-35.

Visitor Information: El Paso Tourist Information Center, 1 Civic Center Plaza (544-0062), next to the Chamber of Commerce at the intersection of Santa Fe St. and San Francisco St. Easily identifiable by the thin, water-filled moat that surrounds it. Well-stocked with brochures; sells **El Paso-Juárez Trolley Co.** tickets for day-long tours across the border ($8 Mon.-Fri., $10 Sat.-Sun). Trolleys run daily 10am-5pm; April-Oct. 9am-4pm; Nov.-March 8am-5pm.

Amtrak, 700 San Francisco St. (545-2247). Walk west away from the border along San Antonio St. to 2001 N. Oregon St. Open daily 9am-5pm except Tues.

Greyhound: 200 San Antonio (542-1355), across from the Civic Center between Santa Fe St. and Chihuaha St. Daily service to and from Dallas, Phoenix, New York, Los Angeles, and other U.S. cities. Lockers $1. Open 24 hrs.

El Paso-Los Angeles Limousine Service, 72 S. Oregon (532-4061). Offers cheaper service to Albuquerque and Tucson en route to Los Angeles. To: Albuquerque ($20), Tucson ($35), Los Angeles ($35).

Public Transport: Sun City Area Transit (SCAT), (533-3333). All routes begin downtown at San Jacinto Plaza (Main at Mesa). Fewer routes in the northwest. Connects with Juárez system. Maps and schedules posted in the Civic Center Park and at public libraries. Most buses stop around 5pm; limited service on Sun. Fare 75¢, seniors 15¢, students with ID 35¢.

Taxi: Yellow Cab, 533-3433. Base fare $1.20, $1.50 per mi.

Car Rental: Dollar-Rent-A-Car, (778-5445). $32 per day, $130 per week with unlimited free mileage. Cars are permitted 10 mi. into Mexico (Juárez); $11 extra charge. Open 24 hrs. They will deliver. Major credit card required; $5 per day extra if you're under 25.

Currency Exchange: Valuta, Mesa and corner of Paisano (544-1152, fax 532-8362). Conveniently near the border. Open 24 hrs. **Traveler's Checks: Bank of the West,** 330 N. Mesa St. (532-1000), on the corner of Main St. and Mesa St. Open Mon.-Thurs. 9am-4pm, Fri. 9am-5pm.

Help Lines: Crisis Hotline, 779-1800. Open 24 hrs. **Lambda** (562-4217) is a Gay/Lesbian Line, with 24 hr. info and counseling Mon., Wed., Fri. 7-9pm.

Post Office: 219 Mills (775-7563). Open Mon.-Fri. 8:30am-5pm, Sat. 8:30am-2pm. **ZIP code:** 79910.

Area Codes: El Paso: 915. To direct dial Ciudad Juárez, dial 011-52-16, followed by the local number.

The geographical intrusion of the **Río Grande River** and the **Franklin Mountains** makes El Paso one of the more confusing cities you'll come across in Texas. Most places have exits off I-40, so call for directions. Follow **Paisano St.** through downtown to drive to Juárez, or park on **Santa Fe,** which runs parallel, and walk. Get yourself a map and get oriented quickly.

ACCOMMODATIONS, CAMPING, AND FOOD

The cheapest hotel rooms land across the border, but downtown El Paso has more appealing offerings. The **Gardner Hotel/Hostel (HI-AYH),** 311 E. Franklin (532-3661), is 2 blocks up Mesa St. from San Jacinto Park, in the heart of downtown. From the airport, take bus #33 to San Jacinto Park, walk 1 block north to Franklin, turn right, and head east 1½ blocks. A friendly group staffs this 75-year-old establishment, which features quiet, clean rooms. Weary travelers obtain money-saving advice and maps for both El Paso and Juárez. (Reception open 24 hrs. Locker rental. Washing machines and dryers available. **Hotel:** TV. Check-out 1pm. (Singles $27.50. Doubles $32.50, with bath $40. **Hostel:** Spotless kitchen, common room, and an array of couches for easy living and casual socializing. Check-out 10am. Bed in 4-person dorm room with sink $12, nonmembers $15.) **Gateway Hotel,** 104 S. Stanton St. (532-2611), at the corner of S. Stanton St. and San Antonio, is a favorite stop for Mexicans; speak Spanish to get respect and a room. Clean rooms with bathrooms. (A/C upstairs. Singles $21 and up. Doubles $27.22 and up. Check-out 4pm. Parking $1.50 per 24 hrs.) A diner downstairs will satiate your budget travel-hunger.

El Paso is a hybrid species with North American and Mexican ancestors. Well-known gringo chains coexist with small mom-and-pop restaurants. **Big Bun,** 500 N. Stanton (533-3926), serves tacos, burritos, and hefty burgers (99 ¢) with salsa on the side. Unlimited refills at the soda machines. (Open Mon.-Sat. 8am-8pm, Sun. 10am-3pm.) **La Chica Maria** (543-6700), on Franklin and Mesa, hypnotizes customers with the ubiquitous sounds of steak sizzling. (Enchiladas $5. Free delivery. Open Mon.-Fri. 7am-4:30pm, Sat. 7:30am-2pm.)

There are a few small RV campgrounds near downtown, but the nicest outdoor lodgings lie miles outside El Paso and are not very accessible by public transportation. The **Hueco Tanks State Park** (857-1135), a 32-mi. hike east of El Paso on U.S. 62/180, is a great place for hiking and rockclimbing but offers meager service. (Sites $8, with electricity $11. Showers and restrooms.)

SIGHTS AND ENTERTAINMENT

The majority of visitors to El Paso are either stopping off on the long drive through the desert or headed across the border for a taste of Mexico. Two pedestrian and motor roads cross the Río Grande: **El Paso,** an overcrowded one-way street, and **Santa Fe,** a parallel road lined with Western wear stores, clothing shops, and decent restaurants. Entry to Mexico is 25¢, and the trip back into the U.S. costs 45¢. Check out the **Border Jumper Trolleys** (544-0062), which depart every hour from 9am-4pm Mon.-Fri. ($10, kids 6-12 $8, under 6 free). Daytrippers, including foreign travelers with a multi-entry visa, need only flash their documents of citizenship in order to pass in and out. A walk across the border is worth your while but try to make it to downtown Juárez and avoid the border area tourist businesses.

Volatile downtown El Paso has more to offer than just a cross-border trip. Historic **San Jacinto Plaza** swarms daily with men and women, young and old. Catch the true flavor of local culture and listen to street musicians perform here where Spanish *conquistadores*, Fort Bliss cavalry men, and *señoritas* once rested. South of the square, **El Paso Street** is another place you don't want to miss. Hundreds of locals hurry along the street and dash into stores trying to grab the best bargain. You can buy a pair of Wranglers for as little as $10. To take in a complete picture of the Río Grande Valley, head northeast of downtown on Rim Rd. (which becomes Scenic Dr.) to **Murchison Park,** at the base of the mountains; the park offers a fine view of El Paso, Juárez, and the Sierra Madre.

For nightlife, try the **Cadillac Bar,** 1170 Sunmount (779-5881; open daily 6pm-2am). The gay hotspot is downtown at **The Old Plantation,** 219 S. Ochoa (533-6055), a dance club/bar (open Thurs.-Sun. 8pm-2am). For a wild time there is, of course, Juárez, with rowdiness, no minimum drinking age, and ubiquitous nightlife.

Strategic timing can make your visit to El Paso more entertaining. The town hosts the **Southwestern Livestock Show & Rodeo** (532-1401) in February, the **World Championship Finals Rodeo** (544-2582) in November, and a **Jazz Festival** (534-6277) in October at the Chamizal Memorial. All three festivals are well worth a visit.

■ NEAR EL PASO: CIUDAD JUÁREZ

Like its sister city north of the border, Juárez has blossomed in the valley carved out of the Rocky Mountains by the Río Grande. Some parts of the city cater to the merry bands of carousing *gringos* that venture down south for wild nights of drinking. Other sections of Juárez (near the Parques Industriales, for instance) are densely packed with the production centers of large North American firms that have relocated to Mexico to take advantage of relatively low labor costs.

Coordinación de Turismo, (tel. 15-23-01) Malecón and Francisco Villa, in the gray Unidad Administrativa Municipal building to the right of the Santa Fe bridge, has plenty of brochures but few that are truly helpful unless you know Spanish. (Open

Mon.-Fri. 8am-8pm, Sat.-Sun. 7am-3pm.) **Emergency** is 06. In Juárez, banks congregate near the bus station, Juárez St., and 16 de Septiembre. (Most are open Mon.-Fri. 9am-1:30pm.) One of the biggest is **Comisiones San Luis,** on the corner of 16 de Septiembre and Juárez (tel. 14-20-33; open Mon.-Sat. 9am-9pm, Sun. 9am-6pm). One of the few places where travelers checks are accepted is **Chequerama,** at Union and Juárez. (Open daily 10am-5:30pm.)

In Juárez, a typical cheap hotel meets only minimal standards and charges some of the highest "budget" rates in Mexico. **Hotel del Río,** 488 Juárez (tel. 12-37-76), is well worth the climb upstairs. Large rooms, thick beds, A/C, and color TVs await. Check-out is at noon. (Singles or doubles 65 pesos. Triples 85 pesos. AmEx, MC.) **Santa Fe,** Lerdo Nte. 673 (tel. 14-02-70, fax 12-56-27) at Tlaxcala, has A/C, well-kept rooms, and large TVs. (Singles US$37.50. Doubles US$43. MC, Visa, AmEx.)

The hungry and prudent will mosey to Av. Juárez and Lerdo. **Garlic and Chili's,** 519 Av. Juárez Nte. (tel. 12-27-21) next to the Plaza de Mariachis. Try the *filet mignon* (25 pesos). (Open Sat.-Thurs. 8am-midnight, Fri.-Sat. 8am-2am.) **Hotel Santa Fe Restaurant** (tel. 14-02-70), has *enchiladas de pollo* for 10 pesos.

The **Aduana Frontensa** (tel. 12-47-07), built in 1889 as a trading outpost, hosts an exhibit on the region's history during the Mexican Revolution (open Tues.-Sun. 10am-6pm; free). The ProNaf center contains the **Museo de Arte** (tel. 16-74-14), which exhibits past and present Mexican art. (Open Tues.-Sun. 11am-7pm; .75 pesos, students free.) Also at the ProNaf center, the **Centro Artesanal** sells handmade goods at maximum prices; haggle here. The "Ruta 8" bus will take you from *el centro* to ProNaf for .70 pesos; a taxi charges 25 times as much.

The *toro* and the *matador* battle in traditional bullfights on occasional evenings during the summer at the **Plaza Monumental de Toros,** República and Huerta (tel. 13-16-56). Seats range in price from 40 to 130 pesos. Call for dates and times. The **Lienzo de Charro,** on Av. Charro off República, also conducts bullfights and a *charreada* (rodeo) on summer Sunday afternoons. Juárez has so many bars that simply counting them can make you dizzy even before you carouse. Many establishments are unsavory, and some downright dangerous. Stick to the glutted strip along Av. Juárez. On weekends, North Americans swarm to Juárez to join their Mexican friends in a 48-hr. quest for fun, fights, and fiestas. **Kentucky Club,** Juárez 629 (tel. 14-99-90), was voted Best Bar 1991 by an El Paso paper (open 11am-midnight). **Mr. Fog Bar,** Juárez Nte. 140 (tel. 14-29-48), is also popular. The walls are decked with pictures of dogs playing pool and sipping beer—possibly a subtle social commentary. (Beer 5 pesos, margaritas 7 pesos. Open daily 11am-2am.)

For more information on Ciudad Juárez, see *Let's Go: Mexico.*

■■■ BIG BEND NATIONAL PARK

Roadrunners, coyotes, wild pigs, mountain lions, and 350 species of birds make their home in Big Bend National Park, a 700,000-acre tract that lies within the curve of the Río Grande. The spectacular canyons of this river, the vast **Chihuahuan Desert,** and the **Chisos Mountains** have all witnessed the 100 million years which molded the park's natural attractions. This place is literally and figuratively far-out.

Practical Information   For **Emergency,** call 477-2251 until 6pm; afterwards call 911. The **park headquarters** (915-477-2251) is at **Panther Junction,** about 20 mi. inside the park. (Open daily 8am-6pm. Vehicle pass $5 per week.) For info, write Superintendent, Big Bend National Park 79834. The **Texas National Park Services** (800-452-9292) provides info on the park and will help you plan your excursion (open winter only). Other **ranger stations** are at Río Grande Village, Persimmon Gap, and Chisos Basin (all open daily 8am-4pm).

Big Bend may be the most isolated spot you'll ever encounter. The park is *only accessible by car* via Rte. 118 or U.S. 385. There are few gas stations along the way;

be sure to gas up before you leave urban areas. **Amtrak** (800-872-7245) serves the town of Alpine, 70 mi. north of Big Bend.

Accommodations and Food The only motel-style lodging within the park is the expensive **Chisos Mountain Lodge** (915-477-2291) is 10 mi. from the headquarters (singles $57, doubles $62, $10 per additional person); lodge units are equipped with shower and baths but no A/C (singles $56, doubles $64, $10 per additional person); and stone cottages come with three double beds ($66, $10 per additional person). Reservations are a must, since the lodge is often booked up a year in advance. The lodge also runs a restaurant and coffee shop, where entrees run $5-12 (open daily 7am-9pm). Cheaper motels line Rte. 118 and Rte. 170 near Terlingua and Lajitas, 21 and 28 mi. respectively from park headquarters. **Groceries** and **gas** are available in Panther Junction, Río Grande Village, and the Chisos Basin at Castolon. The park's only public **shower** (75¢ per 5 min.) is at the Río Grande Village Store.

Hiking and Camping If your stay is brief, take the 43-mi. **scenic drive** to Santa Elena Canyon, and once there swim in the secluded river. Watch for flash floods. For overnight backcountry camping, you must get a free **wilderness permit** at the park headquarters. The park rangers will suggest hikes and places to visit. The **Lost Mine Peaks Trail,** a 3-hr. hike up a peak in the Chisos, leads to an amazing summit view of the desert and the Sierra de Carmen in Mexico. Another easy walk leads up the **Santa Elena Canyon** along the Río Grande. The canyon walls rise up as much as 1000 ft. over the banks of the river. Three companies offer **river trips** down the 133-mi. stretch of the Río Grande owned by the park. Info on rafting and canoeing is available at the park headquarters (see above).

Designated **campsites** within the park are allotted on a first-come, first-served basis. **Chisos Basin** and **Río Grande Village** have sites with running water ($5), while **Cottonwood** has toilets but no water ($3). Free sites along the hiking trails are available with a required permit from any ranger station. Make sure you have plenty of water. The best (and coolest) campsites by far are those in Chisos Basin. Get here early, as the basin sites fill up fast, especially those near the perimeter.

Named for the three languages spoken in the town in the late 1800s (English, Spanish, and an Indian dialect), **Terlingua, TX** is a good base from which to explore Big Bend. Accessible from Road 170 in Study Butte, Terlingua is about 35 mi. from Panther Junction park headquarters but only 7 mi. from the western entrance of the park. The **Easter Egg Valley Motel** (915-371-2430) is a good alternative to park sites (singles $30, doubles $34). Farther up Road 170, the **Starlight Theatre Bar and Grill** (915-371-2326) has cheap food ($3-8) with large portions and free live music. (Open Mon.-Thurs. 5pm-midnight, Fri.-Sun. 5pm-2am.) Next door you can book a Río Grande rafting trip at **Far-Flung Adventures** (800-359-4138). Call for prices.

TEXAS

THE SOUTHWEST

Amidst the vast stretches of austere desert and sculpted sandstone of the Southwest, the myths of the pioneer, the courageous lawman, and the desperate gunman were born. But Americans have played only a small part in the history of the old Southwest. The Anasazi of the 10th and 11th centuries were the first to discover that the arid lands of the Southwest—with proper management—could support an advanced agrarian civilization. The Navajo, Apache, and Pueblo nations later migrated into the region, sharing the land with the Hopi, descendents of the Anasazi. The Native Americans have since been largely displaced, confined to barren reservations, but their influence on this area is everywhere. Spanish conquest came early in the 17th century, bringing European colonists to modern-day Texas and New Mexico. Mexican independence in 1821 was followed by American agitation. The Texan War of Independence in 1836 began as a revolt by U.S. settlers against Santa Anna's dictatorship, and culminated in the Mexican-American War. Santa Fe, Nuevo Mexico, became the first foreign capital ever to fall to the U.S. In 1853, Mexico's defeated government agreed to sell a tract of land south of the Gila River—vital to completion of the Southern Pacific Railway—that today forms a large part of Arizona and New Mexico.

History has seen great conflict, but before the people there was the land. The austere, lonely beauty of the desert stretches for hundreds of miles, and the water- and wind-scored landscape stands in silent testimony to millennia of incessant battles waged by erosion. The steel blue of the Superstition mountains, the amazing rainbows bouncing off the Painted Desert, the cliffs of the Guadalupe Mountains, the gorges of the Grand Canyon, the murky depths of Carlsbad Caverns, and the redstone arches and twisted spires of southern Utah and northern Arizona all await exploration and meditation.

 # New Mexico

From the dunes of White Sands to the underground labyrinth of Carlsbad Caverns, New Mexico is actually one of the most diverse geographic areas; it sits at the meeting place of the Great Plains, the southern Rockies, and the Range and Basin Province of the four corners area. With Native Americans, Mexicans, and transplanted Easterners, New Mexico features a unique cultural fabric. Old ranchers, several generations of soul searchers, and young professionals jetting into Santa Fe and Taos demand a wide range of taste and scenery that only New Mexico can provide.

New Mexico serves as a haven for hikers, backpackers, and mountain-climbers alike. Six national forests lying within the state provide miles and miles of beautiful and challenging opportunities for the outdoorsman at heart, while Sandía, Mogollon, and Sangre de Cristo are all great locales for mountain-climbers.

PRACTICAL INFORMATION

Capital: Santa Fe.
New Mexico Dept. of Tourism, 491 Old Santa Fe Trail, Santa Fe 87501 (800-545-2040). Open Mon.-Fri. 8am-5pm. **Park and Recreation Division,** Villagra Bldg., P.O. Box 1147, Santa Fe 87504 (827-7465). **U.S. Forest Service,** 517 Gold Ave. SW, Albuquerque 87102 (842-3292).
Time Zone: Mountain (2 hr. behind Eastern). **Postal Abbreviation:** NM
Sales Tax: 5.7%.

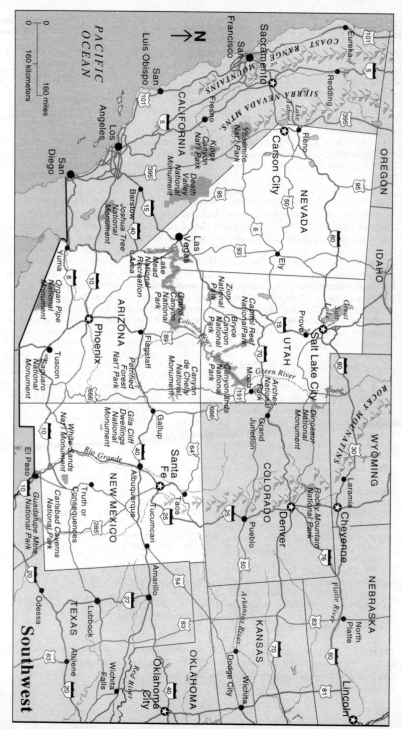

NORTHERN NEW MEXICO

Northern New Mexico is a picturesque canvas of fertile forests and arid canyons, dazzling desert and the Sangre de Cristos Mountains. This is the land that turns painters into artists; Georgia O'Keeffe and many celebrated Taos artists earned fame painting the adobe and desert sun of Northern New Mexico.

■■■ SANTA FE

Coming to New Mexico's capital and visiting its museums and historic town plaza will tell you much less about the town than will a casual *paseo* down Camon Rd., the local artists's turf. Santa Fe's variety extends beyond its population of Pueblo, Mexican, Spanish, and American peoples. The legendary spirit of tolerance and the laws requiring all downtown buildings be in 17th-century adobe-style (and painted in one of 23 approved shades of brown), has attracted scores of artists to work and live amongst the city's earth-toned beauty and mountainous backdrop. New-Age spiritual voyagers coexist with temperamental artists, Native Americans, retirees enjoying the calm of the area, jewelry hawkers, and hordes of tourists.

PRACTICAL INFORMATION

Emergency: 911.

Visitor Information: The Santa Fe Convention and Visitors Bureau, 201 W. Mary St. (800-777-2489), where you can pick up the useful *Santa Fe Visitors Guide.* Open Mon. 8am-5pm. Also there is an **Information Booth** at Lincoln and Palace. (Summer only, open Mon.-Sat. 9am-4:30pm.) Visitors from abroad should gallop down to the **Santa Fe Council on International Relations,** 100 E. San Francisco St., room 281, at the La Fonda Hotel. Open Mon.-Fri. 9am-noon.

Gray Line Tours: 983-6565. Free pickup from downtown hotels. Tours Mon.-Sat. to: Taos and Taos Pueblo (9am, $50); Bandelier and Los Alamos (1pm, $35); around Santa Fe (Mon.-Sat. 9:30am, 3 hr., $15); Puye and Santa Clara (1pm, $45). Walking tours daily at 9:30am and 1:30pm (2½ hr., $10). Also operates the Roadrunner, a sight-seeing trolley around Old Santa Fe leaving from the La Fonda Hotel on the plaza downtown (5 per day, 1½ hr., $8, under 12 $4).

Greyhound: 858 St. Michael's Dr. (471-0008 or 800-321-2222). To: Denver (via Raton, NM; 4 per day; $66); Taos (2 per day, 1½ hr., $15); Albuquerque (4 per day, 1½ hr., $10.50). Open Mon.-Fri. 6am-6pm and 7:30-9pm; station closed on Sat.-Sun so you have to pay the driver.

Amtrak: Nearest station (446-4511 or 800-872-7245) in **Lamy,** 20 mi. away, on Country Rd. 41. Van shuttle to Santa Fe is $14. Open daily noon-5pm.

Shuttle Service: Shuttlejack, 982-4311. Runs from the Albuquerque ($22) and Santa Fe airports; also goes to the opera ($6 round-trip).

Public Transport: Santa Fe Trails (984-6730) has 6 bus routes throughout the city from Mon.-Sat. 6:30am-7:30pm.

Car Rental: Budget Rent-a-Car, 1946 Cerrillos Rd. (984-8028). $28 per day, $129 per week. Must be 25 with major credit card. Open Mon.-Fri. 8am-6pm, Sat.-Sun. 8am-5pm.

Taxi: Capital City Taxi, 438-0000. $1.85 first mi., $1 per additional mi.

New Age Referral Service: 474-0066. Info clearinghouse for holistic healing services and alternative modes of thought.

Post Office: (988-6351), in the Montoya Office Bldg., S. Federal Pl., next to the Courthouse. Open Mon.-Fri. 7:30am-6:30pm, Sat. 9am-noon. **ZIP code:** 87501. **Area Code:** 505.

Except for the museums southeast of the city center, most restaurants and important sights in Santa Fe cluster within a few blocks of the downtown plaza and inside the loop formed by the **Paseo de Peralta.** Because the narrow streets make driving troublesome, park your car and pad the pavement. You'll find adobe parking lots behind Santa Fe Village, near Sena Plaza, and one block east of the Federal Court-house near the plaza. Pick up a *Downtown Parking Guide* at the visitors center.

ACCOMMODATIONS AND CAMPING

For the low down on budget accommodations call the **Santa Fe Detours Accommodations Hotline** (986-0038). Besides hostel accommodations, hotels in Santa Fe tend to be very expensive. Hotels become swamped with requests as early as May for **Fiesta de Santa Fe** week in early September and **Indian Market** the third week of August; make reservations early or plan on sleeping in the street. At other times, look around the **Cerrillos Road** area for the best prices, but *use caution* and evaluate the motel before checking in. At many of the less expensive adobe motels, bargaining is acceptable. The beautiful adobe **Santa Fe Hostel (HI-AYH)**, 1412 Cerrillos Rd. (988-1153), 1 mi. from the adobe bus station, and 2 mi. from the adobe plaza, has a kitchen, library, and very large dorm-style adobe beds. (Office open daily 7am-11pm, reservations accepted with first night deposit. No curfew. Chores. $12, nonmembers $15; linen $2; B&B rooms $25-30.)

To camp around Santa Fe, you'll need a car. The **Santa Fe National Forest** (988-6940) has numerous campsites as well as free backcountry camping in the beautiful Sangre de Cristo Mountains. **New Mexico Parks and Recreation** operates the **Black Canyon Campground** (sites $5), 8 mi. away, on Rte. 475 northeast of Santa Fe. You can also find free camping on Rte. 475, 12 mi. out at **Big Tesuque,** and 15 mi. out at **Aspen Basin** (no reservations). (All three campgrounds open May-Oct.; call the forest service at 988-6940 for info.) Or try **KOA Santa Fe** (982-1419), exit 290 on I-25N and follow signs. (Open March 1-Nov. 1. Sites $15, RV hookup $15.50-20.)

FOOD

Spicy Mexican food served on blue corn tortillas is the staple. The few vegetarian restaurants here are expensive, catering to an upscale crowd. The better restaurants near the plaza dish up their chilis to a mixture of government employees, well-heeled tourists, and local artistic types. Because many serve only breakfast and lunch, you should also look for inexpensive meals along **Cerrillos Road** and **St. Michael's Drive** south of downtown. One little-known fact: the **Woolworth's** on the plaza actually serves a mean bowl of chili ($2.75).

Tomasita's Santa Fe Station, 500 S. Guadalupe (983-5721), near downtown. Locals and tourists line up for their blue corn tortillas and fiery green chili dishes ($4.50-5). Indoor and outdoor seating. Open Mon.-Sat. 11am-10pm.

Josie's, 225 E. Marcy St. (983-5311), in a converted house. Pronounce the "J" in the name like an "H." Family-run for 26 years. Incredible Mexican-style lunches and multifarious mouth-watering desserts worth the 20-min. wait. Specials $4-6. Open Mon.-Fri. 11am-4pm.

The Burrito Company, 111 Washington Ave. (982-4453). Excellent Mexican food at reasonable prices. Burrito plates $2-4.25. Open Mon.-Sat. 7:30am-7pm, Sun. 11am-5pm.

Tortilla Flats, 3139 Cerrillos Rd. (471-8685). Frighteningly bland family atmosphere belies Mexican masterpieces ($4-8). Breakfasts ($3-7), *huevos rancheros* ($4.75). Open daily 7am-10pm; winter Sun.-Thurs. 7am-9pm, Fri.-Sat. 7am-10pm.

San Francisco Street Bar & Grill, 114 W. San Francisco St. (982-2044), 1 block from the plaza. Excellent sandwiches and the best pasta salad ($6) in town. Open daily 11am-11pm.

SIGHTS

Since 1609, **Plaza de Santa Fe** has held religious ceremonies, military gatherings, markets, cockfights, and public punishments. The city also provided a pit-stop on two important trails: the **Santa Fe Trail** from Independence, MO and **El Camino Real** ("Royal Road") from Mexico City. The plaza is a good starting point for exploring the city's museums, sanctuaries, and galleries.

Since the following four museums are commonly operated by **The Museum of New Mexico,** their hours are identical and a 3-day pass bought at one admits you to all. (Open daily 10am-5pm; Jan.-Feb. Tues.-Sun. 10am-5pm. 3-day pass $5, seniors and kids under 17 free on Wed.) For 24-hr. museum info call 827-6465. The **Palace of the Governors,** 100 Palace Ave. (827-6483), the oldest public building in the U.S., on the north side of the plaza, was the seat of seven successive governments after its construction in 1610. The *haciendas* palace is now a museum with exhibits on Native American, Southwestern, and New Mexican history. To buy Native American crafts or jewelry, check out the displays spread out in front of the Governor's Palace each day by artists from the surrounding pueblos; their wares are often cheaper and better quality than those in the "Indian Crafts" stores around town. Across Lincoln St., on the northwest corner of the plaza, lies the **Museum of Fine Arts** (827-4455), a large, adobe building with thick, cool walls. Exhibits include works by major Southwestern artists, including Georgia O'Keeffe and Edward Weston, and an amazing collection of 20th-century Native American art. Two other museums lie southeast of town on **Camino Lejo,** just off Old Santa Fe Trail. The **Museum of International Folk Art,** 706 Camino Lejo (827-6350), 2 mi. south of the plaza, houses the Girard Collection of over 100,000 works of folk art from around the world. Amazingly vibrant but unbelievably jumbled, the collection is incomprehensible without the gallery guide handout. Next door, the **Museum of American Indian Arts and Culture,** 710 Camino Lejo (827-6344), has photographs and artifacts that unveil a multifaceted Native American tradition. Also downtown, the **Institute of American Indian Arts Museum,** 108 Cathedral Place (988-6281), houses an extensive collection of contemporary Indian art. (Open Mon.-Tues. and Thurs.-Sat. 9am-6pm, Wed. 9am-8pm, Sun. noon-5pm; Oct. 1-April 30 Mon.-Fri. 10am-5pm, Sat.-Sun. noon-5pm. Closed Mon. in Jan. and Feb.)

Across Palace Ave. from Sena Plaza at the eastern end of San Francisco St. is the gorgeous **San Francisco Cathedral** (982-5619). About 5 blocks southeast of the Plaza lies the **San Miguel Mission** (983-3974) on the corner of DeVargas and the Old Santa Fe Trail. Built in 1710, the adobe mission is the oldest functioning church in the U.S. Inside, glass windows at the altar look down upon the original "altar" built by Native Americans. (Open Mon.-Sat. 9am-4:30pm, Sun. 1-4:30pm; Nov.-April Mon.-Sat. 10am-4pm, Sun. 1-4:30pm. Free.) Just down DeVargas St. is the adobe **Oldest House** in the U.S. (983-8206), dating from about 1200 AD. Built by the Pueblos, the house contains the remains of a certain Spaniard named Hidalgo, who allegedly bought some love potion from a woman who resided here. Apparently he started kissing everything in sight and was beheaded several days later. (Open Mon.-Sat. Love Potion Number 9am-5pm. $1.)

ENTERTAINMENT AND EVENTS

With numerous musical and theatrical productions, arts and crafts shows, and Native American ceremonies, Santa Fe offers rich entertainment year-round. Fairs, rodeos, and tennis tournaments complement the active theater scene and the world-famous musicians who often play in Santa Fe's clubs. The **El Farol,** 808 Canyon Rd. (983-9912), features excellent up-and-coming rock and R&B musicians (shows nightly 9:30pm; cover $5) Check out the *Santa Fe Reporter*, or *Pasatiempo* magazine, a supplement to the Friday issue of the *Santa Fe New Mexican*.

Don Diego De Vargas's peaceful reconquest of New Mexico in 1692 marked the end of the 12-year Pueblo Rebellion, now celebrated in the traditional three-day **Fiesta de Santa Fe** (988-7575). Held in early September, the celebration reaches its height with the burning of the 40-ft. *papier-mâché* **Zozobra** (Old Man Gloom). Festivities include street dancing, processions, and political satires. Most events are free. The *New Mexican* publishes a guide and schedule for the fiesta's events.

The **Santa Fe Chamber Music Festival** (983-2075) celebrates the works of great baroque, classical, and 20th-century composers. Tickets are not readily available. (Performances July to mid-Aug. Sun.-Mon. and Thurs.-Fri. in the St. Francis Auditorium of the Museum of Fine Arts. Tickets $20-32.) The **Santa Fe Opera,** P.O. Box

2408, Santa Fe 87504-2408 (982-3855), 7 mi. north of Santa Fe on Rte. 84, performs in the open, so bring a blanket. The downtown box office is in the gift and news shop of the El Dorado Hotel, 309 W. San Francisco St. (986-5900). Standing-room only tickets can be purchased for $6. (Performances July-Aug. at 9pm.) **Shuttlejack** (982-4311; see Practical Information) runs a bus from downtown Santa Fe to the opera before each performance.

In August, the nation's largest and most impressive **Indian Market** floods the plaza. Native American tribes from all over the U.S. participate in dancing as well as over 500 exhibits of fine arts and crafts. The **Southwestern Association on Indian Affairs** (983-5220) has more info.

■ NEAR SANTA FE

Pecos National Historical Park, located in the hill country 25 mi. southeast of Santa Fe on I-25 and Rte. 63, features ruins of a pueblo and Spanish mission church. The small monument includes an easy 1-mi. hike through various archaeological sites. Especially notable are Pecos's renovated *kivas*—underground ceremonial chambers used in Pueblo rituals—built after the Rebellion of 1680. Off-limits at other ruins, these *kivas* are open to the public. (Open daily 8am-dusk; Labor Day-Memorial Day 8am-5pm. Entrance fee $1 per person, $3 per car.) The monument's **visitors center** (757-6414 or 757-6032) has a small, informative museum and a 10-min. film shown every ½-hr. (Open daily 8am-6pm; Labor Day-Memorial Day 8am-5pm. Free.) **Greyhound** sends early-morning and late-evening buses daily from Lamy to Pecos, 2 mi. north of the monument (471-0008; call for schedule and prices). Use the campsites, or simply pitch a tent in the backcountry of the **Santa Fe National Forest,** 6 mi. north on Rte. 63 (see Santa Fe Accommodations above).

Bandelier National Monument, 40 mi. northwest of Santa Fe (take U.S. 285 to Rte. 4, then follow signs), features some of the most amazing pueblo and cliff dwellings in the state (accessible by 50 mi. of hiking trails), as well as 50 sq. mi. of dramatic mesas and tumbling canyons. The most accessible of these is **Frijoles Canyon,** site of the **visitors center** (672-3861; open daily 8am-6pm; winter 9am-5:30pm). A 5-mi. hike from the parking lot to the Río Grande descends 600 ft. to the mouth of the canyon, past two waterfalls and fascinating mountain scenery. The **Stone Lions Shrine** (12-mi., 8-hr. round-trip from the visitors center), features two stone statues of crouching mountain lions, and an unexcavated Yapashi pueblo. A 2-day, 20-mi. hike leads from the visitors center past the stone lions to **Painted Cave,** decorated with over 50 Anasazi pictographs, and to the Río Grande. Both hikes are quite strenuous. Free permits are required for backcountry hiking and camping; pick up a topographical map ($6) of the monument area at the visitors center. A less taxing self-guided 1-hr. tour takes you through pueblo cliff dwellings near the visitors center. You can camp at **Juniper Campground,** ¼ mi. off Rte. 4 at the entrance to the monument (sites $6). (Park entrance fee $5 per vehicle.)

Los Alamos, 10 mi. north of Bandelier on NM Loop 4, starkly contrasts nearby Santa Fe and Taos. The U.S. government selected the small mountain village at the outset of World War II, as the site of a top-secret nuclear weapons development program; today, nuclear research continues at the **Los Alamos Scientific Laboratory.** The facility perches eerily atop several mesas connected by highway bridges over deep gorges, supporting a community with more PhDs per capita than any other city in the U.S. The public may visit the **Bradbury Museum of Science** (667-4444) on Diamond Dr., for exhibits on the Manhattan Project, the strategic nuclear balance, and the technical processes of nuclear weapons testing (open Tues.-Fri. 9am-5pm, Sat.-Mon. 1-5pm; free). The **Los Alamos County Historical Museum,** 1921 Juniper St. (662-6272 or 662-4493), off Central, details life in the 1940s when Los Alamos was a government-created "secret city" (open Mon.-Sat. 9:30am-4:30pm, Sun. 1-5pm; Oct.-April Mon.-Sat. 10am-4pm, Sun. 1-4pm).

■■■ TAOS

Lodged between the Sangre de Cristo mountains and the canyon gouged by the Río Grande, Taos has attracted people for hundreds of years. First were the Native American tribes, whose still-vital pueblos are scattered throughout the valley. Spanish missionaries came in the 17th century in a vain attempt to convert the indigenous populace to Christianity. The 20th century saw the town invaded by dozens of artists, such as Georgia O'Keeffe and Ernest Blumenschein, captivated by Taos's untainted beauty. Aspiring artists still flock to the city, accompanied by athletes anxious to ski or hike the nearby mountains, rafters ripe for the whitewaters of the Río Grande, and naturalistic New Agers eager to vibe away. Drivers should park on Placitas Road, one block west of the plaza. In town, Rte. 68 becomes Paseo del Pueblo.

PRACTICAL INFORMATION

Emergency: Police, 758-2216. **Ambulance,** 911.

Visitor Information: Chamber of Commerce, 1139 Paseo del Pueblo Sur (758-3873 or 800-732-8267), just south of town at the intersection of Rte. 68 and Rte. 64. Open May-Oct. daily 9am-6pm; Nov.-April daily 9am-5pm. **Information booth** (no phone) in the center of the plaza. Hours vary by season and the number of volunteers available. Pick up maps and tourist literature from either.

Greyhound: (758-1144), Paseo del Pueblo Sur, 1 mi. south of Taos at Rtes. 68 and 64 east. To: Albuquerque (2 per day, $20); Santa Fe (2 per day, $15); Denver (2 per day, $59). Open Mon.-Fri. 9am-1pm and 3-7pm, Sat.-Sun. 9-11am and 5-7pm.

Public Transport: Pride of Taos Trolley, 758-8340. Serves several hotels and motels as well as the town plaza and Taos Pueblo. Schedules available in the plaza, the chamber of commerce, and most lodgings. Operates daily 10am-3pm. Variable fare depending on destination.

Taxi: Faust's Transportation, 758-3410. Operates daily 7am-10pm.

Post Office: 318 Paseo Del Pueblo Norte (758-2081), ¼ mi. north of the plaza. Open Mon.-Fri. 8:30am-5pm, Sat. 12:30-2pm. **ZIP code:** 87571.

Area Code: 505.

ACCOMMODATIONS AND CAMPING

The **Plum Tree Hostel (HI-AYH)** (758-0090 or 800-999-PLUM), on Rte. 68, 15 mi. south of Taos in Pilar, hankers down next to the Río Grande. This hostel is a flag stop on the Greyhound and airport shuttle routes between Santa Fe and Taos, so getting in and out of town isn't a problem. Kitchen facilities are available, as well as summer arts programs and Río Grande rafting trips; call ahead to reserve a spot. (Office open daily 5am-10pm. Dorm beds $8, nonmembers $11. Private rooms with bath $35 for 2 people, $40 for 3. Also has 2 bungalows available, $15 for 1 person, $24 for 2; must use shared bath in hostel. If you're planning a longer stay, you may be able to negotiate a work-exchange. Breakfast $3.)

Close to Taos Ski Valley, the **Abominable Snowmansion Hostel (HI-AYH)** (776-8298) has been spotted in **Arroyo Seco,** a tiny town 10 mi. northeast of Taos on Rte. 150. Guests may sleep in dorm rooms, bunk houses, or even a teepee. (Office open daily 8-10am and 4-10pm. Inside the hostel $12, outside in a bunkhouse or teepee $8.50; nonmembers $15.50/11.50. Private rooms $35-40.) Another option is the **New Buffalo Bed and Breakfast Retreat Center,** P.O. Box 247, Arroyo Hondo 87513 (776-2015) near Taos (call for directions). This former hippie commune, like many children of the 60s, has been reborn as a B&B (rooms $45-65).There are also teepees ($10) and tent sites ($12.50). No drugs or alcohol permitted in these rooms where Timothy Leary and Janis Joplin once slept. The cheapest hotel rooms are found at the **Taos Motel** (758-2524 or 800-323-6009), on Rte. 68, 3 mi. south of the plaza. (Singles $27-42. Doubles $32-48. Triples $36-52. Quads $38-55. Sextet $49-69.) Next door is the **Taos RV Park** (758-2524 or 800-323-6009) which offers tent sites ($12 for 2 people) and full hookups ($17 for 2 people).

Camping around Taos is easy for those with a car. Up in the mountains on wooded Rte. 64, 20 mi. east of Taos, the **Kit Carson National Forest** operates three campgrounds. Two are free but have no hookups or running water; look for campers and tents and pull off the road at a designated site. **La Sombra,** also on this road, has running water (sites $5). An additional six free campgrounds line the road to Taos Ski Valley. No permit is required for backcountry camping in the national forest. For more info, including maps of area campgrounds, contact the **forest service office** (758-6200; open Mon.-Fri. 8am-4:30pm). On Rte. 64 west of town, next to the awesome campground near the **Río Grande Gorge Bridge** (758-8851; sites with water and porta-potty $7. Porta-visitors center open daily 9am-4:30pm.)

FOOD

Major restaurants congregate at **Taos Plaza** and **Bent Street. Murray's Deli and Takeout,** 115 E. Plaza St (758-4205) in Taos Plaza, caters to the lover of kraut and potato pancakes (2 for $3). (Open Mon.-Tues. 7:30am-6pm, Wed.-Sat. 7:30am-8pm, Sun. 9am-5pm.) In the rear of **Amigo's Natural Foods,** 326 Pueblo Rd. (758-8493), across from Jack Donner's, sits a small but holistic deli serving such politically and nutritionally correct dishes as tofu on polygranulated bread ($3.25). (Open Mon.-Sat. 9am-7pm, Sun. 11am-5pm.) **El Patio de Taos Restaurant and Cantina** (758-2121), on Teresina Lane between Taos Plaza and Bent St., serves excellent New Mexican and Mexican cuisine out of the oldest building in Taos. (Open daily 11:30am-10pm.) **Michael's Kitchen,** 84 N. Pueblo Rd. (758-4178), makes mainstream munchies. Sandwiches are around $4.50. (Open daily 7am-8:30pm.)

SIGHTS AND ACTIVITIES

The spectacle of the Taos area has inspired artists since the days when the Pueblo exclusively inhabited this land. Many early Taos paintings hang at the **Harwood Foundation's Museum,** 238 Ledoux St. (758-9826), off Placitas Rd. (open Mon.-Fri. noon-5pm, Sat. 10am-4pm; free). The plaza features other galleries with works by notable locals such as R.C. Gorman, as do **Kit Carson Road, Ledoux Street,** and **El Prado,** a village just north of Taos. Taos's galleries range from high-quality operations of international renown to upscale curio shops. In early October of each year, the **Taos Arts Festival** celebrates local art.

Taos artists love rendering the **Mission of St. Francis of Assisi,** Ranchos De Taos Plaza (758-2754). The mission has a "miraculous" painting that changes into a shadowy figure of Christ when the lights go out. (Open Mon.-Sat. 9am-4pm. $1 donation.) Exhibits of Native American art, including a collection of beautiful black-on-black pottery, grace the **Millicent Rogers Museum** (758-2462), north of El Prado St., 4 mi. north of Taos off Rte. 522. (Open daily 9am-5pm; Nov.-April Tues.-Sun. 9am-4pm. $4, seniors $3, kids $2, families $8.)

Taos Pueblo (758-9593), remarkable for its five-story adobes, pink-and-white mission church, and striking silhouette, is one of the last inhabited pueblos. The vibrant community unfortunately charges dearly to look around. Much of the pueblo also remains off-limits to visitors; if this is the only one you will see, make the trip—otherwise, skip it. (Open daily 8:30am-4:30pm. $5 per car, $2 per pedestrian. Camera permit $5, sketch permit $10, painting permit $15.) Feast days highlight beautiful tribal dances; **San Gerónimo's Feast Days** (Sept. 29-30) also feature a fair and races. Contact the **tribal office** (758-9593) for schedules of dances and other info. The less-visited **Picuris Pueblo** lies 20 mi. south of Taos on Rte. 75, near Peñasco. Smaller and somewhat friendlier to visitors, Picuris is best known for its sparkling pottery, molded from mica and clay.

Taos Ski Valley (776-2291), about 5 mi. north of town on Rte. 150, is the state's premier ski resort, with powder conditions on bowl sections and "short but steep" downhill runs rivaling Colorado's. Reserve a room well in advance if you plan to come during the winter holiday season. (Lift tickets $37, equipment rental $10 per day. For info and ski conditions, call the Taos Valley Resort Association at 776-2233 or 800-776-1111.) In summer, the ski-valley area offers great hikes.

After a day of strenuous sight-seeing, soak your weary bones in one of the natural **hot springs** near Taos. One of the most accessible bubbles 9 mi. north on Rte. 522

near Arroyo Hondo; turn left onto a dirt road immediately after you cross the river. Following the dirt road for about 3 mi., turn left when it forks just after crossing the Río Grande—the hot spring is just off the road at the first switchback. Though not very private, the spring's dramatic location on the Río Grande Gorge more than compensates. Located 10 mi. west of Taos, the **U.S. 64 Bridge** over the Río Grande Gorge is the nation's second-highest span, affording a spectacular view of the canyon and the New Mexico sunset.

Taos offers every New Age service on earth. Vibrasound relaxation, drum therapy, harmony massage, and cranial therapy are all to be had here. **Taos Drums** (758-3786), 5 mi. south of the plaza on Rte. 68, features the world's largest collection of Native American drums (open Mon.-Sat. 9am-6pm, Sun. 11am-6pm). **Merlin's Garden,** 127 Bent St. (758-0985), has a bulletin board outside the store that lists activities such as drum therapy and massages (open when Jupiter aligns with Mars).

■■■ ALBUQUERQUE

Since the Anasazi tribes who settled here nearly 2000 years ago created sophisticated transportation networks, travelers have always seen Albuquerque as a town to pass through on the way somewhere else. In search of the legendary seven cities of gold, the infamous Spaniard Coronado made the town an established stop on the Camino Real. In 1880, the railroad arrived, and in 1926, the legendary Rte. 66 paved its way through the town. Some lucky travelers, however, have stopped here long enough to experience the youthful spirit surrounding New Mexico University, the historic flavor of the old town, and the dramatic backdrop of the Sandía Mountains.

PRACTICAL INFORMATION

Emergency: 911.

Visitor Information: Albuquerque Convention and Visitors Bureau, 121 Tijeras N.E., 1st floor (243-3696 or 800-284-2282). Free maps and the useful *Albuquerque Visitors Guide.* Open Mon.-Fri. 8am-5pm. After hours, call for recorded events info. **Old Town Visitors Center** (243-3215), Plaza Don Luis on Romero NW across from the church. Open Mon.-Sat. 9am-7pm, Sun. 10am-5pm. They also have an information booth at the airport. Open Mon.-Sat. 9:30am-8pm.

Airport: Albuquerque International, 2200 Sunport Blvd. S.E. (842-4366), south of downtown. Take bus #50 from Yale and Central downtown Mon.-Sat. 6:47am-6:05pm. Taxi to downtown under $10.

Amtrak: 214 1st St. S.W. (842-9650 or 800-872-7245). Open daily 9:30am-5:45pm. 1 train per day to: Los Angeles (13 hr., $91); Kansas City (17 hr., $157); Santa Fe (1 hr., $36); Flagstaff (5 hr., $82). Reservations required.

Buses: 300 2nd St. S.W., 3 blocks south of Central Ave. **Greyhound** (247-0246 or 800-231-2222) and **TNM&O Coaches** (242-4998) go to: Santa Fe (4 per day, 1½ hr., $10.50); Flagstaff (4 per day, 6 hr., $52.50); Oklahoma City (4 per day, $84); Denver (5 per day, $68); Phoenix (4 per day, $39); Los Angeles (4 per day, $59).

Public Transport: Sun-Tran Transit, 601 Yale Blvd. S.E. (843-9200; open Mon.-Fri. 7am-5pm). Most buses run Mon.-Sat. 6am-6pm. Pick up system maps at any visitors center, the transit office, or the main library. Fare 75¢, ages 5-18 and seniors 25¢.

Taxi: Albuquerque Cab, 883-4888. $2.90 the first mi., $1.40 per additional mi.

Car Rental: Rent-a-Wreck, 501 Yale Blvd. S.E. (242-9556 or 800-247-9556). Cars with A/C from $23 per day. 150 free mi. per day, 20¢ each additional mi. $130 per week. Open Mon.-Fri. 7:30am-6pm, Sat. 8am-5pm, Sun. 10am-4pm. Must be 21 with credit card; $3 extra per day if you're under 25.

Help Lines: Rape Crisis Center, 1025 Hermosa S.E. (266-7711). Center open Mon.-Fri. 8am-noon and 1-5pm; hotline open 24 hrs. **Gay and Lesbian Information Line,** 266-8041. Open daily 7am-10pm.

Post Office: 1135 Broadway N.E. (245-9469). Open Mon.-Fri. 8am-6pm. **ZIP code:** 87104.

Area Code: 505.

Central Avenue and the **Santa Fe railroad tracks** create four quadrants used in city addresses: Northeast Heights (N.E.), Southeast Heights (S.E.), North Valley (N.W.), and South Valley (S.W.). The all-adobe campus of the **University of New Mexico (UNM)** stretches along Central Ave. N.E. from University Ave. to Carlisle St.

ACCOMMODATIONS AND CAMPING

Cheap motels line Central Ave., even near downtown, but *use caution as many are dangerous*. Avoid those that are decrepit, have people lounging on the stairs, or seem to house transients. At night, look for bright, outdoor lighting. The **Route 66 Youth Hostel** (247-1813), at 10th St., offers bunks in sparse but clean rooms, as well as beautiful, newly-renovated private rooms. (Office open daily 7-11am and 4-11pm. Check-out 11am. Bunks $10 with any affiliation; private rooms with shared bath: singles $16, doubles $21. Key deposit $5. Linen $1. No reservations or curfew. Small chores may be required.) **Río Grande Inn,** 1015 Río Grande Blvd. NW (843-9500 or 800-959-4726), near the interstate and Old Town, offers a place in a titanic building complex. (Singles $29, doubles $35, $5 each additional person.) **Lorlodge West Motel,** 1020 Central Ave. SW (247-4023), has clean rooms and free local calls. (Singles $20, doubles $24, quads with 2 beds $33.)

 Coronado State Park Campground (867-5589), 1 mi. west of Bernalillo on Rte. 44, about 20 mi. north of Albuquerque on I-25, offers unique camping. Adobe shelters on the sites provide respite from the heat. The Sandía Mountains are haunting, especially beneath a full moon. Sites have toilets, showers, and drinking water. (Open daily 7am-10pm. Sites $7, with hookup $11. 2-week max. stay. No reservations.) The nearby **Albuquerque West Campground,** 5739 Ouray Rd. N.W. (831-1912), has a swimming pool. Take I-40 west from downtown to the Coors Blvd. N. exit, or bus #15 from downtown. (Tent sites $13 per 2 people, each additional person $2.) Rent camping equipment and canoes ($35 per day) at **Mountains & Rivers,** 2320 Central Ave. S.E. (268-4876), across from the university. (Deposit required; reservations recommended; open Mon.-Fri. 9:30am-6:30pm, Sat. 9am-5pm.)

FOOD AND NIGHTLIFE

Tasty, inexpensive eateries border the University of New Mexico, which stretches along Central Ave. N.E. "Feed your Body with Love, Light, and high VIBRATIONAL Food," advises **Twenty Carrots,** 2110 Central Ave. S.E. (242-1320). Wheatgrass smoothies ($2.25) and bulk organic food are, apparently, quite vibratory (open Mon.-Sat. 10am-6:30pm, Fri. until 9pm). The homemade ice cream (one scoop $1.10) and pastries at the nearby (hungry, hungry) **Hippo Ice Cream,** 120 Harvard Dr. S.E. (266-1997), could turn you into one (open Mon.-Thurs. 7:30am-10:30pm, Fri.-Sat. 7:30am-11:30pm, Sun. 9am-9pm). **La Hacienda,** 302 San Felipe NW (243-3131), in Old Town Plaza, offers authentic Mexican al fresco. Delicious fried bread comes with dinners ($5-9). (Open Mon.-Fri. 11am-9:30pm, Sat.-Sun. 11am-10pm.) **The Albuquerque Grill,** 1015 Río Grande Blvd. NW (843-9500) in the Río Grande Inn, has a "disaster burrito" ($3). (Open Mon.-Thurs. 6am-9pm, Fri.-Sat. 6am-10pm, Sun. 6am-3pm.) **Hurricane's** (255-4248), on Lomas and Washington, is a 50s drive-through with Mexican/Southwest fare at affordable prices. (Open Mon.-Fri. 6:30am-9pm, Sat. 6:30am-10pm, Sun. 6:30am-8pm.) Get a mean frank at **The Dog House,** 1216 Central SW (243-1019; open daily 10am-10pm). Crowds materialize at lunchtime at the **M and J Sanitary Tortilla Factory,** 403 2nd St. S.W. (242-4890), at Lead St. (Entrees $4-6. Open Mon.-Sat. 9am-4pm.)

 You can also dig in your spurs at **Caravan East,** 7605 Central Ave. N.E. (265-7877; continuous live music every night 4:30pm-2am; cover weekends $3). Less rurally-inclined music lovers can hear rock, blues, and reggae bands over cheap beer ($1.50) at **El Ray,** 622 Central Ave. S.W. (242-9300), a spacious old theater transformed into a bar and nightclub (open 8am-2am; music daily at 8:30pm; cover $3).

SIGHTS

Old Town, on the western end of downtown, consists of Albuquerque's Spanish plaza surrounded by restaurants and Native American art galleries. Located at the northeast corner of the intersection of Central Ave. and Río Grande Blvd., 1 mi. south of I-40, Old Town presents three great museums. The **Albuquerque Museum of Art, History, and Science,** 2000 Mountain Road NW (242-4600), has some fascinating exhibits on the city's history, New Mexican art, and a new exhibit on the various horsemen of the area: the Conquistadors, the Commanche, the Vaqueros, and the cowboys of the old West. (Open Tues.-Sun. 9am-5pm; free.) The **Rattlesnake Museum,** 202 San Felipe NW (242-6569), houses the world's largest display of different rattlesnake species. (Open daily 10am-8:30pm; $2, kids $1.) The **New Mexico Museum of Natural History,** 1801 Mountain Rd. (841-8837), does the natural wonder thing. (Open daily 9am-5pm. $4.20, kids $3.15, seniors $1.)

While in Old Town don't forget to tour the beautiful adobe **San Felipe de Neri Church,** and the civil war cannons buried in the back. Need some animal lovin'? Waddle over to the **Río Grande Zoological Park,** 903 10th St. (843-7413), a few minutes drive from Old Town. (Open Mon.-Fri. 9am-9:30pm, Sat.-Sun. 9am-5:30pm. $4.25, seniors and kids 3-15 $2.25.)

The **National Atomic Museum,** 20358 Wyoming Blvd. (845-6670), Kirkland Air Force Base, tells the story of the development of the atomic bombs "Little Boy" and "Fat Man," and of the obliteration of Hiroshima and Nagasaki. *Ten Seconds that Shook the World,* a 1-hr. documentary on the development of the atomic bomb, is shown four times daily at 10:30am, 11:30am, 2pm, and 3:30pm. Access is controlled; ask at the visitor control gate on Wyoming Blvd. for a visitors' museum pass. Be prepared to show *several* forms of ID. The Air Force base is several miles southeast of downtown, just east of I-25. (Open daily 9am-5pm. Free.)

For a different feel, the **Indian Pueblo Cultural Center,** 2401 12th St. N.W. (843-7270), just north of I-40 (take bus #36 from downtown), provides a sensitive introduction to the nearby Pueblo reservations. The cafeteria serves authentic Pueblo food (fry-bread $1.75; cafeteria open 7:30am-3:30pm) and hosts colorful Pueblo dance performances on weekends year-round at 11am and 2pm. (Open daily 9am-5:30pm. $2.50, seniors $1.50, students $1.)

■ NEAR ALBUQUERQUE

Indian Petroglyphs National Park (897-8814), located at the edge of suburbia on Albuquerque's west side, includes a trail leading through lava rocks written on by Native Americans. Take the Coors exit on I-40 north to Atristo Rd. to reach this free attraction, or take bus #15 to Coors and transfer to bus #93. (Open daily 9am-6pm; off-season 8am-5pm. Parking $1, weekends and holidays $2.)

The **Sandía Peaks,** from the Spanish for "watermelon," are named for the color they turn at sunset. Take Tramway Rd. from either I-25 or I-40 to the Sandía Peak Aerial Tramway (296-9585, or 298-8518 for recorded info). The longest aerial tramway in the world, it is a thrilling ride to the top of Sandía Crest, allowing you to ascend the west face of Sandía Peak and gaze out over Albuquerque, the Río Grande Valley, and western New Mexico. The ascent is most striking at sunset. (Operates daily 9am-10pm; Sept. 2-May 25 Mon.-Tues. and Thurs.-Sun. 9am-9pm, Wed. 5-9pm; during ski season Mon.-Tues. and Thurs.-Fri. 9am-9pm, Wed. noon-9pm, Sat.-Sun. 8am-9pm. Round-trip $12.50, seniors and students $9.50. Departs every 20-30 min., lasts 1½ hrs. Combination chairlift and tram ticket $14, seniors and kids $11.50.) A 7-mi. toll-road (Rte. 536) leads to the summit of **Sandía Crest.** A dazzling ridge hike covers the 1½ mi. separating the crest and **Sandía Peak** (10,678 ft.).

A trip through the **Sandía Ski Area** makes for a beautiful 58-mi., day-long driving loop. Take I-40 east up Tijeras Canyon 17 mi. and turn north onto Rte. 44, which winds through lovely piñon pine, oak, ponderosa pine, and spruce forests. Rte. 44 descends 18 mi. to Bernalillo, through a gorgeous canyon.Rangers offer guided hikes on Saturdays in both summer and winter. Make reservations for the challenging winter snowshoe hikes (242-9052). In the summer, hiking and mountain-biking trails are often open to the public during specific hours; call for details.

■■■ CHACO CANYON

Sun-scorched and water-poor, **Chaco Canyon** seems an improbable setting for the first great flowering of the Anasazi. At a time when most farmers relied on risky dry farming, Chacoans created an oasis of irrigated fields. They also constructed sturdy five-story rock apartment buildings while Europeans were still living in squalid wooden hovels. By the 11th century, the canyon residents had set up a major trade network with dozens of small satellite towns in the surrounding desert. Around 1150 AD, however, the whole system collapsed; with no food and little water, the Chacoans simply abandoned the canyon for greener pastures.

Chaco Canyon, a 160-mi., 3½-hour drive northwest from Albuquerque, lies 90 mi. south of Durango, CO. When the first official archaeologist left for the canyon at the turn of the century, it took him almost a year to get here from Washington, DC. Today's visitor faces unpaved **Rte. 57,** which reaches the park from paved Rte. 44 (turn off at the tiny town of **Nageezi**) on the north (29 mi.), and from I-40 on the south (about 60 mi., 20 mi. of it unpaved).

Chaco Canyon is now part of the **Chaco Culture National Historical Park.** The **visitors center** (988-6727 or 786-7014; open Labor Day-Memorial Day daily 8am-6pm, in the winter daily 8am-5pm), at the eastern end of the canyon, houses an excellent museum that exhibits Anasazi art and architecture, as well as dsecribes the sophisticated economic network by which the Chacoan Anasazi traded with the smaller Anasazi tribes of modern Colorado and northern Mexico. (Museum open same as the visitors center. Entrance fee $4 per carload.) **Camping** in Chaco costs $5; arrive by 3pm since space is limited to 46 sites. Registration is required. You can also make Chaco a daytrip from **Gallup,** where cheap accommodations are plentiful.

Only ruins remain, but these are the best-preserved sites in the Southwest. **Pueblo Bonito,** the canyon's largest town, demonstrates the skill of Anasazi masons. Among many other structures, one four-story wall still stands. Nearby **Chetro Ketl** houses one of the canyon's largest *kivas,* used in Chacoan religious rituals. Bring water, since even the visitors center occasionally runs dry.

Just west of the Continental Divide on Rte. 53, 12 mi. southeast of the Navajo town of **Ramah,** sits **Inscription Rock National Monument** (505-783-4226), where Native Americans, Spanish *conquistadores,* and later pioneers made their mark while traveling through the scenic valley. Today, self-guided trails allow access to the rock as well as to ruins farther into the park. (Open daily 8am-6pm.) The **visitors center** (open daily 8am-7pm; in winter 8am-5pm) includes a small museum as well as several dire warnings against emulating the graffiti of old and marking the rocks. For those unable to resist the urge to inscribe, an alternate boulder is provided.

■■■ FOUR CORNERS AREA

Land planning is never more prominent than at the **Four Corners,** where **New Mexico, Arizona, Utah,** and **Colorado** meet. The states come together about 40 mi. northwest of **Shiprock,** NM, on the Navajo Reservation. There isn't much to see, but the die-hard tourist will get a perverse thrill out of getting on all fours and putting a limb in each state. A good story for a cocktail party. ($1. Open dawn-dusk).

SOUTHERN NEW MEXICO

Since Billy the Kid ranged through this area, Southern New Mexico has been the model of the Wild West. Enormous caverns, heaping sand dunes, and ghost towns pocket the plains. Many Native Americans once called this area home; their influences remain throughout the region, reminding us of a very different world order.

■■■ GILA CLIFF DWELLINGS NATIONAL MONUMENT

Constructed by the Pueblo people around 1200 AD, the cliff dwellings include over 40 rooms of stone and timber carved into natural caves. The 10 to 15 families who lived here, farming the mesa top, mysteriously disappeared in the early 1300s. Surrounded by Gila National Forest, the Gila Cliff Dwellings (505-536-9461) are absolutely spectacular. The two routes to the monument are also stunning journeys. From I-25, take Rte. 152 west to Rte. 35 northwest to Rte. 15 and head about 70 mi. north. Accessible only by a 44-mi. drive on Rte. 15 from Silver City in the southwest part of the state, the drive to the park winds up and down mountains to the canyon of the Gila River. For maps or info head to the **visitors center** (505-536-9461) at the end of Rte. 15, 1 mi. from the dwellings (open daily 8am-5pm). Or write to the district ranger at Rte. 11, Box 100, Silver City 88601. The 1-mi. round-trip hike to the dwellings moves quickly and provides plenty of opportunities for photographs. The surrounding **Gila National Forest** (388-8201) beckons with great hiking and back-country camping. For lodging, see Silver City (home to a hostel) below. **Camping** in the national forest is free.

■ NEAR THE DWELLINGS: SILVER CITY

When you tire of camping, **Silver City** provides a nice, more urban stop. The city grew in the late 1800s as a mining town; several large open pits still surround the city. Silver City was also home to fabled outlaws such as Billy the Kid and Geronimo. Silver City was recently rated one of the "healthiest places to live and retire in the country." The town is 80 mi. west of I-25 on Rte. 152 west. The **Chamber of Commerce,** 1103 N. Hudson (538-37895), is a good place to start (open Mon.-Sat. 8am-5pm, Sun. 11am-3pm). Bus service to Silver City is offered by **Silver Stage Lines** (388-2856 or 800-522-0162) twice daily from the El Paso airport ($33 each way). **Las Cruces Shuttle Service** (800-288-1784) offers daily service between Silver City and Deming ($15), Las Cruces ($25), and El Paso ($32).

Carter House (HI-AYH), 101 North Cooper St. (505-388-5485), is squeaky-clean. Owner Lucy Dilworth ensures that your stay is enjoyable. The hostel has separate dorm-style rooms, a kitchen, and laundry facilities; upstairs is a B&B. Check-in is officially 4-9pm; if you're going to be later than 9pm, call ahead. ($12, nonmembers $15. B&B doubles from $59.) The **Palace Hotel,** 106 W. Broadway (388-1811), has a beautiful antique rooms (doubles from $30). The **Red Barn,** 708 Silver Heights Blvd. (505-538-5666), offers sandwiches and an all-you-can-eat salad bar for $5.50 (open Mon.-Sat. 11am-10pm, Sun. 11am-9pm). The **Buckhorn Saloon,** on Main St., is a watering hole in the spirit of the old West (open Mon.-Sat. 3-10pm). The **Buffalo Bar,** 211 N. Bullard St., is a boozer's paradise with college night Thursdays, and live music other nights. (Open Mon.-Sat. 10am-2am, Sun. noon-midnight.) The **New Mexico Cowboy Poetry Gathering** is held every August in Silver City.

To get a feel for the history of Silver City just stroll down **Broadway.** The **Silver City Museum,** 312 W. Broadway (538-5921), houses excellent exhibits on the history of the town. (Open Tues.-Fri. 9am-4:30pm, Sat.-Sun. 10am-4pm.) The **Royal Scepter Gem and Mineral Museum,** 1805 Little Walnut Rd., rocks. (Open Mon.-Tues. and Thurs.-Fri. 9am-5:30pm, Wed. noon-5:30pm, Sat. 9am-5pm.) **The Western New Mexico University Museum** (538-6386) contains a huge exhibit of painted pottery. (Open Mon.-Fri. 9am-4:30pm, Sat.-Sun. 10am-4pm. Free.) The **Open Pit Copper Mine and Mill** and the **Phelps Dodge Tyrone Mine** offers free tours of holes. Call 538-5331 for directions to the holes.

The nearby ghost town of **Shakespeare** was less fortunate than Silver City; the town's only modern residents are deer and birds. For tour info, contact **Shakespeare Ghost Town,** P.O. Box 253, Lordsburg, NM 88045 (505-542-9034).

■■■ TRUTH OR CONSEQUENCES

In 1950, the popular radio show "Truth or Consequences" sought to celebrate its tenth anniversary by persuading a small town to change its name to that of the program. Hot Springs, New Mexico was selected and T or C was born. Besides its philosophical name, T or C offers travelers the healing waters of natural hot springs, the recreation of nearby Elephant Butte Park, a land rich in Apache history and ruins, and a fantastic hostel.

Practical Information T or C is accessible from I-25, 150 mi. south of Albuquerque. The drive from Albuquerque is a fantastic trip through the stunning vastness of the desert. T or C is halfway between the Grand Canyon and Carlsbad Caverns. **Greyhound,** 302 S. Jones St. (894-3649), has a station (open Mon.-Fri. 7:30am-noon and 3:30-5:30pm, Sat. 8am-noon). Cheaper bus service is available from **El Paso-Los Angeles Limousine Express,** which offers a daily run from the McDonald's to Albuquerque (247-8036; $10), El Paso (915-532-4061; $20), and Los Angeles (213-623-2323; $35). The **chamber of commerce,** 201 S. Foch (894-3536), has some friendly folk (open daily 8am-noon and 1-5pm). T or C's **post office:** 300 Main St. (894-3137; open Mon.-Fri. 9am-5pm); **ZIP code:** 87901; **area code:** 505.

Accommodations The **Riverbend Hot Springs Hostel (HI-AYH),** 100 Austin St. (894-6183; call for directions), is by far the best hostel in New Mexico, and one of the greatest budget traveler destinations in the country. Owners Sylvia and "T or C" Lee possess more knowledge and love of their state than 10 visitors centers or spiritual yogis combined. The hostel is located on the banks of the Río Grande, and its large earthen tubs on the balcony are filled daily with healing water from T or C's hot springs. With hot outdoor mineral baths, nearby Turtleback Mountain, and sportsperson's paradise Elephant Butte Lake, a stay at Riverbend is a fulfilling vacation all by itself. The hostel offers a series of unique tours to the holy grounds of the Apache, mellow Mexican villages, and rafting trips on the river. Sleep in Apache tepees for $9. Tent sites are $7.50 per person and dorm beds are $11. Rooms for couples are the best privacy $11 can buy. Private suites ($35-42) come with kitchen and private bath.

Cheap hotels line Date St., such as the **Oasis Motel,** 819 N. Date (894-6629), which is clean and quiet with free HBO and local calls (singles $27, doubles $30). Another locally owned motel is the **Red Haven Motel,** 605 Date St. (894-2964), which has free cable TV. (Single $20, each additional person $2-4.)

Food and Sights For good value in a spacious setting, try **Tim Lizzie's,** 1502 Date St. (894-9184; open Sun.-Thurs. 6am-9pm, Fri.-Sat. 6am-10pm). For Southern diner atmosphere, the **Hill-Top Cafe,** 1301 N. Date St. (894-3407), is the place. Standard diner fare, but the menu features a variety of foods. (Mexican dinner plates ($4-6), chicken fried steak ($5.50), and reasonably priced sandwiches. Open daily 6am-9pm.) **TRC's "Big-A" Burger,** 719 Main St. (894-3099), boasts the best burgers in town. Try the Tex-Mex burger ($3.15) or the famous Big-A burger ($2.45). (Open daily 11am-9pm.)

The best of T or C remains virtually untouched by the tourist industry. Also the **Geronimo Springs Museum,** 211 Main St. (894-6600), has vast exhibits of woolly mammoths and the wild West (open Mon.-Sat. 9am-5pm; $2, students $1). If you'd rather absorb the beauty of nature, **Elephant Butte Park** (744-5421), 7 mi. from T or C, has campsites available. (Entrance fee $3 per car, tent sites $7, hookups $11.)

Mescalero Apache Reservation rests east of T or C on Rte. 70, in the town of Mescalero. The Riverbend hostel offers tours here. For info on ceremonies and the area's tourist facilities, inquire at the **community center** in town (671-4491).

■■■ WHITE SANDS NATIONAL MONUMENT

Remember walking in the sand? Located on Rte. 70, 15 mi. southeast of Alamogordo and 52 mi. northeast of Las Cruces, **White Sands National Monument** (505-479-6124) contains the world's largest gypsum sand dunes, composed of 300 sq. mi. of beach without ocean. Located in the Tularosa Basin between the Sacramento and San Andres mountains, the dunes were formed when rainwater dissolved gypsum in a nearby mountain and then collected in the basin's Lake Lucero. As the desert weather evaporated the lake, the gypsum crystals were left behind and eventually formed the continually growing sand dunes. Walking, rolling, or hiking through the dunes can provide hours of mindless fun; the brilliant white sand is especially awe-inspiring at sunset. Tragically, the basin is also home to a missile test range, as well as the **Trinity Site,** where the first atomic bomb was exploded in July 1945. Although a visit today won't make your hair fall out, the road to the park is subject to closures, usually no more than two hours, while missiles are tested. The **Visitors center,** P.O. Box 1086, Holloman AFB, 88330 (505-479-6124) is 15 mi. west of Alamogordo on Rte. 70. (Open 8am-7pm; Labor Day-Memorial Day 8am-4:30pm. Dunes drive open 7am-9pm; off-season 7am-sunset. $4 per vehicle. Disabled access.) To use the park's backcountry **campsites,** you must register at the park headquarters. **Lincoln National Forest** (505-434-7200), 13 mi. to the east, has free backcountry camping as well as at **Aguirre Springs** (505-525-4300), 30 mi. to the west ($3 per vehicle to enter Aguirre Springs). Contact **Forest Supervisor,** Lincoln National Forest, Alamogordo 88310 for info. There is also a campground in **Oliver Lee Memorial State Park** (505-437-8284); go 10 mi. south of Alamogordo on U.S. 54, then 5 mi. east on Dog Canyon Rd. The campground is at the canyon mouth on the west face of the Sacramento Mountains (Sites $7, with wattage $11). (Park open daily 6am-9pm; **visitor center** open daily 9am-4pm. $3 entrance fee per vehicle.)

If you're not camping, make nearby **Alamogordo** your base. The city is home to several motels and restaurants along White Sands Blvd., including ol' faithful: **Motel 6,** Panorama Dr. (505-434-5970), off Rte. 70, with clean, sparse rooms, TV, a pool, HBO, free local calls, and a view (singles $24, doubles $32) and the **All American Inn,** 508 S. White Sands Blvd. (505-437-1850), with clean rooms at reasonable prices, A/C, pool, and adjacent restaurant. (Singles $28, doubles $34.) While you're at it, you might as well check out the **Alameda Park and Zoo,** downtown on U.S. 54 (505-437-8430), a great place for a picnic. (Open daily 9am-5pm. $1, over 62 and under 12 50¢.) Or "reach for the stars" at the nifty **Space Center** (505-437-2840 or 800-545-4021), 2 mi. northeast of U.S. 54 in Alamogordo. (Open June-Aug. daily 9am-6pm; Sept.-May 9am-5pm. $2.25, seniors and kids 6-12 $1.75, family rate $7.)

■■■ CARLSBAD CAVERNS NATIONAL PARK

Imagine the surprise of the first Europeans wandering through southeastern New Mexico when tens of thousands of bats began swarming from out of nowhere at dusk. The legendary bat population of Carlsbad Caverns (a staggering 250,000) is responsible not only for its discovery at the turn of the century, when curious frontiersmen tracked the bats to their home, but also for its exploration. Miners first began mapping the cave in search of bat *guano,* an excellent fertilizer found in 100-ft. deposits in the cave. By 1923, the caverns had been designated a national park, and herds of tourists began flocking to this desolate region. The caverns are one of the world's largest and oldest cave systems. Beneath the surface rests a world of unusual creation that would make even the most jaded spelunker stand in awe.

Practical Information White's City, an expensive, tiny, rather tacky town on U.S. 62/180, 20 mi. southeast of Carlsbad and 7 mi. from the caverns along steep, winding mountain roads, serves as the access point to the caverns. Because flash floods occasionally close roads, call ahead. El Paso, TX is the closest major city, just 150 mi. to the west, past Guadalupe Mountains National Park, which is 35 mi. southwest of White's City. **Greyhound,** in cooperation with **TNM&O Coaches** (887-1108), runs three buses a day from El Paso ($25, $47.50 round-trip) or Carlsbad ($5.75 round-trip) to White's City. Two of these routes use White's City only as a flag stop. From White's City, you can take the overpriced **Carlsbad Cavern Coaches** to the visitors center ($15 round-trip for 1-3 people); buy tickets in the White's City Gift Shop where Greyhound drops you off. Carlsbad's **post office:** next to the Best Western Visitors Center (open Mon.-Fri. 8am-noon and 1-5pm); **ZIP code: 88268-0218; area code: 505.**

Accommodations and Food Backcountry camping is free in the park, get a permit at the visitors center. To stay in White's City, head over to the **Carlsbad Caverns International Hostel** (785-2291), which has six-bed rooms that include a TV, pool, and spa. Membership is required. ($14. Open 24 hrs.) The **Park Entrance Campground** (785-2291) is just outside the park entrance. The campground provides water, showers, restrooms, and pool. (Full hookup $16.) For cheap motels, drive 20 mi. north to Carlsbad's **Motel 6,** 3824 National Parks Hwy. (885-0011). Another joint in Carlsbad, the **La Caverna Motel** (885-4151) is on Main St. Make reservations in summer. (Singles $30. Doubles $36.) More inexpensive motels lie farther down the road. Additional campsites are available at nearby **Guadalupe Mountains National Park** in Texas. Some great and cheap Mexican food can be found in Carlsbad at **Lucy's,** 701 S. Canal (887-7714). Dinners run $2.25-10. (Open Mon.-Sat. 11am-9:30pm.)

Sights Today, the **Carlsbad Visitors Center** (785-2232 or 885-8884; for a 24-hr. recording, call 785-2107) has replaced dung-mining with a gift shop, nursery, and kennel. For 50¢ you can rent a small radio that transmits a guided tour. (Open daily 8am-6:30pm; Labor Day-Memorial Day 8am-5:30pm.) There are two ways to see the caverns. The **Natural Entrance Tour** and the **Big Room Tour** ($5 a pop) are self-guided. There are plaques in the cave explaining as you go along. You may tour the caves during the same hours as the park. A ranger-guided **King's Palace Tour** takes you through four scenic rooms. (Given on the hour. $5, kids $3, seniors $2.50.) Plan your visit to the caves for the late afternoon so as not to miss the magnificent nightly **bat flights**. An army of hungry bats pour out of the cave at the incredible rate of 6000 per minute. (Daily just before sunset May-Oct.) A ranger talk precedes this amazing ritual. (Free *guano* samples.) The pre-dawn return can also be viewed.

For a rugged and genuine caving experience, visit the undeveloped **Slaughter Canyon Cave** (formerly **New Cave**). Two-hour, 1¼-mi. flashlight tours traverse difficult and slippery terrain; there are no paved trails or handrails. Even getting to the cave takes some energy, or better yet, a car; the parking lot is 23 mi. down a dirt road off U.S. 62/180 south (there is no transportation from the visitors center or from White's City), and the cave entrance is a steep, strenuous ½ mi. from the lot. Call 785-2232 at least two days in advance for reservations; the park limits the number of persons allowed inside each day. Bring a flashlight. (Tours daily 9am-12:30pm; Labor Day-Memorial Day weekends only. $8, kids 6-15 $4.) Backcountry hiking is allowed in the Carlsbad Caverns National Park, but talk to rangers first.

Arizona

Arizona remains one of the country's premier tourist destinations. The Grand Canyon, Monument Valley, Saguaro National Monument, and Sunset Crater are just a few of the state's natural masterpieces. Even man-made ones, such as Lake Powell and the Biosphere project, attract much deserved attention. A little rattlesnake venom gets into your blood as you pass through "Wild West" towns such as Tombstone and Jerome. Almost one-seventh of the Native American population of the U.S. lives in Arizona, and one-quarter of the state's land is occupied by reservations—the Navajo Nation of northeastern Arizona is the largest and most influential. The Grand Canyon state features some of the best ruins in the world at Canyon de Chelly, Navajo National Monument, and Wupatki and Walnut Canyons. And next to these ancient cultures stand youthful, modern centers of spirituality and New Age medicine such as Sedona and Flagstaff.

PRACTICAL INFORMATION

Capital: Phoenix.
Arizona Tourism, 1100 W. Washington, Phoenix 85007 (602-542-8687 or 800-842-8257; open Mon.-Fri. 7am-5pm). **Arizona State Parks,** 1300 W. Washington St., Phoenix 85007 (542-4174). Open Mon.-Fri. 8am-5pm.
Time Zone: Mountain (2 hr. behind Eastern). Arizona (with the exception of the reservations) does not follow Daylight Savings Time; in summer it is 1 hr. behind the rest of the Mountain Time Zone. **Postal Abbreviation:** AZ
Sales Tax: 6%.

NORTHERN ARIZONA

■■■ GRAND CANYON

One of the greatest natural wonders in the United States, if not the world, the Grand Canyon is a breathtaking 277 mi. long, 10 mi. wide, and over 1 mi. deep. It is difficult to believe that the Colorado River which trickles along the canyon floor could have created the looming walls and slashing valley of limestone, sandstone, and shale, even over a period of millions of years. The dramatic landscapes of the canyon are home to equally spectacular wildlife, including mountain lions, eagles, deer, and falcons. Don't just peer over the edge—hike down into the gorge to get a genuine feeling for the immensity and beauty of this natural phenomenon.

The **Grand Canyon National Park** consists of three areas: the **South Rim,** including Grand Canyon Village; the **North Rim;** and the canyon gorge itself. The slightly lower, slightly more accessible South Rim draws 10 times more visitors than higher, more heavily forested North Rim. The 13-mi. trail that traverses the canyon floor makes a two-day adventure for sturdy hikers, while the 214 mi. of perimeter road prove a good five-hr. drive for those who would rather explore from above. Despite commercial exploitation, the Grand Canyon is still untamed; every year several careless hikers take what locals morbidly refer to as "the 12-second tour." Please remember to observe all safety precautions and the rules of common sense.

■ SOUTH RIM

In summer, everything on two legs or four wheels converges from miles around on this side of the Grand Canyon. If you plan to visit during this mobfest, make reservations for lodging, campsites, or mules if you want them—and prepare to battle crowds. During the winter there are fewer tourists, however the weather is brisk and many of the canyon's hotels and facilities are closed.

PRACTICAL INFORMATION

Emergency: 911.

Visitor Information: The **visitors center** (638-7888), is 6 mi. north of the south entrance station. Open daily 7:30am-7:30pm. Info on road conditions surrounding the park and programs 24 hr. Also info on tours, taxis, trips, etc. Ask for their *Trip Planner.* For written info ahead of time, write the Superintendent, Grand Canyon National Park, P.O. Box 129, Grand Canyon, AZ 86023.

Lodging Reservations: For booking ahead of time write, call, or fax the Reservations Dept., Grand Canyon National Park Lodges, Grand Canyon AZ 86023 (638-2401, fax 638-9247). For same-day reservations, it's best to call 638-2631 and ask to be connected with the proper lodge.

Nava-Hopi Bus Lines: 800-892-8687. Leaves Flagstaff Amtrak station for Grand Canyon daily at 5:45am, 8:05am, and 3:45pm; departs from Bright Angel Lodge at Grand Canyon for Flagstaff daily at 10:10am, 5:15pm, and 6:45pm. $12.50 each way, 14 and under $6.50; $2 entrance fee for Canyon not included. Times vary by season, so call ahead.

Grand Canyon Railway: (800-THE-TRAIN/800-843-8724). Offers historic steam train rides from Williams. The 2¼ hr. ride each way includes food, strolling musicians, and voice-over explanations of the scenery. ($47 roundtrip, $23.50 for teenagers, and $14.50 for children under 12.)

Accessibility: (638-2631). **Free wheelchairs**, *The Grand Canyon National Park Accessibility Guide*, and free permit for automobile access to the West Rim Drive (summer only). Wheelchair accessible tours are offered by prior arrangement.

Transportation Information Desk: In **Bright Angel Lodge** (638-2631). Reservations for mule rides, bus tours, Phantom Ranch, taxis, even helicopter rides. Open daily 6am-7pm. A **free shuttle bus** system operates along the West Rim Loop (7:30am-sunset daily) and the Village Loop (6:30am-10:30pm daily). A $3 hiker's shuttle offers transport between Grand Canyon village and the South Kaibab Trailhead near Yalci Point (leaves Bright Angel at 6:30am, 8:30am, 11:30am daily).

Equipment Rental: Babbit's General Store, (638-2262 or 638-2234) in Mather Center Grand Canyon Village near Yavapai Lodge. Rents comfortable hiking boots ($8 for the first day, $5 each additional day), sleeping bags ($7-9, $5 each additional day), tents ($15-16, $9 each additional day), and other camping gear. Hefty deposit required on all items. Open daily 8am-8pm.

Car Trouble: Grand Canyon Garage (638-2631) east of the visitors center on the park's main road (near Masuik Lodge), provides 24-hr. emergency service.

Pets: They are allowed in the park, provided they are on a leash. Pets may not go below the rim. There is a **kennel** (638-2631, ext. 6039) on the South Rim.

Medical Care: Grand Canyon Clinic (638-2551 or 638-2469), several miles south on Center Rd. Open Mon.-Fri. 8am-5:30pm, Sat. 9am-noon. After hours emergency care available.

Road Conditions: 638-2631 or 779-2711 for recorded message.

Post Office: (638-2512) next to Babbit's. Open daily 7:30am-5pm. **ZIP code:** 86023.

Area Code: 602.

There are two entrances to the park: the main **south entrance** lies on U.S. 180N, the eastern **Desert View** entrance lies on I-40W. From Las Vegas, the fastest route to the Canyon is U.S. 93S to I-40E, and then Rte. 64N. From Flagstaff, I-40E to U.S. 89N is the most scenic; from there, Rte. 64N takes you to the Desert View entrance. The **entrance fee** to the Grand Canyon is $10 per car and $4 for travelers using other modes of transportation—even bus passengers must pay. Upon arriving in the South Rim, grab a copy of the small but comprehensive *The Guide*, available at the entrance gate and the visitors center (free).

ACCOMMODATIONS AND CAMPING

Compared with the six million years it took the Colorado River to cut the Grand Canyon, the six months it takes to get a room on the South Rim is a blink of an eye. Since the youth hostel closed in 1990, it is nearly impossible to sleep indoors anywhere near the South Rim without reservations or a wad of cash; if you arrive unprepared, check at the visitors center (see Practical Information above) for vacancies.

Most accommodations on the South Rim other than those listed below are very expensive. The campsites listed usually fill by 10am in summer. Campground overflow usually winds up in the **Kaibab National Forest,** adjacent to the park along the southern border, where you can pull off a dirt road and camp for free. No camping is allowed within ¼ mi. of U.S. 64. Sleeping in cars is *not* permitted within the park, but is allowed in the Kaibab National Forest. For more information, contact the Tusayan Ranger District, Kaibab National Forest, P.O. Box 3088, Grand Canyon, AZ 86023, (683-2443). Backcountry campsites within the park require a free Backcountry Use Permit which is available at the Backcountry Reservations Office (638-7884), ¼ mi. south of the visitors center. You must reserve permits and campsites well in advance. Once reserved the permit must be picked up *no later than 9am* the day you plan to camp, or it will be cancelled. The Nava-Hopi bus pauses at Bright Angel Lodge, where you can check your luggage for 50¢ per day. Reservations for **Bright Angel Lodge, Maswik Lodge, Trailer Village,** and **Phantom Ranch** can be made through Grand Canyon National Park Lodges, P.O. Box 699, Grand Canyon 86023 (638-2631). All rooms should be reserved 6 months in advance for the summer.

Lodging

Bright Angel Lodge, Grand Canyon Village. Rustic cabins with plumbing but no heat. Very convenient to Bright Angel Trail and both shuttle buses. Singles or doubles from $37, depending on how much plumbing you want. $7 per additional person. Historic cabins for 1or 2 people are $61, $7 per additional person.

Maswik Lodge, Grand Canyon Village. Small, clean cabins with shower $48 (singles or doubles). $7 per additional person. Reservations required.

Phantom Ranch, on the canyon floor, a 4-hr. hike down the Kaibab Trail. Reservations required 6 months in advance for April-Oct., but check at the Bright Angel Transportation Desk (see above) for last-minute cancellations. Don't show up without reservations made well in advance—they'll send you back up the trail, on foot. Dorm beds $21. Cabins for 1 or 2 people $55, $11 per additional person.

Camping

Camper Village, 7 mi. south of the visitors center in Tusayan, offers both RV and tent sites from $15-22 a night. Call 638-2887 for reservations.

Cottonwood Campground, 16.6 mi. from the Bright Angel trailhead on the North Kaibab trail. 14 free sites; closed Nov.-April.

Indian Garden, 4.6 mi. from the South Rim Bright Angel trailhead, lies 3100 ft. below the rim and offers 15 sites, toilets, water; open year-round; free.

Mather Campground, Grand Canyon Village, 1 mi. south from the visitors center. 320 shady, relatively isolated sites without hookups $10, 7 day limit. Make reservations for Mar.-Nov. (call MISTIX, 800-365-2267, up to 8 weeks in advance). The rest of the year sites go on a first-come, first served basis.

Trailer Village, next to Mather Campground. Clearly designed with the RV in mind. Showers and laundry nearby. Open year-round. 84 sites with hookup $17 for 2 people. $1.50 per additional person. 7 day limit.

Desert View Campsite, 26 mi. east of Grand Canyon Village. No hookups. 50 sites $8. Open mid-May-Oct. No reservations, restrooms and phone; arrive early.

Ten-X Campground (638-2443) in the Kaibab National Forest, 10 mi. south of Grand Canyon Village on Rte. 64. Open May-Sept., first-come, first-served basis. Toilets, water, no hookups, $10. Group sites for up to 100 people available through reservations.

FOOD

Fast food has not sunk its greasy talons into the rim of the Canyon. While you might find meals for fast-food prices, uniformly bland cuisine is harder to locate. **Babbit's General Store** (638-2262), in Maswik Lodge, is more than just a restaurant—it's a supermarket. Stock up on trail mix, water, and gear (open daily 8am-8pm; deli open 8am-7pm). **The Maswik Cafeteria,** also in Maswik Lodge, has a variety of inexpensive options grill-made and served in a delightful cafeteria atmosphere (open daily 6am-10pm). **Bright Angel Dining Room** (638-2631), in Bright Angel Lodge, has hot sandwiches ($4-6; open daily 6:30am-10pm). The soda fountain at Bright Angel Lodge offers 16 flavors of ice cream (1 scoop $1) to hikers emerging from the Bright Angel Trail (open daily 11am-9pm).

SIGHTS AND ACTIVITIES

At your first glimpse of the canyon, you will realize that the best way to see it is to hike down into it, an enterprise that is much harder than it looks. Even the young at heart must remember that what seems to be an easy hike downhill can become a nightmarish 100° incline on the return journey. Heat exhaustion, the second greatest threat after slipping, is marked by a monstrous headache and termination of sweating. You *must* take two quarts of water along; it's absolutely necessary. A list of hiking safety tips can be found in the *Grand Canyon Guide,* available at the entrance gate and the visitors center. Overestimating your limits is a common mistake; parents should think twice about bringing children more than a mile down the trails—kids have good memories and might exact revenge when they get bigger.

The two most accessible trails into the Canyon are the **Bright Angel Trail,** which begins at the Bright Angel Lodge, and **South Kaibab Trail,** originating at Yaki Point. Bright Angel is outfitted for the average tourist, with rest houses stationed strategically 1½ mi. and 3 mi. from the rim. **Indian Gardens,** 4½ mi. down, offers the tired hiker restrooms, picnic tables, and blessed shade; all three rest stops usually have water in the summer. Kaibab is trickier, steeper, and lacks shade or water, but it rewards the intrepid with a better view of the canyon. Remember that hiking back up is much, *much* more arduous and takes *twice as long* as the hike down.

If you've made arrangements to spend the night on the canyon floor, the best route is the **Kaibab Trail** (3-4 hr., depending on conditions) and back up the Bright Angel (7-8 hr.) the following day. The hikes down Bright Angel Trail to Indian Gardens and **Plateau Point,** 6 mi. out, where you can look down 1360 ft. to the river, make excellent daytrips, but start early (around 7am) to avoid the worst heat.

If you're not up to descending into the canyon, follow the **Rim Trail** east to Grandeur Point and the **Yavapai Geological Museum,** or west to **Hermit's Rest,** using the shuttles as desired. Watch your footing. The Eastern Rim Trail swarms at dusk with sunset-watchers, and the Yavapai Museum at the end of the trail has a sweeping view of the canyon during the day from a glassed-in observation deck. The Western Rim Trail leads to several vistas, notably **Hopi Point,** a favorite for sunsets, and the **Abyss,** where the canyon wall drops almost vertically to the **Tonto Plateau** 3000 ft. below. To watch a sunset, show up at your chosen spot 45 min. beforehand and watch the earth-tones and pastels melt into darkness.

The park service rangers present a variety of free informative talks and hikes. Listings are available at the visitors center. A free talk at 8:30pm (7:30pm in winter) in **Mather Amphitheater,** behind the visitors center, highlights the Grand Canyon.

■ NORTH RIM

If you are coming from Utah or Nevada, or if you simply want a more solitary Grand Canyon experience, consider the North Rim. Here the canyon experience is a bit wilder, a bit cooler, and much more serene—with a view as groovy as that from the South Rim. Unfortunately, because it is less frequented, it's tough to get to the North Rim by public transportation.

PRACTICAL INFORMATION

Emergency: 911.

Visitors Information: The **National Park Service Information Desk** (638-2611; open 8am-5pm) is in the lobby of Grand Canyon Lodge.

Health Services: North Rim Clinic, (638-2611 ext. 222), located in cabin #7 at Grand Canyon Lodge. Walk in or make an appointment. Open Mon., Fri., and Sun. 9am-noon and 3-6pm, Tues. 9am-noon, Thurs. 3-6pm.

Public Transportation: Transcanyon, P.O. Box 348, Grand Canyon, AZ 86023 (638-2820), late May-Oct. Buses depart South Rim 1:30pm, arrive North Rim at 6pm, and depart North Rim 7am, arriving at South Rim 11:30am ($60, round-trip $100). Call for reservations.

Accessibility: Many North Rim viewpoints, facilities, and some trails are wheel-chair accessible. Inquire at the Information Desk (638-2611) for more details.

Post Office: Located with everything else in the Grand Canyon Lodge (638-2611; open Mon.-Fri. 8-11am and 11:30am-4pm, Sat. 8am-2pm); **ZIP Code:** 86023.

Area Code: 602.

The **entrance fee** for the North Rim is $10 for cars, $4 for those on foot, bike, bus, or holy pilgrimage. From the South Rim, the North Rim is a 200-plus-mi., stunningly scenic drive. Take Rte. 64 east to U.S. 89 north, which runs into Alt. 89; off Alt. 89, take Rte. 67 south to the edge. Between the first snows at the end of October and May 15, Rte. 67 is closed to traffic. Then, only a snowmobile can get you to the North Rim. Park visitor facilities closed in winter.

ACCOMMODATIONS, CAMPING, AND FOOD

Since camping within the confines of the Grand Canyon National Park is limited to designated campgrounds, only a lucky minority of North Rim visitors get to spend the night "right there." If you can't get in-park lodgings, visit the **Kaibab National Forest,** which runs from north of Jacob Lake to the park entrance. You must be ½ mi. from official campgrounds and ½ mi. from the road. Campsite reservations can be made through **MISTIX** (800-365-2267 or 619-452-5956). If you don't have reservations, mark your territory (not like Fido) by 10am.

Canyonlands International Youth Hostel (HI-AYH), 143 E. 100 South, Kanab, UT 84741 (801-644-5554), 1 hr. north of the Grand Canyon on U.S. 89, an equal distance south of Bryce, Zion, and Lake Powell. Dormitory-style rooms and buffet breakfast, all for the amazingly low price of $9. Reservations recommended.

Premium Motel, 94 S. 100 E. (801-644-9281), right around the corner from the hostel. A/C, phones, TV. Singles $22, doubles $26, triples $30.

Grand Canyon Lodge (638-2611), on the edge of the rim. Call TW Recreational Services (801-586-7686) for reservations. The pioneer cabins are the best deal at $59 for 4 people, $64 for 5. Frontier cabins are $49 for singles or doubles, $54 for triples. Front desk open 24 hrs. Western cabins and motel rooms are available at higher rates. Open daily 8am-7pm; late Oct.-mid-May Mon.-Fri. 8am-5pm.

Jacob Lake Inn (643-7232), 44 mi. north of the North Rim at Jacob Lake. Cabins $57-64 for 2, $67-69 for 3, $72-74 for 4, $77 for 5, $82 for 6. Pricier motel units. Also offers 50 campsites at $10 per vehicle. Half the sites available first-come, first-served; others can be reserved through MISTIX (800-283-2267; $7 fee) or call Jacob Lake RV Park (643-7804). Has dining room and coffee shop. Campground open May-Oct. 15.

North Rim Campground, the only campground in the park, has 82 sites on Rte. 67 near the rim. You can't see into the canyon from the pine-covered site, but you know it's there. Near food store; has laundry facilities, recreation room, and showers. Sites $10. Reserve by calling MISTIX, 800-365-2267. Closes Oct. 21. Max. stay 7 days.

DeMotte Park Campground, 5 mi. north of the park entrance in Kaibab National Forest. 25 sites $8. First-come, first-served.

Both eating options on the North Rim are placed strategically at the **Grand Canyon Lodge** (638-2611; dining room open 6:30am-9:30pm). The restaurant slaps together dinners for $4.50-12 and breakfast for $3.50. A skimpy sandwich at the "buffeteria" extorts $2.50. North Rim-ers are better off eating in Kanab or stopping at the **Jacob Lake Inn** for snacks and great shakes (meal about $5; open daily 6:30am-9pm).

ACTIVITIES

A ½-mi. paved trail takes you from the Grand Canyon Lodge to **Bright Angel Point,** which commands a seraphic view of the Canyon. **Point Imperial,** an 11-mi. drive from the lodge, overlooks **Marble Canyon** and the **Painted Desert.**

The North Rim offers nature walks and evening programs, both at the North Rim Campground and at Grand Canyon Lodge (see Accommodations). Check at the info desk or campground bulletin boards for schedules. Half-day **mule trips** ($35) descend into the canyon from Grand Canyon Lodge (638-2292; open daily 7am-8pm). If you'd prefer to tour the Canyon wet, pick up a *Grand Canyon River Trip Operators* brochure and select among the 20 companies which offer trips.

On warm evenings, the Grand Canyon Lodge fills with an eclectic group of international travelers, U.S. families, and rugged adventurers. A young crowd frequents the **Lodge Saloon** (638-2611) for drinks and a jukebox disco. (Open daily until 10:30pm, last call 10:15.) Others look to the warm air rising from the canyon, a full moon, and the occasional shooting stars for their intoxication at day's end.

■■■ NAVAJO AND HOPI RESERVATIONS

A very lost Christopher Columbus, who thought he had arrived in the Indies, mistakenly called the natives he encountered "Indians." His unfortunate clumping of the 570 different groups of natives living in America has come to dominate popular imagination. Understanding Native America goes far beyond seeing *Dances With Wolves.* If you do want to visit a reservation and actually try to understand the lifestyles and hardships of Native Americans, you can, but when doing so, proceed with caution. When in doubt, *ask questions,* since some people resent tourists.

The largest reservation in America, the Navajo Nation covers 17 million acres of northeastern Arizona, southern Utah, and northwestern New Mexico (larger than all of West Virginia). Of the one and a half million Native Americans in the country today, over 200,000 Navajo ("people of the soil") live on the reservation. "Navajo" is actually a European name for these proud, stoic people, who call themselves "Dinee." The reservation is covered with Anasazi ("Cliff Dwellers") ruins, remnants to the ancestors who lived here centuries before the Navajo arrived. The Navajo, not the U.S. government, have sovereignty over this large but agriculturally unproductive land. For a taste of the Dinee's unusual language and even some Native American ritual songs, tune your radio to 660AM, from Window Rock, "The Voice of the Navajo." Reservation politics are lively but obscure, written up only in the *Navajo Times* or in regional sections of Denver, Albuquerque, or Phoenix newspapers.

Monument Valley, Canyon de Chelly, Navajo National Monument, Rainbow Bridge, and the roads which access these sights, all lie on Navajo land. From your car, you might glimpse a *hogan* (traditional log and clay shelter). Driving off-road without a guide is considered trespassing. Photography requires a permission fee (tourist photography is not permitted among the Hopi). The Navajo Nation has its own police force, and *possession and consumption of alcohol is prohibited* on the reservation. Do not remove anything from the reservation and always respect the privacy of the people who live here. *Discover Navajoland* has a full list of accommodations, jeep and horseback tours, and tourist info, available from the **Navajoland Tourism Department,** P.O. Box 663, Window Rock 86515 (602-871-6436).

Window Rock, as well as being the seat of tribal government, features the geological formation that gives the town its name. In Window Rock, the **Navajo Tribal**

Museum (871-6673), on Rte. 264, has small cultural exhibits (free; open Mon.-Fri. 8am-5pm). The **Navajo Council Tribal Chambers** (871-6417) offers tours of the governing body's meeting place (open Mon.-Fri. 8am-noon and 1-5pm). The **Navajo Nation Zoo and Botanical Park** (871-6573) hosts wildlife domestic to the reservation (open daily 8am-5pm). The limited lodging in town is expensive; it's best to make Window Rock a day trip. The **Hubbell Trading Post** (733-3475), 30 mi. west of Window Rock on Rte. 264, is the oldest trading post in the country and a national historic site. Founded in 1876, the post still functions today as well as house a museum. (Open daily 8am-6pm.)

The "border towns" of **Gallup, NM,** and **Flagstaff** (see above) provide good entry points to the reservations; you can rent cars in one of these towns. Frequent **Greyhound** routes along I-40 serve both.

Within the boundaries of the Navajo Reservation lies the smaller **Hopi Reservation,** home to 6,000 Hopi ("peaceable people"). For info on the Hopi, call the **tribal office** (734-2441, ext. 360), or write or visit the **Hopi Cultural Center,** P.O. Box 67 Second Mesa (734-2401), on Rte. 264 in the community of **Second Mesa.** The center consists of a museum of pottery, photography, and handicrafts, along with four gift shops, a motel, and a restaurant (see below).

Inquire at the cultural center or at the Flagstaff Chamber of Commerce for the dates and sites of the **Hopi village dances.** Announced only a few days in advance, these religious ceremonies last from sunrise to sundown. The dances are highly formal occasions; tourists may come to watch, but should not wear shorts, tank tops, or other casual wear. Photography is strictly forbidden. Several tribal parks have their own small info booths. Pick up the excellent *Visitors Guide to the Navajo Nation* ($3), which includes a detailed map. Hotels charge exorbitant rates, so plan on camping at the national monuments or Navajo campgrounds, some of which also charge guests. The **hotel** at the Hopi Cultural Center (734-2401) is expensive but decent and requires reservations two weeks to a month in advance. (Singles $55. Doubles $60.) The **restaurant** is surprisingly reasonable (open daily 7am-9pm). Alternatively, you can make your visit a day trip from Flagstaff or Gallup.

■■■ CANYON DE CHELLY NATIONAL MONUMENT

While not matching the Grand Canyon's awesome dimensions, Canyon de Chelly more than makes up in beauty what it lacks in size. In the aptly-named **Beautiful Valley,** the canyon's 30- to 1000-ft. sandstone cliffs tower over the sandy, fertile valley created by the Chelly River. The oldest ruins in the eroded walls of the Canyon date back to the Anasazi civilization of the 12th century. In the 1800s, the Navajo sought refuge here during hostilities with white settlers. In what was to become a sickening pattern, dozens of Native American women and children were shot by the Spanish in 1805; the site of the executions is now called **Massacre Cave.** Kit Carson starved the Navajo out of the Canyon in the 1860s. The discovery of Native American burials under the Rio de Chelly gave the main tributary the name "Canyon del Muerto." Today, Navajo farmers once again inhabit the canyon, cultivating the lush soil and living in traditional Navajo dwellings, *hogans.*

The most common route to the park is from Chambers, 75 mi. south, at the intersection of I-40 and U.S. 191, but you can also come from the north via U.S. 191. Entrance to the monument is free. The **visitors center** (674-5500) is 2 mi. east of **Chinle** on Navajo Rte. 64. (Open daily May 1-Sept. 30 8am-6pm; Oct. 1-April 30 8am-5pm.) Chinle is adjacent to U.S. 191. There is no public transportation to the park. For **emergencies,** contact the park ranger at 674-5523, the Navajo Police at 674-5291, or an ambulance at 674-5464.

The land constituting Canyon de Chelly National Monument is owned by the Navajo Nation and is administered by the National Park Service. The Nation has its own police. Alcoholic beverages are prohibited on the reservation. Hiking or cross-country excursions off established roads without permission is trespassing. Permission should also be asked before photographing or drawing people or personal property. A fee is often expected. All but one of the park trails are closed to public travel unless hikers are escorted by Navajo representatives. The park service offers free short tours into the canyon, but the only way to get far into the canyon or close to the Anasazi ruins is to hire a Navajo guide. The staff arranges for guides and tours at any time of day, although guides usually arrive at the visitors center at about 9am. Guides generally charge $10 per hr. to walk or drive into the canyon. Advance reservations are helpful, but you can try dropping in. To drive into the canyon with a guide, you must provide your own four-wheel-drive vehicle which requires a free permit available at the visitors center. Horseback tours can be arranged at **Justin's Horse Rental** (674-5678), on South Rim Dr., at the mouth of the canyon. (Open daily approximately 9am-9pm. Horses $8 per hr.; mandatory guide $8 per hr.)

The 1-mi. trail to **White House Ruin,** 7 mi. from the visitors center off South Canyon Rd., winds down a 400-ft. face, past a Navajo farm and traditional *hogan,* through an orchard, and across a stream. This trail is the only one you can walk without a guide; it's best in the spring when you can hike in the canyon heat with the cool stream swirling about your ankles. Take one of the paved **Rim Drives** (North Rim 44 mi., South Rim 36 mi.), which skirt the edge of the 300- to 700-ft. cliffs; the South Rim is more dramatic. **Spider Rock Overlook,** 16 mi. from the visitors center, is a narrow sandstone monolith towering hundreds of feet above the canyon floor. Native American lore says that the whitish rock at the top of Spider Rock contains bleached bones of victims of the *kachina* spirit Spider Woman. Get booklets on the White House Ruin and Rim Drives (50¢) at the visitors center.

Camp for free in the park's **Cottonwood Campground,** ½ mi. from the visitors center. This giant campground in a pretty cottonwood grove rumbles at night with the din of stray dogs which tend to wander the site. Facilities include restrooms, picnic tables, water (except during winter months), and a dump station. Max. RV length is 35 ft. Sites are first-come, first-served with a 5 day max. stay. Group sites (15-25 people) can be reserved 90 days in advance for a 3 day max.; call 674-5500. Don't expect to find any budget accommodations anywhere in Navajo territory. Farmington, NM, and Cortez, CO, are the closest major cities with cheap lodging.

■■■ MONUMENT VALLEY AND NAVAJO MONUMENT

Monument Valley Navajo Tribal Park You may have seen the red rock towers of Monument Valley in one of numerous westerns filmed here. Rather ironically, the 1000-ft. monoliths helped boost "injun" killer John Wayne to heights of movie slaughter. The best way to see the valley is via the Park's looping 17-mi. **Valley Drive.** This dirt road winds in and out of the most dramatic monuments, including the famous pair of **Mittens** and the slender **Totem Pole.** The gaping ditches, large rocks, and mudholes on this road will do horrible things to your car—drive at your own risk, and hold your breath. Much of the valley can be reached only in a sturdy four-wheel-drive vehicle or by a long hike. In winter, snow laces the rocky towers, and almost all the tourists flee. Inquire about snow and road conditions at the Flagstaff Chamber of Commerce (800-842-7293).

The park entrance is 24 mi. north on U.S. 163 from the town of **Kayenta,** at the intersection with U.S. 160 (park open daily 7am-8pm; Oct.-April 8am-5pm; entrance fee $2.50, seniors $1, kids 7 and under free). The **visitors center** (801-727-3287) at the end of Rte. 564, 9 mi. west of U.S. 160, has a craft shop as well as pottery and artifacts displays (open daily 7am-8pm; Oct.-April 8am-5pm). Remember to advance your watches one hour, since during the summer, the Navajo Nation runs on **Mountain Daylight Time,** while the rest of Arizona remains on Mountain Standard Time.

The **Mitten View Campground,** ¼ mi. southwest of the visitors center, offers 99 sites ($10), coin-op showers, and restrooms. Reservations accepted only for groups of 11 or more, otherwise first-come, first-served. Also see the National Monument.

Navajo National Monument From the park entrance, Rte. 564 takes you 9 mi. to the Navajo National Monument. This stunning site consists of three Anasazi cliff-dwellings, including **Keet Seel,** the best-preserved site in the Southwest (open May 27-Sept. 5). The village requires an 18-mi. round-trip hike or a $53 horseback ride from the visitors center. A free campground near Keet Seel allows hikers to stay overnight.The site at the National Monument has no showers or hookups, but it's free and has the advantage of nightly ranger talks. Inscription House has closed, and entrance into Keet Seel and **Betatakin,** a 135-room complex, is limited to 25 people per day in ranger-led groups. (Tours daily at 9am, noon, and 2pm; try to make reservations at least 2 months in advance.) The Navajo maintain a small **campground** (30 sites, $10) with water and restrooms, next to the visitors center.

Two trails take you around the Betatakin area. The **Sandal Trail** is a 1-mi. round trip paved hike to an overlook of Betatakin, and **Aspen Forest Trail,** another 1-mi. hike, overlooks canyons and aspens but no ruins. On your own, explore the free 17-mi. self-guided **valley drive.** The road is unpaved and could be rough on cars with low bottom clearance. **Jeep tours** are available from the visitors center; most cost around $15. For $50, Navajo guides put you on a horse, lead you down the 8-mi. trail, and leave you with a ranger to explore the 400-year-old Anasazi ruins. Allow a full day for the ride and the strenuous hike. Rangers also lead 5-mi. hikes. You can hike on your own, but you must obtain a permit. Write Navajo National Monument, Tonalea, AZ 86044 for more details.

■ ■ ■ PAGE

Rated one of the best towns in America, Page has come a long way since its founding in 1957 as a construction camp for the federal government. With over 3 million visitors a year, the town serves as the gateway to Lake Powell, the largest man-made lake we know of. To turn the Page from Utah, take **U.S. 89** south and east past Big Water across into Arizona. From Flagstaff, take U.S. 89 north.

The incredibly ebullient **Lake Powell International Hostel,** 141 8th Ave. (645-3898), has free pickup and delivery to Lake Powell, free tea and coffee, free linens and blankets, free local calls, a kitchen, a BBQ grill, TV, a volleyball court, outdoor eating area, nightly videos, and bathrooms in every unit. Also a $15 shuttle to Flagstaff. Ask Jeff, the host, to arrange tours for you. Don't miss the traditional midnight swim. ($12-15 a bunk, doubles $35, quads $45. No curfew.) **Pension at Lake Powell,** next door to the hostel has more upscale rooms with 4-6 person suites of 3 rooms with bathroom, living room with cable TV, and kitchen $60. If the hostel is full try **Bashful Bob's Motel,** 750 S. Navajo Dr. (645-3919), where most rooms have kitchens and cable TV (doubles $39, triples $43).

For "calzones as big as your head," head to **Strombolli's Restaurant and Pizzeria,** 711 N. Navajo Dr. (645-2605; open Mon.-Sat. 11am-10pm, Sun. 11am-midnight). Gulp a margarita at **Salsa Brava** (645-9058) on Elm St. across from "Subway Plaza." (Open Mon.-Wed. 11am-10pm, Thurs.-Sun. 11am-11pm.)

Emergency is 911. To start on the right Page, seek the **chamber of commerce,** 106 S. Lake Powell Blvd. (645-2741; open Mon.-Fri. 8am-9pm, Sat.-Sun. 8am-7pm). **Skywest** (645-4200) flies into the Page airport from Phoenix, Las Vegas, St. George, and Salt Lake City. Page's **area code:** 602.

■ NEAR PAGE: LAKE POWELL AND RAINBOW BRIDGE

When President Dwight Eisenhower said "dammit," they did. Ten years and ten million tons of concrete later, **Glen Canyon Dam,** the second largest dam in the country was made. With no particular place to go, the Colorado River flooded a canyon in northern Arizona and southern Utah to form the 186 mi.-long Lake Powell, named after the first Anglo male to explore the Colorado. The lake offers a stunning 1960 mi. of national recreation shoreline. Many companies offer **Jeep tours** to many of the side canyons including the **Kaleidoscopic Antelope Canyon.** Check pamphlets at the Page Chamber of Commerce for more information.

The **Carl Hayden Visitors Center** (645-8200) is on U.S. 89N adjacent to the dam and 1 mi. north of Page. Here you can also descend into the cool inner-workings of the dam. (Open daily 7am-7pm, 8am-5pm off-season; free guided tours of the dam every hr. on the ½ hr. 8:30am-5:30pm; 8:30am-3:30pm off-season.)

If you want to sleep near the lake, the **Wahweep Lodge,** 100 Lake Shore Dr. (645-2433 or 800-528-6154) will make you cry with its pricey rooms (singles $100, doubles $110, triples $129, quads, $130; off-season singles and doubles are $72-77). Rooms not facing lake are roughly $10 cheaper. If these prices tell you all you need to know about the crying game, the **Wahweep Campground,** adjacent to the lodge, has 200 sites on a first-come, first-served basis ($8.50, group sites available for $2 per person, 9 person min.). The **Wahweep RV Park,** next door, has two-person full hook-ups for $25, $2.30 extra for A/C or heater, $2.50 each additional person.

Accessible from Lake Powell is **Rainbow Bridge National Monument,** the largest natural stone bridge in the world. Sacred to the Navajo, Rainbow Bridge is named after the Navajo work, Nonnezoshi, meaning "rainbow turned to stone." It can be reached only by **boat-trip** or by hiking. Boat tours are available through **ARA Leisure Services** (800-528-6154; full-day $65, $35 kids under 12; ½-day $52, $28 under 12. Call for reservations well in advance.)

■■■ SUNSET CRATER, WUPATKI, AND WALNUT CANYON NATIONAL MONUMENTS

Sunset Crater Volcano National Monument (602-556-7042), 17 mi. north on U.S. 89, contains a volcanic crater which erupted in 1065AD to form cinder cones and lava beds; oxidized iron in the cinder gives the pre-nuclear crater its dramatic dark color. (Visitors center open daily 8am-6pm; in winter 8am-5pm. $4 per car or $2 per person.) The self-guided **Lava Flow Nature Trail** wanders ½ mi. through the plain's surreal lava formations, 1½ mi. east of the visitors center. Lava tube tours have been permanently discontinued because of lava falling on visitors.

Wupatki National Monument, 18 mi. northeast of Sunset Crater National Monument along a stunning scenic road with views of the Painted Desert and the Grand Canyon. The Sinagua moved here over a thousand years ago when they found the black-and-red soil ideal for agriculture. After 300 years, however, droughts, disease, and over-farming precipitated the abandonment of the pueblos. Some of the Southwest's most scenic ruins, these stone houses are perched on the sides of *arroyos* in view of the San Francisco Peaks. Five major abandoned pueblos stretch along the 14-mi. road from U.S. 89 to the visitors center. A different road than the one that leads from Sunset Crater to the ruins begins on U.S. 89 about 30 mi. north of Flagstaff. The largest and most accessible, **Wupatki Ruin,** located on a ½ mi. roundtrip loop trail from the visitors center, rises three stories high. Below the ruins, you can see one of Arizona's two stone ballcourts, the sites of ancient games which employed a rubber ball and a stone hoop in a circular court. Get info at the **Wupatki Ruin Visitors Center** (556-7040; open daily 8am-6pm; off-season 8am-5pm). The monument and visitors center are open dawn to dusk. Trail guides go for 50¢. **Backcountry hiking** is allowed at Wupatki with a free permit available at the visitors center. Admission to Sunset Crater includes Wupatki. When visiting Wupatki or Sunset Crater you can camp at the **Bonito Campground.**

Walnut Canyon National Monument (602-526-3367), 7 mi. east of Flagstaff off I-40, contains 13th-century ruins of more than 300 rooms in Sinagua dwellings constructed within a 400-ft.-deep canyon. From a glassed-in observation deck in the visitors center you can survey the whole canyon; a stunning variety of plants sprout out of its striated grey walls. The self-guided **Island Trail** snakes down from the visitors center past 25 cliff dwellings; markers along the trail describe aspects of Sinagua life and identify the plants the natives used for food, dyes, medicine, and hunting. Rangers lead hikes down this 2-mi. trail to the original Ranger Cabin and many remote cliff dwellings. These mildly strenuous 2½-hr. hikes leave from the visitors center every Saturday morning (call ahead, hours change frequently). Hiking boots and long pants are required. (Monument open daily 7am-6pm; Labor Day-Memorial Day 8am-5pm. Admission $4 per car, $2 per biker or hiker.)

■■■ PETRIFIED FOREST NATIONAL PARK AND METEOR CRATER

The Petrified Forest National Park is titanic and austere, covering over 60,000 acres and including in the northern section a scenic chunk of the **Painted Desert.** Don't expect to see a forest here; that's the *last* thing the Petrified Forest resembles. The park consists of Arizona desert dotted with tree logs that turned into rock some 225 million years ago. Petrification involves an unlikely set of circumstances: logs must fall into a swamp, be cut off from air and water rapidly, then have each cell replaced by crystal. The sunset view in the Painted Desert (named for the magnificent multicolored bands of rock inlaid with quartz and amethyst crystals that scatter across the desert floor and change color) is spectacular.

To enter the Petrified Forest section of the park, exit I-40 at Holbrook and take U.S. 180 west to the **Rainbow Forest Museum** (524-6228). The museum serves as a visitors center and has quite a lot of fossils and petrified stuff. A 27-mi. park road connects the two entrances, winding past piles of petrified logs and Native American ruins. Stop to look at oddly-named **Newspaper Rock,** covered with Native American petroglyphs. At **Blue Mesa,** a hiking trail winds through the desert. **Long Logs Crystal** and **Jasper Forest** contain some of the most exquisite fragments of petrified wood. Picking up fragments of petrified wood in the park is illegal and traditionally unlucky; if the demons don't getcha then the district attorney will. Those who *must* take a piece home should buy one at a store along I-40. Although there are no established campgrounds in the park, **free backcountry camping** is allowed in several areas with a free permit from the Rainbow Forest Museum.

To enter the Painted Desert section of the park, take I-40 to exit 311 (107 mi. east of Flagstaff). Less than 5 mi. from the exit, is the **Painted Desert Visitors Center** (524-6228, ext. 236; open in summer daily 7am-7pm; 8am-5pm the rest of the year).

There is no public transportation to either park. **Nava-Hopi Bus Lines, Gray Line Tours,** and **Blue Goose Backpacker Tours** offer services (see Flagstaff Practical Information). Entrance to the parks is $5 per vehicle, $2 by foot or bike. The fee includes access to both the Painted Desert and the Petrified Forest. Lodging is available in **Holbrook** (27 mi. from the museum), but prices are fairly high. Budgeteers should return to Flagstaff.

Meteor Crater (774-8350), 35 mi. east of Flagstaff off I-40 on the Meteor Crater Rd. exit, is a great stop on the way from Flagstaff to the Petrified Forest. This privately-owned meteor crater, one of the world's largest, was originally believed to be just another ancient volcanic cone. Once scoffed at, geologic tests in the crater and on rock fragments from the surrounding desert proved the hypothesis that about 50,000 years ago a huge nickel-iron meteorite plummeted through the atmosphere and onto the desert to create the 570-ft. deep pothole. The site was used to train the Apollo astronauts in the 1960s. Visitors cannot hike down into the crater, but must peer over the guard-railed edge. A museum in the building near the center (free with paid entrance to the crater) patriotically celebrates the U.S. space program and the sciences of astronomy and mineralogy. This museum is pricey and only for space nuts. (Open daily 6am-6pm; in winter 8am-5pm. $7, seniors $6, students $4.)

■■■ FLAGSTAFF

Eager with the call of manifest destiny, the early pioneers of this town celebrated their settlement by hoisting the stars and stripes up a tall pine on Independence Day in 1876. Named after this action, the town and its flag evolved into an established spot on a well-worn western trail that became the famous Route 66. Today, Flagstaff has a personality that is difficult to define—15,000 college students, retired cowboys, yuppies, and soul searchers all call Flagstaff home. Add the thousands of Grand Canyon tourists and the town is bustling and schizophrenic in a great way.

PRACTICAL INFORMATION

Emergency: 911. **Sheriff,** 774-4523.

Visitor Information: Flagstaff Visitors Center, 1 E. Rte. 66 (800-842-7293 or 774-9541), inside the Amtrak station. Open March 16-Oct. 15 Mon.-Sat. 8am-9pm, Sun. 8am-5pm; rest of the year Mon.-Sat. 8am-6pm, Sun. 8am-5pm.

Tours: Blue Goose Backpacker Tours and Travels, (800-332-1944, or in AZ 774-6731). Run out of the Motel DuBeau International Hostel at 19 W. Phoenix Ave. (See Accommodations below). Full-day round-trip guided tours to: the Grand Canyon ($36); Sedona and Oak Creek ($15); Page and Lake Powell ($25). **Gray Line/Nava-Hopi,** 144 W. Rte. 66, (774-5003 or 800-892-8687 outside AZ). 1-day sight-seeing tours year-round to: the Grand Canyon south rim ($38); Sunset Crater, Walnut and Wupatki Canyons, and the Museum of Northern Arizona ($34); Navajo Reservation and Monument Valley ($74); Petrified Forest and Meteor Crater ($58); Oak Creek Canyon, Sedona, Jerome, and Montezuma Castle ($36); Hopi Reservation, Navajo Reservation, and Painted Desert ($62). Some tours seasonal. Free pick-up at most hotels. Reserve a spot 12 hr. ahead. Kids 5-15 ride ½-price on all tours. Reservations required. Get tickets at the Amtrak or Greyhound station.

Amtrak: 1 E. Santa Fe Ave. (774-8679 or 800-872-7245). 1 train daily to Los Angeles (11 hr., $87) and Albuquerque (6 hr., $82). 1 connecting shuttle bus to the Grand Canyon ($12). Open daily 5:30am-1:30pm and 2-5:45pm and 7pm-midnight.

Buses: Greyhound, 399 S. Malpais Lane (774-4573), across from NAU campus, 5 blocks southwest of the train station on U.S. 89A. To: Phoenix (5 per day, $18); Albuquerque (6 per day, $46); Los Angeles (5 per day, $76); Las Vegas (3 per day via Kingman, AZ, $43). Terminal open 24 hrs. **Gray Line/Nava-Hopi,** 144 W. Rte. 66, (774-5003 or 800-892-8687). Buses leave and arrive at both the Nava-Hopi terminal (address above) and Amtrak station. Use caution in this area at night. Shuttle buses to the Grand Canyon (3 per day, $25 round-trip) and Phoenix (3 per day, $43 round-trip).

Public Transport: Pine Country Transit, 970 W. Rte. 66 (779-6624). 3 routes covering most of town. Fare 75¢. Runs once per hr. **Flagstaff Trolley** (774-5003) runs the hotel pickup route (daily 8:30am-4:10pm) and a museum-shopping-history route (daily 9:30am-5:20pm). $4 to ride all day.

Camping Equipment Rental: Peace Surplus, 14 W. Rte. 66 (779-4521), 1 block from the hostel. Daily rental of dome tents ($5-8), packs ($5), stoves ($3), plus a good stock of cheap outdoor gear. 3-day min. rental on all equipment. Credit card or cash deposit required. Open Mon.-Fri. 8am-9pm, Sat. 8am-7pm, Sun. 9am-6pm.

Bike Rental: Cosmic Cycles, 113 S. San Francisco St. (779-1092), downtown. Mountain bikes $13 per ½ day, $20 per day, $35 per weekend, $75 per week. Open Mon.-Sat. 9am-7pm, Sun. 11am-4pm.

Taxi: Dream Taxi (774-2934). Open 24 hrs.; airport to downtown about $10.

Car Rental: Budget Rent-A-Car, 100 N. Humphreys St. (774-2763), within walking distance of the hostels. Guarantees the lowest rates. Economy cars from $33 per day, with 100 free mi., 25¢ per additional mi. $145 weekly with 1050 free mi. Open daily 7am-9pm. Must be 21 or older with a major credit card or at least $200 cash deposit. Under 25 surcharge $5 per day. Ask Tom for *Let's Go* discount rates.

Post Office: 2400 N. Postal Blvd. (527-2440), for general delivery. Open Mon.-Fri. 9am-5pm, Sat. 9am-noon. **ZIP code:** 86004.
Area Code: 602.

Flagstaff is 138 mi. north of Phoenix (take I-17) and 26 mi. north of Sedona (take U.S. 89A). The Grand Canyon's south rim is 81 mi. north on U.S. 180. Downtown lies at the intersection of **Beaver Street** and **Route 66** (formerly Santa Fe Ave.). Within ½-mi. of this spot are both bus stations, the three youth hostels, the chamber of commerce, and several inexpensive restaurants. Other commercial establishments lie on **South San Francisco Street.** Because Flagstaff is a mountain town, it stays cooler than much of the rest of the state and receives frequent afternoon thundershowers. You can walk around most of downtown, but to get anywhere worth seeing, rent a car or take a tour bus.

ACCOMMODATIONS AND CAMPING

When swarms of tourists descend upon Flagstaff in the summer, accommodation prices shoot up. However, the town is blessed with excellent hostels. For cheap motels cruise historic Rte. 66. Camping in **Coconino National Forest** surrounding the city is a pleasant and inexpensive alternative.

Motel Du Beau, 19 W. Phoenix (774-6731 or 800-332-1944), just behind the train station. A registered National Landmark which once hosted L.A. film stars and Chicago gangsters. Now a top-rated hostel in the Southwest, offering superlative service to hostelers. Non-stop party atmosphere. Free rides to and from airport, bus, and train stations. Free breakfast and coffee all day. Kitchen, library, and nightly videos. Dorm beds $12, private rooms $25. Beautiful, refurbished camping area $6 per person. Reservations accepted. Open 24 hrs.

The Weatherford Hotel (HI-AYH), 23 N. Leroux (774-2731). Friendly management and convenient location. Dorm rooms, baths in rooms and halls, kitchen, and a cozy common area; ride board in lobby. Curfew 1am. $10. Required sleep-sheet $1. Private singles $22. Doubles $28. Open daily 7-10am and 5-10pm. Guests enjoy free cover charge at **Charley's,** downstairs, which has live music.

Hotel Monte Vista, 100 N. San Francisco St. (779-6971) in the heart of downtown. Quiet, in a hotel with restaurant and lounge with live music. 30 dorm beds $12. Rooms with shared bath $30-55 for 1 or 2 people. Rooms with 2 double beds $45-85 for up to 4 people. Open 24 hrs.

The Grand Canyon International Youth Hostel in Flagstaff, 809 W. Riordan (779-9421), ½ block off historic Rte. 66 on the west corner at Metzwalk, a brand-new facility specifically designed to be a hostel with 250 beds. Scheduled to open in April 1995. Dormitory-style with 4 to 6 beds per unit. Laundry, free linen, free tea and coffee, free continental breakfast, access to the kitchen facilities, 2 lounges with pool tables, videos, TV, and a jacuzzi. 4 blocks from the Greyhound station and ½ mi. from the Amtrak Station make this hostel a nice alternative from the noisier downtown hostels. Free pickup from Greyhound and Amtrak stations. Shuttles to Page ($15), Sedona ($15), and Grand Canyon ($26; $36 for a full-day guided tour). No curfew. Bunks $12, private doubles $30, $5 per additional person. Reservations accepted. Open 24 hrs.

KOA, 5803 N. U.S. 89 (526-9926), 6 mi. northeast of Flagstaff. Municipal bus routes stop near this beautiful campground. Showers, restrooms, and free nightly movies. Tent sites for 2 $20. "Kamping Kabins" $28. Each additional person $4.

You'll probably need a car to reach the **public campgrounds** in Coconino National Forest. All open on a first-come, first-served basis. Campgrounds at higher elevations close during the winter; many are small and fill up quickly during the summer, particularly on weekends when Phoenicians flock to the mountains. If you stake out your site by 1pm you shouldn't encounter problems. National forest sites are usually $2-3 per night. Pick up a forest map ($2) in Flagstaff at the chamber of commerce (see above). **Lake View** (527-3650), 13 mi. southeast on Forest Hwy. 3 (U.S. 89A), has 30 sites ($10). **Bonito** (527-3630), 2 mi. east on Forest Rd. 545, off U.S. 89, has

If you're going to

SAN FRANCISCO

Forget wearing flowers in your hair!! (This is the 90's.)

Just bring the incredible coupon on the other side of this page!

Your Hostelling International card will allow you stay at over 5,000 hostels in 70 countries for only $5 to $30 per night.

Please sign me on for a full 12 months as a:
☐ youth (under 18) $10
☐ adult $25
☐ family $35,
☐ senior (over 54) $15
☐ Life $250

My payment is enclosed via:
☐ Check
☐ MC/VISA # _____--_____--_____--_____ __/_

☐ **I do not want to join yet; please send me more information**
Please allow 3 weeks for delivery. For faster delivery options call 1-800-444-6111.

Name _____

Address _____

City _____ | State _____ | Zip _____ | Birth Date (m/y) _____

Phone _____ | Departure Date _____ | Destination _____

IF YOU CAN'T AFFORD TO TRAVEL, JOIN THE CLUB.

HOSTELLING INTERNATIONAL

The new seal of approval of the International Youth Hostel Federation.

HOSTELLING INTERNATIONAL®

431

44 sites at Sunset Crater ($8). (Both are open May-Sept.; max. stay 7 days.) All have running water and flush toilets. Those who can live without amenities can camp free in any national forest outside the designated campsites, unless otherwise marked. For info call the **Coconino Forest Service** (527-7400; open Mon.-Fri. 7:30am-4:30pm). **Fort Tuthill Park** (774-5139), 3 mi. south of Flagstaff on U.S. 89A, has 335 acres of ponderosa pines. **Fort Tuthill Campground** (774-3464) offers 100 sites. (Open May 1-Sept. 30; $8, $12 with hookup; reservations accepted.)

FOOD AND ENTERTAINMENT

To suit every taste, Flagstaff offers an odd blend of cafés and diners. Downtown eateries serve great sandwiches for as little as $4, but real meals will cost much more.

Macy's, 14 S. Beaver St. (774-2243), behind Motel Du Beau. This hippy, happy, tourist and college student hangout serves fresh pasta ($3.25-5.25), plus a wide variety of vegetarian entrees, pastries, and espresso-based drinks. Open daily 6am-8pm, Thurs. and Sat. until 10pm; food served until 7pm.

Café Espress, 16 N. San Francisco St. Fine danishes, plus various sandwiches and coffees ($1). The artsy staff makes a cult of healthy food, dimmed lighting, and light-hearted angst. Open Mon.-Thurs. and Sun. 7am-10pm, Fri.-Sat. 7am-11pm.

Alpine Pizza, 7 Leroux St. (779-4109) and 2400 E. Santa Fe Ave. (779-4138). A popular spot for beer, pool, and pizza. Excellent, huge calzones ($5.25) and strombolis ($6.55). Open Mon.-Sat. 11am-11pm, Sun. noon-11pm.

Main St. Bar and Grill, 4 S. San Francisco St. (774-1519), across from Downtown. When the vegetarian meals and non-alcoholic drinks of the cafes get too healthy, try the delicious barbecued dishes ($2-11), complete with Buttery Texas Toast. Excellent selection of beers. Live music Tues.-Sat. at 8pm. No cover. Open Mon.-Sat. 11am-midnight, Sun. noon-10pm.

While there isn't much to see within Flagstaff proper, the nights you spend here could be full of lively entertainment. Party animals with a taste for the wild West will enjoy the **Museum Club,** 3404 E. Rte. 66 (526-9434). Known locally as the **Zoo,** it rocks with live country-western and cowboys and cowgirls (open daily noon-1am). The cover charge is $3 but you can call **Dream VIP Taxi** (774-2934) for a free round-trip ride. Below the Weatherford Hotel, **Charley's,** 23 N. Leroux (779-1919), plays great blues. Hostelers staying at the Weatherford get in free. (Open daily 11am-3pm and 5-9pm, bar open daily 11am-1am.)

■ NEAR FLAGSTAFF

The Lowell Observatory, 1400 W. Mars Hill Rd. (774-3358), just west of downtown off Rte. 66, has 8 telescopes used in breakthrough studies of Mars and Pluto. Visitors get a tour of the facility and hands-on astronomy exhibits. On a clear night, they might even let you peek through the big telescope and see the little green men in Los Angeles. Call about special viewing evenings. (Open April-Oct. daily 9am-5pm; Nov.-March Mon.-Sat. 10am-5pm, Sun. noon-5pm. $2.50, ages 5-17 $1.)

The Museum of Northern Arizona (774-5211), on Fort Valley Rd. off U.S. 180 just north of town, features one of the largest collections of Southwestern Native American art. Nava-Hopi bus lines and the trolley offer service to the museum (see Practical Information). (Open daily 9am-5pm. $4, seniors $3, college students $2.)

The **San Francisco Peaks** are the huge, snow-capped mountains visible to the north of Flagstaff. **Humphrey's Peak**—the highest point in Arizona at 12,670 ft.—is sacred to the Hopi, who believe that the Kachina spirits live there. Nearby **Mt. Agassiz** has the area's best skiing. The **Arizona Snow Bowl** operates four lifts from mid-Dec. to mid-April; its 32 trails receive an average of 8½ ft. of powder each winter. Lift tickets cost $29. Call the switchboard (779-1951; 24 hrs.) for information on ski conditions, transportation, and accommodations. During the summer, the peaks are perfect for hiking. You can see the North Rim of the Grand Canyon, the Painted Desert, and countless square miles of Arizona and Utah from the top of Humphrey's

Peak when the air is clear. Those not up to the hike should take the **chairlift** (20-30 min.) up the mountain (779-1951; runs daily 10am-4pm; Labor Day-June 18 Sat.-Sun. 10am-4pm; $8.50, seniors $6, kids 6-12 $4.50). The vista from the top of the lift proves almost as stunning. Picnic facilities and a cafeteria are open from May-Oct. Since the mountains occupy national forest land, camping is free, but no established campsites are available. To reach the peaks, take U.S. 180 about 7 mi. north to the Fairfield Snow Bowl turnoff.

Old Route 66 When travelling along I-40 between Northern Arizona and Nevada, take a breather and cruise along a museum of American dreams, **Old Route 66.** Between **Kingman** and **Seligman,** Arizona, runs 90 mi. of pleasurable detour. Constructed in the 20s along long-established trading routes, the highway stretched from Chicago to Los Angeles. The construction of I-40 has outdated the highway and the colorful road culture it created. In the small town of **Hackberry,** less than 30 mi. east of Kingman, **The Old Route 66 Visitors Center and Preservation Foundation** (769-2605) makes its home in an old general store. Outside, elms and Joshua trees provide shade to travelers who can sit on the old couches and chairs beneath them. (Center open daily 10am-dark; if no one is there sit and wait a spell.)

■■■ JEROME

Built into the Mingus Mountains, Jerome began as a copper-mining boom town in the late 1800s. Miners from around the world spent their life extracting ore from the rich Cleopatra Hill. Later they just blasted the whole thing, and labor unrest during the 50s turned Jerome into a ghost town. Exit industry, enter counterculture—artists and idealists renovated Jerome into their home. Today, Jerome is in a transitional period between quiet shire and luxury resort getaway. The budget traveler should visit Jerome as a day trip.

U.S. 89A slinks its way to Jerome 30 mi. southwest of Sedona. The drive between the two is simply gorgeous. With no chamber of commerce, **The Station** (634-9621), on U.S. 89A across from the high school, serves as the unofficial visitors center (open daily 11am-6pm). Jerome's **area code:** 602.

Learn more about the area by heading over to **Jerome State Historic Park** (634-5381), ½ mi. off U.S. 89A just as you enter town. Housed in the 80-year-old house of mine owner James Douglas, the museum is crammed full of exhibits on mining, minerals, and the early years of the town (open daily 8am-5pm; $2, kids under 17 $1). From the park, visitors get a panoramic view of town and its various and sundry architecture complete with helpful tidbit placards. **The Gold King Mine and Ghost Town** (634-0053), also on U.S. 89A just past Main, is, guess what, an abandoned mine and ghost town. Fun for its period cars, trucks, machines, and props. Feel free to explore all you want (open daily 9am-5pm; $3, seniors and kids under 12 $2.50). **The Mine Museum,** 200 Main St. (634-5477), has a stock of rocks viewable for 50¢ (open daily 9am-4:30pm). Visit Lance the friendly hermit in his **hermit's cave,** a cabin he built out of old wood and outhouse doors.

If you have to stay the night in Jerome, **The Inn at Jerome,** 309 Main St. (634-5094), is one of the lower-priced joints in town. Rooms run about $55-75. For food, **The English Kitchen,** 119 Jerome Ave. (634-2132), is the oldest restaurant in Arizona and has a large array of salads and sandwiches under $5. (Open Tues.-Sun. 8am-3:30pm.) **Marcy's,** 363 Main St. (634-0417), offers ice cream, soups, and sandwiches (under $4) in a pleasant ambience. (Open Fri.-Wed. 11am-5pm.) A bit pricey, **The House of Joy** (634-5339), on Hull Ave., was formerly a brothel, and now offers some of Arizona's finest food. At night, float over to **The Spirit Room** (634-8809), on Main and Jerome, for live music and mayhem (open daily 10am-1am). Get sloppy at **Paul and Jerry's Saloon** (634-2603), also on Main, a watering hole that has served Jerome for three generations (open daily 10:30am-1am).

■■■ SEDONA

The pines of the Coconino National Forest blanket Sedona's red sandstone formations, offering some of Arizona's most sensational scenery. Ignore the upper-class shopping mall that is the town and concentrate on the state parks, fine dining, and the good vibes at this point of "psychic energy convergence."

Sedona lies 120 mi. north of Phoenix (take I-17 north to Rte. 179 west) and 30 mi. south of Flagstaff (take I-17 south to Rte. 179 west or use U.S. 89A southwest). The **Sedona-Phoenix Shuttle** (282-2066) offers three trips daily ($30 one way, $55 round-trip). The **Sedona Chamber of Commerce** (282-7722) is at Forest Rd. and Rte 89A. (Open Mon.-Sat. 8:30am-5pm, Sun. 9am-3pm.) Sedona's **area code** is 602.

Sedona is an expensive town with a few budget lodgings. **The White House Inn** (282-6680) has singles ($38-50) and doubles ($40-75) depending on the season and the day of the week. The **Star Motel,** 295 Jordan Rd. (282-3641), or **La Vista,** 500 N. Rte 89A, both have comfy rooms with cable TV (1 bed $55-59, 2 beds $65-79). There are a number of **campgrounds** within **Coconino National Forest** (282-4119) along Oak Creek Canyon on U.S. 89A. With 78 sites, the largest campsite is **Cave Springs,** 20 mi. north of town. First-come, first-served. Sites for all campgrounds all $10 per vehicle. For more info on Coconino, visit the **ranger station,** 250 Brewer Rd. (turn off U.S. 89A at Burger King; open Mon.-Sat. 7:30am-4:30pm, closed on Sat. in the winter). **Backcountry camping** is allowed within the forest for free as long as you're outside of Oak Creek and more than 1 mi. from any official campground. There are also plenty of commercial campgrounds and RV parks near town that you can get details on at the chamber of commerce.

Locals hang at **The Sedona Coffee House and Bakery,** 293 N. Highway (282-2241), which has fine homemade pastries and sandwiches (open daily 8am-5pm). The **Coffee Pot Restaurant,** 2050 W. U.S. 89A (282-6626), serves up 101 varieties of omelettes (open daily 5:30am-9pm). **Cups Bistro and Gallery,** 1670 W. U.S. 89A (282-2531), in west Sedona, serves the organic, karmic food with live music. (Open daily 8am-4pm in the summer, a bit later in the winter.)

Meditate amidst the splendor at **Red Rock State Park** (282-6907), on U.S. 89A about 15 mi. southwest of town. The **visitors center** in the park is open daily 8am to 5pm. There are day hikes into the nearby red rocks, including ranger-led nature and bird walks (call for times). There are no campsites. (Park open April-Oct. daily 8am-6pm; rest of the year 8am-5pm. $5 per vehicle, $1 per pedestrian or cyclist.)

Slide Rock Park, 10 mi. north of Sedona on U.S. 89A, has a natural stone slide into the waters of Oak Creek that is popular during the summertime. (Open daily 8am-7pm in the summer; closed earlier in the winter. $3 per car, $1 pedestrian.) An architectural wonder, the **Chapel of the Holy Cross** (282-4069), on Chapel Rd., is just outside a 1000-ft. rock wall in the middle of the red sandstone (call for hours).

Scenic driving happens naturally in Sedona. Tour **Oak Creek Canyon** along U.S. 89A north of town. For an off-road experience into the rugged backcountry, try the 13-mi. **Schnebley Hill Road** east of downtown. If you have a chauffeur fetish call **Earth Wisdom Tours,** 293 N. U.S. 89A (282-4714), in uptown Sedona, which has jeep tours including the groovy "Earth Wisdom Vortex Tour." (Tour rates $20-65 per person depending on length. Open daily, hours vary.)

■ NEAR SEDONA

Tuzigoot National Monument (634-5564), 20 mi. southwest of Sedona (take U.S. 89A to Rte. 279 and continue through the town of Cottonwood), stands as a dramatic Sinaguan ruin overlooking the Verde Valley. (Open daily 8am-7pm. $2, 62 and over and the rest of the car free, under 17 free.) **Montezuma Castle National Monument** (567-3322), 10 mi. south of Sedona on I-17, is a 20-room adobe abode. The dwellings were constructed around 1100AD, when overpopulation in the Flagstaff area forced the Sinagua south into the Verde Valley along Beaver Creek. Visitors can view the "castle" from a path below. (Open daily 8am-7pm. $2, 62 and over the rest of the car free, under 16 free.) The **Montezuma Well,** 11 mi. from the Castle, springs up on I-17 at the Wall exit. Then drive east and find a beautiful lake formed by the collapse of an underground cavern; at one time, it served as a source of water for the Sinagua who lived here (open daily 7am-7pm; free).

When finally completed, **Arcosanti** (632-7135) will be a self-sufficient community embodying Italian architect Paolo Soleri's concept of an "arcology," defined as "architecture and ecology working together as one integral process." Budgetarians will appreciate the architect's vision of a city where cars are obsolete. The complete city, with its subterranean parks, will surprise the most imaginative Legoland architect. (Tours daily every hr. 10am-4pm. Open to the public daily 9am-5pm. $5 donation.) For more info, contact Arcosanti, HC 74, P.O. Box 4136, Mayer AZ 86333.

SOUTHERN ARIZONA

■■■ PHOENIX

Originally inhabited by the Hohokam peoples, then "settled" by the Spanish Conquistadors, Phoenix (named for the mythic bird that rose from its ashes) was incorporated in 1860 in the hopes that a magnificent city would arise. Today Phoenix is the eighth largest city in the country.

Forget genetics—Phoenix is a product of its environment. Rising out of the aptly-named Valley of the Sun, it is a winter haven for frostbitten tourists and sun-loving students. During these balmy months, golf, spring-training baseball, and the Fiesta Bowl flourish. During the summer, the city crawls into its air-conditioned shell; visitors should carry water with them if they plan on walking for *any* length of time. Despite the average summer temperature of 100°F, the 50-70% drop in hotel rates in the summer make things cool. Unlike Sedona and Flagstaff which have summer peaks, Phoenix provides an inexpensive base from which to explore the Southwest.

PRACTICAL INFORMATION

Emergency: 911.

Visitor Information: Phoenix and Valley of the Sun Convention and Visitors Center, 400 E. Van Buren St. (254-6500), on the 6th floor of the Arizona Center. Ask for the pamphlet on affordable accommodations and a Valley Pass to save up to 50% at resorts, hotels, and attractions. Open Mon.-Fri. 8am-5pm. **Weekly Events Hotline,** 252-5588. 24-hr. recording.

Amtrak: 401 W. Harrison (253-0121 or 800-872-7245), 2 blocks south of Jefferson St. NOT safe at night. *See Mileage Chart.* Station open Sun.-Wed. 5:45am-11:30pm, Thurs. and Sat. 3-9:30pm.

Greyhound: 525 E. Washington St. (800-231-2222). *See Mileage Chart.* Open 24 hrs. Lockers $1.

Public Transport: Valley Metro, 253-5000. Most lines run to and from the **City Bus Terminal,** Central and Washington. Most routes operate Mon.-Fri. 5am-9:30pm; severely reduced service on Sun. Fare $1; disabled persons, seniors, and kids 50¢. 10-ride pass $10, all-day $2.50; disabled persons and seniors ½-price. Pick up free timetables, maps of the bus system, and bus passes at the terminal. City bus #13 runs to the **Sky Harbor International** (273-3300), only minutes southeast of downtown.

Car Rental: Rent-a-Wreck, 2422 E. Washington St. (254-1000). Economy cars from $21 per day; 100 mi per day free. Open Mon.-Fri. 7am-6:30pm, Sat.-Sun. 9am-5pm. Must be 21 with credit card or cash deposit.

Auto Transport: Auto Driveaway, 3530 E. Indian School Rd. (952-0339). 1st tank of gas free. Open Mon.-Fri. 9am-4:30pm. Must be 21, $250 deposit.

Taxi: Ace Taxi, 254-1999. $2.45 base fare, $1.10 per mi. **Yellow Cab,** 252-5252. $2.05 base fare, $1.30 per mi.

Help Lines: Center Against Sexual Assault, 241-9010. Open 24 hrs. **Gay/Lesbian Hotline** and **Community Switchboard,** 234-2752. Daily 10am-10pm.
Post Office: 522 N. Central (407-2051), downtown. Open Mon.-Fri. 8:30am-5pm, Sat. 8:30am-noon. General Delivery at 4949 E. Van Buren St (225-3158). Open Mon.-Fri. 8am-5pm. **ZIP code:** 85026.
Area Code: 602.

The **bus terminal** at Central Ave. and Washington St. is in the heart of downtown. **Central Avenue** runs north-south; "avenues" are numbered west from Central and "streets" are numbered east. **Washington Street** divides streets north-south.

ACCOMMODATIONS AND CAMPING

Summer is the best season for the budget traveler to visit Phoenix. Almost all motels near downtown have vacancies and slash their rates by up to 70%. In the winter, when temperatures and vacancy signs go down, prices go up; be sure to make reservations if possible. The reservationless should cruise the row of motels on **Van Buren Street** or on **Main Street** (Apache Trail) in Tempe and Mesa. The strip is full of 50s ranch-style motels with names like "Deserama," as well as the requisite modern chains. But be advised that portions of these areas *can be quite dangerous* and you should investigate a hotel thoroughly before checking in. **Bed and Breakfast in Arizona,** Gallery 3 Plaza, 3819 N. 3rd St. (265-9511), can help you find accommodations in homes in Phoenix and throughout Arizona. (Preferred 2-night min. stay. Singles $25; doubles $35. Reservations recommended.)

> **Metcalf House (HI-AYH),** 1026 N. 9th St. (254-9803), a few blocks northeast of downtown. From the city bus terminal, take bus #7 down 7th St. to Roosevelt St., then walk 2 blocks east to 9th St. and turn left—the hostel is ½ block north. Dorm-style rooms, wooden bunks, and common showers. Kitchen, porch, common room, and laundry. Sleep sack required. Check-in 7-10am and 5-10pm. $10, nonmembers $13. Linen $1.
>
> **Quality Inn Airport,** 3541 E. Van Buren St. (273-7121), has quality singles $29-43, doubles $35-57, depending on the season.
>
> **Comfort Inn Airport,** 4120 E. Van Buren St. (275-5746), is comfortable. Singles $28-53, doubles $33-58 depending on the season.
>
> **The American Lodge,** 965 Van Buren St. (252-6823), is truly American. 1 bed $22-25, 2 beds $30-33.
>
> **KOA Phoenix West** (853-0537), on Citrus Rd. Take I-10 to exit 124 and go ¾ mi. south to Van Buren, then 1 mi. west to Citrus. 11 mi. west of Phoenix. Heated pool and jacuzzi, and other perks. Sites $13, With hookup $14.50-19.

FOOD

Besides the malls, you will rarely find several restaurants together amid Phoenix's sprawl. Downtown is fed mainly by small coffeeshops, most of which close on weekends. For more variety, drive down McDowell St. The **Arizona Center** (271-4000) on 3rd and Van Buren, is a new mall with fountains and palm trees. **The Mercado** (256-6322), on E. Van Buren between 5th and 7th, has ethnic fare in a mall.

> **Tacos de Juárez,** 1017 N. 7th St. (258-1744), near the hostel. Mexican fare at rock-bottom prices. Specializes in tacos. A la carte items all under $3. Open Mon.-Thurs. 11am-9pm, Fri. 11am-10:30pm, Sat. 8am-10:30pm, Sun. 8am-8pm.
>
> **The Matador,** 125 E. Adams St. (254-7563), downtown. Standard Mexican dinners $5-8. The deep-fried ice cream is a novelty. Live music Fri. and Sat. nights. Open daily 7am-11pm. Lounge open until 1am.
>
> **The Purple Cow Deli,** 200 N. Central (253-0861), in the San Carlos Hotel; also in the Park Central Mall (265-8431). Great sandwiches ($4) and frozen yogurt. Kosher food available. Open Mon.-Fri. 6am-6pm, Sat.-Sun. 8am-2pm.
>
> **Tee Pee's,** 4144 E. Indian School Rd. (956-0178). Great Mexican food at low prices. Try the beef or chicken *burros* ($4.50) or the many combination plates ($4-6). Open daily 11am-whenever.

Bill Johnson's Big Apple, 3757 E. Van Buren (275-2107), 1 of 4 locations. A down-south delight with sawdust on the floor. Sandwiches ($4-6), hearty soups ($2-3). Open Mon.-Sat. 6am-11pm.

Gourmet House of Hong Kong, 1438 E. McDowell Rd. (253-4859), has lunch specials under $5 from 11am-4pm. Near the hostel. Open daily 11am-10pm.

SIGHTS

Phoenix offers many museums to those interested in the arts, Native American culture, wildlife, technology, and architecture. The **Heard Museum,** 22 E. Monte Vista Rd. (252-8848 or 252-8840), 1 block east of Central Ave. near the hostel, has outstanding collections of Navajo handicrafts and promotes the work of contemporary Native American artists, many of whom give free demonstrations. The museum also sponsors occasional lectures and Native American dances. (Guided tours daily. Open Mon.-Tues. and Thurs.-Sat. 9:30am-5pm, Wed. 9:30am-9pm, Sun. noon-5pm. $5, seniors and students $4, kids 3-12 $4; free Wed. 5-9pm.) The **Phoenix Art Museum,** 1625 N. Central Ave. (257-1222), 3 blocks south, has exhibits of European, modern, and U.S. folk art (open Tues. and Thurs.-Sat. 10am-5pm, Wed. 10am-9pm, Sun. noon-5pm; $4, seniors $3, students $1.50, kids under 6 free; free Wed.). The **Pueblo Grande Museum and Cultural Park,** 4619 E. Washington St. (495-0900), offers over 100 acres of exhibits on Native Americans of the Southwest. (Open Mon.-Sat. 9am-4:45pm, Sun. 1-4:45pm; 50¢.)

The **Desert Botanical Gardens,** 1201 N. Galvin Pkwy. (941-1225), in Papago Park 5 mi. east of the downtown area, grows a beautiful and colorful collection of cacti and other desert plants. Visit in the morning or late afternoon to avoid the midday heat. (Open daily 7am-10pm; winter 8am-sunset. $5, seniors $4, kids 5-12 $1. Take bus #3 east to Papago Park.) Also within the confines of Papago Park is the **Phoenix Zoo** (273-1341), at 62nd and E. Van Buren, which presents exhibits and a children's zoo. Walk around or take a guided tour via tram. (Open May 1-Labor Day daily 7am-4pm, otherwise 9am-5pm; $6, seniors $5, kids $3.) The **Arizona Museum of Science and Technology,** 80 N. 2nd St. (256-9388), has interactive science exhibits such as a transparent talking anatomical mannequin such that you can see its guts. (Open Mon.-Sat. 9am-5pm, Sun. noon-5pm; $3.50, seniors and kids 4-12 $2.50.) The **Champlia Fighter Museum,** 4636 Fighter Aces Dr. (830-4540), in nearby Mesa, offers aircrafts. (Open daily 10am-5pm; $6, kids under 14 $3.)

Taliesin West (860-8810 or 860-2700), on Frank Lloyd Wright Blvd. in nearby Scotttsdale, served as the architectural studios and residence of Frank Lloyd Wright. Designed by Wright, the studio seeks to blend into the surrounding desert. (Open June-Sept. daily 10am-4pm; $10, students and seniors $8, kids $3. Guided tour included.) To see Wright's work check out the **Arizona Biltmore** (955-6600), on 24th St. and Missouri. Another Wright creation is the **Gammage Memorial Auditorium** (965-3434), at Mill Ave. within Arizona State University, is one of the last major buildings designed by the architect. Painted pink and beige to match the surrounding desert, the eccentric edifice's coloration is sure to either astound or nauseate you. (20-min. tours daily in winter. Take bus #60 or #22 on weekends.)

South of Phoenix across the dry Salt River lie Tempe's **Arizona State University (ASU)** and its sunny college atmosphere. Cafes and art galleries abound in this area.

ENTERTAINMENT

Phoenix has an active nightlife. **Toolie's Country Saloon and Dance Hall,** 4231 W. Thomas Rd. (272-3100), was recently rated the nation's best country nightclub. (Country-western music nightly. Free dance lessons Mon., Wed., and Sun. Open Mon.-Thurs. 8am-1am, Fri.-Sat. 7am-1am, Sun. 10am-1am; cover Thurs.-Sat. $4, other days $2.) **Phoenix Live,** 455 N. 3rd St. (252-2112), at Arizona Center, quakes the complex with four bars and clubs. For the hefty $5 cover you'll have access to the entire building. On Fri.-Sat. **LTL Ditty's** plays piano and encourages sing-alongs and wild fans. **Char's Has the Blues,** 4631 N. 7th Ave. (230-0205), is self-explanatory. Dozens of junior John Lee Hookers rip it up nightly. (Music nightly at 9pm. Cover from $4.) Headbangers find their black leather, big guitar Eldorado in the bottom of the **Mäson Jar,** 2303 E. Indian School (956-6271). (*Heavy* jams nightly at 9pm. Cover $3 weekdays, $5 weekends.) The free *New Times Weekly* (271-0040), on local magazine racks, lists club schedules. Pick up a copy of the *Cultural Calendar of Events,* a guide covering three months of area entertainment activities.

Phoenix also has plenty for the sports-lover. Catch NBA action with the **Phoenix Suns** (379-7867) at the America West Arena, or root for the NFL's **Phoenix Cardinals** (379-0101). Phoenix also hosts professional indoor tennis tournaments, a professional baseball team, and a hockey team. Call the visitors center for more info.

■■■ FROM PHOENIX TO TUCSON

Biosphere 2 Do not tap on the glass. It disturbs the scientists of this giant, hermetic greenhouse which holds seven life-size, man-made ecosystems—a savannah, tropical rainforest, marsh, 25-ft.-deep ocean and coral reef, desert, an intensive agricultural area, and a 7-11. In 1991, the Biosphere officially sealed eight research scientists within the dome to cultivate their own food and knit their own socks with no aid from the outside world for anywhere from three months to a year.

The Biosphere is an hour from Tucson. Take I-10 west to the "Miracle Mile" exit, follow the miracles to Oracle Rd. north until it becomes Rte. 77N. From Phoenix take I-10 to exit 185, follow Rte. 387 to Rte. 79 (Florence highway), ride Rte. 79 to Oracle Juntio, where you turn left onto Rte. 77. You can't go inside but there are 50-min. **guided tours** on the hour. Visitors can enter "analog greenhouses" which are model ecosystems used to design the Biosphere. The tour also has films and exhibits. Come early, as lines can be long. Visitors to Biosphere 2 are welcome daily 9am-5pm. ($13, seniors $11, ages 5-17 $6. AAA discount.) The **Inn at the Biosphere** (825-6222) offers deluxe accommodations on the same ranch as the Biosphere. (Cable TV, giant beds, and huge patios overlooking the Catalina mountains. $49 for two, a hefty $20 for each additional person.) Guests are sealed into their room at 8pm and are taken out the subsequent leap year. Rates soar to $80 from Oct. 1 to May 1. There is also a **Biosphere Cafe** in the complex.

Aravaipa Canyon A true natural wonder off the beaten path. From the Biosphere travel roughly 20 mi. north on Rte. 77. Just past the wooly town of **Mammoth,** take a right at the sign for Central Arizona College. Follow this road about 11 mi., half of which is unpaved, and you're there. The canyon is perfectly centered in a panorama of desert, mountains, and cacti. Overseen by the Bureau of Land Management, the canyon is allowed only 50 visitors per day. **Permits** ($1.50) are required in advance. Reserve permits and get instructions for picking them up by calling 428-4040. In 1993, winter storms knocked the road to the ranger station off the face of a cliff, so hike 3 mi. to the fee station and another mile to the wilderness area. There are some primitive **campsites** and backcountry camping available (2-day max. stay, no more than 10 people). Take the posted warnings seriously, camp on high ground, beware of flash floods, don't camp on railroad tracks, and don't play with rattlesnake tails. Hydrate yourself frequently and with zeal.

Apache Junction A small mining town at the junction of Rte. 88 and U.S. 60 (40 mi. east of Phoenix), Apache Junction is the "gateway to the Superstition Mountains." Steep, gray, and haunting, the mountains derived their name from Pima Native American legends. In the 1800s the Apache used the mountains as a stronghold against settlers and invading tribes.

The **Apache Trail** follows Rte. 88 from Apache Junction into the mountains and around the man-made **Lake Canyon, Lake Apache,** and **Lake Roosevelt.** The trail loops around to the town and U.S. 60 and is about 6-8 driving hrs. **Apache Trail Tours** (982-7662) offers a variety of jeep tours along the trail ($25 per person for 1½ hrs., or $75 per person for 8 hrs.). For more info head to **Apache Junction Chamber of Commerce,** 1001 N. Idaho (982-3141; open Mon.-Fri. 8am-5pm, Sat. 9am-1pm).

Some of the loop around the mountains is unpaved, and many attractions along the way vie for your attention. Among the best is the **Goldfield Ghost Town Mine Tours** (983-0333) on Rte. 88, 3½ mi. north of the U.S. 60 junction. The refurbished ghost town offers tours of the nearby mines and some goldpanning (open daily 10am-6pm; mine tours $4, kids $2, goldpanning $3). "Where the hell am I?" said Jacob Waltz when he came upon **Lost Dutchman State Park** (982-4485), on Rte. 88 5 mi. north of the junction. At the base of the Superstitions, the park offers **nature trails, picnic sites,** and **campsites** (day use entrance fee $3 per vehicle, night camping is first-come, first-served at $8 a night). **Tortilla Flat** (984-1776) is an old ghost town 18 mi. north of the junction on Rte. 88. The ghosts keep busy with a restaurant, ice cream shop, and saloon. 5 mi. east of Roosevelt Lake on Rte. 88W lies **Tonto National Monument** (467-2241), a 700-year-old masonry and pueblo ruins of the prehistoric Salado people. (Visitors center and monument open daily 8am-5pm.)

■■■ TUCSON AND ENVIRONS

Settled by the Hohokam and Pima tribes, the Tucson region witnessed the arrival of the Spanish in 1776, who built a collection of forts and missions in this dry valley (which boasts over 350 days of sun). Immortalized in song by Little Feat ("I've been from Tucson to Tucumcari, Tehachapi to Tonopah") as a western outpost for those willin' to be movin', Tucson at first glance appears indeed to be little more than a glorified truck stop. But stick around and enjoy the zip and zing of the University of Arizona (UA), or cavort with the cacti at Saguaro National Monument.

PRACTICAL INFORMATION

Emergency: 911.

Visitor Information: Metropolitan Tucson Convention and Visitors Bureau, 130 S. Scott Ave. (624-1817 or 800-638-8350). Ask for a bus map, the *Official Visitor's Guide,* and an Arizona campground directory. Open Mon.-Fri. 8am-5pm, Sat.-Sun. 9am-4pm.

Airport: Tucson International (573-8000), on Valencia Rd., south of downtown. Bus #25 runs every hr. to the Laos Transit Center, where bus #16 goes downtown. Last bus daily at 7:17pm. **Arizona Stagecoach** (889-1000) has a booth at the airport and will take you downtown for $11. Open 24 hrs. Reserve ahead.

Amtrak: 400 E. Toole (623-4442 or 800-872-7245), at 5th Ave., across from the Greyhound station. Open Sun.-Wed. 7:45am-8:30pm, Thurs. 1:15-8:30pm, Sat. 7:45am-3pm. 3 trains per week to: Phoenix ($28); Los Angeles ($104).

Greyhound: 2 S. 4th Ave. (882-4386 or 800-231-2222), between Congress St. and Broadway. To: Phoenix (11 per day, 2 hr., $14); Los Angeles (7 per day, 10 hr., $47); Albuquerque (6 per day, $71); El Paso (7 per day, $49). Open 24 hrs.

Taxi: Yellow Cab, 624-6611. 24 hrs.

Sun-Tran: 792-9222. Buses run from the Ronstadt terminal downtown at Congress and 6th. Approximate operating times are Mon.-Fri. 5:30am-10pm, Sat.-Sun. 8am-7pm. Fare 75¢, students 18 and under 50¢ (student ID required), seniors 25¢.

Car Rental: Care Free, 1760 S. Craycroft Rd. (790-2655). For the car free. $18 per day with 100 free mi. per day; within Tucson only. Open Mon.-Fri. 9am-5pm, Sat. 9am-3pm. Must be 21 with major credit card.

Bike Rental: The Bike Shack, 835 Park Ave. (624-3663), across from UA campus. $20 for day, $30 for 2 days, $40 for 3 days. Open Mon.-Fri. 9am-7pm, Sat. 10am-5pm, Sun. noon-5pm.

Help Lines: Rape Crisis, 327-7273. Takes calls 24 hrs.

Post Office: 141 S. 6th St. (622-8454). Open Mon.-Fri. 8:30am-5pm, Sat. 9am-noon. General Delivery at 1501 Cherry Bell (620-5157). **ZIP code:** 85726.

Area Code: 602.

Tucson's downtown area is just east of I-10, around the intersection of Broadway (running east-west) and Stone Ave., and includes the train and bus terminals. The **University of Arizona** studies 1 mi. northeast of downtown at the intersection of

Park and Speedway Blvd. Avenues run north-south, streets east-west; because some of each are numbered, intersections such as "6th and 6th" are possible—and probable. **Speedway** and **Broadway Blvds.** are the best east-west routes through town. To go north-south follow either **Campbell Ave.** on the west side, or **Craycroft Rd.** on the east. **Oracle Rd.** heads north-south through the heart of the city.

ACCOMMODATIONS AND CAMPING

When summer arrives, Tucson opens its arms to budget travelers. For motel bargains, browse through the stack of accommodation leaflets at the visitors center. Motel row lies along **South Freeway,** the frontage road along I-10, just north of the junction with I-19. **Old Pueblo Homestays Bed and Breakfast,** P.O. Box 13603, Tucson 85732 (800-333-9776; open daily 8am-8pm), arranges overnight stays in private homes. (Singles $35. Doubles $45. Winter reservations usually required 2 weeks in advance.)

Hotel Congress and Hostel (Rucksackers), 311 E. Congress (622-8848), is conveniently located across from the Greyhound and Amtrak stations. The hotel is the site where the long arm of the law finally arrested the ruthless and Byronic John Dillinger. Prices are $3 more in winter or for a renovated room. A cafe, bar, and club swing downstairs. ($12, nonmembers $14. Hotel singles $32. Doubles $36. Students receive 20% discount on hotel rooms.) **The Tucson Desert Inn** (624-8151), I-10 at Congress, has the "largest pool in Tucson." Large, clean rooms have good furnishings and plenty of sun. (Singles $24. Doubles a re $34. Seniors 10% discount. Light breakfast included.) **Mount Lemmon Recreation Area** in the **Coronado National Forest** offers beautiful campgrounds and free off-site camping in certain areas. Campgrounds and picnic areas are two minutes to two hours outside Tucson via the Catalina Hwy. **Rose Canyon,** at 7000 ft., is heavily wooded, comfortably cool, and has a small lake. Sites at the higher elevations fill quickly on summer weekends. (Sites $7 at Rose and Spencer Canyons; General Hitchcock Campground free, but no water available.) For more info, contact the **National Forest Service,** 300 W. Congress Ave. (670-4552), at Granada, 7 blocks west of Greyhound (open Mon.-Fri. 7:45am-4:30pm). Among the commercial campgrounds near Tucson, try **Cactus Country RV Park** (574-3000), 10 mi. southeast of Tucson on I-10 off the Houghton Rd. exit. It has showers, restrooms, and a pool. (Sites $12 for 1 or 2 people, with full hookup $18.50. Each additional person $2.50.)

FOOD

The downtown business district and the area farther east around the University feature some of the best and most affordable Mexican cuisine in the Southwest. Those homesick for institutional food can get their fill at any of the eateries at UA's student union (open 7am-5pm in summer).

El Charro, 311 N. Court Ave. (622-5465), 4 blocks north of the Civic Center. The oldest Mexican restaurant in Tucson. Tasty but not fiery sun-dried *carne seca* in various forms. Open Sun.-Thurs. 11am-9pm, Fri.-Sat. 11am-10pm.

El Minuto, 354 S. Main Ave. (882-4145), just south of the community center. Tucson's best late-night restaurant packed with locals. Open daily 11am-11pm.

Big Red's Cafe, 6372 S. Nogales Hwy. (889-8294). Welcome to the real deal. Big Ray's has some of the friendliest service in town and damn good BBQ sandwiches ($2.50-4). Open Mon.-Fri. 5am-2pm, Sat. 5am-1pm, Sun. 6am-5pm.

Café Poca Cosa, 20 S. Scott St. Near the visitors center, the intimate, casual setting is perfect for their lunch specials ($5). Open Mon.-Fri. 7:30am-2:30pm.

Mama Louisa's Lacantina Restaurant, 2041 S. Craycroft Rd. (790-4702). Palatable Italian at palatable prices. Open Sun.-Thurs. 11am-9pm, Fri.-Sat. 11am-10pm.

ENTERTAINMENT

Tucson is a musical smorgasboard. While UA students rock and roll on Speedway Blvd., more subdued folks do the two-step in several country music clubs on North

Oracle. Pick up a copy of the free *Tucson Weekly* or the weekend sections of *The Star* or *The Citizen* for current entertainment listings. Throughout the year, the city of the sun presents **Music Under the Stars,** a series of sunset concerts by the Tucson Symphony Orchestra. Call 792-9155 for concert dates and times. For milling and moseying head to **Downtown Saturday Night.** Blockaded on the first and third Saturdays of each month, Congress St. celebrates the arts with outdoor singers, crafts, and galleries. Call the Tucson Arts District (624-9977) for info.

Hotel Congress Historic Tap Room, 311 E. Congress (622-8848). Frozen in its 1938 incarnation. Eclectic—perhaps even weird—crowd, but very friendly. Open daily 11am-1am. Across the hall, the **Club Congress** has DJs with live music every night. Drink specials $1.25. Club opens 8pm.

Wild Wild West, 4385 W. Ina Rd. (744-7744), not accessible by public transportation. An authentic Old West saloon with continuous country-western music and the largest dance floor in Arizona. An acre of dancin' and romancin'. Buffet ($2) 5-7:30pm. Cover Fri.-Sat. $2 for women, $3 for men. Open daily 4pm-1am.

Berkey's, 5769 E. Speedway (296-1981). A smoke-filled blues and rock club. Open daily noon-1am. Live music nightly. Cover Fri.-Sat. $3.

Sweetwater Café, 340 E. 6th St. (622-6464). Cheap eats and live music. Open Mon.-Thurs. 11am-10pm, Fri.-Sat. 11am-11pm.

SIGHTS

The best place for a stroll in town is **4th Ave.** Lined with cafes, restaurants, galleries, and vintage clothing shops, the street is an alternative and artsy magnet. Between Speedway and Broadway, 4th Ave. becomes a historic shopping district with more touristy shops. The **Tucson Museum of Art,** 140 N. Main Ave. (624-2333), downtown, has an impressive collection of pre-Columbian art (open Mon.-Sat. 10am-4pm, Sun. noon-4pm; $2, seniors and students $1; free Tues.).

The **University of Arizona,** whose "mall" sits where E. 3rd St. should be, parades another main concentration of in-town attractions. The mall itself is lovely, less for the architecture than for the varied—and elaborately irrigated—vegetation. The **UA Visitors Center** (621-3621), at Cherry and the Mall, offers tours of campus. (Tours fall-spring Mon.-Fri.10am-2pm, Sat. at 10am; summer Mon.-Sat. at 10am.) Across the Mall, the **Flandrau Planetarium** (621-7827) has a museum and a public telescope, plus planetarium shows. (Eccentric hours for museum and shows; call ahead. Museum free; shows $4.50, seniors and students $4, kids 3-12 $2.50.) At the west end of campus, **University Blvd.** is jammed with shops catering to student needs.

A vibrant local event, the **mariachi mass,** thrills at **St. Augustine Church,** 192 S. Stone Ave. (623-6351), downtown. The singing and dancing take place in Tucson's old white Spanish cathedral, but is not intended as a tourist attraction. (Sun. 8am mass in Spanish.) **The Reid Park Zoo** (791-4022), on Broadway and Lake Shore Lane, is big with animals. (Open daily 9am-4pm. $3, seniors $2, kids 5-14 75¢.)

■ NEAR TUCSON

Pima's **Titan II Missile Museum,** 1580 W. Duvall Mine Rd. (791-2929), in Green Valley, 25 mi. south of Tucson, is a chilling monument built around a deactivated missile silo. (Open Wed.-Sun. 9am-4pm; Nov.-April daily 9am-5pm. $5, seniors and active military $4, ages 10-17 $3. Reservations advised.) The Southwest is the desert graveyard for many an outmoded aircraft; low humidity and sparse rainfall combine to preserve the relics. Over 20,000 warplanes, from WWII fighters to Vietnam War jets, are parked in ominous, silent rows at the **Davis-Monthan Air Force Base** (750-4570), 15 mi. southeast of Tucson. Take the Houghton exit off I-10, then travel west on Irvington to Wilmont. (Free tours Mon. and Wed. at 9am. Call ahead for reservations.) You can also view the 2-mi. long graveyard through the airfield fence.

Saguaro National Monument (296-8576), east of Tucson, is home base to those tall, gangly cacti you always see in Westerns and on the Arizona license plate. The park has an east and west wing. The visitors center in the east is at the **Rincon**

Mountain Unit (296-8576), on the Old Spanish Trail. (Open daily 8am-5pm. $4 per vehicle, $2 per pedestrian.) This section of Saguaro offers an 8-mi. scenic loop as well as trails. Backcountry campsites are available to those with free permits from the visitors center. To reach Saguaro East, take I-10 east to exit 279 and follow Vail Rd. to the Old Spanish Trail. The **Colossal Cave** (647-7275) on Vail Rd. is the only "dormant" cave in the U.S. 45-min. guided tours are given with flagstone walking and fluorescent lights. (Open Mon.-Sat. 8am-6pm, Sun. 8am-7pm; winter Mon.-Sat. 9am-5pm, Sun. 9am-6pm. $6.50, kiddies 11-16 $5, 6-10 $3.50.)

Saguaro's western half is called the **Tucson Mountain Unit** (883-6366), on N. Kinney Rd. at Rte. 9. This portion of the park has limited hiking trails for day-use only and an auto loop. (Visitors center open daily 8am-5pm.) Just south of this unit is the **Arizona-Sonora Desert Museum,** 2021 N. Kinney Rd. (883-2702), a naturalist's dream, which gives an up-close look at the flora and fauna of the Sonoran desert, including an excellent walk-though aviary, an underwater look at otters, and a beaver the size of a small cow. Take at least two hours to see the museum; the best time to visit is the cool morning hours when the animals have not begun their afternoon siesta. (Open daily 7:30am-6pm; winter 8:30am-5pm. $8, kids 6-12 $1.50.) The way to the Tucson Mountain Unit and the Desert Museum goes through **Gates Pass,** whose vistas make it a great spot for watching sunrises and sunsets.

Old Tucson Studios, 201 S. Kinney Rd. (883-0100), just south of the Desert Museum, is the Disneyland of the Southwest (open daily 9am-8pm; $12, kids 4-11 $8, after 5pm $8). The entire theme park was built as a set for the movie *Arizona.*

Sabino Canyon (749-2861), north of Tucson, has cliffs and waterfalls—an ideal spot for picnics and day hikes. (Tram through the canyon daily every ½ hr. 9am-4:30pm.) Call the canyon folk for best directions. **Sabino Canyon Tours,** 5900 N. Sabino Canyon Rd. (749-2327), runs a shuttle bus through the canyon ($5 Sat.-Sun. 9am-4:30pm every ½ hr., in summer Mon.-Fri. 9am-4pm every hr. on the hr.).

■■■ TOMBSTONE

One of most enjoyable tourist experiences in the country, "the town too tough to die" was founded by a gold and silver rush in the 1870s. Soon after, the Earp brothers rolled into town and, in the name of liberty and justice for all, had their shoot-out at the O.K. Corral with the Clanton gang. Once home to gunslingers Bat Masterson and Doc Holliday, Tombstone has lost little of its fire and ire.

To get to Tombstone, career your Conestoga to the Benson exit off I-10 and then south on Rte. 80. The **Tombstone Chamber of Commerce and Visitors Center** (457-3929) welcomes y'all at 4th and Allen (open daily 9am-5pm). The nearest **Greyhound** station (457-4390) is in **Benson** at The Sewing Basket on 4th St. **Amtrak** (800-872-7245) choochoos across the street. **Mr. Reynolds Taxi** (457-3897) drives from Benson to Tombstone ($15). Tombstone's **area code** is 602.

Old West fans can hit the hay at the **Hacienda Huachuca Motel,** 320 Bruce St. (457-2201 or 800-893-2201). John Wayne slept in room 4 during the 1963 shooting of *McLintock* (singles or doubles $27). You no longer need to sleep with a pistol under your pillow at **Trail Rider's Inn,** 13 N. 7th St. (457-3573; singles $25-32, $5 each additional person). The **Round-up Trailer Ranch,** 201 W. Allen St. (457-3738), has sites for $10 and RV spots for $12.50. Or try the **Tombstone KOA** (457-3829 or 800-348-3829) on Rte. 80 just north of town (sites $17, RV spots $18-21).

Get some victuals at **Ol' Miner's BBQ and Cafe,** 10 S. 5th St. (457-3488; fickle hours). **Blake's Char-Broiled Burgers and BBQ Ranch,** 511B Allen St. (457-3646), slaps the cow on the bun starting at $3. (Open Tues.-Sat. 11am-7pm, Sun.-Mon. 11am-6pm.) **Don Teodoro's,** 15 N. 4th St. (457-3647), has Mexican plates for less than $5 (open daily 11am-9pm). For a bit of moonshine and country music, smell your way to **Big Nose Kate's Saloon** (457-3107) on Allen. Named for "the girl that loved Doc Holliday and everyone else too." (Open daily 10am-midnight.)

Browse through the saloons, western wear, and curio shops on Allen St. **The O.K. Corral** (457-3456), on Allen next to City Park, is where it all happened (open daily

8:30am-5pm; $2). The tastefully-named **Tombstone Historama** (457-3456) depicts the town history with animated figures on a revolving (did someone say revolver? DRAW!) stage. The whole deal is powered by the "miracle of missile-age electronics" (shows every hr. on the hr. daily 9am-4pm, $2). "Bargain special" tickets will get you into this and most of the town's sights for $4. The **Tombstone Courthouse** (457-3311), on 3rd and Toughnut, is where marshals such as John Slaughter battled scores of outlaws. (Open daily 8am-5pm. $2, kids 12-18 $1, kids free.) The **Rose Tree Museum** (457-3326), on 4th and Toughnut, has the largest rose tree in the world. (Open daily 9am-5:30pm. $1.50, under 14 free.) See the **tombstones** of Tombstone on Rte. 80 just north of town (open daily 7:30am-7pm; free).

Re-enactments of famous gunfights are performed by the **Boothill Gunslingers,** the **Wild Bunch,** and the **Vigilantes/Vigilettes.** Arrange with one of these groups to treat a friend or relative to a **public mock hanging.** Mock gunfights occur every Sunday at 2pm in the streets or at the O.K. Corral. Call the visitors center for more info on these groups. Many **ghost towns** lie within short driving distance of Tombstone. Empty and haunting, they are not to be missed; pick up a map at the visitors center.

Utah

Once home to dinosaurs, Utah now beckons bipedal mammals to its variegated landscape, which ranges from a vast salt lake to a multitude of bizarre rock formations. Southern Utah has an amazing array of redstone canyons, deep river gorges, arches, spires, and columns carved out of the terrain by wind and water. Northeastern and central Utah feature the Uinta Mountains, dotted with lakes and speckled with aspens and ponderosa pine. Finally, the dinosaurs are still with us at Dinosaur National Monument, on the border with Colorado. Utah's human history is equally colorful. Driven westward by religious persecution, the Mormons began settling Utah—which they called *Deseret*—in 1848. Today, Mormons make up over 70% of the state's population.

PRACTICAL INFORMATION

Capital: Salt Lake City.

Utah Travel Council, 300 N. State St., Salt Lake City 84114 (538-1030), across the street from the capitol building. Information on national and state parks, campgrounds, and accommodations. Open summer Mon.-Fri. 8am-5pm. Pick up a free copy of the *Utah Travel Guide*, with a complete listing of motels, national parks, and campgrounds. **Utah Parks and Recreation,** 1636 W. North Temple, Salt Lake City 86116 (538-7220). Open Mon.-Fri. 8am-5pm.

Alcohol: Utah has weird alcohol laws. Beer for take-out can be purchased at food stores and convenience stores only. Because of licenses and zoning laws, you may have to move down a bar 10 ft. to get a mixed drink. No alcohol may be taken into Utah from another state.

Time Zone: Mountain (2 hr. behind Eastern). **Postal Abbreviation:** UT
Sales Tax: 6.25%.

NORTHERN UTAH

■■■ SALT LAKE CITY

On July 24, 1847, Brigham Young led a group of Mormon pioneers to find a place where they could practice their religion free from the persecution they faced in the

East. When Young first saw the valley of the Great Salt Lake, he said, "This is the right place." Today, the "This is the Place" monument commemorates the famous utterance. Salt Lake City is the spiritual center of the Church of Latter Day Saints, and the home of the Mormon Temple and the Tabernacle Choir. Despite its commitment to preserving traditions, Salt Lake is a booming modern city whose proximity to the mountains makes it a favorite base town for skiers and outdoor enthusiasts.

PRACTICAL INFORMATION

Emergency: 911.

Visitor Information: Salt Lake Valley Convention and Visitors Bureau, 180 S. West Temple (521-2868), 2 blocks south of Temple Sq. Open Mon.-Sat. 8am-6pm; off-season Mon.-Sat. 8am-5:30pm. Pick up the *Salt Lake Visitors Guide.*

Airport: Salt Lake City International, 776 N. Terminal Dr. (575-2600), 4 mi. west of Temple Sq. UTA buses provide the best means of transport to and from the airport. Bus #50 serves the terminal directly to and from downtown.

Amtrak: 325 S. Río Grande (364-8562). To: Las Vegas ($89), L.A. ($111). Tickets sold Mon.-Sat. 4-9:30am, 10am-12:30pm and 4:15pm-1am; Sun. 4pm-1am.

Greyhound: 160 W. South Temple (800-231-2222), 1 block west of Temple Sq. To Las Vegas ($50), L.A. ($82). Tickets sold daily 5am-10pm. Terminal open 24 hrs.

Public Transport: Utah Transit Authority, 600 S. 700 West (287-4636 until 7pm). Frequent service to the University of Utah campus; buses to Ogden (#70/72 express), suburbs, airport, and east to the mountain canyons and Provo (#4 local or #1 express; fare $1.50). Buses every ½ hr. or more 6:30am-11pm. Fare 65¢, seniors 30¢ under 5 free. Get maps at libraries or the visitors bureau.

Taxi: Ute Cab, 359-7788. **Yellow Cab,** 521-2100. $1.25 base fare, $1.50 per mi., about $14 from the airport to Temple Sq.

Car Rental: Payless Car Rental, 1974 W. North Temple (596-2596). $25 per day with 200 free mi., $120 per week with 1200 free mi.; 14¢ per additional mi. Open Sun.-Fri. 6am-10pm, Sat. 8am-6pm. Must be 21 with a major credit card.

Bike Rental: Wasatch Touring, 702 E. 100 South (359-9361). 21-speed mountain bikes $20 per day. Open Mon.-Sat. 9am-7pm.

Help Lines: Rape Crisis, 467-7273. 24 hrs.

Post Office: 230 W. 200 South (974-2200), 1 block west of the visitors bureau. Open Mon.-Fri. 8am-5:30pm, Sat. 9am-2pm. **ZIP code:** 84101.

Area Code: 801.

Salt Lake's grid system makes navigation simple. Brigham Young designated **Temple Square** as the heart of downtown. Street names indicate how many blocks east, west, north, or south they lie from Temple Square. **Main Street,** running north-south, and **South Temple Street,** running east-west, are the "0" points. Local address listings exclude the hundred at the end of each numbered street—800 E. 13 South means 800 E. 1300 South. Smaller streets and streets that do not fit the grid pattern often have non-numeric names. Occasionally, a numbered street reaches a dead end, only to resume a few blocks farther on. The downtown is equipped with audible traffic lights for the convenience of blind pedestrians.

ACCOMMODATIONS AND CAMPING

The Avenues (HI-AYH), 107 F St. (363-8137), 7 blocks east of Temple Sq. Bright rooms with 4 bunks each or private singles and doubles. Popular with British and German students. Blankets and linens provided. Kitchen and laundry available. Check-in daily 8am-2:30pm and 6-10pm. Dorm rooms with shared bath $12, non-members $14. Singles with private bath $22. Doubles $32.

Ute Hostel, 19 E. Kelsey Ave. (595-1645). Free pickups can be arranged from Amtrak, Greyhound, or the visitors information center. Free tea and coffee, parking, linen, and safety deposit. Check-in 24 hrs. Dorm rooms are $13, doubles $35.

Kendell Motel, 667 N. 300 West (355-0293), 10 blocks northwest of Temple Sq. From airport take #50 bus to N. Temple, then #70 bus. From Greyhound or downtown, take #70. Well-kept rooms with kitchens, color TV, and A/C $25, doubles $35. Huge dorm-style rooms with kitchen and nice bath for $15 per person.

Motel 6, 3 locations: 176 W. 600 South (531-1252); 1990 W. North Temple (364-1053), 2½ mi. from the airport (take bus #50); and 496 N. Catalpa (561-0058), just off I-15. Singles $32. Doubles $39.

Dean's Motor Lodge, 1821 S. Main (486-7495). Basic rooms with A/C, heat, and TV with HBO. Check out the cute lobby. Singles and doubles $30-40.

Camping is available outside the city. The **Wasatch-Cache National Forest** (524-5030) skirts Salt Lake City on the east, offering many established sites. Make reservations through MISTIX (800-283-2267). The terrain by the city is quite steep, making the best sites those on the far side of the mountains. Three of the closest campgrounds are in the **Mount Olympus Wilderness** (within the W-C National Forest), off of Rte. 210 east of the city: **Box Elder** (35 sites), **Terraces** (25 sites), and **Bigwater Trailhead** (45 sites). Just north of the city on I-15, outside of the towns of Bountiful and Farmington, there are four campgrounds: **Sunset** (32 sites), **Bountiful Park** (79 sites), **Buckland Flat** (26 sites), and **Mueller Park** (63 sites). Go early on weekends to ensure a space (sites $7-8). The **Utah Travel Council** (538-1030) has detailed information on all campsites in the area. **East Canyon State Park** (829-6866), 30 mi. from Salt Lake, near the junction of Rtes. 65 and 66, has 31 sites by East Canyon Reservoir—a good place to go boating and fishing (sites $9). If you need a hookup, try the **KOA,** 1400 W. North Temple (355-1192; 60 tent sites, 290 RV sites $18, with water and electricity $21, full hookup $23).

FOOD

Affordable food abounds in Salt Lake City. Fill up on **scones,** adopted from the British and made into a Utah specialty. Otherwise stick to ethnic food downtown or the cheap, slightly greasy eateries on the outer fringe. The two (literally) opposing main shopping malls, ZCMI Mall, and Crossroads Mall on Main St., have food courts.

Río Grande Cafe, 270 Río Grande (364-3302), in the Río Grande Railroad depot, 4 blocks west of the Temple, near Amtrak and the Historical Society. Take bus #16 or 17. Stylish, fun Mexican restaurant with neon-and-glass decor. Huge combination plates $6. Open for lunch Mon.-Sat. 11:30am-2:30pm and for dinner Mon.-Thurs. 5-10pm, Fri-Sat. 5-10:30pm, Sun. 4-10pm.

Park Café, 604 E. 1300 South (487-1670), near Liberty Park. A classy little joint with a patio and a view of a park. Lunches about $6, dinners a bit pricier ($10), but they offer "light" meals like chicken quesadillas ($6). Open for breakfast Mon.-Fri. 7-11:30am, Sat.-Sun. 7am-3pm. Lunch Mon.-Sat. 11:30am-3pm. Dinner Mon.-Thurs. 5-9pm, Fri.-Sat. 5-10pm.

Bill and Nada's Cafe, 479 S. 600th St. (354-6984), right by Trolley Sq. One of Salt Lake's most revered cafes. Patsy Cline on the jukebox and paper placemats of U.S. presidents on the tables. Two eggs, hash browns, toast $3. Roast leg of lamb, salad, soup, vegetable, roll, and potatoes $5.35. Open 24 hrs.

Salt Lake Roasting Company, 249 E. 400 South (363-7572). Funky jazz and classical music amidst burlap bags of coffee beans. Caters to the twentysomething set. Coffee (85¢); quiche ($3); soup ($1.50). Open Mon.-Sat. 6:45am-midnight.

The Sconecutter, 2040 S. State St. (485-9981). The Elvis of sconemakers. Your favorite flavor of fluffy, stuffing scone ($1). Try the cinnamon and butter. Restaurant open Sun.-Thurs. 7am-midnight, Fri.-Sat. 7am-3am. Drive-thru open 24 hrs.

MORMON SIGHTS

Salt Lake City is home to the **Church of Jesus Christ of Latter Day Saints,** whose followers hold both the *Book of Mormon* and the *Bible* to be the word of God. The highest Mormon authority and the central temple reside here. **Temple Square** (240-2534) is the symbolic center of the Mormon religion. Feel free to wander around the flowery and pleasant 10-acre square, but the sacred temple is off-limits to non-Mormons. Alighting on the highest of the building's three towers, a golden statue of the angel Moroni watches over the city. The square has two **visitors centers** (north and south), and a 45-min. **Historical Tour** leaves from the south visitors center every 10 min. 30-min. **Book of Mormon Tours** and **Purpose of Temple Tours** leave alternately every 30 min. and explain the religious meaning behind Temple Square. (Visitors centers open daily 8am-10pm; off-season 9am-9pm.)

Visitors on any tour in Temple Square may visit the **Mormon Tabernacle,** which houses the famed Choir. Built in 1867, the structure is so acoustically sensitive that a pin dropped at one end can be heard 175 ft. away at the other end. Rehearsals on Thursday evening (8pm) and Sunday morning broadcasts from the tabernacle are open to the public (9:30-10am; doors close at 9:15am). Though supremely impressive, the Choir can't match the size and sound of the 11,623-pipe organ that accompanies it. (Recitals Mon.-Sat. at noon; summer Sun. 2pm as well.) **Assembly Hall,** next door, also hosts various concerts almost every summer evening.

Around the perimeter of Temple Sq. stand several other buildings commemorating Mormon history. The **Genealogical Library,** 35 N. West Temple (240-2331), provides resources for Mormons and others to research their lineage, in accordance with Mormon belief that ancestors must be baptized by proxy to seal them into an eternal family. If you've ever wanted to research your roots, this is the place; the library houses the largest collection of genealogical documents in the world. An orientation film is available. (Open Mon. 7:30am-6pm, Tues.-Sat. 7:30am-10pm Free.)

The **Museum of Church History and Art,** 45 N. West Temple (240-3310), houses Mormon memorabilia from 1820 to the present. (Open Mon.-Fri. 9am-9pm, Sat.-Sun. and holidays 10am-7pm. Free.) Once the official residence of Brigham Young while he served as "governor" of the Deseret Territory (unrecognized by the U.S. government) and president of the Church, the **Beehive House,** (240-2671) N. Temple, at State St., two blocks east of Temple Sq., gives half-hour guided tours every 10-15 min. (Open Mon.-Fri. 9:30am-6:30pm, Sat. 9:30am-4:30pm, Sun. 10am-1pm; Sept.-May Mon.-Sat. 9:30am-4:30pm, Sun. 10am-1pm. Closes 1pm on all holidays. Free.)

The city of Salt Lake encompasses the **Pioneer Trail State Park,** 2601 Sunnyside Ave. (584-8391), in Emigration Canyon on the eastern end of town. Take bus #4 or follow 8th South St. until it becomes Sunnyside Ave., then take Monument Rd. The **"This is the Place" Monument** commemorates Brigham Young's decision to settle here. A **visitors center** will tell you all about the Mormons' long march through Ohio, Illinois, and Nebraska. Tour **Brigham Young's forest farmhouse** (open daily 11am-5pm), where the leader held court with his numerous wives. (Park grounds open in summer daily 8am-8pm, but visit 9am-7:30pm for the best reception. Entrance fee charged from 10:30am-4:30pm, $1.50, ages 6-15 $1.)

SECULAR SIGHTS AND ACTIVITIES

The grey-domed **capitol** lies behind the spires of Temple Square. (538-1563; tours are offered Mon.-Fri. 9am-3pm.) For more info, contact the **Council Hall Visitors Center** (538-1030), across from the main entrance. (Open Mon.-Fri. 8am-5pm, Sat.-Sun. and holidays 10am-5pm.) While in the capitol area, hike up City Creek Canyon to **Memory Grove,** savoring the shade as you gaze out over the city, or stroll down to the **Church of Jesus Christ of Latter Day Saints Office Building,** 50 E. North Temple, and take the elevator to the 26th-floor **observation deck** (240-3789) from which you can see the Great Salt Lake to the west, and the Wasatch Mountain Range to the east (open Mon.-Sat. 9am-4:30pm). Also on capitol hill is the **Hansen Planetarium,** 15 S. State St. (538-2098 or 538-2104). Even if you don't pay for a show, enjoy the fabulous free exhibits. (Open Sun.-Thurs. 9am-10pm, Fri.-Sat. 9am-1am.) Head for the **Children's Museum,** 840 N. 300 West (328-3383), to pilot a 727 jet or implant a Jarvik artificial heart in a life-sized "patient." (Open Mon. 9:30am-9pm, Tues.-Sat. 9:30am-5pm, Sun. noon-5pm. $3, ages 2-13 $2.15. Adult $1.50, kids $1 after 5pm Mon. Take bus #61.) You also can walk through the University of Utah campus to the **Utah Museum of Natural History,** 215 South and 1350 East (581-4303), which catalogues the variety of flora and fauna that has lived on the Salt Lake plain. (Open Mon.-Thurs. 9:30am-5:30pm, Fri. 9:30am-9pm, Sat. 9:30am-5:30pm, holidays noon-5pm. $6, under 14 $3.) Next door is the yard-sale-like collection at the **Utah Museum of Fine Arts** (581-7332; open Mon.-Fri. 10am-5pm, Sat.-Sun. 2-5pm;

free). For university happenings, contact the **Information Desk** in the U. of Utah Park Administration Building (581-6515; open Mon.-Fri. 9am-4pm), or the **Olpin Student Center** (581-5888; open Mon.-Sat. 8am-9pm).

Pioneer Memorial Museum, 300 North Main St. (538-1050), next to the state capitol, has relics of the earliest settlers in the valley (guns, books, clothing) and gives insight into the two most prominent Mormon leaders: Brigham Young and his first counselor, Heber C. Kimball. (Open Mon.-Sat. 9am-5pm, Sun. 1-5pm; Sept.-May Mon.-Sat. 9am-5pm. Free.) Next to the Amtrak station, the **Utah State Historical Society,** 300 Río Grande (533-3500), hosts an interesting series of exhibits, including pre-Mormon photographs and quilts. (Open Mon.-Fri. 8am-5pm. Free.)

The **Utah Symphony Orchestra** (533-6407) performs in Abravanel Hall, 123 W. South Temple. (Concert tickets $13-19 in summer, $14-35 in winter; student rush tickets $6.) Dance and opera performances occur at the neighboring **Salt Lake Art Center** (328-4201; open Mon.-Sat. 10am-5pm, Sun. 1-5pm; donation).

ALCOHOL AND NIGHTLIFE

A number of hotels and restaurants have licenses to sell mini-bottles and splits of wine, but consumers must make drinks themselves. Most restaurants serve just beer, and public bars serve only beer. Only private clubs requiring membership fees are allowed to serve mixed drinks. Some clubs have two-week trial memberships for $5; others will give a free, temporary membership to visitors in town for a night or two. In most cases you need a sponsor to become a member or guest. Most locals are aware that the laws of their state are unusual and offer their sponsorship to friendly strangers. The drinking age of 21 is well-enforced. (State liquor stores open Mon.-Sat. 10am-10pm. There are 6 within 3 mi. of downtown Salt Lake City.)

Despite the alcohol restrictions, there are several fun downtown bars and clubs. Pick up a free copy of *Private Eye Weekly* or *The Event,* both available at bars and restaurants, for local club listings and events. The **Dead Goat Saloon,** 165 S. West Temple (328-4628), attracts tourists and locals alike. (Open Mon.-Fri. 11:30am-2am, Sat. 6pm-2am, Sun. 7pm-1am. Beer served until 1am. No BYOB. Cover $2-4, Fri.-Sun. $5.) Head over to the **X Wife's Place,** 465 S. 700 East (532-2353), to shoot stick. (Open Mon.-Fri. 11:30am-1am, Sat. 5pm-1am. Beer and mixed drinks served.) No cover, but you'll need a club membership ($15 per year) or get a member to sponsor you. **Club DV8,** 115 S. West Temple (539-8400), deviates from the straight and narrow. Friday is college night. From 9-10pm on Saturday, drafts are 25¢. (Open Thurs.-Sat. 9pm-2am; ½-price drafts from 9-10pm; Thurs. is modern music night. Cover $1.) **The Zephyr,** 79 W. 300 South (355-2582), blows with live rock and reggae nightly. (Open daily 7pm-2am; off-season daily 7pm-1am. Cover $5-10.) **Junior's Tavern,** 202 E. 500 South (322-0318), is the favorite local watering hole for jazz and blues aficionados. (Open daily noon-1am. Music starts at 9pm. No cover.)

■ NEAR SALT LAKE CITY

The **Great Salt Lake,** 17 mi. west of town on I-80 (exit 104), a remnant of primordial Lake Bonneville, is a bowl of salt water in which only blue-green algae and brine shrimp can survive. The salt content varies from 5-15% and provides such buoyancy that it is almost impossible for the human body to sink; only the Dead Sea has a higher salt content. Unfortunately, flooding sometimes closes the state parks and beaches on the lakeshore, but you can still try **Saltair Beach,** 17 mi. to the west, or head north 40 min. to fresh-water **Willard Bay.** Bus #37 ("Magna") will take you within 4 mi. of the lake. Be warned that the aroma around the lake ain't rosy. Contact the visitors center (see Practical Information) or the **Great Salt Lake State Park** (250-1898) for how to access the lake, as it is difficult to reach without a car.

In the summer, escape the heat with a drive or hike to the cool breezes and icy streams of the nearby mountains. One of the prettiest roads over the Wasatch Range is **Route 210.** Heading east from Sandy, 12 mi. southeast of the city, this road goes up **Little Cottonwood Canyon** to the Alta ski resort. The **Lone Peak Wilderness**

Area stretches away southward from the road, around which the range's highest peaks tower, at over 11,000 ft. **City Creek, Millcreek,** and **Big Cottonwood** also make good spots for a picnic or hike.

Of the seven **ski resorts** within 40 min. of Salt Lake City, **Snowbird** (521-6040; lift tickets $39) and **Park City** (649-8111; lift tickets $44) are two of the classiest. For a more affordable alternative, try nearby **Alta** (742-3333; lift tickets $25). The **Alta Peruvian Lodge** (328-8589) is a great place to pass the night. They offer a $125 package which includes a bed, all meals, service charge, tax, and lift tickets. You can ski Snowbird, Deer Valley, and Alta from the **Alpine Prospectors Lodge,** 151 Main St. (649-3483 or 800-457-3591), in Park City. (Singles $25-49, doubles $35-59, depending on season; more for private bath. Also offers packages including 3 lift tickets and 4 nights for $198 per person; breakfast included.) **UTA** (see Practical Information above) runs buses from Salt Lake City to the resorts in winter, with pick-ups at downtown motels; **Lewis Bros. Stages** (800-826-5844) is one of many shuttle services providing transport to Park City, departing the airport every 30 min. in winter and five times per day in summer ($18, $36 round-trip). You can rent equipment from **Breeze Ski Rentals** (800-525-0314), at Snowbird and Park City ($15; 10% discount if reserved; lower rates for rentals over 3 days). Call or write the Utah Travel Council (see Utah: Practical Information above). Ask for the free *Ski Utah* for listings of ski packages and lodgings.

Some resorts offer summer attractions as well. You can rent mountain bikes at **Snowbird** (see above) for $22 per day or $15 per half-day. Snowbird's **aerial tram** climbs to 11,000 ft., offering a spectacular view of the Wasatch Mountains and the Salt Lake Valley below. (Open daily 11am-8pm. $8, kids 5-16 $6, seniors and under 5 free.) Mountain bikes can ride the tram for $4 a trip, $9 a day, or with a $32 10-ride punch card. During the summer, **Park City** offers a thrilling ½ mi. of curves and drops on their **alpine slide**. (Open Mon.-Fri. noon-10pm, Sat.-Sun. 10am-10pm. $5.50, seniors and kids $4. Take I-80 east 30 mi. from Salt Lake.)

■■■ DINOSAUR NATIONAL MONUMENT

Dinosaur National Monument is more than just a heap of bones. The Green and Yampa Rivers have here created vast, colorful gorges and canyons, and the harsh terrain evokes eerie visions of its reptilian past. Pick up the monument visitors guide *Echoes* for more detailed information.

Practical Information The park **entrance fee** is $5 per car, $2 for bikers, pedestrians, and those in tour buses. The more interesting western side lies along Rte. 149 off U.S. 40 just outside of **Jensen,** 30 mi. east of Vernal. The eastern side of the park is accessible only from a road off U.S. 40, outside **Dinosaur, CO.** The **Dinosaur National Monument Headquarters,** (303-374-2216) on U.S. 40 in Dinosaur, CO, at the intersection with the park road, provides orientation for exploring the canyonlands of the park and information on nearby river rafting. (Open daily 8am-4:30pm; Sept.-May Mon.-Fri. 8am-4:30pm.) For more information on the eastern side of the park, write to the **Monument Superintendent,** P.O. Box 210, Dinosaur, CO 81610. For additional info and maps, call 800-845-3466.

Greyhound makes daily runs east and west along U.S. 40 (2 per day each way), stopping in Vernal and Dinosaur en route from Denver and Salt Lake City. Jensen is a flag stop, as is the monument headquarters, 2 mi. west of Dinosaur. In an **emergency,** call 789-2115 (Utah) or 374-2216 (Colorado). Dino's **post office:** 198 Stegosaurus Dr. (303-374-2353; open Mon.-Fri. 8:30am-12:30pm and 1-5pm); **ZIP code:** 81610; **area code:** 801.

Camping and Accommodations For the low-down on campgrounds call 789-2115. A few miles beyond the Quarry Center on Rte. 149 you'll find the shady

Green River Campground (80 sites) with flush toilets, drinking water, and tent and RV sites. (Open late spring-early fall. Sites $8.) There are also several free primitive campsites in and around the park; call the visitors center for info. A rugged 13 mi. east of Harper's Corner, in the park's eastern half, is **Echo Campground** (9 sites), the perfect location for a crystalline evening under the stars. Watch for signs near Harper's Corner leading to a dirt road into the valley below (free). For **backcountry camping,** obtain a free permit from the headquarters or from Quarry Center.

The **Park Motel,** 105 E. Brontosaurus Blvd. (303-374-2267), offers singles for $20, doubles for $22, and two beds for $26 (closed Nov. 15-April).

Sights and Activities The **Dinosaur Quarry** (789-2115), 7 mi. from the intersection with U.S. 40 on the western side of the park, is accessible from the road by free shuttle bus or a fairly strenuous ½-mi. walk (cars prohibited in summer). A hill inside the center has been partially excavated to reveal the hulking remains of dinosaurs. (Center open daily 8am-4:30pm, in summer until 7pm. You can drive your car in after closing.) Winter finds the park lonely, cold, and fossilized with neither shuttle service nor the possibility of self-guided tours.

Past the campgrounds on Rte. 149, just beyond the end of the road, you can see one of the best examples of the monument's many Native American **petroglyphs.** The most accessible rock art is at **Club Creek** (a few miles east of Quarry Visitors Center), but the finest petroglyph panels are at **McKee Spring.** You can also see relics of ancient cultures, such as pot shards at **Jones Hole Trail,** and remains of granaries and other storage structures at **Yampa Canyon.**

The 25-mi. road (closed in winter) to majestic **Harper's Corner,** at the junction of the Green and Yampa River gorges, begins 2 mi. east of Dinosaur. From the road's terminus, a 2-mi. round-trip nature hike leaves for the corner itself. It's worth the sweat; the view is one of the most spectacular in all of Utah.

■■■ FLAMING GORGE NATIONAL RECREATION AREA

Wild horses roam the north desert of Flaming Gorge country, a reminder of mountain pioneers who once settled here on the western frontier. A combination of the Uinta Mountains and the Wyoming deserts, Flaming Gorge offers hiking, fishing, and climbing. The Flaming Gorge National Recreation Area is part of the Ashley National Forest, which expands across southwest Wyoming and northeast Utah. The area's center is marked by the Flaming Gorge Reservoir, a 91-mi.-long lake created by a towering dam built on the Green River in the 1960s.

Practical Information From Wyoming, the most scenic route to the gorge is the amazing **U.S. 191** south from I-80 (exit between Rock Springs and Green River). Rte. 530 closely parallels the reservoir's western shore, but the scenery is not as compelling. Take this route only if you want to camp on the flat beaches of the lake's Wyoming section. To reach Flaming Gorge from the south, take U.S. 191 north from Vernal, over the gorgeous flanks of the Uinta Mountains (see below), to **Dutch John, UT.** Much of the recreation area is in Wyoming, but Utah has the most scenic and best-developed area of the park, at the base of the Uinta Range. The **Flaming Gorge Visitors Center** (885-3135), on U.S. 191 right on the top of Flaming Gorge Dam, offers guided tours of the dam area along with maps of the area (open daily 8am-6pm; off-season 9am-5pm; $1). The **Red Canyon Visitors Center** (889-3713), a few mi. off U.S. 191 on Rte. 44 to Manila, perches 1360 ft. above Red Canyon and Flaming Gorge Lake. (Open daily 10am-5pm; closed winter.)

Camping and Accommodations Inexpensive **campgrounds** abound in the Flaming Gorge area; reservations for large groups can be made by calling MISTIX (800-283-2267). You can camp next to the Red Canyon Visitors Center in **Canyon**

Rim Campground (18 sites, $8), or in one of the numerous national forest camp-grounds along U.S. 191 and Rte. 44 in the Utah portion of the park (sites $7-10; 2-week max. stay). **Buckboard Crossing** (307-875-6927; 68 sites, $8) and **Lucerne Valley** (801-784-3293; 143 sites, $10), located further north, tend to be drier and unshaded, but are close to the marinas on the reservoir. Either visitors center can offer you heaps of information on camping. There are a number of free, primitive campgrounds in the high country. You do not necessarily have to camp at a devel-oped site; just check with the rangers to make sure the spot you pick is kosher.

If you'd rather sleep indoors, **Red Canyon Lodge** (889-3759), west on Rte. 44, 2 mi. before the visitors center, offers reasonably priced rustic cabins. Frontier cabins share bath facilities (singles $28, doubles $38); deluxe cabins have a private bath (singles $42, doubles $52; $5 for a roll-away). **Flaming Gorge Lodge,** near the dam in Dutch John (889-3773), offers upscale rooms, with A/C and cable TV, for upscale prices (singles $49, doubles $55; Nov.-Feb. singles $33, doubles $39).

Sights and Activities Try your hand at fishing along the Green River Gorge below the dam. More than ½ million trout are stocked annually in Flaming Gorge Lake. The Green River offers some of the best fly-fishing in the country. For Green River fishing you must obtain a **permit** (available at Flaming Gorge Lodge and at sev-eral stores in Manila). For more information, call the **Utah Department of Wildlife Resources,** 152 E. 100 North (789-3103; open Mon.-Fri. 8am-5pm) in Salt Lake City. You can rent fishing rods and boats at **Cedar Springs Marina** (889-3795), 3 mi. before the dam in Dutch John. (Fishing boats $40 for 3 hr., $55 for 6 hr., $65 daily. Rods $5 with a boat. Pontoons also available. Open May-Sept. Mon.-Fri. 8am-6:30pm.) At **Lucerne Valley Marina** (784-3483), in Manila, you can get small, 14-ft. fishing boats for $35 a day (open Mon.-Fri. 8am-6:30pm). **Dan River Hatch Expedi-tions,** 55 E. Main (789-4316 or 800-342-8243), in Vernal, offers a wide variety of summer rafting trips (1-day voyage $55, under 12 $45).

For a hide-out from tourists, the large valley of **Brown's Park,** 23 mi. east of Flam-ing Gorge, is the answer. Four-wheel drive is recommended. The valley's isolation was a magnet for 19th century western outlaws—Butch Cassidy and his Wild Bunch found it ideally located near three state lines for evading the law. Free campsites (no water) are located within ¼ mi. of the park in either direction: **Indian Crossing,** just up the Green River, and **Indian Hollow,** just downstream. The river's shore is an idyllic place to camp or just stop for a while. To get to Brown's Park from Dutch John, head north about 10 mi. on U.S. 191 until you reach Minnie's Gap, from here follow the signs to Clay Basin (13 mi.) and to the park (23 mi.).

■■■ VERNAL

Vernal, 16 mi. west of Dinosaur National Monument on U.S. 40, is a popular base for exploring the attractions Flaming Gorge and the Uinta Mountains. Lest you forget how close it is to Dinosaur National Monument, thousands of plastic replicas lining the strip of highway that makes up this town will remind you. Stop in at the **visitors center** at the Utah Fieldhouse of Natural History and Dinosaur Garden, 235 W. Main St. (789-4002), which offers brochures and helpful advice on day trips in the area (open daily 8am-9pm). The **Ashley National Forest Service,** 355 N. Vernal Ave. (789-1181), has jurisdiction over much of this area, including most campgrounds. (Open Mon.-Fri. 8am-5pm, Sat. 8am-4:30pm.)

The **Sage Motel,** 54 W. Main St. (789-1442), has big, clean rooms and cable TV. (Singles $30. Doubles $42.) **Dine-A-Ville Motel,** 801 W. Main St. (789-9571), at the far west end of town, is less centrally located, but the cheapest in town. Nice rooms with color TV and kitchenettes. (Singles $26. Doubles $32.)

Camping might be a better alternative for those on a tight budget. **Vernal KOA,** 1800 W. Sheraton Ave. (789-8935), off U.S. 40 south of town, has a store, laundry, pool, and all the amenities of the typical KOA. (Tent sites $13, with water and elec-tricity $14, full hookup $17.) **Campground Dina RV Park,** 930 N. Vernal Ave., about 1 mi. north of Main St. on U.S. 191 (789-2148), is more basic. (Tent sites about $6.50 per person, with water and electricity $17.50, full hookup $19.)

The **Open Hearth Donut Shop,** 360 E. Main St. (789-0274), has homemade donuts (37¢ each, $3.70 per dozen) and large sub sandwiches ($2.75). (Open Mon.-Fri. 5:30am-6pm, Sat. 5:30am-1pm.) The **7-11 Ranch Restaurant,** 77 E. Main St. (789-1170), serves good food, including a big breakfast consisting of two eggs, hash-browns, and toast ($2.50) and entrees with salad, vegetable, and bread from $6.

In town, the **Utah Fieldhouse of Natural History and Dinosaur Garden,** 235 Main St. (789-3799), offers excellent displays on the state's geological and natural history. The dinosaur garden features life-size models. Check out the geological dis-plays where fluorescent minerals make your shoelaces glow in the dark. (Open daily 8am-9pm; off-season daily 9am-5pm. $1.50, ages 6-15 $1.)

SOUTHERN UTAH

Gaping canyons, sculpted mountains, towering ridges, and a stunning terrain of sandstone arches and mesas cover Southern Utah. These are the lands that were home to the Anasazi, Ute, and Navajo, and are still home to the Navajo reservation. The terra is definitely hotta, but is also some of the most breathtaking on earth. Retrace the steps of natural history through the miles of fabulously-colored rock which tell a story millions of years old.

Finding the Fab Five Follow these roads to and through the five National Parks that cover this majestic area. From Moab take U.S. 191 north to **Arches.** Back on U.S. 191 continue north to Rte. 313 south which takes you to **Canyonlands, Islands in the Sky** (60 mi.). Again on 191 north take I-70 west, exit 147, follow Rte. 24 south to Hanksville and then west to **Capitol Reef.** Take Rte. 24 west to Torrey and then scenic Rte. 12 south and west through **Dixie National Forest** to **Bryce Canyon.** Continue on Rte. 12 west to U.S. 89 south through Mt. Carmel Junction and pick up Rte. 9 west to **Zion.**

There are two national forests in Southern Utah. Both are divided into districts near and far from the national parks and serve as excellent places to stay on a cross-country jaunt. **Manti La Sal National Forest** has two sections near Arches and the Needles section of Canyonlands. **Dixie National Forest** stretches from Capitol Reef, through Bryce, all the way to the western side of Zion. Check below in the Camping sections of these parks for additional sites and information.

■■■ MOAB

Originally founded by the Mormons, Moab flourished in the 1950s due to its abun-dance of uranium. The town has since adapted itself to the tourist industry; perhaps too well—the golden arches of McDonald's on Main St. are as prominent as the sandstone arches of the town's environs. Big Macs aside, Moab attracts a multitude of hippies and hyper-athletes alike. With its proximity to Arches and Canyonlands, and its youthful, "crunchy" character, the town of Moab provides a great base for exploring southern Utah, either by car, mountain bike, or raft on the Green River.

Practical Information Moab is 50 mi. southeast of I-70 on U.S. 191, 5 mi. south of Arches. There is no public transportation to Moab. The nearest **Amtrak** stops at Thompson, 41 mi. northeast of town, and **Greyhound** rides out to Green River, 52 mi. northwest of Moab. Some buses will stop along I-70, in Crescent Junc-tion, 30 mi. north of town. From these distant points your best bet is a taxi, or check to see if your hotel or hostel will pick you up for a small fee. **Redtail Aviation** (259-7421) also offers flights into Moab from the surrounding areas.

The **Moab Information Center,** 805 N. Main St. (259-8825 or 800-635-6622; open Mon.-Sat. 8am-5pm, Sun. 10am-7pm), can provide information on Moab. Moab's **post office:** 39 S. Main St. (644-2760; open Mon.-Fri. 8:30am-4pm, Sat. 9am-noon); **ZIP code:** 84532; **area code:** 801.

Accommodations and Camping Chain motels clutter Main St. In the summer, Moab fills up fast, especially on weekends; call ahead to guarantee your reservations. But if you brave the cold, off-season rates can drop as much as 50%. The owners of the **Lazy Lizard International Hostel (Rucksackers),** 1213 S. U.S. 191 (259-6057; look for the "A1 Storage" sign when going north on U.S. 191), go out of their way to be helpful and will pick you up (usually for $10-15). The kitchen, VCR, laundry, and hot tub are at your beck and call. (Bunks $8. Singles and doubles $22, triples $27. Cabins $25 for 1 or 2 people, $5 each additional person up to 5. Campsites with water, $4 per person. Tepees $10 for 1 or 2 people.) The owners will help arrange rafting, bicycling, and horseback riding trips through local companies.

To find **Hotel Off Center,** 96 E. Center St. (259-4244 or 800-237-4685), travel towards Arches on Main St., turn right onto Center; the hotel is half a block down on the right. Quirky rooms have theme decorations, TVs, and shared baths. (Dorms $10 per person; singles $35, doubles $45, $3 additional person.) **The Silver Sage Inn,** 840 S. Main (259-4420), operated by a Lutheran church, has sparse but clean rooms with cable TV. (Singles $35, doubles $39, $4 per additional person. Office closes at 10pm.) **The Prospector Lodge,** 186 N. 1st W. (259-5145), 1 block west of Main St., offers cool, comfy rooms with TV and free java. (Singles $30 with a double bed, $40 with queen size; doubles $50, and triples $60, each additional person $6.)

The best **camping** lies amidst the sandstone in Arches National Park (see Arches). The **Canyonlands Camp Park,** 555 S. Main St. (259-6848), has a pool (sites $14, electricity and water $17, full hookup $19, each additional person $2). **Slickrock Campground,** 1302 ½ N. U.S. 191 (259-7660 or 259-4152), offers a pool, 3 hot tubs, and a laundry (singles sites $13.50, doubles $22; full hookup $19.25; sparse cabins with A/C for 4 people $27).

Food Eclectic dining experiences abound in Moab, but due to strict Utah laws, if you need a drink, the only place to purchase alcohol above 3.2% is at the **Moab Liquor Store,** 260 S. Main St. (259-5314; open Mon.-Sat. 11am-9pm). The only place for mixed drinks without food is the private club **The Rio,** 2 S. 100 West (259-6666), off Center St. Ask to be sponsored by a member or buy a 2-week pass ($5) good for up to 8 people. (Open Sun.-Thurs. 11:30am-11pm, Fri.-Sat. 10:30am-12:30am.)

The **Poplar Place Pub and Eatery,** 100 N. Main St. (259-6018; open daily 11:30am-11pm), serves great pizzas, Mexican dishes, and fresh salads (around $5). **The Moab Diner,** 189 S. Main St. (259-4006; open 6am-10pm daily, Fri.-Sat. until 10:30pm), is a top-notch campy diner with veggie specials. **Eddie McStiff's,** 57 S. Main St. (259-BEER/2337; open daily 3-10pm), has 12 homemade brews from "chestnut brown" to "passion fruit pale." **Honest Ozzie's Café and Desert Oasis,** 60 N. 100 W. (259-8442), delivers breakfast combos, a plethora of fruity drinks, and vegetarian dishes (open daily 6:30am-10:30pm).

Sights and Activities Although the main sights have sculpted themselves for eons in the nearby national parks, Moab has two museums worth a gander. Particularly enjoyable is **The Hollywood Stuntmen's Hall of Fame,** 111 E. North St. (259-6100), with exhibits ranging from John Wayne to *Thelma and Louise.* Owner-stuntman John Hagner will balance a plastic fish on his nose for you. (Open Mon.-Fri. 10am-6pm, Sat. noon-5pm. $3, seniors and students $2, kids $1.) For a more traditional look at the history and geology of the area, peruse the **Dan O'Laurie Museum,** 118 E. Center St. (254-7445; open Mon.-Sat. 1-5pm and 7-9pm).

The majority of activities centers on moving and being moved: horseback, motorboat, raft, canoe, jeep, even helicopter. **Park Creek Ranch** (259-5505) offers **trail rides** into the La Sal Mountains (1 hr. $15 per person; 2 hr. $25 per person) or into the Arches (1 hr. $20 per person; 2 hr. $35 per person). **Navtech Expeditions,** 321 N. Main St. (259-7983), offers raft, powerboat, and jeep tours into the Colorado River and canyons ($38-175 per person). **Trapax, Inc.** (259-5261) presents **Canyonlands by Night,** an evening boat ride along the Colorado River with a sound and light show which ricochets off the canyon walls ($18, ages 6-16 $9, under 6 free).

■■■ ARCHES NATIONAL PARK

"This is the most beautiful place on earth," park ranger and novelist Edward Abbey wrote of Arches. Abbey is not alone in that opinion; Arches is indeed stunning. Massive expanses of red rock testify to the grandeur of nature and overwhelm visitors with their extraordinary spires, pinnacles, and, of course, arches. Arches National Park has more than 200 natural arches. Because of their nearly perfect form, explorers first thought that they were the ruins of a lost civilization.

Practical Information Emergency is 911. The park entrance is on U.S. 191, 5 mi. north of Moab. There is no public transportation to Arches, but buses run along I-70, stopping in Crescent Junction. The **visitors center** (259-8161) is to the right of the entrance station (open daily 8am-6pm; off-season daily 8am-4pm). An **entrance pass** ($4 per carload; pedestrians and bikers $2) is valid for a week. Water is available in the park. For more info, write to the **Superintendent,** Arches National Park, P.O. Box 907, Moab, UT 84532 (801-259-8161). Utah's **area code: 801.**

Camping The park's only campground, **Devil's Garden,** has 54 sites (one reserved for handicapped visitors) and doesn't take reservations, so get there early since sites go very quickly in season. Get in line at the visitors center at 7:30am when the mad rush begins. The campground is 18 mi. from the visitors center. (No wood-gathering; running water April-Oct.; 2-week max. stay; sites $8.) **Backcountry camping** in Arches is free. Register at the National Park Service office in Moab (2 blocks west of the Ramada Inn on Main St.), and pick up a map to avoid getting lost. Bring plenty of water and bug spray, and avoid hiking on summer afternoons. Camping is also available in nearby Moab.

Escape the summer heat, crowds, and biting gnats by heading to the **Moab Range District** of the Manti-La Sal National Forest. Campgrounds here (30 mi. southeast of Moab off U.S. 191) are about 4000 ft. higher than those of Arches. All cost $5, except free **Oowah. Oowah Lake,** 3 mi. down a dirt road, is a rainbow trout heaven (fishing permit $5 per day). For more info, contact the Manti-La Sal National Forest Service office in Moab, 125 W. 200 South (259-7155; open Mon.-Fri. 8am-4:30pm).

Sights and Activities Plenty of scenic wonders embellish the 18-mi. road between the visitors center and Devil's Garden. No matter how short your stay, be sure to see the **Windows** at **Panorama Point,** about halfway along the road. Cyclists will enjoy the ride in spring or fall, but steep inclines make the trip almost unbearable in the summer heat. **Rim Cyclery,** 94 W. 100 North (259-5333), offers rimming bikes for $20 per day, including helmet and water bottle (open daily 9am-6pm). At the end of the paved road, **Devil's Garden** boasts an astounding 64 arches. A challenging hike from the **Landscape Arch** leads across harrowing exposures to the secluded **Double O Arch.** The highlight of your visit should be **Delicate Arch,** the symbol of the monument. Take the Delicate Arch turn-off from the main road, 2 mi. down a graded unpaved road (impassable after rainstorms). Once you reach Wolfe Ranch, go down a 1½-mi. foot trail to the free-standing Delicate Arch. Beyond, you can get a glimpse of the Colorado River gorge and the La Sal Mountains. If you're lucky, you may come across petroglyphs on the stone walls left by the Anasazi and Ute who wandered the area centuries ago.

Arches aren't the only natural wonders here. One of the most popular trails, the moderately strenuous 2-mi. **Fiery Furnace Trail,** leads downward into the canyon bottoms, providing views of the imposing cliffs and monoliths above. Only experienced hikers should attempt the Fiery Furnace Trail alone (ranger-lead group tours into the labyrinth at 10am and 4pm daily; make reservations 48 hrs. in advance).

■■■ CANYONLANDS NATIONAL PARK

Those who make it to Canyonlands National Park will be rewarded with a pleasant surprise: an absence of that overabundant, pestering species, *homo Winnebagiens.* The Green and Colorado Rivers divide the park into three sections, each with its own **visitors center.** (All three open daily 8am-5pm; hours subject to change in off-season, so call ahead.) **The Needles** are a region of spires, arches, canyons, and Native American ruins (not as rough as the Maze area, see below, but still Moon Rover country). To get to Needles (visitors center 259-2652), take Rte. 211 west from U.S. 191, about 40 mi. south of Moab. Farther north, **Island in the Sky,** a towering mesa, sits within the "Y" formed by the two rivers. Take Rte. 313 west from U.S. 191 about 10 mi. north of Moab. Island in the Sky (visitors center 259-4351) is accessible by car and provides a bird's eye view of the surrounding canyons and mountains. The most remote district of the park is the rugged **Maze** area, a hurly-burly of twisted canyons made for rugged *über*-pioneers with four-wheel-drive vehicles only (visitors center 259-2652). Once you've entered a section of the park, you're committed to it—unless you're flying a helicopter. Getting from one section to the next involves retracing your steps and re-entering the park, a tedious trip lasting from several hours to a full day.

Practical Information Outside the park, there are two visitors centers. Monticello's **Interagency Visitors Center,** 32 S. 1st E. St. (587-3235; open Mon.-Fri. 8am-4:30pm), sells area maps ($3-6). In **Moab,** visit the **Information Center** (259-8825) at the corner of Center and Main (open daily 8am-9pm), or the **Park Service,** 125 W. 200 S. (259-7164; open Mon.-Fri. 8am-4:30pm). Both can provide info in French, Spanish, German, and Italian. The park entrance fee is $4 per car, $2 per hiker or cyclist. Neither gas nor water is available within the park. There are no food services in the park. Just outside the boundary in the Needles district, however, the **Needles Outpost** houses a limited, expensive grocery store and gas pump. Hauling groceries, water, and first-aid supplies in from Moab or Monticello is the best budget alternative. For more information, write to the **Superintendent,** Canyonlands National Park, 125 W. 200 S., Moab, UT 84532 (259-7164).

Camping and Hiking Before backcountry camping or hiking, register for a permit at the proper visitors center ($10 except at the Maze, limited number available). Four-wheel drivers should also register at the visitors center and inquire about possible fees and backcountry parking sites. Each visitors center has a brochure of possible hikes including length and difficulty, so you can pick your own and start out from there. With summer temperatures regularly climbing over 100°F, be sure to bring at least one gallon of water per person per day.

Hiking options from the Needles area are probably the best, though Island in the Sky offers some spectacular views. Cyclists should check at the visitors centers for lists of trails. If hiking in desert heat doesn't appeal to you, you can rent Jeeps and mountain bikes in Moab, or take a 1-hr. airplane flight from **Red Tail Aviation** (259-7421) that can cost as little as $45 per person for a group of four.

Each region has its own official **campground.** In the Needles district, **Squaw Flat's** 26 sites are situated in a sandy plain surrounded by giant sandstone towers, 35 mi. west of U.S. 191 on Rte. 211. Avoid this area in June, when insects swarm. Bring fuel and water, although the latter is usually available from April through September ($6 fee year-round). **Willow Flat Campground,** in the Island in the Sky district, sits high atop the mesa on Rte. 313, 41 mi. west off U.S. 191. You must bring your own water; the sites (12 in all) are free, but again, bring insect repellent. Willow Flat and

Squaw Flat both have picnic tables, grills, and pit toilets. All campgrounds operate on a first-come, first-served basis. The backcountry campground at the **Maze Overlook** has no amenities at all. (See Arches for more camping info.)

For some great overlooks at elevations over 8000 ft. head to the **Monticello District** of Manti La Sal National Forest south of Needles. This section of the forest has two campgrounds on **Blue Mountain: Buckboard** (9 sites and 2 group areas), and **Dalton Springs** (9 sites). Reservations for areas in Buckboard can be made at the **visitors center** in Monticello, 117 S. Main St. (587-3235). From Moab head south on U.S. 191 to Monticello and then west on state Rte. 1S. For more info on the Monticello District, call the Manti-La Sal National Forest Service office in Monticello, 496 E. Central (587-2041) on U.S. 666 just east of Monticello (open Mon. 8am-4:30pm).

Farther away is **Dead Horse Point State Park** (entrance fee $3), perched on the rim of the Colorado Gorge south of Arches and 14 mi. south of U.S. 191, accessible from Rte. 313 (modern restrooms, water, hookups, and covered picnic tables; sites $8; half can be reserved and half are first-come, first-served; open year-round). For more info, contact the Park Superintendent, Dead Horse Point State Park, P.O. Box 609, Moab, UT 84532 (259-2614 or 800-322-3770; open Mon.-Fri. 8am-5pm).

■■■ CAPITOL REEF NATIONAL PARK

A geologist's fantasy, this 100-mi. wrinkle in time snakes through the park and presents visitors 65 million years of stratified natural history. The sheer cliffs bisect the state's southern region and were originally called a "reef" not for their oceanic origins, but because they posed a barrier to travel. Spiny and forbidding, like the backbone of an immense prehistoric sea creature, Capitol Reef's **Waterpocket Fold** dominates the terrain of south-central Utah with its vaulted rock rotundas. To the west lie Zion and Bryce Canyon; to the east lie Arches and Canyonlands. Major bus lines don't serve the park itself.

You'll want to make at least a brief stop at the park's **visitors center** (425-3791), on Rte. 24 for information on the Capitol Reef and daily activities (open daily 8am-7pm, Sept.-May daily 8am-4:30pm). The center offers waterproof topographic maps ($7), regular maps ($4), and free brochures on trails. Check the bulletin boards for ranger-led jaunts and campfire talks. The **entrance fee** for the park is $4 per vehicle, $1 per hiker, $6 for overnight camping. For more info on the park, contact the **Superintendent,** Capitol Reef National Park, Torrey, UT 84775 (425-3791).

From the seat of your car, you can explore the 25-mi. (round trip) **scenic drive**; the 90-min. jaunt takes you out along the reef itself. Also pause at the **Fruita Schoolhouse** and **Petroglyphs Panoramic Point** along Rte. 24 when entering the park. When hiking, keep in mind that summer temperatures average 95° F, and most water found in seep springs and rain-holding water pockets is contaminated and can only be used if purified.

For **backcountry camping,** register at the visitors center or at the campsites. There are three campgrounds available on a first-come, first-served basis. The main campground and Utah's version of Versailles is **Fruita** which has drinking water, toilets, and a nearby orchard from which you can pick at a price. Its 73 sites (one reserved for the handicapped) are located 1.3 mi. south off Rte. 24 ($6). **Cedar Mesa Campground** in the north end of the park and **Cathedral Valley** in the south both have only five sites, and neither has water or a paved road, but they are free. With plenty of water affixed to their person, backcountry hikers should stop at the visitors center for maps and advice.

For accommodations in the region, try **Torrey,** 11 mi. west of the visitors center on Rte. 24. The **Rim Rock Motel and RV Park** (425-3843) also on Rte. 24, 3 mi. east of Torrey, is perched dramatically on top of a cliff (singles $45, doubles $50-55; sites $8.50, full hookup $11). The **Chuck Wagon General Store** (425-3288), in the center of Torrey on Rte. 24 west, proudly offers a splendid selection of groceries, sporting goods, and picnic implements (open daily 7am-10pm). For repast, try **Brink's Burgers,** 165 E. Main (425-3710; open 11am-8pm daily). **The Redrock Restaurant and Campground** (542-3235), in Hanksville, 37 mi. from the visitors center on Rte. 24, is the main tourist service in the region (cheeseburgers $2.15, daily special $4.75; open daily 7am-10pm; sites $8 with electricity and water, full hookup $12). For couples, there's **Joy's Bed and Breakfast,** 296 South Center (542-3252 or 542-3235), in Hanksville. Room and bath begin at $35 for two.

Betwixt Boulder and Capitol Reef lies a stretch of Dixie National Forest with three lovely campgrounds, all off scenic Rte. 12 between Boulder and Torrey. All three have an elevation over 8000 ft., are open from May through September, have drinking water and toilets, and are available on a first-come, first-served basis. **The Oak Creek Campground** has 7 sites, the **Pleasant Creek Campground** has 16 sites, and **Single Tree Campground** has 22 sites, with 2 group sites (800-280-CAMP for reservations) and 2 family sites, one of which can be reserved ahead of time. For more info, call the **Interagency** in Escalante (826-5499).

■■■ BRYCE CANYON NATIONAL PARK

The fragile, slender spires of pink and red limestone that rise out of Bryce's canyons often seem more like the subjects of surrealist painting than the natural results of wind and water currents. Etched by millennia of erosion, these canyons made life very difficult for the Anasazi, Fremont, Paiute, and white settlers who had to navigate the area. Ebenezer Bryce, the first white man to glimpse the canyon, called it "one hell of a place to lose a cow." For a solitary experience, hike into the canyons or visit Oct.15-April 15, when accommodation rates drop to as little as half.

Practical Information Emergency is 911 or 676-2411. From the west, Bryce Canyon lies 1½ hrs. east of Cedar City. Take Rte. 14 to U.S. 89. From the east, take I-70 to U.S. 89. From U.S. 89 at Bryce Junction (7 mi. south of Panguitch), turn east on Rte. 12 and drive 14 mi. to the Rte. 63 junction, then turn south and go 4 mi. to the park entrance (entrance fee $5 per car, $3 per pedestrian). There is no public transportation to the park, but a **shuttle bus** travels to the developed areas of the park from Ruby's Inn (runs daily summer 8am-7pm, $4, kids and seniors $2).

The park's **visitors center** (834-5322) is the place to begin any tour. Pick up a copy of the free Bryce Canyon *Hoo Doo,* listing all park services, events, suggested hikes, and sight-seeing drives. (Open daily 8am-8pm; April-May and Sept.-Oct. daily 8am-6pm; Nov.-March daily 8am-4:30pm.)

Accommodations North and Sunset Campgrounds, both within 3 mi. of the visitors center, offer 210 sites on a first-come, first-served basis. Both have toilets, picnic tables, and potable water ($7, show up in early morning to reserve a spot). Those who enjoy **backcountry camping** should stop by the **Nature Center** (834-5322) near **Sunrise Point** for a free permit (open daily in summer 8am-6pm). Winter permits are available through the visitor's center. **Bryce Lodge** (586-7686), open April-Nov. 1, is very expensive ($65 for singles and doubles—heck, might as well get a double), but may be a good deal for a group of 3 ($73), 4 ($78), or 5 ($83). For provisions within the park, try the **grocery store** at Sunrise Point (831-5361; open mid-April-late Oct., 7am-7pm). Behind the store are **showers** ($1.75 for 10 min.; available 7am-10pm). The lodge also houses a **post office** (834-5361).

Canyonlands International Youth Hostel, 143 E. 100th S. (801-644-5554), is 60 mi. south of Bryce in the town of **Kanab.** The hostel offers roomy bunks ($9), free coffee, buffet breakfast, laundry, kitchen, TV, and car parking.

There are two campgrounds just west of Bryce on scenic Rte. 12, in the Dixie National Forest. At an elevation of 7400 ft., the **Red Canyon Campground** has 36 sites for $7; first-come, first-served. The **King Creek Campground** is 11 mi. from

Bryce on a dirt road off Rte. 12. Look for the signs to the Tropic Reservoir. (Sites $6; first-come, first-served.) Group sites available with reservations (800-280-2267). For more sites in the Bryce area, see below under East of Bryce and West of Bryce.

If you arrive too late to get a site in Bryce, try the **Panguitch District** of the Dixie National Forest, which has six campgrounds (most near Rte. 14, none more than an hour away; sites $7, includes toilets, running water, swimming, boating, and fishing, except at Navajo Lake). The most favored forest campgrounds are **TE-AH, Spruces,** and **Navajo Lake.** Inquire at the visitors center or call the forest service office in Panguitch, 225 E. Center St. (676-8815; open Mon.-Fri. 8am-4:30pm).

Hiking and Driving The most popular scenery is concentrated within 2 mi. of the visitors center. Sunrises here are particularly rewarding. The section between Sunrise and Sunset Points is wheelchair-accessible. The 3-mi. loop of the **Navajo** and **Queen's Garden** trails winds you into the canyon itself. If you are up to the challenge, branch off onto the **Peek-A-Boo Trail,** a 4-mi. round-trip. **Trail to the Hat Shop** is a strenuous 4-mi. journey on an extremely steep descent. (And if you think climbing down is tough. . .) Check out these and other trails at the visitors center. By car or shuttle bus (see Practical Information), drive along the 15-mi. main road to spectacular look-outs such as **Sunrise Point, Sunset Point, Inspiration Point,** and **Bryce Point.** Due to construction, the park is closed at **Farview Point;** inquire at the visitors center for more details.

At Bryce Lodge, you can reserve a **1938 Limousine Tour** along the main road ($7, teens $3.50, under 12 free), or arrange for a guided horseback tour through **Canyon Trail Rides** (834-2519, off-season 679-8665) at $25-35 per person. From Memorial Day to Labor Day, **Ruby's Inn Rodeo** (834-5341) pits human against beast every night at 7:30pm except Sunday ($6, kids $3). Another popular event, the **Fiddler's Association Contest,** tunes up in early July.

East of Bryce To hike into the desert environment of the ominously named **Phipps Death Hollow Outstanding Natural Area,** part of a network of sandstone canyons just north of **Escalante,** contact the **Escalante Interagency Office,** 755 W. Main St., Escalante 84726 (826-5499), on Rte. 12, just west of town (open daily 7am-6pm; off-season Mon.-Fri. 8am-5pm). Popular **Calf Creek** camping grounds, 15 mi. east of Escalante on Rte. 12, has a great hike near a cascading waterfall (sites $6, including drinking water and fresh toilets). **Boulder** has the **Anasazi State Park and Museum** off Rte. 12 (335-7308), which displays a reconstructed Anasazi village dating from about 1100AD (open daily 8am-6pm; off-season 9am-5pm). The Anasazi ("ancient ones") disappeared almost completely around 1300AD, but are believed to be the predecessors of the modern Hopi, Zuni, and Pueblo. If you don't mind dodging cows and driving on dirt roads, head out 5 mi. to **Lower Bowns Reservoir Lake** (826-4221; pit toilets, no drinking water).

West of Bryce Wandering out of Bryce to the west, on Rte. 14 to Cedar City, you'll come across the refreshing and surprisingly green **Cedar Breaks National Monument** ($4 per car, $2 per pedestrian). The rim of this giant amphitheater is a lofty 10,350 ft. above sea level. 2000 ft. of flowered slopes separate the rim from the chiseled depths. At **Point Supreme** you'll find a 30-site **campground** (sites $7) and the **visitors center** (586-0787; open summer daily 8am-6pm). For more information, contact the Superintendent, Cedar Breaks National Monument, 82 N. 100 E., Cedar City 84720 (586-9451).

Cedar City's Iron Mission State Park, 585 N. Main St. (586-9290), has an amazing horse-drawn vehicle collection which merits a visit (open daily 9am-7pm; off-season daily 9am-5pm; $1.50, ages 7-16 $1). The **Economy Motel,** 443 S. Main St. (586-4461), has very plain rooms; try to get one with a book-sized window (singles $30, doubles $35). For more info, contact the **Cedar City Chamber of Commerce Visitors Center,** 286 N. Main St. (586-4484; open Mon.-Fri. 8am-5pm).

■■■ ZION NATIONAL PARK

Some 13 million years ago, the cliffs and canyons of Zion made up the sea floor. That sea has been reduced to the lone, powerful Virgin River, which today carves fingers through the Navajo sandstone. Cut into the Kolob Terrace, the walls of Zion now tower thousands of feet above the river. In the 1860s, Mormon settlers came to this area and enthusiastically proclaimed they had found the promised land. But Brigham Young thought otherwise and declared to his followers that the place was awfully nice, but "not Zion." The name "not Zion" stuck for years until a new wave of entranced explorers dropped the "not," giving the park its present name.

Practical Information From the west, Zion National Park can be reached from I-15, via Rte. 9 (at Hurricane), or coming east, from U.S. 89, via Rte. 9 (at Mount Carmel Junction). For **emergency assistance,** call 772-3256 during the day, 772-3322 after hours. The main entrance to the park is in **Springdale,** on Rte. 9, which bounds the park to the south along the Virgin River. **Greyhound** runs in St. George (43 mi. southwest of the park on I-15); the bus station (673-2933) is in the McDonald's at 1235 S. Bluff St., at St. George Blvd. Buses run to: Salt Lake City (2 per day, 6 hr., $52); Provo (2 per day, 5 hr., $42); Los Angeles (6 per day, 15 hr., $53); Las Vegas (6 per day, 2 hr., $25). The main **Zion Canyons Visitors Center** (772-3256), in the southeast corner of the park, ½ mi. off Rte. 9, has an introductory slide program and a small but interesting museum (open daily 8am-8pm, off-season 8am-6pm). The **Kolob Canyons Visitors Center** (586-9548) lies in the northwest corner of the park, off I-15 (open daily 8am-5pm; off-season daily 8am-4:30pm). The park entrance fee is $5 per car, $2 per pedestrian.

Camping and Accommodations Over 300 sites are available on a first come, first-served basis (come early) at the **South** and **Watchman Campgrounds.** Both are at the south gate. (Sites $7; 2-week max. stay. Always open.) The park's only other campground is a primitive area at **Lava Point,** accessible from a hiking trail in the mid-section of the park or from the gravel road that turns off Rte. 9 in **Virgin** (6 sites; open May-Oct.; toilets but no water; free).

    Zion Canyon Campground, 479 Zion Park Blvd. (772-3237), in Springdale, just south of the park, has a convenience store, a restaurant, a grocery store (772-3402; open daily 8am-8pm), showers, and coin-op laundry for the weary, hungry, and filthy. (Sites $13 for 2 people, full hookup $16. Extra adult $3.50, extra child under 15 50¢. Open daily 8am-9pm.) The **Zion Canyon Lodge** (772-3213) along the park's main road, offers premium rooms at premium prices. The lodge offers a snack shop (open daily 7am-9pm) and a dining room (772-3213; reservations for dinner). For reservations at the lodge call 586-7686. (Singles and doubles $67, each additional person up to 5 $5. Motel suite singles and doubles $102, each additional person up to 4 $5. Cabin singles and doubles $74, each additional person up to 4 $5.) For lodging alternatives, try **Springdale** or **Rockville,** 2-5 miles south of the park.

    You need a free permit from a visitors center for **backcountry camping. Observation Point** is one of the only canyon rim spots where you can pitch a tent. Many backpackers spend a few nights on the 27-mi. **West Rim Trail** (too long for a day hike) or in the **Kolob Canyons,** where crowds never converge. Zion campgrounds don't take reservations and often fill on holiday and summer weekends; if you don't get in, try one of the 6 campgrounds in Dixie National Forest (see Bryce Canyon).

    To the west of Zion lies another district of the Dixie National Forest—**Pine Valley.** With an elevation of 6683 ft., Pine Valley offers 57 sites (open May-Sept., water, toilets, $9 entrance fee). There are group sites you can reserve (800-280-CAMP); call the National Forest Service of this district (673-3431) for more details.

    If you don't want to spend the night under the stars, spend it at **O'Toole's,** 980 Zion Park Blvd. (772-3457), in Springdale. New ownership has upgraded this stucco and sandstone house with a beautiful garden. Make reservations early; these gorgeous rooms, featuring stained glass windows and queen size beds, go quickly. Perfect for couples and small families; includes a hot tub and a full breakfast. (Rooms for 2 people from $55-95, $15 per additional person.)

Canyonlands International Youth Hostel, 143 E. 100th S. (801-644-5554), is 40 mi. south of Zion in the town of **Kanab.** The hostel offers roomy bunks ($9), free coffee, buffet breakfast, laundry, kitchen, TV, and car parking.

Sights If you love to walk or hike, you're in the right place. The **Angel's Landing** trail (5 mi. round trip) takes you 1488 feet above the canyon; the last ½ mile of the trail is a terrifying climb on a narrow ridge with guide chains blasted into the rock. An easier trail (1.2 mi. round trip), called the **Emerald Pools** is refreshing and accessible to the handicapped. Overnight hikers can spend days on the 27-mi. **West Rim Trail.** Short hikes to the base of the cliffs can be made on foot and by wheelchair. Even if you wisely plan to visit **Kolob Canyon's** backcountry, be sure to make the pilgrimage to **Zion Canyon.** Drive along the 7-mi. dead-end road that follows the floor of the canyon or take the upper canyon tour (summer only; $2.75, kids $1.75). You'll ride through the giant formations of **Sentinel, Mountain of the Sun,** and the overwhelming symbol of Zion, the **Great White Throne.** A challenging trail takes you to **Observation Point,** where steep switchbacks let you explore an impossibly gouged canyon. For fun without the sweat, follow by car the **scenic drive,** a 7-mi. road through Zion Canyon with plenty of vistas. A **guided tour** by foot of the same area leaves from Zion Lodge every hour on the hour (9am-5pm; $2.75, kids $1.75). Horseback tours leave the lodge and are arranged by **Canyon Trail Rides** (772-3967) for $12-35 per person. Or you can rent an **inner tube** ($3) from the Canyon grocery store and float down the ravishing Virgin River.

■■■ NATIONAL MONUMENTS AND VALLEY OF THE GODS

Natural Bridges National Monument Nearly 3000 years ago, the Paiutes who inhabited this region called it "Ma-Vah-Talk-Tump" ("under the horse's belly"). In 1909, President Taft renamed each bridge with Hopi terms like "Sipapu" ("place of desolation") and "Kachina" ("ghost dancer"). Named in the less-imaginative present day, Utah's first national monument is simply called Natural Bridges. Nonetheless, these water-sculpted bridges that stretch up to 250 ft. high and across, cannot be summarized in any name.

To reach Natural Bridges from northern Utah, follow U.S. 191 south from Moab to the junction with **Scenic Rte. 95W** (north of Bluff and 4 mi. south of Blanding). From Colorado follow Rte. 66 south out of Cortez to U.S. 191S (the junction is in Monticello). From Arizona, take Rte. 163 north through Monument Valley. At the junction just past Mexican Hat, catch Rte. 261 north to Scenic Rte. 95W.

The 13-site **campground** near the visitors center is open year round on a first-come, first-served basis (sites $5). There is a 21-ft. combined length limit for RVs and vehicles with trailers. Each site can accommodate up to nine people with a grill, tent pad, and picnic table. Water is only available at the visitors center. Ranger-led campfire talks are offered daily at 9pm in summer at the amphitheater.

Hiking from overlooks down to the bridges allows visitors to truly comprehend the size of the monuments. Hikes range from .4 to 1.5 mi. round-trip, except for the "loop" trail (8.6 mi. round-trip). Check in at the **visitors center** (259-5174), on Rte. 95E, which offers a slide show, small bookstore, and exhibits (open daily 8am-6pm; Nov.-Feb. 9am-4:30pm; entrance fee $4 per vehicle, $2 per hiker or bicyclist; good for 7 days). There are no telephones at the monument. For further info contact the Superintendent, Natural Bridges, Box 1, Lake Powell, UT 84533 (259-5174).

Hovenweep National Monument Time travel is possible after all. Hovenweep, from the Ute meaning "deserted valley" consists of six groups of Pueblo ruins dating back over 1000 years. The valley remains pretty much deserted today with only two rangers (one in Utah, one in Colorado) covering 784 acres of the monument. Immune to a peak season or even small crowds, Hovenweep provides visitors plenty of space and time to ponder.

Getting to Hovenweep is a desolate but wonderful experience. In Utah or Arizona, the journey begins on U.S. 191 to Rte. 262 east (the junction is 14 mi. south of Blanding, 11 mi. north of Bluff). After about 30 mi. watch for signs to the monument. The road in is unpaved for 2½ mi. but still accessible to all vehicles. From Cortez, CO, turn south on U.S. 166/160 to country road 6 (the airport road), then follow Hovenweep signs for 45 mi. The route includes 15 mi. of gravel road. You may want to call ahead to check road accessibility at the **visitors center** (303-749-0510; open daily 8am-5pm), which is accessible from both the Utah and Colorado sides. If it's locked, the ranger is out on patrol. There is no gasoline or telephone at the monument; entrance is free. For more information, contact the Superintendent, Hovenweep National Monument, McElmo Rte., Cortez, CO 81321 (303-749-0510). The 31-site **campground** near the center operates on a first-come, first-served basis. The grounds include drinking water and restrooms ($6 March-mid-Nov.).

Footsteps from the visitors center are the best preserved and most impressive **Square Tower Ruins.** The **Square Tower Loop Trail,** 2 mi. round-trip, is an easy hike which leads to all the ruins in this section, such as the **Hovenweep Castle** and the two-story apartment houses called the **Twin Towers.** A shorter trail, the ½-mi. **Tower Point Loop,** leads only to the ruins of a tower perched on a canyon. The outlying ruins—**Cujon Ruins** and **Huckberry Canyon** in Utah, and **Cutthroat Castle** and **Goodman Point Ruins** in Colorado—are isolated and difficult to reach. Inquire at the visitors center for more info on road conditions and access to these ruins.

Valley of the Gods and Environs Valley of the Gods is the scenery from *Thelma and Louise*—gigantic, austere, monolithic sandstone sculptures. The 17-mi. scenic drive on U.S. 163W, 15 mi. south of Bluff on the right side of the road, goes right through the valley (the roads are tough, 4-wheel drive is best). Though not a park or a monument, it is perhaps the greatest roadside attraction ever.

Three small Utah towns provide lodging and services for travelers to the monuments. In the agricultural town of **Blanding** (45 mi. from Hovenweep, 60 mi. from Natural Bridges), you can spend the night at the **Prospector Motor Lodge,** 591 U.S. 191S (singles $35, $27 off-season; doubles $39, $32 off-season). Or try the **Blanding Sunset Inn,** 88 W. Center St. (678-3323; rooms from $22 to $42). Coffee is served up at the **Elk Ridge Cafe,** 120 E. Center St. (678-3390; open daily 6am-10pm). Saddle up to **The Cedar Pony** (678-2715) on U.S.191N (open daily 10:30am-9:30pm).

Perched amidst the sandstone canyons, **Bluff** (40 mi. from Hovenweep, 65 mi. from Natural Bridges) is a tiny town that can be grand for the budget traveler. Several cheap motels line U.S. 191 including **The Recapture Lodge** (672-2281; singles $30-38, doubles $32-44). Try the Navajo's sheepherder sandwich ($5) at the **Turquoise Cafe** (672-2219), on U.S.191S (open 7am-9pm, winter until 8pm).

Named for a rock formation that looks just like one, **Mexican Hat** (60 mi. from Hovenweep, 45 mi. from Natural Bridges, 21 mi. south of the Arizona border on U.S. 163) is a comatose desert town near the San Juan River. Sit a spell at the **Canyonlands Motel** (683-2230) on U.S. 163. (Rooms from $28-40.) The place for Navajo specialties is **The Old Bridge Bar and Grille** (683-2220) on U.S. 163.

Nevada

Nevada once walked the straight and narrow. Explored by Spanish missionaries and settled by Mormons, the Nevada Territory's arid land and searing climate seemed a perfect place for ascetics to strive for moral uplift. But the discovery of gold in 1850 and silver in 1859 won the state over permanently to the worship of filthy lucre. When the precious metal ran out, Nevadans responded by shirking the last vestiges of virtue, and gambling and marriage-licensing became the state industries. In a final break with the rest of the country, Silver Staters legalized prostitution on a county by county basis and began paying Wayne Newton enormous amounts of cash.

But a different Nevada exists outside the gambling towns of Las Vegas and Reno. The forested slopes of Lake Tahoe, shared with California, offer serenity in little resorts a far cry away from the casinos of the south shore. Lake Mead National Recreation Area, only 25 mi. from Las Vegas, features an amazing oasis in stunning desert surroundings. Nevada also hosts a large Basque population which originally came from the Pyrenees to herd sheep in Nevada.

PRACTICAL INFORMATION

Capital: Carson City.

Nevada Commission on Tourism, Capitol Complex, Carson City 89710, (702-687-4322). **Nevada Division of State Parks,** 123 W. Nye Lane, Carson City 89701 (687-4384). Open Mon.-Fri. 8am-5pm.

Gay and lesbian travelers should know that it is illegal for homosexual couples to display public affection in Nevada and the law is enforced. Members of the same sex sharing a hotel room may be required to book a room containing two beds.

Time Zone: Pacific (3 hr. behind Eastern). **Postal Abbreviation:** NV

Sales Tax: 5.75-6%.

■■■ LAS VEGAS

The American dream—a new life for the pioneer on the plain—has been stripped of spirituality, tubed in neon, and manifested in the raw promise of every pull of the slot machine. Even the jaded traveler will be impressed, if only by contemplating the electric bills generated by a town which runs non-stop 24 hours a day, 365 days a year. Since Bugsy Segal built his dream of a then-extravagant casino-hotel, the Flamingo Hilton, Las Vegas has only continued to exploit the American dream. But what this means for the budget traveler is a dream come true: all-you-can-eat buffets and luxurious hotel rooms for unbelievable prices. Most of the entertainment is free, as each casino is a self-contained amusement park with its own theme—circus, medieval castle, Roman Empire. For an education in tacky American culture, Las Vegas is crash course 101.

PRACTICAL INFORMATION

Emergency: 911. **Police department:** 795-3111.

Visitor Information: Las Vegas Convention and Visitors Authority, 3150 Paradise Rd. (892-7575 or 892-0711), at the gigantic Convention Center, 4 blocks from the Strip, by the Hilton. Up-to-date info on hotel bargains and buffets. Open Mon.-Fri. 8am-6pm, Sat.-Sun. 8am-5pm.

Helpful Publications: *What's On In Las Vegas, Today in Las Vegas, Vegas Visitor, Casino Player, Tour Guide Magazine, Insider Viewpoint of Las Vegas.* All free and available at visitors centers, most hotels, and attractions. Up-to-date info on shows and events. For more coupons, ask for **funbooks** at hotels and casinos.

Tours: Gambler's specials number among the cheapest and most popular ways to reach Las Vegas. These bus tours leave early in the morning and return at night or the next day; ask in L.A., San Francisco, or San Diego tourist offices. You can also call casinos for info. Prices include everything except food and gambling. **Gray Line,** 1550 S. Industrial Rd. (384-1234). Bus tours: Hoover Dam/Lake Mead Express (2 per day at 8am and noon, 5 hr., $18); the South Rim of the Grand Canyon (2 days, one night lodging and park admission included; bus leaves Mon., Wed, Fri at 7am; $147 with a single room, $111 doubles, $99 triple or quad.; runs March-Oct. 31; reservations required).; Mini City Tours (1 per day, ½-day, $17.50). **Ray and Ross Tours,** 300 W. Owens St. (646-4661 or 800-338-8111).

Bus tours to Hoover Dam (daily, 6 hr., $19) and Hoover Dam/Lake Mead (daily, 7 hr., $32). Other tours available. Pick-up and drop-off at most hotels.

Airport: McCarran International (798-5410), at the southeast end of the Strip. Main terminal on Paradise Rd. Within walking distance of the University of Nevada campus and the southern casinos. Taxi to downtown $23. Vans run to hotels on the Strip and Downtown ($5-7).

Amtrak: 1 N. Main St. (386-6896), in Union Plaza Hotel. To: L.A. ($68, 8 hrs.), San Francisco ($117). Ticket office open daily 6am-7:30pm.

Greyhound: 200 S. Main St. (304-4561 or 800-752-4841), at Carson Ave. downtown. To: L.A. ($39, 5 hrs.), San Francisco ($61, 15 hrs.). Ticket office open daily 6am-1am; terminal open 24 hrs.

Public Transportation: CAT, 228-7433. Route #301 serves Downtown and the Strip 24 hrs. Route #302 serves the airport. Both are $1.50, seniors and kids under 17 50¢. All other routes are $1 and 50¢ and operate daily 5:30am-1:30am.

Car Rental: Rebel Rent-a-Car, 5466 Paradise Rd. (597-0427 or 800-372-1981), $20 per day; unlimited mi. within Clark County. Must be 21 with major credit card; $7 per day surcharge if you're under 25. $100 deposit. Like accommodations and restaurants, car rental agencies offer discounts in tourist publications.

Taxi: Yellow and **Checker Taxis** (873-2000); $2.20 flat, $1.50 per mi.

Tying the Knot: Marriage License Bureau, 200 S. 3rd St. (455-3156). Must be 18. Available Mon.-Thurs. 8am-midnight, Fri.-Sun. 24 hrs. $35.

Help Lines: Rape Crisis Center Hotline, 366-1640. **Gamblers Anonymous,** 385-7732. 24 hrs. **Suicide Prevention:** 731-2990. **Gay and Lesbian Community Center,** 912 E. Sahara Ave. (733-9800).

Post Office: 301 E. Stewart (385-8944). Open Mon.-Fri. 9am-5pm, Sat. 9am-1pm. General delivery open Mon.-Fri. 10am-3pm. **ZIP code:** 89114.

Area Code: 702.

Getting to Vegas from Los Angeles is a straight, 300-mi. shot on I-15. From Arizona, take I-40 west to Kingman and then U.S. 93/95 north. Vegas has two major casino areas. The **downtown** area, around Fremont and 2nd St., is foot-friendly; casinos cluster close together, and some of the sidewalks are even carpeted (man, oh man). The other main area, known as the **Strip,** is a collection of mammoth casinos on both sides of **Las Vegas Boulevard South.** Other casinos lie on Paradise Blvd., parallel to Las Vegas Blvd. As in all cities where money reigns supreme, many areas of Las Vegas are unsafe. Always stay on brightly lit pathways and do not wander too far from the major casinos and hotels. The neighborhoods just north and west of downtown are especially dangerous.

ACCOMMODATIONS AND CAMPING

Room rates at most hotels in Vegas fluctuate all the time. A room that costs $20 during a promotion can cost hundreds during a convention. For a painless experience, check local publications and *make reservations as far in advance as possible.* The earlier you reserve, the more chances you have of snagging a special rate. Coming to town on a Friday or Saturday night without reservations is flirting with disaster. Even though Vegas has over 90,000 rooms, most hotels fill on weekend nights. If you do get stuck call the **Room Reservations Hotline** (800-332-5333). Hotels use two rate ranges—one for week nights, the other weekend nights.

Hostels and Downtown Hotels

Las Vegas Hostel, 1208 Las Vegas Blvd. S. (385-9955). Spartan, airy rooms with foam mattresses. Free breakfast; ride board in kitchen. Check-out 7-10am. Tours to Zion, Bryce, and the Grand Canyon ($125). Office open daily 7am-11pm. Shared room and bath $9, private room and shared bath $20. Winter rates lower. Key deposit $5. Free T-shirt with 3-night stay.

Las Vegas International Hostel (735-4050 or 735-2911). Call for the address, free pickup and reservation to the newly-moved hostel (address unavailable at press time). Common room with pool table, TV, and kitchen. Free BBQ several times weekly. Free breakfast. Tours to Death Valley, Grand Canyon, Bryce, and Zion

($49-$85). Dorm rooms with A/C and private bath $14 in the summer, $10 in the winter, $75 per week. Private rooms with TV and A/C $28, doubles $35.

Gold Spike, 400 E. Ogden Ave. in the downtown area a few blocks from Fremont. Only 109 rooms but 422 slots, find the least common multiple. Fixed rate of $22.

Sam's Town, 5111 Boulder Hwy. (456-7777 or 800-634-6371), a short trip from the Strip. 650 rooms and 3000 slots. Sun.-Thurs. $32-36, Fri.-Sat. $35-39.

Nevada Palace, 5255 Boulder Hwy., is a quick *drive* from the Strip and downtown. 220 rooms, 640 slots. Sun.-Thurs. $33, Fri.-Sat. $45, barring conventions.

Hotel-Casinos

The strip hotels are the center of the action, and within walking distance of each other. Remember to reserve a room as far as in advance as possible.

Circus Circus, 2880 Las Vegas Blvd. South. (734-0410 or 800-634-3450). A major casino with 2800 rooms but some of the best prices. Rooms with TV for 1-4 people. Sun.-Thurs. $21-42, Fri.-Sat. $55-75; holidays $65-85. Roll-away bed $7.

Frontier, 3120 Las Vegas Blvd. South. A giant hotel-casino with nearly 1000 rooms and among the best rates on the Strip. Sun.-Thurs. $35, Fri.-Sat. $55.

Excalibur, 3850 Las Vegas Blvd. (597-7777 or 800-937-7777). A giant white castle complete with over 4000 rooms. When paged, guests are referred to as "Lady" or "Lord." They beat this medieval thing into the ground twice-over. Sun-Thurs. $39-60, Fri.-Sat. $79-90.

Stardust, 3000 Las Vegas Blvd. South (732-6111 or 800-824-6033). 1680 slots and 2300 rooms. Sun.-Thurs. $36-150, Fri.-Sat. $60-150.

Camping

Lake Mead National Recreation Area (293-8906), 25 mi. south of town on U.S. 93/95, offers $8 campgrounds (see Near Las Vegas: Lake Mead).

KOA Las Vegas (451-5527). Take U.S. 93/95 south to the Boulder exit and turn left. Free casino shuttle. Pool, laundry, slots, and video poker. Sites $22, RV spots $25, A/C $3 extra.

Circusland RV Park, 500 Circus Circus Dr. (734-0410), a part of the Circus Circus hotel on the strip. Laundry, shower, pool, jacuzzi, and convenience store. Sun.-Thurs. $13, Fri.-Sat. $17.

BUFFET BONANZA

The hungry budget traveler is right at home in Vegas. Almost every hotel-casino in Vegas courts tourists with cheap all-you-can-eat invitations. In most cafeterias, buffet food is served nonstop 11am-10pm. Alcoholic drinks in most casinos cost 75¢-$1, but are free to those who look like they're playing.

Circus Circus, 2800 Las Vegas Blvd. (734-0410), has the cheapest buffet in town; breakfast $3 (6-11:30am), brunch $4 (noon-4pm), dinner $5.

Excalibur, 3850 Las Vegas Blvd. South (597-7777), has the Roundtable Buffet; breakfast $3.50 (7-11am), lunch $4.50 (11am-4pm), dinner $6 (4-10pm).

Luxor, 3900 Las Vegas Blvd. South (262-4000), is a bit classier with a Manhattan Buffet; breakfast $4 (7:30-11am), lunch $5 (11am-4pm), dinner $7 (4-11pm).

Treasure Island, 3300 Las Vegas Blvd. South (894-7111), a couple bucks more of elegance with a choice of American, Italian, and Chinese; breakfast $5 (7-10:45am), lunch $7 (11am-3:45pm), dinner $9 (4-11pm).

CA$INO-HOPPING AND NIGHTLIFE

Gambling is illegal for those under 21. Casinos, nightclubs, and wedding chapels stay open 24 hrs. Hotels and most casinos give "funbooks," with alluring gambling coupons that can stretch your puny $5 into $50 worth of wagering. And always remember: *in the long run, you will almost definitely lose money.* Do not bring more money than you're prepared to lose cheerfully. Keep your wallet in your front pocket, and beware of the thieves who prowl casinos to nab big winnings from unwary jubilants. Some casinos offer free gambling lessons (Circus Circus and Caesar's); more patient dealers may offer a tip or two (in exchange for one from you).

Caesar's Palace, 3570 Las Vegas Blvd. (731-7110), is by far the most enjoyable casino in town. Marble statues grace hallways and lobby. Actors dressed in Roman garb wander through the hotel all day and night posing for pictures and uttering proclamations. A giant moving walkway sucks people into the palace from Las Vegas Blvd. The Forum Shops is an upscale mall inside the hotel with a "sky" which changes color to mimic the outside day. During the **Festival Fountain show,** statues stand, move, talk, battle, and shout amid a fantastic laser-light show—ah, all the trappings and decorum of old Rome (shows every ½ hr. 10am-11pm). Next door, **Mirage,** 3400 Las Vegas Blvd. S. (791-7111), includes among its attractions, tigers, a Dolphin habitat, an indoor tropical rain forest, and a "volcano" that erupts in fountains and flames every ½ hr. from 8pm-1am, barring bad weather. The new **Treasure Island,** 3300 Las Vegas Blvd. South (894-7111), features pirate battles with cannons staged on giant wooden ships in a "bay" on Las Vegas Blvd. (Daily every hour and a half from 4:30pm-midnight. Free.) **Luxor,** 3900 Las Vegas Blvd. (262-4000), has boat rides through the Nile River and hotel lobby (every 20 min. daily 9am-12:30am; $3). Or head to the **King Tut Tomb and Museum** which houses replicas of the artifacts uncovered at the king's grave (open Sun.-Thurs. 9am-11pm, Fri.-Sat. until 11:30pm; $3). The three, 3-D **holographic films,** *Search of the Obelisk,* *Luxor Live,* and *The Theater of Time* have dazzling special effects. The **MGM Grand,** 3799 Las Vegas Blvd. South (891-1111), has themes centered on Hollywood, especially the *Wizard of Oz.* **MGM Grand Adventures** has Disney-esque attractions that make me think Todo that we're not in Kansas anymore (open daily 10am-10pm; $15, ages 4-12 $10, seniors $9). **Circus Circus,** 2880 Las Vegas Blvd. S. (734-0410), attempts to cultivate a (dysfunctional) family atmosphere; while parents run to the card tables and slot machines downstairs, their children can spend 50¢ tokens upstairs on the souped-up carnival midway and enjoy the titanic video game arcade. Two stories above the casino floor, tightrope-walkers, fire-eaters, and rather impressive acrobats perform 1pm-midnight. Within the hotel complex is the **Grand Slam Canyon,** a Grand Canyon theme park with rollercoasters and other rides—all enclosed in a glass shell. (Open Sun.-Thurs. 10am-10pm, until midnight on Fri.-Sat. $15, under 12 $12.) **Excalibur,** 3850 Las Vegas Blvd. S. (800-937-7777), has a medieval England theme that may make you nostalgic for the Black Plague. The list goes on and on in a gaudy assemblage of Americana.

Extra bucks will buy you a seat at a made-in-the-U.S.A. phenomenon—the Vegas spectacular. The overdone but stunning twice-nightly casino-sponsored productions feature marvels such as waterfalls, explosions, fireworks, and casts of thousands (including animals). You can also see Broadway plays and musicals, ice revues, and individual entertainers in concert. Some "production shows" are topless; most are tasteless. To see a show by the musical stars who haunt the city, such as Diana Ross or Frank Sinatra, you may have to fork over $35 or more. Far more reasonable are the many "revues" featuring imitations of (generally deceased) performers. In Vegas you can't turn around without bumping into an aspiring Elvis clone, or perhaps the real Elvis, pursuing anonymity in the brilliant disguise of an Elvis impersonator. A cheaper alternative might be a more intimate lounge act, some charging only a drink minimum. All hotels have city-wide ticket booths in their lobbies.

Nightlife in Vegas gets rolling around midnight and keeps going until everyone drops or runs out of money. The casino lounge at the **Las Vegas Hilton,** 3000 Paradise Rd. (732-5111), has a disco every night (no cover, 2-drink min.). At Caesars Palace (731-7110) you can rock the boat at **Cleopatra's Barge,** a huge ship-disco (open Tues.-Sun. 10pm-4am; free). The **Hard Rock Café,** 4475 Paradise Rd. (733-8400), features its trademark Cadillac awning and rock-and-roll memorabilia. (Meals served Mon.-Fri. 11:30am-11:30pm, Sat.-Sun. 7am-midnight; bar open as long as humanity continues to drink.) The **Fremont Street Blues and Reggae Club** (594-7111) on Fremont and 4th, rocks the casbar with live music every night (open Sun.-Thurs. 7pm-3am, Fri-Sat. 7pm-5am). A popular disco, **Gipsy,** 4605 Paradise Rd. (731-1919), southeast of the Strip, may look deserted at 11pm, but by 1am the medium-sized dance floor packs in a gay, lesbian, and straight crowd. **Carrow's,** 1290 E. Flamingo Rd. (796-1314), has three outdoor patios, plus plenty of people and plants. During happy hour (4-7pm), the filling hors d'oeuvres are free. Laughter may be the best medicine for a painful losing streak. The **Comedy Stop at the Trop,** in the Tropicana, 3101 Las Vegas Blvd. (739-2714 or 800-634-4000), offers three comedians for $16 (includes 2 drinks); two shows every night (8 and 10:30pm).

Fans of classical music and kitsch will be delighted by the **Liberace Museum,** 1775 E. Tropicana Ave. (798-5595), devoted to the flamboyant late "Mr. Showmanship." There's fur, velvet, and rhinestone in combinations that boggle the rational mind, and outstrips the Strip. (Open Mon.-Sat. 10am-5pm, Sun. 1-5pm. $6.50, seniors $4.50, ages 6-12 $2.) **The Guinness World Records Museum,** 2870 Las Vegas Blvd. (792-3766), showcases freaky stuff and displays describing the most tattooed lady and the largest pizza (open daily 9am-9pm; $4.45, seniors, military, students $4). Join the flyin' Elvises at the **Las Vegas Skydiving Center** (877-1010) which will take you on a free-fall almost 2 mi. down at 120mph (call for more info).

■■■ LAKE MEAD NATIONAL RECREATION AREA

Hoover Dam, the Western Hemisphere's highest concrete dam and the brainchild of President Herbert Hoover, straddles Nevada and Arizona. The 4.4 million cubic yards of concrete holds back the Colorado River, creating man-made **Lake Mead.** Built in the 1930s, the dam stretches 226 ft. high and 1244 ft. across the Black Canyon. U.S. 93/95 runs right over the Hoover Dam. There is no public transportation to the dam. **Gray Line** buses and **Ray and Ross Tours** offers service from Las Vegas (see Las Vegas Practical Information). **Guided tours** into the powerplant bowels of the dam are offered continuously throughout the day. The tour lasts 45 min. (Tours given in the summer 8am-6:45pm; rest of the year 9am-4:15pm. Wheelchairs available. $3, kids under 11 free.) The **visitors center** (293-8367) lies on the Nevada half of the dam (open daily 8am-7pm in the summer; 9am-4:30pm rest of the year). There are several parking lots (free) at intervals along U.S. 93/95. Shuttle bus service is available from the more remote lots. Numerous National Park Service **campgrounds** lie within the recreation area. All cost $8 per night and are first-come, first-served. None have showers. Backcountry camping is permitted and free in most areas. The most popular campground is **Boulder Beach** (293-8906), accessible by Lakeshore Rd. off U.S. 93/95.

■■■ RENO

Reno, the "biggest little city in the world," is not much more than a branch of Las Vegas. With the same non-stop environment (the casinos are immune to the rhythm of the sun), Reno feeds on gambling and its proximity to Lake Tahoe and California.

Practical Information Contact the **Reno-Sparks Convention and Visitors Center,** 4590 Virginia St. (800-367-7366), at Kitsky (open Mon.-Sat. 7am-8pm, Sun. 9am-6pm). **Amtrak** gambles at 135 E. Commercial Row and Lake St. (329-8638 or 800-872-7245; open 8- 11:30am and 1-4:30pm). Trains to: San Francisco (1 per day, $58); Salt Lake City (1 per day, $111); Chicago (1 per day, $217). **Greyhound** bets at 155 Stevenson St. (322-2970; open 24 hrs.), ½ block from W. 2nd St. Buses to: San Francisco (14 per day, $34); Salt Lake City (3 per day, $49); L.A. (10 per day, $39). **Arrow Trans** (786-2376) and **Reno-Tahoe Connection** (825-3900) both offer bus service to S. Lake Tahoe ($18 per person, 4-person min., or $72 base fare). Reno's **post office:** 50 S. Virginia St. (786-5523; open Mon.-Fri. 9am-5pm, Sat. 10am-2pm); **ZIP code:** 89501; **area code:** 702.

Accommodations and Camping **El Cortez,** 239 W. 2nd St. (322-9161), 2 blocks east of Greyhound station, is run by pleasant management and offers terrific bargains. Rarely are city block hotels so clean. (Rooms $27; off-season $20. Add $3 on weekends and holidays.) The hall showers and rooms at **Windsor Hotel,** 214 West St. (323-6171), 1½ blocks from the Greyhound Station toward Virginia St., are wonderfully clean. Fans turn lazily overhead in compensation for the lack of A/C. (Singles $22, with bath $24. Doubles $28; Fri.-Sat. add $4.) Some of the best deals in town can be found in the major casinos, where all sorts of hidden discounts exist. Be nosy and ask enough questions and you just may find yourself paying $35 for a room on the 20th floor of the Hilton. Thursday night specials abound. Most casinos have welcome centers which can give advice on discounts.

Park your RV at the **Reno Hilton,** 2500 E. 2nd St. (789-2000), full hookup $18.50. The **Toiyabe National Forest,** only a few miles southwest of Reno, has camping. Also drive to the woodland sites of **Davis Creek Park** (849-0684), 17 mi. south on U.S. 395 then ½ mi. west (follow the signs). (Full service, including showers, but no hookups. Sites $9, each extra vehicle $3. Picnic area open 8am-9pm.)

Food Casinos offer a range of all-you-can-eat buffets, and 99¢ breakfasts. Local Basque food is spicy and delicious. **Louis' Basque Corner,** 301 E. 4th St. (323-7203), at Evans Ave., 3 blocks east of Virginia, is a local institution. The friendly bar, family-style dining, and hearty full-course dinner with wine make the price ($14, under 10 $6.50) happily bearable. (Open Mon.-Sat. 10am-2:30pm and 5:30-10pm, Sun. 4:30-9:30pm.) **Cal Neva,** 38 E. 2nd St. (323-1046), has 2-egg breakfasts with ham, toast, and jelly (99¢), 1-lb. prime rib dinner served 4-10pm ($7), includes rolls, all-you-can-eat salad bar, vegetable, and potato. Midnight sirloin steak special starts at 10:30pm, ($1.99). Seafood lovers will appreciate the lobster dinner (3 tails $9.60). **The Blue Heron,** 1091 S. Virginia St. (786-4110), at Vassar St., offers all-vegetarian, healthy cuisine. (Open Mon.-Fri. 11am-9pm, Sat.-Sun. noon-8pm.)

Gambling Those new to the gambling scene might try the **Behind the Scenes Gaming Tour** (333-2858), which takes you to the other side of the one-way mirrors, and instructs you in the rudiments of the games, teaching you exactly how they take your money. The 2-hr. tours show the surveillance at Calvera, and the tourists get a chance to play a few practice games. ($6. Tours leave from Ticket Station, 135 N. Sierra, daily 12:30pm.) Don't forget: *gambling is illegal for persons under 21 years of age*; if you win the jackpot at age 20, it'll be the casino's lucky day, not yours. Many casinos offer free gaming lessons and minimum bets vary between establishments—the best gamblers shop around before plunking down. Beer is usually free if you look as if you're gambling. Most casinos charge heftily for admission to their live shows, but **Circus Circus,** 500 N. Sierra (329-0711), has free 15-min. "big-top" performances (daily 11:15am-4:45pm and 6:10-11:40pm every ½-hr.).

Pyramid Lake Thirty mi. outside Reno off Pyramid Way on the Paiute Indian Reservation lies emerald green Pyramid Lake. Named for the pyramidal rock island in its midst, the lake is open for day use and camping. **Camping** is allowed anywhere on the lakeshore, but only some areas have toilets. A $5 **permit** is required for use of the park and the area is carefully patrolled by the Paiute tribe. Permits are available at the **Ranger Station** (476-1155; open Mon.-Sat. 9am-5pm) and at **Long's Drugs** (590 E. Prater Way; 900 E. Plumb Ln.; 2300 Odie Blvd.; 5019 S. McCurran Blvd.) in Reno/Sparks. Surrounded by sagebrush-covered hills, this remnant of an ancient sea is a local escape from city life. It contains a hot spring and a series of rocks on the north shore which beg to be climbed. Those looking for solitude should try the south and east shores; north of the ranger station is clogged with RVs.

ROCKY MOUNTAINS

Whether you're crossing from the western desert or the midwestern plain, these "purple mountain majesties" soar unexpectedly. Sagebrush, ponderosa, and mountain lupine replace corn and wheat as grassland yields to open pine forest, and then, at the timberline, the forest gives way to the peerless peaks of the Rockies. This continental divider stretches from northern Canada to central Utah, all the while blushing with pristine alpine meadows, forbidding rocky gorges, and unpolluted streams.

The whole Rocky Mountains area supports less than five percent of the population of the U.S., and much of the land is preserved in national parks, forests, and wilderness areas. The Waterton-Glacier International Peace Park straddles Montana's border with Alberta; Wyoming and Colorado are the landlords of Yellowstone and Rocky Mountain National Parks; Idaho encompasses two back-country regions, as well as acre upon acre of state and national forest. The area boasts stunningly scenic trails for car, foot, or bike—there's a way for everyone to experience the Rockies.

Not surprisingly, most residents of the mountain states live close to the land; even in Colorado, agriculture is still bigger business than tourism. Denver, the only major metropolis in the region, combines sophistication with an appreciation for the area's rich natural endowment. Most other cities are oil or mining towns, ski villages, or university seats—commercial centers are in short supply in the mountains.

 # Colorado

For millions of years, Colorado has been eroded into beauty. The Gunnison and Colorado Rivers have carved terrific museums of "natural history," such as the Black Canyon and the Colorado National Monument. In a shorter and less interesting amount of time, Europeans settlers came here and chiseled the region for its silver and gold. Even today, the U.S. military has dug enormous "intelligence" installations into the mountains around Colorado Springs.

But from its depths rise extraordinary heights. Hikers, skiers, and climbers worship Colorado's peaks, giving rise to cool enclaves from the wild such as Grand Junction and Crested Butte. As the hub of the state and the entire Rocky Mountain region, Denver provides both an ideal resting place for cross-country travelers and a "culture fix" for people heading to the mountains.

PRACTICAL INFORMATION

Capital: Denver.

The Colorado Board of Tourism (800-265-6723) *was closed for an indefinite period of time* at press. Call the chamber of commerce in the area you plan to visit. **U.S. Forest Service,** Rocky Mountain Region, 740 Sims St., Lakewood 80225 (275-5360). Free tour maps; forest maps $3. Open Mon.-Fri. 7:30am-4:30pm. **Ski Country USA,** 1560 Broadway #1440, Denver 80202 (837-0793, open Mon.-Fri. 8am-5pm; recorded message 831-7669). **National Park Service,** 12795 W. Alameda Pkwy., P.O. Box 25287, Denver 80255 (969-2000). For reservations for Rocky Mountain National Park, call 800-365-2267. Open Mon.-Fri. 7:30am-5pm. **Colorado State Parks and Recreation,** 1313 Sherman St. #618, Denver 80203 (866-3437). Guide to state parks and metro area trail guide. Open Mon.-Fri. 8am-5pm.

Time Zone: Mountain (2 hr. behind Eastern). **Postal Abbreviation:** CO

Sales Tax: 7.3% in Denver but varies from city to city.

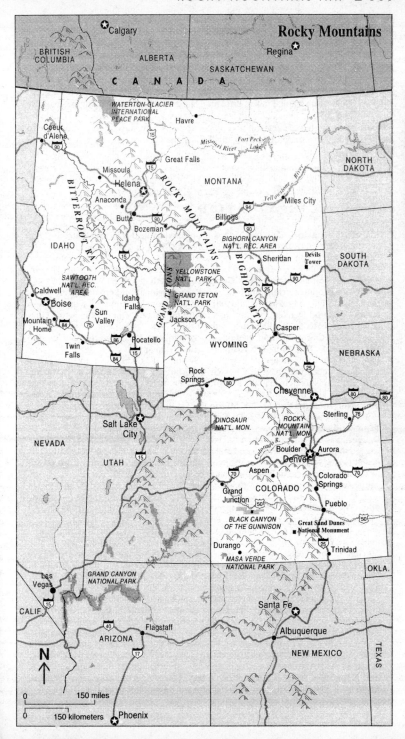

■■■ DENVER

In 1858 the discovery of a small amount of gold at the base of the Rocky Mountains brought a premature rush of eager miners to northern Colorado. The town prospered with the patronage of desperadoes who searched the mountains for the mother-lode. Three separate towns fought over the right to name the city until peace was restored when the name "Denver" was bought with a barrel of whiskey.

Today, Colorado's capital is the Rockies's largest and fastest growing metropolis. Centrally located between Colorado's eastern plains and western ski resorts, Denver serves as the commercial and cultural nexus of the region, and has recently gone to the big show with a major league baseball team, the Colorado Rockies. The city has doubled in population since 1960 and continues to attract diversity—ski bums, sophisticated city-slickers from the coasts, and, of course, the old-time cowpokes. The gold mines may be depleted, but Denver retains its best asset—a combination of big city sophistication and the laid-back attitude of the West.

PRACTICAL INFORMATION

Emergency: 911.

Visitor Information: Denver Metro Convention and Visitors Bureau, 225 West Colfax Ave. (892-1112 or 892-1505), near Civic Center Park just south of the capitol. Open Mon.-Sat. 8am-5pm, Sun. 10am-2pm; winter Mon.-Fri. 8am-5pm, Sat. 9am-1pm. Pick up a free copy of the comprehensive *Denver Official Visitors Guide.* **Big John's Information Center,** 1055 19th St. (892-1505 or 892-1112), at the Greyhound station. Big John, an ex-professional basketball player, offers enthusiastic info on hosteling and activities in Colorado. Stop by for information on tours around Denver and day trips to the mountains. Open Mon.-Sat. 7-11am and 1-3pm. **16th St. Ticket Bus,** in the 16th St. Mall at Curtis St. Double-decker bus with visitor information, half-price tickets to local theater performances, and RTD bus info. Open Mon.-Fri. 10am-6pm, Sat. 11am-3pm.

Airports: Stapleton International (398-3844 or 800-247-2336), in northeast Denver. Easily accessible from downtown. RTD bus lines #28, 32, 38 serve the airport. For buses to Denver, take a right out of Door 12 (E concourse); wait at sign #2. Buses A and B go to Boulder. Cab fare to downtown $8-12. **Ground Transportation Information** (270-1750) on the 1st floor can arrange transport to surrounding areas such as Estes Park, Vail, and other nearby resorts. Open daily 7am-11pm. Still not officially opened, **Denver International** (342-2000), in northeast Denver, was scheduled to open in Dec. 1993, but due to problems with the luggage system, it will remain closed at least through the fall of 1994. When it opens it will be the largest airport in the world (53 square miles). 30 min. from downtown, it will be accessible by both taxi and bus.

Trains: Amtrak, Union Station (534-2812 or 800-872-7245), at 17th St. and Wynkoop, in the nw corner of downtown. *See Mileage Chart.* Ticket office open 7am-9pm. The **Río Grande Ski Train,** 555 17th St. (296-4754). Leaves from Amtrak Union Station and treks through the Rockies, stopping in Winter Park (Dec.-April only). Departs Denver at 7:15am, Winter Park at 4:15pm; 2 hr.; $30 round-trip.

Buses: Greyhound, 1055 19th St. (800-231-2222 or 293-6555), downtown. *See Mileage Chart.* Ticket office open 6:10am-10pm. **Gray Line Tours:** At the bus station, 19th and Curtis St. (289-2841). In the summer, daily to Rocky Mountain National Park (10 hr.; $38, under 12 $29), the U.S. Air Force Academy (7½ hr.; $29, under 12 $15). Year-round tours of Denver Mountain Parks (3½ hr.; $20, under 12 $10) and of the city (2½ hr.; $17, under 12 $9), twice daily in summer.

Public Transport: Regional Transportation District (RTD), 1600 Blake St. (299-6000). Service within Denver and to Longmont, Evergreen, Conifer, Golden, and suburbs. Route hours vary; Many shut down by 9pm or earlier. Fare Mon.-Fri. 6-9am and 4-6pm $1; all other times 50¢; over 65 15¢. Have exact fare. Free 16th Street Mall Shuttle covers 14 blocks downtown. Over 20 buses per day to Boulder (45 min.; $2.50). Call Mon.-Fri. 6am-8pm, Sat.-Sun. 8am-8pm. Bus maps $1.

Taxi: Metro Taxi, 333-3333. **Yellow Cab,** 777-7777. **Zone Cab,** 444-8888. All $1.40 base fare, $1.40 per mi. Numbers for the memory impaired.

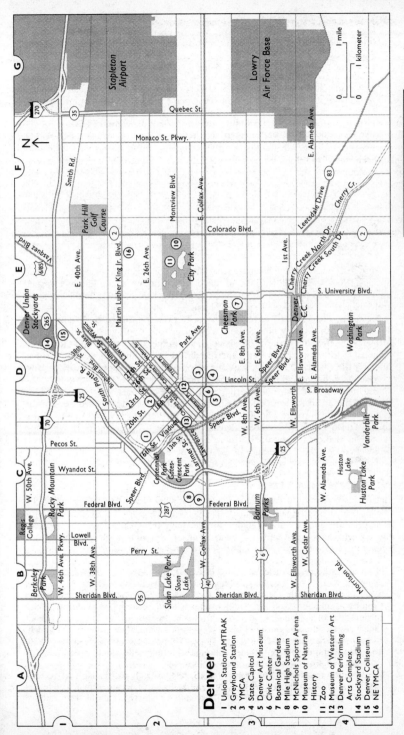

Stapleton Airport

Lowry Air Force Base

Quebec St.

Monaco St. Pkwy.

Smith Rd.

Vasquez Blvd.

Park Hill Golf Course

Montview Blvd.

E. Colfax Ave.

E. Alameda Ave.

Colorado Blvd.

Leetsdale Drive

Cherry Cr.

S. University Blvd.

City Park

Denver C.C.

Cherry Creek North Dr.

Cherry Creek South Dr.

Martin Luther King Jr. Blvd.

E. 40th Ave.

E. 26th Ave.

1st Ave.

Cheesman Park

Washington Park

Denver Union Stockyards

South Platte R.

Blake St.

Walnut St.

Lawrence St.

Larimer St.

Brighton Blvd.

Park Ave.

E. 8th Ave.

E. 6th Ave.

Speer Blvd.

Speer Blvd.

Lincoln St.

S. Broadway

E. Ellsworth Ave.

E. Alameda Ave.

20th St.

23rd St.

16th St. / Viaduct

13th St.

Curtis St.

Champa St.

Lawrence St.

Speer Blvd.

W. 8th Ave.

W. 6th Ave.

W. Ellsworth

Vanderbilt Park

Pecos St.

Wyandot St.

Centennial Park

Gates-Crescent Park

Huston Lake

Huston Lake Park

W. 50th Ave.

Rocky Mountain Park

Federal Blvd.

Federal Blvd.

W. Alameda Ave.

Regis College

Lowell Blvd.

Speer Blvd.

Barnum Parks

W. 46th Ave. Pkwy.

W. 38th Ave.

Perry St.

W. Colfax Ave.

W. Ellsworth Ave.

W. Cedar Ave.

Morrison Rd.

Berkeley Park

Sloan Lake Park

Sloan Lake

Sheridan Blvd.

Sheridan Blvd.

Sheridan Blvd.

0   1 mile

0   1 kilometer

Denver

1 Union Station/AMTRAK
2 Greyhound Station
3 YMCA
4 State Capitol
5 Denver Art Museum
6 Civic Center
7 Botanical Gardens
8 Mile High Stadium
9 McNichols Sports Arena
10 Museum of Natural History
11 Zoo
12 Museum of Western Art
13 Denver Performing Arts Complex
14 Stockyard Stadium
15 Denver Coliseum
16 NE YMCA

Car Rental: Be wary of renting clunkers in the mountains; check out the car before accepting it. More expensive car rentals like Hertz and Avis may be worth it if you are going to remote areas. **Rent-a-Heap,** 7900 E. 40th Ave. (698-0345). $18 per day, $108 per week, unlimited free mi., but you must remain in the metro area. Open Mon.-Fri. 8am-6pm, Sat. 8am-1pm. Must have $50 deposit and proof of liability insurance. **Cheap Heaps Rent-a-Car,** 6005 E. Colfax Ave. (393-0028). $17-25 per day, $110-125 per week, $389 per month, 50 free mi. per day; 500 free mi. per week, 1500 free mi. per month. Open Mon.-Fri. 8am-6pm, Sat. 8am-2pm. Must have at least $100 deposit and proof of liability insurance or $7 additional insurance charge per day. For both, must be at least 21 and stay in CO.

Auto Transport Company: Auto Driveaway, 5777 E. Evans Ave. (757-1211); take bus #21 to Holly and Evans. Open Mon.-Fri. 8:30am-5pm. Must have a $250 cash deposit, a valid drivers license, and be at least 21. There is a $10 fee.

Help Lines: Contact Lifeline, 758-1123, 24 hrs. **Comitus** (general crisis line) 343-9390. 24 hrs. **Rape Crisis Center,** 329-9922. 24 hrs. Office open Mon.-Fri. 9am-5pm. **Rape Emergency Hotline,** 322-7273. **Gay and Lesbian Community Center,** 831-6268. Open Mon.-Fri. 10am-10pm, Sat. 10am-1pm. **Gay and Lesbian Help Line,** 837-1598.

Post Office: 951 20th St. (297-6000). Open Mon-Fri. 9am-5pm, Sat. 9am-noon. **ZIP code:** 80202.

Area Code: 303.

During rush hour, traffic sits at a virtual standstill between Denver and Colorado Springs. I-70 links Denver with Grand Junction (250 mi. west) and Kansas City (600 mi. east). Rte. 285 cuts south through the central Rockies, opening up the Saguache and Sangre de Cristo Ranges to easy exploration.

Broadway divides east Denver from west Denver and **Ellsworth Avenue** forms the north-south dividing line. Streets west of Broadway progress in alphabetical order, while the streets north of Ellsworth are numbered. Streets downtown run diagonal to those in the rest of the metropolis. Keep in mind that many of the avenues on the eastern side of the city become numbered *streets* downtown. Most even-numbered thoroughfares downtown run only east-west.

The hub of downtown is the **16th Street Mall.** Few crimes occur in the immediate area, but avoid the west end of Colfax Ave., the east side of town beyond the capitol, and the upper reaches of the **Barrio** (25th-34th St.) at night. **Lower downtown** ("Lo Do" to locals), a 22-block area from 20th St. to Speer, and from Wynkoop St., S.E. to Market St., is on the northern edge of downtown Denver. The Victorian buildings reflect the architecture of the silver boom era at the turn of the century, and today house trendy restaurants, art galleries, offices, and shops.

ACCOMMODATIONS

Denver offers many affordable accommodations within easy reach of downtown by foot or bus. Hostelers with specific interests (or no ideas at all) can see "Big John" Schrant at the Greyhound bus station for information and directions. The hotels in the downtown area are fairly expensive, but for discount packages that include events and tours, call **Mile High Lights** (800-489-4888; open Mon.-Fri. 8am-5pm).

Melbourne International Hostel (HI-AYH), 607 22nd St. (292-6386), downtown at Welton St., yet a bit outside the well-traversed downtown area—women and lone travelers should be cautious. Owned by WWII pilot Leonard Schmitt and run by his nephew Gary, the Melbourne is a clean, well-run hostel, just 6 blocks from the 16th St. Mall. Ask Gary (the office is in the laundromat downstairs) about local restaurants and music clubs. Every room has a fridge; communal kitchen. Check-in 7am-midnight. No curfew. Dorms $8, private rooms $15, couples $20; nonmembers: dorms $9, private room $18, doubles $24. Sheet rental $2. Key deposit $10. Call ahead for reservations June-Oct.

Denver International Youth Hostel (Rucksackers), 630 E. 16th Ave. (832-9996), 10 blocks east of the bus station, 4 blocks north of downtown. The hostel is outside the well-traversed area, women and lone travelers should be cautious.

Take bus #15 to Washington St., 1 block away or take free 16th St. shuttle to Broadway and walk east on 16th Ave. for 6 blocks. Office open daily 8am-10am and 5pm-10:30pm. Dorm-style rooms with its own bathroom and kitchen. Laundry facilities and communal fridge occasionally stocked. $8.50, $1 discount with a copy of this guide. Sheet rental $1. Call to arrange arrival plans during office hours. "Professor K's" full-day tour of Denver and the surrounding mountains leaves from the hostel Mon.-Sat. at 9:15am ($12).

Franklin House B&B, 1620 Franklin St. (331-9106). European-style inn within walking distance of downtown. Clean and spacious rooms, free breakfast. Not for late-night arrivals. Singles $20. Doubles $32, with private bath $42. $10 for each additional person. MC, Visa, and travelers checks welcome.

YMCA, 25 E. 16th St. (861-8300) at Lincoln St. Divided into 3 parts for men, women, and families. Laundry and TV rooms. Singles $20 per day, $81 weekly. With a shared bath $22.50, private bath $27. Doubles with bath $40.25, with shared bath $38 per day, $148 weekly, with shared bath $136. Key deposit $12.

Motel 6, 8 locations in the greater Denver area, all with A/C, pool, and TV. All are accessible by local bus. North: 6 W. 83rd Pl. (429-1550); Northwest: 10300 S. I-70 Frontage Rd. (467-3172), 3050 W. 49th Ave. (455-8888); East (near Stapleton Airport): 12020 E. 39th Ave. (371-1980), 12033 E. 38th Ave. (371-0740); South: 480 S. Wadsworth Blvd. (232-4924), 9201 E. Arapahoe Rd. (790-8220). Singles $20-30, each additional person $6. All major credit cards accepted.

CAMPING

There are plenty of places to camp in the Denver area. Contact the Metro-Regional office of the **Colorado Division of Parks and Recreation** (791-1957; open Mon.-Fri. 9am-5pm) for more information on campgrounds, or **Denver Mountain Parks Reservations** (331-4029). For reservations at any campground in the Denver area call (470-1144 or 800-678-2267).

Cherry Creek Lake Recreation Area (699-3860). Take I-25 to exit 200, then west on Rte. 225 for about 1½ mi. and south on Parker Rd.—follow the signs, or take the "Parker Road" bus. The 102 sites fill only on summer weekends. Sites $7, with electricity $10. Daily entrance fee $4. $6.75 reservation fee. Max. 90 days advance for reservations, min. 14 days if reserve by check, 3 days for credit cards.

Chatfield Reservoir (791-7275). Take I-75 or I-85 south to Rte. 470 W. to Wadsworth. Then turn south for 2 stoplights and follow the signs. 153 well-developed sites. Sites $7, with electricity $10. Open mid-April to mid-Oct. Make reservations for weekends. Daily entrance fee $3.

Aspen Meadows Campground (642-3856). Take I-70 west to 6th Ave. Take 6th Ave. west towards Central City to Rte. 119. Follow this road 19 mi. north to signs for park's entrance. 35 sites, no electricity. Sites $6. Daily entrance fee $3.

National Forest Campgrounds (275-5350) are plentiful in the mountains 25 mi. west of Denver near **Idaho Springs,** Rte. 103 and Rte. 40, and in the region around **Deckers,** 30 mi. southwest of downtown on Rte. 67. **Lone Rock** (in the Deckers area) has 19 marked sites that are difficult to find. Call ahead for directions. **Painted Rocks Campground** (719-636-1602), on Rte. 67, in the Pikes Peak Ranger District. Sites $4. **Top of the World** (275-5610), off Pine Junction on Rte. 126. Look down on creation from 7 free sites with no water. Most campgrounds open May-Sept. Call ahead or pick up maps at the **National Forest's Rocky Mountain Regional Headquarters,** 11177 W. 8th Ave., Lakewood (236-9431; open Mon.-Fri. 8am-5pm).

FOOD

Downtown Denver is great for inexpensive Mexican and Southwestern food. Eat al fresco and people-watch at the cafes along the **16th St. Mall. Larimer Square,** 1½ southwest from the mall on Larimer St, has several more gourmet eateries. **Sakura Square,** at 19th St. and Larimer, offers Japanese cuisine in restaurants and a market.

Colorado's distance from the ocean may make you wonder about *Rocky Mountain oysters.* This delicacy of fried bull testicles and other buffalo-meat specialties can be found at the **Denver Buffalo Company,** 1109 Lincoln St. (832-0080). They are expensive, but it may be worth—if only for the story.

The Market, 1445 Larimer Sq. (534-5140), downtown. Popular with a young artsy crowd that people-watches alongside suits and hippies. Cappuccino $2, sandwiches $4-5, and exotic salads $5-8 per lb. Open Mon.-Thurs. 6:30-11pm, Fri.-Sat. 7:30am-midnight, Sun. 7:30-6pm.

City Spirit Café, 1434 Blake St. (575-0022), a few blocks from the north end of the 16th St. Mall. Check out the funky decor with waitstaff to match. Serving delicious salads ($6), vegetarian dishes (try the City Smart Burrito $6.25), and homemade desserts. Acid jazz on Tue. nights, a disco party on Fri. Open Mon.-Thurs. 11am-midnight, Fri.-Sat. 11am-2am.

Mead St. Station, 3625 W. 32nd Ave. (433-2138). Take bus #32 between Mead and Lowell. A slightly artsy pub for locals north of the city. Try the John Bull, a gourmet cheesecake ($5.95), or the MacGregor sandwich ($4.95) for vegetarians. Live music Sun. and Tues. nights. Open Tues.-Sat. 11am-midnight, Sun. 2pm-midnight, Mon. 4pm-midnight.

Wynkoop Brewery (297-2700), at 18th St. and Wynkoop across from Union Station. An American pub in a renovated warehouse that serves beer (pint $3), Alfalfa mead, and homemade root beer. Serves lunch and dinner too (burgers $5). Pool tables upstairs. Happy hour 3-6pm, $1.50 pints. Brewery open Mon.-Sat. 11am-2am, Sun. 11am-midnight. Free brewery tours Sat. 1-5pm.

Mercury Café, 2199 California (294-9281). Just across from the Melbourne Hostel. Inside is decorated like an old tea parlor. Homebaked wheat bread and reasonably priced lunch and dinner items. 10-oz. sirloin with bread and vegetable $10. Mon.-Fri. 11:30am-2:30pm and 5:30pm-2am, Sat.-Sun. 9am-3pm and 5:30pm-2am. Nightly events include live bands, open stage, and poetry readings until 2am.

Goldie's Deli, 511 16th St. (623-6007), at the Glenarm on the Mall. Great for picnic-fixings—or eat at outside tables. Sandwiches and salads $4, with low-fat, low-cholesterol options. Open Mon.-Sat. 11am-4pm.

Reese Coffee House, 1435 Curtis St. (534-4304) between 14th and 15th. In the basement of an apartment building across from the Denver Performing Arts Complex. Cheap but good breakfast 24 hrs.

SIGHTS

Denver's mild, dry climate and 300 days of sunshine (sorry, no money-back guarantees) promises pleasant days. The **Denver Metro Visitors Bureau,** (see Practical Information above) across from the U.S. Mint, is a good place to plan tours in the city or to the mountains. A great deal is the **Cultural Connection Trolley** where $2 takes you to over 20 of the city's main attractions. The 1-hr. tour runs daily every 20 min. from 9:20am to 5:50pm; buy your tickets from the driver. The tour begins at the **Denver Performing Arts Complex** (follow the arches to the end of Curtis, at 14th St.), but can be picked up near any of the attractions or the visitors bureau. Look for the green and red sign. The fare entitles you to a full day of transportation, so feel free to get off at any or all of the sights.

A modern reminder of Colorado's old silver mining days, the **U.S. Mint,** 320 W. Colfax (844-3582), issues U.S. coins with a small "D" for Denver embossed beneath the date. Free 15-min. tours, every 15-20 min. in summer and every 30 min. in winter, will lead you past a million-dollar pile of gold bars and expose you to the deafening roar of money-making machines that churn out a total of 20 million shiny coins per day. And, no, they do not give free samples. Arrive early; summer lines often reach around the block. (Tours Mon.-Fri. 8am-2:45pm, sales Mon.-Fri. 8am-3:30pm. Tickets must be bought in person the day of the tour.)

Don't be surprised if the 15th step on the west side of the **State Capitol Building** is crowded—it is exactly 5280 ft. (1 mi.) above sea level. The gallery under the 24-karat-gold-covered dome gives a great view of the Rocky Mountains. Free tours include visits to the Senate and House of Representatives chambers. (Tours every 30 min., summer Mon.-Sat. 9:30am-5:30pm, winter Mon.-Fri. 9:30am-2pm.)

Just a few blocks from the capitol and the U.S. Mint stands the **Denver Art Museum,** 100 W. 14th Ave. (640-2793). Architect Gio Ponti designed this six-story "vertical" museum in order to accommodate totem poles and period architecture. The museum's collection of Native American art rivals any in the world. The fabulous third floor of pre-Columbian art of the Americas resembles an archeological excavation site with temples, huts, and idols. Call for information on special exhibits. (Open Tues.-Sat. 10am-5pm, Sun. noon-5pm. $3, seniors and students $1.50, Sat. free for everyone.) Housed in the Navarre Building, the **Museum of Western Art,** 1727 Tremont Place (296-1880), holds a stellar collection of Russell, Benton, O'Keeffe, and Grant Wood paintings and drawings. (Open Tues.-Sat. 10am-4:30pm.) You can still see the tunnel which connects this one-time brothel to the **Brown Palace,** across the street at 321 17th St. (297-3111), a historic grand hotel that once hosted presidents, generals, and movie stars. Step in to see the beautiful atrium lobby. **The Black American West Museum and Heritage Center,** 91 California St. (292-2566), will show you a side of frontier history left unexplored by John Wayne movies. Come here to learn that one-third of all cowboys were African-American, and discover other details left out of textbooks. (Open Mon.-Fri. 10am-3pm, Sat. noon-5pm, Sun. 2-5pm. $2, seniors $1.50, ages 12-17 75¢, under 12 50¢.)

The **Natural History Museum,** 2001 Colorado Blvd. (322-7009), in City Park, presents lifelike wildlife sculptures and dioramas (open daily 9am-5pm; $4.50, ages 4-12 and seniors $2.50). The Natural History Museum complex includes the **Gates Planetarium** with its "Laserdrive" show and an **IMAX theater** (370-6300; call for shows, times and current prices). Across the park roars the **Denver Zoo** (331-4100), at E. 23rd St. and Steele, where you can view the live versions of the museum specimens. (Open daily 9am-6pm, gates close at 5:30pm; $6, seniors and kids 4-12 $3.)

Red Rocks Amphitheater and Park, 12 mi. southwest of Denver on I-70, is carved into red sandstone. As the sun sets over the city, even the best performers must compete with the natural spectacle behind them. (For tickets call 694-1234, Mon.-Fri. 9:30-5:30pm. Park admission free. Shows $15-40.) West of Denver in nearby Golden is the **Coors Brewery** (277-2337), 3rd and Ford St., founded by brewer Adolf Coors (free 30-min. tours every 20-30min. Mon.-Sat. 10am-4pm). Go and take a tour.

For outdoor enthusiasts Denver has many public parks for bicycling, walking, or lolling about in the sun. **Cheesman Park** (take bus #6 or #10), one of the 205 parks in Denver, offers a view of the snow-capped peaks of the Rockies. For Denver Parks information, call 698-4900. For a wilder park experience from June-September, take I-70 from Golden to Idaho Springs, and then pick up Rte. 103 south over the summit (14,260 ft.) of **Mt. Evans.** Check with **Colorado Division of Parks and Outdoor Recreation** (866-3437) about road conditions in fall and winter (open Mon.-Fri. 8am-5pm). A paved bike and foot trail runs along Cherry Creek for 20 mi.

ENTERTAINMENT AND NIGHTLIFE

Denver's local restaurants and bars cater to a college-age and slightly older singles crowd. Pick up a copy of *Westword* for details on the downtown club scene and local events. At **Muddy's Java Café**, 2200 Champa St. (298-1631), you can spend nights listening to live music or reading a novel from their bookstore while you eat dinner. Muddy's will even serve you an early breakfast after a long night of partying. (Open daily 4pm-4am, Happy Hour 4-7pm.) **My Brother's Bar**, 2376 15th St. at Platte (455-9991) is a "bar of conversation." That means no sports TVs or pool tables but a friendly, chatty atmosphere. Beer on tap is $2.50 for imported, $1.50 for domestic. Live music plays every Saturday. No cover and outdoor seating make it a local favorite. The "Hill of the Grasshopper," **El Chapultepec** (295-9126), 20th and Market St., is an authentic hole-in-the-wall with live music every night (open daily 7am-2am; one drink min. per set). **Lane's Tavern**, 11400 W. Colfax in Lakewood (233-9723), serves only Coors but quantity replaces quality—ask for one and you get a platter of ten 10 oz. glasses. (Open Mon.-Sat. 3pm on.) At **Bangles**, 4501 E. Virginia (377-2702), live bands blare in the evening, and the afternoon volleyball matches often become jubilant free-for-alls after a few pitchers of beer ($5). (Open daily 8pm-2am. Volleyball games Tues.-Fri. at 5:30pm. Cover $1-4.) **Ex Hole,** 2936 Fox St. (265-8505), is a popular gay bar but is not in a very safe neighborhood. Other gay bars can be found located on S. Broadway just between 1st Ave. and Alameda Ave.

Every January, Denver hosts the world's largest rodeo, the **National Western Stock Show** (297-1166). Cowfolk compete for prize money while over 10,000 head of cattle compete for "Best of Breed." **A Taste of Colorado** takes place during the last weekend in August, featuring a large outdoor celebration at Civic Center Park, near the capitol, with food vendors and open-air concerts from Colorado's own.

In April of 1995, the baseball **Colorado Rockies** (292-0200) will open their season in the brand new **Coors Stadium** at 20th and Blake. (Tickets $12, $1 on game day to sit in the Rock Pile.) In the fall the **Denver Broncos** (433-7466) reclaim **Mile High Stadium** and football fever spreads throughout the state. Denver's NBA team, the **Nuggets,** are on the rise. Catch them at **McNichols Arena** (572-4703).

■ MOUNTAIN RESORTS NEAR DENVER

Summit County Skiers, hikers, and mountain bikers will find a sportman's paradise in the six towns of Summit County, about 55 mi. west of Denver on I-70. All six towns fall under the jurisdiction of the **Summit County Chamber of Commerce,** 110 Summit Blvd., P.O. Box 214, Frisco 80443 (668-5800 or 668-2051), which provides information on current area events (open daily 9am-5pm). **Breckenridge, Dillon, Copper Mountain, Keystone, Frisco,** and **Silverthorne** are extremely popular with skiers and outdoorsmen from in-state, but provide somewhat of a respite from the expensive and adulterated resorts of Aspen and Vail.

Even if you aren't a sportsman, stay at the fantastic, incredible, amazing, perfect **Alpen Hütte (HI-AYH),** 471 Rainbow Dr. (468-6336), in Silverthorne. The Greyhound bus from Denver stops just outside the door, as does the **Summit Stage** shuttle bus, which provides free transportation to and from any on the Summit County towns. This immaculate and delightful hostel is a bargain of unsurpassed quality. (Office open 7am-noon, 4pm-midnight, and is located across the street from an immense recreation center.) Guest rooms are closed 9:30am-3:30pm. Curfew is midnight. Rates vary seasonally; summer rates are lowest ($10, nonmembers $12), while winter rates are highest, peaking at $23. (Discounts for groups. On-site parking, TV, wheelchair accessible. Lockers $5 deposit. Free sheets and towels. Reservations recommended.) **Breckenridge,** only 15 min. away by car, is a more fashionable town than Silverthorne. Despite the many expensive restaurants and stores, you can still find reasonable accommodations at the **Fireside Inn,** 114 N. French St. (453-6456), one block east of Main St. Indoor hot-tub is great for *apresski.* (Closed in May. Rates vary seasonally; dormitory $15, private rooms $40-60 in summer, up to $27/$80-130 in winter.) Reservation deposit fee (first two nights lodging) due within 10 days of reservation; balance is due thirty days before your arrival.

Winter Park 68 mi. northwest of Denver on U.S. 40, Winter Park slaloms among delicious-smelling mountain pines, surrounded by 600 square miles of skiing, hiking, and biking trails. The **Winter Park-Fraser Valley Chamber of Commerce,** 50 Vasquez Rd. (726-4118; in Denver 422-0666), provides information about skiing at the Winter Park Mary Jane Ski Area (open daily 9am-5pm). The chamber also serves as the **Greyhound** depot (2 buses per day from Denver, 2 hr., $10). The nearest **Amtrak** station is in Fraser (726-8816). **Home James Transportation Services** (726-5060 or 800-451-4844), runs door-to-door shuttles to and from Denver Airport (1 per day, 2 Sundays mid-April-mid-Nov.; 6 per day mid-Nov.-mid-Dec. and in early April; 11 per day mid-Dec.-April 1; $30 each way). Call ahead for reservations. From December to April, the **Río Grande Ski Train** (296-4754) leaves from

Denver's Union Station Saturday-Sunday at 7:15am, arriving in Winter Park at 9:30am, and departing Winter Park at 4:15pm ($30 round-trip).

On the town's southern boundary, Polly and Bill run the **Winter Park Hostel (HI-AYH)** (726-5356), 2½ blocks from the Greyhound stop and 2 mi. from Amtrak (free shuttle if you call ahead). The hostel is made up of converted trailer units, each with its own kitchen, bathroom, and living area (32 beds including 2-, 4-, and 6-person bunkrooms and 3 double-bed rooms). In winter, free shuttles run to the ski area and supermarket. Hosteler's discounts save you money on bike and ski rentals, raft trips, and restaurants. (Nov.-April $12, nonmembers $15; May-Oct. $8, nonmembers $10. Private room $3 more, $1 per extra person. Linens $2 for the sleep-sackless. Check-in 8-11:30am; 4-7pm. Closed April 15-June 15.) Call for reservations. **Le Ski Lab,** 7894 U.S. 40 (726-9841), conveniently next door, offers discounts for hostelers (mountain bikes $9 per day; ski rentals $8). **Timber Rafting** offers an all-day rafting trip ($39 for hostelers, includes transportation and lunch). The **Alpine Slide,** at 1½ mi., is Colorado's longest. (Open daily June 5-Sept. 6, weekends through Sept. 10am-7pm; $5, seniors and kids $3.) You and your bike can ride the **Zephyr Express** chairlift to the more challenging trails. (Open June 19-Sept. 6 10am-5pm; June 26-Aug. 15 until 6:30pm; $15 per day.) Every Saturday at 6pm in July and August get trampled underfoot at the **High Country Stampede Rodeo** at the John Work Arena, west of Fraser on County Road 73 (adults $6, children $3).

■■■ BOULDER

Almost painfully hip, Boulder lends itself to the pursuit of both higher knowledge and better karma. It is home to the central branch of the University of Colorado (CU) and the only accredited Buddhist university in the U.S., the Naropa Institute. Only here can you take summer poetry and mantra workshops lead by Beat guru Allen Ginsberg at the Jack Kerouac School of Disembodied Poets.

Boulder is an aesthetic and athletic mecca. The nearby Flatiron Mountains, rising up in charcoal-colored slabs on the western horizon, beckon rock climbers, while a system of paths make Boulder one of the most bike- and pedestrian-friendly areas around. For those motorists seeking a pacific retreat into nature, Boulder is *on the road* (Colorado Rte. 36) to Rocky Mountain National Park, Estes Park, and Grand Lake.

PRACTICAL INFORMATION

Emergency: 911.

Visitor Information: Boulder Chamber of Commerce/Visitors Service, 2440 Pearl St. (442-1044 or 800-444-0447), at Folsom about 10 blocks from downtown. Take bus #200. Open Mon. 9am-5pm, Tues.-Fri. 8:30am-5pm. **University of Colorado Information** (492-6161), 2nd floor of University Memorial Center (UMC) student union. Campus maps. Open Mon.-Thurs. 7am-11pm, Fri.-Sat. 7am-midnight, Sun. 11am-11pm. The **CU Ride Board,** UMC, Broadway at 16th, advertises lots of rides and lots of riders—even in the summer.

Public Transport: Boulder Transit Center (299-6000), 14th and Walnut St. Routes to Denver and Longmont as well as intra-city routes. Buses run Mon.-Fri. 6am-8pm, Sat.-Sun. 8am-8pm. Fare 50¢, Mon.-Fri. 6-9am and 4-6pm $1. To Nederland ("N" bus) and Lyons ("Y" bus) $1.50; to Golden ("G" bus) and to Boulder Foothills or Denver ("H" bus) $2.50. Several other lines link up with the Denver system (see Denver Practical Information). Get a bus map ($1) at the terminal.

Taxi: Boulder Yellow Cab, 442-2277. $1.50 base fare, $1.20 per mi.

Car Rental: Budget Rent-a-Car, 1545 28th St. (444-9054), near the Clarion Harvest House. Rates begin at $30 per day; $150 per week. Must be at least 25. Open Mon.-Fri. 8am-6pm, Sat. 8am-1pm, Sun. 9am-2pm.

Bike Rental: University Bicycles, 839 Pearl St. (444-4196), downtown. 12 and 14 speeds and mountain bikes $14 per 4 hr., $18 per 8 hr., $22 overnight, with helmet and lock. Open Mon.-Sat. 9am-7pm, Sun. 10am-6pm.

Help Lines: Rape Crisis, 443-7300. 24 hrs. **Crisis Line,** 447-1665. 24 hrs. **Gays, Lesbians, and Friends of Boulder,** 492-8567, no regular hrs. during summer but has info on recorded message.

Post Office: 1905 15th St. (938-1100), at Walnut across from the RTD terminal. Open Mon.-Fri. 7:30am-5:30pm, Sat. 10am-2pm. **ZIP code:** 80302.

Area Code: 303.

Boulder (pop. 83,000) is a small, manageable city. The most developed part of Boulder lies between **Broadway** (Rte. 93) and **28th Street** (Rte. 36), two busy streets running parallel to each other north-south through the city. **Baseline Road,** which connects the Flatirons with the eastern plains, and **Canyon Boulevard** (Rte. 7), which follows the scenic Boulder Canyon up into the mountains, border the main part of the **University of Colorado** (CU) campus. The school's surroundings are known locally as **"the Hill."** The pedestrian-only **Pearl Street Mall,** between 11th and 15th St. centers hip life in Boulder. Most east-west roads have names, while north-south streets have numbers; Broadway is a conspicuous exception.

ACCOMMODATIONS AND CAMPING

After spending your money at the Pearl St. Mall on tofu and yogurt, you may find yourself strapped for cash and without a room—Boulder doesn't offer many inexpensive places to spend the night. In summer, you can rely on the hostels.

Boulder International Youth Hostel (Rucksackers), 1107 12th St. (442-0522, summer 7am-1am, desk closed 11am-4pm but a machine will pick up), two blocks west of the CU campus and 15 min. south of the RTD station. From Denver take the A or B bus as close to College Ave. as possible. Located in the heart of CU housing and fraternities, the BIYH is a loud, youthful place. Shared hall bathrooms, kitchen, laundry, and TV. Curfew Sun.-Thurs. 1am, Fri. and Sat. 2:30 am. Lockout for dorms 10am-5pm. Dorm beds $11; private singles $25 per night, $110 per week; doubles $30 per night, $130 per week; additional person $5. Linen $3, towel and showers $3. Key deposit $5.

Big Al's International Youth Hostel, 3171 Valmont (440-7754), is a bit out of the way—call for a free pick up from the Walnut and 14th St. bus station or call for directions. A small, newly-opened, privately-owned Victorian house. The owners are amiable. They'll ask you to take your shoes off before entering. 2 bathrooms for 20 or so people. Communal kitchen and laundromat across the street. Dorm rooms only $15, $12 with a foreign passport.

Chautauqua Association (442-3282), off Baseline Rd., turn at the Chautauqua Park sign and follow Kinnikinic to the administrative office, or take bus #203. Set at the foot of the Flatirons. Stay in one of their lodges: $42 for two, $52 for a suite for four, or in a private cottage with room enough for 4 people $45; 10-person cottage $88; 4-night min. stay. Make reservations months in advance.

The Boulder Mountain Lodge, 91 Four Mile Canyon Rd. (444-0882), a 2-mi. drive west on Canyon Rd., near creek-side bike and foot trails. Facilities include phone and TV; 2 hot tubs and seasonal pool are a nice plus. Check-in after 10am for campsites. 2-week max. stay. Sites with or without hookup $14 for up to 3 people, each additional person $2; $80 per week.

Camping information for **Arapahoe Roosevelt National Forest** is available from the **Forest Service Station** at 2995 Baseline Rd. #16, Boulder 80303 (444-6600; open Mon.-Fri. 8am-5pm). Make reservations for any campground by calling 800-280-CAMP (800-280-2267). All sites $9 (except $5 for Rainbow Lakes). Maps $3. **Kelly Dahl,** 3 mi. south of Nederland on Rte. 119, has 46 sites. **Rainbow Lakes,** 6 mi. north of Nederland on Rte. 72, and 5 mi. west on rough and unmaintained Arapahoe Glacier Rd., has 18 sites, but no water (campgrounds open late May to mid-Sept.). **Peaceful Valley** (15 sites) and **Camp Dick** (34 sites), are both north on Rte. 72, and have cross-country skiing in the winter. First-come, first-served; $8 per site.

FOOD AND HANGOUTS

The streets on "the Hill" surrounding CU and those along the Pearl St. Mall burst with good eateries, natural foods markets, cafes, and colorful bars. Many more restaurants and bars line Baseline Rd. As one might expect, given the peace-love-nature-touchy-feely climate, Boulder has more restaurants for vegetarians than for carnivores. For an abundance of fresh produce, homemade breads, and pies, head for the **Boulder County Farmer's Market** at 13th and Canyon, which operates May-October Wednesday 2-6pm, Saturday 8am-2pm. Get there early.

The Sink, 1165 13th St. (444-7465). When the word went out in 1989 that the Sink had reopened, throngs of former "Sink Rats" commenced their pilgrimage back to Boulder; the restaurant still awaits the return of its former janitor, Robert Redford, who quit his job and headed out to California back in the late 1950s. Burgers $4. Vegetarian and Mexican specialties too. Call for info on live music nights (Tues. and Fri.). Food served until 10pm. Open Mon.-Sun. 11am-2am.

Mountain Sun Pub and Brewery, 1535 Pearl St. (546-0886). A 21-tap salute to micro-breweries near and far, plus burgers ($4), veggie selections, and pizza. Open Mon.-Sat. 11:30am-1am, Sun. 2pm-midnight.

Sushi Zanmai, 1221 Spruce (440-0733), next to the Hotel Boulderado. Best Japanese food in Boulder, served by wacky knife-throwing chefs. Chicken teriyaki lunch special $6.80. Lunch Mon.-Fri. 11:30am-2pm, dinner daily 5-10pm.

The Walrus Café, 1911 11th St. (443-9902). Universally popular night spot. Alas, Paul McCartney is nowhere to be found. Beer $1-3.50. Burgers $4.50. Open Mon.-Fri. 4pm-2am, Sat.-Sun. 2pm-2am. Free pool and $1 during Happy Hours, Wed. 4-8pm, Sat. and Sun. 2-8pm. Coo coo ka choo.

SIGHTS AND ACTIVITIES

University of Colorado's intellectuals collaborate with wayward poets and back-to-nature crunchers to find innovative things to do. Check out the perennially outrageous street scene on the Mall and the Hill and watch the university's kiosks for the scoop on downtown happenings.

The university's **Cultural Events Board** (492-8409) has the latest word on all CU-sponsored activities. The **University Memorial Center** (492-6161) at Euclid and Broadway, is an event hub (open Mon.-Sat. 10am-6pm). The **Colorado Shakespeare Festival** (492-0554) takes place from late June to mid-August. (Previews $9, tickets $10-30, student discounts available.) The **Chautauqua Association** (442-3282) hosts the **Colorado Music Festival** (449-2413) from mid-July to August, tickets $10-29. The **Boulder Blues Festival** (443-5858; for tickets 444-3601, $10-15) is held the second week of September. The **Parks and Recreation Department** (441-3400; open Mon.-Fri. 8am-5pm) sponsors free summer performances in local parks; dance, classical and modern music, and children's theater are staples. **The Boulder Center for the Visual Arts,** 1750 13th St. (443-2122), focuses on contemporary regional art. (Open Tues.-Fri. 11am-5pm, Sat. 9am-3pm, Sun. noon-4pm. Free.)

Boulder Public Library, 1000 Canyon Rd. (441-3197), and CU's **Muenzinger Auditorium,** near Folsom and Colorado Ave. (492-1531), both screen international films. Call for times and prices. The intimate and impressive **Leanin' Tree Museum,** 6055 Longbow Dr. (530-1442), presents an interesting array of Western art and sculpture. (Open Mon.-Fri. 8am-4:30pm, Sat. 10am-4pm. Free.) The small **Naropa Institute** is located at 2130 Arapahoe Ave. (444-0202). Drop by and drop off at one of their many free meditation sessions with Tibetan monks. (Open daily 9am-5pm.)The **Rockies Brewing Company,** 2880 Wilderness Place (444-8448), offers tours and free beer. (25-min. tours Mon.-Sat. at 2pm; open Mon.-Sat. 11am-10pm.)

Running and **biking** competitions far outnumber any other sports events around Boulder. Call the Boulder Roadrunners (499-2061; open daily 9am-6pm).

Flatiron Mountains Rising up from Green Mountain, the Flatirons offer countless variations on walking, hiking, and biking. Take a stroll or cycle along **Boulder Creek Path,** a beautiful strip of park that lines the creek for 15 mi. Farther back in the mountains lie treacherous, less accessible rocky outcroppings. Trails weave through the 6000-acre **Boulder Mountain Park,** beginning from several sites on the western side of town. **Flagstaff Road** winds its way to the top of the mountains from the far western end of Baseline Rd. The **Boulder Creek Canyon,** accessible from Rte. 119, offers splendid rocky scenery. Nearby **Eldorado Canyon,** as well as the Flatirons themselves, has some of the best **rock climbing** in the world.

■■■ ROCKY MOUNTAIN NATIONAL PARK

Since French fur traders Joel and Milton Estes landed in the valley that now bears their name, millions have followed their footsteps to **Estes Park,** the gateway to this nature lover's paradise. Although purists disparage its overpopularity, this sanctuary makes even the slickest city dweller don a flannel shirt and take in some of the Rockies. The lack of mineral resources may have been a disappointment to the hopeful miners who attacked the mountains with a vengeance in the 1880s, but it is only because the land was so profitless that today we are able to appreciate the park's beauty. Visitors often find that they need a week or more to fully explorethe park.

The mountain wilds are made accessible by tourist towns on the park's borders and by **Trail Ridge Rd. (U.S. 34),** the highest continuously paved road in the U.S., which runs 45 mi. through the park from the town of **Grand Lake** to the town of **Estes Park.** The Ute shied away from **Grand Lake,** believing that mists rising from its surface were the spirits of rafters who had drowned in a storm. Today, this glacial lake and its namesake town sit in the west end of the park. At the road's peak of over two vertical miles, oxygen is rare and an eerie silence prevails among the low vegetation of the tundra. Closed in winter for obvious reasons (like lots of snow).

PRACTICAL INFORMATION

Emergency: 911. **Park Emergency,** 586-1333. **Estes Park police,** 586-4465; **Grand Lake police,** 627-3322.

Visitor Information: Estes Park Chamber of Commerce, P.O. Box 3050, Estes Park 80517, at 500 Big Thompson Hwy. (586-4431 or 800-443-7837). Slightly east of downtown. Open daily 8am-8pm, 8am-5pm in winter. **Grand Lake Area Chamber of Commerce,** 14700 U.S. 34 (800-531-1019), just outside of the park's west entrance. Open daily 9am-5pm; off-season Mon.-Fri. 10am-5pm.

Park Entrance Fees: $5 per vehicle, $3 per biker or pedestrian, under 16 free, and over 61 ½-price. Valid for 7 days.

Park Visitor and Ranger Stations: Park Headquarters and Visitors Center, on Rte. 36 2½ mi. west of Estes Park, at the Beaver Meadows entrance to the park. Call 586-1206 for park info, or to make sure the Trail Ridge Rd. is open. Headquarters and visitors center open daily 8am-9pm; off-season 8am-5pm. **Kawuneeche Visitors Center** (627-3471), just outside the park's western entrance, 1¼ mi. north of Grand Lake. Open daily 8am-5pm; July 2-Labor Day 7am-7pm. **Moraine Park Visitors Center and Museum** (586-3777), on the Bear Lake Rd. Open daily 8am-5pm. Closed Nov.-April. **Alpine Visitors Center,** at the crest of Trail Ridge Rd. Check out the view of the tundra from the back window. Call area chamber of commerce for details. Open Memorial Day-closing day of Trail Ridge Rd. (mid-Oct.) daily 9am-5pm. **Lily Lake,** open Memorial Day-Labor Day daily 9am-5pm.

Horse Rental: Sombrero Ranch, 1895 Big Thompson Rd. (586-4577), in Estes Park 2 mi. from downtown on U.S. 34 east, and on Grand Ave. in Grand Lake (627-3514). $15 for 1 hr., $25 for 2 hr. The breakfast ride (at 7am, $25) includes a 2-hr. ride and a huge breakfast. Call ahead. Hostelers get 10% discount; special rates for those staying at the H Bar G Ranch. Both open daily 7am-5:30pm.

Help Lines: Roads and Weather, 586-1333.

Post Office: Grand Lake, 520 Center Dr. (627-3340). Open Mon.-Fri. 8:30am-5pm. **Estes Park,** 215 W. Riverside Dr. (586-8177). Open Mon.-Fri. 8:30am-5:30pm, Sat. 10am-2pm. **ZIP code:** 80517.

Area Code: 303.

You can reach the National Park most easily from Boulder via U.S. 36 or from Loveland up the Big Thompson Canyon via U.S. 34. Busy during the summer, both routes lead to Estes Park and are biking trails. From Denver, take the RTD bus (20 per day, 45 min., $2.50) to its last stop in Boulder, and transfer (free) to bus #202 or 204 which will drop you off on U.S. 36 west. From there, you'll have to hike 30 mi. In Boulder you can find the entrance to U.S. 36 at 28th and Baseline Rd. Perhaps an easier way to get to Estes Park from Boulder is to call the **Hostel Hauler** (586-3688) before 9pm and arrange a shuttle ($10).

Estes Park parks 65 mi. from Denver, 39 mi. from Boulder, and 31 mi. from Loveland. With a car, "loop" from Boulder by catching U.S. 36 through Estes Park, pick up Trail Ridge Rd. (U.S. 34), go through Rocky Mountain National Park (45 mi.), stop in Grand Lake, and take U.S. 40 to Winter Park and I-70 back to Denver.

Reach the western side of the park from Granby (50 mi. from I-70/U.S. 40). One of the most scenic entrances, Rte. 7 approaches the park from the southeast out of Lyons or Nederland, accessing the **Wild Basin Trailhead,** the starting point for some glorious hikes. When Trail Ridge Rd. (open May-Oct.) closes, you can drive around the park from Walden and Fort Collins, via Rte. 125 out of Granby and then Rte. 14 to Fort Collins. Or take the more traveled U.S. 40 over spectacular **Berthoud Pass** to I-70, then Rtes. 119 and 72 north to the park. Note: when Trail Ridge Rd. is closed, the drive jumps from 48 to 140 mi.

ACCOMMODATIONS

Although Estes Park and Grand Lake have an overabundance of expensive lodges and motels, there are few good deals on indoor beds near the national park, especially in winter when the hostels close down.

Estes Park

H Bar G Ranch Hostel (HI-AYH), 3500 H Bar G Rd., P.O. Box 1260, Estes Park 80517 (586-3688, fax 586-5004). Hillside cabins, tennis courts, kitchen, and a spectacular view of the front range. Proprietor Lou drives you to the park entrance or into town every morning at 7:30am, and picks you up again at the chamber of commerce. Members only, $7.50. Rent a car for $26 per day. Open late May to mid-Sept. Call ahead.

YMCA of the Rockies, 2515 Tunnel Rd., Estes Park Center 80511 (586-3341), 2 mi. south of the park headquarters on Rte. 66 and 5 mi. from the chamber of commerce. Caters largely to clan gatherings and conventions. Extensive facilities on the 1400-acre complex, as well as daily hikes and other events. 4 people can get a cabin from $48, kitchen and bath included. Lodge with bunk beds that sleep up to 5 $41. Guest membership $3. Families $5. This large resort has plenty of room for recreation; great for kids. Call ahead; very busy in summer.

The Colorado Mountain School, 351 Moraine Ave. (586-5758). Dorm-style accommodations open to travelers unless already booked by mountain-climbing students. Wood bunks with comfortable mattresses and shower $16. Shower only $2. Reservations are recommended at least 1 week in advance. Open in summer daily 8am-5pm. Check-out 10am.

Grand Lake

Camp on the shores of adjacent **Shadow Mountain Lake** and **Lake Granby.** Grand Lake draws fewer crowds in the summer, and though inaccessible without a car in the winter, the town offers hair-raising snowmobile and cross-country routes. Ask at the visitors center about seasonal events..

Shadowcliff Hostel (HI-AYH), P.O. Box 658, Grand Lake 80447 (627-9220). Near the western entrance to the park. Entering Grand Lake, take the left fork after the visitors center on West Portal Rd.; their sign is ¾-mi. down the road on the left. Hand-built pine lodge on a cliff overlooking the lake. Offers access to the trails on the western side of the park and to the lakes of Arapahoe National Recreation Area. Kitchen. Hall showers. $8, nonmembers $10. Private rooms $28 for 2, $4

ROCKY MOUNTAINS

each extra person. Cabins all have fireplaces, stoves, refrigerators, and private bath. 6-day min. stay. 2 cabins sleep up to 8 ($55); 1 sleeps up to 20 ($60). Rates are for 5 people—$4 per additional person. Open June-Oct.

Sunset Motel, 505 Grand Ave. (627-3318). Friendly owners and cozy singles and doubles will warm your stay in Grand Lake. 1 or 2 people $44; 3 or 4 people $50.

CAMPING

Sites fill up right quick in summer; call ahead or arrive early. Make reservations from eight to 12 weeks in advance through **MISTIX** P.O. Box 85705, San Diego, CA 92138-5705, (800-365-2267). In addition there is a seven-day limit to all campgrounds. The exception is Long's Peak which is three days.

National Park Campgrounds: Moraine Park (5½ mi. from Estes) requires reservations in summer. Open May 29-Sept. 6, sites $10. **Glacier Basin** (9 mi. from Estes) also requires reservations in summer. Open May 29-Sept. 6, sites $10. **Aspenglen** (5 mi. west of Estes Park near the Fall River entrance) operates on first-come, first-served basis. Open May 8-Sept. 30, sites $8. **Longs Peak** (11 mi. south of Estes Park and 1 mi. off Rte. 7), operates on a first-come, first-served basis. Open year-round (in winter, no water, no charge), tents only, sites $8. **Timber Creek** (10 mi. north of Grand Lake—the only campground on the western side of the park) operates on a first-come, first-served basis. Open year-round (in winter, no water, no charge), sites $8. **Spring Lake Handicamp** (586-1242 for information and reservations, daily 7am-7pm.) is the park's backcountry campsite for the disabled; 7 mi. from Estes Park Headquarters at Sprague Lake Picnic Area.

Backcountry camping: Offices at **Park Headquarters** (586-2371) and **Kawuneeche Visitors Center** (627-1242), on the western side of the park at Grand Lake. Open daily 7am-7pm. Get reservations at these offices or write the **Backcountry office,** Rocky Mountain National Park, Estes Park 80517 (586-1242). Many areas are in no-fire zones, and it's a good idea to bring a campstove.

Olive Ridge Campground, 15 mi. south of Estes Park on Rte. 7, in Roosevelt National Forest. Call 800-280-2267 for reservations. First-come, first-served sites $8. Contact the **Arapaho-Roosevelt National Forest Service Headquarters,** 161 2nd St., Estes Park (586-3440). Open daily 9am-noon and 1-5pm; in Aug.-May, call main office in Ft. Collins (498-2775).

Indian Peaks Wilderness, just south of the park, jointly administered by Arapaho and Roosevelt National Forests. Permit required for backcountry camping during the summer. On the east slope, contact the **Boulder Ranger District,** 2915 Baseline Rd. (444-6600). Open Mon.-Fri. 8am-5pm. Last chance permits ($4) are available in Nederland at Coast to Coast Hardware (take Rte. 7 to 72 south). Open Mon.-Sat. 9am-9pm. On the west slope, contact the **Sulphur Ranger District,** 62429 Hwy. 40 (887-3331) in Granby. Open May 27-Sept. 2 daily 8am-5pm.

FOOD

Both towns near the park have several grocery stores where you can stock up on trail snacks. Look for "bulk foods" at **Safeway** in Estes's Stanley Village Mall across from the chamber of commerce—they are ideal. If you are aiming to get away from the kitchen on your vacation, the following establishments offer inexpensive and tasty food so you don't have to cook.

Johnson's Café (586-6624), 2 buildings to the right of Safeway, across from the Chamber of Commerce. Must try Mike's waffles (from $1.95) made from scratch and served all day long. Open Mon.-Sat. 7am-2:30pm, Sun. 7am-1pm.

Ed's Cantina, 362 E. Elkhorn Ave. (586-2919). Fastest Mexican food in the park area. Combination plate (cheese enchilada, bean burrito, and bean tostada) $6.75. Open daily 7am-10pm, breakfast until 11am.

Poppy's, 342 E. Elkhorn Ave. (586-8282), in Barlow Plaza shopping area. A variety of your basic popular items. 15" pizza $10, sandwiches $4-8, all-you-can-eat salad bar $5. Open daily 11am-8pm.

The Terrace Inn, 813 Grand Ave. (627-3079), in Grand Lake. Homemade, home-made, homemade! Debby's special Italian sauce and huge fluffy pancakes ($3.50) are definite favorites. Open summer Mon.-Fri. 8am-9pm, Sat.-Sun. 8am-10pm.

SIGHTS AND ACTIVITIES

The star of this park is **Trail Ridge Road**. At its highest point, this 50-mi.-long stretch reaches 12,183 ft. above sea level; much of the road rises above timberline. The round-trip drive takes three hours by car, 12 hours by bicycle (if you have buns of steel and abs of iron). For a closer look at the fragile tundra environment, walk from roadside to the **Forest Canyon Overlook,** or take the half-hour **Tundra Trail** round-trip. **Fall River Road,** a one-way dirt road going from east to west merging with Trail Ridge Rd. at the alpine center, basks in even more impressive scenery, but also sharp cliffs and tight switchbacks along the road.

Rangers can help plan a **hike** to suit your interests and abilities. Since the trail-heads in the park are already high, just a few hours of hiking will bring you into unbeatable alpine scenery along the Continental Divide. Be aware that the 12,000- to 14,000-ft. altitudes can make your lungs feel as if they're constricted by rubber bands; give your brain enough time to adjust to the reduced oxygen levels before starting up the higher trails. Some easy trails include the 3.6-mi. round-trip from Wild Basin Ranger Station to **Calypso Cascades** and the 2.8-mi. round-trip from the Long Peaks Ranger Station to **Eugenia Mine.** From the nearby **Glacier Gorge Junction** trailhead, take a short hike to **Mills Lake** or up to the **Loch.**

From Grand Lake, a trek into the scenic and remote **North** or **East Inlets** should leave camera-toting crowds behind. Both of these wooded valleys swim with excellent trout fishing. The park's gem is prominent **Longs Peak** (14,255 ft.), dominating the eastern slope. The peak's monumental east face, a 2000-ft. vertical wall known simply as the **Diamond,** is the most challenging rock-climbing spot in Colorado.

You can traverse the park on a mountain bike as a fun and challenging alternative to hiking. **Colorado Bicycling Adventures,** 184 E. Elkhorn (586-4241), Estes Park, rents bikes ($5 per hr., $9 for 2 hr., $14 per ½-day, $19 per day; discounts for hostelers; helmets included). Guided mountain bike tours are also offered (2 hr. $20, 4 hr. $35, ½-day $40-60; open daily 10am-9pm; off-season 10am-5pm).

During the summer, the three major campgrounds (Moraine Park, Glacier Basin, and Aspenglen) have nightly amphitheater programs that examine the park's ecology. The visitors centers have information on these and on many ranger-led interpretive activities, including nature walks, birding expeditions, and artist's forays.

■ ■ ■ ASPEN

A world-renowned asylum for musicians and skiers, Aspen looms as the budget traveler's worst nightmare. In this upper-class playground, low-budget living is virtually non-existent. *Let's Go* suggests lodging in **Glenwood Springs,** only 40 mi. north on Rte. 82, and making a daytrip here. Pick up the free *What to do in Aspen and Snow-mass* at the **visitors center,** 320 E. Hyman Ave. (Open daily 9am-7pm; winter 9am-5pm.) For info on campgrounds and a map ($3) of the area, call (925-3445; open daily 8am-5pm, winter Mon.-Fri. 3-5pm). Aspen's **area code:** 303.

Some reasonably priced skiers's dorms double as guest houses in summer. The largest crowds and highest rates arrive during winter. The **Little Red Ski Haus,** 118 E. Cooper (925-3333), two blocks west of downtown, has winter rates from $42 for a quad with shared bath to $62 for double with private bath; summer rates are $23-$45. Breakfast included. Unless 6 ft. of snow cover the ground, try **camping** in the mountains nearby. Hike well into the forest and camp for free, or use one of the ten **National Forest Campgrounds** within 15 mi. of Aspen. **Maroon Lake** (44 sites), **Silver Bar** (4 sites), **Silver Bell** (7 sites), and **Silver Queen** (6 sites) are on Maroon Creek Rd. just west of Aspen. (3-5 day max. stay. Sites fill well before noon. Open July-early Sept.) Southeast of Aspen on Rte. 82 toward Independence Pass are six campgrounds: **Difficult** (11 sites), **Lincoln Gulch** (7 sites), **Lincoln Creek Dispersed**

Sites (28 sites), **Weller** (11 sites), **Lost Man** (9 sites), and **Portal** (7 sites). For reservations and fee info at Silver Bar, Silver Bell, Silver Queen, and Difficult, contact MIS-TIX (800-280-2267; open Mon.-Fri. 8am-5pm, Sat.-Sun. 8am-3pm.)

The Main Street Bakery, 201 E. Main St. (925-6446), offers gourmet soups ($3.50), homemade granola ($3.85), and three-grain pancakes ($4). (Open Mon.-Sat. 7am-9pm, Sun. 7am-2pm.) The **In and Out House,** 233 E. Main St. (925-6647), is just that—a virtual revolving door of customers in an outhouse-sized space. Huge sandwiches on fresh-baked bread ($2-5). (Open Mon.-Fri. 8am-7pm, Sat.-Sun. 8am-4pm.)

The *après*-ski hours and nightlife of Aspen may be forbidden to the budget traveler (or anyone not worth millions of dollars). Budget voyeurs will find Aspen a great place to just sit and watch. A popular local hangout for the beautiful people is the **Cooper Street Pier,** 500 Cooper Ave. (925-7758; restaurant open daily 11:30am-10pm, bar until 1am). The **Flying Dog Brew Pub,** 424 E. Cooper Ave. (925-7464), just a few blocks down, is a mini-brewery serving American food. Try a four-beer sampler for $3 (open Mon.-Sun. 11:30am-10pm). Off Rte. 82 towards Glenwood Springs, you'll find **Woody Creek Tavern,** 2 Woody Creek Pl. (923-4285), with hefty burgers ($6), and great Mexican specialties. Journalist Hunter S. Thompson used to be a regular here. (Open daily 11:30am-10pm.)

Skiing is the main attraction in Aspen. The hills surrounding town contain four ski areas: **Aspen Mountain, Aspen Highland, Tiehack Mountain,** and **Snowmass Ski Area** (925-1220). The resorts sell interchangeable lift tickets ($50, ages over 70 free, kids $29, under 6 free; daily hours: Aspen Mtn. 9am-3pm, You can enjoy the mountains without going into debt paying for lift tickets. In the summer, ride the **Silver Queen Gondola** (925-1220, $12.50, kids 3-12 $6) to the top of Aspen mountains (open daily 9:30am-4pm). **Hiking** in the Maroon Bells and Elk Mountains is permitted when the snow isn't too deep. Undoubtedly Aspen's most famous event, the **Aspen Music Festival** (925-9042) holds sway over the town from late June-Aug. Free bus transportation goes from Rubey Park downtown to "the Tent," south of town, before and after all concerts. (Tickets $17-50; Sun. rehearsals $2.)

■■■ GLENWOOD SPRINGS

Glenwood Springs, 40 mi. north on Colorado Rte. 82, is the smarter choice than Aspen for the budget traveler. Renown for its steaming hot springs and vapor caves, Glenwood is stocked with budget-friendly markets, cafes, and a great hostel. The **Aspen/Glenwood Bus** offers four buses between Aspen and Glenwood, Monday-Friday. (Last bus leaves Glenwood at 3:15pm; Aspen at 5:15pm, and five buses Sat.-Sun. $5 one way, children and seniors $4, 50¢ within Glenwood.)

Nearby **Glenwood Hot Springs,** 401 N. River Rd. (945-6571), provides most of the town's income (open daily 7:30am-10pm; day pass $6, after 9pm $3.75, ages 3-12 $3.75). Just one block from the large pools is the **Yampah Spa and Vapor Caves,** 709 E. 6th St. (945-0667), where hot mineral waters flow through the cave walls, creating a relaxing 125°F heat ($6.75, $3.75 for hostelers; open daily 9am-9pm). Ski 10 mi. west of town at **Sunlight,** 10901 County Rd. 117 (945-7491 or 800-445-7931). (4-5 lifts. Ski passes $26 per day for hostelers, including access to the springs. Cross-country skiing trail pass $4. Downhill rentals $10 for hostelers.)

Within walking distance of the springs you'll find the **Glenwood Springs Hostel (HI-AYH),** 1021 Grand Ave. (945-8545 or 8-9-HOSTEL), a former Victorian home with spacious dorm and communal areas as well as a full kitchen. The newly-renovated building next door is now equipped with its own kitchen, deluxe dorms, and private rooms. Ask Gary to play one of his collection of 2000 records. At night, groups go to the hot springs or the local pool halls. Gary also leads caving expeditions ($15), a trip to Independence Pass ($15), and an $80 kayak package for novices. You can also rent mountain bikes for $9 per day and receive a free ride (by car) from train and bus stations. (Hostelers can ski at Sunlight Ski Area for $16 Mon.-Fri., $21 Sat.-Sun., or get a 10% discount at Aspen or Vail, or go white-water rafting for $22, or visit the vapor caves for $3.75. Hostel closed 10am-4pm. $9.50. $12 for deluxe dorms, $18 for private single, $24 for a private double. Linen included. Free pasta, rice, potatoes.) The Victorian B&B next door is **Adducci's Inn,** 1023 Grand Ave. (945-9341). Private rooms cost $28-65 for a single, $38-65 for a double; $10 per additional person. Prices are negotiable according to room availability. Includes breakfast every morning and wine in the evenings. Hot tub. Call for free pick-up from bus and train stations. Cheap motels line the main drag of 6th St.

For a good, cheap breakfast or lunch, try the **Daily Bread Café and Bakery,** 729 Grand Ave. (945-6253). (Open Mon.-Fri. 7am-2pm, Sat. 8am-2pm, Sun. 8am-noon.) **Doc Holliday's,** 724 Grand Ave. (945-9050), is the place for burgers ($6). Weekdays from 5-7pm, the Doc offers dollar drafts and food (open daily 10am-2am).

The **Amtrak** station thinks it can at 413 7th St. (800-872-7245 or 945-9563). One daily train chugs east to Denver (6 hrs., $54) and one west to Salt Lake City (8 hrs. 40 min., $84). (Station open daily 9am-5pm. Ticket office open daily 9:30am-4:30pm.) **Greyhound** runs from 118 W. 6th St. (945-8501). Three buses run daily to Denver (4 hr., $18) and Grand Junction (2 hr., $8). (Open Mon.-Fri. 7am-5pm, Sat. 8am-1pm.) For more town info, contact **Glenwood Springs Chamber Resort Association,** 1102 Grand Ave. (945-6589; open Mon.-Fri. 8:30am-5pm).

■■■ GRAND JUNCTION

Grand Junction gets its hyperbolic name from its seat at the confluence of the Colorado and Gunnison Rivers and the conjunction-junction of the Río Grande and Denver Railroads. This city serves as a base from which to explore **Colorado National Monument, Grand Mesa,** the Gunnison Valley, and the western San Juans.

Grand Junction lies at the present juncture of U.S. 50 and U.S. 6 in northwestern Colorado. Denver is 228 mi. to the east; Salt Lake City 240 mi. to the west. For literature on the area, visit the **visitors center,** 740 Horizon Dr. (244-1480). Ask about their weekly lecture and slide show programs which feature the history and culture of southwest Colorado (open daily 8:30am-8pm, in the winter open daily 8:30am-5pm). The **Greyhound station,** 230 S. 5th St. (242-6012), has service to: Denver (5 per day, 7 hr., $24); Durango (1 per day, 4 hr., $26); Salt Lake City (1 per day, $47); Los Angeles (5 per day, $91). (Open Mon.-Fri. 9pm-6pm, Sat.-Sun. 3-8am and 11am-6pm and 9-11pm.) **Amtrak,** 337 S. 1st St. (241-2733 or 800-872-7245), chugs once a day to Denver ($68) and Salt Lake City ($69). (Open daily 10am-6pm.)

Many of the sites are difficult to get to without a car, but the tours from the Melrose Hostel (see below) are fantastic. If you've got moola and are 21, you can rent a car. **Thrifty Car Rental,** 752 Horizon Dr. (243-7556 or 800-367-2277), rents compact cars for $36 per day, $180 per week with unlimited mileage. The Melrose has discount rental coupons. Grand Junction's **post office:** 241 N. 4th St. (244-3401; open Mon.-Fri. 8am-5:30pm, Sat. 9am-12:30pm); **ZIP code:** 81502; **area code:** 303.

One reason to go to Grand Junction is the **Melrose Hotel (HI-AYH),** 337 Colorado Ave. (242-9636 or 800-430-4555), between 3rd and 4th St. Owners Marcus and Sabrina will make you feel at home and direct you to the best deals in town. Marcus's tours to Arches National Park, Colorado National Monument, and Grand Mesa are a must-see, taking you off tourist paths for some serious sight-seeing. His cohort Andy leads novice and expert mountain biking tours—bring your own or use one of the hostel's (prices vary according to trip—5 nights at the hostel and 3 fully supported tours $110). In the winter they offer discount ski trips to Boulderhorn ($22) and Aspen ($37) including lift ticket, ski rental, shuttle to and from the hostel, and outerware. A super-value package ($89) includes 4 nights at the hostel and 3 tours (Arches, Colorado, and Grand Mesa). (Dorms $10, including tax, breakfast, and kitchen facilities. Singles $20, with private bath $25. Doubles $25, with TV and private bath $30. Call for winter rates. Visa/MC.) **Lo Master Motel,** 2858 North Ave. (243-3230), has singles $28, doubles $32. Camp in **Highline State Park** (858-7208), 22 mi. from town and 7 mi. north of exit 15 on I-70 with 25 sites, fishing access, and restrooms ($10), or **Island Acres State Park** (464-0548), 15 mi. east on the banks of the Colorado River, 32 sites ($9 per site plus $3 day pass to enter the park).

Dos Hombres Restaurant, 421 Brach Dr. (242-8861), just south of Broadway (Rte. 340) on the southern bank of the Colorado River, serves great Mexican food in a casual setting. (Combination dinners $3-8. Open daily 11am-10pm.) **Pufferbelly Station Restaurant,** 337 S. 1st St. (242-1600), by the Amtrak station, has generous portions. Try the pancake special (6 pancakes, 2 strips of bacon, and an egg—$3). Sunday buffet ($5) is served from 7am to noon. (Open daily 6am-2pm.) For all the fixins' head to **City Market,** 1909 N. 1st St. (243-0842; open daily 5am-1am).

Grand Junction also offers wineries and a few interesting museums. The **Museum of Western Colorado,** 248 S. 4th St. (242-0971), traces the history of western Colorado. ($2, ages 2-17 $1; open Mon.-Sat. 10am-4:45pm; closed Mon. during winter.) **Dinosaur Valley,** an extension of the museum, is located two blocks away at 362 Main St. Moving and growling dinosaurs entertain children, while displays of serious paleontological research cater to adults. (Open daily 9am-5:30pm; Sept.-May. Tues.-Fri. 10am-4:30pm; $4, ages 2-12 $2.50.)

■■■ COLORADO NATIONAL MONUMENT

Thanks to John Otto, the arid, red, canyons, and striated sandstone of the land west of Grand Junction was declared a national monument in 1911, with 32 square miles of scenic hiking trails, rock-climbing face, and bike paths. **Saddlehorn Campground** offers campsites in the monument on a first-come, first-served basis, with picnic tables, grills, and restrooms (sites $7; free in winter). The **Bureau of Land Management** (244-3000; open Mon.-Fri. 7:30am-5pm) maintains three free "campgrounds" near **Glade Park** at Mud Springs. Bring your own water. **Little Dolores Fall,** 10½ mi. west of Glade Park, has fishing and swimming. The monument charges an additional admission fee of $4 per vehicle, $2 per cyclist or hiker, and is free for the disabled and seniors. Check in at the monument **headquarters and visitors center** (858-3617), near the campground on the Fruita side, and see the 12-min. slideshow (every ½ hr., 8am-7:30pm in the peak season; in the off-season by request). No camping permit is needed. (Open daily 8am-8pm; off-season Mon.-Fri. 8am-4:30pm.)

■■■ GRAND MESA

Grand Mesa, "the great table" which is the world's largest flat-top mountain, looms 50 mi. east of Grand Junction. Dominating the landscape from miles around, Grand Mesa has long been subject to speculation. A Native American story tells how the Mesa's many lakes were formed by fragments of a serpent torn to bits by a mad mother eagle who believed her young to be inside the serpent's belly. Recently geologists have estimated that a 300 ft. thick lava flow covered the entire region 6000 million years ago and that the Mesa is the only portion to have survived the erosion.

Whatever the Mesa's origin, this area offers outdoor attractions, including fine **backcountry hiking.** To reach Grand Mesa from Grand Junction, take I-70 eastbound to Plateau Creek, where Rte. 65 cuts off into the long climb through the spruce trees to the top of the mesa. Near the top is the Land's End turn-off to the very edge of Grand Mesa, some 12 mi. down a well-maintained dirt road (closed in winter). On a clear day, you can see halfway across Utah. The higher areas of the Mesa remain cool into summer, so be sure to bring a sweater and long pants.

The Mesa not only has an excellent view, but excellent camping as well. The Grand Mesa National Forest Service maintains **campsites** on the Mesa. Island Lake (41 sites, $8) and Ward Lake (27 sites, $8) are both on the water and have good fishing; Jumbo (26 sites $8), Little Bear (37 sites, $8), and Cottonwood (42 sites, $6) are good, large campgrounds; Crag Crest (11 sites, $7) and Spruce Grove (16 sites, $7) are smaller and more intimate; Eggleston (6 sites, $7) is for group camping; and there are also 10 free campgrounds. Call the visitors center (856-4153) for more info on any site. The district **forest service,** 764 Horizon Dr. (242-8211), in Grand Junction, has maps and info (open Mon.-Fri. 8am-5pm). **Vega State Park** (487-3407), 12 mi. east of Colbrain off Rte. 330, also offers camping in the high country. (Park entrance fee $3 per vehicle; campsites $6 per night.)

The **Alexander Lake Lodge** (856-6700), off scenic Rte. 65, is a good place to stop if you're cold, tired, or hungry. This old hunting lodge serves up burgers ($5), pasta dinners with salad and bread ($9), and hot cocoa to warm you up ($1). The Lodge also runs a general store and rents out seven cabins (3 with kitchenettes) for $45 ($15 per additional person). Motor boats are available at $9 per hour. There are over 200 lakes full of rainbow trout around the Mesa. The **Alexander Lake stables** (856-7323) across the street offers horseback riding for $15 per hour.

■■■ COLORADO SPRINGS

Colorado Springs sprawls among several natural wonders. 300 million years ago the earth's inner turmoil created Pikes Peak and the surrounding mountain rangers to the west while uplifting the floor of an inland ocean basin made out of red rocks. This is now called the Garden of the Gods and has hypnotized many travelers passing through the region. The Ute Indians came here for the healing mineral waters and believed the red rocks were the bodies of their enemies thrown down by the gods. The view from Pikes Peak inspired Katherine Lee Bates to write "America the Beautiful."

Home to the United States Olympic Team, the Springs churn out champion lugers and synchronized swimmers. While tourists pour millions into the Colorado Springs economy, the U.S. government pours in even more: North American Air Defense Command Headquarters (NORAD) lurks beneath nearby Cheyenne Mountain.

PRACTICAL INFORMATION

Emergency: 911.
Visitor Information: Colorado Springs Convention and Visitors Bureau, 104 S. Cascade #104, 80903 (635-7506 or 800-368-4748), at Colorado Ave. Check out the *Colorado Springs Pikes Peak Park Region Official Visitors Guide* and the city bus map. Open Mon.-Fri. 8:30am-6pm, Sat.-Sun. 8:30am-5pm; Nov.-March Mon.-Fri. 8:30am-5pm.
Greyhound: 120 S. Weber St. (635-1505). To: Denver (8 per day, 2 hrs., $10); Pueblo (9 per day, 50 min., $6.25); Albuquerque (5 per day, 7-9 hr., $60). Tickets sold daily 5:15am-11:30pm.
Public Transport: Colorado Springs City Bus Service, 125 E. Kiowa (475-9733) at Nevada, 3 blocks from the Greyhound station. Serves the city, Widefield, Manitou Springs, Fort Carson, Garden of the Gods, and Peterson AFB. Service Mon.-Sat. 5:45am-6:15pm every ½ hr., evening service 6-10pm every hr. Fare 75¢, seniors and kids 35¢, ages 5 and under free; long trips 25¢ extra. Exact change required.
Tours: Gray Line Tours, 3704 Colorado Ave. (633-11810 or 800-345-8197), at the Garden of the Gods Campgrounds. Trips to the U.S. Air Force Academy and Garden of the Gods (4 hrs., $15, kids $7.50), Pikes Peak (4 hrs., $20, kids $10). Also offers 10 mi. whitewater rafting trip (7 hrs., includes lunch, $50). Must be at least 50 lbs. Office open daily 7am-10pm.
Taxi: Yellow Cab, 634-5000. $3 first mi., $1.35 each additional mi.
Car Rental: Ugly Duckling, 2021 E. Platte (634-1914). $18 per day, $108 per week. Open Mon.-Fri. 9am-5:30pm, Sat. 9am-1pm. Must stay in-state and be 21 with major credit card or $250 deposit.
Help Lines: Crisis Emergency Services, 635-7000. 24 hrs.
Post Office: 201 Pikes Peak Ave. (570-5336), at Nevada Ave. Open Mon.-Fri. 7:30am-5:30pm, Sat. 7:30am-1pm. **ZIP code:** 80903.
Area Code: 719.

Colorado Springs is laid out in a grid of broad thoroughfares. The mountains are to the west. **Nevada Ave.** is the main north-south strip, known for its bars and restaurants. **Pikes Peak Ave.** serves as the east-west axis, running parallel to **Colorado**

Ave., which connects with **U.S. 24** on the city's west side. **U.S. 25** from Denver plows through downtown. East of Nevada Ave. there are basically only residential homes and large shopping centers. The streets west of Nevada are numbered, with the numbers increasing as you move west.

ACCOMMODATIONS AND CAMPING

Avoid the mostly shabby motels along Nevada Ave. If the youth hostel fails you, head for a nearby campground or the establishments along W. Pikes Peak Ave.

Garden of the Gods Youth Hostel and Campground (HI-AYH), 3704 W. Colorado Ave. (475-9450 or 800-345-8197). Take bus #1 west to 37th St. 4-bunk shanties. Showers and bathrooms shared with campground. Immaculate facilities. Bunkrooms are not heated; bring your sleeping bag! Swimming pool, jacuzzi, laundry. $11; members only. Linen included. Open April-Oct.

Apache Court Motel, 3401 W. Pikes Peak Ave. (471-9440). Take bus #1 west down Colorado Ave. to 34th St., walk 1 block north. Pink adobe rooms. A/C and TV, hot tub. Summer singles $33 for one person, $40 for two; doubles $54 for two, $5 each additional person; Sept. 15-April $26/$30/$39/$41. No pets.

Motel 6, 3228 N. Chestnut St. (520-5400), at Fillmore St. just west of I-25 exit 145. Take bus #8 west. TV, pool, A/C. Some rooms with unobstructed view of Pikes Peak. Some rooms with unobstructed view of parking lot. Singles $34-40, doubles $43-46. Oct.-May roughly $8 less.

Amarillo Motel, 2801 W. Colorado Ave. (635-8539). Take bus #1 west down Colorado Ave. to 28th St. Ask for rooms in the older National Historic Register section. Bunker-like rooms lack windows, but have kitchens and TV. Laundry available. Singles $24-38. Doubles $38-40. Off-season from $20.

Located in the city itself is the four-star **Garden of the Gods Campground** (see hostel above). As most of the sites are on a gravel parking lot, this is better for RVs than tents. Enjoy flapjack breakfasts (Sundays), or coffee and doughnuts (25¢ each). (Sites $17, additional person over 3 $2, with electricity and water $20, full hookup $22.) Several **Pike National Forest** campgrounds lie in the mountains flanking Pikes Peak (generally open May-Sept.). No local transportation serves this area. Campgrounds clutter Rte. 67, 5-10 mi. north of **Woodland Park,** which is 18 mi. northwest of the Springs on U.S. 24. Others fringe U.S. 24 near the town of Lake George. (Sites at all, $7-10.) You can always camp off the road on national forest property for free if you are at least 100 yds. from a road or stream. The **Forest Service Office,** 601 S. Weber (636-1602), has maps ($3) of the area (open Mon.-Fri. 7:30am-4:30pm). Farther afield, you can camp in the **Eleven Mile State Recreation Area** (748-3401 or 800-678-2267), off a spur road from U.S. 24 near Lake George. (Sites $6, full hookup $9. Entrance fee $3. Reserve on weekends at least 3 days in advance, at the most 90 days in advance.) A last resort is the **Peak View Campground,** 4954 N. Nevada Ave. (598-1545; sites $14, water and electricity $15.50; full hookup $16-18).

FOOD

Poor Richard's Restaurant, 324½ North Tejon (632-7721). The local coffeehouse/college hangout. Pizza ($1.75 per slice; $8.75 per pie) and veggie food. Open daily 11am-10pm. **Poor Richard's Espresso and Dessert Bar** (577-4291) is right next door. Bagels and sinful desserts. Open daily 6:30am-midnight.

Meadow Muffins, 2432 W. Colorado Ave. (633-0583), in a converted opera house. Neon lights, smoke, beer, and the "Mighty burger" ($4.50). Open daily 11am-2am.

Henri's, 2427 W. Colorado Ave. (634-9031). Genuine, excellent Mexican food. Popular with locals for 40 years. Fantastic margaritas. Meat-and-cheese enchiladas $2.50. Open Tues.-Sat. 11:30am-10pm, Sun. noon-10pm.

GAMES, GUNS, AND THE GREAT OUTDOORS

From any part of the town, one can't help noticing the 14,110-ft. summit of **Pikes Peak** on the western horizon. You can climb the peak via the 13-mi. **Barr Burro**

Trail. The trailhead is in Manitou Springs by the "Manitou Incline" sign. Catch bus #1 to Ruxton. Don't despair if you don't reach the top—explorer Zebulon Pike never reached it either, and they named the whole mountain after him. Otherwise, pay the fee to drive up the **Pikes Peak Highway** (684-9383), administered by the Colorado Department of Public Works. (Open May-June 10 daily 9am-3pm, June 11-Sept. 2 7am-7:30pm; hours dependent on weather. $5, kids 6-11 $2.) You can also reserve a seat on the **Pikes Peak Cog Railway,** 515 Ruxton Ave. (685-5401; open May-Oct. 8 daily 8am-5:20pm with departures every 80 min.; round-trip $21, ages 5-11 $9, under 5 free if held on lap). At the summit, you'll see Kansas, the Sangre de Cristo Mountains, and ranges along the Continental Divide. Expect cold weather; even when it is in the 80s in Colorado Springs; the temperature at the summit reaches the mid-30s. Roads often remain icy through the summer.

Eat amid other Olympians in 300-million-year-old **Garden of the Gods City Park,** 1401 Recreation Way (578-6640). Take Colorado Ave. to 30th St. and then north on Gateway Rd. The park contains many secluded picnic and hiking areas. (Visitors center 578-6939; open daily 9am-5pm; Sept.-June 10am-4pm. Free.) The oft-photographed "balanced rock" is at the park's south entrance. The best vantage point for pictures is from Mesa Rd., off 30th St. on the opposite side of the park. For more strenuous hiking, head for the contorted caverns of the **Cave of the Winds** (685-5444), 6 mi. west of exit 141 off I-25 on Rte. 24 (guided tours daily every 15 min. 9am-9pm; off-season 10am-5pm). Just above Manitou Springs on Rte. 24 lies the **Manitou Cliff Dwellings Museum** (685-5242), U.S. 24 bypass, where you can wander through a pueblo of ancient Anasazi buildings dating from 1100-1300AD (open daily June-Aug. 9am-8pm; $4.50, seniors $3.50).

Buried in a hollowed-out cave 1800 ft. below Cheyenne Mountain, the **North American Air Defense Command Headquarters (NORAD)** (554-2241) was designed to survive even a direct nuclear hit. A 3-mi. tunnel leads to this center, which monitors every plane in the sky. The **Peterson Air Force Base,** on the east side of the city has a **visitors center** and the **Edward J. Peterson Space Command Museum** (556-4915; open Tues.-Fri. 8:30am-4:30pm, Sat. 9:30am-4:30pm; free).

The **United States Air Force Academy** marches 12 mi. north of town on I-25 and is the most popular attraction of the area, with over 1 million visitors each year. Its chapel (472-4515) is made of aluminum, steel, and other materials used in airplanes (open Mon.-Sat. 9am-5pm). On weekdays during the school year, cadets gather at 12:10pm near the chapel for the cadet lunch formation—a big production just to chow down. The **visitors center** (472-2555 or 472-2025) has self-guided tour maps, info on special events, and a 12-min. movie every ½-hr. (open daily 9am-6pm).

The **Pioneers' Museum,** downtown at 215 S. Tejon St. (578-6650), covers the settling of Colorado Springs, including a display on the techniques and instruments of a pioneer doctor (open Tues.-Sat. 10am-5pm, Sun. 1-5pm; free). Mining awaits at the **Western Museum of Mining and Industry,** 1025 N. Gate Rd. (488-0880). Learn how to pan for gold. (Open Mon.-Sat. 9am-4pm, Sun. noon-4pm. $5, students and seniors $4, kids under 13 $2; closed Dec.-Feb.) Take exit 156-A off I-25 and all your questions about those famous Olympians will be answered at the **U.S. Olympic Complex,** 750 E. Boulder St. (632-4618; tour hotline 578-4644), which offers informative 1-hr. tours every ½ hr. with a tear-jerking film. Watch Olympic hopefuls in the afternoons. (Open in the summer Mon.-Sat. 9am-5pm, Sun. 10am-4pm, in the off-season open Mon.-Sat. 9am-4pm, Sun. noon-4pm.) Take bus #1 east to Farragut.

A fun, hokey way to spend an evening is at the **Flying W Ranch,** 3330 Chuckwagon Rd. (598-4000 or 800-232-3599). Grab a tin plate and chow down at the huge chuckwagon supper ($12) while you watch a Wild West show. (Summer chuckwagon, $12.50 includes show and dinner, kids under 8, $6.50. In Oct.-May, the winter steakhouse is offered on Fri.-Sat. nights. The Ranch is closed in Jan. and Feb. Every evening a blacksmith shoes a horse—now that's entertainment!)

At night, Colorado College's literati find comfortable reading at **Poor Richard's Espresso Bar** (577-4291), adjacent to the bookstore (see Food above). The bar occasionally hosts comedy, acoustic performances, and readings. (Open Mon.-Thurs.

7am-midnight, Fri.-Sat. 7am-1:30am.) A theater next door (through the coffee shop) usually plays artsy films. The **Dublin House,** 1850 Dominion Way (528-1704) at Academy St., is a popular sports bar, with Sunday night blues downstairs (open daily 11am-2am; no cover). Call Funfare for current events (see Practical Information).

■■■ GREAT SAND DUNES NATIONAL MONUMENT

When Colorado's mountains begin to look the same, make a path to the waves of grainy sand at the northwest edge of the **San Luis Valley.** The 700-ft. dunes lap at the base of the **Sangre de Cristo Range,** representing thousands of years of wind-blown accumulation. The progress of the dunes at passes in the range is checked by the shallow **Medano Creek.** The **Medano Pass Primitive Road** shows the terrain for those with four-wheelers. Visitors can wade across the creek from April to mid-July. For a short hike, head out **Mosca Trail,** a 3½-mi. jaunt over the mountains and into the woods. Try to avoid the intense afternoon heat. Also the trail to **Escape Dunes** and **Ghost Forest** (nearly a mi. each way) leads to exciting, yet desolate dune shifts.

Rangers preside over daily activities. Full schedules are at the **visitors center** (719-378-2312), ½-mi. past the entrance gate, where you can also view a 15-minute film on the dunes, shown every ½-hour. (Open daily 8am-7pm; Memorial Day-Labor Day 8am-5pm. Entrance fee for vehicles $4, pedestrians and bikers $2.) For more info contact the Superintendent, Great Sand Dunes National Monument, Mosca, CO 81146 (378-2312). The **Oasis** complex (378-2222) on the southern boundary also provides four-wheel-drive tours of the backcountry. The two-hour tour takes the rugged Medano Pass Primitive Road into the nether regions of the monument. (2 tours daily; $14, kids 5-11 $8.)

Pinyon Flats (378-2312), the monument's primitive **campground,** fills quickly in summer. Camping here among the prickly pear cacti is on a first-come, first-served basis. Bring mosquito repellent in June. (88 Sites $8. Group sites reservable, $2 per person, $26 min.) Also within the monument are eight free backcountry sites that require a free permit available at the visitors center. If the park's sites are full, you can camp at Oasis. (Sites $9 for 2 people, with hookup $13.50. Each additional person $2.50. Showers included. Cabins and tepees $20 for 2 people.) For info on nearby National Forest Campgrounds, contact the Río Grande National Forest Service Office, 1803 W. U.S. 160, Monte Vista, CO 81144 (852-5941). All sites are $8.

Great Sand Dunes National Monument blows 32 mi. northeast of Alamosa and 112 mi. west of Pueblo, on Rte. 150 off U.S. 160. **Greyhound** sends one bus per day out of Denver to Alamosa (5 hrs., $40, see Denver: Practical Information), with a depot at 8480 Stockton St. (589-4948; open Mon.-Fri. 10am-4:30pm, Sat. 3-4:30pm). The country road from Mosca on Rte. 17 is strictly for four-wheel-drive vehicles. In case of an **emergency** within the park, call 911. The Dunes's **area code:** 719.

SAN JUAN MOUNTAINS

Ask Coloradans about their favorite mountain retreats, and they'll most likely name a peak, lake, stream, or town in the San Juan Range of southwestern Colorado. Four **national forests**—the **Uncompahgre** (un-cum-PAH-gray), the **Gunnison,** the **San Juan,** and the **Río Grande**—encircle this sprawling range.

Durango is an ideal base camp for forays into these mountains. In particular, the **Weminuche Wilderness,** northeast of Durango, tempts the hardy backpacker with a particularly large expanse of hilly terrain. You can hike for miles where wild, sweeping vistas are the rule. Get maps and info on hiking in the San Juans from **Pine Needle Mountaineering,** Main Mall, Durango 81301 (247-8728; open Mon.-Sat. 9am-9pm, Sun. 11am-4pm; maps $2.50).

The San Juan area is easily accessible on U.S. 50, traveled by hundreds of thousands of tourists each summer. **Greyhound** serves the area, but very poorly. Car travel is the best option in this region. On a happier note, the San Juans are loaded with HI-AYH hostels and campgrounds, making them one of the most economical places to visit in Colorado. Overall, the San Juans are a paradise for hikers, bikers, and just outdoorsy people who appreciate scenic America.

■■■ BLACK CANYON OF THE GUNNISON NATIONAL MONUMENT

Native American parents used to tell their children that the light-colored strands of molten material streaking through the walls of the Black Canyon were the hair of a blond woman—and that if they got too close to the edge they would get tangled in it and fall. With or without folklore, the edge of the Black Canyon is a scary place. The 53-mi. canyon has been carved for 2 million years by the Gunnison River. The result is a 2500-ft.-deep gorge. The Empire State Building, if placed at the bottom of the river, would not even rise half-way up the canyon walls. Dark shadows and rays of sunlight fall upon the walls of the canyon and the river at the bottom, inviting many tourists to take in the awesome view, and a few hardy souls to explore below. Those who stay on the beaten track will not be disappointed—along with a variety of tremendous views, there is plenty of wildlife to see along the road.

There is only one 12-mi. dirt road to the **North Rim,** the most remote area of the canyon, with less tourists and arguably the best views. This route is closed in winter. From Montrose, take U.S. 50 west and Rte. 92 west through Curecanti National Recreation Area to Crawford. From the west side of the monument, take U.S. 50 west and Rte. 92 east through Delta to Crawford. From Crawford, a graveled county road takes you to the North Rim. The better-developed **South Rim** is reached from U.S. 50, via Rte. 347 just outside of Montrose. There are 10 "overlooks" along the rim, and a nature trail starts from the campground. The 8-mi. scenic drive along this rim boasts spectacular **Chasm View,** where you can peer 2000 ft. down a sheer vertical drop. Although this view may seem like enough, don't miss the view of the **Painted Wall** (56 yds. away), the highest cliff in Colorado, and over a billion years old.

Practical Information The closest town to the Gunnison National Monument is **Montrose,** with administrative offices for the monument located at 2233 E. Main St. (249-7036; open Mon.-Fri. 8am-4:30pm, shorter hours in the off-season). **Greyhound** serves Montrose, 132 N. 1st St. (249-6673), and Gunnison, 711 Rio Grande (641-0060), at the Gunnison county airport. Gunnison lies about 55 mi. east of Montrose on U.S. 50. Fare between Gunnison and Montrose is $10. The bus will drop you off at the junction of U.S. 50 and Rte. 347, 6 mi. from the canyon. **Western Express Taxi** (249-8880) will drive you in from Montrose for about $30.

The town's **visitors center** assists at 2490 S. Townsend Ave. (249-1726; open May-Oct. daily 9am-7pm). The Canyon has two **visitors centers**—one on the South Rim (249-1915; open daily 8am-7:30pm), and the other on the North Rim (open daily 11:30am-2:30pm). Montrose's **ZIP code:** 81401; **area code:** 303.

Accommodations and Food Many inexpensive motels line **Main Street (U.S. 30). The Log Cabin Motel,** 1034 E. Main St. (249-7610), is toward the end of town closest to the Monument, and offers clean rooms (singles $32, doubles $38). The **Stockmen's Cafe and Bar,** 320 E. Main St. (249-9946), serves Mexican and western food (open Thurs., Sun., Mon.-Tues. 7am-10pm, Fri.-Sat. 7am-midnight). **Starvin' Arvin's,** 1320 S. Townsend Ave. (249-7787; open daily 6am-10pm), serves generous portions. You can't go wrong at a place that serves breakfast all day. Feast on 3-egg omelettes with hashbrowns and hotcakes ($4).

Hiking and Camping Inspired hikers can descend to the bottom of the canyon; the least difficult trail (more like a controlled fall) drops 1800 ft. over a distance of 1 mi. The hike up is a *tad* more difficult. At certain points you must hoist yourself up on a chain in order to gain ground. Suffice it to say, this hike is *not* to be undertaken lightly. A **backcountry permit** is available at the South Rim visitors center (249-1915), a self-registration system is in place on the North Rim. Get advice from a ranger before any descent. The visitors center offers 40-min. guided nature walks at 11am and 2pm. Free narrated evening programs are given at the park's entrance daily in summer at 8:45pm. (Park entrance fee $4 per car charged only on the South Rim; if one of the passengers is 62 or over, entrance fee is half-price, so be sure to bring grandma along.) A short walk down from the visitors center affords a view startling enough in its steepness to require chest-high rails.

Each rim has one **campground.** The North Rim has 13 sites, the South Rim has 102 sites. Each has pit toilets and charcoal grills; the one in the **South Rim** has an amphitheater with summer programs at 8:45pm. Water is available, but sparse. Both campgrounds are open May-Nov. (sites $7). Since wood gathering is not allowed, bring your own wood/charcoal or pick up some at the Information/Gift Shop at the turn-off to the park on U.S. 50. (Open May-mid-Nov.) Backcountry camping and driftwood fires in the canyon bottom are permitted. Call the National Park Service in Montrose at 249-7036 or the **South Rim Visitor Info Center** at 249-1915 for details.

If you hunger, head to the **Crystal Dam** via the E. Portal Rd. off S. Rim Rd. before South Rim Campground. The road is long, steep, and winding, but the picnic tables and the beautiful setting of the Gunnison River will make you forget your swearing on the way down at whoever wrote this part of *Let's Go: USA and Canada.*

The **Ute Indian Museum,** 17253 Chipeta Dr. (249-3098), a few miles south of Montrose on U.S. 550, displays exhibits from the Bear Dance and the bilingual letters of chief Ouray (leader of the Southern Ute tribe). (Open mid-May-Sept. Mon.-Fri. 9am-6pm, Sun. 1-5pm. $2.50, 65 and over $2, ages 6-16 $1.50.)

■ NEAR GUNNISON: CRESTED BUTTE

Crested Butte (CREST-uh-BÛT, not Crusty Butt you meddling kids) used to be a mining town. Luckily for the snow bunnies, the coal was exhausted by the 1950s, and Crested Butte is now frequented by skiers and mountain bikers. Crested Butte is 27 mi. north of **Gunnison** and U.S. 50 on Rte. 135. The ski area is on a mountain ergo, **Mt. Crested Butte,** 3 mi. north, is where to enjoy the snow. During the summer, a small **visitor information booth** sits inconspicuously at the four-stop in the middle of town (open daily 9am-5pm). The **Crested Butte Chamber of Commerce,** 7 Emmons Rd. (349-6438), near the bus stop in Mt. Crested Butte, can answer queries (open daily 9am-5pm). Crested Butte's **post office:** on Elk Ave. (349-5568; open Mon.-Fri. 8am-4:30pm, Sat. 9am-1pm); **ZIP Code:** 81224; **area code:** 303.

Finding budget lodging here is like getting an elk into formal wear—it's tough. **The Forest Queen Hotel and Restaurant** (349-5336 or 800-937-1788), on 2nd and Elk, offers pleasant rooms in an old brothel. (Doubles with shared bath $40, with private bath $50, $10 higher during holidays.) **The White Rock Lodge** (349-6669 or 800-783-7052), on Whiterock Ave. and Rte. 135, has one bunk room with six bunks ($20 a night). Call the reservations hotline at 800-215-2226. **Gunnison National Forest** (641-0471) contains a plethora of campgrounds. Within the forest are the **Lake Irwin Campground** (32 sites, $8), the **Cement Creek Campground** (13 sites, $7), and the **Almont Campground** (10 sites, $7).

During the winter, **Mt. Crested Butte** (800-544-8448) offers great trails, racing, ski schools, and snowboarding. Many package deals are available such as $99 for three nights lodging and three days skiing. Call for details. The resort offers endless activities such as **dog-sled** tours (641-1636), **fondue** parties (349-2211), and **hot air balloon** rides (349-6335). During the summer, the main activities are hiking, camping, and biking on the mountain and in Gunnison National Forest. Talk to the friendly chaps at the visitors center for their ideas on summer to-dos.

Stephanie's Country Store serves burgers ($3) and savory lunch specials. (Open Mon.-Thurs. 7am-6pm, Fri. 7am-9pm, Sat. 8am-9pm, Sun. 9am-4pm; call for winter hrs.) The Crested Butte Brewery, 265 Elk Ave. (349-5026), features homemade beers such as "Rodeo Stout" and "Buck's Wheat." 16 oz. for $2.75, as well as BBQ, Tex-Mex fare, and live music (open daily 11:30am-10pm).

■■■ TELLURIDE

Site of the first bank Butch Cassidy ever robbed (the San Miguel), Telluride has a history right out of a 1930s black-and-white film. Prizefighter Jack Dempsey used to wash dishes in the Athenian Senate, a popular saloon/brothel that frequently required Dempsey to double as bouncer between plates. The Sheridan Theatre (see below) hosted actresses Sarah Bernhardt and Lillian Gish on cross-country theater tours. Presidential candidate William Jennings Bryan delivered his "Cross of Gold" speech in silver-scooping Telluride from the front balcony of the Sheridan Hotel. Not so rare (especially after its devaluation) was the silver that attracted all the less aesthetically inclined hoodlums to Telluride in the first place.

Skiers, hikers, and vacationers now come to Telluride to put gold and silver *into* these mountains. Telluride is becoming more popular and may become the Aspen of the future. Still, a small-town feeling prevails in the rows of lightly painted, wood-shingled houses with rocking chairs on porches, and dogs tied to porches on store fronts.

Practical Information The visitors center is upstairs at Rose's, near the entrance to town at demonic 666 W. Colorado Ave. (728-3041 or 800-525-3455; open daily 9am-9pm). Telluride is only accessible by car, on U.S. 550 or Rte. 145. The closest Greyhound stop is in Montrose, 132 N. 1st St. (249-6673), a 60-mi. drive from here. Telluride's post office: 101 E. Colorado Ave. (728-3900; open Mon.-Fri. 9am-5pm, Sat. 10am-noon); ZIP code: 81435; area code: 303.

Accommodations and Food The Oak Street Inn, 134 N. Oak St. (728-3383), offers dorm-style lodging complete with a sauna. (Singles with shared bath $35, doubles $49, 3 people $63, 4 people $76. Showers $3. More expensive during festivals.) You can camp in the east end of town in a town-operated facility with water, restrooms, and showers (728-3071; 2-week max. stay; sites $8, except during the festivals). If visiting Telluride for a festival, bring a sleeping bag; the cost of a bed is outrageous. Sunshine, 4 mi. southwest on Rte. 145 toward Cortez, is a well-developed national forest campground. (2-week max. stay. Sites $8.) For information on all National Forest Campgrounds call the Forest Service (327-4261). Accessible by jeep roads, several free primitive sites huddle nearby. During festival times, you can crash just about anywhere, and hot showers are available at the local high school ($2).

Baked in Telluride, 127 S. Fir St. (728-4775), has enough rich coffee and delicious pastry, pizza, salad, and 50¢-bagels to get you through a festival weekend even if you *aren't* baked in Telluride. (Open daily 5:30am-10pm.) For delicious Italian fare, head to Eddie's Cafe, 300 W. Colorado (728-5335), for eight-inch pizzas ($5) and hefty pasta entrees under $10. (Open daily 11:30am-10pm.) A good breakfast is found at Sofio's Mexican Café, 110 E. Colorado (728-4882). Hashbrowns are $3.25, most breakfast items start at $4. (Open 7am-11:30am for breakfast; 5:30-10pm for dinner.)

Get a beer at The House, A Tavern, 131 N. Fir St. (728-6207), where most college students gone ski bums hang out. (Open daily 3pm-2am). Improve your beer gut at the Last Dollar Saloon (728-4800), at the corner of E. Colorado and Pine (open daily 3pm-2am). The ski crowd hangs at Leimgruber's, 573 W. Pacific Ave. (728-4663; open in the summer Wed.-Sun. 4-10pm; in the winter daily 4-10pm). Hear good live music at the One World Café, 114 E. Colorado (728-5530; open daily 4pm-2am) or at Fly Me to the Moon Saloon, 132 E. Colorado Street (728-6666; open daily 8pm-2am).

Festivals and Activities The quality and number of summer arts festivals seem staggering when you consider that only 1500 people call the town home. While get-togethers occur just about every weekend in summer and fall, the most renowned is the **Bluegrass Festival** (800-624-2422) in late June—in recent years the likes of James Taylor and the Indigo Girls have attracted crowds of 19,000 although the capacity is limited to 16,000. Festival Headquarters sell tickets for about $35 per night. On the weekend of the festivals, you can volunteer to usher or sell sandwiches in exchange for tickets to the show. Telluride also hosts a **Talking Gourds** poetry fest (early June; call 327-4767 or 800-525-3455 for info), and a **Jazz Festival** (early Aug.; 800-525-3455), among others. You can often hear the music festivals all over town, all day, and deep into the night as you try to sleep. Above all, the **Telluride International Film Festival** (603-643-1255) on Labor Day weekend, draws famous actors and directors from all over the globe, including Daniel Day Lewis, Clint Eastwood, and director David Lynch.

Two blocks from the visitors center lies the **Coonskin Chairlift,** which will haul you up 10,000 ft. for an excellent view of Pikes Peak and the La Sal Mountains. (Open June 11-Sept. 14 Thurs.-Mon. 10am-2pm. $7, seniors and kids 7-12 $4.) Biking, hiking, and backpacking opportunities are endless; ghost towns and lakes are tucked behind mountain crags. For an enjoyable day hike, trek up the San Miguel River Canyon to **Bridal Veil Falls.** Drive to the end of Rte. 145 and hike the steep dirt road to the waterfall. In winter, self-proclaimed atheists can be spied crossing themselves before hitting the "Spiral Stairs" and the "Plunge," two of the Rockies' most gut-wrenching slopes. For more info, contact the **Telluride Ski Resort,** P.O. Box 307, Telluride, CO 81435 (728-3856).

For a copy of the *Skier Services Brochure*, call 800-525-3455. A free shuttle connects the mountain village with the rest of the town. Pick up a current schedule at the visitors center (see above). **Paragon Ski and Sport,** 213 W. Colorado Ave. (728-4525), has camping supplies, bikes, skis, and roller blades. (Open daily 9am-7:30pm; winter daily 8am-9pm.)

■■■ DURANGO

As Will Rogers once put it, Durango is "out of the way and glad of it." Despite its popularity as a tourist destination, Durango retains a relaxed atmosphere. Come here to see Mesa Verde and to raft down the Animas River.

Practical Information Emergency is 911. Durango parks at the intersection of U.S. 160 and U.S. 150. Streets run perpendicular to avenues, but everyone calls Main Avenue "Main Street." The **Durango Lift** (259-5438) provides hourly bus service beginning at Main Ave. and Earl St. from 8am-5:15pm (75¢). **Greyhound,** 275 E. 8th Ave. (259-2755), serves Grand Junction ($31), Denver ($51), and Albuquerque ($35). (Open Mon.-Fri. 7:30am-noon and 3:30-5pm, Sat. 7:30am-noon; holidays 7:30-10am.) The **Durango Area Chamber Resort Association,** 111 S. Camino del Rio (247-0312 or 800-525-8855), across from Gateway Dr., is extremely helpful, and will answer questions about camping. (Open Mon.-Fri. 8am-5pm, Sat.-Sun. 11am-5pm; winter Mon.-Fri. 8am-5pm.) Durango's **post office:** 228 8th St. (247-3434; open Mon.-Fri. 8:30am-5:30pm, Sat. 9am-1pm); **ZIP code:** 81301; **area code:** 303.

Accommodations, Food, and Nightlife Durango Youth Hostel, 543 E. 2nd Ave. (247-9905), has simple bunks and kitchen facilities. Bare-bones, but only one block from downtown and the only reasonably-priced joint in the area. (Check-in 7-10am and 5-10pm. Check-out 7-10am. Bunks $10.) Since prices change so often, it's best to check ahead with the chamber resort association. Be ready to spend at least $40 for a double during the summer. Even the **Budget Inn,** 3077 Main Ave. (247-5222), charges a lot for the spacious rooms and a nice pool and hot tub (singles $50, doubles $53; less during off-season). The **Cottonwood Camper Park,** on U.S. 160 (247-1977), ½ mi. west of town, has tent sites $14, full hookup $18.

You may decide to stay in the quieter and cheaper town of **Silverton.** Though less popular as a destination, this small mining town is situated at the base of some of the most beautiful mountains and hiking trails. The **Teller House Hotel,** 1250 Greene St. (387-5423 or 800-342-4338), right next to the French Bakery (which provides the hotel's complementary breakfast), has comfortable rooms in a well-maintained 1896 hotel. (Singles $25, with private bath $37. Doubles $31/$47, $8 per additional person.) Silverton is at the end of the Durango & Silverton RR (see below).

For fixins', head to **City Market,** on U.S. 550 one block down 9th St., or at 3130 Main St., both open 24 hrs. The **Durango Diner,** 957 Main St. (247-9889), serves up mongo cheeseburgers ($2.75) and scrumptious, plate-sized pancakes cooked by a singing chef. (Open Mon.-Sat. 6am-2pm, Sun. 6am-1pm.) Or breakfast with locals at **Carver's Bakery and Brewpub,** 1022 Main Ave. (259-2545), which has good bread, breakfast specials ($2-4.50), veggie burritos ($5), and other vegetarian dishes. Brew-Jitas (beef fajitas sauteed in tequila) are $6.50. (Fri.-Sat. pitchers of beer $5. Open Mon.-Sat. 6:30am-10pm, Sun. 6am-1pm.) **Farquhart's,** 725 Main Ave. (247-9861), serves up good burritos for $5.75. They also have the best live music in town. (Sun.-Tues. free bluegrass; Sun.-Mon. rock n' roll; $3-5 cover. Open daily 11am-2am.)

Activities Winter is Durango's busiest season, when nearby **Purgatory Resort** (247-9000), 20 mi. north on U.S. 550, hosts skiers of all levels. (Lift tickets $37, kids 13-18 $19, kiddies under 12, one free child per adult.) When the heat is on, trade in your skis for a sled and test out the **Alpine Slide** ($4, under 6 must ride with an adult; open summer daily 9:30am-6pm). Or take the **Scenic Chairlift Ride** ($6).

Durango is best known for the **Durango and Silverton Narrow Gauge Train,** 479 Main St. (247-2733), which runs along the Animas River Valley to the glistening tourist town of **Silverton.** Old-fashioned, 100% coal-fed locomotives wheeze and cough through the San Juans, making a 2-hr. stop in Silverton before returning to Durango. (5 per day, at 7:30, 8:30, 9:15, and 10:15am, and 4:40pm; 6 hr., $43; ages 5-11 $21.50. Office open daily Aug.-Oct. 7am-7pm; Nov.-May 8am-3pm; the rest of the time 6am-9pm.) Or buy a one-way train ticket ($24.75), and take a bus back from Silverton along U.S. 550. **Buses** wait at the train station to service the weary (1½-hr.).

To backpack into the scenic **Chicago Basin,** purchase a round-trip ticket to Needleton ($34, ages 5-11 $17). To get into the **New York Basin,** you'll need $36 and a ticket to Elk Park. The train will drop you off here on its trip to Silverton. When you decide to leave the high country, return to Needleton and flag the train, but you must have either a return pass or $24 in cash to board. The train chugs through at 4:43pm. For more info on the train and its services for backpackers, contact the Durango & Silverton Narrow Gauge RR, 479 Main St., Durango 81301. (Offices open daily 6am-9pm; Aug.-Oct. 7am-7pm; Nov.-May 8am-5pm.)

For river rafting, **Rivers West,** 520 Main St. (259-5077), has good rates (1-hr. $12, 2-hr. $19; kids 20% discount; open daily 8am-9pm). **Durango Rivertrippers,** 720 Main St. (259-0289), organizes trips (2-hr. $19, for kids $15, 4-hr. $29, kids $23; open daily 8:30am-8:30pm). Biking gear is available from **Hassle Free Sports,** 2615 Main St. (259-3874 or 800-835-3800; bikes $8 per hr., $25 per day; open Mon.-Sat. 8:30am-6pm, Sun. 10:30am-5pm; must have driver's license and major credit card).

■ NEAR DURANGO: PAGOSA SPRINGS

The Ute were the first to discover the waters of Pagosa and believed that the springs were a gift of the Great Spirit. Today they remain the hottest and largest springs in the world. Pagosa springs from the San Juan Mountains on Rte. 160, 62 mi. east of Durango. The principal hot baths are located in two motels. The **Spring Inn** (264-4168) on Hot Springs Blvd., offers outside baths at $6.50 a bather. There is no time limit—the baths are open 24 hrs. The **Spa Motel** (264-54910) features stewing for $5 (open 8am-9pm daily). The **visitors center** (264-2360) is at the intersection of San Juan St. and Hot Springs Blvd. (open Mon.-Sat. 8am-5pm in summer; 9am-5pm winter). Except for the occasional mudslide and wildebeest stampede, there is no public transportation in Pagosa Springs. Pagosa's **post office:** 155 Hot Springs Blvd. (open Mon.-Fri. 7:30am-5;30pm, Sat. 9am-2pm); **ZIP code:** 81147; **area code:** 303.

Cheap lodging is available. The **Sky View Motel** (263-5803), 1 mi. west of town on Rte. 160, offers single with cable TV for $30, doubles $40, quads $50. The **First Inn Motel** (264-4161), just east of town on Rte. 160, provides singles for $40, doubles $45, and sweet suites for up to eight for $69 (winter rates $5-10 cheaper). The **High Country Lodge** (264-4181), 3 mi. east on Rte. 160, has high country, but low prices. (Singles $45, $5 each additional personal up to 4. Cabin for 1 $60, $5 each additional person up to 4. Winter rates $5 less.)

The **Malt Shoppe,** 124 Pagosa St. (264-2784), has 14 flavors of shakes as well as burgers and sandwiches. The **Moose River Pub,** 20 Village Dr. (731-5451), serves up southwest chop-lickin' goodies. (Open Mon.-Fri. 11am-2pm and 5-9pm, Sat. 5-9pm.) **The Hogs Breath Saloon,** 157 Navajo Trail Dr. (731-2626), near Rte. 160W, features country western dancing and a surf n' turf menu (open daily 11am-2am).

During the winter, **Wolf Creek**, 20 mi. east of the town, claims to have the most snow in Colorado. (Lift tickets $30, children $10. Rates subject to voguish changes.) **Chimney Rock Archeological Area** (264-2268), 20 mi. west of Pagosa Springs on U.S. 160 and Rte. 151S, contains the ruins of a high-mesa Anasazi village. (2-hr. guided tour from May 15-Sept. 15 at 9:30am, 10:30am, 1pm, and 2pm. $3, under 12 $2.) The **San Juan National Forest** (247-4874) surrounds the whole area and offers hiking, fishing, and camping. Call for more info. Spend quality time with mountain lions, black bears, bull elk, and other mammalia at the **Rocky Mountain Wildlife Park** (264-4515), 3 mi. south of Pagosa on Rte. 84 (open daily 9am-6pm).

■■■ MESA VERDE NATIONAL PARK

Long ago, Native American tribes cultivated the desert mesas of southwestern Colorado. In the year 1200, they constructed the cliff dwellings which they mysteriously abandoned in 1275. Navajo tribes arriving in the area in 1450 named the former inhabitants the Anasazi or "ancient ones." Today only 5 of the 1000 archeological sites are open to touring because the sandstone wears quickly under human feet.

Practical Information For emergencies, call 529-4469. The park's main entrance is off U.S. 160, 36 mi. from Durango and 10 mi. from Cortez. The **Far View Visitors Center** (529-4543), 20 mi. from the gate on the main road, is open daily during the summer from 8am-5pm. During the winter, your best bet for the low down is the **Chapin Mesa Museum** (529-4475) at the south end of the park (open daily 8am-5pm) or the **Colorado Welcome Center/Cortez Chamber of Commerce,** 928 E. Main (800-253-1616 or 565-3414; open daily 9am-6pm; winter 8am-5pm), in Cortez. **Mesa Verde Tours** (259-4818 in Durango; 565-1278 in Cortez) picks up in Durango or Cortez and take you on a 9-hr. tour of the park, leaving at 8:30am ($28, under 12 $14); bring a lunch. Make reservations the night before as tours fill up. Since sights lie up to 40 mi. apart, a car is helpful. Van transport is available at the Far View Lodge (see above) for self-guided tours (provide 24-hr. notice). Mesa Verde's **ZIP code:** 81330; **area code:** 303. For more info call 529-4461.

Accommodations and Camping Mesa Verde's only lodging, **Far View Motor Lodge** (529-4421), across from the visitors center, is extremely expensive, but a few nearby motels can put you up for under $30. Try the **Ute Mountain Motel,** 531 S. Broadway (565-8507), in Cortez, CO. (Singles from $35. Doubles from $42. Rates drop in winter.) Your best bet is to stay at the nearby **Durango Hostel** (see Durango). The only camping in Mesa Verde is 4 mi. inside the park at **Morfield Campground** (529-4400; off-season 533-7731). The second largest campground in America *has never been full,* and boasts some beautiful, secluded sites. In summer, go early to beat the crowds. (450 sites $8, only 15 RV spots that can be reserved, full hookup $16. Showers 75¢ for 5 min.)

Activities The southern portion of the park divides into the **Chapin Mesa** and the **Wetherill Mesa.** On Wetherill Mesa, tours leave from Far View Lodge. (June-Sept. 3-hr. tours at 9:30am and 1:30pm, $12, under 12 $5; 5-hr. tours at 9:30am, $15, under 12 $5.) You may take guided tours up ladders and through the passageways of Anasazi dwellings. **Cliff Palace** is the largest cliff dwelling in North America. Free tickets for tours are necessary and available at visitors center. **Spruce Tree House** is one of the better-preserved ruins. **Balcony House,** a dwelling of almost 40 rooms 600ft. above the floor of Soda Canyon, is a must see. (Open in summer only.) Free tickets are required for ranger-guided entry into the site and are available at the visitors center, first-come, first-served (tours every ½ hr., daily 9am-6pm). To get an overview of the Anasazi lifestyle, visit the **Chapin Mesa Museum** (529-4475), at the south end of the park (open daily 8am-6:30pm; winter 8am-5pm).

Idaho

Although most of the U.S. associates Idaho with "Famous Potatoes" (until recently its motto), Idaho ain't just tubers. The state's proximity to the Pacific Northwest lends it a feel distinct from its cowboy neighbors. The Northern panhandle is filled with dense pine forests and several spectacular lakes; Coeur d'Alene is the jewel of the region. The western border is lined with rushing rivers providing some of the wildest whitewater rafting in the country. The Snake River's serpentine waters have carved out Hell's Canyon, the deepest gorge in North America. The U.S. government quietly guards Idaho's most spectacular parts in the Selway-Bitteroot Wilderness and the Idaho Primitive Area, through which rushes the meandering Salmon. At the bottom of Sawtooth National Recreation Area, the chi-chi Ketchum hosts movie stars, but is not far from the old general store and tackle shop in Stanley.

PRACTICAL INFORMATION

Capital: Boise.
Idaho Information Line, 800-635-7820. **Boise Convention and Visitors Bureau** (344-7777), corner of 9th and Idaho, 2nd floor. Open daily 8:30am-5pm. **Parks and Recreation Department,** 5657 Warm Springs Ave., Boise 83720 (334-4199). **Idaho Outfitters and Guide Association,** P.O. Box 95, Boise 83701 (342-1438). Info on companies leading whitewater, packhorse, and backpacking expeditions in the state. Free vacation directories.
Time Zones: Mountain and Pacific. The dividing line runs east-west at about the middle of the state; if you straddle it, you'll break the bonds of time.
Postal Abbreviation: ID
Sales tax: 5%.

■■■ BOISE

Boise is a booming, surprisingly hip town in the middle of rural Idaho. The city's proximity to natural splendor adds to its value. Idaho's capital also contains numerous grassy parks, making this small city both a verdant residential bulwark amid the state's dry southern plateau and a relaxing way-station on a cross-country jaunt. Most of the city's sights lie between the capitol and I-84 a few miles south; you can manage pretty well on foot.

Practical Information Amtrak (800-872-7245) serves Boise from the beautiful Spanish-mission-style **Union Pacific Depot,** 1701 Eastover Terr. (336-5992), easily visible from Capitol Blvd. Three trains a week go to Salt Lake City (7¾ hr., $70); one goes west to Portland (10½ hr., $83) and Seattle (15½ hr., $111). **Greyhound** has I-84 schedules from its terminal at 1212 W. Bannock (343-3681), a few blocks west of downtown. Three buses per day head to Portland (8-10 hr., $57) and Seattle (11 hr., $101). **Boise Urban Stages** (336-1010) runs several routes through the city, with maps available from any bus driver and displayed at each stop. (Buses operate Mon.-Fri. 5:15am-8:45pm, Sat. 6:45am-6:45pm. Fare 75¢, seniors 35¢.) To get around in Boise more athletically, rent at **McU's Sports,** 822 W. Jefferson (342-7734) which offers rollerblades ($4 per hour, $12 per day, $15 overnight) and mountain bikes ($14 per ½-day, $22 per day) as well as equipment for sports of all seasons. Boise's main **post office:** 770 S. 13th St. (383-4211; open Mon.-Fri. 7:30am-5:30pm, Sat. 10am-2pm); **ZIP code:** 83707; **area code:** 208.

Accommodations and Camping Finding lodging in Boise is harsh; neither the YMCA nor the YWCA provide rooms, and even the cheapest hotels charge more than $20 per night. The more reasonable places tend to fill quickly, so make reservations. The friendly **Boisean,** 1300 S. Capitol Ave. (343-3645 or 800-365-3645), has modest rooms and a friendly staff. (Singles $32. Doubles $47. Additional person $6.) The enormous **Capri Motel,** 2600 Fairview Ave. (344-8617), offers air-conditioned rooms, coffee, and queen-sized beds. (Singles $28. Doubles $34.) The **Forest Service Campground** lies 3 mi. north of town. Contact **Boise National Forest,** 1715 Front St. (364-4100), for a map ($3), or for mushroom permits (3 days, $10). (Open Mon.-Fri. 7:30am-4:30pm.) Other campgrounds include **Boise KOA Kampground,** 7300 S. Federal Way (345-7673; sites $17.50, full hookup $20); **Americana Kampground,** 3600 American Terrace Blvd. (344-5733; 90 sites, $17, with water and wattage $20.50); and **Fiesta Park,** 11101 Fairview Ave. (375-8207; sites $16, hookup with water and electricity $18.50, full hookup $19.50).

Food and Nightlife Food in Boise is more than just potatoes. The downtown area, centered around 6th and Main St., is bustling with lunchtime delis, coffee shops, ethnic cuisine, and several stylish bistros. A local tradition is **Moon's Kitchen,** 815 W. Bannock St. (385-0472; soup, sandwich, drink special $5; huge breakfast $2.75; open Mon.-Fri. 7am-3pm, Sat. 8am-3pm). A more innovative menu and tastier sandwiches can be found at the **Raintree Deli,** 210 North Capitol Blvd. (336-4611), where half a sandwich is $3 and a stuffed baked potato is $4 (open Mon.-Fri. 9am-3:30pm). For a sit-down Italian meal go to **Louise's,** 620 W. Idaho (344-5200), and slurp up shrimp fettucini for $9, or create-your-own-pizza starting at $6. (Open Mon.-Thurs. 11am-10pm, Fri. 11am-11pm, Sat. noon-11pm, Sun. 3-10pm.) Long live *Casablanca* at the combination restaurant and movie theater at **Rick's Café American/The Flicks,** 646 Fulton St. (342-4222). Huge portions are $6-13. (Kitchen open 5-9:30pm, movies daily 5, 7, and 9:45pm, weekends and summer matinees daily at 1pm.) For a pub ambience, stroll along Main St. from 5th to Capitol and check out the bar scene—**Hannah's,** 621 Main, is a good choice with live music most nights. (Open Tues.-Fri. 3pm-2am, Sat.-Sun. 5pm-close.) Treat all your senses to a musical hot spot called the **Blues Bouquet,** 1010 Main St. (345-6605), which has $1.50 drafts Tues.-Thurs. and live music nightly. Call about Blues sisters's nights when women's drinks are reduced. (Open Tues.-Sun. 5pm until the blues take a walk.)

Sights The **Boise Tour Train** (342-4796) shows you 75 sites around the city in one hour. Tours start and end in the parking lot of **Julia Davis Park,** departing every 75 min. (Summer 3 tours per day, Mon.-Sat. 10am-3pm, Sun. noon-5pm, evening tour Fri.-Sat. 7pm; off-season Wed.-Sun. afternoons only. $6, seniors $5.50, ages 3-12 $3.50. Arrive 15 min. early.) To learn about Idaho and the Old West at your own pace, walk through the **Historical Museum** (334-2120), in Julia Davis Park. (Open Mon.-Sat. 9am-5pm, Sun. 1-5pm. Free, donations encouraged.) Also in the park, the

Boise Art Museum, 670 Julia Davis Dr. (345-8330), displays international and local works. (Open Tues.-Fri. 10am-5pm, Sat.-Sun. noon-5pm. $3, students and seniors $2, under 6 free. Free the first Thurs. of every month.) Take a self-guided tour through the country's only **state capitol** to be heated with natural geothermal hot water. (Open Mon.-Fri. 8am-5pm, Sat. 9am-5pm.) The tiny and crowded **Boise Zoo** (384-4260) roars and howls beyond these two buildings. (Open Mon.-Wed. and Fri.-Sun. 10am-5pm, Thurs. 10am-9pm. $3, seniors and ages 4-12 $1.25, under 4 free, Thurs. ½-price.) Taloned avians perch and dive at the **World Center for Birds of Prey** (362-3716), 6 mi. south of I-84 on Cole Rd. You must call ahead to arrange a tour (donations of $4). For more back-to-nature fun, try the 22-mi. **Boise River Greenbelt,** a pleasant path ideal for a leisurely walk or picnic.

Bask in the region's cultural history at the **Basque Museum and Cultural Center** (343-2671), at 6th and Grove St. in downtown Boise, where you'll find out about the surprisingly rich Basque heritage in the Great Basin and the Western Rockies. (Open Tues.-Fri. 10am-4pm, Sat. 11am-3pm.)

■■■ KETCHUM AND SUN VALLEY

In 1935, Union Pacific heir Averill Harriman sent Austrian Count Felix Schaffgotsch to scour the U.S. for a site to develop a ski resort area rivaling Europe's best. The Count settled on the small mining and sheep-herding town of Ketchum in Idaho's Wood River Valley, which has since become Sun Valley, a ski resort for the American rich and famous. The town of Ketchum serves as the area's metropolis—the term Sun Valley only applies to the resort outside of town. Ketchum's streets are lined with fashionable shops and galleries, but a quick glance up and you realize that the town is sandwiched between hills—the Smokies to the west, the Pioneers to the east, and the Boulders to the north. The budget traveler should avoid the Valley and head for these hills which provide endless warm-weather opportunities for camping, hiking, biking, and fishing.

The best time to visit the area is during "slack" (late Oct.-Thanksgiving and May-early June), when the tourists magically vanish. For local info, visit the **Sun Valley/Ketchum Chamber of Commerce** (800-634-3347), at 4th and Main St., Ketchum, where a well-informed, helpful staff shines. (Open daily 9am-5pm, less when slacking.) The **Ketchum Ranger Station,** 206 Sun Valley Rd. (622-5371), four blocks east of Rte. 75, is the place to go for information on national forest land around Ketchum, and tapes and maps on the Sawtooth Recreation Area. (Open Mon.-Fri. 8am-5pm.) Ketchum's **post office:** 301 1st Ave. (726-5161; open Mon.-Fri. 8:30am-5:30pm, Sat. 11am-1pm); **ZIP code:** 83340; **area code:** 208.

The food may be cheap; the same cannot be said for indoor accommodations. From early June to mid-October, **camping** is the best option for cheap sleep. The **Sawtooth National Forest** surrounds Ketchum—drive or hike along the forest service road and camp for free. There are also several nearby campgrounds in the Sawtooth National Recreation Area, call the SNRA headquarters (726-7672). The **North Fork** (26 sites) and **Wood River** (31 sites) campgrounds lie 7 and 10 mi. north of Ketchum, respectively, and cost $3 per site. Wood River has an amphitheater and flush toilets. You must bring your own water to the three **North Fork Canyon** campgrounds 7 mi. north of Ketchum (free).

Though it's a small town, Ketchum has plenty of inexpensive, enjoyable restaurants (**Irving's,** across from the tourist info center, is the legendary local hot-dog stand; open daily 11:30am-3pm.) Have this guidebook and eat it too at the **Main St. Bookcafe,** 211 Main St. (726-3700), which we grudgingly admit sells other books, as well as standard café fare (espresso $1.25, hummus plate $4.50, veggie burger $6). (Open Mon.-Tues. 7am-6pm, Wed.-Fri. 7am-10pm, Sat.-Sun. 7am-midnight.) Find HUGE food at **Mama Inez** (726-4213), at 7th and Warm Springs, including bean burritos ($2.30) and beef enchiladas ($6). The nachos ($6.85) require dextrous utensil skill to eat. (Open Mon.-Sat. 11:30am-2pm and 5:30-10pm, Sun. 5-10pm.)

The best in town is dollar night for beer and mixed drinks at **Whiskey Jacques,** 209 N. Main St. (726-3200; open daily 5pm-1am). **Lefty's** (726-2744), on the corner of 6th and Washington, serves up the bar munchies and big ol' beers. (Grill closes at 10:30pm, open daily 11:30am-1am or whenever it slows up.)

The Outdoors and Hot Springs The hills of Ketchum have more natural **hot springs** than any spot in the Rockies except Yellowstone; bathing is free and uncrowded in most of the springs. Like the ghost towns of the surrounding mountains, many springs can be reached only by foot; for maps, inquire at **Chapter One Bookstore** (726-5425) on Main St. next to Pedro's Market, or **Elephant's Perch,** on Sun Valley Rd. (726-3497). "The Perch" is also the best source for mountain bike rentals and trail info. (Bikes $12 per ½-day, $18 per day.)

More accessible, non-commercial springs include **Warfield Hot Springs** on Warm Springs Creek, 11 mi. west of Ketchum on Warm Springs Rd., and **Russian John Hot Springs,** 8 mi. north of the SNRA headquarters on Rte. 75, just west of the highway. For the best information on fishing conditions and licenses, as well as equipment rentals, stop by **Silver Creek Outfitters,** 507 N. Main St. (726-5282; open daily 8am-6pm). The fly-fishing bible, *Curtis Creek Manifesto,* is available here ($7).

■■■ CRATERS OF THE MOON NATIONAL MONUMENT

Craters of the Moon, 60 mi. south of Sun Valley on U.S. 20/26/93, is a black lava plateau that rises from the surrounding fertile plains. Windswept and remarkably quiet, the stark, twisted lava formations are speckled with sparse, low vegetation. Volcanic eruptions occurred here as recently as 2000 years ago.

Park admission is $4 per car, $2 per individual, and the bizarre black campsites cost $8 (52 sites without hookup). Wood fires are prohibited but charcoal fires are permitted. You can also camp for free in the adjacent **Bureau of Land Management** properties. The park's sites often fill by 4pm on summer nights. Unmarked sites in the monument are free with free backcountry permits, but even with the topographical map ($4), it may be hard to find a comfortable spot; the first explorers couldn't sleep in the lava fields for lack of bearable places to bed down. You can camp in only one designated area, after a 4-mi. hike.

The **visitors center** (527-3257), just off U.S. 20/26/93, has displays and videotapes on the process of lava formation, and printed guides for hikes to all points of interest within the park. They also distribute backcountry camping permits and sell the maps mentioned above. Rangers lead evening strolls and programs at the campground amphitheater (daily mid-June to mid-Sept.). (Open daily 8am-6pm; off-season Mon.-Fri. 8am-4:30pm.) Explore nearby **lava tubes,** caves formed when a surface layer of lava hardened and the rest of the molten rock drained out, creating a tunnel. If a ranger does not escort you, bring a flashlight. From nearby Arco, Blackfoot, or Pocatello you can connect with **Greyhound**. There is, however, neither transportation to the national monument nor food available when you get there.

■■■ SAWTOOTH NATIONAL RECREATION AREA

Rough mountains pack the 756,000 acres of wilderness in this recreation area. Home to the **Sawtooth** and **White Cloud Mountains** in the north and the **Smokey** and **Boulder** ranges in the south, the **Sawtooth National Recreation Area (SNRA)** is surrounded by four national forests, encompassing the headwaters of five of Idaho's major rivers. If you have a car, getting to the heart of the SNRA is easy. Make sure to pause at the **Galena Summit,** 25 mi. north of Ketchum on Rte. 75. The 8701-ft. peak provides an excellent introductory view of the range. If you don't have a car, take the bus to Missoula (250 mi. north on U.S. 93) or Twin Falls (120 mi. south on Rte. 75); from there, rent a car or plan for a long and beautiful hike.

Practical Information Information centers in the SNRA are almost as plentiful as the peaks themselves. Stop by the **Stanley Chamber of Commerce** (774-3411), on Rte. 21 about three-quarters of the way through town. (Open daily 10am-6pm; winter hours vary.) Topographical maps ($2.50) and various trail books are available at McCoy's Tackle (see below) and at the **Stanley Ranger Station** (774-3681), 3 mi. south on Rte. 75 (open Mon.-Fri. 8am-5pm, Sat.-Sun. 8:30am-5pm). The **Redfish Visitors Center** (774-3376) lies 8 mi. south and 2 mi. west of Stanley at the **Redfish Lake Lodge** (774-3536). (Both open June 19-Sept. 2 daily 9am-6pm.) Whatever you can't find at these three places awaits at **SNRA Headquarters** (726-7672), 53 mi. south of Stanley off Rte. 75, 8 mi. north of Ketchum. The building itself mimics the peaks of the Sawtooths. (Open daily 8am-5:30pm; fall and spring Wed.-Sun. 8am-5:30pm, winter Mon.-Fri. 8am-4:30pm, Sat.-Sun. 9am-4:30pm.) All the info centers have maps of the Sawtooths ($3) and free taped auto tours of the impressive Ketchum-Stanley trip on Rte. 75. Stanley's **post office:** (774-2230) is on Ace of Diamonds St. (open Mon.-Fri. 8am-noon, 1-5pm); **ZIP code:** 83278; **area code:** 208.

Food and Camping In the heart of Stanley, on Ace of Diamonds St., the **Sawtooth Hotel and Cafe** (774-9947) is a perfect place to stay after a wilderness sojourn (singles $24, with private bath $40; doubles $27, with private bath $45). More scenic is **McGowan's Resort** (800-447-8141), 1 mi. down Rte. 75 in Lower Stanley. Hand-built cabins here sit directly on the banks of the Salmon River, house up to six people each, and usually contain kitchenettes. They also offer a terrific view of the Sawtooths and unmatched hospitality. ($50-85; Sept.-early June $40-75.) Campgrounds line Rte. 75; clusters are at **Redfish Lake** at the base of the Sawtooths at **Stanley Lake** farther north on Rte. 75; at **Alturas Lake** in the Smokies; at **Salmon River Canyon** along the Salmon to the east of Stanley; and at the **Wood River Corrido** farther south on Rte. 75. At Redfish, the catch of the day is the small campground at the Point, which has its own beach. The two campgrounds on nearby Little Redfish Lake are the best spots for trailers. Each cluster has at least three campgrounds—**Redfish, Stanley,** and **Salmon River** have the most campgrounds. Sites at Red Fish are $8, everywhere else $6. Most operate on a first-come, first-served basis—Elk Creek (3 sites), Sheep Trail (3 sites), and Trap Creek (3 sites) in the **Stanley area;** Point and Glacier View in the **Redfish Area;** and Easley (9 sites) in the **Wood River Corridor** require reservations (800-280-2267). For general info on all campgrounds call the SNRA Headquarters (726-7672). Overflow camping, primitive but free, is available in several spots. Two good areas are **Redfish Overflow,** just off Rte. 75, and **Decker Flats,** just north of 4th of July Rd. on Rte. 75.

Activities and Sights Places for **hiking, boating,** and **fishing** in all four of the SNRA's little-known ranges are unbeatable and innumerable. 2 mi. northwest of Stanley on Rte. 21, take the 3-mi. Iron Creek Rd. which leads to the trailhead of the **Sawtooth Lake Hike.** This 5½-mi. trail is steep but well-worn, and not overly difficult if you stop to rest. Bolder hikers who want to survey the White Cloud Range from above should head southeast of Stanley to the **Casino Lakes** trailhead. This trek terminates at **Lookout Mountain,** 3000 ft. higher than far-away Stanley itself. (Groups of 10-20 need to acquire free wilderness permits for sojourning into the wilderness area, on the western side of the SNRA. If you want a big bonfire, get a burning permit, and always check with a ranger where you can light fires.) The long and gentle loop around **Yellow Belly, Toxaway,** and **Petit Lakes** is recommended for novice hikers or any tourists desiring a leisurely overnight trip. For additional hiking information, consult the detailed topographic maps in any of Margaret Fuller's **Trail Guides** ($13 for the Sawtooths and White Cloud guide), available at McCoy's Tackle Shop (see below). Stock up on food at the **Mountain Village Grocery Store** (774-3350) before venturing into the mountains (open daily 7am-9pm).

In the heat of summer, the cold rivers beg for **fishing**, **canoeing**, or **whitewater rafting**. **McCoy's Tackle Shop** (774-3377), on Ace of Diamonds St. in Stanley, rents gear, sells a full house of outdoor equipment, and has a gift shop (fly rod $10 per day, $42 per 6 days; spinning rod $6 per day, $27 per 6 days; open daily 8am-8pm). The **Redfish Lake Lodge Marina** (774-3536) rents paddleboats ($4-5 per ½ hr.), canoes ($5 per hr., $15 per ½ day, $25 per day), and power boats ($10 per hr., $33.50 for ½ day, $60 per day; open in summer daily 7am-9pm). **The River Company** (774-2244), based in Ketchum (726-8890) with an office in Stanley, arranges whitewater rafting and float trips. (Ketchum office open daily 8am-6pm. Stanley office open in summer daily 7:30am-4pm unless a trip is in progress.)

The most inexpensive way to enjoy the SNRA waters is to visit the **hot springs** just east of Stanley. Watch for the rising steam on the roadside, often a sign of hot water. **Sunbeam Hot Springs,** 13 mi. from town, is the best of the batch. Be sure to bring a bucket or cooler to the stone bathhouse; you'll need to add about 20 gallons of cold Salmon River water before you can get into these hot pools. The SNRA headquarters has information on all hot springs in the area. For evening entertainment, try to get in on the regionally famous **Stanley Stomp,** when fiddlers in **Casanova Jack's Rod and Gun Club** (774-9920) keep the foot-stomping going all through the night. (Open daily to 2am; live music Thurs.-Sat. evenings.)

■■■ HELL'S CANYON NATIONAL RECREATION AREA

Along the western border of Idaho rush several of the country's wildest rivers, providing a whitewater rafting and kayaking paradise. It is here that the **Snake River** has carved out Hell's Canyon, the deepest gorge in North America. The canyon descends deceptively in rising and falling slopes. Still, the **Hell's Canyon National Recreation Area** offers spectacular camping, hiking, rafting, kayaking, and fishing opportunities. The area's **headquarters,** 88401 Highway 82, Enterprise, OR 97828 (508-426-4978), are in Oregon, but there is also an office in Riggins, ID on U.S. 945 (523-6391; both open Mon.-Fri. 9am-5pm). There are several viewing points of the canyon in Idaho, the most spectacular being **Heavens Gate Overlook,** 17 mi. southwest of Riggins on Rte. 517, and **Pittsburgh Landing,** southwest of White Bird off of Rte. 493. To access the Snake River within the canyon travel to either Winston to the north or Hell's Canyon Dam in the south. Jet boat and raft trips are available through **Hell's Canyon Adventures, Inc.** in Oxbow, OR (800-422-3568 or 505-785-3352). A 3-hr. lunch tour on jet boat is $25. A full-day rafting trip, including lunch and a jet boat trip back to Hell's Canyon Dam is $90 per person.

Though popular because of its name and the astounding depth, the Snake River through Hell's Canyon is only one of the many areas good for **whitewater rafting.** Arguably the highest quality river to float on is the **Selway,** which cuts horizontally across the center of the state. The **Middle Fork of the Salmon** is a high quality river with a larger carrying capacity and easier accessibility. The **Middle Main Salmon** is good for the do-it-your-selfers, but for those passing through looking for a short jaunt led by experts, **Riggins, ID** has what you need. Nestled along the main fork of the Salmon, Riggins is home to more whitewater outfitters than restaurants and hotels combined. Two of the most reputable are **Epley's** (800-233-1813 or 628-3533) where ½-day trips start at $30, $40 with lunch; full-day trips are $55, with dinner $60; and **Discovery** (800-755-8894 or 628-3319), where ½-day trips are $35, full day $60. Both companies are on Rte. 95 as you drive into Riggins.

■■■ COEUR D'ALENE

When the French fur trappers passed through northern Idaho in the late 1800s, they attempted to trade their goods with the local Native Americans, who weren't interested. Offended at their indifference, the French told the Indians that they had hearts as small as awls—and that's how the area and its magnanimous natives got the name Coeur d'Alene. These days the locals still don't accept trades—it takes a lot of cold, hard cash to vacation at the city by the lake. Still, the budget traveler can perservere and enjoy the serene beauty of the area.

PRACTICAL INFORMATION

Emergency: 911.

Visitor Information: Chamber of Commerce, 1621 N. 3rd St. (664-3194), at Spruce. Open Mon.-Fri. 8am-5pm. **Visitors center** (664-0587), corner of First and Sheridan St. Open Mon.-Fri. 9am-5pm, Sat.-Sun. 10am-3pm. **Toll-free Visitors Info:** 800-232-4068.

Bus Station: 1527 Northwest Blvd. (664-3343), 1 mi. north of the lake. **Greyhound** serves Boise (12 hr., $50); Spokane (1 hr., $9.75); Lewiston (1 per day, $28); and Missoula (5 hr., $34). **Empire Lines** connects to Sandpoint at 5th and Cedar St. (1 per day, $8.30). Open Mon.-Sat. 8-10am and 4-8pm, Sun. 8-10am.

Car Rental: Auto of Couer d'Alene Rental, 120 Anton Ave. (667-4905), $27 per day, $180 per week; 100 free mi. per day, 25¢ per extra mi. Open Mon.-Sat. 8:30am-5:30pm. Must be 21. Credit card or $100 cash deposit required. **U-Save Auto Rental,** 302 Northwest Blvd. (664-1712). $22 per day with 150 free mi, 20¢ each additional mi. Open Mon.-Fri. 8am-6pm, Sat. 8am-3pm, Sun. 10am-4pm.

Help Line: Crisis Services, 664-1443. 24 hrs.

Time Zone: Pacific (3 hr. behind Eastern).

Post Office: 111 N. 7th St. (664-8126), 5 blocks east of the Chamber of Commerce off Sherman. Open Mon.-Fri. 8:30am-5pm. **ZIP code:** 83814.

Area Code: 208.

ACCOMMODATIONS, CAMPING, AND FOOD

Cheap lodgings are hard to find in this booming resort town. You'll have your best luck in the eastern outskirts of the city. Budget motels line **Sherman Ave.** on the outside of town. One of the cheapest is **El Rancho,** 1915 Sherman Ave. (664-8794 or 800-359-9791), which has a TV and coffeemaker filled with grounds in each room. (In the summer singles $46-49, doubles $53-58; off-season $25-35.) A bit closer to town, the **Star Motel,** 1516 Sherman Ave. (667-5035), has large, furnished rooms with TV, free HBO, phones, and fridges (singles $45, doubles $65; off-season all rooms $40-60). Near Silver Mt., about 35 mi. east of Coeur d'Alene, is a **youth hostel,** 834 W. McKinley Ave., Kellogg, ID (783-4171); it has laundry, TV, VCR, and 40 beds. (April-Oct. $10; Nov.-March $12.)

Camping is the way to go for cheap lodging in Coeur d'Alene. There are five **public campgrounds** within 20 mi. of Coeur d'Alene. The closest is **Robin Hood RV Park,** 703 Lincoln Way (664-2306); it has showers, laundry, hookups, no evil sheriffs, and is within walking distance of downtown. (Sites $15.50.) **Beauty Creek,** a forest service site 10 mi. south along the lake, is the next closest. Camp alongside a lovely stream trickling down the side of a mountain. Drinking water and pit toilets. (Sites $12. Open May 5-Oct. 15.) **Honeysuckle Campground,** 25 mi. northeast, has nine sites with drinking water and toilets ($8; open May 15-Oct. 15). **Bell Bay,** on Lake Coeur d'Alene (off U.S. 95 south, then 14 mi. to Forest Service Rd. 545) offers 26 sites, a boat launch, and good fishing (sites $5; open May 5-Oct. 15). Call the Fernan Ranger District Office (765-7381), for info on these and other campgrounds. (Open Mon.-Fri. 7:30am-4:30pm, Sat. 8:30am-3pm.) **Farragut State Park** (683-2425), 20 mi. north on U.S. 95, is an extremely popular 4000-acre park dotted with hiking trails and beaches along Lake Pend Oreille (pon-do-RAY). (Sites $9, with hookup $12. $2 day-use fee for motor vehicles. Open May 27-Sept. 2.)

There are oysters aplenty in Coeur d'Alene, but if you like your snacks to come without shells, sit at the sidewalk tables at the "Wake up and Live" **Java Café,** 324 Sherman Ave. (667-0010). Sip their gourmet coffee, eat confetti eggs for breakfast ($3.50), or gourmet pizza for lunch ($4-5). (Open Mon.-Sat. 7am-11pm, Sun. 7am-6pm.) Create your own sandwich at **Spooner's,** 215 Sherman Ave. (667-7666), for $4.25. Ice cream is $1-2 (open daily 10am-8:30pm). **Tito Macaroni,** 210 Sherman

Ave. (667-2782), oven bakes its pizza ($4-14). (Open daily 11am-10pm.) Breakfast at **Jimmy D's,** 320 Sherman Ave. (664-9774), sets you back only $2-6, lunch $5-7, dinner $5-13 (open daily 9am-11pm; winter 9am-10pm).

SIGHTS AND ACTIVITIES

The lake is Coeur d'Alene's *raison d'être*. Hike 2 mi. up **Tubbs Hill** to a scenic vantage point, or head for the **Coeur d'Alene Resort** and walk along the **world's longest floating boardwalk** (3300 ft.). You can tour the lake on a **Lake Coeur d'Alene Cruise** (765-4000) departing from the downtown dock every afternoon June-Sept. (1:30, 3:30, and 6:30pm, 90 min., $9.75, seniors $8.75, kids $5.75). Rent a canoe from **Eagle Enterprises** (664-1175) at the city dock to explore the lake ($7 per hr., $20 per ½-day, $35 first whole day, $15 per day thereafter). A 3-mi. bike/foot path circles the lake. **Four Seasons Outfitting,** 105 Sherman Ave. (765-2863), organizes rafting (½-day $45, full day $89), horse rides ($13 first 45 min., $21 for 3 hrs. or over), and fly fishing (½-day walk $125, full-day float trip $195). Call well in advance.

The **Old Mission at Cataldo** (682-3814), 20 mi. east of town on I-90, is now contained in a day-use state park. Built in 1850 by Native Americans, the mission is the oldest extant building in Idaho. (Free tours daily. Open June-July daily 8am-6pm. Vehicle entry fee $2.) Near Sandpoint, about 50 mi. north of Coeur d'Alene, the **Roosevelt Grove of Ancient Cedars** has trees up to 12 ft. in diameter.

Continue another 35 mi. east on I-90 through mining country to the town of **Wallace,** for retail shops shaped like mining helmets and the **Wallace Mining Museum,** 509 Bank St. (556-1592), which features turn-of-the-century mining equipment. (Open daily 8am-8pm; off-season Mon.-Sat. 9am-6pm. $1.50, seniors $1, and kids 50¢.) Next door, take the **Sierra Silver Mine Tour** (752-5151; leaves from museum) through a depleted silver mine. (1-hr. tours May-Sept. daily every 30 min. 9am-4pm; July-Aug. 9am-6pm. $7, seniors and under 12 $6.) Ride the **world's largest gondola** up Silver Mountain 20 mi. north on U.S. 95. The gondola can transport mountain bikes. (783-1111; $10, students and seniors $8, kids under 6 free; chairlift rides $2.) "Rise and dine" packages (gondola ride and dinner) are also popular. (Open midMay to early Oct. Mon.-Thurs. 10am-6pm, Fri.-Sat. 10am-10pm, Sun. 10am-9pm.)

 # Montana

In Big Sky country, the populations of elk, deer, and pronghorn antelope outnumber the human population. Despite the recent acquisition of large amounts of acreage by such Eastern celebrities as Ted Turner, Tom Brokaw, and Liz Claiborne, Montana still has 25 million acres of national forest and public lands. Cattle ranches bespeckle the eastern plains, while grizzlies and glaciers grace the Rockies of the western region. The state has a few booming college towns—Missoula the most booming of them all. Copious fishing lakes, 500 species of wildlife (not including millions of insect types), and thousands of ski trails make Montana a nature-lover's paradise.

PRACTICAL INFORMATION

Capital: Helena.
Travel Montana, P.O. Box 200533, Helena 59620 (444-2654 or 800-541-1447). Write for a free *Montana Travel Planner*. **National Forest Information,** Northern Region, Federal Bldg., 200 E. Broadway, Box 7669, Missoula 59801 (329-3511). Gay and lesbian tourists can write **Lambda Alliance**, P.O. Box 7611, Missoula, MT 59807, for Montana gay community activities.
Time Zone: Mountain (2 hrs. behind Eastern). **Postal Abbreviation:** MT
Sales Tax: 0%.

■■■ BILLINGS

Named after Northern Pacific Railroad President Frederick Billings, the town started out in 1882 as a rail stop. Despite its size today (pop. 80,000), Billings maintains a deserted and very industrial atmosphere. There are very few sights to behold here.

Billings lies at the junction of Rte. 90 and 94. Street naming and numbering is confusing; three streets will have the same name, distinguished only by direction. Definitely invest in the $1 city map at the **visitors center** at the Chamber of Commerce, 815 S. 27th St. (252-4016), which also has an electronic map highlighting areas with good hiking and fishing. (Open daily 8:30am-7:30pm, off season Mon.-Fri. 8:30am-5pm.) **Rent-a-Wreck** (252-0219) has cheap cars, from $28 per day ($28.50 winter), or $130 per week (winter $160), with 100 free mi./day, 19¢ (17¢ in winter) per additional mi. (Open Mon.-Fri. 8am-5:30pm, Sat. 9am-2pm, Sun. by appt. Must be 21 with credit card and have liability insurance.) Both **Greyhound** and **Rimrock Trailways** run from 2502 1st Ave. N. (245-5116). Buses run to Bozeman (4 per day, $19), Missoula (3 per day, $41), Bismarck (3 per day, $57.50), Seattle (3 per day, $105), and Cheyenne (2 per day, $99). The station is open 24 hrs. **PRIDE!** (gay and lesbian hotline), 800-610-9322 (in MT). Open 24 hrs. Billings's **post office:** 2602 1st Ave. N. (657-5732; open Mon.-Fri. 8am-5:30pm); **ZIP code:** 59101; **area code:** 406.

Rooms in Billings don't come cheap. Most have easy access to downtown, however. **Motel 6** has two locations, one at 5400 Midland (252-0093; singles $32, doubles $38), another at 5353 Midland (248-7551; same prices). **Picture Court,** 5146 Laurel Rd. (252-8478), lets their singles ($26) and doubles ($31). Or try the **Rainbow Motel,** 421 St. Johns (259-4949; singles $28, doubles $30, pot of gold not included). Women and lone travelers should be advised that this motel is not in the safest area.

There are a number of casino/fast-food joints (hamburgers and pizza with slot machines) downtown. For more interesting food, try the strips outside of town. Excellent Mexican is found at **Dos Machos** (652-2020), 24th St. W. at Phyllis. Cajun steak sandwich $6.50. Tacos, enchiladas, and burritos $1.50-9.50. A pitcher of margaritas $10. (Open Mon.-Sat. 11am-10pm, Sun. 9am-9pm.) For "the best Chinese in Montana," the **Great Wall,** 1309 Grand Ave. (245-8601), has lunch dishes ($4-8) and dinner ($7-11). (Open Sun.-Thurs. 11am-10pm, Fri.-Sat. 11am-10:30pm.) The **Happy Diner,** 1045 Grand Ave. (248-5100), has burgers from $2.15 and slices of pies for $1.60. (Open Mon.-Thurs. 11am-10pm, Fri. and Sat. 11am-10:30pm.)

The **Yellowstone Art Center,** 401 N. 27th St. (256-6804), houses an interesting collection of Western art created by Montana artists. (Open Tues.-Wed. and Fri.-Sun. 10am-5pm, Thurs. 10am-8pm. Free.) The **Billings Night Rodeo** (248-1080), rides at the Four Cross Arena next to the Fireside Inn. (June-Aug. daily at 8pm. $7, seniors $5, youth $4.) **Eastern Montana College** (657-2882), on Rimrock Rd., on the way to the airport, offers canoeing classes and other outdoor activities. Continue along this road up the hill for a fantastic view of Billings and the surrounding valley. Look for the **Billings Summer Fair** the third weekend in July.

■■■ BOZEMAN

Bozeman keeps on growing in Montana's broad Gallatin River Valley, wedged between the Bridger and Madison Mountains. The valley, originally settled by farmers who sold food to Northern Pacific Railroad employees living in the neighboring town of Elliston, is still chock full of farmlands and supplies food to a large portion of southern Montana. Bozeman's expansion and the presence of Montana State University invokes a slightly cosmopolitan air peppering the town with green-leafy trees, cafes, farmhouse kitchens, and college students.

Practical Information Greyhound and **RimRock Stages** serve Bozeman from 625 N. 7th St. (587-3110). Greyhound runs to: Butte (3 per day, $12) and Billings (3 per day, $14). RimRock runs two buses per day to Helena ($16.50) and Missoula ($24). (Open Mon.-Sat. 7:30am-5:30pm and 8:30-10pm, Sun. 12:30-5:30pm and 8:30-10pm.) **Rent-a-Wreck,** 112 N. Tracey St. (587-4551), rents well-worn autos from $29 per day, with 100 free mi., 18¢ each additional mi. Must be 21 with major credit card (open Mon.-Fri. 8am-6pm, Sat. 8am-5pm, Sun. by appointment). The **Bozeman Area Chamber of Commerce,** 1205 E. Main St. (586-5421), provides ample info on local events (open Mon.-Fri. 8am-5pm). **PRIDE!** (gay hotline), 800-610-9322 (in MT). Open 24 hrs. Bozeman's **post office:** 32 E. Babcock St. (586-1508; open Mon.-Fri. 9am-5pm); **ZIP code:** 59715; **area code:** 406.

Accommodations Summer travelers in Bozeman support a number of budget motels along Main St. and on 7th Ave. north of Main. The **Sacajawea International Backpackers Hostel,** 405 West Olive St. (586-4659), services travelers with showers, laundry, full kitchen facilities, and transport to trailheads. Owners offer advice on where to eat, drink, hangout, hike, and rent bikes. Call ahead as there are only 10 beds ($9, kids $5). The **Ranch House Motel,** 1201 E. Main St. (587-4278), has free cable TV and A/C (singles $22, doubles $24). At the **Rainbow Motel,** 510 N. 7th Ave. (587-4201), the owners disburse good travel advice and offer large, pleasant rooms (singles $36-48, doubles $55-65, prices drop a bit in the winter). The **Alpine Lodge,** 1017 E. Main St. (586-0356), has fairly clean but rather small rooms. (Singles $30, doubles $42. Cabins with kitchen summer $55, winter $45.)

Food A friendly MSU student will make you a delicious, filling sandwich on freshly-baked sourdough bread at the **Pickle Barrel,** 809 W. College (587-2411), across from the MSU campus. Even half a sandwich ($4) is hard to finish (open daily 10:30am-10pm; winter 11am-10:30pm). In the **Baxter Hotel,** 105 W. Main St. (586-1314), the **Bacchus Pub** provides cocktails, ample soup, and salad plates for Bozeman's intellectual and yuppie crowds. (Both open daily 7am-10pm. Reservations advised.) Have a sloppy slice of joy at **McKenzie's River Pizza** (587-0055), at E. Main St. Create your own deep dish starting at $11.50 (open Mon.-Sat. 11:30am-10pm, Sun 5-9pm). Led Zeppelin's Robert Plant recommends the Black Dog Ale at **Spanish Peaks Brewery,** 1290 N. 19th Ave. (585-2296). Pints are $2.50, $5 for a sampler of all their beers. Eat cheaply and well at the **Western Cafe,** 443 E. Main St. (587-0436), which boasts the best chicken-fried steak in the West ($7.25). (Open Mon.-Fri. 5am-7:30pm, Sat. 5am-2pm.)

Fishing Livingston, a small town about 20 mi. east of Bozeman off I-90, is an angler's heaven; the town is near the Yellowstone, Madison, and Gardiner rivers, all of which are known for their abundance of trout. The **Yellowstone Angler,** P.O. Box 660, U.S. 89S. (222-7130), will equip you with fishing gear and wear, and answer queries about fishing conditions (open Mon.-Sat. 7am-6pm, Sun. 7am-5pm; Oct.-March Mon.-Sat. 7am-5pm). After a day of flyfishing, cast a line to **Livingston's Bar and Grill,** 130 N. Main St. (222-7909), where the vast quantities of imported and domestic beer will hook you (open Mon.-Sat. 11:30am-11pm, Sun. 4-11pm).

■■■ LITTLE BIG HORN NATIONAL MONUMENT

Little Big Horn National Monument, until recently known as the Custer Battlefield National Monument, marks the site where Sioux and Cheyenne warriors, fighting on June 25, 1876, to protect land ceded to them by the Laramie Treaty, defeated Lt. Col. George Armstrong Custer and five companies, over 200 of his soldiers from the Seventh Cavalry. Fittingly, the monument is located on what is now the Crow Reservation, 60 mi. southeast of Billings off I-90. A 5-mi. self-guided car tour takes you past the area where Custer made his "last stand" ($5). White stone graves mark where the U.S soldiers fell. The locations of the Sioux casualties are not known, as their families and fellow warriors removed their bodies from the battlefield almost immediately. You can also see the park on a 45-min. bus tour ($4). The **visitors center**

(638-2621) has a small museum that includes 100-year-old eyewitness drawings depicting the Native American warriors' view of the battle. (Museum and visitors center open daily 8am-8pm; fall daily 8am-6pm, winter daily 8am-4:30pm. Free. Monument open daily 8am-7:30pm. Entrance $4 per car, $2 per person.)

■■■ MISSOULA

Home to the University of Montana, Missoula is Montana's most happening college town. Nature lovers, artists, students, and outdoor enthusiasts all congregate here, on the mountainous west side of the state along the Clark Fork River. Health food and used bookstores abound, as well as some funky delis and restaurants.

Practical Information The **Missoula Chamber of Commerce,** 825 E. Front St. (543-6623) at the corner of Van Buren, provides bus schedules. (Open daily 8:30am-7pm, Sat. 10am-7pm, Sun. noon-7pm, in the winter daily 8:30am-5pm.) Traveling within Missoula is easy thanks to reliable city **buses** (721-3333; buses operate Mon.-Fri. 6am-7pm, Sat. 9:30am-6pm; fare 50¢). The **Greyhound terminal,** 1660 W. Broadway (549-2339) pants to: Bozeman (3 per day, $26) or Spokane (3 per day, $36). **Intermountain Transportation** serves Whitefish (1 per day, $22) and **Rim-Rock Stages** serves Helena (1 per day, $15) and Bozeman (1 per day, $22) from the same terminal. **Rent-a-Wreck,** 2401 W. Broadway (721-3838), offers humble autos ($36 per day, $220 per week, 150 free mi. per day, 20¢ each additional mi.; local cars $20 per day in winter, $25 in summer with 50 free mi. per day, 25¢ each additional mi. Must be 21; credit card deposit required.) **Rape Crisis Line,** 543-7606. **PRIDE!** (gay and lesbian hotline), 800-610-9322 (in MT). Both are open 24 hrs. Missoula's **post office:** 1100 W. Kent (329-2200), at Brooks and South St. (open Mon.-Fri. 8am-6pm, Sat. 9am-1pm); **ZIP code:** 59801; **area code:** 406.

Accommodations Spend the night in Missoula at the **Birchwood Hostel (HI-AYH),** 600 S. Orange St. (728-9799), 13 blocks east of the bus station on Broadway, then 8 blocks south on Orange. The spacious, immaculate dormitory room sleeps 22. Laundry, kitchen, and bike storage facilities are available, and the friendly owner knows the area. ($7 for members and cyclists, $9 otherwise. Open daily 5-10pm. Closed for 2 weeks in late Dec.) The **Canyon Motel,** 1015 E. Broadway (543-4069 or 543-7251), has rooms at prices that won't gouge your wallet. (Singles $20-25. Doubles $25-30.) Near the bus station, the **Sleepy Inn,** 1427 W. Broadway (549-6484), has soporific singles for $29 and doubles for $41. The year-round **Outpost Campground** (549-2016), 2 mi. north of I-90 on U.S. 93, has showers, laundry and scattered shade from its trees (sites $10, full hookup).

Food and Nightlife Missoula's dining scene offers much more than the West's usual steak and potatoes. Many great and thrifty eateries line the downtown, particularly between Broadway and Railroad Streets, and north of the Clark Fork River. A few other places are scattered about the perimeter of the university campus, on the other side of the river. Many a Montana grizzly eats and thinks at the **Food for Thought Café,** 540 Daly Ave., where creative sandwiches, salads, and veggie dishes run $3-6. (Open daily 7am-10pm.) Every breakfast dish you ever dreamed of is under $5 at the **Old Town Café,** 127 W. Alder St. (728-9742; open daily 6am-5pm). **Torrey's** restaurant and natural food store, 1916 Brooks St. (721-2510), serves health food at absurdly low prices. Seafood stir-fry $3.50. (Restaurant open Mon.-Sat. 11:30am-8:30pm; store open Mon.-Sat. 10am-8:30pm.) If you'd rather be happy than healthy, slurp up creamy smoothees at **Goldsmith's Premium Ice Cream Shop,** 809 E. Front St. (721-6732), near the chamber of commerce ($1.50-$2.75; open Sun.-Thurs. 7am-10:30pm, Fri.-Sat. 7am-11pm).

The **Iron Horse Brew Pub,** 100 W. Railroad Ave. (721-8705), at Higgins Ave., is part of a triad of entertainment—restaurant, bar, and brewery. The pub merges the best of both worlds with good local beer and cheap barfood/dinner. (Open daily noon-midnight.) A bit more rowdy is a local favorite, the **Rhinoceros (Rhino's),** 158 Ryman Ave. (721-6061; open daily 11am-2am). Or perchance **Bodega's,** 221 Ryman Ave. (549-0455) just down the street (open daily 11am-2am).

Outdoor Activities   The outdoors are really Missoula's greatest sight. Cycling enthusiasts have put the town on the map with the rigorous **Bikecentennial Route. Adventure Cycling,** 150 E. Pine St. (721-1776), provides info about the route. To participate in Missoula's most popular sport, visit the **Braxton Bike Shop,** 2100 South Ave. W. (549-2513), and procure a bike for a day ($12), overnight ($15), or a week ($75). (Open Mon.-Sat. 10am-6pm; leave credit card deposit.)

Ski trips, raft trips, backpacking, and day hikes are other popular Missoula diversions. The **University of Montana Department of Recreation,** University Center #164 (243-2802) organizes day hikes and overnight trips (open Mon.-Fri. 7:30am-5pm). The university's outdoor program (243-5172) at Field House 116, gives classes in outdoor activities, as well as renting equipment and leading excursions. (Open Mon.-Thurs. 9am-5pm, during the school year Mon.-Fri. 9am-5pm, Sat. 9am-2pm, Sun 9am-noon.) The **Rattlesnake Wilderness National Recreation Area** hisses a few miles northeast of town off the Van Buren St. exit from I-90 and makes for a great day of hiking. Wilderness maps ($3) are available from the **U.S. Forest Service Information Office,** 200 E. Broadway (329-3511; open Mon.-Fri. 9am-4pm). The Clark Fork, Blackfoot, and Bitterroot Rivers provide gushing opportunities for float trips. For float maps ($3.50), visit the **Montana State Regional Parks and Wildlife Office,** 3201 Spurgin Rd. (542-5500; open Mon.-Fri. 8am-5pm). For rafting trips to a time when this continent thing wasn't so complicated, visit **Pangaea Expeditions,** 180 S. 3rd (721-7719; $15 for 2 hr., $25 ½-day, $45 per day).

For a touch of Missoula culture, on the first Friday of every month all of the local museums and galleries (15 total) have open houses. Artists are present at some. The **Historical Museum at Fort Missoula** (728-3476) on Fort Rd. off Reserve St., offers exhibits and lectures on forestry, agriculture, mining, and community life. (Open Memorial Day-Labor Day Tues.-Sat. 10am-5pm, Sun. noon-5pm. Winter hours vary.)

The hottest sight in town is the **Aerial Fire Depot Visitors Center** (329-4934), 7 mi. west of town on Broadway (Rte. 10, past the airport), where you'll learn to appreciate the courage and folly aerial firefighters need to jump into flaming, roadless forests. (Open daily 8:30am-5pm; Oct.-April by appointment for large groups. Free tours every hr. in summer, except noon-1pm.)

■■■ FROM MISSOULA TO GLACIER

One of the greatest collections of Americana in the country lies on U.S. 93 between Missoula and Glacier. Don't miss the **Miracle of America Museum,** right off the highway before you enter the town of **Polson.** What at first glance may seem to be a crowded attic full of junky souvenirs is really a crowded museum full of classic American kitsch. Look for the reconstructed general store, saddlery shop, barber shop, and gas station. (Open April-Sept. Mon.-Sat. 8am-5pm, Sun. 2-6pm, any other time by chance or appointment. $2.)

■■■ WATERTON-GLACIER PEACE PARK

Waterton-Glacier transcends international boundaries to unite two of the most pristine but relatively accessible wilderness areas on the continent. Symbolizing the peace between the United States and Canada, the park provides sanctuary for many endangered bears, bighorn sheep, moose, mountain goats, and now the grey wolf.

Technically one park, Waterton-Glacier is, for all practical purposes, two distinct areas: the small Waterton Lakes National Park in Alberta, and the enormous Glacier National Park in Montana. Each park charges its own admission fee (in Glacier, $5 per week; in Waterton Lakes, CDN$5 per day, CDN$10 for 4 days), and you must go through customs to pass from one to the other. Several **border crossings** pepper the park: **Chief Mountain** (open mid-Sept.-mid-May daily 9am-6pm, June-mid-Sept. daily 7am-10pm); **Piegan/Carway** (in U.S., year-round daily 7am-11pm; in Canada, open March-Oct. 7am-11pm, call for off-season hours); **Trail Creek** (open June-Oct. daily 9am-5pm); and **Roosville** (open year-round 24 hrs.).

Since snow melt is an unpredictable process, the parks are usually in full operation only from late May to early September. To find the areas of the park, hotels, and campsites that will be open when you visit, contact the headquarters of either Waterton or Glacier (406-888-5441). The *Waterton Glacier Guide* has dates and times of trail, campground, and border crossing openings.

■ GLACIER NATIONAL PARK, MONTANA

PRACTICAL INFORMATION

Glacier's layout is simple: one road enters through West Glacier on the west side, and three roads enter from the east—at Many Glacier, St. Mary, and Two Medicine. West Glacier and St. Mary provide the two main points of entry into the park, connected by **Going-to-the-Sun Road** ("The Sun"), the only road traversing the park. **U.S. 2** runs between West and East Glacier along 82 mi. of the southern park border. Look for the "Goat Lick" signs off Rte. 2 near **Walton.** Mountain goats often descend to the lick for a salt fix in June and July.

Stop in at the **visitors centers** at **St. Mary,** at the east entrance to the park (732-4424; open daily early June 8am-5pm, late June-early Sept. 8am-9pm), or at **Apgar,** at the west park entrance (open daily early June 8am-5pm, late June-early Sept. 8am-8pm). A third visitors center graces **Logan Pass** on Going-to-the-Sun Rd. (open daily mid-June 9am-5pm, late June-early Sept. 9am-6pm). Alberta's **info center** (888-5743) is in West Glacier; ask any questions there before hiking (open daily 8am-7pm).

Amtrak (226-4452 or 800-872-7245) traces a dramatic route along the southern edge of the park. Daily trains huff and puff to West Glacier from Whitefish ($7), Seattle ($126), and Spokane ($63); Amtrak also runs from East Glacier to Chicago ($213) and Minneapolis ($189). **Intermountain Bus Lines** (862-6700) is the only line that comes near the park (Kalispell). As with most of the Rockies, a car is the most convenient mode of transport, particularly within the park. **Rent-a-Wreck** rents used cars from Kalispell, 1194 U.S. 2 E. (755-4555; $25 per day), and East Glacier, at the Sears Motel (226-9293; $50 per day). You must be over 21; major credit card required, 125 mi. free per day, 25¢ each additional mi. Glacier's **post office:** Lake McDonald Lodge, in the park (open Mon.-Fri. 9am-3:45pm); **ZIP code:** 59921; **area code:** 406.

ACCOMMODATIONS

Staying indoors within Glacier is absurd and expensive. **Glacier Park, Inc.** handles all lodging within the park and offers only the **Swiftcurrent Motor Inn** in Many Glacier Valley for budget travelers. The Swiftcurrent has cabins without bathrooms for $26, and two bedrooms for $35 (each additional person $5; open late June-early Sept.). Motel rooms are available, but they cost twice as much. All reservations can be made through Glacier Park, Inc. From mid-September to mid-May, contact them at 925 Dial Tower Mail Station, Phoenix, AZ 85077 (602-207-6000); from early May to late September at East Glacier Park 59434 (406-226-5551). Other than the Swiftcurrent, the company operates seven pricier lodges which open and close on a staggered schedule. Apgar opens first, in mid-May.

East Side of the Park

Excellent, affordable lodging can be found just across the park border in **East Glacier,** which sits on U.S. 2, 30 mi. south of the St. Mary entrance, and about 5 mi. south of the Two Medicine entrance. **Brownies Grocery (HI-AYH),** 1020 Rte. 49 (226-4426), in East Glacier, offers comfortable dorms in what is rumored to have once been a brothel. There are usually yummy goods in the bakery. Offers a great view from the porch. Rent bunks ($11, nonmembers $13), private rooms (singles $15, nonmembers $18; doubles $20/23), or a family room ($30, 4-6 people). The **Backpackers Inn Hostel,** 29 Dawson Ave. (226-9392), packs a home-away-from-home behind **Serrano's,** a tasty Mexican restaurant (entrees $4-11). The Inn offers clean beds and hot showers for only $8 per night (bring a sleeping bag or rent one for $1). The owners of the Inn and restaurant, Pat and Renée Schur, offer excellent advice about trails and activities. Also, the young adults who work at the restaurant befriend travelers and are knowledgeable about the park.

West Side of the Park

The **Kalispell/Whitefish Hostel,** 2155 Whitefish Stage Rd., Kalispell 59901 (756-1908), beckons 25 mi. from Glacier's west entrance, between U.S. 93 and U.S. 2. Located within a home, there are 4 rooms with comfortable beds (linen provided), a kitchen, stereo, and available mountain bikes. Also has a small in-house self-repair bike and ski shop. ($10 one night, more than 3 nights $9, more than a week $8.)

East of the town of Hungry Horse, 9 mi. from the park entrance, is the **Mountain Meadow RV Park and Campground** (387-9125), off U.S. 2. The campground has secluded sites and hot showers (sites $12, with hookup $16).

Those up for a truly rustic experience should trek to a town called **Dolebridge.** The **North Fork Hostel** (888-5241), located at the end of Beaver Dr. in Dolebridge, is furnished with propane lamps, stoves, and outhouses. (Dorm beds $12, $10 after 2 nights. In the back are two cabins $26. Linen $2. Log homes $35, weekly $175.) There are only two other buildings in town—the general store (also the post office) and the **Northern Lights Saloon** (open 4-9pm for food and 9-12pm for drinks). Nearby are secluded campgrounds: Bowman Lake and Kintla (see Camping below).

CAMPING

Camping is a cheaper and more scenic alternative to indoor accommodations. All developed campsites are available on a first-come, first-camped basis; the most popular sites fill by noon. However, "Campground Full" signs sometimes stay up for days on end; look carefully for empty sites. All 11 campgrounds accessible by car are easy to find. Just follow the map distributed as you enter the park. **Sprague Creek** on Lake McDonald has 25 peaceful sites near the lake; arrive early to avoid those near the road. **Bowman Lake** and **Kintla Lake** rarely fill and offer scenic, lakeside sites (Bowman has 48 sites, Kintla 13). Neither have flush toilets, but are the cheapest thing going ($8). The rest of the campgrounds cost $10 and you can flush away. **Two Medicine,** nearer to East Glacier, at the southeast corner of the park, has 99 sites. **Apgar** (196 sites) and **Fish Creek** (180 sites) are in the southwest corner, near Lake McDonald. Some sites at Sprague, Apgar, and Avalanche remain reserved for bicyclists; towed units are prohibited. Campgrounds without running water in the surrounding national forests offer sites for $5. Check at the Apgar or St. Mary visitors centers for up-to-date information on conditions and vacancies at established campgrounds. Weather and the grizzlies can adjust the operating dates as they desire.

THE OUTDOORS

Backcountry trips are the best way to appreciate the mountain scenery and the wildlife which make Glacier famous. The **Highline Trail** from Logan Pass is a good day hike through prime bighorn sheep and mountain goat territory, although locals consider it too crowded. The visitors center's free *Nature with a Naturalist* pamphlet has a hiking map marked with distances and backcountry campsites. All backcountry travelers who camp overnight must obtain in person a free wilderness permit from a visitors center or ranger station 24 hrs. in advance; backcountry camping is allowed only at designated campgrounds. The **Two Medicine** area in the southeast corner of the park is well traveled, while the trek to **Kintla Lake** rewards you with fantastic views of nearby peaks. Before embarking on any hike, familiarize yourself with the precautions necessary to avoid a run-in with a bear (see Bear

Necessities in the Essentials section). Rangers at any visitors center or ranger station will instruct you on the finer points of noise-making and food storage.

Going-to-the-Sun Rd. is a beautiful 52-mi. traverse of the park. Even on cloudy days, the constantly changing views of the peaks will have you struggling to keep your eyes on the road. Snow keeps the road closed until June, so check with rangers for exact dates. All vehicles must be under 21 ft. long and under 8 ft. wide.

Although "The Sun" is a popular **bike route,** only experienced cyclists with appropriate gear and legs of titanium should attempt this grueling stint. The sometimes nonexistent shoulder of the road creates a hazardous situation for cyclists: in the summer (June 15-Sept. 2), bike traffic is prohibited from the Apgar turn-off at the west end of Lake McDonald to Sprague Creek, and from Logan Creek to Logan Pass, 11am-4pm. The east side of the park has no such restrictions. Bikes are not permitted on any hiking trails. **Equestrian** explorers should check to make sure trails are open; fines for riding on closed trails are steep.

While in Glacier, don't overlook the interpretive programs offered through the park. Ask about "jammers," the red buses that snake around the park. Inquire at any visitors center for the day's menu of guided hikes, lectures, bird-watching walks, and children's programs. At the Backpacker's Inn, ask about **Sun Tours,** guides through the park with the Native American interpretation of events. The tour guide is extremely knowledgable about wildlife and vegetation.

BOATING AND FISHING

Boat tours explore all of Glacier's large lakes. At Lake McDonald and Two Medicine Lake, 1-hr. tours leave throughout the day. (Tours at Lake McDonald $6.50, ages 4-12 $3.25; at Two Medicine $6 and $3.) The tours from St. Mary (90 min.) and Many Glacier (75 min.) provide access to Glacier's backcountry (from St. Mary $8, ages 4-12 $4; from Many Glacier $7.50, $3.75). The $7 sunset cruise proves a great way to see this quotidian phenomenon which doesn't commence until about 10pm in the middle of the summer. Call Lake McDonald (888-5727), Many Glacier (732-4480), or St. Mary (732-4430) for information. **Glacier Raft Co.,** in West Glacier (800-332-9995 or 888-5454) hawks full- and half-day trips down the middle fork of the Flathead River. A full-day trip (lunch included) costs $60, under 13 $28; ½-day trips ($30, $18) leave in the morning and the afternoon. Call for reservations.

Rent **rowboats** ($6 per hr., $30 per 10 hr.) at Lake McDonald, Many Glacier and Two Medicine; **canoes** ($6 per hr.) at Two Medicine and Many Glacier; and **outboards** ($11 per hr., $55 per 10 hr.) at Lake McDonald. All require a $50 deposit. Fishing is excellent in the park—cutthroat trout, lake trout, and even the rare Arctic Grayling challenge the angler's skill and patience. No permit is required—just be familiar with the rules, as explained by the pamphlet *Fishing Regulations,* available at all visitors centers. Right outside the park, however, on Blackfoot Indian land, you need a special permit. Anywhere else in Montana you need a Montana permit.

■ WATERTON LAKES NATIONAL PARK, ALBERTA

The Canadian section of Waterton-Glacier is only a fraction of the size of its U.S. neighbor, but it nonetheless offers much of the same scenery and many similar activities without Glacier's crowds.

Practical Information The only road from Waterton's park entrance leads 5 mi. south to **Waterton.** On the way, grab a copy of the *Waterton-Glacier Guide* to local services and activities, at the **Waterton Visitor Centre,** 215 Mountain View Rd. (859-2224), 5 mi. south of the park entrance (open mid-May-June daily 10am-5:30pm; July-mid-Sept.; 8am-8:30pm). If you're on four wheels, drive either the **Akamina Parkway** or the less traveled **Red Rock Canyon Road.** Rent bikes from **Pat's Texaco and Cycle Rental,** Mount View Rd., Waterton townsite (859-2266; mountain bikes $5.50 per hr. or $27 per day, plus $20 damage deposit; motor scooters cost $13 per hr. or $60 per day). In an **emergency,** call (859-2636). Waterton's **post office:** Fountain Ave. at Windflower (open Mon., Wed., and Fri. 8:30am-4:30pm, Tues. and Thurs. 8:30am-4pm); **postal code:** T0K 2M0; **area code:** 403.

Accommodations, Camping, and Food As you enter the park, marvel at the enormous **Prince of Wales Hotel** (859-2231), where you can have tea while maintaining a proper distance from the common townsite. Pitch a tent at one of the park's three campgrounds. **Crandell** (sites $10.50), on Red Rock Canyon Rd., and **Belly River** (sites $7.25), on Chief Mountain Hwy., are cheaper and farther removed from the hustle and bustle characteristic of town life. **Backcountry camping** is free but requires a permit from the Visitor Center (see above) or from **Park Headquarters and Information,** Waterton Lakes National Park, 215 Mount View Rd., (859-2224; open Mon.-Fri. 8am-4pm). The backcountry campsites are rarely full, and several, including beautiful **Crandell Lake,** are less than an hour's walk from the trailhead. If you insist on having a bed in Waterton, drop by the **Waterton Pharmacy,** on Waterton Ave. (859-2335), and ask to sleep in one of the nine rooms of the **Stanley Hotel** (singles or doubles $45; no shower or private bath).

Waterton is lacking in budget restaurants; the most attractive option in the Townsite is **Zum's,** 116B Waterton Ave. (859-2388), which serves good cheeseburgers for $4 (open daily 8am-9pm). Save money and buy groceries outside the park. Stock up on dried meat and granola at the Rocky Mountain Foodmart (859-2526) on Windflower Ave. (open daily 8am-10pm; hours vary). Nothing gets cheaper by being trucked out to Waterton. Buy your groceries outside the park for substantial savings.

Outdoors If you've brought only hiking boots to Waterton, you can set out on the **International Lakeside Hike,** which leads along the west shore of Upper Waterton Lake and delivers you to Montana some 5 mi. after leaving the town. The **Crypt Lake Hike,** voted Canada's best hike in 1981, leads past waterfalls in a narrow canyon, and through a 20m natural tunnel bored through the mountainside to arrive after 4 mi. at icy, green Crypt Lake, which straddles the international border. To get to the trailhead, you must take the water taxi run by **Emerald Bay Marina** (85902632). The boat runs 4 times per day ($9, ages 4-14 $5). The Marina also runs a 2-hr. boat tour of Upper Waterton Lake (mid-May-mid-Sept.; 5 per day July-Aug., fewer outside these months. $15, ages 13-17 $11, ages 4-12 $7).

Anglers will appreciate Waterton's **fishing;** a **license** is required ($6 per 7 days), available from the Park offices, campgrounds, wardens, and service stations in the area. A boat tour of Upper Waterton Lake leaves from the **Emerald Bay Marina** (859-2362), in the townsite (5 per day mid-May to mid-Sept.; 2 hr.; $15, ages 4-12 $7). You can also rent a rowboat at Cameron Lake ($10 per hr.) You can rent a **rowboat** or **paddleboat** at Cameron Lake for $8 per hour, or a canoe for $10 per hour. **Alpine Stables,** 2½ mi. north of the Townsite (859-2462, in winter 908-968-0247), conducts trail rides of varying lengths. (1-hr. ride $12.50, all-day $64.)

In the evening, take in an **interpretive program** at the **Falls** or **Crandell Theatre.** "The Fall of the Roamin' Empire" examines the annihilation of the great buffalo herds; "Salamander Suicides and Other My-newt Tragedies" exposes the soft white underbellies of the park's tiniest residents. (Programs in summer daily at 8:30pm; contact the Information Office for schedule information. Free.)

■ Wyoming

The ninth largest state in the Union, Wyoming is also the least populated. This is a place where men wear cowboy hats and boots for *real,* and livestock outnumber the citizens. Yet this rugged land was more than just a frontier during westward expansion; it was the first state to grant women the right to vote and contains the country's first national monument (Devil's Tower) and first national park (Yellowstone). Wyoming has everything you'd ever want to see in a state in the Rockies region: a Frontier Days festival, national parks, spectacular mountain ranges (the Bighorns and the Tetons), breath-taking panoramas, and, of course, cattle and beer.

PRACTICAL INFORMATION

Capital: Cheyenne.
Wyoming Travel Commission, I-25 and College Dr. at Etcheparc Circle, Cheyenne 82002 (777-7777 or 800-225-5996). Write for their free *Wyoming Vacation Guide.* **Wyoming Recreation Commission,** 2301 Central Ave., Cheyenne 82002 (777-7695). Information on Wyoming's 10 state parks. Open Mon.-Fri. 8am-5pm. **Game and Fish Department,** 5400 Bishop Blvd., Cheyenne 82002 (777-4600). Open Mon.-Fri. 8am-5pm.
Time Zone: Mountain (2 hr. behind Eastern). **Postal Abbreviation:** WY
Sales Tax: 5-6% depending on the city.

■■■ YELLOWSTONE NATIONAL PARK

Legendary mountain man John Colter's descriptions of his 1807 trek into the Yellowstone area—boiling, sulfuric pits, spouting geysers, and smelly mudpots—inspired a half-century of popular stories about "Colter's Hell." In 1870 the first official survey party, the Washburn Expedition, reached the area. As they crested a ridge, the explorers were greeted by a fountain of boiling water and steam spurting 130 ft. into the air. Members of the expedition watched it erupt nine times and named it "Old Faithful" before leaving the Upper Geyser Basin. A year later, President Grant declared Yellowstone a national park, the world's first.

Visitors in Grant's time might have encountered only a handful of other adventurers amidst Yellowstone's 3472 square mi. Today's visitors will find the park cluttered with the cars, RVs, and detritus of some 50,000-odd tourists. The park's main attractions are huge, tranquil Yellowstone Lake, the 2100-ft.-deep Yellowstone River Canyon, and the world's largest collection of reeking, sputtering geysers, mudpots, hot springs, and fumaroles (steam-spewing holes in the ground). In the backcountry, you can stand far from the crowds and observe the park's abundant bear, elk, moose, bison, and bighorn sheep.

In 1988 Yellowstone was ravaged by a blaze that charred one third of the park. Surprisingly, crowds in Yellowstone doubled in 1989. The fire damage does make for interesting, if somewhat bleak, viewing; rangers have erected exhibits throughout the park to better explain the fire's effects.

PRACTICAL INFORMATION

Emergency: 911.
Park Information and Headquarters: Superintendent, Mammoth Hot Springs, Yellowstone National Park 82190 (344-7381). General information, campground availability, and emergencies. Headquarters open Mon.-Fri. 9am-5pm.
Park Entrance Fee: $10 for non-commercial vehicles, $4 for pedestrians and bikers. Good for 1 week and also valid at Grand Teton National Park.
Visitors Centers and Ranger Stations: Most regions in this vast park have their own center/station. The district rangers have a good deal of autonomy in making regulations for hiking and camping, so check in at each area. All centers have guides for the disabled and give backcountry permits, or have a partner ranger station that does. Each center's display focuses on the attributes of its region of the park. All centers open daily. Hours vary, especially after Labor Day, so call ahead. **Albright Visitors Center** at **Mammoth Hot Springs** (344-2263): natural and human history. Open late May-June 6 9am-3pm; mid-May-June 7 8am-7pm. **Grant Village** (242-2650): wilderness. Open mid-May-June 6 9am-5pm; June 7-Labor Day 8am-7pm. **Old Faithful/Madison** (545-2750): geysers. Open mid-May-

June 6 9am-4:30pm; June 7-Labor Day 8am-8pm; call for hours after Labor Day. **Fishing Bridge** (242-2450): wildlife and Yellowstone Lake. Open mid-may-June 6 9am-5pm; June 7-Labor Day 8am-7pm. **Canyon** (242-2550): natural history and history of canyon area. Open mid-May-June 6 9am-5pm; open June 7-Labor Day 8am-7pm. **Norris** (344-2812): park museum. Open mid-May-June 6 9am-5pm; June 7-Labor Day 8am-9pm. **Tower/Roosevelt Ranger Station** (344-7746): temporary exhibits. Open 8am-5pm. *Yellowstone Today,* the park's activities guide, has a thorough listing of tours and programs.

Radio Information: Tune to 1610AM for service information.

West Yellowstone Chamber of Commerce: 100 Yellowstone Ave., West Yellowstone, MT 59758 (406-646-7701). Located 2 blocks west of the park entrance. Open daily 8am-6pm.

Greyhound: 633 Madison Ave., West Yellowstone, MT (406-646-7666). To: Bozeman (1 per day, 2 hr., $13); Salt Lake City (1 per day, 9 hr., $46). Open summer only, daily 10:30am-1:30pm and 4:30-7pm.

TW Services, Inc: (344-7311). Monopolizes concessions within the park. 9-hr. bus tours of the lower portion of the park leave daily from lodges ($25, ages 12-16 $12, under 12 free). Similar tours of the northern region leave Gardiner, MT and the lodges at Mammoth Lake and Fishing Bridge ($15-22). Individual legs of this extensive network of tour loops can get you as far as the Grand Tetons or Jackson, but the system is inefficient and costs much more than it's worth.

Gray Line Tours: 633 Madison Ave., West Yellowstone, MT (406-646-9374). Offers full-day tours from West Yellowstone around the upper and lower loop ($36, under 12 $21), and Grand Tetons and Jackson ($46, under 12 $26). Open daily 7:30am-6:30pm.

Car Rental: Big Sky Car Rental, 429 Yellowstone Ave., West Yellowstone, MT (406-646-9564 or 800-426-7669). $30-35 per day, unlimited mileage. Must be 21 with a credit card or passport.

Bike Rental: Yellowstone Bicycles, 132 Madison Ave., West Yellowstone, MT (406-646-7815). 10-speeds $9.50 per day; mountain bikes $10.50 per ½-day, $17.50 per day. Open daily 9am-8pm.

Horse Rides: Mammoth Hot Springs Hotel, Roosevelt Lodge, and **Canyon Lodge,** late May-early Sept. $11.85 per hr., $22 for 2 hrs. Call TW Services (344-7311) for more information.

Medical Facilities: Lake Clinic, Pharmacy, and **Hospital** (242-7241) at Lake Hotel. Clinic open late May-mid-Sept. daily 8:30am-8:30pm. Emergency Room open May-Sept. 24 hrs., clinic 8:30am-8:30pm. **Old Faithful Clinic,** at Old Faithful Inn (545-7325), open mid-May-mid-Oct. daily 8:30am-5pm. **Mammoth Hot Springs Clinic** (344-7965), open year-round Mon.-Fri. 8:30am-5pm. Can always contact a ranger at 344-7381.

Post Offices: Mammoth Hot Springs (334-7764), near the park headquarters. Open Mon.-Fri. 8:30am-5pm, in July and Aug. on Sat. 10-11am. **ZIP code:** 82190. Also at **West Yellowstone, MT,** 7 Madison Ave. (646-7704). Open Mon.-Fri. 8:30am-5pm. **ZIP code:** 59758.

Area Codes: 307 (in the park), 406 (in West Yellowstone and Gardiner). Unless otherwise listed, phone numbers have a 307 area code.

The bulk of Yellowstone National Park lies in the northwest corner of Wyoming with slivers slicing into Montana and Idaho. **West Yellowstone, MT,** at the park's western entrance, and **Gardiner, MT,** at the northern entrance, are the most built-up and expensive towns along the edge of the park. For a rustic stay, venture northeast to **Cooke City, MT.** The southern entry to the park is through Grand Teton National Park. The eastern entrance to the park from Cody is via Rte. 14/20. The northeast entrance to the park leads to U.S. 212, a gorgeous stretch of road known as **Beartooth Highway,** which climbs to **Beartooth Pass** at 11,000 ft. and descends to **Red Lodge,** a former mining town. (Road open summer only because of heavy snowfall; ask at the chamber of commerce for exact dates.)

Yellowstone's extensive system of roads circulates its millions of visitors. Side roads branch off to park entrances and some of the lesser-known sights. It's unwise to bike or walk around the deserted roads at night since you may risk startling large wild animals. The best time to see the animals is at dawn or dusk. You'll know when they're out when traffic stops and cars pull over. Approaching any wild beast at any time is illegal and extremely unsafe, and those who don't remain at least 100 ft. from bison, bear, or moose risk being mauled, gored to death, or made the victim of a Far Side cartoon. Another danger is falling trees; dead trees can fall into a campsite or road with little or no warning. Near thermal areas, stay on marked trails, because "scalding water can ruin your vacation."

The park's high season extends from about June 15 to September 15. If you visit during this period expect large crowds, clogged roads and motels, and campsites filled to capacity.

ACCOMMODATIONS

Camping is far cheaper but cabin-seekers will find many options within the park. Standard hotel and motel rooms for the nature-weary also abound, but if you plan to keep your budget in line, stick to the towns near the park's entry-points.

In The Park

TW Services (344-7311) controls all of the accommodations within the park, and uses a special set of classifications for budget cabins: "Roughrider" means no bath, no facilities; "Western Frontier" means with bath, somewhat furnished. All cabins or rooms should be reserved well in advance of the June to September tourist season.

Old Faithful Inn and Lodge, near the west Yellowstone entrance. Offers pleasant Roughrider cabins ($21) and Western Frontier cabins ($33). Well-appointed hotel rooms from $39, with private bath $60.

Roosevelt Lodge, in the northwest corner. A favorite campsite of Roughrider Teddy Roosevelt. Provides the cheapest and most scenic indoor accommodations around. Rustic shelters $19, each with a wood-burning stove (bring your own bedding and towel). Also Roughrider cabins ($24, bring your own towel) and more spacious "family" cabins with toilet ($37).

Mammoth Hot Springs, 18 mi. west of Roosevelt area, near the north entrance. Unremarkable budget cabins $28. Frontier cabins from $57.

Lake Yellowstone Hotel and Cabins, near the south entrance. Overpriced, but with a nice view of the lake. Spacious, frontier cabins $45-76.

Canyon Village, middle of the figure eight of the park loop, is a less authentic and more expensive than Roosevelt Lodge's cabins, but slightly closer to the popular Old Faithful area. Frontier cabins $45-76.

West Yellowstone, MT

West Yellowstone International Hostel (Rucksackers) at the Madison Hotel and Motel, 139 Yellowstone Ave. (406-646-7745 or 800-646-7745 outside MT). Friendly manager presides over old but clean, wood-adorned hotel. Hostel honors all memberships. Singles $24, with bath $35; doubles with bath $40. Rooms $2 cheaper in the spring. Hostelers stay in more crowded rooms; no kitchen. $15, nonmembers $17. Open May 27-mid-Oct.

Alpine Motel, 120 Madison (406-646-7544). Clean rooms with cable TV, a pool, and hand-crafted bed frames. Singles $38, doubles $52. $3 less in off-season.

Traveler's Lodge, 225 Yellowstone Ave. (406-646-9561). Comfortable, large rooms; ask for one away from the hot tub. Singles $58, off-season $40; doubles $75. $5 discount if you rent a car from them (see Practical Information above).

Ho-Hum Motel, 126 Canyon Rd. (406-646-7746). Small, dark, ho-hum, but clean rooms. Open the windows. Singles $36, doubles $40, triples $45, quadruples $50.

Gardiner, MT

Located about 90 min. northeast of West Yellowstone, Gardiner served as the original entrance to the park and is smaller and less tacky than its neighbor.

Wilson's Yellowstone River Motel, 14 Park St. (406-848-7303). Large, well-decorated rooms overseen by friendly manager. Singles $30, doubles $34. Off-season singles $35, doubles $39.

Hillcrest Cottages (406-848-7353), on U.S. 89 near the crossing of the Yellowstone River. Singles $40, doubles $50. $6 each additional adult, $3 each under 12.

The Town Motel, Lounge, and Gift Shop (406-848-7322), on Park St. across from the park's northern entrance. Pleasant, wood-paneled, carpeted rooms. TVs and baths but no showers or phones. Singles $40, doubles $50.

Cooke City, MT

Cooke City is located at the northeast corner of the park. The Nez Perce slipped right by the U.S. cavalry, Lewis and Clark deemed the area impassible, and many tourists today miss it as well. The lodging is cheap and breakfast at Joan and Bill's **Family Restaurant** is delicious. Drive to the Red Lodge and over the Bear Tooth Pass (Rte. 212), for mean plates of homefries and breakfast combos $2.95.

After a day of tracking Yogi Bear, rest at **Antler's Lodge** (406-838-2432), at the eastern end of town (there's only one street in Cooke, Rte. 212). A renovated U.S. Cavalry outpost, singles $35, doubles $45 with larger cabins for families equipped with kitchens from $55. Ernest Hemingway supposedly completed *For Whom the Bell Tolls* in cabin 17.

CAMPING

All developed campsites are available on a first-come, first-served basis except for the **Bridge Bay Campground,** which reserves sites up to eight weeks in advance through MISTIX (800-365-2267; 619-452-5956 outside U.S.). During summer, most campgrounds fill by 2pm. All sites $6-8. Arrive very early, especially on weekends and holidays. If all sites are full, try the $8 campgrounds outside the park in the surrounding National Forest land. Bring a stove or plan to search for or buy firewood. Except for **Mammoth Campground,** all camping areas close in winter.

Two of the most beautiful and tranquil areas are **Slough Creek Campground,** 29 sites, 10 mi. northeast of Tower Junction (open late May-Oct.), and **Pebble Creek Campground,** 36 sites, 15 mi. farther down the same road (no RVs, open mid-June-early Sept.). Both offer relatively uncrowded spots and have good fishing. You can also try **Canyon Village** with 208 sites. **Fishing Bridge Campgrounds** (344-7311 for reservations) has hookup only ($18; open late May-early Sept.). The popular and scenic campgrounds at **Norris** (116 sites; open May-Sept.) and **Madison** (292 sites, open May-Oct.) fill early (by 1pm), while others, such as **Canyon** and **Pebble Creek,** may have sites until 6pm. **Bridge Bay** (420 sites, open late May-mid-Sept.), **Indian Creek** (75 sites, open June-Sept.), and **Mammoth** (85 sites, open year-round) campgrounds are treeless and non-scenic. A better bet is camping in the **Gallatin National Forest** to the northwest. Good sites line U.S. 20, 287, 191, and 89. Call the Park Headquarters (344-7381) for info on any of Yellowstone's campgrounds.

The campgrounds at Grant, Village Lake, Fishing Bridge, and Canyon all have coin-op laundries and pay showers ($1.50 plus 25¢ for towel or soap). The lodges at Mammoth and Old Faithful have no laundry facilities but have showers for $1.50.

More than 95% (almost two million acres) of the park is backcountry. To venture overnight into the wilds of Yellowstone, you must obtain a free **wilderness permit** from a ranger station or visitors center. It is always best to consult a ranger before any hike. Be sure you understand the most recent instructions regarding the closure of campgrounds and trails due to bears and other wildlife. Other backcountry regulations include: sanitation rules, pet and firearms restrictions, campfire permits, and firewood rules. The more popular areas fill up in high season, but you can reserve a permit up to 48 hrs. in advance, in person; campfire permits are not required, but ask if fires at your site are allowed.

Note: most people are not as smart as your average bear—campers should keep clean camps and store food in a locked car or suspended 10 ft. above ground, 4 ft. horizontally from a post or tree trunk.

FOOD

Be very choosy when buying food in the park, as the restaurants, snack bars, and cafeterias are quite expensive. If possible, stick to the **general stores** at each lodging location (open daily 7:30am-10pm). Harvest from the vast amounts of inexpensive food at **Food Farm**, 710 Scott St. W., Gardiner, MT (406-848-7524), across from the Super 8, or lasso some chow at the **Food Round-Up Grocery Store**, 107 Dunraven St., W. Yellowstone, MT (406-646-7501).

SIGHTS AND ACTIVITIES

TW Services, for unbelievable amounts of money, will sell you tours, horseback rides, and chuckwagon dinners until the cows come home. But given enough time, your eyes and feet will do an even better job than TW's tours, and won't bankrupt you. Hiking to the main attractions is much easier if you make reservations at the cabins closest to the sights you most want to see.

The **geysers** that made Yellowstone famous are clustered on the western side of the park, near the West Yellowstone entrance. Geysers are holes in the earth's crust into which water slowly trickles, then turns to steam; when the pressure reaches a certain point, the steam bursts out to the surface. The duration of the explosion depends on how much water has leaked into the hole and how hot the steam is. **Old Faithful,** while neither the largest, the highest, nor the most regular geyser, is certainly the most popular; it gushes in the **Upper Geyser Basin,** 16 mi. south of **Madison Junction** where the entry road splits north-south. Since its discovery in 1870, the granddaddy of geysers has consistently erupted with a whoosh of spray and steam (5000-8000 gallons worth) every 45 to 70 min. Avoiding crowds here in summer is nearly impossible unless you come for the blasts at dusk or dawn. Enjoy other geysers as well as elk in the surrounding **Firehole Valley.** Swimming in any hot springs or geysers is prohibited, but you can swim in the **Firehole River,** three-quarters of the way up Firehole Canyon Drive (turn south just after Madison Jct.), or in the **Boiling River,** 2½ mi. north of Mammoth, which is not really hot enough to cook pasta. Still, do not swim alone, and beware of strong currents.

From Old Faithful, take the easy 1½-mi. walk to **Morning Glory Pool,** a park favorite, or head 8 mi. north to the **Lower Geyser Basin,** where examples of all four types of geothermal activity (geysers, mudpots, hot springs, and fumaroles) steam, bubble, and spray together in a cacophonous symphony. The regular star here is **Echinus,** which erupts about every hour from a large basin of water. If you are lucky enough to witness it, the biggest show on earth is put on by **Steamboat,** the largest geyser in the world. Eruptions can last 20 minutes and top 400 ft. The last such enormous eruption occurred on Oct. 2, 1991; they used to occur about once a year. Don't hold your breath waiting for another one, but you might get lucky.

Whether you're waiting for geysers to erupt or watching them shoot skyward, don't go too close, as the crust of earth around a geyser is only two ft. thick, and the Surgeon General has determined that falling into a boiling sulfuric pit *may* be hazardous to your health. Pets are not allowed in the basin. Check out the squirrel-type animals roaming around without much fur to understand why.

Mammoth Hot Springs has famous hot spring terraces, built of multicolored striated limestone deposits which enlarge 6 in. every year. Wildlife is quite abundant in the northern part of the park, both along the road from Mammoth to Roosevelt—perhaps on the road itself—and past Roosevelt in the Lamar Valley.

The pride of the park's western side is the **Grand Canyon of the Yellowstone,** carved through glacial deposits and volcanic bedrock. For the best views, hike or drive to the 308-ft. Lower Falls at Artist Point, on the southern rim, or Lookout Point on the northern rim. All along the canyon's 19-mi. rim, keep an eye out for bighorn sheep; at dawn or dusk the bear-viewing area (at the intersection of Northern Rim and Tower roads) should be loaded with opportunities to use your binoculars.

Yellowstone Lake, 16 mi. south of the Canyon's rim at the southeastern corner of the park, contains tons o' trout, but requires a Yellowstone fishing permit. ($5 weekly, $10 annually for 16 and up, 12-15 must get a free permit, 11 and under may fish without a permit. Permits are available at ranger and visitors centers.) Catch a few and have the chef fry them for you in the Lake Yellowstone Hotel Dining Room. Most other lakes and streams allow catch-and-release fishing only. The expensive **Lake Yellowstone Hotel,** built in 1891 and renovated in 1989, merits a visit, if only for the magnificent view of the lake through the lobby's large windows. Walks around the main body of the lake, as well as those that take you around one of the lake's three fingers, are scenic and serene rather than strenuous. Nearby **Mud Volcano,** close to Yellowstone Lake, features boiling sulfuric earth and the **Dragon's Mouth,** a vociferous steaming hole that early explorers reportedly heard all the way from the lake. You'll smell it that far away for sure.

Most of the spectacular sights in the park are accessible by car, but only a hike will get you up close and personal with the multilayered petrified forest of **Specimen Ridge** and the geyser basins at **Shoshone** and **Heart Lake. Cascade Corner,** in the southwest, is a lovely area accessible by trails from Belcher. Over 1200 mi. of trails crisscross the park, but many are poorly marked. When planning a hike, pick up a topographical trail map ($7) at any visitors center and ask a ranger to describe forks in the trail. Allow yourself extra time (at least 1 hr. per day) in case you lose the trail.

■■■ CODY

William F. "Buffalo Bill" Cody was more than just a Pony Express rider, scout, hunter, sportsman, and entrepreneur. Buffalo Bill started "Buffalo Bill's Wild West Show," an extravaganza that catapulted the image of the cowboy into the world's imagination. Cody's show traveled all over the U.S. and Europe, even attracting the attention of royalty and statesmen. Founded in 1896 by Cody, this "wild west" town still hasn't come down off that Cowboy high.

The **Buffalo Bill Historical Center,** 720 Sheridan Ave., (587-4771), is known affectionately as the "Smithsonian of the West." The center is actually four museums under one roof: **The Buffalo Bill Museum** documents the life of guess who; the **Whitney Gallery of Western Art** shows off Western paintings including a few Russells and Remingtons; the **Plains Indian Museum** contains several exhibits about indigenous peoples; the **Cody Firearms Museum** shows off the rifles that the white man brought here—the world's largest collection of American firearms.

At night, Cody turns into "The Rodeo Capital of the World" with one every night (587-5155; tickets $7-9, kids $4-6). On July 4th weekend the **Cody Stampede** rough rides on into town (587-5155, $11). For fun without the bullshit, drive about 6 mi. west on Rte. 20/14/16 towards Yellowstone and see the mighty **Buffalo Bill Dam.** Completed in 1910, at which time it was the highest dam in the world.

Cody lies at the junction of Rte. 120 and Rte. 14. The eastern entrance to Yellowstone Park is 5.3 mi. to the west; the Montana border is about 40 mi. north on Rte. 120. The town's main street is **Sheridan Ave.** Otherwise, the streets running east-west have names, those running north-south are numbered. The friendly **Chamber of Commerce,** 836 Sheridan Ave. (587-2297), can give the low down. For public transportation, the **Cody Trolley** stops throughout the town, as well as for anyone who flags it down ($1 one way, $1.75 round trip, kids 75¢, seniors $1.50.) Car rental is available through **Rent-a-Wreck,** 1139 Ramsey Ave. (587-4993 or 800-452-0396). Small cars are $15 with 100 free mi. a day. Must be 24 with major credit card. Call ahead. Cody's **post office:** 1301 Stampede Ave. (527-7161; open Mon.-Fri. 8am-5:30pm, Sat. 9am-noon); **ZIP code:** 82414; **area code:** 307.

There is a veritable slew of budget hotels which fill up quickly in the summertime when the livin' is easy. The **Skyline Motel,** 1919 19th St. (587-4201), has some decent, clean rooms, cable TV, a pool, and a restaurant. (Summer singles from $36, doubles from $48. Winter singles from $26, doubles from $34.) **Rainbow Park Motel,** 1136 17th St. (587-6257), has cable TV and laundry. (In summer, singles $36, doubles $52. Off-season, singles $25-29, doubles $32-39.) **The Ponderosa Campground,** 1815 Yellowstone Highway (587-9203), is not far from town and is quite near the Buffalo Bill Historical Center. (102 tent sites $12. RV hookup available.)

Anyone passing through Cody cannot miss the **Irma Hotel and Restaurant,** 1192 Sheridan Ave. (587-4221), named after Buffalo Bill Cody's youngest daughter. Originally Buffalo Bill's own saloon; don't miss the original cherrywood bar, sent as a gift from Queen Victoria. (Open daily 6am-10pm, Oct.-March daily 6am-8pm.)

■■■ GRAND TETON NATIONAL PARK

When French fur trappers first peered into Wyoming's wilderness from the eastern border of Idaho, they found themselves facing three craggy peaks, each over 12,000 ft. In an attempt to make the rugged landscape seem more trapper-friendly, they dubbed the mutant mountains "Les Trois Tetons," French for "the three tits." When they found that these triple nipples had numerous smaller companions, they named the entire range "Les Grands Tetons." Today the snowy heights of Grand Teton National Park delight modern hikers and cyclists with miles of strenuous trails. The less adventurous will appreciate the rugged appearance of the Tetons; the craggy pinnacles and glistening glaciers possess stunning beauty.

PRACTICAL INFORMATION

Emergency: 911. Also 733-3300 or 543-2581; **sheriff's office,** 733-2331.

Park Headquarters: Superintendent, (733-3300), Grand Teton National Park, P.O. Drawer 170, Moose 83012. Office at the Moose Visitors Center (see below). Open daily 8am-7pm. General info line, 739-3600.

Park Entrance Fee: $10 per car, $4 per pedestrian or bicycle, $5 per family (non-motorized), under 16 (non-motorized) free. Good for 7 days in both the Tetons and Yellowstone.

Visitors Centers: Moose (733-3399), Teton Park Rd. at the southern tip of the park. Open June-Aug. daily 8am-7pm; Sept.-May daily 8am-5pm. **Jenny Lake** (739-3392) next to the Jenny Lake Campground. Open June-Aug. daily 8am-6pm. **Colter Bay** (739-3594), on Jackson Lake in the northern part of the park. Open early June-early Sept. daily 8am-8pm; May and late Sept.-early Oct. daily 8am-5pm. Park information brochures available in Braille, French, German, Japanese, Spanish, Serbo-Croatian, Farsi, and Hebrew. Topographical maps ($3.95, waterproof $5). Pick up the *Teewinot* newspaper (free) at any entrance or at the visitors center for a list of park activities, lodgings, and facilities.

Park Information and Road and Weather Conditions: 733-3611; 24-hr. recording. **Wyoming Highway Info Center,** 733-3316.

Bike Rental: Mountain Bike Outfitters, Inc. (733-3314), at Dornan's in Moose. Adult mountain bikes $6 per hr., $24 per day; kids $3.50 per hr., $14 per day; includes helmet. Open daily 9am-6pm. Credit card or deposit required.

Medical Care: Grand Teton Medical Clinic, Jackson Lake Lodge (543-2514 or 733-8002 after hours), near the Chevron station. Open June-mid-Sept. daily 10am-6pm. In a dire emergency, contact **St. John's Hospital** (733-3636), in Jackson.

Post Office: In **Moose,** across from the Park HQ. Open Mon.-Fri. 8:30am-1pm and 1:30-5pm, Sat. 9-10:30am. **ZIP Code:** 83012.

Area Code: 307.

The national park occupies most of the space between Jackson to the south and Yellowstone National Park to the north. **Rockefeller Parkway** connects the two parks and is open year-round. The park is directly accessible from all directions except the west, as those poor French trappers found out centuries ago. There are several recreational areas; the most developed is **Colter Bay,** the most beautiful is **Jenny Lake** (sorry, no swimmy in the Jenny). For a cool, secluded dip, drive north to the **Lizard Creek Campground** and grab one of the highly prized lakeside camping spots.

ACCOMMODATIONS

If you want to stay indoors, grit your teeth and pry open your wallet. **The Grand Teton Lodge Co.** has a monopoly on lodging within the park. Make reservations for any Grand Teton Lodge establishment by writing the Reservations Manager, Grand Teton Lodge Co., P.O. Box 240, Moran 83013 (543-2855 or 800-628-9988 outside WY). Accommodations are available late May through early October and are most expensive late June to early August. Reservations are recommended and can be made up to a year in advance. (See Jackson for accommodations outside the park.)

Colter Bay Tent Cabins (543-2855) has the cheapest indoor accommodations in the park, but not the place to stay in extremely cold weather. Canvas shelters with wood-burning stoves, tables, and 4-person bunks. Sleeping bags, wood, cooking utensils, and ice chests available for rent. Office open June-early Sept. daily 7am-10pm, or call Maintenance, 543-2811. 66 cabins $21 for 2, each additional person $2.50, cots $4. Restrooms and showers ($2) nearby.

Colter Bay Log Cabins (543-2855) maintains 208 quaint log cabins near Jackson Lake. Room with semi-private bath $26, with private bath $51-75. 2-room cabins with bath $75-97. Open mid-May-early Oct.

Flagg Ranch Village, P.O. Box 187, Moran 83013 (543-2861 or 800-443-2311), on the Snake River near the park's northern entrance. 52 simple cabins for 2 with private bath $69.

CAMPING

Camping is the way to see the Tetons without emptying your savings account. The park service maintains five campgrounds, all on a first-come, first-served basis (sites $8). In addition, there are two trailer parks and some designated backcountry open to visitors whenever the snow's not too deep. RVs are welcome in all but the Jenny Lake area, but no hookups. Call 739-3399 for campground information.

Park Campgrounds all have rest rooms, cold water, fire rings, dump stations, and picnic tables. Large groups can go to Colter Bay and Gros Ventre; all others allow a maximum of 6 people and 1 vehicle per site. Extremely popular **Jenny Lake:** 49 highly coveted sites; *arrive early*. No RVs. **Signal Mountain:** a few miles south of Colter Bay. 86 spots, usually full by 10am. **Colter Bay:** 310 sites, showers, grocery store, and laundromat. Usually full by noon. **Gros Ventre:** on the park's southern border, 360 sites. A good bet if you arrive late. **Lizard Creek:** 60 sites in the north end of the park, convenient to Yellowstone. Max. stay in Jenny Lake 7 days, all others 14 days. Reservations required for camping groups. All sites $8.

Colter Bay RV Park has 112 sites, electrical hookups. Reserved through Grand Teton Lodge Co. (733-2811 or 543-2855). Grocery store and eateries. Sites $22; May 15-June 7 and Sept.-Oct. 4 $17. Showers $2.

Flagg Ranch Village Camping is operated by Flagg Ranch Village (543-2861 or 800-443-2311). Right next to Yellowstone, so fills quickly. Grocery and eateries. Sites $16 for 2, $22 with hookup. Make reservations.

For **backcountry camping,** reserve a spot in a camping zone in a mountain canyon or on the shores of a lake by submitting an itinerary to the permit office at **Moose Ranger Station** (739-3303) from January 1 to June 1. Pick up the permit on the morning of the first day of your hike. You can make reservations by mail, but two-thirds of all spots are left open for reservation on a first-come, first-served basis; get a permit up to 24 hrs. before setting out at the Moose, Colter Bay, or Jenny Lake Ranger Stations. (Moose and Colter Bay open daily 8am-7pm, Jenny Lake mid-May-late Sept. daily 8am-6pm.) Camping is unrestricted in some off-trail backcountry areas (though you must have a permit). Wood fires are not permitted above 7000 ft.; check with rangers about fires in the lower regions. The weather can be severe, even in the summer. All backcountry campers should take precautions.

FOOD

The best way to eat in the Tetons is to bring your own grub. If this isn't possible, stick to what non-perishables you can pick up at the **Flagg Ranch Grocery Store** (543-2861 or 800-443-2311; open daily 7am-10pm; reduced winter hours), or **Dor-**

nan's **Grocery** in Moose (733-2415; open daily 8am-8pm). In Jackson, you can stock up on provisions at **Albertson's** supermarket (733-5950; open daily 6am-midnight).

SIGHTS AND ACTIVITIES

While Yellowstone wows visitors with its geysers and mudpots, Grand Teton's geology boasts some of the most scenic mountains in the U.S., if not the world. The youngest mountain range in North America, the Tetons provide hikers, climbers, rafters, and sightseers with vistas not found in more weathered peaks. The Grandest Teton rises to 13,771 ft. above sea level, virtually without foothills.

Cascade Canyon Trail, one of the least arduous (and therefore most popular) hikes, originates at Jenny Lake. To start, take a boat trip (operated by monopolistic Grand Teton Lodge Co.) across Jenny Lake (one way $3.75, round-trip $4; kiddies 7-12 $2.25, under 7 free), or hike the 2-mi. trail around the lake. Trail guides (free) are available at the trailhead, at the west boatdock. The **Hidden Falls Waterfall** plunges ½-mi. from the trail entrance; only the lonely can trek 6¾ mi. further to **Lake Solitude.** Another pleasant day hike, popular for its scope of wildlife, is the 4-mi. walk from Colter Bay to **Hermitage Point.** The **Amphitheater Lake Trail,** which begins just south of Jenny Lake at the Lupine Meadows parking lot, will take you 4.6 breathtaking miles to one of the park's many glacial lakes. Those who were bighorn sheep in past lives can butt horns with **Static Peak Divide,** a 15-mi. steep trail up 4020 ft. from the Death Canyon trailhead (4½ mi. south of Moose Visitors Center) and offers some of the best lookouts in the park. All information centers (see Practical Information above) provide pamphlets about the day hikes and sell the *Teton Trails* guide ($2). Call **National Park Tours** (733-4325) for tours as well (open 7am-9pm, reservations required, prices vary greatly depending on where you want to start).

For a leisurely afternoon on Jackson Lake, rent boats at the **Signal Mountain Marina** (543-2831; open early May-mid-Oct.). (Rowboats and canoes $8 per hr. Motorboats $15 per hr. Water-ski boats $45 per hr. plus gas and oil. Pontoons $40 per hr. plus gas and oil. Open daily 8am-7pm.) **Colter Bay Marina** has a somewhat smaller variety of boats at similar prices. (Open daily 7am-8pm, rentals stop at 6pm.) **Grand Teton Lodge Co.** (733-2811 or 543-2811) can also take you on scenic Snake River float trips within the park. (10½-mi. ½-day trip $28, ages 6-16 $18. 10½-mi. with lunch, $32, ages 6-16 $22, or supper trips $36, ages 6-16 $26.) **Triangle X Float Trips** (733-5500) can float you on a 5-mi. river trip for less ($19, under 12 $14). **Fishing** in the park's lakes, rivers, and streams is excellent. A Wyoming license ($5) is required; get one in Jackson, at Moose General Store, at Signal Mt., at Colter Bay, in Flagg Ranch, or at Dornan's. **Horseback riding** is available through the Grand Teton Lodge Co. (1-4 hr. rides, $16-34 per person).

The **American Indian Art Museum** (739-3594), next to the Colter Bay Visitors Center, offers an extensive private collection of Native American artwork, artifacts, movies, and workshops. (Open June-Sept. daily 8am-7pm; late May and late Sept. daily 8am-5pm. Free.) During July and August you can see Cheyenne, Cherokee, Apache, and Sioux dances at Jackson Lake Lodge (Fri. at 8:30pm). At the **Moose** and **Colter Bay Visitors Centers,** June through September, rangers lead a variety of activities aimed at educating visitors about such subjects as the ecology, geology, wildlife, and history of the Tetons. Check the *Teewinot* for exact times.

In the winter, all hiking trails and the unploughed sections of Teton Park Road are open to cross-country skiers. Pick up the trail map *Winter in the Tetons* or the *Teewinot* at the Moose Visitors Center. From January through March, naturalists lead **snowshoe hikes** from the Moose Visitors Center (739-3300; snowshoes distributed free). Call for reservations. **Snowmobiling** along the park's well-powdered trails and up into Yellowstone is a noisy but popular winter activity. Grab a map and guide at the Jackson Chamber of Commerce, 10 mi. south of Moose. For a steep fee you can rent snowmobiles at **Signal Mt. Lodge, Flagg Ranch Village,** or down in **Jackson;** an additional $10 registration fee is required for all snowmobile use in the park. There is a new, well-developed snowmobile trail from Moran to Flagg Ranch. All campgrounds close during the winter. The Colter Bay and Moose parking lots are available for RVs and cars, and backcountry snow camping (only for those who know what they're doing) is allowed with a free permit from Moose. Check with a ranger station for current weather conditions—many early trappers froze to death in the 10-ft. drifts—and avalanche danger.

■ ■ ■ JACKSON

Named after fur trapper David Jackson, "Jackson Hole" describes the valley bounded by the Teton and Gros Ventre Ranges; it was called a hole rather than a valley due to its high elevation. Since Jackson Hole is the only major ski resort in Wyoming, and a major whitewater rafting center in summer, the nearby town of Jackson is packed with expensive shops and eateries as well as many outdoorsy folk who make a living off the year-round tourism. Despite the crowds, the beauty of the surroundings is astounding; the Snake River winds by the town, Jenny Lake spins nearby, and the Grand Tetons crop up in the distance. Between Ralph Lauren outlets and rock climbing there is something for everyone to do in Jackson.

PRACTICAL INFORMATION

Emergency: 911.

Visitor Information: Jackson Hole Area Chamber of Commerce, 532 N. Cache St. (733-3316), in a modern, wooden split-level with grass on the roof. A crucial information stop. Open mid-June-mid-Sept. daily 8am-8pm; off-season daily 8am-5pm. **Bridger-Teton National Forest Headquarters,** 340 N. Cache St. (739-5500), 2 blocks south of the chamber of commerce. Maps $4 paper, $7 waterproof. Open Mon.-Fri. 8am-4:30pm.

Bus Tours: Grayline Tours, 332 N. Glenwood St. (733-4325), in front of Dirty Jack's Theatre. Full-day tours of Grand Teton National Park ($36) and Yellowstone National Park lower loop ($39). Call for reservations.

Public Transportation: Jackson START (733-4521), $1 per ride, $2 out of the county. **Grand Teton Lodge Co.** (733-2811) runs a shuttle twice daily in summer to Jackson Lake Lodge ($10).

Car Rental: Rent-A-Wreck, 1050 U.S. 89 (733-5014). $27 per day, $154 per week; mid-size $34 per day, $188 per week; 150 free mi. per day, 1000 free mi. weekly, 20¢ each additional mi. Must be 21 with credit card; over 25, credit card or $300 cash deposit. Must stay within 500 mi. of Jackson. Open daily 8am-6pm.

Ski and Bike Rental: Hoback Sports, 40 S. Millward (733-5335). 10-speeds $5 per 2 hr., $16 per day; mountain bikes $11 per 2 hr., $22 per day; lower rates for longer rentals. Skis, boots, and poles $13 per ½-day, $16 per day. Open peak summer daily 9am-7pm, peak winter daily 8am-9pm, off-season daily 9am-7pm. Must have drivers license or credit card. **Skinny Skis,** 65 W. Deloney St. (733-6094). Cross country skis $8 per ½ day, $12 per day; rollerblades $12 per day; camping equipment also available. Major credit card or deposit for value of equipment required. Open daily 9am-8pm.

Help Lines: Rape Crisis Line, 733-7466. **Road Information,** 733-9966, outside WY 800-442-7850. **Weather Line,** 733-1731. 24-hr. recording.

Post Office: 220 W. Pearl St. (733-3650), 2 blocks east of Cache St. Open Mon.-Fri. 8:30am-5pm. **ZIP code:** 83001.

Area Code: 307.

Although most services in Jackson are expensive, the town makes an ideal base for trips into the **Tetons,** 10 mi. north, or the **Wind River Range,** 70 mi. southeast. U.S. 191, the usual southern entry to town, ties Jackson to I-80 at Rock Springs (180 mi. south). This road continues north into Grand Teton Park and eventually reaches Yellowstone, 70 mi. to the north. The streets of Jackson are centered around **Town Square,** a small park on Broadway and Cache St. Teton Village refers to the skiing area directly towards the mountains from downtown, by Teton Village Road off Rte. 22. The ski resort visible from town is not the famed Jackson Hole, but **Snow King**

Mountain. The Jackson Hole resort is 12 mi. from town, on Teton Village Road (off Rte. 22). **Teton Village** is the shops, restaurants, and hotel area at its base.

ACCOMMODATIONS AND CAMPING

Jackson's constant influx of tourists ensures that if you don't book ahead, rooms will be small and expensive at best and non-existent at worst. Fortunately you can sleep affordably in one of two local hostels. **The Bunkhouse,** 215 N. Cache St. (733-3668), in the basement of the Anvil Motel, has a lounge, kitchenette, laundromat, ski storage, and, as the name implies, one large but quiet sleeping room with comfortable bunks. ($18. Linens included.) **The Hostel X,** P.O. Box 546, Teton Village 83025 (733-3415), near the ski slopes, 12 mi. northwest of Jackson, is a budgetary oasis among the wallet-parching condos and lodges of Teton Village, and a favorite of skiers because of its location. It also has a game room, TV room, ski waxing room, and movies nightly in winter. Accommodations range from dorm-style rooms. (4 beds in each, in summer honors HI-AYH cards. $15 for members, $37 for 2 non-members, $47 for 3 or 4; in winter, no member discount, $43 for 1 or 2, $56 for 3 or 4.) If you prefer to stay in a Jackson motel, **The Pioneer,** 325 N. Cache St. (733-3673), offers lovely rooms with teddy bears and stupendous hand-made quilts during the summer. (Singles $60, doubles $70, off-peak $36/$42.) Old faithful **Motel 6,** 1370 W. Broadway (733-1620), has rates that rise steadily as the peak season approaches. (Singles from $39. Each additional person $6.)

While it doesn't offer scenery, Jackson's RV/tent campground, the **Wagon Wheel Village,** 435 N. Cache St. (733-4588), operates on a first-come, first-served basis (32 sites $15, RVs $21.60). Cheaper sites and more pleasant surroundings are available in the **Bridger-Teton National Forest** surrounding Jackson. Drive toward Alpine Junction on U.S. 26/89 to find spots. Check the map at the chamber of commerce for a complete list of campgrounds. (Sites $6, no showers.)

FOOD

The Bunnery, 130 N. Cache St. (733-5474), in the "Hole-in-the-Wall" mall, has hearty breakfasts—two eggs, homefries, chili, cheese, and sprouts go for $5.25. Sandwiches are $4-6. (Open daily 7am-9:30pm.) When the moon hits your eye, climb **Mountain High Pizza Pie,** 120 W. Broadway (733-3646). (10-incher $5.75; open daily 11am-midnight; in winter will stay open 'til the pie hits the fan.) Call ahead for good eats at the **Sugarfoot Café,** 145 N. Glenwood (733-9148), where three friendly owners change the menu and hours every season. When open, the food is excellent and set in the decor of a renovated saddle shop. If you ask for the "Bump-n-Grind" combo at **Bombers** (739-2295) in the Grand Teton Plaza, you'll get a home-made muffin (the bump) and a grinder for $6. (Open Mon. 6:30am-3pm, Tues.-Fri. 6:30am-10pm, Sat. 7am-10pm, Sun. 7am-3pm.) Chow down on barbecued chicken and spare ribs ($7) at **Bubba's,** 515 W. Broadway (733-2288). No reservations, so come early. (Open daily 7am-10pm.) Have a grand visit at **Vista Grande,** on Teton Village Rd. (733-6964), where all items, including veggie burritos, enchiladas *magnifico,* and corn tacos are $3-11. (Open daily 5pm-10pm.)

OUTDOOR ADVENTURES

Whitewater rafting is enormously popular; between May 15 and Labor Day, over 100,000 city slickers and backwoods folk float out of Jackson. **Mad River Boat Trips,** 1060 S. Hwy. 89 (U.S. 89) (733-6203 or 800-458-7238) 25 mi. from Jackson, offers the cheapest whitewater and scenic raft trips (3 mi. trip $21, river rat special for early risers $19; with dinner $26). **Lone Eagle Expeditions** (377-1090) gives you a meal on your 8-mi. raft trip (breakfast and lunch trips $21 per person; afternoon and evening dinner trips $29 per person). **Black Diamond Llamas,** Star Route Box 11-G (733-2877), offers hikes in the company of these South American furry friends (they carry your packs; $50 day hike with meals, $125 per day overnight). Cheaper thrills include a lift 10,452 ft. up Rendez-Vous Mountain on the **Jackson Hole Aerial Tram** (733-2292; $14, seniors $12, teens $7, ages 6-12 $2, brochure has coupons).

In winter, the **Jackson Hole Ski Resort** (733-2292) at Teton Village offers some of the steepest, most challenging skiing in the country.

Cultural activities in Jackson fall into two camps—the rowdy, foot-stomping Western celebrations and the more formal, sedate presentations of music and art. Every summer evening except Sunday, the Town Square hosts a kitschy episode of the 37-year-old **Longest-Running Shoot-Out in the World.** For $2.50 on Friday evenings at 6:30pm, you can join in at the **Teton Twirlers Square Dance** (733-5269 or 543-2825) in the fair building on the rodeo grounds. Each June, the town celebrates the opening of the **Jackson Hole Rodeo** (733-2805; open June-Aug. Wed. and Sat. 8pm; tickets $7, ages 4-12 $4.50, under 4 free, family rate $21). Eat and watch at the **Bar J Chuckwagon** supper and western show (733-3370) on Teton Village Rd. Show, steak or grilled chicken, and foil-wrapped potatoes $13, under 8 $4.50, lap-sized free. The **Grand Teton Music Festival** (733-1128) blows and bows in Teton Village in mid-July and August. (Performances weeknights at 8pm, Sat.-Sun. 8:30pm; student tickets $3-5. Fri. and Sat. symphony at 8:30pm; $20, student tickets $9. Reserve in advance.) On Memorial Day, the town bursts its britches as tourists, locals, and nearby Native American tribes pour in for the dances and parades of **Old West Days.** Throughout September, the **Jackson Hole Fall Arts Festival** attracts crafters, painters, dancers, actors, and musicians to town.

ENTERTAINMENT

If you're in town Sunday night, two step on over to the **Stagecoach Bar** (733-4407) on Rte. 22 in Wilson. (Open Mon.-Sat. 10am-2am, Sun noon-10pm.) Down the street is the **Otto Brothers Brewery** (733-9000), which offers free tours and tastings. (Open Mon.-Fri. 8am-8pm, Sat.-Sun. 4-8pm.) For more local ales check out the new **Jackson Hole Pub and Brewery,** 765 S. Millward St. (739-2337), Wyoming's first micro-brewery with a public house. The "Zonkers Stout" is guaranteed to put hair on your chest ($3 pints, $10 pitchers). They also serve yummy pasta, sandwiches, and gourmet pizzas all under $3. (Open Mon.-Thurs. until midnight, Fri.-Sat. until 1am, Sun. until 10pm.) Western saddles serve as bar stools at the **Million Dollar Cowboy Bar,** 25 N. Cache St. (733-2207), Town Square. This Jackson institution is mostly for tourists, but attracts some rodeo goers and local cowboys. (Open Mon.-Sat. 10am-2am, Sun. noon-10pm. Live music Mon.-Sat. 9pm-2am. Cover $2-5 after 8pm.) The **Mangy Moose,** Teton Village (733-4913), is a great place for live moosic, food, and frolicking. (Dinner daily 5:30-10:30pm, bar open 10pm-2am. 21 and over.)

■■■ BUFFALO AND SHERIDAN

Most travelers will want to use either Buffalo or Sheridan as a base town from which to explore the mountains. At the junction of I-90 (east to the Black Hills area and north to Billings, MT) and I-25 (south to Casper, Cheyenne, and Denver), **Buffalo** is much easier to reach. **Sheridan** is just 30 mi. to the north of Buffalo.

PRACTICAL INFORMATION

The **Buffalo Chamber of Commerce** is at 55 N. Main St. (684-5544 or 800-227-5122), 1 mi. west of the bus station (open Mon.-Sat. 8am-6pm; Sept.-June Mon.-Fri. 9am-5pm). The **U.S. Forest Service Offices,** 300 Spruce St. (684-7981), will answer questions about the Buffalo District in the Bighorns and sell you a road/trail map of the area for three greenbacks (open Mon.-Fri. 8am-4:30pm, Sat.-Sun. 9am-6pm). At **Alabam's,** 421 Fort St. (684-7452), you can buy topographical maps ($2.50), hunting, fishing, and camping supplies, and fishing licenses (1 day $5, 5 days $20). (Open daily 7am-8pm; off-season daily 8am-6pm.) Sheridan's **U.S. Forest Service Office,** 1969 S. Sheridan Ave. (672-0751), offers maps of the Bighorns ($3), along with numerous pamphlets on how to navigate them safely (open Mon.-Fri. 8am-5pm). The **Sheridan Chamber of Commerce** (672-2485), 5th St. at I-90, can also provide info on the national forest (open May 15-Oct. 15 daily 8am-8pm).

Powder River Transportation serves Buffalo from a terminal at **Big Horn Travel Plaza**, 207 South By-Pass (684-5246), where twice daily you can catch a bus north to Sheridan ($8.40) and Billings ($33), or south to Cheyenne ($45). Buffalo, as the crossroads of north-central Wyoming, remains a popular place for hitchhikers to catch rides to the southern cities of Casper and Cheyenne; getting a lift on the freeway in Sheridan is more difficult. *Let's Go* does not recommend hitchhiking. **Powder River buses** run from the depot at the **Energy Inn Motel**, 580 E. 5th St. (674-6188), to Billings (2 per day, $28), Buffalo (2 per day, $8), and Cheyenne (2 per day, $44). Buffalo's **ZIP code:** 82801. The **area code** for the Bighorns is 307.

ACCOMMODATIONS AND FOOD

In Buffalo, budget motels line Main St. (Rte. 90) and Fort St. The **Mountain View Motel** (684-2881) is by far the most appealing pine cabins with TV, A/C, and heating (singles $30, doubles $34; winter $20/24). Also try the **Z-Bar Motel** next door (684-5535), with HBO, refrigerator or kitchen, and A/C. (Singles $37, doubles $45; winter $29; for kitchen add $5. Reservations recommended.)

The **Stagecoach Inn**, 845 Fort St. (684-2507), has Singer sewing machine tables with bandana napkins and cowboy table cloths. Huge portions, specials with soup or salad, potato, pie, and miraculous bread for $9-12. (Open Mon.-Fri. 11:30am-2pm and 5-9pm, Sat. 5-9pm.) Stock up on sandwiches at the **Breadboard,** 190 E. Hart (684-2318), where an eight-inch-long "Freight Train" (roast beef and turkey with all the toppings) knows it can for $3.50 (open daily 11am-10pm). Or try **Dash Inn,** 620 E. Hart St. (684-7930), for scrumptious fried chicken (2 pieces $3.75). (Open Tues.-Sun. 11am-10pm, winter 11am-8:30pm.)

SIGHTS

The Jim Gatchell Museum of the West, 10 Fort St. (684-9331; $2, under 17 free), or the museum and outdoor exhibits at the former site of **Fort Phil Kearny** (684-7629), on U.S. 87 between Buffalo and Sheridan serves those hankerin' after a bit o' frontier history (open daily 8am-6pm; Oct. 16-May 14 Wed.-Sun. noon-4pm; $2, students $1). Drive by the historic **Occidental Hotel,** 10 N. Main St. (684-2788), the town hall since 1880 (open daily 10:30am-4:30pm and 6:30-8:30pm; free).

Sheridan's claim to fame is that Buffalo Bill Cody used to sit on the porch of the once luxurious **Sheridan Inn,** at 5th and Broadway, as he interviewed cowboy hopefuls for his *Wild West Show.* The Inn now gives tours ($3, seniors $2, under 12 free).

■■■ BIGHORN MOUNTAINS

The Bighorns erupt from the hilly pastureland of northern Wyoming, a dramatic backdrop to the grazing cattle and sprawling ranch houses at their feet. In the 1860s, violent clashes occurred here between incoming settlers and the Sioux, who were defending their traditional hunting grounds. Cavalry posts such as Fort Phil Kearny, on U.S. 87 between Buffalo and Sheridan, could do little to protect the settlers. The war reached a climax at the Fetterman Massacre, which forced settlers temporarily out of the Bighorns. Now peaceful, the mountain range offers naturelovers miles and miles of wilderness recreation.

Hiking and Camping Hike through the woods or follow **scenic highways U.S. 14** and **U.S. 16** and discover waterfalls, layers of prehistoric rock, and the mysterious Medicine Wheel stone formation, which even had the earliest Native Americans guessing. For sheer solitude, you can't beat the Bighorns's **Cloud Peak Wilderness,** in the **Bighorn National Forest.** To get to **Cloud Peak,** a 13,175-ft. summit in the range, most hikers enter at **West Tensleep,** accessible from the town of **Tensleep,** 70 mi. west of Buffalo on the western slope, due west on Rte. 16. Tensleep was so named because it took the Sioux 10 sleeps to travel from there to their main winter camps. The most convenient access to the wilderness area, though, is from the trailheads near U.S. 16, 25 mi. west of Buffalo. From the **Hunter Corrals** trailhead, move to beautiful **Seven Brothers Lake,** an ideal base for forays into the high peaks beyond. You can also enter the wilderness area from U.S. 14 out of Sheridan in the north.

Campgrounds fill the forest (sites $5-8). Near the Buffalo entrance, **Lost Cabin** (14 sites, water and toilets; 28 mi. southwest of Buffalo on U.S. 16; open mid-May-Nov.; 14-day limit; for reservations call 800-280-CAMP; altitude 8200 ft.) and **Crazy Woman** (6 sites; 25 mi. from Buffalo on U.S. 16; open mid-May-Oct.; altitude 7600 ft.) boast magnificent scenery, as do **Cabin Creek** and **Porcupine** campgrounds near Sheridan. You can spend only one night free just off Coffeen St. in Sheridan's grassy **Washington Park.** You can also camp along the Bighorn River at Afterbay, Two Leggins, Bighorn, and Mallards Landing.

■■■ DEVIL'S TOWER NATIONAL MONUMENT

No, it's not a shrine to an almighty Freudian phallus—Devil's Tower is actually an extinct volcanic core. Sixty million years ago, in northeastern Wyoming, fiery magma forced its way through sedimentary rocks and cooled without breaking the surface. Centuries of wind, rain, and snow eroded the surrounding sandstone, leaving a stunning spire that was named the first national monument in the U.S. in 1906. If looking at this stone obelisk inspires you to play with mashed potatoes or gives you an eerie feeling of déjà vu, you will be comforted to know that Devil's Tower was the cinematic landing strip for extra-terrestrials in *Close Encounters of the Third Kind* ($4 entrance fee per car; $2 per pedestrian). The only way to get to the top is by climbing; over 5000 people attempt it yearly. Those interested in making the climb must register with a ranger at the **visitors center** (307-467-5263), 3 mi. from the entrance (open daily 8am-7:45pm). There are more than 150 established routes. For the base hikers, there are several **hiking trails** that provide an excellent view of the Tower. The park maintains a **campground.** (Sites $7; water, bathrooms, fireplaces, picnic tables, no showers; open May 15-Nov.) But watch out for rattlesnakes and don't feed the prairie dogs. **KOA** (307-467-5395) camps right next to the park entrance ($16, full hookup $19). From I-90 take U.S. 14 25 mi. north to Rte. 24.

■■■ CASPER AND ENVIRONS

Built primarily as a stop for the Union Pacific Railroad, Casper has a history characteristic of hundreds of other similar railroad towns. Casperites are proud of their city's *raison d'être* and their chief claim to fame: nine of the pioneer trails leading west, including the Oregon and Bozeman trails, intersected at a point not far from what is today the city's southern limit. Mountain men, fur trappers, friendly ghosts, Mormons, Shoshone, and Sioux all lived in the Casper area during the mid-1880s. The convergence of those famous paths lives in the minds of those who call Casper by its nicknames, "the Hub" and "the Heart of Big Wyoming," and who also seem to have forgotten that most of those pioneers kept moving on.

PRACTICAL INFORMATION

The helpful **Casper Area Convention and Visitors Bureau,** 500 N. Center St. (234-5311 or 800-852-1889, fax 265-2643), will help you find your way in Casper, and even provide suggestions for trips to neighboring states. (Open Mon.-Fri. 8am-7pm, Sat.-Sun. 8am-6pm; off-season Mon.-Fri. 8am-5pm.) **Powder River Transportation Services,** (266-1904; 800-433-2093 outside WY), at I-25 and Center St. in the Parkway Plaza Hotel, Room 1159, sends one bus per day to: Buffalo ($21), Sheridan ($26), Rapid City ($44); and two per day to: Cheyenne ($30) and Billings ($46). **Casper Affordable Used Car Rental,** 131 E. 5th St. (237-1733), rents cars for $22 per day, with 50 free mi., 15¢ per additional mi.; $149 per week, 350 free mi., 15¢ per additional mi. (Open Mon.-Fri. 8am-5:30pm. Must be 22 to rent; $200 or credit card deposit required.) Casper's **post office:** 150 E. B St. (266-4000; open Mon.-Fri. 7am-6pm); **ZIP code:** 82601; **area code:** 307.

ACCOMMODATIONS AND CAMPING

Unforgiven high plains drifters can bunk down at **The Royal Inn,** 440 E. A St. (234-3501). Folks from the inn will pick pale riders up at the bus station for free. Rooms have showers, baths, cable, and phones. Outdoor heated pool. Pets allowed. (Singles $19, with fridge and TV $26. Doubles $27/$29. Extra person $5.) Just up the street, step out of the high noon sun into **The Virginian Motel,** 830 E. A St. (266-9731; singles $19, $70 per week; doubles $23, $82 per week; key deposit $2).

Campers can settle down at the **Fort Caspar Campground,** 4205 W. 13th St. (234-3260; tents $10; full hookup $13.50). The **Natrona County Parks Office,** 4621 CY Ave. (234-6821), provides information about camping in the greater Casper area (open Mon.-Fri. 8am-5pm). The parks office presides over several campgrounds, including **Casper Mountain** (237-8098), 12 mi. south of Casper on Rte. 251, near Ponderosa Park, and **Alcova Lake Campground** (237-7052), 35 mi. southwest of Casper on Country Rd. 407 off Rte. 220, a popular recreation area with beaches, boats, and private cabins. (Tent sites $5; RV hookups at Alcova $12.) The **Hell's Half Acre Campground** (472-0018), 45 mi. west on U.S. 20/26, proves more inviting than its name implies, offering more amenities than the primitive park sites, including showers and hookups (tent sites $2 per person; full hookup $11).

FOOD

When you've kicked up enough dust for one day and are hankerin' for a hunk of cheese, mosey on into the **Cheese Barrel,** 544 S. Center St. (235-5202), for a hearty and affordable breakfast or lunch. Try the pita veghead ($3.95) and be sure to have at least one order of cheese bread (85¢ for two slices). (Open Mon.-Sat. 6:30am-2:30pm.) **Anthony's,** 241 S. Center St. (234-3071), serves huge portions of Italian food by candlelight (spaghetti $5.50; open daily 11:30am-10pm). The best Chinese food in town is at **The Peking Restaurant,** 333 E. A St. (266-2207). Lunch specials from $3.75. A lot of dishes to choose from in a refreshing non-Western setting (open Mon.-Fri.11am-2pm, Sun.-Thurs. 5-8pm, Fri.-Sat. 5-9pm).

SIGHTS AND ACTIVITIES

Casper's pride and joy, **Fort Caspar,** 4001 Ft. Caspar Rd. (235-8462), is a reconstruction of an old army fort on the western side of town. There is an informative museum on the site. (Open Mon.-Sat. 8am-7pm, Sun. noon-7pm; mid-Sept.-mid.-May Mon.-Fri. 8am-5pm, Sun. 1-4pm. Free.) From Ft. Caspar you can hike to **Muddy Mountain** or **Lookout Point** to survey the terrain that hosted some of the last conflicts between the Native Americans and the pioneers.

Devil's Kitchen (also called Hell's Half-Acre), 45 mi. northwest of Casper on U.S. 20/26, is a 320-acre bowl serving up hundreds of crazy colorful spires and caves. **Independence Rock,** 55 mi. southwest on Rte. 220, still welcomes travelers to the entrance of a hellish stretch of the voyage across Wyoming. In 1840, Father Peter DeSmet nicknamed it the "Great Registry of the Desert," honoring the godless renegades and Mormon pioneers who etched their name into the rock as they passed by. Explore the abandoned prospecting town on Casper Mountain or follow the **Lee McCune Braile Trail** through Casper Mountain's Skunk Hollow.

If you are here in early August, check out the week-long **Central Wyoming Fair and Rodeo,** 1700 Fairgrounds Rd. (235-5775), which keeps the town in an extended state of Western hoopla replete with parades, demolition derbies, livestock shows, and rodeos.

In winter, consider surrendering to the snowy slopes of Casper Mountain, 11 mi. south of Casper, which hosts the **Hogadon Ski Area** (235-8499), 60 acres of downhill, cross-country, and snowmobile trails and runs rising 8000 ft. above sea level. For equipment, **Mountain Sports,** 543 S. Center St. (266-1136), rents downhill and cross-country skis. Credit card deposit or cost of equipment in cash required. (Open

Mon.-Sat. 9am-6pm, Nov.-Dec. Mon.-Fri. 9am-8pm, Sat. 9am-6pm, Sun. noon-5pm.)
For info on other activities, contact **Community Recreation, Inc.** (235-8383; open
Mon.-Thurs. 6am-10pm, Fri. 6am-8pm, Sat. 8am-8pm, Sun. 1-7pm).

■■■ CHEYENNE AND ENVIRONS

Originally the name of the Native American tribe that once roamed the wilderness
surrounding the city, "Cheyenne" was considered a prime candidate for the name of
the Wyoming Territory. This moniker was struck down by vigilant Senator Sherman, who pointed out that the pronunciation of Cheyenne closely resembled that
of the French word *chienne* meaning, shall we say, female dog.

PRACTICAL INFORMATION

Emergency is 911. To recointer yourself, check with the **Cheyenne Area Convention and Visitors Bureau,** 309 W. Lincolnway (778-3133; 800-426-5009 outside
WY), just west of Capitol Ave., for extensive accommodations and restaurant listings (open daily 8am-6pm, in winter Mon.-Fri. 8am-5pm), or the **Wyoming Information and Division of Tourism,** I-25 and College drive (777-7777; 800-225-5996
outside WY; open daily 8am-5pm). *There no longer is an Amtrak station in Cheyenne,* although there is a waiting room in the lobby of the Plains Hotel from which
a shuttle bus will transport you to the station nearest Cheyenne. Trains chug daily
to: Denver ($24), Salt Lake City ($86), San Francisco ($161), and Chicago ($188).
(Open daily 9:30am-5:30pm.) **Greyhound,** 1503 Capitol Ave. (634-7744) at 15th St.,
has two buses daily to: Salt Lake City (9 hrs., $61), Chicago ($129), Laramie ($9),
Rock Springs ($36), and Denver ($22). (Station open daily 10am-12:30pm and 5pm-
2am, but subject to change.) **Powder River Transportation** (635-1327), in the Greyhound terminal, runs buses south to Rapid City once daily ($61), and north to
Casper ($30.45) and Billings ($66) twice daily. Greyhound passes are honored.

The **Rape Crisis Line** (637-7233) is open 24 hrs. Cheyenne's **post office:** 2120
Capitol Ave. (772-6580), 6 blocks north of the bus station (open Mon.-Fri. 7:30am-
5:30pm, Sat. 7:30am-noon); **ZIP code:** 82001; **area code:** 307.

ACCOMMODATIONS AND CAMPING

It's not hard to land a cheap room here among the lariats, plains, and pioneers,
unless your visit coincides with Wyoming's enormous hootenanny **Frontier Days**,
the last full week of July (see Sights and Entertainment). In days approaching this
week, beware of doubling rates.

Many budget motels line **Lincolnway** (U.S. 30). Just a few blocks from the bus station, the old **Plains Hotel,** 1600 Central Ave. (638-3311), offers very attractive, large
rooms with marble sinks, HBO, and phones in grand-lobbied splendor (singles $28,
doubles $37, extra person $5). The **Guest Ranch Motel,** 1100 W. 16th St. (634-
2137), a short hike west from the bus stop, has large, tidy rooms with cable, phones,
shower, and bath (singles with 1 queen bed $26, doubles $32).

For campers, spots are plentiful (except during Frontier Days) at the **Restway
Travel Park,** 4212 Whitney Rd. (634-3811), 1½ mi. east of town. (150 sites; $12.50
for up to 4 people, with electricity and water $15.50, full hookup $16.50; prices rise
slightly in July. Laundry, heated pool, FREE MINI-GOLF!) You might also try **Curt
Gowdy State Park,** 1319 Hynds Lodge Rd. (632-7946), 23 mi. west of Cheyenne on
Rte. 210. This year-round park has shade, scenery, 280 sites, fishing, hiking, an
archery range, and land for horseback riding—BYO horse. (Entrance fee $2; out-of-
state visitors $3; sites $4 per night, annual camping permit $25.)

FOOD AND NIGHTLIFE

Cheyenne is basically a meat n' potatoes place, but there are also a few good ethnic
eateries sprinkled around downtown. For a taste of some home cookin', float into

the **Driftwood Cafe,** 200 E. 18th St. (634-5304), and try the pies and specials ($4.25 and under) concocted daily in the diner's small kitchen (open Mon.-Fri. 7am-4pm).

Lexie's Cafe, 216 E. 17th (638-8712), serves breakfast and lunch, including Mexican and Italian specialties, towering stack of pancakes ($2.75), and huge burgers ($3.75). (Open Mon.-Sat. 7am-3pm.) **Los Amigos,** 620 Central Ave. (638-8591), serves burritos ($2-4) and humongous dinners (from $7.25). You might want to go with a half-order (60% of the price), or swing by for the $4 lunch specials (open Mon.-Thurs. 11am-8:30pm, Fri.-Sat. 11am-9pm).

Those weary of the deer and antelope can play in **Joe Pages Bookstore and Coffeehouse,** 207 W. 17th St. (778-7134 or 800-338-7428), which offers occasional live music and poetry readings. **The Cheyenne Club,** 1617 Capitol Ave. (635-7777), is a country nightspot for a 21+ crowd, hosting live bands nightly at 9pm. When the urge to guzzle consumes you, look for a pink elephant above **D.T.'s Liquor and Lounge,** 2121 Lincolnway (open Mon.-Sat. 7am-2am, Sun. noon-10pm).

SIGHTS AND ENTERTAINMENT

If you're within 500 mi. of Cheyenne during the last week in July, make every possible effort to attend the **Cheyenne Frontier Days,** nine days of non-stop Western hoopla. The town doubles in size as anyone worth a grain of Western salt comes to see the world's oldest and largest rodeo competition and partake of the free pancake breakfasts (every other day in the parking lot across from the chamber of commerce), parades, and square dances. Most remain inebriated for the better part of the week. Reserve accommodations in advance or camp nearby. For information, contact Cheyenne Frontier Days, P.O. Box 2477, Cheyenne 82003 (800-227-6336, fax 778-7213; open Mon.-Fri. 9am-5pm).

Throughout June and July the **Cheyenne Gunslingers** perform a mock gunfight at W. 16th and Carey St. (Shows Mon.-Fri. at 6pm, Sat. at noon. Free. For info call the Cheyenne Area Convention and Visitors Bureau at 773-3133.) The **Cheyenne Frontier Days Old West Museum** (778-7290), in Frontier Park at 8th and Carey St., chronicles the rodeo's history from 1897 to the present. (Open Mon.-Fri. 8am-6pm, Sat.-Sun. 10am-5pm; in winter Tues.-Fri. 9am-5pm, Sat. 11am-4pm. $3, seniors $2, under 12 free, families $6.)

The **Wyoming State Museum,** 2301 Central Ave. (777-7024) at 24th St., presents an especially digestible history of Wyoming's cowboys, sheepherders, and suffragettes, along with exhibits on the Oglala, Cheyenne, and Shoshone who preceded them. (Open Mon.-Fri. 8:30am-5pm, Sat. 9am-4pm, Sun. noon-4pm; off-season closed Sun. Free.) The **Wyoming State Capitol Building** (777-7220), at the base of Capitol Ave. on 24th St., shows off its stained glass windows and yellowed photographs (open Mon.-Fri. 8:30am-4:30pm; summer tours every 15 min., free).

■ LARAMIE

Not just a frontier shire, Laramie is the hoppin' home to the University of Wyoming (the state's only four-year college) and much cowboy country. With all the trappings of a western college town, minus the overdevelopment, Laramie has been called "the hippest little cowboy town in the West." From Cheyenne, take the **"Happy Jack Road" (Rte. 210)** for the scenic tour, or Rte. 80W for expedience. Drop by the **chamber of commerce,** 800 S. 3rd St. (745-4195 or 800-445-5303) for the low down on skiing, snowmobiling, biking, hiking, and other sports (open Mon.-Fri. 8am-5pm).

Look for the funky restaurants, bars, and shops on **Ivinson St.** between 1st and 3rd St. You can find students and Harleys at the **Buckhorn Bar,** 114 Ivinson (742-3554; open daily 6am-2am). **The Home Bakery and Café,** 304 S. 2nd St. (742-2721), has been around for 100 years (open Mon.-Sat. 5am-5:30pm).

Cheap board is hard to find in Laramie. Budget motels muster around 3rd St. (Rte. 287). **The Travel Inn,** 262 N. 3rd St. (745-0896), boasts pink and turquoise painted beds, a pool, cable TV, and small fridges in each room (singles $31-39, doubles $34-

45). Or flop for more at **Annie Moore's Guest House,** 819 University Ave. (721-4177). Prices range from $40-65 for 1-2 people.

■ MEDICINE BOW NATIONAL FOREST

From Laramie, take the **Snowy Range Scenic Byway (Rte. 130)** through Medicine Bow National Forest. The area is named after two Native American Indian practices: conducting ceremonial powwows for curing disease, and making bows from the mahogany they found here. Medicine Bow is less toured than other attractions, but offers all the fun.

There are 23 developed campsites within the **Snowy Range Area** (and many others more remote in the forest). Campgrounds are open in the summer only; most are $5, and only a few require reservations. Two ideal settings are **Nash Fork,** off Snowy Range Pass on the eastern side of the forest (27 sites, first-come, first-served, $7), and **Silver Lake,** also off Snowy Range Pass, in the center of the forest (19 sites, first come, first-served, $7). Call ahead for information or visit **Bush Creek's Visitors Center** (326-5258), located on the western side of the forest on Rte. 130.

■ SARATOGA

On the far side of Medicine Bow from Laramie, Saratoga, like its New York sister, is known for its **hot mineral springs** (open 24 hrs., free). After curing your aches, Saratoga's proximity to the **North Platte River** makes for great, great **fishing.** No full-moon discounts, but still a howlin' good time is the **Hotel Wolf** (326-5525) at the corner of Rte. 130 and E. Bridge St. The Wolf is a renovated Victorian inn with budget motel prices (singles $26, doubles $30). Find a good cup of coffee at **Lolly-pops** (326-5020), next door to the Wolf. For a hearty meal, try **Wally's** (326-8472) also on Bridge St. (open Mon.-Fri. 10am-2:30pm and 6-9pm, Sat.-Sun. 11am-9pm).

THE PACIFIC NORTHWEST

The drive of "manifest destiny" brought 19th-century pioneers to the Pacific Northwest, some of the most beautiful and awe-inspiring territory in the United States. Lush rainforests, snow-capped peaks, and the deepest lake on the continent all reside in this corner of the country. Oregon's Mt. Hood and Columbia River Gorge, Washington's Cascade Mountains, miles and miles of the Pacific Crest Trail, and a long, stormy coast inhabited by sea lions and giant redwoods draw the rugged individualist and the novelty-seeking city-slicker alike. Moving up from California, Coastal Highway 101 hugs the Pacific Ocean, rising above the mist with over 200 miles of salty spray and breath-taking scenery.

Settled like jewels amid the wet and wild lands of the Pacific Northwest, the cities of this region sparkle with all the urban flair of their Northeastern counterparts. But unlike New York, Washington, D.C., or Boston, the cosmopolitan communities of Seattle and Portland have spectacular mountain ranges in their backyards. The Northwestern traveler can hike the Cascade Range by day and club-hop by night, ride Seattle's monorail or raft down southern Oregon's wild river rapids.

For more comprehensive coverage of the Pacific Northwest, consult the handsome and intrepid *Let's Go: Alaska & The Pacific Northwest.*

 # Oregon

Have you ever wondered why, over 150 years ago, entire families sank their life savings into covered wagons, oxen, horses, flour, bacon, and small arms, and trekked 1500 mi. from the edge of civilization (Missouri) across harsh, hostile, and totally unfamiliar country to get to Oregon? Once you visit Oregon, you'll realize why. Thousands of visitors are drawn each year by unparalleled natural beauty, including North America's deepest gorge and the towering Wallowa Mountains in the northeast; the vast, desolate Steens country in the southeast, begging for outdoor exploration; the forested peaks of the Cascade Range, with Crater Lake, Mt. Hood, and the Pacific Crest Trail; the awesome Columbia River Gorge; and the rugged coast with its brilliant tide pools. Hikers, cyclists, anglers, climbers, skiers, windsurfers, trekkers, and explorers all find themselves reveling in Oregon.

The waves and cliffs of the gorgeous Oregon's Pacific coast are indeed amazing. However, you should also venture inland to see some of Oregon's greatest attractions—fabulous Mt. Hood, the volcanic cinder-cones near Crater Lake, the Shakespeare festival in Ashland, and world-class yet easy-going Portland.

PRACTICAL INFORMATION

Capital: Salem.
State Tourist Office, 775 Summer St. NE, Salem 97310 (800-547-7842). **Oregon State Parks,** 1115 Commercial St. SE, Salem 97310-1001 (378-6305). **Department of Fish and Wildlife,** P.O. Box 59, Portland 97207 (229-5404). **Oregon State Marine Board,** 435 Commercial St. NE, Salem 97310 (378-8587).
Time Zone: Mountain and Pacific. **Postal Abbreviation:** OR
Sales Tax: 0%

■■■ PORTLAND

Casual and tolerant, Portland is the mellowest big city on the West Coast. Unhurried, uncongested, and without pretension, the downtown area is spotless and building height is regulated to preserve views of the river, hills, and mountains. Funded by a one-percent tax on new construction, Portland's varied artistic scene is anchored by Portland's venerable Symphony Orchestra, the oldest in the country. On a July day you can ski Mt. Hood in the morning, watch the sun drop into the Pacific Ocean from the cool sand of an empty beach, and still return to town in time to catch an outdoor jazz concert at the zoo. Portland's first-rate flock of small breweries pump out barrels of some of the nation's finest ale.

The award-winning **Tri-Met bus system** weaves together Portland's districts and suburbs. In the transit mall, 31 covered passenger shelters serve as both stops and information centers. Southbound buses pick up passengers along SW 5th Ave.; northbound passengers board on SW 6th Ave. Bus routes fall into seven regional service areas, each with its own individual "Lucky Charm": orange deer, yellow rose, green leaf, brown beaver, blue snow, red salmon, and purple rain. Shelters and buses are color-coded for their regions. A few buses with black numbers on white backgrounds cross town north-south or east-west, ignoring color-coded boundaries.

Most of downtown, from NW Irving St. in the north to I-405 in the west and south and the Willamette River in the east, constitutes **"Fareless Square."** As the name suggests, the buses and MAX are free in this zone. For fares outside this zone, see Practical Information. Pick up monthly passes, bus maps, and schedules at the visitors center (see Practical Information), or at the Tri-Met Customer Assistance Office.

PRACTICAL INFORMATION

Emergency: 911.

Visitors Information: Portland/Oregon Visitors Association, 25 SW Salmon St. (222-2223 or 800-962-3700), at Front St., in the Two World Trade Center complex. From I-5, follow the signs for City Center. Pick up copy of *Portland Book*. Open Mon.-Fri. 8am-6:30pm, Sat. 8:30am-5pm, Sun. 10am-4pm; in winter Mon.-Fri. 8:30am-5pm, Sat. 9am-3pm.

Airport: Portland International, 7000 NE Airport Way (335-1234). Take Tri-Met bus #12 (a 45-min. ride), which arrives going south on SW 5th Ave. (95¢). **Raz Tranz** (246-3301 for taped info) has a shuttle that stops at most major hotels downtown. Fare $7, ages 6-12 $1. Taxis to downtown $21-24.

Amtrak, 800 NW 6th Ave. (273-4866 or 800-872-7245, Union Station 273-4865), at Hoyt St. To: Seattle (4 per day, $23); Eugene (1 per day, $24); Spokane (1 per day, $67), Boise (1 per day, $83). Open daily 6:45am-6pm.

Greyhound, 550 NW 6th Ave. (800-231-2222) at Glisan. To: Seattle (12 per day; $19); Eugene (11 per day, $13); Spokane (5 per day, $42). Lockers available, $2 for 6 hrs. Ticket window daily open 5am-midnight. Station open 24 hrs.

Public Transportation: Tri-Met, Customer Service Center, #1 Pioneer Courthouse Sq., 701 SW 6th Ave. (238-7433; open Mon.-Fri. 7:30am-5:30pm). Several 24-hr. recorded info lines; fare info (231-3198); updates, changes, and weather-related problems (231-3197); senior and disabled services (238-4952). Service generally 5am-midnight, reduced Sat.-Sun. Fare 95¢-$1.25, ages 7-18 70¢, over 65 and handicapped 45¢; no fare in Fareless Square downtown. All-day pass $3.25. All buses have bike racks (a $5 2-year permit can be obtained at an area bike store) and are wheelchair accessible. **MAX** (228-7246) is an efficient rail running between Gresham to the east and downtown, using same fare system as buses.

Taxi: Broadway Cab, 227-1234. **New Rose City Cab Co.,** 282-7707. 24 hrs.

Car Rental: Avis Rent-A-Car, at airport (800-331-1212 or 249-4950). $30 per day, unlimited free mi. $120 weekly rate. Must be 25 or older with credit card.

Crisis Line: 223-6161. **Women's Crisis Line:** 235-5333. Both 24 hrs. **Phoenix Rising** (gay/lesbian) (223-8299). Open Mon.-Fri. 9am-5pm.

Post Office: 715 NW Hoyt St. (294-2300). **ZIP Code:** 97208-9999. Open Mon.-Sat. 7am-6:30pm.

Area Code: 503.

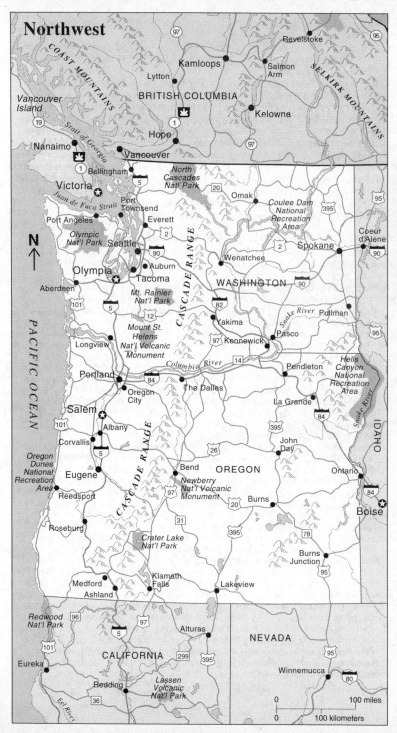

Northwest

Portland is in the northwest corner of Oregon, near where the Willamette (wi-LAM-it) River flows into the Columbia River. By car, Portland lies about 70 mi. from the Pacific Ocean, 635 mi. north of San Francisco, and 170 mi. south of Seattle. I-5 connects Portland with San Francisco and Seattle; I-84 follows the route of the Oregon Trail through the Columbia River Gorge toward Boise.

Portland is divided into five districts. **Burnside St.** divides the city north and south; the Willamette River separates east and west. **Williams Ave.** cuts off a corner of the northeast which is called "North." All street signs are labeled by their districts: N, NE, NW, SE, and SW. **Southwest** district is the city's hub, encompassing the downtown area and the southern end of historic Old Town. The heart of downtown is between SW 5th and 6th Ave., where car traffic is prohibited. The **Northwest** district contains **Old Town** and the swanky West Hills. The **Southeast** is the hippest part of the city. The city's best ethnic restaurants line **Hawthorne Boulevard,** along with small cafes and theaters catering to the artsy crowd, mostly supported by nearby Reed College's students. The **North** and **Northeast** districts are chiefly residential, punctuated by a few quiet, small parks.

Parking is plentiful but expensive: meters are 75¢ per hour.

ACCOMMODATIONS AND CAMPING

It's always wise to make reservations early, because places can fill in a flash, especially during the Rose Festival or a convention. Camping, though distant, is plentiful.

Portland International Hostel (HI-AYH), 3031 SE Hawthorne Blvd. (236-3380), at 31st Ave, is the place to meet cool folks. Take bus #14 (brown beaver). Sleep inside or on the back porch. Kitchen; laundromat across the street. Fills up early in the summer, so make reservations (credit card required) or plan to arrive at 5pm to get one of the 12-15 beds saved for walk-ins. Don't miss the all-you-can-eat pancakes every morning ($1). Open daily 7:30-10am and 5-11pm. No curfew. $12, nonmembers $15.

Ondine, 1912 SW 6th Ave. (725-4336), at Portland State University between College and Hall St., is the budget travel experience of a lifetime. 5 clean, spacious rooms, each with 2 twin beds. Linen and towels provided. Private bathrooms. Microwaves available; no kitchen. Laundry facilities. The dormitory is in Fareless Square, so you can hop on the bus and be downtown in a minute. Parking nightmarish. Reservations required 1-2 wks. in advance. One person $20, two $25.

Aladdin Motor Inn, 8905 SW 30th St. (246-8241 or 800-292-4466; fax 244-1939), behind the shopping center at Barbur Blvd., 10-min. from downtown. Take bus #12 (yellow rose) from 5th Ave., exit 294 from northbound I-5, or exit 296A and turn left off the exit if coming south. Stellar rooms with cable TV, free local calls, A/C, kitchens. Mention *Let's Go* for a discount. Singles $35-40. Doubles $39-49.

YWCA, 1111 SW 10th St. (223-6281) is women only. Clean and one of the safest options. Small rooms. Bathroom, shower, laundry, and small kitchen down hall. Hostel has 7 beds ($10); singles $19, with semi-private bath $24. Key deposit $2.

McMenamins Edgefield Hostel, 2126 SW Halsey St., Troutdale (669-8610 or 800-669-8610) is 20 min. east of Portland off I-84. 2 vast rooms, single-sex, each with 12 beds. Showers down the hall in claw-footed tubs. $18 per night.

Ben Stark Hotel International Hostel, 1022 SW Stark St. (274-1223; fax 274-1033). Ascend the imposing, dark staircase to find 3 decent hostel rooms, mostly for international travelers. 12 beds. $15, $12 in winter. No curfew; 24-hr. desk service. Fantastic location, just blocks from downtown. Call for reservations.

Milo McIver State Park is 25 mi. southeast of Portland, off Rte. 211, 5 mi. west of the town of Estacada. Fish, swim, or bicycle along the Clackamas River. (Hot showers, flush toilets. Sites $12.) Hike, bike, or visit the historic home and log cabin museum at **Champoeg State Park,** 8239 Champoeg Rd. NE (678-1251; sites $16, "primitive" tent sites $9). **Ainsworth State Park,** 37 mi. east of Portland off I-84, in the Columbia Gorge, has hot showers, flush toilets, and hiking trails. (Sites with full hookup $13.)

FOOD

Portland has more restaurants per capita than any other American city. You'll never get tired of eating out in Portland, and you'll also never go broke. Espresso bars are everywhere.

Western Culinary Institute Chef's Corner, 1239 SW Jefferson (242-2422). The testing ground for the cooking school's creative adventures. Students in tall white hats will whip up a delicious, cheap meal. All lunches under $6. For breakfast, try the gourmet hash browns. Open Mon. 8am-2:30pm, Tues.-Fri. 8am-6pm.

Brasserie Montmartre, 626 SW Park Ave. (224-5552). Paper tablecloths and crayons and live jazz nightly offer diversions for dull dates and similarly-awkward social situations. Lunch entrees around $6, dinner $9 for chicken or steak. Open Mon.-Thurs. 11:30am-2am, Fri. 11:30am-3am, Sat. 10am-3am, Sun. 10am-2am.

Food Front, 2375 NW Thurman St. (223-6819), offers a wonderland of natural foods, fruit, and baked goods. Open daily 9am-9pm, summer 9am-10pm.

Kornblatt's, 628 NW 23rd Ave. (242-0055), is a deli haven for homesick New Yorkers. Take bus #15 (red salmon). Menu includes matzo ball soup ($3) and knishes ($2.25). Open Mon.-Fri. 7am-9pm, Sat. 7:30am-10pm, Sun. 7:30am-9pm.

Cafe Lena, 2239 SE Hawthorne Blvd. (238-7087), is known for its open-mike poetry every Tues. at 7:30pm. Live music accentuates an appetizing menu. Try the Birkenstock Submarine ($5). Open Tues.-Sat. 7am-11pm, Sun. 8am-2pm.

Thanh Thao Restaurant, 4005 SE Hawthorne Blvd. (238-6232) serves up fabulous Thai. There's often a wait for dinner, so go early. (Open Mon.-Fri. 11am-2:30pm and 5-10pm, Sat.-Sun. 11am-10pm.)

Pied Cow Coffeehouse, 3244 SE Belmont St. (230-4866). Take bus #15 (brown beaver). Bring that hot date from the hostel, 6 blocks away, for latte and chocolate cake by candlelight in the outdoor garden. Open Tues.-Thurs. 6pm-midnight, Fri. 6pm-1am, Sat. 10am-1am, Sun. 10am-11pm.

Kent's, 1022 SW Morrison St. (221-4508). Of the dozen *bento* (Japanese: "in a box") places that have opened recently in Portland, Kent's is *ichi-ban*. Chicken and vegetable bento $5. Pretend you're an on-the-go *sarariman* in need of refueling and guzzle the vitamin beverage Lipovitan-D ($1.75). Open Mon.-Sat. 11:30am-9pm.

Chang's Mongolian Grill, 1 SW 3rd St. (243-1991), at Burnside. All-you-can-eat lunches ($6) or dinners ($9). Select your meal from a buffet of fresh vegetables, meat, and fish, mix your own sauce to taste, and watch your chef make a wild show of cooking it on a domed grill the size of a Volkswagen beetle. Rice and hot-and-sour soup included. Open daily 11:30am-2:30pm and 5-10pm.

SIGHTS AND ACTIVITIES

Parks, gardens, museums, galleries, and open-air markets beckon the city's tourists and residents alike. Catch the best of Portland's art every **"First Thursday"** (of each month) when many small galleries in the Southwest and Northwest stay open until 9pm. For info contact the **Metropolitan Arts Commission,** 1120 SW 5th Ave. (823-5111). Take a **Public Art Walking Tour** from the **Portland Art Museum,** 1219 SW Park Ave. (226-2811; open Tues.-Sat. 11am-5pm, Sun. 1-5pm).

Portland's downtown area is centered on the **mall,** running north-south between 5th and 6th Ave., bounded on the north by W. Burnside St. and on the south by SW Madison St. At 5th Ave. and Morrison St. sits **Pioneer Courthouse,** the original downtown landmark. The monument is still a Federal courthouse, and is the centerpiece for **Pioneer Courthouse Square,** 701 SW 6th Ave. (223-1613), which opened in 1983. Portland and area citizens purchased personalized bricks to support the construction of an amphitheater in the square for live jazz, folk, and ethnic music. During the summer (Tues. and Thurs. noon-1pm) the **Peanut Butter and Jam Sessions** draw thousands to enjoy the music.

Certainly the most controversial building in the downtown area is Michael Graves's postmodern **Portland Building** (823-4000), located on the mall. The building's 1984 opening was attended by King Kong (full-sized when inflated), perched on the roof. Since then, this amazing confection of pastel tile and concrete has been both praised to the stars and condemned as an overgrown jukebox.

There is room for romping just west of the mall on the **South Park Blocks,** a series of cool, shaded parks down the middle of Park Ave., enclosed on the west by **Portland State University.** Facing the parks is the **Oregon Art Institute,** 1219 SW Park Ave. (226-2811), at Jefferson St., which houses the **Portland Art Museum,** the **Pacific Northwest College of Art** (226-4391), and the **Northwest Film Center** (221-1156), which shows classics and offbeat flicks. Tickets are available at the box office, 921 SW Morrison. The Art Museum has a fine exhibit of Pacific Northwest Native American art, including masks, textiles, and sacred objects. (Open Tues.-Sat. 11am-5pm, Sun. 1-5pm. $4.50, seniors $3.50, students $2.50. 2 for 1 AAA discount. 1st Thurs. of each month free from 4-9pm. Thurs. seniors free.)

Old Town, north of the mall, resounded a century ago with the clamor of sailors whose ships filled the ports. The district has been revived by the large-scale restoration of store fronts, new "old brick," polished iron and brass, and a bevy of recently opened shops and restaurants. Old Town also marks the end of **Waterfront Park.** This 20-block-long swath of grass and flowers along the Willamette River provides locals with an excellent place to picnic, fish, stroll, and enjoy major community events. At **Where's the Art!!!,** 219 SW Ankeny (226-3671), for just 25¢ you can pray at the church of Elvis, view the world's first 24-hr. coin-operated art gallery, or get marriage counseling. The largest open-air crafts market in the country, **Saturday Market,** 108 W. Burnside St. (222-6072), under the Burnside Bridge between 1st and Front St., is overrun with street musicians, artists, craftspeople, chefs, and greengrocers (March-Christmas Sat. 10am-5pm, Sun. 11am-4:30pm).

Less than 2 mi. west of downtown, the posh neighborhoods of **West Hills** form a manicured buffer zone between the soul-soothing parks and the turmoil of the city below. Take the animated "zoo bus" (#63) or drive up SW Broadway to Clay St. and turn right onto U.S. 26 (get off at zoo exit). **Washington Park** and its nearby attractions are perhaps the most soulful sites in Portland. The park's gates are open daily 7am to 9pm. **Hoyt Arboretum,** 4000 SW Fairview Blvd. (228-8733 or 823-3655), at the crest of the hill above the other gardens, features 200 acres of trees and trails. Free nature walks (April-Nov. Sat.-Sun. at 2pm) last 60-90 min. and cover 1-2 mi. The **Rose Garden,** 400 SW Kingston Ave., on the way to the zoo entrance, is a gorgeous place to stroll on a lazy day or cool evening. Clear days afford a spectacular view of the city and distant **Mount Hood.** Stunning views are also seen at the **Japanese Gardens,** 611 SW Kingston Ave., the most authentic outside Japan.

Below the Hoyt Arboretum stands Portland's favorite attractions. The **Washington Park Zoo,** 4001 SW Canyon Rd. (226-1561 or 226-7627), is renowned for its successful elephant-breeding and its scrupulous recreation of natural habitats. Take the #63 "zoo" bus from the park to SW Morrison St. in the downtown mall. A miniature **railway** also connects the Washington Park gardens with the zoo. (Rail $2.50, seniors and ages 3-11 $1.75. Zoo open summer daily 9:30am-6pm. $5.50, seniors $4, children $3.50. 2nd Tues. of each month free 3-6pm.) In June, July, or August, head to the Washington Park amphitheater to catch **Your Zoo and All That Jazz** (234-9695 or 226-1561), a nine-week series of open-air jazz concerts (Wed. 7-9pm), free with zoo admission. **Rhythm and Zoo Concerts** (234-9694) also features a series of concerts free with admission (Thurs. 7-9pm). The **World Forestry Center,** 4033 SW Canyon Rd. (228-1367), specializes in exhibits on Northwestern forestry and logging. Warning: the Forestry Center's 70-ft. "talking tree" never shuts up. (Open daily 9am-5pm, Labor Day-Memorial Day 10am-5pm. $3, students $2.)

The funky students in the cafes, theaters, and restaurants on Hawthorne Blvd. belong to **Reed College,** 3203 SE Woodstock (771-1112). Founded in 1909, Reed sponsors many cultural events. The ivy-draped grounds, which encompass a lake and a wildlife refuge, make up one of the most attractive campuses in the country. One-hour tours, geared to prospective students, leave Eliot Hall #220, 3203 Woodstock Blvd. at SE 28th, twice per day during the school year (Mon.-Fri. 10am and 2pm; individual tours are available by appointment in summer. Call 777-7511).

Farther southeast is **Mt. Tabor Park,** SE 60th Ave. and Salmon St., one of two city parks in the world on the site of an extinct volcano. Take bus #15 (brown beaver).

ENTERTAINMENT AND NIGHTLIFE

Once an uncouth and rowdy port town, Portland manages to maintain an irreverent attitude. Many waterfront pubs have evolved into upscale bistros and French bakeries. Nightclubs cater to everyone from the casual college student to the hard-core rocker. The best entertainment listings are in the Friday edition of the *Oregonian* and in a number of free handouts: *Willamette Week* (put out each evening and catering to students), the *Main Event,* and the *Downtowner* are available in restaurants downtown and in boxes on street corners.

Portland has its share of good, formal concerts, but why bother with admission fees? You'll find the most exciting talent playing for free in various public facilities around the city. Call the Park Bureau (796-5193) for info, and check the *Oregonian* for **Brown Bag Concerts,** free public concerts given around the city in a six-week summer series (at noon during the week and Tues. evenings). The **Oregon Symphony Orchestra** plays classical and pop in Arlene Schnitzer Concert Hall, 1111 SW Broadway Ave. (800-228-7343 or 228-1353, Sept.-June. Tickets $8-46. "Symphony Sunday" afternoon concerts $18), while **Chamber Music Northwest** performs summer concerts from late June through July at Reed College Commons, 3203 SE Woodstock Ave. (223-3202; Mon., Thurs., and Sat. at 8pm. $17, ages 7-14 $9).

Portland's many fine theaters produce everything from off-Broadway shows to experimental drama. **Portland Center Stage** (274-6588), at the Intermediate Theater of **PCPA,** at SW Broadway and SW Main. features classics from Oct.-April. (Tickets: Fri.-Sat. $11-33, Sun. and Tues.-Thurs. 10% higher. Half-price tickets sometimes available at the Intermediate Theater 1 hr. before showtime.)

Neighborhood taverns and pubs have the most character and best music, but are harder to find. The clubs closest to downtown are in Northwest Portland.

Produce Row Cafe, 204 SE Oak St. (232-8355), has 28 beers on tap, 72 bottled domestic and imported beers. Bus #6 (red salmon) to SE Oak and SE Grand, then walk west along Oak towards the river. Live music Sat.-Mon., $1 cover. Open Mon.-Fri. 11am-midnight or 1am, Sat. noon-1am, Sun. noon-midnight.

La Luna, 215 SE 9th Ave. (241-5862). Take bus #20 (purple rain), get off at 9th, walk 2 blocks south with live concerts, 2 bars and a Generation X crowd. Open Thurs.-Sat. 8pm-2:30am, concerts and special events other nights.

Bridgeport Brew Pub, 1313 NW Marshall (241-7179). A great beer and pizza joint. Open Mon.-Thurs. 2-11pm, Fri. 2pm-midnight, Sat. noon-midnight, Sun. 1-9pm.

Lotus Card Room and Cafe, 932 SW 3rd Ave. (227-6185), at SW Salmon St., plays techno, house, and hip-hop, attracting collegiate crowd on Fri. and Sat. Dance floor open Wed.-Sun. 10pm-2am. Cover $3, Thurs.-Sun. $1. Open daily 7am-2am.

Red Sea, 318 W. 3rd Ave. (241-5450), has live reggae Thurs. Bring an escort; it's a seedy area. Cover $2-3. Open Thurs. 9pm-1:30am, Fri.-Sat. 9pm-2:30am.

The Space Room, 4800 SE Hawthorne Blvd. (235-8303). Take bus #14 (brown beaver). Judy Jetson smoked way too many cigarettes inside this space-age joint. The cutting-edge crowd contemplate the vintage-clothing possibilities. One bloody mary ($3) will put you over the edge. Open daily 6am-2:30am.

Brigg and Boxx's Video Bar, 1035 SW Stark (226-4171). Male-dominated, primarily gay bar with dancing beginning at 9pm. Boxx open daily, noon-2:30am, Brigg open daily 8am-2:30am.

OREGON COAST

The renowned coastal highway **U.S. 101** hugs the shore, sometimes rising in elevation to lofty viewpoints. From **Astoria** in the north to **Brookings** in the south, the highway laces together the resorts and fishing villages that cluster around the mouths of rivers flowing into the Pacific. Its most breathtaking stretch lies between the coastal towns, where hundreds of miles of state parks allow direct access to the beach. Wherever the highway leaves the coast, look for a beach loop road—these quiet byways afford some of the finest scenery on the coast. **Greyhound** offers only two coastal runs from Portland per day; one of those takes place at night, when the coast's beautiful scenery is hidden. Gasoline and grocery **prices** on the coast are about 20% higher, so stock up and fill up before reaching the coastal highways.

Astoria   Astoria was Lewis and Clark's final stop at the end of their transcontinental trek; they reached the Pacific here in 1805. Six years later, John Astor, scion of one of 19th-century America's most wealthy families, established a fur-trading post, making Astoria the first permanent U.S. settlement on the West Coast. Today Astoria is a scenic getaway for inlanders and city-dwellers. The **chamber of commerce,** 111 W. Marine Dr. (325-6311; fax 325-6311), just east of the bridge to Washington, is stocked with area info. (Open Mon.-Sat. 8am-6pm, Sun. 9am-5pm; Sept.-May Mon.-Fri. 8am-5pm, Sat.-Sun. 11am-4pm.)

Astoria is the most convenient connection between the Oregon coast and Washington. Two bridges run from the city: the **Youngs Bay Bridge,** to the southwest, on which Marine Drive becomes U.S. 101, and the **Astoria Bridge,** a 4-mi. span over the Columbia River into Washington. The Astoria Bridge has extremely narrow and hazardous bike lanes. Motels are crowded and expensive. The great, almost unknown **Fort Columbia State Park Hostel (HI-AYH),** Fort Columbia, Chinook, WA (206-777-8755), within Fort Stevens State Park, is across the 4-mi. bridge into Washington, then 3 mi. north on U.S. 101. This hospital-turned-hostel has 50¢ stuff-your-face pancakes, coffee, tea, and snacks in the kitchen, and laundry and barbecue facilities. (Lockout 9:30am-5pm, check-in 5-10pm. $9, nonmembers $12, bicyclists $7, under 18 with parent $4.50. Open March 1-Oct. 3.) The area is also a haven for campers; U.S. 101, south of Astoria, is littered with campgrounds. **Fort Stevens State Park** is by far the best (sites $16-18).

Tillamook   Ever seen a cheese factory at work? Some of Oregon's finest, most famous cheeses are cultured on the shore of Tillamook Bay, where cow pastures predominate. Most visitors hanker for a hunk of cheese at the **Tillamook Cheese Factory.** Watch from glass windows of this temple to dairy delights as cheese is made, stirred, cut, weighed, and packaged. Sample a tidbit in the tasting room. Try their ice cream too (open daily 8am-8pm; Sept.-mid-June 8am-6pm).

Tillamook lies 49 mi. south of Seaside and 44 mi. north of Lincoln City on U.S. 101. The most direct route from Portland is U.S. 26 to Rte. 6 (74 mi.). U.S. 101 is the main drag, and splits into two one-way streets in the downtown area. The Tillamook Cheese Factory is almost a downtown in itself, but is north of the major shops. The **visitors center** (842-7525), next to the cheese factory, has a map of all the camping spots in the area; it's worth a look. For a cheap bed try the **Tillamook Inn,** 1810 U.S. 101N (842-4413), between the center of town and the Tillamook Cheese Factory. (Singles $34. Doubles $46. Winter rates lower. Call a few days in advance.)

Newport   Part tourist mill, part fishing village, and part logging town, Newport offers the sights and smells of a classic seaport with kitschy shops. Newport's **chamber of commerce,** 555 SW Coast Hwy. (265-8801 or 800-262-7844) has a helpful office (open Mon.-Fri. 8:30am-5pm, Sat.-Sun. 10am-4pm; Oct.-April no weekends.

The strip along U.S. 101 provides plenty of affordable motels, with predictably noisy consequences. The **Brown Squirrel Hostel (HI-AYH),** 44 SW Brook St. (265-3729), has a cavernous living room adjacent to the kitchen. You can be out the door and at the beach in 2 min. (Lockout 10am-4pm. Doors locked at 11:30pm, mid-Sept.-May at 10pm. Laundry and kitchen. $10.) Campers should escape Newport to the many state campgrounds along U.S. 101. Just north of town lies the best option, **Beverly Beach State Park,** 198 N. 123rd St., Newport (265-9278), which has 151 tent sites ($14) and 53 full hookup sites; reserve ahead of time. **South Beach State**

Park, 5580 S. Coast Hwy., South Beach 97366 (867-4715), 2 mi. south of town, has 254 electrical hookups ($12) and showers.

The Chowder Bowl, 728 NW Beach Dr. (265-7477), at Nye Beach, has renowned chowder ($2.75). The "Mate's Portion" of Fish & Chips is $6 (open June-mid-Sept. 11am-8pm, Fri.-Sat. 11am-9pm). Then head over to the **Oregon Coast Aquarium,** 2820 SE Ferry Slip Rd. (867-3474), a vast building featuring 2½ acres of exhibits. ($7.75, seniors and ages 13-18 $4.50, under 13 $3.30. Open daily 9am-6pm; winter 10am-4:30pm.) Some of the sheltered coves in the area, especially those north around Depoe Bay, are excellent for **scuba diving.** Rent equipment from **Newport Water Sports,** 1441 SW 26th St., South Beach (867-3742), at the south end of the bridge. (Open daily Mon.-Thurs. 9am-6pm, Fri. 8am-6pm, Sat.-Sun. 8am-8pm. Top-of-the-line gear rental about $25 during the week, $30 on weekends.)

Oregon is famous for its microbreweries. **Rogue Ale Brewery,** 2320 SE Oregon State University Dr. (867-3663), across the bay bridge, brews a local favorite. Request a tour. (Open daily 11am-8pm; winter hours less.) The second week in October, the **Microbrew Festival** features beers of the Northwest.

Oregon Sand Dunes For 50 mi. between Florence and Coos Bay, the beach widens to form the **Oregon Dunes National Recreation Area.** Shifting hills of sand rise to 500 ft. and extend up to 3 mi. inland (often to the shoulder of U.S. 101), clogging streams and forming many small lakes. Hiking trails wind around the lakes, through the coastal forests, and up to the dunes.

Siuslaw National Forest administers the national recreation area. **Campgrounds** fill up early with dune buggy and motorcycle junkies, especially on summer weekends. The blaring radios, thrumming engines, and staggering swarms of tipsy tourists might drive you into the sands to seek eternal truth, or at least a quiet place to crash. The campgrounds that allow dune buggy access, **Spinreel, Lagoon, Waxmyrtle,** parking-lot style **Driftwood II,** and **Horsfall** (with showers), are generally loud and rowdy in the summer (sites $10). (Limited reservations for summer weekends are available; call 800-280-2267 more than 10 days prior to arrival.) **Carter Lake** (22 sites) and **Tah Kenitch** (36 sites), both $10, are quiet sites for tenters and small RVs. The sites closest to Reedsport are in Winchester Bay and are either ugly, RV-infested, or both. The best campgrounds are between 1 and 4 mi. south of the Bay.

The dunes' shifting grip on the coastline is broken only once along the expanse, when the Umpqua and Smith Rivers empty into Winchester Bay about 1 mi. north of town. **Reedsport,** 21 mi. south of Florence, is a typical small highway town of motels, banks, and flashy restaurants, neatly subdivided by U.S. 101 and Rte. 38. In Reedsport, the **National Recreation Area Headquarters** (271-3611), just south of the Umpqua River Bridge, will happily provide you with a map ($3) or *Sand Tracks,* the area recreation guide. (Open daily 8am-4:30pm; Sept.-May Mon.-Fri. 8am-4:30pm.) **Winchester Bay,** just south of Reedsport, has inexpensive rooms. The **Harbor View Motel** (271-3352), on U.S. 101, has clean, comfortable rooms. (Singles $26. Doubles $29. Rooms with 2 beds $34. Off-season rates $4 lower.)

Those with little time or low noise tolerance should at least stop at the **Oregon Dunes Overlook,** off U.S. 101, about halfway between Reedsport and Florence. Steep wooden ramps lead to the gold and blue swells of the dunes and the Pacific. Trails wander off from the overlook, as they do at several other points on U.S. 101. An excellent, easy trail is the **Taylor Dunes,** a gentle, ½-mi. trail that brings you to a good view of the dunes without the crowds.

For a true dune experience, venture out on wheels on a **dune buggy** or a guided tour. **Oregon Dunes Tours** (759-4777) on Wildwood Dr., 10 mi. south of Reedsport off U.S. 101, gives 30-minute ($18) and hour-long ($30) dune-buggy rides (open daily 9am-6pm). If you really want to tear up the dunes, shell out $25 for one hour on your own dune buggy. Rent from **Dune's Odyssey,** on U.S. 101 in Winchester Bay (271-4011; open Mon.-Sat. 8am-5:30pm, Sun. 9am-5:30pm, in winter closed Wed.) or **Sandland Adventures** (997-8087) at 10th St. and U.S. 101 (open daily).

THE PACIFIC NW

Inside **Umpqua Lighthouse State Park,** 6 mi. south of Reedsport, the Douglas County Park Department operates the **Coastal Visitor Center** (271-4631), in the old Coast Guard administration building, which has exhibits on the shipping and timber industries at the turn of the century (open May-Sept. Wed.-Sat. 10am-5pm, Sun. 1-5pm; free). **Bird watching** and **whale watching** are also popular diversions.

CENTRAL AND EASTERN OREGON

■■■ ASHLAND

With an informal, rural setting near the California border, Ashland mixes hippiness and history, making it the perfect locale for the world-famous **Shakespeare festival.** The brainchild of local college teacher Angus Bowmer, the festival began with two plays performed in the Chautauqua theater by schoolchildren as a complement to daytime boxing matches. Today, professional actors perform eleven plays—Shakespeare's share has shrunk to three; the other eight are classical and contemporary dramas. Performances run from mid-February through October on three Ashland stages—the **Elizabethan Stage,** the **Angus Bowmer,** and the **Black Swan.**

Due to the productions's popularity, ticket purchases are recommended six months in advance. General mail-order ticket sales begin in January, but phone orders are not taken until February ($17-23 spring and fall, $20-26 in summer). For complete ticket info, write Oregon Shakespeare Festival, P.O. Box 158, Ashland 97520; call 482-4331; or fax 482-8045. Though obtaining tickets can be difficult in summer, spontaneous theater-goers should not abandon hope. The **box office**, 15 S. Pioneer St., opens at 9:30am and releases any unsold tickets for the day's performances. Local patrons have been known to leave their shoes to hold their places in line; you should respect this tradition. **Backstage tours** provide a wonderful glimpse of the festival from behind the curtain leaving from the Black Swan (2 hrs.; Tues.-Sun.10am-3pm; $8, ages 5-7 $6). The Shakespeare festival also includes special events, such as the **Feast of Will** in mid-June, a celebration honoring the opening of the Elizabethan Theater (tickets $16; call 482-4331 for exact date).

The **Ashland Hostel (HI-AYH),** 150 N. Main St. (482-9217), is well-kept, cheery, and run by a wonderful staff that is ready to advise you on the ins and outs of Shakespeare ticket-hunting. Laundry facilities, game room. ($11, non-members $13. Check-in 5-11pm. Curfew midnight. Lockout 10am-5pm. Reservations essential March-Oct.; large groups sometimes fill the hostel.) **Jackson Hot Springs,** 2253 Rte. 99N (482-3776), off exit 19 from I-5, down Valley View Rd. to Rte. 99N for about ½ mi., is the campground nearest to downtown. (Laundry facilities, hot showers, and mineral baths $5 per person, $8 per couple. Sites $12, with full hookup $17.)

■■■ EUGENE

Situated between the **Siuslaw** (see-YU-slaw) and the **Willamette** (wil-LAM-it) **National Forests,** Oregon's second-largest city sits astride the Willamette River. Home to the **University of Oregon,** Eugene teems with museums, pizza joints, and all the trappings of a college town. The fleet-footed and free-spirited have dubbed Eugene "the running capital of the universe." Only in this city could the annual **Bach Festival,** in late June, be accompanied by the "Bach Run."

The **Eugene-Springfield Visitors Bureau,** 305 W. 7th (484-5307; outside OR 800-547-5445), at Lincoln St. off Lawrence downtown, has it all (open June-Aug. Mon.-Fri. 8am-5pm, Sat. and Sun. 10am-4pm.). Info on the area forests can be found at **Willamette National Forest Service,** 211 E. 7th Ave. (465-6522; open Mon.-Fri. 8am-4:30pm). Both **Amtrak,** 433 Willamette St. (800-872-7245), and **Greyhound,** 987 Pearl St. (344-6265 or 800-231-222; open daily 6am-10pm) roll through town.

Eugene is 111 mi. south of Portland on the I-5 corridor. The University of Oregon campus lies in the southeastern corner of town, bordered on the north by Franklin Blvd., which runs from the city center to I-5. **Willamette Ave.** is the main drag and is interrupted by the **pedestrian mall** on 7th, 8th, and 9th St. The city is a motorist's nightmare of one-way streets; free parking is virtually nonexistent downtown.

The cheapest motels are on E. Broadway and W. 7th St. **Lost Valley Educational Center (HI-AYH),** 81868 Lost Valley Lane, near Dexter (937-3351; fax 937-3646) is an educational experience. Take Rte. 58 east for 8 mi. toward Oakbridge, turn right on Rattlesnake Creek Rd.; after 4 mi., turn right on Lost Valley Lane, and 1 mi. later you're there. Come in at night for the organic dinner. Call ahead for reservations. ($7, non-members $10. Campsites $5 per person. Dinner Mon.-Fri. $6.) Unfortunately, KOAs and RV-only parks monopolize the camping scene around Eugene, but farther east on Rtes. 58 and 126 the immense **Willamette National Forest** is packed with forested campsites. The **Black Canyon Campground,** 28 mi. east of Eugene on Rte. 58 ($3-7), is another option.

If you just have an afternoon hour to spare, canoe or kayak the **Millrace Canal,** which parallels the Willamette for 3 mi. Rent canoes or kayaks from **The Canoe Shack,** 1395 Franklin Blvd. (346-4386), run by University of Oregon students (open summer Mon.-Fri. 12:30-dusk, Sat.-Sun. 10:30am-dusk. $4 per hour, $15 per 24 hrs.). For a taste of the town, head to the **Saturday Market** (686-8885), at 8th and Oak, held weekly April through December.

The granola crowd shops at **Sundance Natural Foods,** 748 E. 24th Ave. (343-9142), at 24th and Hilyard (open daily 9am-11pm). **Keystone Cafe,** 395 W. 5th St. (342-2075), is an eclectic co-op serving vegetarian and vegan food (open daily 7am-3pm). Locals also love **The Glenwood Restaurant,** 1340 Alder (687-0355), at 13th St. (open 24 hrs., except Sun. until 9pm). For some mellow nightlife, head to the **High St. Brewery Cafe,** 1243 High St. (345-4905; open Mon.-Sat. 11am-1am, Sun. noon-1am). **Doc's Pad,** 165 W. 11th St. (683-8101), has good (strong) drinks and live music (open daily 10am-2:15am).

■■■ CRATER LAKE NATIONAL PARK

Mirror-blue Crater Lake, Oregon's only national park, was regarded as sacred by Native American shamans, who forbade their people to look upon it. Iceless in winter and flawlessly circular, the lake plunges from its 6000-ft. elevation to a depth of nearly 2000 ft., making it the nation's deepest lake. This fantastic depth combined with the extreme clarity of the water creates a serene, intensely beautiful effect.

Practical Information Emergency is 911. **Park admission** for cars is $5; hikers and bikers are charged $3 only in summer. **William G. Steel Center** (594-2211), next to the park headquarters, provides free **backcountry camping permits,** details on the area, and road conditions. (Open daily 9am-5pm.) Find **Amtrak** at S. Spring St. depot (884-2822; open daily 7-10:30am and 8:45-10pm), and **Greyhound** at 1200 Klamath Ave. (882-4616; open Mon.-Fri. 6am-5pm, Sat. 6am-4pm).

To get to the park from Portland, take I-5 to Eugene, then Rte. 58 east to U.S. 97 south for 18 mi., then west on Rte. 138. **Rte. 62** cuts through Crater Lake National Park's southwest corner and then heads southwest to **Medford** or southeast to **Klamath Falls,** 24 mi. south of the Rte. 62/U.S. 97 intersection.

Accommodations and Food The park contains two campsites: **Mazama Campground** (594-2511) has 200 sites with no hookups ($11). **Lost Creek Campground** (594-2211), at the southwest corner of the park, has only 16 sites ($5). You may be wise to make your foray to Crater Lake from the **Fort Klamath Lodge Motel** (381-2234), on Rte. 62, 6 mi. from the southern entrance to Crater Lake National Park. (Singles $30. Doubles $35.)

Eating inexpensively in the Crater Lake area is difficult. Buying food at the **Old Fort Store** (381-2345; open summer daily 9am-7pm) in **Fort Klamath,** is the best bet. In Klamath Falls, shop at the 24-hr. grocery store **Safeway** (882-2660) at Pine and 8th St., or try the sandwiches ($4-6) at **Llao Rock Cafe,** in the Rim Village (open daily 8am-8pm). Upstairs, **The Watchman Eatery and Lounge** has burgers ($6 with potato salad) you can munch while looking out on the stillness of Crater Lake, plus a salad bar—all you can eat $6 (open June 10-Sept. 4 daily noon-10pm).

Sights   About 7700 years ago, Mt. Mazama created this pacific scene through one of the Earth's most destructive cataclysms. A massive eruption buried thousands of square miles in the western U.S. under a thick layer of ash and left a deep caldera to be filled with the still waters of **Crater Lake.** This splendid lake is rightfully the center of attention and activity in the park.

   Rim Drive, open only in summer, is a 33-mi. loop high above the lake and leads to some great trails, including **Discovery Point Trail,** where the first pioneer saw the lake in 1853 (1.3 mi. one way), **Garfield Peak Trail** (1.7 mi. one way), and **Watchman Lookout** (.8 mi. one way). If pressed for time, walk the easy 100 yd. from the visitors center down to the **Sinnott Memorial Overlook.** The view is the area's most panoramic and accessible. The steep but rewarding hike up **Mt. Scott** (2½ mi. one way), the park's highest peak (a tad under 9000 ft.), begins from the drive near the lake's eastern edge. The **Cleetwood Trail,** a 1-mi. switchback, is the only route to the lake's edge. From here, the **Lodge Company** (594-2511) offers 2-hr. boat tours on the lake. (Tour schedule varies; 3-9 tours leave per day June 18-Sept. 17; fare $10, under 12 $6.) If you take an early tour, you can be left on **Wizard Island** to be picked up later. Picnics and fishing are allowed, as is swimming, but the surface temperature reaches a maximum of 50°F (10°C). Park rangers lead free walking tours daily in the summer and periodically during the winter. Call the Steel Center for schedules (see Practical Information).

■■■ BEND

Bend yields the best of both weather worlds with temperatures as high as 100°F (36°C) in summer and over 5 ft. of snow in the winter. Bordered by Mt. Bachelor, tthe Deschutes River, and a national forest, the city is an ideal focal point for hikers, bikers, rafters, and adventure-seekers. Put on the map in the 1820s by pioneers who found "Farewell Bend" a convenient river ford, the city has grown to become the cultural mecca east of the Cascades. Bend's young, athletic crowd make the town one of the liveliest and most inexpensife in the Northwest.

Practical Information   Central Oregon Welcome Center, 63085 N. U.S. 97 (382-3221), has good info and free maps (open Mon.-Sat. 9am-5pm, Sun. 11am-3pm). **Deschutes National Forest Headquarters,** 1645 E. U.S. 20 (388-2715), can inform you on forests, recreation, and the wilderness (open Mon.-Fri. 7:45-4:30pm). **Greyhound,** 2045 E. U.S. 20 (382-2151), a few mi. east of town, runs one bus per day to Portland ($20.50) and Klamath Falls ($19.50). (Open Mon.-Fri. 7:30am-noon and 12:30-5:30pm, Sat. 7:30am-noon, Sun. 8-11:30am.) **Hot Lines** include **Central Oregon Battering and Rape Alliance** (800-356-2369 and **Teen Crisis Line** (800-660-0934). Bend's **post Office:** 2300 NE 4th St. (388-1971), at Webster (open Mon.-Fri. 8:30am-5:30pm, Sat. 10am-1pm); **ZIP code:** 97701; **area code:** 503.
   U.S. 97 (3rd St.) bisects Bend. The downtown area lies to the west along the Deschutes River; Wall and Bond St. are the two main arteries.

Accommodations   Most of the cheapest motels are just outside town on 3rd St. **Bend Alpine Hostel (HI/AYH),** 19 SW Century Dr., (389-3813) is 2 blocks from ski and bike rentals and the free shuttle to Mt. Bachelor. From 3rd St., take Franklin west, and follow the Cascade Lakes Tour signs to Century Drive (14th St.). (Laundry and kitchen, linen rental available. Lockout 9:30am-4:30pm, curfew 11pm. Members $12, nonmembers $15.) **Mill Inn,** 642 NW Colorado (389-9198), on the corner of Bond St., is a bed & breakfast in a recently rebuilt hotel and boarding house. Hearty home-cooked breakfast is included. $15 gets you a bunk in the dorm-style "Locker Room" (capacity 4), or splurge for a trim, elegant private room for $32 for one or $36 for two, with shared bath. Reservations are recommended. Go to the brand new and impeccably clean **Deschutes National Forest** which maintains a huge number of campgrounds in the Cascades to the west of town. All have pit toilets; those with drinking water cost $8-12 per night; those without are free. Contact the **Bend Ranger District Office** at 1230 NE 3rd St., Suite A-262 (388-5664).

Food While downtown Bend offers many pleasant cafés, 3rd St. also proffers a variety of good eateries. **Nature's General Store,** in the Wagner Mall on 3rd St. (382-6732), has bulk food, organic produce, and healthy sandwiches (open Mon.-Fri. 9:30am-9pm, Sat. 9:30am-6pm, Sun. 11am-6pm). **West Side Bakery and Cafe,** 1005 NW Galveston (382-3426), is locally famous for its breakfasts and lunches. Virtually everything here is homemade, including the delicious bread. (Open breakfast and lunch only, Mon.-Sat. 7am-3pm, Sun. 7am-2pm.) **Pilt Butte Drive-In Restauarant,** 917 NE Greenwood (U.S. 20) (382-2972), is home of the 18-oz. "Pilot Butte Burger" ($9.50), and many of more manageable size. Breakfasts are huge—for example, #3 (2 eggs and 2 hotcakes for $2.75). (Open daily 6am-9pm.)

Sights The **High Desert Museum** (382-4754), 6 mi south of Bend on U.S. 97, is great, offering exhibits on the fragile ecosystem of the Oregon plateau, realistic and audio-visual exhibitions of the West in days past, and refreshing temporary exhibitions. Coming early in the day is your only hope of beating the crowds. Allow at least a few hours for the visit. Lack of funding has kept the price of admission high, but it's worth it. (Open daily 9am-5pm. $5.50, seniors $5, ages 5-12 $2.75.)

In November, 1990, **Newberry National Volcanic Monument** was established to link together and preserve the volcanic features south of Bend. For an introduction to the area, visit the **Lava Lands Visitor Center** (593-2421), 5 mi. south of the High Desert Museum on U.S. 97. The center has exhibits on the volcanism that created the Cascade Range and shaped the local geography. (Open March to mid-Oct. daily 10am-4pm; Memorial Day-Labor Day 9am-5pm.)

Immediately behind the visitor center is **Lava Butte**, a 500-ft. cinder cone from which many of the nearby lava flows can be viewed. Between Memorial Day and Labor Day, one can take a shuttle bus ($1.50) or walk the 1.5-mi. road. South of the visitor center on U.S. 97 is **Lava River Cave** (593-1456), a 1-mi.-long subterranean lava tube. The entrance to the cave is in a stand of gigantic ponderosa pines, perfect for a picnic. The cave temperature hovers at 42°F (5°C) year-round, so come bundled in warm clothes, and bring a flashlight or propane lantern. (Open May-Oct. 10 daily 9am-6pm. $2, ages 13-17 $1.50, under 13 free. Lantern rental $1.50.)

The central component of the monument is **Newberry Crater**, 18 mi. south of Lava Butte on U.S. 97, then about 15 mi. east on Rte. 21. This diverse volcanic region was formed by many eruptions of Newberry Volcano over millions of years (Newberry is one of three volcanoes in Oregon expected to possibly erupt again "soon"). The caldera in the center of the volcano covers some 500 sq. mi. and contains two lakes, **Paulina Lake** and **East Lake,** whose azure waters are popular for fishing and boating. The crater also contains an enormous **Obsidian Flow,** deposited by an eruption only 1300 years ago; a 1-mi. trail winds among the huge chunks of volcanic glass. Over 150 mi. of trails cross the area, including a 21-mi. loop that circumnavigates the caldera rim. Five campgrounds line the shores of the lakes.

West of Bend, **Century Drive** (Cascade Lakes Hwy.; follow the signs throughout town) makes a dramatic 89-mi. loop past Mt. Bachelor, through the forest, and past the Crane Prairie Reservoir before rejoining U.S. 97. Thirty campgrounds, trout fishing areas, and hiking trails dot the countryside. Allow a full day for the spectacular drive, and pack a picnic lunch.

If you can ski the 9075-ft. **Mt. Bachelor,** with its 3100-ft. vertical drop, you're in good company; Mt. Bachelor is one of the home mountains of the U.S. Ski Team.

(Daily lift passes $33, ages 7-12 $18. Call 800-829-2442 for more info. Chairlifts are open for sightseers during the summer (open daily 10am-4pm; $9, kids $4.50, seniors $6.50) and in the summer a U.S. Forest Service naturalist gives free presentations on local natural history on the summit daily at 11:30am and 2:30pm.

The Three Sisters Wilderness Area, north and west of the Cascade Lakes Highway, is one of Oregon's largest and most popular wilderness areas. A free permit is required to go into the wilderness, but day-hikers can issue themselves permits at most trailheads. No bikes allowed in the wilderness.

Whitewater rafting, although costly, is the number one local recreational activity. Most resorts offer half- to three-day whitewater rafting expeditions, and most companies will pick you up in town. Trips usually run around $65 per person per day, $25 per half day. Two of the most highly regarded are **Hunter Expeditions** (389-8370; ½ day $27, full day $65) and **Inn of the Seventh Mountain** (382-8711; ½ day $22, ages 12 and under $18).

■ NEAR BEND: SISTERS

Nestled against the Cascades, 20 mi. northwest of Bend, is the charming, restored western village of Sisters. Somehow, the tiny town has managed to take an Old West look in order to attract tourist dollars without falling victim to tacky commercialism.

From Sisters, Rte. 126 heads east to Redmond (20 mi.) and Prineville (39 mi.), and joins U.S. 20 for the trip over the Cascades to the west. Rte. 242 heads southwest out of town and over McKenzie Pass to rejoin Rte. 126 on the other side of the Cascades. The highways all blend in town into one street, Cascade St. Almost everything in Sisters is within a block or two of it. The **Sisters Ranger District Station (Deschutes National Forest)** (549-2111), on Cascade St. at the west edge of town, is the place to go for all kinds of recreation info, including a list of nearby campgrounds and the *Day Hike Guide* (free), a catalogue of five nearby hikes from 2 to 10 mi. long (open Mon.-Fri. 7:45am-4:30pm, Sat. 11am-3pm).

A cheap bed is hard to find in Sisters. One option is the **Silver Spur Motel,** on the highway at the west end of town (549-6591), an old building with dim, undistinguished rooms, some with free kitchens. (Singles $33, doubles $36.) Next door, the **Sisters Motor Lodge,** 600 W. Cascade (549-2551), is a step up in both quality and price, with clean, classy rooms for $43-60 in summer, $36-50 in winter. Groups of 3-7 people can rent a room at **Conklin's Guest House,** 69013 Camp Polk Rd. (549-0123), off Cascade at the east end of town for a flat $90 (breakfast included).

The Sisters Ranger District (see above) maintains 26 **campgrounds.** Many of these cluster near **Camp Sherman,** a small community on the Metolius River, 15 mi. northwest of Sisters. The Metolius River campgrounds tend to be the most crowded, and virtually all charge an $8 fee. For free and less frequented camping spots, take Elm St. south from Sisters. The street becomes Forest Rd. 16 and leads to two free campgrounds, **Black Pine Springs** (8 mi. out; 4 sites) and **Driftwood** (17 mi. out; 16 sites). Better yet, cruise 14 mi. west on Rte. 242 to **Lava Camp Lake,** a magnificently isolated, free campground just off of the lava fields of McKenzie Pass.

The **Sisters Rodeo,** the "Biggest Little Show in the World," takes place annually on the second weekend in June and packs an astonishing purse: some $170,000 total attracts big-time wranglers for three days and nights of saddle bronco riding, calf-roping, and steer wrestling, among other events. Tickets are $8-12, and the show usually sells out. (Write the Sisters Rodeo Association, P.O. Box 1018, Sisters, OR 97759, or call 549-0121 for more informatio; 800-827-7522 for tickets.)

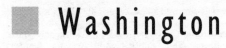
Washington

Geographically, politically, and culturally, Washington is divided by the Cascade Mountains. The personality difference between the state's eastern and western halves is pervasive and long-standing. To "wet-siders" who live near Washington's coast, the term "dry-siders" conjures images of rednecks tearing through the eastern deserts in their Chevy trucks. In the minds of dry-siders, the residents of Seattle and the rest of western Washington are yuppified, liberal freaks too wealthy to respect rural livelihoods or wildlife. What does unify Washingtonians is an independent frame of mind. Like its ideological spectrum, Washington's terrain is all-encompassing: deserts, volcanoes, and the world's only non-tropical rain forest all lie within state boundaries. You can raft on Washington's rivers, sea kayak around the San Juan Islands, and build sand castles on the Strait of Juan de Fuca. Mount Rainier has fantastic hiking, while the Cascades boast perfect conditions for nearly every winter recreational activity. Seattle and Spokane are draped in handsome, green landscapes, proving that natural beauty can be its own selling point.

PRACTICAL INFORMATION

Capital: Olympia.
Visitor Information: Dept. of Economic Development, Tourism Development Division, P.O. Box 42500, Olympia 98504-2500 (206-586-2088 or 206-586-2102, 800-544-1800 for vacation planning guide). Open Mon.-Fri. 9am-5pm. **Washington State Parks and Recreation Commission,** 7150 Cleanwater Lane, KY-11, Olympia 98504 (206-753-5755, May-Aug. in WA 800-562-0990).
Time Zone: Pacific (3 hr. behind Eastern). **Postal Abbreviation:** WA
Sales Tax: 6.5%

■■■ SEATTLE

It seems everybody wants to come to Seattle, the Northwest's largest and most cosmopolitan city. It may be for the setting; Seattle is an isthmus, nearly surrounded by water, with mountain ranges to the east and west. Every hilltop offers an impressive view of Puget Sound, Lake Washington, Mt. Olympus, Mt. Baker, Mt. Rainier, or Mt. St. Helens. Residents spend as much time as possible outdoors, biking in the parks or hiking, climbing, or skiing in the nearby Cascades and Olympic Peninsula. Incredible, sublime outdoor experiences are within a day's drive.

Even those who do stay indoors do so with energetic abandon; Seattle is internationally known for its alternative music scene. The city has spawned musicians such as Jimi Hendrix and Mudhoney. The roar of the "Seattle Sound"—best exemplified by groups like Nirvana, Pearl Jam, Screaming Trees, and Soundgarden—has outshined all other recent developments in rock and roll. The theater community supports Broadway shows and alternative vaudeville, while the opera consistently sells out. Seattle also supports a palette of large-scale museums and parks, small galleries, and personable bistros throughout the downtown.

Whatever you do, don't be dismayed by the drizzle. Although the clouds may seem as permanent as the mountains they mask, the temperature is constant, too, hovering between 40°F and 70°F year-round. Even in winter, light drizzle is standard; it rarely snows. Occasionally the skies clear and Seattlites run to the country.

PRACTICAL INFORMATION

Emergency: 911.
Visitor Information: Seattle-King County Visitors Bureau, 8th and Pike St. (461-5840; fax 461-5855), on the 1st floor of the convention center. Open Mon.-Fri. 8:30am-5pm; summer Mon.-Fri. 8:30am-5pm, Sat.-Sun. 10am-4pm. **National**

Park Service, Pacific Northwest Region, 915 2nd Ave. #442 (220-7450). Open Mon.-Fri. 8am-4:30pm.

Airport: Seattle-Tacoma International (Sea-Tac) (433-5217 for general info) on Federal Way, south of Seattle proper. **Sea-Tac Visitors Information Center** (433-5218), near the central baggage claim, helps with transportation concerns.

Amtrak (800-872-7245), King St. Station, 3rd and Jackson St. *See Mileage Chart.* Station open daily 6am-5:30pm; ticket office open daily 6:30am-5pm.

Greyhound (800-231-2222 or 628-5526), 8th Ave. and Stewart St. *See Mileage Chart.* Ticket office open daily 5:30am-9pm and midnight-2am.

Public Transportation: Metro Transit, 821 2nd Ave. (24-hr. information 553-3000; TTD service 684-1739), in the Exchange Building downtown. Open Mon.-Fri. 8am-5pm. Fares are based on a 2-zone system. Zone 1 includes everything within the city limits ($1.10 during peak hours, 85¢ off-peak); Zone 2 comprises anything outside the city limits ($1.45 peak, $1.10 off-peak). Ages 5-18 75¢. With reduced fare permits ($1), over 64 and disabled pay 25¢ to go anywhere at any time. Peak hours in both zones are generally Mon.-Fri. 6-9am and 3-6pm. Exact fare required. Transfers valid for 2 hrs. and for Waterfront Streetcars. Weekend all-day passes $1.70. Ride free 4am-9pm within the **"Magic Carpet"** area downtown, bordered by Jackson St. on the south, 6th Ave. and I-5 on the east, Battery St. on the north, and the waterfront on the west.

Ferries: Washington State Ferries, (800-84-FERRY in WA, or 464-6400) Colman Dock, Pier 52, downtown. Service from downtown to: Bainbridge Island, Bremerton in the Kitsap Peninsula, and Vashon Island. Service from Fauntleroy in West Seattle to: Southworth in the Kitsap Peninsula and Vashon Island. Ferries leave daily, and frequently, about 5am-about 2am.

Car Rental: A-19.95-Rent-A-Car, 804 N. 145th St. (365-1995). $20 per day ($25 if under 21); 10¢ per mi. after 100 mi. Free delivery. Drivers under 21 welcome, but must have verifiable auto insurance. Credit card required. **Auto Driveaway** (235-0880) hires people to drive their cars to various locations across the U.S.

Bike Rentals: The Bicycle Center, 4529 Sand Point Way (523-8300). $3 per hr. (2-hr. min.), $15 per day. Credit card or license required as deposit. Open Mon.-Fri. 10am-6pm, Sat. 9am-6pm, Sun. 10am-5pm.

Crisis Clinic: 461-3222. 24 hrs. **Seattle Rape Relief:** 1905 S. Jackson St., #102 (632-7273). Crisis counseling, advocacy, and prevention training. 24 hrs.

Post Office: (442-6340), Union St. and 3rd Ave. downtown. Open Mon.-Fri. 8am-5:30pm. **ZIP Code:** 98101.

Area Code: 206.

Seattle is a long, skinny city stretched out north to south between long, skinny **Puget Sound** on the west and long, skinny **Lake Washington** on the east. The city is split by Lake Union and a string of locks, canals, and bays. These link the saltwater of Puget Sound with the freshwater of Lake Washington. Downtown, avenues run northwest to southeast and streets southwest to northeast. After Western Ave., the avenues run numerically up the hill. Downtown streets run south to north in pairs. Outside downtown, avenues run north to south and streets east to west, with only a few exceptions. The city is split into **quadrants:** 1000 1st Ave. NW is a long hike from 1000 1st Ave. S.

The city is easily accessible by **car** via **I-5,** running north-south through the city, east of downtown; and by **I-90** from the east, ending at I-5 southeast of downtown. From I-5, get to downtown by taking any of the exits from James to Stewart St. (including **Pioneer Square, Pike Place Market,** and the **waterfront**). Take the Mercer St./Fairview Ave. exit to the **Seattle Center.** The Denny Way exit leads to **Capitol Hill,** and farther north, the 45th St. exit will take you to the **University District. Rte. 99** is less crowded than I-5, and is often the better choice downtown.

ACCOMMODATIONS

The **Seattle International Hostel** is the best option for the budget traveler staying downtown. For those tired of the urban scene, the **Vashon Island Hostel** (sometimes called "Seattle B") is ideal (see Near Seattle: Vashon Island). **Pacific Bed and**

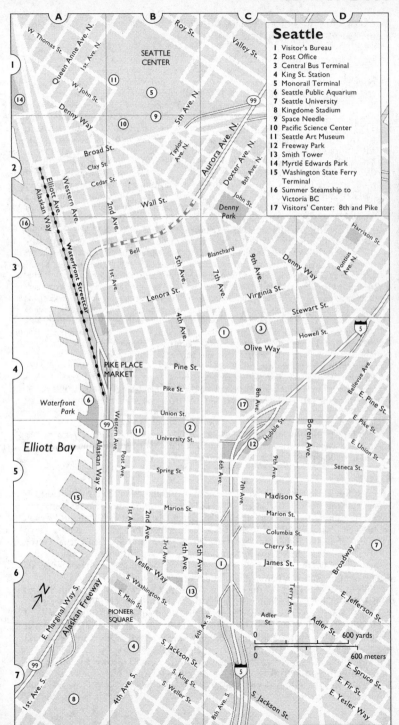

Seattle

1 Visitor's Bureau
2 Post Office
3 Central Bus Terminal
4 King St. Station
5 Monorail Terminal
6 Seattle Public Aquarium
7 Seattle University
8 Kingdome Stadium
9 Space Needle
10 Pacific Science Center
11 Seattle Art Museum
12 Freeway Park
13 Smith Tower
14 Myrtle Edwards Park
15 Washington State Ferry Terminal
16 Summer Steamship to Victoria BC
17 Visitors' Center: 8th and Pike

Breakfast, 701 NW 60th St., Seattle 98107 (784-0539), can set you up with a single room in a B&B in the $40-70 range (open Mon.-Fri. 9am-5pm).

Seattle International Hostel (HI-AYH), 84 Union St. (622-5443), at Western Ave. Take Metro #174, 184, or 194 from the airport. 139 beds, common kitchen open 24 hrs., immaculate facilities, modern amenities, and a friendly, knowledgeable staff. In summer, the hostel is always full and members receive priority. Make reservations early. In summer, there is a supplemental hostel for overflow. Offers discount tickets for Aquarium and Omnidome. Sleep sacks required (linen rental $2). 5-day max. stay in summer. Front desk open 7am-2am. Check-out 10:30am. Room lock-out 11am-2pm, but common room open at all times. No curfew. IBN reservations available. $14, nonmembers $17.

YMCA, 909 4th Ave. (382-5000), near the Madison St. intersection. Men and women welcome; must be over 18. Small, well-kept rooms. TV lounge on each floor, laundry facilities, and swimming pool and fitness facilities. Bring your own bedding and lock. Check-out by noon. No curfew. HI-AYH members: bunk in a 4-person room $18, singles $30, doubles $34. Nonmembers: singles $34, with bath $46, doubles $43.50, with bath $51.

Green Tortoise Backpacker's Guesthouse, 715 2nd Ave. N. (322-1222; fax 282-9075), on the southern slope of Queen Anne Hill, 3 blocks from the Space Needle. 40 beds in 11 rooms and a common kitchen with adjoining deck and garden. Library/reading room with view of the city. No curfew. Quiet hours after 11pm. Laundry $1. Rooms $11. Shared doubles $20. Private doubles $30. Call for pickup.

YWCA, 1118 5th Ave. (461-4888), near the YMCA. Take any 4th Ave. bus to Seneca St. *Women only,* ages under 18 require advance arrangement. Great security; front desk staffed 24 hrs. Good, central location. Shared kitchen facilities. 2-week max. stay. No curfew. Singles $31, with bath $36. Doubles $42, with bath $48. Weekly: singles $186, with bath $216. Health center use $5. Key deposit $2.

Commodore Hotel, 2013 2nd Ave. (448-8868), at Virginia. Clean, feels safe. Singles $42, with bath $47, with 2 beds and bath $54.

Moore Motel, 1926 2nd Ave. (448-4851 and 448-4852), at Virginia. Next to the historic Moore Theater. Big rooms include 2 beds, bath, and TV. Singles $34. Doubles $39. HI-AYH member overflow from the full hostel: singles $30, doubles $35.

Park Plaza Motel, 4401 Aurora Ave. N (632-2101). Just north of the Aurora bridge; take bus #6 to 46th Ave. or #5 to 43rd and Fremont. Friendly and surprisingly quiet. Bare rooms and halls. Singles $30. Doubles from $32.

Nites Inn, 11746 Aurora Ave. N (365-3216). Take bus #6. One of the many motels that line Aurora north of 85th St., but the rooms are larger than most. Cable TV and free local calls. Singles $38. Doubles $42.

FOOD

The best fish, produce, and baked goods can be purchased in the crowd-filled **Pike Place Market** since 1907 (open Mon.-Sat. 6:30am-6pm, Sun. 6:30am-5pm). For excellent ethnic food, head for the **International District,** along King and Jackson St., between 5th and 8th Ave., which crowds together immigrants—some of them excellent chefs—from China, Japan, the Philippines, and Southeast Asia. Fierce competition keeps prices low and quality high. Great food and interesting clubs abound in the **U District** near the University of Washington. Washington's famous fishing industries and orchards offer wonderful salmon, apples, and cherries.

You can buy fish right off the boats at **Fisherman's Wharf,** at NW 54th St. and 30th Ave. NW in Ballard, along the route of bus #43. The wharf is usually open from 8am to 3 or 4pm. Or visit one of Seattle's active **food coops,** such as those at 6518 Fremont Ave. N (in Green Lake) and at 6504 20th NE (in the Ravenna District north of the university). Also in Ravenna is a fine produce stand, **Rising Sun Farms and Produce,** 6505 15th Ave. NE (524-9741; open daily 8am-8pm).

Seattle boasts more coffee shops than any other city. **Uptown Espresso,** 525 Queen Anne Ave. N (281-8669) at the base of Queen Anne, has a well-established reputation. Most Seattlites develop strict loyalties to several obscure street corner carts for their espresso; brand-wise, the best bet is the locally roasted **Starbucks** or **SBC** (Stuart Bros. or "Seattle's Best"). Both have many shops downtown.

Soundview Cafe (623-5700), on the mezzanine level in the Main Arcade, just to the left of the largest fish stall. This wholesome self-serve sandwich-and-salad bar offers fresh food. Get a View Special (eggs and potatoes) for $2.90, egg salad for $3.25, or bring a bag lunch: the cafe offers public seating and a pleasant atmosphere. Open daily 7am-5pm.

Three Girls Bakery (622-1045), at Post and Pike Pl. Order to go or sit in the cafe. The rows of bread and pastry will make you drool, not to mention the fresh-bread aroma. Mammoth apple fritters (95¢). Open Mon.-Sat. 7am-6pm, Sun. 8am-6pm.

Tai Tung, 655 S. King St. (622-7372). A Chinese diner. The busiest hours at Tai Tung are 1-3am, when the munchies take hold of university students. Waiters here rise to the occasion; they're likely to learn your name by the second night you're in. Entrees $7-8. Open Mon.-Sat. 10am-3:30am, Sun. 10am-1:30am.

Hamburger Mary's, 401 Broadway E (325-6565), in the ritzy Broadway Market. This branch of Portland's famous H.M. is a hot-spot for the gay crowd. Hamburgers around $5. Entrees under $12. Open Mon.-Fri. 10am-2am, Sat.-Sun. 9am-2am.

Cafe Paradiso, 1005 E. Pike (322-6960). A bit off the geographical beaten-path, this proud-to-be-alternative cafe gives you your RDA of both caffeine and counterculture. Muffin and croissant fare. Open Mon.-Sat. 7am-1am, Sun. 9am-1am.

Asia Deli, 4235 University Way NE (632-2364). Quick service and generous portions of delicious Vietnamese and Thai food. Almost all the dishes are under $4, and all are prepared without MSG. Open daily 11am-9pm.

Phnom Penh Noodle Soup House, 414 Maynard Ave. S (682-5690). Phnomenal Cambodian cuisine. Head to the tiny upstairs dining room for a view of the park and a large bowl of noodles. Try the Phnom Penh Noodle Special; some people come here weekly and never order anything else (well, there are only six items on the menu). Everything $3.90. Open Mon.-Tues. and Thurs.-Sun. 8:30am-6pm.

Viet My Restaurant, 129 Prefontaine Pl. S (382-9923), near 4th and Washington. Hard to find, but the consistently delicious Vietnamese food at great prices is worth the search. Try *bo la lot* (beef in rice pancakes, $3.50) or shrimp curry ($4.25). Avoid the lunch rush. Open Mon.-Sat. 11am-9pm.

House of Hong Restaurant, 409 8th Ave. S (622-7997), at Jackson. The most popular *dim sum* in town at $1.80-3 per dish; served daily 11am-3pm. Open Mon.-Thurs. 11am-10pm, Fri. 11am-midnight, Sat. 10:30am-midnight, Sun. 10:30am-10pm. Reservations and semi-formal dress recommended. Cocktail lounge Mon.-Fri. 11am-midnight, Sat. 10:30am-midnight, Sun. 10:30am-11pm.

SIGHTS AND ACTIVITIES

The best way to take in the city and its skyline is from one of the **ferries** that leave the waterfront at frequent intervals (see Practical Information above). You can get a good look at most sights in one day—most are walking distance from each other, within the Metro's free zone. You can explore Pike Place, waterfront, Pioneer Square, and the International District in one easy excursion. Or skip the downtown thing altogether and take a rowboat out onto Lake Union, bike along Lake Washington, or hike through Discovery Park.

The new **Seattle Art Museum,** 100 University Way (654-3100 for a recording, 345-3121 Wed.-Fri. 1-5pm for a live voice), near 1st and University Way, boasts a stunning design by Philadelphia architect Robert Venturi. There's art *inside* the building, too. (Call for free tour schedule. Open Fri.-Wed. 10am-5pm, Thurs. 10am-9pm. $6, students and seniors $4, under 12 free.) One block north of the museum on 1st Ave., inside the Alcade Plaza Building, is the **Seattle Art Museum Gallery,** featuring current art, sculpture, jewelry, and prints by local artists. Browse for free.

Lunatic fish- and produce-mongers bellow at customers and at each other while street performers offer their own entertainment to the crowds at **Pike Place Market.** Visit between 7 and 9am, when the fish are yawning and the fruit is freshest. In summer (10am-5pm) tourists and locals flood the market, providing excellent people-watching opportunities. At **86 Pike Place** on the corner (you can't miss it), the famous fish flingers will sing your order in chorus—and you thought fish couldn't fly. At the south end of the Market begins the **Pike Place Hillclimb,** a set of staircases leading down past chic shops and ethnic restaurants to Alaskan Way and the waterfront. (An elevator is also available.) The waterfront docks once accepted shiploads of gold from the 1897 Klondike gold rush. The excellent **Seattle Aquarium** (386-4320) sits at the base of the Hillclimb at Pier 59, near Union St. Outdoor tanks recreate the ecosystems of salt marshes and tide pools. (Open daily 10am-5pm. $6.75, seniors $5.25, ages 6-18 $4.25, ages 3-5 $1.75.)

Westlake Park, on Pike St. between 5th and 4th Ave., with its Art Deco patterns and Wall of Water, is a good place to kick back and listen to steel drums. This small park is bordered by the original **Nordstrom's** and the new **Westlake Center.** (*Let's Go* travelers may find **Nordstrom's Rack,** at 2nd and Pine, more appealing.) Take the **monorail** from the Westlake Center; for 90¢ (ages 5-12 60¢, seniors 35¢) to the **Seattle Center,** every 15 min. from 9am to midnight. Between Denny Way and W. Mercer St., and 1st and 5th Ave., the Center has eight gates, each with a locating map. The **Pacific Science Center** (443-2001), within the park, houses some of Seattle's best entertainment: a laserium (443-2850) and an IMAX theater (443-4629). Evening IMAX shows run Wednesday through Sunday (tickets to IMAX *and* the museum $8, seniors and ages 6-13 $7, ages 2-5 $5.50). The evening laser shows quake to music by groups like U2, Genesis, Metallica, and Led Zeppelin (Tues. $2.50; Wed.-Sun. $5.50). Left over from the 1962 World's Fair, the **Space Needle** (443-2111), houses an observation tower and dizzy, mediocre restaurant.

From the waterfront or downtown, it's just a few blocks to historic **Pioneer Square,** where 19th-century warehouses and office buildings were restored in the 1970s. The *Complete Browser's Guide to Pioneer Square,* available in area bookstores, includes a short history and walking tour of the area, plus listings of all the shops, galleries, restaurants, and museums in the square. The earliest Seattlites settled on the site of Pioneer Square. "Doc" Maynard, a notorious early resident, gave a plot of land here to one Henry Yesler on t he condition that he build a steam-powered lumber mill. Logs dragged down the steep grade of Yesler Way fed the mill, earning that street the epithet "Skid Row." Years later, the center of activity moved north, precipitating the decline of Pioneer Square and giving the term "skid row" its present meaning as a neighborhood of poverty and despair. The **Klondike Gold Rush National Historic Park,** 117 S. Main St. (553-7220), is not so much a park as an "interpretive center" that depicts the lives and fortunes of miners. To add some levity to this history of shattered dreams, the park screens Charlie Chaplin's 1925 classic, *The Gold Rush,* on the first Sunday of every month at 3pm (open daily 9am-5pm; free). While in Pioneer Square, browse through the local art galleries, distributors for many of the Northwest's prominent artists. The first Thursday evening of each month, the art community sponsors **First Thursday,** a well-dressed and well-attended gallery walk. Call a Pioneer Square gallery for info; **Flury and Co. Gallery,** 322 1st Ave. S (587-0260), has vintage photo portraits of Native American life.

When Seattle nearly burned to the ground in 1889, an ordinance was passed to raise the city 35 ft. At first, shops below the new elevated streets remained open for business and were connected to the upper city by an elaborate network of ladders. In 1907 the city moved upstairs permanently, and the underground city was sealed off. Tours of the vast underworld are now given by **Bill Speidel's Underground Tours** (682-4646). Make reservations at least one day in advance.

Capitol Hill's leftist and gay communities set the tone for its nightspots. The hill's coffee shops and restaurants offer the great people-watching. Explore Broadway and its cross streets, or stroll down the blocks east and north to see the Victorian homes of the hill's residential area. Bus #10 runs on 15th St.; #7 cruises Broadway.

University District

The immense **University of Washington** (colloquially known as "U-Dub"), north of downtown between Union and Portage Bays, supports a colorful array of funky shops, ethnic restaurants, and a slew of coffeehouses. Most of the good restaurants, jazz clubs, cinemas, and cafes are within a few blocks of **University Way.** Ask for "University Way," however, and be prepared for puzzled looks; it's known around here as **"Th'Ave"** (one contracted syllable). To reach the University, take any one of buses #70-74 from downtown, or bus #7 or 43 from Capitol Hill. Join the other 33,000 students milling around, the **"U District,"** but first stop by the friendly, helpful **visitors center,** 4014 University Way NE (543-9198), to pick up a campus map and to obtain info about the University (open Mon.-Fri. 8am-5pm). On the campus, visit the **Thomas Burke Memorial Washington State Museum** (543-5590), at NE 45th St. and 17th Ave. NE, in the northwest corner of the campus. The museum exhibits a superb collection about the Pacific Northwest's Native nations. (Open daily 10am-5pm. Suggested donation $3, seniors and students $2.) The **Henry Art Gallery,** 15th Ave. NE and NE 41st St. (543-2280), has excellent exhibits. Stop in before you stroll the campus lawns. (Open Tues.-Wed. and Fri.-Sun. 11am-5pm, Thurs. 10am-9pm. $3.50, seniors and students $2, under 12 and Thurs. free.) The **UW Arts Ticket Office,** 4001 University Way NE (543-4880), has tickets for all events (open Mon.-Fri. 10:30am-4:30pm).

Students often cross town for drinks in the **Queen Anne** neighborhood, and the intervening neighborhood, **Fremont,** basks in the jovial atmosphere. Fremont is the home of **Archie McPhee's,** 3510 Stone Way (545-8344), a shrine to pop culture and plastic absurdity. People of the punk and funk persuasion make pilgrimages from as far as the record stores of Greenwich Village in Manhattan just to handle the notorious **slug selection.** You can get to Archie's on the Aurora Hwy. (Rte. 99), or take bus #26. The store is east of the Hwy. between 35th and 36th, two blocks north of Lake Union (open Mon.-Fri. 10am-6pm, Sat. 10am-5pm).

The International District

Three blocks east of Pioneer Square, up Jackson on King St., is Seattle's International District. Though sometimes still called "Chinatown" by Seattlites, this area is now home to immigrants from all over Asia, and their descendants. Start off your tour of the district by ducking into the **Wing Luke Memorial Museum,** 414 8th St. (623-5124). This tiny museum houses a permanent exhibit on the different Asian nationalities in Seattle, and temporary exhibits by local Asian artists. Thursdays are always free. (Open Tues.-Fri. 11am-4:30pm, Sat.-Sun. noon-4pm. $2.50, seniors and students $1.50, ages 5-12 75¢.) Other landmarks include the **Tsutakawa sculpture** at the corner of S Jackson and Maynard St. and the gigantic dragon mural in **Hing Hay Park** at S King and Maynard St. The community gardens at Main and Maynard St. provide a peaceful and well-tended retreat from the downtown sidewalks.

Waterways, Parks and the Great Outdoors

A string of attractions festoon the waterways linking Lake Washington and Puget Sound. Houseboats and sailboats fill **Lake Union.** Here, the **Center for Wooden Boats,** 1010 Valley St. (382-2628; open daily 11am-6pm), rents rowboats ($8-12 per hr.), and sailboats ($10-15 per hr.). **Kelly's Landing,** 1401 NE Boat St. (547-9909), below the UW campus, rents canoes on Lake Union. (Sailboats $10-20 per hr., also day rates. 2-hr. min. Open normally Mon.-Fri. 10am-dusk, Sat.-Sun. 9am-dusk.)

Climb over to the **fish ladder** on the south side of the locks to watch trout and salmon hurl themselves over 21 concrete steps on their journey from the sea. Take bus #43 from the U District or #17 from downtown. On the northwestern shore of the city lies the **Golden Gardens Park,** in the Loyal Heights neighborhood, between NW 80th and NW 95th St., an ideal spot for a picnic. Several expensive restaurants line the piers to the south, and unobstructed views of the Olympic Mountains almost justify the prices of their uniformly excellent seafood.

Directly across town, on Puget Sound, is **Alki Beach Park,** a thin strip of beach wrapped around residential West Seattle. Take bus #36. The water is chilling, but the **views** of downtown and the Olympic Mountains are outstanding.

Directly north of Lake Union, exercisers run, ride, and skate around **Green Lake.** Take bus #16 from downtown Seattle to Green Lake. Whoever named Green Lake wasn't kidding; even a quick dunk results in gobs of green algae clinging to your body. Next to the lake is Woodland Park and the **Woodland Park Zoo,** 5500 Phinney Ave. N (684-4034), best reached from Rte. 99 or N. 50th St. Take bus #5 from downtown. The park itself is shaggy, but the animals's habitats seem realistic. (Open daily 9:30am-6pm, $6.50; ages 6-17, seniors and disabled $5, ages 3-5 $4.)

Many **whitewater rafting** outfitters are based in the Seattle area, even though the rapids are hours away by car. Over 50 companies compete for a growing market. A good way to secure an inexpensive trip is to call outfitters and quote competitors's prices at them; they are often willing to undercut one another. Scour the "Guides" section in the Yellow Pages. In recent years rafting companies have attempted to subject themselves to a regulatory bureaucracy of their own making, **River Outfitters of Washington (ROW)** (485-1427), which sets safety guidelines for its members. Even if your outfitter does not belong to ROW, be sure it lives up to ROW's basic safety standards. Don't hesitate to spend the extra dollars to ensure the highest level of safety. Private boaters should remember that whitewater is unpredictable and potentially dangerous; *always* scout out new rivers before running them. ROW has a list of tips for private boaters, and outfitters can give you the scoop on navigable Washington rivers.

The **Northwest Outdoor Center,** 2100 Westlake Ave. (281-9694), on Lake Union, holds instructional programs in **whitewater** and **sea kayaking** during the spring, summer, and fall. (Two-evening introduction to sea kayaking $40 if you have your own boat. Equipment rentals available.) The center also leads excursions, sea kayaking through the San Juan Islands, or **backpacking and paddling** through the North Cascades (open Mon.-Fri. 10am-8pm, Sat.-Sun. 10am-6pm).

Skiing near Seattle is great. **Alp Rental, Ski-Acres,** and **Snoqualmie** co-sponsor an info number (232-8182), which gives out conditions and lift ticket rates for all three. **Crystal Mountain** (663-2265) is reached by Rte. 410 south out of Seattle.

Since the Klondike gold rush, Seattle has been one of the foremost cities in the world for outfitting wilderness expeditions. Besides Army-Navy surplus stores and campers' supply shops (try **Federal Army and Navy Surplus,** 2112 1st Ave.; 443-1818; open Mon.-Sat. 9:30am-6pm), the city is home to many world-class outfitters. **Recreational Equipment Inc. Coop (REI Coop),** 1525 11th Ave. (323-8333), is the favored place to buy high-quality mountaineering and water recreation gear. Take bus #10. The salespeople are very knowledgeable about hiking in the area. For a few dollars you can join the Coop and receive a year-end rebate on your purchases. REI has a bulletin board where lone hikers advertise for hiking companions. The company also offers its own backpacking and climbing trips. (Open Mon.-Tues. 10am-6pm, Wed.-Fri. 10am-9pm, Sat. 9:30am-6pm, Sun. noon-5pm.)

ENTERTAINMENT

The **Seattle Opera** (389-7676, open Mon.-Fri. 9am-5pm, or TicketMaster at 292-2787) performs in the Opera House in the Seattle Center throughout the winter. The popularity of the program requires that you order tickets well in advance; rush tickets are sometimes available 15 min. before curtain ($8 and up). Write to the Seattle Opera, P.O. Box 9248, Seattle 98109. During lunch hours in the summertime, the free, city-sponsored **"Out to Lunch"** series (623-0340) brings everything from reggae to folk dancing to the parks and squares of Seattle.

With the second-largest number of professional companies in the U.S., Seattle hosts an exciting array of first-run plays and alternative works. You can often get **rush tickets** at nearly half price on the day of the show (with cash only) from **Ticket/Ticket** (324-2744). The **Seattle Repertory Theater,** 155 Mercer (443-2222), performs in the **Bagley Wright Theater** in Seattle Center. (Tickets for weekends and opening nights $16-32. Other nights and Sun. matinee $14-30. Student and senior rush tickets 10 min. before show with ID for $7.) Other theaters to check out: **A Contemporary Theater (ACT),** 100 W. Roy (285-5110), at the base of Queen Anne Hill; the **Annex Theatre,** 1916 4th Ave. (728-0933); **The Empty Space Theatre,** 3509 Fremont Ave. N (547-7500; tickets $7-23).

THE PACIFIC NW

Seattle is also a *cinema paradiso*. Most of the theaters that screen non-Hollywood films are on Capitol Hill and in the University District. Most matinee shows (before 6pm) cost $4—after 6pm, expect to pay $6.50. **The Egyptian,** 801 E. Pine St. (323-4978), on Capitol Hill, is best known for hosting the **Seattle Film Festival.** Half the fun of seeing a movie at **The Harvard Exit,** 807 E. Roy (323-8986), on Capitol Hill, is the theater itself, a converted residence—the lobby was once someone's living room. Arrive early for complimentary cheese and crackers over a game of chess, checkers, or backgammon. (Tickets at both $6.50, seniors and kids $4.)

At the **Kingdome,** 201 S. King St. (340-2100 or 340-2128), down 1st Ave., the **Mariners** play baseball. Tickets $15 on the 3rd base line (206-628-0888 or 292-5454; open Mon.-Sat. 8am-9pm, Sun. 8am-6pm). Sunday is senior discount day. The **Seahawks** play football here. The **Seattle Supersonics** (281-5800) is the only Seattle team ever to win a national title, and their basketball games in the Coliseum in Seattle Center attract a religious following.The **University of Washington Huskies** football team has dominated recently. Call (543-2200) for ticket info.

NIGHTLIFE

The best spot to go for guaranteed good beer, live music, and big crowds is **Pioneer Square.** Most of the bars around the Square participate in a **joint cover** ($10) that will let you wander from bar to bar and sample the bands you like. **Fenix Cafe and Fenix Underground** (343-7740), **Central Tavern** (622-0209), and the **Swan Cafe** (343-5288) all rock and roll, while **Larry's** (624-7665) and **New Orleans** (622-2563) feature great jazz and blues nightly. All the Pioneer Square clubs shut down at 2am Friday and Saturday nights, and at around midnight on weeknights. The Northwest produces a variety of local beers, some sold in area stores but most only on tap in bars. Popular brews include **Grant's, Imperial Russian Stout, India Pale Ale, Red Hook, Ballard Bitter, Black Hook,** and **Yakima Cider.**

The Trolleyman Pub, 3400 Phinney Ave. N (548-8000). In the back of the Red Hook Ale Brewery, which rolls the most popular kegs on campus to U of W students. Early hours make it a mellow spot to listen to good acoustic music and contemplate the newly-made bubbles in a fresh pint, especially a pint of Nut Brown Ale. Open Mon.-Thurs. 8:30am-11pm, Fri. 8:30am-midnight, Sat. noon-midnight, Sun. noon-7pm.

Off Ramp, 109 Eastlake Ave. E (628-0232). Among the most popular venues of the local music scene. Always loud; wild at times. Open 5pm-2am daily. Cover varies.

Under the Rail (448-1900), 5th and Battery. This newest and largest downtown club offers local music (cover $4-5) and the occasional national tour. DJ and dancing on nights without concerts. Loud. Hours change nightly according to show times. Often open past 2am. Always open Sat. midnight-5am.

OK Hotel, 212 Alaskan Way S (621-7903). One cafe, one bar, one building. All-ages establishment serves beer, wine, coffee, and dessert. Just below Pioneer Square toward the waterfront. Open Sun.-Thurs. 6am-3am, Fri.-Sat. 8am-4am. Occasional cover charge up to $6. Call 386-9934 for the coffee house.

Weathered Wall, 1921 5th Ave. (448-5688). An audience as diverse and artistic as its offerings (poetry readings to punk). The Weathered Wall is always interesting, and promotes audience interaction. Open Tues.-Sun. 9pm-2am. Cover $3-7.

Comet Tavern, 922 E Pike (323-9853), in the Capitol Hill area. Mixed crowd, no cover, and you can add your tip to the growing sculpture of dollar bills stuck to the ceiling. Open daily noon-2am.

The Vogue, 2018 1st Ave. (443-0673). A rockin' dance place for the black-clad and/or angst-ridden. Features local alternative music. Open daily 9pm-2am

The University Bistro, 4315 University Way NE (547-8010). Live music (everything from blues to reggae) nightly. Happy hours (4-7pm) feature pints of Bud for $1.25, pitchers $4. Cover $2 Tues., $3-5 Wed.-Sat., free Sun.-Mon. Open Mon.-Fri. 11am-2am, Sat. 6pm-2am.

Murphy's Pub (634-2110), at Meridian Ave. N and N. 45th St., in Wallingford, west of the U District. Take bus #43. A classic Irish pub with a mile-long beer list. Popular with a young crowd, Murphy's has live Irish and folk music Fri. and Sat. (cover $2). Open mike on Wed. Open daily 11:30am-2am.

Re-Bar, 1144 Howell (233-9873). A gay bar for those who like dancing on the wild side, depending on the night. Open daily 9pm-2am. Cover $5.

■ NEAR SEATTLE: VASHON ISLAND

Only a short ferry ride from Seattle and an even shorter ferry hop from Tacoma, Vashon Island remains inexplicably invisible to most Seattlites—green forests of Douglas firs, rolling cherry orchards, strawberry fields, and wildflowers cover the island during the summer. Four different **Washington State Ferries** can get you to Vashon Island. Call 800-84-FERRY for all the details.

The island is wonderful for **biking**, and **Point Robinson Park** is a gorgeous spot for a picnic (from Vashon Hwy. take Ellisburg to Dockton to Pt. Robinson Rd.). More than 500 acres of hiking trails weave their way through the woods in the middle of the island, and several lovely walks start from the **Vashon Island Ranch/Hostel (HI-AYH)** 12119 SW Cove Rd. (463-2592). The hostel, sometimes called **Seattle B,** is really the island's only accommodation, and it is itself one of the main reasons to come here. Judy will come pick you up if the hour is reasonable, and she has never turned a hosteler away. "Seattle B" has free pancakes for breakfast, free use of old bikes, free campfire wood, free volleyball games in the afternoon, and a caring manager. When all beds are full, you can pitch a tent (open year-round; tents and beds $9, nonmembers $12). Most hostelers get creative in the kitchen with supplies from **Thriftway** downtown (open daily 8am-9pm). For **B&B** info, call 463-3556.

■■■ SAN JUAN ISLANDS

The San Juan Islands are an accessible treasure. Bald eagles spiral above haggard hillsides, pods of orcas spout offshore, and despite the lush vegetation it never seems to rain. An excellent guide to the area is *The San Juan Islands Afoot and Afloat* by Marge Mueller ($10), available on the islands and in Seattle.

Ferries depart Anacortes on the mainland about nine times per day on a route that stops at **Lopez, Shaw, Orcas,** and **San Juan Islands.** Purchase ferry tickets in Anacortes. You pay only on westbound trips to or between the islands; no charge is levied on eastbound traffic. Save money by traveling directly to the westernmost island on your itinerary, and then make your way back to the mainland island by island. Foot passengers travel in either direction between the islands free of charge. For specific departure times and rates, call **Washington State Ferries** (464-6400; in WA 800-542-0810). On peak travel days, arrive with your vehicle at least 1 hour prior to scheduled departure. The ferry authorities accept only cash. San Juan Islands's **area code:** 206.

■ SAN JUAN ISLAND

San Juan may be the last stop on the ferry route, but it is still the most frequently visited island, providing the traveler with all the beauty of San Juan and all the comforts of **Friday Harbor,** the largest town in the archipelago. Since the ferry docks right in town, this island is also the easiest to explore. The **Whale Museum,** 62 1st St. (378-4710), displays skeletons, sculptures, and information on new research. (Open daily 10am-5pm; in winter daily 11am-4pm. $3, seniors and students $2.50, under 12 $1.50.) **Lime Kiln State Park** provides the best ocean vista for **whale-watching** of all of the islands. Part of the **San Juan National Historical Park** is the **British Camp,** which lies on West Valley Rd. on the sheltered **Garrison Bay** (take Mitchell Bay Rd. east from West Side Rd.). Here, four original buildings have been preserved, including the barracks, now used as an **interpretive center.** If you're eager to **fish** or **clam,** pick up a free copy of *Salmon, Shellfish, Marine Fish Sport Fishing Guide,* for details on regulations and limits at **Friday Harbor Hardware and Marine,** 270 Spring St. (378-4622; open Mon.-Sat. 8am-6pm, Sun. 10am-4pm). They also give hunting and fishing licenses, which are required on the islands. For the low down on bike rentals, tours, and the island's sights check with the **chamber of commerce** (468-3663), on Front St. at the Ferry Terminal.

San Juan County Park, 380 Westside Rd. (378-2992), 10 mi. west of Friday Harbor on Smallpox and Andrews Bays, has cold water and flush toilets, but no RV hookups. Sites for those with vehicles are $14. Hiker/biker sites are $4.50. **Lakedale Campgrounds,** 2627 Roche Harbor Rd. (378-2350), 4 mi. from Friday Harbor, has attractive grounds surrounded by 50 acres of lakes; boat rentals and swimming available. (Sites for 1-2 people $15, July-Aug. $18, plus $3.50 per each additional person. Open April 1-Oct. 15.) Hard to find, but worth it, **Katrina's,** 65 Nichols St. (378-7290), behind the Funk 'n Junk "antique" store, has local organic salads, freshly baked bread, and gigantic cookies (50¢). (Open Mon.-Sat. noon-5pm.)

■ ORCAS ISLAND

Mt. Constitution overlooks Puget Sound from its 2409-ft. summit atop Orcas Island, the largest island of the San Juan group. In the mountain's shadow dwells a small population of retirees, artists, and farmers in understated homes surrounded by the red bark of madrona trees and greenery. Orcas has perhaps the best budget tourist facilities of all the islands. Unfortunately, the beach access is occupied by private resorts and is closed to the public. The trail to **Obstruction Pass Beach** is the best way to clamber down to the rocky shores. Because Orcas is shaped like a horseshoe, getting around is a chore. The ferry lands on the southwest tip. The island's main town, **Eastsound,** is 9 mi. northeast. Stop in a shop to get a free **map** (most are open daily 8:30am-6:30pm).

Moran State Park, Star Rte. 22, Eastsound 98245 (376-2326), is Orcas's greatest attraction. Over 21 mi. of hiking trails cover the park, ranging in difficulty from a one-hour jaunt around Mountain Lake to a day-long constitutional up the south face of Mt. Constitution, the highest peak on the islands. Pick up a copy of the trail guide from the **ranger station** (376-2837). From the summit of Constitution, you can see other islands, the Olympic and Cascade Ranges, Vancouver Island, and Mt. Rainier. Swim in two freshwater lakes easily accessible from the highway, or rent rowboats ($8 per hr.) and paddleboats ($9 per hr.) from the park. **Camping** in the park offers all the best of San Juan fun: swimming, fishing, and hiking. There are four different campgrounds with a total of 151 sites. About 12 sites remain open year-round, as do the restrooms. Backcountry camping is prohibited. Rowboats and paddleboats $8-9 for the first hr., $6 per hr. thereafter. Standard sites have hot showers for $12. Hiker/biker sites are $5. The **information booth** at park entrance is open Memorial Day-Labor Day daily 2-11pm. (Park open daily 6:30am-dusk; Sept.-March 8am-dusk. Reservations strongly recommended May-Labor Day.)

For **visitors information** call 206-468-3663, or contact the **chamber of commerce** (376-2273). For **Bike Rental** go to **Wildlife Cycle** (376-4708), A St. and North Beach Rd., in Eastsound. (21-speeds $5 per hr. Open Mon.-Sat. 10:30am-5pm.) For **lodging,** call the hotline at 376-8888.

OLYMPIC PENINSULA

In the fishing villages and logging towns of the Olympic Peninsula, locals joke about having webbed feet and using Rustoleum instead of suntan oil. The Olympic Mountains wring the area's moisture (up to 200 in. of rain per year fall on Mt. Olympus) out of the heavy Pacific air. While this torrent supports genuine rain forests in the peninsula's western river valleys, towns such as Sequim in the range's eastern rain shadow are the driest in Washington, with as little as 17 in. of rain per year.

Extremes of climate are matched by extremes of geography. The beaches along the Pacific strip are a hiker's paradise—isolated, windy, and wildly sublime. The seaports of the peninsula's northern edge crowd against the Strait of Juan de Fuca, hemmed in by the glaciated peaks of the Olympic range. Most visitors, however, come here for one reason: the spectacularly rugged scenery of Olympic National Park, which lies at the Peninsula's center. Though the park's network of trails now covers an area the size of Rhode Island, these rough and wooded mountains resisted exploration until well into the 20th century. For information on the area, contact the **Tourist Regional Information Program,** SW Washington, P.O. Box 128, Longview 98632. In **emergencies** call the state **police** at 911 or 206-577-2050.

■■■ PORT TOWNSEND

The Victorian splendor of Port Townsend's buildings, unlike the salmon industry, has survived the progression of time and weather. The entire business district has been restored and declared a national landmark. Port Townsend is a cultural oasis on an otherwise untamed peninsula. Walk down Water Street, and you'll be lured by cafes, book shops, and an immense ice cream parlor. By land, Port Townsend can be reached either from **U.S. 101** or from the **Kitsap Peninsula** across the Hood Canal Bridge. **Greyhound**'s daily Seattle-to-Port Angeles run connects with Jefferson County Transit in Port Ludlow for the last leg to Port Townsend.

The Port Townsend area boasts two hostels. **Fort Worden Youth Hostel (HI-AYH),** Fort Worden State Park (385-0655), 2 mi. from downtown, has bulletin boards and trekkers's logs, which are good, if dated, sources of information on budget travel around the Olympics. The hostel also has kitchen facilities. (Open Feb.-Dec. 21. Call ahead for Nov.-Feb. Check in 5-10pm; check-out 9:30am; no curfew. $9, non-members $12. Cyclists $7-10. Family rates available.) **Fort Flagler Youth Hostel (HI-AYH),** Fort Flagler State Park (385-1288), lies on handsome Marrowstone Island, 20 mi. from Port Townsend. From Port Townsend head south on Rte. 19, which connects to Rte. 116 east and leads directly into the park. It's fantastic for cyclists and solitude-seekers. (Open year-round by reservation only. Check in 5-10pm, lockout 10am-5pm. $8.50, nonmembers $11.50. Cyclists $6.)

Port Townsend has its share Queen Anne and Victorian mansions. Of the over 200 restored homes in the area, some have been converted into bed and breakfasts; others are open for tours. The 1868 **Rothschild House** (355-2722), at Franklin and Taylor St., has period furnishings and herbal and flower gardens. (Open daily 10am-5pm; Sept. 16-May 14 Sat.-Sun. 11am-4pm. Requested donation $2.) Or peek into the **Heritage House** at Pierce and Washington (open daily 12:30-3pm; $1.50).

Point Hudson, the hub of the small shipbuilding area, forms the corner of Port Townsend, where Admiralty Inlet and Port Townsend Bay meet. North of Point Hudson are several miles of beach, **Chetzemolka Park,** and the larger **Fort Worden State Park.** Port Townsend's **chamber of commerce,** 2437 E. Sims Way (385-2722), lies 10 blocks from the center of town on Rte. 20. Ask the helpful staff for a map and visitors guide. (Open Mon.-Fri. 9am-5pm, Sat. 10am-4pm, Sun. 11am-4pm.)

■■■ OLYMPIC NATIONAL PARK

Amid the august Olympic Mountains, Olympic National Park unites 900,000 acres of velvet-green rainforest, jagged snow-covered peaks, and dense evergreen woodlands. This enormous region at the center of the peninsula allows limited access to four-wheeled traffic. There is no scenic loop, and only a handful of secondary roads attempt to penetrate the interior. The roads that do exist serve as trailheads for over 600 mi. of hiking. The enormous amount of rain on the western side of the mountains supports rainforests dominated by Sitka spruce and western red cedars in the Hoh, Queets, and Quinault river valleys. The only people who seem not to enjoy this diverse and wet wilderness are those who come unprepared; a parka, good boots, and a waterproof tent are essential here.

Vancouver Island

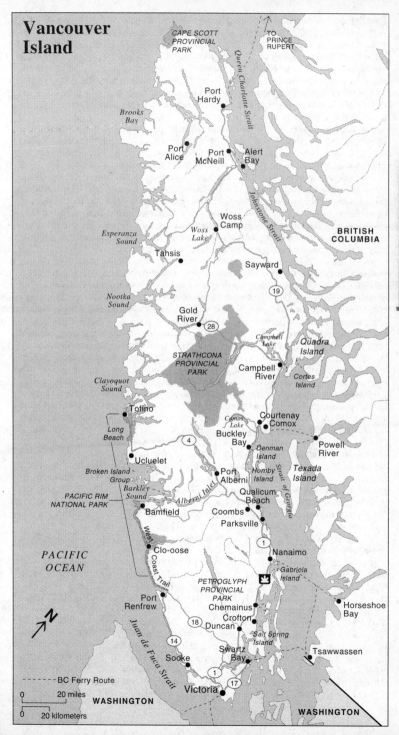

CAPE SCOTT
PROVINCIAL
PARK

TO
PRINCE
RUPERT

*Brooks
Bay*

Queen Charlotte Strait

Port
Hardy

Port
Alice

Port
McNeill

Alert
Bay

Johnstone Strait

**BRITISH
COLUMBIA**

Woss
Camp

*Esperanza
Sound*

*Woss
Lake*

Tahsis

Sayward

19

*Nootka
Sound*

Gold
River

28

*Campbell
Lake*

*Quadra
Island*

STRATHCONA
PROVINCIAL
PARK

Campbell
River

*Cortes
Island*

*Clayoquot
Sound*

Tofino

*Comox
Lake*

Courtenay
Comox

*Long
Beach*

4

Buckley
Bay

*Denman
Island*

Powell
River

Ucluelet

*Broken Island
Group*

Port
Alberni

*Hornby
Island*

*Texada
Island*

PACIFIC RIM
NATIONAL PARK

*Barkley
Sound*

Alberni Inlet

Qualicum
Beach

Strait of Georgia

Bamfield

Coombs

Parksville

West Coast Trail

Clo-oose

1

Nanaimo

*PACIFIC
OCEAN*

*Gabriola
Island*

PETROGLYPH
PROVINCIAL
PARK

Horseshoe
Bay

Port
Renfrew

Chemainus

Crofton

18

Duncan

*Salt Spring
Island*

Tsawwassen

14

Juan de Fuca Strait

Sooke

Swartz
Bay

1

17

- - - - - BC Ferry Route

0   20 miles

WASHINGTON

0   20 kilometers

Victoria

WASHINGTON

THE PACIFIC NW

Practical Information The **Olympic Visitors Center,** 3002 Mt. Angeles Rd., Port Angeles (452-0330), off Race St., fields questions about the whole park, including camping, backcountry hiking, and fishing, and displays a map of locations of other park ranger stations (open daily July-Aug. 8:30am-6pm; Sept.-May 9am-4pm). This is the only reason to visit Port Angeles, a cheerless industrial complex dominated by paper and plywood mills. The park charges an **entrance fee** of $3 per car, $1 per hiker or biker, at the more built-up entrances, such as the Hoh, Heart o' the Hills, and Elwha—all of which have paved roads and toilet facilities. Entrance permit is good for 7 days. In an **emergency,** call 911.

The Park Service runs **interpretive programs** such as guided forest walks, tidal pool walks, and campfire programs out of its ranger stations (all free). For a schedule of events look in the park newspaper from ranger stations or the visitors center. The map distributed at the park's gates is detailed and extremely helpful.

July, August, and September are the best months to visit Olympic National Park, since much of the backcountry often remains snowed-in until late June, and only the summer provides rainless days with any regularity. Be prepared for a potpourri of weather conditions at any time. Make sure hiking boots are waterproof and have good traction, because trails can transform into rivers of slippery mud. **Backcountry camping** requires a free **wilderness permit,** available at ranger stations. The Park Service's backcountry shelters are for emergencies only.

Never drink the untreated **water** in the park. *Giardia,* a *very* nasty microscopic parasite, lives in all these waters, and causes severe diarrhea, gas, and abdominal cramps. Carry your own water supply, or boil local water for five minutes before drinking it. You can also buy water purification tablets at the visitors center (see above) or at most camping supply stores. **Dogs** are not allowed in the backcountry, and must be leashed at all times within the park.

Mountain climbing is tricky in the Olympic Range. Although the peaks are not high in absolute terms, they are steep, and their proximity to the sea makes them prone to nasty weather. Climbers are required to check in at a ranger station before any summit attempt. The rangers urge novices to buddy up with experienced climbers who are "wise in the ways of Northwest mountaineering."

Fishing within park boundaries requires no permit, but you must obtain a state game department punch card for salmon and steelhead trout at outfitting and hardware stores locally, or at the game department in Olympia. The Elwha River is best for **trout,** and the Hoh is excellent for **salmon.**

Camping Olympic National Park, Olympic National Forest, and the State of Washington all maintain free campgrounds. Pick up the **map** of the area from a ranger station for comprehensive information. The free **National Park campgrounds** include **Deer Park, Dosewallips, Graves Creek, July Creek, Ozette** (all with drinking water), and **Queets** (no water). In addition, the National Park has many standard campgrounds (sites $8). Fees in the **National Forest campgrounds** range from $4 to $12; six campgrounds in the Hood Canal Ranger District are free. Reservations can be made for three Forest Service campgrounds: **Seal Rock, Falls View,** and **Klahowga,** by calling 800-280-CAMP/2267. Any ranger station can provide a list of both Park and Forest Service campgrounds, fees, and facilities. Several **State Parks** are scattered along Hood Canal and the eastern rim of the peninsula (sites $10-16; occasionally only $4-5). **Dosewallips** (doh-see-WALL-ups), on a road that leaves U.S. 101 27 mi. north of Hoodsport, has 32 free but less developed sites for cars. The **ranger station** (summer only), has no electricity or telephones. **Heart o' the Hills Campground** (452-2713; 105 sites), 5½ mi. from Port Angeles up Race Rd. inside Olympic National Park, is filled with vacationers poised to take **Hurricane Ridge** by storm the next day (sites $8, plus the $5 entrance fee), where interpretive programs and a ranger station await. Farther west on U.S. 101, **Elwha Valley** (452-9191; 41 sites), 5 mi. south off U.S. 101, has a ranger station accessible also to nearby **Altaire** (30 sites). Both have drinking water (sites $8). **Fairholm Campground** (928-3380; 87 sites), 30 mi. west of Port Angeles at the western tip of Lake Crescent, has sites with drinking water ($8). **The Storm King Information Station** (open June-Aug. daily 9am-5pm) runs interpretive evening programs.

Farther west on U.S. 101, an entrance fee of $5 and 13 mi. of paved road will get you through to the **Sol Duc Hot Springs Campground** (327-3534), which has sites for $8. Get free backcountry permits at the **Sol Duc Ranger Station** (327-3534; open July-Aug. daily 8am-5pm). At nearby **Sol Duc Hot Springs** (327-3583; $5.50 per day, seniors $4.50), the cement docks, chlorine smell, and "shower before you enter" signs detract from this pristine source of naturally hot water (open mid-May-Sept. daily 9am-9pm; closes at 8pm in Sept.; April and Oct. 9am-5pm). A better and less well-known way to harness the region's geothermal energy is to hike up to **Olympic Hot Springs.** Turn off at the Elwha River Road and follow it 12 mi. to the trailhead. The natural springs are about a 2½-mi. hike, but well worth it.

Outdoors and the Rainforest Olympic National Park is home to one of the **world's only temperate rainforests.** Gigantic, thick old-growth trees, ferns, and mosses blanket the valleys of the Hoh, Queets, and Quinault Rivers, all on the west side of the Park. Although the forest floor is thickly carpeted with unusual foliage and fallen trees, rangers keep the many walking trails clear and well-marked. Many travelers seek out the **Hoh Rainforest Trail** for an incredible rainforest experience. Perfect for longer expeditions, the trail parallels the Hoh River for 18 mi. to Blue Glacier on the shoulder of Mount Olympus. Shy Roosevelt elk and Northern spotted owl inhabit the area. The first two campgrounds along the Hoh River Rd., which leaves U.S. 101 13 mi. south of the town of Forks, are administered by the Department of Natural Resources (DNR), accept no reservations, and are free. Drinking water is available at the **Minnie Peterson** site only. DNR sites are usually uncrowded; stay at one and drive to the Hoh trailhead to get a map and begin your rainforest exploration. You can obtain a separate map of the Hoh-Clearwater Multiple Use Area from the DNR main office, just off U.S. 101 on the north side of Forks, or at Minnie Peterson. The **Hoh Rainforest Visitors Center** (374-6925) provides posters and permits (open July-Aug. daily 9am-6:30pm, winter 9am-5pm). Just south of Hoh River Rd., the Oil City Rd. leads west to the coast.

Trailheads to seek out for relative solitude are **Queets, North Fork,** and **Graves Creek,** in the west and southwest of the Park. Queets Trail follows the Queets River east from a free campground (20 sites for tents only; open June-Sept.). The Park and Forest Services and the Quinalt Reservation, which owns the lake, share the land surrounding **Quinault Lake.** The Forest Service operates a day-use beach and an information center in the **Quinault Ranger Station,** South Shore Rd. (288-2444; open daily 9am-4:30pm; winter Mon.-Fri. 9am-4:30pm). From the Quinalt Ranger Station, it's 20 mi. to the North Fork trailhead; enterprising hikers can journey 44 mi. north across the entire park, finishing up at Whiskey Bend.

Hurricane Ridge, is 5½ mi. from Port Angeles up Race Rd. Auto-lovers can drive right up the mountain; just make sure you hide the car in your pictures on top. Clear days bring splendid views of Mt. Olympus and Vancouver Island. The ridge can be crowded; the ideal time to go is sunrise. Many trails that originate here, including some for seniors and the disabled. On winter weekends the Park Service organizes **snowshoe walks** atop the ridge. Call the Visitors Center (452-0330) for details.

The Olympic Peninsula contains Cape Flattery, the northwesternmost point in the contiguous U.S. At the westernmost point on the strait is Neah Bay, the only town in the **Makah Reservation.** Rte. 112 leads there west from Port Angeles. In Neah Bay, the **Makah Cultural and Research Center** (645-2711) on Hwy. 112 houses artifacts from the archaeological site at Cape Alava, where a huge mudslide 500 years ago buried and preserved an entire settlement. The downstairs of a 70-ft.-long house, with a sloped roof ideally suited to the rainy environment, has been replicated at the museum. (Open daily 10am-5pm; Oct.-April Wed.-Sun. 10am-5pm. $4, seniors and students $3.)

Coastal Beaches Piles of driftwood, imposing sea stacks, sculptured arches and abundant wildlife lie along 57 mi. of rugged and deserted beaches. Bald eagles are often out on windy days, and whales and seals tear through the sea. Where U.S. 101 hugs the coast between the Hoh and Quinault Reservations, the beaches are easily accessible. The 15-mi. stretch of beaches begins in the north with **Ruby Beach** near Mile 165 on U.S. 101. South of Ruby Beach at Mile 160 is **Beach #6,** a favorite whale-watching spot. Another three mi. south is Beach #4, with its beautiful tidepools. South of Beaches #4 and #6 is **Kalaloch** (KLAY-lok) **Center,** with 177 sites near the ocean, including a lodge, a general store, a gas station, and a ranger station. Gather in the morning hours for interpretive talks on the tidepools.

■■■ OLYMPIA

While still peaceful and easy-going, Olympia has smoothly made the transition from small fishing-and-oyster port to growing state capital. The sprawling Capitol Campus dominates the downtown, but Olympia also draws on its natural environment and growing alternative rock scene. Located where I-5 meets U.S. 101, Olympia is a logical stopping point for those heading north to the Olympic Peninsula or Seattle, or south to the Cascade peaks or Portland.

Emergency is 911. Olympia's **Chamber of Commerce,** 1000 Plum St. (357-3362 or 800-753-8474), is next to the City Hall (open Mon.-Fri. 9am-5pm). An information booth is set up at the **Farmer's Market,** 401 N. Capitol Way. **Amtrak,** 6600 Yelm Hwy. (800-872-7245) toots to Seattle and Portland three times a day. **Greyhound,** 107 E. 7th Ave. (357-5541), at Capitol Way, is open daily 6:30am-8pm. Olympia's **post office:** 900 S. Jefferson SE (357-2286; open Mon.-Fri. 7:30am-6pm, Sat. 9am-4pm); **ZIP code:** 98501; **area code:** 206.

The motels in Olympia generally cater to lobbyists and lawyers rather than to budget tourists. Camping is the cheapest option. The **Bailey Motor Inn,** 3333 Martin Way (491-7515), exit 107 off I-5 has clean, comfortable rooms. (Singles from $34. Doubles from $41.) **Millersylvania State Park,** 12245 Tilly Rd. S (753-1519), is 10 mi. south of Olympia. Take Exit 99 off I-5, then head south on Rte. 121, or exit 95 off I-5 and head north on Rte. 121. The park offers 216 tree-shrouded, reasonably spacious sites with pay showers and flush toilets (standard sites $11, RV hookups $16). **Capital Forest Multiple Use Area,** 15 mi. southwest of Olympia, off I-5 exit 95, is 50 free campsites scattered among 6 campgrounds. The area is unsupervised; lone travelers and women might be better off paying the $11 for Millersylvania.

There is potential for good eating along bohemian 4th Ave., east of Columbia, especially when the pace picks up during the school year. The **Olympia Farmer's Market,** 401 N. Capitol Way (352-9096), has a great selection of in-season fruits and berries; you can buy a fantastic cheap lunch here. (Open early May-Sept. Thurs.-Sun.10am-3pm; April Sat.-Sun. 10am-3pm; Oct.-mid-Dec. Fri.-Sun. 10am-3pm.) Try a grilled oyster sandwich ($6) or a Spar burger ($5.50) at **The Spar Cafe & Bar,** 111 E. 4th Ave. (357-6444; open daily 6am-9pm; bar open daily 11am-2am). Or dig the deluxe burrito ($4.50) and the vegetarian and vegan options at the **Smithfield Cafe,** 212 W. 4th Ave. (786-1725; open Mon.-Fri. 7am-8pm, Sat.-Sun. 8am-8pm).

The focal point of Olympia is the **State Capitol Campus.** Take a free tour of the **Legislative Building** (586-8677) to sneak a peek of the public sphere. Only the tours can usher you in to the legislative chambers, which are otherwise off-limits. (45-min. tours daily 10am-3pm; building open Mon.-Fri. 8am-5pm, Sat.-Sun. 10am-4pm.)

Capitol Lake Park is a favorite retreat for runners, sailors, and swimmers. Or stroll on the boardwalk at **Percival Landing Park** (743-8379); various boats jam the Port, a reminder of Olympia's oyster-filled past. The **Yashiro Japanese Garden** (753-8380; open daily from 10am to dusk), is tiny but beautiful, a perfect spot for a picnic.

The **Nisqually National Wildlife Refuge** (753-9467), off I-5 between Olympia and Tacoma (at exit 114), has recently pitted environmentalists against developers in the quiet Nisqually delta. For the time being, you can still view the protected wildlife from blinds or walk the trails that wind through the preserve. Trails open daily during daylight hours (office open Mon.-Fri. 7:30am-4pm; $2).

Wolfhaven, 3111 Offut Lake Rd. (264-4695 or 800-448-9653) 10 mi. south of Olympia, now preserves 40 wolves of six different species. Tour the grounds ($5, children $2) or take part in the **Howl-In** (every Fri. and Sat. 6-9pm; $6, children $4).

CASCADE RANGE

The Northwestern Native Americans summed up their admiration succinctly, dubbing the Cascades "The Home of the Gods." Intercepting the moist Pacific air, the Cascades have divided the eastern and western parts of Oregon and Washington into the lush green of the west and the high, dry plains of the east.

The tallest of these mountains—the white-domed peaks of Baker, Vernon, Glacier, Rainier, Hood, Adams, and Mount St. Helens—have been made accessible by four major roads offering good trailheads and impressive scenery. **U.S. 12** through White Pass approaches Mt. Rainier most closely; **I-90** sends four lanes past the major ski resorts of Snoqualmie Pass; scenic **U.S. 2** leaves Everett for Stevens Pass and descends the Wenatchee River, a favorite of whitewater rafters; **Route 20,** the **North Cascades Hwy.,** provides access to North Cascades National Park. These last two roads are often traveled in sequence as the **Cascade Loop.**

Greyhound covers the routes over Stevens and Snoqualmie Passes to and from Seattle (3 hr. round-trip), while **Amtrak** cuts between Ellensburg and Puget Sound. Rainstorms and evening traffic can slow hitchhiking; locals warn against thumbing along Rte. 20, as a few hitchers apparently have vanished over the last few years. Let's Go does not recommend hitching here. This corner of the world can only be explored properly with a car. The mountains are most accessible in July, August, and September; many high mountain passes are snowed in the rest of the year. The best source of information on the Cascades is the joint **National Park/National Forest Information Service,** 915 2nd Ave., Seattle 98174 (206-220-7450).

■■■ NORTH CASCADES

A favorite stomping ground for deer, mountain goats, and bears, the North Cascades—an aggregation of dramatic peaks in the northern part of the state—remain one of the last great expanses of untouched land in the continental U.S. The **North Cascades Hwy. (Rte. 20)** provides the major access to the area, as well as astounding views awaiting each twist in the road. Use the information below to follow the road eastward from Burlington (exit 230 on I-5) along the Skagit River to the Skagit Dams (whose hydroelectric energy powers Seattle), then across the Cascade Crest at Rainy Pass (4860 ft.) and Washington Pass (5477 ft.), finally descending to the Methow River and the dry Okanogan rangeland of eastern Washington. **Rte. 9** branches off of Rte. 20 and leads north through the rich farmland of **Skagit Valley,** offering roundabout access to **Mt. Baker** via forks at the Nooksack River and Rte. 542. Mt. Baker (10,778 ft.) has been belching since 1975, and in winter jets of steam often snort from its dome.

Greyhound stops in Burlington once per day, and **Empire Lines** (affiliated with Greyhound) serves Okanogan, Pateros, and Chelan on the eastern slope. No public transportation lines run within the North Cascades National Park or along the North Cascades Highway. Avoid hitching in this area. Information on **North Cascades National Park** (surrounding Rte. 20 and the Ross Lake Recreation Area between Marblemount and Ross Dam) is available at 2105 Rte. 20, Sedro Wooley (206-856-5700; open Sun.-Thurs. 8am-4:30pm, Fri.-Sat. 8am-6pm). To know more about the **Okanogan National Forest** (surrounding Rte. 20 east of Ross Dam), go to 1240 2nd Ave. S, (509-422-2704); for the **Wenatchee National Forest** (south of Okanogan National Forest and north of U.S. 2), try 301 Yakima St. (509-662-4335).

■ NORTH CASCADES NATIONAL PARK

Newhalem is the first town on Rte. 20 as you cross into the **Ross Lake National Recreation Area,** a buffer zone between the highway and North Cascades National Park. A small grocery store and **hiking** trails to the dams and lakes nearby are the highlights of Newhalem. The **visitors center** (386-4495) is on Rte. 20 (open late June-early Sept. daily 8:30am-5:30pm; late Sept. 9am-4:30pm; call for winter hours).

The artificial expanse of **Ross Lake,** behind Ross Dam, extends into the mountains as far as the Canadian border. The lake is ringed by 15 campgrounds, some accessible by trail, others only by boat. The trail along **Big Beaver Creek,** at Mile 134 on Rte. 20, leads from Ross Lake over Ross Dam into the Picket Range and eventually all the way to Mt. Baker. The **Sourdough Mountain** and **Desolation Peak lookout towers** near Ross Lake offer eagle-eye views of the range.

The National Park's **Goodell Creek Campground,** just south of Newhalem, has 22 sites for tents and trailers with drinking water and pit toilets, and a launch site for **whitewater rafting** on the Skagit River (sites $7; after Oct., no water, and sites are free). **Colonial Creek Campground,** 10 mi. to the east, is a fully developed, vehicle-accessible campground with flush toilets, a dump station, and campfire programs every evening. Colonial Creek is also a trailhead for the southern unit of the North Cascades National Park (open mid-May to Nov.; 164 sites, $7). **Newhalem Creek Campground,** near the visitors center, is another similarly developed National Park facility (129 sites, $7).

Diablo Lake lies southwest of Ross Lake; the foot of Ross Dam acts as its eastern shore. Diablo Lake Town is the main trailhead for hikes into the southern unit of the Park. The **Thunder Creek Trail** traverses Park Creek Pass to Stehekin River Rd., in Lake Chelan National Recreation Area south of the park. For some areas, a free **backcountry permit** is required and available from park ranger stations.

■ ROUTE 20 EAST TO MAZAMA AND WINTHROP

Thirty mi. of jaw-dropping views east on Rte. 20, the **Pacific Crest Trail** crosses **Rainy Pass** on one of the most scenic and difficult legs of its 2500-mi. Canada-to-Mexico route. The trail leads north through **Pasayten Wilderness** and south past **Glacier Peak** (10,541 ft.) in the **Glacier Peak Wilderness.** Near Rainy Pass, groomed **scenic trails** 1 to 3 mi. long can be hiked in sneakers, provided the snow has melted (about mid-July). An overlook at **Washington Pass** rewards a short hike with one of the state's most dramatic panoramas, a flabbergasting view of the red rocks of upper **Early Winters Creek's Copper Basin.** The popular 2.2-mi. walk to **Blue Lake** begins just east of Washington Pass. An easier 2-mi. hike to **Cutthroat Lake** departs from an access road 4.6 mi. east of Washington Pass. From the lake, the trail continues 4 mi. further and almost 2,000 ft. higher to **Cutthroat Pass,** giving the persevering hiker a breathtaking view of towering peaks. The spectacular, hair-raising 19-mi. gravel road snakes up to **Hart's Pass,** the highest pass crossed by any road in the state. The road begins at **Mazama,** 10 mi. east of Washington Pass.

The Forest Service maintains a string of campgrounds along Rte. 20 (sites $8), between Washington Pass and Mazama. Explore the other, more remote campgrounds along the Forest Rd. northwest of Mazama. The **Early Winters Visitor Center** (996-2534), just outside Mazama, is aflutter with information about the **Pasayten Wilderness,** an area whose rugged terrain and mild climate endear it to hikers and equestrians. Take yourself on a hard-core five-day backcountry excursion to really experience it (open daily 9am-5pm; in winter, Sat.-Sun. 9am-5pm).

■ WINTHROP TO TWISP

Farther east is the town of **Winthrop,** child of an unholy marriage between the old television series *Bonanza* and Long Island yuppies who would eagerly claim a rusty horseshoe as an antique. Find the **Winthrop Information Station** (996-2125), on the corner of Rte. 20 and Riverside (open early May-mid-Oct. daily 10am-5pm). For homemade soups and great sandwiches, stop in at the **Trail's End Way Station** (996-2303), tucked into a corner of the Trail's End Motel. Follow Riverside from Rte. 20; the Trail's End is the last old-west style building on the right. Delicious sandwiches run about $4 to $5. Most entrees are $8 to $9 (open daily 7am-9pm).

You can take a guided trail ride at the **Rocking Horse Ranch** (996-2768), 9 mi. north of Winthrop on the North Cascade Hwy. ($20 per 1½ hrs.), rent a bike ($5 per hr., $20 per day), or try you hand at an indoor climbing wall at **Winthrop Mountain Sports,** 257 Riverside Ave. (996-2886). The **Winthrop Ranger Station,** P.O. Box 579 (996-2266), at 24 W. Chewuch Rd., off Rte. 20 in the west end of town, knows all about campgrounds, hikes, and fishing spots (open Mon.-Fri. 7:45am-5pm, Sat. 8:30am-5pm; closed Sat. in winter).

Flee Winthrop's prohibitively expensive hotels and sleep in **Twisp,** 9 mi. south of Winthrop on Rte. 20. This peaceful hamlet offers low prices and far fewer tourists than its neighbor. Stay at **The Sportsman Motel,** 1010 E. Rte. 20 (997-2911), a hidden jewel, where a barracks-like facade masks tastefully decorated rooms and kitchens (singles $31, doubles $36). The **Twisp Ranger Station,** 502 Glover St. (997-2131), employs a helpful staff ready to pelt you with trail and campground guides (open Mon.-Sat. 7:45am-4:30pm; winter Mon.-Fri. 7:45am-4:30pm). From Twisp, Rte. 20 continues east to Okanogan, and Rte. 153 south to **Lake Chelan.**

Locals frequent **Rosey's Branding Iron,** 123 Glover St. (997-3576), in the center of town. The Iron usually has really cheap specials on the menu (under $3.50) and offers special menus for dieters, seniors, and children. All-you-can-eat soup and salad is only $6 (open Mon.-Sat. 5am-8pm, Sun. 6am-3pm).

■■■ MOUNT RAINIER NATIONAL PARK

Rising 2 mi. above the surrounding foothills, 14,411-ft.-high Mt. Rainier (ray-NEER) presides regally over the Cascade Range. Native Americans once called it "Tahoma," meaning "mountain of God." Today, Rainier is simply "The Mountain" to most Washingtonians. Rainier even creates its own weather, jutting up into the warm ocean air and pulling down vast amounts of snow and rain. Clouds mask the mountain up to 200 days per year. Some 76 glaciers patch the slopes and combine with sharp ridges and steep gullies to make Rainier an inhospitable place for the 3000 determined climbers who clamber to its summit each year. Even for those who don't feel up to scaling The Mountain, with over 305 mi. of trails, there is plenty to explore.

Practical Information Mt. Rainier is 60 mi. from Tacoma and 70 mi. from Seattle. To reach the park from the west, drive south from Seattle on I-5 to Tacoma, then go east on Rte. 512, south on Rte. 7, and east on Rte. 706. **Rte. 706** is the only access road open throughout the year; snow usually closes all other park roads Nov.-May. The park **entrance fee** is $5 per car, $3 per hiker; the gates are open 24 hrs. For **visitor information,** stop in at the **Longmire Hiker Information Center,** which distributes backcountry permits (open Sun.-Thurs. 8am-4:30pm, Fri. 8am-7pm, Sat. 7am-7pm; closed in winter); **Paradise Visitors Center** (589-22275) offers lodging, food, and souvenirs (open daily 9am-7pm; late Sept. to mid-Oct. 9:30am-6pm; mid-Oct.-winter 10am-5pm); the **Sunrise Visitors Center** contains exhibits, snacks, and a gift shop (open daily June 25-mid-Sept. 9am-6pm); and the **Ohanapecosh Visitors Center** offers information and wildlife displays (open summer daily until mid-Oct. 9am-6pm and Sat.-Sun. May-June 9am-6pm). All centers can be contacted by writing c/o Superintendent, Mt. Rainier National Park, Ashford 98304, or by telephoning the park's central operator (569-2211).

Rainier Mountaineering Inc. (RMI) (569-2227), in Paradise, rents ice axes ($7), crampons ($7.25), boots ($15), packs ($15), and helmets ($5) by the day. Expert

RMI guides also lead summit climbs, seminars, and special schools and programs. (Open May-Oct. daily 10am-5pm. Winter office: 535 Dock St. #209, Tacoma 98402 627-6242.) In a park **emergency,** call 569-2211. Ranier's **area code: 206.**

Accommodations and Food **Longmire, Paradise,** and **Sunrise** offer hotels and food that are often very costly. Stock up and stay in **Ashford** or **Packwood.** The **Hotel Packwood,** 104 Main St. (494-5431), has good prices (singles $20, with bath $38, doubles $30). The **Gateway Inn Motel,** 38820 Rte. 706, Ashford (569-2506), has cabins for two ($49; singles and doubles with bath $40; shared bath $35).

Camping at the auto-accessible campsites from June through Sept. requires a permit ($5-8), available at campsites. Go to **Ohanapecosh** for the serene high ceiling of old-growth trees, to **Cougar Rock** for the strict quiet hours, and to **White River** or **Sunshine Point** for the panoramas. All are open on a first-come, first-camped basis. Sunshine Point is the only auto site open year-round.

Alpine and **cross-country camping** require free permits year-round and are subject to restrictions. Be sure to pick up a copy of the *Wilderness Trip Planner* pamphlet at any ranger station before you set off. With a **backcountry permit,** cross-country hikers can use any of the free, well-established **trailside camps** scattered throughout the park's backcountry. Most camps have toilet facilities and a nearby water source, and some have shelters as well. *Fires are prohibited,* and the size of a party is limited. **Glacier climbers** and **mountain climbers** intending to go above 10,000 ft. must register in person at ranger stations to be granted permits.

Outdoors All major roads offering scenic views of the mountain have numerous roadside sites for viewing. The roads to Paradise and Sunrise are especially picturesque. **Stevens Canyon Road** connects the southeast corner of the national park with Paradise, Longmire, and the Nisqually entrance, unfolding spectacular vistas of Rainier and the rugged Tatoosh Range. The accessible roadside attractions of **Box Canyon, Bench Lake,** and **Grove of the Patriarchs** line the route.

Mt. Adams and Mount St. Helens, not visible from the road, can be seen clearly from such **mountain trails** as **Paradise** (1½ mi.), **Pinnacle Peak** (2½ mi.), **Eagle Peak** (7 mi.), and **Van Trump Peak** (5½ mi.). For more information on these trails, pick up *Viewing Mount St. Helens* at one of the visitors centers.

A segment of the **Pacific Crest Trail (PCT),** running between the Columbia River and the Canadian border, crosses through the southeast corner of the park. The PCT is maintained by the U.S. Forest Service. Primitive **campsites** and **shelters** line the trail as it snakes through delightful wilderness areas.

A trip to the **summit** of Mt. Rainier requires special preparation and substantial expense. The ascent is a vertical rise of more than 9000 ft. over a distance of 8 or more mi.—usually taking two days. Experienced climbers may form their own expeditions upon satisfactory completion of a detailed application; novices can sign up for a **summit climb** with **Rainier Mountaineering, Inc. (RMI).** For more information, contact **Park Headquarters** or **RMI** (see Practical Information).

Hardcore hikers will also be thrilled by the 95-mi. **Wonderland Trail,** which circumscribes Rainier. The entire circuit takes 10 to 14 days and includes several brutal ascents and descents. Rangers can provide information on weather and trail conditions; they also can store food caches for you at ranger stations along the trail.

If you are llooking to spend an unusual day in a llovely llocation, **Llama Wilderness Pack Trips,** Tatoosh Motel, Packwood (491-5262) offers a llunch with the llamas in the park for $25 per person (4 to 5-hr. trip).

■■■ MOUNT ST. HELENS

On the morning of May 18, 1980, Mount St. Helens exploded violently, shaking the entire state of Washington out of bed. In the three days that followed, a hole 2 mi. long and 1 mi. wide opened in the mountain. Ash blackened the sky for hundreds of miles and blanketed the streets of nearby towns with inches of soot. Debris from the volcano flooded Spirit Lake, choked rivers with mud, and sent house-sized boulders tumbling down the mountainside. The blast leveled entire forests, leaving a stubble of trunks on the hills and millions of trees pointing arrow-like away from the crater.

Mount St. Helens National Volcanic Monument is slowly recovering from that explosion. Fourteen years later, the devastated landscape has signs of returning life—saplings press up, insects flourish near newly formed waterfalls, and small rodents scurry among burrows. Nature's power of destruction, it seems, is exceeded only by her power of regeneration.

Practical Information Start any trip to the mountain at the **Mount St. Helens National Volcanic Monument Visitors Center** (274-6644; 274-4038 for 24-hr. recording), on Rte. 504, 5 mi. east of Castle Rock (exit 49 off of I-5). Interpretive talks and displays recount the mountain's eruption and regeneration, and are augmented by a 22-min. film, a 10-min. slide show, and many hands-on activities. The center also provides camping and mountain access info. (Open 9am-6pm; Oct.-March 9am-5pm.) If time permits, plan to spend the whole day in the monument and visit either the **Pine Creek Information Center** in the south or the **Woods Creek Information Center** in the north. While not as large as the main center near Castle Rock, these two are each within 1 mi. of excellent viewpoints and offer displays, maps, and brochures on the area. (Open May-Oct. 9am-5pm.) In case of an **emergency** in the park, head to one of these centers.

From the north, get on U.S. 12 and go south on Forest Road 25 at the town of Randle. From the south, take Rte. 503, which becomes Forest Road 90 at Yale; follow 90 to Pine Creek. Drivers should fill up their gas tanks before starting the journey, as fuel is not sold within the park. Drivers of trailers or RVs should avoid Road 26, which turns east from Road 25; it's a one-lane, steep, and curvy road. **Gray Line,** 400 NW Broadway, Portland, OR (503-226-6755 or 800-426-7532) runs buses from Seattle to Mount St. Helens (round-trip $37). Mount St. Helens's **area code:** 206.

Camping For those who want an early start touring the mountain, there are two primitive **campgrounds** relatively near the crater. **Iron Creek Campground,** just south of the Woods Creek Information Center on Forest Road 25, has 98 sites ($8 each, call 800-283-2267 for reservations), and **Swift Campground,** just west of the Pine Creek Information Center on Forest Road 90, has 93 sites ($8 each, no reservations). Just west of Swift Campground on Yale Reservoir lie **Beaver Bay** and **Cougar Campgrounds,** both of which have flush toilets and showers and are run by Pacific Power & Light (sites $8; for reservations call 503-464-5035). **Free camping** is dispersed in the monument—if you stumble across a site on an old Forest Service road, you can camp there. Contact a ranger or the **Gifford Pinchot National Forest Headquarters,** 6926 E. Fourth Plain Blvd., Vancouver, WA (696-7500), for info.

Sights Road 99 leads visitors along 17 mi. of curves, clouds of ash, and precipices, past **Spirit Lake,** to a point just 3½ mi. from the crater. Without stops it takes nearly an hour to travel out and back, but the numerous interpretive talks and walks, and the spectacular views along the way, are definitely worth exploring. Check with one of the visitors centers or in the free newsletters for times and meeting places of these interpretive activities. Continue 25 mi. south on Road 25, 12 mi. west on Road 90, then 2 mi. north on Road 83 to **Ape Cave,** a broken, 2½-mi.-long lava tube formed in an ancient eruption, which is now open for visitors to explore. Be sure to wear a jacket and sturdy shoes; you can rent a lantern for $3. Interpreters lead cave walks daily; check at the center there for times.

The **Coldwater Ridge Visitors Center** (274-2131; fax 274-2129), 43 mi. east of Castle Rock and I-5 on Rte. 504, is an angular triumph of modern architecture, and practically a free museum unto itself. The deck, flooded with photographs, has a superb view of the cavity where the mountain's north side used to be and two lakes created by the eruption's aftermath. Check out the hiking and picnic areas, interpretive talks, snack bar, and gift shop (open daily 9am-6pm; Oct.-March 9am-5pm).

■■■ SPOKANE

Spokane was the first pioneer settlement in the Northwest, and is now one of the area's major trade centers. Spokane graces eastern Washington with inexpensive accommodations and lots of delicious, cheap food.

Emergency is 911. The **Spokane Area Convention and Visitors Bureau,** W. 926 Sprague Ave. (747-3230), exit 280 off I-90, is overflowing with Spokane info (open Mon.-Fri. 8:30am-5pm, and most summer weekends, Sat. 8am-4pm, Sun. 9am-2pm). **Amtrak,** W. 221 1st St. (624-5144, after business hours 800-872-7245), runs out at Bernard St., downtown (open Mon.-Fri. 11am-3:30am, Sat.-Sun. 7:15pm-3:30am). **Greyhound,** W. 1125 Sprague (624-5251), at 1st Ave. and Jefferson St., downtown, shares its terminal with **Empire Lines** (624-4116) and **Northwest Stage Lines** (800-826-4058 or 838-4029), which serve other parts of Eastern Washington, Idaho, and British Columbia (station open 24 hrs.). Spokane's **post office:** W. 904 Riverside (459-0230; open Mon.-Fri. 8:30am-5pm); **ZIP Code:** 99210; **area code:** 509.

Spokane lies 280 mi. east of Seattle on I-90. The **Spokane International Airport** (624-3218) is off I-90, 8 mi. southwest of town. Avenues run east-west parallel to the river, streets north-south, and both alternate one-way. The city is divided north and south by **Sprague Ave.,** east and west by **Division St.**

Climb up Lincoln to **Hosteling International Spokane (HI-AYH),** 930 Lincoln (838-5968), with its spacious porch, delightfully creaky wooden floorboards, a kitchen, and laundry in a large Victorian house. The hostel fills in July and Aug., so make reservations. (22 beds. Check-in 4-10pm, no curfew. $10, nonmembers $13.)

Spokane's best sights are the outdoors. **Riverside State Park** (456-3964) embroiders the Spokane River with 12 sq. mi. of volcanic outcroppings, hiking trails (especially good in **Deep Creek Canyon,** the fossil beds of a forest that grew there seven million years ago), and equestrian trails in nearby Trail Town (horse rides $12.50 per hr., by appointment only; 456-8249). A July, 1994 wildfire charred much of the park, but the blackened trees blend in well with the volcanic rock, yielding a stark and beautiful effect. You can also camp at one of the 100 sites in Riverside ($11). **Mount Spokane State Park** (456-4169) stands 35 mi. to the northeast of the city. A well-paved road extends to the summit, affording views of the Spokane Valley and, on clear days, the distant peaks of the Rockies and Cascades. Mt. Spokane is a **skiing** center with free cross-country trails and downhill ski packages (from $20). The area is also good for hiking, horseback riding (no rentals), and camping (12 sites, $11).

Lucky visitors may catch a glimpse of trumpeter swans at the **Turnbull National Wildlife Refuge** (235-4723), 21 mi. south of Spokane. Take the Four Lakes exit off I-90 in Cheney, left on Badger Rd. (Open daily until dusk. $2 per vehicle.)

The **Spokane County Market** at Division St. and Riverside Ave. (482-2627) sells fresh fruit, vegetables, and baked goods (open May-Oct. Wed. 9am-5pm, Sat.-Sun. 11am-4pm). A takeout burger phenom, **Dick's,** E. 103rd Ave. (747-2481), at Division, is an inexplicably inflation-free pocket of Washington. (Burgers 55¢, fries 43¢, sundaes 65¢. Open daily 9am-1:30am.) **Cyrus O'Leary's,** W. 516 Main St. (624-9000), in the Bennetts Block complex at Howard St., is another Spokane legend. Sandwiches are $5.75 and up. (Happy hour 4:30-6:30pm. Open Mon.-Thurs. 11:30am-11pm, Fri.-Sat. 11:30am-midnight, Sun. 11:30am-10pm.) For a bit of nightlife, **Mother's Pub,** W. 230 Riverside Ave. (624-9828), is the place for live rock Fri.-Sat. nights. (Cover charge varies from $2-6 depending on the band; draft beer $1.50-25; open Wed.-Sat. 7pm-2am.)

California

California is the most populous state in the U.S., and in terms of diversity and size, it is practically a nation unto itself. Indeed, its citizens often come across as blithely ignorant of the existence of the other 49 states. Californians firmly believe that they have found the best living space on the planet. Yet beyond the natural beauty, the opportunities for economic success, and the toleration of different lifestyles, the Californian spirit nurtures a strong streak of narcissism—California almost demands celebration of individuality. Only here could self-realization be an industry.

Don't come to the Golden State looking for America. You won't find it. You will find a culture and lifestyle that is peculiarly Californian, from sprawling Los Angeles to compact San Francisco. The small towns and countryside in the hinterland of the two megalopoli have characters of their own, from the quiet beach settlements on the coast, to the agribusiness centers of the Central Valley, to the boom-and-bust towns of the Sierra Nevada. You will find low, sweltering deserts and cool alpine ski country. On coastal highways 101 and 1, you will find towering redwoods and drifting sands. And in the end, you will perhaps understand how Californians can still exhibit vestiges of provincialism in the age of the global village—with a whole world right in their backyard, why would they look any further?

PRACTICAL INFORMATION

Capital: Sacramento.
Visitors Information: California Office of Tourism, 801 K St. #1600, Sacramento 95814 (call 800-862-2543 ext. A1003 to have a package of tourism materials sent to you). **National Park Information:** 415-556-0560.
Time Zone: Pacific (3 hrs. behind Eastern). **Postal Abbreviation:** CA
Sales Tax: 7.5%

> Our coverage is awesome, but even more excellent and entertaining prose can be found in *Let's Go: California*.

■■■ LOS ANGELES

Los Angeles embodies much of what many find wrong with the United States, but millions of people would never live anywhere else. Since L.A.'s most celebrated industry is the production and dissemination of images, it is not surprising that Angelenos are often accused of confusing perception and reality. Increasingly, however, they have been forced to look beyond the glitter of Universal Studios and the opulence of Rodeo Drive, and acknowledge a growing range of social and environmental problems. In the past few years, L.A. has had to contend not only with its overcrowded freeways, smog, and drought, but with riots triggered by the verdicts in the Rodney King case, the sensational murder trials of the Menendez brothers and O.J. Simpson, fires, and an earthquake measuring 6.6 on the Richter scale.

However battered, L.A. keeps growing. A drive into the far reaches of the L.A. Basin, to Simi Valley, to San Bernardino, and even up Rte. 14 toward Lancaster and Palmdale and the Mojave Desert, reveals wooden frames of new tract houses and the creeping tendrils of outer suburbia. Even Bakersfield, over 100 mi. to the northwest, plans to build a light-rail connection to L.A. and anticipates the day when it forms just another of the proverbial "suburbs in search of a city."

PRACTICAL INFORMATION

Emergency: 911.
Basic Orientation: Los Angeles is enormous; it is wise to acquaint yourself with its layout before you arrive. L.A. is best understood as a set of five distinctive regions;

Downtown, Hollywood, the **Westside** (including West Hollywood, Westwood, Century City, and Beverly Hills), **Coast** (including Malibu, Santa Monica, Venice, and the southern beaches), and the **Valley region** (including the San Fernando Valley, San Gabriel, and Pasadena).

Visitors Information: Los Angeles Convention and Visitors Bureau, 685 S. Figueroa St. 90017 (213-689-8822), between Wilshire and 7th St. downtown. Hundreds of brochures. Multi-lingual staff. Good maps. Pick up the free *Destination Los Angeles*. Open Mon.-Fri. 8am-5pm, Sat. 8:30am-5pm. Also in **Hollywood** at 6541 Hollywood Blvd. (213-461-4213; open Mon.-Sat. 9am-5pm).

Airport: Los Angeles International (LAX), (310-646-5252) in Westchester, about 15 mi. southwest of downtown. Travelers Aid, for major emergencies, is available in all terminals (open daily 7am-10pm). **Metropolitan Transit Authority** (MTA) service stops at the transfer terminal at Sepulveda and 96th St. To: downtown, bus #439 (Mon.-Fri. rush hr. only) or #42 (from LAX daily 5:30am-11:15pm; from downtown daily 5:30am-12:10am); Westwood/UCLA, express #560; Long Beach, #232; West Hollywood and Beverly Hills, #220. **Taxi** to downtown $27; Hollywood $30. **Shuttle vans** offer door-to-door service from the terminal to different parts of L.A. for a flat rate. Prices vary widely. Typical rates are $15 downtown, $16 to Santa Monica, $35 to San Fernando Valley.

Amtrak: Union Station, 800 N. Alameda (213-624-0171), at the northwestern edge of the heart of downtown. *See Mileage Chart.*

Buses: Greyhound, 716 E. 7th St. (800-231-2222), downtown, in a rough neighborhood. Continue to other area stations—it's safer than getting off downtown, especially after dark. *See Mileage Chart.* Lockers $1 per day. In **Hollywood:** 1409 N. Vine St. (213-466-6381), 1 block south of Sunset Blvd. Station open daily 6:30am-11pm. Lockers available. In **Santa Monica:** 1433 5th St. (310-394-1648), Broadway and Santa Monica Blvd. Open Mon.-Sat. 9:30am-5pm. **Green Tortoise** (310-392-1990), leaves L.A. every Sunday night with stops in Venice, Hollywood, and downtown. Call for reservations and information.

City Buses: MTA Bus Information Line: 213-626-4455. Customer Service Center at 5301 Wilshire Blvd. Open Mon.-Fri. 8:30am-5pm. Free info, maps, timetables. Open Mon.-Fri. 10am-6pm. Important buses: #1 along Hollywood Blvd., #2 and 3 along Sunset Blvd., #4 along Santa Monica Blvd., #10 along Melrose. Fare $1.10, transfers 25¢. 1-month pass $42, ½-month $23. **Santa Monica Municipal (Big Blue) Bus Lines:** 1660 7th St. (310-451-5444), at Olympic. Open Mon.-Fri. 8am-5pm. Faster and cheaper than the MTA. Fare 50¢ for most routes, and 25¢ transfer tickets for MTA buses. Transfers to other Big Blue buses are free. Important buses: #1 and #2 connect Santa Monica and Venice. Bus #10 provides express service from downtown Santa Monica (at 7th and Grand) to downtown L.A.

Taxi: Checker Cab (213-482-3456), **Independent** (213-385-8294) Call if you need a cab—cabbies don't search for fares on the street. From LAX to downtown $27.

Car Rentals: Avon Rent-A-Car, 8459 Sunset Blvd. (213-654-5533; fax 654-4979). Rent economy-size cars to ages 18 and over. $15 per day with 100 free mi.; 20¢ each additional mi. $90 per week. Drivers 18-20 surcharge $15 per day, 21-24 $5 per day. Open Mon.-Fri. 7:30am-8pm, Sat.-Sun. 9:30am-4pm. **Penny Rent-A-Car,** 12425 Victory Blvd., N. Hollywood (818-786-1733). $25 per day with 75 free mi., 15¢ per additional mi. $150 per week with 500 free mi. CDW $9 per day. Must be at least 18. Open Mon.-Fri. 8am-6pm, Sat. 8am-2pm, Sun. 10am-noon. **Thrifty Car Rental** (800-367-2277), at LAX. $26 per day, unlimited mileage. $140 per week. Must be 21 with credit card, under 25 surcharge $15 per day. Open 24 hrs.

Beach Information: 310-457-9701, recording for Malibu, Santa Monica, and South Bay. Most FM radio stations have a surf report at noon.

Weather: 213-554-1212. An excruciatingly detailed region-by-region report.

Highway Conditions: 213-626-7231. May help you stave off an afternoon stuck on the freeway. AM radio stations offer frequent reports.

Hotlines: AIDS Hotline, 800-922-2437. For recorded info: 976-4700 (small service charge). **Rape Crisis,** 310-392-8381. 24-hr. **Crisis Response,** 310-855-3506.

Post Office: 900 N. Alameda, at 9th St. (310-431-6546). Open Mon.-Fri. 9am-5pm, Sat. 9am-noon. **ZIP Code:** 90086. In **Hollywood:** 1615 Wilcox Ave. (213-464-2194). Open Mon.-Fri. 8am-5pm, Sat. 8am-1pm. **ZIP Code:** 90028. In **Santa**

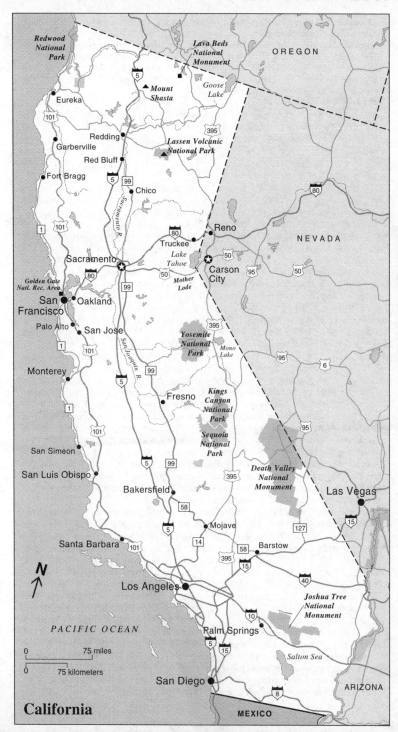

California

Monica: 5th and Arizona (310-576-2626). Open Mon.-Fri. 9am-6pm, Sat. 9am-1pm. **ZIP Code:** 90406.
Area Codes: Downtown L.A., Hollywood, Huntington Park, Vernon, and Montebello: 213. Malibu, Pacific Coast Highway, Westside, southern and eastern L.A. County: 310. Northern L.A. County, San Fernando Valley, and Pasadena: 818. Orange County: 714. San Diego County: 619. Ventura County: 805.

ORIENTATION

A car is a vital necessity in L.A. The city was made to be driven in. Before you even think about navigating Los Angeles's 6500 mi. of streets and 40,000 intersections, get yourself a good **map**—Los Angeles defies all human comprehension otherwise. A sound investment is the *Thomas Guide; Los Angeles County Street Guide and Directory* ($15). Travelers should also purchase regional maps for the neighborhoods in which they plan to stay.

L.A. is a city of distinctive boulevards; its shopping areas and business centers are distributed along these broad arteries. Streets throughout L.A. are designated east, west, north, and south from First and Main St. at the center of downtown.

Once the sun sets, those on foot anywhere, especially outside West L.A. and off well-lit main drags, should exercise caution. It is unwise to walk in many areas alone after dark. Be aware of the character of the neighborhood you are traveling in and be extra cautious when necessary. In L.A. there are certain neighborhoods that are better avoided altogether. When exploring, plan your route carefully, and remember—it is worth a detour to avoid passing through particularly crime-ridden areas.

A legitimate **downtown** Los Angeles does exist, but it won't help orient you toward the rest of the city. Streets running east-to-west in downtown are numbered for the most part and are crossed by streets such as Figueroa, Flower, Broadway, and Main. Most of *Let's Go's* lodgings are found in the heart of downtown, which is reasonably safe on weekdays. Park your car in a paid lot rather than on the street, not only for safety, but because a quarter will buy a mere 7½ min. of parking time on the street. The generously dispensed parking violations are some of L.A.'s less beloved souvenirs. Avoid walking around downtown after the workday or on weekends.

The predominately Latino section of L.A. begins east of downtown's Western Ave., with the districts of **Boyle Heights, Montebello,** and **El Monte.** South of downtown are the **University of Southern California (USC), Exposition Park,** and the districts of **Watts** and **Compton,** home to a large concentration of African Americans. **South Central,** the area south of downtown, suffered the brunt of the fires and looting that erupted in 1992 following the acquittal of four white police officers videotaped beating African-American Rodney King. These primarily residential districts east and south of downtown, known as South Central and **East L.A.,** are considered crime-ridden and dangerous. If you decide you must visit, go during the day and if you park, don't leave anything valuable in the car.

Northwest of downtown is **Hollywood,** whose most significant east-west thoroughfares (from south to north) are Beverly, Melrose Ave., Sunset, and Hollywood. Sunset Boulevard, which runs from the ocean to downtown, presents a cross-section of virtually everything L.A. has to offer: beach communities, lavish wealth, famous nightclubs along "the strip," sleazy motels, the old elegance of Silver Lake, and Chicano murals. Hollywood Boulevard runs just beneath the Hollywood Hills, home to the movie industry's screenwriters, actors, and producers.

The next major region, known informally as the **Westside,** encompasses West Hollywood, Westwood, Century City, Culver City, Crenshaw, Bel Air, Brentwood and (for our purposes) the independent city of **Beverly Hills.** Containing some of L.A.'s most affluent communities, the Westside also is home to the University of California at Los Angeles (UCLA, in Westwood Village), and the trendy, off-beat Melrose Avenue hangouts. The area west of downtown is known as the **Wilshire District** after its main boulevard. **Hancock Park,** a green and affluent residential area, covers the northeast portion of the district—the 5900 area—and harbors the Los Angeles County Museum of Art and the George C. Page Fossil Museum.

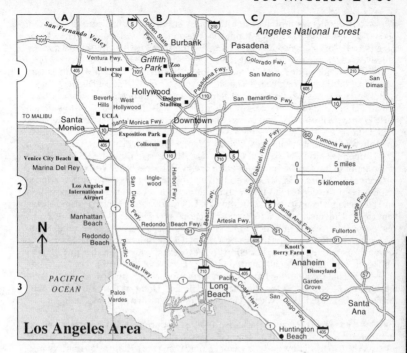

Los Angeles Area

The **Valley Region** spreads north of the Hollywood Hills and the Santa Monica Mountains. For most people, *the* valley is the **San Fernando Valley,** where more than a million people live in the suburbs of a basin bounded in the north and west by the Santa Susanna Mountains and the Simi Freeway, in the south by the Ventura Freeway, and to the east by the Golden State Freeway. The valleys also contain the suburbs of **San Gabriel** and **Pasadena.**

Beach lines L.A.'s **Coastal Region** for 80 mi. **Zuma** is northernmost, followed by **Malibu,** which lies 15 mi. up the coast from **Santa Monica.** Just a bit farther south is the funky and famous beach community of **Venice.** The beach towns south of Santa Monica, comprising the area called the **South Bay,** are Marina del Rey, El Segundo, and Manhattan, Hermosa, and Redondo Beaches. South across the **Palos Verdes Peninsula** is **Long Beach,** a port city of a half-million people. Finally, farthest south are the **Orange County** beach cities: Seal Beach, Sunset Beach, Huntington Beach, Newport Beach, and Laguna Beach. Confused yet? Invest in good maps.

TRAVELING IN LOS ANGELES

The great god of Automobile rules L.A.

Public Transportation Most Angelenos will insist that it's impossible to live in or visit Los Angeles without a car, but public transportation does exist in the form of the **Metropolitan Transit Authority** (once known as the Southern California Rapid Transit District). Using the MTA to sightsee in L.A. can be frustrating because the attractions are very spread out. Those determined to see everything in L.A. should get hold of a car. Bus service is dismal in the outer reaches of the city.

To familiarize yourself with the MTA write for a **Rider's Kit,** MTA, Los Angeles 90001, or stop by one of the 10 **customer service centers.** There are three downtown: in ARCO Plaza, 505 S. Flower St., Level B; at 419 S. Main St.; and at 1016 S. Main St. The MTA prints **route maps** for the different sections of the city. *MTA Self-*

Guided Tours details how to reach the most important sights from downtown. (800-252-7433 from 5:30am-11:30pm for transit info and schedules.) MTA's **basic fare** is $1.10, passengers with disabilities 45¢; transfers 25¢, 10¢ for seniors and disabled; exact change required. Transfers operate from one MTA line to another or to other transit authorities such as Santa Monica Municipal Bus Lines, Culver City Municipal Bus Lines, Long Beach Transit, or Orange County Transit District.

Bus service is best downtown and along the major thoroughfares west of downtown. (There is 24-hr. service, for instance, on Wilshire Blvd.) The downtown **DASH shuttle** is only 25¢ and serves Chinatown, Union Station, Olvera Street, City Hall, Little Tokyo, the Music Center, ARCO Plaza, and more, including Sunset Blvd. in Hollywood, Pacific Palisades, Fairfax, Venice Beach, and Watts. (Downtown DASH operates Mon.-Fri. 6:30am-6:30pm, Sat. 10am-5pm; other DASH shuttles do not run on Sat.) **All route numbers given are MTA unless otherwise designated.**

Gray Line Tours, 6541 Hollywood Blvd., Hollywood (213-856-5900), is a more expensive but easier way to reach distant attractions. Costs include transportation and admission: Disneyland ($62 for the day, $69 for day and evening); Magic Mountain ($53); Universal Studios ($56); San Diego Zoo ($55); Sea World ($59). Tours leave from the Gray Line office for 200 different locations in summertime. Some larger hostels offer bus trips to area beaches and attractions for reasonable fees.

In a desperate, expensive, last effort to alleviate the congestion that threatens to choke the city, L.A. has finally started building a **subway.** The first leg of L.A.'s 300-mi. Metro Rail Plan, the Blue Line, presently runs from 7th St. in Downtown to Long Beach (call 213-626-4455 for information). The Red Line currently runs from Mac-Arthur Park Station in Westlake to Union Station downtown (5 stops, 7 min.).

Freeways The freeway is perhaps the most enduring of L.A.'s images. When uncongested, these 10- and 12-lane concrete behemoths offer speed and convenience; the trip from downtown to Santa Monica can take as little as 20 min. No matter how crowded the freeway is, it's almost always quicker and safer than taking surface streets to your destination. Californians refer to the highways by names rather than by numbers. For freeway info, call **CalTrans** (213-897-3693). The main freeways are the **San Diego Freeway (I-405),** the **Santa Monica Freeway (I-10), San Bernardino Freeway** east of downtown), the **Golden State Freeway (I-5; Santa Ana** south of downtown), the **Ventura Freeway (U.S. 101; Hollywood Freeway** in Hollywood), and the $2 billion **Glen Anderson Freeway (I-105).** Travelers should not be fooled into thinking that freeways head toward the cities for which they are named; often they do not.

ACCOMMODATIONS

If you arrive at LAX, do *not* accept an offer of free transportation to an unknown hostel. As in any large city, cheap accommodations in Los Angeles are often unsafe. Be suspicious of unusually low posted rates, they are rarely the bargains they seem. Hotels in L.A. should cost at least $35 or they're probably not the kind of hotels most travelers would feel secure in. Americans should be aware that some hostels accept international travelers only or may require international passports.

In choosing where to stay, the first consideration should be how much access you have to a car. If you don't have wheels, you would be wise to decide what element of L.A. appeals to you the most. Those visiting for the beaches would do well to choose lodgings in Venice or Santa Monica. Avid sightseers will probably be better off in Hollywood or the slightly more expensive (but cleaner and nicer) Westside. Downtown has more public transportation but an eerie lack of nightlife. Even those with a car should weigh whether they care more for the seaside or the studio tours, and choose accordingly. Listed prices do not include L.A.'s 14% hotel tax.

CALIFORNIA

L.A. Westside

1 Armand Hammer Museum of Art and Cultural Center
2 Century City
3 Beverly Hills Hotel
4 Pacific Design Center
5 Schindler House
6 Beverly Center
7 Farmer's Market
8 Los Angeles County Museum of Art
9 La Brea Tar Pits
10 Max Factor Museum
11 Mann's Chinese Theater
12 Hollywood Wax Museum
13 Frederick's of Hollywood
14 Barnsdall Park
15 I. Magnin BW Wilshire

N ←

TO GRIFFITH PARK

Vermont Ave.
Franklin Ave.
Hollywood Frwy.
HOLLYWOOD
Santa Monica Blvd.
Western Ave.
3rd St.
Olympic Blvd.
Crenshaw Blvd.
Hollywood Blvd.
Sunset Blvd.
WEST HOLLYWOOD
Highland Ave.
La Brea Blvd.
Melrose Ave.
Beverly Blvd.
Fairfax Ave.
San Vincente Blvd.
Kings Rd.
La Cienega Blvd.
Pico Blvd.
Venice Blvd.
Santa Monica Frwy.
3rd St.
Wilshire Blvd.
BEVERLY HILLS
Sunset Blvd.
Rodeo Dr.
Olympic Blvd.
WESTWOOD
Westwood Blvd.
BEL AIR
Sunset Blvd.
University of California Los Angeles
WESTWOOD VILLAGE
San Diego Frwy.

TO SANTA MONICA AIRPORT

TO SANTA MONICA AND VENICE

Downtown

Though busy and relatively safe by day, the downtown area empties and becomes dangerous when the workday ends and on weekends. Both men and women should travel in groups after dark, especially between Broadway and Main.

Royal Host Olympic Motel, 901 W. Olympic Blvd. (213-626-6255; fax 488-3481). A ritzy budget hotel—great rooms with bathtubs, telephone, radio, and cable TV. Singles $30, doubles $35, with kitchenettes $45. Students can sometimes get a double room for as low as $25. Discounts for stays longer than 3 days.

Hotel Stillwell, 838 S. Grand Ave. (800-553-4774 or 213-627-1151). Recently refurbished, this ultra-clean hotel is one of the most sensible downtown options. A/C, color TV. Singles $35, $175 per week. Doubles $45, $225 per week.

Milner Hotel, 813 S. Flower St. (213-627-6981 or 800-827-0411; fax 623-4751), Central location and good upkeep compensate for the slightly shabby decor. Pub, grill, and pleasant lounge area in lobby. A/C, color TV. Singles $35. Doubles $45.

Park Plaza Hotel, 607 S. Park View St. (213-384-5281; fax 488-3481), on the west corner of 6th St. across from sometimes noisy MacArthur Park. This Art Deco giant with a 3-story marble-floored lobby once entertained Bing Crosby and Eleanor Roosevelt, but now caters mainly to semi-permanent residents. A/C (in some rooms) and TV. Olympic pool. Singles from $50. Doubles $55.

Motel de Ville, 1123 W. 7th St. (213-624-8474; fax 624-7652), next door to the City Center Motel. Pool, clean rooms with free HBO. Singles $35. Doubles $43.

Hollywood

Epitomizing L.A. for many, Hollywood combines convenience and excitement for tourists; it is well-connected to other areas of the city and contains the most famous sights, restaurants, and night spots. Be cautious on Hollywood or Sunset Blvds.—especially east of the main strips, the area can be frightening, particularly at night.

Banana Bungalow Hollywood, 2775 Cahuenga Blvd. (213-851-1129 or 800-4-HOSTEL, 467735; fax 851-1569), in Hollywood, just past the Hollywood Bowl on Highland Ave. A rambunctious place good for partiers. The hostel runs free shuttle service from the airport, as well as to area beaches and attractions (including Disneyland, Magic Mountain, and Universal Studios). Free nightly movies, arcade, and frequent parties. Pool, basketball court, and weight room on premises. Full restaurant serving breakfast ($1-3), lunch ($2), and dinner ($3-5) daily. 24-hr. check-in. Check-out 10:30am. Standard bunks with bathroom and TV. Rooms are coed. Linen included. $15. Doubles $45.

Hollywood International Guest House and Hostel, 6561 Franklin Ave. (213-850-6287, 800-750-6561 in CA), 2 blocks north of Hollywood Blvd. A beautiful house close to Hollywood attractions. Shuttle service to LAX, beaches, tourist attractions. Full kitchen, living room, free coffee. Shared rooms for 2-4 people. Linen included. Check-in 9am-8pm. No curfew. $12. Make reservations early.

Hollywood Wilshire YMCA International Hostel, 1553 N. Hudson Ave. (213-467-4161), 1½ blocks south of Hollywood Blvd. The dorm-style rooms are clean and light. Common room with cable TV, full kitchen, pool table, laundry facilities, and storage lockers. Complimentary use of the adjacent Y facilities: two pools, aerobic classes, high-tech weights and exercise machines. Must be over 18 and out of state. No curfew. Single sex rooms $11, plus refundable $4 deposit. Free linen and breakfast. Reservations recommended 2 weeks ahead.

Hollywood International Hostel, 7038½ Hollywood Blvd. (213-463-0797 or 800-750-6561 in CA only), across from Hollywood Galaxy Center. Small, low-key, 2nd-floor hostel in the heart of Hollywood Blvd. Shuttle service to beach, LAX, and amusement parks. Clean and new, though facilities limited. Small common room with a TV and microwave. 3-4 people in rooms $12, $75 per week. Doubles $30.

Hollywood Hills Hostel, 1921 Highland Ave. (213-850-7733; fax 310-301-2537), 3 blocks from Hollywood Blvd. Free pickup from airport, Greyhound, and Amtrak. Free linen and free transportation to area attractions. Large common room with TV. Laundry facilities and game room. 24-hr. check-in, 11am check-out. No curfew. Complimentary breakfast and coffee. Single-sex rooms $15.50. Doubles $45.

Westside: Beverly Hills, Westwood, Wilshire District

The Westside is an attractive and safer part of town, but for the most part, room rates are out of sight. Call the **UCLA Off-Campus Housing Office** (310-825-4491; 100 Sproul Hall; open Mon.-Fri. 8am-5pm) and see if they can put you in touch with students who have a spare room through their "roommate share board."

Century City-Westwood Motel, 10604 Santa Monica Blvd. (310-475-4422), on the southern part of the boulevard. Clean rooms have elegantly tiled bathrooms, refrigerators, TVs, A/C, and occasional futon for extra guests. More than you usually get at this price. Singles $35-50, each additional person $5, up to 5 in a room.

Hotel Del Flores, 409 N. Crescent Dr., Beverly Hills (310-274-5115), only 3 blocks east of chic Rodeo Dr. and 1 block south of Santa Monica Blvd. You actually can do Beverly Hills cheaply. Communal microwaves and refrigerators. Some rooms with color TV and ceiling fans. Singles $42, with private bath $45. Doubles $55.

Bevonshire Lodge Motel, 7575 Beverly Blvd. (213-936-6154; fax 934-6640). Near Farmers Market and Beverly Center. Clean, attractive motel with quiet, enclosed pool area. A/C, color TV, telephones. Singles $38.50. Doubles $42.50.

Wilshire Orange Hotel, 6060 W. 8th St. (213-931-9533), in West L.A. near Wilshire Blvd. and Fairfax Ave. Buses #20, 21, and 22 serve Wilshire Blvd. from downtown. One of L.A.'s best-located accommodations, but not the cheapest. Near many major sights. Most rooms have refrigerators, TV, and private bath. Weekly housekeeping. Many semi-permanent residents. Singles $45. Doubles $54. Reservations recommended 2 weeks in advance, especially in summer.

Coastal: Santa Monica and Venice

The hostels at Venice Beach are havens for the young, sociable budget traveler whose highest priority is to meet other people and have a good time. You may miss the Sunset Strip, but in return you'll find well-populated beaches, kinky architecture, and a mellow and unpretentious community devoted to worshiping the sun and cultivating its own eccentricities. The hostels attract many foreign students, who are lured by Venice's lively blend of indulgent beach culture (beaches *are not* safe at night) and relentless nightlife. Some hostels cater exclusively to foreigners. Nearby Santa Monica is far more upscale, but offers a nice hostel.

Santa Monica International HI-AYH Hostel, 1436 2nd St., (310-393-9913; fax 393 1769), Santa Monica. Only hostel guests with receipts are allowed in. Tighter security than most hostels in the area. Take MTA bus #33 from downtown to 2nd and Broadway, or take Blue Bus #3 from airport to 4th and Broadway, Blue Bus #10 from downtown. 2 blocks from beach. Kitchen, laundry facilities, and weekend BBQs. TV room, nightly movies, storage room, and lockers. Sunny courtyard. Linen rental $2. 2-week max. stay. Dorm-style room $16, nonmembers $19. Doubles $43/46. IBN reservations available.

Venice Marina Hostel, 2915 Yale Ave. (310-301-3983), Marina del Rey. Located at the end of a quiet residential street, this hostel offers a respite from the manic pace closer to the shore. Free shuttle from LAX, Amtrak, etc. TV room, laundry, and kitchen. No curfew. 24-hr. check-in. Flexible check-out. Includes linen, breakfast, and local phone calls. $13. $84 per week gets you a bed, but be prepared to share the room with 3-8 others. Reservations helpful.

Venice Beach Hostel, 1515 Pacific Ave. (310-452-3052; fax 821-3469), Venice, on the corner of Windward Ave. Not to be confused with the Venice Beach Hostel on Washington Blvd. Take the #1 or #2 Big Blue Bus or MTA #3. Recipient of the Venice Historical Society's Annual Award in 1994 for its renovations, this hostel used to be the Trolley Hotel building. Game room with pool, darts, video poker, cable TV. Kitchen. Sauna in the works. Free coffee and breakfast. Occasional free dinner and beer. Linen provided. Laundry facilities. 24-hr. check-in. Check-out 10am. No curfew. 4-person dorm rooms; $10-11 per person. Doubles $30-35.

Cadillac Hotel, 401 Ocean Front Walk (310-399-8876), Venice. A beautiful Art deco landmark directly on the beachfront. Call for airport shuttle service. Limited parking. Sundeck and gym. 1-week max. stay. Check-out 11am. No curfew. Free linen and lockers. Shared accommodations $18. Private ocean-view rooms $55 and up. Reservations for groups of 4 only. Wheelchair accessible.

Stardust Motor Hotel, 3202 Wilshire Blvd., (310-828-4584), Santa Monica. Well-kept accommodations with cable TV, telephone, A/C, and a tiny pool. Singles from $36. Doubles $45. Room with kitchen $45-50.

Jim's at The Beach, 17 Brooks Ave., Venice (310-399-4018; fax 399-4216). Outstanding location ½ block off the boardwalk. **International Passport required.** No more than 6 beds per room. Kitchen. No curfew. Linen included. Free breakfast, and BBQs on weekends. Clean and sunny rooms $15, $90 per week.

Venice Beach Hostel, 701 Washington Blvd. (508-306-5180), near a somewhat noisy street. **International passport required.** Free shuttle bus from airport. Relaxed atmosphere and large common room. Rooftop deck is popular with sun-lovers. Full kitchen. Keg parties Thurs. night. Lockers available. No curfew or lock-out. Reception open 24 hrs. $12 per night, $70 per week. One room for couples available at $30 per night.

Airport Interclub Hostel, 2221 Lincoln Blvd., Venice (310-305-0250; fax 305-8590), near Venice Blvd. Take MTA #3 from LAX or #33 from downtown. **International passport required.** Festive after-hours common-room atmosphere in which many nationalities bump elbows. Free airport pick-up, bike and skate rental, pool table, and TV. Psychedelic decor. Mixed- or single-sex accommodations. Kitchen with stove and fridge. Linen. Laundry room. Check-out 10:30am. Rooms sleep 6, or you can sleep in the prison-like 25-bed dorm for the same price. $14, $84 per week. Doubles $32, $200 per week. $5 deposit.

Inglewood

Inglewood is far from most attractions and *should not be covered by public transportation or on foot.* The following accommodations have fantastic services, but have not been visited by a *Let's Go* researcher. **Backpackers Paradise,** 4200 W. Century Blvd. (310-419-0999), is located in the **California Trade Winds Hotel.** Their offer of free shuttle transportation from airport or Venice Beach is useful—you don't want to walk in this neighborhood. The hostel has semi-private rooms for $16. The hotel has 2-room suites for $35, 3-room suite for $55. For both, TV, continental breakfast, nightly champagne party, and movies are included in price. Laundry facilities, lockers, pool, jacuzzi, and game room are available; no curfew at either.

FOOD

The range of culinary options in L.A. is directly proportional to the city's ethnic diversity—Angelenos speak 116 different languages. Certain types of food are concentrated in specific areas. Jewish and Eastern European food is most prevalent in the **Fairfax** area; Mexican in **East L.A.;** Japanese, Chinese, Vietnamese, and Thai around **Little Tokyo** and **Chinatown,** and seafood along the coast. Hawaiian, Indian, and Ethiopian restaurants are scattered throughout the city. Los Angeles elevates fast-food and chain restaurants to heights virtually unknown in the rest of the country. For the optimal burger-and-fries experience, try **In 'n' Out Burger** (various locations, call 818-287-4377 for the one nearest you), a family-operated chain only in the L.A. area. **Johnny Rocket's** returns you to the lost era of American diners. **California Pizza Kitchen,** (CPK) spawned the now-national interest in wood-fired, well-decorated pizza. The restaurant at 121 N. La Cienega Blvd. (213-854-6555), is a good place to start. L.A. restaurants tend to shut down early, often by 11pm. Even fast-food chains are rarely open past midnight.

Downtown

Lunch specials are easy to find in the financial district, however finding a reasonably priced dinner can be a challenge. Nearby, **Chinatown** has standard restaurants with as well as generally inexpensive delis; **Weller Court** by the New Ofani Hotel and Garden surrounds several Japanese restaurants, a few of which are in budget range.

The Pantry, 877 S. Figueroa St. (213-972-9279). Open since the '20s, the Pantry defies culinary trendiness. The restaurant seats only 84 yet serves 2500-3000 meals a day. Be prepared to wait for the enormous breakfast specials ($6), especially on weekends. Sun. brunch at the Pantry is an L.A. tradition. Open 24 hrs.

Philippe's, The Original, 1001 N. Alameda (213-628-3781), 2 blocks north of Union Station. A great place for lunch. Philippe's claims to have originated the French-dipped sandwich ($3-4). Open daily 6am-10pm.

La Luz Del Día, 1 W. Olvera St. (213-628-7495). This authentic and inexpensive Mexican restaurant is hidden amidst the many tourist-trap Mexican joints along historic Olvera St. Combination plates $4-5. Open Tues.-Sun. 11am-10pm.

Café China, 1123 W. 7th St. (213-689-9898). Filling combination plates, like spicy shrimp and almond chicken, served with soup, egg roll, and rice ($4.50). Eat in or take out. American breakfasts. Open Mon.-Fri. 8am-7pm. Sat 9am-2am.

Thank Vi, 422 Ord St. (213-687-3522). A favorite spot among Chinatown denizens for Vietnamese cuisine and justifiably so; the clean, light setting matches the eats. Everything under $7.75; most items under $5. Open Thurs.-Tues. 7:30am-6:30pm.

Hollywood and West Hollywood

Most of Hollywood and West Hollywood's residents are young, single, hungry, and near broke after paying the rent on their bungalows. As a result, Hollywood has the best budget dining in L.A. Look on Hollywood and Sunset Boulevards for diverse cuisines, while Fairfax (the traditionally Jewish area of town) has Mediterranean-style restaurants and delis. Melrose is full of chic cafés and eateries; many with outdoor seating perfect for people-watching.

Lucy's El Adobe Café, 5536 Melrose Ave. (213-462-9421), 1 block east of Gower St., in Hollywood. This family-run restaurant is a favorite among downtown politicians and Paramount executives. Indulge in some of the best Mexican food in town. Former California governor Jerry Brown and Linda Ronstadt allegedly met here. Full dinners $10-11. Open Mon.-Sat. 11:30am-11pm.

Duke's, 8909 Sunset Blvd. (310-652-3100), at San Vicente, in West Hollywood. Hangout for L.A.'s music industry bigwigs; its walls are a kaleidoscope of posters and autographed album covers. Perfect for brunch—carry a copy of *Spin* to pass the time while you wait for a table. Entrees $4-7. Open Mon.-Fri. 7:30am-9pm, Sat.-Sun. 8am-4pm.

Pink's Famous Chili Dogs, 711 N. la Brea Ave. (213-931-4223), in Hollywood. The chili dogs are good and cheap ($2.10) and that's why this friendly stand has been around since 1939. They're a better bargain now, if you factor in inflation and the shrinking dollar. Open Sun.-Thurs. 8am-2am, Fri.-Sat. 8am-3am.

Chin Chin, 8618 Sunset Blvd. (310-652-1818), in West Hollywood. Other locations in Brentwood, Studio City, and Woodland Hills. Immensely popular with the lunchtime set for its handmade "dim sum and then sum" (averages $5). The shredded chicken salad ($6) is a perfect example of California-ized Chinese cuisine. Outdoor seating. Open Sun.-Thurs. 11am-11pm, Fri.-Sat. 11am-midnight.

Wilshire District and Beverly Hills

Although inexpensive, quality food is difficult to find in the Wilshire District, both La Brea Ave. and Pico Blvd. offer an assortment of restaurants worth exploring. Beverly Hills has some of the finest dining in the country, but don't expect any bargains.

The Apple Pan, 10801 W. Pico Blvd. (310-475-3585), in West L.A. between Westwood and Overland. From downtown, take bus #431. This little building is easily overshadowed by the mammoth Westside Pavilion shopping center across the street, but since 1927 it continues to draw crowds for large, juicy hamburgers ($3.60). Almost legendary status. Frequented by locals. Open Sun. and Tues.-Thurs. 11am-midnight, Fri.-Sat. 11am-1am. Closed the first 2 weeks in July.

El Nopal, 10426 National Blvd. (310-559-4732), in West L.A., between Motor and Overland, just south of the Santa Monica Fwy. "Home of the pregnant burrito."

The famed *embarrasado* ($6.25), stuffed with chicken and avocado, lives up to its name. Smaller burritos $2-4. Open Sun.-Thurs. 11am-9pm, Fri.-Sat. 11am-10pm.

The Cheesecake Factory, 364 N. Beverly Dr. (310-278-7270), also in Brentwood (310-826-7111). Very, very popular—expect to stand in line. Once you get in, you'll be treated to ridiculously huge portions. Half-sandwich with soup or salad $6. The scrumptious cheesecakes come in dozens of flavors. Open Sun. 10:30am-11pm, Mon.-Thurs. 11am-11:30pm, Fri.-Sat. 11am-12:30am.

Dragon Garden, 2625 S. Robertson (310-837-3626). Not the best Chinese food in L.A., but you can't beat the $1.20-per-item lunch special (11:30am-4:30pm).

Westwood

Westwood is filled with chic and convenient eateries perfect before a movie or while shopping, and you'll find everything from falafel to gelato in corner shops.

Mongols B-B-Q, 1064 Gayley Ave. (310-824-3377). Follow the lunchtime crowd as they stream into this colorful little joint. In the center of it all, a glass-enclosed chef sizzles up various specialties. Full of people slurping up big bowls of noodles. Buffet-style lunch (Mongolian BBQ, $5.45). Come early. Open Sun.-Thurs. 11:30am-10pm, Fri.-Sat. 11:30am-11pm.

Sphinx, 1779 A Westwood Blvd. (310-477-2358), ½ block north of Santa Monica Blvd. A bit out of the way from Westwood proper, but the clientele of locals is evidence it's worth the trip. Excellent Middle Eastern cuisine. Delectable BBQ chicken kebab $3.50. Open Mon.-Fri. 10am-10pm, Sat. 11am-10pm.

Santa Monica and Venice

Unfortunately, many of Santa Monica's eateries are quite expensive. Venice runs the gamut from greasy to health-conscious, as befits its beachy-hippie population. **EATZ Café** in Santa Monica Pl. (at the end of the 3rd St. Promenade on Broadway) has 17 different types of mall food—many of which are tasty and reasonably priced.

Ye Olde King's Head, 116 Santa Monica Blvd. (310-451-1402), in Santa Monica. An authentic British pub owned by a Manchester expatriate. Fish and chips $7.50. A broad assortment of English beers and ales. Open Mon.-Thurs. 11am-11pm, Fri.-Sat. 11am-midnight, Sun. noon-11:30pm.

Skorpio's, 109 Santa Monica Blvd. (310-393-9020), ½ block from Ocean Ave. Standard and solid Greek fare for under $6. Giant gyro sandwiches ($3.50) and great spanakopitas ($5.50). Beer, wine, and cappuccino. Open daily 11am-11pm.

Benita's Frites, 1437 3rd St. Promenade (310-458-2889), in Santa Monica. French fries are the fare here. They're served the Belgian way, in a paper cone with any of the 20 sauces—try the garlic-lemon-mayonnaise. Open Sun. noon-8pm, Mon. 11:30am-4pm., Tues.-Thurs. 11:30am-10pm, Fri.-Sat. 11:30am-10:30pm.

Tito's Tacos, 11222 Washington Place (310-391-5780), a bit out of the way in Culver City at Sepulveda, 1 block north of Washington Blvd., virtually *beneath* the San Diego Fwy. The name should have been Tito's Burritos, since the burrito, with its huge hunks of shredded beef, is the star attraction (at $2.10, it's also the most expensive thing on the menu). Plenty of parking. Open daily 9am-11:30pm.

San Fernando Valley

Ventura Blvd. is filled with restaurants. Eating lunch near the studios in **Studio City** is your best stargazing opportunity. The famous are willing to dine outside the studios because of Studio City's unwritten law—you can stare all you want, but don't bother them, *and don't ask for autographs.* **Dalt's Grill,** 3500 W. Olive Ave. (818-953-7752) in Burbank at Olive and Riverside, is a swank grill next door to Warner Studios. A chicken fajita Caesar salad is $7. Burgers and sandwiches are $4-5. (Open Mon.-Thurs. 11am-midnight, Fri.-Sat. 11am-1am, Sun. 10am-midnight.)

SIGHTS

Major Museums

Los Angeles County Museum of Art (LACMA), 5905 Wilshire Blvd. (213-857-6000), at the west end of Hancock Park. A distinguished, comprehensive collection, representing most major periods and styles. The LACMA is the largest museum in the West. Five major buildings cluster around the Times-Mirror Central Court. The museum offers a variety of tours and free talks. For schedules, check with the information desk in the Central Court (ticket office 857-6010) or contact the Docent Council at 857-6108. Open Mon. and Wed. 10am-5pm, Fri. 10am-9pm, Sat.-Sun. 11am-6pm. $6, seniors and students $4, ages 6-17 $1. Free 2nd Wed. of each month.

J. Paul Getty Museum, 17985 PCH (310-458-2003), set back on a cliff above the ocean north of Santa Monica. Getty, an oil magnate, built this mansion as a re-creation of the first-century Villa dei Papiri in Herculaneum. The museum owns an incredible variety of artwork. With a $2.9 billion endowment (New York's Metropolitan Museum of Art has "only" $350 million), the trustees can afford to keep their purse wide open. Access to the museum is tricky. The parking lot is small and reservations are needed at least a day in advance, and weeks in advance in summer. Take MTA #434 to the museum. Ask for a free **museum pass** from the bus driver or you will not be admitted. The museum gate is a ½ mi. from the bus stop, so be prepared to walk. Open Tues.-Sun. 10am-5pm; free.

Norton Simon Museum of Art, 411 W. Colorado Blvd. (213-681-2484), at Orange Grove Blvd. in Old Pasadena. Houses numerous Rodin and Brancusi bronzes, and paintings by Rembrandt, Raphael, and Picasso. From downtown take bus #483 from Olive St., anywhere between Venice Blvd. and 1st St., to Colorado Blvd. and Fair Oaks Ave. in Pasadena. Then take #180 or 181. The museum is 4 blocks west. Open Thurs.-Sun. noon-6pm. $4, seniors and students $2, under 12 free.

Beit HaShoa Museum of Tolerance, 9786 W. Pico Blvd. (310-553-9036), corner of Roxbury just outside of Beverly Hills. Previously known as the Simon Wiesenthal Center, the museum has received $5 million from former Governor Deukmejian to build a larger structure. The museum includes displays on the Armenian and Native American genocides, as well as the Jewish Holocaust. Mandatory tours leave at 10-min. intervals and last 2½ hrs. Tickets cannot be reserved and often sell out on Fri. and Sun. last tours leave 2½ hrs. before closing. Open Mon.-Wed. 10am-5pm, Thurs. 10am-8pm, Fri. 10am-3pm, Sun. 10:30am-5pm. $7.50, seniors $5.50, students $4.50, ages 3-12 $2.50.

Southwest Museum, 234 Museum Dr. (213-221-2163), in Pasadena. Collection includes contemporary Native American art. Housed in a palatial Hispano-Moorish home on a hill fairly close to the east side of downtown. Take bus #83 along Broadway to Museum Dr. and trek up the hill. Drivers, take the Pasadena Fwy. (Rte. 110) to Ave. 43 and follow the signs. Open Tues.-Sun. 11am-5pm. $5, seniors and students $3, ages 7-18 $2. Library open Wed.-Sat. 11am-5pm.

Museum of Contemporary Art (MOCA), 250 S. Grand Ave. (213-626-6222), at California Plaza, downtown. Showcases art from 1940 to the present. Focuses on abstract expressionism, and includes works by Pollock, Calder, Miró, and Giacometti. MOCA open Tues.-Wed. and Fri.-Sun. 11am-5pm, Thurs. 11am-8pm. $6, seniors and students with ID $4; under 12 free. Free Thurs. 5-8pm.

Museum of African-American Art, 4005 Crenshaw Blvd., 3rd floor (213-294-7071), in downtown. The first of its kind in the American West, thoughtfully contextualizes pieces within their proper historical framework. Open Wed.-Sat. 11am-6pm, Sun. noon-5pm. Free.

Hollywood Studio Museum, 2100 N. Highland Ave. (213-874-2276), across from the Hollywood Bowl. A refreshing look at the history of early Hollywood filmmaking. Antique cameras, costumes, props, vintage film clips, and other memorabilia clutter the museum. Open Sat. and Sun. 10am-4pm. $4, seniors and students $3, ages 6-12 $2. Tours for $3 per person. Ample free parking.

Gene Autry Western Heritage Museum, 4700 Zoo Dr. (213-667-2000), within Griffith Park at the junction of Golden State (I-5) and Ventura Fwy. (Rte.134). Covers the facts and fictions of the Old West. Exhibits on pioneer life and Westerns. Open Tues.-Sun. 10am-5pm. $7, seniors and students $5, children $3.

California Museum of Science and Industry, 700 State Dr. (213-744-7400), in Exposition Park. Enter at the corner of Figueroa and Exposition next to the United DC-8. Some corporate propaganda. IBM, Bell Telephone, and McDonald's all sponsor displays. The Aerospace Building exhibits $8 million worth of aircraft. Museum open daily 10am-5pm. Free. Parking $3; bring quarters.

Los Angeles County Natural History Museum, 900 Exposition Blvd. (213-744-3466), in Exposition Park. The museum exhibits pre-Columbian cultures, North American and African mammals, American history, and dinosaurs. Open Tues.-Sun. 10am-5pm. $5, seniors and students $2.50, ages 5-12 $1, under 5 free.

Downtown L.A.

The Los Angeles downtown area alone is larger than most cities. The downtown provides a theoretical, if not geographical, centerpoint for Los Angeles's dispersed neighborhoods. Financiers who flee to valley domiciles every evening and a substantial street population that retires and rises on the street coexist here. An uneasy truce prevails, but visitors should be cautious; the area is especially unsafe after business hours and on weekends. Don't bring valuables with you and leave nothing costly in your car. Park in a secure lot, rather than on the streets.

The **Financial District** is where the gigantic offices crowd the busy downtown center (an area bounded roughly by 3rd and 6th St., Figueroa St., and Grand Ave.). The district's skyline includes some of L.A.'s most magnificent buildings. The I.M. Pei-designed **First Interstate World Center,** 633 W. 5th St., perched atop Bunker Hill, dominates the skyline; at 73 stories and 1017 ft., it's the tallest building west of the Mississippi River. With the exception of its 1970s addition, the **Times-Mirror Building** at 220 W. 1st is the area's most impressive building.

To the north of the financial district is L.A.'s **Music Center,** 135 N. Grand Ave. (213-972-7211), comprised of the **Dorothy Chandler Pavillion** (site of the Oscars), the **Mark Taper Forum,** and the **Ahmanson Theatre.** The center is home to the Los Angeles Philharmonic Orchestra and the Joffrey Ballet. The **Civic Center,** a solid wall of bureaucratic architecture bounded by the Hollywood Fwy. (U.S. 101), Grand, 1st, and San Pedro St., runs east from the Music Center. It ends at **City Hall,** 200 N. Spring St., which has a great **observation deck** on the 27th floor.

El Pueblo neighborhood lies farther north as the historic birthplace of Los Angeles, bounded by Spring St., Arcadia St., and Macy St. In the place where the original city center once stood, **El Pueblo de Los Angeles State Historic Park** (213-680-2525; open daily 10am-3pm) preserves a number of historically important buildings from the Spanish and Mexican eras. Start out at the **Visitors Center,** 622 N. Main, in the Sepulveda House (213-628-1274). The center offers free walking tours (Tues.-Sat. hourly 10am-noon; call to check). The **Old Plaza,** with its century-old Moreton Bay fig trees and huge bandstand, is at the center of the pueblo. Tours start here and wind their way past the **Avila Adobe,** 10 E. Olvera St., the oldest house in the city (the original adobe has been replaced with concrete in order to meet earthquake regulations), followed by **Pico House,** 500 N. Main St., once L.A.'s most luxurious hotel. **Olvera Street,** one of L.A.'s original roads, is now called Tijuana North by the locals. The street is packed with touristy little stands selling Mexican handicrafts. Olvera St. is the sight of the Cinco de Mayo celebrations of L.A.'s Chicano population. Across Alameda St. from El Pueblo is the grand old **Union Station.** The station is being renovated through L.A. Conservancy efforts, but is ready to be opened to the public.

Chinatown lies north of this area, roughly bordered by Yale, Spring, Ord, and Bernard St. From downtown, take the DASH shuttle. Roman Polanski's *Chinatown,* starring Jack Nicholson, was filmed in this once vice-ridden neighborhood. **Little Tokyo** is centered on 2nd and San Pedro St. on the eastern edge of downtown. The **New Otani Hotel,** 120 S. Los Angeles St., 1 block south of the Civic Center between 1st and 2nd, rents lavish Meiji-style rooms for up to $700 per night. For slightly less, you can have a drink in the elegant rooftop garden. The **Japanese Village Plaza**

(213-620-8861), in the 300 block of E. 2nd St., is the center of the district and is a florid fusion of American shopping mall and Japanese design. The **Japanese-American Cultural and Community Center** was designed by Buckminster Fuller and Isamu Noguchi, who crafted a monumental sculpture for the courtyard. (Administrative offices open Mon.-Fri. 9am-5pm.)

Exposition Park

At the turn of the century, this area was an upscale suburb of downtown; it deteriorated in the '20s but was renewed when the Olympiad first came to town in 1932. This neighborhood was revitalized yet again by the 1984 Olympics, and today it is one of the few parts of L.A. where a number of important attractions are clustered together. The museums are generally safe and well-visited, and keep early hours. The park is southwest of downtown, just off the Harbor Fwy., and is bounded by Exposition Blvd., Figueroa St., Vermont Ave., and Santa Barbara Ave. From downtown, take bus #40 or 42 (from Broadway between 5th and 6th St.) to the park's southern edge. From Hollywood, take #204 down Vermont. *Exposition Park is not a safe area, particularly at night.*

Exposition Park also includes the **Los Angeles Memorial Coliseum,** 2601 S. Figueroa St., home of the **Los Angeles Raiders** and the **USC Trojan** football teams, and the **Sports Arena,** home of the **Los Angeles Clippers** NBA team and a venue for rock concerts. The colossal Coliseum, which seats over 100,000, was a main venue during the 1932 and 1984 Summer Olympic Games.

The **University of Southern California (USC)** campus sits opposite Exposition Park on Exposition Blvd. The campus is beautiful and generally safe, although exercise caution after dark. (213-740-2300; walking tours of the campus are available on the hr., Mon.-Fri. 10am-2pm.) The **Fisher Gallery,** 823 Exposition Blvd. (213-740-4561), includes portions of the Armand Hammer collection of Dutch paintings. (Open early Sept. to summer Tues.-Fri. noon-5pm, Sat. 11am-3pm. Free.)

Watts, a neighborhood made notorious by riots in 1965, rests 7 mi. southeast of the USC campus. Tourists will probably feel unwelcome or unsafe here. The only tourist attraction per se is the **Watts Towers,** 1765 E. 107th St. (213-569-8181), which is reasonably safe if you remain aware and responsible. The towers of glistening fretwork, decorated with mosaics of broken glass, ceramic tile, and sea shells, are a testament to one man's extraordinary vision and dedication. (On-the-spot tours $1, children free if accompanied by adult; open Sat.-Sun. 10am-4pm.) Next door, at 1727 E. 107th St. the **Watts Tower Arts Center** (213-847-4646), houses a permanent exhibit of folk instruments (open Tues.-Sun. 10am-4pm).

Wilshire District and Hancock Park

The cosmopolitan Wilshire District contains a wide variety of attractions from art museums to a baseball stadium. Most of the action centers around sprawling Wilshire Boulevard which connects downtown Los Angeles with Santa Monica. Wilshire Boulevard, especially the "Miracle Mile" between Highland and Fairfax Ave., played a starring role in Los Angeles's westward suburban expansion. On what was then the end of the boulevard, the Bullocks Corporation gambled on attracting shoppers from downtown and in 1929 erected one of L.A.'s few architecturally significant buildings, the massive, bronze-colored **Bullocks Wilshire** at 3050 Wilshire Blvd., near Vermont Ave., now called the **I. Magnin BW Wilshire.**

La Brea Tar Pits, one of the most popular hangouts in the world for fossilized early mammals, bubbles only a few miles farther down Wilshire, in **Hancock Park,** next to L.A. country. Most of the one million bones recovered from the pits between 1913 and 1915 have found a new home in the **George C. Page Museum of La Brea Discoveries,** 5801 Wilshire Blvd., at Curson and Wilshire (recording 213-936-2230, operator 213-857-6311). (Open daily 10am-5pm. $5, seniors and students $3.50, ages 5-10 $2, under 5 free. Free admission 1st Tues. of month. Parking $4. Museum tours Wed.-Sun. 2pm. Tours of grounds 1pm.)

Elysian Park, about 3 mi. northeast of downtown, has 525 acres of greenery ideal for picnicking. The park curves around the northern portion of Chavez Ravine, home of the well-designed and sparkling-clean **Dodger Stadium** (213-224-1400) and the **Los Angeles Dodgers** baseball team. (See Sports below)

Hollywood

For decades, this tiny chunk of massive L.A. has defined glamour for the world. Countless young people have crossed land and oceans for a chance to share in the glitz and fame associated with this capital of the movie industry. For years, Hollywood has symbolized the American desire to "make it"—to forget one's past and fabricate an instant persona of sophistication and wealth. For years, it succeeded, generating the image and style associated with California, and with America itself.

Hollywood today has lost much of its sparkle. To catch a fleeting glimpse of the orange groves and farm lands that first lured movie men, travel into the Hollywood Hills north of the more urban and grittier world of central Hollywood. The major studios have moved over the mountains into the roomier San Fernando Valley and blockbusters are increasingly shot "on location" elsewhere in the U.S. or overseas. Hollywood Boulevard and other thoroughfares, once glittering and glamorous, are now run-down and rated X. Hollywood is still fascinating, but a far cry from the Emerald City it was once thought to be.

The **HOLLYWOOD sign**—those 50-ft.-high, slightly erratic letters perched on Mt. Cahuenga north of Hollywood—stands with New York's Statue of Liberty and Paris's Eiffel Tower as universally recognized civic symbols. The original 1923 sign, which read HOLLYWOODLAND, was an advertisement for a new subdivision in the Hollywood Hills. By 1978 the city had acquired the sign and reconstructed the crumbling letters, leaving off the last syllable. The sign has been a target of pranksters (USC frat boys and Cal Tech hackers) who have made it read everything from "Hollyweed" to "Ollywood," after the infamous Lt. Col. Oliver North. For a closer look at the site, follow Beachwood Dr. up into the hills (bus #208; off Franklin Ave. between Vine St. and Western Ave.).

Drive along the narrow, twisting streets of the Hollywood Hills for glimpses of the multi-colored homes and lifestyles of the Rich and Famous. **Hollywood Boulevard** itself, lined with souvenir shops, clubs, and theaters, is busy day and night. Most sights in this area now focus around the intersection of Highland Ave. and Hollywood Blvd., and then west down Hollywood. To the east, things turn seedier. The facade of **Mann's Chinese Theater** (formerly Grauman's), 6925 Hollywood Blvd. (213-464-8111), between Highland and La Brea, is a garish rendition of a Chinese temple. There's always a crowd of tourists in the courtyard, worshiping impressions made by movie stars in the cement outside the theater. The impressions are of parts of the stars' anatomy or trademark possessions. (Al Jolson's knees, Trigger's hooves, R2D2's wheels, Jimmy Durante's nose, George Burns's cigar, etc.) Passersby can sometimes get free passes to sit in the audience of live TV shows from studio workers standing outside the theater.

If you want to stroll among the stars, have a look at the **Walk of Fame** along Hollywood Blvd. and Vine St. More than 2500 bronze-inlaid stars are embedded in the sidewalk, inscribed with the names of the famous. Film, television, and radio celebrities are commemorated, but many names will be meaningless to the under-40 generation. To catch a glimpse of today's (or yesterday's) stars in person, call the Hollywood Chamber of Commerce (213-469-8311) for the times and locations of upcoming star-unveiling ceremonies.

Two blocks east of Mann's is the **Hollywood Wax Museum,** 6767 Hollywood Blvd. (213-462-5991), where you'll meet 200 figures, from Jesus to Elvis. (Open Sun.-Thurs. 10am-midnight, Fri.-Sat. 10am-2am. $9, children $7.) Across the street from the Wax Museum you'll find two touristy "Odd-itoriums," **Frederick's of Hollywood** (including the museum of lingerie with classic ads extorting you to "put your breasts on a shelf"), and the **Max Factor Museum,** which features dozens of glamourous photos paying tribute to the most celebrated make-up artist of all time. (Open Mon.-Sat. 10am-4pm; free.)

The **Hollywood Studio Museum,** 2100 N. Highland Ave. (213-874-2276), across from the Hollywood Bowl, provides a refreshing look at the history of early Hollywood film-making. Back in 1913, when it was a barn, famed director Cecil B. DeMille rented this building as a studio and shot Hollywood's first feature film, *The Squaw Man,* there. Antique cameras, costumes, props, vintage film clips, and other memorabilia clutter the museum. (Open Sat. and Sun. 10am-4pm. $4, seniors and students $3, ages 6-12 $2. Tours for $3 per person. Ample free parking.)

Music is another industry that, like film, finds a center in Los Angeles. The pre-eminent monument of the modern record industry is the 1954 **Capitol Records Tower,** 1750 Vine St., just north of Hollywood Blvd. The building, which was designed to look like a stack of records, is cylindrical with fins sticking out at each floor (the "records") and a needle on top. If you're still not sated, visit the **Hollywood Cemetery,** 6000 Santa Monica Blvd. (213-469-1181), between Vine St. and Western Ave., which has the remains of Rudolph Valentino, Douglas Fairbanks, Sr., and other Hollywood legends (open daily 8am-5pm; mausoleums close at 4:30pm).

Barnsdall Park, 4800 Hollywood Blvd., relatively small and discreet, contains the **Municipal Art Gallery,** 4804 Hollywood Blvd. (213-485-4581), a modern building that displays the works of Southern California artists in a low-key setting. (Open Tues.-Sun. 12:30-5pm. $1, under 13 free.) Adjacent to the museum, the **Hollyhock House,** 4808 Hollywood Blvd. (213-662-7272), commands a 360° view of Los Angeles and the mountains. Completed in 1922 for eccentric oil heiress Aline Barnsdall, the house remains one of Frank Lloyd Wright's most important works. The name of the house derives from Barnsdall's favorite flower, which she had Wright reproduce (grudgingly) in abstract all over the house. (Tours Tues.-Sun. on the hr. from noon-3pm. $1.50, seniors $1, under 12 free. Buy tickets at the Municipal Art Gallery.)

West Hollywood

Once considered a no-man's land between Beverly Hills and Hollywood, West Hollywood was incorporated in 1985 and was one of the first cities in the country to be governed by openly gay officials. West Hollywood and Hollywood have distinctly different characters. The *LA Weekly* has a list of weekly events in West Hollywood.

In the years before incorporation, lax zoning and other liberal laws gave rise to today's **Sunset Strip.** Long the nightlife center of L.A., the Strip was originally lined with posh nightclubs frequented by stars. Today the strip plays host to several rock clubs. Many world-famous bands from The Doors to Guns 'n Roses got their start here. Restaurants and comedy clubs flourish here as well. The **billboards** on the Strip are vividly hand-painted, many heralding the latest motion pictures.

Melrose Avenue, running through the southern portion of West Hollywood, is lined with restaurants, ultra-trendy boutiques, and art galleries. Punk clothing pits like **Retail Slut** and novelty shops like **Condom Mania** outfit clubbies for the evening. The choicest stretch is between La Brea and Fairfax, but the entire way between Highland and Doheny is packed with a stylish set.

Although now an international chain, the Los Angeles **Hard Rock Café** (310-276-7605), on the corner of Beverly and San Vicente Blvd., is still fun. Indiana Jones's leather jacket, one of Pete Townsend's guitars, and a 6-ft.-tall martini glass adorn the interior. Expect to wait for a table most nights—over an hour on weekends. (Open Sun.-Thurs. 11:30am-11:30pm, Fri.-Sat. 11:30am-midnight.)

Griffith Park

The L.A. Zoo, the Greek Theater, Griffith Observatory and Planetarium, Travel Town, a bird sanctuary, tennis courts, two golf courses, campgrounds, and various hiking trails decorate the dry hills and mountains of Griffith Park (open daily 5:30am-10pm). This formidable recreational region stretches from the hills above North Hollywood to the intersection of the Ventura and Golden State Freeways. Pick up a map at any of the entrance points. Several of the mountain roads through the park, especially Vista Del Valle Dr., offer panoramic (though often smog-obscured) views of Los Angeles, looking south over downtown, Hollywood, and the Westside. For information, stop by the **Visitors Center and Ranger Headquarters,** 4730 Crystal Spring Dr. (213-665-5188; open 24 hrs.).

The white stucco and copper domes of the Art Deco **Observatory and Planetarium** (213-664-1181, for a recording 664-1191) structure are visible from around the park. A telescope with a 12-in. lens is open to the public every clear night (dusk-9:45pm; winter Tues.-Sun. 7-10pm; sky report and information 213-663-8171). The planetarium also presents popular **Laserium** light shows (818-997-3624), psychedelic symphonies of lasers and music. (Observatory open daily 12:30pm-10pm; winter Tues.-Sun. 2-10pm. Planetarium show Mon.-Fri. at 3 and 7:30pm, Sat.-Sun. also at 4:30pm; in winter Tues.-Fri. 3 and 7:30pm, Sat.-Sun. also at 4:30 pm. $4, seniors $3, under 12 $2, under 5 not admitted. Laser shows Sun. and Tues.-Sat. 6 and 8:30pm, summer also Fri.-Sat 9:45pm. $6.50, children $5.50.)

A large **bird sanctuary** at the bottom of the observatory hill is nice, but if you crave a wider assortment of animal life, you might prefer the **L.A. Zoo,** 5332 Western Heritage Way, at the park's northern end (213-666-4090). (Open daily 10am-5pm. $8, seniors $5, ages 2-12 $3.) To get to the Observatory take bus #203 from Hollywood. To reach the Zoo and Travel Town, take bus #97 from downtown.

Forest Lawn Cemetery, 1712 Glendale Ave., Glendale (818-241-4151), was analyzed by Jessica Mitford as the showy emblem of the "American Way of Death." Its grounds include reproductions of many of Michelangelo's works, the "largest religious painting on earth" (the famous 195-ft. version of the *Crucifixion*), a stained-glass *Last Supper,* and innumerable other works of art. (Grounds open daily 8am-6pm, mausoleum until 4:30.) From downtown, take bus #90 or 91 and disembark just after the bus leaves San Fernando Rd. to turn onto Glendale Ave. Forest Lawn is easily approached via the Golden State Fwy. or Glendale Fwy. (Rte. 2).

Beverly Hills

Located in the north of Greater Los Angeles, about two-thirds of the way between downtown L.A. and the coast, Beverly Hills remains a steadfast enclave of wealth. Beverly Hills seceded from L.A. in 1914 and has remained distinct (physically and ideologically) ever since. Before you hop on a stargazing tour bus, be forewarned that the only people visible on the streets are gardeners, and many of them don't even know whom they're working for. Celebrity-hungry visitors should have plenty of time and pride to spare before buying a street corner *Star Map.* Hawkers do their best to convince you that every map besides theirs is fraudulent. Believe all of them.

There is nothing understated about this city's riches. Walk along Rodeo Dr. for 15 minutes, and count how many BMWs, Porsches, and Rolls purr past you; the Beverly Hills Post Office (on Beverly Dr.) must be the only one in the country with valet parking. The heart of the city is in the **Golden Triangle,** a wedge formed by Wilshire and Santa Monica Blvd. centering on **Rodeo Drive,** known for its many opulent clothing boutiques and jewelry shops. Beverly Hills's European aspirations consume the Golden Triangle, where signs proudly proclaim Cannes as the sister-city of Beverly Hills. One particularly outlandish attempt to make customers believe they have strayed into Europe is the cobblestoned street of **Via Rodeo.** Faking antiquity, the entire street and hill, lampposts and all, was constructed in the last decade. Across the way is the venerable **Beverly Wilshire Hotel** (310-275-5200), whose old and new wings are connected by **El Camino Real,** a cobbled street with Louis XIV gates. Inside, hall mirrors reflect the glitter of crystal chandeliers and marble floors.

The new **Beverly Hills City Hall** (310-285-1000), looks a bit out of place, on Crescent Dr. just below Santa Monica Blvd. This Spanish Renaissance building was erected during the heart of the Great Depression, and is now engulfed in Beverly Hills's new **Civic Center.** The **Beverly Hills Library,** 444 N. Rexford Dr. (213-228-2220), is a case study in the city's overriding concerns—the interior is adorned with marble imported from Thailand, but contains a paltry collection of books.

Fans of *Beverly Hills 90210* will be disappointed to find that West Beverly High, alas, is only a television construct. They can, however, cruise **Beverly Hills High** (located on Moreno, between Olympic and Spalding). Beverly Hills High must be the only high school in the country with its own **oil well.** The **indoor swimming pool** is open for public use in summer (310-550-4796; open Mon.-Thurs. 1pm-5pm, Fri. 2-4pm). This is where Jimmy Stewart and Donna Reed danced the aquatic Charleston in *It's a Wonderful Life.* Just west of Beverly Hills High is **Century City.**

Westwood and UCLA

The university has left a clear impact on this region of Los Angeles. Many of the activities in the area are directed at the energetic student body. However, enclaves of more reserved attractions persist in the halls of Armand Hammer's museum and the tree-lined streets of Bel Air. The gargantuan **University of California at Los Angeles** campus (it covers over 400 acres in the foothills of the Santa Monica Mountains, bounded by Sunset, Hilgard, Le Conte, and Gayley) and the dearth of parking spaces make it virtually impossible to park. UCLA, described in *Let's Go: USA 1969* as where "most of Playboy's pin-up beauties ripen," is not the uni-dimensional, hedonistic colony of blond, deep-tanned party animals it was once thought to be. On the contrary, it is one of the top research universities in the world, and among California's highly-regarded public universities, second only to U.C. Berkeley.

Start a tour of UCLA at the **Visitors Center,** 10945 Le Conte Ave., #147 (310-206-8147), located in the Ueberroth Olympic Office Building. At the northernmost reach of the campus, the **Dickson Art Center** (310-825-1462) houses the Wight Art Gallery, home to the Grunwald Center for the Graphic Arts, as well as internationally recognized exhibitions, many of which are being moved to the Armand Hammer building (call 310-443-7097 for the details). (Open Sept.-June Tues. 11am-8pm, Wed.-Fri. 11am-5pm, Sat.-Sun. 1-5pm. Free.) The **Murphy Sculpture Garden,** containing over 70 pieces scattered through five acres, lies directly in front of the Art Center. Opposite the sculpture garden is **MacGowen Hall,** which contains the **Tower of Masks.** UCLA's **Inverted Fountain** is located between Knudsen Hall and Schoenberg Hall, directly south of Dickson Plaza. The **Botanical Gardens** (310-825-3620), bloom in the southeast corner of the campus. Their Zen Buddhist-inspired Japanese Garden can be viewed only by appointment. (Open Tues. 10am-1pm, Wed. noon-3pm. Call 310-825-4574 two weeks in advance to arrange for a tour.)

Westwood Village, just south of the campus, with its myriad of movie theaters, trendy boutiques, and upscale bistros, is geared more toward the residents of L.A.'s Westside than UCLA students. Like most college neighborhoods, however, Westwood is humming on Friday and Saturday nights. For the most part, Westwood is safe, and generally overrun by the high school and college crowd. The **Armand Hammer Museum of Art and Cultural Center,** 10899 Wilshire Blvd. (310-443-7000), houses a large collection of European and American works. (Parking in Westwood $2.75; open Tues.-Sat. 11am-7pm, Sun. 11am-6pm; tours Sun. and Thurs. at 1pm. $4.50, students and seniors $3, under 17 free.) Directly across from UCLA is the opulent community of **Bel Air,** where Ronald Reagan has retired.

Santa Monica

Santa Monica, the Bay City of Raymond Chandler's novels, was once known as the "Gold Coast" because of the fabulously wealthy stars who called it home. It takes about half an hour (with no traffic) on express bus #10 or on the Santa Monica Fwy. (I-10) from downtown to reach Santa Monica.

Santa Monica's beach is the closest to Los Angeles proper and is thus crowded and dirty. Still, the lure of sun, surf, and sand causes nightmarish summer traffic jams on I-10 and I-405. There are much prettier and cleaner beaches to visit to the north and south. The colorful **Santa Monica Pier** is a nostalgic and popular, if a bit sleazy, spot. **Palisades Park,** on the bluff overlooking the pier, offers a magnificent view of the ocean, especially at sunset. With the creation of the **Third Street Promenade** in 1989, and the recent remodeling of **Santa Monica Place,** Santa Monica has become one of L.A.'s major walking, movie-seeing, and yuppie-gathering areas. The Third Street Promenade sports some cool cafés, a couple of L.A.'s better bookshops, popular bars and restaurants, and a variety of street artists.

Venice

Venice is Los Angeles to the max—it perpetuates the image that evokes L.A. for so many people. A perennial favorite among foreigners, Venice is wacky on weekdays and wild on weekends. A typical Sunday includes trapeze artists, spontaneous Rollerblade dancing competitions, clowns, jugglers, comedians, glass-eaters, and bodybuilders, bikini-clad skaters, fortune tellers, and Angelenos cruising the boardwalk and taking it all in stride. Don't let yourself be distracted by the excitement to the point of forgetting about personal safety, and if you stop to watch a street act, you may be *strongly* encouraged to make a donation.

Ocean Front Walk, Venice's main beachfront drag, is a dramatic demographic departure from Santa Monica's promenade. Street people converge on shaded clusters of benches, yelping evangelists drown out off-color comedians, and bodybuilders of both sexes pump iron in skimpy spandex outfits at the original **Muscle Beach** (1800 Ocean Front Walk, closest to 18th and Pacific Ave.). This is where the roller-skating craze began. Collect your wits and people-watch at one of the cafés or juice bars. The **Sidewalk Café,** 1401 Ocean Front Walk (310-399-5547), with free live music most evenings, is nearly always packed (open daily 7am-11pm). If your feet don't move you through the crowds fast enough, rent skates or a bike. **Skatey's Sports,** 102 Washington (310-823-7971), rents in-line skates ($5 per hr., $10 per day) and bikes ($15 per day; open Mon.-Fri. 9am-7pm, Sat.-Sun. 9am-6pm).

Venice's **street murals** are another free show. Don't miss the brilliant, graffiti-disfigured homage to Botticelli's *Birth of Venus* on the beach pavilion at the end of Windward Ave.: a woman of ostensibly divine beauty, wearing short shorts, a Band-aid top, and roller skates, boogies out of her seashell.

To get to Venice from downtown L.A., take bus #33 or 333 (or 436 during rush hour). From downtown Santa Monica, take Santa Monica bus #1 or 2. Drivers can avoid hourly meter-feedings by parking in the $5 per day lot at Pacific and Venice.

San Fernando Valley

The end of the Ventura Freeway marks the spiritual center of American suburbia—a long series of communities with tree-lined streets, cookie-cutter homes, lawns, and shopping malls. A third of L.A.'s population resides here. The portion of the valley incorporated into the City of Los Angeles alone covers 140 million acres. **Ventura Boulevard,** the main commercial thoroughfare, today combines business and recreation with its office buildings, restaurants, and shops. The sprawling valley viewed from the foothills at night, particularly from Mulholland Drive, is spectacular. It's a nice place to live, but you wouldn't want to visit. Aside from the major attractions of Magic Mountain and tours of nearby movie studios, the valley is best known as the land of the infamous and stereotypical valley girls and dudes.

Once you've finished searching Ventura Blvd. for the ultimate valley hangout (try a Denny's on a weekend night between 2 and 4am), you may want to check out the **Museum of Neon Art,** 1000 Universal Dr. (818-761-MONA, -6662), at the City Walk in Universal City. (Open daily 11am-11pm. Free.)

After about an hour's drive along the San Fernando Freeway you'll reach **Simi Valley,** home to the **Ronald Reagan Presidential Library,** 40 Presidential Dr. (805-522-8444). (Open Mon.-Sat. 10am-5pm, Sun. noon-5pm. $4, seniors $2, under 15 free.)

ENTERTAINMENT

Film and Television Studios

All of the major TV studios offer free tickets to shows' tapings. Some are available on a first-come, first-serve basis from the **Visitors Information Center** of the Greater L.A. Visitor and Convention Bureau or by mail. Most networks won't send tickets to out-of-state addresses but will send a guest card or letter that can be redeemed for tickets. Be sure to enclose a self-addressed, stamped envelope. Write: Tickets, Capital City/**ABC** Inc., 4151 Prospect, Hollywood 90027 (213-557-7777); **CBS** Tickets, 7800 Beverly Blvd., Los Angeles 90036 (310-852-2624); **NBC**-TV Tickets, 3000 W. Alameda Ave., Burbank 91523 (818-840-3537); or **FOX** Tickets, through Audiences Unlimited at 100 Universal City Plaza, Bldg. 153, Universal City 91608 (818-506-0067). Tickets are also available to shows produced by **Paramount Television,** 860 N. Gower St., Hollywood 90038 (213-956-5575). Tickets don't guarantee admittance; arrive a couple of hours early, as seating is also first-come, first-served. The minimum age for many tapings is 16. The **L.A. City Film and Video Permit Office,** 6922 Hollywood Blvd. Suite 602 (213-485-5324), has lists of shooting locations for films being made around Los Angeles (open Mon.-Fri. 9am-5pm).

Universal Studios, Universal City (818-508-9600). Hollywood Fwy. to Lankershim. Take bus #424 to Lankershim Blvd. For a hefty fee, the studio will take you for a ride; visit *Psycho*'s Bates Hotel, movie sets, watch Conan the Barbarian flex his pecs, be attacked by Jaws, get caught in a flash flood, experience an 8.3 earthquake, and witness a variety of special effects. Reservations not accepted; it's best to arrive *early* to secure a ticket—despite the price, the tour is a lot of fun. Allow 2½ hrs. for the tour and at least 1 hr. to wander around afterward. Tours in Spanish daily. Open summer and holidays daily 8am-8pm (last tram leaves at 5pm); Sept.-June 9am-6:30pm. $31, ages 3-11 and over 60 $25. Parking $5.

NBC Television Studios Tour, 3000 W. Alameda Ave. (818-840-3572), at Olive Ave. in Burbank, 2 mi. from Universal. Hollywood Fwy. north, exit east on Barham Blvd., which becomes Olive Ave. Take bus #96 or 97 on Olive going northbound. Open Mon.-Fri. 9am-3pm, Sat. 10am-2pm. $6, ages 6-12 $3.75.

Warner Bros. VIP Tour, 4000 Warner Blvd., Burbank (818-954-1744). Personalized, unstaged tours (max. 12 people) through the Warner Bros. studios. These are technical, 2-hr. treks which chronicle the detailed reality of the movie-making craft. No children under 10. Tours every ½-hr. Mon.-Fri. 9am-4:30pm, additional tours in summer. Reservations recommended in advance. $27 per person.

Movies

In the technicolor heaven of Los Angeles, you'd expect to find as many movie theaters as stars on the Walk of Fame. You won't be disappointed. Numerous theaters show films the way they were meant to be seen: in a big space, on a big screen, and with high-quality sound. Watching a movie at one of the **Universal City** or **Century City** theaters is an amazing experience. The theaters in **Westwood Village** near UCLA are also incredibly popular, especially on weekends. Devotees of second-run, foreign-language, and experimental films are rewarded by the Santa Monica theaters away from the Promenade. Foreign films play consistently at the six **Laemmle Theaters** in Beverly Hills, West L.A., Santa Monica, Pasadena, Encino, and downtown. For film-screening information, dial 213-777-FILM (213-777-3456).

Music and Theater

L.A.'s concert venues range from small to massive. The **Wiltern Theater** (213-380-5005) has presented artists such as Suzanne Vega and The Church. The **Hollywood Palladium** (213-962-7600) is of comparable size with 3500 seats. Mid-size acts head for the **Universal Amphitheater** (818-777-3931) and the **Greek Theater** (213-665-1927). Huge indoor arenas, such as the **Sports Arena** (213-748-6131) or the **Forum** (310-419-3182), double as concert halls for large shows. Few dare to play at the 100,000+-seat **L.A. Coliseum.** The famous **Hollywood Bowl** and the **Music Center** are popular sites for classical music, ballet, and opera performances.

Los Angeles is blessed with one of the most active theater circuits on the West Coast. The *LA Weekly* has comprehensive listings of big and small L.A. theaters. **Pasadena Playhouse,** 39 S. El Molino Ave. (818-356-PLAY, -7529), in Pasadena, is California's premier theater and historical landmark. It has spawned Broadway careers and productions. Call for rush tickets, and info on Sat. and Sun. matinees. Find Big

Broadway shows at the **Shubert Theatre,** 2020 Ave. of the Stars, Century City (800-233-3123) and **Pantages,** 6233 Hollywood Blvd. (213-480-3232). **Santa Monica Playhouse,** 1211 4th St. (394-9779), is a non-profit theater. Look for the hors d'oeuvres or buffet suppers which often precede their matinees.

NIGHTLIFE

Bars

The bar scene in L.A. is ever-growing. Bars on Santa Monica Promenade are currently some of the most popular in L.A. **Molly Malone's,** 575 S. Fairfax (213-935-1579), is not your typical Irish pub—showcasing some of L.A.'s big up-and-coming bands. (Cover varies. Open 10am-2am.) **Al's Bar,** 305 S. Hewitt St. (213-625-9703), downtown, is one of L.A. nightlife's best-hidden secrets, with a wide range of nightly entertainment: traditional rock 'n' roll, poetry, experimental bands, performance art and more. (Open daily 6pm-2am.) **Yankee Doodle's,** 1410 3rd St. (310-394-4632), on the Santa Monica Promenade, has a lively bi-level sports bar has 32 (count 'em) pool tables and the de rigeur big screen TV. (Outdoor seating for the intense action. Open daily 11am-2am.) Also check out **The Snake Pit,** 7529 Melrose Ave. (213-852-9390), in W. Hollywood, an unpretentious little hole amid many poseur bars. It's crowded with a young, affable jetset. (Open Sun.-Thurs. 4:30pm-2am, Sat.-Sun. 11:30am-2am.)

Clubs

L.A.'s nightlife is famous for its club scene. With the highest number of bands per capita in the world, most clubs are able to book top-notch acts night after night. Most music clubs have DJs a couple times a week. Underground clubs are generally cheaper, more fun, and more elite. Coupons in *LA Weekly* can save you a bundle. To enter the club scene it's best to be at least 21—or to look it. Most of the best clubs are in Hollywood or along Sunset Blvd. A few to check out are: **Whisky A Go-Go,** 8901 Sunset Blvd. (310-652-4205); **Roxy,** 9009 Sunset Blvd. (310-276-2222); **The Palace,** 1435 N. Vine St. (213-462-3000), in West Hollywood; and **Anti-Club,** 4658 Melrose Ave. (213-661-3913), in East Hollywood. **The Palms,** 8572 Santa Monica Blvd. (310-652-6188), is West Hollywood's oldest women's bar. Top-40 dancing every night. (Full bar. Low cover, if any. 21 and over.) **Rage,** 8911 Santa Monica Blvd., West Hollywood (310-652-7055), throbs with dance and R&B sounds for a gay male crowd. (Full bar. Cover varies. 21 and over.) **Coconut Teaszer,** 8117 Sunset Blvd. (213-654-4773). Dingy, grungy, loud, and popular. Peace and green decor provide odd background for live bands (Sun.), DJ with dancing (Fri.-Sat.), and excellent drink specials. (Full bar. No cover. Official policy is 21 and over. **Club Lingerie,** 6507 Sunset Blvd., Hollywood (213-466-8557),has normously varied bookings and lots of indie rock. Come early. (2 full bars. Open Mon.-Sat. 9pm-2am. 21 and over.)**Kingston 12,** 814 Broadway (310-451-4423), Santa Monica. L.A.'s only full-time reggae club presents both local and foreign acts. (Jamaican food, dance floor, 2 bars. Open Thurs.-Sun. 8:30pm-2am. Cover varies. 21 and over.) **Florentine Gardens,** 5951 Hollywood Blvd. (213-464-0706), is Hollywood's giant dance club for an 18-and-over crowd. (Open Fri.-Sat. 8pm-4am. $8 cover before 10:30pm, higher after.)

Coffeehouses

Espresso bars are the latest, largest fad in L.A. nightlife, and for good reason: they offer a cheap, quiet alternative to L.A.'s buzzing club scene, often with entertainment gratis. They range from the obscure to the franchised. One popular chain is the **Coffee Bean and Tea Leaf.** There are locations in Santa Monica, Westwood (near UCLA), and Beverly Hills. Buy ten beverages and get another free—you might scoff at this deal, but wait 'til you taste their Vanilla Ice Blended, the most delicious drink in the entire world ($2.75). It won't take you long to down ten. Call 800-TEA-LEAF, -832-5323, to find a location near you. Some other coffeehouses worth a visit are: **Insomnia Café,** 7286 Beverly Blvd. (213-931-4943; open Sun.-Thurs. 9:30am-

2am, Fri.-Sat. 9:30am-3am); **Bourgeois Pig,** 5931 Franklin Ave. (213-962-6366; open Mon.-Fri. noon-2am, Sat.-Sun. 8am-2am); and **The Living Room,** 110 S. la Brea (213-933-2933; open Sun.-Thurs. 9am-midnight, Fri.-Sat. 9am-2:30am). Walking into **Nova Express,** 426 N. Fairfax Ave. (213-658-7533) is is like walking into the bar scene in Star Wars. The wacky space-art was created by the owner. Espresso is around $2. (Live rock music Fri., acoustic Sat. Open daily 5pm-4am.) **Highland Grounds,** 742 N. Highland Ave. (213-466-1507), in Hollywood, features live entertainment every night from 8pm and poetry readings on Tues. There's also an outdoor patio with continuously burning fire pit. (Open Sun.-Thurs. 9am-12:30am, Fri-Sat. 9am-1am.)

Sports

L.A. sports, even those on ice, benefit from the warm climate of the region; there are solid professional teams in every sport, as well as numerous collegiate programs through USC and UCLA. For tickets to events at the **Great Western Forum** (310-673-1300) in Inglewood, call the box office (310-419-3182; open daily 10am-6pm) or **Ticketmaster** (213-480-3232). The Forum itself has become a symbol of the city, partially because the worthy **L.A. Lakers** shoot hoops there. The **L.A. Dodgers** throw strikes at Dodger Stadium (213-224-1400) in Elysian Park, 3 mi. northeast of downtown. Tickets are about $6-11.Hockey's **Los Angeles Kings** skate at the Forum (310-673-1300). Football fans can watch the **Los Angeles Raiders** and the **USC Trojans** rumble and fumble at the Los Angeles Memorial Coliseum, 2601 S. Figueroa St.

■■■ ROUTE I: THE PACIFIC COAST HIGHWAY

Originating among the surfer beaches south of L.A., Rte. 1—or the Pacific Coast Highway (PCH)—sweeps grandly along the California coast. Never straying more than a few miles from the sea, the highway ends in the magnificent wave-splattered redwood groves near **Garberville,** more than 200 mi. north of San Francisco. Along the way, its two lanes of blacktop offer a taste of the California experience. PCH traverses a cross-section of the state's landscape. Many of the numerous bridges on the route were architectural wonders in their day; and some—such as the Bixby Creek Bridge, one of the longest single-span bridges in the world—still are. Some segments of the highway have been rebuilt more than once; earthquake damage forced a stretch of Rte. 1 in Marin County to close for nearly a year. But too much of California's identity is tied to this highway for locals to give it up.

After skirting the coastal communities of **Los Angeles,** slowly and spectacularly, the Pacific Coast Hwy. (Rte. 1) curves north from **Ventura** and **Oxnard** to genteel **Santa Barbara.** PCH winds by vineyards, fields of wildflowers, and miles of beach on the journey northward to **San Luis Obispo. San Simeon,** north of San Luis Obispo, anchors the southern end of **Big Sur,** the legendary 90-mi. strip of sparsely inhabited coastline. Climbing in and out of Big Sur's mountains, Rte. 1 inches motorists to the edge of jutting cliffs hanging precipitously over the surf. On the Monterey Peninsula, **Carmel** and **Monterey** cater to waves of tourists intent on seeing rural Carmel and Steinbeck's Cannery Row. Just above Monterey, and 79 mi. south of San Francisco, **Santa Cruz** breeds a youthful surfer and university culture with **San Francisco's** off-beat quirkiness, resulting in a uniquely conscious beach community. From Ventura to Santa Cruz, state parks and national forests offer peaceful campgrounds and daring recreation.

■■■ ORANGE COUNTY

Orange County, Los Angeles's neighbor to the south, was part of Los Angeles County until 1861, when "O.C." seceded over a tax dispute. Since then, it has managed to organize itself quite efficiently into a region that contrasts sharply with L.A.'s heterogeneous sprawl. Orange County has a higher per capita income and a less ethnically diverse population than Los Angeles. Millions of visitors flock to the Anaheim area each year to catch California Angels and L.A. Rams games or, most of all, to visit the perpetually happy Disneyland.

Visitors Information is found at **Anaheim Area Visitors and Convention Bureau,** 800 W. Katella Ave., Anaheim 92802 (999-8999), in the Anaheim Convention Center. (Open Mon.-Fri. 8:30am-5pm.) **Amtrak** (800-872-7245) has stations at 120 E. Santa Fe Ave. (992-0530), in Fullerton; 1000 E. Santa Ana (547-8389), in Santa Ana; and Santa Fe Depot (240-2972), in San Juan Capistrano. **Greyhound** stations are at 2080 S. Harbor (999-1256), in Anaheim, 3 blocks south of Disneyland (open daily 6:30am-8pm); 1000 E. Santa Ana Blvd. (542-2215), Santa Ana (open daily 7am-8pm); and 510 Avenida de la Estrella (492-1187), San Clemente (open Mon.-Thurs. 7:45am-6:30pm, Fri. 7:45am-8pm). The **Orange County Transit District (OCTD)** is at 11222 Acacia Parkway (636-7433), in Garden Grove. Thorough service. Bus #1 travels the coast from Long Beach down to San Clemente. (Fare $1, transfers 5¢. MTA Information: 800-252-7433; open daily 4:55am-10:45pm.) Anaheim's **post office:** 701 N. Loara (520-2600), 1 block north of Anaheim Plaza (open Mon.-Fri. 8:30am-5pm, Sat. 8:30am-2pm); **ZIP Code:** 92803; **area code:** 714; 310 in Seal Beach.

ACCOMMODATIONS, CAMPING, AND FOOD

Disneyland single-handedly grants **Anaheim** a thriving tourist trade. Because it's fairly remote from L.A.'s other sights, there is no reason to stay here unless you plan to linger in the Magic Kingdom. Start with the Anaheim Visitors Center, which will match you with a room. There are state beaches with campgrounds in Orange County. Reservations can be made through **MISTIX** (800-365-2267).

Fullerton Hacienda Hostel (HI-AYH), 1700 N. Harbor Blvd. (738-3721), in Fullerton, 15-min. drive north of Disneyland. Shuttle from LAX $18. OCTD bus #43 runs up and down Harbor Blvd. to Disneyland. This big, Spanish-style house complete with porch swing is set back from the road on a quiet hill. Modern kitchen, clean communal bathrooms, and spiffy single- and mixed-sex accommodations. 5-day max. stay. No curfew. Registration daily 7:30-10:30am and 5-11pm. $14,non-members $17. Reservations accepted.

Huntington Beach Colonial Inn Youth Hostel, 421 8th St. (536-3315), in Huntington Beach, 4 blocks inland at Pecan. Wooden house shaded by huge palm trees. Common showers, bathroom, large kitchen. Reading/TV room. Check-in 7am-11pm. No lockout. After 11pm, entry requires late-night key, free with $20 deposit. Multi-person dorms $12 per person. Doubles $14. Must have picture ID. Call 2 days in advance for summer weekends.

Motel 6, 4 Anaheim locations, and 2 more in adjacent suburbs at 921 S. Beach Blvd. (220-2866), and 7450 Katella Ave. (891-0717), both within a 10-min. drive of Disneyland. Both have pools and are filled with couples and their rambunctious, Mickey Mouska-eared children. Most rooms have HBO. All offer A/C and free local calls. The S. Beach Blvd. location is the best deal for groups ($32 for 1-4 persons). The Katella Ave. motel is in better shape and a steal: Singles $25. Doubles $29.

San Clemente (492-3156), I-5, get off on Avenida del Presidente and follow the state beach signs (there are no signs for the campground itself). Heavy on sites (a total of 157, 85 with hookups) and RVs, short on trees. Great vistas of ocean, and, unfortunately, of the adjacent neighborhoods as well. Sites $16.

Bolsa Chica (848-1566), Rte. 1, 3 mi. west of Huntington Beach. Self-contained RVs only. No hookups. 7-day max. stay. $14 per vehicle, $13 for seniors.

Standard, cheap food is easily found in Anaheim; there are countless fast-food restaurants and many hotels offer all-you-can-eat buffets. Try one of the various inexpensive ethnic restaurants tucked into the strip malls. Many have only take-out.

BEACHES

Orange County **beaches** are generally cleaner, less crowded, and more charming than those in L.A. County. **Huntington Beach** served as a port of entry for the **surf-**

ing craze, which transformed the California coast life in the early 1900s. Riding or shredding the waves remains the activity of choice and the newly remodeled pier provides a perfect vantage point for oglers. Nightlife here is scant, and most locals head to 2nd Street in Long Beach for after-hours fun.

Newport Beach and the surrounding inland cities are the jewels of Orange County. Stunning multimillion dollar homes line **Newport Harbor,** the largest leisure craft harbor in the world. The beach itself displays few signs of ostentatious wealth; it is crowded with young, frequently rowdy hedonists in neon-colored bikinis and trunks. In the shadow of a giant Ferris wheel, the area around Newport Pier is a haven for families; the streets from 30th to 56th give way to students. To appreciate the shoreline from the water, you can rent a **party pontoon boat** for $30 per hour. Each holds up to six adults. Contact Anchors Away Boat Rentals at 673-3372.

The sands of Newport Beach run south onto the **Balboa Peninsula,** separated from the mainland by Newport Bay. The peninsula itself is only two to four blocks wide and can be reached from Pacific Coast Hwy. (PCH) by Balboa Blvd. The ornate **Balboa Pavilion** at the end of Main St., once a sounding ground for Big Band great Benny Goodman, is now a hub for harbor tours and winter whale-watching. The **Ocean Front Walk** extends the length of the peninsula and provides excellent views of the ocean and numerous waterfront homes. At the end of the peninsula, **The Wedge,** seasonally pounded by storm-generated waves up to 20 ft. tall, is a **bodysurfing** mecca. Advanced surfers risk life and limb for a monster ride.

Melt into the crowd on Newport Beach or the Balboa Peninsula by hopping on a bicycle or strapping on a pair of in-line skates. Rental shops cluster around the Newport Beach pier and at the end of the peninsula. (Bike rentals run $5 per hr., $15 per day. Skates $3-6 per hr., $15 per day. Boogie-boards $5-6 per day.)

Once you have reached the end of the peninsula, from the harbor side you can see **Balboa Island,** largest of the three islands sheltered by the peninsula.Balboa Island is expensive and covered with chic eateries, boutiques, and bikini shops. A vintage **ferryboat** (673-1070) will take you there from the peninsula. (Ferry runs every 3-5 min., Sun.-Thurs. 6:30am-midnight, Fri.-Sat. 6:30am-2am. Car and driver $1, additional passengers 35¢, children 15¢.) Balboa Island can also be reached from PCH by a bridge on Jamboree Rd.

North of Newport Beach, **Costa Mesa** houses the dazzling **Orange County Performing Arts Center,** 600 Town Center Dr. (556-2121), on Bristol St. off I-405. The opulent, 3000-seat structure was constructed in 1986 at a cost of $70 million and has hosted the American Ballet Theatre and the Kirov Ballet, among others.

Laguna Beach, 4 mi. south of Newport, is nestled between canyons on the coast. Back in the old days, Laguna was a Bohemian artists' colony, but is no longer for the starving set. Punctuated by rocky cliffs, coves, and lush hillside vegetation, the town is decidedly Mediterranean in character. South of Laguna Beach, the California coastline takes on a dry, dusty appearance—there's a significant change in the landscape. **Main Beach** and the shops nearby are the prime parading areas, though there are other, less crowded spots as well. One accessible beach (with a sizable gay crowd) is **Westry Beach,** which spreads out south of Laguna just below **Aliso Beach Park.** Park on Pacific Coast Hwy. or residential streets to the east and look for "Public Access" signs between private properties.

Laguna Beach's artwork is displayed at the **Laguna Beach Museum of Art,** 307 Cliff Dr. (494-8971), which houses recent works by important Californian artists including an excellent collection of early 20th-century Impressionist works. (Open Tues.-Fri. 11am-5pm, Sat. 11am-9pm, Sun. 10am-7pm. $4, seniors and students $3, under 12 free. Tours Tues.-Wed. and Sun. 2pm.)

■ DISNEYLAND

Though Disney's empire is vast, the spiritual heart of it all is still found where Walt wanted it, in the former orange groves of Anaheim. "The Happiest Place on Earth" has delighted hundreds of millions of visitors over the last 39 years. The attractions are inspired testaments to the charm and wit of child-like creativity, but the crowds of 75,000 young-at-heart per day jamming into the park can be a little unnerving, even though most of the rides are fairly tame. The **Unlimited Use Passport** (1 day $31, ages 3-11 $25) grants admission and use of all rides. (Park open Sun.-Fri. 9am-midnight, Sat. 8am-1am. Hours may change, so call 999-4565 for info.)

Disneyland is located at 1313 Harbor Blvd., in Anaheim in Orange County. From L.A. take bus #460 from 6th and Flower St. downtown, about 1½ hours to the Disneyland Hotel. From the hotel take the free shuttle to Disneyland's portals. If you're driving, take the Santa Ana Fwy. (I-5) to the Katella Ave. exit. Parking is $6.

Visitors enter the Magic Kingdom by way of **Main Street, USA,** a collection of shops, arcades, and even a movie theater. The broad avenue leads to a replica of Sleeping Beauty's castle at the center of the park. Definitely pick up the essential and free map of the park at the information booth. Rent strollers and wheelchairs for $6 per day as you enter the park. The **Disneyland Railroad** arrives every five to 10 min. and takes its passengers on a ride that circles the park with limited stops. The long line for seats should encourage you to explore on foot. Disneyland is more compact than the grandiose rhetoric would lead you to believe.

Disneyland is best at night. During the day, the park can be hot and crowded, but at night the **Main Street Electrical Parade** transforms the masses into an excited, unified whole. Each summer night at 8:50pm and 10:25pm floats and humans generate a thrilling nighttime display. To the right of Main St. lies **Tomorrowland—** futuristic home to two of Disney's premier attractions: **Space Mountain,** arguably the park's most thrilling ride; less frightening, but more high-tech is the George Lucas-produced **Star Tours.**

Recrossing the tracks and moving counter-clockwise around the park, **Fantasyland** sports numerous fairy tale-inspired kids' rides. The most dominating feature is the **Matterhorn Mountain,** through and around which winds a high-speed bobsled. Sadly, the Matterhorn offers little in the way of thrills. Nearby is the ever popular **It's a Small World** cruise (be prepared to be brainwashed by the theme song).

Frontierland, features the **Thunder Mountain Railroad** coaster and **Tom Sawyer Island.** Tucked in behind Tom's Island are **Critter Country** and **New Orleans Square. Splash Mountain,** the newest of the super-rides, climaxes with a wet, five-story drop, but the rest of the water-bound cruise is relatively tame. **Pirates of the Caribbean** showcases Disney magic at its finest. **Haunted Mansion** is a must-see.

■■■ BIG BEAR

Hibernating in the **San Bernardino Mountains,** the town of **Big Bear Lake** entertains visitors with winter skiing and summer boating. The consistent winds make the lake one of the best for sailing in the state. The **Big Bear Chamber of Commerce,** 630 Bartlett Rd. (mailing address: P.O. Box 2860), Big Bear Lake 92315 (909-866-4607), dispenses glossy ski brochures and arranges accommodations/ski packages (open Mon.-Fri. 9am-5pm, Sat.-Sun. 10am-5pm). The **Big Bear Ranger Station,** Rte. 38 (909-866-3437), 3 mi. east of Fawnskin, on the opposite side of the lake, has camping and trail info (open Mon.-Sat. 8am-4:30pm).

To reach Big Bear Lake, take I-10 to Junction 30/330. Follow Rte. 30 to Rte. 330, also known as Mountain Rd., and continue to Rte. 18. About halfway up the mountain, Rte. 18 becomes Big Bear Blvd., the main route encircling the lake.

Public transportation to Big Bear Lake is currently unavailable. **Big Bear Shuttle** (866-9493 or 585-7427) schedules service from the mountain communities to San Bernardino and desert areas. (Round-trip to Yucca Valley $29. Door-to-door service around Big Bear $1 per mile.) **Rim of the World Transit Bus** (866-4444; 60¢) connects Big Bear with Running Springs, Snow Valley, and Lake Arrowhead. The **Big Bear Valley Transit** trolley (866-4444) covers stops around Big Bear (75¢) and provides **Dial-A-Ride** service for seniors and the disabled ($1).

Big Bear has few budget accommodations, especially in the winter. Big Bear Blvd., the main drag on the lake's South Shore, is lined with lodging possibilities but finding bargains is a challenge. Groups can find the best deals by sharing a cabin. Things fill up quickly; call ahead and make reservations. **Hillcrest Lodge,** 40241 Big Bear Blvd. (909-866-7330) offers cozy rooms with an expensive feel at a budget price. ($32-39 singles; $64 for a 4-person unit).

Camping is permitted at U.S. Forest Service sites throughout the area. Several of the grounds accept reservations (through 800-280-2267). Most are open from May to November. For camping, check out **Pineknot** (7000 ft.), from Big Bear go south on Summit Blvd. to end, then left ¼ mi. to sites. (Surprisingly isolated. 48 heavily wooded spots, half of which accept reservations. Wheelchair accessible, flush toilets, water. Sites $11.) **Food** is pricey in the mountains. Cook your own if you have a kitchen. Groceries are available at **Slater Bros.,** 42171 Big Bear Blvd. (866-5211; open 7am-10pm daily).

Mountain biking is a popular activity in Big Bear when the snow melts. Both **Big Bear Mountain** and **Snow Mountain** operate lifts in summer so thrill-seeking bikers can plummet downhill without the grueling uphill ride. ($7 per ride or $16 for a day pass (helmet required). Beautiful national forest land to the east and wēst of ski country invites exploration. Bikes can be rented from **Big Bear Bikes,** 41810 Big Bear Blvd. (866-2224) for $6 per hour or $21 per half-day.

Fishing, boating, and **horseback riding** are also popular Big Bear summer activities. No license is required at **Alpine Trout Lake** (866-4532) ¼ mi. off Big Bear Lake Blvd. Fishing boats can be rented at **Gray's Landing** (866-2443) on North Shore Dr., for $12 per hour or $25 per half-day. Call Big Bear Lake's **Fishing Association** (866-6260) for answers to your fishing questions. Inexpensive horseback tours are available in the evening from **Big Bear Riding Stable** (585-1260) in Big Bear City (tours $10 per hr. on weekdays, $12 weekends).

Skiers and snowboarders pack area slopes during the winter. Driving the crowded mountain roads to destinations of choice can challenge both vehicle and driver. Gas up completely before heading onto the mountain routes as stations are scarce. Use tire chains when they are required by posted signs. Call 800-427-7623 for information on road conditions and closures. Ski area's include: **Bear Mountain Ski (and Golf) Resort** (909-585-2517), 1½ mi. southeast of downtown Big Bear Lake; **Snow Summit** (909-866-5766), about 4 mi. south of Big Bear Lake; and **Snow Valley** (714-867-2751; snow report 714-867-5151), near Running Springs.

■ ■ ■ SAN DIEGO

San Diego, settled by the Spanish in 1769, did not become a major metropolis until the economic boom of the 1940s and 1950s. Today, the city has matured into a metropolis that now sprawls for miles over the once-dry, rolling hills of chaparral. San Diego has ample tourist attractions—a world-famous zoo, Sea World, and Old Town—but the most enjoyable destination might simply be a patch of sand at one of the area's superb beaches. There is also much to see outside the city proper. Explore the nearby mountains and deserts and the surrounding communities such as La Jolla and Ocean Beach, or head for Mexico, right next door.

PRACTICAL INFORMATION

Emergency: 911.

International Visitors Information Center: 11 Horton Plaza (236-1212), downtown at 1st Ave. and F St. Multilingual staff. Open Mon.-Sat. 8:30am-5pm. Also Sun. 11am-5pm in summer.

Airport: San Diego International lies at the northwestern edge of downtown, across from Harbor Island. San Diego Transit bus #2 ("30th and Adams") goes downtown ($1.50); transfer to other routes. #2 buses run Mon.-Fri. 4:30am-1:10am, Sat.-Sun. 4:45am-1:05am. Cab fare downtown $7.

Amtrak: Santa Fe Depot, 1050 Kettner Blvd. (239-9021, for schedules and information 800-872-7245), at Broadway. To: L.A. (Mon.-Fri. 8 per day 5:05am-9pm; one way $24, round-trip $32). To: L.A. ($24, 4 hrs.), San Francisco ($77). Information on bus, trolley, car, and boat transportation available at the station. Ticket office open 4:45am-9:15pm.

Greyhound: 120 W. Broadway (239-8082), at 1st Ave. To L.A. (every 45 min. 2:30am-11:45pm; $12, round-trip $24). To: L.A. ($19, 3 hrs.), San Francisco ($59, 12 hrs.). Open for ticket sales 2am-midnight.

Public Transportation: The **regional transit systems** cover the area from Oceanside in the north to Tijuana in Mexico, and inland to Escondido, Julian, and other towns. Call for **public transit information** (233-3004; Mon.-Fri. 5:30am-8:25pm, Sat.-Sun. 8am-5pm. Fare $1.05 for North County and local routes, $1.75-2 for express routes, and $2-3 for commuter routes. One transfer free in San Diego. Exact change; many accept dollar bills.) **Day Tripper passes** allow unlimited travel on buses, trolleys, and even the Bay Ferry ($4 for 1 day, $15 for 4 days). The **San Diego Trolley** runs two lines from a starting point near the Santa Fe Depot on C St., at Kettner. To: El Cajon, daily 4:45am-1:15am; San Ysidro "the Tijuana Trolley," 5am-1am. Wheelchair accessible. Fare $1-1.75.

Car Rental: Aztec Rent-A-Car, 2401 Pacific Hwy. (232-6117 or 800-231-0400). $22-50 per day with unlimited mi. (in California only). Must be 21 with major credit card. With purchase of Mexican insurance ($16 per day), cars may venture as far as Ensenada, Mexico (80 mi.). Open Mon.-Fri. 6am-8pm, Sat.-Sun. 8am-5pm.

Bike Rental: Rent-A-Bike, 1st and Harbor Dr. (232-4700). Bike, helmet, and lock $8 per hour, $28 per day. Open Mon.-Fri. 8am-6pm, Sat.-Sun. 7am-6pm.

Help Lines: Rape Crisis Hotline: 233-3088. 24 hrs. **Gay Crisis Line:** 692-4297, Mon.-Sat. 6am-10pm. **Crime Victims Help Line:** 236-0101. 24 hrs.

Post Office: Main Branch, 2535 Midway Dr. (627-0915), between downtown and Mission Beach. Bus #6, 9, or 35. Open Mon.-Fri. 7am-1am, Sat. 8am-4pm. **ZIP Code:** 92138.

Area Code: 619.

San Diego rests in the extreme southwestern corner of California, 127 mi. south of L.A. and only 15 mi. north of the Mexican border. **I-5** runs south from Los Angeles and skirts the eastern edge of downtown. **I-15** runs northeast to Nevada. The major downtown thoroughfare, **Broadway,** runs east-west. A group of skyscrapers in the blocks between Broadway and I-5 defines the downtown. On the northeastern corner of downtown lies **Balboa Park.** To the north and east of Balboa Park are the main residential areas. **Hillcrest,** San Diego's most cosmopolitan district and a center for the gay community, lies at the park's northwestern corner. **University Heights** and **North Park** sit along University Ave., El Cajon Blvd., and Adams Ave. West of downtown is the bay, 17 mi. long and formed by the Coronado Peninsula (jutting northward from Imperial Beach) and Point Loma (dangling down from Ocean Beach). North of Ocean Beach are Mission Beach, Pacific Beach, and La Jolla.

ACCOMMODATIONS AND CAMPING

Lodging rates skyrocket in summer, particularly on weekends, so make reservations. If you have a car, consider camping outside of San Diego. For information on state park camping, call the enthusiastic people at San Elijo Beach (753-5091; reservations through MISTIX (800-444-7275) as well as by individual campgrounds.)

Banana Bungalow, 707 Reed Ave. (237-1440 or 800-5-HOSTEL, -467835), just off of Mission Blvd., on Mission Beach. Take Bus #34 to Mission Blvd. and Reed Ave. Opened in July of 1993, the Bungalow has become the most popular hostel in the city. Offers a long list of amenities: great location, (directly on a beautiful beach) friendly staff, free breakfast, cheap keg parties ($3 all-you-can-drink), and bonfires and BBQs on the beach. Located near bars and restaurants. No curfew. Check-out 10:15am. Dorm $11-15, private double $45. Common room with cable TV and porch overlooking the beach. Linen included. Blankets and overnight key require $10 deposit. Call in advance.

Downtown Hotel at Baltic Inn, 521 6th Ave. (237-0387). Well-equipped, clean rooms (each has toilet, sink, microwave, mini-fridge, table TV, closets). Clean communal showers. No curfew, 24-hr. security. Laundry facilities. Great location for downtown connections. Singles $15. Doubles $20. Weekly rates from $80.

Hostel on Broadway (HI-AYH), 500 W. Broadway (232-1133), in the core of downtown, close to train and bus stations. Shared bathrooms, common room with TV. Laundry and game room (pool table and video). Panhandlers cluster outside but security cameras and guards monitor the hostel. Desk open 8am-11pm. No curfew. $12, nonmembers $15. Doubles (with bunk) $13 per person, regular doubles $14. Storage fee $1. Use of YMCA facilities $5. IBN reservations available.

Jim's San Diego, 1425 C St. (235-0234), south of the park, 2 blocks from "City College" trolley. Spruce, hostel-type rooms for 4 with wooden bunks and free linen. Kitchen, sun deck, common room, laundry. Check-out noon. $13 per night, $11 in winter, $77-80 per week. Breakfast and Sunday BBQ included. No reservations.

Elliot-Point Loma Hostel (HI-AYH), 3790 Udall St., Point Loma (223-4778). Take bus #35 from downtown; get off at the first stop on Voltaire and walk across the street. If driving a car, take I-5 to Sea World exit, then left to Sunset Cliffs Blvd. Take left on Voltaire, right on Warden and look for hostel sign painted on a remodeled church. The airy 2-story building is 1½ mi. from Ocean Beach. Wooden bunks for 60, common room, large kitchen, and patio. Check-out 10am. Office open 8-10am and 4:30-10pm. Lockout 10:30am-4:30pm. No curfew. 3-night max. stay; reserve 48 hrs. in advance. $12, nonmembers $15.

The Maryland Hotel, 630 F St. (239-9243; fax 235-8968). Well-located and affordable, this hotel's clean rooms and dapper staff make up for some absent amenities. Lots of long-term residents. Laundry facilities, cable TV available. Singles $17, $22 with half bath, $25 with full bath, second guest $8. Weekly rates $85, with half bath $95, with full bath $115, second guest $40.

Downtown Inn Hotel, 660 G St. (238-4100), just east of the Gaslamp District. Comfortable, tastefully furnished rooms with microwave or toaster oven, refrigerator, TV, and ceiling fan. Convenient to buses. Laundry facilities. Check-out 1pm. Singles $27, weekly $99. Doubles $27, weekly $117.

Hillcrest Inn, 3754 5th Ave., Hillcrest (293-7078). Sunny garden, jacuzzi, and spiffy rooms. Each room has a kitchenette with microwave, bar, sink, and fridge. Updates on local entertainment, and staff is trained to direct tourists around San Diego's attractions and nightlife. Young clientele. Ask for handy map of Hillcrest. Singles $49-55. No official weekly rates.

Campland on the Bay, 2211 Pacific Beach Dr. (581-4212). Take I-5 to Grand Ave. exit and follow the signs, or take bus #30 and get off on Grand at the campground sign on the left. Expensive and crowded because it's the only central place to pitch a tent or plug in an RV. The cheapest sites are in a "dirt area" with nothing to block the wind coming off the water. Scheduled family activities. Some wooded areas, a pool, and a boat launch. Market, laundry, and game room on grounds. Sites $22-52; in winter $19-37.

South Carlsbad Beach State Park (431-3143), Rte. 21 near Leucadia, in north San Diego County. 215 sites, half for tents. On cliffs over the sea. Showers, laundry facilities. No hiking trails. Sites $16-21. Reservations necessary in summer.

FOOD

San Diego has hundreds of fast-food joints, an achievement befitting the birthplace of the genre. The lunchtime business crowd has nurtured scores of restaurants speccializing in well-made, inexpensive meals. Purchase high-quality fruits and vegetables at the **Farmer's Market,** 1 Horton Plaza (696-7766).

Anthony's Fishette, 555 Harbor Ln. (232-2933), at the foot of Market St. on the bay. A downscale version of **Anthony's** posh restaurants. A catch, with bay view and a bar. Dinners $5-10. Open Sun.-Thurs. 11am-8pm, Fri.-Sat. 11am-8:30pm.

The Golden Dragon, 414 University Ave., Hillcrest (296-4119; delivery 275-7500), in Balboa Park. Varied menu offers over a hundred dishes and a special vegetarian menu. Almost all under $8. Perfect for late-night dining. Open daily 3pm-3am.

Machos, 1125 6th Ave. (231-1969), downtown. Some of the best, cheapest, and most authentic Mexican food around. Endless chips and salsa. Daily specials. Two beef enchiladas $2.85. Open Mon.-Fri. 7am-7pm, Sat.-Sun. 8am-5pm.

El Indio, 3695 India St. (299-0333), in India St. Colony. El Indio opened its doors in 1940. A half-century later, folks are still lining up for the delicious food. Counter-style service is speedy and quality remains high. Sizable portions; combination plates around $3-5.50, a la carte tacos and burritos from $2. Open daily 7am-9pm.

Caffe Italia, 1704 India St. (234-6767), in Little Italy. This Eurocafé has excellent coffee and sells foreign and domestic periodicals. *Formaggi* sandwich $4. Open Mon.-Thurs. 7am-10pm, Fri. 7am-11pm, Sat. 8am-11pm, Sun. 8am-10pm.

Corvette Diner Bar & Grill, 3946 5th Ave. (542-1001), in Balboa Park. '50s decor includes a real Corvette and booming oldies. Old-fashioned shake $3. Open Sun.-Thurs. 11am-11pm, Fri.-Sat. 11am-midnight.

SIGHTS

The inland neighborhoods of San Diego form a tangible record of the city's history. **Old Town** is home to many early 19th-century Spanish-style adobe buildings. Extending south from Broadway is the **Gaslamp Quarter,** home to pre-1910 commercial buildings now being resurrected as upscale shops and restaurants. Downtown San Diego bears witness to the city's naval background with the Embarcadero. Sprawling **Balboa Park** encloses museums and the San Diego Zoo while holding the lion's share of cultural attractions in the city. When planning museum visits, be aware that San Diego has a "free Tuesdays" program—lots of museums offer discounts or free admission on certain Tuesdays. Call your destination for info. The sky-scrapers of San Diego's central business district coexist with the ships and museums that line the waterfront.

Downtown

Moored windjammers, cruise ships, and the occasional naval destroyer face the boardwalk shops and museums along the **Embarcadero,** the Spanish name for a dock. The magnificently restored 1863 sailing vessel *Star of India* is docked in front of the touristy **Maritime Museum,** 1306 N. Harbor Dr. (234-9153). Alongside are anchored both the 1904 British steam yacht *Medea* and the 1898 ferryboat *Berkeley*, a bay ferry that slunk away from its mooring after the 1906 earthquake. (Open daily 9am-9pm. $6, ages 13-17 and over 55 $4, 6-12 $2, families $12.). From Harbor Drive, the **Coronado Bridge** stretches westward from Barrio Logan to the Coronado Peninsula. From the bridge, one can see San Diego's skyline to the north and the main naval base to the south. (Toll $1. Bus #901 and other routes also cross.) When the bridge was built in 1969, its eastern end cut a swath through San Diego's largest Chicano community. In response, the community created **Chicano Park and** painted splendid murals on the bridge's piers. Walk around the park to appreciate the murals, which are both heroic in scale and theme. Take bus #11 or the San Ysidro trolley to Barrio Logan station. **Horton Plaza,** at Broadway and 4th Ave, is an open-air, multi-leveled shopping center encompassing seven city blocks.

Balboa Park

Balboa Park was the creation of pioneering horticulturists whose plantings trans-formed a once-treeless pueblo tract into a botanical montage. Thousands are drawn each year to Balboa Park for its concerts, cultural events, Spanish architecture, lush vegetation, and of course, its zoo. Balboa Park is accessible by bus #7, or by driving east from downtown on Laurel St. Parking is free at museums and zoo lots.

With over 100 acres of exquisite fenceless habitats, the **San Diego Zoo** (234-3153) deserves its reputation as one of the finest in the world. It even attracts more than animal lovers; its flora is as exotic as its fauna. The zoo recently moved to a system of "bioclimatic" areas, in which animals and plants are grouped together by habitat, rather than by taxonomy. Joining the stunning **Tiger River** and **Sun Bear Forest** is the **Gorilla Tropics** enclosure, housing lowland gorillas and plant species imported from Africa. In addition to the usual elephants and zebras, the zoo houses such unusual creatures as Malay tapirs and everybody's favorite, koalas. The most efficient way to tour the zoo is to arrive as early as possible and take the 40-min.

open-air **double-decker bus tour,** which covers 70% of the park. ($3, ages 3-11 $2.50. Sit on the left, given a choice.) The **Skyfari Aerial Tramway** rises 170 feet above the park. (Both free with admission.) (Main zoo entrance open Mon.-Wed. 9am-5pm, exit by 9pm; Thurs.-Sun. 9am-9pm, exit by 10pm; Labor Day-Memorial Day open daily 9am-4pm, exit by 6pm. $13, ages 3-11 $6. Group rates available. Free Oct. 1.) Look for discount coupons for zoo entrance in guidebooks.

Balboa Park has the greatest concentration of museums in the U.S. outside of Washington, DC. The park centers on the **Plaza de Panama,** where the Panama California Exposition of 1915-16 took place. Before exploring El Prado on your own, you might want to stop by the **House of Hospitality** at 1549 El Prado St., which contains the park **information center** (239-0512). The center sells simple maps and the **Passport to Balboa Park** ($13), which contains nine coupons for a week's worth of entry to all of the park's museums. (Passports are also available at participating museums. Open daily 9:30am-4pm.) The star of the western axis of the Plaza de Panama is Goodhue's California State Building, now the **Museum of Man** (239-2001). Inside, human evolution is traced through permanent exhibits on primates and early man. (Open daily 10am-4:30pm. $4 or 2 coupons, ages 13-18 $2, 6-12 $1.) Behind the Museum of Man is the **Old Globe Theater** (239-2255), the oldest professional theater in California. Classical and contemporary plays are performed nightly (Tues.-Sun.), with weekend matinees. Across the Plaza de Panama is the **San Diego Museum of Art** (232-7931), which maintains a comprehensive collection, ranging from ancient Asian to contemporary Californian. (Open Tues.-Sun. 10am-4:30pm. $7, seniors $6, military with ID $5, ages 6-18 and students with ID $2, under 6 free. Free 3rd Tues. of each month.)

South of El Prado is the **Reuben H. Fleet Space Theater** and **Science Center** (238-1233), with two **OmniMax** projectors, 153 speakers, and a hemispheric planetarium. (10-14 per day; Sat. 10 and 11am shows are subtitled in Spanish. $6, senior citizens $4.50, ages 5-15 $3.50, military and students with ID $4.80. Call 232-6860 for advance tickets.) The **Laserium** features Pink Floyd's "Dark Side of the Moon" (9 and 11pm; $6, seniors $4.50, children $3.50, under 5 not admitted). Tickets to the space theater include admittance to the **Science Center,** where visitors can play with a cloud chamber, telegraph, light-mixing booth, and other gadgets. (Open Sun.-Tues. 9:30am-9:30pm, Sat. 9:30am-10:30pm. $2.50, ages 5-15 $1.25.)

Sea World, Old Town, and Presidio Park

Sea World (226-3901) may be a commercial venture, but the Mission Park attraction is far more educational than your average amusement park. Sea World offers 20 major attractions, as well as numerous daytime and nighttime shows which range from educational to exploitative. There are well-lit, state-of-the-art aquaria and open pools, which allow astonishingly clear views of all types of marine life. Sea World's landmark **Skytower** ride (approx. 10 min.) offers spectacular views of San Diego County and the sea ($2). The most recent and high-tech addition to the park is **Mission Bermuda Triangle,** a virtual reality underwater adventure video. To get to Sea World, take I-5 or W. Mission Bay Dr. to Sea World Dr. (Bus #9 runs right to the entrance, but stops running in the early evening—you will miss the night show. Open Sun.-Thurs. 9am-10pm, Fri.-Sat. 9am-11pm, ticket sales end 1½ hr. before closing. $28, ages 3-11 $20. Shorter hours off-season. Parking $5 for cars, $7 RVs.)

To find San Diego's roots, look in **Old Town,** northwest from downtown on I-5 or bus #5. Southern California's first Europeans settled here in the late 1700s and built the county courthouse, the town gallows, and a busy commercial district here. The state park offers free daily walking tours, starting from their office at San Diego Ave. and Wallace St. at 2pm (237-6770). To appreciate Old Town's buildings on your own, get the visitors center's indispensable walking tour/history book ($2).

The Spanish **Presidio,** or military post, was established in 1769 in what is now **Presidio Park.** Presidio Park, next to and north of Old Town, now houses the **Serra Museum** (297-3258). Built in 1929, the museum is styled after the original San Diego mission on the site. (Open Tues.-Sat. 10am-4:30pm, Sun. noon-4:30pm; museum admission $3, under 12 free; park admission free.)

Mission Basilica San Diego de Alcalá (281-8449) was moved 6 mi. in 1774 to its present location in the hills north of the Presidio, in order to be closer to the Native American villages. (Take I-8 east to Mission Gorge Rd. and follow the signs, or bus #43.) Still an active parish church where mass is held (daily 7am and 5:30pm), the Mission has a chapel, a garden courtyard, a small museum of artifacts, and a reconstruction of the living quarters of mission-builder extraordinaire Junípero Serra.

West of the mission is Jack Murphy Stadium, home of the **San Diego Chargers** (280-2121) football team and baseball's **San Diego Padres** (525-8282).

NIGHTLIFE

San Diego's nightlife is found scattered throughout the city. The Gaslamp Quarter is home to numerous upscale restaurants and bars that feature live music nightly. Hillcrest draws a young, largely gay crowd to its clubs and restaurants once the sun has set. The beach areas (especially Garnet Ave. at Pacific Beach) are host to dozens of dance clubs, bars, and cheap eateries, which attract college-age revelers in masses. **Arts Tix,** 121 Broadway (238-3810), at 1st Ave., offers cheap same-day tickets.

Pacific Beach Grill and Club Tremors, 860 Garnet Ave., in Pacific Beach (2-PB-PARTY, 2-72-72779). A flight of steps connects the club and the restaurant. Attracting the young and unattached with a nightly DJ, Club Tremors is open nightly 8:30pm-2am. Cover varies $1-5. The upstairs bar is quieter and has an ever-changing menu of cheap food specials (open 11am-2am, kitchen 'til 11pm).

Dick's Last Resort, 345 4th Ave. (231-9100), in the Gaslamp Quarter. Visitors and natives alike turn out in droves for buckets o' Southern chow and a wildly irreverent atmosphere. Dick's stocks beers from around the globe, from Dixieland Blackened Voodoo lager to Pete's Wicked Ale. No cover for the nightly rock or blues. Burgers under $4, other dinners $10-15. Open daily 11am-1:30am.

Velvet, 2812 Kettner Blvd. (692-1080), near Old Town. Live and loud, the Velvet hosts San Diego's rock 'n' roll up-and-comers, as well as more established bands. Alternative rock 6 nights a week. Cover Wed.-Sat. $3-10. Pool table. Must be 21. Open daily 4pm-2am.

Croce's Top Hat Bar and Grille and Croce's Jazz Bar, 802 Fifth Ave., at F St. in Gaslamp District (233-6945). A rock/blues bar and classy jazz bar side by side. Live music nightly, up to $5 cover. Open daily 7:30am-2am.

Popular **lesbian** and **gay clubs** include: **The Flame** (3780 Park Blvd. in Hillcrest, 295-4163), a lesbian dance club; **West Coast Production Company** (2028 Hancock St. in Middletown, 295-3724), a gay club offering dancing, billiards, and a patio; and **Bourbon Street,** 4612 Park Blvd. (291-0173), in University Heights,

■ NEAR SAN DIEGO

Beaches San Diego has 70 mi. of beaches. While the ocean witnesses an endless stream of surfers and boogie-boarders, the sand from Imperial Beach in the south to La Jolla in the north is choked with sun-worshippers. Come prime sunning time on summer weekends, chic places like Mission Beach and La Jolla are likely to be as packed as funky Ocean Beach. The coastal communities do have more to offer than waves and white sand; wander inland a few blocks and explore.

La Jolla La Jolla means "the jewel" and this gilded city fulfills all the expectations its name inspires. Situated on a small rocky promontory, La Jolla (pronounced la HOY-a) in the 1930s and 40s was a hideaway for wealthy Easterners who built luxurious houses and gardens atop the bluffs over the ocean. To reach La Jolla, turn from I-5 and take a left at the Ardath exit or take buses #30 or 34 from downtown.

The coastline buckles against **Prospect St.'s** lavish hideaways. La Jolla claims some of the finest beaches in the city. Surfers are especially fond of the waves at

Tourmaline Beach and **Windansea Beach.** The waves at these beaches can be too much for non-surfers. **La Jolla Shores,** has gentler waves ideal for bodysurfers. **Black's Beach** is a public beach, not *officially* a nude beach, but you wouldn't know it from the sun-kissed hue of most beachcombers' buns. The northern part of the beach generally attracts gay patrons. Take I-5 to Genesee Ave., go west and turn left on N. Torrey Pines Rd. until you reach the **Torrey Pines Glider Port** (where the young and foolhardy "cliff dive" into the high tide).

THE DESERT

Mystics, misanthropes and hallucinogenophiles have long been fascinated by the desert's vast spaces, austere scenery, and brutal heat. In the winter the desert is a pleasantly warm refuge, in the spring a floral landscape, and in the summer a blistering wasteland. A barren place of overwhelming simplicity, the desert's beauty lies not so much in what it contains, but in what it lacks—congestion, pollution, and throngs of visitors.

Southern California's desert lies at the fringe of the North American Desert, a 500,000-square-mi. territory stretching east into Arizona and New Mexico, northeast into Nevada and Utah, and south into Mexico. Despite receiving only six inches of rain each year, the desert supports an astonishing array of plant and animal life.

California's desert divides roughly into two zones. The **Sonoran,** or **Low Desert,** occupies southeastern California from the Mexico north to Needles and is flat, dry, and barren. The oases in this area are essential to the existence of human, animal, and plant life; the largest of them supporting the super-resort of **Palm Springs.** Points of interest include **Anza-Borrego Desert State Park.**

The **Mojave,** or **High Desert,** spans the south central part of the state, bounded by the Sonoran Desert to the south and the Sierra Nevada Mountains to the north, and Death Valley to the east. The High Desert consists of foothills and plains nestled within mountain ranges approaching 5000 ft. Consequently, it is cooler (by about 10°F in summer) and wetter. **Joshua Tree National Park** is a popular destination for campers. **Barstow** is the central city of the High Desert and an important rest stop on the way from L.A. to Las Vegas or the Sierras.

Death Valley represents the eastern boundary of the Mojave but could be considered a region unto itself, since it has both high and low desert areas. Major highways cross the desert east-west: I-8 hugs the California-Mexico border, I-10 goes through Blythe and Indio on its way to Los Angeles, and I-40 crosses Needles to Barstow, where it joins I-15, running from Las Vegas and other points west to L.A.

For special health and safety precautions in the desert, see Desert Survival in the Health section of the General Introduction to this book.

■■■ PALM SPRINGS

The lackadaisical brand of decadence offered by Palm Springs has attracted people from all walks of life. Many year-round residents are retirees, however Palm Springs is also a popular spring break destination for students and a winter destination for middle-aged, monied golfers and hip, young scene-seekers from coastal communities. Memorial Day weekend and Labor Day weekend are the busiest times of year. Palm Springs lies off I-10, 120 miles east of L.A. The budget method for taking a sight-seeing of **celebrity homes** is to buy a map downtown and guide oneself.

Visitor information can be obtained at 190 W. Amado (325-1577; Mon.-Fri. 8:30am-4:30pm). **Greyhound,** 311 N. Indian Canyon (800-231-2222), runs 7 buses per day to L.A. ($17, $32.30 round-trip). The local **Sun Bus** system (343-3451) connects all Coachella Valley cities (6am-6pm; 75¢). **Desert Cab** is at 325-2868. Palm Spring's **post office:** 333 E. Amado Rd. (325-9631; open Mon.-Fri. 8am-5pm, Sat. 9am-1pm.) **ZIP code:** 92263; **area code:** 619.

Palm Springs' cheapest accommodations are at nearby state parks and national forest campgrounds. In you need a roof, try the **Budget Host Inn,** 1277 S. Palm Canyon Dr. (800-829-8099 or 325-5575), with large, clean rooms with refrigerators, phones and pool access. ($29 for 1-4 persons on weekdays, $39 on summer weekends.)

Picnicking is a great idea in Palm Springs, but for good Mexican food, try **Las Casuelas—The Original,** 368 N. Palm Canyon Dr. (325-3213; Open Sun.-Thurs. 10am-10pm, Fri.-Sat. 10:30am-11pm.) Bars offer nightly drink specials to lure revelers. **La Taqueria,** 125 E. Tahquitz Way (778-5391), attracts customers by spritzing its lovely tile patio with mist and serving Moonlight Margaritas for $2.25.

Rising nearly 6000 ft., the **Palm Springs Aerial Tramway** (325-1391) climbs up the side of Mt. San Jacinto to an observation deck that affords excellent views. The tramway station is located on Tramway Dr., just north of Palm Springs. (Trams runs at least every ½ hr. Mon.-Fri. starting at 10am, Sat.-Sun. starting at 8am. Last car leaves at 9pm; Nov.-April at 8pm. Round-trip fare $16, seniors $12, under 12 $10.) The **Desert Museum,** 101 Museum Dr. (325-0189), offers an impressive collection of Native American art, talking desert dioramas, and live animals. (Museum open late Sept.-early June Tues.-Fri. 10am-4pm, Sat.-Sun. 10am-5pm. $4, seniors $3, students and under 17 $2, under 6 free. Free first Tues. of each month.) The **Living Desert Reserve** in Palm Desert, located 1½ mi. south of Rte. 111 at 47900 Portola Ave. (346-5694), houses Arabian oryxes, iguani, desert unicorns, and Grevy's zebras alongside indigenous flora in the **Botanical Gardens.** The twilight reptile exhibit is a must-see. (Open daily Sept.-mid-June 9am-5pm. $7, seniors $6, under 15 $3.50. Wheelchair access.) The **Indian Canyons** (325-5673), once home to the Agua Caliente Cahuilla Indians, are oases that contain a wide variety of desert life and remnants of the human communities they once supported. All four canyons can be accessed at the end of S. Palm Canyon Dr., 5 mi. from the center of town. (Open daily Sept. 5-July 4, 8am-6pm. $5, students $2.50, seniors $2, ages 6-12 $1.)

Cabot's Old Indian Pueblo, 67616 E. Desert View Ave. (329-7610), 1 mi. east of Palm Dr. in **Desert Hot Springs,** is a Hopi-style pueblo built from materials found in the desert from 1941 to 1964. Take bus #19 from downtown Palm Springs to Desert View Ave. (Open 10am-4pm daily. $2.50, seniors $2, ages 5-16 $1.)

■■■ JOSHUA TREE NATIONAL PARK

When the Mormons crossed the desert in the 1800s, they named the enigmatic desert tree they encountered after the Biblical prophet Joshua, who beckoned the weary traveler to the promised land. The Joshua trees of the Mojave desert meet the wildflowers of the Sonoran desert at this spectacular preserve. Sparse forests of gangly Joshuas extend for miles in the high central and eastern portions of the park, punctuated by great piles of quartz monzonite boulders, some over 100 ft. high. This bizarre landscape emerged over millenia as shoots of hot magma pushed to the surface and erosion wore away the supporting sandstone. Together, the two forces have created fantastic textures, shapes, and rock albums. Alongside the natural environment appear vestiges of human existence: ancient rock pictographs, dams built in the 19th century in order to catch the meager rainfall for livestock, and the ruins of gold mines that operated as late as the 1940s.

Practical Information Joshua Tree National Park covers 558,000 acres northeast of Palm Springs, about 160 mi. (3-3½ hr. by car) east of L.A. It is ringed by three highways: **I-10** to the south, **Rte. 62** (Twentynine Palms Hwy.) to the west and north, and **Rte. 177** to the east. From I-10, the best approaches are via Rte. 62 from the west, leading to the towns of Joshua Tree and **Twentynine Palms** on the northern side of the park, and via an unnumbered road that exits the interstate about 25 mi. east of Indio. Visitor info is available at the **Headquarters and Oasis Visitor**

Center, 74485 National Monument Dr., Twentynine Palms 92277 (367-7511), ¼ mi. off Rte. 62. (Open daily 8am-4:30pm.) Also check out the **Cottonwood Visitor Center,** at the southern gateway, located approximately 7 mi. north of I-10; exit 4 mi. west of the town of Chiriaco Summit, 25 mi. east of Indio. (Open daily 8am-3:30pm, but hours are sometimes irregular.) **Desert Stage Lines,** (251-6162), based in Palm Springs, stops in Twentynine Palms (from Palm Springs $8.80).

You can rent a car at **Tropical Car Rental,** 6136 Adobe Rd. (361-8000), in Twentynine Palms. (From $130 per week. Must be 21 with major credit card.) In case of **emergency,** call 911 or 367-3523 for a ranger. For the 24-hr. dispatch center, call 714-383-5651 collect. Joshua Tree's **post office:** 73839 Gorgonio Dr. (367-3501), in Twentynine Palms (open Mon.-Fri. 9am-5pm.); **ZIP Code:** 92277; **area code:** 619.

Camping Most campgrounds in the park operate on a first-come, first-camped basis and accept no reservations. Exceptions are the group sites at Cottonwood, Sheep Pass, and Indian Cove, and family sites at Black Rock Canyon. Call MISTIX (800-365-2267). All campsites have tables, fireplaces, and pit toilets, and are free unless otherwise noted. Water (hence flush toilets) is available only at Black Rock Canyon and Cottonwood campgrounds. Bring your own firewood, because burning anything you find in the park is a major offense. **Backcountry camping** is unlimited, but be sure to register first at a backcountry board found along the park's main roads so park staff knows where you are. The best wooded campground is **Hidden Valley** (4200 ft.), in the center of the park off of Quail Springs Rd. It has secluded alcoves in which to pitch a tent, and shade provided by enormous boulders—39 sites in the Wonderland of Rocks. It's a haven for rock-climbers and near Barker Dam Trail. **Jumbo Rocks** (4400 ft.), near Skull Rock Trail on the eastern edge of Queen Valley, has 125 well-spaced sites (65 in summer) surrounding jumbo rocks. Front spots have best shade and protection; all are wheelchair accessible. Take Quail Springs Rd. 15 mi. south of the visitors center. **Black Rock Canyon** (4000 ft.) has 100 sites in a woodland environment on Joshua Lane off of Rte. 62, 2 mi. north of Yucca Valley. (Sites $10. Reservations accepted. Wheelchair accessible.)

Sights Over 80% of the park (mostly the southern and eastern areas) has been designated by Congress as a wilderness area—meaning trails but no roads, toilets, or campfires. For those seeking backcountry desert hiking and camping, Joshua Tree offers fantastic opportunities to explore truly remote territory. There is no water in the wilderness except when a flash flood comes roaring down a wash (beware your choice of campsite), and even then, it doesn't stay long. Carry lots of water. The most temperate weather is in late fall (Oct.-Dec.) and early spring (March-April). Temperatures in other months often span uncomfortable extremes.

Joshua Tree draws thousands of climbers each year and is one of the most popular destinations in the world for **rock-climbing.** The visitors center can provide info on established top rope routes and will identify where placement of new bolts is restricted. For instruction and equipment rentals contact **Ultimate Adventures** (366-4758) or **Wilderness Connection** (366-4745).

A drive is an easy way to explore the magic of Joshua Tree without specialized equipment (although 4-wheel-drive wouldn't hurt). Paved roads branch through the park's varied sights. A 34-mi. stretch crosses the center of the park from Twentynine Palms to the town of Joshua Tree. The longer drive through the park, between Twentynine Palms and I-10, traverses a sampling of both high and low desert landscapes. One sight that must not be missed is **Key's View** (5185 ft.), 5 mi. off the park road just west of Ryan Campground. On a clear day, you can see Palm Springs and the Salton Sea; it's also a fabulous spot to watch the sunrise. The **Palm Oases: Twentynine Palms, Fortynine Palms, Cottonwood Spring, Lost Palms,** and **Monson Canyon** merit a visit, as does the **Cholla Cactus Garden,** off Pinto Basin Rd.

Hiking through the park's trails is perhaps the best way to experience Joshua Tree. The **Barker Dam Trail** is packed with tourists, but the painted petroglyphs make the reservoir worth a trip. Get an early start. Rusted machinery and abandoned mineshafts eerily clutter the **Lost Horse Mine,** reached by a 1½-mi. trail, and evokes the region's gold prospecting days. Wildflowers, cooler temperatures, and the indelible picture of the encircling valleys reward the hardy hiker who climbs the 3 mi. to the summit of **Ryan Mountain** (5461 ft.). Bring plenty of water for this strenuous, unshaded climb. Pack extra water on all hikes. **Wildflower season** (mid-March-mid-May) is an especially colorful season in the park.

■■■ BARSTOW

Do not expect to revel in Barstow—this is the place to stock up for forays into the desert. Barstow is midway between Los Angeles and Las Vegas on I-15; it is the western terminus of I-40.The **California Desert Information Center,** 831 Barstow Rd., Barstow 92311 (256-8313), has the best tourist info on the area. (Open daily 9am-5pm.) The **Amtrak** station lies at 7685 N. 1st St. (800-872-7245), well past Main St., over the bridge that crosses the railroad tracks. Buy tickets on board or at a travel agency. (To: L.A., 2 per day, $34). **Greyhound,** 681 N. 1st St. (256-8757), has buses to L.A. (11 per day, $21.50) and Las Vegas (10 per day, $32). (Open daily 8am-2pm, 3:30-6pm, and 8-11:30pm.) **Yellow Cab** is at 256-6868. **Dial-A-Ride** (256-0311) is Barstow's limited bus service with routes throughout the city. (Mon.-Sat. 7am-5pm. Sun. service for seniors and people with disabilities only. Service is a bit unpredictable. 75¢.) **Enterprise Car Rental,** 620 W. Main St. (256-0761), offers economy cars for $130 per week with 1050 free mi. Drivers must be 21 with credit card. **Emergency** is 911. Barstow's **post office:** 425 S. 2nd Ave. (256-8494; open Mon.-Fri. 9am-5pm, Sat. 10am-noon); **ZIP Code:** 92312; **area code:** 619.

What Barstow lacks in charm it makes up for by its abundant inexpensive motels and eateries. **Motel 6,** 150 N. Yucca Ave. (256-1752), is relatively close to Greyhound and Amtrak stations, and only a block from a 24-hr. grocery and drugstore. Standard, clean rooms have cable TV. (Singles $22. Doubles $26.) **Motel Calico,** 35556 Yermo Rd. (254-2419), at I-15 and Ghost Town Rd. in Yermo, 8 mi. east of Barstow, offers seven attractive rooms decorated with desert photographs taken by the owner. (Singles $24. Doubles $30.) **Barstow/Calico KOA** (254-2311), 7 mi. northeast of Barstow on north side of Outer Rte. 15, between Ft. Irwin Rd. and Ghost Town Rd. exits caters to corporate campers with a pool, showers, and snack bar. It can get uncomfortably crowded. (Tent sites for 2 $17, additional person $2.50. RVs $20, with electric and water hookup. Sewer hookup $2 extra.)

Carlo's and Toto's, 901 W. Main. St. (256-7513) is a favorite local diner. (Huge platters of Mexican $4-7). (Open Sun.-Thurs. 11am-10pm, Fri.-Sat. 11am-11pm.)

Barstow is also home to the **Factory Merchants Outlet Plaza,** 2837 Lenwood Rd. (253-7342), an outlet shopping mecca just south of town off I-15.

■■■ DEATH VALLEY NATIONAL PARK

Dante and Milton could have found inspiration for their visions of hell in Death Valley. No place in the Old World approaches the searing temperatures of summer here. Much of the landscape resembles photographs of the surface of Mars, with its stark, desolate reddish crags and canyons. The highest temperature ever recorded in the Western Hemisphere (134°F in the shade) was measured at the Valley's Furnace Creek Ranch on July 10, 1913. Of that day, the ranch caretaker Oscar Denton said, "I thought the world was going to come to an end. Swallows in full flight fell to the ground dead, and when I went out to read the thermometer with a wet Turkish towel on my head, it was dry before I returned."

Although the fatal threshold of 130°F is rarely crossed—the *average* high temperature in July is 116°F, with a nighttime low of 88°F. Nature focuses all of its extremes and varieties here at a single location, resulting in a landscape that is at once harshly majestic and delicate. Few venture to the valley floor during the summer and it is foolish to do so; ground temperatures hover near an egg-frying 200°F. When visiting Death Valley in any season, check at the visitors center for the free pamphlet, *Hot Weather Hints*. To enjoy the park, visit in winter, *not* summer.

Late November through February are the coolest months (40-70°F in the valley, freezing temperatures and snow in the mountains) and also the wettest, with infrequent but violent rainstorms. Desert wildflowers bloom in March and April, accompanied by moderate temperatures and tempestuous winds that whip sand and dust into an obscuring curtain for hours or even days. Over 50,000 people crowd into Death Valley's facilities during the **49ers Encampment** festival, held the last week of October and the first two weeks of November. Traffic jams and congested trails also plague the area on three-day winter weekends and most major holidays.

Practical Information Visitor Information is found at the **Furnace Creek Visitor Center** (786-2331), on Rte. 190 in the east-central section of the valley. For information by mail, write the Superintendent, Death Valley National Park, Death Valley 92328. Purchase guides and topographic maps (the park service map/guide is "free" with payment of the entrance fee), and get a schedule of activities and guided ranger hikes. (Open summer daily 8am-4pm, winter 8am-7pm.) The park **fee** is $5. **Ranger Stations** are: **Grapevine,** junction of Rte. 190 and 267 near Scotty's Castle; **Stovepipe Wells,** on Rte. 190; **Wildrose,** Rte. 178, 20 mi. south of Emigrant via Emigrant Canyon Dr.; **Shoshone,** outside the southeast border of the valley at the junction of Rtes. 178 and 127; and **Beatty,** on Rte. 374 in Beatty, NV. Weather report, weekly naturalist program, and park info posted at each station. They also provides emergency help and are all closed during most of the summer. **Tank up** with gasoline outside Death Valley at Olancha, Shoshone, or Beatty, NV. Otherwise, you'll pay about 20¢ per gallon more at the stations across from the Furnace Creek Visitors Center, in Stove Pipe Wells Village, and at Scotty's Castle. **Propane gas, and diesel fuel** are available at the Furnace Creek Chevron; **gas** at the Furnace Creek Ranch and Stove Pipe Wells Village stores. **Groceries and Supplies** can be had at the **Furnace Creek Ranch Store,** which is well-stocked but expensive. (Open daily 7am-9pm.) **Emergency:** 911. **Post Office:** Furnace Creek Ranch (786-2223; open Mon.-Fri. 8:30am-5pm, June-Sept. Mon.-Fri. 8:30am-3pm); **ZIP Code:** 92328; **area code:** 619.

Getting Around There is no regularly scheduled public transportation into Death Valley. Bus tours are monopolized by **Fred Harvey's Death Valley Tours.** They begin at Furnace Creek Ranch, which also handles reservations (786-2345, ext. 222), and are offered from early October to late May. A two-hour tour of the lower valley ($20, children $12) leaves at 9am, stopping briefly at Zabriskie Point, Mushroom Rock, Devil's Golf Course, Badwater, and Artists' Drive. The best way to get into and around Death Valley is by car. The nearest rental agencies are in Las Vegas, Barstow, and Bishop.

Of the 13 **park entrances,** most visitors choose Rte. 190 from the east. The road is well-maintained, the pass is less steep, and you arrive more quickly at the visitors center, located about midway along the 130-mi. north-south route through the valley. But since most of the major sights adjoin not Rte. 190 but the north-south road, the daytripping visitor with a trusty vehicle will be able to see much of the park by entering from the southeast (Rte. 178 west from Rte. 127 at Shoshone) or the north (direct to Scotty's Castle via NV Rte. 267 from U.S. 95). Unskilled mountain drivers should not attempt to enter via the smaller Titus Canyon or Emigrant Canyon Drive roads; neither has guard rails to keep cars from going over the cliffs.

Twenty-wheelers have replaced 20-mule teams, but driving in Death Valley still takes stubborn determination. **Radiator water** (*not* for drinking) is available at critical points on Rte. 178 and 190 and NV Rte. 374, but not on any unpaved roads. Believe the signs that say "Four-Wheel-Drive Only." Those who do bound along the backcountry trails by four-wheel-drive should carry chains, extra tires, gas, oil, water (both to drink and for the radiator), and spare parts. Know how to make minor repairs, bring along appropriate topographic maps, leave an itinerary with the visitors center, and bring a CB radio. Check ahead for road closings—especially in summer. Do not drive on wet backcountry roads.

Accommodations Budget travelers should be wary of the high prices at **Fred Harvey's Amfac Consortium** at the **Furnace Creek Ranch** complex (786-2345, for reservations 800-528-6367). Older cabins with A/C and two double beds will set you back $76. Remodeled motel-style accommodations start at $98 for a double. Look for cheaper places in the towns near Death Valley: **Olancha** (west), **Shoshone** (southwest), **Tecopa** (south), and **Beatty, NV** (northwest).

The National Park Service maintains nine **campgrounds**, only one of which accepts reservations. Call ahead to check availability and be prepared to battle for a space if you come during peak periods. All campsites have toilets. Water availability is not completely reliable; always pack water and your own supplies. Collecting wood, be it alive or dead, is forbidden everywhere in the park; carry in your own firewood. Roadside camping is not permitted, but **backcountry camping** is free and legal, provided you check in at the visitors center and pitch tents at least 1 mi. from main roads and 5 mi. from any established campsite.

Sights Death Valley has **hiking** trails to challenge the mountain lover, the desert daredevil, the backcountry camper, and the fair-weather day hiker. Backpackers and day hikers alike should inform the visitors center of their trip, and take along the appropriate topographic maps. During the summer, the National Park Service recommends that valley floor hikers plan a route along roads where assistance is readily available, and outfit a hiking party of at least two people with another person following in a vehicle to monitor the hikers' progress. Carrying salve to treat feet parched by the nearly 200°F earth is also wise (do not wear sandals or lightweight footwear). Better yet, reschedule your trip for a cooler time of year. Check the weather forecast before setting out—roads and trails can disappear during a winter rainstorm. Canyon and valley floors are transformed into deadly torrents during heavy rains.

The **Visitor Center and Museum** is the place to expand your knowledge of tours and hikes. If you're interested in astronomy, speak to one of the rangers; some set up telescopes at Zabriskie Point and offer free-lance stargazing shows. In **wildflower season** (Feb.-mid-April), tours are lead to some of the best places for viewing the display. **Hell's Gate** and **Jubilee Pass** are beautiful, and **Hidden Valley** even more so, though it is accessible only by a difficult, 7-mi., four-wheel-drive only route from **Teakettle Junction** (25 mi. south of Ubehebe Crater). Both the **Harmony Borax Works** and the **Borax Museum** are a short drive from the visitors center.

Artist's Drive is a one-way loop off Rte. 178, beginning 10 mi. south of the visitors center. The road twists and winds its way through rock and dirt canyons on the way to **Artist's Palette**, a rainbow of green, yellow, and red mineral deposits in the hillside. About 5 mi. south, you'll reach **Devil's Golf Course**, a plane of spiny salt crust made up of the precipitate left from the evaporation of ancient Lake Manly.

Zabriskie Point is a marvelous place from which to view Death Valley's corrugated badlands. Perhaps the most spectacular sight in the entire park is the vista at **Dante's View**, reached by a 15-mi. paved road from Rte. 190. Just as the Italian poet stood with Virgil looking down on the damned, so the modern observer gazes upon a vast inferno punctuated only by the virginal-white expanse of the salt flats. On a really clear day, you can see the highest point in the continental United States (Mt. Whitney, 14,494 ft.) and the lowest (Badwater, 282 ft. below sea level). It can be snowy here in mid-winter and cold anytime but summer.

CENTRAL COAST

The Central Coast offers what many fail to find in Los Angeles. Here, as one winds along the coast, the smog lifts, the freeways narrow, and the traffic jams loosen, bringing into stark relief the California that has inspired New Agers, surfers, good and bad poets, and lovers of nature. The Central Coast has the most dramatic scenery and relaxed cosmopolitanism the state has to offer.

■■■ SANTA BARBARA

In 1782, Spanish missionaries chose this site for a mission. In subsequent years many of the native Chumash were converted, and many more died from diseases the friars inadvertently carried. Over the ruins of the extinct Chumash, the Spanish, followed by the Americans, built Santa Barbara into a prosperous port town. In the 1920s, Santa Barbarans discovered an oil deposit and the city boomed even louder. Today, most foreigners know it for its namesake soap opera. Santa Barbara's alluring display of red tile and white stucco, gentle climate, and unaggressive lifestyle attract wealthy vacationers, the homeless, European tourists, and students.

PRACTICAL INFORMATION

Emergency: 911.

Visitors Information: Chamber of Commerce, 504 State St. (965-3021). Mailing address: Santa Barbara Conference and Visitors Bureau, 510A State St., Santa Barbara 93101. Open Mon.-Fri. 9am-5pm. Open Mon.-Sat. 9am-6pm, Sun. 10am-6pm; Oct.-April Mon.-Sat. 9am-4pm, Sun. 10am-5pm.

Amtrak: 209 State St. (963-1015; for schedule and fares, 800-872-7245), downtown. Be careful after dark. Open daily 7am-1:45pm, 2:30-6:30pm, and 7-11pm. Tickets sold until 9:30pm. To L.A. ($20) and San Francisco ($67).

Greyhound: 34 W. Carrillo St. (966-3962), at Chapala. To L.A. (11 per day, $10.50) and San Francisco (7 per day, $43.75). Open daily 5:45am-11:30pm.

Santa Barbara Metropolitan Transit District: Transit Center, 1020 Chapala St. (683-3702), at Cabrillo, behind the Greyhound station.Get bus maps at the visitor center or at the transit center on Chapala. (Fare 75¢, disabled and over 61 30¢, under 5 free. Free transfers.) A 25¢ **downtown/waterfront shuttle** runs along State St. (Sun.-Thurs. 10:10am-5:40pm, Fri.-Sat. 10:10am-8:40pm; every 10 min. 11am-5:40pm, otherwise every 30 min.). Stops area at circular blue signs.

Taxi: Yellow Cab Company, (965-5111). 24 hrs.

Car Rental: U-Save Auto Rental, 510 Anacapa (963-3499). $20 per day with 100 free mi., $109 per week with 700 free mi.; 15¢ per additional mi. Must be 21 with major credit card. Open Mon.-Fri. 8am-5:30pm, Sat.-Sun. 9am-1pm.

Bike Rental: Cycles-4-Rent, 101 State St. (966-3804), 1 block from the beach. Rent a 1-speed beach cruiser for $4 per hr., $17 per day. 21-speed $7 per hr., $30 per day. Open Mon.-Fri. 9am-6:30pm, Sat.-Sun. 8:30am-7:30pm.

Crisis Hotline: 569-2255. 24 hrs.

Post Office: 836 Anacapa St. (564-2266), 1 block east of State St. Open Mon.-Fri. 8am-5:30pm. **ZIP Code:** 93102.

Area Code: 805.

Santa Barbara is 96 mi. northwest of Los Angeles and 27 mi. past Ventura on **U.S. 101.** The beach lies at the southern end of the city, and **State Street,** the main street in Santa Barbara, runs northwest from the waterfront.

ACCOMMODATIONS AND CAMPING

U.S. 101 is lined with cheap, though bland lodgings. As always, **Motel 6** is an option.

Santa Barbara International Backpackers Hostel, 409 State St. (963-0154), 5-min. walk from beach and 2 blocks from Amtrak terminal. Passport, AYH or student ID required. Relatively safe and clean, located in one of the most happening parts of town. International clientele. $16 for 4 bed room. $17 8 bed room.

The Schooner Inn, 533 State St. (965-4572; fax 962-2412), central downtown. Sizable hotel in a beautiful building. Singles and doubles $40, with bath $50-65. For weekend stays, make reservations at least a week in advance.

Hotel State Street, 121 State St. (966-6586; fax 962-8459), just off the beach. Cable TV. Continental breakfast included. Private bedrooms; shared bath. $45 for one double bed, $55 for two. A room with two twin beds is $45. In winter, rooms are $5 less. Reservations recommended.

Californian Hotel, 35 State St. (966-7153), near beach. One of S.B.'s older hotels. TV, phone, private bath, good location. Singles $35-50. Doubles $45-70.

The *Santa Barbara Campsite Directory* lists prices, directions to sites, and reservation numbers for all **campgrounds** in the area. It's free and available at the visitors center. State sites can be reserved through MISTIX (800-444-7275). **Carpinteria Beach State Park** (684-2811), 12 mi. southeast of Santa Barbara along U.S. 101, has 262 developed tent sites with hot showers. (Sites $16, $20-25 with hookups.) There are three state beaches under 30 mi. west of Santa Barbara (sites at all three $16): **El Capitan** (968-3294), **Gaviota** (968-3294), and **Refugio** (968-1350).

FOOD

Restaurants cluster on State St., Milpas St., and E. Canon Perdido St. State St. tends to be a little more upscale. There's a **farmer's market** on old town State St. (Tues. 4-7:30pm), and another at Santa Barbara St., downtown (Sat. 8:30am-noon).

Flavor of India, 3026 State St. (682-6561). This clean, friendly establishment is the place to go for astoundingly good tandoor and vegetarian dishes. Great all-you-can-eat lunch buffet ($6). Curry dishes are about $8. Buffet Mon.-Sat. 11:30am-3pm. Open for dinner Sun.-Thurs. 5:30-10pm, Fri.-Sat. 5:30-10:30pm.

La Super-rica Taquería, 622 N. Milpas (963-4940). Julia Child's favorite Mexican restaurant. Popular place to chat. Dishes $1.30-5.10. Open Sun.-Thurs. 11am-9:30pm, Fri.-Sat. 11am-10pm.

The Natural Café, 508 State St. (962-9494). Oak interior with lots of plants. Healthy, attractive clientele dines on healthy, attractive food. Smoothies ($3) and sandwiches ($3.50-5). Veggie Grill ($5). Open daily 11am-11pm.

SIGHTS

For a great view of the city, climb to the observation deck of the **Santa Barbara County Courthouse** at 1100 Anacapa St. (962-6464). The courthouse itself is one of the West's great public buildings. (Building open Mon.-Fri. 8am-5pm, Sat.-Sun. 9am-5pm. Tower closes at 4:45pm. Free.) Pick up "Santa Barbara's Red Tile Tour," a map and walking tour guide, at the Chamber of Commerce.

The **Public Library** and the **Santa Barbara Museum of Art** blend different styles of architecture into an eye-pleasing ensemble. The library, 40E Anapamu St. (962-7653), and the museum, 1130 State St. (963-4364), are linked by a pedestrian plaza. Inside the library, the **Faulkner Gallery** usually displays works for sale by local artists. (Open Mon.-Thurs. 10am-9pm, Fri.-Sat. 10am-5:30pm, Sun. 1-5pm. Free.) The art museum prides itself on its American art. (Open Tues.-Wed. and Fri.-Sat. 11am-5pm, Thurs. 11am-9pm, Sun. noon-5pm. Tours Tues.-Sun. 1pm. $3, seniors $2.50, ages 6-16 $1.50. Free Thurs.) The **Arlington Center for Performing Arts,** 1317 State St. (box office 963-4408), is a rarity—a uniplex.

The beach west of State St. is called **West Beach.** The longer stretch in the other direction, **East Beach,** with its volleyball and biking trails, is universally popular. The beach at **Summerland,** east of Montecito (bus #20), is frequented by the gay and hippie communities. **Rincon Beach,** 3 mi. southeast of Carpinteria, has the best surfing in the county. **Gaviota State Beach,** 29 mi. west of Santa Barbara, offers good surf, and the western end is a (sometimes) clothing-optional beach. **Whale-watching** takes place from late November to early April, as the grays migrate.

Chase Palm Park acts as a buffer between East Beach and Cabrillo Blvd. The park has nearly 2 mi. of bike and foot paths. At the far end of Palm Park is the **Santa Barbara Zoo,** 500 Niños Dr. (962-6310), off Cabrillo Blvd. From U.S. 101, take either Milpas St. or Cabrillo Blvd. exits to Cabrillo Blvd., then turn toward the mountains at

Niños Dr. You can also take bus #21. (Open daily 10am-5pm; Labor Day-June daily 9am-6pm. $5, seniors and ages 2-12 $3, under 2 free. Free parking.)

Mission Santa Barbara (682-4713), is at the end of Laguna St. on the northern side of town (Take bus #22.) Praised as the "Queen of Missions" when built in 1786, the mission assumed its present majestic incarnation in 1820. (Open daily 9am-5pm. Museum $2, under 16 free.) Two blocks north of the mission is the **Santa Barbara Museum of Natural History,** 2559 Puesta del Sol Rd. (682-4711); follow the signs. (Open Mon.-Sat. 9am-5pm, Sun. 10am-5pm. Planetarium shows summer; observatory 682-3224. $5, seniors and ages 13-17 $4, under 12 $3; off-season $1 less.)

NIGHTLIFE

Most clubs and bars are located in the square formed by State, Ortega, Cota, and Haley Streets. For the scoop, pick up a free copy of *The Independent* or *The Metro,* available at the Chamber of Commerce, in restaurants, or in boxes on the street.

Joseppi's, 434 State St. (962-5516). Jazz and blues nightly in a tiny club (the oldest jazz club in Santa Barbara) that occasionally spills into the street. Shows begin at 8pm. Cover $2-3. Open whenever Joe, the owner, feels like it. Smoke-free.

Alex's Cantina, 633 State St. (966-0032), downtown. Also at 5918 Hollister Ave. (683-2577), in Goleta between downtown and UCSB. The Happiest Hour in town, 3:30-8pm daily with drink specials. Dancing nightly 9pm-2am. Live bands 6 nights per week, alternative music Sat. Cover varies, usually less than $5. Hollister location has comedy and sports Fri.-Sat.; also has more DJ time.

Calypso, 514 State St. (966-1388). Tropical theme. Crowded with local frat-types. Live performances every night: blues, jazz, rock, reggae. 14-oz. Coors Light 50¢ every night 7-10pm. Open daily 11am-2am.

Green Dragon Art Studio and Espresso Bar, 22 W. Mission (687-1902). A coffeehouse with poetry or music. Open Sun.-Thurs. 7am-11pm, Fri.-Sat. 7am-1am.

■■■ BIG SUR

In 1542 Cabrillo, sailing off the coast of Big Sur, wrote "here there are mountains which seem to reach the heavens, and the sea beats on them." He was a master of understatement. Big Sur's 90-mi. stretch of coast and the cliffs that tower over it, backdropped by fields of wildflowers and mist-laden mountains, are bound to win over even those most oblivious to nature's beauty.

Practical Information Monterey's Spanish settlers simply called the entire region below their town "El Sur Grande"—the large South. Today, "Big Sur" signifies a more exact coastal region bordered on the south by San Simeon and on the north by Carmel. For visitors info, go to the **Big Sur Station:** 667-2315, on Rte. 1, inside **Big Sur State Park.** This is a multi-agency station that provides info on all area State Parks, U.S. Forest Service campgrounds, and local transit. (Open daily 8am-5:30pm.) Big Sur's **post office:** on Rte. 1, next to the Center Deli in Big Sur Center; (667-2305; open Mon.-Fri. 8:30am-5pm); **ZIP Code:** 93920; **area code:** 408.

Camping Places to camp are abundant and beautiful. The cheapest way to stay in Big Sur is to camp for free in the Ventana Wilderness (pick up a permit at Big Sur Station). Ventana, at the northern end of Los Padres National Forest, is a backpack-only area—no automobiles. The **Big Sur Campgrounds and Cabins** (667-2322), 26 mi. south of Carmel, near the Big Sur River has campsites ($22, with hookup $25) and tent cabins in summer ($40). (Store, laundry, playground, volleyball courts, and hot showers.) The **Los Padres National Forest** has several U.S. Forest Service Campgrounds: **Plaskett Creek** (667-2315), south of Limekiln, near Jade Cove (43 sites) and **Kirk Creek,** about 5 mi. north of Jade Cove (33 beautiful spots, but they're close to the highway; no showers, only toilets and cold running water; open 24 hrs; check-out 2pm; sites $15, hikers and bikers $3; no reservations).

CALIFORNIA

Food Grocery stores are located at River Inn, Ripplewood, Fernwood, Big Sur Lodge, Pacific Valley Center, and Gorda, but it's better to arrive prepared; prices are high. The **Center Deli** (667-2225), right beside the Big Sur Post Office, has the most reasonably priced goods in the area (sandwiches $2.75), plus a broad selection of groceries. (Open daily 8am-9pm; winter 8am-8pm.) Or try the **Fernwood Burger Bar** (667-2422), Rte. 1, 2 mi. north of post office. There's a homey bar as well as a grocery store. The gas is slightly less expensive here. (Open daily 11:30am-10pm.)

Activities The **state parks** and **wilderness areas** are exquisite settings for dozens of outdoor activities. **Hiking** on Big Sur is fantastic: the state parks and **Los Padres National Forest** all have trails that penetrate redwood forests and cross low chaparral, offering even grander views of Big Sur than those available from Rte. 1. The northern end of Los Padres National Forest has been designated the **Ventana Wilderness** and contains the popular **Pine Ridge Trail.** Grab a map and a required permit at the Big Sur station (See Practical Information).

Within **Pfeiffer Big Sur State Park** are eight trails of varying lengths (50¢ map available at park entrance). Try the **Valley View Trail,** a short, steep path overlooking the valley below. **Buzzard's Roost Trail** is a rugged two-hour hike up tortuous switchbacks. Big Sur's most jealously guarded treasure is USFS-operated **Pfeiffer Beach**, 1 mi. south of Pfeiffer State Park. Turn off Rte. 1 at the stop sign and the "Narrow Road not suitable for trailers" sign. Follow the road 2 mi. to the parking area; take the footpath to the beach. North of this, the 1889 **Lighthouse Station** (625-4419) perches atop Point Sur. (Tours Sat.-Sun., weather permitting. $5, ages 13-17 $3, ages 5-12 $2. Arrive 1 hr. early; be prepared for a steep hike.)

■ NEAR BIG SUR: HEARST CASTLE

The **Hearst San Simeon Historic Monument** (927-2010) lies 5 mi. east of Rte. 1 near San Simeon. William Randolph Hearst, infamous millionaire-*cum*-yellow journalist and instigator of the Spanish-American War, began building this Hispano-Moorish indulgence in 1919. Much of the castle's "art" is fake: concrete statuary, plaster pilasters, artificially aged tiles. Yet genuine treasures remain: the world's largest private collection of Greek vases lines the library shelves; medieval tapestries grace the halls; and ancient Chinese ceramics perch on the mantelpieces of Gothic fireplaces. Visitors have a choice of five **tours**, each 1¾-2 hours long. It's possible to take them all in one day, but each costs $14 (ages 6-12). You must take a tour to see the castle; wandering around on your own is not allowed. Tours are offered at least every hour from 8:20am to 3pm. To see the Castle in summer, advance reservations are a must (800-444-4445). The gates to the visitors center open in summer at 6am, in winter at 7am. Tickets go on sale daily at 8am.

■■■ MONTEREY

In the 1940s, Monterey was a coastal town geared toward sardine fishing and canning. But the sardines disappeared in the early '50s, and when John Steinbeck revisited his beloved Cannery Row around 1960, he wrote scornfully of how the district had become a tourist trap. Today, few traces of the Monterey described in *Cannery Row* remain; along the famous Row and Fisherman's Wharf, packing plants have been converted to multiplex souvenir malls, and the old bars where sailors used to drink and fight now feature wax recreations. Still, the ineradicable beauty of the coastline, the seafood, and a world-class aquarium justify a journey to Monterey.

Practical Information The Monterey Peninsula, 115 mi. south of San Francisco, contains Monterey, Pacific Grove, a residential community, and Pebble Beach, an exclusive nest of mansions. Motorists can approach Monterey from **U.S. 101** (Munras Ave. exit), which runs north-south slightly inland from the peninsula, or **Rte. 1.** First stop at the **Monterey Peninsula Chamber of Commerce,** 380 Alvarado St. (649-1770), downtown. (Open Mon.-Fri. 8:30am-5pm.) **Greyhound** (800-231-2222) has no station, but does stop at 351 Del Monte Ave., site of the old office with a schedule posted on the door. Tickets may be purchased from the driver or at another station (like Salinas or Santa Cruz). For a taxi, call **Yellow Cab** (646-1234, $1.50 plus $1.75 per mi). **Emergency** is 911. Monterey's **post office**: 565 Hartnell (372-5803; open Mon.-Fri. 8:45am-5:10pm); **ZIP Code:** 93940; **area code:** 408.

Accommodations and Camping Accommodations prices vary by day, month, and proximity to a popular event, such as the Jazz Festival. Look for reasonably priced hotels on the 2000 block of Fremont St. in Monterey (bus #9 or 10) and Lighthouse Ave. in Pacific Grove (bus #2 or some #1 buses). The **Monterey Peninsula Youth Hostel (HI-AYH)** (649-0375), theoretically, does not have a fixed location, but the hostel has been in the Monterey High School for the past few summers. To reach the high school, take Pacific away from the water, turn right on Madison and left on Larkin St. Mattresses are put on the floor along the gymnasium walls. Staff tries to make up for the lack of amenities by providing lots of info. (Ample parking. Lockout 9:30am-6pm. Curfew 11pm. $6, nonmembers $9. Under 18 50% off. Open daily mid-June to mid-Aug.) The **Del Monte Beach Inn,** 1110 Del Monte (649-4410), close to downtown, across from the beach, offers pleasant rooms (shared bath) and a hearty breakfast for $45-60. *Let's Go* travelers get a 10% discount on weekdays. The **Veterans Memorial Park Campground** (646-3865), Via Del Rey (1½ mi. from the town center), is perched on a hill with a view of the bay. Take Skyline Dr. off the section of Rte. 68 called W.R. Holman Hwy. From downtown, take Pacific St. south, turn right on Jefferson, and follow the signs, or take bus #3. (40 sites, hot showers. First-come, first-camped. Arrive before 3 pm in summer and on winter weekends. Sites $15, hikers $3.)

Food The sardines may be gone, but the unpolluted Monterey Bay teems with squid, crab, rock cod, sand dab, red snapper, and salmon. You can enjoy your seafood as Sicilian marinated octopus, English fish & chips, Thai sweet-and-sour snapper, or artfully wrapped sushi. **Casa de Gutiérrez,** 590 Calle Principal (375-0095), at the south end of the street, offers huge portions of traditional fare and good vegetarian dishes. (2 tacos $2.75; combination plate $6-10; open Mon.-Thurs. 11am-9pm, Fri.-Sun. 10am-10pm.) **Tutto Buono Gastronomic Specialties,** 469 Alvarado (372-1880) is large and Californian, with track lighting. (Homemade pastas and sauce; fresh brick-oven pizzas from $6; open daily 11am-10pm.)

SIGHTS
Cannery Row lies along the waterfront south of the aquarium. Once a depressed street of languishing sardine packing plants, this ¾-mi. row has been converted into glitzy mini-malls, bars, and discos. All that remains of the earthiness and gruff camaraderie celebrated by John Steinbeck in *Cannery Row* and *Sweet Thursday* are a few building façades: 835 Cannery Row once was the Wing Chong Market, the bright yellow building next door is where *Sweet Thursday* took place, and Doc Rickett's Lab at 800 Cannery Row is now owned by a private men's club.

At the northwest end of Cannery Row, the renowned **Monterey Bay Aquarium,** 866 Cannery Row (648-4800), stands all but open to the bay. Taking advantage of the bay's ocean-swept purity, valves continually pump in raw, unfiltered seawater. This not only guarantees a genuine ocean environment in the tanks, but it also lets in eggs and larvae which eventually join the exhibits. After 3pm the crowds dwindle. (Open daily 9:30am-6pm. $11.25; students and over 65 $8.25; ages 3-12 $5.)

Built in 1846 by prisoners, military deserters, and a "volunteer" crew of Native Americans, **Fisherman's Wharf** was for decades the center of one of the largest fishing and whaling industries in the West. Since WWII, however, fishermen have followed the fish to Moss Landing, south of Monterey Bay. Fisherman's Wharf is currently awash with tourists, junkfood, and shops. Located at the base of Fisherman's Wharf in the Historic Customs House Plaza is the **Stanton Center's Mari-**

time Museum of Monterey (373-2469). (Open daily 10am-5pm. $5, seniors and disabled $4, ages 13-18 $3, ages 6-12 $2.) For **sight-seeing boat trips** around Monterey Bay, **Monterey Sport Fishing**, 96 Fisherman's Wharf (372-2203), provides 25-min. tours every half-hour ($7, under 12 $5).

Most of the town's historical buildings downtown now belong to the **Monterey State Historic Park.** Each house is clearly marked by a sign and can provide information and free maps of walking tours. If you plan to visit more than one of the houses which charge admission, you'll want to purchase a $5 pass which allows you to enter all historic park buildings and participate in any or all of the walking tours. Buy your ticket at the **Visitors Center** (649-7118) inside the Park Headquarters in the Customs House Plaza (open daily 10am-5pm, in winter 10am-4pm).

Nearby **Pacific Grove** has Victorian houses, a beautiful coastline, numerous lunch counters, and lots of funky shops. Pacific Grove also houses thousands of **monarch butterflies** which annually flee Canada to winter in its cypress groves from October to March. Look, but don't touch; harming butterflies is a $1000 fine.

Monterey's nightly entertainment centers around the same areas that click with cameras by day; bars downtown attract fewer tourists. One option is to tire yourself biking, hiking, or kayaking in the beautiful peninsula and go to bed early. **Planet Gemini,** 625 Cannery Row (373-1449), on the 3rd floor, is a comedy and dance club that features rock on Tues., country on Wed., and comedy Thurs.-Sat. Doors open at 8pm, shows start at 9pm. (Dancing Thurs.-Sat. !0:30pm-2am. Cover varies.) The famous **Monterey Jazz Festival** (373-3366), rules the third week of September.

■ NEAR MONTEREY: PINNACLES NATIONAL MONUMENT

South of Salinas, U.S. 101 runs through the Salinas Valley, the self-styled "salad bowl of the nation." The stunning, mysterious peaks of Pinnacles National Monument make a visit to this land of produce worth your while. **Gonzales, Soledad, Greenfield,** and **King City** are the four towns in the Salinas Valley. This area is essentially accessible only by car. But it's worth the trip. Towering dramatically over the chaparral east of Soledad, **Pinnacles National Monument** contains the spectacular remnants of an ancient volcano. Set aside as a national park by Teddy Roosevelt in 1908, the park preserves the erratic and unique spires and crags that millions of years of weathering carved out of prehistoric lava flows. Over 30 mi. of hiking trails wind through the park's low chaparral, boulder-strewn caves, and pinnacles of rock. For info. check out the **King City Chamber of Commerce and Agriculture,** 203 Broadway, King City, CA 93930 (385-3814; open Mon.-Fri. 10am-noon, 1-4pm). The park headquarters is located at the east side entrance (Rte. 25 to Rte. 146; 389-4485), but there is also a ranger station on the west side (U.S. 101 to Rte. 146). **Area code:** 408.

The **High Peaks Trail** runs a strenuous 5.3 mi. across the park between the east and west entrances, and offers amazing views of the surrounding rock formations. For a less exhausting trek, try the **Balconies Trail,** a 1½-mi. promenade from the west entrance up to the Balconies Caves. If you visit during the week, you will have the park nearly to yourself. The park also has the widest range of wildlife of any park in California, including a number of rare predator mammals: mountain lions, bobcats, coyote, gold eagles, and peregrine falcons (park admission $4). **Camping** is to be found only at the monument. The campground is walk-in, but some of the sites are just 50 yds. from the parking lot. Reservations are not accepted, and with only 23 sites, it's best to show up early if you're trying to camp on a weekend. The campground has firepits, restrooms, and picnic tables. (Sites $10.)

■■■ SANTA CRUZ

Santa Cruz sports the kind of mellow hipness of which other coastal towns can only dream. The city was born as one of Father Junípero Serra's missions in 1791 (the name means "holy cross"), but today, Santa Cruz is nothing if not liberal. One of the few places where the old '60s catch-phrase "do your own thing" still applies, it simultaneously embraces macho surfers and a large lesbian community.

PRACTICAL INFORMATION

Emergency: 911

Visitors Information: Santa Cruz Conference and Visitor's Council, 701 Front St. (425-1234 or 800-833-3494). Pick up the *Visitors Guide, Dining Guide,* or the *Accommodations Guide* (all free). Open Mon.-Sat. 9am-5pm, Sun. 10am-4pm.

Greyhound/Peerless Stages: 425 Front St. (423-1800 or 800-231-2222). To San Francisco (3 per day, $10). To L.A. via Salinas (4 per day, $47). Luggage lockers. Open Mon.-Fri. 7:45am-11am, 2-7:45pm., Sat.-Sun. 7-11am, 3-4pm, 6-7:45pm.

Santa Cruz Metropolitan District Transit (SCMDT): 920 Pacific Ave. (425-8600 or 688-8600), at the Metro Center in the Pacific Garden Mall. Pick up a free copy of *Headways* for route info. Bus fare is $1 (no bills accepted); day passes obtained at the Metro Center are $3 (over 61 40¢, day pass $1.10; under 5 free).

Taxi: Yellow Cab, 423-1234. 24 hrs. $1.75 plus $1.75 per mi.

Bicycle Rental: The Bicycle Rental Center, 415 Pacific Ave. (426-8687), at Front St. Mountain bikes and cruisers. 1st hour $6, $4 per additional hr. $25 per day, Helmets and locks provided. Open daily 10am-6pm, winter daily 10am-5pm.

Post Office: 850 Front St. (426-5200). Open Mon.-Fri. 8:30am-5pm. Sat. 9am-4pm.

ZIP Code: 95060.

Area Code: 408

Santa Cruz is about one hour south of San Francisco on the northern lip of Monterey Bay. Take **U.S. 101** or **Rte. 1** from S.F. The Santa Cruz beach and its boardwalk run roughly east-west, with Monterey Bay to the south. The narrow San Lorenzo River runs mainly north-south, bisecting the city. Chestnut, Front, and Ocean St. run roughly parallel with the river while Laurel-Broadway, Lincoln-Soquel, and Water cross it. Pacific Ave. lies to the west of Front St.

ACCOMMODATIONS AND CAMPING

Like many a beach town, Santa Cruz gets crowded during the summer and on weekends and doubly crowded on summer weekends when room rates skyrocket and availability plummets. Fortunately, a number of hotels on the winding San Lorenzo-East Cliff-Murray Dr. offer a few unreservable rooms for about $30. Show up early.

Carmelita Cottage (HI-AYH), 321 Main St. (429-8541), 4 blocks from Greyhound and 2 blocks from the beach. 24 beds. Kitchen, common room. 3-day max. stay. Curfew 11pm. Lock-out 9am-5pm. Office hours 5-10pm. $12, nonmembers $15. Reservations by mail only to P.O. Box 1241, Santa Cruz, CA 95061.

Harbor Inn, 645 7th Ave. (479-9731), near the harbor and a few blocks north of Eaton St. A small and beautiful hotel well off the main drag. 1 queen bed per room (1 or 2 people). Check-out 11am. Rooms $30, with bath $45. Weekends $45, with bath $70. Reservations important on summer weekends.

Salt Air, 510 Leibrant (423-6020). 2 blocks from the beach, the boardwalk, and the wharf. Swimming pool. Singles and doubles $40-50. During promotions $28.

Santa Cruz Inn, 2950 Soquel Ave. (475-6322), located just off Rte. 1. 20 clean and comfortable rooms and amiable management. Coffee and pastries for guests. Check-out 11am. Singles $35-59. Doubles $45-69. Prices may vary, call for details.

Reservations for all state campgrounds can be made through MISTIX (800-283-2267). The **Manresa Uplands State Beach Park** (761-1795) is 12 mi. south of Santa Cruz. Take Rte. 1 and exit Larkin Valley. Veer right and follow San Andreas Rd. for 4 mi. then turn right on Sand Dollar. (64 sites, tents only. $16, winter $14.) The **New Brighton State Beach** (475-4850 or 444-7275) is 4 mi. south of Santa Cruz off Rte. 1. Take SCMDT bus #54 "Aptos". Fall asleep to the murmur of the breakers in one of 112 campsites on a bluff overlooking the beach. Tall pines and shrubs maintain privacy between sites. (Showers get crowded 7-9am. 1-week max. stay. No hookups. Check-out noon. Sites $16, winter $14. Reservations required.)

FOOD

Santa Cruz sports an astounding number of restaurants in budget range. There's the normal spread of chain burger joints, but better food (served just as fast) is available at the Pacific Mall's **Food Pavilion** at Lincoln and Cedar (open daily 8am-9pm).

Zachary's, 819 Pacific Ave. (427-0646). Bustling and happy, with hot coffee. In the morning locals crowd in for Mike's Mess: 3 scrambled eggs with bacon, mushrooms, and home fries topped with cheese, sour cream, tomatoes, and green onions served on toast ($5.50). Open Tues.-Sun. 7am-2:30pm. Come before 9am on weekends to avoid long waits.

Royal Taj, 270 Soquel Ave. (427-2400). Exquisite and exotic Northern Indian dishes in a comfortable, batik setting. Lunch buffet 11:30am-2:30pm for $6.50 offers all-you-can-eat from 25 items. Open daily 11:30am-2:30pm and 5:30-10pm.

Saturn Café, 1230 Mission St. (429-8505). A few blocks from downtown, but you're rewarded with vegetarian meals at their Santa Cruz best (generally under $4). Wheat germ is right-wing at this busy mixed hangout. Women's music Wed. 6:30-8:30pm. Open Mon.-Fri. 11:30am-midnight, Sat.-Sun. noon-midnight.

Zoccoli's Pasta House, 2017 N. Pacific Ave. (423-1717). Hearty and zesty helpings of pasta—you choose what sauce goes with which noodles. Most entrees $8-13, including baskets of fresh sourdough and soup or salad. You'll leave stuffed. Open Tues.-Sun. 11:30am-2pm, Tues.-Thurs. and Sun. 5-9pm, Fri.-Sat. 5-10pm.

SIGHTS AND ACTIVITIES

The **Boardwalk** (426-7433), a three-block arcade of caramel apples, ice-cream, and taco joints dominates the Santa Cruz beach area and provided the setting for teen vampire flick *The Lost Boys.* Video games, pinball, and shooting galleries complement miniature golf and amusement-park rides. The classiest rides are two veterans, both national historic landmarks: the **Looff Carousel** and the 1924 **Giant Dipper** roller coaster, one of the largest surviving wooden coasters in the country, which has miraculously weathered numerous quakes undamaged. A 3-min. ride is $3. (Tickets for unlimited rides $17. Discounts often available. Open Memorial Day-Labor Day daily; weekends and some holidays the rest of the year.)

The **Santa Cruz Beach** (officially named Cowell Beach) is broad and sandy, and generally packed with students. If you're seeking solitude, try the banks of the San Lorenzo River immediately east of the boardwalk. If you are craving nude sunbathing, head for the **Red White and Blue Beach.** Take Rte. 1 north to just south of Davenport and look for the cars to your right ($7 per car). Do not go here alone.

A pleasant 10-min. walk along the beach toward the southwest will take you to two unusual Santa Cruz museums, both worth short visits. The **Shroud of Turin Museum,** 1902 Ocean St. Extension (426-1601), at St. Joseph's shrine, is where science and faith clash over whether this famous piece of linen bearing the image of a man was used to bury Jesus. (Open Mon.-Sat. 1-4pm. Donation requested. Call ahead before visiting.) Just south of this museum lies Lighthouse Point, home to the **Santa Cruz Surfing Museum** (429-3429). Opened in 1986, the museum was the first of its kind. The main room of the lighthouse displays vintage wooden boards, early wetsuits, and surfing videos, while the tower contains the ashes of Mark Abbott, a local surfer who drowned in 1965 and to whom the museum is dedicated. (Open Wed.-Mon. noon-5pm; winter Thurs.-Mon. noon-4pm; $1.)

The 2000-acre **University of California at Santa Cruz (UCSC)** campus lies 5 mi. northwest of downtown. The campus is accessible by public bus, auto, and bicycle. (From the Metro Center, bus #1 leaves Mon.-Fri. 6:30am-12:45am, Sat.-Sun. 7:30am-12:45am every 15 to 30 min.). Then-governor Ronald Reagan's plan to make UCSC a "riot-proof campus," resulted instead in a stunning, sprawling campus. Guided tours start from the **visitors center** at the base of campus. On weekdays, make sure you have a parking permit. Trails behind the campus are perfect for day hikes, but it is not safe to go alone. (Get parking permits and maps at the police station, 429-2231.) The **UCSC arboretum** is one of the state's finest (open daily 9am-5pm; free).

ENTERTAINMENT AND NIGHTLIFE

Good Times and UCSC's *City on a Hill* are informative free weeklies. Pick up the free *Summer Activity Guide* (useful for long-range planning) at the **Parks and Recreation Department,** 307 Church St. (429-3663; open Mon.-Fri. 9am-6pm).

Kuumbwa Jazz Center, 320-2 Cedar St. (427-2227). Great jazz, renowned throughout the region. Under 21 welcome in this simple setting. The big names play here Mon. ($12-17); Fri. is the locals' turn (about $5). Most shows at 8pm.

The Catalyst, 1011 Pacific Ave. (423-1336). This 700-seat hall draws national acts, college favorites, and local bands. Big, boisterous, beachy bar and dance club. Cover $1 until 9pm, $2 after. Must be 21. Shows at 9:30pm. Open daily 9am-2am.

Front St. Pub, 516 Front St. (429-8838). Hip brewery. Three-glass beer sampler $2.50. Happy hour Mon.-Fri. 3-6pm offers $2 pints. Open daily 11:30am-midnight.

Blue Lagoon, 923 Pacific Ave. (423-7117). Relaxed gay bar. Sun.-Wed. dancing; no cover. Thurs.-Sat. DJ, $1 cover. Drinks about $1.50. Open daily 4pm-2am.

SAN FRANCISCO BAY AREA

■■■ SAN FRANCISCO

San Francisco — a city that evokes images of gold, cable cars, LSD, or gay liberation—began its life in 1776 as the Spanish mission of *San Francisco de Asis* (St. Francis of Assisi). The area remained sparsely populated until 1848, when gold was discovered in the Sierra Nevada's foothills. San Francisco's 800 or so residents realized that in addition to living a short river trip from the gold fields, they were also sitting on one of the greatest natural ports in the world. That year 10,000 people passed through San Francisco to get to the gold and a city was born.

The city's growth was neither smooth nor stable. Most famously, a massive 8.3 earthquake rocked the city on April 18, 1906, setting off three days of fire and looting. Unfazed, residents rebuilt their city within three years. The 1936 and '37 openings of the Golden Gate and Bay Bridges ended the city's isolation from the rest of the Bay Area. The city served as home to the Beat Generation in the 1950s; the 60s saw Haight-Ashbury become the hippie capital of the cosmos; and in the 70s, the gay population emerged as one of the city's most visible groups. To understand San Francisco one must get to know its neighborhoods, which pack an amazing level of diversity into a small area. Today, San Francisco continues to rest on mutual tolerance and appreciation of the different people who call this city home.

PRACTICAL INFORMATION

Visitor Information Center, Hallidie Plaza (391-2000), Market at Powell St., beneath street level in Benjamin Swig Pavillion. Open Mon.-Fri. 9am-5:30pm, Sat. 9am-3pm, Sun. 10am-2pm. Event recordings in English (391-2001), French (391-2003), German (391-2004) Spanish (391-2122).**Travelers' Aid Society,** at the airport (877-0118) and at 1049 Market St. between 6th and 7th (255-2252), can provide meals and limited funds for travelers who have been robbed.

Airport: San Francisco International (general information 761-0800) is located on a small peninsula in San Francisco Bay about 15 mi. south of the city center via U.S. 101. SFO has luggage lockers ($1 first day, $2 per additional day). **San Mateo County Transit** (800-660-4287), runs two buses from SFO to downtown. (#7F; 35 min.; runs 6-9am and 4-6pm every 30-60 min., 9am-4pm less frequently; $1.75, off-peak 85¢, under 18 85¢, over 64 60¢.) Taxi to downtown $25.

Train: Amtrak (800-872-7245) on 16th in Oakland. (Amtrak open daily 6:45am-10:45pm; to L.A. $75.) Amtrak also has a desk at Transbay Terminal, 425 Mission St., downtown. *See Mileage Chart.* **CalTrain** (800-660-4287 for voice or TDD) is a regional commuter train that runs south to Palo Alto, San Jose, and Santa Cruz. The depot at 4th and Townsend St. is served by **MUNI** buses #15, 30, 32, and 42.

Bus: Greyhound (800-231-2222) serves the **Transbay Terminal,** 425 Mission St. (495-1551), between Fremont and 1st St. downtown (open 5am-12:35am; to L.A. $39). The terminal is a transportation hub; buses from **Golden Gate Transit, AC Transit** (East Bay), and **samTrans** (San Mateo County) all stop here. *See Mileage Chart.*

Public Transportation: See Driving and Public Transportation below.

Taxi: Yellow Cab, 626-2345. **Luxor Cabs,** 282-4141. **DeSoto Cab,** 673-1414. For each, $1.70 plus $1.80 per additional mi. Open 24 hrs.

Car Rental: Budget (415-875-6850) has several conveniently located branches, including Pier 39 and 321 Mason St. in Union Sq. Compacts are about $25 per day, $150 per week. Unlimited mi. $15 per day surcharge for drivers under 25.

Ride Boards: Berkeley Ride Board (510-642-5259) has free, 24-hr. listings. **San Francisco International Hostel** (771-7277) at Fort Mason in the Marina and **San Francisco State University** (469-1842, in the student union; open Mon.-Fri. 7am-10pm, Sat. 10am-4pm). **KALX Radio** (642-5259) broadcasts a ride list (Mon.-Sat. 10am and 10pm). Call to put your name on the air for free.

Help Lines: Rape Crisis Center, 647-7273. **United Helpline,** 772-4357.

Post Office: 101 Hyde St., at Golden Gate Ave. Open Mon.-Fri. 7am-5:30pm, Sat. 7am-3pm. **ZIP Code:** 94142. General Delivery open Mon.-Sat. 10am-2pm.

Area Code: 415.

ORIENTATION

San Francisco is 403 mi. north of Los Angeles and 390 mi. south of the Oregon border. The city proper lies at the northern tip of a peninsula that sets off San Francisco Bay from the Pacific Ocean. From the south, the city can be reached by car via U.S. 101, via I-5 to I-580, or via Rte. 1. If approaching from the east on I-580 or I-80, go directly over the Bay Bridge into downtown. From the north, U.S. 101 leads directly into the city over the Golden Gate Bridge (toll $3).

San Francisco radiates outward from its docks, on the northeast edge of the peninsula. Many of San Francisco's shining attractions are found within a wedge formed by **Van Ness Avenue** running north-south, **Market Street** running northeast-southwest, and the **Embarcadero** (waterfront road) curving along the coast. Market Street takes a diagonal course and interrupts the regular grid of streets.

At the top of this wedge lies **Fisherman's Wharf** and slightly below, around **Columbus Avenue,** is **North Beach.** Across Columbus Ave. begin the **Nob Hill** and **Russian Hill** areas, home of the city's old money. Below Nob Hill and North Beach, and north of Market, **Chinatown** covers around 24 square blocks between Broadway in the north, Bush St. in the south, Powell St. in the west, and Kearny St. in the east. The heavily developed **Financial District** lies between Washington St. in the north and Market in the south, east of Chinatown and south of North Beach. Down Market from the Financial District, toward the bottom of the wedge, you pass through the core downtown area centered on **Union Square** and then, beyond Jones St., the **Civic Center.** Below Market St. lies the **South-of-Market-Area (SoMa),** largely deserted during the day but home to much of the city's nightlife.

On the north end of the peninsula, Van Ness Ave. leads to the commercially developed **Marina. Fisherman's Wharf** lies immediately to the east of the Marina and to the west lie the **Presidio** and **The Golden Gate Bridge.** Inland from the Marina rise the wealthy hills of **Pacific Heights.** Farther west is the rectangular **Golden Gate Park,** which extends to the Pacific and is bounded by Fulton Street to the north and Lincoln Street to the south. At its eastern end juts a skinny panhandle bordered by the **Haight-Ashbury** district.

DRIVING AND PUBLIC TRANSPORTATION

Unlike L.A., a **car** here is not a necessity. Parking in the city is *hell* and very expensive. On steep hills, make sure your car's wheels point towards the curb. *Always* set the emergency brake. Think twice about attempting to use a **bike** to climb up and down the hills of San Francisco. Golden Gate Park is a more sensible location for biking. Even **walking** in this city is an exciting exertion—some of the sidewalks are so

San Francisco

N

1 miles
1 kilometer

PACIFIC OCEAN

San Francisco Bay

TO ALCATRAZ
Fisherman's Wharf
Pier 39

Golden Gate Bridge

Lincoln Blvd.
Baker Beach
China Beach
Doyle Dr.

PRESIDIO

Crissy Field
Palace of Fine Arts/ Exploratorium
Richardson Ave.
West Pacific Ave.

Fort Mason
Marina Park
Marina Blvd.
MARINA
Chestnut St.
Lombard St.
Union St.

PACIFIC HEIGHTS
Alta Park
California St.
Pine St.
Bush St.
Pacific Ave.
Broadway
Divisadero St.
Steiner St.

RUSSIAN HILL
Bay St.
Beach St.
Columbus Ave.
Taylor St.
Powell St.
Van Ness Ave.
Franklin St.
Gough St.
Washington St.

NORTH BEACH
TELEGRAPH HILL
Coit Tower
Montgomery St.
Kearny St.
Transamerica Pyramid
Jackson Square
The Embarcadero

Ferry Building
S.F.-Oakland Bay Bridge
Main St.
1st St.
2nd St.
3rd St.
4th St.
5th St.
6th St.

China Basin
Central Basin
CHINA BASIN
3rd St.
Indiana St.
Mariposa St.
20th St.

CHINATOWN
NOB HILL
California St.
Hyde St.
Larkin
Union Square
Visitor's Information
Geary St.
Turk St.
Market St.
Mission St.
Howard St.
Folsom St.
Harrison St.
7th St.
8th St.
9th St.
10th St.
SOMA
Transbay Terminal
Townsend
King St.
Brannan St.

JAPAN-TOWN
Lafayette Park
Geary Expressway
Laguna St.

Central Freeway
Potrero St.
Harrison St.
S. Van Ness Ave.
Treat Ave.
16th St.
20th St.

Alamo Square
WESTERN ADDITION
Turk St.
Golden Gate Ave.
Oak St.
Duboce Ave.
Mission Dolores
Mission Dolores Park
MISSION
Market St.

Masonic Ave.
Presidio Ave.
Geary Blvd.
University of San Francisco
Stanyan St.
HAIGHT-ASHBURY
Fell St.
Frederick St.
Clayton St.
Panhandle
Buena Vista Park
Castro St.
CASTRO
Clarendon Ave.

Arguello Blvd.
Conservatory
Parnassus Ave.
UC Medical Center
7th Ave.

8th Ave.
10th Ave.
Balboa St.
Park Presidio Blvd.
Funston Ave.
10th Ave.

RICHMOND
Lake St.
California St.
Clement St.
25th St.
34th Ave.
19th St.
Geary Blvd.

SEA CLIFF
Palace of the Legion of Honor
Lincoln Park

GOLDEN GATE PARK
Museums
Stow Lake
Fulton St.
Lincoln Way
Kennedy Dr.
Middle Dr.
19th Ave.
25th Ave.
28th Ave.
Judah St.
Sunset Blvd.
SUNSET

80
280
101
1

CALIFORNIA

steep they have steps cut into them. There are many **walking tours** of the city. Some even promise "no steep hills." **City Guides** (332-9601) has free summer tours. The *San Francisco Street and Transit Map* is a valuable purchase ($2).

San Francisco Municipal Railway (MUNI) (673-6864) operates buses, cable cars, and a combined subway/trolley system. Fares for buses and trolleys $1, seniors and ages 5-17 35¢. Ask for a free transfer. (MUNI PASSPORTS valid on all MUNI vehicles: 1 day, $6; 3 days, $10; 7 days, $15; 1 month, $35. **MUNI Metro** runs **streetcars** along five lines serving points south and west of downtown.

Cable cars, national historic landmark in 1964, have been transporting San Franciscans since 1873. The cars are noisy, slow, and crowded with tourists. Use them to sight-see, not to get from point A to point B. Ride them early. Of the three lines, the California (C) line is by far the least crowded; it runs from the Financial District up Nob Hill. The Powell-Hyde (PH) line, however, might be the most fun, for it has the steepest hills and the sharpest turns. (Runs daily 7am-1am. $2, seniors $1 9pm-7am. 3-hr. unlimited transfers.)

Bay Area Rapid Transit (BART) (778-2278) does not (alas) serve the entire Bay Area, but it does operate modern and carpeted trains along four lines connecting San Francisco with the East Bay, including Oakland, Berkeley, Concord, and Fremont. BART is not a local transportation system within the city of San Francisco; use the MUNI system for that. (BART trains run Mon.-Sat. 6am-1:30am, Sun. 8am-1:30am. One way 80¢ to $3.) Maps and schedules are available at all stations. All stations and trains are wheelchair accessible.

ACCOMMODATIONS

There are a tremendous number of reasonable and convenient places to stay in San Francisco. The Tenderloin and the Mission District can be particularly unsafe.

Hostels

Pacific Tradewinds Guest House, 680 Sacramento St. (433-7970), in the Financial District between Montgomery and Kearny. This is one of the best hostels around. Laundry ($4, they do it), kitchen, free tea and coffee. No smoking. Check-in 8am-midnight. Check-out 10:30am. No curfew. 14-day max. stay. $14.

San Francisco International Hostel (HI-AYH), Bldg. 240, Fort Mason (771-7277), in the Marina west of Fisherman's Wharf. Entrance at Bay and Franklin St., 1 block west of Van Ness Ave. Beautiful location. Free movies, walking tours, kitchens, dining room, laundry. Registration 7am-2pm and 3pm-midnight daily. *Lines start at 6am.* $13. IBN reservations available.

Green Tortoise Guest House, 1116 Kearny St. at Broadway (834-9060) in the colorful place where North Beach and Chinatown meet. Clean, nicely finished rooms in an old Victorian building. Friendly atmosphere. Lockers under each bed, bring your own lock. Sauna, laundry room ($1.25 wash, 75¢ dry), kitchen. 25-day max. stay. $12 per bed in shared room. Singles $19.50. Doubles $30-35. $20 key deposit. Reserve and pay for rooms in advance.

Hostel at Union Square (HI-AYH), 312 Mason St. (788-5604), 1 block from **Union Square**. 3rd largest hostel in the country. Acceptable neighborhood. Big, common areas, TV. Key deposit $5. Some rooms reserved by phone with credit card or show up at noon. IBN reservations available. $14, nonmembers $17.

Globetrotter's Inn, 225 Ellis St. (346-5786), Downtown at Mason St. On the border of a dangerous neighborhood; caution is advised. Small and intimate. Large kitchen adjoins common room with piano and TV. Check-in summer 8am-11pm; winter 8am-1pm and 5-11pm. Check-out 11am. No curfew. $12 per night; $75 per week. Call to reserve a bed and confirm 2 days ahead.

San Francisco International Student Center, 1188 Folsom St. (255-8800), in SoMa. Bay windows, brick walls, and a big comfy couch. Only 17 rooms. Free coffee and tea. 2 week max. stay in summer. Registration 9am-11pm. No curfew. $12.Key deposit $10. Pre-paid reservations required.

San Francisco International Guest House, 2976 23rd St. (641-1411), at Harrison in the Mission District. **International passport required.** Warm atmosphere in a beautiful Victorian house. Hardwood floors, wall tapestries, and houseplants. Two large kitchens. 5-day min. stay. All beds $13; after 10 days $11.

Interclub Globe Hostel, 10 Hallam Place (431-0540), in SoMa off Folsom St. between 7th and 8th. **International passport required.** Catering to an "adventurous crowd." The common room is home to a pool table, some pretty wild parties, and the Globe Cafe, which serves breakfast and dinner. Free sheets, blankets and pillows. $15. A $10 deposit is required for a reservation.

Hotels

Accommodations costing more than $20 must charge a 12% bed tax which is not included in the prices listed below. Hotels are busy during the summer—call ahead.

Downtown

Adelaide Inn, #5 Isadora Duncan (441-2261; fax 441-0161), at the end of a little alley off Taylor near Post St., 2 blocks west of Union Square. Perhaps the most charming of San Francisco's many "European-style" hotels. Kitchenette with microwave and fridge. Continental breakfast included. Doors close at 11pm. Office hours Tues.-Fri. 9am-1pm, 4-9pm, Sat.-Mon. flexible. 18 rooms. Hall baths. Singles $38. Twin beds or doubles $48. Reservations encouraged.

Sheehan Hotel, 620 Sutter St. (775-6500 or 800-848-1529), at Mason St. near Union Sq. Excellent location. International students galore. 68 rooms, cable TV, phone. Indoor swimming pool. Exercise room. Continental breakfast included. Singles $45, with bath $60. Doubles $55, with bath $75. $10 per additional.

The Amsterdam, 749 Taylor St. (673-3277 or 800-637-3444; fax 673-0453), between Bush and Sutter St., 2 blocks from Nob Hill, 3½ blocks from Union Sq. Beautiful rooms in a very central location. Check-out 11am. Continental breakfast included. Singles $45, with bath $60. Doubles $50, with bath $69.

Golden Gate Hotel, 775 Bush St. (392-3702), between Powell and Mason St., 2 blocks north (uphill) of Union Square. Comfy, beautiful rooms. Spotless hall toilets and bath. Check-out noon. Rooms $59, with bath $89. Continental breakfast included. Garage parking $14 per 24 hrs. 2-week advance reservations advisable.

Allison Hotel, 417 Stockton St. (986-8737, outside CA 800-628-6456, within CA 800-344-6030), just south of the Stockton St. tunnel, 2 blocks north of Union Sq.—a prime location. Recently renovated. Pleasant rooms with cable TV, phones. Check-out 11am. Singles and doubles $50, with bath $59. Triples $65. Quads $75. Reserve ahead in summer.

Chinatown

Gum Moon Women's Residence, 940 Washington (421-8827), at Stockton in Chinatown's center. *Women only.* Bright, spacious rooms with shared bath. Kitchen and laundry facilities. Call ahead to make sure there are rooms available. Registration 9am-6pm. Check-out noon. Singles $24. Doubles $20 per bed.

YMCA Chinatown, 855 Sacramento St. (982-4412), between Stockton St. and Grant Ave. Convenient location. *Men over 18 only.* Pool, and gym. Registration Mon.-Fri. 6:30am-10pm, Sat. 9am-5pm, Sun. 9am-1pm. Check-out 1pm. No curfew. Singles $28, with bath $38. Doubles $36. 7th day free. No reservations.

Grant Plaza, 465 Grant Ave. (434-3883 or 800-472-6899), at Pine St. 1 block from the Chinatown gate. Excellent location. Clean, bright rooms with bath, phones, and TV. Parking $8.50 per day. Check-in after 2:30pm. Check-out noon. Singles $42. Doubles $52. Make reservations 3 weeks in advance.

Haight-Ashbury

The Red Victorian Bed and Breakfast Inn, 1665 Haight St. (864-1978), 3 blocks west of Masonic Ave., 2 blocks east of Golden Gate Park. 18 lovely rooms. Downstairs, a café and market will be open soon. Check-in 3-6pm. Check-out 11am. Fresh breakfast included. Complimentary tea, coffee, popcorn, and cheese in the afternoons. 2-night stay usually required on weekends. Discounts on stays longer than 3 days. Doubles $76-200, with discount $64-134. Reserve well in advance.

Near the Civic Center

Harcourt Residence Club, 1105 Larkin (673-7720). Rooms by the week or by the month. Maid service, TV room, 2 meals a day, and Sunday brunch. Traveling students and local residents. Occasional barbecues. Office hours 9am-5pm. Weekly rates $130-200 per person, depending on size of room and private or hall bath.

YMCA Hotel, 220 Golden Gate Ave. (885-0460), at Leavenworth St., 2 blocks north of Market St. on the edge of the infamous Tenderloin. Men and women allowed. Double locks on all doors and policy requiring visitors to stay in the lobby enhance security. Pool, gym, and racquetball court. Breakfast included. Laundry. No curfew. Singles $28, with bath $37.50. Doubles $38. Triples $60. Hostel beds for HI-AYH members only are $15. $5 key deposit. No reservations for hostel beds. For room reservations, send money order for first night.

Hotel Essex, 684 Ellis St. (474-4664; within CA 800-44-ESSEX, -37739; outside CA 800-45-ESSEX), at Larkin, north of Civic Center. Just renovated. Free coffee and tea. Clean and charming rooms with TVs and phones. Surprisingly elegant lobby. Person at front desk 24 hrs. Check-out noon. Singles $39, with bath $49. Doubles $44, with bath $59. Weekly rates $175-250.

FOOD

San Francisco is home to almost 4000 restaurants, but don't be daunted. The neighborhoods are listed in an order which reflects their potential for those seeking an inexpensive, satisfying meal. Your odds are best in the Mission District.

Mission District

The Mission is the one of the best places in the city to find good, cheap food, and the city's best and cheapest produce. Great Mexican, Salvadoran, and other Latin American restaurants are found on 24th St. (east of Mission St.). After a meal, nearby Castro Street is a great place for an evening coffee or drink.

La Cumbre, 515 Valencia St. (863-8205) between 16th and 17th St. As you stand in line, your mouth-watering, steak is brought in from the kitchen, dripping in marinade, ready to be made into a superlative burrito. ($2.50 for a regular; $4 for a "super"). Open Mon.-Sat. 11am-midnight, Sun. noon-midnight.

New Dawn Café, 3174 16th St. (553-8888), at Guerrero. Hip restaurant with a menu consisting mainly of breakfast food and burgers. Enormous servings. Vegetarian chili $3.50. Open Wed.-Thurs., Sun. 8:30am-8:30pm, Fri.-Sat. 8:30am-9pm.

Café Macondo, 3159 16th St. (863-6517), between Guerrero and Valencia. Appetizing Central American food and coffee in an eccentrically decorated café. Chicken tamale $3.50. Open Mon.-Thurs. 11am-10pm, Fri.-Sun. 11am-11pm.

Manora, 3226 Mission (550-0856). This attractive Thai restaurant serves delicious cuisine at reasonable prices. The red beef curry garners high praise from locals ($5.75). Most dishes under $10. Open Tues.-Sun. 5-10pm.

Chinatown

Chinatown abounds with downright cheap restaurants; in fact, their multitude and incredible similarity can make a choice nearly impossible.

House of Nanking, 919 Kearny St. between Columbus and Jackson (421-1429). Outstanding Chinese food in a crowded, but pleasant atmosphere. Long lines, particularly at lunch. *Moo-shu* vegetables $5, onion cakes $1.75. Tsing Tao beer sauce is essential. Open Mon.-Sat. 11am-10pm, Sun. 4-10pm.

Sam Wo, 813 Washington at Grant (982-0596). The late hours and BYOB policy, not to mention the exceptionally cheap prices, make this restaurant a favorite among students from all over the Bay Area. If you want to hang with the really rowdy crowd, ask to be seated on the 3rd floor. Most dishes $2-5. Open Mon.-Sat. 11am-3am; summer Mon.-Sat. 11am-3am, Sun. 12:30-9:30pm.

Brandy Ho's, 217 Columbus Ave. (788-7527). The food is SPICY! Order everything mild or extra mild if you're feeling timid. Large interior. Very service-oriented. Entrees a la carte $6-10. *Gon pou* shrimp $9. Open daily 11:30am-midnight.

North Beach

North Beach is home to oodles of noodles served in a wide variety of ways in traditional (and not so traditional) pasta restaurants. Save room for homemade *cannoli* and cappuccino. North Beach restaurants can be pricey; choose wisely.

U.S. Restaurant, 431 Columbus Ave. (362-6251), at Stockton St. Once a hangout for Kerouac and buddies, now popular with young San Franciscans. Long wait at dinner. Titanic, tasty portions. Most dishes under $10. Open Tues.-Sat. 6:30am-9:30pm. Closed for 2-3 weeks in June or July (vacation time).

The Stinking Rose, 325 Columbus Ave. (781-ROSE, -7673). "We season our garlic with food" is their motto. Excellent, *very* aromatic garlic chowder, salads, pastas, and pizettes. Try the delicious, no garlic "vampire fare" lasagna. Open Sun.-Thurs. 11am-11pm, Fri.-Sat. 11am-midnight. Reservations recommended.

Richmond District

Some locals claim that the Chinese restaurants in Richmond are better than the ones in Chinatown. In addition, the area contains fine Thai, Burmese, Cambodian, Japanese, Italian, Russian, Korean, and Vietnamese restaurants.

The Red Crane, 1115 Clement St. (751-7226), between Park Presidio Blvd. and 12th Ave., is an award-winning Chinese vegetarian and seafood restaurant. Lunch special Mon.-Fri. 11:30am-2:30pm includes entree with soup and rice for just $3.50. Open daily 11:30am-10pm.

Ernesto's, 2311 Clement St. (386-1446), at 24th Ave. A well-kept San Francisco culinary secret. Dinners at this family-run Italian restaurant are awesome (entrees $8-11.25). Open Tues.-Sun. 4-10pm.

Civic Center

Hayes Street offers an extensive selection of cafés. In the summer, load up on produce at the **Farmers Market** in the U.N. Plaza (every Wed. and Sun.).

Pendragon Bakery, 450 Hayes St. (552-7017), at Gough St. Natural ingredients go into the excellent, handmade pastries, soups, and vegetarian dishes. Open Mon. and Thurs. 6:30am-5pm, Tues.-Wed., Fri. 7am-4pm, Sat. 8am-4pm, Sun. 8am-3pm.

Nyala Ethiopian Restaurant, 39A Grove St. (861-0788), east of Larkin St.Combination of Ethiopian and Italian cuisine. Vegetarian all-you-can-eat buffet. Buffet Mon.-Sat. 11am-3pm ($5) and 4pm-closing ($7). Open Mon.-Sat. 11am-10pm.

Tommy's Joynt, 1101 Geary Blvd. (775-4216), at Van Ness Ave. Outrageously painted San Francisco landmark with a stunning selection of beers. A carnivore's delight. Thick pastrami sandwich $4. Open daily 10am-1:50am.

Haight-Ashbury

The Haight boasts a terrific selection of bakeries. There are also some great ethnic restaurants with reasonable prices, but quality varies between establishments.

Cha Cha Cha, 1801 Haight St. (386-5758). Love-children line up with upwardly mobile professionals for a chance to eat at this trendy Latin restaurant, thought to be the best in the Haight. Entrees $6.50-13. Open Mon.-Thurs. 11:30am-3pm and 5-11:30pm, Fri. 11:30am-3pm and 5:30-11:30pm, Sat. 9am-3pm and 5:30-11:30pm, Sun. 9am-3pm and 5-11pm. The wait is up to 2 hrs., no reservations.

Ganges, 775 Frederick St. (661-7290), not exactly in the Haight, but close. Traditional, low Indian seating in back. Try the mashed banana *pakoda*, and don't miss the delicious raisin-tamarind chutney. Dinners $8.50-12.50. Live music Fri.-Sat. starting at 7:15pm. Open Tues.-Sat. 5-10pm. Reservations a good idea.

Tassajara Bread Bakery, 1000 Cole St. (664-8947), at Parnassus, a bit of a trek from Haight but well worth it. Tassajara is one of the city's best bakeries. Day-old pastries 30-50% off. Open Mon.-Sat. 7am-11pm, Sun. 8am-11pm.

Marina and Pacific Heights

Pacific Heights and the Marina abound in high-quality restaurants serving good, fresh food. Some are expensive, but it is fairly easy to find a great meal for under $10. Most of the restaurants in this area lie on the main commercial streets.

Leon's Bar*B*Q, 1911 Fillmore St. (922-2436), between Pine and Bush. At the southern end of yuppified Fillmore, Leon's has been serving up Cajun jambalaya ($5) and the like since 1963. Dinner plates with ribs or seafood and fixin's for $8-15.25. Open daily 11am-9:30pm for table service, until 10pm for take out.

Sweet Heat, 3324 Steiner St. (474-9191), between Chestnut and Lombard. A spunky little place serving Mexican food to a health-conscious Marina crowd. Veggie burrito ($4). Open Sun.-Thurs. 11am-midnight, Fri.-Sat. 11am-2am.

Jackson Fillmore Trattoria, 2506 Fillmore St. (346-5288). Count on great southern Italian cuisine and a lively atmosphere at this hip *trattoria*. Large portions. Eat bread sticks to fill up. Reservations recommended. Open Mon. 5:30-10pm, Tues.-Thurs. 5:30-10:30pm, Fri.-Sat. 5:30-11pm, Sun. 5-10pm.

SIGHTS

Any resident will tell you that this city is not made of landmarks or "sights," but of neighborhoods. If you blindly rush from the Golden Gate Bridge to Coit Tower to Mission Dolores, you'll be missing the point—the city itself. Whether defined by ethnicity, tax brackets, topography, or a shared spirit, these neighborhoods present off-beat bookstores, Chinatown's *dim sum,* Pacific Heights' architecture, SoMa's nightlife, Japantown's folk festivals, Golden Gate Park's Strawberry Hill, North Beach's Club Fugazi, and Haight-Ashbury simply for being itself.

Museums

San Francisco Museum of Modern Art, 151 3rd St. between Mission and Howard, in SoMa. The museum's new site in the Yerba Buena Gardens was one of the largest building projects ever undertaken by an American museum. Open Tues.-Wed. and Fri.-Sun. 11am-6pm, Thurs. 11am-9pm. $7, over 61 and students $3.50, under 13 free. Thurs. 5-9pm half price. 1st Tues. of month free.

California Academy of Sciences, (221-5100; 750-7145 for a recording) in Golden Gate Park. One of the nation's largest institutions of its kind—houses several smaller museums that specialize in different bodies of science. The **Steinhart Aquarium** (home to members of over 14,000 aquatic species) is more lively than the natural history exhibits. The Academy's **Morrison Planetarium** (750-7141) re-creates the heavens above with an impressive show ($2.50, seniors and students $1.25). The **Laserium** (750-7138) orients its argon laser show to such rocking themes as Pink Floyd's "The Wall" and several U2 albums. $6, over 65 and 6-12 $4, 5pm matinee $5; call for schedule. Academy open daily 10am-5pm; Sept. 2-July 3 10am-5pm. $7, $5 with MUNI Fast Pass or transfer, seniors and ages 12-17 $3, 6-11 $1.50. Free 1st Wed. of month until 8:45pm.

Ansel Adams Center, 250 4th St. (495-7000), at Howard and Folsom, in the Civic Center area. Houses a permanent collection of the master's photographs, as well as temporary shows by other photographers. $4, students $3, over 64 and ages 13-17 $2, under 13 free. Open Tues.-Sun. 11am-6pm.

Wells Fargo History Museum, 420 Montgomery St. (396-2619), between California St. and Sacramento St. in the financial district. An impressive display of Gold Rush exhibits. Open Mon.-Fri. 9am-5pm.

San Francisco Women Artists Gallery, 370 Hayes St. (552-7392), between Franklin and Gough, near Civic Centera. Exhibits women's photographs, paintings, prints, and crafts. Open Tues.-Wed. and Fri.-Sat. 11am-6pm, Thurs. 11am-8pm.

M. H. de Young Memorial Museum (750-3600), in Golden Gate Park. Takes visitors through a 21-room survey of American painting, from the colonial period to the early 20th century. Also noteworthy is the museum's glass collection, which features ancient, European, Tiffany, and Steuben pieces. The **Asian Art Museum** (668-7855) in the west wing of the building is the largest museum outside Asia dedicated entirely to Asian artwork. Both museums open Wed.-Sun. 10am-5pm.

Admission to both $5; $3 with MUNI Fast Pass or transfer; seniors and ages 12-17 $2; under 12, 1st Wed. of month, and Sat. 11am-noon free.

Presidio Army Museum (556-0856), Lincoln Blvd. at Funston Ave. Heavy on guns, uniforms, and sepia-toned photographs. Open Wed.-Sun. 10am-4pm; free.

Tattoo Art Museum, 841 Columbus (775-4991; open Mon.-Sat. noon-1pm, Sun. noon-8pm), displays a fantastic collection of tattoo memorabilia, including hundreds of designs and exhibits on different tattoo techniques. $50 will buy a quick, glowing rose on the hip; larger tattoos are $100 an hour.

Cable Car Powerhouse and Museum, 1201 Mason St. (474-1887), at Washington in Russian Hill. The building is the working center of the cable-car system. You can look down on the operation from a gallery or view displays to learn more about the picturesque cars, some of which date back to 1873. Open daily 10am-6pm; Nov.-March 10am-5pm; free.

Downtown and Union Square

Union Square is the center of San Francisco. Now an established shopping area, the square has a rich and somewhat checkered history. During the Civil War, a large public meeting was held here to decide whether San Francisco should secede. The square became the rallying ground of the Unionists, who bore placards reading "The Union, the whole Union, and nothing but the Union"—hence its name.

The sounds of Union Square today are far removed from politics. The clanging of the cable cars mixes with the contented cooing of overfed pigeons. At the turn of the century, murders in Union Square averaged one per week, and prostitutes waved to their favorite customers from second-story windows. After the 1906 earthquake and fire destroyed most of the flophouses, a group of merchants moved in and renamed the area **Maiden Lane** in hopes of changing the street's image. Surprisingly enough, the switch worked. Today Maiden Lane—extending 2 blocks from Union Square's eastern side—is home to smart shops and ritzy boutiques.

One of the Maiden Lane's main attractions is the **Circle Gallery,** 140 Maiden Lane. The only Frank Lloyd Wright building in San Francisco, the gallery sells some of the city's most expensive art (open Mon.-Sat. 10am-6pm, Sun. noon-5pm; free). The best free ride in town is on the outside elevators of the **Westin St. Francis Hotel** on Powell at Geary. As you glide up the building, the entire Bay Area stretches out before you. For another ride with an excellent view, take the Powell St. cable cars. To relax and enjoy a potable, go to the 30th floor of the **Holiday Inn,** 480 Sutter St. (398-8900; take MUNI bus #2, 3, or 4), where the **Sherlock Holmes Esquire Public House** has been meticulously decorated to the specifications of 221B Baker St.

Financial District

North of Market and east of Kearny, snug against the Bay, beats the West's financial heart, or at least one of its ventricles. **Montgomery Street,** the Wall Street of the West, is of only passing interest to the visitor and is best seen before the workday ends. After 7:30pm, the heart stops, only to be resuscitated the next morning. During the day parking is next to impossible. If you must drive, park your car South-of-Market (SoMa) and walk from there. It's better to take any MUNI Metro line, BART to the Montgomery or Embarcadero station, or hop on the California St. cable car.

In the east end of the district, at the foot of Sacramento St., stands **Embarcadero Center** (772-0500), a three-level complex housing over a hundred expensive and mostly trivial shops. At the foot of Market St. is **Justin Herman Plaza** and its famous geodesic **Vallaincourt Fountain.** You can walk through the fountain and remain dry while the water flows overtop. The area is often rented out by bands or for rallies during lunch from noon to 1:30pm. One such free lunchtime concert, performed by U2 in the fall of 1987, resulted in lead singer Bono's arrest for spray painting "Stop the Traffic—Rock and Roll" on the fountain. Connected to the $300-million complex is the **Hyatt Regency** hotel (788-1234), whose glass elevator up leads to the 20th floor and the **Equinox Revolving Rooftop Restaurant and Lounge.** There is a lovely view of the bay from this fabulous revolving cocktail lounge every 45 min. Buy a drink and ample dawdling time for $3. (Open Mon.-Thurs. 4pm-midnight, Fri. 4pm-1:15am, Sat. noon-1:15am, Sun. noon-midnight.)

San Francisco's tallest and most distinctive structure, the defining element of the city's skyline, is the **Transamerica Pyramid** at Montgomery St. between Clay and Washington St. (take MUNI bus #15). The building's pyramidal shape and subterranean concrete "anchor" base make it one of the city's most stable, earthquake-resistant buildings. The Pyramid was once the site of the Montgomery Block, a bar lured the likes of Mark Twain, Robert Louis Stevenson, Bret Harte, and Jack London.

The **Golden Gate Ferries** (332-6600) sends boats from the Ferry Building at Market St. on the Embarcadero across the street from Justin Herman Plaza. Although primarily for commuters, the ferries offer a pleasing view of San Francisco's skyline and bay. (Fare to Sausalito $4, ages 6-12 $3; to Larkspur $2.50, ages 6-12 $1.90. Seniors and people with disabilities ½-price. Family rates available.)

South-of-Market (SoMa)

The area south of Market St. to about 10th St. is now home to the city's hottest nightlife: yesterday's leather bars are today's stylish nightclubs. During the day the area fills with workers from the encroaching Financial District. At night, SoMa is the place for hip young professionals to dine at chic restaurants before hitting the club scene. SoMa is one of the easiest areas of the city in which to park your car, but lock it securely, and don't leave valuables inside. On public transportation take samTrans bus #1A or 1L (weekends and holidays) or #1C, 22D, 10L, or 10T (8-10am and 4-6pm only), or MUNI bus #9x, 12, 14, 15, 26, 27, 30, 45, or 71.

The **Old Mint** (744-6830), on 5th St. at Mission St., is worth a look. In one room, a lone, placid guard watches over a stack of gold bullion, coins, and raw gold worth more than $150,000. The other rooms house assorted historical artifacts. (Tours on the hr., 10am-3pm. Mint open Mon.-Fri. 10am-4pm. Free.)

The **San Francisco Chronicle building** is at 901 Mission St. The *Chronicle*, the newspaper with the largest paid circulation west of the Mississippi, has been printed here since construction on the building finished in 1924.

Civic Center

The vast Civic Center is a collection of massive buildings arranged around two expansive plazas. Street people and itinerant travelers used to camp out on the lawns surrounding the plazas, but the city has worked to move them out of the area. By public transportation, take MUNI Metro to the Civic Center/City Hall stop or MUNI bus #5, 16X, 19, 21, 26, 42, 47, or 49. You can also take the J, K, L, M, or N lines to Van Ness station or Golden Gate Transit bus #10, 20, 50, or 70.

The largest gathering of *Beaux Arts* architecture in the U.S. is centered on the palatial **San Francisco City Hall,** which was modeled after St. Peter's Cathedral. The city hall was the site of the tragic 1978 double murder of Mayor George Moscone and City Supervisor Harvey Milk, the first openly gay politician to be elected to public office in the U.S. At the eastern end is the United Nations Plaza and public library, at the western end the Opera House and Museum of Modern Art.

In the evenings, the **Louise M. Davies Symphony Hall,** 201 Van Ness Ave. (431-5400), at Grove St., rings with the sounds of the San Francisco Symphony. Next door, the **War Memorial Opera House,** 301 Van Ness Ave. (864-3330), between Grove and McAllister, hosts the well-regarded **San Francisco Opera Company** (864-3330) and the **San Francisco Ballet** (621-3838 for info). Also in the block of Van Ness between Grove and McAllister is the **Veterans Building** (252-4000). Within you'll find the **Herbst Theatre** (392-4400), which hosts concerts and lectures. Between the Opera House and the Veterans Building lies **Opera Plaza,** a beautifully maintained grassy lawn planted with rows of trees and encased by gilded gates with hanging lamps. (Tours of the Davies Symphony Hall, the War Memorial Opera House, and Herbst Auditorium leave every ½ hr. from the Grove St. entrance to Davies Hall Mon. 10am-2pm. Tours of Davies Hall are offered Wed. 1:30-2:30pm, Sat. 12:30-1:30pm. $3, seniors and students $2. Call 552-8338.)

Mission District

The Mission, which lies south of the Civic Center area, is roughly bordered by 16th St. to the north, Noe St. to the west, Army St. to the south, and U.S. 101 to the east. The area is laced with MUNI bus routes, including #9, 12, 22, 26, 27, 33, and 53. Take BART to the 16th or 24th St. stops and walk south down Mission St. The Germans and Scandinavians who inhabited the Mission District in the 1800s have been replaced by Latinos, Filipinos, and Southeast Asians. The colorful **murals** along 24th St. in the Mission District reflect the rich cultural influence of Latin America.

Celebrating its 202nd birthday this year, **Mission Dolores,** at 16th and Dolores St. in the old heart of San Francisco, is considered the oldest building in the city. Exotic poppies and birds-of-paradise bloom in the cemetery, which was featured in Hitchcock's *Vertigo* (open daily 9am-4:30pm, Nov.-April 9am-4pm; $1).

The Mission is best seen by strolling during the day. The **Mission Cultural Center,** 2868 Mission St. (821-1155), between 24th and 25th St., includes a graphics workshop, a theater, and often-stunning art exhibitions. (Open Tues.-Fri. noon-6pm, Sat. 10am-4pm. Free. Box office 695-6970.)

For spiritual and physical rejuvenation, women might enjoy a plunge into the waters at **Osento,** 955 Valencia St. (282-6333), between 20th and 21st St. Osento is a women's bathhouse in the Mission with wet and dry sauna, jacuzzi, and pool. (Sliding entrance fee $7-11, unlimited time. $1 towel rental. $1 refundable locker deposit. Open daily 1pm-1am.)

A few blocks' walk east down 24th Street will give you the best sights, sounds, and tastes of the Mission district. **La Galeria de la Raza,** 2857 24th St. (826-8009) at Bryant, is small but shows excellent exhibitions of Chicano and Latino art by local and international artists. The gift shop next door sells impressive pieces of folk art from Mexico and Latin America. (Gallery free. Open Tues.-Sat. noon-6pm.)

Castro

Castro and the Mission District enjoy the city's best weather, often while fog blankets nearby Twin Peaks. Much of San Francisco's gay community calls the area home. As AIDS has taken its toll, the scene has mellowed considerably from the wild days of the '70s, but **Castro Street** remains a proud and assertive emblem of gay liberation. Most of the action takes place along Castro St. to the south of Market Street, although the neighborhood itself extends south from Market to Noe Valley and west from the Mission to Portola Drive and Twin Peaks.

The best way to see Castro is through the district's shops and bars. Two popular hangouts are **Café Flore,** 2298 Market St. (621-8579), and **The Café,** 2367 Market St. (861-3846). Down the street, **The Names Project,** 2362 Market St. (863-1966), sounds a more somber note. This is the headquarters of an organization that has accumulated over 12,000 3 ft. x 6 ft. panels for the **AIDS Memorial Quilt,** including ones from 30 other countries. (Open Mon. noon-6:30pm, Tues.-Wed. and Fri. noon-7pm, Sat.-Sun. noon-5pm.)

Cruisin' Castro gives **walking tours** of Castro St. (Daily at 10am. Tours are $30, including brunch at the famed Elephant Walk Restaurant. Call Trevor at 550-8110 for reservations.) MUNI bus #24 runs along Castro St. from 14th to 26th.

West of Castro, the peninsula swells with several large hills. On rare fogless nights, you can get a breathtaking view of the city from **Twin Peaks,** between Portola Dr., Market St., and Clarendon Ave. West of the Mt. Davidson is the **San Francisco Zoo** (753-7061), on Sloat Blvd. The zoo is distant and unremarkable. (Open daily 10am-5pm. $6.50, seniors and ages 12-16 $3, under 12 free.)

Haight-Ashbury

Long live the 60s in Haight-Ashbury. The Haight, located at the eastern edge of Golden Gate Park and surrounding its panhandle, willfully preserves an era that many seek to experience, others desire to forget, and some can't quite remember. Originally a quiet lower-middle-class neighborhood, the Haight's large Victorian houses—perfect for communal living—and the district's proximity to the University of California in San Francisco (UCSF) drew a massive hippie population in the mid and late 1960s. LSD—possession of which was not yet a felony—pervaded the neighborhood. The hippie voyage reached its apogee in 1966-67 when Janis Joplin, the Grateful Dead, and the Jefferson Airplane all lived and made music in the neighborhood. During 1967's "Summer of Love," young people from across the country converged on the grassy panhandle for the celebrated "be-ins." Despite recent gentrification, the past lives on in Haight-Ashbury. Many of the bars and restaurants are remnants of yesteryear. The Haight is great for browsing; bookstores are everywhere, as are vintage clothing stores and inexpensive cafés. Take MUNI bus #6, 7, 16x, 43, 66, 71, and 73; Metro line N runs along Carl St., four blocks south.

The **Love 'n' Haight Tour** takes visitors past the **Psychedelic Shop** and the one-time residence of the Grateful Dead (2½ hr.; $20; call for reservations). Northeast of the Haight, at Hayes and Steiner St., lies **Alamo Square,** the vantage point of a thousand postcards. Climb the gentle, grassy slope and you'll understand why it's a favorite with photographers. The view seems to capture the essence of the entire city.

The **Red Victorian Movie House,** 1727 Haight St. (668-3994), between Cole and Shrader, shows foreign, student, and Hollywood films. **Wasteland,** 1660 Haight St. (863-3150), is an immense used clothing store, deserving of notice, if only for its wonderful facade and window displays. (Open Mon.-Fri. 11am-6pm, Sat. 11am-7pm, Sun. noon-6pm.) Vintage meets rummage sale at **Buffalo Exchange,** 1555 Haight St. (431-7733; open Mon.-Sat. 11am-7pm, Sun. noon-6pm). Resembling a dense green mountain in the middle of the Haight, **Buena Vista Park** predictably, has a reputation for free-wheeling lawlessness. (Of course it may all be hype.) Enter at your own risk, and once inside, be prepared for those doing their own thing.

Golden Gate Park

No visit to San Francisco is complete without a visit to Golden Gate Park. Frederick Law Olmsted—designer of New York's Central Park—said it couldn't be done. Engineer William Hammond Hall and Scottish gardener John McLaren proved him wrong. Hall designed the 1000-acre park—gardens and all—when the land was still just shifting sand dunes, and then constructed a mammoth breakwater along the oceanfront to protect the seedling trees and bushes from the sea's burning spray.

To get to the park from downtown, hop on bus #5 or 21. Bus #44 passes right by the major attractions and serves 6th Ave. to California Ave. to the north and the MUNI Metro to the south. Most of the park is bounded by Fulton St. to the north, Stanyan St. to the east, Lincoln Way to the south, and the Pacific Ocean to the west. The **Panhandle,** a thin strip of land bordered by Fell and Oak St. on the north and south respectively, is the oldest part of the park and extends into Haight-Ashbury.

Park Headquarters (666-7200), offers info and maps in McLaren Lodge at Fell and Stanyan St., on the eastern edge of the park (open Mon.-Fri. 8am-5pm). The California Academy of Sciences, the M. H. de Young Memorial Museum and the Asian Art Museum are in the eastern side of the park (see museums above).

Despite its sandy past, the soil of Golden Gate Park appears rich enough today to rival the fertile soil of the San Joaquin Valley. Flowers bloom all around, particularly in spring and summer. The **Conservatory of Flowers,** erected in 1879, is the oldest building in the park, allegedly constructed in Ireland and shipped from Dublin via Cape Horn. (752-8080. Open daily 9am-6pm; Nov.-April 9am-5pm. $1.50, seniors and ages 6-12 75¢, under 6 free. Free daily 9:30-10am and 5:30-6pm, 1st Wed. of month, and holidays.) The **Strybing Arboretum,** on Lincoln Way at 9th Ave. (661-1316), southwest of the academy, is home to 5000 varieties of plants. Near the Music Concourse on a path off South Dr., the **Shakespeare Garden** contains almost every flower and plant ever mentioned by the herbalist of Stratford-upon-Avon (open daily dawn-dusk; in winter closed Mon.; free). Rent a **boat** ($9.50-14.50 per hour), or cross the footbridge and climb the hill for a dazzling view of the San Francisco peninsula. At Lincoln Way and South Dr., the **Japanese Cherry Orchard** blooms intoxicatingly during the first week in April; it remains beautiful year-round.

Created for the 1894 Mid-Winter Exposition, the elegant **Japanese Tea Garden** is a serene collection of dark wooden buildings, small pools, graceful footbridges, carefully pruned trees, and plants. Buy tea and cookies for $2 and watch the giant carp circle the central pond. (Open daily 9am-6:30pm; Oct.-Feb. 8:30am-dusk. $2, seniors and ages 6-12 $1, under 6 free. Free 1st and last ½ hr. and on holidays.)

What could be more American than a herd of **buffalo?** A dozen of the shaggy beasts roam a spacious paddock at the western end of John F. Kennedy Dr., near 39th Ave. On Sundays traffic is banned from park roads, and bicycles and in-line skates come out in full force. Rent bikes at **Stow Lake** ($7 per hour or $28 per day).

Richmond (New Chinatown)

The region enclosed by these streets and 28th and 5th Ave. on the west and east is known as the Richmond District, a largely residential neighborhood north of Golden Gate Park. This quiet district contains many ethnic neighborhoods and restaurants for exploration. "Inner Richmond," the area east of Park Presidio Blvd. has a large Chinese population, earning it the nickname "New Chinatown."

Lincoln Park, at the northwest extreme of the San Francisco, is Richmond's biggest attraction (MUNI bus #1 or 38). The park grounds offer a romantic view of the Golden Gate Bridge. The **Palace of the Legion of Honor** is closed for renovations, and should reopen in November 1995. Southwest of Lincoln Park sits the precarious **Cliff House,** the third to occupy this picturesque spot (the previous two burned down before the present structure was erected in 1909). The nearby **National Park Service Visitors Center** (556-8642), dispenses info on the wildlife of the cliffs area, as well as on the history of the Cliff Houses. (Open 10am-4:30pm daily. Free.)

Turning out to sea from the western cliffs along Point Lobos Ave., you can see **Seal Rocks,** often occupied by the sleek animals. **Ocean Beach,** the largest and most popular of San Francisco's beaches, begins south of Point Lobos and extends down the city's coast line. The undertow along the point is so strong that swimming is prohibited and even wading is dangerous. Swimming is allowed at **China Beach** at the end of Seacliff Ave. on the eastern edge of Lincoln Park. The water is COLD here too, but the views of the Golden Gate Bridge are stunning.

Chinatown

The largest Chinese community outside of Asia (over 100,000 people), Chinatown is also the most densely populated of San Francisco's neighborhoods. Chinatown was founded in the 1880s when, after the gold had been dug and the tracks laid, bigotry fueled by unemployment engendered a racist outbreak against what was then termed the "Yellow Peril." In response, Chinese-Americans banded together to protect themselves in a small section of the downtown area. As the city grew, Chinatown gradually expanded, but remains almost exclusively Chinese. Most visitors come to Chinatown for the food, but there are plenty of other attractions. **Grant Avenue** is the most picturesque part of Chinatown.

Watch fortune cookies being shaped by hand in the **Golden Gate Cookie Company,** 56 Ross Alley (781-3956; huge bag of cookies $2), between Washington and Jackson St., just west of Grant Ave. Nearby **Portsmouth Square,** at Kearny and Washington St., made history in 1848 when Sam Brennan first announced the discovery of gold at Sutter's Mill from the square. Now the square is filled with Chinese men playing lively card games. A stone bridge leads from this square to the **Chinese Culture Center,** 750 Kearny St., 3rd floor of the Holiday Inn (986-1822), which houses exhibits of Chinese-American art and sponsors a heritage and a culinary **walking tour** of Chinatown. The **Chinese Historical Society,** 650 Commercial St. (391-1188), between Kearny and Montgomery, relates the tale of the Chinese who came to California through some remarkable artifacts, including a 1909 parade dragon head (open Tues.-Sat. noon-4pm; donation).

At Grant and Bush stands the ornate, dragon-crested **Gateway to Chinatown,** given by the Republic of China in 1969. Some noteworthy buildings include **Buddha's Universal Church** (720 Washington), the **Kong Chow Temple** (855 Stockton), and **Old St. Mary's,** (660 California St. at Grant), which was built in 1854 of granite cut in China and was San Francisco's only cathedral for almost four decades.

The Presidio and the Golden Gate Bridge

The **Presidio,** established in 1776, is a sprawling army-owned preserve that extends all the way from the Marina in the east to the wealthy Sea Cliff area in the west, provides endless opportunities for perambulating through the trees or along the beach. The preserve also supports the southern end of San Francisco's world-famous Golden Gate Bridge. Take MUNI bus #28, 29, or 76.

At the northern tip of the Presidio (and the peninsula), under the tower of the Golden Gate Bridge, **Fort Point** (556-1693) stands guard over the entrance to San Francisco Bay. The fort was built in 1853 as one of a series of bunker defenses designed to protect San Francisco from invasion by the British during the tense dispute over the Oregon boundary. Guided tours are given by National Park Rangers. (Museum open Wed.-Sun. 10am-5pm. Free 1-hr. **walks** with presentation 10:30am, 1:30, and 3:30pm with extra 12:30pm walk on weekends.)

The **Golden Gate Bridge,** the rust-colored symbol of the West's bounding confidence, sways above the entrance to San Francisco Bay. Built in 1937 under the direction of chief engineer Joseph Strauss, the bridge is almost indescribably beautiful from any angle on or around it. The bridge's overall length is 8981 ft., the main span is 4200 ft. long. The stolid towers are 746 ft. high. Built to swing, the bridge was undamaged by the 1989 quake. Just across the bridge, **Vista Point** is just that, providing an incredible view of the city.

Marina, Pacific Heights, and Presidio Heights

The Marina, Pacific Heights, and the adjoining Presidio Heights are the most sought-after addresses in San Francisco for young, urban professionals. **Fillmore Street, Union Street,** and **Chestnut St.** are the centers of activity for the upwardly mobile folk who make this area their home. Despite the chi-chi boutiques, thrifty *Let's Go*ers will enjoy the impressive mansions, well-kept parks, and pristine paths.

Pacific Heights, centered about Union and Sacramento Sts., boasts the greatest number of **Victorian buildings** in the city. The 1906 earthquake and fire destroyed most of the northeast part of San Francisco, but left the Heights area west of Van Ness Ave. unscathed. The Marina was the hardest hit in 1989, but the Heights area was not as lucky this time around and sustained serious damage. The **Octagon House,** 2645 Gough St. (441-7512), at Union St., is currently the headquarters of the National Society of Colonial Dames. (Open 2nd Sun. and 2nd and 4th Thurs. except Jan.; group tours by arrangement.) The **Haas-Lilienthal House,** 2007 Franklin St. (441-3004), is another grand example of Victorian architecture run rampant. (Open Wed. noon-4pm, Sun. 11am-4pm. $5, seniors and under 18 $3.)

Marina District is down from Pacific Heights toward the bay and past Union. **Chestnut Street,** once a neighborhood lane of small grocers, has recently become the destination of choice for a young crowd of shoppers, diners, and drinkers. To the east of Marina Green at Laguna and Marina lies **Fort Mason Center** (441-5706). The army's former embarkation facility has been converted into a center for nonprofit organizations and a place for young people to meet. The **San Francisco Museum of Modern Art Rental Gallery** (441-4777), Building A, provides prospective collectors with the opportunity to view art and then rent it on a trial basis. Works of all different media by several hundred artists are on display. (Open Tues.-Sat. 11:30am-5:30pm; closed Aug.) The **San Francisco Craft and Folk Art Museum** (775-0990), Building A, is smart and self-explanatory. (Open Tues.-Fri. and Sun. 11am-5pm, Sat. 10am-5pm. $1.) The **African-American Historical and Cultural Society Museum** (441-0640), Building C, Room 165, focuses on contemporary African arts and crafts (open Wed.-Sun. noon-5pm; donation requested). **Museo Italo Americano** (673-2200), Building C #100, displays work created by artists with Italian heritage (open Wed.-Sun. noon-5pm; $2, students and seniors $1).

A walk eastward over the hill of Fort Mason takes you to Ghirardelli Square and Fisherman's Wharf. To the west lies the **Palace of Fine Arts,** on Baker St. between Jefferson and Bay St. The beautiful domed structure and the two curving colonnades are reconstructed remnants of the 1915 Panama Pacific Exposition, which commemorated the opening of the Panama Canal and signalled San Francisco's recovery from the great earthquake. Next to the domed building is the **Exploratorium,** 3601 Lyon St. (561-0360). Hundreds of interactive exhibits expound the wonders of science from giant bubble makers to shadow machines. (Open Sun.-Tues. and Thurs.-Sat. 10am-6pm, Wed. 10am-9:30pm. $8.50, students and seniors $6.50, ages 6-17 $4.50. First Wed. of every month free.)

Fisherman's Wharf and Ghirardelli Square

Traveling eastward, along the waterfront, one arrives at the most popular tourist destination in San Francisco. Stretching from Pier 39 in the east to Ghirardelli Square in the west is "Fisherman's Wharf," home to ¾ mi. of porcelain figurines, gifts for lefties, and enough t-shirts to have kept Washington's army snug at Valley Forge. This area can be very crowded and expensive, but don't let that keep you away. Enjoy the street performances, the prime people-watching, and the shopping. The best way to appreciate the wharf is to wake up at 4am, put on a warm sweater, and go down to the piers to see why it's called Fisherman's Wharf. **Pier 39** (981-7437), built on pilings that extend several hundred yards into the harbor, was designed to recall old San Francisco (shops open daily 10:30am-8:30pm). Toward the end of the pier is **Center Stage,** where mimes, jugglers, and magicians do their thing.

Tour boats and ferries dock just west of Pier 39. The two main tour fleets, the Blue and Gold Fleet and the Red and White Fleet, were named after the colors of UC Berkeley and Stanford University to symbolize the long-running rivalry between the two Bay Area schools. The **Blue and Gold Fleet** (781-7877) offers 1¼-hour tours on 400-passenger sight-seeing boats. The tours cruise under both the Golden Gate and Bay Bridges, past Angel Island, Alcatraz, and Treasure Islands, and provide sweeping views of the San Francisco skyline (tours begin at 10am, last boat 5:30pm; $15, seniors, ages 5-18, and military $8). The **Red and White Fleet** (546-2700 or 800-229-2784) at Pier 41 offers 45-min. ferry rides leaving from Piers 41 and 43½ and goes under the Golden Gate Bridge and past Alcatraz and Angel Islands. ($15, over 62 and ages 12-18 $12, ages 5-11 $8; ask about multi-lingual narratives.)

Easily visible from boats and the waterfront is **Alcatraz Island.** Named in 1775 for the *alcatraces* (pelicans) that flocked to it, this former federal prison looms over the San Francisco Bay, 1½ mi. from Fisherman's Wharf. Of the 23 men who attempted to escape, all were recaptured or killed, except for five who were "presumed drowned" although their bodies were never found. The film *Escape from Alcatraz* is about the most probable escape. Robert Stroud, "The Birdman of Alcatraz," spent 17 years in solitary confinement. Although sentenced to death for killing a prison guard, he was spared by President Wilson and went on to write two books on bird diseases. In 1962, Attorney General Robert Kennedy closed the prison. Alcatraz is currently a part of the **Golden Gate National Recreation Area,** the largest park in an urban area in the United States, administered by the National Park Service. The **Red and White Fleet** (546-2896) runs boats to Alcatraz from Pier 41. Once on Alcatraz, you can wander by yourself or take a two-hour audiotape-guided tour, full of clanging chains and the ghosts of prisoners past. (Boats depart every ½ hr. from Pier 41; summer 9:15am-4:15pm, winter 9:45am-2:45pm. Fare $5.75, seniors $4.75, ages 5-11 $3.25; tours cost $3.25 extra, ages 5-11 $1.25 extra. Passengers can remain on the island until the final 6:30pm ferry departs.) Reserve tickets in advance through Ticketron (392-7469) for $1 extra or confront long lines and risk missing the boat.

As you continue along the waterfront and pass the shops and restaurants on Jefferson Street, don't neglect to veer from the tourist-ridden sidewalks and explore the docks and old fish houses. The **Maritime National Historic Park** (929-0202), at the Hyde Street Pier where Hyde meets Jefferson, displays the *Balclutha,* a swift trading vessel that plied the Cape Horn route in the 1880s and '90s and was featured in the

CALIFORNIA

first Hollywood version of *Mutiny on the Bounty*. The vessel was recently restored. (Open daily 9am-6pm. $3, ages 12-17 $1, over 61 and under 12 free.)

Ghirardelli Square (GEAR-ah-deh-lee), 900 N. Point St. (info booth 775-5500; open daily 10am-9pm) is the most famous of the shopping malls around Fisherman's Wharf and rightfully so—it houses some of the best chocolate in the world. Today, the only remains of the machinery from Ghirardelli's original **chocolate factory** are in the rear of the **Ghirardelli Chocolate Manufactory,** an old-fashioned ice cream parlor. The old Ghirardelli factory's square is now a popular and scenic destination, with acclaimed restaurants and an elegant mermaid fountain. Pricey boutiques fill the old factory's brick buildings, and musicians and magicians entertain the masses. (Stores open Mon.-Sat. 10am-9pm, Sun. 10am-6pm.)

North Beach

As one walks north along Stockton St. or Columbus Ave., there is a gradual transition from supermarkets displaying ginseng to those selling provolone. North Beach today is an old Italian neighborhood filled with restaurateurs, shoe repairers, bakers, and cappuccino makers. In the '50s, this area was home to the Bohemian Beats (Allen Ginsberg, Jack Kerouac, Lawrence Ferlinghetti, and others).

Lying between Stockton and Powell is **Washington Square** (North Beach's *piazza* and the wedding site of Joe DiMaggio and Marilyn Monroe), a lush lawn edged by trees and watched over by a statue of Benjamin Franklin. In the square itself is the **Volunteer Firemen Memorial,** donated by Mrs. Lillie Hitchcock Coit, who was rescued from a fire in childhood. Coit's most famous gift to the city is **Coit Tower** (often called "the candle"), which stands a few blocks east on **Telegraph Hill.** Coit Tower's spectacular 360° view makes it one of the most romantic spots in the city. An elevator takes you to the top. (362-0808; open daily 10am-7pm; Oct.-May 9am-4pm. $3, over 64 $2, ages 6-12 $1, under 6 free.)

North Beach Bohemianism flourished when the Beat artists moved in. Drawn here by low rents and cheap bars, the group came to national attention when Ferlinghetti's **City Lights Bookstore,** 261 Columbus Ave. (362-8193), published Allen Ginsberg's poem *Howl.* Banned in 1956, the book was found "not obscene" after an extended trial, but the publicity turned North Beach into a must-see for tourists.

Nob Hill and Russian Hill

Before the earthquake and fire of 1906, Nob Hill was home to the mansions of the great railroad magnates. Today, Nob Hill remains one of the nation's most prestigious addresses. The streets are lined with many fine buildings, and the aura is that of idle and settled wealth, sitting atop a hill and peering down upon the *hoi polloi*.

Grace Cathedral, 1051 Taylor St. (776-6611), the most immense Gothic edifice west of the Mississippi, crowns Nob Hill. The castings for its portals are such exact imitations of Ghiberti's on the Baptistry in Florence that they were used to restore the originals. Visitors should respect that the Cathedral is still used for worship.

Once the site of the enormous and majestic mansions of the four mining and railroad magnates who "settled" Nob (Charles Crocker, Mark Hopkins, Leland Stanford, and Collis Huntington), the hilltop is now home to upscale hotels and bars. Nearby Russian Hill is named after Russian sailors who died during an expedition in the early 1800s and were buried on the southeast crest. At the top of Russian Hill, the notorious **Lombard Street curves,** on Lombard (the most crooked street in the world) between Hyde and Leavenworth St. afford a fantastic view of the city and harbor—that is, if you dare allow your eyes to stray from the road down this plunge.

Nihonmachi (Japantown)

Nihonmachi encompasses an area three blocks long by three blocks wide. This small neighborhood 1.1 mi. from downtown San Francisco is bounded by Fillmore, Laguna and Bush Sts. Nihonmachi is centered around the aptly named **Japanese Cultural and Trade Center** at Post and Buchanan. Similar to the Tokyo Ginza, the five-acre center includes Japanese *udon* houses, sushi bars, and a massage center and bathhouse. Japan gave as a gift to the 12,000 Japanese-Americans of San Francisco the **Peace Pagoda,** a magnificent 100-ft. tall, five-tiered structure which graces the heart of Japantown. The **Kabuki Complex** (931-9800) at Post St. and Fillmore shows current films. During early May it is the main site of the San Francisco International Film Festival. The weary traveler with some money to spend might want to invest in a rejuvenating *Shiatsu* massage at **Fuji Shiatsu,** 1721 Buchanan Mall (346-4484; (open Mon.-Fri. 9am-8pm, Sat. 9am-7pm, Sun. 10am-6pm; $30 per hr.).

ENTERTAINMENT AND NIGHTLIFE

San Fran offers great entertainment. Call the **Entertainment Hotline** at 391-2001 or 391-2002. The *Bay Guardian* and *SF Weekly* always have a thorough listing of dance clubs and live music. North America's largest Chinese community celebrates with cultural festivities, a parade, lots of fireworks, and the crowning of Miss Chinatown USA at the **Chinese New Year Celebration** (982-3000), late Feb. in Chinatown. **San Francisco International Film Festival** (931-3456), in mid-April to mid-May, is the oldest film festival in North America. More than 100 films of all genres from around the world are shown. **San Francisco ExaminerBay to Breakers,** mid-May, is the largest road race (7.1 mi.) in the United States, done in inimitable San Francisco style. Runners win not only on their times but on their costumes as well. The **Haight Street Fair** (661-8025), in early June, has bands, vendors, and masses of people in the streets between Masonic and Stanyan. **18th San Francisco International Lesbian & Gay Film Festival** (703-8650), mid- to late June, is the world's largest presentation of lesbian and gay media, centered around the Roxie Cinema (16th St. at Valencia), and the Castro Theatre (Castro St. at Market). People come from all over the country to join the **Lesbian-Gay Freedom Parade** (864-3733), in late June.

Sports enthusiasts should see the San Francisco **Giants** and **49ers** play baseball and football at notoriously windy **Candlestick Park** (467-8000), 8 mi. south of the city via the Bayshore Freeway (U.S. 101).

Bars

Café du Nord (861-5016), on Market St. between Church and Sanchez. Painfully hip. Expansive bar. Dinner served Wed.-Sat. Pool tables 75¢. Live jazz or world music nightly. Beer $3.25. Cover $1 on the weekends. Open 4pm-2am.

Perry's, 1944 Union St. (922-9022), at Laguna, in Pacific Heights. San Francisco's most famous pick-up joint is a comfortable, vaguely old-fashioned place. Ten beers on tap, large draft beer $3.25. Food until midnight. Open daily 7:30am-1am.

The Elbo Room, 647 Valencia St. (552-7788), near 17th in the Mission. Cover (usually $3) for the music and dancing upstairs only. This place is becoming less and less roomy while getting more and more popular. Open daily 5pm-2am.

The Savoy-Tivoli, 1434 Grant Ave. (362-7023), in North Beach. Sit outside and watch the passersby or play pool. Wear black. Reggae music. Crowded, so don't expect speedy service. Open Tues.-Wed. 5pm-2am, Thurs.-Sun. 3pm-2am.

Clubs

The Paradise Lounge, 1501 Folsom St. (861-6906), at 11th St., in SoMa. With 3 stages, 2 floors, 5 bars, and up to 5 different bands a night, this club is one of those unique places where you feel equally comfortable in spike heels or Birkenstocks. Pool tables upstairs. Open daily 3pm-2am. Must be 21.

Club DV8, 540 Howard St. (957-1730), in SoMa. 3 floors of sheer dance mania. One of those "in places to be." 18 and over on Tues.-Wed. Disco flashbacks on Thurs. Cover ranges from free to $10. Open Tues.-Sun. 8pm-4am.

CRASH Palace, 628 Divisadero (931-1914). This hot new club features lots of jazz. Worldbeat on Sun., speakeasy on Tues. Live music nightly. No cover Mon.-Tues., $5-10 otherwise. Open daily 5pm-2am.

Slims, 333 11th St. (621-3330), between Folsom and Harrison, in SoMa. Blues and jazz. Legendary house for American Roots Music. Open nightly. Must be 21.

DNA Lounge, 375 11th St. (626-1409), at Harrison, in SoMa. Both live music and dancing. The best night for dancing is Wed. Funk, house, and soul. Cover varies but usually doesn't exceed $10. Open daily until 4am. Must be 21.

The Holy Cow, 1531 Folsom (621-6087), between 11th and 12th St, in SoMa. A life-size plastic cow marks the spot. This bar/dance club attracts the trendy mainstream with music to match. No cover. Tough carding. Open Wed.-Sun. 9am-2am.

The Mad Dog in the Fog, 530 Haight St. (626-7279). Very relaxed. Guinness served. Bands (mostly acoustic) on Sun. Open mike on Tues. Dancing (with DJ) to soul and funk on Wed. No cover. Open daily 11:30am-2am.

The Top, 424 Haight St. (864-7386). Close to the housing projects; go with friends. Small, dark, and trendy. Sat. is gay, cover $3. Open daily 8pm-2am.

Gay and Lesbian Clubs

Gay nightlife in San Francisco flourishes. Most of the popular bars can be found in the city's two traditionally gay areas—the Castro (around the intersection of Castro St. and Market St., see Sights) and Polk St. (several blocks north of Geary St.). Most "straight" dance clubs in San Francisco feature at least one gay night a week. Consult the *San Francisco Bay Guardian* or the **Gay Switchboard** (510-841-6224).

The I-Beam, 1748 Haight St. (668-6006). Tea Dance every Sun. 6pm. Every Fri. is industrial alternative. Happy hour 6-8pm. Cover $5-7. Open daily 8pm-2am.

The Café, 2367 Market St. (861-3846), the Castro. San Francisco's most popular bar for women. 2 levels with pinball, pool tables, and sundeck. DJs lay down fierce music. No cover. Open daily noon-2am.

End Up, 401 6th St. (543-7700), at Harrison. San Francisco's original Tea Dance 6am-9pm, $3. Fri. night is men's night. Sat. night is women's night. Cover $4 (except for Tea Dance). Open daily 9pm-2am, sometimes 3:30am.

The Stud, 399 9th St. (863-6623). A classic gay club with great dance music. Mon. night is funk night. Wed. night is oldies night featuring cheap beer. Thurs. is women's night. Cover $2-4. Open daily 5pm-2am, Fri.-Sat. after hours.

■■■ BERKELEY

Almost 30 years ago, Mario Savio climbed on top of a police car and launched Berkeley's free speech movement. Today, Berkeley is still a national symbol of political activism and social iconoclasm. The site of the country's most renowned public university, Berkeley is as famous for its street people and chefs as for its political cadres and academics. Chez Panisse, the restaurant owned by Alice Waters, is believed to have originated the elusive concept of California cuisine. Telegraph Avenue—the Champs Elysées of the '60s—remains the home of street-corner soothsayers, funky bookstores, aging hippies, countless cafés, and itinerant street musicians. Berkeley revels in the bourgeois while maintaining its idealistic spirit.

PRACTICAL INFORMATION

Emergency: 911.

Visitors Information: Berkeley Convention and Visitors Bureau, 1834 University Ave. (549-7040), at Martin Luther King, Jr. Way. Open Mon.-Fri. 9am-noon and 1-4pm. 24-hr. Visitor Hotline 549-8710. **U.C. Berkeley Visitor Center,** 101 University Hall, 2200 University Ave. (642-5215). Open Mon.-Fri. 8am-5pm.

Greyhound: Information 800-231-2222. Closest station is in Oakland.

Amtrak: Information 800-872-7245. Closest station is in Oakland.

Public Transportation: Bay Area Rapid Transit (BART): 465-2278. The Berkeley station is at Shattuck Ave. and Center St., close to the western edge of the university, about 7 blocks from the Student Union. $1.80 to downtown San Francisco. The university **Perimeter Shuttle** (642-5149) connects the BART station with the university campus (Sept.-June Mon.-Fri. 7am-7pm every 8 min., except on holidays; 25¢). BART also stops at Virginia and Sacramento St. (north) and at Ashby St. (west).

Alameda County Transit (AC Transit): 800-559-4636 or 839-2882. Buses #14, 40, 43, and 51 run from the Berkeley BART stop to downtown Oakland, via M.L. King Jr. Way, Telegraph Ave., Shattuck Ave., and College Ave., respectively. Fare $1.10, seniors, ages 5-12, and disabled 55¢, under 5 free. Transfers 25¢, valid for 1 hr. **Berkeley TRiP,** 2033 Center St. (643-7665), informs on public transport, bikes, and carpools. Open Mon.-Wed. and Fri. 8:30am-5:30pm, Thurs. 9am-6pm.

Taxi: Yellow A l Cab, 843-1111. Open 24 hrs.

Car Rental: Budget (524-7237), Gilman St. and 2nd. Compact car $40 per day with unlimited mi. Must be 21, under 25 pay additional $15. Open Mon.-Thurs. 8am-4:30pm, Fri. 8am-5:30pm, Sat. 8:30am-2:30pm, Sun. 9am-1pm.

Post Office: 2000 Allston Way (649-3100). Open Mon.-Fri. 8:30am-6pm, Sat. 10am-2pm. **ZIP Code:** 94704.

Area Code: 510.

Berkeley lies across the bay northeast of San Francisco, just north of Oakland. Reach the city by BART from downtown San Francisco or by car (**I-80** or **Rte. 24**). Berkeley is sandwiched between a series of rolling hills to the east and San Francisco Bay to the west. The **University of California** campus stretches into the hills, but most of the university's buildings are in the westernmost section of campus, near BART. **Telegraph Avenue,** which runs south from the Student Union, is the spiritual center of town. Undergraduates tend to hang out on Telegraph and other streets on the south side of campus, while the north side is dominated by graduate students. The **downtown** area, around the BART station, contains several businesses as well as the public library and post office. The **Gourmet Ghetto** encompasses the area along Shattuck Ave. and Walnut St. between Virginia and Rose St. The **Fourth Street Center,** west of campus and by the bay, is home to great eating and window shopping. Northwest of campus, **Solano Ave.** offers countless ethnic restaurants, bookstores, and movie theaters. Avoid walking alone on Berkeley's streets at night.

Driving in the Bay Area is frustrating. Crossing the bay by **BART** ($1.80-2) is quick and easy. Both the university and Telegraph Ave. are short walks from the station.

ACCOMMODATIONS

It is surprisingly difficult to sleep cheaply in Berkeley. The **Bed and Breakfast Network** (540-5123) coordinates 20 B&Bs in the East Bay, some of which offer reasonable rates. You can stay in San Francisco and make daytrips to Berkeley.

YMCA International Youth Hostel, 2001 Allston Way (848-9622), at Milvia St. New hostel offers a clean, cheap, secure place to stay. Rooms have one bunk bed. TV room, hall baths. Registration 6:30pm. Lockout 9am-6pm. Bring linens. Men and women ages 18-30 only. $12.60 per night, $10.60 for AYH members.

YMCA, 2001 Allston Way (848-6800), at Milvia St. Clean, adequate rooms are available in this hotel-portion of the YMCA. Co-ed by floor. Registration daily 8am-9:30pm. Check-out noon. No curfew. Prices include tax and use of pool and basic fitness facilities. 14-day max. stay. Singles $25, doubles $30. All share hall baths.

University Conference Services, 2601 Warring St. (642-4444; fax 642-2888; after June 1 call 442-5925). Spacious, clean dorm rooms in Stern Hall. Phones available in summer to "university visitors" (i.e. everybody). Make reservations through Conference Services Mon.-Fri. 10am-5:30pm. Singles $34. Doubles $44.

Travel Inn, 1461 University Ave. (848-3840), 2 blocks from North Berkeley BART station, 7 blocks west of campus. Rooms are clean and comfortable. TV and phones. Singles $32-35, doubles $42-50 depending on season. Key deposit $1-5.

Golden Bear Motel, 1620 San Pablo Ave. (525-6770), at Cedar. Located farther away from campus but with recently painted bedrooms and clean white bedspreads. Check-out noon. Room with queen-size bed (for 1 or 2) $41, room with 2 beds $46, room with 2 queen-size beds $49.

FOOD

Berkeley is a relatively small area with a wide range of excellent budget eateries. Consult *Bayfood* (652-6115; available free in Berkeley's cafés and restaurants).

CALIFORNIA

Telegraph Avenue has lots of pizza, coffee, and frozen yogurt. For the best food in Berkeley head downtown to **Shattuck Avenue** or north to **Solano Avenue.**

Anne's Soup Kitchen, 2498 Telegraph (548-8885), at Dwight. *The* place for breakfast in Berkeley and a favorite with students. Towering portions more than compensate for crowded dining. Weekday special includes 2 whole wheat pancakes with bacon and eggs ($3) or with homefries ($2.75). Open daily 8am-7pm.

Café Fanny, 1603 San Pablo Ave. (524-5447). Alice Water's most recent venture, this tiny café offers limited seating, lots of standing room, and benches under pleasant outdoor trellis. Great sandwiches ($5.25-6.25). Famous for giant bowls of *café au lait* ($2.08). Open Mon.-Fri. 7am-3pm, Sat. 8am-4pm, Sun. 9am-3pm.

Plearn, 2050 University Ave. at Shattuck (841-2148), 1 block west of campus. Constant winner of best Thai in the Bay Area. Very hot, very good curries ($7). Plentiful vegetarian options. The *Thai Song Kran* brew eases the heat of the spices. Lunch specials 11:30am-3:30pm $4.25. Open daily 11:30am-10pm.

Brennan's, 720 University Ave. (841-0960), at 4th St. Established in 1959, Brennan's is a Berkeley institution. Locals flock here for huge plates of traditional food. Open 11am-9:30pm. Bar open Sun.-Thurs. 11am-11:30pm, Fri.-Sat. 11am-1:30am.

SIGHTS

In 1868, the privately run College of California and the publicly run Agricultural, Mining, and Mechanical Arts College coupled to give birth to the **University of California.** Because Berkeley was the first of the nine University of California campuses, it is permitted the nickname "Cal." The school has an enrollment of over 30,000 students and more than 1000 full professors. Berkeley also boasts more Nobel laureates per capita than any other city. Berkeley's student body is celebrated for its diversity.

Pass through **Sather Gate** (one of the sites of student sit-ins) into **Sproul Plaza** (another such site) and enter the university. Berkeley covers 160 acres, bounded by Bancroft Way, Oxford St., Hearst Ave., and parkland. The staff at the **Visitor Information Center,** 101 University Hall, 2200 University Ave. (642-5215; open Mon.-Fri. 8am-5pm), happily provides free maps and info. (Campus tours 1½ hrs. Mon., Wed., Fri. 10am and 1pm.)

The most dramatic campus attraction is **Sather Tower** (much better known as the **Campanile,** Italian for "bell tower"), a 1914 monument to Berkeley benefactor Jane Krom Sather. It was created by campus architect John Galen Howard who designed it after the clock tower in Venice's St. Mark's Square. You can ride to the observation level of the 307-ft.-tall tower (the tallest building on campus) for a stupendous view (50¢). The tower's 61-bell carillon is played most weekdays, often by University Carillonist Ronald Barnes, at 7:50am, noon, and 6pm. **Bancroft Library,** across from the *Campanile,* has exhibits which change frequently and range from California history to folio editions of Shakespeare's plays. A gold nugget purported to be the first one plucked from Sutter's Mill is on display. The 7 million volumes of books are open to the public. (Open Mon.-Fri. 9am-5pm, Sat. 1-5pm. Free.)

The **University Art Museum (UAM),** 2626 Bancroft Way at College (642-0808), holds a diverse and enticing permanent collection and hosts different exhibits yearly. Within the museum, the **Pacific Film Archives (PFA)** (642-1124), is one of the nation's largest film libraries. (Museum open Wed. and Fri.-Sun. 11am-5pm, Thurs. 11am-9pm. $6; students, over 64 and ages 6-17 $4. Free Thurs. 11am-noon and 5-9pm. PFA shows films in the evening.)

The **Lawrence Hall of Science** (642-5132), a concrete octagon standing above the northeast corner of campus, shares honors with San Francisco's Exploratorium as the finest science museum in the Bay Area. (Open Mon.-Fri. 10am-4:30pm, Sat.-Sun. 10am-5pm. $5; seniors, students, and ages 7-18 $4, ages 3-6 $2.)

The **Botanical Gardens** (642-3343) in Strawberry Canyon contain over 10,000 varieties of plant life. Berkeley's Mediterranean climate, moderated by coastal fog, provides an outstanding setting for this 33-acre garden. Agatha Christie is said to have come here to examine a rare poisonous plant whose deadly powers she wished to utilize in one of her mystery novels (open daily 9am-4:30pm; free, parking permit $1 for 2 hrs.). The **Berkeley Rose Garden** on Euclid Ave. at Eunice St., north of campus contains a lovely collection of roses. (Open May-Sept. dawn-dusk.)

Outside of Berkeley's campus. The **Judah Magnes Museum,** 2911 Russell St. (849-2710), displays a leading collection of Judaica (open Sun.-Thurs. 10am-4pm; free). The **Julia Morgan Theater,** 2640 College Ave. (box office 845-8542), is housed in a beautiful former church designed by Morgan and notable for its graceful and unusual mix of materials.

People's Park, on Haste St., one block off Telegraph Ave., is a kind of unofficial museum. A mural depicts the '60s struggle between the city and local activists over whether to develop it commercially. During the conflict, then-governor Ronald Reagan sent in the National Guard, an action which led to the death of a Berkeley student. Three years ago, despite heated protests, the city and the university bulldozed part of the park to build sand volleyball courts, basketball courts, and restrooms. The park is patrolled by police officers 24 hours a day.

Tilden Regional Park presents hiking, biking, running, and riding trails. Swim in **Lake Anza,** in the center of the park, during the summer (10am-dusk.) The park also contains a botanical garden that teaches about California's plant life.

NIGHTLIFE

Hang out with procrastinating students in front of or inside the **Student Union** (642-4636). **The Underground** contains a ticket office, an arcade, bowling alleys, foosball tables, and pool tables, all run from a central blue desk (642-3825; open Mon.-Fri. 8am-6pm, Sat. 10am-6pm; winter Mon.-Fri. 8am-10pm, Sat. 10am-6pm). The **Bear's Lair,** a student pub with live music on Thursday and Friday is next door at 2425 Bancroft. It's *the* popular campus hangout on sunny Friday afternoons when quarts of beer are $2.75. (843-0373; open Mon.-Thurs. noon-midnight, Fri. 11am-8pm; summer hours vary, usually Sat.-Wed. 11am-6pm). **Henry's,** 2600 Durant Ave. (845-8981), in the Durant Hotel, is a somewhat upscale frat hangout. (Open daily 11am-2am.) **Blakes,** 2367 Telegraph Ave. (848-0886), at Durant, is also worth seeing. Named "best bar in Berkeley" by the *Daily Californian,* Blake's has 3 stories, 2 happy hours, and one classic-packed CD jukebox. (Cover $2-5. Open Mon.-Sat. 11:30am-2am, Sun. 4pm-2am.) Also check out **Jupiter,** 2181 Shattuck Ave. (843-8277), across the street from the BART station, which boasts table-bowling, beer garden, and terrific pizza ($6). (Open Mon.-Thurs. 11:30am-1am, Fri. 11:30am-1:30am, Sat. 1pm-1:30am, Sun. 1-11pm. Live music Fri.-Sun., no cover.)

■■■ MARIN COUNTY

Home to Jerry Garcia, Dana Carvey, and 560 acres of spectacular redwood forest, Marin County (mah-RIN) boasts a bizarre blend of outstanding natural beauty, trendiness, liberalism, and wealth. Marinites love their real estate values as much as their open space and organic food. Neighboring communities grumble about Marin's excesses, but Marin residents believe they have learned how to reconcile eco-conscious habits and a self-indulgent lifestyle. Much of Marin can be explored in a daytrip from San Francisco. The area can be reached by car, bus, or ferry. Muir Woods National Monument with its coastal redwoods, Marin Headlands, Mt. Tamalpais State Park, and the Point Reyes National Seashore offer mountain bikers and hikers a day's adventure, a two-week trek, or anything in between.

PRACTICAL INFORMATION

Emergency: 911.

Visitors Information: Marin County Chamber of Commerce, 30 N. San Pedro Rd. #150 (472-7470). Open Mon.-Fri. 8:30am-4:30pm. **Sausalito Chamber of Commerce,** 333 Caledonia St. (332-7262). Open Mon.-Fri. 9am-5pm. **San Rafael Chamber of Commerce,** 818 5th Ave. (454-4163). Open Mon.-Fri. 9am-5pm.

Greyhound: 850 Tamalpais (453-0795), in San Rafael. To San Francisco: 2 buses per day, $5, leaving at 4:45am and 5pm.

Bay Area Transportation: Golden Gate Transit (453-2100; 332-6600 in San Francisco). Daily bus service between San Francisco and Marin County via the Golden Gate Bridge, as well as local service in Marin. Buses #10, 20, 28, 30, and 50 provide service to Marin from San Francisco's Transbay Terminal. The **Golden Gate Ferry** (see numbers above) provides transportation between Sausalito or Larkspur and San Francisco from the Ferry Bldg. at the end of Market St.
Taxi: Radio Cab (800-464-7234). Serves all of Marin County.
Car Rental: Budget, 20 Bellam Blvd. (457-4282), San Rafael. $30 per day, unlimited mileage. Will rent to ages 21-25 at no extra charge.
Crisis Lines: Rape Crisis, 924-2100. 24 hrs.
Post Office: San Rafael Main Office, 40 Bellam Ave. (459-0944). Open Mon.-Fri. 8:30am-5pm, Sat. 10am-1pm. **ZIP Code:** 94915.
Area Code: 415.

The Marin peninsula lies at the north end of San Francisco Bay, and is connected to the city by **U.S. 101** via the Golden Gate Bridge. **Rte. 1** creeps north along the Pacific to the Sonoma Coast. The Richmond-San Rafael Bridge connects Marin County to the East Bay via **I-580.** The eastern side of the county cradles the towns of **Sausalito, Larkspur, San Rafael, Terra Linda, Ignacio,** and **Novato.** These towns line U.S. 101, which runs north-south through Marin. West Marin is more rural, with rolling hills and fog-bound coastal valleys. **Rte 1,** runs through **Stinson Beach, Bolinas, Olema, Inverness,** and **Pt. Reyes National Seashore** (from south to north). **Sir Francis Drake Boulevard** runs from U.S. 101 in Larkspur west through the San Geronimo Valley. It passes through the towns of Greenbrae, Kentfield, Ross, San Anselmo, Fairfax, Woodacre, and San Geronimo on the way to Pt. Reyes and its rendezvous with Rte. 1.

ACCOMMODATIONS AND CAMPING

Golden Gate Youth Hostel (HI-AYH) (331-2777). 6 mi. south of Sausalito and 10 mi. from downtown San Francisco. No bus service. From the north, take the Sausalito exit off U.S. 101 (the last one before the bridge) and follow the signs into the Golden Gate Recreation Area. From San Francisco, take U.S. 101 to the Alexander Ave. exit. Game room with pool table, spacious kitchen, common room, and laundry facilities. 24-hr. check-in. Curfew 12:30am. Dormitory and family-style rooms. Linen rental $1. Members and nonmembers $10. Children under 18 with parent $5. Reservations suggested in summer—or show up early.
Point Reyes Hostel (HI-AYH) (663-8811), sits off Limantour Rd. in the Pt. Reyes National Seashore. By car take the Seashore exit west from Rte. 1, then take Bear Valley Rd. to Limantour Rd. and drive 6 mi. in to the park. Reservations are advised on weekends. Reservations must be made by mail with a deposit (Box 247, Point Reyes Station, CA 94956) or by phone with credit card. Spectacular site. Hiking, wildlife, bird-watching, and Limantour Beach are all within walking distance. Kitchen. Cozy common room with a wood stove. Registration 4:30-9:30pm. Hostel closed 9:30am-4:30pm. Sleep sheet and towel $1 each. Members and nonmembers $10; chore also expected.
Marin Headlands, northwest of the Golden Gate Bridge. 15 campsites. Most are primitive with only picnic tables and chemical toilets. Some running water. Reserve as much as 90 days in advance by calling the **visitors center** (331-1540; 9:30am-noon). Permits are required, but sites are free. The Golden Gate Youth Hostel (see above) permits use of showers and kitchen ($2 each). Free cold showers available at Rodeo Beach (located in the Headlands).
Mt. Tamalpais State Park, 801 Rte. 1 (388-2070). 16 campsites ($14; first-come, first-served), a group camp, and **Steep Ravine,** an "environmental camp" with cabins ($30 for up to 5 people) and tent sites ($9). Tent sites with no showers. Cabins have wood-burning stoves. No running water or electricity. Make cabin reservations 90 days in advance (MISTIX 800-444-7275). Reservations $6.75.

FOOD

Gourmet, health-conscious Marinites take their fruit juices, tofu, and nonfat double-shot cappuccino very seriously. A fun, more economical option is to raid one of the many organic groceries and picnic in one of Marin's countless parks.

Mama's Royal Cafe, 387 Miller Ave. (388-3261), in downtown Mill Valley. Heartily recommended by locals. Unusual but very good dishes. Brunch with live music Sat. and Sun. Poetry readings Tues. Some outdoor seating. Open for breakfast/lunch Mon.-Fri. 7:30am-2:30pm, Sat.-Sun. 8:30am-3pm. Dinner Tues.-Sat. 6-10pm.

Stuffed Croissant, etc..., 43 Caledonia St. (332-7103), in Sausalito. Way laid-back bakery-style sandwich shop (sandwiches $3-6). An amazing array of goods. Open Mon. 6:30am-9pm, Tues.-Sat. 6:30am-10pm, Sun. 7:30am-9pm.

The Town's Deli, 501 Caledonia (331-3311), in Sausalito. Sandwiches $2.50-3.75. Known for their roasted chicken (half-chicken $3). Vegetarian options. Open Mon.-Sat. 8am-7pm, Sun. 8am-6pm.

SIGHTS

Marin's attractions range from the excellent hiking trails and beaches to unique shopping and dining opportunities in the pleasant towns of Tiburon and Sausalito. Marin's proximity to San Francisco makes it an ideal area for daytrips.

Sausalito lies at the extreme southeastern tip of Marin. Initially a fishing center, the city traded its sea-dog days for a bevy of retail boutiques. For beautiful views of San Francisco and a relaxing daytrip, take the ferry from San Francisco to Sausalito.

The undeveloped, fog-shrouded hills just to the west of the Golden Gate Bridge comprise the **Marin Headlands,** which are oddly populated by abandoned machine gun nests, missile sites, and soldiers' quarters, now converted into picnic spots, the Golden Gate Hostel, and the **Marine Mammal Center** (289-7325; open daily 10am-4pm; donation requested). The headlands (and the viewpoints) are easily accessible by car: take the Alexander Ave. exit off U.S. 101 from San Francisco, or if coming from the north take the last exit before the Golden Gate Bridge.

Muir Woods National Monument, a 560-acre stand of primeval coastal redwoods, is located about 5 mi. west along Rte. 1 off U.S. 101. The **visitors center** (388-2595) near the entrance keeps the same hours as the monument. Nearby are **Muir Beach** and **Muir Beach Lookout** (open sunrise-9pm). Adjacent to Muir Woods is the isolated, largely undiscovered, and utterly beautiful **Mount Tamalpais State Park** (tam-ull-PIE-us). Also in the park is **Stinson Beach,** a local favorite for sunbathing. Encompassing 100 mi. of coastline along most of the western side of Marin, the **Point Reyes National Seashore** juts into the Pacific from the eastern end of the submerged Pacific Plate. Sir Francis Drake Blvd. runs from San Rafael through Olema. **Limantour Beach,** at the end of Limantour Rd., west of the seashore headquarters, is one of the area's nicest beaches. **San Rafael,** the largest city in Marin County, lies along U.S. 101 on the bay. Architecture buffs may want to check out the **Marin Civic Center,** 3501 Civic Center Dr. (499-7407), off U.S. 101. Frank Lloyd Wright designed this highly unusual, but functional open-air building.

■■■ WINE COUNTRY: NAPA AND SONOMA VALLEYS

Wine is what brings most visitors to the quiet vineyards of the Napa and Sonoma valleys, and with good reason—the area's wines are regarded highly by connoisseurs both in the U.S. and abroad. Napa is better known; Sonoma is older and less crowded. The crowds will thin and you'll receive the most personal attention as you move into the Russian River Valley. The valleys themselves are beautiful and rural. Green fields of gnarled grape vines stretch in all directions and scenic mountain views tower along the horizon.

If you have a hankering for a non-alcoholic activity, 10 mi. south of Napa is 160-acre **Marine World Africa USA** (643-6722), an enormous zoo-oceanarium-theme park (which is often mobbed on summer weekends). (The park is accessible by BART Mon.-Sat.; call 415-788-2278 for more info. Open daily 9:30am-6:15pm. $25, seniors $21, ages 4-12 $17. Parking $4. Wheelchair and stroller access.)

PRACTICAL INFORMATION

Emergency: 911.

Visitors Information: Napa Visitor Center, 1310 Town Center (226-7459), on 1st St. Eager staff offers much info. Open Mon.-Fri. 9am-5pm, Sat.-Sun. 9am-3pm. Pick up a copy of *California Visitors Review* (free) for maps, winery listings, and weekly events guide. In Sonoma, the **Sonoma Valley Visitors Bureau,** 453 E. 1st St. (996-1090), in the central plaza, provides info. Open daily 10am-4pm.

Greyhound: 2 per day through the valley. It stops in Napa at 9:45am and 6pm in front of Napa State Hospital, 2100 Napa-Vallejo Hwy. Also stops in Yountville, St. Helena, and Calistoga. Closest bus station: Vallejo (643-7661).

Local Buses: Napa City Bus, 1151 Pearl St. (255-7631). Provides transport throughout the valley and to Vallejo. Buses run Mon.-Sat. 5:30am-7:30pm. Fare varies: Napa to Calistoga $2, to Yountville $1, to Vallejo $1.50. Discounts available for children and seniors. In Sonoma, the **Sonoma County Transit** (576-7433 or 800-345-7433) serves the entire county. (Mon.-Fri., 3 on Sat.; $1.90, students $1.55, over 60 and disabled 95¢, under 6 free).

Car Rental: Budget, 407 Soscol Ave. (224-7845), in Napa. Must be 21 with credit card. $29 per day.

Bicycle Rental: Napa Valley Cyclery, 4080 Byway East (255-3377), in Napa. Bicycles $4 per hr., $20 per day, $70 per week. Tandem bikes $28 per day. Major credit card required for deposit. Open Mon.-Sat. 9am-6pm, Sun. 10am-5pm; in winter Sun. hours are 10am-4pm.

Taxi: Taxi Cabernet (963-2620), in St. Helena. $2 per mi.

Police: 1539 First St. (253-4451).

Post Office: 1625 Trancas St. (255-1621). Open Mon.-Fri. 8:30am-5pm. **ZIP Code:** 94558. **Sonoma,** 617 Broadway (996-2459), at Patten St. Open Mon.-Fri. 8:30am-5pm. **ZIP Code:** 95476. **Area Code:** 707.

Rte. 29 runs through the middle of Napa valley from **Napa** at its southern end, to **Calistoga** in the north, passing **St. Helena** and **Yountville** in between. Napa is 25 min. from Sonoma on Rte. 12. The best way to see Napa is by **bicycle** since the valley is dead flat and only 30 mi. long. The Sonoma Valley runs between **Sonoma** in the south and **Glen Ellen** in the north, with **Rte. 12** traversing its length.

ACCOMMODATIONS AND CAMPING

Bed and breakfasts, and most hotels, are a budget breaking $55-225 per night. A few resorts have rooms under $40, but they go fast and are inaccessible without a car. If you do have a car, it's better to stay in Santa Rosa, Sonoma, or Petaluma. Without a reservation or a car, plan on camping; there are many excellent sites.

Triple S Ranch, 4600 Mountain Home Ranch Rd. (942-6730). Beautiful setting in the mountains above Calistoga. Take Rte. 29 toward Calistoga, and turn left past downtown, onto Petrified Forest Rd. Light, woodsy cabins. The best deal in the valley. Pool, restaurant, and bar. Check-in 3pm. Check-out noon. Singles $37. Doubles $49. $7 per additional person. Call in advance. Open April-Dec. 31.

Silverado Motel, 500 Silverado Trail (253-0892), in Napa near Soscol Ave. Clean, fresh, newly remodeled rooms with kitchenette and cable TV. Registration noon-6pm. Check-out 11am. Singles $40-45. Doubles $40-48.

Motel 6, 5135 Montero Way (664-9090), in Petaluma. Take the Old Redwood/Petaluma Blvd. exit off U.S. 101. Small pool. Singles $30. $6 per additional person.

Sugarloaf Ridge State Park, 2605 Adobe Canyon Rd. (833-5712), near Kenwood. 50 sites. By far the most beautiful place to camp in Sonoma Valley. Pretty views and open field for frisbee. Drive carefully up the mountain road. Flush toilets, running water, no showers. Sites $14. Call MISTIX (800-444-7275) to reserve.

Napa County Fairgrounds, 1435 Oak St. (942-5111), in Calistoga. First-come, first-camped. Shaded sites, with showers and electricity. $15 covers 2 adults. Closed June 28-July 5 for county fair. Check-out noon. Open 24 hrs.

FOOD

Sit-down meals are often expensive, but Napa and its neighboring communities support numerous delis where you can buy inexpensive picnic supplies. The **Sonoma Market,** 520 W. Napa St. (996-0563), in the Sonoma Valley Center, is an old-fashioned grocery store with deli sandwiches ($3-4.25) and very fresh produce.

Villa Corona Panaderia-Tortilleña, 3614 Bel Aire Plaza (257-8685), in Napa. Off of Trancas, behind Citibank, in an alley. Impressive selection of Mexican beers. Large burrito with the works $4.35. Open Mon.-Sat. 9am-8pm, Sun. 8am-8pm.

Taylor's Refresher (963-3486), on Rte. 29 across from the Merryvale Winery, near the heart of the wine country. A burger stand with vegetarian and traditional burgers, Mexican dishes, and ice-cream. Outdoor seating. Open daily 11am-8pm.

Quinley's, 310 D St. at Petaluma Blvd. (778-6000), in Sonoma. Newly remodeled burger counter first opened its doors in 1952. Listen to '50s tunes and enjoy your meal outdoors. Open daily 11am-9pm.

WINERIES

Napa Valley is home to the wine country's heavyweights; vineyards include national names such as Inglenook, Christian Brothers, and Mondavi. There are more than 250 wineries in Napa County, nearly two-thirds of which are in Napa Valley. Many wineries now charge for wine tastings, but free tours and tastings are still available. The fee is usually small ($3-6), and includes a tour with three or four tastes. Sonoma Valley's wineries are less tourist-ridden and offer more free tasting than those in Napa. The majority of smaller wineries require that visitors phone ahead. You must be 21 or older to purchase or drink alcohol, which includes tastings at vineyards.

Robert Mondavi Winery, 7801 St. Helena Hwy. (963-9611), 8 mi. north of Napa in Oakville. Spanish-style buildings, beautiful grounds. The best free tour with tasting for the completely unknowledgeable, and the wine itself is decent. Tours 10am-4pm on the hour. Reservations required. You should call ahead; they fill fast, especially in the summer. Open daily 10:30am-5pm; Oct.-April 11am-4:30pm.

Domaine Chandon, 1 California Dr. (944-2280), in Yountville. One of the finest tours in the valley. Owned by Moët Chandon of France, this is the place to learn the secrets of making sparkling wine. 45-min. tours hourly 11am-5pm. Tastings by the glass ($3-5; includes bread and cheese) or by the bottle in the restaurant. Open daily 11am-6pm; Nov.-April Wed.-Sun. 11am-6pm.

Sterling Vineyards, 1111 Dunaweal Lane (942-3345), in Calistoga, 6 mi. north of St. Helena (go right on Dunaweal from Rte. 29N). Perhaps the most visually arresting of the valley's vineyards. Mounted on top of a small hill, surrounded by vines, with a view of the valley below. Aerial tram to vineyard, tour, and tasting $6. Open daily 10:30am-4:30pm.

Beringer Vineyards, 2000 Main St. (963-7115), off Rte. 29 in St. Helena. One of the more popular vineyards. Free tours include Rhine House, a landmark mansion, and a tasting session. In summer, the tours are a mob scene. Try the reserve room on the second floor of the Rhine House. Generous samples in the reserve room cost $2-3. Open daily 9:30am-6pm; winter 9:30am-5pm.

Sebastiani, 389 E. 4th St. (938-5532), a few blocks from the northwest corner of Sonoma's central plaza. This giant mass-producer draws 250,000 visitors per year, and is a perfect place to get an introduction to the noble drink. Interesting 20-min. tour of the aging rooms. Free tasting and tours daily 10am-5pm.

Ravenswood, 18701 Gehricke Rd. (938-1960), off Lovall Valley Rd., in Sonoma. Produces some of the valley's best *vino,* strongly recommended by the locals. The picnic area and the view alone are worth the trip. Summer weekend BBQs ($4.75-8.75); free tasting and tours by appointment. Open daily 10am-4:30pm.

CALIFORNIA

■■■ THE SAN MATEO COAST

Route 1, the **Pacific Coast Highway** winds along the San Mateo County Coast south from San Francisco to the Big Basin Redwoods State Park. Charming old towns like Half Moon Bay, San Gregorio, and Pescadero, complete with family-run country stores, complement the secluded and beautiful beaches. Although most people find it too cold for swimming (even in summer), the sands offer a royal stroll along the water's edge. State beaches charge $4, with admission valid for the entire day at all state parks—keep your receipt. About 2 mi. south of Pacifica (take samTrans bus #1L) is **Gray Whale Cove State Beach,** a privately owned nudist beach off Rte. 1. You must be 18 and pay $5 to join the fun (but where do you keep your ID?).

At the **San Mateo County Coast Convention and Visitors Center,** Seabreeze Plaza, 111 Anza Blvd., #410 (800-288-4748), in Burlingame, ask for other pamphlets besides those on display. (Open Mon.-Fri. 8:30am-5pm.) **San Mateo County Transit (samTrans),** 945 California Dr. (800-660-4287), has service from Burlingame (adjacent to San Francisco) to Half Moon Bay. (Fare 85¢, seniors 25¢, ages 5-17 35¢. Operates daily 6am-7pm. San Mateo's **area code:** 415.

The fishing and farming hamlet of **San Gregorio** rests 10 mi. south of Half Moon Bay. Walk to its southern end of **San Gregorio Beach** to find little caves in the shore rocks, and a stream warm enough to swim in. (Open 8am-sunset.) **Unsigned Turnout, Marker 27.35** is an undeveloped beach off Rte. 1. A few decades ago locals of **Pescadero** created the **olallieberry** (oh-la-la-BEHR-ree) by crossing a blackberry, a loganberry, and a youngberry. Pick a pint at **Phipp's Ranch,** 2700 Pescadero Rd. (879-0787; open mid-June-Aug. 1 10am-7pm.) The **Pescadero Marsh** shelters various migratory birds including the blue heron, often seen poised in search of fish.

Año Nuevo State Reserve (379-0595), 7 mi. south of Pigeon Point and 27 mi. south of Half Moon Bay, is the mating place of the 18-ft.-long **elephant seal.** December to April is breeding season, when males compete for beach space next to the females. It is not unusual for 2000 seals to crowd on the beach together. To see this unforgettable show (Dec. 15-Mar. 31), you must make reservations (8 weeks in advance recommended) by calling MISTIX (800-444-7275). Tickets go on sale November 15 and are generally sold out by the end of the month. (2½-hr. guided tours, $2 per person, 8am-sunset). samTrans (348-7325) runs a special shuttle bus from December-March From April to November the reserve is open and free (parking $4). You will need a hiking permit from the park ranger, however. Arrive before mid-August to catch the last of the "molters" and the young who've yet to find their sea-legs. Don't get too close—they may be fat but they're fast, and mothers are intolerant of strangers who appear to threaten their young. The beach is always cold and windy, so dress warmly. (Open daily 8am-6pm; last permits issued 4pm.)

An absolutely breathtaking hostel which is an attraction itself is the **Pigeon Point Lighthouse Hostel (HI-AYH)** (879-0633), 6 mi. south of Pescadero on the highway and 20 mi. south of Half Moon Bay, near the second-tallest lighthouse on the West Coast. This 50-bed hostel operates a hot tub in the old lightkeeper's quarters. (Check-in 4:30-9:30pm. Curfew 11pm. Check-out and chores completed by 9:30am. Lock-out 9:30am-4:30pm. $9-11, nonmembers $12-14.) **Point Montara Lighthouse Hostel (HI-AYH)** (728-7177), is a wholesome 45-bed facility on windswept Lighthouse Point 25 mi. south of San Francisco, 4 mi. north of Half Moon Bay. There's a samTrans stop one block north at 14th St. and Rte. 1 (#1C, 1L, 90H). They have two kitchens and laundry facilites. Bikes and hot tubs ($5 per hr.) for rent. (Check-in 4:30-9:30pm. Curfew 11pm-7am. $9, nonmembers $12. $5 extra for couple's room. Reservations recommended for weekends, group and private rooms.

3 Amigos, 200 N. Cabrillo Hwy. (Rte. 1), at Kelly Ave. (726-6080). Nearly everyone in the area wholeheartedly recommends the savory Mexican fare. (Open daily 9am-midnight.) **Ketch Joanne Fish Market & Captain's Deck** (728-7850), at Pillar Point Harbor, serves great seafood. they will also smoke what you catch for $2 per lb. (Open Mon.-Thurs. 11am-5pm, Fri.-Sun. 11am-9pm.)

NORTHERN CALIFORNIA

■■■ AVENUE OF THE GIANTS

About 6 mi. north of **Garberville** off U.S. 101, the **Avenue of the Giants** winds its way through a 31-mi.-long canopy of the largest living creatures this side of sea level. The tops of the mammoth trees cannot be seen from inside a car—pull over and get out of your car to avoid straining your neck, wrecking your vehicle, and looking ridiculous. A slow meander through the forest is the best way to experience the redwoods' grandeur. The less crowded trails are found in the Northern Section of the park around **Rockefeller Forest,** which contains the largest grove of old-growth redwoods (200 years plus) in the world. You should be sure to pay your respects to the **Dyerville Giant,** located in the redwood graveyard at Founder's Grove, about midway through the Avenue of the Giants. The Dyerville Giant rests on its side, over 60 human body-lengths long. Leggett, 16 mi. south of Garberville, is home of the **Drive-Thru-Tree.** This 315-ft. redwood has a 21-ft. base which you can drive through ($3). The **Garberville Chamber of Commerce,** 733 Redwood Dr. (923-2613; open daily 10am-6pm), will supply you with a free list of businesses on the Avenue. The **Eel River Redwoods Hostel,** 70400 U.S. 101 (925-6469)—16 mi. south on U.S. 101 in Leggett—is *the* place to hang your hat. This hosteling wonderland is located in an aromatic redwood grove right on the South Fork Eel River and provides access to a sauna, a jacuzzi, and a swimming hole (complete with inner tubes). If you're traveling by bus, ask the driver to stop at the hostel or get off at **Standish Hickey State Park;** the hostel is a ½-mi. walk north from there. ($12, nonmembers $14.)

■■■ REDWOOD NATIONAL PARK

Redwood National Park encompasses some of California's most impressive trees. A visitor cannot help but be awed by the towering giants and the astounding biodiversity they help to support. Steinbeck called the redwoods "ambassadors from another time." Elk and black bears roam the Prairie Creek area as whales swim by the coast (migrating southward Nov.-Jan. and returning March-May), and birds are everywhere. The park begins just south of the Oregon border and extends down the coast for almost 40 mi., encompassing three state parks while avoiding the tiny coastal towns which cling to Rte. 101. The region is famous for its fishing, and the variegated terrain is ideal for hikers and backpackers. The lack of public transportation within the park, however, requires extreme perseverance from those without cars. The ideal time to visit is mid-April to mid-June or September to mid-October. The park is less crowded during these months and is free of summer fog. Call MISTIX (800-365-2267) for camping reservations, essential in the summer.

The park divides into five segments (Orick, Prairie Creek, Klamath, Crescent City, and Hiouchi) ranging north to south along U.S. 101. **Crescent City,** with park headquarters and a few basic services, stands at the park's northern end. Klamath serves the middle. The small town of **Orick** is situated at the southern limit and harbors an extremely helpful ranger station, a state park headquarters, and a handful of motels. Rte. 101 connects the two, traversing most of the park.

PRACTICAL INFORMATION

Emergency: 911.

Visitors Information: Redwood National Park Headquarters and Information Center, 1111 2nd St., Crescent City 95531 (464-6101). Open daily 8am-5pm. Headquarters of the entire national park, but the ranger stations are just as well-informed. **Redwood Information Center** (488-3461), on U.S. 101, 1 mi. south of Orick. **Crescent City Chamber of Commerce,** 1001 Front St., Crescent City (464-3174) provides plenty of information. Open Mon.-Fri. 8am-7pm, Sat.-Sun. 9am-5pm; Labor Day-Memorial Day Mon.-Fri. 9am-5pm.

Greyhound: 1125 Northcrest Dr. (464-2807), in Crescent City. 2 buses per day headed north and 2 going south. Open Mon.-Fri. 7-10am and 5-7pm, Sat. 7-10am and 6:30-7:30pm.Buses can supposedly be flagged down at 3 places within the park: at the **Shoreline Deli** (488-5761), 1 mi. south of Orick on U.S. 101; at **Paul's Cannery** in Klamath on U.S. 101; and in front of the **Redwood Hostel**.

Post Office: 751 2nd St. (464-2151), in **Crescent City.** Open Mon.-Fri. 8:30am-5pm, Sat. noon-3pm. **ZIP Code:** 95531. Open Mon.-Fri. 8:30am-noon, 1-5pm.

Park Activity Information: 464-6101 (recorded information, 24 hrs.) Also tune in at **1610 AM** on your radio in Hiouchi and Orick areas.

Area Code: 707.

ACCOMMODATIONS

The most pleasant roost is the **Redwood Youth Hostel (HI-AYH),** 14480 U.S. 101, Klamath 95548 (482-8265), at Wilson Creek Rd. This hostel combines ultramodern facilities with a certain ruggedness. ($1.25 per load, free for passing cyclists). Affording a spectacular view of the ocean and an ideal location, the hostel asks that you take your shoes off when you're inside the building. (Check-in 4:30-9:30pm. Curfew 11pm. Closed 9:30am-4:30pm, so you'll have to be an early riser. $10, under 18 with parent $5. Linen $1.50.0) Reservations are recommended, and must be made by mail 3 weeks in advance. See Sights for info about park campgrounds.

SIGHTS

You can see Redwood National Park in just over an hour by car, but there's no reason to. Get out and stroll around or do not come at all—the redwoods should be experienced in person, not through tempered glass windows. The National Park Service conducts a symphony of organized activities for all ages. Pick up a detailed list of Junior Ranger programs and nature walks at any of the park's ranger stations (see Practical Information, page 777). From Memorial Day to Labor Day, the Jedediah Smith, Mill Creek, and Prairie Creek Campfire Centers all host nightly campfires and sing-alongs. Roving Rangers cruise the park's popular areas from 11am to 3pm in season to answer questions and tell stories. If you're lucky, you may bump into Jeff and Christie, two wonderfully helpful and entertaining rangers. Call the **Redwood Information Center** (488-3461) for details on park programs. Most activities are described in a seasonal newsletter, the *Redwood Visitor Guide,* available throughout the park. There's also an excellent booklet ($1.50) which details all trails in both the national and state parks, but the rangers can supply you with information about the trails most suited to your preferences free of charge.

Orick Area

This region covers the southernmost section of the park. Its **visitors center** lies about 1 mi. south of Orick on U.S. 101 and ½ mi. south of the Shoreline Deli (the Greyhound bus stop). The main attraction is the **tall trees grove,** a 2½-mi. trail which begins 6 mi. from the ranger station. If you're driving, you'll need a permit; only 35 per day are issued on a first-come, first-served basis until 2pm. A minimum of three to four hours should be allowed for the trip. A **shuttle bus** ($7 donation per person) runs from the station to the tall trees trail (June 13-Sept. 7, 2 per day; May 23-June 12 and Sept. 8-20, 1 per day). From there, it's a 1.3-mi. hike down (about 30 min.) to the tallest redwoods in the park and, in fact, to the **tallest known tree in the world** (367.8 ft., one-third the height of the World Trade Center.)

   Orick itself (pop. 650) is a friendly town, overrun with souvenir stores selling "burl sculptures" (wood carvings pleasing to neither eye nor wallet). The rampant commercialism of the small town contrasts sharply with the surrounding natural beauty. Along U.S. 101 are some motels, a **post office,** and the reasonably-priced **Orick Market** (488-3225; open daily from 8am to 7pm and delivers groceries to Prairie Creek Campground at 7:30pm daily. Phone in your order before 6pm; minimum order $10; delivery free). The **Park Woods Motel,** 121440 Rte. 101 (488-5175), has singles and doubles for $35, and a two-bedroom unit with full kitchen is only $40.

Prairie Creek and Klamath Areas

The Prairie Creek Area, equipped with a **ranger station** and **state park campgrounds,** is perfect for hikers, who can experience 75 mi. of trails in the park's 14,000 acres. The **James Irvine Trail** (4.5 mi. one way) starts at the Prairie Creek Visitors Center and winds through magnificent redwoods, around clear and cold creeks, past numerous elk, through **Fern Canyon** (famed for its 50-ft. fern walls and crystalline creek), and by a stretch of the Pacific Ocean (wear shoes that you don't mind getting wet). The **Elk Prairie Trail** (1.4 mi. one way) skirts the prairie and can be made into a loop by hooking up with the nature trail. (Elk may look peaceful, but they are best left unapproached.)

There are three **campgrounds** in Prairie Creek; make reservations through (MIS-TIX 800-365-2267). **Elk Prairie** allows RVs and has hookups, hot showers, flush toilets, and drinking water. **Gold Bluffs Beach** does not allow RVs (cars are okay), but has all the same amenities except the showers are solar, making hot water conspicuously finite. Both sites are $14. **Butler Creek,** an isolated, primitive campground without amenities (sites $3), is a 2-mi. hike from Fern Canyon.

In Klamath, **Camp Marigold,** 16101 U.S. 101 (482-3585 or 800-621-8513) has well-kept, woodsy cabins with kitchenettes ($34) and is the cleanest and safest place after the Redwood Hostel. There is no ranger station here.

Crescent City Area

Crescent City calls itself the city "where the Redwoods meet the Sea." In 1964, it met the sea for real, when a *tsunami* caused by oceanic quakes brought 500mph winds and leveled the city. Nine blocks into the town, the powerful wave was still two stories high. Today the rebuilt city offers an outstanding location from which to explore the National Park. The **Crescent City Visitors Center,** in the Chamber of Commerce at 1001 Front St. (464-3174), has lots of brochures (open Mon.-Fri. 8am-7pm, Sat.-Sun. 9am-5pm; Labor Day-Memorial Day Mon.-Fri. 9am-5pm). Seven mi. south of the city lies the Del Norte Coast Redwoods State Park's **Mill Creek Campground** (464-9533), a state-level extension of the Redwood Forest. (Sites $14, hiker/biker $3, day use $5.) **El Patio,** 655 H St. (464-5114), offers decent rooms with an early '70s look for a modest price. Some rooms have kitchenettes; all have TVs. (Singles $24.20, doubles $30.80; $2 key deposit.) Crescent City is loaded with inexpensive restaurants. Your craving for buffalo meat can be satisfied at **Three Feathers Fry Bread,** 451 U.S. 101 (464-6003). These lean, tasty burgers will set you back $6. Forego the fries in favor of delicious, authentic fry bread $1.50. (Open daily 11am-7pm.) **Torero's,** 200 U.S. 101 (464-5712), dishes out filling, flavorful Mexican food (entrees $4-8). (Open Sun.-Thurs. 11am-8:30pm, Fri.-Sat. 11am-9:30pm).

Hiouchi Area

This inland region sits in the northern part of the park along Rte. 199 and contains several excellent hiking trails. The **Stout Grove Trail** can be found by traveling 2 mi. north of Jedediah State Park on U.S. 101, and then 3 mi. along South Fork Rd., which becomes Douglas Park Dr. It's an easy ½-mi. walk, passing the park's widest redwood, (18 ft. in diameter). The path is also accessible to people with disabilities; call 458-3310 for arrangements. Just 2 mi. south of the Jedediah State Park on U.S. 101 lies the **Simpson-Reed Trail.** A tour map (25¢ from the rangers station) will guide you on this pleasant trek. **Kayak** trips on the Smith River leave from the ranger station. The four-hour trip covers some challenging rapids. (2 trips daily Wed.-Sun. at 9am, approx. dates June 17-Aug. 2. Low water may force premature cancellation of the program. $6, ages under 10 not allowed.) Participants must weigh under 220 lbs. and be able to swim. Make reservations at the rangers station (see Practical Information, page 777). The **Howland Hill Road** skirts the Smith River as it travels through redwood groves. The scenic stretch of road (no RVs or trailers allowed) begins near the Redwood Forest information center and ends at Crescent City.

Six Rivers National Forest and the corresponding recreation area lie directly east of Hiouchi. The Smith River rushes through rocky gorges as it winds its way from the mountains to the coast. This last "wild and scenic" river in California is the state's only major undammed river. Consequently, its cool, clear water flows extraordinarily fast and provides excellent salmon, trout, and steelhead fishing.

■■■ SACRAMENTO VALLEY

The Sacramento Valley is the California that few know. Right in the middle of the state, visitors will pass through the Valley on I-80 or I-5. The pace of life is considerably slower than along the coast and tourists are scarce. Thus, except in Sacramento, residents wake up early and are quiet by nightfall. The state capital is worth a visit only if you're into early California history and state government. Chico, Red Bluff, and Redding are useful as bases for exploring the nearby marvels of the Lassen National Forest, Mt. Shasta, and the Lava Beds.

Sacramento (pop. 385,000) is located at the center of the Sacramento Valley, and is the indistinctive capital of a highly distinctive state. Although it's the seventh largest city in California, Sacramento has a small-town U.S.A. feel. Five major highways converge on the city: **I-5** and **Rte. 99** run north-south, **I-80** runs east-west between San Francisco and Reno, and **U.S. 50** and **Rte. 16** bring traffic from the Gold Country into the capital. Worth seeing in Sacramento are: Old Sacramento, the California State Railway Museum, the Crocker Art Museum, the State Capitol, the Old Governor's Mansion, and Sutter's Fort. For accommodations and sights info, contact the **Sacramento Convention and Visitors Bureau,** 1421 K St. (916-264-7777).A drive 20 min. west of Sacramento will bring you to **Davis,** a quaint town with 45,000 bicycles, a branch of the University of California, wonderful public transportation—and not much else. Don't come out of your way to go to small-town **Chico,** but beneath the quiet surface lurks Chico State, formerly the nation's foremost party school. The university in the eastern section of town fuels a dynamic party scene on weekends.

Lassen Volcanic National Park is accessible by **Rte. 36** from Red Bluff to the south, and **Rte. 44** from Redding to the north. In 1914, the earth radiated destruction as tremors, lava flows, black dust, and a series of enormous eruptions continued over several months, climaxing in 1915 when Lassen sneezed a 7-mi.-high cloud of ashes. Lassen is less crowded than neighboring parks and is therefore an excellent destination for serious hikers seeking solitude amidst the forests and mountains. Visitor info is available at the **Lassen Volcanic National Park Headquarters,** in Mineral (595-4444).

Mt. Shasta is located 60 mi. north of Redding on **I-5** and about 50 mi. west of Lassen Volcanic National Park. For centuries, residents of this part of the world have believed that Mt. Shasta (14,162 ft.) possesses mystical powers. The Shasta Indians worshipped a Great Spirit whom they believe created the snow-capped volcano as her own permanent residence. If you are skeptical of the mountain's communicative abilities, sit a spell on Shasta's isolated, majestic, and snow-capped slopes—few travelers leave unconvinced. **Shasta-Trinity National Forest Service,** 204 W. Alma St. (926-4511 or 926-4596, TDD 926-4512), 1½ blocks across the railroad tracks from the intersection of Mt. Shasta Blvd. and Alma St., has visitor information.

Lava Beds National Park has two entrances, both located off Rte. 139 south of the farming community of **Tulelake** (TOO-lee-lake). The southeast entrance (25 mi. south of town) is closer to the visitors center. Beneath the unpromising surface of the park lies a complex network of lava-formed caves and tunnels unlike anything else on earth. Cool, quiet, and often eerie, caves created by the lava range from 18-in. crawl spaces to 80-ft. awe-inspiring cathedrals. While Lava Beds' landscape lacks the drama of the Sierra Nevada or the Pacific coast, its unique formations have a special appeal. Pick up free maps from the well-informed staff at **Lava Beds Visitors Center,** 30 mi. south of Tulelake on Rte. 139 (667-2282).

■■■ GOLD COUNTRY

In 1848 California was a rural backwater of only 15,000 people. The same year, saw-mill operator James Marshall wrote in his diary: "This day some kind of met-tle...found in the tailrace...looks like goald." In the next four years some 90,000 people from around the world headed for California and the 120 mi. of gold-rich seams called the Mother Lode. Ultimately, California's gilded terrain proved most profitable to the merchants who outfitted the miners. Five years later, the panning gold was gone. Today the towns of Gold Country make their money mining the tourist traffic. These "Gold Rush Towns," solicit tourists traveling along the appro-priately numbered **Rte. 49,** which runs through the foothills, connecting dozens of small Gold Country settlements. If you tire of Gold Country lore, don't despair. Vine-yards, river rafting, and cave exploring are popular and don't involve the "g-word".

Unsuspecting **Calaveras County** turned out to be sitting on a literal gold mine—the richest part of the Mother Lode—when the big rush hit. Over 550,000 pounds of gold were pulled out of the county's earth. Calaveras County hops with small towns. **Angels Camp,** at the juncture of Rtes. 49 and 4, is the county hub and (not very big) population center. Throughout the rest of the county are **Alteville, Cop-peropolis, Sheep Ranch, San Andreas,** and other small towns. Just south of Angels Camp is **Tuttletown,** Mark Twain's one-time home, now little more than an historic marker and a grocery store. **Mokelumne Hill,** 7 mi. north of San Andreas, is a ghost story town—this town's modern claim to fame is an affinity for spooky tales. Spirited minstrels haunt the **Leger Bar** on Main St. along Rte. 49 (286-1401).

About 20 mi. due east of Angels Camp lies **Calaveras Big Trees State Park** (795-3840; open dawn-dusk; day use $5). Here the *Sequoiadendron giganteum* (Giant Sequoia) reigns over all. These magnificent trees aren't as huge as those on the coast, but they do reach heights of 325 ft.

The ravines and hillsides now known as **Sonora** were once the domain of the Mi-wok Indians, but the arrival of the gold rushers changed this section of the Sierra foothills into a bustling mining camp. Sonora can make a good rest stop between Lake Tahoe and Yosemite. However, travelers faced with a choice between Cala-veras County and Sonora-Columbia may want to opt for the former, because of its proximity to Stanislaus National Forest, caves, and wineries. The **visitors center** in Sonora (800-446-1333 or 533-4420) has guides to Columbia State Park.

Columbia State Park (532-0150) dedicates itself to the whole-hearted practice of thinly veiled artifice. The "miners" here peel off their beards at night, the out-house is nailed shut, and the horse and buggy carriage spend the nights in a nearby parking lot. Visitors to the park can pan for gold and peer into the town's numerous historical buildings as part of the "living history" environment. Entrance to the park and the mining museum (532-4301) within is free.

Stanislaus National Forest is 900,000 acres of forests of Ponderosa pines and wildflower meadows, well-maintained roads and campsites, craggy peaks, and doz-ens of cool aquamarine lakes. Here, peregrine falcons, bald eagles, mountain lions, and bears sometimes surprise the lucky traveler. Stanislaus remains popular as a place to camp when cousin Yosemite is full. **Park headquarters** are at 19777 Greenly Rd. (532-3671; open summer 8am-5pm, call for winter hours). No camping permit is required.

Every gold miner's life was rough, but none had it rougher than those who worked the **northern half** of the Mother Lode. Here, granite peaks kept a rigid grip on the nuggets, while merciless winters punished persistent miners for their efforts. Today, the small towns of the Northern Gold Country are far removed from the less authentic "Main Street" scenes of the Southern Gold Country, and the natural beauty of this region handsomely rewards exploration. The miniature towns of **Downieville, Sierra City, Forest City,** and **Alleghany** are remnants of the Northern Gold Country's past and do little to cater to tourists; depending on your point of view, they may be either appealingly or discouragingly rural. In friendly relaxed **Downieville,** the **Downieville Bakery** vends delicious breads and pastries. The basics are available at the **Downieville Grocery Store** (289-3596) on Main St. The **Downieville Motor Inn** (289-3243) and its kindly management provide simple, cozy accommodations. (Singles and doubles $36.)

SIERRA NEVADA

The Sierra Nevada is the highest, steepest, and most physically stunning mountain range in the contiguous United States. Thrust skyward 400 million years ago by plate tectonics and shaped by erosion, glaciers, and volcanoes, this enormous hunk of granite stretches 450 mi. north from the Mojave Desert to Lake Almanor. The heart-stopping sheerness of Yosemite's rock walls, the craggy alpine scenery of Kings Canyon and Sequoia National Parks, and the abrupt drop of the Eastern Slope into Owens Valley are unparalleled sights.

Temperatures in the Sierra Nevada are as diverse as the terrain. Even in the summer, overnight lows can dip into the 20s. Check local weather reports. Normally, only U.S. 50 and I-80 are kept open during the snow season. Exact dates vary from year to year, so check with a ranger station for local road conditions, especially from October through June. Come summer, protection from the high elevations' ultraviolet rays is necessary; always bring sunscreen, and a hat is a good idea.

■■■ YOSEMITE NATIONAL PARK

In 1868 a young Scotsman named John Muir arrived by boat in San Francisco and asked for directions to "anywhere that's wild." He was pointed toward the Sierra Nevada. The natural wonders that awaited Muir inspired him to a lifetime of conservationism. In 1880 he succeeded in securing national park status for Yosemite. Today, few of the park's 3.5 million annual visitors know of his efforts, but most leave with an appreciation and love for Yosemite's awe-inspiring granite cliffs, thunderous waterfalls, lush meadows, rock monoliths, and thick pine forests. The park covers 1189 sq. mi. of mountainous terrain. **El Capitán, Half Dome,** and **Yosemite Falls** lie in the Yosemite Valley, an area carved out by glaciers over thousands of years. Once you've seen these main attractions, though, head out to the other parts of the park. **Little Yosemite Valley,** accessible by hiking trails, offers two spectacular waterfalls: **Vernal** and **Nevada Falls. Tuolumne Meadows** (pronounced ta-WALL-um-ee) in the northeastern corner of the park is an Elysian expanse of alpine meadows surrounded by granite cliffs and rushing streams. **Mariposa Grove** is a forest of giant sequoia trees at the park's southern end.

PRACTICAL INFORMATION

Emergency: 911; park rangers can be found throughout the park.

Visitors Information: A map of the park and a copy of the informative *Yosemite Guide* are available for free at visitors centers. Wilderness **permits** are available at all visitors centers. All hours listed are valid mid-May-mid-Sept., unless otherwise noted; call for off-season hours. **General Park Information,** 372-0265; 24-hr. recorded information 372-0200. Open Mon.-Fri. 9am-5pm. **Campground information:** 372-0200 (recorded). **Yosemite Valley Visitors Center,** Yosemite Village (372-0229). Open daily 8am-8pm; winter 8am-5pm.

Park Admission: $3 if you enter on foot, bicycle, or bus. $5 for 7-day vehicle pass.

Park Transportation: See below.

Delaware North Co. Room Reservations, 5410 E. Home, Fresno 93727 (252-4848, TTY users 255-8345).

Equipment Rental: Yosemite Mountaineering School (372-1224), Rte. 120 at Tuolumne Meadows. Open daily 8:30am-5pm.

Post Office: Yosemite Village, next to visitors center. Open Mon.-Fri. 8:30am-5pm; Sept.-May Mon.-Fri. 8:30am-12:30pm and 1:30-5pm. **ZIP Code:** 95389.

Area code: 209.

Yosemite lies 200 mi. due east of San Francisco and 320 mi. northeast of Los Angeles. It can be reached by taking **Rte. 140** from Merced, **Rte. 41** north from Fresno, and **Rte. 120** east from Manteca or west from Lee Vining. Of the five major park approaches, Rte. 120 to the Big Oak Flat entrance is most challenging to the stability of your stomach. The easiest route from the west is Rte. 140 into Yosemite Valley.

Yosemite runs public **buses** that connect the park with Merced, Fresno, and Lee Vining. In Merced, **Yosemite VIA,** 300 Grogan Ave., (742-5211 or 800-VIA-LINE, 842-5463), makes two round-trips per day from the Amtrak station to Yosemite ($15, round-trip $28; discount for seniors). **Yosemite Transportation System (YTS)** connects the park with Greyhound in Lee Vining (July through Labor Day; 372-1240; one way $20.25). You need to buy your ticket on the bus. A comfortable free **shuttle bus** runs through the valley daily at 10-min. intervals from 7:30am to 10pm. Although crowded, the buses have broad viewing windows.

ACCOMMODATIONS, CAMPING, AND FOOD

Lodgings in Yosemite Valley are monopolized by the Delaware North Company and range from simple canvas tent cabins to the luxurious Ahwahnee Hotel. Restaurants in Yosemite are expensive and dreary. Bring your own food for a campfire feast. Overpriced groceries are available from the **Yosemite Lodge, Wawona,** or the **Village Stores** (open daily 8am-10pm; Oct.-May 8am-9pm).

All lodgings have access to dining and laundry facilities, showers, and supplies. Reservations (252-4848) required for all park lodgings, some as far as a year in advance. Camping is the best (and cheapest) way to experience Yosemite. Reservations to Yosemite Valley's drive-in campgrounds are required April to November; call MISTIX (800-365-2267) up to eight weeks ahead. Or show up at the **Campground reservations office** in Curry Village at 9am or 4pm to catch a cancellation.

Yosemite Lodge, in Yosemite Valley west of Yosemite Village. Small, spruce, sparsely furnished cabins under surveillance by deer. To catch cancellations, inquire before 4pm. Singles and doubles $48, with bath $63.

Curry Village, southeast of Yosemite Village. The flashing neon sign heralds the crowded camp area. Back-to-back cabins are noisy but clean. Ice cream and pizza only a minute away. $48, with bath $63. Canvas-sided cabins $38.

Backpacker's Camp, 1½ mi. east of Yosemite Village across the river, behind North Pine Campground. Must have a wilderness permit and be a backpacker without a vehicle to camp here. Unadvertised. Low on facilities, high on camaraderie. Fishing is popular. Running water, toilets, and showers nearby. 2-night max. stay. $3 per person. Open May-Oct.

Sunnyside, at the west end of Yosemite Valley past the Yosemite Lodge Chevron station. A walk to the climber's camp, called **Camp 4** by regulars. Water, toilets, and tables. $3 per person. Often fills up early with visitors without reservations.

Wawona, Rte. 41 in the southern end of the park. 100 sites beautified by tables, toilets, and water. No showers. Sites $10.

White Wolf, off Rte. 120 E. Water, toilets, tables, fire pits. Pets allowed. 87 sites. $10 per site. Open June-mid-Sept.

Porcupine Flat, off Rte. 120 E. RV access to front section only. Pit toilets, potable stream water. 52 sites. $6 per site. Open June-Oct.

Hodgdon Meadow, on Rte. 120 near Big Oak Flat entrance. Suitable for winter camping or for finding solitude year-round. Water, tables, and toilets. Sites $12.

Lower Pines, in the busy eastern end of Yosemite Valley. Slick, commercial, and crowded, the campground has toilets, water, showers, and tables. Sites $14. This is the designated **winter camping** spot.

SIGHTS AND THE OUTDOORS

By Car or Bike You can see a large part of Yosemite from the bucket seat. The *Yosemite Road Guide* ($3.25 at every visitors center) is keyed to the roadside markers, and outlines a superb tour of the park—it's almost like having a ranger tied to the hood. The drive along **Tioga Road** (Rte. 120 E) presents one panorama after another. Driving west from the Pass brings you to **Tuolumne Meadows** and its open, alpine spaces, shimmering **Tenaya Lake,** and innumerable scenic views of granite slopes and canyons. A drive into the heart of the valley leads to thunderous 2425-ft. **Yosemite Falls** (the highest in North America), **Sentinel Rock,** and **Half Dome.**

For a different perspective on the valley, drive to **Glacier Point,** off Glacier Point Rd. Hovering 3214 ft. above the valley floor, this gripping overlook is guaranteed to impress the most jaded of travelers. Half Dome rests majestically across the valley, and the sight and sound of **Vernal Falls** and **Nevada Falls** punctuate the silence.

Walk among the giant sequoias at **Mariposa Grove,** off Rte. 41. The short hiking trail begins at the **Fallen Monarch,** a massive trunk lying on its side, and continues to the 209-ft., 2700-year-old **Grizzly Giant,** and the fallen **Wawona Tunnel Tree.** Ancient Athens was in its glory when many of these trees were saplings.

Bicyclists can pick up a brochure which indicates the safest roads at the visitors center. Roads are fairly flat near the villages, more demanding farther afield. Those near **Mirror Lake,** open only to hikers and bikers, guarantee a very good ride, and the valley roads, filled with traffic, are easily circumvented by the bike paths. Make bike inquiries at Yosemite Lodge (372-1208) or Curry Village (372-1200).

Day Hiking in the Valley Experience Yosemite the way it was meant to be and travel on foot, even if just for a day. Day-use trails are usually fairly busy, crowded, and occasionally (July 4th) the site of human traffic jams. A colorful trail map with difficulty ratings and average hiking times is available at the visitors center for 50¢. **Swimming** is allowed in the park except where posted. Misty **Bridalveil Falls** is an easy ¼-mi. walk from the shuttle bus stop. The **Mirror Lake Loop** is a level, 3-mi. walk to the glassy lake, which is slowly silting up to become a meadow. These trails, as well as pretty **Lower Yosemite Falls,** are wheelchair accessible.

One of the most popular trails in Yosemite begins at **Happy Isles.** From this point, you can trek 211-mi. and reach Mt. Whitney via the John Muir Trail, but you might prefer the 1½-mi. **Mist Trail** past Vernal Falls to the top of Nevada Falls, a steep and strenuous climb up hundreds of tiny stairs. Take the **free shuttle** from the valley campgrounds to Happy Isles; there is no parking available. The Mist Trail continues to the base of **Half Dome,** a monolithic testament to the power of glaciation.

The wildflower-laden **Pohon Trail** starts from Glacier Point, crossing Sentinel River (spectacular Sentinel Falls, the park's second largest cascade, lies to the north) on its way to Taft Point and other secluded lookouts. For a taste of "real" rock-climbing without requisite equipment and training, Yosemite day hikers scramble up **Lembert Dome** above Tuolumne Meadows.

The world's greatest climbers come to Yosemite to test themselves at angles past vertical. If you've got the courage (and the cash), you can join the stellar Yosemite rock climbers by taking a lesson with the **Yosemite Mountaineering School** (372-1335; Sept.-May 372-1244; open 8:30am-5pm). The basic **rock-climbing classes,** offered daily in mid-April to September, teach you the basics, then take you 80 ft. up a cliff to learn bouldering and rappelling ($48 plus $6 for rock shoes rental)

BEYOND YOSEMITE VALLEY: BACKCOUNTRY

Some folks never leave the valley, but a wilder, lonelier Yosemite awaits those who do. The visitors center has day-hike fliers for areas outside Yosemite Valley, but there are many more trails than shown on the map. Preparation is key before an backcountry adventure. Plan ahead and obtain a **topographical map** of the region you plan to explore, (learn to read it) and plan your route. **Backcountry camping** is prohibited in the valley (you'll get slapped with a stiff fine if caught), but it's generally permitted along the high-country trails with a free **wilderness permit** (call 372-0310). Each trailhead limits the number of permits available. Reserve by mail between March 1 and May 31 (write Wilderness Office, P.O. Box 577, Yosemite National Park 95389), or take your chances with the 50% quota held on 24-hr. notice at the Yosemite Valley Visitors Center, the Wawona Ranger Station, and Big

Oak Flat Station. Popular trails like **Little Yosemite Valley, Clouds Rest,** and **Half Dome** fill their quotas regularly. To receive a permit, you must show a "planned" itinerary. Many hikers stay at the undeveloped mountain campgrounds in the high country for the **bear lockers,** used for storing food. Hikers can use plastic **canisters,** which may be mandatory on more popular hiking routes in 1995. Check with rangers. By keeping bears away from human food, you're protecting the bear more than the food—bears who forage for human food are frequently shot. There are five High Sierra walk-in campsites; ask the Wilderness Office.

A free shuttle bus to **Tuolumne Meadows** will deposit you at the heads of several trails. **Lembert Dome** has a trail to its peak that is ideal for inexperienced hikers eager to test their skills. The **Pacific Crest Trail** follows a series of awe-inspiring canyons. South Yosemite is home to the **Giant Sequoia and Mariposa Grove,** the park's largest. Some of these trails continue as far as Washington State.

■■■ MONO LAKE

As fresh water from streams and springs drains into the "inland sea" of Mono Lake (MOE-no) it evaporates, leaving behind a mineral-rich,13-mi. wide expanse that Mark Twain called "the Dead Sea of the West." Although Mono supports no fish, brine flies and shrimp provide a buffet for migratory birds. The lake derives its moon-like appearance from remarkable towers of calcium carbonate called *tufa,* which form when calcium-rich freshwater springs well up in the carbonate-filled salt water. At over 700,000 years old, this extraordinary lake remains the Western Hemisphere's oldest enclosed body of water.

The town of **Lee Vining** provides the best access to Mono Lake and the ghost town of **Bodie** (see below). Lee Vining is located 70 mi. north of **Bishop** on U.S. 395 and 10 mi. west of the Tioga Pass entrance to **Yosemite.** For area information, call the **Mono Lake Visitors Center and Lee Vining Chamber of Commerce,** (647-6595 or 647-6629) on Main St. in Lee Vining, in the large orange and blue building. **Greyhound** stops in the Lee Vining Market (647-6301; 800-231-2222 for fares and routes). To: L.A. (11am, 1 per day); Reno (at 1:50am, 1 per day). Buy your ticket at the next stop; they don't sell them here. (Open daily 8am-9pm.) **Area Code:** 619.

It can be difficult to find affordable lodging and meals in Lee Vining. Explore camping and picnics as alternatives to the jaw-dropping rates at hotels and restaurants. There are six Inyo National Forest **campgrounds** ($0-8) within 15 mi. of town. Make reservations for these campgrounds well in advance with the Lee Vining District Ranger. Less than 6 mi. north of town. **Sawmill Campground** (free) and **Tioga Lake Campground** ($8) are 9000 ft. up, at the edge of Yosemite.

In 1984, Congress set aside 57,000 acres of land surrounding Mono Lake and called it the **Mono Basin National Forest Scenic Area** (647-6525). **South Tufa Grove,** 10 mi. from Lee Vining, harbors an awe-inspiring collection of calcium carbonate formations. (Take U.S. 395 south to Rte. 120, then go 4 mi. east and take the Mono Lake Tufa Reserve turn-off 1 mi. south of Tufa Grove.) The **Mono Lake Foundation** offers excellent guided canoe tours of the lake on weekends that include a crash course on Mono Lake's natural history, ecology, and conservation. Arrange tours through the visitors center ($12, ages 4-12 $6). **June Lake,** a canyon carved by glaciers and now filled with water, is 10 mi. south of Lee Vining on U.S. 395. If you have time, take the scenic loop along Rte. 158. The sparkling lake and its surrounding ring of mountains are prized as a wayward slice of the Alps. During the summer, June Lake is an angler's heaven, with brook, golden, rainbow, and brown trout stocked weekly. **Campsites** in the area are plentiful (sites $8-10; few have showers).

Tucked away in the desert, **Bodie** is a real ghost town, even if it does charge admission ($5; self-guide booklet $1). Described as "a sea of sin, lashed by the tempests of lust and passion," in 1880 the town was home to 10,000 people, 65 saloons, and one homicide per day. Today the streets and buildings are strewn with abandoned furniture, automobiles, wagons, and train engines, well-preserved by the dry climate and by the state of California. Bodie is accessible by a paved road off U.S. 395, 15 mi. north of Lee Vining, and by a dirt road from Rte. 167 out of Mono Inn. (647-6445. Ghost town open daily 9am-7pm; Labor Day-Memorial Day 9am-4pm.)

■■■ MAMMOTH LAKES

Home to one of the most popular ski resorts in the United States, the town of Mammoth Lakes is rapidly transforming itself into a giant, year-round playground. Mountain biking, rock-climbing, and hiking now complement the traditional snow-bound pursuits. The nightlife on weekends is lively, as the young and athletic locals mingle with the constant stream of visitors who come for sports and a good time.

Practical Information Mammoth Lakes is on **U.S. 395,** 160 mi. south of Reno and 40 mi. southeast of the eastern entrance to Yosemite National Park. **Rte. 203** runs through the town as **Main Street.** Stop by the the **Visitors Center and Chamber of Commerce** (934-2712 or 800-367-6572), on Main St. inside Village Center Mall West, across from the post office. Pick up the free *Mammoth Times.* Open Sat.-Thurs. 8am-6pm, Fri. 8am-8pm; winter daily 8am-6pm. **Greyhound** (213-620-1200) stops in the parking lot behind McDonald's on Main St. One bus runs daily to Reno (at 1:05am) and to L.A. (at 12:30pm). Board here and buy your ticket at the next station. Mammoth Lakes's **post office:** Main St. across from the visitors center. (934-2205; open Mon.-Fri. 8:30am-5pm); **ZIP Code:** 93546; **area code:** 619.

Accommodations and Food There are nearly 20 Inyo Forest public **campgrounds** in the area, at **Mammoth Lakes, Mammoth Village, Convict Lake,** and **Reds Meadow.** All sites have piped water. Call the Mammoth Ranger District (924-5500) for more info. Reservations are taken for all group sites ($20-$35), as well at nearby Sherwin Creek, through MISTIX (800-283-2267). For indoor lodging, check out the **Hilton Creek International Hostel (HI-AYH)** (935-4989), about 10 mi. south of town, a converted park station with 22 beds including a family room. ($10, nonmembers $13. Under 18 with parents and seniors half-price. Add $2 in winter.) Another option is the **ULLR Lodge** (934-2454); turn left from Main St. onto Minaret Rd., a ski-chalet style place with sauna and shared kitchen. Dorm-style rooms have a hall bathroom and some rooms have television and private bath ($15-58). For a bite to eat, **Angel's** (934-7427), at Main St. and Sierra, is a local favorite with great BBQ and a wide selection of beers (open Mon.-Fri. 11:30am-10pm, Sat.-Sun. 5-10pm).

After hours, revelers can be found at **Grumpy's** on 37 Old Main St. (934-8587), shooting pool until 1am on weekdays, 2am on weekends. **Whiskey Creek** (934-2555), at Main and Minaret, is open (and usually lively) until 1:30am every night.

Sights and Activities Most things in Mammoth Lakes are accessible only by car. **Devil's Postpile National Monument,** an intriguing geological oddity, was formed when lava flows oozed through Mammoth Pass thousands of years ago and then cooled to form columns 40 to 60 ft. high. A pleasant 3-mi. walk away from the center of the monument is **Rainbow Falls,** where the middle fork of the San Joaquin River drops 140 ft. past dark cliffs into a glistening green pool. From U.S. 395, the monument and its nearby bubbling **hot springs** can be reached by a 15-mi. drive past Minaret Summit on paved Rte. 203.

Although there are over 100 lakes near town (60 of them within a 5-mi. radius), not one actually goes by the name of "Mammoth Lake." The most mammoth lake in the basin, the 1-mi.-long **Lake Mary,** is popular for boating, fishing, and sailing. **Twin Lakes** is the closest lake to the village, only 3 mi. down Rte. 203. **Lake Mamie** has a picturesque picnic area, and many short hikes lead out to **Lake George,** where exposed granite sheets attract climbers.

You can ride the **Mammoth Mountain Gondola** (934-2571) during the summer for a spectacular view of the area. (Open daily 11am-3pm. Round-trip $10, children $5.) **Obsidian Dome** lies 14 mi. north of Mammoth Junction and 1 mi. west of U.S.

395 on Glass Flow Rd. (follow the sign to "Lava Flow"). Hot-air balloons, climbing walls, mountain bike paths, and even dogsled trails attract visitors to Mammoth. You can evaluate your options at the **Mammoth Adventure Connection** (800-228-4947), in the Mammoth Mountain Inn. Courageous cyclists can take the gondola to the top of **Mammoth Mountain Bike Park,** where trails start from 11,053 ft. and head straight *down* the thawed winter-time ski trails, bared to expose many, many sharp rocks. Get tickets and information at the **Mammoth Mountain Bike Center** at the base of the mountain (934-0606; $5 per day for helmet rentals, bike rental $25 for 4 hrs., $35 per 8-hr. day; open daily 9:30am-6pm).

Skiing calls in the winter. With 132 downhill runs, over 26 lifts (plus 2 gondolas), and miles of nordic skiing trails, Mammoth is one of the country's premier resorts. Mammoth Mountain lift tickets can be purchased at the **Main Lodge** at the base of the mountain on Minaret Rd. (934-2571; open Mon.-Fri. 8am-3pm, Sat.-Sun. 7:30am-3pm), at **Stormriders** at Minaret Rd. and Canyon Blvd. (open 8am-9pm daily), or at **Warming Hut II** at the end of Canyon and Lakeview Blvds. (934-0787; open Mon.-Fri. 8am-3pm, Sat.-Sun. and holidays 7:30am-3pm). A free **shuttle bus** (934-0687) transports skiers between lifts, town, and the Main Lodge. The Forest Service can provide information on the area's cross country trails.

■■■ SEQUOIA AND KINGS CANYON NATIONAL PARKS

Though they may not attract the throngs of visitors that Yellowstone, Yosemite, and the Grand Canyon do each summer, the twin parks of Kings Canyon and Sequoia can go sight-for-sight with any park in the U. S. The terrain here has been alternately tortured and healed by ambivalent nature; cool waters knit scars left by glaciers while a snowy gauze bandages mountains that have broken the skin of the earth and thrust themselves heavenward. Meadow life buzzes, blooms, and breeds in expanses that were once cleared by fire. Uncertain Sequoia saplings cower beside the stumps and felled remains of their ancestors, suggesting that even the blight left by men may someday be erased.

Glacier-covered **Kings Canyon** displays a stunning array of imposing cliffs and sparkling waterfalls. Home to the deepest canyon walls in the country, turn-outs along the roads offer breathtaking vistas into gaping near-vertical declivities. The sights of this region, like lodging and food, are organized around **Grant Grove** and **Cedar Grove.** Predictably, the two greatest attractions correspond to the names of the parks; most of the visitors are here to see the sequoia trees and breathtaking Kings River Canyon. In **Sequoia,** the Sierra Crest lifts itself to its greatest heights. Several 14,000-ft. peaks scrape the clouds along the park's eastern border, including **Mt. Whitney,** the tallest mountain in the contiguous U.S. (14,495 ft.). Facilities in Sequoia center around **Giant Forest** and **Mineral King.** Both parks contain impressive groves of massive sequoia trees in addition to a large bear population. Visitors like to cluster around the largest sequoias near the entrances to the parks; the vast backcountry remains relatively empty. **Road's End** in Kings Canyon or the **High Sierra Trail** across Sequoia offer wilderness without the crowds.

The two parks are accessible to vehicles from the west only. From Fresno follow **Rte. 180** east into the foothills; it's about 60 mi. to the entrance of **Grant Grove** section of Kings Canyon, 30 mi. more to **Cedar Grove.** This road is closed in winter. From **Visalia,** take **Rte. 198** to Sequoia. This road, which passes Lake Kaweah and runs alongside the Kaweah River, presents scenic views and turnouts. **Generals Highway** (Rte. 198) connects the Ash Mountain entrance to the **Giant Forest** in Sequoia, and continues to Grant Grove in Kings Canyon. In summer, allow two hours for the stunning yet treacherous road to **Mineral King,** which opens up southern Sequoia. From Visalia, take **Rte. 198** and turnoff 3 mi. past Three Rivers.

Practical Information The **Kings Canyon and Sequoia Main Line** (565-3341) offers 24-hr. direct contact with a park ranger in addition to dispatch service to any office within the parks. The **Parks General Information Line** is 565-3134. **Park Admission** for 7-day vehicle pass valid in both parks is $5; a 1-yr. pass valid in all national parks and monuments is $25. **Park shuttle buses** operate out of Giant Forest in Sequoia National Park and take visitors to and from Lodgepole, Moro Rock, Sherman Tree, and Crescent Meadow from 8am-5:30pm. (Single ride $1, $3 per family. Day pass $3, $6 per family.) There are many visitors centers throughout the parks. In Sequoia, try the **Foothills Visitors Center:** Three Rivers 93271 (565-3134), at the park headquarters 1 mi. beyond the Three Rivers entrance, on Rte. 198 out of Visalia. (Open daily 8am-5pm; Nov.-April 8am-4pm.) In Kings Canyon, opt for the **Grant Grove Visitors Center** (335-2856), Grant Grove Village, 2 mi. east of the Big Stump Entrance by Rte. 180. (Open daily 8am-6pm, winter 9am-5pm.) Sequoia's **post office:** in Lodgepole (open Mon.-Fri. 8am-1pm and 1:30-4pm); **ZIP code:** 93262. Kings Canyon's **post office:** in Grant Grove Village. across from the Visitors Center (open June-Sept. Mon.-Fri. 8:30am-1:30pm and 2:30-4:30pm, Sat. 8:30am-1:30pm); **ZIP code:** 93633. **Area Code:** 209.

Accomodations and Food Sequoia Guest Services, Inc. (S.G.S.), P.O. Box 789, Three Rivers, CA 93271 (561-3314), monopolizes indoor accommodations and food in the parks. **Giant Forest** and **Grant Grove** offer "rustic sleeping cabins" with canvas tops during the summer season (May-Oct.) for $32; add $6.50 for a wooden roof. Just outside of the park boundaries Kings Canyon Lodge and the Montecito-Sequoia Lodge will place a large dent in your budget. If you need electricity, for about $50, the **Best Western** and **Sierra Lodge** in Three Rivers can help. Most campgrounds are open from mid-May to October (2-week max. stay in summer).

For **camping** in Sequoia, try **Lodgepole,** 4 mi. northeast of Giant Forest Village in the heart of Sequoia National Park by Kaweah River and **Buckeye Flat,** past park headquarters, a few mi. into the park from the Ash Mountain entrance on Rte. 198, are your best bets. Lodgepole allows RVs; Buckeye Flat is cheaper, and has no RVs. (Sites $10-$12.) Reserve sites through MISTIX (800-365-2267) mid-May-mid-Sept.

In Kings Canyon, **Sunset, Azalea,** and **Crystal Springs** are within a stone's throw of Grant Grove Village but are still relatively quiet. Azalea is open year-round and is free in winter. Sunset features flat tenting spots, brilliant views of the San Joaquin Valley, and an amphitheater with daily programs. Crystal Springs is the smallest and the quietest. All have restrooms and water. (Sites $10.) **Sheep Creek, Sentinel, Canyon View,** and **Moraine,** are at the Kings River near Cedar Grove. All have restrooms and water; sites $10. Canyon View accepts reservations from organized groups only. (Very full on weekends. Access roads and campgrounds closed mid-Oct. to mid-May.)

Park food, like lodging, is monopolized by SGS. Tempting culinary alternatives lie in nearby Three Rivers. **Noisy Water Cafe** (561-4517), along Rte. 180 in Three Rivers, is nicknamed "The Home of the Hummingbirds" for the frequent visitors to the feeders out back. Unique, tasty sandwiches ($4.50-6) make this the overwhelming favorite among the townfolk. (Open daily 6am-10pm.)

SIGHTS

Giant Forest is the center of activities in Sequoia and host to one of the world's greatest concentrations of giant sequoia trees. The grove was named by John Muir, who explored the area and fought for its preservation. The tallest marvel is **General Sherman,** discovered and named in 1879 and believed to be the world's largest living thing. The tree stands 275 ft. tall and measures 102 ft. around at its base; its trunk is estimated to weigh 1385 tons. This 2700-year-old creature is at last mature, and, while still growing, gains only a millimeter in height each year. The 2-mi. **Congress Trail,** the park's most popular (and crowded) trail, boomerangs around General Sherman. Perhaps the most spectacular sight in the Giant Forest area is the view from atop **Moro Rock,** 1½ mi. from the village. A rock staircase winds ¼ mi. up this granite monolith to the top, which offers a stunning 360° view of the southern Sierras. **Crystal Cave,** 9 mi. from Giant Forest Village on Rte. 198, is one of the few caves on the western side of Sequoia open to the public. (Naturalists lead tours late June to Labor Day daily every ½-hr.; May-June and Sept. Fri.-Mon. every hour. Open 10am-3pm. $4, ages 6-12 $2. Buy tickets in advance at Lodgepole.)

The most developed portion of Kings Canyon National Park is **Grant Grove.** The **General Grant Tree,** the third-largest of the sequoias, gives the region its name. At 267.4 ft. tall, it is perhaps the most aesthetically pleasing, displaying "classic" sequoia form. Just north of the park entrance on Rte. 180 lies the **Big Stump Basin Trail,** a self-guided walk through an old logging camp. Here remain scars left by early loggers who erroneously viewed the enormous sequoia as a timber gold mine. They abandoned their efforts after unsuccessfully assailing the unyielding trees.

Hidden in the visitors center parking lot behind the post office is the steep, switchback-riddled road to **Panoramic Point.** In addition to affording fantastic views of the nearby mountains, the point serves as the trailhead for **Park Ridge Trail,** one of the prettiest in the park. One of the more secluded regions of the two parks is the **Cedar Grove** area, which rests inside the towering granite walls of Kings Canyon. The drive on Rte. 180 is scenic and mountainous. In the budding grove, explore the Kings River's banks and marvel at the depth of the canyon (8000 ft. in some spots, surpassing even the Grand Canyon). **Road's End** brings you to the **backcountry.** Foray from there on the **Rae Lakes Loop,** which traverses a sampling of the Sierra's best: glaciated canyons, gentle meadows, violent rapids, and inspiring lake vistas. Campgrounds pace the five-day trek at about 7-mi. intervals. Obtain backcountry permits at the Cedar Grove Ranger Station or the Road's End Kiosk.

In the summer, **rent horses** at Wolverton Pack Station, Grant Grove, and Cedar Grove (565-3341). **Bicycles** are not permitted on hiking trails or in the backcountry.

■■■ LAKE TAHOE

Lake Tahoe is neither one big casino nor an untamed paradise; careful planning here has balanced the natural and civilized worlds. The budget traveler's best bet is to eat cheap in **Stateline,** sleep cheap in **South Lake Tahoe,** and head to **North Lake Tahoe** to enjoy the splendor of the waves or woods. Activity in North Lake Tahoe centers around **Tahoe City,** where Western families come season after season, year after year, to enjoy the lake's extraordinary recreational and natural resources. Tahoe City is not the most economical place to find a motel in Lake Tahoe, but it is rich with campsites and excellent trails. Tahoe City also offers an alternative to casinos with an active club and bar scene.

PRACTICAL INFORMATION

Emergency: 911.

Visitors Information: South Lake Tahoe Visitors Center, 3066 U.S. 50 (541-5255), at Lion's Ave. A local map, coupons, and a lengthy directory can be found in *101 Things to Do in Lake Tahoe* (free). Open Mon.-Fri. 8:30am-5pm, Sat. 9am-4pm. **Lake Tahoe Visitor Center,** 4018 Lake Tahoe Blvd. (544-3133), near Stateline. **Visitors Bureau,** 950 North Lake Blvd. (581-6900), in Tahoe City.

Buses: Greyhound, 1098 U.S. 50 in Harrah's Hotel Casino (588-9645), by Raley's in S. Lake Tahoe. To San Francisco (5 per day, $20) and Sacramento (5 per day, $18). All rates subject to seasonal price changes. No lockers. Open daily 8am-5pm. **Tahoe Casino Express** (800-446-6128) provides shuttle service between Reno airport and casinos (8am-midnight; $15).

Tahoe Area Regional Transport (TART): 581-6365. Connects the western and northern shores from Tahoma to Incline Village. 12 buses daily 7am-6pm. Fare $1.

South Tahoe Area Ground Express (STAGE): 573-2080. 24-hr. bus service around town, service to the beach (every hr.).

Car Rental: Tahoe Rent-a-Car (544-4500), U.S. 50 at Tahoe Keys Blvd. in S. Lake Tahoe. 100 free mi. Cars from $29 per day. Must be 24.

CALIFORNIA

Bicycle Rental: Anderson's Bicycle Rental, 645 Emerald Bay Rd. (541-0500), convenient to the well-maintained west shore bike trail. Mountain bikes $6 per hr., ½-day $18, full day $22. Deposit (usually an ID) required. Open daily 8am-6:30pm, Sept.-May 9am-6:30pm.

Public Pool and Recreation Center: 1180 Rufus Allen Blvd. (542-6056), across from Campground by the Lake. $2.75, children $1.50, seniors $1.75. Weight room same price as pool. Open Mon.-Sat. 8am-8pm, Sun. 11:30am-5:30pm.

24-Hr. Hotlines: Rape Crisis, 544-4444. **Mental Health,** 573-3251. **Gamblers Anonymous,** 800-287-8670. **Alcoholics Anonymous,** 546-1126.

Post Office: Stateline Station, 1085 Park Ave. (544-6162), next to Greyhound. Open Mon.-Fri. 8:30am-5pm.

Area Code: 916 in CA, 702 in NV.

Lake Tahoe is located 118 mi. northeast of Sacramento and 35 mi. southwest of Reno. **U.S. 50, Rte. 89,** and **Rte. 28** overlap to form a ring of asphalt around the lake. The versatile Rte. 89 is also known as Lake Tahoe Blvd., W. Lake Blvd., and Emerald Bay Rd. Rte. 28 masquerades as N. Lake Blvd. and Lakeshore Dr.

ACCOMMODATIONS AND CAMPING

The strip off U.S. 50 on the California side of the border supports the bulk of Tahoe's 200 motels. Others line Park Avenue and Pioneer Trail off U.S. 50, which is quieter. The Forest Service at the visitors bureau provides info on camping. **Bayview** is the only free campground for miles (544-5994; 2-night max.; open June-Sept.). Advance reservations are essential for all sites (800-365-2267).

Edwards Lodge, (525-7207) on Tahoma along Rte. 89. 11 cabins during the summer, 7 in winter. A good option for 4-6 people, the cabins have several beds, a kitchen, a big deck, and TV. Convenient to many ski areas. Pool. Cash only. Cabins $70-85.

El Nido, 2215 Lake Tahoe Blvd. (541-2711). Pleasant and newly refurbished. TV, VCR (rent movies from the front desk for $3.50), hot tub, and casino shuttle to Stateline. Singles $35, summer and winter $45 (includes a continental breakfast).

Lake Shore Lodge, 3496 Lake Tahoe Blvd. (544-2834). Cheap during the week but beware of seasonal and weekend rate increases. TV, pool. Mon.-Thurs.: singles $20; doubles $25. Fri.-Sat.: $25; $30.

Nevada Beach (573-2600), 1 mi. from Stateline on U.S. 50. Flush toilets and drinking water. Popular with families. Sites are 100 yds. from shore. Sites $14-16.

D.L. Bliss State Park, Rte. 89 (525-7277), a few mi. west of Emerald Bay. Hot showers, blissful beach. 14-day max. 168 sites; $14, near-beach sites $19. Open June to Labor Day. Popular day-use beach. Arrive by 10am to stake your claim.

Emerald Bay State Park, Rte. 89 (541-3030), 10 mi. west of town. 14-day max. stay. 5-min.Sites $14. Day use $5, seniors $4. Open June-Labor Day.

FOOD

The casinos offer perpetual low-priced buffets, but there are restaurants along the lakeshore with reasonable prices, similar large portions, and much better food.

The Bridgetender, 30 West Lake Blvd. (583-3342), in Tahoe City. Lots of burgers. Enjoy yours on the outdoor patio and watch the Truckee River roll by.Wide range of beers on tap, festive atmosphere, and late hours make the bar a hopping night spot. Open daily 11am-10pm. Bar open until 2am.

Cantina Los Tres Hombres, Rte. 89 at 10th St. (544-1233) and Rte. 28 in Kings Beach (546-4052). $7.75 margarita pitchers (the standard flavors plus some exotic ones, kiwi, passionfruit, raspberry, etc.), free chips and salsa during happy hour (4-6pm). Dinners from $7. Lunch specials $6.Open 11am-10:30pm; bar until 1am

Firesign, 1785 W. Lake Blvd. (583-0871). The stone hearth, wood tables, and homey country-style feeling make this a popular restaurant. Out-of-the-ordinary cooking and outdoor seating. Dill and artichoke omelette, with home fries, toast, and muffin $6.50. Sandwiches $4.25. Open daily 7am-3pm.

ACTIVITIES

Lake Tahoe supports numerous beaches. On the south shore, **Pope Beach,** off Rte. 89, is wide and shaded by pines. **Nevada Beach** is close to the casinos off U.S. 50, offering a quiet place to reflect on your losses. Campsites are available. Farther along Rte. 28, you will likely see cars parked on the shoulder away from beach access roads. It's a popular custom with locals to hike down the steep, wooded hill to the secluded shores below, often leaving their clothes behind. **Zephyr Cove Beach** is a favorite spot for the younger college crowd. Magnificent **Emerald Bay** in the lake's southwest corner contains Tahoe's only island, **Fannette** (the most photographed sight in the area). No trip to Tahoe is complete without a visit to Emerald Bay. The park offers **hiking** and **biking trails** of varying difficulty, **camping,** (both open and designated), and terrain for **rock-climbing.**

Cycling is a popular area activity. The region supports numerous bike rental shops (usually lined up used-car-lot-style along the major roads). The forest service office at Taylor Creek and bike rental places can give advice on safer and often more scenic routes. Rental rates run about $5 per hour, $20 per full day. South Lake Tahoe boasts a variety of scenic trails for bikers. **Angora Ridge** (4 mi.) is a moderate trail accessible from Rte. 89 that meanders past Fallen Leaf Lake to the Angora Lakes. For serious mountain bikers, **Mr. Toad's Wild Ride** (3 mi.) is a strenuous, winding trail that climbs to 9000 ft. It can be reached from U.S. 50 or Rte. 89.

River rafting is an exciting and refreshing way to appreciate the Tahoe scenery. Unfortunately, the quality (and existence) of rafting on the American and the Truckee Rivers depends on the amount of snowfall during the preceding winter. Consequently, late spring and early summer are the best times to hit the rapids. If water levels are high, keep a look out for raft rental places along the Truckee. (Call 800-466-7238 for more information.) If California droughts continue to make conventional rafting scarce, all need not be lost. Floating around in an **inner tube** is popular with many would-be rafters. Make sure inner tubes are permitted on the body of water you select, don't go alone, and always know what lies downstream before you shove off.

In the summer, **Windsurf Tahoe** will rent you a board ($14 for first hr., $10 per additional hr.) and a wetsuit ($10 per day). You'll want to rent a wetsuit, since the average temperature of the lake remains a chilly 39°F year-round (though in the shallows it can warm up to 70°F). Most drowned bodies are never recovered, one tourist leaflet cheerfully reveals, because the cold prevents the decomposition that usually makes corpses float to the surface. **Wildlife enthusiasts** should visit the Profile Chamber near the Taylor Creek Visitors Center (see Practical Information, page 789), especially in late September and October. The creek literally turns red with tens of thousands of **salmon** swimming upstream. Several marinas rent out **fishing boats** and **paddle boats**. Stop by the Visitor Center for the latest information on fishing regulations. Licenses are available at local sporting good stores. Tahoe is a difficult lake to fish; be prepared to walk away empty-handed. If you feel the need for speed, get a group of people together and rent a **motorboat** and **water-skis** ($54 per hour) or a **jet-ski** ($45 per hour) at **Zephyr Cove** on U.S. 50 (702-588-3833). Zephyr Cove also rents out fishing boats and paddle boats. Incidentally, you're more likely to run into friendly monster "Tahoe Tessie" in gift shops than in the water.

Hiking is one of the best ways to explore the beautiful Tahoe Basin. Detailed information including trail maps is available at the visitors center. Experienced hikers may want to test their mettle on the moderate to strenuous trails on the West and the South Shores. Backcountry users must obtain a (free) **Wilderness Permit** for any hike into the Desolation Wilderness. **River rafting** is also an exciting and refreshing way to appreciate the Tahoe scenery. Keep a look out for raft rental places along the Truckee. (Call 800-466-7238 for more info.)

When the snow falls, **skiers** in Tahoe get psyched. There are approximately twenty ski resorts in the Tahoe area. The visitors center has prices and maps. Some better ski areas are: **Alpine Meadows** (800-824-6348); **Squaw Valley** (583-6985); **Northstar** (587-0257); **Heavenly** (702-586-7000); and **Ski Homeward** (525-2992).

CALIFORNIA

Hawaii

Hawaii, 2400 mi. off mainland America, is both physically and psychologically set apart from the rest of the United States. Here, as nowhere else, you will find lush vegetation, expansive beaches, towering surf, and sultry breezes. Acres of untainted tropical forest border luxurious resort areas while active volcanoes release billows of grey into the air. With no clear racial majority, Hawaii's cultural geography is as varied as that of the land and one of the most ethnically diverse regions in the world

The Hawaii chain is comprised of 132 islands, though only seven are inhabited. Honolulu resides on the island of **Oahu,** as do most of the state's residents and tourists. Oahu is the most accessible island in the chain, but as a consequence, there are few unexplored and unexploited places. The **Big Island** (officially called **Hawaii**) is famed for its Kona coffee, macadamia nuts, black sand beaches, open space and Volcanoes National Park. **Maui's** strong winds have made it one of the premier windsurfing destinations in the world, and with the windsurfers comes a hopping nightlife. Maui also boasts the historic whaling village of Lahaina, fantastic surfing, and the dormant volcanic crater of Haleakala. The green isle of **Kauai,** at the northwestern end of the inhabited islands, ranks first for sheer beauty. **Molokai,** with 6,000 inhabitants, is for the solitude-seeking traveler. The "Friendly Isle" still moves to the slow, quiet rhythms of the Pacific. On tiny **Lanai** exclusive resorts have replaced pineapples as the primary commodity. The seventh populated isle, **Niihau,** is closed to most visitors, supporting just a few hundred plantation families who still converse in the Hawaiian language. Together, the Hawaii islands present, in the words of Mark Twain, "the loveliest fleet of islands that lies anchored in any ocean."

PRACTICAL INFORMATION

Capital: Honolulu.
Hawaii Visitors Bureau, 2270 Kalakaua Ave., 7th floor, Honolulu 96815 (923-1811).The ultimate source for information on Hawaii. (Open Mon.-Fri. 8am-4:30pm.) The other islands staff offices at major towns, as listed in the appropriate sections. **Camping and Parks: Department of Land and Natural Resources,** 1151 Punchbowl St., Room 310, Honolulu 96813 (587-0301). Open Mon.-Fri. 8am-4pm. Information and permits for camping in state parks and trail maps. **National Park Service,** Prince Kuhio Federal Bldg., #6305, 300 Ala Moana Blvd., Honolulu 96850 (541-2693). Permits are given at individual park headquarters. Open Mon.-Fri. 7:30am-4pm.
Time Zone: Hawaii (6 hr. behind Eastern in spring and summer; 5 hr. otherwise).
Postal Abbreviation: HI.
Area Code: 808 for all of Hawaii.
Sales Tax: 4.167%; hotel rooms 10.167%. **Road Tax:** $2 per day for rented cars.

GETTING AROUND AND SLEEPING AROUND

From Los Angeles round-trip tickets on many major carriers start at $300. **Cheap Tickets** (947-3717 in Hawaii; 800-234-4522 on the mainland) in Honolulu, offers low fares. Regular **ferry** service exists only between Maui, Molokai, and Lanai. **Airlines** are faster, cheaper, and often offer special deals on car rentals. The major inter-island carriers, **Hawaiian** and **Aloha Airlines,** can jet you quickly (about 40 min.) from Honolulu to any of the islands. Travel agents, such as **Pali Tour and Travel, Inc.** 1300 Pali Hwy. Suite 1004, Honolulu, 96813 (533-3608), sell Hawaiian Air inter-island coupon books that are extremely convenient for island-hopping (6 flights for $312). Hawaiian Airlines also sells 5-15-day **passes** offering unlimited inter-island flights for $169-269. The **Hotel Exchange,** 1946 Ala Moana Blvd. (942-8544), sells inter-island Aloha Airlines tickets for $103. On flights, surfboards cost an extra $20.

Sands and Seaside Hotels, (800-451-6754 from the islands, 800-367-7000 from the mainland), manages some of the cheapest (and only locally owned) resort hotels

Hawaii

PACIFIC OCEAN

N ←

KAUAI

Na Pali
Coast

Kilauea
Wailua
Lihue

Waimea
Poipu

NIIHAU

OAHU

Waimea Bay
Wai-a-lua

Mākaha

La'ie
Kane-'ohe
Bay

Honolulu
Wai-kiki
Beach

Pearl
Harbor

Mauna
Loa

MOLOKAI
Kalaupapa N.P.

Kaunakakai
Garden of the Gods
Lanai City

LANAI

KAHOOLAWE

D. T. Fleming Beach Park
Hookipa Beach Park
Kaanapali
Iao Valley
State Park
Keanae
Waianapanapa
State Park
Hana
Oheo Stream (Seven Pools)
Haleakala Crater

Kahului
Kihei

Lahaina

MAUI

HAWAII
(The Big Island)

Mauna
Kea

Hilo

Waimea

Kohala Mt.

VOLCANOES
NATIONAL
PARK

Mauna
Loa

Kilauea
Caldera

Kalapana
Black Sand
Beach

Naalehu

KONA

Kailua-
Kona

Kealakekua
Bay

Hapuna Beach
Park

50 miles

50 km

Oahu

PACIFIC OCEAN

N →

10 miles

10 kilometers

5

5

KOOLAU
RANGE

La'ie

Hau-'ula

Puna-lu'u

Wai-mea

Wai-a-lua

Kai-ena
Point

Waimea Bay

Wai-a-lua

Mākaha

Nānā-kuli

WAIANAE RANGE

KOOLAU RANGE

Wahi-a-wā

Ka-mehameha Hwy

Pearl City

U.S.S. Arizona
Memorial

Pearl
Harbor
Entrance

Honolulu
Harbor

Diamond
Head

Wai-kiki Beach

Mauna-lua
Bay

Hanauma Bay
Beach Park

Wai-'alae
Beach
Park

Honolulu

KOOLAU
RANGE

Kai-lua

Wai-mānalo
Bay

Kāne-'ohe
Bay

Wai-Kāne

Wai-Kāne

($70 and up). For B&B reservations, try **B&B Hawaii** (822-7771 on Kauai; 800-733-1632 on the other islands), **B&B Honolulu (Statewide)** (595-7533; fax 595-2030), and **All Islands B&B** (800-542-0344 or 263-2342). **Camping** will save you money and bring you closer to the natural beauty. The national campgrounds on Maui and The Big Island require no permit, but they do enforce a 3-day maximum stay. Free **camping permits** are required (applicants must be at least 18 years old; available from the Dept. of State Parks in Honolulu). Camping is limited to five nights per 30 days. Sites are open Friday through Wednesday on Oahu, daily on the other islands.

> For a more in-depth understanding of Hawaii, please refer to *Let's Go: California, Including Hawaii.*

OAHU

At the time of explorer Captain Cook's landing, Oahu was untouched by the West. Oahu's importance increased as Honolulu's commercial traffic expanded and the U.S. Navy acquired exclusive rights to the inlet at Pearl Harbor. Oahu can be roughly divided into four sections. **Honolulu** is a vibrant city inhabited by native Hawaiians, Caucasians, Japanese, Chinese, Samoans, Koreans, and Filipinos, and the metropolitan heart of the island. **Waikiki Beach,** 3 mi. from downtown Honolulu, extends outward toward the volcanic crater of **Diamond Head,** the island's southernmost extremity. The **North Shore,** from Kahuku to Kaena Point, is the home of the winter swells of which surfers around the world dream. The **Windward Coast** (on the east), especially around Hanauma Bay, is rife with tropical fish and coral reefs. The **Leeward Coast** (on the west) is raw and rocky. The slopes of two now-extinct volcanic mountain ridges, **Waianae** in the west and **Koolau** in the east, run parallel from northwest to southeast and make up the bulk of Oahu's 600 square mi.

■■■ HONOLULU

Honolulu is the cultural, commercial, and political locus of Hawaii. Its industrial-strength harbor and concrete-and-glass business district attest to its status as a capital city (pop. 370,000) and major Pacific seaport. At the same time, acres of white sand beaches make it one of the world's premier tropical vacation getaways. Waikiki, the quintessential tourist haven, boasts an abundance of glitzy restaurants and nightclubs interspersed among 70,000 hotel rooms. Honolulu offers a varied nightlife and bargains are available from establishments competing fiercely for your dollar.

Practical Information Visitors information is available at the **Hawaii Visitors Bureau,** 2270 Kalakaua Ave., 7th Floor, Honolulu 96815 (923-1811). (Open Mon.-Fri. 8am-4:30pm; closed holidays.) **Buses** (848-5555) cover the entire island, but different lines start and stop running at different times. (Fare 85¢.) **Taxi: Sida,** 439 Kalewa St. (836-0011). **Car Rental: Discover Rent-a-Car** 1920 Ala Moana Blvd. (949-4767). $25 per day for drivers 21 and older. Honolulu's **post office:** Main Office, 3600 Aolele Ave. (423-3990; open Mon.-Fri. 8am-7:30pm, Sat. 8am-2:30pm); **ZIP Code:** 96813; **area code:** 808.

Honolulu International Airport is 20 min. west of downtown, off the Lunalilo Freeway (H-1). The **Nimitz Hwy.** (Rte. 92) will take you all the way to Waikiki. Buses #19 and #20, among others, go the 9 mi. to Waikiki, but you won't be able to bring your luggage unless it can fit on your lap. **Airport Motorcoach** (839-0911) offers continuous service from the airport to Waikiki and hotels ($6). 24-hr. advance return reservations are required (call 6:30am-10:30pm). **EM Tours and Transportation** (836-0210) will pick up at any time ($7).

Accommodations Honolulu, especially Waikiki, caters to affluent tourists, but there *are* bargains. Guests must show an airline ticket to stay at **Interclub Waikiki,** 2413 Kuhio Ave. (924-2636. Female or mixed dorms. Laundry, refrigerators, and outdoor grill. No curfew; reception open 24 hrs. Check-out 10am. Bunks $15; doubles $45. Key deposit $10.) Single-sex rooms and free use of snorkeling gear are available at **Hale Aloha (HI-AYH),** 2417 Prince Edward St. (926-8313), in Waikiki, 2 blocks from the beach. Take Waikiki #8 bus to Kuhio and Uluniu. (Beds guaranteed 3 nights although you might be allowed to stay longer. 24-hr. check-in. Check-out 11am. No lockout or curfew. Dorm bunks $15; doubles $35. Sleep sack rental $1. Key deposit $5. Make reservations.) Small and peaceful, though somewhat remote is **Honolulu International (HI-AYH),** 2323A Seaview Ave. (946-0591). 1½ mi. north of Waikiki. Take bus #6 from Ala Moana Shopping Center to Metcalf and University Ave. (Kitchen, locker, and clean single-sex facilities. Windows are netting; watch your belongings. Beds guaranteed for 3 nights. Reception open 7:30-10am and 5pm-midnight. Check-out 10am. Lights out 11pm; rooms locked noon-4:30pm. $12, nonmembers $15. Reservations recommended.) **Hawaiian Seaside Hostel,** 419 Seaside Ave. (924-3306), two blocks from the beach is for the international backpacker ready to party. *Overseas airline ticket or foreign passport required.* (Rooms always unlocked. Kitchen in each room. Open 24 hrs. Co-ed bunks $9.75 first night, $13 thereafter.) **B&B Pacific Hawaii,** 19 Kai Nani Place (262-6026), will book B&B rooms all over the island from $45 per couple.

Food and Nightlife The **Kapahulu, Kaimuki, Moiliili,** and **downtown** districts are all within 10 min. of Waikiki by bus, and with a good map, you can walk from one district to the next quite easily. Small Chinese and other Asian food counters serve excellent, authentic, and affordable lunches and *dim sum* all over Chinatown, especially on **Hotel Street.** A variety of ethnic restaurants, including Hawaiian, Japanese, Thai, and French, are located between the 500 and 1000 blocks of **Kapahulu Avenue. The Wave,** 1877 Kalakaua Ave. (941-0424), on the edge of Waikiki, has loud music and dancing for a mixed crowd. (Open daily 9pm-4am. Cover for live bands.) **Pink Cadillac,** 478 Ena (942-5282), is one of the few dancing options for the 18-21 set. Neo-rave and neon lights blend with hip-hop and progressive music. (Open 9pm-1:45am. Cover: under 21 $10; 21 and over $5, Fri.-Sat. $3.)

Sights **Chinatown,** found at the intersection of Nuuanu Ave. and Hotel St., is worth seeing. The **Iolani Palace** (538-1471), at King and Richard St., the only royal residence ever built in America, was first the home of King Kalakaua and his sister Queen Liliuokalani. (45-min. tours begin every 15 min. Wed.-Sat. 9am-2:15pm; $4, ages 5-12 $1, under 5 not admitted.) At the corner of Beretania and Richard St. stands Hawaii's postmodern **State Capitol,** an architectural mosaic of Hawaii's landscape (open Mon.-Fri. 9am-4pm; free). Nearby, the **Honolulu Academy of Arts,** 900 S. Beretania St. (532-8701), houses one of the finest collections of Asian art in the U.S. (Open Tues.-Sat. 10am-4:30pm, Sun. 1-5pm. Tours Tues.-Sat. 11am, Sun. 1pm. Suggested donation $4, students and seniors $2.)

On December 7, 1941 a stunned nation listened to the reports of the Japanese bombing of the U.S. Pacific Fleet in **Pearl Harbor.** Today, the **U.S.S. Arizona National Memorial** (422-2771) commemorates that event.The **visitors center** is open Monday through Sunday 7:30am to 5pm with the last commemorative program starting at 3pm. Take the #20 bus from Waikiki, the #50, 51, or 52 bus from Ala Moana, or the $2 shuttle from the major Waikiki hotels (839-0911). Tickets to the memorial are free, but two-hour-plus waits are not unusual. (Bring a book.)

Waikiki Visitors of all ages flock to the Waikiki Beach area for rest, relaxation, sun, surf, nightlife, tacky souvenirs, and romance. Originally a marshy swampland and hideaway for Hawaiian royalty, Waikiki's wetlands were drained into the Ala Canal to launch the island's tourist industry. Farthest to the east is the **Sans Souci Beach,** in front of the Kaimona Otani Hotel. The **Queen's Surf Beach,** closer to

HAWAII

downtown, attracts swimmers, skaters, and an increasing number of rollerbladers. If you seek more secluded beaches, go east on Diamond Head Rd. (a moped will do) until you hit Kahala Ave. For a break from sun and surf, hike the 1 mi. into the **Diamond Head Crater.** To get there, take bus #58 from Waikiki. Bring a flashlight to guide you through a pitch-dark section of the tunnel. The view of Waikiki is spectacular, and if you go on the right day, you might catch a rainbow arching over the U.S. military base in the center of the crater. The **Waikiki Trolley** (591-2561) stops at major sites and museums in Waikiki and downtown Honolulu. Trolley leaves the Royal Hawaiian Shopping Center every 15 min. from 8am to 4:30pm. (Day pass $15, under 11 $5; 5-day pass $25, under 11 $10.)

■■■ THE REST OF THE ISLAND

Everything on Oahu outside Honolulu is considered "the other side." In general, the farther from the city you scoot, the fewer tourists you will encounter. Concrete and glass quickly fade into pineapple and sugarcane fields sprinkled with small outlying communities. **H-2** going north traverses a fertile plateau before descending at the sugar-and-surfer town of Haleiwa on the North Shore. Well-maintained highways lead east from Haleiwa and the scenic windward coast. To the west you can only travel as far as Kaena Point, where the paved road ends and a rough, rocky trail begins. You can see the Leeward Coast by traveling west on **H-1** from Honolulu until it becomes **Farrington Highway (Rte. 93).**

A drive around the perimeter of the island can be done in five hours, but it's best to give yourself at least a full day. Start on the Windward Coast and work your way around the perimeter. To reach the southern Windward Coast, take bus #55 from Ala Moana. To see the North Shore, hop on bus #52 at Ala Moana. Both buses run every hour daily from 7am until 6pm. The **Kamehameha Hwy. (Rte. 83)** skirts most of the Windward Coast and North Shore. The drive is absolutely spectacular; if it's sunny, consider renting a convertible.

There is a smaller pool of accommodations in these less densely populated areas. Look along the Kamehameha Hwy. for "hostel" signs, but if you stay with these, remember they are not licensed. Camping can be beautiful along the coast, but unfortunately, there have been reports of violence against tourists at some campgrounds in recent years. Remember that rangers patrol the beach to roust illegal campers. Don't risk it; get a permit. There are alternatives to camping. **Backpacker's Vacation Inn and Plantation Villas,** 59-788 Kamehameha Hwy. (638-7838), ¼-mi. north of Waimea Bay, is adjacent to placid Three Table Bay and neighboring Shark's Cove. The inn caters to an international crowd of travelers and water sport enthusiasts. Plantation Village consists of cottages with bunks, bathroom, shared kitchen and laundry facilities, and color TV. (Co-ed bunks and rooms. Free use of boogieboards and snorkeling equipment. 50% discounts on some nearby sights. Bunks $16. Doubles $35-45. Summer rates $96 per week. Key deposit $20.) Another option is the **Punaluu Guest House** (293-8539), a beautiful, one-level, remote waterfront home on the northeast side of Oahu and north of Kahana Bay. The house is small and quiet. (Kitchen and TV room. Beds have sheets and pillows. $18 per night, small chore required. $10 key deposit. Contact Honolulu International for required reservations at 946-0591.)

■ WINDWARD OAHU AND HANAUMA BAY

Miles of beaches and rural towns span the 40-mi. coast, running from Laie in the north to Mokapu Point in the south; the result is the most scenic drive on the island. The Koolau Range rises out of the ocean and the highway slices through the mountains, skirting the cliffs along the sea. Farther south, Kalanianaole Hwy. wraps around a rugged 2-mi. stretch to Koko Head, the eastern boundary of Honolulu.

Fruit vendors, plate lunches, and shaved ice are plentiful on the Windward Coast. Try the **Bueno Nalo,** 41-865 Kalanianaole Hwy. (259-7186), in Waimanalo, the best restaurant for miles. Delicious Mexican meals are the specialty ($6-8). Try the absolutely incredible cheese enchiladas. (Open daily 11:30am-9pm.) **Frankie's Drive-Inn,** 41-1610 Kalanianaole Hwy. (259-7819), Waimanalo, is also worth a visit. Frankie has been serving up cheeseburgers (95¢) at this take-out since 1953. A good bet is a yummy ice cream shake. (Take-out only. Open Mon.-Sat. 9:30am-4:30pm.)

MAUI

Maui has sun, sand, waves, and more than 2 million visitors each year. The island's resort areas are crowded and the beaches and waters are filled with families on vacation. But with a little effort (and a car), one can find unspoiled stretches of sand.

Maui is like several islands in one. The **West Maui Mountains** slope down to an arid coastline of drowsy little towns (including **Kaanapali,** the resort haven). A land bridge between two ancient volcanoes supports the **Wailuku-Kahului** sprawl (pop. 63,000), as well as acres of wind-blown sugarcane. Home of the mystifying **Haleakala volcano,** the **East Mountains** contain an imperiled native ecosystem, while Paia's aggressively '60s feel foreshadows the laid-back lushness of the **Hana coast.** The island's western side is dry and mountainous. The east is a rainforest enveloped by the famous Hana Highway. A large, semi-permanent population of windsurfers provides a more youthful, laid-back alternative to Maui's tourists.

Practical Information Visitors should visit the **Visitor Information Kiosk** (877-3894), at the Kahului Airport terminal. (Open daily 6am-9pm.) **Trans Hawaiian** (877-7308) offers hourly service between Kahului Airport and the major Lahaina-Kaanapali $13; reservation is necessary only for return. Runs daily 7am-7pm on the hr. The **Lahaina Express** provides free transport between the Kaanapali Resorts and Lahaina. Get the schedule in the *Lahaina Historical Guide* (available at the tourist stands in Lahaina). **Department of Parks and Recreation,** War Memorial Gym, 1580 Kaahumanu Ave. (243-7389), between Kahului and Wailuku, has information and permits ($3) for county parks. (Open Mon.-Fri. 8am-4pm. You may have to knock on the window.) **Ferries** are an ideal way to go from Maui to Molokai and Lanai. Going by boat is more exciting and cheaper than flying. The **Maui Princess** (661-8397) runs daily from Lahaina to Kaunakakai (Molokai) at 7am and from Molokai, to Lahaina at 3:55pm. Crossing takes about 1¾ hr. and costs $25 one way. **Expeditions** (661-3756) runs daily between Lahaina and Manele, Lanai, $25 one way. **Resort Taxi** (661-5285) offers a $9 ride into Kahului or Wailuku from the airport. **Rent a car** at **VIP,** Haleakala Hwy. (877-2054), near Kahului Airport. ($25 per day.)

Maui consists of two mountains joined at an isthmus. The highways follow the shape of the island in a broken figure-eight pattern. **Rte. 30** leads to hot and dry **Lahaina** and **Kaanapali,** the major resort area. **Rte. 34** leads counterclockwise around the same loop from the isthmus to where the paved road ends at **Kapuna.** Circling the slopes of Haleakala southbound along the eastern loop, **Rte. 31** runs past **Kihei** and **Wailea. Rte. 36** winds through rainy terrain, over 54 one-lane bridges and 600 hairpin curves, to **Hana.**

Accommodations The **Banana Bungalow Hotel and International Hostel,** 310 N. Market St., Wailuku (244-5090 or 800-846-7835), is a basic hostel supercharged with youthful energy. Windsurfers and international guests will plug you into the local tourist subculture with daytrips, night trips to clubs, athletic games, dart tournaments. (TV room with A/C, VCR. Laundry. Kitchen. Airport pick-up. Bunks $15. Singles with double bed $32. Doubles $39. (Key deposit $5.) Another option is the **Northshore Inn,** 2080 Vineyard St. (242-8999), which is secure and clean. There's a fan and fridge in each room, a full kitchen, laundry, and occasional barbecues. (Hostel bunks $10. Singles $26. Doubles $35. $10 key deposit.)

Haleakala Featuring a fantastic volcanic crater, **Haleakala National Park** is open 24 hrs. and costs $4 per car for a seven-day pass. The **Park Headquarters** (572-9300; open daily 7:30am-4pm), about 1 mi. up from the entrance, provides camping **permits,** displays on Haleakala wildlife, and funky postcards. **Haleakala Visitors Center** (572-9172), near the summit, has a few exhibits on the region's geology, archaeology, and ecology, as well as one of the best views of the crater. **Haleakala Crater Campground** (572-9306), 4 mi. from Halemauu parking lot, has camping and cabins within the crater itself. The park allocates cabins by a highly competitive lottery. You must apply 3 months prior to your visit. Holua and Paliku areas also serve as campgrounds. Free camping permits are issued at park headquarters (1 mi. up from park entrance). (2-night max. stay in cabins, 3 in campgrounds.)

Hana The **Hana Coast** spans from the Keanae Peninsula to Kaupo. The **Hana Highway,** leading to the Hana coast, may be the world's most beautiful stretch of road; carved from cliff faces and valley floors, its alternate vistas of smooth sea and lush terrain are made only somewhat less enjoyable by its tortuous curves. Be prepared to spend an entire day on the trip. Wild ginger plants and fruit trees laden with mangos, guavas, and bananas perfume the air of the twisted drive.

THE BIG ISLAND

The Big Island emerged from the confluence of five major volcanoes on top of a hot spot in the Pacific Plate. Two are still active: "Long Mountain," **Mauna Loa** (13,677 ft.), and **Kilauea** (4000 ft.), home of **Halemaumau Crater.** Kilauea is currently in its 51st phase of eruption without showing any signs of exhaustion, and crowds flock daily to the island to tread on newly created earth. Although the eruptions are powerful, the volcanoes do not emit dangerous ash clouds, and the lava flow is quick only near the summit and in underground lava tubes. The towns of **Hilo** and **Kailua-Kona,** on opposite sides of the island, are the main tourist gates.

The two mountains in **Volcanoes National Park** continue to spout and grow, adding acres of new land each year. **Kilauea Caldera,** with its steaming vents, sulfur fumes, and periodic "drive-in" eruptions, is the star of the park, although the less active **Mauna Loa** and its dormant northern neighbor, **Mauna Kea,** are in some respects more amazing. Each towers nearly 14,000 ft. above sea level and drops some 16,000 ft. to the ocean floor. Mauna Loa is the largest volcano in the world, while Mauna Kea, if measured from its ocean floor base, would be the tallest mountain on earth. (Park entrance $5 per car, valid for 7 days.) At the **visitors center** in **Kilauea,** Crater Rim Rd. (967-7311; open daily 7:45am-5pm), receive bulletins of the latest volcanic activity. Trails of varying difficulty lead around Kilauea and to the summit of Mauna Loa; speak to a ranger before setting out.

Staying in the volcano area is expensive because of the limited number of hotels. From Hilo, take Rte. 11 almost to the National Park, turn right at Haunani Rd. in Volcano Village, then left on Kalani Holua Rd, 2 mi. from the visitors center, to the **Holo Holo Inn,** 19-4036 Kalani Holua Rd., (967-7950), which offers several large, clean rooms. (Bunk $15. Call after 4:30pm and reserve in advance.) **Volcano House,** in the Hawaii Volcanoes National Park 96718 (967-7321), is expensive, you can sleep on the rim of an active volcano ($79 and up). Also try the **Namakani Paio** cabins, 3 mi. behind the Volcano House in an *ohia* forest. (Check-in after 3pm. Singles or doubles $32.) In **Volcanoes National Park** (967-7311), find free campsites at **Kipuka Nene, Namakani Paio** (near Kilauea Crater), and **Kamoamoa** (on the coast)—each with shelters and fireplaces, but no wood. (7-day max. No reservations.)

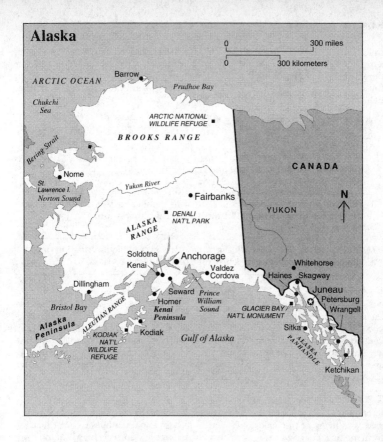

Alaska

Alaska's beauty is born of extremes. By far the largest of the 50 states, it comprises fully one-fifth of America's land mass. The 33,000-mi. coastline stretches 11 times the distance from New York to San Francisco. Nineteen Alaskan peaks reach over 14,000 ft., more than three million lakes are larger than 20 acres, and several glacial ice fields occupy areas larger than the state of Rhode Island. Alaska has the highest mountain in North America (20,320-ft.-tall Mt. McKinley in Denali National Park), the largest American National Park (13-million-acre Wrangell-St. Elias National Park), the hugest carnivore in North America (the Kodiak brown bear), and the greatest collection of bald eagles in the world. At the height of summer, Alaska becomes the "Land of the Midnight Sun," where you can play softball at 2am; in the depths of winter it is land of the noonday moon, where shimmering curtains of spectral color—the *aurora borealis*—dance like smoke in the darkened midday sky.

Alaska's history, like the state itself, is larger than life. The first humans to colonize North America crossed the Bering Strait into Alaska via a now-sunken land bridge. Russian-sponsored Danish navigator Vitus Bering was the first European to arrive, bringing in his wake a wave of Russian fur traders who exhausted the fur supply within a century. In 1867, when Secretary of State James Seward negotiated the United States's acquisition of the territory from Russia for a trifling $7,200,000 (about 2¢ per acre). He became the laughingstock of the nation—the purchase was

ALASKA

called "Seward's Folly,"—but within 20 years Alaska showed its worth by revealing a mother lode of gold ore. In 1968, long after the gold rush had slowed to a trickle, the state's fortunes rebounded yet again, with the discovery of "black gold" (oil) on the shore of the Arctic Ocean. By 1981, $7,200,000 worth of crude oil flowed from the Arctic oil field every four-and-a-half hours.

PRACTICAL INFORMATION

Capital: Juneau.
Alaska Division of Tourism, 33 Willoughby St. (465-2010). Mailing address: P.O. Box 110801, Juneau 99811-0801. Open Mon.-Fri. 8am-5pm. **Alaska State Division of Parks,** 3601 C St., Anchorage 99510 (762-2617). Open Mon.-Fri. 8am-4:30pm. **United States Forest Service,** 1675 C. St., Anchorage, AK 99501-5198 (271-4126). General info on parks and reserves. Open Mon.-Fri. 8am-5pm.
Time Zones: Alaska (most of the state; 4 hr. behind Eastern); Aleutian-Hawaii (Aleutian Islands; 6 hr. behind Eastern). **Postal Abbreviation:** AK
Sales Tax: 0%

> *Let's Go: Alaska & The Pacific Northwest* has invaluable information on the Aleutians, the Interior, the Alaskan West Coast, and Arctic Alaska.

CLIMATE

No single climatic zone covers the whole state. Fairbanks, Tok, and the Bush frequently enjoy 95°F hot spells, receiving less than eight inches of precipitation annually. The Interior freezes with -50°F temperatures in winter. Farther south, the climate is milder and rainier. Cordova rusts with 167 inches of precipitation annually. Anchorage and other coastal towns in the southcentral are blessed with the Japanese Current, which has a moderating effect on the climate. Average temperatures for Anchorage range from 13°F in January to 57°F in July.

TRAVEL

Driving in Alaska is not for the faint of heart. Roads reach only a quarter of the state's area, and many of the major ones remain in deplorable condition. "Frost heaves" from melting and contracting permafrost cause dips and surreal "twists" in the road. Radiators and headlights should be protected from flying rocks with wire screens, and a fully functioning spare tire and a good set of shocks are essential. Winter can actually offer a smoother ride. At the same time, the danger of avalanches and ice is cause for major concern. Anyone venturing onto Alaska's roads should own a copy of *The Milepost,* available for $10 from Vernon Publications, Inc., 300 Northrup Way, #200, Bellevue, WA 98004 (800-726-4707).

Given Alaska's size, **air travel** is often a necessity, albeit an exorbitantly expensive one (the hourly rate exceeds $100). Several intrastate airlines, almost exclusively based at the Anchorage airport, transport passengers and cargo virtually to every village in Alaska: **Alaska Airlines** (to larger Bush towns and Cordova; 800-426-5292); **Mark Air** (to larger Bush towns, Kodiak, and the Aleutians; 800-426-6784); **ERA Aviation** (southcentral; 243-6633); **Southcentral Air** (southcentral; 243-2761); **Reeve Aleutian Airways** (Aleutians; 243-4700); and **Ryan Air Service** (practically anywhere in the Bush; 561-2090). Many other charters and flight-seeing services are available. Write **Ketchum Air Service Inc.,** P.O. Box 190588, Anchorage 99519 (243-5525), on the North Shore of Lake Hood, to ask about their charters. One-day flights and overnight or weekend trips to isolated lakes, mountains, and tundra usually range from $165 up.

AlaskaPass offers unlimited access to Alaska's railroad, ferry, and bus systems; a 15-day pass sells for $569, a 30-day pass for $799. The pass extends from Bellingham, WA to Dutch Harbor on the Aleutian Islands, and is a good deal for those who want to see a lot of Alaska in a short amount of time. Call 800-248-7598 for details.

■■■ KETCHIKAN

"People don't tan in Ketchikan," according to a local proverb, "they rust." Fourteen feet of rain per year explain the ubiquitous awnings projecting over the streets. Cradled at the base of Deer Mountain, Ketchikan is also the first stopping point in Alaska for northbound cruise ships and ferries, which disgorge loads of tourists and dump hordes of students in search of the summer bucks offered at the canneries.

Practical Information The **Ketchikan Visitors Bureau,** 131 Front St. (225-6166 or 800-770-3300), on the cruise ship docks downtown, offers a **map** of a good walking tour (open Mon.-Fri. 7:30am-4:30pm, Sat.-Sun. depending on cruise ship arrival times). The **U.S. Forest Service,** Ranger District Office, Federal Building at 648 Mission St. (225-3101), offers informative packets on hiking and paddling in Misty Fjords and the Ketchikan area (free). (Open in summer Mon.-Fri. 7:30am-4:30pm, Sat.-Sun. 8am-4:30pm; closed weekends in off-season.) Ketchikan's **airport** is located across from the city on Gravina island. A small ferry runs from the airport to just above the state ferry dock ($3). **Alaska Airlines** (225-2141 or 800-426-0333) provides flight information from Ketchikan. Daily flights to Juneau are $124. (Open Mon.-Fri. 9:30am-5pm.) Ketchikan's **post office:** (225-9601) is next to the ferry terminal (open Mon.-Fri. 8:30am-5pm); **ZIP code:** 99901; **area code:** 907.

Accommodations and Food Besides hostels, rooms here are relatively expensive. The **Ketchikan Bed and Breakfast Network,** Box 3213, Ketchikan 99901 (225-8550), provides rooms from $65-75. **Ketchikan Youth Hostel (HI-AYH),** P.O. Box 8515 (225-3319), is at Main and Grant St. in the basement of the First Methodist Church. Although there are no beds, 4-in.-thick foam mats on the floor are comfortable if you have a sleeping bag. Clean kitchen, common area, 2 showers, tea, and coffee. (Lockout 9am-6pm. Lights out at 10:30pm, on at 7am. Curfew 11pm. Call ahead if arriving on a late ferry. $7, nonmembers $10. 3-day max. stay subject to availability. Open June 1-Sept. 1. No reservations.) If you plan in advance, camping provides an escape from Ketchikan's high prices. **Ketchikan Ranger District** (225-2148) runs the **Signal Creek Campground** 6 mi. north on Tongass Hwy. from the ferry terminal, which has 25 units on the shores of Ward Lake with water and pit toilets (sites $5; open in summer). The supermarket most convenient to downtown is **Tatsuda's,** 633 Stedman (225-4125), at Deermount St., just beyond the Thomas Basin (open daily 7am-11pm). The **5 Star Cafe,** 5 Creek St. (247-7827), has salads and sandwiches for $5-10 (open Mon.-Wed. 8am-5pm, Thurs.-Sat. 8am-8pm, Sun. 8am-8pm).

SIGHTS AND THE OUTDOORS

Fortune-seeking prospectors turned Ketchikan into a mining boom-town, and some of this history is preserved on **Creek Street,** once a thriving red-light district where sailors and salmon went upstream to spawn. Creek St. itself is a wooden boardwalk on pilings lined with shops along Ketchikan Creek; there is no actual street. Older women in black fishnets and red-tasseled silk still beckon passersby into **Dolly's House,** 24 Creek St. (225-6329), a former-brothel-turned-museum. Countless antiques from the 1920s and 30s are set amidst bawdy colors and secret caches. Hours vary with cruise ship arrivals; call ahead ($2.50).

Also on the walking tour is the **Totem Heritage Center,** 601 Deermount St. (225-5900), the largest collection of authentic totem poles in the world. The center houses 33 well-preserved totem poles from Tlingit, Haida, and Tsimshian villages, composing the largest collection of authentic totem poles in the U.S. (Open daily 8am-5pm. $2, under 18 free, Sun. afternoon free.) Across the creek, at the **Deer Mountain Fish Hatchery** (225-6760), a self-guided tour explains artificial salmon sex. (Open daily 8am-4:30pm. Free.) The **Tongass Historical Museum** (225-5600), on Dock St., explains the town's historical pastiche of Native Americans, rain, salmon, and prostitutes. (Open mid-May-Sept. daily 8am-5pm. $2, under 13 free;

ALASKA

Sun. afternoon free.) Under the same roof as the museum, the **Ketchikan Library,** overlooking a waterfall and rapids, is the best place to pass a rainy day (open Mon. and Wed. 10am-8pm; Tues., Thurs., Fri.-Sat. 10am-6pm, Sun. 1-5pm). A free **funicular** ascends the street slope behind Creek St. near the library. Enjoy the amazing **view** of the harbor from the top of the Westmark Hotel.

Some of the finest ancient and contemporary totems inhabit Ketchikan and the surrounding area. Pick up the guided walking totem tour at the visitors bureau. World-renowned totem carver Nathan Jackson lives here; his work stands in front of the Federal Building. If you can see only one thing in Ketchikan, visit the best and largest totem park in the world—the **Saxman Native Village,** 2½ mi. southwest of Ketchikan on Tongass Hwy. ($8 by cab), including an open studio where artisans carve new totems. (Open daily 9am-5pm.) Also, 13½ mi. north of Ketchikan on Tongass Hwy. is **Totem Bight,** featuring 13 totems. Entry to both parks is free; visitors are welcome during daylight hours.

A good day-hike from Ketchikan is 3001-ft. **Deer Mountain** (10-mi. roundtrip). Walk on Fair St. up the hill towards the town dump; the trail branches off left just behind the dump. A steep but manageable ascent leads 2 mi. up the mountain and above treeline along a sometimes steep-sided ridge. **Blue Lake,** an alpine pond stocked with trout, lies at the middle of the walk.

Many of the boats and planes continually buzzing through Ketchikan's harbor travel to nearby **Misty Fjords National Monument.** Only 20 mi. from Ketchikan, this region of narrow waterways and old-growth forests, home to both whales and mountain goats, invites hikers and kayakers to play in a small state-sized wilderness.

■■■ JUNEAU

The only state capital in the nation inaccessible by road, Juneau was not founded for the convenience of the location but instead for the lucrative mining that once occurred here. In 1880, Tlingit Chief Kowee led Joe Juneau and Richard Harris to the gleaming "mother lode" in the hills up Gold Creek. Within 25 years, Juneau replaced Sitka as capital of the Alaska territory. Today, this tiny strip of land at the base of imposing Mt. Juneau offers jumbled architecture and a wharf-side tourist mecca, which have garnered it the nickname "Little San Francisco."

Practical Information Emergency is 911. **Davis Log Cabin,** 134 3rd St., Juneau 99801 (586-2284 or 586-2201, fax 586-6304), at Seward St., is the visitors center (open Mon.-Fri. 8:30am-5pm, Sat.-Sun. 9am-5pm; Oct.-May Mon.-Fri. 8:30am-5pm). **Forest and National Park Services,** 101 Egan Dr. (586-8751), in Centennial Hall, provides info on hiking and fishing in the area (open daily 8am-5pm; winter Mon.-Fri. 8am-5pm). **Juneau International Airport,** 9 mi. north of Juneau on Glacier Hwy., is serviced by Alaska Air, Delta, and local charters. **Alaska Marine Highway,** 1591 Glacier Ave., P.O. Box 25535, Juneau 99802-5535 (800-642-0066 or 465-3941, fax 277-4829), has ferries that dock at the Auke Bay terminal 14 mi. from the city on the Glacier Hwy. Call **MGT Ferry Express** (789-5460) from 6-8pm to reserve a ride from any major hotel to the airport or ferry for $5. Also offers a 2½-hr. guided tour of Mendenhall Glacier ($12.50). Juneau's **post office:** 709 W. 9th St. (586-7138; open Mon.-Fri. 8:30am-5pm, Sat. 1-3pm); **ZIP code:** 99801; **area code:** 907.

Accommodations and Food If you can't get into Juneau's hostel, the **Alaska Bed and Breakfast Association,** P.O. Box 3/6500 #169, Juneau 99802 (586-2959), provides info on rooms. **Juneau International Hostel (HI-AYH),** 614 Harris St. (586-9559), at 6th atop a steep hill, is a spotless, highly efficient hostel. (Kitchen available 7-8:30am and 5-10:30pm; common area, smoking area. Chores assigned. 48 beds. Will store packs during the day. Free showers, laundry (wash $1.25, dry 75¢), small charges for sheets, towels, soap, and detergent. (3-day max. stay if beds are full. Lockout 9am-5pm. The 11pm curfew is not negotiable. Beds $10. Popular; make reservations by May for expected stays in July and Aug.) For sleeping under the stars, try the **Mendenhall Lake Campground,** Montana Creek Rd. Take Glacier Hwy. north 9 mi. to Mendenhall Loop Rd.; continue 3½ mi. and take the right fork. If asked, the bus driver will let you off within walking distance (2 mi.) of camp (7am-10:30pm only). (60 sites. Fireplaces, water, pit toilet, picnic tables, free firewood. 14-day max. stay. Sites $5. Call the Forest Service in Juneau at 907-586-8800, or reserve for an extra $7.50 by calling 800-280-2267.) **Auke Village Campground,** on Glacier Hwy., 15 mi. from Juneau, has 12 sites near a scenic beach, 1.5 mi. west of ferry terminal. (Fireplaces, water, flush toilets, picnic tables.) Call the Forest Service, Juneau Ranger District (907-586-8800) for information. (No reservations. 14-day max. stay. Sites $5.)

Fresh fish is the key food in Juneau. Seafood lovers haunt **Merchants Wharf,** next to Marine Park. **Fiddlehead Restaurant and Bakery,** 429 W Willoughby Ave. (586-3150), a half block from the State Museum, lures mobs with its beef, salads, seafood, exquisite desserts, and fresh Alaskan sourdough. (Open daily 6-10pm; Sun.-Thurs. 11:30am-2pm.) The **Fireweed Room** upstairs has weekend jazz throughout the summer. (Open daily 6:30-10pm.) Buy groceries at the **Foodland Supermarket,** 631 Willoughby Ave. (586-3101) will ship food anywhere (open daily 7am-9pm).

Sights The **Alaska State Museum,** 395 Whittier St. (465-2901), leads you through the history, ecology, and cultures of Alaska's four major indigenous groups (Tlingit, Athabascan, Aleut, and Inuit). (Open Mon.-Fri. 9am-6pm, Sat.-Sun. 10am-6pm; Sept. 18-May 17 Tues.-Sat. 10am-4pm. $2, seniors and students free.) Check out the gold-onion-domed 1894 **St. Nicholas Russian Orthodox Church** on 5th St. between N. Franklin and Gold St. Services, held Sat. at 6am and Sun. at 10am, are conducted in English, Old Slavonic, and Tlingit. Tours are open to the public ($1 donation requested; open daily 9am-5pm). The **House of Wickersham,** 213 7th St. (586-9001), was home to one of the Alaska's founding fathers, Judge James Wickersham. As a U.S. District Court judge, Wickersham steamed and sledded around Alaska from Fort Yukon to the Aleutian Islands. His contributions to the state include founding the Alaska Railroad, establishing the University of Alaska, and pushing for statehood as early as 1917 (open May-Sept. Sun.-Fri. noon-5pm; free).

Juneau is a top hiking center in southeast Alaska. **Perseverance Trail,** which leads past the ruins of the **Silverbowl Basin Mine** behind Mt. Roberts and to waterfalls, makes for a pleasant day's trek. Pick up a free **map** from the Forest Service office. To reach this trailhead, follow Gold St. uphill until it turns into Basin Rd.

In winter, the slopes of the **Eaglecrest Ski Area,** 155 S. Seward St., Juneau 99801, on Douglas Island, offer decent **alpine skiing** (586-5284 or 586-5330; $24 per day, children grades 7-12 $17, up to 6th grade $12; rental of skis, poles, and boots $20, children $14). In the summer, the Eaglecrest "Alpine Summer" trail is a good way to soak in the mountain scenery of virtually untouched Douglas Island.

The 38 glaciers of the **Juneau Icefield** cover an area larger than Rhode Island. The most visited glacier is the **Mendenhall Glacier,** about 10 mi. north of downtown Juneau. The **Glacier Visitors Center** (789-0097), will explain everything about the glacier (open daily late May-mid Sept. 8:30am-5:30pm). The rangers also give an interesting walking tour Sun.-Fri. at 9:30am, beginning from the flagpole. The best view of the glacier is from the 3½-mi. **West Glacier Trail.** If pressed for time, the 3½-mi. **East Glacier Loop Trail** affords a way to catch a side view of the glacier.

■■■ ANCHORAGE

Only 80 years ago, cartographers wasted no ink on what is now Alaska's major metropolis, located in southcentral Alaska. Approximately half the state's popula-tion lives in "Los Anchorage," the term that some rural residents use to mock the city's urban pretensions. More than merely a decentralized jumble of fast-food joints and liquor stores, Anchorage supports semi-professional baseball and basketball teams, performances by internationally known orchestras and music stars, theater, and opera. Although moose and bear not only occasionally wander downtown but are hunted legally within the municipality, this is as close to "big city" as Alaska gets.

Practical Information Emergency is 911. The **Log Cabin Visitor Informa-tion Center,** W. 4th Ave. (274-3531), at F St., has plenty of **maps** and brochures (open daily 7:30am-7pm; May and Sept. 9am-6pm; Oct.-April 9am-4pm). The **Alaska International Airport,** P.O. Box 190649-VG, Anchorage 99519-0649 (266-2525), is serviced by 8 international carriers and 3 Alaskan carriers, including **Reeve Aleu-tian, Pen Air,** and **Era.** Nearly every airport in Alaska can be reached from Anchor-age, either directly or through Fairbanks. **Alaska Railroad,** 411 W. 1st Ave., Anchorage 99510-7500 (265-2494; 800-544-0552 out of state), runs to Denali ($88), Fairbanks ($125), and Seward ($50). (In winter, 1 per week to Fairbanks; no service to Seward.) A summertime "flag-stop" runs to Anchorage and Hurricane (a stop between Talkeetna and Denali) on Sat. and Sun. ($88). For more info write to Pas-senger Service, P.O. Box 107500, Anchorage. (Office open daily 6am-10pm; ticket sales Mon.-Fri. 5:30am-5:30pm, Sat. 5:30am-4pm, Sun. 5:30am-2:30pm.)

Alaska Backpacker Shuttle (344-8775) has van service to towns and trailheads in the vicinity. Buses into Denali ($35, $60 round trip, $5 bike). Leaves daily from the youth hostel at 8am. Buses also go to: Talkeetna ($30), Girdwood ($15), Portage Train Station ($17.50), and trailheads north and south of Anchorage ($5-10 depend-ing on distance). Call to arrange pick-up. **Moon Bay Express** (274-6454) goes to Denali (1 per day, $35, $60 round-trip, $10 bike). Pickup is at Anchorage Youth Hos-tel at 8am. **Fireweed Express** (452-0521) runs to Denali ($25, $45 round-trip, $5 bike). Several pickups, including the visitors center. Call for reservations. **Homer and Seward Bus Lines** (800-478-8280) buses to Seward (1 per day, $30) and Homer (1 per day, $38). Leaves from the Alaskan Samovar Inn, 720 Gambell St. **Alaskon Express** (800-544-2206) heads to Valdez ($59, leaves daily at 8am), Haines ($194, leaves Sun., Tues., and Fri. at 7am), and Fairbanks ($109, leaves Sun., Tues., and Fri. at 7am). **Alaska Direct** (277-6652) goes to Whitehorse, YT (Mon., Wed., and Sat. at 6am, $145). **Alaska Marine Highway,** 333 W. 4th St. (272-4482), in the Post Office Mall, sells ferry tickets and reservations (open Mon.-Fri. 8am-4:30pm). **Affordable Car Rental,** 4707 Spenard Rd. (243-3370), rents cars across from the Regal Alaskan Hotel ($24 per day, 40 free mi., 30¢ each additional mi.) or try **Budget** (243-0150). ($39 per day, unlimited mileage.) For both, must be at least 21 with major credit card. Both are at the **airport.** Ask about a free drop-off and pick-up downtown. For **road conditions,** call 243-7675. Anchorage's **post office:** W. 4th Ave. and C St. (279-3062), is in the lower level in the mall (open Mon.-Fri. 10am-5:30pm, Sat. 10am-4pm); **ZIP Code:** 99510; **area code:** 907.

From its seat 114 mi. north of Seward on the Seward Hwy., 304 mi. west of Valdez on the Glenn and Richardson Hwy., and 358 mi. south of Fairbanks on the George Parks Hwy., Anchorage is the hub of Southcentral Alaska. The **downtown area** of Anchorage is laid out in a grid. Numbered avenues run east-west, and addresses are designated East or West from **C Street.** North-south streets are lettered alphabeti-cally west of **A Street,** and named alphabetically east of A Street. The rest of Anchor-age spreads out—*way* out—along the major highways.

Accommodations, Camping, and Food Although Anchorage is blessed with affordable lodgings, few are downtown. The best option is the **Anchorage International Youth Hostel (HI-AYH),** 700 H St. (276-3635), at 7th, 1 block south of the Transit Center downtown. (3 kitchens, 2 balconies, and scads of info on trav-eling throughout the state. Family and couple rooms available. Frequently filled in summer; write ahead for reservations. Bring a sleeping bag. Lockout noon-5pm. Cur-few midnight; watchman can check you in until 3am. 4-day max. stay in summer. $12, nonmembers $15; photo ID required. Weekly and monthly rates during the off-season.) The quiet, family-run **International Backpackers Inn,** 3601 Peterkin (274-3870 or 272-0297), at Mumford, has 45 dorm-style beds, common kitchens, bathrooms, TVs, and free linen. Take bus #45 to Bragaw and Peterkin, turn left and walk 3 blocks. A chore is required. (Key deposit $10. Beds $12-15. Tent sites $10.)

Among the best of the state campgrounds are **Eagle River** (688-0998) and **Eklutna** (EE-kloot-nah; 694-2108), which are 12.6 mi. and 26.5 mi. northeast of Anchorage, respectively, along Glenn Hwy. For more information on these and other campsites, contact the **State Parks Service** (762-2261) or the **Alaska Parks and Recreation Dept.** (762-2617). **Centennial Park,** 5300 Glenn Hwy. (333-9711), is north of town off Muldoon Rd.; look for the park sign. Take bus #3 or #75 from downtown. (90 sites for tents and RVs. Showers, dumpsters, fireplaces, pay phones, and water. 7-day max. stay. Check-in daily 7am-midnight. Flexible noon check-out. Sites $13, Alaskans $11. Open May 1-Sept. 30.) **Lions' Camper Park,** 800 Boniface Pkwy. (333-9711), south of the Glenn Hwy. i n Russian Jack Springs Park across from the Municipal Greenhouse. Take bus #12 or 45 to the mall and walk. (50 campsites with showers, dumpsters, fireplaces, pay phones, and water. 7-day max. stay. Office at Centennial Park. Sites $13, Alaskans $11. Open June 15-Sept. 30.)

Anchorage presents budget travelers with the most affordable and varied culinary fare in the state. **Phyllis' Cafe and Salmon Bake,** 436 D St. (274-6576), has all-day breakfast (2 eggs, sausage, hash browns, and toast, $6). Dinners, served with salad, vegetable, potato, beans, and a roll, also satisfies (open daily 7am-11pm). The best breakfast spot in town, **Alaska Flapjacks,** 1230 W. 27th Ave. (274-2241) offers three eggs, bacon, biscuit, and gravy, and hash browns for $6 (open daily 6am-8pm).

Sights and Nightlife Watching over Anchorage from Cook Inlet is **Mt. Susitna,** known to locals as the "Sleeping Lady." For a view of Susitna, head about 4 mi. from downtown to **Point Warzenof,** on the western end of Northern Lights Blvd. **Earthquake Park** recalls the 1964 Good Friday earthquake, a day Alaskans refer to as "Black Friday." The quake was the strongest ever recorded in North America, registering 9.2 on the Richter scale. For a little less shakin', drive, walk, skate, or bike along the **Tony Knowles Coastal Trail,** an 11-mi. paved track that skirts Cook Inlet on one side and the backyards of Anchorage's upper-crust on the other.

A four-hour **walking tour** of downtown Anchorage begins at the visitors center. Or get it all in one place at the public **Anchorage Museum of History and Art,** 121 W. 7th Ave. (343-4326), at A St. The museum features exhibits of Alaskan Native artifacts and art, and a Native dance three times per day in the summer ($4). The gallery gives free tours daily at 10am, 11am, 1pm, and 2pm. (Open daily 9am-6pm; Sept. 16-May 14 Tues.-Sat. 10am-6pm, Sun. 1-5pm. $4, seniors $3.50, under 18 free.) The **Alaska Aviation Heritage Museum,** 4721 Aircraft Dr. (248-5325), provides a fun look at Alaska's pioneer aviators (open daily 9am-6pm; $5, seniors $3.75, youths $2).

To counteract urban claustrophobia, hike to the summit of **Flattop Mountain** in the "Glenn Alps" of the Chugach Range near Anchorage. The view of the city and, if it's clear, sun-soaked Denali, is well worth the hour-long hike. To reach the trailhead, jump on bus #92 to the intersection of Hillside Rd. and Upper Huffman Rd. From there walk ¾ mi. along upper Huffman Rd. and take a right on Toilsome Hill Dr. Proceed for 2 mi. Trail signs point the way up the 4500-ft. mountain.

Six bars and a rockin' dance floor fill **Chilkoot Charlie's,** 2435 Spenard Rd. (272-1010), at Fireweed. Take bus #7 or 60. (Open Mon.-Thurs. 10am-2:30am, Fri.-Sat. 10am-3am, Sun. noon-2:30am.) Less crowded and more interesting is **Mr. Whitekey's Fly-by-Night Club,** 3300 Spenard Rd. (279-7726). Take bus #7. Mr. Whitekey's is a "sleazy bar serving everything from the world's finest champagnes to a damn fine plate of Spam." Try Spam nachos or Spam on a bagel ($3-7). Nightly music ranges from rock to jazz to blues. (Bar open Tues.-Sat. 4pm-2:30am.)

■■■ DENALI NATIONAL PARK

Established in 1917 to protect wildlife, Denali National Park is also the home of **Denali** (Athabascan for "The Great One"), the highest mountain in North America. Anglicized as **Mt. McKinley,** Denali towers as the tallest mountain in North America

A L A S K A

and the greatest vertical relief in the world from base to summit. More than 18,000 ft. of rock scrapes upward toward the sky—even mighty Mt. Everest rises only 11,000 ft. from its base on the Tibetan Plateau. Denali is so big it manufactures its own weather (earning it the nickname "Weathermaker"). But even if you can't see the peak, you can still experience the park's tundra, taiga, and wildlife.

Practical Information Emergency is 911. All travelers stop at the **Denali Visitor Center** (683-1266 or 683-2294; 24-hr. emergency number 683-9100), 1 mi. from Rte. 3 for orientation. It is also headquarters of the **shuttle-bus** (see below). Park **entrance fee** is $3, families $5. Also at the center are **maps,** shuttle-bus schedules, free permits for backcountry camping, and the indispensable publication *Alpenglow* (free). (Center open summer daily 7am-6pm. Lockers outside 50¢.)

Shuttle buses leave the visitors center daily (5:30am-2:30pm). Go for the less frequent Wonder Lake bus if you can, as the best views of Denali are beyond Eielson. **Camper buses** move faster, transporting *only* people with **campground permits** and **backcountry permits.** However, camper buses will stop to pick up dayhikers along the road. Camper buses leave the visitors center five times daily. The final bus stays overnight at Wonder Lake and returns at 7:10am. You can get on and off these buses **anywhere along the road;** flag the next one down when you want to move on or back. This is a good strategy for dayhiking and convenient for Park explorers.

Eielson Visitors Center, 66 mi. into the park, is staffed by helpful rangers and is accessible by shuttle bus (open summer daily 9am-dusk). For info write to **Denali National Park and Preserve,** P.O. Box 9, Denali Park, AK 99755 (683-1266).

Denali National Park can be easily reached by air, road, or rail. The best place to catch a flightseeing tour is **Talkeetna.** The **George Parks Hwy.** (Rte. 3), the road connecting Anchorage (240 mi. south of Denali) and Fairbanks (120 mi. north), offers direct access to the Denali Park Rd. Leading east away from Denali is Rte. 8, the gravel **Denali Hwy.,** connecting the towns of Cantwell and Paxson. Closed in winter, the Denali Hwy. is one of Alaska's most scenic drives. Several bus companies have service connecting Denali with Anchorage and Fairbanks. **Moon Bay Express** (274-6454) has 1 bus daily to Anchorage ($35 one-way, $60 round-trip). **Fireweed Express** (452-0251) provides daily van service to Fairbanks ($25 one way). **Alaska Direct** (277-6652) has service from Fairbanks to Anchorage via Denali ($23). The **Alaska Backpacker Shuttle** runs a bus one-way from Anchorage to Denali ($35). The **Alaska Railroad,** P.O. Box 107500, Anchorage 99510 (683-2233, out of state 800-544-0552), makes stops at Denali station 1½ mi. from the entrance. Denali's **post office:** (683-2291), next to the Denali Hotel, 1 mi. from the V.C. (open Mon.-Fri. 8:30am-5pm, Sat. 10am-1pm; Oct.-May Mon.-Sat. 10am-1pm); **ZIP code:** 99755; **area code:** 907.

Accommodations, Camping, and Food The **Denali Hostel,** P.O. Box 801 Denali Park 99755 (683-1295), is 9.6 mi. north of the park entrance. Take a left on Otto Lake Rd.; it's the second house on the right. They offer bunks, showers, kitchen facilities, and morning shuttles into and out of the park ($22).

There are six **campgrounds** within the park that line Denali Park Rd. Most have water and some form of toilet facilities (sites $12). Backpackers waiting for a backcountry permit or a campsite are assured a space in **Morino Campground** ($3), next to the hostel. Permits are distributed on a first-come, first-served basis.

Food in Denali is expensive. Try to bring groceries into the park with you. Meager provisions in the park are available at **Mercantile Gas and Groceries,** 1½ mi. along Denali Park Rd. (683-2215; open daily 7am-10pm). The **Lynx Creek Grocery** (683-2548) has similarly priced items 1 mi. north of the park entrance and is open 24 hrs.

Exploring the Backcountry Denali National Park has no trails, and it is not a park that can be covered in one day. Although dayhiking is unlimited, only 2-12 hikers can camp at one time in each of the park's 44 units. Select a few different areas in the park in case your first choice is booked. The first third of the park is varying degrees of taiga forest and tundra which is hellish to hike—imagine walking on old wet mattresses with bushes growing out of them. The last third of the park is infested with mosquitoes in July and biting "no-see-ums" in August. The prime hiking and back-country camping spots are in the middle third. Although rangers at the backcountry desk will not give recommendations for specific areas (they want to disperse hikers as widely as possible), especially good locations are along the **Toklat River, Marmot Rock,** and **Polychrome Pass.** You'll want to take the 10-hr. round-trip bus ride to Wonder Lake Campground for your best chance at a glimpse of Denali *sans* clouds, but if you're planning to camp there, reserve the last bus out to the campground and the first bus back in the morning, and bring protective netted head gear (available in the convenience store). Also beware of bears—see Bear Necessities in the Essentials section.

■■■ THE ALASKA HIGHWAY

Built during World War II, the Alaska Highway maps out an astonishing 2647-km route between Dawson Creek, BC, and Fairbanks, AK. After the Pearl Harbor attack in 1941, worried War Department officials were convinced that an overland route was necessary to supply the U.S. Army bases in Alaska. The U.S. Army Corps of Engineers completed the daunting task in just eight months and 12 days.

Travelers on the highway should be prepared for heavy-duty driving. For much of the route, pavement gives way to chip-seal, a layer of packed gravel held in place by hardened oil. In summer, dust and rocks fly freely, guaranteeing shattered headlights and a chipped windshield. Drivers should fit their headlights with plastic or wire-mesh covers. Most locals protect their radiators from bug splatter with large screens mounted in front of the grill. Travel with at least one **spare tire** and some **spare gas;** if you're crazy enough to drive the highway in winter, bring along a full set of arctic clothing and prepare your four-wheel-drive for subzero conditions.

Before setting out on your epic Alaskan journey, pick up the exhaustive listing of *Emergency Medical Services* and Canada Highway's *Driving the Alaska Highway* at a visitors bureau, or write the Department of Health and Social Services, P.O. Box H-06C, Juneau, AK 99811 (907-465-3027). The free pamphlet *Help Along the Way* lists emergency numbers along the road from Whitehorse to Fairbanks.

■■■ WRANGELL-ST. ELIAS NATIONAL PARK

Wrangell-St. Elias National Park and Preserve is Alaska's best-kept secret.If you have any time at all to spend in Alaska, come *here.* The largest national park in the U.S., it could swallow more than 14 Yosemites. Four major mountain ranges converge within the park: the Wrangells, the Alaskas, the Chugach, and the St. Elias Mountains. Nine peaks tower at more than 14,000 ft. within the park, including the second highest mountain in the U.S. (18,008-ft. **Mt. St. Elias**). The park is located in the southeast corner of Alaska's mainland and is bounded by the Copper River to the west and Kluane National Park in the Yukon to the east. Park access is through two roads: the **McCarthy Road,** which enters the heart of the park, and the **Nabesna Road,** which enters from the northern park boundaries. The **visitors center** (822-5234) can be found 1 mi. off the Richardson Highway on the side road toward **Copper Center.** (Open daily 8am-6pm, in winter Mon.-Fri. 8am-5pm.) Informed rangers will give you the low-down on all the to-dos and to-sees in the park. There are also **ranger stations** in **Chitina** (CHIT-na; 823-2205; open Fri.-Mon. 9:30am-4:30pm) and in **Slana** on the northern park boundary (822-5238; open daily 8am-5pm).

SIGHTS

Most travelers head to McCarthy, a small town in the middle of the park. To reach McCarthy, turn onto the Edgarton Hwy. at its junction with the Richardson Hwy. 33

ALASKA

mi. south of Glenallen, and follow the Edgarton east for 34 mi. to the town of **Chitina**, which has a single cafe (open daily 6am-10pm), a general store (823-2111; open daily June-Aug. 8am-11pm; spring and fall 9am-8pm; winter 10am-7pm), and a ranger station (see below). From Chitina, the **McCarthy Road** follows the old road-bed of the **Copper River and Northwestern Railway** for 58 mi. to the Kennicott River. This road is arguably the roughest state road in Alaska. The road terminates on the western edge of the Kennicott River, a silt-laden river originating within the Kennicott Glacier. The only way across the river is by a hand-operated **tram** (a metal "cart" with two seats, running on a cable). McCarthy is an easy ½-mi. walk from the opposite side of the river.

McCarthy, 5 mi. south of Kennicott, was developed for miners's recreation. From 1900-38, both women and alcohol were prohibited in Kennicott and abundant in McCarthy. Today, McCarthy retains a distinctive, if less bawdy, charm.

Getting to McCarthy isn't too difficult. Drive on your own if you want to test your car's suspension. **Backcountry Connections** (822-5292; in AK 800-478-5292) will take you aboard their roomy, comfortable vans complete with friendly and knowledgeable drivers. One way from Glenallen is $69, from Chitina $35. Vans depart Mon.-Sat. from Glenallen (7:15am) and Chitina (8:30am) and return from McCarthy (4:30pm). **Wrangell Mountain Air** (see below in the Outdoors section) flies here daily from Chitina ($60 each way).

There are no **phones** in McCarthy. Telecommunication is via the "bush phone" (a CB system) and most businesses have "phone bases" elsewhere. To reach a **business** in town, phone 333-5402, and they will be dispatched by CB. The McCarthy Lodge has **showers** for $5. There is no **post office**; local mail is delivered in weekly.

Beds in the bunk house at the **McCarthy Lodge** (333-5402), in downtown ($20). **Camping** is free on the west side of the Kennicott River (no water, pit toilets).

Walking from the river, the **McCarthy-Kennicott Historical Museum** has artifacts and documents from the mining days (open daily 8am-6pm). Get general info about the area here and pick up a walking tour map ($1 donation).

If you go **flightseeing** anywhere in Alaska, do it here. **Wrangell Mountain Air** (800-478-1160 for reservations), based in downtown McCarthy, has several flights over the area ($40-100). There is a 3-person minimum on all flights. **McCarthy Air** (800-245-6909), also in McCarthy, offers similar flights and rates.

St. Elias Alpine Guides (277-6867) organizes daytrips (a ½-day glacier walk $55). You can rent bikes here to explore some of the old, obscure roads that are everywhere around town ($25 per day, ½ day $15). **The Bike Shop** also rents bikes ($8 per hour, $20 per day). **Copper Oar** (522-1670), at the end of the McCarthy Rd., offers a 2-hr. whitewater trip down the Kennicott River for $40. For those on a serious shoestring, just walking around McCarthy and Kennicott is plenty interesting. A **shuttle bus** runs out to Kennicott from McCarthy on a regular schedule ($8 round-trip). It's a 5-mi. hike between the two towns. Most **hikers and trekkers** use the McCarthy Rd. or McCarthy as a base. The park maintains no trails, but miners and other travelers from decades past have established various pathways. The most common route, a hike out past Kennicott to the Root Glacier, takes from 1-3 days for the 16-mi. round-trip and follows roadbed and glacial moraine with three moderate stream crossings. For any overnight trip, the park service requests a written itinerary; though it's not required, it's in your own best interest.

■■■ FAIRBANKS

If E.T. Barnette hadn't gotten stuck with his load of trade goods at the junction of the Tanana and Chena Rivers just when Felix Pedro, Italian immigrant-turned-prospector, unearthed a golden fortune nearby, and if territorial Judge James Wickersham hadn't been trying to woo political favors from an Indiana senator (Charles Warren Fairbanks by name), then this town might never even have existed—it certainly wouldn't have been named for somebody who never even set foot in Alaska.

Practical Information   Fairbanks lies 358 mi. north of Anchorage via the **George Parks Hwy.**, and 480 mi. south of Prudhoe Bay on the gravelly **Dalton Highway. Emergency** is 911. Fairbanks's **Convention and Visitors Bureau** (456-5774 or 800-327-5774) is at 550 1st Ave. (open daily 8am-8pm; Oct.-April Mon.-Fri. 8am-5pm, Sat.-Sun. 10am-4pm). The **Alaska Public Lands Information Center (APLIC)** (451-7352), at 3rd and Cushman St., has info on parks and protected areas of Alaska (open daily 9am-6pm; winter Tues.-Sat. 10am-6pm). Fairbanks is headquarters for nearby **Gates of the Arctic National Park,** 201 1st Ave. (456-0281; open Mon.-Fri. 8am-4:30pm) and the **Arctic National Wildlife Refuge,** 101 12th St., Room 266 (456-0250; open Mon.-Fri. 8am-4:30pm).

Fairbanks's **airport** is 5 mi. from downtown on Airport Way (George Parks Hwy.). **Alaska Air** (452-1661) flies to Anchorage ($184) and Juneau ($283); **Mark Air** (455-5104), to Bush towns, including Barrow ($235). The **Alaska Railroad,** 280 N. Cushman (456-4155), is a good way to see the wilderness. May-Sept., there is one train daily to: Nenana ($18), Anchorage ($120), and Denali National Park ($45). Ages 2-11 ride ½-price. During the winter, a train leaves for Anchorage every Sun. ($70). (Depot open Mon.-Fri. 7am-9:45pm, Sat.-Sun. 6-10pm.) Take **Denali Express** (800-327-7651) daily to Denali ($25). **Alaskan Express** (800-544-2206) speeds daily to Anchorage ($109) and 4 times a week to Haines ($169; a room for overnight in Beaver Creek not included). Fairbanks's **post office:** 315 Barnette St. (452-3203; open Mon.-Fri. 9am-6pm, Sat. 10am-2pm); **ZIP code:** 99707; **area code:** 907.

Accommodations, Camping, and Food   For information on bed and breakfasts, go to the visitors bureau or write **Fairbanks B&B,** 902 Kellum St., Anchorage (452-4967). **Fairbanks Youth Hostel (HI-AYH),** 400 Acadia St. (456-4159), on Birch Hill, has moved around a lot but has settled for the time being at the home of Walter Weesem, who hopes to buy a new hostel building in the upcoming year. There are 6 beds ($12) and plenty of tent space ($6). (No curfew, no lockout, free showers, bike rental ($5 per day). Write P.O. Box 72196, Fairbanks 99707 for information.) **Billie's Backpackers Hostel** (479-2034), has 4 beds in a simple, clean cabin and 8 beds in the main house. Take Westridge Rd. is 1 block off College to Mack Rd. Look for the "Billie's B&B" sign. With showers and kitchen runs $13.50. **Tanana Valley Campground,** 1800 College (456-7956), next to the Aurora Motel and Cabins, is noisy, but the closest campground to the downtown. (Free showers, laundromat. Tent sites for travelers with no vehicle $6, with vehicle $10.) Just about every fast-food chain in existence can be found along Airport Way and College Road. **The Whole Earth,** 1157 Deborah St. (479-2052), behind College Corner Mall, is a health food store, deli, and restaurant all in one. (Store and seating open Mon.-Sat. 8am-8pm, Sun. noon-6pm. Hot food served 11am-3pm and 5-7pm.) **Souvlaki,** 112 N. Turner (452-5393), across the bridge from the visitors center, has succulent stuffed grape leaves (3 for $1.15). Salad in a pita ($3). (Open summer Mon.-Fri. 10am-9pm, Sat. 10am-6pm; winter Mon.-Sat. 10am-6pm.)

Sights and Entertainment   The **University of Alaska-Fairbanks** is at the top of a hill overlooking the flat cityscape. Both bus lines stop at the **Wood Campus Center** (474-7033). The **University of Alaska Museum** (474-7505), a 10-min. walk up Yukon Dr. from the Campus Center, houses exhibits ranging from Russian Orthodox vestments to a mummified prehistoric bison. The most popular exhibit is a 7-min. video of the *aurora borealis* (northern lights). (Open daily 9am-8pm; May & Sept 9am-5pm; Oct-April noon-5pm. $4, seniors & students $3, families $12.50. Oct-April free Fri.) View a technological wonder of the world, the **Trans-Alaska Pipeline,** at Mile 8 of Steese Hwy. heading out of Fairbanks. The Pipeline is elevated on super-cooled posts to protect the tundra's frozen eco-system from the 108°F oil. With nothing but black spruce to keep them company, Fairbanksians turn to bars at night. Carouse with rugged types fresh from the North Slope oil fields. UAF students head for the **Howling Dog Saloon** (457-8780), 11½ mi. down Steese Hwy., for live rock-and-roll (open Tues.-Fri. 5pm-5am, Sat.-Sun. noon-5am).

■ CANADA

O Canada! Encompassing almost 10 million square kilometers (3.85 million square miles), Canada stands proudly behind Russia as the second largest country in the world. It is also one of the most sparsely populated; ten provinces and two territories sprawl over six time zones. But numbers don't tell Canada's story; geography does. Framed by the Atlantic coastline to the east and the Rockies to the west, Canada spreads north from farmland and urbanized lakeshores to barren, frozen tundra.

The name Canada derives from the Huron-Iroquois world "kanata," meaning "village" or "community." However the Canadian community is anything but unified. Periodically, ethnic, linguistic, and cultural tensions flare into actual conflict. The division between Canada's two dominant cultures—the French and the English—is so strong that Canadian society has been described as "two solitudes." Although the grounds of the conflict shift from linguistic to philosophical, or from religious to economic, it persists. Recently, the collapse of the Meech Lake Accord—which would have given French-speaking regions such as Québec and New Brunswick increased autonomy—has strengthened *québecois* separatist movements.

Another persistent schism divides the dominant Euro-colonist cultures and the aboriginal tribes. The treatment of Native Americans has been as sensitive an issue in Canada as it has been in the United States. A headline-grabbing conflict involved *québecois* Mohawks, who spent weeks under police siege to prevent sacred burial grounds from being converted into a golf course. Aboriginal representatives in resource-laden Northern Québec have also hinted at splitting the province in half should Québec secede from the rest of Canada.

The division between West and East also tears at the Canadian fabric. French and English set root in the Eastern provinces and their intellectual descendants, who are politically dominant in Ontario and Québec, are comfortable with Canada's active federal government. But the Western provinces probably have more in common with the America's libertarian West—from which came many of their settlers—than with the rest of Canada; here, opposition parties led by anti-government politicos such as Preston Manning are growing in popularity.

Finally, the blurring between the United States and Canada must be mentioned. The U.S./Canadian border is the largest undefended border in the world; it is also perhaps the most irrelevant border in the world. Canadian nationalists have become concerned that the ubiquity of American culture and mass communication in the provinces threatens the survival of indigenous attributes. Steps have been taken to protect genuine Canadian media and cultural products from "Americanization." At the same time, recent approval of the North American Free Trade Association (NAFTA) involving the United States and Canada (as well as Mexico) has threatened to further erode the distinctions between the two national identities.

Much crucial information concerning Canada can be found in the Essentials section at the front of the book. Only information specific to Canada is contained here.

■ Canadian Culture

Culturally, Canada is often overshadowed by its neighbor to the south. Canada actually is a mixture of many different cultures, including the Native cultures, English-Canadian culture, and a vibrant French-speaking culture mainly in Québec. Today, Canada is officially bilingual, and this blend has created a heritage in which most Canadians take vociferous pride.

HISTORY

Native Canadians

It seems Canada was first settled 25,000 years ago when a stream of hunters flowed over the Alaska land bridge in search of better lands. Their descendants flooded the continent, breaking up into the various tribes that met European Settlers upon their arrival. Dominant tribes in the Great Lakes region included the Five Nations, composed of members of the Seneca, Mohawk, Onondaga, Oneida, and Cayuga tribes, and the Hurons, who normally opposed these people in a kind of scattered warfare. In the Prairies settled the Ojibwa, Blackfoot, and Cree, to the north swept the Inuit peoples, and further to the west gathered the Oneida, who reached as far as the towering forests on the Pacific Coast. As Europeans encroached, these nations often traded furs for guns, which made inter-tribal warfare even more vicious than it had been before. Tribes entered into alliances with would-be colonial powers, providing a vast knowledge of the land and enabling the rapid vanquishing of enemies. In the area around Niagara Falls, Indians helped the British annihilate the Americans in a decisive battle of the War of 1812, just as the Dutch had supplied the Five Nations with firepower to allow them to eradicate the Huron midway through the 17th century. The tribes' bargain, of course, did not pay off. As the English and French became more familiar with the land, they squeezed the Indians out by force and by less-than-desirable land agreements. Natives found themselves confined to large settlements such as Moose Factory in Ontario or Oka in Québec. In recent years, the tribes have begun to assert more authority through the Assembly of First Nations, which theoretically speaks for all Canadian Aboriginals. Developments such as the Federal granting of a semi-autonomous parcel of the Northwest Territories to Inuit tribes may speak to a bettering of times for Canada's first peoples.

The French and British Empires

Jacques Cartier landed on the gulf of the St. Lawrence River in 1534, ostensibly founding Canada. England may have gotten to it earlier when John Cabot sighted Newfoundland, yet the Vikings trod the same turf centuries before. And before them were the Native Americans and Inuit. In 1608 the explorer Champlain established Québec City. By the mid-1600s, colonization was well underway due to the fur-trade; the Company of New France was declared a colony of France in 1663. Meanwhile, Britain was gobbling up territory, forming the Hudson Bay Company in 1670. A rivalry for land persisted for a century until the Seven Years War, when the British captured Québec in 1759 and the rest of New France in 1763, giving their global rivals the boot from North America.

On the heels of this acquisition came the American Revolution, in which the British lost her more southern colonies. Canada, as secure British territory, became crucially involved in the war. General Gage withdrew his forces to Halifax, Nova Scotia after he was forced to abandon Boston in 1775, and General Burgoyne launched his ill-fated offensive against the Americans from Québec in 1777. Thousands of Tory loyalists fled north into Canada, and some of them established New Brunswick in 1784. In 1791, Québec was divided into two colonies, Upper and Lower Canada; after an open rebellion by the French Canadians in 1837, Québec was reunited as a single colony called Canada in 1841. The drive for sovereignty was accelerating. In 1847, the colonies were given the right to self-government under the watchful eye of the British monarchy. This only fueled the confederation movement.

The Dominion of Canada

The desire for a unified country was in part sparked by first-hand witnessing of the American Civil War. Some feared that the U.S. might turn its aggressions outwards, as it had in the War of 1812, and try to absorb British North America (including Canada). For many, greater Canadian unity was an imperative. The Colonial Secretary struggled to establish the Confederation, working quickly to oust reluctant colony heads. The first Confederation proposal (1865) was nixed by the two maritime colonies of Nova Scotia and New Brunswick, both of which feared that they were too remote from the other colonies to gain equal representation in a federal system. Over the next two years, though, sufficient support was swiftly consolidated (a Confederation resolution was passed through the Nova Scotia legislature in the same month that a pro-Confederation government replaced an anti-Confederation one). The appropriate legislation made its way to British Parliament, where, despite anti-Confederation lobbyists, the four colonies of Québec, Ontario, Nova Scotia, and New Brunswick were united as the Dominion of Canada. The British North America (BNA) Act, as it was called, was signed by Queen Victoria on March 29, 1867, and proclaimed on July 1, Canada Independence Day. Canada had its country, but was still a dominion of the British throne.

Westward Ho!

Following the passage of the BNA Act, Conservatives rode the crest of the consolidation wave into power; Sir John MacDonald in the English colonies and Sir George-Etienne Cartier in Québec. The government was dedicated to national expansion through three methods: pumping money into economic growth, encouraging mass settlement in the west, and creating high protective tariffs. As a result, Canada quickly grew to encompass most of the land it consists of today: Manitoba and the Northwest Territories were molded from Rupert's Land in 1870, a purchase from the Hudson Bay Company; British Columbia, fearing American expansionism, hopped on board in 1871, after being promised a trans-Canada railway; and Prince Edward Island signed on in 1873. By 1885, British Columbia had its railroad and the economy boomed. Increased wheat production and immigration to the west sparked the addition of Alberta and Saskatchewan to the provincial list in 1905.

Just as in the United States, this westward growth displaced natives. In the Arctic, the Inuit were largely left alone, and their lands were tacitly incorporated into the growing Canadian territory. But in the west, the Native Americans and the Metis (mixed-blood children of Native American women and French fur-traders who inhabited Manitoba) lost their way of life as the European settlers moved in. Western land was gathered for the Dominion in return for treaty and reservation rights for the natives. The acquisition of the west was peaceful and largely unchallenged, a situation far different from that south of the 49th parallel.

Turn of the Century Politics and WWI

A steadfast nationalism and a newfound imperialism drove Prime Minister Sir Wilfrid Laurier, leader of the Liberal Party and the first French-speaking Prime Minister, to send troops to aid Britain in the Boer War from 1899-1902 and to create a national navy in 1910. Laurier lost the election of 1911, however, because he proposed reciprocal trade agreements with the U.S. which would have lowered Canada's high trading tariffs.

Though a new party ruled after 1911, the tide of imperialism did not abate, and the Dominion sent hordes of troops to aid Britain in the Great War. Canada split along an entirely new line—the question of the draft. The conservatives, a proconscription party, maintained their hold through the 1917 election. Though her sacrifice was great, Canada gained significantly from the Great War. The Dominion acquired new international status as a signator of the Treaty of Versailles and a charter member of the League of Nations. Further, women made headway on account of their war efforts, receiving the right to vote in 1918, two years before their American sisters received the same right.

The Inter-War Years

But hard times hit. Returning vets from the war and post-war slumps fueled high inflation and unemployment; protesting farmers ousted governments in the west and in Ontario, and the provincial economies collapsed. In 1919, with 3 million employed in the Dominion, over 4 million working days were lost due to strikes, the most famous of which was the Winnipeg General Strike. Almost the entire labor force responded to aid the ailing metal-trades workers who had been denied wage increases. The government stepped in with police and troops, and the strike collapsed. The strike was effective only in bringing the workers to political action; they have since been sending their own representatives to the federal Parliament.

Like many other countries, Canada experienced an economic and cultural boom in the 20s and 30s. But wheat prices plummeted, and the Great Depression moved in. Unemployment skyrocketed to 20% in 1933. Provincial governments tried to assist the troubled farmers, but their relief was limited and drought exacerbated the problems of the agricultural community. The liberals gained power in 1935 under Mackenzie King. As in the U.S., the government initiated direct relief programs and regulated businesses; both the Bank of Canada and the Canadian Wheat Board were established during the depression. King sponsored bills on family allowance and unemployment insurance, as well. Following in the footsteps of the U.S., the workers formed a multitude of unions, and Canada was able to drag itself out of the depression with the assistance of World War II.

Cold War Party-Hopping

Louis St. Laurent took the helm of the Liberal party in 1948, just after the war. The Liberals held office from 1935 to 1957, largely due to their relief programs of the late 30s (again, akin to the U.S.), and later to the prosperity of the early Cold War years. Political decisions which would have otherwise irked the populace were deemed permissible because of the Cold War; thus, Canada joined the United Nations in 1945, hopped into the North Atlantic Treaty Organization in August, 1949, and sent troops to Europe in 1951. With inspiring visions of a "new" Canada, the conservatives, led by John Diefenbaker, grabbed precarious control in June, 1957. A new party, the growing, left-wing National Democratic Party, introduced Medicare to Saskatchewan in 1962. This program quickly spread nationally and became the popular and successful national health care program Canada has today. Impaired by high unemployment rates (again) and record budget deficits (foreshadowing the U.S.'s similar problems), the Prime Ministership fell to Lester Pearson of the minority Liberal party in April, 1963.

Québec had always been a thorn in the side of the mainly British Dominion. In an attempt to unite Québec and the rest of the Dominion, Pierre Trudeau was selected to head the Liberal party in 1968. Trudeau espoused bilingualism and biculturalism, and brought many Québecois to his government. But the move toward biculturalism apparently threatened the English Canadians; Liberal victory in 1972 was slim, and the New Democratic Party held the deciding votes in Parliament. The Liberals bowed to the radicals and shifted left to acquire their support—this dramatically affected the party and its positions thereafter. The Liberals were dependent on Québec and urban Ontario for their support; the Conservatives on western Canada and Ontario. The NDP relied on unskilled workers for its less significant support.

In the late 70s came the drive for French separatism. Under the banner Parti Québecois, separatist René Lévesque gained power in Québec in 1976, stunning Canadians across the country. Under Bill 101, the Parti Québecois established French as the only official language seen and heard in Québec, forcing everyone there to use French. Trudeau rose to the occasion and took head-on the rising separatism movement by fighting for a united Canada. In 1979, Québec stood solidly behind Trudeau, but the rest of the nation backed the Conservative head, Joe Clark, who won the election in May. Clark floundered early, and with the defeat of his budget and a no-confidence motion in December, Trudeau and the liberals returned in early 1980. This election marked perhaps the greatest national division of the century; the liberals swept Québec but won no seats west of Manitoba, and only two there. Trudeau succeeded in preventing Québec from seceding in a 1980 referendum, and the country remained united if torn through early 1982.

The Canada Act of 1982

Finally, Britain let go. On March 25, 1982, Canada's constitution was ratified by British Parliament. Queen Elizabeth II gave her royal assent on March 29, exactly 115 years to the day after Queen Victoria assented to the BNA Act of 1867. The Canada Act was proclaimed by her majesty three weeks later, and the BNA Act was patriated to Canada, releasing Canada from the legal bonds of England. The act was a compromise between the vision of "one Canada with two official languages" and provincial concerns. The constitution includes an unusual Charter of Rights and Freedoms, akin to the Bill of Rights, but more tepid in its provisions—in order to preserve parliamentary supremacy, individual rights may be superseded by federal Parliament or provincial legislatures via "notwithstanding clauses" for periods of up to five years. True to form, Québec tried to claim veto power over the constitution, but was rejected by courts at every level, including the Supreme Court of Canada, on December 6, 1982.

Mulroney, Meech Lake, and NAFTA

In 1983 the conservatives chose a new leader, the president of the Iron Ore Company of Canada, Brian Mulroney, an amiable Montréal lawyer. Conservative support rose as Mulroney pronounced social programs "a sacred trust" and supported an NDP attempt to provide bilingual support in Manitoba. When Trudeau resigned in 1984 and Turner took his place, the stage was set for a conservative comeback. Turner buckled under pressure to Mulroney, and lost money and support. Mulroney rolled to a landslide victory, claiming 211 of 281 seats in the Parliament, a clear mandate for conservative change. Mulroney and his conservatives supported privatazation, increased armed forces, and reduction of the deficit. Government had not changed, however, and Mulroney could do little to rally support in the west. By 1986, Mulroney lagged last in the polls as elections neared. As a result, Mulroney's government entered two massive endeavors—rolling the dice for the Meech Lake Accord and the North American Free Trade Agreement (NAFTA).

The Meech Lake Accord was, in the final analysis, an attempt to keep Québec in Canada and to gain *québecois* support for the conservatives. The Accord would have provided constitutional protection for the French language and culture in Québec. English Canadians feared the Accord gave Québec too much power in relation to the Charter of Rights and Freedoms, while not guaranteeing similar powers for other minority groups. The Accord was defeated in June 1990, when Newfoundland and Manitoba failed to approve it. A patchwork replacement went to national referendum in 1993, but failed miserably.

NAFTA is, in most ways, a success. By finally lowering trade tariffs between the economic giants of the western hemisphere, NAFTA promises to allow the economy to thrive in a free-market system. After years of negotiations (the roots for NAFTA stretch back to 1987), the central agreement was signed in May, 1992, and approved by the U.S. Senate in 1994.

Even the promise of the benefits of free trade was not enough to prevent Mulroney's fall from popularity in 1992. Just as he was finishing up NAFTA, the country was finishing with him. In a cloud of incompetence, scandal, and distrust, Mulroney was ousted from power in April 1993, as Kim Campbell became the first woman Prime Minister of Canada. Campbell's tenure was short—her party quickly dissolved from a decent majority in the House of Commons to a paltry two-seat total. Though Jean Chrétien and his Liberal Party won power, two new parties caught all the attention: the far-right Reform Party, led by former evangelist Preston Manning, blitzed Campbell's Tories in the West; and in Québec reigned the new opposition, the Bloc Québeqois, elected with a mandate to wrest their province from Canada's clutches.

LITERATURE

The very first expressions of the Canadian literary mind were poetry, descriptive verses composed by the first settlers in the early 17th century; Canadian fiction did not come into its own until almost 200 years later. Much of the early work detailed the difficulties of settling in a wild, new land or satirized the existence of life in the colonies. *The Literary Garland*, published in Montréal from 1838 to 1851, served as a forum for all sorts of fiction, including historical romances. The opening of the northwest and the Klondike Gold Rush led the way for the blossoming of the adventure story. Jack London penned stories of wolves and prospectors based on his experiences of the time, while the Bard of the Yukon, Robert Service, composed the ballad "The Cremation of Sam McGee." Back east, L.M. Montgomery authored the *Anne of Green Gables* series, which have delighted generations of young readers from the corners of the earth. The onset of the 20th century brought a shift in emphasis to the cities and led to works exposing the dark side of urban conditions. Novelist and playwright Robertson Davies arose from Toronto's Upper Canada College to chronicle the roving Canadian identity in the *Deptford Trilogy*, and Margaret Laurence detailed the difficult lives of prairie women in such novels as *A Jest of God* and *The Stone Angel*. Two of Canada's best authors, Malcolm Lowry and Hugh McLellan, also produced their most significant works, *Under the Volcano* and *Barometer Rising* (respectively), during this period. On the critical side, Canada boasted three of the world's most prominent cultural and literary authorities: Northrop Frye, Hugh Kenner, and Marshall McLuhan. Prominent contemporary authors include Margaret Atwood, best known for the futuristic bestseller *The Handmaid's Tale;* Alice Munro *(Lives of Girls and Women),* and Sri Lankan-born poet and novelist Michael Ondaatje, who recently won the prestigious Booker Prize for *The English Patient.*

MOVIES, TELEVISION, AND MUSIC

Canadian films have yet to achieve the commercial success of Canadian literature. Québecois filmmakers have captured the world's attention, producing Oscar-nominated movies like *Le declin de l'empire americain,* directed by Denys Arcand, who also directed the striking *Jesus de Montréal;* art-flick *Léolo* was deemed a classic by critics. François Girard has made audiences gasp with his recent *Thirty-two Short Films about Glenn Gould,* and actress Sheila McCarthy shone in *I Have Heard the Mermaids Singing*.

Canada has also made some notable contributions to the American entertainment industry; there are many famous actors and comedians of Canadian origin, including Dan Aykroyd, Jim Carrey *(The Mask),* Mike Myers of *Saturday Night Live* and *Wayne's World* fame, Michael J. Fox *(Family Ties, Back to the Future),* newscaster Peter Jennings, *Jeopardy* host Alex Trebek, and William Shatner (Captain James T. Kirk himself). The Canadian comedy troupe SCTV spawned the careers of many famous comedians, such as Martin Short, John Candy, Rick Moranis, Eugene Levy, and more. In an effort to hold down production costs, many American TV shows and movie companies shoot in Canadian cities, such as Toronto and Vancouver.

Canada has made a major contribution to popular music, lending the world's airwaves a range of artists such as Neil Young, Joni Mitchell, Bruce Cockburn, Rush, Cowboy Junkies, Bare Naked Ladies, k.d. lang, and the Crash Test Dummies. Today, Canadian popular music shows even stronger signs of life, as MuchMusic, the Canadian version of MTV, has been inspiring bands all over the country to capture the national identity on vinyl and on video. Canada is also home to world-class orchestras, including the Montréal, Toronto, and Vancouver Symphonies.

C A N A D A

 Canada Essentials

Below is some essential information about Canada (on currency, travel, and mail), but further information can be found in the main Essentials section at the front of the book.

■■■ CURRENCY AND EXCHANGE

US$1 = CDN$1.36	CDN$1 = US$0.73
UK£1 = CDN$2.11	CDN$1 = UK£0.47
IR£1 = CDN$2.08	CDN$1 = IR£0.48
AUS$1 = CDN$1.00	CDN$1 = AUS$1.00
NZ$1 = CDN$0.83	CDN$1 = NZ$1.21

The main unit of currency in Canada is the **dollar**, which is identical to the U.S. dollar in name only. You will need to exchange your currency when you go over the border. As in the U.S., Canadian currency uses a decimal system, with the dollar divided into 100 cents (¢); fractions are represented in the same way: 35¢. Paper money comes in denominations of $2, $5, $10, $20, $50, and $100, which are all the same size but color-coded by denomination. Several years ago, the Canadian government phased out the $1 bill and replaced it with a $1 coin, known as the **loony** for the loon which graces its reverse.

Many Canadian shops, as well as vending machines and parking meters, accept U.S. coins at face value (which is a small loss for you). Many stores will even convert the price of your purchase for you, but they are under no legal obligation to offer you a fair exchange. During the past several years, the Canadian dollar has been worth roughly 20% less than the U.S. dollar.

Prices tend to be higher in Canada than in the U.S., as are taxes; you'll quickly notice the 7% **goods and services tax (GST)** and an additional **sales tax** in some provinces. See the provincial introductions for info on local taxes. Oddly enough, you will find yourself being taxed on taxes; in Québec, for example, provincial sales tax of 8% is computed on the price including GST, so that the total tax will be 15.56%. Visitors can claim a rebate of the GST they pay on accommodations of less than one month and on most goods they buy and take home, so be sure to save your receipts and pick up a GST rebate form while in Canada. The total claim must be at least CDN$7 of GST (equal to $100 in purchases) and must be made within one year of the date on which you purchased the goods and/or accommodations for which you are claiming your rebate. A brochure detailing restrictions is available from local tourist offices or through **Revenue Canada, Customs, Excise, and Taxation, Visitor's Rebate Program,** Ottawa, Ontario, Canada K1A 1J5 (800-668-4748 in Canada, 613-991-3346 outside Canada). Québec and Manitoba offer refunds of provincial sales tax as well; contact the Provincial Tourist Information Centres for details (see Practical Information listing of each province). All prices in the Canada section of this book are listed in Canadian dollars unless otherwise noted.

■■■ GETTING AROUND CANADA

For information on money, traveling by plane or bus in Canada, or on driving, bicycling, or hitchhiking, see Getting There and Getting Around in the beginning Essentials section. Note: it is legal in Canada, but not in the U.S., to bicycle on most limited-access highways.

VIA Rail, Place Ville Marie, Lobby Level, Montréal, Québec H3B 2G6 (800-561-3949), is Amtrak's Canadian analogue, with routes as scenic as Amtrak's but more affordable fares. If you'll be traveling by train a great deal or across great distances you may save money with the **Canrail Pass,** which allows travel on 12 days within a 30-day period; distance traveled is unlimited. Between early June and late September, passes cost $546, and, for senior citizens and youths under 24, $492. Off-season passes cost $342, $374 for youths and senior citizens.

Remember when pricing VIA Rail tickets that a discount of 40% is applied to all tickets purchased at least 7 days in advance. Fares vary, rising during the high summer season. During the peak season, a one-way ticket from Montréal to Halifax sells for $189; a one-way ticket between Toronto and Vancouver sells for $492; a one-way ticket between Montréal and Toronto sells for $90. Call for specific details.

CANADA

A number of **discounts** apply on full-fare tickets: children ages two to 11 accompanied by an adult (half-fare); children under two (free on the lap of an adult); students and seniors (10% discount). Passengers with disabilities and their companions together are charged a single fare, although a letter from a physician stating the companion is necessary for travel is required (see Specific Concerns in Essentials).

■■■ KEEPING IN TOUCH

In Canada, mailing a letter (or a postcard, which carries the same rate as a letter) to the U.S. costs 50¢ for the first 30 grams and $1.13 if the letter is between 31-100 grams. To every other foreign country, a 20-gram letter costs 88¢, a 21-50 gram letter $1.33, and a 51-100 gram letter $2.20. The domestic rate is 43¢ for a 30-gram letter, and 88¢ for a letter between 31-100 grams. Aerogrammes can be mailed only to other locations in Canada (88¢). **Note:** The postal rates quoted here are accurate as of September, 1994, but rates are expected to be considered again by Parliament in October, and may rise slightly at that time.

Letters take from three to eight working days to reach the U.S. and a week or two to get to an overseas address. Guaranteed next-day delivery exists between any two Canadian cities; the cost depends on the provinces involved; for the purposes of Priority Courier, Québec and Ontario represent one region.

In Canada, **postal codes** are the equivalent of U.S. ZIP codes and contain letters as well as numbers (for example, H4P 1B8). Postal codes vary within cities; you can get information on postal codes from anywhere in Canada at 800-267-1133. The normal form of address is nearly identical to that in the U.S.; the only difference is that the apartment or suite number can *precede* the street address along with a dash. For example, 23-40 Sherbrooke St. refers to Room #23 at 40 Sherbrooke St. Mailboxes in Canada are red and look something like space-age garbage chutes.

General Delivery *(Poste Restante)* mail can be sent to any post office and will be held for 15 days; it can be held for longer at the discretion of the Postmaster if such a request is clearly indicated on the front of the envelope. General Delivery letters should be labeled like this:

Ms. Eve <u>Rothbart</u> (underline last name for accurate filing)
c/o General Delivery
Hollander Station C
274 Riverhead St.
St. John's, Newfoundland, A1C 5H1
CANADA

American Express offices throughout Canada will act as a mail service for cardholders, *if* you contact them in advance. Under this free "Client Letter Service," they will hold mail for 30 days, forward upon request, and accept telegrams. For a complete list of offices and instructions on how to use the service, call 800-528-4800.

Telephones and telegrams in Canada work exactly as in the United States. See Keeping in Touch in the Essentials section.

CANADA

New Brunswick

New Brunswick prides itself on its natural scenery: deep forests, vast spaces, and a spectacular coast. The tremendous Bay of Fundy gives rise to the world's highest tides, at 48 feet. Other natural oddities include the Reversing Falls in St. John and Moncton's Magnetic Hill. Mixing with New Brunswick's natural beauty are two dominant cultures. The Acadians, French pioneers who had originally settled in Nova Scotia in the 17th century, migrated to the northern and eastern coasts and established the farming and fishing nation of *l'Acadie,* or Acadia. When the British took control of the area in 1755, they expelled many of these farmers who then drifted all the way down to the Gulf of Mexico to found Acadiana amidst their compatriots in Louisiana. The southern region of New Brunswick was settled by the Loyalists, British subjects who fled in the wake of the American Revolution. Although over a third of the province's population is French-speaking, it is rare to encounter someone in the larger cities who doesn't speak English.

PRACTICAL INFORMATION

Capital: Fredericton.

Department of Economic Development and Tourism, P.O. Box 12345, Fredericton, NB E3B 5C3, distributes free publications including the *Official Highway Map, Outdoor Adventure Guide, Craft Directory, Fish and Hunt Guide,* and *Travel Guide* (with accommodation and campground directory). Call **Tourism New Brunswick** (800-561-0123) from anywhere in Canada Mon.-Fri. 8am-9pm, Sat.-Sun. 9am-6pm.

Alcohol: Legal drinking age 19. Bars close at 2am.

Time Zone: Atlantic (1 hr. ahead of Eastern). **Postal Abbreviation:** NB

Provincial Sales Tax: 11%.

■■■ FREDERICTON

In the early 1780s the American Revolution sent some 2000 British Loyalists up the St. John River Valley to Ste. Anne's Point. They renamed the settlement "Frederics-town," in honor of King George III's second son. It was selected provincial capital two years later because of its ready access to the Atlantic Ocean via the St. John River and its defensible location in the heart of New Brunswick.

Today, Fredericton maintains its importance as New Brunswick's governmental and administrative center, despite its small size and small-town atmosphere. This "celestial city," so-named because of the presence of Canada's first observatory at the local University of New Brunswick, seems to have two faces. Don't let the any-old-town shops, the quiet residential areas, and the fast-food joints fool you; there is plenty to do and see in Fredericton that is one-of-a-kind.

PRACTICAL INFORMATION

Emergency: 911.

Visitor Information: Visitor Information Centre (452-9500), City Hall, on the corner of Queen and York. The exceptionally courteous and ready-to-help staff provides the *Street Index Map/Transit Guide* and the invaluable *Fredericton Visitor Guide* (both free) with complete listings of area accommodations and attractions. Out-of-province plates also make you eligible for a free, three-day parking pass which can be claimed here. Open daily 8am-8pm; early Sept.-mid-May daily 8:15am-4:30pm.

Student Travel Agency: Travel CUTS (453-4850), in the student Union Bldg. of the University of New Brunswick. Ride-showing board posted. Open Mon.-Fri. 9am-4pm, mid-Sept.-May Mon.-Fri. 9am-5pm.

Eastern Canada

NEWFOUNDLAND

Channel-Port-aux-Basques

TO ARGENTIA, NEWFOUNDLAND

Cape Breton Island

Sydney

Cape Breton Highlands Nat'l Park

Îles de la Madeleine

Gulf of St. Lawrence

Antigonish

NOVA SCOTIA

Ile d'Anticosti

Charlottetown
Wood Islands

PRINCE EDWARD ISLAND

Caribou

Dartmouth
Halifax

Borden

Lunenburg

Reserve de Sept-Îles

Gaspé
Percé

Bayfield

Amherst

Fundy N.P.

Digby

Yarmouth

Sept-Îles

Baie des Chaleurs

Gaspé Peninsula

Parc de la Gaspésie

Matane

Bathurst
Dalhousie

NEW BRUNSWICK

Moncton

Saint John

Bay of Fundy

ATLANTIC OCEAN

Fleuve St-Laurent

Mont-Joli
Trois-Pistoles

Edmundston

Fredericton

Calais

Bar Harbor

TO LABRADOR CITY

Baie-Comeau

Rivière-du-Loup

Presque Isle

MAINE

Bangor

Portland

Forestville
Les Escoumins

St-Siméon

Ste Anne de Beaupré

Québec

Sherbrooke

Berlin

Augusta

Montpelier

N.H. Concord

Alma
Jonquiere

Réserve des Laurentides

Grand-Mère

Trois Rivières

Granby

Lake Champlain

V.T.

Lac St-Jean

Mistassini

Parc du Mont-Tremblant

Montréal

Laval

Burlington

Adirondacks Park

Chibougamau

Mont-Tremblant

Mont-Laurier

Cornwall

Ottawa River

Val-d'Or

Réserve la Vérendrye

Ottawa

Kingston

NEW YORK

QUÉBEC

Algonquin Provincial Park

ONTARIO

Huntsville

Lake Ontario

Toronto

N

100 kilometers

100 miles

Trains: VIA Rail (368-7818 or 800-561-3952), on Hwy. 101 in Fredericton Junction, about 50 min. from Fredericton. A VIA Rail shuttle bus will pick you up in front of the **Sheraton Inn,** 225 Woodstock Rd. (457-7000). Buy this ticket along with your VIA Rail fare and it will cost less than the lone shuttle fare of $10.70, students $9.70. To: Montréal (Mon., Thurs., and Sat., 11½ hr., $98, students $88; 7 days in advance $73/$63); Halifax (Tues., Fri., and Sun., 9 hr., $70/$63; 5 days in advance, students traveling any day and adults traveling on Tues. $42/$35). Advance purchase discounts have limited availability. These prices do not include the shuttle. (Open Mon., Thurs., Sat. 6:30-10pm, Sun., Tues., Fri. 6:30-10am.)

Bus: SMT, 101 Regent St. (458-6000). On-time service to: Saint John (2 per day, 1½hr., $15); Edmunston (2 per day, 3½hr., $35); Moncton (2 per day, 2-3 hr., $25). Connections to Halifax and Charlottetown (P.E.I.) in Moncton.(Open Mon.-Fri. 7:30am-8:30pm, Sat.-Sun. 9am-8:30pm.)

Public Transport: Fredericton Transit, 470 St. Mary's (454-6287), circulates around town every hr. Mon.-Sat. 7am-10pm. Fare $1, seniors and students over 12 75¢, kids 6-12 50¢, kids under 6 free. All buses stop downtown on King St. in front of King's Place. Office open Mon.-Fri. 7:15am-4:30pm. Sat. 7:15am-4pm.

Taxi: Budget, 450-1199. **Student,** 454-0000, driven by hired students; discounts for students and seniors. Both function 24 hrs. and average about $3 per trip.

Car Rental: Delta, 304 King St. (458-8899). Rents economy cars at $25 per day with 100km free, 12¢ per additional km. Insurance $10 per day. Must be 21 with major credit card. Open Mon.-Fri. 7:30am-8pm, Sat. 8am-5pm, Sun. 10am-5pm.

Bike Rental: Savage's, 449 King St. (458-8985), will provide you wheels for $3 per hr. or $15 per day. Must have some sort of ID. Open Mon.-Wed. 8:30am-6pm, Thurs.-Fri. 8:30am-9pm, Sat. 9am-5pm.

Help lines: Rape Crisis Center, 454-0437. **CHIMO** (emotional distress) 450-4357. Both operate 24 hrs.

Post Office: Station "A," 527 Queen St. (452-3345), next to Officer's Sq. Open Mon.-Fri. 8am-5:15pm. **Postal Code:** E3B 4Y1.

Area Code: 506.

Traffic congestion is rare downtown, and almost all areas of interest can easily be reached on foot. Parking meters are read only on Mon.-Fri. 9am-5pm, so claim a space for the weekend and walk around. **Officer's Square,** a small park between Queen St. and the river, is the geographic heart of activity.

ACCOMMODATIONS AND CAMPING

Cheap housing, though not plentiful, is generally not too hard to find in the summer. Most motels and B&Bs run $35-50, and campgrounds are plentiful. A comprehensive listing of accommodations and prices is available in the *Fredericton Visitor Guide.* Ideally positioned down-town, the **York House Hostel (HI-C),** 193 York St. (454-1233), has 30 beds in single-sex dorms, a kitchen and lounge, but no access between 9:30am and 4pm. The zealous young staff makes sure you are in by midnight and out by 9:30am. Breakfast 7:30-8:30am ($1.50-3). Reception open 4pm-midnight. $10, nonmembers $12. Open June-Aug. The **University of New Brunswick,** Residential Administration Bldg. (453-4835), Baily Drive on campus, rents good clean dorm rooms with free local phones and coin laundry facilities. From downtown, follow Brunswick St. to its end and take a right on University St., which goes right to the gates, or take bus #16 South. The **Student Hotel** is open to any students, $12.75 per day, $69 per week. The **Tourist Hotel** is pricier but open to all. Singles $28, doubles $41. Open May-late Aug. For year-round lodging, you'll have to go to the motels outide of town. The **Norfolk Motel** (472-3278), on the Trans-Canada Highway East on the north shore of the river, is 3km east of downtown. Bus #15 North passes by near the end of the route. Here the rooms are standard motel issue with clean, private bathrooms. (Singles $29, doubles $32.)

Fredericton's closest camping, **Hartt Island Campground** (450-6057), is hidden within an amusement park (the Bucket Club) on the Trans-Canada Highway, 5km west of town. 125 riverside sites, pool, laundry, showers. Sites $15, with hookup

$17-20; $2 per person in groups larger than 4 people. Free coffee and donuts 7am-11am. Reservations highly recommended July-Aug. Open May-Oct.

FOOD

Decently-priced places to eat abound in Fredericton. At **Molly's Coffee House,** 422 Queen St. (457-9305), you can buy anything in the shop including gourmet coffee, scrumptious breads baked on the premises, and the antique chairs you sit in. Perfect for breakfast or a light lunch (soup with home-made bread $2.25-2.95). (Open Mon.-Wed. 8am-6pm, Thurs.-Fri. 8am-9pm, Sat. 10am-5pm, Sun. noon-4pm.) **Trumpers,** 349 King St. (444-0819), serves a wide variety of vegetarian and vegan sandwiches ($2.75, and fresh-baked Banana Chocolate Chip Cake ($2). (Open Mon.-Thurs. 8am-6pm, Fri. 8am-8pm, Sat. 10am-5pm.) **Mexicali Rosa's,** 546 King St. (451-0686), offers lunch specials $5-7 (Mon.-Fri. 11:30am-4pm, Sat. noon-4pm) in a decor strewn with cowboy figurines and fake cacti (open Mon.-Fri. 11:30am-1am, Tues. and Wed. 11:30am-11:30pm, Thurs. 11:30am-midnight, Sat. noon-1am, Sun. noon-11pm). The **Boyce Farmers Market** (451-1815), located behind the Old York County Gaol between Regent and St. John St., has over 140 stalls selling farm-fresh foods, crafts, and other goodies (open Sat. 6am-1pm).

SIGHTS

Just inside the entrance to the **Beaverbrook Art Gallery,** 703 Queen St. (458-85845), hangs Salvador Dalí's awe-inspiring, largest (13x10 ft.) masterpiece, *Santiago el Grande.* A gift of local-boy Lord Beaverbrook, the gallery also houses a collection of Anglo paintings including works by Gainsborough, Turner, and Constable. (Open Sun.-Wed. 10am-5pm, Thurs.-Sat. 10am-7pm; Sept.-June Sun.-Mon. noon-5pm, Tues.-Sat. 10am-5pm. $3, seniors $2, students $1.) Across the street, New Brunswick's provincial government meets in the **Legislative Assembly Building** (453-2527), where visitors can view hand-colored copper engravings by John James Audubon in the New Brunswick **Legislative Library.** Tours of the building, including the Assembly Chamber when the Legislature isn't spending money, leave every half-hour. (Open daily 9am-8pm, Sept.-early June Mon.-Fri. 9am-4pm.) In July and August, pageantry-lovers can witness the **Changing of the Guard** (452-9500)—specifically the Royal New Brunswick Regiment—in Officers' Sq. (Tues.-Sat. at 11am and 7pm. Sentries change every hr. Inspection of the guard Thurs. at 11am.)

The quirky **York-Sunbury Historical Society Museum** (455-6041) operates within the Old Officers' Quarters in Officers' Square. Exhibits detail aspects of New Brunswick life from the Micmac natives to the recreation of a World War I trench. Also in residence is the famous 42-lb. Coleman Frog. Old Fred Coleman supposedly fed his pet croaker bran and ox blood, although it had a liking for scotch, rum, and gin. To preserve the enigma of the frog, museum officials have forbidden scientific examination of the specimen. $1, students and seniors 50¢, families $2.50. (Open May-Mabor Day Mon.-Sat. 10am-6pm; Labor Day to mid-Oct. Mon.-Fri. 9am-5pm, Sat. noon-4pm; mid-Oct. to April Mon., Wed., Fri. 11am-3pm or by appointment.)

The green which borders the river's banks offers 5 km. of groomed pathways perfect for a walk or bike ride. Those of more aquatic taste can rent a **canoe** from the **Small Craft Aquatic Center** (458-5513), off Woodstock Rd., on the river bank behind the Victoria Health Center. (Canoes, kayaks, and rowing shells for a beastly $7 per hr. A $5 registration fee per season is necessary. Open Mon.-Fri. 6-9am and 4:30-9pm, Sat.-Sun. 10am-6pm.) Paddle along the St. John, stopping at the **Fredericton Lighthouse** (459-2515 or 800-561-4000), where the public is allowed access all the way to the top. (Open daily 10am-9pm; June and Sept. Mon.-Fri. 9am-4pm, Sat.-Sun. noon-4pm, Oct.-May Mon.-Fri. 9am-4pm. $2, kids under 12 $1.) The *Fredericton Visitor Guide's* **walking tour** hits all the attractions in central Fredericton or during July and Aug. a member of the Calithumpians, a local theater group, will give you a free guided walking tour complete with colonial costumes. (Tours begin at City Hall. Mon.-Fri. 10am, 2, 4, and 7pm; Sat. and Sun. 10am, 4 and 7pm.)

Kings Landing Historical Settlement, 37km west of Fredericton, off exit #259 off the Trans-Canada Highway (Hwy. 2), is a living, breathing museum, staffed by period actors whose daily chores from buttermaking to blacksmithing. This replica of an early Loyalist township is actually a completely self-sufficient village. The saw and grist mills particularly stand out in the 300-acre expanse of Kings Landing. Leave several hours for exploration. (Open June-Oct. daily 10am-5pm; $7.50, seniors $6, youths 6-18 $4.50, under 6 free, families $18.) There is no public transportation to Kings Landing.

ENTERTAINMENT AND NIGHTLIFE

In the summer, Fredericton moves entertainment into the open with a free **outdoor summer theater** (452-9500), sponsored by the Calithumpians on the lawn of Officer's Square (Mon.-Fri. shows at 12:15pm, Sat. and Sun. 2pm.) Also catch Officers' Square's open-air concerts in July and August on Tues. and Thurs. evenings at 7:30, featuring everything from pipe bands to bluegrass. The **Harvest Blues and Jazz Festival** rolls into town in mid-Sept. with late-night jam sessions and free performances all over town. If you prefer a roof over your head, your best bet would be **The Playhouse,** 686 Queen St. (458-8344) and the resident Theatre New Brunswick Company, who, when not touring, put on the best shows in town, for a price.

Much of Fredericton's nightlife is inspired by students of the University of New Brunswick and St. Thomas College, which together import 10,000 young people to the city each fall. **The Hilltop Pub,** 152 Prospect St. (458-9057), serves heaping portions of steak ($8-14) and an ample lunch buffet ($6.50; Mon.-Fri. 11am-2pm) by day and seriously cheap drafts by night ($1.90, Sat. 8-10pm; 50¢ gets "ladies" a draft Thurs. after 8pm). Local youth boogie to country music in this cavernous barn-like saloon. (Open Mon. and Wed. 11am-1am; Tues., Thurs., and Fri. 11am-2am, Sat. 10am-2am. Dining room closes at 9pm.) **The Lunar Rogue Pub,** 625 King St. (450-2065), offers the eclectic live Irish, contemporary, and folk music. No cover Thurs.-Sat. (Open Mon.-Sat. 11am-1am, Sun. noon-midnight.) For dancing, the **Chestnut Pub,** 440 York St. (450-1230), is one of the few establishments in Fredericton which qualifies as a club, not a pub. (Open Mon.-Sat. 11:30am-2pm, Sun. 6pm-2am.)

■■■ FUNDY NATIONAL PARK

Fundy National Park is characteristically New Brunswickian in that its main attractions are its natural wonders. Approximately every 12 hours, the world's largest tides draw back over 1km into the Bay of Fundy, allowing visitors to explore a vast, usually hidden territory. Don't get caught too far out without your running shoes though. The water rises 1 foot per minute when the tide comes in. Thankfully, Fundy offers more than enough dry-land activities to keep you busy for another 12 hours. Fundy's extensive hiking tails, forests, campgrounds, and recreational facilities occupy 260 square kilometers on New Brunswick's coast, only an hour's drive southeast of Moncton on Hwy. 114.

Practical Information **Park Headquarters** (887-6000), P.O. Box 40, Alma, NB, E0A 1B0, is made up of a group of buildings in the southeastern corner of the Park facing the Bay, across the Upper Salmon River from the town of Alma. The area includes the administration building, the assembly building, an amphitheater, and the **Visitors Reception Center,** which sits at the east entrance (open daily 8am-9pm; mid-Sept. to late May Mon.-Fri. 8:15am-4:30pm). **Wolfe Lake Information** (432-6026), the park's other visitors center, lurks at the northwest entrance, off Hwy. 114 (open mid-June to Sept. Sat.-Thurs. 10am-6pm, Fri. 9am-9pm). In the off-season, contact Park Headquarters (open Mon.-Fri. 8:15am-4:30pm). No public transportation serves Fundy, and the nearest bus depots are in Moncton and Sussex. The park extracts a car entrance fee of $5 per day and $10 for four days from mid-June to Labor Day, but is free year-round for bicyclists and hikers. The free and invaluable park newspaper *Salt and Fir,* available at the park entrance stations and info centers, includes a map of all hiking trails, campgrounds, and interpretive programs and activities.

Fundy weather can be unpleasant for the unprepared. Evenings are often chilly, even when days are warm. It's best to always bring a wool sweater or jacket, as well as a can of insect repellent for the warm, muggy days. **Weather** forecasts are available from the info centers by calling 887-2000. Fundy's nearest **post office:** Main St. in Alma. (887-2272; open Mon.-Fri. 9am-noon and 12:30-5pm, Sat. 9am-noon); **postal code:** EOA 1BO; **area code:** 506.

Camping, a Hostel, and Food

The park operates four **campgrounds** totalling over 600 sites; getting a site is seldom a problem, although landing one at your campground of choice may be a little more difficult. Reservations are *not* accepted; all sites are first-come, first-grabbed. **Headquarters Campground** is in highest demand due to its proximity to facilities. When the campground is full, put your name on the waiting list, and sleep somewhere else for the night. Return the next day at noon when names of those admitted for the night are read. (Open mid-May to Labor Day. Sites $10, with hookup $15.50.) **Chignecto North Campground,** off Hwy. 114, 5km inland from the headquarters, is the other campground with electrical hookups. Here, the forest and distance between campsites affords more privacy. Ten sites offer three-way hookup, 106 offer electricity and water, 56 offer electricity only, and 120 have no hookup at all. (Open mid-June to mid-Oct. Sites $8, with varying degrees of hookup $14-16.) **Point Wolfe Campground,** scenically located along the coast 7km west of Headquarters, stays cooler and more insect-free than the inland campgrounds. (Open July-Aug. Sites $7.75.) All three campgrounds have showers and washrooms. The **Wolfe Lake Campground** offers primitive sites near the northwest park entrance. About a minute's walk from the lake; no showers or washrooms. (Open late May-early Oct. Sites $6, $18 for 4 nights, $30 per week.) Wilderness camping is also available in some of the most scenic areas of the park, especially at **Goose River** along the coast. The campsites are open year-round, require a $2 per person per night permit fee, and all have fireplaces, wood, and an outhouse. Reservations are needed year-round, and should be made one or two weeks in advance; call 887-6000.

The **Fundy National Park Hostel (HI-C)** (887-2216), near Devil's Half Acre about 1km south of the park headquarters, has a full kitchen and showers, although in separate buildings from the bunkrooms. Ask the staff for the lowdown on park staff nightlife ($8.50, nonmembers $10; open June-Aug. Handicapped accessible.) For a cheap, home-cooked meal, try **Harbor View Market and Coffee Shop** (887-2450), on Main St. in Alma, where you can get do-it-yourself groceries or let the owner cook for you. A breakfast special of two eggs, toast, bacon, and coffee is $3; fantastic strawberry shortcake $2. (Open daily 7am-10pm; Sept.-May daily 7:30am-8pm.)

Activities

About 120km of park trails are open year-round. Descriptions of all trails are detailed in *Salt and Fir*. A handful are open to mountain bikes, which can be rented at the youth hostel (887-2216; 1hr. $7, 5hrs. $15; rates decrease over time). Look for the many spectacular sights, including waterfalls, ocean views, and wild animals. Though declining in numbers, deer are still fairly common, and raccoons are thick as thieves around the campsites. Catching a glimpse of a moose or a peregrine falcon will require considerably more patience.

Most recreational facilities open only during the summer season (mid-May to early Oct.), including free, daily, interpretive programs designed to help visitors get to know the park. The park staff lead beach walks, evening programs (in the Amphitheater), and weekly campfire programs. Visit the park in September and October to avoid the crush of vacationers and to catch the fall foliage. Those seeking quiet, pristine nature would be wise to visit in the chillier off-season.

CANADA

■■■ MONCTON

Formerly a thriving English shipbuilding settlement, Moncton is the unofficial capital city of the province's Acadian population. Its demographics accurately reflect New Brunswick's cultural schizophrenia; the francophone one-third and anglophone two-thirds of Moncton's population coexist without tension. English predominates except around the campus of the Université de Moncton, Canada's only French-language university outside of Québec. The city's inexpensive B&Bs and restaurants, and its central location to the Fundy and Kouchibouguac National Parks, the Rocks Provincial Park, the town of Shediac on the coast, and Halifax farther east in Nova Scotia, make it an excellent base for exploring the region.

PRACTICAL INFORMATION

Emergency: 911.
Visitor Information: City Hall's Convention and Visitor Services, 774 Main St. (853-3590), handles tourists Mon.-Fri. 9am-4:30pm.
Trains: VIA Rail, 1240 Main St. (857-9830), behind the mall. Ask for student discounts. To: Halifax (6 per week, 4½ hr., $40); Montréal (6 per week, 14 hr., $122). Open Mon.-Fri. 9:30am-7pm, Sat.-Sun. 10am-7pm.
Buses: SMT, 961 Main St. (859-2170), downtown at Bonaccord St. To: Halifax (2 per day, 5 hr., $33); Saint John (2 per day, 2 hr., $20); Charlottetown, P.E.I. (2 per day, 4½ hr., $29); connects to Acadian Lines, Amherst. Open Mon.-Fri. 7:30am-6.
Public Transport: Codia Transit, 280 Pacific Ave. (857-2008), provides service through Greater Moncton Mon.-Wed. and Sat. 7am-7pm, Thurs.-Fri. 7am-11pm. Buses congregate downtown at Highfield Square. Fare $1, students and seniors 70¢; exact change only. Office open Mon.-Fri. 6:30am-4:30pm.
Car Rental: Econo, 740 Mountain Rd. (858-9100), rents for $23 per day, with 200km free, 10¢ per km thereafter. Insurance $10. Must be 25 with major credit card. Open Mon.-Fri. 8:30am-5:30pm, Sat. 9am-1pm.
Help line: Help-24-au secours, 857-9782, 24hrs.
Post Office: 281 St. George St. (857-7240), near Highfield St. Open Mon.-Fri. 8am-5:30pm. **Postal code:** E1C 8K4.
Area Code: 506.

ACCOMMODATIONS AND FOOD

Moncton's dozen or so B&Bs definitely offer the best accommodation rates in town (singles $28-40), as well as clean, comfortable rooms. Try to plan in advance, as these are unlikely to be available without a reservation. A number of motels line up along the Trans-Canada Hwy., preying on those who drive through the area to experience Magnetic Hill.

The **McCarthy Bed and Breakfast,** 82 Peter St. (383-9152), is a jewel. Gerry and Marge will welcome you with genuine warmth and unforgettable hospitality. Talk to Gerry about his philanthropic activities or simply look at his St. Patrick Card Collection, the largest in the world (singles $28, doubles $38. Full breakfast included. Open May-Sept.; reservations are highly recommended). Gerry will pick you up at the bus or train station. The **Université de Moncton** (858-4015 or 858-4014) opens two dorms for summer lodging. The LaFrance building—the tallest structure on campus—provides spacious, newly renovated rooms with kitchenette units. (Singles $35, students $28.) The Lefevre building is more low-key, more student-like, and more affordable (singles $25, students $19; doubles $35/30). Laundry facilities are available in both. From Queen St. downtown, follow Archibald St. all the way out (10 min. drive). From downtown, take bus 5 ("Elmwood A"). (Open May-Aug.) The **YWCA,** 35 Highfield St. (855-4349), one block from Main St. behind the bus station, also provides good-sized, clean rooms upstairs for women only (singles $20, doubles $30; kitchen and laundry; check-out 11am). Reservations highly recommended. From mid-May to mid-Sept. the Y doubles as a **HI-C hostel,** renting 5 beds to women and 8 cot-like bunks to men ($7, nonmembers $8; linen rental $4, so bring a sleeping-bag; check-in until 11pm curfew time; check-out 9am). Breakfast ($3), large noontime dinner ($7.50), and supper ($4) are available.

The only area campground is **Camper's City** (384-7867), located off the Trans-Canada Hwy. on Mapleton Rd., only 5km north of downtown. (177 sites, with showers, toilets, pool, grocery, and laundry; sites $14, with hookup $18; office open daily 7:30am-11pm.)

Jean's Restaurant, 368 St. George St. (885-1053), has home-cooked dinner specials for $6, including main course, vegetable, potato, roll, and coffee (open daily 5:45am-11pm). **Fancy Pocket,** 589 Main St. (858-7898), is an elegant Lebanese restaurant, carrying a wide variety of pita pockets ($5-6) and brochettes ($8.25-11). (Open daily 11am-9pm.) **Club Cosmopolitan,** 700 Main St. (857-9117), is the place to boogie off your dinner. Live jazz on Fridays. ($2 cover 5:30-9:30pm only. Open daily 8pm-2am, open at 5:30pm on Fri.) Moncton's American League **hockey** franchise, the **Hawks,** play at the Maritime Coliseum Complex (Oct.-April; 859-2689; 857-4100 for tickets).

TIDAL BORE AND MAGNETIC HILL

Moncton is deservedly proud of its two natural wonders, which are both more impressive in person than on paper. The **Tidal Bore,** best viewed from Tidal Bore Park near the corner of Main St. and King St., is an awesome product of the Bay of Fundy tides. Twice a day the incoming tide surges up the Petitcodiac River, a muddy river bottom along whose banks Moncton is situated, and within an hour or so fills up to the 25-ft.-high river banks. Then the flow of water reverses direction, and over the next two hours the mighty river recedes back into Chignecto Bay. It's best to arrive 15 min. before posted Tidal Bore times (consult the city guide), in case it hits early. Spring and fall are the best seasons during which to catch the phenomenon at full force, as well as at a full or new moon.

Magnetic Hill (384-9527) on Mountain Rd., just off the Trans-Canada Hwy. (Hwy. 2) northwest of central Moncton, has recently become one in a long line of natural phenomena co-opted by the tourist industry. This once-free attraction now costs $2, but is worth it. Drive your car down to the bottom of the hill, put it in neutral, and feel it inexplicably roll back up to the top of the hill. Several tries allowed. (Feel free to supply your own explanation. The park has no party line, and locals support the optical illusion theory; open daily 7am-9pm.)

■ NEAR MONCTON

The Rocks Provincial Park, at Hopewell Cape, off Hwy. 114, 34km south of Moncton, are 50-ft.-high sandstone formations with trees on top. At high tide, they look like little islands off the coast, but at low tide they resemble gigantic flowerpots. Tourists are free to explore the Rocks on foot. ($3.50; open 24 hr. May 9-Columbus Day.) Call the information center (734-3429) or **Tourism New Brunswick** (800-561-0123) for tide info.

The Acadian town of **Shediac,** 30km north of Moncton on Hwy. 15, stakes its claim as the Lobster Capital of the World by holding their annual **Shediac Lobster Festival** in mid-July. For more info about scheduled events, write to **Shediac Information,** P.O. Box 969, Shediac E0A 3G0 (532-1500; open June-Aug. daily 9am-9pm). More important to sun worshipers is the popular **Parlee Beach Provincial Park** (533-8813), in Shediac Bay near the warm salt waters of the Northumberland Strait (open July-Aug. daily 8am-midnight; June and Sept.1-Labor Day 8am-10pm:).

Fort Beauséjour National Historical Park is located near the Nova Scotia border off the Trans-Canada Hwy. in Aulac, 40km southeast of Moncton (536-0720). One of the numerous forts built by the French and captured by the British, Fort Beauséjour is not much more than rubble these days. The real reason to visit the site is the panoramic view it provides on a clear day. One can see southward to the Cumberland Basin of the Chignecto Bay, and northward to the Tantramar River Valley. (Site always open. Museum open June to mid-Oct. daily 9am-5pm. Free.)

CANADA

Kouchibouguac Unlike Fundy's rugged forests and the high tides along the Loyalist coast, Kouchibouguac (meaning "river of the long tides" in Micmac) proudly shows off its warm lagoon waters, salt marshes, peat bogs, and white sandy beaches. Sun along the 25km stretch of barrier islands and sand dunes, or swim through canoe waterways that were once highways for the Micmacs. You can rent canoes and bikes at **Ryans Rental Center** (876-2571) in the park between the South Kouchibouguac Campground and Kellys Beach. (Open late May-early June Sat.-Sun. 9am-5pm; early June-early Sept. daily 8am-9pm.) The park operates two camp-grounds in the summer, neither with hookups (sites $8-11.75). **South Kouchibou-guac** has 219 sites with showers, and **Côte-à-Fabien** has 32 sites with no showers. Primitive sites within the park and several nearby commercial campgrounds just outside of the park are available for off-season campers. Kouchibouguac National Park charges a vehicle permit fee of $5 per day, $10 per four days, or $20 per year. The **Park Information Centre** is located at the Park Entrance on Hwy. 117 just off Hwy. 11, 90km north of Moncton. (Open mid-May to mid-June daily 10am-6pm; mid-June to early Sept. daily 10am-6pm; early Sept. to mid-Oct. daily 9am-5pm.) The park administration (876-2443) is open year-round Mon.-Fri. 8:15am-4:30pm.

■■■ SAINT JOHN

The city of Saint John was founded literally overnight on May 18, 1783, by a band of about 10,000 American colonists (known as the United Empire Loyalists) loyal to the British crown. Saint John's long loyalist tradition is apparent in its architecture, festivals, and institutions; the walkways of King and Queen Squares in central Saint John (never abbreviated so as to prevent confusion with St. John's, Newfoundland) were laid out to resemble the Union Jack. The city rose to prominence in the 19th century as a major commercial and shipbuilding port. Now home to 125,000 peo-ple, Canada's oldest incorporated city maintains a small town atmosphere uncharac-teristic of a city its size. Saint John's location on the Bay of Fundy ensures cool summers and mild winters, albeit foggy and wet; locals joke that Saint John is where you go to get your car, and yourself, washed for free.

PRACTICAL INFORMATION

Emergency: 911.

Visitor Information: Saint John Visitors and Convention Bureau, 15 Market Sq. (658-2990), on the 11th floor of City Hall at the foot of King St., operates year-round. Open Mon.-Fri. 8:30am-4:30pm. The **City Center** information center, alias **The Little Red Schoolhouse** (658-2855), offers info in Loyalist Plaza by the Market Slip uptown. Open mid-May to early June and Labor Day to mid-Oct. daily 9am-6pm; early June-Labor Day daily 9am-7pm.

Trains: VIA Rail, 125 Station St. (642-2916), next to Hwy. 1 north of Market Square. To: Halifax (Fri., Sun., and Tues.; 7 hr.; $58, students $53; at least 5 days in advance $35, Tues. only $29); Montréal (Mon., Thurs., and Sat.; 12 hr. $107/ $97, 7 days in advance $86/$70). Station and ticket office open Tues., Fri., and Sun. 7:30am-12:30pm, Mon., Thurs., and Sat. 4-9pm.

Buses: SMT, 300 Union St. (648-3555), provides service to: Montréal (2 per day, 14 hr., $80); Moncton (2 per day, 2 hr., $20); Halifax (2 per day, 8 hr., $52). Station and ticket office open daily 9am-6pm.

Public Transport: Saint John Transit (658-4700), runs until roughly 11:30pm. $1.25, under 14 $1. Also gives a 3-hr. guided tour of historic Saint John leaving from Loyalist Plaza and Reversing Falls June 15-Sept. Tour fare $15, ages 6-14 $5.

Ferry: Marine Atlantic (636-4048 or 800-341-7981 from the continental U.S.), on the Lancaster St. extension in West Saint John, near the mouth of Saint John Har-bor. Crosses to Digby, Nova Scotia (1-3 per day, 2½ hr., $21, seniors $16, ages 5-12 $10.50, bike $10, car $45; Oct.-May $15/$12/$7.50/$5/$40). To get to the ferry, take the Saint John Transit West-Saint-John bus, then walk 10 min.

Taxi: Royal Taxi, 800-561-8294; **Diamond,** 648-8888. Both open 24 hrs.

Car Rental: Downey Ford, 10 Crown St. (632-6000). $24 per day, with 100km free, 11¢ per additional km. Must be 25 with major credit card. No charge for insurance, but the deductible is a hefty $1500. $8 for zero deductible. All cars are automatics. (Open Mon.-Fri. 7am-6pm, Sat. 8am-5pm, Sun. 9am-5pm.)
Weather: 636-4991. **Dial-a-Tide:** 636-4429. Both 24 hrs.
Post Office: Main Office, 125 Rothesay Ave. (800-565-0726). Open Mon.-Fri. 7:30am-5:15pm. **Postal Code:** E2L 3W9. For stamps, go to the postal outlet in Lawton's Drugs, 39 King St. (652-4956), in Brunswick Sq. Open Mon.-Wed. 9am-5:30pm, Thurs.-Fri. 9am-9pm, Sat. 10am-5pm.
Area Code: 506.

Saint John is divided from West Saint John by the Fort Latour Harbor Bridge (toll 25¢), on Hwy. 1. Saint John's busy downtown (Saint John Centre) is bounded by Union St. to the north, Princess St. to the south, King Square on the east, and Market Square and the harbor on the west. Find free 3-hr. parking outside the city's malls.

ACCOMMODATIONS AND CAMPING

Finding lodging for under $35 per night is difficult, especially in summer. A number of nearly identical motels cover the 1100 to 1300 blocks of **Manawagonish Road** in West Saint John (take the Fairville bus), usually charging $35-45 for a single. Avoid the bridge toll when driving to this area by taking Hwy. 100 into West Saint John. Take a right on Main St. west, which quickly turns into Manawagonish Rd.

Saint John YMCA/YWCA (HI-C), 19-25 Hazen Ave. (634-7720), from Market Square, 2 blocks up Union St. on left. Drab, bare, but clean rooms. Access to YMCA recreational facilities. Pool, work-out room. Reservations recommended in the summer. $25, nonmembers and nonstudents $30. Open daily 5:30am-11pm. Guests arriving on the evening ferry can be checked in later.
Tartan B&B, 968 Manawagonish Rd. (672-2592). No frills, but clean and well-decorated. Stay here in off-season; with the full breakfast included, it's a good deal. Shared baths. Singles $35, doubles $40. Oct.-June $30/$35.
Hillside Motel, 1131 Manawagonish Rd. (672-1273). Standard clean motel room with TV and private bath. Kitchenettes available at no extra cost. $35 for one bed, $45 for two beds; Sept.-April $28/35.
Rockwood Park Campground (652-4050), at the southern end of Rockwood Park, off Hwy. 1, 2km north of uptown in a partly wooded area. RV sites in cramped parking area. Sites $12, with hookup $14; 2 days $21/$26; weekly $50/$75. Take University bus to Park entrance, then walk 5 min. Open mid-May to May-Sept.

FOOD AND ENTERTAINMENT

For cheap, fresh produce and seafood, your best bet is the **City Market,** 47 Charlotte St. (658-2820), between King and Brunswick Squares. The oldest building of its kind in Canada, City Market is opened and closed by the ringing of the 83-year-old Market Bell. It is also your best source for **dulse,** or sun-dried seaweed picked in the Bay of Fundy's waters, a local specialty not found outside New Brunswick, best described as "Ocean jerky." A $1 bag is more than a sample serving. (Market open Mon.-Thurs. 7:30am-6pm, Fri. 7:30am-7pm, Sat. 7:30am-5pm.) At **Slocum and Ferris** (652-2260), in the market, you can sample everything from Argentinian *empanadas* ($1) to Indian *samosas* (75¢), and wash it down with a glass of fantastic peach juice. **Reggie's Restaurant,** 26 Germain St. (657-6270), provides fresh, homestyle cooking of basic North American fare. Reggie's uses famous smoked meat from Ben's Deli in Montréal, but their sandwiches are too small to constitute a full meal. The best deal in the house is breakfast. From 6am-11am, two eggs, sausage, homefries, toast, and coffee is $3.25. (Open daily 6am-9pm; Nov.-May Mon.-Wed. 6am-6pm, Thurs.-Fri. 6am-7pm, Sat. 6am-5pm, Sun. 7am-3pm.) In 1995 the best time to be in Saint John will be July 9-15, when the unique **Loyalist Days** festival (634-8123) celebrates the long-ago arrival of the Tories, complete with re-enactment, costumes, and street parade. The **Festival By the Sea** (632-0086), August 11-20, 1995, brings in a number of stage and musical productions.

SIGHTS

Saint John's main attraction is **Reversing Falls,** but before you start imagining 100-ft. walls of gravity-defying water, read on. The "falls" are actually beneath the surface of the water; what patient spectators will see is the flow of water at the nexus of the St. John River and Saint John Harbor slowly halting and changing direction due to the powerful Bay of Fundy tides. More amazing may be the number of people captivated by the phenomenon. (24 hrs. Free.) Pick up a tide schedule or watch the thrill-a-minute 12-min. film on the phenomenon at the **Reversing Falls Tourist Centre** (658-2937), located at the west end of the Hwy.100 bridge crossing the river; unfortunately, the film does not show the Big Event. (Center open May-Oct. daily 8am-8pm; film $1.25; kids under 12 free; screenings every ½ hr. To reach the viewpoint and tourist center, take the west-bound East-West bus.)

Moosehead Breweries, 49 Main St. (635-7020), in West Saint John, offers free 1-hr. tours of the factory Mon.-Fri. twice daily, June through August, leaving from their Country Store. Since tours are limited to 20 people, make reservations one or two days ahead. (The tours, of course, include samples.)

Three self-guided **walking tours** are mapped out by the city, each lasting about 2 hr. The walking tour brochures can be picked up at any tourist info center. **The Victorian Stroll** takes you past some of the old homes in Saint John, most dating to the late 1800s; **Prince William's Walk** details commerce in the port city; **The Loyalist Trail** traces the places frequented by the Loyalist founders. All of the walking tours heavily emphasize history, architecture, and nostalgia. **Trinity Church,** 115 Charlotte St. (693-8558), on the Loyalist Trail tour, displays some amazing stained-glass windows, as well as the Royal Coat of Arms of the House of Hanover (to which George III belonged), stolen (or "rescued") from the walls of the old Boston Council Chamber by fleeing Loyalists during the American Revolution (tours and viewing Mon. 10am-4pm, Tues.-Sat. 10am-5pm, Sun. 9:30-10:30am and 1-5pm).

Fort Howe Lookout affords a fine view of the city and its harbor. Originally erected to protect the harbor from American privateers, the landmark bristles with cannon. Shooting still occurs here—though predominantly with tripod-mounted cameras rather than with the huge, now-defunct guns. To visit the Lookout, walk a few blocks in from the north end of the harbor and up the hill; look for the wooden blockhouse atop the hill. (Open 24 hrs. Free.)

The **Cherry Brook Zoo** (634-1440), north of downtown on Sandy Point Rd., provides a chance to see over 100 species of animals. ($3.50, seniors and students $2.50, kids 3-5 $1.50, under 3 free; open daily 10am-dusk.)

Nova Scotia

Since 1605, when French colonists known as Acadians began sharing the Annapolis Valley and Cape Breton's shores with the indigenous Micmac Indians, Nova Scotia has possessed a unique cultural diversity. Despite strong trading ties with Massachusetts, Nova Scotia declined the opportunity to become the 14th state in the early American Republic. Instead, the colony established itself as a refuge for fleeing British loyalists. Subsequent immigration brought the Scottish, English, and Irish, who have all left their mark on the social melange. A strong Scottish identity has been preserved in Pictou and Antigonish Counties. In 1867, to protect itself against a feared American invasion, Nova Scotia joined three other provinces to form the Dominion of Canada.

Four distinct geographies dominate the province: the rugged Atlantic coast, the agriculturally lush Annapolis Valley, the calm coast of the Northumberland Strait, and the magnificent highlands and lakes of Cape Breton Island. Each of these areas offers breathtaking scenery unique to its geography. However, one thing remains constant: the people of Nova Scotia are proud of their province and happy to help visitors who have come to enjoy it.

PRACTICAL INFORMATION

Capital: Halifax.

Economic Renewal Agency, Tourism Nova Scotia, Historic Properties, P.O. Box 456, Halifax, NS B3J 2R5. A dozen provincial info centers are scattered throughout Nova Scotia. Call 800-565-0000 (from Canada) or 800-341-6096 (from the continental U.S.) to make reservations with participating hostels and to get most tourist information.

Time Zone: Atlantic (1 hr. ahead of Eastern time). **Postal abbreviation:** NS

Drinking Age: 19.

Provincial Sales Tax: 11%, plus 7% GST (see Canada Essential for details on obtaining a refund of the GST).

■■■ ANNAPOLIS VALLEY

Green and fertile, the Annapolis Valley stretches along the **Bay of Fundy** between **Yarmouth** and the **Minas Basin.** Its calm, sunny weather draws harried city-folk seeking a relaxed lifestyle. The Annapolis River Valley runs slightly inland, but parallel to the coast, flanked by the imaginatively named North and South Mountains. Charming towns scatter along the length of the Valley connected by scenic Hwy. 1. In spring, orchards covered with aromatic pink apple blossoms perfume the Valley.

French Acadian farmers settled this serene valley in the 17th century. Their expulsion from there by the British in 1755 was commemorated by Henry Wadsworth Longfellow's tragic epic poem "Evangeline," and although Longfellow himself never actually visited this "forest primeval," the title "Land of Evangeline" has nevertheless stuck. Rushing from sight to sight is not the most satisfying method of exploring the Valley. Bicycling is an ideal means of transport between the towns, but beware of long, uninhabited stretches which look deceptively shorter on a map.

Northern Coast   Digby, home of the famous Digby scallops, harbors one of the world's largest scallop fleets and hosts the annual August **Scallop Days** festival. About 104km up the coast from Yarmouth, Digby is connected by the **Marine Atlantic Ferry** (245-2116 or 800-341-7981 from the Continental U.S.), to Saint John, New Brunswick, which lies across the Bay of Fundy. (1-2 trips daily, 2-3 daily late June-Columbus Day; 3 hr. $21, seniors $16, ages 5-12 $10.50, car $45; Columbus Day-late June $16/$12.25/$8/$40.) Terminal open 24 hrs.

Brier Island, the home of Joshua Slocum (the first person to sail around the world solo), forms the tips off Digby Neck, a 90-min. drive south from Digby on Hwy. 217. Whale watching in the island's surrounding waters is so successful that **Brier Island Whale and Seabird Cruises** (839-2995) in **Westport** guarantees whale sightings or you go again free. The guides are scientific researchers from the Brier Island Ocean Study or from local universities. (Voyages, weather permitting, last 4 hr. $33, ages 6-12 $16, under 6 free, 10% senior discount. Reserve at least 1 week in advance.)

The **Habitation Port-Royal,** founded by French explorer Samuel de Champlain in 1605, was the earliest permanent European settlement in North America north of Florida. It served as the capital of French Acadia for nearly a century until its capitulation to the British in 1710, who renamed it Annapolis Royal in honor of Queen Anne. The original town later fell into ruin but has been restored faithfully in the form of the **Port-Royal National Historical Park** (532-2898) across the Annapolis Basin, 12km from modern-day Annapolis Royal. The restoration affords a rare glimpse of the wooden palisades and stone chimneys typical in early French fur-trading posts. To get to the Habitation, turn off Hwy. 1 at the Granville Ferry and go 10km. (Open May 15-Oct. 15 daily 9am-6pm. $2, kids under 5 free, families $6.) **Kejimkujik National Park** (682-2772), Hwy. 8, about 60km inland from Annapolis Royal and 160km west of Halifax, lies relatively close by. Called "Keji," the park is remote, densely wooded, and liberally peppered with small lakes and unspoiled waterways best explored by canoe. Fee for bringing vehicles into the park: $5 for 1 day, $10 for 4 days. The park has a **campground** with hot showers and 329 sites ($10.50, no hookup). The park's **information center** is in the northeast corner on the Mersey River (open daily 8:30am-9pm, Sept. 6 to mid-June 8:30am-4:30pm).

For a less historical park experience, seek out the new amusement park, **Upper Clements Theme Park** (532-7557), 6km west of Annapolis Royal on Hwy. 1. Yes, there are roller coasters, water rides, and a mini-golf course, but you'll also find petting farms, artisans, storytellers, and craftspeople plying their trade. (Open late June-early Sept. daily 10am-7pm. Park admission $5, but pass for attractions $12; kids under 6 free; fees good for 2 consecutive days.) Of note to engineers and "tido-philes" is the **Annapolis Tidal Generating Station,** just off Hwy. 1 (532-5454), the first attempt to generate electrical energy by harnessing the powerful Bay of Fundy tides. (Open daily 8am-8pm; off-season daily 9:30am-5:30pm. Free.) The station is paired with a Provincial **visitors center** (same hours).

Eastern Annapolis Valley   **Wolfville,** 55km north of Annapolis Royal, was renamed in 1830 at the urging of postmaster de Wolf, whose nieces were ashamed of saying that they were from the town of Mud Creek. The town still commemorates its muckier appellation with **Mud Creek Days** (542-7000; Oct.-May 542-2400), the first weekend in August. The most panoramic Valley view is from **The Lookoff,** Hwy. 358, 20km north of Hwy. 1, perched on a mountain top.

Grand Pré, or **Great Meadow,** stands at the north-eastern head of Annapolis Valley, 100km northwest of Halifax. The highlight is the **Grand Pré National Historic Site** (542-3631), a memorial of the deportation of the Acadians in 1755. After refusing to take oaths of allegiance, the Acadians of Grand Pré were imprisoned in the Stone Church before their deportation from the British colonies. The refugees later resettled further south, establishing communities in modern-day Louisiana, where time and accents have transformed "Acadians" into "Cajuns." (Grounds always open. Buildings open mid-May to mid-Oct. daily 9am-6pm. Free.) Canada's best wines ferment in the Annapolis Valley; the **Grand Pré Wine Estate Vineyard** (542-1753) gives three daily tours. (Open May-Sept. daily 9am-5pm. Free.)

Yarmouth   The port of **Yarmouth,** 339km from Halifax, on the southwestern tip of Nova Scotia, has a major **ferry terminal** at 58 Water St., with ships departing across the **Bay of Fundy** to Maine (open daily 8am-5pm). **Marine Atlantic** (742-6800 or 800-341-7981 from continental U.S.) provides service to Bar Harbor (1 per day, Oct.-May 3 per week; 6-7 hr.; $47, seniors $35, ages 5-12 $23.50, car $60; Oct.-May $32/$24/$15.50/$55). **Prince of Fundy Cruises** (800-341-7540 in USA and Canada), sail from Yarmouth's port to Portland, ME. (Departs May-Oct. daily at 10am; 10 hr.; early May to mid-June and mid-Sept. to mid-Oct. US$55, ages 5-14 US$27.50; car US$80; mid-June to mid-Sept. US$75/US$37.50.) Renting a car in Yarmouth is a very popular idea, so reserve ahead. **Avis,** 44 Starr's Rd. (742-3323), and at a desk in the ferry terminal, rents cars for $48 per day plus $9 for insurance with 100 free km. (Extra km. 15¢; must be 23.)

An **information center,** 288 Main St., uphill and visible from the ferry terminal, houses both **Nova Scotia Information** (742-5033) and **Yarmouth Town and County Information** (742-6639; both open daily 8am-7pm).

■■■ HALIFAX

The Halifax Citadel was erected in 1749 as a British garrison to counter the French Fortress of Louisbourg on the northeastern shoulder of Cape Breton Island. Never captured or even attacked during the era of the colonial empires, the Citadel has seen more French tourists in its lifetime than it has French soldiers. Halifax's placid history is marred by only one horrific event—in 1917, miscommunication between a Belgian relief ship and a French ship carrying picric acid and 400,000 tons of TNT resulted in a collision in Halifax Harbor, hurling sparks into the picric acid. One hour later, Halifax was rocked by the largest man-made explosion before the atomic bomb. Approximately 11,000 people were killed or injured, north Halifax was razed, and windows were shattered up to 50 mi. away. Long recovered from the disaster, Halifax has grown to be the largest city in Atlantic Canada, with a population of 320,000. The city's universities are a cosmopolitan magnet for the province's youth. With an active nightlife, Halifax is all the more attractive as a base for travel throughout the villages lining the coast.

PRACTICAL INFORMATION

Emergency: 4105.

Visitor Information: Halifax Tourist Information (421-8736), City Hall on the corner of Duke and Barrington. Open Mon.-Wed. 8:30am-7pm, Thurs.-Fri. 8:30am-8pm, Sun. 9am-6pm; early Sept.-May Mon.-Fri. 9am-5pm. Another branch (421-2772) on the corner of Sackville and S. Park, across from the Public Garden. Open mid-June to Labor Day, same hours. Find **Tourism Nova Scotia,** 1869 Lower Water St. (424-4247), in a red building on the downtown harbor boardwalk. (Open daily 8:30am-7pm; mid-Oct. to early June Mon.-Fri. 8:30am-4:30pm.)

Student Travel Agency: Travel CUTS, Dalhousie University Student Union Building 1st floor (494-2054). Open Mon.-Fri. 9am-4pm. **Rideboard** posted near Travel CUTS, near the cafeteria.

Airport: Halifax International, 40km from the city on Hwy. 102. The **Airbus** (873-2091) runs to downtown (18 per day, 7:45am-10:45pm; $11, round-trip $18, under 10 free with adult). **Ace Y Share-a-cab** (429-4444) runs service to the airport 5am-9pm. Phone 3 hr. ahead of pick-up time. Fare $18 ($30 for 2) from anywhere in Halifax. From airport, fare $20.

Trains: VIA Rail, 1161 Hollis St. (429-8421), on the corner of South St. in the South End near the harbor. Service to: Montréal ($150, student or senior $135, under 11 $75; discounts with 7 day advance purchase). Open daily 9am-5:30pm.

Buses: Acadian Lines and **MacKenzie Bus Line** share the same terminal, at 6040 Almon St. (454-9321), near Robie St. To get downtown from the bus terminal, take bus 7 or 80 on Robie St., or any of the 6 buses running on Gottingen St., 1 block east of the station. MacKenzie runs service along the Atlantic coast to: Yarmouth (1 per day, 6 hr., $29). Ask about stops at the small towns en route. Acadian covers most of the remainder of Nova Scotia, with connections to the rest of Canada: Annapolis Royal (2 per day, 3-5 hr., $23); Charlottetown (2 per day, 8½ hr., $47); North Sydney (3 per day, 6-8 hr., $42). Senior discount 25%. Kids 5-11 50% discount, under 5 free with adult. Ticket office open daily 7am-7pm; station open Sun.-Fri. 6:30am-midnight, Sat. 6:30am-11pm.

Public Transport: Metro Transit (421-6600; info line open Mon.-Fri. 7:30am-10pm, Sat.-Sun. 8am-10pm). Efficient and thorough. Pick up route map and schedules at any info center. Fare $1.25, seniors 90¢, and ages 5-15 75¢. Fare from Sackville St. $1.50. Buses run daily, roughly 7am-midnight.

Dartmouth-Halifax Ferry (464-2639), on the harborfront. 15-min. harbor crossings depart both terminals every 15-30 min. Mon.-Fri. 6:30am-midnight; every 30 min. Sat. 6:30am-midnight and Sun. noon-5:30pm. Fare $1.10, kids 5-12 75¢. Call 464-2142 for parking info.

Taxi: Aircab, 456-0373; **Ace Y Cab,** 429-4444. $2.40 base fee, $1.50 per mi.

Car Rental: Rent-a-Wreck, 2823 Robie St. (454-2121), at Almon St. $30 per day, 200km free, 12¢ per extra km. Insurance $9 per day, ages 21-25 $11. Must be 21 with credit card. Open Mon.-Fri. 8am-5pm, Sat. 8am-1pm.

Bike Rental: Pedal and Sea, 1253 Barrington St. (492-0116), downstairs from the Halifax Hostel. Mountain bikes $6 per hr., $5 for hostel members; ½ day $13/11; full day $22/15; week $80/60. Open daily May to mid.-Oct. 9am-6pm.

Driver/Rider Services: Alternative Passage, 5945 Spring Garden Rd. (429-5169), promotes ecological rides. To: Montréal ($50); North Sydney ($21); Fredericton ($28); Cape Tourmentine ($16). $7 yearly membership required with 3 character references and positive I.D. Open Mon.-Fri. 8:30am-7:30pm, Sat.-Sun. 10am-5pm. **Auto-Driveaway,** 752 Bedford Hwy. (457-7111). $50 application fee, $300 security deposit ($350 to the U.S.), and you only pay for the gas. Open Mon.-Fri. 9am-6:30pm, Sat. noon-3pm.

Help Lines: Sexual Assault: 425-0122, 24 hrs. **Crisis Centre:** 421-1188, 24 hrs. **Gayline:** 423-7129, Thurs.-Sat. 7-10pm.

Post Office: Station "A," 6175 Almon St. (494-4712), in the North End, 2.5km from downtown. Open Mon.-Fri. 8am-5:15pm. **Postal Code:** B3K 5M9.

Area Code: 902.

Barrington is the major north-south street. **Sackville Street,** approaching the Citadel and the Public Garden, runs east-west parallel to **Spring Garden Road,** Halifax's shopping thoroughfare. Flanking downtown are the less affluent **North End** and the mostly quiet and arboreal **South End,** on the ocean. Downtown traffic is bearable, but parking difficult. If you visit in the winter, do *not* park on the street; it's prohibited in case snowplows are needed. Heed this warning even if it is sunny and warm or meters go unread on weekends.

ACCOMMODATIONS AND CAMPING

You will have no trouble finding affordable summer accommodations in Halifax, unless you happen upon a major event, such as the Tattoo Festival or the Moosehead Grand Prix. Free at tourism offices, the impressive *Doer's and Dreamer's Complete Guide* lists over 300 pages of Nova Scotia accommodations. Call **Check-In** (800-565-0000) to reserve a space in nearly 90% of the province's accommodations. Halifax's closest camping is actually in Hammond's Plain, a 20-min. drive north on Hwy. 102. Take exit 3 off Rte. 213 and follow the signs to **Wood Havens Park** (835-2271; 95 sites, $14, hookup $17-18.50; open May-Oct.).

Halifax Heritage House Hostel (HI-C), 1253 Barrington St. (422-3863), 1 block from the train station, 3-min. walk from the heart of downtown. Clean rooms. Lounge with TV. Kitchen and laundry. Ask for a room on the 1st floor where bathrooms are not shared by many people. Free linen. IBN reservations available. No curfew. Closed noon-3pm. Check-in 3-11pm. $12.75, nonmembers $15.75, non-Canadian nonmembers $16.75.

Technical University of Nova Scotia, M. M. O'Brien Bldg., 5217 Morris St. (420-7780), at Barrington. Refinished dorms right downtown. Free laundry and parking. Kitchen access. Check-in daily 9am-midnight. Singles $23, doubles $36; students $18/32; kids $10/16. Reservations recommended July-Aug. Open May-Aug.

Dalhousie University (494-3401, after 8pm 494-2108), Howe Hall on Coburg Rd. at LaMarchant, 3km southwest of downtown. Usually packed, so arrive early. Laundry and Dal recreation facilities extra. Singles $29, doubles $43 (breakfast and parking included), student singles $20 ($5 extra for breakfast). Under 11 free. Make July-Aug. reservations 1 week in advance. Open early May-late Aug., 24 hrs.

Gerrard Hotel, 1234 Barrington St. (423-8614), between South and Morris St. Subdued live-in clientele and elaborate rooms. Kitchen and parking. Must check in Mon.-Fri. 8am-8:30pm, Sat. 8am-7:30pm. Singles $30, with private bath $44; doubles $39/49. $5 per extra person.

FOOD

Downtown pubs provide cheap grub and vitality. Try the local mussels (about $3), served on generous platters. Though the pubs stay open late, kitchens close down around 10pm. For fresh local produce and baked goods, visit the **farmer's market** (492-4043) in the old brewery on Lower Water St. (open May-Sept. Sat. 7am-1pm.)

Granite Brewery, 1222 Barrington St. (423-5660). The best pub food in town and its own microbrewery to boot, which produces three labels; the Old Peculiar is strangely good ($2.30 for 9-oz. glass). Try some with the shrimp and sausage *jambalaya* ($9.50) and finish up with blueberry shortcake ($3.50). Open Mon.-Sat. 11:30am-12:30pm, Sun. noon-11pm.

Lawrence of Oregano, 1726 Argyle St. (425-8077). Called "Larry O's" by the regulars. Satisfying Italian and seafood dishes around $5, daily specials $3-4. Open daily 11am-2am. Kitchen closes at 10pm.

Mediterraneo Café, 1571 Barrington St. (423-6936), where long-haired, somber students engage in obviously profound conversation over Middle Eastern dishes. Coffee's filled twice for 80¢, so relax and stay awhile. Tabouli with 2 huge pita pockets $2.50, falafel sandwich $3. Filling daily specials $3.25-5. Open daily Mon.-Fri. 6am-8pm, Sat.-Sun. 7:30am-8pm.

SIGHTS

The star-shaped **Halifax Citadel National Historic Park** (426-5080) in the heart of Halifax, and the old **Town Clock** at the foot of Citadel Hill are Halifax traditions. A walk along the walls affords a fine view of the city and harbor. Come any day between June 15 and Labor Day at 11:40am to see the pageantry of preparation for the **noonday cannon firing.** Small exhibits and a 1-hour film inside the fortress will catch you up on the relevant history. (Open May 15-June 15 daily 10am-5pm; June 15-Labor Day daily 9am-6pm; Labor Day-Oct. daily 9am-5pm. Grounds are open all year, daily 10am-5pm off-season. Admission charged June 15-Labor Day only: $2, ages 5-16 and students $1. Seniors and kids under 5 free. Families $5.)

The **Halifax Public Gardens,** across from the Citadel near the intersection of South Park and Sackville St., provide a relaxing spot for a lunch break. Overfed loons on the pond, Roman statues, a Victorian bandstand, gas lamps, and exquisite horticulture are very properly British in style. From July to September, concerts are given Sundays at 2pm. (Gates open daily 8am-sunset.)

Point Pleasant Park, a car-free, wooded tract of land encompassing the southern tip of Halifax, is one of England's last imperial holdings. Encompassing 186 acres, the park is leased to the city of Halifax for 999 years at the bargain rate of 1 shilling per year. Inside the park, the **Prince of Wales Martello Tower,** an odd fort built by the British in 1797, stands as testimony to one of Prince Edward's two fascinations: round buildings and his mistress, both of which he kept in Halifax. To reach the park, take bus #9 from downtown Barrington St. Much farther south, overlooking the mouth of Halifax Harbor, is another example of British architecture, the **York Redoubt.** Built to defend British holdings against the French, this fort was used until World War II. The tower commands a gorgeous view of the harbor. To get to the fort, take bus #15 to Purcell's Cove.

Reconstructed early-19th-century architecture covers the **Historic Properties** district (429-0530), downtown on lower Water St. The charming stone-and-wood facades, however, are only sheep's clothing disguising wolfishly overpriced boutiques and restaurants of tourist-trap commercialism. One remaining vestige of colonial tradition is preserved in the person of Peter Cox, Halifax's official Town Crier. Meet him at **Tea with the Mayor** (421-8736), Town Hall on the corner of Duke and Barrington, where you can feel important in the company of, yes, the mayor, free tea, and free food (July-Aug. Mon.-Thurs. 3:30-4:30pm; free). **Province House** (424-4661) on the corner of Granville and George St., can be quite a show during parliament. Inside the small, Georgian brownstone, the Assembly Speaker and Sergeant-at-Arms don elegant top hats and black cloaks for sometimes lively debate. (Open Mon.-Fri. 9am-5pm, Sat.-Sun. 10am-4pm; Sept.-June Mon.-Fri. 9am-4pm.)

Museums in Halifax don't stack up to the competition within Nova Scotia. However, die-hard museum-goers might enjoy the **Maritime Museum of the Atlantic,** 1675 Lower Water St. (424-7490), which has an interesting display on the Halifax Explosion. (Open Mon. and Wed.-Sat. 9:30am-5:30pm, Tues. 9:30am-8pm, Sun. 1-5:30pm. Closed Mon. mid-Oct.-May. $2.25, under 17 50¢. Free Tues. 5:30-8pm and mid-Oct. to May.) The **Nova Scotia Museum,** 1747 Summer St. (424-7353), behind Citadel Hill, offers exhibits on the natural history, geology, and native cultures of the province. (Open Mon. and Wed.-Sat. 9:30am-5:30pm, Tues. 9:30am-8pm, Sun. 1-5:30pm; mid-Oct. to May Wed.-Sun. 9:30am-5pm. $3, ages 5-16 50¢, under 5 free, families $6. Free Wed. 5:30-8pm.)

ENTERTAINMENT AND NIGHTLIFE

Numerous pubs and clubs pack downtown Halifax; bar-hopping is common. Purple-haired students meet lawyers at the **Seahorse Pub,** 1665 Argyle St. (423-7200), in a dark basement room with carved woodwork (open Mon.-Wed. 11:30am-12:30am, Thurs.-Sat. 11:30am-1am). The **Lower Deck** (425-1501), in the Historic Properties, offers excellent Irish folk music along with nautical pub decor. (Cover $2-4. Open Mon.-Sat. 11am-12:30am, Sun. 11am-11pm. No music and no cover on Sun.) **Peddler's Pub** (423-5033), in Barrington Place Mall on Granville St., is huge and always packed; favored for good pub food, including wings ($4.50) and steamed mussels ($3.75). Fridays after 4pm you can get 99¢ specials, from pizza to shrimp. (Open Mon.-Sat. 11am-11pm, Sun. noon-10pm.) **J.J. Rossy's,** 1887 Granville St. (422-4411), across the street from Peddler's, attracts nocturnal crowds with its dance floor and tremendous drink specials, which are best during the "power hours" (Wed.-Sat. 10-11pm and midnight-1am) when a draft falls to 70¢. Rossy's also offers all-you-can eat lunch specials Friday noon-2pm ($4.50). Dancing daily. (Cover charge after 8pm Thurs.-Sat. $2.50. Open Mon.-Sat. 11am-2am, kitchen closes 10pm.) The **Double Deuce,** 1560 Hollis St. (422-4033), has been called the "hottest alternative rock bar east of Montréal." However, a change of management has locals wondering if it will ever be quite the same. Live music still packs in crowds, so check it out and judge for yourself. (Open stage Monday nights; cover charge $1-5; open Mon.-Fri. 11am-2am, Sat. noon-2am.) Find some of the city's best dance music at **The Studio** (423-6866), at Barrington and Spring Garden, an unrestricted gay and lesbian club. (Cover Thurs.-Sat. $2-3. Open Mon.-Sat. 4pm-2am, Sun. 6pm-2am.)

The **Nova Scotia International Tattoo Festival** (420-1114 or 451-1221 for tickets), is possibly Halifax's biggest summer event. Presented by the Province of Nova Scotia and the Canadian Maritime Armed Forces, and running through the first week of July, the festival features international musicians, bicyclists, dancers, acrobats, gymnasts, and military groups. At noon, the Metro area spawns lots of free entertainment. Later, a two-hour show, featuring 1800 performers, is held in the Halifax Metro Centre. (Tickets for the show $11-25, seniors and kids under 13 $2 off.)

The **Neptune Theatre,** 5216 Sackville St. (429-7070), presents the area's most noteworthy professional stage productions. The theater's season runs from September to mid-May and features classics as well as contemporary selections. At **Wormwood's Dog and Monkey Cinema,** 2015 Gottingen St. (422-3700), Canadian and international art films have been known to prompt sell-outs and sizable lines. Go early to beat the intellectual masses. (Tickets $7, members $3.50. Shows around 7 and 9:30pm each evening with matinees on Sundays.)

The **DuMaurier Atlantic Jazz Festival** (492-2225 or 800-567-5277) fests for a week in mid-July with both ticketed and free concerts throughout the city. **Festival 95** (421-2900) will celebrate Halifax's birthday during the first weekend in August. Don't miss the **Natal Day** parade and fireworks which close this celebration. For ten days in mid-August, **Buskerfest** (425-4329) showcases street performers from around the world. The **Atlantic Film Festival** (422-3456) wraps up the festival season at the end of September with a showcase of Canadian and international films.

■■■ CAPE BRETON ISLAND

"I have traveled around the globe," said Alexander Graham Bell, "I have seen the Canadian and American Rockies, the Andes, and the Alps, and the Highlands of Scotland; but for simple beauty, Cape Breton outrivals them all." Bell backed his boast by building Bein Bhreagh, the estate where he spent the waning years of his life, in Cape Breton. Breathtaking coastline, loch-like finger-lakes, dramatic cliffs, and lush hills have prompted people to call Cape Breton Scotland's missing west coast. But this reference runs deeper than geography. Immigrants from the Scottish Highlands began settling the area in 1805 and their cultural imprint on the island is deep. Today, the Gaelic College of Celtic Arts and Crafts in St. Ann's is the only institution in North America where students can major in bagpiping, Highlands dancing, and Gaelic song. However, the Scots were not the only people attracted by Cape Breton's inviting highlands; a healthy French Acadian population thrives in and around the town of Cheticamp. Set aside ample time to savor both the island's rich cultural heritage and its legendary beauty.

Practical Information Cape Breton Island, the northeastern portion of Nova Scotia, connects to the mainland by the **Trans-Canada Highway** across the **Canso Causeway,** 280km from Halifax. **Port Hastings** is the first town you'll encounter in Cape Breton; it supports a **Provincial Tourism Nova Scotia** center (625-1717), on the right-hand side of the road after crossing the causeway. (Open July-Aug. daily 8:30am-8pm, May 15-June and Sept.-Oct. 15 9am-5pm.) **Acadian Lines,** 99 Terminal Drive, Sydney (564-5533), services many small towns along Rte. 4 on the way to and from Halifax. Call to find out where, when, and for how much. The limited service bus can be flagged down in a town near you; then be prepared to stop the driver when you want to get off (open daily 7am-midnight). The **Bras d'Or Lake,** an 80km-long inland sea, roughly divides Cape Breton in two. The larger western section includes the scenic Cape Breton Highlands and the Cabot Trail. The industrial eastern section has been developed with revenues mined from steel and coal. **Sydney** and **Glace Bay,** Cape Breton's two largest cities, are depressed industrial centers.

The Cabot Trail and Cape Breton Highlands National Park
Named after English explorer John Cabot, who landed in the Highlands in 1497, the **Cabot Trail** is the most scenic marine drive in Canada—the Canadian answer to California's Rte. 1. The 300km-long loop winds precipitously around the perimeter of northern Cape Breton. A photographer's dream, the Trail takes seven to 10 hours to enjoy (allowing for a lunch break, stops at overlooks, and slow traffic). The land extending across the northern tip of Cape Breton and wedged within the northern loop of the Cabot Trail belongs to the 950 square kilometers of highlands and ocean wilderness of the **Cape Breton Highlands National Park.** For a more relaxing experience, drive or bike the park's trail clockwise, shying away from the sheer cliffs. One **park information center** (224-2306) is located along the Cabot Trail 5km north of **Cheticamp,** at the southwest park entrance, and another is at the southeast entrance in **Ingonish Beach** (285-2535). (Both centers open daily 8am-8pm; mid-May to late June and early Sept.-Columbus Day 9am-5pm; mid-Oct. to mid-May Mon.-Fri. 8am-4pm for phone inquiries only.) For **bike rentals,** contact **Les Amis Du Plein Air** (224-3814), or inquire in the bookstore at the southwest park information center where fees are paid and bikes picked up ($4 per hr., $25 per day).

Lodging is expensive along the Trail, generally $50-60 for a double. The **Glenmore International Hostel (HI-C)** (258-3622; call for directions), is in Twin Rock Valley on Rte. 395 west of Whycocomagh. The only reasonably priced way to put a roof over your head within 140km, this hostel is a rough but comfortable cabin surrounded by wild daisies. (Full kitchen; $10, nonmembers $12; tent sites $7; linen rental $1.50.) Very few B&Bs line the Cabot Trail. However, the park provides six **campgrounds** within its boundaries, totalling 548 first-come, first-served sites. Weekdays yield the best selection. (Sites $8-11, with fireplace $13, hookup $17; if you pay for 3 days, you can camp for 4. Backcountry camping permits $7 per night. Camping mid-Oct to mid-May is free. Park motor vehicle admission $5 per day, $10 per 4 days. Open mid-May to mid-Oct.)

On the southern loop of the Cabot Trail, the resort village of **Baddeck** lies on the shore of Lake Bras d'Or. **The Alexander Graham Bell National Historic Site** (295-2069), Chebucto St. (Rte. 205) in the east end of Baddeck, provides a spectacular view of the lake from its roof gardens. Inside the building is a fascinating museum dedicated to the life and inventions of Bell. More than just the inventor of the telephone, Bell introduced such creations as medical tools, hydrofoils, and airplanes. Bell's humanitarian spirit inspired him to assist the deaf and sailors lost at sea. Talks on his life and works provide all the details. (Mid-May to mid-Oct. $2, kids 6-12 and seniors $1, families $5, under 6 free. Open daily 9am-8pm; Sept. 9am-6pm; Oct.-June 9am-5pm exhibits only. Handicapped accessible.)

Sydney North Sydney, Sydney Mines, Sydney River, and Sydney all conglomerate within a 20km radius, 430km northeast of Halifax. **North Sydney** stands out as the departure point for ferries to **Newfoundland** (see Newfoundland: Getting There). The Marine Atlantic Ferry Terminal sits at the end of the Trans-Canada Hwy.

Get helpful info at the **North Sydney Tourist Bureau**, 1 Purves St. (794-7719), next to the Marine Atlantic Terminal, in a little house decorated with question marks. Accommodations information is available. (Open July-early Sept. daily 8am-8pm.) Lodging is expensive on Cape Breton Island, and the Sydney area is no exception. The town's two B&Bs ask $45 for a single and $55 for a double. The best deal in North Sydney is the **Seaview Inn**, 30 Seaview Dr. (794-3066), 2km from the Ferry Terminal. (Clean singles with shared bath $24, doubles $28.) To circulate within North Sydney, use your feet or take a taxi. **Blue & White Taxi**, 794-4767, charges $3.25 from any point within town to the Ferry Terminal for 1-2 passengers ($1 per additional passenger; kids under 13 free). Accommodation reservations are highly recommended, especially on those nights preceding the departure of the ferry to Argentia, when the whole area can be booked solid.

Glace Bay Not all of Cape Breton is scenic. The grimy, industrial city of **Glace Bay** once drew innumerable immigrants for hazardous jobs in the Sydney coalfields. Although coal mining has now ceased, the **Miners' Museum** (849-4522), 42 Birkley St. off South St. east of downtown, preserves its history with exhibits on coal mining and the plight of organized labor, as well as a reconstructed miners' village and films on life as a coal miner. The highlight of the museum is the ¼-mi. tour of an underground coal mine, guided by experienced miners who paint a bleak picture of their hard days' toil. (Open Wed.-Mon, 10am-6pm, Tues. 10am-7pm; museum only early Sept.-early June Mon.-Fri. 9am-4pm; $6, without tour $3.25; kids $3/1.75.) Don't miss the **Men of the Deeps**, the local miners singing group, perform at the museum during July and August.

Louisbourg The **Fortress of Louisbourg** was the King of France's most ambitious military project in the Colonies, his "New World Gibraltar"—the launching pad from which France would regain the Americas. A small band of New Englanders laid siege to and quickly captured Louisbourg in 1745. A treaty soon returned it to France, but then the British took the fortress back in 1758, with even greater ease. The $25 million rebuilding of Louisbourg, the largest historic reconstruction in North America, resulted in **Fortress of Louisbourg National Historic Park** (733-2280), 37km southeast of Sydney on Rte. 22. The fortress has been far more successful as a tourist attraction than it ever was as a military outpost. Every attempt has been made to recreate the atmosphere of 1744. From the visitors center, where tickets are purchased and cars parked, a shuttle bus takes you to the fortress gates. The fort offers 2-4 guided walking tours daily, in English or French. The buildings feature period rooms, staffed by costumed actors doing their 1744 thing, and historical museums depicting fortress life. The scope is startling, the re-creation convincing. (Open July-Aug. 9am-6pm; June and Sept. 9:30am-5pm; May and Oct. 9am-5pm. $6.50, students and youths $3.25, families $16, seniors and kids under 5 free.)

The **Hôtel de la Marine** within the fortress prepares full-course meals ($9) from authentic 1744 French recipes—lots of fun, but be forewarned that the 18th century had no Cordon Bleu chefs. No red meat is served Fri.-Sat.—it was outlawed as a religious observance. Peek at the kitchen, if you can skirt the actors. The 80% whole wheat/20% rye bread from the **King's Bakery** ($2.50) looks like a cannonball and is almost as hard. 1995 marks multiple anniversaries in Louisbourg's history, both the fort's and the town's; the festivals will last all summer, so be sure to check the schedule during your visit. For more information, contact the **Louisbourg Tourist Bureau** (733-2720), off Rte. 22 near the fortress. (Open May-Oct. daily 9am-7pm.)

■■■ ATLANTIC COAST

Gulf Stream waters crash onto the rocky Atlantic Coast, settling the pace of life along the shore. Follow Nova Scotia's **Lighthouse Route** south on Hwy. 3 from Halifax to coastal villages boasting not only beacons but all of the picturesque trappings of oceanside life. Here, boats and lobster traps are the tools of a trade, not just props for the tourists. **MacKenzie Bus Lines** (543-2491) runs between Halifax and Yarmouth with few stops. Call for details Mon.-Sat. 9am-5pm. A beautiful lighthouse can be found at **Peggy's Cove,** off Hwy. 333, 43 km. southwest of Halifax. No public transportation serves Peggy's Cove, but most bus companies offer packages which include the village. These buses, coupled with the throngs of cars that arrive in the summer, and the cruise lines which bring visitors on Wednesday. and Sunday, make a mockery of the cove's declared population of 60. Arrive early in the morning to avoid the crowds, and wake up with espresso ($1.25) and fresh baked goods from **Beal's Bailiwick** (823-2099). The café is on the back terrace. (Open May-Oct. daily 9am-dusk). For info on the cove, contact the new **DeGarthe Gallery** (823-2256; open May to mid-Oct. daily 10am-6pm).

Return to Hwy. 3 and continue south for about 50km to **Mahone Bay,** a slightly larger town, quaint enough to attract proportional crowds. The **tourist office,** 165 Edgewater St. (624-6151), provides information on the area's attractions, accommodations, campgrounds, and beaches. (Open May-June, Sept.-early Oct. daily 10am-6pm, July-Aug. daily 9am-7pm.) Mahone Bay's big event comes at the end of July with the **Wooden Boat Festival** (624-8443), a celebration of the regions ship-building heritage, which includes a parade of a number of old-style schooners.

Lunenburg, a shipbuilding center 11km east of Mahone Bay on Hwy. 3, produced the undefeated racing schooner Bluenose, which graces the back of the Canadian dime and the Nova Scotia license plate. The **Fisheries Museum of the Atlantic** (634-4794) on Bluenose Drive of the harborfront, brings the fishing industry to life. The highlight is a chance to explore the schooner and trowler docked at the museum (open daily 9:15am-5:30pm, Oct. 15-May by appointment only Mon.-Fri. $3, kids 5-12 50¢, under 5 free, families $6.50). The **Lunenburg Hostel (HI-C),** 9 King St. (634-9146), consists of 5 beds in a lived-in-looking room in a small inn. (Kitchen access, parking; $12.50, nonmembers $16. Curfew midnight, check-in 8am-noon, 4-8pm.) For info on camping and other accommodations and attractions, visit the **tourist office** (634-8100), in the faux lighthouse on Blockhouse Hill Rd. (open late May to mid-June, daily 10am-6pm, mid-June to early Oct. daily 9am-8pm).

From Lunenburg, follow the signs to the **Ovens Natural Park** (766-4621), a 16km trip west on Hwy. 3 then south and east on Hwy. 332. The park features a spectacular set of natural caves as well as the region's best **campground.** Noncampers pay $3 (kids 5-12 $2.50) to hike in the caves for a day. (75 sites, some overlook the ocean; access to caves, free hot showers, restrooms, grocery stores, and a restaurant; open mid-May to mid-Oct.; $15, with hook-up $16; ½ of sites are first-come, first served.)

Hwy. 332 continues along the shore and into the town of **East LaHave.** There, a **ferry** runs across the LaHave River and into **LaHave,** a great and incredibly cheap way to move along the coast without doing a lot of extra driving (9 daily, on the ½ hr., 6am-midnight; 50¢ fare including car). About 1000 ft. from the ferry dock on the left is the **LaHave Bakery** (daily 9am-6:30pm, mid-Sept to June 10am-5pm). Follow the incredible smell of cheese and herb bread ($2.50) inside in order to check in for a night at the **LaHave Marine Hostel (HI-C).** Located upstairs in an apartment with a wood-burning stove, the hostel is run by the bakery proprietor. Try to call ahead or arrive during the bakery hours (9 beds; open June-Oct. $9, nonmembers $10). **Cresent Beach** is just a 10-min. drive south down Hwy. 331 from LaHave. You can drive a car down onto the beach, but be sure the tide isn't coming in.

CANADA

Newfoundland and Labrador

The relatively undeveloped, unknown expanses of Newfoundland and Labrador are especially surprising when one considers the vast length of time during which humans have been "discovering," settling, and rediscovering these areas. Inuit presence stretches back some 9000 years on both the island and the mainland, and confirmed European exploration dates to around 1000 AD, when Norse Vikings settled, if only briefly, at L'Anse aux Meadows on the island's northern tip. But relative newcomer John Cabot, who sailed into present-day St. John's harbor in 1497, has long been credited with finding Newfoundland.

PRACTICAL INFORMATION

Capital: St. John's.

Department of Tourism and Culture: P.O. Box 8730, St. John's, NF A1B 4K2 (729-2830 or 800-563-6353). Staffed Mon.-Fri. 9:30am-6pm with an answering service 24 hrs.

Time Zones: Atlantic (Labrador, except for the coast south of Cartwright, is 1 hr. ahead of Eastern) and Newfoundland (on the island and Labrador's southern coast; 1½ hr. ahead of Eastern). **Postal Abbreviation:** NF

Drinking Age: 19.

Provincial Sales Tax: 12%, plus 7% GST.

NEWFOUNDLAND ISLAND

The island of Newfoundland was formed by collisions of the earth's tectonic plates. Its mountains rise unexpectedly from the Atlantic to tower above rocky shores and waters that were once blessed with the earth's most plentiful cod stocks. Newfoundland's breathtaking, if daunting, landscape is a natural wonder, alternately featuring deep fjords and granite cliffs, barren rock, and gentle forests. The central region, hardly accessible, combines lowlands, boggy forests, and rolling hills. Gros Morne National Park in the west and Terra Nova National Park in the east offer geological samplings dating back to the Earth's Precambrian period, and diverse wildlife populations from the land, sea, and air. The island's interior is scarcely inhabited.

A British Dominion since 1855, Newfoundland became Canada's tenth province in 1949. "Newfies" may speak in a deep, often incomprehensible drawl which combines both accent and idiom with an Irish or western English quality. The people of "the rock" are strong, weathered by the ocean which isolates and nourishes them.

Newfies are characterized by a sense of humor and friendliness virtually unparalleled on the mainland. The food and drink for which they are notorious are equally unpretentious, hearty, sturdy, and in the case of "screech," the locally made rum, downright overwhelming.

Getting There and Getting Around There are two ways to reach Newfoundland: boat or plane. Taking the boat is the cheaper option. **Marine Atlantic** (800-341-7981 from the Continental U.S.; 794-5700 from North Sydney or Nova Scotia; 695-7081 from Port-aux-Basques; 772-7701 from St. John's) ferries depart from North Sydney to Port-aux-Basques (2-3 per day, 5 hr., $17, ages 5-12 $8.50, seniors $12.75, cars $53) and Argentia (Tues. and Fri. 7am, 14 hr., $47.50, ages 5-12 $23.50, seniors $35.25, cars $103). Reservations are required, especially for the

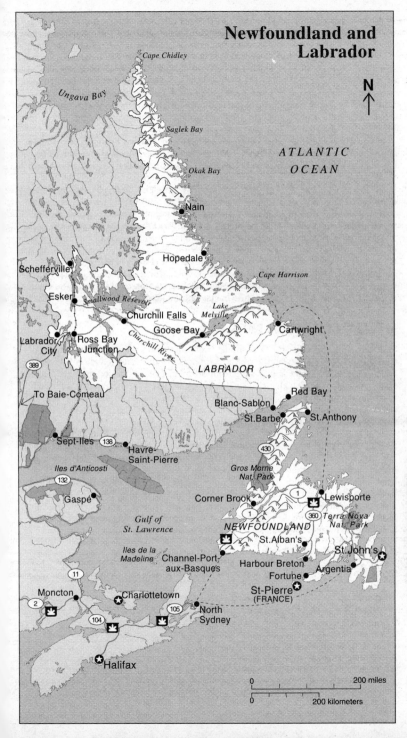

Newfoundland and Labrador

N

Cape Chidley

Ungava Bay

Saglek Bay

Okak Bay

ATLANTIC OCEAN

Nain

Hopedale

Schefferville

Cape Harrison

Esker

Smallwood Resevoir

Lake Melville

Churchill Falls

Goose Bay

Cartwright

Labrador City

Ross Bay Junction

Churchill River

LABRADOR

389

Red Bay

To Baie-Comeau

Blanc-Sablon

St.Barbe

St.Anthony

Sept-Iles

138

Havre-Saint-Pierre

430

Gros Morne Nat. Park

Iles d'Anticosti

132

Corner Brook

1

Lewisporte

Gaspé

1

360

Terra Nova Nat. Park

Gulf of St. Lawrence

NEWFOUNDLAND

St.Alban's

St.John's

Iles de la Madeline

Channel-Port-aux-Basques

Harbour Breton

Argentia

Fortune

11

Moncton

Charlottetown

St-Pierre (FRANCE)

2

104

105

North Sydney

Halifax

0   200 miles

0   200 kilometers

CANADA

Argentia Ferry. Carless travelers can usually get on without a reservation, but be at the terminal at least 2 hours in advance. **CN Roadcruiser** (737-5912) services the whole island, and goes from Port-aux-Basques to St. John's (1 per day, 14 hr., $80). The bus leaves early in the morning; try taking a night ferry if you don't want to be stranded overnight in barren Port-aux-Basques. **Grand J Transportation** (682-6245) runs a minibus service between Argentia and St. John's. Call and the owner will pick you up anywhere in either town for the trip. ($12. Departs St. John's 9am, returns 5pm, once daily.) Newfoundland's severely limited transportation and formidable size make exploration nearly impossible without a car—consider driving.

Accommodations For a comprehensive, town-by-town listing of Newfoundland's accommodations, pick up the *Newfoundland & Labrador Travel Guide* at any visitors center, including the one in the Marine Atlantic Ferry Terminal in North Sydney, NS (open before ferry departures). Rooms at hotels, motels, and B&Bs tend to go for $35-55, but they are few and far between. **The Coffey House Bed and Breakfast** (227-2262 or 227-7303), located on Rte. 100 in Freshwater, is conveniently placed just 6km from the Argentia ferry landing, perfect for the lag time between an evening arrival and a next-day bus to St. John's. (Singles $38, doubles $45. Breakfast included and other meals available.) Staying at one of the island's 74 campgrounds allows more flexibility and closer contact with the area's superb nature. Newfoundland has one hostel, **Woody Point (HI-C)** (453-2442), offering a roof over your head and a prime location in Gros Morne National Park. (Kitchen without refrigerator, and laundry facilities. $12, nonmembers $14; open June-Sept. daily 10am-10pm; after hours call the manager at 453-2470).

■■■ ST. JOHN'S

St. John's, an oasis of civilization amidst Newfoundland's picturesque expanses of caribou and conifers, sits on the southeastern coast of the island's Avalon Peninsula. Legend has it that John Cabot, sailing from Bristol in 1497, stumbled upon St. John's Harbor on St. John's Day. Despite Sir Humphrey Gilbert's 1583 claim that the newly found land was English, St. John's was often besieged by coveting European nations and free-lancing pirates. Final victory went to the British in 1762, when they recaptured St. John's from the French after the Seven Years' War.

Most of St. John's claims to fame are related to its geographic location as the continent's easternmost point—it received the first transatlantic wireless signal in 1901 and saw the first successful nonstop trans-Atlantic flight take off in 1919—and its historical significance as one of North America's oldest European settlements. However, St. John's has more to offer than important dates and names. Located almost halfway between Europe and Montréal, St. John's is typically "Newfie" for its distinct culture and character. A population of nearly 162,000, exceedingly friendly locals, a unique culture and tradition, and an unexpected, rather impressive nightlife combine to make St. John's a memorable vacation destination.

PRACTICAL INFORMATION
Emergency: 911.

Visitor Information: The City of St. John's Economic Development and Tourism Division (576-8106 or 576-8455), on New Gower St. across from City Hall (open Mon.-Fri. 9am-4:30pm, early Sept.-May Mon.-Fri. 9am-5pm), and the **Rail Car Tourist Chalet** (576-8514), on Harbor Drive (you can't miss it, it's the only rail car in town; open early June-Labor Day 8:30am-6:30pm).

Student Travel Agency: Travel CUTS (737-7926 or 737-7936; fax 737-4743), in the Thomson Student Center, Memorial University. Open Mon.-Thurs. 9am-4:30pm, Fri. 9am-4pm, Labor Day-late May Mon.-Fri. 9am-5pm.

Airport: St. John's International, (726-7888) 10km from downtown off Portugal Cove Rd. (Rte. 40). No buses go there and **Bugdon's Taxi** (726-4400) will charge $11-13 for the ride. **Air Canada** (726-7880) has excellent stand-by rates for youths under 25 who are willing to take the chance on flights within Canada. ($125 to Montréal and $375 to Vancouver instead of normal rates of $341/1038.)

Buses: CN Roadcruiser, 495 Water St. (737-5912), serves the entire island. To: Port-aux-Basques (1 per day, 14 hr., $80); Lewisporte (3 per week, 6 hr., $45). Discount of 50% for kids 5-11 and 15% for students and seniors. Kids under 5 free. Open daily 7am-5:30pm. A minibus service called **G and J Transportation** runs between Argentia and St. John's, a route unserviced by CN Roadcruiser(682-6245; see "Newfoundland Island: Getting there and Getting Around" for details).

Taxi: Bugdon's Taxi, 726-4400. 24 hrs. $2 base fare, $1.60 per mi.

Public Transportation: Metrobus, 245 Freshwater Rd. (722-9400), provides service 6:30am-11:30pm throughout the city. Fare: $1.50, kids 4-18 $1. Office open daily 7am-11pm.

Car Rental: Rent-a-Wreck, 43 Pippy Pl. (753-2277). $32 per day, 100km free, 12¢ per km thereafter. Insurance $10 per day, under 25 $12. Must be 21 with major credit card or $300 cash deposit. Open Mon.-Fri. 8am-5pm, Sat. 9am-1pm. Also try **Discount,** 350 Kenmount Rd. (722-6699). $36 per day, 130km free, 14¢ per km thereafter. Insurance $8 per day. Must be 21 with major credit card. Open Mon.-Fri. 8am-5pm, Sat. 9am-1pm.

Help Lines: Rape Crisis and Information Center, 726-1411, 24 hrs. **Crisis Line Telecare,** 579-1601, 24 hrs.

Post Office: Postal Station C, 354 Water St. (758-1003). Open Mon.-Fri. 8am-5pm. **Postal Code:** A1C 5H1.

Area Code: 709.

St. John's is located on a hill, the bottom of which is **St. John's Harbour. Harbour Drive** borders the water and is paralleled by downtown's two main streets, **Water Street** and **Duckworth Street. Freshwater Road** (which later becomes Kenmount Rd., and, eventually, the **Trans-Canada Highway**) and **New Cove Road** (farther out, Portugal Cove Rd.) extend up the hill towards Memorial University and the airport, connecting Portugal Cove Rd. with Kenmount Rd. Price Phillip Drive, in the west Confederation Parkway, passes directly in front of the university and C.A. Pippy Park.

ACCOMMODATIONS AND CAMPING

B&Bs tend to be cheaper ($40-60 for a single) and more enjoyable than hotels and motels. However, cheap lodgings do exist. For a more complete listing, consult *St. John's Tourist Information Guide,* available in the city's visitors centers.

Memorial University Residences, at Hatcher House (737-7933, or Mon.-Fri. 9am-4:30pm call the housing office at 737-7590), off Elizabeth Ave. From downtown take bus 3 or walk 45 min. Clean dorm rooms with basic student amenities. Definitely the best prices around. Singles $16, students $13; doubles $25/$20. Open 24 hrs., but the phone is rarely answered. Go directly to Hatcher house and find the on-guard clerk's phone number on the conference office booth. Call the clerk if necessary. Rooms reputedly never run out. Open mid-April to late Aug.

Catherine Booth House Traveler's Hostel, 18 Springdale St. (738-2804). Off Water St., 3 min. from the heart of downtown. From bus station, walk down Water St. and turn left on Springdale. Run by the Salvation Army, this hostel functions like a B&B and offers 32 comfortable beds in spotless rooms. Singles $36, doubles $42. Breakfast (7:30-9:30am) and late night snack (8:30-10pm) included. 12:30am curfew, closing, and quiet time. Free parking and laundry facilities. Must be at least 20 or accompanied by an adult.

Southcott Hall, 100 Forest Rd. (737-6448), 10 min. walk from downtown. The nurses' residence of St. John's General Hospital rents 30 singles ($27.50) in a 12-story high-rise with a great view. Open 24 hrs.

Pippy Park Trailer Park, (737-3669), on Nagles Pl. off Prince Philip Pkwy., offers nicely wooded campsites in the heart of St. John's picnic and barbecue areas. Hiking, fishing, and a convenience store within the park. 180 sites. Sites $5.50, RV sites $11-15, depending on service. Open May-Sept.

A Gower Street House B&B, 180 Gower St. (800-563-3959). Located in the center of the old city, near downtown shopping and nightlife, one block from the cathedral of St. Johns. Private rooms, telephones, A/C, off-street parking, and separate lounge. Singles $45 in-season, $35 off-season, including full breakfast.

FOOD

Don't leave before having sampled traditional Newfie foods, such as jigg's dinner or fish 'n' brewis (basically fish mixed with soaked and boiled hardbread; it's better than it sounds), scrunchions, and hot-fried dough toutons with blackstrap molasses. **House of Hayne's,** 207 Kenmount Rd. (754-4937), will set you up with plentiful portions of any of these delicacies. (Jigg's dinner $6, fish 'n' brewis with scrunchions $6.30, touton $1.50. Open daily 6:15am-10pm.)

Cafe Duckworth, 190 Duckworth St. (722-1444), is where you'll find coffee-sipping long-haired musicians drawing long puffs from imported cigarettes, blue-haired women reading *The New Yorker,* and sandwiches ($3.75-4.50), breakfast specials ($3-4.25), and coffees. Open Mon.-Sat. 8am-9pm, Sun. 10am-8pm.

Ches's, 9 Freshwater St. (722-4083). Fish & chips ($5-6, depending on cod availability) are superbly greased and fried. Don't be put off by the fast-food setting; the food is good. Open Sun.-Thurs. 9am-2am, Fri.-Sat. 9am-3am.

Magic Wok Eatery, 402 Water St. (753-6907), offers Szechuan, Cantonese, and Peking dishes at friendly prices. Lunch specials ($5.50-7), dinner specials ($5-6), and entrees ($7-9). Open Mon.-Sat. noon-midnight, Sun. 3pm-midnight.

Classic Cafe, 364 Duckworth St. (579-4444), serves classic café food and drink. Sandwiches ($4.50-7) and the "Big Hungry Human" ($10). Open 24 hrs.

SIGHTS

One of the oldest cities in North America, St. John's is steeped in history. Downtown is full of architectural landmarks, most prominently **St. John the Baptist Anglican Cathedral** (726-5677), Gower St. at Church Hill, one of the finest examples of ecclesiastical Gothic architecture in North America (tours available May to mid-Oct. Mon.-Sat. 10am-5pm, Sun. noon-5pm), and **Commissariat House** (729-6730), King's Bridge Rd., a late Georgian style building where guides in period costumes show you around (open June to mid-Sept. daily 10am-6pm).

Uphill and to the east from the waterfront are **Signal Hill** and the **Cabot Tower.** The French and English fought several times for control of the hill and Marconi received the first trans-Atlantic cable transmission here in 1901. Today the Hill offers a great view of St. John's and features a **Military Tatoo,** in which actors recreate the everyday drills and procedures of the fort's heyday (July-Aug. Wed.-Thurs. and Sat.-Sun. 3pm and 7pm). At the **Visitor Information and Interpretation Center** (772-5367) collect facts or enjoy their exhibit on the history of the hill (open June daily 8:30am-8pm; July-Labor Day daily 8:30am-9pm). Look to the south from Signal Hill and see **Cape Spear,** the easternmost point of land on North America.

Museum junkies can get a fix at the **Newfoundland Museum,** 285 Duckworth St. (729-2329), which displays chronicle 900 years of Newfoundland history. (Free. Open daily 9am-4:30pm, Labor Day-June 9am-noon and 1-4:30pm.) During July and August, take in free concerts at this museum where local musicians perform in both modern and traditional styles. (sun. 2:30-4pm).

ENTERTAINMENT AND NIGHTLIFE

Culture in St. John's centers around the small but lively **LPSU Hall Theatre and Resource Center for the Arts,** 3 Victoria St. (752-4531), which has performances by local troupes, theatrical productions, and a permanent art gallery (free).

For a taste of more typical Newfie fun, head to the waterfront, where **Adventure tours** (726-5000; 2½ hr.; $20, under 12 $10, students $15, seniors $10 on Mon). involves whale sightings, cod-jigging, drinking screech rum, kissing a cod, and receiving a screechers certificate. You'll also find Bosun, an enormous Newfoundland dog. (Open daily 10am-5pm, Thurs.-Sat. additional evening hours for the

9:30pm Moonlight Tour $15.) The annual **St. John's Regatta**, North America's oldest continuing sporting event (since 1825) happens the first Wednesday of August (weather permitting); the city shuts down while everyone gathers at Quidi Vidi Lake. Call the **Regatta Museum** (576-8058) in the boathouse at Quidi Vidi Lake for details. The **George Street Festival** (576-8106) lets contemporary and traditional local musicians strut their stuff the last weekend in July on Prince Edward Plaza.

St. John's is transformed by the setting of the sun, as quiet streets come alive with the vibrancy of a young partying crowd. **George Street** in particular becomes one continuous strip of clubs where loud music and drinking youths congregate. Most clubs and bars close at 2am and have cover charges. To avoid the long lines, show up before 10pm. Become initiated into Newfie culture with an official screeching-in ceremony at **Trapper John's Museum and Pub,** 2 George St. (579-9630). The $5.45 double screech is free for cod-kissing first-timers. ($2 cover Fri. and when bands play; open Mon.-Sat. 10am-2am, Sun. 10am-midnight.) **The Sundance Saloon,** 33 George St. (753-7822), has noteworthy food and drink specials and an active dance floor. Go Thursday for 9¢ wings and Friday for Karaoke (5-9pm). The line at the door can be more than 200 people long, so plan early. ($3 cover Fri.-Sat. 8pm-1am. Open Mon.-Sat. noon-2am, Sun. noon-midnight.) For live entertainment every night of the week, including a Wednesday night talent show and the area's best Irish folk music, stop in at **Erin's Pub,** 186 Water St. (722-1916). Bands strike up at 10:30 to the delight of locals ranging in age from 19 to 90. (Cover $1-3. Open Mon.-Sat. noon-2am, Sun. noon-midnight; May-Aug. opens at 7pm Wed., Fri., Sat., and some Thurs.)

■■■ THE REST OF THE ISLAND

Caribou rather than people roam Newfoundland's interior. Communities and roads tend to concentrate along the island's rugged coast. Heading west from St. John's, take the time to stray from the beaten path and explore Cape Bonavista, where charming villages speckle the coastline. Central Newfoundland's towns are mostly industrial and provide an unglamorized view of the logger lifestyle. **Corner Brook,** in the west, and **Gander,** east of center, are the island's main towns after St. John's.

Passing directly through Terra Nova and within ½ hr. of Gros Morne, the **Trans-Canada Highway (Rte. 1)** provides convenient access to Newfoundland's two sensational national parks. Both parks extract a car entrance fee ($5 per day, $10 for 4 days, $20 per season mid-June to Labor Day), but only when you stop to use the park facilities. Driving through and staring in awe are both free.

Gros Morne National Park Where receding glaciers once created spectacular fjords, UNESCO has designated a World Heritage Site. The ancient formations, which have earned the park the appellation "the Galapagos of geology," show rock, instead of life, preserved in forms unknown to most of the world. Look in the park's southwest corner near Woody Point for an unusual flat-topped mountain known as the Serpentine Tableland; it was forced upward by the interactions of the earth's mantle, a layer usually hidden miles beneath the surface. Hiking is dazzling here. In particular, the James Callaghan Trail ascends Gros Morne Mountain, offering a 16km, world-exhausting panorama at the top. The hike is strenuous, steep, and saturated with black furry spiders. The park advises allotting 7 to 8 hours to make the hike and distributes backcountry camping passes if you choose to take a more leisurely pace ($3 per person per night). The **visitor center** (458-2714) distributes camping passes, free trail guides and information on other attractions. (3km west of Rocky Harbor on Rte. 430, one hour from the Trans-Canada Highway. Open daily 9am-10pm, Labor Day-May Mon.-Fri. 9am-5pm.)

Gros Morne is blessed with five **campgrounds** totaling 296 sites: Berry Hill, Green Point, Lomond, Shallow Bay, and Trout River. (Sites $7.25-11.25. No electrical hookup available. Green Point is open year-round.) **Berry Hill,** with 156 wooded sites, is popular thanks to the three hiking trails within the campground, its proximity to Gros Morne Mountain, and its fuller services (sites $11.25; showers, kitchen shelters, and fireplaces; open mid-May to Oct.).

Terra Nova National Park Along the shores of Newman Sound and the beaches of Sandy Pond, and throughout the forests in between, Terra Nova's 400 square kilometers find room for lynx, moose, ospreys, and eagles, with whales passing just off the coast. If you want to meet these locals, try one of the park's 16 hiking trails (45 min. to 6 hr. long). Less strenuous enjoyment lies on the fine sands of Sandy Pond, where you can swim, picnic, or rent canoes and kayaks ($5). **Twin Rivers Visitors Center** (543-2354) can aid you (open mid-June to early Sept. daily 10am-6pm). Another visitors center (533-2801, same hrs.) operates at the entrance to the main campground at **Newman Sound** (387 semi-serviced sites; showers, laundry, bike rental, convenience store; sites $10, $30 for 4 nights, $50 for 1 week; open year round). Primitive campgrounds are located at Minchin Cove, South Broad Cove, Overs Island, and Dumphy's Pond. You must register at a visitors center and buy a permit for $3 per person each night before staking your claim. The park is about 400km from Gros Morne, on the other side of the island.

LABRADOR

Labrador in the winter is a snowy wonderland full of snow and caribou and snow and musk oxen and snow and 30,000 people, and snow. In summer, it beckons nature lovers with virgin forests and untouched wilderness and lures the very wealthy with excellent fishing. **Marine Atlantic** (800-341-7981 for U.S., 772-7701 from St. John's) runs ferries June-Sept. from Lewisporte, Newfoundland to Goose Bay, Labrador with an optional stop in Cartwright (2 per week, 35 hr., $81, ages 5-12 $41, seniors $61, cars $132). **CN Roadcruiser,** 495 Water St. in St. John's (737-5912) runs from St. John's to Lewisporte (3 per week, 6 hr., $45. students $40) and Notre Dame Junctions, 4 miles to the south (1 per day, 6 hr., $42, students $38.) Return service only from Notre Dame Junction (open daily 7am-5:30pm.)

Another ferry service, the **Northern Cruiser Ltd.,** with offices in St. John's (for info only, 726-0015 or 722-4000; 23 Springdale St., St. John's; open Mon.-Fri. 9am-5:30pm), Québec (418-461-2056), and Labrador (709-931-2309), provides ferry service from St. Barbe on the north coast of Newfoundland Island to Blanc Sablon. From Blanc Sablon, it's a quick drive along Hwy. 510 up to Red Bay, Labrador, where the paved roads end. Flying is another option, though hideously expensive. Adventurous souls should contact the **Vacances-Inter** (418-962-9411) to book a ticket on the **Québec North Shore and Labrador Railroad** (418-968-7803; 968-7805 for Labrador). This agency handles all ticket sales for the railroad's trains from Sept-Iles, to Labrador City ($50) and Schefferville ($65).

Check out the *Newfoundland and Labrador Official Highway Map,* which provides inset town maps, campsite and practical info. Labrador's **Department of Tourism and Culture,** P.O. Box 8730, St. John's A1B 4K2 (800-563-6353 or 729-2830), provides basic info on Labrador (open Mon.-Fri. 9:30am-6pm).

Prince Edward Island

Prince Edward Island, now more commonly called "P.E.I." or "the Island," began as St. John's Island. In 1799, residents renamed the area for Prince Edward, son of King George III, in thanks for his interest in the territory's welfare. In actuality, such appreciation may have been more convenient than anything, as the change cleared up the exasperating confusion between the island and St. John's, Newfoundland; St. John, Labrador; and Saint John, New Brunswick.

The smallest province in Canada attracts visitors with promises of relaxation and beauty; the Island's soil, made red by its high iron-oxide content, complements the ubiquitous green crops and shrubbery, azure skies and turquoise waters, and purple roadside lupin. On the north and south shores, some of Canada's finest beaches extend for miles alternately displaying red and white sands. Always small, the Island towns seem to exist more for visitors than for residents and consist mainly of restaurants and shopping areas. The largest "city" is Charlottetown, the provincial capital, with a whopping 15,000 residents. Effusively hospitable, the Island's population is 17% Acadian French and 80% British.

Public transportation on P.E.I. is sadly inadequate, and the island is too vast to be covered on foot. Fortunately, distances are manageable and the scenic network of highways and country roads is superb for bikers.

PRACTICAL INFORMATION

Capital: Charlottetown.
Time Zone: Atlantic (1 hr. ahead of Eastern time). **Postal Abbreviation:** P.E.I.
Drinking Age: 19.
Provincial Sales Tax: 10%.
Visitor Information: P.E.I. Visitor Information Centre, P.O. Box 940, C1A 7M5 (368-4444 or 800-463-4734), on the corner of University Ave. and Summer St. in Charlottetown. Courtesy calls for reservations. Open daily 8am-10pm, Sept.-May daily 9am-5pm. The **Charlottetown Visitors Bureau,** 199 Queen St. (566-5548), inside City Hall. Open Mon.-Fri. 9am-9pm.
Tours: Abegweit Tours, 157 Nassau St. (894-9966), offers sightseeing tours on a London double-decker bus departing from Confederation Center in Charlottetown. Tours of town (6 per day, 1 hr., $6, kids under 12 $1), the North Shore including Green Gables (1 per day, 7 hr., $30, kids $15), and the South Shore (1 per day, 5 hr., $27, kids $13). Tours run June-Sept.
Buses: SMT, 330 University Ave., Charlottetown (566-9744), provides service to: Moncton (1-2 per day, 5 hr., $29); Amherst (2 per day, 4-7 hr., $23); Halifax (2 per day, 10 hr., $47), via **Acadian Lines** connections in Amherst. Station open daily 9:30-10pm, and Mon.-Fri. 7am-6:15pm, Sat. 7am-1pm and 5:30-6:30pm, Sun. 7-8am and 11:30am-1pm and 5:30-6:30pm. **Trius Lines,** on Garfield St. (566-5664), runs 2 buses daily to Summerside ($10; open ½ hr. before and after departures and arrivals).
Beach Shuttles: Sherwood Beach Shuttle (566-3243) picks up at the P.E.I. Visitor Information Centre and drops off in Cavendish (9am-5:15pm, 2 per day June and Sept., 4 per day July and August; $8, round-trip $12).
Ferries: Marine Atlantic (855-2030 or 800-341-7981 from U.S.), in Borden, 56km west of Charlottetown on Trans-Canada Hwy., makes runs to Cape Tormentine, New Brunswick (12-18 per day; 1 hr., round-trip $7.75, seniors $6, ages 5-12 $4, cars $18.50, not including driver). **Northumberland Ferries** (566-3838 or 800-565-0201 from P.E.I. and Nova Scotia), in Wood Islands 61km east of Charlottetown on Trans-Canada Hwy., goes to Caribou, Nova Scotia (15 per day, 1½ hr., round-trip $8.50, seniors $6.50, ages 5-12 $4.50, cars $27.50). For both ferries, fares are only round-trip and only collected leaving P.E.I. Thus, it is cheaper to leave from Borden than from Wood Islands, no matter how you come over.
Taxi: City Cab, 892-6567. **Star Cab,** 892-6581. Both open daily 24 hrs; no credit cards accepted. Service from Borden ferry to downtown Charlottetown $45.
Car Rental: Rent-a-Wreck, 57A St. Peter's Rd. (566-9955). $32 per day, with 200km free, 12¢ per additional km, damage waiver $9 per day, ages 21-25 $12. Must be 21 with credit card or $250 deposit. Mon.-Fri. 8:30am-5:30pm, Sat. 8:30am-1pm, Sun. on call. **Hillside Autohost,** 207 Mt. Edward Rd. (894-7037), rents for $43 per day, 250km free, 15¢ per additional km; insurance $10-14 per day; must be 21 with major credit card. Open Mon.-Fri. 8:30am-5pm, Sat.-Sun. 8am-3pm.

CANADA

Bike Rental: MacQueens, 430 Queen St. (368-2453), rents road and mountain bikes, $20 per day, $80 per week. Must have credit card or $75 deposit. Open Mon.-Sat. 8:30am-5pm, Sun. 10am-3pm.
Charlottetown Police: 368-26778. **Royal Canadian Mounted Police:** 566-7111.
Help lines: Crisis Centre, 566-8999. 24 hrs.
Post Office: 135 Kent St. (566-4400). Open Mon.-Fri. 8am-5:15pm. **Postal Code:** C1A 7N1.
Area code: 902.

Queen St. and University Ave. are Charlottetown's main thoroughfares, straddling **Confederation Centre** along the west and east, respectively. The most popular beaches, **Cavendish, Brackley,** and **Rustico Island,** lie on the north shore in the middle of the province, opposite but not far from Charlottetown. Hamlets and fishing villages dot the Island landscape of **Kings County** on the east and **Prince County** on the west. Acadian communities thrive on the south shore of Prince County. **Rte. I (TCH)** follows the southern shore from ferry terminal to ferry terminal, passing through Charlottetown.

ACCOMMODATIONS AND CAMPING

B&Bs and **country inns** crowd every nook and cranny of the province; many are open year-round. Rates are generally around $28 for singles and $35 for doubles. 26 farms participate in a provincial **Farm Vacation** program, in which tourists spend some time with a farming family. Call the **Tourist Industry Association of P.E.I.** (566-5008) for info, or pick up a brochure at the Visitor Information center.

P.E.I. has one hostel, the **Charlottetown International Hostel (HI-C),** 153 Mt. Edward Rd. (894-9696), across the yard from the University of P.E.I., in a big, green barn one long block east of University Ave. and a 45-min. walk from the bus station. Neat, spacious rooms, friendly staff, and diverse clientele are all great reasons to stay. (Bike rentals $5. Max. stay 3 nights. Check-in 7-10am and 4pm-midnight. Curfew midnight. $12.50, nonmembers $15. Blanket rental $1. Open June-Labor Day.) The **University of Prince Edward Island,** 550 University Ave. (566-0442), in Blanchard Hall in the southwestern end of campus overlooking Belvedere St., offers fully serviced and furnished two-bedroom apartments with dorm rooms, a kitchen, a living room, and a hall laundry room—a great value for four people. ($60, nonstudents $55 plus tax for up to 4 people, extra cot $5. Weekly and monthly rates also available. Open May 20-Aug.) The University also runs a B&B in **Marion Hall,** with a full all-you-can-eat breakfast included. (Singles $26/21, doubles $36/31. Open July-Aug. Check-in for both at Blanchard Hall 8:30am-10pm.)

Prince Edward Island National Park (672-6350 or 963-2391) operates 3 campgrounds (148 primitive sites $8.75; 330 sites with showers, toilets, kitchen access and laundry facilities $13.50; 92 sites with hookup $19), and 14 of the 30 provincial parks offer camping. Additionally, there are over 30 other private campgrounds scattered throughout the Island, ensuring that there will always be a campsite available. (Campgrounds open different dates, but one is always open mid-June to Sept.)

FOOD

The search for a meal of P.E.I. is essentially the search for a reasonably-priced **lobster.** At market, the coveted crustaceans go for $6 (canning quality) to $8 (restaurant quality) per pound. Boiling them at home is not difficult, especially since any local you meet should have considerable experience. Try boiling lobsters in saltwater for easy seasoning and delicious results. Die-hard bargain hunters take note: some tourists tell tales of a day spent on a lobster boat, a unique experience in itself, which can also yield several of the day's catch free of charge. There's no organized "Tourist goes Lobstering" program, so just ask around at the waterfront or with locals if you're interested. Another option is the traditional **lobster supper,** usually thrown by churches and community centers. These feasts generally include all-you-can-eat extras. The P.E.I. Visitor Information Center (see above) has brochures on this year's scheduled dinners; be ready to pay $18-26, depending on the size of the lobster. Fresh seafood, including the world famous **Malpeque oysters,** is sold along the shores of the island, especially in North Rustico on the north shore. The back of the *P.E.I. Visitor's Guide* lists fresh seafood outlets. For the freshest food around, shop the **Charlottetown Farmers' Market** (368-4444), on Belvedere St. opposite U.P.E.I. (open July-Sept. Sat 9am-2pm and Wed. 10am-5pm).

Cedar's Eatery, 81 University Ave., in Charlottetown (892-7377). A local favorite serving Lebanese and Canadian cuisine. Try their sizeable lunch specials 11am-2pm ($5). Open Mon.-Thurs. 11am-midnight, Fri.-Sat. 11am-1am, Sun. 4-10pm.

Peake's Quay (368-1330), Great George St., below Lower Water St. on the Charlottetown waterfront overlooking the Marina (pronounced PEEKS KEY). An upscale restaurant with a great location and *some* reasonable prices. Seafood sandwich and salad $5-9. Supper entrees $13-23. Open daily 11:30am-3am.

J.R.'s Place, 22 Weymouth St., serves the cheapest lobster dinner in town, with ample trimmings ($9).

SIGHTS

The **Prince Edward Island National Park** (672-2259 or 963-2391), a coastal strip of 32 square kilometer, embraces some of Canada's finest beaches and over a fifth of P.E.I.'s northern coast. It is the most popular Canadian national park east of Banff. Along with the beaches, heap-big sand dunes and salt marshes rumple the park's terrain. The park is home to many of the Island's 300-odd species of birds, including the endangered **piping plover;** birdwatchers should pick up the *Field Check List of Birds* (free) from any National or Provincial Park office. Park campgrounds, programs, and services operate mid-June to Labor Day, with **Cavendish campground** staying open until late September. At the entrance kiosks, receive a copy of the park guide *Blue Heron.* (Vehicle permits $5 per day, $10 per 4 days.)

Green Gables House (672-6350), is located off Rte. 6 in Cavendish near Rte. 13. Popularized by Lucy Maud Montgomery's novel, *Anne of Green Gables,* this house is a mecca for adoring readers, a surprising number of whom come all the way from Japan. The House and Haunted Woods are certain to be recognized by fans but will appear to be just a nice little estate for the uninitiated. Green Gables can get very crowded between late July and September, so it's best to arrive in the early morning or the evening. Tours are available in English and French. (Free. Open mid-May to late July and early Sept.-Oct. daily 9am-5pm; late June-early Sept. daily 9am-8pm; Nov. to mid-May by request, 894-4246.)

Woodleigh (836-3401), just off Rte. 234 in Burlington midway between Cavendish and Summerside, will satisfy the monarchist in you. It contains miniature but still sizeable replicas of British architectural landmarks including St. Paul Cathedral, Tower of London, and Lord Nelson's Trafalgar Square statue—all available for exploration. Yes, the Crown Jewels are replicated inside the Tower. The craftsmanship is striking, but the cuteness of the whole concept can rankle after a while. ($8, seniors $7, 6-15 $4.50, under 6 free, open late May- late June and early Sept.-Columbus Day; daily 9am-5pm; late June-early Sept. daily 9am-8pm.)

Off the Island's northwest point, an unusual and fleeting sight known as **Elephant Rock** can be found off the shores of the town of Norway. Here wind and tides have carved a massive replica of an elephant in P.E.I.'s soft coastal rocks. The elephant is expected to be destroyed by the same natural forces which created it, and within the next five years should be indistinguishable.

Charlottetown prides itself on being the "Cradle of Confederation." The brownstone **Province House** (566-7626), on the corner of Great George and Richmond St., was where delegates from the British North American colonies met to discuss the union which would become the Dominion of Canada in 1867. Chambers of historical importance are open for viewing, as are special exhibits and the modern-day legislative chambers. (Open daily 9am-8pm; mid-Oct. to June Mon.-Fri. 9am-5pm. Free.) Adjoining the Province House is the **Confederation Centre for the Arts** (628-

CANADA

1864), located on the corner of Queen and Grafton St., a modern performing-arts complex with theaters, displays, a library, and an art gallery. Free hour-long guided tours of the Centre are conducted July to August. (Open daily 9am-8pm, Sept.-June Mon.-Sat. 9am-5pm, Sun. 2-5pm.) Every summer, a musical production of **Anne of Green Gables** takes the Mainstage as part of the Charlottetown Festival. (Performances July-early Sept. Mon and Wed.-Fri. at 8pm. Tickets $22-30. Matinees Wed. and Sat. 1:30pm; tickets $17-25. For ticket info, call 566-0278 or 800-565-1267.) Proof that some Islanders aren't so reverent when it comes to *her*, **Annekenstein 5** (566-1267) gibes the girl and the island. Call for details. **P.E.I. House Parties** (800-461-4734) are all the rage in the summer; local musicians will perform traditional music across the island for anyone who will pay to party ($5, kids under 12 $2; refreshments included).

Québec

Home to 90% of Canada's French-speaking citizenry, Québec continues to fight for political and legal recognition of its separate cultural identity. Originally populated by French fur trading settlements along the St. Lawrence River, Québec was ceded to the British in 1759. Ever since, proud *québecois* have strove to remain distinct from their largely-Anglicized country. French is spoken by 95% of Québec's population, and all the signs are in French only. However, despite the failure of the 1990 Meech Lake Accord intended to recognize Québec as a "distinct society," the atmosphere in the province is not antagonistic. The *Québecois* provincial motto, *Je me souviens,* promises a prosperous future as well as a remembered past.

PRACTICAL INFORMATION
Capital: Québec City.
Tourisme Québec, C.P. 20,000, Québec G1K 7X2 (800-363-7777; 514-873-2015 in Montréal). Open daily 8:30am-7:30pm; Labor Day to mid-June 9am-5pm. **Canadian Parks Service, Québec Region,** 3 Buade St. P.O. Box 6060, Québec GIR 4V7 (800-463-6769; 418-648-4177 in Québec City).
Time Zone: Eastern. **Postal abbreviation:** QU
Alcohol: Legal drinking age 18.
Sales Tax: 8% on goods and 4% on services, plus a 7% GST.

ACCOMMODATIONS INFORMATION
For assistance in locating accommodations, try the following organizations.

Bed and Breakfast: Vacances-Familles, 1291, boul. Charest Ouest, Québec JIR 2C9 (418-682-5484; in Montréal 514-251-8811). $40 yearly club membership. Provides discounts of 10-40% (usually around 15%) on province lodgings.
Camping: Association des terrains du camping du Québec, 2001, rue de la Metropole, Bureau 700 Longueil, Québec J4G 1S9 (514-651-7396), and **Fédération québecoise du camping et de caravaning,** 4545, ave. Pierre-de-Coubertin, Stade Olympique, C.P. 1000, succursale "M," Montréal H1V 3R2 (514-252-3003). Mon.-Fri. 8:30.
Hostels: Regroupement Tourisme Jeunesse (HI-C), at the Fédération address (514-252-3117). For reservations in any Québec hostel call 800-461-8585 at least 24 hrs. in advance, with a credit card.

■■■ MONTRÉAL

This island city, named for the Mont-Royal in its midst, has been coveted territory for over 300 years. Wars and sieges have brought governments in and out like the tide,

Montreal

1 Notre Dame
2 Place Jacques-Cartier
3 Chateau Ramezay
4 City Hall
5 Montreal History Center/
Place d'Youville
6 Tourisme Quebec
7 Place des Arts
8 Vieux Montreal
9 Museum of Fine Arts
10 Post Office House
11 McCord Museum
12 Christ Church Cathedral
13 Grey Nuns' Museum
14 Notre Dame de Bon-Secours
15 Marie Reine du Monde/
Place du Canada
16 Windsor Station
17 Central Station
18 Voyageur Bus Terminal
19 Sir George William Art
Galleries

Parc Mont-Royal

Parc
Helene-de-Champlain

St. Lawrence River

including a brief take-over by American revolutionaries in late 1775. Amidst it all, Montréal has grown into a diverse city with a cosmopolitan air seen in few other cities on the continent. Above and beyond the Québecois and English cultures which often still chafe, the city hosts large enclaves of Chinese, Italian, and Greek. Whether you credit the international flavor or the large student population of the city, it is hard not to be swept up by the energy, vibrancy, and fun which course through Montréal's *centre-ville*.

PRACTICAL INFORMATION

Emergency: 911.

Visitors Information: Infotouriste, 1001, rue de Square-Dorchester (873-2015 or outside Montréal 800-363-7777), on Dorchester Sq. between rue Peel and rue Metcalfe. Metro: Peel. Free city maps and guides, and extensive food and housing listings. Open daily 8:30am-7:30pm; Labor Day-June 9am-6pm. A branch office in **Old Montréal,** 174, rue Notre-Dame Est at Place Jacques Cartier, is open at the same hours and seasons as the main branch.

Tourisme Jeunesse (youth tourist info), **Boutique Temps Libre,** 3063, rue St-Denis (252-3117). Métro: Sherbrooke. Free maps; youth hostel info available. A non-profit organization that inspects and ranks all officially recognized youth hostels in Québec; has travel gear and helpful suggestions. Open Mon.-Wed. 10am-6pm, Thurs.-Fri. 10am-9pm, Sat. 10am-5pm. Mailing address: c.p. 1000, Succursale "M," Montréal P.Q., H1V 3R2. **Travel CUTS,** a student travel agency at the McGill Student Union, 3480, rue McTavish (398-0647). Métro: McGill. They specialize in budget travel for college students. Open Mon.-Fri. 9am-5pm.

Consulates: U.S., 1155, rue St-Alexander (398-9695). Open Mon.-Fri 8:30am-1pm for passports; for visas Mon.-Fri. 8:30am-noon. **U.K.,** 1155, rue de l'Université, suite 901 (866-5863). Open for info Mon.-Fri. 9am-5pm. For consular help, open Mon.-Fri. 9am-12:30pm and 2-4:30pm. **France,** Place Ville-Marie, 26th (878-4281). Open 8:30am-1pm.

Currency Exchange: Currencies International, 1230, rue Peel (392-9100). Métro: Peel. Open Mon.-Fri. 8:30am-6pm, Sat.-Sun. 9am-5pm. **Thomas Cook,** 625, boul. René-Lévesque Ouest (397-4029). Métro: Square-Victoria. Open Mon.-Fri. 9am-5pm. **FORESCO,** 1250, rue Peel at Ste-Catherine (879-1300). Métro: Peel. Open Mon.-Fri. 8:30am-5pm. Another office at 382, rue St-Jacques (843-6922). Métro: Square-Victoria. Open Mon.-Fri. 8am-6pm, Sat. 8:30am-5pm. Although many cafés will take U.S. dollars, you'll get a better deal from a currency exchange agent. Most **bank machines** are on the PLUS system and charge only the normal transaction fee for withdrawals in foreign countries.

Airports: Dorval (info service: 633-3105), 20-30 min. from downtown by car. From the Lionel Groulx Métro stop, take bus 211 to Dorval Shopping Center, then transfer to bus 204 (total fare $1.75). Taxi from downtown $24. **Connoisseur Grayline** (934-1222) runs bus service daily to Dorval from the Queen Elizabeth Hotel at the corner of René-Lévesque and Mansfield. Other stops include the Château Champlain, the Sheraton Center, and the Voyageur Terminal. (Buses run Mon.-Fri. every ½ hr., 5:20-7:20am, every 20 min. 7:20am-11:20pm, Sat.-Sun. every ½ hr. 7am-1am. $9 one way; under age 5 free.) **Mirabel International** (476-1224), 45 min. from downtown by car ($60 for a taxi), handles all flights from outside North America. Grayline buses service Mirabel (daily 1, 4, 6, and 8am, 9am-noon hourly, noon-8pm every ½ hr., 8pm-1am every hr., $14.50).

Trains: Central Station, 895, rue de la Gauchetière under the Queen Elizabeth Hotel. Métro: Bonaventure. Served by **VIA Rail** (871-1331) and **Amtrak** (800-872-7245). VIA discounts a limited number of tickets booked at least 5 days in advance for students traveling on any day and adults traveling Mon.-Thurs. or Sat. *See Mileage Chart.* VIA ticket counters open Mon.-Sat. 6:30am-8:45pm, Sun. 8am-8:45pm. Amtrak ticket counters open Mon.-Sat. 7:30am-7:30pm, Sun. 8am-7:30pm. Baggage check $2, and station open 24 hrs. for baggage pick-up.

Buses: Terminus Voyageur, 505, boul. de Maisonneuve Est (287-1580). Métro: Berri-UQAM. Voyageur offers 14-consecutive-day tour passes for $192.50 May-Oct., which will take you all over Québec and Ontario. Voyage to: Toronto (5 per day, 6½ hr., $64.50); Ottawa (17 per day, 2½ hr., $26.60); Québec City (17 per day, 3 hr., $35). The Ottawa Bus also leaves from **Dépanneur Beau-soir,** 2875, boul. St-Charles (630-4836). **Greyhound** (287-1580) serves New York City (7 per day, 8¾ hr., $91). **Vermont Transit** (842-2281) serves Boston (2 per day, 8½ hr., $77.60) and Burlington, VT (2 per day, 3 hr., $31.70).

Public Transport: STCUM Métro and Bus, (288-6287). A generally safe and extremely efficient network. The four Métro lines and most buses operate daily 5:30am-12:30am; some have night schedules as well. Get network maps at the tourist office, or at any Métro station booth. Maps have locations of shops and malls as well. Downtown ticketing is rampant so take the Métro. Buses are also part of the system, so remember to take a transfer ticket from the bus driver; it's good as a subway ticket. Fare for trains or bus $1.75, 6 tickets $7.

Taxis: Taxi Pontiac, 761-5522. **Champlain Taxi Inc.,** 273-2435. Both operate 24 hrs. at the city's regulated rates. Meters start at $2.45.

Car Rental: Via Route, 1255, rue MacKay at Ste-Catherine (871-1166). $29 per day, 200km free, 12¢ each additional km. Insurance for those over 25 $13 per day, ages 21-24 $63 per day. Must be 21 with credit card. Open Mon.-Fri. 8am-7pm, Sat. 8am-5pm, Sun. 9am-5pm.

Driver/Rider Service: Allo Stop, 4317, rue St-Denis (985-3032), matches you with a driver (part of the fee goes to the driver, who must be a member) heading for Québec City ($15), Ottawa ($10), Toronto ($26), Sherbrooke ($9), New York City ($50), or Boston ($42). Riders and drivers fix their own fees for rides over 1000 miles. Annual membership fee required ($6, drivers $7). Open Mon.-Wed. 9am-5pm, Thurs.-Fri. 9am-7pm, Sat. 10am-5pm, Sun. 10am-7pm.

Bike Rental: Cycle Pop, 978, Rachel Est (524-7102). Métro: Sherbrooke. Rent an 18-speed; $20 per day, weekends $50. Open Mon.-Wed. 9:30am-6pm, Thurs.-Fri. 9:30am-9pm, Sat.-Sun. 9:30am-5pm. Credit card or $250 deposit required.

Ticket Agencies: Ticketmaster (790-2222). Open Mon.-Sat. 9am-9pm, Sun. noon-6pm. Also try **Admission Ticket Network** (790-1245 or 800-361-4595). Open daily 8am-11pm. Credit card number required.

Help Lines: Tel-aide, 935-1101. **Sexual Assault,** 934-4504. **Suicide-Action,** 723-4000. All three open 24 hrs. **Rape Crisis,** 278-9383 (Mon.-Fri. 9:30am-4:30pm). **Gay Info,** 768-0199 (Fri.-Sat. 7:30-10:30pm). **Gay Line,** 931-8668.

Post Office: Succursale "A," 1025, St-Jacques Ouest (846-5390). Open Mon.-Fri. 8am-5:45pm. **Postal code:** H3C 1T1.

Area Code: 514.

Two major streets divide the city, making orientation convenient. The **boulevard St-Laurent** (also called "The Main") stretches north-south, splitting the city and streets east-west (traffic here runs one-way: north). The Main also serves as the unofficial French/English divider: English **McGill University** lies to the west while slightly east is **St-Denis,** a parallel two-way thorough-fare which defines the **French student quarter** (also called the *quartier latin* or the student ghetto). **Rue Sherbrooke** which is paralleled by de Maisonneuve and Ste-Catherine downtown, runs east-west almost the entire length of Montréal. Parking is often difficult in the city, particularly during winter when snowbanks narrow the streets and slow traffic. Meters cost 25¢ for 10 min. downtown and $30 parking tickets are common. Take the **Métro** to avoid the hassle. 85% off Montréal's population is French-speaking, but most are bilingual. Speak French if you know it.

ACCOMMODATIONS AND CAMPING

The **Québec Tourist Office** is the best resource for info about hostels, hotels, and *chambres touristiques* (rooms in private homes or small guest houses). B&B singles cost $25-40, doubles $35-75. The most extensive B&B network is **Bed & Breakfast à Montréal,** P.O. Box 575, Snowdon St., Montréal H3X 3T8 (738-9410), which recommends that you reserve by mail ($15 per night deposit upon confirmation). (Singles from $35, doubles from $55. Leave a message on the answering machine if the owners are out.) The **Downtown Bed and Breakfast Network,** 3458, ave. Laval, Montréal H2X 3C8 (289-9749 or 800-267-5180), at Sherbrooke, lists about 80 homes downtown. (Singles $40, doubles $55. Open spring and summer daily 9am-9pm; fall and winter 9am-6pm.) For cheaper B&B listings, check with the **Marbel Guest House,** 3507, boul. Décarie, H4A 3J4. Métro: Vendôme (486-0232; singles $25; doubles $30. Breakfast $5). Make reservations by sending a check for the first night as a deposit. Virtually all B&Bs have bilingual hosts.

Many of the least expensive *maisons touristiques* and hotels are around rue St-Denis, and they range from quaint to seedy. The area flaunts lively nightclubs, a number of funky cafés and bistros, and abuts Vieux Montréal. Two blocks east of St-Denis, **Hotel Le Breton,** 1609, rue St-Hubert (524-7273), is a particular gem in this set of accommodations. Though the neighborhood is not particularly wholesome, the 13 rooms are clean and comfortable and have TV and A/C. Around the corner from bus station. Métro: Berri-UQAM. Singles $30-55. Doubles $55-70. The hotel fills up quickly—make reservations.

Montréal Youth Hostel (HI-C), 1030, rue MacKay (843-3317). Métro: Lucien-L'Allier. Recently moved to a new, larger, and extremely convenient location in an old hotel, the place continues to have great service. The friendly, upbeat staff will give you the nightlife lowdown in addition to their own free tours and outings. Rooms have 2-6 beds (250 total). Kitchen, laundry, carpet, A/C, and extensive ride board. Continental breakfast special $2.25. Linen $1.75. Some parking available. Open 24 hrs., no curfew. Max stay 1 week (10 days in winter). $16, Canadian nonmembers $18, non-Canadian nonmembers $20.56. Reservations by credit card accepted with 24 hr. notice. IBN reservations available. Tell the airport shuttle driver where you're going and he'll make a special stop.

Résidences "Quartier Latin," 3475, St-Urbain (288-3366); rents small, bare apartments with full kitchenettes right off of rue Sherbrooke. Rooms are clean and have private baths. No singles. Parking available. June-Aug. 55 beds in rooms of 2-4. Aug.-June 260 beds. $12.50 per person, $15.50 each for a double. Office open Mon.-Fri. 1-6pm, Sat. 1-4pm, Sun. 9am-noon by apt. Reservations recommended.

Collège Français, 5155, ave. de Gaspé, H2T 2A1 (495-2581). Métro: Laurier, then walk west on Laurier and ½ block north on Gaspé. Rooms year-round. Clean and well-located. Access to gym. Young clientele. Prices vary from $13 depending on the number of beds in the room (4-7) and whether the showers are in the room or down the hall. Free parking off-school hrs. Summer breakfast $3.25. Open July-Aug. 24 hrs.; Sept.-June Mon.-Fri. 7:30am-1am, Sat.-Sun. 7:30am-2am. More beds inconveniently located at 1391, rue Beauregard Longueuil (Métro: Longueuil, then take Bus 71 up Taschereau and Ségin), open July-Aug.

McGill University, Bishop Mountain Hall, 3935, rue de l'Université, H3A 2B4 (398-6367). Métro: McGill. Follow Université through campus (bring your hiking boots; it's a long haul). Ideally located singles. Kitchenettes and payphones on each floor. Common room with TV, and laundry. Ask for Gardner building, where the views are best. Desk open Mon.-Fri. 7am-10:30pm, Sat.-Sun. 8am-10pm; a guard will check you in late at night. $27.50, non-students $36.50. $50 per 2 nights. Weekly $135. Continental breakfast ($2.90) served Mon.-Fri. 7:30-9am. Open May 15-Aug. 15. Reservations by mail (1-night deposit) needed July- Aug.

Université de Montréal, Residences, 2350, rue Edouard-Montpetit, H2X 2B9, off Côte-des-Neiges (343-6531). Métro: Edouard-Montpetit. Located on the edge of a beautiful campus; try the East Tower for great views. Singles $35, students, $24. Laundry. Phone and sink in each room. Desk open 24 hrs. Cafeteria open Mon.-Fri. 7am-7pm. Open May 6 to mid-Aug.

YWCA, 1355, rue René-Lévesque Ouest (866-9941). Métro: Lucien l'Allier. Clean, safe rooms in the heart of downtown. Women only. Newly-renovated. Access to Y facilities. Kitchen, TV on every floor. Doors lock at 10pm but the desk will buzz you in all night. Singles $35, with shared bathroom $40, with private bath $45. Doubles $50, with semi-private bath $60. $5 deposit. Reservations accepted.

YMCA, 1450, rue Stanley (849-8393), downtown. Métro: Peel. 331 rooms. Co-ed. Singles: men $35, women $38. Doubles $54. Triples $62. Quads $71. Students and seniors $2 off. Cafeteria open daily 7am-8pm. Access to Y facilities. TV and phone in every room. Usually fills up June-Aug.

Maison André Tourist Rooms, 3511, rue Université (849-4092). Métro: McGill. Mme. Zanko will rent you a room in her old, well-located house and spin great yarns, but only if you don't smoke. Guests have been returning to this bastion of European cleanliness and decor for over 30 years. Singles $26-35, doubles $38-45, $10 per extra person in room. Reservations recommended.

Manoir Ambrose, 3422, rue Stanley (288-6922), is somewhat upscale both in price and decor. Located just off of Sherbrooke in an old Victorian mansion. 22 rooms, TV, A/C, most with private baths, free continental breakfast. Singles from $40, doubles from $50.

Those with a car and time can camp at **Camping Parc Paul Sauvé** (479-8365), 45 min. from downtown. Take Autoroutes 20 west to 13 north to 640 west and follow the signs to the park. There are 850 beautiful sites on the **Lac des Deux Montagnes.** (Sites $16, beachside $17, with hookup $21.) For private sites, try **KOA Montréal-South,** 130, boul. Monette, St-Phillipe J0L 2K0 (659-8626), a 15-min. drive from the city. Follow Autoroute 15 south over Pont Champlain, take exit 38, turn left at the stop sign, and go straight for about 1 mi. (1.6km)—it's on your left. (Sites $17, with hookup $21. Both accommodate 2 people; $3 per each additional person up to 6.) If these don't wet your camping whistle try **Camping Pointe-des-Cascades,** 2 ch. du Canal, Pte. des Cascades (455-9953). Take Autoroute 40 west, exit 41 at Ste. Anne de Bellevue, junction 20, direction west to Dorion. In Dorion, follow "Théâtre des Cascades" signs. (140 sites, many near water. Sites $15, with hookup $20.)

FOOD

Restaurants pack in along **boul. St-Laurent** and on the western half of **Ste-Catherine,** with prices ranging from affordable to astronomical. While in the Latin Quarter, scout out energetic **rue Prince Arthur,** which vacuum-packs Greek, Polish, and Italian restaurants into a tiny area. Here maître-d's stand in front of their restaurants and attempt to court you toward their cuisine. Street performers and colorful wall murals further enliven this ethnic neighborhood. The accent changes slightly at **avenue Duluth,** where Portuguese and Vietnamese establishments prevail. **Rue St-Denis,** the main thoroughfare in the French student quarter, has many small restaurants and cafés, most of which cater to student pocketbooks.

French-Canadian cuisine is unique but generally expensive. When on a tight budget, look for *tourtière,* a traditional meat pie with vegetables and a thick crust, or *crêpes québecois,* stuffed with everything from scrambled eggs to asparagus with *béchamel* (a cream sauce). Wash it down with *cidre* (hard cider). Other Montréal specialties include French bread (the best on the continent), smoked meat, Matane salmon, Gaspé shrimp, lobster from the Iles de la Madelene, and *poutine,* a gooey concoction of French fries *(frites),* cheese curds, and gravy, which you can find everywhere. For *québecois* food in an authentic atmosphere, try **La Planéte Bleue,** 361 rue St.-Paul Est. (879-1278). Traditional dinners $8-10. (Open daily noon-1am.)

Montréal offers many ethnic options. See "sights" for details on finding Chinese, Italian, and Greek neighborhoods. A thriving Jewish community offers a few Jewish delis and bagel bakeries north of downtown around boul. St-Laurent. Don't leave without savoring a bagel baked before your eyes in brick ovens at **La Maison de l'Original Fairmount Bagel,** 74, rue Fairmount Ouest (272-0667; Métro: Laurier; open 24 hrs).

You'll be charged 13% tax for meals totaling more than $3.25. All restaurants are required by law to post their menus outside, so shop around. Consult the free *Restaurant Guide,* published by the Greater Montréal Convention and Tourism Bureau (844-5400), which lists more than 130 restaurants by type of cuisine (available at the tourist office). When preparing your own grub, look for produce at the **Atwater Market** (Metro: Lionel-Groulx); the **Marché Maisonneuve,** 4375, rue Ontario Est (Métro: Pie-IX); the **Marché St-Jacques** (Metro: Berri-UQAM, at the corner of Ontario and Amherst); or the **Marché Jean-Talon** (Métro: Jean Talon). (For info on any of these markets call 277-1873 Mon.-Wed., Sat. 7am-6pm; Thurs. 7am-8pm, Fri. 7am-9pm, Sun. 7am-5pm.; all open Sat.-Wed. 8am-6pm, Thurs.-Fri. 8am-9pm.)

CANADA

Café Santropol, 3990, rue Duluth (842-3110), at St-Urbain. Métro: Sherbrooke, then walk north on St-Denis and west on Duluth. *"Bienvenue à la planète Santropol!"* Student hangout, complete with aquarium and outdoor terrace for schmoozing. Eclectic menu: huge veggie sandwiches with piles of fruit ($6-8). Cream cheese, cottage cheese, yogurt, and nuts are staples. Open Mon.-Thurs. 11:30am-midnight, Fri.-Sat. noon-3am, Sun. noon-midnight.

Terasse Lafayette, 250, rue Villeneuve Ouest (288-3915), at rue Jeanne Mance, west of the Mont-Royal Métro at the southern boundary of Little Greece. Pizza, pasta, souvlaki, and salad $7.50-10; gyro plate $9.70. One of the better Greek restaurants, with a huge outdoor terrace. BYOB. 10% discount on pick-up orders. Open daily 11am-1am. Free delivery.

La Muraille Chine, 1017, boul. St-Laurent (875-8888), serves Canton and Szechuan food in the heart of Chinatown. More expensive than some, but quality is above average. Dinner around $10. Open daily 10am-11pm.

Peel Pub, 1107, rue Ste-Catherine Ouest, (844-6769), has the consummate pub food. Huge plates of spaghetti are a mere 99¢. The waiters rush about with three pitchers of beer in each hand to keep up. Another location at 1106, boulevard de Maisonneuve (845-9002.) (Both open daily 11am-3am.)

Le Mazurka, 64, rue Prince Arthur (844-3539). Métro: Sherbrooke, cross St-Denis and dance through the park. Prince Arthur is on the other side. Classy décor belies great prices. Fine Polish fare. *Pierogis* with soup, $4.25-5. Specials abound, especially Mon.-Thurs. after 9pm; it gets crowded. Dine on the terrace. Open daily 11:30am-midnight.

Etoile des Indes, 1806, Ste-Catherine Ouest (932-8330), near St-Matthieu. Métro: Guy-Concordia. Split-level dining room with tapestries covering the walls. The best Indian fare in town. Dinner entrees $7-17, daily lunch specials $7 (11:30am-2:30pm). The brave should try their bang-up *bangalore phal* dishes. Open Mon.-Sat. 11:30am-2:30pm and 5-11pm, Sun. 5-11pm.

Wilensky's, 34, rue Fairmount Ouest (271-0247). Métro: Laurier. A great place for a quick lunch. Pull out a book from Moe Wilensky's shelf, note the sign warning "We always put mustard on it," and linger. Hot dogs $1.60, sandwiches $1.85. Open Mon.-Fri. 9am-4pm.

Dunn's, 892, Ste-Catherine Ouest (866-3866). Arguably the best smoked meat in town, served in monstrous slabs tucked between bread and slathered with mustard (sandwiches $4.50, larger meat plates $7.10). Well-known for its strawberry cheesecake ($4). Open 24 hrs.

Da Giovanni, 572, Ste-Catherine Est, Métro: Berri. Serves generous portions of fine Italian food; don't be put off by the lines or the diner atmosphere. The sauce and noodles are cooked up right in the window. (842-8851; open daily 7am-2am.)

SIGHTS

Montréal has matured from a riverside settlement of French colonists into a hip metropolis. The city's ethnic pockets and architectural diversity give it a cosmopolitan flair. Museums, Vieux Montréal (Old Montréal), and the new downtown may be fascinating, but Montréal's greatest asset is its cultural vibrancy. Wander aimlessly and often—and *not* through the high-priced boutiques touted by the tourist office. A small **Chinatown** orients itself along rue de la Gauchetière, near Vieux Montréal's Place d'Armes. Between 11:30am and 2:30pm, most of its restaurants offer mouthwatering Canton and Szechuan lunch specials ranging from $3.50 to $5. Baklava abounds in **Little Greece,** a bit farther than you might care to walk from downtown just southeast of the Outremont Métro stop around rue Hutchison between ave. Van Horne and ave. Edouard-Charles. At the northern edge of the town's center, **Little Italy** occupies the area north of rue Beaubien between rues St-Hubert and Louis-Hémon. Walk east from Métro Beaubien and look for pasta. For a **walking tour** approach to the city, stick to the downtown area. Many attractions between Mont Royal and the Fleuve St-Laurent are free: from parks (Mont Royal and Lafontaine) and universities (McGill, Montréal, Concordia, Québec at Montréal) to architectural spectacles of all sorts.

Walk or bike down **boulevard St-Laurent,** north of Sherbrooke. Originally settled by Jewish immigrants, this area now functions as a sort of multi-cultural welcome wagon, home to Greek, Slavic, Latin American, and Portuguese immigrants. **Rue St-Denis,** abode of the city elite around the turn of the century, still serves as the **Latin Quarter's** mainstreet (Metro: Berri-UQAM). Jazz fiends command the street the first 10 days of July during the annual **Montréal International Jazz Festival** (871-1881) with over 350 outdoor shows. Also visit **rue Prince-Arthur** (Métro: Sherbrooke), which has street performers in the summer, **Carré St-Louis** (Métro: Sherbrooke), with its fountain and sculptures, and **Le Village,** a gay village in Montréal from rue St-Denis Est to Papineau along rue Ste-Catherine Est.

The **McGill University** campus (main gate at the corner of rue McGill and Sherbrooke; Métro: McGill) runs up Mont Royal and boasts Victorian buildings and pleasant greens in the midst of downtown. More than any other sight in Montréal, the university illustrates the impact of British tradition in the city. The campus also contains the site of the 16th-century Native-American village of Hochelaga and the **Redpath Museum of Natural History** (398-4086), with rare fossils and two genuine Egyptian mummies. (Open June-Sept. Mon.-Thurs. 9am-5pm; Sept.-June Mon.-Fri. 9am-5pm. Free.) Guided tours of the campus are available (daily year-round 9am-4pm with 1-day advance notice; 398-6555).

About five blocks west of the McGill entrance, Montréal's **Musée des Beaux-Arts** (Fine Arts Museum), 1379 and 1380, rue Sherbrooke Ouest (285-1600; Métro: Peel or Guy-Concordia), houses a small permanent collection that touches upon all major artistic periods and includes Canadian and Inuit work. (Open Tues.-Sun. 11am-6pm, Wed. and Sat. closes at 9pm, $9.50, students and seniors $4.75, under 12 $2.) Inquire about their impressive visiting exhibits. The newly renovated and expanded **McCord Museum of Canadian History,** 690, rue Sherbrooke Ouest (398-7100; Métro: McGill), presents a collection of textiles, costumes, paintings, prints, and 700,000 pictures spanning 133 years in their photographic archives. (Archives open by appointment only; contact Nora Hague.) (Open Tues.-Wed. and Fri. 10am-6pm, Thurs. 10am-9pm, Sat.-Sun. 10am-5pm; $5, students $2, seniors $3. Free Thurs. 6-9pm.) Opened in May 1989, the **Centre Canadien d'Architecture,** 1920, ave. Baile (939-7026; Métro: Guy-Concordia), houses one of the world's most important collections of architectural prints, drawings, photographs, and books. (Open Tues.-Sun. 11am-6pm, Thurs. 11am-8pm; Oct.-May Wed. and Fri. 11am-6pm, Thurs. 11am-8pm, Sat.-Sun. 11am-5pm; $5, students and seniors $3, children under 12 free. Students free all day long, everyone free Thurs. 6-8pm.)

Musée d'Art Contemporain (Museum of Contemporary Art), 185, Ste-Catherine Ouest at Jeanne-Mance (847-6226; Métro: Place-des-Arts), has the latest by *québecois* artists, as well as textile, photography, and avant-garde exhibits (open Tues. and Thurs.-Sun. 11am-6pm, Wed. 11am-6pm; $4.75, seniors $3.75, students $2.75, under 12 free; free Wed. 6-9pm). Outside of the downtown museum circuit, the **Montréal Museum of Decorative Arts,** 2929, rue Jeanne-d'Arc (259-2575; Metro: Pie-IX), houses innovatively designed decorative pieces dating from 1935 to the present and from the functional to the ridiculous. ($3, students under 26 $1.50, under 12 free; open Wed.-Sun. 11am-5pm.)

Olympic Park, 4141, ave. Pierre-de-Coubertin (252-4737; Métro: Pie-IX or Viau), hosted the 1976 Summer Olympic Games. Its daring architecture, uncannily reminiscent of the *U.S.S. Enterprise,* includes the world's tallest inclined tower and a stadium with one of the world's only fully retractable roofs. Despite this, baseball games *still* get rained out because the roof cannot be put into place with crowds in the building (small goof, really). (Guided tours daily at 12:40 and 3:40pm; more often May-Sept., $5.25, ages 5-17 $4.25, under 5 free.) Take the *funiculaire* to the top of the tower for a panoramic view of Montréal and a guided tour of the observation deck. (Every 10 min., Mon.-Thurs. 10am-9pm, Fri.-Sun. 10am-11pm; off-season daily 10am-6pm; $10.25, kids $7.50.) The most recent addition to the attractions at the Olympic Park is the **Biodôme,** 4777, ave. Pierre-de-Coubertin (868-3000). Housed in the building which was once the Olympic Vélodrome, the Biodôme is a "living museum" in which four complete ecosystems have been reconstructed: the Tropical Forest, the Laurentian Forest, the St-Laurent marine ecosystem, and the Polar World. The goal is environmental awareness and conservation; the management stresses repeatedly that the Biodôme is *not* a zoo; rather, it is intended to be a means for people to connect themselves with the natural world. (Open daily 9am-8pm. $8.50, students and seniors $6, ages 6-17 $4.25, under 6 free.) In the summer, a train will take you across the park to the **Jardin Botanique** (Botanical Gardens), 4101, rue Sherbrooke Est (872-1400; Métro: Pie-IX), one of the most important gardens in the world. The Japanese and Chinese areas house the largest *bonsai* and *penjing* collections outside of Asia. (Gardens open daily 9am-8pm; Sept.-April daily 9am-4:30pm. $7, students and seniors $5, ages 6-17 $3.50, under 6 free. 30% less Sept.-April.) Package tickets are available for Biodôme and Gardens. Parking in the complex starts at $5.

Montréal's more natural approach to a park, **Parc du Mont-Royal,** Centre de la Montagne (844-4928; Métro: Mont-Royal), climbs up to the mountain from which the city took its name. From rue Peel, hardy hikers can take a foot path and stairs to the top, or to the lookouts on Camillien-Houde Parkway and the Mountain Chalet. The 30-foot cross at the top of the mountain commemorates the 1643 climb by de Maisonneuve, founder of Montréal. In winter, *montréalais* congregate here to ice-skate, toboggan, and cross-country ski. In summer, Mont-Royal welcomes joggers, cyclists, picnickers, and amblers. (Officially open 6am-midnight.) **Parc Lafontaine** (872-2644; Métro: Sherbrooke), bordered by Sherbrooke, Rachel, Papineau, and ave., has picnic facilities, an outdoor puppet theater, seven tennis courts (hourly fee), ice-skating in the winter, and an international festival of public theater in June.

The Underground City

Montréal residents aren't speaking cryptically of a sub-culture or a hideout for dissidents when they rave about their Underground City. They literally mean *under the ground:* 29km of tunnels link Métro stops and form a subterranean village of climate-controlled restaurants and shops—a haven in Montréal's sub-zero winter weather. The ever-expanding network connects railway stations, two bus terminals, restaurants, banks, cinemas, theaters, hotels, two universities, two department stores, 1700 businesses, 1615 housing units, and 1600 boutiques. Somewhat frighteningly hailed by the city as "the prototype of the city of the future," these burrows give the word "suburban" a whole new meaning. Enter the city from any Métro stop, or start your adventure at the **Place Bonaventure,** 901, rue de la Gauchetière Ouest (397-2205; Métro: Bonaventure), Canada's largest commercial building. Inside, the **Viaduc** shopping center contains a mélange of shops, each selling products imported from a different country. The tourist office supplies city guides that include treasure maps of the tunnels and underground attractions. (Shops open Mon.-Wed. 9:30am-6pm, Thurs.-Fri. 9:30am-9pm, Sat. 9:30am-5pm, Sun. 9am-noon.) Poke your head above ground to see **Place Ville-Marie** (Métro: Bonaventure), a 1960s office-shopping complex. Revolutionary when first built, the structure triggered Montréal's architectural renaissance.

Back in the underworld, ride the train that made it all happen, the Métro, to the McGill stop and enjoy some of the underground city's finest offerings. Here, beneath the Christ Church Cathedral, 625, Ste-Catherine Ouest, waits **Promenades de la Cathédrale** (849-9925), where you can not only shop but enjoy theatrical presentation in the complex's central atrium. (Call for details). Three blocks east, passing through **Centre Eaton,** of grand department store fame, the **Place Montréal Trust** is famous for its modern architecture and unfortunately expensive shopping area. There's certainly no charge for looking around though.

Vieux Montréal (Old Montréal) and Fleuve St-Laurent Islands

'n the 17th century, the city of Montréal struggled with Iroquois tribes for control of ˈrea's lucrative fur trade, and erected walls circling the settlement as a defensive measure. Today the remnants of those ramparts do no more than delineate the boundaries of Vieux Montréal, the city's first settlement, on the stretch of river bank between rues McGill, Notre-Dame, and Berri. The fortified walls that once protected the quarter have crumbled, but the beautiful 17th- and 18th-century mansions of politicos and merchants retain their splendor. Take the Métro to Place d'Armes, or get off at Bonaventure and check out Cathédrale Marie Reine du Monde (Mary Queen of the World Cathedral), at the corner of René-Lévesque and Mansfield (866-1661), before walking to the port. A scaled-down replica of St. Peter's in Rome, the church was definitely built in the heart of Montréal's Anglo-Protestant area. (Open daily 7am-7:30pm; off-season Sun.-Fri. 9:30am-7:30pm, Sat. 8am-8:30pm.)

The 19th-century church **Notre-Dame-de-Montréal,** 116, rue Notre-Dame Ouest (842-2925), towers above the Place d'Armes and the memorial to de Maisonneuve. Historically the center for the city's Catholic population, the neo-Gothic church once hosted separatist rallies. It seats 4000 and is one of the largest and most magnificent churches in North America. Concerts are held here throughout the year. After suffering major fire damage, the **Wedding Chapel** behind the altar re-opened in 1982, complete with an enormous bronze altar. (Open daily 7am-8pm; Labor-Day-June 24 7am-6pm. Guided tours offered.)

From Notre-Dame walk next door to the **Sulpician Seminary,** Montréal's oldest building (built in 1685) and still a functioning seminary. The clock over the facade is the oldest public timepiece in North America and has recorded the passage of over nine billion seconds since it was built in 1700. A stroll down rue St-Sulpice will bring you to the old docks along the **rue de la Commune,** on the banks of the Fleuve St-Laurent. Proceed east along rue de la Commune to **rue Bonsecours.** At the corner of rue Bonsecours and the busy rue St-Paul stands the 18th-century **Notre-Dame-de-Bonsecours,** 400, rue St-Paul Est (845-9991; Métro: Champ-de-Mars), founded on the port as a sailors' refuge by Marguerite Bourgeoys, leader of the first congregation of non-cloistered nuns. Sailors thankful for their safe pilgrimages presented the nuns and priests with the wooden boat-shaped ceiling lamps in the chapel. The church also has a museum in the basement and a bell tower with a nice view of Vieux Montréal and the Fleuve St-Laurent. (Chapel open Mon.-Sat. 9am-5pm, Sun. 9am-6pm; Nov.-April Mon.-Fri. 10am-3pm, Sat. 10am-5pm, Sun. 10am-6pm. Free. Tower and museum open the same hours. $4, under 4 50¢.)

Opening onto rue St-Paul is **Place Jacques Cartier,** site of Montréal's oldest market. Here the modern European character of Montréal is most evident; cafés line the square and street artists strut their stuff during the summer. Visit the grand **Château Ramezay,** 280, rue Notre-Dame Est (861-3708; Métro: Champ-de-Mars), built in 1705 to house the French viceroy, and its museum of Québecois, British, and American 18th-century artifacts. (Open Tues.-Sun. 10am-4:30pm. $5, students and seniors $3, families $10. Guided tours available on Wed.) Check out the **Vieux Palais de Justice,** built in 1856 in Place Vaugeulin. Across from it stands **City Hall. Rue St-Jacques** in the Old City, established in 1687, is Montréal's answer to Wall Street.

There are many good reasons to venture out to **Île Ste-Hélène,** an island in the Fleuve St-Laurent, just off the coast of Vieux Montréal. The best is **La Ronde** (872-6222; bus 167), Montréal's popular amusement park. It's best to go in the afternoon and buy an unlimited pass. From late May to July on Wednesday and Saturday, stick around La Ronde until 10pm to watch the **International Fireworks Competition** (872-8714). (Park open June-Labor Day Sun.-Thurs. 11am-11pm, Fri.-Sat. 11am-midnight. $18, under 12 $9, families $42.) If you don't want to pay admission to the park, watch the fireworks from people-packed Pont Jacques-Cartier.

Le Vieux Fort ("The Old Fort," also known as the **David M. Stewart Museum;** 861-6701), was built in the 1820s to defend Canada's inland waterways. Now primarily a military museum, the fort displays artifacts and costumes detailing Canadian colonial history. (Open Wed.-Mon. 10am-6pm; Sept.-April Wed.-Mon. 10am-5pm. 3 military parades daily June-Aug. $5, seniors, students, and kids $3, under 6 free, families $10.) Take the Métro under the St-Laurent to the Île Ste-Hélène stop.

The other island in Montréal's Parc des Iles is **Ile Notre-Dame,** where the recently opened **Casino de Montréal,** 1, ave. de Casino (392-2746 or 800-665-2274), awaits those who wish to push their luck. Don't bet against the house sticking to its dress code. T-shirts and running shoes allowed June-Labor Day; no athletic wear or jeans in any size, shape, or color, ever. (Admission free. Parking free, with shuttles from the parking lot every 10-15 min. Open daily 11am-3am.)

Whether swollen with spring run-off or frozen over during the winter, the **Fleuve St-Laurent** (St. Lawrence River) can be one of Montréal's most thrilling attractions, but the whirlpools and 15-ft. waves of the **Lachine Rapids** once precluded river travel. No longer—now St-Laurent and Montréal harbor cruises depart from Victoria Pier (842-3871) in Vieux Montréal (mid-May to mid-Oct., 3 per day, 2 hr., $18.75). Tours of the Lachine Rapids (284-9607) leave five times per day (May-Sept. 10am-6pm; 1½-hr. cruise $45, seniors $40, ages 13-19 $35, ages 8-12 $25). For a close-up and personal introduction to the river, contact **Rafting Montréal,** 8912, boul. LaSalle (983-3707). Two 1½-hr. white water trips are available, at differing levels of shock-induction. Reservations are necessary. ($34, students and seniors $28, kids 6-12 $17. Open May-Oct. daily 9am-5:30pm.)

NIGHTLIFE, NIGHTLIFE, AND NIGHTLIFE

Montréal has a very happening nightlife. Even in the dead of winter, the bars are full. *The drinking age in Montréal is 18.* You can save money by buying your own wine at a *dépanneur* or at the **SAQ** (Sociéte des alcohols du Québec) and bringing it to one of the unlicensed restaurants, concentrated on the **boul. St-Laurent,** north of Sherbrooke, and on the pedestrian precincts of **rue Prince Arthur** and **rue Duluth.** Should you choose to ignore the massive neon lights flashing "films érotiques" and "Château du sexe," you can find lots and lots of nightlife in Québec's largest city—either in **brasseries** (with food as well as beer, wine, and music), in **pubs** (with more hanging out and less eating), or in the multitude of **dance clubs.**

Though intermingled with some of the city's hottest dance venues, the establishments of **rue Ste-Catherine Ouest** and the near-by side streets tend to feature drink as the primary entertainment (Metro: Peel.) Downstairs at 1107, rue Ste-Catherine Ouest, the **Peel Pub** (844-6769), provides live rock bands and good, cheap food nightly, but more noted are its exceptional drink prices. Here waiters rush about with three pitchers of beer in each hand to keep up with the mötley crüe of university students and suited types. Happy hour (Mon.-Fri. 2-8pm) floods the joint with $6 pitchers. Another location is at 1106, boul. de Maisonneuve (845-9002.) (Both open daily 11am-3am.) For slightly older and more subdued drinking buddies, search the side streets and the touristy English strongholds around **rue Crescent** and **rue Bishop** (Métro: Guy), where bar-hopping is a must. **Déjà-Vu,** 1224, Bishop near Ste-Catherine (866-0512), has live bands each night at 10pm. (Open daily 3pm-3am; happy hour 3-10pm. No cover.) Set aside Thursday for a night at **D.J.'s Pub,** 1443, Crescent (287-9354), when $12 gets you drinks for the night after 9pm. (Open noon-3am.) **Sir Winston Churchill's,** 1459, Crescent (288-0616), is another hotspot. (Open daily 11:30am-3am.)

Rue Prince Arthur at St-Laurent is devoted solely to pedestrians who mix and mingle at the outdoor cafés by day and clubs by night. **Café Campus,** 57, Prince Arthur (844-1010), features live rock and other genres. (Cover up to $3. Open Sun.-Fri. 8pm-1am.) **The Shed Café,** 3515, St-Laurent (842-0220; open Mon.-Fri. 11am-3am, Sat.-Sun. 9am-3am), the **Zoo Bar,** 3556, St-Laurent (848-6398; open daily 9pm-3am; Wed. is the night here), and **Angel's,** 3604, St-Laurent (282-9944; open Thurs.-Sat. 8pm-3am) all boast a young student clientele, charge a small to no cover, and are all within a few blocks around **St-Laurent** (Métro: St-Laurent or Sherbrooke). The density of nightlife makes this a great area to wander through. Farther up St-Laurent on the corner of rue Bernard (farther than most people care to walk), lies **Eugene Patin,** 5777, St-Laurent (278-6336), one of the city's hidden jewels (cover ~ until 2am; open Wed.-Sat. 9pm-3am).

French nightlife also parleys in the open air cafés on **rue St-Denis** (Métro: UQAM). **Bar Passeport,** 4156, rue St-Denis (842-6063), at Rachel, doubles as a store by day and a crowded dance club by night. (No cover. Open daily 10am-3am.)

In the gay village of Montréal there are plenty of clubs for both women and men. (Métro: Papineau or Beaudry). For lots of gay men and lots of good dance music try **Max,** 1156, Ste-Catherine Est (866-8667; open Mon.-Fri. 4pm-3am, Sat.-Sun. 2pm-3am). The **Loubar,** 1368, Ste-Catherine Est (523-9325), caters to lesbians and has slightly more subdued music. (Open daily 5pm-3am.)

Vieux Montréal, too, is best seen at night. Street performers, artists, and *chanson-niers* in various *brasseries* set the tone for lively summer evenings of clapping, stomping, and singing along. The real fun goes down on St-Paul, in the *brasseries* near the corner of St-Vincent. For a sweet Sunday in the park, saunter over to **Parc Jeanne-Mance** for bongos, dancing, and handicrafts (May-Sept. noon-7pm).

The city has a wide variety of theatrical groups: the **Théâtre du Nouveau Monde,** 84, Ste-Catherine Ouest (861-0563; Métro: Place-des-Arts) and the **Théâtre du Rideau Vert,** 4664, rue St-Denis (844-1793), stage *québecois* works (all productions in French). For English language plays, try the **Centaur Theatre,** 453, rue St-François-Xavier (288-1229; Métro: Place-d'Armes), which has a season running mainly Oct.-June. The city's exciting **Place des Arts,** 260, boul. de Maisonneuve Ouest (842-2112 for tickets), houses the **Opéra de Montréal** (985-2258), the **Montréal Symphony Orchestra** (842-9951), and **Les Grands Ballets Canadiens** (849-8681). **The National Theatre School of Canada,** 5030, rue St-Denis (842-7954), stages excellent student productions during the academic year. **Théâtre Saint-Denis,** 1594, rue St-Denis (849-4211), hosts traveling productions like *Cats* and *Les Misérables.* Check the *Calendar of Events* (available at the tourist office and reprinted in daily newspapers), or call **Ticketmaster** (790-2222) for ticket info.

SPORTS

Montréalais are rabid sports fans, and their home team support runs deep. In order to see professional sports, call well in advance to reserve tickets. The **Expos,** Montréal's baseball team, swing in Olympic Stadium (see address in Sights above; for Expos info call 846-3976). Between October and April, be sure to attend a **Montréal Canadiens** hockey game: the **Montréal Forum,** 2313, Ste-Catherine Ouest (Métro: Atwater), is the shrine to hockey and **Les Habitants** (nickname for the Canadiens) are its acolytes. In 1993 they roughed-up everyone and sailed home with the Stanley Cup. Games are usually sold out, so call for tickets as early as possible. (For more info, call 932-2582.) *Montréalais* don't just watch: their one-day **Tour de l'île,** consisting of a 64km circuit of the island, is the largest participatory cycling event in the world, with 45,000 mostly amateur cyclists pedaling their wares. (Call 847-8687 to see how you can take part, too. Registration for the ride in early June must be completed in April.) During the second weekend in June, the **Circuit Gilles-Villeneuve** on the Ile Notre-Dame hosts the annual **Molson Grand Prix,** a Formula 1 race (392-0000 or 800-567-8687), and this August, **Tennis Canada** will host the world's best tennis players at Jarry Park. This tournament features men and women in alternating years and will host men in 1995. (Metro: De Castelnau; 273-1515 ticket info.)

■■■ QUÉBEC CITY

High on the rocky heights of Cape Diamond, where the Fleuve St-Laurent narrows and joins the St. Charles River, Québec City has been called the "Gibraltar of America" because of the stone escarpments and military fortifications protecting the port. When passing through the portals of North America's only walled city, one seems to pass through time. Narrow streets and horse-drawn carriages greet visitors to the Old City, and there are enough sights and museums to satisfy the most voracious historical buff. Along with the historical attachment, Canada's oldest city boasts a thriving French culture; never assume that the locals speak English. Fully steeped in their

CANADA

cultural history, the *Québecois* and their city retain vitality, energy, and *joie de vivre,* as well as modern-day fun.

PRACTICAL INFORMATION

Emergency: Police, 911 (city); 623-6262 (province). **Info-santé:** 648-2626, 24-hr. service with info from qualified nurses.

Visitor Information: Centre d'information de l'office du tourisme et des congrés de la communauté urbaine de Québec, 60, rue d'Auteuil (692-2471), in the Old City. Visit here for accommodations listings, brochures, free maps, and friendly bilingual advice. Ask for the annual *Greater Québec Area Guide.* Free local calls. Open June-Labor Day daily 8:30am-8pm; April-May and Sept.-Oct. Mon.-Fri. 8:30am-5:30pm; winter Mon.-Fri. 8:30am-5pm. **Maison du tourisme de Québec,** 12, rue Ste-Anne (800-363-7777), deals specifically with provincial tourism, distributing accommodations listings for the entire province and free road and city maps. Some bus tours and Budget Rent-a-Car also have desks. Open 8:30am-7:30pm; Labor Day to mid-June 9am-5pm.

Youth Tourist Information: Boutique Temps-Libre of Regroupement tourisme jeunesse, 2700, boul. Laurier (800-461-8585), in Ste-Fo, in the Place Laurier. Sells maps, travel guides, ISICs and HI-C memberships, and health insurance. Makes reservations at any hostel in the Québec province. (Open Mon.-Wed. 10am-5:30pm, Thurs.-Fri. 10am-9pm, Sat. 10am-5pm, Sun. noon-5pm.)

Airlines: Air Canada (692-0770 or 800-361-7413) and **Canadian International** (692-1031 or 800-361-7413). Special deals available for ages 12-21 (with ID) willing to go standby and fly only in Canada. The airport is far out of town and inaccessible by public transport. Taxi to downtown $22. By car, turn right onto Rte. de l'aéroport and then take either boul. Wilfred-Hamel or, beyond it, Autoroute 440 to get into the city. **Maple Leaf Sightseeing Tours** (649-9226) runs a shuttle service between the airport and the major hotels of the city. (Mon.-Fri. 5 per day to the airport and 8 per day from the airport, 8am-5:30pm; Sat.-Sun. 4 per day to the airport and 5 per day from the airport, 10am-3pm. $8.50.)

Trains: VIA Rail Canada, 450, rue de la Gare du Palais in Québec City (524-6452). To: Montréal (3 per day; 3 hr., $41, students $37). 40% discounts if booked at least 5 days in advance; applicable for students traveling on any day and for adults not traveling on Fri., Sun., or a holiday. Open Mon.-Fri. 6am-8:45pm, Sat. 7am-8:45pm, Sun. 9am-8:45pm. Nearby stations at 3255, ch. de la Gare in Ste-Foy (658-8792; open same hours as Québec City station) and 5995, St-Laurent Autoroute 20 Lévis (833-8056; open Thurs.-Mon. 4-5am, 8:15-10:45pm; Tues. 4-5am; Wed. 8:15-10:45pm). Call 800-361-5390 anywhere in Canada or the U.S. for reservations.

Buses: Voyageur Bus, 320 Abraham Martin (525-3000). Open daily 5:30am-1am. Outlying stations at 2700, ave. Laurier, in Ste-Foy (651-7015; open daily 6am-1am), and 63, Hwy. Trans-Canada Ouest (Hwy. 132), in Lévis (837-5805; open daily 24 hrs). To Montréal (every hr. 6am-9pm and 11pm, 3 hr., $35.50) and Ste-Anne-de-Beaupré (2 per day, 25 min., $5). Connections to U.S. via Montréal or Sherbrooke.

Public Transport: Commission de transport de la Communauté Urbaine de Québec (CTCUQ), 270, rue des Rocailles (627-2511 for route and schedule info; open Mon.-Fri. 6:30am-10pm, Sat.-Sun. 8am-10pm. Buses operate daily 5:30am-12:30am although individual routes vary. Fare $1.95, students $1.45, seniors and children $1.25, children under 6 free.

Taxis: Coop Taxis Québec, 525-5191. $2.25 base fee, $1 each additional km.

Driver/Rider Service: Allo-Stop, 467, rue St-Jean (522-0056), will match you with a driver heading for Montréal ($15) or Ottawa ($29). Must be a member ($6 per year, drivers $7). Open Mon.-Wed. 9am-5pm, Thurs.-Fri. 9am-7pm, Sat. 10am-5pm, Sun. 10am-7pm.

Car Rental: Pelletier, 900, boul. Pierre Bertrand (681-0678). $39 per day; unlimited km, $15 insurance. Must be 25 with credit card deposit of $350. Open Mon.-Fri. 7:30am-8pm, Sat.-Sun. 8am-5pm.

Bike Rental: Promo-Vélo (687-3301), located in a tent in the tourist center parking lot on Rue d'Auteuil. One hour $6, 4 hr. $14, 24 hrs. $23; $40 deposit with credit card required. Open daily May-Oct. 8am-9pm, weather permitting.

CANADA

Help Lines: Tél-Aide, 683-2153. Open daily noon-midnight. **Viol-Secours** (sexual assault line), 522-2120. Counselors on duty Mon.-Fri. 9am-4pm and on call 24 hrs. for emergencies. **Center for Suicide Prevention,** 522-4588. Open 24 hrs.

Post Office: 3, rue Buade (694-6102). **Postal Code:** G1R 2J0. Also at 300, rue St-Paul (694-6175). **Postal code:** G1K 3W0. Both open Mon.-Fri. 8am-5:45pm.

Area Code: 418.

Québec's main thoroughfares run though both the Old City (*Vieux Québec*) and outside it, generally parallel in an east-west direction. Within **Vieux Québec,** the main streets are **St-Louis, Ste-Anne,** and **St-Jean.** Most streets in Vieux Québec are one way, the major exception being rue d'Auteuil, which borders the walls and which is the best bet for parking during the busy times of day. Outside the walls of Vieux Québec, both St-Jean and St-Louis continue (St-Jean eventually joins Chemin Ste-Foy and St-Louis becomes **Grande Allée**). **Boul. René-Lévesque,** the other major street outside the walls, runs between them. The Basse-ville (lower town) is separated from the Haute-ville (upper town, Old Québec) by an abrupt cliff which is roughly paralleled by rue St-Vallier Est.

ACCOMMODATIONS AND CAMPING

Gîte Québec is Québec City's only referral service. Contact Thérèse Tellier, 3729, ave. Le Corbusier, Ste-Foy, Québec G1W 4P5 (651-1860). Singles run $30-40, doubles $60-65. (Call 8am-1pm or after 6pm.) Hosts are usually bilingual and the service inspects the houses for cleanliness and convenience of location.

You can obtain a list of nearby campgrounds from the Maison du Tourisme de Québec (see Practical Information), or by writing Tourisme Québec, c.p. 20,000 Québec, Québec G1K 7X2 (800-363-7777; open daily 9am-5pm).

Centre international de séjour HI-C, 19, Ste-Ursule (694-0755), between rue St-Jean and Dauphine. Follow Côte d'Abraham uphill from the bus station until it joins ave. Dufferin. Turn left on St-Jean, pass through the walls, and walk uphill, to your right, on Ste-Ursule. If you're driving, follow St-Louis into the Old City and take the second left past the walls onto Ste-Ursule. The rooms are cramped, but a friendly staff, youthful clientele, and fabulous location should make it your first choice. Laundry, microwave, TV, pool, ping-pong tables, living room, kitchen (open 7:30am-11pm), cafeteria in basement. Breakfast served 7:30-10am ($3.75). Check-out 10am, check-in starting at noon. Doors lock at 11pm, but front desk will let you in if you flash your key. 300 beds. One bed in a 2-bed room $17, in a 4-to 8-person room $15, in an 8- to 16-person room $13; nonmembers pay $3 more; kids under 8 free; ages 8-13 $8. HI-C memberships sold. Usually full July-Aug., so make reservations or arrive early. IBN reservations available.

Auberge de la Paix, 31, rue Couillard (694-0735). Has neither the activity nor the facilities of the Centre; stay here when the Centre is full. Both offer great access to the restaurants and bars on rue St-Jean. Rooms a bit roomier and mattresses a bit better than those at the Centre; rooms are co-ed. 56 beds, 2-8 beds per room, most have 3-4 occupants. Curfew 2am with all-day access. $16. Breakfast of toast, cereal, coffee, and juice included (8-10am). Kitchen open all day. Linen $2 for entire stay. Reservations necessary July-Aug.

Montmartre Canadien, 1675, ch. St-Louis, Sillery (681-7357), on the outskirts of the city, in the Maison du Pelerin; a small white house behind the main building at 1671. Take bus 25 or 1. Clean house in a religious sanctuary overlooking the Fleuve St-Laurent run by Assumptionist monks. Relaxed, almost ascetic, setting—don't expect to meet tons of exciting new people here. Mostly used by groups. Common showers. Dorm-style singles $15. Doubles $26. Triples $36. Bed in 7-person dormitory $11; groups of 20 or more $13. Breakfast (eggs, cereal, bacon, and pancakes) $3.50. Reserve 2-3 weeks in advance.

Manoir La Salle, 18, rue Ste-Ursule (692-9953), opposite the youth hostel. Clean private rooms fill up quickly, especially in the summer. Reservations necessary. Cat-haters beware: felines stalk the halls. Singles $25-30; doubles $40-55 depending on bed-size and status of facilities.

CANADA

Le Petit Hôtel, 3, ruelle des Ursulines (694-0965), just off of rue Ste-Ursule. This tidy little hotel is a great deal for two people, with a TV, free local phone, private bath, and refrigerator in each room. Astoundingly combines a downtown location with free parking. May-Oct. $50 for 1 or 2 occupants, off-season $30-35.

Maison Demers, 68, rue Ste-Ursule, GIR 4E6 (692-2487), up the road from the youth hostel. Clean, comfortable rooms with TV and live conversation with Jean-Luc Demers; all rooms have a sink, some have a private bath. Singles $33-35, doubles with shower $45-65, 2-bed, 4-person room $70. Breakfast of coffee and fresh croissants included. Parking available. Reservations recommended.

Camping Canadien, 6030, rue Ancienne-Lorette (872-7801). 17 sites. $17.50, with hookup $18.50. Showers, laundry. Open May 15-Oct. 15. Take Autoroute 173 out of the city to Boul. Wilfred-Hamel and follow the signs.

Municipal de Beauport, Beauport (666-2228). Take Autoroute 40 east, exit #321 at rue Labelle onto Hwy. 369, turn left, and follow the signs marked "camping." Bus 800 will also take you to this campground overlooking the Montmorency River. Swimming pool and canoes ($6 per hr.) are available. Showers, laundry. 135 sites. $15, with hookup $20; weekly $85/120. Open June-Labor Day.

FOOD

In general, rue Buade, St-Jean, and Cartier, as well as the **Place Royale** and **Petit Champlain** areas offer the widest selection of food and drink. The **Grande Allée,** a 2km-long strip of nothing but restaurants on either side, might seem like heaven to the hungry, but its steep prices make it a place to visit rather than to eat. (There are a few exceptions, see the Vieille Maison below.)

Traditional Québecois food is usually affordable and appetizing. One of the most filling yet inexpensive meals is a *croque-monsieur,* a large, open-faced sandwich with ham and melted cheese (about $5), usually served with salad. Be sure to try *québecois* French onion soup, slathered with melted cheese and generally served with bats of French bread or *tourtière,* a thick meat pie. Other specialties include the *crêpe,* stuffed differently to serve as either an entree or a dessert. The **Casse-Crepe Breton,"** 1136, St-Jean, offers many choices of fillings in their "make your own combination" crepes for dinner ($3-5), as well as scrumptious dessert options ($2.25-$2.50). (Open daily 7:30am-1am.) Finally, seek out the French-Canadian "sugar pie," made with brown sugar and butter. Don't be fooled into thinking that your best bet for a simple and affordable meal is to line up behind one of the many fast-food joints which proliferate throughout the city. Instead experience culinary excellence at the **Pâtisserie au Palet d'Or,** 60, rue Garneau (692-2488), a quaint French bakery where $2.75 will get you a salmon sandwich and $1.50 a crisp, golden baguette. (Open daily 8am-10pm.) Remember that some of these restaurants do not have non-smoking sections.

For those doing their own cooking, **J.A. Moisan,** 699, rue St-Jean (522-8268) sells groceries in an old country-style store. (Open daily 8:30am-10pm.) **Dépanneurs** are Québec's answer to the corner store, selling milk, bread, snack food, and booze.

Café Mediterranée, 64, boul. René Lévesque (648-1849 lunchtime; 648-0768 dinner). Take the 25 bus or walk for about 10 min. outside the walls. Elegant surroundings for a Mediterranean buffet. Enjoy vegetable platters, *couscous,* spicy chicken dishes—or all three: the ideal, filling lunch. Soup, dessert, coffee, and as much as you want for a main meal for $8 (lunch) or $15 (dinner). Open Mon.-Thurs. noon-2pm; Fri.-Sat. noon-2pm and 6-11pm; Sun. 9am-2:30pm. Arrive early for the best of the buffet. Reservations recommended.

Kyoto, 560, Grande Allée (529-6141). By night an expensive Japanese restaurant with authentic garden decor; by day a cheap buffet with authentic garden decor. Buffet $6.50 Mon.-Fri. 11:30am-2pm. Open daily 5:30-9pm as well.

Mille-Feuille, 32, rue Ste-Angèle (692-2147). Vegetarian meals ($5-9) served in a chic restaurant with an outdoor terrace to boot. Try *tourtière* or vegetable quiche ($4). Open daily 8am-11pm.

Fleur de Lotus, 38, Côte de la Fabrique (692-4286), across from the Hôtel de ~~·~~e. Cheerful and unpretentious. Thai, Cambodian, Vietnamese, and Japanese dishes $8.75-14. Open Mon.-Wed. 11:30am-10:30pm, Thurs.-Fri. 11:30am-11pm, Sat. 5-11pm, Sun. 5-10:30pm.

Chez Temporel, 25, rue Couillard (694-1813). Stay off the tourist path while remaining within your budget at this genuine *café québecois,* discreetly tucked in a side alley off rue St-Jean. Besides the usual café staples, it offers exotic coffee and liquor drinks ($4.50). You can sip Irish coffee while listening to Edith Piaf. Linger as long as you like. Open Sun.-Thurs. 7am-1:30am, Fri.-Sat. 7am-2:30am.

Restaurant Liban, 23, rue d'Auteuil, off rue St-Jean (694-1888). Great café for lunch or a late-night bite. Tabouli and hummus plates $3.50, both with pita bread. Excellent felafel ($4) and baklava ($1.75). Open 11am-4am.

SIGHTS

Confined within walls built by the English, *Vieux Québec* (Old City) contains most of the city's historic attractions. Though monuments are clearly marked and explained, you'll get more out of the town if you consult the tourist office's *Greater Québec Area Tourist Guide,* which contains a walking tour of the Old City. (Available from all 3 tourist offices listed in Practical Information above.) It takes one or two days to explore Vieux Québec on foot, but you'll learn more than on the many guided bus tours. Be forewarned, any map of the city which isn't typographical is somewhat misleading; everything in Old Québec is either up or downhill.

Begin your walking tour of Québec City by climbing to the top of **Cap Diamant** (Cape Diamond), just south of the **Citadelle,** where the view of both inside and outside the walls is best. A magnificent complex and home to the Royal 22 Regiment, the **Citadelle** is the largest North American fortification still guarded by troops. Visitors can witness the **changing of the guard** (mid-June to Labor Day daily 10am) and the **beating of the retreat** (July-Aug. Tues. and Thurs. and Sat.-Sun. 7pm). Tours are given every 55 min. (Citadelle open daily 9am-6pm; Labor Day-Oct. and May-June 9am-4pm; mid-March to April 10am-3pm; Nov. to mid-March open by reservation only. $4, ages 7-17 $2, disabled and under 7 free.)

From the Citadelle take Promenade des Gouverneurs downhill to **Terrasse Dufferin.** Built in 1838 by Lord Durham, this popular promenade offers excellent views of the Fleuve St-Laurent, the Côte de Beaupré (the "Avenue Royale" Highway), and Ile d'Orléans across the Channel. The promenade passes the landing spot of the European settlers, marked by the **Samuel de Champlain Monument,** where Champlain secured French settlement by building Fort St-Louis in 1620. Today, the promenade is a favorite location for performers of all flavors—clowns, bagpipers, and banjo and clarinet duos alike.

At the bottom of the promenade, towering above the *terrasse* next to rue St-Louis, you'll find **le Château Frontenac** (692-3861), built on the ruins of two previous châteaux. The immense, baroque Frontenac, named for Comte Frontenac, governor of *Nouvelle-France,* was built in 1893 by the Canadian Pacific Company. The château was the site of two historic meetings between Churchill and Roosevelt during World War II, and is now a luxury hotel. Although budget travelers must forego staying here, you can take a guided tour of Québec's pride and joy. ($4, seniors $3, children 6-16 $2, children under 6 free. (Tours leave daily on the hour 9am-6pm.)

Near Château Frontenac, between rue St-Louis and rue Ste-Anne, lies the **Place d'Armes.** The *calèches* (horse-drawn buggies) that congregate here in summer provide atmosphere, and especially strong scents in muggy weather. A carriage will give you a tour of the city for $56, but your feet will do the same for free. From the Place d'Armes, the pedestrian and artist-ridden rue du Trésor leads to rue Buade, were stands the **Notre-Dame Basilica** (692-2533). The clock and outer walls date back to 1647; the rest of the church has been rebuilt twice (most recently after a fire in 1922). (Open daily 6:30am-6pm. Tours in multiple languages, mid-May to mid-Oct. daily 9am-4:30pm.) In addition to the ornate gold altar and impressive religious artifacts (including a chancel lamp given to the congregation by Louis XIV), the basilica is home to a 3D historical **sound and light show** (692-3200, daily at 6:30, 7:45, and 9pm; Tues. and Fri. 4pm and 5:15pm, Oct.-May twice a week; tickets $5, ages 12-17 $3, under 12 free). Notre-Dame, with its odd mix of architectural styles, contrasts sharply with the adjacent **Seminary of Québec,** an excellent example of 17th-century *québecois* architecture. Founded in 1663 as a Jesuit training ground, the seminary became the *Université de Laval* in 1852. The **Musée du Séminaire,** 9, rue de l'Université (692-2843), is found nearby. (Open daily 10am-5:30pm; Oct.-May Tues.-Sun. 10am-5pm; $3, seniors $2, students $1.50, under 16 $1.)

The **Musée du Fort,** 10, rue Ste-Anne (692-2175), presents a sound and light show that narrates the history of Québec City and the series of six battles fought between 1629 and 1775 for control of it. (Open daily June-Sept. 10am-6pm; $4.75, seniors $3.75, students 7-25 $2.75.) Ask at the tourist office for their sporadic schedule.

The **post office,** 3, rue Buade, now called **the Louis St-Laurent Building** (after Canada's second French Canadian Prime Minister), was built in the late 1890s and towers over a statue of Monseigneur de Laval, the first bishop of Québec. Across the Côte de la Montagne, a lookout park provides an impressive view of the Fleuve St-Laurent. A statue of Georges-Etienne Cartier, one of the key French-Canadian fathers of the Confederation, presides over the park.

Walk along rue St-Louis to see its 17th- and 18th-century homes. The surrender of Québec to the British occurred in 1759 at **Maison Kent,** 25, rue St-Louis, built in 1648. The Québec government now uses and operates the house. At the end of rue St-Louis is **Porte St-Louis,** one of the oldest entrances to the fortified city.

Outside The Walls

From the old city, the **promenade des Gouverneurs** and its 310 steps lead to the **Plains of Abraham** (otherwise known as the **Parc des Champs-de-Bataille**). Hike or bike through the Plains, site of the 1759 battle between General James Wolfe's British troops and General de Montcalm's French forces. Both leaders died during the decisive 15-min. confrontation, won by the British. A beautiful park, the Plains now serve as drill fields and the Royal Québec Golf Course. A **tourist reception center** (648-4071) at 390, ave des Berniéres, offers maps and pamphlets about the park. (Open Thurs. and Tues. 10am-5:45pm, Wed. 10am-9:45pm; the park is handicapped accessible.)

At the far end of the Plains of Abraham you'll find the newly transformed **Musée du Québec,** 1, ave. Wolfe-Montcalm, parc des Champs-de-Bataille (643-2150), which contains (surprise!) a collection of *québecois* paintings, sculptures, decorative arts, and prints. The Gérard Morisset pavilion, greets you with the unlikely *mélange à trois* of Jacques Cartier, Neptune, and Gutenberg, houses the Musée's permanent collection. The renovated old "prison of the plains," the Baillarce Pavilion, displays temporary exhibits. (Open Thurs.-Tues. 10am-5:45pm, Wed. 10am-9:45pm; Labor Day to mid-May Tues. and Thurs.-Sun. 10am-6pm, Wed. 10am-10pm. $4.75, seniors $3.75, students and disabled persons $2.75, under 16 free. Free Wed.) At the corner of la Grande Allée and rue Georges VI, right outside Porte St-Louis, stands **l'Assemblée Nationale** (643-7239). Built in the style of French King Louis XIII's era and completed in 1886, the hall merits a visit. You can view debates from the visitors gallery. Anglophones and Francophones both have recourse to simultaneous translation earphones. (Free 30-min. tours daily 9am-4:30pm; Labor Day to late June Mon.-Fri. 9am-4:30pm. Call ahead to ensure a space.)

For those who shy from the stairmaster method, a *funiculaire* (cable car) connects Upper Town with Lower Town and Place Royale, the oldest section of Québec (692-1132; operates June-Labor Day daily 8am-midnight; $1, under 6 free). This way leads to **rue Petit-Champlain,** the oldest road in North America. Many of the old buildings that line the street have been restored or renovated and now house craft shops, boutiques, cafés, and restaurants. The **Café-Théâtre Le Petit Champlain,** 68, rue Petit-Champlain (692-2613), presents *québecois* music, singing, and theater. From here, just continue west (right, from the bottom of the *funiculaire)* to reach the Plains of Abraham.

From the bottom of the *funiculaire* you can also take rue Sous-le-Fort and then turn left to reach **Place Royale,** built in 1608, where you'll find the small but beautiful l'Eglise Notre-Dame-des-Victoires (692-1650), the oldest church in Canada, dating from the glorious year of 1688. (Open Mon.-Sat. 9am-4:30pm, closed on Sat. if a wedding is being held; Oct. 16-April Mon.-Sat. 9am-noon, Sun. 7:30am-1pm. Free.) The houses surrounding the square have been restored to late 18th-century styles. Considered one of the birthplaces of French civilization in North America, the Place Royale is now the site of fantastic outdoor summer theater and concerts. Also along the river stands the recently opened Musée de la Civilisation, 85, rue Dalhousie (643-2158), which celebrates Québec's past, present, and future with giant phone booths, satellites, videos, and recreated moon landings. This thematic museum targets French Canadians, though English tours and exhibit notes are available. (Open daily 10am-7pm; early Sept.-late June Tues.-Sun. 10am-5pm, Wed. 10am-9pm; $5, seniors $4, students $3, kids under 7 free.)

ENTERTAINMENT AND NIGHTLIFE

Locals follow the Nordiques, Québec's hockey team, with near-religious fanaticism; they play from mid-September to April in the Coliseum. (For info, call 529-8441; for tickets call Nordtel 523-3333 or 800-463-3333). The raucous Winter Carnival (626-3716), parties through mid-February. Québec's Summer Festival (692-4540) boasts a number of free outdoor concerts in mid-July. The Plein Art (694-0260) exhibition of arts and crafts takes over the Pigeonnier on Grande-Allée in early August. Les nuits Black (849-7080), Québec's rapidly growing jazz festival, bebops the city for two weeks in late June. But the most festive day of the year is June 24, la Fête nationale du Québec (Saint-Jean-Baptiste Day) (681-7011), a celebration of *québecois* culture with free concerts, a bonfire, fireworks, and five million drunk francophones.

The Grande Allée's many restaurants are interspersed with a number of *Bar Discothèques,* where the early 20s mainstream crowd gathers. Chez Dagobert, 600 Grande Allée (522-0393), saturates its two dance floors while plentiful food and drink pour onto the streetside patio. Dagobert is *the* place to be seen (open daily 11am-3am, no cover). Down the block at O'Zone, 564 Grande Allée (529-7932), the tempo is a little slower and more pub-like (open daily 10am-3am).

Quebéc City's visible, young punk contingent clusters around rue St-Jean. La Fourmi Atomik, 33, rue d'Auteuil (694-1463), features underground rock. Monday is reggae only and Wednesday is rap only (open 10am-3am, Oct.-May 2pm-3am, no cover). At L'Ostradamus, 29, rue Couillard (694-9560), you can listen to live jazz and intellectual conversations in a smoke-drenched pseudo-spiritual and artsy Thai decor (open daily 4pm-3am, Oct.-May 5pm-3am, $1-3 cover when band is playing). A more traditional Québec evening can be found at Les Yeux Bleux, 1117½, rue St-Jean (694-9118), a local favorite where *chansonniers* perform nightly (open daily 8pm-3am, no cover).

The gay scene in Québec City isn't huge but also isn't hard to find. Le Ballon Rouge, 811, St-Jean (647-9227), is a popular dance club for gay men near the walls of the Old City. (No cover. Open daily 10:30pm-3am.) Farther from downtown at 157 Chemin Ste-Foy, Studio 157 (529-9958), caters to a crowd of women only.

■ NEAR QUÉBEC CITY

Ile-d'Orléans on the St-Laurent is untouched by Québec City's public transport system, but its proximity to Québec (about 10km downstream) makes it an ideal short side trip by car or bicycle (see Practical Information for rentals). Take Autoroute 440 Est., and cross over the only bridge leading to the island (Pont de l'Ile). A tour of the island covers 64km. Originally called *Ile de Bacchus* because of the plethora of wild grapes fermenting here, the Ile-d'Orléans remains a sparsely populated retreat of several small villages. Strawberries are its main crop. The Manoir Mauvide-Genest, 1451, ch. Royal (829-2630), dates from 1734, and is now a private museum housing crafts and traditional colonial furniture. (Open daily June 10am-5pm; July-Aug. 10am-8pm; Sept.-Oct. weekends by reservation; $3, ages 10-18 $1.50.)

CANADA

Exiting Ile-d'Orléans, turn right (east) onto Hwy. 138 (boul. Ste-Anne) to view the splendid **Chute Montmorency** (Montmorency Falls), which are substantially taller than Niagara Falls. In winter, vapors from the falls freeze completely to form a frozen shadow of the running falls. About 20km along 138 lies **Ste-Anne-de-Beaupré** (Voyageur buses link it to Québec City, $5). This small town's entire *raison d'être* is the famous **Basilique Ste-Anne-de Beaupré**, 10018, ave Royale (827-3781). Since 1658, this double-spired basilica has contained a Miraculous Statue and the alleged forearm bone of Saint Anne (mother of the Virgin Mary). Every year, more than one million pilgrims come here in the hopes that their prayers will be answered, and legend has it that some have been quite successful. (Open early May to mid-Sept. daily 8:30am-5pm.) Go to Ste-Anne in the winter months (Nov.-April) for some of the best skiing in the province. (Lift tickets $38 per day.) Contact **Parc du Mont Ste-Anne**, P.O. Box 400, Beaupré, G0A IE0 (827-4561), which has a 625m/2050 ft. vertical drop and night skiing to boot.

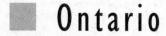

Ontario

First claimed by French explorer Samuel de Champlain in 1613, Ontario soon became a center of English influence within Canada. Hostility and famine in Europe drove hordes of Scottish and Irish immigrants to this territory. This mixture of British people asserted control with a takeover of New France in 1763 during the Seven Years War; twenty years later, a flood of Loyalist emigres from the newly-forged United States streamed into the province, fortifying its Anglo character. To this day, Ontario counterbalances Québec as a strong reminder of Canada's British heritage.

Ontario is not a melting pot—the different populations cling more to their distinct traditions than assimilation as "Canadians." However, Ontarians might agree in refuting the claim that Ontario is the most "American" of the Provinces. In the south you'll find world-class Toronto—multicultural, enormous (3 million plus, by *far* the largest city in sparse Canada), vibrant, clean, and safe. Surrounding this sprawling megalopolis are yuppified suburbs, the occasional college town, and farms. In the east, capital Ottawa sits on Ontario's frontier with Québec. The North is as French and Indian as it is British. Here the layers of cottage country and ski resorts yield to Canadian wilderness, national parks, and beautiful lakes.

PRACTICAL INFORMATION

Capital: Toronto.

Ontario Ministry of Culture, Tourism, and Recreation, Customer Service Brance, 77 Bloor St. W., 9th floor, Toronto M7A 2R9 (800-668-2746; open Mon.-Sat. 9am-8pm, Sun. 10am-5pm;, winter Mon.-Sat. 9am-6pm, Sun. 10am-5pm). Free brochures, guides, maps, and info on upcoming special events.

Alcohol: Legal drinking age 19.

Time Zone: Eastern. **Postal Abbreviation:** ONT

Sales Tax: 8%, plus 7% GST.

■■■ OTTAWA

Legend has it that Queen Victoria chose this capital of Canada by closing her eyes and poking her finger at a map. But perhaps political savvy and not mere chance guided the Queen to this once-remote logging town, which, as a stronghold for neither camp, became a perfect compromise capital between French and English interests. Today Ottawa continues in the role of cultural ambassador to its own country, bridging the divisions between these two unique and separate elements. Every year,

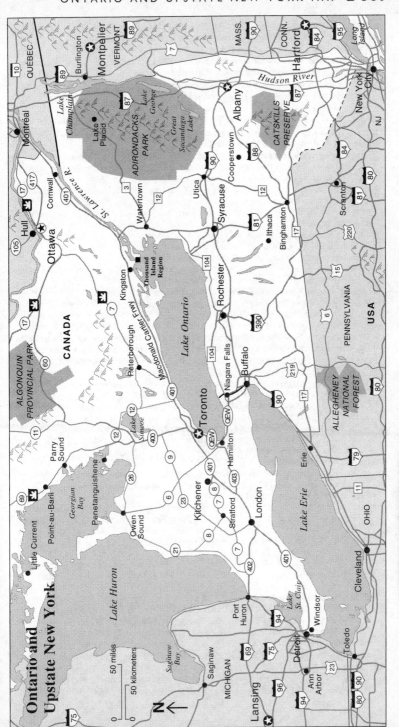

Ontario and Upstate New York

each of the provinces sends representatives to the capital with the increasingly tricky task of forging a national unity while preserving local identity.

Ottawa's rough-hewn character was not polished until the turn of the century when then-Prime Minister Sir Wilfred Laurier called on urban planners to create a "Washington of the North." Millions of dollars and nearly a century of conscientious grooming has left Ottawa with museums, cultural facilities, and parks which its sister capital on the Potomac can seriously envy.

PRACTICAL INFORMATION

Emergency: 911. **Ontario Provincial Police:** 592-4878, infoline 800-267-2677. **Ottawa Police:** 230-6211; infoline 236-0311.

Visitor Information: National Capital Commission Information Center, 14 Metcalfe St. (239-5000 or 800-465-1867 across Canada), at Wellington opposite the Parliament Buildings. Open summer daily 8:30am-9pm; Sept. 3-May 5 Mon.-Sat. 9am-5pm, Sun. 10am-4pm. **Ottawa Tourism and Convention Authority Visitor Information Centre,** National Arts Centre, 65 Elgin St. (237-5158). Open summer daily 9am-9pm; Sept. 7-April 30 Mon.-Sat. 9am-5pm, Sun. 10am-4pm. Both provide free maps and the detailed, annually-updated *Ottawa Visitors Guide* to restaurants, hotels, and sights. Free 30-min. parking in the Arts Centre lot with ticket validation at the Visitor Centre. For info on Hull and Québec province, turn to the **Association Touristique de l'Outaouais,** 25 rue Laurier, Hull, on the corner of rue Victoria (819-778-2222). Open mid-June to Sept. Mon.-Fri. 8:30am-8:30pm, Sat.-Sun. 9am-5pm; off-season Mon.-Fri. 8:30am-5pm.

Student Travel Agencies: Travel CUTS, 1 Stewart St., Suite #203 (238-8222), at Waller, just east of Nicholas two block north of the Université d'Ottawa, or on the 1st level of the Unicentre, Carleton Univ. (238-5493). Experts in student travel, youth hostel cards, cheap flights, VIA Rail and Eurail passes. Open Mon.-Tues. and Thurs.-Fri. 9am-5pm, Wed. 9am-4:30pm. **Hosteling International-Canada (HI-C), Ontario East Region,** 18 Byward Market (241-1400). Eurail and youth hostel passes, travel info and equipment. Open Mon.-Fri. 9:30am-5:30pm, Sat. 9:30am-5pm. (See Essentials Section..

Embassies: U.S., 100 Wellington St. (238-5335), directly across from Parliament. Open daily 8:30am-5pm. **U.K.,** 80 Elgin St. (237-1530), at the corner of Queen. Open Mon.-Fri. 9am-5pm. **Australia,** 50 O'Connor St. (236-0841), at Queen St., #710. Open Mon.-Fri. 9am-noon and 2-4pm for visas and info. **New Zealand,** 99 Bank St. suite 727 (238-5991). Open Mon.-Fri. 8:30am-4:30pm. **Ireland,** 170 Metcalfe St. (233-6281). Open Mon.-Fri. 10am-1pm, 2:30-4pm. **France,** 42 Sussex Dr. (789-1795). Open for information Mon.-Fri. 9:30am-1:30pm.

American Express: 220 Laurier W. (563-0231), between Metcalfe and O'Connor in the heart of the business district. Open Mon.-Fri. 8:30am-5pm. In case of lost Traveler's checks, call 800-221-7282; for lost cards call 800-268-9805.

Airport: Ottawa International (998-3151), 20 min. south of the city off Bronson Ave. Take bus 96 from the MacKenzie King Bridge. Tourist info available daily 9am-9pm in arrival area. Express airport **Pars Transport** buses (523-8880) from Lord Elgin Hotel, 100 Elgin Blvd. at Slater, and from 10 other hotels including the Delta, the Westin, Château Laurier, and the Hotel Novotel, one block north of the Ottawa Int'l Hostel. Call by phone for pick-up from 14 other hotels. Fare $9, ages 7-12 $5, under 7 free, seniors 10% off. Daily every ½-hr. 5am-midnight. Call for later pick-up and schedule specifics. Service from airport too. **Air Canada** (237-1380) has youth standby rates for those 12-24 with ID.

VIA Rail Station: 200 Tremblay Rd. (244-8289 for reservations or recorded departure info), off Alta Vista Rd. To: Montréal (4 per day, 2 hr., $34, student $31); Toronto (4 per day, 4 hr., $72/65). Also to Québec City, must travel via Montréal ($63/57). 40% discount for reservations at least 5 days in advance for students for traveling on any day (while tickets last) and for adults traveling Sat. or Mon.-Thurs. Ticket office open Mon.-Fri. 5am-9pm, Sat. 6:30am-9pm, Sun. 8:30am-9pm.

Voyageur Bus: 265 Catherine St. (238-5900), between Kent and Lyon. Service throughout Canada. To: Montréal (on the hr. 6am-10pm, 2½ hr., $25; Toronto (7 per day, 4½ hr., $53); Québec City (13 per day, 6 hr., $59). For service to the U.S.

you must first go to Montréal or Toronto; connections made through Greyhound. Open daily 5am-midnight. Purchase tickets at station or at Ottawa Int'l Hostel.

Public Transport: OC Transport, 1500 St. Laurent (741-4390). Excellent bus system. Buses congregate on either side of Rideau Centre. $1.60, rush hour (3-5:30pm) $2.10, express routes (green buses) rates $2.70. Seniors $1.60 at all times. Under 5 free. For info on the blue **Hull City Buses,** call 819-770-3242.

Taxi: Blue Line Taxi, 238-1111. **A-1,** 746-1616. $2 base fare. 24 hrs.

Car Rental: Hertz, 30 York St. in Byward Market (238-7681). $30 per day with unlimited km. Insurance $13 per day with $1500 deductible. Must be 21 with credit card. Open Mon.-Fri. 7:30am-7pm, Sat.-Sun. 8am-6pm. **Budget,** 443 Somerset W. at Kent (232-1526). $33 per day. 200km free, 12¢ each additional km. Insurance $12 per day with no deductible. Must be 21 with credit card. Open Mon.-Fri. 7am-7pm, Sat.-Sun. 8am-6pm.

Rider/Driver Matching Agency: Allostop, 238 Dalhousie at St. Patrick (562-8248). To: Toronto ($24), Québec City ($29), Montréal ($10), and New York City ($50). Membership ($6 yearly, drivers $7) required. Open Mon.-Wed. 9am-5pm, Thurs.-Fri. 9am-7pm, Sat.-Sun. 10am-5pm. There is also an active rideboard on the 2nd floor of the University of Ottawa's University center.

Bike Rental: Rent-A-Bike-Vélocationo, 1 Rideau St. (241-4140), behind the Château Laurier Hotel. $6 per hr., $18 per day. Family deals. Escorted tours for a price. Maps, locks free. Tandems available. Open mid-May to Oct. daily 9am-7:30pm. Credit card required.

Alcohol: Legal ages 19 (Ottawa) and 18 (Hull). Shutdown 1am (Ottawa) and 3am (Hull).

Help Line: Gayline-Telegai, 238-1717. Info on local bars, special events and meetings, as well as counseling. Open daily 7-10pm. **Ottawa Distress Centre,** 238-3311, English-speaking. **Tel-Aide,** 741-6433, French-speaking. **Rape Crisis Centre,** 729-8889. All 3 lines open 24 hrs.

Post Office: Postal Station "B," 59 Sparks St. at Elgin St. (844-1545). Open Mon.-Fri. 8am-6pm. **Postal Code:** K1P 5A0.

Area Code: 613 (Ottawa); 819 (Hull).

The **Rideau Canal** divides Ottawa into the eastern lower town and the western upper town. West of the canal, Parliament buildings and government offices line **Wellington Street,** one of the city's main east-west arteries, which runs directly into the heart of downtown and crosses the canal. **Laurier** is the only other east-west street which permits traffic from one side of the canal to the other. East of the canal, Wellington St. becomes **Rideau Street,** surrounded by a fashionable new shopping district. North of Rideau Street lies the **Byward Market,** a recently renovated shopping area, which hosts a summertime open-air market and much of Ottawa's nightlife. **Elgin Street,** a primary north-south artery, stretches from the **Queensway** (Hwy. 417) to the War Memorial just south of Wellington, in front of **Parliament Hill. Bank Street,** another main street, runs parallel to Elgin, three blocks to the east, and services the town's older shopping area. The canal itself is a major access route: in winter, thousands of Ottawans skate to work on this, the world's longest skating rink; in summer, power boats breeze by regularly. Bike paths and pedestrian walkways also line the canals. Parking is painful downtown; meters cost up to 25¢ for 10 min. Residential neighborhoods east of the canal have longer limits and the police ticket less often than on main streets.

Hull, Québec, across the Ottawa River, is most notable for its less strict drinking laws and 18 year old drinking age. Many bars and clubs rock nightly until 3am. Close to Gatineau Provincial Park, Hull is accessible by several bridges and the blue Hull buses from downtown Ottawa.

ACCOMMODATIONS AND CAMPING

Clean, inexpensive rooms and campsites are not difficult to find in Ottawa, except during May and early June, when student groups and conventioneers come to claim their long-reserved rooms, or during July and August, when the tourism season is at its peak. The area boasts a number of B&Bs for those who can afford them. An

CANADA

extensive listing can be found in the *Ottawa Visitor Guide*, available at the National Capital Commission Information Center (see above). One particular value is the **Ottawa Bed and Breakfast** (563-0161), an association of ten guesthouses in the Ottawa area, all of which rent singles ($40) and doubles ($50).

Ottawa International Hostel (HI-C), 75 Nicholas St., K1N 7B9 (235-2595), in downtown Ottawa. The site of Canada's last public hanging, this trippy hostel now "incarcerates" travelers in the cells of the former Carleton County Jail. Rooms contain 4-8 bunks and minimal storage space. Communal showers (hot only in the thermal sense), kitchen, laundry, large and comfortable lounges, and a cast of friendly, personable regulars. Due to the centrality of its location, a funky international crowd, and a plethora of organized activities (biking, canoeing, tours), you won't regret your stay. IBN reservations available. Doors locked 2-7am. 153 beds. $14, nonmembers $18.

University of Ottawa Residences, 100 University St. (564-5400), in the center of campus directly across from the University Center. Take bus 1, 7, or 11 on Bank St. to the Rideau Centre from the bus station and walk up Nicholas to the U of O campus. Bus 95 west from the train station or an easy walk from downtown. Clean dorm rooms. Shared hall showers. Free local hall phone. Check-in 4:30pm, but they'll store your luggage until then. Linen, towels free. Access to university student center (with bank machines). Continental breakfast $2. Singles $31. Doubles $39.50. Any student with ID: $19.50/34.50. Open early May-late Aug.

Centre Town Guest House Ltd., 502 Kent St. (233-0681), just north of the bus station, a 10- to 15-min. walk from downtown. Impeccably clean rooms in a friendly, comfortable house. Free breakfast (eggs, cereal, bacon, toast) in a cozy dining room. Singles from $15. Doubles from $25. 2 twin beds $40. Monthly rates from $400. Reservations recommended. Parking available.

YMCA/YWCA, 180 Argyle St. (237-1320), at O'Connor. Close to the bus station; walk left on Bank and right on Argyle. Nice-sized (though unattractively decorated) rooms in a modern high-rise. Free local phones in every room. Kitchen with microwave available until midnight. Guests can use gym facilities. Singles with shared bath $37.40, with private bath $43.30. Doubles $44. Weekly and group rates available. Payment must be made in advance. Cafeteria (breakfast $2.75) open Mon.-Fri. 7am-7pm, Sat.-Sun. 8am-2:30pm. Indoor parking available to guests at an extra charge (Mon.-Fri. $6.50 per day, Sat.-Sun. $2.75 per day, evenings 4:30pm-8:30am, $2.75).

Camp Le Breton (943-0467), at the corner of Fleet and Booth. Urban tent-only camping within sight of Parliament, a 15-min. walk from downtown. Washrooms, showers, free wood. 5-day max. stay. Check-in 24 hrs. Sites $7.50 per person, seniors $3.75, under 12 free. No reservations—they'll squeeze you in.

Gatineau Park (reservations 456-3016; info 827-2020), northwest of Hull. Map available at visitors center. (Open daily 9am-6pm, winter Sat. and Sun. 9am-6pm.) Three rustic campgrounds within 45 min. of Ottawa: **Lac Philippe Campground,** 248 sites with facilities for family camping, trailers, and campers; **Lac Taylor Campground,** with 34 "semi-wilderness" sites; and **Lac la Pêche,** with 36 campsites accessible only by canoe. All the campgrounds are off Hwy. 366 northwest of Hull—watch for signs. From Ottawa, take the Cartier-MacDonald Bridge, follow Autoroute 5 north to Scott Rd., turn right onto Hwy. 105 and follow it to 366. To reach La Pêche continue on 366 to Eardley Rd. on your left. Camping permits for Taylor and Philippe available at the entrance to the campground. $16, seniors $8. Pay for a site at La Pêche on Eardley Rd. $13. All sites available mid.-May to mid.-Oct.

FOOD

No stranger to the notorious Canadian breakfast, Ottawa has more than its share of greasy spoons offering up eggs, potatoes, meat, toast, and coffee for a more-than-reasonable price. Try **Tony's Restaurant,** 380 Dalhousie St. (241-9762), for an especially good rendition of this stand-by. ($2.35. Open 24 hrs.) A more refined morning alternative can be found across the street at **For the Love of Waffles,** 373 Dalhousie

St. (271-7939), where sweet liège waffles ($1.90) and fluffy Belgian waffles ($2.00) can be smothered with your choice of fresh fruits and toppings (85¢ each; open Mon.-Fri. 7:30am-10pm, Sat.-Sun. 8am-11pm). During summer days, fresh fruit, vegetables, and flowers as well as occasional street music is available at the lively open-air **Byward Market** on Byward between York and Rideau (open daily 8am-6pm). In the evenings, look for restaurant/bars in Ottawa serving dirt-cheap food to lure you into their dens of high-priced beer. **Tramps,** 53 William St. (241-5523), serves 20¢ chicken wings daily after 4pm (open daily 11am-1am).

After eating, relax at **Café Wim,** 537 Sussex Dr. (241-1771), with no fear of being run out too soon. This Dutch café encourages lingering and serves sumptuous Colombian brown coffee ($1.40), and decadent desserts ($2-6). (Open daily 9am-midnight.) For even later nourishment, check out **Dunn's,** 126 George St. (562-3866), a 24-hour deli popular with the after-clubbing crowd (deli fare $3.50-9).

Sunset Grill, 47 Clarence St. (241-9497). Sit on the huge outdoor terrace and grapple with an infamously large club sandwich ($8). The less ambitious appetite and wallet can tackle the "in a hurry-on a diet-or just broke" meal ($6). Open Sun.-Tues. 11am-10pm, Thurs.-Sat. 11am-1am.

Las Palmas, 111 Parent Ave. (241-3728). This outstanding Mexican restaurant recently discontinued its nightclub entertainment in order to concentrate on the dinner business. The effect is less samba and even better salsa. Dinners $5-13. Open Mon.-Thurs. and Sat. 11:30am-10:30pm, Fri. 11:30am-midnight.

Blue Cactus, 2 Byward Mkt. (238-7061), at Clarence, specializes in Tex-Mex dishes with an exotic twist. For a new experience, try the brie and papaya quesadilla ($6-7). Their bowl of soup ($2.50) comes with two slices of Mexican bread and constitutes a hearty meal. Open Mon.-Wed. 11:30am-midnight, Thurs.-Sat. 11:30am-1am, Sun. 11:30am-11pm.

Boko Bakery, 87 George St. (241-2656), in the Byward Market Mall, is a local favorite. Sit down and enjoy a breakfast special (7:30-11am): 2 eggs, ham, coffee, and croissant ($2.95); or go to the take-out counter and enjoy the delicious aroma of freshly baked muffins (80¢). Open Sun.-Fri. 7:30am-5pm, Sat. 7:30am-6pm.

The International Cheese and Deli, 40 Byward St. (241-5411). Deli and Middle Eastern sandwiches to go. Vegetable *samosa* or $1.25. Turkey and cheese $4, falafel on pita $2.30. Open Sat.-Thurs. 8am-6pm, Fri. 8am-8pm.

Father and Sons, 112 Osgoode St. (233-6066), at the eastern edge of the U of O campus. Student favorite for tavern-style food with some Lebanese dishes thrown in. Try the falafel platter ($6.50) or a triple-decker sandwich ($6.50). Drink-encouraging specials daily 8-11pm, Mon. and Sat., 8-11pm wings 15¢. Open Mon.-Fri. 7am-1am, Sat. and Sun. 8am-1am. Kitchen until midnight.

SIGHTS AND PARKS

Although overshadowed by Toronto's size and Montréal's cosmopolitan color, Ottawa's status as capital of Canada is shored up by its cultural attractions. Since the national museums and political action are packed in tightly, most sights can be reached on foot. **Parliament Hill,** on Wellington St. at Metcalfe, towers over downtown as the city's focal point, set apart by its Gothic architecture. Warm your hands, and your herat over the **Centennial Flame** at the south gate, lit in 1967 to mark the 100th anniversary of the Dominion of Canada's inaugural session of Parliament. The central parliament structure, **Centre Block,** contains the House of Commons, the Senate, and the Library of Parliament, and is where the Prime Minister can occasionally be spotted. The Library was the only part of the original (1859-66) structure to survive the 1916 fire. On display behind the library is the original bell from Centre Block, which, according to legend, crashed to the ground after chiming at midnight on the night of the fire. The bell's replacement is a carillon of 53 bells which range in side from ½ ounce to several tons and play each day at 11:45am, to the delight of sightseers and the chagrin of late sleepers. Free, worthwhile tours of Centre Block (in English or French) depart every 10 min. from the Infotent. (Group reservations year-round 996-0896. Public information 992-4793. Open mid-May to early Sept.

Mon.-Fri. 9am-8:30pm, Sat.-Sun. 9am-5:30pm; off-season daily 9am-4:30pm. Last tour begins 40 min. before closing time.) Watch Canada's Prime Minister and his government squirm on the verbal hot seat during the official **Question Period** in the House of Commons chamber (Mon.-Thurs. 2:15-3pm, Fri. 11:45am-12:30pm). Far less lively or politically meaningful, the sessions of the **Senate of Canada** (992-4791) also welcome spectators. See (while you can) the body of "sober second thought," on which some Canadians are ready to lock the doors and throw away the gavel. After all but the last tour of the day, visitors can ascend into the **Peace Tower** and see Ottawa from its observation desk—302.6 feet above the ground. The tower, recently renovated, houses the bells of Centre Block and the white marble **Memorial Chamber,** which honors Canadian war dead. Those interested in trying to make a number of statuesque soldiers giggle should attend the **Changing of the Guard** (993-1811), on the broad lawns in front of Centre Block (June 26-Aug. 28 daily at 10am, weather permitting). At dusk, Centre Block and its lawns transform into the set for *Sound and Light,* which relates the history of the Parliament Buildings and the development of the nation (early May-early Sept. daily 9:30 and 10:30pm; performances alternate between French and English). A 5-minute walk west along Wellington St. is the **Supreme Court of Canada** (995-5361), where nine justices preside. Worthwhile 30-minute tours of the Federal Court and the Supreme Court, both housed in this building, are offered. (Open May-Aug. daily 9am-5pm; Sept.-April Mon.-Fri. 9am-5pm. Free.) One block south of Wellington, Sparks St. is home to one of North America's first pedestrian malls, hailed as an innovative experiment in 1960. The **Sparks Street Mall** recently received a $5-million face lift, rejuvenating many of Ottawa's banks and upscale retail stores. The **Rideau Centre,** south of Rideau St. at Sussex Dr., is the city's primary shopping mall as well as one of the main OC Transport stations. The sidewalks in front of Rideau Street's numerous stores are enclosed by glass, making them bearable during the cold winter months.

East of the Parliament Buildings at the junction of Sparks, Wellington, and Elgin stands **Confederation Square** with its enormous **National War Memorial,** dedicated by King George VI in 1939. The towering structure symbolizes the triumph of peace over war, an ironic message on the eve of World War II. **Nepean Point** (239-5000), several blocks northwest of Rideau Centre and the Byward Market behind the National Gallery of Canada, provides a panoramic view of the capital.

The Governor-General, the Queen's representative in Canada, opens the grounds of **Rideau Hall,** his official residence, to the public. Tours leave from the main gate at One Sussex Drive. (Call 998-7113, 998-7114 or 800-465-6890 for tour info; free.) Dress up nicely on New Year's Day or Canada Day and they'll even let you see the interior. At nearby **24 Sussex Drive** resides the Prime Minister. Gawk from afar or use a scope; you can't get any closer to the building than the main gates.

Ottawa's reputation for ignoring cultural difference extends beyond the conflict between French and English. Many nationalities are well-integrated in this city, leaving ethnically-grouped neighborhoods somewhat sparse. There is a small **Chinatown** clustered around Somerset St. between Kent St. and Bronson Ave. From downtown, walk south on Elgin St. until you reach Somerset; then go west on Somerset until fruit stands line the streets and signs change from French and English to Chinese and English (about a 20 min. walk). **Little Italy** is just around the corner on Bronson Ave., south of Somerset down to the Queensway (Hwy. 417).

Ottawa is home to many of Canada's huge national museums. **The National Gallery,** 380 Sussex Dr. (990-1985), in a spectacular glass-towered building adjacent to Nepean Point, contains the world's most comprehensive collection of Canadian art, as well as outstanding European, American, and Asian works. The building's exterior is a parody of the facing neo-Gothic buttresses of the Library of Parliament. (Open Fri.-Wed. 10am-6pm, Thurs. 10am-8pm; mid-Oct. to April Tues.-Sun. 10am-5pm, Thurs. until 8pm. Permanent collection free; special events $8, seniors and group members $5, under 18 and students free.) The gallery is free on Thursday and is wheelchair-accessible, as are most of Ottawa's public museums and galleries. The **Canadian Museum of Contemporary Photography,** 1 Rideau Canal (990-8257), between the Chateau Laurier and the Ottawa Locks, opened its doors for the first time in 1992. The museum allows a glimpse of life in modern Canada frozen in time by today's photographers. (Open Fri.-Tues. 11am-5pm, Wed. 4-8pm, Thurs. 11am-8pm; mid-Oct. to April Wed.-Thurs. 11am-8pm, Fri.-Sun. 11am-5pm. Free.) A space-ship-like structure across the river in Hull houses the **Canadian Museum of Civilization,** 100 Laurier St. (776-7000). Admire the architecture but be wary of overly ambitious exhibits that attempt to put perspective on 1000 years of Canadian history. Don't miss the breathtaking films screened in **CINEPLUS** (776-7010 for show-times), the first theater in the world capable of projecting both IMax and OmniMax. (Open May-June Fri.-Wed. 9am-5pm, Thurs. 9am-8pm; July-early Sept. Fri.-Wed. 9am-6pm, Thurs. 9am-8pm; winter Tues.-Wed. and Fri.-Sun. 9am-5pm, Thurs. 9am-8pm. Museum $4.50, seniors and youths $3, under 15 free; Thurs. free from 5-8pm for museum only. CINEPLUS $7, seniors and students $5.) The **Canadian Museum of Nature** (996-3102), at McLeod St. at Metcalf, explores the natural world from dinosaur skeletons to minerals through multi-media displays. (Daily 9:30am-5pm, Thurs. 9:30am-8pm; Oct.-April daily 10am-5pm, Thurs. 10am-8pm. $4, students $3, ages 6-16 and seniors $2, under 6 free; Thurs. ½-price 10am-5pm, free 5-8pm.)

Canadian history buffs could easily lose themselves in the **National Library Archives,** 395 Wellington St. at Bay St. (995-5138), which houses oodles of Canadian publications, old maps, photographs, letters, and historical exhibits. (Library open daily 9am-9pm and will provide group tours for those with professional interest only. Exhibit area open daily 9am-9pm.) Anyone who enjoys an occasional guffaw at the government's expense (and who doesn't?) will double up with laughter at the new **Canadian Museum of Caricature,** 136 Patrick St. at Sussex (995-3145). (Open Sat.-Tues. 10am-6pm, Wed.-Fri. 10am-8pm. Free.) Walk to the elegant **Laurier House,** 335 Laurier Ave. E. (692-2581), from which Liberal Prime Minister William Lyon Mackenzie King governed Canada for most of his lengthy tenure. Admire at your leisure the antiques accumulated by King, as well as the crystal ball he used to consult his long-dead mother on matters of national importance. (Open Tues.-Sat. 9am-5pm, Sun. 2-5pm; Oct.-March Tues.-Sat. 10am-5pm, Sun. 2-5pm. Free.)

Farther out of town, the **National Museum of Science and Technology,** 1867 St. Laurent Blvd. at Smyth (991-3044), lets visitors explore the developing world of tech and transport with touchy-feely exhibits. The museum entrance is on Lancaster, 200m east of St. Laurent, accessible by bus routes 85 and 148 from downtown. (Open daily 9am-5pm, Thurs. 9am-9pm; Sept.-April closed Mon.; $4.30, students and seniors $3.50, ages 6-15 $1.50, under 6 free. Free Thurs. 5-9pm.) The **National Aviation Museum** (993-2010), at the Rockcliffe Airport off St. Laurent Blvd. north of Montréal St., illustrates the history of flying, and displays more than 100 aircrafts. Take bus 95, then switch to 198. (Open daily 9am-5pm, Thurs. 9am-9pm; Labor Day-April, closed Mon. $5, students and seniors $4, ages 6-15 $1.75; free on Thurs. after 5pm.)

Ottawa is pleasantly unaffected by the traditionally urban vices of pollution and violent crime; a multitude of parks and recreational areas will make you forget you're in a city at all. **Gatineau Park** extends 356 square km into the northwest and is a favorite destination for Ottawans who want to cycle, hike, or fish. **Dow's Lake** (232-1001), accessible by means of the Queen Elizabeth Driveway, is an artificial lake on the Rideau Canal, 15 min. south of Ottawa. Pedal boats, canoes, and bikes are available at the Dow's Lake Pavilion, at 101 Queen Elizabeth Driveway, near the corner of Preston St. (Rentals by the ½ hr. and the hr. Prices vary. Open daily 11:30-1am.)

ENTERTAINMENT AND NIGHTLIFE

In Ottawa, the **Byward Market** area contains most of the action. Ottawa clubs close at 1am (many at 11pm on Sun.) but most, in an effort to keep people from going, offer free admission. **Château Lafayette,** 42 York St. (241-4747), the oldest tavern in Ottawa, lures the budgeteer with $3 pints. The regulars are hard-core beer drinkers who pound a beer, slam the mug down on the bar, and say "Mr. Keeper, I'll hava 'nuther." (Open daily noon-1am.) Possibly the cheapest beer on the continent can be found at **Grand Central,** 141 George St. (241-2727), where $2 gets 20 oz. of draft beer. (Thurs.-Sat. $2 cover with live bands. Open Mon.-Sun. 11:30am-1am.) **Joe Bloze,** 407 Dalhousie St. (562-4747), with a sports grill motif and $2 munchies on Monday and Tuesday, is becoming a popular hangout. (Open Mon.-Sat. 11:30am-1am, Sun. noon-1am.) For no-frills pool try the **Orange Monkey**, 880 Wellington St. (230-2850; open Mon.-Sat. 10am-2am, Sun. noon-2am).

The music in Ottawa is plentiful and diverse, whether for dancing or for listening. Check out **Woodsy's** (562-7335), 62 William St., for bright lights, dance music, and a huge outdoor terrace. (Formerly the Peel Pub. Open daily 11am-1am.) For a taste of life, the universe, and a bit of everything else, head to **Zaphod Beeblebrox,** 27 York in Byward Market, (562-1010), a popular alternative club with live bands Tuesday and Thurs.-Sat. nights. Be advised that the cover is usually hiked up to $10 on nights with bands. Famous for their $5.50 Pangalactic Gargle Blasters. (Open noon-1am daily.) Celtic music and jazz can be appreciated at **Cock Robin Deli Ltd.,** 56 Byward Mkt. (241-5404), with no cover. (Thurs. and Sun. Celtic; Tues. jazz. Open daily 11am-1pm.) **The Rainbow Bistro,** 76 Murray St. (241-5123), is dark and smoky like a blues joint should be, while the staff is anything but grim. (Open daily 11am-1pm.) A popular, up-scale gay club, **Tak Tiks,** 150 George St. is unrestricted and great for dancing. (Cover $2, 11pm-midnight, $3 midnight-1am, $1 1am-close. Open Sun. Thurs. 9pm-1:30am, Fri.-Sat. 9pm-2:30am.)

Hull, Quebec remains the house for the dedicated nightlifer. Right across the border establishments grind and gnash until 3am every day of the week and the legal drinking age is 18. Over 20 popular nightspots pack the **Promenade du Portage** in Hull (a.k.a The Strip), just west of Place Portage, the huge government office complex. **Le Coquetier** (771-6560) is one of the more peaceful places on the promenade to treat a friend to a "brewski"($3.25). (Open daily 11:30am-3am.) Not so peaceful, but certain to be a blast is **Broadstreet,** #86 Broadstreet (772-1225), where dancing is the primary entertainment. (Cover $5, open daily 9pm-1am.)

The **National Arts Centre,** 53 Elgin St. at Albert St. (tickets 755-1111; info 996-5051), houses an excellent small orchestra and theater company and frequently hosts international entertainers. (Box office open Mon.-Sat. noon-9pm.) **Odyssey Theatre** (232-8407) holds open-air comedy at **Strathcona Park,** at the end of Laurier Ave. at Charlotte St., well east of the canal. The shows are bawdy enough that they don't recommend using the children's discount. (Shows July to mid-Aug. Tues.-Sun. 8:30pm; $15, students and seniors $12, under 12 $6.)

Ottawans seem to have a celebration for just about everything, even the bitter Canadian cold. During early February, **Winterlude** (239-5000) lines the Rideau Canal with a number of ice sculptures which illustrate how it feels to be an Ottawan in the winter—frozen. In mid-May the **Tulip Festival** (567-5757) explodes around Dow's Lake in a colorful kaleidoscope of more than 100,000 blooming tulips. Summer brings music to Ottawa both in the form of the **Dance Festival** (996-5051 or 947-7000) in mid-June and the **Jazz Festival** (594-3580) in mid-July. Performers come from all over the country to perform in free recitals and concerts, among other pricier events. Labor Day weekend the politicians over on Parliament Hill lend some of their bombast to the **Hot Air Balloon Festival** (243-2330), which sends aloft hundreds of beautiful balloons from Canada, the U.S., and Europe.

If you're looking to escape the city, try a **beach** on the Ottawa River. Beaches lie west of town by way of the Ottawa River Parkway (follow the signs). **Mooney's Bay,** one popular strip of river bank, is about 15 min. out of Ottawa by car.

■ ■ ■ ALGONQUIN PROVINCIAL PARK

The wilder Canada of endless rushing rivers and shimmering lakes awaits in Algonquin Provincial Park, about 250 km west of Ottawa. From the city take Hwy. 417

(the Queensway) west until the Renfrew exit, then follow Rte. 60 west to the park. At the **East Gate Information Center** (705-633-5572) you can obtain the necessary camping permits and info on the park. (Open daily June-Labor Day 7am-10pm; off-season 9am-6pm.) Experience Algonquin through one of two venues: the Hwy. 60 Corridor, where tents and trailers crowd the roadsides (permits $15.25 per person each night), or the park interior, the "essence of Algonquin," (permits $25 per person per night). Reservations for either area can be made through the **Algonquin Reservation Network** (705-633-5538), which handles 1200 sites on the corridor, all with free showers and bathrooms, but none with hook-up, and limitless primitive campsites in the interior accessible only by hiking or canoe. (In service 5:45 daily June-Labor Day, though there is limited camping year round.) You can rent gear for a backcountry adventure at several outfitting stores around and inside the park. Closest to the eastern entrance is **Opeongo Algonquin Outfitters** (613-637-2075), on Rte. 60 near Opeongo Lake, about 15 min. into the park. Here tents rent for $6 (two-person) to $10 (six-person) per night, sleeping bags ($3.50-4.50), and canoes ($15-20). (Open daily; 8am-6pm, July-Aug. daily 8am-8pm.)

■■■ TORONTO

Once a prim and proper Victorian city where even window-shopping was prohibited on the Sabbath, Toronto today has shed much of its conservative provincialism and become an economic and cultural capital. This transition, led largely by the opening of the St. Lawrence Seaway and later prodded along indirectly by the perceived threat of Québecois nationalism in the late 1970s, brought big business to the Ontarian capital. Immigrants from all over the world resettled in Toronto, which today is home to over 60 minorities, gaining it the United Nations title as the world' most multi-cultural city.

Toronto has spent millions in recent decades to improve its image by creating superlative architecture such as the world's biggest "free-standing" structure (the CN tower), the biggest retractable roof (the Sky Dome), an outstanding lakefront development, and a significant sponsorship of arts and museums. Torontonians maintain an efficient and safe public transportation system, promote recycling virtually everywhere, and keep the city impeccably clean and safe. Two film crews learned this the hard way. One crew, after dirtying a Toronto street to make it look more like a typical "American" avenue, went on a coffee break and returned a short time later only to find their set spotless again, swept by the ever-vigilant city maintenance department. Another crew, filming an attack scene, was twice interrupted by Toronto residents hopping out of their cars to "rescue" the actress.

PRACTICAL INFORMATION

Emergency: 911.

Visitor Information: Metropolitan Toronto Convention and Visitors Association (MTCVA), 207 Queens Quay W (203-2500 or 800-363-1990), at Harbourfront Centre. Open daily 9:30am-5pm. **Ontario Travel,** (800-668-2746). Enter Eatons at 220 Yonge at Dundas, go down 2 flights to level one, exit the store, and it's on the right. Information on all of Ontario. Open Mon.-Fri. 10am-9pm, Sat. 10am-6pm, Sun. noon-5pm.

Student Travel Agency: Travel CUTS, 187 College St. (979-2406), just west of University Ave. Subway: Queen's Park. Smaller office at 74 Gerrard St. E. (977-0441). Subway: College. Both open Mon.-Fri. 9am-5pm.

Traveler's Aid: Each terminal at Pearson Airport, and Union Station (366-7788). Mon.-Fri. 9am-9pm.

Consulates: U.S., 360 University Ave. (595-0228 or 595-1700 for visa information). Subway: St. Patrick. Open Mon.-Fri. 8:30am-1pm for consular services. **Australia,** 175 Bloor St. E., suite #314-6 (323-1155). Subway: Bloor St. Open Mon.-Fri. 9am-5pm for info; 9am-1pm and 2-4pm for visas. **U.K.,** 777 Bay St. #1910 (593-1267). Subway: College. Open Mon.-Fri. 9:30am-3:30pm; 9am-4:50pm for info.

Currency Exchange: Visitors should note that only banks and exchange houses guarantee the official exchange rate. **Toronto Currency Exchange,** 313 Yonge St. (598-3769) and 2 Walton (599-5821), gives the best rates around, and doesn't charge a service fee. Both open daily 9am-6pm. **Royal Bank of Canada** has exchange centers at Pearson Airport (676-322; open daily 5am-11:30pm) and throughout the city. Headquarters at 200 Bay St. (974-5340 or 974-5533). For 24-hr. service, head to **Money Mart,** 684 Younge St. (924-1000), but expect to pay a service fee.

Airport: Pearson International (247-7678), about 20km west of Toronto via Hwy. 427, 401, or 409. Take Bus #58 west from Lawrence W. subway. **T.W. Transportation** (905-672-0293) runs buses every 20 min. directly to downtown hotels ($11, round-trip $19). Buses also serve the Yorkdale ($6.70), York Mills ($7.75), and Islington ($6.20) subway stations every 40 min. 5:45am-12:25am. The **Hotel Airporter** also runs transportation from select, downtown hotels (798–2424). $11 one way, $18 round-trip. **Air Canada** (925-2311 or 800-422-6232) flies to Montréal, Calgary, New York City, and Vancouver. Student discounts available. See Essentials Section.

Trains: All trains chug from **Union Station,** 61 Front St. (366-8411), at Bay. Subway: Union. **VIA Rail** (366-8411) cannonballs to: Montréal (4-6 per day, $79); Windsor (4-5 per day, $59); Vancouver (3 per week, ; $460). Student and senior discounts available; 40% discount for 6-day pre-reservation on all trains except those to Vancouver. VIA also offers a CanRail Pass good for 12 days of coach travel within a 30-day period, anywhere in Canada. (June-Sept. $510; Oct.-May $350). **Amtrak** (800-872-7245) goes to: New York City (1 per day, 12 hr. US$86); Chicago (1 per day, 11 hr., US$100). Seniors 10% discount. Ticket office open Mon.-Sat. 7am-9pm, Sun. 8am-9pm. Station open daily 7am-11:30pm.

Buses: Voyageur (393-7911) and **Greyhound** (367-8747), 610 Bay St., just north of Dundas. Subway: St. Patrick or Dundas. Voyageur has service to Montréal (5-6 per day, 7 hr., $61). Greyhound takes you west or south to Calgary ($240), Vancouver ($279), or New York City ($89). No reservations; show up 30 min. prior to departure. A 7 day advance-purchase, unlimited ticket can be used anywhere in Canada ($190 one way). Ticket office open daily 5:30am-1am.

Public Transport: Toronto Transit Commission (TTC) (393-4000). Network includes 2 subway lines and numerous bus and streetcar routes. Free pocket maps at all stations. Some routes 24 hrs. New policy requires buses running after dark to stop anywhere along the route at a female passenger's request. Free transfers among subway, buses, and streetcars, but only within stations. Fare $2, 5 tokens $6.50, seniors 50% off with ID, under 13 50¢, 8 for $2.50. Unlimited travel day pass, good for subway, bus, and streetcar, $5. Monthly pass $67.

Toronto Island Ferry Service (392-8193; 392-8194 for recording). Numerous ferries to Centre Island, Wards Island, and Hanlans Point leave daily from Bay St. Ferry Dock at the foot of Bay St. Service approximately every ½ hr. to 1 hr. 8am-midnight. $3 round-trip; seniors, students, ages 15-19 $1.50, under 15 $1.

Taxi: Co-op Cabs, 364-7111. $2.20 base.

Car Rental: Wrecks for Rent, 77 Nassau St. (585-7782). Subway: Spadina or Bathurst. $29 per day; first 100km free, 9¢ each additional km. Insurance $9.50 if over 25 with credit card, $15 without. Surcharge $3, ages 23-25 $5, ages 21-23. Open Mon.-Fri. 6am-6pm, Sat. 9am-4pm. **Hertz** (800-263-0600), **Tilden** (922-2000), **Budget** (673-3322), and **Discount** (961-8006) also serve Toronto.

Auto Transport: Allostop, 663 Yonge St., Suite 301 (531-7668), at Bloor. Matches riders and drivers. Membership $6 for passengers, $7 for drivers. Passengers pay drivers for trips. To: Ottawa ($24), Montréal ($26), Québec City ($41), New York ($40). Open Mon.-Wed. 9am-5pm, Thurs.-Fri. 9am-7pm, Sat.-Sun. 10am-5pm.

Bike Rental: Brown's Sports and Bike Rental, 2447 Bloor St. W. (763-4176). $17 per day, $34 per weekend, $44 per week. $200 deposit or credit card required. Open Mon.-Wed. 9:30am-6pm, Thurs.-Fri. 9:30am-8pm, Sat. 9:30am-5:30pm.

Help Lines: Rape Crisis, 597-8808. 24 hrs. **Services for the Disabled,** Ontario Travel, 314-0944. **Toronto Gay and Lesbian Phone Line,** 964-6600. Open Mon.-Sat. 7-10pm.

Toronto

1 Harbour Square
2 Toronto Island Ferry Terminal
3 Skydome
4 CN Tower
5 Union Station
6 O'Keefe Centre
7 St. Lawrence Market
8 Post Office
9 Roy Thomson (concert) Hall
10 Toronto City Hall

11 Toronto International Hostel
12 Infobooth
13 Bay Street Bus Terminal
14 World's Biggest Bookstore
15 Art Gallery of Ontario
16 Kensington Market
17 Neill-Wycik College-Hotel
18 Ontario Provincial Parliament Building
19 Knox College

20 Hart House
21 Trinity College
22 McLaughlin Planetarium
23 Royal Ontario Museum (ROM)
24 The Annex

◇◇◇◇◇ Subway Line and Station

Post Office: Toronto Dominion Centre (360-7105), at King and Bay St. General Delivery at Postal Station K, 2384 Yonge St. (483-1334). Subway: Eglington. Open Mon.-Fri. 8am-5:45pm. **Postal Code:** M4P 2E0.
Area Code: 416 (city), 905 (outskirts).

The city maps available at tourism booths only show major streets and may prove inadequate for getting around. A better bet is to go to any drugstore or postcard shack and buy the indispensable *Downtown and Metro Toronto Visitor's Map Guide* in the yellowish-orange cover ($1.50). The pocket *Ride Guide,* free at all TTC stations and tourism information booths (see Practical Information), shows the subway and bus routes for the metro area.

There is no one spot downtown that can be called the heart of the action. Instead, there are many decentralized neighborhoods; each has its own distinctive character. Zoning regulations require that Toronto developers include housing and retail space in commercial construction; this has kept downtown from becoming a barren canyon of glass boxes at night; people actually live there.

The city streets lie in a grid pattern. The addresses on north-south streets increase as you head north, away from Lake Ontario. **Yonge Street** is the main artery, dividing the city and the streets perpendicular to it into east and west. Numbering for both sides starts at Yonge and increases as you move in either direction. Heading west from Yonge St., the main streets are **Bay Street, University Avenue, Spadina Avenue,** and **Bathurst.** From the water, northwards, the major east-west routes are **Front Street, Queen Street, Dundas, College, Bloor,** and **Edlington.**

Traffic is heavy in Toronto—avoid rush hour (4-7pm). Parking on the street is hard to find and usually limited to one hour, except on Sundays when street parking is free and abundant. Street parking is free at night, but your car must be gone by 7am. The parking officials are extremely zealous about enforcing parking violations—don't tempt them. Day parking is free at outlying subway stations, the best bet for inbound day-trippers, yet parking overnight at the subway stations is prohibited. If you park within the city, expect to pay at least $12 for 24 hours (7am-7am).

GETTING AROUND

There are many neighborhoods worth exploring. One of the most distinctive is **Chinatown,** on Dundas St. W. between Bay St. and Spadina Ave. This area can be a little dangerous at night. **Kensington Market** is found on Kensington Ave., Augusta Ave., and the western half of Baldwin St.—previously the Jewish market in the 1920s, now a largely Portuguese neighborhood, has many good restaurants, vintage clothing shops, and an outdoor bazaar of produce, luggage, spices, nuts, clothing, and shoes. **Queen Street West,** from University Ave. to Bathurst St., is a strip of old factories, stores, and warehouses that now contains a fun mix of shopping from upscale, uptight boutiques to reasonable used book stores, restaurants, and cafés. Listen to street musicians. The **University of Toronto** campus with its old ivy-covered Gothic buildings and magnificent quadrangles, occupies about 200 acres in the middle of downtown. The law-school cult-flick *The Paper Chase* was filmed here because the campus supposedly looked more Ivy League than Harvard, where the movie was set. **The Annex,** Bloor St. W. at the Spadina subway, has an artistic and literary ambiance, and excellent budget restaurants serving a variety of ethnic cuisines (see Food). This is the best place to come at night when you're not sure exactly what you're hungry for; afterwards, stay and hit the nightclubs.

Yorkville, just north of Bloor between Younge and Avenue, has been renovated since its days as the crumbling communal home of flower children and folk guitarists. Today, most can only afford to windowshop at stores like Tiffany's and Hermés. **Cabbagetown,** just east of Younge, bounded by Gerrard St. east, Wellesley, and Sumach, takes its name from the Irish immigrants who used to plant the vegetable in their yards. Today, its renowned Victorian housing is occupied by professionals and quite probably, the only crowing rooster in the city. The **Gay and Lesbian Village** is located around Church and Wellesley, and offers numerous options for fine dining or outdoor cafés. The **Theatre District,** on Front St. between Sherbourne and Younge, is home to enough venues to feed anyone's cultural and physical appetites. Music, food, ferry rides, dance companies, and art all dock at the **Harborfront** on Queen's Quay W. from York St. to Bathurst, on the lake. Call 973-3000 for information. There are three main **Toronto Islands,** all accessible by ferry (see Practical Info above). The islands offer beaches, bike rental, and an amusement park. Just east, the **beaches** along and south of Queen's St. E. between Woodbine and Victoria, boasts a lot of shops and a very popular boardwalk. Farther east still, about 5 km from the city center, the **Scarborough Bluffs** are a rugged, 16-km. long section of cliffs jutting up from the lakeshore.

Only 30-45 min. by public transit from downtown lie three ethnic enclaves. **Corso Italia** is on St. Clair W. at Dufferin St.; take the subway to St. Clair W. and bus #512 west. **Little India** is on Gerrard St. E. at Coxwell. Subway: Coxwell; bus #22 south to 2nd Gerrard stop. **Greektown** (better known as **"the Danforth"**) is on Danforth Ave., at Pape Ave. (subway: Pape). All three have bilingual street signs, cater to locals, not tourists, and are worth the ride.

ACCOMMODATIONS AND CAMPING

Budget travelers in Toronto have a staggering number of first-rate lodging choices in Toronto. The hostels and U. of Toronto dorms are remarkable for their towering quality to price ratio. Avoid the cheap hotels concentrated around Jarvis and Gerrard St. You can call the Visitors Bureau to obtain a B&B or call one of two B&B agencies: the **Downtown Association of Bed and Breakfast Guest Houses** (690-1724), which places guests in renovated Victorian homes (singles $40-60), or the **Metropolitan B&B Registry** (964-2566), which has locations all over the city (singles from $35). Always visit a B&B before you commit, as it is difficult to regulate these registries.

Toronto International Hostel (HI-C), 223 Church St. (368-1848 or 368-0207), 5 min. from Eaton Centre. Subway: Dundas. 175 beds, no TV. Huge lounge, excellent kitchen, laundry facilities, tourist info, and an HI retail store stocked exclusively with *Let's Go* guides. Daily organized activities run the gamut from dart tournaments to bar-hopping. Check-out 10am. Quiet hours midnight-7am. Bed in 10-person dorm $15, in 6-bed dorm $17, in 4-bed dorm $22, in 2-bed dorm $24.50. Mixed and single-sex rooms. No curfew. 24-hr. office. Reservations essential. Ask about discount coupons for local cafés. IBN reservations available. The recommended Canadian Experience tour leaves from here—see "near Toronto" for details.

Leslieville Home Hostel, 185 Leslie St. (461-7258). Subway: Queen. Take any Queen streetcar from the subway stop and get off at Leslie; walk left to hostel. Inviting home setting. Friendly owners will work hard to place all comers. Dorm-style bed $12; $15 with a huge breakfast; mixed and single sex rooms. Singles $35. Doubles $45. Price includes linens, towels, soap, and breakfast. No curfew. No smoking. During the winter, singles $27, doubles $34 (add $3 per person for breakfast). Check out of bedrooms 10am, but travelers are welcome to hang out all day in the common area.

Trinity College and St. Hilda's College Residences, 6 Hoskin Ave. (978-2523), near Knox; check-in at bursar's office in Queen's Park Crescent on U of T campus. Subway: Museum. Prices $28 and up. Office open Mon.-Fri. 9am-4pm.

Knox College, 59 St. George St. (978-2793). Subway: Queen's Park. Huge rooms with wood floors around an idyllic courtyard. Many rooms refinished by the crew of *Class of '96.* This gothic residence is U of T's most coveted. Common rooms and baths on each floor. Great location in the heart of U of T's campus. Singles $25. Doubles $35. Call for reservations Mon.-Fri. 9am-5pm. Available June-Aug.

Neill-Wycik College Hotel, 96 Gerrard St. E. (800-268-4358 or 977-2320). Subway: College. Rooms impeccably clean, some with beautiful views of the city. Kitchen on every floor, but no utensils. Check-in after 1pm (locked storage room provided). Check-out 11am. Singles (including simple breakfast) $9.50, doubles $36. Family room $47. Dorm bunks for backpackers $18. 10% discount for 7-night stay if you pay up front; student discount available. Will cancel reservations after 6:30pm unless arrangements are made. Open early May-late Aug.

Karabanow Guest House and Tourist Home, 9 Spadina Rd. (phone and fax 923-4004), at Bloor St. 6 blocks west of Yonge. Subway: Spadina. Good location by subway stop. Small and intimate. 20 rooms with desks (mostly doubles) in a renovated Victorian house. TV, free parking, free local calls. Office open Mon.-Tues. 10am-8pm, Wed. and Sat. 10am-9pm, Sun. 10am-6pm; check-out 11am. No curfew. Singles $46. Doubles $56. $10 key deposit. Rooms $5 less Oct.-April. No kids under 12 please. Reservations recommended.

The Allenby Bed and Breakfast, 223 Strathmore Blvd. (461-7095). Subway: Greenwood. Spacious, pristine rooms in a quiet neighborhood. Subway stop next door adds convenience, not noise. Private-use kitchens and bathrooms abound. Long-term and groups stays encouraged. Singles $35 during winter, $40 during summer. Doubles $45/50.

Hotel Selby, 592 Sherbourne St. (921-3142 or 800-387-4788). Subway: Sherbourne. Hotel Selby has seen many changes but today is a registered historic spot and a thriving guest house. Completely refurbished, including cable TV, A/C, and phones. Special period suites have been set up to capture the splendor of the 1920's Selby as Hemingway lived it (his desk is still there). Some private baths. Singles start at $49.

Indian Line Tourist Campground, 7625 Finch Ave. W. (678-1233 off-season call 661-6600, ext. 203), at Darcel Ave. Follow Hwy. 427 north to Finch and go west. The closest campground to metropolitan Toronto. Discounts available to some local attractions. Showers, laundry. Close to Pearson Airport. Sites $15, with hookup $19. Open May 10-early Oct.

YWCA - Woodlawn Residence, 80 Woodlawn Ave. (923-8454), off Yonge St. Subway: Summerhill. 115 rooms for women only with complimentary breakfast. TV lounges and laundry facilities. Singles $44, doubles $59.

FOOD

A burst of immigration from around the world has made Toronto a haven for good ethnic food that is rivaled in North America only by New York City. Over 5000 restaurants squeeze into metropolitan Toronto; you could eat at a different place every night for the next 15 years. Best bets are Bloor St. W. and Chinatown. For fresh produce, go to Kensington Market (see Getting Around) or the St. Lawrence Market at King St. E. and Sherbourne, six blocks east of the King subway stop. The budget traveler staying in town for more than a few days will want *Toronto Dinners for $7.95 or Less,* by PBG Productions, a pocket guide to 100 restaurants ($6, available at **World's Biggest Bookstore,** 20 Edward St. (977-7709), which boasts 27 km. of shelves with over 143,000 titles (subway: Dundas; open Mon.-Sat. 9am-10pm, Sun noon-10pm.) "L.L.B.O" posted on the window of a restaurant means that it has a liquor license.

Real Peking Restaurant, 355 College St. (920-7952), at Augusta Ave. The effort many Chinese restaurants put into decorations here goes into the food instead. Understanding server explains the menu. Entrees $6.50-8.50. Open Mon.-Fri. 5pm-2am, Sat. 5-11pm, Sun. 5-10pm.

Shopsy's, 33 Yonge St. (365-3333), at Front St., 1 block from Union Station. *The* definitive Toronto deli. 300 seats, quick service. Try the famous hot corned beef on a Reuben ($7.65). Open Sun. 8am-11pm, Mon.-Wed. 7am-11pm, Thurs.-Fri. 7am-midnight, Sat. 8am-midnight.

Mr. Greek, 568 Danforth Ave. (461-5470), at Carlaw. Subway: Pape. A friendly, bustling café serving shish kabobs, salads, steak, chicken, Greek music, and wine. Family atmosphere, fast service. Gyros or souvlaki $3.80. Open Sun.-Thurs. 10-1am, Fri.-Sat. until 3am.

Country Style Hungarian Restaurant, 450 Bloor St. W. (537-1745). Hearty stews, soups, and casseroles. Entrees come in small and large portions; better terms would be "more than enough" and "stop, lest I burst." Entrees $3-8. Open daily 11am-10pm.

Renaissance Cafe, 509 Bloor St. W. (968-6639). Subway: Spadina. Fun for tofu-lovers and other hip health eccentrics. Moon burger (tofu, spices, and *tahini* sauce) $7. Lite bites (noon-4pm) $5-7. Luncheon specials $6. Open Mon.-Thurs. 11:30am-midnight, Fri.-Sun. 11:30am-1am.

Vanipha, 193 Augusta Ave. (340-0491), off Dundas St. W., across from playground. Standard Thai including curry, poultry, meat, and vegetarian dishes. Entrees $7-9. Open Tues.-Sun. noon-11pm.

Saigon Palace, 454 Spadina Ave. (963-1623), at College St. Subway: Queen's Park. Popular with locals. Great spring rolls. Beef, chicken, or vegetable dishes over rice or noodles ($4-7). Open Mon.-Thurs. 9am-10pm, Fri.-Sat. until 10pm.

Alley Katz Café, 386 Bloor St. W. (923-1091). Good soup and sandwiches. Raw drinks $2 (try a carrot-romaine or carrot-celery). Best known for the gelato; the raspberry is exquisite ($2.50). Open daily 10:30am-midnight.

Furture's Bakery and Café, 483 Bloor St. W (922-5887). Have an espresso and hang out on the popular outdoor patio. Sinful desserts like the phantom cake ($3.25) can follow a lunch of spinach crepes ($5.25). Open daily 7:30am-3pm.

Chez Cappuccino, 3 Charles St. E. (925-6142). Jazz music provides the backdrop for this 24-hr. café. 3 or 4 soups daily ($2.95), quiches ($4.35), and scrumptious muffins baked fresh ($1.50). Upper Canada beer on tap.

The Old Fish Market Restaurant, 12 Market St. (363-FISH/363-3474), just off the Esplanade. Somewhat pricey but excellent seafood. Dinners normally run $6-14, but look for special deals. At lunch, try the halibut fish and chips with chowder ($5.99). Monday features all-you-can-eat mussels ($6.99), and Wednesday has the same deal with shrimp ($9.99). There is a half-price menu after nine. Open Mon.-Thurs. 11:45am-2:30pm and5-10pm; Fri 11:45am-2:30pm and 5-11pm; Sat 8:30am-11am, 11:30am-3pm an d 4:30-11pm; Sun. noon-3pm and 4-10pm.

The Organ Grinder, 58 the Esplanade (364-6517), treats your ears as well as your stomach, as jingles dance forth from the 1925 theater pipe organ, assembled from pieces of over 50 pipe organs. Pizzas $7-9. Open Sun.-Thurs. 11:30am-10pm, Fri.-Sat. 11:30am-midnight.

Mövenpick Marché, (366-8986) in the BCE Place at Younge and Front St., offers a 1620 sq. meter market. Browse through and pick your meal from the various culinary stations, including a bakery, wine shop, pastas, seafood, and salad counters, and a grill. A main entree runs $5-8. Open daily 9am-2am.

The Midtown Café, 552 College St. W (920-4533), sounds alternative music while you play pool or just relax and eat from the large *tapas* menu ($2.50-3). Sandwiches ($3.50-5). Open daily 10am-1am.

Bar Italia, 584 College St. W. (535-3621). Excellent Italian food in a jazzy ambiance. A favorite is the *panino terracina* sandwich ($6). Open daily 8am-1am.

SIGHTS

Exploring the **ethnic neighborhoods** on foot is one of the most enjoyable (and cheapest) activities in Toronto. As you pass between neighborhoods, the signs change languages, different food aromas waft through the air, and your ears are greeted by the lively conversation of foreign tongues. Life takes place on the streets here: watch locals haggling at outdoor produce markets, or sit and sample the local cuisine at an outdoor café. For a more organized expedition, join one of the seven free **walking tours** operated by the **Royal Ontario Museum** (Wed. at 6pm, Sun. at 2pm, June-Aug.). Destinations vary on different dates, as do meeting places. Call for specific information at 586-5513 or 556-5514. The **University of Toronto** conducts free, hour-long walking tours of Canada's largest university. Meet at the Map Room of Hart House for tours June-Aug. Mon.-Fri. at 10:30am, 1pm, and 2:30pm (978-5000). Available in English, French, Portuguese, or Hindi; call ahead for the latter two. Other guided trips within the city revolve around the themes of architecture, sculptures, or ghost-infested Toronto haunts. (Contact the Visitors Bureau for info. Tours $10.) Modern architecture aficionados should visit **City Hall** (392-7341) at the corner of Queen and Bay St. between the Osgoode and Queen subway stops, with its curved twin towers and 2-story rotunda. (Free tours offered Mon.-Fri. at 3:15pm.) In front of City Hall, Nathan Phillips Square is home to the reflecting pool (which

CANADA

becomes a skating rink in winter) and numerous special events. Call the **Events Hotline** (392-0458) for information. A few blocks away, the **Toronto Stock Exchange,** 2 First Canadian Place on York between Adelaide St. W. and King St. W, serves as Canada's leading stock market, where over $250 million are exchanged daily. Presentations given Tues.-Fri.at 2pm. The visitors center has a viewing gallery and is open Mon.-Fri. 9am-4:30pm (947-4676). The Ontario government legislates in the **Provincial Parliament Buildings** (325-7500), at Queen's Park in the city center. (Subway: Queen's Park. Free guided tours Mon.-Fri. by request, Sat.-Sun. 9am-4pm every ½ hr. excluding lunch time. Free visitors gallery passes available at info desk in main lobby at 1:30pm. Building open 8:30am-6pm Mon.-Fri., 9am-4pm Sat.-Sun., chambers close 4:30pm. Parliament in session Oct.-Dec. and March-June, Mon.-Thurs. 1:30-6pm, and Thurs. 10am-noon.) Queen's Park itself holds outdoor summer concerts and events; on non-event days it provides a terrific picnic site.

At 553m, the **CN Tower** (360-8500; subway: Union, and follow the skywalk) does not quite pierce the ozone layer, but the ride to the top, at a towering $12 (seniors $8, children $6.50), will poke a big hole in your wallet. (Open June-Labor Day Mon.-Sat. 9-midnight, Sun. 10am-10pm; Labor Day-May Sun.-Thurs. 10am-10pm, Fri.-Sat. 10am-11pm.) Some people say that free passage to the top is given at night to those who at least claim to be heading for the Horizons bar at the top (you can even get a drink there). Another classic tourist attraction is the 98-room **Casa Loma** (923-1171), Davenport Rd. at 1 Austin Terrace, near Spadina a few blocks north of the Dupont subway stop. The outside of the only real turreted castle in North America belongs in a fairy tale, and the inside contains secret passageways and an underground tunnel. (Open daily 10am-4pm. $8, seniors and ages 5-16 $4.50, under 5 free with parent.) The **Royal Ontario Museum (ROM),** 100 Queen's Park (586-5551; subway: Museum), has artifacts from ancient civilizations (Greek, Chinese, Egyptian), a floor of life sciences (kids will love the preserved stuffed animals and bugs), plus a bat cave, and an autopsy of a mummified Egyptian. (Open in summer daily 10am-6pm, Tues. and Thurs. until 8pm; closed Mon. in winter. $7, seniors and students $4, children $3.50. Free all day Tuesday for seniors; after 4:30 for everyone; includes entry to the **George M. Gardiner Museum of Ceramic Art** across the street.) Also in the museum complex, the **McLaughlin Planetarium** (586-5736) showcases presentations on astronomy and laser shows. (Open Tues.-Sun. 10am-6pm, Tues. and Thurs. until 8pm. Tickets $5.50, seniors/students $4, children $3.50. ROM admission includes a discount to the Planetarium.

One of the top 10 museums in North America, the **Art Gallery of Ontario (AGO),** 3170 Dundas St. W. (979-6648; Subway: St. Patrick), three blocks west of University Ave. in the heart of Chinatown, houses an enormous collection of Western art spanning from the Renaissance to the 1980s, with a particular concentration on Canadian artists. (Open Tues.-Sun. 10am-5:30pm; $7.50, seniors and students $4, under 12 free, families $15. Free Wed. 5-10pm. Seniors free on Fri.) Budget travelers who have spent all day on their feet may enjoy the **Bata Shoe Museum,** 131 Bloor St. W. (924-7463), 2nd floor, two blocks from the Museum subway stop. A fascinating collection of footwear from many cultures and ages: the moon boot worn by Buzz Aldrin, Hindu ivory stilted sandals, Elton John's sparkling sliver platform boots, and two-inch slippers once worn by Chinese women with bound feet. (Open Tues.-Sun. 11am-6pm. $3, students and seniors $1, families $6. Visitors get 2 hrs. free underground parking.) In the spring of 1995, the Bata will be relocating to the corner of Bloor and St. George. The new phone number is unknown, but visitors should definitely make the effort to seek out this museum.

The newest addition to the museum circuit showcases Canada's favorite sport: the **Hockey Hall of Fame** (360-7765), on the concourse level of BCE, 30 Yonge St. at Front St. Head first to the Bell Great Hall, where the plaques of hockey greats such as Bobby Orr and Bobby Clarke are displayed, then make sure to catch all of the exhibits, including the evolution of skates, uniforms, and sticks, the goalie mask collection, and the replica dressing room. Flick a few pucks or test your goalie skills on the inter-active video games. Two theaters present films on great hockey moments.

(Open Mon.-Wed. and Sat. 9am-6pm; Thurs.-Fri. 9am-9:30pm; Sun. 10am-6pm. $6, seniors/children $5.50.)

The **Holocaust Education and Memorial Center of Toronto,** 4600 Bathurst St. (635-22883; take the Bathurst bus north to the Joseph Latimer Library), runs a museum and two audio-visual presentations portraying the lives of Jews in Europe before, during, and after WWII. A sobering experience for visitors to commemorate the six million Jews murdered by Germany's Nazi regime. (Open daily 9am-4pm. Free.) Smaller Toronto museums include: the **Marine Museum of Upper Canada,** Exhibition Place (392-1765; open Tues.-Fri. 9:30am-5pm, Sat.-Sun. noon-5pm; $3.25, seniors and students $2.50, children $2.25); the **Museum for Textiles,** 55 Center Ave. (599-5321; open Tues.-Fri. 11am-5pm, Sat.-Sun. noon-5pm; $5, seniors and student $4, children free); and the **Redpath Sugar Museum,** 95 Queens Quay E. (366-3561; call for hours).

The **Upper Canada Brewing Company,** 2 Atlantic Ave. (534-9281), get off the subway at King or St. Andrews and take the King street car west to Atlantic and Jefferson. Free tours and tastings Mon.-Sat. at 1pm, 3pm, and 5:30pm and Sun. at 1pm, and 3pm. Reservations required. (Open Mon.-Sat. 10am-8pm, Sun. 10am-6pm.)

Biking and **hiking** trails abound in Toronto. For a map of the trails, write the **Metro Parks and Property Department,** 365 Bay St., 8th floor, Toronto, M5H 2V1, or call the **Parks and Recreation Department** at 392-1111. (Mon.-Fri. 8:30am-4:30pm for info on local facilities and activities.) For a relaxing afternoon, go to **High Park** (392-7251; subway: High Park) and you may well find a free summer Shakespeare performance (fishing pond and sports facilities also available). On the southeast end of Toronto, the **beaches** are now a permanent community in what was once a summer resort. The 4-km boardwalk is bordered by park lands and sandy beach, a perfect area for weekend strolling or picnicking. The **Beaches Recreation Center,** 6 Williamson Rd. (392-0740), gives information on the **Toronto Islands Park,** a 4-mi. strip of connected islands just opposite downtown (15-min. ferry trip; 392-8193 for ferry info, see Practical Information). A popular "vacationland," they have a boardwalk, bathing beaches, canoe and bike rentals, a Frisbee golf course, and an amusement park. Ferries leave from the Bay Street Ferry Dock at Bay St.

From April to October, the **Toronto Blue Jays** (info 341-1000; 341-1234 for tickets) knock balls at the hotel behind center field in the four-year-old **Sky Dome,** Front and Peter St. (subway: Union and follow the signs). The dome is more of an entertainment center than a ballpark; it lacks the charm and tradition of Fenway Park or Wrigley Field, but boasts a retractable roof, a 348-room hotel next to the field, and retail outlets and offices. Most games sell out, but before the game the box office usually has some obstructed view seats. (Tickets $4-17.50.) Scalpers sell tickets for far beyond face value; latecomers wait until the game starts and then haggle like crazy. To get a behind-the-scenes look at the Sky Dome, take the tour (341-2770; July-August Mon.-Fri. 10am-6pm, Sept.-June Mon.-Fri. 10am-4pm; $8, seniors and under 16 $5.50.) For information on concerts and other Sky Dome events, call 341-3663. Hockey fans should head for **Maple Leaf Gardens,** 60 Carlton St., (977-1641; Subway: College), to see the knuckle-crackin', puck-smackin' **Maple Leafs**. Tours of the gardens leave daily at 11am, 1pm, 2:30pm, and 4pm. Tickets required. Call for details.

Farther out from the city are many attractions about 1-hr. from downtown and accessible by public transportation. **Canada's Wonderland,** 9580 Jane St. (832-7000), is Canada's answer to Disneyland. Splash down the water rides or dare to ride the backwards, looping, and suspended roller coasters. (Open fall weekends, daily May-Labor Day; opens at 10am, closing times vary. Late June-Labor Day open daily 10am-10pm. $31.50, ages 3-6 $15.40. The **Ontario Science Center,** 770 Don Mills Rd. (696-3127) at Eglington Ave. E ., presents more than 650 exhibits for visitors to interact with. The museum showcases man's greatest discoveries and innovations. (Open daily 10am-6pm, Fri. 10am-9pm. $7.50, youths 11-17 $5.50, seniors/children $3.) The **Metro Toronto Zoo** (392-5900), Meadowvale Rd., off exit 389 on Hwy. 401 north, is home to over 5000 animals in a 710 acre park containing sec-

CANADA

tions representing the world's seven geographic regions. (Open late May-Labor Day 9am-7:30pm; rest of the year 9:30am-4:30pm. Last entry 1 hr. before closing. $9.75, seniors/ages 12-17 $7, children 4-11 $5.)

NIGHTLIFE

Some of Toronto's clubs and pubs remain closed on Sundays because of liquor laws. The more formal clubs maintain dress code. The city shuts down alcohol distribution at 1am, so most clubs close down then. To mingle with students try **The Brunswick House** or **Lee's Palace** (see below). The interesting new clubs are on trendy **Queen Street West, College Street West,** and **Bloor Street West.** The gay scene centers around Wellesley and Church. Two comprehensive free entertainment magazines, *Now* and *Eye,* are published every Thursday. Monthly *Where Toronto,* available free at tourism booths, gives a good art and entertainment run-down.

Bamboo, 312 Queen St. W. (593-5771), 3 blocks west of the Osgoode subway stop. Popular with students. Live reggae, jazz, rock, and funk daily. Great dancing. Patio upstairs. Open Mon.-Sat. noon-1am. Hefty cover (Mon.-Thurs. $5-8, Fri.-Sat. $10) varies band to band.

Brunswick House, 481 Bloor St. W. (964-2242), between the Bathurst and Spadina subway stops. Reeling with students. Beer $2.95. Upstairs is **Albert's Hall,** famous for its blues. Open Mon.-Fri. 11:30-1am, Sat. noon-1am.

Lee's Palace, 529 Bloor St. W. (532-7383), just east of the Bathurst subway stop. Amazing crazy creature art depicting rock n' roll frenzy. Live music nightly downstairs. DJ dance club upstairs. Pick up a calendar of bands. Cover $3-12 downstairs. Box office opens 8pm, shows begin at 10pm. Downstairs open daily noon-1am; upstairs open Tues. and Thurs.-Sat. 8pm-3am, cover after 10pm $4.

George's Spaghetti House, 290 Dundas St. E. (923-9887), at Sherbourne St. (subway: Dundas). Take the streetcar east to Sherbourne. Restaurant downstairs. Upstairs, the city's best jazz club attracts the nation's top ensembles. Don't forget your jacket and tie or you may feel out of place. Dinner entrees from $9. Restaurant open Mon.-Thurs. 11am-11pm, Fri. 11am-midnight, Sat. 5pm-midnight. Jazz club open Mon.-Sat. 6:30pm-1am. Cover Wed.-Thurs. $4, Fri.-Sat. $5; free on Mon. and Tues., at the bar, or during last set.

Second City, 110 Lombard St. (863-1111), in The Old Firehall, at Jarvis, 2 blocks east and 2 short blocks south of Queen's Park subway stop. One of North America's wackiest and most creative comedy clubs. Spawned comics Dan Akroyd, John Candy, Gilda Radner, Dave Thomas, Rick Moranis, Martin Short, a hit TV show (SCTV), and the legendary "Great White North." Dinner and theater $22-39. Theater without dinner $13-20, students $9. Free improv sessions Mon.-Thurs. at 10:15pm. Shows Mon.-Thurs. at 6 and 8:30pm, Fri.-Sat. at 8 and 11pm. Reservations required.

Sneaky Dee's, 431 College St. W. (368-5090), at Bathurst. A hip new Toronto hotspot tapping the most inexpensive brew ($8.20 for 60-oz pitcher of Ontario microbrewery drought). The downstairs restaurant/bar offers Tex-mex food with a daily half-price special. Mon.-Fri. before 6pm, domestic beer runs only $2 per bottle. Open Sun.-Wed. 11am-3am, Thurs.-Sat. 11am-4am. Upstairs, punk and alternative bands play nightly. Open daily 8pm-1:30am.

College St. Bar, 574 College St. W. (533-2417), with its brick interior, has a mellow atmosphere and serves its own bitter stout, as well as other suds. Sun. night is its trademark, when live blues or funk sounds pack the place. Open Mon.-Fri. 4pm-1am, Sat., Sun. 11:30am-1am.

Bistro 422, 422 College St. W. (963-9416), is a small (often cramped) downstairs bar catering to the Doc Martens crowd. Typical bar food with daily specials $4.99. Open daily 4pm-1am.

FESTIVALS AND CULTURAL EVENTS

The city offers a few first-class freebies. **Ontario Place,** 955 Lakeshore Blvd. W. (314-9811; 314-9900 recording), features top-notch cheap entertainment in the summer—the Toronto Symphony, the National Ballet of Canada, the Ontario Place

Pops, and top pop artists perform here free with admission to the park. (Park open mid-May to early Sept. daily 10:30am-midnight. Free except for special events. Call for schedule.) Spectacular IMAX movies can be seen at the six-story **Cinesphere** (870-8000; $4, seniors and kids $2; call for screening schedule). The mix of old and new talents at the **du Maurier Ltd. Downtown Jazz Festival** (363-5200 for info) mesmerizes the city in late June. More than 1500 artists from 17 countries participate in this 10-day extravaganza. Also in June, the **Toronto International Dragon Boat Race Festival** continues a 2000-year. old Chinese tradition, finishing at Toronto's Ceter Island and including various cultural performances and food (364-0046). Budget travelers will appreciate the abundance of free, outdoor concerts at lunchtime and in the early evening.

On five evenings in early July watch the **Benson and Hedges Symphony of Fire** blaze in the Toronto skies off Ontario Place (870-8000 for seats, 314-9900 for info). From mid-August through Labor Day, the **Canadian National Exhibition (CNE)** brings a country carnival atmosphere to Ontario Place as the world largest annual fair comes to town. (393-6000; $8.50, seniors $4.25, children $3. Special price days do exist, call for information. Grounds open daily 10am-midnight.) Enjoy superb performances of contemporary theater by **Canadian Stage** (367-8243) amid the greenery of High Park, on Bloor St. W. at Parkside Dr. (subway: High Park). Performances include new Canadian works and time-honored classics, including annual Shakespeare performances. Bring something to sit on or perch yourself on the 45° slope which faces the stage. ($5 donation requested. Call for schedules.)

Roy Thomson Hall, 60 Simcoe St. (872-4255), at King St. W. (subway: St. Andrews), is both Toronto's premier concert hall and the home of the Toronto Symphony Orchestra. Tickets are expensive ($19-50), but rush tickets for the symphony ($8-10) go on sale at the box office the day of the concert (at 11am for concerts Mon.-Fri., 1pm Sat.). Or order ticket by phone (593-4828; Mon.-Fri. 8:45am-8pm, Sat. noon-5pm; summer hours Mon.-Fri. noon-6pm; office open 2 hrs. before Sun. performances). Ask about discounts. The same ticket office serves **Massey Hall,** 178 Victoria St. (593-4828), near Eaton Centre (Subway: Dundas), a great hall for rock and folk concerts and musicals. The opera and ballet companies perform at **O'Keefe Centre,** 1 Front St. E. (872-2262; ballet tickets from $55, opera from $27), at Yonge. Rush tickets (for the last row of orchestra seats) go on sale at 11am Prices range upward from $10. A limited number of half-price tickets are available for seniors and students. Selected shows also have student dress rehearsals ($12). (Box office open Mon.-Sat. 11am-6pm or until 1 hr. after curtain.) Next door, **St. Lawrence Centre,** 27 Front St. E. (366-7723), presents excellent drama and chamber music recitals in two different theaters. Ask for possible student and senior discounts. (Box office open Mon.-Sat. 10am-6pm; in winter Mon.-Fri. 10am-8pm.)

You can beat the high cost of culture by seeking out standby or student discount options. **T.O. Tix** (596-8211) sells ½-price tickets for theater, music, dance, and opera on the day of performance; their booth at Dundas and Yonge in front of Eaton Centre opens at noon, so arrive before 11:45am for first dibs. (Subway: Dundas. Open Tues.-Sat. noon-7:30pm, Sun. 11am-3pm.) **Ticketmaster** (870-8000) will supply you with tickets to many events. Film fans looking for good classic and contemporary cinema should head to **Bloor Cinema,** 506 Bloor St. W. (532-6677), at Bathurst or to **Cinématheque Ontario,** 317 Dundas St. W. (923-3456).

■ NEAR TORONTO

Onation's Niagara Escarpment passes west of Toronto as it winds its way from Niagara Falls to Tobermory at the tip of Bruce Peninsula, and it merits exploration by all who visit the Toronto area. Along this 724 km rocky ridge runs the **Bruce Trail,** which snakes through parks and private land. Hikers are treated to spectacular waterfalls, breathtaking cliffs along the **Georgian Bay,** and an abundance of unusual animals and plants, including an old growth forest. Since the escarpment recently became a world biosphere reserve, future land development will be limited to that capable of existing symbiotically with the natural environment. For maps and Escarpment info, write: Niagara Escarpment Commission, 232 Guelph St., George-town, Ontario L7G4B1, or call: 905-877-5191 or 905-453-2468 (in Toronto). Specif-ics on the Bruce Trail can be obtained by writing: Bruce Trail Association, P.O. Box 857, Hamilton, Ontario L8N3N9. Since the area is unreachable by public transporta-tion, a phenomenal way to get out and explore the Ontarian countryside is with **The Canadian Experience** (368-1848 or 800-668-4487, daily 9am-9pm), which is fully endorsed by Toronto International Hostel. Guides Kellie and Larry Casey Shaw, an Olympic skier and a former pro hockey player respectively, take small groups on a 2½ day journey along the Bruce Trail and Escarpment, including stops at Niagara Falls, Elora (home of limestone Elora Gorge), Sante Marie (a native Huron settle-ment), St. Jacobs (a mennonite community), and Wasaga Beach (the world's largest fresh water beach). All food and transportation (including pick-up and drop-off at HI-Toronto), along with a 2-night stay at their 70-acre farm, is included in the $195 per person price. Two trips weekly: Mon. 8am-Wed. 2pm, and Wed 2pm-Fri. 8pm.

■■■ STRATFORD

Filling the coffers since 1953, the **Stratford Shakespeare Festival** has proven to be the life-blood of this picturesque town. Stratford-born scribe Tom Patterson founded the festival, which opened its inaugural season with Sir Alec Guiness in the title role of *Richard III*. Since then, both the town and the festival have become inextricably entwined. The **Shakespeare Festival** runs from late April, when pre-views begin, through early November. In high season there are up to six different shows per day (none on Mon.). Matinees commence at 2pm and evening perfor-mances begin at 8pm each of the three theaters: the crown-shaped **Festival The-atre,** the **Avon Theatre,** once a vaudeville house, and the intimate **Tom Patterson Theatre.** Complete information about casts, performances and other aspects of the Festival can be obtained by phone (free call from Toronto 363-4471, from London 227-1352, and from other areas 800-567-1600) or by writing the Stratford Festival, P.O. Box 520, Stratford, Ont. N5A 6V2. Ticket prices are expensive ($30-60), but good deals are to be had. Some **rush tickets** are reserved for every performance and are sold at 9am on the morning of the show at the Festival Theatre Box Office, or ½ hour before the show at the appropriate theater ($15-40). Certain mid-week mati-nee performances have been specifically designated for senior and students ($15.50-16.50). However, for any performance, students can purchase a ticket for $20 two weeks prior to any preview show. Seniors can obtain any remaining seat for $20. On Tues. and Thurs., save 50 % on tickets to some theater performances. Look for free Jazz on the River (mid-June to mid-Sept. Mon.-Fri. 6:30-8pm, on the Avon River). Stretch your legs on the 100km **Avon Trail,** which crosses through Stratford at the T.J. Dolan Natural Area (near where John St. intersects Centre St.).

To get to Stratford, travelers can go by train on **VIA Rail** (273-3234 or 800-361-1235), whose depot is on Shakespeare St., or by bus on **Chaco Trails** (271-7870), owned by Greyhound, which connects cities including Kitchener and Toronto. Head in town to the **Tourism Stratford Information Booth,** 30 York St. (273-3352 or 800-561-7926), on the river. If you call ahead, they will send a free 106-page visi-tors guide. (Open Sun.-Mon. 9am-5pm, Tues.-Sat. 9am-8pm.) Stratford's **post office:** 34 Wellington St. (271-5712; open Mon.-Fri. 8am-5pm), in Blowes Stationary; **postal code:** N5A 7M3; **area code:** 519.

The budget traveler's best bet for lodging is the **Burnside Guest Home and Hos-tel,** 139 William St., Stratford, Ont. N5A 4X9 (271-7076), which overlooks Lake Vic-toria from an Edenic perch. a Hearty breakfast is included in the room charge. B&Bs range from $40-60; hostel rooms are $25. The **Festival Accommodations Bureau** (273-1600) can book you into many local B&Bs ($35-100) and some hotels. Not all B&B owners cater to the younger crowd. Those who don't mind a few bugs can camp at the **Wildwood Conservation Area** (519-284-2292), on Hwy. 7, 11 km SW of Stratford; access to beach, pool, and marina, sites $15.75-19.25).

■ Prairie Provinces

■■■ MANITOBA

Manitoba marks the beginning of the Canadian West. Frontier prairie dominates this vast land, which is also pocketed with tens of thousands of lakes. To the north, tundra and the lush forests grow out of the wooded park lands of the central region. Farther west, the rolling mountains, replete with grain- and wheat-rich fields, belie the misconception that Manitoba is a flat prairie.

Manitoba lacks sophistication, but has its own peculiar midwestern quality. Its largest city and capital, **Winnipeg**, combines cosmopolitan elements with a local folksy atmosphere. The Royal Winnipeg Ballet is one of the best in North America, and its museums and art galleries are celebrated nationally. Contact **Tourism Winnipeg,** 302-25 Forks Market Rd., R3C 4S8 (800-665-0204 or 204-943-1970), or **Travel Manitoba** (800-665-0040, ext. 36, or 204-945-3777). Two youth hostels lodge in Winnipeg. **Ivey House International Hostel (HI-AYH),** 210 Maryland St. (204-772-3022; $12) and **Guest House International,** 168 Maryland St. (204-772-1272; $11).

Farther north are the prairie areas, still largely inhabited by Native Americans. Take the train up north to **Churchill,** on **Hudson Bay,** itself quite an attraction and worth the trip. A summer seaport operates out of Churchill which becomes the "Polar Bear Capital of the World" in the winter. Beluga whales, seals, and caribou live in and along Churchill's coast. The northern lights here are spectacular.

Around Winnipeg, **Lake Manitoba** offers excellent facilities, and **Riding Mountain National Park** displays forest, open grassland, meadows, prairies, and mountains. The fishing is superb and you are guaranteed to see bison, moose, and bears. Call **Wasagaming Visitors Center** (204-848-2811; open daily 9am-9pm) for details.

Manitoba is on Central time (1 hr. behind Eastern). **Postal Abbreviation:** MAN **Sales Tax:** 7% plus a 7% GST.

■■■ SASKATCHEWAN

Saskatchewan (a Native term meaning "the river that flows swiftly") produces over 60% of Canada's wheat, thus earning its nickname, "Heartland of North America." It also houses Canada's only training academy for the Royal Canadian Mounted Police (in Regina). Saskatchewan's diverse terrain also is made up of southern highlands (Cypress Hills reach a higher elevation than Banff, Alberta), water-covered valleys (the Qu'Appelle Valley with eight lakes and multiple gardens and parks), muddy Badlands (Butch Cassidy had a station here), and northern deserts. The north also boasts nearly 100,000 lakes and 80 million acres of forests. Queen City of the plains, and Saskatchewan's capital city, Regina is home to the training academy for the Canadian Mounties (306-780-5900). Ukrainian is Regina's second language, the French are a proud and assertive group, and Reginians are loyal subjects of the Queen.

For more info, contact **Tourism Regina,** (306-789-5099; open May-Sept. Mon.-Fri. 8am-7pm, Sat.-Sun. 10am-6pm, Oct.-April Mon.-Fri. 8:30am-4:30pm.) In Regina, stay at the **Turgeon International Hostel (IYHF-CHA),** 2310 MacIntyre St. (306-791-8165), in a beautifully restored old mansion. (Kitchen, lockers. 50 beds. $12, nonmembers $14. Open after 5pm.)

Saskatchewan is on Mountain Time (2 hr. behind Eastern). **Postal Abbreviation:** SK. **Sales Tax:** 9%, plus a 7% GST.

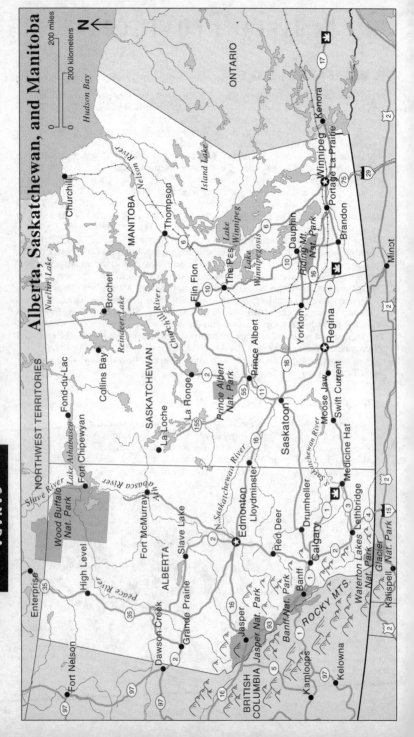

Alberta, Saskatchewan, and Manitoba

 Alberta

Alberta's glitter is concentrated in the west of the province; the icy peaks and turquoise lakes of Banff and Jasper National Parks reign as Alberta's most prominent landscapes. To the east, less sublime vistas of farmland, prairie, and oil fields fill the yawning expanses. Alberta boasts thousands of prime fishing holes, world-renowned fossil fields, and centers of Native American culture. Calgary caught the world's eye when it hosted the XV Winter Olympics in 1988, and is annual host to the wild and wooly Stampede.

Hwy. 16 connects Jasper with Edmonton, while the **Trans-Canada Hwy.** (Hwy. 1) connects Banff with Calgary, 120km to the east. **Hwy. 3** runs from Medicine Hat to Vancouver, BC. **Greyhound** runs from Calgary to Edmonton to Jasper, as well as from Calgary to Banff. **Brewster**runs an express bus between Banff and Jasper.

PRACTICAL INFORMATION

Capital: Edmonton.
Visitors Information: Alberta Tourism, 3rd floor, 10155 102 St., Edmonton T5J 4L6 (800-661-8888, 427-4321 in Alberta). **Provincial Parks Information,** Standard Life Centre #1660, 10405 Jasper Ave., Edmonton T5J 3N4 (944-0313). **Parks Canada,** Box 2989, Station M, Calgary T2P 3H8 (292-4401).
Time Zone: Mountain (2 hr. behind Eastern).
Postal Abbreviation: AB
Drinking Age: 18.

Alberta receives even more complete coverage in *Let's Go: Alaska & The Pacific Northwest.* Check it out!

■■■ EDMONTON

Beyond Edmonton's superficial drabness, there is plenty to see and do. Edmonton boasts one of the few existing shops devoted exclusively to budget travel, and a funky conservatory which exhibits a large collection of tropical and desert plants north of 53°N latitude. Toss in a toy museum and a great alternative music festival, and it shouldn't take long for Edmonton to lose its dull image.

Practical Information Emergency is 911. **Edmonton Tourism,** City Hall, 1 Sir Winston Churchill Square (426-4715), at 102A Ave., west of 99 St. has info, maps, brochures, and directions. (Open Victoria Day-Labor Day Mon.-Fri. 9am-4pm, Sat.-Sun. 11am-5pm.) For details about the rest of the province, head to **Alberta Tourism,** Commerce Court, 10155 102 St. (427-4321; postal code T5J 4L6), on the 3rd floor. (Open Mon.-Fri. 8:15am-4:30pm.) **Greyhound,** 10324 103 St. (421-4211), runs to: Calgary (nearly every hr., 8am-8pm, $32); Jasper (4 per day, $43); and Vancouver (3 per day direct via Jasper-Kamloops, 2 per day via Calgary, $111). (Open daily 5:30am-1am. Locker storage $1.50 per 24 hrs.) **VIA Rail,** 10004 104 Ave. (422-6032 or 800-501-863), in the CN Tower, thunders away to: Jasper ($82, students $73) and Vancouver ($194, students $175). (Open Mon., Thurs., and Sat. 7am-3:30pm, Tues. and Fri. 8:30am-9pm, Wed. 8:30am-4pm, Sun. 10:30am-9pm.) **Edmonton Transit,** (423-4636 for schedule info) operates buses and light rail transit **(LRT)** run frequently all over this sprawling metropolis. The LRT is free in the downtown area (Mon.-Fri. 9am-3pm and Sat. 9am-6pm. Fare $1.60, over 65 and under 15 80¢. No bikes on LRT during peak hours Mon.-Fri. 7:30-8:30am, 4-5pm.) Edmonton's **post office:** 9808 103A Ave. (495-4105; open Mon.-Fri. 8am-5:45pm); **postal code:** T5J 2G8; **area code:** 403.

Accommodations, Food, and Sights The liveliest place to stay in Edmonton is the **Edmonton International Youth Hostel (HI-C),** 10422 91 St. (429-0140), off Jasper Ave. Take bus #1 or 2; it's a long walk from the bus station. The area surrounding the hostel is a bit seedy. The hostel offers air-conditioned with common room, snack bar, showers, kitchen, and laundry facilities. (Open daily 8am-midnight. $10, nonmembers $14.) **St. Joseph's College** (492-7681), 89 Ave. at 114 St., in the University of Alberta neighborhood, has small, quiet, and cheap rooms. Take bus #43, or take the LRT and get off at University. In the summer, make reservations; rooms fill up fast. (Singles $21.75, weekly $131. Full board plan available. Singles with full board $34.75, or pay for meals separately: breakfast $3.25, lunch $4.50, dinner $6.50. Library facilities, TV, pool table. Check-in desk open Mon.-Fri. 9am-5pm.) **The Travel Shop,** 10926 88 Ave. (travel 439-3096, retail 439-3089, is the regional office for **Alberta Hostels.** The shop is a travel agency serving youth and student travelers. The staff will make hostel reservations. (Open Mon.-Wed. and Fri.-Sat. 9am-6pm, Thurs. 9am-8pm.)

The **Silk Hat,** 10251 Jasper Ave. (428-1551), is beside the Paramount theater. One of the oldest restaurants in Edmonton serves two eggs with two Northwest Territories-scale pancakes for $3.25. (Hamburger Deluxe with choice of fries or potato salad $4.25. Open Mon.-Fri. 6:30am-10pm, Sat. 8am-9pm, Sun. and holidays 11am-7pm.) **The Next Act,** 8224 104 St. (433-9345), in Old Strathcona, has cheap daily lunch specials (Mon.-Fri. On Saturdays, draft beer is $1.25 a glass. Small stage features local bands every Wed.; used during the jazz festival in June. Open Sun.-Wed. 11:30am-midnight; Thu.-Sat. 11:30am-2am.)

The "oh-my-god-that's-*obscenely*-huge" **West Edmonton Mall** (444-5200 or 800-661-8890) sprawls across the general area of 170 St. and 87 Ave. The World's Second-Biggest Mall appears even Bigger than It is thanks to the mirrors plastered on nearly every wall. Among Its many attractions, The Mall boasts twice as many submarines as the Canadian Navy, a full-scale replica of Columbus' *Santa Maria,* and **Lazermaze,** the world's first walk-through video game. You can get to The Mall via bus #10. (Open Mon.-Fri. 10am-9pm, Sat. 10am-6pm, Sun. noon-5pm.)

After sampling the achievements of late 20th-century malls, the Victorian era will seem a welcome relief as you head for **Fort Edmonton Park** (428-2992), off Whitemud Dr. near the Quesnell Bridge.

■■■ CALGARY

Calgary was founded in 1875 as the summer outpost of the Northwest Mounted Police. The discovery of oil in 1947 transformed this cowtown into a wealthy, cosmopolitan city, and in 1988, Calgary hosted the Winter Olympics. The oil may be crude, but the city is refined. Skyscrapers overshadow oil derricks, business people scurry about, and a modern transport system threads soundlessly through immaculate downtown streets. In July, Calgarians forget the oil business and get all gussied up in cowboy boots, jeans, Western shirts, and ten-gallon hats for the "Greatest Outdoor Show on Earth," the **Calgary Stampede.**

PRACTICAL INFORMATION
Emergency: 911.
Visitors Information: Calgary Convention and Visitors Bureau, 237 8th Ave. SE, Calgary, AB T2G 0K8 (263-8510). Open daily 8am-5pm.
Airport: Calgary International (292-8477), about 5km northwest of the city center. Bus #57 provides sporadic service to the city. The **Airporter Bus** (291-3848) offers frequent and friendly service for $7.50.
Greyhound, 877 Greyhound Way SW (outside Calgary 800-661-8747; 265-9111 in Calgary). Frequent service to Edmonton ($31) and Banff ($15). **Brewster Tours** (221-8242) runs buses to: Banff (3 per day, $26); Jasper (1 per day, $50).
Calgary Transit, 240 7th Ave. SW. Bus schedules, passes, and maps. Open Mon.-Fri. 8:30am-5pm. Fare $1.50, ages 6-14 90¢, under 6 free. Exact change required.

Day pass $4.50, children $2.50. Book of 10 tickets $12.50, children $8.50. **Information line** (262-1000) open Mon.-Fri. 6am-11pm, Sat.-Sun. 8am-9:30pm.
Taxi: Checker Cab, 299-9999. **Yellow Cab,** 974-1111.
Car Rental: Dollar, 221-1888 at airport, 269-3777 downtown (123 5th Ave. SE). Cars start at $37 per day with unlimited mileage. Weekend special for $29 per day. Must be 23 with a major credit card. Under 25 surcharge $9 per day. Open daily 7am-midnight at airport; Mon.-Fri. 7am-7pm, Sat. and Sun. 8am-7pm downtown. **Rent-A-Wreck,** 112 5th Ave, SE (287-9703). Cars start at $30 per day, 200km free, 13¢ each additional km. $5 per day discount to HI members. Under 25 surcharge $16 per day. Open Mon.-Fri. 8am-6pm, Sat.-Sun. 9am-5pm.
Bike Rental: Sports Rent, 9250 Macleod Trail (252-2055). $17 per day.
Help Lines: Crisis Line: 266-1605. **Sexual Assault Centre:** 237-5888. Open daily 9:30am-5pm. **Gay Lines Calgary:** (234-8973). Open Mon.-Fri. 10am-10pm, Sat.-Sun. 10am-5pm.
Post Office: 220 4th Ave. SE (292-5512). Open Mon.-Fri. 8am-5:45pm. **Postal Code:** T2P 180.
Area Code: 403.

Calgary is divided into quadrants: **Centre Street** is the east-west divide; the **Bow River** divides the north and south sections. The rest is simple: avenues run east-west, streets run north-south. Pay careful attention to the quadrant distinctions (NE, NW, SE, SW) at the end of each address.

ACCOMMODATIONS AND FOOD

Cheap lodging in Calgary is rare only when packs of tourists Stampede into the city's hotels. Contact the **B&B Association** of Calgary (531-0065) for info on this type of lodging. Prices for singles begin around $30, doubles around $45. The **Calgary International Hostel (HI-C),** 520 7th Ave. SE (269-8239), is conveniently located several blocks east of downtown with access to the 3rd St. SE C-Train station and public buses. Facilities include snack bar, meeting rooms, barbecue, laundry, and a cycle workshop. Make reservations for the Stampede *way* in advance. (Wheelchair accessible. Open 24 hrs., but the front desk closes at midnight. $13, nonmembers $18.) The **University of Calgary,** in the NW quadrant, out of the way, but easily accessible via bus #9 or the C-Train. U of C was the Olympic Village home to 1988 competitors and offers clean, inexpensive rooms. Booking for all rooms through **Kananaskis Hall,** 3330 24th Ave. (220-3203), a 12-min. walk from the University C-Train stop (open 24 hrs.). Rooms available May-Aug. only. (22 rooms are first-come, first-served for those with student ID: singles $21, doubles $31.50. Advance reserved rooms are often booked solid: singles $30, doubles $38.) **St. Regis Hotel,** 124 7th Ave. SE (262-4641) offers comfortable rooms (singles $37, with TV $40).

Ethnic and cafe-style dining spots line the **Stephen Avenue Mall,** 8th Ave. S between 1st St. SE and 3rd St. SW. Good, reasonably-priced food is also readily available in the **"+15" Skyway System** (look for the blue and white "+15" signs on street level). If you're at the University, the **MacEwen Student Centre** has a food court on the 2nd floor with every kind of cheap, quick food imaginable. Fresh fruits, vegetables, seafood, and baked goods grace the upscale **Eau Claire Market** (264-6450), on 3rd St. SW near Prince's Island Park. **4th Street Rose,** 2116 4th St. SW (228-5377), is a fashionable restaurant on the outskirts of town. The house specialty is the "pro-size" Caesar Salad ($4.50), served in a large Mason jar. (Open Mon.-Thurs. 11am-1am, Fri. 11am-2am, Sat. 10am-2am, Sun. 10am-midnight.)

SIGHTS AND THE STAMPEDE

Don't just gaze at the **Calgary Tower,** 101 9th Ave. SW (266-7171); ride an elevator to the top for a spectacular view of the Rockies ($5, seniors $3, ages 13-18 $3.25, ages 3-12 $2). The **Glenbow Museum,** 130 9th Ave. SE (268-4100), is just across the street. From rocks and minerals to Native American lifestyles to the art of Asia to the history of the Canadian West, the Glenbow has it all. (Open Tues.-Sun. 10am-6pm. $4.50, seniors, students and children $3; under 7 free; free on Sat.) Five blocks down 8th Ave. to the west and about 50 ft. straight up are the **Devonian Gardens,** a cool, quiet oasis in an often hot and noisy city (open daily 9am-9pm, free).

Prince's Island Park can be reached by footbridges from either side of the Bow River. Many evenings in summer at 7:30pm a local college puts on free Shakespeare plays in the park. Calgary's other island park, **St. George's Island,** is accessible by the river walkway to the east and is home to the marvelous **Calgary Zoo** (232-9300). No matter how strongly you might disapprove of caging wild animals, you'll be impressed by the habitats's authenticity, the variety of animals, and how cute a baby hippo can be. (Gates open in summer 9am-6:30pm; winter 9am-4pm; grounds open in summer until 8:30pm; winter until 5:30pm. $7.50, seniors $4.75, children $3.75. Seniors $2 on Tues. Refund if you leave within ½ hr. of arriving.) The **Energeum,** 640 5th Ave. SW (297-4293), is Calgary's shrine to oil (open Mon.-Fri. 10:30am-4:30pm, June-Aug. also open Sun.; always free).

Stampede lovers join Calgarians in their "Greatest Outdoor Show on Earth." The Stampede draws millions from across the province, the country, and the world to don ten-gallon hats and yell "yahoo" in the least likely of circumstances. The Stampede takes place July 7-16 in 1995 and July 5-14 in 1996. Make the trip out to **Stampede Park,** southeast of downtown, for a glimpse of steer wrestling, bull riding, and the famous chuckwagon races. For information and ticket order forms, contact the **Calgary Exhibition and Stampede,** Box 1860, Station M, Calgary T2P 2L8 (800-661-1260; 261-0101 in Calgary; tickets are $16-42; inquire about rush tickets, available for $8; youth $7, seniors and children $4.)

■■■ HEAD-SMASHED-IN BUFFALO JUMP

Coveted as a source of fresh meat, sustenance, tools, and shelter, the buffalo was the victim of one of history's most innovative forms of mass slaughter: the buffalo jump. For 0ver 5500 years, Native Americans in Southern Alberta maneuvered the herd into position, while a few extremely brave young men, disguised in coyote skins among the buffalo, would spook hundreds of nearly-blind bison into a fatal stampede over a 10m cliff. Usually highly successful, though occasionally grotesquely fatal, this created an instant all-you-can-eat-or-use buffet at the bottom of the cliff. The area earned its name 150 years ago in memory of a young thrill-seeker who was crushed against the cliff by a pile of buffalo as he watched the event from the base.

Although UNESCO will fine you $50,000 if you forage for souvenirs in the 10m-deep beds of bone, you can learn about buffalo jumps and local Native culture at the **Interpretive Centre** (553-2731), a $10-million, 7-story facility built into the cliff itself. 2km of walking trails lead to the top of the cliff and the kill site below.

■■■ BANFF NATIONAL PARK

Banff is Canada's best-loved and best-known natural preserve. It offers 2543 sq. mi. (6600 sq. km) of peaks and canyons, white foaming rapids, brilliant turquoise lakes, dense forests, and open meadows. Yet it was not simple love of natural beauty that motivated Prime Minister Sir John MacDonald to establish Canada's first national park in 1885. Rather, officers of the Canadian Pacific Railroad convinced him of Banff's potential for "large pecuniary advantage," and were quick to add, "since we can't export the scenery, we shall have to import the tourists."

PRACTICAL INFORMATION AND ORIENTATION

Emergency: Banff Warden Office (762-4506), **Lake Louise Warden Office** (522-3866). Open 24 hrs. **Police:** (762-2226), on Railway St. by the train depot. **Visitors Information: Banff Information Centre,** 224 Banff Ave. (762-1550). Includes **Chamber of Commerce** (762-8421) and **Canadian Parks Service** (762-4256). Open daily 8am-8pm; Oct.-May 9am-5pm. **Lake Louise Information**

Centre (522-3833). Open mid-May-mid-June daily 10am-6pm; mid-June-Aug. 8am-8pm; Sept.-Oct. 10am-6pm; winter 9am-5pm.

Greyhound, 100 Gopher St. (762-6767). From the Brewster terminal. To: Lake Louise (5 per day, $7), Calgary (6 per day, $15), Vancouver (5 per day, $96).

Brewster Transportation, 100 Gopher St. (762-6767), near the train depot. Monopoly on tours of the area; runs 1 express daily to Jasper ($37). Does not honor Greyhound Ameripasses. Depot open daily 7:30am-10pm.

Post Office: 204 Buffalo St. (762-2586). Open Mon.-Fri. 9am-5:30pm. **Postal Code:** T0L 0C0.

Area Code: 403.

Banff National Park hugs the Alberta-British Columbia border, 120km west of Calgary. The **Trans-Canada Hwy.** (Hwy. 1) runs east-west through the park; **Icefields Parkway** (Hwy. 93) connects Banff to Jasper National Park in the north. Greyhound links the park to major points in Alberta and British Columbia. Civilization centers around the towns of Banff and **Lake Louise,** 55km northwest on Hwy. 1.

ACCOMMODATIONS, CAMPING, AND FOOD

Finding a cheap place to stay is easy in Banff. Fifteen residents of the townsite offer rooms in their own homes, often at reasonable rates, especially in the off-season. Check the list in the back of the *Banff and Lake Louise Official Visitor's Guide,* available free at the information center. There's a chain of hostels stretching from Calgary to Jasper, anchored by the ones at Banff and Lake Louise. The **Pika Shuttle** (800-363-0096) offers transport among these hostels. To reserve a shuttle spot, you must have a reservation at your destination hostel. Shuttle rates vary from $5 to $51.

Banff International Hostel (HI-C), Box 1358, Banff T0L 0C0 (762-4122 or 800-363-0096), 3km from Banff townsite on Tunnel Mountain Rd. BIH has the look and setting of a ski lodge. Clean quads with 2-4 bunk beds. Cafeteria, laundry facilities, TVs, hot showers. Wheelchair-accessible. Accommodates 154. Open all day. No curfew; front desk closes at midnight. $16, nonmembers $21. Linen $1.

Castle Mountain Hostel (HI-C), on Hwy. 1A, 1.5km east of the junction of Hwy. 1 and Hwy. 93 between Banff and Lake Louise. Accommodates 36. Call Banff International Hostel (see above) for reservations.$10, nonmembers $16.

Lake Louise International Hostel (HI-C), Village Rd. (522-2200 or 800-363-0096), ½km from Samson Mall in Lake Louise townsite. Accommodates 100. Cafeteria, full-service kitchen, hot showers. Wheelchair-accessible. $16, nonmembers $24. Private rooms $21.50, nonmembers $28.

Mosquito Creek Hostel (HI-C), 103km south of the Icefield Centre and 26km north of Lake Louise. Close to Icefield Centre. Accommodates 38. Fireplace, sauna, full-service kitchen. $10, nonmembers $15. Call BIH for reservations.

Rampart Creek Hostel (HI-C), 34km south of the Icefield Centre. Accommodates 30 in rustic cabins. Full-service kitchen, wood-heated bathtub. $9, nonmembers $14. Call BIH for reservations.

Hilda Creek Hostel (HI-C), 8.5km south of the Icefield Centre on the Icefields Parkway. Full-service kitchen. Accommodates 21. Excellent hiking and skiing nearby at Parker's Ridge. $8, nonmembers $13. Call BIH for reservations.

None of the park's popular camping sites accepts reservations, so arrive early. Many campgrounds reserve sites for bicyclists and hikers; inquire at the office. Rates range from $7.25 to $13. Park facilities include (listed from north to south): **Waterfowl** (116 sites), **Lake Louise** (220 sites), **Protection Mountain** (89 sites), **Johnston Canyon** (132 sites), **Two Jack Main** (381 sites) and **Tunnel Mountain Village** (620 sites). Each site holds a maximum of two tents and six people.

Restaurants in Banff generally serve expensive, mediocre food. Luckily, the Banff **(Cafe Aspenglow)** and Lake Louise **(Bill Peyto's Cafe)** International Hostels serve affordable, wholesome meals for $3 to $7. Shop at **Safeway** (762-5378), at Marten and Elk St., just off Banff Ave. (open daily 8am-10pm; winter 9am-9pm). If you're 18, some of the bars offer daily specials at reasonable prices.

CANADA

OUTDOORS

Hike to the **backcountry** for privacy, beauty, and over 1600km of trails. For info on day and overnight hikes in the Lake Louise and Banff areas, get the free pamphlet *Drives and Walks*, available at the Information Centers. Also available at the centers are free backcountry permits, which are required for overnight stays. Also bring a propane stove; no wood may be chopped in the parks. The Park Information Center has the *Canadian Rockies Trail Guide,* with excellent information and maps.

Two easy but rewarding trails lie within walking distance of the townsite. **Fenland** winds 2km through an area creeping with beaver, muskrat, and waterfowl. Follow Mt. Norquay Rd. out of Banff and look for signs. About 25km out of Banff toward Lake Louise, **Johnston Canyon** offers a popular ½-day hike. The 1.1km hike to the canyon's lower falls and the 2.7km trip to the canyon's upper falls consist mostly of a catwalk along the edge of the canyon. Don't stop here, though; continue along the trail for another 3.1km to seven blue-green cold-water springs known as the **Inkpots.**

Your car will find **Tunnel Mountain Drive** and **Vermilion Lakes** particularly scenic places to cough fumes into the clear air. Turn right onto Tunnel Mountain Rd. to see the **hoodoos,** long, finger-like projections of limestone once part of the cliff wall and thought by Native Americans to encase sentinel spirits.

The **Sulphur Mountain Gondola** (762-5438), next to the Upper Hot Springs pool, lifts you 700m to a view of the Rockies normally reserved for birds and mountain goats (open daily 8:30am-8pm; $8.50, kids 5-11 $3.75, under 5 free.) **Brewster Tours** (762-6767) offers an extensive array of bus tours with knowledgeable and entertaining guides. If you don't have a car, these tours may be the only way to see some of the main attractions, such as the Athabasca Glacier and the spiral railroad tunnel. (One way $60, 9½-hr. round-trip $83. Purchase tickets at the bus depot.) Taking a **gondola** to the top of a peak is an expensive way to see the park, but it saves your legs for hiking at the summit.

The **Sulphur Mountain Gondola** (762-5438), next to the Upper Hot Springs pool, lifts you 700m to a view of the Rockies normally reserved for birds and mountain goats. You can hike all the way back down on a 6-km trail that deposits you right back at the parking lot (open daily 8:30am-8pm. Fare $8.50, ages 5-11 $4, under 5 free.) The **Summit Restaurant** (Canada's highest), perched atop Sulphur Mountain, serves an "Early Morning Lift" breakfast special for $4. Grab a table by the window.

Fishing is legal virtually anywhere you can find water, but you must hold a National Parks fishing permit, available at the Information Centre ($6 for a 7-day permit, $13 for an annual permit). Those who prefer more vigorous water sports can **raft** the white waters of the **Kootenay River.** A particularly good deal is offered by the Banff International Hostel—rafting on the **Kicking Horse River** for $44.

Bicycling is permitted on public roads and highways and on certain trails in the park. *Trail Bicycling in National Parks in Alberta and British Columbia,* available at the Information Centres in Banff and Lake Louise, lists appropriate trails. Horseback riding is available at the **Banff Springs Hotel,** Spray Ave. (daily 9am-5pm; $18 for 1 hr., $28 for 2 hrs., $34 for 3 hrs.; reservations are strongly recommended during the high season).

■■■ JASPER NATIONAL PARK

Before the Icefields Parkway was built, few travelers dared venture north from Banff into the untamed wilderness of Jasper. But those bushwhackers who returned came back with stunning reports, and the completion of the Parkway in 1940 paved the way for everyone to appreciate Jasper's astounding beauty. In contrast to its glitzy southern peer, Jasper townsite manages to maintain the feel of a real small town.

Practical Information RCMP emergency is 852-4848; **ambulance and fire** is 852-3100. **Park Information Centre,** 500 Connaught Dr. (852-6176), has trail

maps and info on all aspects of the park. (Open daily 8am-8pm; early Sept. to late Oct. and late Dec. to mid-May 9am-5pm; mid-May-mid-June 8am-5pm.) **VIA Rail,** 314 Connaught Dr. (800-852-3168), runs to: Vancouver (Mon., Thurs., Sat.; $130), Edmonton (Tues., Fri., Sun.; $76), and Winnipeg (Tues., Fri., Sun.; $207). **Greyhound,** 314 Connaught Dr. (852-3926), in the VIA station, buses to: Edmonton (4 per day; $43), Kamloops ($45), and Vancouver ($84). **Brewster Transportation Tours,** 314 Connaught Dr. (852-3332), in the VIA station, journeys to Banff (daily; 4¼hr.; $37) and Calgary (daily; 8hrs.; $49.50). Jasper's **post office:** 502 Patricia St. (852-3041; open Mon.-Fri. 9am-5pm); **postal code:** T0E 1E0; **area code:** 403.

All of the above addresses are found in **Jasper townsite,** which is near the center of the park, 362km west of Edmonton and 287km northwest of Banff. **Hwy. 16** transports travelers through the northern reaches of the park, while the **Icefields Parkway** (Hwy. 93) connects to Banff National Park in the south. Buses run to the townsite daily from Edmonton, Calgary, Vancouver, and Banff.

Accommodations and Camping Hotels in Jasper are expensive. You may, however, be able to stay cheaply at a **B&B** (singles $20-35, doubles $25-45). If you have a car, head for one of Jasper's hostels (listed below from north to south). Reservations are made through the Edmonton-based **Northern Alberta Hostel Association** (439-3139; fax 433-7781).

> **Maligne Canyon Hostel (HI-C),** (852-3584), 11km east of the townsite on Maligne Canyon Rd. Small, recently renovated cabins on the bank of the Maligne River. Accommodates 24. $9, nonmembers $12. Winter closed Wed.
>
> **Whistlers Mountain Hostel (HI-C),** (852-3215), on Sky Tram Rd., 7km south of the townsite. Closest to the townsite, this is the park's most modern (and crowded) hostel. Accommodates 69. Curfew midnight. $13, nonmembers $18.
>
> **Mt. Edith Cavell Hostel (HI-C),** on Edith Cavell Rd., off Hwy. 93A. The road is closed in winter, but the hostel welcomes anyone willing to ski 11km from Hwy. 93A; see reservations number above. Accommodates 32. $8, nonmembers $12. Open mid-June to early Oct., "key system" in winter.
>
> **Athabasca Falls Hostel (HI-C),** on Hwy. 93 (852-5959), 30km south of Jasper townsite, 500m from Athabasca Falls. Huge dining/recreation room with wood-burning stove. Accommodates 40. $9, nonmembers $14. Closed Tues. in winter.
>
> **Beauty Creek Hostel (HI-C),** on Hwy. 93, 78km south of Jasper townsite. Next to the stunning Sunwapta River. Accommodates 24. "Key system" in winter (groups only). $8, nonmembers $12. Open May-mid-Sept. Thurs.-Tues.

For camping updates, tune to **1450 AM** near Jasper Townsite. The park has sites at 10 campgrounds, including (north to south): **Pocahontas** (140 sites), **Snaring River** (56 sites), **Whistlers** (781 sites), **Wapiti** (366 sites), **Wabasso** (238 sites), **Columbia Icefield** (33 sites), and **Wilcox Creek** (46 sites). Sites from $7.25-17.50.

Food For grocery supplies at any time of night or day, stop at **Wink's Food Store,** 617 Patricia St. (852-4223), or **Super A Foods,** 601 Patricia St. For bulk grains, nuts, and dried fruits, try **Nutter's,** 622 Patricia St. (852-5844). They also sell deli meats, canned goods, and freshly ground coffee. (Open Mon.-Sat. 9am-10pm, Sun. 10am-8pm.) **Mountain Foods and Cafe,** 606 Connaught Dr. (852-4050), has both hot and cold sandwiches ($3), soups, and desserts (open daily 8am-10pm). **Smitty's,** 109 Miette Ave. (852-3111) is a diner with all-day breakfast (open summer 6:30am-10:30pm; winter 6:30am-6:45pm).

Outdoors An extensive network of trails connects most of Jasper, many starting at the townsite. Information Centres distribute *Day Hikes in Jasper National Park* (free) and a summary of longer hikes. **Mt. Edith Cavell** will shake you to the bone with the thunderous roar of avalanches off the Angel Glacier. Take the 1.6km loop trail Path of the Glacier to the top or the 8km hike through **Cavell Meadows.** Edith rears her enormous head 30km south of the townsite on Mt. Edith Cavell Rd.

CANADA

Maligne Lake, the largest glacier-fed lake in the Canadian Rockies, is located 50km southeast of the townsite at the end of Maligne Lake Rd. Farther north in the valley and 30km east of the townsite, the Maligne River flows into **Medicine Lake.** The water escapes underground through tunnels re-emerging 16km downstream in the **Maligne Canyon,** 11km east of the townsite on Maligne Canyon Rd. This is the longest known underground river in North America. **Whitewater Rafting (Jasper) Ltd.** (852-7238) offers several rafting trips (from $35; 2-hr. trip down the Maligne River $45). Register by phone or stop at the Esso station in the townsite.

Trout abound in Jasper's spectacular lakes during the month of May—but so do anglers. **Beaver Lake,** however, located about 1km from the main road at the tip of Medicine Lake, is never crowded, and even novice fisherfolk can hook themselves a dinner. Rent equipment at **Currie's,** in **The Sports Shop** at 416 Connaught Dr. (852-5650; rod, reel, and line $10; one-day boat rental $25, $18 if rented after 2pm).

Three-hour **guided horseback rides** at Maligne Lake cost $45, $30 at the Jasper Park Lodge (852-5794). Guided rides at Pyramid Lake are $17 per hour (852-3562). The saddle-sore can revive at **Miette Hot Springs** (866-3939), off Hwy. 16 along the clearly marked, 15km Miette Hotsprings Rd. Intrepid hikers should attempt the 11km **Mystery Lake Trail,** leading uphill from the pools.

■ British Columbia

Larger in area than California, Oregon, and Washington combined, British Columbia attracts so many visitors that tourism has become the province's second largest industry after logging. Although skiing is excellent year-round, most tourists arrive in summer, flocking to Vancouver and Victoria, and the pristine lakes and beaches of the hot Okanagan Valley.

As you head north, clouds begin to replace the crowds. Temperate BC receives even more rain than the American Northwest, and little snow. Thick forests, low mountains, and occasional patches of high desert are interrupted only by such supply and transit centers as Prince George and Prince Rupert. Farther north, even these outposts of civilization defer to thick spruce forests. BC's extensive and accessible park system allows for an affordable escape from urbandom.

PRACTICAL INFORMATION

Capital: Victoria.
Visitors Information: Call 800-663-6000 or write the **Ministry of Tourism and Provincial Secretary,** Parliament Bldgs., Victoria V8V 1X4 (604-387-1642). **Parks Canada,** 220 4th Ave. SE, P.O. Box 2989, Station M, Calgary, AB T2P 3H8.
Time Zone: Pacific and Mountain. **Postal Abbreviation:** BC
Drinking Age: 19.

For even more thorough coverage of British Columbia, refer to *Let's Go: Alaska & The Pacific Northwest,* carried by reputable booksellers worldwide.

■ ■ ■ VANCOUVER

Canada's third-largest city will thrill even the most jaded metropolis-hopping traveler. Vancouver has a seamless public transit system, spotless sidewalks, and good safety record rare in a city this size. A multi-ethnic metropolis, Vancouver is Canada's gateway to the Pacific, hosting scores of immigrants from China, Hong Kong, and the Far East. With nature walks among 1000-year-old virgin timber, wind-surfing, and the most technologically advanced movie theater in the world all downtown, Vancouver offers an astounding range of things to do.

British Columbia and the Yukon Territory

NATIONAL PARKS
1 Banff
2 Glacier
3 Jasper
4 Kluane
5 Kootenay
6 Mt. Revelstoke
7 Pacific Rim
8 Yoho

PROVINCIAL PARKS
9 Atlin
10 Garibaldi
11 Kwadacha Wilderness
12 Mt. Edziza
13 Mt. Robson
14 Muncho Lake
15 Spatsizi Plateau Wilderness
16 Stone Mountain
17 Strathcona
18 Tweedsmuir
19 Wells Gray
20 Willmore Wilderness

ALASKA

Beaufort Sea

Inuvik

Fort Mcpherson

Arctic Red River

Dawson City

YUKON TERRITORY

Carmacks

Ross River

Haines Junction

Whitehorse

Carcross

Johnson's Crossing

Skagway

Haines

Watson Lake

Juneau

NORTHWEST TERRITORIES

Alaska Hwy.

Cassiar Highway

Fort Nelson

Meziadin Jct.

BRITISH COLUMBIA

Dawson Creek

ALBERTA

Masset

Port Clements

Tlell

Queen Charlotte

Sandspit

QUEEN CHARLOTTE ISLANDS

Prince Rupert

Prince George

Edmonton

Barkerville

Quesnel

CANADA

PACIFIC OCEAN

Port Hardy

Williams Lake

Cariboo Highway

Cache Creek

Revelstoke

Vancouver Island

Garabaldi

Lytton
Yale

Salmon Arm

Penticton

0   150 miles
0   150 kilometers

N

Nanaimo

Victoria

Hope

Vancouver

WASHINGTON

PRACTICAL INFORMATION

Emergency: 911.

Visitors Information: Travel Infocentre, 1055 Dunsmuir St. (683-2000), near Burrard St., in the West End. Open daily 8am-6pm. **Parks and Recreation Board,** 2099 Beach Ave. (681-1141). Open Mon.-Fri. 8:30am-4:30pm.

Airport: Vancouver International, on Sea Island, 11km south of the city center. To reach downtown from the airport, take BC bus #100 to the intersection of Granville and 70th Ave. Transfer there to bus #20, which arrives downtown heading north on the Granville Mall. The private **Airport Express** (273-9023) bus leaves from airport level #2 and heads for downtown hotels and the Greyhound station (6am-midnight, 4 per hr., $8.25 per person).

VIA Rail, 1150 Station St. (800-561-8630 or 669-3050), at Main St. Sky Train stop. *See Mileage Chart.*

Greyhound, 1150 Station St. (662-3222), in the VIA Rail, see below. Service to the south and across Canada. *See Mileage Chart.* Open daily 4am-10pm.

BC Transit Information Centre, 261-5100. Fare $1.50, exact change. BC Transit subdivides the city into three concentric zones for fare purposes. You can ride in BC Transit's central zone for two hours for $1.50 (seniors and ages 5-11 80¢) at all times. During peak hours (6:30-9:30am and 3-6:30pm), it costs $2 (seniors and ages 5-11 $1) to travel between two zones, and $2.75 to travel through three zones. During off-peak hours, passengers pay only the one-zone price. **Day-passes** are $4.50, and transfers are free. Single fares, passes, and transfers are also good for the **SeaBus** (running from the Granville Waterfront Station, at the foot of Granville St. in downtown Vancouver, to the Lonsdale Quay at the foot of Lonsdale Ave. in North Vancouver) and **SkyTrain** (running southeast from downtown to New Westminster).

Taxis: Yellow Cab, 681-3311. **Vancouver Taxi,** 255-5111. Both 24 hrs.

Car Rental: Rent-A-Wreck, 180 W. Georgia St. (688-0001). Also 340 W. 4th at Manitoba. From $30 a day; 300km free, 10¢ per added km. Must be 19 with credit card. Open Mon.-Fri. 7am-7pm, Sat. 8am-5pm, Sun. 8am-5pm.

Bike Rental: Bayshore, 745 Denman St. (689-5071). Good bikes $5.60 per hr., $20 per 12 hrs., $25 per day. Open May-Sept. daily 9am-9pm. Winter hours vary.

Help Lines: Vancouver Crisis Center, 733-4111. 24 hrs. **Rape Crisis Center,** 255-6344. 24 hrs. **Gay and Lesbian Switchboard,** 684-6869. Open daily 7-10pm.

Post Office: Main branch, 349 W Georgia St. (662-5725). Open Mon.-Fri. 8am-5:30pm. **Postal Code:** V6B 3P7.

Area Code: 604.

Vancouver looks like a hand with the fingers together pointing west, and the thumb to the north. South of the mitten flows the Fraser River. Beyond the fingertips lies the Georgia Strait. Downtown is on the thumb. At the thumb's tip lie the residential **West End** and **Stanley Park.** Burrard Inlet separates the downtown from North Vancouver; the bridges over False Creek (the space between the thumb and the rest of the hand) link downtown with **Kitsilano** ("Kits"), **Fairview, Mount Pleasant,** and the rest of the city. East of downtown, where the thumb is attached, lie **Gastown** and **Chinatown.** The **airport** lies south, at the pinkie-tip; the University of British Columbia lies at the tip of the index finger (**Point Grey**). Kitsilano and Point Grey are separated by north-south Alma Ave., Hwy. 99, and the Trans-Canada Hwy. Most of the city's attractions are concentrated on the thumb peninsula and in the fingers.

ACCOMMODATIONS AND CAMPING

Greater Vancouver offers many B&Bs. Rates average about $45 to $60 for singles and $55 to $75 for doubles. The visitors bureau has a list of B&Bs, or contact **Town and Country Bed and Breakfast** (731-5942) or **Best Canadian** (738-7207).

Vancouver International Hostel (HI-C), 1515 Discovery St. (224-3208), in Jericho Beach Park. Turn north off 4th Ave., following the signs for Marine Dr., or take bus #4 from Granville St. downtown. 285 beds in dorm rooms and 8 family rooms. Kitchen, TV room, laundry. In summer 5-day max. stay. Registration

7:30am-midnight. Bedding $1.50. $14.50, nonmembers $18.50. Reserve 2 weeks ahead during summer. Rent top-quality mountain bikes for $20 per day.

University of British Columbia Conference Centre, 5959 Student Union Mall, Walter Gage Residence (822-1010), at the end of Vancouver's largest peninsula. Take bus #4 or 10 from the Granville Mall. Dorm-style rooms available May-Aug. Check-in after 2pm. Dorm-style singles with shared bath $19, doubles $38; B&B-style singles with shared bath $22, doubles $44; private singles $29, doubles $68.

Paul's Guest House, 345 W. 14th Ave. (872-4753), at Alberta. Take bus #15. Shared baths. Complimentary full breakfast. If Paul's is booked, they can arrange your stay at one of these other B&Bs. Check-in before 11pm. Call ahead for reservations. Singles $40. Doubles $50-60. Rates $5 lower in winter.

Vincent's Backpackers Hostel, 927 Main St. (682-2441), next to the VIA Rail station. Take bus #3 (Main St.) or #8 (Fraser). Not as clean or as structured as the HI-C hostel. Narrow, dark hallways, with exposed pipes. Kitchen, TV, laundry. Mountain bikes $5 per day. Office open 8am-midnight. Shared rooms $10. Singles with shared bath $20. Doubles with shared bath $25. Weekly: shared rooms $60, singles $100, doubles $130. Pay before 10am of first morning for 20% discount.

Richmond RV Park, 6200 River Rd. (270-7878), near Holly Bridge in Richmond. Take Hwy. 99 to Westminster Hwy., then follow the signs. Sites $15, with hookup $19-21. Open April-Oct.

Hazelmere RV Park and Campground, 18843 8th Ave. (538-1167), in Surrey. Off Hwy. 99A, head east on 8th Ave. Showers 50¢. Sites for 1-2 people $14, with hookups $17; add $2 for each additional person.

FOOD

The city's best eateries are the ethnic and natural-foods restaurants. Vancouver's **Chinatown** is second in size only to San Francisco's in North America, and the Indian areas along Main, Fraser, and 49th St. serve up spicy dishes. The **Granville Island Market,** southwest of downtown under the Granville Bridge, off W. 4th Ave. across False Creek, offers countless produce stands. Take bus #50 from Granville St. downtown. (Open daily 9am-6pm; Labor Day-Victoria Day Tues.-Sun. 9am-6pm.)

The Green Door, 111 E. Pender St. (685-4194). Follow the alley off Columbia St. to find the hidden entrance. Huge portions of slightly greasy Chinese ($8-10). No liquor license. Open daily noon-10pm.

Nuff-Nice-Ness, 1861 Commercial Dr. (255-4211), at 3rd. Vegetable and meat patties ($1.87 each). Jerk chicken with salad and rice $6.25. Daily specials offered in the late afternoon for $5. Open Mon.-Fri. 11am-8pm, Sat. noon-8pm, Sun. 1-6pm.

Isadora's Cooperative Restaurant, 1540 Old Bridge Rd. (681-8816). This natural foods restaurant sends its profits to community service organizations. Sandwiches $7, dinner entrees $10-13. Open Mon.-Thurs. 7:30am-9pm, Fri.-Sun. 9am-9pm.

The Naam, 2724 W. 4th Ave. (738-7151), at Stephens. Take bus #4 or 7 from Granville. Tofu-nut-beet burgers ($5.50), spinach enchiladas ($8.95), and salad bar ($1.25 per 100g). Live music nightly from 7-10pm. Open 24 hrs.

Nirvana, 2313 Main St. (876-2911), at 7th. Take bus #8, 3, or 9. Spiritual Indian cuisine. Find or lose yourself in the chicken curry ($7.25) or vegetable *biryani* ($8.75). Open Mon.-Fri. 11:30am-11pm, Sat.-Sun. noon-11pm.

SIGHTS AND ACTIVITIES

The remaining landmark of the Expo '86 World's Fair is a 17-story, metallic, geodesic sphere which houses **Science World,** 1455 Québec St. (687-7832), at Terminal Ave. The big-screen star is the **Omnimax Theatre,** a 27m sphere that is the largest, most technologically advanced theatre in the world. The Canada Pavilion, now called **Canada Place,** is about ½km away and can be reached by SkyTrain from the main Expo site. The shops are expensive, but the promenades are terrific vantage points for gawking at one of the 200 luxury liners that dock here annually. At 8 W. Penter St. is squeezed the **world's skinniest building**.

Newly renovated, the **Lookout!** at 555 W. Hastings St. (689-0421), offers fantastic 360° views of the city! Tickets are expensive! But they're good for the whole day!

CANADA

($6!, seniors $5!, students $4!; open daily 8:30am-10:30pm, in winter 8:30am-9pm; 50% off with HI membership or receipt from the Vancouver International Hostel)!

Gastown, named for "Gassy Jack" Deighton, the con man who opened Vancouver's first saloon, is a tourist snare disguised as a restored turn-of-the-century neighborhood. Listen for the continent's only steam-powered clock on the corner of Cambie and Water St.—it whistles every 15 min. **Chinatown,** replete with restaurants and shops, also lies within walking distance of downtown, but you can take bus #22 on Burrard St. northbound to Pender St. at Carrall St. and return by bus #22 westbound along Pender St.

One of the city's most alluring sites is **Stanley Park,** on the western end of the city-center peninsula (take bus #19). Surrounded by a **seawall promenade,** this thickly wooded park is crisscrossed with cycling and hiking trails. Within the park's boundaries lie various restaurants, tennis courts, the **Malkin Bowl** (an outdoor theater), and equipped beaches. Cavort alongside beluga whales at the **Vancouver Aquarium** (682-1118), on the eastern side of the park near the entrance (open daily 9:30am-8pm; $10, seniors and students $8.50, under 12 $6.50).

During the summer, a tiny **ferry** (684-7781) carries passengers from the Aquatic Centre across False Creek to **Vanier** (van-YAY) **Park** and its museum complex. (Ferries daily, every 15 min. 10am-8pm. Fare $1.25, youth 50¢.) Another **ferry** runs from the Maritime Museum in Vanier Park to **Granville Island** ($2.50). Vanier Park can also be reached by bus #22, heading south on Burrard St. from downtown. Once you reach the park, visit the circular **Vancouver Museum,** 1100 Chestnut St. (736-4431), which displays artifacts from Native Canadian and American cultures in the Pacific Northwest and several rotating exhibits. (Open daily 10am-9pm, Oct.-April Tues.-Sun. 10am-5pm. $5, students, seniors, and kids under 18 $2.50, families $10.)

For a large city, Vancouver has remarkably clean beaches. Follow the western side of the Stanley Park seawall south to **Sunset Beach Park** (738-8535). At the southern end of Sunset Beach is the **Aquatic Centre,** 1050 Beach Ave. (665-3424), a public facility with a 50m indoor saltwater pool, sauna, gymnasium, and diving tank. (Open Mon.-Thurs. 7am-10pm, Sat. 8am-9pm, Sun. 11am-9pm; pool opens Mon.-Thurs. at 7am. Gym use $3.50, pool use $3.)

Kitsilano Beach (731-0011), known to residents of Vancouver as "Kits," on the other side of Arbutus St. from Vanier, is a local favorite. Its heated outdoor saltwater pool has lockers and a snack bar. (Pool open June.-Sept. Mon.-Fri. 7am-9pm, Sat.-Sun. 10am-8:30pm. $3.25, seniors $1.60, children $2.10.)

Students hang at **Jericho Beach,** to the west, which tends to be less heavily used than Kits Beach. Jericho has free showers. North Marine Dr. runs along the beach, and a great cycling path at the edge of the road leads to the westernmost edge of the **University of British Columbia (UBC)** campus. Bike and hiking trails cut through the campus and crop its edges. From the UBC entrance, several marked trails lead down to the unsupervised, inauspicious **Wreck Beach.** The high point of a campus visit is the university's **Museum of Anthropology,** 6393 NW Marine Dr. (822-3825 for a recording, 822-5087 for an operator). To reach the campus, take bus #4 or #10 from Granville. Be sure to find the renowned work "The Raven and the First Man," by Bill Reid, an artistic allusion to the Haida creation myth. (Open Tues. 11am-9pm, Mon. and Wed.-Sun. 11am-5pm. Sept.-June closed Mondays. $5, seniors and students $2.50, families $12, under 6 free. Tues. after 5pm free.)

With pseudo-European delicatessens and shops, the **Robsonstrasse** shopping district, on Robson St. between Howe and Broughton St., tempts tourists to throw around their money under kaleidoscopic awnings. The recently renovated **Pacific Centre,** 700 W Georgia St., is near the Granville SkyTrain station. For more reasonable prices and "idiosyncratic" offerings, stroll down Commercial Dr., or browse through the numerous boutiques lining 4th Ave. and Broadway. **Granville Mall,** on Granville Ave. between Smithe and Hastings St., is Vancouver's pedestrian and bus mall. From Hastings St. to the Orpheum Theatre, most shops and restaurants on the mall cater to young professionals and business executives on their power-lunch hours. A few blocks to the west, the **Harbour Centre,** 555 W Hastings St., flaunts a mall with distinctly non-budget restaurants, and a fantastic **skylift** providing uplifting views of the cityscape. If you are dying to fill your matching luggage set with chic purchases, head to the ritziest mall west of Long Island: the **Park Royal Shopping Centre** on Marine Dr. in West Vancouver. Take bus #250, 251, or 252 on Georgia St. downtown.

ENTERTAINMENT AND NIGHTLIFE

To keep abreast of the entertainment and nightlife, pick up a copy of the weekly *Georgia Straight* or the new monthly *AF Magazine,* both free at newsstands and record stores. The **Vancouver Symphony Orchestra** (VSO, 684-9100) plays in the refurbished **Orpheum Theater,** 884 Granville St. (280-4444; ticketline 280-3311). The 52-year-old **Vancouver Bach Choir** (921-8012) sometimes performs with the VSO in the Orpheum.

Vancouver theatre is renowned throughout Canada. The **Arts Club Theatre** (687-1644) hosts big-name theatre and musicals, and the **Theatre in the Park** program (687-0174 for ticket information), in Stanley Park's Malkin Bowl, plays a summer season of musical comedy. The annual **Vancouver Shakespeare Festival** (734-0194; June-Aug. in Vanier Park) often needs volunteer ticket-takers and program-sellers, who work for free admission to the critically acclaimed shows. **UBC Summer Stock** (822-2678) puts on four plays in summer at the **Frederick Wood Theatre.**

The famed **Vancouver Folk Music Festival** (879-2931) jams in mid-July in Jericho Park. For three days the best acoustic performers in North America give concerts and workshops. Tickets can be purchased for each day or for the whole weekend. (Tickets $26 per day, $70 per weekend. Prices increase at the gate.) Enjoy 10 days of hot jazz at the annual **Du Maurier International Jazz Festival Vancouver** (682-0706) in the third week of June. Call 682-0706 or write to 435 W. Hastings, Vancouver V6V 1L4 for details. Ask about the free concerts at the Plaza, in Gastown, and on Granville Island. Vancouver's Chinese community celebrates **Chinese New Year** (usually early to mid-Feb.) with fireworks, music, parades, and dragons. All kinds of music is enjoyed in Vancouver's pubs and clubs. Most shut down at 2am.

The Fringe Cafe, 3124 W. Broadway (738-6977), in Kitsilano. Working-class crowd mixes with UBC students. Open daily noon-1am.

The Arts Club Lounge, Granville Island (687-1354). Have a mixed drink ($4.50-6.50) on the terrace overlooking False Creek. Live music (with a $5 cover) Wed., Fri., and Sat. nights. Open Mon.-Sat. 9pm-2am.

Graceland, 1250 Richards St. (688-2648), downtown. House music on Fri. and Sat. nights, reggae on Wed. Open Mon.-Sat. noon-2am, Sun. noon-midnight.

Luv-A-fair, 1275 Seymour St. (685-3288), downtown. Trendy dance space pipes alternative music into the ears of black-clad clubsters. Experiment with the live underground bands Wed. night. Open Mon.-Sat. 9pm-2am, Sun. 9am-midnight.

Celebrities, 1022 Davie St. (689-3180), downtown. Very big, very hot, and very popular with the gay community. Open Mon.-Sat. 9pm-2am, Sun. 9pm-midnight.

■■■ VICTORIA

Set among the rough-hewn logging and fishing towns of Vancouver Island, the capital of British Columbia evinces enough reserve to chill even the Windsors. On warm summer days, Anglophile residents sip their teas on the lawns of Tudor-style homes in the suburbs, while downtown, horse-drawn carriages clatter in the streets.

Practical Information Emergency is 911. **Tourism Victoria,** 336 Government St., (382-2127), on the corner of Wharf St. has the low-down (open daily 9am-9pm; winter daily 9am-5pm). **Pacific Coast Lines (PCL)** and its affiliate, **Island Coach Lines,** 700 Douglas St. at Belleville (385-4411), connect all major points and most minor ones; to: Vancouver (11 per day, $22); Seattle (daily 10am, $28.60). **BC Ferry,** (656-0757 for a recording, 386-3431 for an operator between 7am-10pm), runs between Swartz Bay (Victoria) and Tsawwassen (Vancouver); (20 per day 5:30am-10pm $6.25, bikes $2.50, cars $24.50). **Washington State Ferries,** (381-1551) makes waves from Sidney, BC to Anacortes, WA, via the San Juan Islands: 2 per day in summer, 1 per day in winter. Fares vary by season, so call for exact rates and schedules. Take bus #70 ($1.75) to reach the ferry terminal. **Victoria Regional Transit** (382-6161) provides city bus service, with connections downtown at the corner of Douglas and Yates St. Travel in the single-zone area costs $1.35, multi-zone (north to Sidney and the Butchart Gardens) $2. Daily passes for unlimited single-zone travel are available at the visitors center and 7-11 stores for $4 (over 65 and under 12 $3). Victoria's **post office:** 714 Yates (363-3887; open Mon.-Fri. 8:30am-5pm); **postal code:** V8W 1L0; **area code:** 604.

Ferries and buses connect Victoria to many cities in British Columbia and Washington. The city of Victoria enfolds the Inner Harbour; **Government Street** and **Douglas Street** are the main north-south thoroughfares.

Accommodations, Camping, and Food Victoria Youth Hostel (HI-C), 516 Yates St., (385-4511), at Wharf St. downtown, has 104 beds in the newly remodeled Victoria Heritage Building. (Desk open until 11pm; curfew 2:30am. $14, nonmembers $18.50.) **Cherry Bank Hotel,** 825 Burdett Ave. (385-5380), at Blanchard, is a 90-year-old bed and breakfast (singles from $43, doubles from $51). **McDonald Park** (655-9020), less than 3km south of the Swartz Bay Ferry Terminal, 30km north of downtown on Hwy. 17, offers primitive sites with neither showers nor beach access (30 tent and RV sites, $9.50). **Thetis Lake Campground,** 1938 Trans-Canada Hwy. (478-3845), 10km north of the city center, serves traffic entering Victoria from northern Vancouver Island (sites $15 for 2 people; full hookups $17).

Eugene's, 1280 Broad St. (381-5456), souvlaks vegetarian souvlaki ($3). *Rizogalo* or *bougatsa* is a nice change for breakfast ($2). (Open Mon.-Fri. 8am-8pm, Sat. 10am-8pm.) **Ferris' Oyster and Burger Bar,** 536 Yates St. (360-1824), next to the hostel, has smoked oysters for $2 each along with traditional pub fare and a number of vegetarian options. (Open Mon.-Wed. 8:30am-8pm, Thurs.-Fri. 8:30am-10pm, Sat. 8:30am-11pm. HI members discount.) **Fan Tan Cafe,** 549 Fisgard St. (383-1611), in Chinatown, boasts fantastic food at reasonable prices. Combo plates are $6 (open Mon.-Thurs. 11am-1am, Fri. 11am-2:30am, Sat. 2pm-2:30am, Sun. 2-10pm).

Sights and Nightlife Victoria is a small city; you can wander the **Inner Harbour,** watch the boats come in, and take in many of the city's main attractions, all on foot. The first stop for every visitor should be the **Royal British Columbian Museum,** 675 Belleville St. (387-3014 for a recording, 387-3701 for an operator, 800-661-5411). One of the best museums in Canada, it chronicles the geological, biological, and cultural history of the province, and showcases detailed exhibits on logging, mining, and fishing. (Open daily 9:30am-7pm; Oct.-April 10am-5:30pm. $5; seniors, handicapped, and students with ID or HI card $3; ages 6-18 $2. Free after 5:45pm and Oct.-April on Mon. Hang on to your ticket; it's good for 2 days.) Behind the museum, **Thunderbird Park** is a striking thicket of totems and longhouses.

Across the street from the museum are the imposing **Parliament Buildings,** 501 Belleville St. (387-3046), home of the Provincial government since 1898. The 10-story dome and vestibule are gilded with almost 50 oz. of gold. Free tours leave from the main steps daily 9am to 5pm, every 30 minutes in summer, every hour in winter (open Mon.-Fri. 8:30am-5pm, on weekends for tours only).

South of the Inner Harbour, **Beacon Hill Park** surveys the Strait of Juan de Fuca (take bus #5). East of the Inner Harbour, **Craigdarroch Castle,** 1050 Joan Crescent (592-5323; take bus #11 or 14), was built in 1890 by Robert Dunsmuir, a coal and railroad tycoon, to lure his wife from their native Scotland to Victoria. (Open daily 9am-7pm; winter 10am-4:30pm. $6, students $5, ages 6-12 $2, under 6 $1.)

The stunning **Butchart Gardens,** 800 Benvenuto, 22km north of Victoria (652-5256 for a recording or 652-4422 for an operator Mon.-Fri. 9am-5pm), are a maze of pools and fountains. Take bus #75 from Douglas and View northbound right into the Gardens, or #70 and walk 1km. Motorists should consider approaching Butchart Gardens via the **Scenic Marine Drive,** following the coastline. (Gardens open 9am; call for closing times. Summer $11, ages 13-17 $8, ages 5-12 $3.50; winter $7.50, $5.50, and $2.50. Hang on to your ticket: readmission within 24 hrs. only $1.)

You can get an exhaustive listing of what's where when in the free weekly *Monday Magazine.* For an eclectic mix of music, check out **Harpo's Cabaret,** 15 Bastion Sq. (385-5333), at Wharf St. (open Mon.-Sat. 9pm-2am, Sun. 8pm-midnight; cover $5). **The Forge,** 919 Douglas St. (383-7137), in the Strathcona Hotel, specializes in loud 70s rock (open Tues.-Sat. 8pm-2am). **Rumors,** 1325 Government St. (385-0566), has drinking and dancing for a gay clientele (open Mon.-Sat. 9pm-3am).

■■■ GLACIER NATIONAL PARK

For a $5000 salary bonus and immortality on the map, Major A.B. Rogers discovered a route through the Columbia Mountains which finally allowed Canada to build its first transcontinental railway. Completed in 1885, the railway was a dangerous enterprise; more than 200 lives were lost to avalanches during its first 30 years of operation. Today, **Rogers Pass** lies in the center of Glacier National Park, and 1350 sq. km commemorate the efforts of Rogers and other hardy explorers who bound British Columbia to the rest of Canada.

Practical Information The Trans-Canada Hwy.'s many **scenic turn-offs** offer picnic facilities and historical plaques. For a detailed description of the park's 19 hiking trails, contact the **Park Administration Office** (837-7500), at 3rd and Boyle, west of the park in Revelstoke (open Mon.-Fri. 8:30am-noon, 1pm-4:30pm), or pick up a copy of *Footloose in the Columbias* at the **Rogers Pass Information Centre,** located along the highway in Glacier (open daily 8am-6pm; in winter hours vary). **Park passes** are required if you don't drive straight through ($5 per day, $10 for 4 days, $30 per year, and good in all National Parks). For more info about Glacier National Park, write the Superintendent, P.O. Box 350, Revelstoke, BC V0E 2S0.

Glacier lies right on the Trans-Canada Hwy., 262km west of Calgary and 723km east of Vancouver. **Greyhound** (837-5874) makes four trips daily from Revelstoke to Glacier ($7). In an **emergency,** call the **Park Warden Office** (837-6274; open daily 7am-11pm; winter daily 24 hrs.). Glacier's **area code:** 604.

Accommodations, Camping, and Food There are two campgrounds in Glacier: **Illecillewaet** (ill-uh-SILL-uh-watt) and **Loop Brook.** Both offer flush toilets, kitchen shelters with cook stoves, drinking water, and firewood (open mid-June-Sept.; sites for both $10.50). Illecillewaet stays open in winter without plumbing; winter guests must register at the Park Administration Office at Rogers Pass. **Backcountry campers** must pitch their tents at least 5km from the pavement and register with the Administration Office beforehand. For **food,** you'd do well to drop by a supermarket in Golden or Revelstoke before you enter the park.

Outdoors A century after Rogers's discovery, Glacier National Park remains an unspoiled and remote wilderness. The jagged peaks and steep, narrow valleys of the Columbia Range prevent development. One would literally have to move mountains to build here. The Trans-Canada Highway cuts a thin ribbon through the park, affording spectacular views of over 400 glaciers. More than 140km of challenging trails lead away from the highway, inviting rugged mountain men and women to penetrate the near-impenetrable. Try to visit the park in late July or early August, when brilliant explosions of mountain wildflowers offset the deep green of the forests. Glacier receives measurable precipitation every other day in summer, but the clouds of mist that encircle the peaks and blanket the valleys only add to the park's beauty. Unless you're Sir Edmund Hillary, avoid the park in winter, as snowfalls and the constant threat of avalanches often restrict travel to the Trans-Canada Hwy.

CANADA

Eight popular **hiking trails** begin at the Illecillewaet campground, 3.4km west of Rogers Pass. The relaxing, 1km **Meeting of the Waters** trail leads to the confluence of the Illecillewaet and Asulkan Rivers. The 4.2-km **Avalanche Crest** trail offers spectacular views of Rogers Pass, the Hermit Range, and the Illecillewaet River Valley; the treeless slopes below the crest testify to the destructive power of winter snowslides. From early July to late August, the Information Centre runs daily **interpretive hikes** through the park beginning at 9am. Come prepared for one of these four- to six-hour tours with a picnic lunch, a rain jacket, and a sturdy pair of walking shoes. Regulations prohibit biking on the trails in Glacier.

■■■ PRINCE RUPERT

Most visitors come to Prince Rupert either for fishing or ferries. An afternoon in a guided fishing boat costs upwards of $100; pass the hours before your ship comes in browsing the 15 downtown blocks. The **Travel Infocentre,** 1st Ave. and McBride St. (624-5637), has maps for a self-guided tour, including the Infocentre's free museum, a cornucopia of totem poles, the manicured Sunken Gardens, and a Native Canadian **carving shed** (open May 15-Labor Day daily 9am-9pm; winter Mon.-Sat. 10am-5pm). The only major road into town is **Hwy. 16,** or McBride at the city limits, curving left to become 2nd Ave. downtown. **Prince Rupert Bus Service** (624-3343) provides local service downtown Mon.-Sat. (fare $1, seniors 60¢, students 75¢; day pass $2.50, seniors and students $2). The #52 bus runs from 2nd Ave. and 3rd St. to within a five-min. walk of the ferry terminal. Or try **Skeena Taxi,** (624-2185; open 24 hrs.). The **Alaska Marine Highway** (627-1744) runs ferries north from Prince Rupert to Ketchikan (US$38, car US$75), Wrangell (US$56, car US$117), Petersburg (US$68, car US$145), Juneau (US$104, car US$240), and Haines (US$118, car US$273). **BC Ferries** (624-9627), at the end of Hwy. 16, serves the Queen Charlotte Islands (6 per week, $20.75, car $79) and Port Hardy (4 per week; $93.50, car $192). Vehicle reservations required 3 wks. in advance. Ferrygoers may not leave cars parked on the streets of Prince Rupert. Some establishments charge a daily rate for storage; pick up a list at the Infocentre (see above). In an **emergency,** call 911. Prince Rupert's **post office** is at 2nd Ave. and 3rd St. (624-2383; open Mon.-Fri. 8:30am-4:30pm); **postal code:** V8J 3P3; **area code:** 604.

Nearly all of Prince Rupert's hotels are within the six-block area defined by 1st Ave., 3rd Ave., 6th St., and 9th St. Everything fills when the ferries dock, so call a day or two ahead. Few visitors realize that Prince Rupert harbor has the highest concentration of archaeological sites in North America. Large piles of discarded clam shells on nearly every island in the harbor attest to the 10,000-year inhabitance of indigenous peoples and their mollusk-intensive diets. Three-hour **archaeological boat tours** leave from the Infocentre daily. A local expert will take you to **Digby Island;** unfortunately, some of the most interesting petroglyphs are inaccessible to the tour boat, and the tour leaves you staring at your feet too much of the time. (Tours depart June 14-30 daily 12:30pm; July to mid-Sept. 1pm. $20, children $12, under 5 free.)

The grassy hills of **Service Park,** off Fulton St., offer a panoramic view of downtown Prince Rupert and the harbor beyond. **Diana Lake Park,** 16km east of town along Hwy. 16, provides a picnic area set against an enticing lake.

■ Yukon Territory

Native Americans recognized the majesty of this land when they dubbed the Yukon River "Yuchoo," or Big River. Gold-hungry white settlers streamed in at the end of the 19th century, interested in more metallic aspects of the land, and left almost as quickly. Although the Yukon and Northern British Columbia were the first regions of North America to be settled some 20,000 years ago, today they remain largely untouched and inaccessible. With an average of only one person per 15 sq. km, the loneliness of the area is overwhelming—as is its sheer physical beauty, a reward for those willing to deal with unpredictable winter weather and poor road conditions.

> *Let's Go: Alaska & The Pacific Northwest* has golden info on the Yukon.

■■■ WHITEHORSE

Named for the once perilous Whitehorse Rapids (now tamed by a dam) that was said to resemble an entourage of galloping pale mares, Whitehorse marks the first navigable point on the Yukon River. Capital of the Yukon since 1953, Whitehorse now boasts a population of more than 20,000 and is as cosmopolitan as one might expect a city of its size to be—yet it still maintains much of its century-old gold rush architecture, and it serves as a gateway to the surrounding country.

Practical Information The **Whitehorse Visitor Reception Centre,** on the Alaska Hwy. next to the airport (667-2915), has an entire forest's worth of free brochures and maps. (Open mid-May-mid-Sept. daily 8am-8pm.) Or, get info by writing **Tourism Yukon,** P.O. Box 2703, Whitehorse, YT Y1A C26.

Canadian Airlines (668-4466, for reservations 668-3535) soars to: Calgary (2-3 per day, $519); Edmonton (3 per day, $519); Vancouver (3 per day, $448). **Greyhound** runs buses from 2191 2nd Ave. (667-2223) on Tues., Thurs., and Sat. at noon to: Vancouver ($291); Edmonton ($225); Dawson Creek ($155). (Open Mon.-Fri. 8:30am-5:30pm, Sat. 8am-noon, Sun. 5-9am.) **Alaskan Express** also operates from the Greyhound depot (667-2223). Buses run late May-mid-Sept. to: Anchorage (4 per week, US$184); Haines (4 per week, US$79); Fairbanks (4 per week, US$149).

There is no main **post office** in Whitehorse. For general services, go to 211 Main St. (668-5847; open Mon.-Fri. 8am-6pm, Sat. 9am-5pm). For general delivery, head for 3rd and Wood, in the Yukon News Bldg. (668-3824; open Mon.-Sat. 7am-7pm). General Delivery **Postal Code** for last names beginning with the letters A-L is Y1A 3S7; for M-Z it's Y1A 3S8. Whitehorse's **area code:** 403.

Accommodations, Camping, and Food Call the **Northern Network of Bed and Breakfasts** (993-5649), in Dawson City, to reserve a room in a Klondike household. Singles start at $50 and doubles at $60. **High Country Inn (HI-C),** 4051 4th Ave. (667-4471), offers long- and short-term housing. This residence boasts cooking and laundry facilities, good security, and free use of the city pool next door. (Hostel beds (in a shared twin) $18, nonmembers $20. Private singles $50. Doubles $75. Call to reserve a bed.) **Roadside Inn,** 2163 2nd Ave. (667-2594), near shopping malls and Greyhound, has bare-bones accommodations (singles from $40, doubles from $45). Camping in Whitehorse is a problem: there is only one RV campground and one tenting park near the downtown area. **Robert Service Campground,** 1km from town on South Access Rd. on the Yukon River, is convenient with firewood, fire pits, playground, picnic area, drinking water, toilets, metered showers (open late May-early Sept.; gate closed midnight-6am. 40 sites, $14).

No Pop Sandwich Shop, 312 Steele (668-3227), is popular with Whitehorse's small suit-and-tie crowd. You can order a Beltch (BLT and cheese, $4.50). (Open Mon.-Thurs. 8am-9pm, Fri. 8am-10pm, Sat. 10am-8pm, Sun. 10am-3pm.) **Talisman Cafe,** 2112 2nd Ave. (667-2736) delivers good food in a nondescript environment. (Burgers from $5 and breakfasts around $5.50. Open daily 6am-10pm.)

Sights The restored *Klondike,* on South Access Rd. (667-4511), is a dry-docked sternwheeler that recalls the days when the Yukon River was the city's sole artery of survival. Pick up a ticket for a free and fascinating guided tour at the information booth at the parking lot entrance (open June 20-Aug. 13 9am-7:30pm). The **Whitehorse Rapids Fishway** (633-5965), at the end of Nisutlin Drive, 2km southeast of town, allows salmon to bypass the dam and continue upstream in the world's longest salmon migration (open daily mid-June to mid-Sept. 8am-10pm; free). **Miles Canyon** whispers 2km south of town on Miles Canyon Rd. off of South Access Rd. Once the location of the feared Whitehorse rapids, this dammed stretch of the Yukon now swirls silently under the first bridge to span the river's banks. The **MacBride Museum,** 1st Ave. and Wood St. (667-2709), features memorabilia from the early days of the Yukon, including photographs of Whitehorse as a tent city. (Open daily May and Sept. noon-4pm; June and Aug. 10am-6pm; July 9am-6pm. $3.25, seniors and students $2.25, families $7.50.) From June to September, the **Youcon Kat** (668-2927; 668-1252 for tickets) will take you downstream from the dam. Boats leave daily at 1, 4, and 7pm from the pier at 1st and Steele ($15, children $7.50).

■■■ KLUANE NATIONAL PARK

On St. Elias' Day 1741, Vitus Bering, a Danish captain in the Russian service, sighted the mountains of what is now Kluane National Park. "Kluane" (kloo-AH-nee) is a Tutchone Native word, meaning "place of many fish." Kluane is Canadian wilderness at its most rugged, unspoiled, and beautiful. The "Green Belt" along the eastern park boundary, at the foot of the Kluane Range, supports the greatest diversity of plant and animal species in northern Canada. Beyond the Kluane loom the glaciers of the Icefield Range, home to Canada's highest peaks, including the tallest, 19,850-ft. Mt. Logan. The Alaska Highway, near the northeastern boundary of the park, provides generally convenient park access.

Practical Information Pick up plenty of free information at the **Haines Junction Visitor Centre,** on Logan St. in Haines Junction (Canadian Park Service 634-2251; Tourism Yukon 634-2345; open mid-May to mid-Sept. daily 9am-9pm), or at the **Sheep Mountain Visitor Centre,** at Alaska Hwy. Km 1707 (841-5161; open June to mid-Sept. daily 9am-6:30pm). Visitors may also write to Superintendent, Kluane National Park and Preserve, Parks Service, Environment Canada, Haines Junction, YT Y0B 1L0 for information. **Alaska Direct** (800-770-6652, in Whitehorse 668-4833) runs three buses per week from Haines Junction to Anchorage (US$125), Fairbanks (US$100), Whitehorse (US$20), and Skagway (US$55). The **visitor radio** station is FM 96.1. **Emergency numbers** in Haines Junction include: **medical,** 634-2213; **fire,** 634-2222; and **police,** 635-5555 (if no answer, call 1-667-5555). Kluane's **post office:** (634-2706) in Madley's General Store (open Mon., Wed., and Fri. 9-10am and 1-5pm, Tues. 9am-1pm, Thurs. 9am-noon, 1-5pm); **postal code:** Y0B 1L0; **area code:** 403.

Kluane's 22,015 sq. km are bounded by Kluane Game Sanctuary and the Alaska Hwy. to the north, and the Haines Hwy. (Hwy. 3) to the east. The town of **Haines Junction** is at the eastern park boundary, 158km west of Whitehorse.

Camping, Accommodations, and Food Kathleen Lake Campground (634-2251), 27km south of Haines Junction off Haines Rd., is close to good hiking and fishing and features water, flush toilets, fire pits, firewood, and occasional "campfire talks" (sites $7.25; open June-Oct.). The Yukon government runs four campgrounds, all with hand-pumped cold water and pit toilets (sites $8; call Tourism Yukon at 634-2345 for more information): **Pine Lake,** 7km east of Haines Jct. on the Alaska Hwy.; **Congdon Creek,** 85km west of Haines Jct. on the Alaska Hwy.; **Dezadeash Lake,** 50km south of Haines Junction on Haines Rd.; and **Million Dollar Falls,** 90km south of Haines Jct. on Haines Rd., near the BC border.

Indoor accommodations can be found at **Kathleen Lake Lodge,** 25km south of Haines Jct. (634-2319), which has enormous rooms and private bathtubs (singles $37, doubles $47; showers $3 or free with room). **The Gateway Inn** (634-2371), at Haines Rd. and the Alaska Hwy. in Haines Junctio, offers clean, spare rooms with private bath and TV (singles $53.50, doubles $59, 8 RV sites $12.50).

Haines Junction restaurants offer standard highway cuisine; for groceries, head for **Madley's General Store,** at Haines Rd. and Bates (634-2200; open daily 8am-8pm; Oct.-April 8am-6:30pm). You could live for days on a monster croissant ($1) or tasty sourdough loaf ($2.25) from the **Village Bakery and Deli** (634-2867), on Logan St. across from the visitor centre. (Open May-June and Sept. daily 9am-6pm; July-Aug. 9am-9pm.)

Outdoors in the Park There are few actual trails in the park; the major ones are the 4km **Dezadeash River Loop** (dez-a-DEE-ush), beginning at the Haines Junction Visitor Centre, the 15km **Auriol Trail** starting from Haines Hwy. (an excellent overnight hike), and the 85km **Cottonwood Trail,** a four-to-six-day trek beginning either 27 or 55km south of Haines Junction on Haines Hwy. Cottonwood is a loop trail offering 25km of trail above tree-line and a short detour up an adjacent ridge providing a view of the Icefield Ranges and Mount Logan on clear days.

The park also offers many **"routes"** following no formal trail and not maintained by the park. These are reserved for more experienced hikers, since route finding, map reading, and compass skills may all be called for. Perhaps the most popular are the **Slims East** and **Slims West** routes, both beginning 3km south of the Sheep Mountain Information Center (see above); both follow the Slims River (each on its respective side) for 23-30km (one-way) to ridges overlooking the mighty **Kaskawalsh Glacier.** Both routes take 3-5 days; due to increased bear activity in this area, the park mandates the use of **bear canisters** for the storage of food on all overnight trips. All trekkers camping in the backcountry must register at one of the visitor centres. The park strongly encourages day-hikers to do the same, especially in the **north end** and **Slims Valley** section of the park where trails are not as well marked and bear activity is more frequent. For the less adventurous, the park offers shorter **day-hikes** and **walks** led by wardens concentrating on specific themes, ranging from bear habitats to the park's wildflowers.

The **Kluane Park Adventure Center** (634-2313) is the central booking office for all outdoor activities going on in and around the park (open daily 9am-6pm). The centre has **mountain bikes** ($5 per hr.) and canoes ($15 per ½ day) for rent. For $100, travelers can go from Copper Mine, BC to Dalton Post, YT through Class III and IV rapids along the Tatshenshini River. For the more serene, the centre offers a 2-hr. scenic float trip illustrating the park's ecology, fauna, and geology for $25.

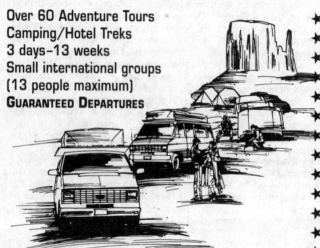

INDEX

★ FREE T-SHIRT ★

JUST ANSWER THE QUESTIONS ON THE FOLLOWING PAGES AND MAIL TO:

> Attn: Let's Go Survey
> St. Martin's Press
> 175 Fifth Avenue
> New York, NY 10010

WE'LL SEND THE FIRST 1,500 RESPONDENTS A LET'S GO T-SHIRT!

(Make sure we can read your address.)

■ LET'S GO 1995 READER ■ QUESTIONNAIRE

1) Name _____

2) Address _____

3) Are you: female   male

4) How old are you?   under 17   17-23   24-30   31-40   41-55   over 55

5) Are you (circle all that apply):   in high school   in college   in grad school
                                      employed   retired   between jobs

6) What is your personal yearly income?
 Under $15,000 $15,000 - $25,000 $26,000 - $35,000 $36,000 - $50,000
 $51,000 - $75,000 $76,000 - $100,000   over $100,000   not applicable

7) How often do you normally travel
   with a guidebook?
   This is my first trip
   Less than once a year
   Once a year
   Twice a year
   Three times a year or more

8) Which *Let's Go* guide(s) did you buy
   for your trip?
   _____
   _____

9) Have you used *Let's Go* before?
   Yes   No

10) How did you first hear about
    Let's Go? (Choose one)
    Friend or fellow traveler
    Recommended by store clerk
    Display in bookstore
    Ad in newspaper/magazine
    Review or article in newspaper/
       magazine
    Radio

11) Why did you choose *Let's Go*?
    (Choose up to three)
    Updated every year
    Reputation
    Easier to find in stores
    Better price
    "Budget" focus
    Writing style
    Attitude
    Better organization
    More comprehensive
    Reliability
    Better Design/Layout
    Candor
    Other _____
    _____
    _____

12) Which of the following guides have
    you used, if any?
    Frommer's $-a-Day
    Fodor's Affordable Guides
    Rough Guides/Real Guides
    Berkeley Guides/On the Loose
    Lonely Planet
    None of the above

13) Is *Let's Go* the best guidebook?
    Yes
    No (which is?) _____
    Haven't used other guides

14) When did you buy this book?
    Jan   Feb   Mar   Apr   May   Jun
    Jul   Aug   Sep   Oct   Nov   Dec

15) When did you travel with this
    book? (Circle all that apply)
    Jan   Feb   Mar   Apr   May   Jun
    Jul   Aug   Sep   Oct   Nov   Dec

16) How long was your trip?
    1 week   2 weeks
    3 weeks   1 month
    2 months   over 2 months

17) Where did you spend most of your
    time on this trip? (Circle one)
    cities   small towns   rural areas

18) How many travel companions did
    you have?   0 1 2 3 4 over 4

19) Roughly how much did you spend
    per day on the road?
    $0-15 $51-70
    $16-30 $71-100
    $31-50 $101-150
                    over $150

...t was the purpose of your trip?
..rcle all that apply)
Pleasure   Business
Study   Volunteer
Work/internship

21) What were the main attractions of your trip? (Circle top three)
Sightseeing
New culture
Learning Language
Meeting locals
Camping/Hiking
Sports/Recreation
Nightlife/Entertainment
Meeting other travelers
Hanging Out
Food
Shopping
Adventure/Getting off the beaten path

22) How reliable/useful are the following features of *Let's Go*?
v = very, u = usually, s = sometimes
n = never, ? = didn't use

Accommodations	v u s n ?
Camping	v u s n ?
Food	v u s n ?
Entertainment	v u s n ?
Sights	v u s n ?
Maps	v u s n ?
Practical Info	v u s n ?
Directions	v u s n ?
"Essentials"	v u s n ?
Cultural Intros	v u s n ?

23) On the list above, please circle the top 3 features you used the most.

24) Would you use *Let's Go* again?
Yes
No (why not?) _____
_____

25) Do you generally buy a phrasebook when you visit a foreign destination?
Yes   No

26) Do you generally buy a separate map when you visit a foreign city?
Yes   No

27) Which of the following destinations are you planning to visit as a tourist ..n the next five years?
..rcle all that apply)

..ta   Hong Kong
..and   Vietnam
Malaysia
Singapore
India

Nepal   U.S. Nat'l Parks
Middle East   Rocky Mtns.
Israel   The South
Egypt   New Orleans
Africa   Florida
Turkey   Mid-Atlantic
Greece   States
Scandinavia   Boston/New
Portugal   England
Spain   The Midwest
Switzerland   Chicago
Austria   The Southwest
Berlin   Texas
Russia   Arizona
Poland   Colorado
Czech/Slovak   Los Angeles
   Rep.   San Francisco
Hungary   Seattle
Baltic States   Hawaii
Caribbean   Alaska
Central America   Canada
Costa Rica   British Columbia
South America   Montreal/
Ecuador   Quebec
Brazil   Maritime
Venezuela   Provinces
Colombia

28) Please circle the destinations you visited on your trip:

ME	NH	VT	MA	CT	RI
NY	NJ	DE	MD	PA	VA
WV	NC	SC	GA	FL	AL
MS	LA	AR	TN	KY	OH
MI	IN	IL	WI	MN	IA
MO	ND	SD	NE	KS	OK
TX	NM	CO	WY	MT	ID
UT	AZ	CA	NV	OR	WA
AK	HI		B.C.	Alberta	

Ontario   Quebec
Newfoundland   New Brunswick
Nova Scotia
Prince Edward Island

29) How did you get around on your trip?
Car   Train   Plane
Bus   Ferry   Hitching
Bicycle   Motorcycle

30) Which of these do you own?
(Circle all that apply)
Computer   CD-ROM
Modem   On-line Service

Mail this to:
Attn: Let's Go Survey
St. Martin's Press
175 Fifth Avenue
New York, NY 10010
Thanks For Your Help!

Downtown Washington, D.C.

Central Washington, D.C.

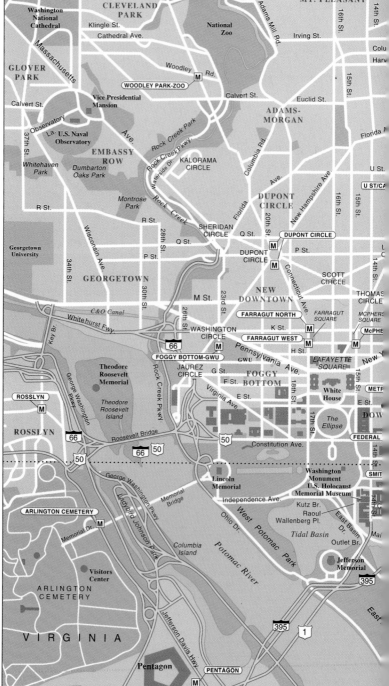

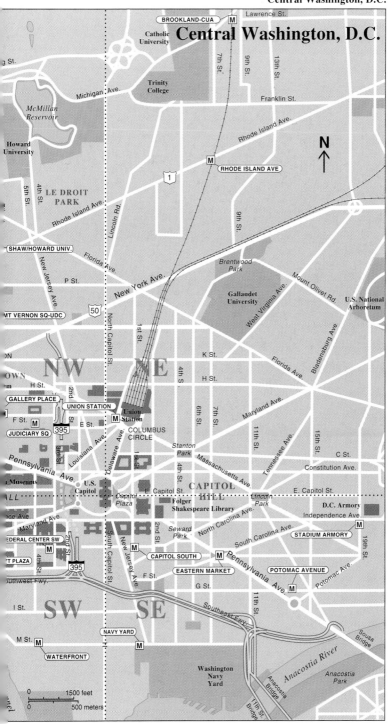

The Mall Area, Washington, D.C.

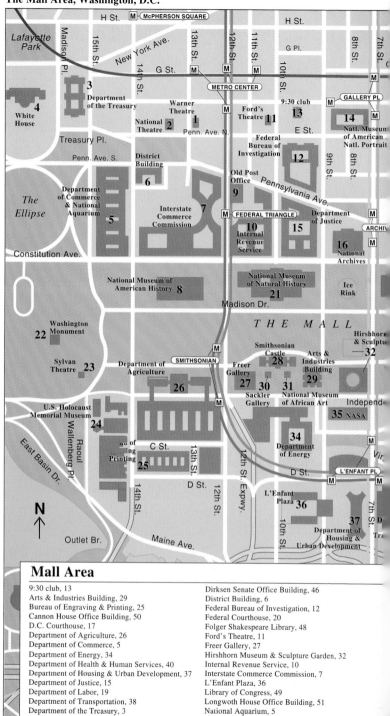

Mall Area

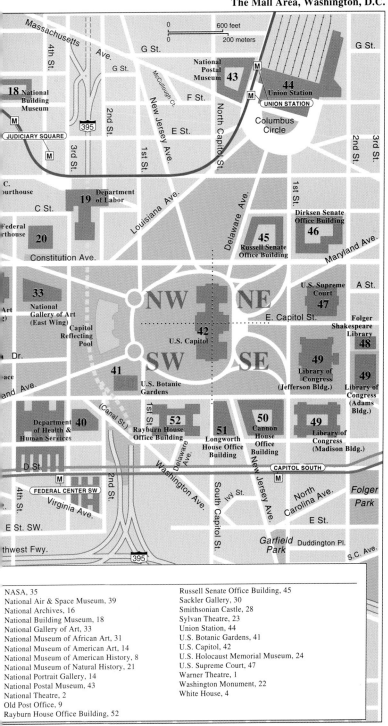

The Mall Area, Washington, D.C.

White House Area, Foggy Bottom, and Nearby Arlington

N↑

GEORGETOWN

Prospect St.
N St.
Olive St.
33rd St.
31st St.
Old Stone House
M St.
Rock Creek
24th St.
C&O Creek
South St.
Whitehurst Fwy.
K St. (under expressway)
29
26th St.
25th St.
L St.
WASH CIR

Potomac River

FOGGY BOTTOM-GW
66

Thompson Boat Center
Watergate Hotel
Watergate Hotel Complex
JUAREZ CIRCLE
24th St.
FC BO

Francis Scott Key Br.

George Washington Pkwy.

Theodore Roosevelt Memorial

Rock Creek Pkwy.

Kennedy Center for the Performing Arts

Theodore Roosevelt Island

Fort Myer Dr.
N. Lynn St.
N. Moore St.
19th St.
N. Kent St.
ROSSLYN
M
Wilson Blvd

ROSSLYN
Fairfax Dr.

Arlington Ridge Rd.
66

Theodore Roosevelt Br.
66 50

N. Nash St.
Mead Dr.
50

NW
SW

Marine Corps War Memorial (Two Jima Statue)

12th St.

George Washington Memorial Pkwy.

Arlington Memorial Br.

Ericsson Memori

Netherlands Carillon

ARLINGTON

Ladybird Johnson Park

Columbia Island

M
Memorial Dr.
ARLINGTON CEMETERY

Grave of President John F. Kennedy

Arlington House

Robert E. Lee Memorial

Visitor Center

Jefferson Davis Hwy.

ARLINGTON NATIONAL CEMETERY

Tomb of the Unknown Soldier

Lyndon B. Johnson Memorial

VIRGINIA

0   1500 feet
0   500 meters

Pentagon, National Airport

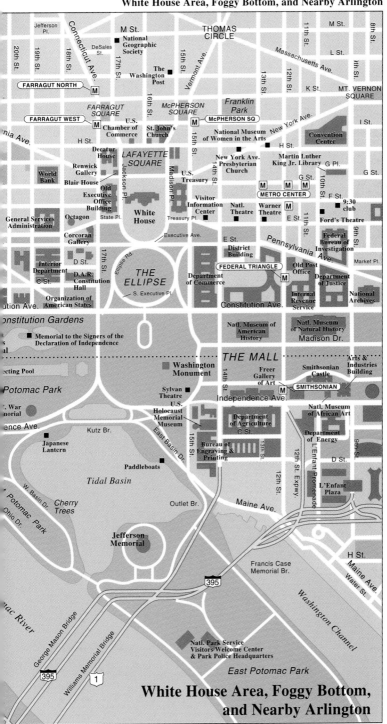

White House Area, Foggy Bottom, and Nearby Arlington

Metrorail System, Washington, D.C.

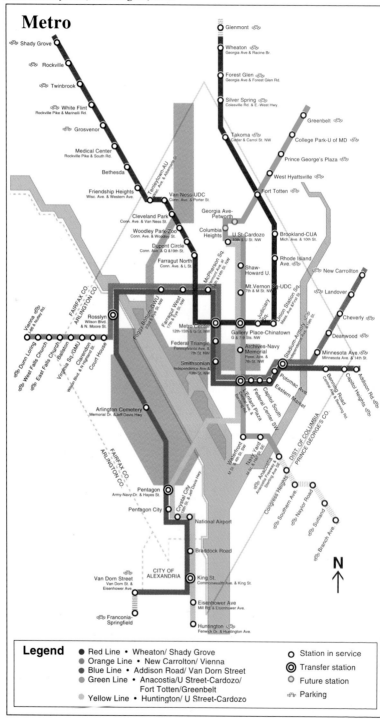

Metro

Legend

- ● Red Line • Wheaton/ Shady Grove
- ● Orange Line • New Carrolton/ Vienna
- ● Blue Line • Addison Road/ Van Dorn Street
- ● Green Line • Anacostia/U Street-Cardozo/ Fort Totten/Greenbelt
- ● Yellow Line • Huntington/ U Street-Cardozo

- ○ Station in service
- ◎ Transfer station
- ○ Future station
- 🚲 Parking

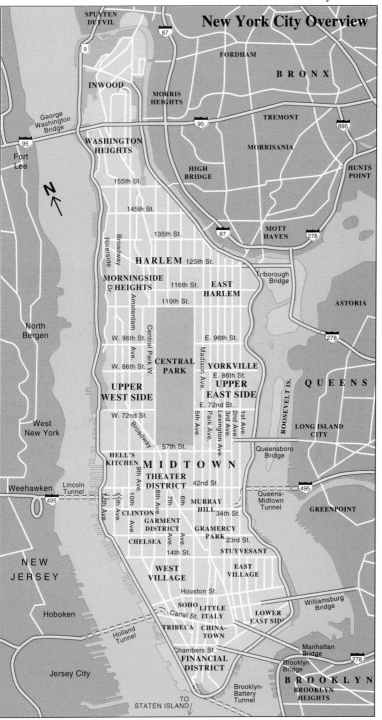

New York City Overview

New York City Subways

Subways

Stops are not served by all trains at all times.
Refer to Transit Authority map for descriptions
of express, local, and limited service.

Downtown Manhattan

New Museum of
 Contemporary Art, 31
New School of Social
 Research, 46
New York Stock
 Exchange, 14
New York University, 37
Puck Building, 32
St. John's Episcopal
 Methodist Church, 19
St. Luke's Chapel, 35
St. Mark's in the Bowery
 Church, 40
St. Paul's Chapel, 20
South Street Seaport
 Museum, 18
Staten Island Ferry
 Terminal, 7
Statue of Liberty and Ellis
 Island Ferry Terminal, 3
Strand Bookstore, 42
Tower Records, 36
Trinity Church, 12
Umberto's Clam House, 30
U.S. Customs House, 11
Woolworth Building, 23
World Financial Center, 22
World Trade Center, 21

Downtown

Alternative Museum, 28
Anthology Film
 Archives, 33
Buddhist Temple, 27
Castle Clinton, 1
Cherry Lane Theatre, 34
Chinatown Fair, 26
Church of the
 Ascension, 44
Church of Our Lady of the
 Rosary, 8
City Hall, 24
Clocktower Gallery, 25
Cooper Union, 39
Downtown Heliport, 9
East Coast Memorial, 2
Federal Hall, 15
Federal Reserve Bank, 16
Forbes Magazine
 Galleries, 47
Forbidden Planet, 43
Fraunces Tavern, 10
Fulton Fish Market, 17
Grace Church, 41
Jefferson Market
 Library, 45
Joseph Papp Public
 Theater, 38
Morgan Guaranty Trust
 Company, 13
Museum of Holography, 29

Midtown Manhattan

Map of Midtown Manhattan showing numbered landmarks, avenues, and streets from the East River to Twelfth Avenue.

Labels on map:

East River
Queens-Midtown Tunnel
FDR Dr.
Queensboro Bridge
First Ave.
Second Ave.
Third Ave.
Lexington Ave.
Park Ave.
Madison Ave.
Fifth Ave.
Sixth Ave.
Seventh Ave.
Broadway
Eighth Ave.
Ninth Ave.
Tenth Ave.
Eleventh Ave.
Twelfth Ave.
Central Park South
Grand Army Plaza
Park Ave. South

TURTLE BAY
United Nations
MURRAY HILL
GARMENT DISTRICT
HERALD SQUARE
HELL'S KITCHEN
COLUMBUS CIRCLE
TIMES SQUARE

Carnegie Hall
Museum of Modern Art
Rockefeller Center
Grand Central Terminal
New York Public Library
Bryant Park
Empire State Building
Citicorp Center
New York Convention & Visitors Bureau
Port Authority Bus Terminal
General Post Office
Lincoln Tunnel
Dyer Ave.

Streets:
W. 60th St., W. 59th St., W. 58th St., W. 57th St., W. 56th St., W. 55th St., W. 54th St., W. 53rd St., W. 52nd St., W. 51st St., W. 50th St., W. 49th St., W. 48th St., W. 47th St., W. 46th St., W. 45th St., W. 44th St., W. 43rd St., W. 42nd St., W. 41st St., W. 40th St., W. 39th St., W. 38th St., W. 37th St., W. 36th St., W. 35th St., W. 34th St.

E. 60th St., E. 59th St., E. 58th St., E. 57th St., E. 56th St., E. 55th St., E. 54th St., E. 53rd St., E. 52nd St., E. 51st St., E. 50th St., E. 49th St., E. 48th St., E. 47th St., E. 46th St., E. 45th St., E. 44th St., E. 43rd St., E. 42nd St., E. 41st St., E. 40th St., E. 39th St., E. 38th St., E. 37th St., E. 36th St., E. 35th St., E. 34th St., E. 33rd St.

Subway lines:
A,B,C,D 1,2,3,9
N,R
B,Q
4,5,6
E,F
6
4,5,6,S
7
B,D,F,Q,7
1,2,3,N,R,9
C,E
A,C,E
B,D,E

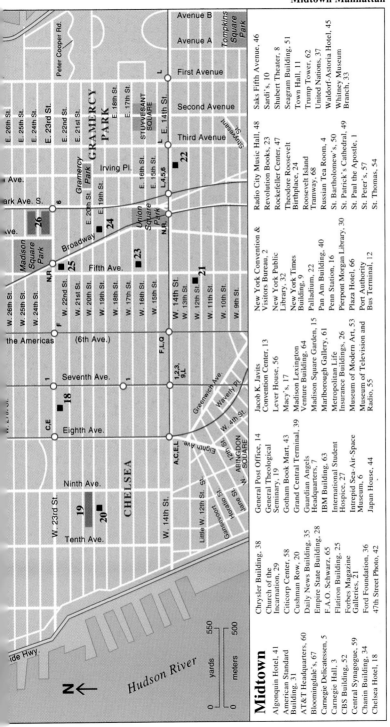

Uptown

American Museum of Natural History, 53
The Ansonia, 55
The Arsenal, 25
Asia Society, 14
Belvedere Castle, 36
Bethesda Fountain, 33
Blockhouse No. 1, 42
Bloomingdale's, 22
Bridle Path, 30
Cathedral of St. John the Divine, 47
Central Park Zoo, 24
Chess and Checkers House, 28
Children's Museum of Manhattan, 51
Children's Zoo, 26
China House, 19

Cleopatra's Needle, 38
Columbia University, 46
Conservatory Garden, 2
Cooper-Hewitt Museum, 7
The Dairy, 27
Dakota Apartments, 56
Delacorte Theater, 37
El Museo del Barrio, 1
Fordham University, 60
Frick Museum, 13
Gracie Mansion, 10
Grant's Tomb, 45
Great Lawn, 39
Guggenheim Museum, 9
Hayden Planetarium (at the American Museum of Natural History), 53
Hector Memorial, 50
Hotel des Artistes, 57

Hunter College, 16
International Center of Photography, 5
Jewish Museum, 6
The Juilliard School (at Lincoln Center), 59
Lincoln Center, 59
Loeb Boathouse, 34
Masjid Malcolm Shabazz , 43
Metropolitan Museum of Art, 11
Mt. Sinai Hospital, 4
Museum of American Folk Art, 58
Museum of American Illustration, 21
Museum of the City of New York, 3
National Academy of Design, 8
New York Convention & Visitors Bureau, 61

New York Historical Society, 54
New York Hospital, 15
Plaza Hotel, 23
Police Station (Central Park), 40
Rockefeller University, 20
7th Regiment Armory, 17
Shakespeare Garden, 35
Soldiers and Sailors Monument, 49
Strawberry Fields, 32
Studio Museum in Harlem, 44
Symphony Space, 48
Tavern on the Green, 31
Temple Emanu-El, 18
Tennis Courts, 41
Whitney Museum of American Art, 12
Wollman Rink, 29
Zabar's, 52

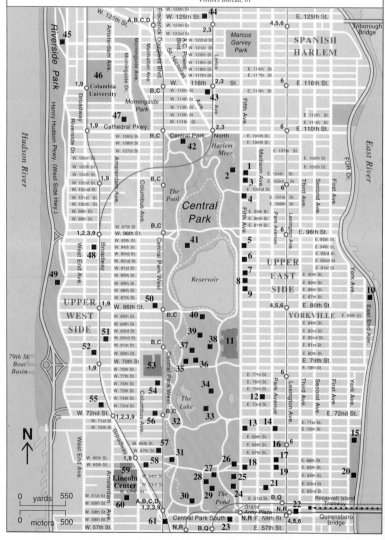